Masters of British Literature

VOLUME A

David Damrosch
COLUMBIA UNIVERSITY

Kevin J. H. Dettmar
SOUTHERN ILLINOIS UNIVERSITY

Christopher Baswell
UNIVERSITY OF CALIFORNIA, LOS ANGELES

Clare Carroll
QUEENS COLLEGE, CITY UNIVERSITY OF NEW YORK

Heather Henderson

Constance Jordan
CLAREMONT GRADUATE UNIVERSITY

Peter J. Manning
STATE UNIVERSITY OF NEW YORK, STONY BROOK

Anne Howland Schotter
WAGNER COLLEGE

William Chapman Sharpe
BARNARD COLLEGE

Stuart Sherman
FORDHAM UNIVERSITY

Susan J. Wolfson
PRINCETON UNIVERSITY

Masters of British Literature

David Damrosch and Kevin J. H. Dettmar
General Editors

VOLUME A

THE MIDDLE AGES
Christopher Baswell *and* Anne Howland Schotter

THE EARLY MODERN PERIOD
Constance Jordan *and* Clare Carroll

THE RESTORATION AND THE 18TH CENTURY
Stuart Sherman

PEARSON
Longman

New York   San Francisco   Boston
London   Toronto   Sydney   Tokyo   Singapore   Madrid
Mexico City   Munich   Paris   Cape Town   Hong Kong   Montreal

Editor-in-Chief: *Joseph Terry*
Senior Development Editor: *Mikola De Roo*
Director of Development: *Mary Ellen Curley*
Executive Marketing Manager: *Ann Stypuloski*
Senior Supplements Editor: *Donna Campion*
Media Supplements Editor: *Jenna Egan*
Production Manager: *Denise Phillip*
Project Coordination, Text Design, and Page Makeup: *GGS Book Services*
Cover Designer/Cover Design Manager: *Nancy Danahy*
On the Cover: Joshua Reynolds, *Mrs. Abington as "Miss Prue." 1771.* Yale Center for British Art,
    Paul Mellon Collection.
Photo Researcher: *Julie Tesser*
Manufacturing Buyer: *Lucy Hebard*
Printer and Binder: RR Donnelley Crawfordsville, In
Cover Printer: *The Lehigh Press, Inc.*

For permission to use copyrighted material, grateful acknowledgment is made to the copyright
holders on pages 1489–1490, which are hereby made part of this copyright page.

Library of Congress Cataloging-in-Publication Data

Masters of British literature.
    p. cm.
    Vol. A general editors David Damrosch and Kevin J. H. Dettmar.
    Includes index.
    ISBN-13: 978-0-321-33399-5 (v. A)
    ISBN-10: 0-321-33399-3 (v. A)
    ISBN-13: 978-0-321-33400-8 (v. B)
    ISBN-10: 0-321-33400-0 (v. B)
  1. English literature. 2. Great Britain—Literary collections. 3. English literature—History
and criticism. I. Damrosch, David. II. Dettmar, Kevin J. H., 1958-
    PR1109.M373 2007
    820.8—dc22

                                                                        2006102396

Visit us at www.ablongman.com

ISBN-13: 978-0-321-33399-5
ISBN-10:   0-321-33399-3

7 8 9 0—DOC—16 15 14 13

CONTENTS

The Early Modern Period   411

The Restoration and the Eighteenth Century   1017

───┤ PERSPECTIVES ├───
Reading Papers   1171

LIST OF ILLUSTRATIONS

The Middle Ages

The Early Modern Period

Color Plates   *following page 416*

Black-and-White Images

The Restoration and the Eighteenth Century

Color Plates   *following page 1024*

Black-and-White Images

PREFACE

Literature has a double life. Born in one time and place and read in another, literary works are at once products of their age and independent creations, able to live on long after their original world has disappeared. The goal of this anthology is to present a wealth of poetry, prose, and drama from the literary masters of Great Britain and its empire, and to do so in ways that will bring out these classic works' original cultural contexts and their lasting aesthetic power. These aspects are, in fact, closely related: Form and content, verbal music and social meanings, go hand in hand. This double life makes literature, as Aristotle said, "the most philosophical" of all the arts, intimately connected to ideas and to realities that the writer transforms into moving patterns of words. The challenge is to show these core works in the contexts in which, and for which, they were written, while at the same time not trapping them within those contexts. The warm response this anthology has received from instructors who have reviewed it reflects the growing consensus that we do not have to accept an "either/or" choice between the literature's aesthetic and cultural dimensions. This preface can serve as a road map to this text and the ways in which it reveals the masters of the British literary tradition in a whole new light.

A GENEROUS REPRESENTATION OF MAJOR CLASSIC TEXTS

Major works in all three genres are included in their entirety—among them *Beowulf*, Shakespeare's *The Tempest*, Dickens' *A Christmas Carol*, Wilde's *The Importance of Being Earnest*, Conrad's *Heart of Darkness*, and Beckett's *Endgame*. The book also offers a wealth of significant poetry selections, from Chaucer, Spenser, and Milton to Blake, Keats, and Yeats—and beyond. In addition, enduring works that are taught most frequently have been included:

- J. R. R. Tolkien's translation of *Sir Gawain and the Green Knight*

- the modern translation of Chaucer's General Prologue from *The Canterbury Tales* (appearing on facing pages from the Middle English)

- a generous selection of poems from Sidney's *Astrophil and Stella*

- poems by Lady Mary Wroth

- an extensive excerpt of Milton's *Paradise Lost,* including Books 1 and 9 in their entirety

- chapters from the third voyage and the complete fourth voyage from Swift's *Gulliver's Travels*

- a broad selection of poems from Blake's *Songs of Innocence and of Experience*

- numerous poems by Wordsworth and Keats

- a plethora of World War I poems, including an expansive selection of women poets

- a wide range of works touching on issues of post-colonialism by such authors as Chinua Achebe, Salman Rushdie, Lorna Goodison, Derek Walcott, and Agha Shahid Ali.

LITERATURE IN ITS TIME—AND IN OURS

When we engage with a rich literary history that extends back over a thousand years, we often encounter writers who assume their readers know all sorts of things that are little known today: historical facts, social issues, literary and cultural references. Beyond specific information, these works will have come out of a very different literary culture than our own. Even the contemporary British Isles present a cultural situation—or a mix of cultures—very different from what North American readers encounter at home, and these differences only increase as we go further back in time. A major emphasis of this anthology is to bring the works' original cultural moment to life: not because the works simply or naively reflect that moment of origin, but because they do refract it in fascinating ways. British literature is both a major heritage for modern North America and, in many ways, a very distinct culture; reading British literature will regularly give an experience both of connection and of difference. Great writers create imaginative worlds that have their own compelling internal logic, and a prime purpose of this anthology is to help readers to understand the formal means—whether of genre, rhetoric, or style—with which these writers have created works of haunting beauty. At the same time, as Virginia Woolf says in *A Room of One's Own*, the gossamer threads of the artist's web are joined to reality "with bands of steel." This anthology pursues a range of strategies to bring out both the beauty of these webs of words and their points of contact with reality.

Masters of British Literature brings related authors and works together in several ways:

☞ PERSPECTIVES: Broad groupings that illuminate underlying issues in a variety of the major works of a period.

☞ AND ITS TIME: A focused cluster that illuminates a specific cultural moment or a debate to which an author is responding.

☞ RESPONSES: One or more texts in which later authors in the tradition respond creatively to the challenging texts of their forebears.

For example, Tracts on Women and Gender in the Early Modern section presents Erasmus on marriage, Rachel Speght's defense of womanhood, and a pair of humorous texts on gender and style of dress.

These groupings provide a range of means of access to the literary culture of each period. The Perspectives sections do much more than record what major writers thought about an issue: they give a variety of views in a range of voices, to illustrate the wider culture within which the literature was being written. These and many other vivid readings give rhetorical as well as social contexts for the poems, plays, and stories around them. Perspectives sections typically relate to several major authors of the period, as with a section on The Abolition of Slavery and the Slave-Trade that relates broadly to the work of William Wordsworth and Lord Byron. Many of the writers included in Perspectives sections are important figures of the period who might be neglected if they were listed on their own with just a few pages each; grouping them together has proven to be useful pedagogically as well as intellectually. Perspectives sections may also include work by a major author whose primary listing appears elsewhere in the period, so as to give a rounded presentation of the issue in ways that can inform the reading of those authors in their individual sections.

When we present a major work "And Its Time," we give a cluster of related materials to suggest the context within which the work was written. Thus Jonathan Swift's "A Modest Proposal" is accompanied by a reading showing the tensions that were raging at the time between England and Ireland. Some of the writers in these groupings and in our Perspectives sections have not traditionally been seen as literary figures, but all have produced lively and intriguing works, from medieval writers of King Arthur, to a polemical seventeenth-century tract giving *The Arraignment of Lewd, Idle, Froward, and Unconstant Women*, to the Gang of Four's punk rock anthem derived from Conrad's *Heart of Darkness*.

Also, we include "Responses" to significant texts in the British literary tradition, demonstrating the sometimes far-reaching influence these works have had over the decades and centuries, and sometimes across oceans and continents. *Beowulf* and John Gardiner's *Grendel*, for example, are separated by the Atlantic ocean, perhaps eleven- or twelve-hundred years—and, most notably, their attitude toward the poem's monster.

Cultural Editions

The publication of *Masters of British Literature* finds eighteen volumes of the Longman Cultural Editions now in print, which carry further the anthology's emphases by presenting major texts along with a generous selection of contextual material. Included in those volumes are frequently taught texts ranging from *Beowulf* and *Hamlet* to *Frankenstein* and *Northanger Abbey;* nearly three dozen new titles are currently being developed, bringing the list of available titles up to the early twentieth century. In some instances, dedicating a full, separate volume to major texts (like *Othello/Miriam* and *Frankenstein*)—available at no additional charge, for course use, with the anthology itself—has helped to free up space for our many additions in this new edition. Taken together, our new edition and the Longman Cultural Editions offer an unparalleled set of materials for the enjoyment and study of British literary culture from its earliest beginnings to the present.

Illustrating Visual Culture

Another important context for literary production has been a different kind of culture: the visual. This edition includes a suite of color plates in each volume, along with one hundred black-and-white illustrations throughout the anthology, chosen to show artistic and cultural images that figured importantly for literary creation. Sometimes, a poem refers to a specific painting, or more generally emulates qualities of a school of visual art. At other times, more popular materials like advertisements may underlie scenes in Victorian or Modernist writing. In some cases, visual and literary creation have merged, as in Blake's illustrated engravings of his *Songs of Innocence and of Experience*, several of whose plates are reproduced in color in Volume B. A thumbnail portrait of major authors in each period marks the beginning of author introductions.

AIDS TO UNDERSTANDING

We have attempted to contextualize our selections in suggestive rather than exhaustive ways, trying to enhance rather than overwhelm the experience of reading the texts themselves. Thus, when difficult or archaic words need defining in poems, we use glosses in the margins, so as to disrupt the reader's eye as little as possible; footnotes are intended to be concise and informative, rather than massive or interpretive. Important literary and social terms are defined when they are used; for convenience of reference, there is also an extensive glossary of literary and cultural terms at the end of each volume, together with useful summaries of British political and religious organization, and of money, weights, and measures. For further reading, carefully selected, up-to-date bibliographies for each period and for each author can be found in each volume.

LOOKING—AND LISTENING—FURTHER

Beyond the boundaries of the anthology itself, we have incorporated a pair of CDs, one for each volume, giving a wide range of readings of texts in the anthology and of selections of music from each period. It is only in the past century or two that people usually began to read literature silently; most literature has been written in the expectation that it would be read aloud, or even sung in the case of lyric poetry ("lyric" itself means a work meant to be sung to the accompaniment of a lyre or other instruments). The aural power and beauty of these works is a crucial dimension of their experience. For further explorations, we have also expanded our Web site, available to all users at www.ablongman.com/damroschbritlit3e; this site gives a wealth of information, annotated links to related sites, and an archive of texts for further reading. Links to relevant pages are appended to anthology selections. For instructors, we have revised and expanded our popular companion volume, *Teaching British Literature*, written directly by the anthology editors, 600 pages in length, available free to everyone who adopts the anthology.

WHAT IS BRITISH LITERATURE?

Turning now to the book itself, let us begin by defining our basic terms: What is "British" literature? What is literature itself? And just what should an anthology of this material look like at the present time? The term "British" can mean many things, some of them contradictory, some of them even offensive to people on whom the name has been imposed. If the term "British" has no ultimate essence, it does have a history. The first British were Celtic people who inhabited the British Isles and the northern coast of France (still called Brittany) before various Germanic tribes of Angles and Saxons moved onto the islands in the fifth and sixth centuries. Gradually the Angles and Saxons amalgamated into the Anglo-Saxon culture that became dominant in the southern and eastern regions of Britain and then spread outward; the old British people were pushed west, toward what became known as Cornwall, Wales, and Ireland, which remained independent kingdoms for centuries, as did Celtic Scotland to the north. By an ironic twist of linguistic fate, the Anglo-Saxons began to appropriate the term British from the Britons they had displaced, and they took as a national hero the early, semi-mythic Welsh King Arthur. By the seventeenth century, English monarchs had extended their sway over Wales, Ireland, and Scotland, and they began to refer to their holdings as "Great Britain." Today, Great Britain includes England, Wales, Scotland, and Northern Ireland, but does not include the Republic of Ireland, which has been independent from England since 1922.

This anthology uses "British" in a broad sense, as a geographical term encompassing the whole of the British Isles. For all its fraught history, it seems a more satisfactory term than to speak simply of "English" literature, for two reasons. First: most speakers of English live in countries that are not the focus of this anthology; second, while the English language and its literature have long been dominant in the British Isles, other cultures in the region have always used other languages and have produced great literature in these languages. Important works by Irish, Welsh, and Scots writers appear regularly in the body of this anthology, some of them written directly in their languages and presented here in translation, and others written in an English inflected by the rhythms, habits of thought, and modes of expression characteristic of these other languages and the people who use them.

We use the term "literature" in a similarly capacious sense, to refer to a range of artistically shaped works written in a charged language, appealing to the imagination at least as much as to discursive reasoning. It is only relatively recently that creative writers have been able to make a living composing poems, plays, and novels, and only in the past hundred years or so has creating "belles lettres" or high literary art been thought of as a sharply separate sphere of activity from other sorts of writing that the same authors would regularly produce. Sometimes, Romantic poets wrote sonnets to explore the deepest mysteries of individual perception and memory; at other times, they wrote sonnets the way a person might now write an Op-Ed piece, and such a sonnet would be published and read along with parliamentary debates and letters to the editor on the most pressing contemporary issues.

WOMEN'S WRITING, AND MEN'S

Literary culture has always involved an interplay between central and marginal regions, groupings, and individuals. A major emphasis in literary study in recent years has been the recovery of writing by women writers, some of them little read until recently, others major figures in their time. This anthology emphasizes the presence of women writers with selections by writers like Lady Mary Wroth and Eliza Haywood, as well as by including new voices like the contemporary Welsh poet Gwyneth Lewis and a cluster of women poets writing out of their response to World War I. Attending to these voices gives us a new variety of compelling works, and helps us rethink the entire periods in which they wrote. The first third of the nineteenth century, for example, can be defined more broadly than as a "Romantic Age" dominated by six male poets; looking closely at women's writing as well as at men's, we can deepen our understanding of the period as a whole, including the specific achievements of Blake, William Wordsworth, Coleridge, Keats, Percy Shelley, and Byron, all of whom continue to have a major presence in these pages as most of them did during the nineteenth century.

VARIETIES OF LITERARY EXPERIENCE

Above all, we have striven to give as full a presentation as possible to the varieties of great literature produced over the centuries in the British Isles, by women as well as by men, in outlying regions as well as in the metropolitan center of London, and in prose, drama, and verse alike. We have taken particular care to do justice to prose fiction: we include entire novels or novellas by Charles Dickens and Joseph Conrad, as well as a wealth of short fiction from the eighteenth century to the present. For the earlier periods, we give major space to narrative poetry by Chaucer and Spenser, and to Milton's *Paradise Lost* and Swift's *Gulliver's Travels,* among others. Drama appears throughout the anthology, from the medieval *Second Play of the Shepherds* to William Wycherley's *The Country Wife* to Samuel Beckett's *Endgame*. Finally, lyric poetry appears in profusion throughout the anthology, from early lyrics by anonymous Middle English poets to the powerful contemporary voices of Seamus Heaney, Eavan Boland, and Derek Walcott—himself a product of colonial British education, heir of Shakespeare and James Joyce.

As topical as these contemporary writers are, we hope that this anthology will show that the great works of earlier centuries can also speak to us compellingly today, their value only increased by the resistance they offer to our views of ourselves and our world. To read and reread the full sweep of this literature is to be struck anew by the degree to which the most radically new works are rooted in centuries of prior innovation. Even this preface can close in no better way than by quoting the words written eighteen hundred years ago by Apuleius of Madaura—both a consummate artist and a kind of anthologist of extraordinary tales—when he concluded the prologue to his masterpiece *The Golden Ass*: Attend, reader, and pleasure is yours.

David Damrosch & Kevin Dettmar

ACKNOWLEDGMENTS

In planning and preparing this anthology, the editors have been fortunate to have the support, advice, and assistance of many people. Our editor, Joe Terry, has been unwavering in his enthusiasm for the book and his commitment to it; he and his associates Roth Wilkofsky, Mary Ellen Curley, and Ann Stypuloski have supported us in every possible way throughout the process, ably assisted by Alison Main, Christine Halsey, and Abby Lindquist. Our developmental editor Mika De Roo guided us and our manuscript from start to finish with unfailing acuity and Wildean wit. Our copyeditor marvelously integrated the work of a dozen editors. Jenna Egan, Mika De Roo, Teresa Ward, and Heidi Jacobs have devoted enormous energy and creativity to our Web site and audio CD. Natalie Giboney cleared our many permissions, and Julie Tesser cleared our illustrations. Finally, Valerie Zaborski and Denise Phillips oversaw the production with sunny good humor and kept the book successfully on track on a very challenging schedule, working closely with GGS Book Services.

We are also grateful for the guidance of the reviewers who advised us on the creation of this book. Robert Barrett, University of Illinois-Urbana-Champaign; Bryan P. Davis, Georgia Southwestern State University; Maria Doyle, University of West Georgia; Alison L. Ganze, Valparaiso University; Kevin Gustafson, University of Texas-Arlington; Ruth Jenkins, California State University-Fresno; Tamara Ketabgian, Beloit College; Mary Kramer, University of Massachusetts-Lowell; Jim McKeown, McLennan Community College; Rebecca M. Mills, Hillsborough Community College; Emily H. Moorer, Hinds Community College; Patricia G. Morgan, Louisiana State University; Barry R. Nowlin, University of South Alabama; and Jackie Walsh, McNeese State University.

Other colleagues brought our developing book into the classroom, teaching from portions of the work-in-progress. Our thanks go to Lisa Abney (Northwestern State University), Charles Lynn Batten (University of California, Los Angeles), Brenda Riffe Brown (College of the Mainland, Texas), John Brugaletta (California State University, Fullerton), Dan Butcher (Southeastern Louisiana University), Lynn Byrd (Southern University at New Orleans), David Cowles (Brigham Young University), Sheila Drain (John Carroll University), Lawrence Frank (University of Oklahoma), Leigh Garrison (Virginia Polytechnic Institute), David Griffin (New York University), Rita Harkness (Virginia Commonwealth University), Linda Kissler (Westmoreland County Community College, Pennsylvania), Brenda Lewis (Motlow State Community College, Tennessee), Paul Lizotte (River College), Wayne Luckman (Green River Community College, Washington), Arnold A. Markely (Pennsylvania State University, Delaware County), James McKusick (University of Maryland, Baltimore), Eva McManus (Ohio Northern University), Manuel Moyrao (Old Dominion University), Kate Palguta (Shawnee State University, Ohio), Paul Puccio (University of Central Florida), Sarah Polito (Cape Cod Community

College), Meredith Poole (Virginia Western Community College), Tracy Seeley (University of San Francisco), Clare Simmons (Ohio State University), and Paul Yoder (University of Arkansas, Little Rock).

As if all this help weren't enough, the editors also drew directly on friends and colleagues in many ways, for advice, for information, sometimes for outright contributions to headnotes and footnotes, even (in a pinch) for aid in proofreading. In particular, we wish to thank David Ackiss, Marshall Brown, James Cain, Cathy Corder, Jeffrey Cox, Michael Coyle, Pat Denison, Tom Farrell, Andrew Fleck, Jane Freilich, Laurie Glover, Lisa Gordis, Joy Hayton, Ryan Hibbet, V. Lauryl Hicks, Nelson Hilton, Jean Howard, David Kastan, Stanislas Kemper, Andrew Krull, Ron Levao, Carol Levin, David Lipscomb, Denise MacNeil, Jackie Maslowski, Richard Matlak, Anne Mellor, James McKusick, Melanie Micir, Michael North, David Paroissien, Stephen M. Parrish, Peter Platt, Cary Plotkin, Desma Polydorou, Gina Renee, Alan Richardson, Esther Schor, Catherine Siemann, Glenn Simshaw, David Tresilian, Shasta Turner, Nicholas Watson, Michael Winckleman, Gillen Wood, and Sarah Zimmerman for all their guidance and assistance.

The pages on the Restoration and the eighteenth century are the work of many collaborators, diligent and generous. Michael F. Suarez, S. J. (Campion Hall, Oxford) edited the Swift and Pope sections; Michael Caldwell (University of Chicago) edited the portions of "Reading Papers" on *The Craftsman* and the South Sea Bubble. Steven N. Zwicker (Washington University) co-wrote the period introduction, and the headnotes for the Dryden section. Bruce Redford (Boston University) crafted the footnotes for Dryden, Gay, Johnson, and Boswell. Susan Brown, Janice Cable, Christine Coch, Marnie Cox, Tara Czechowski, Susan Greenfield, Mary Nassef, Paige Reynolds, and Andrew Tumminia helped with texts, footnotes, and other matters throughout; William Pritchard gathered texts and wrote notes. To all, abiding thanks.

It has been a pleasure to work with all of these colleagues in the ongoing collaborative process that has produced this book and brought it to this new stage of its life and use. This book exists for its readers, whose reactions and suggestions we warmly welcome, as these will in turn reshape this book for later users in the years to come.

David Damrosch & Kevin Dettmar

David Damrosch
COLUMBIA UNIVERSITY

Kevin J. H. Dettmar
SOUTHERN ILLINOIS UNIVERSITY

Christopher Baswell
UNIVERSITY OF CALIFORNIA, LOS ANGELES

Clare Carroll
QUEENS COLLEGE, CITY UNIVERSITY OF NEW YORK

Heather Henderson

Constance Jordan
CLAREMONT GRADUATE UNIVERSITY

Peter J. Manning
STATE UNIVERSITY OF NEW YORK, STONY BROOK

Anne Howland Schotter
WAGNER COLLEGE

William Chapman Sharpe
BARNARD COLLEGE

Stuart Sherman
FORDHAM UNIVERSITY

Susan J. Wolfson
PRINCETON UNIVERSITY

Masters of
British Literature

＊━❖━＊

VOLUME A

Laurence, Prior of Durham, depicted as a scribe, from a 12th-century manuscript.

The Middle Ages

At the present time, there are five languages in Britain, just as
the divine law is written in five books, all devoted to seeking out
and setting forth one and the same kind of wisdom, namely the
knowledge of sublime truth and of true sublimity. These are the
English, British, Irish, Pictish, as well as the Latin languages;
through the study of the scriptures, Latin is in general use among
them all.

—Bede, *Ecclesiastical History of the English People*

The Venerable Bede's famous and enormously influential *Ecclesiastical History of the English People*, written in the early 700s, reflects a double triumph. First, its very title acknowledges the dominance by Bede's day of the Anglo-Saxons, who, centuries earlier, had established themselves on an island already inhabited by Celtic Britons and by Picts. Second, the Latin of Bede's text and his own life as a monk point to the presence of ancient Mediterranean influences in the British Isles, earlier through Rome's military colonization of ancient Britain and later through the conversion of Bede's people to Roman Christianity.

In this first chapter of his first book, Bede shows a complex awareness of the several populations still active in Britain and often resisting or encroaching on Anglo-Saxon rule, and much of his *History* narrates the successive waves of invaders and missionaries who had brought their languages, governments, cultures, and beliefs to his island. This initial emphasis on peoples and languages should not be taken as early medieval multiculturalism, however: Bede's brief comparison to the single truth embodied in the five books of divine law also shows us his eagerness to draw his fragmented world into a coherent and transcendent system of Latin-based Christianity.

It is useful today, however, to think about medieval Britain, before and long after Bede, as a multilingual and multicultural setting, densely layered with influences and communities that divide, in quite different ways, along lines of geography, language, and ethnicity, as well as religion, gender, and class. These elements produced extraordinary cultures and artistic works, whose richness and diversity challenge the modern imagination. The medieval British Isles were a meeting place, but also a point of resistance, for wave after wave of cultural and political influences. Awareness of these multiple origins, moreover, persisted. In the mid-thirteenth century, Matthew Paris's map of England (Color Plate 4) reflects an alertness to the complex geography of history and settlement on his island. Six hundred years after Bede we encounter a historian like Sir Thomas Gray complaining that recent disorders were "characteristic of a medley of different races. Wherefore some people are of the opinion that the diversity of spirit among the English is the cause of their revolutions" (*Scalacronica*, c. 1363).

This complex mixture sometimes resulted from systematic conquest, as with the Romans and, three centuries after Bede, the famous Norman Conquest of 1066; sometimes it was from slower, less unified movements of ethnic groups, such as the Celts, Anglo-Saxons, the Irish in Scotland, and the Vikings. Other important influences arrived more subtly: various forms of Christianity, classical Latin literature and learning, continental French culture in the thirteenth century, and an imported Italian humanism toward the close of the British Middle Ages.

Our understanding of this long period and our very name for it also reflect a long history of multiple influences and cultural and political orders. The term "medieval" began as a condescending and monolithic label, first applied by Renaissance humanists who were eager to distinguish their revived classical scholarship from what they interpreted as a "barbarous" past. They and later readers often dismissed the Middle Ages as rigidly hierarchical, feudal, and Church-dominated. Others embraced the period for equally tendentious reasons, rosily picturing "feudal" England and Europe as a harmonious society of contented peasants, chivalrous nobles, and holy clerics. It is true that those who exercised political and religious control during the Middle Ages—the Roman church and the Anglo-Norman and then the English monarchy—sought to impose hierarchy on their world and created explicit ideologies to justify doing so. They were not unopposed, however; those who had been pushed aside continued to resist—and to contribute to Britain's multiple and dynamic literatures.

The period that we call "the Middle Ages" is vast and ungainly, spanning eight hundred years by some accounts. Scholars traditionally divide medieval English literature into the Old English period, from about 700 to 1066 (the date of the Norman Conquest), and the Middle English period, from 1066 to about 1500. Given the very different state of the English language during the two periods and given the huge impact of the Norman Conquest, this division is reasonable; there were substantial continuities, nevertheless, before and after the Conquest, especially in the Celtic areas beyond the Normans' immediate control.

THE CELTS

It is with the Celts, in fact, that the recorded history of Britain begins, and their literatures continue to the present day in Ireland and Wales. The Celts first migrated to Britain about 400 B.C., after spreading over most of Europe in the two preceding centuries. In England these "Brittonic" Celts absorbed some elements of Roman culture and social order during Rome's partial occupation of the island from the first to the fifth centuries A.D. After the conversion of the Roman emperor Constantine in the fourth century and the establishment of Christianity as the official imperial religion, many British Celts adopted Christianity. The language of these "British" to whom Bede refers gave rise to Welsh. The Celts maintained contact with their people on the Continent, who were already being squeezed toward what is now Brittany, in the west of France. The culture of the Brittonic Celts was thus not exclusively insular, and their myths and legends came to incorporate these cross-Channel memories, especially in the stories of King Arthur.

Celts also arrived in Ireland; and as one group, the "Goidelic" Celts, achieved linguistic and social dominance there, their language split off from that of the

Britons. Some of these Irish Celts later established themselves in Argyll and the western isles of Scotland, "either by friendly treaty or by the sword," says Bede, and from them the Scottish branch of the Celtic languages developed. Bede mentions this language as the "Irish" that is spoken in Britain. The Irish converted to Christianity early but slowly, without the pressure of a Christianized colonizer. When the great Irish monasteries flourished in the sixth century, their extraordinary Latin scholarship seems to have developed alongside the traditional learning preserved by the rigorous schools of vernacular poetry, as we see in the section "Early Irish Verse" (pages 101–10). If anything, Irish monastic study was stimulated by these surviving institutions of a more poetic and priestly class. The Irish monasteries in turn became the impetus behind Irish and Anglo-Saxon missionaries who carried Christianity to the northern and eastern reaches of Europe. Both as missionaries and as scholars, insular Christians had great impact on continental Europe, especially in the eighth and ninth centuries.

By 597 when Pope Gregory the Great sent Augustine (later "of Canterbury") to expand the Christian presence in England, there was already a flourishing Christian Celtic society, especially in Ireland. Ensuing disagreements over Celtic versus Roman ways of worship were ultimately resolved in favor of the Roman liturgy and calendar, but the cultural impact of Celts on British Christianity remained enormous. The Irish *Book of Kells* (page 10), and the Lindisfarne Gospels (Color Plate 1), produced in England, are enlivened by the swirls, interlace, and stylized animals long evident in the work of pagan Celtic craftsmen on the Continent. The monks who illuminated such magnificent gospel books also copied classical Latin texts, notably Virgil's *Aeneid* and works by Cicero and Seneca, thereby helping keep ancient Roman literature alive when much of continental Europe fell into near chaos during the Germanic invasions that led to the fall of Rome.

Included in this anthology are examples from the two great literatures written in Celtic languages, Irish and Welsh. Episodes included in "Early Irish Narrative" reveal a heroic spirit and an acceptance of the magical which can be compared with aspects of *Beowulf*. Like much Irish heroic narrative, though, these episodes also reveal a far more prominent and assertive role for women, some of whom retain resemblances to the goddess figures of Ireland's pagan era. Welsh literature is represented first by lyrics attributed to the early, shadowy poet Taliesin and second by a much later story about his accomplishments which serves to show some of these continuities of Welsh literary culture. Wales also absorbed Latin and later European influences.

THE GERMANIC MIGRATIONS

While Celtic culture flourished in Ireland, the British Celts and their faith suffered a series of disastrous reversals after the withdrawal of the Romans and the aggressive incursions of the pagan Angles, Saxons, and Jutes from the Continent. The Picts and Scots in the north, never Romanized, had begun to harass the Britons, who responded by inviting allies from among the Germanic tribes on the Continent in the mid-fifth century. These protectors soon became predators, demanding land and establishing small kingdoms of their own in roughly the eastern half of modern-day England. Uneasy and temporary treaties followed. The Britons retained a presence in the northwest, in the kingdoms of Rheged and of the Strathclyde Welsh; others were slowly pressed toward present-day Wales in the southwest.

The Angles, Saxons, and Jutes were not themselves a monolithic force, though. Divided into often warring states, they faced resistance, however diminishing, from the Britons and still had to battle the aggressive Picts and Scots, who were the original reason for their arrival. Their own culture was further changed as they converted to Christianity. The piecemeal Anglo-Saxon colonization of England in the sixth and seventh centuries and the island's conversion and later reconversion to Christianity present a complex picture, then—one that could be retold very differently depending on the perspectives of later historians. As the Angles and Saxons settled in and extended their control, the emerging "English" culture drew on new interpretations of the region's history. The most influential account of all was Bede's *Ecclesiastical History*, completed in 731. Our most reliable and eloquent source for early British history, Bede nonetheless wrote as an Anglo-Saxon. He presented his people's history from a providential perspective, seeing their role in Britain and their conversion to Christianity as a crucial part of a divine plan. King Alfred extended this world view when, in the late ninth century, he wrote of his people's struggle against the invading pagan Vikings.

Bede thus adopts an approach to history that reflects his own devout Christian faith and the disciplined religious practices of his monastic brethren in Northumberland. Nevertheless, Bede lived in a wider culture still deeply imbued with the tribal values of its Germanic and pagan past, a culture that maintained at least a nostalgic regard for the kind of individual heroic glory that rarely looks beyond this world. Even in Bede's day, most kings died young and on the battlefield. And natural disasters such as those in 664 (a plague, and the deaths of a king and an archbishop occurring on the day of an eclipse) could send the Anglo-Saxons back to pagan worship. The two worlds, one with its roots in Mediterranean Christianity and the other in Germanic paganism, overlapped and interpenetrated for generations.

The pagan culture that is the setting for the epic *Beowulf* still strongly resembled that of the Germanic "barbarians" described by the Roman historian Tacitus in the first century. The heroic code of the Germanic warrior bands—what Tacitus called the "*comitatus*"—valued courage in battle above all, followed by loyalty to the tribal leader and the warband. These formed the core of heroic identity. A warrior whose leader fell in battle was obliged to seek vengeance at any cost; it was an indelible shame to survive an unavenged leader. Family links were also profound, however, and a persistent tragic theme in Germanic and Anglo-Saxon heroic narrative pits the claims of vengeance against those of family loyalty.

Early warrior culture in the British Isles, as elsewhere, was fraught with violence, as fragile truces between warring tribes and clans were continually broken. The tone of Old English poetry (as of much of Old Irish heroic narrative) is consequently somber, often suffused with a sense of doom. Even moments of high festivity are darkened by allusions to later disasters. Humor often occurs through a kind of ironic understatement: a poet may state that a warrior strode less swiftly into battle, for example, when the warrior in fact is dead. Similarly Cet, an Irish warrior, claims that if his brother were in the house, he would overcome his opponent, Conall. Conall replies, "But he is in the house," and almost casually flings the brother's head at Cet. A lighter tone is found mostly in shorter forms, such as the playful Anglo-Saxon riddles and in some Old Irish poetry.

The Angles and Saxons had come to England as military opportunists, and they in turn faced attacks and settlement from across the Channel. Their increasingly ordered political world and their thriving monastic establishments, such as Bede's monastery of Jarrow, were plundered by Vikings in swift attacks by boat as early as the end of the eighth century. Irish monastic culture faced similar depradations. This continued for a hundred years, and eventually resulted in widespread Scandinavian settlements north of the Thames, in areas called the Danelaw, and around modern-day Dublin. By the 890s Christian Viking kings reigned at York and in East Anglia, extending a history of independence from the southern kingdoms. The period of raids and looting was largely over by 900, but even King Alfred (d. 899) faced Viking incursions in Wessex and consciously depicted himself as a Christian hero holding the line against pagan invaders. Only his kingdom, in fact, resisted their attacks with complete success. Vikings also intermarried with Anglo-Saxons and expanded their influence by political means. Profiting from English dynastic disorder around the turn of the eleventh century, aristocrats in the Danelaw became brokers of royal power. From 1016 to 1035 the Danish Cnut (Canute) was king of both England and Denmark, briefly uniting the two in a maritime empire. The Scandinavian presence was not exclusively combative, however. They sent peaceful traders to the British Isles—among them Ohthere; they also left their mark on literature and language, as in the early Middle English romance *Havelock the Dane*, which contains many words borrowed from Old Norse.

PAGAN AND CHRISTIAN: TENSION AND CONVERGENCE

Given that writing in the Roman alphabet was introduced to pre-Conquest England by churchmen, it is not surprising that most texts from the period are written in Latin on Christian subjects. Most writing even in the Old English language was also religious. In Anglo-Saxon England and in the Celtic cultures, vernacular literature tended at first to be orally composed and performed. The body of written vernacular Anglo-Saxon poetry that survives is thus very small indeed, although there are plenty of prose religious works. It is something of a miracle that *Beowulf*, which celebrates the exploits of a pagan hero, was deemed worthy of being copied by scribes who were almost certainly clerics. (In fact, almost all the greatest Anglo-Saxon poetry survives in only a single copy—so tenuous is our link to that past.) Yet the copying of *Beowulf* also hints at the complex interaction of the pagan and Christian traditions in Anglo-Saxon culture.

The conflict between the two traditions was characterized (and perhaps exaggerated) by Christian writers and readers as a struggle between pagan violence and Christian values of forgiveness. The old, deep-seated respect for treasure as a sign of power and achievement seemed to conflict with Christian contempt for worldly goods. In fact, however, pagan Germanic and Christian values were alike in many respects and coexisted with various degrees of mutual influence.

Old English poets explored the tensions as well as the overlap between the two sets of values in two primary poetic modes—the heroic and the elegiac. The heroic mode, of which *Beowulf* is the supreme example, celebrates the values of bravery, loyalty, vengeance, and desire for treasure. The great buckle from Sutton Hoo burial (Color Plate 2) is a surviving artifact of such treasure. The elegiac mode, by contrast, calls the value of these things into question, as at best transient and at worst a worldly distraction from spiritual life. The elegiac speaker, usually an exile, laments the loss of earthly goods—his lord, his comrades, the joys of the mead hall—and, in the case of the short poem known as *The Wanderer*, turns his thoughts to heaven. *Beowulf*, composed most likely by a Christian poet looking back at the deeds of his pagan Scandinavian ancestors, uses elements of both the heroic and the elegiac to focus on the overlap of pagan and Christian virtues. A similar, though less adversarial, interaction of a heroic code and the new religion is also encountered in medieval Irish literature, such as the examples of early Irish verse offered here.

The goals of earthly glory and heavenly salvation that concern Old English poetry are presented primarily as they affect men. Recent scholarship, however, reveals the active roles played in society by Anglo-Saxon women, particularly aristocratic ones. One of these is Aethelflaed, daughter of King Alfred, who co-ruled the kingdom of Mercia with her brother Edward at the turn of the tenth century, taking an active military role in fighting off the Danes. Better known today is Abbess Hilda, who founded and ran the great monastery at Whitby from 657 until her death in 680; five Whitby monks became bishops across England during her rule. Nevertheless, women generally take a marginal role in Old English poetry. In secular works marriages are portrayed as being arranged to strengthen military alliances, in efforts (often doomed) to heal bloody rifts between clans. Women thus function primarily as "peace weavers," a term referring occasionally to their active diplomacy in settling disputes but more often to their passive role in marriage exchanges. This latter role was fraught with danger, for if a truce were broken between the warring groups, the woman would face tragically conflicting loyalties to husband and male kin.

The effect of the Germanic heroic code on women is explored in two tantalizingly short poems that invest the elegiac mode with women's voices: *Wulf and Eadwacer* and *The Wife's Lament*. In both, a woman speaker laments her separation from her lord, whether husband or lover, through some shadowy events of heroic warfare. More indicative of the actual power of aristocratic and religious women in Anglo-Saxon society, perhaps, is the Old English poem *Judith*, a biblical narrative which uses heroic diction reminiscent of that in *Beowulf* to celebrate the heroine's military triumph over the pagan Holofernes.

ORAL POETRY, WRITTEN MANUSCRIPTS

For all their deep linguistic differences and territorial conflicts, the Celts and Anglo-Saxons had affinities in the heroic themes and oral settings of their greatest surviving narratives and in the echoes of a pre-Christian culture that endure there. Indeed, these can be compared to conditions of authorship in oral cultures worldwide, from Homer's Greece to parts of contemporary Africa. In a culture with little or no writing, the singer of tales has an enormously important role as the conservator of the past. In *Beowulf*, for instance, the traditional content and verbal formulas of the poetry of praise are swiftly reworked to celebrate the hero's killing of the monster Grendel:

> Meanwhile a man
> skilled as a singer,   versed in old stories,
> wove a new lay   of truly-linked words.
> So the scop started   his song of Beowulf's

wisdom and strength,   setting his spell
with subtle staves.

A poet of this kind (in Anglo-Saxon, a *scop* or "shaper") does not just enhance the great warrior's prestige by praising his hero's ancestors and accomplishments. He also recalls and performs the shared history and beliefs of the entire people, in great feats of memory that make the poet virtually the encyclopedia of his culture. A poet from the oral tradition might also become a singer of the new Christian cosmology, like the illiterate herdsman Caedmon, whom Bede describes as having been called to monastic vows by the Abbess Hilda, in honor of his Christian poems composed in the vernacular oral mode.

In Celtic areas, oral poets had even greater status. The ancient class of learned Irish poets were honored servants of noblemen and kings; they remained as a powerful if reduced presence after the establishment of Christianity. The legal status of such a poet (a *fili*) was similar to that of a bishop, and indeed the *fili* carried out some functions of spells and divination inherited from the pagan priestly class, the druids. The ongoing influence of these poets in Irish politics and culture is reflected in the body of surviving secular literature from medieval Ireland, which is considerably larger than that from Anglo-Saxon England. A comparable situation prevailed in Wales. Even in the quite late Welsh *Tale of Taliesin*, the poet Taliesin appears as a public performer before the king as well as a possessor of arcane wisdom, magic, and prophecy.

This attitude of awe toward the word as used by the oral poet was only enhanced by the arrival of Christianity, a faith that attributes creation itself to an act of divine speech. Throughout the Middle Ages and long after orally composed poetry had retreated from many centers of high culture, the power of the word also inhered in its written form, as encountered in certain prized books. Chief among these were the Bible and other books of religious story, especially by such church fathers as Saints Augustine and Jerome, and books of the liturgy. Since these texts bore the authority of divine revelation, the manuscripts that contained them shared in their charisma.

The power of these manuscripts was both reflected and aided by their visual grandeur. Among the highest expressions of the fervor and discipline of early insular monasticism is its production of beautifully copied and exquisitely decorated books of the Bible. The extreme elaboration of their production and the great labor and expense lavished on them suggest their almost holy status. Figures depicted holding a book in the late eighth-century *Book of Kells* (page 10), or writing in the Lindisfarne Gospels, indicate this importance; a fascination with the new technology is suggested by Old English riddles whose answers are "a hand writing," "a book worm," or "a bookcase."

The cost and effort of making manuscript books and their very scarcity contributed to their aura. Parchment was produced from animal skins, stretched and scraped. The training and discipline involved in copying texts, especially sacred texts, were great. The decoration of the most ambitious manuscripts involved rare colors, gold leaf, and often supreme artistry. Thus these magnificent manuscripts could become almost magical icons: Bede, for example, tells of scrapings from Irish manuscripts which mixed with water cured the bites of poisonous snakes.

Manuscripts slowly became more widely available. By the twelfth century we hear more of manuscripts in private hands and the beginning of production outside ecclesiastical settings. By the fourteenth century merchants and private scholars were buying books from shops that resembled modern booksellers. The glamour and

Saint John, from the *Book of Kells.* Late 8th century.

prestige of beautiful manuscripts remained, though, even if the sense of their magic faded to a degree. Great families would donate psalters and gospels to religious foundations, with the donor carefully represented in the decoration presenting the book to the Virgin Mary or the Christ child. Spectacular books of private devotion were at once a medium for spiritual meditation and proof of great wealth (see Color Plate 10). Stories of epic conquest like the *Aeneid* would sometimes feature their aristocratic owners' coat of arms.

THE NORMAN CONQUEST

By the time of these developments in book production, though, a gigantic change had occurred. In a single year, 1066, England witnessed the death of the Anglo-Saxon King Edward and the coronation of his disputed successor King Harold, the invasion and triumph of the foreigner William of Normandy, and his own coronation as King William. These events are recorded, from very different perspectives, in *The Anglo-Saxon Chronicle* and the Bayeux Tapestry. The Normans conquered, with relative ease, an Anglo-Saxon kingdom disordered by civil strife. The monastic movement had lost much of its earlier fervor and discipline, despite reform in the tenth century. Baronial interests had weakened severely the reign of the late King Edward "the Confessor." On an island that already perceived itself as repeatedly colonized, 1066 nonetheless represented a climactic change, experienced and registered at virtually all levels of social, religious, and cultural experience.

One sign of how great a breach had been opened in England, paradoxically, is the multifaceted effort put forth by conquerors and conquered to maintain—or invent—continuity with the pre-Conquest past. In religious institutions, in dynastic genealogies, in the intersection of history and racial myth, in the forms and records of social institutions, the generations after 1066 sought to absorb a radically changed world yet to ground their world in an increasingly mythicized Anglo-Saxon or Briton antiquity. The Normans and their dynastic successors the Angevins eagerly took up and adapted to their own preoccupations ancient Briton political myths such as that of King Arthur and his court, and the stories of such saintly Anglo-Saxon kings as Oswald and Edward the Confessor.

They promoted narratives of their ancestors, like Wace's *Roman de Rou*, the story of the Normans' founder Rollo, commissioned by Henry II. Geoffrey of Monmouth dedicated his *History of the Kings of England* partly to Henry II's uncle, Robert Duke of Gloucester. In that work Geoffrey links the Celtic myths of King Arthur and his followers to an equally ancient myth that England was founded by descendants of the survivors of Troy; he makes his combined, largely fictive but enormously appealing work available to a Norman audience by writing it in Latin. Geoffrey's story was soon retold in "romance," the French from which vernacular texts took their name. The Angevin court also supported the "romances of antiquity," poems in French that narrate the story of Troy (the *Roman de Troie*), its background (*Roman de Thèbes*), and its aftermath (*Roman d'Eneas*), thus creating a model in the antique past for the Normans and their westward conquest of England. And the *Song of Roland*, the great crusading narrative celebrating the heroic death of Charlemagne's nephew as he protected Christendom from the Spanish Moslems, was probably written in the milieu of Henry II's court.

The Normans brought with them a new system of government, a freshly renovated Latin culture, and most important a new language. Anglo-Saxon sank into relative insignificance at the level of high culture and central government. Norman French became the language of the courts of law, of literature, and of most of the nobility. By the time English rose again to widespread cultural significance, about 250 years later, it was a hybrid that combined Romance and Germanic elements.

Latin offered a lifeline of communication at some social levels of this initially fractured society. The European clerics who arrived under the immigrant archbishops Lanfranc and Anselm brought a new and different learning, and often new and deeply unwelcome religious practices: a celibate priesthood, skepticism about local saints, and newly disciplined monasticism. Yet despite these differences and the tensions that accompanied them, clerics of European or British origin were linked by a common liturgy, a considerable body of shared reading, and most of all a common learned language. Secular as well as religious society were coming to be based more and more on the practical use of the written word: the letter, the charter, the documentary record, and the written book. Whereas Anglo-Saxon England had been governed by the word enacted and performed—a law of oral witness and a culture of oral poets— Norman England increasingly became a land of documents and books.

The Three Living and the Three Dead, from *The De Lisle Psalter.* The transience of life, especially of worldly glory, was never far from the medieval imagination. In this image from a Psalter made in the early 14th century for Baron Robert de Lisle, three kings in elegant courtly array face three rotting corpses. While most of the Psalter is in French and Latin, this scene has a "caption" in rhymed Middle English at the top. The kings say in turn (in modernized form), "I am afeared. Lo, what I see! I think that here are devils three." The corpses reply, "I was well fair. Such shall thou be. For God's love beware by me."

SOCIAL AND RELIGIOUS ORDER

The famed Domesday Book is a first instance of many of these developments. The Domesday survey was a gigantic undertaking, carried out with a speed that still astonishes between Christmas 1085 and William the Conqueror's death in September 1087. A county-by-county survey of the lands of King William and those held by his tenants-in-chief and subtenants, Domesday also records the obligations of landholders and thus reflects a new feudal system by which, increasingly, land was held in post-Conquest England.

Under the Normans, a nobleman held land from the king as a fief, in exchange for which he owed the king certain military and judicial services, including the provision of armed knights. These knights in turn held land from their lord, to whom they also owed military service and other duties. Some of this land they might keep for their own farming and profit, and the rest they divided among serfs (who were obliged, in theory, to stay on the land to which they were born) and free peasantry. Both groups owed their knight or lord labor and either a portion of their agricultural produce or rents in cash. This system of land tenure was surely more complex and irregular in practice than in the theoretical model called feudalism. For instance, services at all levels were sometimes (and increasingly) commuted to cash payment, and while fiefs were theoretically held only by an individual for a lifetime, increasingly there were expectations that they would be inherited. Royal power gradually grew during the thirteenth and fourteenth centuries, yet the local basis of landholding and social order always acted as a counterbalance, even a block, to royal ambition.

The Domesday Book was only one piece of the multifaceted effort by which the Norman and later kings sought to extend and centralize royal power in their territories. William and his successors established a system of royal justices who traveled throughout the realm and reported ultimately to the king, and an organized royal bureaucracy began to appear. The most powerful and learned of these Anglo-Norman kings was William the Conqueror's great-grandson, Henry II, who ruled from 1154 to 1189. Under Henry, royal justice, bureaucracy, and record-keeping made great advances; the production of documents was centralized and took on more standardized forms, and copies of these documents (called "pipe rolls") began to be produced for later reference and proof.

Along with a stronger royal government, the Normans brought a clergy invigorated both by new learning and by the spirituality of recent monastic reforms. Saint Anselm, the second of the Norman archbishops of Canterbury, was a great prelate and the writer of beautiful and widely influential texts and prayers of private devotion. The Victorines and the Cistercians (inspired in part by Saint Bernard of Clairvaux) also brought a strong mystical streak to English monasticism. All these would bear fruit once again in the fourteenth century in a group of mystics writing in Latin and in English.

On the other hand, the Norman prelates, like their kings, brought an urge toward centralized order in the church and a belief that the church and its public justice (the "canon law") should be independent of secular power. This created frequent conflict with kings and aristocrats, who wanted to extend their judicial power and expected to wield considerable influence in the appointment of church officials.

The most explosive moment in this ongoing controversy occurred in the disagreements between Henry II and Thomas Becket, who was Henry's Chancellor and then Archbishop of Canterbury. Becket's increasingly public refusal to accommodate the king, in either the judicial sphere or the matter of clerical appointments, finally led to his murder by Henry's henchmen in 1170 at the altar of Canterbury Cathedral and his canonization very soon thereafter. A large body of hagiography (narratives of his martyrdom and posthumous miracles) swiftly developed, adding to an already rich tradition of writing about the lives of English saints. As Saint Thomas, Becket became a powerful focus for ecclesiastical ambition, popular devotion and pilgrimage, and religious and secular narrative. In fact, the characters of Chaucer's *Canterbury Tales* tell their stories while making a pilgrimage to his shrine.

At least in theory, feudal tenure involved an obligation of personal loyalty between lord and vassal that was symbolically enacted in the rituals of enfeoffment, in which the lord would bestow a fief on his vassal. This belief was elaborated in a large body of secular literature in the twelfth century and after. Yet feudal loyalty was always fragile and ideologically charged. Vassals regularly resisted the wills of their lord or king when their interests collided, sometimes to the extent of officially withdrawing from the feudal bond. Connected to feudal relations was the notion of a chivalric code among the knightly class (those who fought on horses, *chevaliers*), which involved not just loyalty to the lord but also honorable behavior within the class, even among enemies. Chivalric literature is thus full of stories of captured opponents being treated with the utmost politeness, as indeed happened when Henry II's son Richard was held hostage for years in Germany, awaiting ransom.

Similarly, although medieval theories of social order had some basis in fact, they exercised shifting influence within a much more complex social reality. For instance,

The Murder of Thomas Becket, from Matthew Paris's *Historia Major,* mid-13th century.

medieval society was often analyzed by the model of the "three estates"—those who fought (secular aristocrats), those who prayed (the clergy), and those who worked the land (the free and servile peasantry). This model appears more or less explicitly in the poetry of William Langland and Chaucer. Such a system, though, did not allow for the gradual increase in manufacturing (weaving, pottery, metalwork, even the copying of books) or for the urban merchants who traded in such products. As society became more complex, a model of the "mystical social body" gained popularity, especially in the fourteenth century. Here a wider range of classes and jobs was compared to limbs and other body parts. Even this more flexible image was strictly hierarchical, though. Peasants and laborers were the feet, knights (on the right) and merchants (on the left) were hands, and townspeople were the heart, but the head was made up of kings, princes, and prelates of the church.

CONTINENTAL AND INSULAR CULTURES

The arrival of the Normans, and especially the learned clerics who came then and after, opened England to influences from a great intellectual current that was stirring on the Continent, the "renaissance of the twelfth century," which was to have a significant impact in the centuries that followed. A period of comparative political stability and economic growth made travel easier, and students and teachers were on the move, seeking new learning in Paris and the Loire valley, in northern Italy, and in Toledo with its Arab and Jewish cultures. Schools were expanding beyond the monasteries and into the precincts of urban cathedrals and other religious foundations. Along with offering traditional biblical and theological study, these schools sparked a revived interest in elegant Latin writing, Neoplatonic philosophy, and science deriving from Aristotle.

Because the Normans and Angevins ruled large territories on the Continent, movement across the Channel was frequent; by the mid-twelfth century learned English culture was urbane and international. English clerics like John of Salisbury studied at Chartres and Paris, and texts by eminent speculative and scientific writers like William of Conches and Bernard Silvestris came to England. As these foreign works entered England, education became more ambitious and widely available, and its products show growing contact with the works of classical Latin writers such as Horace, Virgil, Terence, Cicero, Seneca, and Ovid in his erotic as much as in his mythological poetry.

The renewed attention to these works went along with a revival of interest in the *trivium*, the traditional division of the arts of eloquence: grammar, rhetoric, and dialectic. The most aggressive of these was dialectic, a form of logic developed by the Greeks and then rediscovered by Christian Europe from Arab scholars who had preserved and pursued Greek learning. John of Salisbury, who promoted dialectic in his *Metalogicon*, described it with metaphors of military prowess, as though it were an extension of knightly jousting. "Since dialectic is carried on between two persons," he writes, Aristotle's *Topics* "teaches the matched contestants whom it trains and provides with reasons and topics, to handle their proper weapons and engage in verbal, rather than physical conflict." Rhetoric was elaborately codified in technical manuals of poetry. Though in one sense it was merely ornamental, teaching how to flesh out a description or incident with figures of speech, rhetoric could be as coercive as dialectic, though, since it specified strategies of persuasion in a tradition deriving from ancient oratory. Rhetorical texts also instructed the student in letter-writing, increasingly important as an administrative skill and as a form of elevated composition.

The study of the *trivium* generated many Latin school texts and helped foster a high level of Latinity and a self-consciously sophisticated, classicizing literature in the second half of the twelfth century. Some school texts had great influence on vernacular literature, such as the *Poetria Nova* by Geoffrey of Vinsauf, a rhetorical handbook filled with vivid poetic examples. More intriguing is *Pamphilus*, a short Ovidian poem about a seduction, aided by Venus, which turns into a rape. It is thought to have been an exercise in *disputatio*, the oral form that dialectic assumed in the classroom. The poem was immensely popular in the next few centuries and was translated into many vernacular languages. *Pamphilus* was a conduit at once for Ovidian eroticism and for the language of debate on love. Chaucer mentions it as a model of passionate love and seems to have adapted some of its plot devices in his *Troilus and Criseyde*.

While classical Latin literature was often read with a frank interest in pagan ideas and practices, commentators also offered allegorical interpretations that drew pagan stories into the spiritual and cosmological preoccupations of medieval Christianity. Ovid's *Metamorphoses* were thus interpreted in a French poem, the *Ovide Moralisé*, that was clearly known to Chaucer, and in Latin commentaries such as the *Ovidius moralizatus* of Pierre Bersuire. For instance, Ovid describes Jupiter, in the form of a bull, carrying the Tyrian princess Europa into the sea to rape her. Bersuire interprets this as Christ taking on human flesh in order to take up the human soul he loves. Alternatively, he offers an explicitly misogynist allegory, casting Europa as young women who like to see handsome young men—bulls: "They are drawn through the stormy sea of evil temptations and are raped." Neither text is often very subtle in the extraction of Christian or moral analogies from Ovid's stories, yet both were popular and influential, if only because they also tell Ovid's tales before allegorizing them.

Allegory became a complex and fruitful area of the medieval imagination, with profound implications not only for reading, but for artistic production as well. In its simplest sense, an allegorical text takes a metaphor and extends it into narrative, often personifying a quality as a character. For instance, the enormously popular dream vision the *Roman de la Rose* by Guillaume de Lorris and Jean de Meun (which Chaucer translated into English) presents a lady's ambivalence toward courtship as the conflict between such personifications as "Reserve" and "Fair Welcome," both aspects of her own mind. When Christine de Pizan came to challenge the misogynist texts of Western tradition—the *Roman de la Rose* among them—she too chose the allegorical mode. In the *Book of the City of Ladies*, it is three virtues personified as ladies—Reason, Rectitude, and Justice—who refute the slanders of men and who encourage the poet to build a city celebrating female achievements. (The continuing influence of this text is reflected by the English translation printed in 1521.) The English morality play *Mankind* uses allegory to portray external forces, presenting its hero as tempted by the vices of the modern age, "New-Guise" (trendy behavior), "Nowadays," and "Nought." Medieval writers also employed an allegorical method known as typology, derived from biblical interpretation, in which Old Testament events are seen as literally true but also symbolically predictive of, and fulfilled by, events in the New Testament. An example of this occurs in *Piers Plowman*, which, among all its other allegorical devices, presents Abraham both as an Old Testament Patriarch, and, in his willingness to sacrifice his son, a type of Faith.

The Continent, particularly France, provided a variety of vernacular influences. French was the international language of aristocratic culture and an important literary language in England; continental French literature was crucial in the rise of courtly literature in Middle English. Many English Arthurian works, including *Sir Gawain and the Green Knight* and Sir Thomas Malory's *Morte Darthur*, are less indebted to English sources than to French romances, whether written on the Continent or in England by authors such as Marie de France and Thomas of Britain. Chaucer borrowed the conventions and imagery of the love poetry of Guillaume de Machaut and Eustache Deschamps, and even the meter of his earlier poetry derives from their French octosyllabic couplets. To a lesser extent, influences from Italy can be seen in Chaucer's use of Dante's *Divine Comedy*, and his extensive borrowing from Petrarch and Boccaccio. Such continental vernacular literatures infiltrated even the Celtic cultures.

If such writers and records reflect the higher achievements of education in England of the twelfth century and later, literacy was also diffusing in wider circles and new venues. In a society like England's that continued to produce considerable oral and public literature, indeed, the divide between literacy and illiteracy was always unstable and permeable. A secular aristocrat might have a clerk read to him or her; an urbanite could attend and absorb parts of public rituals that involved poems and orations; even a peasant would be able to pick up Latin tags from sermons or the liturgy. Thus a fourteenth-century writer like William Langland could expect his wide and mixed audience to recognize at least some of the Latin phrases he used along with English; and Chaucer could imagine a character like the Wife of Bath who, at best semiliterate, could still quote bits of the Latin liturgy. Access to texts and the self-awareness fostered by private reading may have helped promote the social ambitions and disruptions within the mercantile and even peasant classes during the later Middle Ages.

WOMEN, COURTLINESS, AND COURTLY LOVE

Access to books also increased the self-awareness of women. Possession of books that encouraged prayer and private devotion, such as psalters and Books of Hours, appears to have facilitated early language training in the home. The many images in manuscripts of women reading—especially the Virgin Mary and her mother, Saint Anne—have interesting implications for our understanding of women's literacy and cultural roles. (See for instance the illumination from the *Bedford Hours*, Color Plate 10.) A number of aristocratic Norman and Angevin women received good educations at convents. Women in the holy life possessed at least some literacy, though this often may have been minimal indeed. Even well-educated women were more likely to read English or French than Latin, with the exception of liturgical books.

The roles of women in the society and cultural imagination of post-Conquest England are complex and contradictory. No Anglo-Norman woman held ecclesiastical prestige like the Anglo-Saxon Abbess Hilda or other Anglo-Saxon holy women. Women's power seems to have declined in the long term, both in worldly affairs and in the church, as the Normans consolidated their hold on England and imposed their order on society. Nevertheless, ambitious women could have great influence, especially when they seized upon moments of disruption. In civil strife over the succession to King Henry I, the Empress Matilda organized an army, issued royal writs, and in the end guaranteed the accession of her son Henry II. If Henry II's wife, Eleanor of Aquitaine, spent the latter decades of her husband's reign under virtual house arrest, it was largely because she had conspired with her sons to raise an army against her own husband.

Despite the limitations of their actual power, women were the focus, often the worshiped focus, of much of the best imaginative literature of the twelfth and thirteenth centuries; and women were central to the social rituals we associate with courtliness and the idea of courtly love. Despite her later imprisonment, Eleanor of Aquitaine was a crucial influence in the diffusion of courtly ideas from the Continent, especially the south of France; and among the great writers of the century was Marie de France, who was probably related to Henry II. Scholars continue to debate whether the observances of "courtly love" were in fact widely practiced and whether its worship of women was empowering or restrictive: the image of the distant, adored lady implies immobility and even silence on her part. Certainly lyrics and narratives that embody courtly values are widespread, even if they often question what they celebrate; and the ideals of courtliness may have had as great an impact through these imaginative channels as through actual enactment.

The ideas and rituals of courtliness reach back to Greek and Roman models of controlled and stylized behavior in the presence of great power. In the Middle Ages, values of discretion and modesty also may have filtered into the secular world from the rigidly disciplined setting of the monasteries. As the society of western Europe took on a certain degree of order in the eleventh and twelfth centuries, courtly attainments began to converge and even compete with simple martial prowess in the achievement

Grotesques and a Courtly Scene, from the *Ormesby Psalter,* c. 1310–1325.

of worldly power. The presence of large numbers of armed and ambitious men at the great courts provided at once an opportunity for courtly behavior and the threat of its disruption.

Whatever its historical reality, courtly love as a literary concept had an immense influence. In this it adopted the vocabulary of two distinct traditions: the veneration of the Virgin Mary and the love poetry of Ovid and his heirs. Mariolatry, which has a particularly rich tradition in England, celebrates the perfection of Mary as a woman and mother, who undid the sins of Eve and now intercedes for fallen mankind. Ovid, with his celebration of sensuality and cynical instructions for achieving the lover's desire, provided medieval Europe with a whole catalog of love psychology and erotic persuasion.

The self-conscious command of fine manners, whether the proper way of hunting, dressing, addressing a superior, or wooing a lady, became a key mark of an aristocrat. Great reputations grew around courtly attainment, as in the legends that circulated about Richard I. Centuries later, the hero of *Sir Gawain and the Green Knight* is tested as much through his courtly behavior as through his martial bravery. A literature of etiquette emerged as early as the reign of Henry I in England and continued through the thirteenth century. In the court of Henry II, Daniel of Beccles wrote *Urbanus Magnus,* a verse treatise in Latin on courtesy. In this poem he offers detailed advice in many arenas of specific behavior at court: avoiding frivolity, giving brief counsel, and especially comporting oneself among the wealthy:

> Eating at the table of the rich, speak little
> Lest you be called a chatterbox among the diners.
> Be modest, make reverence your companion.

In a mildly misogynist passage, Daniel especially warns against becoming involved with the lord's wife, even if she makes an overture, as occurs in Marie de France's *Lanval.* Should this happen, Daniel offers polite evasive strategies, skills we see demonstrated in *Sir Gawain and the Green Knight.*

A Knight, early 14th century. This rubbing from a funerary brass depicts a knight as he presented himself to eternity, sheathed in chain mail and fully armed but with his hands joined in prayer. The dog at his feet is a symbol of fidelity.

ROMANCE

Courtliness was expressed both in lyric poetry and in a wide range of vernacular narratives that we now loosely call "romances"—referring both to their genre and to the romance language in which they were first written. The Arthurian tradition, featured in this anthology, is only one of many romance traditions; others include the legends of Tristan and Isolde, Alexander, and Havelock the Dane. In romances that focus on courtly love, the hero's devotion to an unapproachable lady tends to elevate his character. Although many courtly romances conclude in a happy and acceptable marriage of hero and heroine, others begin with such a marriage and move to complications (as does Chaucer's *Franklin's Tale*) or warn of the dangers of transgressive love (as does Marie's *Lanval*). To the extent that they portray women as disruptive agents of erotic desire, some romances take on elements of the misogynist tradition that persisted in clerical thought alongside the adoration of the Virgin. Near the end of *Sir Gawain and the Green Knight*, even the courtly Gawain explodes in a virulent diatribe against women.

Love was not the only subject of romance, however. Stories of love and war typically lead the protagonists into encounters with the uncanny, the marvelous, the taboo. This is not so surprising when we recall the practices of medieval Christianity that brought the believer into daily contact with such miracles as the Eucharist; even chronicles of saints' lives regularly showed the divine will breaking miraculously into everyday life. We may say today that romance looses the hero and heroine onto the landscape of the private or social subconscious; a medieval writer might have stressed that nature itself is imbued with mystery both by God and by other, more shadowy, spiritual forces.

In romances, the line between the mundane and the extraordinary is often highly permeable: an episode may move swiftly from a simple ride to a meeting with a magical lady or malevolent dwarf, as often occurs in Thomas Malory. In *The Franklin's Tale*, Chaucer pokes gentle fun at this tendency by having a magician agree to create the illusion of rocks disappearing from the sea, and then bargain with his client over the price of this service. Romance also seems to be a form of imaginative literature in which medieval society could acknowledge the transgressions of its own ordering principles: adultery, incest, unmotivated martial violence. And it often revisits areas of belief and imagination that official culture long had put aside: *Sir Gawain and the Green Knight*, for instance, features a magical knight who can survive having his head cut off and a powerful aged woman who is called a goddess. Both characters reach back, however indirectly, to pre-Christian figures encountered in early Irish and Welsh stories.

THE RETURN OF ENGLISH

The romances are another of the dense points of contact among the many languages and ethnicities of the medieval British Isles. These powerful and evocative narratives often feature figures of Celtic origin like the British King Arthur and his court who came to French- and English-language culture through the Latin *History* of Geoffrey of Monmouth. Such transmission is typical of the linguistic mix in post-Conquest England. The language of the aristocracy was French, used in government and law as well as in the nascent vernacular literature. A few conservative monasteries continued the famed *Anglo-Saxon Chronicle* in its original language after the Conquest. But increasingly English or an evolving form of Anglo-Saxon was the working language of the peasantry. Mixed-language households must have appeared as provincial Anglo-Saxon gentry began, quite quickly, to intermarry with the Normans and their descendants. The twelfth-century satirist Nigel of Canterbury (or "Wireker"), author of the *Mirror of Fools*, came from just such a mixed family.

Few writings in Middle English survive from the late twelfth century, and very little of value besides the extraordinary *Brut* of Layamon, which retranslates much of Geoffrey of Monmouth's *History* from a French version. A manuscript containing the earliest English lyric in this collection, the thirteenth-century *Cuckoo Song*, can suggest the linguistic complexity of the era: it contains lyrics in English and French, and instructions for performance in Latin.

English began to reenter the world of official discourse in the thirteenth century. Communications between the church and the laity took place increasingly in English, and by the late 1250s, Archbishop Sewal of York tended to reject papal candidates for bishoprics if they did not have good English. In 1258 King Henry III issued a proclamation in Latin, French, and English, though the circumstances were unusual. Teaching glossaries included a growing number of English words, as well as the French traditionally used to explain difficult Latin.

The fourteenth century inaugurated a distinct change in the status of English, however, as it became the language of parliament and a growing number of governmental activities. We hear of Latin being taught in the 1340s through English rather than French. In 1362 a statute tried (but failed) to switch the language of law courts from French to English, and in 1363 Parliament was opened in English. The period also witnesses tremendous activity in translating a wide range of works into English, including Chaucer's version of Boethius' *Consolation of Philosophy* and the Wycliffite translations of the Bible, completed by 1396. Finally, at the close of the century, the Rolls of Parliament record in Latin the overthrow of Richard II, but they feature Henry IV (in what was probably a self-consciously symbolic gesture) claiming the throne in a brief, grave speech in English and promising to uphold "the gude lawes and custumes of the Rewme."

The reemergence of English allowed an extraordinary flowering of vernacular literature, most notably the achievements of Chaucer, Langland, and the anonymous genius who wrote *Sir Gawain and the Green Knight*. It would be more accurate, nevertheless, to speak of the reemergence of "Englishes" in the second half of the fourteenth century. The language scholars now call Middle English divides into four quite distinct major dialects in different regions of the island. These dialects were in many ways mutually unintelligible, so that Chaucer, who was from London in the Southeast Midlands, might have been hard-pressed to understand *Sir Gawain and the Green Knight*, written in the West Midlands near Lancashire. (Certainly Chaucer was aware of dialects and mimics some northern vocabulary in his *Canterbury Tales*.) London was the center of government and commerce in this era and later the place of early book printing, which served to stabilize the language. Thus Chaucer's dialect ultimately dominated and developed into modern English. Therefore English-speaking students today can read Chaucer in the original without much difficulty, whereas Langland's *Piers Plowman* is very challenging and *Sir Gawain* may seem virtually a foreign tongue. As a result, the latter two works are offered in translation in this anthology. (For a practical guide to Chaucer's Middle English, also helpful in reading some of the lyrics and plays in this section, see pages 216–18.)

Not only are *Piers Plowman* and *Sir Gawain* written in dialects different from that of Chaucer's London, they also employ a quite distinct poetic style which descends from the alliterative meter of Old English poetry, based on repetitions of key consonants and on general patterns of stress. By contrast, the rhymed syllabic style used by poets like Chaucer developed under the influence of medieval French poetry and its many lyric forms. Fourteenth-century alliterative poetry was part of a revival that occurred in the North and West of the country, at a time when the form would have seemed old fashioned to many readers in the South. In the next two centuries, in a region even more distant from London, alliterative poetry or its echoes persisted in the Middle Scots poetry of William Dunbar, Robert Henryson, and Gavin Douglas.

POLITICS AND SOCIETY IN THE FOURTEENTH CENTURY

The fourteenth-century authors wrote in a time of enormous ferment, culturally and politically as well as linguistically. During the second half of the fourteenth century, new social and theological movements shook past certainties about the divine right of kings, the division of society among three estates, the authority of the church, and the role of women. An optimistic backward view can see in that time the struggle of the peasantry for greater freedom, the growing power of the Commons in Parliament, and the rise of a mercantile middle class. These changes often appeared far darker at the time, though, with threatening, even apocalyptic implications, as can be seen in *Piers Plowman*.

The forces of nature also cast a shadow across the century. In a time that never produced large agricultural surpluses, poor harvests led to famine in the second and third decades of the century, and an accompanying deflation drove people off the land. In 1348 the Black Death arrived in England, killing at least 35 percent of the population by 1350. Plague struck violently three more times before 1375, emptying whole villages. Overall, as much as half the population may have died.

The kingship was already in trouble. After the consolidation of royal power under Henry II and the Angevins in the twelfth century, the regional barons began to reassert their power. In a climactic confrontation in 1215, they forced King John to sign the Magna Carta, guaranteeing (in theory at least) their traditional rights and privileges as well as due process in law and judgment by peers. In the fourteenth century the monarchy came under considerable new pressures. Edward II (1307–1327) was deposed by one of his barons, Roger de Mortimer, and with the connivance of his own queen, Isabella. His son Edward III had a long and initially brilliant reign, marked by great military triumphs in a war against France, but the conflict dragged on so long that it became known as the Hundred Years' War. Edward III's reign was marked at home by famine, deflation, and then, most horribly, plague. His later years were marked by premature senility and control by a court circle. These years were further darkened by the death of that paragon of chivalry, Edward's son and heir-apparent, Edward "The Black Prince." Edward's successor, the Black Prince's son Richard II, launched a major peace initiative in the Hundred Years' War and became a great patron of the arts, but he was also capable of great tyranny. In 1399 like his great-grandfather, he was deposed. An ancient and largely creaky royal bureaucracy had difficulty running a growing mercantile economy, and when royal justice failed to control crime in the provinces, it was increasingly replaced by local powers.

The aristocracy too experienced pressures from the increased economic power of the urban merchants and from the peasants' efforts to exploit labor shortages and win better control over their land. The aristocrats responded with fierce, though only partly successful, efforts to limit wages and with stricter and more articulate divisions within society, even between the peerage and gentry. It is not clear, however, that fourteenth-century aristocrats perceived themselves as a threatened order. If anything, events may have pressed them toward a greater class cohesion, a more self-conscious pursuit of chivalric culture and values. The reign of Edward III saw the foundation of the royal Order of the Garter, a select group of nobles honored for their chivalric accomplishments as much as their power (the order is almost certainly evoked at the close of *Sir Gawain and the Green Knight*). Edward further exploited the Arthurian myth in public rituals such as tournaments and Round Tables. The ancient basis of the feudal tie, land tenure, began to give way to contract and payment in the growing, hierarchicalized retinues of the period. These were still lifelong relationships between lord and retainer, nevertheless, and contemporary historians of aristocratic sympathies like Jean Froissart idealize an ongoing community of chivalric conduct that could reach even across combating nations.

The second estate, the church, was also troubled—in part, paradoxically, because of the growing and active piety of the laity. Encouraged by the annual confession that had been required since the Fourth Lateran Council of 1215, laymen increasingly took control of their own spiritual lives. But the new emphasis on confession also led to clerical corruption. Mendicant (begging) friars, armed with manuals of penance, spread across the countryside to confess penitents in their own homes and sometimes accepted money for absolving them. Whether or not these abuses were truly widespread, they inspired much anticlerical satire—as is reflected in the works of Chaucer and Langland—and the Church's authority diminished in the process. The traditional priesthood, if better educated, was also more worldly than in the past, increasingly pulled from parish service into governmental bureaucracy; it too faced widespread literary satire. Well aware of clerical venality, the church nevertheless fearfully resisted the criticisms and innovations of "reforming clerics" like John Wycliffe and his supporters among the gentry, the "Lollard knights." The church's control over religious experience was further complicated and perhaps undermined by the rise of popular mysticism, among both the clergy and the laity, which was difficult to contain within the traditional ecclesiastical hierarchy. Mystical writing by people as varied as Richard Rolle, Julian of Norwich, the anonymous author of *The Cloud of Unknowing*, and the emotive Margery Kempe all promulgate the notion of an individual's direct experience of the divine. Many of these developments—and the efforts to stop them—appear in the section "Vernacular Religion" (pages 373–78). Finally, and on a much broader scale, all of Christian Europe was rocked by the Great Schism of 1378, when believers faced the disconcerting spectacle of two popes ruling simultaneously.

The third estate, the commoners, was the most problematic and rapidly evolving of the three in the fourteenth century. The traditional division of medieval society into three estates had no place for the rising mercantile bourgeoisie and grouped them with the peasants who worked the land. In fact the new urban wealthy formed a class quite of their own. Patrons and consumers of culture, they also served in the royal bureaucracy under Edward III, as is illustrated by the career of Geoffrey Chaucer who came from just such a background. Yet only the wealthiest married into the landed gentry, and poor health conditions in the cities made long mercantile dynasties uncommon. Cities in anything like a modern sense were few and retained rural features. Houses often had gardens, even orchards, and pigs (and pig dung) filled the narrow, muddy streets. Only magnates built in stone; only they and ecclesiastical institutions had the luxury of space and privacy. Otherwise, cities were crowded and dirty—the suburbs especially disreputable—and venues for communicable disease.

The peasants too had a new sense of class cohesion. Events had already loosened the traditional bond of serfs to the land on which they were born, and the plagues further shifted the relative economic power of landowning and labor. As peasants found they could demand better pay, fiercely repressive laws were passed to stop them. These and other discontents, like the arrival of foreign labor and technologies, led to the Rising of 1381 (also known as the Peasants' Revolt). Led by literate peasants and renegade priests, the rebels attacked aristocrats, foreigners, and some priests. They were swiftly and violently put down, but the event was nevertheless a watershed and haunted the minds of the English.

When one leader of the revolt, the priest John Ball, cited Langland's fictional character Piers Plowman with approval, Langland reacted with dismay and revised his poem to emphasize the proper place of peasants. Even more conservative, Chaucer's friend John Gower wrote a horrified Latin allegory on the revolt, *Vox Clamantis* (*The Voice of One Crying*), where he compared the rebels to beasts. By contrast, Chaucer virtually ignored the revolt, aside from a brief comic reference in *The Nun's Priest's Tale*; it remains unclear, though, whether Chaucer's silence reflects comfortable bourgeois indifference or stems from deep anxiety and discomfort. At the same time, these disruptions introduced a period of cultural ferment, and the mercantile middle class also provided a creative force, appearing (though not without some nervous condescension) in some of Chaucer's most enduring characters like *The Canterbury Tales*' Merchant, the Wife of Bath, and the Miller.

It is both from this new middle class and from the established upper class that wider choices in the lives of women emerged in the later Middle Ages. Their social and political power had been curtailed both by clerical antifeminism and by the increasingly centralized government during the twelfth and thirteenth centuries. Starting in the fourteenth century, however, women began to regain an increased voice and presence. Among the aristocracy, Edward II's wife Isabella was an important player in events that brought about the king's deposition. And at the end of the century, Edward III's mistress Alice Perrers was widely criticized for her avarice and her influence on the aging king (for instance by William Langland who refers to her in the allegorical figure Lady Meed).

Women were also important in the spread of lay literacy among the middle class. In France, Christine de Pizan reexamined whole areas of her culture, especially ancient and biblical narrative, from a feminist perspective; her work was known and translated in England. Important autobiographical works were composed in Middle English by Julian of Norwich and Margery Kempe. Julian was an anchoress, living a cloistered religious life but able to speak to visitors such as Margery herself; Margery was an illiterate but prosperous townswoman, daughter of a mayor, who dictated to scribes her experiences of wifehood and rebellion against it, of travel to holy places, and of spiritual growth. Still, for the representation of women's voices in this period we are largely dependent on the fictional creations of men. Chaucer's famous Wife of Bath, for instance, strikes many modern readers as an articulate voice opposing women's repression and expressing their ambitions, but for all her critique of the antifeminist stereotypes of the church, she is in many ways their supreme embodiment. And in a number of Middle English lyrics, probably by men, the woman's voice may evoke scorn rather than pity as she laments her seduction and abandonment by a smooth-talking man, usually a cleric.

THE SPREAD OF BOOK CULTURE IN THE FIFTEENTH CENTURY

Geoffrey Chaucer died in 1400, a convenient date for those who like their eras to end with round numbers. Certainly literary historians have often closed off the English Middle Ages with Chaucer and left the fifteenth century as a sort of drab and undefined waiting period before the dawn of the Renaissance. Yet parts of fifteenth-century England are sites of vital and burgeoning literary culture. Book ownership spread more and more widely. Already in the late fourteenth century, Chaucer had imagined a fictional Clerk of Oxford with a solid collection of university texts despite his relative poverty. More of the urban bourgeoisie bought books and even had appealing collections assembled for them. When printing came to England in the later fifteenth century, books became even more available, though still not cheap.

Whether in manuscript or print, a swiftly growing proportion of these books was in English. The campaigns of Henry V in the second decade of the fifteenth century and his death in 1422 mark England's last great effort to reclaim the old Norman and Angevin territories on the Continent. With the loss of all but a scrap of this land and the decline of French as a language of influence, these decades consolidate a notion of cultural and nationalistic Englishness. The Lancastrian kings, Henry the Fourth, Fifth, and Sixth, seem to have adopted English as the medium for official culture and patronized translators like Lydgate. Later in the period William Caxton made a great body of French and English texts available to aristocratic and middle-class readers, both by translating and by diffusing them in the new medium of print.

Ancient aristocratic narratives continued to evolve, as in Thomas Malory's retelling of the Arthurian story in his *Morte Darthur*, one of the books printed by Caxton. Malory works mostly from French prose versions but trims back much of the exploration of love and the uncanny; the result is a recharged tale of chivalric battle and familial and political intrigue. Other continental and local traditions are revived in another courtly setting by a group of Scots poets including William Dunbar.

As more and more commoners had educational and financial access to books, they also participated in a lively public literary culture in towns and cities. The fifteenth century sees the flowering of the great dramatic "mystery cycles," sets of plays on religious themes produced and in part performed by craft guilds of larger towns in the Midlands and North. Included here is a brilliant sample, *The Second Play of the Shepherds* from Wakefield. Probably written by clerics, these plays are nonetheless dense with the preoccupations of contemporary working people and enriched by implicit analogies between the lives of their actors and the biblical events they portray. Lyrics and political poems continue to flourish. Sermons remain a popular and widespread form of religious instruction and literary production. And highly literary public rituals, such as Henry V's triumphal civic entries as he returned from his French campaigns, are part of Lancastrian royal propaganda.

By the time Caxton was editing and printing Malory in 1485 with an eye to sales and profit, over eight hundred years had passed since Caedmon is said to have composed his first Christian hymn under angelic direction. The idea of the poet had moved from a version of magician and priest to something more like a modern author; and the dominant model of literary transmission was shifting from listening to an oral performance to reading a book privately. Chaucer, that most bookish of poets, is a case in point. Many of his early poems refer to the pleasures of reading, not only for instruction but even as a mere pastime, often to avoid insomnia. He opens the dream vision *The Parliament of Fowls* with the poet reading a classical Latin text, Cicero's *Dream of Scipio*. Chaucer, of course, read his books and disseminated his own work in handwritten manuscript; in his humorous lyric *To His Scribe Adam* he expresses his frustration with copyists who might mistranscribe his words.

Despite such private bookishness, however, a more public and oral literary culture never disappeared from medieval Britain. Considerable interdependence between oral and literate modes of communication remained; poetry was both silently read and orally performed. In *The Canterbury Tales*, for instance, when the pilgrim Chaucer apologizes for the bawdiness of *The Miller's Tale*, he suggests that if the listener/reader does not like what he *hears*, he should simply turn the *page* and choose another tale. At the same time, literate clerics practiced what we might call learned orality, through lectures or disputations at Oxford and Cambridge or from the pulpit in a more popular setting. Langland imitates such sophisticated oral practice in the theological debates in *Piers Plowman*, and Chaucer uses the sermon form in *The Wife of Bath's Prologue*, *The Pardoner's Tale*, and *The Parson's Tale*. The popular orality of minstrel performance, harking back however distantly to the world of the Anglo-Saxon *scop* and the Irish *fili*, was also exploited with great self-consciousness by literate poets. Langland expresses harsh disapproval of those minstrels who were mere entertainers, undercutting the serious work of preachers. *Sir Gawain and the Green Knight* presents itself as an oral performance, based on a tale that the narrator has heard recited. By contrast, Chaucer gently twits minstrels in his marvelous parody of popular romance, *Sir Thopas*. Chaucer remains a learned poet whose greatest achievement, paradoxically, was the presentation of fictional oral performances—the tale-telling of the Canterbury pilgrims.

The speed with which communication technologies are changing in our own era has heightened our awareness of such changes in the past. We are now closing the era of the book and moving into the era of the endlessly malleable electronic text. In many ways the means by which we have come to receive and transmit information—television, radio, CD-ROM, Internet—mix orality and literacy in a fashion wholly new yet also intriguingly reminiscent of the later Middle Ages. In contrast to the seeming fixity of texts in the intervening centuries, contemporary literary culture may be recovering the sense of textual and cultural fluidity that brought such dynamism to literary creation in the Middle Ages.

BEFORE THE NORMAN CONQUEST

Beowulf

Beowulf has come down to us as if by chance, for it is preserved only in a single manuscript now in the British Library, Cotton Vitellius A.xv, which almost perished in a fire in 1731. An anonymous poem in the West Saxon dialect of Old English, it may stretch back as early as the late eighth century, although recent scholars think the version we now have was composed within one hundred years of its transcription in the late tenth century. If the later date is correct, this first "English epic" could have appealed to one of the Viking kings who ruled in northern and eastern England. This would help explain a king's burial at sea, a Viking practice, that occurs early in the poem (page 32), and the setting of most of the poem's action in Scandinavia (see map, page 28). Although it was studied by a few antiquarians during the early modern period, *Beowulf* remained virtually unknown until its first printing in 1815, and it was only in the twentieth century that it achieved a place in the canon, not just as a cultural artifact or a good adventure story but as a philosophical epic of great complexity and power.

Several features of *Beowulf* make its genre problematic: the vivid accounts of battles with monsters link it to the folktale, and the sense of sorrow for the passing of worldly things mark it as elegiac. Nevertheless, it is generally agreed to be the first postclassical European epic. Like the *Iliad* and the *Odyssey*, it is a primary epic, originating in oral tradition and recounting the legendary wars and exploits of its audience's tribal ancestors from the heroic age.

The values of Germanic tribal society are indeed central to *Beowulf*. The tribal lord was held to ideals of extraordinary martial valor. More practically, he rewarded his successful followers with treasure that symbolized their mutual obligations. A member of the lord's *comitatus*—his band of warriors—was expected to follow a rigid code of heroic behavior stressing bravery, loyalty, and willingness to avenge lord and comrades at any cost. He would suffer the shame of exile if he should survive his lord in battle; the speaker of *The Wanderer* (pages 116–18) may be such a man. Such values are explicitly invoked at the end of *Beowulf*, when Wiglaf, the hero's only loyal retainer, upbraids his comrades for having abandoned Beowulf to the dragon: he says that their prince wasted his war gear on them, and predicts the demise of their people, the Geats, once their ancient enemies, the Swedes, hear that Beowulf is dead.

Beowulf offers an extraordinary double perspective, however. First, for all its acceptance of the values of pagan heroic code, it also refers to Christian concepts that in many cases conflict with them. Although all characters in the poem—Danes, Swedes, and Geats, as well as the monsters— are pagan, the monster Grendel is described as descended from Cain and destined for hell. It is the joyous song of creation at Hrothgar's banquet, reminiscent of Genesis 1, that inspires Grendel to renew his attacks. Furthermore, while violence in the service of revenge is presented as the proper way for Beowulf to respond to inhuman assailants such as Grendel's mother, the narrator expresses a regretful view, perhaps influenced by Christianity, of the unending chain of violence engaged in by feuding tribes. And although the Danish king Hrothgar uses wealth as a kind of social sacrament when he lavishly rewards Beowulf for his military aid, he simultaneously invokes God in a "sermon" warning him against excessive pride in his youthful strength. This rich division of emotional loyalty probably arises from a poet and audience of Christians who look back at their pagan ancestors with both pride and grief, stressing the intersection of pagan and Christian values in an effort to reconcile the two. By restricting his biblical references to events in the Old

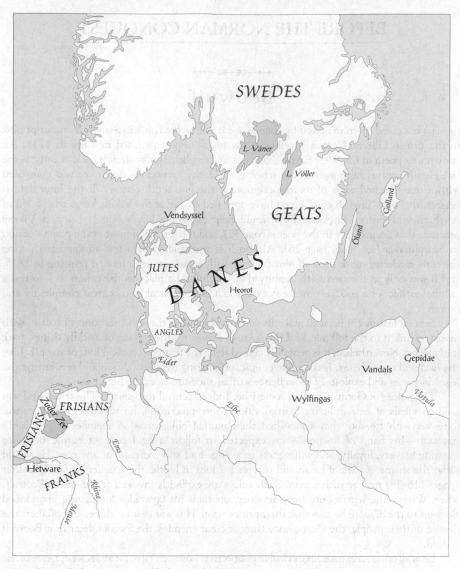

Peoples and places in *Beowulf,* after F. Klaeber.

Testament, the poet shows the Germanic revenge ethic as consistent with the Old Law of retribution, and leaves implicit its conflict with the New Testament injunction to forgive one's enemies.

The style *of Beowulf* is simultaneously a challenge and a reward to the modern reader. Some of its features, such as the variation of an idea in different words—which would have been welcomed by a listening, and often illiterate, audience—can seem repetitious to a literate audience. The poem's somewhat archaic diction can make it seem difficult as well, although the translators of the version included here have adopted a more straightforward and colloquial style than was often used in the past. By rendering the opening word "Hwaet!" as "So!" rather than "Hark!" or "Lo!" they have avoided the stuffiness of earlier versions. They have also tried to reduce the confusion arising from the poem's use of patronymics—phrases identifying a character by his father's name. Though they generally retain the designations of Beowulf as "Ecgtheow's son," they often substitute the name of a minor character for the poem's patronymic, rendering "Ecglaf's son" as "Unferth," for instance.

Two other stylistic features that are indebted to the poem's oral origin are highly admired today. First, like other Old English poems, *Beowulf* uses alliteration as a structural principle, beginning three of the four stressed words in a line with the same letter. The translators have sought the same effect, even when departing considerably from the original language, as when they render the line, "waes se grimma gaest Grendel haten" in the passage below as "a horror from hell, hideous Grendel." The poet also uses compound words, such as *mearcstapa* ("borderland-prowler") and *fifelcynnes* ("of monsterkind"), with unusual inventiveness and force. A specific type of compound used for powerful stylistic effects is the "kenning," a kind of compressed metaphor, such as "swan-road" for "ocean" or "wave-courser" for ship. The kennings resemble the Old English riddles in their teasing, enigmatic quality.

On a larger narrative level is another stylistic feature, also traceable to the poem's oral roots: the tendency to digress into stories tangential to the action of the main plot. The poet's digressions, however, actually contribute to his artistry of broad contrasts—youth and age, joy and sorrow, good and bad kingship. For instance, Hrothgar, while urging humility and generosity on the victorious Beowulf, tells the story of the proud and parsimonious King Heremod. Similarly, when Beowulf returns home in glory to the kingdom of the Geats, the poet praises his uncle Hygelac's young Queen Hygd by contrasting her with the bad Queen Modthryth, who lost her temper and sent her suitors to death.

These episodes also return to prominent themes like nobility, heroic glory, and the distribution of treasure. Such return to key themes, as well as the poem's formulaic repetition and stylistic variation, all bear comparison to insular art of its time. As seen in the page from the *Book of Kells* illustrated on page 10, the dense repetition of lines and intertwined curves, even zoomorphic shapes (often called interlace) competes for attention with the central image of Saint John. This intricately crafted biblical image, like the royal treasure from Sutton Hoo ship burial (Color Plate 2), help remind us that the extraordinary artistic accomplishments of Anglo-Saxon culture went hand-in-hand with its nostalgia for heroic violence.

The poet uses digression and repetition in an especially subtle way to foreshadow dark events to come. To celebrate Beowulf's victory over Grendel, the Scop at Hrothgar's hall sings of events of generations earlier, in which a feud caused the deaths of a Danish princess's brother and son. Although this story has nothing to do with the main plot of the poem, there is an implied parallel a few lines later, when, ominously, Hrothgar's queen Wealtheow hints that her husband's nephew Hrothulf should treat her young sons honorably, remembering the favors Hrothgar has shown him, and soon after, urges Beowulf also to be kind them. The original audience would have known that after Hrothgar's death, his queen will suffer a disaster like that of the princess in the song. The poet thus applies his broad principle of comparison and contrast to complex narrative situations as well as to simpler concepts such as good and bad kings. The often tragic tenor of these digressions contributes to the dark mood that suffuses *Beowulf*, even in its moments of heroic triumph.

The following passage from the original Old English, and the literal translation after it, correspond to lines 89–100 in full translation. It illustrates some of the stylistic features of *Beowulf* discussed above.*

> Swā ðā drihtguman   drēamum lifdon,
> 100   ēadiglīce,   oð ðæt ān ongan
> fyrene fre(m)man   fēond on helle;

*The passage is taken from *Beowulf and the Fight at Finnsburg*, 3d ed., ed. Frederick Klaeber (Boston: D. C. Heath, 1950). The translation is by Anne Schotter.

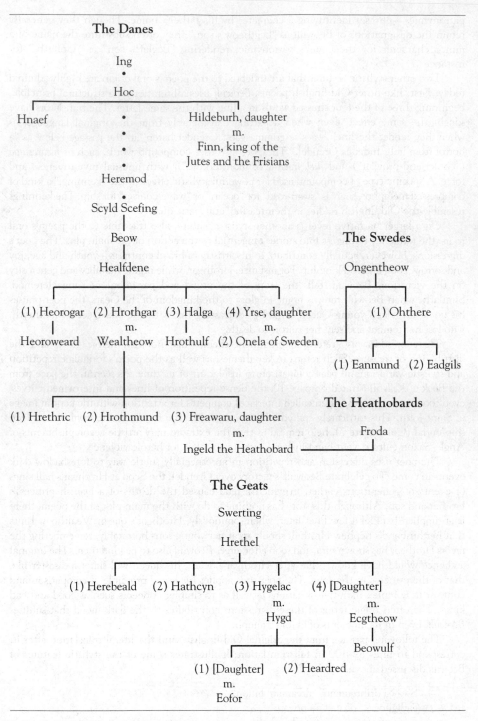

The Danes

Ing

•

Hoc

Hnaef   •   Hildeburh, daughter
                                   •   m.
                                   •   Finn, king of the
                                   •   Jutes and the Frisians

Heremod

•

Scyld Scefing

Beow   **The Swedes**

Healfdene   Ongentheow

(1) Heorogar (2) Hrothgar (3) Halga (4) Yrse, daughter   (1) Ohthere
                    m.   m.
Heoroweard   Wealtheow   Hrothulf (2) Onela of Sweden

                                                   (1) Eanmund (2) Eadgils

                                                  The Heathobards

(1) Hrethric (2) Hrothmund (3) Freawaru, daughter
                                        m.   Froda
                              Ingeld the Heathobard

The Geats

Swerting

Hrethel

(1) Herebeald (2) Hathcyn (3) Hygelac (4) [Daughter]
                                   m.   m.
                                  Hygd   Ecgtheow

                                                     Beowulf

                    (1) [Daughter]   (2) Heardred
                          m.
                        Eofor

Royal genealogies of the Northern European tribes according to the *Beowulf* text.

wæs se grimma gǣst   Grendel hāten,
mǣre mearcstapa, sē þe mōras hēold,
fen ond fæsten; fifelcynnes eard
105   wonsǣeli wer weardode hwile,
siþðan him Scyppend forscrifen haefde
in Cāines cynne— þone cwealm gewraec
ēce Drihten, þaes þe hē Ābel slōg;
ne gefeah hē þǣre fǣðe, ac hē hine feor forwraec,
110   Metod for þȳ māne mancynne fram.

      And so the warriors   lived in joy
100   happily until one began
the commit crimes, a fiend from hell
the grim demon was called Grendel,
notorious borderland-prowler who dwelt in the moors
fen and stronghold; the home of monsterkind
105   this cursed creature occupied for a long while
since the Creator had condemned him
as the kin of Cain— he punished the killing,
the Eternal Lord, because he slew Abel;
He did not rejoice in that evil deed, but He banished him far
110   from mankind, God, in return for the crime.

Beowulf[1]

1. Grendel

So! The Spear Danes in days of old
were led by a lord famed for his forays.
We heard of that prince's power and prowess.
Often Scyld Scefing[2] ambushed enemies,
5   took their mead-benches, mastered their troops,
though first he was found forlorn and alone.[3]
His early sorrows were swiftly consoled:
he grew under heaven, grew to a greatness
renowned among men of neighboring lands,
10   his rule recognized over the whale-road,
Danegeld[4] granted him. That was a good king!

      Afterward God gave him an heir,
a lad in the hall to lighten all hearts.
The Lord had seen how long and sorely
15   Denmark had languished for lack of a leader.
Beow[5] was blessed with boldness and honor;

1. The modern English translation is by Alan Sullivan and Timothy Murphy (2002).
2. The traditional founder of the Danish royal house. His name means "shield" or "protection" of the "sheaf," suggesting an earlier association in Norse mythology with the god of vegetation. The Danes are known afterward as "Scyldings," descendants of Scyld.
3. Scyld Scefing arrives among the Danes as a foundling, a dangerous position in both Norse and Anglo-Saxon cultures. Solitaries and outcasts were generally regarded with suspicion; it is a tribute to Scyld Scefing that he surmounted these obstacles to become the leader and organizer of the Danish people.
4. Gold paid as tribute to the Danes.
5. The manuscript reads "Beowulf" here, the copyist's mind having skipped ahead to the story's protagonist.

throughout the North   his name became known.
A soldierly son   should strive in his youth
to do great deeds,   give generous gifts
20   and defend his father.   Then in old age,
when strife besets him,   his comrades will stand
and his folk follow.   Through fair dealing
a prince shall prosper   in any kingdom.

Still hale on the day   ordained for his journey,
25   Scyld went to dwell   with the World's Warder.
His liegemen bore   his bier to the beach:
so he had willed   while wielding his words
as lord of the land,   beloved by all.
With frost on its fittings,   a lordly longboat
30   rode in the harbor,   ring-bowed and ready.
They propped their prince,   the gold-giver,
in the hollow hull   heaped with treasures,
the famous man   at the foot of the mast.
No ship ever sailed   more splendidly stocked
35   with war-weapons,   arms and armor.
About his breast   the booty was strewn,
keepsakes soon to be   claimed by the sea.
So he was sent   as a child chosen
to drift on the deep.   Now the Danes granted
40   treasures no less   than those they had taken,
and last they hoisted   high overhead
a golden banner   as they gave the great one
back to the Baltic   with heavy hearts
and mournful minds.   No man can say,
45   though clever in council   or strong under sky,
who might have landed   that shipload of loot.

But the son of Scyld   was hailed in the strongholds
after the father   had fared far away,
and he long ruled   the lordly Scyldings.
50   A son was born   unto Beow also:
proud Healfdene,   who held his high seat,
battle-hardened   and bold in old age.
Four offspring   descended from Healfdene,
awake in the world: Heorogar, Hrothgar,
55   kindly Halga;   I have heard that the fourth
was Onela's queen[6]   and slept with the sovereign
of haughty Swedes.
                    Hrothgar was granted
swiftness for battle   and staunchness in strife.[7]

---

6. The daughters of Germanic royal families were married to the heads of opposing tribes in an attempt to cement military alliances. Often, as here, they are not named in the poem.

7. Significantly, Hrothgar is not the first-born of his generation. Leadership of the tribe was customarily conferred by acclamation upon the royal candidate who showed the greatest promise and ability.

Color Plate 1 First page of the Gospel of Matthew, from the *Lindisfarne Gospels*, c. 698. This illustrated gospel book was made on the "holy island" of Lindisfarne off the coast of Northumberland, partly in honor of St. Cuthbert, who had died there 11 years earlier and whose cult was fast developing at the time. The manuscript reflects an extraordinary flowering of artistic production during these years, and the meeting of world cultures that occurred in Northumbrian monastic life: Mediterranean Latin language and imagery, Celtic interlace, and Germanic animal motifs. In the 10th century an Anglo-Saxon translation was added in the margins and between the lines. *(By permission of The British Library, Cott. Nero. D.IV f.27.)*

Color Plate 2 Gold buckle, from the Sutton Hoo ship-burial, c. 625–630. Fragments of a remarkably preserved ship-burial, probably for an Anglo-Saxon king, were discovered among other burial mounds at Sutton Hoo, in Suffolk, England, in 1939. The burial mound contained numerous coins and 41 objects in gold, among them this magnificent buckle. Stylized animal heads (including two dragons in the circle at bottom) invite comparison with the powerful animal imagery in *Beowulf.* Other objects in the ship include two silver spoons inscribed "Saul" and "Paul," signs of the mixing of pagan practices and Christian influences in this era. *(Copyright The British Museum.)*

Color Plate 3 The Ardagh Chalice, c. 9th century. This greatest surviving piece of medieval Celtic metalwork was found near the site of an ancient fort at Ardagh, in County Limerick in the southwest of Ireland. Measuring 9.5 inches across and 7 inches tall, the chalice was probably used for wine on great holidays like Easter, when laypeople took Communion. In the 7th century, the learned Irish monk Adamnan had described the chalice of the Last Supper as a silver cup with two opposite handles. The Ardagh Chalice is very similar. It is made of silver alloy, magnificently decorated with gilt and enamel. Its elaborate interlace decoration uses a wide range of Celtic motifs, including fearsomely toothed animal heads. In a band running around the entire bowl are the names of the 12 apostles, further linking its liturgical role to the Last Supper. *(National Museum of Ireland.)*

Color Plate 4 Map of England, from Matthew Paris's *Historia Major*, mid-13th century. A monk of St. Albans, Matthew Paris wrote a monumental *History of England*, of which two illustrated copies in his own hand survive. Matthew's richly detailed map of England, including counties and major towns, illustrates the geographical knowledge of his day. It further suggests how alert he was to the ethnic divisions that still crossed his island and to the settlements and invasions, both mythic and actual, that had given rise to them. His inscription near the depiction of Hadrian's Wall, for example, informs us that the wall "once divided the English and the Picts." Recalling the claim that the original Britons were Trojan refugees, he writes about Wales (left center): "The people of this region are descended from the followers of Brutus." The story of Arthur's conception may have led Paris to identify Tintagel ("Tintaiol," lower left). Matthew also links geography and racial character, as in his comment on northern Scotland (top center): "A mountainous, woody region producing an uncivilized people." *(By permission of The British Library, Cott. Claud. D.IV f.12v.)*

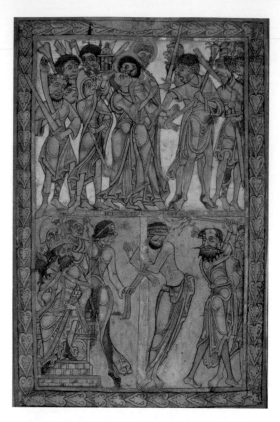

Color Plate 5 *Passion Scenes,* from the *Winchester Psalter,* 1150–1160. A series of full-page miniatures of crucial scenes from the Bible precedes the Psalter texts of this manuscript. The page reproduced here depicts scenes of the betrayal and flagellation of Christ. The vividly drawn images show the clinging drapery and exaggerated expressions typical of the manuscript; equally exaggerated are the African and Semitic features of some of the tormentors, associating them with peoples who were exotic or reviled in 12th-century England. Some of the original richness of color of this manuscript has been lost through damp, but also because blue pigment has been scraped off, presumably for reuse—a sign of how costly was the making of such manuscripts. *(By permission of The British Library, Cott. Nero. C.IV f.21.)*

Color Plate 6 *King Arthur and His Knights,* from a manuscript of the *Prose Lancelot,* late 13th century. This miniature appears in a manuscript of French prose Arthurian romances, which were also widely known in England. Here, King Arthur asks his knights to tell about their adventures on the quest for the Holy Grail. *(Beinecke Rare Book and Manuscript Library, Yale University.)*

Color Plate 7 *Annunciation to the Shepherds* (top) and *Nativity Scene* (bottom), from *The Holkham Bible Picture Book*, c. 1325–1330. This vividly illustrated manuscript depicts episodes from the Bible, adding events from later Christian legends. Crowded scenes are vigorous and full of gesture; they may reflect contact with liturgical drama and look forward to vernacular enactments such as the *Second Play of the Shepherds*. Short rhyming narratives above each picture mix up the major languages of early 14th-century England. At first the shepherds cannot understand the angel's Latin *"Gloria in excelsis"*; in Anglo-French they say "Glum? Glo? That means nothing. Let's go there, we'll understand better." At the scene of the Nativity, below, Middle English breaks in and "Songen alle with one stevene [voice]," though the shepherds can now sing famous Latin hymns: *"Gloria in excelsis deo"* and *"Te deum laudamus."* Both the images and French and Middle English text mediate between the learned clerical class and the wealthy lay people who were the manuscript's intended audience. *(By permission of The British Library, Add. 18850 f.257v.)*

Color Plate 8 *Richard II with His Regalia*, 1394–1395. Richard himself commissioned this splendid life-size and unusually lifelike portrait soon after the death of his beloved first wife, Anne of Bohemia. It was probably mounted at the back of the King's private pew at Westminster Abbey in London, but it also may suggest his wish to be perpetually near Anne, who was entombed nearby. At the same time, the throne, crown, orb, and scepter are all signs of Richard's sense of kingship and secular authority. *(Copyright: Dean and Chapter of Westminster.)*

Color Plate 9 Opening page of *The Wife of Bath's Tale,* from the Ellesmere manuscript of Chaucer's *Canterbury Tales,* 1405–1410. One of the two earliest surviving manuscripts of the *Tales,* it was owned for centuries by the Egerton family, who became Earls of Ellesmere in the nineteenth century. The Ellesmere Chaucer was probably made in London, by then the center of book production in England. Its elaborate decoration and illustration are all the more striking, given how few Middle English texts received such treatment. The portrait of the Wife of Bath is positioned to highlight the beginning of her tale. Her red clothing, whip, and large hat follow details of her description in the *General Prologue* of the *Tales,* and her own words in the prologue to her tale. The grandeur of the treatment of text and decoration in this manuscript—clearly meant both for display and reading—reflect the speed with which Chaucer became a "canonical" author in the years after his death in 1400, and perhaps the wish of wealthy patrons to associate themselves and their interests with his work. It is partly the same wish that ultimately led the American railroad tycoon Henry E. Huntington to buy the manuscript in 1917 and leave it to his library in San Marino, California. *(This item is reproduced by permission of The Huntington Library, San Marina, California. EL26C9F72r.)*

Color Plate 10 *Anne, Duchess of Bedford, Kneeling Before the Virgin Mary and Saint Anne*, from the *Bedford Hours*, early 15th century. A book of hours was a prayerbook used by laypeople for private devotion. The *Bedford Hours* was produced in a Paris workshop for the Duke of Bedford, a brother of Henry V, and his wife, Anne of Burgundy. Here, Saint Anne is shown teaching her daughter, the Virgin Mary, to read; another book lies open on a lectern in front of the kneeling Anne of Burgundy. *(By permission of The British Library, Add. 18850 f.257v.)*

Friends and kinfolk   followed him freely;
60   his band of young soldiers   swelled to a swarm.
In his mind he mulled   commanding a meadhall
higher than humankind   ever had heard of,
and offering everyone,   young and old,
all he could give   that God had granted,
65   save common land   and the commoners' lives.
Then, I am told,   he tackled that task,
raising the rafters   with craftsmen summoned
from many kingdoms   across Middle-Earth.
They covered it quickly   as men count the time,
70   and Hrothgar whose word   held the land whole
named it Heorot,[8]   highest of houses.
The prince did not fail   to fulfill his pledge:
feasts were given,   favor and fortune.
The roof reared up;   the gables were great,
75   awaiting the flames   which would flare fiercely
when oaths were broken,   anger awakened;
but Heorot's ruin   was not yet at hand.[9]

Each day, one evil   dweller in darkness
spitefully suffered   the din from that hall
80   where Hrothgar's men   made merry with mead.
Harp-strings would sound,   and the song of the scop
would recount the tales   told of time past:
whence mankind had come,   and how the Almighty
had fashioned the world   with its fair fields
85   set in wide waters,   with sun and moon
lifted on high   and lighting the lands
for Earth's first dwellers,   with forests everywhere
branching and blooming,   with life breathing
in all kinds of creatures.
                              So the king's thanes
90   gathered in gladness;   then crime came calling,
a horror from hell,   hideous Grendel,
wrathful rover   of borders and moors,
holder of hollows,   haunter of fens.
He had lived long   in the land of the loathsome,
95   born to the band   whom God had banished
as kindred of Cain,   thereby requiting
the slayer of Abel.[1]   Many such sprang
from the first murderer: monsters and misfits,
elves and ill-spirits,   also those giants
100   whose wars with the Lord   earned them exile.

---

8. The name of Hrothgar's hall in Anglo-Saxon literally means "hart" or "stag," a male deer. The epithet "adorned with horns," which is applied to Heorot later, may further suggest its function as a hunting lodge.
9. The peace concluded between the Danes and the

Heathobards through intermarriage is already doomed before it has taken place. The events foreshadowed here will occur long after the time of the poem.
1. See Genesis 4.3–16.

After nightfall   he nosed around Heorot,
saw how swordsmen   slept in the hall,
unwary and weary   with wine and feasting,
numb to the sorrows   suffered by men.
105   The cursed creature,   cruel and remorseless,
swiftly slipped in.   He seized thirty thanes
asleep on their couches,   carried away
what trophies he would,   and took to his lair
pleased with the plunder,   proud of his murders.

110   When daylight dawned   on the spoils of slaughter,
the strength of the fiend   was readily seen.
The feast was followed   by fits of weeping,
and cries of outrage   rose in the morning.
Hrothgar the strong   sank on his throne,
115   helpless and hopeless   beholding the carnage.
This foe was too fierce,   too steadfast in rage,
ancient and evil.   After one evening
he murdered again   with no more remorse,
so fixed was his will   on that wicked feud.
120   Henceforth the fearful   were easily found
elsewhere, anywhere   far from the fiend,
bedding in barns,   for the brutal hall-thane
was truly betokened   by terrible signs,
and those who escaped   stayed safer afar.

125   So wrath fought alone   against rule and right;
one routed many;   the mead-hall stood empty.
Strongest of Spear-Danes,   Hrothgar suffered
this fell affliction   for twelve winters' time.
As his woes became known   widely and well,
130   sad songs were sung   by the sons of men:
how season on season,   with ceaseless strife,
Grendel assailed   the Scylding's sovereign.
The monster craved   no kinship with any,
no end to the evil   with wergeld[2] owed;
135   nor might a king's   council have reckoned
on quittance come   from the killer's hand.
The dark death-shadow   daunted them all,
lying in ambush   for old and young,
secretly slinking   and stalking by night.
140   No man knows where   on the misty moor
the heathen keepers   of hell-runes[3] wander.

2. A cash payment for someone's death. *Wergeld* was regarded as an advance over violent revenge, and Grendel is marked as uncivilized because he refuses to acknowledge this practice.
3. By rendering the Old English *helrunan*, which means "those adept in the mysteries of hell," as "heathen keepers of hell-runes," the translators are taking the liberty of suggesting that "demons" such as Grendel are familiar with runes—the letters of the early Germanic alphabet.

So over and over   the loathsome ogre
mortally menaced   mankind with his crimes.
Raising by night,   he reigned in the hall,
145 and Heorot's high   adornments were his,
but God would not grant   throne-gifts to gladden
a scourge who spurned   the Sovereign of Heaven.

Stricken in spirit,   Hrothgar would often
closet his council   to ponder what plan
150 might be deemed best   by strong-minded men.
Sometimes the elders   swore before altars
of old war-idols,   offering prayers
for the soul-slayer   to succor their people.[4]
Such was their habit,   the hope of heathens:
155 with hell in their hearts,   they were lost to the Lord.
They never would know   the Almighty's mind
or worship the world's   one true protector.
Sorry are those   who sear their souls,
afflicted by flames   they freely embraced.
160 No cheer for the chastened!   No change for the better!
But happy is he   who trusts in heaven
and lives to his last   in the Lord's keeping.

So in his sorrow   the son of Healfdene[5]
endlessly weighed   how a wise warrior
165 might fend off harm.   The hardship this foe
of his folk inflicted   was fierce and long-lasting,
most ruinous wrath   and wracking night-evil.

A thane[6] of Hygelac   heard in his homeland
of Grendel's deeds.   Great among Geats,[7]
170 this man was more mighty   than any then living.
He summoned and stocked   a swift wave-courser,
and swore to sail   over the swan-road
as one warrior should   for another in need.
His elders could find   no fault with his offer,
175 and awed by the omens,   they urged him on.
He gathered the bravest   of Geatish guardsmen
and strode to his ship   with those skilled sailors
as first of fifteen   whom he led from that land.

He was keen to embark: his keel was beached
180 under the cliff   where sea-currents curled
surf against sand;   his soldiers were ready.
Over the longboat's   bow they boarded,

---

4. In their fear, the Danes resume heathen practices. In Christian belief, the pagan gods were transformed into devils.
5. Hrothgar. He is referred to by his patronymic, his father's name, as is frequent with male characters in the poem.

6. One of the king's principal retainers, chief among these being the earls.
7. A Germanic tribe who lived along the southwestern coast of what is now Sweden.

bearing below   their burnished weapons
and gilded gear   to hoard in the hull.
185   Other men shoved   the ship from the shore,
and off went the band,   their well-braced vessel
bound for the venture   with wind on the waves
and foam under bow,   like a fulmar in flight.[8]

On the second day   their upswept prow
190   slid into sight   of a steep-sided coast,
the goal of their voyage,   gained in good time.
Sea-cliffs and stacks   shone before them,
flat-topped capes   at the close of their crossing.
Swiftly the sailors   steered for the shore,
195   moored their boat   and debarked on the berm.
Clad in corselets   of clattering mail,
they saluted the Lord   for their smooth sailing.

From the post he held   high on the headland,
a Scylding had spied   the strangers bearing
200   bright bucklers   and battle-armor
over their gangplank.   Avid for answers
and minded to know   what men had come hence,
Hrothgar's thane   hastened on horseback
down to the beach   where he brusquely brandished
205   spear-haft in hand   while speaking stern words:

"What warriors are you,   wearers of armor,
bearers of byrnies,   daring to bring
your lofty longboat   over the sea-lane?
Long have I looked   out on the ocean
210   so foreign foes   might never float hither
and harry our homeland   with hostile fleets.
No men have ever   more brazenly borne
shields to our shores,   nor have you sought
leave from our lords   to land in this place,
215   nor could you have known   my kin would consent.
I have never beheld   an earl on this earth
more mighty in arms   than one among you.
This is no hall-warmer,   handsome in harness,
showy with shield,   but the noblest of knights
220   unless looks belie him.   Now let me know
who are your fathers   before you fare further
or spy on the Danes.   I say to you, sailors
far from your homes: hear me and hasten
to answer me well.   Whence have you wandered?
225   Why have you come?"
                    Wisest with words,

8. Gull-like sea bird of the far north Atlantic.

the eldest offered   an answer for all:
"From Geat-land we come;   we are Geatish men,
sharers of Hygelac's   hearth and hall.
My father was famous   among our folk
230   as a lordly leader   who lived many winters
before, full of years,   he departed our fastness.
His name was Ecgtheow.   All over Earth
every wise man   remembers him well.
We have landed in friendship   to look for your lord,
235   the son of Healfdene,   sovereign of Scyldings.
Give us good guidance: a great errand
has driven us hence   to the holder of Danes.
Our purpose is open;   this I promise;
but you could attest   if tales tell the truth.
240   They speak of some scourge,   none can say what,
secretly stalking   by night among Scyldings,
the shadowy shape   of his malice to men
shown by a shameful   shower of corpses.
I offer Hrothgar,   with honest heart,
245   the means to make   an end to this menace.
Wise and good,   he will win his reward
if ever such awful   evil is vanquished.
So his sorrows   shall swiftly be soothed
or else his anguish   haunt him, unaltered,
250   as long as his house   holds on the hilltop."

Astride his steed,   the guard spoke again:
"A sharp-witted warrior   often must weigh
words against works   when judging their worth.
This I have learned: you honor our lord.
255   Thus you may come,   though clad in corselets
and weaponed for war.   I shall show you the way.
Meanwhile those thanes   who are mine to command
shall stand by the ship   you steered to our shore.
No looter will trouble   your newly-tarred craft
260   before you return   and take to the tide.
A swan-necked bow   will bear you back
to your windward coast.   Most welcome of men,
may you be granted   good fortune in battle,
enduring unharmed   the deed you would do."
265   So they set out   while the ship sat at rest,
the broad-beamed longboat   bound to the beach,
lashed by its lines.   Lustrous boar-icons
glinted on head-guards.   Adorned with gold,
the flame-hardened helms   defended their lives.
270   Glad of their mettle   while marching together,
the troop hastened   until they beheld
the highest of halls   raised under heaven,
most famed among folk   in foreign lands.

Boar, from a bas-relief carving on Saint Nicholas Church, Ipswich, England. Although this large and vigorous boar dates from the 12th century, it retains stylistic elements of earlier Anglo-Saxon and Viking art. An ancient totem of power, boars were often depicted on early medieval weapons and helmets.

Sheathed with gold   and grandly gabled,
275   the roof of the ruler   lit up his realm.
The foremost warrior   waved them forward
and bade the band   go straight to that building,
court of the king   and his brave kinsmen.
Reining his steed,   he spoke a last word:
280   "It is time I returned.   May All-Ruling Father
favor your errand.   I ride for the ocean
to watch and ward off   troops of intruders."

A stone-paved street   steered the men hence.
They strode on together,   garbed in glinting
285   jackets of chain-mail   whose jingling rings,
hard and hand-linked,   sang on harnesses
borne toward the hall   by that battle-armed band.
Still sea-weary,   they set down their shields
of well-seasoned wood   against Heorot's wall.
290   Their byrnies clanged   as they bent to a bench
and stood their sturdy   spears in a row,
gray from the ash grove,   ground to sharp points.
This was a war party   worthy of weapons.

Then a proud prince   questioned their purpose:
295   "Where are you bringing   these burnished bosses,
these gray mail-shirts,   grimly-masked helms
and serried spears?   I am Hrothgar's
herald and door-ward.   I have never beheld
a band of wanderers   with bearings so brave.

300 I believe that boldness   has brought you to Hrothgar,
     not banishment's shame."
                         The eldest answered,
     hard and hardy   under his helmet,
     a warlike prince   of the Weder[9] people:
     "We are Hygelac's   hearth-companions.
305 My name is Beowulf;   my purpose, to bear
     unto Healfdene's son,   your lordly leader,
     a message meant   for that noblest of men,
     if he will allow us   leave to approach."

     Wise Wulfgar,   man of the Wendels,
310 known to many   for boldness in battle,
     stoutly spoke out: "I shall ask our sovereign,
     well-wisher of Danes   and awarder of wealth,
     about this boon   you have come to request
     and bear you back,   as soon as may be,
315 whatever answer   the great man offers."

     He went straightaway   where Hrothgar waited,
     old and gray-bearded,   with earls gathered round.
     Squarely he stood   for his king to assess him.
     Such was the Scylding   custom at court,
320 and so Wulfgar spoke   to his sovereign and friend:
     "Far-sailing Geats   have come to our kingdom
     across the wide water.   These warriors call
     their leader *Beowulf*   and bid me bring
     their plea to our prince,   if it pleases him
325 to allow them entrance   and offer them audience.
     I hope you will hear them,   hear and be glad,
     for I deem them worthy   of wearing their armor
     and treating with earls.   Truly the elder
     who led them hither   is a lord of some stature."

330 Helm of the Scyldings,   Hrothgar held forth:
     "I knew him once.   He was only a lad.
     His honored father,   old Ecgtheow,
     was dowered the daughter   of Hrethel the Geat.
     His son now seeks us   solely from friendship.
335 Often seafarers,   fond of that people,
     have praised his strength   after sailing hence
     with gifts for the Geats.   They claimed his hand-grip
     would match the might   of thirty strong men.
     The West Danes[1] have long   awaited God's grace.
340 Here is our hope   against Grendel's dread,
     if I reckon rightly   the cause of his coming.

---

9. An alternate name for Geat.
1. Hrothgar is, in fact, king of all the Danes: North, South, East, and West. The different terms merely conform to the Anglo-Saxon alliterative pattern established in each line.

I shall give this brave man   boons for boldness.
Bring him in quickly.   The band of my kinsmen
is gathered together.   Welcome our guest
345   to the dwelling of Danes."
                                        Then Wulfgar went
through the hall's entry   with word from within:
"I am ordered to answer   that the lord of East Danes
honors your father   and offers you welcome,
sailors who sought us   over the sea-waves,
350   bravely bent   on embarking hither.
Now you may march   in your mail and masks
to behold Hrothgar.   Here you must leave
war-shields and spears   sharpened for strife.
Your weapons can wait   for words to be spoken."

355   The mighty one rose   with many a man
marshaled about him,   though some were bidden
to stay with the weapons   and stand on watch.
Under Heorot's roof   the rest hastened
when Beowulf brought them   boldly before
360   the hearth of Hrothgar.   Helmed and hardy,
the war-chief shone   as he stood in skillfully
smithed chain-mail   and spoke to his host:

"Hail to you, Hrothgar!   I am Hygelac's
kinsman and comrade,   esteemed by the king
365   for deeds I have done   in the years of youth.
I heard in my homeland   how Grendel grieves you.
Seafarers say   that your splendid hall
stands idle and useless   after the sun
sinks each evening   from Heaven's height.
370   The most honored among us,   earls and elders,
have urged me to seek you,   certain my strength
would serve in your struggle.   They have seen me return
bloody from binding   five brutish giants,
a family of foes   destroyed in our strife;
375   and under the surf   I have slain sea-monsters,
nightmarish nixies[2]   noxious to Geats.
Hardship I had,   but our harms were avenged,
our enemies mastered.   Now I shall match
my grip against Grendel's   and get you an end
380   to this feud with the fiend.   Therefore one favor
I ask from you, Hrothgar,   sovereign of Spear-Danes,
shelter of shield-bearers,   friend to your folk:
that I and my officers,   we and no others,
be offered the honor   of purging your hall.
385   I have also heard   that the rash thing reckons

2. Fabulous sea creatures, probably walruses.

the thrust of a weapon   no threat to his thews.[3]
Thus I foreswear   my sword and strong shield.
Instead I shall grab   and grapple with Grendel,
fighting for life   with that fearsome foe.
390 Whomever death takes,   his doom is doubtless
decreed by the Lord.   If I let the creature
best me when battle   begins in this building,
he will freely feast   as he often has fed
on men of much mettle.   My corpse will require
395 no covering cloth.   He will carry away
a crushed carcass   clotted with gore,
the fiend's fodder   gleefully eaten,
smearing his lonesome   lair on the moor.
No need to worry   who buries my body
400 if battle takes me.   Send back to my sovereign
this best of shirts   which has shielded my breast,
this choice chain-mail,   Hrethel's heirloom
and Weland's work.[4]   Fate goes as it will."

Helm of the Scyldings,   Hrothgar answered:
405 "It is fair that you seek   to defend us, my friend,
in return for the favor   offered your father
when a killing fanned   the fiercest of feuds
after he felled   the Wylfing, Heatholaf.
Wary of war,   the Weder-Geats wanted
410 Ecgtheow elsewhere,   so over the sea-swells
he sought the South Danes,   strong Scyldings.
I had lately become   king of my kinsmen,
a youth ruling   this jewel of a realm,
this store-house of heroes.   Heorogar was dead,
415 my brother and better,   born of Healfdene.
I calmed your father's   quarrel with wergeld
sent over sea   straight to the Wylfings,
an ancient heirloom;   and Ecgtheow's oath
I took in return.
            "It pains me to tell
420 what grief Grendel   has given me since,
what harm in Heorot,   hatred and shame
at his sudden onset.   My circle is shrunken;
my guardsmen are gone,   gathered by fate
into Grendel's grip.   How simply the Sovereign
425 of Heaven could hinder   deeds of this hell-fiend!
Beer-swollen boasters,   brave in their ale-cups,
often have sworn   to stay with their swords
drawn in the dark,   to strike down the demon.
Then in the morning   the mead-hall was drenched,
430 blood on the bench-boards,   blood on the floor,

---

3. Well-developed sinew or muscle.   4. Legendary blacksmith of the Norse gods.

the highest of houses   a horror at dawn.
Fewer were left   to keep faith with their lord
since those dear retainers   were taken by death.
But sit now to sup   and afterward speak
435   of soldierly pride,   if the spirit prompts you."

A bench was cleared,   there in the beer-hall
So all of the Geats   could gather together,
sturdy soldiers,   proud and stout-hearted.
Dutiful Danes   brought them bright ale-cups
440   and poured sweet mead   while the scop was singing
high-voiced in Heorot.   That host of warriors,
Weders and Scyldings,   shared in the wassails.

But envious Unferth,[5]   offspring of Ecglaf,
spat out his spite   from the seat he took
445   at his sovereign's feet.   The seafarer's quest
grieved him greatly,   for he would not grant
any man ever,   in all middle-earth,
more fame under heaven   than he himself had.

"Are you that Beowulf   Breca bested
450   when both of you bet   on swimming the straits,
daring the deep   in a dire struggle,
risking your lives   after rash boasting?
Though friend or foe,   no man could deflect
your foolhardy foray.   Arms flailing,
455   you each embraced   the billowing stream,
spanned the sea-lane   with swift-dipping hands
and wended over   the warring ocean.
Winter-like waves   were roiling the waters
as the two of you toiled   in the tumult of combers.
460   For seven nights   you strove to outswim him,
but he was the stronger   and saw at sunrise
the sea had swept him   to Heathoraeme[6] shores.
Breca went back   to his own homeland,
his burg on the bluff,   stronghold of Brondings,
465   fair folk and wealthy.   The wager was won;
Beanstan's son   had brought off his boast.
However you fared   in onslaughts elsewhere,
I doubt you will live   the length of a night
if you dare to linger   so near Grendel."

470   Then Beowulf spoke,   son of Ecgtheow:
"Listen, Unferth,   my fuddled friend
brimful of beer,   you blabber too much
about Breca's venture.   I tell you the truth:

---

5. Hrothgar's spokesman or court jester; his rude behavior
toward Beowulf is consistent with other figures in epics
and romances who taunt the hero before he undertakes
his exploits. "Unferth" may mean "strife."
6. Coastal tribe of central Sweden near the Norwegian
border.

my force in the flood   is more than a match
475   for any man   who wrestles the waves.
Boys that we were,   brash in our youth
and reckless of risk,   both of us boasted
that each one could swim   the open ocean.
So we set forth,   stroking together
480   sturdily seaward   with swords drawn
hard in our hands   to ward off whale-fish.
No swifter was he   in those heaving seas;
each of us kept   close to the other,
floating together   those first five nights.
485   Then the storm-surges   swept us apart:
winter-cold weather   and warring winds
drove from the north   in deepening darkness.
Rough waves rose   and sea-beasts raged,
but my breast was wound   in a woven mail-shirt.
490   Hard and hand-linked,   hemmed with gold,
it kept those creatures   from causing me harm.
I was drawn to the depths,   held fast by the foe,
grim in his grasp;   yet granted a stab,
I stuck in my sword-point,   struck down the horror.
495   The mighty sea-monster   met his unmaker.

"Often afterward   snatchers of swimmers
snapped at my heels.   With my strong sword
I served them fitly.   I would fatten no foes,
feed no man-banes   munching their morsels
500   when setting to feast   on the floor of the sea.
Instead at sunrise   the sword-stricken
washed up in windrows   to lie lifelessly,
lodged by the tide-line,   and nevermore trouble
sailors crossing   the steep-cliffed straits.
505   As God's beacon   brightened the East,
I spied a cape   across calming seas,
a wall to windward.   So I was spared,
for fate often favors   an unmarked man
if he keeps his courage.   My sword was the slayer
510   of nine nixies.   I have not heard of many
who fought a more fearsome   assault in the night
while hurled by the waves   under heaven's vault.
Yet I broke the beasts' grip   and got off alive,
weary of warfare.   Swiftly surging
515   after the storm,   the sea-current swept me
to Finland's coast.   "Such close combat
or stark sword-strokes   you have not seen,
you or Breca.   No yarn has boasted
how either of you two   ever attempted
520   so bold a deed   done with bright sword,
though I would not bruit   a brother's bane

if the killing of kin   were all I accomplished.
For that you are certain   to suffer in Hell,
doomed with the damned   despite your swift wit.
525   I say straight out,   son of Ecglaf,
that ghastly Grendel,   however gruesome,
would never have done   such dreadful deeds,
harming your lord   here in his hall,
if your spirit were stern,   your will, warlike,
530   as you have affirmed.   The foe has found
that he need not reckon   with wrathful swords
or look with alarm   on the likes of you,
Scylding victor.   He takes his tribute,
sparing no man,   snatching and supping
535   whenever he wishes   with wicked delight,
expecting no strife   with spear-bearing Danes.
But soon, very soon,   I shall show him the strength
and boldness of Geats   giving him battle.
When morning comes   to light up the land,
540   you may go again   and gladly get mead
as the bright sun   beams in the South
and starts a new day   for the sons of men."

Gray-haired Hrothgar,   giver of hoard-wealth,
was happy to hear   Beowulf bolster
545   hope for his folk   with forthright avowal.
About the Bright Danes'   battle-leader
rang warriors' laughter   and winsome words.
The queen, Wealtheow,[7]   courtly by custom,
greeted the party   aglitter with gold
550   and bore the full cup   first to her lord,
the keeper of East Danes,   dear to his people,
bidding him drink   and be glad of his beer.
That soldierly sovereign   quaffed and supped
while his Helming princess   passed through the hall
555   offering everyone,   young man and old,
the dole he was due.   Adorned with rings,
she bore the burnished   mead-bowl to Beowulf,
last of them all,   and honored the Geat
with gracious words,   firm in her wisdom
560   and grateful to God   for granting her wish.
Here was the prayed-for   prince who would help
to end the ill deeds.   He emptied the cup
Wealtheow offered;   then the willing warrior,
Ecgtheow's son,   spoke as one ready
565   for strife and slaughter:

---

7. "Weal theow" means "foreign slave," and she may be British or Celtic in origin. Even after her marriage to Hrothgar, she continues to maintain her identity as the "lady of the Helmings," an epithet recalling her father Helm.

               "When I set my ship
to sail on the sea   and hunched in her hull
with my squadron of swords,   I swore to fulfill
the will of the Scyldings   or die in the deed,
fall with the slain,   held fast by the foe,
570   my last day lived out   here in your hall."

The wife was well-pleased   with Beowulf's words,
this oath from the Geat;   and glinting with gold
the queen, Wealtheow,   went to her king.
Boasts were bandied   once more in the beer-hall,
575   the hearty words   of a hopeful household,
a forceful folk.   But soon the sovereign,
son of Healfdene,   hankered for sleep.
He knew the brute   brooded on bloodshed
all day from dawn   until deepening dusk.
580   Covered by darkness,   the creature would creep,
a shade among shadows;   so everyone stood
as Hrothgar saluted   his hardy house-guard
and wished him well   watching the wine-hall:

"So long as my hand   has hefted a shield,
585   I never have yielded   the Danes' mansion
to any man else,   whatever his mettle.
Now you shall hold   this highest of houses.
Be mindful of fame;   make your might known;
but beware of the brute.   You will lack no boon
590   if you tackle this task   and live to request it."

Hrothgar and his princes   departed the hall;
the warder of Danes   went to his woman,
couched with his queen.   The King of Glory
had granted a guard   against Grendel's wrath,
595   as all had now learned.   One man had offered
to take on this task   and watch for the terror.
The gallant Geat   trusted in God
to buttress his boldness.   He stripped off his byrnie,
then handed his helmet   and inlaid sword
600   to the squire assigned   safe-keeping of iron
and gilded war-gear.   Again the bold
Beowulf boasted   while bound for his bed:

"I am no weaker   in works of war,
no less a grappler   than Grendel himself.
605   Soon I shall sink him   into his death-sleep,
not with my sword   but solely by strength.
He is unschooled in skills   to strike against me,
to shatter my shield,   though feared for his fierceness.
So I shall bear   no blade in the night
610   if he sees fit   to fight without weapons.
May God in His wisdom   grant whom He wills

blessing in battle."
                  The brave soldier
settled in bed,   and a bolster pillowed
his proud cheekbone.   About him were stretched
615   the strong sea-warriors,   each one wondering
whether he ever   would walk once again
his beloved land,   or find his own folk
from childhood's time   in an untroubled town.
All had been told   how often before
620   dreadful death   had swept up the Danes
who lay in this hall.   But the Lord lent them
aid in their anguish,   weaving their war-luck,
for one man alone   had the might and main
to fight off the fiend,   crush him in combat,
625   proving who ruled   the races of men,
then and forever: God, the Almighty.[8]

Cunningly creeping,   a spectral stalker
slinked through the night.   The spearmen were sleeping
who ought to have held   the high-horned house,
630   all except one,   for the Lord's will
now became known: no more would the murderer
drag under darkness   whomever he wished.
Wrath was wakeful,   watching in hatred;
hot-hearted Beowulf   was bent upon battle.

635   Then from the moor   under misty hillsides,
Grendel came gliding,   girt with God's anger.
The man-scather sought   someone to snatch
from the high hall.   He crept under cloud
until he caught sight   of the king's court
640   whose gilded gables   he knew at a glance.
He often had haunted   Hrothgar's house;
but he never found,   before or after,
hardier hall-thanes   or harder luck.
The joyless giant   drew near the door,
645   which swiftly swung back   the touch of his hand
though bound and fastened   with forge-bent bars.
The building's mouth   had been broken open,
and Grendel entered   with ill intent.
Swollen with fury,   he stalked over flagstones
650   and looked round the manse   where many men lay.
An unlovely light   most like a flame
flashed from his eyes,   flared through the hall
at young soldiers dozing   shoulder to shoulder,
comradely kindred.   The cruel creature laughed

---

8. This interpolation of Christian belief into what is essentially a pagan tradition has been taken as evidence of a conscious rewriting of much earlier material. The narrative assures its reader that Christian beliefs were still valid, regardless of what the characters in the story may have believed.

655 in his murderous mind, thinking how many
now living would die before the day dawned,
how glutted with gore he would guzzle his fill.
It was not his fate to finish the feast
he foresaw that night.
                              Soon the Stalwart,
660 Hygelac's kinsman, beheld how the horror,
not one to be idle, went about evil.
For his first feat he suddenly seized
a sleeping soldier, slashed at the flesh,
bit through bones and lapped up the blood
665 that gushed from veins as he gorged on gobbets.
Swiftly he swallowed those lifeless limbs,
hands and feet whole; then he headed forward
with open palm to plunder the prone.
One man angled up on his elbow:
670 the fiend soon found he was facing a foe
whose hand-grip was harder than any other
he ever had met in all Middle-Earth.
Cravenly cringing, coward at heart,
he longed for a swift escape to his lair,
675 his bevy of devils. He never had known
from his earliest days such awful anguish.

The captain, recalling his speech to the king,
straightaway stood and hardened his hold.
Fingers fractured. The fiend spun round;
680 the soldier stepped closer. Grendel sought
somehow to slip that grasp and escape,
flee to the fens; but his fingers were caught
in too fierce a grip. His foray had failed;
the harm-wreaker rued his raid on Heorot.
685 From the hall of the Danes a hellish din
beset every stalwart outside the stronghold,
louder than laughter of ale-sharing earls.
A wonder it was the wine-hall withstood
this forceful affray without falling to earth.
690 That beautiful building was firmly bonded
by iron bands forged with forethought
inside and out. As some have told it,
the struggle swept on and slammed to the floor
many mead-benches massive with gold.
695 No Scylding elders ever imagined
that any would harm their elk-horned hall,
raze what they wrought, unless flames arose
to smother and swallow it. Awful new noises
burst from the building, unnerved the North Danes,
700 each one and all who heard those outcries
outside the walls. Wailing in anguish,
the hellish horror, hateful to God,

sang his dismay,   seized by the grip
of a man more mighty   than any then living.

705 That shielder of men   meant by no means
to let the death-dealer   leave with his life,
a life worthless   to anyone elsewhere.
Then the young soldiers   swung their old swords
again and again   to save their guardian,
710 their kingly comrade,   however they could.
Engaging with Grendel   and hoping to hew him
from every side,   they scarcely suspected
that blades wielded   by worthy warriors
never would cut   to the criminal's quick.
715 The spell was spun   so strongly about him
that the finest iron   of any on earth,
the sharpest sword-edge   left him unscathed.
Still he was soon   to be stripped of his life
and sent on a sore   sojourn to Hell.
720 The strength of his sinews   would serve him no more;
no more would he menace   mankind with his crimes,
his grudge against God,   for the high-hearted kinsman
of King Hygelac   had hold of his hand.
Each found the other   loathsome while living;
725 but the murderous man-bane   got a great wound
as tendons were torn,   shoulder shorn open,
and bone-locks broken.   Beowulf gained
glory in war;   and Grendel went off
bloody and bent   to the boggy hills,
730 sorrowfully seeking   his dreary dwelling.
Surely he sensed   his life-span was spent,
his days upon days;   but the Danes rejoiced:
their wish was fulfilled   after fearsome warfare.

Wise and strong-willed,   the one from afar
735 had cleansed Heorot,   hall of Hrothgar.
Great among Geats,   he was glad of the work
he had done in darkness,   his fame-winning feat,
fulfilling his oath   to aid the East Danes,
easing their anguish,   healing the horror
740 they suffered so long,   no small distress.
As token of triumph,   the troop-leader hung
the shorn-off shoulder   and arm by its hand:
the grip of Grendel   swung from the gable!

Many a warrior   met in the morning
745 around Hrothgar's hall,   so I have heard.
Folk-leaders fared   from near and far
over wide wolds   to look on the wonder,
the track of the terror,   glad he had taken
leave of his life   when they looked on footprints

750 wending away   to the mere of monsters.
     Weary and weak,   defeated in war,
     he dripped his blood-spoor   down to dark water,
     tainting the terrible   tide where he sank,
     spilling his lifeblood   to swirl in the surge.
755 There the doomed one   dropped into death
     where he long had lurked   in his joyless lair,
     and Hell harrowed   his heathen soul.
     Many went hence: young men and old
     mounted white mares   and rode to the mere,
760 a joyous journey   on brave battle-steeds.
     There Beowulf's   prowess was praised
     and applauded by all.   Everyone said
     that over the Earth   and under bright sky,
     from north to south   between sea and sea,
765 no other man   was more worthy of wearing
     corselet or crown,   though no one denied
     the grace of Hrothgar: that was a good king.

     Sometimes they galloped   great-hearted bays;
     races were run   where roads were smooth
770 on open upland.   Meanwhile a man
     skilled as a singer,   versed in old stories,
     wove a new lay   of truly-linked words.
     So the scop started   his song of Beowulf's
     wisdom and strength,   setting his spell
775 with subtle staves.   Of Sigemund[9] also
     he said what he knew: many marvels,
     deeds of daring   and distant journeys,
     the wars of Waels' son,   his wildness, his sins,
     unsung among men   save by Fitela,
780 Sigemund's nephew,   who knew his secrets
     and aided his uncle   in every conflict
     as comrade-at-need.   A whole clan of ogres
     was slain by the Waelsing   wielding his sword.
     No small esteem   sprang up for Sigemund
785 after his death-day.   Dauntless in war,
     he struck down a serpent   under gray stone
     where it held its hoard.   He fared alone
     on this fearsome foray,   not with Fitela;
     but fate allowed him   to lunge with his blade,
790 spitting the scaly   worm to the wall.
     His pluck repaid,   Sigemund was pleased
     to take his pick   of the piled-up treasure
     and load bright arms   in his longboat's breast
     while the molten worm   melted away.

9. The story of Sigemund is also told in the Old Norse *Volsunga Saga* and with major variations in the Middle High German *Niebelungenlied*. The scop's comparison of Sigemund with Beowulf is ironic in that the order and the outcome of Beowulf's later encounter with a dragon will be reversed.

795   Thus that wayfarer   famed far and wide
          among nations of men,   that mighty war-maker,
          shelter of shield-bearers,   outshone another:
          unhappy Heremod,[1]   king of the Danes,
          whose strength, spirit,   and courage were spent.
800   He fell among foes,   was taken by traitors
          and swiftly dispatched.   So his sorrows
          ended at last.   Too long had lords
          and commoners suffered,   scourged by their king,
          who ought to have honored   his father's office,
805   defending his homeland,   his hoard and folk.
          Evil had entered him.   Dearer to Danes
          and all humankind   was Hygelac's kinsman.

          Still running heats,   the horses hurtled
          on sandy lanes.   The light of morning
810   had swung to the south,   and many men sped,
          keen to behold   the hall of the king,
          the strange sights inside.   Hrothgar himself,
          keeper of treasures   and leader of troops,
          came from the queen's   quarters to march
815   with measured tread   the track to his mead-hall;
          the queen and her maidens   also came forth.
          He stopped on the stairs   and gazed at the gable,
          glinting with gold   behind Grendel's hand.

          "My thanks for this sight   go straight to Heaven!
820   Grendel has given me   grief and grievance;
          but God often works   wonders on wonders.
          Not long ago   I had no hope at all
          of living to see   relief from my sorrows
          while slaughter stained   the highest of houses,
825   wide-spilling woes   the wisest advisors
          despaired of stanching.   None of them knew
          how to fend off the foe,   the fearful demon
          afflicting our folk   here in our fastness.
          Now, praise Heaven,   a prince has proven
830   this deed could be done   that daunted us all.
          Indeed the mother   who bore this young man
          among mankind   may certainly say,
          if she still is living,   that the Lord of Old
          blessed her child-bearing.   Henceforth, Beowulf,
835   best of the brave,   I shall hold you in heart
          as close as a son.   Keep our new kinship,
          and I shall award you   whatever you wish
          that is mine to command.   Many a time
          I have lavished wealth   on lesser warriors,

1. Heremod, an earlier Danish king, was the stock illustration of the unjust and unwise ruler. After bringing bloodshed upon his own house, Heremod took refuge among the Jutes, who eventually put him to death.

840   slighter in strife.   You have earned your esteem.
May the All-Wielder   reward you always,
just as He gives you   these goods today."

Beowulf spoke,   son of Ecgtheow:
"We gladly engaged   in this work of war
845   and freely faced   the unknowable foe,
but I greatly regret   that you were not granted
the sight of him stricken   here in your hall.
I sought to grip him   swiftly and strongly,
wrestle him down   to writhe on his death-bed
850   as life left him,   unless he broke loose.
It was not my fate   to fasten the man-bane
firmly enough.   The fiend was so fierce
he secured his escape   by leaving this limb
to ransom his life,   though little the wretch
855   has gained for his hurt,   held in the grip
of a dire wound,   awaiting death
as a savage man,   besmirched by his sins,
might wait to learn   what the Lord wills."

Unferth was silent.   He spoke no more boasts
860   about works of war   when warriors gazed
at the hand   hanging from Heorot's roof,
the fiend's fingers   jutting in front,
each nail intact,   those terrible talons
like spikes of steel.   Everyone said
865   that the strongest sword   from smithies of old,
the hardest iron   edge ever forged,
would never have harmed   that heathen horror,
those bloody claws   crooked for combat.

2. Grendel's Mother

Inside Heorot   many hands hastened
870   at Hrothgar's command: men and women
washed out the wine-hall,   unfurled on the walls
gold-woven hangings   to gladden their guests,
each of whom gazed   wide-eyed in wonder.
Though badly battered,   with door-bolts broken,
875   the building was bound   with bands of iron.
Only the roof   had escaped unscathed
before the fell creature   twisted and fled,
stained by his sin   and despairing of life.
Flee it who will,   a well-earned fate
880   is not often altered,   for every earth-dweller
and soul-bearing son   must seek out a spot
to lay down his body,   lie on his death-bed,
sleep after feasting.
                So it was fitting
for Healfdene's son   to stride through his hall:

885   the king would come   to sup with his kin.
        I have never heard   in any nation
        of such a great host   so graciously gathered,
        arrayed on benches   around their ruler,
        glad of his fame   and glad for the feast.
890   Many a mead-cup   those masterful kinsmen
        Hrothgar and Hrothulf   raised in the hall.
        All were then friends   who filled Heorot,
        treason and treachery   not yet contrived.[1]
        Crowning his conquest,   the King of the Danes
895   bestowed on the Stalwart   a battle-standard
        embroidered with gold,   a helmet, a byrnie,
        and an unblemished blade   borne out while ranks
        of warriors watched.   Then Beowulf drank
        a flagon before them: he would feel no shame
900   facing bold spearmen   with boons such as these.
        Not many men   on mead benches
        have given another   four golden gifts
        in friendlier fashion.   The head-guard was flanged
        with windings of wire.   Facing forward,
905   it warded off harm   when the wearer in war
        was obliged to bear shield   against enemy blades
        that were hammer-hardened   and honed by files.
        The sovereign ordered   eight swift steeds
        brought to the court   on braided bridles.
910   One bore a saddle   studded with gems
        and glinting gold-work: there the great king,
        son of Healfdene,   would sit during sword-strife,
        never faltering,   fierce at the front,
        working his will   while the wounded fell.
915   Then Hrothgar awarded   horses and weapons
        both to Beowulf,   bade that he keep them
        and wield them well.   So from his hoard
        he paid the hero   a princely reward
        of heirlooms and arms   for braving the battle;
920   no man could fairly   or truthfully fault them.

        That lord also lavished   gifts on the Geats
        whom Beowulf brought   over broad seas,
        and wergeld he gave   for the one Grendel
        had wickedly killed,   though the creature would surely
925   have murdered more   had God in his wisdom,
        man in his strength   failed to forestall it.
        So the Almighty   has always moved men;
        but man must forever   strive to discern
        good from evil,   evil from good,
930   while drunk with days   he dwells in this world.

---

1. Possibly an allusion to the later usurpation of the Danish throne by Hrothgar's nephew Hrothulf.

Song and story   now sounded together
as Hrothgar's bard   declaimed over benches
a tale often told   when harp was held:
how Finn's followers,[2]   faithless Jutes,
935   fell to fighting   friends in his fortress;
how Hnaef the Half-Dane,   hero of Scyldings,
was fated to fall   in Frisian warfare;
how by shield-swagger   harmless Hildeburh,
faithful to Finn   though daughter of Danes,
940   lost her beloved   brother and son
who were both born   to be struck by spears.
Not without cause   did Hoc's daughter
bewail the Lord's will   when morning awoke:
she who had known   nothing but happiness
945   beheld under heaven   the horror of kin-strife.

War had taken   its toll of attackers;
few men remained   for Finn to muster,
too few to force   the fight against Hengest,
a dutiful earl   who had rallied the Danes.
950   As tokens of truce   Finn offered these terms:
a haven wholly   emptied of foes,
hall and high seat,   with an equal share
in gifts given   his own gathered kin.
Each time he treated   his sons to treasures
955   plated with gold,   a portion would go
to sweeten Hengest's   stay in his hall.
The two sides swore   a strict treaty;
and Finn freely   affirmed to Hengest
that all would honor   this oath to the Danes,
960   as his council decreed,   and further declared
no Frisian would ever,   by word or work,
challenge the peace   or mention with malice
the plight of survivors   deprived of their prince
and wintered-in   at the slayer's stronghold.
965   Should any Frisian   enter in anger,
the sword's edge   would settle the quarrel.

That oath offered,   the hoard was opened
for gold to array   the greatest of War-Danes.
Iron-hard guardians   gilded with gold,
970   bloody byrnies   and boar-tusked helms
were heaped on his bier,   awaiting the balefire.
Many a warrior,   weakened by wounds,
had faltered and fallen   with foes he had slain.

2. The following episode is one of the most obscure in *Beowulf*. It seems that Hnaef and Hildeburh are both children of an earlier Danish king named Hoc and that Hildeburh has been sent to marry Finn, the son of Folcwalda and king of the Jutes and Frisians, in order to conclude a marriage alliance and thus settle a prior blood feud between the two tribes. Upon going to visit her sister and her husband, Hnaef is treacherously ambushed and killed by Finn's men; Hildeburh's son by Finn is also killed. In her role as peace-weaver, Hildeburh is torn by conflicting allegiances, foreshadowing the fate of Hrothgar's own daughter Freawaru in her marriage to Ingeld.

Hildeburh ordered   her own dear son
975   be placed on the pyre,   the prince and his uncle
shoulder to shoulder.   Their bodies were burned
while the stricken lady   sang out her sorrow.
Streamers of smoke   burst from the bier
as corpses kindled   with cruelest of flames.
980   Faces withered,   flesh-wounds yawned
and blood boiled out   as the blaze swallowed
with hateful hunger   those whom warfare
had borne away,   the best of both houses.
Their glory was gone.
                    The Frisians were fewer
985   heading for home;   their high stronghold
was empty of allies.   For Hengest also
that winter was woeful,   walled up in Frisia,
brooding on bloodshed   and yearning to leave,
though knowing his longboat   never could breast
990   the wind-darkened swells   of a wide ocean
seething with storms,   or break the ice-bindings
that barred his bow   from the bitter waters.
Constrained to wait   for kindlier weather,
he watched until spring,   season of sunlight,
995   dawned on men's dwellings   as ever it did
and still does today.   Winter withdrew
and Earth blossomed.   Though the exile was eager
to end his visit,   he thought more of vengeance
than sailing homeward.   Loathe to foreswear
1000   the way of this world,   he schemed to assail
the sons of slayers.   So Hengest heeded
Hunlaf's son,   who laid on his lap
the sword War-Flame,   feared by all foes,
asking its edge   be offered the Jutes.
1005   His heart was hot;   he could hold back no more;
gladly he answered   Guthlaf and Oslaf,
who wrathfully spoke   of the wrong they suffered,
the shame of Scyldings   sharing their plight.
Then fierce-hearted Finn   fell in his turn,
1010   stricken by swords   in his own stronghold.
The building was bloody   with bodies of foemen:
the king lay slain,   likewise his kin;
and the queen was captured.   Scyldings carried
off in their ship   all of the chattels
1015   found in Finn's fortress,   gemstones and jewels.
The lady was borne   to the land of her birth.

So that story   was sung to its end,
then mirth once more   mounted in Heorot.
Revelry rang   as wine-bearers brought
1020   finely-wrought flagons   filled to the brim.

Wearing her circlet,   Wealtheow walked
where uncle and nephew,   Hrothgar and Hrothulf,
were sitting in peace,   two soldiers together,
each still believing   the other was loyal.

1025   Likewise the officer,   Unferth, was honored
to sit at the feet   of the Scylding sovereign.
Everyone thought him   honest and trustworthy,
blameless and brave,   though his blade had unjustly
stricken a kinsman.

So the queen spoke:

1030   "Share now this cup,   king of the Scyldings,
giver of gold;   share and be glad;
greet the Geats mildly   as well a man might,
mindful of gifts   graciously given
from near and far,   now in your keeping.

1035   They say you would name   that knight as a son
for purging the ring-hall.   Employ as you please
wealth and rewards,   but bequeath to your kin
rule of this realm   when the Ruler of All
holds that you must.   I know that Hrothulf

1040   will honor our trust   and treat these youths well
if you have to leave   this world before him.
I am counting on him   to recall our kindness
when he was a child   and repay our children
for presents we gave   and pleasures we granted."

1045   She turned to the bench   where her sons were seated,
Hrethric and Hrothmund.   Between the two brothers
Beowulf sat;   and the cup-bearer brought him
words of welcome,   willingly gave him
as tokens of favor   two braided arm-bands,

1050   jerkin, corselet,   and jeweled collar[3]
grander than any   other on Earth.
I have heard under heaven   of no higher treasure
hoarded by heroes   since Hama stole off
to his fair fortress   with Freya's necklace,

1055   shining with stones   set by the Fire-Dwarves.
So Hama earned   Eormanric's anger,
and fame for himself.   Foolhardy Hygelac,
grandson of Swerting   and sovereign of Geats,
would wear it one day   on his final foray.

1060   He fell in the fray   defending his treasure,
the spoils he bore   with his battle-standard.

---

3. The narrative jumps ahead beyond Beowulf's return home to the Geats. His uncle, Hygelac, the king, will not only receive the collar from Beowulf but will die with it in battle among the Frisians. The collar thus connects different events at different times.

Recklessly raiding   the realm of Frisia,
the prince in his pride   had prompted misfortune
by crossing the sea   while clad in that collar.
1065 He fell under shield,   fell to the Franks,
weaker warriors   stripping the slain
of armor and spoil   after the slaughter.
Hygelac held   the graveyard of Geats.

The hall applauded   the princely prize
1070 bestowed by the queen,   and Wealtheow spoke
for the host to hear: "Keep this collar,
beloved Beowulf;   and bear this byrnie,
wealth of our realm;   may it ward you well.
Swear that your strength   and kindly counsel
1075 will aid these youngsters,   and I shall reward you.
Now your renown   will range near and far;
your fame will wax wide,   as wide as the water
hemming our hills,   homes of the wind.
Be blessed, Beowulf,   with abundant treasures
1080 as long as you live;   and be mild to my sons,
a model admired.   Here men are courtly,
honest and true,   each to the other,
all to their ruler;   and after the revels,
well-bolstered with beer,   they do as I bid."

1085 The lady left him   and sat on her seat.
The feast went on;   wine was flowing.
Men could not know   what fate would befall them,
what evil of old   was decreed to come
for the earls that evening.   As always, Hrothgar
1090 headed for home,   where the ruler rested.
A great many others   remained in the hall,
bearing bright benches   and rolling out beds
while one drunkard,   doomed and death-ripened,
sprawled into sleep.   They set at their heads
1095 round war-shields,   well-adorned wood.
Above them on boards,   their battle-helms rested,
ringed mail-shirts   and mighty spear-shafts
waiting for strife.   Such was their wont
at home or afield,   wherever they fared,
1100 in case their king   should call them to arms.
That was a fine folk.
                            They sank into slumber,
but one paid sorely   for sleep that evening,
as often had happened   when grim Grendel
held the gold-hall,   wreaking his wrongs
1105 straight to the end: death after sins.
It would soon be perceived   plainly by all

that one ill-wisher   still was alive,
maddened by grief: Grendel's mother,
a fearsome female   bitterly brooding
1110   alone in her lair   deep in dread waters
and cold currents   since Cain had killed
the only brother   born of his father.
Marked by murder,   he fled from mankind
and went to the wastes.   Doomed evil-doers
1115   issued from him.   Grendel was one,
but the hateful Hell-walker   found a warrior
wakefully watching   for combat in Heorot.
The monster met there   a man who remembered
strength would serve him,   the great gift of God,
1120   faith in the All-Wielder's   favor and aid.
By that he mastered   the ghastly ghoul;
routed, wretched,   the hell-fiend fled,
forlornly drew near   his dreary death-place.
Enraged and ravenous,   Grendel's mother
1125   swiftly set out   on a sorrowful journey
to settle the score   for her son's demise.

She slipped into Heorot,   hall of the Ring-Danes,
where sleeping earls   soon would suffer
an awful reversal.   Her onslaught was less
1130   by as much as a maiden's   mettle in war
is less than a man's   wielding his weapon:
the banded blade   hammered to hardness,
a blood-stained sword   whose bitter stroke
slashes a boar-helm   borne into battle.
1135   In the hall, sword-edge   sprang from scabbard;
broadshield was swung   swiftly off bench,
held firmly in hand.   None thought of helmet
or sturdy mail-shirt   when terror assailed him.

Out she hastened,   out and away,
1140   keen to keep living   when caught in the act.
She fastened on one,   then fled to her fen.
He was Hrothgar's   highest counselor,
boon companion   and brave shield-bearer
slain in his bed.   Beowulf slept
1145   elsewhere that evening,   for after the feast
the greatest of Geats   was given lodging.
Howls of outrage   rose from Heorot:
the gory hand   was gone from the gable.
Dread had retaken   the Danes' dwelling.
1150   That bargain was bad   for both barterers,
costing each one   a close comrade.

It was grim for the sovereign,   the grizzled soldier,
to learn his old thane   was no longer living,
to know such a dear one   was suddenly dead.
1155   Swiftly he sent   servants to fetch
battle-blessed Beowulf   early from bed,
together with all   the great-hearted Geats.
He marched in their midst,   went where the wise one
was wondering whether   the All-Wielder
1160   ever would alter   this spell of ill-fortune.
That much-honored man   marched up the floor,
and timbers dinned   with the tread of his troop.
He spoke soberly   after the summons,
asking how soundly   the sovereign had slept.

1165   Hrothgar answered,   head of his house:
"Ask not about ease!   Anguish has wakened
again for the Danes.   Aeschere is dead.
He was Yrmenlaf's   elder brother,
my rune-reader   and keeper of counsel,
1170   my shoulder's shielder,   warder in war
when swordsmen struck   at boar-headed helms.
Whatever an honored   earl ought to be,
such was Aeschere.   A sleepless evil
has slipped into Heorot,   seized and strangled.
1175   No one knows where   she will wander now,
glad of the gory   trophy she takes,
her fine fodder.   So she requites
her kinsman's killer   for yesterday's deed,
when you grabbed Grendel   hard in your hand-grip.
1180   He plagued and plundered   my people too long.
His life forfeit,   he fell in the fray;
but now a second   mighty man-scather
comes to carry   the feud further,
as many a thane   must mournfully think,
1185   seeing his sovereign   stricken with grief
at the slaying of one   who served so well.

"I have heard spokesmen   speak in my hall,
country-folk saying   they sometimes spotted
a pair of prodigies   prowling the moors,
1190   evil outcasts,   walkers of wastelands.
One, they descried,   had the semblance of woman;
the other, ill-shapen,   an aspect of man
trudging his track,   ever an exile,
though superhuman   in stature and strength.
1195   In bygone days   the border-dwellers
called him *Grendel*.   What creature begot him,
what nameless spirit,   no one could say.
The two of them trek   untraveled country:
wolf-haunted heights   and windy headlands,
1200   the frightening fen-path   where falling torrents

dive into darkness,   stream beneath stone
amid folded mountains.   That mere[4] is not far,
as miles are measured.   About it there broods
a forest of fir trees   frosted with mist.

1205   Hedges of wood-roots   hem in the water
where each evening   fire-glow flickers
forth on the flood,   a sinister sight.
That pool is unplumbed   by wits of the wise;
but the heath-striding hart   hunted by hounds,

1210   the strong-antlered stag   seeking a thicket,
running for cover,   would rather be killed
than bed on its bank.   It is no pleasant place
where water-struck waves   are whipped into clouds,
surging and storming,   swept by the winds,

1215   so the heights are hidden   and Heaven weeps.
Now you alone   can relieve our anguish:
look, if you will,   at the lay of the land;
and seek, if you dare,   that dreadful dale
where the she-demon dwells.   Finish this feud,

1220   and I shall reward you   with the wealth of ages,
twisted-gold treasures,   if you return."

Beowulf spoke,   son of Ecgtheow:
"Grieve not, good man.   It is better to go
and avenge your friend   than mourn overmuch.

1225   We all must abide   an end on this earth,
but a warrior's works   may win him renown
as long as he lives   and after life leaves him.
Rise now, ruler;   let us ride together
and look on the spoor   of Grendel's mother.

1230   I swear to you this: she shall not escape
in chasm or cave,   in cliff-climbing thicket
or bog's bottom,   wherever she bolts.
Endure your dread   this one day only;
I wish you to wait,   wait and be patient."

1235   The elder leapt up and   offered his thanks
for such hopeful speech.   Then Hrothgar's horse,
a steed with mane braided,   was brought on its bridle.
The sage sovereign   set out in splendor
with shield-bearing soldiers   striding beside him.

1240   Tracks on the trail   were easy to trace:
they wound from woodland   out to the open,
heading through heather   and misty moors
where the best of thanes   was borne off unbreathing.
He would live no longer   in Hrothgar's house.

1245   Crossing the moorland,   the king mounted
a stony path   up steepening slopes.

---

4. A small lake.

With a squad of scouts   in single file,
he rode through regions   none of them knew,
mountains and hollows   that hid many monsters.
1250   He suddenly saw   a forest of fir-trees
rooted on rock,   with trunks tipping
over a tarn   of turbulent eddies.
Danes were downcast,   and Geats, grim;
every soldier   was stricken at heart
1255   to behold on that height   Aeschere's head.

As they looked on the lake,   blood still lingered,
welled to the surface.   A war-horn sounded
its bold battle-cry,   and the band halted.
Strange sea-dragons   swam in the depths;
1260   sinuous serpents   slid to and fro.
At the base of the bluff   water-beasts lay,
much like monsters   that rise in the morning
when seafarers sail   on strenuous journeys.
Hearing the horn's   high-pitched challenge,
1265   they puffed up with rage   and plunged in the pool.
One Geatish lad   lifted his bow
and loosing an arrow,   ended the life
of a wondrous wave-piercer.   War-shaft jutting
hard in its heart,   the swimmer slowed
1270   as death seized it.   With startling speed
the waters were torn   by terrible tuskers.
They heaved the hideous   hulk to the shore
with spear-hooked heads   as warriors watched.
Undaunted, Beowulf   donned battle armor.
1275   His woven war-corselet,   wide and ornate,
would safeguard his heart   as he searched underwater.
It knew how to armor   the beast of its bearer
if an angry grappler   grasped him in battle.
The bright war-helm   would hold his head
1280   when he sought the seafloor   in swirling flood.
A weapon-smith   had skillfully worked
its gilding of gold   in bygone days
and royally ringed it.   He added afterward
figures of boars   so blades of foemen
1285   would fail to bite.   One further aid
Beowulf borrowed: Unferth offered
the hilt of Hrunting,   his princely sword,
a poisoned war-fang   with iron-edged blade,
blood-hardened   in battles of old.
1290   It never had failed   in any man's grasp
if he dared to fare   on a dreadful foray
to fields of foes.   This was not the first time
it was forced to perform   a desperate deed.

Though strong and sly,   the son of Ecglaf
1295   had somehow forgotten   the slander he spoke,

bleary with beer.   He loaned his blade
to a better bearer,   a doer of deeds
that he would not dare.   His head never dipped
under wild waves,   and his fame waned
1300   when bravery failed him   as battle beckoned.
Not so, the other,   armed and eager.

Beowulf spoke,   son of Ecgtheow:
"Remember, wise master,   mover of men
and giver of gold,   since now I begin
1305   this foray full-willing,   how once before
you pledged to fill   the place of a father
if I should be killed   acquitting your cause.
Guard these young earls,   my partners in arms,
if death takes me.   The treasures you dealt,
1310   Hrothgar, my lord,   I leave to Hygelac.
Let the king of Geats   gaze on the gold
and see that I found   a fair bestower,
a generous host   to help while I could.
And let Unferth have   his heirloom, Hrunting,
1315   this wonderful weapon,   wavy-skinned sword
renowned among men.   Now I shall conquer
or die in the deed."
                       So saying, he dived,
high-hearted and hasty,   awaiting no answer.
The waters swallowed   that stout soldier.
1320   He swam for hours   before seeing sea-floor.
Straightaway someone   spied him as well:
she that had hidden   a hundred half-years
in the void's vastness.   Grim and greedy,
she glimpsed a creature   come from above
1325   and crept up to catch him,   clutch him, crush him.
Quickly she learned   his life was secure;
he was hale and whole,   held in the ring-mail.
Linked and locked,   his life-shielding shirt
was wrapped around him,   and wrathful fingers
1330   failed to rip open   the armor he wore.
The wolf of the waters   dragged him away
to her den in the deep,   where weapons of war,
though bravely wielded,   were worthless against her.
Many a mere-beast   banded about him,
1335   brandishing tusks   to tear at his shirt.

The soldier now saw   a high-roofed hall:
unharmed, he beheld   the foe's fastness
beyond the reach   of the roiling flood.
Fire-light flared;   a blaze shone brightly.
1340   The lordly one looked   on the hellish hag,
the mighty mere-wife.   He swung his sword
for a swift stroke,   not staying his hand;
and the whorled blade   whistled its war-song.

But the battle-flame   failed to bite her;
1345   its edge was unable   to end her life,
though Hrunting had often   hacked through helmets
and slashed mail-shirts   in hand-to-hand strife.
For the first time   the famous blade faltered.

Resolve unshaken,   courage rekindled,
1350   Hygelac's kinsman   was keen for conquest.
In a fit of fury,   he flung down the sword.
Steely and strong,   the ring-banded brand
rang on the stones.   He would trust in the strength
of his mighty hand-grip.   Thus should a man,
1355   unmindful of life,   win lasting renown.
Grabbing the tresses   of Grendel's mother,
the Geats' battle-chief,   bursting with wrath,
wrestled her down: no deed to regret
but a favor repaid   as fast as she fell.
1360   With her grim grasp   she grappled him still.
Weary, the warrior   stumbled and slipped;
the strongest foot-soldier   fell to the foe.
Astraddle the hall-guest,   she drew her dagger,
broad and bright-bladed,   bent on avenging
1365   her only offspring.   His mail-shirt shielded
shoulder and breast.   Barring the entry
of edge or point,   the woven war-shirt
saved him from harm.   Ecgtheow's son,
the leader of Geats,   would have lost his life
1370   under Earth's arch   but for his armor
and Heaven's favor   furnishing help.
The Ruler of All   readily aided
the righteous man   when he rose once more.
He beheld in a hoard   of ancient arms
1375   a battle-blessed sword   with strong-edged blade,
a marvelous weapon   men might admire
though over-heavy   for any to heft
when finely forged   by giants of old.
The Scyldings' shielder   took hold of the hilt
1380   and swung up the sword,   though despairing of life.
He struck savagely,   hit her hard neck
and broke the bone-rings,   cleaving clean through
her fated flesh.   She fell to the floor;
the sword sweated;   the soldier rejoiced.

1385   The blaze brightened,   shining through shadows
as clearly as Heaven's   candle on high.
Engorged with anger,   Hygelac's guardsman
glanced round the room   and went toward the wall
with his weapon raised,   holding it hard
1390   by the inlaid hilt.   Its edge was not useless
for quickly requiting   the killings of Grendel.

Too many times   he had warred on the West-Danes.
He had slain Hrothgar's   hearth-mates in sleep,
eagerly eaten   fifteen of those folk
1395 and as many more borne   for his monstrous booty.
He paid their price   to the fierce prince,
who looked on the ground   where Grendel lay limp,
wound-weary,   worn out by warfare.
The lifeless one lurched   at the stroke of the sword
1400 that cleaved his corpse   and cut off his head.

At once the wise men   waiting with Hrothgar
and watching the waters   saw the waves seethe
with streaks of gore.   Gray-haired and glum,
age around honor,   they offered their counsel:
1405 they doubted the brave man   would ever emerge
and seek out the sovereign,   for all were certain
the mere-wolf had mauled him.   It was mid-afternoon,
and the proud Danes   departed the dale;
generous Hrothgar   headed for home.
1410 The Geats lingered   and looked on the lake
with sorrowful souls,   wistfully wishing
they still might see   their beloved leader.

The sword shrank   from battle-shed blood;
its blade began melting,   a marvel to watch,
1415 that war-icicle   waning away
like a rope of water   unwound by the Ruler
when Father releases   fetters of frost:
the true Sovereign   of seasons and times.
Among many treasures,   the Weders' warlord
1420 took only two: the head and the hilt,
studded with gems.   The sword had melted.
Its banded blade   was burnt by the blood,
so hot was the horror,   so acid the evil
that ended thereon.   Soon he was swimming:
1425 the strife-survivor   drove up from the deep
when his foe had fallen.   The foaming waves,
the wide waters   were everywhere cleansed;
that dire demon   had passed her life-days
and left the loaned world.
                          Landward he swam;
1430 the strong-minded savior   of sea-faring men
was glad of his burden,   the booty he brought.
Grateful to God,   the band of brave thanes
hastened gladly   to greet their chieftain,
astonished to see him   whole and unharmed.
1435 His helm and hauberk   were swiftly unstrapped.
Calm under clouds,   the lake lay quietly,
stained by the slain.   They found the foot-path
and marched manfully,   making their way

back through the barrens.   Proud as princes,
1440   they hauled the head   far from the highland,
an effort for each   of the four who ferried it
slung from spear-shafts.   They bore their booty
straight to the gold-hall.   Battle-hardened,
all fourteen strode   from the field outside,
1445   a bold band of Geats   gathered about
their leader and lord,   the war-worthy man,
peerless in prowess   and daring in deeds.
He hailed Hrothgar   as Grendel's head
was dragged by the hair,   drawn through the hall
1450   where earls were drinking.   All were awe-stricken:
women and warriors   watched in wonder.

Beowulf spoke,   son of Ecgtheow:
"Hail, Hrothgar,   Healfdene's son.
Look on this token   we took from the lake,
1455   this glorious booty   we bring you gladly.
The struggle was stark;   the danger, dreadful.
My foe would have won   our war underwater
had the Lord not looked   after my life.
Hrunting failed me,   though finely fashioned;
1460   but God vouchsafed me   a glimpse of a great-sword,
ancient and huge,   hung from the wall.
All-Father often   fosters the friendless.
Wielding this weapon,   I struck down and slew
the cavern's keeper   as the moment permitted.
1465   My banded war-blade   was burned away
when blood burst forth   in the heat of battle.
I bore the hilt here,   wrested from raiders.
Thus I avenged   the deaths among Danes
as it was fitting,   and this I promise you:
1470   henceforth in Heorot   heroes shall sleep
untroubled by terror.   Your warrior troop,
all of your thanes,   young men and old,
need fear no further   evil befalling,
not from that quarter,   king of the Scyldings."

1475   He gave the gold hilt   to the good old man;
the hoary war-chief   held in his hand
an ancient artifact   forged by giants.
At the devils' downfall,   this wondrous work
went to the Danes.   The dark-hearted demon,
1480   hater of humans,   Heaven's enemy,
committer of murders,   and likewise his mother,
departed this Earth.   Their power passed
to the wisest world-king   who ever awarded
treasure in Denmark   between the two seas.

1485   Hrothgar spoke   as he studied the hilt,
        that aged heirloom   inscribed long ago
        with a story of strife: how the Flood swallowed
        the race of giants   with onrushing ocean.
        Defiant kindred,   they fared cruelly,
1490   condemned for their deeds   to death by water.
        Such were the staves   graven in gold-plate,
        runes rightly set,   saying for whom
        the serpent-ribbed sword   and raddled hilt[5]
        were once fashioned   of finest iron.
1495   When the sage spoke,   all were silent.

        "Truth may be told   by the homeland's holder
        and keeper of kinfolk,   who rightly recalls
        the past for his people: this prince was born
        bravest of fighters.   My friend, Beowulf,
1500   your fame shall flourish   in far countries,
        everywhere honored.   Your strength is sustained
        by patience and judgement.   Just as I promised,
        our friendship is sealed,   a lasting alliance.
        So you shall be   a boon to your brethren,
1505   unlike Heremod   who ought to have helped
        Ecgwela's sons,   honored Scyldings.
        He grew up to grief   and grim slaughter,
        doling out death   to the Danish people.
        Hot-tempered at table,   he cut down comrades,
1510   slew his own soldiers   and spurned humankind,
        alone and unloved,   an infamous prince,
        though mighty God   had given him greatness
        and raised him in rank   over all other men.
        Hidden wrath   took root in his heart,
1515   bloodthirsty thoughts.   He would give no gifts
        to honor others.   Loveless, he lived,
        a lasting affliction   endured by the Danes
        in sorrow and strife.   Consider him well,
        his life and lesson.
                            "Wise with winters,
1520   I tell you this tale   as I mull and marvel
        how the Almighty   metes to mankind
        the blessings of reason,   rule and realm.
        He arranges it all.   For a time He allows
        the mind of a man   to linger in love
1525   with earthly honors.   He offers him homeland
        to hold and enjoy,   a fort full of folk,
        men to command   and might in the world,
        wide kingdoms   won to his will.

---

5. On the sword hilt is the story of the flood, written in runes (letters of the early Germanic alphabet), and a decorative pattern of twisted serpent shapes. A similar pattern can be seen on the great buckle of the Sutton Hoo ship burial, Color Plate 2.

In his folly, the fool   imagines no ending.
1530 He dwells in delight   without thought of his lot.
Illness, old age,   anguish or envy:
none of these gnaw   by night at his mind.
Nowhere are swords   brandished in anger;
for him the whole world   wends as he wishes.
1535 He knows nothing worse   till his portion of pride
waxes within him.   His soul is asleep;
his gate, unguarded.   He slumbers too soundly,
sunk in small cares.   The slayer creeps close
and shoots a shaft   from the baneful bow.
1540 The bitter arrow   bites through his armor,
piercing the heart   he neglected to guard
from crooked counsel   and evil impulse.
Too little seems all   he has long possessed.
Suspicious and stingy,   he refuses to share
1545 gold-plated gifts.   He forgets or ignores
what fate awaits him,   for the world's Wielder
surely has granted   his share of glory.
But the end-rune   is already written:
the loaned life-home   collapses in ruin;
1550 some other usurps   and openly offers
the hoarded wealth,   heedless of worry.

"Beloved Beowulf,   best of defenders,
guard against anger   and gain for yourself
perpetual profit.   Put aside pride,
1555 worthiest warrior.   Now for awhile
your force flowers,   yet soon it shall fail.
Sickness or age   will strip you of strength,
or the fangs of flame,   or flood-surges,
the sword's bite   or the spear's flight,
1560 or fearful frailty   as bright eyes fade,
dimming to darkness.   Afterward death
will sweep you away,   strongest of war-chiefs.
"I ruled the Ring-Danes   a hundred half-years,
stern under clouds   with sword and spear
1565 that I wielded in war   against many nations
across Middle-Earth,   until none remained
beneath spacious skies   to reckon as rivals.
Recompense happened   here in my homeland,
grief after gladness   when Grendel came,
1570 when the ancient enemy   cunningly entered.
Thereafter I suffered   constant sorrows
and cruelest cares.   But God has given me
long enough life   to look at this head
with my own eyes,   as enmity ends
1575 spattered with gore.   Sit and be glad,
war-worthy one: the feast is forthcoming,
and many gifts   will be granted tomorrow."

Gladly the Geat   went to his seat
as the Ancient asked.   With all of his men,
1580   the famous one feasted   finely once more.
The helm of Heaven   darkened with dusk,
and the elders arose.   The oldest of Scyldings
was ready to rest   his hoary-haired head
1585   at peace on his pillow.   Peerless with shield,
the leader of Geats   was equally eager
to lie down at last.   A thane was appointed
to serve as his squire.   Such was the courtesy
shown in those days   to weary wayfarers,
soldiers sojourning   over the ocean.

1590   Beneath golden gables   the great-hearted guest
dozed until dawn   in the high-roofed hall,
when the black raven   blithely foretold
joy under Heaven.   Daybreak hastened,
sun after shadow.   The company stirred:
1595   soldiers were eager   to seek out their ship
and start homeward.   The Stalwart would sail
forth to his folk.   But first he bade
that Hrunting be sent   to the son of Ecglaf,
a treasure returned   with thanks for the loan
1600   of precious iron.   He ordered the owner
be told he considered   the sword a fine friend,
blameless in battle.   That was a knight!
Keen for the crossing,   his weapons secure,
the warrior went   to the worthy Dane;
1605   the thane sought the throne   where a sovereign sat,
that steadfast hero,   Hrothgar the Great.

Beowulf spoke,   son of Ecgtheow:
"Now we must say   as far-sailing seamen,
we wish to make way   homeward to Hygelac.
1610   Here we were well   and warmly received.
If anything further   would earn your favor,
some deed of war   that remains to be done
for the master of men,   I shall always be ready.
Should word ever wend   over wide ocean
1615   that nearby nations   menace your marches,
as those who detest you   sometimes have tried,
I shall summon a thousand   thanes to your aid.
I know Hygelac,   though newly-anointed
the nation's shepherd,   will surely consent
1620   to honor my offer   in word and action.
If you ever need men,   I shall muster at once
a thicket of spears   and support you in strength.
Should Hrethric, your son,   sail overseas,
he shall find friends   in the fort of the Geats.
1625   It is well for the worthy   to fare in far countries."

Hrothgar spoke   these words in response:
"Heaven's Sovereign   has set in your heart
these thoughts to be voiced.   I have never known
someone so young   to pronounce more wisely.
1630   You are peerless in strength,   princely in spirit,
straightforward in speech.   If a spear fells
Hrethel's son,   if a hostile sword-stroke
kills him in combat   or after, with illness,
slays your leader   while you still live,
1635   the Sea-Geats surely   could name no better
to serve as their king   and keeper of treasure,
should you wish to wield   rule in your realm.
I sensed your spirit   the instant I saw you,
precious Beowulf,   bringer of peace
1640   for both our peoples: War-Danes and Weders,
so often sundered   by strife in the past.
While I wield the rule   of this wide realm
men will exchange   many more greetings
and riches will ride   in ring-bowed ships
1645   bearing their gifts   where the gannets bathe.
I know your countrymen   keep to old ways,
fast in friendship,   and war as well."

Then the hall's holder,   Healfdene's son,
gave his protector   twelve more treasures,
1650   bidding he bear   these tokens safely
home to his kin,   and quickly return.
The good king kissed   that noblest of knights;
the hoary-haired warrior   hugged him and wept,
too well aware   with the wisdom of age
1655   that he never might see   the young man again
coming to council.   He had grown so close,
so strong in esteem,   he could scarcely endure
the secret longing   that surged in his heart,
the flame of affection   burned in his blood.
1660   But Beowulf walked   away with his wealth;
proud of his prizes,   he trod on the turf.
Standing at anchor,   his sea-courser
chafed for its captain.   All the way home
Hrothgar's gifts   were often honored.
1665   That was a king   accorded respect
until age unmanned him,   like many another.

High-hearted,   the band of young braves
strode to the sea,   wrapped in their ring-mesh,
linked and locked shirts.   The land-watcher spied
1670   the fighters faring,   just as before.
He called no taunts   from the top of the cliff
but galloped to greet them   and tell them the Geats

would always be welcome,   armored warriors
borne on their ship.   The broad longboat
1675   lay on the beach,   laden with chain-mail,
chargers and treasures   behind its tall prow.
The mast soared high   over Hrothgar's hoard.

The boat-guard was given   a gold-hilted sword;
thereafter that man   had honor enhanced,
1680   bearing an heirloom   to Heorot's mead-bench.
They boarded their vessel,   breasted the deep,
left Denmark behind.   A halyard hoisted
the sea-wind's shroud;   the sail was sheeted,
bound to the mast,   and the beams moaned
1685   as a fair wind wafted   the wave-rider forward.
Foamy-throated,   the longboat bounded,
swept on the swells   of the swift sea-stream
until welcoming capes   were sighted ahead,
the cliffs of Geat-land.   The keel grounded
1690   as wind-lift thrust it   straight onto sand.

The harbor-guard hastened   hence from his post.
He had looked long   on an empty ocean
and waited to meet   the much-missed men.
He moored the broad-beamed   bow to the beach
1695   with woven lines   lest the backwash of waves
bear off the boat.   Then Beowulf ordered
treasures unloaded,   the lordly trappings,
gold that was going   to Hygelac's hall,
close to the cliff-edge,   where the ring-giver kept
1700   his comrades about him.
                        That building was bold
at the hill's crown;   and queenly Hygd,
Haereth's daughter,   dwelt there as well.
Wise and refined,   though her winters were few,
she housed in her bower,   enclosed by the keep,
1705   and granted generous   gifts to the Geats,
most unlike Modthryth,[6]   a maiden so fierce
that none but her father   dared venture near.
The brave man who gazed   at Modthryth by day
might reckon a death-rope   already twisted,
1710   might count himself quickly   captured and killed,
the stroke of a sword   prescribed for his trespass.
Such is no style   for a queen to proclaim:
though peerless, a woman   ought to weave peace,
not snatch away life   for imagined slights.

6. The "Modthryth" may mean "arrogant in temper"; it may be a reference to an arrogant woman rather than a proper name.

1715 Modthryth's madness   was tamed by marriage.
     Ale-drinkers say   her ill-deeds ended
     once she was given   in garlands of gold
     to Hemming's kinsman.   She came to his hall
     over pale seas,   accepted that prince,
1720 a fine young heir,   at her father's behest.
     Thenceforth on the throne,   she was famed for fairness,
     making the most   of her lot in life,
     sustained by loving   her lordly sovereign.
     That king, Offa,   was called by all men
1725 the ablest of any   ruling a realm
     between two seas,   so I am told.
     Gifted in war,   a wise gift-giver,
     and widely honored,   the spear-bold soldier
     held his homeland   and also fathered
1730 help for the heroes   of Hemming's kindred:
     war-worthy Eomer,   grandson of Garmund.

     Brave Beowulf   marched with his band,
     strode up the sands   of the broad beach
     while the sun in the south   beamed like a beacon.
1735 The earls went eagerly   up to the keep
     where the strong sovereign,   Ongentheow's slayer,
     the young war-king   was doling out rings.
     Beowulf's coming   was quickly proclaimed.
     Hygelac heard   that his shoulder-shielder
1740 had entered the hall,   whole and unharmed
     by bouts of battle.   The ruler made room
     for the foot-guest crossing   the floor before him.

     Saluting his lord   with a loyal speech
     earnestly worded,   the winner in war
1745 sat facing the king,   kinsman with kinsman.
     A mead-vessel moved   from table to table
     as Haereth's daughter,   heedful of heroes,
     bore the wine-beaker   from hand to hand.
     Keen to elicit   his comrade's account
1750 in the high-roofed hall,   Hygelac graciously
     asked how the Sea-Geats   fared on their foray:
     "Say what befell   from your sudden resolve
     to seek out strife   over salt waters,
     to struggle in Heorot.   Have you helped Hrothgar
1755 ward off the well-known   cares of his kingdom?
     You have cost me disquiet,   angst and anguish.
     Doubting the outcome,   dearest of men,
     for anyone meeting   that murderous demon,
     I sought to dissuade you   from starting the venture.
1760 The South Danes themselves   should have settled their feud
     with ghastly Grendel.   Now I thank God
     that I see you again,   safe and sound."

Beowulf spoke,   son of Ecgtheow:
"For a great many men   our meeting's issue
1765   is hardly hidden,   my lord Hygelac.
What a fine fracas   passed in that place
when both of us battled   where Grendel had brought
sore sorrow   on scores of War-Scyldings!
I avenged them all,   so that none of his kin
1770   anywhere need   exult at our night-bout,
however long   the loathsome race lives,
covered with crime.   When Hrothgar came
and heard what had happened   there in the ring-hall,
he sat me at once   with his own two sons.

1775   "The whole of his host   gathered in gladness;
all my life long   I never have known
such joy in a hall   beneath heaven's vault.
The acclaimed queen,   her kindred's peace-pledge,
would sometimes circle   the seated youths,
1780   lavishing rings   on delighted young lords.
Hrothgar's daughter   handed the elders
ale-cups aplenty,   pouring for each
old trooper in turn.   I heard the hall-sitters
calling her Freaware   after she proffered
1785   the studded flagon.   To Froda's fair son
that maiden is sworn.   This match seems meet
to the lord of Scyldings,   who looks to settle
his Heatho-Bard feud.   Yet the best of brides
seldom has stilled   the spears of slaughter
1790   so soon after spears   have stricken a sovereign.

"Ingeld and all   his earls will be rankled,
watching that woman   walk in their hall
with high-born Danes   doing her bidding.
Ancient heirlooms   will adorn her escorts,
1795   Heatho-Bard swords   with braided steel blades,
weapons once wielded   and lost in war
along with the lives   of friends in the fray.
Eyeing the ring-hilts,   an old ash-warrior
will brood in his beer   and bitterly pine
1800   for the stark reminders   of men slain in strife.
He will grimly begin   to goad a young soldier,
testing and tempting   a troubled heart,
his whispered words   waking war-evil:

"My friend, have you spotted   the battle-sword
1805   that your father bore   on his final foray?
Wearing his war-mask,   Withergeld fell
when foemen seized   the field of slaughter:
his priceless blade   was plundered by Danes.
Now some son   of the Scylding who slew him

1810   struts on our floor,   flaunting his trophy,
       an heirloom that you   should rightfully own.'

       "He will prick and pique   with pointed words
       time after time   till the challenge is taken,
       the maiden's attendant   is murdered in turn,
1815   blade-bitten   to sleep in his blood,
       forfeit his life   for his father's feat.
       Another will run,   knowing the road.
       So on both sides   oaths will be broken;
       and afterward Ingeld's   anger will grow
1820   hotter, unchecked,   as he chills toward his wife.
       Hence I would hold   the Heatho-Bards likely
       to prove unpeaceable   partners for Danes.

       "Now I shall speak   of my strife with Grendel,
       further acquainting   the kingdom's keeper
1825   with all that befell   when our fight began.
       Heaven's gem   had gone overhead;
       in darkness the dire   demon stalked us
       while we stood guard   unharmed in Heorot.
       Hondshioh was doomed   to die with the onslaught,
1830   first to succumb,   though clad for combat
       when grabbed by Grendel,   who gobbled him whole.
       That beloved young thane   was eaten alive.
       Not one to leave   the hall empty-handed,
       the bloody-toothed terror   intended to try
1835   his might upon me.   A curious creel
       hung from his hand,   cunningly clasped
       and strangely sewn   with devilish skill
       from skin of a dragon.   The demon would stuff me,
       sinless, inside   like so many others;
1840   but rising in wrath,   I stood upright.
       It is too long a tale,   how the people's plaguer
       paid for his crimes   with proper requital;
       but the feat reflected   finely, my lord,
       on the land you lead.   Though the foe fled
1845   to live awhile longer,   he left behind him
       as spoor of the strife   a hand in Heorot.
       Humbled, he fell   to the floor of the mere.

       "The warder of Scyldings   rewarded my warfare
       with much treasure   when morning arrived,
1850   and we sat for a feast   with songs and sagas.
       He told many tales   he learned in his lifetime.
       Sometimes a soldier   struck the glad harp,
       the sounding wood;   sometimes strange stories
       were spoken like spells,   tragic and true,
1855   rightly related.   The large-hearted lord
       sometimes would start   to speak of his youth,

his might in war.   His memories welled;
ancient in winters,   he weighed them all.

"So we delighted   the livelong day
1860   until darkness drew   once more upon men.
Then Grendel's mother,   mourning her son,
swiftly set out   in search of revenge
against warlike Geats.   The grisly woman
wantonly slew   a Scylding warrior:
1865   aged Aeschere,   the king's counselor,
relinquished his life.   Nor in the morning
might death-weary Danes   bear off his body
to burn on a bier,   for the creature clutching him
fled to her fastness   under a waterfall.
1870   This was the sorest   of sorrows that Hrothgar
suffered as king.   Distraught, he beseeched me
to do in your name   a notable deed.
If I dived in the deep,   heedless of danger,
to war underwater,   he would reward me.

1875   "Under I went,   as now is well-known;
and I found the hideous   haunter of fens.
For a time we two   contested our hand-strength;
then I struck off her head   with a huge sword
that her battle-hall held,   and her hot blood
1880   boiled in the lake.   Leaving that place
was no easy feat,   but fate let me live.
Again I was granted   gifts that the guardian,
Healfdene's son,   had sworn to bestow.
The king of that people   kept his promise,
1885   and I kept all   he had earlier offered:
meed for my might,   with more treasures,
my choice from the hoard   of Healfdene's son.
These, my lord,   I deliver to you,
as proof of fealty.   My future depends
1890   wholly on you.   I have in this world
few close kin   but my king, Hygelac."

He bade the boar-banner   now be brought in,
the high helmet,   hard mail-shirt,
and splendid sword,   describing them thus:
1895   "When Hrothgar gave me   this hoarded gear,
the sage sovereign   enjoined me to tell
the tale of his gift: this treasure was held
by Heorogar, king,   who long was the lord
of Scylding people.   It should have passed
1900   to armor the breast   of bold Heoroweard,
the father's favorite,   faithful and brave;
but he willed it elsewhere,   so use it well."

I have heard how horses   followed that hoard,

four dappled mounts,   matching and fleet.
1905 He gave up his gifts,   gold and horses.
Kinsmen should always   act with honor,
not spin one another   in snares of spite
or secretly scheme   to kill close comrades.
Always the nephew   had aided his uncle;
1910 each held the other's   welfare at heart.
He gave to Queen Hygd   the golden collar,
wondrously wrought,   Wealtheow's token,
and also three steeds,   sleek and bright-saddled.
Thereafter her breast   was graced by the gift.

1915 So Ecgtheow's son   won his repute
as a man of mettle,   acting with honor,
yet mild-hearted   toward hearth-companions,
harming no one   when muddled with mead.
Bold in battle,   he guarded the guerdon
1920 that God had granted,   the greatest strength
of all humankind,   though once he was thought
weak and unworthy,   a sloucher and slacker,
mocked for meekness   by men on the mead-bench,
and given no gifts   by the lord of the Geats.
1925 Every trouble   untwined in time
for the glory-blessed man.
                              A blade was brought
at the king's request,   Hrethel's heirloom
glinting with gold.   No greater treasure,
no nobler sword   was held in his hoard.
1930 He lay that brand   on Beowulf's lap
and also bestowed   a spacious estate,
hall and high seat,   since land and lordship
were left to them both.   By birthright and law,
the wide realm's ruler   was one who ranked higher.

3. The Dragon

1935 It happened long after,   with Hygelac dead,
that war-swords slew   Heardred, his son,
when battle-Scylfings   broke his shield-wall
and hurtled headlong   at Hrethel's nephew.
So Beowulf came   to rule the broad realm.
1940 For fifty winters   he fostered it well;
then the old king,   keeper of kinfolk,
heard of a dragon   drawn from the darkness.
He had long lain   in his lofty fastness,
the steep stone-barrow,   guarding his gold;
1945 but a path pierced it,   known to no person
save him who found it   and followed it forward.
That stranger seized   but a single treasure.
He bore it in hand   from the heathen hoard:
a finely-worked flagon   he filched from the lair

1950   where the dragon dozed.   Enraged at the robber,
the sneaking thief   who struck while he slept,
the guardian woke   glowing with wrath,
as his nearest neighbors   were soon to discern.

It was not by choice   that the wretch raided
1955   the wondrous worm-hoard.   The one who offended
was stricken himself,   sorely distressed,
the son of a warrior   sold as a slave.
Escaping his bondage,   he braved the barrens
and guiltily groped   his way below ground.
1960   There the intruder   trembled with terror
hearing the dragon   who drowsed in the dark,
an ancient evil   sleepily breathing.
His fate was to find   as fear unmanned him
his fingers feeling   a filigreed cup.

1965   Many such goblets   had gone to the earth-house,
the legacies left   by a lordly people.
In an earlier age   someone unknown
had cleverly covered   those costly treasures.
A thane held the hoard   for the lifetime allowed him,
1970   but gold could not gladden   a man in mourning.
Newly-built   near the breaking waves,
a barrow stood   at the base of a bluff,
its entrance sculpted   by secret arts.
Earthward he bore   the best of the bounty.
1975   As golden giltwork   went below ground,
the ringkeeper spoke   staves for the dead:

"Hold now, Earth,   what men may not,
the hoard of the heroes,   earth-gotten wealth
when it first was won.   War-death has felled them,
1980   an evil befalling   each of my people.
The long-house is mirthless   when men are lifeless.
I have none to wear sword,   none to bear wine
or polish the precious   vessels and plates.
Gone are the brothers   who braved many battles.
1985   From the hard helmet   the hand-wrought gilding
drops in the dust.   Asleep are the smiths
who knew how to burnish   the war-chief's mask
or mend the mail-shirts   mangled in battle.
Shields and mail-shirts   molder with warriors
1990   and follow no foes   to faraway fields.
No harp rejoices   to herald the heroes,
no hand-fed hawk   swoops through the hall,
no stallion stamps   in the keep's courtyard.
Death has undone   many kindreds of men."

1995   Stricken in spirit,   he spoke of his sorrow
as last of his line,   drearily drifting

through day and dark   until death's flood-tide
stilled his heart.   The old night-scather
was happy to glimpse   the unguarded hoard.
2000   Balefully burning,   he seeks out barrows.
Naked and hateful   in a raiment of flame,
the dragon dreaded   by outland dwellers
must gather and guard   the heathen gold,
no better for wealth   but wise with his winters.

2005   For three hundred winters   the waster of nations
held that mighty   hoard in his earth-hall
till one man wronged him,   arousing his wrath.
The wretched robber   ransomed his life
with the prize he pilfered,   the plated flagon.
2010   Beholding that marvel   men of old made,
his fief-lord forgave   the skulker's offense.
One treasure taken   had tainted the rest.
Waking in wrath,   the worm reared up
and slid over stones.   Stark-hearted,
2015   he spotted the footprints   where someone had stepped,
stealthily creeping   close to his jaws.
The fortunate man   slips swiftly and safely
through the worst dangers   if the World's Warder
grants him that grace.
                          Eager and angry,
2020   the hoard-guard hunted   the thief who had haunted
his hall while he slept.   He circled the stone-house,
but out in that wasteland   the one man he wanted
was not to be found.   How fearsome he felt,
how fit for battle!   Back in his barrow
2025   he tracked the intruder   who dared to tamper
with glorious gold.   Fierce and fretful,
the dragon waited   for dusk and darkness.
The rage-swollen holder   of headland and hoard
was plotting reprisal: flames for his flagon.
2030   Then day withdrew,   and the dragon, delighted,
would linger no longer   but flare up and fly.
His onset was fearful   for folk on the land,
and a cruel ending   soon came for their king.

The ghastly specter   scattered his sparks
2035   and set their buildings   brightly burning,
flowing with flames   as homesteaders fled.
He meant to leave   not one man alive.
That wreaker of havoc   hated and harried
the Geatish folk   fleeing his flames.
2040   Far and wide   his warfare was watched
until night waned   and the worm went winging
back to the hall   where his hoard lay hidden,
sure of his stronghold,   his walls and his war,
sure of himself,   deceived by his pride.

2045   Then terrible tidings   were taken to Beowulf:
how swiftly his own   stronghold was stricken,
that best of buildings   bursting with flames
and his throne melting.   The hero was heart-sore;
the wise man wondered   what wrong he had wrought
2050   and how he transgressed   against old law,
the Lord Everlasting,   Ruler of All.
His grief was great,   and grim thoughts
boiled in his breast   as never before.
The fiery foe   had flown to his coastlands,
2055   had sacked and seared   his keep by the sea.
For that the bold war-king   required requital.
He ordered a fender   be fashioned of iron,
better for breasting   baleful blazes
than the linden-wood   warding his warriors.
2060   Little was left   of the time lent him
for life in the world;   and the worm as well,
who had haughtily held   his hoard for so long.
Scorning to follow   the far-flying foe
with his whole host,   the ring-giver reckoned
2065   the wrath of a dragon   unworthy of dread.
Fearless and forceful,   he often had risked
the straits of struggle,   blessed with success.
Beowulf braved   many a battle
after ridding Hrothgar's   hall of its horrors
2070   and grappling with Grendel's   gruesome kin.

Not least of his clashes   had come when the king
Hygelac fell   while fighting the Frisians
in hand-to-hand combat.   His friend and fief-lord,
the son of Hrethel,   was slain in the onslaught,
2075   stricken to death   by a blood-drinking blade.
Beowulf battled   back to the beach
where he proved his strength   with skillful swimming,
for he took to the tide   bearing the trophies
of thirty earls   he had felled in the field.
2080   None of the Hetware   needed to boast
how bravely they fared   flaunting their shields
against that fierce fighter,   for few remained
after the battle   to bear the tale home.

Over wide waters   the lone swimmer went,
2085   the son of Ecgtheow   swept on the sea-waves
back to his homeland,   forlorn with his loss,
and hence to Hygd   who offered her hoard:
rings and a kingdom,   a throne for the thane.
With Hygelac dead   she doubted her son
2090   could guard the Geats   from foreigners' forays.
Refusing her boon,   Beowulf bade
the leaderless lords   to hail the lad
as their rightful ruler.   He chose not to reign

by thwarting his cousin   but to counsel the king
2095   and guide with good will   until Heardred grew older.

It was Heardred who held   the Weder-Geats' hall
when outcast Scylfings   came seeking its safety:
Eanmund and Eadgils,   nephews of Onela.
That strongest of sea-kings   and spender of treasures
2100   sailed from Sweden   pursuing the rebels
who challenged his right   to rule their realm.
For lending them haven,   Hygelac's son
suffered the sword-stroke   which spilled out his life.
The Swede headed home   when Heardred lay dead,
2105   so the feud among Scylfings   granted the Geats
a greater guardian,   giving them Beowulf.
That was a good king,   kindly to kin;
yet Heardred's death   dwelled in his thoughts
until he befriended   destitute Eadgils.
2110   He summoned an army   for Othere's son,
sent weapons and warriors   over wide waters,
a voyage of vengeance   to kill off a king.

Such were the struggles   and tests of strength
the son of Ecgtheow   saw and survived.
2115   His pluck was proven   in perilous onslaughts
till that fateful day   when he fought the dragon.
As leader of twelve   trailing that terror,
the greatest of Geats   glowered with rage
when he looked on the lair   where the worm lurked.
2120   By now he had found   how the feud flared,
this fell affliction   befalling his kingdom,
for the kingly cup   had come to his hand
from the hand of him   who raided the hoard.
That sorry slave   had started the strife,
2125   and against his will   he went with the warriors,
a thirteenth man   bringing the band
to the barrow's brink   which he alone knew.
Hard by the surge   of the seething sea
gaped a cleft cavern   glutted with golden
2130   medals and chains.   The murderous manbane
hunkered within,   hungry for warfare.
No taker would touch   his treasures cheaply:
the hoard's holder   would drive a hard bargain.

Then the proud war-king   paused on the sea-point
2135   to lighten the hearts   of his hearth-companions,
though his heart was heavy   and hankered for death.
It was nearing him now.   That taker of treasure
would sunder the soul   from his old bones and flesh.
So Beowulf spoke,   the son of Ecgtheow,

2140   recalling the life   he was loathe to lose:

        "From boyhood I bore   battles and bloodshed,
        struggles and strife: I still see them all.
        I was given at seven   to house with King Hrethel,
        my mother's father   and friend of our folk.
2145   He kept me fairly   with feasts and fine gifts.
        I fared no worse   than one of his sons,
        Hathcyn, Herebeald   or princely Hygelac
        who was later my lord.   The eldest, Herebeald,
        unwittingly went   to a wrongful death
2150   when Hathcyn's horn-bow   hurled an arrow.
        Missing the mark,   it murdered the kinsman;
        a brother was shot   by the blood-stained shaft.
        This blow to the heart   was brutal and baffling.
        A prince had fallen.   The felon went free.[1]

2155   "So it is sore   for an old man to suffer
        his son swinging   young on the gallows,
        gladdening ravens.   He groans in his grief
        and loudly laments   the lad he has lost.
        No help is at hand   from hard-won wisdom
2160   or the march of years.   Each morning reminds him
        his heir is elsewhere,   and he has no heart
        to sire a second   son in his stronghold
        when death has finished   the deeds of the first.
        He ceaselessly sees   his son's dwelling,
2165   the worthless wine-hall,   the windswept grave-sward
        where swift riders   and swordsmen slumber.
        No harp-string sounds,   no song in the courtyard.
        He goes to his bed   sighing with sorrow,
        one soul for another.   His home is hollow;
2170   his field, fallow.
                        "So Hrethel suffered,
        hopeless and heart-sore   with Herebeald gone.
        He would do no deed   to wound the death-dealer
        or harrow his household   with hatred and anger;
        but bitter bloodshed   had stolen his bliss,
2175   and he quit his life   for the light of the Lord.
        Like a luckier man,   he could leave his land
        in the hands of a son,   though he loved him no longer.

        "Then strife and struggle   of Geats and Swedes
        crossed the wide water.   Warfare wounded
2180   both sides in battle   when Hrethel lay buried.
        Ongentheow's sons,   fierce and unfriendly,
        suddenly struck   at Hreosna-Beorh

---

1. Even in cases of involuntary manslaughter, punishment was required to avenge the dead. In this instance, it seems that a ritual, sacrificial hanging was performed to spare Hathcyn for murdering his brother Herebeald.

and bloodied the bluff   with baneful slaughter.
Our foes in this feud   soon felt the wrath
2185 of my kinsman the king   claiming our due,
though the counterblow   cost his own life.
Hathcyn was killed,   his kingship cut short;
The slayer himself   was slain in the morning.
I have heard how Eofer   struck the old Scylfing.
2190 Sword-ashen,   Ongentheow sank,
with his helm split: heedful of harm,
to kinsman and king,   the hand would not halt
the death-blow it dealt.
                              "My own sword-arm
repaid my prince   for the gifts he granted.
2195 He gave me a fiefdom,   the land I have loved.
He never had need   to seek among Spear-Danes,
Gifthas or Swedes   and get with his gifts
a worse warrior.   I wielded my sword
at the head of our host;   so shall I hold
2200 this blade that I bear   boldly in battle
as long as life lasts.   It has worn well
since the day when Daeghrefn   died by my hand,
the Frankish foe   who fought for the Frisians,
bearing their banner.   He broke in my grip,
2205 never to barter   the necklace he robbed
from Hygelac's corpse.   I crushed that killer;
his bones snapped,   and his life-blood spilled.
I slew him by strength,   not by the sword.
Now I shall bear   his brand into battle:
2210 hand and hard sword   will fight for the hoard."

Now Beowulf spoke   his last battle-boast:
"In boyhood I braved   bitter clashes;
still in old age   I would seek out strife
and gain glory   guarding my folk
2215 if the man-bane comes   from his cave to meet me."

Then he turned to his troop   for the final time,
bidding farewell   to bold helmet-bearers,
fast in friendship: "I would wear no sword,
no weapon at all   to ward off the worm
2220 if I knew how to fight   this fiendish foe
as I grappled with Grendel   one bygone night.
But here I shall find   fierce battle-fire
and breath envenomed,   therefore I bear
this mail-coat and shield.   I shall not shy
2225 from standing my ground   when I greet the guardian,
follow what will   at the foot of his wall.
I shall face the fiend   with a firm heart.
Let every man's Ruler   reckon my fate:

words are worthless   against the war-flyer.
2230   Bide by the barrow,   safe in your byrnies,
and watch, my warriors,   which of us two
will better bear   the brunt of our clash.
This war is not yours;   it is meted to me,
matching my strength,   man against monster.
2235   I shall do this deed   undaunted by death
and get you gold   or else get my ending,
borne off in battle,   the bane of your lord."

The hero arose,   helmed and hardy,
a war-king clad   in shield and corselet.
2240   He strode strongly   under the stone-cliff:
no faint-hearted man,   to face it unflinching!
Stalwart soldier   of so many marches,
unshaken when shields   were crushed in the clash,
he saw between stiles   an archway where steam
2245   burst like a boiling   tide from the barrow,
woeful for one   close to the worm-hoard.
He would not linger long   unburned by the lurker
or safely slip   through the searing lair.
Then a battle-cry broke   from Beowulf's breast
2250   as his rightful rage   was roused for the reckoning.
His challenge sounded   under stark stone
where the hateful hoard-guard   heard in his hollow
the clear-voiced call   of a man coming.
No quarter was claimed;   no quarter given.
2255   First the beast's breath   blew hot from the barrow
as battle-bellows   boomed underground.
The stone-house stormer   swung up his shield
at the ghastly guardian.   Then the dragon's grim heart
kindled for conflict.   Uncoiling, he came
2260   seeking the Stalwart;   but the swordsman had drawn
the keen-edged blade   bequeathed him for combat,
and each foe confronted   the other with fear.
His will unbroken,   the warlord waited
behind his tall shield,   helm and hauberk.
2265   With fitful twistings   the fire-drake hastened
fatefully forward.   His fender held high,
Beowulf felt   the blaze blister through
hotter and sooner   than he had foreseen.
So for the first time   fortune was failing
2270   the mighty man   in the midst of a struggle.
Wielding his sword,   he struck at the worm
and his fabled blade   bit to the bone
through blazoned hide: bit and bounced back,
no match for the foe   in this moment of need.

2275 The peerless prince   was hard-pressed in response,
for his bootless blow   had maddened the monster
and fatal flames   shot further than ever,
lighting the land.   No praise for the warlord's
prowess in battle: the blade he brandished
2280 had failed in the fray   though forged from iron.
No easy end   for the son of Ecgtheow:
against his will   he would leave this world
to dwell elsewhere,   as every man must
when his days are done.   Swiftly the death-dealer
2285 moved to meet him.   From the murderous breast
bellows of breath   belched fresh flames.
Enfolded in fire,   he who formerly
ruled a whole realm   had no one to help him
hold off the heat,   for his hand-picked band
2290 of princelings had fled,   fearing to face
the foe with their lord.   Loving honor
less than their lives,   they hid in the holt.
But one among them   grieved for the Geats
and balked at quitting   his kinsman, the king.

2295 This one was Wiglaf,   son of Weostan,
beloved shield-bearer   born in Scylf-land.
Seeing his liege-lord   suffering sorely
with war-mask scorched   by the searing onslaught,
the thankful thane   thought of the boons
2300 his kinsman bestowed: the splendid homestead
and folk-rights his father   formerly held.
No shirker could stop him   from seizing his shield
of yellow linden   and lifting the blade
Weostan won   when he slew Eanmund,
2305 son of Othere.   Spoils of that struggle,
sword and scabbard,   smithwork of giants,
a byrnie of ring-mail   and bright burnished helm
were granted as gifts,   a thane's war-garb,
for Onela never   acknowledged his nephews
2310 but struck against both   of his brother's sons.
When Eadgils avenged   Eanmund's death,
Weostan fled.   Woeful and friendless,
he saved that gear   for seasons of strife,
foreseeing his son   someday might crave
2315 sword and corselet.   He came to his kinsman,
the prince of the Geats,   and passed on his heirlooms,
hoping Wiglaf   would wear them with honor.
Old then, and wise,   he went from the world.

This war was the first   young Wiglaf would fight
2320 helping the king.   His heart would not quail
nor weapon fail   as the foe would find
going against him;   but he made his grim mood

known to the men: "I remember the time
when taking our mead   in the mighty hall,
2325 all of us offered   oaths to our liege-lord.
We promised to pay   for princely trappings
by staunchly wielding   sword-blades in war
if need should arise.   Now we are needed
by him who chose,   from the whole of his host,
2330 twelve for this trial,   trusting our claims
as warriors worthy   of wearing our blades,
bearing keen spears.   Our king has come here
bent on battling   the man-bane alone,
because among warriors   one keeper of kinfolk
2335 has done, undaunted,   the most deeds of daring.
But this day our lord   needs dauntless defenders
so long as the frightful   fires keep flaring.
God knows I would gladly   give my own body
for flames to enfold   with the gold-giver.
2340 Shameful, to shoulder   our shields homeward!
First we must fell   this fearsome foe
and protect the life   of our people's lord.
It is wrong that one man   be wrathfully racked
for his former feats   and fall in this fight,
2345 guarding the Geats.   We shall share our war-gear:
shield and battle-shirt,   helm and hard sword."

So speaking, he stormed   through the reek of smoke,
with helmet on head,   to help his lord.
"Beloved Beowulf,   bear up your blade.
2350 You pledged in your youth,   powerful prince,
never to let   your luster lessen
while life was left you.   Now summon your strength.
Stand steadfast.   I shall stand with you."

After these words   the worm was enraged.
2355 For a second time   the spiteful specter
flew at his foe,   and he wreathed in flames
the hated human   he hungered to harm.
His dreadful fire-wind   drove in a wave,
charring young Wiglaf's   shield to the boss,
2360 nor might a byrnie   bar that breath
from burning the brave   spear-bearer's breast.
Wiglaf took cover   close to his kinsman,
shielded by iron   when linden was cinder.
Then the war-king,   recalling past conquests,
2365 struck with full strength   straight at the head.
His battle-sword, Naegling,   stuck there and split,
shattered in combat,   so sharp was the shock
to Beowulf's great   gray-banded blade.
He never was granted   the gift of a sword
2370 as hard and strong   as the hand which held it.

I have heard that he broke   blood-hardened brands,
so the weapon-bearer   was none the better.

The fearful fire-drake,   scather of strongholds,
flung himself forward   a final time,
2375   wild with wounds   yet wily and sly.
In the heat of the fray,   he hurtled headlong
to fasten his fangs   in the foe's throat.
Beowulf's life-blood   came bursting forth
on those terrible tusks.   Just then, I am told,
2380   the second warrior   sprang from his side,
a man born for battle   proving his mettle,
keen to strengthen   his kinsman in combat.
He took no heed   of the hideous head
scorching his hand   as he hit lower down.
2385   The sword sank in,   patterned and plated;
the flames of the foe   faltered, faded.
Though gored and giddy,   Beowulf gathered
strength once again   and slipped out his sheath-knife,
the keen killing-blade   he kept in his corselet.
2390   Then the Geats' guardian   gutted the dragon,
felling that fiend   with the help of his friend,
two kinsmen together   besting the terror.
So should a thane   succor his sovereign.

That deed was the king's   crowning conquest;
2395   Beowulf's work   in the world was done.
He soon felt his wound   swelling and stinging
where fell fangs   had fastened upon him,
and evil venom   enveloped his heart.
Wisely he sought   a seat by the stone-wall,
2400   and his gaze dwelled   on the dark doorway
delved in the dolmen,   the straight stiles
and sturdy archway   sculpted by giants.
With wonderful kindness   Wiglaf washed
the clotting blood   from his king and kinsman;
2405   his hands loosened   the lord's high helm.
Though banefully bitten,   Beowulf spoke,
for he knew his lifetime   would last no longer.
The count of his days   had come to a close.
His joys were done.   Death drew near him.

2410   "Now I would wish   to will my son
these weapons of war   had I been awarded
an heir of my own,   holder of heirlooms.
I fathered our folk   for fifty winters.
No warlike lord   of neighboring lands
2415   dared to assail us   or daunt us with dread.
A watchful warden,   I waited on fate
while keeping the Geats   clear of quarrels.

I swore many oaths;   not one was wrongful.
So I rejoice,   though sick with my death-wound,
2420 that God may not blame me   for baseless bloodshed
or killing of kin   when breath quits my body.
Hurry below   and look on the hoard,
beloved Wiglaf.   The worm lies sleeping
under gray stone,   sorely stricken
2425 and stripped of his gold.   Go swiftly and seize it.
Get me giltwork   and glittering gems:
I would set my sight   on that store of wealth.
Loath would I be   to leave for less
the life and lordship   I held for so long."

2430 I have heard how swiftly   the son of Weostan
hastened to heed   his wounded and weakening
war-lord's behest.   In his woven mail-shirt,
his bright byrnie,   he entered the barrow;
and passing its threshold,   proud and princely,
2435 he glimpsed all the gold   piled on the ground,
the walled-in wealth   won by the worm,
that fierce night-flyer.   Flagons were standing,
embossed wine-beakers   lying unburnished,
their inlays loosened.   There were lofty helmets
2440 and twisted arm-rings   rotting and rusting.
Gold below ground   may betray into grief
any who find it,   hide it who will.

Wiglaf saw also   a gold-woven standard,
a wonder of handiwork,   finger-filigreed
2445 high above ground.   It gave off a glow
that let him behold   the whole of the hoard.
I am told he took   from that trove of giants
goblets and platters   pressed to his breastplate,
and the golden banner   glinting brightly.
2450 He spotted no sign   of the stricken worm.
The iron-edged brand   old Beowulf bore
had mortally wounded   the warder of wealth
and fiery foe   whose flames in the night
welled so fiercely   before he was felled.

2455 Bent with his burden,   the messenger hastened
back to his master,   burning to know
whether the brave   but wound-weakened
lord of the Weders   was lost to the living.
Setting his spoils   by the storied prince
2460 whose lifeblood blackened   the ground with gore,
Wiglaf wakened   the war-lord with water,
and these words thrust   like spears through his breast
as the ancient one grimly   gazed on the gold:

"For these precious things   I look upon last,
2465   I thank the Lord,   eternal World-Ruler.
Bright is this boon   my life's loss has bought,
to lighten my death-day.   Look to our people,
for you shall be leader;   I lead no longer.
Gather my guard   and raise me a grave-mound
2470   housing my ashes   at Hronesnaesse,
reminding my kin   to recall their king
after his pyre   has flared on the point.
Seafarers passing   shall say when they see it
'Beowulf's Barrow'   as bright longboats
2475   drive over darkness,   daring the flood."

So the stern prince   bestowed on his sword-thane
and keen spear-wielder   the kingly collar,
his gold-plated helm   and hammered hauberk.
He told him to bear them   bravely in battle:
2480   "Farewell, Wiglaf,   last Waegmunding.
I follow our fathers,   foredestined to die,
swept off by fate,   though strong and steadfast."
These heartfelt words   were the warrior's last
before his body   burned in the bale-fire
2485   and his soul sought   the doom of the truthful.

Smitten with sorrow,   the young man saw
the old lord he loved   lying in pain
as life left him.   Slain and slayer
died there together: the dread earth-dragon,
2490   deprived of his life,   no longer would lurk
coiled on the hoard.   Hard-hammered swords
had felled the far-flyer   in front of his lair.
No more would he sport   on the midnight sky,
proud of his wealth,   his power and pomp.
2495   He sprawled on stone   where the war-chief slew him.
Though deeds of daring   were done in that land,
I have heard of no man   whose might would suffice
to face the fire-drake's   fuming breath
or help him escape   if he handled the hoard
2500   once he had woken   its warder from sleep.
Beowulf paid   for that lode with his life;
his loan of days   was lost to the dragon.

Before long the laggards   limped from the woods,
ten cowards together,   the troth-breakers
2505   who had failed to bare   their blades in battle
at the moment their master   needed them most.
In shame they shouldered   their shields and spears.
Armored for war,   they went to Wiglaf
who sat in sorrow   beside their old sovereign.
2510   No soldier's water   would waken the Stalwart,
nor wishes win life   for a lifeless leader.

The World's Warden   decided what deeds
a man might achieve   in those days and these.
A hard answer   was easily offered
2515 by young Wiglaf,   Weostan's son.
With little love   he looked on the shirkers:

"I tell you in truth,   takers of treasure,
bench-sitting boasters   brave in the hall:
Beowulf gave you   the gear that you wear,
2520 the best helms and hauberks   found near or far
for a prince to proffer   his thankless thanes;
but he wasted his wealth   on a worthless troop
who cast off their king   at the coming of war.
Our lord had no need   to laud his liege-men;
2525 yet God, giver   of glory and vengeance,
granted him strength   to stand with his sword.
I could do little   to lengthen his life
facing that foe,   but I fought nonetheless:
beyond my power   I propped up my prince.
2530 The fire-drake faltered   after I struck him,
and his fuming jaws   flamed less fiercely,
but too few friends   flew to our king
when evil beset him.   Now sword-bestowing
and gold-getting   shall cease for the Geats.
2535 You shall have no joy   in the homeland you love.
Your farms shall be forfeit,   and each man fare
alone and landless   when foreign lords
learn of your flight,   your failure of faith.
Better to die   than dwell in disgrace."

2540 Then Wiglaf bade   that the battle-tidings
be sent to the camp   over the sea-cliff
where warriors waited   with shields unslung,
sadly sitting   from dawn until noon
to learn if their lord   and beloved leader
2545 had seen his last sunrise   or soon would return.
The herald would leave them   little to doubt;
he sped up the headland   and spoke to them all:

"Now the wish-granter,   warlord of Weders,
lies on his death-bed.   The leader of Geats
2550 stays in the slaughter-place,   slain by the worm
sprawled at his side.   Dagger-stricken,
the slayer was felled,   though a sword had failed
to wound the serpent.   Weostan's son,
Wiglaf is waiting   by Beowulf's body;
2555 a living warrior   watches the lifeless,
sad-heartedly   sitting to guard
the loved and the loathed.   Look now for war
as Franks and Frisians   learn how the king
has fallen in combat.   Few foreigners love us,

2560   for Hygelac angered   the harsh Hugas
         when his fleet forayed   to far-off Frisia.
         Fierce Hetware   met him with forces
         bigger than his.   They broke him in battle;
         that mail-clad chieftain   fell with his men.
2565   Hygelac took   no trophies to thanes;
         no Meroving king   has since wished us well.

         "I also foresee   strife with the Swedes,
         feud without end,   for all know Ongentheow
         slew Hrethel's son   when hot-headed Hathcyn
2570   first led the Geats   beyond Ravenswood
         and raided the realm   of Scylf-land's ruler.
         That fearsome old foe,   father of Othere,
         quickly struck back.   He cut down our king
         to rescue the queen   Hathcyn had captured.
2575   Her captors had shorn   the crone of her gold,
         dishonored the aged   mother of Onela.
         Ongentheow followed   hard on their heels.
         Wounded, weary   and fiercely-harried,
         those left unslain   by Swedish swords
2580   limped off leaderless,   hid in the holt.
         A huge army   beleaguered them there.
         All night long   Ongentheow taunted
         the wretched raiders.   At daybreak, he swore,
         he would slice them to slivers.   Some would swing
2585   slung on his gallows,   sport for the ravens.
         But gladness came   again to grim Geats
         hearing Hygelac's   horns in the morning,
         the trumpet calls   of the troop that tracked them.
         Hathcyn's brother,   bold with his band,
2590   had rallied for battle.
                             "A bloody swath
         Scylfings and Geats   left on the landscape,
         everywhere gored   with spoor of the stricken.
         So the two folks   stirred further feuds.
         Wise in warfare,   old Ongentheow
2595   grimly stood off,   seeking the safety
         of higher ground.   He had heard of Hygelac's
         strength in struggles,   his pride and prowess.
         Mistrusting his force   to fend off the foray,
         he feared for his family   and fell back to guard
2600   the hoard hidden   behind his earthworks.
         Then Hrethel's people   pressed the pursuit:
         the standards of Hygelac   stormed the stronghold.
         There the Swede   was snared between swords.
         Eofer humbled   that hoary-haired leader,
2605   though Wulf struck first,   fierce with his weapon,
         and a cut vein colored   the king's white head.
         Undaunted, Ongentheow   warded him off;

Wulf was wounded   the worse in return:
Ongentheow's blow   broke open his helm,
2610   hurled him headlong,   helpless and bleeding
though not destined   to die on that day.
Then Eofer faced   the folk-lord alone.
Sternly he stood   when his brother slumped:
Hygelac's soldier   with broadsword in hand
2615   and helmet on head,   hoarded smithwork
shaped by old crafts,   shattered the shield-wall.
The king crumpled,   struck to the quick.

"Now the Geats gathered   after the slaughter.
Some bound the wound   of Eofer's brother
2620   and bundled him off   the field of battle.
Meanwhile one warrior   looted the other:
Eofer stripped   the hard-hilted sword,
helm and corselet   from Ongentheow's corpse.
He handed that heap   of armor to Hygelac.
2625   Glad of the plunder,   the prince pledged in turn
to reward war-strokes   as lord of the Weders.
He gave great riches   to Wulf and Eofer.
Once they were home,   he honored each one
with a hundred thousand   in land and linked rings.
2630   No man in middle-earth   ever begrudged them
the favor and fortune   bestowed for their feat.
Yet a further honor   was offered Eofer:
the king's only daughter   adorned his house,
awarded in wedlock   to Wonred's son.

2635   "Full of this feud,   this festering hatred,
the Swedes, I am certain,   will swiftly beset us,
as soon as they learn   our lord lies lifeless
who held his hoard,   his hall and his realm
against all foes   when heroes had fallen,
2640   who fostered his folk   with fair kingship.
Now must we hasten,   behold our sovereign,
and bear him for burial.   The brave one shall not
be beggared of booty   to melt on his bier.
Let funeral flames   greedily fasten
2645   on gold beyond measure,   grimly gotten,
lucre our leader   bought with his life.
No earl shall take   tokens to treasure
nor maiden be made   fairer with finery
strung at her throat.   Stripped of their wealth,
2650   they shall wander woefully   all their lives long,
lordless and landless   now that their king
has laid aside laughter,   sport and song.
Their hands shall heft   many a spear-haft,
cold in the morning.   No call of the harp
2655   shall waken warriors   after their battles;
but the black raven   shall boast to the eagle,

crowing how finely   he fed on the fated
when, with the wolf,   he went rending the slain."

Thus the terrible   tidings were told,
2660   and the teller had not   mistaken the truth.
The warriors all rose   and woefully went
to look on the wonder   with welling tears.
They found on the sand   under Earnanaesse
their lifeless lord   laid there to rest,
2665   beloved giver   of gifts and gold rings,
the war-king come   at the close of his days
to a marvelous death.   At first the monster
commanded their gaze: grim on the ground
across from the king   the creature had crumpled,
2670   scaly and scorched,   a fearsome fire-drake
fifty feet long.   He would fly no more,
free in the darkness,   nor drop to his den
at the break of dawn.   Death held the dragon;
he never would coil   in his cavern again.
2675   Beyond the serpent   stood flagons and jars,
plated flatware   and priceless swords
rotting in ruin,   etched out with rust.
These riches had rested   in Earth's embrace
for a thousand winters,   the heritage held
2680   by warders of old,   spell-enwoven
and toilfully tombed   that none might touch them,
unless God Himself,   granter of grace,
true Lord of glory,   allotted release
to one of His choosing   and opened the hoard.

2685   It little profited   him who had wrongfully
hidden the hand-wrought   wealth within walls.
His payment was scant   for slaying the one
with courage to claim it: the kill was quickly
and harshly requited.   So the kingly
2690   may come to strange ends   when their strength is spent
and time meted out.   They may not remain
as men among kin,   mirthful with mead.
Beowulf goaded   the gold's guardian,
raised up the wrath,   not reckoning whether
2695   his death-day had dawned,   not knowing the doom
solemnly sworn   by princes who placed
their hoard in that hollow: the thief who held it
would fall before idols,   forge himself hell-bonds,
waste in torment   for touching the treasure.
2700   He failed to consider   more fully and sooner
who rightfully owned   such awesome riches.
So spoke Wiglaf,   son of Weostan:
"By the whim of one man,   many warriors
sometimes may suffer,   as here has happened.

2705 No means were at hand   to move my master;
     no counsel could sway   the kingdom's keeper
     never to trouble   the treasure's taker,
     but leave him lying   where long he had hidden,
     walled with his wealth   until the world's ending.
2710 He kept to his course,   uncovered the hoard.
     Fate was too strongly   forcing him hither.
     I have entered that hall,   beheld everything
     golden within,   though none too glad
     for the opening offered   under its archway.
2715 In haste I heaved   much from the hoard,
     and a mighty burden   I bore from the barrow
     straight to my sovereign.   He still was alive;
     his wits were clear;   his words came quickly.
     In anguish, the Ancient   asked that I say
2720 he bade you to build   a barrow for him
     befitting the deeds   of a fallen friend.
     You shall heap it high   over his ashes,
     since he was the world's   worthiest warrior,
     famed far and wide   for the wealth of his fortress.

2725 "Now let us hurry   hence to the hoard.
     For a second time   I shall see that splendor
     under the cliff-wall,   those wonders of craft-work.
     Come, I shall take you   close to the trove.
     where you may behold   heaps of broad gold.
2730 Then let a bier   be readied to bear
     our beloved lord   to his long dwelling
     under the watch   of the world's Warder."

     Then Weostan's heir   ordered the earls,
     heads of houses   and fief holders,
2735 to fetch firewood   fit for the folk-leader's
     funeral pyre.   "Flames shall now flare,
     feed on the flesh   and fade into darkness,
     an ending for him   who often endured
     the iron showers   shot over shield-walls
2740 when string-driven storms   of arrows arose
     with fletches affixed   to steer them in flight
     with barbed arrowheads   eager to bite."

     Wisely Wiglaf,   son of Weostan,
     summoned the seven   most steadfast thanes.
2745 They went in together,   eight earls entering
     under the evil   arch of the earth-house
     with one man bearing   a blazing torch.
     No lot was cast   to learn which liege-man
     would plunder the loot   which lay unguarded,
2750 as each searcher   could see for himself;
     yet none was unhappy   to hurry that hoard
     out into daylight.   They heaved the dragon

over the sea-cliff   where surges seized him:
the treasure's keeper   was caught by the tide.
2755   Then they filled a wain   with filigreed gold
and untold treasures;   and they carried the king,
their hoary-haired warlord,   to Hronesnaesse.

There the king's kinsmen   built him a bier,
wide and well-made   just as he willed it.
2760   They hung it with helmets,   shields and hauberks,
then laid in its midst   their beloved lord,
renowned among men.   Lamenting their loss,
his warriors woke   the most woeful fire
to flare on the bluff.   Fierce was the burning,
2765   woven with weeping,   and wood-smoke rose
black over the blaze,   blown with a roar.
The fire-wind faltered   and flames dwindled,
hot at their heart   the broken bone-house.
Sunken in spirit   at Beowulf's slaying,
2770   the Geats gathered   grieving together.
Her hair waving,   a woebegone woman
sang and resang   her dirge of dread,
foretelling a future   fraught with warfare,
kinfolk sundered,   slaughter and slavery
2775   even as Heaven   swallowed the smoke.

High on the headland   they heaped his grave-mound
which seafaring sailors   would spy from afar.
Ten days they toiled   on the scorched hilltop,
the cleverest men   skillfully crafting
2780   a long-home built   for the bold in battle.
They walled with timbers   the trove they had taken,
sealing in stone   the circlets and gems,
wealth of the worm-hoard   gotten with grief,
gold from the ground   gone back to Earth
2785   as worthless to men   as when it was won.
Then sorrowing swordsmen   circled the barrow,
twelve of his earls   telling their tales,
the sons of nobles   sadly saluting
deeds of the dead.   So dutiful thanes
2790   in liege to their lord   mourn him with lays
praising his peerless   prowess in battle
as it is fitting   when life leaves the flesh.
Heavy-hearted   his hearth-companions
grieved for Beowulf,   great among kings,
2795   mild in his mien,   most gentle of men,
kindest to kinfolk   yet keenest for fame.

RESPONSE
John Gardner: from *Grendel*[1]
CHAPTER ONE

The old ram stands looking down over rockslides, stupidly triumphant. I blink. I stare in horror. "Scat!" I hiss. "Go back to your cave, go back to your cowshed—whatever." He cocks his head like an elderly, slow-witted king, considers the angles, decides to ignore me. I stamp. I hammer the ground with my fists. I hurl a skull-size stone at him. He will not budge. I shake my two hairy fists at the sky and I let out a howl so unspeakable that the water at my feet turns sudden ice and even I myself am left uneasy. But the ram stays; the season is upon us. And so begins the twelfth year of my idiotic war.

The pain of it! The stupidity!

"Ah, well," I sigh, and shrug, trudge back to the trees.

Do not think my brains are squeezed shut, like the ram's, by the roots of horns. Flanks atremble, eyes like stones, he stares at as much of the world as he can see and feels it surging in him, filling his chest as the melting snow fills dried-out creekbeds, tickling his gross, lopsided balls and charging his brains with the same unrest that made him suffer last year at this time, and the year before, and the year before that. (He's forgotten them all.) His hindparts shiver with the usual joyful, mindless ache to mount whatever happens near—the storm piling up black towers to the west, some rotting, docile stump, some spraddle-legged ewe. I cannot bear to look. "Why can't these creatures discover a little dignity?" I ask the sky. The sky says nothing, predictably. I make a face, uplift a defiant middle finger, and give an obscene little kick. The sky ignores me, forever unimpressed. Him too I hate, the same as I hate these brainless budding trees, these brattling birds.

Not, of course, that I fool myself with thoughts that I'm more noble. Pointless, ridiculous monster crouched in the shadows, stinking of dead men, murdered children, martyred cows. (I am neither proud nor ashamed, understand. One more dull victim, leering at seasons that never were meant to be observed.) "Ah, sad one, poor old freak!" I cry, and hug myself, and laugh, letting out salt tears, he he! till I fall down gasping and sobbing. (It's mostly fake.) The sun spins mindlessly overhead, the shadows lengthen and shorten as if by plan. Small birds, with a high-pitched yelp, lay eggs. The tender grasses peek up, innocent yellow, through the ground: the children of the dead. (It was just here, this shocking green, that once when the moon was tombed in clouds, I tore off sly old Athelgard's head. Here, where the startling tiny jaws of crocuses snap at the late-winter sun like the heads of baby watersnakes, here I

---

1. John Gardner was a best-selling American novelist and professor of medieval literature who died in a motorcycle accident in 1982 at the age of 49. His first popular success came with the 1971 publication of *Grendel*, a rewriting of *Beowulf* from the monster's point of view. Alienated from traditional morality and the comforts of the beer hall, Grendel gorges himself gleefully on the bodies he has carried off from Hrothgar's hall, and fondly recalls the places where he "tore off sly old Athelgard's head" or ate an old woman who "tasted of urine and spleen." Though Gardner does not portray him entirely sympathetically, Grendel can be seen in the romantic tradition of the outsider hero, like the monster in Mary Shelley's *Frankenstein* or Satan in Blake's rereading of Milton's *Paradise Lost*.

While Gardner's interpretation of the monster is distinctly modern, the style of the novel reveals his background as a medievalist: he imitates the Old English of *Beowulf* in his use of alliteration and of Germanic compound words such as "falconswift," "whalecocks," and "earth-rim-rover."

killed the old woman with the irongray hair. She tasted of urine and spleen, which made me spit. Sweet mulch for yellow blooms. Such are the tiresome memories of a shadow-shooter, earth-rim-roamer, walker of the world's weird wall.) "Waaah!" I cry, with another quick, nasty face at the sky, mournfully observing the way it is, bitterly remembering the way it was, and idiotically casting tomorrow's nets. "Aargh! Yaww!" I reel, smash trees. Disfigured son of lunatics. The big-boled oaks gaze down at me yellow with morning, beneath complexity. "No offense," I say, with a terrible, sycophantish smile, and tip an imaginary hat.

It was not always like this, of course. On occasion it's been worse.

No matter, no matter.

The doe in the clearing goes stiff at sight of my horridness, then remembers her legs and is gone. It makes me cross. "Blind prejudice!" I bawl at the splintered sunlight where half a second ago she stood. I wring my fingers, put on a long face. "Ah, the unfairness of everything," I say, and shake my head. It is a matter of fact that I have never killed a deer in all my life, and never will. Cows have more meat and, locked up in pens, are easier to catch. It is true, perhaps, that I feel some trifling dislike of deer, but no more dislike than I feel for other natural things—discounting men. But deer, like rabbits and bears and even men, can make, concerning my race, no delicate distinctions. That is their happiness: they see all life without observing it. They're buried in it like crabs in mud. Except men, of course. I am not in a mood, just yet, to talk of men.

So it goes with me day by day and age by age, I tell myself. Locked in the deadly progression of moon and stars. I shake my head, muttering darkly on shaded paths, holding conversation with the only friend and comfort this world affords, my shadow. Wild pigs clatter away through brush. A baby bird falls feet-up in my path, squeaking. With a crabby laugh, I let him lie, kind heaven's merciful bounty to some sick fox. So it goes with me, age by age. (Talking, talking. Spinning a web of words, pale walls of dreams, between myself and all I see.)

The first grim stirrings of springtime come (as I knew they must, having seen the ram), and even under the ground where I live, where no light breaks but the red of my fires and nothing stirs but the flickering shadows on my wet rock walls, or scampering rats on my piles of bones, or my mother's fat, foul bulk rolling over, restless again—molested by nightmares, old memories—I am aware in my chest of tuberstirrings in the blacksweet duff of the forest overhead. I feel my anger coming back, building up like invisible fire, and at last, when my soul can no longer resist, I go up—as mechanical as anything else—fists clenched against my lack of will, my belly growling, mindless as wind, for blood. I swim up through the firesnakes, hot dark whalecocks prowling the luminous green of the mere, and I surface with a gulp among churning waves and smoke. I crawl up onto the bank and catch my breath.

It's good at first to be out in the night, naked to the cold mechanics of the stars. Space hurls outward, falconswift, mounting like an irreversible injustice, a final disease. The cold night air is reality at last: indifferent to me as a stone face carved on a high cliff wall to show that the world is abandoned. So childhood too feels good at first, before one happens to notice the terrible sameness, age after age. I lie there resting in the steaming grass, the old lake hissing and gurgling behind me, whispering patterns of words my sanity resists. At last, heavy as an ice-capped mountain, I rise and work my way to the inner wall, beginning of wolfslopes, the edge of my realm.

I stand in the high wind balanced, blackening the night with my stench, gazing down to cliffs that fall away to cliffs, and once again I am aware of my potential: I could die. I cackle with rage and suck in breath.

"Dark chasms!" I scream from the cliff-edge, "seize me! Seize me to your foul black bowels and crush my bones!" I am terrified at the sound of my own huge voice in the darkness. I stand there shaking from head to foot, moved to the deep-sea depths of my being, like a creature thrown into audience with thunder.

At the same time, I am secretly unfooled. The uproar is only my own shriek, and chasms are, like all things vast, inanimate. They will not snatch me in a thousand years, unless, in a lunatic fit of religion, I jump.

I sigh, depressed, and grind my teeth. I toy with shouting some tidbit more—some terrifying, unthinkable threat, some blackly fuliginous riddling hex—but my heart's not in it. "Missed me!" I say with a coy little jerk and a leer, to keep my spirits up. Then, with a sigh, a kind of moan, I start very carefully down the cliffs that lead to the fens and moors and Hrothgar's hall. Owls cross my path as silently as raiding ships, and at the sound of my foot, lean wolves rise, glance at me awkwardly, and, neat of step as lizards, sneak away. I used to take some pride in that—the caution of owls when my shape looms in, the alarm I stir in these giant northern wolves. I was younger then. Still playing cat and mouse with the universe.

I move down through the darkness, burning with murderous lust, my brains raging at the sickness I can observe in myself as objectively as might a mind ten centuries away. Stars, spattered out through lifeless night from end to end, like jewels scattered in a dead king's grave, tease, torment my wits toward meaningful patterns that do not exist. I can see for miles from these rock walls: thick forest suddenly still at my coming—cowering stags, wolves, hedgehogs, boars, submerged in their stifling, unmemorable fear; mute birds, pulsating, thoughtless clay in hushed old trees, thick limbs interlocked to seal drab secrets in.

I sigh, sink into the silence, and cross it like wind. Behind my back, at the world's end, my pale slightly glowing fat mother sleeps on, old, sick at heart, in our dingy underground room. Life-bloated, baffled, long-suffering hag. Guilty, she imagines, of some unremembered, perhaps ancestral crime. (She must have some human in her.) Not that she thinks. Not that she dissects and ponders the dusty mechanical bits of her miserable life's curse. She clutches at me in her sleep as if to crush me. I break away. "Why are we here?" I used to ask her. "Why do we stand this putrid, stinking hole?" She trembles at my words. Her fat lips shake. "Don't ask!" her wiggling claws implore. (She never speaks.) "Don't ask!" It must be some terrible secret, I used to think. I'd give her a crafty squint. She'll tell me, in time, I thought. But she told me nothing. I waited on. That was before the old dragon, calm as winter, unveiled the truth. He was not a friend.

And so I come through trees and towns to the lights of Hrothgar's meadhall. I am no stranger here. A respected guest. Eleven years now and going on twelve I have come up this clean-mown central hill, dark shadow out of the woods below, and have knocked politely on the high oak door, bursting its hinges and sending the shock of my greeting inward like a cold blast out of a cave. "Grendel!" they squeak, and I smile like exploding spring. The old Shaper, a man I cannot help but admire, goes out the back window with his harp at a single bound, though blind as a bat. The drunkest of Hrothgar's thanes come reeling and clanking down from their wall-hung beds, all shouting their meady, outrageous boasts, their heavy swords aswirl like eagles' wings. "Woe, woe, woe!" cries Hrothgar, hoary with winters, peeking in, wide-eyed, from his bedroom in back. His wife, looking in behind him, makes a scene. The thanes in the meadhall blow out the lights and cover the wide stone fireplace with shields. I laugh, crumple over; I can't help myself. In the darkness, I alone see clear as day. While they squeal and screech and bump into each other, I silently sack up my dead and withdraw to the woods. I eat and laugh and eat until I can barely walk, my chest-hair matted with dribbled blood, and then the roosters on the hill crow, and dawn comes over the roofs of the houses, and all at once I am filled with gloom again.

"This is some punishment sent us," I hear them bawling from the hill.

My head aches. Morning nails my eyes.

"Some god is angry," I hear a woman keen. "The people of Scyld and Herogar and Hrothgar are mired in sin!"

My belly rumbles, sick on their sour meat. I crawl through bloodstained leaves to the eaves of the forest, and there peek out. The dogs fall silent at the edge of my spell, and where the king's hall surmounts the town, the blind old Shaper, harp clutched tight to his fragile chest, stares futilely down, straight at me. Otherwise nothing. Pigs root dully at the posts of a wooden fence. A rumple-horned ox lies chewing in dew and shade. A few men, lean, wearing animal skins, look up at the gables of the king's hall, or at the vultures circling casually beyond. Hrothgar says nothing, hoarfrost-bearded, his features cracked and crazed. Inside, I hear the people praying—whimpering, whining, mumbling, pleading—to their numerous sticks and stones. He doesn't go in. The king has lofty theories of his own.

"Theories," I whisper to the bloodstained ground. So the dragon once spoke. ("They'd map out roads through Hell with their crackpot theories!" I recall his laugh.)

Then the groaning and praying stop, and on the side of the hill the dirge-slow shoveling begins. They throw up a mound for the funeral pyre, for whatever arms or legs or heads my haste has left behind. Meanwhile, up in the shattered hall, the builders are hammering, replacing the door for (it must be) the fiftieth or sixtieth time, industrious and witless as worker ants—except that they make small, foolish changes, adding a few more iron pegs, more iron bands, with tireless dogmatism.

Now fire. A few little lizard tongues, then healthy flames reaching up through the tangled nest of sticks. (A feeble-minded crow could have fashioned a neater nest.) A severed leg swells up and bursts, then an arm, then another, and the red fire turns on the blackening flesh and makes it sizzle, and it reaches higher, up and up into greasy smoke, turning, turning like falcons at warplay, rushing like circling wolves up into the swallowing, indifferent sky. And now, by some lunatic theory, they throw on golden rings, old swords, and braided helmets. They wail, the whole crowd, women and men, a kind of song, like a single quavering voice. The song rings up like the greasy smoke and their faces shine with sweat and something that looks like joy. The song swells, pushes through woods and sky, and they're singing now as if by some lunatic theory they had won. I shake with rage. The red sun blinds me, churns up my belly to nausea, and the heat thrown out of the bone-fire burns my skin. I cringe, clawing my flesh, and flee for home.

Early Irish Narrative

Ireland had long been Christian when its huge tradition of heroic tales was created and written down, but Irish storytellers remained largely comfortable with their pagan myths and legends. Their tales look back, sometimes with playful doubt, to an ancient world of gods and goddesses, warring heroes, magical weapons, shape shifters, and wondrous beasts, in which the line between mortals and gods was blurry and often crossed. Heroes and powerful women often have both human and divine qualities, such as Cú Chulainn (*coo-HULL-in*) and Macha in the brief episodes included here. Cú Chulainn's father may be a human husband or a pagan god, while Macha draws her name and some powers from a war goddess yet suffers the pains of childbirth. Part of the impact of these stories, indeed, is the way that the uncanny in them emerges, subtly if sometimes suddenly, from the mundane.

These episodes reflect other qualities typical of the far longer narrative groups from which they are drawn. Written and repeatedly revised in a literate world of hand-copied manuscripts, from as early as the sixth century, the stories still echo the prestige of an older, oral narrative tradition. Heroic warriors like Conall Cernach also appear as great storytellers; other heroes are both poets and prophets. The stories are equally concerned with genealogies and the mythic resonance of geography. Each episode here concerns the history of the Ulaid, the "men of Ulster" who serve king Conchobor (*CON-cho-ver*), and each story reminds its listeners of some piece of their legendary lineage or the mythic events behind place names. Together these and other tales act like an encyclopedia. They help recall, even if they do not promote, their listeners' ancient beliefs and values.

"The Labour Pains of the Ulaid" explains the sudden and debilitating weakness of the Ulstermen at times of military crisis. The most famous such moment is in the epic *The Cattle Raid of Cooley*, when Cú Chulainn has to protect the borders of Ulster against an invading army in a series of single combats until his countrymen recover their strength. At the same time, it links the name of the seat of the kings of Ulster to a wondrous, perhaps divine woman, and to her husband's disastrous indiscretion. "The Birth of Cú Chulainn" reflects more a logic of association than of narrative resolution. The tale invokes several versions of the hero's paternity, almost playfully, each time frustrating the expected moment of wondrous birth; yet it leaves Cú Chulainn linked to paternity through magic, a god, incest, or legal marriage. "The Naming of Cú Chulainn" both relates an early instance of his superhuman strength and offers a legendary explanation for the name of this preeminent hero of Irish tradition.

The Labour Pains of the Ulaid[1]

Crunniuc son of Agnoman of the Ulaid was a hospitaller with many lands. He lived in the wildernesses and the mountains, and his sons lived with him; his wife was dead. One day, when he was alone in his house, he saw a woman coming towards him, and she seemed beautiful to him. She settled in at once and went to her tasks, just as if she had always been there, and, when evening came, she set the household in order without being asked. That night, she slept with Crunniuc. She was with him

1. Translated by Jeffrey Gantz.

a long time after that, and there was no prosperity that she did not bring him, no want of food or clothing or wealth.

Not long afterwards, the Ulaid held a fair, and they all went, men and women, sons and daughters. Crunniuc set out as well, with good clothes on him and a great bloom in his face. "Take care to say nothing foolish," she said to him. "Not likely that," he replied. The fair was held, and at the end of the day the king's chariot was brought on to the field, and his chariot and horses were victorious. The hosts said "Nothing is as fast as those horses are": Crunniuc said "My wife is that fast." He was taken to the king at once, and the news was taken to his wife. "A great misfortune my having to go and free him now, when I am with child," she said. "Misfortune or no," said the messenger, "he will die if you do not come."

She went to the fair, then, and her labour pains seized her. "Help me," she said to the hosts, "for a mother bore every one of you. Wait until my children are born." She failed to move them, however. "Well then," she continued, "the evil you suffer will be greater, and it will afflict Ulaid for a long time." "What is your name?" asked the king. "My name and that of my children will mark this fairground for ever—I am Macha daughter of Sainrith son of Imbath,"[2] she said. She raced against the chariot, then, and, as the chariot reached the end of the field, she gave birth in front of it, and she bore a son and a daughter. That is why the place is called Emain Macha.[3] At her delivery, she screamed that any man who heard her would suffer the pains of birth for five days and four nights. All the Ulaid who were there were so afflicted, and their descendants suffered for nine generations afterwards. Five days and four nights, or five nights and four days—that was the extent of the labour pains of the Ulaid; and, for nine generations, the Ulaid were as weak as a woman in labour. Three classes of people, however, did not suffer this affliction: the women and the children of Cú Chulainn. This was the inheritance of Ulaid from the time of Crunniuc son of Agnoman son of Curir Ulad son of Fíatach son of Urmi until the time of Furcc son of Dallán son of Manech son of Lugaid.

The Birth of Cú Chulainn

One time, when Conchobo[1] and the chieftains of Ulaid were at Emain Macha, a flock of birds frequented the plain outside Emain, and it grazed there until not so much as a root or a stalk or a blade of grass remained. The Ulaid were distressed to see the land so devastated, and thus, one day, they harnessed nine chariots and set out to drive the birds away, for it was their custom to hunt birds. Conchobor sat in his chariot together with his grown daughter Deichtine,[2] for she was his charioteer; and the other champions of the Ulaid sat in their chariots, Conall and Lóegure and everyone else, even Bricriu. Before them the birds flew, over Slíab Fúait, over Edmund, over Brega,[3] and the Ulaid were enchanted by the birds' flight and by their singing. There were nine score birds in all, each score flying separately, and each pair of birds was linked by a silver chain.

2. "Strange son of the ocean"; these parental names suggest Macha's magical or quasi-divine powers.
3. EV-in MA-ha, "the twins of Macha," legendary capital of the Ulstermen.
1. CON-cho-ver, legendary king of the Ulstermen.

2. DECH-ti-ne.
3. Slíab Fúait, a mountain in Armagh and site of many episodes in heroic legends; Edmund, a region to the south of it; Brega, a fertile plain, site of Tara, the seat of legendary high kings of Ireland.

Towards evening three birds broke away and made for Bruig na Bóinde.[4] Then night came upon the Ulaid, and a great snow fell, so Conchobor told his people to unyoke their chariots, and he sent a party to seek shelter. Conall and Bricriu[5] searched the area and found a single house, new; they went inside and were welcomed by the couple there, and then they returned to their people. Bricriu complained that it would not be worthwhile to go to a house that had neither food nor clothing and was narrow into the bargain. All the same, the Ulaid went; they took their chariots with them, but they did not take much inside. Suddenly, they discovered a storehouse door before them. Then it came time to eat, and the Ulaid grew merry with drink, and their disposition was good. The man of the house told them that his wife was in labour in the storehouse, so Deichtine went back to help, and soon a son was born. At the same time, a mare that was at the entrance to the house gave birth to two foals. The Ulaid gave the colts to the boy as a gift, and Deichtine nursed him.

When morning came, the Ulaid found themselves east of the Bruig—no house, no birds, only their horses and the boy with his colts. They returned to Emain Macha, and the boy was nursed until he was a young lad, but then he fell ill and died. Tears were shed, and Deichtine was greatly saddened by the death of her foster-son. Finally, when she had left off sighing, she felt thirsty and requested drink from a copper vessel, and that was brought. Every time she put the vessel to her mouth, a tiny creature would leap from the liquid towards her lips; yet, when she took the vessel from her mouth, there was nothing to be seen. That night, she had a dream: a man spoke to her and said that he had brought her towards the Bruig, that it was his house she had entered, that she was pregnant by him and that it was a son that would be born. The man's name was Lug son of Eithliu;[6] the boy's name was to be Sétanta,[7] and it was for him that the colts were to be reared.

Thereafter, Deichtine indeed became pregnant. The Ulaid were troubled since they did not know the father, and they surmised that Conchobor had fathered the child while drunk, for Deichtine used to sleep next to him. Conchobor then betrothed his daughter to Súaltam son of Roech. Deichtine was greatly embarrassed at having to go to Súaltam's bed while being pregnant, so, when the time came, she lay down in the bed and crushed the child within her. Then she went to Súaltam, and at once she became pregnant by him and bore him a son.

The Naming of Cú Chulainn

'We knew that boy, indeed,' said Conall Cernach,[1] 'and we were none the worse for knowing him. He was our fosterling. Not long after the deeds Fergus has just related he performed another feat.

'When Culann the smith offered Conchobor his hospitality, he said that a large host should not come, for the feast would be the fruit not of lands and possessions but

---

4. An otherworldly residence, home to several Irish deities, especially Angus Og, the god of youth and of poetry.
5. Conall Cernach, foster brother of Cú Chulainn, is a great champion who serves Conchobor; another warrior, Bricriu "of the poison tongue," is equally famed for promoting strife among his fellows.

6. LOOG, a pre-Christian deity, also imagined as a hero and chief of the Túatha Dé Danann, first of the legendary founding peoples of Ireland, and source of its arts.
7. Cú Chulainn's name as a boy.
1. Conall adds to a series of stories about the hero's origins.

of his tongs and his two hands. Conchobor went with fifty of his oldest and most illustrious heroes in their chariots. First, however, he visited the playing field, for it was his custom when leaving or returning to seek the boys' blessing; and he saw Cú Chulainn driving the ball past the three fifties of boys and defeating them.[2] When they drove at the hole, Cú Chulainn filled the hole with his balls, and the boys could not stop them; when the boys drove at the hole, he defended it alone, and not a single ball went in. When they wrestled, he overthrew the three fifties of boys by himself, but all of them together could not overthrow him. When they played at mutual stripping, he stripped them all so that they were stark naked, while they could not take so much as the brooch from his mantle.

"Conchobor thought all this wonderful. He asked if the boy's deeds would be similarly distinguished when he became a man, and everyone said that they would be. He said to Cú Chulainn, then, "Come with me to the feast, and you will be a guest." "I have not had my fill of play yet," replied the boy. "I will come after you."

'When everyone had arrived at the feast, Culann said to Conchobor "Do you expect anyone else?" "I do not," answered Conchobor, forgetting that his fosterling was yet to come. "I have a watchdog," said Culann, "with three chains on him and three men on every chain. I will loose him now to guard our cattle and our herds, and I will close the courtyard."

'By that time, the boy was on his way to the feast, and when the hound attacked him he was still at play. He would throw his ball up and his hurley[3] after it, so that the hurley struck the ball and so that each stroke was the same; he would also throw his javelin on ahead and catch it before it could strike the ground. The hound's attack did not distract the boy from his play; Conchobor and his people, however, were so confounded they could not move. They could not believe that, when the courtyard doors were opened, they would find the boy alive. But, when the hound attacked him, the boy threw away his ball and hurley and went at it with his bare hands: he put one hand on the hound's throat and the other on its back and struck it against a pillar until every limb fell apart.

'The Ulaid rose to rescue him, some to the courtyard and some to the door of the courtyard, and they took him in to Conchobor. Everyone was greatly alarmed that the son of the king's sister had nearly been killed. But Culann entered the house and said "Welcome, lad, for the sake of your mother's heart. As for myself, however, this was an evil feast. My life is lost, and my household are out on the plain, without our hound. It secured life and honour; it protected our goods and cattle and every creature between field and house. It was the man of the family." "No great matter that," replied the boy. "I will rear for you a whelp from the same litter, and, until it is grown and capable of action, I will be the hound that protects your cattle and yourself. I will protect all Mag Muirthemni,[4] and neither herd nor flock will be taken without my knowledge." "Cú Chulainn[5] will be your name henceforth," said Cathbad.[6] "I prefer my own name," said Cú Chulainn.

'The boy who did that when he was six would not surprise by doing heroic deeds when he was seventeen,' said Conall Cernach.

---

2. Three boy-troops play, and train in mock battles, around Emain Macha.

3. A stick like that used in field hockey.

4. A coastal plain in eastern Ireland, home of Culann.

5. "Hound of Culann."

6. Druid (sage, prophet) in Conchobor's service.

Early Irish Verse

Although copied by clerics in a world of written manuscripts, the stories above look backward to an age of oral tales about legendary heroes and heroines, many of them still closely linked to the native gods and goddesses of pre-Christian Ireland. The following samples of Irish verse from the ninth and tenth centuries suggest some of the complex but enormously fruitful interactions of those native Irish traditions and the new Christian culture.

Ireland began to be Christianized from the mid-fifth century, but Christianity came to Ireland more by genuine and gradual conversion than by the point of a sword. The learned monks and hermits, well established by the ninth and tenth centuries, encountered far more disruption from the raids of Vikings, beginning in A.D. 795, than from surviving Irish pre-Christian cultures. Instead, the ancient native dynasties of learned poets, genealogists, and diviners interacted with the new learning of Latin Christianity. Indeed, Saint Columba (c. 521–597) was partly educated by the *fili* Gemmán, the chief poet of Leinster. (*Fili*, plural *filid*, was the highest class of poet in medieval Ireland.) One of Columba's few returns to Ireland after founding his monastery on the isle of Iona was to defend the native poets from clerical forces that wanted them suppressed. In fact we know that many monks were also vernacular poets; and conversely, secular *filid* wrote praise poems to clerics, most famously to Saint Columba himself. Their cultural prestige and preservation of ancient learning continued, even as their religious and quasi-magical activity dwindled. All this led to a rich and persistent convergence (not without competition) of native and Christian elements in medieval Irish culture.

The figure addressed in *To Crinog*, for instance, is at once a wise crone—a traditional figure of initiation—and a book of Christian wisdom, perhaps a Latin primer. Irish myths report instruction in craft or battle by a wise woman, with whom the apprentice also enjoys physical intimacy (as a youthful Cú Chulainn had with the woman warrior Scáthach), although in this poem Crinog's teaching is explicitly chaste. Monks also began using the resources of Irish poetry to record religious study—the Word, to which their faith was so attached—and the making of written books. *Pangur the Cat* explores the solitary pleasures of the monk or hermit, and the challenge of textual interpretation, in contrast with the more heroic mold of many saints' lives or contemporary heroic tales: "Fame comes second to the peace / Of study. . . ." *Writing in the Wood* is a poem of labor, but undertaken in a holiday spirit, away from the monastic scriptorium where books were usually copied.

Other voices look to the legendary past with open regret. *A Grave Marked with Ogam* evokes a disastrous battle in which the speaker, now quite alone, fought on the losing side. *Findabair Remembers Fróech* is a yearning lament for a lost lover. It is quite unconnected to monasticism, but a similar history of passions that efface the present also informs the powerful monologue *The Old Woman of Beare*; there the contrast also involves the shift from a lost world of secular heroes to declining mortality in a convent. Her name, and the memories she has of past generations and eras, may link the Old Woman of Beare to a mythic figure of sovereignty, rejuvenated by each man to whom she gives her body and her powers. At the same time, she is a voice of wise lament on the passing of greater times (not unlike many moments in *Beowulf*); she is a rich concubine who has lost her beauty and become a nun; and—in a land where women's powers were usually quite limited—she is a woman who has gone her own way and made choices that now leave her poor, unprotected, and rueful, but not regretful. *The Old Woman of Beare* records the unresolved dialogue between the era of heroic legend and the era of Christ, between joys mortal and immortal: "for Mary's Son / too soon redeems."

The Voyage of Máel Dúin shows us, perhaps most clearly of all, how native secular genres and attitudes persisted, but were revised, under the influence of Christianity. Both in structure and detail, the *Voyage* echoes the *immrana*, native tales of wondrous voyages to otherworldly islands, places both of terror and sybaritic pleasures. Máel Dúin and his companions visit many such islands, but they also pause at the island homes of four Christian hermits, themselves not without magical qualities. Máel Dúin's own genealogy mirrors this meeting of traditions; he is the illegitimate child of a nun and a great warrior. His father has been killed by raiders, he learns, and his voyage is a quest to find them and take obligatory vengeance in the heroic style. The fourth hermit he meets, though, convinces Máel Dúin to forgive his father's murderers and return home in peace. At the levels of genre, genealogy, and narrative, then, the *Voyage* enacts at once a preservation and revision of native traditions under Christian influence.

To Crinog[1]

Crinog, melodious is your song.
Though young no more you are still bashful.
We two grew up together in Niall's[2] northern land,
When we used to sleep together in tranquil slumber.

5   That was my age when you slept with me.
O peerless lady of pleasant wisdom:
A pure-hearted youth, lovely without a flaw,
A gentle boy of seven sweet years.

We lived in the great world of Banva[3]
10   Without sullying soul or body,
My flashing eyes full of love for you,
Like a poor innocent untempted by evil.

Your just counsel is ever ready,
Wherever we are to seek it:
15   To love your penetrating wisdom is better
Than glib discourse with a king.

Since then you have slept with four men after me,
Without folly or falling away:
I know, I hear it on all sides,
20   You are pure, without sin from man.

At last, after weary wanderings,
You have come to me again,
Darkness of age has settled on your face:
Sinless your life draws near its end.

25   You are still dear to me, faultless one,
You shall have welcome from me without stint:
You will not let us be drowned in torment;
We will earnestly practice devotion with you.

The lasting world is full of your fame.
30   Far and wide you have wandered on every track:

1. Translated by Kuno Meyer.
2. Legendary Irish king, whose dynasty ruled Ulster and other areas.

3. An early name for Ireland.

If every day we followed your ways,
We should come safe into the presence of dread God.

You leave an example and a bequest
To every one in this world,
35   You have taught us by your life:
Earnest prayer to God is no fallacy.

Then may God grant us peace and happiness!
May the countenance of the King
Shine brightly on us
40   When we leave behind us our withered bodies.

Pangur the Cat[1]

Myself and Pangur, cat and sage
Go each about our business;
I harass my beloved page,
He his mouse.

5   Fame comes second to the peace
Of study, a still day.
Unenvious, Pangur's choice
Is child's play.

Neither bored, both hone
10   At home a separate skill,
Moving, after hours alone,
To the kill.

On my cell wall here,
His sight fixes. Burning.
15   Searching. My old eyes peer
At new learning.

His delight when his claws
Close on his prey
Equals mine, when sudden clues
20   Light my way.

So we find by degrees
Peace in solitude,
Both of us—solitaries—
Have each the trade

25   He loves. Pangur, never idle
Day or night
Hunts mice. I hunt each riddle
From dark to light

1. Translated by Eavan Boland.

Writing in the Wood[1]

Overwatched by woodland wall
    merles make melody full well;
above my book—lined, lettered—
    birds twittered a soothing spell.

5   Cuckoos call clear—fairest phrase—
    cloaked in grays, from leafy leas.
Lord's love, what blessings show' ring!
    Good to write 'neath tow' ring trees.

The Viking Terror[1]

Bitter is the wind to-night,
It tosses the ocean's white hair:
To-night I fear not the fierce warriors of Norway
Coursing on the Irish Sea.

The Old Woman of Beare[1]

The ebbing that has come on me
is not the ebbing of the sea.
What knows the sea of grief or pain?—
Happy tide will flood again.

5   I am the hag of Bui and Beare—[2]
the richest cloth I used to wear.
Now with meanness and with thrift
I even lack a change of shift.

It is wealth
10   and not men that you love.
In the time that we lived
it was men that we loved.

Those whom we loved, the plains
we ride today bear their names;
15   gaily they feasted with laughter
nor boasted thereafter.

To-day they gather in the tax
but, come to handing out, are lax;
the very little they bestow
20   be sure that everyone will know.

1. Translated by Ruth P. M. Lehmann. This translation aims to reproduce much of the complex internal rhyme and end-rhyme, assonance, and alliteration of the original; it takes minor liberties with the literal sense.
1. Translated by Kuno Meyer.
1. Translated by James Carney. The speaker's name, "caillech," "veiled one," can mean old woman, hag,

widow, and nun. The hag figure has resonance with teachers of crafts and wisdom, as well as early mythic female figures of sovereignty and initiation, rejuvenated when they are embraced by a chosen hero.
2. A peninsula in Munster, in the far southwest of Ireland, or a tiny island off its coast. "Bui" may be the small nearby island of Dursey.

Chariots there were, and we
had horses bred for victory.
Such things came in a great wave;
pray for the dead kings who gave.

25   Bitterly does my body race
seeking its destined place;
now let God's Son come and take
that which he gave of his grace.

These arms, these scrawny things you see,
30   scarce merit now their little joy
when lifted up in blessing
       over sweet student boy.

These arms you see,
       these bony scrawny things,
35   had once more loving craft
       embracing kings.

When Maytime comes
       the girls out there are glad,
and I, old hag, old bones,
40   alone am sad.

No wedding wether killed for me,
an end to all coquetry;
a pitiful veil I wear
on thin and faded hair.

45   Well do I wear
plain veil on faded hair;
many colors I wore
and we feasting before.

Were it not for Feven's plain[3]
50   I'd envy nothing old;
I have a shroud of aged skin,
       Feven's crop is gold.

Ronan's city there in Bregon[4]
       and in Feven the royal standing stone,
55   why are their cheeks not weathered,
       only mine alone?

Winter comes and the sea will rise
       crying out with welcoming wave;
but no welcome for me from nobleman's son
60   or from son of a slave.

3. In inland Munster; connected with power and wealth.
4. Probably an 8th-century king who ruled in the area of Feven.

What they do now, I know, I know:
    to and fro they row and race;
but they who once sailed Alma's ford[5]
    rest in a cold place.

65   It's more than a day
        since I sailed youth's sea,
    beauty's years not devoured
        and sap flowing free.

It's more than a day, God's truth,
70   that I'm lacking in youth;
I wrap myself up in the sun—
I know Old Age, I see him come.

There was a summer of youth
    nor was autumn the worst of the year,
75   but winter is doom
        and its first days are here.

God be thanked, I had joy in my youth.
    I swear that it's true,
if I hadn't leapt the wall
80   this old cloak still were not new.

The Lord on the world's broad back
    threw a lovely cloak of green;
first fleecy, then it's bare,
    and again the fleece is seen.

85   All beauty is doomed.
        God! Can it be right
to kneel in a dark prayer-house
    after feasting by candlelight?

I sat with kings drinking wine and mead
90   for many a day,
and now, a crew of shriveled hags,
    we toast in whey.

Be this my feast, these cups of whey;
    and let me always count as good
95   the vexing things that come of Christ
    who stayed God's ire with flesh and blood.

The mind is not so clear,
    there's mottling of age on my cloak,
gray hairs sprouting through skin,
100   I am like a stricken oak.

For deposit on heaven
    of right eye bereft,

5. An unidentified site.

       I conclude the purchase
         with loss of the left.

105   Great wave of flood
         and wave of ebb and lack!
       What flooding tide brings in
         the ebbing tide takes back.

       Great wave of flood
110   and wave of ebbing sea,
       the two of them I know
         for both have washed on me.

       Great wave of flood
         brings no step to silent cellar floor;
115   a hand fell on all the company
         that feasted there before.

       The Son of Mary knew right well
         he'd walk that floor one day;
       grasping I was, but never sent
120   man hungry on his way.

       Pity Man!—
         If only like the elements he could
       come out of ebbing in the very way
         that he comes out of flood.

125   Christ left with me on loan
         flood tide of youth, and now it seems
       there's ebb and misery, for Mary's Son
         too soon redeems.

       Blessed the island in the great sea
130   with happy ebb and happy flood.
       For me, for me alone, no hope:
         the ebbing is for good.

Findabair Remembers Fróech[1]

       This, thereafter, is what Findabair used to say,
       seeing anything beautiful:
       it would be more beautiful for her
       to see Fróech crossing the dark water,
5   body for shining whiteness,
       hair for loveliness,
       face for shapeliness,

---

1. Translated by James Carney. Findabair (*FIN-a-wer*) was a daughter of Medb and Ailill (central characters in the *Táin*). She falls in love with the famously handsome warrior Fróech (Froich, guttural -ch) but her parents resist their marriage. When Fróech is killed by Cú Chulainn, Findabair ultimately dies of heartbreak.

eye for blue-grayness,
a well-born youth
10   without fault or blemish,
face broad above, narrow below,
and he straight and perfect,
the red branch with its berries
between throat and white face.
15   This is what Findabair used to say:
She had never seen
anything a half
or a third as beautiful as he.

A Grave Marked with Ogam[1]

Ogam in stone on grave stead,
     where men sometimes tread on course;
king's son of Ireland cut low,
     hit by spear's throw hurled from horse.

5   Cairpre let a quick cast fly
     from high on horseback, stout steed;
ere he wearied his hand struck,
     cut down Oscar, cruel deed.[2]

Oscar hurled a hard throw, crude,
10   like a lion, rude his rage;
killed Con's kin, Cairpre proud,
     ere they bowed on battle stage.

Tall, keen, cruel were the lads
     who found their death in the strife,
15   just before their weapons met;
     more were left in death than life.

I myself was in the fight
     on right, south of Gabair green;
twice fifty warriors I killed,
20   my skilled hand slew them, clear, clean.

I'd play for pirates in bale,
     the while the trail I must tread,
in holy holt boar I'd fell,
     or would snatch the snell bird's egg.

1. Translated by Ruth P. M. Lehmann. This translation
again aims to reproduce much of the rhyme, assonance,
and alliteration of the original; it takes minor liberties
with the literal sense. Ogam is the earliest Irish alphabet,
used before the Latin alphabet was applied to Irish. It is
a system of long lines marked with short dashes, cross-
hatches, and small figures. Most often found in inscriptions or associated with secret messages and divination, it
is too awkward an alphabet for writing longer texts.
2. Characters from the "Finn Cycle," a group of tales even
more popular than the Ulster Cycle and its central epic
the *Táin*. Oscar is Finn's grandson and the cycle's greatest
warrior. He and Cairpre, high king of Ireland, kill one another at the Battle of Gabair (GAV-*ar*), which ends the
power of Finn's people.

25   That ogam there in the stone,
      around which the slain fall prone,
  if Finn the fighter could come,
      long would he think on ogam.

from The Voyage of Máel Dúin[1]

They went to an island with a high enclosure of the color of a swan
In which they found a noble pavilion, a dwelling of brightness.
Silver brooches, gold-hilted swords, large necklets,
Beautiful beds, excellent food, golden rows.
5   Strengthening delicate food in the midst of the house, sound savory liquor;
With fierce greediness upon a high pillar a seemly very quick cat.
It leapt then over the pillars, a speedy feat;
Not very big was the guardian of the meat, it was not repulsive.
One of the three foster brothers of the powerful chief, it was a
    courageous action,
10 Takes with him—it was a proud ounce-weight—a golden necklet.[2]
The fiery claw of the mysterious cat rent his body,
The guilty body of the unfortunate man was burnt ash.
The large necklet was brought back, it created friendship again,
The ashes of the unfortunate man were cast into the ocean.

* * *

Then they saw in a small island a psalm-singing old man;
Excellent was his dignified noble appearance, holy were his words.
Hair of his noble head—delightful the bright covering—a garment
    with whiteness,
A brilliant large mantle; bright-covered coloring covering was around him.
5   The excellent chief said to him: "Whence were you sent?"
"I shall not hide from you what you ask: from Ireland.
My pilgrimage brought me without any penance
In the body of a boat over the swift sea; I did not regret it.
My prowed boat came apart under me on the very violent sea;
10 A bitter, twisting, active, big-waved course put me ashore.
I cut a sod from the gray-green surface of my fatherland;
To the place in which I am a breeze brought me: small is the fame.
The star-strong King established under me out of the miraculous sod
A delightful island with the color of a seagull over the dark sea.
15 A foot was added to the island every year—
It is a victorious achievement—and a tree above the sea's crest.
A clear well came to me—everlasting food—
By the grace of angels, sound beautiful food—a holy gathering.
You will all reach your countries, a fruitful company along the ocean's track,

---

1. Verse redaction of chs. 11, 19, and 34, translated by H. P. A. Oskamp. Máel Dúin (*Moil Doon*), the illegitimate son of a nun and a warrior, is brought up by a queen. Learning at the same time of his father's death, he sets out on a sea journey to find and take vengeance on his father's killers. Máel Dúin and his companions came upon a series of islands, each with its marvel or danger.
2. Máel Dúin's foster brothers had swum to his boat as it departed, violating a druid's prohibition; none return from the journey.

20   Though it will be a long journey; all except one man."[3]
        By the grace of the angels to each single man of them
        Came a complete half-loaf and a noble morsel of fish as provision.

* * *

        Then they went to an island full of flocks, a famed halting-place,
        A victorious achievement; they found there an Irish falcon.
        Then they rowed after it, swift to encounter,
        Over the crest of the waves to an island in which was their enemy.
5   They made peace there with the swift Máel Dúin, in the presence of
            every swift man;
        After true pledging they went to their country, a prosperous journey.
        Many remarkable things, many marvels, many mysteries
        Was their pleasant story, as swift Máel Dúin told.
        A long life and peace while I am in the famous world,
10   May I have cheerful company with virtue from my King of Kings.
        When I die may I then reach heaven past the fierce, violent host of demons
        In the Kingdom of angels, a famous affair, a very high dwelling.

⟶ ⋈ ⟵

The Dream of the Rood

The Dream of the Rood is a remarkable tenth-century poem, a mystical dream vision whose narrator tells of his dream that the rood—Christ's cross—appeared to him and told the story of its unwilling role in the crucifixion. The poem is an excellent illustration of how the conventions of Old English heroic poems like *Beowulf* were adapted to the doctrines of Christianity. Christ's Passion is converted into a heroic sacrifice as the cross reports that it watched him— the young hero—strip himself naked, as if preparing for battle, and bravely ascend it. In the same vein, the cross presents itself as a thane (retainer) forced into disloyalty, as it watches— and participates in—the crucifixion, unable to avenge its beloved Lord.

In addition to heroic poetry, *The Dream of the Rood* recalls Old English genres such as the riddle and the elegy. In riddle fashion, the cross asks, "What am I?"—that started as a tree, became an instrument of torture, and am now a beacon of victory, resplendent with jewels. In the manner of elegies like *The Wanderer*, the speaker, stained with sin, presents himself as a lonely exile whose companions have left him and gone to heaven. After his vision, he resolves to seek the fellowship of his heavenly Lord and his former companions, which he pictures as taking place in a celestial mead hall: "the home of joy and happiness, / where the people of God are seated at the feast / in eternal bliss."

One of the most striking poetic effects of *The Dream of the Rood* is its focus on the Incarnation, God's taking on human flesh. The poet often juxtaposes references to Christ's humanity and divinity in the same line, thereby achieving a powerful effect of paradox, as when he tells of the approach of "the young warrior, God Almighty." It is noteworthy that the aspect of Christ's humanity which the poet stresses is the heroism rather than the pathos which was to become so prominent in later medieval poetry and art. This heroism provides a context for a cryptic passage at the end of the poem, where the dreamer refers to Christ's "journey" to bring "those who before suffered burning" victoriously to heaven. In *The Harrowing of Hell* (based on

---

3. One of the three foster brothers still remains with the voyagers at this point. A later hermit prophesies, "though you will meet your enemies, you will not slay them."

the apocryphal Gospel of Nicodemus), Christ heroically freed the virtuous Old Testament patriarchs from damnation and led them to eternal bliss.

The fame of *The Dream of the Rood* appears to have been widespread in its own time. Our knowledge of it comes from three sources: the huge stone Ruthwell Cross in southern Scotland built in the eighth century (on which a short version is inscribed in runic letters); the silver Brussels Cross, made in England in the tenth century; and the manuscript found in Vercelli in northern Italy, also written in the tenth century—the only complete version of the poem. These varied locations are a testament to the wide influence of Anglo-Saxon scholars, not only in the British Isles but on the Continent as well.

The Dream of the Rood[1]

Listen! I will describe the best of dreams
which I dreamed in the middle of the night
when, far and wide, all men slept.
It seemed that I saw a wondrous tree
5   soaring into the air, surrounded by light,
the brightest of crosses; that emblem was entirely
cased in gold; beautiful jewels
were strewn around its foot, just as five
studded the cross-beam. All the angels of God,
10   fair creations, guarded it. That was no cross
of a criminal, but holy spirits and men on earth
watched over it there—the whole glorious universe.

Wondrous was the tree of victory, and I was stained
by sin, stricken by guilt. I saw this glorious tree
15   joyfully gleaming, adorned with garments,
decked in gold; the tree of the Ruler
was rightly adorned with rich stones;
yet through that gold I could see the agony
once suffered by wretches, for it had bled
20   down the right hand side. Then I was afflicted,
frightened at this sight; I saw that sign often change
its clothing and hue, at times dewy with moisture,
stained by flowing blood, at times adorned with treasure.
Yet I lay there for a long while
25   and gazed sadly at the Savior's cross
until I heard it utter words;
the finest of trees began to speak:
"I remember the morning a long time ago
that I was felled at the edge of the forest
30   and severed from my roots. Strong enemies seized me,
bade me hold up their felons on high,
made me a spectacle. Men shifted me
on their shoulders and set me on a hill.
Many enemies fastened me there. I saw the Lord of Mankind
35   hasten with such courage to climb upon me.

1. Translated by Kevin Crossley-Holland.

The Ruthwell Cross, north side, top section, 7th–8th century. Preserved in a church in southern Scotland, this 18-foot stone cross is carved with many Christian scenes, including this depiction of Saint John the Baptist, bearded and holding the Lamb of God. The Latin inscription beneath the saint is written in runes—the traditional Germanic alphabet, used for ritualistic purposes. Runic inscriptions elsewhere on the cross reproduce portions of *The Dream of the Rood* in Old English. Still other inscriptions are in Latin and employ the Roman alphabet. Thus, like *The Dream of the Rood* itself, whose Christlike hero resembles a Germanic warrior, the Ruthwell Cross illustrates the fusion of Mediterranean and Germanic traditions in Anglo-Saxon Christian culture.

I dared not bow or break there
against my Lord's wish, when I saw the surface
of the earth tremble. I could have felled
all my foes, yet I stood firm.
40   Then the young warrior, God Almighty,
stripped Himself, firm and unflinching. He climbed
upon the cross, brave before many, to redeem mankind.
I quivered when the hero clasped me,
yet I dared not bow to the ground,
45   fall to the earth. I had to stand firm.
A rood was I raised up; I bore aloft the mighty King,
the Lord of Heaven. I dared not stoop.
They drove dark nails into me; dire wounds are there to see,
the gaping gashes of malice; I dared not injure them.
50   They insulted us both together; I was drenched in the blood
that streamed from the Man's side after He set His spirit free.

"On that hill I endured many grievous trials;
I saw the God of Hosts stretched
on the rack; darkness covered the corpse
55   of the Ruler with clouds, His shining radiance.
Shadows swept across the land, dark shapes
under the clouds. All creation wept,
wailed for the death of the King; Christ was on the cross.
Yet men hurried eagerly to the Prince
60   from afar; I witnessed all that too.
I was oppressed with sorrow, yet humbly bowed to the hands of men,
and willingly. There they lifted Him from His heavy torment,
they took Almighty God away. The warriors left me standing there,
stained with blood; sorely was I wounded by the sharpness of spear-shafts.
65   They laid Him down, limb-weary; they stood at the corpse's head,
they beheld there the Lord of Heaven; and there He rested for a while,
worn-out after battle. And then they began to build a sepulchre;
under his slayers' eyes, they carved it from the gleaming stone,
and laid therein the Lord of Victories. Then, sorrowful at dusk,
70   they sang a dirge before they went, weary,
from their glorious Prince, He rested in the grave alone.
But we still stood there, weeping blood,
long after the song of the warriors
had soared to heaven; the corpse grew cold,
75   the fair human house of the soul. Then our enemies
began to fell us; that was a terrible fate.
They buried us in a deep pit; but friends
and followers of the Lord found me there
and girded me with gold and shimmering silver.

80   "Now, my loved man, you have heard
how I endured bitter anguish
at the hands of evil men. Now the time is come
when men far and wide in this world,
and all this bright creation, bow before me;
85   they pray to this sign. On me the Son of God
suffered for a time; wherefore I now stand on high,
glorious under heaven; and I can heal
all those who stand in awe of me.
Long ago I became the worst of tortures,
90   hated by men, until I opened
to them the true way of life.
Lo! The Lord of Heaven, the Prince of Glory,
honored me over any other tree
just as He, Almighty God, for the sake of mankind
95   honored Mary, His own mother,
before all other women in the world.
Now I command you, my loved man,
to describe your vision to all men;
tell them with words this is the tree of glory

100   on which the Son of God suffered once
    for the many sins committed by mankind,
    and for Adam's wickedness long ago.
    He sipped the drink of death. Yet the Lord rose
    with His great strength to deliver man.
105   Then He ascended into heaven. The Lord Himself,
    Almighty God, with His host of angels,
    will come to the middle-world again
    on Domesday to reckon with each man.
    Then He who has the power of judgment
110   will judge each man just as he deserves
    for the way in which he lived this fleeting life.
    No-one then will be unafraid
    as to what words the Lord will utter.
    Before the assembly, He will ask where that man is
115   who, in God's name, would undergo the pangs of death,
    just as He did formerly upon the cross.
    Then men will be fearful and give
    scant thought to what they say to Christ.
    But no-one need be numbed by fear
120   who has carried the best of all signs in his breast;
    each soul that has longings to live with the Lord
    must search for a kingdom far beyond the frontiers of this world."

    Then I prayed to the cross, eager
    and light-hearted, although I was alone
125   with my own poor company. My soul
    longed for a journey, great yearnings
    always tugged at me. Now my hope in this life
    is that I can turn to that tree of victory
    alone and more often than any other man
130   and honor it fully. These longings master
    my heart and mind, and my help comes
    from holy cross itself. I have not many friends
    of influence on earth; they have journeyed on
    from the joys of this world to find the King of Glory,
135   they live in heaven with the High Father,
    dwell in splendor. Now I look day by day
    for that time when the cross of the Lord,
    which once I saw in a dream here on earth,
    will fetch me away from this fleeting life
140   and lift me to the home of joy and happiness
    where the people of God are seated at the feast
    in eternal bliss, and set me down
    where I may live in glory unending and share
    the joy of the saints. May the Lord be a friend to me,
145   He who suffered once for the sins of men
    here on earth on the gallows-tree.

He has redeemed us; He has given life to us,
and a home in heaven.
                         Hope was renewed,
blessed and blissful, for those who before suffered burning.
150   On that journey the Son was victorious,
strong and successful. When He, Almighty Ruler,
returned with a thronging host of spirits
to God's kingdom, to joy among the angels
and all the saints who lived already
155   in heaven in glory, then their King,
Almighty God, entered His own country.

The Wanderer

In the Exeter Book, a manuscript copied about 975 and donated to the Bishop of Exeter, are preserved some of the greatest short poems in Old English, including a number of poems referred to as elegies—laments that contrast past happiness with present sorrow and remark on how fleeting is the former. Along with *The Wanderer*, the elegies include its companion piece *The Seafarer*; *The Ruin*; *The Husband's Message*; *The Wife's Lament*; and *Wulf and Eadwacer*. While the last two are exceptional in dealing with female experience, elegies for the most part focus on male bonds and companionship, particularly the joys of the mead hall. Old English poetry as a whole is almost entirely devoid of interest in romantic love between men and women and focuses instead on the bond between lord and retainer; elegiac poems such as *The Wanderer* have in fact been called "the love poetry of a heroic society."

The Wanderer opens with an appeal to a Christian concept, as the third-person narrator speaks of the wanderer's request for God's mercy. The body of the poem, however—primarily a first-person account in the wanderer's voice—reflects more pagan values in its regret for the loss of earthly joys. Though the poem's structure is somewhat confusing, one can discern two major parts. In the first, the wanderer laments his personal situation: he was once a member of a warrior band, but his lord—his beloved "gold-friend"—has died, leaving him a homeless exile. He dreams that he "clasps and kisses" his lord, but he then wakes to see only the dark waves, the snow, and the sea birds.

The second part of the poem turns from personal narrative to a more general statement of the transitoriness of all earthly things. The speaker (possibly someone other than the wanderer at this point), looking at the ruin of ancient buildings, is moved to express the ancient Roman motif known as "*ubi sunt*" (Latin for "where are"): "Where has the horse gone? Where the man? Where the giver of gold? / Where is the feasting place? And where the pleasures of the hall?" In the concluding five lines, the reader is urged to seek comfort in heaven.

There has been much debate about the degrees of Christianity and paganism in this tenth-century poem. The positions range from the view that the Christian opening and closing are totally extraneous to the poem and have been tacked on by a monkish copyist, to the view that the poem is a Christian allegory about a soul exiled from his heavenly home, longing for his lord Jesus Christ. It is now generally held that the poem is authentically Christian, in a literal rather than an allegorical way, but that the values of pagan society still exert a powerful pull in it.

The Wanderer[1]

Often the wanderer pleads for pity
and mercy from the Lord; but for a long time,
sad in mind, he must dip his oars
into icy waters, the lanes of the sea;
5   he must follow the paths of exile: fate is inflexible.

Mindful of hardships, grievous slaughter,
the ruin of kinsmen, the wanderer said:
"Time and again at the day's dawning
I must mourn all my afflictions alone.
10   There is no one still living to whom I dare open
the doors of my heart. I have no doubt
that it is a noble habit for a man
to bind fast all his heart's feelings,
guard his thoughts, whatever he is thinking.
15   The weary in spirit cannot withstand fate,
a troubled mind finds no relief:
wherefore those eager for glory often
hold some ache imprisoned in their hearts.
Thus I had to bind my feelings in fetters,
20   often sad at heart, cut off from my country,
far from my kinsmen, after, long ago,
dark clods of earth covered my gold-friend;
I left that place in wretchedness,
plowed the icy waves with winter in my heart;
25   in sadness I sought far and wide
for a treasure-giver, for a man
who would welcome me into his mead-hall,
give me good cheer (for I boasted no friends),
entertain me with delights. He who has experienced it
30   knows how cruel a comrade sorrow can be
to any man who has few loyal friends:
for him are the ways of exile, in no wise twisted gold;
for him is a frozen body, in no wise the fruits of the earth.
He remembers hall-retainers and treasure
35   and how, in his youth, his gold-friend
entertained him. Those joys have all vanished.
A man who lacks advice for a long while
from his loved lord understands this,
that when sorrow and sleep together
40   hold the wretched wanderer in their grip,
it seems that he clasps and kisses
his lord, and lays hands and head
upon his lord's knee as he had sometimes done
when he enjoyed the gift-throne in earlier days.
45   Then the friendless man wakes again
and sees the dark waves surging around him,

the sea-birds bathing, spreading their feathers,
frost and snow falling mingled with hail.
"Then his wounds lie more heavy in his heart,
50   aching for his lord. His sorrow is renewed;
the memory of kinsmen sweeps through his mind;
joyfully he welcomes them, eagerly scans
his comrade warriors. Then they swim away again.
Their drifting spirits do not bring many old songs
55   to his lips. Sorrow upon sorrow attend
the man who must send time and again
his weary heart over the frozen waves.
"And thus I cannot think why in the world
my mind does not darken when I brood on the fate
60   of brave warriors, how they have suddenly
had to leave the mead-hall, the bold followers.
So this world dwindles day by day,
and passes away; for a man will not be wise
before he has weathered his share of winters
65   in the world. A wise man must be patient,
neither too passionate nor too hasty of speech,
neither too irresolute nor too rash in battle;
not too anxious, too content, nor too grasping,
and never too eager to boast before he knows himself.
70   When he boasts a man must bide his time
until he has no doubt in his brave heart
that he has fully made up his mind.
A wise man must fathom how eerie it will be
when all the riches of the world stand waste,
75   as now in diverse places in this middle-earth
old walls stand, tugged at by winds
and hung with hoar-frost, buildings in decay.
The wine-halls crumble, lords lie dead,
deprived of joy, all the proud followers
80   have fallen by the wall: battle carried off some,
led them on journeys; the bird carried one
over the welling waters; one the gray wolf
devoured; a warrior with downcast face
hid one in an earth-cave.
85   Thus the Maker of Men laid this world waste
until the ancient works of the giants stood idle,
hushed without the hubbub of inhabitants.
Then he who has brooded over these noble ruins,
and who deeply ponders this dark life,
90   wise in his mind, often remembers
the many slaughters of the past and speaks these words:
Where has the horse gone? Where the man? Where the giver of gold?
Where is the feasting-place? And where the pleasures of the hall?
I mourn the gleaming cup, the warrior in his corselet,
95   the glory of the prince. How that time has passed away,

darkened under the shadow of night as if it had never been.
Where the loved warriors were, there now stands a wall
of wondrous height, carved with serpent forms.
The savage ash-spears, avid for slaughter,
100   have claimed all the warriors—a glorious fate!
Storms crash against these rocky slopes,
sleet and snow fall and fetter the world,
winter howls, then darkness draws on,
the night-shadow casts gloom and brings
105   fierce hailstorms from the north to frighten men.
Nothing is ever easy in the kingdom of earth,
the world beneath the heavens is in the hands of fate.
Here possessions are fleeting, here friends are fleeting,
here man is fleeting, here kinsman is fleeting,
110   the whole world becomes a wilderness."
So spoke the wise man in his heart as he sat apart in thought.
Brave is the man who holds to his beliefs; nor shall he ever
show the sorrow in his heart before he knows how he
can hope to heal it. It is best for a man to seek
115   mercy and comfort from the Father in heaven, the safe home that awaits us all.

Wulf and Eadwacer *and* The Wife's Lament

Old English literature focuses largely on masculine and military concerns and lacks a concept of romantic love—what the twelfth-century French would later call "*fine amour.*" Against this backdrop *Wulf and Eadwacer* and *The Wife's Lament* stand out, first, by their use of woman's voice and second, by their treatment of the sorrows of love.

Though the exact genre of these poems is problematic, some scholars classify them as riddles and others as religious allegories, most group them with a class of Old English poems known as elegies, with which they are preserved in the same manuscript, the Exeter Book. The elegies lament the loss of earthly goods, comradeship, and the "hall joys," often, as in *The Wanderer* and *The Seafarer*, by a speaker in exile. *The Wife's Lament* and *Wulf and Eadwacer* differ from the other elegies in that the speakers, as women, had no experience of comradeship to lose, as their main function was to be exchanged in marriage to cement relationships between feuding tribes. They are in a sense twice exiled, first from the noble brotherhood by their gender, and second from their beloved by their personal history. Furthermore, unlike the speakers in *The Wanderer* and *The Seafarer*, they do not look forward to the consolation of a heavenly kingdom imagined as a warlord with his group of retainers.

Although the two elegies in woman's voice are unique in the Old English corpus, they have analogues within the larger tradition of continental woman's song, which flourished in medieval Latin and the vernaculars from the eleventh century on. Their composition was so early—990 at the latest—that this tradition could not have influenced them, although the Roman poet Ovid's *Heroides* (verse letters of abandoned heroines to their faithless lovers) could have done so. One critic has raised the question of female authorship, on the grounds that continental nuns in the eighth century were criticized for writing romantic songs. As the critic

Marilynn Desmond has suggested, perhaps Virginia Woolf's speculation that "anonymous was a woman" is true of these poems.

Though scholars agree that *Wulf and Eadwacer* is "heartrending" and "haunting," they cannot agree on the dramatic situation—each translation is an act of interpretation. The present translator, Kevin Crossley-Holland, sees the poem as involving the female speaker; her husband (Eadwacer); her lover (Wulf), from whom she is separated; and her child (a "cub"). Although what transpired before is unclear, she wistfully concludes, "men easily savage what was never secure, our song together." The dramatic setting of *The Wife's Lament* is similarly ambiguous; it is not clear whether the woman's anger is directed toward her husband or to a third person who plotted to separate them.

Wulf and Eadwacer[1]

Prey, it's as if my people have been handed prey.
They'll tear him to pieces if he comes with a troop.

O, we are apart.

Wulf is on one island, I on another,
5   a fastness that island, a fen-prison.
Fierce men roam there, on that island;
they'll tear him to pieces if he comes with a troop.

O, we are apart.

How I have grieved for my Wulf's wide wanderings.
10 When rain slapped the earth and I sat apart weeping,
when the bold warrior wrapped his arms about me,
I seethed with desire and yet with such hatred.
Wulf, my Wulf, my yearning for you
and your seldom coming have caused my sickness,
15 my mourning heart, not mere starvation.
Can you hear, Eadwacer? Wulf will spirit
our pitiful whelp to the woods.
Men easily savage what was never secure,
our song together.

The Wife's Lament[1]

I draw these words from my deep sadness,
my sorrowful lot. I can say that,
since I grew up, I have not suffered
such hardships as now, old or new.

5 I am tortured by the anguish of exile.
First my lord forsook his family
for the tossing waves; I fretted at dawn
as to where in the world my lord might be.
In my sorrow I set out then,

---

1. Translated by Kevin Crossley-Holland.

10   a friendless wanderer, to search for my man.
      But that man's kinsmen laid secret plans
      to part us, so that we should live
      most wretchedly, far from each other
      in this wide world; I was seized with longings.

15   My lord asked me to live with him here;
      I had few loved ones, loyal friends
      in this country; that is reason for grief.
      Then I found my own husband was ill-starred,
      sad at heart, pretending, plotting
20   murder behind a smiling face. How often
      we swore that nothing but death should ever
      divide us; that is all changed now;
      our friendship is as if it had never been.
      Early and late, I must undergo hardship
25   because of the feud of my own dearest loved one.
      Men forced me to live in a forest grove,
      under an oak tree in the earth-cave.
      This cavern is age-old; I am choked with longings.
      Gloomy are the valleys, too high the hills,
30   harsh strongholds overgrown with briars:
      a joyless abode. The journey of my lord so often
      cruelly seizes me. There are lovers on earth,
      lovers alive who lie in bed,
      when I pass through this earth-cave alone
35   and out under the oak tree at dawn;
      there I must sit through the long summer's day
      and there I mourn my miseries,
      my many hardships; for I am never able
      to quiet the cares of my sorrowful mind,
40   all the longings that are my life's lot.

      Young men must always be serious in mind
      and stout-hearted; they must hide
      their heartaches, that host of constant sorrows,
      behind a smiling face.
                            Whether he is master
45   of his own fate or is exiled in a far-off land—
      sitting under rocky storm-cliffs, chilled
      with hoar-frost, weary in mind,
      surrounded by the sea in some sad place—
      my husband is caught in the clutches of anguish;
50   over and again he recalls a happier home.
      Grief goes side by side with those
      who suffer longing for a loved one.

2. Translated by Kevin Crossley-Holland.

Riddles

Riddles were a popular genre in Anglo-Saxon England, appealing to a taste for intellectual puzzles, which we also see in *Beowulf*, with its kennings; *The Dream of the Rood*, with its speaking cross; and *Wulf and Eadwacer*, with its cryptic dramatic situation. In the Exeter Book, one of the four major manuscripts containing Anglo-Saxon poetry (including *The Wanderer*, *The Wife's Lament*, and *Wulf and Eadwacer*) there are nearly a hundred riddles in Old English, dating from the seventh to the tenth centuries. They were in some cases modeled on collections of a hundred Latin riddles by the seventh-century Anglo-Saxon scholar Aldhelm, but they also derive in large part from indigenous folk tradition. In fact, they mark an important point of intersection between literate and oral culture in Anglo-Saxon England: though designed to be recited, they are written and sometimes focus on the technology of writing.

The three Anglo-Latin riddles by Aldhelm included here reveal an attitude of awe toward writing, conceived as an almost magical act, partly because of its novelty in a recently oral culture, but more because of its ownership by a priestly class in control of Christianity, the religion of "the Book." Aldhelm gives a sense of the tremendous effort that went into bookmaking—scratching treated animal skins with a quill pen or cutting into tablets made of wax, wood, and leather—and the resultant splendid object, adorned with "artful windings," cut into a "fair design." In the *Alphabet*, he makes the personified letters express their pride in the paradox of writing as voiceless speech: "We / in silence quickly bring out hoarded words." The pen in the riddle of that name speaks of its origin as a bird's feather and of its ability, despite its present earthbound state, to help lead the virtuous to heaven.

Of the Old English riddles included here, four also have to do with writing, an activity important in the daily life of priests. Old English Riddle 2 traces the making of a book by speaking as a sheep slain for its skin to make parchment, describing the "bird's feather" leaving tracks on its surface, and concluding in the person of the Bible itself, decorated with "the wondrous work of smiths," sacred and useful at the same time. Old English Riddle 5 similarly traces a tool from its origin in nature to its status as a manufactured thing. The narrator speaks of its life growing by the water (as a plant), the paradox that, though "mouthless," it should "sing / to men sitting at the mead-bench" (as a flute), and the "miracle" by which it can send a private message (as a pen).

In contrast to those Old English riddles concerned with writing, the majority deal with aspects of Anglo-Saxon secular life, with answers such as a shield, a storm, an iceberg, or a ship. The poem of this sort included here, Old English Riddle 1, explores areas of experience usually ignored by Old English epic, elegiac, and religious poetry. Beginning traditionally, "I'm a strange creature," it treats domestic activity—the storage and preparation of food—by a lower-class woman, a churl's daughter. One of several sexual riddles in the Exeter Book, it is a finely sustained *double entendre*, showing that there was indeed humor in Old English poetry.

(Following the manuscripts, Aldhelm's riddles are printed with the titles that state their solutions, while those from the Exeter Book—which offers no solutions—are followed by solutions given by modern editors.)

Three Anglo-Latin Riddles by Aldhelm[1]
Alphabet

We seventeen sisters, voiceless all, declare
Six others bastards are, and not of us.

---

1. Translated by James Hall Pitman.

Of iron we are born, and find our death
Again by iron; or at times we come
From pinion of a lofty-flying bird.
Three brothers got us of an unknown mother.
To him who thirsts for instant counsel, we
In silence quickly bring out hoarded words.

Writing Tablets

Of honey-laden bees I first was born,
But in the forest grew my outer coat;
My tough backs came from shoes. An iron point
In artful windings cuts a fair design,
And leaves long, twisted furrows, like a plow.
From heaven unto that field is borne the seed
Or nourishment, which brings forth generous sheaves
A thousandfold. Alas, that such a crop,
A holy harvest, falls before grim war.

Pen

The shining pelican, whose yawning throat
Gulps down the waters of the sea, long since
Produced me, white as he. Through snowy fields
I keep a straight road, leaving deep-blue tracks
Upon the gleaming way, and darkening
The fair champaign with black and tortuous paths;
Yet one way through the plain suffices not,
For with a thousand bypaths runs the road,
And them who stray not from it, leads to heaven.

Five Old English Riddles[2]
1

I'm a strange creature, for I satisfy women,
a service to the neighbors! No one suffers
at my hands except for my slayer.
I grow very tall, erect in a bed,
5   I'm hairy underneath. From time to time
a good-looking girl, the doughty daughter
of some churl dares to hold me,
grips my russet skin, robs me of my head
and puts me in the pantry. At once that girl
10   with plaited hair who has confined me
remembers our meeting. Her eye moistens.

---

2. Translated by Kevin Crosly Holland.

2

An enemy ended my life, took away
of my bodily strength; then he dipped me
in water and drew me out again,
15   and put me in the sun where I soon shed
all my hair. The knife's sharp edge
bit into me once my blemishes had been scraped away;
fingers folded me and the bird's feather
often moved across my brown surface,
20   sprinkling useful drops; it swallowed the wood-dye
(part of the stream) and again traveled over me
leaving black tracks. Then a man bound me,
he stretched skin over me and adorned me
with gold; thus I am enriched by the wondrous work
25   of smiths, wound about with shining metal.
Now my clasp and my red dye
and these glorious adornments bring fame far and wide
to the Protector of Men, and not to the pains of hell.
If the sons of men would make use of me
30   they would be the safer and more sure of victory,
their hearts would be bolder, their minds more at ease,
their thoughts wiser, they would have more friends,
companions and kinsmen (true and honorable,
brave and kind) who would gladly increase
35   their honor and prosperity, and heap
benefits upon them, holding them fast
in love's embraces. Ask what I am called,
of such use to men. My name is famous,
of service to men and sacred in itself.

3

A moth devoured words. When I heard
of that wonder it struck me as a strange event
that a worm should swallow the song of some man,
a thief gorge in the darkness on fine phrases
and their firm foundation. The thievish stranger
was not a whit the wiser for swallowing words.

4

I watched four curious creatures
traveling together; their tracks were swart,
each imprint very black. The birds' support
moved swiftly; it flew in the air,
dived under the wave. The toiling warrior

worked without pause, pointing the paths
to all four over the beaten gold.

5

I sank roots first of all, stood
near the shore, close by the dyke
and dash of waves; few men
saw my home in that wilderness,
5   but each dawn, each dusk,
the tawny waves surged and swirled
around me. Little did I think
that I, mouthless, should ever sing
to men sitting at the mead-bench,
10   varying my pitch. It is rather puzzling,
a miracle to men ignorant of such arts,
how a knife's point and a right hand
(mind and implement moving as one)
could cut and carve me—so that I
15   can send you a message without fear,
and no one else can overhear
or noise abroad the words we share.

Solutions: 1. Penis or onion; 2. Bible; 3. Book worm; 4. Pen and fingers; 5. Reed.

ARTHURIAN ROMANCE

◄—► ⚏◆⚏ ◄—►

Marie de France
fl. 2nd half of the 12th century

In a famous line from the prologue to her *Lais*, Marie de France suggested that serious readers could approach an obscure old book and "supply its significance from their own wisdom." The original French text, "*de lur sen le surplus mettre*," implies that such readers add on something that is missing. In part a gesture of respect toward the study of pagan Latin literature in a Christian setting, this statement also seems to permit Marie herself a dramatically new perspective when she encounters long-established Arthurian stories such as *Lanval*, and the related tale of Tristan and Isolt in *Chevrefoil*. Starting with a scene of war that readers of Geoffrey of Monmouth might recognize, Marie swiftly brings into play elements that had been largely absent in the historicizing stories of Arthur: bodily desire and its dangers, romantic longing, the realm of the uncanny, the power of women, the force of wealth and influence in even the noblest courts. Similarly, in *Chevrefoil* the lovers' brief, ecstatic meeting occurs as a crowd of courtiers awaits her.

Marie's specific identity remains obscure, but it is clear that she was a woman of French background writing in England in the later decades of the twelfth century, widely educated, and in touch with the royal court. She dedicates her book of *Lais* to a "noble King" who was probably Henry II, and she may have been his kinswoman. Marie's works draw into that courtly culture the languages and traditions of the English and Celtic past. She rewrote a Latin narrative about the origin of "Saint Patrick's Purgatory" and the adventure of an Irish knight there; and she retold the fables of Aesop using an English translation that she attributed to King Alfred. The *Lais*, she says, came to her through oral transmission, and she connects them with the Bretons. Indeed, the best early copy of the *Lais*, Harley manuscript 978 in the British Library, is itself a multilingual compilation that includes the early Middle English poem *The Cuckoo Song* ("Sumer is icumen in"; see page 386).

Writing a generation after Geoffrey of Monmouth and not long before Gerald of Wales, Marie brings a quite different and rather critical set of preoccupations to her Arthurian stories. She opens her tale with a realistic and admirable occasion of male power and strong kingship: Arthur's battle for territory and his reward of faithful vassals. A bleaker side of that courtly world, and perhaps of Marie's own, is also implicit, however. With a terseness and indirection typical of her *lais*, Marie shows women as property in the king's gift, knights forgotten when their wealth runs out, and the perversion of judicial process. In *Chevrefoil*, again, Isolt has only the title she gained by marriage, "the queen," never her own name.

Marvels and erotic desire dominate her tales, though, and women's power, for good or ill, is their primary motivating force. Guinevere, in a hostile portrait of adulterous aggression and vengeful dishonesty, nonetheless manages to manipulate Arthur and his legal codes when Lanval rejects her advances. The queen is countered by Lanval's supernatural mistress, who commands luxurious riches that dwarf Arthur's; she rescues Lanval by being an unimpeachable legal witness in his defense. Indeed, she arrives on her white palfrey as the moment of judgment nears, almost like a knightly champion in a trial by battle. Lanval vanishes into a timeless world of fulfilled desire and limitless wealth that has analogies in much older Celtic tradition—for instance, in *The Voyage of Máel Dúin* (pages 109–10). This closing scene defies the reintegration of male courtly order that is typical even in the erotic romances of Marie's contemporary Chrétien de Troyes.

The realm of eroticism and women's power in *Lanval*, though, is not automatically any more virtuous or stable than the ostentatious wealth and corruptible law of the world of Arthurian men. If Lanval's mysterious lady is beautiful and generous, she also takes his knightliness from him. Lanval is last seen riding behind the lady, and not on a warhorse but on a palfrey. Guinevere swiftly reduces Arthur to a weak and temporizing king. And in her initial explosion after Lanval rejects her, Guinevere accuses him of homosexuality. For all its absurdity, the moment articulates unnerving implications of the profound bonds among men in the Arthurian world, implications that could interrupt genealogical transmission of wealth and power. Marie's Guinevere again voices fears the tradition has left unsaid.

Chevrefoil ("Honeysuckle") involves romantic desires far more elevated than those in *Lanval*, but equally dangerous to the social order, and ultimately disastrous to the lovers. Even in this brief episode, the lovers' one intimate moment is hedged about by an anxious sense of a public and hostile world nearby, as well as a more distant royal power that crushes private love. Marie can assume her readers know the story of Tristan and Isolt and their tragic love. Tristan is sent to Ireland to fetch Isolt, the fiancée of his uncle, King Mark. On a boat returning to Cornwall, Tristan and Isolt share a love potion that had been meant to seal her marriage with Mark. The adulterous (and, from a medieval Catholic perspective, incestuous) affair that follows entangles all three in a web of desire, dependency, and family loyalty. The intense joy of the lovers' brief encounter in this episode, then, is complicated and darkened by the many echoes of other famous moments in their affair: a meeting under a tree, joint exile in a forest, and the intertwining vine and rose that later grow from their adjacent graves. And Marie's readers would have known that the reconciliation Isolt promises never, in fact, takes place. This tone of superabundant meaning—perhaps another version of the "*surplus*" mentioned above—is mirrored in the *lai* by the long message Isolt can interpret from a single word, Tristan's name carved on a piece of wood.

Marie de France may be trying less to propound a critique of the received stories of Arthur and Tristan than to recall her readers' attention to elements that tradition has left aside, as she suggests in her prologue. Some of this is no more troubling than a delightful fantasy of wealth and pleasure, outside time and without consequences. Other elements imply, with startling economy, forces that (in the hands of later romancers) tear the Arthurian world to pieces.

from LAIS[1]

Prologue

Whoever has received knowledge
and eloquence in speech from God
should not be silent or secretive
but demonstrate it willingly.
5   When a great good is widely heard of,
then, and only then, does it bloom,
and when that good is praised by many,
it has spread its blossoms.
The custom among the ancients—
10   as Priscian[2] testifies—
was to speak quite obscurely
in the books they wrote,
so that those who were to come after
and study them
15   might gloss the letter
and supply its significance from their own wisdom.[3]
Philosophers knew this,
they understood among themselves
that the more time they spent,
20   the more subtle their minds would become
and the better they would know how to keep themselves
from whatever was to be avoided.
He who would guard himself from vice
should study and understand
25   and begin a weighty work
by which he might keep vice at a distance,
and free himself from great sorrow.
That's why I began to think
about composing some good stories
30   and translating from Latin to Romance;[4]

1. Translated by Robert Hanning and Joan Ferrante.
2. A famed grammarian of the late Roman empire, Priscian remained widely influential in the study of Latin language and literature in the 12th century.
3. Marie refers to the practice of supplying glosses—

explanatory notes such as this one—to school texts; she also implies that later readers bring their own perspective to earlier works, a point relevant to her own free adaptation of earlier Arthurian stories.
4. That is, to French.

Marie de France Writing, from an illuminated manuscript of her works. While most images of writing feature men, women were also writers and copyists as well as readers (see Color Plate 10). Here, in a late-13th-century manuscript of her poems, Marie de France is shown at her writing desk, strikingly similar in posture and detail (and in authority) to Laurence of Durham more than a century earlier (see page 2).

but that was not to bring me fame:
too many others have done it.
Then I thought of the *lais* I'd heard.[5]
I did not doubt, indeed I knew well,
35   that those who first began them
and sent them forth
composed them in order to preserve
adventures they had heard.
I have heard many told;
40   and I don't want to neglect or forget them.
To put them into word and rhyme
I've often stayed awake.

In your honor, noble King,[6]
who are so brave and courteous,
45   repository of all joys
in whose heart all goodness takes root,
I undertook to assemble these *lais*
to compose and recount them in rhyme.
In my heart I thought and determined,
50   sire, that I would present them to you.
If it pleases you to receive them,
you will give me great joy;
I shall be happy forever.

5. A *lai* was typically a short verse narrative, meant for oral performance with music. A particular group of these, often including Arthurian tales, was especially connected with Brittany.

6. Probably Henry II.

Do not think me presumptuous
55   if I dare present them to you.
Now hear how they begin.

Lanval

I shall tell you the adventure of another *lai*,
just as it happened:
it was composed about a very noble vassal;
in Breton, they call him Lanval.[1]

5   Arthur, the brave and the courtly king,
was staying at Cardoel,[2]
because the Scots and the Picts
were destroying the land.[3]
They invaded Logres°   England
10   and laid it waste.
At Pentecost, in summer,[4]
the king stayed there.
He gave out many rich gifts:
to counts and barons,
15   members of the Round Table—
such a company had no equal in all the world—
he distributed wives and lands,
to all but one who had served him.
That was Lanval; Arthur forgot him,
20   and none of his men favored him either.
For his valor, for his generosity,
his beauty and his bravery,
most men envied him;
some feigned the appearance of love
25   who, if something unpleasant happened to him,
would not have been at all disturbed.
He was the son of a king of high degree
but he was far from his heritage.
He was of the king's household
30   but he had spent all his wealth,
for the king gave him nothing
nor did Lanval ask.
Now Lanval was in difficulty,
depressed and very worried.
35   My lords, don't be surprised:
a strange man, without friends,
is very sad in another land,

---

1. Marie seems to imply knowledge of Breton, a Celtic language related to Welsh. In other works, she shows knowledge of English as well, and excellent Latin.
2. Carlisle, in the north of England.
3. Scots and Picts were Arthur's traditional enemies.

4. "Summer" here refers to late spring. The feast of Pentecost commemorates the descent of the Holy Spirit among Christ's apostles; it is often the occasion of Arthurian stories, especially those that involve marvels.

when he doesn't know where to look for help.
The knight of whom I speak,
40   who had served the king so long,
one day mounted his horse
and went off to amuse himself.
He left the city
and came, all alone, to a field;
45   he dismounted by a running stream
but his horse trembled badly.
He removed the saddle and went off,
leaving the horse to roll around in the meadow.
He folded his cloak beneath his head
50   and lay down.
He worried about his difficulty,
he could see nothing that pleased him.
As he lay there
he looked down along the bank
55   and saw two girls approaching;
he had never seen any lovelier.
They were richly dressed,
tightly laced,
in tunics of dark purple;
60   their faces were very lovely.
The older one carried basins,
golden, well made, and fine;
I shall tell you the truth about it, without fail.
The other carried a towel.
65   They went straight
to where the knight was lying.
Lanval, who was very well bred,
got up to meet them.
They greeted him first
70   and gave him their message:
"Sir Lanval, my lady,
who is worthy and wise and beautiful,
sent us for you.
Come with us now.
75   We shall guide you there safely.
See, her pavilion is nearby!"
The knight went with them;
giving no thought to his horse
who was feeding before him in the meadow.
80   They led him up to the tent,[5]
which was quite beautiful and well placed.
Queen Semiramis,
however much more wealth,
power, or knowledge she had,

---

5. Elaborate tents are often found in contemporary narratives of kings going out to battle.

85   or the emperor Octavian[6]
       could not have paid for one of the flaps.
       There was a golden eagle on top of it,
       whose value I could not tell,
       nor could I judge the value of the cords or the poles
90   that held up the sides of the tent;
       there is no king on earth who could buy it,
       no matter what wealth he offered.
       The girl was inside the tent:
       the lily and the young rose
95   when they appear in the summer
       are surpassed by her beauty.
       She lay on a beautiful bed—
       the bedclothes were worth a castle—
       dressed only in her shift.
100   Her body was well shaped and elegant;
       for the heat, she had thrown over herself,
       a precious cloak of white ermine,
       covered with purple alexandrine,°   *embroidery*
       but her whole side was uncovered,
105   her face, her neck and her bosom;
       she was whiter than the hawthorn flower.
       The knight went forward
       and the girl addressed him.
       He sat before the bed.
110   "Lanval," she said, "sweet love,
       because of you I have come from my land;
       I came to seek you from far away.
       If you are brave and courtly,
       no emperor or count or king
115   will ever have known such joy or good;
       for I love you more than anything."
       He looked at her and saw that she was beautiful;
       Love stung him with a spark
       that burned and set fire to his heart.
120   He answered her in a suitable way.
       "Lovely one," he said, "if it pleased you,
       if such joy might be mine
       that you would love me,
       there is nothing you might command,
125   within my power, that I would not do,
       whether foolish or wise.
       I shall obey your command;
       for you, I shall abandon everyone.
       I want never to leave you.
130   That is what I most desire."

6. Semiramis, legendary queen of Assyria and builder of Babylon, led armies of conquest; she is also a conventional figure of uncontrolled sexual desire. She is interestingly placed here as a female counterpart to Octavian (Augustus Caesar), the first Roman emperor.

When the girl heard the words
of the man who could love her so,
she granted him her love and her body.
Now Lanval was on the right road!

135   Afterward, she gave him a gift:
he would never again want anything,
he would receive as he desired;
however generously he might give and spend,
she would provide what he needed.

140   Now Lanval is well cared for.
The more lavishly he spends,
the more gold and silver he will have.
"Love," she said, "I admonish you now,
I command and beg you,

145   do not let any man know about this.
I shall tell you why:
you would lose me for good
if this love were known;
you would never see me again

150   or possess my body."
He answered that he would do
exactly as she commanded.
He lay beside her on the bed;
now Lanval is well cared for.

155   He remained with her
that afternoon, until evening
and would have stayed longer, if he could,
and if his love had consented.
"Love," she said, "get up.

160   You cannot stay any longer.
Go away now; I shall remain
but I will tell you one thing:
when you want to talk to me
there is no place you can think of

165   where a man might have his mistress
without reproach or shame,
that I shall not be there with you
to satisfy all your desires.
No man but you will see me

170   or hear my words."
When he heard her, he was very happy,
he kissed her, and then got up.
The girls who had brought him to the tent
dressed him in rich clothes;

175   when he was dressed anew,
there wasn't a more handsome youth in all the world;
he was no fool, no boor.
They gave him water for his hands
and a towel to dry them,

180 and they brought him food.
 He took supper with his love;
 it was not to be refused.
 He was served with great courtesy,
 he received it with great joy.
185 There was an entremet°   *side dish*
 that vastly pleased the knight
 for he kissed his lady often
 and held her close.
 When they finished dinner,
190 his horse was brought to him.
 The horse had been well saddled;
 Lanval was very richly served.
 The knight took his leave, mounted,
 and rode toward the city,
195 often looking behind him.
 Lanval was very disturbed;
 he wondered about his adventure
 and was doubtful in his heart;
 he was amazed, not knowing what to believe;
200 he didn't expect ever to see her again.
 He came to his lodging
 and found his men well dressed.
 That night, his accommodations were rich
 but no one knew where it came from.
205 There was no knight in the city
 who really needed a place to stay
 whom he didn't invite to join him
 to be well and richly served.
 Lanval gave rich gifts,
210 Lanval released prisoners,
 Lanval dressed jongleurs,°   *performers*
 Lanval offered great honors.
 There was no stranger or friend
 to whom Lanval didn't give.
215 Lanval's joy and pleasure were intense;
 in the daytime or at night,
 he could see his love often;
 she was completely at his command.
 In that same year, it seems to me,
220 after the feast of Saint John,
 about thirty knights
 were amusing themselves
 in an orchard beneath the tower
 where the queen was staying.
225 Gawain was with them
 and his cousin, the handsome Yvain;[7]

7. Gawain and Yvain serve to place Marie's hero in the context of more famous Arthurian episodes. Gawain, nephew of Arthur and distinguished both for bravery and courtesy, increasingly acts as Lanval's sponsor in the rest of the *lai*.

Gawain, the noble, the brave,
who was so loved by all, said:
"By God, my lords, we wronged
230   our companion Lanval,
who is so generous and courtly,
and whose father is a rich king,
when we didn't bring him with us."
They immediately turned back,
235   went to his lodging
and prevailed on Lanval to come along with them.
At a sculpted window
the queen was looking out;
she had three ladies with her.
240   She saw the king's retinue,
recognized Lanval and looked at him.
Then she told one of her ladies
to send for her maidens,
the loveliest and the most refined;
245   together they went to amuse themselves
in the orchard where the others were.
She brought thirty or more with her;
they descended the steps.
The knights came to meet them,
250   because they were delighted to see them.
The knights took them by the hand;
their conversation was in no way vulgar.
Lanval went off to one side,
far from the others; he was impatient
255   to hold his love,
to kiss and embrace and touch her;
he thought little of others' joys
if he could not have his pleasure.
When the queen saw him alone,
260   she went straight to the knight.
She sat beside him and spoke,
revealing her whole heart:
"Lanval, I have shown you much honor,
I have cherished you, and loved you.
265   You may have all my love;
just tell me your desire.
I promise you my affection.
You should be very happy with me."
"My lady," he said, "let me be!
270   I have no desire to love you.
I've served the king a long time;
I don't want to betray my faith to him.
Never, for you or for your love,
will I do anything to harm my lord."
275   The queen got angry;

in her wrath, she insulted him:
"Lanval," she said, "I am sure
you don't care for such pleasure;
people have often told me
280 that you have no interest in women.
You have fine-looking boys
with whom you enjoy yourself.
Base coward, lousy cripple,
my lord made a bad mistake
285 when he let you stay with him.
For all I know, he'll lose God because of it."
When Lanval heard her, he was quite disturbed;
he was not slow to answer.
He said something out of spite
290 that he would later regret.
"Lady," he said, "of that activity
I know nothing,
but I love and I am loved
by one who should have the prize
295 over all the women I know.
And I shall tell you one thing;
you might as well know all:
any one of those who serve her,
the poorest girl of all,
300 is better than you, my lady queen,
in body, face, and beauty,
in breeding and in goodness."
The queen left him
and went, weeping, to her chamber.
305 She was upset and angry
because he had insulted her.
She went to bed sick;
never, she said, would she get up
unless the king gave her satisfaction
310 for the offense against her.
The king returned from the woods,
he'd had a very good day.
He entered the queen's chambers.
When she saw him, she began to complain.
315 She fell at his feet, asked his mercy,
saying that Lanval had dishonored her;
he had asked for her love,
and because she refused him
he insulted and offended her:
320 he boasted of a love
who was so refined and noble and proud
that her chambermaid,
the poorest one who served her,
was better than the queen.

325 The king got very angry;
    he swore an oath:
    if Lanval could not defend himself in court
    he would have him burned or hanged.
    The king left her chamber
330 and called for three of his barons;
    he sent them for Lanval
    who was feeling great sorrow and distress.
    He had come back to his dwelling,
    knowing very well
335 that he'd lost his love,
    he had betrayed their affair.
    He was all alone in a room,
    disturbed and troubled;
    he called on his love, again and again,
340 but it did him no good.
    He complained and sighed,
    from time to time he fainted;
    then he cried a hundred times for her to have mercy
    and speak to her love.
345 He cursed his heart and his mouth;
    it's a wonder he didn't kill himself.
    No matter how much he cried and shouted,
    ranted and raged,
    she would not have mercy on him,
350 not even let him see her.
    How will he ever contain himself?
    The men the king sent
    arrived and told him
    to appear in court without delay:
355 the king had summoned him
    because the queen had accused him.
    Lanval went with his great sorrow;
    they could have killed him, for all he cared.
    He came before the king;
360 he was very sad, thoughtful, silent;
    his face revealed great suffering.
    In anger the king told him:
    "Vassal, you have done me a great wrong!
    This was a base undertaking,
365 to shame and disgrace me
    and to insult the queen.
    You have made a foolish boast:
    your love is much too noble
    if her maid is more beautiful,
370 more worthy, than the queen."
    Lanval denied that he'd dishonored
    or shamed his lord,
    word for word, as the king spoke:

he had not made advances to the queen;
375   but of what he had said,
he acknowledged the truth,
about the love he had boasted of,
that now made him sad because he'd lost her.
About that he said he would do
380   whatever the court decided.
The king was very angry with him;
he sent for all his men
to determine exactly what he ought to do
so that no one could find fault with his decision.
385   They did as he commanded,
whether they liked it or not.
They assembled,
judged, and decided,
that Lanval should have his day;
390   but he must find pledges for his lord
to guarantee that he would await the judgment,
return, and be present at it.[8]
Then the court would be increased,
for now there were none but the king's household.
395   The barons came back to the king
and announced their decision.
The king demanded pledges.
Lanval was alone and forlorn,
he had no relative, no friend.
400   Gawain went and pledged himself for him,
and all his companions followed.
The king addressed them: "I release him to you
on forfeit of whatever you hold from me,
lands and fiefs, each one for himself."
405   When Lanval was pledged, there was nothing else to do.
He returned to his lodging.
The knights accompanied him,
they reproached and admonished him
that he give up his great sorrow;
410   they cursed his foolish love.
Each day they went to see him,
because they wanted to know
whether he was drinking and eating;
they were afraid that he'd kill himself.
415   On the day that they had named,
the barons assembled.
The king and the queen were there
and the pledges brought Lanval back.
They were all very sad for him:

---

8. Marie introduces judicial procedures that may have recalled those in Henry's reign: summons and accusation, setting a day for judgment, the rise of royal jurisdiction, the possibility of a champion, and trial by battle.

420 I think there were a hundred
     who would have done all they could
     to set him free without a trial
     where he would be wrongly accused.
     The king demanded a verdict
425 according to the charge and rebuttal.
     Now it all fell to the barons.
     They went to the judgment,
     worried and distressed
     for the noble man from another land
430 who'd gotten into such trouble in their midst.
     Many wanted to condemn him
     in order to satisfy their lord.
     The Duke of Cornwall said:
     "No one can blame us;
435 whether it makes you weep or sing
     justice must be carried out.
     The king spoke against his vassal
     whom I have heard named Lanval;
     he accused him of felony,
440 charged him with a misdeed—
     a love that he had boasted of,
     which made the queen angry.
     No one but the king accused him:
     by the faith I owe you,
445 if one were to speak the truth,
     there should have been no need for defense,
     except that a man owes his lord honor
     in every circumstance.
     He will be bound by his oath,
450 and the king will forgive us our pledges
     if he can produce proof;
     if his love would come forward,
     if what he said,
     what upset the queen, is true,
455 then he will be acquitted,
     because he did not say it out of malice.
     But if he cannot get his proof,
     we must make it clear to him
     that he will forfeit his service to the king;
460 he must take his leave."
     They sent to the knight,
     told and announced to him
     that he should have his love come
     to defend and stand surety for him.
465 He told them that he could not do it:
     he would never receive help from her.
     They went back to the judges,
     not expecting any help from Lanval.

The king pressed them hard
470 because of the queen who was waiting.
When they were ready to give their verdict
they saw two girls approaching,
riding handsome palfreys.
They were very attractive,
475 dressed in purple taffeta,
over their bare skin.
The men looked at them with pleasure.
Gawain, taking three knights with him,
went to Lanval and told him;
480 he pointed out the two girls.
Gawain was extremely happy, and begged him
to tell if his love were one of them.
Lanval said he didn't know who they were,
where they came from or where they were going.
485 The girls proceeded
still on horseback;
they dismounted before the high table
at which Arthur, the king, sat.
They were of great beauty,
490 and spoke in a courtly manner:
"King, clear your chambers,
have them hung with silk
where my lady may dismount;
she wishes to take shelter with you."
495 He promised it willingly
and called two knights
to guide them up to the chambers.
On that subject no more was said.
The king asked his barons
500 for their judgment and decision;
he said they had angered him very much
with their long delay.
"Sire," they said, "we have decided.
Because of the ladies we have just seen
505 we have made no judgment.
Let us reconvene the trial."
Then they assembled, everyone was worried;
there was much noise and strife.
While they were in that confusion,
510 two girls in noble array,
dressed in Phrygian silks
and riding Spanish mules,
were seen coming down the street.
This gave the vassals great joy;
515 to each other they said that now
Lanval, the brave and bold, was saved.
Gawain went up to him,

bringing his companions along.
"Sire," he said, "take heart.
520 For the love of God, speak to us.
Here come two maidens,
well adorned and very beautiful;
one must certainly be your love."
Lanval answered quickly
525 that he did not recognize them,
he didn't know them or love them.
Meanwhile they'd arrived,
and dismounted before the king.
Most of those who saw them praised them
530 for their bodies, their faces, their coloring;
each was more impressive
than the queen had ever been.
The older one was courtly and wise,
she spoke her message fittingly:
535 "King, have chambers prepared for us
to lodge my lady according to her need;
she is coming here to speak with you."
He ordered them to be taken
to the others who had preceded them.
540 There was no problem with the mules.
When he had seen to the girls,
he summoned all his barons
to render their judgment;
it had already dragged out too much.
545 The queen was getting angry
because she had fasted so long.
They were about to give their judgment
when through the city came riding
a girl on horseback:
550 there was none more beautiful in the world.
She rode a white palfrey,
who carried her handsomely and smoothly:
he was well apportioned in the neck and head,
no finer beast in the world.
555 The palfrey's trappings were rich;
under heaven there was no count or king
who could have afforded them all
without selling or mortgaging lands.
She was dressed in this fashion:
560 in a white linen shift
that revealed both her sides
since the lacing was along the side.
Her body was elegant, her hips slim,
her neck whiter than snow on a branch,
565 her eyes bright, her face white,
a beautiful mouth, a well-set nose,

dark eyebrows and an elegant forehead,
her hair curly and rather blond;
golden wire does not shine
570   like her hair in the light.
Her cloak, which she had wrapped around her,
was dark purple.
On her wrist she held a sparrow hawk,
a greyhound followed her.
575   In the town, no one, small or big,
old man or child,
failed to come look.
As they watched her pass,
there was no joking about her beauty.
580   She proceeded at a slow pace.
The judges who saw her
marveled at the sight;
no one who looked at her
was not warmed with joy.
585   Those who loved the knight
came to him and told him
of the girl who was approaching,
if God pleased, to rescue him.
"Sir companion, here comes one
590   neither tawny nor dark;
this is, of all who exist,
the most beautiful woman in the world."
Lanval heard them and lifted his head;
he recognized her and sighed.
595   The blood rose to his face;
he was quick to speak.
"By my faith," he said, "that is my love.
Now I don't care if I am killed,
if only she forgives me.
600   For I am restored, now that I see her."
The lady entered the palace;
no one so beautiful had ever been there.
She dismounted before the king
so that she was well seen by all.
605   And she let her cloak fall
so they could see her better.
The king, who was well bred,
rose and went to meet her;
all the others honored her
610   and offered to serve her.
When they had looked at her well,
when they had greatly praised her beauty,
she spoke in this way,
she didn't want to wait:
615   "I have loved one of your vassals:

you see him before you—Lanval.
He has been accused in your court—
I don't want him to suffer
for what he said; you should know
620 that the queen was in the wrong.
He never made advances to her.
And for the boast that he made,
if he can be acquitted through me,
let him be set free by your barons."
625 Whatever the barons judged by law
the king promised would prevail.
To the last man they agreed
that Lanval had successfully answered the charge.
He was set free by their decision
630 and the girl departed.
The king could not detain her,
though there were enough people to serve her.
Outside the hall stood
a great stone of dark marble
635 where heavy men mounted
when they left the king's court;
Lanval climbed on it.
When the girl came through the gate
Lanval leapt, in one bound,
640 onto the palfrey, behind her.
With her he went to Avalun,
so the Bretons tell us,
to a very beautiful island;
there the youth was carried off.
645 No man heard of him again,
and I have no more to tell.

Chevrefoil (The Honeysuckle)

I should like very much
to tell you the truth
about the *lai* men call *Chevrefoil*—
why it was composed and where it came from.
5   Many have told and recited it to me
and I have found it in writing,
about Tristan and the queen
and their love that was so true,
that brought them much suffering
10   and caused them to die the same day.
King Mark was annoyed,
angry at his nephew Tristan;

he exiled Tristan from his land
because of the queen whom he loved.
15 Tristan returned to his own country,
South Wales, where he was born,
he stayed a whole year;
he couldn't come back.
Afterward he began to expose himself
20 to death and destruction.
Don't be surprised at this:
for one who loves very faithfully
is sad and troubled
when he cannot satisfy his desires.
25 Tristan was sad and worried,
so he set out from his land.
He traveled straight to Cornwall,
where the queen lived,
and entered the forest all alone—
30 he didn't want anyone to see him;
he came out only in the evening
when it was time to find shelter.
He took lodging that night,
with peasants, poor people.
35 He asked them for news
of the king—what he was doing.
They told him they had heard
that the barons had been summoned by ban.[1]
They were to come to Tintagel[2]
40 where the king wanted to hold his court,
at Pentecost they would all be there,
there'd be much joy and pleasure,
and the queen would be there too.
Tristan heard and was very happy;
45 she would not be able to go there
without his seeing her pass.
The day the king set out,
Tristan also came to the woods
by the road he knew
50 their assembly must take.
He cut a hazel tree in half,
then he squared it.
When he had prepared the wood,
he wrote his name on it with his knife.
55 If the queen noticed it—
and she should be on the watch for it,
for it had happened before
and she had noticed it then—

---

1. A royal summons to feudal service.   In Arthurian legend, it is the site of Arthur's conception.
2. One of Mark's castles, on the north coast of Cornwall.

she'd know when she saw it,
60   that the piece of wood had come from her love.
This was the message of the writing[3]
that he had sent to her:
he had been there a long time,
had waited and remained
65   to find out and to discover
how he could see her,
for he could not live without her.
With the two of them it was just
as it is with the honeysuckle
70   that attaches itself to the hazel tree:
when it has wound and attached
and worked itself around the trunk,
the two can survive together;
but if someone tries to separate them,
75   the hazel dies quickly
and the honeysuckle with it.
"Sweet love, so it is with us:
You cannot live without me, nor I without you."
The queen rode along;
80   she looked at the hillside
and saw the piece of wood; she knew what it was,
she recognized all the letters.
The knights who were accompanying her,
who were riding with her,
85   she ordered to stop:
she wanted to dismount and rest.
They obeyed her command.
She went far away from her people
and called her girl
90   Brenguein,[4] who was loyal to her.
She went a short distance from the road;
and in the woods she found him
whom she loved more than any living thing.
They took great joy in each other.
95   He spoke to her as much as he desired,
she told him whatever she liked.
Then she assured him
that he would be reconciled with the king—
for it weighed on him
100   that he had sent Tristan away;
he'd done it because of the accusation.[5]
Then she departed, she left her love,
but when it came to the separation,

3. From Tristan's name alone, or possibly a few words in code or runic letters, Isolt can elicit the entire message that follows.
4. Isolt's maid, who earlier substituted herself for Isolt in the marriage bed with King Mark.
5. Envious courtiers had plotted to expose the lovers' affair to the king.

they began to weep.
105   Tristan went to Wales,
       to wait until his uncle sent for him.
       For the joy that he'd felt
       from his love when he saw her,
       by means of the stick he inscribed
110   as the queen had instructed,
       and in order to remember the words,
       Tristan, who played the harp well,
       composed a new *lai* about it.
       I shall name it briefly:
115   in English they call it *Goat's Leaf*
       the French call it *Chevrefoil*.
       I have given you the truth
       about the *lai* that I have told here.

Sir Gawain and the Green Knight

As a subject of literary romance, Arthurian tradition never had the centrality in later medieval England it had gained in France. It was only one of a wide range of popular topics like Havelok the Dane, King Horn, and the Troy story. Nevertheless Arthur and his court played an ongoing role in English society, written into histories and emulated by aristocrats and kings. And in the later fourteenth or early fifteenth century, several very distinguished Arthurian poems appeared, such as the alliterative *Morte Arthure* and the *Awntyrs* (Adventures) *off Arthure*.

Sir Gawain and the Green Knight is the greatest of the Arthurian romances produced in England. The poem embraces the highest aspirations of the late medieval aristocratic world, both courtly and religious, even while it eloquently admits the human failings that threaten those values. A knight's troth and word, a Christian's election and covenant, the breaking point of a person's or a society's virtues, all come in for celebration and painful scrutiny during Gawain's adventure.

Like *Beowulf*, *Sir Gawain and the Green Knight* comes down to us by the thread of a single copy. Its manuscript contains a group of poems (*Sir Gawain, Pearl, Purity,* and *Patience*) that mark their anonymous author as a poet whose range approaches that of his contemporary Chaucer, and whose formal craft is in some ways more ambitious than Chaucer's.

Gawain is the work of a highly sophisticated provincial court poet (likely in the northwest Midlands), working in a form and narrative tradition that is conservative in comparison with Chaucer's. The poet uses the alliterative long line, a meter with its roots in Anglo-Saxon poetry; the unrhymed alliterative stanzas, of irregular length, each end with five shorter rhymed lines often called a "bob-and-wheel" stanza. (For a further discussion of the alliterative style, see the introduction to William Langland, pages 328–30.) Within these traditional constraints, however, the poem achieves an apex of medieval courtly literature, as a superlatively crafted and stylized version of quest romance.

The romance never aims to detach itself from society or history, though. It opens and closes by referring to Troy, the ancient, fallen empire whose survivors were legendary founders of Britain, a connection well known through Geoffrey of Monmouth. Arthur, their ultimate heir, went on later in his myth to pursue imperial ambitions that, like those of Troy, were foiled by adulterous desire and political infidelity. *Sir Gawain* also echoes its contemporary world in the technical language of architecture, crafts, and arms. This helps draw in the kind of conservative, aristocratic court for which the poem seems to have been written, probably in Cheshire or Lancashire, a somewhat backward region whose nobles remained loyal to Richard II. Along with the pleasure it takes in fine armor and courtly ritual, the poem seems to enfold anxieties about the economic pressures of maintaining chivalric display in a period of costly new technology, inflation, and declining income from land.

By the time this poem was written, toward the close of the fourteenth century, Gawain was a famous Arthurian hero. His reputation was ambiguous, though; he was both Arthur's faithful retainer and nephew, but also a suave seducer. Which side of Gawain would dominate in this particular poem? Would he stand for a civilization of Christian chivalry or one of cynical sophistication?

The test that begins to answer this question occurs during Arthur's ritual celebrations of Christmas and the New Year, and within the civilized practices of Eucharist and secular feast. A gigantic green knight interrupts Arthur's banquet to offer a deadly game of exchanged ax-blows, to be resolved in one year's time. Although the Green Knight, with his ball of holly leaves, seems at first to come from the tradition of the Wild Man—a giant force of nature itself—he is also a sophisticated knight, gorgeously attired. He knows, too, just how to taunt a young king without quite overstepping the bounds of courtly behavior. Gawain takes up the challenge, but a still greater marvel ensues.

As the term of the agreement approaches, Gawain rides off, elaborately armed, to find the Green Knight and fulfill his obligation, even if that means his death. What Gawain encounters first, though, are temptations of character and sexuality even trickier and more crucial than they at first seem.

Sir Gawain and the Green Knight is remarkable not only for the intricacy of its plot but also for the virtuosity of its descriptions, such as the almost elegiac review of the passing seasons ("And so the year runs away in yesterdays many"). The poem rejoices in the masterful exercise of skill as the mark of civilization. Beautifully crafted knots appear everywhere, and we encounter artisanal craft as well in narrative elements like the Green Knight's dress (a dazzling mixture of leafy green and jeweler's gold), Gawain's decorated shield and arms, and the expertise of the master of the hunt who carves up the prey of Gawain's host with ritual precision. Even Gawain's exquisite courtly manners appear as a civilizing artifice.

The ambition of the poem's own craft is equally evident in its extraordinary range of formal devices. Preeminent among these is the symbolic register of number. The poem can be seen as a single unit, circling back to the Trojan scene with which it begins. It has a double structure, too, as it shifts between the courts of Arthur and Gawain's mysterious host. In the manuscript it is divided into four parts ("fits") that respond to the seasonal description at the opening of Part 2. The narrative proper ends by echoing the very start of the poem, at line 2525 (in the original Middle English), itself a multiple of fives that recalls the pentangle on Gawain's shield symbolizing his virtues. The final rhyming stanza, with its formula of grace and salvation, brings the line total to 2530, whose individual digits add up to ten, a number associated with the divine in medieval numerology.

This symbolic structure can seem sometimes overdetermined. A range of elements, however, invites the reader to come at the poem from other perspectives. The poem's very circularity, narrative and formal, allows it to be viewed from beginning or ending. From the front it is a poem of male accomplishment, largely celebrating *men's* courts and *men's* virtues (even men's horses). At the other end, however, it focuses on a court presided over by an old woman (later called a goddess), a court whose irruption into the Arthurian world is explained as the playing out of an old and mysterious rivalry between two queens. Male, even patriarchal from one direction, the poem seems matriarchal, almost pagan, from the other. For all its formal cohesion and celebration of craft, the poem also pulls the reader back and keeps its mysteries intact by leaving many narrative loose ends and unanswered questions.

Unresolvable ambiguities reside most clearly in the pentangle on Gawain's shield and in the "green girdle" whose true owner remains uncertain. For all their differences, both are figures that insist on repetition, end where they begin, and possess a geometry that can be traced forward or backward. Yet the static perfection of the pentangle is subtly set against the protean green girdle, which passes through so many hands, alters its shape (being untied and retied repeatedly), and connects with so many issues in the poem: mortality, women's power, Gawain's fault and the acceptance of that fault by the whole Arthurian court. The girdle becomes an image both of flaw and triumph and of all the loose ends in this early episode of the Arthurian myth.

The girdle also serves to link *Sir Gawain* to political and social issues of the poet's own time, particularly efforts to revalidate a declining system of chivalry. After the last line in the manuscript, a later medieval hand has added "Hony Soyt Qui Mal Pence" ("shamed be he who thinks ill thereof"), the motto of the royal Order of the Garter, founded by Edward III in 1349 to promote a revival of knighthood. The Arthurian myth had already been redeployed to buttress royal power when Edward III refounded a Round Table in 1344. King Arthur's wisdom at the close of Gawain's adventure lies in transforming Gawain's shame, rage, and humiliated sense of sin into an emblem at once of mortal humanity and aristocratic cohesion. This is the place—back with the king and ritually connected with the Order of the Garter—where the closed circle of the poem opens to the social, historical world of empire, court, and kingship.

Sir Gawain and the Green Knight[1]
Part 1

When the siege and the assault had ceased at Troy,
and the fortress fell in flame to firebrands and ashes,
the traitor who the contrivance of treason there fashioned
was tried for his treachery, the most true upon earth—
5   it was Aeneas[2] the noble and his renowned kindred
who then laid under them lands, and lords became
of well-nigh all the wealth in the Western Isles.[3]
When royal Romulus to Rome his road had taken,
in great pomp and pride he peopled it first,
10   and named it with his own name that yet now it bears;
Tirius[4] went to Tuscany and towns founded,
Langaberde[5] in Lombardy uplifted halls,
and far over the French flood Felix Brutus
on many a broad bank and brae[6] Britain established
15   full fair,
where strange things, strife and sadness,
at whiles in the land did fare,
and each other grief and gladness
oft fast have followed there.

---

1. This translation, remarkably faithful to the original alliterative meter and stanza form, is by J. R. R. Tolkien.
2. Aeneas led the survivors of Troy to Italy, after a series of ambiguous omens and misadventures. In medieval tradition, he was also said to have plotted to betray his own city. "The traitor" in 1.3, though, may refer to the Trojan Antenor, also said to have betrayed Troy.
3. Perhaps Europe, or just the British Isles. Many royal houses traced their ancestry to Rome and Troy.
4. Possibly Titus Tatius, ancient king of the Sabines.
5. Ancestor of the Lombards, and a nephew of Brutus.
6. The steep bank bounding a river valley.

20 And when fair Britain was founded by this famous lord,[7]
 bold men were bred there who in battle rejoiced,
 and many a time that betid they troubles aroused.
 In this domain more marvels have by men been seen
 than in any other that I know of since that olden time;
25 but of all that here abode in Britain as kings
 ever was Arthur most honoured, as I have heard men tell.
 Wherefore a marvel among men I mean to recall,
 a sight strange to see some men have held it,
 one of the wildest adventures of the wonders of Arthur.
30 If you will listen to this lay but a little while now,
 I will tell it at once as in town I have heard
   it told,
   as it is fixed and fettered
   in story brave and bold,
35   thus linked and truly lettered,
   as was loved in this land of old.

 This king lay at Camelot[8] at Christmas-tide
 with many a lovely lord, lieges most noble,
 indeed of the Table Round[9] all those tried brethren,
40 amid merriment unmatched and mirth without care.
 There tourneyed many a time the trusty knights,
 and jousted full joyously these gentle lords;
 then to the court they came at carols to play.
 For there the feast was unfailing full fifteen days,
45 with all meats and all mirth that men could devise,
 such gladness and gaiety as was glorious to hear,
 din of voices by day, and dancing by night;
 all happiness at the highest in halls and in bowers
 had the lords and the ladies, such as they loved most dearly.
50 With all the bliss of this world they abode together,
 the knights most renowned after the name of Christ,
 and the ladies most lovely that ever life enjoyed,
 and he, king most courteous, who that court possessed.
 For all that folk so fair did in their first estate[1]
55   abide,
   Under heaven the first in fame,
   their king most high in pride;
   it would now be hard to name
   a troop in war so tried.

---

7. According to Geoffrey of Monmouth and others, a great-grandson of Aeneas, exiled after accidentally killing his father and later the founder of Britain.
8. Arthur's capital, probably in Wales, perhaps at Caerleon-on-Usk where Arthur had been crowned. Knights were expected to gather at his court, in celebration and homage, on the five liturgical holidays on which Arthur wore his crown: Easter, Ascension, Pentecost, All Saints' Day, and Christmas.
9. Its shape symbolized the unity of Arthur's knights but also avoided disputes over precedence.
1. Arthur is emphatically a young king here, even "boyish." The phrase may also recall the Golden Age, an era of uncorrupted happiness.

60 While New Year was yet young that yestereve had arrived,
    that day double dainties on the dais were served,
    when the king was there come with his courtiers to the hall,
    and the chanting of the choir in the chapel had ended.
    With loud clamour and cries both clerks and laymen
65 Noel announced anew, and named it full often;
    then nobles ran anon with New Year gifts,
    Handsels,° handsels they shouted, and handed them out,   *gifts*
    Competed for those presents in playful debate;
    ladies laughed loudly, though they lost the game,
70 and he that won was not woeful, as may well be believed.[2]
    All this merriment they made, till their meat was served;
    then they washed, and mannerly went to their seats,
    ever the highest for the worthiest, as well held to be best.
    Queen Guinevere the gay was with grace in the midst
75 of the adorned dais[3] set. Dearly was it arrayed:
    finest sendal° at her sides, a ceiling above her   *thin silk*
    of true tissue of Toulouse, and tapestries of Tharsia
    that were embroidered and bound with the brightest gems
    one might prove and appraise to purchase for coin
80   any day.
        That loveliest lady there
        on them glanced with eyes of grey;
        that he found ever one more fair
        in sooth might no man say.

85 But Arthur would not eat until all were served;
    his youth made him so merry with the moods of a boy,
    he liked lighthearted life, so loved he the less
    either long to be lying or long to be seated:
    so worked on him his young blood and wayward brain.
90 And another rule moreover was his reason besides
    that in pride he had appointed: it pleased him not to eat
    upon festival so fair, ere he first were apprised
    of some strange story or stirring adventure,
    or some moving marvel that he might believe in
95 of noble men, knighthood, or new adventures;
    or a challenger should come a champion seeking
    to join with him in jousting, in jeopardy to set
    his life against life, each allowing the other
    the favour of fortune, were she fairer to him.
100 This was the king's custom, wherever his court was holden,
    at each famous feast among his fair company
            in hall.

---

2. The distribution of New Year's gifts displayed the
king's wealth and power; it was also the occasion here of
some courtly game of exchange, in which the loser perhaps gave up a kiss.

3. A medieval nobleman's hall typically had a raised platform at one end, on which the "high table" stood.

So his face doth proud appear,
and he stands up stout and tall,
105   all young in the New Year;
much mirth he makes with all.

Thus there stands up straight the stern king himself,
talking before the high table of trifles courtly.
There good Gawain was set at Guinevere's side,
110   with Agravain a la Dure Main on the other side seated,
both their lord's sister-sons, loyal-hearted knights.
Bishop Baldwin had the honour of the board's service,
and Iwain Urien's[4] son ate beside him.
These dined on the dais and daintily fared,
115   and many a loyal lord below at the long tables.
Then forth came the first course with fanfare of trumpets,
on which many bright banners bravely were hanging;
noise of drums then anew and the noble pipes,[5]
warbling wild and keen, wakened their music,
120   so that many hearts rose high hearing their playing.
Then forth was brought a feast, fare of the noblest,
multitude of fresh meats on so many dishes
that free places were few in front of the people
to set the silver things full of soups on cloth
125   so white.
Each lord of his liking there
without lack took with delight:
twelve plates to every pair,
good beer and wine all bright.

130   Now of their service I will say nothing more,
for you are all well aware that no want would there be.
Another noise that was new drew near on a sudden,
so that their lord might have leave at least to take food.
For hardly had the music but a moment ended,
135   and the first course in the court as was custom been served,
when there passed through the portals a perilous horseman,
the mightiest on middle-earth in measure of height,
from his gorge to his girdle so great and so square,
and his loins and his limbs so long and so huge,
140   that half a troll upon earth I trow° that he was,   trust; believe
but the largest man alive at least I declare him;
and yet the seemliest for his size that could sit on a horse,
for though in back and in breast his body was grim,
both his paunch and his waist were properly slight,
145   and all his features followed his fashion so gay
in mode;

4. Another nephew of Arthur. The relationship of uncle
and nephew is close in many Arthurian romances, and
noble youths were often sent to be raised by an uncle on

the mother's side.
5. Holiday banquets were formalized, almost theatrical.

for at the hue men gaped aghast
in his face and form that showed;
as a fay-man fell he passed,
150   and green all over glowed.

All of green were they made, both garments and man:
a coat tight and close that clung to his sides;
a rich robe above it all arrayed within
with fur finely trimmed, shewing fair fringes
155   of handsome ermine gay, as his hood was also,
that was lifted from his locks and laid on his shoulders;
and trim hose tight-drawn of tincture alike
that clung to his calves; and clear spurs below
of bright gold on silk broideries banded most richly,
160   though unshod were his shanks, for shoeless he rode.
And verily all this vesture was of verdure clear,
both the bars on his belt, and bright stones besides
that were richly arranged in his array so fair,
set on himself and on his saddle upon silk fabrics:
165   it would be too hard to rehearse one half of the trifles
that were embroidered upon them, what with birds and with flies
in a gay glory of green, and ever gold in the midst.
The pendants of his poitrel,° his proud crupper,   *breast-plate*
his molains,° and all the metal to say more, were enamelled,   *mouthpiece*
170   even the stirrups that he stood in were stained of the same;
and his saddlebows in suit, and their sumptuous skirts,
which ever glimmered and glinted all with green jewels;
even the horse that upheld him in hue was the same,
          I tell:
175   a green horse great and thick,
a stallion stiff to quell,
in broidered bridle quick:
he matched his master well.

Very gay was this great man guised all in green,
180   and the hair of his head with his horse's accorded:
fair flapping locks enfolding his shoulders,
a big beard like a bush over his breast hanging
that with the handsome hair from his head falling
was sharp shorn to an edge just short of his elbows,
185   so that half his arms under it were hid, as it were
in a king's capadoce[6] that encloses his neck.
The mane of that mighty horse was of much the same sort,
well curled and all combed, with many curious knots
woven in with gold wire about the wondrous green,
190   ever a strand of the hair and a string of the gold;
the tail and the top-lock were twined all to match
and both bound with a band of a brilliant green:

6. Probably a hooded cape, fastened under the chin.

with dear jewels bedight° to the dock's ending,   *fastened*
and twisted then on top was a tight-knitted knot
195   on which many burnished bells of bright gold jingled.
Such a mount on middle-earth, or man to ride him,
was never beheld in that hall with eyes ere that time;
       for there
      his glance was as lightning bright,
200   so did all that saw him swear;
      no man would have the might,
      they thought, his blows to bear.

And yet he had not a helm, nor a hauberk[7] either,
not a pisane,[8] not a plate that was proper to arms;
205   not a shield, not a shaft, for shock or for blow,
but in his one hand he held a holly-bundle,
that is greatest in greenery when groves are leafless,
and an axe in the other, ugly and monstrous,
a ruthless weapon aright for one in rhyme to describe:
210   the head was as large and as long as an ellwand,°   *yardstick*
a branch of green steel and of beaten gold;
the bit, burnished bright and broad at the edge,
as well shaped for shearing as sharp razors;
the stem was a stout staff, by which sternly he gripped it,
215   all bound with iron about to the base of the handle,
and engraven in green in graceful patterns,
lapped round with a lanyard that was lashed to the head
and down the length of the haft was looped many times;
and tassels of price were tied there in plenty
220   to bosses of the bright green, braided most richly.
Such was he that now hastened in, the hall entering,
pressing forward to the dais—no peril he feared.
To none gave he greeting, gazing above them,
and the first word that he winged: "Now where is," he said,
225   "the governor of this gathering? For gladly I would
on the same set my sight, and with himself now talk
      in town."
      On the courtiers he cast his eye,
      and rolled it up and down;
230   he stopped, and stared to espy
      who there had most renown.

Then they looked for a long while, on that lord gazing;
for every man marvelled what it could mean indeed
that horseman and horse such a hue should come by
235   as to grow green as the grass, and greener it seemed,
than green enamel on gold glowing far brighter.
All stared that stood there and stole up nearer,

---

7. A tunic of chain mail.   8. A piece of armor to protect the upper part of the chest
and neck.

watching him and wondering what in the world he would do.
For many marvels they had seen, but to match this nothing;
240   wherefore a phantom and fay-magic folk there thought it,
and so to answer little eager was any of those knights,
and astounded at his stern voice stone-still they sat there
in a swooning silence through that solemn chamber,
as if all had dropped into a dream, so died their voices
245   away.
Not only, I deem, for dread;
but of some 'twas their courtly way
to allow their lord and head
to the guest his word to say.

250   Then Arthur before the high dais beheld this wonder,
and freely with fair words, for fearless was he ever,
saluted him, saying: "Lord, to this lodging thou'rt welcome!
The head of this household Arthur my name is.
Alight, as thou lovest me, and linger, I pray thee;
255   and what may thy wish be in a while we shall learn."
"Nay, so help me," quoth the horseman, "He that on high is throned,
to pass any time in this place was no part of my errand.
But since thy praises, prince, so proud are uplifted,
and thy castle and courtiers are accounted the best,
260   the stoutest in steel-gear that on steeds may ride,
most eager and honourable of the earth's people,
valiant to vie with in other virtuous sports,
and here is knighthood renowned, as is noised in my ears:
'tis that has fetched me hither, by my faith, at this time.
265   You may believe by this branch that I am bearing here
that I pass as one in peace,[9] no peril seeking.
For had I set forth to fight in fashion of war,
I have a hauberk at home, and a helm also,
a shield, and a sharp spear shining brightly,
270   and other weapons to wield too, as well I believe;
but since I crave for no combat, my clothes are softer.
Yet if thou be so bold, as abroad is published,
thou wilt grant of thy goodness the game that I ask for
by right."
275   Then Arthur answered there,
and said: "Sir, noble knight,
if battle thou seek thus bare,
thou'lt fail not here to fight."

"Nay, I wish for no warfare, on my word I tell thee!
280   Here about on these benches are but beardless children.
Were I hasped in armour on a high charger,
there is no man here to match me—their might is so feeble.

---

9. A holly branch could symbolize peace and was used in games of the Christmas season.

And so I crave in this court only a Christmas pastime,
since it is Yule and New Year, and you are young here and merry.

285 If any so hardy in this house here holds that he is,
if so bold be his blood or his brain be so wild,
that he stoutly dare strike one stroke for another,
then I will give him as my gift this guisarm[1] costly,
this axe—'tis heavy enough—to handle as he pleases;

290 and I will abide the first brunt, here bare as I sit.
If any fellow be so fierce as my faith to test,
hither let him haste to me and lay hold of this weapon—
I hand it over for ever, he can have it as his own—
and I will stand a stroke from him, stock-still on this floor,

295 provided thou'lt lay down this law: that I may deliver him another.
        Claim I!
        And yet a respite I'll allow,
        till a year and a day go by.
        Come quick, and let's see now

300   if any here dare reply!"

If he astounded them at first, yet stiller were then
all the household in the hall, both high men and low.
The man on his mount moved in his saddle,
and rudely his red eyes he rolled then about,

305 bent his bristling brows all brilliantly green,
and swept round his beard to see who would rise.
When none in converse would accost him, he coughed then loudly,
stretched himself haughtily and straightway exclaimed:
"What! Is this Arthur's house," said he thereupon,

310 "the rumour of which runs through realms unnumbered?
Where now is your haughtiness, and your high conquests,
your fierceness and fell mood, and your fine boasting?
Now are the revels and the royalty of the Round Table
overwhelmed by a word by one man spoken,

315 for all blench now abashed ere a blow is offered!"
With that he laughed so loud that their lord was angered,
the blood shot for shame into his shining cheeks
        and face;
        as wroth as wind he grew,

320   so all did in that place.
        Then near to the stout man drew
        the king of fearless race,

And said: "Marry! Good man, 'tis madness thou askest,
and since folly thou hast sought, thou deservest to find it.

325 I know no lord that is alarmed by thy loud words here.
Give me now thy guisarm, in God's name, sir,
and I will bring thee the blessing thou hast begged to receive."

---

1. A long-handled axe with a spike at the end.

Quick then he came to him and caught it from his hand.
Then the lordly man loftily alighted on foot.
330   Now Arthur holds his axe, and the haft grasping
sternly he stirs it about, his stroke considering.
The stout man before him there stood his full height,
higher than any in that house by a head and yet more.
With stern face as he stood he stroked at his beard,
335   and with expression impassive he pulled down his coat,
no more disturbed or distressed at the strength of his blows
than if someone as he sat had served him a drink
        of wine.
    From beside the queen Gawain
340   to the king did then incline:
    "I implore with prayer plain
    that this match should now be mine."

"Would you, my worthy lord," said Gawain to the king,
"bid me abandon this bench and stand by you there,
345   so that I without discourtesy might be excused from the table,
and my liege lady were not loth to permit me,
I would come to your counsel before your courtiers fair.
For I find it unfitting, as in fact it is held,
when a challenge in your chamber makes choices so exalted,
350   though you yourself be desirous to accept it in person,
while many bold men about you on bench are seated:
on earth there are, I hold, none more honest of purpose,
no figures fairer on field where fighting is waged.
I am the weakest, I am aware, and in wit feeblest,
355   and the least loss, if I live not, if one would learn the truth.
Only because you are my uncle is honour given me:
save your blood in my body I boast of no virtue;
and since this affair is so foolish that it nowise befits you,
and I have requested it first, accord it then to me!
360   If my claim is uncalled-for without cavil shall judge
        this court."
    To consult the knights draw near,
    and this plan they all support;
    the king with crown to clear,
365   and give Gawain the sport.

The king then commanded that he quickly should rise,
and he readily uprose and directly approached,
kneeling humbly before his highness, and laying hand on the weapon;
and he lovingly relinquished it, and lifting his hand
370   gave him God's blessing, and graciously enjoined him
that his hand and his heart should be hardy alike.
"Take care, cousin," quoth the king, "one cut to address,
and if thou learnest him his lesson, I believe very well
that thou wilt bear any blow that he gives back later."

375   Gawain goes to the great man with guisarm in hand,
and he boldly abides there—he blenched not at all.
Then next said to Gawain the knight all in green:
"Let's tell again our agreement, ere we go any further.
I'd know first, sir knight, thy name; I entreat thee
380   to tell it me truly, that I may trust in thy word."
"In good faith," quoth the good knight, "I Gawain am called
who bring thee this buffet, let be what may follow;
and at this time a twelvemonth in thy turn have another
with whatever weapon thou wilt, and in the world with none else
385   but me."
     The other man answered again:
     "I am passing pleased," said he,
     "upon my life, Sir Gawain,
     that this stroke should be struck by thee.

390   "Begad," said the green knight, "Sir Gawain, I am pleased
to find from thy fist the favour I asked for!
And thou hast promptly repeated and plainly hast stated
without abatement the bargain I begged of the king here;
save that thou must assure me, sir, on thy honour
395   that thou'lt seek me thyself, search where thou thinkest
I may be found near or far, and fetch thee such payment
as thou deliverest me today before these lordly people,"
"Where should I light on thee," quoth Gawain, "where look for thy place?
I have never learned where thou livest, by the Lord that made me,
400   and I know thee not, knight, thy name nor thy court.
But teach me the true way, and tell what men call thee,
and I will apply all my purpose the path to discover:
and that I swear thee for certain and solemnly promise."
"That is enough in New Year, there is need of no more!"
405   said the great man in green to Gawain the courtly.
"If I tell thee the truth of it, when I have taken the knock,
and thou handily hast hit me, if in haste I announce then
my house and my home and mine own title,
then thou canst call and enquire and keep the agreement;
410   and if I waste not a word, thou'lt win better fortune,
for thou mayst linger in thy land and look no further—
       but stay!
     To thy grim tool now take heed, sir!
     Let us try thy knocks today!"
415   "Gladly," said he, "indeed, sir!"
     and his axe he stroked in play.

The Green Knight on the ground now gets himself ready,
leaning a little with the head he lays bare the flesh,
and his locks long and lovely he lifts over his crown,
420   letting the naked neck as was needed appear.
His left foot on the floor before him placing,
Gawain gripped on his axe, gathered and raised it,

from aloft let it swiftly land where 'twas naked,
so that the sharp of his blade shivered the bones,
425 and sank clean through the clear fat and clove it asunder,
and the blade of the bright steel then bit into the ground.
The fair head to the floor fell from the shoulders,
and folk fended it with their feet as forth it went rolling;
the blood burst from the body, bright on the greenness,
430 and yet neither faltered nor fell the fierce man at all,
but stoutly he strode forth, still strong on his shanks,
and roughly he reached out among the rows that stood there,
caught up his comely head and quickly upraised it,
and then hastened to his horse, laid hold of the bridle,
435 stepped into stirrup-iron, and strode up aloft,
his head by the hair in his hand holding;
and he settled himself then in the saddle as firmly
as if unharmed by mishap, though in the hall he might wear
       no head.
440   His trunk he twisted round,
           that gruesome body that bled,
           and many fear then found,
           as soon as his speech was sped.

For the head in his hand he held it up straight,
445 towards the fairest at the table he twisted the face,
and it lifted up its eyelids and looked at them broadly,
and made such words with its mouth as may be recounted.
"See thou get ready, Gawain, to go as thou vowedst,
and as faithfully seek till thou find me, good sir,
450 as thou hast promised in this place in the presence of these knights.
To the Green Chapel go thou, and get thee, I charge thee,
such a dint as thou hast dealt—indeed thou hast earned
a nimble knock in return on New Year's morning!
The Knight of the Green Chapel I am known to many,
455 so if to find me thou endeavour, thou'lt fail not to do so.
Therefore come! Or to be called a craven thou deservest."
With a rude roar and rush his reins he turned then,
and hastened out through the hall-door with his head in his hand,
and fire of the flint flew from the feet of his charger.
460 To what country he came in that court no man knew,
no more than they had learned from what land he had journeyed.
       Meanwhile,
           the king and Sir Gawain
           at the Green Man laugh and smile;
465   yet to men had appeared, 'twas plain,
           a marvel beyond denial.

Though Arthur the high king in his heart marvelled,
he let no sign of it be seen, but said then aloud
to the queen so comely with courteous words:

470   "Dear Lady, today be not downcast at all!
    Such cunning play well becomes the Christmas tide,
    interludes,² and the like, and laughter and singing,
    amid these noble dances of knights and of dames.
    Nonetheless to my food I may fairly betake me,
475   for a marvel I have met, and I may not deny it."
    He glanced at Sir Gawain and with good point he said:
    "Come, hang up thine axe, sir!³ It has hewn now enough."
    And over the table they hung it on the tapestry behind,
    where all men might remark it, a marvel to see,
480   and by its true token might tell of that adventure.
    Then to a table they turned, those two lords together,
    the king and his good kinsman, and courtly men served them
    with all dainties double, the dearest there might be,
    with all manner of meats and with minstrelsy too.
485   With delight that day they led, till to the land came the night
        again.
        Sir Gawain, now take heed
        lest fear make thee refrain
        from daring the dangerous deed
490   that thou in hand hast ta'en!

Part 2

    With this earnest of high deeds thus Arthur began
    the young year, for brave vows he yearned to hear made.
    Though such words were wanting when they went to table,
    now of fell work to full grasp filled with their hands.
495   Gawain was gay as he began those games in the hall,
    but if the end be unhappy, hold it no wonder!
    For though men be merry of mood when they have mightily drunk,
    a year slips by swiftly, never the same returning;
    the outset to the ending is equal but seldom.
500   And so this Yule passed over and the year after,
    and severally the seasons ensued in their turn:⁴
    after Christmas there came the crabbed Lenten
    that with fish tries the flesh and with food more meagre;
    but then the weather in the world makes war on the winter,
505   cold creeps into the earth, clouds are uplifted,
    shining rain is shed in showers that all warm
    fall on the fair turf, flowers there open,
    of grounds and of groves green is the raiment,
    birds are busy a-building and bravely are singing
510   for sweetness of the soft summer that will soon be on
        the way;

---

2. Brief performances between the courses of the banquet.
3. A literal suggestion, but also an invitation to put the matter aside.

4. This famous passage on the cycle of seasons draws both on Germanic conventions of the battle of Winter and Summer, and on Romance springtime lyrics, the *reverdies*.

and blossoms burgeon and blow
in hedgerows bright and gay;
then glorious musics go
515   through the woods in proud array.

After the season of summer with its soft breezes,
when Zephyr goes sighing through seeds and herbs,
right glad is the grass that grows in the open,
when the damp dewdrops are dripping from the leaves,
520   to greet a gay glance of the glistening sun.
But then Harvest hurries in, and hardens it quickly,
warns it before winter to wax to ripeness.
He drives with his drought the dust, till it rises
from the face of the land and flies up aloft;
525   wild wind in the welkin° makes war on the sun,   *the sky*
the leaves loosed from the linden alight on the ground,
and all grey is the grass that green was before:
all things ripen and rot that rose up at first,
and so the year runs away in yesterdays many,
530   and here winter wends again, as by the way of the world
           it ought,
until the Michaelmas moon[5]
has winter's boding brought;
Sir Gawain then full soon
535   of his grievous journey thought.

And yet till All Hallows[6] with Arthur he lingered,
who furnished on that festival a feast for the knight
with much royal revelry of the Round Table.
The knights of renown and noble ladies
540   all for the love of that lord had longing at heart,
but nevertheless the more lightly of laughter they spoke:
many were joyless who jested for his gentle sake.
For after their meal mournfully he reminded his uncle
that his departure was near, and plainly he said:
545   "Now liege-lord of my life, for leave I beg you.
You know the quest and the compact; I care not further
to trouble you with tale of it, save a trifling point:
I must set forth to my fate without fail in the morning,
as God will me guide, the Green Man to seek."
550   Those most accounted in the castle came then together,[7]
Iwain and Eric and others not a few,
Sir Doddinel le Sauvage, the Duke of Clarence,
Lancelot, and Lionel, and Lucan the Good,

---

5. The harvest moon at Michaelmas, on September 29.
6. All Saints' Day, on November 1, another holiday on which Arthur presided, crowned, over his court.
7. The list that follows would have recalled, especially to readers of French romances, other great quests and challenges encountered by Arthur's knights. The list's order may also suggest later and more tragic episodes in the Arthurian narrative, ending with Bedivere who throws Excalibur into a lake after Arthur is mortally wounded.

Sir Bors and Sir Bedivere that were both men of might,
555 and many others of mark with Mador de la Porte.
All this company of the court the king now approached
to comfort the knight with care in their hearts.
Much mournful lament was made in the hall
that one so worthy as Gawain should wend on that errand,
560 to endure a deadly dint and deal no more
     with blade.
   The knight ever made good cheer,
   saying, "Why should I be dismayed?
   Of doom the fair or drear
565   by a man must be assayed."

He remained there that day, and in the morning got ready,
asked early for his arms, and they all were brought him.
First a carpet of red silk was arrayed on the floor,
and the gilded gear in plenty there glittered upon it.
570 The stern man stepped thereon and the steel things handled,
dressed in a doublet of damask of Tharsia,
and over it a cunning capadoce that was closed at the throat
and with fair ermine was furred all within.
Then sabatons[8] first they set on his feet,
575 his legs lapped in steel in his lordly greaves,
on which the polains° they placed, polished and shining   *knee-guards*
and knit upon his knees with knots all of gold;
then the comely cuisses that cunningly clasped
the thick thews of his thighs they with thongs on him tied;
580 and next the byrnie,° woven of bright steel rings   *coat of mail*
upon costly quilting, enclosed him about;
and armlets well burnished upon both of his arms,
with gay elbow-pieces and gloves of plate,
and all the goodly gear to guard him whatever
585   betide;
   coat-armour richly made,
   gold spurs on heel in pride;
   girt with a trusty blade,
   silk belt about his side.

590 When he was hasped in his armour his harness was splendid:
the least latchet or loop was all lit with gold.
Thus harnessed as he was he heard now his Mass,
that was offered and honoured at the high altar;
and then he came to the king and his court-companions,
595 and with love he took leave of lords and of ladies;
and they kissed him and escorted him, and to Christ him commended.
And now Gringolet stood groomed, and girt with a saddle
gleaming right gaily with many gold fringes,
and all newly for the nonce nailed at all points;

8. A foot-covering worn by warriors in armor.

600   adorned with bars was the bridle, with bright gold banded;

that apparelling proud of poitrel° and of skirts,   *breast-plate*

and the crupper and caparison[9] accorded with the saddlebows:

all was arrayed in red with rich gold studded,

so that it glittered and glinted as a gleam of the sun.

605   Then he in hand took the helm and in haste kissed it:

strongly was it stapled and stuffed within;

it sat high upon his head and was hasped at the back,

and a light kerchief was laid o'er the beaver,°   *visor*

all braided and bound[1] with the brightest gems

610   upon broad silken broidery, with birds on the seams

like popinjays depainted, here preening and there,

turtles and true-loves, entwined as thickly

as if many sempstresses had the sewing full seven winters

        in hand.

615   A circlet of greater price

        his crown about did band;

        The diamonds point-device

        there blazing bright did stand.

    Then they brought him his blazon° that was of brilliant gules°   *shield / red*

620   with the pentangle[2] depicted in pure hue of gold.

By the baldric° he caught it and about his neck cast it: *strap*

right well and worthily it went with the knight.

And why the pentangle is proper to that prince so noble

I intend now to tell you, though it may tarry my story.

625   It is a sign that Solomon once set on a time

to betoken Troth, as it is entitled to do;

for it is a figure that in it five points holdeth,

and each line overlaps and is linked with another,

and every way it is endless; and the English, I hear,

630   everywhere name it the Endless Knot.

So it suits well this knight and his unsullied arms;

for ever faithful in five points, and five times under each,

Gawain as good was acknowledged and as gold refinéd,

devoid of every vice and with virtues adorned.

635   So there

        the pentangle painted new

        he on shield and coat did wear,

        as one of word most true

        and knight of bearing fair.

640   First faultless was he found in his five senses,

and next in his five fingers he failed at no time,

and firmly on the Five Wounds all his faith was set

---

9. A cloth or covering spread over the saddle or harness of a horse, often gaily ornamented.
1. The technical language of armor is now joined by an equally technical description of needlework, for which English women were famous.

2. A five-pointed star and symbol of perfection and eternity, since it can be drawn with an uninterrupted line ending at the point of the star where it begins. Inscribed within a circle, it was called Solomon's seal.

that Christ received on the cross, as the Creed tells us;
and wherever the brave man into battle was come,
645 on this beyond all things was his earnest thought:
that ever from the Five Joys all his valour he gained
that to Heaven's courteous Queen once came from her Child.[3]
For which cause the knight had in comely wise
on the inner side of his shield her image depainted,
650 that when he cast his eyes thither his courage never failed.
The fifth five that was used, as I find, by this knight
was free-giving and friendliness first before all,
and chastity and chivalry ever changeless and straight,
and piety surpassing all points: these perfect five
655 were hasped upon him harder than on any man else.
Now these five series, in sooth, were fastened on this knight,
and each was knit with another and had no ending,
but were fixed at five points that failed not at all,
coincided in no line nor sundered either,
660 not ending in any angle anywhere, as I discover,
wherever the process was put in play or passed to an end.
Therefore on his shining shield was shaped now this knot,
royally with red gules upon red gold set:
this is the pure pentangle as people of learning
665   have taught.
    Now Gawain in brave array
    his lance at last hath caught.
    He gave them all good day,
    for evermore as he thought.

670 He spurned° his steed with the spurs and sprang on his way   *struck*
so fiercely that the flint-sparks flashed out behind him.
All who beheld him so honourable in their hearts were sighing,
and assenting in sooth one said to another,
grieving for that good man: "Before God, 'tis a shame
675 that thou, lord, must be lost, who art in life so noble!
To meet his match among men, Marry, 'tis not easy!
To behave with more heed would have behoved one of sense,
and that dear lord duly a duke to have made,
illustrious leader of liegemen in this land as befits him;
680 and that would better have been than to be butchered to death,
beheaded by an elvish man for an arrogant vaunt.
Who can recall any king that such a course ever took
as knights quibbling at court at their Christmas games!"
Many warm tears outwelling there watered their eyes,
685 when that lord so beloved left the castle
     that day.
    No longer he abode,

---

3. Poems and meditations on the Virgin's joys and sorrows were widespread. Her five joys were the Annunciation, Nativity, Resurrection, Ascension, and Assumption.

but swiftly went his way;
bewildering ways he rode,
690   as the book I heard doth say.

Now he rides thus arrayed through the realm of Logres,[4]
Sir Gawain in God's care, though no game now he found it.
Oft forlorn and alone he lodged of a night
where he found not afforded him such fare as pleased him.
695   He had no friend but his horse in the forests and hills,
no man on his march to commune with but God,
till anon he drew near unto Northern Wales.
All the isles of Anglesey he held on his left,
and over the fords he fared by the flats near the sea,
700   and then over by the Holy Head to high land again
in the wilderness of Wirral: there wandered but few
who with good will regarded either God or mortal.
And ever he asked as he went on of all whom he met
if they had heard any news of a knight that was green
705   in any ground thereabouts, or of the Green Chapel.
And all denied it, saying nay, and that never in their lives
a single man had they seen that of such a colour
could be.
The knight took pathways strange
710   by many a lonesome lea,
and oft his view did change
that chapel ere he could see.

Many a cliff he climbed o'er in countries unknown,
far fled from his friends without fellowship he rode.
715   At every wading or water on the way that he passed
he found a foe before him, save at few for a wonder;
and so foul were they and fell that fight he must needs.
So many a marvel in the mountains he met in those lands
that 'twould be tedious the tenth part to tell you thereof.
720   At whiles with worms he wars, and with wolves also,
at whiles with wood-trolls that wandered in the crags,
and with bulls and with bears and boars, too, at times;
and with ogres that hounded him from the heights of the fells.
Had he not been stalwart and staunch and steadfast in God,
725   he doubtless would have died and death had met often;
for though war wearied him much, the winter was worse,
when the cold clear water from the clouds spilling
froze ere it had fallen upon the faded earth.
Wellnigh slain by the sleet he slept ironclad
730   more nights than enow in the naked rocks,
where clattering from the crest the cold brook tumbled,

---

4. Identified with England in Geoffrey of Monmouth, elsewhere a vaguer term for Arthur's kingdom. Here, Gawain is heading northward through Wales, then along the coast of the Irish Sea and into the forest of Wirral in Cheshire—a wild area and resort of outlaws in the 14th century.

and hung high o'er his head in hard icicles.
Thus in peril and pain and in passes grievous
till Christmas-eve that country he crossed all alone
735   in need.
     The knight did at that tide
     his plaint to Mary plead,
     her rider's road to guide
     and to some lodging lead.

740   By a mount in the morning merrily he was riding
into a forest that was deep and fearsomely wild,
with high hills at each hand, and hoar woods beneath
of huge aged oaks by the hundred together;
the hazel and the hawthorn were huddled and tangled
745   with rough ragged moss around them trailing,
with many birds bleakly on the bare twigs sitting
that piteously piped there for pain of the cold.
The good man on Gringolet goes now beneath them
through many marshes and mires, a man all alone,
750   troubled lest a truant at that time he should prove
from the service of the sweet Lord, who on that selfsame night
of a maid became man our mourning to conquer.
And therefore sighing he said: "I beseech thee, O Lord,
and Mary, who is the mildest mother most dear,
755   for some harbour where with honour I might hear the Mass
and thy Matins[5] tomorrow. This meekly I ask,
and thereto promptly I pray with Pater and Ave
     and Creed."[6]
     In prayer he now did ride,
760   lamenting his misdeed;
     he blessed him oft and cried,
     "The Cross of Christ me speed!"

The sign on himself he had set but thrice,
ere a mansion he marked within a moat in the forest,
765   on a low mound above a lawn, laced under the branches
of many a burly bole° round about by the ditches: *tree trunk*
the castle most comely that ever a king possessed
placed amid a pleasaunce with a park all about it,
within a palisade of pointed pales° set closely   *stakes*
770   that took its turn round the trees for two miles or more.
Gawain from the one side gazed on the stronghold
as it shimmered and shone through the shining oaks,
and then humbly he doffed his helm, and with honour he thanked
Jesus and Saint Julian,[7] who generous are both,

---

5. First of the canonical hours of prayer and praise in monastic tradition, observed between midnight and dawn.
6. The Paternoster ("Our Father . . ."). Ave Maria ("Hail Mary . . ."), and Creed (the articles of the Christian faith).
7. Patron saint of hospitality.

775   who had courtesy accorded him and to his cry harkened.
        "Now bon hostel," quoth the knight, "I beg of you still!"
        Then he goaded Gringolet with his gilded heels,
        and he chose by good chance the chief pathway
        and brought his master bravely to the bridge's end
780   at last.
            That brave bridge was up-hauled,
            the gates were bolted fast;
            the castle was strongly walled,
            it feared no wind or blast.

785   Then he stayed his steed that on the steep bank halted
        above the deep double ditch that was drawn round the place.
        The wall waded in the water wondrous deeply,
        and up again to a huge height in the air it mounted,
        all of hard hewn stone to the high cornice,
790   fortified under the battlement in the best fashion
        and topped with fair turrets set by turns about
        that had many graceful loopholes with a good outlook:
        that knight a better barbican had never seen built.[8]
        And inwards he beheld the hall uprising,
795   tall towers set in turns, and as tines° clustering   *pinnacles*
        the fair finials, joined featly, so fine and so long,
        their capstones all carven with cunning and skill.
        Many chalk-white chimneys he chanced to espy
        upon the roofs of towers all radiant white;
800   so many a painted pinnacle was peppered about,
        among the crenelles of the castle clustered so thickly
        that all pared out of paper it appeared to have been.[9]
        The gallant knight on his great horse good enough thought it,
        if he could come by any course that enclosure to enter,
805   to harbour in that hostel while the holy day lasted
                with delight.
            He called, and there came with speed
            a porter blithe and bright;
            on the wall he learned his need,
810   and hailed the errant knight.

        "Good sir," quoth Gawain, "will you go with my message
        to the high lord of this house for harbour to pray?"
        "Yes, by Peter!"[1] quoth the porter, "and I promise indeed
        that you will, sir, be welcome while you wish to stay here."
815   Then quickly the man went and came again soon,
        servants bringing civilly to receive there the knight.
        They drew down the great drawbridge, and duly came forth,
        and on the cold earth on their knees in courtesy knelt

---

8. The poet again revels in technical vocabulary, here architectural; this is a fashionable (if exaggerated) building of the 14th century.

9. Models in cut paper sometimes decorated elaborate feasts such as that at the beginning of the poem.
1. Swearing by St. Peter, keeper of the keys to heaven.

to welcome this wayfarer with such worship as they knew.
820   They delivered him the broad gates and laid them wide open,
and he readily bade them rise and rode o'er the bridge.
Several servants then seized the saddle as he alighted,
and many stout men his steed to a stable then led,
while knights and esquires anon descended
825   to guide there in gladness this guest to the hall.
When he raised up his helm many ran there in haste
to have it from his hand, his highness to serve;
his blade and his blazon both they took charge of.
Then he greeted graciously those good men all,
830   and many were proud to approach him, that prince to honour.
All hasped in his harness to hall they brought him,
where a fair blaze in the fireplace fiercely was burning.
Then the lord of that land leaving his chamber
Came mannerly to meet the man on the floor.
835   He said: "You are welcome at your wish to dwell here.
What is here, all is your own, to have in your rule
        and sway."
     "Grammercy!" quoth Gawain,
     "May Christ you this repay!"
840   As men that to meet were fain
        they both embraced that day.

Gawain gazed at the good man who had greeted him kindly,
and he thought bold and big was the baron of the castle,
very large and long, and his life at the prime:
845   broad and bright was his beard, and all beaver-hued,
stern, strong in his stance upon stalwart legs,
his face fell as fire, and frank in his speech;
and well it suited him, in sooth, as it seemed to the knight,
a lordship to lead untroubled over lieges trusty.
850   To a chamber the lord drew him, and charged men at once
to assign him an esquire to serve and obey him,
and there to wait on his word many worthy men were,
who brought him to a bright bower where the bedding was splendid:
there were curtains of costly silk with clear-golden hems,
855   and coverlets cunning-wrought with quilts most lovely
of bright ermine above, embroidered at the sides,
hangings running on ropes with red-gold rings,
carpets of costly damask that covered the walls
and the floor under foot fairly to match them.
860   There they despoiled him, speaking to him gaily,
his byrnie doing off and his bright armour.
Rich robes then readily men ran to bring him,
for him to change, and to clothe him, having chosen the best.
As soon as he had donned one and dressed was therein,
865   as it sat on him seemly with its sailing skirts,
then verily in his visage a vision of Spring

to each man there appeared, and in marvellous hues
bright and beautiful was all his body beneath.
That knight more noble was never made by Christ
870   they thought.
     He came none knew from where,
     but it seemed to them he ought
     to be a prince beyond compare
     in the field where fell men fought.

875 A chair before the chimney where charcoal was burning
was made ready in his room, all arrayed and covered
with cushions upon quilted cloths that were cunningly made.
Then a comely cloak was cast about him
of bright silk brocade, embroidered most richly
880 and furred fairly within with fells of the choicest
and all edged with ermine, and its hood was to match;
and he sat in that seat seemly and noble
and warmed himself with a will, and then his woes were amended.
Soon up on good trestles a table was raised[2]
885 and clad with a clean cloth clear white to look on;
there was surnape, salt-cellar, and silvern spoons.
He then washed as he would and went to his food,
and many worthy men with worship waited upon him;
soups they served of many sorts, seasoned most choicely,
890 in double helpings, as was due, and divers sorts of fish;
some baked in bread, some broiled on the coals,
some seethed, some in gravy savoured with spices,
and all with condiments so cunning that it caused him delight.
A fair feast he called it frankly and often,
895 graciously, when all the good men together there pressed him:
          "Now pray,
     this penance deign to take;
     'twill improve another day!"[3]
     The man much mirth did make,
900   for wine to his head made way.

Then inquiry and question were carefully put
touching personal points to that prince himself,
till he courteously declared that to the court he belonged
that high Arthur in honour held in his sway,
905 who was the right royal King of the Round Table,
and 'twas Gawain himself that as their guest now sat
and had come for that Christmas, as the case had turned out.
When the lord had learned whom luck had brought him,
loud laughed he thereat, so delighted he was,
910 and they made very merry, all the men in that castle,

2. A castle's great hall had many uses; tables were set up
for dining and then put aside or hung.
3. An exchange of courtesies. Gawain has politely praised
the many fish dishes; his hosts demur, remind him that
Christmas Eve is a fast day, and promise him better meals
later.

and to appear in the presence were pressing and eager
of one who all profit and prowess and perfect manners
comprised in his person, and praise ever gained;
of all men on middle-earth he most was admired.
915   Softly each said then in secret to his friend:
"Now fairly shall we mark the fine points of manners,
and the perfect expressions of polished converse.
How speech is well spent will be expounded unasked,
since we have found here this fine father of breeding.
920   God has given us His goodness, His grace now indeed,
Who such a guest as Gawain has granted us to have!
When blissful men at board for His birth sing blithe
          at heart,
        what manners high may mean
925   this knight will now impart.
        Who hears him will, I ween,
        of love-speech learn some art."[4]

When his dinner was done and he duly had risen,
it now to the night-time very near had drawn.
930   The chaplains then took to the chapel their way
and rang the bells richly, as rightly they should,
for the solemn evensong of the high season.
The lord leads the way, and his lady with him;
into a goodly oratory gracefully she enters.
935   Gawain follows gladly, and goes there at once
and the lord seizes him by the sleeve and to a seat leads him,
kindly acknowledges him and calls him by his name,
saying that most welcome he was of all guests in the world.
And he grateful thanks gave him, and each greeted the other,
940   and they sat together soberly while the service lasted.
Then the lady longed to look at this knight;
and from her closet she came with many comely maidens.
She was fairer in face, in her flesh and her skin,
her proportions, her complexion, and her port than all others,
945   and more lovely than Guinevere to Gawain she looked.
He came through the chancel to pay court to her grace;
leading her by the left hand another lady was there
who was older than she, indeed ancient she seemed,
and held in high honour by all men about her.
950   But unlike in their looks those ladies appeared,
for if the younger was youthful, yellow was the elder;
with rose-hue the one face was richly mantled,
rough wrinkled cheeks rolled on the other;
on the kerchiefs of the one many clear pearls were,
955   her breast and bright throat were bare displayed,
fairer than white snow that falls on the hills;

4. Though Gawain is engaged on a serious quest, his reputation as a graceful courtier and master in the arts of love has preceded him.

the other was clad with a cloth that enclosed all her neck,
enveloped was her black chin with chalk-white veils,
her forehead folded in silk, and so fumbled all up,
960 so topped up and trinketed and with trifles bedecked
that naught was bare of that beldame but her brows all black,
her two eyes and her nose and her naked lips,
and those were hideous to behold and horribly bleared;
that a worthy dame she was may well, fore God,
965   be said!
  short body and thick waist,
  with bulging buttocks spread;
  more delicious to the taste
  was the one she by her led.

970 When Gawain glimpsed that gay lady that so gracious looked,
with leave sought of the lord towards the ladies he went;
the elder he saluted, low to her bowing,
about the lovelier he laid then lightly his arms
and kissed her in courtly wise with courtesy speaking.
975 His acquaintance they requested, and quickly he begged
to be their servant in sooth, if so they desired.
They took him between them, and talking they led him
to a fireside in a fair room, and first of all called
for spices, which men sped without sparing to bring them,
980 and ever wine therewith well to their liking.
The lord for their delight leaped up full often,
many times merry games being minded to make;
his hood he doffed, and on high he hung it on a spear,
and offered it as an honour for any to win
985 who the most fun could devise at that Christmas feast—
"And I shall try, by my troth, to contend with the best
ere I forfeit this hood, with the help of my friends!"
Thus with laughter and jollity the lord made his jests
to gladden Sir Gawain with games that night
990   in hall,
  until the time was due
  that the lord for lights should call;
  Sir Gawain with leave withdrew
  and went to bed withal.

995 On the morn when every man remembers the time
that our dear Lord for our doom to die was born,
in every home wakes happiness on earth for His sake.
So did it there on that day with the dearest delights:
at each meal and at dinner marvellous dishes
1000 men set on the dais, the daintiest meats.
The old ancient woman was highest at table,
meetly to her side the master he took him;
Gawain and the gay lady together were seated

in the center, where as was seemly the service began,
1005 and so on through the hall as honour directed.
When each good man in his degree without grudge had been served,
there was food, there was festival, there was fullness of joy;
and to tell all the tale of it I should tedious find,
though pains I might take every point to detail.
1010 Yet I ween that Gawain and that woman so fair
in companionship took such pleasure together
in sweet society soft words speaking,
their courteous converse clean and clear of all evil,
that with their pleasant pastime no prince's sport
1015   compares.
Drums beat, and trumps men wind,
many pipers play their airs;
each man his needs did mind,
and they two minded theirs.

1020 With much feasting they fared the first and the next day,
and as heartily the third came hastening after:
the gaiety of Saint John's day[5] was glorious to hear;
[with cheer of the choicest Childermas followed,]
and that finished their revels, as folk there intended,
1025 for there were guests who must go in the grey morning.
So a wondrous wake they held, and the wine they drank,
and they danced and danced on, and dearly they carolled.[6]
At least when it was late their leave then they sought
to wend on their ways, each worthy stranger.
1030 Good-day then said Gawain, but the good man stayed him,
and led him to his own chamber to the chimney-corner,
and there he delayed him, and lovingly thanked him,
for the pride and pleasure his presence had brought,
for so honouring his house at that high season
1035 and deigning his dwelling to adorn with his favour.
"Believe me, sir, while I live my luck I shall bless
that Gawain was my guest at God's own feast."
"Gramercy, sir," said Gawain, "but the goodness is yours,
all the honour is your own—may the High King repay you!
1040 And I am under your orders what you ask to perform,
as I am bound now to be, for better or worse,
      by right."
Him longer to retain
the lord then pressed the knight;
1045 to him replied Gawain
that he by no means might.

Then with courteous question he enquired of Gawain
what dire need had driven him on that festal date

5. December 27, traditionally given over to drinking and   6. Danced in a ring.
celebration.

Courtly Women Hunting, from the *Taymouth Hours,* 14th century. Women in courtly dress dismember a stag, usually the work of aristocratic men.

with such keenness from the king's court, to come forth alone
1050   ere wholly the holidays from men's homes had departed.
"In sooth, sir," he said, "you say but the truth:
a high errand and a hasty from that house brought me;
for I am summoned myself to seek for a place,
though I wonder where in the world I must wander to find it.
1055   I would not miss coming nigh it on New Year's morning
for all the land in Logres, so our Lord help me!
And so, sir, this question I enquire of you here:
can you tell me in truth if you tale ever heard
of the Green Chapel, on what ground it may stand,
1060   and of the great knight that guards it, all green in his colour?
For the terms of a tryst were between us established
to meet that man at that mark, if I remained alive,
and the named New Year is now nearly upon me,
and I would look on that lord, if God will allow me,
1065   more gladly, by God's son, than gain any treasure.
So indeed, if you please, depart now I must.
For my business I have now but barely three days,
and I would fainer fall dead than fail in my errand."
Then laughing said the lord: "Now linger you must;
1070   for when 'tis time to that tryst I will teach you the road.
On what ground is the Green Chapel—let it grieve you no more!

In your bed you shall be, sir, till broad is the day,
without fret, and then fare on the first of the year,
and come to the mark at midmorn, there to make what play
1075   you know.
    Remain till New Year's day,
    then rise and riding go!
    We'll set you on your way,
    'tis but two miles or so."

1080   Then was Gawain delighted, and in gladness he laughed:
"Now I thank you a thousand times for this beyond all!
Now my quest is accomplished, as you crave it, I will
dwell a few days here, and else do what you order."
The lord then seized him and set him in a seat beside him,
1085   and let the ladies be sent for to delight them the more,
for their sweet pleasure there in peace by themselves.
For love of him that lord was as loud in his mirth
as one near out of his mind who scarce knew what he meant.
Then he called to the knight, crying out loudly:
1090   "You have promised to do whatever deed I propose.
Will you hold this behest here, at this moment?"
"Yes, certainly, sir," then said the true knight,
"while I remain in your mansion, your command I'll obey."
"Well," returned he, "you have travelled and toiled from afar,
1095   and then I've kept you awake: you're not well yet, not cured;
both sustenance and sleep 'tis certain you need.
Upstairs you shall stay, sir, and stop there in comfort
tomorrow till Mass-time, and to a meal then go
when you wish with my wife, who with you shall sit
1100   and comfort you with her company, till to court I return.
    You stay,
    and I shall early rouse,
    and a hunting wend my way."
    Gawain gracefully bows:
1105   "Your wishes I will obey."

"One thing more," said the master, "we'll make an agreement:
whatever I win in the wood at once shall be yours,
and whatever gain you may get you shall give in exchange.
Shall we swap thus, sweet man—come, say what you think!—
1110   whether one's luck be light, or one's lot be better?"
"By God," quoth good Gawain, "I agree to it all,
and whatever play you propose seems pleasant to me."
"Done! 'Tis a bargain! Who'll bring us the drink?"
So said the lord of that land. They laughed one and all;
1115   they drank and they dallied, and they did as they pleased,
these lords and ladies, as long as they wished,
and then with customs of France and many courtly phrases
they stood in sweet debate and soft words bandied,

and lovingly they kissed, their leave taking.
1120   With trusty attendants and torches gleaming
       they were brought at the last to their beds so soft,
             one and all.
             Yet ere to bed they came,
             he the bargain did oft recall;
1125   he knew how to play a game
             the old governor of that hall.

Part 3

       Before the first daylight the folk uprose:
       the guests that were to go for their grooms they called;
       and they hurried up in haste horses to saddle,
1130   to stow all their stuff and strap up their bags.
       The men of rank arrayed them, for riding got ready,
       to saddle leaped swiftly, seized then their bridles,
       and went off on their ways where their wish was to go.
       The liege-lord of the land was not last of them all
1135   to be ready to ride with a rout of his men;
       he ate a hurried mouthful after the hearing of Mass,
       and with horn to the hunting-field he hastened at once.[1]
       When daylight was opened yet dimly on earth
       he and his huntsman were up on their high horses.
1140   Then the leaders of the hounds leashed them in couples,
       unclosed the kennel-door and cried to them "out!",
       and blew boldly on bugles three blasts full long.
       Beagles bayed thereat, a brave noise making;
       and they whipped and wheeled in those that wandered on a scent;
1145   a hundred hunting-dogs, I have heard, of the best were they.
             To their stations keepers passed;
             the leashes were cast away,
             and many a rousing blast
1150   woke din in the woods that day.

       At the first burst of the baying all beasts trembled;
       deer dashed through the dale by dread bewildered,
       and hastened to the heights, but they hotly were greeted,
       and turned back by the beaters, who boldly shouted.
1155   They let the harts go past with their high antlers,
       and the brave bucks also with their branching palms;
       for the lord of the castle had decreed in the close season
       that no man should molest the male of the deer.
       The hinds were held back with hey! and ware!,
1160   the does driven with great din to the deep valleys:
       there could be seen let slip a sleet of arrows;

---

1. The hunts that follow, for all their violent energy, are as ritualized in their procedure as the earlier feasts and games. The poet delights in describing still another area of knightly lore. A number of contemporary treatises on hunting survive.

at each turn under the trees went a twanging shaft
that into brown hides bit hard with barbéd head.
Lo! they brayed, and they bled, and on the banks they died;
1165   and ever the hounds in haste hotly pursued them,
and hunters with high horns hurried behind them
with such a clamour and cry as if cliffs had been riven.
If any beast broke away from bowmen there shooting,
it was snatched down and slain at the receiving-station;
1170   when they had been harried from the height and hustled
         to the waters,
the men were so wise in their craft at the watches below,
and their greyhounds were so great that they got them at once,
and flung them down in a flash, as fast as men could see
         with sight.
1175   The lord then wild for joy
         did oft spur and oft alight,
         and thus in bliss employ
         that day till dark of night.

Thus in his game the lord goes under greenwood eaves,
1180   and Gawain the bold lies in goodly bed,
lazing, till the walls are lit by the light of day,
under costly coverlet with curtains about him.
And as in slumber he strayed, he heard stealthily come
a soft sound at his door as it secretly opened;
1185   and from under the clothes he craned then his head,
a corner of the curtain he caught up a little,
and looked that way warily to learn what it was.
It was the lady herself, most lovely to see,
that cautiously closed the door quietly behind her,
1190   and drew near to his bed. Then abashed was the knight,
and lay down swiftly to look as if he slept;
and she stepped silently and stole to his bed,
cast back the curtain, and crept then within,
and sat her down softly on the side of the bed,
1195   and there lingered very long to look for his waking.
He lay there lurking a long while and wondered,
and mused in his mind how the matter would go,
to what point it might pass—to some surprise, he fancied.
Yet he said to himself: "More seemly 'twould be
1200   in due course with question to enquire what she wishes."
Then rousing he rolled over, and round to her turning
he lifted his eyelids with a look as of wonder,
and signed him with the cross, thus safer to be kept
         aright.
1205   With chin and cheeks so sweet
         of blended red and white,
         with grace them him did greet
         small lips with laughter bright.

"Good morning, Sir Gawain!" said that gracious lady.
1210 "You are a careless sleeper, if one can creep on you so!
Now quickly you are caught! If we come not to terms,
I shall bind you in your bed, you may be assured."
With laughter the lady thus lightly jested.
"Good morning to your grace!" said Gawain gaily.
1215 "You shall work on me your will, and well I am pleased;
for I submit immediately, and for mercy I cry,
and that is best, as I deem, for I am obliged to do so."
Thus he jested in return with much gentle laughter:
"But if you would, lady gracious, then leave grant me,
1220 and release your prisoner and pray him to rise,
I would abandon this bed and better array me;
the more pleasant would it prove then to parley with you."
"Nay, for sooth, fair sir," said the sweet lady,
"you shall not go from your bed! I will govern you better:
1225 here fast shall I enfold you, on the far side also,
and then talk with my true knight that I have taken so.
For I wot° well indeed that Sir Gawain you are,   know
to whom all men pay homage wherever you ride;
your honour, your courtesy, by the courteous is praised,
1230 by lords, by ladies, by all living people.
And right here you now are, and we all by ourselves;
my husband and his huntsmen far hence have ridden,
other men are abed, and my maids also,
the door closed and caught with a clasp that is strong;
1235 and since I have in this house one that all delight in,
my time to account I will turn, while for talk I chance
          have still.
     To my body will you welcome be
     of delight to take your fill;
1240   for need constraineth me
     to serve you, and I will."

"Upon my word," said Gawain, "that is well, I guess;
though I am not now he of whom you are speaking—
to attain to such honour as here you tell of
1245 I am a knight unworthy, as well indeed I know—
by God, I would be glad, if good to you seemed
whatever I could say, or in service could offer
to the pleasure of your excellence—it would be pure delight."
"In good faith, Sir Gawain," said the gracious lady,
1250 "the prowess and the excellence that all others approve,
if I scorned or decried them, it were scant courtesy.
But there are ladies in number who liever would now
have thee in their hold, sir, as I have thee here,
pleasantly to play with in polished converse,
1255 their solace to seek and their sorrows to soothe,
than great part of the goods or gold that they own.

But I thank Him who on high of Heaven is Lord
that I have here wholly in my hand what all desire,
     by grace."
1260   She was an urgent wooer,
        that lady fair of face;
        the knight with speeches pure
        replied in every case.

"Madam," said he merrily, "Mary reward you!
1265   For I have enjoyed, in good faith, your generous favour,
and much honour have had else from others' kind deeds;
but as for the courtesy they accord me, since my claim is not equal,
the honour is your own, who are ever well-meaning."
"Nay, Mary!" the lady demurred, "as for me, I deny it.
1270   For were I worth all the legion of women alive,
and all the wealth in the world at my will possessed,
if I should exchange at my choice and choose me a husband,
for the noble nature I know, Sir Knight, in thee here,
in beauty and bounty and bearing so gay—
1275   of which earlier I have heard, and hold it now true—
then no lord alive would I elect before you."
"In truth, lady," he returned, "you took one far better.
But I am proud of the praise you are pleased to give me,
and as your servant in earnest my sovereign I hold you,
1280   and your knight I become, and may Christ reward you."
Thus of many matters they spoke till midmorn was passed,
and ever the lady demeaned her as one that loved him much,
and he fenced with her featly, ever flawless in manner.
"Though I were lady most lovely," thought the lady to herself,
1285   "the less love would he bring here," since he looked for his bane,
        that blow
        that him so soon should grieve,
        and needs it must be so.
        Then the lady asked for leave
1290   and at once he let her go.

Then she gave him "good day," and with a glance she laughed,
and as she stood she astonished him with the strength of her words:
"Now He that prospers all speed for this disport repay you!
But that you should be Gawain, it gives me much thought."
1295   "Why so?", then eagerly the knight asked her,
afraid that he had failed in the form of his converse.
But "God bless you! For this reason," blithely she answered,
"that one so good as Gawain the gracious is held,
who all the compass of courtesy includes in his person,
1300   so long with a lady could hardly have lingered
without craving a kiss, as a courteous knight,
by some tactful turn that their talk led to."
Then said Gawain, "Very well, as you wish be it done.
I will kiss at your command, as becometh a knight,

1305   and more, lest he displease you, so plead it no longer."
      She came near thereupon and caught him in her arms,
      and down daintily bending dearly she kissed him.
      They courteously commended each other to Christ.
      Without more ado through the door she withdrew and departed,
1310   and he to rise up in haste made ready at once.
      He calls to his chamberlain, and chooses his clothes,
      and goes forth when garbed all gladly to Mass.
      Then he went to a meal that meetly awaited him,
      and made merry all day, till the moon arose
1315   o'er earth.
        Ne'er was knight so gaily engaged
        between two dames of worth,
        the youthful and the aged:
        together they made much mirth.

1320   And ever the lord of the land in his delight was abroad,
      hunting by holt and heath after hinds that were barren.
      When the sun began to slope he had slain such a number
      of does and other deer one might doubt it were true.
      Then the fell° folk at last came flocking all in,   *fierce*
1325   and quickly of the kill they a quarry assembled.
      Thither the master hastened with a host of his men,
      gathered together those greatest in fat
      and had them riven open rightly, as the rules require.
      At the assay they were searched by some that were there,
1330   and two fingers' breadth of fat they found in the leanest.
      Next they slit the eslot,° seized on the arber,°   *throat / gullet*
      shaved it with a sharp knife and shore away the grease;
      next ripped the four limbs and rent off the hide.
      Then they broke open the belly, the bowels they removed
1335   (flinging them nimbly afar) and the flesh of the knot;
      they grasped then the gorge, disengaging with skill
      the weasand° from the windpipe, and did away with the guts.   *esophagus*
      Then they shore out the shoulders with their sharpened knives
      (drawing the sinews through a small cut) the sides to keep whole;
1340   next they burst open the breast, and broke it apart,
      and again at the gorge one begins thereupon,
      cuts all up quickly till he comes to the fork,
      and fetches forth the fore-numbles;[2] and following after
      all the tissues along the ribs they tear away quickly.
1345   Thus by the bones of the back they broke off with skill,
      down even to the haunch, all that hung there together,
      and hoisted it up all whole and hewed it off there:
      and that they took for the numbles, as I trow is their name
        in kind.

---

2. Internal organs such as heart, liver, lungs.

1350   Along the fork of every thigh
           the flaps they fold behind;
           to hew it in two they hie,
           down the back all to unbind.

           Both the head and the neck they hew off after,
1355   and next swiftly they sunder the sides from the chine,°   *backbone*
           and the bone for the crow they cast in the boughs.[3]
           Then they thrust through both thick sides with a thong by the rib,
           and then by the hocks of the legs they hang them both up:
           all the folk earn the fees that fall to their lot.
1360   Upon the fell of the fair beast they fed their hounds then
           on the liver and the lights° and the leather of the paunches   *lungs*
           with bread bathed in blood blended amongst them.
           Boldly they blew the prise,[4] amid the barking of dogs,
           and then bearing up their venison bent their way homeward,
1365   striking up strongly many a stout horn-call.
           When daylight was done they all duly were come
           into the noble castle, where quietly the knight
                   abode
               in bliss by bright fire set.
1370   Thither the lord now strode;
               when Gawain with him met,
               then free all pleasure flowed.

           Then the master commanded his men to meet in that hall,
           and both dames to come down with their damsels also;
1375   before all the folk on that floor fair men he ordered
           to fetch there forthwith his venison before him,
           and all gracious in game to Gawain he called,
           announced the number by tally of the nimble beasts,
           and showed him the shining fat all shorn on the ribs.
1380   "How does this play please you? Have I praise deserved?
           Have I earned by mine art the heartiest thanks?"
           "Yea verily," the other averred, "here is venison the fairest
           that I've seen in seven years in the season of winter!"
           "And I give it you all, Gawain," said the good man at once,
1385   "for as our covenant accorded you may claim it as your own."
           "That is true," he returned, "and I tell you the same:
           what of worth within these walls I have won also
           with as good will, I warrant, 'tis awarded to you."
           His fair neck he enfolded then fast in his arms,
1390   and kissed him with all the kindness that his courtesy knew.
           "There take you my gains, sir! I got nothing more.
           I would give it up gladly even if greater it were."
           "That is a good one!" quoth the good man. "Greatly I thank you.
           'Tis such, maybe, that you had better briefly now tell me

---

3. The gristle at the end of the breastbone was left for the   4. A thing seized or requisitioned for the king's use or for
crows, still another of the prescribed rituals of the hunt.   the use of the garrisons in his castles.

1395   where you won this same wealth by the wits you possess."
"That was not the covenant," quoth he. "Do not question me more!
For you've drawn what is due to you, no doubt can you have
    'tis true."
    They laugh, and with voices fair
1400   their merriment pursue,
    and to supper soon repair
    with many dainties new.

Later by the chimney in chamber they were seated,
abundant wine of the best was brought to them oft,
1405 and again as a game they agreed on the morrow
to abide by the same bond as they had bargained before:
chance what might chance, to exchange all their trade,
whatever new thing they got, when they gathered at night.
They concluded this compact before the courtiers all;
1410 the drink for the bargain was brought forth in jest;
then their leave at the last they lovingly took,
and away then at once each went to his bed.
When the cock had crowed and cackled but thrice,
the lord had leaped from his bed, and his lieges each one;
1415 so that their meal had been made, and the Mass was over,
and folk bound for the forest, ere the first daybreak,
      to chase.
    Loud with hunters and horns
    o'er plains they passed apace,
1420   and loosed there among the thorns
    the running dogs to race.

Soon these cried for a quest in a covert by a marsh;
the huntsman hailed the hound that first heeded the scent,
stirring words he spoke to him with a strident voice.
1425 The hounds then that heard it hastened thither swiftly,
and fell fast on the line, some forty at once.
Then such a baying and babel of bloodhounds together
arose that the rock-wall rang all about them.
Hunters enheartened them with horn and with mouth,
1430 and then all in a rout rushed on together
between a fen-pool in that forest and a frowning crag.
In a tangle under a tall cliff at the tarn's° edges,   *mountain pond*
where the rough rock ruggedly in ruin was fallen,
they fared to the find, followed by hunters
1435 who made a cast round the crag and the clutter of stones,
till well they were aware that it waited within:
the very beast that the baying bloodhounds had spoken.
Then they beat on the bushes and bade him uprise,
and forth he came to their peril against folk in his path.
1440 'Twas a boar without rival that burst out upon them;
long the herd he had left, that lone beast aged,
for savage was he, of all swine the hugest,

grim indeed when he grunted. Then aghast were many;
for three at the first thrust he threw to the ground,
1445   and sprang off with great speed, sparing the others;
and they hallooed on high, and ha! ha! shouted,
and held horn to mouth, blowing hard the rally.
Many were the wild mouthings of men and of dogs,
as they bounded after this boar, him with blare and with din
1450   to quell.
    Many times he turns to bay,
    and maims the pack pell-mell;
    he hurts many hounds, and they
    grievously yowl and yell.

1455   Hunters then hurried up eager to shoot him,
aimed at him their arrows, often they hit him;
but poor at core proved the points that pitched on his shields,
and the barbs on his brows would bite not at all;
though the shaven shaft shivered in pieces,
1460   back the head came hopping, wherever it hit him.
But when the hurts went home of their heavier strokes,
then with brain wild for battle he burst out upon them,
ruthless he rent them as he rushed forward,
and many quailed at his coming and quickly withdrew.
1465   But the lord on a light horse went leaping after him;
as bold man on battle-field with his bugle he blew
the rally-call as he rode through the rough thickets,
pursuing this wild swine till the sunbeams slanted.
This day in such doings thus duly they passed,
1470   while our brave knight beloved there lies in his bed
at home in good hap, in housings so costly
        and gay.
    The lady did not forget:
    she came to bid good day;
1475   early she on him set,
    his will to wear away.

She passed to the curtain and peeped at the knight.
Sir Gawain graciously then welcomed her first,
and she answered him alike, eagerly speaking,
1480   and sat her softly by his side; and suddenly she laughed,
and with a look full of love delivered these words:
"Sir, if you are Gawain, a wonder I think it
that a man so well-meaning, ever mindful of good,
yet cannot comprehend the customs of the gentle;
1485   and if one acquaints you therewith, you do not keep them in mind:
thou hast forgot altogether what a day ago I taught
by the plainest points I would put into words!"
"What is that?" he said at once. "I am not aware of it at all.
But if you are telling the truth, I must take all the blame."
1490   "And yet as to kisses," she quoth, "this counsel I gave you:

wherever favour is found, defer not to claim them:
that becomes all who care for courteous manners."
"Take back," said the true knight, "that teaching, my dear!
For that I dared not do, for dread of refusal.

1495   Were I rebuffed, I should be to blame for so bold an offer."
"Ma fay!"° said the fair lady, "you may not be refused;   *"My faith"* (Fr.)
you are stout enough to constrain one by strength, if you like,
if any were so ill bred as to answer you nay."
"Indeed, by God," quoth Gawain, "you graciously speak;

1500   but force finds no favour among the folk where I dwell,
and any gift not given gladly and freely.
I am at your call and command to kiss when you please.
You may receive as you desire, and cease as you think
      in place."

1505   Then down the lady bent,
      and sweetly kissed his face.
      Much speech then there they spent
      of lovers' grief and grace.

"I would learn from you, lord," the lady then said,

1510   "if you would not mind my asking, what is the meaning of this:
that one so young as are you in years, and so gay,
by renown so well known for knighthood and breeding,
while of all chivalry the choice, the chief thing to praise,
is the loyal practice of love: very lore of knighthood[5]—

1515   for, talking of the toils that these true knights suffer,
it is the title and contents and text of their works:
how lovers for their true love their lives have imperilled,
have endured for their dear one dolorous trials,
until avenged by their valour, their adversity passed,

1520   they have brought bliss into her bower by their own brave virtues—
and you are the knight of most noble renown in our age,
and your fame and fair name afar is published,
and I have sat by your very self now for the second time,
yet your mouth has never made any remark I have heard

1525   that ever belonged to love-making, lesser or greater.
Surely, you that are so accomplished and so courtly in your vows
should be prompt to expound to a young pupil
by signs and examples the science of lovers.
Why? Are you ignorant who all honour enjoy?

1530   Or else you esteem me too stupid to understand your courtship?
      But nay!
      Here single I come and sit,
      a pupil for your play;
      come, teach me of your wit,

1535   while my lord is far away."

---

5. The lady compares Gawain's behavior to descriptions of courtly love in romances; the poem is mirrored within itself.

"In good faith," said Gawain, "may God reward you!
Great delight I gain, and am glad beyond measure
that one so worthy as you should be willing to come here
and take pains with so poor a man: as for playing with your knight,
1540   showing favour in any form, it fills me with joy.
But for me to take up the task on true love to lecture,
to comment on the text and tales of knighthood
to you, who I am certain possess far more skill
in that art by the half than a hundred of such
1545   as I am, or shall ever be while on earth I remain,
it would be folly manifold, in faith, my lady!
All your will I would wish to work, as I am able,
being so beholden in honour, and, so help me the Lord,
desiring ever the servant of yourself to remain."
1550   Thus she tested and tried him, tempting him often,
so as to allure him to love-making, whatever lay in her heart.
But his defence was so fair that no fault could be seen,
nor any evil upon either side, nor aught but joy
      they wist.°   *knew*
1555   They laughed and long they played;
      at last she him then kissed,
      with grace adieu him bade,
      and went whereso she list.

Then rousing from his rest he rose to hear Mass,
1560   and then their dinner was laid and daintily served.
The livelong day with the ladies in delight he spent,
but the lord o'er the lands leaped to and fro,
pursuing his fell swine that o'er the slopes hurtled
and bit asunder the backs of the best of his hounds,
1565   wherever to bay he was brought, until bowmen dislodged him,
and made him, maugre° his teeth, move again onward,   *despite*
so fast the shafts flew when the folk were assembled.
And yet the stoutest of them still he made start there aside,
till at last he was so spent he could speed no further,
1570   but in such haste as he might he made for a hollow
on a reef beside a rock where the river was flowing.
He put the bank at his back, began then to paw;
fearfully the froth of his mouth foamed from the corners;
he whetted his white tusks. Then weary were all
1575   the brave men so bold as by him to stand
of plaguing him from afar, yet for peril they dared not
      come nigher.
      He had hurt so many before,
      that none had now desire
1580   to be torn with the tusks once more
      of a beast both mad and dire.

Till the knight himself came, his courser spurring,
and saw him brought there to bay, and all about him his men.

Nothing loth he alighted, and leaving his horse,
1585   brandished a bright blade and boldly advanced,
striding stoutly through the ford to where stood the felon.
The wild beast was aware of him with his weapon in hand,
and high raised his hair; with such hate he snorted
that folk feared for the knight, lest his foe should worst him.
1590   Out came the swine and set on him at once,
and the boar and the brave man were both in a mellay°   *struggle*
in the wildest of the water. The worse had the beast,
for the man marked him well, and as they met he at once
struck steadily his point straight in the neck-slot,
1595   and hit him up to the hilts, so that his heart was riven,
and with a snarl he succumbed, and was swept down the water
       straightway.
      A hundred hounds him caught,
      and fiercely bit their prey;
1600   the men to the bank him brought,
      and dogs him dead did lay.

There men blew for the prise in many a blaring horn,
and high and loud hallooed all the hunters that could;
bloodhounds bayed for the beast, as bade the masters,
1605   who of that hard-run chase were the chief huntsmen.
Then one that was well learnéd in woodmen's lore
with pretty cunning began to carve up this boar.
First he hewed off his head and on high set it,
then he rent him roughly down the ridge of the back,
1610   brought out the bowels, burned them on gledes,°   *coals*
and with them, blended with blood, the bloodhounds rewarded.
Next he broke up the boar-flesh in broad slabs of brawn,
and haled forth the hastlets° in order all duly,   *innards*
and yet all whole he fastened the halves together,
1615   and strongly on a stout pole he strung them then up.
Now with this swine homeward swiftly they hastened,
and the boar's head was borne before the brave knight himself
who felled him in the ford by force of his hand
       so great.
1620   Until he saw Sir Gawain
      in the hall he could hardly wait.
      He called, and his pay to gain
      the other came there straight.

The lord with his loud voice and laughter merry
1625   gaily he greeted him when Gawain he saw.
The fair ladies were fetched and the folk all assembled,
and he showed them the shorn slabs, and shaped his report
of the width and wondrous length, and the wickedness also
in war, of the wild swine, as in the woods he had fled.
1630   With fair words his friend the feat then applauded,
and praised the great prowess he had proved in his deeds;

for such brawn on a beast, the brave knight declared,
or such sides on a swine he had never seen before.
They then handled the huge head, and highly he praised it,
1635   showing horror at the hideous thing to honour the lord.
"Now, Gawain," said the good man, "this game is your own
by close covenant we concluded, as clearly you know."
"That is true," he returned, "and as truly I assure you
all my winnings, I warrant, I shall award you in exchange."
1640   He clasped his neck, and courteously a kiss he then gave him
and swiftly with a second he served him on the spot.
"Now we are quits," he quoth, "and clear for this evening
of all covenants we accorded, since I came to this house,
       as is due."
1645   The lord said: "By Saint Gile,[6]
       your match I never knew!
       You'll be wealthy in a while,
       such trade if you pursue."

Then on top of the trestles the tables they laid,
1650   cast the cloths thereon, and clear light then
wakened along the walls; waxen torches
men set there, and servants went swift about the hall.
Much gladness and gaiety began then to spring
round the fire on the hearth, and freely and oft
1655   at supper and later: many songs of delight,
such as canticles of Christmas, and new carol-dances,
amid all the mannerly mirth that men can tell of;
and ever our noble knight was next to the lady.
Such glances she gave him of her gracious favour,
1660   secretly stealing sweet looks that strong man to charm,
that he was passing perplexed, and ill-pleased at heart.
Yet he would fain not of his courtesy coldly refuse her,
but graciously engaged her, however against the grain
       the play.
1665   When mirth they had made in hall
       as long as they wished to stay,
       to a room did the lord them call
       and to the ingle° they made their way.   *hearth*

There amid merry words and wine they had a mind once more
1670   to harp on the same note on New Year's Eve.
But said Gawain: "Grant me leave to go on the morrow!
For the appointment approaches that I pledged myself to."
The lord was loth to allow it, and longer would keep him,
and said: "As I am a true man I swear on my troth
1675   the Green Chapel thou shalt gain, and go to your business
in the dawn of New Year, sir, ere daytime begins.

6. A hermit and patron saint of woodlands.

So still lie upstairs and stay at thine ease,
and I shall hunt in the holt here, and hold to my terms
with thee truly, when I return, to trade all our gains.
1680   For I have tested thee twice, and trusty I find thee.
Now 'third time pays for all,' bethink thee tomorrow!
Make we merry while we may and be mindful of joy,
for the woe one may win whenever one wishes!"
This was graciously agreed, and Gawain would linger.
1685   Then gaily drink is given them and they go to their beds
        with light.
        Sir Gawain lies and sleeps
        soft and sound all night;
        his host to his hunting keeps,
1690   and is early arrayed aright.

After Mass of a morsel he and his men partook.
Merry was the morning. For his mount then he called.
All the huntsmen that on horse behind him should follow
were ready mounted to ride arrayed at the gates.
1695   Wondrous fair were the fields, for the frost clung there;
in red rose-hued o'er the wrack° arises the sun,   *mist*
sailing clear along the coasts of the cloudy heavens.
The hunters loosed hounds by a holt-border;°   *grove's edge*
the rocks rang in the wood to the roar of their horns.
1700   Some fell on the line to where the fox was lying,
crossing and re-crossing it in the cunning of their craft.
A hound then gives tongue, the huntsman names him,
round him press his companions in a pack all snuffling,
running forth in a rabble then right in his path.
1705   The fox flits before them. They find him at once,
and when they see him by sight they pursue him hotly,
decrying him full clearly with a clamour of wrath.
He dodges and ever doubles through many a dense coppice,
and looping oft he lurks and listens under fences.
1710   At last at a little ditch he leaps o'er a thorn-hedge,
sneaks out secretly by the side of a thicket,
weens he is out of the wood and away by his wiles from the hounds.
Thus he went unawares to a watch that was posted,
where fierce on him fell three foes at once
1715   all grey.
        He swerves then swift again,
        and dauntless darts astray;
        in grief and in great pain
        to the wood he turns away.

1720   Then to hark to the hounds it was heart's delight,
when all the pack came upon him, there pressing together.
Such a curse at the view they called down on him
that the clustering cliffs might have clattered in ruin.
Here he was hallooed when hunters came on him,

1725   yonder was he assailed with snarling tongues;
        there he was threatened and oft thief was he called,
        with ever the trailers at his trail so that tarry he could not.
        Oft was he run at, if he rushed outwards;
        oft he swerved in again, so subtle was Reynard.
1730   Yea! he led the lord and his hunt as laggards behind him
        thus by mount and by hill till mid-afternoon.
        Meanwhile the courteous knight in the castle in comfort slumbered
        behind the comely curtains in the cold morning.
        But the lady in love-making had no liking to sleep
1735   nor to disappoint the purpose she had planned in her heart;
        but rising up swiftly his room now she sought
        in a gay mantle that to the ground was measured
        and was fur-lined most fairly with fells well trimmed,
        with no comely coif° on her head, only the clear jewels   *close-fitting cap*
1740   that were twined in her tressure° by twenties in clusters;   *hairnet*
        her noble face and her neck all naked were laid,
        her breast bare in front and at the back also.
        She came through the chamber-door and closed it behind her,
        wide set a window, and to wake him she called,
1745   thus greeting him gaily with her gracious words
               of cheer:
            "Ah! man, how canst thou sleep,
            the morning is so clear!"
            He lay in darkness deep,
1750   but her call he then could hear.

        In heavy darkness drowsing he dream-words muttered,
        as a man whose mind was bemused with many mournful thoughts,
        how destiny should his doom on that day bring him
        when he at the Green Chapel the great man would meet,
1755   and be obliged his blow to abide without debate at all.
        But when so comely she came, he recalled then his wits,
        swept aside his slumbers, and swiftly made answer.
        The lady in lovely guise came laughing sweetly,
        bent down o'er his dear face, and deftly kissed him.
1760   He greeted her graciously with a glad welcome,
        seeing her so glorious and gaily attired,
        so faultless in her features and so fine in her hues
        that at once joy up-welling went warm to his heart.
        With smiles sweet and soft they turned swiftly to mirth,
1765   and only brightness and bliss was broached there between them
               so gay.
            They spoke then speeches good,
            much pleasure was in that play;
            great peril between them stood,
1770   unless Mary for her knight should pray.

        For she, queenly and peerless, pressed him so closely,
        led him so near the line, that at last he must needs

either refuse her with offence or her favours there take.
He cared for his courtesy, lest a caitiff° he proved,   *coward*
1775   yet more for his sad case, if he should sin commit
and to the owner of the house, to his host, be a traitor.
"God help me!" said he. "Happen that shall not!"
Smiling sweetly aside from himself then he turned
all the fond words of favour that fell from her lips.
1780   Said she to the knight then: "Now shame you deserve,
if you love not one that lies alone here beside you,
who beyond all women in the world is wounded in heart,
unless you have a lemman,° more beloved, whom you like better,   *lover*
and have affianced faith to that fair one so fast and so true
1785   that your release you desire not—and so I believe now;
and to tell me if that be so truly, I beg you.
For all sakes that men swear by, conceal not the truth
        in guile."
        The knight said: "By Saint John,"
1790   and softly gave a smile,
        "Nay! lover have I none,
        and none will have meanwhile."

"Those words," said the woman, "are the worst that could be.
But I am answered indeed, and 'tis hard to endure.
1795   Kiss me now kindly, and I will quickly depart.
I may but mourn while I live as one that much is in love."
Sighing she sank down, and sweetly she kissed him;
then soon she left his side, and said as she stood there:
"Now, my dear, at this parting do me this pleasure,
1800   give me something as thy gift, thy glove it might be,
that I may remember thee, dear man, my mourning to lessen."
"Now on my word," then said he, "I wish I had here
the loveliest thing for thy delight that in my land I possess;
for worthily have you earned wondrously often
1805   more reward by rights than within my reach would now be,
save to allot you as love-token thing of little value.
Beneath your honour it is to have here and now
a glove for a guerdon° as the gift of Sir Gawain   *reward*
and I am here on an errand in unknown lands,
1810   and have no bearers with baggage and beautiful things
(unluckily, dear lady) for your delight at this time.
A man must do as he is placed; be not pained nor aggrieved,"
        said he.
        Said she so comely clad:
1815   "Nay, noble knight and free,
        though naught of yours I had,
        you should get a gift from me."

A rich ring she offered him of red gold fashioned,
with a stone like a star standing up clear
1820   that bore brilliant beams as bright as the sun:

I warrant you it was worth wealth beyond measure.
But the knight said nay to it, and announced then at once:
"I will have no gifts, fore God, of your grace at this time.
I have none to return you, and naught will I take."

1825 She proffered it and pressed him, and he her pleading refused,
and swore swiftly upon his word that accept it he would not.
And she, sorry that he refused, said to him further:
"If to my ring you say nay, since too rich it appears,
and you would not so deeply be indebted to me,

1830 I shall give you my girdle, less gain will that be."
She unbound a belt swiftly that embracing her sides
was clasped above her kirtle under her comely mantle.
Fashioned it was of green silk, and with gold finished,
though only braided round about, embroidered by hand;

1835 and this she would give to Gawain, and gladly besought him,
of no worth though it were, to be willing to take it.
And he said nay, he would not, he would never receive
either gold or jewelry, ere God the grace sent him
to accomplish the quest on which he had come thither.

1840 "And therefore I pray you, please be not angry,
and cease to insist on it, for to your suit I will ever
        say no.
    I am deeply in debt to you
    for the favour that you show,
1845   to be your servant true
    for ever in weal or woe."

"Do you refuse now this silk," said the fair lady,
"because in itself it is poor? And so it appears.
See how small 'tis in size, and smaller in value!
1850 But one who knew of the nature that is knit therewithin
would appraise it probably at a price far higher.
For whoever goes girdled with this green riband,
while he keeps it well clasped closely about him,
there is none so hardy under heaven that to hew him were able;

1855 for he could not be killed by any cunning of hand."
The knight then took note, and thought now in his heart,
'twould be a prize in that peril that was appointed to him.
When he gained the Green Chapel to get there his sentence,
if by some sleight he were not slain, 'twould be a sovereign device.

1860 Then he bore with her rebuke, and debated not her words;
and she pressed him on the belt, and proffered it in earnest;
and he agreed, and she gave it very gladly indeed,
and prayed him for her sake to part with it never,
but on his honour hide it from her husband; and he then agreed

1865 that no one ever should know, nay, none in the world
        but they.
    With earnest heart and mood
    great thanks he oft did say.

She then the knight so good

1870   a third time kissed that day.

Then she left him alone, her leave taking,
for amusement from the man no more could she get.
When she was gone Sir Gawain got him soon ready,
arose and robed himself in raiment noble.

1875   He laid up the love-lace that the lady had given,
hiding it heedfully where he after might find it.
Then first of all he chose to fare to the chapel,
privately approached a priest, and prayed that he there
would uplift his life, that he might learn better

1880   how his soul should be saved, when he was sent from the world.
There he cleanly confessed him and declared his misdeeds,
both the more and the less, and for mercy he begged,
to absolve him of them all he besought the good man;
and he assoiled him and made him as safe and as clean

1885   as for Doom's Day indeed, were it due on the morrow.[7]
Thereafter more merry he made among the fair ladies,
with carol-dances gentle and all kinds of rejoicing,
than ever he did ere that day, till the darkness of night,
     in bliss.

1890   Each man there said: "I vow
    a delight to all he is!
    Since hither he came till now,
    he was ne'er so gay as this."

Now indoors let him dwell and have dearest delight,

1895   while the free lord yet fares afield in his sports!
At last the fox he has felled that he followed so long;
for, as he spurred through a spinney° to espy there the villain,   *grove*
where the hounds he had heard that hard on him pressed,
Reynard on his road came through a rough thicket,

1900   and all the rabble in a rush were right on his heels.
The man is aware of the wild thing, and watchful awaits him,
brings out his bright brand and at the beast hurls it;
and he blenched at the blade, and would have backed if he could.
A hound hastened up, and had him ere he could;

1905   and right before the horse's feet they fell on him all,
and worried there the wily one with a wild clamour.
The lord quickly alights and lifts him at once,
snatching him swiftly from their slavering mouths,
holds him high o'er his head, hallooing loudly;

1910   and there bay at him fiercely many furious hounds.
Huntsmen hurried thither, with horns full many
ever sounding the assembly, till they saw the master.
When together had come his company noble,
all that ever bore bugle were blowing at once,

---

7. Gawain's confession and absolution are problematic, since he has just accepted the green girdle and resolved to break the covenant of exchange with his host.

1915   and all the others hallooed that had not a horn:
        it was the merriest music that ever men harkened,
        the resounding song there raised that for Reynard's soul
                awoke.
            To hounds they pay their fees,
1920   their heads they fondly stroke,
            and Reynard then they seize,
            and off they skin his cloak.

        And then homeward they hastened, for at hand was now night,
        making strong music on their mighty horns.
1925   The lord alighted at last at his beloved abode,
        found a fire in the hall, and fair by the hearth
        Sir Gawain the good, and gay was he too,
        among the ladies in delight his lot was most joyful.
        He was clad in a blue cloak that came to the ground;
1930   his surcoat well beseemed him with its soft lining,
        and its hood of like hue that hung on his shoulder:
        all fringed with white fur very finely were both.
        He met indeed the master in the midst of the floor,
        and in gaiety greeted him, and graciously said:
1935   "In this case I will first our covenant fulfil
        that to our good we agreed, when ungrudged went the drink."
        He clasps then the knight and kisses him thrice,
        as long and deliciously as he could lay them upon him.
        "By Christ!" the other quoth, "you've come by a fortune
1940   in winning such wares, were they worth what you paid."
        "Indeed, the price was not important," promptly he answered,
        "whereas plainly is paid now the profit I gained."
        "Marry!" said the other man, "mine is not up to't;
        for I have hunted all this day, and naught else have I got
1945   but this foul fox-fell°—the Fiend have the goods!—   *fox-skin*
        and that is price very poor to pay for such treasures
        as these you have thrust upon me, three such kisses
                so good."
            "'Tis enough," then said Gawain.
1950   "I thank you, by the Rood,"
            and how the fox was slain
            he told him as they stood.

        With mirth and minstrelsy and meats at their pleasure
        as merry they made as any men could be;
1955   amid the laughter of ladies and light words of jest
        both Gawain and the good man could no gayer have proved,
        unless they had doted indeed or else drunken had been.
        Both the host and his household went on with their games,
        till the hour had approached when part must they all;
1960   to bed were now bound the brave folk at last.
        Bowing low his leave of the lord there first

the good knight then took, and graciously thanked him:[8]
"For such a wondrous welcome as within these walls I have had,
for your honour at this high feast the High King reward you!
1965   In your service I set myself, your servant, if you will.
For I must needs make a move tomorrow, as you know,
if you give me some good man to go, as you promised,
and guide me to the Green Chapel, as God may permit me
to face on New Year's day such doom as befalls me."
1970   "On my word," said his host, "with hearty good will
to all that ever I promised I promptly shall hold."
Then a servant he assigns him to set him on the road,
and by the downs to conduct him, that without doubt or delay
he might through wild and through wood ways most straight
1975   pursue.
         Said Gawain, "My thanks receive,
         such a favour you will do!"
         The knight then took his leave
         of those noble ladies two.

1980   Sadly he kissed them and said his farewells,
and pressed oft upon them in plenty his thanks,
and they promptly the same again repaid him;
to God's keeping they gave him, grievously sighing.
Then from the people of the castle he with courtesy parted;
1985   all the men that he met he remembered with thanks
for their care for his comfort and their kind service,
and the trouble each had taken in attendance upon him;
and every one was as woeful to wish him adieu
as had they lived all their lives with his lordship in honour.
1990   Then with link-men and lights he was led to his chamber
and brought sweetly to bed, there to be at his rest.
That soundly he slept then assert will I not,
for he had many matters in the morning to mind, if he would,
         in thought.
1995   There let him lie in peace,
         near now is the tryst he sought.
         If a while you will hold your peace,
         I will tell the deeds they wrought!

Part 4

Now New Year draws near and the night passes,
2000   day comes driving the dark, as ordained by God;
but wild weathers of the world awake in the land,
clouds cast keenly the cold upon earth
with bitter breath from the North biting the naked.
Snow comes shivering sharp to shrivel the wild things,

8. Gawain's highly stylized leave-taking is typical of courtly romance and again emphasizes his command of fine manners.

2005	and whistling wind whirls from the heights
	and drives every dale full of drifts very deep.
	Long the knight listens as he lies in his bed;
	though he lays down his eyelids, very little he sleeps:
	at the crow of every cock he recalls well his tryst.
2010	Briskly he rose from his bed ere the break of day,
	for there was light from a lamp that illumined his chamber.
	He called to his chamberlain, who quickly him answered,
	and he bade him bring his byrnie° and his beast saddle. *chain-mail coat*
	The man got him up and his gear fetched him,
2015	and garbed then Sir Gawain in great array;
	first he clad him in his clothes to keep out the cold,
	and after that in his harness that with heed had been tended,
	both his pauncer and his plates° polished all brightly, *leg armor*
	the rings rid of the rust on his rich byrnie:
2020	all was neat as if new, and the knight him thanked
	with delight.
	He put on every piece
	all burnished well and bright;
	most gallant from here to Greece
2025	for his courser called the knight.
	While the proudest of his apparel he put on himself:
	his coat-armour, with the cognisance of the clear symbol
	upon velvet environed with virtuous gems
	all bound and braided about it, with broidered seams
2030	and with fine firs lined wondrous fairly within,
	yet he overlooked not the lace that the lady had given him;
	that Gawain forgot not, of his own good thinking;
	when he had belted his brand° upon his buxom haunches, *sword*
	he twined the love-token twice then about him,
2035	and swiftly he swathed it sweetly about his waist,
	that girdle of green silk, and gallant it looked
	upon the royal red cloth that was rich to behold.
	But he wore not for worth nor for wealth this girdle,
	not for pride in the pendants, though polished they were,
2040	not though the glittering gold there gleamed at the ends,
	but so that himself he might save when suffer he must,
	must abide bane without debating it with blade or with brand
	of war.
	When arrayed the knight so bold
2045	came out before the door,
	to all that high household
	great thanks he gave once more.
	Now Gringolet was groomed, the great horse and high,
	who had been lodged to his liking and loyally tended:
2050	fain to gallop was that gallant horse for his good fettle.
	His master to him came and marked well his coat,

and said: "Now solemnly myself I swear on my troth
there is a company in this castle that is careful of honour!
Their lord that them leads, may his lot be joyful!
2055 Their beloved lady in life may delight befall her!
If they out of charity thus cherish a guest,
upholding their house in honour, may He them reward
that upholds heaven on high, and all of you too!
And if life a little longer I might lead upon earth,
2060 I would give you some guerdon° gladly, were I able."   *reward*
Then he steps in the stirrup and strides on his horse;
his shield his man showed him, and on shoulder he slung it,
Gringolet he goaded with his gilded heels,
and he plunged forth on the pavement, and prancing no more
2065   stood there.
     Ready now was his squire to ride
     that his helm and lance would bear.
     "Christ keep this castle!" he cried
     and wished it fortune fair.

2070 The bridge was brought down and the broad gates then
unbarred and swung back upon both hinges.
The brave man blessed himself, and the boards crossing,
bade the porter up rise, who before the prince kneeling
gave him "Good day, Sir Gawain!", and "God save you!"
2075 Then he went on his way with the one man only
to guide him as he goes to that grievous place
where he is due to endure the dolorous blow.
They go by banks and by braes° where branches are bare,[1]   *hillsides*
they climb along cliffs where clingeth the cold;
2080 the heavens are lifted high, but under them evilly
mist hangs moist on the moor, melts on the mountains;
every hill has a hat, a mist-mantle huge.
Brooks break and boil on braes all about,
bright bubbling on their banks where they bustle downwards.
2085 Very wild through the wood is the way they must take,
until soon comes the season when the sun rises
          that day.
     On a high hill they abode,
     white snow beside them lay;
2090   the man that by him rode
     there bade his master stay.

"For so far I have taken you, sir, at this time,
and now you are near to that noted place
that you have enquired and questioned so curiously after.
2095 But I will announce now the truth, since you are known to me,
and you are a lord in this life that I love greatly,

1. The grimness of this landscape, reminiscent of wastelands in Anglo-Saxon poetry, swiftly returns the poem from the courtly world to the elemental challenge Gawain now faces.

if you would follow my advice you would fare better.
The place that you pass to, men perilous hold it,
the worst wight in the world in that waste dwelleth;
2100   for he is stout and stern, and to strike he delights,
and he mightier than any man upon middle-earth is,
and his body is bigger than the four best men
that are in Arthur's house, either Hector[2] or others.
All goes as he chooses at the Green Chapel;
2105   no one passes by that place so proud in his arms
that he hews not to death by dint of his hand.
For he is a man monstrous, and mercy he knows not;
for be it a churl or a chaplain that by the Chapel rideth,
a monk or a mass-priest or any man besides,
2110   he would as soon have him slain as himself go alive.
And so I say to you, as sure as you sit in your saddle,
if you come there, you'll be killed, if the carl has his way.
Trust me, that is true, though you had twenty lives
        to yield.
2115   He here has dwelt now long
        and stirred much strife on field;
        against his strokes so strong
        yourself you cannot shield.

And so, good Sir Gawain, now go another way,
2120   and let the man alone, for the love of God, sir!
Come to some other country, and there may Christ keep you!
And I shall haste me home again, and on my honour I promise
that I swear will by God and all His gracious saints,
so help me God and the Halidom,[3] and other oaths a plenty,
2125   that I will safe keep your secret, and say not a word
that ever you fain were to flee for any foe that I knew of."
"Gramercy!" quoth Gawain, and regretfully answered:
"Well, man, I wish thee, who wishest my good,
and keep safe my secret, I am certain thou wouldst.
2130   But however heedfully thou hid it, if I here departed,
fain in fear now to flee, in the fashion thou speakest,
I should a knight coward be, I could not be excused.
Nay, I'll fare to the Chapel, whatever chance may befall,
and have such words with that wild man as my wish is to say,
2135   come fair or come foul, as fate will allot
        me there.
        He may be a fearsome knave
        to tame, and club may bear;
        but His servants true to save
2140   the Lord can well prepare."

---

2. Chief hero among the defenders of Troy and, like
Arthur, one of the "Nine Worthies" celebrated for their

heroic valor: or perhaps Arthur's knight Hector De Maris.
3. "By my holy relics."

"Marry!" quoth the other man, "now thou makest it so clear
that thou wishest thine own bane to bring on thyself,
and to lose thy life hast a liking, to delay thee I care not!
Have here thy helm on thy head, thy spear in thy hand,
2145   and ride down by yon rock-side where runs this same track,
till thou art brought to the bottom of the baleful valley.
A little to thy left hand then look o'er the green,
and thou wilt see on the slope the selfsame chapel,
and the great man and grim on ground that it keeps.
2150   Now farewell in God's name, Gawain the noble!
For all the gold in the world I would not go with thee,
nor bear thee fellowship through this forest one foot further!"
With that his bridle towards the wood back the man turneth,
hits his horse with his heels as hard as he can,
2155   gallops on the greenway, and the good knight there leaves
              alone.
         Quoth Gawain: "By God on high
         I will neither grieve nor groan.
         With God's will I comply,
2160   Whose protection I do own."

Then he puts spurs to Gringolet, and espying the track,
thrust in along a bank by a thicket's border,
rode down the rough brae right to the valley;
and then he gazed all about: a grim place he thought it,
2165   and saw no sign of shelter on any side at all,
only high hillsides sheer upon either hand,
and notched knuckled crags with gnarled boulders;
the very skies by the peaks were scraped, it appeared.
Then he halted and held in his horse for the time,
2170   and changed oft his front the Chapel to find.
Such on no side he saw, as seemed to him strange,
save a mound as it might be near the marge of a green,
a worn barrow⁴ on a brae by the brink of a water,
beside falls in a flood that was flowing down;
2175   the burn° bubbled therein, as if boiling it were.   *brook*
He urged on his horse then, and came up to the mound,
there lightly alit, and lashed to a tree
his reins, with a rough branch rightly secured them.
Then he went to the barrow and about it he walked,
2180   debating in his mind what might the thing be.
It had a hole at the end and at either side
and with grass in green patches was grown all over,
and was all hollow within: nought but an old cavern,
or a cleft in an old crag; he could not it name
2185   aright.
         "Can this be the Chapel Green,
         O Lord?" said the gentle knight.

4. Perhaps a burial mound, which seems to link the moment to ancient, probably pagan, inhabitants.

"Here the Devil might say, I ween,
his matins about midnight!"

2190 "On my word," quoth Gawain, "'tis a wilderness here!
This oratory looks evil. With herbs overgrown
it fits well that fellow transformed into green
to follow here his devotions in the Devil's fashion.
Now I feel in my five wits the Fiend 'tis himself
2195 that has trapped me with this tryst to destroy me here.
This is a chapel of mischance, the church most accursed
that ever I entered. Evil betide it!"
With high helm on his head, his lance in his hand,
he roams up to the roof of that rough dwelling.
2200 Then he heard from the high hill, in a hard rock-wall
beyond the stream on a steep, a sudden startling noise.
How it clattered in the cliff, as if to cleave it asunder,
as if one upon a grindstone were grinding a scythe!
How it whirred and it rasped as water in a mill-race!
2205 How it rushed, and it rang, rueful to harken!
Then "By God," quoth Gawain, "I guess this ado
is meant for my honour, meetly to hail me
          as knight!
     As God wills! Waylaway!
2210   That helps me not a mite.
     My life though down I lay,
     no noise can me affright."

Then clearly the knight there called out aloud:
"Who is master in this place to meet me at tryst?
2215 For now 'tis good Gawain on ground that here walks.
If any aught hath to ask, let him hasten to me,
either now or else never, his needs to further!"
"Stay!" said one standing above on the steep o'er his head,
"and thou shalt get in good time what to give thee I vowed."
2220 Still with that rasping and racket he rushed on a while,
and went back to his whetting, till he wished to descend.
And then he climbed past a crag, and came from a hole,
hurtling out of a hid nook with a horrible weapon:
a Danish axe[5] newly dressed the dint to return,
2225 with cruel cutting-edge curved along the handle—
filed on a whetstone, and four feet in width,
'twas no less—along its lace of luminous hue;
and the great man in green still guised as before,
his locks and long beard, his legs and his face,
2230 save that firm on his feet he fared on the ground,
steadied the haft on the stones and stalked beside it.
When he walked to the water, where he wade would not,

5. A long-bladed axe, associated with Viking raiders.

he hopped over on his axe and haughtily strode,
fierce and fell on a field where far all about
2235   lay snow.
          Sir Gawain the man met there,
          neither bent nor bowed he low.
          The other said: "Now, sirrah fair,
          I true at tryst thee know!

2240   "Gawain," said that green man, "may God keep thee!
On my word, sir, I welcome thee with a will to my place,
and thou hast timed thy travels as trusty man should,
and thou hast forgot not the engagement agreed on between us:
at this time gone a twelvemonth thou took'st thy allowance,
2245   and I should now this New Year nimbly repay thee.
And we are in this valley now verily on our own,
there are no people to part us—we can play as we like.
Have thy helm off thy head, and have here thy pay!
Bandy me no more debate than I brought before thee
2250   when thou didst sweep off my head with one swipe only!"
"Nay," quoth Gawain, "by God that gave me my soul,
I shall grudge thee not a grain any grief that follows.
Only restrain thee to one stroke, and still shall I stand
and offer thee no hindrance to act as thou likest
2255   right here."
          With a nod of his neck he bowed,
          let bare the flesh appear;
          he would not by dread be cowed,
          no sign he gave of fear.

2260   Then the great man in green gladly prepared him,
gathered up his grim tool there Gawain to smite;
with all the lust in his limbs aloft he heaved it,
shaped as mighty a stroke as if he meant to destroy him.
Had it driving come down as dour as he aimed it,
2265   under his dint would have died the most doughty man ever.
But Gawain on that guisarm° then glanced to one side,   axe
as down it came gliding on the green there to end him,
and he shrank a little with his shoulders at the sharp iron.
With a jolt the other man jerked back the blade,
2270   and reproved then the prince, proudly him taunting.
"Thou'rt not Gawain," said the green man, "who is so good reported,
who never flinched from any foes on fell or in dale;
and now thou fleest in fear, ere thou feelest a hurt!
Of such cowardice that knight I ne'er heard accused.
2275   Neither blenched I nor backed, when thy blow, sir, thou aimedst,
nor uttered any cavil in the court of King Arthur.
My head flew to my feet, and yet fled I never;
but thou, ere thou hast any hurt, in thy heart quailest,
and so the nobler knight to be named I deserve
2280   therefore."

"I blenched once," Gawain said,
"and I will do so no more.
But if on floor now falls my head,
I cannot it restore.

2285   But get busy, I beg, sir, and bring me to the point.
Deal me my destiny, and do it out of hand!
For I shall stand from thee a stroke and stir not again
till thine axe hath hit me, have here my word on't!"
"Have at thee then!" said the other, and heaved it aloft,
2290   and watched him as wrathfully as if he were wild with rage.
He made at him a mighty aim, but the man he touched not,
holding back hastily his hand, ere hurt it might do.
Gawain warily awaited it, and winced with no limb,
but stood as still as a stone or the stump of a tree
2295   that with a hundred ravelled roots in rocks is embedded.
This time merrily remarked then the man in the green:
"So, now thou hast thy heart whole, a hit I must make.
May the high order now keep thee that Arthur gave thee,
and guard thy gullet at this go, if it can gain thee that."
2300   Angrily with ire then answered Sir Gawain:
"Why! lash away, thou lusty man! Too long dost thou threaten.
'Tis thy heart methinks in thee that now quaileth!"
"In faith," said the fellow, "so fiercely thou speakest,
I no longer will linger delaying thy errand
2305   right now."
        Then to strike he took his stance
        and grimaced with lip and brow.
        He that of rescue saw no chance
        was little pleased, I trow.

2310   Lightly his weapon he lifted, and let it down neatly
with the bent horn of the blade towards the neck that was bare;
though he hewed with a hammer-swing, he hurt him no more
than to snick him on one side and sever the skin.
Through the fair fat sank the edge, and the flesh entered,
2315   so that the shining blood o'er his shoulders was shed on the earth;
and when the good knight saw the gore that gleamed on the snow,
he sprang out with spurning° feet a spear's length and more,   *thrusting*
in haste caught his helm and on his head cast it,
under his fair shield he shot with a shake of his shoulders,[6]
2320   brandished his bright sword, and boldly he spake—
never since he as manchild of his mother was born
was he ever on this earth half so happy a man:
"Have done, sir, with thy dints! Now deal me no more!
I have stood from thee a stroke without strife on this spot,
2325   and if thou offerest me others, I shall answer thee promptly,

---

6. Gawain, who has displayed so much courtly refinement and religious emotion, now shows himself a practiced fighter, swiftly pulling his armor into place.

and give as good again, and as grim, be assured,
    shall pay.
    But one stroke here's my due,
    as the covenant clear did say
2330   that in Arthur's halls we drew.
    And so, good sir, now stay!"

From him the other stood off, and on his axe rested,
held the haft to the ground, and on the head leaning,
gazed at the good knight as on the green he there strode.
2335 To see him standing so stout, so stern there and fearless,
armed and unafraid, his heart it well pleased.
Then merrily he spoke with a mighty voice,
and loudly it rang, as to that lord he said:
"Fearless knight on this field, so fierce do not be!
2340 No man here unmannerly hath thee maltreated,
nor aught given thee not granted by agreement at court.
A hack I thee vowed, and thou'st had it, so hold thee content;
I remit thee the remnant of all rights I might claim.
If I brisker had been, a buffet, it may be,
2345 I could have handed thee more harshly, and harm could have done thee.
First I menaced thee in play with no more than a trial,
and clove thee with no cleft: I had a claim to the feint,
for the fast pact we affirmed on the first evening,
and thou fairly and unfailing didst faith with me keep,
2350 all thy gains thou me gavest, as good man ought.
The other trial for the morning, man, I thee tendered
when thou kissedst my comely wife, and the kisses didst render.
For the two here I offered only two harmless feints
    to make.
2355   The true shall truly repay,
    for no peril then need he quake.
    Thou didst fail on the third day,
    and so that tap now take!

"For it is my weed that thou wearest, that very woven girdle:
2360 my own wife it awarded thee, I wot° well indeed.   *know*
Now I am aware of thy kisses, and thy courteous ways,
and of thy wooing by my wife: I worked that myself!
I sent her to test thee, and thou seem'st to me truly
the fair knight most faultless that e'er foot set on earth!
2365 As a pearl than white pease is prized more highly,
so is Gawain, in good faith, than other gallant knights.
But in this you lacked, sir, a little, and of loyalty came short.
But that was for no artful wickedness, nor for wooing either,
but because you loved your own life: the less do I blame you."
2370 The other stern knight in a study° then stood a long while,   *thinking*
in such grief and disgust he had a grue° in his heart;   *shudder*
all the blood from his breast in his blush mingled,

and he shrank into himself with shame at that speech.
The first words on that field that he found then to say
2375 were: "Cursed be ye, Coveting, and Cowardice also!
In you is vileness, and vice that virtue destroyeth."
He took then the treacherous thing, and untying the knot
fiercely flung he the belt at the feet of the knight:
"See there the falsifier, and foul be its fate!
2380 Through care for thy blow Cowardice brought me
to consent to Coveting, my true kind to forsake,
which is free-hand and faithful word that are fitting to knights.
Now I am faulty and false, who afraid have been ever
of treachery and troth-breach: the two now my curse
2385   may bear!
      I confess, sir, here to you
      all faulty has been my fare.
      Let me gain your grace anew,
      and after I will beware."

2390 Then the other man laughed and lightly answered:
"I hold it healed beyond doubt, the harm that I had.
Thou hast confessed thee so clean and acknowledged thine errors,
and hast the penance plain to see from the point of my blade,
that I hold thee purged of that debt, made as pure and as clean
2395 as hadst thou done no ill deed since the day thou wert born.
And I give thee, sir, the girdle with gold at its hems,
for it is green like my gown. So, Sir Gawain, you may
think of this our contest when in the throng thou walkest
among princes of high praise; 'twill be a plain reminder
2400 of the chance of the Green Chapel between chivalrous knights.
And now you shall in this New Year come anon to my house,
and in our revels the rest of this rich season
            shall go."
      The lord pressed him hard to wend,
2405   and said, "my wife, I know,
      we soon shall make your friend,
      who was your bitter foe."

"Nay forsooth!" the knight said, and seized then his helm,
and duly it doffed, and the doughty man thanked:
2410 "I have lingered too long! May your life now be blest,
and He promptly repay you Who apportions all honours!
And give my regards to her grace, your goodly consort,
both to her and to the other, to mine honoured ladies,
who thus their servant with their designs have subtly beguiled.
2415 But no marvel it is if mad be a fool,
and by the wiles of women to woe be brought.
For even so Adam by one on earth was beguiled,
and Solomon by several, and to Samson moreover
his doom by Delilah was dealt; and David was after

2420   blinded by Bathsheba, and he bitterly suffered.[7]
Now if these came to grief through their guile, a gain 'twould be vast
to love them well and believe them not, if it lay in man's power!
Since these were aforetime the fairest, by fortune most blest,
eminent among all the others who under heaven bemused
2425   were too,
     and all of them were betrayed
     by women that they knew,
     though a fool I now am made,
     some excuse I think my due.

2430   "But for your girdle," quoth Gawain, "may God you repay!
That I will gain with good will, not for the gold so joyous
of the cincture, nor the silk, nor the swinging pendants,
nor for wealth, nor for worth, nor for workmanship fine;
but as a token of my trespass I shall turn to it often
2435   when I ride in renown, ruefully recalling
the failure and the frailty of the flesh so perverse,
so tender, so ready to take taints of defilement.
And thus, when pride my heart pricks for prowess in arms,
one look at this love-lace shall lowlier make it.
2440   But one thing I would pray you, if it displeaseth you not,
since you are the lord of yonder land, where I lodged for a while
in your house and in honour—may He you reward
Who upholdeth the heavens and on high sitteth!—
how do you announce your true name? And then nothing further."
2445   "That I will tell thee truly," then returned the other.
"Bertilak de Hautdesert hereabouts I am called,
[who thus have been enchanted and changed in my hue]
by the might of Morgan le Fay[8] that in my mansion dwelleth,
and by cunning of lore and crafts well learned.
2450   The magic arts of Merlin she many hath mastered;
for deeply in dear love she dealt on a time
with that accomplished clerk, as at Camelot runs
     the fame;
     and Morgan the Goddess
2455   is therefore now her name.
     None power and pride possess
     too high for her to tame.

   She made me go in this guise to your goodly court
to put its pride to the proof, if the report were true
2460   that runs of the great renown of the Round Table.
She put this magic upon me to deprive you of your wits,
in hope Guinevere to hurt, that she in horror might die

---

7. Gawain suddenly erupts in a brief but fierce diatribe, including this list of treacherous women recognizable from contemporary misogynist texts.
8. Morgan is Arthur's half-sister and ruler of the mysterious Avalon; she learned magical arts from Merlin. Her presence can bode good or ill. In some stories she holds a deep grudge against Guinevere, yet she carries off the wounded Arthur after his final battle, perhaps to heal him. The earlier Celtic Morrigan, possibly related, is queen of demons, sower of discord, and goddess of war.

aghast at that glamoury° that gruesomely spake   *enchanted one*
with its head in its hand before the high table.

2465 She it is that is at home, that ancient lady;
she is indeed thine own aunt, Arthur's half-sister,
daughter of the Duchess of Tintagel on whom doughty Sir Uther
after begat Arthur, who in honour is now.[9]
Therefore I urge thee in earnest, sir, to thine aunt return!

2470 In my hall make merry! My household thee loveth,
and I wish thee as well, upon my word, sir knight,
as any that go under God, for thy great loyalty."
But he denied him with a "Nay! by no means I will!"
They clasp then and kiss and to the care give each other

2475 of the Prince of Paradise; and they part on that field
      so cold.
         To the king's court on courser keen
         then hastened Gawain the bold,
         and the knight in the glittering green

2480   to ways of his own did hold.

Wild ways in the world Gawain now rideth
on Gringolet: by the grace of God he still lived.
Oft in house he was harboured and lay oft in the open,
oft vanquished his foe in adventures as he fared

2485 which I intend not this time in my tale to recount.
The hurt was healed that he had in his neck,
and the bright-hued belt he bore now about it
obliquely like a baldric[1] bound at his side,
under his left arm with a knot that lace was fastened

2490 to betoken he had been detected in the taint of a fault;
and so at last he came to the Court again safely.
Delight there was awakened, when the lords were aware
that good Gawain had returned: glad news they thought it.
The king kissed the knight, and the queen also,

2495 and then in turn many a true knight that attended to greet him.
About his quest they enquire, and he recounts all the marvels,
declares all the hardships and care that he had,
what chanced at the Chapel, what cheer made the knight,
the love of the lady, and the lace at the last.

2500 The notch in his neck naked he showed them
that he had for his dishonesty from the hands of the knight
      in blame.
         It was torment to tell the truth:
         in his face the blood did flame;

2505   he groaned for grief and ruth°   *remorse*
         when he showed it, to his shame.

---

9. The poem now recalls an earlier transgression of guest-host obligations, when Uther began to lust for Ygerne while her husband, Gorlois, was at his court; he later killed Gorlois and married Ygerne.
1. A belt for a sword or bugle, worn over one shoulder and across the chest.

"Lo! Lord," he said at last, and the lace handled,
"This is the band! For this a rebuke I bear in my neck!
This is the grief and disgrace I have got for myself
2510   from the covetousness and cowardice that o'ercame me there!
This is the token of the troth-breach that I am detected in,
and needs must I wear it while in the world I remain;
for a man may cover his blemish, but unbind it he cannot,
for where once 'tis applied, thence part will it never."
2515   The king comforted the knight, and all the Court also
laughed loudly thereat, and this law made in mirth
the lords and the ladies that whoso belonged to the Table,
every knight of the Brotherhood, a baldric should have,
a band of bright green obliquely about him,
2520   and this for love of that knight as a livery should wear.
For that was reckoned the distinction of the Round Table,
and honour was his that had it evermore after,
as it is written in the best of the books of romance.
Thus in Arthur his days happened this marvel,
2525   as the Book of the Brut beareth us witness;
since Brutus the bold knight to Britain came first,
after the siege and the assault had ceased at Troy,
　　　　I trow,
　　many a marvel such before,
2530   　has happened here ere now.
　　To His bliss us bring Who bore
　　the Crown of Thorns on brow!   AMEN

HONY SOYT QUI MAL PENCE[2]

<hr />

Sir Thomas Malory
c. 1410–1471

The full identity of Sir Thomas Malory shimmers just beyond our grasp. In several of his colophons—those closing formulas to texts—the author of the *Morte Darthur* says he is "a knyght presoner, sir Thomas Malleorré," and prays that "God sende hym good delyveraunce sone and hastely." Scholars have traced a number of such names in the era, among whom two seem particularly likely: Sir Thomas Malory of Newbold Revell, and Thomas Malory of Papworth. The former Thomas Malory had a scabrous criminal record and was long kept prisoner awaiting trial, while the latter had links to a rich collection of Arthurian books.

Another colophon provides the more useful information that "the hoole book of kyng Arthur and of his noble knyghtes of the Rounde Table" was completed in the ninth year of King Edward IV, that is 1469 or 1470. So whichever Malory wrote the *Morte Darthur*, he was

<hr />

2. "Let them be ashamed who think ill of it" (French), the English royal motto.

certainly working in the unsettled years of the War of the Roses, in which the great ducal families of York and Lancaster battled for control of the English throne. As one family gained dominance, adherents of the other were often jailed on flimsy charges. The spectacle of a nation threatening to crumble into clan warfare provides much of the thematic weight of the *Morte Darthur*, while the declining chivalric order of the later fifteenth century underlies Malory's increasingly elegiac tone.

Whether he gained his remarkable knowledge of French and English Arthurian tradition in or out of jail, Malory infused his version of these stories with a darkening perspective very much his own. Malory sensed the high aspirations, especially the bonds of honor and fellowship in battle, that held together Arthur's realm. Yet he was also bleakly aware of how tenuous those bonds were and how easily undone by tragically competing pressures. These include the centuries-old Arthurian preoccupation with transgressive love, but Malory is more concerned with the conflicting claims of loyalty to clan or king, the urge to avenge the death of a fellow knight, and the resulting alienation even among the best of knights. Still more unnerving, agents of a virtually unmotivated or unexplained malice have ever more impact as the *Morte Darthur* progresses.

For all his initial energy and control, Malory's Arthur is increasingly a king forced to suppress knightly grievances, to deplore religious quest, even to overlook the adultery of his wife and his greatest knight, all in the interest of his fading hopes for chivalric honor and unity. Arthur's commitment to courtesy finally undoes his honor in the eyes of his own knights. As the Round Table is broken (an image Malory uses repeatedly) Arthur is put in the agonizing position of acting as judge in his wife's trial, making war on his early companion Lancelot, and finally engaging in single combat with his own treacherous son Mordred.

Malory would have found many of these themes in his sources. Twelfth-century Arthurian romances in French verse had explored the elevation and danger of courtly eroticism, and the theme was extended in the enormous French prose versions of the thirteenth century that Malory had read in great detail. In these prose romances, too, religious and chivalric themes converged around the story of the Grail. Malory also knew the *Morte Arthur* poems of fourteenth-century England, with their emphases on conquest, treachery, and the military details of Arthur's final battles.

Malory regularly acknowledges these sources, but his powers of synthesis and the stamp of his style make his *Morte Darthur* unique. While he occasionally writes a complex, reflective sentence, Malory's prose is typically composed of simple, idiomatic narrative statements, and speeches so brief as to be almost gnomic. On hearing of his brother's death, Gawain faints, then rises and says only "Alas!" Yet the grief of his cry resonates across the closing episodes of the work. Malory's imagery is similarly resonant. He tends to strip it of the explanations that had become frequent in the French prose works, and he concentrates its impact by an almost obsessive repetition. The later episodes of the work become almost an incantation of breakage and dispersal, blood and wounds, each image cluster reaching alternately toward religious experience or secular destruction.

These versions of chivalric ambition, sacred or secular, do not divide easily in the *Morte Darthur*. The saintly Galahad and the scheming Mordred may represent extremes of contrary ambition, but Malory is more preoccupied by the sadly mixed motives of Lancelot or Arthur himself. In three late episodes offered below, the reader is drawn into the perspective of lesser knights like Bors and Bedivere, who witness great moments while affecting them only marginally. They bring back to the world of lesser men stories of uncanny experience and oversee their conversion from verbal rumor to written form, whether in books or on tombs. Much of Malory's power and his continuing appeal come from his unresolved doubleness of perspective. Whether by way of his characters or his style, resonant and mysterious elements emerge from a narrative of gritty realism.

from **Morte Darthur**
from **Caxton's Prologue**[1]

After that I had accomplysshed and fynysshed dyuers hystoryes as
wel of° contemplacyon as of other hystoryal and worldly actes of   *both about*
grete conquerours and prynces, and also certeyn bookes of
ensaumples° and doctryne, many noble and dyuers gentylmen of   *moral tales*
thys royame° of Englond camen and demaunded me many and   *realm*
oftymes, wherefore that I haue not do made and enprynte the noble
hystorye of the Sayntgreal° and of the moost renomed° Crysten   *Holy Grail /*
kyng, fyrst and chyef of the thre best Crysten[2] and worthy, Kyng   *famed*
Arthur, whyche ought moost to be remembred emonge vs Englysshe-
men tofore° al other Crysten kynges. * * *   *before*
    To whome I answerd that dyuers men holde oppynyon that
there was no suche Arthur, and that alle suche bookes as been maad
of hym ben° but fayned and fables, bycause that somme cronycles   *are*
make of hym no mencyon ne° remembre hym noothynge ne of his   *nor*
knyghtes.
    Wherto they answerd, and one in specyal sayd, that in hym that
shold say or thynke that there was neuer suche a kyng callyd Arthur
myght wel be aretted° grete folye and blyndenesse; for he sayd that   *presumed*
there were many euydences of the contrarye. Fyrst ye may see his
sepulture° in the monasterye of Glastyngburye. And also in Poly-   *tomb*
cronycon,[3] * * * where his body was buryed and after founden and
translated into the sayd monasterye. Ye shal se also in th'ystory of
Bochas, in his book De Casu Principum,[4] parte of his noble actes and
also of his falle; also Galfrydus in his Brutysshe book[5] recounteth his
lyf. And in dyuers places of Englond many remembraunces ben yet
of hym and shall remayne perpetuelly, and also of his knyghtes. Fyrst
in the Abbey of Westmestre at Saynt Edwardes Shryne remayneth
the prynte of his seal in reed waxe closed in beryll, in which is wryton, PATRICIUS ARTHURUS BRITANNIE GALLIE GERMANIE DACIE IMPER-
ATOR.[6] Item° in the Castel of Douer ye may see Gauwayns skulle and   *also*
Cradoks mantel; at Wynchester, the Round Table; in other places,
Launcelottes swerde, and many other thynges.
    Thenne, al these thynges consydered, there can no man reson-
ably gaynsaye but there was a kyng of thys lande named Arthur. * * *
    Thenne al these thynges forsayd aledged, I coude not wel denye
but that there was suche a noble kynge named Arthur, and reputed

---

1. The first English printer, William Caxton exerted a
major literary influence through his translations of
French works and his pioneering editions of English writers, including Chaucer and Gower. In 1485 he published
a version of *Le Morte Darthur*, probably based on a revision by Malory himself but different from the text edited
by Eugene Vinaver (1947, 1975) and used here. Caxton's
Prologue is interesting in its own right as an early response
to Malory, even as Caxton takes the opportunity to
promote interest in his book. To give a sense of early
printed English, the passages from Caxton's *Prologue* are
presented in unaltered spelling.

2. Arthur appears in the traditional list of "nine worthies," three heroes each from pagan, Jewish, and Christian narratives.
3. The *Polychronicon*, a universal history by the monk
Ranulph Higden (d. 1364).
4. Boccaccio's *On the Fall of Princes*.
5. Geoffrey of Monmouth, *History of the Kings of Britain*,
whose later versions were often called simply *Brut*.
6. The Noble Arthur, Emperor of Britain, Gaul, Germany,
Dacia.

one of the ix worthy, and fyrst and chyef of the Cristen men. And many noble volumes be made of hym and of his noble knyghtes in Frensshe, which I haue seen and redde beyonde the see, which been not had in our maternal tongue. But in Walsshe ben many, and also in Frensshe, and somme in Englysshe, but nowher nygh alle. Wherfore suche as haue late ben drawen oute bryefly° into Englysshe, I haue, after the symple connyng° that God hath sente to me, vnder the fauour and correctyon of al noble lordes and gentylmen, enprysed° to enprynte a book of the noble hystoryes of the sayd Kynge Arthur and of certeyn of his knyghtes, after a copye vnto me delyuerd, whyche copye Syr Thomas Malorye dyd take oute of certeyn bookes of Frensshe and reduced it into Englysshe. And I, accordyng to my copye, haue doon sette it in enprynte, to the entente° that noble men may see and lerne the noble actes of chyualrye, the ientyl° and vertuous dedes that somme knyghtes used in tho° dayes, by whyche they came to honour, and how they that were vycious were punysshed and ofte put to shame and rebuke. Humbly bysechyng al noble lordes and ladyes, wyth al other estates° of what estate or degree they been of, that shal see and rede in this sayd book and werke, that they take the good and honest actes in their remembraunce and to folowe the same, wherin they shalle fynde many ioyous and playsaunt hystoryes and noble and renomed actes of humanyte, gentylness, and chyualryes. For herein may be seen noble chyualrye, curtosye, humanyte, frendlynesse, hardynesse, loue, frendshyp, cowardyse, murdre, hate, vertue, and synne. Doo after the good and leue the euyl, and it shal brynge you to good fame and renommee.°

And for to passe the tyme thys book shal be plesaunte to rede in, but for to gyue fayth and byleue that al is trewe that is conteyned herin, ye be at your lyberte. But al is wryton for our doctryne and for to beware that we falle not to vyce ne synne, but t'excersyse° and folowe vertu, by whyche we may come and atteyne to good fame and renomme in thys lyf, and after thys shorte and transytorye lyf to come vnto euerlastyng blysse in heuen, the whyche He graunte vs that reygneth in heuen, the Blessyd Trynyte. Amen.

Marginal glosses:
abridged
wit

undertaken

with the aim

noble / those

ranks

renown

in practice

The Miracle of Galahad[1]

Now saith the tale that Sir Galahad rode many journeys in vain, and at last he came to the abbey where King Mordrains was. And when he heard that, he thought he would abide to see him.

And so upon the morn, when he had heard mass, Sir Galahad came unto King Mordrains. And anon the king saw him, which had

1. From *The Holy Grail*, in *King Arthur and His Knights*, ed. Eugène Vinaver (1975). Earlier in the text, Lancelot's saintly son Galahad had come to the Round Table and precipitated a brief apparition of the Holy Grail (the cup or dish with which Christ had celebrated the Last Supper). One hundred fifty of Arthur's knights then took a vow to seek a fuller vision of the Grail, but in the mysterious adventures that followed, many died or despaired. Malory's attention now narrows to Lancelot and his partial vision of the Grail, and the continuing quest of Galahad, Perceval, and Bors. The blind King Mordrains is one of several maimed or aged kings cured by Galahad's presence.

lain blind of long time, and then he dressed him against° him and
said,   *rose to meet*

"Sir Galahad, the servant of Jesu Christ and very° knight, whose   *true*
coming I have abiden° long, now embrace me and let me rest on thy   *awaited*
breast, so that I may rest° between thine arms! For thou art a clean   *die*
virgin above all knights, as the flower of the lily in whom virginity is
signified. And thou art the rose which is the flower of all good
virtue, and in colour of fire.[2] For the fire of the Holy Ghost is taken
so in thee that my flesh, which was all dead of oldness, is become
again young."

When Galahad heard these words, then he embraced him and
all his body. Then said he,°   *Mordrains*

"Fair Lord Jesu Christ, now I have my will! Now I require Thee,
in this point° that I am in, that Thou come and visit me."   *state*

And anon Our Lord heard his prayer, and therewith the soul departed from the body. And then Sir Galahad put him in the earth as
a king ought to be, and so departed and came into a perilous forest
where he found the well which boiled with great waves, as the tale
telleth tofore.°   *earlier*

And as soon as Sir Galahad set his hand thereto it ceased, so
that it brent° no more, and anon the heat departed away. And cause   *burned*
why it brent, it was a sign of lechery that was that time much used.
But that heat might not abide his pure virginity. And so this was
taken in the country for a miracle, and so ever after was it called
Galahad's Well.

So by adventure he came unto the country of Gore, and into the
abbey where Sir Lancelot had been toforehand and found the tomb
of King Bagdemagus; but he was founder thereof.[3] For there was the
tomb of Joseph of Arimathea's son and the tomb of Simeon, where
Lancelot had failed.[4] Then he looked into a croft° under the   *crypt*
minster,° and there he saw a tomb which brent full marvellously.   *church*
Then asked he the brethren what it was.

"Sir," said they, "a marvellous adventure that may not be
brought to an end but by him that passeth of bounty and of knighthood all them of the Round Table."

"I would," said Sir Galahad, "that ye would bring me thereto."

"Gladly," said they, and so led him till° a cave. And he went   *to*
down upon greses° and came unto the tomb. And so the flaming   *steps*
failed, and the fire staunched° which many a day had been great.   *was quenched*

Then came there a voice which said,

2. Galahad's physical and spiritual purity are shown in a number of earlier episodes.
3. Gore, the mysterious realm of Bagdemagus, who had been gravely wounded when he presumed to take a shield intended for Galahad. Words may be missing from the final phrase.
4. In Arthurian tradition, Joseph of Arimathea was keeper of the Grail and used it to catch Christ's blood at the Crucifixion. His son Joseph was the first Christian bishop and carried both the faith and the Grail to England. Galahad is the last of their lineage. Lancelot's failure refers to an episode in the French source that Malory never tells, either inadvertently or because he assumed that many readers would know the story.

"Much are ye beholden to thank God which hath given you a good hour,° that ye may draw out the souls of earthly pain and to put them into the joys of Paradise. Sir, I am of your kindred, which hath dwelled in this heat this three hundred winter and four-and-fifty to be purged of the sin that I did against Arimathea Joseph."

  good luck

Then Sir Galahad took the body in his arms and bare it into the minster. And that night lay Sir Galahad in the abbey; and on the morn he gave him his service and put him in the earth before the high altar.

So departed he from thence, and commended the brethren to God, and so he rode five days till that he came to the Maimed King. And ever followed Perceval the five days asking where he had been, and so one told him how the adventures of Logres were achieved.[5] So on a day it befell that he came out of a great forest, and there they met at traverse with Sir Bors[6] which rode alone. It is no need to ask if they were glad! And so he salewed them, and they yielded to him° honour and good adventure, and everych told other how they had sped. Then said Sir Bors,

  wished him

"It is more than a year and a half that I ne lay° ten times where men dwelled, but in wild forests and in mountains. But God was ever my comfort."

  have not slept

Then rode they a great while till they came to the castle of Corbenic. And when they were entered within, King Pelles knew them. So there was great joy, for he wist well by their coming that they had fulfilled the Sankgreall.[7]

Then Eliazar, King Pelles' son, brought tofore them the broken sword wherewith Joseph was stricken through the thigh.[8] Then Bors set his hand thereto to essay if he might have sowded° it again; but it would not be. Then he took it to Perceval, but he had no more power thereto than he.

  joined

"Now have ye it again," said Sir Perceval unto Sir Galahad, "for an° it be ever achieved by any bodily man, ye must do it."

  if

And then he took the pieces and set them together, and seemed to them as it had never be broken, and as well as it was first forged. And when they within espied that the adventure of the sword was achieved, then they gave the sword to Sir Bors, for it might no better be set,° for he was so good a knight and a worthy man.

  used

And a little before even the sword[9] arose, great and marvellous, and was full of great heat, that many men fell for dread. And anon alight a voice among them and said, "They that ought not to sit at the table of Our Lord Jesu Christ, avoid° hence! For now there shall very° knights be fed."

  withdraw
  true

So they went thence, all save King Pelles and Eliazar, his son, which were holy men, and a maid which was his niece. And so there

---

5. Perceval has followed Galahad's movements. Malory reduces a five-year period in his source to five days and omits the two knights' meeting.
6. Sir Bors has also been wandering in search of the Grail.
7. Pelles is the maimed king and keeper of Corbenic, the

Grail Castle. The past tense looks forward to events not yet achieved.
8. This sword had wounded Joseph of Arimathea; joining its broken halves is part of the Grail quest.
9. Malory misconstrues a phrase meaning "a wind."

abode these three knights and these three; else were no more. And
anon they saw knights all armed come in at the hall door, and did off
their helms and their arms, and said unto Sir Galahad,

"Sir, we have hied° right much for to be with you at this table   *hastened*
where the holy meat shall be departed.°"   *distributed*

Then said he, "Ye be welcome! But of whence be ye?"

So three of them said they were of Gaul, and other three said
they were of Ireland, and other three said they were of Denmark.

And so as they sat thus, there came out a bed of tree° of° a   *wood / from*
chamber, which four gentlewomen brought; and in the bed lay a
good man sick, and had a crown of gold upon his head. And there, in
the midst of the palace, they set him down and went again. Then he
lift up his head and said,

"Sir Galahad, good knight, ye be right welcome, for much have
I desired your coming! For in such pain and in such anguish as I have
no man else° might have suffered long. But now I trust to God the   *no other man*
term is come that my pain shall be allayed, and so I shall pass out of
this world, so as it was promised me long ago."

And therewith a voice said, "There be two among you that be
not in the quest of the Sankgreall, and therefore departeth!"

Then King Pelles and his son departed. And therewithal
beseemed them° that there came an old man and four angels from   *it seemed*
heaven, clothed in likeness of a bishop, and had a cross in his hand.
And these four angels bare him up in a chair and set him down
before the table of silver whereupon the Sankgreall was. And it
seemed that he had in midst of his forehead letters which said: "See
ye here Joseph, the first bishop of Christendom, the same which Our
Lord succoured[1] in the city of Sarras in the spiritual palace." Then
the knights marvelled, for that bishop was dead more than three
hundred year tofore.

"Ah, knights," said he, "marvel not, for I was sometime an
earthly man."

So with that they heard the chamber door open, and there they
saw angels; and two bare candles of wax, and the third bare a towel,[2]
and the fourth a spear which bled marvellously, that the drops fell
within a box which he held with his other hand. And anon they set
the candles upon the table, and the third the towel upon the vessel,
and the fourth the holy spear even° upright upon the vessel.   *straight*

And then the bishop made semblaunt as though he would have
gone to the sacring° of a mass, and then he took an ubblie° which   *consecration /*
was made in likeness of bread. And at the lifting up there came a fig-   *wafer*
ure in likeness of a child, and the visage was as red and as bright as
any fire, and smote himself° into the bread, that all they saw it that *impressed itself*
the bread was formed of a fleshly man. And then he put it into the
holy vessel again, and then he did that longed° to a priest to do mass. *what was right*

And then he went to Sir Galahad and kissed him and bade him
go and kiss his fellows. And so he did anon.

---

1. Joseph of Arimathea was blessed by Christ.   2. In the French source, a veil of samite.

"Now," said he, "the servants of Jesu Christ, ye shall be fed afore this table with sweet meats that never knights yet tasted."

And when he had said he vanished away. And they set them at the table in great dread and made their prayers. Then looked they and saw a Man come out of the holy vessel that had all the signs of the Passion of Jesu Christ, bleeding all openly, and said,

"My knights and my servants and my true children which be come out of deadly life into the spiritual life, I will no longer cover me from you, but ye shall see now a part of my secrets and of my hid things. Now holdeth and receiveth the high order and meat which ye have so much desired."

Then took He himself the holy vessel and came to Sir Galahad. And he kneeled down and received his Saviour. And after him so received all his fellows, and they thought it so sweet that it was marvellous to tell. Then said He to Sir Galahad,

"Son, wotest thou what I hold betwixt my hands?"

"Nay," said he, "but if ye tell me."

"This is," said He, "the holy dish wherein I ate the lamb on Easter Day, and now hast thou seen that thou most desired to see. But yet hast thou not seen it so openly as thou shalt see it in the city of Sarras, in the spiritual palace. Therefore thou must go hence and bear with thee this holy vessel, for this night it shall depart from the realm of Logres, and it shall nevermore be seen here. And knowest thou wherefore? For he° is not served nother worshipped to his right° by them of this land, for they be turned to evil living, and therefore I shall disinherit them of the honour which I have done them. And therefore go ye three to-morn unto the sea, where ye shall find your ship ready, and with you take the sword with the strange girdles,° and no more with you but Sir Perceval and Sir Bors. Also I will that ye take with you of this blood of this spear for to anoint the Maimed King, both his legs and his body, and he shall have his heal."

"Sir," said Galahad, "why shall not these other fellows go with us?"

"For this cause: for right as I depart° my apostles one here and another there, so I will that ye depart. And two of you shall die in my service, and one of you shall come again and tell tidings."

Then gave He them His blessing and vanished away.

And Sir Galahad went anon to the spear which lay upon the table and touched the blood with his fingers, and came after to the maimed knight and anointed his legs and his body. And therwith he clothed him anon, and start upon his feet out of his bed as an whole man, and thanked God that He had healed him. And anon he left the world and yielded himself to a place of religion of white monks,[3] and was a full holy man.

And that same night, about midnight, came a voice among them which said,

_it_

properly

belts

separate

3. The white monks were Cistercians, whose spirituality had some role in Malory's French sources.

"My sons, and not my chief sons,[4] my friends, and not mine enemies, go ye hence where ye hope best to do, and as I bade you do."

"Ah, thanked be Thou, Lord, that Thou wilt whightsauf° to call   *vouchsafe*
us Thy sons! Now may we well prove that we have not lost our
pains."

And anon in all haste they took their harness and departed; but
the three knights of Gaul (one of them hight Claudine, King Clau-
das' son, and the other two were great gentlemen) then prayed° Sir   *asked*
Galahad to everych of them, that an° they come to King Arthur's   *if*
court, "to salew my lord Sir Lancelot, my father and them all of the
Round Table"; and prayed them, an they came on that party,° not to   *to that region*
forget it.

Right so departed Sir Galahad, and Sir Perceval and Sir Bors
with him, and so they rode three days. And then they came to a
rivage° and found the ship whereof the tale speaketh of tofore. And   *shore*
when they came to the board° they found in the midst of the bed the   *on board*
table of silver which they had left with the Maimed King, and the
Sankgreall which was covered with red samite.° Then were they glad   *silk*
to have such things in their fellowship; and so they entered and
made great reverence thereto, and Sir Galahad fell on his knees and
prayed long time to Our Lord, that at what time he asked he might
pass out of this world. And so long he prayed till a voice said,

"Sir Galahad, thou shalt have thy request, and when thou asketh the death of thy body thou shalt have it, and then shalt thou
have the life of thy soul."

Then Sir Perceval heard him a little, and prayed him of° fellow-   *for the sake of*
ship that was between them wherefore he asked such things.

"Sir, that shall I tell you," said Sir Galahad. "This other day,
when we saw a part of the adventures of the Sankgreall, I was in such
a joy of heart that I trow° never man was that was earthly. And   *believe*
therefore I wot° well, when my body is dead, my soul shall be in great   *know*
joy to see the Blessed Trinity every day, and the majesty of Our Lord,
Jesu Christ."

And so long were they in the ship that they said to Galahad,

"Sir, in this bed ye ought to lie, for so saith the letters.°"   *writings*

And so he laid him down, and slept a great while. And when he
awaked he looked tofore him and saw the city of Sarras. And as they
would have landed they saw the ship wherein Sir Perceval had put
his sister in.

"Truly," said Sir Perceval, "in the name of God, well hath my
sister holden us covenant."[5]

Then they took out of the ship the table of silver, and he took it
to Sir Perceval and to Sir Bors to go tofore, and Sir Galahad came
behind, and right so they went into the city. And at the gate of the
city they saw an old man crooked, and anon Sir Galahad called him
and bade him help "to bear this heavy thing."

---

4. A confusing phrase, perhaps in error for "stepsons."
5. Kept her promise to us. In an earlier episode Perceval's
sister died after giving a basin of her blood to heal a leper
woman.

"Truly," said the old man, "it is ten year ago that I might not go but with crutches."

"Care thou not," said Galahad, "and arise up and show thy good will!"

And so he essayed, and found himself as whole as ever he was. Then ran he to the table and took one part against° Galahad. *beside*

Anon arose there a great noise in the city that a cripple was made whole by knights marvellous that entered into the city. Then anon after the three knights went to the water and brought up into the palace Sir Perceval's sister, and buried her as richly as them ought a king's daughter.

And when the king of that country knew that and saw that fellowship (whose name was Estorause), he asked them of whence they were, and what thing it was that they had brought upon the table of silver. And they told him the truth of the Sankgreall, and the power which God hath set there.

Then this king was a tyrant, and was come of the line of paynims,° and took them and put them in prison in a deep hole. But *pagans* as soon as they were there Our Lord sent them the Sankgreall, through whose grace they were alway fulfilled° while that they were *fed* in prison.

So at the year's end it befell that this king lay sick and felt that he should die. Then he sent for the three knights, and they came afore him, and he cried them mercy of that he had done to them, and they forgave it him goodly, and he died anon.

When the king was dead all the city stood dismayed and wist° not *knew* who might be their king. Right so as they were in council there came a voice among them, and made them choose the youngest knight of three to be their king, "for he shall well maintain you and all yours."

So they made Sir Galahad king by all the assent of the whole city, and else they would have slain him. And when he was come to behold his land he let make° above the table of silver a chest of gold *had made* and of precious stones that covered the holy vessel, and every day early the three knights would come before it and make their prayers.

Now at the year's end, and the self Sunday after that Sir Galahad had borne the crown of gold, he arose up early and his fellows, and came to the palace, and saw tofore them the holy vessel and a man kneeling on his knees in likeness of a bishop that had about him a great fellowship of angels, as it had been Jesu Christ himself. And then he arose and began a mass of Our Lady. And so he came to the sacring, and anon made an end. He called Sir Galahad unto him and said,

"Come forth, the servant of Jesu Christ, and thou shalt see that thou hast much desired to see."

And then he began to tremble right hard when the deadly° flesh *mortal* began to behold the spiritual things. Then he held up his hands toward heaven and said,

"Lord, I thank Thee, for now I see that that hath been my desire many a day. Now, my Blessed Lord, I would not live in this wretched world no longer, if it might please Thee, Lord."

And therewith the good man took Our Lord's Body[6] betwixt his hands, proffered it to Sir Galahad, and he received it right gladly and meekly.

"Now wotest thou what I am?" said the good man.

"Nay, Sir," said Sir Galahad.

"I am Joseph, the son of Joseph of Arimathea, which Our Lord hath sent to thee to bear thee fellowship. And wotest thou wherefore He hath sent me more than any other? For thou hast resembled me in two things: that thou hast seen, that is the marvels of the Sankgreall, and for thou hast been a clean maiden° as I have been and am."

chaste virgin

And when he had said these words Sir Galahad went to Sir Perceval and kissed him and commended him to God. And so he went to Sir Bors and kissed him and commended him to God, and said,

"My fair lord, salew me° unto my lord Sir Lancelot, my father, and as soon as ye see him bid him remember of this world unstable."

give my greeting

And therewith he kneeled down tofore the table and made his prayers. And so suddenly departed his soul to Jesu Christ, and a great multitude of angels bare it up to heaven, even in the sight of his two fellows.

Also these two knights saw come from heaven an hand, but they saw not the body, and so it came right to the vessel, and took it, and the spear, and so bare it up to heaven. And sithen° was there never man so hardy to say that he had seen the Sankgreall.

since then

So when Sir Perceval and Sir Bors saw Sir Galahad dead they made as much sorrow as ever did men. And if they had not been good men they might lightly° have fallen in despair. And so people of the country and city, they were right heavy. But so he was buried, and soon as he was buried Sir Perceval yielded him to an hermitage out of the city and took religious clothing. And Sir Bors was alway with him, but he changed never his secular clothing, for that he purposed him to go again into the realm of Logres.

easily

Thus a year and two months lived Sir Perceval in the hermitage a full holy life, and then passed out of the world. Then Sir Bors let bury him by[7] his sister and by Sir Galahad in the spiritualities.°

consecrated ground

So when Bors saw that he was in so far° countries as in the parts of Babylon, he departed from the city of Sarras and armed him and came to the sea, and entered into a ship. And so it befell him, by good adventure, he came unto the realm of Logres, and so he rode a pace° till he came to Camelot where the king was.

remote

swiftly

And then was there made great joy of him in all the court, for they weened all he had been lost forasmuch as he had been so long out of the country. And when they had eaten, the king made great clerks to come before him, for cause they should chronicle of° the high adventures of the good knights. So when Sir Bors had told him of the high adventures of the Sankgreall such as had befallen him and his three fellows, which were Sir Lancelot, Perceval, Sir

record

---

6. The wafer of the Eucharist.   7. Had him buried next to.

Galahad and himself, then Sir Lancelot told the adventures of the Sankgreall that he had seen. All this was made in great books and put up in almeries° at Salisbury.   *libraries*

And anon Sir Bors said to Sir Lancelot,

"Sir Galahad, your own son, salewed you by me, and after you my lord King Arthur and all the whole court, and so did Sir Perceval. For I buried them with both mine own hands in the city of Sarras. Also, Sir Lancelot, Sir Galahad prayed you to remember of this unsiker° world, as ye behight him° when ye were together more than half a year."   *uncertain /*
                                                                                           promised

"This is true," said Sir Lancelot; "now I trust to God his prayer shall avail me."

Then Sir Lancelot took Sir Bors in his arms and said,

"Cousin, ye are right welcome to me! For all that ever I may do for you and for yours, ye shall find my poor body ready at all times while the spirit is in it, and that I promise you faithfully, and never to fail. And wit ye well, gentle cousin Sir Bors, ye and I shall never depart in sunder while our lives may last."

"Sir," said he, "as ye will, so will I."

THUS ENDETH THE TALE OF THE SANKGREALL THAT WAS BRIEFLY
DRAWN OUT OF FRENCH, WHICH IS A TALE CHRONICLED FOR ONE OF
THE TRUEST AND OF THE HOLIEST THAT IS IN THIS WORLD, BY SIR
THOMAS MALEORRÉ, KNIGHT.

O BLESSED JESU HELP HIM THROUGH HIS MIGHT! AMEN.

Geoffrey Chaucer
c. 1340–1400

On Easter weekend 1300, the Italian poet Dante Alighieri had a vision in which he descended to hell, climbed painfully through purgatory, and then attained a transcendent experience of paradise. He tells his tale in his visionary, passionately judgmental *Divine Comedy*. One hundred years later, on 25 October 1400, Geoffrey Chaucer—the least judgmental of poets—died quietly in his house at the outskirts of London. By a nice accident of history, these two great writers bracket the last great century of the Middle Ages.

Of Chaucer's own life our information is abundant but often frustrating. Many documents record the important and sensitive posts he held in government, but there are only faint hints of his career as a poet. During his lifetime, he was frequently in France and made at least two trips to Italy, which proved crucial for his own growth as a writer and indeed for the history of English literature. He also served under three kings: the aging Edward III, his brilliant and sometimes tyrannical grandson Richard II, and—at the very end of his life—Richard's usurper Henry IV.

Chaucer was born into a rising mercantile family, part of the growing bourgeois class that brought so much wealth to England even while it disrupted medieval theories of social order. Chaucer's family fit nowhere easily in the old model of the three estates: those who pray (the clergy), those who fight (the aristocracy), and those who work the land (the peasants). Yet like many of their class, they aspired to a role among the aristocracy, and in fact Chaucer's parents

7. Here lies Arthur, once and future king.

succeeded in holding minor court positions. Chaucer himself became a major player in the cultural and bureaucratic life of the court, and Thomas Chaucer (who was very probably his son) was ultimately knighted.

Geoffrey was superbly but typically educated. He probably went to one of London's fine grammar schools, and as a young man he very likely followed a gentlemanly study of law at one of the Inns of Court. He shows signs of knowing and appreciating the topics debated in the university life of his time. His poems reflect a vast reading in classical Latin, French, and Italian (of which he was among the earliest English readers). *The Parliament of Fowls*, for instance, reveals the influence not only of French court poetry but also of Dante's *Divine Comedy*; and the frame-story structure of *The Canterbury Tales* may have been inspired by Boccaccio's *Decameron*.

By 1366 Chaucer had married Philippa de Roet, a minor Flemish noblewoman, and a considerable step up the social hierarchy. Her sister later became the mistress and ultimately the wife of Chaucer's great patron, John of Gaunt. Thus, when Gaunt's son Henry Boling-broke seized the throne from Richard II, the elderly Geoffrey Chaucer found himself a distant in-law of his king. Chaucer had been associated with Richard II and suffered reverses when Richard's power was restricted by the magnates. But he was enough of a cultural figure that Henry IV continued (perhaps with some prompting) the old man's royal annuities. Whatever Western literature owes to Chaucer (and its debts are profound), in his own life his writing made a place in the world for him and his heirs.

Despite his lifelong productivity as a writer, and despite the slightly obtuse narrative voice he consistently uses, Geoffrey Chaucer was a canny and ambitious player in the world of his time. He was a soldier, courtier, diplomat, and government official in a wide range of jobs. These included controller of the customs on wool and other animal products, a lucrative post, and later controller of the Petty Custom that taxed wine and other goods. Chaucer's frequent work overseas extended his contacts with French and Italian literature. He was ward of estates for several minors, a job that also benefited the guardian. Chaucer began to accumulate property in Kent, where he served as justice of the peace (an important judicial post) and then Member of Parliament in the mid-1380s.

Despite the comfortable worldly progress suggested by such activities, these were troubled years in the nation and in Chaucer's private life. Chaucer's personal fortunes were affected by the frequent struggles between King Richard and his magnates over control of the government. From another direction there exploded the Rising of 1381, rocking all of English society. The year before that, Chaucer had been accused of *raptus* by Cecilia Chaumpaigne, daughter of a baker in London. A great deal of nervous scholarship has been exercised over this case, but it becomes increasingly clear that in legal language *raptus* meant some form of rape. The case was settled, and there are signs of efforts to hush it up at quite high levels of government. The somewhat bland and bumbling quality of Chaucer's narrative persona would probably have seemed more artificially constructed and more ironic to Chaucer's contemporaries than it does at first glance today.

Chaucer was a Janus-faced poet, truly innovative at the levels of language and theme yet deeply involved with literary and intellectual styles that stretched back to Latin antiquity and twelfth- and thirteenth-century France. His early poems—the dream visions such as *The Parliament of Fowls* and the tragic romance *Troilus and Criseyde*—derive from essentially medieval genres and continental traditions: the French poets Deschamps and Machaut and the Italians Dante, Boccaccio, and Petrarch. Yet in his reliance on the English vernacular, Chaucer was in a vanguard generation along with the *Gawain* poet and William Langland. English was indeed gaining importance in other parts of this world, such as in Parliament, in some areas of education, and in the "Wycliffite" translations of the Bible. Chaucer's own exclusive use of English was particularly ambitious, though, for a poet whose patronage came from the court of the francophile Richard II.

The major work of Chaucer's maturity, *The Canterbury Tales*, founds an indisputably English tradition. While he still uses the craft and allusions he learned from his continental masters, he also experiments with the subject matter of everyday English life and the vocabularies of the newly valorized English vernacular. Moreover, starting with traditional forms and largely traditional models of society and the cosmos, Chaucer found spaces for new and sometimes

Portrait of Geoffrey the Canterbury Pilgrim, from the Ellesmere manuscript of The Canterbury Tales, early 15th century. This carefully produced and beautifully decorated manuscript reflects the speed with which Chaucer's works took on wide cultural prestige and were enshrined in luxury books for a wealthy, probably aristocratic audience.

disruptive perspectives, especially those of women and the rising mercantile class into which he had been born. Though always a court poet, Chaucer increasingly wrote in ways that reflected both the richness and the uncertainties of his entire social world. The Tales include a Knight who could have stepped from a twelfth-century heroic poem, yet they also offer the spectacle of the Knight's caste being aped, almost parodied, and virtually shouted down by a sword-carrying peasant, the Miller. And the entire notion of old writings as sources of authoritative wisdom is powerfully challenged by the illiterate or only minimally literate Wife of Bath.

The Canterbury Tales also differ from the work of many of Chaucer's continental predecessors in their deep hesitation to cast straightforward judgment, either socially or spiritually. Here we may return to Chaucer's connection with Dante. Dante's Divine Comedy presented mortal life as a pilgrimage and an overt test in stable dogma, a journey along a dangerous road toward certain damnation or the reward of the heavenly Jerusalem. The Canterbury Tales are literally about a pilgrimage, and Chaucer presents the road as beautiful and fascinating in its own right. The greatness of the poem lies in its exploration of the variousness of the journey and that journey's reflection of a world pressured by spiritual and moral fractures. In depicting a mixed company of English men and women traveling England's most famous pilgrimage route and telling one another stories, Chaucer suggests not only the spiritual meaning of humankind's earthly pilgrimage, but also its overflowing beauties and attractions as well as the evils and temptations that lie along the way. The vision of the serious future, the day of judgment, is constantly attended in The Canterbury Tales by the troubling yet hilarious and distracting present.

Unlike Dante, however, Chaucer almost never takes it upon himself to judge, at least not openly. He records his characters with dizzying immediacy, but he never tells his reader quite what to think of them, leaving the gaps for us as readers to fill. He does end the Tales with a kind of sermon, the Parson's long prose treatise on the Christian vices and virtues. That coda by no means erases the humor and seriousness, sentiment and ribaldry, high spiritual love and unmasked carnal desire, profound religious belief and squalid clerical corruption that have been encountered along the way. Indeed, Chaucer's genius is to transmute the disorder of his world almost into an aesthetic of plenitude: "foyson" in Middle English. His poem overflows constantly with rich detail, from exquisite visions to squabbling pilgrims. His language overflows with its multiple vocabularies, Anglo-Saxon, Latin, and French. And finally, the tales themselves are notable for the range of genres used by the pilgrims: the Miller's bawdy fabliau, the Wife of Bath's romance, the Franklin's story of courtly love and clerkly magic, the Nun's Priest's beast fable, the Pardoner's hypocritical cautionary tale, as well as the Parson's sermon. *The Canterbury Tales* are an anthology embracing almost every important literary type of Chaucer's day.

None of this celebratory richness, however, fully masks the unresolved social and spiritual tensions that underlie the *Tales*. The notion of spiritual pilgrimage is deeply challenged by the very density of characterization and worldly detail that so enlivens the work. And the model of a competitive game, which provides the fictional pretext for the tales themselves, is only one version of what the critic Peggy Knapp has called Chaucer's "social contest" in the work as a whole. The traditional estates such as knight and peasant openly clash during the pilgrimage, and the estate of the clergy is more widely represented by its corrupt than by its virtuous members. Women, merchants, common landowners, and others from outside the traditional three estates bulk large in the tales. And their stories cast doubt upon such fundamental religious institutions as penance and such social institutions as marriage. For all their pleasures, *The Canterbury Tales* have survived, in part, because they are so riven by challenge and doubt.

CHAUCER'S MIDDLE ENGLISH

Grammar

The English of Chaucer's London, and particularly the English of government bureaucracy, became the source for the more standardized vernacular that emerged in the era of print at the close of the Middle Ages. As a result, Chaucer's English is easier to understand today than the dialect of many of his great contemporaries such as the *Gawain* poet, who worked far to the north. The text that follows preserves Chaucer's language, with some spellings slightly modernized and regularized by its editor, E. Talbot Donaldson. To help beginners, we include David Wright's fine translation of the General Prologue on facing pages with the original text.

The marginal glosses in the readings are intended to help the nonspecialist reader through Chaucer's language without elaborate prior study. It will be helpful, though, to explain a few key differences from Modern English.

Nouns: The possessive is sometimes formed without a final *-s*.

Pronouns: Readers will recognize the archaic *thou, thine, thee* of second-person singular, and *ye* of the plural. Occasional confusion can arise from the form *hir*, which can mean "her" or "their." *Hem* is Chaucer's spelling for "them," and *tho* for "those." Chaucer uses *who* to mean "whoever."

Adverbs: Formed, as today, with *-ly*, but also with *-liche*. Sometimes an adverb is unchanged from its adjective form: *fairly, fairliche, faire* can all be adverbs.

Verbs: Second-person singular is formed with *-est* (*thou lovest*, past tense *thou lovedest*); third-person singular often with *-eth* (*he loveth*); plurals often with *-n* (*we loven*); and infinitive with *-n* (*loven*).

Strong verbs/impersonal verbs: Middle English has many "strong verbs," which form the past and perfect by changing a vowel in their stem; these are usually recognizable by analogy with surviving forms in Modern English (*go, went, gone; sing, sang, sung;* etc.). Middle English also often uses "impersonal verbs" (*liketh*, "it pleases"; *as me thinketh*, "as I think"), in which case sometimes no obvious subject noun or pronoun occurs.

Pronunciation

A few guidelines will help approximate the sound of Chaucer's English and the richness of his versification. For fuller discussion, consult sources listed in the bibliography.

Pronounce all consonants: *knight* is "k/neecht" with a guttural *ch*, not "nite"; *gnaw* is "g/naw." Middle English consonants preserve many of the sounds of the language's Germanic roots: guttural *gh*; sounded *l* and *w* in words like *folk* or *write*. (Exceptions occur in some words that derive from French, like *honour* whose *h* is silent.)

Final *-e* was sounded in early Middle English. Such pronunciation was becoming archaic by Chaucer's time, but was available to aid meter in the stylized context of poetry.

The distinction between short and long vowels was greater in Middle English than today. Middle English short vowels have mostly remained short in Modern English, with some shift in pronunciation: short *a* sounds like the *o* in *hot*, short *o* like a quick version of the *aw* in *law*, short *u* like the *u* in *full*.

Long vowels in Middle English (here usually indicated by doubling, when vowel length is unclear by analogy to modern spelling) are close to long vowels in modern Romance languages. The chart shows some differences in Middle English long vowels.

Middle English	pronounced as in	Modern English
a (as in *name*)		*father*
open *e* (*deel*)		*swear, bread*
close *e* (*sweet*)		*fame*
i (*whit*)		*feet*
open *o* (*holy*)		*law*
close *o* (*roote*)		*note*
u (as in *town*, *aboute*)		*root*
u (*vertu*)		*few*

Open and close long vowels are a challenge for modern readers. Generally, open long *e* in Middle English (*deel*) has become Modern English spelling with *ea* (*deal*); close long *e* (*sweet*) has become Modern English spelling with *ee* (*sweet*). Open long *o* in Middle English has come to be pronounced as in *note*; close long *o* in Middle English has come to be pronounced *root*. This latter case illustrates the idea of "vowel shift" across the centuries, in which some long vowels have moved forward in the throat and palate.

Versification

All of Chaucer's poetry presented here is in a loosely iambic pentameter line, which Chaucer was greatly responsible for bringing into prominence in England. He is a fluid versifier, though, and often shifts stress, producing metrical effects that have come to be called trochees and spondees. Final *-e* is often pronounced within lines to provide an unstressed syllable and is typically pronounced at the end of each line. Yet final *-e* may also elide with a following word that begins with a vowel. The following lines from *The Nun's Priest's Tale* have a proposed scansion, but the reader will see that alternate scansions are possible at several places.

> "Avoi," quod she, "fy on you, hertelees!
> Allas," quod she, "for by that God above,
> Now han ye lost myn herte and al my love!
> I can nat love a coward, by my faith.

For certes, what so any womman saith,
We alle desiren, if it mighte be,
To han housbondes hardy, wise, and free,
And secree, and no nigard, ne no fool,
Ne him that is agast of every tool,
Ne noon avauntour. By that God above,
How dorste ye sayn for shame unto youre love
That any thing mighte make you aferd?
Have ye no mannes herte and han a beerd?

from THE CANTERBURY TALES

THE GENERAL PROLOGUE   The twenty-nine "sondry folke" of the Canterbury company gather at the Tabard Inn, ostensibly with the pious intent of making a pilgrimage to England's holiest shrine, the tomb of Saint Thomas Becket at Canterbury. From the start in the raffish and worldly London suburb of Southwark, though, the pilgrims' attentions and energy veer wildly between the sacred and the profane. The mild story-telling competition proposed by the Host also slides swiftly into a contest among social classes. Set in Chaucer's own time and place, *The Canterbury Tales* reflect both the dynamism and the uncertainties of a society still nostalgic for archaic models of church and state, yet riven by such crises as plague, economic disruption, and the new claims of peasants and mercantile bourgeoisie—claims expressed and repressed most violently in the recent Rising, or "Peasants' Revolt," of 1381.

Chaucer's *Prologue* has roots in the genre known as "estates satire." Such writings criticized the failure of the members of the three traditional "estates" of medieval society—the aristocracy, the clergy, and the commons—to fulfill their ordained function of fighting, praying, and working the land, respectively. From the beginning the pilgrims' portraits are couched in language fraught with class connotations. The Knight, the idealized (if archaic) representative of the aristocracy, is called *gentil* (that is, "noble, aristocratic") and is said never to have uttered any *vileynye*—speech characteristic of peasants or *villeyns*. Many of the pilgrims in the other two estates display aristocratic manners, among the clergy notably the Prioress, with her "cheere of court," and the Monk, who lives like a country gentleman, hunting with greyhounds and a stable full of fine horses. Both pilgrims contrast with the ideal of their estate, the Parson, who, though *"povre"* is "rich" in holy works.

The commons are traditionally the last of the "three estates," yet they bulk largest in the Canterbury company and fit least well in that model of social order. There are old-fashioned laborers on the pilgrimage, but many more characters from the emerging and disruptive world of small industry and commerce. They are commoners, but have ambitions that lead them both to envy and to mock the powers held by their aristocratic and clerical companions.

Among the group that traditionally comprised the commons, the peasants, Chaucer singles out one ideal, the Plowman, who is, significantly, the Parson's brother. He is characterized as a diligent *swynkere* (worker), in implicit contrast to the lazy peasants castigated in estates satire. Most of the rest of the commons, however, such as the Miller and the Cook, are presented as "churlish," and their tales have a coarse vigor that Chaucer clearly relishes even as he disassociates himself from their vulgarity.

In theory, women were treated as a separate category, defined by their sexual nature and marital role rather than by their class. Nevertheless, the Prioress and the Wife of Bath are both satirized as much for their social ambition as for the failings of their gender. The Prioress prides herself on her courtesy, and the commoner Wife of Bath aspires to the same social recognition as the guildsmen's upwardly mobile wives. Her portrait is complex, however, for she is simultaneously satirized and admired for challenging the expected roles of women at the time, with her economic independence (as a rich widow and a cloth-maker) and her resultant freedom to travel. The narrator's suggestion that she goes on many pilgrimages in order to find a sixth husband bears out the stereotype of unbridled female sexuality familiar from estates satire, as her fondness of talking and laughing bears out the stereotype of female garrulousness.

Chaucer's satire is pointed but also exceptionally subtle, largely because of the irony achieved through his use of the narrator, seemingly naive and a little dense. His deadpan narration leaves the readers themselves to supply the judgment.

from THE CANTERBURY TALES

The General Prologue[1]

Whan that April with his showres soote°   *sweet*
The droughte of March hath perced to the roote,
And bathed every veine in swich licour,°   *such liquid*
Of which vertu° engendred is the flowr;   *by whose strength*
5   Whan Zephyrus[2] eek° with his sweete breeth   *also*
Inspired hath in every holt and heeth°   *wood and field*
The tendre croppes, and the yonge sonne
Hath in the Ram° his halve cours yronne,   *the zodiac sign Aries*
And smale fowles maken melodye
10 That sleepen al the night with open yë°—   *eye*
So priketh hem Nature in hir corages°—   *hearts, spirits*
Thanne longen folk to goon on pilgrimages,
And palmeres[3] for to seeken straunge strondes°   *shores*
To ferne halwes,° couthe° in sondry londes;   *far-off shrines / known*
15 And specially from every shires ende
Of Engelond to Canterbury they wende,°   *go*
The holy blisful martyr[4] for to seeke
That hem hath holpen° whan that they were seke.°   *helped / sick*
    Bifel that in that seson on a day,
20 In Southwerk[5] at the Tabard as I lay,
Redy to wenden on my pilgrimage
To Canterbury with ful devout corage,

---

1. Each page of The General Prologue in Middle English is followed by its modern English translation by David Wright on the facing page. Because the number of verse lines in the modern translation does not always match the Middle English precisely—for example, Wright translates Chaucer's first 36 lines of The General Prologue in 35 lines—no line numbers have been included in Wright's translation.
2. In Roman mythology Zephyrus was the demigod of the west wind, herald of warmer weather.
3. Pilgrims who had traveled to the Holy Land.

4. St. Thomas Becket, murdered in Canterbury Cathedral in 1170.
5. Southwark, a suburb of London south of the Thames and the traditional starting point for the pilgrimage to Canterbury in Kent, was notorious as a center of gambling and prostitution. The Tabard Inn was an actual public house at the time, named for the shape of its sign which resembled the coarse, sleeveless outer garment worn by members of the lower classes, monks, and foot soldiers alike.

The General Prologue

When the sweet showers of April have pierced
The drought of March, and pierced it to the root,
And every vein is bathed in that moisture
Whose quickening force will engender the flower;
And when the west wind too with its sweet breath
Has given life in every wood and field
To tender shoots, and when the stripling sun
Has run his half-course in Aries, the Ram,
And when small birds are making melodies,
That sleep all the night long with open eyes,
(Nature so prompts them, and encourages);
Then people long to go on pilgrimages.
And palmers to take ship for foreign shores,
And distant shrines, famous in different lands;
And most especially, from all the shires
Of England, to Canterbury they come,
The holy blessed martyr there to seek,
Who gave his help to them when they were sick.

   It happened at this season, that one day
In Southwark at the Tabard where I stayed
Ready to set out on my pilgrimage
To Canterbury, and pay devout homage,

At night was come into that hostelrye
Wel nine and twenty in a compaignye
25   Of sondry folk, by aventure yfalle
In felaweshipe, and pilgrimes were they alle
That toward Canterbury wolden ride.
The chambres° and the stables weren wide,   guestrooms
And wel we weren esed° at the beste.   accommodated
30   And shortly, whan the sonne was to reste,
So hadde I spoken with hem everichoon
That I was of hir felaweshipe anoon,
And made forward° erly for to rise,   agreed
To take oure way ther as I you devise.°   relate
35   But nathelees, whil I have time and space,°   opportunity
Er that I ferther in this tale pace,°   proceed
Me thinketh it accordant to resoun
To telle you al the condicioun°   circumstances
Of eech of hem, so as it seemed me,
40   And whiche they were, and of what degree,°   social status
And eek in what array that they were inne:
And at a knight thanne wol I first biginne.
A Knight ther was, and that a worthy man,
That fro the time that he first bigan
45   To riden out, he loved chivalrye,
Trouthe and honour, freedom and curteisye.[6]
Ful worthy was he in his lordes werre,°   war
And therto hadde he riden, no man ferre,°   farther
As wel in Cristendom as hethenesse,°   heathen lands
50   And evere honoured for his worthinesse.
At Alisandre[7] he was whan it was wonne;
Ful ofte time he hadde the boord bigonne[8]
Aboven alle nacions in Pruce;
In Lettou had he reised,° and in Ruce,   campaigned
55   No Cristen man so ofte of his degree;
In Gernade at the sege eek hadde he be
Of Algezir, and riden in Belmarye;
At Lyeis was he, and at Satalye,
Whan they were wonne; and in the Grete See
60   At many a noble arivee° hadde he be.   military landing
At mortal batailes[9] hadde he been fifteene,
And foughten for oure faith at Tramissene
In listes° thries, and ay° slain his fo.   duels / always
This ilke° worthy Knight hadde been also   same
65   Somtime with the lord of Palatye

---

6. Fidelity and good reputation, generosity, and courtliness.
7. The place-names Chaucer lists over the next 15 lines were primarily associated with 14th-century Crusades against both Muslims and Eastern Orthodox Christians. Alisandre: Alexandria in Egypt; Pruce: Prussia; Lettou: Lithuania; Ruce: Russia; Gernade and Algezir: Granada and Algeciras in Spain; Belmarye: Ben-Marin near Morocco; Lyeis: Ayash in Turkey; Satalye: Atalia in Turkey; Grete See: Mediterranean; Tramissene: Tlemcen near Morocco; Palatye: Balat in Turkey.
8. Held the place of honor at feasts.
9. Tournaments waged to the death.

There came at nightfall to the hostelry
Some nine-and-twenty in a company,
Folk of all kinds, met in accidental
Companionship, for they were pilgrims all;
It was to Canterbury that they rode.
The bedrooms and the stables were good-sized,
The comforts offered us were of the best.
And by the time the sun had gone to rest
I'd talked with everyone, and soon became
One of their company, and promised them
To rise at dawn next day to take the road
For the journey I am telling you about.

But, before I go further with this tale,
And while I can, it seems reasonable
That I should let you have a full description
Of each of them, their sort and condition,
At any rate as they appeared to me;
Tell who they were, their status and profession,
What they looked like, what kind of clothes they dressed in;
And with a knight, then, I shall first begin.

There was a knight, a reputable man,
Who from the moment that he first began
Campaigning, had cherished the profession
Of arms; he also prized trustworthiness,
Liberality, fame, and courteousness.
In the king's service he'd fought valiantly,
And travelled far; no man as far as he
In Christian and in heathen lands as well,
And ever honoured for his ability.

He was at Alexandria when it fell,
Often he took the highest place at table
Over the other foreign knights in Prussia;
He'd raided in Lithuania and Russia,
No Christian of his rank fought there more often.
Also he'd been in Granada, at the siege
Of Algeciras; forayed in Benmarin;
At Ayas and Adalia he had been
When they were taken; and with the great hosts
Freebooting on the Mediterranean coasts;

Fought fifteen mortal combats; thrice as champion
In tournaments, he at Tramassene
Fought for our faith, and each time killed his man.

This worthy knight had also, for a time,
Taken service in Palatia for the Bey,

Again° another hethen in Turkye;   *against*
And everemore he hadde a soverein pris.°   *reputation*
And though that he were worthy, he was wis,
And of his port° as meeke as is a maide.   *bearing*
70   He nevere yit no vilainye° ne saide   *rudeness*
In al his lif unto no manere wight:°   *no kind of man*
He was a verray,° parfit,° gentil° knight.   *true / perfect / noble*
But for to tellen you of his array,°   *equipment*
His hors were goode, but he was nat gay.°   *gaily attired*
75   Of fustian° he wered a gipoun°   *coarse cloth / tunic*
Al bismotered with his haubergeoun,[1]
For he was late come from his viage,°   *expedition*
And wente for to doon his pilgrimage.
     With him ther was his sone, a yong Squier,
80   A lovere and a lusty bacheler,[2]
With lokkes crulle° as they were laid in presse.   *curled*
Of twenty yeer of age he was, I gesse.
Of his stature he was of evene° lengthe,   *average*
And wonderly delivere,° and of greet strengthe.   *agile*
85   And he hadde been som time in chivachye°   *cavalry expedition*
In Flandres, in Artois, and Picardye,[3]
And born him wel as of so litel space,°   *time*
In hope to stonden in his lady grace.°   *lady's favor*
     Embrouded° was he as it were a mede,°   *embroidered / meadow*
90   Al ful of fresshe flowres, white and rede;
Singing he was, or floiting,° al the day: *playing the flute*
He was as fressh as is the month of May.
Short was his gowne, with sleeves longe and wide.
Wel coude he sitte on hors, and faire ride;
95   He coude songes make, and wel endite,°   *compose*
Juste° and eek daunce, and wel portraye° and write.   *joust / draw*
So hote he loved that by nightertale°   *nighttime*
He slepte namore than dooth a nightingale.
Curteis he was, lowely,° and servisable,°   *humble / attentive*
100 And carf° biforn his fader° at the table   *carved / father*
     A Yeman[4] hadde he° and servants namo   *i.e., the Knight*
At that time, for him liste° ride so;   *he liked*
And he was clad in cote and hood of greene.
A sheef of pecok arwes,° bright and keene,   *peacock arrows*
105 Under his belt he bar ful thriftily;
Wel coude he dresse° his takel° yemanly: *arrange / gear*
His arwes drouped nought with fetheres lowe.
And in his hand he bar a mighty bowe.
A not-heed° hadde he with a brown visage.°   *short haircut / face*

---

1. Rust-stained from his coat of mail.
2. An unmarried and unpropertied younger knight.
3. Regions in the north of France and in what is now Belgium, where the English and the French were fighting

out the Hundred Years' War.
4. A yeoman was a freeborn servant (not a peasant), who looked after the affairs of the gentry. This particular yeoman was a forester and gamekeeper for the Knight.

Against another heathen in Turkey;
And almost beyond price was his prestige.
Though eminent, he was prudent and sage,
And in his bearing mild as any maid.
He'd never been foul-spoken in his life
To any kind of man; he was indeed
The very pattern of a noble knight.
But as for his appearance and outfit,
He had good horses, yet was far from smart.
He wore a tunic made of coarse thick stuff,
Marked by his chainmail, all begrimed with rust,
Having just returned from an expedition,
And on his pilgrimage of thanksgiving.

    With him there was his son, a young squire,
A lively knight-apprentice, and a lover,
With hair as curly as if newly waved;
I took him to be twenty years of age.
In stature he was of an average length,
Wonderfully athletic, and of great strength.
He'd taken part in cavalry forays
In Flanders, in Artois, and Picardy,
With credit, though no more than a novice,
Hoping to stand well in his lady's eyes.

    His clothes were all embroidered like a field
Full of the freshest flowers, white and red.
He sang, or played the flute, the livelong day,
And he was fresher than the month of May.
Short was his gown, with sleeves cut long and wide.
He'd a good seat on horseback, and could ride,
Make music too, and songs to go with it;
Could joust and dance, and also draw and write.
So burningly he loved, that come nightfall
He'd sleep no more than any nightingale.
Polite, modest, willing to serve, and able,
He carved before his father at their table.

    The knight had just one servant, a yeoman,
For so he wished to ride, on this occasion.
The man was clad in coat and hood of green.
He carried under his belt, handily,
For he looked to his gear in yeoman fashion,
A sheaf of peacock arrows, sharp and shining,
Not liable to fall short from poor feathering;
And in his hand he bore a mighty bow.
He had a cropped head, and his face was brown;

110	Of wodecraft° wel coude he al the usage.	*forestry*
	Upon his arm he bar a gay bracer,°	*archer's armguard*
	And by his side a swerd and a bokeler,°	*small shield*
	And on that other side a gay daggere,	
	Harneised wel and sharp as point of spere;	
115	A Cristophre⁵ on his brest of silver sheene;	
	An horn he bar, the baudrik° was of greene.	*shoulder strap*
	A forster° was he soothly,° as I gesse.	*gamekeeper / truly*
	Ther was also a Nonne, a Prioresse,	
	That of hir smiling was ful simple and coy.°	*quiet, shy*
120	Hir gretteste ooth was but by Sainte Loy!⁶	
	And she was cleped° Madame Eglantine.°	*called / Brier-rose*
	Ful wel she soong the service divine,	
	Entuned in hir nose ful semely;°	*becomingly*
	And Frenssh she spak ful faire and fetisly,°	*elegantly*
125	After the scole of Stratford at the Bowe⁷	
	For Frenssh of Paris was to hire unknowe.	
	At mete° wel ytaught was she withalle:	*meals*
	She leet no morsel from hir lippes falle,	
	Ne wette hir fingres in hir sauce deepe;	
130	Wel coude she carye a morsel, and wel keepe°	*safeguard*
	That no drope ne fille upon hir brest.	
	In curteisye was set ful muchel hir lest.°	*her great pleasure*
	Hir over-lippe° wiped she so clene	*upper lip*
	That in hir coppe ther was no ferthing⁸ seene	
135	Of grece,° whan she dronken hadde hir draughte;	*grease*
	Ful semely after hir mete she raughte.°	*reached for her food*
	And sikerly° she was of greet disport,°	*certainly / good cheer*
	And ful plesant, and amiable of port,	
	And pained hire to countrefete cheere°	*appearance*
140	Of court, and to been estatlich° of manere,	*stately*
	And to been holden digne° of reverence.	*worthy*
	But, for to speken of hir conscience,	
	She was so charitable and so pitous	
	She wolde weepe if that she saw a mous	
145	Caught in a trappe, if it were deed or bledde.	
	Of smale houndes hadde she that she fedde	
	With rosted flessh,° or milk and wastelbreed;⁹	*meat*
	But sore wepte she if oon of hem were deed,	
	Or if men smoot° it with a yerde° smerte;°	*hit / rod / painfully*
150	And al was conscience and tendre herte.	
	Ful semely hir wimpel¹ pinched was,	
	Hir nose tretis,° hir yën greye as glas,	*shapely*

5. Medal of St. Christopher, patron saint of travelers.
6. St. Eligius, patron saint of metalworkers, believed never to have sworn an oath in his life.
7. From the school (i.e., after the manner) of Stratford, a suburb of London where the prosperous convent of St. Leonard's was located; her French is Anglo-Norman as opposed to the French spoken on the Continent.
8. Spot the size of a farthing.
9. Bread of the finest quality.
1. A pleated headdress covering all but the face, such as nuns and married women wore.

Of woodcraft he knew all there was to know.
He wore a fancy leather guard, a bracer,
And by his side a sword and a rough buckler,
And on the other side a fancy dagger,
Well-mounted, sharper than the point of spear,
And on his breast a medal: St Christopher,
The woodman's patron saint, in polished silver.
He bore a horn slung from a cord of green,
And my guess is, he was a forester.
　　There was also a nun, a prioress,
Whose smile was unaffected and demure;
Her greatest oath was just, "By St Eloi!"
And she was known as Madame Eglantine.
She sang the divine service prettily,
And through the nose, becomingly intoned;
And she spoke French well and elegantly
As she'd been taught it at Stratford-at-Bow,
For French of Paris was to her unknown.
Good table manners she had learnt as well:
She never let a crumb from her mouth fall;
She never soiled her fingers, dipping deep
Into the sauce; when lifting to her lips
Some morsel, she was careful not to spill
So much as one small drop upon her breast.
Her greatest pleasure was in etiquette.
She used to wipe her upper lip so clean,
No print of grease inside her cup was seen,
Not the least speck, when she had drunk from it.
Most daintily she'd reach for what she ate.
No question, she possessed the greatest charm,
Her demeanour was so pleasant, and so warm;
Though at pains to ape the manners of the court,
And be dignified, in order to be thought
A person well deserving of esteem.
But, speaking of her sensibility,
She was so full of charity and pity
That if she saw a mouse caught in a trap,
And it was dead or bleeding, she would weep.
She kept some little dogs, and these she fed
On roast meat, or on milk and fine white bread.
But how she'd weep if one of them were dead,
Or if somebody took a stick to it!
She was all sensitivity and tender heart.
Her veil was pleated most becomingly;
Her nose well-shaped; eyes blue-grey, of great beauty;

Hir mouth ful smal, and therto softe and reed—
But sikerly she hadde a fair forheed:

155　It was almost a spanne[2] brood, I trowe,°　　　　　　*believe*
For hardily,° she was nat undergrowe.°　　　　*assuredly / short*
Ful fetis° was hir cloke, as I was war;　　　　　　*elegant*
Of smal coral aboute hir arm she bar
A paire of bedes, gauded al with greene,[3]

160　And theron heeng a brooch of gold ful sheene,
On which ther was first writen a crowned A.[4]
And after, *Amor vincit omnia*.[5]
　　Another Nonne with hire hadde she
That was hir chapelaine,° and preestes three.　　　*secretary*

165　　A Monk ther was, a fair for the maistrye,°　　*very good-looking*
An outridere[6] that loved venerye,°　　　　　　*hunting*
A manly° man, to been an abbot able.　　　　　*courageous*
Ful many a daintee° hors hadde he in stable,　　　*fine*
And whan he rood, men mighte his bridel heere

170　Ginglen° in a whistling wind as clere　　　　　*jingling*
And eek as loude as dooth the chapel belle
Ther as this lord was kepere of the celle.[7]
The rule of Saint Maure or of Saint Beneit,[8]
By cause that it was old and somdeel strait°—　　*somewhat strict*

175　This ilke Monk leet olde thinges pace,
And heeld after the newe world the space.°　　*the times (customs)*
He yaf nought of that text° a pulled° hen　　*regulation / plucked*
That saith that hunteres been nought holy men,
Ne that a monk, whan he is recchelees,°　　　　*careless*

180　Is likned til a fissh that is waterlees—
This is to sayn, a monk out of his cloistre;
But thilke° text heeld he nat worth an oystre.　　*that same*
And I saide his opinion was good:°
What sholde he studye and make himselven wood°　　*crazy*

185　Upon a book in cloistre alway to poure,
Or swinke° with his handes and laboure,　　　　*work*
As Austin[9] bit?° How shal the world be served?　　*orders*
Lat Austin have his swink° to him reserved!　　　*toil*
Therfore he was a prikasour° aright.　　　*hunter on horseback*

190　Grehoundes he hadde as swift as fowl in flight.
Of priking and of hunting for the hare
Was al his lust,° for no cost wolde he spare.　　*pleasure*
I sawgh his sleeves purfiled° at the hand　　　*fur-lined*
With gris,° and that the fineste of a land;　　　*gray fur*

2. A hand's width, 7 to 9 inches.
3. A set of rosary beads, marked off by larger beads (gauds) to indicate where the Paternosters should be said.
4. The letter "A" with a crown on top.
5. Love conquers all (Virgil, *Eclogues*, 10.69). Though pagan and secular in origin, the phrase was often used to refer to divine love as well.
6. A monk who worked outside the confines of the monastery.

7. Supervisor of the outlying cell of the monastery.
8. St. Benedict (Beneit) was the founder of Western monasticism, and his Rule prohibited monks from leaving the grounds of the monastery without special permission. St. Maurus introduced the Benedictine order into France.
9. St. Augustine recommended that monks perform manual labor.

And her mouth tender, very small, and red.
And there's no doubt she had a fine forehead,
Almost a span in breadth, I'd swear it was,
For certainly she was not undersized.
Her cloak, I noticed, was most elegant.
A coral rosary with gauds of green
She carried on her arm; and from it hung
A brooch of shining gold; inscribed thereon
Was, first of all, a crowned "A,"
And under, *Amor vincit omnia.*

   With her were three priests, and another nun,
Who was her chaplain and companion.

   There was a monk; a nonpareil was he,
Who rode, as steward of his monastery,
The country round; a lover of good sport,
A manly man, and fit to be an abbot.
He'd plenty of good horses in his stable,
And when he went out riding, you could hear
His bridle jingle in the wind, as clear
And loud as the monastery chapel-bell.
Inasmuch as he was keeper of the cell,
The rule of St Maurus or St Benedict
Being out of date, and also somewhat stricter,
This monk I speak of let old precepts slide,
And took the modern practice as his guide.
He didn't give so much as a plucked hen
For the maxim, "Hunters are not pious men,"
Or "A monk who's heedless of his regimen
Is much the same as a fish out of water,"
In other words, a monk out of his cloister.
But that's a text he thought not worth an oyster;
And I remarked his opinion was sound.
What use to study, why go round the bend
With poring over some book in a cloister,
Or drudging with his hands, to toil and labour
As Augustine bids? How shall the world go on?
You can go keep your labour, Augustine!
So he rode hard—no question about that—
Kept greyhounds swifter than a bird in flight.
Hard riding, and the hunting of the hare,
Were what he loved, and opened his purse for.
I noticed that his sleeves were edged and trimmed
With squirrel fur, the finest in the land.

195	And for to festne his hood under his chin	
	He hadde of gold wrought a ful curious° pin:	*elaborate*
	A love-knotte[1] in the grettere° ende ther was.	*larger*
	His heed was balled,° that shoon as any glas,	*bald*
	And eek his face, as he hadde been anoint:	
200	He was a lord ful fat and in good point;°	*in good shape*
	His yën steepe,° and rolling in his heed,	*bright*
	That stemed as a furnais of a leed;[2]	
	His bootes souple,° his hors in greet estat[3]—	*supple*
	Now certainly he was a fair prelat.[4]	
205	He was nat pale as a forpined° gost:	*tormented*
	A fat swan loved he best of any rost.	
	His palfrey° was as brown as is a berye.	*saddle horse*
	A Frere° ther was, a wantoune[5] and a merye,	*Friar*
	A limitour,[6] a ful solempne man.	
210	In alle the ordres foure[7] is noon that can°	*knows*
	So muche of daliaunce° and fair langage:	*flirtation*
	He hadde maad ful many a mariage	
	Of yonge wommen at his owene cost;	
	Unto his ordre he was a noble post.°	*pillar*
215	Ful wel biloved and familier was he	
	With frankelains[8] over al in his contree,	
	And with worthy wommen of the town—	
	For he hadde power of confessioun,	
	As saide himself, more than a curat,°	*parish priest*
220	For of his ordre he was licenciat.[9]	
	Ful swetely herde he confessioun,	
	And plesant was his absolucioun.	
	He was an esy man to yive penaunce	
	Ther as he wiste to have a good pitaunce;[1]	
225	For unto a poore ordre for to yive	
	Is signe that a man is wel yshrive;°	*absolved*
	For if he yaf, he dorste make avaunt°	*boast*
	He wiste that a man was repentaunt;	
	For many a man so hard is of his herte	
230	He may nat weepe though him sore smerte:°	*hurts*
	Therfore, in stede of weeping and prayeres,	
	Men mote yive silver to the poore freres.	
	His tipet° was ay farsed° ful of knives	*scarf / packed*
	And pinnes, for to yiven faire wives;	
235	And certainly he hadde a merye note;	
	Wel coude he singe and playen on a rote;°	*fiddle*
	Of yeddinges° he bar outrely the pris.[2]	*singing ballads*

1. An elaborate knot.
2. Glowed like a furnace under a cauldron.
3. Excellent condition.
4. Prelate, important churchman.
5. Jovial, pleasure-seeking.
6. Friar licensed by his order to beg for alms within a given district.

7. The four orders of friars were the Carmelites, Augustinians, Dominicans, and Franciscans.
8. Franklins, important property holders.
9. Licensed by the Church to hear confessions.
1. Where he knew he would get a good donation.
2. Utterly took the prize.

For fastening his hood beneath his chin,
He wore an elaborate golden pin,
Twined with a love-knot at the larger end.
His head was bald and glistening like glass
As if anointed; and likewise his face.
A fine fat patrician, in prime condition,
His bright and restless eyes danced in his head,
And sparkled like the fire beneath a pot;
Boots of soft leather, horse in perfect trim:
No question but he was a fine prelate!
Not pale and wan like some tormented spirit.
A fat roast swan was what he loved the best.
His saddle-horse was brown as any berry.

　　There was a begging friar, a genial merry
Limiter and a most imposing person.
In all of the four Orders there was none
So versed in small talk and in flattery:
And many was the marriage in a hurry
He'd had to improvise and even pay for.
He was a noble pillar of his Order,
And was well in and intimate with every
Well-to-do freeman farmer of his area,
And with the well-off women in the town;
For he was qualified to hear confession,
And absolve graver sins than a curate,
Or so he said; he was a licentiate.
How sweetly he would hear confession!
How pleasant was his absolution!
He was an easy man in giving shrift,
When sure of getting a substantial gift:
For, as he used to say, generous giving
To a poor Order is a sign you're shriven;
For if you gave, then he could vouch for it
That you were conscience-stricken and contrite;
For many are so hardened in their hearts
They cannot weep, though burning with remorse.
Therefore, instead of weeping and prayers,
They should give money to the needy friars.
The pockets of his hood were stuffed with knives
And pins to give away to pretty wives.
He had a pleasant singing voice, for sure,
Could sing and play the fiddle beautifully;
He took the biscuit as a ballad-singer,

His nekke whit was as the flowr-de-lis;[3]
Therto he strong was as a champioun.

240 He knew the tavernes wel in every town,
And every hostiler and tappestere,°   *innkeeper and barmaid*
Bet than a lazar or a beggestere.°   *a leper or a beggar*
For unto swich a worthy man as he
Accorded nat, as by his facultee,°[4]   *official position*

245 To have with sike° lazars aquaintaunce: *such*
It is nat honeste,° it may nought avaunce,°   *dignified / profit*
For to delen with no swich poraile,°   *poor people*
But al with riche, and selleres of vitaile;°   *food*
And over al ther as profit sholde arise,

250 Curteis he was, and lowely° of servise.   *humble*
Ther was no man nowher so vertuous:°   *capable*
He was the beste beggere in his hous.
And yaf a certain ferme for the graunt:[5]
Noon of his bretheren cam ther in his haunt.°   *territory*

255 For though a widwe hadde nought a sho,
So plesant was his *In principio*[6]
Yit wolde he have a ferthing er he wente;
His purchas° was wel bettre than his rente.°   *income / expense*
And rage° he coude as it were right a whelpe;°   *flirt / puppy*

260 In love-dayes[7] ther coude he muchel helpe,
For ther he was nat lik a cloisterer,
With a thredbare cope, as is a poore scoler,
But he was lik a maister° or a pope.   *professor*
Of double worstede was his semicope,[8]

265 And rounded as a belle out of the presse.°   *bell-mold*
Somwhat he lipsed for his wantounesse
To make his Englissh sweete upon his tonge;
And in his harping, whan that he hadde songe,
His yën twinkled in his heed aright

270 As doon the sterres in the frosty night.
This worthy limitour was cleped° Huberd.   *called*

   A Marchant was ther with a forked beerd,
In motlee,° and hye on hors he sat,   *multicolored fabric*
Upon his heed a Flandrissh° bevere hat,   *Flemish*

275 His bootes clasped faire and fetisly.°   *elegantly*
His resons° he spak ful solempnely,   *opinions*
Souning° alway th'encrees of his winning.   *announcing*
He wolde the see were kept for any thing°   *protected at all costs*
Bitwixen Middelburgh and Orewelle.[9]

280 Wel coude he in eschaunge sheeldes[1] selle.

---

3. Lily, emblem of the royal house of France.
4. It was unbecoming to his official post.
5. And gave a certain fee for the license to beg.
6. "In the beginning," the opening line in Genesis and
the Gospel of John, popular for devotions.
7. Holidays for settling disputes out of court.
8. His short cloak was made of thick woolen cloth.

9. Middleburgh in the Netherlands and Orwell in Suffolk
were major ports for the wool trade.
1. Unit of exchange, a credit instrument for foreign
merchants.

This worthy man ful wel his wit bisette:°   *employed*
And though his neck was whiter than a lily,
Yet he was brawny as a prize-fighter.
He knew the taverns well in every town,
And all the barmaids and the innkeepers,
Better than lepers or the street-beggars;
It wouldn't do, for one in his position,
One of his ability and distinction,
To hold acquaintance with diseased lepers.
It isn't seemly, and it gets you nowhere,
To have any dealings with that sort of trash,
Stick to provision-merchants and the rich!
And anywhere where profit might arise
He'd crawl with courteous offers of service.
You'd nowhere find an abler man than he,
Or a better beggar in his friary;
He paid a yearly fee for his district,
No brother friar trespassed on his beat.
A widow might not even own a shoe,
But so pleasant was his *In principio*
He'd win her farthing in the end, then go.
He made his biggest profits on the side.
He'd frolic like a puppy. He'd give aid
As arbitrator upon settling-days,
For there he was not like some cloisterer
With threadbare cape, like any poor scholar,
But like a Master of Arts, or the Pope!
Of the best double-worsted was his cloak,
And bulging like a bell that's newly cast.
He lisped a little, from affectation,
To make his English sweet upon his tongue;
And when he harped, as closing to a song,
His eyes would twinkle in his head just like
The stars upon a sharp and frosty night.
This worthy limiter was called Hubert.

   A merchant was there, on a high-saddled horse:
He'd a forked beard, a many-coloured dress,
And on his head a Flanders beaver hat,
Boots with expensive clasps, and buckled neatly.
He gave out his opinions pompously,
Kept talking of the profits that he'd made,
How, at all costs, the sea should be policed
From Middleburg in Holland to Harwich.
At money-changing he was an expert;
He dealt in French gold florins on the quiet.
This worthy citizen could use his head:

	Ther wiste° no wight° that he was in dette,	knew / person
	So estatly° was he of his governaunce,°	dignified / management
	With his bargaines, and with his chevissaunce.°	borrowing
285	Forsoothe° he was a worthy man withalle;	in truth
	But, sooth to sayn, I noot° how men him calle.	do not know
	A Clerk ther was of Oxenforde also	
	That unto logik hadde longe ygo.°	gone (studied)
	As lene was his hors as is a rake,	
290	And he was nought right fat, I undertake,	
	But looked holwe,° and therto sobrely.	emaciated
	Ful thredbare was his overeste courtepy,°	outer cloak
	For he hadde geten him yit no benefice,°	church income
	Ne was so worldly for to have office.°	secular employment
295	For him was levere° have at his beddes heed	he preferred
	Twenty bookes, clad in blak or reed,	
	Of Aristotle and his philosophye,	
	Than robes riche, or fithele,° or gay sautrye.°	fiddle / harp
	But al be that he was a philosophre[2]	
300	Yit hadde he but litel gold in cofre;	
	But al that he mighte of his freendes hente,°	get
	On bookes and on lerning he it spente,	
	And bisily gan for the soules praye	
	Of hem that yaf him wherwith to scoleye.°	study
305	Of studye took he most cure° and most heede.	care
	Nought oo° word spak he more than was neede,	one
	And that was said in forme° and reverence,	formally
	And short and quik, and ful of height sentence:°	lofty meaning
	Souning in° moral vertu was his speeche,	consonant with
310	And gladly wolde he lerne, and gladly teche.	
	A Sergeant of the Lawe,[3] war and wis,	
	That often hadde been at the Parvis[4]	
	Ther was also, ful riche of excellence.	
	Discreet he was, and of greet reverence—	
315	He seemed swich, his wordes weren so wise.	
	Justice he was ful often in assise[5]	
	By patente and by plein commissioun.[6]	
	For his science° and for his heigh renown	knowledge
	Of fees and robes hadde he many oon.	
320	So greet a purchasour° was nowher noon;	buyer of land
	Al was fee simple[7] to him in effect—	
	His purchasing mighte nat been infect.°	invalidated
	Nowher so bisy a man as he ther nas;	
	And yit he seemed bisier than he was.	
325	In termes hadde he caas and doomes° alle	lawsuits and judgments
	That from the time of King William[8] were falle.	

2. A philosopher could be a scientist or an alchemist.
3. A lawyer of the highest rank.
4. The porch of St. Paul's Cathedral, a meeting place for lawyers.
5. He was often judge in the court of assizes (civil court).

6. By letter of appointment from the king and by full jurisdiction.
7. Owned outright with no legal impediments.
8. Since the introduction of Norman law in England under William the Conqueror.

No one could tell whether he was in debt,
So impressive and dignified his bearing
As he went about his loans and bargaining.
He was a really estimable man,
But the fact is I never learnt his name.
    There was a scholar from Oxford as well,
Not yet an MA, reading Logic still;
The horse he rode was leaner than a rake,
And he himself, believe me, none too fat,
But hollow-cheeked, and grave and serious.
Threadbare indeed was his short overcoat:
A man too unworldly for lay office,
Yet he'd not got himself a benefice.
For he'd much rather have at his bedside
A library, bound in black calf or red,
Of Aristotle and his philosophy,
Than rich apparel, fiddle, or fine psaltery.
And though he was a man of science, yet
He had but little gold in his strongbox;
But upon books and learning he would spend
All he was able to obtain from friends;
He'd pray assiduously for their souls,
Who gave him wherewith to attend the schools.
Learning was all he cared for or would heed.
He never spoke a word more than was need,
And that was said in form and decorum,
And brief and terse, and full of deepest meaning.
Moral virtue was reflected in his speech,
And gladly would he learn, and gladly teach.
    There was a wise and wary sergeant-at-law,
A well-known figure in the portico
Where lawyers meet; one of great excellence,
Judicious, worthy of reverence,
Or so he seemed, his sayings were so wise.
He'd often acted as Judge of Assize
By the king's letters patent, authorized
To hear all cases. And his great renown
And skill had won him many a fee, or gown
Given in lieu of money. There was none
To touch him as a property-buyer; all
He bought was fee-simple, without entail;
You'd never find a flaw in the conveyance.
And nowhere would you find a busier man;
And yet he seemed much busier than he was.
From yearbooks he could quote, chapter and verse,
Each case and judgement since William the First.

Therto he coude endite and make a thing,[9]

Ther coude no wight° pinchen° at his writing;   *person / find fault with*

And every statut coude he plein by rote.[1]

330   He rood but hoomly° in a medlee° cote,   *simply / multicolored*

Girt with a ceint° of silk, with barres° smale.   *belt / stripes*

Of his array telle I no lenger tale.

   A Frankelain[2] was in his compaignye:

Whit was his beerd as is the dayesye;°   *daisy*

335   Of his complexion he was sanguin.[3]

Wel loved he by the morwe a sop in win.[4]

To liven in delit° was evere his wone,°   *pleasure / custom*

For he was Epicurus owene sone,

That heeld opinion that plein° delit   *complete*

340   Was verray felicitee parfit.[5]

An housholdere and that a greet was he:

Saint Julian[6] he was in his contree.

His breed, his ale, was always after oon;°   *just as good*

A bettre envined° man was nevere noon.   *stocked with wine*

345   Withouten bake mete was nevere his hous,

Of fissh and flessh, and that so plentevous°   *plentiful*

It snewed° in his hous of mete and drinke,   *snowed*

Of alle daintees that men coude thinke.

After the sondry sesons of the yeer

350   So chaunged he his mete and his soper.[7]

Ful many a fat partrich° hadde he in mewe,°   *partridge / cage*

And many a breem,° and many a luce° in stewe.°   *carp / pike / pond*

Wo was his cook but if his sauce were

Poinant° and sharp, and redy al his gere.   *pungent*

355   His table dormant[8] in his halle alway

Stood redy covered al the longe day.

At sessions[9] ther was he lord and sire.

Ful ofte time he was Knight of the Shire.[1]

An anlaas° and a gipser° al of silk   *dagger / purse*

360   Heeng at his girdel, whit as morne milk.

A shirreve hadde he been, and countour.[2]

Was nowher swich a worthy vavasour.[3]

   An Haberdasshere° and a Carpenter,   *hat-maker*

A Webbe, a Dyere, and a Tapicer[4]—

365   And they were clothed alle in oo liveree°   *in the same uniform*

Of a solempne and a greet fraternitee.°   *parish guild*

Ful fresshe and newe hir gere apiked was;[5]

---

9. Compose and draw up a deed.
1. He knew entirely from memory.
2. A large landholder, freeborn but not belonging to the nobility.
3. In temperament he was sanguine (optimistic, governed by blood as his chief humor).
4. In the morning a sop of bread soaked in wine.
5. True and perfect happiness.
6. Patron saint of hospitality.

7. For health he changed his diet according to the different seasons.
8. Left standing rather than dismantled between meals.
9. Meetings of the justices of the peace.
1. A representative of the district at Parliament.
2. He had been sheriff and auditor of the county finances.
3. Lower member of the feudal elite.
4. A weaver, dyer, and tapestry-maker, all members of the same commercial guild.
5. Their gear was decorated.

And he knew how to draw up and compose
A deed; you couldn't fault a thing he wrote;
And he'd reel all the statutes off by rote.
He was dressed simply, in a coloured coat,
Girt by a silk belt with thin metal bands.
I have no more to tell of his appearance.

　　A franklin—that's a country gentleman
And freeman landowner—was his companion.
White was his beard, as white as any daisy;
Sanguine his temperament; his face ruddy.
He loved his morning draught of sops-in-wine,
Since living well was ever his custom,
For he was Epicurus' own true son
And held with him that sensuality
Is where the only happiness is found.
And he kept open house so lavishly
He was St Julian to the country round,
The patron saint of hospitality.
His bread and ale were always of the best,
Like his wine-cellar, which was unsurpassed.
Cooked food was never lacking in his house,
Both meat and fish, and that so plenteous
That in his home it snowed with food and drink,
And all the delicacies you could think.
According to the season of the year,
He changed the dishes that were served at dinner.
He'd plenty of fat partridges in coop,
And kept his fishpond full of pike and carp.
His cook would catch it if his sauces weren't
Piquant and sharp, and all his equipment
To hand. And all day in his hall there stood
The great fixed table, with the places laid.
When the justices met, he'd take the chair;
He often served as MP for the shire.
A dagger, and a small purse made of silk,
Hung at his girdle, white as morning milk.
He'd been sheriff, and county auditor:
A model squireen, no man worthier.

　　A haberdasher and a carpenter,
A weaver, dyer, tapestry-maker—
And they were in the uniform livery
Of a dignified and rich fraternity,
A parish-guild: their gear all trim and fresh,

	Hir knives were chaped° nought with bras,	*mounted*
	But al with silver; wrought ful clene° and weel	*quite nicely made*
370	Hir girdles and hir pouches everydeel.°	*entirely*
	Wel seemed eech of hem a fair burgeis°	*townsperson*
	To sitten in a yeldehalle° on a dais.	*guildhall*
	Everich, for the wisdom that he can,°	*knows*
	Was shaply° for to been an alderman.°	*fit / mayor*
375	For catel° hadde they ynough and rente,°	*property / income*
	And eek hir wives wolde it wel assente—	
	And elles certain were they to blame:	
	It is ful fair to been ycleped° "Madame,"	*called*
	And goon to vigilies⁶ al bifore,	
380	And have a mantel royalliche ybore.	
	A Cook they hadde with hem for the nones,°	*for the occasion*
	To boile the chiknes with the marybones,°	*marrowbones*
	And powdre-marchant tart and galingale.°	*aromatic spices*
	Wel coude he knowe a draughte of London ale.	
385	He coude roste, and seethe,° and broile, and frye,	*boil*
	Maken mortreux,° and wel bake a pie.	*stews*
	But greet harm was it, as it thoughte me,	
	That on his shine a mormal° hadde he.	*ulcer*
	For blankmanger,° that made he with the beste.	*thick stew*
390	A Shipman was ther, woning° fer by weste—	*dwelling*
	For ought I woot,° he was of Dertemouthe.⁷	*know*
	He rood upon a rouncy° as he couthe,	*nag*
	In a gowne of falding° to the knee.	*coarse brown cloth*
	A daggere hanging on a laas° hadde he	*strap*
395	Aboute his nekke, under his arm adown.	
	The hote somer hadde maad his hewe al brown;	
	And certainly he was a good felawe.	
	Ful many a draughte of win hadde he drawe	
	Fro Burdeuxward, whil that the chapman° sleep:⁸	*merchant*
400	Of nice° conscience took he no keep;°	*scrupulous / care*
	If that he faught and hadde the hyer hand,	
	By water he sente hem hoom to every land.	
	But of his craft, to rekene wel his tides,	
	His stremes° and his daungers° him bisides,	*currents / hazards*
405	His herberwe° and his moone, his lodemenage,°	*harboring / navigation*
	Ther was noon swich from Hulle to Cartage.⁹	
	Hardy he was and wis to undertake;	
	With many a tempest hadde his beerd been shake;	
	He knew alle the havenes as they were	
410	Fro Gotlond to the Cape of Finistere,¹	
	And every crike° in Britaine° and in Spaine.	*inlet / Brittany*
	His barge ycleped was the Maudelaine.	

6. Feasts held the night before a holy day.
7. Dartmouth, a port on the southwestern coast.
8. On the trip back from Bordeaux while the merchant slept.
9. Hull, on the northeastern coast in Yorkshire; Cartage:

Carthage in North Africa or Cartagena on the Mediterranean coast of Spain.
1. Gotland in the Baltic Sea; Finistere: Land's End in western Spain.

Knives silver-mounted, none of your cheap brass;
Their belts and purses neatly stitched as well,
All finely finished to the last detail.
Each of them looked indeed like a burgess,
And fit to sit on any guildhall dais.
Each was, in knowledge and ability,
Eligible to be an alderman;
For they'd income enough and property.
What's more, their wives would certainly agree,
Or otherwise they'd surely be to blame
It's very pleasant to be called "Madam"
And to take precedence at church processions,
And have one's mantle carried like a queen's.
　　They had a cook with them for the occasion,
To boil the chickens up with marrowbones,
Tart powdered flavouring, spiced with galingale.
No better judge than he of London ale.
And he could roast, and seethe, and boil, and fry,
Make a thick soup, and bake a proper pie;
But to my mind it was the greatest shame
He'd got an open sore upon his shin;
For he made chicken-pudding with the best.
　　A sea-captain, whose home was in the west,
Was there—a Dartmouth man, for all I know
He rode a cob as well as he knew how,
And was dressed in a knee-length woollen gown.
From a lanyard round his neck, a dagger hung
Under his arm. Summer had tanned him brown.
As rough a diamond as you'd hope to find,
He'd tapped and lifted many a stoup of wine
From Bordeaux, when the merchant wasn't looking.
He hadn't time for scruples or fine feeling,
For if he fought, and got the upper hand,
He'd send his captives home by sea, not land.
But as for seamanship, and calculation
Of moon, tides, currents, all hazards at sea,
For harbour-lore, and skill in navigation,
From Hull to Carthage there was none to touch him.
He was shrewd adventurer, tough and hardy.
By many a tempest had his beard been shaken.
And he knew all the harbours that there were
Between the Baltic and Cape Finisterre,
And each inlet of Britanny and Spain.
The ship he sailed was called "The Magdalen."

With us ther was a Doctour of Physik:°   *Medicine*
In al this world ne was ther noon him lik
415 To speken of physik and of surgerye.
For he was grounded in astronomye,°   *astrology*
He kepte his pacient a ful greet deel
In houres° by his magik naturel.   *astronomical hours*
Wel coude he fortunen the ascendent[2]
420 Of his images° for his pacient.   *talismans*
He knew the cause of every maladye,
Were it of hoot or cold or moiste or drye,[3]
And where engendred° and of what humour:[4]   *originated*
He was a verray parfit praktisour.°   *practitioner*
425 The cause yknowe, and of his harm the roote,
Anoon he yaf the sike man his boote.°   *remedy*
    Ful redy hadde he his apothecaries
To senden him drogges and his letuaries,°   *medicines*
For eech of hem made other for to winne:
430 Hir frendshipe was nought newe to biginne.
Wel knew he the olde Esculapius,[5]
And Deiscorides and eek Rufus,
Olde Ipocras, Hali, and Galien,
Serapion, Razis, and Avicen,
435 Averrois, Damascien, and Constantin,
Bernard, and Gatesden, and Gilbertin.
Of his diete mesurable° was he,   *moderate*
For it was of no superfluitee,
But of greet norissing and digestible.
440 His studye was but litel on the Bible.
In sanguin° and in pers° he clad was al,   *red / Persian blue*
Lined with taffata and with sendal;°   *silks*
And yit he was but esy of dispence;°   *thrifty*
He kepte that he wan in pestilence.
445 For gold in physik is a cordial,°   *tonic*
Therfore he loved gold in special.
    A good Wif was ther of biside Bathe,
But she was somdeel deef,° and that was scathe.°   *somewhat deaf / a pity*
Of cloth-making she hadde swich an haunt,°   *practice*
450 She passed hem of Ypres and of Gaunt.[6]
In al the parissh wif ne was ther noon
That to the offring[7] bifore hire sholde goon,
And if ther dide, certain so wroth° was she   *angry*
That she was out of alle charitee.

2. Calculate the ascendent (propitious moment).
3. The qualities of the four natural elements, corresponding to the humors of the body and the composition of the
universe, needed to be kept in perfect balance.
4. Bodily fluids, or "humors," thought to govern moods
(blood, phlegm, black bile, yellow bile).
5. The Physician is acquainted with a full range of
medical authorities from among the ancient Greeks
(Aesculapius, Dioscorides, Rufus, Hippocrates, Galen,

and Serapion), the Persians (Hali and Rhazes), the Arabs
(Avicenna and Averroes), the Mediterranean transmit-
ters of Eastern science to the West (John of Damascus,
Constantine the African), and later medical school professors (Bernard of Gordon, who taught at Montpellier;
John of Gaddesden, who taught at Merton College; and
Gilbertus Anglicus, an early contemporary of Chaucer's).
6. Centers of Flemish cloth-making.
7. The collection of gifts at the consecration of the Mass.

With us there was a doctor, a physician;
Nowhere in all the world was one to match him
Where medicine was concerned, or surgery;
Being well grounded in astrology
He'd watch his patient with the utmost care
Until he'd found a favourable hour,
By means of astrology, to give treatment.
Skilled to pick out the astrologic moment
For charms and talismans to aid the patient,
He knew the cause of every malady,
If it were "hot" or "cold" or "moist" or "dry,"
And where it came from, and from which humour.
He was a really fine practitioner.
Knowing the cause, and having found its root,
He'd soon give the sick man an antidote.
Ever at hand he had apothecaries
To send him syrups, drugs, and remedies,
For each put money in the other's pocket—
Theirs was no newly founded partnership.
Well-read was he in Aesculapius,
In Dioscorides, and in Rufus,
Ancient Hippocrates, Hali, and Galen,
Avicenna, Rhazes, and Serapion,
Averroës, Damascenus, Constantine,
Bernard, and Gilbertus, and Gaddesden.
In his own diet he was temperate,
For it was nothing if not moderate,
Though most nutritious and digestible.
He didn't do much reading in the Bible.
He was dressed all in Persian blue and scarlet
Lined with taffeta and fine sarsenet,
And yet was very chary of expense.
He put by all he earned from pestilence;
In medicine gold is the best cordial.
So it was gold that he loved best of all.

There was a business woman, from near Bath,
But, more's the pity, she was a bit deaf;
So skilled a clothmaker, that she outdistanced
Even the weavers of Ypres and Ghent.
In the whole parish there was not a woman
Who dared precede her at the almsgiving,
And if there did, so furious was she,
That she was put out of all charity.

455	Hir coverchiefs ful fine were of ground[8]—	
	I dorste swere they weyeden° ten pound	*weighed*
	That on a Sonday weren upon hir heed.	
	Hir hosen° weren of fin scarlet reed,	*stockings*
	Ful straite yteyd,° and shoes ful moiste° and newe.	*tightly laced / supple*
460	Bold was hir face and fair and reed of hewe.	
	She was a worthy womman al hir live:	
	Housbondes at chirche dore she hadde five,	
	Withouten other compaignye in youthe—	
	But therof needeth nought to speke as nouthe.°	*for now*
465	And thries hadde she been at Jerusalem;	
	She hadde passed many a straunge streem;	
	At Rome she hadde been, and at Boloigne,[9]	
	In Galice at Saint Jame, and at Coloigne:	
	She coude° muchel of wandring by the waye.	*knew*
470	Gat-toothed° was she, soothly for to saye.	*gap-toothed*
	Upon an amblere[1] esily she sat,	
	Ywimpled[2] wel, and on hir heed an hat	
	As brood as is a bokeler or a targe,°	*small shields*
	A foot-mantel° aboute hir hipes large,	*riding skirt*
475	And on hir feet a paire of spores° sharpe.	*spurs*
	In felaweshipe wel coude she laughe and carpe:	
	Of remedies of love she knew parchaunce,[3]	
	For she coude of that art the olde daunce.°	*tricks*
	A good man was ther of religioun,	
480	And was a poore Person° of a town,	*parson*
	But riche he was of holy thought and werk.	
	He was also a lerned man, a clerk,	
	That Cristes gospel trewely wolde preche;	
	His parisshens° devoutly wolde he teche.	*parishioners*
485	Benigne he was, and wonder diligent,	
	And in adversitee ful pacient,	
	And swich he was preved ofte sithes.	
	Ful loth were him to cursen for his tithes,[4]	
	But rather wolde he yiven, out of doute,	
490	Unto his poore parisshens aboute	
	Of his offring and eek of his substaunce:°	*possessions*
	He coude in litel thing have suffisaunce.	
	Wid was his parissh, and houses fer asonder,	
	But he ne lafte nought for rain ne thonder,	
495	In siknesse nor in meschief, to visite	
	The ferreste in his parissh, muche and lite,[5]	
	Upon his feet, and in his hand a staf.	

---

8. Her linen kerchiefs were fine in texture.
9. Rome, Boulogne, Santiago Compostela, and Cologne were major European pilgrimage sites.
1. A horse with a gentle pace.
2. Wearing a large headdress that covers all but the face.
3. She knew cures for lovesickness, as it happened.

4. And so was he shown to be many times. / He was most unwilling to curse parishioners (with excommunication) if they failed to pay his tithes (a tenth of their income due to the Church).
5. The furthest away in his parish, great and small.

Her headkerchiefs were of the finest weave,
Ten pounds and more they weighed, I do believe,
Those that she wore on Sundays on her head.
Her stockings were of finest scarlet red,
Very tightly laced; shoes pliable and new.
Bold was her face, and handsome; florid too.
She had been respectable all her life,
And five times married, that's to say in church,
Not counting other loves she'd had in youth,
Of whom, just now, there is no need to speak.
And she had thrice been to Jerusalem;
Had wandered over many a foreign stream;
And she had been at Rome, and at Boulogne,
St James of Compostella, and Cologne;
She knew all about wandering—and straying:
For she was gap-toothed, if you take my meaning.
Comfortably on an ambling horse she sat,
Well-wimpled, wearing on her head a hat
That might have been a shield in size and shape;
A riding-skirt round her enormous hips,
Also a pair of sharp spurs on her feet.
In company, how she could laugh and joke!
No doubt she knew of all the cures for love,
For at that game she was a past mistress.
   And there was a good man, a religious.
He was the needy priest of a village,
But rich enough in saintly thought and work.
And educated, too, for he could read;
Would truly preach the word of Jesus Christ,
Devoutly teach the folk in his parish.
Kind was he, wonderfully diligent;
And in adversity most patient,
As many a time had been put to the test.
For unpaid tithes he'd not excommunicate,
For he would rather give, you may be sure,
From his own pocket to the parish poor;
Few were his needs, so frugally he lived.
Wide was his parish, with houses far asunder,
But he would not neglect, come rain or thunder,
Come sickness or adversity, to call
On the furthest of his parish, great or small;
Going on foot, and in his hand a staff.

This noble ensample° to his sheep he yaf   *example*
That first he wroughte,° and afterward he taughte.   *did*
500   Out of the Gospel he tho° wordes caughte,   *those*
And this figure° he added eek therto: *saying*
That if gold ruste, what shal iren do?
For if a preest be foul, on whom we truste,
No wonder is a lewed° man to ruste.   *uneducated*
505   And shame it is, if a preest take keep,°   *is concerned*
A shiten° shepherde and a clene sheep.   *shit-covered*
Wel oughte a preest ensample for to yive
By his clennesse how that his sheep sholde live.
He sette nought his benefice to hire[6]
510   And leet his sheep encombred in the mire
And ran to London, unto Sainte Poules,
To seeken him a chaunterye for soules,
Or with a bretherhede to been withholde,
But dwelte at hoom and kepte wel his folde,
515   So that the wolf ne made it nought miscarye:
He was a shepherde and nought a mercenarye.
And though he holy were and vertuous,
He was to sinful men nought despitous,°   *scornful*
Ne of his speeche daungerous ne digne,°   *haughty*
520   But in his teching discreet and benigne,
To drawen folk to hevene by fairnesse
By good ensample—this was his bisinesse.
But it were any persone obstinat,
What so he were, of heigh or lowe estat,
525   Him wolde he snibben° sharply for the nones:°   *rebuke / on the spot*
A bettre preest I trowe° ther nowher noon is.   *believe*
He waited after° no pompe and reverence,   *expected*
Ne maked him a spiced° conscience,   *overly critical*
But Cristes lore° and his Apostles twelve   *teaching*
530   He taughte, but first he folwed° it himselve.   *followed*
    With him ther was a Plowman, was his brother,
That hadde ylad of dong ful many a fother.[7]
A trewe swinkere° and a good was he,   *worker*
Living in pees° and parfit° charitee.   *peace / perfect*
535   God loved he best with al his hoole herte
At alle times, though him gamed or smerte,[8]
And thanne his neighebor right as himselve.
He wolde thresshe, and therto dike and delve,°   *make ditches and dig*
For Cristes sake, for every poore wight,°   *person*

---

6. The priest did not rent out his parish to another in order to take a more profitable position saying masses for the dead at the chantries of St. Paul's in London or to serve as chaplain to a wealthy guild (bretherhede).
7. That had carried many a cartload of manure.
8. Enjoyed himself or suffered pain.

540   Withouten hire,° if it laye in his might.   *pay*
     His tithes payed he ful faire and wel,
     This was the good example that he set:
     He practised first what later he would teach.
     Out of the gospel he took that precept;
     And what's more, he would cite this saying too:
     "If gold can rust, then what will iron do?"
     For if a priest be rotten, whom we trust,
     No wonder if a layman comes to rust.
     It's shame to see (let every priest take note)
     A shitten shepherd and a cleanly sheep.
     It's the plain duty of a priest to give
     Example to his sheep; how they should live.
     He never let his benefice for hire
     And left his sheep to flounder in the mire
     While he ran off to London, to St Paul's
     To seek some chantry and sing mass for souls,
     Or to be kept as chaplain by a guild;
     But stayed at home, and took care of his fold,
     So that no wolf might do it injury.
     He was a shepherd, not a mercenary.
     And although he was saintly and virtuous,
     He wasn't haughty or contemptuous
     To sinners, speaking to them with disdain,
     But in his teaching tactful and humane.
     To draw up folk to heaven by goodness
     And good example, was his sole business.
     But if a person turned out obstinate,
     Whoever he was, of high or low estate,
     He'd earn a stinging rebuke then and there.
     You'll never find a better priest, I'll swear.
     He never looked for pomp or deference,
     Nor affected an over-nice conscience.
     But taught the gospel of Christ and His twelve
     Apostles; but first followed it himself.
       With him there was his brother, a ploughman,
     Who'd fetched and carried many a load of dung;
     A good and faithful labourer was he,
     Living in peace and perfect charity.
     God he loved best, and that with all his heart,
     At all times, good and bad, no matter what;
     And next he loved his neighbour as himself.
     He'd thresh, and ditch, and also dig and delve,
     And for Christ's love would do as much again
     If he could manage it, for all poor men,
     And ask no hire. He paid his tithes in full,

Bothe of his propre swink⁹ and his catel.°   *possessions*
In a tabard° rood upon a mere.°   *smock / mare*
   Ther was also a Reeve° and a Millere,   *estate manager*
545 A Somnour, and a Pardoner¹ also,
A Manciple,° and myself—ther were namo.   *Steward*
   The Millere was a stout carl° for the nones.   *fellow*
Ful big he was of brawn and eek of bones—
That preved wel, for overal ther he cam
550 At wrastling he wolde have alway the ram.²
He was short-shuldred, brood, a thikke knarre.°   *bully*
Ther was no dore that he nolde heve of harre,°   *push off its hinges*
Or breke it at a renning with his heed.
His beerd as any sowe or fox was reed,
555 And therto brood, as though it were a spade;
Upon the cop° right of his nose he hade   *tip*
A werte, and theron stood a tuft of heres,
Rede as the bristles of a sowes eres;
His nosethirles° blake were and wide.   *nostrils*
560 A swerd and a bokeler° bar° he by his side.   *small shield / carried*
His mouth as greet was as a greet furnais.
He was a janglere and a Goliardais,³
And that was most of sinne and harlotries.°   *obscenities*
Wel coude he stelen corn and tollen thries⁴—
565 And yit he hadde a thombe of gold,⁵ pardee.°   *by God*
A whit cote and a blew hood wered he.
A baggepipe wel coude he blowe and soune,
And therwithal he broughte us out of towne.
   A gentil Manciple was ther of a temple,°   *law school*
570 Of which achatours° mighte take exemple   *buyers*
For to been wise in bying of vitaile;°   *food*
For wheither that he paide or took by taile,°   *on credit*
Algate he waited so in his achat⁶
That he was ay biforn° and in good stat.°   *always ahead / well off*
575   Now is nat that of God a ful fair grace°   *blessing*
That swich a lewed° mannes wit shal pace°   *uneducated / surpass*
The wisdom of an heep of lerned men?
Of maistres° hadde he mo than thries ten   *scholars*
That weren of lawe expert and curious,°   *skillful*
580 Of whiche ther were a dozeine in that house
Worthy to been stiwardes of rente° and lond   *managers of revenues*
Of any lord that is in Engelond,
To make him live by his propre good°   *own wealth*
On what he earned and on his goods as well.
He wore a smock, and rode upon a mare.

9. Money earned from his own work.
1. A Summoner, a server of summonses for the ecclesiastical courts; Pardoner: a seller of indulgences.
2. Awarded as a prize for wrestling.
3. He was a teller of dirty stories and a reveller.
4. Collect three times as much tax as was due.

5. It was proverbial that millers were dishonest and that
an honest miller was as rare as one who had a golden
thumb. The statement is meant ironically.
6. He was always so watchful for his opportunities to
purchase.

There was a reeve as well, also a miller,
A pardon-seller and a summoner,
A manciple, and myself—there were no more.
    The miller was a burly fellow—brawn
And muscle, big of bones as well as strong,
As was well seen—he always won the ram
At wrestling-matches up and down the land.
He was barrel-chested, rugged and thickset,
And would heave off its hinges any door
Or break it, running at it with his head.
His beard was red as any fox or sow,
And wide at that, as though it were a spade.
And on his nose, right on its tip, he had
A wart, upon which stood a tuft of hairs
Red as the bristles are in a sow's ears.
Black were his nostrils; black and squat and wide.
He bore a sword and buckler by his side.
His big mouth was as big as a furnace.
A loudmouth and a teller of blue stories
(Most of them vicious or scurrilous),
Well versed in stealing corn and trebling dues,
He had a golden thumb—by God he had!
A white coat he had on, and a blue hood.
He played the bagpipes well, and blew a tune,
And to its music brought us out of town.
    A worthy manciple of the Middle Temple
Was there; he might have served as an example
To all provision-buyers for his thrift
In making purchase, whether on credit
Or for cash down: he kept an eye on prices,
So always got in first and did good business.
    Now isn't it an instance of God's grace,
Such an unlettered man should so outpace
The wisdom of a pack of learned men?
He'd more than thirty masters over him,
All of them proficient experts in law,
More than a dozen of them with the power
To manage rents and land for any peer
So that—unless the man were off his head—

In honour dettelees but if he were wood,°   *unless he were crazy*
585 Or live as scarsly° as him list° desire,   *thriftily / pleases*
And able for to helpen al a shire
In any caas° that mighte falle° or happe,   *event / befall*
And yit this Manciple sette hir aller cappe!°   *made fools of them all*
    The Reeve was a sclendre° colerik° man;   *lean / ill-tempered*
590 His beerd was shave as neigh° as evere he can;   *close*
His heer was by his eres ful round yshorn;
His top was dokked° lik a preest biforn;°   *clipped / in front*
Ful longe were his legges and ful lene,
Ylik° a staf, ther was no calf yseene.°   *like / visible*
595 Wel coude he keepe a gerner° a binne—   *granary*
Ther was noon auditour coude on him winne.[7]
Wel wiste he by the droughte and by the rain
The yeelding of his seed and of his grain.
His lordes sheep, his neet,° his dayerye,°   *cattle / dairy cattle*
600 His swim, his hors, his stoor,° and his pultrye   *livestock*
Was hoolly in this Reeves governinge,
And by his covenant° yaf the rekeninge,°   *contract / gave account*
Sin that his lord was twenty yeer of age.
Ther coude no man bringe him in arrerage.°   *financial arrears*
605 Ther nas baillif, hierde, nor other hine,[8]
That he ne knew his sleighte° and his covine°—   *tricks / plotting*
They were adrad of him as of the deeth.
His woning° was ful faire upon an heeth;°   *dwelling / meadow*
With greene trees shadwed was his place.
610 He coude bettre than his lord purchace.°   *buy property*
Ful riche he was astored prively.°   *stocked in secret*
His lord wel coude he plesen subtilly,
To yive and lene° him of his owene good,°   *lend / possessions*
And have a thank,° and yit a cote and hood.   *gratitude*
615 In youthe he hadde lerned a good mister:°   *profession*
He was a wel good wrighte, a carpenter.
This Reeve sat upon a ful good stot°   *stallion*
That was a pomely° grey and highte° Scot.   *dappled / named*
A long surcote° of pers° upon he hade,   *overcoat / blue*
620 And by his side he bar a rusty blade.
Of Northfolk[9] was this Reeve of which I telle,
Biside a town men clepen° Baldeswelle.   *call*
Tukked[1] he was as is a frere aboute,
And evere he rood the hindreste° of oure route.°   *hindmost / group*
625   A Somnour was ther with us in that place
That hadde a fir-reed° cherubinnes° face,   *fire-red / cherub's*
For saucefleem° he was, with yën narwe,   *pimply*
And hoot he was, and lecherous as a sparwe,°   *sparrow*

7. Gain anything (by catching him out).
8. There was no foreman, herdsman, or other farmhand.
9. Norfolk in the north of England. The Reeve is notable

for his northern dialect and regionalisms.
1. He wore his clothes tucked up with a cinch as friars
did.

He could live honourably, free of debt,
Or sparingly, if that were his desire;
And able to look after a whole shire
In whatever emergency might befall;
And yet this manciple could hoodwink them all.

    There was a reeve, a thin and bilious man;
His beard he shaved as close as a man can;
Around his ears he kept his hair cropped short,
Just like a priest's, docked in front and on top.
His legs were very long, and very lean,
And like a stick; no calf was to be seen.
His granary and bins were ably kept;
There was no auditor could trip him up.
He could foretell, by noting drought and rain,
The likely harvest from his seed and grain.
His master's cattle, dairy, cows, and sheep,
His pigs and horses, poultry and livestock,
Were wholly under this reeve's governance.
And, as was laid down in his covenant,
Of these he'd always rendered an account
Ever since his master reached his twentieth year.
No man could ever catch him in arrears.
He was up to every fiddle, every dodge
Of every herdsman, bailiff, or farm-lad.
All of them feared him as they feared the plague.
His dwelling was well placed upon a heath,
Set with green trees that overshadowed it.
At business he was better than his lord:
He'd got his nest well-feathered, on the side,
For he was cunning enough to get round
His lord by lending him what was his own,
And so earn thanks, besides a coat and hood.
As a young man he'd learned a useful trade
As a skilled artisan, a carpenter.
The reeve rode on a sturdy farmer's cob
That was called Scot: it was a dapple grey.
He had on a long blue-grey overcoat,
And carried by his side a rusty sword.
A Norfolk man was he of whom I tell,
From near a place that they call Bawdeswell.
Tucked round him like a friar's was his coat;
He always rode the hindmost of our troop.

    A summoner was among us at the inn,
Whose face was fire-red, like the cherubim;
All covered with carbuncles; his eyes narrow;
He was as hot and randy as a sparrow.

	With scaled° browes blake and piled² beerd:	*scabby*
630	Of his visage children were aferd.°	*frightened*
	Ther nas quiksilver, litarge, ne brimstoon,	
	Boras, ceruce, ne oile of tartre noon,³	
	Ne oinement that wolde clense and bite,	
	That him mighte helpen of his whelkes° white,	*blotches*
635	Nor of the knobbes° sitting on his cheekes.	*lumps*
	Wel loved he garlek, oinons, and eek leekes,	
	And for to drinke strong win reed as blood.	
	Thanne wolde he speke and crye as he were wood;°	*crazy*
	And whan that he wel dronken hadde the win,	
640	Thanne wolde he speke no word but Latin:	
	A fewe termes hadde he, two or three,	
	That he hadde lerned out of som decree;	
	No wonder is—he herde it al the day,	
	And eek ye knowe wel how that a jay°	*parrot*
645	Can clepen "Watte°" as wel as can the Pope—	*call "Walter"*
	But whoso coude in other thing him grope,°	*examine*
	Thanne hadde he spent all his philosophye;	
	Ay *Questio quid juris*⁴ wolde he crye.	
	He was a gentil harlot° and a kinde;	*rascal*
650	A bettre felawe sholde men nought finde:	
	He wolde suffre,° for a quart of win,	*allow*
	A good felawe to have his concubin°	*mistress*
	A twelfmonth, and excusen him at the fulle;	
	Ful prively a finch eek coude he pulle.⁵	
655	And if he foond owher° a good felawe	*anywhere*
	He wolde techen him to have noon awe	
	In swich caas of the Ercedekenes curs,⁶	
	But if a mannes soule were in his purs,°	*wallet*
	For in his purs he sholde ypunisshed be.	
660	"Purs is the Ercedekenes helle," saide he.	
	But wel I woot° he lied right in deede:	*know*
	Of cursing° oughte eech gilty man him drede,°	*excommunication / fear*
	For curs wol slee° right as assoiling° savith—	*will kill / absolving*
	And also war him of a *significavit*.⁷	
665	In daunger hadde he at his owene gise⁸	
	The yonge girles of the diocise,	
	And knew hir conseil,° and was al hir reed.°	*secrets / advice*
	A gerland hadde he set upon his heed	
	As greet as it were for an ale-stake;°	*tavern sign*
670	A bokeler hadde he maad him of a cake.°	*loaf of bread*
	With him ther rood a gentil Pardoner	
	Of Rouncival,⁹ his freend and his compeer,°	*companion*

2. With hair falling out.
3. There was not mercury, lead ointment, or sulphur, / Borax, white lead, nor any oil of tartar that could clean him.
4. "The question as to what point of law (applies)"; often used in ecclesiastical courts.

5. And secretly he also knew how to fool around.
6. In case of excommunication by the archdeacon.
7. Order of transfer from ecclesiastical to secular courts.
8. Under his control he had at his disposal.
9. A hospital at Charing Cross in London.

He'd scabbed black eyebrows, and a scraggy beard,
No wonder if the children were afraid!
There was no mercury, white lead, or sulphur,
No borax, no ceruse, no cream of tartar,
Nor any other salves that cleanse and burn,
Could help with the white pustules on his skin,
Or with the knobbed carbuncles on his cheeks.
He'd a great love of garlic, onions, leeks,
Also for drinking strong wine, red as blood,
When he would roar and gabble as if mad.
And once he had got really drunk on wine,
Then he would speak no language but Latin.
He'd picked up a few tags, some two or three,
Which he'd learned from some edict or decree—
No wonder, for he heard them every day.
Also, as everybody knows, a jay
Can call out "Wat" as well as the Pope can.
But if you tried him further with a question,
You'd find his well of learning had run dry;
"*Questio quid juris*" was all he'd ever say.
     A most engaging rascal, and a kind,
As good a fellow as you'd hope to find:
For he'd allow—given a quart of wine—
A scallywag to keep his concubine
A twelvemonth, and excuse him altogether.
He'd dip his wick, too, very much sub rosa.
And if he found some fellow with a woman,
He'd tell him not to fear excommunication
If he were caught, or the archdeacon's curse,
Unless the fellow's soul was in his purse,
For it's his purse must pay the penalty.
"Your purse is the archdeacon's Hell," said he.
     Take it from me, the man lied in his teeth:
Let sinners fear, for that curse is damnation,
Just as their souls are saved by absolution.
Let them beware, too, of a "*Significavit*."
     Under his thumb, to deal with as he pleased,
Were the young people of his diocese;
He was their sole adviser and confidant.
Upon his head he sported a garland
As big as any hung outside a pub,
And, for a shield, he'd a round loaf of bread.
     With him there was a peerless pardon-seller
Of Charing Cross, his friend and his confrère,

That straight was comen fro the Court of Rome.
Ful loude he soong, "Com hider, love, to me."[1]
675 This Somnour bar to him a stif burdoun:°   *a strong baritone*
Was nevere trompe° of half so greet a soun.   *trumpet*
    This Pardoner hadde heer as yelow as wex,
But smoothe it heeng as dooth a strike of flex;°   *clump of flax*
By ounces° heenge his lokkes that he hadde,   *thin strands*
680 And therwith he his shuldres overspradde,
But thinne it lay, by colpons,° oon by oon;   *strands*
But hood for jolitee° wered he noon,   *fanciness*
For it was trussed up in his walet:°   *pack*
Him thoughte he rood al of the newe jet.°   *fashion*
685 Dischevelee° save his cappe he rood al bare.   *loose-haired*
Swiche glaring yën hadde he as an hare.
A vernicle[2] hadde he sowed upon his cappe,
His walet biforn him in his lappe,
Bretful of pardon,[3] comen from Rome al hoot.
690 A vois he hadde as smal° as hath a goot;°   *high-pitched / goat*
No beerd hadde he, ne nevere sholde have;
As smoothe it was as it were late yshave:
I trowe he were a gelding or a mare.[4]
But of his craft,° fro Berwik into Ware,[5]   *skill*
695 Ne was ther swich another pardoner;
For in his male° he hadde a pilwe-beer°   *bag / pillowcase*
Which that he saide was Oure Lady veil;
He saide he hadde a gobet° of the sail   *chunk*
That Sainte Peter hadde whan that he wente
700 Upon the see, til Jesu Crist him hente.°   *grabbed*
He hadde a crois of laton,° ful of stones,   *brass cross*
And in a glas he hadde pigges bones,
But with thise relikes whan that he foond
A poore person° dwelling upon lond,   *parson*
705 Upon a day he gat him more moneye
Than that the person gat in monthes twaye;°   *two*
And thus with feined flaterye and japes°   *tricks*
He made the person and the peple his apes.°   *dupes*
But trewely to tellen at the laste,
710 He was in chirche a noble ecclesiaste;
Wel coude he rede a lesson and a storye,°   *liturgical texts*
But alderbest° he soong an offertorye,   *best of all*
For wel he wiste whan that song was songe,
He moste preche and wel affile° his tonge   *sharpen*
715 To winne silver, as he ful wel coude—
Therfore he soong the merierly and loude.
    Now have I told you soothly° in a clause°   *truly / briefly*
Th'estaat, th'array, the nombre, and eek the cause

---

1. A popular ballad.
2. A pilgrim badge, reproducing St. Veronica's veil bearing the imprint of Christ's face.
3. Full to the brim with indulgences.

4. I believe he was a gelding (eunuch) or a mare (perhaps a passive homosexual).
5. Towns north and south of London.

Who'd come straight from the Vatican in Rome.
Loudly he sang, "Come to me, love, come hither!"
The summoner sang the bass, a loud refrain;
No trumpet ever made one half the din.
    This pardon-seller's hair was yellow as wax,
And sleekly hanging, like a hank of flax.
In meagre clusters hung what hair he had;
Over his shoulders a few strands were spread,
But they lay thin, in rat's tails, one by one.
As for a hood, for comfort he wore none,
For it was stowed away in his knapsack.
Save for a cap, he rode with head all bare,
Hair loose; he thought it was the *dernier cri*.
He had big bulging eyes, just like a hare.
He'd sewn a veronica on his cap.
His knapsack lay before him, on his lap,
Chockful of pardons, all come hot from Rome.
His voice was like a goat's, plaintive and thin.
He had no beard, nor was he like to have;
Smooth was his face, as if he had just shaved.
I took him for a gelding or a mare.
As for his trade, from Berwick down to Ware
You'd not find such another pardon-seller.
For in his bag he had a pillowcase
Which had been, so he said, Our Lady's veil;
He said he had a snippet of the sail
St Peter had, that time he walked upon
The sea, and Jesus Christ caught hold of him.
And he'd a brass cross, set with pebble-stones,
And a glass reliquary of pigs' bones.
But with these relics, when he came upon
Some poor up-country priest or backwoods parson,
In just one day he'd pick up far more money
Than any parish priest was like to see
In two whole months. With double-talk and tricks
He made the people and the priest his dupes.
But to speak truth and do the fellow justice,
In church he made a splendid ecclesiastic.
He'd read a lesson, or saint's history,
But best of all he sang the offertory:
For, knowing well that when that hymn was sung.
He'd have to preach and polish smooth his tongue
To raise—as only he knew how—the wind,
The louder and the merrier he would sing.
    And now I've told you truly and concisely
The rank, and dress, and number of us all,

Why that assembled was this compaignye
720   In Southwerk at this gentil hostelrye
That highte the Tabard, faste by the Belle;[6]
But now is time to you for to telle
How that we baren us that like° night   *same*
Whan we were in that hostelrye alight;
725   And after wol I telle of oure viage,°   *trip*
And al the remenant of oure pilgrimage.
    But first I praye you of youre curteisye
That ye n'arette° it nought my vilainye°   *consider / rudeness*
Though that I plainly speke in this matere
730   To telle you hir wordes and hir cheere,°   *comportment*
Ne though I speke hir wordes proprely;°   *accurately*
For this ye knowen also wel as I:
Who so shal telle a tale after a man
He moot reherce,° as neigh as evere he can,   *must repeat*
735   Everich a word, if it be in his charge,
Al speke he nevere so rudeliche° and large,°   *crudely / freely*
Or elles he moot telle his tale untrewe,
Or feine° thing, or finde wordes newe;   *invent, falsify*
He may nought spare although he were his brother:
740   He moot as wel saye oo word as another.
Crist spak himself ful brode° in Holy Writ,   *plainly*
And wel ye woot° no vilainye is it;   *know*
Eek Plato saith, who so can him rede,
The wordes mote be cosin° to the deede.   *closely related*
745   Also I praye you to foryive it me
Al° have I nat set folk in hir degree°   *although / rank*
Here in this tale as that they sholde stonde:
My wit is short, ye may wel understonde.
    Greet cheere made oure Host us everichoon,
750   And to the soper sette he us anoon.
He served us with vitaile at the beste.
Strong was the win, and wel to drinke us leste.°   *it pleased*
A semely° man oure Hoste was withalle   *apt*
For to been a marchal° in an halle;   *master of ceremonies*
755   A large man he was, with yën steepe;°   *glaring eyes*
A fairer burgeis was ther noon in Chepe°—   *Cheapside (in London)*
Bold of his speeche, and wis, and wel ytaught,
And of manhood him lakkede° right naught.   *he lacked*
Eek therto he was right a merye man,
760   And after soper playen he bigan,
And spak of mirthe amonges othere thinges—
Whan that we hadde maad oure rekeninges°—   *paid the bill*
And saide thus, "Now, lordinges, trewely,
Ye been to me right welcome, hertely.

6. Another tavern in Southwark.

765   For by my trouthe, if that I shal nat lie,
And why we gathered in a company
In Southwark, at that noble hostelry
Known as the Tabard, that's hard by the Bell.
But now the time has come for me to tell
What passed among us, what was said and done
The night of our arrival at the inn;
And afterwards I'll tell you how we journeyed,
And all the remainder of our pilgrimage.
      But first I beg you, not to put it down
To my ill-breeding if my speech be plain
When telling what they looked like, what they said,
Or if I use the exact words they used.
For, as you all must know as well as I,
To tell a tale told by another man
You must repeat as nearly as you can
Each word, if that's the task you've undertaken,
However coarse or broad his language is;
Or, in the telling, you'll have to distort it
Or make things up, or find new words for it.
You can't hold back, even if he's your brother:
Whatever word is used, you must use also.
Christ Himself spoke out plain in Holy Writ,
And well you know there's nothing wrong with that.
Plato, as those who read him know, has said,
"The word must be related to the deed."
      Also I beg you to forgive it me
If I overlooked all standing and degree
As regards the order in which people come
Here in this tally, as I set them down:
My wits are none too bright, as you can see.
      Our host gave each and all a warm welcome,
And set us down to supper there and then.
The eatables he served were of the best;
Strong was the wine; we matched it with our thirst.
A handsome man our host, handsome indeed,
And a fit master of ceremonies.
He was a big man with protruding eyes
—You'll find no better burgess in Cheapside—
Racy in talk, well-schooled and shrewd was he;
Also a proper man in every way.
And moreover he was a right good sort,
And after supper he began to joke,
And, when we had all paid our reckonings,
He spoke of pleasure, among other things:
"Truly," said he, ladies and gentlemen,
Here you are all most heartily welcome.
Upon my word—I'm telling you no lie—

I sawgh nat this yeer so merye a compaignye
At ones in this herberwe° as is now.   *inn*
Fain wolde I doon you mirthe, wiste I how.
And of a mirthe I am right now bithought,
770   To doon you ese, and it shal coste nought.
        Ye goon to Canterbury—God you speede;
The blisful martyr quite° you youre meede.°   *repay / reward*
And wel I woot° as ye goon by the waye   *know*
Ye shapen° you to talen° and to playe,   *intend / tell tales*
775   For trewely, confort ne mirthe is noon
To ride by the waye domb as stoon;
And therfore wol I maken you disport
As I saide erst,° and doon you som confort;   *before*
And if you liketh alle, by oon assent,
780   For to stonden at my juggement,
And for to werken as I shal you saye,
Tomorwe whan ye riden by the waye—
Now by my fader soule that is deed,
But° ye be merye I wol yive you myn heed!   *unless*
785   Holde up youre handes withouten more speeche."
        Oure conseil was nat longe for to seeche;°   *seek*
Us thoughte it was nat worth to make it wis,°   *deliberate*
And graunted him withouten more avis,°   *opinions*
And bade him saye his voirdit° as him leste.   *verdict*
790   "Lordinges," quod he, "now herkneth for the beste;
But taketh it nought, I praye you, in desdain.
This is the point, to speken short and plain,
That eech of you, to shorte with oure waye
In this viage, shal tellen tales twaye°—   *two*
795   To Canterburyward, I mene it so,
And hoomward he shal tellen othere two,
Of aventures that whilom° have bifalle;   *long ago*
And which of you that bereth him best of alle—
That is to sayn, that telleth in this cas
800   Tales of best sentence° and most solas°—   *substance / pleasure*
Shal have a soper at oure aller cost,
Here in this place, sitting by this post,
Whan that we come again fro Canterbury.
And for to make you the more mury
805   I wol myself goodly° with you ride—   *gladly*
Right at myn owene cost—and be youre gide.
And who so wol my juggement withsaye°   *contradict*
Shal paye al that we spende by the waye.
And if ye vouche sauf° that it be so,   *grant*
810   Telle me anoon, withouten wordes mo,
And I wol erly shape° me therfore."   *prepare*
        This thing was graunted and oure othes swore
With ful glad herte, and prayden him also

All year I've seen no jollier company
At one time in this inn, than I have now.
I'd make some fun for you, if I knew how.
And, as it happens, I have just now thought
Of something that will please you, at no cost.
   "You're off to Canterbury—so Godspeed!
The blessed martyr give you your reward!
And I'll be bound, that while you're on your way,
You'll be telling tales, and making holiday;
It makes no sense, and really it's no fun
To ride along the road dumb as a stone.
And therefore I'll devise a game for you,
To give you pleasure, as I said I'd do.
And if with one accord you all consent
To abide by my decision and judgement,
And if you'll do exactly as I say,
Tomorrow, when you're riding on your way,
Then, by my father's soul—for he is dead—
If you don't find it fun, why, here's my head!
Now not another word! Hold up your hands!"
   We were not long in making up our minds.
It seemed not worth deliberating, so
We gave our consent without more ado,
Told him to give us what commands he wished,
   "Ladies and gentlemen," began our host,
"Do yourselves a good turn, and hear me out:
But please don't turn your noses up at it.
I'll put it in a nutshell: here's the nub:
It's that you each, to shorten the long journey,
Shall tell two tales *en route* to Canterbury,
And, coming homeward, tell another two,
Stories of things that happened long ago.
Whoever best acquits himself, and tells
The most amusing and instructive tale,
Shall have a dinner, paid for by us all,
Here in this inn, and under this roof-tree,
When we come back again from Canterbury.
To make it the more fun, I'll gladly ride
With you at my own cost, and be your guide.
And anyone who disputes what I say
Must pay all our expenses on the way!
And if this plan appeals to all of you,
Tell me at once, and with no more ado,
And I'll make my arrangements here and now."
   To this we all agreed, and gladly swore
To keep our promises; and furthermore
We asked him if he would consent to do

That he wolde vouche sauf for to do so,
815   And that he wolde been oure governour,
And of oure tales juge° and reportour,°   *judge / recordkeeper*
And sette a soper at a certain pris,°   *price*
And we wol ruled been at his devis,°   *plan*
In heigh and lowe; and thus by oon assent
820   We been accorded to his juggement.
And therupon the win was fet° anoon;   *fetched*
We dronken and to reste wente eechoon°   *everyone*
Withouten any lenger taryinge.
        Amorwe° whan that day bigan to springe   *next morning*
825   Up roos oure Host and was oure aller cok,°   *cock, wake-up call*
And gadred us togidres in a flok,
And forth we riden, a litel more than pas,°   *slow walk*
Unto the watering of Saint Thomas;⁷
And ther oure Host bigan his hors arreste,°   *stop*
830   And saide, "Lordes, herkneth if you leste:°   *it please*
        "Ye woot youre forward° and it you recorde:°   *agreement / remember*
If evensong and morwesong accorde,
Lat see now who shal telle the firste tale.
As evere mote I drinken win or ale,
835   Who so be rebel to my juggement
Shal paye for al that by the way is spent.
Now draweth cut° er that we ferrer twinne:°   *lots / separate further*
He which that hath the shorteste shal biginne.
        "Sire Knight," quod he, "my maister and my lord,
840   Now draweth cut, for that is myn accord.°   *wish*
Cometh neer," quod he, "my lady Prioresse,
And ye, sire Clerk, lat be youre shamefastnesse°—   *modesty*
Ne studieth nought. Lay hand to, every man!"
        Anoon to drawen every wight° bigan,   *person*
845   And shortly for to tellen as it was,
Were it by aventure, or sort, or cas,°   *luck, fate or chance*
The soothe° is this, the cut fil° to the Knight;   *truth / fell*
Of which ful blithe° and glad was every wight,   *happy*
And telle he moste his tale, as was resoun,
850   By forward and by composicioun,°   *agreement*
As ye han herd. What needeth wordes mo?
And whan this goode man sawgh that it was so,
As he that wis was and obedient
To keepe his forward by his free assent,
855   He saide, "Sin I shal biginne the game,
What, welcome be the cut, in Goddes name!
Now lat us ride, and herkneth what I saye."
And with that word we riden forth oure waye,
And he bigan with right a merye cheere°   *expression*
860   His tale anoon, and saide as ye may heere.

As he had said, and come and be our leader,
And judge our tales, and act as arbiter,
Set up our dinner too, at a fixed price;
And we'd obey whatever he might decide
In everything. And so, with one consent,
We bound ourselves to bow to his judgement.
And thereupon wine was at once brought in.
We drank; and not long after, everyone
Went off to bed, and that without delay.
   Next morning our host rose at break of day:
He was our cockcrow; so we all awoke.
He gathered us together in a flock,
And we rode, at little more than walking-pace
Till we had reached St Thomas' watering-place,
Where our host began reining in his horse.
"Ladies and gentlemen, attention please!"
Said he. "All of you know what we agreed,
And I'm reminding you. If evensong
And matins are in harmony—that's to say,
If you are still of the same mind today—
Let's see who'll tell the first tale, and begin.
And whosoever baulks at my decision
Must pay for all we spend upon the way,
Or may I never touch a drop again!
And now let's draw lots before going on.
The one who draws the short straw must begin.
   Sir Knight, my lord and master," said our host,
"Now let's draw lots, for such is my request.
Come near," said he, "my lady Prioress,
And, Mister Scholar, lay by bashfulness,
Stop dreaming! Hands to drawing, everyone!"
   To cut the story short, the draw began,
And, whether it was luck, or chance, or fate,
The truth is this: the lot fell to the knight,
Much to the content of the company.
Now, as was only right and proper, he
Must tell his tale, according to the bargain
Which, as you know, he'd made. What more to say?
And when the good man saw it must be so,
Being sensible, and accustomed to obey
And keep a promise he had freely given,
He said, "Well, since I must begin the game,
Then welcome to the short straw, in God's name!
Now let's ride on, and listen to what I say."
And at these words we rode off on our way,
And he at once began, with cheerful face,
His tale. The way he told it was like this.

THE MILLER'S TALE   *The Miller's Tale* both answers and parodies *The Knight's Tale*, a long aristocratic romance about two knights in rivalry for the hand of a lady. While the Miller tells a nearly analogous story of erotic competition, his tale is radically shorter and explicitly sexual. Such brevity and physicality fit his tale's genre—a fabliau, or short comic tale, usually bawdy and often involving a clerk, a wife, and a cuckolded husband. Following the convention (if not the reality) that romances were written by and for the nobility and fabliaux by and for the commons, Chaucer suits *The Miller's Tale* to its teller as aptly as he does the Knight's. Slyly disclaiming responsibility for the tale, he explains its bawdiness by the Miller's class status: "the Millere is a cherle" and like his peer the Reeve who follows and "requites" him, tells "harlotrye."

The drunken Miller's insistence on telling his tale to requite the Knight's tale has been called a "literary peasants' revolt." Although the Miller, a free man, was not actually a peasant, yeomen of his status were active in the Rising of 1381, and millers in particular played a symbolic role in it (see the letters of John Ball, pages 347–48). In fact, this tale is highly literate, with its echoes of the Song of Songs and its parody of the language of courtly love: an actual miller would have had neither the education nor the social sophistication to tell it. Yet a parody implies some degree of attachment to the very model being ridiculed, and *The Miller's Tale* is as much a claim upon the Knight's world as a repudiation of it. The Miller wants to "quiten" the Knight's tale, he says, using a word that can mean to repay or avenge, but also to fulfill. The tale's several plots converge brilliantly upon a single cry: "Water!" The tale's impact derives as well from its plenitude of pleasures (sexual, comic, even religious) after the austere and rigid desires of *The Knight's Tale*.

The Miller's Tale
The Introduction

	Whan that the Knight hadde thus his tale ytold,	
	In al the route° nas ther yong ne old	*group*
	That he ne saide it was a noble storye,	
	And worthy for to drawen° to memorye,	*recall*
5	And namely the gentils° everichoon.	*upper class*
	Oure Hoste lough° and swoor, "So mote I goon,[1]	*laughed*
	This gooth aright: unbokeled is the male.[2]	
	Lat see now who shal telle another tale.	
	For trewely the game is wel bigonne.	
10	Now telleth ye, sire Monk, if that ye conne,°	*know*
	Somwhat to quite° with the Knightes tale."	*repay*
	The Millere, that for dronken was al pale,	
	So that unnethe° upon his hors he sat,	*barely*
	He nolde avalen° neither hood ne hat,	*would not remove*
15	Ne abiden no man for his curteisye,	
	But in Pilates[3] vois he gan to crye,	
	And swoor, "By armes and by blood and bones,°	*(of Christ)*
	I can° a noble tale for the nones,	*know*
	With which I wol now quite the Knightes tale."	
20	Oure Hoste sawgh that he was dronke of ale,	
	And saide, "Abide,° Robin, leve° brother,	*wait / dear*

---

1. Thus I may proceed.
2. The bag is opened (i.e., the games are begun).

3. The role of Pilate was traditionally played in a loud and raucous voice in the mystery plays.

Som bettre man shal telle us first another.
Abide, and lat us werken thriftily.°"   *properly*
   "By Goddes soule," quod he, "that wol nat I,
25 For I wol speke or elles go my way."
   Oure Host answerde, "Tel on, a devele way!°   *in the devil's name*
Thou art a fool; thy wit is overcome."
   "Now herkneth," quod the Millere, "alle and some.°   *one and all*
But first I make a protestacioun
30 That I am dronke: I knowe it by my soun.°   *sound*
And therfore if that I mis speke or saye,
Wite it° the ale of Southwerk, I you praye;   *blame it on*
For I wol telle a legende and a lif[4]
Bothe of a carpenter and of his wif,
35 How that a clerk hath set the wrightes cappe."[5]
   The Reeve answerde and saide, "Stint thy clappe!°   *hold your tongue*
Lat be thy lewed° dronken harlotrye.°   *unlearned / obscenity*
It is a sinne and eek a greet folye
To apairen° any man or him defame,   *injure*
40 And eek to bringen wives in swich fame.
Thou maist ynough of othere thinges sayn."
   This dronken Millere spak ful soone again,
And saide, "Leve brother Osewold,
Who hath no wif, he is no cokewold.°   *cuckold*
45 But I saye nat therfore that thou art oon.
Ther ben ful goode wives many oon,
And evere a thousand goode ayains oon badde.°   *against one bad*
That knowestou wel thyself but if thou madde.°   *go insane*
Why artou angry with my tale now?
50 I have a wif, pardee,° as wel as thou,   *by God*
Yet nolde I, for the oxen in my plough,[6]
Take upon me more than ynough
As deemen° of myself that I were oon:°   *judge / one (a cuckold)*
I wol bileve wel that I am noon.
55 An housbonde shal nought been inquisitif
Of Goddes privetee,° nor of his wif.   *secrets*
So he may finde Goddes foison° there,   *plenty*
Of the remenant needeth nought enquere."
   What sholde I more sayn but this Millere
60 He nolde° his wordes for no man forbere,   *would not*
But tolde his cherles° tale in his manere.   *commoner's*
M'athinketh° that I shal reherce° it here,   *I regret / repeat*
And therfore every gentil wight° I praye,   *person*
Deemeth nought, for Goddes love, that I saye
65 Of yvel entente, but for° I moot° reherse   *because / must*
Hir tales alle, be they bet or werse,
Or elles falsen som of my matere.

---

4. The story of a saint's life.
5. Made a fool of the carpenter.

6. Yet I wouldn't, not even (in wager) for the oxen in my plough.

And therfore, whoso list it nought yheere
Turne over the leef,° and chese° another tale,   *page / choose*
70   For he shal finde ynowe,° grete and smale,   *enough*
Of storial° thing that toucheth gentilesse,°   *historical / nobility*
And eek moralitee and holinesse:
Blameth nought me if that ye chese amis.
The Millere is a cherl, ye knowe wel this,
75   So was the Reeve eek, and othere mo,
And harlotrye they tolden bothe two.
Aviseth you,° and putte me out of blame: *be warned*
And eek men shal nought maken ernest of game.°   *treat jokes seriously*

The Tale

Whilom° ther was dwelling at Oxenforde   *long ago*
80   A riche gnof° that gestes heeld to boorde,°   *fool / took in boarders*
And of his craft he was a carpenter.
With him ther was dwelling a poore scoler,
Hadde lerned art,[7] but al his fantasye°   *fancy*
Was turned for to lere° astrologye,   *learn*
85   And coude a certain of conclusiouns,°   *predictions*
To deemen by interrogaciouns,[8]
If that men axed° him in certain houres   *asked*
Whan that men sholde have droughte or elles showres,
Or if men axed him what shal bifalle
90   Of every thing—I may nat rekene° hem alle.   *count*
    This clerk was cleped° hende[9] Nicholas.   *called*
Of derne° love he coude, and of solas,[1]   *secret*
And therto he was sly and ful privee,°   *secretive*
And lik a maide meeke for to see.
95   A chambre hadde he in that hostelrye°   *inn*
Allone, withouten any compaignye,
Ful fetisly ydight with herbes swoote,[2]
And he himself as sweete as is the roote
Of licoris or any setewale.[3]
100   His Almageste[4] and bookes grete and smale,
His astrelabye,[5] longing for° his art,   *belonging to*
His augrim stones,° layen faire apart   *abacus beads*
On shelves couched° at his beddes heed;   *arranged*
His presse° ycovered with a falding° reed;   *dresser / coarse cloth*
105   And al above ther lay a gay sautrye,°   *harp*
On which he made a-nightes melodye
So swetely that al the chambre roong,
And *Angelus ad Virginem*[6] he soong,

7. The arts curriculum (trivium).
8. To estimate by consulting (the stars).
9. Handsome, courteous, handy.
1. Pleasure, (sexual) comforts.
2. Elegantly decked out with sweet herbes.

3. Setwall, a gingerlike spice used as a stimulant.
4. An astrological treatise by Ptolemy.
5. Astrolabe, an astrological instrument.
6. A prayer commemorating the Annunciation.

　　　　And after that he soong the *Kinges Note:*[7]
110　　Ful often blessed was his merye throte.
　　　　And thus this sweete clerk his time spente
　　　　After his freendes finding and his rente.[8]
　　　　　　This carpenter hadde wedded newe a wif
　　　　Which that he loved more than his lif.
115　　Of eighteteene yeer she was of age;
　　　　Jalous he was, and heeld hire narwe in cage,
　　　　For she was wilde and yong, and he was old,
　　　　And deemed° himself been lik a cokewold.　　　　　　　　*supposed*
　　　　He knew nat Caton,[9] for his wit was rude,
120　　That bad men sholde wedde his similitude:°　　　　*equal in age*
　　　　Men sholde wedden after hir estat,°　　　　　　　　*station in life*
　　　　For youthe and elde is often at debat.
　　　　But sith that he was fallen in the snare,
　　　　He moste endure, as other folk, his care.
125　　　　Fair was this yonge wif, and therwithal
　　　　As any wesele hir body gent and smal.[1]
　　　　A ceint° she wered, barred° al of silk;　　　　　　　　*belt / striped*
　　　　A barmcloth° as whit as morne milk　　　　　　　　　　*apron*
　　　　Upon hir lendes,° ful of many a gore;°　　　　　　　*loins / flounce*
130　　Whit was hir smok,° and broiden° al bifore　　　*slip / embroidered*
　　　　And eek bihinde, on hir coler aboute,°　　　　　*around her collar*
　　　　Of col-blak silk, withinne and eek withoute;
　　　　The tapes° of hir white voluper°　　　　　　　　　　*ribbons / cap*
　　　　Were of the same suite° of hir coler;　　　　　　　　*pattern*
135　　Hir filet° brood° of silk and set ful hye;　　　*headband / broad*
　　　　And sikerly she hadde a likerous yë;[2]
　　　　Ful smale ypulled° were hir browes two,　　　　　　　*plucked*
　　　　And tho° were bent, and blake as any slo.°　　　　　*they / plum*
　　　　She was ful more blisful on to see
140　　Than is the newe perejonette° tree,　　　　　　　　　　*pear*
　　　　And softer than the wolle is of a wether;°　　　　　　　*ram*
　　　　And by hir girdel° heeng a purs of lether,　　　　　　　*belt*
　　　　Tasseled with silk and perled° with latoun.°　　*decorated / brass*
　　　　In al this world, to seeken up and down,
145　　Ther nis no man so wis that coude thenche°　　　　*imagine*
　　　　So gay a popelote° or swich a wenche.[3]　　　　　　　*doll*
　　　　Ful brighter was the shining of hir hewe
　　　　Than in the Towr the noble° yforged newe.[4]　　　*gold coin*
　　　　But of hir song, it was as loud and yerne°　　　　　　*lively*
150　　As any swalwe sitting on a berne.
　　　　Therto she coude skippe and make game

---

7. A popular song.
8. According to what his friends gave him and his income.
9. Cato, Latin author of a book of maxims used in elementary education.
1. Her body as delicate and slender as any weasel.
2. And certainly she had a wanton eye.
3. Woman of the working class.
4. Than the new-forged gold coin in the Tower (of London, the royal mint).

As any kide or calf folwing his dame.°   *mother*
Hir mouth was sweete as bragot or the meeth,°   *honey drinks*
Or hoord of apples laid in hay or heeth.°   *heather*
155   Winsing° she was as is a joly° colt,   *skittish / spirited*
Long as a mast, and upright° as a bolt.°   *strait / arrow*
A brooch she bar upon hir lowe coler
As brood as is the boos° of a bokeler;°   *boss / shield*
Hir shoes were laced on hir legges hye.
160   She was a primerole,° a piggesnye,[5]   *primrose*
For any lord to leggen in his bedde,
Or yet for any good yeman to wedde.

     Now sire, and eft° sire, so bifel the cas   *again*
That on a day this hende Nicholas
165   Fil with this yonge wif to rage° and playe,   *sport*
Whil that hir housbonde was at Oseneye°   *Osney, near Oxford*
(As clerkes been ful subtil and ful quainte°),   *clever*
And prively he caughte hire by the queinte,[6]
And saide, "Ywis,° but if ich have my wille,   *certainly*
170   For derne° love of thee, lemman,° I spille,"°   *secret / sweetheart / die*
And heeld hire harde by the haunche-bones,
And saide, "Lemman, love me al atones,°   *at once*
Or I wol dien, also° God me save."   *so*
And she sproong as a colt dooth in a trave,[7]
175   And with hir heed she wried° faste away;   *twisted*
She saide, "I wol nat kisse thee, by my fay.°   *faith*
Why, lat be," quod she, "lat be, Nicholas!
Or I wol crye 'Out, harrow, and allas!'
Do way youre handes, for your curteisye!"
180   This Nicholas gan mercy for to crye,
And spak so faire, and profred him° so faste,   *pressed his case*
That she hir love him graunted atte laste,
And swoor hir ooth by Saint Thomas of Kent
That she wolde been at his comandement,
185   Whan that she may hir leiser° wel espye.   *opportunity*
"Myn housbonde is so ful of jalousye
That but ye waite wel and been privee,[8]
I woot° right wel I nam but deed,"° quod she.   *know / am no more than*
"Ye moste been ful derne° as in this cas."   *secret*
190   "Nay, therof care thee nought," quod Nicholas.
"A clerk hadde litherly biset his while,°   *wasted his time*
But if he coude a carpenter bigile."
And thus they been accorded and ysworn
To waite a time, as I have told biforn.
195   Whan Nicholas hadde doon this everydeel,
And thakked° hire upon the lendes° weel,   *patted / loins*
He kiste hire sweete, and taketh his sautrye,

---

5. Pig's eye, a flower.
6. Literally "dainty part," slang for the female genitals.

7. A restraint for horses when they are being shod.
8. That unless you're very cautious and discreet.

And playeth faste, and maketh melodye.
Thanne fil it thus, that to the parissh chirche,

200 Cristes owene werkes for to wirche,
This goode wif wente on an haliday:°   holy day
Hir forheed shoon as bright as any day,
So was it wasshen whan she leet° hir werk.   left off
Now was ther of that chirche a parissh clerk,

205 The which that was ycleped° Absolon: called
Crul° was his heer, and as the gold it shoon,   curly
And strouted as a fanne[9] large and brode;
Ful straight and evene lay his joly shode.°   part in his hair
His rode° was reed, his y'n greye as goos.   complexion

210 With Poules window[1] corven° on his shoos,   carved
In hoses rede he wente fetisly.°   elegantly
Yclad he was ful smale° and proprely,   fine
Al in a kirtel° of a light waget°—   tunic / blue
Ful faire and thikke been the pointes° set—   laces

215 And therupon he hadde a gay surplis,°   clerical robe
As whit as is the blosme upon the ris.°   twig
A merye child° he was, so God me save.   lad
Wel coude he laten blood,[2] and clippe,° and shave,   cut hair
And maken a chartre of land, or acquitaunce;°   legal release

220 In twenty manere coude he trippe and daunce
After the scole of Oxenforde tho,
And with his legges casten° to and fro,   fling
And playen songes on a smal rubible;°   fiddle
Therto he soong somtime a loud quinible,°   high treble

225 And as wel coude he playe on a giterne:°   guitar
In al the town nas brewhous ne taverne
That he ne visited with his solas,[3]
Ther any gailard tappestere° was.   saucy barmaid
But sooth to sayn, he was somdeel squaimous°   somewhat squeamish

230 Of farting, and of speeche daungerous.°   haughty
This Absolon, that joly was and gay,
Gooth with a cencer° on the haliday,   incense bowl
Cencing the wives of the parissh faste,
And many a lovely look on hem he caste,

235 And namely on this carpenteres wif:
To looke on hire him thoughte a merye lif.
She was so propre and sweete and likerous,°   sexy
I dar wel sayn, if she hadde been a mous,
And he a cat, he wolde hire hente° anoon.   catch

240 This parissh clerk, this joly Absolon,
Hath in his herte swich a love-longinge
That of no wif ne took he noon offringe—

9. And spread out like a winnowing fan (for separating
wheat from chaff).
1. The windows of St. Paul's Chapel were intricately
patterned.

2. Let blood (a medical treatment performed by barbers).
3. Entertainment (also with sexual connotations).

For curteisye he saide he wolde noon.
The moone, whan it was night, ful brighte shoon,
245 And Absolon his giterne hath ytake—
For paramours he thoughte for to wake[4]—
And forth he gooth, jolif° and amorous,   *pretty*
Til he cam to the carpenteres hous,
A litel after cokkes hadde ycrowe,
250 And dressed° him up by a shot-windowe°   *placed / hinged window*
That was upon the carpenteres wal.
He singeth in his vois gentil and smal,°   *high*
"Now dere lady, if thy wille be,
I praye you that ye wol rewe° on me,"   *take pity*
255 Ful wel accordant° to his giterninge.   *harmonizing*
This carpenter awook and herde him singe,
And spak unto his wif, and saide anoon,
"What, Alison, heerestou nought Absolon
That chaunteth thus under oure bowres° wal?"   *bedroom's*
260 And she answerde hir housbonde therwithal,
"Yis, God woot,° John, I heere it everydeel."°   *knows / every bit*
      This passeth forth. What wol ye bet than weel?[5]
Fro day to day this joly Absolon
So woweth° hire that him is wo-bigoon: *woos*
265 He waketh al the night and al the day;
He kembed° his lokkes brode° and made him gay;   *combed / wide-spreading*
He woweth hire by menes and brocage,[6]
And swoor he wolde been hir owene page;°   *attendant*
He singeth, brokking° as a nightingale;   *trilling*
270 He sente hire piment,° meeth,° and spiced ale,   *spiced wine / mead*
And wafres° piping hoot out of the gleede;°   *pastries / coals*
And for she was of towne, he profred meede°—   *bribes*
For som folk wol be wonnen for richesse,
And som for strokes,° and som for gentilesse.   *by force*
275 Somtime to shewe his lightnesse° and maistrye,°   *agility / skill*
He playeth Herodes[7] upon a scaffold° hye.   *platform*
But what availeth him as in this cas?
She loveth so this hende Nicholas
That Absolon may blowe the bukkes horn;[8]
280 He ne hadde for his labour but a scorn.
And thus she maketh Absolon hir ape,°   *fool*
And al his ernest turneth til a jape.°   *joke*
Ful sooth° is this proverbe, it is no lie;   *true*
Men saith right thus: "Alway the nye slye°   *sly one nearby*
285 Maketh the ferre leve to be loth."[9]
For though that Absolon be wood° or wroth,°   *crazy / angry*

4. For the sake of love he thought to keep a vigil.   as a bully.
5. What more would you want?   8. Undertake a useless endeavor.
6. He woos her with go-betweens and mediation.   9. Makes the distant beloved seem hateful.
7. In the English mystery plays, Herod was often portrayed

By cause that he fer was from hir sighte,

This nye Nicholas stood in his lighte.°   *in the way*

   Now beer thee wel, thou hende Nicholas,

290   For Absolon may waile and singe allas.

   And so bifel it on a Saterday

This carpenter was goon til Oseney,

And hende Nicholas and Alisoun

Accorded been to this conclusioun,

295   That Nicholas shal shapen hem a wile°   *devise them a trick*

This sely° jalous housbonde to bigile,   *innocent*

And if so be this game wente aright,

She sholden sleepen in his arm al night—

For this was his desir and hire also.

300   And right anoon, withouten wordes mo,

This Nicholas no lenger wolde tarye,

But dooth ful softe unto his chambre carye

Bothe mete and drinke for a day or twaye,

And to hir housbonde bad hire for to saye,

305   If that he axed after Nicholas,

She sholde saye she niste° wher he was—   *did not know*

Of al that day she sawgh him nought with yë:

She trowed° that he was in maladye,   *believed*

For for no cry hir maide coude him calle,

310   He nolde° answere for no thing that mighte falle.°   *would not / happen*

   This passeth forth al thilke° Saterday   *that same*

That Nicholas stille in his chambre lay,

And eet, and sleep, or dide what him leste,°   *he liked*

Til Sonday that the sonne gooth to reste.

315   This sely carpenter hath greet mervaile°   *wonder*

Of Nicholas, or what thing mighte him aile,

And saide, "I am adrad,° by Saint Thomas,   *afraid*

It stondeth nat aright with Nicholas.

God shilde° that he deide sodeinly!   *forbid*

320   This world is now ful tikel,° sikerly:°   *changeable / surely*

I sawgh today a corps yborn to chirche

That now a Monday last I sawgh him wirche.°   *working*

Go up," quod he unto his knave° anoon,   *manservant*

"Clepe° at his dore or knokke with a stoon.   *call*

325   Looke how it is and tel me boldely."

   This knave gooth him up ful sturdily,

And at the chambre dore whil that he stood

He cride and knokked as that he were wood,

"What? How? What do ye, maister Nicholay?

330   How may ye sleepen al the longe day?".

But al for nought: he herde nat a word.

An hole he foond ful lowe upon a boord,

Ther as the cat was wont in for to creepe,

And at that hole he looked in ful deepe,

335   And atte laste he hadde of him a sighte.

This Nicholas sat evere caping° uprighte   *staring*
As he hadde kiked° on the newe moone.   *gazed*
A down he gooth and tolde his maister soone
In what array° he saw this ilke° man.   *condition / same*
340   This carpenter to blessen him[1] bigan.
And saide, "Help us, Sainte Frideswide![2]
A man woot litel what him shal bitide.
This man is falle, with his astromye,
In som woodnesse° or in som agonye.°   *madness / fit*
345   I thoughte ay° wel how that it sholde be: *always*
Men sholde nought knowe of Goddes privetee.
Ye, blessed be alway a lewed° man   *unlearned*
That nought but only his bileve can.°   *knows his creed*
So ferde° another clerk with astromye: *fared*
350   He walked in the feeldes for to prye°   *gaze*
Upon the sterres, what ther sholde bifalle,
Til he was in a marle-pit° yfalle—   *clay-pit*
He saw nat that. But yet, by Saint Thomas,
Me reweth sore° for hende Nicholas.   *feel sorry*
355   He shal be rated° of his studying,   *scolded*
If that I may, by Jesus, hevene king!
Get me a staf that I may underspore,°   *pry upward*
Whil that thou, Robin, hevest up the dore.
He shal out of his studying, as I gesse."
360   And to the chambre dore he gan him dresse.°   *placed himself*
His knave was a strong carl° for the nones,°   *fellow / purpose*
And by the haspe° he haaf° it up atones: *hinge / heaved*
Into the floor the dore fil anoon.
This Nicholas sat ay as stille as stoon,
365   And evere caped up into the air.
This carpenter wende° he were in despair,   *thought*
And hente° him by the shuldres mightily,   *grabbed*
And shook him harde, and cride spitously,°   *vigorously*
"What, Nicholay, what, how! What! Looke adown!
370   Awaak and thenk on Cristes passioun![3]
I crouche° thee from elves and fro wightes."°   *bless / evil spirits*
Therwith the nightspel° saide he anoonrightes   *charm*
On foure halves° of the hous aboute,   *sides*
And on the threshfold on the dore withoute:
375   "Jesu Crist and Sainte Benedight,[4]
Blesse this hous from every wikked wight!
For nightes nerye° the White Pater Noster.[5]   *protect*
Where wentestou, thou Sainte Petres soster?"°   *sister*
And at the laste this hende Nicholas
380   Gan for to sike° sore, and saide, "Allas,   *sigh*

---

1. Bless himself (with the sign of the cross).
2. A saint venerated for her healing powers.
3. Thinking about Christ's death and resurrection was supposed to ward off evil spells.
4. St. Benedict, founder of Western monasticism.
5. The Lord's Prayer, used as a charm.

Shal al the world be lost eftsoones° now"?   *immediately*
　　This carpenter answerde, "What saistou?
What, thenk on God as we doon, men that swinke."°   *work*
　　This Nicholas answerde, "Fecche me drinke,
385　And after wol I speke in privetee
Of certain thing that toucheth me and thee.
I wol telle it noon other man, certain."
　　This carpenter gooth down and comth again,
And broughte of mighty ale a large quart,
390　And whan that eech of hem hadde dronke his part,
This Nicholas his dore faste shette,°   *shut*
And down the carpenter by him he sette,
And saide, "John, myn hoste lief° and dere,   *beloved*
Thou shalt upon thy trouthe° swere me here   *word of honor*
395　That to no wight thou shalt this conseil° wraye;°   *advice / disclose*
For it is Cristes conseil that I saye,
And if thou telle it man, thou art forlore,°   *lost*
For this vengeance thou shalt have therfore,
That if thou wraye° me, thou shalt be wood."°   *reveal / mad*
400　　"Nay, Crist forbede it, for his holy blood,"
Quod tho this sely man. "I nam no labbe,°   *am no blabbermouth*
And though I saye, I nam nat lief° to gabbe.   *do not like*
Say what thou wilt, I shal it nevere telle
To child ne wif, by him that harwed helle."[6]
405　　"Now John," quod Nicholas, "I wol nought lie.
I have yfounde in myn astrologye,
As I have looked in the moone bright,
That now a Monday next, at quarter night,°   *near dawn*
Shal falle a rain, and that so wilde and wood,°   *furious*
410　That half so greet was nevere Noees° flood.   *Noah's*
This world," he saide, "in lasse than an hour
Shal al be dreint,° so hidous is the showr.   *drowned*
Thus shal mankinde drenche° and lese hir lif."°   *drown / lose their lives*
　　This carpenter answerde, "Allas, my wif!
415　And shal she drenche? Allas, myn Alisoun!"
For sorwe of this he fil almost adown,
And saide, "Is there no remedye in this cas?"
　　"Why yis, for Gode," quod hende Nicholas,
"If thou wolt werken° after lore° and reed°—   *act / learning / advice*
420　Thou maist nought werken after thyn owene heed;
For thus saith Salomon that was ful trewe,
'Werk al by conseil and thou shalt nought rewe.'°   *regret*
And if thou werken wolt by good conseil,
I undertake, withouten mast or sail,
425　Yet shal I save hire and thee and me.
Hastou nat herd how saved was Noee

---

6. Christ, who harrowed hell upon his resurrection, releasing captive souls.

Whan that Oure Lord hadde warned him biforn
That al the world with water sholde be lorn?"°   *lost*
"Yis," quod this carpenter, "ful yore° ago."   *long*
430   "Hastou nat herd," quod Nicholas, "also
The sorwe° of Noee with his felaweshipe?°   *sorrow / companions*
Er that he mighte gete his wif to shipe,
Him hadde levere,° I dar wel undertake,   *would have preferred*
At thilke° time than alle his wetheres blake°   *that / black rams*
435   That she hadde had a ship hirself allone.[7]
And therfore woostou° what is best to doone?   *do you know*
This axeth haste, and of an hastif° thing   *urgent*
Men may nought preche or maken tarying.
Anoon go gete us faste into this in°   *inn*
440   A kneeding trough or elles a kimelin°   *brewing trough*
For eech of us, but looke that they be large,
In whiche we mowen swimme as in a barge,
And han therinne vitaile suffisaunt°   *enough food*
But for a day—fy on the remenaunt!
445   The water shal aslake° and goon away   *recede*
Aboute prime° upon the nexte day.   *6 A.M.*
But Robin may nat wite° of this, thy knave,   *know*
Ne eek thy maide Gille I may nat save.
Axe nought why, for though thou axe me,
450   I wol nought tellen Goddes privetee.
Suffiseth thee, but if thy wittes madde,°   *go mad*
To han° as greet a grace as Noee hadde.   *have*
Thy wif shal I wel saven, out of doute.
Go now thy way, and speed thee heraboute.
455   But whan thou hast for hire and thee and me
Ygeten° us thise kneeding-tubbes three,   *gotten*
Thanne shaltou hangen hem in the roof ful hye,
That no man of oure purveyance° espye.   *preparations*
And whan thou thus hast doon as I have said,
460   And hast oure vitaile faire in hem ylaid,
And eek° an ax to smite° the corde atwo,   *also / cut*
Whan that the water comth that we may go,
And broke an hole an heigh° upon the gable   *on high*
Unto the gardinward,° over the stable,   *toward the garden*
465   That we may freely passen forth oure way,
Whan that the grete showr is goon away,
Thanne shaltou swimme as merye, I undertake,
As dooth the white doke° after hir drake.   *female duck*
Thanne wol I clepe,° 'How, Alison? How, John?   *call out*
470   Be merye, for the flood wol passe anoon.'
And thou wolt sayn, 'Hail, maister Nicholay!
Good morwe, I see thee wel, for it is day!'

---

7. Noah's wife was traditionally portrayed in the mystery plays as a complaining wife who resisted boarding the ark.

And thanne shal we be lordes al oure lif
Of al the world, as Noee and his wif.
475 But of oo thing I warne thee ful right:
Be wel avised on that ilke night
That we been entred into shippes boord
That noon of us ne speke nought a word,
Ne clepe,° ne crye, but been in his prayere,   call out
480 For it is Goddes owene heeste° dete.   commandment
Thy wif and thou mote° hange fer atwinne,°   must / apart
For that bitwixe you shal be no sinne—
Namore in looking than ther shal in deede.
This ordinance is said: go, God thee speede.
485 Tomorwe at night whan men been alle asleepe,
Into oure kneeding-tubbes wol we creepe,
And sitten there, abiding Goddes grace.
Go now thy way, I have no lenger space°   time
To make of this no lenger sermoning.
490 Men sayn thus: 'Send the wise and say no thing.'
Thou art so wis it needeth thee nat teche:
Go save oure lif, and that I thee biseeche."
        This sely° carpenter gooth forth his way: hapless
Ful ofte he saide allas and wailaway,
495 And to his wif he tolde his privetee,
And she was war,° and knew it bet° than he,   aware / better
What al this quainte cast° was for to saye.°   clever trick / mean
But nathelees she ferde° as she wolde deye,   acted
And saide, "Allas, go forth thy way anoon.
500 Help us to scape,° or we been dede eechoon.   escape
I am thy trewe verray wedded wif:
Go, dere spouse, and help to save oure lif."
        Lo, which a greet thing is affeccioun!°   emotion
Men may dien,° of imaginacioun,°   die / fantasy
505 So deepe may impression be take.
This sely carpenter biginneth quake;
Him thinketh verrailiche° that he may see   truly
Noees flood come walwing° as the see   rolling in
To drenchen Alison, his hony dere.
510 He weepeth, waileth, maketh sory cheere;°   expression
He siketh° with ful many a sory swough,°   sighs / breath
And gooth and geteth him a kneeding-trough,
And after a tubbe and a kimelin,
And prively he sente hem to his in,
515 And heeng hem in the roof in privetee;
His owene hand he made laddres three,
To climben by the ronges and the stalkes°   uprights
Unto the tubbes hanging in the balkes,°   rafters
And hem vitailed, bothe trough and tubbe,
520 With breed and cheese and good ale in a jubbe,°   jug
Suffising right ynough as for a day.

But er that he hadde maad al this array,
He sente his knave, and eek his wenche also,
Upon his neede° to London for to go.   *errand*
525 And on the Monday whan it drow to nighte,
He shette his dore withouten candel-lighte,
And dressed° alle thing as it sholde be,   *arranged*
And shortly up they clomben alle three.
They seten stille wel a furlong way.[8]
530   "Now, Pater Noster, clum,"[9] saide Nicholay,
And "Clum" quod John, and "Clum" saide Alisoun.
This carpenter saide his devocioun,
And stille he sit and biddeth his prayere,
Awaiting on the rain, if he it heere.
535   The dede sleep, for wery bisinesse,
Fil on this carpenter right as I gesse
Aboute corfew time,° or litel more.   *dusk*
For travailing of his gost° he groneth sore,   *spirit*
And eft he routeth,° for his heed mislay.   *snores*
540   Down of the laddre stalketh Nicholay,
And Alison ful softe adown she spedde:
Withouten wordes mo they goon to bedde
Ther as the carpenter is wont to lie.
Ther was the revel and the melodye,
545 And thus lith Alison and Nicholas
In bisinesse of mirthe and of solas,
Til that the belle of Laudes[1] gan to ringe,
And freres° in the chauncel° gonne singe.   *friars / chapel*
   This parissh clerk, this amorous Absolon,
550 That is for love always so wo-bigoon,
Upon the Monday was at Oseneye,
With compaignye him to disporte and playe,
And axed upon caas° a cloisterer[2]   *by chance*
Ful prively after John the carpenter;
555 And he drow him apart out of the chirche,
And saide, "I noot:° I sawgh him here nought wirche°   *don't know / working*
Sith Saterday. I trowe that he be went
For timber ther oure abbot hath him sent.
For he is wont for timber for to go,
560 And dwellen atte grange° a day or two.   *outlying farm*
Or elles he is at his hous, certain.
Where that he be I can nought soothly° sayn."   *truly*
   This Absolon ful jolif was and light,°   *amorous and happy*
And thoughte, "Now is time to wake al night,
565 For sikerly,° I sawgh him nought stiringe   *surely*
Aboute his dore sin° day bigan to springe.°   *since / break*
So mote I thrive,° I shal at cokkes crowe   *may I prosper*

---

8. The length of time to travel a furlong.
9. Say the Lord's Prayer and hush.

1. Lauds, daily church service before sunrise.
2. Member of the monastery.

Ful prively knokken at his windowe
That stant ful lowe upon his bowres° wal.   *bedroom's*
570   To Alison now wol I tellen al
My love-longing, for yet I shal nat misse
That at the leeste way I shal hire kisse.
Som manere confort shal I have, parfay.°   *indeed*
My mouth hath icched° al this longe day: *itched*
575   That is a signe of kissing at the leeste.
Al night me mette° eek I was at a feeste.   *dreamed*
Therfore I wol go sleepe an hour or twaye,
And al the night thanne wol I wake and playe."
    Whan that the firste cok hath crowe, anoon
580   Up rist this joly lovere Absolon,
And him arrayeth gay at point devis.°   *fastidiously*
But first he cheweth grain[3] and licoris,
To smellen sweete, er he hadde kembd his heer.
Under his tonge a trewe-love[4] he beer.
585   For therby wende° he to be gracious.°   *supposed / attractive*
He rometh to the carpenteres hous,
And stille he stant under the shot-windowe—
Unto his brest it raughte,° it was so lowe —   *reached*
And ofte he cougheth with a semisoun.°   *soft noise*
590   "What do ye, hony-comb, sweete Alisoun,
My faire brid,° my sweete cinamome?   *bird or bride*
Awaketh, lemman° myn, and speketh to me.   *sweetheart*
Wel litel thinken ye upon my wo
That for your love I swete° ther I go.   *dissolve*
595   No wonder is though that I swelte° and swete: *swelter*
I moorne as dooth a lamb after the tete.
Ywis,° lemman, I have swich love-longinge,   *certainly*
That lik a turtle° trewe is my moorninge: *turtle-dove*
I may nat ete namore than a maide."
600   "Go fro the windowe, Jakke fool," she saide.
"As help me God, it wol nat be com-pa-me.°   *come kiss me*
I love another, and elles I were to blame,
Wel bet than thee, by Jesu, Absolon.
Go forth thy way or I wol caste a stoon,
605   And lat me sleepe, a twenty devele way."[5]
    "Allas," quod Absolon, "and wailaway,
That trewe love was evere so yvele biset.°   *badly done to*
Thanne kis me, sin that it may be no bet,
For Jesus love and for the love of me."
610   "Woltou thanne go thy way therwith?" quod she.
    "Ye, certes, lemman," quod this Absolon.
    "Thanne maak thee redy," quod she. "I come anoon."
And unto Nicholas she said stille,

---

3. Grain of paradise, an aromatic spice.   5. In the name of 20 devils.
4. Four-leafed herb in the shape of a love knot.

"Now hust,° and thou shalt laughen al thy fille."   *hush*
615 This Absolon down sette him on his knees,
And saide, "I am a lord at alle degrees,°   *in every way*
For after this I hope ther cometh more.
Lemman, thy grace, and sweete brid, thyn ore!"°   *mercy*
The windowe she undooth, and that in haste.
620 "Have do," quod she, "com of and speed thee faste,
Lest that oure neighebores thee espye."
This Absolon gan wipe his mouth ful drye:
Derk was the night as pich or as the cole,
And at the windowe out she putte hir hole.
625 And Absolon, him fil no bet ne wers,
But with his mouth he kiste hir naked ers,
Ful savoury,° er he were war of this.   *enthusiastically*
Abak he sterte, and thoughte it was amis,
For wel he wiste a womman hath no beerd.
630 He felte a thing al rough and longe yherd,°   *haired*
And saide, "Fy, allas, what have I do?"
"Teehee," quod she, and clapte the windowe to.
And Absolon gooth forth a sory pas.°   *with downcast step*
"A beerd, a beerd!" quod hende Nicholas,
635 "By Goddes corpus,° this gooth faire and weel."   *body*
This sely Absolon herde everydeel,
And on his lippe he gan for anger bite,
And to himself he saide, "I shal thee quite."°   *repay*
Who rubbeth now, who froteth now his lippes
640 With dust, with sond, with straw, with cloth, with chippes,
But Absolon, that saith ful ofte allas?
"My soule bitake° I unto Satanas,   *hand over*
But me were levere than⁶ all this town," quod he,
"Of this despit° awroken° for to be.   *insult / avenged*
645 Allas," quod he, "allas I ne hadde ybleint!"°   *turned aside*
His hote love was cold and al yqueint,°   *quenched*
For fro that time that he hadde kist hir ers
Of paramours he sette nought a kers,⁷
For he was heled of his maladye.
650 Ful ofte paramours he gan defye,°   *renounce*
And weep as dooth a child that is ybete.°   *beaten*
A softe paas he wente over the streete
Until a smith men clepen daun Gervais,°   *call Sir*
That in his forge smithed plough harneis:°   *equipment*
655 He sharpeth shaar° and cultour° bisily.   *plowshare / plough-blade*
This Absolon knokketh al esily,°   *softly*
And saide, "Undo,° Gervais, and that anoon."   *open up*
"What, who artou?" "It am I, Absolon."
"What, Absolon? What, Cristes sweete tree!

6. I would rather than (have).   7. Did not value as much as a piece of cress.

660	Why rise ye so rathe?° Ey, benedicite,°	*early / bless me*
	What aileth you? Som gay girl, God it woot,	
	Hath brought you thus upon the viritoot.°	*on the prowl*
	By Sainte Note,[8] ye woot wel what I mene."	
	This Absolon ne roughte nat a bene°	*did not care a bean*
665	Of al his play. No word again he yaf:°	*gave*
	He hadde more tow on his distaf[9]	
	Than Gervais knew, and saide, "Freend so dere,	
	This hote cultour in the chimenee° here,	*fireplace*
	As lene it me:[1] I have therwith to doone.	
670	I wol bringe it thee again ful soone."	
	Gervais answerde, "Certes, were it gold,	
	Or in a poke nobles alle untold,[2]	
	Thou sholdest have, as I am trewe smith.	
	Ey, Cristes fo,[3] what wol ye do therwith?"	
675	"Therof," quod Absolon, "be as be may.	
	I shal wel telle it thee another day,"	
	And caughte the cultour by the colde stele.°	*handle*
	Ful softe out at the dore he gan to stele,	
	And wente unto the carpenteres wal:	
680	He cougheth first and knokketh therwithal	
	Upon the windowe, right as he dide er.°	*before*
	This Alison answerde, "Who is ther	
	That knokketh so? I warante° it a thief."	*bet*
	"Why, nay," quod he, "God woot, my sweete lief,°	*dear*
685	I am thyn Absolon, my dereling.	
	Of gold," quod he, "I have thee brought a ring—	
	My moder yaf it me, so God me save;	
	Ful fin it is and therto wel ygrave:°	*engraved*
	This wol I yiven thee if thou me kisse."	
690	This Nicholas was risen for to pisse,	
	And thoughte he wolde amenden al the jape:[4]	
	He sholde kisse his ers er that he scape.	
	And up the windowe dide he hastily,	
	And out his ers he putteth prively,	
695	Over the buttok to the haunche-boon.°	*thigh*
	And therwith spak this clerk, this Absolon,	
	"Speek, sweete brid, I noot nought wher thou art."	
	This Nicholas anoon leet flee° a fart	*let fly*
	As greet as it hadde been a thonder-dent°	*thunderbolt*
700	That with the strook he was almost yblent,°	*blinded*
	And he was redy with his iren hoot,	
	And Nicholas amiddle the ers he smoot:	
	Of gooth the skin an hande-brede° aboute;	*hand's width*

8. St. Noet, a ninth-century saint, with possible pun on Noah.
9. Flax on his distaff (i.e., cares on his mind).
1. Be so good as to lend it to me.

2. Or in a pouch of uncounted gold coins.
3. By Christ's foe (i.e., the Devil).
4. Make the joke even better.

The hote cultour brende so his toute°   *backside*
705 That for the smert° he wende° for to die;   *pain / thought*
As he were wood for wo he gan to crye,
"Help! Water! Water! Help, for Goddes herte!"
    This carpenter out of his slomber sterte,
And herde oon cryen "Water!" as he were wood,
710 And thoughte, "Allas, now cometh Noweles° flood!"   *Noah's*
He sette him up withoute wordes mo,
And with his ax he smooth the corde atwo,
And down gooth al: he foond neither to selle
Ne breed ne ale til he cam to the celle,[5]
715 Upon the floor, and ther aswoune° he lay.   *stunned*
    Up sterte° hire Alison and Nicholay,   *leaped*
And criden "Out" and "Harrow" in the streete.
The neighebores, bothe smale and grete,[6]
In ronnen for to gauren° on this man   *stare*
720 That aswoune lay bothe pale and wan,
For with the fal he brosten° hadde his arm;   *broken*
But stonde he moste unto his owene harm,
For whan he spak he was anoon bore down°   *restrained*
With° hende Nicholas and Alisoun: *by*
725 They tolden every man that he was wood°—   *crazy*
He was agast° so of Noweles flood,   *afraid*
Thurgh fantasye, that of his vanitee°   *folly*
He hadde ybought him kneeding-tubbes three,
And hadde hem hanged in the roof above,
730 And that he prayed hem, for Goddes love,
To sitten in the roof, *par compaignye*.°   *for fellowship*
    The folk gan laughen at his fantasye.
Into the roof they kiken° and they cape,°   *peer / gape*
And turned al his harm unto a jape,
735 For what so that this carpenter answerde,
It was for nought: no man his reson herde;
With othes grete he was so sworn adown,°   *refuted by oaths*
That he was holden wood in al the town,
For every clerk anoonright heeld with other:
740 They saide, "The man was wood, my leve brother,"
And every wight° gan laughen at this strif.   *person*
Thus swived° was the carpenteres wif   *screwed*
For al his keeping and his jalousye,
And Absolon hath kist hir nether° yë,   *lower*
745 And Nicholas is scalded in the toute:
This tale is doon, and God save al the route!

---

5. He found no time to sell either bread or ale until he reached the floor (i.e., he fell to the ground too quickly to be aware of what was happening).

6. Lower- and upper-class people alike.

THE WIFE OF BATH'S PROLOGUE AND TALE   Dame Alison, the Wife of Bath, is Chaucer's greatest contribution to the stock characters of Western culture. She has a long literary ancestry, most immediately in the Duenna of the thirteenth-century French poem, *The Romance of the Rose,* and stretching back to the Roman poet Ovid. Dame Alison stands out in bold relief, even among the vivid Canterbury pilgrims, partly because Chaucer gives her so rebellious and explicitly self-created a biography. She has outlived five husbands, accumulated wealth from the first three, and made herself rich in the growing textile industry of her time. At once a great companion and greatly unnerving, Alison lives in constant battle with a secular and religious world mostly controlled by men and yet has a keen appetite both for the men and for the battle.

The Wife of Bath's *Prologue* and *Tale* seem only the current installments of a multifaceted struggle in which Dame Alison has long been engaged, at first through her body and social role and now, in the face of advancing years, through the remaining agency of retrospective story-telling. She battles a society in which many young women are almost chattels in a marital market, as was the twelve-year-old version of herself who first was married off to a wealthier, much older man. She battles him and later husbands for power within the marriage, and her ambition to social dominance, as the *General Prologue* reports, extends to life in her urban parish.

By the moment of the Canterbury pilgrimage, though, the Wife's adversaries are more daunting, less easily conquered. The *Wife's Prologue*, for all its autobiographical energy, is primarily a debate with the clergy and with "auctoritee"—the whole armature of learning and literacy by which the clergy (like her clerically educated fifth husband, Jankyn) seeks to silence her.

The Wife's *Tale*, too, can be seen as an angry riposte to the secular fantasies of Arthurian chivalry and genetic nobility. The Wife's well-born Arthurian knight is a common rapist, who finds himself at the mercy of a queen and then in the arms of a crone. The tale turns Arthurian conventions on their head, lays sexual violence in the open, and puts legal and magical power in the hands of women. It is explicitly a fantasy, but a powerful one.

Alison's final enemy, mortality itself, is what makes her both most desperate and most sympathetic. The husbands are gone. Even the fondly recalled Jankyn slips into a rosy glow and the past tense; so does her own best friend and "gossip," the odd mirror-double "Alisoun." The Wife of Bath keeps addressing other "wives" in her *Prologue*, but there are no others on the pilgrimage. Her very argument with the institutionalized church distances her from its comforts, and she is deeply aware that time is stealing her beauty as it has taken away the companions who made up her earlier life. If Alison's *Tale* closes with a delicious fantasy of restored youth, it is only a pendant to the much longer *Prologue* and its cheerful yet poignant acceptance of age.

The Wife of Bath's Prologue

Experience, though noon auctoritee[1]
Were in this world, is right ynough for me
To speke of wo that is in mariage:
For lordinges,° sith I twelf yeer was of age—   *gentlemen*
5   Thanked be God that is eterne on live—
Housbondes at chirche dore I have had five
(If I so ofte mighte han wedded be),
And alle were worthy men in hir° degree.   *their*
But me was told, certain, nat longe agoon is,
10   That sith that Crist ne wente nevere but ones°   *once*

1. Even if no authority, textual precedent.

To wedding in the Cane of Galilee,[2]
That by the same ensample taughte he me
That I ne sholde wedded be but ones.
Herke eek, lo, which a sharp word for the nones,°   *for the purpose*
15   Biside a welle, Jesus, God and man,
Spak in repreve° of the Samaritan:[3]   *reproof*
"Thou hast yhad five housbondes," quod he,
"And that ilke° man that now hath thee   *same*
Is nat thyn housbonde." Thus saide he certain.
20   What that he mente therby I can nat sayn,
But that I axe why that the fifthe man
Was noon housbonde to the Samaritan?
How manye mighte she han in mariage?
Yit herde I nevere tellen in myn age
25   Upon this nombre diffinicioun.
Men may divine° and glosen° up and down,   *guess / interpret*
But wel I woot,° expres,° withouten lie,   *know / manifestly*
God bad us for to wexe° and multiplye: *increase*
That gentil text can I wel understonde.
30   Eek wel I woot he saide that myn housbonde
Sholde lete° fader and moder and take to me,   *leave*
But of no nombre mencion made he—
Of bigamye or of octogamye:
Why sholde men thanne speke of it vilainye?°   *as churlish*
35   Lo, here the wise king daun° Salomon: *Lord*
I trowe° he hadde wives many oon,   *believe*
As wolde God it leveful° were to me   *lawful*
To be refresshed half so ofte as he.
Which yifte° of God hadde he for alle his wives!   *what a gift*
40   No man hath swich that in this world alive is.
God woot° this noble king, as to my wit,°   *knows / understanding*
The firste night hadde many a merye fit
With eech of hem, so wel was him on live.
Blessed be God that I have wedded five,
45   Of whiche I have piked° out the beste,   *picked*
Bothe of hir nether purs and of hir cheste.[4]
Diverse° scoles maken parfit° clerkes,   *different / accomplished*
And diverse practikes in sondry werkes
Maken the werkman° parfit sikerly:°   *craftsman / surely*
50   Of five housbondes scoleying° am I.   *studying*
Welcome the sixte whan that evere he shal!
For sith I wol nat keepe me chast in al,
Whan myn housbonde is fro the world agoon,
Som Cristen man shal wedde me anoon.
55   For thanne th'Apostle[5] saith that I am free

2. Cana, where Jesus performed his first miracle at a wedding feast (John 2.1).
3. The story of Jesus and the Samaritan woman is related

4. Money chest, with a pun on body parts.
5. St. Paul, in Romans 7.2.in John 4.6 ff.

To wedde, a Goddes half,[6] where it liketh° me.   *please*
He said that to be wedded is no sinne:
Bet° is to be wedded than to brinne.°   *better / burn (in hell)*
What rekketh° me though folk saye vilainye   *do I care*
60   Of shrewed° Lamech[7] and his bigamye?   *cursed*
I woot wel Abraham was an holy man,
And Jacob eek, as fer as evere I can,°   *know*
And eech of hem hadde wives mo than two,
And many another holy man also.
65   Where can ye saye in any manere age
That hye God defended° mariage   *prohibited*
By expres word? I praye you, telleth me.
Or where comanded he virginitee?
I woot as wel as ye, it is no drede,°   *doubt*
70   Th'Apostle, whan he speketh of maidenhede,°   *virginity*
He saide that precept° therof hadde he noon: *command*
Men may conseile a womman to be oon,°   *single*
But conseiling nis no comandement.
He putte it in oure owene juggement.
75   For hadde God comanded maidenhede,
Thanne hadde he dampned° wedding with the deede;   *condemned*
And certes, if ther were no seed ysowe,
Virginitee, thanne wherof sholde it growe?
Paul dorste nat comanden at the leeste
80   A thing of which his maister yaf no heeste.°   *commandment*
The dart° is set up for virginitee: *prize*
Cacche whoso may, who renneth° best lat see.   *runs*
But this word is nought take° of every wight,°   *required / person*
But ther as God list° yive it of his might.   *pleases*
85   I woot wel that th'Apostle was a maide,°   *virgin*
But nathelees, though that he wroot or saide
He wolde that every wight were swich as he,
Al nis but° conseil to virginitee;   *it is only*
And for to been a wif he yaf me leve
90   Of indulgence; so nis it no repreve
To wedde me if that my make° die,   *mate*
Withouten excepcion° of bigamye—   *legal objection*
Al were it good no womman for to touche
(He mente as in his bed or in his couche,
95   For peril is bothe fir and tow t'assemble[8]—
Ye knowe what this ensample may resemble).
This al and som,° he heeld virginitee   *all told*
More parfit than wedding in freletee.°   *due to weakness*
(Freletee clepe° I but if° that he and she   *call / except*
100   Wolde leden al hir lif in chastitee).

---

6. From God's perspective.   8. To bring together fire and flax.
7. The earliest bigamist in the Bible (Genesis 4.19).

I graunte it wel, I have noon envye
Though maidenhede preferre° bigamye: *surpasses*
It liketh hem to be clene in body and gost.°   *soul*
Of myn estaat° ne wol I make no boost;   *condition*
105 For wel ye knowe, a lord in his houshold
Ne hath nat every vessel al of gold:
Some been of tree,° and doon hir lord servise.   *wood*
God clepeth° folk to him in sondry wise,   *calls*
And everich hath of God a propre yifte,
110 Som this, som that, as him liketh shifte.⁹
Virginitee is greet perfeccioun,
And continence eek with devocioun,
But Crist, that of perfeccion is welle,°   *source*
Bad nat every wight° he sholde go selle   *person*
115 Al that he hadde and yive it to the poore,
And in swich wise folwe° him and his fore:°   *follow / footsteps*
He spak to hem that wolde live parfitly°—   *perfectly*
And lordinges, by youre leve, that am nat I.
I wol bistowe the flour of al myn age
120 In th'actes and in fruit of mariage.

     Telle me also, to what conclusioun°   *end*
Were membres maad of generacioun
And of so parfit wis a wrighte ywrought?¹
Trusteth right wel, they were nat maad for nought.
125 Glose whoso wol, and saye bothe up and down
That they were maked for purgacioun
Of urine, and oure bothe thinges smale
Was eek to knowe a femele from a male,
And for noon other cause—saye ye no?
130 Th'experience woot wel it is nought so.
So that the clerkes be nat with me wrothe,°   *angry*
I saye this, that they maked been for bothe—
That is to sayn, for office° and for ese°   *use / pleasure*
Of engendrure,° ther we nat God displese.   *procreation*
135 Why sholde men elles in hir bookes sette
That man shal yeelde° to his wif hir dette?°   *pay / marriage debt*
Now wherwith sholde he make his payement
If he ne used his sely° instrument?   *innocent*
Thanne were they maad upon a creature
140 To purge urine, and eek for engendrure.
     But I saye nought that every wight is holde,°   *bound*
That hath swich harneis° as I to you tolde,   *equipment*
To goon and usen hem in engendrure:
Thanne sholde men take of chastitee no cure.°   *heed*
145 Crist was a maide and shapen as a man,
And many a saint sith that the world bigan,
Yit lived they evere in parfit° chastitee.   *perfect*

---

9. As it pleases him to provide.   1. And created by so perfectly wise a Creator?

I nil envye no virginitee:

Lat hem be breed° of pured° whete seed,   *bread / refined*

150   And lat us wives hote° barly breed —   *be called*

And yit with barly breed, Mark telle can,

Oure Lord Jesu refresshed many a man.

In swich estaat as God hath cleped° us   *called*

I wol persevere: I nam nat precious.°   *am not fussy*

155   In wifhood wol I use myn instrument

As freely° as my Makere hath it sent.   *generously*

If I be daungerous,° God yive me sorwe:°   *withholding / sorrow*

Myn housbonde shal it han both eve and morwe,°   *morning*

Whan that him list come forth and paye his dette.

160   An housbonde wol I have, I wol nat lette,°   *forgo*

Which shal be bothe my dettour and my thral,°   *slave*

And have his tribulacion withal

Upon his flessh whil that I am his wif.

I have the power during al my lif

165   Upon his propre° body, and nat he: *own*

Right thus th'Apostle tolde it unto me,

And bad oure housbondes for to love us weel.

Al this sentence° me liketh everydeel.   *interpretation*

An Interlude

Up sterte° the Pardoner and that anoon: *started*

170   "Now dame," quod he, "by God and by Saint John,

Ye been a noble prechour° in this cas.   *preacher*

I was aboute to wedde a wif: allas,

What° sholde I bye° it on my flessh so dere?   *why / buy*

Yit hadde I levere° wedde no wif toyere."°   *rather / this year*

175   "Abid," quod she, "my tale is nat bigonne.

Nay, thou shalt drinken of another tonne,°   *barrel*

Er that I go, shal savoure wors than ale.

And whan that I have told thee forth my tale

Of tribulacion in mariage,

180   Of which I am expert in al myn age—

This is to saye, myself hath been the whippe—

Thanne maistou chese° wheither thou wolt sippe   *may you choose*

Of thilke° tonne that I shal abroche:°   *that same / open*

Be war of it, er thou too neigh approche,

185   For I shal telle ensamples mo than ten.

'Whoso that nile° be war by othere men,   *will not*

By him shal othere men corrected be.'

Thise same wordes writeth Ptolomee:[2]

Rede in his Almageste and take it there."

190   "Dame, I wolde praye you if youre wil it were,"

Saide this Pardoner, "as ye bigan,

---

2. Ptolemy, ancient Greek astronomer and author of the *Almageste*.

Telle forth youre tale; spareth for no man,
And teche us yonge men of youre practike."
    "Gladly," quod she, "sith it may you like;

195 But that I praye to al this compaignye,
     If that I speke after my fantasye,°   *fancy*
     As taketh nat agrief° of that I saye,   *amiss*
     For myn entente nis but° for to playe."   *intent is only*

The Wife Continues

Now sire, thanne wol I telle you forth my tale.

200 As evere mote I drinke win or ale,
     I shal saye sooth:° tho° housbondes that I hadde,   *truth / those*
     As three of hem were goode, and two were badde.
     The three men were goode, and riche, and olde;
     Unnethe° mighte they the statut holde   *scarcely*

205 In which they were bounden unto me—
     Ye woot wel what I mene of this, pardee.°   *by God*
     As help me God, I laughe whan I thinke
     How pitously anight I made hem swinke;°   *work*
     And by my fay,° I tolde of it no stoor:°   *faith / gave it no heed*

210 They hadde me yiven hir land and hir tresor;°   *wealth*
     Me needed nat do lenger diligence
     To winne hir love or doon hem reverence.
     They loved me so wel, by God above,
     That I ne tolde no daintee° of hir love.   *set no value on*

215 A wis womman wol bisye hire evere in oon°   *constantly*
     To gete hire love, ye, ther as she hath noon.
     But sith I hadde hem hoolly in myn hand,
     And sith that they hadde yiven me al hir land,
     What sholde I take keep° hem for to plese,   *care*

220 But it were for my profit and myn ese?
     I sette hem so awerke, by my fay,°   *faith*
     That many a night they songen wailaway.
     The bacon was nat fet° for hem, I trowe,   *collected*
     That some men han in Essexe at Dunmowe.³

225 I governed hem so wel after my lawe
     That eech of hem ful blisful was and fawe°   *glad*
     To bringe me gaye thinges fro the faire;
     They were ful glade whan I spak to hem faire,
     For God it woot, I chidde° hem spitously.°   *scolded / cruelly*

230   Now herkneth how I bar me proprely:
     Ye wise wives, that conne understonde,
     Thus sholde ye speke and bere him wrong on honde°—   *wrongly accuse*
     For half so boldely can ther no man
     Swere and lie as a woman can.

235 I saye nat this by wives that been wise,

---

3. At Dunmowe, spouses who had spent a year without quarrelling were awarded a side of bacon.

	But if it be whan they hem misavise.°	*err*
	A wis wif, if that she can hir good,⁴	
	Shal bere him on hande the cow is wood,⁵	
	And take witnesse of hir owene maide	
240	Of hir assent.° But herkneth how I saide:	*as her accomplice*
	"Sire olde cainard,° is this thyn array?	*dotard*
	Why is my neighebores wif so gay?	
	She is honoured overal ther she gooth:	
	I sitte at hoom; I have no thrifty° cloth.	*decent*
245	What doostou at my neighebores hous?	
	Is she so fair? Artou so amorous?	
	What roune° ye with oure maide, benedicite°?	*whisper / bless us*
	Sire olde lechour, lat thy japes° be.	*tricks*
	And if I have a gossib° or a freend,	*confidante*
250	Withouten gilt ye chiden as a feend,	
	If that I walke or playe unto his hous.	
	Thou comest hoom as dronken as a mous,	
	And prechest on thy bench, with yvel preef.°	*bad luck to you*
	Thou saist to me, it is a greet meschief	
255	To wedde a poore womman for costage.°	*expense*
	And if that she be riche, of heigh parage,°	*breeding*
	Thanne saistou that it is a tormentrye	
	To suffre hir pride and hir malencolye.	
	And if that she be fair, thou verray knave,	
260	Thou saist that every holour° wol hire have:	*whoremonger*
	She may no while in chastitee abide	
	That is assailed upon eech a side.	
	"Thou saist som folk desiren us for richesse,	
	Som for oure shap, and som for oure fairnesse,	
265	And som for she can outher° singe or daunce,	*either*
	And som for gentilesse and daliaunce,°	*conversation*
	Som for hir handes and hir armes smale—	
	Thus gooth al to the devel by thy tale!⁶	
	Thou saist men may nat keepe a castel wal,	
270	It may so longe assailed been overal.	
	And if that she be foul, thou saist that she	
	Coveiteth° every man that she may see;	*desires*
	For as a spaniel she wol on him lepe,	
	Til that she finde som man hire to chepe.°	*take*
275	Ne noon so grey goos gooth ther in the lake,	
	As, saistou, wol be withoute make;°	*mate*
	And saist it is an hard thing for to weelde°	*control*
	A thing that no man wol, his thankes,° heelde.°	*willingly / hold*
	Thus saistou, lorel,° whan thou goost to bedde,	*scoundrel*
280	And that no wis man needeth for to wedde,	
	Ne no man that entendeth° unto hevene—	*expects (to go)*

4. Knows what's good for her.   6. According to what you say.
5. Shall convince him the chough is mad. The chough, a
crow-like bird, was fabled to reveal wives' infidelities.

With wilde thonder-dint° and firy levene°   *thunderclap / lightning*
Mote° thy welked° nekke be tobroke!°   *may / withered / broken*
Thou saist that dropping° houses and eek smoke   *leaking*
285 And chiding wives maken men to flee
Out of hir owene houses: a, benedicite,
What aileth swich an old man for to chide?
Thou saist we wives wil oure vices hide
Til we be fast,° and thanne we wol hem shewe—   *bound (in marriage)*
290 Wel may that be a proverbe of a shrewe!°   *scoundrel*
Thou saist that oxen, asses, hors, and houndes,
They been assayed° at diverse stoundes;°   *tested / times*
Bacins,° lavours,° er that men hem bye,   *basins / wash bowls*
Spoones, stooles, and al swich housbondrye,
295 And so be pottes, clothes, and array—
But folk of wives maken noon assay°   *trial*
Til they be wedded—olde dotard shrewe!
And thanne, saistou, we wil oure vices shewe.
Thou saist also that it displeseth me
300 But if° that thou wolt praise my beautee,   *unless*
And but thou poure alway upon my face,
And clepe° me 'Faire Dame' in every place,   *call*
And but thou make a feeste on thilke° day   *that*
That I was born, and make me fressh and gay,
305 And but thou do to my norice° honour,   *nurse*
And to my chamberere° within my bowr,°   *chambermaid / bedroom*
And to my fadres folk, and his allies°—   *kinsmen*
Thus saistou, olde barel-ful of lies.
And yit of our apprentice Janekin,
310 For his crispe heer,° shining as gold so fin,   *curly hair*
And for he squiereth° me bothe up and down,   *chaperones*
Yit hastou caught a fals suspecioun;
I wil° him nat though thou were deed tomorwe.   *desire*
   "But tel me this, why hidestou with sorwe
315 The keyes of thy cheste away fro me?
It is my good as wel as thyn, pardee.°   *by God*
What, weenestou° make an idiot of oure dame?   *do you suppose*
Now by that lord that called is Saint Jame,[7]
Thou shalt nought bothe, though that thou were wood,°   *enraged*
320 Be maister of my body and of my good:
That oon thou shalt forgo, maugree thine yën.[8]
   "What helpeth it of me enquere and spyen?
I trowe thou woldest loke° me in thy cheste.   *lock*
Thou sholdest saye, 'Wif, go wher thee leste.°   *it pleases*
325 Taak youre disport.° I nil leve° no tales: *amusement / believe*
I knowe you for a trewe wif, dame Alis.'
We love no man that taketh keep° or charge   *notice*

---

7. Santiago de Compostela, whose shrine in Spain the   8. In spite of your eyes (an oath).
Wife of Bath has already made a pilgrimage to visit.

Wher that we goon: we wol been at oure large.°   *liberty*
Of alle men yblessed mote he be
330 The wise astrologen daun Ptolomee,
That saith this proverbe in his Almageste:
'Of alle men his wisdom is the hyeste
That rekketh° nat who hath the world in honde.'   *cares*
By this proverbe thou shalt understonde,
335 Have thou ynough, what thar° thee rekke° or care   *need / be concerned*
How merily that othere folkes fare?°   *go about*
For certes, olde dotard, by youre leve,
Ye shal han queinte° right ynough at eve: *sex*
He is too greet a nigard that wil werne°   *refuse*
340 A man to lighte a candle at his lanterne;
He shal han nevere the lasse lighte, pardee.°   *by God*
Have thou ynough, thee thar nat plaine thee.°   *complain*
     "Thou saist also that if we make us gay
With clothing and with precious array,
345 That it is peril of oure chastitee,
And yit with sorwe thou moste enforce thee,[9]
And saye thise wordes in th'Apostles name:
'In habit° maad with chastitee and shame   *clothing*
Ye wommen shal apparaile you,' quod he,
350 'And nat in tressed heer° and gay perree,°   *styled hair / jewels*
As perles ne with gold ne clothes riche.'
After thy text, ne after thy rubriche,[1]
I wol nat werke as muchel as a gnat.
Thou saidest this, that I was lik a cat:
355 For whoso wolde senge° a cattes skin,   *singe*
Thanne wolde the cat wel dwellen in his in;°   *inn*
And if the cattes skin be slik° and gay,   *sleek*
She wol nat dwelle in house half a day,
But forth she wol, er any day be dawed,°   *dawned*
360 To shewe her skin and goon a-caterwawed.°   *caterwauling*
This is to saye, if I be gay, sire shrewe,
I wol renne out, my borel° for to shewe.   *coarse cloth*
Sire olde fool, what helpeth thee t'espyen?
Though thou praye Argus[2] with his hundred yën
365 To be my wardecors,° as he can best,   *bodyguard*
In faith, he shal nat keepe me but me lest:
Yit coude I make his beerd,[3] so mote I thee.°   *so may I prosper*
     "Thou saidest eek that ther been thinges three,
The whiche thinges troublen al this erthe,
370 And that no wight° may endure the ferthe.°   *person / fourth*
O leve sire shrewe, Jesu shorte thy lif!
Yit prechestou and saist an hateful wif

9. Reinforce (your position).
1. Rubric, interpretive heading on a text.
2. Mythical hundred-eyed monster employed by Juno to
guard over Io, one of Jove's many lovers, whom the goddess turned into a cow.
3. Deceive him.

Yrekened° is for oon of thise meschaunces.   *accounted*
Been ther nat none othere resemblaunces
375 That ye may likne youre parables to,
But if a sely° wif be oon of tho?   *innocent*
    "Thou liknest eek wommanes love to helle,
To bareine land ther water may nat dwelle;
Thou liknest it also to wilde fir—
380 The more it brenneth,° the more it hath desir   *burns*
To consumen every thing that brent wol be;
Thou saist right as wormes shende° a tree,   *destroy*
Right so a wif destroyeth hir housbonde—
This knowen they that been to wives bonde."
385   Lordinges, right thus, as ye han understonde,
Bar I stifly° mine olde housbondes on honde°   *firmly / swore*
That thus they saiden in hir dronkenesse—
And al was fals, but that I took witnesse
On Janekin and on my nece° also.   *kinswoman*
390 O Lord, the paine I dide hem and the wo,
Ful giltelees, by Goddes sweete pine!°   *suffering*
For as an hors I coude bite and whine;
I coude plaine and° I was in the gilt,°   *when / wrong*
Or elles often time I hadde been spilt.°   *ruined*
395 Whoso that first to mille comth first grint.°   *grinds*
I plained first: so was oure werre° stint.°   *war / stopped*
They were ful glad to excusen hem ful blive°   *quickly*
Of thing of which they nevere agilte° hir live.   *offended (in)*
Of wenches wolde I beren hem on honde,
400 Whan that for sik they mighte unnethe° stonde,   *barely*
Yit tikled I his herte for that he
Wende° I hadde had of him so greet cheertee.°   *supposed / fondness*
I swoor that al my walking out by nighte
Was for to espye wenches that he dighte.°   *had sex with*
405 Under that colour° hadde I many a mirthe.   *pretense*
For al swich wit is yiven us in oure birthe:
Deceite, weeping, spinning God hath yive
To wommen kindely° whil they may live.   *by nature*
And thus of oo thing I avaunte° me: *boast*
410 At ende I hadde the bet in eech degree,
By sleighte° or force, or by som manere thing,   *deception*
As by continuel murmur° or grucching;°   *complaining / grumbling*
Namely abedde° hadden they meschaunce:°   *in bed / misfortune*
Ther wolde I chide and do hem no plesaunce;
415 I wolde no lenger in the bed abide
If that I felte his arm over my side,
Til he hadde maad his raunson° unto me;   *amends*
Thanne wolde I suffre him do his nicetee.°   *lust*
And therfore every man this tale I telle:
420 Winne whoso may, for al is for to selle;
With empty hand men may no hawkes lure.

	For winning° wolde I al his lust endure,	*profit*
	And make me a feined appetit—	
	And yit in bacon° hadde I nevere delit.	*old meat*
425	That made me that evere I wolde hem chide;	
	For though the Pope hadde seten° hem biside,	*sat*
	I wolde nought spare hem at hir owene boord.°	*table*
	For by my trouthe, I quitte° hem word for word.	*repaid*
	As help me verray God omnipotent,	
430	Though I right now sholde make my testament,	
	I ne owe hem nat a word that it nis quit.°	*is not repaid*
	I broughte it so aboute by my wit	
	That they moste yive it up as for the beste,	
	Or elles hadde we nevere been in reste;	
435	For though he looked as a wood leoun,°	*crazed lion*
	Yit sholde he faile of his conclusion.°	*purpose*
	Thanne wolde I saye, "Goodelief,° taak keep,	*Sweetheart*
	How mekely looketh Wilekin, oure sheep!	
	Com neer my spouse, lat me ba° thy cheeke—	*kiss*
440	Ye sholden be al pacient and meeke,	
	And han a sweete-spiced conscience,	
	Sith ye so preche of Jobes[4] pacience;	
	Suffreth alway, sin ye so wel can preche;	
	And but ye do, certain, we shal you teche	
445	That it is fair to han a wif in pees.	
	Oon of us two moste bowen, doutelees,	
	And sith a man is more resonable	
	Than womman is, ye mosten been suffrable.°	*patient*
	What aileth you to grucche thus and grone?	
450	Is it for ye wolde have my queinte allone?	
	Why, taak it al—lo, have it everydeel.	
	Peter,° I shrewe° you but ye love it weel.	*by St. Peter / curse*
	For if I wolde selle my bele chose,[5]	
	I coude walke as fressh as is a rose;	
455	But I wol keepe it for youre owene tooth.°	*taste*
	Ye be to blame. By God, I saye you sooth!"	
	Swiche manere wordes hadde we on honde.	
	Now wol I speke of my ferthe housbonde.	
	My ferthe housbonde was a revelour—	
460	This is to sayn, he hadde a paramour°—	*lover*
	And I was yong and ful of ragerye,°	*wantonness*
	Stibourne° and strong and joly as a pie:°	*stubborn / magpie*
	How coude I daunce to an harpe smale,°	*gracefully*
	And singe, ywis,° as any nightingale,	*certainly*
465	Whan I hadde dronke a draughte of sweete win.	
	Metellius,[6] the foule cherl,° the swin,	*ruffian*

4. The biblical Job, who suffers patiently the trials imposed by God.
5. "Beautiful thing," a euphemism for female genitals.

6. Egnatius Metellius, whose actions are described in Valerius Maximus's *Facta et dicta memorabilia*, 6.3.

That with a staf birafte his wif hir lif
For she drank win, though I hadde been his wif,
Ne sholde nat han daunted me fro drinke;
470 And after win on Venus moste I thinke,
For also siker° as cold engendreth hail,   *certainly*
A likerous° mouth moste han a likerous° tail: *gluttonous / lecherous*
In womman vinolent° is no defence—   *drunken*
This knowen lechours by experience.
475   But Lord Crist, whan that it remembreth me
Upon my youthe and on my jolitee,
It tikleth me aboute myn herte roote°—   *bottom of my heart*
Unto this day it dooth myn herte boote°   *good*
That I have had my world as in my time.
480 But age, allas, that al wol envenime,°   *poison*
Hath me biraft my beautee and my pith°—   *vigor*
Lat go, farewel, the devel go therwith!
The flour is goon, ther is namore to telle:
The bren° as I best can now moste I selle;   *bran*
485 But yit to be right merye wol I fonde.°   *try*
Now wol I tellen of my ferthe housbonde.
    I saye I hadde in herte greet despit
That he of any other hadde delit,
But he was quit,° by God and by Saint Joce:°   *repaid / St. Judocus*
490 I made him of the same wode a croce°—   *cross*
Nat of my body in no foul manere—
But, certainly, I made folk swich cheere
That in his owene grece° I made him frye,   *grease*
For angre and for verray jalousye.
495 By God, in erthe I was his purgatorye,
For which I hope his soule be in glorye.
For God it woot, he sat ful ofte and soong
Whan that his sho° ful bitterly him wroong.°   *shoe / pinched*
Ther was no wight° save God and he that wiste   *person*
500 In many wise how sore I him twiste.
He deide whan I cam fro Jerusalem,
And lith ygrave° under the roode-beem,°   *buried / crossbeam*
Al is his tombe nought so curious°   *carefully made*
As was the sepulcre of him Darius,[7]
505 Which that Appelles wroughte subtilly:
It nis but wast to burye him preciously.°   *expensively*
Lat him fare wel, God yive his soule reste;
He is now in his grave and in his cheste.
    Now of my fifthe housbonde wol I telle—
510 God lete his soule nevere come in helle—
And yit he was to me the moste shrewe:
That feele I on my ribbes al by rewe,°   *in a row*

---

7. Persian Emperor defeated by Alexander the Great, whose tomb was elaborately designed by the Jewish craftsman Apelles.

	And evere shal unto myn ending day.	
	But in oure bed he was so fressh and gay,	
515	And therwithal so wel coude he me glose°	*flatter*
	Whan that he wolde han my bele chose,°	*pretty thing*
	That though he hadde me bet° on every boon,°	*beaten / bone*
	He coude winne again my love anoon.	
	I trowe I loved him best for that he	
520	Was of his love daungerous° to me.	*hard to get*
	We wommen han, if that I shal nat lie,	
	In this matere a quaint fantasye:	
	Waite° what thing we may nat lightly° have,	*note that / easily*
	Therafter wol we crye al day and crave;	
525	Forbede us thing, and that desiren we;	
	Presse on us faste, and thanne wol we flee.	
	With daunger oute we al oure chaffare:[8]	
	Greet prees° at market maketh dere ware,°	*crowd / costly goods*
	And too greet chepe° is holden at litel pris.	*bargain*
530	This knoweth every womman that is wis.	
	My fifthe housbonde—God his soule blesse!—	
	Which that I took for love and no richesse,	
	He somtime was a clerk of Oxenforde,	
	And hadde laft scole° and wente at hoom to boorde	*left school*
535	With my gossib,° dwelling in oure town—	*close friend*
	God have hir soule!—hir name was Alisoun;	
	She knew myn herte and eek my privetee°	*secrets*
	Bet than oure parissh preest, as mote I thee.	
	To hire biwrayed° I my conseil° al,	*revealed / thoughts*
540	For hadde myn housbonde pissed on a wal,	
	Or doon a thing that sholde han cost his lif,	
	To hire, and to another worthy wif,	
	And to my nece which that I loved weel,	
	I wolde han told his conseil everydeel;	
545	And so I dide ful often, God it woot,	
	That made his face often reed° and hoot°	*red / hot*
	For verray shame, and blamed himself for he	
	Hadde told to me so greet a privetee.	
	And so bifel that ones in a Lente—	
550	So often times I to my gossib wente,	
	For evere yit I loved to be gay,	
	And for to walke in March, Averil, and May,	
	From hous to hous, to heere sondry tales—	
	That Janekin clerk and my gossib dame Alis	
555	And I myself into the feeldes wente.	
	Myn housbonde was at London al that Lente:	
	I hadde the better leiser° for to playe,	*opportunity*
	And for to see, and eek for to be seye°	*seen*

8. With coyness we spread out all our merchandise.

560	Of lusty° folk—what wiste I wher my grace°	*merry / luck*
	Was shapen° for to be, or in what place?	*destined*
	Therfore I made my visitaciouns	
	To vigilies⁹ and to processiouns,	
	To preching eek, and to thise pilgrimages,	
	To playes of miracles and to mariages,	
565	And wered upon my gaye scarlet gites°—	*robes*
	Thise wormes ne thise motthes ne thise mites,	
	Upon my peril, frete° hem neveradeel:	*devoured*
	And woostou why? For they were used weel.	
	Now wol I tellen forth what happed me.	
570	I saye that in the feeldes walked we,	

Of lusty° folk—what wiste I wher my grace°   *merry / luck*
560 Was shapen° for to be, or in what place?   *destined*
     Therfore I made my visitaciouns
     To vigilies⁹ and to processiouns,
     To preching eek, and to thise pilgrimages,
     To playes of miracles and to mariages,
565 And wered upon my gaye scarlet gites°—   *robes*
     Thise wormes ne thise motthes ne thise mites,
     Upon my peril, frete° hem neveradeel: *devoured*
     And woostou why? For they were used weel.
           Now wol I tellen forth what happed me.
570 I saye that in the feeldes walked we,
     Til trewely we hadde swich daliaunce,°   *flirtation*
     This clerk and I, that of my purveyaunce°   *providence*
     I spak to him and saide him how that he,
     If I were widwe, sholde wedde me.
575 For certainly, I saye for no bobaunce°   *boast*
     Yit was I nevere withouten purveyaunce
     Of mariage n'of othere thinges eek:
     I holde a mouses herte nought worth a leek
     That hath but oon hole for to sterte° to,   *flee*
580 And if that faile thanne is al ydo.
     I bar him on hand he hadde enchaunted me
     (My dame taughte me that subtiltee);
     And eek I saide I mette° of him al night: *dreamed*
     He wolde han slain me as I lay upright,°   *facing up*
585 And al my bed was ful of verray blood—
     "But yit I hope that ye shul do me good;
     For blood bitokeneth gold, as me was taught."
     And al was fals, I dremed of it right naught,
     But as I folwed ay° my dames lore°   *always / teaching*
590 As wel of that as of othere thinges more.
     But now sire—lat me see, what shal I sayn?
     Aha, by God, I have my tale again.
           Whan that my ferthe housbonde was on beere,°   *funeral bier*
     I weep algate,° and made sory cheere,   *constantly*
595 As wives moten, for it is usage,°   *custom*
     And with my coverchief covered my visage;
     But for that I was purveyed° of a make,°   *provided / mate*
     I wepte but smale, and that I undertake.°   *vouch*
           To chirche was myn housbonde born amorwe°   *next morning*
600 With neighebores that for him maden sorwe,
     And Janekin oure clerk was oon of tho.
     As help me God, whan that I saw him go
     After the beere, me thoughte he hadde a paire
     Of legges and of feet so clene and faire,

9. Services on the eve of holy days.

605   That al myn herte I yaf unto his hold.°   *possession*
       He was, I trowe, twenty winter old,
       And I was fourty, if I shal saye sooth°—   *truth*
       But yit I hadde alway a coltes tooth:°   *youthful tastes*
       Gat-toothed° was I, and that bicam me weel;   *gap-toothed*
610   I hadde the prente° of Sainte Venus seel.°   *imprint / beauty mark*
       As help me God, I was a lusty oon,
       And fair and riche and yong and wel-bigoon,°   *well situated*
       And trewely, as mine housbondes tolde me,
       I hadde the beste quoniam° mighte be.   *you-know-what*
615   For certes I am al Venerien[1]
       In feeling, and myn herte is Marcien:°   *governed by Mars*
       Venus me yaf my lust, my likerousnesse,
       And Mars yaf me my sturdy hardinesse.
       Myn ascendent° was Taur° and Mars therinne—   *zodiac sign / Taurus*
620   Allas, allas, that evere love was sinne!
       I folwed ay my inclinacioun
       By vertu of my constellacioun;
       That made me I coude nought withdrawe°   *withhold*
       My chambre of Venus from a good felawe.
625   Yit have I Martes° merk upon my face,   *Mars's*
       And also in another privee place.
       For God so wis° be my savacioun,°   *surely / salvation*
       I loved nevere by no discrecioun,
       But evere folwede° myn appetit,   *followed*
630   Al were he short or long or blak or whit;
       I took no keep, so that he liked° me,   *pleased*
       How poore he was, ne eek of what degree.
           What sholde I saye but at the monthes ende
       This joly clerk Janekin that was so hende°   *courteous*
635   Hath wedded me with greet solempnitee,
       And to him yaf I al the land and fee°   *property*
       That evere was me yiven therbifore—
       But afterward repented me ful sore:
       He nolde suffre° no thing of my list.°   *would allow / pleasure*
640   By God, he smoot° me ones on the list°   *struck / ear*
       For that I rente° out of his book a leef,°   *tore / page*
       That of the strook myn ere weex° al deef.   *grew, became*
       Stibourne I was as is a leonesse,
       And of my tonge a verray jangleresse,°   *chatterbox*
645   And walke I wolde, as I hadde doon biforn,
       From hous to hous, although he hadde it sworn;°   *prohibited*
       For which he often times wolde preche,
       And me of olde Romain geestes° teche,   *Latin stories*
       How he Simplicius Gallus[2] lafte his wif,
650   And hire forsook for terme of al his lif,

---

1. Governed by Venus, the planet.   2. Narrated in Valerius Maximus, *Facta et dicta memorabilia*
                                         6.3.

Nought but for open-heveded° he hire sey°   *bareheaded / saw*
Looking out at his dore upon a day.
 Another Romain³ tolde he me by name
That, for his wif was at a someres° game   *summer's*
655 Withouten his witing,° he forsook hire eke;   *knowledge*
And thanne wolde he upon his Bible seeke
That ilke proverbe of Ecclesiaste⁴
Where he comandeth and forbedeth faste
Man shal nat suffre his wif go roule° aboute;   *roam*
660 Thanne wolde he saye right thus withouten doute:
"Whoso that buildeth his hous al of salwes,°   *willow branches*
And priketh° his blinde hors over the falwes,° *rides / open fields*
And suffreth his wif to go seeken halwes,°   *shrines*
Is worthy to be hanged on the galwes."
665 But al for nought—I sette nought an hawe⁵
Of his proverbes n'of his olde sawe;
N'I wolde nat of him corrected be:
I hate him that my vices telleth me,
And so doon mo, God woot, of us than I.
670 This made him with me wood al outrely:°   *utterly*
I nolde nought forbere° him in no cas.   *would not submit*
 Now wol I saye you sooth, by Saint Thomas,
Why that I rente out of his book a leef,
For which he smoot me so that I was deef.
675 He hadde a book that gladly night and day
For his disport° he wolde rede alway.   *amusement*
He cleped° it Valerie and Theofraste,⁶   *called*
At which book he lough° alway ful faste;   *laughed*
And eek ther was somtime a clerk at Rome,
680 A cardinal, that highte Saint Jerome,
That made a book again Jovinian;
In which book eek ther was Tertulan,
Crysippus, Trotula, and Helouis,
That was abbesse nat fer fro Paris;
685 And eek the Parables of Salomon,
Ovides Art, and bookes many oon—
And alle thise were bounden in oo volume.
And every night and day was his custume,°   *custom*
Whan he hadde leiser and vacacioun
690 From other worldly occupacioun,
To reden in this book of wikked wives.

---

3. P. Sempronius Sophus, as related in Valerius Maximus, *Facta* 6.3.
4. Ecclesiasticus 25.25.
5. Hawthorn berry (i.e., little value).
6. Janekin's book is a collection of different works, nearly all of which are directed against women: Walter Map's fictitious letter entitled *Valerius's Dissuasion of Rufinus from Marrying* (Valerius); Theophrastus's *Golden Book on Marriage* (Theofraste); Saint Jerome's *Against Jovinian*;

Tertullian's misogynist tracts on sexual continence (Tertulan); Crysippus's writings, mentioned by Jerome but otherwise unknown; *The Sufferings of Women*, an 11th-century book on gynecology by Trotula di Ruggiero, a female physician from Sicily (Trotula); the letters of the abbess Heloise to her lover Abelard (Helouis); the biblical Book of Proverbs (Parables of Salomon), and Ovid's *Art of Love*.

He knew of hem mo legendes and lives
Than been of goode wives in the Bible.
For trusteth wel, it is an impossible°   *impossibility*
695   That any clerk wol speke good of wives,
But if it be of holy saintes lives,
N'of noon other womman nevere the mo—
Who painted the leon, tel me who?[7]
By God, if wommen hadden writen stories,
700   As clerkes han within hir oratories,
They wolde han writen of men more wikkednesse
Than al the merk of° Adam may redresse.   *mark, sex*
The children of Mercurye and Venus[8]
Been in hir werking° ful contrarious:°   *deeds / contradictory*
705   Mercurye loveth wisdom and science,
And Venus loveth riot° and dispence;°   *celebration / expense*
And for hir diverse disposicioun
Each falleth in otheres exaltacioun,[9]
And thus, God woot, Mercurye is desolat°   *powerless*
710   In Pisces wher Venus is exaltat,
And Venus falleth ther Mercurye is raised:
Therfore no womman of no clerk is praised.
The clerk, whan he is old and may nought do
Of Venus werkes worth his olde sho,°   *shoe*
715   Thanne sit he down and writ in his dotage
That wommen can nat keepe hir mariage.
    But now to purpos why I tolde thee
That I was beten for a book, pardee:°   *by God*
Upon a night Janekin, that was oure sire,°   *master of our house*
720   Redde on his book as he sat by the fire
Of Eva[1] first, that for hir wikkednesse
Was al mankinde brought to wrecchednesse,
For which that Jesu Crist himself was slain
That boughte° us with his herte blood again—   *redeemed*
725   Lo, heer expres of wommen may ye finde
That womman was the los° of al mankinde.   *ruin*
    Tho° redde he me how Sampson loste his heres:°   *then / hair*
Sleeping his lemman° kitte° it with hir sheres,   *lover / cut*
Thurgh which treson loste he both his yën.
730   Tho redde he me, if that I shal nat lien,
Of Ercules and of his Dianire,[2]
That caused him to sette himself afire.

7. In one of Aesop's fables, a lion asked this question when confronted by a painting of a man killing a lion, indicating that if a lion had painted the picture, the scene would have been very different.
8. Followers of Mercury, the god of rhetoric (scholars, poets, orators); followers of Venus (lovers).
9. Astrologically, one planet diminishes in influence as the other ascends.

1. Eve's temptation by the serpent was blamed for humanity's fall from grace and thus required Christ's incarnation to redeem the world.
2. Deianira gave her husband, Hercules, a robe which she believed was charmed with a love potion, but once he put it on, it burned his flesh so badly that he died.

No thing forgat he the sorwe and wo
That Socrates hadde with his wives two—
735   How Xantippa[3] caste pisse upon his heed:
This sely man sat stille as he were deed;
He wiped his heed, namore dorste he sayn
But "Er° that thonder stinte,° comth a rain."   *before / stops*
Of Phasipha[4] that was the queene of Crete—
740   For shrewednesse° him thoughte the tale sweete—   *wickedness*
Fy, speek namore, it is a grisly thing
Of hir horrible lust and hir liking.
Of Clytermistra[5] for hir lecherye
That falsly made hir housbonde for to die,
745   He redde it with ful good devocioun.
He tolde me eek for what occasioun
Amphiorax[6] at Thebes loste his lif:
Myn housbonde hadde a legende of his wif
Eriphylem, that for an ouche° of gold   *trinket*
750   Hath prively unto the Greekes told
Wher that hir housbonde hidde him in a place,
For which he hadde at Thebes sory grace.
Of Livia[7] tolde he me and of Lucie:
They bothe made hir housbondes for to die,
755   That oon for love, that other was for hate;
Livia hir housbonde on an even late
Empoisoned hath for that she was his fo;
Lucia likerous loved hir housbonde so
That for he sholde alway upon hire thinke,
760   She yaf him swich a manere love-drinke
That he was deed er it were by the morwe.
And thus algates° housbondes han sorwe.   *continually*
Thanne tolde he me how oon Latumius
Complained unto his felawe Arrius
765   That in his gardin growed swich a tree,
On which he saide how that his wives three
Hanged hemself for herte despitous.°   *cruel*
"O leve brother," quod this Arrius,
"Yif° me a plante of thilke° blessed tree,   *give / that same*
770   And in my gardin planted shal it be."
Of latter date of wives hath he red
That some han slain hir housbondes in hir bed
And lete hir lechour dighte° hire al the night,   *screw*
Whan that the cors° lay in the floor upright;°   *corpse / face up*
775   And some han driven nailes in hir brain
Whil that they sleepe, and thus they han hem slain;

3. Xanthippe was famous for nagging her husband, the philosopher Socrates.
4. Pasiphae, wife of Minos, became enamored of a bull, engendering the Minotaur.
5. Clytemnestra, queen of Mycenae, slew her husband Agamemnon when he returned from the Trojan War.
6. Amphiaraus died at the Siege of Thebes after listening to the advice of his wife, Eriphyle.
7. Livia poisoned her husband, Drusus, to satisfy her lover Sejanus; Lucia unwittingly poisoned her husband, the poet Lucretius, with a potion meant to keep him faithful.

Some han hem yiven poison in hir drinke.
He spak more harm than herte may bithinke,
And therwithal he knew of mo proverbes
780   Than in this world ther growen gras or herbes:
"Bet is," quod he, "thyn habitacioun
Be with a leon or a foul dragoun
Than with a wommman using° for to chide."   *accustomed*
"Bet is," quod he, "hye in the roof abide
785   Than with an angry wif down in the hous:
They been so wikked and contrarious,
They haten that hir housbondes loveth ay."°   *always*
He saide, "A womman cast hir shame away
Whan she cast of hir smok,"° and ferthermo,   *slip*
790   "A fair womman, but she be chast also,
Is lik a gold ring in a sowes nose."
Who wolde weene, or who wolde suppose
The wo that in myn herte was and pine?
     And whan I sawgh he wolde nevere fine°   *end*
795   To reden on this cursed book al night,
Al sodeinly three leves have I plight°   *plucked*
Out of his book right as he redde, and eke
I with my fist so took° him on the cheeke   *struck*
That in oure fir he fil bakward adown.
800   And up he sterte as dooth a wood° leoun,   *enraged*
And with his fist he smoot me on the heed
That in the floor I lay as I were deed.
And whan he sawgh how stille that I lay,
He was agast,° and wolde have fled his way,   *afraid*
805   Til atte laste out of my swough° I braide:°   *faint / arose*
"O hastou slain me, false thief?" I saide,
"And for my land thus hastou mordred me?
Er I be deed yit wol I kisse thee."
     And neer he cam and kneeled faire adown,
810   And saide, "Dere suster Alisoun,
As help me God, I shal thee nevere smite.
That I have doon, it is thyself to wite.°   *blame*
Foryif it me, and that I thee biseeke."
And yit eftsoones° I hitte him on the cheeke,   *immediately*
815   And saide, "Thief, thus muchel am I wreke.°   *avenged*
Now wol I die: I may no lenger speke."
     But at the laste with muchel care and wo
We fille accorded by us selven two.
He yaf me al the bridel° in myn hand,   *bridle, control*
820   To han the governance of hous and land,
And of his tonge and his hand also;
And made him brenne his book anoonright tho.
And whan that I hadde geten unto me
By maistrye° al the sovereinetee,°   *skill / dominance*
825   And that he saide, "Myn owene trewe wif,

Do as thee lust° the term of al thy lif,   *please*
Keep thyn honour, and keep eek myn estat,"
After that day we hadde nevere debat.
God help me so, I was to him as kinde
830   As any wif from Denmark unto Inde,
And also trewe, and so was he to me.
I praye to God that sit in majestee,
So blesse his soule for his mercy dere.
Now wol I saye my tale if ye wol heere.

Another Interruption

835   The Frere lough whan he hadde herd al this:
"Now dame," quod he, "so have I joye or blis,
This is a long preamble of a tale."
And whan the Somnour herde the Frere gale,°   *exclaim*
"Lo," quod the Somnour, "Goddes armes two,
840   A frere wol entremette him° everemo!   *interfere*
Lo, goode men, a flye and eek a frere
Wol falle in every dissh and eek matere.
What spekestou of preambulacioun?
What, amble or trotte or pisse or go sitte down!
845   Thou lettest° oure disport in this manere."   *hinder*
     "Ye, woltou so, sire Somnour?" quod the Frere.
"Now by my faith, I shal er that I go
Telle of a somnour swich a tale or two
That al the folk shal laughen in this place."
850   "Now elles, Frere, I wol bishrewe thy face,"
Quod this Somnour, "and I bishrewe me,
But if I telle tales two or three
Of freres, er I come to Sidingborne,[8]
That I shal make thyn herte for to moorne—
855   For wel I woot thy pacience is goon."
     Oure Hoste cride, "Pees, and that anoon!"
And saide, "Lat the womman telle hir tale:
Ye fare° as folk that dronken been of ale.   *behave*
Do, dame, tel forth youre tale, and that is best."
860   "Al redy, sire," quod she, "right as you lest°—   *it pleases*
If I have licence of this worthy Frere."
"Yis, dame," quod he, "tel forth and I wol heere."

The Wife of Bath's Tale

In th'olde dayes of the King Arthour,
Of which that Britouns° speken greet honour,   *Bretons*
865   Al was this land fulfild° of faïrye: *filled*
The elf-queene° with hir joly compaignye   *fairy queen*

8. Sittingbourne, a town about 40 miles from London.

Daunced ful ofte in many a greene mede°—   *meadow*
This was the olde opinion as I rede;
I speke of many hundred yeres ago.
870   But now can no man see none elves mo,
For now the grete charitee and prayeres
Of limitours,[1] and othere holy freres,
That serchen every land and every streem,
As thikke as motes° in the sonne-beem,   *dust particles*
875   Blessing halles, chambres, kichenes, bowres,°   *bedrooms*
Citees, burghes,° castels, hye towres,   *boroughs*
Thropes,° bernes,° shipnes,° dayeries—   *villages / barns / stables*
This maketh that ther been no faïries.
For ther as wont° to walken was an elf   *where there used*
880   Ther walketh now the limitour himself,
In undermeles° and in morweninges,°   *afternoons / mornings*
And saith his Matins° and his holy thinges,   *morning prayers*
As he gooth in his limitacioun.°   *prescribed district*
Wommen may go saufly° up and down: *safely*
885   In every bussh or under every tree
Ther is noon other incubus[2] but he,
And he ne wol doon hem but dishonour.
        And so bifel it that this King Arthour
Hadde in his hous a lusty bacheler,°   *young knight*
890   That on a day cam riding fro river,°   *hunting waterfowl*
And happed that, allone as he was born,
He sawgh a maide walking him biforn;
Of which maide anoon, maugree hir heed,°   *against her will*
By verray force he rafte° hir maidenheed;   *stole*
895   For which oppression was swich clamour,
And swich pursuite° unto the King Arthour,   *petitioning*
That dampned° was this knight for to be deed   *condemned*
By cours of lawe, and sholde han lost his heed—
Paraventure° swich was the statut tho°—   *as it happens / then*
900   But that the queene and othere ladies mo
So longe prayeden the king of grace,
Til he his lif him graunted in the place,
And yaf him to the queene, al at hir wille,
To chese° wheither she wolde him save or spille.°   *decide / destroy*
905   The queene thanked the king with al hir might,
And after this thus spak she to the knight,
Whan that she saw hir time upon a day:
"Thou standest yit," quod she, "in swich array°   *situation*
That of thy lif yit hastou no suretee.°   *guarantee*
910   I graunte thee lif if thou canst tellen me
What thing it is that wommen most desiren:
Be war and keep thy nekke boon° from iren.°   *bone / iron*

---

1. Friars licensed to beg within set districts.   2. Demon who fornicates with women.

And if thou canst nat tellen me anoon,
Yit wol I yive thee leve for to goon
915   A twelfmonth and a day to seeche° and lere°   seek out / learn
An answere suffisant° in this matere,   satisfactory
And suretee° wol I han er that thou pace,°   pledge / pass
Thy body for to yeelden° in this place."   surrender
Wo was this knight, and sorwefully he siketh.°   sighs
920   But what, he may nat doon al as him liketh,
And atte laste he chees him° for to wende,°   decided / travel
And come again right at the yeres ende,
With swich answere as God wolde him purveye,°   provide
And taketh his leve and wendeth forth his waye.
925   He seeketh every hous and every place
Wher as he hopeth for to finde grace,
To lerne what thing wommen love most.
But he ne coude arriven in no coost°   country
Wher as he mighte finde in this matere
930   Two creatures according in fere.°   agreeing together
Some saiden wommen loven best richesse;
Some saide honour, some saide jolinesse;°   pleasure
Some riche array, some saiden lust abedde,
And ofte time to be widwe and wedde.
935   Some saide that oure herte is most esed
Whan that we been yflatered and yplesed—
He gooth ful neigh the soothe,° I wol nat lie: near the truth
A man shal winne us best with flaterye,
And with attendance and with bisinesse°   attentive service
940   Been we ylimed,° bothe more and lesse.   ensnared
And some sayen that we loven best
For to be free, and do right as us lest,°   pleases
And that no man repreve° us of oure vice,   scold
But saye that we be wise and no thing nice.°   foolish
945   For trewely, ther is noon of us alle,
If any wight wol clawe us on the galle,°   rub a sore spot
That we nil kike° for he saith us sooth:°   kick / the truth
Assaye° and he shal finde it that so dooth.   try
For be we nevere so vicious withinne,
950   We wol be holden° wise and clene of sinne.   considered
And some sayn that greet delit han we
For to be holden stable° and eek secree,°   constant / discreet
And in oo purpos stedefastly to dwelle,
And nat biwraye° thing that men us telle—   reveal
955   But that tale is nat worth a rake-stele.°   rake handle
Pardee,° we wommen conne no thing hele:°   by God / conceal
Witnesse on Mida.³ Wol ye heere the tale?
Ovide, amonges othere thinges smale,

3. Midas's story is recounted in Ovid's *Metamorphoses* 9.

960	Saide Mida hadde under his longe heres,	
	Growing upon his heed, two asses eres,	
	The whiche vice° he hidde as he best mighte	*fault*
	Ful subtilly from every mannes sighte,	
	That save his wif ther wiste of it namo.°	*no one else knows*
	He loved hire most and trusted hire also.	
965	He prayed hire that to no creature	
	She sholde tellen of his disfigure.°	*deformity*
	She swoor him nay, for al this world to winne,	
	She nolde° do that vilainye or sinne	*would not*
	To make hir housbonde han so foul a name:	
970	She nolde nat telle it for hir owene shame.	
	But nathelees, hir thoughte that she dyde°	*would die*
	That she so longe sholde a conseil° hide;	*secret*
	Hire thoughte it swal so sore aboute hir herte	
	That nedely° som word hire moste asterte,°	*surely / come out*
975	And sith she dorste nat telle it to no man,	
	Down to a mareis° faste° by she ran—	*marsh / close*
	Til she cam there hir herte was afire—	
	And as a bitore° bombleth° in the mire,	*heron / squawks*
	She laide hir mouth unto the water down:	
980	"Biwray° me nat, thou water, with thy soun,"°	*betray / sound*
	Quod she. "To thee I telle it and namo:	
	Myn housbonde hath longe asses eres two.	
	Now is myn herte al hool, now is it oute.	
	I mighte no lenger keepe it, out of doute."	
985	Here may ye see, though we a time abide,	
	Yit oute it moot:° we can no conseil hide.	*must*
	The remenant of the tale if ye wol heere,	
	Redeth Ovide, and ther ye may it lere.°	*learn*
	This knight of which my tale is specially,	
990	Whan that he sawgh he mighte nat come therby—	
	This is to saye what wommen loven most—	
	Within his brest ful sorweful was his gost,°	*spirit*
	But hoom he gooth, he mighte nat sojurne:°	*linger*
	The day was come that hoomward moste he turne.	
995	And in his way it happed him to ride	
	In al this care under a forest side,	
	Wher as he sawgh upon a daunce go	
	Of ladies foure and twenty and yit mo;	
	Toward the whiche daunce he drow° ful yerne,°	*drew / gladly*
1000	In hope that som wisdom sholde he lerne.	
	But certainly, er he cam fully there,	
	Vanisshed was this daunce, he niste° where.	*did not know*
	No creature sawgh he that bar lif,	
	Save on the greene he sawgh sitting a wif—	
1005	A fouler wight° ther may no man devise.°	*creature / imagine*
	Again the knight this olde wif gan rise,	
	And saide, "Sire knight, heer forth lith no way.°	*road*

Telle me what ye seeken, by youre fay.°   *faith*
Paraventure it may the better be:
1010 Thise olde folk conne° muchel thing," quod she.   *know*
       "My leve moder,"° quod this knight, "certain,   *dear mother*
I nam but° deed but if that I can sayn   *am no more than*
What thing it is that wommen most desire.
Coude ye me wisse,° I wolde wel quite youre hire."°   *inform / repay you*
1015   "Plight° me thy trouthe° here in myn hand," quod she,   *pledge / promise*
"The nexte thing that I require thee,
Thou shalt it do, if it lie in thy might,
And I wol telle it you er it be night."
       "Have heer my trouthe," quod the knight. "I graunte."
1020   "Thanne," quod she, "I dar me wel avaunte°   *brag*
Thy lif is sauf, for I wol stande therby.
Upon my lif the queene wol saye as I.
Lat see which is the pruddeste° of hem alle   *proudest*
That wereth on a coverchief or a calle°   *headdress*
1025 That dar saye nay of that I shal thee teche.
Lat us go forth withouten lenger speeche."
Tho rouned° she a pistel° in his ere,   *whispered / message*
And bad him to be glad and have no fere.
       Whan they be comen to the court, this knight
1030 Saide he hadde holde his day as he hadde hight,°   *promised*
And redy was his answere, as he saide.
Ful many a noble wif, and many a maide,
And many a widwe—for that they been wise—
The queene hirself sitting as justise,°   *judge*
1035 Assembled been this answere for to heere,
And afterward this knight was bode appere.
To every wight comanded was silence,
And that the knight sholde telle in audience
What thing that worldly wommen loven best.
1040 This knight ne stood nat stille° as dooth a best,°   *silent / beast*
But to his question anoon answerde
With manly vois that al the court it herde.
       "My lige° lady, generally," quod he,   *liege*
"Wommen desire to have sovereinetee
1045 As wel over hir housbonde as hir love,
And for to been in maistrye him above.
This is youre moste desir though ye me kille.
Dooth as you list: I am here at youre wille."
       In al the court ne was ther wif ne maide
1050 Ne widwe that contraried that he saide,
But saiden he was worthy han his lif.
       And with that word up sterte that olde wif,
Which that the knight sawgh sitting on the greene;
"Mercy," quod she, "my soverein lady queene,
1055 Er that youre court departe, do me right.
I taughte this answere unto the knight,

For which he plighte me his trouthe there
The firste thing I wolde him requere
He wolde it do, if it laye in his might.
1060 Bifore the court thanne praye I thee, sire knight,"
Quod she, "that thou me take unto thy wif,
For wel thou woost° that I have kept° thy lif.   *know / saved*
If I saye fals, say nay, upon thy fay."
    This knight answerde, "Allas and wailaway,
1065 I woot° right wel that swich was my biheeste.°   *know / promise*
For Goddes love, as chees° a newe requeste: *choose*
Taak al my good and lat my body go."
    "Nay thanne," quod she, "I shrewe° us bothe two.   *curse*
For though that I be foul and old and poore,
1070 I nolde° for al the metal ne for ore   *would not wish*
That under erthe is grave° or lith above,   *buried*
But if thy wif I were and eek thy love."
    "My love," quod he, "Nay, my dampnacioun!
Allas, that any of my nacioun°   *lineage*
1075 Sholde evere so foule disparaged° be."   *degraded*
But al for nought, th'ende is this, that he
Constrained was: he needes moste hire wedde,
And taketh his olde wif and gooth to bedde.
    Now wolden some men saye, paraventure,
1080 That for my necligence I do no cure
To tellen you the joy and al th'array
That at the feeste was that ilke day.
To which thing shortly answere I shal:
I saye ther nas no joye ne feeste at al;
1085 Ther nas but hevinesse and muche sorwe.
For prively he wedded hire on morwe,°   *in the morning*
And al day after hidde him as an owle,
So wo was him, his wif looked so foule.
    Greet was the wo the knight hadde in his thought:
1090 Whan he was with his wif abedde brought,
He walweth° and he turneth to and fro.   *rolls over*
His olde wif lay smiling everemo,
And saide, "O dere housbonde, benedicite,°   *bless us*
Fareth° every knight thus with his wif as ye?   *behaves*
1095 Is this the lawe of King Arthures hous?
Is every knight of his thus daungerous?°   *reserved*
I am youre owene love and youre wif;
I am she which that saved hath youre lif;
And certes yit ne dide I you nevere unright.°   *injustice*
1100 Why fare° ye thus with me this firste night?   *behave*
Ye faren like a man hadde lost his wit.
What is my gilt? For Goddes love, telle it,
And it shal been amended if I may."
    "Amended!" quod this knight. "Allas, nay, nay,
1105 It wol nat been amended neveremo.

Thou art so lothly° and so old also,   *loathsome*
And therto comen of so lowe a kinde,°   *breeding*
That litel wonder is though I walwe and winde.°   *turn*
So wolde God myn herte wolde breste!"°   *burst*
1110   "Is this," quod she, "the cause of youre unreste?"
"Ye, certainly," quod he. "No wonder is."
"Now sire," quod she, "I coude amende al this,
If that me liste,° er it were dayes three,   *it pleased me*
So° wel ye mighte bere you° unto me.   *provided that / behave*
1115   "But for ye speken of swich gentilesse°   *nobility*
As is descended out of old richesse—
That therfore sholden ye be gentilmen—
Swich arrogance is nat worth an hen.
Looke who that is most vertuous alway,
1120   Privee and apert,° and most entendeth ay   *privately and publicly*
To do the gentil deedes that he can,
Taak him for the gretteste gentilman.
Crist wol° we claime of him oure gentilesse,   *wishes*
Nat of oure eldres for hir 'old richesse.'
1125   For though they yive us al hir heritage,
For which we claime to been of heigh parage,°   *noble lineage*
Yit may they nat biquethe for no thing
To noon of us hir vertuous living,
That made hem gentilmen ycalled be,
1130   And bad us folwen° hem in swich degree.   *to follow*
"Wel can the wise poete of Florence,
That highte° Dant,[4] speken in this sentence;°   *was called / opinion*
Lo, in swich manere rym is Dantes tale:
'Ful selde° up riseth by his braunches[5] smale   *seldom*
1135   Prowesse° of man, for God of his prowesse   *excellence*
Wol that of him we claime oure gentilesse.'
For of oure eldres may we no thing claime
But temporel thing that man may hurte and maime.
Eek every wight woot° this as wel as I,   *person knows*
1140   If gentilesse were planted natureelly
Unto a certain linage down the line,
Privee and apert, thanne wolde they nevere fine°   *end*
To doon of gentilesse the faire office°—   *duty*
They mighte do no vilainye or vice.
1145   "Taak fir and beer° it in the derkeste hous   *bring*
Bitwixe this and the Mount of Caucasus,
And lat men shette° the dores and go thenne,°   *shut / thence*
Yit wol the fir as faire lie and brenne
As twenty thousand men mighte it biholde:
1150   His° office natureel ay° wol it holde,   *its / always*
Up peril of my lif, til that it die.

4. Dante Alighieri, the 13th-century Italian poet, ex-   5. Branches (of his family tree).
pressed similar views in his *Convivio*.

Heer may ye see wel how that genterye°   *gentility*
Is nat annexed° to possessioun,   *connected*
Sith° folk ne doon hir operacioun°   *since / their work*
1155 Alway, as dooth the fir, lo, in his kinde.°   *nature*
For God it woot, men may wel often finde
A lordes sone do shame and vilainye;
And he that wol han pris° of his gentrye,°   *esteem / noble birth*
For he was boren of a gentil hous,
1160 And hadde his eldres noble and vertuous,
And nil° himselven do no gentil deedes,   *will not*
Ne folwen his gentil auncestre that deed is,
He nis nat gentil, be he duc or erl—
For vilaines sinful deedes maken a cherl.°   *ruffian*
1165 Thy gentilesse nis but renomee°   *reputation*
Of thine auncestres for hir heigh bountee,°   *generosity*
Which is a straunge° thing for thy persone.   *foreign*
For gentilesse cometh fro God allone.
Thanne comth oure verray gentilesse of grace:
1170 It was no thing biquethe us with oure place.
Thenketh how noble, as saith Valerius,[6]
Was thilke° Tullius Hostilius[7]   *that*
That out of poverte roos to heigh noblesse.
Redeth Senek,[8] and redeth eek Boece:
1175 Ther shul ye seen expres that no drede° is   *doubt*
That he is gentil that dooth gentil deedes.
And therfore, leve housbonde, I thus conclude:
Al were it that mine auncestres weren rude,°   *lowborn*
Yit may the hye God—and so hope I—
1180 Graunte me grace to liven vertuously.
Thanne am I gentil whan that I biginne
To liven vertuously and waive° sinne.   *avoid*
    "And ther as ye of poverte me repreve,
The hye God, on whom that we bileve,
1185 In wilful poverte chees to live his lif;
And certes every man, maiden, or wif
May understonde that Jesus, hevene king,
Ne wolde nat chese a vicious living.
Glad poverte is an honeste° thing, certain;   *honorable*
1190 This wol Senek and othere clerkes sayn.
Whoso that halt him paid of his poverte,[9]
I holde him riche al° hadde he nat a sherte.°   *although / shirt*
He that coveiteth is a poore wight,
For he wolde han that is nat in his might;

---

6. The Roman historian Valerius Maximus, in his *Facta et dicta memorabilia* 3.4.
7. The legendary third king of Rome who started as a shepherd.
8. Seneca, the Stoic author, in his *Epistle* 44; Boece: Boethius in his *Consolation of Philosophy*.
9. Whoever is satisfied with poverty.

1195   But he that nought hath, ne coveiteth have,
        Is riche, although we holde him but a knave.°   *servant*
        Verray poverte it singeth proprely.
        Juvenal[1] saith of poverte, 'Merily
        The poore man, whan he gooth by the waye,
1200   Biforn the theves he may singe and playe.'
        Poverte is hateful good, and as I gesse,
        A ful greet bringere out of bisinesse;°   *worldly cares*
        A greet amendere eek of sapience°   *wisdom*
        To him that taketh it in pacience;
1205   Poverte is thing, although it seeme elenge,°   *miserable*
        Possession that no wight wol chalenge;
        Poverte ful often, whan a man is lowe,
        Maketh his God and eek himself to knowe;
        Poverte a spectacle° is, as thinketh me,   *eyeglass*
1210   Thurgh which he may his verray freendes see.
        And therfore, sire, sin that I nought you greve,
        Of my poverte namore ye me repreve.
            "Now sire, of elde° ye repreve me: *old age*
        And certes sire, though noon auctoritee
1215   Were in no book, ye gentils of honour
        Sayn that men sholde an old wight° doon favour,   *person*
        And clepe° him fader for youre gentilesse—   *call*
        And auctours° shal I finden, as I gesse.   *authorities*
            "Now ther ye saye that I am foul and old:
1220   Thanne drede you nought to been a cokewold,°   *cuckold*
        For filthe and elde, also mote I thee,
        Been grete wardeins° upon chastitee.   *guardians*
        But nathelees, sin I knowe your delit,
        I shal fulfille youre worldly appetit.
1225   "Chees° now," quod she, "oon of thise thinges twaye: *choose*
        To han me foul and old til that I deye
        And be to you a trewe humble wif,
        And nevere you displese in al my lif,
        Or elles ye wol han me yong and fair,
1230   And take youre aventure° of the repair°   *chances / visits*
        That shal be to youre hous by cause of me—
        Or in som other place, wel may be.
        Now chees youreselven wheither° that you liketh."   *whichever*
            This knight aviseth him° and sore siketh;°   *considers / sighs*
1235   But atte laste he saide in this manere:
        "My lady and my love, and wif so dere,
        I putte me in youre wise governaunce:
        Cheseth youreself which may be most plesaunce
        And most honour to you and me also.
1240   I do no fors° the wheither of the two,   *do not care*

1. The misogynist Roman poet in his Satires 10.21, 10.22.

For as you liketh it suffiseth° me."   *satisfies*
        "Thanne have I gete of you° maistrye," quod she,   *won from you*
"Sin I may chese and governe as me lest?"°   *it pleases*
        "Ye, certes, wif," quod he. "I holde it best."
1245   "Kisse me," quod she. "We be no lenger wrothe.°   *opposed*
For by my trouthe, I wol be to you bothe—
This is to sayn, ye, bothe fair and good.
I praye to God that I mote sterven wood,°   *die mad*
But I to you be al so good and trewe
1250   As evere was wif sin that the world was newe.
And but I be tomorn° as fair to seene   *in the morning*
As any lady, emperisse, or queene,
That is bitwixe the eest and eek the west,
Do with my lif and deeth right as you lest:
1255   Caste up the curtin, looke how that it is."
        And whan the knight sawgh verraily al this,
That she so fair was and so yong therto,
For joye he hente° hire in his armes two;   *seized*
His herte bathed in a bath of blisse;
1260   A thousand time arewe° he gan hire kisse,   *in a row*
And she obeyed him in every thing
That mighte do him plesance or liking.
And thus they live unto hir lives ende
In parfit° joye. And Jesu Crist us sende   *perfect*
1265   Housbondes meeke, yonge, and fresshe abedde—
And grace t'overbide° hem that we wedde.   *outlive*
And eek I praye Jesu shorte hir lives
That nought wol be governed by hir wives,
And olde and angry nigardes of dispence°—   *misers in spending*
1270   God sende hem soone a verray pestilence!

THE NUN'S PRIEST'S TALE Of all his varied and ambitious output, *The Nun's Priest's Tale* may be Chaucer's most impressive tour de force. At its core is a wonderful animal fable, free of the conventionality and sometimes easy moralities this ancient form had taken on by the fourteenth century. The fable of Chauntecleer and Pertelote achieves quite extraordinary density, further, because of the multiple frames—structural and thematic—that surround it.

As part of the Canterbury tale-telling competition, the priest's fable plays a role in that broadest contest of classes and literary genres. More locally, it is one of many moments in which the Host, Harry Bailey, demands a tale from a male pilgrim in a style that also suggests a sexual challenge, and then adjusts his estimate of the teller's virility (even his social position) to suit. The fable itself is surrounded by an intimate portrait of Chauntecleer's peasant owner and her simple life, content with "hertes suffisaunce," a marked contrast to courtly values.

The central story of Chauntecleer's dream, danger, and escape works within a subtle and funny exploration of relations between the sexes. This is conditioned by courtly love conventions, literacy and education, and even the vocabulary of Pertelote's mostly Anglo-Saxon diction and Chauntecleer's love of French. This linguistic competition has its high point when Chauntecleer condescendingly mistranslates a misogynist Latin tag. Linguistic vanity, though, is exactly what puts Chauntecleer most in jeopardy. It is not the destiny Chauntecleer thinks he glimpses in his dream that almost costs his life, but rather another verbal competition, and an almost Oedipal challenge to his father.

Much of the story's energy, however, derives not from its frames but from the explosion of those frames—literary, spatial, even social—enacted and recalled at the heart of the tale. The chickens are simultaneously, and hilariously, both courtly lovers and very realistic fowl. When Chauntecleer is carried off, the whole world of the tale—widow, daughters, dogs, even bees—bursts outward in pursuit. In the midst of mock-epic and mock-romance comparisons to this joyful disorder, Chaucer even inserts one of his very few direct references to the greatest disorder of his time, the Rising of 1381.

The Nun's Priest's Tale is a comedy as well as a fable, reversing a lugubrious series of tragedies in the preceding Monk's Tale. In the end, it is a story of canniness, acquired self-knowledge, and self-salvation. Woven into the priest's humor are a gentle satire and a quiet assertion that free will is the final resource of any agent, avian or human.

The Nun's Priest's Tale
The Introduction

	"Ho!" quod the Knight, "good sire, namore of this:	
	That ye han said is right ynough, ywis,°	*indeed*
	And muchel more, for litel hevinesse	
	Is right ynough to muche folk° I gesse:[1]	*for most folks*
5	I saye for me it is a greet disese,	
	Wher as men han been in greet welthe and ese,	
	To heeren of hir sodein° fal, allas;	*sudden*
	And the contrarye is joye and greet solas,°	*comfort*
	As whan a man hath been in poore estat,	
10	And climbeth up and wexeth° fortunat,	*becomes*
	And there abideth in prosperitee:	
	Swich thing is gladsom, as it thinketh° me,	*seems to*
	And of swich thing were goodly for to telle."	
	"Ye," quod oure Host, "by Sainte Poules° belle,	*Paul's*
15	Ye saye right sooth:° this Monk he clappeth° loude.	*truly / chatters*
	He spak how Fortune covered with a cloude—	
	I noot nevere what.° And als of a tragedye	*I don't know what*
	Right now ye herde, and pardee,° no remedye	*by God*
	It is for to biwaile ne complaine	
20	That that is doon, and als° it is a paine,	*also*
	As ye han said, to heere of hevinesse.	
	"Sire Monk, namore of this, so God you blesse:	
	Youre tale anoyeth al this compaignye;	
	Swich talking is nat worth a boterflye,	
25	For therinne is ther no disport ne game.	
	Wherfore, sire Monk, or daun° Piers by youre name,	*Master*
	I praye you hertely telle us somwhat elles:	
	For sikerly, nere clinking of youre belles,[2]	
	That on youre bridel hange on every side,	
30	By hevene king that for us alle dyde,	
	I sholde er this have fallen down for sleep,	
	Although the slough° hadde nevere been so deep.	*mud*

---

1. The Monk has just told a series of stark and repetitive "tragedies"—the falls of men both ancient and modern.
2. For truly, were it not for the jingling of your bells.

Thanne hadde youre tale al be told in vain;
For certainly, as that thise clerkes sayn,
35 Wher as a man may have noon audience,
Nought helpeth it to tellen his sentence;°   *statement*
And wel I woot° the substance is in me,   *know*
If any thing shal wel reported be.
Sire, saye somwhat of hunting, I you praye."
40   "Nay," quod this Monk, "I have no lust° to playe.   *wish*
Now lat another telle, as I have told."
    Thanne spak oure Host with rude speeche and bold,
And saide unto the Nonnes Preest anoon,
"Com neer, thou Preest,³ com hider, thou sire John:
45 Tel us swich thing as may oure hertes glade.°   *gladden our hearts*
Be blithe,° though thou ride upon a jade!°   *happy / nag*
What though thyn hors be bothe foul and lene?°   *thin*
If he wol serve thee, rekke nat a bene.°   *don't care a bean*
Looke that thyn herte be merye everemo."
50   "Yis, sire," quod he, "yis, Host, so more I go,
But I be merye, ywis, I wol be blamed."
And right anoon his tale he hath attamed,°   *begun*
And thus he saide unto us everichoon,
This sweete Preest, this goodly man sire John.

The Tale

55 A poore widwe somdeel stape° in age   *well along*
Was whilom° dwelling in a narwe cotage,   *once upon a time*
Biside a grove, stonding in a dale:
This widwe of which I telle you my tale,
Sin° thilke° day that she was last a wif,   *since / that*
60 In pacience ladde a ful simple lif.
For litel was hir catel° and hir rente,°   *property / income*
By housbondrye° of swich as God hire sente   *management*
She foond° hirself and eek hir doughtren two.   *provided for*
Three large sowes hadde she and namo,
65 Three kin,° and eek a sheep that highte° Malle.   *cows / was named*
Ful sooty was hir bowr° and eek hir halle,   *bedroom*
In which she eet ful many a slendre meel;
Of poinant° sauce hire needed neveradeel: *pungent*
No daintee morsel passed thurgh hir throte—
70 Hir diete was accordant to hir cote.°   *cottage*
Repleccioun° ne made hire nevere sik: *gluttony*
Attempre° diete was al hir physik,   *moderate*
And exercise and hertes suffisaunce.
The goute lette hire nothing for to daunce,⁴
75 N'apoplexye shente° nat hir heed.   *hurt*

3. The Host uses the familiar, somewhat condescending   4. Did not keep her from dancing.
"thou," then contemptuously calls the priest "Sir John."

No win ne drank she, neither whit ne reed:
Hir boord° was served most with whit and blak,   *table*
Milk and brown breed, in which she foond no lak;°   *fault*
Seind° bacon, and somtime an ey° or twaye,°   *singed / egg / two*
80   For she was as it were a manere daye.°   *dairy maid*
A yeerd° she hadde, enclosed al withoute   *yard*
With stikkes, and a drye dich aboute,
In which she hadde a cok heet° Chauntecleer: *called*
In al the land of crowing nas his peer.
85   His vois was merier than the merye orgon
On massedayes that in the chirche goon;°   *is played*
Wel sikerer° was his crowing in his logge°   *surer / dwelling*
Than is a clok or an abbeye orlogge;°   *timepiece*
By nature he knew eech ascensioun
90   Of th'equinoxial[5] in thilke town:
For whan degrees fifteene were ascended,
Thanne crew he that it mighte nat been amended.°   *surpassed*
His comb was redder than the fin coral,
And batailed° as it were a castel wal;   *crenellated*
95   His bile° was blak, and as the jeet° it shoon;   *beak / jet*
Like asure° were his legges and his toon;°   *azure / toes*
His nailes whitter than the lilye flowr,
And lik the burned° gold was his colour.   *burnished*
This gentil cok hadde in his governaunce
100   Sevene hennes for to doon al his plesaunce,
Whiche were his sustres and his paramours,°   *lovers*
And wonder like to him as of colours;
Of whiche the faireste hewed° on hir throte   *colored*
Was cleped° faire damoisele Pertelote: *called*
105   Curteis she was, discreet, and debonaire,°   *gracious*
And compaignable,° and bar hirself so faire,   *sociable*
Sin thilke° day that she was seven night old,   *that*
That trewely she hath the herte in hold
Of Chauntecleer, loken in every lith.[6]
110   He loved hire so that wel was him therwith.
But swich a joye was it to heere hem singe,
Whan that the brighte sonne gan to springe,
In sweete accord "My Lief is Faren in Londe"[7]—
For thilke time, as I have understonde,
115   Beestes and briddes° couden speke and singe.   *birds*
    And so bifel that in a daweninge,
As Chauntecleer among his wives alle
Sat on his perche that was in the halle,
And next him sat this faire Pertelote,
120   This Chauntecleer gan gronen in his throte,

---

5. The points marking the celestial hours.   7. A popular ballad, "My Love Has Gone to the Country."
6. Locked in every limb (i.e., thoroughly).

As man that in his dreem is drecched° sore.   *disturbed*
　And whan that Pertelote thus herde him rore,
She was agast, and saide, "Herte dere,
What aileth you to grone in this manere?
125　Ye been a verray° slepere, fy, for shame!"   *true*
　And he answerde and saide thus, "Madame,
I praye you that ye take it nat agrief.°   *amiss*
By God, me mette° I was in swich meschief   *I dreamed*
Right now, that yit myn herte is sore afright.
130　Now God," quod he, "my swevene recche aright,[8]
And keepe my body out of foul prisoun!
Me mette how that I romed up and down
Within oure yeerd, wher as I sawgh a beest,
Was lik an hound and wolde han maad arrest°   *taken captive*
135　Upon my body, and han had me deed.
His colour was bitwixe yelow and reed,
And tipped was his tail and bothe his eres
With blak, unlik the remenant of his heres;°   *the rest of his hair*
His snoute smal, with glowing yën twaye.
140　Yit of his look for fere almost I deye:
This caused me my groning, douteleec."
　"Avoi,"° quod she, "fy on you, hertelees!°   *Have done! / coward*
Allas," quod she, "for by that God above,
Now han ye lost myn herte and al my love!
145　I can nat love a coward, by my faith.
For certes, what so any womman saith,
We alle desiren, if it mighte be,
To han housbondes hardy, wise, and free,°   *generous*
And secree,° and no nigard, ne no fool,   *discreet*
150　Ne him that is agast° of every tool,°   *afraid / weapon*
Ne noon avauntour.° By that God above,   *braggart*
How dorste ye sayn for shame unto youre love
That any thing mighte make you aferd?
Have ye no mannes herte and han a beerd?
155　Allas, and conne ye been agast of swevenes?
No thing, God woot,° but vanitee° in swevene is!   *knows / illusion*
Swevenes engendren of replexiouns,°   *surfeits*
And ofte of fume° and of complexiouns,°   *gas / bodily humors*
Whan humours been too habundant in a wight.°   *creature*
160　Certes, this dreem which ye han met tonight
Comth of the grete superfluitee
Of youre rede colera,[9] pardee,°   *by God*
Which causeth folk to dreden in hir dremes
Of arwes,° and of fir with rede lemes,°   *arrows / flames*
165　Of rede beestes, that they wol hem bite,

---

8. Intepret my dream correctly.　　　　　　9. Choleric bile, thought to overheat the body.

Of contek,° and of whelpes° grete and lite—   *strife / dogs*
Right as the humour of malencolye[1]
Causeth ful many a man in sleep to crye
For fere of blake beres or boles° blake,   *bulls*
170 Or elles blake develes wol hem take.
Of othere humours coude I telle also
That werken many a man in sleep ful wo,
But I wol passe as lightly as I can.
Lo, Caton,[2] which that was so wis a man,
175 Saide he nat thus? 'Ne do no fors° of dremes.'   *pay no attention to*
Now, sire," quod she, "whan we flee° fro the bemes,°   *fly / rafters*
For Goddes love, as take som laxatif.
Up° peril of my soule and of my lif,   *upon*
I conseile you the beste, I wol nat lie,
180 That bothe of colere and of malencolye
Ye purge you; and for ye shal nat tarye,
Though in this town is noon apothecarye,
I shal myself to herbes techen you,
That shal been for youre hele° and for youre prow,°   *health / profit*
185 And in oure yeerd tho° herbes shal I finde,   *then*
The whiche han of hir propretee by kinde°   *nature*
To purge you binethe and eek above.
Foryet nat this, for Goddes owene love.
Ye been ful colerik of complexioun;
190 Ware° the sonne in his ascencioun   *beware lest*
Ne finde you nat repleet° of humours hote;°   *full / hot*
And if it do, I dar wel laye[3] a grote°   *fourpence*
That ye shul have a fevere terciane,[4]
Or an agu° that may be youre bane.°   *fever / death*
195 A day or two ye shul han digestives
Of wormes, er ye take youre laxatives
Of lauriol, centaure, and fumetere,[5]
Or elles of ellebor that groweth there,
Of catapuce, or of gaitres beries,
200 Of herbe-ive growing in oure yeerd ther merye is.°   *where it is pleasant*
Pekke hem right up as they growe and ete hem in.
Be merye, housbonde, for youre fader kin!
Dredeth no dreem: I can saye you namore."
          "Madame," quod he, "graunt mercy of youre lore.°   *learning*
205 But nathelees, as touching daun Catoun,
That hath of wisdom swich a greet renown,
Though that he bad no dremes for to drede,
By God, men may in olde bookes rede
Of many a man more of auctoritee

---

1. Black bile, thought to produce dark thoughts.
2. Marcus Porcius Cato, ancient author of a book of proverbs used by schoolchildren.
3. Bet (with a pun on egg-laying).

4. Recurring fever.
5. These and the following are bitter herbs that produce hot and dry sensations and lead to purging.

210	Than evere Caton was, so mote I thee,°	*so may I prosper*
	That al the revers sayn of his sentence,°	*opinion*
	And han wel founden by experience	
	That dremes been significaciouns	
	As wel of joye as tribulaciouns	
215	That folk enduren in this lif present.	
	Ther needeth make of this noon argument:	
	The verray preve° sheweth it in deede.	*proof*
	"Oon of the gretteste auctour that men rede	
	Saith thus, that whilom two felawes wente	
220	On pilgrimage in a ful good entente,	
	And happed so they comen in a town,	
	Wher as ther was swich congregacioun	
	Of peple, and eek so strait of herbergage,°	*short of lodging*
	That they ne founde as muche as oo° cotage	*one*
225	In which they bothe mighte ylogged be;	
	Wherfore they mosten of necessitee	
	As for that night departe compaignye.	
	And eech of hem gooth to his hostelrye,	
	And took his logging as it wolde falle.	
230	That oon of hem was logged in a stalle,	
	Fer in a yeerd, with oxen of the plough;	
	That other man was logged wel ynough,	
	As was his aventure or his fortune,	
	That us governeth alle as in commune.	
235	And so bifel that longe er it were day,	
	This man mette in his bed, ther as he lay,	
	How that his felawe gan upon him calle,	
	And saide, 'Allas, for in an oxes stalle	
	This night I shal be mordred° ther I lie!	*murdered*
240	Now help me, dere brother, or I die!	
	In alle haste com to me,' he saide.	
	"This man out of his sleep for fere abraide,°	*bolted up*
	But whan that he was wakened of his sleep,	
	He turned him and took of this no keep:°	*heed*
245	Him thoughte his dreem nas° but a vanitee.	*was not*
	Thus twies in his sleeping dremed he,	
	And atte thridde time yit his felawe	
	Cam, as him thoughte, and saide, 'I am now slawe:°	*slain*
	Bihold my bloody woundes deepe and wide.	
250	Aris up erly in the morwe tide°	*morning time*
	And atte west gate of the town,' quod he,	
	'A carte ful of dong° ther shaltou see,	*dung*
	In which my body is hid ful prively:	
	Do thilke° carte arresten° boldely.	*that / have seized*
255	My gold caused my mordre, sooth° to sayn'—	*truth*
	And tolde him every point how he was slain,	
	With a ful pitous face, pale of hewe.	

And truste wel, his dreem he foond ful trewe,
For on the morwe as soone as it was day,

260   To his felawes in he took the way,
And whan that he cam to this oxes stalle,
After his felawe he bigan to calle.
    "The hostiler° answerde him anoon,   *innkeeper*
And saide, 'Sire, youre felawe is agoon:

265   As soone as day he wente out of the town.'
    "This man gan fallen in suspecioun,
Remembring on his dremes that he mette;
And forth he gooth, no lenger wolde he lette,°   *delay*
Unto the west gate of the town, and foond

270   A dong carte, wente as it were to donge° lond,   *spread manure on*
That was arrayed in that same wise
As ye han herd the dede man devise;
And with an hardy herte he gan to crye,
'Vengeance and justice of this felonye!

275   My felawe mordred is this same night,
And in this carte he lith gaping upright!°   *facing up*
I crye out on the ministres,"° quod he,   *magistrates*
'That sholde keepe and rulen this citee.
Harrow, allas, here lith my felawe slain!'

280   What sholde I more unto this tale sayn?
The peple up sterte and caste the carte to grounde,
And in the middel of the dong they founde
The dede man that mordred was al newe.°   *just recently*
    "O blisful God that art so just and trewe,

285   Lo, how that thou biwrayest° mordre alway!   *reveal*
Mordre wol out, that see we day by day:
Mordre is so wlatsom° and abhominable   *loathsome*
To God that is so just and resonable,
That he ne wol nat suffre it heled° be,   *concealed*

290   Though it abide a yeer or two or three.
Mordre wol out: this my conclusioun.
And right anoon ministres of that town
Han hent° the cartere and so sore him pined,°   *seized / tortured*
And eek the hostiler so sore engined,

295   That they biknewe° hir wikkednesse anoon,   *confessed*
And were anhanged by the nekke boon.
Here may men seen that dremes been to drede.
    "And certes, in the same book I rede—
Right in the nexte chapitre after this—

300   I gabbe° nat, so have I joye or blis—   *lie*
Two men that wolde han passed over see
For certain cause into a fer contree,
If that the wind ne hadde been contrarye
That made hem in a citee for to tarye,

305   That stood ful merye upon an haven° side—   *harbor*
But on a day again° the even tide   *toward*

The wind gan chaunge, and blewe right as hem leste:° *they wanted*
Jolif° and glad they wenten unto reste, *merry*
And casten hem° ful erly for to saile. *decided*
310   "But to that oo man fil a greet mervaile;
That oon of hem, in sleeping as he lay,
Him mette a wonder dreem again the day:
Him thoughte a man stood by his beddes side,
And him comanded that he sholde abide,
315   And saide him thus, 'If thou tomorwe wende,° *travel*
Thou shalt be dreint:° my tale is at an ende.' *drowned*
      "He wook and tolde his felawe what he mette,
And prayed him his viage to lette;° *put off his journey*
As for that day he prayed him to bide.
320   His felawe that lay by his beddes side
Gan for to laughe, and scorned him ful faste.
'No dreem,' quod he, 'may so myn herte agaste
That I wol lette for to do my thinges.° *business*
I sette nat a straw by thy dreminges,
325   For swevenes been but vanitees and japes:° *tricks*
Men dreme alday° of owles or of apes, *constantly*
And of many a maze° therwithal — *delusion*
Men dreme of thing that nevere was ne shal.
But sith° I see that thou wolt here abide, *since*
330   And thus forsleuthen° wilfully thy tide, *waste due to sloth*
Good woot, it reweth me; and have good day.'
And thus he took his leve and wente his way.
But er that he hadde half his cours ysailed —
Noot° I nat why ne what meschaunce it ailed°— *know / went wrong*
335   But casuelly° the shippes botme rente,° *by accident / split apart*
And ship and man under the water wente,
In sighte of othere shippes it biside,
That with hem sailed at the same tide.
And therfore, faire Pertelote so dere,
340   By swiche ensamples olde maistou lere° *may you learn*
That no man sholde been too recchelees° *careless*
Of dremes, for I saye thee doutelees
That many a dreem ful sore is for to drede.
      "Lo, in the lif of Saint Kenelm[6] I rede—
345   That was Kenulphus sone, the noble king
Of Mercenrike—how Kenelm mette a thing
A lite° er he was mordred on a day. *little while*
His mordre in his avision° he sey.° *dream / saw*
His norice° him expounded everydeel *nurse*
350   His swevene, and bad him for to keepe him° weel *guard against*
For traison, but he nas but seven yeer old,
And therfore litel tale hath he told° *he cared little for*

---

6. St. Cenhelm, son of Cenwulf, a 9th-century child-king in Mercia who was murdered at his sister's orders.

Of any dreem, so holy was his herte.

By God, I hadde levere than my sherte°   *would give my shirt*

355   That ye hadde rad his legende as have I.

    "Dame Pertelote, I saye you trewely,

Macrobeus,[7] that writ the Avisioun

In Affrike of the worthy Scipioun,

Affermeth° dremes, and saith that they been   *confirms*

360   Warning of thinges that men after seen.

    "And ferthermore, I praye you looketh wel

In the Olde Testament of Daniel,

If he heeld dremes any vanitee.[8]

    "Rede eek of Joseph and ther shul ye see

365   Wher° dremes be somtime—I saye nat alle—   *whether*

Warning of thinges that shul after falle.

    "Looke of Egypte the king daun Pharao,

His bakere and his botelere° also,   *butler*

Wher they ne felte noon effect in dremes.[9]

370   Whoso wol seeke actes of sondry remes°   *various kingdoms*

May rede of dremes many a wonder thing.

    "Lo Cresus, which that was of Lyde° king,   *Lydia*

Mette he nat that he sat upon a tree,

Which signified he sholde anhanged be?

375   "Lo here Andromacha, Ectores° wif,   *Hector of Troy*

That day that Ector sholde lese° his lif,   *lose*

She dremed on the same night biforn

How that the lif of Ector sholde be lorn,

If thilke day he wente into bataile;

380   She warned him, but it mighte nat availe:

He wente for to fighte nathelees,

But he was slain anoon of Achilles.

But thilke tale is al too long to telle,

And eek it is neigh day, I may nat dwelle.

385   Shortly I saye, as for conclusioun,

That I shal han of this avisioun

Adversitee, and I saye ferthermoor

That I ne telle of laxatives no stoor,°   *hold no regard for*

For they been venimes,° I woot° it weel: *poisons / know*

390   I hem defye, I love hem neveradeel.

    "Now lat us speke of mirthe and stinte° al this.   *stop*

Madame Pertelote, so have I blis,

Of oo thing God hath sente me large grace:

For whan I see the beautee of youre face—

395   Ye been so scarlet reed aboute youre yën—

It maketh al my drede for to dien.

---

7. Macrobius, a 4th-century author, wrote an extensive commentary on Cicero's *Dream of Scipio*.
8. Daniel interprets the pagan King Nebuchadnezzar's

dream, which foretells his downfall (Daniel 4).
9. Joseph interpreted dreams for the pharaoh's chief baker and butler (Genesis 40–41).

For also siker° as *In principio*,[1]   *certain*
Mulier est hominis confusio.[2]
Madame, the sentence° of this Latin is,   *meaning*
400   'Womman is mannes joye and al his blis.'
For whan I feele anight youre softe side—
Al be it that I may nat on you ride,
For that oure perche is maad so narwe, allas—
I am so ful of joye and of solas°   *delight*
405   That I defye bothe swevene and dreem."
And with that word he fleigh down fro the beem,
For it was day, and eek° his hennes alle,   *also*
And with a "chuk" he gan hem for to calle,
For he hadde founde a corn lay in the yeerd.
410   Real° he was, he was namore aferd:°   *regal / afraid*
He fethered Pertelote twenty time,
And trad° hire as ofte er it was prime.[3]   *mounted*
He looketh as it were a grim leoun,°   *lion*
And on his toes he rometh up and down:
415   Him deined nat to sette his foot to grounde.
He chukketh whan he hath a corn yfounde,
And to him rennen thanne his wives alle.
Thus royal, as a prince is in his halle,
Leve I this Chauntecleer in his pasture,
420   And after wol I telle his aventure.
        Whan that the month in which the world bigan,
That highte March, whan God first maked man,
Was compleet, and passed were also,
Sin March biran,° thritty days and two,[4]   *finished*
425   Bifel that Chauntecleer in al his pride,
His sevene wives walking him biside,
Caste up his yën to the brighte sonne,
That in the signe of Taurus hadde yronne
Twenty degrees and oon and somwhat more,
430   And knew by kinde,° and by noon other lore,   *nature*
That it was prime, and crew with blisful stevene.°   *voice*
"The sonne," he saide, "is clomben up on hevene
Fourty degrees and oon and more, ywis.°   *indeed*
Madame Pertelote, my worldes blis,
435   Herkneth thise blisful briddes° how they singe,   *birds*
And see the fresshe flowres how they springe:
Ful is myn herte of revel and solas."
But sodeinly him fil a sorweful cas,°   *event*
For evere the latter ende of joye is wo—
440   God woot that worldly joye is soone ago,

1. "In the beginning," the opening verse of the Book of   3. First hour of the day.
Genesis and the Gospel of John.   4. The date is thus May 3.
2. "Woman is the ruination of mankind."

And if a rethor° coude faire endite,°   *rhetorician / compose*
He in a cronicle saufly° mighte it write,   *safely*
As for a soverein notabilitee.
Now every wis man lat him herkne me:
445   This storye is also° trewe, I undertake,   *as*
As is the book of Launcelot de Lake,[5]
That wommen holde in ful greet reverence.
Now wol I turne again to my sentence.°   *topic*
            A colfox° ful of sly iniquitee,   *black fox*
450   That in the grove° hadde woned° yeres three,   *woods / lived*
By heigh imaginacion forncast,[6]
The same night thurghout the hegges brast°   *burst*
Into the yeerd ther Chauntecleer the faire
Was wont, and eek his wives, to repaire;
455   And in a bed of wortes° stille he lay   *cabbages*
Til it was passed undren° of the day,   *midmorning*
Waiting his time on Chauntecleer to falle,
As gladly doon thise homicides alle,
That in await liggen to mordre men.
460   O false mordrour, lurking in thy den!
O newe Scariot! Newe Geniloun![7]
False dissimilour°! O Greek Sinoun,[8]   *dissembler*
That broughtest Troye al outrely° to sorwe!   *entirely*
O Chauntecleer, accursed be that morwe
465   That thou into the yeerd flaugh fro the bemes!
Thou were ful wel ywarned by thy dremes
That thilke day was perilous to thee;
But what that God forwoot moot° needes be,   *foreknew must*
After the opinion of certain clerkes:
470   Witnesse on him that any parfit° clerk is   *accomplished*
That in scole is greet altercacioun
In this matere, and greet disputisoun,
And hath been of an hundred thousand men.
But I ne can nat bulte it to the bren,[9]
475   As can the holy doctour Augustin,
Or Boece, or the bisshop Bradwardin[1]—
Wheither that Goddes worthy forwiting°   *foreknowledge*
Straineth° me nedely for to doon a thing   *compels*
("Nedely" clepe I simple necessitee),
480   Or elles if free chois be graunted me
To do that same thing or do it nought,
Though God forwoot it er that I was wrought;°   *made*

---

5. The adventures of the Arthurian knight.
6. Predicted (in Chauntecleer's dream).
7. Judas Iscariot, who handed Jesus over to the Roman
authorities for execution; Ganelon, a medieval traitor
who betrayed the hero Roland to his Saracen enemies.
8. The Greek who tricked the Trojans into accepting the

Trojan horse behind the city walls.
9. Sift it from the husks (i.e., discriminate).
1. St. Augustine, the ancient writer Boethius, and the
14th-century Archbishop of Canterbury Thomas Brad-
wardine attempted to explain how God's predestination
of events still allowed for humans to have free will.

Or if his witing straineth neveradeel,
But by necessitee condicionel[2]—
485 I wol nat han to do of swich matere:
My tale is of a cok, as ye may heere,
That took his conseil of his wif with sorwe,
To walken in the yeerd upon that morwe
That he hadde met the dreem that I you tolde.
490 Wommenes conseils been ful ofte colde,°   *disastrous*
Wommanes conseil broughte us first to wo,
And made Adam fro Paradis to go,
Ther as he was ful merye and wel at ese.
But for I noot° to whom it mighte displese   *do not know*
495 If I conseil of wommen wolde blame,
Passe over, for I saide it in my game—
Rede auctours° where they trete of swich matere,   *authors*
And what they sayn of wommen ye may heere—
Thise been the cokkes wordes and nat mine:
500 I can noon harm of no womman divine.°   *guess at*
     Faire in the sond° to bathe hire merily,   *sand*
Lith° Pertelote, and alle hir sustres by,   *lies*
Again the sonne, and Chauntecleer so free
Soong merier than the mermaide in the see—
505 For Physiologus[3] saith sikerly
How that they singen wel and merily.
     And so bifel that as he caste his yë
Among the wortes on a boterflye,°   *butterfly*
He was war of this fox that lay ful lowe.
510 No thing ne liste him° thanne for to crowe,   *he wanted*
But cride anoon "Cok cok!" and up he sterte,
As man that was affrayed in his herte—
For naturelly a beest desireth flee
Fro his contrarye° if he may it see,   *natural enemy*
515 Though he nevere erst° hadde seen it with his yë.   *before*
This Chauntecleer, whan he gan him espye,
He wolde han fled, but that the fox anoon
Saide, "Gentil sire, allas, wher wol ye goon?
Be ye afraid of me that am youre freend?
520 Now certes, I were worse than a feend°   *devil*
If I to you wolde harm or vilainye.
I am nat come youre conseil for t'espye,
But trewely the cause of my cominge
Was only for to herkne how that ye singe:
525 For trewely, ye han as merye a stevene°   *voice*
As any angel hath that is in hevene.
Therwith ye han in musik more feelinge

2. Boethius argued only for conditional necessity, which still permitted for much exercise of free will.   3. Said to have written a bestiary.

Than hadde Boece,[4] or any that can singe.
My lord your fader—God his soule blesse!—
530   And eek youre moder, of hir gentilesse,°   *gentility*
Han in myn hous ybeen, to my grete ese.
And certes sire, ful fain° wolde I you plese.   *gladly*
    But for men speke of singing, I wol saye,
So mote I brouke° wel mine yën twaye,   *use*
535   Save ye, I herde nevere man so singe
As dide youre fader in the morweninge.
Certes, it was of herte° al that he soong.   *heartfelt*
And for to make his vois the more strong,
He wolde so paine him that with bothe his yën
540   He moste winke,° so loude wolde he cryen;   *shut his eyes*
And stonden on his tiptoon therwithal,
And strecche forth his nekke long and smal;
And eek he was of swich discrecioun
That ther nas no man in no regioun
545   That him in song or wisdom mighte passe.°   *surpass*
I have wel rad in Daun Burnel the Asse.[5]
Among his vers how that ther was a cok,
For° a preestes sone yaf him a knok   *because*
Upon his leg whil he was yong and nice,°   *foolish*
550   He made him for to lese his benefice.[6]
But certain, ther nis no comparisoun
Bitwixe the wisdom and discrecioun
Of youre fader and of his subtiltee.
Now singeth, sire, for sainte° charitee!   *holy*
555   Lat see, conne ye youre fader countrefete?"°   *imitate*
    This Chauntecleer his winges gan to bete,
As man that coude his traison nat espye,
So was he ravisshed with his flaterye.
    Allas, ye lordes, many a fals flatour
560   Is in youre court, and many a losengeour,°   *deceiver*
That plesen you wel more, by my faith,
Than he that soothfastnesse° unto you saith!   *truth*
Redeth Ecclesiaste[7] of flaterye.
Beeth war, ye lordes, of hir trecherye.
565   This Chauntecleer stood hye upon his toos,
Strecching his nekke, and heeld his yën cloos,
And gan to crowe loude for the nones;°   *for the purpose*
And daun Russel the fox sterte up atones,°   *at once*
And by the gargat° hente° Chauntecleer,   *throat / seized*
570   And on his bak toward the wode him beer,
For yit ne was ther no man that him sued.

---

4. In addition to theology, Boethius also wrote a music
textbook
5. The hero of a 12th-century satirical poem , Speculum
Stultorum, by Nigel Wirecker, Brunellus was a donkey

who traveled around Europe trying to educate himself.
6. Lose his commission (because he overslept).
7. The Book of Ecclesiasticus.

O destinee that maist nat been eschued!°   *avoided*
Allas that Chauntecleer fleigh fro the bemes!
Allas his wif ne roughte° nat of dremes!   *cared*
575   And on a Friday[8] fil al this meschaunce!
    O Venus that art goddesse of plesaunce,
Sin that thy servant was this Chauntecleer,
And in thy service dide al his power—
More for delit than world° to multiplye—   *population*
580   Why woldestou suffre him on thy day to die?
    O Gaufred,[9] dere maister soverein,
That, whan thy worthy king Richard was slain
With shot,° complainedest his deeth so sore,   *(of an arrow)*
Why ne hadde I now thy sentence and thy lore,
585   The Friday for to chide as diden ye?
For on a Friday soothly° slain was he.   *truly*
Thanne wolde I shewe you how that I coude plaine°   *lament*
For Chauntecleres drede and for his paine.
    Certes, swich cry ne lamentacioun
590   Was nevere of ladies maad whan Ilioun°   *Troy*
Was wonne, and Pyrrus[1] with his straite° swerd,   *drawn*
Whan he hadde hent King Priam by the beerd
And slain him, as saith us Eneidos,°   *Virgil's Aeneid*
As maden alle the hennes in the cloos,°   *yard*
595   Whan they hadde seen of Chauntecleer the sighte.
But sovereinly Dame Pertelote shrighte°   *shrieked*
Ful louder than dide Hasdrubales wif[2]
Whan that hir housbonde hadde lost his lif,
And that the Romains hadden brend Cartage:
600   She was so ful of torment and of rage
That wilfully unto the fir she sterte,
And brende hirselven with a stedefast herte.
    O woful hennes, right so criden ye
As, whan that Nero[3] brende the citee
605   Of Rome, criden senatoures wives
For that hir housbondes losten alle hir lives:
Withouten gilt this Nero hath hem slain.
Now wol I turne to my tale again.
    The sely° widwe and eek hir doughtres two   *innocent*
610   Herden thise hennes crye and maken wo,
And out at dores sterten they anoon,
And sien° the fox toward the grove goon,   *saw*
And bar upon his bak the cok away,
And criden, "Out, harrow, and wailaway,

---

8. Venus's day, but also an ominous day of the week.
9. Geoffrey of Vinsauf, who wrote a poem when King Richard the Lion-Hearted died, cursing the day of the week on which he died, a Friday.
1. Pyrrhus, the son of Achilles, who slew Troy's King Priam.

2. Hasdrubal was King of Carthage when it was defeated by the Romans during the Punic Wars.
3. The Emperor Nero set fire to Rome, killing many of his senators.

615   Ha, ha, the fox," and after him they ran,
     And eek with staves many another man;
     Ran Colle oure dogge, and Talbot and Gerland,[4]
     And Malkin with a distaf in hir hand,
     Ran cow and calf, and eek the verray hogges,
620   Sore aferd for berking of the dogges
     And shouting of the men and wommen eke.
     They ronne so hem thoughte hir herte breke;
     They yelleden as feendes doon in helle;
     The dokes° criden as men wolde hem quelle;°   *ducks / kill*
625   The gees for fere flowen over the trees;
     Out of the hive cam the swarm of bees;
     So hidous was the noise a, benedicite,
     Certes, he Jakke Straw[5] and his meinee
     Ne made nevere shoutes half so shrille
630   Whan that they wolden any Fleming kille,
     As thilke day was maad upon the fox:
     Of bras they broughten bemes° and of box,°   *trumpets / boxwood*
     Of horn, of boon, in whiche they blewe and pouped,°   *puffed*
     And therwithal they skriked and they houped—
635   It seemed as that hevene sholde falle.
        Now goode men, I praye you herkneth alle:
     Lo, how Fortune turneth sodeinly
     The hope and pride eek of hir enemy.
     This cok that lay upon the foxes bak,
640   In al his drede unto the fox he spak,
     And saide, "Sire, if that I were as ye,
     Yit sholde I sayn, as wis° God helpe me,   *certainly*
     'Turneth ayain, ye proude cherles° alle!   *ruffians*
     A verray pestilence upon you falle!
645   Now am I come unto this wodes side,
     Maugree° your heed,° the cok shal here abide.   *despite / planning*
     I wol him ete, in faith, and that anoon.'"
        The fox answerde, "In faith, it shal be doon."
     And as he spak that word, al sodeinly
650   The cok brak from his mouth deliverly,°   *nimbly*
     And hye upon a tree he fleigh anoon.
        And whan the fox sawgh that he was agoon,
     "Allas," quod he, "O Chauntecleer, allas!
     I have to you," quod he, "ydoon trespas,
655   In as muche as I maked you aferd
     Whan I you hente and broughte out of the yeerd.
     But sire, I dide it in no wikke° entente: *wicked*
     Come down, and I shal telle you what I mente.
     I shal saye sooth to you, God help me so."

---

4. Common names for dogs.
5. Jack Straw was one of the leaders of the Peasants'   Revolt of 1381, which was directed in part against the
       Flemish traders in London.

660   "Nay thanne," quod he, "I shrewe° us bothe two: *curse*
     But first I shrewe myself, bothe blood and bones,
     If thou bigile me ofter than ones;
     Thou shalt namore thurgh thy flaterye
     Do° me to singe and winken with myn yë.°   *make*
665   For he that winketh whan he sholde see,
     Al wilfully, God lat him nevere thee.°"   *prosper*
        "Nay," quod the fox, "but God yive him meschaunce
     That is so undiscreet of governaunce
     That jangleth° whan he sholde holde his pees."   *chatters*
670   Lo, swich it is for to be recchelees°   *careless*
     And necligent and truste on flaterye.
     But ye that holden this tale a folye
     As of a fox, or of a cok and hen,
     Taketh the moralitee, goode men.
675   For Saint Paul saith that al that writen is
     To oure doctrine° it is ywrit, ywis:°   *instruction / indeed*
     Taketh the fruit, and lat the chaf be stille.
     Now goode God, if that it be thy wille,
     As saith my lord, so make us alle goode men,
680   And bringe us to his hye blisse. Amen

The Epilogue

     "Sire Nonnes Preest," oure Hoste saide anoon,
     "Yblessed be thy breech° and every stoon:°   *buttocks / testicle*
     This was a merye tale of Chauntecleer.
     But by my trouthe, if thou were seculer°   *a layman*
685   Thou woldest been a tredefowl° aright: *a cock*
     For if thou have corage° as thou hast might   *desire*
     Thee were neede of hennes, as I weene,°   *suppose*
     Ye, mo than sevene times seventeene.
     See whiche brawnes° hath this gentil preest—   *muscles*
690   So greet a nekke and swich a large breest.
     He looketh as a sperhawk° with his yën;   *sparrowhawk*
     Him needeth nat his colour for to dyen
     With brasil ne with grain of Portingale.[6]
     Now sire, faire falle you for youre tale."
695   And after that he with ful merye cheere
     Saide unto another as ye shul heere.

THE PARSON'S TALE   Although *The Canterbury Tales* remain unfinished and even the order of the tales is unclear, we know that Chaucer's plan was to end them with *The Parson's Tale*, just as it was to begin them with the pilgrimage to Canterbury in *The General Prologue*. Thus, when the Parson responds to the Host's request for a final tale by praying Jesus to show the way to the "glorious pilgrimage" called "Jerusalem celestial," there is a sense of

---

6. Two types of red dye, the latter from Portugal.

closure in his return to an idea that has been obscured during the tale-telling. His shift of the destination from Canterbury to the heavenly city, however, gives us pause. The view that life on earth is a pilgrimage to heaven was a Christian commonplace, but was it Chaucer's view? The three parts of *The Parson's Tale* included here raise questions about how Chaucer's religious beliefs relate to his art. What is his final judgment of the artful, but often sinful, tales he has been telling?

In the introduction, the Parson rejects the idea of poetry entirely, scornfully refusing to tell a "fable" or to adorn his tale with alliteration or rhyme; instead, he will tell what he refers to as a "merye tale in prose," which turns out to be a forty-page treatise on penitence. Thus Chaucer specifically attributes to him an ascetic view of art which is hard to reconcile with his own extraordinary poetry. Does the Parson speak for Chaucer? Although he has a measure of authority as the only exemplary member of the clergy on the pilgrimage, he is nevertheless a fictional character. Since, however, Chaucer is thought to have written the introduction to this tale as well as the *Retraction* at the same time at the end of his life, perhaps he could have come to share the Parson's aesthetic views.

The Parson begins his tale proper with a second reference to celestial Jerusalem, stating that the route to it is through penitence. The tale, which Chaucer had translated at an earlier period, belongs to a common type of manual of confession for either clergy or laity. Included in it is an analysis of the seven deadly sins—pride, envy, anger, sloth, avarice, gluttony, and lechery—in an order that suggests that Chaucer, like Dante, considered the last to be the least serious, although still worthy of damnation. The passage on lechery excerpted here offers an opportunity to measure *The Parson's Tale* against the tales that have gone before, particularly such "sinful" works as *The Miller's Tale* and *The Wife of Bath's Prologue*.

Whatever conclusion we draw about the relevance of *The Parson's Tale* to the tales preceding, the *Retraction* appended to it is troubling yet intriguing. In it Chaucer repudiates much of the work for which he is most loved and admired, such "worldly vanitees" as *Troilus and Criseyde*, *The Parliament of Fowls*, and those of the *Canterbury Tales* that "sounen [lead] into sinne." On the other hand, he thanks God for his works of "moralitee," including his translation of Boethius and his saints' legends, works that are seldom read today. He himself is engaged in penance—repentance, confession, and satisfaction—thus connecting his own spiritual experience with the manual he has translated. However disappointing it is to read this rejection of his most artistically satisfying tales, we must remember that a concept of art for art's sake would have been historically unavailable to him. Perhaps his last tale was indeed his last word.

from The Parson's Tale
The Introduction

By that° the Manciple hadde his tale al ended,		*by that time*
The sonne fro the south line[1] was descended		
So lowe, that he nas nat to my sighte		
Degrees nine and twenty as in highte.		
5 Four of the clokke it was, so as I gesse,		
For elevene foot,° or litel more or lesse,		*feet*
My shadwe was at thilke° time as there,		*that*
Of swich feet as my lengthe parted were		
In sixe feet equal of proporcioun.		

1. Astronomical marking parallel to the celestial equator.

10	Therwith the moones exaltacioun°—	*dominant influence*
	I mene Libra²—alway gan ascende,	
	As we were entring at a thropes ende.°	*village boundary*
	For which oure Host, as he was wont to gie°	*lead*
	As in this caas oure joly compaignye,	
15	Saide in this wise, "Lordinges everichoon,	
	Now lakketh us no tales mo than oon:	
	Fulfild is my sentence° and my decree;	*design*
	I trowe° that we han herd of eech degree;	*believe*
	Almost fulfild is al myn ordinaunce.	
20	I praye to God, so yive him right good chaunce	
	That telleth this tale to us lustily.	
	Sire preest," quod he, "artou a vicary,°	*vicar*
	Or arte a Person°? Say sooth, by thy fay.°	*parish priest / faith*
	Be what thou be, ne breek thou nat oure play,	
25	For every man save thou hath told his tale.	
	Unbokele and shew us what is in thy male!°	*bag*
	For trewely, me thinketh by thy cheere°	*expression*
	Thou sholdest knitte up wel a greet matere.	
	Tel us a fable anoon, for cokkes bones!"³	
30	This Person answerde al atones,	
	"Thou gerest fable noon ytold for me,	
	For Paul, that writeth unto Timothee,⁴	
	Repreveth hem that waiven soothfastnesse,°	*truth*
	And tellen fables and swich wrecchednesse.	
35	Why sholde I sowen draf° out of my fest,°	*chaff / fist*
	Whan I may sowen whete if that me lest?°	*it pleases*
	For which I saye that if you list to heere	
	Moralitee and vertuous matere,	
	And thanne that ye wol yive me audience,	
40	I wol ful fain,° at Cristes reverence,	*gladly*
	Do you plesance leveful° as I can.	*lawfully*
	But trusteth wel, I am a southren man:⁵	
	I can nat geeste° Rum-Ram-Ruf by lettre—	*tell stories*
	Ne, God woot,° rym holde° I but litel bettre.	*knows / appreciate*
45	And therfore, if you list, I wol nat glose;°	*adorn my speech*
	I wol you telle a merye tale in prose,	
	To knitte up al this feeste and make an ende.	
	And Jesu for his grace wit me sende	
	To shewe you the way in this viage°	*journey*
50	Of thilke parfit° glorious pilgrimage	*that perfect*
	That highte Jerusalem celestial.	
	And if ye vouche-sauf,° anoon I shal	*agree*

2. Seventh sign in the Zodiac, the Scales.
3. Cock's bones, a euphemism for God's bones.
4. St. Paul's Epistle to Timothy.
5. The parson, like Chaucer himself, comes from the south of England and so is not accustomed to telling stories in the alliterative meter used traditionally in the north. Rum-Ram-Ruf is an example of alliteration.

Biginne upon my tale, for which I praye
Telle youre avis:° I can no bettre saye.   *opinion*
55   But nathelees, this meditacioun
I putte it ay° under correccioun   *always*
Of clerkes, for I am nat textuel:°   *a literalist*
I take but the sentence,° trusteth wel.   *sense*
Therfore I make protestacioun
60   That I wol stonde to correccioun."
     Upon this word we han assented soone,
For, as it seemed, it was for to doone
To enden in som vertuous sentence,°   *topic*
And for to yive him space° and audience;   *time*
65   And bede oure Host he sholde to him saye
That alle we to telle his tale him praye.
     Oure Hoste hadde the wordes for us alle:
"Sire preest," quod he, "now faire you bifalle:
Telleth," quod he, "youre meditacioun.
70   But hasteth you, the sonne wol adown.
Beeth fructuous, and that in litel space,
And to do wel God sende you his grace.
Saye what you list, and we wol gladly heere."
And with that word he saide in this manere.

from *The Tale*

Oure sweete Lord God of Hevene, that no man wol perisse[1] but wol
that we comen alle to the knowliche of him and to the blisful lif that is
perdurable,° amonesteth° us by the prophete Jeremie[2] that saith in this   *enduring /*
wise: "Stondeth upon the wayes and seeth and axeth of olde pathes   *warns*
(that is to sayn, of olde sentences°) which is the goode way, and   *opinions*
walketh in that way, and ye shul finde refresshing for youre soules."
     Manye been the wayes espirituels that leden folk to oure
Lord Jesu Crist and to the regne of glorye: of whiche wayes ther is
a ful noble way and a ful covenable° which may nat faile to man ne to   *suitable*
womman that thurgh sinne hath misgoon fro the righte way
of Jerusalem celestial; and this way is cleped° Penitence. ***   *called*

THE REMEDY FOR THE SIN OF LECHERY

Now cometh the remedye agains Lecherye, and that is generally
Chastitee and Continence that restraineth alle the desordainee
mevinges° that comen of flesshly talents.° And evere the gretter   *impulses / desires*
merite shal he han that most restraineth the wikkede eschaufinges°   *inflammations*
of the ardure of this sinne. And this is in two maneres: that is to
sayn, chastitee in mariage and chastitee of widwehood.

---

1. Who wishes no man to perish.   2. Jeremiah 6.16.

Now shaltou understonde that matrimoine is leeful° assembling   *lawful*
of man and of womman that receiven by vertu of the sacrement the
bond thurgh which they may nat be departed in al hir life—that is to
sayn, whil that they liven bothe. This, as saith the book, is a ful greet
sacrement: God maked it, as I have said, in Paradis, and wolde himself be born in mariage. And for to halwen° mariage, he was at a   *bless*
wedding where as he turned water into win, which was the firste
miracle that he wroughte in erthe biforn his disciples. Trewe effect
of mariage clenseth fornicacion and replenisseth Holy Chirche of
good linage° (for that is the ende of mariage), and it chaungeth   *offspring*
deedly sinne³ into venial sinne bitwixe hem that been ywedded, and
maketh the hertes al oon° of hem that been ywedded, as wel as the   *united*
bodies.

This is verray mariage that was establissed by God er that sinne
bigan, whan naturel lawe was in his right point° in Paradis; and it   *order*
was ordained that oo man sholde have but oo womman, and oo
womman but oo man (as saith Saint Augustine) by manye resons:
First, for mariage is figured° bitwixe Crist and Holy Chirche; and   *represented*
that other is for a man is heved° of a womman—algate,° by ordi-   *head / at least*
nance it sholde be so. For if a womman hadde mo men than oon,
thanne sholde she have mo hevedes than oon, and that were an horrible thing biforn God; and eek a womman ne mighte nat plese to
many folk at ones. And also ther ne sholde nevere be pees ne reste
amonges hem, for everich wolde axen his owene thing. And
fortherover, no man sholde knowe his owene engendrure,° ne who   *offspring*
sholde have his heritage, and the womman sholde been the lesse
biloved fro the time that she were conjoint to manye men.

Now cometh how that a man sholde bere him with his wif, and
namely in two thinges, that is to sayn, in suffrance° and in rever-   *obedience*
ence, as shewed Crist whan he made first womman. For he ne made
hire nat of the heved of Adam for she sholde nat claime too greet
lorshipe: for ther as womman hath the maistrye she maketh too greet
desray° (ther needen none ensamples of this: the experience of day   *disorder*
by day oughte suffise). Also, certes, God ne made nat womman of
the foot of Adam, for she ne sholde nat be holden too lowe, for she
can nat paciently suffre. But God made womman of the rib of Adam
for womman sholde be felawe unto man. Man sholde bere him to his
wif in faith, in trouthe, and in love, as saith Sainte Paul, that a man
sholde loven his wif as Crist loved Holy Chirche, that loved it so wel
that he deide for it. So sholde a man for his wif, if it were neede.

Now how that a womman sholde be subjet to hir housbonde,
that telleth Sainte Peter: First, in obedience. And eek, as saith the
decree, a womman that is a wif, as longe as she is a wif, she hath
noon auctoritee° to swere ne to bere witnesse withoute leve of hir   *power*
housbonde that is hir lord—algate, he sholde be so by reson. She
sholde eek serven him in alle honestee, and been attempree° of hir   *moderate*
array; I woot wel that they sholde setten hir entente° to plesen hir   *purpose*

---

3. Sex remains a minor sin even within marriage, but it is a more serious sin outside of marriage.

housbondes, but nat by hir quaintise of array:° Saint Jerome saith *flamboyant attire*
that wives that been apparailed in silk and in precious purpre ne
mowe nat clothen hem in Jesu Crist. What saith Saint John eek in
this matere? Saint Gregorye eek saith that no wight° seeketh   *person*
precious array but only for vaine glorye to been honoured the more
biforn the peple. It is a greet folye a womman to have a fair array
outward and in hireself be foul inward. A wif sholde eek be
mesurable° in looking and in bering and in laughing, and discreet in   *modest*
alle hir wordes and hir deedes. And aboven alle worldly thinges she
sholde loven hir housbonde with al hir herte, and to him be trewe
of hir body (so sholde an housbonde eek be to his wif): for sith that°   *since*
al the body is the housbondes, so sholde hir herte been, or elles ther
is bitwixe hem two as in that no parfit mariage.

Thanne shul men understonde that for three thinges a man and
his wif flesshly mowen° assemble. The firste is in entente of engen-   *may*
drure of children to the service of God: for certes, that is the cause
final of matrimoine. Another cause is to yeelden everich° of hem to   *each*
other the dette of hir bodies, for neither of hem hath power of his
owene body. The thridde is for to eschewe lecherye and vilainye.
The ferthe is, for soothe, deedly sinne. As to the firste, it is merito-
rye; the seconde also, for, as saith the decree, that she hath merite
of chastitee that yeeldeth to hir housbonde the dette of hir body,
ye, though it be again hir liking and the lust of hir herte. The
thridde manere is venial sinne—and, trewely, scarsly may any of
thise be withoute venial sinne, for the corrupcion and for the delit.
The ferthe manere is for to understonde if they assemble only for
amorous love and for noon of the forsaide causes, but for to accomplice thilke brenning delit—they rekke° nevere how ofte—soothly,   *care*
it is deedly sinne. And yit with sorwe some folk wol painen hem°   *trouble themselves*
more to doon than to hir appetit suffiseth. * * *

Another remedye agains lecherye is specially to withdrawen
swiche thinges as yive occasion to thilke vilainye, as ese,° eting, and   *leisure*
drinking: for certes, whan the pot boileth strongly, the beste remedye is to withdrawe the fir. Sleeping longe in greet quiete is eek a
greet norice° to lecherye. Another remedye agains lecherye is that a   *nurse*
man or a womman eschewe the compaignye of hem by whiche he
douteth° to be tempted: for al be it so that the deede be withston-   *suspects*
den, yit is ther greet temptacion. Soothly, a whit wal,° although it ne   *wall*
brenne nought fully by stiking of a candele, yit is the wal blak of the
leit.° Ful ofte time I rede that no man truste in his owene perfeccion   *from the flame*
but he be stronger than Sampson, holier than David, and wiser than
Salomon.

Chaucer's Retraction

Here Taketh the Makere of This Book His Leve

Now praye I to hem alle that herkne this litel tretis° or rede,° that if   *treatise / advice*
ther be any thing in it that liketh° hem, that therof they thanken   *pleases*
oure Lord Jesu Crist, of whom proceedeth al wit and al goodnesse.

And if ther be any thing that displese hem, I praye hem also that they arrette° it to the defaute of myn unconning,° and nat to my wil, *attribute / inability* that wolde ful fain° have said bettre if I hadde had conning. For oure *gladly* book saith, "Al that is writen is writen for oure doctrine," and that is myn entente. Wherfore I biseeke you mekely, for the mercy of God, that ye praye for me that Crist have mercy on me and foryive me my giltes,° and namely of my translacions and enditinges° of worldly *sins / writings* vanitees, the whiche I revoke in my retraccions:[4] as is the book of Troilus; the book also of Fame; the book of the five and twenty Ladies; the book of the Duchesse; the book of Saint Valentines Day of the Parlement of Briddes; the tales of Canterbury, thilke that sounen° into sinne; the book of the Leon; and many another book, if *lead* they were in my remembrance, and many a song and many a lecch- erous lay: that Crist for his grete mercy foryive me the sinne. But of the translacion of Boece *de Consolatione*, and othere bookes of legen- des of saintes, and omelies, and moralitee, and devocion, that thanke I oure Lord Jesu Crist and his blisful Moder and alle the saintes of hevene, biseeking hem that they from hennes forth unto my lives ende sende me grace to biwaile° my giltes and to studye to *repent* the salvacion of my soule, and graunte me grace of verray penitence, confession, and satisfaccion to doon in this present lif, thurgh the benigne grace of him that is king of kinges and preest over alle preestes, that boughte° us with the precious blood of his herte, so *redeemed* that I may been oon of hem at the day of doom° that shulle be saved. *judgment* *Qui cum patre et Spiritu Sancto vivis et regnas Deus per omnia saecula. Amen.*[5]

To His Scribe Adam[1]

Adam scrivain,° if evere it thee bifalle   *copyist*
Boece[2] or Troilus for to writen newe,
Under thy longe lokkes thou moste have° the scalle,°   *may you get / mange*
But after my making thou write more trewe,[3]
So ofte a day I moot° thy werk renewe,   *must*
It to correcte, and eek to rubbe and scrape:
And al is thurgh thy necligence and rape.°   *haste*

---

4. Here Chaucer repents having written most of his major works: *Troilus and Criseyde*, *The Book* (or *House*) *of Fame*, *The Legend of Good Women*, *The Book of the Duchess*, *The Parliament of Fowls*, and various of *The Canterbury Tales*. *The Book of the Lion* has not been preserved. Chaucer's translation of Boethius's *Consolation of Philosophy* is excepted.
5. You who live with the Father and the Holy Spirit and reign as God through all the centuries. Amen.
1. Given his position at court, Chaucer was asked to write many lyrics and occasional poems, such as this poem and the one that follows. In both, he wittily bemoans the conditions of authorship under which he was forced to work, depending on scribes to reproduce his poetry and on patrons to support it. In *To His Scribe Adam*, he strikes a pose of affectionate raillery toward his scribe, whose

occupation writers widely scorned. Perhaps he sees it as fitting to curse Adam with a skin disease which will make him scratch his scalp, just as Chaucer has had to scratch out the errors from his manuscripts. However, the poem has a serious undertone too. In fearing that Adam will miscopy his great romance, *Troilus and Criseyde*, he echoes a concern for the accurate reproduction of his work, which he voiced at the end of *Troilus* itself: he prays God that, in view of the great dialectal "diversitee / in Englissh," and in writing of oure tonge," no one "mis-write" his book (5.1793–94).
2. Chaucer's translation of Boethius's *Consolation of Philosophy*.
3. Unless you make a more reliable copy of what I have composed.

Complaint to His Purse[1]

To you, my purs, and to noon other wight,°   creature
Complaine I, for ye be my lady dere
I am so sory, now that ye be light,°   empty, wanton
For certes, but if° ye make me hevy cheere,[2]   unless
5 Me were as lief° be laid upon my beere;°   I would prefer / bier
For which unto youre mercy thus I crye:
Beeth hevy again, or elles moot° I die.   must

Now voucheth sauf° this day er it be night   grant
That I of you the blisful soun may heere,
10 Or see youre colour, lik the sonne bright,
That of yelownesse hadde nevere peere.
Ye be my lif, ye be myn hertes steere,°   guide
Queene of confort and of good compaignye:
Beeth hevy again, or elles moot I die.

15 Ye purs, that been to me my lives light
And saviour, as in this world down here,
Out of this tonne° helpe me thurgh your might,   dark situation
Sith that ye wol nat be my tresorere;
For I am shave as neigh° as any frere.[3]   close
20 But yit I praye unto youre curteisye:
Beeth hevy again, or elles moot I die.

Envoy to Henry IV[4]

O conquerour of Brutus Albioun,[5]
Which that by line° and free eleccioun   inheritance
Been verray king, this song to you I sende:
25 And ye, that mowen° alle oure harmes amende,   may
Have minde upon my supplicacioun.

⊷ ⋈ ⊶

William Langland
c. 1330–1387

Little is known of William Langland. On the basis of internal evidence in *Piers Plowman*, he is thought to have been a clerk in minor orders whose career in the church was curtailed by his marriage. He may have come from the Malvern Hills in the west of England, but he spent

1. This is a traditional "begging" poem, based on French models. The request for money is presented humorously, as a parody of a courtly love complaint to a cruel mistress. The parallel takes on ironic force when one recalls Chaucer's presentation of himself, in such early poems as *The Parliament of Fowls*, as a failed lover. This is one of Chaucer's last poems, written a year before his death. It was addressed to Henry IV when he took the throne in 1399, to request a renewal of the annuity Chaucer had received from the deposed Richard II. The flattering "envoy" to Henry at the end alludes to the tradition dat-

ing from Geoffrey of Monmouth that Britain was founded by Brutus, the grandson of Aeneas, the exiled prince of Troy and founder of Rome.
2. Serious expression (in a person); full weight (in a purse).
3. Friar (with a bald tonsure).
4. The "envoy" is the traditional close of a ballad, usually directed to its addressee.
5. According to legend, Brutus conquered the kingdom of Albion and renamed it "Britain," after himself.

much of his professional life in London. He was clearly learned, using many Latin quotations from the Bible (given below primarily in English translation, designated by italics and unnumbered), and the style of his poem in many ways resembles sermon rhetoric.

Piers Plowman is an ambitious and multilayered allegory, an attempt to combine Christian history, social satire, and an account of the individual soul's quest for salvation. It is presented as a dream vision whose hero is a humble plowman, and whose narrator, the naive dreamer named Will, may be only a convenient fiction. Even its first audience sometimes reacted to this mysterious poem in surprising ways. *Piers Plowman* was so inspiring to the leaders of the Rising of 1381 that they saw Piers not as a fictional character but as an actual seditious person. This interpretation of the poem is remarkable given Langland's profound conservatism; despite his scathing social satire, he offers no program for social change. In fact, he supports the traditional model of the three estates, whereby the king and knights protect the body politic, the clergy prays for it, and the commons provide its food. Although he was sympathetic toward the poor and scornful of the rich and powerful, he felt that what ailed society was that *none* of the three estates was performing its proper role.

Piers Plowman survives in many manuscripts, a fact that suggests a large audience, which most likely included secular readers in the government and law as well as the clergy. Most of John Ball's followers would have been unable to read it. The poem exists in three versions—known as the A-, B-, and C-texts—and their history throws light on the poem's role in the Rising of 1381. The short A-text was expanded into the B-text some time between 1377 and 1381, when John Ball and other rebel leaders referred to it, while the C-text (which is translated in the excerpts below) is generally agreed to reflect Langland's attempt to distance himself from the radical beliefs of the rebels. Nevertheless, the poem remained popular for the next two centuries as a document of social protest and was ultimately regarded as a prophecy of the English Reformation. Langland's social criticism, however, is only part of his project, for he considered individual salvation to be equally important. A strictly political reading of *Piers Plowman*—whether in the fourteenth century or the twenty-first—misses a great deal of its originality and its power.

Piers Plowman is a challenge to read: it is almost surrealistic in its rapid and unexplained transitions, its many dreams, and its complex use of allegory. It is as confusing to people reading it in its entirety as to those reading it in excerpts, as here. Nevertheless, the poem does have a kind of unity, of a thematic rather than a narrative sort. It is held together by the dreamer's vision of the corruption of society and his personal quest to save his own soul. This quest is loosely structured by the metaphor of the journey, which is reflected in the poem's subdivision into parts called *passūs*—Latin for "steps." The poem is further unified by the allegorical character of Piers the plowman: a literal fourteenth-century English farmer when we first meet him, in the course of the poem he becomes a figural representation of Saint Peter, the first pope and founder of the church, and of Christ himself.

The four passages included here suggest the connection between the social and spiritual aspects of the poem. In the *Prologue*, the dreamer has a vision of a tower on a hill (later explained as the seat of Truth, i.e., God), a hellish dungeon beneath, and between them, a "field full of folk," representing various professions from the three estates, who are later said to be more concerned with their material than their spiritual welfare.

Passus 2 is the first of three on the marriage of Lady Meed, an ambiguous allegorical figure whose name can mean "just reward," "bribery," or the profit motive generally, the last being a cause for anxiety as England moved from a barter economy to one based on money. The dreamer is invited by Lady Holy Church to Meed's marriage to "False Fickle Tongue." Members of all three estates attend this event, a sign of corruption on every social level.

Langland sees greed as a sin of the poor as well as the rich, and in a comic passage of personification allegory represents the seven deadly sins as members of the commons. Included here from *Passus 6* is the vividly realized portrait of Glutton, who revels in his sin as he confesses it. Langland discusses the issues of poverty and work most directly in *Passus 8*, where Piers Plowman insists that the assembled people help him plow his half-acre before he will agree to lead them on a pilgrimage to Truth. Piers supports the traditional division of labor, explicitly exempting the knight from producing food, as long as he protects the commons and clergy from "wasters"—lazy shirkers. He insists, however, that the knight treat peasants well—in part because roles may be reversed in heaven, and earthly underlings can become heavenly masters. Yet Langland is not simply taking the workers' side. The knight turns out to be too courteous to control wasters, and Hunger must be called in to offer an incentive to work. When Piers takes pity on the poor and sends Hunger away, Waster refuses to work and the laborers demand more money, cursing the king for the statutes that have instituted wage freezes.

Langland did not write French-inspired rhymed poetry, which was fashionable in London and used by Chaucer, but rather he composed old-fashioned alliterative poetry, which survived from Old English. The so-called Alliterative Revival was divided into two traditions, one based in the north of England and featuring romances in the alliterative "high" style, such as *Sir Gawain and the Green Knight*, and the other based in the south and west, and tending to social protest poems in a plain style. Langland's subject matter and style link him to the latter tradition, which includes satirical poems such as *Richard the Redeless, Mum and the Sothsegger,* and *Jack Upland.* In Middle English alliterative poetry, each line contains at least four major stressed syllables, with the first three usually beginning with the same sound. The translations of alliterative poems in this anthology—including *Beowulf* and *Sir Gawain*, as well as *Piers Plowman*—all sufficiently retain the alliteration to convey its flavor in modern English. The following passage from *Piers Plowman* in Middle English, the description of Lady Meed in her gaudy clothes, makes the point more clearly. The dreamer, with naive admiration, reports that he

> . . . was war of a womman wonderliche yclothed,
> Purfiled with Pelure, the pureste on erthe,
> Ycorouned in a coroune, the kyng hath noon bettre.
> Fetisliche hire fyngres were fretted with gold wyr
> And theron riche Rubyes as rede as any gleede,
> And Diamaundes of derrest pris and double manere saphires,
> Orientals and Ewages enuenymes to destroye.
> Hire Robe ful riche, of reed scarlet engreyned,
> With Ribanes of reed gold and of riche stones.
> Hire array me rauysshed; swich richesse saugh I neuere.

Although Langland generally uses the plainer alliterative style of southern protest poetry, here he uses the high style of northern alliterative romances, for satirical purposes. Meed's dress recalls that of Bercilak's lady in *Sir Gawain*, in "rich red rayled" (line 952), as well as the elegant clothing of the Green Knight, "with pelure pured apert, the pane ful clene" (154). In contrast to the clothing of Lady Holy Church, whom Langland introduces in *Passus 1* simply as "a lady lovely of look, clothed in linen," the robes of lady Meed seem dangerously seductive, thus underscoring a sexual metaphor for bribery which Langland consistently develops. Thus, in a more subtle fashion than some of his followers, such as the Wycliffite author of *Pierce the Ploughman's Crede*, Langland was able to use the specialized language of alliterative poetry in the service of social criticism.

from **Piers Plowman**[1]
Prologue

In a summer season when the sun shone softly
I wrapped myself in woolens as if I were a sheep;
In a hermit's habit, unholy in his works,
I went out into the world to hear wonders
5   And to see many strange and seldom-known things.
But on a May morning in the Malvern Hills[2]
I happened to fall asleep, worn out from walking;
And in a meadow as I lay sleeping,
I dreamed most marvelously, as I recall.
10   All the world's wealth and all of its woe,
Dozing though I was, I certainly saw;
Truth and treachery, treason and guile,
Sleeping I saw them all, as I shall record.
    I looked to the East toward the rising sun
15   And saw a tower—I took it Truth was inside.
To the West then I looked after a while
And saw a deep dale—Death, as I believe,
Dwelled in that place, along with wicked spirits.
Between them I found a fair field full of folk
20   Of all manner men, the common and the poor,
Working and wandering as this world asks us.
    Some put themselves to the plow, and seldom played,
To work hard as they can at planting and sowing
And won what these wasters through gluttony destroy.
25   And some put themselves in pride's ways and apparel
Themselves accordingly in clothes of all kinds.
Many put themselves to prayers and penances,
All for love of our lord they live so severely
In hope of good ending and heaven-kingdom's bliss;
30   As anchorites and hermits[3] that keep to their cells,
With no great desire to cruise the countryside
Seeking carnal pleasures and luxurious lives.
    And some turned to trade—they made out better,
As it always seems to us that such men thrive;
35   And some know as minstrels how to make mirth,
Will neither work nor sweat, but swear out loud,
Invent sleazy stories and make fools of themselves
Though it's in their power to work if they want.
What Paul preached about them I surely can prove;

---

1. Translated by George Economou.
2. These hills in the west of England were probably Langland's original home.

3. Both were vowed to a religious life of solitude, hermits in the wilderness and anchorites walled in a tiny dwelling.

40   *Qui turpiloquium loquitur*[4] is Lucifer's man.
      Beggars and moochers moved about quickly
Till their bags and their bellies were crammed to the top,
Faking it for food and fighting over ale.
In gluttony those freeloaders go off to bed
45   And rise to rob and run off at the mouth.
Sleep and sloth are their steady companions.
      Pilgrims and palmers[5] pledged to travel together
To seek Saint James[6] and the saints of Rome,
Went on their way with many wise tales
50   And took leave to lie about it for a lifetime.
A heap of hermits with their hooked staves
Went to Our Lady of Walsingham,[7] with wenches in tow;
Great deadbeats that hated a good day's work
Clothed themselves in hooded cloaks to stand apart
55   And proclaimed themselves hermits, for the easy life.
      I found there friars from all four orders,[8]
Preaching to people to profit their gut,
And glossing the gospel to their own good liking;
Coveting fine copes,° some of these doctors° contradicted   *monk's capes /*
    authorities.   *of divinity*
60   Many of these masterful mendicant° friars   *begging*
Bind their love of money to their proper business.
And since charity's become a broker and chief agent for lords'
    confessions[9]
Many strange things have happened these last years;
Unless Holy Church and charity clear away such confessors
65   The world's worst misfortune mounts up fast.
      A pardoner[1] preached there as if he were a priest
And brought forth a bull° with the bishops' seals,   *papal license*
Said that he himself could absolve them all
Of phony fasts and of broken vows.
70   Illiterates believed him and liked what they heard
And came up and kneeled to kiss his pardons;
He bonked them with his bulls and bleared their eyes
And with this rigmarole raked in their brooches and rings.
Thus you give your gold to help out gluttons
75   And lose it for good to full-time lechers.
If the bishop were true and kept his ear to the ground
He'd not consign his seal to deceit of the people.
But it's not through the bishop that this guy preaches,

---

4. Who speaks filthy language; not Paul, though (cf. Ephesians 5.3–4).
5. "Professional" pilgrims who took advantage of the hospitality offered them in order to travel.
6. That is, his shrine at Compostela, in Spain.
7. English town, site of a famous shrine to the Virgin Mary.
8. The four orders of friars—Franciscans, Dominicans, Carmelites, and Augustinians. In 14th-century England

they were much satirized for their corruption (cf. the friar in the *General Prologue* to Chaucer's *Canterbury Tales*).
9. Confession and the remission of sins is cynically sold by the friars.
1. An official empowered to pass on from the Pope absolution for the sins of people who had given money to charity.

For the parish priest and pardoner split the silver
80   That, if not for them, the parishoners would have.

* * *

Still I kept dreaming about poor and rich,
220   Like barons and burgesses and village bondmen,[2]
All I saw sleeping as you shall hear next:
Bakers and brewers, butchers and others,
Weavers and websters, men that work with their hands,
Like tailors and tanners and tillers of earth,
225   Like dike and ditch diggers that do their work badly
And drive out their days with *Dew vous saue, dame Emme*.[3]
Cooks and their helpers cried, "Get your hot pies!
Good geese and pig meat! Come on up and eat!"
And taverners touted in much the same way:
230   "White wine of Alsace and wine from Gascony,
Wash down your roast with La Reole and La Rochelle!"
All this, and seven times more, I saw in my sleep.

Passus 2
[THE MARRIAGE OF LADY MEED]

And then I kneeled before her[1] and cried to her for grace,
"Mercy, madame, for the love of Mary in heaven
That bore the blessed child that bought us on the cross,
Teach me the way to recognize Falsehood."
5   "Look to your left and see where he stands.
Falsehood and Fave[2] and fickle-tongued Liar
And many more men and women like them."
I looked to my left as the lady said
And saw a woman wonderfully clothed.
10   She was trimmed all in fur, the world's finest,
And crowned with a coronet as good as the king's;
On all five fingers were the richest rings
Set with red rubies and other precious gems.
Her robes were richer than I can describe,
15   To talk of her attire I don't have time;
Her raiment and riches ravished my heart.
Whose wife she was and her name I wanted to know,
"Dear lady," I then asked, "conceal nothing from me."
"That is the maid Meed[3] who has hurt me many times
20   And lied against my beloved who is called Loyalty
And slanders him to the lords that keep all our laws,
In the king's court and the commons' she contradicts my teaching,

---

2. Barons were members of the higher aristocracy; burgesses were town-dwellers with full rights as citizens; and bondmen were peasants who held their land from a lord in return for services or rent.
3. Presumably a popular song.
1. Lady Holy Church.

2. "Lying"; the name of characters representing deceit in Old French literature.
3. A richly ambiguous word referring to a wide variety of "reward," both positive and negative, including just reward, heavenly salvation, recompense, the profit motive, graft, and bribery.

In the pope's palace is privy as I,
But Truth would she weren't for she's a bastard.
25   Favel was her father who has a fickle tongue
And seldom speaks truth unless it's a trick,
And Meed takes after him, as men remark on kin:
     Like father, like daughter.
For never shall a briar put forth berries
Nor on a rough, crooked thorn a real fig grow:
     A good tree bringeth forth good fruit.[4]
30   I should be higher, for I come from better stock;
He that fathered me *filius dei*° is named,   son of God
Who never lied or laughed in his entire life,
And I am his dear daughter, duchess of heaven,
The man that loves me and follows my will
35   Shall have grace a-plenty and a good end,
And the man that loves Meed, I'll bet my life,
Will lose for her love a morsel of charity.
What is man's most help to heaven Meed will most hinder—
I base this on King David, whose book[5] does not lie:
     Lord, who shall dwell in thy tabernacle.[6]
40   And David himself explains, as his mute book shows:
     And not taken bribes against the innocent.[7]
     Tomorrow Meed marries a miserable wretch,
One False Faithless of the Fiend's lineage.
With flattery Favel's fouly enchanted Meed
And Liar's made all the arrangements for the match.
45   Be patient and you will see those that are pleased
By Meed's marriage, tomorrow you'll view it.
Get to know them if you can and avoid all those
Who love her lordship, both the high and the low.
Don't fault them but let them be till Loyalty's judge
50   And has power to punish them, then do your pleading.
Now I commend you to Christ and his pure mother,
And never load your conscience with coveting meed."
     Thus the lady left me lying asleep
And still dreaming I saw Meed's marriage.
55   All the rich retinue rooted in false living
Were bid to the bridal from the entire country,
All kinds of men that were Meed's kin,
Knights, clerics, and other common people,
Like jurors, summoners, sheriffs and their clerks,
60   Beadles, bailiffs, businessmen, and agents,
Purveyors, victualers, advocates of the Arches,[8]
I can't keep count of the crowd that ran with Meed.

4. Matthew 7.17.
5. The Book of Psalms.
6. Psalms 14.1.

7. Psalms 14.5.
8. The officials in this and the two preceding lines had jobs that made them particularly open to bribery.

But Simony and Civil⁹ and his jurymen
Were tightest with Meed it seemed of all men.
65 But Favel was first to fetch her out of chamber
And like a broker brought her to be joined with False.

from *Passus 6*
[THE CONFESSION OF GLUTTON]

350 Now Glutton heads for confession
And moves towards the Church, his *mea culpa*¹ to say.
Fasting on a Friday he made forth his way
By the house of Betty Brewer, who bid him good morning
And where was he going that brew-wife asked.
355 "To Holy Church," he said, "to hear mass,
And then sit and be shriven and sin no more."
"I have good ale, Glutton, old buddy, want to give it a try?"
"Do you have," he asked, "any hot spices?"
"I have pepper, peony, and a pound of garlic,
360 A farthing-worth of fennel seed² for fasting days I bought it."
Then in goes Glutton and great oaths after.
Cissy the shoemaker sat on the bench,
Wat the game warden and his drunken wife,
Tim the tinker and two of his workmen,
365 Hick the hackney-man and Hugh the needler,
Clarice of Cock's Lane³ and the clerk of the church,
Sir Piers of Pridie and Purnel of Flanders,
A hayward, a hermit, the hangman of Tyburn,
Daw the ditchdigger and a dozen rascals
370 In the form of porters and pickpockets and bald tooth-pullers,
A fiddler, a rat-catcher, a street-sweeper and his helper,
A rope-maker, a road-runner, and Rose the dish-seller,
Godfrey the garlic-man and Griffith the Welshman,
And a heap of secondhand salesmen, early in the morning
375 Stood Glutton with glad cheers to his first round of ale.
Clement the cobbler took off his cloak
And put it up for a game of New Fair⁴
Hick the hackney-man saw with his hood
And asked Bart the butcher to be on his side.
380 Tradesmen were chosen to appraise this bargain,
That whoso had the hood should not have the cloak,
And that the better thing, according to the arbiters, compensate the
    worse.
They got up quickly and whispered together
And appraised these items apart in private,

9. Simony is the buying and selling of church offices or spiritual functions; Civil is civil as opposed to criminal law (especially noted for its bribery and corruption).
1. By my own fault; formula used in Christian prayers and confession.
2. An herb thought to be good for someone drinking on an empty stomach.
3. Clarice and Parnel (of the next line) are prostitutes.
4. An elaborate game involving the exchange of clothing.

385   And there was a load of swearing, for one had to get the worse.
      They could not in conscience truthfully accord
      Till Robin the rope-maker they asked to arise
      And named him umpire so that all arguing would stop.
         Hick the hostler got the cloak
390   On condition that Clement should fill the cup
      And have Hick the hostler's hood and rest content;
      And whoever took it back first had to get right up
      And greet Sir Glutton with a gallon of ale.
         There was laughing and louring and "please pass the cup!"
395   Bargaining and drinking they kept starting up
      And sat so till evensong[5] and sang from time to time,
      Until Glutton had gobbled down a gallon and a gill°   *1/4 pint*
      His guts began to rumble like two greedy sows;
      He pissed half a gallon in the time of a *pater noster*,[6]
400   He blew his round bugle at his backbone's bottom,
      So that all who heard that horn had to hold their noses
      And wished it had been well plugged with a wisp of briars.
      He could neither step nor stand unless he held a staff,
      And then he moved like a minstrel's performing dog,
405   Sometimes sideways and sometimes backwards,
      Like some one laying lines in order to trap birds.
         And when he reached the door, then his eyes dimmed,
      And he stumbled on the threshold and fell to the ground,
      And Clement the cobbler grabbed him by the waist
410   And in order to lift him up set him on his knees.
      But Glutton was a huge boor and troubled in the lifting
      And barfed up a mess into Clement's lap;
      There is no hound so hungry in Hertfordshire
      That he'd dare lap up that leaving, so unlovely it smacked.°   *tasted*
415   With all the woe in this world his wife and his daughter
      Bore him to his bed and put him in it,
      And after all this excess he had a bout of sloth;
      He slept through Saturday and Sunday till sundown.
      Then he awoke pale and wan and wanted a drink;
420   The first thing he said was "Who's got the bowl?"
      His wife and his conscience reproached him for his sin;
      He became ashamed, that scoundrel, and made quick confession
      To Repentance like this: "Have pity on me," he said,
      "Lord who are aloft and shape all that lives!
425   To you God, I, Glutton, acknowledge my guilt
      Of how I've trespassed with tongue, how often I can't tell,
      Sworn 'God's soul and his sides!' and 'So help me God, Almighty!'
      There was no need for it so many times falsely;
      And overate at supper and sometime at noon
430   More than my system could naturally handle,

5. Vespers, the evening prayer service said just before   6. The time it takes to say the Paternoster, the Lord's
sunset.   Prayer.

And like a dog that eats grass I began to throw up
And wasted what I might have saved—I can't speak for my shame
Of the depravity of my foul mouth and maw—
And on fasting days before noon I fed myself ale
435   Beyond all reason, among dirty jokesters, their dirty jokes to hear.
    For this, good God, grant me forgiveness
For my worthless living during my entire lifetime.
For I swear by the true God, despite any hunger or thirst,
Never shall on Friday a piece of fish digest in my stomach
440   Till my aunt Abstinence has given me leave—
And yet I've hated her all my lifetime."

Passus 8
[Piers Plowing the Half-Acre]

Perkin[1] the plowman said, "By Saint Peter of Rome!
I have a half-acre to plow by the highway;
Had I plowed this half-acre and afterwards sown it
I'd go along with you and teach you the way."
5   "That would be a long delay," said a lady in a veil,
"What should we women work on meanwhile?"
    "I appeal to you for your profit," said Piers to the ladies,
"That some sew the sack to keep the wheat from spilling,
And you worthy women with your long fingers
10   That you have silk and sandal[2] to sew when you've time
Chasubles° for chaplains to the church's honor.   *robes*
Wives and widows spin wool and flax;
Conscience counsels you to make cloth
To benefit the poor and for your own pleasure.
15   For I shall see to their sustenance, unless the land fail,
As long as I live, for love of the Lord of heaven.
And all manner of men who live off the land
Help him work well who obtains your food."
    "By Christ," said a knight then, "he teaches us the best;
20   But truly on the plow theme I was never taught.
I wish I knew how," said the knight, "by Christ and his mother;
I'd try it sometime for fun as it were."
    Certainly, sir knight," said Piers then,
"I shall toil and sweat and sow for us both
25   And labor for those you love all my lifetime,
On condition you protect Holy Church and me
From wasters and wicked men who spoil the world,
And go hunt hardily for hares and foxes,
Boars and bucks that break down my hedges,
30   And train your falcons to kill the wild birds
Because they come to my croft° and defile my corn."°   *field / grain*
    Courteously the knight then commenced with these words:

---

1. A nickname for Piers, or Peter.   2. A thin, rich form of silk.

Plowmen, from the *Luttrell Psalter*, early 14th century.

"By my power, Piers, I pledge you my truth
To defend you faithfully, though I should fight."
35   "And still one point," said Piers, "I ask of you further:
Try not to trouble any tenant unless Truth agrees
And when you fine any man let Mercy be assessor
And Meekness your master, despite Meed's moves.
And though poor men offer you presents and gifts
40 Don't take them on the chance you're not deserving,
For it may be you'll have to return them or pay for them dearly.
Don't hurt your bondman, you'll be better off;
Though he's your underling here, it may happen in heaven
He'll be sooner received and more honorably seated.
    Friend, go up higher[3]
45 At church in the charnel[4] it's hard to discern churls
Or between knight and knave or a queen on a corner[5] and one on the
    throne.
It becomes you, knight, to be courteous and gracious,
True of tongue and loth to hear tales
Unless they're about goodness, battles, or good faith.
50 Don't keep company with crude-mouths or listen to their stories,
And especially at your meals avoid such men
For they are the Devil's entertainers and draw men to sin.
And do not oppose Conscience or the rights of Holy Church."
    "I assent, by Saint Giles," said the knight then,
55 "To work by your wisdom and my wife, too."
    "And I shall dress myself," said Perkin, "in pilgrims' fashion
And go with all those who wish to live in Truth."
And he put on his clothes of all kinds of crafts,
His leggings and mittens, as Common Sense taught him,
60 And hung his seed bag on his neck instead of a satchel;

3. Luke 14.10.
4. Crypt for dead bodies.

5. I.e., "queen," a prostitute.

A bushel of bread grain was brought inside it.
"For I will sow it myself and then start out
On pilgrimage, as palmers[6] do, to win pardon.
My plow-stick shall be my pikestaff and pick apart the roots
65 And help my coulter to cut and clean the furrows.
And all that help me plow or weed
Shall have leave by our Lord to go and glean after me
And make themselves merry with, no matter who grumbles.
And all kinds of craftsmen who know how to live in truth
70 I shall provide them with food who faithfully live,
Except for Jack the juggler and Janet from the whorehouse
And Daniel the dice-player and Denot the pimp
And friar faker and folk of that order,
That loyal men consider lollers and losers,
75 And Robin the foul mouth for his filthy words.
Truth once told me and ordered me to spread it further:
Deleantur de libro viuencium,[7] I should not deal with them,
For Holy Church is obliged to ask no tithes[8] of them
    Because with the just they may not be written.[9]
They've escaped by good luck, now God amend them!"
80   Dame Work-when-it's-time is Pier's wife's name;
His daughter's called Do-just-so-or-your-mother-will-beat-you;
His son's name is Suffer-your-masters-to-have-their-will-
Judge-them-not-for-if-you-do-you'll-pay-for-it-dearly.
"I bid you counsel the commons not to displease the king,
85 And those who have laws to see they not fail them.
Leave it all to God, as holy scripture teaches:
    The scribes and the Pharisees have sitten on the chair of Moses[1]
Masters, as mayors be, and great men, senators,
Whatever they command, just as by the king, never oppose it;
All that they call for, I call on you to endure earnestly
90 And conduct yourself according to their warnings and wordings.
    All things whatsoever they say, observe and do.[2]
But do not follow their practices, my dear son," said Piers.
    "For now that I'm old and gray and have a little something,
To penance and pilgrimage I'll pass with these others.
I will therefore, before leaving, dictate my will.
95   *In dei nomine amen*[3] I make it myself.
He shall have my soul who made all souls
And defend it from the Fiend, and so is my belief,
Till I come to his account as my creed tells
To have remission and release on the rent I still owe.
100 The church shall have my body and keep my bones

---

6. "Professional" pilgrims.
7. Let them be blotted out of the book of the living.
(Psalms 68.29).
8. Because the money they make is illegitimate, they do
not owe the church the customary tithes, or ten percent
of their income.

9. Psalms 68.29.
1. Matthew 23.2.
2. Matthew 23.3.
3. In the name of God, amen; customary beginning of a
will.

For of my corn and cattle the parson required my tithe.
I paid it promptly for peril of my soul;
He's beholden, I hope, to have me in his mass
And keep me in commemoration among all Christians.
105 My wife shall have what I won with truth and no more
And divide it among my daughters and dear children.
For though I die today I have no debt;
I returned what I borrowed before I went to bed.
And with what's left over, by the cross in Lucca![4]
110 I will worship Truth with that all my life
And be a pilgrim at the plow to benefit rich and poor."
    Now Perkin and these pilgrims go to their plowing;
Many helped him to turn over the half-acre.
Ditchers and diggers dug up the strip-ridges;
115 All this pleased Perkin and he paid them good wages.
Other workmen were there who worked very hard,
Each man in his way made himself useful
And some to please Perkin picked weeds in the field.
    At high prime, about nine[5] Piers let the plow stand
120 And oversaw them himself; whoever worked best
Would later be hired when harvest time comes.
    And then, some sat down and sang at ale
And helped plow this half-acre with a "hey trolliloly![6]
Said Piers the plowman in a pure anger:
125 "If you don't get up quickly and rush back to work
No grain that grows here will cheer you in need,
And though you die of grief, the devil take him who cares."
    Then the phonies were frightened and pretended to be blind
And twisted their legs backwards as such losers know how
130 And moaned to Piers about how they couldn't work:
"And we pray for you Piers and for your plow, too,
That God for his grace multiply your grain
And reward you for the alms you give us here.
We may neither sweat nor strain, such sickness ails us,
135 Nor have we limbs to labor with, the Lord God we thank."
    "Your prayers," said Piers, "if you were upright,
Might help, as I hope, but high Truth would
That no fakery were found in people that go begging.
You're wasters, I know well, and waste and devour
140 What true land-tilling men loyally work for.
But Truth shall teach you to drive his team
Or you'll eat barley bread and drink from the brook,
Unless he's blind or broken-legged or braced with iron—
Such poor," said Piers, "shall share in my goods,

4. Ornate crucifix in the Italian city of Lucca, which was
a popular object of pilgrimage.
5. Nine in the morning, after a substantial amount of
work has been done.

6. Probably the refrain of a popular song.

145　　Both of my corn and my cloth to keep them from want.
　　　But anchorites and hermits who eat only at noon
　　　And friars who don't flatter and poor sick people,
　　　Hey! I and mine will provide for their needs."
　　　　Then Waster got angry and wanted to fight
150　　And pressed Piers the plowman to "put 'em up!"
　　　And told him to go piss with his plow, pigheaded creep!
　　　A Breton came bragging and threatened Piers also:
　　　"Whether you like it or not," he said, "we'll have our way,
　　　And take your flour and meat whenever we like
155　　And make merry with it, despite any grumbling."
　　　　Piers the plowman then complained to the knight
　　　To keep him and his property as they had agreed:
　　　"Avenge me on these wasters who bring harm to the world;
　　　Excommunication they take no account of nor fear Holy Church.
160　　There will be no plenty," said Piers, "if the plow stands still."
　　　　Then the knight, as was his nature, courteously
　　　Warned Waster and advised him to improve:
　　　"Or I'll beat you according to the law and put you in the stocks."
　　　　"I'm not used to working," said Waster, "and I won't start now!"
165　　And made light of the law and less of the knight
　　　And sized up Piers as a pea to complain wherever he would.
　　　　"Now by Christ," said Piers the plowman, "I'll punish you all,"
　　　And whooped after Hunger who heard right away.
　　　"I pray you," Piers said then, "Sir Hunger, *pour charite*[7]
170　　Avenge me on these wasters, for the knight will not."
　　　　Hunger in haste then grabbed Waster around the belly
　　　And hugged him so tight that his eyes watered.
　　　He battered the Breton about the cheeks
　　　So that he looked like a lantern the rest of his life,
175　　And he so beat both of them up he nearly busted their guts
　　　Had not Piers with a peas-load[8] called him off.
　　　"Have mercy on them, Hunger," said Piers, "and let me give them
　　　　　beans,
　　　And what was baked for Bayard[9] may come to their relief."
　　　　Then the fakers were frightened and flew into Piers' barns.
180　　And flapped with flails from morning till evening,
　　　So that Hunger was less intent on looking upon them.
　　　For a potful of pottage that Piers' wife had made
　　　A heap of hermits took up spades,
　　　Dug and spread dung to despite Hunger.
185　　They cut up their capes and made them short coats
　　　And went as workmen to weeding and mowing
　　　All for fear of death, so hard did Hunger hit.
　　　The blind and broken-legged he bettered by the thousand
　　　And lame men he healed with animal entrails.

7. For charity's sake.
8. Cheapest kind of bread, standard fare for the poor.

9. A generic name for a horse; a bread made of beans and bran was fed to horses.

190   Priests and other people drew towards Piers
        And friars from all five orders,[1] all for fear of Hunger.
        For what was baked for Bayard relieved many hungry,
        Dross and dregs were drink for many beggars.
        There was no lad living that wouldn't bow to Piers
195   To be his faithful servant though he had no more
        Than food for his labor and his gift at noon.
            Then Piers was proud and put them all to work
        At daubing and digging, at dung bearing afield,
        At threshing, at thatching, at whittling pins,
200   At every kind of true craft that man can devise.
        There was no beggar so bold, unless he were blind,
        Dared oppose what Piers said for fear of Sir Hunger.
        And Piers was proud of that and put them all to work
        And gave them food and money according to their deserts.
205   Then Piers had pity for all poor people
        And bade Hunger hurry up out of the country
        Back home to his own yard and stay there forever.
        "I'm well avenged on wasters thanks to your might.
        But I pray you," Piers said, "Hunger, before you go,
210   What's best to do about beggars and bidders?[2]
        For I know well, if Hunger went, they'd work very badly.
        Misfortune makes them so meek now
        And for want only these guys follow my orders.
        It's not for love, believe it, they labor this hard
215   But for fear of famine, in faith," said Piers.
        "There is no filial love in these people, for all their fair speech;
        And they're my blood brothers, for God bought us all.
        Truth taught me once to love each one of them
        And to help them in all things always as needed.
220   Now I'd like to know before you go what's best,
        How can I govern them to love and to labor
        For their livelihood, teach me now, Sir Hunger."
            "Listen now," said Hunger, "and hold it for wisdom.
        Big bold beggars that can work for their bread,
225   Heal their hunger with hound's bread and horse's bread
        And hold them off with beans to keep their stomachs from swelling;
        And if the men grumble tell them to get to work
        And he shall sup the sweeter when he's deserved it.
        But if you find people who've been impaired by false men
230   Comfort them with your goods for so Truth commands;
        Love them and give to them, as the law of nature asks:
            Bear ye one another's burdens.[3]
        And all manner of men that you might see

---

1. See Prologue, n.8 (line 56) on the four orders. The fifth order referred to here may be the Crutched Friars, a minor order.

2. Paid prayer-sayers.
3. Galatians 6.2.

In misfortune or disease, and you can help them,
Look to it on your life that you not let them perish.
235 If you've gained anything wickedly, make use of it wisely,
   Make unto you friends of the mammon of iniquity."[4]
   "I would not grieve God," said Piers, "for all the goods on
      earth!
Might I sinless do as you say?" asked Piers the plowman.
   "Yes, I guarantee it," said Hunger, "or else the Bible lies.
Go to our beginning when God made the world,
240 As wise men have written and as Genesis testifies,
That says with toil and sweat and sweating face
You'll till and travail truly for your living:
   In labor and in the sweat of thy face shalt thou eat bread.[5]
And Solomon the sage agrees with this:
The sluggard that grows no corn because of the cold
245 In the summer for his sloth shall suffer want
And go a-begging and begging and no man abates his hunger.
   *Because of the cold the sluggard would not plough; he shall beg
   therefore in the winter, and it shall not be given him.*[6]
Matthew mentions a man that lent
His silver to three kinds of men intending they should
Trade and achieve with it through hot and cold,
250 And those that worked best were praised best
And put in charge for their efforts over all the lord's goods.
But he that was despicable and didn't work hard
The lord for his idleness and his bad sloth
Took away from him all he had and gave it to his fellow
255 Who had labored loyally, and then the lord said:
'He who has shall have and be helped where he pleases
And he who has not shall not have and further no man help him
And whatever he thinks well to have I will take it away.'
And look, what the psalter says to manual laborers:
260 'Blessed be all those who work for their faith
Through any loyal labor as through limbs and hands.'
   Thou shalt eat the labors of thy hands.[7]
This is evidence," said Hunger, "for those who won't work
That their means of life will be lean and worth as little as their
      clothes."
   "By Christ," said Piers the plowman then, "I'll show this
      proverb
265 To beggars and old boys that have an aversion for work.
But still I pray you," said Piers, "*pour charite,*[8] Sir Hunger,
If you can treat or know of any kind of medicine,
For some of my servants and myself, too,

---

4. Luke 16.9.   7. Psalms 127.2.
5. Genesis 3.19.   8. For charity.
6. Proverbs 20.4, substituting "winter" for the Vulgate's
"summer."

Don't work a whole week, our stomachs hurt so."
270   "I know well," said Hunger, "what sickness ails you.
You've overeaten—and that makes you sick.
But don't eat, I tell you, before hunger grabs you
And sends you some of his sauce to savor with your lips.
And keep some till suppertime and don't sit too long
275   At noon or any other time, and especially at your supper
Don't let Sir Surfeit sit at your table,
And see that you don't drink any day before you've eaten somewhat.
And consider that Dives[9] for his delicate life went to the devil
And Lazarus the lean beggar who longed after crumbs—
280   And yet he had none, for I, Hunger, killed him,
And afterwards I saw him sit as if he were an elder
In all manner ease and in Abraham's lap.
And if you have the power, Piers, I advise you,
All who cry out in your direction for food for God's love,
285   Share with them some of your bread, soup, or spread,
Give them some of your loaf though there's less for you to chew.
And if liars and latch-pickers and lollers knock,
Let them wait till the table's taken but give them no crumbs
Till all your needy neighbors have had their noon meal.
290   And if you follow this diet I'll bet my ears
That the Doctor man shall sell his fur hoods for his food
And pledge his Calabrian cloak for his provisions
And be glad, by my faith, to abandon his practice
And learn to work on the land lest livelihood fail him.
295   There are many bad doctors but few true physicians;
They prescribe men's deaths before destiny knocks."
  "By Saint Paul," said Piers, "you point near the truth
And speak faithfully, I believe, the Lord reward you for it!
Go now whenever you like and good luck to you always.
300   For you've avenged me well and also taught me."
  "I promise you," said Hunger, "I won't go away
Before I have this day both dined and drunk."
  "I've no penny," said Piers, "with which to buy pullets,
Nor goose or pork but two green cheeses
305   And a few curds and cream and an oat cake
And bean and pea bread for my kids.
And still I say, by my soul, I've no salt bacon
Nor any egg, by Christ, to fry up together.
But I have leeks, parsley and scallions,
310   Chives and chervil and half-ripe cherries,
And a cow with a calf and a cart-mare
To draw my dung afield during dry spells.

9. Latin for "rich"; was taken as the name of the rich man who in the parable in Luke 16.19–31 goes to the hell because he does not feed the beggar Lazarus (who ends up in the bosom of Abraham).

And we must live by this means of life till Lammas time[1]
And by then I hope to have harvest in my fields;
315 Then may I make dinner just as I like."
    All the poor people then fetched peascods;
Beans and baked apples they brought by the lapful,
And offered Piers this present with which to please Hunger.
Hunger ate it all in haste and asked for more.
320 For fear then poor folk fed Hunger quickly
With cream and curds, with cress and other herbs.
By then harvest drew near and new corn came to market
And people were happy and fed Hunger deliciously,
And then Glutton with good ale put Hunger to sleep.
325   And then Waster refused to work and wandered around,
Nor'd any beggar eat bread in which there were beans,
But the finest white breads and of pure wheat,
Nor no way would they drink half-penny ale
But the best and brownest that brewsters sell.
330 Laborers with no land to live on but their own hands
Wouldn't deign to dine today on last night's veggies;
No penny-ale or piece of bacon pleased them
But it had to be fresh meat or fish, fried or baked,
And that *chaud* or *plus chaud*[2] against a chilled stomach.
335 And unless he's hired for high pay he'll otherwise argue
And curse the time he was made a workman.
He begins to grumble against Cato's counsel:
Paupertatis onus paciencier ferre memento.[3]
And then he curses the king and all his justices
340 For teaching such laws that grieve workingmen[4]
But as long as Hunger was master none of them would bitch,
Nor strive against his statute, he looked so stern.
    I warn you workmen, get ahead while you can,
For Hunger's hurrying this way fast as he can.
345 He shall awake through water, wasters to punish,
And before a few years finish famine shall arise,
And so says Saturn[5] and sends us warning.
Through floods and foul weather fruits shall fail;
Pride and pestilence shall take out many people.
350 Three ships and a sheaf with an 8 following
Shall bring bane and battle under both halves of the moon.
And then death shall withdraw and dearth be the judge
And Dave the ditcher° die of hunger   ditch-digger
Unless God of his goodness grant us a truce.

1. The harvest festival, August 1, when a loaf made from
the first wheat of the season was offered at mass.
2. Hot or very hot.
3. Remember to bear your burden of poverty patiently.
From Cato's *Distichs*, a collection of phrases used to teach
Latin to beginning students.
4. A reference to the Statutes of Laborers, passed after
1351, when the Black Death depopulated the countryside
and a labor shortage ensued. They were intended to control the mobility and the wages of laborers.
5. Planet thought to influence the weather, generally perceived to be hostile.

✦ "PIERS PLOWMAN" AND ITS TIME ✦

The Rising of 1381

The event previously known as the "Peasants' Revolt" is generally referred to by today's historians as the "Rising of 1381," since it is now recognized that it included many members of the commons who were not peasants but rather middle-class landholders, artisans, and so forth. William Langland had a rather ambiguous relation to the rising, for while deploring the conditions that caused it, he refused to endorse its radical social program. When the rebels invoked his character Piers as a cultural hero, he revised *Piers Plowman* for a second time (the so-called C-text), thus disassociating himself from them. This section brings together a number of documents that record the events of the rising, and more importantly, reveal the subjective responses of contemporary writers to it.

The causes of the rising were varied. Among them was the "Statute of Laborers" enacted by Parliament in 1351 to freeze wages and restrict laborers' mobility, both of which had been increasing as a result of the depopulation caused by the Black Death. The more immediate catalyst, however, was a flat poll tax enacted in 1380, which hurt the poor disproportionately and which the government collected in a particularly ruthless way.

The rising itself was astonishingly brief, beginning at the end of May 1381 and collapsing by the end of July. From the prosperous southern counties of Essex and Kent the rebels marched to London, swearing loyalty to one another and to Richard II. Their hostility was directed against the church hierarchy and the feudal lords rather than against the monarchy. In London they burned the Savoy Palace, the local residence of the powerful John of Gaunt, Duke of Lancaster and uncle of King Richard. The king, then only fourteen years old, found his advisers ineffectual, and so retreated with them to the Tower of London.

Having agreed to meet the Essex contingent outside the city, at Mile End, the king acceded to their demands of an end to villeinage (serfdom), and ordered his office of chancery to make multiple copies of charters to that effect. During this meeting, some rebels broke into the Tower of London and beheaded two of the most hated men in the kingdom, Simon Sudbury (the king's chancellor and Archbishop of Canterbury) and Robert Hales (his treasurer). Afterward, they displayed their heads on London Bridge, as a sign that they were traitors to the commons.

The next day the king met with the Kentish rebels, again outside the city, at Smithfield. Here their captain Wat Tyler demanded not only the abolition of villeinage but fixed rents, partial disendowment of the church and dispersal of its goods to the poor, and punishment of all "traitors" held to be responsible for the poll tax. In the course of a scuffle, the Lord Mayor of London, William Walworth, stabbed Tyler and mortally wounded him; thereupon, the king rode before the rebels and declared himself their new captain, successfully leading them off the field.

Tyler's death broke the will of the rebels, and the king promptly revoked the charters freeing the serfs. In a series of trials, he prosecuted the instigators, among them John Ball, the priest who had shortly before preached to the rebels at Blackheath the famous sermon challenging the division of society into three estates: "Whan Adam dalf and Eve span, / who was thanne a gentilman?" Ball was found guilty of treason, and drawn, hanged, and quartered. Aside from such punishments, there were few apparent effects of the rising, although the nobles and the clergy relented in their treatment of the commons, and in the long run, the institution of villeinage declined. For the ruling class itself, the rising caused intense anxiety. John Gower, in his allegorized account, *The Voice of One Crying*, reports hiding in the woods to escape the peasants. Like him, the monastic chroniclers like Thomas of Walsingham generally present the rebels as mad beasts.

Adam and Eve, detail of a misericord, c. 1379. Misericords were shallow seats in the choir stalls of medieval churches, on which worshipers could rest, still standing, during the long celebrations of the Mass and Daily Office. Their undersides were often carved with animal grotesques and scenes of common life, both seen in this depiction of Adam and Eve from a misericord in Worcester Cathedral. Eve spins and Adam digs, in a moment reminiscent of the couplet from John Ball's sermon: "Whan Adam dalf and Eve span, / who was thanne a gentilman?"

What is perhaps most significant about the written reception of the rising is the languages—Latin, French, and English—in which it occurs. Like Gower's *Voice of One Crying*, the chronicles are generally written in Latin, although the *Anonimalle Chronicle*, from which a passage is included here, is in French. Langland and Chaucer wrote in English, while the short poem below, *The Course of Revolt*, is macaronic, alternating English lines with Latin ones. Although there is little written evidence in the voice of the rebels themselves (who were generally illiterate), there are two tantalizing scraps identified as John Ball's letters, written in English although embedded in hostile Latin chronicle accounts of Ball's trial and execution. It has been suggested recently that the most important fact about the rebel speeches and writings is their "vernacularity"—the fact that they appear in a language that the common people could understand.

Three Poems on the Rising of 1381
John Ball's First Letter[1]

John Ball Saint Mary Priest, greeteth well all manner of men, and biddeth them in name of the Trinitie, Father, Sonne, & holy Ghost, stand manlike together in truth, & helpe truth, and truth shall helpe you:

---

1. This and the piece following can only provisionally be called "poems," despite their rhymed couplets and sporadic alliteration. The court that tried and convicted Ball regarded them as actual directions to his followers, and modern scholarship has tended to concur. If so they are directions in code, for they are, in the words of one chronicler, "full of enigmas." In this poem the complaint about the seven deadly sins running rampant is conventional, but the conclusion, "God do bote for now is time" (God make amends, for now is the time) is highly unusual in its call to action. Significantly, the sin of anger is absent from the list.

now raygneth pride in price,
couetise° is holden° wise   *greed / held*
lechery without shame,
gluttonie without blame,
enuye raygneth° with reason,   *reigns*
and sloath is taken in great season,
God doe boote° for nowe is time. Amen.   *make amends*

John Ball's Second Letter[2]

LITTERA IOHANNIS BALLE MISSA COMMUNIBUS ESTSEXIE
[THE LETTER OF JOHN BALL TO THE ESSEX COMMONS]

Iohan schep, som-tyme seynte marie prest of york, and now of colchestre, Greteth wel Iohan nameles & Iohn the mullere and Iohon cartere, and biddeth hem thei bee war of gyle [treachery] in borugh, and stondeth to-gidere in godes name, and biddeth Pers ploughman / go to his werk and chastise wel hobbe the robbere; and taketh with yow Iohan Trewman and alle hijs felawes and no mo, and loke schappe you to on heued[3] and no mo.

Iohan the mullere hath y-grounde smal, smal, smal.
The kynges sone of heuene schal paye for al.
be war or the be wo.°   *beware or be sorry*
knoweth your freend fro your foo.
haueth y-now & seith hoo!
and do wel and bettre and fleth° synne,   *flee*
and seketh pees and hold yow ther-inne.
and so biddeth Iohan trewaman and alle his felawes.

Hanc litteram Idem Iohannes balle confessus est scripisse, et communibus transmisisse, et plura alia fatebatur et fecit; propter-que, ut diximus, traitus, suspensus, et decollatus apud sanctum albanum Idibus Iulij, presente rege, et cadauer eius quadripertitum quatuor regni cuntatibus missum est. [John Ball confessed that he wrote this letter and sent it to the commons, and said and did many other things. For which reason, as we have said, he was drawn, hanged, and beheaded before the king at Saint Albans, on the ides of July; and his body was quartered and sent to four cities in the kingdom.]

The Course of Revolt[4]

The taxe hath tened° vs alle,   *harmed*
probat hoc mors tot validorum;°   *this death tests so many of the strong[?]*

---

2. According to the chronicle from which this "letter" was taken, Ball sent it to "the leaders of the commons in Essex . . . in order to urge them to finish what they had begun," and it was "afterwards found in the sleeve of a man about to be hanged for disturbing the peace." It appears in Thomas Walsingham's Latin *Historia Anglicana,* where it is included as evidence of the treason for which Ball was hanged. In the prose introduction to the poem, John the "shep," priest of Colchester, is the assumed name of John Ball (as "pastor"), while John Carter and John the Miller are both generic occupational names often ascribed to the leaders of the rebels. The reference to "Pers Ploughman" in the poem's introduction indicates that the rebels interpreted Langland's conservative poem for their own purposes. It presents Piers not as Langland's patient laborer, but as

one who should get to his "work" of punishing "robbers," perhaps "Hobbe" (Robert) Hales, the treasurer of the king, beheaded by the rebels for his role in collecting the poll tax.

3. Take one head for yourself; possibly a reference to the rebels' loyalty to Richard II as opposed to the nobles.

4. Unlike the two preceding letters, there is no doubt that this piece is a poem: it is written in six- or eight-line stanzas of English alternating with Latin, with a rhyme scheme *ababab (ab).* The masculine rhymes of the English (alle, small, etc.) contrast with the feminine rhymes of the Latin (validorum, cupidorum, etc.) to give it a lilting quality. The poem laments the violence of the rising, although it opens with a recognition of the rebels' grievances: the poll tax of 1377, 1379, and 1380–1381 "hath tened [harmed] vs alle."

The Kyng therof had small,
ffuit in manibus cupidorum.°[5]   *it was in the hands of the greedy ones*
5   yt had ful hard hansell,°   *bad omen*
dans causam fine dolorum;°   *giving cause to an end of sorrows*
vengeaunce nedes most° fall,   *must*
propter peccata malorum.°   *on account of the sins of the wicked*

In Kent care° be-gan,[6]   *troubles*
10 *mox infestando potentes;*°   *soon attacking the rulers*
On rowtes° tho Rebawdes° they ran,   *crowds / rascals*
Sua turpida arma ferentes.°   *bearing their shameful weapons*
ffoles° they dred no man,   *fools*
Regni Regem, neque gentes;°   *neither king of the realm, nor the people*
15 laddes° they were there Cheveteyns,°   *churls / captains*
Sine iure fere superantes.°   *lawlessly rising above their station*

laddes° lowde they lowght,°   *churls / laughed*
Clamantes voce sonora,°   *shouting in a loud voice*
The bischop[7] wan they slowght,°   *slew*
20 *Et corpora plura decora.*°   *and many handsome people*
Maners down they drowght,°   *they threw down manor houses*
In regno non meliora;°   *there were none better in the kingdom*
Harmes they dyde y-nowght;°   *enough*
habuerunt libera lora.°   *they had free rein*

25 Iak strawe[8] made yt stowte°   *swaggered*
Cum profusa comitiua,°   *with a captain's munificence*
And seyd al schuld hem lowte,°   *bow down to them*
Anglorum corpora viua.°   *the living community of Englishmen*
Sadly° can they schowte,°   *vigorously / shouted*
30 *pulsant pietatis oliua,*°   *they beat the olive branch of pity*
The wycche were wont to lowte,°   *those who used to skulk*
aratrum traducere stiua°.   *disgrace the plough and plough handle*

Hales,[9] that dowghty° knyght,   *brave*
quo splenduit Anglia tota,°   *in whom all England shone*
35 dolefully° he was dyght,°   *pitiably / cut down*
Cum stultis pace remota.°   *when removed from peace by fools*
There he myght not fyght,
nec Christo soluere vota.°   *nor say his prayers to Christ*

Savoy[1] semely set°   *beautifully built*
40 *heu! funditus igne cadebat.*°   *alas, it was given over to the fire*
Arcan don there they bett,[2]
Et eos virtute premebat.°   *and threatened them with force*

---

5. Much of the tax revenue was diverted to collectors rather than returned to the king.
6. The rising actually began in Essex and spread to Kent.
7. Simon Sudbury, Archbishop of Canterbury.
8. Jack Straw was a fictional character believed to have been a leader of the rising; see Chaucer, *Nun's Priest's Tale*, lines 628–31.
9. Sir Robert Hales, treasurer of England and therefore closely associated with the collection of the poll tax. He was beheaded at the Tower of London during the rising.
1. John of Gaunt's London residence.
2. A reference to Achan (Joshua 7), who transgressed the law of God by stealing valuables from Jericho. Several chronicles mention the rebels' restraint in not looting the houses of the nobles.

deth was ther dewe dett,
    qui captum quisque ferebat.°   *whoever carried off stolen goods*

45 Oure kyng myght have no rest,
    Alii latuere cauerna;°   *others hid in caves*
To ride he was ful prest,
    recolendo gesta paterna°.   *remembering his father's deeds*
Iak straw dovn they cast[3]
50   *Smethefeld virtute superna.*°   *at Smithfield with superior strength*
god, as thou may best,
    Regem defende, guberna.°   *defend the kingdom and govern it*

John Gower
from *The Voice of One Crying*[1]
from PROLOGUE

In the beginning of this work, the author intends to describe how the lowly peasants violently revolted against the freemen and nobles of the realm. And since an event of this kind was as loathsome and horrible as a monster, he reports that in a dream he saw different throngs of the rabble transformed into different kinds of domestic animals. He says, moreover, that those domestic animals deviated from their true nature and took on the barbarousness of wild beasts. In accordance with the separate divisions of this book, which is divided into seven parts (as will appear more clearly below in its headings), he treats furthermore of the causes for such outrages taking place among men. ***

[WAT TYLER AS A JACKDAW INCITING THE PEASANTS TO RIOT][2]

Here he says that in his dream he saw that when all the aforementioned madmen stood herded together, a certain Jackdaw (in English a Jay, which is commonly called Wat) assumed the rank of command over the others. And to tell the truth of the matter, this Wat was their leader.

When this great multitude of monsters like wild beasts stood united, a multitude like the sands of the sea, there appeared a Jackdaw, well instructed in the art of speaking, which no cage could keep at home. While all were looking on, this bird spread his wings and claimed to have top rank, although he was unworthy. Just as the Devil was placed in command over the army of the lower world, so this scoundrel was in charge of the wicked mob. A harsh voice, a fierce expression, a very faithful likeness to a

3. It was not (the fictional) Jack Straw, but Wat Tyler who was mortally wounded at Smithfield.

1. Gower grew up in Kent (one of the counties where the Rising of 1381 started), in a well-connected family, and both Richard II and Henry IV were his patrons. He was a friend of Chaucer, who refers to him as "moral Gower." The immorality of contemporary society, particularly the refusal of the three estates to work together, is in fact the unifying theme of Gower's work. Of his three long poems (written in the three languages of the period, English, Anglo-Norman, and Latin), the Middle English *Lover's Confession* (*Confessio amantis*), though primarily a dream vision exploring the frustrations and folly of human divine love, is set a framing complaint about the three estates, and the Anglo-Norman *Mirror of Man* (*Mirour de l'Omme*) is based on such a complaint.

Gower's Latin *Voice of One Crying* (*Vox Clamantis*)

laments the failure of the three estates in a more prophetic way: the speaker identifies himself with John the Baptist, crying in the wilderness of 14th-century England. Like *Piers Plowman*, the poem rakes the form of an allegorical dream vision. Like Langland, Gower revised his work in response to the revolt. He had written Books 2-7 by 1378 as a general complaint about the three estates, though he blamed the peasants in particular. Their refusal to produce food "by the sweat of their brow" as God decreed shows their laziness, and their demand for higher wages shows their wickedness and greed (bk. 5.9). After the Rising of 1381 occurred, he composed what is now Book 1 to decry the violence, which he saw as led by the devil; in it, he casts the peasants as beasts lacking reason, and their leader, Wat Tyler, as a rabble-rousing jackdaw, or jay (bk. 1.9). Translated by Eric W. Stockton.
2. From Book 1.

death's head—these things gave token of his appearance. He checked the murmuring and all kept silent so that the sound from his mouth might be better heard. He ascended to the top of a tree, and with the voice from his open mouth he uttered such words as these to his compeers:

"O you low sort of wretches, which the world has subjugated for a long time by its law, look, now the day has come when the peasantry will triumph and will force the freemen to get off their lands. Let all honor come to an end, let justice perish, and let no virtue that once existed endure further in the world. Let the law give over which used to hold us in check with its justice, and from here on let our court rule."

The whole mob was silent and took note of the speaker's words, and they liked every command he delivered from his mouth. The rabble lent a deluded ear to his fickle talk, and it saw none of the future things that would result. For when he had been honored in this way by the people, he quickly grabbed all the land for himself. Indeed, when the people had unadvisedly given themselves into servitude, he called the populace together and gave orders. Just as a billow usually grows calm after a stiff breeze, and just as a wave swells by the blast of a whirlwind, so the Jackdaw stirred up all the others with his outrageous shouting, and he drew the people's minds toward war. The stupid portion of the people did not know what its "court" might be, but he ordered them to adopt the laws of force. He said, "Strike," and one man struck. He said, "Kill," and another killed. He said, "Commit crime"; everyone committed it, and did not oppose his will. Everyone he called to in his madness listened with ears pricked up, and once aroused to his voice, pursued the [prescribed] course. Thus many an unfortunate man, driven by his persuasive raving, stuck his hand into the fire again and again. All proclaimed in a loud voice, "So be it," so that the sound was like the din of the sea. Stunned by the great noise of their voice, I now could scarcely lift my trembling feet. Yet from a distance I observed how they made their mutual arrangements by clasping their hands. For they said this, that the mob from the country would destroy whatever was left of the noble class in the world.

With these words, they all marched together in the same fashion, and the wicked ruler of hell led the way. A black cloud mingled with the furies of hell approached, and every wickedness poured into their hearts rained down. The earth was so thoroughly soaked with the dew of hell that no virtue could flourish from that time forth. But every vice that a worthy man abhors flourished and filled men's hearts from that time on. Then at midday the Devil attacked and his hard-shot arrow flew during that painful day. Satan himself was freed and on hand, together with all the sinful band of servile hell. Behold, the untutored heart's sense of shame was lost, and it no longer feared the terrors of crime or punishment. And so when I saw the leaders of hell ruling the world, the rights of heaven were worth nothing. The more I saw them, the more I judged I ought to be afraid of them, not knowing what sort of end would be bound to come.

[THE LAZINESS AND GREED OF PLOUGHMEN][3]

Now that he has spoken of those of knightly rank who ought to keep the state unharmed, it is necessary to speak of those who are under obligation to enter into the labors of agriculture, which are necessary for obtaining food and drink for the sustenance of the human race.

3. From Book 5.

Now you have heard what knighthood is, and I shall speak in addition of what the guiding principle for other men ought to be. For after knighthood there remains only the peasant rank; the rustics in it cultivate the grains and vineyards. They are the men who seek food for us by the sweat of their heavy toil, as God Himself has decreed. The guiding principle of our first father Adam, which he received from the mouth of God on high, is rightly theirs. For God said to him, when he fell from the glories of Paradise, "O sinner, the sweat and toil of the world be thine; in them shalt thou eat thy bread."[4] So if God's peasant pays attention to the plowshare as it goes along, and if he thus carries on the work of cultivation with his hand, then the fruit which in due course the fertile field will bear and the grape will stand abundant in their due seasons. Now, however, scarcely a farmer wishes to do such work; instead, he wickedly loafs everywhere.

An evil disposition is widespread among the common people, and I suspect that the servants of the plow are often responsible for it. For they are sluggish, they are scarce, and they are grasping. For the very little they do they demand the highest pay. Now that this practice has come about, see how one peasant insists upon more than two demanded in days gone by. Yet a short time ago one performed more service than three do now, as those maintain who are well acquainted with the facts. For just as the fox seeks his hole and enters it while the woods are echoing on every side of the hole, so does the servant of the plow, contrary to the law of the land, seek to make a fool of the land. They desire the leisures of great men, but they have nothing to feed themselves with, nor will they be servants. God and Nature have ordained that they shall serve, but neither knows how to keep them within bounds. Everyone owning land complains in his turn about these people; each stands in need of them and none has control over them. The peasants of old did not scorn God with impunity or usurp a noble worldly rank. Rather, God imposed servile work upon them, so that the peasantry might subdue its proud feelings; and liberty, which remained secure for freemen, ruled over the serfs and subjected them to its law.

The experience of yesterday makes us better informed as to what perfidy the unruly serf possesses. As the teasel[5] harmfully thins out the standing crops if it is not thinned out itself, so does the unruly peasant weigh heavily upon the well-behaved ones. The peasant strikes at the subservient and soothes the troublesome, yet the principle which the old order of things teaches is not wrong: let the law accordingly cut down the harmful teasels of rabble, lest they uproot the nobler grain with their stinging. Unless it is struck down first, the peasant race strikes against freemen, no matter what nobility or worth they possess. Its actions outwardly show that the peasantry is base, and it esteems the nobles the less because of their very virtues. Just as lopsided ships begin to sink without the right load, so does the wild peasantry, unless it is held in check.

God and our toil confer and bestow everything upon us. Without toil, man's advantages are nothing. The peasant should therefore put his limbs to work, as is proper for him to do. Just as a barren field cultivated by the plowshare fails the granaries and brings home no crop in autumn, so does the worthless churl, the more he is cherished by your love, fail you and bring on your ruin. The serfs perform none of their servile duties voluntarily and have no respect for the law. Whatever the serf's body suffers patiently under compulsion, inwardly his mind ever turns toward utter wickedness. Miracles happen only contrary to nature; only the divinity of nature can go against its own powers. It is not for man's estate that anyone from the class of serfs should try to set things right.

END OF "PIERS PLOWMAN" AND ITS TIME

MEDIEVAL BIBLICAL DRAMA

Medieval biblical drama entertains with both comedy and pathos, but it was meant to instruct as well. It developed not from classical drama, which was little imitated in the Middle Ages, but from church liturgies, especially those associated with Easter and the feast of Corpus Christi, a holiday celebrating Christ's presence among the faithful through the Eucharist. Although biblical dramas originated on the Continent, in Latin and then the vernacular languages, they also had a great flowering in England from the late fourteenth to the late sixteenth centuries. Two surviving play collections, from Chester and York, were conceived as complete cycles of sacred history from Creation to the Last Judgment, including such events as the fall of Lucifer, Noah's flood, the nativity of Christ, and Christ's crucifixion and resurrection. The York plays were performed, across a single vastly ambitious day, around the feast of Corpus Christi in midsummer. The huge arc of biblical narrative gains coherence in these plays (as in other medieval treatments) by a pattern of typology whereby Old Testament events are understood to be fulfilled in the New Testament. Hence Satan's deception and Adam's fall are redeemed by Christ's sacrifice. At a level of analogy, Old Testament events and characters predict and are fulfilled by New Testament ones—Isaac and Moses, for instance, are seen as "types" of Christ, while Cain and Pharaoh are types of Satan.

Other surviving groups of plays, some individually much longer and more ambitious than those from York and Chester, may have been collected together in play-books without being conceived or performed as a cycle. These include the plays now known only as "N-Town" and the Townley plays. Some of the Townley plays are linked to the town of Wakefield, not far from York. These Middle English biblical plays represent a wide range of styles, staging techniques, and sponsors. The York plays were financed by craft guilds (also called "mysteries," which led to the cycles being called mystery plays); the Townley plays may have been produced individually under parish sponsorship. The York plays were enacted on large carts that rolled from one public space to another, each play performed repeatedly; some Townley plays (like the Second Play of the Shepherds) require a central acting area surrounded by several more specific scenes, perhaps on scaffolds. What the plays have in common is their largely outdoor production, their association with prosperous towns and cities, many (not all) in the north, and their connection with a newly prosperous mercantile class. Often guilds sponsored plays specifically linked to their craft; at York, the Shipwrights produced the play of Noah's Ark, and the Fishers and Mariners the play of the Flood.

The popularity of these dramas—as well as their function as a surrogate Bible for the poor—can be seen in Chaucer's Miller's Tale. The Miller himself insists on telling his tale out of order, and does so in "Pilate's voice," the ranting manner of Pontius Pilate in the Passion Plays, and in the tale, the foppish Absolon woos his beloved Alison by playing the role of the tyrant Herod on a scaffold. Indeed, Chaucer's tale may be our first solid reference to Middle English biblical drama, and the locales both of the Miller's performance (between London and Canterbury) and of Absolon's (Oxford, where the tale is set) suggest the geographical range of these plays, many of which must have been lost when they were discouraged during the Reformation.

The Second Play of the Shepherds

Nowhere are the sacred and the profane paired as brilliantly as in the Nativity play known as the Second Play of the Shepherds, one of the Townley collection of plays probably performed at the prosperous Yorkshire town of Wakefield. The play was written or revised by an artist of

dramatic imagination and poetic skill, often called the Wakefield Master. His great achievement is his ability to make biblical stories relevant to fifteenth-century England in such a way
that daily life takes on typological significance. The key example of this, at once moving and
funny, is the parallel between Mak's stolen sheep, hidden in swaddling clothes in a cradle, and
the newborn Christ child whom the shepherds visit at the end of the play. The mercy that the
shepherds show to Mak by tossing him in a blanket rather than delivering him to be hanged
prefigures the mercy that Christ will bring into the world.

No matter how neatly the typological scheme works, however, the author does not present the birth of Christ as nullifying the complaints of the play's characters. With his guileful
assault on the sheepfold and his concealment of the "horned lad" swaddled in a cradle, Mak
may be a type of the devil, but his complaints of poverty are real: he steals the sheep to feed a
hungry family. Just as real are the complaints of the shepherds, to which the first 180 lines of
the play are devoted. The shepherds grumble about taxes, lords and their condescending servants, and their own nagging, prolific wives.

The plight of the shepherds reflects the impact of the wool and cloth trade; it enriched
England in the fourteenth and fifteenth centuries, but it also impoverished peasant farmers
when landlords enclosed tracts of land for conversion to lucrative sheep farming. These
complaints cannot simply be dismissed as the "moan" of fallen men who fail to understand
their need for divine grace. Nor can the complaints of Mak's wife Gill against women's work
be seen as simply setting her up as a contrast with the patient Virgin Mary at the end of the
play. Nonetheless, the social and musical harmony exhibited as the play closes does suggest
the transformation these shepherds undergo, and into which the play invites its believing
audience.

The Second Play of the Shepherds

[*Scene: Field near Bethlehem.*]

I PASTOR: Lord, what these weathers are cold!   And I am ill happed.[1]

    I am near hand dold,°   so long have I napped;   *almost numb*

    My legs they fold,   my fingers are chapped.

    It is not as I would,   for I am all lapped°   *tied up*

5   In sorrow.

    In storms and tempest,

    Now in the east, now in the west,

    Woe is him has never rest

    Mid-day nor morrow!

10   But we sely° shepherds   that walks on the moor,   *poor*

    In faith we are near hands   out of the door.

    No wonder, as it stands,   if we be poor,

    For the tilthe of our lands   lies fallow as the floor,

    As ye ken°.   *know*

15   We are so hamed°,   *hamstrung*

    For-taxed° and ramed°,   *overburdened / oppressed*

    We are made hand tamed

    With these gentlery men.°   *gentry, aristocrats*

    Thus they reave° us our rest,   our Lady them wary!°   *rob / curse*

20   These men that are lord-fest,[2]   they cause the plow tarry.

---

1. Clothed.   2. Bound to their lords.

That men say is for the best,   we find it contrary.
Thus are husbandys° opprest,   in point to miscarry   *farmhands*
On live.
Thus hold they us hunder;°   *under*
25 Thus they bring us in blonder;°   *trouble*
It were great wonder
And ever should we thrive.

For may he get a paint slefe°   or a broche now on days,   *painted sleeve*
Woe is him that him grefe°   or once again says!   *troubles*
30 Dare noman him reprefe,°   what mastry° he mays,   *reprove / power*
And yet may noman lefe°   one word that he says,   *believe*
No letter.
He can make purveance°   *provision*
With boast and bragance,
35 And all is through maintenance
Of men that are greater.

There shall come a swane   as proud as a po,³
He must borrow my wane,° my plow also,   *wagon*
Then I am full fane°   to grant or he go.   *pleased*
40 Thus live we in pain,   anger, and woe,
By night and day.
He must have if he langed,°   *desired*
If I should forgang° it;   *forgo*
I were better be hanged
45 Then once say him nay.

It does me good, as I walk   thus by mine one,
Of this world for to talk   in manner of moan.
To my sheep will I stalk,   and hearken anone,°   *awhile*
There abide on a balk,°   or sit on a stone,   *ridge*
50 Full soon.
For I trowe,° perde,°   *believe / by God*
True men if they be,
We get more company
Or° it be noon.   *before*

[*The Second Shepherd enters without noticing the First.*]
II PASTOR: Benste and Dominus!⁴ What may this bemean?
Why fares this world thus? Oft have we not seen?
Lord, these weathers are spytus,°   and the winds full keen, *spiteful*
And the frosts so hideous   they water my eyes—
No lie.
60 Now in dry, now in wete,
Now in snow, now in sleet;
When my shoen° freeze to my feet,   *shoes*
It is not all easy.

---

3. A servant as proud as a peacock.   4. Corruption of a Latin blessing, *Benedicite ad Dominum.*

But as far as I ken,   or yet as I go,
65   We sely wedmen   dre mekyll woe;[5]
We have sorrow then and then: it falls oft so.
Sely Copple,[6] our hen,   both to and fro
She cackles;
But begin she to croak,
70   To groan or to cluck,
Woe is him is of our cock,
For he is in the shackels.

These men that are wed have not all their will;
When they are full hard sted,°   they sigh full still;   placed
75   God wayte° they are led full hard and full ill;   knows
In bower° nor in bed   they say nought there till,°   bedroom / thereto
This tide.°   time
My part have I fun;°   found
I know my lesson.
80   Woe is him that is bun,°   bound in marriage
For he must abide.

But now late in our lives a marvel to me,
That I think my heart rives°   such wonders to see.   breaks
What that destiny drives   it should so be;
85   Some men will have two wives   and some men three,
In store;
Some are woe that has any,
But so far can I,
Woe is him that has many,
90   For he felys° sore.   suffers

But young men of a-wooing,   for God that you bought,°   redeemed
Be well ware of wedding,   and think in your thought,
"Had I wist"° is a thing   it serves of nought;   known
Mekyll° still° mourning   has wedding home brought,   much / constant
95   And griefs,
With many a sharp shower;
For thou may catch in an hour
That shall savour fulle sour
As long as thou lives.

100   For, as ever read I pistill[7]   I have one to my fere,°   mate
As sharp as a thistle,   as rough as a brere;
She is browed like a bristle   with a sour-loten cheer;[8]
Had she once wet her whistle   she could sing full clear
Her *Paternoster*.°   Lord's Prayer
105   She is as great as a whale;
She has a gallon of gall.

---

5. We poor, innocent married men suffer much.   7. [St. Paul's] Epistle.
6. A copple is the crest on a bird's head.   8. Sour-looking face.

By him that died for us all,
I would I had run to° I had lost her.   *until*

I PASTOR: God look over the raw!⁹   Full deafly ye stand.
II PASTOR: Yea, the devil in thy maw,°   so tariand.°   *mouth / slow*
Saw thou awre° of Daw?¹   *anywhere*
I PASTOR: Yea, on a ley land°   *fallow ground*
Hard I him blaw.²   He comes here at hand,
Not far.
Stand still.
II PASTOR: Why?
I PASTOR: For he comes, hope I.
II PASTOR: He will make us both a lie
But if° we beware.   *unless*

[*Enter Third Shepherd.*]
III PASTOR: Christ's cross me speed,   and Saint Nicholas!
There of had I need;   it is worse than it was.
120   Whoso could take heed   and let the world pass,
It is ever in dread   and brekill° as glass,   *brittle*
And slithes.°   *slides away*
This world fowre° never so,   *fared*
With marvels mo and mo,
125   Now in weal, now in woe,
And all thing writhes.°   *turns about*

Was never sin° Noah's flood   such floods seen;   *since*
Winds and rains so rude,   and storms so keen;
Some stammerd, some stood   in doubt,° as I ween;   *fear*
130   Now God turn all to good!   I say as I mean,
For° ponder.   *to*
These floods so they drown,
Both fields and in town,
And beats all down,
135   And that is a wonder.

We that walk on the nights,   our cattle to keep,
We see sudden sights   when other men sleep.
Yet me think my heart lights;   I see shrews peep;³
Ye are two ill wights.   I will give my sheep
140   A turn.
But full ill have I meant;
As I walk on this bent,
I may lightly repent,
My toes if I spurn.

---

9. Let God pay attention to his audience (row), i.e., God   2. I just blew by him.
attend me.   3. I see villains peeping out.
1. The Third Shepherd.

145   Ah, sir, God you save,   and master mine!
     A drink fain would I have,   and somewhat to dine
I PASTOR: Christ's curse, my knave,   thou art a leder hine!°   *lazy servant*
II PASTOR: What, the boy list rave!   Abide unto sine;[4]
     We have made it.[5]
150   Ill thrift on thy pate!
     Though the shrew came late,
     Yet is he in state
     To dine, if he had it.

III PASTOR: Such servants as I,   that sweats and swinks,°   *works*
155   Eats our bread full dry,   and that me forthinks;°   *upsets*
     We are oft wet and weary   when master-men winks;°   *sleeps*
     Yet comes full lately   both diners and drinks,
     But nately.°   *thoroughly*
     Both our dame and our sire,
160   When we have run in the mire,
     They can nip° at our hire,°   *trim / wages*
     And pay us full lately.

     But here my troth, master: for the fare that ye make,
     I shall do therafter,   work as I take;
165   I shall do a little, sir,   and emang ever lake,[6]
     For yet lay my supper   never on my stomach
     In fields.
     Whereto should I threpe?°   *wrangle*
     With my staff can I leap,
170   And men say "Light cheap°   *little cost*
     Letherly for-yields."°   *poorly yields*

I PASTOR: Thou were an ill lad   to ride a-wooing
     With a man that had   but little of spending.
II PASTOR: Peace, boy, I bade.   No more jangling,°   *chattering*
175   Or I shall make there full rad,°   by the heavens king!   *quickly*
     With thy gauds°—   *tricks*
     Where are our sheep, boy?—we scorn.°   *despise*
III PASTOR: Sir, this same day at morn
     I them left in the corn,
180   When they rang lauds.[7]

     They have pasture good,   they cannot go wrong.
I PASTOR: That is right, by the roode![8]   these nights are long,
     Yet I would, or we yode,°   one gave us a song.   *went*
II PASTOR: So I thought as I stood,   to mirth us among.
III PASTOR: I grant.

---

4. The boy is crazy; wait a while.
5. We have already eaten.
6. Keep playing besides.
7. The first church service of the day.

8. Cross; the humor here, as with the other oaths, is based on the anachronism that Jesus has not yet been born, much less crucified.

I PASTOR: Let me sing the tenory.

II PASTOR: And I treble so hee.

III PASTOR: Then the meyne° falls to me: *middle*

    Let see how ye chant.

  [*They sing.*]

  Tunc intrat Mak in clamide se super togam vestitus.[9]

MAK: Now, Lord, for thy names vii,[1]   that made both moon and starns°   *stars*

    Well mo then can I neven°   thy will, Lord, of me tharns;[2]   *say*

    I am all uneven,   that moves oft my harness.

    Now would God I were in heaven,   for there weep no barnes°   *babies*

    So still.

I PASTOR: Who is that pipes so poor?

MAK: Would God ye wist how I foor!°   *fared*

    Lo, a man that walks on the moor,

    And has not all his will!

II PASTOR: Mak, where has thou gone?   Tell us tiding

III PASTOR: Is he comme? Then ylkon°   take heed to his thing.   *everyone*

    Et accipit clamidem ab ipso.[3]

MAK: What! Ich be a yoman,[4]   I tell you, of the king;

    The self and the same,   sond° from a great lording,   *messenger*

    And sich.°   *such like*

    Fy on you! Goeth hence

205   Out of my presence!

    I must have reverence;

    Why, who be ich?

I PASTOR: Why make ye it so quaint?[5]   Mak, ye do wrang.

II PASTOR: But, Mak, list ye saint?   I trow that ye lang.[6]

III PASTOR: I trow the shrew can paint,   the devill might him hang!

MAK: Ich shall make complaint, and make you all to thwang[7]

    At a word,

    And tell even how ye doth.

I PASTOR: But, Mak, is that sooth?

215   Now take out that southren tooth,°   *accent*

    And set in a turd!

II PASTOR: Mak, the devil in your eye!   A stroke would I lean° you.   *lend*

III PASTOR: Mak, know ye not me?   By God, I could teen° you.   *rage at*

MAK: God look you all three!   Me thought I had seen you;

220   Ye are a fair company.

I PASTOR: Can ye now mean you?

II PASTOR: Shrew, pepe![8]

---

9. Then Mak enters, wearing a cloak over his garment.

1. Seven (written by the copyist as the roman numeral).

2. Is lacking.

3. And he takes his cloak from him.

4. Freeborn property-holder.

5. Why act so elegant?

6. Do you want to be a saint? I think you long to be.

7. Be beaten.

8. Villain, look around!

Thus late as thou goes,
What will men suppose?
And thou has an ill nose°   *reputation*
225   Of steeling of sheep.

MAK: And I am true as steel,   all men waytt,°   *know*
But a sickness I feel   that holds me full haytt;°   *hot*
My belly fares not weel;   it is out of estate.
III PASTOR: Seldom lies the devil   dead by the gate.[9]
MAK: Therfore
Full sore am I and ill,
If I stand stone still;
I eat not an nedill°   *scrap*
This month and more.

I PASTOR: How fares thy wife? By my hood,   how fares sho?°   *she*
MAK: Lies waltering,° by the rood,   by the fire, lo!   *collapsed*
And a house full of brood.°   She drinks well, too;   *children*
Ill spede° other good   that she will do!   *success*
But sho
240   Eats as fast as she can,
And ilk° year that comes to man   *each*
She brings forth a lakan,°   *baby*
And some years two.

But were I not more gracious   and richer by far;
245   I were eaten out of house   and of harbar;°   *home*
Yet is she a foul dowse,°   if ye come nar;   *wench*
There is none that trowse°   nor knows a war°   *imagines / worse*
Than ken I.
Now will ye see what I proffer,
250   To give all in my coffer
To morn at next to offer
Her hed mas-penny.[1]

II PASTOR: I wote so forwaked°   is none in this shire: *sleepless*
I would sleep if I taked   less to my hire.
III PASTOR: I am cold and naked,   and would have a fire.
I PASTOR: I am weary, for-rakyd,°   and run in the mire.   *exhausted*
Wake thou!
II PASTOR: Nay, I will lyg° down by,   *lie*
For I must sleep truly.
III PASTOR: As good a man's son was I
As any of you.

But, Mak, come hither! Between   shall thou lyg down.
[*Mak lies down with the Shepherds.*]
MAK: Then might I let you bedene   of that ye would rowne,[2]

9. Proverbial: The devil seldom lies dead by the wayside;   2. That way I can readily prevent you from whispering
i.e., the devil is not often an innocent victim.   together.
1. Penny offering for a mass for the dead.

No drede.
265   From my top to my toe,
          Manus was commendo,
          Poncio Pilato,[3]
          Christ cross me speed!
     Tunc surgit, pastoribus dormientibus, et dicit[4]

          Now were time for a man   that lacks what he would
270   To stalk privily than   unto a fold,
          And nimbly to work than,   and be not too bold,
          For he might aby the bargain,   if it were told
          At the ending.
          Now were time for to reyll;°   revel
275   But he needs good counsel
          That fain would fare well,
          And has but little spending.

          But about you a circle,   as round as a moon,
          Too I have done that I will,   till° that it be noon,[5]   until
280   That ye lyg stone still   to that I have done,
          And I shall say theretill   of good words a foyne.°   a few
          "On hight
          Over your heads my hand I lift;
          Out go your eyes! Fordo° your sight!"   ruin
285   But yet I must make better shift,
          And it be right.

          Lord, what they sleep hard!   That may ye all here;
          Was I never a shepherd,   but now will I lere.°   learn
          If the flock be scared,   yet shall I nip near.
290   How, drawes° hitherward!   Now mends our cheer   come
          From sorrow:
          A fat sheep, I dare say,
          A good fleece, dare I lay,
          Eft-whyte when I may,[6]
295   But this will I borrow.
     [*Mak goes home to his wife.*]

          How, Gill, art thou in?   Get us some light.
     UXOR EIUS:[7] Who makes such din   this time of the night?
          I am set for to spin;   I hope not[8] I might
          Rise a penny to win,°   I shrew° them on height!   gain / curse
300   So fares
          A housewife that has been
          To be raised° thus between: disturbed

---

3. An amusing corruption of two Bible verses: "Into
your hands I commend my soul" and "I wash my hands
of this man."
4. Then Mak arises, while the shepherds are sleeping, and
speaks.

5. Mak is casting a spell on the shepherds in the form of a
fairy circle to keep them from waking.
6. I will pay it back when I can.
7. His wife.
8. I don't expect that.

Here may no note° be seen   *scrap*
For such small chares.°   *chores*

MAK: Good wife, open the hek!°   Sees thou not what I bring?   *inner door*
UXOR: I may thole the dray the snek.⁹   Ah, come in, my sweeting!
MAK: Yea, thou thar not rek°   of my long standing.   *care*
UXOR: By the naked neck   art thou like for to hing.
MAK: Do way:
310   I am worthy my meat,°   *supper*
            For in a strait° can I get   *tight spot*
            More than they that swink° and sweat   *work*
            All the long day.

        Thus it fell to my lot,   Gill, I had such grace.
UXOR: It were a foul blot   to be hanged for the case.
MAK: I have skaped, Jelot,¹   oft as hard a glase.°   *blow*
UXOR: But so long goes the pot   to the water, men says,
            At last
            Comes it home broken.
MAK: Well know I the token,
            But let it never be spoken;
            But come and help fast.
            I would he were flayn;°   I lyst° well eat: *skinned / wish*
        This twelvemonth was I not   so fain of one sheep mete.
UXOR: Come they or° he be slain,   and hear the sheep bleat— *before*
MAK: Then might I be tane.°   That were a cold sweat!   *taken*
            Go spar°   *lock*
            The gate-door.
UXOR: Yes, Mak,
            For and° they come at thy back—   *if*
MAK: Then might I buy, for all the pack,²
            The devil of the war.

UXOR: A good bowrde° have I spied,   sin thou can none.   *trick*
            Here shall we him hide   to° they be gone;   *until*
335   In my cradle abide.   Let me alone,
            And I shall lyg beside   in childbed, and groan.
MAK: Thou red;°   *get ready*
            And I shall say thou was light°   *delivered*
            Of a knave child this night.
UXOR: Now well is me day bright,
340   That ever was I bred.

        This is a good gise°   and a far cast;   *way*
        Yet a woman avise   helps at the last.
        I wote° never who spies,   agane° go thou fast.   *know / back*

---

9. I will let you draw the latch.   2. Then I may have the worse, for there are such a pack
1. Affectionate nickname for "Gill."   of them.

MAK: But I come or they rise, else blows a cold blast!
345   I will go sleep.
      [*Mak returns to the Shepherds and lies down.*]
         Yet sleeps all this meneye,°   *household*
         And I shall go stalk privily
         As it had never been I
         That carried there sheep.

I PASTOR: *Resurrex a mortruis!*[3]   Have hold my hand.
         Iudas carnas dominus![4]   I may not well stand:
         My foot sleeps, by Jesus,   and I water fastand.[5]
         I thought that we had laid us   full near England.
II PASTOR: Ah ye!
355   Lord, what I have slept well;
         As fresh as an eel,
         As light I me feel
         As leaf on a tree.

III PASTOR: Benste° be here in!   So my heart quakes,   *a blessing*
360   My heart is out of skin,°   what so it makes.   *(body)*
         Who makes all this din?   So my brows blakes°   *darkens*
         To the door will I win.   Hark, fellows, wakes!
         We were four:
         See ye awre° of Mak now?   *anywhere*
I PASTOR: We were up or thou.
II PASTOR: Man, I give God a vow,
         Yet yede° he nawre.°   *went / nowhere*

III PASTOR: Me thought he was lapt,°   in a wolf skin.   *clothed*
I PASTOR: So are many hapt°   now namely within.   *covered*
II PASTOR: When we had long napped,   me thought with a gyn°   *trap*
         A fat sheep he trapped,   but he made no din.
III PASTOR: Be still:
         Thy dream makes thee woode:°   *mad*
         It is but phantom, by the roode.°   *cross*
I PASTOR: Now God turn all to good,
         If it be his will.

II PASTOR: Rise, Mak, for shame!   Thou lies right long.
MAK: Now Christ's holy name   be us among!
         What is this? For Saint Jame,   I may not well gang!
380   I trow I be the same.   Ah, my neck has lain wrong
         Enough.
         Mekill,° thanks syn° yister even,   *many / since*
         Now, by Saint Steven,
         I was flayd° with a sweven,°   *frightened / dream*
385   My heart out of slough.°   *skin*

3. Corruption from the Latin Bible of "He rose from the   5. Stagger from lack of food.
dead."
4. A corruption into Latin gibberish, "Judas lord of the
flesh."

I thought Gill began to croak   and travail° full sad,   *struggle*
Welner° at the first cock,   of a young lad   *nearly*
For to mend our flock.   Then be I never glad;
I have tow° on my rock°   more then ever I had.   *flax / distaff*
390   Ah, my head!
A house full of young tharms;°   *children*
The devil knock out their harns!°   *brains*
Woe is him has many barns,
And thereto little bread!

395   I must go home, by your leave,   to Gill, as I thought.
I pray you looke,° my sleeve   that I steal nought: *inspect*
I am loath you to grieve, or from you take ought.
III PASTOR: Go forth, ill might thou chefe!° Now would I we sought,   *fare*
This morn,
400   That we had all our store.
I PASTOR: But I will go before;
Let us meet.
II PASTOR: Whore?
III PASTOR: At the crooked thorn.
    [*The Shepherds leave. Mak knocks at his door*.]

MAK: Undo this door! Who is here?   How long shall I stand?
UXOR EIUS: Who makes such a bere?°   Now walk in the wenyand.[6]   *noise*
MAK: Ah Gill, what cheer?   It is I, Mak, your husband.
UXOR: Then may we be here   the devil in a band,
Sir Gyle:[7]
Lo, he comes with a lote°   *noise*
410   As he were holden° in the throat.   *held*
I may not sit at my note,°   *work*
A hand-lang° while.   *little*

MAK: Will ye hear what fare she makes   to get her a glose?[8]
And does nought but lakes°   and claws her toes.   *plays*
UXOR: Why, who wanders, who wakes?   Who commes, who goes?
Who brews, who bakes?   What makes me thus hose?°   *hoarse*
And than,
It is rewthe° to behold,   *pitiful*
Now in hot, now in cold,
420   Full woeful is the household
That wants a woman.

But what end has thou made   with the herds, Mak?
MAK: The last word that thay said   when I turned my back,
They would look that they had   their sheep, all the pack.
425   I hope[9] they will not be well paid   when they their sheep lack,
Perde!

---

6. Waning hour, unlucky time.   8. Make up an excuse.
7. Mister Deceiver (the Devil).   9. Expect.

But how so the game goes,
To me they will suppose,
And make a foul noise,
430   And cry out upon me.

But thou must do as thou hight.°   said
UXOR: I accord me there till.
I shall swaddle him right   in my cradle;
If it were a greater sleight,°   yet could I help till.   trick
I will lyg down straight.   Come hap me.
MAK: I will.
UXOR: Behind!
Come Coll¹ and his maroo,°   mate
They will nyp° us full naroo.°   pinch / hard
MAK: But I may cry out "Haroo!"
The sheep if they find.

UXOR: Harken ay whenthey call;   they will come onone.°   soon
Come and make ready all   and sing by thine one;
Sing "lullay" thou shall,   for I must groan,
And cry out by the wall   on Mary and John,
For sore.
445   Sing "lullay" on fast
When thou hears at the last;
And but I play a false cast,°   trick
Trust me no more.

[At the crooked thorn.]
III PASTOR: Ah, Coll, good morn.   Why sleeps thou not?
I PASTOR: Alas, that ever was I born!   We have a foul blot.
A fat wether° have we lorne.°   ram / lost
III PASTOR: Mary, God's forbot!
II PASTOR: Who should do us that scorn?°   That were a foul spot.   harm
I PASTOR: Some shrewe.°   villain
I have sought with my dogs
455   All Horbury² shrogs,°   hedges
And of xv° hogs   fifteen
Found I but one ewe.

III PASTOR: Now trow me, if ye will,   by Saint Thomas of Kent,
Either Mak or Gill   was at that assent.°   affair
I PASTOR: Peace, man, be still!   I saw when he went;
Thou slanders him ill;   thou ought to repent,
Good speed.
II PASTOR: Now as ever might I the,°   thrive
If I should even here die,
465   I would say it were he,
That did that same deed.

1. The First Shepherd.   2. A town south of Wakefield.

III PASTOR: Go we thither, I read,   and run on our feet.

  Shall I never eat bread   the sothe to I wytt.[3]

I PASTOR: Nor drink in my head   with him till I meet.

II PASTOR: I will rest in no stead   till that I him greet,

  My brother.

  One I will hight:°   *promise*

  Till I see him in sight

  Shall I never sleep one night

475 There I do another.

  [*They approach Mak's house.*]

III PASTOR: Will ye hear how they hack?[4]   Our sire list croon.

I PASTOR: Heard I never none crack   so clear out of toon;

  Call on him.

II PASTOR: Mak,   undo your door soon.

MAK: Who is that spake,   as it were noon

480 On loft?

  Who is that, I say?

III PASTOR: Good felows, were it day.

MAK: As far as ye may,

  Good, speaks soft,

485 Over a sick woman's head   that is at malaise;

  I had lever° be dead   or she had any disease.   *rather*

UXOR: Go to another stead!   I may not well qweasse.°   *breathe*

  Each foot that ye tread   goes through my nese,°   *nose*

  So hee!°   *loudly*

I PASTOR: Tell us, Mak, if ye may,

  How fare ye, I say?

MAK: But are ye in this town to-day?

  Now how fare ye?

  Ye have run in the mire,   and are wet yit:

495 I shall make you a fire,   if you will sit.

  A nurse would I hire.   Think ye on yit,

  Well quit is my hire[5]—   my dream this is it—

  A season.

  I have barns, if ye knew,

500 Well mo then enewe,

  But we must drink as we brew,

  And that is but reason.

  I would ye dined or ye yode.[6]   Me think that ye sweat.

II PASTOR: Nay, neither mends our mood   drink nor meat.

MAK: Why, sir, ails you ought but good?

III PASTOR: Yea, our sheep that we get,

---

3. Until I know the truth.
4. Sing (badly).

5. My wages are paid; i.e., his dream has been fulfilled.
6. I would like you to eat before you go.

	Are stolen as they yode. Our loss is great.	
MAK:	Sirs, drinks!	
	Had I been there,	
	Some should have bought it full sore.	
I PASTOR:	Mary, some men trowes° that ye wore,	*believes*
	And that us forthinks.°	*disturbs*

II PASTOR: Mak, some men trowys   that it should be ye.
III PASTOR: Either ye or your spouse,   so say we.

MAK:	Now if ye have suspowse° to Gill or to me,	*suspicion*
515	Come and ripe° our house, and then may ye see	*search*
	Who had her;	
	If I any sheep for,°	*took*
	Either cow or stot;°	*heifer*
	And Gill, my wife, rose not	
520	Here sin she laid her.	

	As I am true and leal,° to God here I pray,	*loyal*
	That this be the first meal that I shall eat this day.	
I PASTOR:	Mak, as have I ceyll,° advise thee, I say;	*heaven*
	He learned timely to steal that could not say nay.	
UXOR:	I swelt!°	*die*
	Out, thieves, from my wonys!°	*home*
	Ye come to rob us for the nonys.°	*for the purpose*
MAK:	Here ye not how she groans?	
	Your hearts should melt.	

UXOR:	Out, thieves, from my barn! Nigh him not thor!°	*there*
MAK:	Wist ye how she had farn,° your hearts would be sore.	*fared*
	Ye do wrong, I you warn, that thus comes before	
	To a woman that has farn— but I say no more.	
UXOR:	Ah, my medill!°	*middle*
535	I pray to God so mild,	
	If ever I you beguiled,	
	That I eat this child	
	That lies in this cradle.	

MAK:	Peace, woman, for God's pain, and cry not so:	
540	Thou spills thy brain, and makes me full woe.	
II PASTOR:	I trow our sheep be slain. What find ye two?	
III PASTOR:	All work we in vain; as well may we go.	
	But hatters,°	*(an oath)*
	I can find no flesh,	
545	Hard nor nesh,°	*soft*
	Salt nor fresh,	
	But two tome° platters.	*empty*

	Whik° cattle but this, tame nor wild,	*living*
	None, as have I bliss, as loud as he smiled.°	*smelled*
UXOR:	No, so God me bliss, and give me joy of my child!	

I PASTOR: We have marked amiss;   I hold us beguiled.

II PASTOR: Sir, don,°   *it is done*

Sir, our Lady him save,

Is your child a knave?[7]

MAK: Any lord might him have

This child to his son.

When he wakens he kips,°   that joy is to see.   *snatches*

III PASTOR: In good time to his hips,   and in cele.°   *heaven*

But who was his gossips,°   so soon rede?°   *godparents / ready*

MAK: So fair fall their lips!

I PASTOR: Hark now, a le.°   *lie*

MAK: So God them thank,

Parkin, and Gibon Waller I say,

And gentle John Horne,[8] in good fay,

He made all the garray,°   *noise*

565   With the great shank.°   *leg*

II PASTOR: Mak, friends will we be,   for we are all one.

MAK: We? Now I hold for me,   for mends° get I none.   *profit*

Farewell all three!   All glad were ye gone.

[*The Shepherds depart.*]

III PASTOR: Fair words may there be,   but love is there none

570   This year.

I PASTOR: Gave ye the child anything?

II PASTOR: I trow not one farthing.

III PASTOR: Fast again will I fling,°   *hurry*

Abide ye me there.

[*Returns to the house.*]

575   Mak, take it to no grief   if I come to thy barn.°   *baby*

MAK: Nay, thou does me great reproof,   and foul has thou farn.°   *done*

III PASTOR: The child will it not grief,   that little daystarn.[9]

Mak, with your leaf,   let me give your barn

But vi° pence.   *six*

MAK: Nay, do way: he sleeps.

III PASTOR: Me think he peeps.

MAK: When he wakens he weeps.

I pray you go hence.

[*The other Shepherds return.*]

III PASTOR: Give me leave him to kiss,   and lift up the clout.°   *cloth*

585   What the devil is this?   He has a long snout.

I PASTOR: He is marked amiss.   We wat° ill about.   *watch*

II PASTOR: Ill-spun weft, iwys,   ay comes foul out.[1]

7. Boy-child (of the serving-class).
8. Parkin, Gibon Waller, and John Horne are the names of the shepherds in the First Play of the Shepherds, possibly referring to actual townspeople.

9. Little day star; a term also used for the Christ child later in the play, indicating a parallel with Mak's baby.
1. Badly spun thread always makes poor cloth.

Aye, so!
He is like to our sheep!

III PASTOR: How, Gyb,° may I peep?   *the Second Shepherd*
I PASTOR: I trow kind° will creep   *Nature*
 Where it may not go.°   *walk*

II PASTOR: This was a quaint gawde,° and a far cast. *clever trick*
 It was a high fraud.

III PASTOR: Yea, sirs, was't.
595 Let bren° this bawd, and bind her fast.   *burn*
 A false skawd° hang at the last;   *scold*
 So shall thou.
 Will ye see how they swaddle
 His four feet in the middle?
600 Saw I never in a cradle
 A horned lad² or° now.   *before*

MAK: Peace bid I. What, let be youre fare;
 I am he that him gat,° and yond woman him bare. *begat*
I PASTOR: What devil shall he hat,° Mak? Lo, God, Mak's heir. *be called*
II PASTOR: Let be all that. Now God give him cure,
 I sagh.°   *saw*
UXOR: A pretty child is he
 As sits on a woman's knee;
 A dillydown,° perde,   *darling*
610 To gar° a man laugh.   *make*

III PASTOR: I know him by the earn mark: that is a good token.
MAK: I tell you, sirs, hark!— his nose was broken.
 Sithen° told me a clerk that he was forspoken.° *since / bewitched*
I PASTOR: This is a false work; I would fain be wroken.° *avenged*
615 Get wepyn.
UXOR: He was taken with° an elf;   *by*
 I saw it myself.
 When the clock struck twelve
 Was he forshapen.°   *changed*

II PASTOR: Ye two are well feft° sam° in a stead. *endowed / together*
III PASTOR: Sin they maintain their theft, let do them to dead.
MAK: If I trespass eft°, gird° off my head.   *again / cut*
 With you will I be left.
I PASTOR: Sirs, do my read.°   *advice*
 For this trespass,
625 We will neither ban ne flite,°   *curse nor quarrel*
 Fight nor chite,°   *chide*
 But have done as tite,°   *quickly*
 And cast him in canvas.

2. A horned child (devil).

[*They toss Mak in a sheet.*]

Lord, what I am sore, in point for to brist.
630   In faith I may no more; therefore will I rist.
II PASTOR: As a sheep of vii score[3]   he weighed in my fist.
For to sleep ay-whore° me think that I list.   anywhere
III PASTOR: Now I pray you,
Lyg down on this green.
I PASTOR: On these thieves yet I mene.°   speak
III PASTOR: Whereto should ye tene?°   be angry
Do as I say you.
[*The Shepherds sleep.*]
Angelus cantat "Gloria in excelsis"; postea dicat[4]

ANGELUS: Rise, herd-men heynd!° For now is he born   virtuous
That shall take fro the fiend   that Adam had lorn;°   lost
640   That warloo° to shend,°   this night is he born.   devil / destroy
God is made your friend   now at this morn.
He behestys°   orders
At Bedlem° go see: Bethlehem
There lies that fre°   lord
645   In a crib full poorly,
Betwyx two bestys.

I PASTOR: This was a quaint steven°   that ever yet I heard.   voice
It is a marvel to neven,°   thus to be scared.   mention
II PASTOR: Of God's son of heaven   he spake upward.°   on high
650   All the wood on a leven   me thought that he gard
Appear.[5]
III PASTOR: He spake of a barn
In Bedlem, I you warn.
I PASTOR: That betokens yond starn.°   star
655   Let us seek him there.

II PASTOR: Say, what was his song?   Heard ye not how he cracked° it?   roared
Three breves to a long.[6]
III PASTOR: Yea, marry, he hakt° it.   sang
Was no crochett° wrong,   nor nothing that lacked it.   note
I PASTOR: For to sing us among   right as he knacked° it,   sang
660   I can.
II PASTOR: Let se how ye croon.
Can ye bark at the moon?
III PASTOR: Hold your tongues, have done!
I PASTOR: Hark after than.
[*Sings.*]

II PASTOR: To Bedlem he bade   that we should gang:
I am full fard°   that we tarry too lang.   afraid

3. Seven score pounds (140 lbs).
4. The Angel sings "Glory to God in the highest," and afterward says.
5. I thought he lit up the woods like lightning.
6. Three short notes to one long.

III PASTOR: Be merry and not sad;   of mirth is our sang;
        Ever-lasting glad   to mede° may we fang,°   *reward / get*
        Without noise.
I PASTOR: Hie we thither for-thy;°   *therefore*
        If we be wet and weary,
        To that child and that lady,
        We have it not to lose.

II PASTOR: We find by the prophecy—   let be your din—
675   Of David and Isay,[7] and mo than I min,
        They prophesied by clergy   that in a virgin
        Should he light and lie,   to sloken° our sin   *remove*
        And slake it,
        Our kynd° from woc;   *humankind*
680   For Isay said so,
        Ecce virgo
        Concipiet[8] a child that is naked.

III PASTOR: Full glad may we be, and abide that day
        That lovely to see,   that all mights may.
685   Lord, well were me,   for once and for ay,
        Might I kneel on my knee,   some word for to say
        To that child.
        But the angel said
        In a crib was he laid;
690   He was poorly arrayed,
        Both mener° and milde.   *poor*

I PASTOR: Patriarchs that has been, and prophets beforn,
        They desired to have seen   this child that is born.
        They are gone full clean,°   that have they lorn.°   *entirely / lost*
695   We shall see him, I ween,   or it be morn,
        To token.°   *as proof*
        When I see him and feel,
        Then wot I full weel
        It is true as steel
700   That prophets have spoken:

        To so poore as we are   that he would appear,
        First find, and declare   by his messenger.
II PASTOR: Go we now, let us fare;   the place is us near.
III PASTOR: I am ready and yare;°   go we in fere°   *prepared / together*
705   To that bright.
        Lord, if thy wills be,
        We are lewde° all three,   *unschooled*
        Thou grant us somkyns glee°   *some kind of joy*
        To comfort thy wight.°   *creature*
    [They enter the stable.]

---

7. The prophet Isaiah.   8. Behold, a virgin conceives (Isaiah 7.14).

I PASTOR: Hail, comely and clean!   Hail, young child!
   Hail, maker, as I mean,   of a maiden so mild!
   Thou has waryd°, I ween,   the warlo° so wild;   *cursed / devil*
   The false gyler° of teen°   now goes he beguiled.   *deceiver / anger*
   Lo, he merries!
715 Lo, he laughs, my sweeting!
   A well fair meeting!
   I have holden my heting;°   *kept my promise*
   Have a bob° of cherries.   *bunch*

II PASTOR: Hail, sovereign saviour,   for thou has us sought!
720 Hail, freely food and flour,[9]   that all thing has wrought!
   Hail, full of favour,   that made all of nought!
   Hail! I kneel and I cower.   A bird have I brought
   To my barn.
   Hail, little tyne mop!°   *tiny baby*
725 Of our creed thou art crop:°   *fruit, fulfillment*
   I would drink on thy cop,°   *cup*
   Little day starn.°   *star*

III PASTOR: Hail, darling dear,   full of Godhede!
   I pray thee be near   when that I have need.
730 Hail, sweet is thy cheer!   My heart would bleed
   To see thee sit here   in so poor weed,°   *clothing*
   With no pennies.
   Hail, put forth thy dall!°   *hand*
   I bring thee but a ball:
735 Have and play thee with all,
   And go to the tenys.°   *tennis*

MARIA: The Father of heaven,   God omnipotent,
   That set all on seven,[1]   his son has he sent.
   My name could he neven,°   and light or he went. *name*
740 I conceived him full even   through might, as he ment,° *intended*
   And now is he born.
   He keep you from woe!
   I shall pray him so.
   Tell forth as ye go,
745 And myn° on this morn.   *remember*

I PASTOR: Farewell, lady,   so fair to behold,
   With thy child on thy knee.
II PASTOR: But he lies full cold.
   Lord, well is me!   Now we go, thou behold.
III PASTOR: Forsooth already   it seems to be told
750 Full oft.

---

9. Noble child and flower.   1. Made everything in seven days.

I PASTOR: What grace we have fun!°   *found*
II PASTOR: Come forth: now are we won.
III PASTOR: To sing are we bun:°   *bound*
    Let take on loft![2]
    [*They go out singing.*]

Explicit pagina Pastorum.[3]

[END OF MEDIEVAL BIBLICAL DRAMA]

— ❈ —

Vernacular Religion

As Middle English religious writers were fond of pointing out, Christ's apostles preached and wrote in the mother tongues of their audiences. The early Western church used Latin, the dominant world language of late-imperial Rome. With the passing centuries, though, the Latin of the church was less and less accessible to most laypeople. They heard a liturgy they understood mostly through vernacular explanations and visual images in the church. Latin became a protective bulwark for clerical authority and the institutional church. Increasingly, this control of the Bible and doctrine accompanied an anxiety among clerics about laypeople reading or interpreting religious texts in the absence of ecclesiastical oversight. Other aspects of the church, such as its great wealth and varying degrees of clerical corruption, also alienated many laypeople in England and elsewhere.

Throughout the Middle Ages, both the established church and its critics were aware of these problems. One response was a persistent call for more and better preaching in local vernaculars. Yet the learning and energies of parish clergy were very uneven. Such "secular" clergy needed books of simple instruction and sample sermons in English for the whole church year. Toward this end, John Mirk wrote a lively and very popular sermon cycle, the *Festial*, toward the end of the fourteenth century. The later thirteenth and fourteenth centuries also witnessed a growing desire among laypeople for more intimate religious experience: "affective piety" as it has been called. Expressive and intense depictions of scriptural events such as the Crucifixion (see page 375) invited intense and expressive response, such as we will witness, in highly exaggerated form, in *The Book of Margery Kempe*.

In the midst of this religious yearning, dissatisfaction, and incomplete response by the church, there arrived the disruptive brilliance of John Wyclif. Wyclif came to public notice at Oxford by the 1350s, initially as a superb though radical practitioner of the technical scholastic theology of his day. He took increasingly extreme positions on a number of religious issues, key among them the nature of the Eucharist. Wyclif maintained—against established orthodoxy— that eucharistic bread was not utterly transformed into the body of Christ ("transubstantiated") when blessed by the priest. Perhaps more challenging to the everyday work of the church, he held that a man in a state of sin could not be a priest—that the priestly role was vested in the individual, not his enactment of the sacraments.

Wyclif vigorously supported ecclesiastical poverty. He argued that tithes could be with- held and used charitably elsewhere, even that the vast accumulated wealth of the church should be "disendowed" and placed in the hands of the secular government. The first notion appealed to many common people, and the latter intrigued a royal court plagued by debt.

---

2. Let us sing on high.   3. The play of the Shepherds is finished.

Wyclif was brought to London by John of Gaunt in 1376 to preach his views about disendow-ment. The church tried to condemn him as a heretic in 1377, but Gaunt deflected their efforts. Wyclif's evolving view of the Eucharist was harder to defend, though, and another church council in 1381 found that and other positions heretical; Wyclif retired from Oxford to his parish church, where he continued to write at a great pace until his death in 1384. Despite the church's condemnation, though, Wyclif's ideas gained followers (called "Lollards" by the late 1380s) at every level of society, and noble sympathizers were influential in the household of Richard II.

Wyclif insisted throughout his life that laypeople had a right to understand, even enter into, theological debate. And that meant they needed access to the fundamental work of all Christian belief, the Bible, in English. A group of his learned adherents undertook an enor-mous and complex project toward this end. They translated the Bible but also wrote extensive English commentaries based on Latin tradition and produced a full cycle of sermons urging Lollard doctrines. Of course, laypeople had always heard biblical passages in English, since they were the basis of most sermons. The great threat of Wyclif and his followers was that they felt the Bible could be used to criticize and correct the church. Along with the impressively or-ganized text production mentioned above, there were Lollard schools, and a network of house-hold "cells" where Lollard texts and ideas were studied and discussed. Taken all together, the outlines of something like a shadow church emerge. The 1430 "confession" of Hawisia Moone, included here, reflects many of these activities, and suggests the major beliefs that Lollards supported.

All of this was profoundly unnerving to the institutional church. Writing around 1390, the monastic chronicler Henry Knighton mentions the English Bible and comments: "that, which formerly belonged to those clergy who were sufficiently learned and intelli-gent, was made available to any lay person, even women, who knew how to read." It was relatively easy to condemn Wyclif's own beliefs and remove him from Oxford, even to burn other Lollards, but far harder to locate and suppress the network of local Lollard groups. And in a culture where church and state were so intimately linked, Lollard religious beliefs soon posed a political threat. Knighton also says Wyclif was inspired by John Ball, the priest who helped lead the Rising of 1381 (see pages 346–52). The movement lost virtually all its aristocratic support after a rebellion against Henry V in 1413, led by the Lollard Sir John Oldcastle.

Repression of Lollard beliefs had been in the air since the church council that condemned Wyclif in 1381. By 1401, Parliament passed a statute that called for the burning of unrepentant heretics. In the somewhat paranoid atmosphere of a threatened church and a king (Henry IV) who had usurped the throne, almost any vernacular religious writings might smell of heresy and political subversion. "Lollard" came to mean almost anyone outside of holy orders who spoke or acted religiously beyond narrow community norms, as we see in the case of Margery Kempe. The 1409 Constitutions enacted under Archbishop Thomas Arundel officially restricted preaching, writing, or translation in English. All these activities had to be licensed by a bishop or his council. Mere possession of some vernacular books, including the Bible, was a ground for arrest and examination. Rumor too could lead to ecclesiastical inquiry, as happened repeatedly to Margery Kempe.

Archbishop Arundel and the church did not oppose all religious reading in the vernacular, however. For instance, Arundel patronized the translation (by Nicholas Love) of a long tract of meditations on the life of Christ. This was a form of meditation recommended to laypeople because knowing the story of Christ's life did not require direct knowledge of the Bible, nor did it involve questions of doctrine or the institutional church. Nonetheless, popular Lollardy continued through the end of the Middle Ages, and over 240 medieval copies of the Wycliffite Bible survive, more than any other Middle English text.

Crucifixion Scene, from a manuscript of Michael de Massa's *On the Passion of Our Lord*, 1405. This illumination is found at the beginning of a narrative of the Passion written in Latin and Middle English. Delicate yet emotive, it evokes much of the "affective spirituality" of its era. The drawing is in pale brown ink and wash, which only renders more emphatic and disturbing the bright red of Christ's elaborately detailed wounds. The weeping Virgin Mary sways, nearly fainting, while Mary Magdalene kneels and clutches Christ's legs. Even the angels look down in sorrow, though the men at right are more restrained. Late-medieval worshipers were encouraged to imagine themselves as if present at such scenes of high pathos. Here, the author of the text, Michael de Massa, is depicted among the witnesses of Christ's suffering; the scroll hanging from his desk contains the first words of his book: *Angeli pacis. . . .*

from The Wycliffite Bible
John 10.11–18[1]

I am a good shepherd. A good shepherd giveth his life for his sheep. But a hired hyne,[2] and that is not the shepherd, whose are not the sheep his own,[3] seeth a wolf coming, and he leaveth the sheep and fleeth, and the wolf ravisheth and disparpleth[4] the sheep. And the hired hyne fleeth for he is an hired hyne, and it pertaineth not to him of the sheep. I am a good shepherd and I know my sheep and my sheep know me, as the father hath known me and I know the father, and I put[5] my life for my sheep. I have other sheep that are not of this fold; and it behoveth me to bring them together; and they shall hear my voice, and it shall be made one fold and one shepherd. Therefore the father loveth me for I put my life that eftsoon[6] I take it. No man takith it from me, but I put it of myself; I have power to put it, and I have power to take it again. This commandment I have taken of my father.

from A Wycliffite Sermon on John 10.11–18[1]

Ego sum pastor bonus. Johannis X[2]

Christ telleth in his gospel the manners of a good herd,[3] so that hereby we may wit[4] how our herds fail now. And default of such herds is most peril in the church for, as right office of them should most bring men to heaven, so default in this office draweth men most to hell. Christ telleth of himself how *he is a good herd*. For he is the best herd that mankind may have, for he is good by himself and may no way fail, for he is both God and man, and God may no way sin. And thus we have the measure to know a good herd and an evil, for the more that a herd is like to Christ he is the better, and the more that he straungeth[5] from him he is the worse in this office.

And eft,[6] when Christ hath given the measure to know good herds, he telleth the highest property that falleth to a good herd: *a good herd*, as Christ saith, *putteth his life for his sheep*, for more charity may none have than to put his life for his friends, and, if he worketh wisely, for to bring these sheep to heaven, for thus the herd hath most pain and the sheep most profit. Thus may we see who is a good herd and who faileth in this office. For as Christ putteth wisely his own life for his sheep, so Antichrist putteth proudly many lives for his foul life; as, if the fiend led the pope to kill many thousand men to hold his worldly state, he sued[7] Antichrist's manners. * * *

And thus seem our religious[8] to be exempt from charity, for, need a man never so much to have help of such goods, yea if they[9] have stones or jewels that harm them, they will not give such goods nor their value to help their brethren, nor cease to

---

1. The process that resulted in the "Wycliffite" Bible is complex and still unclear. The translation was the work of followers of Wycliffite ideas, but Wyclif himself did not participate in it. It was also a huge and well-organized undertaking, that involved study of the Latin original aided by learned commentaries. The later and more colloquial version is given here. We have modernized spellings but altered vocabulary as little as possible, to retain the syntax and rhythms of the original Middle English.
2. Servant.
3. An awkward construction, derived from close adherence to the Latin.
4. Seizes and scatters.

5. Lay down, commit.
6. Another time.
1. Dating from the later 14th century, this is only one sermon from a huge sermon cycle produced in connection with the Wycliffite Bible. Note the rhetorically effective use of alliteration in parts of the sermon.
2. I am a good shepherd (Latin). John 10.
3. Shepherd, priest.
4. Know.
5. Differs.
6. Again.
7. He (the pope) followed, imitated.
8. Clerics.
9. I.e., the clerics.

annoy[1] themselves in building of high houses, nor to gather such vain goods if it do harm to their brethren. Such avaricious men are far from manners of a good herd. And so these new religious[2] that the fiend hath tolled[3] in, by color to help the former herds, harm them many gates,[4] and letten[5] this office in the church, for true preaching and worldly goods are spoiled by such religious. And therefore teacheth Christ to flee them, for they are ravishing wolves: some will as briars tear the wool of sheep and make them cold in charity, and some will sturdily as thorns slay the sheep of holy church.

And thus is our mother shend[6] for default of man's help. And more meed[7] might no man have than to help this sorry widow, for princes of priests and Pharisees that called Christ a beguiler croched[8] to themselves the choosing of many herds in the church, and they are taught by Antichrist to choose his herds and not Christ's. And thus faileth Christ's church. Lord, since herds should pass[9] their sheep as men pass bleating sheep, how should Christ's church fare if these herds were turned to wolves? But Christ saith thus it fareth among the herds of the church, that many of them *are hired hynes and not herds over the sheep, for the sheep are not their own*, and so they love too little the sheep. For, if they have their temporal hire,[1] they reckon not how their flock fare. And thus do all these curates that tell more by[2] worldly winning than by virtues of their subjects or soul's heal[3] to come to heaven.

Such are not herds of sheep but of the dung and wool of them, and these shall not have in heaven joy of the sheep that they keep. *Such hynes see wolves coming to flocks that they should keep, and they flee* for dread of nought. *And these wolves ravish these sheep and scatter them* for this end, that then they may sooner perish. And this moved Paul to found no order,[4] for Christ's order is enough, and then should all Christian men be more surely in one flock. Lord, if cowardice of such hynes be damned of Christ, how much more should wolves be damned that are put to keep Christ's sheep! But Christ saith a clean[5] cause why *this hired hyne fleeth* thus: *for he is an hired hyne and the sheep pertain not to him*, but the dung of such sheep and this dung sufficeth to him, however the sheep fare. Some are wolves without, and some are wolves within and these are more perilous, for homely[6] enemies are the worst. * * *

But *Christ saith he is a good herd and knoweth his sheep and they him*, for the office that falleth to herds maketh him known among them. *As my father knoweth me and I again know my father, so*, saith Christ, *I put my life to keep my sheep* against wolves. And as this knowing might not quench[7] betwixt Christ and his father, so should these herds watch upon their sheep, and they should know him, not by bodily feasts nor other signs[8] that he doth, but by three offices of a herd that Christ hath limited[9] to him. It falleth to a good herd to lead his sheep in wholesome pastures, and when his sheep are hurt or scabbed to heal them and grease them, and when other evil beasts assail them then help them. And hereto should he put his life to save his sheep from such beasts. The pasture is God's law that evermore is green in truth, and rotten pastures are other laws and other fables without ground. And cowardice of such herds that dare not defend God's law witnesseth that they fail in two offices suing[1] after: for

1. Trouble, injure.
2. Friars.
3. Lured.
4. In many ways.
5. Hinder.
6. Ruined.
7. Reward.
8. Seized.
9. Surpass.

1. Wages.
2. Consider more important.
3. Their salvation.
4. I.e., no religious order such as monks or friars.
5. Simple.
6. Familiar.
7. Be extinguished.
8. I.e., liturgical rituals.
9. Assigned.

he that dare not, for world's dread, defend the law of his God, how should he defend his sheep for love that he hath to them? And if they bring in new laws contrary to God's law, how should they not fail after in other offices that they should have?

But Christ that is head of herds saith that *he hath other sheep that are not yet of this flock, and them must he bring together and teach them to know his voice. And so shall there be one flock and one herd* over them all. These sheep are heathen men or Jews that Christ will convert, for all these shall make one flock, the which flock is holy church—but far from this understanding that all men shall be converted.[2]

[END OF VERNICULAR RELIGION]

❖ ⚬⬦⚬ ❖

Margery Kempe
c. 1373–after 1439

Margery Kempe's religious life—its temptations, visions, ecstasies, and pilgrimages—was unusual in intensity, but not in kind, for her time. She was very much in the mainstream of later medieval affective piety. What gained Margery both admiration and contempt, to the extent of endangering her life, was her drive to express these experiences publicly and have them acknowledged within an official hierarchy that had very little place for her. *The Book of Margery Kempe* is only one aspect of a lifetime of religious performance—from "holy conversation" and the vexed dictation of her book, through the kinds of bodily gestures, weeping, and roaring that Margery knew to be almost theatrical in their impact.

The daughter of a mayor in the prosperous market town of Lynn, Margery began her adult life quite traditionally, married to the burger John Kempe. The mental and religious crisis following the birth of her first child inspired her to pursue a holier form of life. To create this mixed life of secular marriage and sacred quest, Margery Kempe had to struggle and negotiate with a hierarchy of male authority. By canon law, her husband could demand the rights of the marriage bed, and did so for many years. She approached her local confessors for permission to undertake pilgrimages. Only a bishop could allow the weekly Eucharist for which Margery yearned, or officially approve her wearing white clothes. Hostile officials and clerics at all levels repeatedly attempted to misrepresent or silence her. She depended on male readers for her knowledge of other mystics, and on a sequence of recalcitrant male amanuenses for the very writing of her book.

Kempe's activities enraged political and ecclesiastical authorities, alienated her fellow pilgrims, and angered people at home. Yet those same activities gained her many admirers, increasingly among common laypeople. Her weeping and noisy mourning for the sufferings of Christ intruded upon daily life and often interrupted religious ceremonies. Just as daringly in the anxious and repressive religious climate of her day, Kempe spoke about her experiences without clerical mediation, and defended herself effectively before the highest clerics in England, including the Archbishop of York. She did not even hesitate to criticize them. She was repeatedly accused and taken into custody as a Lollard heretic, although she was doctrinally quite conservative (almost radically orthodox), as she ably and repeatedly proved under hostile examination.

Along with this pattern of negotiation and striving with a largely male ecclesiastical establishment, Kempe engaged more quietly with a network of female religious. She knew she had predecessors among married women who experienced visions and moved into a holy life while still living in the secular world. She specifically mentions "Saint Bride"—Bridget of

---

1. Following.

2. The preacher does not agree with the opinion that all mankind will convert.

Sweden (c. 1303–1373), who like Margery had many children and took up the holy life (once widowed), traveled to Rome and Jerusalem, and engaged in prophecy. Margery may also have known about the Blessed Angela of Foligno (1248–1309), whose temptations, weeping, and conversations with Christ are similar to Margery's own. She records a visit and long conversation with the mystic and anchoress Julian of Norwich. During her arrest by agents of the Duke of Bedford, local women sympathize with Margery, bring her wine, and listen to her religious discourse. Indeed, it seems that the Duke had Margery arrested because he suspected her of having encouraged a woman cousin to leave her own husband and pursue a religious life.

It is possible, though, to exaggerate Kempe's struggle with male power, secular and ecclesiastical. She was warmly supported by a number of holy men including the bishop of Lincoln. She met the Archbishop of Canterbury and gained at least his qualified approval. For all the conflicts within her marriage, Margery often expressed a wry and affectionate sense of John Kempe's indulgence, and sympathy for his weakness. Indeed, when John became ill and senile in later years, Margery suspended her life of prayer and returned to their home to care for him. Much of the domestic imagery of the *Book* derives from this fractious but loving relationship with her husband.

Perhaps the most appealing aspects of Kempe's religious imagery derive in fact from urban and domestic life. Money is a constant hindrance to her ambitions, and figures in her conversations with Christ. Her understanding of mystical language is often highly literal. If Jesus becomes her mystic lover, he does so very much as a husband, inviting her embraces; and when Kempe has a vision of Christ's birth she bustles about like a midwife. Her concentration on the Eucharist is continuous with her experience of meals (and fasting) within the family and in society. Indeed, a long negotiation with her husband, crucial to Margery's pursuit of chastity, centers upon the heat and thirst of travel, a cake and a bottle of beer. The humble meal that caps their agreement has clear eucharistic implications. Whatever the spectacle of her religious expression, and the struggle to maintain and record it, Margery Kempe's religion and sense of her own limits are grounded in the very life she was eager to abjure.

from The Book of Margery Kempe[1]
The Preface

A short treatise of a creature set in great pomp and pride of the world, who later was drawn to our Lord by great poverty, sickness, shame, and great reproofs in many diverse countries and places, of which tribulations some shall be shown hereafter, not in the order in which they befell, but as the creature could remember them when they were written.

For it was twenty years and more from the time when this creature had forsaken the world and busily cleaved to our Lord before this book was written, notwithstanding that this creature had much advice to have her tribulations and her feelings written down, and a White Friar[2] freely offered to write for her if she wished. And she was warned in her spirit that she should not write so soon. And many years later she was bidden in her spirit to write.

And then it was written first by a man who could neither write English nor German well, so that it could not be read except by special grace alone, for there was so much obloquy and slander of this creature that few men would believe her.

And so at last a priest was greatly moved to write this treatise, and he could not read it for four years together. And afterwards, at the request of this creature, and

---

1. Translated by B. A. Windeatt.   2. Alan of Lynne, a Carmelite.

compelled by his own conscience, he tried again to read it, and it was much easier than it was before. And so he began to write in the year of our Lord 1436, on the next day after Mary Magdalene,[3] after the information of this creature.

[MEETING WITH BISHOP OF LINCOLN AND ARCHBISHOP OF CANTERBURY]
CHAPTER 15

This creature, when our Lord had forgiven her her sin (as has been written before), had a desire to see those places where he was born, and where he suffered his Passion and where he died, together with other holy places where he was during his life, and also after his resurrection.

While she was feeling these desires, our Lord commanded her in her mind—two years before she went[1]—that she should go to Rome, to Jerusalem, and to Santiago de Compostela, and she would gladly have gone, but she had no money to go with.

And then she said to our Lord, "Where shall I get the money to go to these holy places with?"

Our Lord replied to her, "I shall send you enough friends in different parts of England to help you. And, daughter, I shall go with you in every country and provide for you. I shall lead you there and bring you back again in safety, and no Englishman shall die in the ship that you are in. I shall keep you from all wicked men's power. And, daughter, I say to you that I want you to wear white clothes and no other color, for you shall dress according to my will."[2]

"Ah, dear Lord, if I go around dressed differently from how other chaste women dress, I fear people will slander me. They will say I am a hypocrite and ridicule me."

"Yes, daughter, the more ridicule that you have for love of me, the more you please me."

Then this creature dared not do otherwise than as she was commanded in her soul. And so she set off on her travels with her husband, for he was always a good and easygoing man with her. Although he sometimes—out of groundless fear—left her on her own for a while, yet he always came back to her again, and felt sorry for her, and spoke up for her as much as he dared for fear of other people. But all others that went along with her forsook her, and they most falsely accused her—through temptation of the devil—of things that she was never guilty of.

And so did one man in whom she greatly trusted, and who offered to travel with her, at which she was very pleased, believing he would give her support and help her when she needed it, for he had been staying a long time with an anchorite, a doctor of divinity and a holy man, and that anchorite was this woman's confessor.

And so his servant—at his own inward stirring—took his leave to travel with this creature; and her own maidservant went with her too, for as long as things went well with them and nobody said anything against them.

But as soon as people—through the enticing of our spiritual enemy, and by permission of our Lord—spoke against this creature because she wept so grievously, and said she was a false hypocrite and deceived people, and threatened her with burning, then this man, who was held to be so holy, and in whom she trusted so much, rebuked her with the utmost force and scorned her most foully, and would not go any further with her. Her maidservant, seeing discomfort on every side, grew obstreperous

3. July 23.
1. Probably 1411.

2. White dress implied special holiness or virginity.

with her mistress. She would not do as she was told, or follow her mistress's advice. She let her mistress go alone into many fine towns and would not go with her.

And always, her husband was ready when everybody else let her down, and he went with her where our Lord would send her, always believing that all was for the best, and would end well when God willed.

And at this time, he took her to speak with the Bishop of Lincoln, who was called Philip,[3] and they stayed for three weeks before they could speak to him, for he was not at home at his palace. When the Bishop came home, and heard tell of how such a woman had waited so long to speak to him, he then sent for her in great haste to find out what she wanted. And then she came into his presence and greeted him, and he warmly welcomed her and said he had long wanted to speak with her, and he was very glad she had come. And so she asked him if she might speak with him in private and confide in him the secrets of her soul, and he appointed a convenient time for this.

When the time came, she told him all about her meditations and high contemplations, and other secret things, both of the living and the dead, as our Lord revealed to her soul.[4] He was very glad to hear them, and graciously allowed her to say what she pleased, and greatly commended her feelings and her contemplations, saying they were high matters and most devout matters, and inspired by the Holy Ghost, advising her seriously that her feelings should be written down.

And she said that it was not God's will that they should be written so soon, nor were they written for twenty years afterwards and more.

And then she said furthermore, "My Lord, if it please you, I am commanded in my soul that you shall give me the mantle and the ring, and clothe me all in white clothes. And if you clothe me on earth, our Lord Jesus Christ shall clothe you in heaven, as I understand through revelation."[5]

Then the Bishop said to her, "I will fulfill your desire if your husband will consent to it."

Then she said to the Bishop, "I pray you, let my husband come into your presence, and you shall hear what he will say."

And so her husband came before the Bishop, and the Bishop asked him, "John, is it your will that your wife shall take the mantle and the ring and that you live chaste, the two of you?"

"Yes, my lord," he said, "and in token that we both vow to live chaste I here offer my hands into yours," and he put his hands between the Bishop's hands.

And the Bishop did no more with us on that day, except that he treated us very warmly and said we were most welcome.[6] * * *

CHAPTER 16

Then this creature went on to London with her husband, to Lambeth,[7] where the Archbishop was in residence at that time. And as they came into the hall in the afternoon, there were many of the Archbishop's clerks about and other heedless men,

---

3. Philip Repyngdon, Bishop of Lincoln 1405–1419. This journey occurred after their private agreement of chastity in June 1413.
4. Margery had some prophetic visions, though on a smaller scale than those of her predecessor St. Bridget of Sweden.
5. By clothing her, the Bishop would acknowledge Margery and John's vow of chastity. In the Book of Revelation, the saints in heaven are clothed in white robes.

6. The Bishop instructs Margery to approach the Archbishop of Canterbury, England's highest prelate, and obtain his permission to receive the mantle and ring. She agrees to go but says she will not ask the Archbishop for that particular gift.
7. Lambeth Palace was (and is) the Archbishop's home nearest London.

both squires and yeomen, who swore many great oaths and spoke many thoughtless words, and this creature boldly rebuked them, and said they would be damned unless they left off their swearing and the other sins they practised.[8]

And with that there came forward a woman of that town dressed in a pilch[9] who reviled this creature, cursed her, and said very maliciously to her in this way: "I wish you were in Smithfield,[1] and I would bring a bundle of sticks to burn you with—it is a pity that you are alive."

This creature stood still and did not answer, and her husband endured it with great pain and was very sorry to hear his wife so rebuked.

Then the Archbishop sent for this creature to come to him in his garden.[2] When she came into his presence she made her obeisances to him as best she could, praying him, out of his gracious lordship, to grant her authority to choose her confessor and to receive communion every Sunday—if God would dispose her to this—under his letter and his seal throughout all his province. And he granted her with great kindness her whole desire without any silver or gold, nor would he let his clerks take anything for the writing or sealing of the letter.

When this creature found this grace in his sight, she was much comforted and strengthened in her soul, and so she told this worshipful lord about her manner of life, and such grace as God wrought in her mind and in her soul, in order to discover what he would say about it, and if he found any fault with either her contemplation or her weeping.

And she also told him the cause of her weeping, and the manner in which our Lord conversed with her soul. And he did not find fault at all, but approved her manner of life, and was very glad that our merciful Lord Christ Jesus showed such grace in our times—blessed may he be.

Then this creature spoke to him boldly about the correction of his household, saying with reverence, "My lord, our Lord of all, Almighty God, has not given you your benefice and great worldly wealth in order to maintain those who are traitors to him, and those who slay him every day by the swearing of great oaths. You shall answer for them, unless you correct them or else put them out of your service."

In the most meek and kindly way he allowed her to say what was on her mind and gave her a handsome answer, she supposing that things would then be better. And so their conversation continued until stars appeared in the sky. Then she took her leave, and her husband too.

Afterwards they went back to London, and many worthy men wanted to hear her converse, for her conversation was so much to do with the love of God that those who heard it were often moved to weep very sadly.

And so she had a very warm welcome there—and her husband because of her— for as long as they wished to stay in the city. Afterwards they returned to Lynn, and then this creature went to the anchorite at the Preaching Friars in Lynn and told him how she had been received, and how she had got on while she was travelling round the country. And he was very pleased at her homecoming and held it to be a great miracle, her coming and going to and fro.

And he said to her: "I have heard much evil talk of you since you went away, and I have been strongly advised to leave you and not to associate with you any more,

8. Margery frequently reproaches people for swearing.
9. A garment of animal skin with the hair still on it.
1. This is not an idle threat. Lollard heretics were put to death in Margery's lifetime, beginning in 1401 when

William Sawtry (formerly a priest at Lynn) was burned at Smithfield outside London.
2. Thomas Arundel (Archbishop of Canterbury 1396–1414) was a vigorous opponent of Lollards.

and great friendships are promised me on condition that I give you up. And I answered for you in this way: 'If you were still the same as you were when we parted, I certainly dared say you were a good woman, a lover of God, and highly inspired with the Holy Ghost. I will not forsake her for any lady in this realm, if speaking with the lady means leaving her, for I would rather leave the lady and speak with Margery, if I might not do both, than do the contrary.'" (Read first the twenty-first chapter and then this chapter after that.)

[VISIT WITH JULIAN OF NORWICH]
CHAPTER 17

One day long before this time, while this creature was bearing children and was newly delivered of a child, our Lord Christ Jesus said to her that she should bear no more children, and therefore he commanded her to go to Norwich. * * *

CHAPTER 18

This creature was charged and commanded in her soul that she should go to a White Friar in the same city of Norwich, who was called William Southfield, a good man who lived a holy life, to reveal to him the grace that God had wrought in her, as she had done to the good Vicar before. She did as she was commanded and came to the friar one morning, and was with him in a chapel for a long time, and told him her meditations and what God had wrought in her soul, in order to know if she were deceived by any delusions or not.[3]

This good man, the White Friar, all the time that she told him of her feelings, held up his hands and said, "Jesus, mercy, and thanks be to Jesus."

"Sister," he said, "have no fear about your manner of life, for it is the Holy Ghost plentifully working his grace in your soul. Thank him highly of his goodness, for we are all bound to thank him for you, who now in our times inspires you with his grace, to the help and comfort of all of us who are supported by your prayers and by others such as you. And we are preserved from many misfortunes and troubles which we should deservedly suffer for our trespasses, were there not such good creatures among us. Blessed be Almighty God for his goodness.

"And therefore, sister, I advise you to dispose yourself to receive the gifts of God as lowly and meekly as you can, and put up no obstacle or objections against the goodness of the Holy Ghost, for he may give his gifts where he will, and the unworthy he makes worthy, the sinful he makes righteous. His mercy is always ready for us unless the fault be in ourselves, for he does not dwell in a body subject to sin. He flies from all false pretense and falsehood; he asks of us a low, a meek, and a contrite heart, with a good will.[4] Our Lord says himself, 'My spirit shall rest upon a meek man, a contrite man, and one who fears my words.'[5]

"Sister, I trust to our Lord that you have these conditions either in your will or in your affections or else in both, and I do not consider that our Lord allows to be endlessly deceived those who place their trust in him, and seek and desire nothing but him only, as I hope you do. And therefore believe fully that our Lord loves you and is

---

3. Southfield was a Carmelite friar who received visions of the Virgin Mary. Many mystical texts warn against the possibility that visions may be of demonic origin; see selections from *The Cloud of Unknowing*.

4. Psalm 51.17.
5. Isaiah 66.2.

working his grace in you. I pray God increase it and continue it to his everlasting worship, for his mercy."

The said creature was much comforted both in body and in soul by this good man's words, and greatly strengthened in her faith.

And then she was commanded by our Lord to go to an anchoress in the same city who was called Dame Julian.[6] And so she did, and told her about the grace, that God had put into her soul, of compunction, contrition, sweetness and devotion, compassion with holy meditation and high contemplation, and very many holy speeches and converse that our Lord spoke to her soul, and also many wonderful revelations, which she described to the anchoress to find out if there were any deception in them, for the anchoress was expert in such things and could give good advice.

The anchoress, hearing the marvelous goodness of our Lord, highly thanked God with all her heart for his visitation, advising this creature to be obedient to the will of our Lord and fulfill with all her might whatever he put into her soul, if it were not against the worship of God and the profit of her fellow Christians.[7] For if it were, then it were not the influence of a good spirit, but rather of an evil spirit. "The Holy Ghost never urges a thing against charity, and if he did, he would be contrary to his own self, for he is all charity. Also he moves a soul to all chasteness, for chaste livers are called the temple of the Holy Ghost,[8] and the Holy Ghost makes a soul stable and steadfast in the right faith and the right belief.

"And a double man in soul is always unstable and unsteadfast in all his ways.[9] He that is forever doubting is like the wave of the sea which is moved and borne about with the wind, and that man is not likely to receive the gifts of God.[1]

"Any creature that has these tokens may steadfastly believe that the Holy Ghost dwells in his soul. And much more, when God visits a creature with tears of contrition, devotion or compassion, he may and ought to believe that the Holy Ghost is in his soul. Saint Paul says that the Holy Ghost asks for us with mourning and weeping unspeakable;[2] that is to say, he causes us to ask and pray with mourning and weeping so plentifully that the tears may not be numbered. No evil spirit may give these tokens, for Saint Jerome says that tears torment the devil more than do the pains of hell. God and the devil are always at odds, and they shall never dwell together in one place, and the devil has no power in a man's soul.

"Holy Writ says that the soul of a righteous man is the seat of God,[3] and so I trust, sister, that you are. I pray God grant you perseverance. Set all your trust in God and do not fear the talk of the world, for the more contempt, shame and reproof that you have in this world, the more is your merit in the sight of God.[4] Patience is necessary for you, for in that shall you keep your soul."[5]

Great was the holy conversation that the anchoress and this creature had through talking of the love of our Lord Jesus Christ for the many days that they were together.

This creature revealed her manner of life to many a worthy clerk, to honored doctors of divinity, both religious men and others of secular habit, and they said that

---

6. Julian of Norwich.

7. This concern with the whole community of the faithful, a new note in Kempe's book, is highly characteristic of Julian's spirituality.

8. 1 Corinthians 6.19. The density of biblical reference in this passage suggests not only Dame Julian's learning but also Kempe's powerful memory for Scripture and theology. It is important that such biblical justification comes to

Kempe through another holy woman.

9. James 1.8.

1. James 1.6–7.

2. Romans 8.26.

3. 2 Corinthians 6.16, Revelation 21.3.

4. Luke 6.22–23.

5. Luke 21.19.

God wrought great grace in her and bade her not to be afraid—there was no delusion in her manner of living. They counseled her to be persevering, for their greatest fear was that she would turn aside and not keep her perfection. She had so many enemies and so much slander, that it seemed to them that she might not bear it without great grace and a mighty faith. * * *

Middle English Lyrics

Although many Middle English lyrics have a beguilingly fresh and unselfconscious tone, they owe much to learned and sophisticated continental sources—the medieval Latin lyrics of the "Goliard poets" and the Provençal and French lyrics of the Troubadours and Trouvères. Most authors were clerics, aware of the similarities between earthly and divine love, and fond of punning in Latin or English.

The anonymity of the Middle English lyrics prevents us from seeing them as part of a single poet's *oeuvre*, as we can, for instance, with the poems of Chaucer and Dunbar. Rather, we must rely on more general contexts, such as genre, to establish relationships among poems. One of the most popular genres among the secular lyrics was the *reverdie*, a poem celebrating the return of spring. The early thirteenth-century *Cuckoo Song* ("Sumer is icumen in") joyfully invokes the bird's song, and revels in the blossoming of the countryside and the calls of the animals to their young. A more typical example of the *reverdie* is *Alisoun*, whose male speaker ruefully contrasts the burgeoning of nature with the stinginess of his beloved.

Frustration was not the only attitude in Middle English love lyrics, however. A stance more boasting than adoring or despairing is taken in the witty lyric *I Have a Noble Cock*. Furthermore, clerical misogyny is expressed in *Abuse of Women*, which ostensibly praises women by absolving them of the vices—gossip, infidelity, shrewishness—typically attributed to them in satires against women; yet the refrain first praises women as the best of creatures but then undercuts this claim in Latin, which few women would have been able to understand.

The majority of Middle English lyrics were not secular but religious. Songs in praise of the Virgin Mary or Christ, however, employ the same erotic language as the secular lyrics, often in conjunction with typological figures linking events in the Old Testament to those in the New. In *Adam Lay Ibounden*, for instance, the poet follows a statement of the "fortunate Fall"—that Adam's sin was necessary to permit Christ's redemption— with a courtly compliment to the Virgin Mary. Similarly, *I Sing of a Maiden* draws on the typological significance of Gideon's fleece in Judges 6 (the soaking of the fleece by dew figuring Mary's impregnation by the Holy Spirit) while also employing the courtly imagery of a poet "singing of a maiden" who "chooses" Christ as her son, as if he were a lover. In a much longer poem in praise of the Virgin, the poet—casting himself as Mary's "knight" caught in the bonds of love—begs her mercy and also compliments her by contrasting her with her antitype, Eve.

Occasionally the Middle English religious lyric uses secular motifs and genres in a way that approaches parody. For instance, the second stanza of the Nativity poem *Mary Is with Child* resembles a pregnancy lament by a young girl. Mary, however, explains that her condition will be a source of joy rather than shame, when she will sing a lullaby to her "darling." This Middle English poet, far from blaspheming, was trying to humanize the mystery of the Nativity and relate it to daily life.

Other religious poems either celebrate Christ or reject the world. The poems to Christ, in their tenderness and immediacy, resemble those to Mary. Poets used erotic language in poems to Christ as well as those to Mary, as in *Jesus, My Sweet Lover*. Finally, in a different vein, the *Contempt of the World* questions the values of courtly life, with the "*ubi sunt*" ("where are") motif. "Where beth they biforen us weren?" it asks, evoking the lovely women who enjoyed their paradise on earth and now suffer the eternal fires of hell.

The Cuckoo Song

Sumer is icumen in,°	*spring has come in*
Lhude° sing, cuccu!°	*loudly / cuckoo*
Groweth sed° and bloweth° med°	*seed / blooms / meadow*
And springth° the wude° nu.°	*grows / forest / now*
5 Sing, cuccu!	
Awe° bleteth after lomb,	*ewe*
Lhouth° after calve° cu,°	*lows / calf / cow*
Bulluc sterteth,° bucke ferteth.°	*leaps / farts*
Murie° sing, cuccu!	*merrily*
10 Cuccu, cuccu,	
Wel singes thu, cuccu.	
Ne swik° thu naver° nu!	*cease / never*
Sing cuccu nu, sing cuccu!	
Sing cuccu, sing cuccu nu!	

This page contains the words and music to one of the earliest and best loved of Middle English lyrics, *The Cuckoo Song* ("Sumer is icumen in"). The lyric is a *reverdie*, or spring song, but its joyful description of nature's rebirth is given a more sober allegorical interpretation by the interlinear Latin gloss, apparently to be sung to the same tune. The gloss parallels the lyric's celebration of the reawakening landscape with an account of the "heavenly farmer" (*celicus agricola*) whom "rot on the vine" (*vitis vicio*) leads to sacrifice his Son. The fact that the manuscript was copied at a monastery reminds us that this song, like much other early English secular poetry, survives only because it was seen to have religious relevance.

Alisoun

	Bitwene Mersh° and Averil°	*March / April*
	When spray° biginneth to springe,°	*twig / grow*
	The lutel° fowl° hath hire° will	*little / bird / her*
	On° hire lud° to singe.	*in / language*
5	Ich° libbe° in love-longinge	*I / live*
	For semlokest° of alle thinge:	*fairest*
	He° may me blisse bringe;	*she*
	Ich° am in hire baundoun.°	*I / power*
	An hendy hap ich habbe ihent!¹	
10	Ichot° from hevene it is me sent;	*I know*
	From alle wimmen my love is lent,°	*taken away*
	And light° on Alisoun.²	*settled*
	On hew° hire her° is fair inogh,	*color / hair*
	Hire browe browne, hire eye blake;	
15	With lossum chere he on me logh,³	
	With middel° small and well imake.°	*waist / made*
	Bote° he me wolle° to hire take	*unless / will*
	For to ben hire° owen° make,°	*her / own / mate*
	Longe to liven ichulle° forsake,°	*I will / refuse*
20	And feye° fallen adoun.	*doomed*
	An hendy hap ich habbe ihent!	
	Ichot from hevene it is me sent;	
	From alle wimmen my love is lent,	
	And light on Alisoun.	
25	Nightes° when I wende° and wake—	*at night / turn*
	Forthy min wonges waxeth won⁴—	
	Levedy,° all for thine sake	*lady*
	Longinge is ilent° me on.	*come*
	In world nis non so witer° mon	*wise*
30	That all hire° bounte° telle con:	*her / excellence*
	Hire swire° is whittore° then the swon,	*neck / whiter*
	And feirest may° in toune.	*maiden*
	An hendy hap ich habbe ihent!	
	Ichot from hevene it is me sent;	
35	From alle wimmen my love is lent,	
	And light on Alisoun.	
	Ich am for wowing all forwake,⁵	
	Wery so water in wore⁶	
	Lest eny reve° me my make°	*steal / mate*
40	Ich habbe iyerned yore.⁷	

1. A fair destiny I have received.
2. Alison is a stock name for a country woman, shared by the wife in Chaucer's *Miller's Tale* and by his Wife of Bath.
3. With lovely manner she laughed at me.
4. Therefore my cheeks become pale.
5. I am for wooing all sleepless.
6. Weary as water in a troubled pool.
7. (For whom) I have long yearned.

Betere is tholien while sore[8]
Then mournen evermore.
Geynest° under gore,°   *kindest / petticoat*
Herkne to my roun!°   *song*
45   *An hendy hap ich habbe ihent!*
    Ichot from hevene it is me sent;
    From alle wimmen my love is lent,
    And light on Alisoun.

I Have a Noble Cock

I have a gentil° cok,   *noble*
   Croweth° me day;   *who crows*
He doth° me risen erly,   *makes*
   My matins for to say.

5   I have a gentil cok,
   Comen he is of gret;°   *a great family*
His comb is of red corel,
   His tayel is of jet.

   I have a gentil cok,
10   Comen he is of kinde;°   *good lineage*
His comb is of red corel,
   His tail is of inde.°   *indigo*

His legges ben of asor,°   *azure*
   So gentil and so smale;
15   His spores° arn of silver white,   *spurs*
   Into the worte-wale.°   *root of cock's spur*

His eynen° arn of cristal,   *eyes*
   Loken° all in aumber;   *set*
And every night he percheth him
20   In min ladyes chaumber.

Abuse of Women

   Of all creatures women be best:
   Cuius contrarium verum est.[1]

In every place ye may well see
That women be trewe as tirtil° on tree,   *turtledove*
5   Not liberal° in langage, but ever in secree,°   *licentious / secrecy*
And gret joye amonge them is for to be.

   Of all creatures women be best:
   Cuius contrarium verum est.

---

8. It is better to suffer sorely for a time.   1. Latin for "The opposite of this is true."

The stedfastnes of women will never be don,
10 So jentil, so curtes they be everychon,[2]
Meke as a lambe, still as a stone,
Croked° nor crabbed find ye none!   *perverse*

    Of all creatures women be best:
    Cuius contrarium verum est.

15 Men be more cumbers° a thousand fold,   *troublesome*
And I mervail how they dare be so bold
Against women for to hold,
Seeing them so pacient, softe, and cold.

    Of all creatures women be best:
20 *Cuius contrarium verum est.*

For tell a woman all your counsaile,
And she can kepe it wonderly well;
She had lever go quik° to hell,   *alive*
Than to her neighbour she wold it tell!

25   *Of all creatures women be best:*
    Cuius contrarium verum est.

For by women men be reconsiled,
For by women was never man begiled,
For they be of the condicion of curtes Grisell,[3]
30 For they be so meke and milde.

    Of all creatures women be best:
    Cuius contrarium verum est.

Now say well by° women or elles be still,   *about*
For they never displesed man by ther will;
35 To be angry or wroth they can° no skill,   *have*
For I dare say they think non ill.

    Of all creatures women be best:
    Cuius contrarium verum est.

Trow° ye that women list° to smater,°   *think / like / chatter*
40 Or against ther husbondes for to clater?
Nay, they had lever° fast bred and water,   *rather*
Then for to dele in suche a mater.

    Of all creatures women be best:
    Cuius contrarium verum est.

45 Though all the paciens in the world were drownd,
And non were lefte here on the ground,
Again in a woman it might be found,
Suche vertu in them dothe abound!

---

2. So well-bred, so courteous is each one.
3. Griselda, the long-suffering wife of Chaucer's *Clerk's*   *Tale;* the tale ends with the observation that there are no more Griseldas left.

Of all creatures women be best:
50   *Cuius contrarium verum est.*

To the tavern they will not go,
Nor to the alehous never the mo,°   *more*
For, God wot,° ther hartes wold be wo, knows   *knows*
To spende ther husbondes money so.

55   *Of all creatures women be best:*
Cuius contrarium verum est.

If here were a woman or a maid,
That list for to go freshely arayed,
Or with fine kirchers° to go displayed,   *kerchiefs*
60   Ye wold say, "They be proude": it is ill said.

Of all creatures women be best:
Cuius contrarium verum est.

Adam Lay Ibounden

Adam lay ibounden,°   *bound*
Bounden in a bond;
Foure thousand winter
Thowt° he not too long.   *thought*
5   And all was for an appil,
An appil that he took,
As clerkes finden wreten
In here° book.   *their*
Ne hadde° the appil take° ben,   *had not / taken*
10   The appil taken ben,
Ne° hadde never our lady   *not*
A ben hevene quen.[1]
Blissed be the time
That appil take was!
15   Therfore we moun° singen   *may*
"Deo gracias!"°   *Thanks be to God!*

I Sing of a Maiden

I sing of a maiden
That is makeles,[1]
King of alle kinges
To° here° sone she ches.°   *for / her / chose*

5   He cam also° stille°   *as / quietly*
Ther° his moder was   *where*
As dew in Aprille
That falleth on the gras.

---

1. Have been heaven's queen.   1. Spotless, matchless, and mateless.

He cam also stille
10   To his moderes bowr
As dew in Aprille
That falleth on the flour.

He cam also stille
Ther his moder lay
15   As dew in Aprille
That falleth on the spray.°   *twigs*

Moder and maiden
Was never non but she:
Well may swich° a lady   *such*
20   Godes moder be.

In Praise of Mary

Edi° be thu, Hevene Quene,   *blessed*
Folkes froure° and engles° blis,   *comfort / angels'*
Moder unwemmed° and maiden clene,   *unspotted*
Swich° in world non other nis.°   *such / is*
5   On thee it is well eth° sene°   *easily / seen*
Of alle wimmen thu havest that pris.°   *prize*
My swete Levedy,° her my bene,°   *Lady / prayer*
And rew° of me yif° thy wille is.   *take pity / if*

Thu asteye° so° the dais-rewe°   *climb / as / dawn's ray*
10   The° deleth° from the derke night;   *that / separates*
Of thee sprong a leme° newe   *light*
That all this world haveth ilight.°   *illuminated*
Nis non maide of thine hewe
So fair, so shene,° so rudy, so bright.   *beautiful*
15   Swete Levedy, of me thu rewe,
And have mercy of thine knight.

Spronge° blostme° of one rote,°   *sprung / blossom / root*
The Holy Ghost thee reste upon;
That wes for monkunnes° bote,°   *mankind's / healing*
20   And here° soule to alesen° for on.   *their / deliver*
Levedy milde, softe and swote,°   *sweet*
Ic° crye thee mercy: ic am thy mon,°   *I / man*
Bothe to honde and to fote,
On alle wise° that ic con.°   *way / can*

25   Thu ert° erthe° to° gode sede;   *art / earth / for*
On thee lighte° the Hevene° dews;   *came down / of heaven*
Of thee sprong the edi° blede°—   *blessed / fruit*
The Holy Ghost hire on thee sews.°   *sowed it*
Thu bring us ut of care, of drede,°   *fear*
30   That Eve bitterliche us brews.
Thu shalt us into Hevene lede—
Welle° swete is the ilke° dews.   *most / same*

Moder, full of thewes° hende,°   *virtues / gracious*
Maide, dreigh° and well itaught,°   *patient / taught*
35 Ic em in thine lovebende,°   *bonds of love*
And to thee is all my draught.°   *leaning*
Thu me shilde° from the Fende,°   *shield / Fiend*
Ase thu ert fre,° and wilt° and maught:°   *noble / will / can*
Help me to my lives ende,
40 And make me with thine sone isaught.°   *reconciled*

Thu ert icumen° of heghe° cunne,°   *come / high / lineage*
Of David the riche king.
Nis non maiden under sunne
The° mey be thine evening,°   *that / equal*
45 Ne that so derne° loviye cunne,°   *secretly / can*
Ne non so trewe of alle thing.
Thy love us broughte eche° wunne:°   *eternal / bliss*
Ihered° ibe° thu, swete thing!   *praised / be*

Selcudliche ure Louerd it dighte[1]
50 That thu, maide, withute were,°   *mate*
That all this world bicluppe ne mighte,°   *could not encompass*
Thu sholdest of thine boseme° bere.°   *womb / bear*
Thee ne stighte,° ne thee ne prighte,°   *stabbed / pricked*
In side, in lende° ne elleswhere:°   *loins / elsewhere*
55 That wes° with full muchel° righte,   *was / much*
For thu bere° thine Helere.°   *bore / Savior*

Tho° Godes sune alighte wolde°   *when / wished*
On erthe, all for ure° sake,   *our*
Herre° teyen° he him nolde   *higher / servant*
60 Thene° that maide to ben° his make:°   *than / be / mate*
Betere ne mighte he, thaigh° he wolde,   *though*
Ne swetture thing on erthe take.
Levedy,° bring us to thine bolde°   *Lady / abode*
And shild° us from helle wrake.°   *shield / vengeance*

Amen.

Mary Is with Child

Nowel! nowel! nowel!
Sing we with mirth!
Christ is come well
With us to dwell,
5   *By his most noble birth.*

Under a tree
In sporting me,
Alone by a wod-side,°   *side of a wood*

---

1. Marvellously our Lord arranged it.

I hard° a maid¹   heard
10 That swetly said,
"I am with child this tide.°   time

"Graciously
Conceived have I
The Son of God so swete:
15 His gracious will
I put me till,
As moder° him to kepe.   mother

"Both night and day
I will him pray,
20 And her° his lawes taught,   hear
And every dell°   in every way
His trewe gospell
In his apostles fraught.°   carried

"This ghostly° case°   spiritual / act
25 Doth me embrace,
Without despite or mock;
With my derling,
'Lullay,'° to sing,   lullabye
And lovely him to rock.

30 "Without distress
In grete lightness
I am both night and day.
This hevenly fod°   child
In his childhod
35 Shall daily with me play.

"Soone must I sing
With rejoicing,
For the time is all ronne°   run out
That I shall child,°   give birth to
40 All undefil'd,
The King of Heven's Sonne."

Jesus, My Swect Lover

Jesu Christ, my lemmon° swete,   lover
That diyedest on the Rode Tree,°   Cross
With all my might I thee beseche,
For thy woundes two and three,
That also° faste mot° thy love   as / may
Into mine herte fitched° be   fixed
As was the spere into thine herte,
Whon thou soffredest deth for me.

1. A poem that opens with the speaker in the countryside overhearing a woman's lament raises expectations that we will
hear a *chanson d'aventure*, with erotic connotations.

Contempt of the World

Where beth° they biforen us weren?   *are*
Houndes ladden° and hawkes beren,°   *led / bore*
And hadden feld and wode;
The riche levedies° in here° bour,°   *ladies / their / bower*
5   That wereden° gold in here tressour,°   *wore / head-dress*
With here° brighte rode:°   *their / face*

Eten and drounken and maden hem° glad;   *themselves*
Here lif was all with gamen° ilad.°   *sport / spent*
Men keneleden° hem° biforen;   *kneeled / them*
10   They beren hem well swithe° heye°—   *very / high*
And in a twinkling of an eye
Here soules weren forloren.°   *lost*

Where is that laughing and that song,
That trailing[1] and that proude gong,°   *gait*
15   Tho° hawkes and tho houndes?   *those*
All that joye is went away,
That wele° is comen to weylaway,°   *prosperity / woe*
To manye harde stoundes.°   *times*

Here° paradis hy° nomen° here,   *their / they / took*
20   And now they lien° in helle ifere;°   *lie / together*
The fuir° it brennes° evere.   *fire / burns*
Long is "ah!" and long is "oh!"
Long is "wy!" and long is "wo!"
Thennes° ne cometh they nevere.   *thence*

25   Drey° here, man, thenne, if thou wilt,   *suffer*
A litel pine that me thee bit;[2]
Withdraw thine eyses° ofte.   *comforts*
They° thy pine° be unrede,°   *though / pain / severe*
And° thou thenke° on thy mede,°   *if / think / reward*
30   It shall thee thinken° softe.   *seem*

If that fend,° that foule thing,   *the Devil*
Thorou wikke roun, thorou fals egging,°   *counsel*
Nethere° thee haveth icast,   *down*
Up and be good chaunpioun!
35   Stond, ne fall namore adoun
For a litel blast.

Thou tak the rode° to° thy staf,   *cross / as*
And thenk on him that thereonne gaf°   *gave*
His lif that wes so lef°.   *dear*
40   He it gaf for thee; thou yelde° it him;   *give back*
Agein° his of that staf thou nim°   *against / take*
And wrek° him of that thef.°   *avenge / thief*

---

1. Walking with trailing garments.   2. A little pain that one enjoins.

	Of righte bileve° thou nim that sheld,	*belief*
	The whiles that thou best° in that feld,	*are*
45	Thin hond to strengthen fonde;°	*try*
	And kep thy of with° staves° ord,°	*at / staff's / point*
	And do° that traitre seyen that word.	*make*
	Biget° that murie° londe.	*win / happy*

	Thereinne is day withouten night,	
50	Withouten ende strengthe and might,	
	And wreche° of everich fo;	*punishment*
	Mid° God himselven eche° lif,	*with / eternal*
	And pes° and rest withoute strif,	*peace*
	Wele° withouten wo.	*happiness*

55	Maiden moder,° hevene° quene,	*mother / heaven's*
	Thou might and const and owest to bene[3]	
	Oure sheld agein the fende;°	*Devil*
	Help us sunne° for to flen,°	*sin / flee*
	That we moten° thy sone° iseen°	*may / Son / see*
60	In joye withouten ende.	

⊢·━◆Ⅱ·━⊣

William Dunbar

Of all the Makars ("Makers," or Poets), Dunbar is the greatest virtuoso, intoxicated with language, whether it be the elevated vocabulary borrowed from Latin, or the Germanic diction of alliterative poetry, whose tradition was kept alive in Scotland a century after it had died out in England. He was versatile in his choice of genres, writing occasional poems (such as an allegory in celebration of the marriage of James IV and Princess Margaret), divine poems, and parodies such as *The Tretis of Twa Mariit Wemen and the Wedo*, a bawdy satire on the morals of court ladies written in the traditional alliterative long line. Included here are a meditation on death (*Lament for the Makars*), an Easter hymn (*Done Is a Battell*), and a parody of the courtly genre of the *chanson d'aventure* (*In Secreit Place This Hyndir Nycht*).

Lament for the Makars[1]

I that in heill° wes° and gladnes	*health / was*
Am trublit now with gret seiknes	
And feblit with infermite:	
Timor mortis conturbat me.[2]	

---

3. You may and can and ought to be.
1. This poem reflects the late medieval fascination with death. The speaker wistfully observes that beautiful ladies, brave knights, and wise clerks have had their lives cut short but gives most of his attention to poets. He lists 23 of these—three English (Chaucer, Gower, and Lydgate) and 20 Scots, only half of whom modern scholars can

identify. Since Death has taken all his "brothers," he regards himself as next and resolves to prepare himself for the next world. The poem was printed in 1508 by Walter Chepman and Andrew Myllar, who introduced the printing press to Scotland.
2. Fear of death shakes me (from the liturgical Office of the Dead).

5   Our plesance heir is all vane glory,
      This fals warld is bot transitory,
      The flesche is brukle,° the Fend° is sle:°   *frail / Devil / sly*
        Timor mortis conturbat me.

      The stait of man dois change and vary,
10   Now sound, now seik, now blith, now sary,
      Now dansand mery, now like to dee:°   *die*
        Timor mortis conturbat me.

      No stait in erd° heir standis sickir;°   *on earth / secure*
      As with the wynd wavis the wickir,
15   Wavis this warldis vanite:
        Timor mortis conturbat me.

      On to the ded gois all estatis,
      Princis, prelotis,° and potestatis,°   *prelates / rulers*
      Baith riche and pur of al degre:
20   *Timor mortis conturbat me.*

      He takis the knychtis° in to feild,°   *knights / the field*
      Anarmit° under helme and scheild; armed   *armed*
      Victour he is at all mellie:°   *battles*
        Timor mortis conturbat me.

25   That strang unmercifull tyrand
      Takis, on the moderis° breist sowkand,°   *mother's / sucking*
      The bab full of benignite:
        Timor mortis conturbat me.

      He takis the campion° in the stour,°   *champion / conflict*
30   The capitane closit in the tour,
      The lady in bour° full of bewte: *bower*
        Timor mortis conturbat me.

      He sparis no lord for his piscence,°   *power*
      Na clerk for his intelligence;
35   His awfull strak° may no man fle: *stroke*
        Timor mortis conturbat me.

      Art magicianis and astrologgis,
      Rethoris,° logicianis and theologgis,   *rhetoricians*
      Thame helpis no conclusionis sle:°   *clever*
40   *Timor mortis conturbat me.*

      In medicyne the most practicianis,
      Lechis,° surrigianis,° and phisicianis,   *doctors / surgeons*
      Thame self fra ded° may not supple:°   *death / deliver*
        Timor mortis conturbat me.

45   I se that makaris° amang the laif°   *poets / remainder*
      Playis heir ther pageant, syne gois to graif;°   *grave*
      Sparit° is nocht ther faculte: *spared*
        Timor mortis conturbat me.

50   He hes done petuously devour
      The noble Chaucer of makaris flour,°   *flower of poets*
      The Monk of Bery,[3] and Gower, all thre:
      Timor mortis conturbat me.

      The gude Syr Hew of Eglintoun,[4]
      And eik Heryot, and Wyntoun,[5]
55   He hes tane out of this cuntre:
      Timor mortis conturbat me.

      That scorpion fell° hes done infek°   *fierce / infect*
      Maister Johne Clerk and James Afflek[6]
      Fra ballat making and tragidie:
60   *Timor mortis conturbat me.*

      Holland and Barbour[7] he hes berevit;
      Allace,° that he nocht with us levit   *alas*
      Schir Mungo Lokert of the Le:[8]
      Timor mortis conturbat me.

65   Clerk of Tranent eik he hes tane,
      That maid the Anteris° of Gawane;   *adventures*
      Schir Gilbert Hay endit hes he:[9]
      Timor mortis conturbat me.

      He hes Blind Hary and Sandy Traill
70   Slaine with his schour° of mortall haill,   *shower*
      Quhilk Patrik Johnestoun[1] mycht nocht fle:
      Timor mortis conturbat me.

      He hes reft° Merseir his endite°   *taken from / talent*
      That did in luf so lifly° write,   *in a lively manner*
75   So schort, so quyk, of sentence hie:
      Timor mortis conturbat me.

      He hes tane Roull of Aberdene
      And gentill Roull of Corstorphin;
      Two bettir fallowis did no man se:
80   *Timor mortis conturbat me.*

      In Dunfermelyne he hes done roune°   *held conversation*
      With Maister Robert Henrisoun.[2]
      Schir Johne the Ros enbrast° hes he: *embraced*
      Timor mortis conturbat me.

3. John Lydgate, monk of Bury St. Edmunds, a minor poet who was an imitator of Chaucer. He also used the *"timor mortis"* refrain in a poem on the same subject.
4. Brother-in-law of Robert II and not otherwise known as a poet.
5. Andrew of Wyntoun, author of the *Oryginale Chronykil of Scotland.*
6. These two are unknown, as are the other poets in this list not identified.
7. Sir Richard Holland, author of the allegorical *Buke of the Howlat* (c. 1450), and John Barbour, author of the

patriotic *Actes and Life . . . of Robert Bruce* (1376).
8. This Scotsman (d. 1489?) is not otherwise known as a poet.
9. The "clerk of Tranent" is unknown, but Arthurian romances focusing on Gawain were popular in Scotland; Sir Gilbert Hay (d. 1456) translated the poem *The Buik of Alexander* from French.
1. Blind Harry is credited with writing the Scots epic *Wallace* (c. 1475); Patrick Johnstoune was a producer of stage entertainments at court in the late 1400s.
2. Henryson was a major Middle Scots poet.

85 And he hes now tane last of aw
    Gud gentill Stobo and Quintyne Schaw,[3]
    Of quham all wichtis hes pete:[4]
        Timor mortis conturbat me.

    Gud Maister Walter Kennedy[5]
90 In° poynt of dede° lyis veraly;°   *on / death / truly*
    Gret reuth° it wer that so suld be: *pity*
        Timor mortis conturbat me.

    Sen he hes all my brether tane
    He will nocht lat me lif alane;
95 On forse° I man his nyxt pray be: *of necessity*
        Timor mortis conturbat me.

    Sen for the deid remeid° is none,   *remedy*
    Best is that we for dede dispone°   *prepare*
    Eftir our deid that lif may we:
100   *Timor mortis conturbat me.*

Done Is a Battell[1]

    Done is a battell on° the dragon blak,   *with*
    Our campioun° Chryst confountet hes his force;   *champion*
    The yettis° of hell ar brokin with a crak,   *gates*
    The signe triumphall rasit is of the croce,°   *cross*
5   The divillis trymmillis° with hiddous voce,   *trembles*
    The saulis° ar borrowit° and to the blis can go,   *souls / redeemed*
    Chryst with his blud our ransonis dois indoce:°   *endorse*
    Surrexit dominus de sepulchro.[2]

    Dungin° is the deidly dragon Lucifer,   *beaten*
10 The crewall° serpent with the mortall stang,°   *cruel / sting*
    The auld kene tegir with his teith on char°   *ajar*
    Quhilk° in a wait hes lyne° for us so lang,   *which / lain*
    Thinking to grip us in his clowis strang:
    The mercifull lord wald° nocht that it wer so,   *would*
15 He maid him for to felye° of that fang:°   *fail / booty*
    Surrexit dominus de sepulchro.

    He for our saik that sufferit to be slane
    And lyk a lamb in sacrifice wes dicht,°   *prepared*
    Is lyk a lyone° rissin up agane,   *lion*

3. John Reid, known as Stobo, was priest and secretary to
James II, James III, and James IV; Schaw was a minor
Scots poet.
4. On whom all people have pity.
5. Known for his *Flyting* (poem of ritual insult) with
Dunbar.
1. This Easter hymn heroically portrays Christ's Resurrection
as a battle with the devil, drawing on the account of the
harrowing of hell in the apocryphal Gospel of Nicodemus, in
which Christ journeys to hell to release worthy souls who
had been born before his coming. It gains much of its power
from the juxtaposition of alliterative diction from the Scots
tradition with Latinate vocabulary. As in the *Lament for the
Makars*, the Latin refrain fits within the overall English
rhyme scheme.
2. The Lord is risen from the tomb. From the opening of
the service for matins on Easter Sunday.

20 And as a gyane raxit him on hicht.³
   Sprungin° is Aurora radius° and bricht, *arisen / radiant*
   On loft° is gone the glorius Appollo,⁴ *aloft*
   The blisfull day depairtit° fro the nycht: *separated*
   Surrexit dominus de sepulchro.

25 The grit victour agane is rissin on hicht
   That for our querrell to the deth wes woundit;
   The sone that wox° all paill now schynis bricht, *became*
   And, dirknes clerit, our fayth is now refoundit:° *reestablished*
   The knell of mercy fra the hevin is soundit,⁵
30 The Cristin ar deliverit of thair wo,
   The Jowis° and thair errour ar confoundit: *Jews*
   Surrexit dominus de sepulchro.

   The fo is chasit, the battell is done ceis,° *ceased*
   The presone brokin, the jevellouris fleit and flemit,⁶
35 The weir° is gon, confermit is the peis,° *war / peace*
   The fetteris lowsit° and the dungeoun temit,° *loosed / emptied*
   The ransoun maid, the presoneris° redemit,° *prisoners / redeemed*
   The feild is win°, ourcummin° is the fo, *won / overcome*
   Dispulit° of the tresur that he yemit:° *despoiled / kept*
40 *Surrexit dominus de sepulchro.*

In Secreit Place This Hyndir Nycht¹

   In secreit place this hyndir° nycht *last*
   I hard ane beyrne° say till ane bricht,° *man / fair lady*
   "My huny, my hart, my hoip, my heill,²
   I have bene lang° your luifar° leill° *long / lover / loyal*
5 And can of yow get confort nane:° *none*
   How lang will ye with danger deill?³
   Ye brek my hart, my bony ane."° *pretty one*

   His bony beird was kemmit and croppit,⁴
   Bot all with cale° it was bedroppit,° *soup / smeared*
10 And he wes townysche, peirt and gukit.⁵
   He clappit fast, he kist and chukkit⁶
   As with the glaikis° he wer ouirgane;° *lust / overcome*

---

3. And like a giant stretched himself on high. A reference to Samson, who in bearing off the gates of Gaza was seen as a type of Christ breaking the gates of hell.
4. Christ, the sun (and Son) of righteousness, is identified with Apollo, the sun god, which explains the reference to Aurora, goddess of the dawn.
5. An allusion to the ringing of the bells on Easter morning.
6. The prison broken, the jailers fled and banished.
1. This comic account of the wooing of a kitchen maid by a boorish man parodies the *chanson d'aventure*, a genre in which the speaker overhears a dialogue between two

lovers. Dunbar undercuts the poem's courtly language, which he has used seriously elsewhere, with overtly sexual references. In addition to words familiar to modern readers, the poem features terms of endearment from colloquial Scots which have long since been lost.
2. My honey, my heart, my hope, my salvation.
3. Ladies were expected to be "dangerous" (reluctant) in a courtship situation.
4. His handsome beard was combed and trimmed.
5. And he was townish (uncourtly), pert, and foolish.
6. He fondled fast, kissed, and chucked her under the chin.

Yit be his feirris° he wald have fukkit: *manner*
"Ye brek my hart, my bony ane."

15 Quod he, "My hairt, sweit° as the hunye,   *sweet*
Sen that I borne wes of my mynnye°   *mother*
I never wowit° weycht° bot yow;   *wooed / creature*
My wambe° is of your luif sa fow°   *belly / full*
That as ane gaist° I glour° and grane,°   *ghost / glower / groan*
20 I trymble° sa, ye will not trow:°   *tremble / believe*
Ye brek my hart, my bony ane."

"Tehe,"° quod scho, and gaif ane gawfe;°   *Teehee / guffaw*
"Be still my tuchan⁷ and my calfe,
My new spanit howffing fra the sowk,⁸
25 And all the blythnes° of my bowk;°   *joy / body*
My sweit swanking,° saif yow allane   *fine fellow*
Na leid° I luiffit° all this owk:°   *no man / loved / week*
Full leifis° me° your graceles gane."°   *dear / to me / face*

Quod he, "My claver° and my curldodie,°   *clover / a plant*
30 My huny soppis, my sweit possodie,°   *sheep's head broth*
Be not oure bosteous° to your billie,°   *rough / sweetheart*
Be warme hairtit° and not evill willie;°   *hearted / ill-willed*
Your heylis quhyt as quhalis bane,⁹
Garris ryis° on loft my quhillelillie:°   *makes rise / penis*
35 Ye brek my hart, my bony ane."

Quod scho, "My clype, my unspaynit gyane¹
With moderis° mylk yit in your mychane,°   *mother's / mouth*
My belly huddrun,° my swete hurle bawsy,²   *big-bellied glutton*
My huny gukkis,° my slawsy gawsy,   *sweet fool*
40 Your musing waild perse° ane hart of stane: *would pierce*
Tak gud confort, my grit heidit° slawsy,   *great-headed*
Full leifis me your graceles gane."

Quod he, "My kid, my capirculyoun,°   *woodgrouse*
My bony baib° with the ruch° brylyoun,   *babe / rough*
45 My tendir gyrle, my wallie gowdye,°   *pretty goldfinch*
My tyrlie myrlie, my crowdie mowdie,°   *milky porridge*
Quhone° that oure mouthis dois meit° at ane   *when / do meet*
My stang dois storkyn with your towdie:³
Ye brek my hairt, my bony ane."

50 Quod scho, "Now tak me be the hand,
Welcum, my golk° of Marie° land,   *cuckoo / fairy*
My chirrie and my maikles munyoun,⁴
My sowklar° sweit as ony unyoun,°   *suckling / any onion*

---

7. Calf skin stuffed with straw, to encourage a cow to give milk.
8. My clumsy fellow newly weaned from nursing.
9. Your neck white as whale's bone; a common alliterative phrase in the conventional love poetry.

1. Said she, "My big soft fellow, my unweaned giant."
2. An obscure term of endearment, as are several other phrases in the following lines.
3. My pole does stiffen by your thing.
4. My cherry and my matchless darling.

My strumill stirk yit new to spane,[5]
55 I am applyit° to your opunyoun:°   *inclined / opinion*
I luif rycht weill° your graceles gane."   *love right well*

He gaiff to hir ane apill rubye;°   *apple red*
Quod scho, "Gramercye,° my sweit cowhubye."°   *thanks / fool*
And thai tway to ane play began
60 Quhilk° men dois call the dery dan,[6]   *which*
Quhill° that thair myrthis° met baythe in ane: *while / pleasure*
"Wo is me," quod scho, "Quhair will ye,° man?   *where will you go*
Best now I luif° that graceles gane."   *love*

Christine de Pizan
c. 1364–c. 1430

Christine de Pizan is an epochal figure in the history of European literature, not only for the quality and influence of her many works, but equally because she was Europe's first professional woman of letters. There were many important women writers in the Middles Ages, several of them represented in this anthology, but Christine—widowed in 1389 with three children and no family money—was the first to make writing the sole source of her income. She was well aware of this and wove her unique perspective, as a woman engaged with a largely male (and often misogynist) intellectual tradition, into much of her writing.

Like many late medieval writers, Christine de Pizan spent a good part of her energies translating, adapting, and consolidating earlier works on a wide range of topics. She wrote love poetry in traditional forms such as the ballade, but innovated by writing lyrics on widowhood as well. Like other writers of her time, too, Christine frames many of her books as dream-visions populated by allegorical figures, especially teachers or guides, such as the three ladies (Reason, Rectitude, and Justice) whom she encounters in the *Book of the City of Ladies*. Also like her contemporaries, Christine had to seek patronage in the noble and royal courts of France (where she spent most of her life) and Burgundy, as well as England. She was an innovator here as well, though, carefully supervising the scribes and painters who produced splendid manuscripts of her works for presentation to her patrons.

Christine innovated most of all, however, by persistently reacting to her cultural inheritance from the perspective of women. At the turn of the fifteenth century, she was a major voice in the debate surrounding the famous but often misogynist *Romance of the Rose*. Classical and medieval Latin had an even greater store of works hostile to women. With the *Book of the City of Ladies*, though, Christine offers a systematic response to the depiction of women in biblical and classical texts. The three allegorical ladies who appear to her as the book opens instruct Christine to build a walled city of and for the virtuous women of her cultural past. In doing so, Christine radically reinterprets women's histories as they have been recorded by men, and imagines a symbolic space from which a female literary tradition might emanate.

The works of Christine de Pizan were widely known in England in her own lifetime and well into the early modern period. Splendid manuscripts of her French works came into the hands of English kings and nobles. Her elder son was raised for three years in the household of the Duke of Salisbury, an influential member of the court of Richard II. Christine's *Letter of*

---

5. My stumbling bullock still newly weaned.   6. A dance (i.e., copulation).

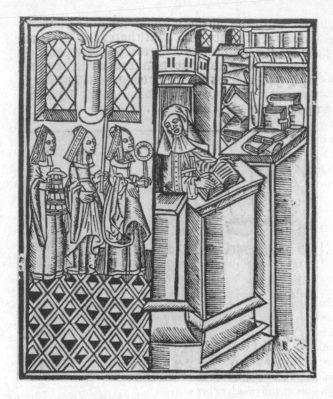

Illustration from Brian Anslay's English translation of *Book of the City of Ladies*, 1521.

Othea was translated three times in the fifteenth century; and Thomas Hoccleve, a late contemporary of Chaucer, adapted her *Letter of the God of Love*—a feminist response to courtly love—as the *Letter of Cupid*. England's first printer, William Caxton, translated and published yet other of her works (some by royal commission) in the 1480s, as did early sixteenth-century printers like Henry Pepwell, who published Brian Anslay's 1521 translation of the *Book of the City of Ladies*.

    Her role in England places Christine de Pizan within several key transitions there. The ongoing translations of her works reflect the importation of continental texts into an increasingly English-language literary and political culture under the Lancastrian and Yorkist kings. The numerous early printings of these translations is part of a massive dissemination of late medieval texts made possible by the rise of print. And in turn, this widespread access to later medieval literary modes carried their influences—not least, that of allegory—into early modern culture in England. Works like the *Book of the City of Ladies* lie behind the allegorized, often female-controlled cities and castles of early modern works like Spenser's *Faerie Queene*. The translation used here is by Earl Jeffrey Richards.

from *Book of the City of Ladies*

[*In the first chapter Christine presents herself surrounded by books in her study, and is dismayed to read philosophers and poets all claiming that women are full of vice. While such a view is contrary to her perception of herself and of other women she has known, she concludes that so many famous men cannot be wrong. She is so over-whelmed by sorrow that she asks God why he created women, if they are so vile, and why he did not make her a man, so that she might serve him better.*]

[PART I, CHAPTER 2]
[*Here Christine describes how three ladies appeared to her and how the one who was in front spoke first and comforted her in her pain.*]

So occupied with these painful thoughts, my head bowed in shame, my eyes filled with tears, leaning on the pommel of my chair's armrest, I suddenly saw a ray of light fall on my lap, as though it were the sun. I shuddered then, as if wakened from sleep, for I was sitting in a shadow where the sun could not have shone at that hour. And as I lifted my head to see where this light was coming from, I saw three crowned ladies standing before me, and the splendor of their bright faces shone on me and throughout the entire room. Now no one would ask whether I was surprised, for my doors were shut and they had still entered. Fearing that some phantom had come to tempt me and filled with great fright, I made the Sign of the Cross on my forehead.

Then she who was the first of the three smiled and began to speak, "Dear daughter, do not be afraid, for we have not come here to harm or trouble you but to console you, for we have taken pity on your distress, and we have come to bring you out of the ignorance which so blinds your own intellect that you shun what you know for a certainty and believe what you do not know or see or recognize except by virtue of many strange opinions. You resemble the fool in the prank who was dressed in women's clothes while he slept; because those who were making fun of him repeatedly told him he was a woman, he believed their false testimony more readily than the certainty of his own identity. Fair daughter, have you lost all sense? Have you forgotten that when fine gold is tested in the furnace, it does not change or vary in strength but becomes purer the more it is hammered and handled in different ways? Do you not know that the best things are the most debated and the most discussed? If you wish to consider the question of the highest form of reality, which consists in ideas or celestial substances, consider whether the greatest philosophers who have lived and whom you support against your own sex have ever resolved whether ideas are false and contrary to the truth. Notice how these same philosophers contradict and criticize one another, just as you have seen in the *Metaphysics* where Aristotle takes their opinions to task and speaks similarly of Plato and other philosophers. And note, moreover, how even Saint Augustine and the Doctors of the Church have criticized Aristotle in certain passages, although he is known as the prince of philosophers in whom both natural and moral philosophy attained their highest level. It also seems that you think that all the words of the philosophers are articles of faith, that they could never be wrong. As far as the poets of whom you speak are concerned, do you not know that they spoke on many subjects in a fictional way and that often they mean the contrary of what their words openly say? One can interpret them according to the grammatical figure of *antiphrasis*, which means, as you know, that if you call something bad, in fact, it is good, and also vice versa. Thus I advise you to profit from their works and to interpret them in the manner in which they are intended in those passages where they attack women. Perhaps this man, who called himself Mathéolus in his own book, intended it in such a way, for there are many things which, if taken literally, would be pure heresy.[1] As for the attack against the estate of marriage—which is a holy estate, worthy and ordained by God—made not only by Mathéolus but also by others and even by the *Romance of the Rose* where greater credibility is averred

---

1. *The Book of the Lamentations of Matheolus*, the misogynist work that most troubled Christine in her study.

because of the authority of its author, it is evident and proven by experience that the contrary of the evil which they posit and claim to be found in this estate through the obligation and fault of women is true. For where has the husband ever been found who would allow his wife to have authority to abuse and insult him as a matter of course, as these authorities maintain? I believe that, regardless of what you might have read, you will never see such a husband with your own eyes, so badly colored are these lies. Thus, in conclusion, I tell you, dear friend, that simple-mindedness has prompted you to hold such an opinion. Come back to yourself, recover your senses, and do not trouble yourself anymore over such absurdities. For you know that any evil spoken of women so generally only hurts those who say it, not women themselves."

[PART I, CHAPTER 3]

[*Here Christine tells how the lady who had said this showed her who she was and what her character and function were and told her how she would construct a city with the help of these same three ladies.*]

The famous lady spoke these words to me, in whose presence I do not know which one of my senses was more overwhelmed: my hearing from having listened to such worthy words or my sight from having seen her radiant beauty, her attire, her reverent comportment, and her most honored countenance. The same was true of the others, so that I did not know which one to look at, for the three ladies resembled each other so much that they could be told apart only with difficulty, except for the last one, for although she was of no less authority than the others, she had so fierce a visage that whoever, no matter how daring, looked in her eyes would be afraid to commit a crime; for it seemed that she threatened criminals unceasingly. Having stood up out of respect, I looked at them without saying a word, like someone too overwhelmed to utter a syllable. Reflecting on who these beings could be, I felt much admiration in my heart and, if I could have dared, I would have immediately asked their names and identities and what was the meaning of the different scepters which each one carried in her right hand, which were of fabulous richness, and why they had come here. But since I considered myself unworthy to address these questions to such high ladies as they appeared to me, I did not dare to, but continued to keep my gaze fixed on them, half-afraid and half-reassured by the words which I had heard, which had made me reject my first impression. But the most wise lady who had spoken to me and who knew in her mind what I was thinking, as one who has insight into everything, addressed my reflections, saying:

"Dear daughter, know that God's providence, which leaves nothing void or empty, has ordained that we, though celestial beings, remain and circulate among the people of the world here below, in order to bring order and maintain in balance those institutions we created according to the will of God in the fulfillment of various offices, that God whose daughters we three all are and from whom we were born. Thus it is my duty to straighten out men and women when they go astray and to put them back on the right path. And when they stray, if they have enough understanding to see me, I come to them quietly in spirit and preach to them, showing them their error and how they have failed, I assign them the causes, and then I teach them what to do and what to avoid. Since I serve to demonstrate clearly and to show both in thought and deed to each man and woman his or her own special qualities and faults, you see me holding this shiny mirror which I carry in my right hand in place of a scepter. I would thus have you know truly that no one can look into this mirror, no matter what kind of creature, without achieving clear self-knowledge. My mirror has such great dignity that not without reason is it surrounded by rich and precious gems, so that you see, thanks to this mirror, the essences, qualities, proportions, and measures of all things are known, nor can anything be done well without it. And because, similarly, you wish to know what are the offices of my other sisters whom you see here, each will reply in her own person about her name and character, and this way our testimony will be all the more certain to you. But now I myself will declare the reason for our coming. I must assure you, as we do nothing without good cause, that our appearance here is not at all in vain. For, although we are not common to many places and our knowledge does not come to all people, nevertheless you, for your great love of investigating the truth through long and continual study, for which you come here, solitary and separated from the world, you have deserved and deserve, our devoted friend, to be visited and consoled by us in your agitation and sadness, so that you might also see clearly, in the midst of the darkness of your thoughts, those things which taint and trouble your heart.

"There is another greater and even more special reason for our coming which you will learn from our speeches: in fact we have come to vanquish from the world the same error into which you had fallen, so that from now on, ladies and all valiant women may have a refuge and defense against the various assailants, those ladies who have been abandoned for so long, exposed like a field without a surrounding hedge, without finding a champion to afford them an adequate defense, notwithstanding those noble men who are required by order of law to protect them, who by negligence and apathy have allowed them to be mistreated. It is no wonder then that their jealous enemies, those outrageous villains who have assailed them with various weapons, have been victorious in a war in which women have had no defense. Where is there a city so strong which could not be taken immediately if no resistance were forthcoming, or the law case, no matter how unjust, which was not won through the obstinance of someone pleading without opposition? And the simple, noble ladies, following the example of suffering which God commands, have cheerfully suffered the great attacks which, both in the spoken and the written word, have been wrongfully and sinfully perpetrated against women by men who all the while appealed to God for the right to do so. Now it is time for their just cause to be taken from Pharaoh's hands, and for this reason, we three ladies whom you see here, moved by pity, have come to you to announce a particular edifice built like a city wall, strongly constructed and well founded, which has been predestined and established by our aid and counsel for you to build, where no one will reside except all ladies of fame and women worthy of praise, for the walls of the city will be closed to those women who lack virtue."

[PART I, CHAPTER 4]

[Here the lady explains to Christine the city which she has been commissioned to build and how she was charged to help Christine build the wall and enclosure, and then gives her name.]

"Thus, fair daughter, the prerogative among women has been bestowed on you to establish and build the City of Ladies. For the foundation and completion of this City you will draw fresh waters from us as from clear fountains, and we will bring you sufficient building stone, stronger and more durable than any marble with cement could be. Thus your City will be extremely beautiful, without equal, and of perpetual duration in the world.

"Have you not read that King Tros founded the great city of Troy with the aid of Apollo, Minerva, and Neptune, whom the people of that time considered gods, and also how Cadmus founded the city of Thebes with the admonition of the gods? And yet over time these cities fell and have fallen into ruin. But I prophesy to you, as a true sybil, that this City, which you will found with our help, will never be destroyed, nor will it ever fall, but will remain prosperous forever, regardless of all its jealous enemies. Although it will be stormed by numerous assaults, it will never be taken or conquered.

"Long ago the Amazon kingdom was begun through the arrangement and enterprise of several ladies of great courage who despised servitude, just as history books have testified. For a long time afterward they maintained it under the rule of several queens, very noble ladies whom they elected themselves, who governed them well and maintained their dominion with great strength. Yet, although they were strong and powerful and had conquered a large part of the entire Orient in the course of their rule and terrified all the neighboring lands (even the Greeks, who were then the flower of all countries in the world, feared them), nevertheless, after a time, the power of this kingdom declined, so that as with all earthly kingdoms, nothing but its name has survived to the present. But the edifice erected by you in this City which you must construct will be far stronger, and for its founding I was commissioned, in the course of our common deliberation, to supply you with durable and pure mortar to lay the sturdy foundations and to raise the lofty walls all around, high and thick, with mighty towers and strong bastions, surrounded by moats with firm blockhouses, just as is fitting for a city with a strong and lasting defense. Following our plan, you will set the foundations deep to last all the longer, and then you will raise the walls so high that they will not fear anyone. Daughter, now that I have told you the reason for our coming and so that you will more certainly believe my words, I want you to learn my name, by whose sound alone you will be able to learn and know that, if you wish to follow my commands, you have in me an administrator so that you may do your work flawlessly. I am called Lady Reason; you see that you are in good hands. For the time being then, I will say no more."

[In the following chapters, the other two ladies identify themselves as Rectitude and Justice. Just as Lady Reason had carried a mirror signifying self-knowledge, Rectitude carries a ruler signifying the distinction of right from wrong, and offers to help Christine measure her City of Ladies with it. Lady Justice carries a gold flask from which she portions out justice to all, and promises to help Christine populate her city. The remainder of the book describes Christine's questions to the three ladies about the achievements of women. Countering charges of physical weakness and cowardice, Lady Reason cites the bravery of the Amazons Hippolyta and Penthesilea. As examples of women's intelligence and learning, she offers the wisdom of Sappho and (more problematically) the cleverness of Medea and Circe. Lady Rectitude absolves women of the charge of lustfulness with the biblical examples of Susannah, Sarah, and Rebecca, and the Greek example of Penelope. After praising Christine's construction work, Lady Justice welcomes the Virgin Mary into the City of Ladies, to rule as queen. In the final chapter, Christine offers advice to women of all marital conditions and social stations on how to bear their lot.]

[PART 3, CHAPTER 19]

THE END OF THE BOOK: CHRISTINE ADDRESSES THE LADIES.

My most honored ladies, may God be praised, for now our City is entirely finished and completed, where all of you who love glory, virtue, and praise may be lodged in great honor, ladies from the past as well as from the present and future, for it has been built and established for every honorable lady. And my most dear ladies, it is natural for the human heart to rejoice when it finds itself victorious in any enterprise and its enemies confounded. Therefore you are right, my ladies, to rejoice greatly in God and in honest mores upon seeing this new City completed, which can be not only the refuge for you all, that is, for virtuous women, but also the defense and guard against your enemies and assailants, if you guard it well. For you can see that the substance with which it is made is entirely of virtue, so resplendent that you may see yourselves mirrored in it, especially in the roofs built in the last part as well as in the other parts which concern you. And my dear ladies, do not misuse this new inheritance like the arrogant who turn proud when their prosperity grows and their wealth multiplies, but rather follow the example of your Queen, the sovereign Virgin, who, after the extraordinary honor of being chosen Mother of the Son of God was announced to her humbled herself all the more by calling herself the handmaiden of God. Thus, my ladies, just as it is true that a creature's humility and kindness wax with the increase of its virtues, may this City be an occasion for you to conduct yourselves honestly and with integrity and to be all the more virtuous and humble.

And you ladies who are married, do not scorn being subject to your husbands, for sometimes it is not the best thing for a creature to be independent. This is attested by what the angel said to Ezra: Those, he said, who take advantage of their free will can fall into sin and despise our Lord and deceive the just, and for this they perish. Those women with peaceful, good, and discreet husbands who are devoted to them, praise God for this boon, which is not inconsiderable, for a greater boon in the world could not be given them. And may they be diligent in serving, loving, and cherishing their husbands in the loyalty of their heart, as they should, keeping their peace and praying to God to uphold and save them. And those women who have husbands neither completely good nor completely bad should still praise God for not having the worst and should strive to moderate their vices and pacify them, according to their conditions. And those women who have husbands who are cruel, mean, and savage should strive to endure them while trying to overcome their vices and lead them back, if they can, to a reasonable and seemly life. And if they are so obstinate that their wives are unable to do anything, at least they will acquire great merit for their souls through the virtue of patience. And everyone will bless them and support them.

So, my ladies, be humble and patient, and God's grace will grow in you, and praise will be given to you as well as the Kingdom of Heaven. For Saint Gregory has said that patience is the entrance to Paradise and the way of Jesus Christ. And may none of you be forced into holding frivolous opinions nor be hardened in them, lacking all basis in reason, nor be jealous or disturbed in mind, nor haughty in speech, nor outrageous in your acts, for these things disturb the mind and lead to madness. Such behavior is unbecoming and unfitting for women.

And you, virgin maidens, be pure, simple, and serene, without vagueness, for the snares of evil men are set for you. Keep your eyes lowered, with few words in your mouths, and act respectfully. Be armed with the strength of virtue against the tricks of the deceptive and avoid their company.

And widows, may there be integrity in your dress, conduct, and speech; piety in your deeds and way of life; prudence in your bearing; patience (so necessary!), strength, and resistance in tribulations and difficult affairs; humility in your heart, countenance, and speech; and charity in your works.

In brief, all women—whether noble, bourgeois, or lower-class—be well-informed in all things and cautious in defending your honor and chastity against your enemies! My ladies, see how these men accuse you of so many vices in everything. Make liars of them all by showing forth your virtue, and prove their attacks false by acting well, so that you can say with the Psalmist, "the vices of the evil will fall on their heads." Repel the deceptive flatterers who, using different charms, seek with various tricks to steal that which you must consummately guard, that is, your honor and the beauty of your praise. Oh my ladies, flee, flee the foolish love they urge on you! Flee it, for God's sake, flee! For no good can come to you from it. Rather, rest assured that however deceptive their lures, their end is always to your detriment. And do not believe the contrary, for it cannot be otherwise. Remember, dear ladies, how these men call you frail, unserious, and easily influenced but yet try hard, using all kinds of strange and deceptive tricks, to catch you, just as one lays traps for wild animals. Flee, flee, my ladies, and avoid their company—under these smiles are hidden deadly and painful poisons. And so may it please you, my most respected ladies, to cultivate virtue, to flee vice, to increase and multiply our City, and to rejoice and act well. And may I, your servant, commend myself to you, praying to God who by His grace has granted me to live in this world and to persevere in His holy service. May He in the end have mercy on my great sins and grant to me the joy which lasts forever, which I may, by His grace, afford to you. Amen.

HERE ENDS THE THIRD AND LAST PART OF THE BOOK OF THE CITY OF LADIES.

Frontispiece from Saxton's *Atlas*, 1579.

The Early Modern Period

We see the past through lenses that show us something of the world we are living in.
How we mark periods in history depends less on an objective evaluation of evidence
than on our sense of its relation to our own present. The centuries between 1500 and
1700 have been termed the "Renaissance," and, more recently, "the early modern
period." They were also centuries in which Europe and England saw a massive change
in Christian religious thought and practice; this has been called the "Reformation."
What do these names mean, and what do they tell us about our understanding of this
single and continuous stretch of time?

However we describe these centuries, they encompassed events that altered the ways
people lived and thought. In 1500 England, and the rest of the nations of Europe, were
Catholic. Apart from its few communities of Jews, Christendom was united by a universal
church whose head was the Pope in Rome, and its faithful prayed according to a common
liturgy in Latin. The shape of the cosmos was determined by Aristotelian physics and what
could be deduced from the scriptural story of creation. It was believed that the earth was
the center of the universe and composed of four elements—earth, air, fire, and water; that
the human body was a balance of these elements; and that nature, read as if it were a book,
revealed a divinely sanctioned moral order. Christian subjects generally respected their national or positive law, which they saw as a mirror of God's law of nature and providentially
guaranteed; they assumed it would protect them from tyranny as well as anarchy. A person's place in society tended to be fixed at birth; the majority of folk lived in country villages, worked the land, and traded in regional markets.

By the end of the seventeenth century, much—though not all—of this way of life
had vanished. Certain of its features would remain in place for the next hundred years,
as historians who study *la longue durée* ("the long term" from the seventeenth to the
nineteenth century) during which social, political and economic structures change
very slowly, remind us: land continued to be farmed by methods followed "time out of
mind"; manufacture was still largely done by individuals on small, handmade machines.
Religion continued to determine every aspect of life; science and art, politics and eco-
nomics were discussed in terms supplied by religious thought and institutions. But
Christianity was no longer of one piece. Europe had become divided by the establishment of Protestantism in the Low Countries, Scandinavia, and most of Germany. England and Scotland were also Protestant, but with a difference: the first conformed to
the doctrine and practices of the Church of England, the second to the requirements of
Presbyterianism. Ireland, speaking its Celtic language and retaining many of its ancient
customs, remained Catholic despite English attempts at conquest and conversion.
Catholics in England, always suspected of subversive intentions, were barely tolerated.
Sects proliferated: among them were Anabaptists, Puritans, and Quakers; commonly,
their religious doctrines called for massive social change. Cosmic order, too, had
changed; it was no longer thought of as geocentric, nor did its elements consist of four
primary materials. A natural philosophy based on experimental methods had begun to
reshape the disciplines of physics, medicine, and biology; such ancient authorities as

Aristotle, Galen, and Pliny were no longer unquestioned. Though sketched in principle by Sir Francis Bacon in his treatise on scientific inquiry, *Novum Organum* ("the new instrument"), published in 1620, a systematic investigation of nature was not underway before the Restoration of the Stuart monarchy in 1660, when scientists in England consolidated their status as intellectuals by forming the Royal Society of London for the Improvement of Natural Knowledge—an organization vigorously supported by the new Stuart king, Charles II. But the worldview that this investigation would help to confirm was already evident early in the seventeenth century. The work of the Italian physicist Galileo Galilei on gravitational force had demonstrated that the most elementary laws of nature were mathematical; the German astronomer Johannes Kepler had confirmed that the universe was heliocentric; the English physician William Harvey had established that the body was energized not by the eccentric flow of "humors" but by a circulation of blood to and from the heart; and the Dutch cosmographer Gerhardus Mercator had discovered the means to navigate the globe safely by accurately mapping latitude and longitude. An international trade, now hugely stimulated by the development of colonies in the Americas, promised wealth to investors willing to take risks and prosperity to the towns and cities in which they lived.

In England, social and political life had been transformed by the activities of city-dwellers, or "burgesses," many of whom were merchants, and also by a civil war. Involving English, Scots, and Irish subjects and parties, it had been fought over religious and social issues but also on a matter of principle. British subjects were to be governed by a monarch whose authority and power were not absolute but limited by law and the actions of Parliament, a legislative assembly representing the monarch's subjects. As a whole, the nation was conceived of as a "mystical body politic"; as the radical Bishop of Winchester John Ponet had declared, the monarch's office—not his person—was sacred. Towns and cities became crowded even as they expanded with new streets, marketplaces, and buildings for private as well as public use. Country folk, flocking to these burgeoning urban centers, succumbed to diseases created by filth and overcrowding and died younger than did their rural relatives. But England was becoming a nation of city dwellers, and everyone knew of "citizens" who had gained wealth and station in these exciting, if also terrifying, cities.

THE HUMANIST RENAISSANCE AND EARLY MODERN SOCIETY

The period from 1500 to 1700 has been understood as a "Renaissance"—literally a "rebirth." Many of its features had already been registered in that earlier renaissance of the twelfth century, particularly an interest in classical authors and their modes of expression in logic and rhetoric. By 1400, however, Italian scholars had begun to reread with fresh eyes the works of Greek and Roman authors such as Plato, Aristotle, Virgil, Ovid, and Horace. What was "reborn" as a result was a sense of the meanings to be discovered in the here and now, in the social, political, and economic everyday world. Writing about the intellectual vitality of the age, the French humanist François Rabelais had his amiable character, the giant Gargantua, confess that his own education had been "darksome, obscured with clouds of ignorance." Gargantua knows, however, that his son will be taught differently:

IMAGO·ERASMI·ROTERODA
MI·AB·ALBERTO·DVRERO·AD
VIVAM·EFFIGIEM·DELINIATA·

ΤΗΝ·ΚΡΕΙΤΤΩ·ΤΑ·ΣΥΓΓΡΑΜ
ΜΑΤΑ·ΔΕΙΞΕΙ

·MDXXVI·

Albrecht Dürer, *Erasmus of Rotterdam*,
1521.

Good literature has been restored unto its former light and dignity, and with such amendment and increase of knowledge, that now hardly should I be admitted unto the first form of the little grammar-school boys ... I see robbers, hangmen, freebooters, tapsters, ostlers, and such like, of the very rubbish of the people, more learned now than the doctors and preachers were in my time.

These comically overstated remarks nevertheless convey the spirit of the Renaissance: learning was no longer to be devoted only to securing salvation but should address the conditions of ordinary life as well. More important, it should be disseminated through all ranks of society.

The writers and scholars responsible for the rebirth of a secular culture, derived in large measure from the pre-Christian cultures of the ancient Mediterranean, have been known as "humanists," because they read "humane" as well as "sacred" letters; their intellectual and artistic practices have been termed "humanism." They cultivated certain habits of thought that became widely adopted by early modern thinkers of all kinds: skill in using language analytically, attentiveness to public and political affairs as well as private and moral ones, and an acute appreciation for differences between peoples, regions, and times. It was, after all, the humanists who began to realize that the classical past required *understanding*. They recognized it as unfamiliar, neither Christian nor European, and they knew, therefore, that it had to be studied, interpreted, and, in a sense, reborn. From its inception in Italy, the work of the humanists traveled north and west, to France, the Low Countries, Germany, the Iberian peninsula, and eventually the British Isles.

At the same time, the cultures of these regions were changing in unprecedented ways. As much as an older world was being reborn, a modern world was being born, and it is in this sense that we can speak of these centuries not only as the Renaissance but also as the "early modern period." Its modernity was registered in various ways, many of them having to do with systems of quantification. Instruments for measuring time and space provided a knowledge of physical nature and its control. Sailing to the new world in 1585, Sir Walter Raleigh made use of Mercator's projection, published in 1568. Means were designed to compute the wealth that was being created by manufacture and trade. Money was used in new and complex ways, its flow managed through such innovations as double-entry bookkeeping and letters of exchange that registered debt and credit in inter-regional markets. The capital that accumulated as a result of these kinds of transactions fueled merchant banks, joint-stock companies, and—notably in England—trading companies that sponsored colonies abroad. Heralded with enthusiasm by William Drayton in 1606, the Virginia colony was reflected in a more muted fashion five years later in Shakespeare's *The Tempest*. In England especially, wealth was increasingly based not on land but on money, and the change encouraged a social mobility that reflected but also exploited the old hierarchy. The effort to ascend the social ladder could prove ruinous, as George Gascoigne's career confirmed. But riches could also make it possible for an artisan's son to purchase a coat of arms and become a gentleman, as Shakespeare did. More important, moneyed wealth supported the artistic and scholarly institutions that allowed the stepson of a bricklayer to attend the best school in London, to profit from the business of the theater, and to compose literary works of sufficient brilliance to make him Poet Laureate—as Ben Jonson did. "Ambition is like choler," warned Francis Bacon; it makes men "active, earnest, full of alacrity and stirring." But if ambition "be stopped and cannot have his way, it becommeth adust, and thereby maligne and venomous." Early modern society was certainly both active and stirring, but the very energy that gave it momentum could also lead to hardship, distress, and personal tragedy.

Urban life flourished in conditions increasingly hospitable to commerce; rural existence became precarious as small farms failed. During the previous century, the nobility had begun to enlarge their estates by the incorporation or "enclosing" of what had formerly been public or common land. They sought to profit from the newest kind of farming: sheep. As Sir Thomas More's *Utopia* illustrates, thousands of men and women who had worked the land on modest estates lost their livelihoods as a result. The situation got worse when Henry VIII broke England's tie to the Catholic Church, for Henry added to the property of the very rich by giving them the land he had confiscated from the church. Many of the poor and dispossessed came to the cities, particularly London; others traveled through the country, looking for odd work, begging and thieving. Some, like Isabella Whitney, would try city life only to find it wanting. By the early 1600s, a few men and women were electing to seek their fortunes in the Americas. Despite such constraints, however, the great centers of commerce—Bristol, Norwich, and London—sustained large populations, employed not only in trade but in many kinds of manufacture. One of the most important was printing. The invention of movable type in 1436 by a German printer, Johann Gutenberg, revolutionized the dissemination of texts. A single illuminated manuscript took years to produce and provided what was often a unique version of a text, an item that might cost as much as a small farm; a printing press could quickly produce multiple copies of a text, all of them identical, for as little as a few shillings.

Both the mentality of the "Renaissance" and the more comprehensive culture of the early modern period are illustrated by the history of the most frequently disseminated and

Jan van der Straet, called Stradanus, Impressio Librorum (Book Printing): Plate 4 of the *Nova Reperta* (New Discoveries), late 16th century.

contested text of these centuries: the Bible. It was the work of humanists to establish what that text was (after centuries of corrupted versions) and then to translate it into the vernacular languages. Desiderius Erasmus provided accurate Hebrew and Greek texts and translated them into Latin. Printed English translations begin with William Tyndale's New Testament, introduced to England in the 1520s. Later versions included the Geneva Bible with its Calvinist commentary; the Bishops' Bible, repudiating much of that commentary; and the King James Bible or "Authorized Version," a work by forty-seven translators published in 1611. Protestant doctrine emphasized the importance of reading Scripture as a means to spiritual enlightenment, and the preface to the King James Bible insists that for this purpose a translation is as good as the original: "No cause why the word translated should be denied to be the word." But the importance of the Bible went beyond its status as the basis for religious belief.

Henry VIII, following his divorce from Queen Catherine of Aragon and marriage to Anne Boleyn, a lady of the court already celebrated by the poet Sir Thomas Wyatt, instituted perhaps the most important feature of Protestant practice in England: that the Bible be read and spoken in English. This, along with the Act in Restraint of Appeals in 1533 making the English church independent of Rome, and the Act of Supremacy in 1534 establishing the monarch as the head of that church, proved to be decisive for Protestants in England. As the Church of England under Elizabeth I and, later, James I came increasingly under criticism from Presbyterians, Puritans, and other sectarians of different kinds, how to read and eventually preach from the text of the Bible became a point of contention. Disputes over doctrine regarding the nature and efficacy of the sacraments and the place of images and icons in religious worship divided communities and even families; occasionally, they even disturbed the peace. Here the story is a grim one. Catholics in the north of England unsuccessfully resisted Henry's imposition of Protestantism in their Pilgrimage of Grace in 1536. Protestants, in turn, were persecuted by Mary I throughout her reign; many of their stories are recounted in John Foxe's *Book of Martyrs*. Catholics were suppressed by Elizabeth I, and sectarians of various denominations were required to adhere to Anglican forms of worship and obey episcopal power under the Stuarts.

Some, seeing the Bible as an eminently useful text, relied on it to argue for the reform of both church and state. This was especially true for a growing number of women writers, who were moved to rethink and resist their customary place as the inferiors of men. While the scholarly Juan Luis Vives had attributed their natures to the disobedient Eve of Genesis, Aemelia Lanyer and others rejected this interpretation. Mary Herbert and Queen Elizabeth each translated the Psalms, in effect turning themselves into interpreters of Scripture; and referring to particular passages in the Bible, agitators like Rachel Speght and Ester Sowernam argued that women were the equal of men. In 1641, women convinced that Scripture granted them the right to protest religious abuses presented their *Petition of the Gentlewomen and Tradesmen's Wives, In and About the City of London* to the House of Commons. Much of the general debate regarding the nature and power of the monarchy and other forms of government reflected interpretations of Scripture. Drawing on biblical representations of conscience, John Ponet insisted that a monarch was obliged to obey the law of the land and thus to adhere to a "constitution"; reflecting the same passages in Scripture, King James VI of Scotland, later James I of England, thought that a monarch should respect only divine law and be considered "absolute." Continued into the next generation of thinkers, this dispute ended in the execution of Charles I. God's word, it turned out, could have a distinctly practical application.

Many features of Renaissance and early modern culture are again in transition today: the printed book, which once superseded the manuscript, is now challenged by computer-generated hypertext; the nation state, which once eclipsed the feudal domain and divided "Christendom," is now qualified by an international economy; and the belief in human progress, which was once applauded as an advance over the medieval faith in divine providence, is now subject to criticism, in large part because of such kinds of injustice and inequity as slavery, colonialism, and the exploitation of wage labor—all factors in the growth of early modern England and other states in Europe. As modern and postmodern readers, we have a special affinity with our early modern counterparts. Like them, we study change.

HISTORY AND EPIC

The political life of the sixteenth century was dominated by the genius of a single dynasty: the Tudors. Its founder was Owen Tudor, a squire of an ancient Welsh family. Employed at the court of Henry V, he eventually married Henry's widow, Catherine of Valois. The first Tudor monarch was their grandson, Henry, Earl of Richmond, who defeated Richard III at Bosworth Field in 1485 to become Henry VII. He married Elizabeth, daughter of Edward IV, whom Richard III had succeeded—a fortunate

Color Plate 11 Rowland Lockey. *Sir Thomas More, His Father, His Household and His Descendants*, fl. 1593–1616 after Hans Holbein, 1497 or 8–1543. Commissioned by Thomas More II, grandson of Sir Thomas More, this painting portrays five generations of this Roman Catholic family. The first seven figures from left to right are modeled on a lost painting by Hans Holbein. Sir Thomas More himself is shown seated at the left, wearing a brown robe. His father, in red, sits next to him, while behind him to either side stand his wife, Anne, and his son, John. His daughters Cecily, Elizabeth, and Margaret are grouped at the center. (*By courtesy of The National Portrait Gallery, London.*)

Color Plate 12 Nicholas Hilliard, *The Young Man Amongst Roses*, c. 1597. Hilliard, the greatest miniaturist of the Elizabethan age, here represents an exquisite aristocratic young man in the pose of melancholic lover. *(Victoria & Albert Museum, London/Art Resource, NY.)*

Color Plate 13 Inigo Jones, *Fiery Spirit*, costume design for a torchbearer in *The Lord's Masque,* performed 14 February 1613. Jones designed this masque as part of the celebrations for the marriage of James I's daughter Elizabeth to Frederick V, the Elector Palatine. The elaborate costume designs were modeled on those created for Florentine court theater. *(The Devonshire Collection, Chatsworth. Reproduced by permission of the Duke of Devonshire and the Chatsworth Settlement Trustees.)*

Color Plate 14 Marcus Gheeraerts II (1561–1636), *Portrait of Captain Thomas Lee*, 1594. Thomas Lee served as an army officer during the Elizabethan colonization of Ireland. This painting portrays him as part barefoot Irish foot soldier and part elaborately accoutered English gentleman. On the tree behind him appears a Latin quotation from Livy, "both to act and to suffer with fortitude is a Roman's part," which is what the Roman patriot Scaevola is supposed to have said when he was captured by rebel Etruscans as he entered their camp disguised in their garb. The painting is thus an elaborate allegory protesting Lee's English loyalty despite his friendship with such Irish chiefs as Hugh O'Neill. On 13 February 1601, Lee died a traitor's death as punishment for his role in the Earl of Essex's rebellion. *(Oil on canvas. © Tate, London 2002.)*

Color Plate 15   *Portrait of John Donne*, c. 1595. *(Private Collection/Bridgeman Art Library.)*

Color Plate 16   Unknown artist, *Portrait of John Milton*, c. 1629. This is very likely the portrait of the great poet at 21, as he appeared at Cambridge, of whom John Aubrey wrote "he was so fair that they called him the lady of Christ's College." *(By courtesy of The National Portrait Gallery, London.)*

Color Plate 17 Peter Paul Rubens, *The Apotheosis of James I*, from the Banqueting House, installed 1636. Idolized and knighted in London, the great Flemish painter Rubens was commissioned by Charles I to celebrate the greatness of his father James I's reign in a series of paintings for the Banqueting House, the ceremonial dining hall of Whitehall Palace. This large oval at the center of the room's ceiling depicts James I with scepter in hand and his foot atop a globe, symbolizing imperial domination. Justice lifts James up in an expression of the Stuart kings' belief in the divine right of kings. The side panels show genii bearing a garland and genii playing with animals. *(Crown copyright: Historic Royal Palaces. Reproduced by permission of Historic Royal Palaces under license from the Controller of Her Majesty's Stationery Office.)*

Color Plate 18 Peter Paul Rubens (1577–1640), *Minerva Protects Pax from Mars (Peace and War)*, 1630. Rubens produced this work for Charles I to commemorate the English-Spanish peace treaty, which the painter himself helped negotiate. The painting optimistically represents both the court of Charles I at its zenith and the hope for European peace that would be dashed ten years later. The painting is charged with movement. A satyr grasps the fruits of peace, while to the right, Minerva, goddess of wisdom, drives out Mars, god of war, and the avenging goddess Fury Allecto. At the center, Peace extends her full breast to the baby Plutus, god of riches. *(Oil [identified] on canvas, 203.5 × 298.0. © National Gallery, London.)*

Color Plate 19 Sir Anthony van Dyck, *Philip, 4th Earl and His Family*, 1635. Born at Antwerp, Van Dyck studied under Rubens for five years. Charles I knighted and appointed Van Dyck as court painter in 1632. This painting was commissioned by the Earl of Pembroke and painted in London in 1634–1635. In 1652 it was moved to Wilton House, where it was placed in the "Double Cube" room designed by Inigo Jones. *(Earl of Pembroke, Wilton House, Wilton, Salisbury, UK.)*

Color Plate 20 Cornelius Johnson (or Jonson) (1593–1661), *The Capel Family*, c. 1640. This painting in the style of Van Dyck portrays the royalist Arthur Capel, who was executed the same year as Charles I. In the background appear gardens, perhaps those of his home at Little Hadham. (*By courtesy of The National Portrait Gallery, London.*)

event for the people of England, as it united the two parties by whom the crown had been disputed for many decades. Once Henry, who represented the House of Lancaster (whose emblem was a red rose) was joined to Elizabeth, a member of the House of York (signified by a white rose), the so-called "Wars of the Roses" were at an end. Henry VII's bureaucratic skills then settled the kingdom in ways that allowed it to grow and become identified as a single nation, however much it also comprised different peoples: the midlands and the north were distinguished from the more populous south by dialectal forms of speech; and to the west, in Cornwall and Wales, many English subjects still spoke Cornish and Welsh. More thoroughly Celtic were Ireland, across the sea to the west, and Scotland, to the north. While the Anglo-Normans had invaded Ireland in the twelfth century, it was not until the reign of Elizabeth that the English pursued the subjugation of Ireland by colonizing plantations and conducting a brutal military campaign that produced famine, massacres, and the forced relocation of people. But this supposed English fiefdom remained rebellious and effectively unconquered for Elizabeth's entire reign. Its resistance to English rule was crushed only in 1603, an event that marked the end of an independent Ireland for three hundred years. Oliver Cromwell's account of the massacre of the city of Drogheda in 1649, related in his *Letters from Ireland*, illustrates a later instance of the brutality typical of the English conquest of Ireland. Scotland, to the far north, was a separate and generally unfriendly kingdom with strong ties to France until James VI of Scotland became James I of England. His accession to the English throne in 1603 began a process that would end with the complete union of the two kingdoms in 1707. And there were even more remote regions to consider: England's colonization of the Americas began under Elizabeth I, progressed under James I, and allowed the English to think of themselves as an imperial power.

Writing history offered a way to reinforce the developing sense of nationhood, a project all the more appealing after the creation of an English church and the beginnings of what was thought to be a British empire. Medieval historians had concentrated on the actions of ambitious men and women whose lives reflected their good or bad qualities; early modern historians wrote about events and their manifold causes. William Camden's *Britannia* and Raphael Holinshed's *Chronicles of England, Scotland, and Ireland* (the source for many of Shakespeare's plays) celebrate the deeds and the character of the early peoples of the British Isles. The land itself became the subject of comment: William Harrison wrote a description of the English counties (included in Holinshed); John Stow surveyed the neighborhoods of London; and Michael Drayton, a Stuart poet, wrote a mythopoetic account of England's towns and countryside entitled *Poly-Olbion*. As a history, however, it is Richard Hakluyt's collection of travel stories, *The Principal Navigations, Voyages and Discoveries of the English Nation*, that has proved most memorable over time. It reports in magnificent detail the exploration of the Americas in the latter half of the sixteenth century. Accounts of this wild and fruitful land fired the imaginations of English readers, who, it was hoped, would decide to promote and even participate in the laborious task of colonization. Describing landfall on the coast of Virginia in 1585, Arthur Barlow evoked the image of a paradise, "where we smelled so sweet and so strong a smell as if we had been in the midst of some delicate garden abounding with all kind of odoriferous flowers. . . . I think in all the world the like abundance is not to be found." Attempts to occupy this land of incredible natural wealth were determined by two principal objectives: securing profitable trade with the Indians, and possessing land from which to extract such resources as timber, furs, fish, and eventually, tobacco. The hope of finding gold was on everyone's mind. The Chesapeake Bay and its environs were settled by men interested in commerce, often at great personal expense. The Massachusetts coast attracted Puritan divines and their flocks, and while these colonists also profited from trade, matters of faith were supposed to be their principal concern. By celebrating a national identity, these and other contemporary narratives reveal their thematic connections with the epic, a genre of poetic fiction. But they do not conform to that genre as contemporary poetry represented it—expressing heroic grandeur not only in action but also in the musical verse form and elevated language of the epic tradition.

The masterpieces of early modern English epic are represented by Edmund Spenser's *The Faerie Queene* and John Milton's *Paradise Lost.* Spenser imitated continental models to create an English Protestant epic-romance, an optimistic projection of Elizabethan culture. The realities of Elizabeth I's reign were indeed far from the poet's vision of things, but they were nonetheless very impressive. England's cities had grown to be centers of world commerce, and the bold explorations of such men as Sir Francis Drake testified to the nation's seafaring power. In the figures of his poem, Spenser embodied the energies producing this expansive growth. His virtuous knights overcome monstrous threats to order, peace, and tranquillity. Aspects of the queen's own genius are reflected in his heroines. Like the warrior maiden Britomart, Elizabeth I assumed a martial character when England was in danger from abroad; like his Queen Mercilla, she was supposed to be gracious to her enemies—a trait somewhat belied by her speeches to Parliament agreeing to the execution of Mary Queen of Scots. Like the virgin Una, she stood for what the poet and most of her readers believed was the one true faith: Protestantism. And like Spenser's enigmatic and distant Queen Gloriana, the Faerie Queene of the title, she exercised her authority and power in unpredictable ways: secrecy and dissimulation were her stock in trade. To her subjects, her majesty was awful and sometimes terrifying. But she was also mortal, and at her death, few could have foreseen the new and divided nation that would come into being with the accession of James I.

The new king was greeted with mixed feelings. On the one hand, his claim to the throne was not disputed; on the other hand, he came from Scotland, long an enemy of England and always a source of anxiety to those who sought dominion over the British Isles as a whole. Although educated by the humanist George Buchanan, whose treatises praising republican government were widely known and read, James, as his own treatise *The True Law of Free Monarchy* shows, favored absolute rule and believed that a monarch should be *lex loquens*, the living spirit of the law, and therefore not bound by the terms of national or positive law. His personal conduct appeared to be dubious. His critics represented him as frequently unkempt and claimed that he preferred to hunt deer rather than to take charge of matters of state. Disputes with the House of Commons over money to support the Crown's activities were frequent. Reports of intrigue with Catholic Spain shattered the nation's sense of security; an attempt in 1605 to blow up the Houses of Parliament, revealed as the Gunpowder Plot, caused a near panic. These and other kinds of unrest grew more intense when James's heir, Charles I, proved to be even more autocratic than his father. Charles's queen, Henrietta Maria, the daughter of Henry IV of France, was a Catholic, and it was rumored that she was treacherous. Religious controversy raged throughout the British

Isles, and the struggle over the authority and power of the monarch culminated in a bloody civil war. Across England and Scotland, forces loyal to the king fought the army of Parliament, led by Oliver Cromwell, a Puritan Member of the Commons. The war, which lasted from 1642 to 1651, ended with the defeat of the royalists.

In 1649 Charles I was captured and executed by order of Parliament, and England began to be governed as a republic. She was no longer a kingdom but a Commonwealth, and this period in her history is known as the Interregnum, the period between kingdoms. The long-advocated change, now a reality, could hardly have begun in a more shocking way. The monarchy had always been regarded as a sacred office and institution, as Shakespeare's Richard II had said:

> Not all the water in the rough rude sea
> Can wash the balm off from an anointed king;
> The breath of worldly men cannot depose
> The deputy elected by the Lord.

But in the course of half a century, the people had proved themselves to be a sovereign power, and it was politically irrelevant that Charles, on the block, exemplified a regal self-control. As the Parliamentarian poet Andrew Marvell later wrote of the King's admirable courage at his execution: "He nothing common did or mean / Upon that memorable scene . . . Nor called the gods with vulgar spite / To vindicate his helpless right."

The conflict itself, its causes and its outcome, have been variously interpreted. As a religious and cultural struggle, the Civil War, also known as the Wars of Three Kingdoms, expressed the resistance of Scots Presbyterians and Irish Catholics to the centralizing control of the English church and government. As a revolution in government, the conflict was defined by common lawyers, energized by Puritan enthusiasm, and marked the nation's transition to a society in which the absolute rule by a monarch was no longer a possibility. The people themselves had acquired a voice. To some extent this was a religious voice. Puritans who professed a belief in congregational church government were generally proponents of republican rule. Their dedication to the ideal of a society of equals under the law was shared by men and women of other sects: the Levellers, led by John Lilburne, who argued for a written constitution, universal manhood suffrage, and religious toleration (for God, Lilburne wrote, "doth not choose many rich, nor many wise"); the Diggers, led by Gerrard Winstanley, who proposed to institute a communistic society in the wastelands they were ploughing and cultivating; the Quakers, led by George Fox, who rejected all forms of church order in deference to the inner light of an individual conscience and, insisting on social equality, refused to take off their hats before gentry or nobility; and the Ranters, who denied the authority of Scripture and saw God everywhere in nature. Without widespread acceptance of the egalitarian concept that had initiated the Protestant reformation—all believers are members of a real though invisible priesthood—it is hard to see how the move from a monarchy to a representative and republican government could have taken place.

The most comprehensive contemporary history of the war, *The True Historical Narrative of the Rebellion and Civil Wars in England,* by Edward Hyde, Earl of Clarendon, was not published before 1704, but the troubled period found an oblique commentary in what is arguably England's greatest and certainly most humanistic epic poem: Milton's *Paradise Lost,* in print by 1667. Milton's career was inextricably bound up with the fate of the Commonwealth. Educated at Cambridge and with his reputation as a poet well established, Milton had begun by 1649 to contribute to a defense of Puritanism and the creation of a republican government. Despite worsening eyesight, he published *The Tenure of Kings and Magistrates*, a sustained and eloquent apology for tyrannicide, after the execution of Charles I; and in his *Eikonoklastes* ("image-breaker"), written after he was made Latin secretary to the new executive, the Council of State, he derided attempts by royalists to celebrate Charles I in John Gauden's pamphlet *Eikon Basilike* ("image of a king"). In 1660, disturbed by the proposed restoration of Charles Stuart, soon to be Charles II, Milton—now completely blind—published his last political treatise, *The Ready and Easy Way to Establish a Commonwealth*. It presented the case for a republicanism that had already lost most of its popularity: the government of the Commonwealth had adopted measures that resembled the autocratic rule of the monarchy it had overthrown. Meanwhile, the composition of *Paradise Lost* was underway. Indebted to many of Spenser's themes in *The Faerie Queene*, Milton infused his subject—the fall of the rebellious angels and the exile from paradise of the disobedient Adam and Eve—with the spirit of the account in Genesis. His poem is the product of a doubly dark vision of life. Sightless and suffering again what he felt were the constraints of a monarchy, Milton's story of exile from paradise spoke to his own and England's loss of innocence and painful acquisition of the knowledge of good and evil during the period of the war and its aftermath. His *Paradise Lost* and its sequel, *Paradise Regained*, express the most provocative ambiguities of contemporary English culture; they were—and still are—praised as rivalling the epics of Homer, Virgil, and Dante in their power and scope.

Drama and Social Satire

Drama provided another perspective on English life. While epics depicted the grander aspirations of the nation, its human character was expressed in stage plays, masques or speaking pageants, and dramatic processions. These forms exploited the material of chronicle to illustrate not only the virtues of heroes but also their foibles and limitations; history's villains warned viewers that evil would be punished, if not by civil authority then by providence. Writing tragedy based on history and legend, Marlowe and Shakespeare complicated the direct moralism of medieval drama. Rather than portraying characters who became victims of their own misdoings, rising to power only to fall in disgrace, the early modern stage showed virtue and vice as intertwined—a hero's tragic error could also be at the heart of his greatness. The origins of evil were seen as mysterious, even obscure. Some sense of this moral ambiguity can be traced to the tragedies of the Roman philosopher Seneca, which were translated into English and published in 1581. English drama reproduced many of their features: the five-act structure, rapid-fire dialogue punctuated by pithy maxims, and images of tyranny, revenge, and fate illustrated by haunting dreams and echoing curses. Shakespeare's *Richard III*, the most frequently performed of his plays in his own time, and Elizabeth Cary's *Tragedy of Mariam*, the first tragedy in English written by a woman, powerfully exemplify the qualities of early modern tragedy.

If tragedy turned away from straightforward piety, so did comedy. The medieval drama of Christian salvation, in which the hero's struggle against sin was ended by his acknowledgment of grace, was replaced with plays about the wars between the sexes and between parents and children. Much of this material was modeled on the comedies of Plautus, a Roman playwright, and on the tales or *novellas* of contemporary Italian writers. Playwrights like Ben Jonson also found a wealth of material in the improvisatory Italian *commedia dell'arte*, with its stock characters of the old dotard, the cuckolded husband, the damsel in distress, and the mountebank or quack. *The Alchemist*, chiefly a satire on confidence men and their credulous victims, those tradesmen and entrepreneurs seeking a quick and easy return on investments (especially in the Americas), concludes somewhat ironically by giving the prize to the burgess Lovewit, who disdains censorious critique in favor of a genial wit. An even more topical form of comedy combined some of these continental traditions with themes and figures specifically drawn from London life. Middleton and Dekker's *The Roaring Girl* dramatizes the urban culture of guildsmen, shopkeepers, city wives, and "coney-catchers"—con artists—as they encounter the city gentry and their servants.

The social criticism implicit in these plays was, of course, one reason why they were so popular. Their pointed censure of various kinds of behavior, including religious practices, showed how ready audiences were to imagine a reform of their society. The end of the century saw a brilliant example of satire in a series of pamphlets secretly published by an anonymous author, known as Martin Marprelate, who disparaged all aspects of the episcopacy and promoted in its place a frankly Presbyterian church, in which authority would reside in Scripture and in congregations rather than in a church hierarchy. But it was the stage that was generally regarded as responsible for both illustrating social failings and stirring up discontent. Although some, like the playwright Thomas Heywood, praised plays as a form of instruction for the unschooled, others, like the Puritan pamphleteer Philip Stubbes, asserted that plays "maintain bawdry, insinuate foolery, and revive the remembrance of heathen idolatry." As Stephen Gosson wrote in *Plays Confuted in Five Actions:*

> If private men be suffered to forsake their calling because they desire to talk gentlemen-like in satin & velvet, with a buckler at their heels, proportion is so broken, unity dissolved, harmony confounded, that the whole body must be dismembered, and the prince or head cannot choose but sicken.

The fear was not only that the tricksters of drama would be the objects of emulation rather than scorn, but also that the actors' masquerade of identities would spur social instability in the public theater's audience, ranging from the groundlings in the pit to the gentry in the higher-priced seats. Parliament had tried to maintain social order by regulating, through sumptuary laws, what style and fabrics persons of a particular rank could wear. A subject's experience of the theater, where commoners played the parts of nobility and dressed accordingly, might discourage observation of these laws, which were repealed in 1633.

Londoners enjoyed two kinds of theater: public and private. The public theaters were open to all audiences for a fee and were generally immune from oversight because they were located outside the City of London, in an area referred to as the Liberties, notorious for prostitution and the sport of bear-baiting. London's two biggest theaters were located there: the Fortune, and the more famous Globe, home to Shakespeare's company. Private theaters—open only to invited guests—were located in the large houses of the gentry, the Inns of Court (the schools of common law), and the guildhalls; the best known, Blackfriars, was housed in an old monastery. Their performances were acted almost exclusively by boy actors, although the popularity of these companies was short-lived. James I, annoyed by the send-up of the Scots court in *Eastward Ho!*, a play that Ben Jonson had a part in writing, dissolved his queen's own company, known as the Queen's Revels Children. The most private and prestigious stage of all remained the royal court. Shakespeare's *The Tempest*, performed at King James's court in 1611, illustrated the resources an indoor stage could provide. By its distinctive framing of dramatic action, it invited the audience to suspend its disbelief and appreciate the illusionism of theater. Of exclusive interest to this audience was the masque, a speaking pageant accompanied by music and dancing, staged with elaborate sets and costumes, and acted by members of the court, including the Queens Anna and Henrietta Maria. But in 1649, a Puritan Parliament, disgusted with what it considered to be the immorality of the drama, banned all stage plays, and the theaters remained closed until the Restoration in 1660.

Lyric Poetry and Romance

In early modern England, epic narratives, stage plays, and satire in all forms were genres designed for audiences and readers the writer did not know, a general public with varied tastes and background. Lyric poetry, prose romances, and tales were more often written for a closed circle of friends. Circulated in manuscript, these genres allowed a writer's wit to play on personal or coterie matters. Here writers could speak of the pain of love or the thrill of ambition, and both reveal and, in a sense, create their own identities in and through language. By imitating and at the same time changing the conventions of the lyric, particularly as they were illustrated by the Italian poet Francesco Petrarch, English poets were able to represent a persona, or fictive self, that became in turn a model for others. Unlike Petrarch, who saw his lady as imbued with numinous power before which he could only submit, Sir Thomas Wyatt and Sir Philip Sidney imagined love in social and very human terms. In the struggle to gain affection and power, their subjectivity took strength from their conquests as well as their resistance to defeat. The origins of the lyric in song are attested in the verse of Thomas Campion, much of which was actually set to music. Its uses in pastoral (whether erotic or spiritual) are illustrated by poets as different as Robert Herrick, John Donne, and Andrew Marvell. At times, its objects of adoration could be divine or mystical, as in the verse of George Herbert and Henry Vaughan. Women poets, such as Lady Mary Wroth and Katherine Philips, reworked the conventions of the love lyric to encompass a feminine perspective on passion and, equally important, on friendship. Sonnet sequences were popular and, reflecting a taste for narrative romance, often dramatized a conflict between lovers. Shakespeare wrote the best-known sonnets of the period. His cast of characters—including the poet as principal speaker, his beloved male friend, a rival poet, and a fickle lady—appear as protagonists in a drama of love, betrayal, devotion, and despair. Some poets embedded their love poetry in prose narratives that told a story, as the Italian poet Dante Alighieri had in his sequence of songs and sonnets to the lady Beatrice entitled *The New Life*. A brilliant tale of seduction frames George Gascoigne's lyrics in his *Adventures of Master F. J.*, and Sidney's eclogues (pastoral poems) punctuate the long and complicated narrative of his prose romance, *Arcadia*.

Prose romances also provided images of new kinds of identity. Stories of marvels surrounded the lives of the powerful and exotic, such as Robert Greene's *Pandosto* (the source for Shakespeare's *The Winter's Tale*) and Thomas Lodge's *Rosalind*, while tales of lower-class artisan-adventurers illustrate the enthusiasm with which early modern writers and readers embraced a freedom to reinvent themselves. The romantic notion of the "marvelous" gained a new meaning in tales of tricksters and of

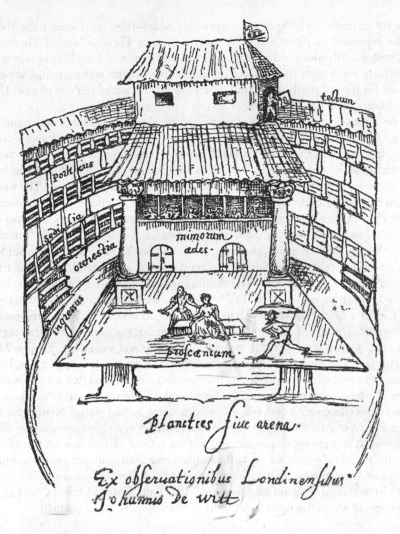

planicies siue arena.

Ex obseruationibus Londinensibus
Johannis de witt

Arend von Buchell, *The Swan Theatre*, after Johannes de Witt, c. 1596. The only extant drawing of
a public theater in 1590s London, this sketch shows what Shakespeare's Globe must have looked
like. The round playhouse centered on the curtainless platform of the stage (*proscenium*), which projected into the yard (*planities sive arena*). Raised above the stage by two pillars, the roof (*tectum*)
stored machinery. At the back of the stage, the tiring house (*mimorum aedes*), where the actors
dressed, contained two doors for entrances and exits. There were no stage sets and only movable
props such as thrones, tables, beds, and benches, like the one shown here. Other documents on the
early modern stage are the contract of the Fortune Theatre, where *The Roaring Girl* was performed,
and stage directions in the plays themselves. Modeled on the Globe, although square in shape, the
Fortune featured a stage forty-three feet broad and twenty-seven and a half feet deep. Stage directions include further clues: sometimes a curtained booth made "discovery" scenes possible; trapdoors
allowed descents; and a space "aloft," such as the gallery above the stage doors, represented a room
above the street. Eyewitness accounts fill out the picture. In the yard stood the groundlings who
paid a penny for standing room, exposed to the sky, which provided natural lighting. For those willing to pay a penny or two more, three galleries (*orchestra, sedilia,* and *porticulus*) provided seats—the
most expensive of which were cushioned. Spectators could buy food and drink during the performance. The early modern theater held an audience of roughly eight hundred standing in the yard,
and fifteen hundred more seated in the galleries. According to Thomas Platter, who had seen
Shakespeare's *Julius Caesar* in 1599, "everyone has a good view."

sturdy entrepreneurs who survived against all odds—they represented the creative energies possessed by plain folk. The short fiction of Thomas Nashe, Thomas Deloney, and the hilarious (and anonymous) *Life and Pranks of Long Meg of Westminster* conclusively break with the delicate sentimentality of pure romance and, appealing to a taste for the ordinarily wonderful, point the way for such later novelists as Daniel Defoe, Henry Fielding, and Charles Dickens.

The spirit of romance infused narratives of travel as well, many of which made little distinction between fact and fantasy. Sir John Mandeville's fifteenth-century *Travels*, in print throughout the sixteenth century, responded to the growing curiosity of Europeans about the wonders of nature in distant lands, which harbored whole peoples who were pictured as utterly different from anything known at home. The wonders reported in popular collections of travel narratives like Samuel Purchas's immensely popular *Purchas His Pilgrimage, or Relations of the World and the Religions Observed in All Ages* (1613) were designed to attract, not repel, readers, but a horror of the "other" was nevertheless implied in many of these accounts. Shakespeare's Othello holds the Venetian senate spellbound when he reports that parts of the world are inhabited by "Cannibals that each other eat, / The Anthropophagi," as well as "men whose heads / Do grow beneath their shoulders." In *The Tempest*, such claims are parodied in the figure of Caliban: despite Prospero's accusations, Caliban bears a very human aspect and is no monster. The lure of distant lands could also attract the social critic who sought to devise images of an ideal world in order to better the real world. Sir Thomas More's *Utopia* projects a fantasy of a communal state that does double duty by pointing both to the inequities of English society *and* to the absurdities of reforms that assume men and women can be consistently reasonable. Literally describing a utopia, a "nowhere," his treatise is also effectively a dystopia, a work describing a "bad place." Neither Sir Francis Bacon's *New Atlantis* (1627) nor James Harrington's *Commonwealth of Oceans* (1656)—each a true utopia suggesting a radical reform of political and intellectual life—emulate More's embrace of both utopian and dystopian perspectives. But the dystopias of later writers, such as Jonathan Swift's *Gulliver's Travels* (1726), Samuel Butler's *Erewhon* (an anagram for "nowhere," 1872) and George Orwell's *1984* (1949), impressively illustrate the hazards of idealistic and visionary social thought.

CHANGING SOCIAL ROLES

The imaginative work of "self-fashioning" in early modern lyric and romance kept pace, to a degree, with actual social change. During this period, a person was born into a place—defined by locale, family, and work—but did not necessarily remain there. The social ladder was traveled in both directions. An impecunious member of the gentry, a second son of a poor squire, or a widow whose noble husband had left her without a suitable jointure or estate could sink below the rank to which they had been born and effectively become a "commoner." In turn, a prosperous artisan, a thrifty yeoman, or an enterprising merchant could eventually become a member of the gentry—folk who were entitled to signal their identity by a coat of arms and were not supposed to do manual work. The new rich were sometimes mocked for seeking advice in conduct books regarding the proper behavior for gentlefolk, but no one could overlook the change in their status. More important, representatives of the "middling sort" were gaining political power. They generally had the right to vote for a member of the House of Commons, and they regularly held local office as bailiffs, magistrates, or sheriffs, and served on juries in towns and villages throughout the kingdom. They administered property, engaged in business, and traded on international markets. Creating much of the wealth of early modern England, they defined the concept of an economic class independent of social rank or family background: "What is Gentry if wealth be wanting, but base servile beggery?" asked Robert Greene. The idea that a person inherited a way of life was undercut by evidence of continuous shifts in both urban and rural society.

The situation for women in particular exhibited a certain ideological ambivalence. Ancient philosophy and medieval theology had insisted that *womankind* was essentially and naturally different from *mankind*, characterized by physical weakness, intellectual passivity, and an aptitude for housework, childcare, and the minor decorative arts. That some women had distinguished themselves in occupations traditionally reserved for men was understood to signal an exception; in general, social doctrine imposed rigid codes of behavior on men and women. This thinking was countered by the text of Scripture—but also and increasingly by evidence from history, which revealed that ordinary women had undertaken all kinds of activity and therefore that a woman had the same range of talents as a man. Literary representation and authorship reflected some of this argument. The gentle defiance of Isabella Whitney contrasts with the vigorous independence of Middleton and Dekker's fictional Moll Cutpurse, the lead character in *The Roaring Girl*, who, it was claimed, was based on an actual woman of the town, Moll Frith. *The Alchemist's* engaging trull, Doll Common, recalls Shakespeare's Doll Tearsheet, but the actions of these Dolls, unacceptable according to conventional canons governing feminine behavior, are not seen as meriting particular reprehension or scorn.

These novel ways of understanding women found corresponding changes in attitudes toward men. Departing from medieval social norms, humanists had stressed that men should be educated in the arts as well as arms, and writers like Sir Philip Sidney, illustrating the sensitivity of men to emotional life, devised characters whose masculinity was amplified by attributes that were conventionally associated with women: passion, sympathy, and a certain self-indulgence. The frustrated lover of his sonnet Sequence *Astrophil and Stella* is both resourceful and humorously pitiable. Flexibility with respect to categories of gender is also a feature of much lyric poetry; the male poet's beloved is sometimes another man. Shakespeare's sonnets are the chief example of homosexual verse in this period, but homoerotic innuendo, often suggested as a feature of a love triangle, is common in all genres of writing. In Marlowe's poem *Hero and Leander*, the youth Leander loves the girl Hero and attracts the sexual attentions of the sea-god Neptune.

Ideas as well as social forms and practices were also changing. The repeated shifts in religious practice—from medieval Catholicism to Henrician Protestantism, then back to the Catholicism dictated by Queen Mary I, and then on to the Anglican Church of Queen Elizabeth I—revealed that divine worship could alter its form without bringing on the apocalypse. More subtly, the emerging capitalist economy produced a conceptual model for cultural exchange. Just as material goods flowed through regional and national markets, entering a particular locale only to move elsewhere, sometimes over great distances, so might ideas, styles, and artistic sensibilities. Drama especially conveyed how fluid were the customs, codes, and practices that gave society its sense of identity. The enthusiasm for stage plays was motivated in part by an interest in role-playing: if an actor who in real life might have been born a servant could perform the part of a king in a play, then might he not also perform the part of a king indeed? Was there more to being than performing? This mutability was both liberating and dangerous, as Shakespeare showed by dramatizing the protean powers of Othello's false friend, Iago, who chillingly boasts, "I am not what I am."

THE BUSINESS OF LITERATURE

It was the business of early modern literature to ask these questions. The idea that social convention was established on a natural order of things was no longer accepted. As Shakespeare's bastard Edmund declares, rejecting the customary inferiority of a person who is born out of wedlock, "Why bastard, Wherefore base? / When my dimensions are as well compact . . . As honest madam's issue." Writers were certainly supposed to educate their readers in virtuous ways. Spenser intended that his epic would "fashion a gentleman or noble person in vertuous and gentle discipline," and Sidney believed that poetry at its finest could "take naughtiness away and plant goodness even in the secretest cabinet of our souls." But literature also questioned matters of being and identity because writers themselves were in the forefront of a class that was in the process of changing its way of life and its means of support.

During the early modern period, an educated man who sought employment as a writer was the object of patronage by the gentry or nobility, often functioning as a tutor or secretary in a prosperous household. The poet John Skelton taught the future Henry VIII; John Donne accompanied his patron Sir William Drury on his European journeys and dedicated his *Anniversaries* to Drury's deceased daughter, Elizabeth; and Andrew Marvell educated Lord Fairfax's daughter, Mary. Men who were employed in other ways—in diplomacy, law, or some aspect of commerce—might be rewarded for their writing by stipends from the rich. Elizabeth I gave Spenser, one of her administrators in Ireland, a single grant of fifty pounds for *The Faerie Queene;* and Ben Jonson, thanks to the generosity of James I, was able to make a successful career for himself as a poet. As a young man, Milton was patronized by the noble Egerton family, for whom he wrote a masque called *Comus.* But as the seventeeth century progressed, writers discovered that they could be supported by a broader public; after the Restoration, the talented playwright Aphra Behn gained a living by selling her literary work to producers and printers. Increasingly, the forces of the market moved to include the business of printing, both liberating and captivating the energies of the nation's writers.

It was obvious to those in power and authority that the printing press was an agent of change; the question they had to answer was how to control it. Under Elizabeth I, all printing was regulated (in effect, subject to censorship) by the Stationer's Company, which had the exclusive right to print and sell literary work. The theater was also controlled. From 1574, all plays had to be licensed by the Master of Revels, a servant and appointee of the monarch, before they could be produced. These conditions bound writers to observe both royal and ecclesiastical policy, at least in their direct statements. Some resorted to coded critique; others openly defied custom. In 1579, John Stubbs wrote a pamphlet against the Queen's proposed marriage to the French king's brother, the Duke of Alençon, entitled *The Discoverie of a Gaping Gulf whereinto England Is Like to be Swallowed;* he was arrested and had his hand cut off as punishment. This situation, in which publication was officially regulated, was altered early in the seventeenth century by the development of a new institution: journalism.

By the middle of James I's reign, a market had emerged for a periodical news-pamphlet known as a "coranto," or current of news, which contained foreign intelligence taken from foreign papers: the first was actually printed in Amsterdam and shipped to England. Within a short time, English printers were publishing their own news in the form of sixteen-page "diurnals," or newsbooks, and by 1646 Londoners could read fourteen different papers in English. The rapid growth of the news industry promoted a public readership increasingly informed about political affairs. Parliament grew alarmed and discussed imposing stringent forms of licensing; in 1649, it sanctioned the publication of only two newspapers, both dedicated to printing official news. Underground presses continued to publish on current affairs, however, some of them from a royalist point of view and others endorsing the position of Parliament. Their writers enjoyed a risky freedom, but it was still a freedom. The boldest of them, Marchamont Nedham, wrote in support of both sides at different times. But journalism did more than provide news; it also created a basis for the freedom of writers in general. The most eloquent attack on a state-controlled press was by Milton, whose *Areopagitica* protested the practice of licensing books before their publication—that is, before readers had a chance to make up their minds about what these books contained. He drew on ideas of democracy that were current in ancient Athens and on the Puritan notion that good emerges only in contact with evil. "I cannot praise a fugitive and cloistered virtue," he announced, because no true virtue is untested, unchallenged, unexamined; it is valid only when it has deliberately and consciously rejected what is false. The journalistic enterprise of this period fostered the right to free speech and a free press that is now the bedrock of modern democracies.

THE LANGUAGES OF LITERATURE: THE NEW SCIENCE AND THE OLD NATURE

Changing ideas of identity, both personal and political, were reflected in changes in the English language, which responded to popular as well as learned culture. An accomplished classicist, Ben Jonson closely modeled his verses on Latin poems and their syntax; at the same time, the language of his poetry and his plays often echoes the cadences of the English spoken by ordinary folk. Authors of popular comic pamphlets, like Dekker and Greene, conveyed the lively language of London rogues and vagabonds, combining local slang with parodic Latin. The writing of English prose was further changed by the study of Latin grammar and rhetoric in the humanist curriculum inspired by the pedagogical reforms of Erasmus and his English followers, John Colet, Roger Ascham (tutor to Elizabeth I), and Richard Mulcaster. Many words of Latin origin were introduced into the English vocabulary, and many writers experimented with analytic prose by adapting Latin syntax, which allowed them to show relations of cause and effect by resorting to clauses beginning with "if," "when," "because," and so forth. The first Latin-English dictionary on humanist principles was compiled by Sir Thomas Elyot, and one of the most important English grammars, Ascham's *The Schoolmaster* (1570), instructed readers in the merits of an eloquent style.

This enrichment of language from various sources inevitably caused debate. Prose composition was especially affected. Proponents of the so-called Ciceronian style (after the Roman orator Cicero), liked long sentences of many clauses exhibiting variation and restatement. Practitioners of the Senecan style favored short, direct, and uncomplicated sentences. Francis Bacon in particular criticized Ciceronian rhetoric for its emphasis on decorative "tropes and figures" rather than descriptive substance or "weight of matter." He argued for a language that would accurately denote what he considered "scientific" data: the measures of the physical world. Bacon's reforms influenced English pedagogy and were further realized in the enterprise of the Royal Academy of Science, founded in 1660 by Charles II, who was determined to give his monarchy a new look and a new purpose. The terse, clear, pointed language of Bacon's *Essays* (1597) more resembles what we might think of as modern than does, for example, the florid style that Robert Burton used a quarter century later for his mythological-historical medical discourse *The Anatomy of Melancholy*.

Language and style were changing notions of the world and of God's design in creating it. Habits of thought that had prevailed during the medieval period now seemed to be incompatible with knowledge derived from the experience of nature. Europeans had inherited from classical philosophy an idea of creation as a vast aggregate of layered systems, or "spheres." Supposedly centered on the densest matter at the earth's core, they emanated outward and upward, ending finally in the sphere of pure spirit, or the ethereal presence of divinity. The entities in these layered spheres had assigned places that determined their natures both within their particular sphere and in relation to other spheres. Thus gold, the most precious metal, was superior to silver, but it was at the same time analogous to a lion, a king, and the sun, each also representing the peak of perfection within its particular class of beings. Human nature was also systematized, with the body and personality alike regulated by a balanced set of "humors," each of which consisted of a primary element. The earth, water, air, and fire that made up the great world, or macrocosm, of nature also composed the small universe, or microcosm, of the individual man or woman, whose personality was ideally balanced between impulses that were melancholic (caused by a kind of bile), phlegmatic (brought on by a watery substance), sanguine (bloody), and choleric (hot tempered). Excessive learning, the contemplation of death, the darkness of night, and isolation were all associated with melancholia, a diseased condition that in more or less severe form is represented in such disparate texts as Marlowe's *Dr. Faustus* and Milton's *Il Penseroso*.

This view of creation was important for artists and writers because it gave them a symbolic language of correspondences by which they could refer to creatures in widely differing settings and conditions. In a sense, it made nature hospitable to poetry by seeing creation as a divine work of art, designed to inspire not only awe but also a kind of familiarity. Things were the likenesses of other things. Particularly in so-called "metaphysical" poetry, whose chief exponent is John Donne, human emotional experience is compared to the realms of astronomy, geography, medicine, Neoplatonic philosophy, and Christian theology. These correspondences are created through strikingly unusual metaphors, which some have called metaphysical conceits, from the Italian *concetto* ("concept"). The result is a pervasive sense of a universal harmony in all human experience.

Such analogies were not always respected, however. Increasingly, they were questioned by proponents of a kind of vision that depended on a quantitative or denotative sense of identity or difference. Poetic metaphor might not be able to account for creation in all its complexity; instead, nature had to be understood through the abstractions of science. By the seventeenth century, it was becoming difficult to regard creation as a single and comprehensive whole; natural philosophers and scientists in the making wanted to analyze it piece by individual piece. As

John Donne wrote of the phenomenon of uniqueness in his elegy for Elizabeth Drury, *The Anniversary*:

> The element of fire is quite put out;
> The Sun is lost, and th' earth, and no man's wit
> Can well direct him, where to look for it.
> And freely men confess, that this world's spent,
> When in the Planets, and the Firmament
> They seek so many new; they see that this
> Is crumbled out again to his Atoms.
> 'Tis all in pieces, all coherence gone;
> All just supply, and all Relation:
> Prince, Subject, Father, Son, are things forgot,
> For every man alone thinks he has got
> To be a Phoenix, and that there can be
> None of that kind, of which he is but he.

The earth had been decentered by the insights of the astronomer Nicholas Copernicus, who in the 1520s deduced that the earth orbits the sun. This "Copernican revolution" was confirmed by the calculations of Tycho Brahe and Johannes Kepler, and our solar system itself was revealed as but one among many. With traditional understandings of the natural order profoundly shaken, many thinkers feared for the survival of the human capacity to order and understand society as well. Ironically, Donne complains of radical individualism by invoking the emblem of the Phoenix, the very sort of traditional metaphor that constituted the coherence he claims has "gone." But whereas the symbol in an emblem book carried with it the myth of the bird's Christ-like death and rebirth, the image of the rare bird takes on a newly skeptical and even satirical meaning in *The Anniversary*: it becomes the sign of a dangerous fragmentation within nature's order. Donne's audience would have been familiar with such symbols from emblem books, poems, and coats of arms, as well as in interior decoration, clothing, and the printers' marks on title pages of books. They were also featured on the standards or flags carried in the Civil War—antique signs in a decidedly modern conflict.

The War and the Modern Order of Things

The Wars of Three Kingdoms ended with the restoration of the Stuart monarchy, but the society that Charles II was heir to was very different from the one his grandfather, James I, had come from Scotland to rule. The terms of modern life were formulated during this period, even though they were only partially and inconsistently realized. They helped to shape these essentially modern institutions: a representative government under law, a market economy fueled by concentrations of capital, and a class system determined by wealth and the power it conferred. They supported a culture in which extreme and opposing points of view were usual. Milton's republican *Tenure of Kings and Magistrates* was followed by Thomas Hobbes's defense of absolute rule, *The Leviathan, or the Matter, Form, and Power of a Commonwealth, Ecclesiastical and Civil* (1651). Hobbes rejected the assumption that had determined all previous political thought—Aristotle's idea that man was naturally sociable—by characterizing the natural condition of human life as "solitary, poor, nasty, brutish and short." A civil state, said Hobbes, depended on the willingness of each and every citizen to relinquish all his or her rights to the sovereign, which is the Commonwealth. The vigorous

Wenceslaus Hollar, *Parliamentarian soldiers in Yorkshire destroying "Popish" paintings, etc*. Illustration to *Sight of the Transactions of these latter yeares*, by John Vicars, 1646.

language of Puritan sermons, preached and published during the 1640s and 1650s, was replicated in the corantos and diurnals of the period. These new forms would eventually lead to the sophisticated commentary of eighteenth-century journalism. Nationalism, however problematic, was registered in history and epic, as well as in attempts to colonize the Americas and to subdue the Gaelic peoples to the west and the north. Irish poems supporting the Stuarts and lamenting the losses of the Cromwellian wars would become rallying cries during the late seventeenth- and eighteenth-century nationalist risings against English control, eventually to result in Ireland's inclusion in the 1801 Union of Great Britain.

Intellectual thought, mental attitudes, religious practices, and the customs of the people fostered new relations to the past and a new sense of self. While Milton was perhaps the greatest humanist of his time, able to read and write Hebrew, Greek, Latin, Italian, and French, his contemporaries witnessed the disappearance of the culture of Petrarch, Erasmus, and More—humanists who had fashioned the disciplines of humanism. As more particularized portraits of individual life emerged, new philosophical trends promoted denotative descriptions and quantitative figurations of the world. Shortly after the Restoration of Charles II, the Royal Academy of Science would form a "committee for improving the English language," an attempt to design a universal grammar and an ideal philosophical language. This project, inspired by the intellectual reforms of Francis Bacon, would have been uncongenial to the skeptical casts of mind exhibited by Erasmus and More. The abstract rationalism of the new science, the growth of an empire overseas, a burgeoning industry and commerce at home, and a print culture spreading news throughout Europe and across the Atlantic, would continue to be features of life in the British Isles through the eighteenth century.

John Skelton

1460?–1529

The first great Tudor satirist, John Skelton illustrates the appeal of the unorthodox. Taking orders at the age of thirty-eight, Skelton already enjoyed an impressive reputation as a writer of satire and love lyrics. His poems must have appealed to Henry VII, who made him responsible for the education of his second son, the future Henry VIII, and they would eventually prompt Erasmus to call Skelton "a light and ornament of British literature." In 1502, following the death of Henry's older brother Arthur, Skelton lost his employment as royal tutor. Henry, now heir apparent to the English throne, was obliged to trade Skelton's gentle instruction in humane and sacred letters for practical training in statecraft and the art of war. At forty-two and already an old man (by contemporary reckoning), Skelton undertook pastoral duties, although he lived away from his rectory for much of the rest of his life. His satires of the clergy in *Colin Clout* and of Cardinal Wolsey in *Why Come Ye Not to Court* may have placed him in some jeopardy; it is said that a threat from the Cardinal forced Skelton to take refuge on the grounds of Westminster Abbey in London. Skelton never got the satisfaction of witnessing Wolsey's disgrace; he died just a few months before Wolsey lost the office of Lord Chancellor for failing to procure a divorce for the king.

Skelton's poetry is as unusual as was his career. His favorite verse form has become known as "skeltonics"; it consists of a series of lines of two or three stresses whose end rhyme repeats itself for an unspecified number of lines. The lines themselves show alliteration and move at a headlong pace. Skelton excused his practice in *Colin Clout* by noting the "pith" or substance it conveys:

> For though my rhyme be ragged,
> Tattered and jagged,
> Rudely rain-beaten,
> Rusty and moth-eaten,
> If ye take well therewith,
> It hath in it some pith.

Skelton's satires poke fun at the pretensions that characterize all forms of public life, including the ways of courtiers and vagabonds. His dream poem, *The Bowge of Court,* and his morality play about wealth and power, *Magnificence,* provide a witty view of court corruption. His verse includes tender tributes to ladies he loves or has loved as well as anticourtly lyrics accusing women of bad behavior and sexual indiscretion. His verse can even be conversational, as when he appears to be addressing a particular person or representing two or more people speaking to each other.

Womanhod, Wanton

Womanhod, wanton,[1] ye want;
Youre medelyng, mastres, is manerles;
Plente of yll, of goodnes skant,
Ye rayll at ryot, recheles:°   *carelessly*
5   To prayse youre porte° it is nedeles;   *bearing*

---

1. The poem addresses mistress Ann, a "wanton" or woman of the town, who lives at an inn called "The Key." The poet's tone disparages Ann's pretensions rather than her way of life.

For all your draffe yet and youre dreggys,°   refuse
As well borne as ye full oft tyme beggys.

Why so koy and full of skorne?
Myne horse is sold, I wene, you say;
10   My new furryd gowne, when it is worne,
Put up youre purs, ye shall non pay.[2]
By crede, I trust to se the day,
As proud a pohen° as ye sprede,   peahen
Of me and other ye may have nede.

15   Though angelyk be youre smylyng,
Yet is youre tong an adders tayle,
Full lyke a scorpyon styngyng
All those by whom ye have avayle:
Good mastres Anne, there ye do shayle:°   mistake
20   What prate° ye, praty pyggysny?°   talk / pretty flower
I truste to quyte° you or° I dy.   revenge myself on / before

Youre key is mete° for every lok,   suited
Youre key is commen and hangyth owte;
Youre key is redy, we nede not knok,
25   Nor stand long wrestyng° there aboute;   twisting
Of youre doregate ye have no doute:
But one thyng is, that ye be lewde:°   common
Holde youre tong now, all beshrewde!°   corrupted

To mastres Anne, that farly swete,°   pretty sweetheart
30   That wonnes° at the Key in Temmys strete.   lives

Lullay

With, Lullay, lullay, lyke a chylde,[1]
Thou slepyst to long, thou art begylde.°   fooled

My darlyng dere, my daysy floure,
Let me, quod he, ly in your lap.
5   Ly styll, quod she, my paramoure,
Ly styll hardely,° and take a nap.   only
Hys hed was hevy, such was his hap,
All drowsy dremyng, dround in slepe,
That of hys love he toke no kepe,°   care
10   With, Hey, lullay, &c.

With ba, ba, ba, and bas, bas, bas,
She cheryshed° hym both cheke and chyn,   stroked
That he wyst never where he was;
He had forgoten all dedely syn.

2. You are scornful because my horse is sold (I am poor
and in need), but you shall have my new gown for nothing
when it is worn out (you are poorer than I am).

1. The poem is an ironic lullaby. It actually warns a man
who is asleep to wake up: he is a fool, and his wife has
gone off with another man.

15   He wantyd wyt her love to wyn;
He trusted her payment,° and lost all hys pray:°   *words / desire*
She left hym slepyng, and stale° away,   *stole*
       Wyth, Hey, lullay, &c.

    The ryvers rowth,° the waters wan;°   *rough / dark*
20   She sparyd not to wete her fete;
She wadyd over, she found a man
That halsyd° her hartely and kyst her swete: *embraced*
Thus after her cold she cought a hete.
My lefe, she sayd, rowtyth° in hys bed;   *snores*
25   I wys he hath an hevy hed,
       Wyth, Hey, lullay, &c.

    What dremyst thou, drunchard, drousy pate!²
Thy lust° and lykyng is from the gone;   *pleasure*
Thou blynkerd blowboll,° thou wakyst to late,   *blinking drunkard*
30   Behold, thou lyeste, luggard, alone!
Well may thou sygh, well may thou grone,
To dele wyth her so cowardly:
I wys,° powle hachet, she bleryd° thyne I.°   *indeed / blinded / eye*

Knolege, Aquayntance

    Knolege, aquayntance, resort,° favour with grace;¹   *love*
Delyte, desyre, respyte wyth lyberte;
Corage wyth lust,° convenient tyme and space;   *pleasure*
Dysdayns, dystres, exylyd° cruelte;   *banished*
5   Wordys well set with good habylyte;°   *skill*
Demure demenaunce,° womanly of porte;°   *appearance / bearing*
Transendyng plesure, surmountyng all dysporte;°   *gratification*

    Allectuary arrectyd° to redres   *medicine designed*
These feverous axys,° the dedely wo and payne   *attacks*
10   Of thoughtfull hertys plungyd in dystres;
Refresshyng myndys° the Aprell shoure of rayne;   *minds*
Condute° of comforte, and well most soverayne;   *stream*
Herber° enverduryd, contynuall fressh and grene;   *arbor*
Of lusty somer the passyng goodly quene;

15   The topas rych and precyouse in vertew;
Your ruddys° wyth ruddy rubys may compare;   *cheeks*
Saphyre of sadnes, envayned wyth indy° blew;   *violet*
The pullyshed perle youre whytenes° doth declare;   *fair skin*
Dyamand poyntyd to rase° oute hartly care;   *erase*
20   Geyne surfetous suspecte the emeraud comendable;²
Relucent smaragd,° objecte imcomperable;   *a bright stone*

---

2. The poet speaks to wake the sleeper.
1. The poem, a series of epithets in praise of a lady, complains of her absence from him. He imagines that she can cure the world's ills by her gracious virtue and that absence will not remove her from his heart.
2. Against excessive suspicion the praiseworthy emerald.

Encleryd° myrroure and perspectyve most bryght,   *shining*
Illumynyd° wyth feturys far passyng my reporte;   *glowing*
Radyent Esperus,° star of the clowdy nyght,   *Hesperus, morning star*
25   Lode star to lyght these lovers to theyr porte,
Gayne dangerous stormys theyr anker of supporte,
Theyr sayll of solace most comfortably clad,[3]
Whych to behold makyth hevy hartys glad:

Remorse have I of youre most goodlyhod,
30   Of youre behavoure curtes° and benynge,   *courteous*
Of your bownte and of youre womanhod,
Which makyth my hart oft to lepe and sprynge,
And to remember many a praty° thynge;   *pleasant*
But absens, alas, wyth tremelyng° fere and drede   *trembling*
35   Abashyth° me, albeit I have no nede.   *shames*

You I assure, absens is my fo,
My dedely wo, my paynfull hevynes;
And if ye lyst° to know the cause why so,   *much*
Open myne hart, beholde my mynde expres:°   *immediately*
40   I wold ye coud! then shuld ye se, mastres,
How there nys thynge that I covet so fayne°   *much*
As to enbrace you in myne armys twayne.

Nothynge yerthly° to me more desyrous   *earthly*
Than to beholde youre bewteouse countenaunce:
45   But, hatefull absens, to me so envyous,°   *distressing*
Though thou withdraw me from her by long dystaunce,°   *absence*
Yet shall she never oute of remembraunce;
For I have gravyd° her wythin the secret wall   *engraved*
Of my trew hart, to love her best of all!

Manerly Margery Mylk and Ale[1]

"Ay, besherewe° yow, be my fay,°   *confound / faith*
This wanton clarkes be nyse all way;
Avent, avent, my popagay!°   *go away, parrot*
What, will ye do no thyng but play?
5   Tully valy, strawe, let be,° I say!"   *stop*
Gup,° Cristian Clowte, gup, Jak of the vale!   *go on*
With, manerly Margery mylk and ale.

"Be Gad, ye be a prety pode,°   *sausage*
And I love you an hole cart lode."
10   "Strawe, Jamys foder,° ye play the fode,°   *ragweed / deceiver*

3. The poet compares the lady's effect to that of the north star guiding a ship to port, the anchor preventing its drifting away, and the sail propelling it forward.
1. The poem is constructed as a dialogue between Margery, who complains of the advances of Christian Clout, and Cristian Clout, who protests that he loves her. Their dialogue is punctuated by the poet's refrain, which encourages Cristian to persist in his courtship. The first stanza is spoken by Margery, the second and third stanzas by Cristian and then Margery, and the final stanza by Cristian, who, having seduced Margery, nevertheless declares he wants to marry her for the love of God.

I am no hakney for your rode;°   *riding*
Go watch a bole,° your bak is brode":   *bull*
Gup, Cristian Clowte, gup, Jak of the vale!
With, manerly Margery mylk and ale.

15 "I wiss ye dele uncurtesly";
What wolde ye frompill° me? now, fy, fy!   *rumple*
What, and ye shalbe my piggesnye?
Be Crist, ye shal not, no, no, hardely;
I will not be japed bodely":°   *fooled, seduced*
20 Gup, Cristian Clowte, gup, Jake of the vale!
With, manerly Margery mylk and ale.

"Walke forth your way, ye cost me nought;
Now have I fownd that I have sought,
The best chepe flessh that evyr I bought.
25 Yet, for his love that all hath wrought,
Wed me, or els I dye for thought!"
Gup, Cristian Clowte, your breth is stale!
With, manerly Margery Mylk and Ale!
Gup, Cristian Clowte, gup, Jak of the vale!
30 With, manerly Margery mylk and ale

from Garland of Laurel[1]

To Maystres Jane Blennerhasset

What though my penne wax faynt,
And hath smale lust° to paint?   *desire*
Yet shall there no restraynt
Cause me to cese,
5 Amonge this prese,°   *crowd*
For to encrese°   *celebrate*
Yowre goodly name.
    I wyll my selfe applye,
Trust me, ententifly,°   *carefully*
10 Yow for to stellyfye;[2]
And so observe
That ye ne swarve°   *swerve*
For to deserve
Inmortall fame.
15   Sith mistres Jane Haiset
Smale flowres helpt to sett
In my goodly chapelet,°   *crown*

1. The next three poems were included in a collection of lyrics entitled *Garland of Laurel*, published in 1523. The first is addressed to Jane Blennerhasset, who was probably the wife of Ralph Blennerhasset; if so, we know that she died in 1501, at the age of 97. The second is addressed to Isabell Pennell, presumably the young daughter of John Paynell. The third is addressed to Margaret Hussey, an unidentified young woman of marriageable age.
2. Place in the sky as a star.

Therefore I render of her the memory
Unto the legend of fare Laodomi.[3]

To Maystres Isabell Pennell

    By saynt Mary, my lady,
Your mammy and your dady
Brought forth a godely babi!
    My mayden Isabell,
5 Reflaring rosabell,°   *sweet rose*
The flagrant camamell;°   *fragrant camomile*
    The ruddy rosary,°   *rosebush*
The soverayne rosemary,
The praty° strawbery;   *pretty*
10   The columbyne, the nepte,°   *catnip*
The jeloffer° well set,   *gillyflower*
The propre vyolet;
    Enuwyd° your colowre   *renewed*
Is lyke the dasy flowre
15 After the Aprill showre;
    Sterre° of the morow gray,   *star*
The blossom on the spray,
The fresshest flowre of May;
    Maydenly demure,
20 Of womanhode the lure;°   *model*
Wherfore I make you sure,°   *assure you*
    It were an hevenly helth,
It were an endeles welth,
A lyfe for God hymselfe,
25   To here this nightingale,[4]
Amonge the byrdes smale,
Warbelynge in the vale,
    Dug, dug,
Jug, jug,
30 Good yere and good luk,
With chuk, chuk, chuk, chuk!

To Maystres Margaret Hussey

Mirry Margaret,
As mydsomer flowre,
Jentill as fawcoun°   *falcon*
Or hawke of the towre;[5]
5   With solace and gladnes,
Moche mirthe and no madnes,

3. The poet remembers a favor Jane Blennerhasset has
done for him and recalls the legend of Laodomia: Just as
Laodomia followed her dead husband to the underworld,
so has the poet's memory followed Jane beyond the grave.

4. The poet imagines Isabell Pennell as a nightingale
whose singing is heavenly.
5. A hawk that towers in the air.

All good and no badnes,
So joyously,
So maydenly,
10   So womanly
Her demenyng°   behavior
In every thynge,
Far, far passynge
That I can endyght,°   recount
15   Or suffyce to wryght
Of mirry Margarete,
As mydsomer flowre,
Jentyll as fawcoun
Or hawke of the towre;
20   As pacient and as styll,[6]
And as full of good wyll,
As fayre Isaphill;
Colyaunder,°   coriander
Swete pomaunder,°   perfume ball
25   Good cassaunder;
Stedfast of thought,
Wele made, wele wrought;
Far may be sought
Erst that ye can fynde
30   So corteise, so kynde
As mirry Margarete,
This midsomer flowre,
Ientyll as fawcoun
Or hawke of the towre.

———— ✠✠✠ ————

Sir Thomas Wyatt
1503–1542

A gifted poet and diplomat, Sir Thomas Wyatt exemplified the ambitious mixture of social and artistic skills that later ages would see as the ideal of the "Renaissance man." Having entered the household of King Henry VIII immediately after his education at Cambridge, Wyatt promoted English interests on missions to France, Venice, Rome, Spain, and the Low Countries. His career was to prove more precarious at home, where he became involved in court politics. He was deeply attached to the Lady Anne Boleyn, who, by 1527, was the object of Henry's affections and a probable pretext for the King's divorce from Catherine of Aragon and England's break from the Roman Catholic Church. Made Henry's queen in 1533, but out of favor by 1536, Anne implicated by association those who were supposed to have been her lovers. Wyatt, who according to several contemporary accounts, admitted to the King that the

6. The poet compares Margaret Hussey to sweet-smelling herbs and strong heroines of classical legend: Isaphill or Hypsipyle, known for her fortitude; and Cassaunder or Cassandra, the prophetess.

Queen had been his mistress, was lucky to suffer no more than imprisonment; the Queen's other favorites were executed. Wyatt subsequently regained political status both at home and abroad, although not without periods of disappointment: His verse letter *Mine Own John Poyns* praises the security of a country life away from London and its intrigues. Wyatt's most protracted mission was from 1537 to 1539, as the King's ambassador to the court of the Holy Roman Emperor in Spain: he tells of his anticipated return to England in the hauntingly brief lyric *Tagus, Farewell*. Despite the execution of his powerful patron, Sir Thomas Cromwell, and a second prison term in 1541 for suspected treason, Wyatt obtained Henry's goodwill at the end of his short life. He died from a fever at the age of thirty-nine while on a diplomatic mission for the king.

By any poetic reckoning, Wyatt is to be valued as a pioneer of English verse. Although many of his poems exhibit irregular meters, they have been praised for their remarkable texture and sense of surprise. His translations of Francesco Petrarch's sonnets established the principal forms of English lyric, the rhyming sonnet with its pentameter line and the more loosely configured song derived from the Italian *canzone*. Wyatt's own poems change the spirit of their Petrarchan themes by giving erotic subjects a satirical and even bitter twist and political topics an inward and personal reference. In one of his best-known sonnets, *Whoso List to Hunt*, he writes of vainly pursuing a "hind" or "deer" (a dear or beloved lady) belonging to "Caesar" (King Henry VIII). Long understood to be a reference to Anne Boleyn, Wyatt's "deer" is quite a different figure than the "deer" in his source, Petrarch's sonnet to a "white doe," who represents his lady, Laura, whom he met in 1327 and loved from a distance until her death in 1350. While Petrarch's lady is imagined as chastely devoted to a heavenly Caesar or God, and therefore as inspiring a religious awe, Wyatt's beloved is the possession of an earthly Caesar, King Henry VIII, and is thus the cause of his immediate frustration.

Wyatt's verse was circulated in manuscript during his lifetime and probably read only by his friends and his acquaintances at court. A few poems were published in 1540, in a collection entitled *The Court of Venus*, but the majority—ninety-seven poems in all—appeared in 1557, in a massive anthology called *Songs and Sonnets*, published by the printer Richard Tottel. This volume, which includes poems by Henry Howard, Earl of Surrey and others, was a milestone in the history of literature. Unlike the earlier sixteenth-century poetry of the British Isles, which remained relatively simple in its genres and diction, *Tottel's Miscellany* (as it has come to be known) exhibited a range of new forms and meters: the sonnet, the song (or *canzone*), the epigram, and rhyming and blank verse. Familiar to writers and readers of Italian and French, these forms allowed poets (now writing a recognizably modern English) to develop a stylistic flexibility and thematic richness previously achieved only by the Middle English poet Geoffrey Chaucer. Before presenting his anthology to the public, however, Tottel did some fairly drastic editing: smoothing out metrical irregularities by adding, subtracting, or changing words, he obviously sought to impress readers with what he judged to be the elegant and up-to-date styles represented by the works in his collection. The poems reprinted here are based not on the *Songs and Sonnets* but on Wyatt's original texts.

The Long Love, That in My Thought Doth Harbor

> The long love, that in my thought doth harbor
> And in mine heart doth keep his residence,
> Into my face presseth with bold pretence,
> And therein campeth, spreading his banner.
> 5 She that me learneth° to love and suffer,   *teaches*
> And will that my trust and lust's negligence

Be reined by reason, shame and reverence,
With his hardiness° taketh displeasure.   *boldness*
Wherewithal, unto the heart's forest he fleeth,
10   Leaving his enterprise with pain and cry,
And there him hideth and not appeareth.
What may I do when my master feareth
But in the field with him to live and die?
For good is the life, ending faithfully.

❧

COMPANION READING
Petrarch, Sonnet 140[1]

Amor, che nel penser mio vive et regna
e 'l suo seggio maggior nel mio cor tene,
talor armato ne la fronte vene;
ivi si loca et ivi pon sua insegna.
5   Quella ch' amare et sofferir ne 'nsegna
e vol che 'l gran desio, l'accesa spene
ragion, vergogna, et reverenza affrene,
di nostro ardir fra se stessa si sdegna.
Onde Amor paventoso fugge al core,
10   lasciando ogni sua impresa, et piange et trema;
ivi s'asconde et non appar più fore.
Che poss' io far, temendo il mio signore,
se non star seco infin a l'ora estrema?
ché bel fin fa chi ben amando more.

Petrarch, Sonnet 140: A Translation

Love, who lives and reigns in my thought and keeps his principal seat in my heart, sometimes comes forth all in armor into my forehead, there camps, and there sets up his banner.

She who teaches us to love and to be patient, and wishes my great desire, my kindled hope, to be reined in by reason, shame, and reverence, at our boldness is angry within herself.

Wherefore Love flees terrified to my heart, abandoning his every enterprise, and weeps and trembles; there he hides and no more appears outside.

What can I do, when my lord is afraid, except stay with him until the last hour? For he makes a good end who dies loving well.

❧

1. Petrarch (1304–1374), known to his fellow Italians as Francesco Petrarca, was the virtual inventor of modern lyric poetry. Comprising sonnets, songs (*canzone*), and odes, his *Rime sparse* or "various poems"—widely circulated during and after his lifetime—were translated and imitated by poets throughout Europe. Petrarch's verse demonstrated to his early modern readers that a lyric poet could invest subjects with a spirituality and a seriousness previously attributed to the epic, the ode, and to philosophical poems. Petrarch's *Sonnet 140* is a good example of what English poets like Wyatt were responding to as they worked to bring the sonnet form into the repertory of English poetry. Translations by Robert M. Durling.

Whoso List to Hunt

Who so list° to hunt, I know where is an hind,°   *wishes / doe*
But as for me, helas, I may no more:
The vain travail° hath wearied me so sore.   *idle labor*
I am of them that farthest cometh behind.
5   Yet may I by no means my wearied mind
Draw from° the deer: but as she fleeth afore,   *forget*
Fainting I follow. I leave off therefore,
Since in a net I seek to hold the wind.
Who list her hunt I put him out of doubt,
10   As well as I may spend his time in vain:
And, graven° with diamonds, in letters plain   *engraved*
There is written her fair neck round about:
Noli me tangere,[1] for Caesar's I am,
And wild for to hold though I seem tame.

❧

COMPANION READING
Petrarch, Sonnet 190

Una candida cerva sopra l'erba
verde m'apparve con duo corna d'oro,
fra due riviere all' ombra d'un alloro,
Levando 'l sole a la stagione acerba.
5   Era sua vista sì dolce superba
ch' i'lasciai per seguirla ogni lavoro,
come l'avaro che 'n cercar tesoro
con diletto l'affanno disacerba.
"Nessun mi tocchi," al bel collo d'intorno
10   scritto avea di diamanti et di topazi.
"Libera farmi al mio Cesare parve."
Et era 'l sol già vòlto al mezzo giorno,
gli occhi miei stanchi di mirar, non sazi,
quand' io caddi ne l'acqua et ella sparve.

Petrarch, Sonnet 190: A Translation

A white doe on the green grass appeared to me, with two golden horns, between two rivers, in the shade of a laurel, when the sun was rising in the unripe season.

Her look was so sweet and proud that to follow her I left every task, like the miser who as he seeks treasure sweetens his trouble with delight.

"Let no one touch me," she bore written with diamonds and topazes around her lovely neck. "It has pleased my Caesar to make me free."

And the sun had already turned at midday; my eyes were tired by looking but not sated, when I fell into the water, and she disappeared.

❧

---

1. "Touch me not," the words the resurrected but not yet risen Christ spoke to Mary Magdalene before his tomb (John 20.17). The "deer" of the poem has often been identified with Anne Boleyn and "Caesar" with Henry VIII.

My Galley

My galley charged° with forgetfulness	loaded
Through sharp seas in winter nights doth pass	
'Tween rock and rock; and eke° mine enemy, alas,	also
That is my lord, steereth with cruelness;	
5 And every oar a thought in readiness,	
As though that death were light° in such a case.	easy
An endless wind doth tear the sail apace.	
Of forced sighs and trusty fearfulness.	
A rain of tears, a cloud of dark disdain	
10 Hath done the wearied cords° great hindrance,	worn rigging
Wreathed with error and eke with ignorance.	
The stars be hid that led me to this pain,	
Drowned is reason that should me comfort,	
And I remain despairing of the port.	

They Flee from Me

They flee from me that sometime did me seek	
With naked foot stalking in my chamber.	
I have seen them gentle tame and meek	
That now are wild and do not remember	
5 That sometime they put themself in danger	
To take bread at my hand; and now they range	
Busily seeking with a continual change.	
Thanked be fortune, it hath been otherwise	
Twenty times better; but once in special,	
10 In thine array after a pleasant guise,°	manner, disguise
When her loose gown from her shoulders did fall,	
And she me caught in her arms long and small;	
Therewithal sweetly did me kiss,	
And softly said, "dear heart, how like you this?"	
15 It was no dream: I lay broad waking.	
But all is turned through my gentleness	
Into a strange fashion of forsaking;	
And I have leave to go of her goodness,	
And she also to use new fangledness.	
20 But since that I so kindly am served,	
I would fain° know what she hath deserved.	wish to

Some Time I Fled the Fire[1]

Some time I fled the fire that me brent°	burned
By sea, by land, by water and by wind;	
And now I follow the coals that be quent°	quenched
From Dover to Calais against my mind.	

1. This poem appears to record Wyatt's attitude as he attended Anne Boleyn on her way to Calais in October 1532. Having been burned by her "fire" (a possible reference to a love affair), he now follows the dead coals of that fire against his will.

5   Lo! how desire is both sprung and spent!
     And he may see that whilom° was so blind;   *formerly*
     And all his labor now he laugh° to scorn,   *may laugh*
     Mashed in the breers° that erst° was all to torn.°   *briars / once / torn up*

My Lute, Awake!

     My lute, awake! perform the last
     Labor that thou and I shall waste
         And end that I have now begun,
     For when this song is sung and past,
5   My lute be still, for I have done.

     As to be heard where ere is none,°   *there is no one*
     As lead to grave in marble stone,
         My song may pierce her heart as sone;°   *soon*
     Should we then sigh, or sing, or moan?
10   No, no, my lute, for I have done.

     The rocks do not so cruelly
     Repulse the waves continually,
         As she my suit and affection,
     So that I am past remedy,
15   Whereby my lute and I have done.

     Proud of the spoil that thou hast got
     Of simple hearts through love's shot,
         By whom, unkind, thou has them won,
     Think not he hath his bow forgot,
20   Although my lute and I have done.

     Vengeance shall fall on thy disdain,
     That makest but game on earnest pain;
         Think not alone under the sun
     Unquit° to cause thy lover's plain,°   *freely / lament*
25   Although my lute and I have done.

     Perchance thee lie weathered and old,
     The winter nights that are so cold,
         Plaining in vain unto the mone;°   *moon*
     Thy wishes then dare not be told,
30   Care then who list,° for I have done.   *wishes*

     And then may chance thee to repent
     The time that thou hast lost and spent
         To cause thy lover's sigh and swoon;
     Then shalt thou know beauty but lent
35   And wish and want as I have done.

     Now cease, my lute, this is the last
     Labor that thou and I shall wast,°   *waste*
         And ended is that we begun;
     Now is this song both sung and past,
40   My lute be still, for I have done.

Tagus, Farewell

Tagus,[1] farewell, that westward with thy streams
Turns up the grains of gold already tried:
With spur and sail for I go seek the Thames,
Gainward° the sun that showeth her wealthy pride;   *toward*
5   And to the town which Brutus[2] sought by dreams
Like bended moon doth lend her lusty side.
My King,° my country, alone for whom I live,   *Henry VIII*
Of mighty love the wings for this me give.

Forget Not Yet

Forget not yet the tried° intent   *proven*
Of such a truth as I have meant,
My great travail° so gladly spent   *effort*
    Forget not yet.

5   Forget not yet when first began
The weary life ye know since whan,°   *when*
The suit, the service none tell can,
    Forget not yet.

Forget not yet the great assays,°   *trials*
10   The cruel wrong, the scornful ways,
The painful patience in denays,°   *denials*
    Forget not yet.

Forget not yet, forget not this,
How long ago hath been and is
15   The mind that never meant amiss,
    Forget not yet.

Forget not then thine own aprovyd,[1]
The which so long hath thee so lovyd,
Whose steadfast faith yet never movyd,
20   Forget not this.

Blame Not My Lute

Blame not my lute for he must sound
    Of this or that as liketh me,
For lack of wit the lute is bound
    To give such tunes as pleaseth me:
5   Though my songs be somewhat strange,
And speaks such words as touch thy change,[1]
    Blame not my lute.

1. The Tagus, or Tajo, River is the longest on the Iberian peninsula and empties into the Atlantic at Portugal. Wyatt was sent to Spain as a diplomat but returned to England in 1539.
2. The legendary Trojan hero Brutus was supposed to have settled the British Isles and founded London, to which he was led by a series of dreams sent to him by the goddess Diana.
1. The poet himself, her "approved" lover.
1. I.e., the lady's change of heart, probably also to be signified by a change of tone in the music to which this lyric was supposedly set.

My lute, alas, doth not offend,
   Though that perforce he must agree
10 To sound such tunes as I intend
   To sing to them that heareth me;
Then though my songs be somewhat plain,
And toucheth some that used to fain,[2]
    Blame not my lute.

15 My lute and strings may not deny,
   But as I strike they must obey;
Break not them then so wrongfully,
   But wreak° thyself some wiser way: *revenge*
And though the songs which I endite°   *write*
20 Do quit° thy change with rightful spite,   *discharge, answer*
    Blame not my lute.

Spite asketh spite and changing change,
   And falsed° faith must needs be known;   *betrayed*
The fault so great, the case so strange,
   Of right it must abroad be blown:
25 Then since that by thine own desart°   *desert*
My songs do tell how true thou art,
    Blame not my lute.

Blame but thyself that hast misdone
30   And well deserved to have blame;
Change thou thy way, so evil begun,
   And then my lute shall sound that same:
But if till then my fingers play
By thy desart their wonted way,
35   Blame not my lute.

Farewell, unknown, for though thou break
   My strings in spite with great disdain,
Yet have I found out for thy sake
   Strings for to string my lute again;
40 And if perchance this folys° rhyme   *foolish*
Do make thee blush at any time,
    Blame not my lute.

Lucks, My Fair Falcon, and Your Fellows All

Lucks, my fair falcon, and your fellows all,
How well pleasant it were your liberty!
Ye not forsake me that fair might ye befall.[1]
But they that sometime liked my company,
5 Like lice away from dead bodies they crawl:

2. Who used to be desirous or who used to feign desire.
1. I.e., "You do not forsake me so that good luck may come your way." Wyatt states that despite the falcon's name, which suggests that he seeks good fortune, Lucks is loyal to his master.

Lo, what a proof in light adversity![2]
But ye my birds I swear by all your bells,
Ye be my friends, and so be but few else.

Stand Whoso List

Stand whoso list° upon the slipper° top   *wishes / slippery*
Of courts' estates, and let me here rejoice;
And use me° quiet without let° or stop,   *my / hindrance*
Unknown in court, that hath such brackish joys:
5   In hidden place, so let my days forth pass,
That when my years be done, withouten noise,
I may die aged after the common trace.[1]
For him death greep' the° right hard by the crop°   *grips / throat*
That is much known of other; and of himself alas,
10 Doth die unknown, dazed with dreadful face.

Mine Own John Poyns

Mine own John Poyns,[1] since ye delight to know
    The cause why that homeward I me draw,
    And flee the press of courts[2] where so they° go,   *courtiers*
Rather then to live thrall° under the awe   *enslaved*
5   Of lordly looks, wrapped within my cloak,
    To will and lust learning to set a law;
It is not for because I scorn or mock
    The power of them to whom fortune hath lent
    Charge over us, of right, to strike the stroke.
10 But true it is that I have always meant
    Less to esteem them than the common sort
    Of outward things that judge in their intent
Without regard what doth inward resort.
    I grant sometime that of glory the fire
15 Doth touch my heart: me list° not to report   *I wish*
Blame by honor and honor to desire.
    But how may I this honor now attain
    That cannot dye the color black a liar?[3]
My Poyns, I cannot frame my tongue to feign,
20   To cloak the truth for praise, without desert,

2. Wyatt may have written this poem during one of his imprisonments; in any event, he complains here that in prison only his falcons visit and befriend him. Falcons wore bells on their legs to let their masters know where they were.
1. In the common or usual manner; from age and sickness rather than murder. Wyatt alludes to the perilous existence of a man in public life.
1. John Poyns, or Poynz, a friend of Wyatt, spent time at

court in the 1520s.
2. Here Wyatt's posing as a retired courtier critical of the court may illustrate his attitude during one of the periods in which he was out of favor with Henry VIII. He had extensive holdings in Kent, to which he could retire and from which he was elected to Parliament shortly before his death.
3. I.e., who cannot change (dye) black another color and hence call black a liar.

Of them that list all vice for to retain.[4]
I cannot honor them that sets their part
   With Venus and Bacchus[5] all their life long;
   Nor hold my piece of them although I smart.
25   I cannot crouch nor kneel nor do so great a wrong,
   To worship them like God on earth alone,
   That are as wolves these sely° lambs among.   *innocent*
I cannot with my words complain and moan
   And suffer nought, nor smart without complaint,
30   Nor turn the word that from my mouth is gone.
I cannot speak and look like a saint,
   Use wiles for wit and make deceit a pleasure,
   And call craft counsel, for profit still to paint.[6]
I cannot wrest the law to fill the coffer,
35   With innocent blood to feed myself fat,
   And do most hurt where most help I offer.
I am not he that can allow the state
   Of high Caesar and damn Cato to die,[7]
   That with his death did scape out of the gate
40   From Caesar's hands, if Livy do not lie,
   And would not live where liberty was lost:
   So did his heart the common weal° apply.°   *state / value*
I am not he such eloquence to boast,
   To make the crow singing as the swan,
45   Nor call the lion of coward beasts the most
That cannot take a mouse as the cat can:
   And he that dieth for hunger of the gold
   Call him Alessaundre;[8] and say that Pan
Passeth Apollo in music manifold;°   *many times*
50   Praise Sir Thopas[9] for a noble tale,
   And scorn the story that the knight told.
Praise him for counsel that is drunk of ale;
   Grin when he laugheth that beareth all the sway,
   Frown when he frowneth and groan when he is pale;
55   On others lust to hang both night and day:
   None of these points would ever frame in me;
   My wit is nought, I cannot learn the way.
And much the less of things that greater be,
   That asken help of colors of device°   *kinds of deception*

---

4. I.e., to lie by praising those who wish to retain vicious ways and therefore do not deserve praise.
5. Venus: the goddess of love; Bacchus: the god of wine (also known as Dionysius). Together they represented lust and excess.
6. I.e., to represent a falsehood as the truth for profit.
7. I.e., I cannot condone the rule of Caesar and damn Cato. Livy: a Roman historian of the republican period; he records the story of Cato of Utica, who opposed the tyrannical impulses of Julius Caesar and committed suicide rather than live under tyranny.
8. I.e., flatter as Alexander the Great a man so greedy for gold that he dies of hunger. Wyatt continues to list the flattery he cannot give: Pan—half-man, half-goat—was god of shepherds and famous for his music on his reed pipe, but the undisputed god of music was Apollo.
9. *The Tale of Sir Thopas*, one of Chaucer's *Canterbury Tales*, was composed to illustrate how not to tell a story; *The Knight's Tale*, by contrast, exemplified the high style of poetic narrative.

60	To join the mean with each extremity,
	With the nearest virtue to cloak alway the vice:
	And as to purpose likewise it shall fall,[1]
	To press° the virtue that it may not rise;
	As drunkenness good fellowship to call;
65	The friendly foe with his double face
	Say he is gentle and courteous therewithal;
	And say that Favel° hath a goodly grace
	In eloquence, and cruelty to name
	Zeal of justice and change in time and place;
70	And he that suffereth offence without blame
	Call him pitiful; and him true and plain
	That raileth reckless° to every man's shame.
	Say he is rude that cannot lie and feign,
	The lecher a lover, and tyranny
75	To be the right of a prince's reign.
	I cannot, I. No, no, it will not be.
	This is the cause that I could never yet
	Hang on their sleeves that weigh as thou mayst see
	A chip of chance more than a pound of wit.[2]
80	This maketh me at home to hunt and to hawk
	And in foul weather at my book to sit.
	In frost and snow then with my bow to stalk;
	No man doth mark whereso I ride or go;
	In lusty lees° at liberty I walk,
85	And of these news I feel nor weal° nor woe,
	Sauf° that a clog doth hang yet at my heel:
	No force for that, for it is ordered so
	That I may leap both hedge and dike full well.
	I am not now in France to judge the wine,
90	With saffry° sauce the delicates to feel;
	Nor yet in Spain where one must him incline
	Rather than to be, outwardly to seem.
	I meddle not with wits that be so fine,
	Nor Flanders' cheer[3] letteth° not my sight to deem°
95	Of black and white, nor taketh my wit away
	With beastliness, they beasts do so esteem;[4]
	Nor I am not where Christ is given in prey°
	For money, poison and treason at Rome,
	A common practice used night and day:
100	But here I am in Kent and Christendom
	Among the muses where I read and rhyme;
	Where if thou list, my Poyns, for to come,
	Thou shalt be judge how I do spend my time.

Glosses (right margin):
- press° — *suppress*
- Favel° — *Flattery, a character*
- reckless° — *carelessly criticizes*
- lees° — *meadows*
- weal° — *happiness*
- Sauf° — *except*
- saffry° — *saffron*
- letteth° ... deem° — *hinders / judge*
- prey° — *in exchange*

1. Also, when occasion permits.
2. I.e., follow those who value a little good fortune more than a lot of intelligence.
3. The Flemish were reputed to love drinking.
4. The Flemish esteem beasts, i.e., drunks.

Henry Howard, Earl of Surrey
1517?–1547

To belong to a rich and powerful family was no guarantee of a secure and prosperous life. Henry Howard, son of the Duke of Norfolk, was one of the most gifted young men in the court of King Henry VIII, yet he was embroiled in factionalism from a very early age. As a boy, he was the companion of Henry Fitzroy, Duke of Richmond, the king's illegitimate son. They spent a year together as guests of the King of France and, after their return to England, continued their friendship at Windsor Castle. After Richmond's death in 1536, Surrey apparently ran afoul of the law and found himself again at Windsor Castle, this time as the king's prisoner. Playing up the irony of his situation in *So Cruel Prison*, he memorializes Windsor, formerly a "place of bliss" but now the site of his sorrow at the loss of his freedom and the greater loss of his friend. Surrey was imprisoned again five years later in London, ostensibly for breaking windows. This punishment occasioned a satire, *London, Thou Hast Accused Me*, on the real corruption in the city. At twenty-seven, Surrey took part in the war against the French, was wounded, and a year later, was made commander of Boulogne. But he fell from favor when he opposed his sister's marriage to the brother of his rival, Edward Seymour, Lord Hertford, and denounced Seymour as guardian of Prince Edward, Henry's heir. Angered beyond all reconciliation, Henry had Surrey tried and executed for treason in 1547.

As a poet, Surrey is often coupled with Wyatt, who was actually a generation older. Many of his poems (like Wyatt's) emulated Petrarchan forms, themes, and imagery and were published initially by Richard Tottel in 1557 in a volume entitled *Songs and Sonnets*. But Surrey's own accomplishments were unique. He perfected English blank or unrhymed verse, characterized by the pentameter or five-stress line, and he was the likely inventor of the form that became the standard for the English sonnet: three quatrains followed by a couplet, rhyming *ababcdcdefefgg*. Some of his poems on social subjects adopt a satirical tone and convey his vigorous rejection of contemporary manners and morals.

Love That Doth Reign and Live within My Thought

Love that doth reign and live within my thought,	
And built his seat within my captive breast,	
Clad in the arms wherein with me he fought	
Oft in my face he doth his banner rest.	
5 But she that taught me love and suffer pain,	
My doubtful hope and eke° my hot desire	*also*
With shamefast° cloak to shadow and refrain,	*ashamed*
Her smiling grace converteth straight to ire.	
And coward love then to the heart apace	
10 Taketh his flight, where he doth lurk and plain°	*complain*
His purpose lost, and dare not show his face.	
For my lord's guilt thus faultless bide° I pain;	*suffer*
Yet from my lord shall not foot remove:	
Sweet is the death that taketh end by love.	

Th'Assyrians' King, in Peace with Foul Desire

Th'Assyrians' king,[1] in peace with foul desire
And filthy lusts that stained his regal heart,
In war that should set princely hearts afire
Vanquished did yield for want of martial art.
5 The dent of swords from kisses seemed strange,[2]
And harder than his lady's side his targe;°   *shield*
From glutton feasts to soldiers' fare a change,
His helmet, far above a garland's charge.[3]
Who scarce the name of manhood did retain,
10 Drenched in sloth and womanish delight;
Feeble of sprite,° unpatient of pain,   *spirit*
When he had lost his honor and his right—
Proud time of wealth, in storms appalled with dread—
Murdered himself to show some manful deed.

Set Me Whereas the Sun Doth Parch the Green

Set me whereas the sun doth parch the green,
Or where his beams may not dissolve the ice,
In temperate heat where he is felt and seen;
With proud people, in presence sad and wise;
5 Set me in base, or yet in high degree,
In the long night or in the shortest day,
In clear weather or where mists thickest be,
In lusty youth, or when my hairs be grey;
Set me in earth, in heaven, or yet in hell,
10 In hill, in dale, or in the foaming flood;
Thrall,° or at large, alive whereso I dwell,   *captive*
Sick, or in health, in ill fame or in good:
Yours will I be, and with that only thought
Comfort myself when that my hap° is nought.   *fortune*

The Soote Season

The soote° season, that bud and bloom forth brings,   *sweet*
With green hath clad the hill and eke the vale:
The nightingale with feathers new she sings:
The turtle to her make° hath told her tale: *mate*
5 Summer is come, for every spray now springs,
The hart° hath hung his old head° on the pale:°   *stag / horns / stake*
The buck in brake° his winter coat he flings: *thicket*

---

1. The king was Sardanapalus, often regarded as dissolute. kisses.
He committed suicide by self-immolation.   3. I.e., his helmet was a greater burden than a garland.
2. I.e., the dent of swords seemed distasteful compared to

The fishes float with new repaired scale:
The adder all her slough away she slings:
10   The swift swallow pursueth the flies small:
The busy bee her honey now she minges:°   *remembers*
Winter is worn° that was the flowers' bale:°   *passed / evil*
And thus I see among these pleasant things
Each care decays, and yet my sorrow springs.

Alas, So All Things Now Do Hold Their Peace

Alas, so all things now do hold their peace.
Heaven and earth disturbed in nothing:
The beasts, the air, the birds their song do cease:
The night's chair° the stars about doth bring: *Ursa Major*
5   Calm is the sea, the waves work less and less:
So am not I, whom love alas doth wring,
Bringing before my face the great increase
Of my desires, whereat I weep and sing
In joy and woe as in a doubtful ease.
10   For my sweet thoughts sometime do pleasure bring:
But by and by the cause of my disease
Gives me a pang, that inwardly doth sting,
When that I think what grief it is again,
To live and lack the thing should rid my pain.

⟨∞⟩

COMPANION READING
Petrarch, Sonnet 164

Or che 'l ciel et la terra e 'l vento tace
et le fere e gli augelli il sonno affrena,
notte il carro stellato in giro mena
et nel suo letto il mar senz' onda giace,

5   vegghio, penso, ardo, piango; et chi mi sface
sempre m'è inanzi per mia dolce pena:
guerra è 'l mio stato, d'ira e di duol piena,
et sol di lei pensando ò qualche pace.

Così sol d'una chiara fonte viva
10   move 'l dolce et l'amaro ond' io mi pasco,
una man sola mi risana et punge;
et perché 'l mio martir non giunga a riva,
mille volte il dì moro et mille nasco,
tanto da la salute mia son lunge.

Petrarch, Sonnet 164: A Translation

Now that the heavens and the earth and the wind are silent, and sleep reins in the beasts and the birds, Night drives her starry car about, and in its bed the sea lies without a wave,

    I am awake, I think, I burn, I weep; and she who destroys me is always before me, to my sweet pain: war is my state, full of sorrow and suffering, and only thinking of her do I have any peace.

    Thus from one clear living fountain alone spring the sweet and the bitter on which I feed; one hand alone heals me and pierces me.

    And that my suffering may not reach an end, a thousand times a day I die and a thousand am born, so distant am I from health.

cˆ∞ˆ

So Cruel Prison

So cruel prison, how could betide,° alas,	*it happen*
As proud Windsor,[1] where I in lust and joy	
With a king's son my childish years did pass,	
In greater feast than Priam's sons of Troy;[2]	

5	Where° each sweet place returns a taste full sour.	*that*
	The large green courts, where we were wont to hove,°	*accustomed to linger*
	With eyes cast up unto the maidens' tower,	
	And easy sighs, such as folk draw in love.	

	The stately sales,° the ladies bright of hue,	*halls*
10	The dances short, long tales of great delight,	
	With words and looks that tigers could but rue,	
	Where each of us did plead the other's right.	

	The palm play,[3] where, despoiled for the game,	
	With dazed eyes oft we by gleams of love	
15	Have missed the ball and got sight of our dame	
	To bait her eyes which kept the leads° above.	*roofs*

	The graveled ground,° with sleeves tied on the helm,[4]	*jousting arena*
	On foaming horse, with swords and friendly hearts,	
	With cheer,° as° though the one should overwhelm,	*joyfully / even*
20	Where we have fought and chased oft with darts.	

	With silver drops the meads yet spread for ruth,°	*pity*
	In active games of nimbleness and strength	

---

1. Surrey was imprisoned in Windsor Castle in 1537. In this poem, his distress at his imprisonment is augmented by his memories of Henry Fitzroy, the Duke of Richmond and bastard son of Henry VIII, with whom he spent time at Windsor when they were young. Richmond married Surrey's sister in 1533; he died in 1536.
2. Priam, King of Troy, was defeated by the Greeks in the Trojan War.

3. Surrey refers to court tennis, a game resembling modern tennis but played against the walls of a court; he remembers that as players, he and Fitzroy watched the ladies who followed the game from the "leads," sheets of metal used to cover roofs.
4. When jousting, a man would tie the sleeve of a lady's garment to his helmet as a sign of her favor.

Where we did strain, trailed by swarms of youth,
Our tender limbs, that yet shot up in length.

25 The secret groves, which oft we made resound
Of pleasant plaint° and of our ladies' praise,   complaint
Recording soft what grace each one had found,
What hope of speed, what dread of long delays.

The wild forest, the clothed holts° with green,   woods
30 With reins avaled° and swift ybreathed° horse,   slackened / panting
With cry of hounds and merry blasts between,
Where we did chase the fearful hart a force.°   ran it down

The void° walls eke, that harbored us each night;   empty
Wherewith, alas, revive within my breast
35 The sweet accord, such sleeps as yet delight,
The pleasant dreams, the quiet bed of rest,

The secret thoughts imparted with such trust,
The wanton talk, the divers change of play,
The friendship sworn, each promise kept so just,
40 Wherewith we passed the winter nights away.

And with this thought the blood forsakes my face,
The tears berain my cheeks of deadly hue;
The which, as soon as sobbing sighs, alas,
Upsupped° have, thus I my plaint renew: absorbed

45 O place of bliss! renewer of my woes!
Give me accompt where is my noble fere,°   companion
Whom in thy walls thou didst each night enclose,
To other lief,° but unto me most dear.   dear

Each wall, alas, that doth my sorrow rue,
50 Returns thereto a hollow sound of plaint.
Thus I, alone, where all my freedom grew,
In prison pine with bondage and restraint,

And with remembrance of the greater grief,
To banish the less, I find my chief relief.

London, Hast Thou Accused Me

London, hast thou accused me
Of breach of laws, the root of strife?[1]
Within whose breast did boil to see,
(So fervent hot) thy dissolute life,
5 That even the hate of sins, that grow

---

1. Surrey was accused of breaking windows with his bow in the city of London in 1543. He states that he was moved to this action by his hatred of the dissolute life within the city (line 4) and that he was responding to an idea of Justice (line 15).

Within thy wicked walls so rife,
For to break forth did convert° so   *convert me*
That terror could it not repress.
The which, by words, since preachers know
10 What hope is left for to redress,
By unknown means it liked me
My hidden burden to express,
Whereby it might appear to thee
That secret sin hath secret spite;
15 From Justice° rod no fault is free;   *Justice's*
But that all such as works unright
In most quiet are next ill rest.[2]
In secret silence of the night
This made me, with a reckless breast,
20 To wake thy sluggards with my bow;
A figure of the Lord's behest,[3]
Whose scourge for sin the scriptures show.
That, as the fearful thunder clap
By sudden flame at hand we know,
25 Of pebble stones the soundless rap,
The dreadful plage° might make thee see   *shore*
Of God's wrath, that doth thee enwrap;[4]
That pride might know, from conscience free,
How lofty works may her defend;[5]
30 And envy find, as he hath sought,
How other seek him to offend;
And wrath taste of each cruel thought
The just shapp hire in the end;[6]
And idle sloth, that never wrought,
35 To heaven his spirit lift° may begin;   *to lift*
And greedy lucre live in dread
To see what hate ill-got goods win;
The lechers, ye that lusts do feed,
Perceive what secrecy is in sin;
40 And gluttons' hearts for sorrow bleed,
Awaked when their fault they find.
In loathsome vice, each drunken wight°   *man*
To stir to God, this was my mind.
Thy windows had done me no spite;
45 But proud people that dread no fall,

---

2. I.e., all those who act wrongly, if they are resting quietly, are nearest to being disturbed.
3. Surrey imagines that he is like a prophet who does the Lord's command (cf. Isaiah 47.11).
4. The phrase is obscure: "just as we know lightening by thunder, so the soundless rap of pebble stones might make you see the dreadful shore of God's wrath that surrounds you."

5. Surrey becomes ironic: "Pride, free from conscience, might know how lofty works may defend her"—i.e., important or prodigious works do not defend from punishment the proud, who are (by definition) without a conscience.
6. I.e., wrath receives, for each of its cruel thoughts, the justly shaped or appointed hire or payment in the end.

Clothed with falsehed° and unright   *falsehood*
Bred in the closures of thy wall,
But wrested to wrath in fervent zeal
Thou hast to strife my secret call.[7]
50   Endured° hearts no warning feel.   *hardened*
Oh shameless whore! is dread then gone
By such thy foes as meant thy weal?[8]
Oh member of false Babylon!
The shop of craft! the den of ire!
55   Thy dreadful dome° draws fast upon;   *judgment*
Thy martyrs' blood, by sword and fire,
In heaven and earth for Justice call.
The Lord shall hear their just desire;
The flame of wrath shall on thee fall;
60   With famine and pest lamentably
Stricken shall be thy lechers all;
Thy proud towers and turrets high,
Enemies to God, beat° stone from stone;   *beaten*
Thine idols burnt that wrought iniquity.
65   When none thy ruin shall bemoan,
But render unto the right wise Lord,
That so hath judged Babylon,
Immortal praise with one accord.

Wyatt Resteth Here

Wyatt resteth here, that quick° could never rest;[1]   *alive*
Whose heavenly gifts increased by disdain
And virtue sank the deeper in his breast:
Such profit he of envy could obtain.

5   A head, where wisdom mysteries did frame;
Whose hammers beat still in that lively brain
As on a stith,° where some work of fame   *anvil*
Was daily wrought, to turn to Britain's gain.

A visage, stern and mild; where both did grow,
10   Vice to condemn, in virtues to rejoice;
Amid great storms whom grace assured so
To live upright and smile at fortune's choice.

A hand that taught what might be said in rhyme;
That reft° Chaucer the glory of his wit;   *took from*
15   A mark the which (unperfited, for time)[2]—
Some may approach, but never none shall hit.

---

7. I.e., you have heard my secret call to strife or struggle.
8. Surrey addresses London as the whore of Babylon, the epitome of iniquity, and asks ironically, "Do you no longer fear those enemies that intend your happiness?"

1. This elegy for the poet Thomas Wyatt was published in 1542, shortly after his death.
2. I.e., was left unperfected for lack of time.

A tongue that served in foreign realms his king;
Whose courteous talk to virtue did enflame
Each noble heart, a worthy guide to bring
20   Our English youth, by travail[3] unto fame.

An eye whose judgment no affect° could blind,   *feeling*
Friends to allure, and foes to reconcile;
Whose piercing look did represent a mind
With virtue fraught, reposed, void of guile.

25   A heart where dread yet never so impressed
To hide the thought that might the truth avaunce;°   *advance*
In neither fortune lift, nor so repressed,[4]
To swell in wealth, or yield unto mischance.

A valiant corps,° where force and beauty met,   *body*
30   Happy, alas! too happy, but for foes,
Lived, and ran the race that nature set;
Of manhood's shape, where she the mold did lose.

But to the heavens that simple soul is fled;
Which left with such, as covet° Christ to know   *desire*
35   Witness to faith that never shall be dead:
Sent for our wealth, but not received so.

Thus, for our guilt, this jewel have we lost;
The earth his bones, the heavens possess his ghost.
Amen.

My Radcliffe, When Thy Reckless Youth Offends

My Radcliffe,[1] when thy reckless youth offends:
Receive thy scourge by others' chastisement
For such calling, when it works none° amends: *no*
Then plagues are sent without advertisement.
5   Yet Salomon[2] said, the wronged shall recure:°   *recover*
But Wyatt said true, the scar doth aye endure.

3. Work, but also travel, in that Surrey describes Wyatt as
a "guide."
4. I.e., neither raised up by fortune to get rich, nor so
depressed (by ill fortune) as to yield to a temptation that
will lead to misfortune.

1. This epigram is probably addressed to Thomas
Radcliffe, third Earl of Essex.
2. Surrey concludes by contrasting an optimistic sentence
of King Solomon, which he probably associated with the
book of Ecclesiasticus, with the dour reflection of Wyatt.

Edmund Spenser
1552?–1599

H. W. Smith, *Edmund Spenser*.

A man whose poetry has come to be known as a monument to Queen Elizabeth's England began life modestly enough. Attending Cambridge as a "sizar," or "poor scholar," he worked as a servant to pay for his fees. Allegiance to the English church was expected of all subjects, and Spenser showed his support of the faith while still a student by contributing anti-Catholic verses to the first emblem book published in England. The genre, consisting of emblems or symbolic scenes explained by clever captions, acquainted the aspiring poet with elements of the mode he was later to master: allegory. Literally a writing that conveys "other" (from the Greek *allos*, "other") than literal meanings, the allegory that Spenser would eventually perfect for his epic poem *The Faerie Queene* produced narrative verse of great flexibility and verve. Building on powerful images, his verse allegories of education in a "virtuous" chivalry convey the challenges he saw attending the creation of a civil society in early modern England.

Shortly after leaving Cambridge in 1576, Spenser found employment as a secretary in the London household of the rich and influential Earl of Leicester, a favorite courtier of Queen Elizabeth and an ardent defender of international Protestantism. There he met Leicester's already famous nephew, Sir Philip Sidney, to whom Spenser dedicated his first work, the deliberately archaic, neo-Chaucerian *The Shepheardes Calender*, a sequence of twelve eclogues or poems on pastoral subjects, one for each month of the year. A work of a paradoxically innovative style, *The Shepheardes Calender* demonstrated a range of metrical forms that had yet to be seen in English poetry; probably more compelling to the general reader was Spenser's use of pastoral motifs and settings to represent opinions on love, poetry, and social order. Sidney's response to the poem was, nevertheless, somewhat ambivalent. While recognizing that Spenser's eclogues had "much poetry" in them, he stated that he disliked verse composed in an "old rustic language"; among earlier and model poets of pastoral, "neither Theocritus in Greek, Virgil in Latin, nor Sannazaro in Italian did affect it." But precisely because this "old rustic language" could be recognized as purely English and independent of European traditions, Spenser would use a modified form of it in *The Faerie Queene*; in this way he hoped to demonstrate that English literature had as rich a past as any in Europe. He probably began the poem while in Leicester's service; the seventeenth-century biographer John Aubrey reported the discovery of "an abundance of cards, with stanzas of the *Faerie Queene* written on them" in the wainscoting of Spenser's London lodging.

From 1580 to the end of his life, Spenser lived in Ireland, serving as secretary to the Lord Deputy of Ireland, Arthur Grey. At such a distance from Queen Elizabeth's court, Spenser could not have secured royal favor. He was rescued from obscurity in 1589 by Sir Walter Raleigh, who, impressed with the first three books of *The Faerie Queene*, invited Spenser to present his poem to the queen. Beside the gallant and charismatic Raleigh, the poet—said to have been a "little man, who wore short hair, little bands (collars) and little cuffs"—must have cut a poor figure. But the queen liked the poem that illustrated her majesty in so many ways, "desired at timely hours to hear" it, and rewarded Spenser with a life pension of £50 a year. When Spenser returned to Ireland in 1590, he met and fell in love with Elizabeth Boyle, a woman much his junior. They were married in 1594, and Spenser celebrated their courtship and wedding in the *Amoretti*, a sonnet sequence describing the poet's quest for his "deer" or dear, and *Epithalamion*, a hymn to each of the twenty-four hours of their wedding day. The second three books of *The Faerie Queene*, published in 1596, proved as popular with readers as the first three, although James VI of Scotland (later James I of England) thought slanderous its portrait of the evil queen Duessa, whom he identified as his mother, Mary Queen of Scots. He demanded that Spenser be "duly tried and punished." Fortunately, however, Spenser's friends at court intervened, and nothing came of the king's displeasure.

The last years of the poet's life were full of grief and bitter disappointment. In 1598 the Irish in the province of Munster, rebelling against the English colonial authorities, burned the castle in which Spenser lived. The poet and his wife fled; their newborn child was reported to have perished in the flames. In December of that year, Spenser went to London to deliver letters to the queen from the Governor of Ireland concerning the uprising. He included a note describing his own assessment of the situation—a note that may have included material in a treatise entitled *A View of the Present State of Ireland*, supporting a militaristic policy to colonize the people of Ireland, which he is supposed to have written. He died a month after arriving in London in January of 1599 and was buried in Westminster Abbey near Geoffrey Chaucer, whose poetry had meant so much to him. The monument placed on his grave is inscribed with these words: "Prince of poets in his time, whose Divine Spirit needs no other witness than the works which he left behind."

Consciously aspiring both to Chaucer's humane dignity and to his vividly colloquial style, Spenser saw himself as fashioning and refashioning a tradition of English and possibly British poetry. As he made a point of using older terms and spelling, his poems are presented here unmodernized. Spenser's choice of language parallels his use of the motifs of knightly romance: turning to the past, he sought a vital perspective on the present. John Milton would later describe him as a "sage and serious" poet, who, in *The Faerie Queene*, wrote of the struggle of good against evil and the triumph of faith over falsehood. The subject, treated by weaving different story lines together to form a vast tapestry, interested not only Milton, who was clearly inspired by Spenser's complex understanding of human psychology, but also the next generation of poets in England, especially Ben Jonson, John Donne, and George Herbert, who turned to Spenser for a poetry of satirical vigor and spiritual insight. Yet other readers have been moved by Spenser's lyrics. His shorter poems and occasional verse show his skillful use of repetitive sounds or verbal echoes and reveal his unerring sense of language as a musical medium.

THE FAERIE QUEENE In 1583 Spenser told guests at a dinner he was attending that he proposed to write a poem in which he would "represent all the moral virtues, assigning to every virtue a knight in whose actions and chivalry the operations of that virtue are to be expressed, and the vices and unruly appetites that oppose themselves to be beaten down." The project, obviously ambitious, recalls the great epics of classical antiquity: the twenty-four books of Homer's *Iliad*, the twelve books of Virgil's *Aeneid*. Spenser must have believed he was prepared for such an undertaking; like Virgil, he had served his apprenticeship by writing pastoral poetry, with the composition of *The Shepheardes Calender*. But whatever his intention, he realized his great work only in part. He depicted the first six virtues in the "legends" of Holiness, Temperance, Chastity, Friendship, Justice, and Courtesy, in which each virtue is perfected by the trials of a particular knight fighting the evil that most threatens his character. He published the first three books in 1590, adding the next three in a second edition in 1596. His plan for a second set of six books resulted in only two cantos—on the virtue of Constancy.

Spenser's moral chivalry is sponsored and sustained by the court of Gloriana, the Faerie Queene, in whom is reflected the imposing figure of Queen Elizabeth. Gloriana's story is illustrated by the actions of a character called Prince Arthur, who intervenes at crucial moments to assist Gloriana's knights and is otherwise bent on seeking out Gloriana herself, the bride he has chosen in a dream. In the mythical genealogy of the Tudors, King Arthur (known to Spenser's readers through Sir Thomas Malory's *Morte Darthur*) was identified as the dynasty's progenitor; thus, in the allegorical schema of the poem, the prospective marriage of the Faerie Queene and Prince Arthur, also the champion of Magnificence, signifies the perfect union of monarch and state.

Book 1 relates the adventures of the knight of Holiness, known as the Redcrosse Knight from the sign on his shield and identified as Saint George, England's patron saint. His mission is to overcome the machinations of spiritual error menacing the English church and to deliver the parents of Una, his lady, who is the Truth, from the demons of false faith. The foes of the Redcrosse Knight are many: the fiendish wizard Archimago, who stands for corrupt doctrine; the cunning queen Duessa, who, as the embodiment of duplicity, is never what she seems; the bloated giant Orgoglio, or Pride; and the loathsome many-headed dragon who is supposed to wield the institutional power of the Catholic Church. The Redcrosse Knight kills Pride and the dragon but, although he at last understands that they are thoroughly sinister, fails to capture Duessa and Archimago. They return in later books to trouble Gloriana's other knights.

The verse form of *The Faerie Queene* is virtually unique to Spenser. It features a sequence of stanzas each comprising nine lines (known to later readers as "Spenserian"), of which the first eight contain five feet or accented syllables and the last contains six feet. They are rhymed in a pattern—*ababbcbcc*—particularly difficult for poets writing in English. Unlike the Romance languages (French, Italian, and Spanish), English has relatively few words ending in vowel sounds, which are easily rhymed. Spenser's ear for the sound of English allowed him to compose verse of a musicality comparable to what was possible in the Romance languages, itself an extraordinary accomplishment. The narrative units of Spenser's epic poem achieve a dramatic coherence by his constructive use of imagery in particular story lines that continuously develop new contexts for their subjects. In other words, a character signifying a special quality in one canto will not signify precisely that quality in another canto: Spenser will change his or her role with the setting the story demands. This gives the reader an active role in the poem's interpretation; in a sense, the reader finds the meaning of the poem in the process of reading it.

from THE FAERIE QUEENE

A Letter of the Authors[1]

A letter of the Authors expounding his whole intention in the course of this worke: which for that it giveth great light to the Reader, for the better understanding is hereunto annexed.

TO THE RIGHT NOBLE, AND VALOROUS, SIR WALTER RALEIGH KNIGHT, LO. WARDEIN OF THE STANNERYES, AND HER MAJESTIES LIEFETENAUNT OF THE COUNTY OF CORNEWAYLL.

Sir knowing how doubtfully all Allegories may be construed, and this booke of mine, which I have entituled the Faery Queene, being a continued Allegory, or darke conceit,[2] I have thought good aswell for avoyding of gealous opinions and misconstructions, as also for your better light in reading thereof, (being so by you commanded,) to discover unto you the general intention and meaning, which in

---

1. Spenser addressed this letter explaining the purpose and plot of *The Faerie Queene* to Sir Walter Raleigh, who had agreed to bring the poem to the attention of Elizabeth I.
2. In Spenser's poetics a series of images or figures that are to be interpreted as metaphor. The narrative understood literally thus implies a second level whose meaning or meanings the reader is to infer.

the whole course thereof I have fashioned, without expressing of any particular purposes or by-accidents therein occasioned. The generall end therefore of all the booke is to fashion a gentleman or noble person in vertuous and gentle discipline: Which for that I conceived shoulde be most plausible and pleasing, being coloured with an historicall fiction, the which the most part of men delight to read, rather for variety of matter, then for profite of the ensample:[3] I chose the historye of king Arthure,[4] as most fitte for the excellency of his person, being made famous by many mens former workes, and also furthest from the daunger of envy, and suspition of present time. In which I have followed all the antique Poets historicall, first Homere, who in the Persons of Agamemnon and Ulysses hath ensampled a good governour and a vertuous man, the one in his Ilias, the other in his Odysseis: then Virgil, whose like intention was to doe in the person of Aeneas: after him Ariosto comprised them both in his Orlando: and lately Tasso dissevered[5] them againe, and formed both parts in two persons, namely that part which they in Philosophy call Ethice, or vertues of a private man, coloured in his Rinaldo: The other named Politice in his Godfredo. By ensample of which excellente Poets, I labour to pourtraict in Arthure, before he was king, the image of a brave knight, perfected in the twelve private morall vertues, as Aristotle hath devised, the which is the purpose of these first twelve bookes: which if I finde to be well accepted, I may be perhaps encoraged, to frame the other part of polliticke vertues in his person, after that hee came to be king. To some I know this Methode will seeme displeasaunt, which had rather have good discipline delivered plainly in way of precepts, or sermoned at large, as they use,[6] then thus clowdily enwrapped in Allegoricall devises.[7] But such, me seeme, should be satisfide with the use of these dayes, seeing all things accounted by their showes, and nothing esteemed of, that is not delightfull and pleasing to commune sence. For this cause is Xenophon preferred before Plato,[8] for that the one in the exquisite depth of his judgement, formed a Commune welth such as it should be, but the other in the person of Cyrus and the Persians fashioned a governement such as might best be: So much more profitable and gratious is doctrine by ensample, then by rule. So have I laboured to doe in the person of Arthure: whome I conceive after his long education by Timon, to whom he was by Merlin delivered to be brought up, so soone as he was borne of the Lady Igrayne, to have seene in a dream or vision the Faery Queen, with whose excellent beauty ravished,[9] he awaking resolved to seeke her out, and so being by Merlin armed, and by Timon throughly instructed, he went to seeke her forth in Faerye land. In that Faery Queene I meane glory in my generall intention,[1] but in my

3. Example.
4. Spenser states that he chose material from the legendary past of Britain: the story of King Arthur and his knights. In fact, apart from a few characters such as Prince Arthur and the magician Merlin, Spenser represented virtually nothing of the Arthurian cycle, known to his readers from Sir Thomas Malory's prose narrative Morte Darthur. More important in a structural and thematic sense were the poets mentioned subsequently: Homer and Virgil; Lodovico Ariosto (1474–1533), who wrote Orlando Furioso; and Torquato Tasso (1544–1595), who wrote Jerusalem Delivered. From these models, Spenser derived the idea of a hero in whom a particular virtue would be exemplified. His division of virtues into moral or ethical on the one hand and political on the other is indebted to Aristotle, who considered the actions of a private person in his Ethics and the organization of a whole society in his Politics.

5. Revealed.
6. Are accustomed to.
7. Figures.
8. Xenophon: the Greek historian (c. 430–355 B.C.), whose account of the Persian king Cyrus creates memorable characters for the reader to emulate; Plato: the Greek philosopher (c. 427–348 B.C.), whose works comprise ethics, politics, and metaphysics. Spenser repeats a conventional excuse for fiction or poetic representation in contrast to philosophy.
9. Overcome.
1. I.e., in the figure of the Faerie Queene Spenser intends to represent glory in general and Queen Elizabeth in particular. He goes on to say that the queen is also represented by the figure of Belphoebe, a nymph who has attributes of Cynthia, or the goddess of the moon, who is herself an aspect of Diana, also the goddess of chastity and the hunt.

particular I conceive the most excellent and glorious person of our soveraine the Queene, and her kingdome in Faery land. And yet in some places els, I doe otherwise shadow her.[2] For considering she beareth two persons, the one of a most royall Queene or Empresse, the other of a most vertuous and beautifull Lady, this latter part in some places I doe expresse in Belphoebe, fashioning her name according to your owne excellent conceipt of Cynthia, (Phoebe and Cynthia being both names of Diana.) So in the person of Prince Arthure[3] I sette forth magnificence in particular, which vertue for that (according to Aristotle and the rest) it is the perfection of all the rest, and conteineth in it them all, therefore in the whole course I mention the deedes of Arthure applyable to that vertue, which I write of in that booke. But of the xii. other vertues, I make xii. other knights the patrones, for the more variety of the history: Of which these three bookes contayn three, The first of the knight of the Redcrosse, in whome I expresse Holynes: The seconde of Sir Guyon, in whome I sette forth Temperaunce: The third of Britomartis a Lady knight, in whome I picture Chastity. But because the beginning of the whole worke seemeth abrupte and as depending upon other antecedents, it needs that ye know the occasion of these three knights severall adventures. For the Methode of a Poet historical is not such, as of an Historiographer.[4] For an Historiographer discourseth of affayres orderly as they were donne, accounting as well the times as the actions, but a Poet thrusteth into the middest, even where it most concerneth him, and there recoursing[5] to the thinges forepaste,[6] and divining of things to come, maketh a pleasing Analysis of all. The beginning therefore of my history, if it were to be told by an Historiographer should be the twelfth booke, which is the last, where I devise[7] that the Faery Queene kept her Annuall feaste xii. dayes, uppon which xii. severall dayes, the occasions of the xii. severall adventures hapned, which being undertaken by xii. severall knights, are in these xii books severally handled and discoursed. The first was this. In the beginning of the feast, there presented him selfe a tall clownishe[8] younge man, who falling before the Queen of Faries desired a boone[9] (as the manner then was) which during that feast she might not refuse: which was that hee might have the atchievement of any adventure, which during that feaste should happen, that being graunted, he rested him on the floore, unfitte through his rusticity for a better place. Soone after entred a faire Ladye in mourning weedes,[1] riding on a white Asse, with a dwarfe behind her leading a warlike steed, that bore the Armes of a knight, and his speare in the dwarfes hand. Shee falling before the Queene of Faeries, complayned that her father and mother an ancient King and Queene, had bene by an huge dragon many years shut up in a brasen[2] Castle, who thence suffred them not to yssew:[3] and therefore besought the Faery Queene to assygne her some one of her knights to take on him that

---

2. Represent.

3. Legendary king of the Britons. Spenser's character is to represent "magnificence," i.e, a splendid and comprehensive generosity, traditionally the virtue most appropriate to royalty. The remaining characters Spenser mentions—the Redcrosse Knight, Sir Guyon, and Britomartis (or Britomart)—represent other virtues and are his own creations.

4. History represents sequential narratives of real events revealing relations of cause and effect; by contrast, poetry constructs narratives governed by the poet's wish to pick and choose among a variety of sources and to speculate on outcomes that may or may not ever come to pass.

5. Having recourse.

6. Passed.

7. Show.

8. Countrified.

9. Wish.

1. Clothes.

2. Brass.

3. Get out.

exployt. Presently that clownish person upstarting, desired that adventure: whereat the Queene much wondering, and the Lady much gainesaying,[4] yet he earnestly importuned[5] his desire. In the end the Lady told him that unlesse that armour which she brought, would serve him (that is the armour of a Christian man specified by Saint Paul v. Ephes.)[6] that he could not succeed in that enterprise, which being forthwith put upon him with dewe furnitures[7] thereunto, he seemed the goodliest man in al that company, and was well liked of the Lady. And eftesoones[8] taking on him knighthood, and mounting on that straunge Courser,[9] he went forth with her on that adventure: where beginneth the first booke, vz.

A gentle knight was pricking on the playne. &c.

The second day ther came in a Palmer[1] bearing an Infant with bloody hands, whose Parents he complained to have bene slayn by an Enchaunteresse called Acrasia: and therfore craved of the Faery Queene, to appoint him some knight, to performe that adventure, which being assigned to Sir Guyon, he presently went forth with that same Palmer: which is the beginning of the second booke and the whole subject thereof. The third day there came in, a Groome who complained before the Faery Queene, that a vile Enchaunter called Busirane had in hand a most faire Lady called Amoretta, whom he kept in most grievous torment, because she would not yield him the pleasure of her body. Whereupon Sir Scudamour the lover of that Lady presently tooke on him that adventure. But being unable to performe it by reason of the hard Enchauntments, after long sorrow, in the end met with Britomartis, who succoured[2] him, and reskewed his love.

But by occasion hereof, many other adventures are intermedled, but rather as Accidents, then intendments.[3] As the love of Britomart, the overthrow of Marinell, the misery of Florimell, the vertuousnes of Belphoebe, the lasciviousnes of Hellenora, and many the like.

Thus much Sir, I have briefly overronne[4] to direct your understanding to the welhead[5] of the History, that from thence gathering the whole intention of the conceit, ye may as in a handfull gripe[6] al the discourse, which otherwise may happily seeme tedious and confused. So humbly craving the continuaunce of your honorable favour towards me, and th'eternall establishment of your happines, I humbly take leave.

23. January, 1589.
Yours most humbly affectionate.
ED. SPENSER.

---

4. Protesting.
5. Begged for.
6. St. Paul's Letter to the Ephesians, often used to justify the spiritual symbolism that from the late Middle Ages had become associated with the practices of chivalry. "Wherefore take unto you the whole armour of God, that ye may be able to withstand in the evil day, and having done all, to stand. Stand therefore, having your loins girt about with truth, and having on the breastplate of righteousness; And your feet shod with the preparation of the gospel of peace; Above all, taking the shield of faith, wherewith ye shall be able to quench all the fiery darts of the wicked. And take the helmet of salvation, and the sword of the Spirit, which is the word of God" (Ephesians 6.13–17).
7. Equipment.
8. Immediately.
9. Warhorse.
1. A pilgrim who carries a palm leaf signifying that he has been to the Holy Land; hence, any pilgrim.
2. Helped.
3. I.e., they are not central to the principal development of the allegory.
4. Outlined.
5. Source.
6. Gather

The First Booke of the Faerie Queene

Contayning The Legende of the Knight of the Red Crosse, or Of Holinesse.

1

Lo I the man, whose Muse whilome° did maske,[1]   *formerly*
As time her taught, in lowly Shepheards weeds,°   *clothing*
Am now enforst a far unfitter taske,
For trumpets sterne to chaunge mine Oaten reeds,
5   And sing of Knights and Ladies gentle deeds;
Whose prayses having slept in silence long,
Me, all too meane,° the sacred Muse areeds°   *lowly / commands*
To blazon broad° emongst her learned throng: *proclaim abroad*
Fierce warres and faithfull loves shall moralize my song.

2

10   Helpe then, O holy Virgin chiefe of nine,[2]
Thy weaker Novice to performe thy will,
Lay forth out of thine everlasting scryne°   *treasure chest*
The antique rolles,° which there lye hidden still,   *scrolls*
Of Faerie knights and fairest Tanaquill,
15   Whom that most noble Briton Prince° so long   *Arthur*
Sought through the world, and suffered so much ill,
That I must rue° his undeserved wrong: *regret*
O helpe thou my weake wit, and sharpen my dull tong.

3

And thou most dreaded impe° of highest Jove,[3]   *child*
20   Faire Venus sonne,° that with thy cruell dart   *Cupid, god of love*
At that good knight° so cunningly didst rove,°   *Arthur / pierce*
That glorious fire it kindled in his hart,
Lay now thy deadly Heben° bow apart,   *ebony*
And with thy mother milde come to mine ayde:[4]
25   Come both, and with you bring triumphant Mart,°   *Mars*
In loves and gentle jollities arrayd,
After his murdrous spoiles and bloudy rage allayd.°   *quelled*

4

And with them eke, O Goddesse heavenly bright,[5]
Mirrour of grace and Majestie divine,

---

1. In this stanza and in the rest of the Proem (introduction), Spenser is announcing his intention to write an epic poem. His earlier *Shepheardes Calender* had been written in the more modest pastoral style, characterized by the "oaten reed" of the shepherd's pipe. Here he casts off the guise of the shepherd to undertake the lofty subject of *The Faerie Queene*.
2. Spenser calls on a muse to inspire him; he may be referring to Clio, the muse of history, or to Calliope, the muse of epic poetry. Tanaquill was a Roman woman famous for her chaste and noble character; here Spenser establishes a symbolic relation between Tanaquill, the Faerie Queene (whom Arthur seeks in the poem), and Queen Elizabeth I, much as he will later refer to other characters—most

prominently, Britomart, Gloriana, and Mercilla—as figuring aspects of the queen, her power and attributes.
3. The king of the pagan gods. Like all the poets of the period who were not writing religious verse, Spenser refers to the classical pantheon as a way of alluding to God and to his various expressions of power.
4. Spenser also invokes Cupid, who combines the loving nature of Venus and the warlike spirit of Mars, to illustrate the mood of his poem.
5. Spenser celebrates the nature of Elizabeth I in grandiose terms: She is a "goddess" whose eyes, like the lamp of Phoebus Apollo (the sun), shine throughout the world and must now illuminate the poet's mind.

30   Great Lady of the greatest Isle, whose light
        Like Phoebus lampe throughout the world doth shine,
        Shed thy faire beames into my feeble eyne,
        And raise my thoughts too humble and too vile,
        To thinke of that true glorious type° of thine,   *the Faerie Queene*
35   The argument of mine afflicted stile:
    The which to heare, vouchsafe,° O dearest dread° a-while.   *grant / power*

Canto 1

The Patron of true Holinesse,
Foule Errour doth defeate:
Hypocrisie him to entrapp;
Doth to his home entreate.

1

A Gentle Knight[6] was pricking° on the plaine,   *riding*
        Y cladd in mightie armes and silver shielde,
        Wherein old dints of deepe wounds did remaine,
        The cruell markes of many a bloudy fielde;
5   Yet armes till that time did he never wield:
        His angry steede did chide his foming bitt,
        As much disdayning to the curbe to yield:
        full jolly knight he seemd, and faire did sitt,
As one for knightly giusts° and fierce encounters fitt.   *jousts*

2

10   But on his brest a bloudie Crosse[7] he bore,
        The deare remembrance of his dying Lord,
        For whose sweete sake that glorious badge he wore,
        And dead as living ever him ador'd:
        Upon his shield the like was also scor'd,°   *represented*
15   For soveraine hope, which in his° helpe he had: *his Lord's*
        Right faithfull true he was in deede and word,
        But of his cheere° did seeme too solemne sad;   *demeanor*
Yet nothing did he dread,° but ever was ydrad.°   *fear / feared*

3

Upon a great adventure he was bond,
20   That greatest Gloriana[8] to him gave,
        That greatest Glorious Queene of Faerie lond,
        To winne him worship, and her grace to have,
        Which of all earthly things he most did crave;

---

6. This gentle or well-born knight, identified as the Red-crosse Knight from the sign on his shield and introduced to the poem in Spenser's prefatory letter, wears the armor of Christianity. The armor itself has been worn by many who fought for the faith, but the Redcrosse Knight is new to the spiritual battlefield and will have to prove himself.
7. The red cross is Spenser's figure for the salvation offered by Christ to humankind through his death on the cross, the sacrifice of his blood, and his resurrection. It was also the badge traditionally worn by St. George, the patron saint of England.
8. The character Spenser most frequently invokes when he alludes to Elizabeth I. Gloriana presides over the action of the poem, although she does not take part in it herself.

And ever as he rode, his hart did earne
25   To prove his puissance° in battell brave   *power*
Upon his foe, and his new force to learne;
Upon his foe, a Dragon horrible and stearne.

4

A lovely Ladie rode him faire beside,
Upon a lowly Asse more white then snow,[9]
30   Yet she much whiter, but the same did hide
Under a vele, that wimpled° was full low,   *gathered*
And over all a blacke stole she did throw,
As one that inly mournd: so was she sad,
And heavie sat upon her palfrey[1] slow:
35   Seemed in heart some hidden care she had,
And by her in a line a milke white lambe she lad.

5

So pure an innocent, as that same lambe,
She was in life and every vertuous lore,
And by descent from Royall lynage came
40   Of ancient Kings and Queenes, that had of yore
Their scepters stretcht from East to Westerne shore,
And all the world in their subjection held;[2]
Till that infernall feend with foule uprore
Forwasted all their land, and them expeld:
45   Whom to avenge, she had this Knight from far compeld.

6

Behind her farre away a Dwarfe[3] did lag,
That lasie seemd in being ever last,
Or wearied with bearing of her bag
Of needments at his backe. Thus as they past,
50   The day with cloudes was suddeine overcast,
And angry Jove an hideous storme of raine
Did poure into his Lemans[4] lap so fast,
That every wight to shrowd° it did constrain,°   *shelter / impel*
And this faire couple eke° to shroud themselves were fain.°   *also / desirous*

7

55   Enforst to seeke some covert° nigh at hand,   *hiding place*
A shadie grove not far away they spide,
That promist ayde the tempest to withstand:
Whose loftie trees yclad with sommers pride,

9. This imagery suggests the role the Lady will play: the ass signifies her humility, the veil her modesty, and the lamb her innocence.
1. A horse suitable for a woman.
2. The Lady traces her lineage to Adam and Eve, who held dominion over Eden before the Fall. The "infernall feend," or Satan, is represented as the destroyer of their realm, which stretched from East to West and was there-

fore truly universal, unlike the regions dominated by Rome or by the Catholic Church. By designating the Knight as the avenger of Adam and Eve, Spenser identifies him with Christ.
3. The servant who serves the Lady, a source of prudence, common sense, and wariness.
4. I.e., his lady love's, or the earth's.

Did spred so broad, that heavens light did hide,
60 Not perceable with power of any starre:
And all within were pathes and alleies wide,
With footing worne, and leading inward farre:
Faire harbour that them seemes; so in they entred arre.

8
And foorth they passe, with pleasure forward led,
65 Joying to heare the birdes sweete harmony,
Which therein shrouded from the tempest dred,
Seemd in their song to scorne the cruell sky.
Much can they prayse the trees so straight and hy,
The sayling° Pine, the Cedar proud and tall,   *soaring*
70 The vine-prop Elme, the Poplar never dry,
The builder Oake, sole king of forrests all,
The Aspine good for staves,° the Cypresse funerall.   *poles*

9
The Laurell, meed° of mightie Conquerours   *reward*
And Poets sage, the Firre that weepeth still,
75 The Willow worne of forlorne Paramours,°   *forsaken lovers*
The Eugh obedient to the benders will,
The Birch for shaftes, the Sallow° for the mill,   *willow*
The Mirrhe sweete bleeding in the bitter wound,
The warlike Beech, the Ash for nothing ill,
80 The fruitfull Olive, and the Platane° round,   *sycamore*
The carver Holme,° the Maple seeldom inward sound.   *holly*

10
Led with delight, they thus beguile° the way,   *make pleasant*
Untill the blustring storme is overblowne;
When weening° to returne, whence they did stray,   *thinking*
85 They cannot finde that path, which first was showne,
But wander too and fro in wayes unknowne,
Furthest from end then, when they neerest weene,
That makes them doubt, their wits be not their owne:
So many pathes, so many turnings seene,
90 That which of them to take, in diverse doubt they been.

11
At last resolving forward still to fare,
Till that some end° they finde or° in or out,   *way / either*
That path they take, that beaten seemd most bare,
And like to lead the labyrinth about;
95 Which when by tract they hunted had throughout,
At length it brought them to a hollow cave,
Amid the thickest woods. The Champion stout
Eftsoones dismounted from his courser brave,
And to the Dwarfe a while his needlesse spere he gave.

12

100 Be well aware, quoth then that Ladie milde,
　　　Least suddaine mischiefe ye too rash provoke:
　　　The danger hid, the place unknowne and wilde,
　　　Breedes dreadful doubts: Oft fire is without smoke,
　　　And perill without show: therefore your stroke
105　　Sir knight with-hold, till further triall made.
　　　Ah Ladie (said he) shame were to revoke
　　　The forward footing for an hidden shade:
Vertue gives her selfe light, through darkenesse for to wade.[5]

13

Yea but (quoth she) the perill of this place
110　　I better wot° then you, though now too late　　　　　　　　know
　　　To wish you backe returne with foule disgrace,
　　　Yet wisedome warnes, whilest foot is in the gate,
　　　To stay° the steppe, ere forced to retrate.°　　　　　　halt / retreat
　　　This is the wandring wood, this Errours den,
115　　A monster vile, whom God and man does hate:
　　　Therefore I read beware. Fly fly (quoth then
The fearefull Dwarfe:) this is no place for living men.

14

But full of fire and greedy hardiment,
　　　The youthfull knight could not for ought° be staide,　　anything
120　　But forth unto the darksome hole he went,
　　　And looked in: his glistring armor made
　　　A litle glooming light, much like a shade,
　　　By which he saw the ugly monster plaine,
　　　Halfe like a serpent horribly displaide,
125　　But th'other halfe did womans shape retaine,[6]
Most lothsom, filthie, foule, and full of vile disdaine.

15

And as she lay upon the durtie ground,
　　　Her huge long taile her den all overspred,
　　　Yet was in knots and many boughtes° upwound,　　　coils
130　　Pointed with mortall sting. Of her there bred
　　　A thousand yong ones, which she dayly fed,
　　　Sucking upon her poisonous dugs, eachone
　　　Of sundry shapes, yet all ill favored:
　　　Soone as that uncouth° light upon them shone,　　　strange
135 Into her mouth they crept, and suddain all were gone.

16

Their dam upstart, out of her den effraide,
　　　And rushed forth, hurling her hideous taile

---

5. Lacking humility and overly confident of his own
virtue, the Redcrosse Knight believes he is strong enough
to withstand the dangers of the wood. In fact, as we learn
in the next stanza, he has stepped into the den of a

monster who personifies Error, one of Satan's many manifestations in the poem.
6. Spenser follows traditional treatments of Error in giving her a woman's face and a serpent's body.

About her cursed head, whose folds displaid
Were stretcht now forth at length without entraile.°   *coiling*
140 She lookt about, and seeing one in mayle°   *armor*
Armed to point, sought backe to turne againe;
For light she hated as the deadly bale,°   *injury*
Ay wont° in desert darknesse to remaine,   *ever used*
Where plaine° none might her see, nor she see any plaine.   *plainly*

17

145 Which when the valiant Elfe° perceiv'd, he lept   *Redcrosse Knight*
As Lyon fierce upon the flying pray,
And with his trenchand blade her boldly kept
From turning backe, and forced her to stay:
Therewith enrag'd she loudly gan to bray,
150 And turning fierce, her speckled taile advaunst,
Threatning her angry sting, him to dismay:
Who nought aghast, his mightie hand enhaunst:°   *raised up*
The stroke down from her head unto her shoulder glaunst.

18

Much daunted with that dint, her sence was dazd,
155 Yet kindling rage, her selfe she gathered round,
And all attonce her beastly body raizd
With doubled forces high above the ground:
Tho wrapping up her wrethed sterne° arownd,   *tail*
Lept fierce upon his shield, and her huge traine°   *tail*
160 All suddenly about his body wound,
That hand or foot to stirre he strove in vaine:
God helpe the man so wrapt in Errours endlesse traine.

19

His Lady sad to see his sore constraint,°   *predicament*
Cride out, Now now Sir knight, shew what ye bee,
165 Add faith unto your force, and be not faint:
Strangle her, else she sure will strangle thee.
That when he heard, in great perplexitie,
His gall did grate° for griefe and high disdaine,   *anger was aroused*
And knitting all his force got one hand free,
170 Wherewith he grypt her gorge with so great paine,
That soone to loose her wicked bands did her constraine.

20

Therewith she spewd out of her filthy maw°   *stomach*
A floud of poyson horrible and blacke,
Full of great lumpes of flesh and gobbets raw,
175 Which stunck so vildly, that it forst him slacke
His grasping hold, and from her turne him backe:
Her vomit full of bookes and papers was,[7]
With loathly frogs and toades, which eyes did lacke,

---

7. Error's vomit is a figurative depiction of the falsehoods that corrupt religion. The vehicles of such lies are both the spoken and written word; hence the material issuing from Error's mouth includes books as well as other poisonous things.

And creeping sought way in the weedy gras:
180   Her filthy parbreake° all the place defiled has.   *vomit*

21

As when old father Nilus° gins to swell   *the river Nile*
    With timely pride aboue the Aegyptian vale,
    His fattie° waves do fertile slime outwell,°   *fertile / pour forth*
    And overflow each plaine and lowly dale:
185   But when his later spring° gins to avale,°   *last waters / subside*
    Huge heapes of mudd he leaves, wherein there breed
    Ten thousand kindes of creatures, partly male
    And partly female of his fruitfull seed;
Such ugly monstrous shapes elswhere may no man reed.°   *know*

22

190   The same so sore annoyed has the knight,
    That welnigh choked with the deadly stinke,
    His forces faile, ne can no longer fight.
    Whose corage when the feend perceiv'd to shrinke,
    She poured forth out of her hellish sinke°   *womb*
195   Her fruitfull cursed spawne° of serpents small,   *offspring*
    Deformed monsters, fowle, and blacke as inke,
    Which swarming all about his legs did crall,
And him encombred sore, but could not hurt at all.

23

As gentle Shepheard in sweete even-tide,
200   When ruddy Phoebus gins to welke° in west,   *sink*
    High on an hill, his flocke to vewen wide,
    Markes which do byte their hasty supper best;
    A cloud of combrous gnattes do him molest,
    All striving to infixe their feeble stings,
205   That from their noyance he no where can rest,
    But with his clownish hands their tender wings
He brusheth oft, and oft doth mar their murmurings.

24

Thus ill bestedd,° and fearefull more of shame,   *situated*
    Then of the certaine perill he stood in,
210   Halfe furious unto his foe he came,
    Resolv'd in minde all suddenly to win,
    Or soone to lose, before he once would lin;°   *surrender*
    And strooke at her with more then manly force,
    That from her body full of filthie sin
215   He raft° her hatefull head without remorse;   *cut off*
A streame of cole black bloud forth gushed from her corse.

25

Her scattred brood, soone as their Parent deare
    They saw so rudely° falling to the ground,   *violently*
    Groning full deadly, all with troublous feare,
220   Gathred themselves about her body round,

Weening their wonted entrance to have found
At her wide mouth: but being there withstood
They flocked all about her bleeding wound,
And sucked up their dying mothers blood,
225   Making her death their life, and eke her hurt their good.

26

That detestable sight him much amazde,
    To see th'unkindly Impes° of heaven accurst,   *unnatural offspring*
    Devoure their dam; on whom while so he gazd,
    Having all satisfide their bloudy thurst,
230   Their bellies swolne he saw with fulnesse burst,
    And bowels gushing forth: well worthy end
    Of such as drunke her life, the which them nurst;
    Now needeth him no lenger labour spend,
His foes have slaine themselves, with whom he should contend.

27

235   His Ladie seeing all, that chaunst, from farre
    Approcht in hast to greet his victorie,
    And said, Faire knight, borne under happy starre,
    Who see your vanquisht foes before you lye:
    Well worthy be you of that Armorie,[8]
240   Wherein ye have great glory wonne this day,
    And proov'd your strength on a strong enimie,
    Your first adventure: many such I pray,
And henceforth ever wish, that like succeed it may.

28

Then mounted he upon his Steede againe,
245   And with the Lady backward sought to wend;
    That path he kept, which beaten was most plaine,
    Ne ever would to any by-way bend,
    But still did follow one unto the end,
    The which at last out of the wood them brought.
250   So forward on his way (with God to frend)
    He passed forth, and new adventure sought;
Long way he travelled, before he heard of ought.

29

At length they chaunst to meet upon the way
    An aged Sire, in long blacke weedes yclad,
255   His feete all bare, his beard all hoarie gray,
    And by his belt his booke he hanging had;
    Sober he seemde, and very sagely sad,
    And to the ground his eyes were lowly bent,
    Simple in shew, and voyde of malice bad,
260   And all the way he prayed, as he went,
And often knockt his brest, as one that did repent.

8. The Lady is proclaiming that by conquering Error, the Redcrosse Knight has become worthy to wear the armor of
Christ; the episode foreshadows the knight's final triumph over the many-headed dragon that represents false faith.

30

He faire the knight saluted, louting° low,   *bowing*
   Who faire him quited,° as that courteous was: *answered*
   And after asked him, if he did know
265   Of straunge adventures, which abroad did pas.
   Ah my deare Sonne (quoth he) how should, alas,
   Silly° old man, that lives in hidden cell,   *simple*
   Bidding° his beades all day for his trespas,   *telling*
   Tydings of warre and worldly trouble tell?
270 With holy father sits not with such things to mell.°   *meddle*

31

But if of daunger which hereby doth dwell,
   And homebred evill ye desire to heare,
   Of a straunge man I can you tidings tell,
   That wasteth° all this countrey farre and neare.   *destroys*
275 Of such (said he)° I chiefly do inquere,   *Redcrosse Knight*
   And shall you well reward to shew the place,
   In which that wicked wight his dayes doth weare:°   *spend*
   For to all knighthood it is foule disgrace,
That such a cursed creature lives so long a space.

32

280 Far hence (quoth he)° in wastfull wildernesse   *the aged Sire*
   His dwelling is, by which no living wight
   May ever passe, but thorough° great distresse.   *through*
   Now (sayd the Lady) draweth toward night,
   And well I wote,° that of your later fight   *know*
285 Ye all forwearied° be: for what so strong,   *exhausted*
   But wanting rest will also want of might?
   The Sunne that measures heaven all day long,
At night doth baite° his steedes the Ocean waves emong.   *nourish*

33

Then with the Sunne take Sir, your timely rest,
290   And with new day new worke at once begin:
   Untroubled night they say gives counsell best.
   Right well Sir knight ye have advised bin,
   (Quoth then that aged man;) the way to win
   Is wisely to advise: now day is spent;
295 Therefore with me ye may take up your In
   For this same night. The knight was well content:
So with that godly father to his home they went.

34

A little lowly Hermitage it was,[9]
   Downe in a dale, hard by° a forests side,   *next to*

9. This stanza illustrates the use of symbol in allegory; taken as a whole, its imagery suggests that the Redcrosse Knight has met the hermit because he suffers from a failing that the hermit will exploit. The hermitage is down in a dale, or valley, because the knight has begun to descend into a false faith, and it is isolated because he is traveling in a strange and unusual direction.

300 Far from resort of people, that did pas
 In travell to and froe: a little wyde
 There was an holy Chappell edifyde,°   *built*
 Wherein the Hermite dewly wont to say
 His holy things each morne and eventyde:
305 Thereby a Christall streame did gently play,
Which from a sacred fountaine welled forth alway.

35

Arrived there, the little house they fill,
 Ne looke for entertainement, where none was:
 Rest is their feast, and all things at their will;
310 The noblest mind the best contentment has.
 With faire discourse the evening so they pas:
 For that old man of pleasing wordes had store,
 And well could file his tongue as smooth as glas;
 He told of Saintes and Popes, and evermore
315 He strowd° an Ave-Mary after and before.[1]   *recited*

36

The drouping Night thus creepeth on them fast,
 And the sad humour° loading their eye liddes,   *moisture*
 As messenger of Morpheus° on them cast   *god of sleep*
 Sweet slombring deaw, the which to sleepe them biddes.
320 Unto their lodgings then his guestes he° riddes: *the aged Sire*
 Where when all drownd in deadly sleepe he findes,
 He to his study goes, and there amiddes
 His Magick bookes and artes of sundry kindes,
He seekes out mighty charmes, to trouble sleepy mindes.

37

325 Then choosing out few wordes most horrible,
 (Let none them read) thereof did verses frame,°   *compose*
 With which and other spelles like terrible,
 He bad awake blacke Plutoes griesly Dame,[2]
 And cursed heaven, and spake reprochfull shame
330 Of highest God, the Lord of life and light;
 A bold bad man, that dar'd to call by name
 Great Gorgon,[3] Prince of darknesse and dead night,
At which Cocytus quakes, and Styx is put to flight.[4]

38

And forth he cald out of deepe darknesse dred
335 Legions of Sprights,° the which like little flyes   *spirits*
 Fluttring about his ever damned hed,

---

1. Despite his pious demeanor, the old man's discourse of saints and popes and his recital of Ave Marias indicate his affiliation with Catholicism; they are therefore intended to signal his corrupt and duplicitous character.
2. Persephone, Pluto's wife and sometimes goddess of the underworld.

3. One of a family of monsters, daughters of the primitive gods of antiquity; Spenser, making her male, identifies the Gorgon with Pluto and also Satan.
4. The Cocytus and the Styx were rivers in the classical underworld.

A-waite whereto their service he applyes,
　　To aide his friends, or fray° his enimies:　　　　　　　　　*frighten*
　　Of those he chose out two, the falsest twoo,
340　　And fittest for to forge true-seeming lyes;
　　The one of them he gave a message too,
The other by him selfe staide other worke to doo.

39

He making speedy way through spersed° ayre,　　　　　　　*empty*
　　And through the world of waters wide and deepe,
345　　To Morpheus[5] house doth hastily repaire.
　　Amid the bowels of the earth full steepe,
　　And low, where dawning day doth never peepe,
　　His dwelling is; there Tethys his wet bed
　　Doth ever wash, and Cynthia still doth steepe
350　　In silver deaw his ever-drouping hed,
Whiles sad Night over him her mantle black doth spred.

40

Whose double gates he findeth locked fast,
　　The one faire fram'd of burnisht Yvory,
　　The other all with silver overcast;
355　　And wakefull dogges before them farre do lye,
　　Watching to banish Care their enimy,
　　Who oft is wont to trouble gentle Sleepe.
　　By them the Sprite doth passe in quietly,
　　And unto Morpheus comes, whom drowned deepe
360　　In drowsie fit° he findes: of nothing he takes keepe.°　　*stupor / notice*

41

And more, to lulle him in his slumber soft,
　　A trickling streame from high rocke tumbling downe
　　And ever-drizling raine upon the loft,
　　Mixt with a murmuring winde, much like the sowne
365　　Of swarming Bees, did cast him in a swowne:°　　　　　*faint*
　　No other noyse, nor peoples troublous cryes,
　　As still are wont t'annoy the walled towne,
　　Might there be heard: but carelesse Quiet lyes,
Wrapt in eternall silence farre from enemyes.

42

370　The messenger approching to him spake,
　　But his wast wordes returnd to him in vaine:
　　So sound he° slept, that nought mought him awake.　　*Morpheus*
　　Then rudely he him thrust, and pusht with paine,
　　Whereat he gan to stretch: but he againe
375　　Shooke him so hard, that forced him to speake.
　　As one then in a dreame, whose dryer braine

5. God of sleep, who lives in the depths of the dark earth: Tethus or the sea washes him; Cynthia or the moon bedews him; Night covers him.

Is tost with troubled sights and fancies weake,
He mumbled soft, but would not all his silence breake.

43

The Sprite then gan more boldly him to wake,
And threatned unto him the dreaded name
Of Hecate:[6] whereat he gan to quake,
And lifting up his lumpish head, with blame
Halfe angry asked him, for what he came.
Hither (quoth he) me Archimago[7] sent,
He that the stubborne Sprites can wisely tame,
He bids thee to him send for his intent
A fit false dreame, that can delude the sleepers sent.°   senses

44

The God obayde, and calling forth straight way
A diverse dreame out of his prison darke,
Delivered it to him, and downe did lay
His heavie head, devoide of carefull carke,°   sorrowful anxiety
Whose sences all were straight benumbd and starke.°   paralyzed
He backe returning by the Yvorie dore,
Remounted up as light as chearefull Larke,
And on his litle winges the dreame he bore
In hast unto his Lord, where he him left afore.

45

Who all this while with charmes and hidden artes,
Had made a Lady of that other Spright,
And fram'd of liquid ayre her tender partes
So lively, and so like in all mens sight,
That weaker sence it° could have ravisht quight: the spright
The maker selfe for all his wondrous witt,
Was nigh beguiled with so goodly sight:
Her all in white he clad, and over it
Cast a blacke stole, most like to seeme for Una[8] fit.

46

Now when that ydle dreame was to him brought,
Unto that Elfin knight he° bad him° fly,   Archimago / the spright
Where he slept soundly void of evill thought,
And with false shewes abuse his fantasy,
In sort as he him schooled privily:
And that new creature borne without her dew,°   unnaturally
Full of the makers guile, with usage sly

---

6. The dark aspect of Cynthia, the moon, and thus also of Diana; Hecate figures the underworld, death, and darkness.
7. The sage Sire is named Archimago, an "arch (or chief) magus (or magician)" and hence a forger or an architect of images rather than real things. Because these images are clever and deceptive imitations of reality, Archimago is associated with hypocrisy and magic, an art that Christians were forbidden to practice.
8. Here the Lady is named Una; she is to symbolize the ideal unity of Truth and the Church whose faith the Redcrosse Knight defends. She is named only when her false double appears.

380

385

390

395

400

405

410

He taught to imitate that Lady trew,
Whose semblance she did carrie under feigned hew.

47

415 Thus well instructed, to their worke they hast,
  And comming where the knight in slomber lay,
  The one upon his hardy head him plast,
  And made him dreame of loves and lustfull play,
  That nigh his manly hart did melt away,
420   Bathed in wanton blis and wicked joy:
  Then seemed him his Lady by him lay,
  And to him playnd, how that false winged boy°   *Cupid*
Her chast hart had subdewd, to learne Dame pleasures toy.

48

And she her selfe of beautie soveraigne Queene,
425   Faire Venus seemde unto his bed to bring
  Her,⁹ whom he waking evermore did weene
  To be the chastest flowre, that ay did spring
  On earthly braunch, the daughter of a king,
  Now a loose Leman to vile service bound:
430   And eke the Graces seemed all to sing,
  *Hymen iõ Hymen,*¹ dauncing all around,
Whilst freshest Flora her with Yvie girlond crownd.

49

In this great passion of unwonted lust,
  Or wonted feare of doing ought amis,
435   He° started up, as seeming to mistrust   *Redcrosse Knight*
  Some secret ill, or hidden foe of his:
  Lo there before his face his Lady is,
  Under blake stole hyding her bayted hooke,
  And as halfe blushing offred him to kis,
440   With gentle blandishment and lovely looke,
Most like that virgin true, which for her knight him took.

50

All cleane° dismayd to see so uncouth sight,   *fully*
  And halfe enraged at her shamelesse guise,
  He thought have slaine her in his fierce despight:°   *indignation*
445   But hasty heat tempring with sufferance° wise,   *patience*
  He stayde his hand, and gan himselfe advise
  To prove his sense,° and tempt° her faigned truth.²   *what he saw / test*

9. I.e., she, impersonating Una, seemed also a Venus; this composite queen of beauty appears to the Redcrosse Knight to have come into his bed.
1. A Roman chant praising Hymen, the god of marriage, sung here by the Graces, handmaids of Venus, who personify the arts of courtesy and courtship. The union they celebrate in this case is not, however, a lawful Christian marriage but rather one provoked by lust and sexuality. In Roman mythology, Flora is the goddess of flowers, but early

modern poets often gave her the role of a harlot. This entire scene uses the imagery of the Roman Bacchanalia (celebration of the god Bacchus) to suggest the mood of an orgy.
2. The Redcrosse Knight unwisely tests his senses rather than his faith. In doing so, he succumbs to the sensuality of the false Una and thus proves himself false to the true Una. The episode illustrates the danger inherent in powerful illusion; in such cases the false and the true may be indistinguishable.

Wringing her hands in wemens pitteous wise,
    Tho° can she weepe, to stirre up gentle ruth,   *then*
450 Both for her noble bloud, and for her tender youth.

51

And said, Ah Sir, my liege Lord and my love,
    Shall I accuse the hidden cruell fate,
    And mightie causes wrought in heaven above,
    Or the blind God, that doth me thus amate,°   *dismay*
455 For hoped love to winne me certaine hate?
    Yet thus perforce he bids me do, or die.
    Die is my dew:° yet rew° my wretched state   *due / pity*
    You, whom my hard avenging destinie
Hath made judge of my life or death indifferently.

52

460 Your owne deare sake forst me at first to leave
    My Fathers kingdome, There she stopt with teares;
    Her swollen hart her speach seemd to bereave,
    And then againe begun, My weaker yeares
    Captiv'd to fortune and frayle worldly feares,
465 Fly to your faith for succour and sure ayde:
    Let me not dye in languor and long teares.
    Why Dame (quoth he) what hath ye thus dismayd?
What frayes° ye, that were wont to comfort me affrayd?   *frightens*

53

Love of your selfe, she said, and deare° constraint°   *dire / danger*
470 Lets me not sleepe, but wast the wearie night
    In secret anguish and unpittied plaint,
    Whiles you in carelesse sleepe are drowned quight.
    Her doubtfull words made that redoubted knight
    Suspect her truth: yet since no'untruth he knew,
475 Her fawning love with foule disdainefull spight
    He would not shend,° but said, Deare dame I rew,   *reproach*
That for my sake unknowne such griefe unto you grew.

54

Assure your selfe, it fell not all to ground;
    For all so deare as life is to my hart,
480 I deeme your love, and hold me to you bound;
    Ne let vaine feares procure your needlesse smart,°   *pain*
    Where cause is none, but to your rest depart.
    Not all content, yet seemd she to appease
    Her mournefull plaintes, beguiled of her art,
485 And fed with words, that could not chuse but please,
So slyding softly forth, she turnd as to her ease.

55

Long after lay he musing at her mood,
    Much griev'd to thinke that gentle Dame so light,

For whose defence he was to shed his blood.
490   At last dull wearinesse of former fight
          Having yrockt a sleepe his irkesome spright,
          That troublous dreame gan freshly tosse his braine,
          With bowres, and beds, and Ladies deare delight:
          But when he° saw his labour all was vaine,   *Archimago*
495   With that misformed spright he backe returnd againe.

Canto 2

The guilefull great Enchaunter parts
The Redcrosse Knight from Truth:
Into whose stead faire falshood steps,
And workes him wofull ruth.

1

By this the Northerne wagoner had set
          His sevenfold teme behind the stedfast starre,[1]
          That was in Ocean waves yet never wet,
          But firme is fixt, and sendeth light from farre
5   To all, that in the wide deepe wandring arre:
          And chearefull Chaunticlere° with his note shrill   *a rooster*
          Had warned once, that Phoebus fiery carre°   *chariot*
          In hast was climbing up the Easterne hill,
          Full envious that night so long his roome° did fill.   *the sky*

2

10   When those accursed messengers of hell,
          That feigning dreame, and that faire-forged Spright
          Came to their wicked maister, and gan° tell   *did*
          Their bootelesse paines,° and ill succeeding night: *fruitless efforts*
          Who all in rage to see his skilfull might
15   Deluded so, gan threaten hellish paine
          And sad Proserpines wrath, them to affright.
          But when he saw his threatning was but vaine,
He cast about, and searcht his balefull° bookes againe.   *evil*

3

Eftsoones° he tooke that miscreated faire,   *soon after*
20   And that false other Spright, on whom he spred
          A seeming body of the subtile aire,
          Like a young Squire, in loves and lusty-hed°   *lechery*
          His wanton dayes that ever loosely led,
          Without regard of armes and dreaded fight:
25   Those two he tooke, and in a secret bed,
          Covered with darknesse and misdeeming° night,   *deceiving*
Them both together laid, to joy in vaine delight.

1. Spenser is referring to a constellation that includes Ursa Major, which contemporary English readers envisioned as a ploughman drawing a wagon. The "stedfast starre" is the Pole Star; it remains at the center of the stars in Ursa Major, which revolve around it and is "never wet" because it never sets into the ocean. The brightest star in this constellation is Arcturus, which the English associated with the mythical King Arthur.

4

Forthwith he runnes with feigned faithfull hast
  Unto his guest, who after troublous sights
30   And dreames, gan° now to take more sound repast,   *began*
  Whom suddenly he wakes with fearefull frights,
  As one aghast with feends or damned sprights,
  And to him cals, Rise rise unhappy Swaine,°   *youth*
  That here wex old in sleepe, whiles wicked wights
35 Have knit themselves in Venus shamefull chaine;
Come see, where your false Lady doth her honour staine.

5

All in amaze he suddenly up start
  With sword in hand, and with the old man went;
  Who soone him brought into a secret part,
40   Where that false couple were full closely ment°   *joined*
  In wanton lust and lewd embracement:
  Which when he saw, he burnt with gealous fire,
  The eye of reason was with rage yblent,°   *blinded*
  And would have slaine them in his furious ire,
45 But hardly was restreined of that aged sire.

6

Returning to his bed in torment great,
  And bitter anguish of his guiltie sight,
  He could not rest, but did his stout heart eat,
  And wast his inward gall° with deepe despight,°   *irritation / malice*
50 Yrkesome° of life, and too long lingring night.   *tired*
  At last faire Hesperus[2] in highest skie
  Had spent his lampe, and brought forth dawning light,
  Then up he rose, and clad him hastily;
The Dwarfe him brought his steed: so both away do fly.

7

55 Now when the rosy-fingred Morning faire,
  Weary of aged Tithones[3] saffron bed,
  Had spred her purple robe through deawy aire,
  And the high hils Titan[4] discovered,
  The royall virgin shooke off drowsy-hed,
60 And rising forth out of her baser bowre,
  Lookt for her knight, who far away was fled,
  And for her Dwarfe, that wont to wait° each houre;   *used to attend*
Then gan she waile and weepe, to see that woefull stowre.°   *plight*

8

And after him she rode with so much speede
65 As her slow beast could make; but all in vaine:
  For him so far had borne his light-foot steede,
  Pricked with wrath and fiery fierce disdaine,

2. The evening and morning star, the planet Venus.   4. The sun. I.e., when the sun revealed the high hills.
3. Husband of the dawn.

That him to follow was but fruitlesse paine;
Yet she her weary limbes would never rest,
70   But every hill and dale, each wood and plaine
Did search, sore grieved in her gentle brest,
He so ungently left her, whom she loved best.

9

But subtill Archimago, when his guests
He saw divided into double parts,
75   And Una wandring in woods and forrests,
Th'end of his drift,° he praisd his divelish arts,   *intention*
That had such might over true meaning harts;
Yet rests not so, but other meanes doth make,
How he may worke unto her further smarts:
80   For her he hated as the hissing snake,
And in her many troubles did most pleasure take.

10

He then devisde himselfe how to disguise;
For by his mightie science he could take
As many formes and shapes in seeming wise,
85   As ever Proteus[5] to himselfe could make:
Sometime a fowle, sometime a fish in lake,
Now like a foxe, now like a dragon fell,°   *deadly*
That of himselfe he oft for feare would quake,
And oft would flie away. O who can tell
90   The hidden power of herbes, and might of Magicke spell?

11

But now seemde best, the person to put on
Of that good knight, his late beguiled° guest: *deceived*
In mighty armes he was yclad anon,°   *presently*
And silver shield: upon his coward brest
95   A bloudy crosse, and on his craven crest°   *cowardly head*
A bounch of haires discolourd diversly:
Full jolly knight he seemde, and well addrest,
And when he sate upon his courser free,
Saint George himself ye would have deemed him to be.[6]

12

100   But he the knight, whose semblaunt° he did beare,   *likeness*
The true Saint George was wandred far away,
Still flying from his thoughts and gealous feare;
Will was his guide, and griefe led him astray.
At last him chaunst to meete upon the way
105   A faithlesse Sarazin[7] all arm'd to point,

---

5. A sea-god, son of two other deities of the sea, Oceanus
and Tethys; Proteus could change his shape at will.
6. Here, Archimago assumes the appearance of the Redcrosse Knight; incidentally, he reveals that the true
knight is actually Saint George.

7. A Saracen, or follower of Islam. Early modern Europeans
commonly represented believers in a non-Christian faith
as infidels or nonbelievers. Sans-Foy (as this knight is later
named—literally, "without faith") is therefore not actually
without a faith, but he is a Saracen and not a Christian.

In whose great shield was writ with letters gay
Sans-Foy:° full large of limbe and every joint   *faithless*
He was, and cared not for God or man a point.°   *bit*

13

He had a faire companion of his way,
110   A goodly Lady[8] clad in scarlot° red,   *a royal cloth*
    Purfled with gold and pearle of rich assay,°   *quality*
    And like a Persian mitre° on her hed   *papal hat*
    She wore, with crownes and owches° garnished,   *jewels*
    The which her lavish lovers to her gave;
115   Her wanton palfrey all was overspred
    With tinsell trappings, woven like a wave,
Whose bridle rung with golden bels and bosses brave.°   *splendid ornaments*

14

With faire disport° and courting dalliaunce°   *teasing / play*
    She intertainde her lover all the way:
120   But when she saw the knight his speare advaunce,
    She soone left off her mirth and wanton play,
    And bad her knight addresse him to the fray:°   *face the challenge*
    His foe was nigh at hand. He prickt° with pride   *spurred on*
    And hope to winne his Ladies heart that day,
125   Forth spurred fast: adowne his coursers side
The red bloud trickling staind the way, as he did ride.

15

The knight of the Redcrosse when him he spide,
    Spurring so hote with rage dispiteous,°   *cruel*
    Gan fairely couch his speare, and towards ride:
130   Soone meete they both, both fell and furious,
    That daunted° with their forces hideous,   *dazed*
    Their steeds do stagger, and amazed stand,
    And eke themselves too rudely rigorous,
    Astonied° with the stroke of their owne hand,   *stunned*
135 Do backe rebut,° and each to other yeeldeth land.   *recoil*

16

As when two rams stird with ambitious pride,
    Fight for the rule of the rich fleeced flocke,
    Their horned fronts so fierce on either side
    Do meete, that with the terrour of the shocke
140   Astonied both, stand sencelesse as a blocke,
    Forgetfull of the hanging victory:
    So stood these twaine, unmoved as a rocke,
    Both staring fierce, and holding idely
The broken reliques of their former cruelty.

8. The description of this Lady associates her with the Whore of Babylon (Revelation 17.4), who was identified by 16th-century Protestants with the Antichrist, i.e., the Pope and his retinue.

17

145 The Sarazin sore daunted with the buffe°   *blow*
        Snatcheth his sword, and fiercely to him flies;
        Who well it wards, and quyteth° cuff° with cuff: *repays / blow*
        Each others equall puissaunce° envies,   *power*
        And through their iron sides with cruell spies
150 Does seeke to perce: repining° courage yields   *exhausted*
        No foote to foe. The flashing fier flies
        As from a forge out of their burning shields,
And streames of purple bloud new dies the verdant fields.

18

Curse on that Crosse (quoth then the Sarazin)
155 That keepes thy body from the bitter fit;°   *pangs of death*
        Dead long ygoe I wote thou haddest bin,
        Had not that charme from thee forwarned° it: *prevented*
        But yet I warne thee now assured sitt,
        And hide thy head. Therewith upon his crest
160 With rigour so outrageous he smitt,°   *struck*
        That a large share it hewd out of the rest,
And glauncing downe his shield, from blame° him fairely blest.°   *injury /*
                                                                                          protected

19

Who thereat wondrous wroth,° the sleeping spark   *angry*
        Of native vertue gan eftsoones revive,
165 And at his haughtie helmet making mark,
        So hugely stroke, that it the steele did rive,°   *cut*
        And cleft his head. He tumbling downe alive,
        With bloudy mouth his mother earth did kis,
        Greeting his grave: his grudging ghost did strive
170 With the fraile flesh; at last it flitted is,
Whither the soules do fly of men, that live amis.

20

The Lady when she saw her champion fall,
        Like the old ruines of a broken towre,
        Staid not to waile his woefull funerall,
175 But from him° fled away with all her powre;   *Redcrosse Knight*
        Who after her as hastily gan scowre,°   *pursue*
        Bidding the Dwarfe with him to bring away
        The Sarazins shield, signe of the conqueroure.
        Her soone he overtooke, and bad° to stay,   *commanded*
180 For present cause was none of dread her to dismay.[9]

21

She turning backe with ruefull° countenaunce,   *pitiful*
        Cride, Mercy mercy Sir vouchsafe to show

9. I.e., he did not mean to frighten her.

        On silly Dame, subject to hard mischaunce,
        And to your mighty will. Her humblesse low
185   In so ritch weedes and seeming glorious show,
        Did much emmove his stout heroïcke heart,
        And said, Deare dame, your suddein overthrow
        Much rueth me;° but now put feare apart,   *I regret*
    And tell, both who ye be, and who that tooke your part.

             22

190   Melting in teares, then gan she thus lament;
        The wretched woman, whom unhappy howre
        Hath now made thrall to your commandement,
        Before that angry heavens list to lowre,°   *scowl*
        And fortune false betraide me to your powre,
195   Was, (O what now availeth° that I was!)   *does it help*
        Borne the sole daughter of an Emperour,
        He that the wide West under his rule has,[1]
    And high hath set his throne, where Tiberis° doth pas.   *Tiber River, in Rome*

             23

        He in the first flowre of my freshest age,
200   Betrothed me unto the onely haire
        Of a most mighty king, most rich and sage;
        Was never Prince so faithfull and so faire,
        Was never Prince so meeke and debonaire;°   *gentle*
        But ere my hoped day of spousall° shone,   *marriage*
205   My dearest Lord fell from high honours staire,
        Into the hands of his accursed fone,°   *foe*
    And cruelly was slaine, that shall I ever mone.

             24

        His blessed body spoild of lively breath,
        Was afterward, I know not how, convaid
210   And fro me hid: of whose most innocent death
        When tidings came to me unhappy maid,
        O how great sorrow my sad soule assaid.°   *afflicted*
        Then forth I went his woefull corse to find,
        And many yeares throughout the world I straid,
215   A virgin widow, whose deepe wounded mind
    With love, long time did languish as the striken hind.°   *doe*

             25

        At last it chaunced this proud Sarazin
        To meete me wandring, who perforce° me led   *forcibly*
        With him away, but yet could never win

---

1. The Lady's story in this and the next two stanzas allegorically describes the corruption of the Holy Roman Empire and its separation from true Christianity. The Lady's father, an emperor, reigned in Rome, the seat of Catholicism (cf. Una's father, who is Adam), and the prince she was to marry was Christ. The Lady's quest to find his corpse suggests that she denies the doctrine of the resurrection of the body. In any case, Protestants in this period were critical of the Catholic emphasis on Christ's dead body in religious art and literature and contrasted it to the Protestant celebration of his resurrection.

220   The Fort, that Ladies hold in soveraigne dread.
       There lies he now with foule dishonour dead,
       Who whiles he liv'de, was called proud Sans-Foy,
       The eldest of three brethren, all three bred
       Of one bad sire, whose youngest is Sans-Joy,
225   And twixt them both was borne the bloudy bold Sans-Loy.[2]

26

In this sad plight, friendlesse, unfortunate,
    Now miserable I Fidessa[3] dwell,
    Craving of you in pitty of my state,
    To do none ill, if please ye not do well.
230   He in great passion all this while did dwell,
    More busying his quicke eyes, her face to view,
    Then his dull eares, to heare what she did tell;
    And said, Faire Lady hart of flint would rew
The undeserved woes and sorrowes, which ye shew.

27

235   Henceforth in safe assuraunce may ye rest,
    Having both found a new friend you to aid,
    And lost an old foe, that did you molest:
    Better new friend then° an old foe is said.   than
    With chaunge of cheare the seeming simple maid
240   Let fall her eyen,° as shamefast to the earth,   eyes
    And yeelding soft, in that she nought gain-said,°   denied
    So forth they rode, he feining seemely merth,
And she coy lookes: so dainty they say maketh derth.[4]

28

Long time they thus together traveiled,
245   Till weary of their way, they came at last,
    Where grew two goodly trees, that faire did spred
    Their armes abroad, with gray mosse overcast,
    And their greene leaves trembling with every blast,
    Made a calme shadow far in compasse round:
250   The fearefull Shepheard often there aghast°   frightened
    Under them never sat, ne wont there sound
His mery oaten pipe, but shund th'unlucky ground.

29

But this good knight soone as he them can spie,
    For the coole shade him thither hastly got:
255   For golden Phoebus now ymounted hie,
    From fiery wheeles of his faire chariot

---

2. Sans-Loy ("without law") and Sans-Joy ("without joy") illustrate other aspects of the infidel attacking the spiritual well-being of the Redcrosse Knight. Spenser draws on Galatians 5.22–23: "But the fruit of the spirit is love, joy . . . faith . . . temperance; against such there is no Law."

3. The Lady in Persian dress calls herself Fidessa, a name that can mean "faithful" in a corrupted kind of Latin. From her association with Sans-Foy, however, the reader knows that she is not representative of the true faith and so only puts on the appearance of fidelity.
4. I.e., such daintiness is costly.

Hurled his beame so scorching cruell hot,
That living creature mote° it not abide;   *might*
And his new Lady it endured not.
260   There they alight, in hope themselves to hide
From the fierce heat, and rest their weary limbs a tide.°   *while*

30

Faire seemely pleasaunce each to other makes,
    With goodly purposes there as they sit:
And in his falsed fancy he her takes
265   To be the fairest wight,° that lived yit;   *creature*
Which to expresse, he bends his gentle wit,
And thinking of those braunches greene to frame
A girlond for her dainty forehead fit,
He pluckt a bough; out of whose rift there came
270 Small drops of gory bloud, that trickled downe the same.[5]

31

Therewith a piteous yelling voyce was heard,
Crying, O spare with guilty hands to teare
My tender sides in this rough rynd embard,°   *enclosed*
    But fly, ah fly far hence away, for feare
275   Least to you hap, that happened to me heare,
And to this wretched Lady, my deare love,
O too deare love, love bought with death too deare.
Astond he stood, and up his haire did hove,
And with that suddein horror could no member move.

32

280 At last whenas the dreadfull passion
    Was overpast, and manhood well awake,
Yet musing at the straunge occasion,
And doubting much his sence, he thus bespake;
What voyce of damned Ghost from Limbo lake,°   *the pit of hell*
285   Or guilefull spright wandring in empty aire,
Both which fraile men do oftentimes mistake,
Sends to my doubtfull eares these speaches rare,
And ruefull plaints, me bidding guiltlesse bloud to spare?

33

Then groning deepe, Nor damned Ghost, (quoth he,)
290   Nor guilefull sprite to thee these wordes doth speake,
But once a man Fradubio,[6] now a tree,
Wretched man, wretched tree; whose nature weake,
A cruell witch her cursed will to wreake,

---

5. Following Dante and Ariosto, Spenser imitates a well-known episode in Virgil's *Aeneid* in which the hero Aeneas, thinking he might have reached the country in which he was to found a new Troy, is warned by a bleeding bush that he must continue his quest. Spenser probably expected that his readers would take pleasure in his own inventive transformation of this powerful image.

6. Brother Doubt (Italian). Because loss of faith through doubt is dehumanizing, Fradubio is cast into the form of a plant. He is intended to convey to the Redcrosse Knight how dangerous a creature Fidessa is.

Hath thus transformd, and plast in open plaines,
295   Where Boreas° doth blow full bitter bleake,   *the north wind*
And scorching Sunne does dry my secret vaines:
For though a tree I seeme, yet cold and heat me paines.

34
Say on Fradubio then, or man, or tree,
Quoth then the knight, by whose mischievous arts
300   Art thou misshaped thus, as now I see?
He oft finds med'cine, who his griefe imparts;
But double griefs afflict concealing harts,
As raging flames who striveth to suppresse.
The author then (said he) of all my smarts,°   *pains*
305   Is one Duessa⁷ a false sorceresse,
That many errant knights hath brought to wretchednesse.

35
In prime of youthly yeares, when corage° hot   *spirit*
The fire of love and joy of chevalree°   *chivalry*
First kindled in my brest, it was my lot
310   To love this gentle Lady, whom ye see,
Now not a Lady, but a seeming tree;
With whom as once I rode accompanyde,
Me chaunced of a knight encountred bee,
That had a like faire Lady by his syde,
315   Like a faire Lady, but did fowle Duessa hyde.

36
Whose forged° beauty he did take in hand,   *artificial*
All other Dames to have exceeded farre;
I in defence of mine did likewise stand,
Mine, that did then shine as the Morning starre:
320   So both to battell fierce arraunged° arre,   *engaged*
In which his harder fortune was to fall
Under my speare: such is the dye° of warre: *hazard*
His Lady left as a prise martiall,
Did yield her comely person, to be at my call.

37
325   So doubly lov'd of Ladies unlike° faire,   *differently*
Th'one seeming such, the other such indeede,
One day in doubt I cast° for to compare,   *sought*
Whether in beauties glorie did exceede;
A Rosy girlond was the victors meede:
330   Both seemde to win, and both seemde won to bee,
So hard the discord was to be agreede.

7. Double-being (Italian), i.e., two-faced or duplicitous. The name contrasts with Una, or the undivided truth. Duessa wears a mask of beauty, although she is actually hideous and evil. Spenser places Duessa, who is not what she appears to be, in opposition to Una, whose beauty is hidden beneath a veil but who signifies wholeness or integrity.

Fraelissa[8] was as faire, as faire mote bee,
And ever false Duessa seemde as faire as shee.

38

The wicked witch now seeing all this while

335
    The doubtfull ballaunce equally to sway,
    What not by right, she cast to win by guile,
    And by her hellish science raisd streight way
    A foggy mist, that overcast the day,
    And a dull blast, that breathing on her face,

340
    Dimmed her° former beauties shining ray,   *Fraelissa's*
    And with foule ugly forme did her disgrace:°   *disfigure*
Then was she faire alone, when none was faire in place.

39

Then cride she out, Fye, fye, deformed wight,

    Whose borrowed beautie now appeareth plaine

345
    To have before bewitched all mens sight;
    O leave her soone, or let her soone be slaine.[9]
    Her loathly visage viewing with disdaine,
    Eftsoones I thought her such, as she me told,
    And would have kild her; but with faigned paine,

350
    The false witch did my wrathfull hand with-hold;
So left her, where she now is turnd to treen mould.°   *a treelike shape*

40

Thens forth I tooke Duessa for my Dame,

    And in the witch unweeting° joyd long time,   *without knowing*
    Ne ever wist, but that she was the same,

355
    Till on a day (that day is every Prime,°   *first (of the month)*
    When Witches wont do penance for their crime)
    I chaunst to see her in her proper hew,
    Bathing her selfe in origane° and thyme: *oregano*
    A filthy foule old woman I did vew,

360
That ever to have toucht her, I did deadly rew.

41

Her neather° partes misshapen, monstruous,   *lower*

    Were hidd in water, that I could not see,
    But they did seeme more foule and hideous,
    Then womans shape man would beleeve to bee.

365
    Thens forth from her most beastly companie
    I gan refraine, in minde to slip away,
    Soone as appeard safe opportunitie:
    For danger great, if not assur'd decay
I saw before mine eyes, if I were knowne to stray.

---

8. Fradubio's lady is Fraelissa, "frail nature" (Italian); she, like Fradubio, is Duessa's victim.

9. Duessa ironically condemns Fraelissa as a witch and tells Fradubio to abandon her.

42

370 The divelish hag by chaunges of my cheare
        Perceiv'd my thought, and drownd in sleepie night,
        With wicked herbes and ointments did besmeare
        My bodie all, through charmes and magicke might,
        That all my senses were bereaved° quight: *departed*
375   Then brought she me into this desert waste,
        And by my wretched lovers side me pight,°   *planted*
        Where now enclosd in wooden wals full faste,
    Banisht from living wights, our wearie dayes we waste.

43

    But how long time, said then the Elfin knight,
380   Are you in this misformed house to dwell?
        We may not chaunge (quoth he) this evil plight,
        Till we be bathed in a living well;[1]
        That is the terme prescribed by the spell.
        O how, said he, mote I that well out find,
385   That may restore you to your wonted well?
        Time and suffised fates to former kynd
    Shall us restore, none else from hence may us unbynd.

44

    The false Duessa, now Fidessa hight,°   *called*
        Heard how in vaine Fradubio did lament,
390   And knew well all was true. But the good knight
        Full of sad feare and ghastly dreriment,°   *terror*
        When all this speech the living tree had spent,°   *finished*
        The bleeding bough did thrust into the ground,
        That from the bloud he might be innocent,
395   And with fresh clay did close the wooden wound:
    Then turning to his Lady, dead with feare her found.

45

    Her seeming dead he found with feigned feare,
        As all unweeting of that well she knew,
        And paynd himselfe with busie care to reare
400   Her out of carelesse° swowne. Her eylids blew   *unconscious*
        And dimmed sight with pale and deadly hew°   *color*
        At last she up gan lift: with trembling cheare
        Her up he tooke, too simple and too trew,[2]
        And oft her kist. At length all passed feare,
405   He set her on her steede, and forward forth did beare.

---

1. The Well of Life: a spring of constantly flowing water, figured in the water of baptism that promises eternal life to the faithful (John 4.14).
2. The Redcrosse Knight fails to connect Fradubio's story to his own; he does not follow the model presented by Virgil's Aeneas, and therefore he remains deceived and on the wrong course.

Canto 3

Forsaken Truth long seekes her love,
And makes the Lyon mylde,
Marres blind Devotions mart, and fals
In hand of leachour vylde.

1

Nought is there under heav'ns wide hollownesse,
    That moves more deare compassion of mind,
    Then beautie brought t'unworthy wretchednesse
    Through envies snares or fortunes freakes unkind:
5   I, whether lately through her brightnesse blind,
    Or through alleageance and fast fealtie,°   *loyalty*
    Which I do owe unto all woman kind,
    Feele my heart perst° with so great agonie,   *pierced*
When such I see, that all for pittie I could die.

2

10 And now it is empassioned° so deepe,   *moved*
    For fairest Unaes sake, of whom I sing,
    That my fraile eyes these lines with teares do steepe,° *soak*
    To thinke how she through guilefull handeling,
    Though true as touch, though daughter of a king,
15 Though faire as ever living wight was faire,
    Though nor in word nor deede ill meriting,
    Is from her knight divorced° in despaire   *separated*
And her due loves° deriv'd to that vile witches share. *the love due her*

3

Yet she most faithfull Ladie all this while
20 Forsaken, wofull, solitarie mayd
    Farre from all peoples prease,° as in exile,   *crowds*
    In wildernesse and wastfull deserts strayd,
    To seeke her knight; who subtilly betrayd
    Through that late vision, which th'Enchaunter wrought,
25 Had her abandond. She of nought affrayd,
    Through woods and wastnesse wide him daily sought;
Yet wished tydings none of him unto her brought.

4

One day nigh wearie of the yrkesome way,
    From her unhastie beast she did alight,
30 And on the grasse her daintie limbes did lay
    In secret shadow, farre from all mens sight:
    From her faire head her fillet she undight,
    And laid her stole aside. Her angels face
    As the great eye of heaven shyned bright,
35 And made a sunshine in the shadie place;
Did never mortall eye behold such heavenly grace.

5

It fortuned out of the thickest wood
  A ramping Lyon[1] rushed suddainly,
  Hunting full greedie after salvage° blood;   *savage*
40 Soone as the royall virgin he did spy,
  With gaping mouth at her ran greedily,
  To have attonce devour'd her tender corse:
  But to the pray when as he drew more ny,
  His bloudie rage asswaged with remorse,
45 And with the sight amazd, forgat his furious forse.

6

In stead thereof he kist her wearie feet,
  And lickt her lilly hands with fawning tong,
  As° he her wronged innocence did weet.   *as if*
  O how can beautie maister the most strong,
50 And simple truth subdue avenging wrong?
  Whose yeelded pride and proud submission,
  Still dreading death, when she had marked long,
  Her hart gan melt in great compassion,
And drizling teares did shed for pure affection.

7

55 The Lyon Lord of everie beast in field,
  Quoth she, his princely puissance° doth abate,   *strength*
  And mightie proud to humble weake does yield,
  Forgetfull of the hungry rage, which late
  Him prickt, in pittie of my sad estate:
60 But he° my Lyon, and my noble Lord,   *Redcrosse Knight*
  How does he find in cruell hart to hate
  Her that him lov'd, and ever most adord,
As the God of my life? why hath he me abhord?

8

Redounding teares did choke th'end of her plaint,
65 Which softly ecchoed from the neighbour wood;
  And sad to see her sorrowfull constraint
  The kingly beast upon her gazing stood;
  With pittie calmd, downe fell his angry mood.
  At last in close hart shutting up her paine,
70 Arose the virgin borne of heavenly brood,
  And to her snowy Palfrey got againe,
To seeke her strayed Champion, if she might attaine.°   *overtake him*

9

The Lyon would not leave her desolate,
  But with her went along, as a strong gard
75 Of her chast person, and a faithfull mate
  Of her sad troubles and misfortunes hard:

---

1. This is the typical heraldic posture of the lion: standing on its hind legs with its paws in the air. A symbol of royal power, the lion was believed to protect virgins and weary pilgrims.

Still when she slept, he kept both watch and ward,
And when she wakt, he waited diligent,
With humble service to her will prepard:
80   From her faire eyes he tooke commaundement,
And ever by her lookes conceived° her intent.   *understood*

10

Long she thus traveiled through deserts wyde,
By which she thought her wandring knight shold pas,
Yet never shew of living wight espyde;
85   Till that at length she found the troden gras,
In which the tract° of peoples footing was,   *trace*
Under the steepe foot of a mountaine hore;°   *barren*
The same she followes, till at last she has
A damzell spyde slow footing her before,
90   That on her shoulders sad a pot of water bore.

11

To whom approching she to her gan call,
To weet, if dwelling place were nigh at hand;
But the rude wench her answer'd nought at all,
She could not heare, nor speake, nor understand;
95   Till seeing by her side the Lyon stand,
With suddaine feare her pitcher downe she threw,
And fled away: for never in that land
Face of faire Ladie she before did vew,
And that dread Lyons looke her cast in deadly hew.

12

100   Full fast she fled, ne° ever lookt behynd,   *nor*
As if her life upon the wager lay,
And home she came, whereas her mother blynd
Sate in eternall night: nought could she say,
But suddaine catching hold, did her dismay
105   With quaking hands, and other signes of feare:
Who full of ghastly fright and cold affray,°   *terror*
Gan shut the dore. By this arrived there
Dame Una, wearie Dame, and entrance did requere.°   *request*

13

Which when none yeelded, her unruly Page
110   With his rude clawes the wicket° open rent,   *small gate*
And let her in; where of his cruell rage
Nigh dead with feare, and faint astonishment,
She found them both in darkesome corner pent;
Where that old woman day and night did pray
115   Upon her beades devoutly penitent;
Nine hundred *Pater nosters* every day,
And thrise nine hundred *Aves* she was wont to say.[2]

2. Spenser's readers would have identified Paternosters and Ave Marias as Catholic prayers.

14

And to augment her painefull pennance more,
   Thrise every weeke in ashes she did sit,
120   And next her wrinkled skin rough sackcloth wore,
   And thrise three times did fast from any bit:°   *bit of food*
   But now for feare her beads she did forget.
   Whose needlesse dread for to remove away,
   Faire Una framed words and count'nance fit:
125   Which hardly doen,° at length she gan them pray,   *done*
That in their cotage small, that night she rest her may.

15

The day is spent, and commeth drowsie night,
   When every creature shrowded is in sleepe;
   Sad Una downe her laies in wearie plight,
130   And at her feet the Lyon watch doth keepe:
   In stead of rest, she does lament, and weepe
   For the late losse of her deare loved knight,
   And sighes, and grones, and evermore does steepe
   Her tender brest in bitter teares all night,
135 All night she thinks too long, and often lookes for light.

16

Now when Aldeboran was mounted hie
   Above the shynie Cassiopeias chaire,[3]
   And all in deadly sleepe did drowned lie,
   One knocked at the dore, and in would fare;
140   He knocked fast, and often curst, and sware,
   That readie entrance was not at his call:
   For on his backe a heavy load he bare
   Of nightly stelths° and pillage severall,   *thefts*
Which he had got abroad by purchase criminall.

17

145 He was to weete° a stout and sturdie thiefe,[4]   *wit*
   Wont to robbe Churches of their ornaments,
   And poore mens boxes of their due reliefe,
   Which given was to them for good intents;
   The holy Saints of their rich vestiments
150   He did disrobe, when all men carelesse slept,
   And spoild the Priests of their habiliments,°   *holy things*
   Whiles none the holy things in safety kept;
Then he by cunning sleights° in at the window crept.   *tricks*

3. Aldeboran and Cassiopeia are stars that appear at midnight during the winter solstice; the references to winter and midnight reflect Una's distress.
4. This thief is later named Kirkrapine, literally "church robber" (see stanza 22). Spenser's Protestant contemporaries complained that the Roman Catholic Church had used English abbeys and monasteries as a means of amassing wealth at the expense of the spiritual well-being of the people that they were supposed to serve.

18

155   And all that he by right or wrong could find,
        Unto this house he brought, and did bestow
        Upon the daughter of this woman blind,
        Abessa daughter of Corceca slow,[5]
        With whom he whoredome usd, that few did know,
160   And fed her fat with feast of offerings,
        And plentie, which in all the land did grow;
        Ne spared he to give her gold and rings:
And now he to her brought part of his stolen things.

19

    Thus long the dore with rage and threats he bet,
        Yet of those fearefull women none durst rize,
165   The Lyon frayed° them, him in to let: *frightened*
        He would no longer stay him to advize,°   *consider*
        But open breakes the dore in furious wize,
        And entring is; when that disdainfull° beast   *indignant*
        Encountring fierce, him suddaine doth surprize,
170   And seizing cruell clawes on trembling brest,
Under his Lordly foot him proudly hath supprest.

20

    Him booteth not° resist, nor succour call,   *it did no good to*
        His bleeding hart is in the vengers hand,
        Who streight him rent° in thousand peeces small,   *tore*
175   And quite dismembred hath: the thirstie land
        Drunke up his life; his corse left on the strand.[6]
        His fearefull friends weare out the wofull night,
        Ne dare to weepe, nor seeme to understand
        The heavie hap,° which on them is alight,   *event*
180   Affraid, least to themselves the like mishappen might.

21

    Now when broad day the world discovered has,
        Up Una rose, up rose the Lyon eke,
        And on their former journey forward pas,
        In wayes unknowne, her wandring knight to seeke,
185   With paines farre passing that long wandring Greeke,[7]
        That for his love refused deitie;
        Such were the labours of this Lady meeke,
        Still seeking him, that from her still did flie,
Then furthest from her hope, when most she weened nie.

---

5. Corceca means "blind of heart"; her daughter, Abessa, who is both deaf and mute, is the offspring of ignorant superstition. Through her name, Spenser associates Abessa with Catholic abbeys and monasteries, which he criticizes in this and the previous two stanzas.

6. Kirkrapine's death signifies a step toward the purification of the Church and thereby an approach to the true Church, which Una represents.

7. Una is compared to Ulysses, whose love for his wife Penelope caused him to reject the goddess Calypso and the promise of immortality she offered him.

22

190 Soone as she parted thence, the fearefull twaine,
 That blind old woman and her daughter deare
 Came forth, and finding Kirkrapine° there slaine,   church-robber
 For anguish great they gan to rend their heare,
 And beat their brests, and naked flesh to teare.
195 And when they both had wept and wayld their fill,
 Then forth they ranne like two amazed deare,
 Halfe mad through malice, and revenging will,°   desire to revenge
To follow her, that was the causer of their ill.

23

 Whom overtaking, they gan loudly bray,
200 With hollow howling, and lamenting cry,
 Shamefully at her rayling° all the way,   accusing
 And her accusing of dishonesty,
 That was the flowre of faith and chastity;
 And still amidst her rayling, she did pray,
205 That plagues, and mischiefs, and long misery
 Might fall on her, and follow all the way,
And that in endlesse error she might ever stray.

24

 But when she saw her prayers nought prevaile,
 She backe returned with some labour lost;
210 And in° the way as she did weepe and waile,   along
 A knight her met in mighty armes embost,
 Yet knight was not for all his bragging bost,°   display
 But subtill Archimag, that Una sought
 By traynes° into new troubles to have tost: tricks
215 Of that old woman tydings he besought,
If that of such a Ladie she could tellen ought.

25

 Therewith she gan her passion to renew,
 And cry, and curse, and raile,° and rend her heare,   accuse
 Saying, that harlot she too lately knew,
220 That causd her shed so many a bitter teare,
 And so forth told the story of her feare:
 Much seemed he to mone her haplesse chaunce,
 And after for that Ladie did inquere;°   inquire
 Which being taught, he forward gan advaunce
225 His fair enchaunted steed, and eke his charmed launce.

26

 Ere long he came, where Una traveild slow,
 And that wilde Champion wayting her besyde,
 Whom seeing such, for dread he° durst not show   Archimago
 Himselfe too nigh at hand, but turned wyde
230 Unto an hill; from whence when she him spyde,
 By his like seeming shield, her knight by name

She weend it was, and towards him gan ryde:[8]
Approching nigh, she wist it was the same,
And with faire fearefull humblesse towards him shee came.

27

235   And weeping said, Ah my long lacked° Lord,   *lost*
Where have ye bene thus long out of my sight?
Much feared I to have bene quite abhord,
Or ought have done, that ye displeasen might,
That should as death unto my deare hart light:°   *come*
240   For since mine eye your joyous sight did mis,
My chearefull day is turnd to chearelesse night,
And eke my night of death the shadow is;
But welcome now my light, and shining lampe of blis.

28

He thereto meeting said, My dearest Dame,
245   Farre be it from your thought, and fro° my will,   *from*
To thinke that knighthood I so much should shame,
As you to leave,° that have me loved still,   *lose*
And chose in Faery court of meere goodwill,
Where noblest knights were to be found on earth:
250   The earth shall sooner leave her kindly skill°   *natural art*
To bring forth fruit, and make eternall derth,°   *famine*
Then I leave you, my liefe, yborne of heavenly berth.

29

And sooth° to say, why I left you so long,   *truly*
Was for to seeke adventure in strange place,
255   Where Archimago said a felon strong
To many knights did daily worke disgrace;
But knight he now shall never more deface:
Good cause of mine excuse; that mote° ye please   *might*
Well to accept, and evermore embrace
260   My faithfull service, that by land and seas
Have vowd you to defend, now then your plaint appease.

30

His lovely words her seemd due recompence
Of all her passed paines: one loving howre
For many yeares of sorrow can dispence:°   *compensate*
265   A dram of sweet is worth a pound of sowre:
She has forgot, how many a wofull stowre°   *hardship*
For him she late endur'd; she speakes no more
Of past: true is, that true love hath no powre
To looken backe; his eyes be fixt before.
270   Before her stands her knight, for whom she toyld so sore.

8. Una recognizes the arms of the Redcrosse Knight but is deceived by appearances; she is actually greeting Archimago.

31

Much like, as when the beaten marinere,
 That long hath wandred in the Ocean wide,
 Oft soust° in swelling Tethys° saltish teare,   *drenched / a sea-goddess*
 And long time having tand his tawney hide
275 With blustring breath of heaven, that none can bide,
 And scorching flames of fierce Orions hound,[9]
 Soone as the port from farre he has espide,
 His chearefull whistle merrily doth sound,
And Nereus° crownes with cups;° his mates him pledg around.   *a sea-god /*
                      of wine

32

280 Such joy made Una, when her knight she found;
 And eke th'enchaunter joyous seemd no lesse,
 Then° the glad marchant, that does vew from ground   *than*
 His ship farre come from watrie wildernesse,
 He hurles out vowes,° and Neptune oft doth blesse: *makes promises*
285 So forth they past, and all the way they spent
 Discoursing of her dreadfull late distresse,
 In which he askt her, what the Lyon ment:
Who° told her all that fell° in journey as she went.   *Una / had happened*

33

They had not ridden farre, when they might see
290 One pricking towards them with hastie heat,
 Full strongly armd, and on a courser free,
 That through his fiercenesse fomed all with sweat,
 And the sharpe yron° did for anger eat,   *iron bit*
 When his hot ryder spurd his chauffed side;
295 His looke was sterne, and seemed still to threat
 Cruell revenge, which he in hart did hyde,
And on his shield Sans-Loy in bloudie lines was dyde.

34

When nigh he drew unto this gentle payre
 And saw the Red-crosse, which the knight did beare,
300 He burnt in fire, and gan eftsoones prepare
 Himselfe to battell with his couched° speare.   *lowered*
 Loth was that other,° and did faint through feare,   *Archimago*
 To taste th'vntryed dint of deadly steele;
 But yet his Lady did so well him cheare,
305 That hope of new good hap he gan to feele;
So bent his speare, and spurnd° his horse with yron heele.   *spurred*

---

9. Sirius, the Dog Star, which marks the hottest days of the year. Nereus is the eldest child of Tethys, a sea-goddess.

35

But that proud Paynim° forward came so fierce,[1]   *pagan*
  And full of wrath, that with his sharp-head speare
  Through vainely crossed shield he quite did pierce,
310 And had his staggering steede not shrunke for feare,
  Through shield and bodie eke he should him beare:
  Yet so great was the puissance of his push,
  That from his saddle quite he did him beare:
  He tombling rudely downe to ground did rush,
315 And from his gored wound a well of bloud did gush.

36

Dismounting lightly from his loftie steed,
  He to him lept, in mind to reave° his life,   *take*
  And proudly said, Lo there the worthie meed
  Of him, that slew Sans-Foy with bloudie knife;
320 Henceforth his ghost freed from repining° strife,   *fretting*
  In peace may passen° over Lethe lake,[2]   *pass*
  When morning altars° purgd with enemies life,   *altars of mourning*
  The blacke infernall Furies doen aslake:°   *satisfy*
Life from Sans-Foy thou tookst, Sans-Loy shall from thee take.

37

325 Therewith in haste his helmet gan unlace,
  Till Una cride, O hold that heavie hand,
  Deare Sir, what ever that thou be in place:
  Enough is, that thy foe doth vanquisht stand
  Now at thy mercy: Mercie not withstand:°   *oppose*
330 For he is one the truest° knight alive,   *the one truest*
  Though conquered now he lie on lowly land,
  And whilest him fortune favourd, faire did thrive
In bloudie field: therefore of life him not deprive.

38

Her piteous words might not abate his rage,
335 But rudely° rending up his helmet, would   *violently*
  Have slaine him straight: but when he sees his age,
  And hoarie head of Archimago old,
  His hastie hand he doth amazed hold,
  And halfe ashamed, wondred at the sight:
340 For the old man well knew he, though untold,°   *i.e., by sight*
  In charmes and magicke to have wondrous might,
Ne ever wont in field, ne in round lists° to fight.   *tournament arenas*

39

And said, Why Archimago, lucklesse syre,
  What doe I see? what hard mishap is this,

---

1. The double deception registered in this episode is characteristic of Spenser's complex allegories: mistaken in his sense of identity, Sans-Loy attacks the very person who is best able to protect him. Archimago, having assumed the guise of the Redcrosse Knight, finds that the cross that should protect him from harm does not in fact do so. In this instance his shield is "vainely crossed."
2. The lake of forgetfulness in the underworld.

345   That hath thee hither brought to taste mine yre?
             Or thine the fault, or mine the error is,
             In stead of foe to wound my friend amis?
             He answered nought, but in a traunce still lay,
             And on those guilefull dazed eyes of his
350   The cloud of death did sit. Which doen away,°   *having passed*
             He left him lying so, ne would no lenger stay.

40

        But to the virgin comes, who all this while
             Amased stands, her selfe so mockt to see
             By him, who has the guerdon° of his guile,   *reward*
355   For so misfeigning her true knight to bee:
             Yet is she now in more perplexitie,°   *distress*
             Left in the hand of that same Paynim bold,
             From whom her booteth° not at all to flie;   *it helped her*
             Who by her cleanly° garment catching hold,   *pure*
360   Her from her Palfrey pluckt, her visage to behold.

41

        But her fierce servant full of kingly awe
             And high disdaine, whenas his soveraine Dame
             So rudely handled by her foe he sawe,
             With gaping jawes full greedy at him came,
365   And ramping on° his shield, did weene the same   *charging at*
             Have reft away with his sharpe rending clawes:
             But he was stout, and lust did now inflame
             His corage more, that from his griping pawes
        He hath his shield redeem'd,° and foorth his swerd he drawes.   *retained*

42

370   O then too weake and feeble was the forse
             Of salvage beast, his puissance to withstand:
             For he was strong, and of so mightie corse,
             As ever wielded speare in warlike hand,
             And feates of armes did wisely understand.
375   Eftsoones he perced through his chaufed° chest   *angered*
             With thrilling° point of deadly yron brand,   *piercing*
             And launcht° his Lordly hart: with death opprest   *pierced*
        He roar'd aloud, whiles life forsooke his stubborne brest.

43

        Who now is left to keepe the forlorne maid
380   From raging spoile of lawlesse victors will?[3]
             Her faithful gard remov'd, her hope dismaid,°   *thwarted*
             Her selfe a yeelded pray to save or spill.°   *destroy*
             He now Lord of the field, his pride to fill,
             With foule reproches, and disdainfull spight

---

3. I.e., who will now protect Una from becoming the spoil or booty of the lawless victor's raging will?

385   Her vildly entertaines,° and will or nill,   *treats*
      Beares her away upon his courser light:
      Her prayers nought prevaile, his rage is more of might.

                              44
      And all the way, with great lamenting paine,
      And piteous plaints she filleth his dull eares,
390   That stony hart could riven have in twaine,
      And all the way she wets with flowing teares:
      But he enrag'd with rancor, nothing heares.
      Her servile beast yet would not leave her so,
      But followes her farre off, ne ought he feares,
395   To be partaker of her wandring woe,
      More mild in beastly kind,° then that her beastly foe.   *animal nature*

                        Canto 4

            To sinfull house of Pride,[1] *Duessa*
                guides the faithfull knight,
            Where brothers death to wreak° *Sans-Joy*   *avenge*
                doth chalenge him to fight.

                              1
      Young knight, what ever° that dost armes professe,   *whoever*
      And through long labours huntest after fame,
      Beware of fraud, beware of ficklenesse,
      In choice, and change of thy deare loved Dame,
5   Least° thou of her beleeve° too lightly blame,   *lest / faith*
      And rash misweening° doe thy hart remove: *rashly mistrusting*
      For unto knight there is no greater shame,
      Then lightnesse and inconstancie in love;
      That doth this Redcrosse knights ensample° plainly prove.   *example*

                              2
10   Who after that he had faire Una lorne,°   *lost*
      Through light misdeeming of her loialtie,
      And false Duessa in her sted had borne,
      Called Fidess', and so supposd to bee;
      Long with her traveild, till at last they see
15   A goodly building, bravely garnished,
      The house of mightie Prince it seemd to bee:
      And towards it a broad high way that led,
      All bare° through peoples feet, which thither traveiled.   *worn bare*

                              3
      Great troupes of people traveild thitherward
20   Both day and night, of each degree and place,
      But few returned, having scaped hard,

---

1. An extended metaphor for the consequences of the sin of Pride. Like the Tower of Babel, which Spenser invokes in this passage, the house of Pride is the product of humanity's art, ambition, and vanity but is devoid of Christian values.

With balefull° beggerie, or foule disgrace,   *wretched*
Which ever after in most wretched case,
Like loathsome lazars,° by the hedges lay.   *lepers*
25   Thither Duessa bad him bend° his pace: *direct*
For she is wearie of the toilesome way,
And also nigh consumed is the lingring day.

4

A stately Pallace built of squared bricke,[2]
Which cunningly was without morter laid,
30   Whose wals were high, but nothing strong, nor thick,
And golden foile all over them displaid,
That purest skye with brightnesse they dismaid:°   *shamed*
High lifted up were many loftie towres,
And goodly galleries farre over laid,°   *built high above*
35   Full of faire windowes, and delightfull bowres;°   *chambers*
And on the top a Diall° told the timely howres.   *sundial*

5

It was a goodly heape° for to behould,   *structure*
And spake the praises of the workmans wit;
But full great pittie, that so faire a mould
40   Did on so weake foundation ever sit:
For on a sandie hill, that still did flit,°   *shift*
And fall away, it mounted was full hie,
That every breath of heaven shaked it:
And all the hinder° parts, that few could spie,   *rear*
45   Were ruinous and old, but painted cunningly.

6

Arrived there they passed in forth right;
For still° to all the gates stood open wide,   *always*
Yet charge of them was to a Porter hight°   *called*
Cald Malvenù,° who entrance none denide: *welcome to evil*
50   Thence to the hall, which was on every side
With rich array and costly arras dight:°   *furnished*
Infinite sorts of people did abide
There waiting long, to win the wished sight
Of her, that was the Lady of that Pallace bright.

7

55   By them they passe, all gazing on them round,
And to the Presence mount; whose glorious vew
Their frayle amazed senses did confound:°   *confuse*
In living Princes court none ever knew
Such endlesse richesse, and so sumptuous shew;
60   Ne° Persia selfe, the nourse° of pompous pride   *not even / nurse*

2. The house of Pride offers a dazzling facade, but its construction is weak, much like the sin of Pride itself, which places outward appearances over inner substance. It is surmounted by a sundial to tell the hours, a sign that Pride has no sense of eternity but lives only for the moment.

Like ever saw. And there a noble crew
Of Lordes and Ladies stood on every side,
Which with their presence faire, the place much beautifide.

8

High above all a cloth of State was spred,
65   And a rich throne, as bright as sunny day,
    On which there sate most brave embellished
    With royall robes and gorgeous array,
    A mayden Queene,[3] that shone as Titans ray,
    In glistring gold, and peerelesse pretious stone:
70   Yet her bright blazing beautie did assay°   *strive*
    To dim the brightnesse of her glorious throne,
As envying her selfe, that too exceeding shone.

9

Exceeding shone, like Phoebus fairest childe,[4]
    That did presume his fathers firie wayne,
75   And flaming mouthes of steedes unwonted° wilde   *unaccustomed*
    Through highest heaven with weaker hand to rayne;°   *guide*
    Proud of such glory and advancement vaine,
    While flashing beames do daze his feeble eyen,
    He leaves the welkin° way most beaten plaine,   *well-known*
80   And rapt with whirling wheeles, inflames the skyen,
With fire not made to burne, but fairely for to shyne.

10

So proud she shyned in her Princely state,
    Looking to heaven; for earth she did disdayne,
    And sitting high; for lowly she did hate:
85   Lo underneath her scornefull feete, was layne
    A dreadfull Dragon with an hideous trayne,
    And in her hand she held a mirrhour bright,
    Wherein her face she often vewed fayne,
    And in her selfe-lov'd semblance° tooke delight;   *image*
90 For she was wondrous faire, as any living wight.

11

Of griesly Pluto she the daughter was,[5]
    And sad Proserpina the Queene of hell;
    Yet did she thinke her pearelesse° worth to pas   *unequaled*
    That parentage, with pride so did she swell,
95   And thundring Jove, that high in heaven doth dwell,

3. "The maiden queen": a reference to the "virgin daughter of Babylon" (Isaiah 47.1). She is later identified as Lucifera, a feminine form of Lucifer, literally "light bringer," but also Satan's name when he was still an angel. Hence the queen shines as brightly as the sun (Titan).
4. Phaeton (son of the sun god Apollo), who stole his father's chariot and perished because he could not manage the horses. He is a figure for the sin of Pride.

5. Lucifera is identified as the daughter of Pluto, king of the underworld, and Proserpina, goddess of the seasons, who is obliged to spend half the year underground with her husband, Pluto. The conflation of mythologies represented in this description of Lucifera is characteristic of Spenser's allegory. Here he associates the biblical figure of the daughter of Babylon with the pagan figures of Pluto and Proserpina. Their "daughter" Lucifera is his own invention.

And wield the world, she claymed for her syre,
 Or if that any else did Jove excell:
 For to the highest she did still aspyre,
Or if ought higher were then° that, did it desyre.   *than*

12

100   And proud Lucifera men did her call,
 That made her selfe a Queene, and crownd to be,
 Yet rightfull kingdome she had none at all,
 Ne heritage° of native° soveraintie,   *inheritance / rightful*
 But did ysurpe° with wrong and tyrannie   *usurp*
105   Upon the scepter, which she now did hold:
 Ne ruld her Realmes with lawes, but pollicie,°   *political cunning*
 And strong advizement of six wisards old,
That with their counsels bad her kingdome did uphold.

13

 Soone as the Elfin knight in presence came,
110   And false Duessa seeming Lady faire,
 A gentle Husher,° Vanitie by name   *usher*
 Made rowme, and passage for them did prepaire:
 So goodly brought them to the lowest staire
 Of her high throne, where they on humble knee
115   Making obeyssance,° did the cause declare,   *submissive bows*
 Why they were come, her royall state to see,
To prove° the wide report of her great Majestee.   *confirm*

14

 With loftie eyes, halfe loth° to looke so low,   *disdaining*
 She thanked them in her disdainefull wise,
120   Ne other grace vouchsafed° them to show   *condescended*
 Of Princesse worthy, scarse them bad arise.
 Her Lordes and Ladies all this while devise
 Themselves to setten forth to straungers sight:
 Some frounce° their curled haire in courtly guise,   *arrange*
125   Some prancke° their ruffes, and others trimly dight   *adjust*
Their gay attire: each others greater pride does spight.

15

 Goodly they all that knight do entertaine,
 Right glad with him to have increast their crew:
 But to Duess' each one himselfe did paine
130   All kindnesse and faire courtesie to shew;
 For in that court whylome° her well they knew: *previously*
 Yet the stout Faerie⁶ mongst the middest crowd
 Thought all their glorie vaine in knightly vew,
 And that great Princesse too exceeding prowd,
135   That to strange knight no better countenance° allowd.   *reception*

6. The Redcrosse Knight. He is designated as a faerie because he is an inhabitant of Faerie Land and also to distinguish him from the inhabitants of the house of Pride.

16

Suddein upriseth from her stately place
    The royall Dame, and for her coche doth call:
    All hurtlen° forth, and she with Princely pace,   *rush*
    As faire Aurora° in her purple pall,   *goddess of the dawn*
140   Out of the East the dawning day doth call:
    So forth she comes: her brightnesse brode° doth blaze;   *abroad*
    The heapes of people thronging in the hall,
    Do ride each other, upon her to gaze:
Her glorious glitterand° light doth all mens eyes amaze.   *glittering*

17

145 So forth she comes, and to her coche does clyme,
    Adorned all with gold, and girlonds gay,
    That seemd as fresh as Flora° in her prime,   *goddess of spring*
    And strove to match, in royall rich array,
    Great Junoes golden chaire, the which they say
150 The Gods stand gazing on, when she does ride
    To Joves high house through heavens bras-paved way
    Drawne of faire Pecocks, that excell in pride,
And full of Argus[7] eyes their tailes dispredden° wide.   *spread out*

18

But this was drawne of six unequall beasts,
155 On which her six sage Counsellours[8] did ryde,
    Taught to obay their bestiall beheasts,°   *urges*
    With like conditions to their kinds° applyde: *natures*
    Of which the first, that all the rest did guyde,
    Was sluggish Idlenesse the nourse of sin;
160 Upon a slouthfull Asse he chose to ryde,
    Arayd in habit blacke, and amis° thin,   *monk's hood*
Like to an holy Monck, the service to begin.

19

And in his hand his Portesse° still he bare,   *prayer book*
    That much was worne, but therein little red,
165 For of devotion he had little care,
    Still drownd in sleepe, and most of his dayes ded;
    Scarse could he once uphold his heavie hed,
    To looken, whether it were night or day:
    May seeme° the wayne was very evill led,   *it may seem that*
170 When such an one had guiding of the way,
That knew not, whether right he went, or else astray.

20

From worldly cares himselfe he did esloyne,°   *withdraw*
    And greatly shunned manly exercise,

---

7. A mythical herdsman with 100 eyes. When Argus died, Juno—goddess of marriage and wife to Jupiter or Jove, king of the gods—set his eyes in the tail of a peacock.

8. The following stanzas describe the procession of Lucifer's wise counsellors, actually the Seven Deadly Sins: Pride (in the person of Lucifera), Idleness, Gluttony, Lechery, Avarice (greed), Envy, and Wrath.

From every worke he chalenged essoyne,°   *claimed exception*
175 For contemplation sake: yet otherwise,
His life he led in lawlesse riotise;°   *unruly conduct*
By which he grew to grievous malady;
For in his lustlesse limbs through evill guise
A shaking fever raignd° continually: *ruled*
180 Such one was Idlenesse, first of this company.

21

And by his side rode loathsome Gluttony,
Deformed creature, on a filthie swyne,
His belly was up-blowne with luxury,
And eke with fatnesse swollen were his eyne,°   *eyes*
185 And like a Crane his necke was long and fyne,
With which he swallowd up excessive feast,
For want whereof poore people oft did pyne;
And all the way, most like a brutish beast,
He spued up his gorge,° that all did him deteast.   *vomited his food*

22

190 In greene vine leaves he was right fitly clad;
For other clothes he could not weare for heat,
And on his head an ivie girland had,
From under which fast trickled downe the sweat:
Still as he rode, he somewhat still did eat,
195 And in his hand did beare a bouzing° can,   *drinking*
Of which he supt so oft, that on his seat
His dronken corse he scarse upholden can,
In shape and life more like a monster, then a man.

23

Unfit he was for any worldly thing,
200 And eke unhable once to stirre or go,
Not meet to be of counsell to a king,
Whose mind in meat and drinke was drowned so,
That from his friend he seldome knew his fo:
Full of diseases was his carcas blew,
205 And a dry dropsie[9] through his flesh did flow:
Which by misdiet daily greater grew:
Such one was Gluttony, the second of that crew.

24

And next to him rode lustfull Lechery,
Upon a bearded Goat, whose rugged haire,
210 And whally° eyes (the signe of gelosy,)   *glaring*
Was like the person selfe,° whom he did beare: *himself*
Who rough, and blacke, and filthy did appeare,
Unseemely man to please faire Ladies eye;

9. A disease characterized by bloating.

Yet he of Ladies oft was loved deare,
215 When fairer faces were bid standen by:
O who does know the bent of womens fantasy?

25

In a greene gowne he clothed was full faire,
Which underneath did hide his filthinesse,
And in his hand a burning hart he bare,
220 Full of vaine follies, and new fanglenesse:
For he was false, and fraught with ficklenesse,
And learned had to love with secret lookes,
And well could daunce, and sing with ruefulnesse,°   melancholy
And fortunes tell, and read in loving bookes,°   books of love
225 And thousand other wayes, to bait his fleshly hookes.

26

Inconstant man, that loved all he saw,
And lusted after all, that he did love,
Ne would his looser life be tide to law,
But joyd weake wemens hearts to tempt and prove°   test
230 If from their loyall loves he might them move;
Which lewdnesse fild him with reprochfull paine
Of that fowle evill, which all men reprove,
That rots the marrow, and consumes the braine:
Such one was Lecherie, the third of all this traine.

27

235 And greedy Avarice by him did ride,
Upon a Camell loaden all with gold;
Two iron coffers hong on cither side,
With precious mettall full, as they might hold,
And in his lap an heape of coine he told;°   counted
240 For of his wicked pelfe° his God he made,   profits
And unto hell him selfe for money sold;
Accursed usurie was all his trade,[1]
And right and wrong ylike in equall ballaunce waide.

28

His life was nigh unto deaths doore yplast,°   i.e., nearly over
245 And thred-bare cote, and cobled° shoes he ware,   patched
Ne scarse good morsell all his life did tast,
But both from backe and belly still did spare,
To fill his bags, and richesse to compare;[2]
Yet chylde ne kinsman living had he none
250 To leave them to; but thorough daily care
To get, and nightly feare to lose his owne,°   his own wealth
He led a wretched life unto him selfe unknowne.

---

1. Usury (lending money for profit) was forbidden by
Scripture but was nevertheless practiced—with certain
restrictions—in early modern Europe and England. High
rates of interest were generally forbidden, but loans could
be made as forms of investment in commerce or industry.
2. I.e., he wore rags and starved himself.

29

Most wretched wight, whom nothing might suffise,
  Whose greedy lust did lacke in greatest store,
255   Whose need had end, but no end covetise,°   *greed*
  Whose wealth was want, whose plenty made him pore,
  Who had enough, yet wished ever more;
  A vile disease, and eke in foote and hand
  A grievous gout tormented him full sore,
260   That well he could not touch, nor go, nor stand:
Such one was Avarice, the fourth of this faire band.

30

And next to him malicious Envie rode,
  Upon a ravenous wolfe, and still did chaw°   *chew*
  Betweene his cankred° teeth a venemous tode,   *infected*
265   That all the poison ran about his chaw;°   *mouth*
  But inwardly he chawed his owne maw°   *guts*
  At neighbours wealth, that made him ever sad;
  For death it was, when any good he saw,
  And wept, that cause of weeping none he had,
270   But when he heard of harme, he wexed° wondrous glad.   *grew*

31

All in a kirtle° of discolourd say°   *gown / fine cloth*
  He clothed was, ypainted full of eyes;
  And in his bosome secretly there lay
  An hatefull Snake, the which his taile uptyes
275   In many folds, and mortall sting implyes.[3]
  Still as he rode, he gnasht his teeth, to see
  Those heapes of gold with griple Covetyse,[4]
  And grudged at the great felicitie
Of proud Lucifera, and his owne companie.

32

280 He hated all good workes and vertuous deeds,
  And him no lesse, that any like did use,°   *perform*
  And who with gracious bread the hungry feeds,
  His almes for want of faith he doth accuse;°   *misrepresent*
  So every good to bad he doth abuse:[5]
285   And eke the verse of famous Poets witt
  He does backebite, and spightfull poison spues
  From leprous mouth on all, that ever writt:
Such one vile Envie was, that fifte in row did sitt.

---

3. Envy's clothing symbolically displays the envious and covetous eyes with which he views the world. The snake he carries in his bosom was a traditional symbol of envy; its "mortall sting" is deadly to Envy himself as well as to others.

4. Grasping Avarice; Envy is envious of Avarice's gold.

5. Envy believes that good deeds reveal a lack of faith. Here Spenser attacks doctrine associated with radical Protestant sects that, rejecting Catholic belief in the merit of good works as a means to salvation, insist that it is only through faith and God's grace that a Christian is saved.

33

290 And him beside rides fierce revenging Wrath,
       Upon a Lion, loth for° to be led;   *reluctant*
       And in his hand a burning brond° he hath,   *brand*
       The which he brandisheth about his hed;
       His eyes did hurle forth sparkles fiery red,
295   And stared sterne on all, that him beheld,
       As ashes pale of hew and seeming ded;
       And on his dagger still his hand he held,
Trembling through hasty rage, when choler° in him sweld.   *anger*

34

       His ruffin° raiment all was staind with blood,   *ruffianly*
       Which he had spilt, and all to rags yrent,
300   Through unadvized rashnesse woxen wood;°   *grown mad*
       For of his hands he had no governement;°   *control*
       Ne car'd for bloud in his avengement:
       But when the furious fit was overpast,
       His cruell facts° he often would repent;   *deeds*
305   Yet wilfull man he never would forecast,°   *foresee*
How many mischieves° should ensue his heedlesse hast.   *evil consequences*

35

Full many mischiefes follow cruell Wrath;
       Abhorred bloudshed, and tumultuous strife,
       Unmanly murder, and unthrifty scath,°   *wasteful harm*
310   Bitter despight,° with rancours rusty knife,   *malice*
       And fretting griefe the enemy of life;
       All these, and many evils moe haunt ire,
       The swelling Splene,° and Frenzy raging rife,   *temper*
       The shaking Palsey, and Saint Fraunces fire:[6]
315 Such one was Wrath, the last of this ungodly tire.°   *procession*

36

And after all, upon the wagon beame°   *shaft*
       Rode Sathan, with a smarting whip in hand,
       With which he forward lasht the laesie teme,
       So oft as Slowth still in the mire did stand.
320   Huge routs of people did about them band,
       Showting for joy, and still° before their way   *always*
       A foggy mist had covered all the land;
       And underneath their feet, all scattered lay
Dead sculs and bones of men, whose life had gone astray.

37

325 So forth they marchen in this goodly sort,
       To take the solace of the open aire,
       And in fresh flowring fields themselves to sport;

---

6. Erysipelas or, as it was actually known, St. Anthony's fire. A common disease of the period, it was characterized by a disfiguring and painful skin rash.

Emongst the rest rode that false Lady faire,
The fowle Duessa, next unto the chaire
330   Of proud Lucifera, as one of the traine:
But that good knight would not so nigh repaire,°   follow
Him selfe estraunging from their joyaunce vaine,
Whose fellowship seemd far unfit for warlike swaine.

38

So having solaced themselves a space
335   With pleasaunce of the breathing fields yfed,[7]
They backe returned to the Princely Place;
Whereas° an errant° knight in armes ycled,   where / wandering
And heathnish shield, wherein with letters red
Was writ Sans-Joy, they new arrived find:
340   Enflam'd with fury and fiers hardy-hed,°   boldness
He seemd in hart to harbour thoughts unkind,
And nourish bloudy vengeaunce in his bitter mind.

39

Who when the shamed shield of slaine Sans-Foy
He spide with that same Faery champions page,
345   Bewraying° him, that did of late destroy   revealing
His eldest brother, burning all with rage
He to him leapt, and that same envious gage°   envious token
Of victors glory from him snatcht away:
But th'Elfin knight, which ought° that warlike wage,   owned
350   Disdaind to loose° the meed° he wonne in fray,   give up / reward
And him recountring° fierce, reskewd the noble pray.[8]   combatting

40

Therewith they gan to hurtlen° greedily,   fight
Redoubted battaile ready to darrayne,°   wage
And clash their shields, and shake their swords on hy,
355   That with their sturre they troubled all the traine;
Till that great Queene upon eternall paine
Of high displeasure, that ensewen° might,   follow
Commaunded them their fury to refraine,
And if that either to that shield had right,
360   In equall lists° they should the morrow next it fight.   tournament

41

Ah dearest Dame, (quoth then the Paynim bold,)
Pardon the errour of enraged wight,
Whom great griefe made forget the raines° to hold   reins
Of reasons rule, to see this recreant° knight,   cowardly
365   No knight, but treachour full of false despight°   indignation
And shamefull treason, who through guile hath slayn

---

7. I.e., having fed themselves with fresh air from the fields, where they momentarily escape the stench of sin.

8. By striving to recover Sans-Foy's shield instead of pursuing his quest to free Una's parents, the Redcrosse Knight exhibits pride and exemplifies a false chivalry.

The prowest knight, that ever field did fight,
Even stout Sans-Foy (O who can then refrayn?)
Whose shield he beares renverst,° the more to heape disdayn.   *upside down*

42

370   And to augment the glorie of his guile,
His dearest love the faire Fidessa loe°   *look*
Is there possessed of° the traytour vile,⁹   *by*
Who reapes the harvest sowen by his foe,
Sowen in bloudy field, and bought with woe:
375   That brothers hand shall dearely well requight°   *repay*
So be, O Queene, you equall favour showe.
Him litle answerd th'angry Elfin knight;
He never meant with words, but swords to plead his right.°   *cause*

43

But threw his gauntlet° as a sacred pledge,   *glove*
380   His cause in combat the next day to try:
So been they parted both, with harts on edge,
To be aveng'd each on his enimy.
That night they pas in joy and jollity,
Feasting and courting both in bowre and hall;
385   For Steward was excessive Gluttonie,
That of his plenty poured forth to all;
Which doen, the Chamberlain° Slowth did to rest them call.   *master of bedchambers*

44

Now whenas° darkesome night had all displayd   *when*
Her coleblacke curtein over brightest skye,
390   The warlike youthes on dayntie couches layd,
Did chace away sweet sleepe from sluggish eye,
To muse on meanes of hoped victory.
But whenas Morpheus had with leaden mace
Arrested° all that courtly company,   *i.e., put to sleep*
395   Up-rose Duessa from her resting place,
And to the Paynims lodging comes with silent pace.

45

Whom broad awake she finds, in troublous fit,
Forecasting, how his foe he might annoy,°   *injure*
And him amoves° with speaches seeming fit: *arouses*
400   Ah deare Sans-Joy, next dearest to Sans-Foy,
Cause of my new griefe, cause of my new joy,
Joyous, to see his ymage in mine eye,
And greev'd, to thinke how foe did him destroy,
That was the flowre of grace and chevalrye;
405   Lo his Fidessa to thy secret faith I flye.

---

9. Sans-Joy accused the Redcrosse Knight of absconding with Fidessa (i.e., Duessa), who actually belonged to his brother, Sans-Foy.

46

With gentle wordes he can° her fairely greet,	*did*
And bad° say on the secret of her hart.	*commanded*
Then sighing soft, I learne that little sweet	
Oft tempred is (quoth she) with muchell smart:°	*much pain*
410 For since my brest was launcht° with lovely dart	*pierced*
Of deare Sans-Foy, I never joyed howre,	
But in eternall woes my weaker hart	
Have wasted, loving him with all my powre,	
And for his sake have felt full many an heavie stowre.°	*sorrowful time*

47

415 At last when perils all I weened past,	
And hop'd to reape the crop of all my care,	
Into new woes unweeting I was cast,	
By this false faytor,° who unworthy ware°	*deceiver / wore*
His° worthy shield, whom he with guilefull snare	*Sans-Foy's*
420 Entrapped slew, and brought to shamefull grave.	
Me silly maid away with him he bare,	
And ever since hath kept in darksome cave,	
For that° I would not yeeld, that to Sans-Foy I gave.	*that which*

48

But since faire Sunne hath sperst° that lowring° clowd,	*dispersed / threatening*
425 And to my loathed life now shewes some light,	
Under your beames I will me safely shrowd,°	*take shelter*
From dreaded storme of his° disdainfull spight:	*Redcrosse Knight's*
To you th'inheritance belongs by right	
Of brothers prayse, to you eke longs his love.	
430 Let not his love, let not his restlesse spright	
Be unreveng'd, that calles to you above	
From wandring Stygian° shores, where it doth endlesse move.	*underworld*

49

Thereto said he, Faire Dame be nought dismaid	
For sorrowes past; their griefe is with them gone:	
435 Ne yet of present perill be affraid;	
For needlesse feare did never vantage none,°	*benefit anyone*
And helplesse hap it booteth° not to mone.	*helps*
Dead is Sans-Foy, his vitall paines° are past,	*troubles in life*
Though greeved ghost for vengeance deepe do grone:	
440 He lives, that shall him pay his dewties last,°	*final debts*
And guiltie Elfin bloud shall sacrifice in hast.	

50

O but I feare the fickle freakes° (quoth shee)	*accidents*
Of fortune false, and oddes of armes in field.	
Why dame (quoth he) what oddes can ever bee,	
445 Where both do fight alike, to win or yield?	
Yea but (quoth she) he beares a charmed shield,	
And eke enchaunted armes, that none can perce,	

Ne none can wound the man, that does them wield.
Charmd or enchaunted (answerd he then fercc)
450   I no whit reck,° ne you the like need to reherce.°   *care nothing / mention*

51

But faire Fidessa, sithens° fortunes guile,   *since*
Or enimies powre hath now captived you,
Returne from whence ye came, and rest a while
Till morrow next, that I the Elfe subdew,
455   And with Sans-Foyes dead dowry you endew.°   *give*
Ay me, that is a double death (she said)
With proud foes sight my sorrow to renew:
Where ever yet I be, my secrete aid
Shall follow you. So passing forth she him obaid.

Canto 5

The faithfull knight in equall field
subdewes his faithlesse foe,
Whom false Duessa saves, and for
his cure to hell does goe.

1

The noble hart, that harbours vertuous thought,
And is with child° of glorious great intent,   *pregnant*
Can never rest, untill it forth have brought
Th'eternall brood of glorie excellent:
5   Such restlesse passion did all night torment
The flaming corage of that Faery knight,
Devizing, how that doughtie° turnament   *worthy*
With greatest honour he atchieven might;
Still did he wake, and still did watch for dawning light.

2

10   At last the golden Orientall° gate   *eastern*
Of greatest heaven gan to open faire,
And Phoebus fresh, as bridegrome to his mate,
Came dauncing forth, shaking his deawie haire:
And hurld his glistring° beames through gloomy aire.   *glistening*
15   Which when the wakeful Elfe perceiv'd, streight way
He started up, and did him selfe prepaire,
In sun-bright armes, and battailous° array: *warlike*
For with that Pagan proud he combat will that day.

3

And forth he comes into the commune hall,
20   Where earely waite him many a gazing eye,
To weet° what end to straunger knights may fall.   *know*
There many Minstrales maken melody,
To drive away the dull melancholy,
And many Bardes, that to the trembling chord

25   Can tune their timely voyces cunningly,
               And many Chroniclers, that can record
          Old loves, and warres for Ladies doen by many a Lord.

4

          Soone after comes the cruell Sarazin,
               In woven maile all armed warily,°   *carefully*
30   And sternly lookes at him, who not a pin
               Does care for looke of living creatures eye.
               They bring them wines of Greece and Araby,°   *Arabia*
               And daintie spices fetcht from furthest Ynd,°   *India*
               To kindle heat of corage privily:°   *internally*
35   And in the wine a solemne oth they bynd
          T'observe the sacred lawes of armes, that are assynd.

5

          At last forth comes that far renowmed° Queene,   *famed*
               With royall pomp and Princely majestie;
               She is ybrought unto a paled greene,°   *enclosed field*
40   And placed under stately çanapee,
               The warlike feates of both those knights to see.
               On th'other side in all mens open vew
               Duessa placed is, and on a tree
               Sans-Foy his shield is hangd with bloudy hew:
45   Both those the lawrell girlonds to the victor dew.[1]

6

          A shrilling trompet sownded from on hye,
               And unto battaill bad them selves addresse:
               Their shining shieldes about their wrestes they tye,
               And burning blades about their heads do blesse,[2]
50   The instruments of wrath and heavinesse:
               With greedy force each other doth assayle,
               And strike so fiercely, that they do impresse
               Deepe dinted furrowes in the battred mayle;
          The yron walles° to ward their blowes are weake and fraile.   *of the armor*

7

55   The Sarazin was stout, and wondrous strong,
               And heaped blowes like yron hammers great:
               For after bloud and vengeance he did long.
               The knight was fiers, and full of youthly heat:
               And doubled strokes, like dreaded thunders threat:
60   For all for prayse and honour he did fight.
               Both stricken strike, and beaten both do beat,
               That from their shields forth flyeth firie light,
          And helmets hewen deepe,° shew marks of eithers might.   *deeply cut*

---

1. I.e., the victor will receive both Sans-Foy's shield and Duessa as his prize.

2. Brandish: They make the sign of the cross in the air with their swords.

8

So th'one for wrong, the other strives for right:
65   As when a Gryfon[3] seized of his pray,
    A Dragon fiers encountreth in his flight,
    Through widest ayre making his ydle way,
    That would his rightfull ravine° rend away: *spoil*
    With hideous horrour both together smight,
70   And souce° so sore, that they the heavens affray: *attack*
    The wise Southsayer seeing so sad sight,
Th'amazed vulgar tels of warres and mortall fight.

9

So th'one for wrong, the other strives for right,
    And each to deadly shame would drive his foe:
75   The cruell steele so greedily doth bight
    In tender flesh, that streames of bloud down flow,
    With which the armes, that earst° so bright did show,   *first*
    Into a pure vermillion now are dyde:
    Great ruth° in all the gazers harts did grow,   *pity*
80   Seeing the gored woundes to gape so wyde,
That victory they dare not wish to either side.

10

At last the Paynim chaunst to cast his eye,
    His suddein eye, flaming with wrathfull fyre,
    Upon his brothers shield, which hong thereby:
85   Therewith redoubled was his raging yre,
    And said, Ah wretched sonne of wofull syre,°   *Sans-Foy*
    Doest thou sit wayling by black Stygian° lake,   *by the river Styx*
    Whilest here thy shield is hangd for victors hyre,
    And sluggish german° doest thy forces slake,   *kinsman*
90   To after-send his foe, that him may overtake?[4]

11

Goe caytive Elfe,[5] him quickly overtake,
    And soone redeeme from his long wandring woe;
    Goe guiltie ghost, to him my message make,
    That I his shield have quit° from dying foe.   *recovered*
95   Therewith upon his crest he stroke him so,
    That twise he reeled, readie twise to fall;
    End of the doubtfull battell deemed tho
    The lookers on, and lowd to him gan call
The false Duessa, Thine the shield, and I, and all.[6]

3. A lion with eagle's wings. Dante used the gryfon as a symbol for the dual nature of Christ, as both spirit and flesh. However, in traditional iconography the gryfon also appeared as a creature who guarded gold and was thus emblematic of greed. The image suggests that the Redcrosse Knight is foolish to engage in a contest for material prizes.
4. Sans-Joy is addressing the dead Sans-Foy, asking if Sans-Foy grieves because his shield is a prize and the strength of his brother, Sans-Joy, which should be wielded to dispatch the Redcrosse Knight to the shores of the Styx, is actually slackening, growing weak.
5. Sans-Joy addresses the Redcrosse Knight. The epithet "caytive," meaning "servile," was especially insulting in the context of chivalry, because it implied weakness and lack of valor.
6. Duessa is calling to Sans-Joy; however, the Redcrosse Knight assumes that she is cheering him on and therefore redoubles his force.

12

100 Soone as the Faerie heard his Ladie speake,
        Out of his swowning dreame he gan awake,
        And quickning faith, that earst was woxen° weake,   *had grown*
        The creeping deadly cold away did shake:
        Tho mou'd with wrath, and shame, and Ladies sake,
105   Of all attonce he cast avengd to bee,
        And with so'exceeding furie at him strake,°   *struck*
        That forced him to stoupe upon his knee;
     Had he not stouped so, he should have cloven° bee.   *cut in half*

13

     And to him said, Goe now proud Miscreant,°   *heathen*
110   Thy selfe thy message doe to german deare,
        Alone he wandring thee too long doth want:°   *lack*
        Goe say, his foe thy shield with his doth beare.
        Therewith his heavie hand he high gan reare,°   *began to raise*
        Him to have slaine; when loe a darkesome clowd
115   Upon him fell: he no where doth appeare,
        But vanisht is. The Elfe him cals alowd,
     But answer none receiues: the darknes him does shrowd.

14

     In haste Duessa from her place arose,
        And to him running said, O prowest° knight,   *most valiant*
120   That ever Ladie to her love did chose,
        Let now abate the terror of your might,
        And quench the flame of furious despight,
        And bloudie vengeance; lo th'infernall powres
        Covering your foe with cloud of deadly night,
125   Have borne him hence to Plutoes balefull° bowres.   *deadly*
     The conquest yours, I yours, the shield, and glory yours.

15

     Not all so satisfide, with greedie eye
        He sought all round about, his thirstie blade
        To bath in bloud of faithlesse enemy;
130   Who all that while lay hid in secret shade:
        He standes amazed, how he thence should fade.
        At last the trumpets Triumph sound on hie,
        And running Heralds humble homage made,
        Greeting him goodly with new victorie,
135   And to him brought the shield, the cause of enmitie.

16

     Wherewith he goeth to that soveraine Queene,
        And falling her before on lowly knee,
        To her makes present of his service seene:
        Which she accepts, with thankes, and goodly gree,°   *courteous goodwill*
140   Greatly advauncing his gay chevalree.
        So marcheth home, and by her takes the knight,

Whom all the people follow with great glee,
  Shouting, and clapping all their hands on hight,°   *high*
That all the aire it fils, and flyes to heaven bright.

17

145 Home is he brought, and laid in sumptuous bed:
  Where many skilfull leaches° him abide,   *doctors*
  To salve° his hurts, that yet still freshly bled.   *dress*
  In wine and oyle they wash his woundes wide,
  And softly can embalme on every side.
150 And all the while, most heavenly melody
  About the bed sweet musicke did divide,°   *modulate*
  Him to beguile of griefe and agony:
And all the while Duessa wept full bitterly.

18

As when a wearie traveller that strayes
155 By muddy shore of broad seven-mouthed Nile,
  Unweeting of the perillous wandring wayes,
  Doth meet a cruell craftie Crocodile,
  Which in false griefe hyding his harmefull guile,
  Doth weepe full sore, and sheddeth tender teares:
160 The foolish man, that pitties all this while
  His mournefull plight, is swallowd up unwares,
Forgetfull of his owne, that mindes° anothers cares.   *attends to*

19

So wept Duessa untill eventide,
  That shyning lampes in Joves high house were light:
165 Then forth she rose, ne lenger° would abide,   *no longer*
  But comes unto the place, where th'Hethen knight
  In slombring swownd nigh voyd of vitall spright,°   *living spirit*
  Lay cover'd with inchaunted cloud all day:
  Whom when she found, as she him left in plight,
170 To wayle his woefull case she would not stay,
But to the easterne coast of heaven makes speedy way.

20

Where griesly Night, with visage deadly sad,
  That Phoebus chearefull face durst never vew,
  And in a foule blacke pitchie mantle clad,
175 She findes forth comming from her darkesome mew,°   *den*
  Where she all day did hide her hated hew.
  Before the dore her yron charet stood,
  Alreadie harnessed for journey new;
  And coleblacke steedes yborne of hellish brood,
180 That on their rustie bits did champ, as they were wood.°   *mad*

21

Who when she saw Duessa sunny bright,
  Adornd with gold and jewels shining cleare,

She greatly grew amazed at the sight,
And th'unacquainted light began to feare:
185   For never did such brightnesse there appeare,
And would have backe retyred to her cave,
Untill the witches speech she gan to heare,
Saying, Yet O thou dreaded Dame, I crave
Abide,° till I have told the message, which I have.   *wait*

22

190   She stayd, and foorth Duessa gan proceede,
O thou most auncient Grandmother of all,[7]
More old then Jove, whom thou at first didst breede,
Or that great house of Gods caelestiall,
Which wast begot in Daemogorgons° hall,   *chaos's*
195   And sawst the secrets of the world unmade,°   *not yet made*
Why suffredst thou thy Nephewes deare to fall
With Elfin sword, most shamefully betrade?
Lo where the stout° Sans-Joy doth sleepe in deadly shade.   *sturdy*

23

And him before, I saw with bitter eyes
200   The bold Sans-Foy shrinke underneath his speare;
And now the pray of fowles in field he lyes,
Nor wayld of friends, nor laid on groning beare,°   *bier*
That whylome was to me too dearely deare.
O what of Gods then boots° it to be borne,   *benefits*
205   If old Aveugles[8] sonnes so evill heare?
Or who shall not great Nightes children scorne,
When two of three her Nephews are so fowle forlorne?°   *foully abandoned*

24

Up then, up dreary Dame, of darknesse Queene,
Go gather up the reliques° of thy race,   *remains*
Or else goe them avenge, and let be seene,
210   That dreaded Night in brightest day hath place,°   *highest rank*
And can the children of faire light deface.
Her feeling speeches some compassion moved
In hart, and chaunge in that great mothers face:
215   Yet pittie in her hart was never proved°   *experienced*
Till then: for evermore she hated, never loved.

25

And said, Deare daughter rightly may I rew
The fall of famous children borne of mee,
And good successes, which their foes ensew:
220   But who can turne the streame of destinee,
Or breake the chayne of strong necessitee,

7. Invoking Night, Duessa recalls that Jove was raised in a dark cave to escape being eaten by his father, Saturn; here, Spenser is implying that darkness gave birth to Jove.

8. Blind (French). Duessa uses the name "Aveugle" to refer to either Night herself or her husband; "Aveugles sonne" is Sans-Joy.

Which fast is tyde to Joves eternall seat?[9]
The sonnes of Day he favoureth, I see,
And by my ruines thinkes to make them great:
225   To make one great by others losse, is bad excheat.°   *exchange*

26

Yet shall they not escape so freely all;
For some shall pay the price of° others guilt: *for*
And he the man that made Sans-Foy to fall,
Shall with his owne bloud price that he hath spilt.
230   But what art thou, that telst of Nephews kilt?°   *killed*
I that do seeme not I, Duessa am,
(Quoth she) how ever now in garments gilt,
And gorgeous gold arayd I to thee came;
Duessa I, the daughter of Deceipt and Shame.

27

235   Then bowing downe her aged backe, she kist
The wicked witch, saying; In that faire face
The false resemblance of Deceipt, I wist
Did closely° lurke; yet so true-seeming grace   *secretly*
It carried, that I scarse in darkesome place
240   Could it discerne, though I the mother bee
Of falshood, and root of Duessaes race.
O welcome child, whom I have longd to see,
And now have seene unwares.° Lo now I go with thee.   *unknowingly*

28

Then to her yron wagon she betakes,
245   And with her beares the fowle welfavourd witch:[1]
Through mirkesome° aire her readie way she makes.   *murky*
Her twyfold° Teme, of which two blacke as pitch,   *twofold*
And two were browne, yet each to each unlich,°   *unlike*
Did softly swim away, ne ever stampe,
250   Unlesse she chaunst their stubborne mouths to twitch;
Then foming tarre, their bridles they would champe,
And trampling the fine element,° would fiercely rampe.°   *air / rear up*

29

So well they sped, that they be come at length
Unto the place, whereas the Paynim lay,
255   Devoid of outward sense, and native° strength,   *natural*
Coverd with charmed cloud from vew of day,
And sight of men, since his late luckelesse fray.°   *fight*
His cruell wounds with cruddy bloud congealed,
They binden up so wisely, as they may,

9. Night reveals her fatalism and therefore her ignorance
of Christian grace. God can forgive a repentant sinner;
hence for Christians there is no "chain of necessity" prior
to God's decision to send the sinner to eternal damnation.

1. Duessa is a foul creature disguised as a beautiful
woman.

260   And handle softly, till they can be healed:
   So lay him in her charet, close° in night concealed.   *hidden*

30

  And all the while she stood upon the ground,
   The wakefull dogs did never cease to bay,°   *howl*
   As giving warning of th'unwonted° sound,   *unaccustomed*
265   With which her yron wheeles did them affray,
   And her darke griesly looke them much dismay;
   The messenger of death, the ghastly Owle
   With drearie shriekes did also her bewray;°   *expose*
   And hungry Wolves continually did howle,
270 At her abhorred face, so filthy and so fowle.

31

  Thence turning backe in silence soft they stole,
   And brought the heavie corse with easie pace
   To yawning gulfe of deepe Avernus° hole.   *a lake in hell*
   By that same hole an entrance darke and bace°   *low*
275   With smoake and sulphure hiding all the place,
   Descends to hell: there creature never past,
   That backe returned without heavenly grace;
   But dreadfull Furies,[2] which their chaines have brast,
  And damned sprights sent forth to make ill° men aghast.   *bad*

32

280 By that same way the direfull° dames doe drive   *dreadful*
   Their mournefull charet, fild° with rusty blood,   *defiled*
   And downe to Plutoes house are come bilive:°   *quickly*
   Which passing through, on every side them stood
   The trembling ghosts with sad amazed mood,
285   Chattring their yron teeth, and staring wide
   With stonie eyes; and all the hellish brood
   Of feends infernall flockt on every side,
  To gaze on earthly wight, that with the Night durst° ride.   *dared*

33

  They pas the bitter waves of Acheron,[3]
290   Where many soules sit wailing woefully,
   And come to fiery flood of Phlegeton,
   Whereas the damned ghosts in torments fry,
   And with sharpe shrilling shriekes doe bootlesse° cry,   *futilely*
   Cursing high Jove, the which them thither sent.
295   The house of endlesse paine is built thereby,
   In which ten thousand sorts of punishment
  The cursed creatures doe eternally torment.

---

2. The three mythical female spirits who live in the underworld and punish people for their crimes; they personified the forces of revenge.

3. Acheron and Phlegeton are two of the four rivers of the underworld.

34

Before the threshold dreadfull Cerberus[4]
   His three deformed heads did lay along,
300   Curled with thousand adders venemous,
   And lilled forth° his bloudie flaming tong: *stuck out*
   At them he gan to reare his bristles strong,
   And felly gnarre,° untill dayes enemy   *deadly snarl*
   Did him appease; then downe his taile he hong
305   And suffered them to passen quietly:
For she in hell and heaven had power equally.

35

There was Ixion[5] turned on a wheele,
   For daring tempt the Queene of heaven to sin;
   And Sisyphus an huge round stone did reele
310   Against an hill, ne might from labour lin;
   There thirstie Tantalus hong by the chin;
   And Tityus fed a vulture on his maw;
   Typhoeus joynts were stretched on a gin,
   Theseus condemned to endlesse slouth by law,
315   And fifty sisters water in leake vessels draw.

36

They all beholding worldly wights in place,
   Leave off their worke, unmindfull of their smart,°   *pain*
   To gaze on them; who forth by them doe pace,
   Till they be come unto the furthest part:
320   Where was a Cave ywrought° by wondrous art,   *built*
   Deepe, darke, uneasie, dolefull, comfortlesse,
   In which sad Aesculapius[6] farre a part
   Emprisond was in chaines remedilesse,
For that Hippolytus rent corse he did redresse.°   *restore*

37

325   Hippolytus a jolly huntsman was,
   That wont° in charet chace the foming Bore;   *often*
   He all his Peeres in beautie did surpas,
   But Ladies love as losse of time forbore:°   *abstained from*
   His wanton stepdame° loved him the more,   *stepmother*
330   But when she saw her offred sweets refused

4. The fierce, three-headed dog who guards the entrance to the underworld.

5. This stanza describes various mythological figures who suffer in the underworld. Ixion, king of Thessaly, sought the love of Juno and was punished by being bound forever on a revolving wheel. Sisyphus, a greedy king of Corinth, was condemned forever to roll up a hill a heavy stone, which always rolled back down again. Tantalus was doomed to stand up to his neck in water with fruit hanging at his fingertips, yet could never reach the fruit or drink the water. Tityus's punishment was to have a vulture constantly feed on his liver, which grew back as soon

as it was devoured. Theseus, hero and eventually king of Athens, was famous for a multitude of exploits and adventures; he was condemned to sit forever in the chair of forgetfulness. The 50 sisters were the daughters of Danaus, king of Argos; they were condemned to collect water in leaky pots because they had murdered their husbands on their wedding night.

6. The god of medicine. In the following stanzas, Spenser tells the story of how Aesculapius revived the corpse of Hippolytus and was punished for exceeding the limits of medical art.

Her love she turnd to hate, and him before
His father fierce of treason false accused,
And with her gealous termes his open eares abused.

38

Who all in rage his Sea-god syre besought,
335   Some cursed vengeance on his sonne to cast:
    From surging gulf two monsters straight were brought,
    With dread whereof his chasing steedes aghast,°   *terrified*
    Both charet swift and huntsman overcast.
    His goodly corps on ragged cliffs yrent,
340   Was quite dismembred, and his members chast°   *virgin, virtuous*
    Scattered on every mountaine, as he went,
That of Hippolytus was left no moniment.°   *trace*

39

His cruell stepdame seeing what was donne,
    Her wicked dayes with wretched knife did end,
345   In death avowing th'innocence of her sonne.
    Which hearing his rash Syre, began to rend°   *tear*
    His haire, and hastie tongue, that did offend:
    Tho gathering up the relicks of his smart°   *pain*
    By Dianes° meanes, who was Hippolyts frend,   *goddess of the hunt*
350   Them brought to Aesculape, that by his art
Did heale them all againe, and joyned every part.

40

Such wondrous science in mans wit to raine°   *rule*
    When Jove avizd,° that could the dead revive,   *found out*
    And fates expired could renew againe,
355   Of endlesse life he might him not deprive,
    But unto hell did thrust him downe alive,
    With flashing thunderbolt ywounded sore:
    Where long remaining, he did alwaies strive
    Himselfe with salves to health for to restore,
360 And slake° the heavenly fire, that raged evermore.   *put out*

41

There auncient Night arriving, did alight
    From her nigh wearie waine, and in her armes
    To Aesculapius brought the wounded knight:
    Whom having softly disarayd of armes,
365   Tho gan to him discover all his harmes,°   *injuries*
    Beseeching him with prayer, and with praise,
    If either salves, or oyles, or herbes, or charmes
    A fordonne° wight from dore of death mote raise,   *dying*
He would at her request prolong her nephews daies.

42

370 Ah Dame (quoth he) thou temptest me in vaine,
    To dare the thing, which daily yet I rew,

And the old cause of my continued paine
With like attempt to like end to renew.[7]
Is not enough, that thrust from heaven dew
375   Here endlesse penance for one fault I pay,
But that redoubled crime with vengeance new
Thou biddest me to eeke?° Can Night defray°   *increase / appease*
The wrath of thundring Jove, that rules both night and day?

43

Not so (quoth she) but sith that heavens king
380   From hope of heaven hath thee excluded quight,
Why fearest thou, that canst not hope for thing,°   *anything*
And fearest not, that more thee hurten might,
Now in the powre of everlasting Night?
Goe to then, O thou farre renowmed sonne
385   Of great Apollo, shew thy famous might
In medicine, that else hath to thee wonne
Great painés, and greater praise, both never to be donne.°   *surpassed*

44

Her words prevaild: And then the learned leach°   *doctor*
His cunning hand gan to his wounds to lay,
390   And all things else, the which his art did teach:
Which having seene, from thence arose away
The mother of dread darknesse, and let stay
Aveugles sonne there in the leaches cure,
And backe returning tooke her wonted way,
395   To runne her timely race, whilst Phoebus pure
In westerne waves his wearie wagon did recure.°   *renew*

45

The false Duessa leaving noyous° Night,   *noxious*
Returnd to stately pallace of dame Pride;
Where when she came, she found the Faery knight
400   Departed thence, albe° his woundes wide   *although*
Not throughly heald, unreadie were to ride.
Good cause he had to hasten thence away;
For on a day his wary Dwarfe had spide,
Where in a dongeon deepe huge numbers lay
405   Of caytive wretched thrals,° that wayled night and day.   *prisoners*

46

A ruefull sight, as could be seene with eie;
Of whom he learned had in secret wise°   *manner*
The hidden cause of their captivitie,
How mortgaging their lives to Covetise,°   *greed*
410   Through wastfull Pride, and wanton Riotise,°   *idle abandon*
They were by law of that proud Tyrannesse

---

7. I.e., to repeat the actions that caused his punishment in the first place and thus to renew the punishment itself.

Provokt with Wrath, and Envies false surmise,°   *suspicion*
Condemned to that Dongeon mercilesse,
Where they should live in woe, and die in wretchednesse.⁸

47

415   There was that great proud king of Babylon,°   *Nebuchadnezzar*
That would compell all nations to adore,
And him as onely° God to call upon,   *the only*
Till through celestiall doome° throwne out of dore,   *heavenly judgment*
Into an Oxe he was transform'd of yore:°   *in ancient times*
420   There also was king Croesus, that enhaunst
His heart too high through his great riches store;
And proud Antiochus, the which advaunst
His cursed hand gainst God, and on his altars daunst.

48

And them long time before, great Nimrod was,
425   That first the world with sword and fire warrayd;°   *ravaged*
And after him old Ninus farre did pas
In princely pompe, of all the world obayd;
There also was that mightie Monarch layd
Low under all, yet above all in pride,
430   That name of native syre° did fowle upbrayd,°   *natural father / denounce*
And would as Ammons sonne be magnifide,
Till scornd of God and man a shamefull death he dide.

49

All these together in one heape were throwne,
Like carkases of beasts in butchers stall.
435   And in another corner wide were strowne°   *strewn*
The antique ruines of the Romaines fall:⁹
Great Romulus the Grandsyre of them all,
Proud Tarquin, and too lordly Lentulus,
Stout Scipio, and stubborne Hanniball,
440   Ambitious Sylla, and sterne Marius,
High Caesar, great Pompey, and fierce Antonius.

---

8. Spenser lists some of the inhabitants of the under-world, the domain of Night, implying that they were damned for their evil deeds and were therefore in a Christian hell. The theology supporting this image is problematic: While Spenser names individuals who were considered to have been proud and malicious, they were also not people who could have known the message of Christianity. Nebuchadnezzar, king of Babylon, set up a golden image to be worshipped as God and was transformed into an ox as a punishment (Daniel 3–6); Croesus was the vastly rich king of Lydia; Antiochus, king of Antioch, was supposed scornfully to have danced on an altar; Nimrod was the first tyrant to emerge after the Flood; Ninus, the founder of Ninevah, conquered India and was the first to make war. "That mightie Monarch" was Alexander the Great, who rejected his father to claim descent from Jove or Jupiter, sometimes called Jupiter Ammon.

9. Spenser lists men who figured prominently in the history of ancient Rome; some were heroes, others were tyrants or wrongdoers. Romulus was the founder and first king of Rome; Tarquin was the last king of Rome before it became a republic; Lentulus attempted to set fire to Rome; Scipio was a Roman general who conquered Africa; Hannibal constantly waged war against Rome; Sylla was a Roman dictator who was engaged in civil war with Marius; Caesar, Pompey, and Antonius fought among themselves for rulership of Rome and its colonies, Caesar eventually winning the office only to be assassinated shortly thereafter.

50

Amongst these mighty men were wemen mixt,[1]
    Proud wemen, vaine, forgetfull of their yoke:°   *place*
    The bold Semiramis, whose sides transfixt
445   With sonnes owne blade, her fowle reproches spoke;
    Faire Sthenoboea, that her selfe did choke
    With wilfull cord, for wanting of her will;
    High minded Cleopatra, that with stroke
    Of Aspes° sting her selfe did stoutly kill: *snakes'*
450 And thousands moe the like, that did that dongeon fill.

51

Besides the endlesse routs° of wretched thralles,   *crowds*
    Which thither were assembled day by day,
    From all the world after their wofull falles,
    Through wicked pride, and wasted wealthes decay.°   *loss*
455   But most of all, which in that Dongeon lay
    Fell from high Princes courts, or Ladies bowres,
    Where they in idle pompe, or wanton play,
    Consumed had their goods, and thriftlesse howres,
And lastly throwne themselves into these heavy stowres.°   *afflictions*

52

Whose case when as the carefull Dwarfe had tould,
460   And made ensample° of their mournefull sight   *description*
    Unto his maister, he no lenger° would   *longer*
    There dwell in perill of like° painefull plight,   *similar*
    But early rose, and ere that dawning light
465   Discovered had the world to heaven wyde,
    He by a privie Posterne° tooke his flight,   *secret back door*
    That of no envious eyes he mote he spyde:
For doubtlesse death ensewd, if any him descryde.°   *discovered*

53

Scarse could he footing find in that fowle way,
470   For° many corses, like a great Lay-stall°   *because of / open grave*
    Of murdred men which therein strowed lay,°   *lay strewn*
    Without remorse, or decent funerall:
    Which all through that great Princesse pride did fall
    And came to shamefull end. And them beside
475   Forth ryding underneath the castell wall,
    A donghill° of dead carkases he spide,   *garbage heap*
The dreadfull spectacle of that sad house of Pride.

---

1. The women in the underworld, like the men, were figures from ancient history and mythology; those who are listed were judged to have been evil. After the death of her husband, King Ninus, Semiramis disguised herself as her son to gain the throne. Her son killed her when she tried to sleep with him. Sthenoboea lusted after her brother-in-law, Bellerophon, and committed suicide when he refused her advances. After Egypt had been defeated by the Roman forces of Octavius (later the Emperor Augustus), Cleopatra, the queen of Egypt, committed suicide by allowing herself to be bitten by asps, a kind of poisonous snake.

Canto 6

From lawlesse lust by wondrous grace
fayre Una is releast:
Whom salvage nation does adore,
and learnes her wise beheast.°   teaching

1

As when a ship, that flyes faire under saile,
    An hidden rocke escaped hath unwares,
    That lay in waite her wrack° for to bewaile,   destruction
    The Marriner° yet halfe amazed stares   sailor
5   At perill past, and yet in doubt ne dares°   dares not
    To joy at his foole-happie° oversight: lucky
    So doubly is distrest twixt joy and cares
    The dreadlesse courage of this Elfin knight,
Having escapt so sad ensamples° in his sight.   warnings

2

10 Yet sad he was that his too hastie speed
    The faire Duess' had forst him leave behind;
    And yet more sad, that Una his deare dreed°   revered one
    Her truth had staind with treason so unkind;°   unnatural
    Yet crime in her could never creature find,
15   But for his love, and for her owne selfe sake,
    She wandred had from one to other Ynd,°   throughout the world
    Him for to seeke, ne ever would forsake,
Till her unwares the fierce Sans-Loy did overtake.

3

Who after Archimagoes fowle defeat,
20   Led her away into a forrest wilde,
    And turning wrathfull fire to lustfull heat,
    With beastly sin thought° her to have defilde,   decided
    And made the vassall° of his pleasures vilde.   slave
    Yet first he cast by treatie,° and by traynes,°   treaty / tricks
25   Her to perswade, that stubborne fort° to yilde: i.e., her chastity
    For greater conquest of hard love he gaynes,
That workes it to his will, then he that it constraines.°   forces

4

With fawning wordes he courted her a while,
    And looking lovely,° and oft sighing sore,   amorously
30   Her constant hart did tempt with diverse guile:°   various deceits
    But wordes, and lookes, and sighes she did abhore,
    As rocke of Diamond stedfast evermore.
    Yet for to feed his fyrie lustfull eye,
    He snatcht the vele, that hong her face before;
35   Then gan her beautie shine, as brightest skye,
And burnt his beastly hart t'efforce° her chastitye.   to force

5

So when he saw his flatt'ring arts to fayle,
   And subtile engines bet from batteree,[1]
   With greedy force he gan the fort assayle,°   *attack*
40   Whereof he weend° possessed soone to bee,   *believe*
   And win rich spoile of ransackt chastetee.
   Ah heavens, that do this hideous act behold,
   And heavenly virgin thus outraged° see,   *violated*
   How can ye vengeance just so long withhold,
45 And hurle not flashing flames upon that Paynim bold?

6

The pitteous maiden carefull° comfortlesse,   *grief-stricken*
   Does throw out thrilling° shriekes, and shrieking cryes,   *piercing*
   The last vaine helpe of womens great distresse,
   And with loud plaints° importuneth the skyes,   *laments*
50   That molten° starres do drop like weeping eyes;   *melting*
   And Phoebus flying so most shamefull sight,
   His blushing face in foggy cloud implyes,°   *hides*
   And hides for shame. What wit of mortall wight
Can now devise to quit a thrall from such a plight?

7

55 Eternall providence exceeding thought,
   Where none appeares can make her selfe a way:
   A wondrous way it for this Lady wrought,
   From Lyons clawes to pluck the griped° pray.   *trapped*
   Her shrill outcryes and shriekes so loud did bray,
60   That all the woodes and forestes did resownd;
   A troupe of Faunes and Satyres° far away   *woodland deities*
   Within the wood were dauncing in a rownd,°   *circle*
Whiles old Sylvanus° slept in shady arber sownd.°   *a wood god / soundly*

8

Who when they heard that pitteous strained voice,
65   In hast forsooke° their rurall meriment,   *abandoned*
   And ran towards the far rebownded° noyce,   *reverberating*
   To weet,° what wight so loudly did lament.   *discover*
   Unto the place they come incontinent:°   *headlong*
   Whom when the raging Sarazin espide,
70   A rude, misshapen, monstrous rablement,
   Whose like he never saw, he durst° not bide,°   *dared / stay*
But got his ready steed, and fast away gan ride.

9

The wyld woodgods arrived in the place,
   There find the virgin dolefull desolate,
75   With ruffled rayments, and faire blubbred° face,   *tear-stained*
   As her outrageous foe had left her late,°   *recently*

---

1. I.e., Sans-Loy's clever devices are overcome by the success of Una's "battery" or repulses.

And trembling yet through feare of former hate;
All stand amazed at so uncouth° sight,   *strange*
And gin to pittie her unhappie state,
80   All stand astonied° at her beautie bright,   *amazed*
In their rude eyes unworthie of so wofull plight.

10

She more amaz'd, in double dread doth dwell;
And every tender part for feare does shake:
As when a greedie Wolfe through hunger fell°   *deadly*
85   A seely° Lambe farre from the flocke does take,   *innocent*
Of whom he meanes his bloudie feast to make,
A Lyon spyes fast running towards him,
The innocent pray in hast he does forsake,
Which quit° from death yet quakes in every lim°   *rescued / limb*
90   With chaunge of feare, to see the Lyon looke so grim.

11

Such fearefull fit assaid° her trembling hart,   *assailed*
Ne word to speake, ne joynt to move she had:
The salvage° nation[2] feele her secret smart,   *wild*
And read her sorrow in her count'nance sad;
95   Their frowning forheads with rough hornes yclad,
And rusticke horror all a side doe lay,°   *put away*
And gently grenning,° shew a semblance° glad   *grinning / expression*
To comfort her, and feare to put away,
Their backward bent knees teach her humbly to obay.[3]

12

100   The doubtfull Damzell dare not yet commit
Her single person to their barbarous truth,°   *allegiance*
But still twixt feare and hope amazd does sit,
Late° learnd what harme to hastie trust ensu'th,°   *recently / follows*
They in compassion of her tender youth,
105   And wonder of her beautie soveraine,
Are wonne with pitty and unwonted° ruth,   *unaccustomed*
And all prostrate upon the lowly plaine,°   *ground*
Do kisse her feete, and fawne on her with count'nance faine.° *glad expressions*

13

Their harts she ghesseth by their humble guise,
110   And yieldes her to extremitie of time;[4]
So from the ground she fearelesse doth arise,
And walketh forth without suspect° of crime:°   *fear / evil*
They all as glad, as birdes of joyous Prime,°   *spring*

---

2. I.e., the wood gods.
3. The fauns and satyrs have goat legs, so when they kneel before Una, their legs bend backward. It is not clear who teaches whom to obey in this line: their own act of kneeling may be teaching the fauns and satyrs to obey Una, or their awkward gestures may be teaching Una to obey them and put away her fear.
4. I.e., she submits to the necessities imposed on her by circumstances and loses her fear of the fauns and satyrs.

Thence lead her forth, about her dauncing round,
115   Shouting, and singing all a shepheards ryme,
And with greene braunches strowing° all the ground,   *strewing*
Do worship her, as Queene, with olive girlond cround.

14

And all the way their merry pipes they sound,
That all the woods with doubled Eccho ring,
120   And with their horned feet do weare° the ground,   *tread*
Leaping like wanton° kids in pleasant Spring.   *playful*
So towards old Sylvanus they her bring;
Who with the noyse awaked, commeth out,
To weet° the cause, his weake steps governing,°   *discover / guiding*
125   And aged limbs on Cypresse stadle stout,[5]
And with an yvie twyne° his wast is girt° about.   *vine / wrapped*

15

Far off he wonders, what them makes so glad,
Or° Bacchus[6] merry fruit° they did inuent,   *whether / grapes*
Or Cybeles[7] franticke rites have made them mad;
130   They drawing nigh, unto their God° present   *Sylvanus*
That flowre of faith and beautie excellent.
The God himselfe vewing that mirrhour rare,
Stood long amazd, and burnt in his intent;
His owne faire Dryope[8] now he thinkes not faire,
135   And Pholoe fowle, when her to this he doth compaire.

16

The woodborne° people fall before her flat,   *born of the woods*
And worship her as Goddesse of the wood;
And old Sylvanus selfe bethinkes not,° what   *cannot tell*
To thinke of wight so faire, but gazing stood,
140   In doubt to deeme° her borne of earthly brood;   *believe*
Sometimes Dame Venus selfe he seemes to see,
But Venus never had so sober° mood;   *serious*
Sometimes Diana he her takes to bee,
But misseth bow, and shaftes,° and buskins° to her knee.   *arrows / boots*

17

145   By vew of her he ginneth to revive
His ancient love, and dearest Cyparisse,[9]
And calles to mind his pourtraiture aliue,°   *living image*
How faire he was, and yet not faire to this,
And how he slew with glauncing dart amisse

---

5. Sylvanus uses a cane made from the trunk of a cypress tree.
6. The Roman god of wine; he is associated with both riot and fertility. Sylvanus suspects the fauns and satyrs of having discovered and drunk too much wine.
7. The goddess of grain and the harvest; the spring festival held in her honor was a fertility rite that resembled a bacchanalia.

8. At this point, Una is still unveiled from her encounter with Sans-Loy. When Sylvanus views her, he sees a mirror reflecting heavenly faith and beauty and hence considers his beloved nymphs, Dryope and Pholoe, ugly by comparison.
9. Cyparisse was a boy whom Sylvanus loved. Here Spenser recounts how Sylvanus accidentally killed Cyparisse's doe, after which the boy became so sad that Apollo turned him into a cypress to relieve his distress.

150 A gentle Hynd, the which the lovely boy
  Did love as life, above all worldly blisse;
  For griefe whereof the lad n'ould after° joy,   *would never afterward*
  But pynd° away in anguish and selfe-wild° annoy.   *wasted / self-willed*

       18
 The wooddy Nymphes, faire Hamadryades°   *tree spirits*
155 Her to behold do thither runne apace,
  And all the troupe of light-foot Naiades,°   *water nymphs*
  Flocke all about to see her lovely face:
  But° when they vewed have her heavenly grace,   *except for*
  They envie her in their malitious mind,
160 And fly away for feare of fowle disgrace:
  But all the Satyres scorne their woody kind,
And henceforth nothing faire, but her on earth they find.

       19
 Glad of such lucke, the luckelesse lucky maid,
  Did her content to please their feeble eyes,
165 And long time with that salvage people staid,
  To gather breath in many miseries.
  During which time her gentle wit she plyes,°   *employs*
  To teach them truth, which worshipt her in vaine,
  And made her th'Image of Idolatryes;
170 But when their bootlesse° zeale she did restraine   *misguided*
From her own worship, they her Asse would worship fayn.° *gladly*

       20
 It fortuned° a noble warlike knight   *happened*
  By just occasion to that forrest came,
  To seeke his kindred, and the lignage right,°   *proper lineage*
175 From whence he tooke his well deserved name:
  He had in armes abroad wonne muchell° fame,   *much*
  And fild far landes with glorie of his might,
  Plaine, faithfull, true, and enimy of shame,
  And ever lou'd to fight for Ladies right,
180 But in vaine glorious frayes° he litle did delight.   *battles*

       21
 A Satyres sonne yborne in forrest wyld,
  By straunge adventure as it did betyde,°   *happen*
  And there begotten of a Lady myld,
  Faire Thyamis the daughter of Labryde,[1]
185 That was in sacred bands of wedlocke tyde
  To Therion, a loose unruly swayne;°   *fellow*
  Who had more joy to raunge the forrest wyde,
  And chase the salvage beast with busie payne,°   *painstakingly*
Then° serve his Ladies love, and wast in pleasures vayne. *than*

---

1. The Greek names reveal the natures of these characters: Thyamis means "passion"; Labryde means "turbulence" or "greed"; and Therion means "wild beast."

22

190 The forlone mayd did with loves longing burne,
And could not lacke° her lovers company,   *do without*
But to the wood she goes, to serve her turne,°   *satisfy her desire*
And seeke her spouse, that from her still° does fly,   *always*
And followes other game and venery:
195 A Satyre chaunst her wandring for to find,
And kindling coles of lust in brutish eye,
The loyall links of wedlocke did unbind,
And made her person thrall° unto his beastly kind.   *prisoner*

23

So long in secret cabin there he held
200 Her captive to his sensuall desire,
Till that with timely fruit her belly sweld,
And bore a boy unto that salvage sire:
Then home he suffred her for to retire,°   *return*
For ransome leaving him the late borne childe;
205 Whom till to ryper yeares he gan aspire,°   *began to grow*
He noursled up° in life and manners wilde,   *raised*
Emongst wild beasts and woods, from lawes of men exilde.

24

For all he taught the tender ymp,° was but   *child*
To banish cowardize and bastard feare;
210 His trembling hand he would him force to put
Upon the Lyon and the rugged Beare,
And from the she Beares teats her whelps° to teare;   *cubs*
And eke wyld roring Buls he would him make
To tame, and ryde their backes not made to beare;°   *be ridden*
215 And the Robuckes° in flight to overtake,   *bucks*
That every beast for feare of him did fly and quake.

25

Thereby so fearelesse, and so fell° he grew,   *deadly*
That his owne sire and maister of his guise°   *behavior*
Did often tremble at his horrid vew,
220 And oft for dread of hurt would him advise,
The angry beasts not rashly to despise,
Nor too much to provoke; for he would learne°   *teach*
The Lyon stoup° to him in lowly wise,   *to bow*
(A lesson hard) and make the Libbard° sterne   *leopard*
225 Leave roaring, when in rage he for revenge did earne.°   *yearn*

26

And for to make his powre approved° more,   *apparent*
Wyld beasts in yron yokes he would compell;°   *command*
The spotted Panther, and the tusked Bore,
The Pardale° swift, and the Tigre cruell;   *female leopard*
230 The Antelope, and Wolfe both fierce and fell;
And them constraine in equall teme to draw.°   *harness together*

Such joy he had, their stubborne harts to quell,°   subdue
And sturdie courage tame with dreadfull aw,
That his beheast° they feared, as a tyrans° law.   command / tyrant's

27

235   His loving mother came upon a day
     Unto the woods, to see her little sonne;
     And chaunst unwares to meet him in the way,
     After his sportes, and cruell pastime donne,
     When after him a Lyonesse did runne,
240   That roaring all with rage, did lowd requere°   demand
     Her children deare, whom he away had wonne:°   taken
     The Lyon whelpes she saw how he did beare,
And lull° in rugged° armes, withouten childish feare.   cradle / hairy

28

The fearefull Dame° all quaked at the sight,   his mother
245   And turning backe, gan fast to fly away,
     Untill with love revokt° from vaine affright,   restrained
     She hardly yet perswaded was to stay,
     And then to him these womanish words gan say;
     Ah Satyrane,[2] my dearling, and my joy,
250   For love of me leave off° this dreadfull play;   stop
     To dally thus with death, is no fit toy,°   pastime
Go find some other play-fellowes, mine own sweet boy.

29

In these and like delights of bloudy game
     He trayned was, till ryper yeares he raught,°   reached
255   And there abode,° whilst any beast of name°   lived / known
     Walkt in that forest, whom he had not taught
     To feare his force: and then his courage haught°   haughty
     Desird of forreine foemen to be knowne,
     And far abroad for straunge° adventures sought: foreign
260   In which his might was never overthrowne,
But through all Faery lond his famous worth was blown.°   broadcast

30

Yet evermore it was his manner faire,
     After long labours and adventures spent,
     Unto those native woods for to repaire,
265   To see his sire and ofspring auncient.
     And now he thither came for like intent;
     Where he unwares the fairest Una found,
     Straunge Lady, in so straunge habiliment,°   surroundings
     Teaching the Satyres, which her sat around,
270   Trew sacred lore, which from her sweet lips did redound.

2. Like a satyr.

31

He wondred at her wisedome heavenly rare,
   Whose like in womens wit he never knew;
   And when her curteous deeds he did compare,
   Gan her admire, and her sad sorrowes rew,
275   Blaming of Fortune, which such troubles threw,
   And joyd to make proofe of° her° crueltie   *test / Fortune's*
   On gentle Dame, so hurtlesse, and so trew:
   Thenceforth he kept her goodly company,
And learnd her discipline of faith and veritie.

32

280 But she all vowd unto the Redcrosse knight,
   His wandring perill closely did lament,
   Ne in this new acquaintaunce could delight,
   But her deare heart with anguish did torment,
   And all her wit in secret counsels spent,
285 How to escape. At last in privie wise°   *secretly*
   To Satyrane she shewed her intent;
   Who glad to gain such favour, gan devise,
How with that pensive Maid he best might thence arise.°   *depart*

33

So on a day when Satyres all were gone,
290 To do their service to Sylvanus old,
   The gentle virgin left behind alone
   He led away with courage stout and bold.
   Too late it was, to Satyres to be told,
   Or ever hope recover her againe:
295 In vaine he seekes that having cannot hold.
   So fast he carried her with carefull paine,°   *skill*
That they the woods are past, and come now to the plaine.

34

The better part now of the lingring day,
   They traveild had, when as they farre espide
300 A wearie wight forwandring° by the way,   *wandering*
   And towards him they gan in hast to ride,
   To weet° of newes, that did abroad betide,°   *learn / occur*
   Or tydings of her knight of the Redcrosse.
   But he them spying, gan to turne aside,
305 For feare as seemd, or for some feigned losse;
More greedy they of newes, fast towards him do crosse.

35

A silly° man, in simple weedes forworne,°   *simple / old clothes*
   And soild with dust of the long dried way;
   His sandales were with toilesome travell torne,
310 And face all tand with scorching sunny ray,
   As he had traveild many a sommers day,
   Through boyling sands of Arabie and Ynde;°   *India*

And in his hand a Iacobs staffe,° to stay   *pilgrim's staff*
  His wearie limbes upon: and eke behind,
315 His scrip° did hang, in which his needments he did bind.   *bag*

36

The knight approching nigh, of him inquerd°   *asked*
  Tydings of warre, and of adventures new;
  But warres, nor new adventures none he herd.
  Then Una gan to aske, if ought he knew,
320   Or heard abroad of that her champion trew,
  That in his armour bare a croslet° red.   *small cross*
  Aye me, Deare dame (quoth he) well may I rew
  To tell the sad sight, which mine eies have red:°   *seen*
These eyes did see that knight both living and eke ded.

37

325 That cruell word her tender hart so thrild,°   *pierced*
  That suddein cold did runne through every vaine,
  And stony horrour all her sences fild
  With dying fit,° that downe she fell for paine.   *deathlike swoon*
  The knight her lightly° reared° up againe,   *quickly / lifted*
330   And comforted with curteous kind reliefe:
  Then wonne° from death,[3] she bad° him tellen plaine   *brought back / ordered*
  The further processe of her hidden griefe;
The lesser pangs can beare, who hath endur'd the chiefe.°   *greater*

38

Then gan the Pilgrim thus, I chaunst this day,
335   This fatall day, that shall I ever rew,
  To see two knights in travell° on my way   *traveling*
  (A sory sight) arraung'd° in battell new,[4]   *engaged*
  Both breathing vengeaunce, both of wrathfull hew:
  My fearefull flesh did tremble at their strife,
340   To see their blades so greedily imbrew,°   *stain themselves*
  That drunke with bloud, yet thristed after life:
What more? the Redcrosse knight was slaine with Paynim knife.

39

Ah dearest Lord (quoth she) how might that bee,
  And he the stoutest° knight, that ever wonne?   *sturdiest*
345 Ah dearest dame (quoth he) how might° I see   *could*
  The thing, that might not be, and yet was donne?
  Where is (said Satyrane) that Paynims sonne,
  That him of life, and us of joy hath reft?°   *deprived*
  Not far away (quoth he) he hence doth wonne°   *stay*
350 Foreby° a fountaine, where I late him left   *nearly*
Washing his bloudy wounds, that through° the steele were cleft.°   *by / cut*

---

3. Recovered from her swoon, Una asks the old man to continue telling her the details of the tale as yet unknown to her that will cause her further grief.
4. The old man is telling the story of Archimago's battle with Sans-Loy; however, because he fabricates a second round of the battle here, the reader knows he is deceitful and should guess that he is himself Archimago.

40

Therewith the knight thence marched forth in hast,
  Whiles Una with huge heavinesse opprest,°   *overcome*
  Could not for sorrow follow him so fast;
355 And soone he came, as he the place had ghest,°   *guessed*
  Whereas° that Pagan proud him selfe did rest,   *where*
  In secret shadow by a fountaine side:
  Even he it was, that earst° would have supprest   *previously*
  Faire Una: whom when Satyrane espide,
360 With fowle reprochfull words he boldly him defide.°   *challenged*

41

And said, Arise thou cursed Miscreaunt,°   *heathen*
  That hast with knightlesse guile and trecherous train°   *tricks*
  Faire knighthood fowly shamed, and doest vaunt°   *boast*
  That good knight of the Redcrosse to have slain:
365 Arise, and with like treason° now maintain°   *treachery / defend*
  Thy guilty wrong, or else thee guilty yield.°   *admit*
  The Sarazin this hearing, rose amain,°   *at once*
  And catching up in hast his three square° shield,   *triangular*
And shining helmet, soone him buckled° to the field.   *prepared*

42

370 And drawing nigh him said, Ah misborne Elfe,
  In evill houre thy foes thee hither sent,
  Anothers wrongs to wreake upon° thy selfe: *bring down*
  Yet ill° thou blamest me, for having blent°   *wrongly / defiled*
  My name with guile and traiterous intent;
375 That Redcrosse knight, perdie,° I never slew,   *by God*
  But had he beene, where earst° his armes were lent,°   *previously / borrowed*
  Th'enchaunter vaine his errour should not rew:
But thou his errour shalt, I hope now proven trew.[5]

43

Therewith they gan, both furious and fell,
380 To thunder blowes, and fiersly to assaile
  Each other bent° his enimy to quell,°   *intending / subdue*
  That with their force they perst both plate and maile,°   *types of armor*
  And made wide furrowes in their fleshes fraile,
  That it would pitty° any living eie.   *inspire pity in*
385 Large floods of bloud adowne their sides did raile;°   *pour*
  But floods of bloud could not them satisfie:
Both hungred after death: both chose to win, or die.

44

So long they fight, and fell revenge pursue,
  That fainting each, themselves to breathen let,°   *to catch their breath*

5. Sans-Loy refers to the action in 3.33–39. He denies killing the Redcrosse Knight, but he also states that had the Red-crosse Knight, and not Archimago, been wearing his own armor, then Sans-Loy would have killed him, and Archimago would not have to regret his, Sans-Loy's, error. But Sans-Loy will make good this error by engaging in judicial combat with Satyrane.

390   And oft refreshed, battell oft renue:
       As when two Bores with rancling malice met,
       Their gory° sides fresh bleeding fiercely fret,°   gored / wound
       Til breathlesse both them selves aside retire,
       Where foming wrath, their cruell tuskes they whet,°   sharpen
395   And trample th'earth, the whiles they may respire;°   so they can breathe
       Then backe to fight againe, new breathed and entire.°   refreshed

                                    45
       So fiersly, when these knights had breathed° once,   rested
       They gan to fight returne, increasing more
       Their puissant° force, and cruell rage attonce,°   powerful / at once
400   With heaped° strokes more hugely, then before,   increased
       That with their drerie° wounds and bloudy gore   bloody
       They both deformed,° scarsely could be known.   disfigured
       By this sad Una fraught° with anguish sore,   afflicted
       Led with their noise, which through the aire was thrown,
405   Arriv'd, where they in erth° their fruitles° bloud had sown.   on the ground /
                                                                        futile

                                    46
       Whom all so soone as that proud Sarazin
       Espide, he gan revive the memory
       Of his lewd lusts, and late attempted sin,
       And left the doubtfull° battell hastily,   undecided
410   To catch her, newly offred to his eie:
       But Satyrane with strokes him turning, staid,
       And sternely bad him other businesse plie,°   attend
       Then hunt the steps of pure unspotted Maid:
       Wherewith he° all enrag'd, these bitter speaches said.   Sans-Loy

                                    47
415   O foolish faeries sonne, what furie mad
       Hath thee incenst,° to hast thy dolefull fate?   enraged
       Were it not better, I that Lady had,
       Then that thou hadst repented° it too late?   regretted
       Most sencelesse man he, that himselfe doth hate,
420   To love another. Lo then for thine ayd
       Here take thy lovers token on thy pate.°   head
       So they to fight; the whiles the royall Mayd
       Fled farre away, of that proud Paynim sore afrayd.

                                    48
       But that false Pilgrim, which that leasing° told,   lie
425   Being in deed old Archimage, did stay
       In secret shadow, all this to behold,
       And much rejoyced in their bloudy fray:
       But when he saw the Damsell passe away
       He left his stond,° and her pursewd apace,°   place / awhile
430   In hope to bring her to her last decay.°   death
       But for to tell her lamentable cace,°   situation
       And eke this battels end, will need another place.

Canto 7

The Redcrosse knight is captive made
By Gyaunt proud opprest,
Prince Arthur meets with Una greatly
with those newes distrest.

1

What man so wise, what earthly wit so ware,°   *alert*
  As to descry° the crafty cunning traine,°   *perceive / guile*
  By which deceipt doth maske in visour° faire,   *mask*
  And cast her colours dyed deepe in graine,
5 To seeme like Truth, whose shape she well can faine,
  And fitting gestures to her purpose frame,°   *suit*
  The guiltlesse man with guile to entertaine?
  Great maistresse of her art was that false Dame,
The false Duessa, cloked with Fidessaes name.[1]

2

10 Who when returning from the drery Night,
  She fownd not in that perilous house of Pryde,
  Where she had left, the noble Redcrosse knight,
  Her hoped pray,° she would no lenger bide,°   *victim / stay*
  But forth she went, to seeke him far and wide.
15 Ere long she fownd, whereas he wearie sate,
  To rest him selfe, foreby a fountaine side,
  Disarmed all of yron-coted Plate,°   *armor*
And by his side his steed the grassy forage ate.

3

He feedes upon the cooling shade, and bayes°   *bathes*
20 His sweatie forehead in the breathing wind,
  Which through the trembling leaves full gently playes
  Wherein the cherefull birds of sundry kind
  Do chaunt sweet musick, to delight his mind:
  The Witch approching gan him fairely greet,
25 And with reproch of carelesnesse unkind
Upbrayd,° for leaving her in place unmeet,   *accused*
With fowle words tempring faire, soure gall° with hony sweet.   *anger*

4

Unkindnesse past, they gan of solace treat,°   *speak of pleasure*
  And bathe in pleasaunce of the joyous shade,
30 Which shielded them against the boyling heat,
  And with greene boughes decking a gloomy glade,
  About the fountaine like a girlond made;
  Whose bubbling wave did ever freshly well,

---

1. Duessa (duplicity) falsely bears the name Fidessa (fidelity).

	Ne ever would through fervent sommer fade:°	dry up
35	The sacred Nymph, which therein wont to dwell,	
	Was out of Dianes favour, as it then befell.°	so happened

5

	The cause was this: one day when Phoebe² fayre	
	With all her band was following the chace,	
	This Nymph, quite tyr'd with heat of scorching ayre	
40	Sat downe to rest in middest of the race:	
	The goddesse wroth gan fowly her disgrace,	
	And bad the waters, which from her did flow,	
	Be such as she her selfe was then in place.	
	Thenceforth her waters waxed dull and slow,	
45	And all that drunke thereof, did faint and feeble grow.³	

6

	Hereof° this gentle knight unweeting was,	of this
	And lying downe upon the sandie graile,°	gravel
	Drunke of the streame, as cleare as cristall glas;	
	Eftsoones his manly forces gan to faile,	
50	And mightie strong was turnd to feeble fraile.	
	His chaunged powres at first them selves not felt,	
	Till crudled° cold his corage° gan assaile,	congealing / vital powers
	And chearefull bloud in faintnesse chill did melt,	
	Which like a fever fit⁴ through all his body swelt.°	raged

7

55	Yet goodly court° he made still to his Dame,	advances
	Pourd out in loosnesse° on the grassy grownd,	licentiousness
	Both carelesse of his health, and of his fame:	
	Till at the last he heard a dreadfull sownd,	
	Which through the wood loud bellowing, did rebownd,	
60	That all the earth for terrour seemd to shake,	
	And trees did tremble. Th'Elfe therewith astownd,	
	Upstarted lightly from his looser make,°	mate
	And his unready weapons gan in hand to take.	

8

	But ere he could his armour on him dight,°	put
65	Or get his shield, his monstrous enimy	
	With sturdie steps came stalking in his sight,	
	An hideous Geant horrible and hye,°	tall
	That with his talnesse seemd to threat the skye,	
	The ground eke groned under him for dreed;	
70	His living like saw never living eye,	

---

2. An aspect or persona of Diana. As Diana, she is goddess of the hunt, but as Phoebe she is also goddess of the moon.
3. The nymph is transformed into a fountain whose waters cause fatigue rather than rejuvenation; paradoxically, this is a fountain that is never dry.

4. Heat is usually associated with strength, but here, the weakening effect of the fountain, associated with cold-ness, turns its forces against the Knight's strength, causing him to suffer both chill and fever.

Ne durst° behold:[5] his stature did exceed   *nor dared*
The hight of three the tallest sonnes of mortall seed.°   *men*

9

The greatest Earth his uncouth° mother was,   *unnatural*
  And blustring Aeolus° his boasted sire,   *god of the winds*
75   Who with his breath, which through the world doth pas,
  Her hollow womb did secretly inspire,°   *impregnate*
  And fild her hidden caues with stormie yre,
  That she conceiv'd; and trebling° the dew time,   *tripling*
  In which the wombes of women do expire,°   *give birth*
80   Brought forth this monstrous masse of earthly slime,
Puft up with emptie wind, and fild with sinfull crime.

10

So growen great through arrogant delight
  Of th'high descent, whereof he was yborne,
  And through presumption of his matchlesse might,
85   All other powres and knighthood he did scorne.[6]
  Such now he marcheth to this man forlorne,
  And left to losse: his stalking steps are stayde°   *supported*
  Upon a snaggy Oke, which he had torne
  Out of his mothers bowelles, and it made
90 His mortall° mace,° wherewith his foemen he dismayde.   *deadly / club*

11

That when the knight he spide, he gan advance
  With huge force and insupportable° mayne,°   *irresistible / force*
  And towardes him with dreadfull fury praunce;
  Who haplesse, and eke hopelesse, all in vaine
95   Did to him pace, sad battaile to darrayne,°   *engage*
  Disarmd, disgrast, and inwardly dismayde,
  And eke so faint in every joynt and vaine,
  Through that fraile fountaine, which him feeble made,
That scarsely could he weeld° his bootlesse° single blade.   *raise / useless*

12

100 The Geaunt strooke so maynly° mercilesse,   *forcefully*
  That could have overthrowne a stony towre,
  And were not heavenly grace, that him did blesse,°   *preserve*
  He had beene pouldred° all, as thin as flowre:°   *pulverized / flour*
  But he was wary of that deadly stowre,°   *attack*
105   And lightly lept from underneath the blow:
  Yet so exceeding was the villeins powre,
  That with the wind it did him overthrow,
And all his sences stound,° that still he lay full low.   *stunned*

---

5. I.e., no living person had ever seen anything like the giant nor would even have dared to look at such a creature.

6. I.e., the giant's ancestry has caused him to grow both
extremely tall and extremely proud.

13

As when that divelish yron Engin° wrought   *the cannon*
110   In deepest Hell, and framd by Furies skill,[7]
      With windy Nitre and quick Sulphur fraught,
      And ramd with bullet round, ordaind to kill,
      Conceiveth° fire, the heavens it doth fill   *catches*
      With thundring noyse, and all the ayre doth choke,
115   That none can breath, nor see, nor heare at will,
      Through smouldry cloud of duskish° stincking smoke,   *dusky*
That th'onely breath him daunts, who hath escapt the stroke.[8]

14

So daunted when the Geaunt saw the knight,[9]
      His heavie hand he heaved up on hye,
120   And him to dust thought to have battred quight,
      Untill Duessa loud to him gan crye;
      O great Orgoglio,[1] greatest under skye,
      O hold° thy mortall hand for Ladies sake,   *stop*
      Hold for my sake, and do him not to dye,
125   But vanquisht thine eternall bondslave make,
And me thy worthy meed unto° thy Leman° take.   *as / beloved*

15

He hearkned, and did stay from further harmes,
      To gayne so goodly guerdon,° as she spake: *prize*
      So willingly she came into his armes,
130   Who her as willingly to grace did take,
      And was possessed of his new found make.
      Then up he tooke the slombred sencelesse corse,
      And ere he could out of his swowne° awake,   *swoon*
      Him to his castle brought with hastie forse,
135   And in a Dongeon deepe him threw without remorse.

16

From that day forth Duessa was his deare,
      And highly honourd in his haughtie° eye,   *proud*
      He gave her gold and purple pall° to weare,   *robe*
      And triple crowne set on her head full hye,
140   And her endowd with royall majestye:
      Then for to make her dreaded more of men,
      And peoples harts with awfull terrour tye,°   *enthrall*
      A monstrous beast ybred° in filthy fen°   *born / swamp*
He chose, which he had kept long time in darksome den.

---

7. According to Renaissance tradition, the cannon was
invented by the devil in hell. "Nitre" (potassium nitrate)
and sulfur are the main ingredients of gunpowder; they
are "windy" because they produce the blast that propels
the cannonball through the air.
8. I.e., those who are not struck by the cannonball are
overcome by the smoke.

9. I.e., when the Giant saw that the Knight was overcome
by the smoke, he raised his heavy hand to beat him down
completely.
1. Pride, haughtiness, disdain (Italian).

17

145 Such one it was, as that renowmed° Snake   *famous*
Which great Alcides in Stremona slew,[2]
Long fostred in the filth of Lerna lake,
Whose many heads out budding ever new,
Did breed him endlesse labour to subdew:
150 But this same Monster much more ugly was;
For seven great heads out of his body grew,
An yron brest, and backe of scaly bras,
And all embrewd° in bloud, his eyes did shine as glas.   *stained*

18

His tayle was stretched out in wondrous length,
155 That to the house of heavenly gods it raught,°   *reached*
And with extorted° powre, and borrow'd strength,   *wrongfully obtained*
The ever-burning lamps from thence it brought,
And prowdly threw to ground, as things of nought;°   *worthless*
And underneath his filthy feet did tread
160 The sacred things, and holy heasts foretaught.°   *previously taught*
Upon this dreadfull Beast with sevenfold head
He set the false Duessa, for more aw and dread.[3]

19

The wofull Dwarfe, which saw his maisters fall,
Whiles he had keeping of his grasing steed,
165 And valiant knight become a caytive thrall,
When all was past, tooke up his forlorne weed,°   *abandoned armor*
His mightie armour, missing most at need;
His silver shield, now idle maisterlesse;
His poynant° speare, that many made to bleed,   *sharp*
170 The ruefull moniments of heavinesse,°   *tokens of grief*
And with them all departes, to tell his great distresse.

20

He had not travaild° long, when on the way   *traveled*
He wofull Ladie, wofull Una met,
Fast flying from the Paynims greedy pray,[4]
175 Whilest Satyrane him from pursuit did let:°   *hinder*
Who when her eyes she on the Dwarfe had set,
And saw the signes, that deadly tydings spake,
She fell to ground for sorrowfull regret,

2. The "snake" Spenser is referring to is the hydra, a creature from Greek mythology with a hundred heads, that lived in the lake of Lerna and was killed by Hercules (Alcides) as one of his 12 labors. The hydra was particularly difficult for Hercules to kill because each time he cut off one of its heads, several new ones grew in its place. Hercules eventually burnt the hydra's neck after each decapitation, thus preventing new heads from sprouting. Stremona is a river in Thrace.
3. Spenser compares the hydra with the Roman Catholic Church. The seven heads of this monster refer to the

seven hills on which Rome was built, as well as the seven deadly sins. Orgoglio mounts Duessa upon the seven-headed monster to make her more dreaded and awe-inspiring. This gesture also associates Duessa with the corrupt Roman Catholic Church, which, represented by the monster, has gained its power through tyranny and defiles true Christian doctrine.
4. I.e., Una is flying from Sans-Loy, who greedily has made her his prey or victim (see 6.42–47). The Dwarf meets Una at this point, while Satyrane is distracting Sans-Loy from his pursuit of her.

And lively breath° her sad brest did forsake,   *breath of life*
180   Yet might her pitteous hart be seene to pant and quake.

21

The messenger of so unhappie newes
        Would faine° have dyde: dead was his hart within,   *rather*
        Yet outwardly some little comfort shewes:
        At last recovering hart, he does begin
185   To rub her temples, and to chaufe° her chin,   *rub*
        And every tender part does tosse and turne:
        So hardly° he the flitted life does win,   *with difficulty*
        Unto her native prison to retourne:⁵
Then gins° her grieved ghost thus to lament and mourne.   *begins*

22

190   Ye dreary instruments of dolefull° sight,⁶   *sorrowful*
        That doe this deadly spectacle behold,
        Why do ye lenger° feed on loathed light,   *longer*
        Or liking find to gaze on earthly mould,°   *shapes*
        Sith cruell fates⁷ the carefull threeds° unfould,   *threads*
195   The which my life and love together tyde?
        Now let the stony dart of senselesse cold
        Perce to my hart, and pas through every side,
And let eternall night so sad sight fro° me hide.   *from*

23

O lightsome day, the lampe of highest Jove,
200   First made by him, mens wandring wayes to guyde,
        When darknesse he in deepest dongeon drove,
        Henceforth thy hated face for ever hyde,
        And shut up heavens windowes shyning wyde:
        For earthly sight can nought but sorrow breed,
205   And late repentance, which shall long abyde.°   *persist*
        Mine eyes no more on vanitie shall feed,
But seeled up with death, shall have their deadly meed.°   *reward of death*

24

Then downe againe she fell unto the ground;
        But he her quickly reared° up againe: *raised*
210   Thrise did she sinke adowne in deadly swownd,
        And thrise he her reviv'd with busie paine:
        At last when life recover'd had the raine,°   *rein, control*
        And over-wrestled his strong enemie,
        With foltring tong,° and trembling every vaine,   *faltering tongue*
215   Tell on (quoth she) the wofull Tragedie,
The which these reliques sad present unto mine eie.

---

5. The native prison of Una's spirit is her body.
6. Here Una is addressing her eyes.

7. Mythical arbiters of human life, who as spinsters measure out the fate of every individual by twisting, winding, and cutting his or her thread of life.

25

Tempestuous fortune hath spent all her spight,
  And thrilling sorrow throwne his utmost dart;
  Thy sad tongue cannot tell more heavy plight,
220   Then that I feele, and harbour in mine hart:
  Who hath endur'd the whole, can beare each part.
  If death it be, it is not the first wound,[8]
  That launched° hath my brest with bleeding smart.°   *pierced / wound*
  Begin, and end the bitter balefull stound;°   *wretched situation*
225 If lesse, then° that I feare, more favour I have found.[9]   *than*

26

Then gan the Dwarfe the whole discourse° declare,   *story*
  The subtill traines° of Archimago old;   *tricks*
  The wanton loves of false Fidessa faire,
  Bought with the bloud of vanquisht Paynim bold:
230   The wretched payre° transform'd to treen mould;°   *pair / tree shape*
  The house of Pride, and perils round about;
  The combat, which he with Sans-Joy did hould;
  The lucklesse conflict with the Gyant stout,°   *sturdy*
Wherein captiv'd, of life or death he stood in doubt.

27

235 She heard with patience all unto the end,
  And strove to maister sorrowfull assay,°   *grief*
  Which greater grew, the more she did contend,°   *struggle*
  And almost rent her tender hart in tway;°   *two*
  And love fresh coles unto her fire did lay:
240   For greater love, the greater is the losse.
  Was never Ladie loved dearer day,
  Then she did love the knight of the Redcrosse;[1]
For whose deare sake so many troubles her did tosse.°   *suffer*

28

At last when fervent° sorrow slaked° was,   *burning / quenched*
245 She up arose, resolving him to find
  A live or dead: and forward forth doth pas,°   *proceed*
  All as the Dwarfe the way to her assynd:°   *indicated*
  And evermore in constant carefull mind
  She fed her wound with fresh renewed bale;°   *bitterness*
250 Long tost with stormes, and bet° with bitter wind,   *beat*
  High over hils, and low adowne the dale,°   *valley*
She wandred many a wood, and measurd° many a vale.°   *crossed / valley*

---

8. I.e., if the Redcrosse Knight has met his death, he would not be the first knight who had died attempting to help Una with her quest, and therefore this would not be the first time that Una has felt the pain of learning of such a death.

9. I.e., if what the Dwarf has to tell is less terrible than Una fears, she will consider herself lucky.

1. I.e., there was never a lady who loved life itself more than Una loved the Redcrosse Knight.

29

At last she chaunced by good hap° to meet   luck
A goodly knight, faire marching by the way
255   Together with his Squire, arayed meet:°   well-dressed
His glitterand armour shined farre away,
Like glauncing° light of Phoebus brightest ray;   dazzling
From top to toe no place appeared bare,
That deadly dint° of steele endanger may: stroke
260   Athwart° his brest a bauldrick brave° he ware,   across / splendid belt
That shynd, like twinkling stars, with stons most pretious rare.

30

And in the midst thereof one pretious stone
Of wondrous worth, and eke of wondrous mights,°   powers
Shapt like a Ladies head, exceeding shone,
265   Like Hesperus[2] emongst the lesser lights,
And strove for to amaze° the weaker sights;   dazzle
Thereby his mortall° blade full comely hong   deadly
In yvory sheath, ycarv'd with curious slights;°   strange designs
Whose hilts were burnisht° gold, and handle strong   polished
270   Of mother pearle, and buckled with a golden tong.° pin

31

His haughtie° helmet, horrid° all with gold,   tall / encrusted
Both glorious brightnesse, and great terrour bred;
For all the crest a Dragon did enfold
With greedie pawes, and over all did spred
275   His golden wings: his dreadfull hideous hed
Close couched° on the bever,° seem'd to throw   crouched / visor
From flaming mouth bright sparkles fierie red,
That suddeine horror to faint° harts did show;   weak
And scaly tayle was stretcht adowne his backe full low.

32

280   Upon the top of all his loftie crest,
A bunch of haires discolourd diversly,°   of many colors
With sprincled pearle, and gold full richly drest,
Did shake, and seem'd to daunce for jollity,
Like to an Almond tree ymounted hye
285   On top of greene Selinis[3] all alone,
With blossomes brave bedecked° daintily;   splendidly ornamented
Whose tender locks do tremble every one
At every little breath, that under heaven is blowne.

---

2. The evening star, associated with Venus. The comparison of the stone on Arthur's breast to Venus suggests that love is central in his quest.
3. From *palmosa Selinis* ("palmy Selinis"), a town in Italy. Spenser suggests that the knight's helmet is topped with palms, signifying victory in battle. This helmet, decorated with a dragon, identifies the knight as Prince Arthur, whose father, Uther Pendragon, was so named because he carried a golden dragon to war with him. "Pendragon" literally means "dragon's head."

33

His warlike shield all closely cover'd° was,   *hidden*

290   Ne might of mortall eye be ever seene;

Not made of steele, nor of enduring bras,

Such earthly mettals soone consumed bene:[4]

But all of Diamond perfect pure and cleene

It framed was, one massie entire mould,°   *solid piece*

295   Hewen° out of Adamant° rocke with engines keene,°   *cut / diamond / sharp*

That point of speare it never percen could,

Ne dint° of direfull° sword divide the substance would.   *stroke / dreadfull*

34

The same to wight° he never wont disclose,[5]   *creature*

But when as monsters huge he would dismay,

300   Or daunt° unequall armies of his foes,   *vanquish*

Or when the flying heavens he would affray;°   *frighten*

For so exceeding shone his glistring ray,

That Phoebus golden face it did attaint,

As when a cloud his beames doth over-lay;

305   And silver Cynthia wexed pale and faint,

As when her face is staynd with magicke arts° constraint.   *witchcraft*

35

No magicke arts hereof had any might,

Nor bloudie wordes of bold Enchaunters call,

But all that was not such, as seemd in sight,

310   Before that shield did fade, and suddeine fall:[6]

And when him list the raskall routes appall,[7]

Men into stones therewith he could transmew,°   *transform*

And stones to dust, and dust to nought at all;

And when him list the prouder lookes subdew,

315   He would them gazing blind, or turne to other hew.[8]

36

Ne let it seeme, that credence this exceedes,[9]

For he that made the same, was knowne right well

To have done much more admirable deedes.

It Merlin[1] was, which whylome° did excell   *formerly*

320   All living wightes in might° of magicke spell: *power*

Both shield, and sword, and armour all he wrought

For this young Prince, when first to armes he fell;

---

4. I.e., steel or brass would soon have been destroyed or disintegrated. The diamond will last forever.

5. Arthur never shows his diamond to anyone except when he uses it to overcome his enemies because it is too dazzling. In this respect, Arthur's diamond functions much like Una's face, whose truth and beauty are so brilliant that she wears a veil to cover it.

6. All that was false, i.e., that was not what it appeared to be, was vanquished in the presence of Arthur's shield.

7. When Arthur wished to subdue vulgar mobs, he would turn them to stone.

8. When Arthur wished to subdue his more elevated opponents, he would blind them.

9. Let it not be thought that this is beyond belief.

1. A magician and prophet in the court of Arthur's father. He created the shield, sword, and armor worn by the young Prince Arthur. By noting that Arthur's armor still exists in Faerie Land, Spenser suggests that Arthur's virtue lives on in England and may be discovered through faith.

But when he dyde, the Faerie Queene it brought
To Faerie lond, where yet it may be seene, if sought.

37

325 A gentle youth, his dearely loved Squire
His speare of heben wood° behind him bare,   *ebony*
Whose harmefull head,° thrice heated in the fire,   *point*
Had riven many a brest with pikehead° square;°   *spear tip / accurately*
A goodly person, and could menage° faire   *manage a horse*
330 His stubborne steed with curbed canon° bit,   *a kind of bit*
Who under him did trample as the aire,
And chauft,° that any on his backe should sit;   *annoyed*
The yron rowels° into frothy fome he bit.   *part of the bit*

38

When as this knight nigh to the Ladie drew,
335 With lovely court° he gan her entertaine;   *attention*
But when he heard her answeres loth,° he knew   *reluctant*
Some secret sorrow did her heart distraine:°   *afflict*
Which to allay,° and calme her storming paine,   *soothe*
Faire feeling words he wisely gan display,
340 And for her humour fitting purpose faine,[2]
To tempt the cause it selfe for to bewray;°   *reveal*
Wherewith emmou'd, these bleeding words she gan to say.

39

What worlds delight, or joy of living speach
Can heart, so plung'd in sea of sorrowes deepe,
345 And heaped with so huge misfortunes, reach?
The carefull cold beginneth for to creepe,
And in my heart his yron arrow steepe,°   *immerse*
Soone as I thinke upon my bitter bale:°   *sorrows*
Such helplesse harmes yts° better hidden keepe,   *it is*
350 Then rip up griefe, where it may not availe,°   *avail*
My last left comfort is, my woes to weepe and waile.

40

Ah Ladie deare, quoth then the gentle knight,
Well may I weene,° your griefe is wondrous great;   *know*
For wondrous great griefe groneth in my spright,
355 Whiles thus I heare you of your sorrowes treat.°   *tell*
But wofull Ladie let me you intrete,°   *entreat*
For to unfold the anguish of your hart:
Mishaps are maistred° by advice discrete,   *mastered*
And counsell° mittigates the greatest smart;   *advice*
360 Found never helpe, who never would his hurts impart.[3]

---

2. Arthur chooses words more appropriate to Una's   3. He who never tells his woes will never find a remedy.
sadness.

41

O but (quoth she) great griefe will not be tould,
And can more easily be thought, then said.
Right so; (quoth he) but he, that never would,
Could never: will to might gives greatest aid.[4]

365 But griefe (quoth she) does greater grow displaid,°   *when displayed*
If then it find not helpe, and breedes despaire.
Despaire breedes not (quoth he) where faith is staid.°   *strong*
No faith so fast° (quoth she) but flesh does paire.°   *firm / weaken*
Flesh may empaire° (quoth he) but reason can repaire.   *impair*

42

370 His goodly reason, and well guided speach
So deepe did settle in her gratious thought,
That her perswaded to disclose the breach,°   *wound*
Which love and fortune in her heart had wrought,
And said; Faire Sir, I hope good hap° hath brought   *luck*
375 You to inquire the secrets of my griefe,
Or that your wisedome will direct my thought,
Or that your prowesse° can me yield reliefe: *valor*
Then heare the storie sad, which I shall tell you briefe.

43

The forlorne Maiden, whom your eyes have seene
380 The laughing stocke of fortunes mockeries,
Am th'only daughter of a King and Queene,
Whose parents deare, whilest equall° destinies   *impartial*
Did runne about,° and their felicities   *run their course*
The favourable heavens did not envy,
385 Did spread their rule through all the territories,
Which Phison and Euphrates floweth by,
And Gehons golden waves doe wash continually.[5]

44

Till that their cruell cursed enemy,
An huge great Dragon[6] horrible in sight,
390 Bred in the loathly lakes of Tartary,°   *Hell*
With murdrous ravine,° and devouring might   *violence*
Their kingdome spoild, and countrey wasted quight:
Themselves, for feare into his jawes to fall,
He forst to castle strong to take their flight,
395 Where fast embard° in mightie brasen° wall,   *imprisoned / brass*
He has them now foure yeres besiegd to make them thrall.

---

4. Desire to overcome adversity is the greatest help. Arthur is preventing Una from falling into a state of hopeless despair and helping her to reaffirm her faith.
5. Una's parents are Adam and Eve, and the territory that they govern is Eden. The Phison, Euphrates, and Gehon are three of the four rivers surrounding Eden and were thought to water the entire world.

6. The dragon is Satan. After the Fall, Adam and Eve were exiled from Eden. The "four years" that Spenser refers to may figuratively represent the 4,000 years that, according to the Geneva Bible, passed between the Fall and the birth of Christ.

45

Full many knights adventurous and stout
    Have enterprizd° that Monster to subdew;   *undertaken*
    From every coast that heaven walks about,
400   Have thither come the noble Martiall[7] crew,
    That famous hard atchievements still pursew,
    Yet never any could that girlond win,
    But all still shronke, and still he greater grew:
    All they for want of faith, or guilt of sin,
405   The pitteous pray of his fierce crueltie have bin.[8]

46

At last yledd° with farre reported praise,   *led by*
    Which flying fame throughout the world had spred,
    Of doughtie° knights, whom Faery land did raise,   *worthy*
    That noble order hight of Maidenhed,°   *virginity*
410   Forthwith to court of Gloriane I sped,
    Of Gloriane great Queene of glory bright,
    Whose kingdomes seat Cleopolis[9] is red,°   *named*
    There to obtaine some such redoubted° knight,   *formidable*
    That Parents deare from tyrants powre deliver might.

47

415   It was my chance (my chance was faire and good)
    There for to find a fresh unproved° knight,   *untried in battle*
    Whose manly hands imbrew'd° in guiltie blood   *stained*
    Had never bene, ne ever by his might
    Had throwne to ground the unregarded right:[1]
420   Yet of his prowesse° proofe he since hath made   *virtue*
    (I witnesse am) in many a cruell fight;
    The groning ghosts of many one dismaide°   *defeated*
    Have felt the bitter dint of his avenging blade.

48

And ye[2] the forlorne reliques of his powre,
425   His byting sword, and his devouring speare,
    Which have endured many a dreadfull stowre,°   *conflict*
    Can speake his prowesse, that did earst° you beare,   *formerly*
    And well could rule: now he hath left you heare,
    To be the record of his ruefull losse,
430   And of my dolefull disaventurous° deare: *unfortunate*
    O heavie record of the good Redcrosse,
    Where have you left your Lord, that could so well you tosse?°   *brandish*

---

7. This stanza refers to the many knights ("the noble Martiall crew") who have undertaken to assist Una in her quest to overcome the Dragon and rescue her parents.
8. Until now, the knights have all failed in their quest because they have lacked faith or have succumbed to sin and have thus become victims of the Dragon's cruelty.
9. The city of fame or glory where the Faerie Queene lives. The knights of her court belong to the order of the

"Maidenhed," or virginity, an order that reflects the Faerie Queene's own virtue as well as that of Queen Elizabeth I, who was known as the "virgin queen."
1. The right for which he had no regard or respect; on the contrary, the Redcrosse Knight promotes and protects the right.
2. Here Una is addressing the Redcrosse Knight's armor.

49

Well hoped I, and faire beginnings had,
 That he my captive langour³ should redeeme,
435 Till all unweeting,° an Enchaunter bad   *unknown to the knight*
 His sence abusd,° and made him to misdeeme°   *distorted / misjudge*
 My loyalty, not such as it did seeme;⁴
 That rather death desire, then° such despight.°   *than / outrage*
 Be judge ye heavens, that all things right esteeme,
440 How I him lov'd, and love with all my might,
So thought I eke of him, and thinke I thought aright.

50

Thenceforth me desolate he quite forsooke,
 To wander, where wilde fortune would me lead,
 And other bywaies he himselfe betooke,
445 Where never foot of living wight did tread,
 That brought not backe the balefull° body dead;   *wretched*
 In which him chaunced false Duessa meete,
 Mine onely foe, mine onely deadly dread,
 Who with her witchcraft and misseeming sweete,
450 Inveigled° him to follow her desires unmeete.°   *tricked / unsuitable*

51

At last by subtill sleights° she him betraid   *tricks*
 Unto his foe, a Gyant huge and tall,
 Who him disarmed, dissolute,° dismaid,°   *weakened / vanquished*
 Unwares surprised, and with mightie mall°   *weapon*
455 The monster mercilesse him made to fall,
 Whose fall did never foe before behold;⁵
 And now in darkesome dungeon, wretched thrall,
 Remedilesse,° for aie° he doth him hold;   *helpless / ever*
This is my cause of griefe, more great, then° may be told. *than*

52

460 Ere she had ended all, she gan° to faint: *began*
 But he her comforted and faire bespake,
 Certes,° Madame, ye have great cause of plaint,   *certainly*
 That stoutest heart, I weene,° could cause to quake. *believe*
 But be of cheare, and comfort to you take:
465 For till I have acquit° your captive knight,   *avenged*
 Assure your selfe, I will you not forsake.
 His chearefull words reviv'd her chearelesse spright,
So forth they went, the Dwarfe them guiding ever right.

---

3. Una is referring to her parents' languishment in captivity but also to the symbolic captivity of humankind whom the Redcrosse Knight, as a figure of Christ, will redeem.

4. The Redcrosse Knight misjudged Una's loyalty, thinking that it was not what it appeared to be.
5. The Redcrosse Knight had never yet been defeated in battle.

Canto 8

Faire virgin to reedeme her deare
brings Arthur to the fight:
Who slayes the Gyant, wounds the beast,
and strips Duessa quight.

1

Ay me, how many perils doe enfold
   The righteous man, to make him daily fall?
   Were not,° that heavenly grace doth him uphold,[1]   *were it not*
   And stedfast truth acquite° him out of all.   *absolve*
5   Her love is firme, her care continuall,
   So oft as he through his owne foolish pride,
   Or weaknesse is to sinfull bands made thrall:
   Else° should this Redcrosse knight in bands have dyde,   *otherwise*
For whose deliverance she this Prince doth thither guide.

2

10   They sadly traveild thus, untill they came
   Nigh to a castle builded strong and hie:
   Then cryde the Dwarfe, lo yonder is the same,
   In which my Lord my liege° doth lucklesse lie,   *master*
   Thrall to that Gyants hatefull tyrannie:
15   Therefore, deare Sir, your mightie powres assay.°   *prove*
   The noble knight alighted by and by
   From loftie steede, and bad the Ladie stay,
To see what end of fight should him befall that day.

3

So with the Squire, th'admirer of his might,
20   He marched forth towards that castle wall;
   Whose gates he found fast shut, ne living wight
   To ward° the same, nor answere commers° call.   *guard / visitor's*
   Then tooke that Squire an horne of bugle small,
   Which hong adowne his side in twisted gold,
25   And tassels gay. Wyde wonders over all
   Of that same hornes great vertues weren told,[2]
Which had approved bene in uses manifold.°   *many*

4

Was never wight, that heard that shrilling sound,
   But trembling feare did feele in every vaine;
30   Three miles it might be easie heard around,
   And Ecchoes three answerd it selfe againe:
   No false enchauntment, nor deceiptfull traine°   *deception*

1. In this stanza, Una is overtly equated with heavenly grace. The Redcrosse Knight originally undertook the quest to help Una redeem her parents, but in this canto it is she who delivers the Redcrosse Knight from captivity. 2. Wonderful stories of the horn's powers were told everywhere.

Might once abide° the terror of that blast,   *tolerate*
But presently was voide and wholly vaine:°   *ineffectual*
35   No gate so strong, no locke so firme and fast,
But with that percing noise flew open quite, or brast.°   *burst*

5

The same before the Geants gate he blew,
That all the castle quaked from the ground,
And every dore of freewill° open flew.   *itself*
40   The Gyant selfe dismaied with that sownd,
Where he with his Duessa dalliance fownd,[3]
In hast came rushing forth from inner bowre,°   *chamber*
With staring° countenance sterne, as one astownd,°   *glaring / confused*
And staggering steps, to weet, what suddein stowre°   *uproar*
45   Had wrought that horror strange, and dar'd° his dreaded powre.   *defied*

6

And after him the proud Duessa came,
High mounted on her manyheaded beast,
And every head with fyrie tongue did flame,
And every head was crowned on his creast,[4]
50   And bloudie mouthed with late cruell feast.
That when the knight beheld, his mightie shild
Upon his manly arme he soone addrest,°   *made ready*
And at him fiercely flew, with courage fild,
And eger greedinesse through every member thrild.

7

55   Therewith the Gyant buckled° him to fight,   *engaged*
Inflam'd with scornefull wrath and high disdaine,
And lifting up his dreadfull club on hight,
All arm'd° with ragged snubbes° and knottie graine,   *covered / roots*
Him thought at first encounter to have slaine.
60   But wise and warie was that noble Pere,
And lightly leaping from so monstrous maine,°   *force*
Did faire° avoide the violence him nere;   *easily*
It booted nought,° to thinke, such thunderbolts to beare.   *it was useless*

8

Ne shame° he thought to shunne so hideous might: *not shameful*
65   The idle stroke, enforcing furious way,
Missing the marke of his misaymed sight
Did fall to ground, and with his heavie sway°   *force*
So deepely dinted° in the driven° clay,   *struck / packed*
That three yardes deepe a furrow up did throw:
70   The sad earth wounded with so sore assay,°   *attack*
Did grone full grievous underneath the blow,
And trembling with strange feare, did like an earthquake show.

---

3. The sound of the horn reached the chamber where the   4. Each head of Duessa's many-headed beast had a crown
Giant and Duessa were engaged in lovemaking.   on it.

9

As when almightie Jove in wrathfull mood,
    To wreake the guilt of mortall sins is bent,°   *determined*
75   Hurles forth his thundring dart with deadly food,°   *hatred*
    Enrold° in flames, and smouldring dreriment,   *engulfed*
    Through riven cloudes and molten firmament;°   *sky*
    The fierce threeforked engin° making way,   *the thunderbolt*
    Both loftie towres and highest trees hath rent,
80   And all that might his angric passage stay,°   *hinder*
And shooting in the earth, casts up a mount° of clay.   *mountain*

10

His boystrous° club, so buried in the ground,   *enormous*
    He could not rearen° up againe so light,°   *raise / easily*
    But° that the knight him at avantage found,   *so*
85   And whiles he strove his combred° clubbe to quight°   *encumbered / free*
    Out of the earth, with blade all burning bright
    He smote° off his left arme, which like a blocke   *struck*
    Did fall to ground, depriv'd of native might;
    Large streames of bloud out of the truncked stocke°   *truncated stump*
90 Forth gushed, like fresh water streame from riven rocke.

11

Dismaied with so desperate deadly wound,
    And eke impatient of unwonted paine,
    He loudly brayd with beastly yelling sound,
    That all the fields rebellowed° againe;   *echoed his bellows*
95   As great a noyse, as when in Cymbrian plaine[5]
    An heard of Bulles, whom kindly rage doth sting,
    Do for the milkie mothers want° complaine,   *absence*
    And fill the fields with troublous bellowing,
The neighbour woods around with hollow murmur ring.

12

100 That when his deare Duessa heard, and saw
    The evill stownd,° that daungerd her estate,°   *peril / situation*
    Unto his aide she hastily did draw
    Her dreadfull beast, who swolne with bloud of late
    Came ramping° forth with proud presumpteous gate,   *bounding*
105   And threatned all his heads like flaming brands.
    But him the Squire made quickly to retrate,°   *retreat*
    Encountring fierce with single sword in hand,
And twixt° him and his Lord did like a bulwarke° stand.   *between / barrier*

13

The proud Duessa full of wrathfull spight,
110   And fierce disdaine, to be affronted so,
    Enforst° her purple beast with all her might   *spurred on*

5. The Cimbri were a savage tribe that invaded Europe in the 1st century B.C.

That stop° out of the way to overthroe,   *obstacle*
Scorning the let° of so unequall° foe: *hindrance / inferior*
But nathemore° would that courageous swayne°   *not at all / fellow*
115 To her yeeld passage, gainst his Lord to goe,
But with outrageous strokes did him restraine,
And with his bodie bard° the way atwixt them twaine.°   *barred / between*

14

Then tooke the angrie witch her golden cup,
Which still she bore, replete° with magick artes;   *filled*
120 Death and despeyre did many thereof sup,°   *drink*
And secret poyson through their inner parts,
Th'eternall bale° of heavie wounded harts;   *destruction*
Which after charmes and some enchauntments said,
She lightly sprinkled on his weaker parts;
125 Therewith his sturdie courage soone was quayd,°   *quelled*
And all his senses were with suddeine dread dismayd.°   *overcome*

15

So downe he fell before the cruell beast,
Who on his necke his bloudie clawes did seize,
That life nigh crusht out of his panting brest.
130 No powre he had to stirre, nor will to rize.
That when the carefull knight gan well avise,°   *notice*
He lightly left the foe, with whom he fought,
And to the beast gan turne his enterprise;°   *attack*
For wondrous anguish in his hart it wrought,
135 To see his loved Squire into such thraldome brought.

16

And high advauncing° his bloud-thirstie blade,   *lifting up*
Stroke one of those deformed heads so sore,
That of his puissance° proud ensample made;   *strength*
His monstrous scalpe downe to his teeth it tore,
140 And that misformed shape mis-shaped more:
A sea of bloud gusht from the gaping wound,
That her gay garments staynd with filthy gore,
And overflowed all the field around;
That over shoes in bloud he waded on the ground.[6]

17

145 Thereat he roared for exceeding paine,
That to have heard, great horror would have bred,[7]
And scourging° th'emptie ayre with his long traine,°   *tearing / tail*
Through great impatience of his grieved hed
His gorgeous ryder from her loftie sted°   *place*
150 Would have cast downe, and trod in durtie myre,

6. The pool of blood is so deep that it reaches over Arthur's shoes.

7. The beast roars so loudly from the pain that anyone who heard it would have been struck with horror.

Had not the Gyant soone her succoured;°   rescued
Who all enrag'd with smart° and franticke yre,   pain
Came hurtling in full fierce, and forst the knight retyre.°   to back off

18

The force, which wont° in two to be disperst,   usually
155   In one alone left hand he now unites,[8]
Which is through rage more strong then both were erst;°   before
With which his hideous club aloft he dites,°   raises
And at his foe with furious rigour° smites,   violence
That strongest Oake might seeme to ouerthrow:
160   The stroke upon his shield so heavie lites,°   falls
That to the ground it doubleth° him full low: collapse
What mortall wight could ever beare so monstrous blow?

19

And in his fall his shield, that covered was,
Did loose his vele° by chaunce, and open flew: its covering
165   The light whereof, that heavens light did pas,°   surpass
Such blazing brightnesse through the aier threw,
That eye mote° not the same endure to vew.   could
Which when the Gyaunt spyde with staring eye,
He downe let fall his arme, and soft withdrew
170   His weapon huge, that heaved° was on hye   raised
For to have slaine the man, that on the ground did lye.

20

And eke the fruitfull-headed° beast, amaz'd   many-headed
At flashing beames of that sunshiny shield,
Became starke blind, and all his senses daz'd,
175   That downe he tumbled on the durtie field,
And seem'd himselfe as conquered to yield.[9]
Whom when his maistresse proud perceiv'd to fall,
Whiles yet his feeble feet for faintnesse reeld,
Unto the Gyant loudly she gan call,
180   O helpe Orgoglio, helpe, or else we perish all.

21

At her so pitteous cry was much amoov'd
Her champion stout, and for to ayde his frend,
Againe his wonted° angry weapon proov'd:°   usual / tried
But all in vaine: for he has read his end°   death
185   In that bright shield, and all their forces spend
Themselves in vaine: for since that glauncing° sight,   dazzling
He hath no powre to hurt, nor to defend;
As where th'Almighties lightning brond° does light,   bolt
It dimmes the dazed eyen, and daunts° the senses quight. stuns

8. The strength that has been divided in the Giant's two hands is now concentrated in his remaining hand.

9. By falling down, the beast seems not only to be conquered but also to submit himself ("yield") to Arthur.

22

190   Whom when the Prince, to battell new addrest,
      And threatning high his dreadfull stroke did see,[1]
      His sparkling blade about his head he blest,°   *brandished*
      And smote off quite his right leg by the knee,
      That downe he tombled; as an aged tree,
195   High growing on the top of rocky clift,
      Whose hartstrings with keene steele nigh hewen be,°   *are nearly cut off*
      The mightie trunck halfe rent, with ragged rift°   *splitting*
Doth roll adowne the rocks, and fall with fearefull drift.°   *force*

23

      Or as a Castle reared° high and round,   *built*
200   By subtile° engins and malitious slight   *clever*
      Is undermined from the lowest ground,
      And her° foundation forst,° and feebled quight,   *the castle's / broken*
      At last downe falles, and with her heaped hight
      Her hastie ruine does more heavie make,
205   And yields it selfe unto the victours might;
      Such was this Gyaunts fall, that seemd to shake
The stedfast globe of earth, as it for feare did quake.

24

      The knight then lightly leaping to the pray,°   *victim*
      With mortall steele him smot° againe so sore,   *struck*
210   That headlesse his unweldy bodie lay,
      All wallowd in his owne fowle bloudy gore,
      Which flowed from his wounds in wondrous store.°   *amounts*
      But soone as breath out of his breast did pas,
      That huge great body, which the Gyaunt bore,
215   Was vanisht quite,° and of that monstrous mas   *completely*
Was nothing left, but like an emptie bladder was.[2]

25

      Whose grievous fall, when false Duessa spide,
      Her golden cup she cast unto the ground,
      And crowned mitre° rudely threw aside;   *papal crown*
220   Such percing griefe her stubborne hart did wound,
      That she could not endure that dolefull stound,°   *dismal situation*
      But leaving all behind her, fled away:
      The light-foot Squire her quickly turnd around,
      And by hard meanes enforcing her to stay,
225   So brought unto his Lord, as his deserved pray.

26

      The royall Virgin, which beheld from farre,
      In pensive plight, and sad perplexitie,

---

1. The Giant is already overcome by the sight of Arthur's shield, but when Arthur sees him raising his weapon to defend Duessa, Arthur renews the battle.

2. A bladder or balloon can be blown up to a great size, although it is actually empty, i.e., full of hot air.

The whole atchievement° of this doubtfull° warre,   *progress / fearful*
Came running fast to greet his victorie,
230   With sober gladnesse, and myld modestie,
And with sweet joyous cheare him thus bespake;
Faire braunch of noblesse, flowre of chevalrie,
That with your worth the world amazed make,
How shall I quite° the paines, ye suffer for my sake?   *repay*

27

235   And you fresh bud of vertue springing fast,
Whom these sad eyes saw nigh unto deaths dore,
What hath poore Virgin for such perill past,
Wherewith you to reward? Accept therefore
My simple selfe, and service evermore;
240   And he that high does sit, and all things see
With equall° eyes, their merites to restore,   *impartial*
Behold what ye this day have done for mee,
And what I cannot quite, requite with usuree.³

28

But sith° the heavens, and your faire handeling°   *since / skill*
245   Have made you maister of the field this day,
Your fortune maister eke with governing,
And well begun end all so well, I pray,⁴
Ne let that wicked woman scape° away;   *escape*
For she it is, that did my Lord bethrall,°   *seduce, enslave*
250   My dearest Lord, and deepe in dongeon lay,
Where he his better dayes hath wasted all.
O heare, how piteous he to you for ayd does call.

29

Forthwith he gave in charge unto his Squire,
That scarlot whore to keepen carefully;
255   Whiles he himselfe with greedie° great desire   *eager*
Into the Castle entred forcibly,
Where living creature none he did espye;
Then gan he lowdly through the house to call:
But no man car'd to answere to his crye.
260   There raignd a solemne silence over all,
Nor voice was heard, nor wight was seene in bowre or hall.

30

At last with creeping crooked pace forth came
An old old man, with beard as white as snow,
That on a staffe his feeble steps did frame,°   *support*

3. What Una cannot completely repay, God will repay with interest. Unlike Duessa, who offers herself as a mistress to those who are victorious in battle, Una, a virgin, can offer only her loyalty and service. She goes on to call on God to restore her champions to a state of grace, with "merites" referring to all that was lost through the Fall of humankind.

4. I.e., while the heavens and skill have made you the "maister of the field this day," now you must also master your fortune through governance, and I pray that what has begun well will also end well.

265 And guide his wearie gate° both too and fro: steps
     For his eye sight him failed long ygo,°   ago
     And on his arme a bounch of keyes he bore,
     The which unused rust did overgrow:
     Those were the keyes of every inner dore,
270 But he could not them use, but kept them still in store.°   handy

                              31
     But very uncouth° sight was to behold,   strange
     How he did fashion his untoward° pace,   awkward
     For as he forward moov'd his footing old,
     So backward still was turnd his wrincled face,
275 Unlike to men, who ever as they trace,
     Both feet and face one way are wont to lead.[5]
     This was the auncient keeper of that place,
     And foster father of the Gyant dead;
     His name Ignaro did his nature right aread.

                              32
280 His reverend haires and holy grauitie
     The knight much honord, as beseemed well,[6]
     And gently askt, where all the people bee,
     Which in that stately building wont° to dwell.   accustomed
     Who answerd him full soft, he could not tell.
285 Againe he askt, where that same knight was layd,
     Whom great Orgoglio with his puissaunce fell°   deadly strength
     Had made his caytive thrall;° againe he sayde,   wretched prisoner
     He could not tell: ne ever other answere made.

                              33
     Then asked he, which way he in might pas:°   enter
290 He could not tell, againe he answered.
     Thereat the curteous knight displeased was,
     And said, Old sire, it seemes thou hast not red°   perceived
     How ill it sits° with that same silver hed   unsuitable
     In vaine to mocke, or mockt in vaine to bee:
295 But if thou be, as thou art pourtrahed
     With natures pen, in ages grave degree,
     Aread° in graver wise, what I demaund of thee.[7]   declare

                              34
     His answere likewise was, he could not tell.
     Whose sencelesse speach, and doted° ignorance   stupid
300 When as the noble Prince had marked well,
     He ghest° his nature by his countenance,°   guessed / behavior
     And calmd his wrath with goodly temperance.

---

5. The steward and doorkeeper of Orgoglio's castle, Ignaro (Ignorance), walks forward but keeps his face turned backward, unlike humans, who look where they go.
6. Arthur treats Ignaro with the respect that his appearance of advanced age warrants.
7. I.e., if you are as old and wise as you appear, respond more seriously to what I ask of you.

Then to him stepping, from his arme did reach
Those keyes, and made himselfe free enterance.
305   Each dore he opened without any breach;°   *breaking in*
There was no barre to stop, nor foe him to empeach.°   *hinder*

35

There all within full rich arayd he found,
With royall arras and resplendent gold.
And did with store of every thing abound,
310   That greatest Princes presence might behold.[8]
But all the floore (too filthy to be told)
With bloud of guiltlesse babes, and innocents trew,
Which there were slaine, as sheepe out of the fold,
Defiled was, that dreadfull was to vew,
315   And sacred ashes[9] over it was strowed new.°   *newly scattered*

36

And there beside of marble stone was built
An Altare, carv'd with cunning imagery,
On which true Christians bloud was often spilt,
And holy Martyrs often doen to dye,
320   With cruell malice and strong tyranny:
Whose blessed sprites from underneath the stone
To God for vengeance cryde continually,
And with great griefe were often heard to grone,
That hardest heart would bleede, to heare their piteous mone.

37

325   Through every rowme he sought, and every bowr,
But no where could he find that wofull thrall:°   *Redcrosse Knight*
At last he came unto an yron doore,
That fast was lockt, but key found not at all
Emongst that bounch, to open it withall;
330   But in the same a little grate was pight,°   *placed*
Through which he sent his voyce, and lowd did call
With all his powre, to weet, if living wight
Were housed therewithin, whom he enlargen° might.   *release*

38

Therewith an hollow, dreary, murmuring voyce
335   These piteous plaints and dolours° did resound;   *laments*
O who is that, which brings me happy choyce
Of death, that here lye dying every stound,°   *moment*
Yet live perforce° in balefull° darkenesse bound?   *constrained / wretched*
For now three Moones have changed thrice their hew,°   *shape*
340   And have beene thrice hid underneath the ground,

---

8. The castle is equipped with everything worthy of the greatest prince.
9. The ashes of martyred saints used here to soak up the blood of innocent Christians. The newly strewn ashes appear to be evidence of a recently performed pagan ritual, as is suggested by the altar in the next stanza.

Since I the heavens chearefull face did vew,
O welcome thou, that doest of death bring tydings trew.[1]

39

Which when that Champion heard, with percing point
    Of pitty deare his hart was thrilled° sore,   *pierced*
345   And trembling horrour ran through every joynt,
    For ruth of gentle knight so fowle forlore:°   *forlorn*
    Which shaking off, he rent that yron dore,
    With furious force, and indignation fell;°   *deadly*
    Where entred in, his foot could find no flore,
350   But all a deepe descent, as darke as hell,
That breathed ever forth a filthie banefull° smell.   *poisonous*

40

But neither darkenesse fowle, nor filthy bands,
    Nor noyous° smell his purpose could withhold,   *noxious*
    (Entire affection hateth nicer hands)[2]
355   But that with constant zeale, and courage bold,
    After long paines and labours manifold,
    He found the meanes that Prisoner up to reare;[3]
    Whose feeble thighes, unhable° to uphold   *unable*
    His pined corse,° him scarse to light could beare,   *wasted body*
360 A ruefull spectacle of death and ghastly drere.°   *misery*

41

His sad dull eyes deepe sunck in hollow pits,
    Could not endure th'unwonted° sunne to view;   *unaccustomed*
    His bare thin cheekes for want° of better bits,°   *lack / food*
    And empty sides deceived° of their dew,   *deprived*
365   Could make a stony hart his hap° to rew;   *situation*
    His rawbone° armes, whose mighty brawned bowrs°   *thin / brawny muscles*
    Were wont to rive steele plates, and helmets hew,
    Were cleane consum'd, and all his vitall powres
Decayd, and all his flesh shronk up like withered flowres.

42

370 Whom when his Lady saw,[4] to him she ran
    With hasty joy: to see him made her glad,
    And sad to view his visage pale and wan,°   *thin*
    Who earst in flowres of freshest youth was clad.°   *dressed*
    Tho when her well of teares she wasted had,
375   She said, Ah dearest Lord, what evill starre
    On you hath found, and pourd his influence bad,[5]

1. Three moons have changed their shape three times; in other words, nine months have passed. The voice they hear rings with despair, wishing for death rather than rescue or salvation.
2. A perfect love disdains great fastidiousness; Prince Arthur could overlook the filth of Orgoglio's prison because he cares so much for the Redcrosse Knight.
3. The Prisoner's legs are too weak to hold him up, so Arthur has to lift him out of the dungeon. The "light" is also a reference to Una.
4. Una recognizes the Prisoner as the Redcrosse Knight.
5. The Redcrosse Knight has ended up in the dungeon through his own folly; however, Una insists here that it must have been an "evill starre," i.e., misfortune, that was responsible for his imprisonment.

That of your selfe ye thus berobbed arre,
And this misseeming hew° your manly looks doth marre?   *appearance*

43

But welcome now my Lord, in wele° or woe,   *prosperity*
380   Whose presence I have lackt too long a day;
And fie° on Fortune mine avowed foe,   *shame*
Whose wrathfull wreakes° them selves do now alay.°   *vengeances / abate*
And for these wrongs shall treble penaunce° pay   *penance*
Of treble good: good growes of evils priefe.°   *trial*
385   The chearelesse man, whom sorrow did dismay,°   *overcome*
Had no delight to treaten° of his griefe;   *tell*
His long endured famine needed more reliefe.

44

Faire Lady, then said that victorious knight,
The things, that grievous were to do, or beare,
390   Them to renew,° I wote, breeds no delight;   *repeat*
Best musicke breeds delight in loathing eare:
But th'onely good, that growes of passed feare,
Is to be wise, and ware° of like agein.   *wary*
This dayes ensample° hath this lesson deare°   *example / dire*
395   Deepe written in my heart with yron pen,
That blisse may not abide in state of mortall men.

45

Henceforth sir knight, take to you wonted strength,
And maister these mishaps° with patient might;   *misfortunes*
Loe where your foe lyes stretcht in monstrous length,
400   And loe that wicked woman in your sight,
The roote of all your care,° and wretched plight,   *trouble*
Now in your powre, to let her live, or dye.
To do her dye (quoth Una) were despight,°   *malice*
And shame t'avenge so weake an enimy;
405   But spoile her of her scarlot robe, and let her fly.[6]

46

So as she bad,° that witch they disaraid,°   *commanded / undressed*
And robd of royall robes, and purple pall,°   *cloak*
And ornaments that richly were displaid;
Ne spared they to strip her naked all.
410   Then when they had despoild her tire and call,°   *attire and headdress*
Such as she was, their eyes might her behold,
That her misshaped parts did them appall,
A loathly, wrinckled hag, ill favoured, old,
Whose secret filth good manners biddeth not be told.

6. Like Christ, who seeks to destroy the works of the devil rather than the devil himself (1 John 3.8), Una seeks to destroy
Duessa's ability to do evil.

47

415   Her craftie head was altogether bald,
         And as in hate of honorable eld,[7]
         Was overgrowne with scurfe° and filthy scald;[8]   *scabs*
         Her teeth out of her rotten gummes were feld,°   *fallen*
         And her sowre breath abhominably smeld;
420   Her dried dugs,° like bladders lacking wind,   *breasts*
         Hong downe, and filthy matter from them weld;°   *oozed*
         Her wrizled° skin as rough, as maple rind,[9]   *wrinkled*
So scabby was, that would have loathd all womankind.

48

         Her neather° parts, the shame of all her kind,   *lower*
425   My chaster Muse for shame doth blush to write;
         But at her rompe° she growing had behind   *rump*
         A foxes taile, with dong all fowly dight;
         And eke her feete most monstrous were in sight;
         For one of them was like an Eagles claw,
430   With griping talaunts° armd to greedy fight,   *talons*
         The other like a Beares uneven° paw: *rough*
More ugly shape yet never living creature saw

49

         Which when the knights beheld, amazd they were,
         And wondred at so fowle deformed wight.
435   Such then (said Una) as she seemeth here,
         Such is the face of falshood, such the sight
         Of fowle Duessa, when her borrowed light
         Is laid away, and counterfesaunce° knowne.   *falsity*
         Thus when they had the witch disrobed quight,
440   And all her filthy feature° open showne,   *body*
They let her goe at will, and wander wayes unknowne.

50

         She flying fast from heavens hated face,
         And from the world that her discovered wide,
         Fled to the wastfull° wildernesse apace,   *desolate*
445   From living eyes her open shame to hide,
         And lurkt in rocks and caves long unespide.
         But that faire crew of knights, and Una faire
         Did in that castle afterwards abide,
         To rest them selves, and weary powres repaire,
450   Where store° they found of all, that dainty was and rare.   *supplies*

7. I.e., Duessa's ugly head is a hateful mockery of old people whose baldness is usually a sign of honorable "eld" or
old age.
8. Scall, a disease that causes scabs to form on the scalp.

9. Maples were often thought to be hard on the outside
but rotten inside. Duessa's diseased appearance also suggests syphilis.

Canto 9

His loves and lignage Arthur tells:
The knights knit friendly bands:
Sir Trevisan flies from Despayre,
Whom Redcrosse knight withstands.

1

O Goodly golden chaine, wherewith yfere°   *together*
   The vertues linked are in lovely wize:
   And noble minds of yore allyed were,
   In brave poursuit of chevalrous emprize,°   *adventure*
5   That none did others safety despize,°   *disregard*
   Nor aid envy to him, in need that stands,
   But friendly each did others prayse devize
   How to advaunce with favourable hands,
As this good Prince redeemd the Redcrosse knight from bands.°   *captivity*

2

10 Who when their powres, empaird° through labour long,   *weakened*
   With dew° repast they had recured° well,   *suitable / recovered*
   And that weake captive wight now wexed° strong,   *grown*
   Them list no lenger there at leasure dwell,
   But forward fare, as their adventures fell,
15 But ere they parted, Una faire besought
   That straunger knight his name and nation tell;
   Least so great good, as he for her had wrought,
Should die unknown, and buried be in thanklesse thought.

3

Faire virgin (said the Prince) ye me require
20 A thing without the compas of my wit:[1]
   For both the lignage° and the certain Sire,   *lineage*
   From which I sprong, from me are hidden yit.
   For all so soone as life did me admit
   Into this world, and shewed heavens light,
25 From mothers pap° I taken was unfit: *breast*
   And streight delivered to a Faery knight,
To be upbrought in gentle thewes° and martiall might.   *manners*

4

Unto old Timon[2] he me brought bylive,°   *immediately*
   Old Timon, who in youthly yeares hath beene
30 In warlike feates th'expertest man alive,
   And is the wisest now on earth I weene;°   *believe*
   His dwelling is low in a valley greene,
   Under the foot of Rauran[3] mossy hore,

---

1. I.e., your question is beyond my ability to answer.   3. A hill in Wales, hoary with moss.
2. Honor (Greek).

From whence the river Dee[4] as silver cleene
His tombling billowes rolls with gentle rore:
There all my dayes he traind me up in vertuous lore.

5

Thither the great Magicien Merlin came,
As was his use,° ofttimes to visit me: *custom*
For he had charge my discipline to frame,[5]
And Tutours nouriture to oversee.
Him oft and oft I askt in privitie,°   *privately*
Of what loines and what lignage I did spring:
Whose aunswere bad me still assured bee,
That I was sonne and heire unto a king,
As time in her just terme° the truth to light should bring.   *due course*

6

Well worthy impe,° said then the Lady gent,°   *offspring / noble*
And Pupill fit for such a Tutours hand.
But what adventure, or what high intent
Hath brought you hither into Faery land,
Aread° Prince Arthur, crowne of Martiall band?[6]   *declare*
Full hard it is (quoth he) to read aright
The course of heavenly cause, or understand
The secret meaning of th'eternall might,
That rules mens wayes, and rules the thoughts of living wight.

7

For whither° he through fatall deepe foresight   *whether*
Me hither sent, for cause to me unghest,°   *unguessed*
Or that fresh bleeding wound, which day and night
Whilome° doth rancle in my riven° brest,   *constantly / wounded*
With forced° fury following his behest,°   *forceful / command*
Me hither brought by wayes yet never found,
You to have helpt I hold my selfe yet blest.
Ah curteous knight (quoth she) what secret wound
Could ever find, to grieve the gentlest hart on ground?[7]

8

Deare Dame (quoth he) you sleeping sparkes awake,
Which troubled once, into huge flames will grow,[8]
Ne ever will their fervent fury slake,°   *cease*
Till living moysture[9] into smoke do flow,
And wasted life do lye in ashes low.
Yet sithens° silence lesseneth not my fire,   *since*

---

4. A river marking the boundary between England and Wales.
5. Merlin was in charge of Arthur's education and made sure Arthur's tutor was properly recompensed.
6. Although Arthur does not declare his name, Una is able to recognize him.
7. I.e., what injury could ever find a way to hurt the gentlest

heart "on ground" (in the world)?
8. Prince Arthur addresses Una; she reminds him of his hidden pain, which once reawakened will continue to grow.
9. A reference to the Renaissance medical theory of the humors that compose the human body.

70   But told it flames, and hidden it does glow,
      I will revele, what ye so much desire:
      Ah Love, lay downe thy bow,[1] the whiles I may respire.°   breathe

                              9
      It was in freshest flowre of youthly yeares,
        When courage first does creepe in manly chest,
75   Then first the coale of kindly heat appeares
        To kindle love in every living brest;
      But me had warnd old Timons wise behest,°   warning
        Those creeping flames° by reason to subdew,   of love
        Before their rage grew to so great unrest,
80   As miserable lovers use to rew,
      Which still wex old in woe, whiles woe still wexeth new.[2]

                              10
      That idle name of love, and lovers life,
        As losse of time, and vertues enimy
      I ever scornd, and joyd to stirre up strife,
85   In middest of° their mournfull Tragedy,   in the midst of
        Ay wont to laugh, when them I heard to cry,
      And blow the fire, which them to ashes brent:°   burned
        Their God himselfe,° griev'd at my libertie,   Cupid
        Shot many a dart at me with fiers intent,
90   But I them warded all with wary government.°   cautious self-control

                              11
      But all in vaine: no fort can be so strong,
        Ne fleshly brest can armed be so sound,°   completely
      But will at last be wonne with battrie° long,   battery
        Or unawares at disavantage found;[3]
95   Nothing is sure, that growes on earthly ground:
        And who most trustes in arme of fleshly might,
      And boasts, in beauties chaine not to be bound,
        Doth soonest fall in disaventrous° fight,   unfortunate
      And yeeldes his caytive° neck to victours most despight.°   servile / malice

                              12
100   Ensampel° make of him your haplesse joy,   example
        And of my selfe now mated,° as ye see;   checked
      Whose prouder vaunt° that proud avenging boy   boast
        Did soone pluck downe, and curbd my libertie.
        For on a day prickt forth with jollitie
105   Of looser life, and heat of hardiment,[4]
        Raunging the forest wide on courser° free,   horse
        The fields, the floods, the heavens with one consent
        Did seeme to laugh on me, and favour mine intent.

1. Cupid shoots arrows of love at people and causes them
to fall in love with the first person they see.
2. Sorrow makes lovers grow old while their sorrow remains forever young.

3. No fort is so strong, or flesh so well protected, that it
cannot be overcome by continual battering.
4. I.e., inspired by the joy of a life of freedom and the heat
of boldness.

13

For-wearied° with my sports, I did alight   *tired*
110   From loftie steed, and downe to sleepe me layd;
         The verdant° gras my couch did goodly dight,°   *green / adorn*
         And pillow was my helmet faire displayd:
         Whiles every sence the humour° sweet embayd,°   *dew of sleep / bathed*
         And slombring soft my hart did steale away,
115   Me seemed,° by my side a royall Mayd   *it seemed to me*
         Her daintie limbes full softly down did lay:
So faire a creature yet saw never sunny day.

14

Most goodly glee° and lovely blandishment   *entertainment*
         She to me made, and bad me love her deare,
120   For dearely sure her love was to me bent,
         As when just time expired should appeare.[5]
         But whether dreames delude, or true it were,
         Was never hart so ravisht with delight,
         Ne living man like° words did ever heare,   *similar*
125   As she to me delivered all that night;
And at her parting said, She Queene of Faeries hight.°   *was called*

15

When I awoke, and found her place devoyd,°   *empty*
         And nought° but pressed gras, where she had lyen,°   *nothing / lain*
         I sorrowed all so much, as earst° I joyd,   *at first*
130   And washed all her place with watry eyen.
         From that day forth I lov'd that face divine;
         From that day forth I cast° in carefull mind,   *resolved*
         To seeke her out with labour, and long tyne,°   *suffering*
         And never vow to rest, till her I find,
135 Nine monethes I seeke in vaine yet ni'll° that vow unbind.   *never will*

16

Thus as he spake, his visage wexed pale,
         And chaunge of hew great passion did bewray;°   *betray*
         Yet still he strove to cloke his inward bale,°   *sorrow*
         And hide the smoke, that did his fire display,
140   Till gentle Una thus to him gan° say;   *did*
         O happy Queene of Faeries, that hast found
         Mongst many, one that with his prowesse may
         Defend thine honour, and thy foes confound:
True Loves are often sown, but seldom grow on ground.°   *on this earth*

17

145   Thine, O then, said the gentle Redcrosse knight,
         Next to that Ladies love, shalbe the place,
         O fairest virgin, full of heavenly light,
         Whose wondrous faith, exceeding earthly race,°   *people*

---

5. Her love was directed as it would appear in the due course of time. Arthur's dream is both lifelike and prophetic.

Was firmest fixt in mine extremest case.
150 And you, my Lord, the Patrone° of my life,   *protector*
Of that great Queene may well gaine worthy grace:
For onely worthy you through prowes priefe[6]
If living man mote° worthy be, to be her liefe.°   *might / beloved*

18

So diversly° discoursing of their loves,   *variously*
155 The golden Sunne his glistring head gan shew,
And sad remembraunce now the Prince amoves,°   *compels*
With fresh desire his voyage to pursew:
Als Una earnd her traveill° to renew.   *quest*
Then those two knights, fast° friendship for to bynd, *firm*
160 And love establish each to other trew,
Gave goodly gifts, the signes of gratefull mynd,
And eke° as pledges firme, right hands together joynd. *also*

19

Prince Arthur gave a boxe of Diamond sure,
Embowd° with gold and gorgeous ornament,   *encircled*
165 Wherein were closd few drops of liquor pure,[7]
Of wondrous worth, and vertue excellent,
That any wound could heale incontinent:°   *immediately*
Which to requite, the Redcrosse knight him gave
A booke, wherein his Saveours testament°   *the Gospels*
170 Was writ with golden letters rich and brave;
A worke of wondrous grace, and able soules to save.

20

Thus beene they parted, Arthur on his way
To seeke his love, and th'other for to fight
With Unaes foe, that all her realme did pray.°   *molest*
175 But she now weighing the decayed plight,
And shrunken synewes of her chosen knight,
Would not a while her forward course pursew,
Ne bring him forth in face of dreadfull fight,
Till he recovered had his former hew:
180 For him to be yet weake and wearie well she knew.

21

So as they traveild, lo they gan espy
An armed knight towards them gallop fast,
That seemed from some feared foe to fly,
Or other griesly thing, that him agast.
185 Still as he fled, his eye was backward cast,
As if his feare still followed him behind;
Als flew his steed, as he his bands had brast,°   *burst*

6. The test of your valor shows that you are the only one   7. The blood of Christ, the wine of the Eucharist.
worthy of her grace.

And with his winged heeles did tread the wind,
As he had beene a fole° of Pegasus[8] his kind.   *foal*

22

190 Nigh as he drew, they might perceive his head
     To be unarmd, and curld uncombed heares
     Upstaring° stiffe, dismayd with uncouth° dread;   *standing / unknown*
     Nor drop of bloud in all his face appeares
     Nor life in limbe: and to increase his feares,
195 In fowle reproch of knighthoods faire degree,
     About his neck an hempen rope he weares,
     That with his glistring armes° does ill agree;   *armor*
But he of rope or armes has now no memoree.

23

     The Redcrosse knight toward him crossed fast,
200 To weet,° what mister° wight was so dismayd: *know / manner of*
     There him he finds all sencelesse and aghast,
     That of him selfe he seemd to be afrayd;
     Whom hardly he from flying forward stayd,[9]
     Till he these wordes to him deliver might;
205 Sir knight, aread who hath ye thus arayd,°   *clothed*
     And eke from whom make ye this hasty flight:
For never knight I saw in such misseeming° plight.   *unseemly*

24

     He answerd nought° at all, but adding new   *not*
     Feare to his first amazment, staring wide
210 With stony° eyes, and hartlesse hollow hew,   *staring*
     Astonisht stood, as one that had aspide
     Infernall furies, with their chaines untide.
     Him yet againe, and yet againe bespake
     The gentle knight; who nought to him replide,
215 But trembling every joynt did inly quake,
And foltring° tongue at last these words seemd forth to shake.   *stammering*

25

     For Gods deare love, Sir knight, do me not stay;°   *detain*
     For loe° he comes, he comes fast after mee.   *here*
     Eft° looking backe would faine° have runne away;   *again / rather*
220 But he him forst to stay, and tellen free°   *freely tell*
     The secret cause of his perplexitie:
     Yet nathemore° by his bold hartie speach,   *not at all*
     Could his bloud-frosen hart emboldned bee,[1]
     But through his boldnesse rather feare did reach,
225 Yet forst, at last he made through silence suddein breach.°   *break*

---

8. A winged horse, belonging to the mythological hero
Perseus.
9. The Redcrosse Knight could hardly keep the frightened knight (earlier identified as Sir Trevisan) from
trying to flee.
1. The Redcrosse Knight's bold words do not encourage
Sir Trevisan; in the end, however, the Redcrosse Knight
forces him to speak.

26

And am I now in safetie sure (quoth he)
  From him, that would have forced me to dye?
  And is the point of death now turnd fro° mee,   *from*
  That I may tell this haplesse° history?   *unlucky*
230 Feare nought: (quoth he) no daunger now is nye.
  Then shall I you recount a ruefull cace,°   *sad situation*
  (Said he) the which with this unlucky eye
  I late beheld, and had not greater grace
Me reft° from it, had bene partaker of the place.[2]   *torn*

27

235 I lately chaunst (Would I had never chaunst)
  With a faire knight to keepen companee,
  Sir Terwin hight, that well himselfe advaunst
  In all affaires, and was both bold and free,
  But not so happie as mote happie bee:
240 He lov'd, as was his lot, a Ladie gent,°   *gentle*
  That him againe° lov'd in the least degree: *in return*
  For she was proud, and of too high intent,°   *ambition*
And joyd to see her lover languish and lament.

28

From whom° returning sad and comfortlesse,   *Terwin's lady*
245 As on the way together we did fare,°   *travel*
  We met that villen (God from him me blesse)
  That cursed wight, from whom I scapt° whyleare,° *escaped / earlier*
  A man of hell, that cals himselfe Despaire:
  Who first us greets, and after faire areedes°   *tells*
250 Of tydings strange, and of adventures rare:
  So creeping close, as Snake in hidden weedes,
Inquireth of our states, and of our knightly deedes.

29

Which when he knew, and felt our feeble harts
  Embost° with bale,° and bitter byting griefe,   *encrusted / sorrow*
255 Which love had launched with his deadly darts,
  With wounding words and termes of foule repriefe°   *scorn*
  He pluckt from us all hope of due reliefe,
  That earst° us held in love of lingring life;   *recently*
  Then hopelesse hartlesse, gan the cunning thiefe
260 Perswade us die, to stint° all further strife: *stop*
To me he lent this rope, to him a rustie knife.

30

With which sad instrument of hastie death,
  That wofull lover, loathing lenger° light,   *longer*
  A wide way° made to let forth living breath.   *cut*
265 But I more fearefull, or more luckie wight,°   *creature*

2. Had not greater grace torn me from the unfortunate events I beheld, I would have been a victim of those events myself.

Dismayd with that deformed dismall sight,
Fled fast away, halfe dead with dying feare:°   *fear of dying*
Ne yet assur'd of life by you, Sir knight,
Whose like infirmitie like chaunce may beare:
270   But God you never let his charmed speeches heare.[3]

31

How may a man (said he) with idle speach
Be wonne,° to spoyle the Castle of his health?   *convinced*
I wote° (quoth he) whom triall late did teach,   *would not*
That like would not for all this worldes wealth:[4]
275   His subtill tongue, like dropping honny, mealt'th°   *melteth*
Into the hart, and searcheth every vaine,
That ere° one be aware, by secret stealth   *before*
His powre is reft,° and weaknesse doth remaine.   *broken*
O never Sir desire to try° his guilefull traine.°   *test / trickery*

32

280   Certes° (said he) hence shall I never rest,   *indeed*
Till I that treachours° art have heard and tride;°   *traitor's / tested*
And you Sir knight, whose name mote I request,
Of grace do me unto his cabin° guide.   *cave*
I that hight° Trevisan (quoth he) will ride   *am called*
285   Against my liking backe, to doe you grace:°   *a favor*
But nor for gold nor glee will I abide
By you, when ye arrive in that same place;
For lever° had I die, then° see his deadly face.   *rather / than*

33

Ere long they come, where that same wicked wight
290   His dwelling has, low in an hollow cave,
Farre underneath a craggie clift ypight,°   *pitched*
Darke, dolefull, drearie, like a greedie grave,
That still° for carrion carcases doth crave: *always*
On top whereof aye° dwelt the ghastly Owle,   *ever*
295   Shrieking his balefull° note, which ever drave   *sorrowful*
Farre from that haunt all other chearefull fowle;
And all about it wandring ghostes did waile and howle.

34

And all about old stockes and stubs of trees,
Whereon nor fruit, nor leafe was ever seene,
300   Did hang upon the ragged rocky knees;°   *hillsides*
On which had many wretches hanged beene,
Whose carcases were scattered on the greene,
And throwne about the cliffs. Arrived there,
That bare-head knight for dread and dolefull teene,°   *grief*

3. May God prevent you from hearing his seductive   4. I would not undergo such a test for all the wealth in
speeches.   the world.

305   Would faine have fled, ne durst° approchen neare,   *dared*
           But th'other forst him stay, and comforted in feare.

                                35
           That darkesome cave they enter, where they find
               That cursed man, low sitting on the ground,
               Musing full sadly in his sullein mind;
310   His griesie lockes, long growen, and unbound,
               Disordred hong about his shoulders round,
               And hid his face; through which his hollow eyne
               Lookt deadly dull, and stared as astound;
               His raw-bone cheekes through penurie° and pine,°   *poverty / starvation*
315   Were shronke into his jawes, as he did never dine.

                                36
           His garment nought but many ragged clouts,°   *rags*
               With thornes together pind and patched was,
               The which his naked sides he wrapt abouts;
               And him beside there lay upon the gras
320   A drearie° corse,° whose life away did pas,   *gory / body*
               All wallowd in his owne yet luke-warme blood,
               That from his wound yet welled fresh alas;
               In which a rustie knife fast fixed stood,
           And made an open passage for the gushing flood.

                                37
325   Which piteous spectacle, approving° trew   *proving*
               The wofull tale that Trevisan had told,
               When as the gentle Redcrosse knight did vew,
               With firie zeale he burnt in courage bold,
               Him to avenge, before his bloud were cold,
330   And to the villein said, Thou damned wight,
               The author of this fact, we here behold,
               What justice can but judge against thee right,
           With thine owne bloud to price° his bloud, here shed in sight?   *pay for*

                                38
           What franticke fit (quoth he) hath thus distraught
335   Thee, foolish man, so rash a doome° to give?   *judgment*
               What justice ever other judgement taught,
               But he should die, who merites not to live?
               None° else to death this man despayring drive,°   *nothing / drove*
               But his owne guiltie mind deserving death.
340   Is then unjust to each his due to give?
               Or let him die, that loatheth living breath?
           Or let him die at ease, that liveth here uneath?°   *unhappily*

                                39
           Who travels by the wearie wandring way,
               To come unto his wished home in haste,
345   And meetes a flood, that doth his passage stay,

Is not great grace to helpe him over past,
Or free his feet, that in the myre sticke fast?
Most envious man, that grieves at neighbours good,
And fond,° that joyest in the woe thou hast,   *foolish*
350 Why wilt not let him passe, that long hath stood
Upon the banke, yet wilt thy selfe not passe the flood?

40

He there does now enjoy eternall rest
And happie ease, which thou doest want and crave,
And further from it daily wanderest:
355 What if some litle paine the passage have,
That makes fraile flesh to feare the bitter wave?
Is not short paine well borne, that brings long ease,
And layes the soule to sleepe in quiet grave?
Sleepe after toyle, port after stormie seas,
360 Ease after warre, death after life does greatly please.

41

The knight much wondred at his suddeine wit,
And said, The terme of life is limited,
Ne may a man prolong, nor shorten it;
The souldier may not move from watchfull sted,°   *post*
365 Nor leave his stand, untill his Captaine bed.°   *command*
Who life did limit by almightie doome,
(Quoth he) knowes best the termes established;
And he, that points the Centonell his roome,
Doth license him depart at sound of morning droome.°   *drum*

42

370 Is not his deed, what ever thing is donne,
In heaven and earth? did not he all create
To die againe? all ends that was begonne.
Their times in his eternall booke of fate
Are written sure, and have their certaine date.
375 Who then can strive with strong necessitie,
That holds the world in his still chaunging state,
Or shunne the death ordaynd by destinie?
When houre of death is come, let none aske whence, nor why.

43

The lenger life, I wote the greater sin,[5]
380 The greater sin, the greater punishment:
All those great battels, which thou boasts to win,
Through strife, and bloud-shed, and avengement,
Now praysd, hereafter deare° thou shalt repent: *dearly*
For life must life, and bloud must bloud repay.
385 Is not enough thy evill life forespent?°   *wasted*

5. The longer the life, the greater the sin.

For he, that once hath missed the right way,
The further he doth goe, the further he doth stray.

44

Then do no further goe, no further stray,
   But here lie downe, and to thy rest betake,
390   Th'ill° to prevent, that life ensewen° may.   *evil / continue*
   For what hath life, that may it loved make,
   And gives not rather cause it to forsake?°   *leave*
   Feare, sicknesse, age, losse, labour, sorrow, strife,
   Paine, hunger, cold, that makes the hart to quake;
395   And ever fickle fortune rageth rife
All which, and thousands mo° do make a loathsome life.   *more*

45

Thou wretched man, of death hast greatest need,
   If in true ballance thou wilt weigh thy state:°   *condition*
   For never knight, that dared warlike deede,
400   More lucklesse disaventures did amate:°   *meet*
   Witnesse the dongeon deepe, wherein of late
   Thy life shut up, for death so oft did call;
   And though good lucke prolonged hath thy date,
   Yet death then, would the like mishaps forestall,
405 Into the which hereafter thou maiest happen fall.[6]

46

Why then doest thou, O man of sin, desire
   To draw thy dayes forth to their last degree?
   Is not the measure of thy sinfull hire°   *employment*
   High heaped up with huge iniquitie,°   *sinfulness*
410   Against the day of wrath, to burden thee?
   Is not enough, that to this Ladie milde
   Thou falsed° hast thy faith with perjurie,   *violated*
   And sold thy selfe to serve Duessa vilde,°   *vile*
With whom in all abuse thou hast thy selfe defilde?

47

415 Is not he just, that all this doth behold
   From highest heaven, and beares an equall eye?
   Shall he thy sins up in his knowledge fold,
   And guiltie be of thine impietie?
   Is not his law, Let every sinner die:
420   Die shall all flesh? what then must needs be donne,
   Is it not better to doe willinglie,
   Then° linger, till the glasse be all out ronne?   *than*
Death is the end of woes: die soone, O faeries sonne.

---

6. If death had come when you called for it, then the misfortunes that await you might have been prevented.

48

The knight was much enmoved° with his speach,   *moved*
425   That as a swords point through his hard did perse,°   *pierce*
And in his conscience made a secret breach,⁷
Well knowing true all, that he did reherse,
And to his fresh remembrance did reverse°   *recall*
The ugly vew of his deformed crimes,
430   That all his manly powres it did disperse,
As° he were charmed with inchaunted rimes,   *as if*
That oftentimes he quakt, and fainted oftentimes.

49

In which amazement, when the Miscreant°   *misbeliever (Despair)*
Perceived him to waver weake and fraile,
435   Whiles trembling horror did his conscience dant,°   *overcome*
And hellish anguish did his soule assaile,
To drive him to despaire, and quite to quaile,
He shew'd him painted in a table° plaine,°   *picture / clearly*
The damned ghosts, that doe in torments waile,
440   And thousand feends that doe them endlesse paine
With fire and brimstone, which for ever shall remaine.

50

The sight whereof so throughly him dismaid,
That nought° but death before his eyes he saw,   *nothing*
And ever burning wrath before him laid,
445   By righteous sentence of th'Almighties law:
Then gan the villein him to overcraw,°   *triumph over*
And brought unto him swords, ropes, poison, fire,
And all that might him to perdition draw;
And bad him choose, what death he would desire:
450   For death was due to him, that had provokt Gods ire.

51

But when as none of them he saw him take,
He to him raught° a dagger sharpe and keene,   *handed*
And gave it him in hand: his hand did quake,
And tremble like a leafe of Aspin greene,
455   And troubled bloud through his pale face was seene
To come, and goe with tydings from the hart,
As it a running messenger had beene.
At last resolv'd to worke his finall smart,°   *pain*
He lifted up his hand, that backe againe did start.

52

460   Which when as Una saw, through every vaine
The crudled cold ran to her well of life,°   *her heart*
As in a swowne: but soone reliv'd° againe,   *revived*

7. Despair's words disrupt the Redcrosse Knight's inner knowledge of God's grace.

Out of his hand she snatcht the cursed knife,
And threw it to the ground, enraged rife,°   *uncontrollably*
465   And to him said, Fie, fie,° faint harted knight,   *shame*
What meanest thou by this reprochfull strife?
Is this the battell, which thou vauntst° to fight   *boast*
With that fire-mouthed Dragon, horrible and bright?

53

Come, come away, fraile, feeble, fleshly wight,
470   Ne let vaine words bewitch thy manly hart,
Ne divelish thoughts dismay thy constant spright.
In heavenly mercies hast thou not a part?
Why shouldst thou then despeire, that chosen art?
Where justice growes, there grows eke greater grace,
475   The which doth quench the brond of hellish smart,
And that accurst hand-writing doth deface.[8]
Arise, Sir knight arise, and leave this cursed place.

54

So up he rose, and thence amounted streight.°   *immediately*
Which when the carle° beheld, and saw his guest   *villain*
480   Would safe depart, for all his subtill sleight,°   *trickery*
He chose an halter° from among the rest,   *noose*
And with it hung himselfe, unbid unblest.
But death he could not worke himselfe thereby;
For thousand times he so himselfe had drest,
485   Yet nathelesse° it could not doe° him die,   *nevertheless / make*
Till he should die his last, that is eternally.

Canto 10

Her faithfull knight faire Una brings
to house of Holinesse,
Where he is taught repentance, and
the way to heavenly blesse.

1

What man is he, that boasts of fleshly might,
And vaine° assurance of mortality,   *empty*
Which all so soone, as it doth come to fight,
Against spirituall foes, yeelds by and by,
5   Or from the field most cowardly doth fly?
Ne let the man ascribe it to his skill,
That thorough° grace hath gained victory.   *through*
If any strength we have, it is to ill,
But all the good is Gods, both power and eke will.

8. Una alludes to heavenly grace and God's mercy toward repentent sinners—an allowance that Despair had omitted from his argument.

2

10 By that, which lately hapned, Una saw,
    That this her knight was feeble, and too faint;
    And all his sinews woxen° weake and raw,   *grown*
    Through long enprisonment, and hard constraint,
    Which he endured in his late restraint,
15 That yet he was unfit for bloudie fight:
    Therefore to cherish° him with diets daint,°   *nourish / dainty foods*
    She cast to bring him, where he chearen° might,   *be cheered*
Till he recovered had his late decayed plight.

3

There was an auntient° house not farre away,   *ancient*
20 Renowmd throughout the world for sacred lore,°   *wisdom*
    And pure unspotted life: so well they say
    It governd was, and guided evermore,
    Through wisedome of a matrone grave and hore;°   *venerable*
    Whose onely joy was to relieve the needes
25 Of wretched soules, and helpe the helpelesse pore:
    All night she spent in bidding of her bedes,°   *saying prayers*
And all the day in doing good and godly deedes.

4

Dame Caelia° men did her call, as thought   *heavenly*
    From heaven to come, or thither to arise,
30 The mother of three daughters, well upbrought
    In goodly thewes,° and godly exercise: *manners*
    The eldest two most sober, chast, and wise,
    Fidelia° and Speranza° virgins were,   *Faith / Hope*
    Though spousd, yet wanting wedlocks solemnize;[1]
35 But faire Charissa° to a lovely fere°   *Charity / loving husband*
Was lincked, and by him had many pledges° dere.   *children*

5

Arrived there, the dore they find fast° lockt;   *tightly*
    For it was warely° watched night and day,   *carefully*
    For feare of many foes: but when they knockt,
40 The Porter opened unto them streight way:°   *right away*
    He was an aged syre, all hory gray,
    With lookes full lowly cast,[2] and gate° full slow,   *pace*
    Wont on a staffe his feeble steps to stay,°   *support*
    Hight Humiltá.° They passe in stouping low;   *named Humility*
45 For streight and narrow was the way, which he did show.

6

Each goodly thing is hardest to begin,
    But entred in a spacious court they see,

---

1. Faith and Hope are each engaged to be married, but their marriages have not yet taken place. The implication is that Faith and Hope are not fulfilled in this life but will be fulfilled in the hereafter through God's promise of salvation.
2. The porter casts his eyes down in an expression of humility.

Both plaine, and pleasant to be walked in,
Where them does meete a francklin[3] faire and free,
50   And entertaines with comely° courteous glee,   *appropriate*
His name was Zele,[4] that him right well became,
For in his speeches and behaviour hee
Did labour lively to expresse the same,
And gladly did them guide, till to the Hall they came.

7

55   There fairely them receives a gentle Squire,
Of milde demeanure,° and rare courtesie,   *manner*
Right cleanly clad in comely sad attire;
In word and deede that shew'd great modestie,
And knew his good to all of each degree,[5]
60   Hight Reverence. He them with speeches meet
Does faire entreat; no courting nicetie,°   *flattery*
But simple true, and eke unfained° sweet,   *honest*
As might become a Squire so great persons to greet.

8

And afterwards them to his Dame he leades,
65   That aged Dame, the Ladie of the place:
Who all this while was busie at her beades:
Which doen,° she up arose with seemely grace,   *done*
And toward them full matronely did pace.°   *walk*
Where when that fairest Una she beheld,
70   Whom well she knew to spring from heavenly race,
Her hart with joy unwonted inly° sweld,   *inwardly*
As feeling wondrous comfort in her weaker eld.°   *age*

9

And her embracing said, O happie earth,
Whereon thy innocent feet doe ever tread,
75   Most vertuous virgin borne of heavenly berth,
That to redeeme thy woeful parents head,
From tyrans° rage, and ever-dying dread,   *tyrant's*
Hast wandred through the world now long a day;
Yet ceasest not thy wearie soles° to lead,   *feet, souls*
80   What grace hath thee now hither brought this way?
Or doen° thy feeble feet unweeting hither stray?   *do*

10

Strange thing it is an errant° knight to see   *wandering*
Here in this place, or any other wight,
That hither turnes his steps. So few there bee,
85   That chose the narrow path, or seeke the right:

---

3. A person who owns his own land and is therefore his own master.
4. The franklin's zeal or enthusiasm is an attribute of his Christian freedom.
5. He knows how to behave courteously toward members of each social rank.

All keepe the broad high way, and take delight
With many rather for to go astray,
And be partakers of their evill plight,
Then with a few to walke the rightest° way;   *righteous*
90 O foolish men, why haste ye to your owne decay?

11

Thy selfe to see, and tyred limbs to rest,
    O matrone sage° (quoth she) I hither came,   *wise*
And this good knight his way with me addrest,°   *directed*
Led with thy prayses and broad-blazed° fame,   *widely reported*
95 That up to heaven is blowne. The auncient Dame
Him goodly greeted in her modest guise,
And entertaynd them both, as best became,
With all the court'sies, that she could devise,°   *think of*
Ne wanted ought, to shew her bounteous° or wise.   *generous*

12

100 Thus as they gan of sundry things devise,
    Loe two most goodly virgins came in place,
Ylinked° arme in arme in lovely wise,[6]   *linked*
With countenance° demure,° and modest grace,   *expression / modest*
They numbred even steps and equall pace:
105 Of which the eldest, that Fidelia hight,
Like sunny beames threw from her Christall face,
That could have dazd the rash° beholders sight,   *foolish*
And round about her head did shine like heavens light.

13

She was araied° all in lilly white,   *dressed*
110 And in her right hand bore a cup of gold,[7]
With wine and water fild up to the hight,°   *brim*
In which a Serpent did himselfe enfold,°   *coil*
That horrour made to all, that did behold;
But she no whit° did chaunge her constant mood: *not a bit*
115 And in her other hand she fast° did hold   *tightly*
A booke, that was both signd and seald with blood,
Wherein darke things were writ, hard to be understood.

14

Her younger sister, that Speranza hight,°   *was called*
    Was clad in blew,[8] that her beseemed° well;   *suited*
120 Not all so chearefull seemed she of sight,
As was her sister; whether dread° did dwell,   *fear*
Or anguish in her hart, is hard to tell:

---

6. Faith and Hope enter the room harmoniously linked, unlike in the House of Pride, where the inhabitants are joined by a yoke of servitude.
7. The sacramental cup of the Holy Communion; it contains the healing blood and baptismal water that poured from Christ's wounds when he was crucified. The serpent here is a symbol of healing and redemption, and the book Fidelia holds is the New Testament, which is sealed with Christ's blood in the sense that Christ's crucifixion assures salvation for all humankind.
8. Blue is the color traditionally associated with the Virgin Mary.

Upon her arme a silver anchor lay,[9]
Whereon she leaned ever, as befell:°   *it happened*
125 And ever up to heaven, as she did pray,
Her stedfast eyes were bent, ne swarved° other way.   *turned*

15

They seeing Una, towards her gan wend,
Who them encounters° with like courtesie;   *greets*
Many kind speeches they betwene them spend,
130 And greatly joy each other well to see:
Then to the knight with shamefast° modestie   *humble*
They turne themselves, at Unaes meeke request,
And him salute with well beseeming glee;
Who faire them quites,° as him beseemed best,   *greets*
135 And goodly gan discourse° of many a noble gest.°   *speak / deed*

16

Then Una thus; But she your sister deare,
The deare Charissa where is she become?[1]
Or wants° she health, or busie is elsewhere?   *lacks*
Ah no, said they, but forth she may not come:
140 For she of late is lightned of her wombe,°   *recently gave birth*
And hath encreast° the world with one sonne more,   *increased*
That her to see should be but troublesome.
Indeede (quoth she) that should her trouble sore,
But thankt be God, and her encrease so evermore.[2]

17

145 Then said the aged Caelia, Deare dame,
And you good Sir, I wote° that of your toyle,   *believe*
And labours long, through which ye hither came,
Ye both forwearied° be: therefore a whyle   *tired*
I read you rest, and to your bowres recoyle.°   *retire*
150 Then called she a Groome, that forth him led
Into a goodly lodge, and gan despoile°   *remove*
Of puissant armes, and laid in easie bed;
His name was meeke Obedience rightfully ared.°   *understood*

18

Now when their wearie limbes with kindly rest,
155 And bodies were refresht with due repast,
Faire Una gan Fidelia faire request,
To have her knight into her schoolehouse plaste,
That of her heavenly learning he might taste,
And heare the wisedome of her words divine.
160 She graunted, and that knight so much agraste,°   *graced*
That she him taught celestiall discipline,
And opened his dull eyes, that light mote° in them shine. *might*

9. Cf. Hebrews 6.19: "which hope we have as an anchor of the soul, both sure and steadfast." Silver is a symbol of purity.
1. What has become of her?
2. May God give her more children.

19

    And that her sacred Booke, with bloud ywrit,°   *written*
      That none could read, except° she did them teach,   *unless*
165   She unto him disclosed every whit,°   *bit*
      And heavenly documents thereout did preach,
      That weaker wit of man could never reach,
      Of God, of grace, of justice, of free will,
      That wonder was to heare her goodly speach:
170   For she was able, with her words to kill,
    And raise againe to life the hart,[3] that she did thrill.°   *pierce*

20

    And when she list° poure out her larger spright,   *chose to*
      She would commaund the hastie Sunne to stay,°   *stop*
      Or backward turne his course from heavens hight;
175   Sometimes great hostes of men she could dismay,°   *defeat*
      Dry-shod to passe, she parts the flouds in tway;°   *two*
      And eke huge mountaines from their native seat
      She would commaund, themselves to beare away,
      And throw in raging sea with roaring threat.°   *threatening roar*
180 Almightie God her gave such powre, and puissance great.[4]

21

    The faithfull knight now grew in litle space,
      By hearing her, and by her sisters lore,
      To such perfection of all heavenly grace,
      That wretched world he gan for to abhore,
185   And mortall life gan loath,° as thing forlore,°   *despise / lost*
      Greev'd with remembrance of his wicked wayes,
      And prickt° with anguish of his sinnes so sore,   *wounded*
      That he desirde to end his wretched dayes:
    So much the dart of sinfull guilt the soule dismayes.°   *overwhelms*

22

190 But wise Speranza gave him comfort sweet,
      And taught him how to take assured hold
      Upon her silver anchor, as was meet;
      Else had his sinnes so great, and manifold
      Made him forget all that Fidelia told.
195   In this distressed doubtfull agonie,
      When him his dearest Una did behold,
      Disdeining life, desiring leave° to die,   *permission*
    She found her selfe assayld with great perplexitie.

23

    And came to Caelia to declare her smart,°   *pain*
200   Who well acquainted with that commune plight,

---

3. Cf. 2 Corinthians 3.6: "for the letter killeth, but the Spirit giveth life."
4. These miracles were attested in Scripture: stopping the sun, Joshua 10.12–13; turning back the sun, 2 Kings 20.10–11; defeating great hosts, Judges 1.21; parting the sea, Exodus 14.22; moving mountains, Matthew 21.21.

Which sinfull horror workes in wounded hart,
Her wisely comforted all that she might,
With goodly counsell and advisement° right;   *advice*
And streightway sent with carefull diligence,

205   To fetch a Leach,° the which had great insight   *doctor*
In that disease of grieved conscience,
And well could cure the same; His name was Patience.

24

Who comming to that soule-diseased knight,
Could hardly him intreat,° to tell his griefe:[5]   *convince*

210   Which knowne, and all that noyd° his heavie spright   *troubled*
Well searcht,° eftsoones he gan apply reliefe   *explored*
Of salves and med'cines, which had passing priefe,°   *surpassing efficacy*
And thereto added words of wondrous might:
By which to ease he him recured briefe,°   *quickly cured*

215   And much asswag'd° the passion° of his plight,   *soothed / suffering*
That he his paine endur'd, as seeming now more light.

25

But yet the cause and root of all his ill,
Inward corruption, and infected sin,
Not purg'd° nor heald, behind remained still,   *cleansed*

220   And festring sore did rankle yet within,
Close creeping twixt the marrow° and the skin.   *bone*
Which to extirpe,° he laid him privily°   *remove / privately*
Downe in a darkesome lowly place farre in,
Whereas he meant his corrosives to apply,

225   And with streight° diet tame his stubborne malady.[6]   *strict*

26

In ashes and sackcloth he did array°   *dress*
His daintie corse,[7] proud humors to abate,[8]
And dieted with fasting every day,
The swelling of his wounds to mitigate,

230   And made him pray both earely and eke late:
And ever as superfluous flesh did rot
Amendment readie still at hand did wayt,
To pluck it out with pincers firie whot,°   *not*
That soone in him was left no one corrupted jot.°   *bit*

27

235   And bitter Penance with an yron whip,
Was wont him once to disple° every day: *discipline*

---

5. Confession is a necessary element of the Redcrosse Knight's recovery.

6. To heal the Redcrosse Knight, Patience returns him to Orgoglio's dungeon. Patience intends to use corrosive medication to remove his "inward corruption."

7. Patience has the Redcrosse Knight assume the role of a penitent.

8. According to Renaissance medicine, the humors, or bodily fluids, must be in balance to achieve good health; here Patience wants to "abate" or diminish them. The Redcrosse Knight's adventure in the House of Pride has left him with an excess of pride, which the doctor seeks to remove through penance and prayer.

And sharpe Remorse his hart did pricke° and nip,   *pierce*
That drops of bloud thence° like a well did play;   *from his heart*
And sad Repentance used to embay°   *drench*
240   His bodie in salt water smarting sore,
The filthy blots of sinne to wash away.
So in short space they did to health restore
The man that would not live, but earst lay at deathes dore.

28

In which his torment often was so great,
245   That like a Lyon he would cry and rore,
And rend his flesh, and his owne synewes° eat.   *muscles*
His owne deare Una hearing evermore
His ruefull shriekes and gronings, often tore
Her guiltlesse garments, and her golden heare,
250   For pitty of his paine and anguish sore;
Yet all with patience wisely she did beare;
For well she wist, his crime could else be never cleare.°   *cleansed*

29

Whom thus recover'd by wise Patience,
And trew Repentance they to Una brought:
255   Who joyous of his cured conscience,
Him dearely kist, and fairely eke besought
Himselfe to chearish, and consuming thought
To put away out of his carefull° brest.   *worried*
By this Charissa, late in child-bed brought,[9]
260   Was woxen strong, and left her fruitfull nest;
To her faire Una brought this unacquainted guest.

30

She was a woman in her freshest age,
Of wondrous beauty, and of bountie° rare,   *generosity*
With goodly grace and comely° personage,   *attractive*
265   That was on earth not easie to compare;
Full of great love, but Cupids wanton snare
As hell she hated, chast in worke and will;
Her necke and breasts were ever open bare,
That ay° thereof her babes might sucke their fill;   *always*
270   The rest was all in yellow robes arayed still.°   *always*

31

A multitude of babes about her hong,
Playing their sports, that joyd her to behold,
Whom still° she fed, whiles they were weake and young,   *always*
But thrust them forth still, as they wexed° old: *grew*
275   And on her head she wore a tyre° of gold,   *crown*
Adornd with gemmes and owches° wondrous faire,   *jewels*

9. Charissa, who had recently given birth.

Whose passing price uneath° was to be told;[1]   *scarcely*
    And by her side there sate a gentle paire
    Of turtle doves, she sitting in an yvorie chaire.

32

280 The knight and Una entring, faire her greet,
    And bid her joy of that her happie brood;
    Who them requites° with court'sies seeming meet,°   *repays / suitable*
    And entertaines with friendly chearefull mood.
    Then Una her besought,° to be so good,   *requested*
285 As in her vertuous rules to schoole her knight,
    Now after all his torment well withstood,
    In that sad house of Penaunce, where his spright
Had past the paines of hell, and long enduring night.

33

She was right joyous of her just° request,   *reasonable*
290 And taking by the hand that Faeries sonne,
    Gan him instruct in every good behest,°   *command*
    Of love, and righteousnesse, and well to donne,°   *good deeds*
    And wrath, and hatred warely° to shonne,   *carefully*
    That drew on men Gods hatred, and his wrath,
295 And many soules in dolours had fordonne:°   *overcome*
    In which when him she well instructed hath,
From thence to heaven she teacheth him the ready° path.   *direct*

34

Wherein his weaker wandring steps to guide,
    An auncient matrone she to her does call,
300 Whose sober lookes her wisedome well descride:°   *revealed*
    Her name was Mercie, well knowne over all,
    To be both gratious, and eke liberall:
    To whom the carefull charge of him she gave,
    To lead aright, that he should never fall
305 In all his wayes through this wide worldes wave,°   *currents*
That Mercy in the end his righteous soule might save.

35

The godly Matrone by the hand him beares°   *leads*
    Forth from her presence, by a narrow way,
    Scattred with bushy thornes, and ragged breares,°   *briars*
310 Which still° before him she remov'd away,   *ever*
    That nothing might his ready° passage stay:°   *direct / stop*
    And ever when his feet encombred were,
    Or gan to shrinke,° or from the right to stray,   *pull back*
    She held him fast,° and firmely did upbeare,°   *firmly / support*
315 As carefull Nourse her child from falling oft does reare.°   *raise*

---

1. Whose surpassing value was incalculable.

36

      Eftsoones unto an holy Hospitall,°   *hostel*
         That was fore° by the way, she did him bring,   *close*
         In which seven Bead-men° that had vowed all   *men of prayer*
         Their life to service of high heavens king
320   Did spend their dayes in doing godly thing:
         Their gates to all were open evermore,°   *always*
         That by the wearie way were traveiling,
         And one sate° wayting ever them before,   *sat*
      To call in commers-by,° that needy were and pore.   *passers-by*

37

325   The first of them that eldest was, and best,
         Of all the house had charge and governement,
         As Guardian and Steward of the rest:
         His office° was to give entertainment°   *duty / provisions*
         And lodging, unto all that came, and went:
330   Not unto such, as could him feast againe,
         And double quite,° for that he on them spent,   *repay*
         But such, as want° of harbour did constraine:[2]   *lack*
      Those for Gods sake his dewty was to entertaine.

38

      The second was as Almner[3] of the place,
335   His office was, the hungry for to feed,
         And thristy give to drinke, a worke of grace:
         He feard not once him selfe to be in need,
         Ne car'd to hoord° for those, whom he did breede:°   *hoard / his children*
         The grace of God he layd up still in store,
340   Which as a stocke he left unto his seede;
         He had enough, what need him care for more?
      And had he lesse, yet some he would give to the pore.[4]

39

      The third had of their wardrobe custodie,
         In which were not rich tyres,° nor garments gay,°   *clothes / trashy*
345   The plumes of pride, and wings of vanitie,
         But clothes meet to keepe keene could° away,   *sharp cold*
         And naked nature seemely° to aray;   *suitably*
         With which bare wretched wights he dayly clad,
         The images of God in earthly clay;
350   And if that no spare cloths to give he had,
      His owne coate he would cut, and it distribute glad.

40

      The fourth appointed by his office was,
         Poore prisoners to relieve with gratious ayd,°   *aid*

---

2. He did not provide for those who could return the favor with an even more lavish reception, but provided only for those who were destitute.
3. One who provides charitable relief to the poor.

4. He did not accumulate worldly goods for the wealth of his family, but gave to the poor, which made him rich in the virtue of charity.

And captives to redeeme° with price of bras,	*ransom*
355	From Turkes and Sarazins, which them had stayd;°	*imprisoned*
And though they faultie were,[5] yet well he wayd,°	*judged*
That God to us forgiveth every howre	
Much more then that, why° they in bands° were layd,	*for which / chains*
And he that harrowd hell with heavie stowre,°	*sorrow*
360 | The faultie soules from thence brought to his heavenly bowre.[6] | |

41

The fift had charge sicke persons to attend,	
	And comfort those, in point° of death which lay;	*at the brink*
	For them most needeth comfort in the end,	
	When sin, and hell, and death do most dismay	
365		The feeble soule departing hence away.	
	All is but lost, that living we bestow,	
	If not well ended at our dying day.[7]	
	O man have mind of that last bitter throw;°	*agony*
For as the tree does fall, so lyes it ever low.	

42

370 | The sixt had charge of them now being dead, | |
	In seemely sort their corses to engrave,°	*bury*
	And deck with dainty flowres their bridall bed,	
	That to their heavenly spouse[8] both sweet and brave	
	They might appeare, when he their soules shall save.	
375		The wondrous workemanship of Gods owne mould,°	*image*
	Whose face he made, all beasts to feare, and gave	
	All in his hand, even dead we honour should.	
Ah dearest God me graunt, I dead be not defould.°	*defiled*

43

| The seventh now after death and buriall done, | |
380 | | Had charge the tender Orphans of the dead | |
	And widowes ayd, least° they should be undone:°	*lest / ruined*
	In face of judgement he their right would plead,	
	Ne ought° the powre of mighty men did dread	*not at all*
	In their defence,[9] nor would for gold or fee	
385		Be wonne° their rightfull causes downe to tread:	*bribed*
	And when they stood in most necessitee,	
He did supply their want, and gave them° ever° free.	*to them / always*

---

5. Christian prisoners of pagans were "faultie" if they had given up their faith, even if they had been tortured in the process. But although succumbing to pagan force was strictly speaking a sin, the fourth Beadman considers that God forgives much greater sins all the time.

6. According to a medieval story, after his crucifixion Christ descended into Hell to release good people who had lived before him and thus had not been able to enter heaven.

7. A lifetime of faith is lost if one gives in to despair at the time of death.

8. In Revelation 21.2, the redeemed are "prepared as a bride adorned for her husband."

9. He would plead their causes in court and did not fear the power of mighty men.

44

There when the Elfin knight arrived was,
  The first and chiefest of the seven, whose care°   *duty*
390 Was guests to welcome, towardes him did pas:°   *go*
  Where seeing Mercie, that his steps up bare,°   *supported*
  And alwayes led, to her with reverence rare
  He humbly louted° in meeke lowlinesse,   *bowed*
  And seemely° welcome for her did prepare: *suitable*
395 For of their order she was Patronesse,°   *protector*
Albe° Charissa were their chiefest founderesse.   *although*

45

There she awhile him stayes, him selfe to rest,
  That to the rest° more able he might bee: *remainder*
  During which time, in every good behest°   *deed*
400 And godly worke of Almes and charitee
  She him instructed with great industree;
  Shortly therein so perfect he became,
  That from the first unto the last degree,
  His mortall life he learned had to frame°   *conduct*
405 In holy righteousnesse,[1] without rebuke or blame.

46

Thence forward by that painfull way they pas,°   *go*
  Forth to an hill, that was both steepe and hy;
  On top whereof a sacred chappell was,
  And eke a litle Hermitage thereby,
410 Wherein an aged holy man did lye,
  That day and night said his devotion,
  Ne other worldly busines did apply;°   *conduct*
  His name was heavenly Contemplation;
Of God and goodnesse was his meditation.

47

415 Great grace that old man to him given had;
  For God he often saw from heavens hight,°   *height*
  All were his earthly eyen both blunt° and bad,   *blurred*
  And through great age had lost their kindly° sight,   *natural*
  Yet wondrous quick and persant° was his spright,   *piercing*
420 As Eagles eye, that can behold the Sunne:
  That hill they scale° with all their powre and might,   *climb*
  That his frayle thighes nigh° wearie and fordonne   *all but*
Gan faile, but by her° helpe the top at last he wonne.°   *Mercy's / reached*

48

There they do finde that godly aged Sire,
425 With snowy lockes adowne his shoulders shed,
  As hoarie frost with spangles° doth attire   *icicles*

---

1. Spenser emphasizes that holy righteousness is not just an inner moral state but is achieved through the active practice of charity.

The mossy braunches of an Oke halfe ded.
Each bone might through his body well be red,°   seen
And every sinew° seene through his long fast: muscle
430   For nought he car'd his carcas long unfed;²
His mind was full of spirituall repast,
And pyn'd° his flesh, to keepe his body low and chast.   starved

49

Who when these two approching he aspide,°   saw
At their first presence grew agrieved sore,°   very upset
435   That forst him lay his heavenly thoughts aside;
And had he not that Dame respected more,
Whom highly he did reverence and adore,
He would not once have moved for the knight.
They him saluted standing far afore;°   at a distance
440   Who well them greeting, humbly did requight,°   return the greeting
And asked, to what end they clomb that tedious height.

50

What end (quoth° she) should cause us take such paine,   said
But that same end, which every living wight
Should make his marke,° high heaven to attaine?   aim
445   Is not from hence the way, that leadeth right
To that most glorious house, that glistreth° bright   shines
With burning starres, and everliuing fire,
Whereof the keyes³ are to thy hand behight°   delivered
By wise Fidelia? she doth thee require,
450   To shew it to this knight, according° his desire.   granting

51

Thrise° happy man, said then the father grave,   thrice
Whose staggering steps thy steady hand doth lead,
And shewes the way, his sinfull soule to save.
Who better can the way to heaven aread,°   show
455   Then thou thy selfe, that was both borne and bred
In heavenly throne, where thousand Angels shine?
Thou doest the prayers of the righteous sead°   the redeemed
Present before the majestie divine,
And his avenging wrath to clemencie incline.⁴

52

460   Yet since thou bidst, thy pleasure shalbe donne.
Then come thou man of earth, and see the way,
That never yet was seene of Faeries sonne,
That never leads the traveiler astray,
But after labours long, and sad delay,
465   Brings them to joyous rest and endlesse blis.

2. He did not care about the hunger of his body.
3. The keys to the kingdom of heaven.

4. Contemplation is addressing Mercy, who turns the Almighty's wrath into forgiveness.

But first thou must a season fast and pray,
Till from her bands° the spright assoiled° is,[5]   bonds / released
And have her strength recur'd° from fraile infirmitis.   restored

53

That done, he leads him to the highest Mount;[6]
470   Such one,[7] as that same mighty man of God,
That bloud-red billowes[8] like a walled front
On either side disparted with his rod,
Till that his army dry-foot through them yod,°   went
Dwelt fortie dayes upon; where writ in stone
475   With bloudy letters by the hand of God,
The bitter doome of death and balefull mone°   moan
He did receive, whiles flashing fire about him shone.[9]

54

Or like that sacred hill, whose head full hie,
Adornd with fruitfull Olives all arownd,[1]
480   Is, as it were for endlesse memory
Of that deare Lord, who oft thereon was fownd,
For ever with a flowring girlond crownd:
Or like that pleasaunt Mount, that is for ay
Through famous Poets verse each where renownd,[2]
485   On which the thrise three learned Ladies[3] play
Their heavenly notes, and make full many a lovely lay.

55

From thence, far off he unto him did shew
A litle path, that was both steepe and long,
Which to a goodly Citie[4] led his vew;
490   Whose wals and towres were builded high and strong
Of perle and precious stone, that earthly tong
Cannot describe, nor wit of man can tell;
Too high a ditty for my simple song;
The Citie of the great king hight it well,°   it is well named
495   Wherein eternall peace and happinesse doth dwell.[5]

56

As he thereon stood gazing, he might see
The blessed Angels to and fro descend[6]
From highest heaven, in gladsome° companee,°   happy / friendship

---

5. The bonds that Contemplation is referring to are the bonds of the flesh.
6. This is the "great and high mountain" of Revelation 21.10, from which God showed John the New Jerusalem.
7. Such a mountain—Sinai—Moses climbed to spend 40 days before receiving the Ten Commandments.
8. Spenser is referring to the Red Sea, which Moses parted to allow the Israelites to escape from Egypt without drowning.
9. Referring to the burning bush through which God appeared to Moses (Deuteronomy 4.11).

1. The Mount of Olives, where Jesus taught.
2. Parnassus, the home of the Greek gods and celebrated by the Greek poets.
3. The nine Muses, goddesses of the arts and sciences.
4. The New Jerusalem, the promised home of the faithful in eternity (Revelation 20.10–21).
5. Cf. Psalms 48.2: "the joy of the whole earth is Mount Zion . . . the city of the great king."
6. The image recalls Jacob's vision of the ladder that extended from earth to heaven (Genesis 28.12).

And with great joy into that Citie wend,
500   As commonly as friend does with his frend.
Whereat he wondred much, and gan enquere,°   asked
What stately building durst° so high extend   dared
Her loftie towres unto the starry sphere,°   heavens
And what unknowen nation there empeopled were.°   inhabited it

57

505   Faire knight (quoth he) Hierusalem that is,
The new Hierusalem, that God has built
For those to dwell in, that are chosen his,
His chosen people purg'd from sinfull guilt,
With pretious bloud,[7] which cruelly was spilt
510   On cursed tree, of that unspotted lam,°   lamb
That for the sinnes of all the world was kilt:
Now are they Saints all in that Citie sam,°   same
More deare unto their God, then younglings to their dam.

58

Till now, said then the knight, I weened well,
515   That great Cleopolis,[8] where I have beene,
In which that fairest Faerie Queene doth dwell,
The fairest Citie was, that might be seene;
And that bright towre all built of christall cleene,
Panthea, seemd the brightest thing, that was:
520   But now by proofe all otherwise I weene;
For this great Citie that does far surpas,
And this bright Angels towre quite dims that towre of glas.

59

Most trew, then said the holy aged man;
Yet is Cleopolis for earthly frame,[9]
525   The fairest peece, that eye beholden can:
And well beseemes all knights of noble name,
That covet in th'immortall booke of fame
To be eternized, that same to haunt,
And doen their service to that soveraigne Dame,[1]
530   That glorie does to them for guerdon° graunt: reward
For she is heavenly borne, and heaven may justly vaunt.[2]

60

And thou faire ymp,° sprong out from English race,   child
How ever now accompted° Elfins sonne,   considered

---

7. The blood spilled by Christ when he was crucified and by which the faithful are redeemed from sin.

8. The Redcrosse Knight compares the New Jerusalem with Cleopolis, the city ruled by the Faerie Queene, and its tower Panthea—literally, in Greek, all sights or the best of sights—together a perfect representation of a political state (as realized by Spenser and perhaps by Plato and others in their political treatises). He finds that the transcendent brilliance of the angels' city surpasses that of the other cities of "glass," i.e., products of a merely human power of reflection.

9. As an earthly as opposed to a heavenly structure.

1. It is fitting that noble knights who seek glory serve in the Faerie Queene's court.

2. Because the Faerie Queene was born in Heaven, Heaven may rightfully boast ("vaunt") that it is her home.

Well worthy doest thy service for her grace,
535   To aide a virgin desolate foredonne.°   *in distress*
But when thou famous victorie hast wonne,
And high emongst all knights hast hong thy shield,
Thenceforth the suit° of earthly conquest shonne,°   *pursuit / shun*
And wash thy hands from guilt of bloudy field:
540   For bloud can nought but sin, and wars but sorrowes yield.

61

Then seeke this path, that I to thee presage,°   *foretell*
Which after all to heaven shall thee send;
Then peaceably thy painefull pilgrimage
To yonder same Hierusalem do bend,°   *go*
545   Where is for thee ordaind a blessed end:
For thou emongst those Saints, whom thou doest see,
Shalt be a Saint, and thine owne nations frend
And Patrone: thou Saint George shalt called bee,
Saint George of mery England, the signe of victoree.

62

550   Unworthy wretch (quoth he°) of so great grace,   *Redcrosse Knight*
How dare I thinke such glory to attaine?
These that have it attaind, were in like cace
(Quoth he°) as wretched, and liv'd in like paine.   *Contemplation*
But deeds of armes must I[3] at last be faine,°   *willing*
555   And Ladies love to leave so dearely bought?
What need of armes, where peace doth ay° remaine,   *ever*
(Said he°) and battailes none are to be fought?   *Contemplation*
As for loose loves are vaine,° and vanish into nought.   *false*

63

O let me not (quoth he) then turne againe
560   Backe to the world, whose joyes so fruitlesse are;
But let me here for aye° in peace remaine,   *ever*
Or streight way° on that last long voyage fare,[4]   *immediately*
That nothing may my present hope empare.°   *diminish*
That may not be (said he) ne maist thou yit
565   Forgo° that royall maides bequeathed care,   *give up*
Who did her cause into thy hand commit,[5]
Till from her cursed foe thou have her freely quit.

64

Then shall I soone, (quoth he) so God me grace,
Abet° that virgins cause disconsolate,   *assist*
570   And shortly backe returne unto this place,
To walke this way in Pilgrims poore estate.°   *condition*
But now aread,° old father, why of late°   *tell me / just now*

3. The Redcrosse Knight asks himself whether he can abandon chivalry and then learns that in the New Jerusalem there are neither wars nor loves.

4. The Redcrosse Knight is referring to death.

5. He may not yet give up Una's quest to which he is committed; he must avenge and free her from her enemy.

Didst thou behight° me borne of English blood,   *call*
Whom all a Faeries sonne doen nominate?[6]
575   That word shall I (said he) avouchen° good,   *prove*
Sith to thee is unknowne the cradle of thy brood.°   *girth*

65

For well I wote, thou springst from ancient race
Of Saxon kings, that have with mightie hand
And many bloudie battailes fought in place°   *in that place*
580   High reard° their royall throne in Britane land,   *erected*
And vanquisht them,° unable to withstand: *the Britons*
From thence a Faerie thee unweeting reft,°   *took*
There as thou slepst in tender swadling band,
And her base Elfin brood° there for thee left.[7]   *child*
585   Such men do Chaungelings° call, so chaungd° by Faeries theft.   *changelings / switched*

66

Thence° she thee brought into this Faerie lond,   *from there*
And in an heaped furrow did thee hyde,
Where thee a Ploughman all unweeting fond,
As he his toylesome teme° that way did guyde,   *toiling oxen*
590   And brought thee up in ploughmans state to byde,
Whereof Georgos° he thee gave to name;   *farmer*
Till prickt° with courage, and thy forces pryde,   *moved*
To Faery court thou cam'st to seeke for fame,
And prove thy puissaunt armes, as seemes thee best became.[8]

67

595   O holy Sire (quoth he) how shall I quight°   *repay*
The many favours I with thee have found,
That hast my name and nation red aright,°   *correctly*
And taught the way that does to heaven bound?
This said, adowne he looked to the ground,
600   To have returnd, but dazed were his eyne,
Through passing brightnesse, which did quite confound°   *bewilder*
His feeble sence, and too exceeding shyne.[9]
So darke are earthly things compard to things divine.

68

At last whenas himselfe he gan to find,
605   To Una back he cast him° to retire;   *decided*
Who him awaited still with pensive mind.

6. The Redcrosse Knight believes he is an inhabitant of Faerie Land, the fictional ground of the poem as Spenser names it to his readers. When Contemplation tells the Redcrosse Knight that he is actually English, Spenser is alerting readers to the fact that St. George (as Spenser apparently believed) was a historical figure, represented in historical record, and not merely a figment of the poet's imagination.

7. I.e., unknown to you, a fairy took you from your cradle and put its own child in your place.
8. The qualities that prompted the Redcrosse Knight to leave the farm—i.e., pride in his chivalric skill—are qualities his faith will have had to modify to conform to a Christian mode of life.
9. The Redcrosse Knight glances down, intending to look back up, but the force of revelation overwhelms him.

Great thankes and goodly meed° to that good syre,   *reward*
He thence departing gave for his paines hyre.[1]
So came to Una, who him joyd to see,
610 And after litle rest, gan him desire,
Of her adventure° mindfull for to bee.   *quest*
So leave they take of Caelia, and her daughters three.

Canto 11

The knight with that old Dragon fights
two dayes incessantly:
The third him overthrowes, and gayns
most glorious victory.

1

High time now gan it wex° for Una faire,   *grow*
To thinke of those her captive Parents deare,
And their forwasted° kingdome to repaire: *desolated*
Whereto whenas they now approched neare,
5 With hartie words her knight she gan to cheare,
And in her modest manner thus bespake;°   *said*
Deare knight, as deare, as ever knight was deare,
That all these sorrowes suffer for my sake,
High heaven behold the tedious toyle, ye for me take.[1]

2

10 Now are we come unto my native soyle,
And to the place, where all our perils dwell;
Here haunts° that feend, and does his dayly spoyle,°   *lurks / evil*
Therefore henceforth be at your keeping well,°   *on your guard*
And ever ready for your focman fell.°   *dangerous enemy*
15 The sparke of noble courage now awake,
And strive your excellent selfe to excell;°   *outdo yourself*
That shall ye evermore renowmed make,
Above all knights on earth, that batteill undertake.

3

And pointing forth, lo yonder is (said she)
20 The brasen towre in which my parents deare
For dread of that huge feend emprisond be,
Whom I from far see on the walles appeare,
Whose sight my feeble soule doth greatly cheare:
And on the top of all I do espye
25 The watchman wayting tydings glad to heare,[2]
That O my parents might I happily
Unto you bring, to ease you of your misery.

---

1. The hire of his pains, the trouble Contemplation took
to instruct the Redcrosse Knight.
1. Una asks the heavens to witness the difficult task that
the Redcrosse Knight undertakes for her.

2. Waiting to hear good news. In the next line, Una addresses her parents, expressing her wish to bring them the
good news of their rescue herself.

⁴

With that they heard a roaring hideous sound,
   That all the ayre with terrour filled wide,
30   And seemd uneath° to shake the stedfast ground.   *almost*
   Eftsoones that dreadfull Dragon they espide,
   Where stretcht he lay upon the sunny side
   Of a great hill, himselfe like a great hill.
   But all so soone, as he from far descryde°   *saw*
35   Those glistring armes, that heaven with light did fill,
He rousd himselfe full blith,° and hastned them untill.°   *joyfully / toward them*

⁵

Then bad the knight his Lady yede aloofe,°   *stand aside*
   And to an hill her selfe with draw aside,
   From whence she might behold that battailles proof
40   And eke be safe from daunger far descryde:°   *seen from a distance*
   She him obayd, and turnd a little wyde.°   *moved aside*
   Now O thou sacred Muse, most learned Dame,³
   Faire ympe of Phoebus, and his aged bride,
   The Nourse of time, and everlasting fame,
45   That warlike hands ennoblest with immortall name;

⁶

O gently come into my feeble brest,
   Come gently, but not with that mighty rage,
   Wherewith the martiall troupes thou doest infest,°   *inspire*
   And harts of great Heroës doest enrage,
50   That nought their kindled courage may aswage,°   *diminish*
   Soone as they dreadfull trompe° begins to sownd;   *trumpet*
   The God of warre with his fiers equipage°   *weapons*
   Thou doest awake, sleepe never he so sownd,
   And scared nations doest with horrour sterne astownd.°   *astonish*

⁷

55   Faire Goddesse lay that furious fit aside,⁴
   Till I of warres and bloudy Mars do sing,
   And Briton fields with Sarazin bloud bedyde,
   Twixt that great faery Queene and Paynim king,
   That with their horrour heaven and earth did ring,
60   A worke of labour long, and endlesse prayse:⁵
   But now a while let downe that haughtie string,
   And to my tunes thy second tenor° rayse,   *accompaniment*
   That I this man of God his godly armes may blaze.°   *proclaim*

⁸

By this the dreadful Beast drew nigh to hand,°   *near*
65   Halfe flying, and halfe footing in his hast,

---

3. Spenser is calling upon Clio, the muse of history, who preserves great events and records glorious deeds.
4. The muse's "furious fit" is music that rouses men to war.

5. The song of war that Spenser refers to here may be some part of the poem he plans to write in the future.

That with his largenesse measured much land,
And made wide shadow under his huge wast;°   *bulk*
As mountaine doth the valley overcast.
Approching nigh, he reared high afore
His body monstrous, horrible, and vast,
Which to increase his wondrous greatnesse more,
Was swolne with wrath, and poyson, and with bloudy gore.

70

9

And over, all with brasen scales was armd,
Like plated coate of steele, so couched neare,°   *closely set*
That nought mote perce, ne might his corse be harmd
With dint of sword, nor push of pointed speare;
Which as an Eagle, seeing pray appeare,
His aery plumes doth rouze, full rudely dight,°   *violently arranged*
So shaked he, that horrour was to heare,
For as the clashing of an Armour bright,
Such noyse his rouzed scales did send unto the knight.

75

80

10

His flaggy° wings when forth he did display,   *drooping*
Were like two sayles, in which the hollow wynd
Is gathered full,[6] and worketh speedy way:
And eke the pennes,[7] that did his pineons° bynd,   *feathers*
Were like mayne-yards,° with flying canvas lynd,   *mainsail ropes*
With which whenas him list the ayre to beat,
And there by force unwonted passage find,[8]
The cloudes before him fled for terrour great,
And all the heavens stood still amazed with his threat.

85

90

11

His huge long tayle wound up in hundred foldes,
Does overspred his long bras-scaly backe,
Whose wreathed boughts° when ever he unfoldes,   *wound-up coils*
And thicke entangled knots adown does slacke,
Bespotted as with shields of red and blacke,
It sweepeth all the land behind him farre,
And of three furlongs does but litle lacke;[9]
And at the point two stings in-fixed arre,
Both deadly sharpe, that sharpest steele exceeden farre.

95

12

But stings and sharpest steele did far exceed
The sharpnesse of his cruell rending clawes;
Dead was it sure, as sure as death in deed,
What ever thing does touch his ravenous pawes,

100

6. The force of the wind fills the sails and makes them billow out.
7. The bones in the Dragon's wings.
8. Although the Dragon cannot fly normally, he does so through the sheer force with which he beats his wings.
9. The Dragon's tail measures nearly three furlongs, 660 yards, a third of a mile.

Or what within his reach he ever drawes.
105   But his most hideous head my toung to tell
Does tremble: for his deepe devouring jawes
Wide gaped, like the griesly mouth of hell,
Through which into his darke abisse° all ravin° fell.   pit / prey

13

And that more wondrous was, in either jaw
110   Threeranckes of yron teeth enraunged were,
In which yet trickling bloud and gobbets° raw   chunks
Of late devoured bodies did appeare,
That sight thereof bred cold congealed feare:
Which to increase, and all atonce° to kill,   suddenly
115   A cloud of smoothering smoke and sulphur seare°   burning
Out of his stinking gorge forth steemed still,
That all the ayre about with smoke and stench did fill.

14

His blazing eyes, like two bright shining shields,
Did burne with wrath, and sparkled living fyre;
120   As two broad Beacons, set in open fields,
Send forth their flames farre off to every shyre,°   district
And warning give, that enemies conspyre,
With fire and sword the region to invade;
So flam'd his eyne with rage and rancorous yre:
125   But farre within, as in a hollow glade,
Those glaring lampes were set, that made a dreadfull shade.

15

So dreadfully he towards him did pas,
Forelifting° up aloft his speckled brest,   raising
And often bounding on the brused gras,
130   As for great joyance of his newcome guest.
Eftsoones he gan advance his haughtie crest,
As chauffed Bore° his bristles doth upreare,   angry boar
And shoke his scales to battell readie drest;[1]
That made the Redcrosse knight nigh quake for feare,
135   As bidding° bold defiance to his foeman neare.   inciting

16

The knight gan fairely couch his steadie speare,
And fiercely ran at him with rigorous might:
The pointed steele arriving rudely theare,
His harder hide would neither perce, nor bight,
140   But glauncing by forth passed forward right;
Yet sore amoved with so puissant push,
The wrathfull beast about him turned light,°   quickly
And him so rudely passing by, did brush
With his long tayle, that° horse and man to ground did rush.°   so that / fall

1. He shook his scales into position for battle.

17

145 Both horse and man up lightly rose againe,
    And fresh encounter towards him addrest:
    But th'idle stroke° yet backe recoyld in vaine,   *futile swordstroke*
    And found no place his deadly point to rest.
    Exceeding rage enflam'd the furious beast,
150   To be avenged of so great despight;
    For never felt his imperceable brest
    So wondrous force, from hand of living wight;
Yet had he prov'd° the powre of many a puissant knight.   *tested*

18

Then with his waving wings displayed wyde,
155   Himselfe up high he lifted from the ground,
    And with strong flight did forcibly divide
    The yielding aire, which nigh° too feeble found   *almost*
    Her flitting partes, and element unsound,
    To beare so great a weight:[2] he cutting way
160   With his broad sayles, about him soared round:
    At last low stouping with unweldie sway,°   *awkward force*
Snatcht up both horse and man, to beare them quite away.

19

Long he them bore above the subject plaine,
    So farre as Ewghen° bow a shaft may send,   *made of yew*
165 Till struggling strong did him at last constraine,
    To let them downe before his flightes end:
    As hagard hauke° presuming to contend   *untamed hawk*
    With hardie fowle, above his hable° might,   *natural*
    His wearie pounces° all in vaine doth spend,   *claws*
170   To trusse° the pray too heavie for his flight;   *carry off*
Which comming downe to ground, does free it selfe by fight.

20

He so disseized° of his gryping grosse,°   *freed / heavy grasp*
    The knight his thrillant speare againe assayd
    In his bras-plated body to embosse,°   *embed*
175   And three mens strength unto the stroke he layd;
    Wherewith the stiffe beame° quaked, as affrayd,   *shaft*
    And glauncing from his scaly necke, did glyde
    Close under his left wing, then broad displayd.
    The percing steele there wrought a wound full wyde,
180 That with the uncouth smart° the Monster lowdly cryde.   *pain*

21

He cryde, as raging seas are wont to rore,
    When wintry storme his wrathfull wreck does threat,
    The rolling billowes beat the ragged shore,

---

2. The air is almost too weak to support the Dragon; in other words, the Dragon is almost too heavy to fly, given the strength of his wings in relation to his overall weight.

As they the earth would shoulder from her seat,
185   And greedie gulfe does gape, as he would eat
His neighbour element° in his revenge: *the earth*
Then gin the blustring brethren boldly threat,
To move the world from off his stedfast henge,°   *hinge*
And boystrous battell make, each other to avenge.

22

190   The steely head stucke fast° still in his flesh,   *firmly*
Till with his cruell clawes he snatcht the wood,°   *shaft*
And quite a sunder broke. Forth flowed fresh
A gushing river of blacke goarie blood,
That drowned all the land, whereon he stood;
195   The streame thereof would drive a water-mill.
Trebly augmented was his furious mood
With bitter sense of his deepe rooted ill,
That flames of fire he threw forth from his large nosethrill.°   *nostril*

23

His hideous tayle then hurled he about,
200   And therewith all enwrapt the nimble thyes°   *thighs*
Of his froth-fomy steed, whose courage stout
Striving to loose the knot, that fast him tyes,
Himselfe in streighter bandes° too rash implyes,   *tighter bondage*
That to the ground he is perforce° constraynd   *thereby*
205   To throw his rider: who can quickly ryse
From off the earth, with durty bloud distaynd,°   *stained*
For that reprochfull fall right fowly he disdaynd.

24

And fiercely tooke his trenchand° blade in hand,   *sharp*
With which he stroke so furious and so fell,
210   That nothing seemd the puissance could withstand:
Upon his crest the hardned yron fell,
But his more hardned crest was armd so well,
That deeper dint therein it would not make;
Yet so extremely did the buffe° him quell,°   *blow / overwhelm*
215   That from thenceforth he shund the like to take,
But when he saw them come, he did them still forsake.°   *avoid*

25

The knight was wrath to see his stroke beguyld,°   *foiled*
And smote againe with more outrageous might;
But backe againe the sparckling steele recoyld,
220   And left not any marke, where it did light;°   *land*
As if in Adamant° rocke it had bene pight.   *hardest*
The beast impatient of his smarting wound,
And of so fierce and forcible despight,°   *injury*
Thought with his wings to stye° above the ground;   *fly*
225   But his late wounded wing unserviceable found.

26

Then full of griefe and anguish vehement,
  He lowdly brayd, that like was never heard,
  And from his wide devouring oven° sent   *mouth*
  A flake of fire, that flashing in his° beard,   *Redcrosse Knight's*
230 Him all amazd, and almost made affeard:
  The scorching flame sore swinged° all his face,   *singed*
  And through his armour all his bodie seard,°   *burned*
  That he could not endure so cruell cace,°   *situation*
But thought his armes to leave, and helmet to unlace.

27

235 Not that great Champion[3] of the antique world,
  Whom famous Poetes verse so much doth vaunt,°   *celebrate*
  And hath for twelve huge labours high extold,°   *praised*
  So many furies and sharpe fits did haunt,
  When him the poysoned garment did enchaunt
240 With Centaures bloud, and bloudie verses charm'd,
  As did this knight twelve thousand dolours daunt,°   *defy*
  Whom fyrie steele now burnt, that carst° him arm'd,   *recently*
That erst° him goodly arm'd, now most of all him harm'd.   *at first*

28

Faint, wearie, sore, emboyled, grieved, brent
245 With heat, toyle, wounds, armes, smart, and inward fire
  That never man such mischiefes did torment;
  Death better were, death did he oft desire,
  But death will never come, when needes require.
  Whom so dismayd when that his foe° beheld,   *the Dragon*
250 He cast to suffer him no more respire,[4]
  But gan his sturdie sterne° about to weld,   *tail*
And him° so strongly stroke, that to the ground him feld.   *Redcrosse Knight*

29

It fortuned (as faire it then befell)
  Behind his backe unweeting, where he stood,
255 Of auncient time there was a springing well,
  From which fast trickled forth a silver flood,
  Full of great vertues, and for med'cine good.
  Whylome, before that cursed Dragon got
  That happie land, and all with innocent blood
260 Defyld those sacred waves, it rightly hot
The well of life, ne yet his vertues had forgot.

30

For unto life the dead it could restore,
  And guilt of sinfull crimes cleane wash away,

---

3. Hercules. After successfully completing his 12 impossible labors, the hero was plagued ("haunted") by "furies": his wife gave him a tunic soaked in the poison blood of a centaur. The blood was meant to work as a love charm but instead burned Hercules' flesh, and he died in agony.
4. The Dragon, seeing how desperate the Redcrosse Knight is, determines to kill him.

Those that with sicknesse were infected sore,
265   It could recure,° and aged long decay   *cure*
Renew, as one were borne that very day.
Both Silo this,[5] and Jordan did excell,
And th'English Bath, and eke the german Spau,
Ne can Cephise, nor Hebrus match this well:
270   Into the same the knight backe overthrowen, fell.

31

Now gan the golden Phoebus for to steepe
    His fierie face in billowes of the west,
    And his faint steedes watred in Ocean deepe,
    Whiles from their journall° labours they did rest,   *daily*
275   When that infernall Monster, having kest°   *cast*
    His wearie foe into that living well,
    Can high advance his broad discoloured brest,
    Above his wonted pitch, with countenance fell,
And clapt his yron wings, as victor he did dwell.°   *remain*

32

280   Which when his pensive° Ladie saw from farre,   *worried*
    Great woe and sorrow did her soule assay,
    As weening that the sad end of the warre,
    And gan to highest God entirely pray,
    That feared chance from her to turne away;[6]
285   With folded hands and knees full lowly bent
    All night she watcht, ne once adowne would lay
    Her daintie limbs in her sad dreriment,°   *plight*
But praying still did wake, and waking did lament.

33

The morrow next gan early to appeare,
290   That Titan rose to runne his daily race;
    But early ere the morrow next gan reare
    Out of the sea faire Titans deawy face,
    Up rose the gentle virgin from her place,
    And looked all about, if she might spy
295   Her loved knight to move his manly pace:
    For she had great doubt° of his safety,   *fear*
Since late she saw him fall before his enemy.

34

At last she saw, where he upstarted brave
    Out of the well, wherein he drenched lay;
300   As Eagle fresh out of the Ocean wave,

---

5. Silo, Jordan, Bath, Spau, Cephise, and Hebrus: all waters reputed to have healing powers. The blind man is cured by bathing in the waters of Siloam (John 9.7), and John baptized Christ in the River Jordan (Matthew 3.16). Cephise and Hebrus are mentioned in classical mythology. Spenser probably wanted his readers to associate the water from "the well of life" with baptism, as in John 4.14.
6. She prayed to God to prevent the event she fears, the death of the Redcrosse Knight.

Where he hath left his plumes all hoary gray,
And deckt himselfe with feathers youthly gay,
Like Eyas hauke[7] up mounts unto the skies,
His newly budded pineons° to assay,   *wings*
305 And marveiles at himselfe, still as he flies:
So new this new-borne knight to battell new did rise.

35

Whom when the damned feend so fresh did spy,
No wonder if he wondred at the sight,
And doubted, whether his late enemy
310 It were, or other new supplied knight.
He,° now to prove his late renewed might,   *Redcrosse Knight*
High brandishing his bright deaw-burning blade,[8]
Upon his crested scalpe so sore did smite,
That to the scull a yawning wound it made:
315 The deadly dint his dulled senses all dismaid.

36

I wote not, whether the revenging steele
Were hardned with that holy water dew,
Wherein he fell, or sharper edge did feele,
Or his baptized hands now greater grew;
320 Or other secret vertue did ensew;°   *result*
Else never could the force of fleshly arme,
Ne molten mettall in his° bloud embrew:°   *the Dragon's / soak*
For till that stownd° could never wight him harme,[9]   *moment*
By subtilty, nor slight, nor might, nor mighty charme.

37

325 The cruell wound enraged him so sore,
That loud he yelded for exceeding paine;
As hundred ramping Lyons seem'd to rore,
Whom ravenous hunger did thereto constraine:°   *torment*
Then gan he tosse aloft his stretched traine,
330 And therewith scourge the buxome° aire so sore,   *yielding*
That to his force to yeelden it was faine;
Ne ought° his sturdie strokes might stand afore,°   *nor anything / before*
That high trees overthrew, and rocks in peeces tore.

38

The same° advauncing high above his head,   *the Dragon*
335 With sharpe intended sting so rude him smot,
That to the earth him drove, as stricken dead,
Ne living wight would have him life behot:°   *predicted*
The mortall sting his angry needle shot
Quite through his shield, and in his shoulder seasd,°   *pierced*

---

7. A young, untamed hawk; a symbol of victory.
8. The Redcrosse Knight's sword is like the sun, which burns up the dew.

9. Until that moment, neither human strength nor human weapons could succeed in piercing the Dragon's flesh.

340   Where fast it stucke, ne would there out be got:
      The griefe thereof him wondrous sore diseasd,
Ne might his ranckling paine with patience be appeasd.

39

But yet more mindfull of his honour deare,
      Then of the grievous smart, which him did wring,°   *afflict*
345   From loathed soile he can° him lightly reare,   *did*
      And strove to loose the farre infixed sting:
      Which when in vaine he tryde with struggeling,
      Inflam'd with wrath, his raging blade he heft,°   *lifted*
      And strooke so strongly, that the knotty string
350   Of his huge taile he quite a sunder cleft,
Five joynts thereof he hewd,° and but the stump him left.   *cut*

40

Hart cannot thinke, what outrage, and what cryes,
      With foule enfouldred[1] smoake and flashing fire,
      The hell-bred beast threw forth unto the skyes,
355   That all was covered with darknesse dire:
      Then fraught with rancour,° and engorged ire,   *malice*
      He cast at once him to avenge for all,
      And gathering up himselfe out of the mire,
      With his uneven wings did fiercely fall
360   Upon his sunne-bright shield, and gript it fast withall.°   *as well*

41

Much was the man encombred with his hold,
      In feare to lose his weapon in his paw,
      Ne wist yet, how his talants to unfold;
      Nor harder was from Cerberus[2] greedie jaw
365   To plucke a bone, then from his cruell claw
      To reave° by strength the griped gage[3] away: *pry*
      Thrise he assayd it from his foot to draw,
      And thrise in vaine to draw it did assay,
It booted nought to thinke, to robbe him of his pray.

42

370   Tho when he saw no power might prevaile,
      His trustie sword he cald to his last aid,
      Wherewith he fiercely did his foe assaile,
      And double blowes about him stoutly laid,
      That glauncing fire out of the yron plaid;°   *leaped*
375   As sparckles from the Anduile° use to fly,   *anvil*
      When heavie hammers on the wedge° are swaid;°   *metal / struck*
      Therewith at last he forst him to unty
One of his grasping feete, him° to defend thereby.   *himself*

---

1. Like a thundercloud filled with lightning bolts.
2. The mythological three-headed dog guarding the gates
of Hell.

3. The prize over which a battle is fought; here, the Redcrosse Knight's shield.

43

The other foot, fast fixed on his shield,

380   Whenas no strength, nor stroks mote him° constraine   *the Dragon*

To loose, ne yet the warlike pledge to yield,

He° smot thereat with all his might and maine,   *Redcrosse Knight*

That nought° so wondrous puissance might sustaine;   *nothing*

Upon the joynt the lucky steele did light,

385   And made such way, that hewd it quite in twaine;

The paw yet missed not his minisht might,°   *diminished strength*

But hong still on the shield, as it at first was pight.°   *fixed*

44

For griefe thereof, and divelish despight,

From his infernall fournace forth he threw

390   Huge flames, that dimmed all the heavens light,

Enrold in duskish smoke and brimstone[4] blew;

As burning Aetna° from his boyling stew   *a volcano in Sicily*

Doth belch out flames, and rockes in peeces broke,

And ragged ribs of mountaines molten new,°   *newly molten*

395   Enwrapt in coleblacke clouds and filthy smoke,

That all the land with stench, and heaven with horror choke.

45

The heate whereof, and harmefull pestilence°   *destruction*

So sore him noyd,° that forst him to retire   *injured*

A little backward for his best defence,

400   To save his bodie from the scorching fire,

Which he° from hellish entrailes did expire.   *the Dragon*

It chaunst (eternall God that chaunce did guide)

As he recoyled° backward, in the mire   *shrank*

His nigh forwearied° feeble feet did slide,   *tired*

405   And downe he fell, with dread of shame sore terrifide.

46

There grew a goodly tree him faire beside,

Loaden with fruit and apples rosie red,

As they in pure vermilion had beene dide,

Whereof great vertues over all were red:

410   For happie life to all, which thereon fed,

And life eke everlasting did befall:

Great God it planted in that blessed sted°   *place*

With his almightie hand, and did it call

The tree of life,[5] the crime of our first fathers fall.

47

415   In all the world like was not to be found,

Save in that soile, where all good things did grow,

---

4. Sulfur, which burns blue.
5. The tree of life was denied to Adam for his "crime"— his defiance of God's commandment not to eat the fruit

of the tree of knowledge of good and evil. As a result, God expelled him from the Garden of Eden where the tree of life grew.

And freely sprong out of the fruitfull ground,
As incorrupted Nature did them sow,
Till that dread Dragon° all did overthrow.   *Satan, the serpent*

420   Another like faire tree eke grew thereby,[6]
Whereof who so did eat, eftsoones did know
Both good and ill: O mornefull memory:
That tree through one mans fault hath doen us all to dy.

48

From that first tree forth flowd, as from a well,
425   A trickling streame of Balme, most soveraine
And daintie deare,° which on the ground still fell,   *very precious*
And overflowed all the fertill plaine,
As it had deawed° bene with timely raine: *sprinkled*
Life and long health that gratious ointment gave,
430   And deadly woundes could heale, and reare againe
The senseless corse appointed for the grave.[7]
Into that same he fell: which did from death him save.

49

For nigh thereto the ever damned beast
Durst° not approch, for he was deadly made,[8]   *dared*
435   And all that life preserved, did detest:
Yet he it° oft adventur'd° to invade.°   *the tree / tried / destroy*
By this the drouping day-light gan to fade,
And yeeld his roome° to sad succeeding night,   *place*
Who with her sable mantle gan to shade
440   The face of earth, and wayes of living wight,
And high her burning torch set up in heaven bright.

50

When gentle Una saw the second fall
Of her deare knight, who wearie of long fight,
And faint through losse of bloud, mov'd not at all,
445   But lay as in a dreame of deepe delight,
Besmeard with pretious Balme, whose vertuous might
Did heale his wounds, and scorching heat alay,
Againe she stricken was with sore affright,
And for his safetie gan devoutly pray;
450   And watch the noyous° night, and wait for joyous day.   *sorrowful*

51

The joyous day gan early to appeare,
And faire Aurora[9] from the deawy bed
Of aged Tithone gan her selfe to reare,
With rosie cheekes, for shame as blushing red;

---

6. The tree of knowledge of good and evil.
7. The balm from the tree of life heals the Redcrosse Knight; its function follows that of the water in baptism. Having been freed of the consequences of original sin in baptism, the baptized are constantly open to restorations of faith in pursuit of good works. Cf. Revelation 22.2: "The leaves of the tree [of life] served to heale the nations."
8. He was allied with Death, not Life.
9. The goddess of the dawn, married to Tithone or Tithonus.

455   Her golden lockes for haste were loosely shed
        About her eares, when Una her did marke
        Clymbe to her charet, all with flowers spred,
        From heaven high to chase the chearelesse darke;
    With merry note her° loud salutes the mounting larke.   *Una*

52

460   Then freshly up arose the doughtie knight,
        All healed of his hurts and woundes wide,
        And did himselfe to battell readie dight;
        Whose early foe awaiting him beside
        To have devourd, so soone as day he spyde,
465   When now he saw himselfe so freshly reare,
        As if late fight had nought him damnifyde,°   *harmed*
        He woxe° dismayd, and gan his fate to feare;   *grew*
    Nathlesse° with wonted rage he him advaunced neare.   *nonetheless*

53

     And in his first encounter, gaping wide,
470   He thought attonce° him to have swallowd quight,   *at once*
        And rusht upon him with outragious pride;
        Who him r'encountring fierce, as hauke in flight,
        Perforce° rebutted° backe. The weapon bright   *necessarily / attacked*
        Taking advantage of his open jaw,
475   Ran through his mouth with so importune° might,   *violent*
        That deepe emperst his darksome hollow maw,°   *mouth*
    And back retyrd,° his life bloud forth with all did draw.   *retracted*

54

     So downe he fell, and forth his life did breath,[1]
        That vanisht into smoke and cloudes swift;
480   So downe he fell, that th'earth him underneath
        Did grone, as feeble so great load to lift;
        So downe he fell, as an huge rockie clift,
        Whose false foundation waves have washt away,
        With dreadfull poyse° is from the mayneland rift,   *force*
485   And rolling downe, great Neptune doth dismay;
    So downe he fell, and like an heaped mountaine lay.

55

     The knight himselfe even trembled at his fall,
        So huge and horrible a masse it seem'd;
        And his deare Ladie, that beheld it all,
490   Durst not approch for dread, which she misdeem'd,
        But yet at last, when as the direfull feend
        She saw not stirre, off-shaking vaine affright,°   *empty fear*
        She nigher drew, and saw that joyous end:
        Then God she praysd, and thankt her faithfull knight,
495   That had atchiev'd so great a conquest by his might.

---

1. The blood that flows from the Dragon takes his life with it.

Canto 12

Faire Una to the Redcrosse knight
*   betrouthed is with joy:*
Though false Duessa it to barre°   prevent
*   her false sleights doe imploy.*

1

Behold I see the haven° nigh at hand,   harbor
    To which I meane my wearie course to bend;
    Vere° the maine shete, and beare up with° the land,   loosen / steer toward
    The which afore is fairely to be kend,°   recognized
5   And seemeth safe from stormes, that may offend;
    There this faire virgin wearie of her way
    Must landed be, now at her journeyes end:
    There eke my feeble barke° a while may stay,   ship
Till merry wind and weather call her thence away.

2

10   Scarsely had Phoebus in the glooming° East   glowing
    Yet harnessed his firie-footed teeme,
    Ne reard above the earth his flaming creast,
    When the last deadly smoke aloft did steeme,
    That signe of last outbreathed life did seeme
15   Unto the watchman on the castle wall;
    Who thereby dead that balefull Beast did deeme,
    And to his Lord and Ladie lowd gan call,
To tell, how he had seene the Dragons fatall fall.

3

Uprose with hastie joy, and feeble speed
20   That aged Sire,° the Lord of all that land,   Una's father
    And looked forth, to weet, if true indeede
    Those tydings were, as he did understand,
    Which whenas true by tryall° he out fond,   investigation
    He bad to open wyde his brazen gate,
25   Which long time had bene shut, and out of hond°   immediately
    Proclaymed joy and peace through all his state;
For dead now was their foe, which them forrayed° late.°   plundered / lately

4

Then gan triumphant Trompets sound on hie,
    That sent to heaven the ecchoed report
30   Of their new joy, and happie victorie
    Gainst him, that had them long opprest with tort,°   wrong
    And fast imprisoned in sieged fort.
    Then all the people, as in solemne feast,
    To him assembled with one full consort,°   in unison
35   Rejoycing at the fall of that great beast,
From whose eternall bondage now they were release.

5

Forth came that auncient Lord and aged Queene,
   Arayd° in antique robes downe to the ground,   *dressed*
   And sad habiliments right well beseene;[1]
40   A noble crew° about them waited round   *crowd*
   Of sage and sober Peres, all gravely gownd;
   Whom farre before did march a goodly band
   Of tall young men, all hable° armes to sownd,°   *able / wield*
   But now they laurell braunches bore in hand;
45 Glad signe of victorie and peace in all their land.

6

Unto that doughtie° Conquerour they came,   *worthy*
   And him before themselves prostrating low,
   Their Lord and Patrone loud did him proclame,
   And at his feet their laurell boughes did throw.
50   Soone after them all dauncing on a row
   The comely virgins came, with girlands dight,°   *prepared*
   As fresh as flowres in medow greene do grow,
   When morning deaw upon their leaves doth light:° *land*
And in their hands sweet Timbrels° all upheld on hight. *tambourines*

7

55 And them before, the fry° of children young   *group*
   Their wanton sports and childish mirth did play,
   And to the Maydens sounding tymbrels sung
   In well attuned notes, a joyous lay,
   And made delightfull musicke all the way,
60   Untill they came, where that faire virgin stood;
   As faire Diana in fresh sommers day
   Beholds her Nymphes, enraung'd° in shadie wood, *spread out*
Some wrestle, some do run, some bathe in christall flood.° *clear waters*

8

So she beheld those maydens meriment
65   With chearefull vew; who when to her they came,
   Themselves to ground with gratious humblesse bent,
   And her ador'd by honorable name,
   Lifting to heaven her everlasting fame:
   Then on her head they set a girland greene,
70   And crowned her twixt earnest and twixt game;[2]
   Who in her selfe-resemblance well beseene,[3]
Did seeme such, as she was, a goodly maiden Queene.

9

And after, all the raskall many° ran,   *playful crowd*
   Heaped together in rude rablement,°   *confusion*

---

1. Their somber clothes were appropriate.
2. Half seriously, half playfully.
3. Una appears appropriately like herself (unlike Duessa,
for instance, who appeared to be something other than
what she was).

75   To see the face of that victorious man:°   *Redcrosse Knight*
      Whom all admired, as from heaven sent,
      And gazd upon with gaping wonderment.
      But when they came, where that dead Dragon lay,
      Stretcht on the ground in monstrous large extent,
80   The sight with idle feare did them dismay,
Ne durst° approch him nigh, to touch, or once assay.[4]   *nor dared*

                    10
      Some feard, and fled; some feard and well it faynd;°   *hid it well*
      One that would wiser seeme, then° all the rest,   *than*
      Warnd him not touch, for yet perhaps remaynd
85   Some lingring life within his hollow brest,
      Or in his wombe might lurke some hidden nest
      Of many Dragonets, his fruitfull seed;
      Another said, that in his eyes did rest
      Yet sparckling fire, and bad thereof take heed;°   *care*
90   Another said, he saw him move his eyes indeed.

                    11
      One mother, when as her foolehardie chyld
      Did come too neare, and with his talants° play,   *claws*
      Halfe dead through feare, her litle babe revyld,
      And to her gossips gan in counsell say;
95   How can I tell, but that his talants may
      Yet scratch my sonne, or rend his tender hand?
      So diversly themselves in vaine they fray;°   *frighten*
      Whiles some more bold, to measure him nigh stand,
To prove how many acres he did spread of land.

                    12
100   Thus flocked all the folke him round about,
      The whiles that hoarie° king, with all his traine,   *aged*
      Being arrived, where that champion stout
      After his foes defeasance° did remaine,   *defeat*
      Him goodly greetes, and faire does entertaine,
105   With princely gifts of yvorie and gold,
      And thousand thankes him yeelds° for all his paine.   *gives*
      Then when his daughter deare he does behold,
Her dearely doth imbrace, and kisseth manifold.°   *many times*

                    13
      And after to his Pallace he them brings,
110   With shaumes,° and trompets, and with Clarions° sweet;   *oboes / trumpets*
      And all the way the joyous people sings,
      And with their garments strowes the paved street:
      Whence mounting up, they find purveyance meet°   *suitable refreshment*
      Of all, that royall Princes court became,

4. They did not dare to approach the dragon, to touch it, or even to try to touch it.

115   And all the floore was underneath their feet
        Bespred with costly scarlot° of great name,   *cloth*
    On which they lowly sit, and fitting purpose frame.°   *converse nicely*

14

    What needs me tell their feast and goodly guize,°   *behavior*
        In which was nothing riotous nor vaine?
120   What needs of daintie dishes to devize,°   *describe*
        Of comely services, or courtly trayne?
        My narrow leaves cannot in them containe
        The large discourse of royall Princes state.
        Yet was their manner then but bare° and plaine: *simple*
125   For th'antique world excesse and pride did hate;
    Such proud luxurious pompe is swollen up but late.°   *only recently*

15

    Then when with meates and drinkes of every kinde
        Their fervent appetites they quenched had,
        That auncient Lord gan fit occasion finde,
130   Of straunge adventures, and of perils sad,
        Which in his travell him befallen had,
        For to demaund of his renowmed° guest: *renowned*
        Who then with utt'rance° grave, and count'nance sad,   *expression*
        From point to point, as is before exprest,
135   Discourst° his voyage long, according his request.   *related*

16

    Great pleasure mixt with pittifull regard,°   *compassion*
        That godly King and Queene did passionate,°   *empathize*
        Whiles they his pittifull adventures heard,
        That oft they did lament his lucklesse state,
140   And often blame the too importune° fate,   *cruel*
        That heapd on him so many wrathfull wreakes:˘   *injuries*
        For never gentle knight, as he of late,°   *recently*
        So tossed was in fortunes cruell freakes;°   *accidents*
    And all the while salt teares bedeawd° the hearers cheaks.   *wetted*

17

145   Then said that royall Pere in sober wise;
        Deare Sonne, great beene the evils, which ye bore
        From first to last in your late enterprise,
        That I note, whether prayse, or pitty more:
        For never living man, I weene, so sore
150   In sea of deadly daungers was distrest;
        But since now safe ye seised° have the shore,   *reached*
        And well arrived are, (high God be blest)
    Let us devize° of ease and everlasting rest.   *speak*

18

    Ah dearest Lord, said then that doughty° knight,   *worthy*
155   Of ease or rest I may not yet devize;

For by the faith, which I to armes have plight,
I bounden am streight after this emprize,°   *enterprise*
As that your daughter can ye well advize,
Backe to returne to that great Faerie Queene,
160   And her to serve six yeares in warlike wize,°   *manner*
Gainst that proud Paynim king, that workes her teene:°   *sorrow*
Therefore I ought crave pardon, till I there have beene.

19

Unhappie falles that hard necessitie,
(Quoth he) the troubler of my happie peace,
165   And vowed foe of my felicitie;
Ne I against the same can justly preace:°   *argue*
But since that band° ye cannot now release,   *bond*
Nor doen undo; (for vowes may not be vaine)
Soone as the terme of those six yeares shall cease,
170   Ye then shall hither backe returne againe,
The marriage to accomplish vowd° betwixt you twain.   *promised*

20

Which for my part I covet° to performe,   *desire*
In sort as through the world I did proclame,
That who so kild that monster most deforme,
175   And him in hardy battaile overcame,
Should have mine onely daughter to his Dame,
And of my kingdome heire apparaunt bee:
Therefore since now to thee perteines the same,
By dew desert of noble chevalree,
180   Both daughter and eke kingdome, lo I yield to thee.

21

Then forth he called that his daughter faire,
The fairest Un' his onely daughter deare,
His onely daughter, and his onely heyre;
Who forth proceeding with sad sober cheare,
185   As bright as doth the morning starre appeare
Out of the East, with flaming lockes bedight,
To tell that dawning day is drawing neare,
And to the world does bring long wished light;
So faire and fresh that Lady shewd her selfe in sight.

22

190   So faire and fresh, as freshest flowre in May;
For she had layd her mournefull stole° aside,   *dark cloak*
And widow-like sad wimple throwne away,
Wherewith her heavenly beautie she did hide,
Whiles on her wearie journey she did ride;
195   And on her now a garment she did weare,
All lilly white, withoutten° spot, or pride,   *without a*

That seemd like silke and silver woven neare,
But neither silke nor silver therein did appeare.

23

The blazing brightnesse of her beauties beame,
200   And glorious light of her sunshyny face
To tell, were as to strive against the streame.
My ragged rimes° are all too rude and bace,   *rhymes*
Her heavenly lineaments° for to enchace.°   *features / display*
Ne wonder; for her owne deare loved knight,
205   All were she dayly with himselfe in place,°   *by his side*
Did wonder much at her celestiall sight:
Oft had he seene her faire, but never so faire dight.

24

So fairely dight, when she in presence came,
She to her Sire made humble reverence,
210   And bowed low, that her right well became,
And added grace unto her excellence:
Who with great wisedome, and grave eloquence
Thus gan to say. But eare he thus had said,
With flying speede, and seeming great pretence,°   *purpose*
215   Came running in, much like a man dismaid,°   *overwhelmed*
A Messenger with letters, which his message said.

25

All in the open hall amazed stood,
At suddeinnesse of that unwarie° sight,   *unexpected*
And wondred at his breathlesse hastie mood.
220   But he for nought would stay his passage right,°   *stop*
Till fast before° the king he did alight;°   *in front of / arrive*
Where falling flat, great humblesse he did make,
And kist the ground, whereon his foot was pight;°   *placed*
Then to his hands that writ° he did betake,°   *message / deliver*
225   Which he disclosing,° red thus, as the paper spake.°   *unfolding / said*

26

To thee, most mighty king of Eden faire,
Her greeting sends in these sad lines addrest,
The wofull daughter, and forsaken heire
Of that great Emperour of all the West;
230   And bids thee be advized for the best,
Ere thou thy daughter linck° in holy band   *join*
Of wedlocke to that new unknowen guest:
For he already plighted° his right hand   *promised*
Unto another love, and to another land.

27

235   To me sad mayd, or rather widow sad,
He was affiaunced° long time before,   *engaged*
And sacred pledges he both gave, and had,

False erraunt° knight, infamous, and forswore:°   *erring / lying*
Witnesse the burning Altars, which° he swore,[5]   *by which*
240 And guiltie heavens of his bold perjury,°   *lie*
Which though he hath polluted oft of yore,
Yet I to them for judgement just do fly,
And them conjure° t'avenge this shamefull injury.[6]   *implore*

28

Therefore since mine he is, or free or bond,
245 Or false or trew, or living or else dead,
Withhold, O soveraine Prince, your hasty hond
From knitting league with him, I you aread;°   *advise*
Ne weene my right with strength adowne to tread,[7]
Through weakenesse of my widowhed,° or woe: *widowhood*
250 For truth is strong, her rightfull cause to plead,
And shall find friends, if need requireth soe,
So bids thee well to fare,° Thy neither friend, nor foe.   *farewell*

29

When he° these bitter byting words had red,°   *the king / heard*
The tydings° straunge did him abashed make,   *news*
255 That still he sate long time astonished
As in great muse,° ne word to creature spake.   *astonishment*
At last his solemne silence thus he brake,
With doubtfull eyes fast fixed on his guest;
Redoubted° knight, that for mine onely sake   *formidable*
260 Thy life and honour late adventurest,
Let nought be hid from me, that ought to be exprest.

30

What meane these bloudy vowes, and idle threats,
Throwne out from womanish impatient mind?
What heavens? what altars? what enraged heates°   *rantings*
265 Here heaped up with termes of love unkind,
My conscience cleare with guilty bands would bind?
High God be witnesse, that I guiltlesse ame.
But if your selfe, Sir knight, ye faultie° find,   *guilty*
Or wrapped be in loves of former Dame,
270 With crime° do not it cover, but disclose the same.   *lies*

31

To whom the Redcrosse knight this answere sent,
My Lord, my King, be nought hereat dismayd,
Till well ye wote by grave intendiment,°   *careful consideration*
What woman, and wherefore° doth me upbrayd   *why*
275 With breach of love, and loyalty betrayd.
It was in my mishaps, as hitherward°   *on my way here*

5. Referring to a pagan marriage ritual in which sacrifices
are burned on an altar to confirm the marriage vows.
6. Although the Redcrosse Knight has polluted the heavens
with his lies, the author of the message nonetheless looks
to them for judgment against him.
7. Do not try to overcome my rights by force.

I lately traveild, that unwares I strayd
Out of my way, through perils straunge and hard;
That day should faile me, ere I had them all declard.

32

280 There did I find, or rather I was found
Of this false woman, that Fidessa hight,
Fidessa hight the falsest Dame on ground,
Most false Duessa, royall richly dight,
That easie° was t'invegle° weaker sight: *eager / blind*
285 Who by her wicked arts, and wylie skill,
Too false and strong for earthly skill or might,
Unwares° me wrought unto her wicked will,   *unknowingly*
And to my foe betrayd, when least I feared ill.

33

Then stepped forth the goodly royall Mayd,
290 And on the ground her selfe prostrating° low,   *bowing*
With sober countenaunce thus to him sayd;
O pardon me, my soveraigne Lord, to show
The secret treasons, which of late° I know   *recently*
To have bene wroght° by that false sorceresse.   *committed*
295 She onely she it is, that earst did throw
This gentle knight into so great distresse,
That death him did awaite in dayly wretchednesse.

34

And now it seemes, that she suborned° hath   *bribed*
This craftie messenger with letters vaine,°   *false*
300 To worke new woe and improvided° scath,   *unforeseen*
By breaking of the band betwixt us twaine;
Wherein she used hath the practicke paine°   *crafty labor*
Of this false footman, clokt° with simplenesse,   *cloaked*
Whom if ye please for° to discover plaine,   *wish*
305 Ye shall him Archimago find, I ghesse,
The falsest man alive; who° tries shall find no lesse.   *whoever*

35

The king was greatly moved at her speach,
And all with suddein indignation fraight,°   *filled*
Bad on that Messenger rude hands to reach.
310 Eftsoones the Gard, which on his state did wait,
Attacht° that faitor false, and bound him strait: *seized*
Who seeming sorely chauffed° at his band,   *annoyed*
As chained Beare, whom cruell dogs do bait,
With idle force did faine° them to withstand,   *attempt*
315 And often semblaunce made° to scape out of their hand.[8]   *pretended*

36

But they him layd full low in dungeon deepe,

---

8. Because Archimago himself is false, his efforts to escape are also false.

And bound him hand and foote with yron chains.
And with continuall watch did warely° keepe;   *carefully*
Who then would thinke, that by his subtile trains
320   He could escape fowle death or deadly paines?
Thus when that Princes wrath was pacifide,
He gan renew the late forbidden banes,°   *banns*
And to the knight his daughter deare he tyde,
With sacred rites and vowes for ever to abyde.[9]

37

325   His owne two hands the holy knots did knit,
That none but death for ever can devide;
His owne two hands, for such a turne most fit,
The housling° fire[1] did kindle and provide,   *domestic*
And holy water thereon sprinckled wide;
330   At which the bushy Teade° a groome did light,   *torch*
And sacred lampe in secret chamber hide,
Where it should not be quenched day nor night,
For feare of evill fates, but burnen ever bright.

38

Then gan they sprinckle all the posts with wine,[2]
335   And made great feast to solemnize that day;
They all perfumde with frankincense divine,
And precious odours fetcht from far away,
That all the house did sweat with great aray:°   *ceremony*
And all the while sweete Musicke did apply
340   Her curious skill, the warbling notes to play,
To drive away the dull Melancholy;
The whiles one sung a song of love and jollity.

39

During the which there was an heavenly noise
Heard sound through all the Pallace pleasantly,
345   Like as it had bene many an Angels voice,
Singing before th'eternall majesty,
In their trinall triplicities[3] on hye;
Yet wist no creature, whence that heavenly sweet
Proceeded, yet eachone felt secretly
350   Himselfe thereby reft of his sences meet,°   *ordinary*
And ravished with rare impression in his sprite.

40

Great joy was made that day of young and old,
And solemne feast proclaimd throughout the land,

9. The King recommences the announcement of marriage that had been recently forbidden by Duessa's false charges against the Redcrosse Knight.
1. Originally Roman marriage rituals, the fire and water used by the King here also suggest baptism and the sanctification of married love.

2. Roman brides sprinkled the doorposts of their new homes with wine in a ritual symbolizing joy and fertility.
3. The triple triad or the nine orders of angels. The music that they play is the music of the spheres, which humankind had been unable to hear since the Fall.

	That their exceeding merth° may not be told:	*joy*
355	Suffice it heare by signes to understand[4]	
	The usuall joyes at knitting of loves band.	
	Thrise° happy man the knight himselfe did hold,	*thrice*
	Possessed of his Ladies hart and hand,	
	And ever, when his eye did her behold,	
360	His heart did seeme to melt in pleasures manifold.	

41

	Her joyous presence and sweet company	
	In full content he there did long enjoy,	
	Ne wicked envie, ne vile gealosy	
	His deare delights were able to annoy:	
365	Yet swimming in that sea of blisfull joy,	
	He nought forgot, how he whilome had sworne,	
	In case he could that monstrous beast destroy,	
	Unto his Faerie Queene backe to returne:	
	The which he shortly did, and Una left to mourne.	

42

370	Now strike your sailes ye jolly Mariners,	
	For we be come unto a quiet rode,°	*haven*
	Where we must land some of our passengers,	
	And light this wearie vessell of her lode.	
	Here she a while may make her safe abode,	
375	Till she repaired have her tackles spent,°	*worn out fittings*
	And wants supplide. And then againe abroad	
	On the long voyage whereto she is bent:	
	Well may she speede° and fairely finish her intent.	*continue*

AMORETTI   Spenser apparently wrote the sequence entitled *Amoretti* for Elizabeth Boyle, whom he married in 1594, although some of its eighty-nine sonnets may be of an earlier date and intended for another woman. The sequence was published in 1595 together with *Epithalamion*, Spenser's marriage hymn in celebration of his wedding. The two works are linked thematically by their allusions to the passage of time. The *Amoretti* refers to seasons of the year, the *Epithalamion* to twenty-four hours of a day that begins at one in the morning and ends at 12 midnight.

from **Amoretti**[1]

1

	Happy ye leaves° when as those lilly hands,	*of the book*
	Which hold my life in their dead doing° might,	*death-dealing*
	Shall handle you and hold in loves soft bands,°	*bonds*

4. I.e., because the happiness of the occasion is beyond the ability of words to express, let it be sufficient to understand it through symbols.

1. "Little loves."

Lyke captives trembling at the victors sight.
5   And happy lines, on which with starry light,
Those lamping° eyes will deigne sometimes to look   *flashing*
And reade the sorrowes of my dying spright,°   *spirit*
Written with teares in harts close bleeding book.
And happy rymes bath'd in the sacred brooke,[2]
10 Of Helicon whence she derived is,
When ye behold that Angels blessed looke,
My soules long lacked foode, my heavens blis.
Leaves, lines, and rymes, seeke her to please alone,
Whom if ye please, I care for other none.

4

New yeare forth looking out of Janus[3] gate,
Doth seeme to promise hope of new delight:
And bidding th'old Adieu, his passed date
Bids all old thoughts to die in dumpish spright°   *low spirits*
5   And calling forth out of sad Winters night,
Fresh love, that long hath slept in cheerlesse bower:
Wils him awake, and soone about him dight
His wanton wings and darts of deadly power.
For lusty spring now in his timely howre,
10 Is ready to come forth him to receive:
And warnes the Earth with divers colord flowre,
To decke hir selfe, and her faire mantle weave.
Then you faire flowre, in whom fresh youth doth raine,°   *reign*
Prepare your selfe new love to entertaine.

13

In that proud port,° which her so goodly graceth,[4]   *bearing*
Whiles her faire face she reares up to the skie:
And to the ground her eie lids low embaseth°   *casts down*
Most goodly temperature° ye may descry,°   *temperament / perceive*
5   Myld humblesse° mixt with awfull° majesty,   *humility / awesome*
For looking on the earth whence she was borne:
Her minde remembreth her mortalitie,
What so is fayrest shall to earth returne.
But that same lofty countenance seemes to scorne
10 Base thing, and thinke how she to heaven may clime:
Treading downe earth as lothsome and forlorne,

---

2. Aganippe, which rises (or is "derived") from Helicon, a mountain that is home to the Muses, goddesses of all the arts but known especially for their inspiration of poets. 3. A Roman god of the new year who has two faces; one looks back at December, the other ahead to January. For Christians the liturgical new year began on March 25, the Feast of the Annunciation, when the Angel Gabriel was thought to have announced the coming of Jesus Christ to the Virgin Mary. Throughout the sequence, Spenser plays with these two concepts of the year, juxtaposing the time dictated by nature, figured by the Roman calendar, with time according to Christian history and celebrated by the fasts and feasts of the church. 4. Spenser describes the lady to whom the sonnet is addressed.

That hinders heavenly thoughts with drossy° slime.   *heavy*
Yet lowly still vouchsafe° to looke on me,   *condescend*
Such lowlinesse shall make you lofty be.

22

This holy season fit to fast and pray,[5]
Men to devotion ought to be inclynd:
Therefore, I lykewise on so holy day,
For my sweet Saynt some service fit will find.
5   Her temple fayre is built within my mind,
In which her glorious ymage placed is,
On which my thoughts doo day and night attend
Lyke sacred priests that never thinke amisse.
There I to her as th'author of my blisse,
10 Will builde an altar to appease her yre:°   *anger*
And on the same my hart will sacrifise,
Burning in flames of pure and chast desyre:
The which vouchsafe O goddesse to accept,
Amongst thy deerest relicks to be kept.

62

The weary yeare his race now having run,
The new[6] begins his compast° course anew: *encompassed*
With shew of morning mylde he hath begun,
Betokening peace and plenty to ensew.
5   So let us, which this chaunge of weather vew,
Chaunge eeke° our mynds and former lives amend,   *also*
The old yeares sinnes forepast° let us eschew,°   *gone by / avoid*
And fly the faults with which we did offend.
Then shall the new yeares joy forth freshly send,
10 Into the glooming° world his gladsome ray: *gloomy*
And all these stormes which now his beauty blend,°   *dim*
Shall turne to caulmes and tymely cleare away.
So likewise love cheare you your heavy spright,
And chaunge old yeares annoy° to new delight.   *grief*

65

The doubt° which ye misdeeme,° fayre love, is vaine,   *fear / misconceive*
That fondly° feare to loose° your liberty,   *foolishly / lose*
When loosing one, two liberties ye gayne,
And make him bond that bondage earst dyd fly.
5   Sweet be the bands, the which true love doth tye,
Without constraynt or dread of any ill:

---

5. The holy season is Lent; the holy day is Ash Wednesday. The sonnet celebrates the poet's admission that his
love has a spiritual dimension; complimenting his heart's
desire is the worship he gives to his lady's image in the
temple of his mind.
6. The Christian new year, the Feast of the Annunciation.

The gentle birde feeles no captivity
Within her cage, but singes and feeds her fill.
There pride dare not approch, nor discord spill
10   The league twixt them, that loyal love hath bound:
But simple truth and mutuall good will,
Seekes with sweet peace to salve° each others wound: heal
There fayth doth fearlesse dwell in brasen towre,
And spotlesse pleasure builds her sacred bowre.

66

To all those happy blessings which ye have,
With plenteous hand by heaven upon you thrown:
This one disparagement they to you gave,
That ye your love lent to so meane a one.[7]
5   Yee whose high worths surpassing paragon,
Could not on earth have found one fit for mate,
Ne but in heaven matchable to none,
Why did ye stoup unto so lowly state.
But ye thereby much greater glory gate,°   got
10   Then° had ye sorted° with a princes pere:°   than / consorted / peer
For now your light doth more it selfe dilate,°   spread
And in my darknesse greater doth appeare.
Yet since your light hath once enlumind° me,   illuminated
With my reflex° yours shall encreased be.   reflected light

68

Most glorious Lord of lyfe that on this day,[8]
Didst make thy triumph over death and sin:
And having harrowd hell, didst bring away
Captivity thence captive us to win.[9]
5   This joyous day, deare Lord, with joy begin,
And grant that we for whom thou diddest dye
Being with thy deare blood clene washt from sin,
May live for ever in felicity.
And that thy love we weighing worthily,
10   May likewise love thee for the same againe:
And for thy sake that all lyke deare° didst buy,   at the same cost
With love may one another entertayne.
So let us love, deare love, lyke as we ought,
Love is the lesson which the Lord us taught.

---

7. Working forward from Sonnet 62 and counting each sonnet as representing a day of love and devotion, Sonnet 66 corresponds to Good Friday. Spenser exploits the idea of humility, consistent with the passion of Christ, to express his own sense of devotion to his lady's virtue.
8. The sonnet addresses the "dear Lord" of the Passion on Easter Day to harmonize the poet's love for his lady and his obligation to follow the lesson of Christ.

9. Christians believed that after his Resurrection, Christ descended into hell to rescue Adam and Eve and the patriarchs and prophets of the Hebrew Bible. The event is often described as the harrowing of hell.

75

One day I wrote her name upon the strand,°   *beach*
But came the waves and washed it away:
Agayne I wrote it with a second hand,
But came the tyde, and made my paynes his pray.
5 Vayne man, sayd she, that doest in vaine assay,°   *attempt*
A mortall thing so to immortalize.
For I my selve shall lyke to this decay,
And eek my name bee wyped out lykewize.
Not so, (quod I) let baser things devize,°   *consent*
10 To dy in dust, but you shall live by fame:
My verse your vertues rare shall eternize,°   *make eternal*
And in the hevens wryte your glorious name:
Where whenas death shall all the world subdew,
Our love shall live, and later life renew.

＋→ ⊰◈⊱ ←＋

Sir Philip Sidney
1554–1586

Reality is often stranger but hardly ever more perfect than fiction. As Sir Philip Sidney tells us, the poets bring forth a "golden world." Exempt from judgments about its truth or falsehood, "poetry" (by which Sidney meant fiction) should construct forms of the ideal to mitigate our suffering and move us to good action. Sidney's own work comments brilliantly on contemporary moral and political issues: his sonnet sequence *Astrophil and Stella* illustrates the lover's paradox (love may require chastity); his prose romance *The Arcadia* describes the politics of love and sexuality, and his *Apology for Poetry* defends poetic and dramatic art from critics who would dismiss it in favor of philosophy and history. Yet to his countrymen, Sidney's most important achievement may have been a life dedicated to a public heroism and shaped by a sense of personal honor.

History has portrayed him as a prodigy. As his friend Fulke Greville wrote, "though I knew him from a child, yet I never knew him other than a man, . . . his very play tending to enrich his mind, so that even his teachers found something in him to observe and learn above that which they had usually read or taught." Play—understood in the Renaissance manner as "serious play"—took up much of Sidney's early career. Leaving Oxford at the age of seventeen but without a degree, Sidney embarked on what in later centuries was known as the Grand Tour. He visited Europe's major cities, seeking men and women who were fashioning the political goals and aesthetic sensibilities of the age. They included the philosopher Hubert Languet, whose Protestantism was linked to a fiercely antityrannical politics; the artists Tintoretto and Paolo Veronese, whose luminous realism was to determine painterly style for more than a generation; and, finally, Henry of Navarre (later King Henry IV of France) and his wife, Margaret of Valois, whose reign would see the worst of the religious wars in Europe. Back in England by 1575, Sidney espoused a politics that challenged authority. Siding with his father, Henry Sidney, Queen Elizabeth's Lord Deputy Governor of Ireland, he argued for imposing a land tax on the Anglo-Irish nobility, citing their "unreasonable and arrogant pretensions" as a cause of civil unrest. And in 1580, seeking to protect the monarchy from foreign influences, he wrote to the Queen cautioning her against a match with Francis, Duke of Alençon and brother to the French king, Henry III. She was furious at his temerity and ordered him to the country, where he was to remain out of touch with court affairs. By 1584 she had relented, sending Sidney to the Netherlands to assess the Protestant resistance to Spanish rule. There, in 1586, fighting for the Queen's interest and the Protestant cause she championed, he died of an abscessed bullet wound in his thigh.

Sidney's first literary work was a brief pastoral masque entitled *The Lady of May*, composed in honor of the Queen in 1578. His subsequent exile from court provided him with extensive time to write. He was often at Wilton, the estate of his sister, Mary Herbert, Countess of Pembroke; it was there that he wrote the first two of his major works, in all likelihood with his sister and her circle as his first readers and critics. *The Apology for Poetry*, a work defending what Sidney called his "unelected vocation," answers attacks on art, poetry, and the theater by such censorious writers as Stephen Gosson. But its argument exceeds the limits of antitheatrical debate to embrace questions about the uses of history and the effectiveness of philosophy—a subject that bears comparison with the poetics of Aristotle and Horace. Readers have remembered most its insistence that "poetry" goes beyond nature to fashion an ideal; it works "not only to make a Cyrus, which had been but a particular excellency as nature might have done, but to bestow a Cyrus upon the world to make many Cyruses." Poetry's creatures—whether heroes, heroines, or villains—cannot misrepresent fact because they exist only in the imagination of readers and listeners: "for the poet," Sidney declared, "he nothing affirms, and therefore never lieth."

Sidney's second work from his period at Wilton, the pastoral prose romance known as *The Arcadia*, was finished in 1581 and circulated in manuscript thereafter (and in print in 1973), depicts the willfulness of a superstitious and lazy duke, Basilius, who sequesters his marriageable daughters, Pamela and Philoclea, in the country where no suitor can meet them. His plans are foiled by two foreign princes, Pyrocles and Musidorus, who, disguised as a woman and a shepherd, manage to court and win the love of these ladies. Interspersed throughout the prose narrative of these events are poems, termed *eclogues*, expressing the joys and sorrows of pastoral life, one of which, *As I my little flock on Ister bank*, has persuaded many readers that Sidney was arguing for a radical, essentially republican politics.

A second version of the *Arcadia*, apparently written two or three years later, very explicitly introduces politics to the plot: Sidney sketches the characters of several rulers, magnificent and tyrannical; includes arguments for resistance and rebellion; and illustrates the nature of justice and equity. This version, revised after Sidney's death by his sister, Mary Herbert, Countess of Pembroke, and published in 1593, contains splendid portraits of queens both good and bad. Especially memorable is the wicked Cecropia, who plots to capture and kill the Arcadian princesses. The mother of Amphialus, who is a kind of moving target for misfortune's arrows, Cecropia has sometimes been understood to figure Catherine de'Medici, the powerful French queen, who many maintained had helped plan the massacre of hundreds of Protestants on Saint Bartholomew's Day, 1572.

Sidney's last work, *Astrophil and Stella*, has often been understood as self-satire, a mockery of adolescent love dismissive of traditional morality yet bent on physical intimacy. Its principal character, the young Astrophil, is frustrated by the marriage of his beloved Stella to a man who is characterized as "rich," an apparent reference to Sidney's disappointment when Penelope Devereux, whom he had courted for several years, married Lord Rich. Sidney derides the young lover's passionate complaints while at the same time transforming the courtly figure of the distant yet beloved lady to reveal a paradox: as "absent," Stella may be present to Astrophil in spirit; as "present," she can only deny him her intimate friendship. Sidney intersperses his lover's sonnets with nine songs describing dramatic attempts at seduction; in the Eighth Song, Sidney interpolates lines spoken by Stella, who denies the lover her favors. As a whole the sequence is a marvelously witty reconceptualization of the principal themes of English Petrarchanism, a style that by the 1580s had become rather trite. Addressing his Stella, Sidney's Astrophil ends a sonnet with these lines:

And not content to be Perfection's heir
Thyself, doest strive all minds that way to move:
Who mark in thee what is in thee most fair.
So while thy beauty draws the heart to love,
As fast thy virtue bends that love to good:
But ah, Desire still cries, give me some food.

Conventionally Petrarchan in his depiction of the lady as a model and inspiration to a moral virtue that would seem to rule out any physical expressions of love, Sidney is at last very unconventional: he refuses to renounce "Desire" and its "food," or sexual gratification. A more imitative poet would not have so rejected Petrarch's idealistic asceticism. But just as Sidney had challenged the authority of church and state to promote better government (as he saw it), so did he exploit the process of "invention," the discovery of new meaning in old matter, to revitalize literary forms and expression.

The Apology for Poetry

When the right virtuous Edward Wotton[1] and I were at the Emperor's court together, we gave ourselves to learn horsemanship of John Pietro Pugliano, one that with great commendation had the place of an esquire in his stable. And he, according to the fertileness of the Italian wit, did not only afford us the demonstration of his practice, but sought to enrich our minds with the contemplations therein, which he thought most precious. But with none I remember mine ears were at that time more laden, than when (either angered with slow payment, or moved with our learner-like admiration) he exercised his speech in the praise of his faculty. He said soldiers were the noblest estate of mankind, and horsemen the noblest of soldiers. He said they were the masters of war and ornaments of peace, speedy goers and strong abiders, triumphers both in camps and courts. Nay, to so unbelieved a point he proceeded as that no earthly thing bred such wonder to a prince as to be a good horseman—skill of government was but a *pedanteria* [pedantry] in comparison. Then would he add certain praises, by telling what a peerless beast the horse was, the only serviceable courtier without flattery, the beast of most beauty, faithfulness, courage, and such more, that if I had not been a piece of a logician before I came to him, I think he would have persuaded me to have wished myself a horse. But thus much at least with his no few words he drave into me, that self-love is better than any gilding to make that seem gorgeous wherein ourselves be parties. Wherein, if Pugliano's strong affection and weak arguments will not satisfy you, I will give you a nearer example of myself, who (I know not by what mischance) in these my not old years and idlest times having slipped into the title of a poet, am provoked to say something unto you in the defense of that my unelected vocation,[2] which if I handle with more good will than good reasons, bear with me, since the scholar is to be pardoned that followeth the steps of his master. And yet I must say that, as I have more just cause to make a pitiful defense of poor poetry, which from almost the highest estimation of learning is fallen to be the laughingstock of children, so have I need to bring some more available proofs: since the former is by no man barred of his deserved credit, the silly latter hath had even the names of

1. Edward Wotton (1548–1626), half-brother of Henry Wotton who saw diplomatic service under James I. Edward Wotton and Sidney undertook a mission to the court of the Emperor Maximilian at Vienna in 1574–1575.

2. Sidney refers to writing poetry as his "unelected vocation" because he would have readers believe that he undertook it only after Elizabeth I had exiled him from court.

philosophers used to the defacing of it, with great danger of civil war among the Muses.[3]

And first, truly, to all them that, professing learning, inveigh against poetry may justly be objected that they go very near to ungratefulness, to seek to deface that which, in the noblest nations and languages that are known, hath been the first light-giver to ignorance, and first nurse, whose milk by little and little enabled them to feed afterwards of tougher knowledges. And will they now play the hedgehog that, being received into the den, drive out his host? Or rather the vipers, that with their birth kill their parents?

Let learned Greece in any of his manifold sciences be able to show me one book before Musaeus, Homer, and Hesiod, all three nothing else but poets.[4] Nay, let any history be brought that can say any writers were there before them, if they were not men of the same skill, as Orpheus, Linus,[5] and some other are named, who, having been the first of that country that made pens deliverers of their knowledge to the posterity, may justly challenge to be called their fathers in learning: for not only in time they had this priority (although in itself antiquity be venerable) but went before them, as causes to draw with their charming sweetness the wild untamed wits to an admiration of knowledge. So, as Amphion[6] was said to move stones with his poetry to build Thebes, and Orpheus to be listened to by beasts—indeed stony and beastly people—so among the Romans were Livius Andronicus and Ennius. So in the Italian language the first that made it aspire to be a treasure-house of science were the poets Dante, Boccaccio, and Petrarch. So in our English were Gower and Chaucer, after whom, encouraged and delighted with their excellent fore-going,[7] others have followed, to beautify our mother tongue, as well in the same kind as in other arts.

This did so notably show itself, that the philosophers of Greece durst not a long time appear to the world but under the masks of poets. So Thales, Empedocles, and Parmenides[8] sang their natural philosophy in verses; so did Pythagoras and Phocylides their moral counsels; so did Tyrtaeus in war matters, and Solon in matters of policy: or rather they, being poets, did exercise their delightful vein in those points of highest knowledge, which before them lay hid to the world. For that wise Solon was directly a poet it is manifest, having written in verse the notable fable of the Atlantic Island, which was continued by Plato. And truly even Plato[9] whosoever well considereth shall

---

3. Mythological figures who were thought to inspire the liberal arts.

4. Musaeus was in fact a poet of the 5th century A.D., reported to be a pupil of the mythical Orpheus, the first musician. Homer was the legendary author of the *Iliad*, an epic poem telling of the seige of Troy by the army of the Greeks led by the hero, Achilles; and of the *Odyssey*, recounting the return of the hero, Odysseus, from Troy to his homeland in Ithaka. Hesiod is known as the poet of the *Theogony*, which tells the story of the gods in Greece; and of *Works and Days*, which describes the rituals and practices of the agricultural year. Both Homer and Hesiod lived in the 8th century B.C.

5. Supposed to have been the teacher of Orpheus.

6. Sidney lists historical and legendary poets to illustrate his claim that they were the founders of civilization and culture. Amphion was supposed to have moved stones by playing his music and thus to have built the walls of Troy; Livius Andronicus (c. 284–204 B.C.) was believed to have been the first Latin poet; Ennius (c. 239–169 B.C.) was traditionally regarded as the greatest of the early Latin poets. Dante, Boccaccio, and Petrarch were the first of

the great Italian poets of the early Renaissance; Chaucer and Gower were the most important of the late medieval poets who wrote in English.

7. Example.

8. Sidney lists the best-known of the Greek philosophers before Plato: Thales, a geometrician; Empedocles, who studied the concepts of change and permanence; Parmenceides, who investigated the nature of being; Pythagoras, a mathematician and astronomer; Phocylides, a moralist; and Tyrtaeus, a poet. Solon (c. 640–558 B.C.) was an Athenian statesman, poet, and constitutional reformer. No trace remains of a poem by Solon telling of Atlantis, an island beyond the pillars of Hercules that vanishes beneath the sea; Sidney recalls Plato's dialogue (*Timaeus*, 21–24), in which Critias tells Socrates that the story of Atlantis originates in an unfinished poem of Solon.

9. Author of many works of philosophy in dialogue form, notably *The Republic*, on the construction of an ideal state, and *The Symposium*, on the nature of love and its association with beauty and truth. He was a key influence on Renaissance thinkers.

find that in the body of his work, though the inside and strength were philosophy, the skin, as it were, and beauty depended most of[1] poetry: for all standeth upon dialogues, wherein he feigneth many honest burgesses of Athens to speak of such matters, that, if they had been set on the rack, they would never have confessed them, besides his poetical describing the circumstances of their meetings, as the well ordering of a banquet,[2] the delicacy of a walk, with interlacing mere tales, as Gyges' ring and others, which who knoweth not to be flowers of poetry did never walk into Apollo's garden.[3]

And even historiographers (although their lips sound of things done, and verity[4] be written in their foreheads) have been glad to borrow both fashion and, perchance, weight of the poets. So Herodotus entitled his History by the name of the nine Muses;[5] and both he and all the rest that followed him either stale[6] or usurped of poetry their passionate describing of passions, the many particularities of battles, which no man could affirm; or, if that be denied me, long orations put in the mouths of great kings and captains, which it is certain they never pronounced.

So that truly neither philosopher nor historiographer could at the first have entered into the gates of popular judgments, if they had not taken a great passport of poetry, which in all nations at this day where learning flourisheth not, is plain to be seen; in all which they have some feeling of poetry.

In Turkey, besides their law-giving divines, they have no other writers but poets. In our neighbor country Ireland, where truly learning goeth very bare, yet are their poets held in a devout reverence. Even among the most barbarous and simple Indians where no writing is, yet have they their poets who make and sing songs, which they call *areytos*,[7] both of their ancestors' deeds and praises of their gods: a sufficient probability that, if ever learning come among them, it must be by having their hard dull wits softened and sharpened with the sweet delights of poetry—for until they find a pleasure in the exercises of the mind, great promises of much knowledge will little persuade them that know not the fruits of knowledge. In Wales, the true remnant of the ancient Britons, as there are good authorities to show the long time they had poets, which they called bards, so through all the conquests of Romans, Saxons, Danes, and Normans, some of whom did seek to ruin all memory of learning from among them, yet do their poets even to this day last; so as it is not more notable in soon beginning than in long continuing.

But since the authors of most of our sciences[8] were the Romans, and before them the Greeks, let us a little stand upon their authorities, but even so far as to see what names they have given unto this now scorned skill.

Among the Romans a poet was called *vates*, which is as much as a diviner, foreseer, or prophet, as by his conjoined words *vaticinium* [prediction] and *vaticinari* [to foretell] is manifest: so heavenly a title did that excellent people bestow upon this heart-ravishing knowledge. And so far were they carried into the admiration thereof, that they thought in the chanceable hitting upon any such verses great foretokens of their following fortunes were placed. Whereupon grew the word of *Sortes Virgilianae*,[9]

---

1. On.
2. A banquet is the setting of *The Symposium*; speakers take a walk in the *The Phaedrus*; and the story of Gyges' ring is told in *The Republic*.
3. Apollo was the god of poetry.
4. Truth.
5. Herodotus, a Greek historian (480–425 B.C.), wrote about the struggle between Asia and Greece; later classical editors divided his work, which he entitled simply *History*, into nine books named after the nine Muses: Calliope, Clio, Euterpe, Melpomene, Terpsichore, Erato,

Polyhymnia, Urania, and Thalia.
6. Stole.
7. A West Indian dance, recorded by José de Acosta in his *Natural and Moral History of the West Indies* (translated into English in 1604).
8. Any body of knowledge, typically natural philosophy and also including ethics and politics.
9. The Virgilian lots, or fortune as it is implied in lines from the *Aeneid*, which the reader chose at random and then subjects to interpretation.

when by sudden opening Virgil's book they lighted upon any verse of his making, whereof the histories of the emperors' lives are full: as of Albinus, the governor of our island, who in his childhood met with this verse

Arma amens capio nec sat rationis in armis[1]

and in his age performed it. Which, although it were a very vain and godless superstition, as also it was to think spirits were commanded by such verses—whereupon this word charms, derived of *carmina* [songs], cometh—so yet serveth it to show the great reverence those wits were held in; and altogether not without ground, since both the oracles of Delphos and Sibylla's prophecies were wholly delivered in verses.[2] For that same exquisite observing of number and measure[3] in the words, and that high flying liberty of conceit proper to the poet, did seem to have some divine force in it.

And may not I presume a little further, to show the reasonableness of this word *vates*, and say that the holy David's Psalms are a divine poem? If I do, I shall not do it without the testimony of great learned men, both ancient and modern. But even the name of Psalms will speak for me, which being interpreted, is nothing but songs; then that it is fully written in meter, as all learned Hebricians agree, although the rules be not yet fully found; lastly and principally, his handling his prophecy, which is merely poetical: for what else is the awaking his musical instruments, the often and free changing of persons, his notable *prosopopoeias* [personifications], when he maketh you, as it were, see God coming in His majesty, his telling of the beasts' joyfulness and hills leaping,[4] but a heavenly poesy, wherein almost he showeth himself a passionate lover of that unspeakable and everlasting beauty to be seen by the eyes of the mind, only cleared by faith? But truly now having named him, I fear me I seem to profane that holy name, applying it to poetry, which is among us thrown down to so ridiculous an estimation. But they that with quiet judgments will look a little deeper into it, shall find the end and working of it such as, being rightly applied, deserveth not to be scourged out of the Church of God.

But now let us see how the Greeks named it, and how they deemed of it. The Greeks called him a "poet," which name hath, as the most excellent, gone through other languages. It cometh of this word ποιεῖν, which is, to make: wherein, I know not whether by luck or wisdom, we Englishmen have met with the Greeks in calling him a maker: which name, how high and incomparable a title it is, I had rather were known by marking the scope of other sciences than by any partial allegation.

There is no art delivered to mankind that hath not the works of nature for his principal object, without which they could not consist, and on which they so depend, as they become actors and players, as it were, of what nature will have set forth. So doth the astronomer look upon the stars, and, by that he seeth, set down what order nature hath taken therein. So doth the geometrician and arithmetician in their diverse sorts of quantities. So doth the musicians in time tell you which by nature agree, which not. The natural philosopher thereon hath his name, and the moral philosopher standeth upon the natural virtues, vices, or passions of man; and follow nature (saith he) therein, and thou shalt not err. The lawyer saith what men have determined; the historian what men have done. The grammarian speaketh only

---

1. "I seize arms madly, nor is there reason in arming" (2.314).
2. The shrine of Apollo at Delphi was presided over by a priestess who was believed to know the god's thoughts about the future; the Sibyls were supposed to be ancient

prophetesses whose words were collected in the *Sibylline Books*.
3. Meter and rhythm.
4. Psalm 29.

of the rules of speech; and the rhetorician and logician, considering what in nature will soonest prove and persuade, thereon give artificial rules, which still are compassed within the circle of a question according to the proposed matter. The physician weigheth the nature of man's body, and the nature of things helpful or hurtful unto it. And the metaphysic,[5] though it be in the second and abstract notions, and therefore be counted supernatural, yet doth he indeed build upon the depth of nature. Only the poet, disdaining to be tied to any such subjection, lifted up with the vigor of his own invention, doth grow in effect another nature, in making things either better than nature bringeth forth, or, quite anew, forms such as never were in nature, as the Heroes, Demigods, Cyclops, Chimeras, Furies,[6] and such like: so as he goeth hand in hand with nature, not enclosed within the narrow warrant[7] of her gifts, but freely ranging only within the zodiac of his own wit. Nature never set forth the earth in so rich tapestry as divers poets have done; neither with so pleasant rivers, fruitful trees, sweet-smelling flowers, nor whatsoever else may make the too much loved earth more lovely. Her world is brazen, the poets only deliver a golden.

But let those things alone, and go to man—for whom as the other things are, so it seemeth in him her uttermost cunning is employed—and know whether she have brought forth so true a lover as Theagenes, so constant a friend as Pylades, so valiant a man as Orlando, so right a prince as Xenophon's Cyrus, so excellent a man every way as Virgil's Aeneas.[8] Neither let this be jestingly conceived, because the works of the one be essential, the other in imitation or fiction; for any understanding knoweth the skill of each artificer standeth in that *idea* or fore-conceit[9] of the work, and not in the work itself. And that the poet hath that *idea* is manifest, by delivering them forth in such excellency as he had imagined them. Which delivering forth also is not wholly imaginative, as we are wont to say by them that build castles in the air; but so far substantially it worketh, not only to make a Cyrus, which had been but a particular excellency as nature might have done, but to bestow a Cyrus upon the world to make many Cyruses, if they will learn aright why and how that maker made him.

Neither let it be deemed too saucy a comparison to balance the highest point of man's wit with the efficacy of nature; but rather give right honor to the heavenly Maker of that maker, who having made man to His own likeness, set him beyond and over all the works of that second nature: which in nothing he showeth so much as in poetry, when with the force of a divine breath he bringeth things forth surpassing her doings—with no small arguments to the credulous of that first accursed fall of Adam, since our erected wit maketh us know what perfection is, and yet our infected will keepeth us from reaching unto it. But these arguments will by few be understood, and

---

5. A philosopher who considered abstractions and aspects of mental and spiritual life entertained in a state of contemplation rather than of action.

6. Furies: supernatural forces figured as mad goddesses pursuing revenge; demigods: male offspring of a god and a mortal, having some divine powers; cyclops: a one-eyed giant; chimeras: imaginary monsters made up of grotesquely disparate parts.

7. Authority.

8. Sidney cites men recognized for their virtues. Theagenes exemplifies the true lover in Heliodorus's romance, the *Aethiopica*; Pylades, who helped Orestes avenge his father Agamemnon's murder, was cited by Renaissance commentators as a perfect friend; Orlando (modeled on Roland, the knight who fought for Charlemagne against

the Basques at the battle of Roncesvalles, A.D. 778) was the hero of Ariosto's *Orlando Furioso* and illustrated the Renaissance idea of valor. The *Anabasis* of Xenophon (himself a general in Cyrus's army) relates how Cyrus the Younger, a Persian prince, helped the Peloponnesians resist the army of Athens and then died in an attempt to take the Persian throne from his brother Artaxerxes in the 5th century B.C. Aeneas, the hero of Virgil's *Aeneid* and the mythical founder of the Roman Empire, was generally considered to be the epitome of the statesman.

9. The element of the literary work that determines how and to what end its subject is conveyed. Sidney later states that an *Idea* works "substantially" because it makes readers want to imitate the virtuous characters represented in a literary work.

by fewer granted. This much (I hope) will be given me, that the Greeks with some probability of reason gave him the name above all names of learning.

Now let us go to a more ordinary opening of him, that the truth may be the more palpable: and so I hope, though we get not so unmatched a praise as the etymology of his names will grant, yet his very description, which no man will deny, shall not justly be barred from a principal commendation.

Poesy therefore is an art of imitation,[1] for so Aristotle termeth it in the word μίμησις—that is to say, a representing, counterfeiting, or figuring forth—to speak metaphorically, a speaking picture—with this end, to teach and delight.

Of this have been three general kinds. The chief, both in antiquity and excellency, were they that did imitate the unconceivable excellencies of God. Such were David in his Psalms; Solomon in his Song of Songs, in his Ecclesiastes, and Proverbs; Moses and Deborah in their Hymns; and the writer of Job: which, beside other, the learned Emanuel Tremellius and Franciscus Junius[2] do entitle the poetical part of the Scripture. Against these none will speak that hath the Holy Ghost in due holy reverence. (In this kind, though in a full wrong divinity, were Orpheus, Amphion, Homer in his Hymns, and many other, both Greeks and Romans.)[3] And this poesy must be used by whosoever will follow St. James's counsel in singing psalms when they are merry, and I know is used with the fruit of comfort by some, when, in sorrowful pangs of their death-bringing sins, they find the consolation of the never-leaving goodness.

The second kind is of them that deal with matters philosophical, either moral, as Tyrtaeus,[4] Phocylides, Cato, or natural, as Lucretius and Virgil's *Georgics*; or astronomical, as Manilius and Pontanus; or historical, as Lucan: which who mislike, the fault is in their judgment quite out of taste, and not in the sweet food of sweetly uttered knowledge.

But because this second sort is wrapped within the fold of the proposed subject, and takes not the course of his own invention, whether they properly be poets or no let grammarians dispute, and go to the third, indeed right poets, of whom chiefly this question ariseth: betwixt whom and these second is such a kind of difference as betwixt the meaner sort of painters, who counterfeit only such faces as are set before them, and the more excellent, who having no law but wit, bestow that in colors upon you which is fittest for the eye to see: as the constant though lamenting look of Lucretia,[5] when she punished in herself another's fault, wherein he painteth not Lucretia whom he never saw, but painteth the outward beauty of such a virtue. For these third be they which most properly do imitate to teach and delight, and to imitate borrow nothing of what is, hath been, or shall be; but range, only reined with

---

1. Aristotle stated that poetry was a mimetic (from *mimesis*) or imitative art; Sidney (following Horace, who sees that poetry is like painting) adds that this imitation is (in some sense) pictorial.
2. Sixteenth-century translators of the Hebrew and Greek Bible into Latin who considered the books here mentioned (all in the Hebrew Bible) to be poetry.
3. Sidney distinguishes the mystical works of Hellenic antiquity as erroneous in their depiction and understanding of divinity.
4. Sidney lists poets who he considers wrote some kind of philosophy and are not altogether "right," that is, pure poets. Tyrtaeus: mid-7th century B.C. Greek poet known for his praise of valor; Phocylides: a moralist of the 6th century B.C.; Cato: Dionysius Cato (c. A.D. 300), a moralist of whom little is known, who wrote a collection of moral

sayings in verse couplets, published by Erasmus for use in schools; Lucretius: the Roman poet of the 1st century B.C. who wrote about the creation of the physical world; Virgil: the poet who stated the principles of farming in his *Georgics*; Manilius: the poet of the 1st century A.D. who wrote a versified treatise on astronomy; Pontanus: Joannes Jovius Pontanus, a late 15th-century poet who wrote a work on astronomy; and Lucan: the Roman poet of the 1st century A.D. who wrote the epic *Pharsalia*, which describes the events in the civil war between Caesar and Pompey up to Caesar's seduction of the Egyptian queen, Cleopatra.
5. Legendary heroine of the ancient Roman republic who committed suicide rather than live in shame after being raped by the tyrant Sextus Tarquinius. Her story was told in versions by Ovid, Livy, Chaucer, Christine de Pisan, Shakespeare, and others.

learned discretion, into the divine consideration of what may be and should be. These be they that, as the first and most noble sort may justly be termed *vates*, so these are waited on in the excellentest languages and best understandings with the fore-described name of poets. For these indeed do merely make to imitate, and imitate both to delight and teach; and delight, to move men to take that goodness in hand, which without delight they would fly as from a stranger; and teach, to make them know that goodness whereunto they are moved—which being the noblest scope to which ever any learning was directed, yet want there not idle tongues to bark at them.

These be subdivided into sundry more special denominations. The most notable be the heroic, lyric, tragic, comic, satiric, iambic, elegiac, pastoral,[6] and certain others, some of these being termed according to the matter they deal with, some by the sorts of verses they liked best to write in; for indeed the greatest part of poets have apparelled their poetical inventions in that numbrous kind of writing which is called verse—indeed but apparelled, verse being but an ornament and no cause to poetry, since there have been many most excellent poets that never versified, and now swarm many versifiers that need never answer to the name of poets. For Xenophon, who did imitate so excellently as to give us *effigiem iusti imperii*, the portraiture of a just empire, under the name of Cyrus (as Cicero saith of him), made therein an absolute heroical poem.[7] So did Heliodorus in his sugared invention of that picture of love in Theagenes and Chariclea;[8] and yet both these wrote in prose: which I speak to show that it is not rhyming and versing that maketh a poet—no more than a long gown maketh an advocate, who though he pleaded in armor should be an advocate and no soldier. But it is that feigning notable images of virtues, vices, or what else, with that delightful teaching, which must be the right describing note to know a poet by; although indeed the senate of poets hath chosen verse as their fittest raiment, meaning, as in matter they passed all in all, so in manner to go beyond them: not speaking (table-talk fashion or like men in a dream) words as they chanceably fall from the mouth, but peising[9] each syllable of each word by just proportion according to the dignity of the subject.

Now therefore it shall not be amiss first to weigh this latter sort of poetry by his works, and then by his parts; and if in neither of these anatomies he be condemnable, I hope we shall obtain a more favorable sentence.

This purifying of wit—this enriching of memory, enabling of judgment, and enlarging of conceit—which commonly we call learning, under what name soever it come forth, or to what immediate end soever it be directed, the final end is to lead and draw us to as high a perfection as our degenerate souls, made worse by their clayey lodgings, can be capable of.

This, according to the inclination of the man, bred many-formed impressions. For some that thought this felicity principally to be gotten by knowledge, and no knowledge to be so high or heavenly as acquaintance with the stars, gave themselves to astronomy; others, persuading themselves to be demigods if they knew the causes of things, became natural and supernatural philosophers; some an admirable delight drew to music; and some the certainty of demonstration to the mathematics. But all, one and other, having this scope: to know, and by knowledge to lift up the mind from the dungeon of the body to the enjoying his own divine essence.

6. Sidney lists the eight genres of poetry; "iambic" was a kind of satiric verse written in iambics, a meter made up of units or feet, each of which consists of a lightly stressed syllable followed by a heavily stressed syllable.
7. Sidney refers to Xenophon's *Cyropaedia*, his history of

Cyrus, the emperor of Persia, a work that he thinks has a heroic quality because it deals with the fate of an empire.
8. Characters in Heliodorus's romance, *Aethiopica*.
9. Weighing.

But when by the balance of experience it was found that the astronomer, looking to the stars, might fall in a ditch, that the inquiring philosopher might be blind in himself, and the mathematician might draw forth a straight line with a crooked heart, then lo, did proof, the overruler of opinions, make manifest that all these are but serving sciences, which, as they have each a private end in themselves, so yet are they all directed to the highest end of the mistress-knowledge, by the Greeks called ἀρχιτεκτονικη, which stands (as I think) in the knowledge of a man's self, in the ethic and politic consideration, with the end of well-doing and not of well-knowing only—even as the saddler's next end is to make a good saddle, but his further end to serve a nobler faculty, which is horsemanship, so the horseman's to soldiery, and the soldier not only to have the skill, but to perform the practice of a soldier. So that, the ending end of all earthly learning being virtuous action, those skills that most serve to bring forth that have a most just title to be princes over all the rest.

Wherein, if we can, show we the poet's nobleness, by setting him before his other competitors. Among whom as principal challengers step forth the moral philosophers, whom, me thinketh, I see coming towards me with a sullen gravity, as though they could not abide vice by daylight, rudely clothed for to witness outwardly their contempt of outward things, with books in their hands against glory, whereto they set their names, sophistically speaking against subtlety, and angry with any man in whom they see the foul fault of anger. These men casting largess as they go, of definitions, divisions, and distinctions, with a scornful interrogative do soberly ask whether it be possible to find any path so ready to lead a man to virtue as that which teacheth what virtue is; and teach it not only by delivering forth his very being, his causes and effects, but also by making known his enemy, vice, which must be destroyed, and his cumbersome servant, passion, which must be mastered; by showing the generalities that containeth it, and the specialities that are derived from it; lastly, by plain setting down how it extendeth itself out of the limits of a man's own little world to the government of families and maintaining of public societies.

The historian scarcely giveth leisure to the moralist to say so much, but that he, laden with old mouse-eaten records, authorizing himself (for the most part) upon other histories, whose greatest authorities are built upon the notable foundation of hearsay; having much ado to accord differing writers and to pick truth out of their partiality; better acquainted with a thousand years ago than with the present age, and yet better knowing how this world goeth than how his own wit runneth; curious for antiquities and inquisitive of novelties; a wonder to young folks and a tyrant in table talk, denieth, in a great chafe,[1] that any man for teaching of virtue, and virtuous actions is comparable to him. "I am *testis temporum, lux veritatis, vita memoriae, magistra vitae, nuntia vetustatis.*[2] The philosopher," saith he, "teacheth a disputative virtue, but I do an active. His virtue is excellent in the dangerless Academy of Plato,[3] but mine showeth forth her honorable face in the battles of Marathon, Pharsalia, Poitiers, and Agincourt.[4] He teacheth virtue by certain abstract considerations, but I

---

1. Heat, fury.
2. Sidney quotes Cicero in his *De Oratore* (*Concerning the Orator*): "I am the witness of time, the light of truth, the life of memory, the governess of life, the herald of antiquity."
3. The olive grove near Athens, where Plato and his successors taught philosophy.
4. Sidney mentions some memorable battles: The Athenians defeated the invading Persians at Marathon in 490 B.C.; Caesar defeated Pompey at Pharsalus in 48 B.C.; the Franks, under Charles Martel, defeated the Moors, led by Spanish emir Abd al-Rahman Ghafiqi in 732; the English, under Edward, the Black Prince, overcame the French army and captured their king, John II in 1356, each time at Poitiers; finally, Henry V defeated the French in 1415 at Agincourt.

only bid you follow the footing of them that have gone before you. Old-aged experience goeth beyond the fine-witted philosopher, but I give the experience of many ages. Lastly, if he make the songbook, I put the learner's hand to the lute; and if he be the guide, I am the light." Then would he allege you innumerable examples, confirming story by stories, how much the wisest senators and princes have been directed by the credit of history, as Brutus, Alphonsus of Aragon,[5] and who not, if need be? At length the long line of their disputation maketh a point in this, that the one giveth the precept, and the other the example.

Now whom shall we find (since the question standeth for the highest form in the school of learning) to be moderator? Truly, as me seemeth, the poet; and if not a moderator, even the man that ought to carry the title from them both, and much more from all other serving sciences. Therefore compare we the poet with the historian and with the moral philosopher; and if he go beyond them both, no other human skill can match him. For as for the divine, with all reverence it is ever to be excepted, not only for having his scope as far beyond any of these as eternity exceedeth a moment, but even for passing each of these in themselves. And for the lawyer, though *Ius* [Right] be the daughter of Justice, and justice the chief of virtues, yet because he seeketh to make men good rather *formidine poenae* than *virtutis amore*;[6] or, to say righter, doth not endeavor to make men good, but that their evil hurt not others; having no care, so he be a good citizen, how bad a man he be: therefore as our wickedness maketh him necessary, and necessity maketh him honorable, so is he not in the deepest truth to stand in rank with these who all endeavor to take naughtiness away and plant goodness even in the secretest cabinet of our souls. And these four are all that any way deal in that consideration of men's manners, which being the supreme knowledge, they that best breed it deserve the best commendation.

The philosopher, therefore, and the historian are they which would win the goal, the one by precept, the other by example. But both, not having both, do both halt.[7] For the philosopher, setting down with thorny arguments the bare rule, is so hard of utterance and so misty to be conceived, that one that hath no other guide but him shall wade in him till he be old before he shall find sufficient cause to be honest. For his knowledge standeth so upon the abstract and general, that happy is that man who may understand him, and more happy that can apply what he doth understand. On the other side, the historian, wanting the precept, is so tied, not to what should be but to what is, to the particular truth of things and not to the general reason of things, that his example draweth no necessary consequence, and therefore a less fruitful doctrine.

Now doth the peerless poet perform both: for whatsoever the philosopher saith should be done, he giveth a perfect picture of it in someone by whom he presupposeth it was done, so as he coupleth the general notion with the particular example. A perfect picture I say, for he yieldeth to the powers of the mind an image of that whereof the philosopher bestoweth but a wordish description, which doth neither strike, pierce, nor possess the sight of the soul so much as that other doth. For as in outward things, to a man that had never seen an elephant or a rhinoceros, who should tell him most exquisitely all their shapes, color, bigness, and particular marks, or of a gorgeous palace, an *architector* [architect], with declaring the full beauties,

---

5. Brutus: Roman statesman, one of Caesar's assassins, who is said to have spent the night before the battle of Pharsalus reading history; Alphonsus: King of Aragon and Sicily who encouraged his soldiers to seize the libraries of those they conquered and to bring their books to him.

6. I.e., rather "from fear of punishment" than "from love of virtue" (Horace, *Epistles* 1.2.62). Sidney distinguishes between staying within the law and moral behavior.
7. Limp.

might well make the hearer able to repeat, as it were by rote, all he had heard, yet should never satisfy his inward conceit[8] with being witness to itself of a true lively knowledge; but the same man, as soon as he might see those beasts well painted, or the house well in model, should straightways grow, without need of any description, to a judicial comprehending of them: so no doubt the philosopher with his learned definitions—be it of virtue, vices, matters of public policy or private government—replenisheth the memory with many infallible grounds of wisdom, which, notwithstanding, lie dark before the imaginative and judging power, if they be not illuminated or figured forth by the speaking picture of poesy.

Tully[9] taketh much pains, and many times not without poetical helps, to make us know the force love of our country hath in us. Let us but hear old Anchises speaking in the midst of Troy's flames,[1] or see Ulysses in the fullness of all Calypso's delights bewail his absence from barren and beggarly Ithaca. Anger, the Stoics said, was a short madness: let but Sophocles bring you Ajax on a stage, killing or whipping sheep and oxen, thinking them the army of Greeks, with their chieftains Agamemnon and Menelaus, and tell me if you have not a more familiar insight into anger than finding in the schoolmen his *genus* [race] and difference.[2] See whether wisdom and temperance in Ulysses and Diomedes, valor in Achilles, friendship in Nisus and Euryalus, even to an ignorant man carry not an apparent shining; and, contrarily, the remorse of conscience in Oedipus, the soon repenting pride in Agamemnon, the self-devouring cruelty in his father Atreus, the violence of ambition in the two Theban brothers, the sour-sweetness of revenge in Medea; and, to fall lower, the Terentian Gnatho and our Chaucer's Pandar so expressed that we now use their names to signify their trades:[3] and finally, all virtues, vices, and passions so in their own natural seats laid to the view, that we seem not to hear of them, but clearly to see through them.

But even in the most excellent determination of goodness, what philosopher's counsel can so readily direct a prince, as the feigned Cyrus in Xenophon; or a virtuous man in all fortunes, as Aeneas in Virgil; or a whole commonwealth, as the way of Sir Thomas More's *Utopia*? I say the way, because where Sir Thomas More erred, it was the fault of the man and not of the poet, for that way of patterning a commonwealth was most absolute, though he perchance hath not so absolutely performed it. For the question is, whether the feigned image of poetry or the regular instruction of philosophy hath the more force in teaching: wherein if the philosophers have more rightly showed themselves philosophers than the poets have attained to the high top of their profession, as in truth

> *Mediocribus esse poetis,*
> *Non dii, non homines, non concessere columnae;*[4]

it is, I say again, not the fault of the art, but that by few men that art can be accomplished.

Certainly, even our Savior Christ could as well have given the moral commonplaces of uncharitableness and humbleness as the divine narration of Dives and

---

8. The listener's mental picture or image.
9. Cicero.
1. In the remainder of this paragraph, Sidney refers to exemplary moments in the lives of mythical figures as illustrated in the literature of antiquity, especially the works of Virgil, Homer, and the Greek and Roman dramatists.

2. Species.
3. Gnatho: a parasite and flatterer in the Roman playwright Terence's *Eunuchus*; Pandar: the go-between for the lovers in Chaucer's *Troilus and Criseyde*.
4. Neither gods, nor men, nor booksellers permit poets to be mediocre; a statement adapted from Horace's *Art of Poetry*.

Lazarus;[5] or of disobedience and mercy, as that heavenly discourse of the lost child and the gracious father; but that His through-searching wisdom knew the estate of Dives burning in hell, and of Lazarus in Abraham's bosom, would more constantly (as it were) inhabit both the memory and judgment. Truly, for myself, meseems I see before mine eyes the lost child's disdainful prodigality, turned to envy a swine's dinner: which by the learned divines[6] are thought not historical acts, but instructing parables.

For conclusion, I say the philosopher teacheth, but he teacheth obscurely, so as the learned only can understand him, that is to say, he teacheth them that are already taught; but the poet is the food for the tenderest stomachs, the poet is indeed the right popular philosopher, whereof Aesop's tales[7] give good proof: whose pretty allegories, stealing under the formal tales of beasts, make many, more beastly than beasts, begin to hear the sound of virtue from these dumb speakers.

But now may it be alleged that if this imagining of matters be so fit for the imagination, then must the historian needs surpass, who bringeth you images of true matters, such as indeed were done, and not such as fantastically or falsely may be suggested to have been done. Truly, Aristotle himself, in his discourse of poesy, plainly determineth this question, saying that poetry is φλοσοφώτερον and σπου-δαιότερον, that is to say, it is more philosophical and more studiously serious than history. His reason is, because poesy dealeth with καθόλου, that is to say, with the universal consideration, and the history with καθέκαστον, the particular: now, saith he, the universal weighs what is fit to be said or done, either in likelihood or necessity (which the poesy considereth in his imposed names), and the particular only marks whether Alcibiades did, or suffered, this or that.[8] Thus far Aristotle: which reason of his (as all his) is most full of reason. For indeed, if the question were whether it were better to have a particular act truly or falsely set down, there is no doubt which is to be chosen, no more than whether you had rather have Vespasian's picture[9] right as he was, or, at the painter's pleasure, nothing resembling. But if the question be for your own use and learning, whether it be better to have it set down as it should be, or as it was, then certainly is more doctrinable the feigned Cyrus in Xenophon than the true Cyrus in Justin, and the feigned Aeneas in Virgil than the right Aeneas in Dares Phrygius:[1] as to a lady that desired to fashion her countenance to the best grace, a painter should more benefit her to portrait a most sweet face, writing Canidia upon it, than to paint Canidia as she was, who, Horace sweareth, was full ill-favored.[2]

If the poet do his part aright, he will show you in Tantalus, Atreus, and such like,[3] nothing that is not to be shunned; in Cyrus, Aeneas, Ulysses, each thing to be followed; where the historian, bound to tell things as things were, cannot be liberal (without he will be poetical) of a perfect pattern, but, as in Alexander or Scipio himself, show doings, some to be liked, some to be misliked. And then how will you discern what to follow but by your own discretion, which you had without reading

5. Sidney cites several parables from scripture. The rich man, Dives, refused to help the beggar Lazarus; Dives was condemned to hell, Lazarus went to heaven (Luke 16.19–31). He then cites the story of the Prodigal Son, welcomed home by his father after a period of dissolution (Luke 15.11–32).
6. Theologians.
7. Moralistic fables reputedly by a Greek slave who lived about 570 B.C.; numerous translations into English of his work were available in the 16th century.
8. Sidney paraphrases Aristotle's Poetics (9.1451b). Alcibiades was a talented if unscrupulous Greek statesman.

9. A Roman emperor (A.D. 70–79) who was described by the historian Suetonius as very ugly.
1. Justinus (2nd–3rd century A.D.), and Dares Phrygius (5th century A.D.) wrote histories that some readers thought were more accurate than the more literary accounts by Xenophon, Homer, and Virgil.
2. Canidia was a prostitute who jilted the Roman poet, Horace; he then attacked her in his poems.
3. Evil figures (Tantalus served the flesh of his son, Pelops, to the gods; Atreus served his nephews' flesh to their father Thyestes).

Quintus Curtius?[4] And whereas a man may say, though in universal consideration of doctrine the poet prevaileth, yet that the history, in his saying such a thing was done, doth warrant a man more in that he shall follow—the answer is manifest: that, if he stand upon that[5] was (as if he should argue, because it rained yesterday, therefore it should rain today), then indeed hath it some advantage to a gross conceit; but if he know an example only informs a conjectured likelihood, and so go by reason, the poet doth so far exceed him as he is to frame his example to that which is most reasonable (be it in warlike, politic, or private matters), where the historian in his bare *Was* hath many times that which we call fortune to overrule the best wisdom. Many times he must tell events whereof he can yield no cause; or, if he do, it must be poetically.

For that a feigned example hath as much force to teach as a true example (for as for to move, it is clear, since the feigned may be tuned to the highest key of passion), let us take one example wherein an historian and a poet did concur. Herodotus and Justin do both testify that Zopyrus, King Darius's faithful servant, seeing his master long resisted by the rebellious Babylonians, feigned himself in extreme disgrace of his king: for verifying of which, he caused his own nose and ears to be cut off, and so flying to the Babylonians, was received, and for his known valor so sure credited, that he did find means to deliver them over to Darius.[6] Much like matter doth Livy record of Tarquinius and his son. Xenophon excellently feigneth such another stratagem performed by Abradatas in Cyrus's behalf.[7] Now would I fain know, if occasion be presented unto you to serve your prince by such an honest dissimulation, why you do not as well learn it of Xenophon's fiction as of the other's verity; and truly so much the better, as you shall save your nose by the bargain: for Abradatas did not counterfeit so far. So then the best of the historian is subject to the poet; for whatsoever action, or faction, whatsoever counsel, policy, or war stratagem the historian is bound to recite, that may the poet (if he list[8]) with his imitation make his own, beautifying it both for further teaching, and more delighting, as it please him: having all, from Dante's heaven to his hell, under the authority of his pen.[9] Which if I be asked what poets have done so, as I might well name some, so yet say I, and say again, I speak of the art, and not of the artificer.

Now, to that which commonly is attributed to the praise of history, in respect of the notable learning is got by marking the success, as though therein a man should see virtue exalted and vice punished—truly that commendation is particular to poetry, and far off from history. For indeed poetry ever sets virtue so out in her best colors, making Fortune her well-waiting handmaid, that one must needs be enamored of her. Well may you see Ulysses in a storm, and in other hard plights; but they are but exercises of patience and magnanimity, to make them shine the more in the near-following prosperity. And of the contrary part, if evil men come to the stage, they ever go out (as the tragedy writer answered to one that misliked the show of such persons) so manacled as they little animate folks to follow them. But the history, being captived to the truth of a foolish world, is many times a terror from well-doing, and an encouragement to unbridled wickedness. For

4. Quintus Curtius (1st century A.D.) wrote a history of Alexander the Great.
5. What.
6. The story of Zopyrus is told in Herodotus's *Histories* (3.153–58) and in Justin's *Histories* (1.10.15–22).
7. Tarquinius Superbus was the last of the Roman kings: his son, Sextus Tarquinius, passed himself off as an ally of the Gabians to spy for Rome (Livy, *Histories* 1.3–4). Abradates (actually Araspes), acted in the same way for the Persian king, Cyrus (Xenophon, *Cyropaedia* 6.1.39).
8. Wishes.
9. Dante's *Divine Comedy* describes his journey through hell, purgatory, and paradise.

see we not valiant Miltiades rot in his fetters?[1] The just Phocion and the accomplished Socrates put to death like traitors? The cruel Severus live prosperously? The excellent Severus miserably murdered? Sulla and Marius dying in their beds? Pompey and Cicero slain then when they would have thought exile a happiness? See we not virtuous Cato driven to kill himself, and rebel Caesar so advanced that his name yet, after 1600 years, lasteth in the highest honor? And mark but even Caesar's own words of the aforenamed Sulla (who in that only did honestly, to put down his dishonest tyranny), *literas nescivit*,[2] as if want of learning caused him to do well. He meant it not by poetry, which, not content with earthly plagues, deviseth new punishments in hell for tyrants, nor yet by philosophy, which teacheth *occidendos esse*; but no doubt by skill in history, for that indeed can afford you Cypselus, Periander, Phalaris, Dionysius, and I know not how many more of the same kennel, that speed well enough in their abominable injustice of usurpation.

I conclude, therefore, that he excelleth history, not only in furnishing the mind with knowledge, but in setting it forward to that which deserveth to be called and accounted good: which setting forward, and moving to well-doing, indeed setteth the laurel crown upon the poets as victorious, not only of the historian, but over the philosopher, howsoever in teaching it may be questionable.

For suppose it be granted (that which I suppose with great reason may be denied) that the philosopher, in respect of his methodical proceeding, doth teach more perfectly than the poet, yet do I think that no man is so much φιλυφιλόσοφος [a lover of philosophy] as to compare the philosopher in moving with the poet. And that moving is of a higher degree than teaching, it may by this appear, that it is well nigh both the cause and effect of teaching. For who will be taught, if he be not moved with desire to be taught? And what so much good doth that teaching bring forth (I speak still of moral doctrine) as that it moveth one to do that which it doth teach? For, as Aristotle saith, it is not γνῶσις [knowing] but πρᾶξις [doing] must be the fruit. And how πρᾶξις can be, without being moved to practice, it is no hard matter to consider.[3]

The philosopher showeth you the way, he informeth you of the particularities, as well of the tediousness of the way, as of the pleasant lodging you shall have when your journey is ended, as of the many by-turnings that may divert you from your way. But this is to no man but to him that will read him, and read him with attentive studious painfulness; which constant desire whosoever hath in him, hath already passed half the hardness of the way, and therefore is beholding to the philosopher

---

1. Sidney demonstrates that the study of history is not conducive to good morals because it does not show virtue rewarded or vice punished. Miltiades: unsuccessful against the Persians in his seige of Paros, he was imprisoned by his own people, the Athenians (Herodotus, *Histories* 6.136). Phocion: an Athenian statesman wrongly put to death for a supposed conspiracy (Plutarch, *Phocion* 38). Plato's teacher Socrates had been put to death for supposed impiety. Lucius Septimius Severus, Emperor of Rome (193–211), was able but termed "most cruel" by his biographer, Aelius Spartianus; by contrast, his virtuous successor, Marcus Aurelius Alexander Severus, was murdered by mutinous soldiers. Lucius Cornelius Sulla was a dictator of Rome, who tyrannized his subjects and yet died peacefully in his bed in 78 B.C.; Caius Marius was also a tyrant and never punished. Pompey opposed Caesar and was murdered after his defeat at Pharsalus; Marcus Tullius Cicero, the most accomplished

of Roman lawyers and orators, was murdered by the order of Marcus Antonius in 43 B.C. Marcus Portius Cato committed suicide after his defeat at the battle of Thapsus rather than be captured by Caesar. Sidney calls Caesar a "rebel" because he invaded the territory of the Roman state (crossing the river Rubicon) without permission from the Roman Senate.
2. He knew no literature. Sidney indicates that the learning Sulla lacked was not of poetry, which reveals the punishments of hell; or of philosophy, which teaches *occidendum esse*—that is, when someone should be put to death, or the punishments inflicted by the state. Sidney argues that Sulla learned his misgovernment from history, which instructed him in the profitable ways of tyrants: Cipselus and Periander, both tyrants of Corinth; Phalaris, tyrant of Agrigentum; and Dionysius, tyrant of Syracuse.
3. *Nicomachean Ethics* 1.1.

but[4] for the other half. Nay truly, learned men have learnedly thought that where once reason hath so much overmastered passion as that the mind hath a free desire to do well, the inward light each mind hath in itself is as good as a philosopher's book; since in nature we know it is well to do well, and what is well, and what is evil, although not in the words of art which philosophers bestow upon us; for out of natural conceit the philosophers drew it. But to be moved to do that which we know, or to be moved with desire to know, *hoc opus, hic labor est*.[5]

Now therein of all sciences (I speak still of human, and according to the human conceit[6]) is our poet the monarch. For he doth not only show the way, but giveth so sweet a prospect into the way, as will entice any man to enter into it. Nay, he doth, as if your journey should lie through a fair vineyard, at the first give you a cluster of grapes, that full of that taste, you may long to pass further. He beginneth not with obscure definitions, which must blur the margin with interpretations, and load the memory with doubtfulness; but he cometh to you with words set in delightful proportion, either accompanied with, or prepared for, the well enchanting skill of music; and with a tale forsooth he cometh unto you, with a tale which holdeth children from play, and old men from the chimney corner. And, pretending no more, doth intend the winning of the mind from wickedness to virtue—even as the child is often brought to take most wholesome things by hiding them in such other as have a pleasant taste, which, if one should begin to tell them the nature of *aloes* or *rhabarbarum*[7] they should receive, would sooner take their physic at their ears than at their mouth. So is it in men (most of which are childish in the best things, till they be cradled in their graves): glad they will be to hear the tales of Hercules, Achilles, Cyrus, Aeneas; and, hearing them, must needs hear the right description of wisdom, valor, and justice; which, if they had been barely, that is to say philosophically, set out, they would swear they be brought to school again.

That imitation whereof poetry is, hath the most conveniency to nature of all other, insomuch that, as Aristotle saith, those things which in themselves are horrible, as cruel battles, unnatural monsters, are made in poetical imitation delightful.[8] Truly, I have known men that even with reading *Amadis de Gaule*[9] (which God knoweth wanteth much of a perfect poesy) have found their hearts moved to the exercise of courtesy, liberality, and especially courage. Who readeth Aeneas carrying old Anchises on his back, that wisheth not it were his fortune to perform so excellent an act? Whom doth not these words of Turnus move, the tale of Turnus having planted his image in the imagination,

> *Fugientem haec terra videbit?*
> *Usque adeone mori miserum est?*[1]

Where the philosophers, as they scorn to delight, so must they be content little to move—saving wrangling whether *virtus* [virtue] be the chief or the only good, whether the contemplative or the active life do excel—which Plato and Boethius well knew, and therefore made mistress Philosophy very often borrow the masking raiment of poesy.[2] For even those hard-hearted evil men who think virtue a school

---

4. Merely.
5. "This is the task, this work"; the words of the Cumaean sybil to the hero Aeneas, who intends to return to earth from the underworld (*Aeneid* 6.128).
6. Way of thinking.
7. Medicines.
8. *Poetics*, 4.1448b.
9. Chivalric romance in Spanish by Vasco de Lobeyra, c. 1325. It appeared in English translation in 1567.
1. In Virgil, Turnus unsuccessfully defended his native

Latium (the region around Rome) against the invading Trojans led by Aeneas. Taking his last stand, Turnus cries: "Shall this ground see [Turnus] fleeing? Is it so hard, then, to die?" (*Aeneid* 12.645–46).
2. The philosophers Plato and Boethius both argued that a retired and contemplative life was superior to the active life or the life in public service. By contrast, the Roman orator Cicero asserted the value of prudence and the importance of contributing to the public good.

name, and know no other good but *indulgere genio* [self-indulgence], and therefore despise the austere admonitions of the philosopher, and feel not the inward reason they
stand upon, yet will be content to be delighted—which is all the good-fellow poet
seemeth to promise—and so steal to see the form of goodness (which seen they cannot but love) ere themselves be aware, as if they took a medicine of cherries.

Infinite proofs of the strange effects of this poetical invention might be alleged;
only two shall serve, which are so often remembered as I think all men know them.
The one of Menenius Agrippa,[3] who, when the whole people of Rome had resolutely
divided themselves from the senate, with apparent show of utter ruin, though he
were (for that time) an excellent orator, came not among them upon trust of figurative speeches or cunning insinuations, and much less with far-fet[4] maxims of philosophy, which (especially if they were Platonic) they must have learned geometry before
they could well have conceived; but forsooth he behaves himself like a homely and
familiar poet. He telleth them a tale, that there was a time when all the parts of the
body made a mutinous conspiracy against the belly, which they thought devoured
the fruits of each other's labor; they concluded they would let so unprofitable a
spender starve. In the end, to be short (for the tale is notorious, and as notorious that
it was a tale), with punishing the belly they plagued themselves. This applied by him
wrought such effect in the people, as I never read that only words brought forth but
then so sudden and so good an alteration; for upon reasonable conditions a perfect
reconcilement ensued. The other is of Nathan the prophet,[5] who, when the holy
David had so far forsaken God as to confirm adultery with murder, when he was to do
the tenderest office of a friend in laying his own shame before his eyes, sent by God
to call again so chosen a servant, how doth he it but by telling of a man whose
beloved lamb was ungratefully taken from his bosom: the application most divinely
true, but the discourse itself feigned; which made David (I speak of the second and
instrumental cause) as in a glass see his own filthiness, as that heavenly psalm of
mercy well testifieth.

By these, therefore, examples and reasons, I think it may be manifest that the
poet, with that same hand of delight, doth draw the mind more effectually than any
other art doth. And so a conclusion not unfitly ensue: that, as virtue is the most excellent resting place for all worldly learning to make his end of, so poetry, being the
most familiar to teach it, and most princely to move towards it, in the most excellent
work is the most excellent workman.

But I am content not only to decipher him[6] by his works (although works, in
commendation or dispraise, must ever hold a high authority), but more narrowly will
examine his parts; so that (as in a man) though all together may carry a presence full
of majesty and beauty, perchance in some one defectuous piece we may find blemish.

Now in his parts, kinds, or species (as you list to term them), it is to be noted
that some poesies have coupled together two or three kinds, as the tragical and
comical, whereupon is risen the tragicomical. Some, in the manner, have mingled
prose and verse, as Sannazaro and Boethius.[7] Some have mingled matters heroical
and pastoral. But that cometh all to one in this question, for, if severed they be good,
the conjunction cannot be hurtful. Therefore, perchance forgetting some and leaving

---

3. Roman consul who calmed rebellious commoners in
494 B.C. (Livy, *Histories* 2.32).
4. Far-fetched.
5. 2 Samuel 12.1–7.
6. Poetry.

7. Sannazaro: Italian poet (1458–1530) whose pastoral of
mixed prose and verse, the *Arcadia*, influenced Sidney's
work of the same name. Boethius (480?–524?): the
Roman and Christian philosopher whose work *The Consolation of Philosophy* contains passages of prose and poetry.

some as needless to be remembered, it shall not be amiss in a word to cite the special kinds, to see what faults may be found in the right use of them.

Is it then the Pastoral poem which is misliked? (For perchance where the hedge is lowest they will soonest leap over.) Is the poor pipe disdained, which sometime out of Meliboeus's mouth can show the misery of people under hard lords or ravening soldiers, and again, by Tityrus, what blessedness is derived to them that lie lowest from the goodness of them that sit highest;[8] sometimes, under the pretty tales of wolves and sheep, can include the whole considerations of wrongdoing and patience; sometimes show that contentions for trifles can get but a trifling victory: where perchance a man may see that even Alexander and Darius, when they strave who should be cock of this world's dunghill, the benefit they got was that the after-livers may say

> Haec memini et victum frustra contendere Thirsin:
> Ex illo Corydon, Corydon est tempore nobis.[9]

Or is it the lamenting Elegiac;[1] which in a kind heart would move rather pity than blame; who bewails with the great philosopher Heraclitus, the weakness of mankind and the wretchedness of the world; who surely is to be praised, either for compassionate accompanying just causes of lamentations, or for rightly painting out how weak be the passions of woefulness? Is it the bitter but wholesome Iambic,[2] who rubs the galled mind, in making shame the trumpet of villainy, with bold and open crying out against naughtiness? Or the Satiric, who

> Omne vafer vitium ridenti tangit amico;[3]

who sportingly never leaveth till he make a man laugh at folly, and at length shamed, to laugh at himself, which he cannot avoid without avoiding the folly; who, while

> circum praecordia ludit,[4]

giveth us to feel how many headaches a passionate life bringeth us to; how, when all is done,

> Est Ulubris, animus si nos non deficit aequus?[5]

No, perchance it is the Comic, whom naughty playmakers and stage-keepers have justly made odious. To the arguments of abuse I will answer after. Only this much now is to be said, that the comedy is an imitation of the common errors of our life, which he representeth in the most ridiculous and scornful sort that may be, so as it is impossible that any beholder can be content to be such a one. Now, as in geometry the oblique must be known as well as the right, and in arithmetic the odd as well as the even, so in the actions of our life who seeth not the filthiness of evil wanteth a great foil to perceive the beauty of virtue. This doth the comedy handle so in our private and domestical matters as with hearing it we get as it were an experience what is to be looked for of a niggardly Demea, of a crafty Davus, of a flattering Gnatho, of a

---

8. Meliboeus and Tityrus are characters in Virgil's *Eclogues*. Sidney responds to the idea that pastoral is the least elevated of the poetic genres; here he declares that it is capable of conveying political and moral ideas.
9. "These things I remember, how vanquished Thrysis tried in vain. Since then it has been Coridon, only Coridon, with us" (Virgil, *Eclogues*, 7.69–70). These lines suggest the futility of ambition.
1. A kind of poetry lamenting loss or remembering what

no longer exists. Heraclitus: a philosopher of conflict and flux, who lived about 500 B.C.
2. A verse form used in satire.
3. "The sly man probes every one of his friend's faults while making his friend laugh" (Persius, *Satires*, 1.116–17).
4. "He plays around the heart" (Persius, *Satires* 1.117).
5. "[Contentment] is at Ulubrae, if a well-balanced mind doesn't fail us" (Horace, *Epistles*, 1.11.30). Ulubrae was a notoriously disagreeable small town.

vainglorious Thraso;[6] and not only to know what effects are to be expected, but to know who be such, by the signifying badge given them by the comedian. And little reason hath any man to say that men learn the evil by seeing it so set out, since, as I said before, there is no man living but, by the force truth hath in nature, no sooner seeth these men play their parts, but wisheth them *in pistrinum;*[7] although perchance the sack of his own faults lie so hidden behind his back that he seeth not himself dance the same measure; whereto yet nothing can more open his eyes than to find his own actions contemptibly set forth.

So that the right use of comedy will (I think) by nobody be blamed; and much less of the high and excellent Tragedy, that openeth the greatest wounds, and showeth forth the ulcers that are covered with tissue; that maketh kings fear to be tyrants, and tyrants manifest their tyrannical humors; that, with stirring the affects of admiration and commiseration, teacheth the uncertainty of this world, and upon how weak foundations gilden roofs are builded; that maketh us know

> *Qui sceptra saevus duro imperio regit*
> *Timet timentes; metus in auctorem redit.*[8]

But how much it can move, Plutarch yieldeth a notable testimony of the abominable tyrant Alexander Pheraeus,[9] from whose eyes a tragedy, well made and represented, drew abundance of tears, who without all pity had murdered infinite numbers, and some of his own blood: so as he, that was not ashamed to make matters for tragedies, yet could not resist the sweet violence of a tragedy. And if it wrought no further good in him, it was that he, in despite of himself, withdrew himself from hearkening to that which might mollify his hardened heart. But it is not the tragedy they do mislike; for it were too absurd to cast out so excellent a representation of whatsoever is most worthy to be learned.

Is it the Lyric that most displeaseth, who with his tuned lyre and well-accorded voice, giveth praise, the reward of virtue, to virtuous acts; who gives moral precepts, and natural problems; who sometimes raiseth up his voice to the height of the heavens, in singing the lauds of the immortal God? Certainly, I must confess my own barbarousness, I never heard the old song of Percy and Douglas[1] that I found not my heart moved more than with a trumpet; and yet is it sung but by some blind crowder,[2] with no rougher voice than rude style; which, being so evil apparelled in the dust and cobwebs of that uncivil age, what would it work trimmed in the gorgeous eloquence of Pindar?[3] In Hungary I have seen it the manner at all feasts, and other such meetings, to have songs of their ancestors' valor, which that right soldierlike nation think one of the chiefest kindlers of brave courage. The incomparable Lacedemonians[4] did not only carry that kind of music ever with them to the field, but even at home, as such songs were made, so were they all content to be singers of them—when the lusty men were to tell what they did, the old men what they had done, and the young what they would do. And where a man may say that Pindar many times praiseth highly

6. Stock characters from the Roman comedies of Terence.
7. At a mill; a customary punishment for criminals and unruly slaves.
8. "The cruel man (i.e., the tyrant) who rules his people with a harsh government fears his fearful people; terror returns to its author" (Seneca, *Oedipus*, 3.705–6).
9. Tyrant of Pherae in Thessaly (369–357 B.C.), described by Plutarch in his *Life of Pelopidas*.

1. Sidney refers to the ballad *Chevy Chase*, which describes the conflict between the Earls of Percy and Douglas.
2. Fiddler.
3. The most famous of Greek lyric poets (c. 522–402 B.C.), whose metrically complex odes celebrate victories in the Panhellenic games, the most famous of which was held every four years at Olympia.
4. Spartans.

victories of small moment, matters rather of sport than virtue; as it may be answered, it was the fault of the poet, and not of the poetry, so indeed the chief fault was in the time and custom of the Greeks, who set those toys at so high a price that Philip of Macedon[5] reckoned a horserace won at Olympus among his three fearful[6] felicities. But as the unimitable Pindar often did, so is that kind most capable and most fit to awake the thoughts from the sleep of idleness to embrace honorable enterprises.

There rests the Heroical—whose very name (I think) should daunt all back-biters: for by what conceit can a tongue be directed to speak evil of that which draweth with him no less champions than Achilles, Cyrus, Aeneas, Turnus, Tydeus, and Rinaldo?[7]—who doth not only teach and move to a truth, but teacheth and moveth to the most high and excellent truth; who maketh magnanimity and justice shine through all misty fearfulness and foggy desires; who, if the saying of Plato and Tully be true, that who could see virtue would be wonderfully ravished with the love of her beauty—this man sets her out to make her more lovely in her holiday apparel, to the eye of any that will deign not to disdain until they understand. But if anything be already said in the defense of sweet poetry, all concurreth to the maintaining the heroical, which is not only a kind, but the best and most accomplished kind of po-etry. For as the image of each action stirreth and instructeth the mind, so the lofty image of such worthies most inflameth the mind with desire to be worthy, and in-forms with counsel how to be worthy. Only let Aeneas be worn in the tablet of your memory, how he governeth himself in the ruin of his country; in the preserving his old father, and carrying away his religious ceremonies; in obeying God's command-ment to leave Dido, though not only all passionate kindness, but even the human consideration of virtuous gratefulness, would have craved other of him; how in storms, how in sports, how in war, how in peace, how a fugitive, how victorious, how besieged, how besieging, how to strangers, how to allies, how to enemies, how to his own; lastly, how in his inward self, and how in his outward government—and I think, in a mind not prejudiced with a prejudicating humor, he will be found in excellency fruitful, yea, even as Horace saith,

> *melius Chrysippo et Crantore.*[8]

But truly I imagine it falleth out with these poet-whippers, as with some good women, who often are sick, but in faith they cannot tell where; so the name of poetry is odious to them, but neither his cause nor effects, neither the sum that contains him, nor the particularities descending from him, give any fast handle to their carping dispraise.

Since then poetry is of all human learning the most ancient and of most fatherly antiquity, as from whence other learnings have taken their beginnings; since it is so universal that no learned nation doth despise it, nor barbarous nation is without it; since both Roman and Greek gave such divine names unto it, the one of prophesy-ing, the other of making, and that indeed that name of making is fit for him, consid-ering that where all other arts retain themselves within their subject, and receive, as it were, their being from it, the poet only bringeth his own stuff, and doth not learn a

5. Father of Alexander the Great, himself a conquering general and hero. Olympus: Sidney's error for Olympia, site of the Olympian Games.
6. Wonderful.
7. Epic heroes and moral exemplars. Tydeus fought to bring Polyneices, the son of Oedipus, to the throne of Thebes (see Statius's *Thebaid*); Rinaldo was one of the French king Charlemagne's knights who fought against the Saracens in Italy (see Ludovico Ariosto's *Orlando Furioso* and Torquato Tasso's *Jerusalem Delivered*).
8. "Better than [the philosophers] Chrysippus and Cran-tor" (Horace, *Epistles*, 1.4).

conceit out of a matter,[9] but maketh matter for a conceit; since neither his description nor end containing any evil, the thing described cannot be evil; since his effects be so good as to teach goodness and to delight the learners; since therein (namely in moral doctrine, the chief of all knowledges) he doth not only far pass the historian, but, for instructing, is well nigh comparable to the philosopher, for moving leaves him behind him; since the Holy Scripture (wherein there is no uncleanness) hath whole parts in it poetical, and that even our Savior Christ vouchsafed to use the flowers of it; since all his kinds are not only in their united forms but in their severed dissections fully commendable; I think (and think I think rightly) the laurel crown appointed for triumphant captains doth worthily (of all other learnings) honor the poet's triumph.

But because we have ears as well as tongues, and that the lightest reasons that may be will seem to weigh greatly, if nothing be put in the counterbalance, let us hear, and, as well as we can, ponder what objections be made against this art, which may be worthy either of yielding or answering.

First, truly I note not only in these μισ′ομονσοι, poet-haters, but in all that kind of people who seek a praise by dispraising others, that they do prodigally spend a great many wandering words in quips and scoffs, carping and taunting at each thing which, by stirring the spleen, may stay the brain from a through-beholding the worthiness of the subject. Those kind of objections, as they are full of a very idle easiness, since there is nothing of so sacred a majesty but that an itching tongue may rub itself upon it, so deserve they no other answer, but, instead of laughing at the jest, to laugh at the jester. We know a playing wit can praise the discretion of an ass, the comfortableness of being in debt, and the jolly commodities of being sick of the plague. So of the contrary side, if we will turn Ovid's verse

Ut lateat virtus proximitate mali,[1]

that good lie hid in nearness of the evil, Agrippa will be as merry in showing the vanity of science as Erasmus was in the commending of folly. Neither shall any man or matter escape some touch of these smiling railers. But for Erasmus and Agrippa,[2] they had another foundation than the superficial part would promise. Marry, these other pleasant faultfinders, who will correct the verb before they understand the noun, and confute others' knowledge before they confirm their own—I would have them only remember that scoffing cometh not of wisdom. So as the best title in true English they get with their merriments is to be called good fools; for so have our grave forefathers ever termed that humorous kind of jesters.

But that which giveth greatest scope to their scorning humor is rhyming and versing. It is already said (and, as I think, truly said), it is not rhyming and versing that maketh poesy. One may be a poet without versing, and a versifier without poetry. But yet, presuppose it were inseparable (as indeed it seemeth Scaliger[3] judgeth), truly it were an inseparable commendation. For if *oratio* next to *ratio*, speech next to reason, be the greatest gift bestowed upon mortality, that cannot be praiseless which

9. I.e., does not take his theme from his material.
1. "That virtue may lie next to evil" (cf. Ovid, *The Art of Love* 2.662).
2. Henry Cornelius Agrippa of Nettesheim (1486–1533), a German philosopher, and Desiderius Erasmus of Rotterdam (1467–1536), the greatest humanist scholar of the early modern period. Sidney refers to their most popular works, *The Uncertainty and Vanity of Knowledge* and *The Praise of Folly*, respectively, both written to satirize human pretensions.
3. Julius Caesar Scaliger (1484–1558), an Italian scholar who wrote a treatise, *Seven Books on Poetry*.

doth most polish that blessing of speech; which considers each word, not only (as a man may say) by his most forcible quality, but by his best measured quantity, carrying even in themselves a harmony—without, perchance, number, measure, order, proportion be in our time grown odious. But lay aside the just praise it hath, by being the only fit speech for music (music, I say, the most divine striker of the senses), thus much is undoubtedly true, that if reading be foolish without remembering, memory being the only treasure of knowledge, those words which are fittest for memory are likewise most convenient for knowledge. Now, that verse far exceedeth prose in the knitting up of memory, the reason is manifest: the words (besides their delight, which hath a great affinity to memory) being so set as one cannot be lost but the whole work fails; which accusing itself, calleth the remembrance back to itself, and so most strongly confirmeth it. Besides, one word so, as it were, begetting another, as, be it in rhyme or measured verse, by the former a man shall have a near guess to the follower. Lastly, even they that have taught the art of memory have showed nothing so apt for it as a certain room divided into many places well and thoroughly known. Now, that hath the verse in effect perfectly, every word having his natural seat, which seat must needs make the word remembered. But what needeth more in a thing so known to all men? Who is it that ever was a scholar that doth not carry away some verses of Virgil, Horace, or Cato, which in his youth he learned, and even to his old age serve him for hourly lessons? But the fitness it hath for memory is notably proved by all delivery of arts: wherein for the most part, from grammar to logic, mathematics, physic, and the rest, the rules chiefly necessary to be borne away are compiled in verses. So that, verse being in itself sweet and orderly, and being best for memory, the only handle of knowledge, it must be in jest that any man can speak against it.

Now then go we to the most important imputations laid to the poor poets. For aught I can yet learn, they are these. First, that there being many other more fruitful knowledges, a man might better spend his time in them than in this. Secondly, that it is the mother of lies. Thirdly, that it is the nurse of abuse, infecting us with many pestilent desires; with a siren's sweetness drawing the mind to the serpent's tail of sinful fancies (and herein, especially, comedies give the largest field to ear,[4] as Chaucer saith); how, both in other nations and in ours, before poets did soften us, we were full of courage, given to martial exercises, the pillars of manlike liberty, and not lulled asleep in shady idleness with poets' pastimes. And lastly, and chiefly, they cry out with open mouth as if they had overshot Robin Hood,[5] that Plato banished them out of his commonwealth. Truly, this is much, if there be much truth in it.

First, to the first. That a man might better spend his time, is a reason indeed; but it doth (as they say) but *petere principium* [beg the question]. For if it be as I affirm, that no learning is so good as that which teacheth and moveth to virtue; and that none can both teach and move thereto so much as poetry: then is the conclusion manifest that ink and paper cannot be to a more profitable purpose employed. And certainly, though a man should grant their first assumption, it should follow (methinks) very unwillingly, that good is not good, because better is better. But I still and utterly deny that there is sprong out of earth a more fruitful knowledge.

4. Sidney refers to an expression in Chaucer's *Canterbury Tales:* "a large feeld to ere," *The Knight's Tale*, line 28.
5. The medieval folk hero, who is said to have lived in Sherwood Forest. Plato banishes poets in his treatise on the ideal state (*The Republic* 3.392).

To the second, therefore, that they should be the principal liars, I answer paradoxically, but truly, I think truly, that of all writers under the sun the poet is the least liar, and, though he would, as a poet can scarcely be a liar. The astronomer, with his cousin the geometrician, can hardly escape, when they take upon them to measure the height of the stars. How often, think you, do the physicians lie, when they aver things good for sicknesses, which afterwards send Charon[6] a great number of souls drowned in a potion before they come to his ferry? And no less of the rest, which take upon them to affirm. Now, for the poet, he nothing affirms, and therefore never lieth. For, as I take it, to lie is to affirm that to be true which is false. So as the other artists, and especially the historian, affirming many things, can, in the cloudy knowledge of mankind, hardly escape from many lies. But the poet (as I said before) never affirmeth. The poet never maketh any circles about your imagination, to conjure you to believe for true what he writes. He citeth not authorities of other histories, but even for his entry calleth the sweet Muses to inspire into him a good invention; in truth, not laboring to tell you what is or is not, but what should or should not be. And therefore, though he recount things not true, yet because he telleth them not for true, he lieth not—without we will say that Nathan lied in his speech before-alleged to David; which as a wicked man durst scarce say, so think I none so simple would say that Aesop lied in the tales of his beasts; for who thinks that Aesop wrote it for actually true were well worthy to have his name chronicled among the beasts he writeth of. What child is there, that, coming to a play, and seeing *Thebes* written in great letters upon an old door, doth believe that it is Thebes? If then a man can arrive to that child's age to know that the poets' persons and doings are but pictures what should be, and not stories what have been, they will never give the lie to things not affirmatively but allegorically and figuratively written. And therefore, as in history, looking for truth, they may go away full fraught with falsehood, so in poesy, looking but for fiction, they shall use the narration but as an imaginative ground-plot of a profitable invention. But hereto is replied, that the poets give names to men they write of, which argueth a conceit of an actual truth, and so, not being true, proves a falsehood. And doth the lawyer lie then, when under the names of *John-a-stiles* and *John-a-nokes*[7] he puts his case? But that is easily answered. Their naming of men is but to make their picture the more lively, and not to build any history: painting men, they cannot leave men nameless. We see we cannot play at chess but that we must give names to our chessmen; and yet, methinks, he were a very partial champion of truth that would say we lied for giving a piece of wood the reverend title of a bishop. The poet nameth Cyrus or Aeneas no other way than to show what men of their fames, fortunes, and estates should do.

Their third is, how much it abuseth men's wit, training it to wanton sinfulness and lustful love: for indeed that is the principal, if not only, abuse I can hear alleged.[8] They say, the comedies rather teach than reprehend amorous conceits. They say the lyric is larded with passionate sonnets; the elegiac weeps the want of his mistress; and that even to the heroical, Cupid hath ambitiously climbed. Alas, Love, I would thou couldst as well defend thyself as thou canst offend others. I would those on whom thou dost attend could either put thee away, or yield good reason why they keep thee. But grant love of beauty to be a beastly fault (although it be very

---

6. According to Greek myth, Charon ferries souls across the river Styx to the underworld.

7. I.e., John Doe, or John Roe of ancient law courts.

8. Sidney refers to contemporary criticism of the drama, the best known of which was Stephen Gosson's *School of Abuse* (1579).

hard, since only man, and no beast, hath that gift to discern beauty); grant that lovely name of Love to deserve all hateful reproaches (although even some of my masters the philosophers spent a good deal of their lamp-oil in setting forth the excellency of it); grant, I say, whatsoever they will have granted, that not only love, but lust, but vanity, but (if they list) scurrility, possesseth many leaves of the poets' books; yet think I, when this is granted, they will find their sentence may with good manners put the last words foremost, and not say that poetry abuseth man's wit, but that man's wit abuseth poetry.

For I will not deny but that man's wit may make poesy, which should be εἰκαστικη [representing real things] (which some learned have defined: figuring forth good things), to be φανταστικη [representing imaginary things] (which doth, contrariwise, infect the fancy with unworthy objects), as the painter, that should give to the eye either some excellent perspective, or some fine picture, fit for building or fortification, or containing in it some notable example (as Abraham sacrificing his son Isaac, Judith killing Holofernes, David fighting with Goliath),[9] may leave those, and please an ill-pleased eye with wanton shows of better hidden matters. But what, shall the abuse of a thing make the right use odious? Nay truly, though I yield that poesy may not only be abused, but that being abused, by the reason of his sweet charming force, it can do more hurt than any other army of words: yet shall it be so far from concluding that the abuse should give reproach to the abused, that, contrariwise, it is a good reason that whatsoever, being abused, doth most harm, being rightly used (and upon the right use each thing conceiveth his title), doth most good. Do we not see the skill of physic, the best rampire[1] to our often-assaulted bodies, being abused, teach poison, the most violent destroyer? Doth not knowledge of law, whose end is to even and right all things, being abused, grow the crooked fosterer of horrible injuries? Doth not (to go to the highest) God's word abused breed heresy, and His name abused become blasphemy? Truly, a needle cannot do much hurt, and as truly (with leave of ladies be it spoken) it cannot do much good: with a sword thou mayst kill thy father, and with a sword thou mayst defend thy prince and country. So that, as in their calling poets fathers of lies they said nothing, so in this their argument of abuse they prove the commendation.

They allege herewith, that before poets began to be in price our nation had set their hearts' delight upon action, and not imagination: rather doing things worthy to be written, than writing things fit to be done. What that before-time was, I think scarcely Sphinx[2] can tell, since no memory is so ancient that hath not the precedent of poetry. And certain it is that, in our plainest homeliness, yet never was the Albion[3] nation without poetry. Marry, this argument, though it be levelled against poetry, yet is it indeed a chainshot[4] against all learning, or bookishness as they commonly term it. Of such mind were certain Goths,[5] of whom it is written that, having in the spoil of a famous city taken a fair library, one hangman (belike fit to execute the fruits of their wits) who had murdered a great number of bodies, would have set fire in it: no, said another very gravely, take heed what you do, for while they are busy about these toys, we shall with more leisure conquer their countries. This indeed is

---

9. Sidney refers to episodes in the Bible (Genesis 22, 1 Samuel 17, Judith 2–14).
1. Rampart.
2. In Greek mythology, a monster with a woman's head and a lion's body who posed riddles to human beings.
3. British.

4. Two cannonballs joined by a chain; it was deployed in naval warfare, usually against the rigging on enemy ships.
5. Northern European tribes, often described as uncivilized by ancient historians. The fate of "a fair library" is told by Michel de Montaigne in his essay Of Pedantry (Essays 1.24.)

the ordinary doctrine of ignorance, and many words sometimes I have heard spent in it. But because this reason is generally against all learning as well as poetry, or rather, all learning but poetry; because it were too large a digression to handle it, or at least too superfluous (since it is manifest that all government of action is to be gotten by knowledge, and knowledge best by gathering many knowledges, which is reading), I only, with Horace, to him that is of that opinion

> *jubeo stultum esse libenter;*[6]

for as for poetry itself, it is the freest from this objection.

For poetry is the companion of camps. I dare undertake, Orlando Furioso, or honest King Arthur, will never displease a soldier; but the quiddity of *ens* and *prima materia* will hardly agree with a corselet;[7] and therefore, as I said in the beginning, even Turks and Tartars are delighted with poets. Homer, a Greek, flourished before Greece flourished. And if to a slight conjecture a conjecture may be opposed, truly it may seem, that as by him their learned men took almost their first light of knowledge, so their active men received their first motions of courage. Only Alexander's example may serve, who by Plutarch is accounted of such virtue, that Fortune was not his guide but his footstool; whose acts speak for him, though Plutarch did not: indeed the phoenix of warlike princes.[8] This Alexander left his schoolmaster, living Aristotle, behind him, but took dead Homer with him. He put the philosopher Callisthenes to death for his seeming philosophical, indeed mutinous, stubbornness, but the chief thing he was ever heard to wish for was that Homer had been alive. He well found he received more bravery of mind by the pattern of Achilles than by hearing the definition of fortitude. And therefore, if Cato misliked Fulvius for carrying Ennius with him to the field,[9] it may be answered that, if Cato misliked it, the noble Fulvius liked it, or else he had not done it; for it was not the excellent Cato Uticensis (whose authority I would much more have reverenced), but it was the former, in truth a bitter punisher of faults (but else a man that had never well sacrificed to the Graces: he misliked and cried out against all Greek learning, and yet, being eighty years old, began to learn it, belike fearing that Pluto understood not Latin). Indeed, the Roman laws allowed no person to be carried to the wars but he that was in the soldiers' roll; and therefore, though Cato misliked his unmustered person, he misliked not his work.[1] And if he had, Scipio Nasica, judged by common consent the best Roman, loved him. Both the other Scipio brothers, who had by their virtues no less surnames than of Asia and Afric, so loved him that they caused his body to be buried in their sepulture. So as Cato's authority, being but against his person, and that answered with so far greater than himself, is herein of no validity.

---

6. "I order [him] to be stupid cheerfully" (Horace, *Satires,* 1.1.63).

7. I.e., soldiers will enjoy reading about knights like Ariosto's Orlando Furioso or Malory's King Arthur, but will balk at philosophers' concerns with "quiddities" (subtleties), "*ens*" (being), and "*prima materia*" (the original matter of the universe).

8. Sidney cites various episodes from Plutarch's accounts of Alexander the Great in his *Lives* (c. A.D. 100), which was translated into English by Sir Thomas North in 1579. The phoenix was a mythic bird thought to be eternally reborn in the ashes of its own funeral pyre.

9. Marcus Portius Cato the Censor (234–184 B.C.),

criticized the general Marcus Flavius Nobilior for carrying the poetry of Quintus Ennius (239–169 B.C.) on a battle campaign. Sidney goes on to distinguish Cato the Censor from his great-grandson, Marcus Porcius Cato, the chief political antagonist of Julius Caesar.

1. In fact, as Sidney states, the poet Ennius in person actually accompanied Flavius; he was "unmustered" in that he was not on the army payroll. Sidney continues to praise Ennius by saying that he was loved by various Scipios: Publius Cornelius Scipio Nasica, Publius Cornelius Scipio Africanus, and Lucius Cornelius Scipio Asiaticus, all notable patriots and generals.

But now indeed my burden is great; now Plato's name is laid upon me, whom, I must confess, of all philosophers I have ever esteemed most worthy of reverence, and with good reason: since of all philosophers he is the most poetical. Yet if he will defile the fountain out of which his flowing streams have proceeded, let us boldly examine with what reasons he did it. First, truly, a man might maliciously object that Plato, being a philosopher, was a natural enemy of poets. For indeed, after the philosophers had picked out of the sweet mysteries of poetry the right discerning true points of knowledge, they forthwith putting it in method, and making a school-art of that which the poets did only teach by a divine delightfulness, beginning to spurn at their guides, like ungrateful prentices, were not content to set up shops for themselves, but sought by all means to discredit their masters; which by the force of delight being barred them, the less they could overthrow them, the more they hated them. For indeed, they found for Homer seven cities strave who should have him for their citizen; where many cities banished philosophers as not fit members to live among them. For only repeating certain of Euripides' verses,[2] many Athenians had their lives saved of the Syracusans, where the Athenians themselves thought many philosophers unworthy to live. Certain poets, as Simonides and Pindar, had so prevailed with Hiero the First,[3] that of a tyrant they made him a just king; where Plato could do so little with Dionysius, that he himself of a philosopher was made a slave. But who should do thus, I confess, should requite the objections made against poets with like cavillations[4] against philosophers; as likewise one should do that should bid one read *Phaedrus* or *Symposium* in Plato, or the discourse of love in Plutarch, and see whether any poet do authorize abominable filthiness, as they do. Again, a man might ask out of what commonwealth Plato did banish them:[5] in sooth, thence where he himself alloweth community of women—so as belike this banishment grew not for effeminate wantonness, since little should poetical sonnets be hurtful when a man might have what woman he listed.[6] But I honor philosophical instructions, and bless the wits which bred them: so as they be not abused, which is likewise stretched to poetry.

St. Paul himself (who yet, for the credit of poets, twice citeth poets, and one of them by the name of "their prophet") setteth a watchword upon philosophy—indeed upon the abuse.[7] So doth Plato upon the abuse, not upon poetry. Plato found fault that the poets of his time filled the world with wrong opinions of the gods, making light tales of that unspotted essence, and therefore would not have the youth depraved with such opinions. Herein may much be said. Let this suffice: the poets did not induce such opinions, but did imitate those opinions already induced. For all the Greek stories can well testify that the very religion of that time stood upon many and many-fashioned gods, not taught so by the poets, but followed according to their nature of imitation. Who list may read in Plutarch the discourses of Isis and Osiris,[8] of

2. Plutarch states that Greek slaves living outside Greece had won their release by teaching their masters the poetry of Euripides (*Life of Nicias*, ch. 29).
3. Tyrant of Syracuse (478–476 B.C.), who patronized Greek poets. Aeschylus was a playwright; Bacchylides a lyric poet; and Simonides a writer of satire. Dionysius the Elder of Syracuse was said to have sold Plato to the Spartan ambassador Pollis as a slave, a situation from which he was later liberated.
4. Objections.
5. I.e., poets. Plato argued that in his ideal republic, all women should be common, that is, not married to a

single man but sexually available to all men (*Republic* 5, 449–462). Sidney observes that Plato banishes poets not because poetry makes men licentious, an impossibility in a state in which women are readily available, but for some other reason.
6. Desired.
7. Paul rejects the assessment of poets by philosophers (Acts 17.18, Colossians 2.8), and he castigates false prophets (Titus 1.12).
8. Isis, the Egyptian goddess of fertility, was sister and wife of Osiris, civilizer of Egypt, god of the dead, and source of life.

the cause why oracles ceased, of the divine providence, and see whether the theology of that nation stood not upon such dreams which the poets indeed superstitiously observed—and truly (since they had not the light of Christ) did much better in it than the philosophers, who, shaking off superstition, brought in atheism. Plato therefore (whose authority I had much rather justly construe than unjustly resist) meant not in general of poets, in those words of which Julius Scaliger saith *Qua authoritate barbari quidam atque hispidi abuti velint ad poetas e republica exigendos;*[9] but only meant to drive out those wrong opinions of the Deity (whereof now, without further law, Christianity hath taken away all the hurtful belief) perchance (as he thought) nourished by the then esteemed poets. And a man need go no further than to Plato himself to know his meaning: who, in his dialogue called *Ion,* giveth high and rightly divine commendation unto poetry. So as Plato, banishing the abuse, not the thing, not banishing it, but giving due honor unto it, shall be our patron, and not our adversary. For indeed I had much rather (since truly I may do it) show their mistaking of Plato (under whose lion's skin they would make an ass-like braying against poesy) than go about to overthrow his authority; whom, the wiser a man is, the more just cause he shall find to have in admiration; especially since he attributeth unto poesy more than myself do, namely, to be a very inspiring of a divine force, far above man's wit, as in the forenamed dialogue is apparent.

Of the other side, who would show the honors have been by the best sort of judgments granted them, a whole sea of examples would present themselves: Alexanders, Caesars, Scipios, all favorers of poets; Laelius, called the Roman Socrates, himself a poet, so as part of *Heautontimorumenos*[1] in Terence was supposed to be made by him; and even the Greek Socrates, whom Apollo confirmed to be the only wise man, is said to have spent part of his old time in putting Aesop's fables into verses. And therefore, full evil should it become his scholar Plato to put such words in his master's mouth against poets. But what need more? Aristotle writes the Art of Poesy;[2] and why, if it should not be written? Plutarch teacheth the use to be gathered of them; and how, if they should not be read? And who reads Plutarch's either history or philosophy, shall find he trimmeth both their garments with guards of poesy. But I list not to defend poesy with the help of his underling historiography. Let it suffice to have showed it is a fit soil for praise to dwell upon; and what dispraise may be set upon it, is either easily overcome, or transformed into just commendation.

So that, since the excellencies of it may be so easily and so justly confirmed, and the low-creeping objections so soon trodden down: it not being an art of lies, but of true doctrine; not of effeminateness, but of notable stirring of courage; not of abusing man's wit, but of strengthening man's wit; not banished, but honored by Plato: let us rather plant more laurels for to engarland the poets' heads (which honor of being laureate, whereas besides them only triumphant captains were, is a sufficient authority to show the price they ought to be held in) than suffer the ill-favored breath of such wrong-speakers once to blow upon the clear springs of poesy.

But since I have run so long a career in this matter, methinks, before I give my pen a full stop, it shall be but a little more lost time to inquire why England, the

---

9. By abuse of whose authority, barbarous and crude men wish to expel poets from the Republic; Scaliger is commenting on Plato's expulsion of poets from an ideal republic in his own treatise on poetry.
1. Gaius Laelius was said to have written parts of a play

called *Heautontimorumenos* (*The Self-Tormenter*), reputed to be by the Roman playwright Terence. Plato reports that Socrates turned Aesop's fables into verse.
2. Sidney refers to Aristotle's *Poetics*.

mother of excellent minds, should be grown so hard a stepmother to poets, who certainly in wit ought to pass all other, since all only proceedeth from their wit, being indeed makers of themselves, not takers of others. How can I but exclaim

Musa, mihi causas memora, quo numine laeso?[3]

Sweet poesy, that hath anciently had kings, emperors, senators, great captains, such as, besides a thousand others, David, Adrian, Sophocles, Germanicus, not only to favor poets, but to be poets;[4] and of our nearer times can present for her patrons a Robert, king of Sicily, the great King Francis of France, King James of Scotland; such cardinals as Bembus and Bibbiena; such famous preachers and teachers as Beza and Melanchthon; so learned philosophers as Fracastorius and Scaliger; so great orators as Pontanus and Muretus; so piercing wits as George Buchanan; so grave counselors as, beside many, but before all, that Hospital of France,[5] than whom (I think) that realm never brought forth a more accomplished judgment, more firmly builded upon virtue: I say these, with numbers of others, not only to read others' poesies, but to poetize for others' reading—that poesy, thus embraced in all other places, should only find in our time a hard welcome in England, I think the very earth lamenteth it, and therefore decketh our soil with fewer laurels than it was accustomed. For heretofore poets have in England also flourished, and, which is to be noted, even in those times when the trumpet of Mars[6] did sound loudest. And now that an overfaint quietness should seem to strew[7] the house for poets, they are almost in as good reputation as the mountebanks[8] at Venice. Truly even that, as of the one side it giveth great praise to poesy, which like Venus (but to better purpose) had rather be troubled in the net with Mars than enjoy the homely quiet of Vulcan:[9] so serves it for a piece of a reason why they are less grateful to idle England, which now can scarce endure the pain of a pen.

Upon this necessarily followeth, that base men with servile wits undertake it, who think it enough if they can be rewarded of the printer. And so as Epaminondas[1] is said with the honor of his virtue to have made an office, by his exercising it, which before was contemptible, to become highly respected; so these men, no more but setting their names to it, by their own disgracefulness disgrace the most graceful poesy. For now, as if all the Muses were got with child to bring forth bastard poets, without any commission they do post over the banks of Helicon,[2] till they make the readers more weary than post-horses; while, in the meantime, they

Queis meliore luto finxit praecordia Titan

are better content to suppress the outflowings of their wit, than, by publishing them, to be accounted knights of the same order. But I that, before ever I durst aspire unto

---

3. "Muse, tell me the cause, by what wounded divinity. . . ." (*Aeneid* 1.8).

4. King David of Israel composed psalms; the emperor Adrian (i.e., Hadrian) wrote verse and prose; Germanicus Caesar, conqueror of Germany, is supposed to have written poetry and plays. Sidney goes on to list a range of modern statesmen-poets.

5. Michel de L'Hôpital (1505–1573), a statesman who favored religious toleration, wrote Latin poems.

6. God of war.

7. Be scattered over.

8. Itinerant quacks peddling fake medicines.

9. Roman god of fire and smiths who caught his adulterous wife, Venus, and Mars, the god of war, in a net he had forged.

1. Theban general (4th century B.C.).

2. Not a very clear paragraph. The mountain named Helicon is sacred to the muses. Here it represents the inspirational springs that are being "post[ed]" over," that is, bypassed, by contemporary "bastard poets" eager to publish, while better writers "whose hearts the Titan [Prometheus] molded out of better clays" (Juvenal, *Satires* 14.36) keep their works private rather than be lumped in with their inferiors. Sidney himself claims, perhaps with false modesty, that as a poet he is classed with the mediocrities, and declares that the reason for poets' low esteem is "want of desert" or lack of worth: They have not been helped by Pallas Athena, goddess of wisdom.

the dignity, am admitted into the company of the paper-blurrers, do find the very true cause of our wanting estimation is want of desert—taking upon us to be poets in despite of Pallas.

Now, wherein we want desert were a thankworthy labor to express; but if I knew, I should have mended myself. But I, as I never desired the title, so have I neglected the means to come by it. Only, overmastered by some thoughts, I yielded an inky tribute unto them. Marry, they that delight in poesy itself should seek to know what they do, and how they do; and especially look themselves in an unflattering glass of reason, if they be inclinable unto it. For poesy must not be drawn by the ears; it must be gently led, or rather it must lead—which was partly the cause that made the ancient-learned affirm it was a divine gift, and no human skill: since all other knowledges lie ready for any that hath strength of wit. A poet no industry can make, if his own genius be not carried into it; and therefore it is an old proverb, *orator fit, poeta nascitur* [the orator is made, the poet born].

Yet confess I always that as the fertilest ground must be manured, so must the highest-flying wit have a Daedalus to guide him.[3] That Daedalus, they say, both in this and in other, hath three wings to bear itself up into the air of due commendation: that is, art, imitation, and exercise. But these, neither artificial rules nor imitative patterns, we much cumber ourselves withal. Exercise indeed we do, but that very fore-backwardly: for where we should exercise to know, we exercise as having known; and so is our brain delivered of much matter which never was begotten by knowledge. For there being two principal parts, matter to be expressed by words and words to express the matter, in neither we use art or imitation rightly. Our matter is *quodlibet* [what you will] indeed, though wrongly performing Ovid's verse,

> *Quicquid conabor dicere, versus erit;*[4]

never marshalling it into any assured rank, that almost the readers cannot tell where to find themselves.

Chaucer, undoubtedly, did excellently in his *Troilus and Criseyde*;[5] of whom, truly, I know not whether to marvel more, either that he in that misty time could see so clearly, or that we in this clear age go so stumblingly after him. Yet had he great wants, fit to be forgiven in so reverent an antiquity. I account the *Mirror of Magistrates* meetly furnished of beautiful parts, and in the Earl of Surrey's lyrics many things tasting of a noble birth, and worthy of a noble mind. The *Shepherd's Calendar* hath much poetry in his eclogues, indeed worthy the reading, if I be not deceived. (That same framing of his style to an old rustic language I dare not allow, since neither Theocritus in Greek, Virgil in Latin, nor Sannazaro in Italian did affect it.) Besides these I do not remember to have seen but few (to speak boldly) printed that have poetical sinews in them; for proof whereof, let but most of the verses be put in prose, and then ask the meaning, and it will be found that one verse did but beget another, without ordering at the first what should be at the last; which becomes a confused mass of words, with a tingling sound of rhyme, barely accompanied with reason.

3. The mythical artisan Daedalus built wings so that he and his son Icarus could escape from Crete, where Minos had confined him in the maze of his own making; but Icarus flew too near the sun, the wax in his wings melted, and he fell into the Aegean Sea and drowned. He is often cited as a figure of ambition.
4. "Whatever I shall try to say shall become verse" (*Tristia* 4.10.26).

5. Sidney gives grudging praise to a number of poets of the early modern period: Chaucer's romance *Troilus and Criseyde* relates the unhappy love affair of two Trojans; the *Mirror of* [i.e., for] *Magistrates*, a poem by various authors and added to at intervals during the 16th century, illustrated exemplary tragedies; the Earl of Surrey is Henry Howard; *The Shepheardes Calender* was written by Edmund Spenser. Theocritus, Virgil, and Sannazaro were poets of pastoral.

Our tragedies and comedies (not without cause cried out against), observing rules neither of honest civility nor skilful poetry—excepting *Gorboduc*[6] (again, I say, of those that I have seen), which notwithstanding as it is full of stately speeches and well-sounding phrases, climbing to the height of Seneca's style, and as full of notable morality, which it doth most delightfully teach, and so obtain the very end of poesy, yet in truth it is very defectuous[7] in the circumstances, which grieveth me, because it might not remain as an exact model of all tragedies. For it is faulty both in place and time, the two necessary companions of all corporal actions. For where the stage should always represent but one place, and the uttermost time presupposed in it should be, both by Aristotle's precept and common reason, but one day, there is both many days, and many places, inartificially[8] imagined.

But if it be so in *Gorboduc,* how much more in all the rest, where you shall have Asia of the one side, and Afric of the other, and so many other under-kingdoms, that the player, when he cometh in, must ever begin with telling where he is, or else the tale will not be conceived? Now you shall have three ladies walk to gather flowers: and then we must believe the stage to be a garden. By and by we hear news of shipwreck in the same place: and then we are to blame if we accept it not for a rock. Upon the back of that comes out a hideous monster with fire and smoke: and then the miserable beholders are bound to take it for a cave. While in the meantime two armies fly in, represented with four swords and bucklers: and then what hard heart will not receive it for a pitched field?

Now, of time they are much more liberal: for ordinary it is that two young princes fall in love; after many traverses, she is got with child, delivered of a fair boy; he is lost, groweth a man, falls in love, and is ready to get another child; and all this in two hours' space: which, how absurd it is in sense, even sense may imagine, and art hath taught, and all ancient examples justified—and at this day, the ordinary players in Italy will not err in. Yet will some bring in an example of *Eunuchus* in Terence, that containeth matter of two days, yet far short of twenty years. True it is, and so was it to be played in two days, and so fitted to the time it set forth. And though Plautus have in one place done amiss, let us hit with him, and not miss with him.[9]

But they will say: How then shall we set forth a story which containeth both many places and many times? And do they not know that a tragedy is tied to the laws of poesy, and not of history; not bound to follow the story, but having liberty either to feign a quite new matter or to frame the history to the most tragical conveniency? Again, many things may be told which cannot be showed, if they know the difference betwixt reporting and representing. As, for example, I may speak (though I am here) of Peru, and in speech digress from that to the description of Calicut;[1] but in action I cannot represent it without Pacolet's horse;[2] and so was the manner the ancients took, by some *Nuntius* [messenger] to recount things done in former time or other place. Lastly, if they will represent a history, they must not (as Horace saith) begin *ab ovo* [from the beginning], but they must come to the principal point of that one action which they will represent.

By example this will be best expressed. I have a story of young Polydorus,[3] delivered for safety's sake, with great riches, by his father Priam to Polymnestor, king of

6. A tragedy by Thomas Sackville and Thomas Norton (1561).

7. Defective.

8. Inartistically.

9. Terence, Plautus: two well-known writers of Roman comedies who influenced the drama in early modern England; Shakespeare took the plot of *The Comedy of Errors* from Plautus's *Menaechmi*.

1. Seaport on the west coast of India.

2. A magic horse in the French romance *Valentine and Orson*.

3. Sidney praises the narrative of the hero Polydorus as told by Euripides, who avoids a lengthy plot in his play on the subject, *Hecuba*.

Thrace, in the Trojan war time; he, after some years, hearing the overthrow of Priam, for to make the treasure his own, murdereth the child; the body of the child is taken up by Hecuba; she, the same day, findeth a sleight to be revenged most cruelly of the tyrant. Where now would one of our tragedy writers begin, but with the delivery of the child? Then should he sail over into Thrace, and so spend I know not how many years, and travel numbers of places. But where doth Euripides? Even with the finding of the body, leaving the rest to be told by the spirit of Polydorus. This need no further to be enlarged; the dullest wit may conceive it.

But besides these gross absurdities, how all their plays be neither right tragedies, nor right comedies, mingling kings and clowns, not because the matter so carrieth it, but thrust in the clown by head and shoulders to play a part in majestical matters with neither decency nor discretion, so as neither the admiration and commiseration, nor the right sportfulness, is by their mongrel tragicomedy obtained. I know Apuleius did somewhat so,[4] but that is a thing recounted with space of time, not represented in one moment; and I know the ancients have one or two examples of tragicomedies, as Plautus hath *Amphitryo*;[5] but, if we mark them well, we shall find that they never, or very daintily, match hornpipes and funerals. So falleth it out that, having indeed no right comedy, in that comical part of our tragedy, we have nothing but scurrility, unworthy of any chaste ears, or some extreme show of doltishness, indeed fit to lift up a loud laughter, and nothing else: where the whole tract of a comedy should be full of delight, as the tragedy should be still maintained in a well-raised admiration.

But our comedians think there is no delight without laughter; which is very wrong, for though laughter may come with delight, yet cometh it not of delight, as though delight should be the cause of laughter; but well may one thing breed both together. Nay, rather in themselves they have, as it were, a kind of contrariety: for delight we scarcely do but in things that have a conveniency to ourselves or to the general nature; laughter almost ever cometh of things most disproportioned to ourselves and nature. Delight hath a joy in it, either permanent or present. Laughter hath only a scornful tickling.

For example, we are ravished with delight to see a fair woman, and yet are far from being moved to laughter; we laugh at deformed creatures, wherein certainly we cannot delight. We delight in good chances, we laugh at mischances: we delight to hear the happiness of our friends, or country, at which he were worthy to be laughed at that would laugh; we shall, contrarily, laugh sometimes to find a matter quite mistaken and go down the hill against the bias in the mouth of some such men—as for the respect of them one shall be heartily sorry, he cannot choose but laugh, and so is rather pained than delighted with laughter.

Yet deny I not but that they may go well together. For as in Alexander's picture well set out we delight without laughter,[6] and in twenty mad antics we laugh without delight; so in Hercules, painted with his great beard and furious countenance, in a

---

4. In his prose romance *The Golden Ass* (c. 155 A.D.); William Adlington translated the work into English in the 16th century.

5. In this play, the tragic element is represented by the heroine Alcmena, tricked into sleeping with the god Jupiter, who is disguised as her husband Amphitrion, and the comic element by the burlesque behavior of the gods who arrange the deception.

6. Sidney distinguishes reactions to different kinds of descriptions: Alexander's portrait delights; mad antics provoke laughter; Hercules, captive and dressed as a woman by Queen Omphale of Lydia, both delights and provokes laughter.

woman's attire, spinning at Omphale's commandment, it breedeth both delight and laughter: for the representing of so strange a power in love procureth delight, and the scornfulness of the action stirreth laughter. But I speak to this purpose, that all the end of the comical part be not upon such scornful matters as stir laughter only, but, mixed with it, that delightful teaching which is the end of poesy. And the great fault even in that point of laughter, and forbidden plainly by Aristotle, is that they stir laughter in sinful things, which are rather execrable than ridiculous, or in miserable, which are rather to be pitied than scorned. For what is it to make folks gape at a wretched beggar and a beggarly clown; or, against law of hospitality, to jest at strangers, because they speak not English so well as we do? What do we learn, since it is certain

> Nil habet infelix paupertas durius in se,
> Quam quod ridiculos homines facit?[7]

But rather, a busy loving courtier and a heartless threatening Thraso;[8] a self-wise-seeming schoolmaster; an awry-transformed traveler. These if we saw walk in stage names, which we play naturally, therein were delightful laughter, and teaching delightfulness—as in the other, the tragedies of Buchanan[9] do justly bring forth a divine admiration.

But I have lavished out too many words of this play matter. I do it because, as they are excelling parts of poesy, so is there none so much used in England, and none can be more pitifully abused; which, like an unmannerly daughter showing a bad education, causeth her mother Poesy's honesty to be called in question.

Other sort of poetry almost have we none, but that lyrical kind of songs and sonnets: which, Lord, if He gave us so good minds, how well it might be employed, and with how heavenly fruit, both private and public, in singing the praises of the immortal beauty: the immortal goodness of that God who giveth us hands to write and wits to conceive; of which we might well want words, but never matter; of which we could turn our eyes to nothing, but we should ever have new-budding occasions. But truly many of such writings as come under the banner of unresistible love, if I were a mistress, would never persuade me they were in love: so coldly they apply fiery speeches, as men that had rather read lovers' writings—and so caught up certain swelling phrases which hang together like a man that once told my father that the wind was at northwest and by south, because he would be sure to name winds enough—than that in truth they feel those passions, which easily (as I think) may be bewrayed by that same forcibleness or energia (as the Greeks call it) of the writer. But let this be a sufficient though short note, that we miss the right use of the material point of poesy.

Now, for the outside of it, which is words, or (as I may term it) diction, it is even well worse. So is that honey-flowing matron Eloquence appareled, or rather disguised, in a courtesan-like painted affectation: one time, with so far-fet words that may seem monsters but must seem strangers to any poor Englishman; another time, with coursing[1] of a letter, as if they were bound to follow the method of a dictionary; another time, with figures and flowers, extremely winter-starved. But I would this fault were only peculiar to versifiers, and had not as large possession among prose-printers;

---

7. "Unfortunate poverty has nothing in itself harder to bear than that it makes men ridiculous" (Juvenal, *Satires* 3.152–53).
8. The braggart soldier of Terence's comedy *Eunuchus*.

9. A Scots humanist (1506–1582) who wrote four tragedies on biblical and classical themes.
1. Alliteration.

and (which is to be marveled) among many scholars; and (which is to be pitied) among some preachers. Truly I could wish, if at least I might be so bold to wish in a thing beyond the reach of my capacity, the diligent imitators of Tully and Demosthenes[2] (most worthy to be imitated) did not so much keep Nizolian paperbooks[3] of their figures and phrases, as by attentive translation (as it were) devour them whole, and make them wholly theirs: for now they cast sugar and spice upon every dish that is served to the table—like those Indians, not content to wear earrings at the fit and natural place of the ears, but they will thrust jewels through their nose and lips, because they will be sure to be fine. Tully, when he was to drive out Catiline, as it were with a thunderbolt of eloquence, often used the figure of repetition, as *Vivit. Vivit? Imo in senatum venit, & c.*[4] Indeed, inflamed with a well-grounded rage, he would have his words (as it were) double out of his mouth, and so do that artificially which we see men in choler do naturally. And we, having noted the grace of those words, hale them in sometimes to a familiar epistle, when it were too too much choler to be choleric. How well store of *similiter cadences* [similar cadences] doth sound with the gravity of the pulpit, I would but invoke Demosthenes' soul to tell, who with a rare daintiness useth them. Truly they have made me think of the sophister[5] that with too much subtlety would prove two eggs three, and though he might be counted a sophister, had none for his labor. So these men bringing in such a kind of eloquence, well may they obtain an opinion of a seeming finesse, but persuade few—which should be the end of their finesse. Now for similitudes, in certain printed discourses, I think all herbarists, all stories of beasts, fowls, and fishes are rifled up,[6] that they come in multitudes to wait upon any of our conceits; which certainly is as absurd a surfeit to the ears as is possible. For the force of a similitude not being to prove anything to a contrary disputer, but only to explain to a willing hearer, when that is done, the rest is a most tedious prattling, rather over-swaying the memory from the purpose whereto they were applied, than any whit informing the judgment, already either satisfied, or by similitudes not to be satisfied. For my part, I do not doubt, when Antonius and Crassus,[7] the great forefathers of Cicero in eloquence, the one (as Cicero testifieth of them) pretended not to know art, the other not to set by it, because with a plain sensibleness they might win credit of popular ears (which credit is the nearest step to persuasion, which persuasion is the chief mark of oratory), I do not doubt (I say) but that they used these knacks very sparingly; which who doth generally use, any man may see doth dance to his own music, and so be noted by the audience more careful to speak curiously than to speak truly. Undoubtedly (at least to my opinion undoubtedly), I have found in divers smally learned courtiers a more sound style than in some professors of learning; of which I can guess no other cause, but that the courtier, following that which by practice he findeth fittest to nature, therein (though he know it not) doth according to art, though not by art: where the other, using art to show art, and not to hide art (as in these cases he should do), flieth from nature, and indeed abuseth art.

2. Athenian statesman and orator (383–322 B.C.).
3. Marius Nizolius, a 16th-century Italian rhetorician and lexicographer, published a collection of phrases by Cicero (i.e., Tully). Sidney complains that contemporary writers use them too often. Cicero, when he prosecuted the traitor Catiline, employed repetition skillfully to heighten the effect of his argument, but writers in Sidney's time are not as discriminating.
4. "He lives. He lives? He still comes into the Senate. . . ."

The sentences paraphrase the opening of Cicero's first oration against Catiline.
5. One who argues by specious reasons.
6. Sidney suggests that the figures in beast fables are all "rifled" or taken by many writers; hence they have become trite.
7. Antonius: Marcus Antonius, consul in 99 B.C.; Crassus: Publius Licinius Crassus Dives Mucianus, consul in 175 B.C. Both men were famous orators.

But what? Methinks I deserve to be pounded for straying from poetry to oratory. But both have such an affinity in the wordish consideration, that I think this digression will make my meaning receive the fuller understanding: which is not to take upon me to teach poets how they should do, but only, finding myself sick among the rest, to show some one or two spots of the common infection grown among the most part of writers, that, acknowledging ourselves somewhat awry, we may bend to the right use both of matter and manner: whereto our language giveth us great occasion, being indeed capable of any excellent exercising of it. I know some will say it is a mingled language.[8] And why not so much the better, taking the best of both the other? Another will say it wanteth grammar. Nay truly, it hath that praise, that it wants not grammar: for grammar it might have, but it needs it not, being so easy in itself, and so void of those cumbersome differences of cases, genders, moods, and tenses, which I think was a piece of the Tower of Babylon's curse,[9] that a man should be put to school to learn his mother-tongue. But for the uttering sweetly and properly the conceits of the mind (which is the end of speech), that hath it equally with any other tongue in the world; and is particularly happy in compositions of two or three words together, near the Greek, far beyond the Latin, which is one of the greatest beauties can be in a language.

Now of versifying there are two sorts, the one ancient, the other modern: the ancient marked the quantity of each syllable, and according to that framed his verse; the modern, observing only number (with some regard of the accent), the chief life of it standeth in that like sounding of the words, which we call rhyme. Whether of these be the more excellent, would bear many speeches: the ancient (no doubt) more fit for music, both words and time observing quantity, and more fit lively to express diverse passions, by the low or lofty sound of the well-weighed syllable; the latter likewise, with his rhyme, striketh a certain music to the ear, and, in fine, since it doth delight, though by another way, it obtains the same purpose: there being in either sweetness, and wanting in neither majesty. Truly the English, before any vulgar language I know, is fit for both sorts. For, for the ancient, the Italian is so full of vowels that it must ever be cumbered with elisions;[1] the Dutch so, of the other side, with consonants, that they cannot yield the sweet sliding, fit for a verse; the French in his whole language hath not one word that hath his accent in the last syllable saving two, called *antepenultima* [third from last]; and little more hath the Spanish, and therefore very gracelessly may they use dactyls.[2] The English is subject to none of these defects. Now for the rhyme, though we do not observe quantity, yet we observe the accent very precisely, which other languages either cannot do, or will not do so absolutely. That *caesura*, or breathing place in the midst of the verse, neither Italian nor Spanish have, the French and we never almost fail of. Lastly, even the very rhyme itself, the Italian cannot put it in the last syllable, by the French named the masculine rhyme, but still in the next to the last, which the French call the female, or the next before that, which the Italian term *sdrucciola* [three-syllable rhyme]. The example of the former is *buono: suono*, of the *sdrucciola* is *femina: semina*. The French, of the other side, hath both the male, as *bon: son*, and the female, as *plaise: taise*, but

8. Sidney describes English as a "mingled" language because it is derived from Anglo-Saxon, brought over by the invading Germanic tribes during the 6th century, and Norman-French, introduced by William the Conqueror in 1066.
9. Early modern writers identified Babylon with Babel (see Genesis 10.10).

1. The suppression of a vowel at the end of a word when the next word begins with a vowel.
2. A metric foot in classical poetry, consisting of one long and two short syllables, as in the words "murmuring," "sensible."

the *sdrucciola* he hath not: where the English hath all three, as *due: true, father: rather, motion: potion*[3]—with much more which might be said, but that already I find the triflingness of this discourse is much too much enlarged.

So that since the ever-praiseworthy Poesy is full of virtue-breeding delightfulness, and void of no gift that ought to be in the noble name of learning; since the blames laid against it are either false or feeble; since the cause why it is not esteemed in England is the fault of poet-apes, not poets; since, lastly, our tongue is most fit to honor poesy, and to be honored by poesy; I conjure you all that have had the evil luck to read this ink-wasting toy of mine, even in the name of the nine Muses, no more to scorn the sacred mysteries of poesy; no more to laugh at the name of poets, as though they were next inheritors to fools; no more to jest at the reverent title of a rhymer; but to believe, with Aristotle, that they were the ancient treasurers of the Grecians' divinity; to believe, with Bembus, that they were first bringers-in of all civility; to believe, with Scaliger, that no philosopher's precepts can sooner make you an honest man than the reading of Virgil; to believe, with Clauserus,[4] the translator of Cornutus, that it pleased the heavenly Deity, by Hesiod and Homer, under the veil of fables, to give us all knowledge, logic, rhetoric, philosophy natural and moral, and *quid non?* [what not]; to believe, with me, that there are many mysteries contained in poetry, which of purpose were written darkly, lest by profane wits it should be abused; to believe, with Landino,[5] that they are so beloved of the gods that whatsoever they write proceeds of a divine fury; lastly, to believe themselves, when they tell you they will make you immortal by their verses. Thus doing, your name shall flourish in the printers' shops; thus doing, you shall be of kin to many a poetical preface; thus doing, you shall be most fair, most rich, most wise, most all, you shall dwell upon superlatives; thus doing, though you be *libertino patre natus* [son of freed slave], you shall suddenly grow *Herculea proles* [a descendant of Hercules],

> *Si quid mea carmina possunt;*[6]

thus doing, your soul shall be placed with Dante's Beatrice, or Virgil's Anchises. But if (fie of such a but) you be born so near the dull-making cataract of Nilus[7] that you cannot hear the planet-like music of poetry; if you have so earth-creeping a mind that it cannot lift itself up to look to the sky of poetry, or rather, by a certain rustical disdain, will become such a mome as to be a Momus[8] of poetry; then, though I will not wish unto you the ass's ears of Midas, nor to be driven by a poet's verses, as Bubonax[9] was, to hang himself, nor to be rhymed to death, as is said to be done in Ireland; yet thus much curse I must send you, in the behalf of all poets, that while you live, you live in love, and never get favor for lacking skill of a sonnet; and, when you die, your memory die from the earth for want of an epitaph.

---

3. *Motion* and *potion* presumably retained three syllables, as the Middle English spelling "mocioun" reveals.
4. Conrad Clauser, a 16th-century German scholar who translated the works of Lucius Annaeus Cornutus, a 1st-century Greek slave who wrote commentaries on Aristotle and Virgil.
5. Cristoforo Landino (1424–1504), an Italian humanist who wrote moral dialogues.
6. "If my songs can do anything" (*Aeneid* 9.446).
7. Cicero claimed that hearing the sound of the cataracts of the Nile River in Egypt caused deafness; the

Neoplatonists thought the movement of the planets produced heavenly music, the music of the spheres.
8. Momus personified the faultfinder in Greek literature; a mome is a blockhead. Apollo changed Midas's ears to those of an ass to signal his stupidity after Midas judged Pan's flute playing to be superior to Apollo's (Ovid, *Metamorphoses* 11.146).
9. Sidney conflates Hipponax, a Greek poet, with Bupalus, a sculptor. The latter had made an unflattering portrait of the former, who took revenge with deadly verses. Irish poets claimed their verses could kill man or beast.

from **Astrophil and Stella**[1]

1

Loving in truth, and fain° in verse my love to show,   *wishing*
That she (dear she) might take some pleasure of my pain:
Pleasure might cause her read, reading might make her know,
Knowledge might pity win, and pity grace obtain,
5   I sought fit words to paint the blackest face of woe,
Studying inventions[2] fine, her wits to entertain:
Oft turning others' leaves, to see if thence would flow
Some fresh and fruitfull showers upon my sun-burned brain.
But words came halting forth, wanting Invention's stay,°   *support*
10 Invention Nature's child, fled step-dame Study's blows,
And others' feet still seemed but strangers in my way.
Thus great with child to speak, and helpless in my throes,°   *agonies*
Biting my trewand° pen, beating my self for spite,   *truant*
Fool, said my Muse to me, look in thy heart and write.

3

Let dainty wits cry on the sisters nine,[3]
That bravely masked, their fancies may be told;
Or, Pindar's apes[4] flaunt they in phrases fine,
Enam'ling with pied flowers their thoughts of gold;
5   Or else let them in statelier glory shine,
Ennobling new-found tropes° with problems° old;   *figures of speech / subjects*
Or with strange similes enrich each line,
Of herbs or beasts which Ind or Afric hold.
For me, in sooth, no Muse but one I know;
10 Phrases and problems from my reach do grow,
And strange things cost too dear for my poor sprites.
How then? Even thus—in Stella's face I read
What love and beauty be; then all my deed
But copying is, what, in her, Nature writes.

7

When Nature made her chief work, Stella's eyes,
In color black, why wrapt° she beams so bright?   *enwrapped*
Would she in beamy° black, like painter wise,   *glowing*
Frame daintiest° luster, mixed of shades and light?   *subtlest*
5   Or did she else that sober hue devise,
In object best to knit and strength° our sight,   *strengthen*

1. This sonnet sequence was composed in 1582 and published in 1591.
2. "Invention" was the term early modern rhetoricians
used to designate the choice of a literary subject and its
development as an argument, in contrast to the forms of
expression, figures of thought and speech, and imagery by
which that subject was conveyed. As Sidney suggests,
"invention" depended on the writer's imaginative intelligence, not on his literary education.
3. The nine Muses, sponsors of the arts, music, and poetry.
4. Poets who slavishly imitated the literary works of the
Greek poet Pindar, A.D. 522–442.

Least if no veil these brave gleams did disguise,
They sun-like should more dazzle then delight?[5]
Or would she her miraculous power show,
10   That whereas black seems beáuty's contrary,
She even in black doth make all beauties flow?
Both so and thus, she minding Love should be
Placed ever there, gave him this mourning weed,
To honor all their deaths, who for her bleed.[6]

24

Rich fools there be whose base and filthy heart
Lies hatching still the goods wherein they flow,
And damning their own selves to Tantal's[7] smart,
Wealth breeding want, more blissed,° more wretched grow.   *blessed*
5   Yet to those fools heaven such wit doth impart
As what their hands do hold, their heads do know,
And knowing, love, and loving, lay apart
As sacred things, far from all danger's show.
But that rich fool who by blind Fortune's lot
10   The richest gem of love and life enjoys,
And can with foul abuse such beauties blot,
Let him, deprived of sweet but unfelt joys,
Exiled for aye from those high treasures which
He knows not, grow in only folly rich![8]

31

With how sad steps, O Moon, thou climb'st the skies,
How silently, and with how wan° a face,   *pale*
What may it be, that even in heavenly place
That busy archer° his sharp arrows tries?   *Cupid*
5   Sure if° that long with Love acquainted eyes   *surely if those*
Can judge of Love, thou feel'st a lover's case;
I read it in thy looks, thy languished grace
To me that feel the like, thy state descries.°   *reveals*
Then even of fellowship, O Moon, tell me
10   Is constant Love deemed there but want of wit?
Are beauties there as proud as here they be?
Do they above love to be loved, and yet
Those lovers scorn whom that Love doth possess?
Do they call Virtue there ungratefulness?

---

5. Did Nature make Stella's eyes black so that their bright beams might be softened to a mixed hue or not blind us with their brilliance?

6. Love is conventionally conveyed by the lady's glance, from her eyes, to the lover's heart, through his eyes; Stella's eyes are dark and in mourning because her glance is lethal.

7. The mythical sinner, condemned forever in Hades to reach for food and drink which were always already out of reach.

8. The sonnet mocks Lord Rich, the husband of Penelope Devereux, the model for Sidney's Stella.

45

Stella oft sees the very face of woe
Painted in my beclouded stormy face:
But cannot skill° to pity my disgrace,   *does not know how*
Not though thereof the cause herself she know:
5   Yet hearing late a fable, which did show
Of lovers never known, a grievous case,°   *situation*
Pity thereof gate° in her breast such place,   *got*
That from that sea derived tears' spring did flow.⁹
Alas, if Fancy drawn by imaged things,
10   Though false, yet with free scope more grace doth breed
Than servants' wrack, where new doubts honor brings;¹
Then think my dear, that you in me do read
Of lovers' ruin some sad tragedy:
I am not I, pity the tale of me.

52

A strife is grown between Virtue and Love,
While each pretends that Stella must be his.
Her eyes, her lips, her all, saith Love, do this,
Since they do wear his badge, most firmly prove.
5   But Virtue thus that title does disprove
That Stella (oh dear name!), that Stella is
That virtuous soul, sure heir of heavenly bliss,
Not this fair outside which our hearts doth move;
And therefore, though her beauty and her grace
10   Be Love's indeed, in Stella's self he may
By no pretense claim any manner place.
Well, Love, since this demur° our suit doth stay,   *objection*
Let Virtue have that Stella's self; yet thus,
That Virtue but that body grant to us.

60

When my good Angel guides me to the place,
Where all my good I do in Stella see,
That heaven of joys throws only down on me
Thundered disdains and lightnings of disgrace:
5   But when the ruggedst step of Fortune's race°   *course*

---

9. I.e., derived from that sea [of pity], a spring of tears did flow.
1. I.e., Fancy with free scope breeds more grace or sympathy than the actual destruction of a servant, a situation in which a sense of honor provokes new doubts about that person's worth.

Makes me fall from her sight, then sweetly she
With words, wherein the Muses' treasures be,
Shows love and pity to my absent case.[2]
Now I wit-beaten long by hardest Fate,
10   So dull am, that I cannot look into
The ground of this fierce love and lovely hate:
Then some good body tell me how I do,
Whose presence, absence, absence presence is;[3]
Blissed° in my curse, and cursed in my bliss.   *blessed*

63

O grammar-rules, O now your virtues show,
So children still read you with awful° eyes,   *respectful*
As my young dove may, in your precepts wise,
Her grant to me by her own virtue know;
5   For late, with heart most high, with eyes most low,
I craved the thing which ever she denies;
She, lightning love, displaying Venus' skies,
Lest once should not be heard, twice said, "No, no!"
Sing then, my muse, now Io Paean sing;[4]
10   Heavens envy not at my high triumphing,
But grammar's force with sweet success confirm,
For grammar says,—oh this, dear Stella, weigh,—
For grammar says,—to grammar who says nay?—
That in one speech two negatives affirm!

68

Stella, the only planet of my light,
Light of my life, and life of my desire,
Chief good whereto my hope doth only aspire,
World of my wealth, and heaven of my delight,
5   Why dost thou spend the treasures of thy sprite°   *spirit*
With voice more fit to wed Amphion's[5] lyre,
Seeking to quench in me the noble fire
Fed by thy worth and blinded by thy sight?
And all in vain; for while they breath most sweet
10   With choicest words, thy words with reasons rare,
Thy reasons firmly set on Virtue's feet,
Labor to kill in me this killing care;
O think I then, what paradise of joy
It is, so fair a virtue to enjoy!

---

2. I.e., when a good angel or good fortune guides the poet to Stella, heaven throws at him only the "joys" of disdain and disgrace. On the other hand, when he is away from her, she shows him love and pity.

3. This paradox is repeated in sonnets 106 and 108.
4. Hymn of thanksgiving.
5. The legendary lyre-player whose music moved the stones that built the walls of Thebes.

71

Who will in fairest book of Nature[6] know,
How Virtue may best lodged in beauty be,
Let him but learn of Love to read in thee,
Stella, those fair lines, which true goodness show.

5   There shall he find all vices overthrow,°   overthrown
Not by rude force, but sweetest sovereignty
Of reason, from whose light those night-birds fly;
That inward sun in thine eyes shineth so.
And not content to be Perfection's heir

10   Thyself, doest strive all minds that way to move:
Who mark in thee what is in thee most fair.
So while thy beauty draws the heart to love,
As fast thy virtue bends that love to good:
But ah, Desire still cries, give me some food.

Second song

Have I caught my heavenly jewel
Teaching sleep most fair to be?
Now will I teach her that she,
When she wakes, is too too cruel.

5   Since sweet sleep her eyes hath charmed
The two only darts of Love,
Now will I with that boy prove
Some play while he is disarmed.[7]

Her tongue, waking, still refuseth,
10   Giving frankly niggard no;
Now will I attempt to know
What no her tongue, sleeping, useth.

See the hand which, waking, guardeth,
Sleeping, grants a free resort.
15   Now will I invade the fort.
Cowards love with loss rewardeth.

But, O fool, think of the danger
Of her just and high disdain!
Now will I, alas, refrain.
20   Love fears nothing else but anger.

Yet those lips, so sweetly swelling,
Do invite a stealing kiss.
Now will I but venture this.
Who will read must first learn spelling.

---

6. All of creation, in effect the second "book" of God and a supplement to the Bible. It was a philosophical commonplace that Nature was the repository of natural law, which all human beings could discover through reason, just as the Bible held divine law, which was revealed to the faithful through grace.
7. Stella's eyes have charmed and disarmed Cupid, leaving him open to the poet's play or contest of wills.

25   O, sweet kiss! But ah, she's waking!
       Louring° beauty chastens me.   *scowling*
       Now will I away hence flee:
       Fool, more fool, for no more taking!

74

     I never drank of Aganippe well,[8]
       Nor ever did in shade of Tempe[9] sit,
       And Muses scorn with vulgar brains to dwell,
       Poor layman I, for sacred rites unfit.
5   Some do I hear of poets' fury[1] tell,
       But, God wot, wot not what they mean by it;
       And this I swear by blackest brook of hell,
       I am no pick-purse of another's wit.
     How falls it then that with so smooth an ease
10   My thoughts I speak; and what I speak doth flow
       In verse, and that my verse best wits doth please?
     Guess we the cause. "What, is it thus?" Fie, no.
     "Or so?" Much less. "How then?" Sure thus it is:
     My lips are sweet, inspired with Stella's kiss.

89

     Now that, of absence, the most irksome night
       With darkest shade doth overcome my day,
       (Since Stella's eyes, wont to give me my day,
       Leaving my hemisphere, leave me in night)
5   Each day seems long and longs for long-stayed night;
       The night, as tedious, woos the approach of day
       Tired with the dusty toils of busy day,
       Languished with horrors of the silent night,
     Suffering the evils both of the day and night,
10   (While no night is more dark than is my day,
       Nor no day hath less quiet than my night)
       With such bad-mixture of my night and day
       That living thus in blackest winter night,
     I feel the flames of hottest summer day.

90

     Stella, think not that I by verse seek fame—
       Who seek, who hope, who love, who live—but thee,
       Thine eyes my pride, thy lips mine history.

---

8. Spring on Mt. Helicon, sacred to the Muses.
9. A valley in Arcadia.

1. Divine frenzy; Sidney identifies it as the poets' inspiration in *The Apology for Poetry*.

If thou praise not, all other praise is shame.
5   Nor so ambitious am I as to frame
A nest for my young praise in laurel tree.[2]
In truth, I swear I wish not there should be
Graved in mine epitaph a poet's name.
Nay, if I would, I could just title make
10 That any laud° to me thereof should grow   *praise*
Without my plumes from others' wings I take,[3]
For nothing from my wit or will doth flow
Since all my words thy beauty doth indite,°   *record*
And Love doth hold my hand, and makes me write.

104

Envious wits,[4] what hath been mine offense,
That with such poisonous care my looks you mark,
That to each word, nay sigh of mine, you hark,
As grudging me my sorrow's eloquence?
5   Ah, is it not enough that I am thence,
Thence, so far thence, that scarcely any spark
Of comfort dare come to this dungeon dark,
Where rigorous exile locks up all my sense?
But if I by a happy° window pass,   *lucky*
10 If I but stars upon mine armor bear[5]—
Sick, thirsty, glad (though but of empty glass),
Your moral notes straight my hid meaning tear
From out my ribs, and, puffing, prove that I
Do Stella love; fools, who doth it deny?

106

O absent presence, Stella is not here;
False flattering hope, that with so fair a face,
Bare° me in hand, that in this orphan place,   *took*
Stella, I say my Stella, should appear.
5   What sayest thou now, where is that dainty cheer,°   *food*
Thou toldst mine eyes should help their famished case?
But thou art gone now that self-felt disgrace
Doth make me most to wish thy comfort near.[6]
But here I do store of fair ladies meet,
10 Who may with charm of conversation sweet,
Make in my heavy mold new thoughts to grow:
Sure they prevail as much with me, as he

2. The laurel tree was identified with Apollo and excellence in poetry.
3. I.e., I do not copy the work of other poets.
4. Poets who identified Sidney as Stella's lover.

5. I.e., Astrophil wears armor decorated with stars in Stella's honor.
6. I.e., you are gone now that that self (my own self) has felt the disgrace of rejection; this makes me wish you here.

That bad his friend but then new maimed,° to be   *wounded*
Merry with him, and not think of his woe.

107

Stella, since thou so right° a princess art   *true*
Of all the powers which life bestows on me,
That ere by them aught undertaken be
They first resort unto the sovereign part;
5   Sweet, for a while give respite to my heart,
Which pants as though it still should leap to thee,
And on my thoughts give thy lieutenancy[7]
To this great cause, which needs both use and art.
And as a queen, who from her presence sends
10   Whom she employs, dismiss from thee my wit
Till it have wrought what thy own will attends.
On servants' shame oft master's blame doth sit.
O let not fools in me thy works reprove,
And scorning say, "See what it is to love!"

108

When sorrow (using mine own fire's might)
Melts down his lead into my boiling breast,
Through that dark furnace to heart oppressed,
There shines a joy from thee my only light;
5   But soon as thought of thee breeds my delight,
And my young soul flutters to thee his nest,
Most rude despair, my daily unbidden guest,
Clips straight my wings, straight wraps me in his night,
And makes me then bow down my head, and say,
10   Ah what doth Phoebus' gold that wretch avail,
Whom iron doors do keep from use of day?
So strangely (alas) thy works[8] in me prevail,
That in my woes for thee thou art my joy,
And in my joys for thee my only annoy.

--- ❦ ---

Isabella Whitney
fl. 1567–1573

Little is known about the life of Isabella Whitney. Biographers agree that she was the sister of Geoffrey Whitney, the author of the first emblem book in England, and that, like him, she was born in Cheshire. The rest is to be deduced from her poetry, which points to an author with

---

7. Dominate my thoughts.   affect me strangely.
8. I.e., "your works," what you have done and meant,

little formal education, a sharp eye for the details of urban life, and some knowledge of classical mythology. The modesty of Whitney's literary background sets her off from such later and accomplished poets as Mary Herbert and Aemilia Lanyer, and her poems on the challenges of love, friendship, and survival in a large city distinguish her from women who wrote devotional verse. Her poems follow the form and conventions of broadside ballads, a feature that may have made them popular with readers who were drawn to stories that gave advice on affairs of the heart and matters of the purse. Of "the middling sort," Whitney probably came to London for employment and diversion, but she seems to have had difficulty supporting herself. In any case, after publishing two collections of verse, *The Copy of a Letter* (c. 1567) and *A Sweet Nosegay* (1573), she left the city, having lived out the dreams as well as the disappointments of many English villagers who went to London to find work.

The Admonition by the Author
to All Young Gentlewomen, and to All Other Maids Being in Love

Ye virgins that from Cupid's tents
    do bear away the foil,[1]
Whose hearts as yet with raging love
    most painfully do boil,

5   To you I speak, for you be they
    that good advice do lack;
Oh, if I could good counsel give,
    my tongue should not be slack.

But such as I can give, I will,
10   here in few words express,
Which if you do observe, it will
    some of your care redress.

Beware of fair and painted talk,
    beware of flattering tongues;
15 The mermaids do pretend no good
    for all their pleasant songs.

Some use the tears of crocodiles
    contrary to their heart,
And if they cannot always weep,
20   they wet their cheeks by art.

Ovid, within his art of love,[2]
    doth teach them this same knack,
To wet their hand and touch their eyes,
    so oft as tears they lack.

1. The reference is obscure. Cupid's weapons were traditionally a bow and arrows; Whitney describes him rather as a fencer who wounds his victims with a foil or sword. By bearing his foil away, Whitney's virgins appear to have experienced unrequited love.

2. The *Ars Amatoria*, a facetious treatise in which the poet advises men how to court and make love to women. Here, Whitney implies that her readers either imitate or avoid the examples of legendary women whose stories she tells.

25   Why have ye such deceit in store?
      have you such crafty wile?
Less craft than this, God knows, would soon
      us simple souls beguile.

And will ye not leave off? But still
30   delude us in this wise?
Since it is so, we trust we shall
      take heed to feigned lies.

Trust not a man at the first sight,
      but try him well before;
35   I wish all maids within their breasts
      to keep this thing in store:

For trial shall declare his truth,
      and show what he doth think,
Whether he be a lover true,
40   or do intend to shrink.

If Scylla[3] had not trust too much
      before that she did try,
She could not have been clean forsake°   *forsaken*
      when she for help did cry.

45   Or if she had had good advice,
      Nisus had lived long;
How durst she trust a stranger, and
      do her dear father wrong?

King Nisus had a hair by fate
50   which hair while he did keep,
He never should be overcome
      neither on land nor deep.

The stranger that the daughter loved
      did war against the King,
55   And always sought how that he might
      them in subjection bring.

This Scylla stole away the hair
      for to obtain her will,
And gave it to the stranger that
60   did straight her father kill.

Then she, who thought herself most sure
      to have her whole desire,

---

3. Daughter of the mythical Nisus, king of Megara, Scylla trusted the love of Minos, king of Crete, who was beseiging her father's city. For love of Minos (whom Whitney refers to as "the stranger"), Scylla betrayed her father by stealing a lock of his hair, a guarantee that Megara would remain free. According to Virgil, Minos, having taken Megara, captured Scylla, tied her to his ship, and dragged her through the sea. She was eventually transformed into a ciris, or sea-bird.

Was clean reject,° and left behind   *rejected*
  when he did home retire.

65 Or if such falsehood had been once
      unto Oenone[4] known,
    About the fields of Ida wood
      Paris had walked alone.

    Or if Demophoon's deceit
70   to Phyllis[5] had been told,
    She had not been transformed so,
      as poets tell of old.

    Hero did try Leander's[6] truth
      before that she did trust,
75 Therefore she found him unto her
      both constant, true, and just.

    For always did he swim the sea
      when stars in sky did glide,
    Till he was drowned by the way
80   near hand unto the side.

    She scratched her face, she tore her hair
      (it grieveth me to tell)
    When she did know the end of him,
      that she did love so well.

85 But like Leander there be few,
      therefore in time take heed;
    And always try before ye trust,
      so shall you better speed.

    The little fish that careless is
90   within the water clear,
    How glad is he, when he doth see
      a bait for to appear.

    He thinks his hap° right good to be,   *luck*
      that he the same could spy,
95 And so the simple fool doth trust
      too much before he try.

    O little fish what hap hadst thou,
      to have such spiteful fate,
    To come into one's cruel hands
100   out of so happy state?

---

4. A nymph of Mount Ida, who was abandoned by Paris, son of Priam, king of Troy.
5. A mythical princess of Thrace and loved by the Greek warrior Demophon (or Demophoon); believing that he would not return to her after the Trojan War, she hanged herself.
6. Hero's lover, Leander, drowned while swimming across the Hellespont to be with her, whereupon she, too, threw herself into the sea.

Thou didst suspect no harm, when thou
 upon the bait didst look;
O that thou hadst had Linceus's[7] eyes
 for to have seen the hook.

105 Then hadst thou with thy pretty mates
 been playing in the streams,
Whereas Sir Phoebus° daily doth   *the sun god Apollo*
 show forth his golden beams.

But since thy fortune is so ill
110 to end thy life on shore,
Of this thy most unhappy end
 I mind to speak no more.

But of thy fellow's chance that late
 such pretty shift did make,
115 That he from fisher's hook did sprint
 before he could him take.

And now he pries on every bait,
 suspecting still that prick
(For to lie hid in every thing)
120 wherewith the fishers strick.°   *strike*

And since the fish that reason lacks
 once warned doth beware,
Why should not we take heed to that
 that turneth us to care?

125 And I who was deceived late
 by one's unfaithful tears,
Trust now for to beware, if that
 I live this hundred years.

Finis.

A Careful Complaint by the Unfortunate Author

Good Dido[1] stint thy tears,
 and sorrows all resign
To me that born was to augment
 misfortune's luckless line.
5 Or using still the same,
 good Dido do thy best,
In helping to bewail the hap
 that furthereth mine unrest.

---

7. A sharp-eyed mythical warrior of Greece.   Aeneas on his way from Troy to Italy.
1. Queen of Carthage, seduced and then abandoned by

For though thy Troyan mate,
10   that Lord Aeneas hight,
Requiting all thy steadfast love,
        from Carthage took his flight,
And foully broke his oath,
        and promise made before
15   Whose falsehood finished thy delight
        before thy hairs were hoar.
Yet greater cause of grief
        compels me to complain,
For Fortune fell° converted hath   *evil*
20   my health to heaps of pain.
And that she[2] swears my death,
        too plain it is (alas),
Whose end let malice still attempt
        to bring the same to pass.
25   O Dido, thou hadst lived
        a happy woman still,
If fickle fancy had not thralled°   *enslaved*
        thy wits to reckless will.
For as the man by whom
30   thy deadly dolors bred,
Without regard of plighted troth
        from Carthage city fled,
So might thy cares in time
        be banished out of thought,
35   His absence might well salve the sore
        that erst° his presence wrought.   *first*
For fire no longer burns
        than faggots° feed the flame,   *except when sticks*
The want of things that breed annoy
40   may soon redress the same.[3]
But I, unhappy most,
        and gripped with endless griefs,
Despair (alas) amid my hope,
        and hope without relief.
45   And as the swelt'ring heat
        consumes the war away,
So do the heaps of deadly harms
        still threaten my decay.
O death delay not long
50   thy duty to declare.
Ye Sisters three[4] dispatch my days
        and finish all my care.

2. I.e., Fortune, whose end or purpose, Whitney's death, malice will bring to pass.
3. I.e., "want," which breeds annoyance, will also end annoyance, as it will eventually result in death.

4. I.e., the three Fates, who determine the length of life and the time of death.

Mary Herbert, Countess of Pembroke

1561–1621

Mary Herbert was like many women of her time in having two phases to her life: a period of service to men, followed by a phase of independent activity. Deeply attached to her brother, Sir Philip Sidney, she spent much of her young adulthood in his company. The estate she presided over as wife to Henry Herbert, Earl of Pembroke, was Sidney's place of refuge after Queen Elizabeth had exiled him from court. At Wilton House and in his sister's company he wrote *The Apology for Poetry* and the first version of his prose romance, *The Arcadia*. Mary Herbert was an interested party in yet another project, his translation of the psalms, and when he died in 1586, she resolved to finish the project. Picking up where he had left off, at Psalm 43, she completed the cycle. Her work was encouraged by the circle of friends that gathered frequently at Wilton House and included such writers and musicians as Francis Mere, Edmund Spenser, Samuel Daniel, Nicholas Breton, Fulke Greville, and Abraham Fraunce. The seventeenth-century biographer John Aubrey spoke of the group as a "college."

Translations of the psalms were popular among Protestant writers of the period; they fulfilled the obligation to know both the Word and the indwelling spirit of God. Poets of religious lyric in the next century, especially George Herbert, would seek and represent a similar knowledge. Mary Herbert dedicated her work to Queen Elizabeth in a poem entitled *Even Now That Care*, which was followed by an elegy for her brother Philip, *To Thee Pure Sprite*. Although riddled with ellipses or words that have been deliberately omitted, they convey the spiritual intensity that characterizes her translations. Some critics think that she did not write a second elegy (here attributed to her), *The Doleful Lay of Clorinda*; it is, however, what we might expect a woman of her station and training to have written about the death of a beloved friend. Milton would later give a profoundly political and religious dimension to the genre in his *Lycidas*, an elegy that is as much for an age and its temperament as it is for a person.

Even Now That Care[1]

Even now that care which on thy crown attends,
And with thy happy greatness daily grows,
Tells me, thrice sacred Queen, my Muse offends,
And of respect to thee the line outgoes.[2]
5 One instant will, or willing can she° lose   *Queen Elizabeth*
I say not reading, but receiving rhymes,
On whom in chief dependeth to dispose
What Europe acts in these most active times?[3]

Yet dare I so, as humbleness may dare
10 Cherish some hope they shall acceptance find;
Not weighing less thy state, lighter thy care,
But knowing more thy grace, abler thy mind.
What heavenly powers thee highest throne assigned,

---

1. This poem prefaces Mary Herbert's translation of the psalms, dedicated to Queen Elizabeth.
2. I.e., my Muse oversteps the boundary of respect that your status demands.

3. I.e., will she or can she lose an instant receiving rhymes—she, who is governing Europe?

Assigned thee goodness suiting that degree,
15   And by thy strength thy burden so defined;
To others' toil, is exercise to thee.[4]

Cares though still great, cannot be greatest still;
Business must ebb, though leisure never flow.
Then these the posts of duty and goodwill
20   Shall press to offer what their senders owe,
Which once in two, now in one subject go,[5]
The poorer left, the richer reft away,
Who better might (O might! Ah, word of woe)
Have given for me what I for him defray.°   pay

25   How can I name whom sighing sighs extend,°   wordlessly amplify
And not unstop my tears' eternal spring?
But he did warp, I weaved this web to end.[6]
The stuff not ours, our work no curious thing,
Wherein yet well we thought the psalmist king,
30   Now English denizened though Hebrew born,
Would to thy music undispleased sing,
Oft having worse, without repining worn.[7]

And I the cloth in both our names present,
A livery robe to be bestowed by° thee,   on
35   Small parcel of that undischarged rent,
From which nor pains, nor payments can us free.
And yet enough to cause our neighbors see
We will our best, though scanted° in our will;   deficient
And those nigh fields where sown thy favors be
40   Unwealthy do, not else unworthy till.[8]

For in our work what bring we but thine own?
What English is, by many names is thine.
There humble laurels in thy shadows grown
To garland others' world, themselves repine.°   are sorrowful
45   Thy breast the cabinet, thy seat the shrine,
Where Muses hang their vowed memories,
Where wit, where art, where all that is divine
Conceived best, and best defended lies.

Which if men did not (as they do) confess,
50   And wronging worlds would otherwise consent,[9]
Yet here° who minds° so meet a patroness   in England / finds
For author's state or writing's argument?

---

4. I.e., thy burden, defined by thy strength, is to others'
toil, [but] to thee exercise.
5. I.e., Herbert and Sidney; the latter is the richer of the
two subjects, the one who could better have offered the
queen duty and good will.
6. I.e., he laid the warp of this web (placed its threads
lengthwise); I wove it to completion (after his death).
7. I.e., you often had worse stuff than our web to wear

(or our poems to listen to), which you did without
complaining.
8. I.e., those near fields where thy favors are sown (as
seed) we, not wealthy but not unworthy, cultivate.
Herbert thanks the queen for her support.
9. I.e., if men did not confess that your breast is the shrine
of the Muses, even unfair worlds would otherwise agree
that this was the case.

A king° should only to a queen be sent.   *King David*
God's loved choice unto his chosen love,
55 Devotion to devotion's president;°   *chief object*
What all applaud, to her whom none reprove.

And who sees aught,° but sees how justly square°   *anything / suitable*
His° haughty ditties to thy glorious days?   *King David's*
How well beseeming thee his triumphs are?
60 His hope, his zeal, his prayer, plaint,° and praise,   *complaint*
Needless thy person to their height to raise,
Less need to bend them down to thy degree;
These holy garments each good soul assays,°   *tries on*
Some sorting° all, all sort to none but thee.   *fitting*

65 For ev'n thy rule is painted° in his reign,   *illustrated*
Both clear in right, both nigh° by wrong oppressed.   *closely*
And each at length (man crossing God in vain)
Possessed of place,° and each in peace possessed.   *office, rule*
Proud Philistines did interrupt his rest,
70 The foes of heav'n no less have been thy foes;
He with great conquest, thou with greater blessed;
Thou sure to win, and he secure to lose.°   *secure against loss*

Thus hand in hand with him thy glories walk,
But who can trace them where alone they go?
75 Of thee two hemispheres on honor talk,
And hands and seas thy trophies jointly show.
The very winds did on thy party° blow,   *ally*
And rocks in arms thy foemen eft defy;[1]
But soft my muse, thy pitch is earthly low,
80 Forbear this heaven, where only eagles fly.

Kings on a queen enforced their states to lay,
Mainlands for empire waiting on an isle;
Men drawn by worth a woman to obey,
One moving all, herself unmoved the while.[2]
85 Truth's restitution, vanity's exile,
Wealth sprung of want, war held without annoy;
Let subject be of some inspired style,
Till then the object of her subject's joy.[3]

Thy utmost can but offer to her sight
90 Her handmaid's task, which most her will endears,
And pray unto thy pains life from that light
Which lively light some court and kingdom cheers.

---

1. I.e., winds blew to help your allies; rocks defied your enemies who were up in arms. Herbert then protests that the level of her poetic skill is low; it must not aspire to a height that only "eagles," or poets of great power, attain.
2. I.e., kings are forced to place their "states" (authority and power) on a queen; mainlands anticipating empire are forced to lay their "states" (conditions, resources) on an island, i.e., England.
3. Herbert defines the subjects of an inspired style of poetry: the restitution of truth, the exile of vanity, a "wealth" created by necessity (i.e., moral virtue), war without harm.

What[4] wish she° may (far past her living peers   *the Queen*
    And rival still to Judah's faithful king,
95 In more than he and more triumphant years),
    Sing what God doth, and do what men may sing.

To Thee Pure Sprite[1]

To thee pure sprite,° to thee alone's addressed   *spirit*
    this coupled work, by double interest thine:
    first raised by thy blessed hand, and what is mine
Inspired by thee, thy secret power impressed.°   *informed by*
5   so dared my Muse with thine itself combine,
        as mortal stuff with that which is divine.
    Thy lightening beams give lustre to the rest,

That heaven's king may deign his own transformed
    in substance no, but superficial tire°   *attire*
10 by thee° put on to praise,[2] not to aspire   *Sidney*
To those high tones so in themselves adorned,
    which angels sing in their celestial choir,
    and all of tongues with soul and voice admire.
    These sacred hymns thy kingly prophet formed.

15 Oh, had that soul which honor brought to rest
        too soon not left, and reft the world of all
        what man could show, which we perfection call,
This half-maimed piece had sorted with° the best.   *matched*
    deep wounds enlarged, long festered in their gall,
20   fresh bleeding smart; not eye- but heart-tears fall.
    Ah memory, what needs this new arrest?°   *delay*

Yet here behold, (oh, wert thou to behold!)
    this[3] finished now, thy matchless Muse begun,
    the rest but pieced, as left by thee undone.
25 Pardon (oh, blessed soul) presumption too too bold,
        if love and zeal such error ill-become,
        'tis zealous love, love which hath never done,
    Nor can enough in world of words unfold.

And since it hath no further scope to go,
30   nor other purpose but to honor thee,
        thee in thy works, where all the Graces[4] be
As little streams with all their all do flow
    to their great sea, due tribute's grateful fee;[5]

---

4. I.e., court and kingdom.
1. Herbert's elegy is for her brother, Sir Philip Sidney. In it she acknowledges his part in the translations.
2. I.e., your intelligence informs this verse not so that the king of heaven will consider his own light transformed substantially; rather it is that your own attire, clothing, is put over that light to praise him. Herbert returns to the idea, expressed earlier in her dedicatory poem to Elizabeth, that the psalms are a web or woven cloth.
3. I.e., the translation.
4. Personifications of the elements of courtesy and courteous expression; typically, they are attributes of poetic and artistic work.
5. I.e., the streams are a tribute to the sea.

so press my thoughts, my burdened thoughts, in me,
35   To pay the debt of infinites I owe

To thy great worth. Exceeding nature's store,
    wonder of men, sole° born perfection's kind,   *alone*
    phoenix[6] thou wert. So rare thy fairest mind,
Heav'nly adorned, Earth justly might adore,
40   where truthful praise in highest glory shined,
    for there alone was praise to truth confined;
And where but there, to live for ever more?

Oh! When to this account, this cast up sum,
    this reckoning made, this audit of my woe,
45   I call my thoughts, whence so strange passions flow,
How works my heart, my senses stricken dumb?
    that° would thee more than ever heart could show,   *my thoughts*
    and all too short,° who knew thee best doth know,   *inadequate*
There lives no wit that may thy praise become.°   *express*

50   Truth I invoke (who scorn elsewhere to move
    or here in aught my blood should partialize),[7]
    Truth, sacred Truth, thee sole to solemnize.
Those precious rights well known best mind's approve;
    and who but doth, hath wisdom's open eyes,
55   not owly° blind the fairest light still° flies,   *owl-like / always*
Confirm no less![8] At least 'tis sealed above.

Where thou art fixed among thy fellow lights,
    my day put out, my life in darkness cast,
    thy angel's soul, with highest angels placed,
60   There blessed sings enjoying heaven, delights°   *delights in*
    thy maker's praise, as far from earthly taste
    as here thy works so worthily embraced
By all of worth, where never envy bites.

As goodly buildings to some glorious end
65   cut off by fate, before the Graces had
    each wond'rous part in all their beauties clad,
Yet so much done, as art would not amend;
    so thy rare works to which no wit can add,
    in all men's eyes, which are not blindly mad,
70   Beyond compare, above all praise extend.

Immortal monuments of thy fair fame,
    though not complete, nor in the reach of thought,
    how on that passing peacetime would have wrought

---

6. A mythical bird, unique in the world, which is miraculously reborn from the ashes of its own funeral pyre.
7. I.e., I scorn that my blood (passion, temperament) should favor anything in a partial or prejudicial way.

8. I.e., who that has wisdom's open eyes and is not owlishly blind, fleeing strong light, does not confirm this?

Had Heav'n so spared the life of life to frame
75   the rest?[9] But ah, such loss! Hath this world aught
      can equal it? Or which like grievance brought?
Yet there will live thy ever-praised name.

To which these dearest offerings of my heart,
      dissolved to ink, while pen's impressions move
80   the bleeding veins of never dying love,
I render here; these wounding lines of smart,
      sad characters indeed of simple love,
      not art nor skill which abler wits do prove,
Of my full soul receive the meanest part.

85 Receive these hymns, these obsequies receive,
      if any mark of thy sweet sprite appear,
      well are they born,[1] no title else shall bear.
I can no more. Dear soul, I take my leave;
      sorrow still strives, would mount thy highest sphere
90   presuming so just cause might meet thee there.[2]
Oh happy change! Could so I take my leave.

Psalm 71: In Te Domini Speravi

On thee my trust is grounded.
    Lord, let me never be
        With shame confounded,
          But set me free
5 And in thy justice rescue me;
      Thy gracious ear to meward° bend   *toward me*
          And me defend.

Be thou my rock, my tower,
    My ever safe resort,
10   Whose saving power
        Hath not been short°   *deficient*
To work my safety, for my fort
    On thee alone is built; in thee
        My strongholds be.

15 Me, O my God, deliver
    From wicked, wayward hand.
      God, my help-giver,
        On whom I stand
And stood since I could understand,
20   Nay, since by life I first became
        What now I am.

9. I.e., had Heaven so spared your life so that you could
frame the life of the rest of mankind.
1. I.e. the hymns are of good parentage.

2. I.e., my sorrow would climb to your sphere in heaven,
presuming that so just a cause would allow my sorrow to
be there.

Since prisoned in my mother,
   By thee I prison brake,°   *broke from*
      I trust no other,
25   No other make
My stay, no other refuge take,
   Void of thy praise no time doth find
      My mouth and mind.

Men for a monster took me,
30   Yet hope of help from thee
      Never forsook me.
        Make then by me
All men, with praise extolled, may see
   Thy glory,[1] thy magnificence,
35   Thy excellence.

When feeble years do leave me
   No stay of other sort,
     Do not bereave me
      Of thy support,
40 And fail not then to be my fort,
   When weakness, in me killing might,°   *strength*
      Usurps his right.[2]

For now against me banded,
   My foes have talked of me;
45   Now unwithstanded,°   *not withstood*
      Who° their spies be   *whoever*
Of me have made a firm decree:
   (Lo!) God to him hath bid adieu,
      Now then pursue.[3]

50 Pursue, say they, and take him;
   No succor can he win,
     No refuge make him.
      O God, begin
To bring with speed thy forces in.
55   Help me, my God, my God, I say
      Go not away.

But let them be confounded
   And perish by whose hate

---

1. I.e., cause all men to see, by my aid, thy glory magnified with praise.
2. I.e., when weakness, having overcome strength, takes the place of strength in my soul.

3. I.e., my enemies' spies have decreed: God has said goodbye to him, so now hunt him down.

My soul is wounded;
60   And in one rate,°   *as a class*
Let them all share in shameful state
     Whose counsels, as their farthest end,°   *goal*
     My wrong intend.

For I will still persevere
65   My hopes on thee to raise,
     Augmenting ever
     Thy praise with praise.
My mouth shall utter forth always
     Thy truths, thy helps, whose sum surmounts
70   My best accounts.

Thy force keeps me from fearing,
     Nor ever dread I aught;
     Thy justice bearing
     In mindful thought
75 And glorious acts which thou hast taught
     Me from my youth;[4] and I have shown
     What I have known.

Now age doth overtake me
     And paint my head with snow;
80   Do not forsake me
     Until I show
The ages which succeeding grow,
     And every afterliving wight,°   *generation of men*
     Thy power and might.

85 How is thy justice raised
     Above the height of thought;
     How highly praised
     What thou hast wrought.
Sought let be all that can be sought,
90   None shall be found, nay none shall be,
     O God, like thee.

What if thou down didst drive me
     Into the gulf of woes;
     Thou wilt revive me
95   Again from those
And from the deep, which deepest goes;
     Exalting me again will make
     Me comfort take.

My greatness shall be greater
100   By thee; by comfort thine
     My good state better.

---

4. I.e., bearing thy justice and glorious acts in mindful thought.

O lute of mine,
To praise his truth thy tunes incline;
My harp extol the Holy One

105   In Judah known.

My voice to my harp join thee,[5]
My soul saved from decay,
My voice conjoin° thee,   *join with*
My tongue each day,

110   In all men's view his justice lay,°   *reveal*
Who° hath disgraced and shamed so,   *those who*
Who work my woe.

∞

COMPANION READING
Miles Coverdale: Psalm 71[1]

In thee, O Lord, is my trust, let me never be put to confusion, but rid me and deliver me through thy righteousness. Incline thine ear unto me and help me. Be thou my stronghold (whereunto I may always fly), thou that hast promised to help me; for thou art my house of defense and my castle. Deliver me (O my God) out of the hand of the ungodly, out of the hand of the unrighteous and cruel man. For thou (O Lord God) art the thing that I long for, thou art my hope even from my youth. I have leaned upon thee ever since I was born, thou art he that took me out of my mother's womb, therefore is my praise always of thee. I am become a wonder unto the multitude, but my sure trust is in thee. Oh, let my mouth be filled with thy praise and honor all the day long. Cast me not away in mine old age, forsake me not when my strength faileth me. For mine enemies speak against me, and they that lay wait for my soul take their counsel together, saying, God hath forsaken him; persecute him, take him, for there is none to help him. Go not far from me, O God; my God haste thee to help me. Let them be confounded and perish that are against my soul; let them be covered with shame and dishonor that seek to do me evil. As for me, I will patiently abide always and will ever increase thy praise. My mouth shall speak of thy righteousness and saving health all the day long, for I know no end thereof. Let me go in (O Lord God) and I will make mention of thy power and righteousness only. Thou (O God) hast learned me from my youth up until now, therefore will I tell of thy wondrous works. Forsake me not (O God) in mine old age, when I am grey-headed; until I have showed thine arm unto children's children, and thy power to all them that are yet for to come. Thy righteousness (O God) is very high, thou that doest great things, O God, who is like unto thee? O what great troubles and adversity hast thou showed me, and yet didst thou turn and refresh me; yea, and broughtest me from the deep of the earth again. Thou hast

---

5. I.e., let my voice, joined to my harp, join thee.
1. Miles Coverdale published his English translation of the Bible (using earlier translations into Latin and German as well as the English translation of William Tyndale) in 1535. Although the King James Bible or Authorized Version, commissioned by James I in 1604 and published in 1611, essentially reproduced Tyndale's translation of the New Testament and portions of the Hebrew Bible, the Prayer Book text of the psalms is considered to be Coverdale's work.

brought me to great honor and comforted me on every side. Therefore will I praise thee and thy faithfulness (O God), playing upon the lute, unto thee will I sing upon the harp, O thou holy one of Israel. My lips would fain sing praises unto thee and so would my soul, whom thou hast delivered.

My tongue talketh of thy righteousness all the day long, for they are confounded and brought unto shame that sought to do me evil.

∾∞∾

Psalm 121: Levavi Oculos

Unto the hills, I now will bend
    And list° with joy my hopeful sight;   *incline*
To him who me doth comfort send,
    My gracious God, the Lord of might.
        Even he (who ever blessed be he named)
        Who Heaven and Earth and all therein hath framed.

By him thy foot, from slip shall stay,°   *prevent*
    Nor will he sleep who thee sustains;
Israel's great God by night or day
    To sleep or slumber aye° disdains.   *always*
        For he is still thy guard forever waking,
        On thy right hand thy safety undertaking.

So undertakes that neither sun
    By day with heat shall thee molest,
Nor moon by night, when day is done,
    Offend thee, or disturb thy rest.
        Yea, from all evil thou still in his protection
        Shalt safely dwell from harm or ill infection.

This Lord (who never fails his flock)
    Shall thee in all thy ways attend
At home, abroad, thy fort, thy rock
    From all annoy shall thee defend.
        Yea, from this time from age to age for ever
        Will be thy God, and thee forsaking never.

5

10

15

20

c. 1590

The Doleful Lay° of Clorinda   *ballad*

Ay me, to whom shall I my case complain
That may compassion° my impatient grief?   *sympathize with*
Or where shall I unfold my inward pain,
That my enriven° ear may find relief?   *dismayed*
    Shall I unto the heavenly powers it show?
    Or unto earthly men that dwell below?

To heavens? Ah they, alas, the authors were
And workers of my unremedied woe;
For they foresee what to us happens here,

5

10   And they foresaw, yet suffered this be so.
       From them comes good, from them comes also ill;
       That which they made, who can them warn to spill.°   destroy

     To men? Ah they, alas, like wretched be
     And subject to the heavens' ordinance;
15   Bound to abide whatever they decree,
     Their best redress is their best sufferance.[1]
       How then can they, like wretched, comfort me,
       The which no less, need comforted to be?[2]

     Then to myself will I my sorrow mourn,
20   Since none alive like sorrowful remains;
     'And to myself my plaints shall back return,
     To pay their usury with doubled pains.
       The woods, the hills, the rivers shall resound
       The mournful accent of my sorrow's ground.°   cause

25   Wood, hills, and rivers now are desolate,
     Since he is gone the which them all did grace;
     And all the fields do wail their widow state,
     Since death their fairest flower did late deface.
       The fairest flower in field that ever grew,
30   Was Astrophel;[3] that was, we all may rue.

     What cruel hand of cursed fate unknown,
     Hath cropped the stalk which bore so fair a flower?
     Untimely cropped, before it were well grown,
     And clean defaced in untimely hour.
35   Great loss to all that ever him did see,
       Great loss to all, but greatest loss to me.

     Break now your garlands, O ye shepherds' lasses,
     Since the fair flower which them adorned is gone;
     The flower which them adorned is gone to ashes,
40   Never again let lass put garland on.
       Instead of garland, wear sad cypress now,
       And bitter elder, broken from the bow.

     Nor ever sing the love-lays which he made,
     Who ever made such lays of love as he?
45   Nor ever read the riddles which he said
     Unto yourselves to make you merry glee.
       Your merry glee is now laid all abed,
       Your merry maker now, alas, is dead.

---

1. I.e., the best recourse for men subject to heaven is to
tolerate its decrees.
2. I.e., how can they comfort me, wretched as I am, who
themselves need to be comforted?

3. Astrophel or Astrophil: the principal speaker and the
lover of "Stella," the figure representing the beloved
woman, in Sir Philip Sidney's sonnet sequence *Astrophil
and Stella*.

Death, the devourer of all world's delight,
50   Hath robbed you and reft from me my joy;
Both you and me and all the world he quite
Hath robbed of joyance and left sad annoy.
     Joy of the world, and shepherds' pride was he,
     Shepherds' hope, never like again to see.

55   Oh death, that hast us of such riches reft,
Tell us at least, what hast thou with it done?
What is become of him whose flower here left
Is but the shadow of his likeness gone,
     Scarce like the shadow of that which he was,
60   Naught° like, but that he like a shade did pass?   *nothing*

But that immortal spirit, which was decked
With all the dowries of celestial grace,
By sovereign choice from the heavenly choirs select,
And lineally derived from angel's race,
65   O what is now of it become, aread°—   *tell*
     Ay me, can so divine a thing be dead?

Ah no, it is not dead, nor can it die,
But lives for aye° in blissful paradise,   *ever*
Where like a newborn babe it soft doth lie,
70   In bed of lilies wrapped in tender wise.°   *manner*
     And compassed all about with roses sweet,
     And dainty violets from head to feet.

There thousand birds all of celestial brood,
To him do sweetly carol day and night,
75   And with strange notes, or him well understood,
Lull him asleep in angel-like delight,
     While in sweet dream to him presented be
     Immortal beauties which no eye may see.

But he them sees and takes exceeding pleasure
80   Of their divine aspects, appearing plain,
And kindling love in him above all measure,
Sweet love still joyous, never feeling pain.
     For what so goodly form he there doth see,
     He may enjoy from jealous rancor free.

85   There liveth he in everlasting bliss,
Sweet spirit never fearing more to die,
Nor dreading harm from any foes of his,
Nor fearing salvage° beasts more cruelty.   *savage*
     While we here, wretches, wail his private lack,
90   And with vain vows do often call him back.

But live thou there still happy, happy spirit,
And give us leave thee here thus to lament.
Not thee that dost thy heaven's joy inherit,

But our own selves that here in dole are drent.°   *drenched*
95   Thus do we weep and wail and wear our eyes,
Mourning others, our own miseries.

⊷ ⚎◆⚏ ⊶

Elizabeth I
1533–1603

No British monarch has left posterity a more dazzling record of accomplishments than Elizabeth Tudor, second daughter of Henry VIII. During the course of her reign, England became a nation to rival France and Spain; England's cities became centers of commerce, her navy controlled the principal routes of trade, and her people pursued lucrative interests in Europe and the New World. Having ruled England for almost half a century, Elizabeth has lived on as a figure of compelling power in the history of her people. What Shakespeare said of his character Cleopatra—"Age cannot wither her, nor custom stale her infinite variety"—conveys something of the fascination the memory of this extraordinary woman has had for the English people as well as for others around the globe. Age did, of course, eventually touch her being; doubtless, too, the brilliant strategies by which she governed subjects who were ever jealous of her royal prerogative must finally have become predictable. But Elizabeth was brought up in the atmosphere of a volatile politics, given to shifts in the winds of chance, susceptible to the heat of violent controversy and even to the flames of rebellion. She did what she had to do to remain on the throne; her father's example, if nothing else, taught her how fragile was the rule of a monarch who depended much more on the loyalty of subjects than on the authority of office or the power of the law.

Elizabeth's birth was itself a disappointment, at least to Henry VIII, who had hoped for a son. Her mother was the king's second wife, the charming Anne Boleyn, whom he married after divorcing Catherine of Aragon, the mother of his first daughter, Mary Tudor. The divorce precipitated the king's break with the Catholic Church, made Mary Tudor illegitimate, and effectively defined Anne's politics as unequivocally Protestant. But the new queen's influence was short-lived. Supporters of Catholicism, those who remained faithful to the memory of Catherine and respected the claims of Mary Tudor, may have been responsible for convincing the king that Anne had been unfaithful to him; in any case, he ordered her execution. Ten days later, he married Jane Seymour, declared Elizabeth illegitimate, and again waited for the birth of a son. Elizabeth's half-brother, the future Edward VI, was born in 1537, when Elizabeth was four years old. Fortunately, at the age of ten, Elizabeth at last acquired a loving stepmother: Henry's sixth wife, Catherine Parr, looked after her interests and education. An excellent student, fluent in Latin, French, and Italian and versed in history, Elizabeth was raised to be the subject of her brother, who became king after Henry's death in 1547. When he died in 1553, she became a pawn in a long and vicious struggle for the crown. Imprisoned in the Tower and then in Woodstock Castle in Oxfordshire by the Catholic supporters of her sister's claim to the throne, Elizabeth wrote lyrics that testify to both her fears and her faith during this dangerous time.

In 1558, Queen Mary died, and Elizabeth was crowned with much rejoicing; in the historian William Camden's words: "neither did the people ever embrace any other Prince with more willing and constant mind." Once on the throne, Elizabeth pursued a policy of exemplary discretion; she rewarded those who were loyal to her and punished those who showed signs of disobedience. In 1568, when her cousin Mary, Queen of Scots, abdicated the throne of Scotland in favor of her son, James VI, Elizabeth granted Mary refuge in England. Yet evidence later suggested that Mary, an ardent Catholic, had plotted to kill Elizabeth and restore

Robert Peake (attr.), *Queen Elizabeth Going in Procession to Blackfriars in 1600*. This splendid painting is linked to no particular event. Its arrangement of figures suggests a Roman imperial triumph, and evokes the success of the queen's monarchy. She appears to be in a litter, but is actually in a chair on wheels pushed by attendants, and protected by a canopy held by courtiers. She is preceded by a knight, perhaps Gilbert Talbot, Earl of Shrewsbury, who carries the sword of state. Though Elizabeth was sixty-eight when this painting was made in 1601, she is shown as a much younger woman. Her wish to be recognized as always desirable and ever the object of courtly devotion is well illustrated by her pale, unlined face, her highly dressed hair and her stylized body, clothed in a bejeweled dress whose puffed sleeves and intricate lace ruff suggest an ethereal and even divine creature. She is attended by six Knights of the Garter; the knight standing directly beside her (with a bald head and stiff grey beard) has been identified as her current favorite, Edward Somerset, Earl of Worcester; his two principal castles, Raglan and Chepstow, are probably those in the background of the painting.

Catholicism in England, and in 1587, Elizabeth ordered her execution with great regret. Reflecting on this action, also the subject of a speech to Parliament, the queen declared: "This death will wring my heart as long as I live."

A woman and reigning monarch, Elizabeth's position was anomalous. As a woman, she retained an important kind of social power only as long as she was an object of desire, to be courted and won; as a reigning monarch, she was expected not only to govern but also to secure the succession. In her speech to Parliament on the subject of marriage early in her reign, Elizabeth provided reasons why she would delay taking a husband. She probably never intended to take one. Continuing the fiction of courtship well past the age at which she could be expected to have a child, she saw to it that she remained at once attractive and unavailable. Most important, she succeeded in commanding the attention of her subjects by transforming her court into a center of literary and artistic activity. Late in life, she met her most serious suitor, the Duke of Alençon, brother to the French king, Henry III. A dwarf whose face was disfigured by smallpox, he was her "little frog," a man she is said to have loved dearly. The problem of succession required another kind of temporizing. She refused to name James VI of

Scotland as the next king of England until shortly before she died—a silence that she maintained was necessary to preserve the peace.

Throughout her long reign she cultivated two personas. As a monarch, she could speak courageously (as she did to her soldiers at Tilbury on the Devon coast while they waited for the Spanish to invade); as a woman, she could convey understanding (as she did to her critics in her so-called Golden Speech curtailing her prerogative to create monopolies). Her government remained a conscientious one to its very end. She cultivated a habit of mind that must have helped to ensure its stability: as her translation of Boethius's *Consolation of Philosophy* (made when she was sixty years old) reminds us, she never allowed herself to forget the vicissitudes of fortune and her own mortality.

Written with a Diamond on Her Window at Woodstock[1]

Much suspected by° me,   *to have been done by*
Nothing proved can be,
   Quoth Elizabeth prisoner.

Written on a Wall at Woodstock

Oh fortune, thy wresting wavering state
Hath fraught with cares my troubled wit,
Whose witness this present prison late
Could bear, where once was joy flown quite.[1]
5   Thou causedst the guilty to be loosed
From lands where innocents were inclosed,
And caused the guiltless to be reserved,°   *bound*
And freed those that death had well deserved.
But all herein° can be nothing caught,   *in prison*
10 So God send to my foes all they have thought.[2]

The Doubt of Future Foes

The doubt° of future foes exiles my present joy,   *fear*
And wit me warns to shun such snares as threaten mine annoy;[1]
For falsehood now doth flow, and subjects' faith doth ebb,
Which should not be if reason ruled or wisdom weaved the web.
5   But clouds of joys untried° do cloak aspiring minds,   *untested*
Which turn to rage of late repent by changed course of winds.[2]
The top of hope supposed the root of rue shall be,
And fruitless all their grafted guile, as shortly ye shall see.[3]
The dazzled eyes with pride, which great ambition blinds,

1. Elizabeth was imprisoned at Woodstock Castle, near Oxford, from 23 May 1554 to sometime late in April 1555. The queen, Mary I, Elizabeth's half-sister, suspected her of treason. This and the following poem are thought to have been written at this time.
1. I.e., this prison could bear witness recently to fortune's wavering state, once joy had flown from it.
2. I.e., nothing can be done by one who is in prison, so

may God send to my foes what they have suspected me of planning.
1. My harm.
2. I.e., because of a change of wind, my enemies' clouds of joy can turn to the rain of repentance.
3. I.e., at their most hopeful, my enemies supposed that the tree of my monarchy would be uprooted, but their grafted limbs of guile will bear no fruit.

10   Shall be unsealed by worthy wights[4] whose foresight falsehood finds.
The daughter of debate that discord aye° doth sow   *ever*
Shall reap no gain where former rule[5] still peace hath taught to know.
No foreign banished wight[6] shall anchor in this port;
Our realm brooks not seditious sects, let them elsewhere resort.
15   My rusty sword through rest shall first his edge employ
To poll their tops[7] that seek such change or gape[8] for future joy.

On Monsieur's Departure[1]

I grieve and dare not show my discontent,
I love and yet am forced to seem to hate,
I do, yet dare not say I ever meant,
I seem stark mute but inwardly do prate.
5   I am and not,° I freeze and yet am burned,   *am not*
    Since from myself another self I turned.

My care is like my shadow in the sun,
Follows me flying, flies when I pursue it,
Stands and lies by me, doth what I have done.
10   His too familiar care doth make me rue° it.   *regret*
    No means I find to rid him from my breast,
    Till by the end of things° it be supprest.   *death*

Some gentler passion slide into my mind,
For I am soft and made of melting snow;
15   Or be more cruel, love, and so be kind.
Let me or° float or sink, be high or low.   *either*
    Or let me live with some more sweet content,
    Or die and so forget what love ere meant.

SPEECHES   The speeches of Elizabeth I exemplify early modern public oratory at its most effective. But they are also marked by features uniquely derived from her sense of herself as a monarch who wished (and probably needed) to convince her subjects that their welfare was more important to her than her own. In the excerpts that follow, Elizabeth emphasizes that although nature made her a woman and therefore of the weaker sex, divine right has made her a "prince," a person endowed with a masculine persona whose function it is to command not obey. She further emphasizes that her principal care is for her subjects, who are her charges and in some sense her children. In her public dealings throughout her reign, she played the gender card for all it was worth; in so doing, she transformed the fact that she was a woman, potentially a liability, into an instrument of policy.

4. Men.
5. The rule of Elizabeth's father, Henry VIII, and brother, Edward VI, both Protestants.
6. Any supporter of Philip II, king of Spain and consort of Mary I.
7. Cut their heads off.

8. Smile.
1. The poem expresses Elizabeth's regret at the departure of the Duke d'Alençon, who had sought her hand in marriage. After four years of visits and inconclusive negotiations, the courtship ended in 1583.

On Marriage[1]

I may say unto you that from my years of understanding, sith[2] I first had consideration of myself to be born a servitor of Almighty God, I happily chose this kind of life in which I yet live, which I assure you for mine own part hath hitherto best contented myself and I trust hath been most acceptable to God. From the which, if either ambition of high estate offered to me in marriage by the pleasure and appointment of my prince[3]—whereof I have some records in this presence, as you our Lord Treasurer[4] well know; or if the eschewing of the danger of mine enemies or the avoiding of the period of death, whose messenger or rather continual watchman, the prince's indignation, was not little time daily before mine eyes—by whose means, although I know or justly may suspect, yet I will not now utter; or if the whole cause were in my sister herself, I will not now burthen her therewith, because I will not charge the dead: if any of these I say, I had not now remained in this estate wherein you see me. But so constant have I always continued in this determination— although my youth and words may seem to some hardly to agree together—yet is it most true that at this day I stand free from any other meaning that either I have had in times past or have at this present. With which trade of life I am so thoroughly acquainted that I trust God, who hath hitherto therein preserved and led me by the hand, will not now of His goodness suffer me to go alone. * * *

Nevertheless if any of you be in suspect—whensoever it may please God to incline my heart to another kind of life, ye may well assure yourselves my meaning is not to do or determine anything wherewith the realm may or shall have just cause to be discontented. And therefore put that clean out of your heads.[5] For I assure you—what credit my assurance may have with you I cannot tell, but what credit it shall deserve to have the sequence shall declare—I will never in that matter conclude anything that shall be prejudicial to the realm, for the weal, good, and safety whereof I will never shun to spend my life. And whomsoever my chance shall be to light upon, I trust he shall be as careful for the realm and you—I will not say as myself, because I cannot so certainly determine of any other; but at the least ways, by my good will and desire he shall be such as shall be as careful for the preservation of the realm and you as myself.

And albeit it might please Almightly God to continue me still in this mind to live out of the state of marriage, yet it is not to be feared but He will so work in my heart and in your wisdoms as good provision by His help may be made in convenient time, whereby the realm shall not remain destitute of an heir that may be a fit governor, and peradventure more beneficial to the realm than such offspring as may come of me. For, although I be never so careful of your well doings and mind ever so to be,

1. In 1559, a year after she had acceded to the throne at the age of twenty-five, Elizabeth addressed Parliament on the subject of marriage. Because the monarchy passed on by inheritance, it was expected that a monarch would marry and have children. In this speech, Elizabeth hints that she will never marry and also that she trusts God to provide for her successor who, she guesses, may be more "beneficial" to the kingdom than any child of her own would be. She probably intended to convey to her subjects that she would never abandon the kingdom either to the rule of a foreign prince (as Mary I had) or to a succession crisis.
2. Since.

3. The "prince" Elizabeth refers to is probably not Philip II, the consort of Mary I, but rather Mary herself, who in her official capacity as queen regnant might have offered her sister's hand in marriage to a suitable consort. Elizabeth can refer to Mary as her "sister" when she alludes to a "cause" that has no implications for the state but is rather personal, "in my sister herself."
4. The Marquis of Winchester.
5. Elizabeth emphasizes that her subjects and their representatives in Parliament have no authority to force her into marriage, however desirable they may think marriage is for the future of the kingdom.

yet may my issue grow out of kind and become perhaps ungracious. And in the end, this shall be for me sufficient, that a marble stone shall declare that a Queen, having reigned such a time, lived and died a virgin.

On Mary, Queen of Scots[1]

The bottomless graces and immeasurable benefits bestowed upon me by the Almighty are and have been such, as I must not only acknowledge them but admire them, accounting them as well miracles as benefits; not so much in respect of His Divine Majesty—with whom nothing is more common than to do things rare and singular—as in regard of our weakness, who cannot sufficiently set forth His wonderful works and graces, which to me have been so many, so diversely folded and embroidered one upon another, as in no sort am I able to express them.

And although there liveth not any that may more justly acknowledge themselves infinitely bound unto God than I, whose life He hath miraculously preserved at sundry times (beyond my merit) from a multitude of perils and dangers, yet is not that the cause for which I count myself the deepliest bound to give Him my humblest thanks, or to yield Him greatest recognition; but this which I shall tell you hereafter, which will deserve the name of wonder, if rare things and seldom seen be worthy of account. Even this it is: that as I came to the crown with the willing hearts of subjects, so do I now, after twenty-eight years' reign, perceive in you no diminution of good wills, which, if haply I should want, well might I breathe but never think I lived.

And now, albeit I find my life hath been full dangerously sought, and death contrived by such as no desert procured it, yet am I thereof so clear from malice—which hath the property to make men glad at the falls and faults of their foes, and make them seem to do for other causes, when rancor is the ground—as I protest it is and hath been my grievous thought that one, not different in sex, of like estate, and my near kin, should be fallen into so great a crime. Yea, I had so little purpose to pursue her with any color of malice, that as it is not unknown to some of my Lords here—for now I will play the blab—I secretly wrote her a letter upon the discovery of sundry treasons, that if she would confess them, and privately acknowledge them by her letters unto myself, she never should need be called for them into so public question. Neither did I it of mind to circumvent her, for then I knew as much as she could confess; and so did I write.

And if, even yet, now the matter is made but too apparent, I thought she truly would repent—as perhaps she would easily appear in outward show to do—and that for her none other would take the matter upon them; or that we were but as two milkmaids, with pails upon our arms; or that there were no more dependency upon us, but mine own life were only in danger, and not the whole estate of your religion and well doings; I protest—wherein you may believe me, for although I may have many vices, I hope I have not accustomed my tongue to be an instrument of untruth—I would most willingly pardon and remit this offence. Or if by my death other

---

1. The text is Elizabeth's answer to a petition from Parliament to execute Mary, Queen of Scots, who was reported to have conspired to depose her cousin Elizabeth and who had been a prisoner of the English queen for ten years. In August 1586, evidence of a new plot came to light, and the conspirators, led by Sir Thomas Babington, were executed. On the evidence in letters to Babington, Mary was then formally tried and convicted of treason by a special court of peers, counsellors, and judges. Elizabeth answered Parliament in October by asking for delay and divine enlightenment.

nations and kingdoms might truly say that this realm had attained an ever prosperous and flourishing estate, I would (I assure you) not desire to live, but gladly give my life, to the end my death might procure you a better prince. And for your sakes it is that I desire to live: to keep you from a worse. For, as for me, I assure you I find no great cause I should be fond to live. I take no such pleasure in it that I should much wish it, nor conceive such terror in death that I should greatly fear it. And yet I say not but, if the stroke were coming, perchance flesh and blood would be moved with it, and seek to shun it.

I have had good experience and trial of this world. I know what it is to be a subject, what to be a sovereign, what to have good neighbors, and sometime meet evil-willers. I have found treason in trust, seen great benefits little regarded, and instead of gratefulness, courses[2] of purpose to cross. These former remembrances, present feeling, and future expectation of evils, (I say), have made me think an evil is much the better the less while it dureth,[3] and so them happiest that are soonest hence;[4] and taught me to bear with a better mind these treasons, than is common to my sex—yea, with a better heart perhaps than is in some men. Which I hope you will not merely impute to my simplicity or want of understanding, but rather that I thus conceived—that had their purposes taken effect, I should not have found the blow, before I had felt it; nor, though my peril should have been great, my pain should have been but small and short. Wherein, as I would be loath to die so bloody a death, so doubt I not but God would have given me grace to be prepared for such an event; which, when it shall chance, I refer to His good pleasure.

And now, as touching their treasons and conspiracies, together with the contriver of them. I will not so prejudicate myself and this my realm as to say or think that I might not, without the last statute, by the ancient laws of this land have proceeded against her; which[5] was not made particularly to prejudice her, though perhaps it might then be suspected in respect of the disposition of such as depend that way. It was so far from being intended to entrap her, that it was rather an admonition to warn the danger thereof. But sith it is made, and in the force of a law, I thought good, in that which might concern her, to proceed according thereunto rather than by course of common law. Wherein, if you the judges have not deceived me, or that the books you brought me were not false—which God forbid—I might as justly have tried her by the ancient laws of the land.

But you lawyers are so nice and so precise in sifting and scanning every word and letter, that many times you stand more upon form than matter, upon syllables than the sense of the law. For, in this strictness and exact following of common form, she must have been indicted in Staffordshire, been arraigned at the bar, holden up her hand, and then been tried by a jury: a proper course, forsooth, to deal in that manner with one of her estate! I thought it better, therefore, for avoiding of these and more absurdities, to commit the cause to the inquisition of a good number of the greatest and most noble personages of this realm, of the judges and others of good account, whose sentence I must approve.[6]

---

2. Plans.
3. Lasts.
4. I.e., out of this world.
5. I.e., the Parliamentary statute of 1584–1585, known as the Act for the Queen's Surety, which provided for the trial of Mary, Queen of Scots, should she be accused of treason.

6. Elizabeth claims that Mary could have been tried as a criminal in a common law court but that this would have been an improper way to proceed as Mary remained a Queen of Scotland and her liability under English law was open to question.

And all little enough: for we Princes, I tell you, are set on stages, in the sight and view of all the world duly observed. The eyes of many behold our actions; a spot is soon spied in our garments, a blemish quickly noted in our doings. It behoveth us, therefore, to be careful that our proceedings be just and honorable.

But I must tell you one thing more: that in this late Act of Parliament you have laid an hard hand on me—that I must give direction for her death, which cannot be but most grievous, and an irksome burden to me. And lest you might mistake mine absence from this Parliament—which I had almost forgotten: although there be no cause why I should willingly come amongst multitudes (for that amongst many, some may be evil), yet hath it not been the doubt of any such danger or occasion that kept me from thence, but only the great grief to hear this cause spoken of, especially that such one of state and kin should need so open a declaration, and that this nation should be so spotted with blots of disloyalty. Wherein, the less is my grief for that I hope the better part is mine; and those of the worse not much to be accounted of, for that in seeking my destruction they might have spoiled their own souls.

And even now could I tell you that which would make you sorry. It is a secret; and yet I will tell it you (although it be known I have the property to keep counsel but too well, often times to mine own peril). It is not long since mine eyes did see it written that an oath was taken within few days either to kill me or to be hanged themselves; and that to be performed ere one month were ended. Hereby I see your danger in me, and neither can or will be so unthankful or careless of your consciences as to take no care for your safety.

I am not unmindful of your oath made in the Association,[7] manifesting your great good wills and affections, taken and entered into upon good conscience and true knowledge of the guilt, for safeguard of my person; done (I protest to God) before I ever heard it, or ever thought of such a matter, till a thousand hands, with many obligations, were showed me at Hampton Court, signed and subscribed with the names and seals of the greatest of this land. Which, as I do acknowledge as a perfect argument of your true hearts and great zeal to my safety, so shall my bond be stronger tied to greater care for all your good.

But, for that this matter is rare, weighty and of great consequence, and I think you do not look for any present resolution—the rather for that, as it is not my manner in matters of far less moment to give speedy answer without due consideration, so in this of such importance—I think it very requisite with earnest prayer to beseech His Divine Majesty so to illuminate mine understanding and inspire me with His grace, as I may do and determine that which shall serve to the establishment of His Church, preservation of your estates, and prosperity of this Commonwealth under my charge. Wherein, for that I know delay is dangerous, you shall have with all conveniency our resolution delivered by our message. And what ever any prince may merit of their subjects, for their approved testimony of their unfeigned sincerity, either by governing justly, void of all partiality, or sufferance of any injuries done (even to the poorest), that do I assuredly promise inviolably to perform, for requital of your so many deserts.

---

7. The Oath (or Bond) of Association was taken by the Queen's Council in October 1582. It provided for Mary's arrest and execution without a trial; in essence, it sanctioned a lynching.

On Mary's Execution[1]

Full grievous is the way whose going on and end breeds cumber[2] for the hire of a laborious journey. I have strived more this day than ever in my life whether I should speak or use silence. If I speak and not complain, I shall dissemble; if I hold my peace, your labor taken were full vain.

For me to make my moan were strange and rare, for I suppose you shall find few that, for their own particular, will cumber you with such a care. Yet such, I protest, hath been my greedy desire and hungry will that of your consultation might have fallen out some other means to work my safety, joined with your assurance, than that for which you are become so earnest suitors, as I protest I must needs use complaint[3]—though not of you, but unto you, and of the cause; for that I do perceive, by your advices, prayers, and desires, there falleth out this accident, that only my injurer's bane must be my life's surety.

But if any there live so wicked of nature to suppose that I prolonged this time only pro forma, to the intent to make a show of clemency, thereby to set my praises to the wire-drawers[4] to lengthen them the more, they do me so great a wrong as they can hardly recompense. Or if any person there be that think or imagine that the least vainglorious thought hath drawn me further herein, they do me as open injury as ever was done to any living creature—as He that is the maker of all thoughts knoweth best to be true. Or if there be any that think that the Lords, appointed in commission, durst do no other, as fearing thereby to displease or to be suspected to be of a contrary opinion to my safety, they do but heap upon me injurious conceits. For, either those put in trust by me to supply my place have not performed their duty towards me, or else they have signified unto you all that my desire was that every one should do according to his conscience, and in the course of these proceedings should enjoy both freedom of voice and liberty of opinion, and what they would not openly, they might privately to myself declare. It was of a willing mind and great desire I had, that some other means might be found out, wherein I should have taken more comfort than in any other thing under the sun.

And since now it is resolved that my surety cannot be established without a princess's head, I have just cause to complain that I, who have in my time pardoned so many rebels, winked at so many treasons, and either not produced[5] them or altogether slipped them over with silence, should now be forced to this proceeding, against such a person. I have besides, during my reign, seen and heard many opprobrious books and pamphlets against me, my realm and state, accusing me to be a tyrant. I thank them for their alms. I believe therein their meaning was to tell me news: and news it is to me indeed. I would it were as strange to hear of their impiety. What will they not now say, when it shall be spread that for the safety of her life a maiden queen could be content to spill the blood even of her own kinswoman? I may therefore full well complain that any man should think me given to cruelty; whereof I am so guiltless and innocent as I should slander God if I should say He gave me so vile a mind. Yea, I protest, I am so far from it that for mine own life I would not touch

1. Parliament had determined that Elizabeth's safety and the future of Protestantism in England could be secured only by Mary's execution; it sent a delegation to Elizabeth asking for her approval. Again Elizabeth demurred. It was only in February 1587, after a new conspiracy was discovered, that Elizabeth signed Mary's death warrant.
2. Distress.
3. Express regret.
4. One who draws metal into wire.
5. Acted upon.

her. Neither hath my care been so much bent how to prolong mine, as how to preserve both: which I am right sorry is made so hard, yea so impossible.

I am not so void of judgment as not to see mine own peril; nor yet so ignorant as not to know it were in nature a foolish course to cherish a sword to cut mine own throat; nor so careless as not to weigh that my life daily is in hazard. But this I do consider, that many a man would put his life in danger for the safeguard of a king. I do not say that so will I; but I pray you think that I have thought upon it.

But sith so many hath both written and spoken against me, I pray you give me leave to say somewhat for myself, and, before you return to your countries, let you know for what a one you have passed so careful thoughts. And, as I think myself infinitely beholding unto you all that seek to preserve my life by all the means you may, so I protest that there liveth no prince—nor ever shall be—more mindful to requite so good deserts. Wherein, as I perceive you have kept your old wont[6] in a general seeking the lengthening of my days, so am I sure that never shall I requite it, unless I had as many lives as you all; but for ever I will acknowledge it while there is any breath left me. Although I may not justify, but may justly condemn, my sundry faults and sins to God, yet for my care in this government let me acquaint you with my intents.

When first I took the sceptre, my title made me not forget the giver, and therefore [I] began as it became me, with such religion as both I was born in, bred in, and, I trust, shall die in; although I was not so simple as not to know what danger and peril so great an alteration might procure me—how many great princes of the contrary opinion would attempt all they might against me, and generally what enmity I should thereby breed unto myself. Which all I regarded not, knowing that He, for whose sake I did it, might and would defend me. Rather marvel that I am, than muse that I should not be if it were not God's holy hand that continueth me beyond all other expectation.

I was not simply trained up, nor in my youth spent my time altogether idly; and yet, when I came to the crown, then entered I first into the school of experience, bethinking myself of those things that best fitted a king—justice, temper, magnanimity, judgment. As for the two latter, I will not boast. But for the two first, this may I truly say: among my subjects I never knew a difference of person, where right was one;[7] nor never to my knowledge preferred for favor what I thought not fit for worth; nor bent mine ears to credit a tale that first was told me; nor was so rash to corrupt my judgment with my censure, ere I heard the cause. I will not say but many reports might fortune[8] be brought me by such as must hear the matter, whose partiality might mar the right; for we princes cannot hear all causes ourselves. But this dare I boldly affirm: my verdict went with the truth of my knowledge.

But full well wished Alcibiades[9] his friend, that he should not give any answer till he had recited the letters of the alphabet. So have I not used over-sudden resolutions in matters that have touched me full near: you will say that with me, I think. And therefore, as touching your counsels and consultations, I conceive them to be wise, honest, and conscionable; so provident and careful for the safety of my life (which I wish no longer than may be for your good), that though I never can yield

---

6. Desire.

7. I.e., my justice was impartial; it did not regard rank, occupation, or property as factors in determining what was right.

8. By chance.

9. An Athenian statesman who took part in the Peloponnesian War; changed sides to support Athen's enemy, Sparta; and was finally assassinated by Persians with whom he sought an alliance. The source of Elizabeth's reference is unknown.

you of recompense your due, yet shall I endeavor myself to give you cause to think your good will not ill bestowed, and strive to make myself worthy for such subjects. And as for your petition: your judgment I condemn not, neither do I mistake your reasons, but pray you to accept my thankfulness, excuse my doubtfulness, and take in good part my answer-answerless. Wherein I attribute not so much to my own judgment, but that I think many particular persons may go before me, though by my degree I go before them. Therefore, if I should say, I would not do what you request, it might peradventure be more than I thought; and to say I would do it, might perhaps breed peril of that you labor to preserve, being more than in your own wisdoms and discretions would seem convenient,[1] circumstances of place and time being duly considered.

To the English Troops at Tilbury, Facing the Spanish Armada[1]

My loving people, we have been persuaded by some that are careful of our safety, to take heed how we commit ourselves to armed multitudes, for fear of treachery. But I assure you, I do not desire to live to distrust my faithful and loving people. Let tyrants fear. I have always so behaved myself that, under God, I have placed my chiefest strength and safeguard in the loyal hearts and good will of my subjects; and therefore I am come amongst you, as you see, at this time, not for my recreation and disport,[2] but being at this time resolved, in the midst and heat of the battle, to live or die amongst you all, to lay down for my God, and for my kingdom, and for my people, my honor and my blood, even in the dust. I know I have the body of a weak and feeble woman, but I have the heart and stomach of a king, and of a king of England too, and think foul scorn[3] that Parma or Spain, or any prince of Europe should dare to invade the border of my realm; to which rather than any dishonor shall grow[4] by me, I myself will take up arms, I myself will be your general, judge, and rewarder of every one of your virtues in the field. I know, already for your forwardness[5] you have deserved rewards and crowns;[6] and we do assure you, in the word of a prince, they shall be duly paid you.

The Golden Speech[1]

Mr. Speaker, we have heard your declaration and perceive your care of our estate, by falling into a consideration of a grateful acknowledgment of such benefits as you have received; and that your coming is to present thanks to us, which I accept with no less joy than your loves can have desire to offer such a present.

I do assure you there is no prince that loves his subjects better, or whose love can countervail our love. There is no jewel, be it of never so rich a price, which I set before this jewel: I mean your love. For I do esteem it more than any treasure or riches;

---

1. Elizabeth equivocates nicely. She refuses to disagree with Parliament, lest she not respect her own misgivings; she refuses to agree with Parliament, lest its policy not be in her own interest.

1. In 1588, with the Spanish fleet threatening the south coast of England, Elizabeth went to Tilbury, in Dorset, to speak to the troops who were guarding England against an invasion.
2. Amusement.
3. Shameful.
4. Be caused.

5. Courage.
6. Recompense.

1. The queen had the prerogative or absolute power to grant favored subjects a patent for an exclusive manufacture. But the monopolies so created were disliked by those who would otherwise have competed for business, and a move to limit them was begun in Parliament. In response, in 1601, Elizabeth met with a committee of the House of Commons, led by the Speaker, thanked them for the subsidies recently granted the crown by the Commons, and promised to reform her practice.

for that we know how to prize, but love and thanks I count unvaluable. And, though God hath raised me high, yet this I count the glory of my crown, that I have reigned with your loves. This makes me that I do not so much rejoice that God hath made me to be a queen, as to be a queen over so thankful a people. Therefore, I have cause to wish nothing more than to content the subject; and that is a duty which I owe. Neither do I desire to live longer days than I may see your prosperity; and that is my only desire. And as I am that person that still yet under God hath delivered you, so I trust, by the almighty power of God, that I shall be His instrument to preserve you from every peril, dishonor, shame, tyranny and oppression; partly by means of your intended helps which we take very acceptably, because it manifesteth the largeness of your good loves and loyalties unto your sovereign.

Of myself I must say this: I never was any greedy, scraping grasper, nor a strait, fast-holding prince, nor yet a waster. My heart was never set on any worldly goods, but only for my subjects' good. What you bestow on me, I will not hoard it up, but receive it to bestow on you again. Yea, mine own properties I account yours, to be expended for your good; and your eyes shall see the bestowing of all for your good. Therefore, render unto them, I beseech you, Mr. Speaker, such thanks as you imagine my heart yieldeth, but my tongue cannot express.

Since I was queen, yet did I never put my pen to any grant but that, upon pretext and semblance made unto me, it was both good and beneficial to the subject in general, though a private profit to some of my ancient servants who had deserved well at my hands. But the contrary being found by experience, I am exceedingly beholding to such subjects as would move the same at the first. And I am not so simple to suppose, but that there be some of the Lower House whom these grievances never touched: and for them, I think they spake out of zeal to their countries,[2] and not out of spleen or malevolent affection as being parties grieved; and I take it exceeding gratefully from them, because it gives us to know that no respects or interest had moved them, other than the minds they have to suffer no diminution of our honor and our subjects' love unto us. The zeal of which affection, tending to ease my people and knit their hearts unto me, I embrace with a princely care, for above all earthly treasure I esteem my people's love, more than which I desire not to merit.

That my grants should be grievous to my people and oppressions privileged under color of our patents, our kingly dignity shall not suffer[3] it. Yea, when I heard it, I could give no rest unto my thoughts until I had reformed it. Shall they, think you, escape unpunished that have thus oppressed you, and have been respectless of their duty, and regardless of our honor?[4] No, I assure you, Mr. Speaker, were it not more for conscience' sake than for any glory or increase of love that I desire, these errors, troubles, vexations and oppressions, done by these varlets and lewd persons, not worthy the name of subjects, should not escape without condign punishment. But I perceive they dealt with me like physicians who, ministering a drug, make it more acceptable by giving it a good aromatical savor, or when they give pills do gild them all over.[5]

I have ever used to set the Last-Judgment Day before mine eyes, and so to rule as I shall be judged to answer before a higher Judge, to whose judgment seat I do appeal, that never thought was cherished in my heart that tended not unto my people's good. And now, if my kingly bounties have been abused, and my grants turned to the hurt

---

2. I.e, those members who protested monopolies in behalf of their constituents, or "countries," and not on their own account.
3. Allow.
4. I.e., those who benefited from a monopoly without

regard to the welfare of the general public.
5. Elizabeth compares unscrupulous patentees to physicians who coat bitter pills with sugar; in this case she is the patient who did not realize what was being given to her.

of my people, contrary to my will and meaning, and if any in authority under me have neglected or perverted what I have committed to them, I hope God will not lay their culps[6] and offences to my charge; who, though there were danger in repealing our grants, yet what danger would I not rather incur for your good, than I would suffer them still to continue?

I know the title of a king is a glorious title; but assure yourself that the shining glory of princely authority hath not so dazzled the eyes of our understanding, but that we well know and remember that we also are to yield an account of our actions before the great Judge. To be a king and wear a crown is a thing more glorious to them that see it, than it is pleasant to them that bear it. For myself, I was never so much enticed with the glorious name of a king or royal authority of a queen, as delighted that God hath made me His instrument to maintain His truth and glory, and to defend this kingdom (as I said) from peril, dishonor, tyranny and oppression.

There will never queen sit in my seat with more zeal to my country, care for my subjects, and that will sooner with willingness venture her life for your good and safety, than myself. For it is my desire to live nor reign no longer than my life and reign shall be for your good. And though you have had and may have many princes more mighty and wise sitting in this seat, yet you never had nor shall have any that will be more careful and loving.

Shall I ascribe anything to myself and my sexly weakness? I were not worthy to live then; and, of all, most unworthy of the mercies I have had from God, who hath given me a heart that yet never feared any foreign or home enemy. And I speak it to give God the praise, as a testimony before you, and not to attribute anything to myself. For I, oh Lord! what am I, whom practices and perils past should not fear? Or what can I do? That I should speak for any glory, God forbid.

This, Mr. Speaker, I pray you deliver unto the House, to whom heartily recommend me. And so I commit you all to your best fortunes and further counsels. And I pray you, Mr. Comptroller,[7] Mr. Secretary,[8] and you of my Council, that before these gentlemen go into their countries, you bring them all to kiss my hand.

~&~

RESPONSE

Sir Walter Raleigh, *from* The 21st and Last Book of the Ocean to Cynthia[1]

> Sufficeth to you, my joys interred,
> In simple words that I my woes complain;
> You that then died when first my fancy erred—[2]
> Joys under dust that never live again.

6. Sins.
7. Sir William Knollys.
8. Sir Robert Cecil.
1. This lyric complaint, a fragment of what was projected as a much longer work, is the most important of Raleigh's poems. It tells of his despair at losing the Queen's favor and reproaches her for indifference to his devoted service. Adopting the conventions of pastoral, Raleigh styles himself "The Shepherd of the Ocean," perhaps to draw attention to his first name, which he pronounced "Water." "Cynthia" is, of course, Elizabeth, figured here (as she was so often) as the moon, ever changeful, as well as Diana,

the goddess of the moon and of chastity. Characterizing Cynthia as the moving force in his life, Raleigh's verse illustrates how conventions of courtly love could acquire a political reference: both Elizabeth and her courtiers were accustomed to conveying their hopes and desires in the coded language of erotic compliment. Spenser's poem *Colin Clout's Come Home Again* (1591) notes that the subject of Raleigh's "Cynthia" is "the great unkindness" and "usage hard" of the "Lady of the Sea," who has "from her presence faultless him (i.e., the Shepherd) debarred."
2. The poet complains to his own "joys" that are now dead and buried.

If to the living were my muse addressed,
Or did my mind her own spirit still inhold,
Were not my living passion so repressed
As to the dead° the dead did these unfold,   *i.e., joys*

Some sweeter words, some more becoming verse
10   Should witness my mishap in higher kind;
But my love's wounds, my fancy in the hearse,
The idea but resting of a wasted mind,

The blossoms fallen, the sap gone from the tree,
The broken monuments of my great desires—
15   From these so lost what may the affections° be?   *passions*
What heat in cinders of extinguished fires?

Lost in the mud of those high-flowing streams,
Which through more fairer fields their courses bend,
Slain with self-thoughts, amazed in fearful dreams,
20   Woes without date, discomforts without end.

From fruitless trees I gather withered leaves,
And glean° the broken ears° with miser's hand,   *harvest / of grain*
Who sometime did enjoy the weighty sheaves;
I seek fair flowers amid the brinish° sand.   *salty*

25   All in the shade, even in the fair sun days,
Under those healthless trees I sit alone,
Where joyful birds sing neither lovely lays,
Nor Philomen° recounts her direful moan.   *the nightingale*

No feeding flocks, no shepherd's company,
30   That might renew my dolorous conceit,°   *imagination*
While happy then, while love and fantasy
Confined my thoughts on that fair flock to wait;

No pleasing streams fast to the ocean wending,
The messengers sometimes of my great woe;
35   But all on earth, as from the cold storms bending,
Shrink from my thoughts in high heavens or below.

Oh, hopeful love, my object and invention,
Oh, true desire, the spur of my conceit,
Oh, worthiest spirit, my mind's impulsion,°   *force*
40   Oh, eyes transpersant,° my affection's bait,   *that penetrate*

Oh princely form, my fancy's adamant,°   *magnet*
Divine conceit,° my pains' acceptance,   *image*
Oh, all in one! Oh, heaven on earth transparent!
The seat of joys and love's abundance!

45   Out of that mass of miracles, my muse
Gathered those flowers, to her pure senses pleasing;

Out of her eyes, the store of joys, did choose
Equal delights, my sorrow's counterpoising.

Her regal looks my vigorous sighs suppressed,
50 Small drops of joys sweetened great worlds of woes,
One gladsome day a thousand cares redressed—
Whom love defends, what fortune overthrows?

When she did well, what did there else amiss?
When she did ill, what empires would have pleased?
55 No other power affecting woe or bliss,
She gave, she took, she wounded, she appeased.

The honor of her love, love still devising,
Wounding my mind with contrary conceit,
Transferred itself sometime to her aspiring,
60 Sometime the trumpet of her thought's retreat.[3]

To seek new worlds for gold, for praise, for glory,
To try° desire, to try love severed far,   *test*
When I was gone, she sent her memory,
More strong than were ten thousand ships of war,

65 To call me back; to leave great honor's thought;
To leave my friends, my fortune, my attempt;
To leave the purpose[4] I so long had sought,
And hold both cares and comforts in contempt.

Such heat in ice, such fire in frost remained,
70 Such trust in doubt, such comfort in despair,
Which, like the gentle lamb, though lately weaned,
Plays with the dug, though finds no comfort there.

But as a body, violently slain,
Retaineth warmth although the spirit be gone,
75 And by a power in nature moves again
Till it be laid below the fatal stone;

Or as the earth, even in cold winter days,
Left for a time by her life-giving sun,
Doth by the power remaining of his rays
80 Produce some green, though not as it hath done;

Or as a wheel, forced by the falling stream,
Although the course be turned some other way,
Doth for a time go round upon the beam,
Till, wanting strength to move, it stands at stay;

3. The honor of being loved by her creating love (in me), wounding me with a contrary (twofold) conception, sometimes aspiring to (please) her, sometimes heralding the withdrawal of her attention. In other words, the poet is constantly aware that his love makes him have a conflicted conception of how to approach Cynthia: sometimes he pleases her, sometimes what he does causes her disdain.
4. Raleigh's "purpose" was to find gold for England in the wilderness of the New World; he continued to hope for success in this venture until 1617, when his last voyage to Guiana ended in nothing.

85   So my forsaken heart, my withered mind—
      Widow of all the joys it once possessed,
      My hopes clean out of sight with forced wind—
      To kingdoms strange, to lands far off, addressed,

      Alone, forsaken, friendless, on the shore
90   With many wounds, with death's cold pangs embraced,
      Writes in the dust, as one that could no more,
      Whom love, and time, and fortune, had defaced,

      Of things so great, so long, so manifold,
      With means so weak, the soul even then depicting
95   The weal, the woe, the passages of old,
      And worlds of thoughts descried° by one last sighing.   *discerned*

      As if, when after Phoebus° is descended,   *the sun*
      And leaves a light much like the past day's dawning,
      And every toil and labor wholly ended,
100   Each living creature draweth to his resting,

      We should begin by such a parting light
      To write the story of all ages past,
      And end the same before approaching night.

      Such is again the labor of my mind,
105   Whose shroud, by sorrow woven now to end,
      Hath seen that ever shining sun declined,
      So many years that so could not descend,

      But that the eyes of my mind held her beams
      In every part transferred by love's swift thought,
110   Far off or near, in waking or in dreams,
      Imagination strong in lustre brought.

      Such force her angelic appearance had
      To master distance, time, or cruelty,
      Such art to grieve, and after to make glad,
115   Such fear in love, such love in majesty.

      My weary lines her memory embalmed;
      My darkest ways her eyes make clear as day.
      What storms so great but Cynthia's beams appeased?
      What rage so fierce, that love could not allay?

120   Twelve years entire I wasted in this war,[5]
      Twelve years of my most happy younger days;
      But I in them, and they now wasted are,
      "Of all which past, the sorrow only stays."

                          * * *

      Yet as the air in deep caves underground
125   Is strongly drawn when violent heat hath vent

5. The 12 years of service to Elizabeth began with his command of troops in Ireland in 1580 and ended, in the terms the
poem supplies, with his marriage and imprisonment in 1592. Raleigh was only 36 at the time.

Great clefts therein, till moisture do abound,
And then the same, imprisioned and up-pent,°   *pent up*

Breaks out in earthquakes, tearing all asunder,
So in the center of my cloven heart—
130   My heart, to whom her beauties were such wonder—
Lies the sharp, poisoned head of that love's dart

Which, till all break and dissolve to dust,
Thence drawn it cannot be, or therein known,
There, mixed with my heart-blood, the fretting rust
135   The better part hath eaten and outgrown.

But what of those or these? Or what of aught
Of that which was, or that which is, to treat?
What I possess is but the same I sought;
My love was false, my labors were deceit.

140   Nor less than such they are esteemed to be,
A fraud bought at the price of many woes,
A guile, whereof the profits unto me—
Could it be thought premediate° for those?   *plead*

Witness those withered leaves left on the tree,
145   The sorrow-worn face, the pensive mind,
The external shows, what may the internal be;
Cold care hath bitten both the root and rind.

But stay, my thoughts, make end, give fortune way;
Harsh is the voice of woe and sorrow's sound;
150   Complaints cure not, and tears do but allay
Griefs for a time, which after more abound.

To seek for moisture in the Arabian sand
Is but a loss of labor and of rest,
The links which time did break of hearty bands

155   Words cannot knit, or wailings make anew,
Seek not the sun in clouds when it is set . . .
On highest mountains, where those cedars[6] grew,
Against whose banks the troubled ocean beat,

And were the marks to find thy hoped port,
160   Into a soil far off themselves remove.
On Sestos' shore, Leander's late resort,
Hero hath left no lamp to guide her love.[7]

Thou lookest for light in vain, and storms arise,
She sleeps thy death, that erst thy danger sighed,

6. The cedar was identified as a tree of royalty; so Raleigh can speak of the ocean beating against banks over which the cedar presides.
7. Leander and Hero were two lovers who lived on opposite shores of the Hellespont. When Leander swam at night from Abydos to visit Hero in Sestos, she hung out a lantern to guide him.

165   Strive then no more, bow down thy weary eyes—
      Eyes which to all these woes thy heart have guided.

      She is gone, she is lost, she is found, she is ever fair;
      Sorrow draws weakly where love draws not too,
      Woe's cries sound nothing, but only in love's ear.
170   Do then by dying what life cannot do.

      Unfold thy flocks and leave them to the fields,
      To feed on hills or dales, where likes them best,
      Of what the summer or the springtime yields,
      For love and time hath given thee leave to rest.

175   Thy heart which was their fold, now in decay
      By often storms and winter's many blasts,
      All torn and rent, becomes misfortune's prey,
      False hope, my shepherd's staff, now age hath brast.°   *broken*

      My pipe, which love's own hand gave my desire
180   To sing her praises and my woe upon—
      Despair hath often threatened to the fire,
      As vain to keep now all the rest are gone.

      Thus home I draw, as death's long night draws on,
      Yet every foot, old thoughts turn back mine eyes;
185   Constraint me guides, as old age draws a stone
      Against a hill, which over-weighty lies

      For feeble arms or wasted strength to move.
      My steps are backward, gazing on my loss,
      My mind's affection and my soul's sole love,
190   Not mixed with fancy's chaff or fortune's dross.

      To God I leave it,° who first gave it me,   *my soul*
      And I her gave, and she returned again,
      As it was hers; so let His mercies be
      Of my last comforts the essential mean.°   *factor*

195   But be it so or not, the effects are past;
      Her love hath end, my woes must ever last.

Aemilia Lanyer
1569–1645

Aemilia Lanyer was born Aemilia Bassano, the daughter of Queen Elizabeth's court musician, Baptista Bassano. Acquaintance with the nobility surrounding the Queen allowed her an education that was typically reserved for women of high station. At eighteen, shortly after her mother's death, she became the mistress of Henry Cary Hunsdon, the Lord Chancellor. Her position increased her presence at court until, at twenty-three, she became pregnant and was forced to marry a court musician. Their son, conspicuously named Henry, was born three months after the wedding. The first years of her married life were not auspicious. Alfonso Lanyer was a spendthrift, and the money Aemilia had acquired as Hunsdon's mistress was soon exhausted. Desperate for reassurance, she visited the astrologer Simon Forman to learn whether the stars indicated that Alfonso would gain a knighthood. The disreputable Forman appears to have had other ideas. His casebook records that on one occasion, he "went and supped with her and stayed all night, and she was familiar and friendly to him in all things. But only she would not halek [have intercourse] . . . he never obtained his purpose and she was a whore and dealt evil with him."

Lanyer's character is more accurately represented in the record of her long friendship with Margaret Clifford, Countess of Cumberland, and her daughter Anne. In 1610, partly in tribute to the loyal support of her patroness, Lanyer published a volume of poetry entitled *Salve Deus Rex Judaeorum*; this included a verse defense of women and a poem to Cookham, a country house leased by Margaret Clifford's brother, William Russell, and visited frequently by Lanyer until 1605. She particularly records two critical transformations in her sense of herself: a spiritual awakening, inspired by the piety of the Countess, and a confirmation of herself as a poet. Her impressions of Cookham express a unity among aesthetic elements that are usually opposed and antithetical: pagan culture and Christian vision, temporal experience and spiritual knowledge, and the erotic pleasure in the discipline of chastity.

The Description of Cookham

	Farewell (sweet Cookham) where I first obtained	
	Grace from that Grace where perfit° grace remained;	*perfect*
	And where the Muses[1] gave their full consent,	
	I should have power the virtuous to content;	
5	Where princely Palace willed me to indite,°	*write*
	The sacred story[2] of the soul's delight.	
	Farewell (sweet place) where virtue then did rest,	
	And all delights did harbor in her breast;	
	Never shall my sad eyes again behold	
10	Those pleasures which my thoughts did then unfold:	
	Yet you (great Lady),[3] Mistress of that place,	
	From whose desires did spring this work of grace;	
	Vouchsafe° to think upon those pleasures past,	*agree*
	As fleeting worldly joys that could not last,	
15	Or, as dim shadows of celestial pleasures,	
	Which are desired above all earthly treasures.	
	Oh how (me thought) against you thither came,[4]	
	Each part did seem some new delight to frame!	
	The house received all ornaments to grace it,	
20	And would endure no foulness to deface it.	
	The walks put on their summer liveries,°	*uniforms*
	And all things else did hold like similies:°	*comparisons*
	The trees with leaves, with fruits, with flowers clad,	
	Embraced each other, seeming to be glad,	
25	Turning themselves to beauteous canopies,	
	To shade the bright sun from your brighter eyes.	
	The crystal streams with silver spangles graced,	

1. Divinities who presided over the arts and courtesy.
2. Possibly the story of the Passion, recounted in the poem *Salve Deus Rex Judaeorum*.

3. Margaret Clifford, the Countess of Cumberland.
4. In preparation for your arrival.

While by the glorious sun they were embraced,
The little birds in chirping notes did sing,
30   To entertain both you and that sweet spring.
And Philomela[5] with her sundry lays,°   songs
Both you and that delightful place did praise.
Oh, how me thought each plant, each flower, each tree
Set forth their beauties then to welcome thee:
35   The very hills right humbly did descend,
When you to tread upon them did intend.
And as you set your feet, they still did rise,
Glad that they could receive so rich a prize.
The gentle winds did take delight to be
40   Among those woods that were so graced by thee.
And in sad° murmur uttered pleasing sound,   deep
That pleasure in that place might more abound:
The swelling banks delivered all their pride,
When such a Phoenix[6] once they had espied.
45   Each arbor, bank, each seat, each stately tree,
Thought themselves honored in supporting thee.
The pretty birds would oft come to attend thee,
Yet fly away for fear they should offend thee:
The little creatures in the burrow by°   nearby
50   Would come abroad to sport them in your eye;
Yet fearful of the bow in your fair hand,
Would run away when you did make a stand.
Now let me come unto that stately tree,
Wherein such goodly prospects you did see;
55   That oak that did in height his fellows pass,
As much as lofty trees, low growing grass
Much like a comely cedar straight and tall,
Whose beauteous stature far exceeded all.
How often did you visit this fair tree,
60   Which seeming joyful in receiving thee,
Would like a palm tree spread his arms abroad,
Desirous that you there should make abode:
Whose fair green leaves much like a comely veil,
Defended Phoebus when he would assail:[7]
65   Whose pleasing boughs did yield a cool fresh air,
Joying his happiness when you were there.
Where being seated, you might plainly see,
Hills, vales, and woods, as if on bended knee
They had appeared, your honor to salute,
70   Or to prefer some strange unlooked for suit:
All interlaced with brooks and crystal springs,

5. In Greek mythology, a woman who was transformed into a swallow; in Latin versions of her story she becomes a nightingale.
6. A mythical bird, always unique on earth, that regenerates

itself in its own funeral pyre and therefore signifies eternity; here it figures the Countess.
7. The leaves of the palm tree protected the Countess from Phoebus, the god of the sun.

A prospect fit to please the eyes of kings:
And thirteen shires appeared all in your sight,
Europe could not afford much more delight.
75   What was there then but gave you all content,
While you the time in meditation spent,
Of their Creator's power, which there you saw,
In all his creatures held a perfit law;
And in their beauties did you plain descry,°   *discern*
80   His beauty, wisdom, grace, love, majesty.
In these sweet woods how often did you walk,
With Christ and his apostles there to talk;
Placing his holy writ in some fair tree,
To meditate what you therein did see:
85   With Moses you did mount his holy hill,[8]
To know his pleasure, and perform his will.
With lovely David[9] you did often sing
His holy hymns to heaven's eternal king.
And in sweet music did your soul delight,
90   To sound his praises, morning, noon, and night.
With blessed Joseph you did often feed
Your pined° brethren, when they stood in need.[1]   *poor*
And that sweet lady sprung from Clifford's race,[2]
Of noble Bedford's blood, fair stream of grace,
95   To honorable Dorset now espoused,
In whose fair breast true virtue then was housed.
Oh, what delight did my weak spirits find
In those pure parts of her well framed mind,
And yet it grieves me that I cannot be
100   Near unto her, whose virtues did agree
With those fair ornaments of outward beauty,
Which did enforce from all both love and duty.
Unconstant Fortune, thou art most to blame,
Who casts us down into so low a frame,
105   Where our great friends we cannot daily see,
So great a diffrence is there in degree.
Many are placed in those orbs of state,
Parters° in honor, so ordained by Fate;   *participants*
Nearer in show, yet farther off in love,
110   In which, the lowest always are above.[3]
But whither am I carried in conceit?°   *imagination*
My wit too weak to conster of° the great.   *understand*
Why not? although we are but born of earth,
We may behold the heavens, despising death;

8. Moses climbed Mount Sinai to receive the law of God (Exodus 24,25).
9. King David the psalmist.
1. Sold by his jealous brothers into slavery, Joseph became Pharoah's right-hand man and granted these same brothers food and money during a famine many years later (Genesis 42.1–28).

2. The Lady is the Countess's daughter Anne, descended from Margaret Russell of Bedford and her father George Clifford, Duke of Cumberland. Anne married the Earl of Dorset in 1609 and is thus referred to as Dorset.
3. I.e., persons of low station or rank love more than those who are of the gentry or nobility.

115   And loving heaven that is so far above,
    May in the end vouchsafe us entire love.
    Therefore sweet memory do thou retain
    Those pleasures past, which will not turn again;
    Remember beauteous Dorset's former sports,
120   So far from being touched by ill reports;
    Wherein myself did always bear a part,
    While reverend Love presented my true heart.
    Those recreations let me bear in mind,
    Which her sweet youth and noble thoughts did find,
125   Whereof deprived, I evermore must grieve,
    Hating blind Fortune, careless to relieve.
    And you sweet Cookham, whom these ladies leave,
    I now must tell the grief you did conceive
    At their departure; when they went away,
130   How everything retained a sad dismay;
    Nay long before, when once an inkling came,
    Methought each thing did unto sorrow frame:
    The trees that were so glorious in our view,
    Forsook both flowers and fruit, when once they knew
135   Of your depart,° their very leaves did wither,   *departure*
    Changing their colors as they grew together.
    But when they saw this had no power to stay you,
    They often wept, though speechless, could not pray° you;   *beg*
    Letting their tears in your fair bosoms fall,
140   As if they said, "Why will ye leave us all?"
    This being vain, they cast their leaves away,
    Hoping that pity would have made you stay,
    Their frozen tops like age's hoary hairs,
    Shows their disasters, languishing in fears;
145   A swarthy riveled rine° all overspread,   *bark*
    Their dying bodies half alive, half dead.
    But your occasions called you so away,
    That nothing there had power to make you stay:
    Yet did I see a noble grateful mind,
150   Requiting each according to their kind,
    Forgetting not to turn and take your leave
    Of these sad creatures, powerless to receive
    Your favor when with grief you did depart,
    Placing their former pleasures in your heart;
155   Giving great charge to noble memory,
    There to preserve their love continually:
    But specially the love of that fair tree,
    That first and last you did vouchsafe to see:
    In which it pleased you oft to take the air,
160   With noble Dorset, then a virgin fair:
    Where many a learned book was read and scanned
    To this fair tree, taking me by the hand,
    You did repeat the pleasures which had passed,
    Seeming to grieve they could no longer last.

165 And with a chaste, yet loving kiss took leave,
     Of which sweet kiss I did it soon bereave:[4]
     Scorning a senseless creature should possess
     So rare a favor, so great happiness.
     No other kiss it could receive from me,
170 For fear to give back what it took of thee:
     So I ungrateful creature did deceive it,
     Of that which you vouchsafed in love to leave it.
     And though it oft° had given me much content,   *often*
     Yet this great wrong I never could repent:
175 But of the happiest made it most forlorn,
     To show that nothing's free from Fortune's scorn,
     While all the rest with this most beauteous tree,
     Made their sad consort° sorrow's harmony.   *music*
     The flowers that on the banks and walks did grow,
180 Crept in the ground, the grass did weep for woe.
     The winds and waters seemed to chide together,
     Because you went away they know not whither:
     And those sweet brooks that ran so fair and clear,
     With grief and trouble wrinkled did appear.
185 Those pretty birds that wonted° were to sing,   *accustomed*
     Now neither sing, nor chirp, nor use their wing;
     But with their tender feet on some bare spray,
     Warble forth sorrow, and their own dismay.
     Fair Philomela leaves her mournful ditty,
190 Drowned in dead sleep, yet can procure no pity:
     Each arbor, bank, each seat, each stately tree,
     Looks bare and desolate now for want of thee;
     Turning green tresses into frosty gray,
     While in cold grief they wither all away.
195 The sun grew weak, his beams no comfort gave,
     While all green things did make the earth their grave;
     Each briar, each bramble, when you went away,
     Caught fast your clothes, thinking to make you stay;
     Delightful Echo[5] wonted° to reply   *used*
200 To our last words, did now for sorrow die:
     The house cast off each garment that might grace it,
     Putting on dust and cobwebs to deface it.
     All desolation then there did appear,
     When you were going whom they held so dear.
205 This last farewell to Cookham here I give,
     When I am dead thy name in this may live,
     Wherein I have performed her noble hest,°   *request*
     Whose virtues lodge in my unworthy breast,
     And ever shall, so long as life remains,
210 Tying my heart to her by those rich chains.

---

4. I.e., I took their kiss from the tree on which they had put it.

5. A nymph who can only repeat what she has heard; in the absence of voices, she dies.

from Salve Deus Rex Judaeorum
To the Doubtful Reader

Gentle reader, if thou desire to be resolved, why I give this title, *Salve Deus Rex Judaeorum*, know for certain; that it was delivered unto me in sleep many years before I had any intent to write in this manner, and was quite out of my memory, until I had written the Passion of Christ, when immediately it came into my remembrance, what I had dreamed long before; and thinking it a significant token, that I was appointed to perform this work, I gave the very same words I received in sleep as the fittest title I could devise for this book.

To the Virtuous Reader[1]

Often have I heard, that it is the property of some women, not only to emulate the virtues and perfections of the rest, but also by all their powers of ill speaking, to eclipse the brightness of their deserved fame. Now contrary to this custom, which men I hope unjustly lay to their charge, I have written this small volume, or little book, for the general use of all virtuous ladies and gentlewomen of this kingdom; and in commendation of some particular persons of our own sex, such as for the most part are so well known to myself, and others, that I dare undertake fame dares not to call any better. And this have I done, to make known to the world that all women deserve not to be blamed, though some—forgetting they are women themselves and in danger to be condemned by the words of their own mouths—fall into so great an error as to speak unadvisedly against the rest of their sex; which if it be true, I am persuaded they can show their own imperfection in nothing more: and therefore could wish (for their own ease, modesties, and credit) they would refer[2] such points of folly to be practiced by evil disposed men, who forgetting they were born of women, nourished of women, and that if it were not by the means of women, they would be quite extinguished out of the world and a final end of them all, do like vipers deface the wombs wherein they were bred, only to give way and utterance to their want of discretion and goodness. Such as these, were they that dishonored Christ his apostles and prophets, putting them to shameful deaths. Therefore we are not to regard any imputations, that they undeservedly lay upon us, no[3] otherwise than to make use of them to our own benefits as spurs to virtue, making us fly all occasions that may color their unjust speeches to pass current,[4] especially considering that they have tempted even the patience of God himself, who gave power to wise and virtuous women, to bring down their pride and arrogance: As was cruel *Caesar* by the discreet counsel of noble *Deborah*,[5] judge and prophetess of Israel; and resolution of *Jael*, wife of *Heber* the Kenite; wicked *Haman*, by the divine prayers and prudent proceedings of beautiful *Hester*; blasphemous *Holofernes*, by the invincible courage, rare wisdom, and

---

1. This preface is Lanyer's general introduction to her poem *Salve Deus Rex Judaeorum* (Hail, Lord God, King of the Jews). Three excerpts follow: the invocation, an argument against beauty without virtue, and Pilate's wife apologizes for Eve.
2. Assign.
3. Not.
4. To avoid occasions in which their unjust speeches might appear to have some truth.
5. Lanyer lists virtuous women who benefited their people:

Deborah, a wise judge and prophet of Israel, who urged the warrior Barak to attack their enemy, Sisera [Cesarus]; Jael, who killed Sisera with a blow to the head (both figures from Judges 4); Hester [Esther], the queen of the Israelites, who hanged Haman (Esther 5–7); the Jewish heroine Judith, who saved her town by killing King Nebuchadnezzar's general Holofernes (the Apocryphal Book of Judith 8–12); and Susanna, whose chastity was proved by the prophet Daniel (the Apocryphal History of Daniel and Susanna).

confident carriage of *Judith;* and the unjust judges, by the innocence of chaste *Susanna;* with infinite others, which for brevity's sake I will omit. As also in respect it pleased our Lord and Savior Jesus Christ, without the assistance of man, being free from original and all other sins from the time of his conception till the hour of his death, to be begotten of a woman, born of a woman, nourished of a woman, obedient to a woman; and that he healed woman,[6] pardoned women, comforted women; yea, even when he was in his greatest agony and bloody sweat, going to be crucified, and also in the last hour of his death, took care to dispose of a woman;[7] after his resurrection, appeared first to a woman, sent a woman to declare his most glorious resurrection to the rest of his disciples.[8] Many other examples I could allege of divers faithful and virtuous women, who have in all ages, not only been confessors, but also endured most cruel martyrdom for their faith in Jesus Christ. All which is sufficient to enforce all good Christians and honorable-minded men to speak reverently of our sex, and especially of all virtuous and good women. To the modest censures of both which, I refer these my imperfect endeavors, knowing that according to their own excellent dispositions, they will rather, cherish, nourish, and increase the least spark of virtue where they find it, by their favorable and best interpretations, than quench it by wrong constructions. To whom I wish all increase of virtue, and desire their best opinions.

[INVOCATION]

Sith *Cynthia*[9] is ascended to that rest
Of endless joy and true eternity,
That glorious place that cannot be expressed
By any wight° clad in mortality,   *person*
5   In her almighty love so highly blest,
And crowned with everlasting sovereignty;
    Where saints and angels do attend her throne,
    And she gives glory unto God alone.

To thee great Countess[1] now I will apply
10   My pen, to write thy never dying fame;
That when to heaven thy blessed soul shall fly,
These lines on earth record thy reverend name:
And to this task I mean my muse to tie,
Though wanting skill I shall but purchase blame:
15   Pardon (dear Lady) want of woman's wit
    To pen thy praise, when few can equal it.

[AGAINST BEAUTY WITHOUT VIRTUE]

185   That outward beauty which the world commends
    Is not the subject I will write upon,

---

6. Womankind.

7. Jesus, from the cross, ordered a disciple (traditionally understood to be John) to care for his mother (John 19.25–27).

8. After his resurrection, Jesus appeared first to Mary Magdalene and "the other Mary," who then told the

other disciples of this event (Matthew 28.8–10).

9. Goddess of the moon, also known as Diana; here she represents Queen Elizabeth I.

1. Lady Margaret Clifford, the Countess of Cumberland. Lanyer declares that the poem she is writing will be a memorial to her.

Whose date expired, that tyrant Time soon ends;
Those gaudy colors soon are spent and gone;
But those fair virtues which on thee attends,
190   Are always fresh, they never are but one:
    They make thy beauty fairer to behold,
    Than was that queen's[2] for whom proud Troy was sold.

As for those matchless colors red and white,
Or perfit° features in a fading face,   *perfect*
195   Or due proportion pleasing to the sight;
All these do draw but dangers and disgrace;
A mind enriched with virtue, shines more bright,
Adds everlasting beauty, gives true grace,
    Frames an immortal goddess on the earth,
200   Who though she dies, yet fame gives her new birth.

That pride of nature which adorns the fair,
Like blazing comets to allure all eyes,
Is but the thread, that weaves their web of care,
Who glories most, where most their danger lies;
205   For greatest perils do attend the fair,
When men do seek, attempt, plot and devise,
    How they may overthrow the chastest dame,
    Whose beauty is the white[3] whereat they aim.

'Twas beauty bred in Troy the ten years' strife,
210   And carried *Helen* from her lawful lord;
'Twas beauty made chaste *Lucrece*[4] lose her life,
For which proud *Tarquin's* fact° was so abhorr'd: *deed*
Beauty the cause *Antonius*[5] wronged his wife,
Which could not be decided but by sword:
215   Great *Cleopatra's* beauty and defects
    Did work *Octavia's* wrongs, and his neglects.

What fruit did yield that fair forbidden tree,
But blood, dishonor, infamy, and shame?
Poor blinded queen,[6] could'st thou no better see,
220   But entertain disgrace, instead of fame?
Do these designs with majesty agree?
To stain thy blood, and blot thy royal name.
    That heart that gave consent unto this ill,
    Did give consent that thou thyself should'st kill.

2. Helen of Troy, wife of King Menelaus of Sparta. Renowned for her beauty, she was kidnapped by Paris, son of Priam, King of Troy. This brought about the Trojan War.
3. The "white" at which hunters aim is the breast of the deer (or dear), a common figure for the beloved lady.
4. Wife of the Roman nobleman Collatinus. She was raped by Sextus Tarquinius, son of Superbus, King of Rome. The crime aroused the people of Rome to overthrow the tyranny of the Tarquins and institute a republic.
5. Marc Antony, who married Octavia, sister to Octavius, who would become the Emperor Augustus; Antony later abandoned her in favor of Cleopatra, queen of Egypt.
6. Cleopatra, figuratively blinded by her passion for Marc Antony. The couple committed suicide after Marc Antony's defeat by Octavius at the battle of Actium.

[PILATE'S WIFE APOLOGIZES FOR EVE]

745   Now *Pontius Pilate*[7] is to judge the cause
       Of faultless *Jesus*, who before him stands;
       Who neither hath offended prince, nor laws,
       Although he now be brought in woeful bands:°   *bonds*
       "O noble governor, make thou you a pause,
750   Do not in innocent blood imbrue° thy hands;   *stain*
          But hear the words of thy most worthy wife,
          Who sends to thee, to beg her Saviour's life.

       Let barbarous cruelty far depart from thee,
       And in true justice take affliction's part;
755   Open thine eyes, that thou the truth mayest see;
       Do not the thing that goes against thy heart,
       Condemn not him that must thy Saviour be;
       But view his holy life, his good desert."
          Let not us women glory in men's fall,
760   Who had power given to overrule us all.

       Till now your indiscretion sets us free,
       And makes our former fault much less appear;[8]
       Our Mother *Eve*, who tasted of the tree,
       Giving to *Adam* what she held most dear,
765   Was simply good, and had no power to see,
       The after-coming harm did not appear:[9]
          The subtle serpent that our sex betrayed,
          Before our fall so sure a plot had laid.

       That undiscerning ignorance° perceived   *i.e., of Eve*
770   No guile, or craft that was by him intended;
       For had she known, of what we were bereaved,
       To his request she had not condescended.
       But she (poor soul) by cunning was deceived,
       No hurt therein her harmless heart intended:
775   For she alleged God's word, which he denies,
          That they should die, but even as gods, be wise.

       But surely *Adam* cannot be excused,
       Her fault though great, yet he was most to blame;
       What weakness offered, strength might have refused,
780   Being Lord of all, greater was his shame:

---

7. The Roman governor of Jerusalem, A.D. 26–36. He was the judge at the trial of Jesus, who was accused of violating the laws of Rome. His wife warned him against condemning Jesus, saying, "Have thou nothing to do with that just man: for I have suffered many things this day in a dream because of him" (Matthew 27.19).
8. Lanyer recapitulates points raised by many writers who denied that Eve should have all the blame for the loss of Eden and paradise. Lanyer stresses Eve's innocence, and emphasizes that Adam should have exercised authority over Eve. This latter point is central to Milton's representation of Adam's sin in *Paradise Lost*, exonerating Eve while also making her Adam's subordinate.
9. She could not foresee the harm that would follow her disobedience.

Although the serpent's craft had her abused,
God's holy word ought all his actions frame,
   For he was lord and king of all the earth,
   Before poor *Eve* had either life or breath.

785 Who being framed by God's eternal hand,
The perfectest man that ever breathed on earth;
And from God's mouth received that strait° command,   *stern*
The breach whereof he knew was present death:
Yea, having power to rule both sea and land,
790 Yet with one apple won to lose that breath
   Which god had breathed in his beauteous face,
   Bringing us all in danger and disgrace.

And then to lay the fault on Patience° back,   *Patience's*
That we (poor women) must endure it all;
795 We know right well he did discretion lack,
Being not persuaded thereunto at all;
If *Eve* did err, it was for knowledge sake,
The fruit being fair, persuaded him to fall:
   No subtle serpent's falsehood did betray him,
800   If he would eat it, who had power to stay him?

Not *Eve*, whose fault was only too much love,
Which made her give this present to her dear,
That what she tasted, he likewise might prove,
Whereby his knowledge might become more clear;
805 He never sought her weakness to reprove,
With those sharp words, which he of God did hear:
   Yet men will boast of knowledge, which he took
   From *Eve's* fair hand, as from a learned book.

If any evil did in her remain,
810 Being made of him, he was the ground of all;
If one of many worlds[1] could lay a stain
Upon our sex, and work so great a fall
To wretched man, by Satan's subtle train;
What will so foul a fault amongst you all?
815   Her weakness did the serpent's words obey;
   But you in malice God's dear Son betray.

Whom, if unjustly you condemn to die,
Her sin was small, to what you do commit;
All mortal sins that do for vengeance cry,
820 Are not to be compared unto it:
If many worlds would altogether try,
By all their sins the wrath of God to get;
   This sin of yours, surmounts them all as far
   As doth the sun, another little star.

---

1. I.e., Adam who, as the father of all humankind, was of many people.

825   Then let us have our liberty again,

And challenge° to your selves no sovereignty;[2]   *attribute*

You came not in the world without our pain:

Make that a bar against your cruelty;

Your fault being greater, why should you disdain

830   Our being your equals, free from tyranny?

      If one weak woman simply did offend,

       This sin of yours, hath no excuse, nor end.

To which (poor souls) we never gave consent,

Witness thy wife (O *Pilate*) speaks for all,

835   Who did but dream, and yet a message sent,

That thou should'st have nothing to do at all

With that just man; which, if thy heart relent,

Why wilt thou be a reprobate° with *Saul?*   *sinner*

      To seek the death of him that is so good,

840   For thy soul's health to shed his dearest blood.

⊷⊷ ⊰◊⊱ ⊶⊶

Christopher Marlowe
1564–1593

When Christopher Marlowe began his career as a dramatist, the Elizabethan stage was at the height of its popularity and sophistication. Marlowe's plays were an immediate success, fascinating audiences with dazzling characters, exotic settings, and controversial subjects. Throughout his career—and even after his sudden death at the age of twenty-nine—Marlowe was Shakespeare's principal commercial and artistic rival.

    A shoemaker's son, Marlowe went to Cambridge on a scholarship that was intended to prepare him for holy orders. His interests proved to be literary rather than religious, however, and he left Cambridge for London. As a student, he had composed a number of poems, notably the brilliant but unfinished *Hero and Leander*, a narrative of heterosexual and homosexual passion, but public recognition came with the production of his first play, *Tamburlaine the Great*, in 1587. This was followed by *The Second Part of Tamburlaine the Great, The Jew of Malta, Edward II, Dr. Faustus, Dido, Queen of Carthage,* and finally, *The Massacre at Paris,* all composed within a period of six years. Marlowe's bold and inventive language captivated audiences; his blank verse, in which the sense of a sentence is not interrupted at the end of each line by the constraints of rhyme, brought the rhythms of natural speech to the language of theater. His characterizations of heroes were equally astonishing: driven by an incandescent desire that no conquest could satisfy, they revealed the torment and tragedy that were occasioned by pride.

    Marlowe himself may have been employed in subversive activities. While still at Cambridge, he became a spy for Queen Elizabeth's secret service, dedicated to the infiltration and exposure of Catholic groups in England and abroad. How much activity he was responsible for remains guesswork. At the very least, the manner in which he died suggests his involvement in

2. Because men are afflicted with the weakness of Adam, they forfeit their original sovereignty over creation; their rule over woman is therefore a tyranny.

clandestine politics. In May 1593, the Queen's Privy Council issued a warrant for his arrest. The charge against him—blasphemy—seems to have come from Thomas Kyd, a fellow playwright with whom Marlowe shared lodgings. While in London waiting for a hearing, Marlowe, who was drinking in an alehouse, got into a fight with three men (all government spies), one of whom was Ingram Friser. Marlowe raised a dagger to stab Friser, but Friser, warding off the blow, managed to turn the dagger against Marlowe. It pierced his eye "in such sort that his brains coming out at the dagger point, he shortly after died." The affair did not end there; two days after Marlowe's death, Richard Baines (himself a former spy) accused him before the Privy Council of atheism, treason, and the opinion "that they that love not tobacco and boys were fools." Whether or not these accusations held any truth, they referred to views that were not unusual in the circles Marlowe frequented; they indicate a skepticism in matters of religion and an indifference to social decorum that authorities responsible for political order would have considered dangerous. Some scholars think that Marlowe was murdered by government command. Although the mystery surrounding his death may never be solved, the mercurial brilliance of his work remains undisputed.

With the exception of the two parts of *Tamburlaine*, published in 1590, Marlowe's works were published after his death: *Edward II* and *Dido, Queen of Carthage* in 1594; *Hero and Leander* in 1598; *Dr. Faustus* in 1604; and *The Jew of Malta* in 1633. The celebrated lyric entitled *The Passionate Shepherd to His Love* first appeared in 1599 in an unauthorized collection of verse called *The Passionate Pilgrim* published by William Jaggard.

The Passionate Shepherd to His Love

Come live with me, and be my love,
And we will all the pleasures prove,
That valleys, groves, hills, and fields,
Woods, or steepy mountain yields.

5   And we will sit upon the rocks,
Seeing the shepherds feed their flocks,
By shallow rivers, to whose falls,
Melodious birds sing madrigals.

And I will make thee beds of roses,
10   And a thousand fragrant poesies,
A cap of flowers, and a kirtle,
Embroidered all with leaves of myrtle.

A gown made of the finest wool,
Which from our pretty lambs we pull,
15   Fair lined slippers for the cold,
With buckles of the purest gold.

A belt of straw, and ivy buds,
With coral clasps and amber studs,
And if these pleasures may thee move,
20   Come live with me, and be my love.

The shepherd swains shall dance and sing,
For thy delight each May morning,
If these delights thy mind may move,
Then live with me and be my love.

RESPONSE

Sir Walter Raleigh: The Nymph's Reply to the Shepherd[1]

If all the world and love were young,
And truth in every shepherd's tongue,
These pretty pleasures might me move,
To live with thee, and be thy love.

5 Time drives the flocks from field to fold,
When rivers rage, and rocks grow cold,
And Philomel° becometh dumb,   *the nightingale*
The rest complain of cares to come.

The flowers do fade, and wanton fields,
10 To wayward winter reckoning yields,
A honey tongue, a heart of gall,
Is fancy's spring, but sorrow's fall.

Thy gowns, thy shoes, thy beds of roses,
Thy cap, thy kirtle, and thy poesies,
15 Soon break, soon wither, soon forgotten;
In folly ripe, in reason rotten.

Thy belt of straw and ivy buds,
Thy coral clasps and amber studs,
All these in me no means can move,
20 To come to thee, and be thy love.

But could youth last, and love still breed,
Had joys no date, nor age no need,
Then these delights my mind might move,
To live with thee, and be thy love.

THE TRAGICAL HISTORY OF DR. FAUSTUS Marlowe's play is the first dramatic rendition of the medieval legend of a man who sold his soul to the devil. Sixteenth-century readers associated him with a necromancer named Dr. Faustus, and Marlowe exploited this identification when he reworked the medieval plot for his play. Rejecting the usual learning available to ambitious men—philosophy, medicine, law, and theology—Marlowe's Faustus signs a contract with the devil, represented in this case by his servant, Mephostophilis; in exchange for his soul, Faustus gains superhuman powers for twenty-four years. He uses these powers to conjure the Pope in Rome into giving the Protestant Emperor Charles V authority over the church through a surrogate Pope, Bruno; but his powers are also deployed in the banal trickery of simple and even criminal characters. The play is enigmatic on points of doctrine. Mephostophilis describes hell not as a locale but rather as the state of mind of one who has rejected God—a description that Milton will later amplify—telling Faustus: "this is hell, nor am I out of it." And Faustus, having worshipped the devil, is nevertheless offered a chance to repent and find salvation even at the very end of his alloted life. But he rejects God's love in favor of a night with Helen of Troy, praising her in lines that are now famous: "Was this the face that launched a thousand ships, / And burnt the topless towers of Ilium?" The play concludes with a report of Faustus' mangled body, torn to bits by the demon to whom he had given his soul.

1. Raleigh's *Reply* was published together with Marlowe's poem in Jaggard's collection.

The textual history of the play is very vexed, and the extent of Marlowe's own authorship remains unclear. A short version of the play was published in 1604; known as the A text, it was probably used by touring companies. The longer B text, given here, was published in 1616, probably based on Marlowe's original manuscript but also incorporating revisions and additions by Marlowe and others as the play continued to evolve in performance.

Although playtexts in this period quite often show variants from one edition to another, the case of *Dr. Faustus* is an extreme one; lacking an authoritative version, it has generally been read in various conflations of A and B. Even so, it has continued to prove popular with audiences, both for the fatal drama of Faustus's bargain with the devil and for the magnificent blank verse in which the drama plays out.

The Tragical History of Dr. Faustus
Dramatis Personae

CHORUS	THE POPE
FAUSTUS	BRUNO
WAGNER, *SERVANT TO FAUSTUS*	RAYMOND, *KING OF HUNGARY*
GOOD ANGEL AND EVIL ANGEL	CHARLES, *THE GERMAN EMPEROR*
VALDES ⎫ *Friends to Faustus*	MARTINO
CORNELIUS ⎭	FREDERICK
MEPHOSTOPHILIS	BENVOLIO
LUCIFER	SAXONY
BELZEBUB	DUKE OF VANHOLT
THE SEVEN DEADLY SINS	DUCHESS OF VANHOLT
CLOWN/ROBIN	SPIRITS IN THE SHAPES OF ALEXANDER
DICK	THE GREAT, DARIUS, PARAMOUR, AND
RAFE	HELEN
VINTNER	AN OLD MAN
CARTER	SCHOLARS, SOLDIERS, DEVILS, COURTIERS,
HOSTESS	CARDINALS, MONKS, CUPIDS

[*Enter Chorus.*]

CHORUS: Not marching in the fields of Thrasimene,[1]
　　　　　Where Mars did mate the warlike Carthigens,
　　　　　Nor sporting in the dalliance of love
　　　　　In courts of kings where state is overturned,
5　　　　　Nor in the pomp of proud audacious deeds,
　　　　　Intends our muse to vaunt his heavenly verse.[2]
　　　　　Only this, gentles: we must now perform
　　　　　The form of Faustus' fortunes, good or bad.
　　　　　And now to patient judgments we appeal,
10　　　　And speak for Faustus in his infancy.

---

1. Trasimeno, a lake in Italy near Rome. The Carthaginian general Hannibal conquered Roman forces at Trasimeno in 217 B.C.; Marlowe's "Mars" is probably a reference to the Roman army, which "mated" or engaged the enemy opposition there.

2. These lines may refer to plays Marlowe had previously staged and whose subjects were war (*Tamburlaine*) and love (*Edward II*, *Dido, Queen of Carthage*).

Title Page, 1620 edition of Marlowe's *The Tragical History of Dr. Faustus*.

Now is he born, of parents base of stock,
In Germany, within a town called Rhodes.
At riper years to Wittenberg he went,
Whereas his kinsmen chiefly brought him up.
15 So much he profits in divinity,
The fruitful plot° of scholarism graced,   *field*
That shortly he was graced with Doctor's name,
Excelling all; and sweetly can dispute
In th' heavenly matters of theology.
20 Till swol'n with cunning of a self-conceit,
His waxen wings did mount above his reach,
And melting, heavens conspired his overthrow.³
For falling to a devilish exercise,
And glutted now with learning's golden gifts,
25 He surfeits upon cursed necromancy.
Nothing so sweet as magic is to him,
Which he prefers before his chiefest bliss:
And this the man that in his study sits.

---

3. Faustus is compared to the legendary figure of Icarus, whose father, the master craftsman Daedalus, made him a pair of wings that were attached to his body with wax. Icarus flew too near the sun, the wax supporting his wings melted, and he fell to the sea. The legend is generally understood to signify the consequences of pride and presumption.

ACT 1

Scene 1

[*Faustus in his study.*]

FAUSTUS: Settle thy studies, Faustus, and begin
                To sound the depth of that thou wilt profess.
                Having commenced, be a divine in show,
                Yet level at the end of every art
5   And live and die in Aristotle's works.
                Sweet Analytics, 'tis thou hast ravished me.[4]
                Bene disserere est finis logices.
                Is "to dispute well logic's chiefest end"?
                Affords this art no greater miracle?
10   Then read no more: thou hast attained that end.
                A greater subject fitteth Faustus' wit.
                Bid *on cai me on*° farewell. And Galen,[5] come.   *being and non-being*
                Seeing, *ubi desinit philosophus, ibi incipit medicus.*
                Be a physician, Faustus: heap up gold
15   And be eternized for some wondrous cure.
                Summum bonum medicinae sanitas:
                "The end of physic is our body's health."
                Why, Faustus, hast thou not attained that end?
                Is not thy common talk sound aphorisms?°   *wise sayings*
20   Are not thy bills hung up as monuments,
                Whereby whole cities have escaped the plague,
                And thousand desperate maladies been cured?
                Yet art thou still but Faustus and a man.
                Couldst thou make men to live eternally,
25   Or being dead, raise them to life again,
                Then this profession were to be esteemed.
                Physic, farewell. Where is Justinian?[6]
                Si una eademque res legatur duobus,
                Alter rem, alter valorem rei etc.,
30   A petty case of paltry legacies!
                Exhaereditare filium non potest pater, nisi—
                Such is the subject of the institute
                And universal body of the law.
                This study fits a mercenary drudge,
35   Who aims at nothing but external trash,
                Too servile and illiberal for me.
                When all is done Divinity is best.

4. Aristotle (384–322 B.C.), the best known of the Greek philosophers, wrote on the natural and social sciences. His *Analytics* dealt with logic.
5. Greek physician (A.D. 130–200) whose works on medicine were studied through the early modern period. Faustus welcomes his change of authorities with "where the philosopher ends, the physician begins."

6. Justinian, Emperor of Byzantium (483–565), codified all of Roman law; his *Institutes* provided the basis for civil law in England as well as on the Continent. Faustus cites a principle of estate law: "if one and the same thing is bequeathed to two people, one of them should have the thing itself, and the other the value of it"; and "the father may not disinherit the son."

	Jerome's Bible![7] Faustus, view it well.
	Stipendium peccati mors est. Ha! Stipendium etc.,
40	"The reward of sin is death."[8] That's hard.
	Si pecasse negamus, fallimur, et nulla est in nobis veritas.
	"If we say that we have no sin
	We deceive ourselves, and there is no truth in us."[9]
	Why then, belike, we must sin,
45	And so consequently die.
	Ay, we must die, an everlasting death.
	What doctrine call you this? *Che sera, sera.*
	"What will be, shall be." Divinity, adieu!
	These necromantic books are heavenly,
50	Lines, circles, scenes, letters and characters:
	Ay, these are those that Faustus most desires.
	Oh, what a world of profit and delight,
	Of power, of honor, of omnipotence,
	Is promised to the studious artisan!
55	All things that move between the quiet poles
	Shall be at my command. Emperors and kings
	Are but obeyed in their several provinces.
	Nor can they raise the wind or rend the clouds.
	But his dominion that exceeds in this
60	Stretcheth as far as doth the mind of man:
	A sound magician is a demi-god.

Here, tire° my brains to get° a deity.   use / engender
[*Enter Wagner.*]

	Wagner, commend me to my dearest friends,
	The German Valdes and Cornelius.
65	Request them earnestly to visit me.

WAGNER: I will, sir.

[*Exit.*]

FAUSTUS: Their conference will be a greater help to me
     Than all my labors, plod I ne'er so fast.
[*Enter the Good and Evil Angels.*]

GOOD ANGEL: Oh Faustus, lay that damned book aside,
70   And gaze not on it lest it tempt thy soul
     And heap God's heavy wrath upon thy head.
     Read, read the scriptures: that is blasphemy.

EVIL ANGEL: Go forward, Faustus, in that famous art
     Wherein all nature's treasure is contained.
75   Be thou on earth as Jove[1] is in the sky,
     Lord and commander of these elements.

[*Exeunt Angels.*]

FAUSTUS: How am I glutted with conceit° of this!   idea
     Shall I make spirits fetch me what I please,

---

7. Jerome (347–420), a theologian who translated the Greek Bible and some of the Hebrew Bible into Latin, also wrote on Christian doctrine.

8. Romans 6.23.
9. 1 John 1.8.
1. Roman god of the heavens and king of the gods.

Resolve me of all ambiguities,
80   Perform what desperate enterprise I will?
I'll have them fly to India for gold,
Ransack the ocean for orient pearl,
And search all corners of the new-found world
For pleasant fruits and princely delicates.
85   I'll have them read me strange philosophy,
And tell the secrets of all foreign kings.
I'll have them wall all Germany with brass,
And make swift Rhine circle fair Wittenberg.
I'll have them fill the public schools° with silk,   *college lecture halls*
90   Wherewith the students shall be bravely clad.
I'll levy soldiers with the coin they bring,
And chase the Prince of Parma from our land,
And reign sole king of all the provinces.
Yea, stranger engines for the brunt of war
95   Than was the fiery keel[2] at Antwerp's bridge
I'll make my servile spirits to invent.
Come, German Valdes and Cornelius,
And make me blest with your sage conference.

[*Enter Valdes and Cornelius.*]

Valdes, sweet Valdes and Cornelius!
100   Know that your words have won me at the last
To practice magic and concealed arts.
Yet not your words only but mine own fantasy
That will receive no object° for my head,   *idea*
But ruminates on necromantic skill.
105   Philosophy is odious and obscure.
Both law and physic are for petty wits.
Divinity is basest of the three,
Unpleasant, harsh, contemptible and vile.
'Tis magic, magic that hath ravished me.
110   Then, gentle friends, aid me in this attempt,
And I, that have with subtle syllogisms
Gravelled the pastors of the German Church
And made the flowering pride of Wittenberg
Swarm to my problems as the infernal spirits
115   On sweet Musaeus[3] when he came to hell,
Will be as cunning as Agrippa was,
Whose shadow made all Europe honor him.

VALDES: Faustus, these books, thy wit and our experience
Shall make all nations to canonize us,
120   As Indian moors obey their Spanish lords.
So shall the spirits of every element

---

2. In 1585 a fire ship destroyed the Duke of Parma's bridge across the river Scheldt in the city of Antwerp.
3. Faustus wants to model himself on Musaeus, a legendary poet, said to have been a student of Orpheus, and

Cornelius Agrippa of Nettesheim (1486–1535), a philosopher known for his works on skepticism and the occult.

Be always serviceable to us three.
Like lions shall they guard us when we please;
Like Almain rutters° with their horsemen's staves;   *German knights*
125   Or Lapland giants trotting by our sides.
Sometimes like women or unwedded maids,
Shadowing more beauty in their airy brows
Than has the white breasts of the queen of love.
From Venice shall they drag huge argosies,°   *merchant ships*
130   And from America the golden fleece[4]
That yearly stuffs old Philip's treasury
If learned Faustus will be resolute.

FAUSTUS: Valdes, as resolute am I in this
As thou to live, therefore object° it not.   *reject*

CORNELIUS: The miracles that magic will perform
Will make thee vow to study nothing else.
He that is grounded in Astrology,
Enriched with tongues,° well seen° in minerals,   *languages / educated*
Hath all the principles magic doth require.
140   Then doubt not, Faustus, but to be renowned,
And more frequented° for this mystery   *sought after*
Than heretofore the Delphian oracle.[5]
The spirits tell me they can dry the sea,
And fetch the treasure of all foreign wracks,°   *wrecks*
145   Yea, all the wealth that our forefathers hid
Within the massy° entrails of the earth.   *massive*
Then tell me, Faustus, what shall we three want?

FAUSTUS: Nothing, Cornelius! Oh, this cheers my soul.
Come, show me some demonstrations magical,
150   That I may conjure in some bushy grove,
And have these joys in full possession.

VALDES: Then haste thee to some solitary grove,
And bear wise Bacon's and Albanus'[6] works,
The Hebrew Psalter and New Testament;
155   And whatsoever else is requisite
We will inform thee e're our conference cease.

CORNELIUS: Valdes, first let him know the words of art,
And then, all other ceremonies learned,
Faustus may try his cunning by himself.

VALDES: First I'll instruct thee in the rudiments,
And then wilt thou be perfecter than I.

FAUSTUS: Then come and dine with me, and after meat
We'll canvass every quiddity° thereof,   *question*

<hr>

4. The "golden fleece" refers to the treasure (the gold wool of a divine ram) sought and won by the legendary hero, Jason, and his companions, known as the Argonauts (from the name of their ship, the Argo). Faustus alludes to this treasure when he refers to the gold the King of Castile, Philip II, was taking from lands in the New World.
5. A shrine of Apollo, the god of the sun, music, and medicine, in his temple at Delphi, where his priestess,

called the Pythia, spoke incoherent phrases that a priest later interpreted as prophecies.
6. Roger Bacon (1214–1294) was an English Franciscan monk and a lecturer at Oxford University who was interested in natural science, particularly alchemy. Albanus is perhaps Pietro D'Abano (1250–1360), who was supposed to be a sorcerer and was burned in effigy by the Inquisition after his death.

For ere I sleep, I'll try what I can do.
165   This night I'll conjure, though I die therefore.   *[Exeunt.]*

Scene 2

[Enter two Scholars.]

FIRST SCHOLAR: I wonder what's become of Faustus, that was wont to make our
schools ring with *sic probo*.[7]

[Enter Wagner.]

SECOND SCHOLAR: That shall we presently know. Here comes his boy.

FIRST SCHOLAR: How now, sirrah, where's thy master?

WAGNER: God in heaven knows.

SECOND SCHOLAR: Why, dost not thou know then?

WAGNER: Yes, I know, but that follows not.

FIRST SCHOLAR: Go to, sirrah. Leave your jesting and tell us where he is.

WAGNER: That follows not by force of argument, which you, being licentiates,[8]
10   should stand upon. Therefore, acknowledge your error and be attentive.

SECOND SCHOLAR: Then you will not tell us?

WAGNER: You are deceived, for I will tell you. Yet if you were not dunces, you
would never ask me such a question. For is he not *Corpus naturale*?[9] And is
not that *mobile*? Then wherefore should you ask me such a question? But
15   that I am by nature phlegmatic, slow to wrath and prone to lechery (to love,
I would say), it were not for you to come within forty foot of the place of
execution, although I do not doubt but to see you both hanged the next sessions. Thus, having triumphed over you, I will set my countenance like a
precision,[1] and begin to speak thus: "Truly, my dear brethren, my master is
20   within at dinner with Valdes and Cornelius, as this wine, if it could speak
would inform your worships. And so the Lord bless you, preserve you and
keep you, my dear brethren."

[Exit.]

FIRST SCHOLAR: Oh Faustus, then I fear that which I have long suspected:
That thou art fallen into that damned art
25   For which they two are infamous through the world.

SECOND SCHOLAR: Were he a stranger, not allied to me,
The danger of his soul would make me mourn.
But come, let us go, and inform the Rector.
It may be his grave counsel may reclaim him.

FIRST SCHOLAR: I fear me nothing will reclaim him now.

SECOND SCHOLAR: Yet let us see what we can do.   *[Exeunt.]*

Scene 3

[Thunder. Enter Lucifer and Four Devils. Faustus to them with this speech.]

FAUSTUS: Now that the gloomy shadow of the night,
Longing to view Orion's drizzling look,
Leaps from th'Antarctic world unto the sky,
And dims the welkin° with her pitchy breath,   *heaven*
5   Faustus, begin thine incantations

---

7. "Thus I prove."   9. A natural body.
8. Postgraduates.   1. Puritan.

And try if devils will obey thy hest,°   command
Seeing thou hast prayed and sacrificed to them.
Within this circle is Jehovah's name
Forward and backward anagrammatized:
10   The abbreviated names of holy saints,
Figures of every adjunct to the heavens,
And characters of signs and evening stars,
By which the spirits are enforced to rise.
Then fear not, Faustus, to be resolute
15   And try the utmost magic can perform.[2]
[Thunder.]

*Sint mihi dei acherontis propitii, valeat numen triplex Jehovae, ignei areii, aquatani
spiritus salvete: orientis princeps Belzebub, inferni ardentis monarcha et
demigorgon, propitiamus vos, ut appareat, et surgat Mephostophilis (Dragon)[3]
quod tumeraris: per Jehovam, gehennam, et consecratam aquam quam nunc*
20   *spargo; signumque crucis quod nunc facio; et per vota nostra ipse nunc surgat
nobis dicatus Mephostophilis.*
[Enter a Devil.]
I charge thee to return and change thy shape.
Thou art too ugly to attend on me.
Go, and return an old Franciscan friar:
25   That holy shape becomes a devil best.

                                             [Exit Devil.]

I see there's virtue in my heavenly words.
Who would not be proficient in this art?
How pliant is this Mephostophilis!
Full of obedience and humility,
30   Such is the force of magic and my spells.
Now, Faustus, thou art conjuror laureate:[4]
Thou canst command great Mephostophilis.
Quin redis Mephostophilis fratris imagine.
[Enter Mephostophilis.]
MEPHOSTOPHILIS: Now, Faustus, what wouldst thou have me do?
FAUSTUS: I charge thee wait upon me whilst I live,
To do whatever Faustus shall command,
Be it to make the moon drop from her sphere,
Or the ocean to overwhelm the world.
MEPHOSTOPHILIS: I am a servant to great Lucifer,
40   And may not follow thee without his leave.
No more than he commands must we perform.

2. Faustus styles himself an accomplished magician. He
now repeats, in Latin, his command to Mephostophilis to
appear in the guise of a friar: "May the gods of the underworld be kind to me; may the triple deity of Jehovah be
gone; to the spirits of fire, air, and water, greetings. Prince
of the east, Beelzebub, monarch of the fires below, and
Demogorgon, we appeal to you so that Mephostophilis
may appear and rise. Why do you delay? By Jehovah, hell
and the hallowed water which I now sprinkle, and the

sign of the cross, which I now make, and by our vows, let
Mephostophilis himself now arise to serve us."
3. This appears to be a stage direction that was inserted
into the playtext; it probably indicates that at this point
the figure of a dragon should come on stage.
4. Faustus, stating he is a "conjurer laureate" or honored
magician, asks again, in Latin: "Why do you not return,
Mephostophilis, in the guise of a friar?"

FAUSTUS: Did not he charge thee to appear to me?

MEPHOSTOPHILIS: No, I came now hither of mine own accord.

FAUSTUS: Did not my conjuring speeches raise thee? Speak.

MEPHOSTOPHILIS: That was the cause, but yet *per accidens;*°   *by accident*
    For when we hear one rack the name of God,
    Abjure the scriptures and his saviour Christ,
    We fly in hope to get his glorious soul.
    Nor will we come unless he use such means
50   Whereby he is in danger to be damned.
    Therefore the shortest cut for conjuring
    Is stoutly to abjure all godliness
    And pray devoutly to the price of hell.

FAUSTUS: So Faustus hath already done, and holds this principle:
55   There is no chief but only Belzebub,
    To whom Faustus doth dedicate himself.
    This word "damnation" terrifies not me,
    For I confound hell in elysium.°   *heaven*
    My ghost be with the old philosophers.
60   But leaving these vain trifles of men's souls,
    Tell me, what is that Lucifer, thy lord?

MEPHOSTOPHILIS: Arch-regent and commander of all spirits.

FAUSTUS: Was not that Lucifer an angel once?

MEPHOSTOPHILIS: Yes, Faustus, and most dearly loved of God.

FAUSTUS: How comes it then that he is prince of devils?

MEPHOSTOPHILIS: Oh, by aspiring pride and insolence,
    For which God threw him from the face of heaven.

FAUSTUS: And what are you that live with Lucifer?

MEPHOSTOPHILIS: Unhappy spirits that fell with Lucifer,
70   Conspired against our God with Lucifer,
    And are for ever damned with Lucifer.

FAUSTUS: Where are you damned?

MEPHOSTOPHILIS: In hell.

FAUSTUS: How comes it then that thou art out of hell?

MEPHOSTOPHILIS: Why, this is hell, nor am I out of it.
    Think'st thou that I that saw the face of God
    And tasted the eternal joys of heaven,
    Am not tormented with ten thousand hells
    In being deprived of everlasting bliss?
80   Oh, Faustus, leave these frivolous demands,
    Which strike a terror to my fainting soul.

FAUSTUS: What, is great Mephostophilis so passionate
    For being deprived of the joys of heaven?
    Learn thou of Faustus manly fortitude,
85   And scorn those joys thou never shalt possess.
    Go, bear these tidings to great Lucifer,
    Seeing Faustus hath incurred eternal death
    By desperate thoughts against Jove's deity.
    Say he surrenders up to him his soul,
90   So he will spare him four and twenty years,

Letting him live in all voluptuousness,
Having thee ever to attend on me,
To give me whatsoever I shall ask,
To tell me whatsoever I demand,
95   To slay mine enemies and to aid my friends
And always be obedient to my will.
Go, and return to mighty Lucifer,
And meet me in my study at midnight,
And then resolve me of thy master's mind.

MEPHOSTOPHILIS: I will, Faustus.   [*Exit.*]

FAUSTUS: Had I as many souls as there be stars,
I'd give them all for Mephostophilis.
By him I'll be great emperor of the world,
And make a bridge through the air
105   To pass the ocean. With a band of men
I'll join the hills that bind the Affrick shore,
And make that country continent to Spain,
And both contributory to my crown.
The Emperor shall not live but by my leave,
110   Nor any potentate of Germany.
Now that I have obtained what I desired,
I'll live in speculation of this art
Till Mephostophilis return again.   [*Exit.*]

Scene 4

[*Enter Wagner and the Clown.*]

WAGNER: Come hither, sirrah boy.

CLOWN: Boy? Oh, disgrace to my person! Zounds! "Boy" in your face! You have
seen many boys with beards, I am sure.

WAGNER: Sirrah, hast thou no comings in?

CLOWN: Yes, and goings out too, you may see, sir.

WAGNER: Alas, poor slave. See how poverty jests in his nakedness. I know the villain's out of service and so hungry that I know he would give his soul to the
devil for a shoulder of mutton though it were blood-raw.

CLOWN: Not so neither. I had need to have it well roasted, and good sauce to it, if
10   I pay so dear, I can tell you.

WAGNER: Sirrah, wilt thou be my man and wait on me? And I will make thee go
like *Qui mihi discipulus*.[5]

CLOWN: What, in verse?

WAGNER: No, slave, in beaten silk and stavesacre.[6]

CLOWN: Stavesacre? That's good to kill vermin. Then belike, if I serve you I shall
be lousy.

WAGNER: Why, so thou shalt be whether thou dost it or no. For, sirrah, if thou
dost not presently bind thyself to me for seven years, I'll turn all the lice
about thee into familiars,[7] and make them tear thee in pieces.

5. One who is my disciple.   7. Spirits.
6. A poison.

CLOWN: Nay, sir, you may save yourself a labor, for they are as familiar with me as if they paid for their meat and drink, I can tell you.

WAGNER: Well, sirrah, leave your jesting and take these guilders.[8]

CLOWN: Yes, marry, sir, and I thank you too.

WAGNER: So, now thou art to be at an hour's warning, whensoever and whereso
25   ever the devil shall fetch thee.

CLOWN: Here, take your guilders.

WAGNER: Truly, I'll none of them.

CLOWN: Truly but you shall.

WAGNER: Bear witness I gave them him.

CLOWN: Bear witness I give them you again.

WAGNER: Not I. Thou art pressed. Prepare thyself, for I will presently raise up two devils, to carry thee away: Banio, Belcher!

CLOWN: Belcher? And Belcher come here, I'll belch him! I am not afraid of a devil.

   [*Enter Two Devils and the Clown runs up and down crying.*]

WAGNER: How now, sir, will you serve me now?

CLOWN: Ay, good Wagner. Take away the devil then.

WAGNER: Baliol and Belcher, spirits, away!

                                                                    [*Exeunt Devils.*]

CLOWN: What, are they gone? A vengeance on them! They have vile long nails. There was a he-devil and a she-devil. I'll tell you how you shall know them:
40   all he-devils has horns, and all she-devils has clifts[9] and cloven feet.

WAGNER: Well, sirrah, follow me.

CLOWN: But, do you hear, if I should serve you, would you teach me to raise up Banio's and Belcheo's?

WAGNER: I will teach thee to turn thyself to anything, to a dog, or a cat, or a
45   mouse, or a rat, or anything.

CLOWN: How? A Christian fellow to a dog or a cat, a mouse or a rat? No, no, sir, if you turn me into anything, let it be in the likeness of a little pretty frisking flea, that I may be here and there and everywhere. Oh, I'll tickle the pretty wenches' plackets![1] I'll be amongst them, i'faith.

WAGNER: Well, sirrah, come.

CLOWN: But do you hear, Wagner?

WAGNER: How? Baliol and Belcher!

CLOWN: Oh Lord, I pray, sir, let Banio and Belcher go sleep.

WAGNER: Villain, call me Master Wagner, and see that you walk attentively and
55   let your right eye be always diametrically fixed upon my left heel, that thou mayest *Quasi vestigias nostras insistere.*[2]   [*Exit.*]

CLOWN: God forgive me, he speaks Dutch fustian![3] Well, I'll follow him. I'll serve him, that's flat.   [*Exit.*]

---

8. Coins.
9. Clefts.
1. Petticoats.
2. Wagner mocks the Clown by telling him to walk "as if

to tread in our footsteps," knowing that the clown's magic will never be as powerful as his own.
3. Nonsense.

Scene 5

[*Enter Faustus in his study.*]

FAUSTUS: Now, Faustus, must thou needs be damned?
     And canst thou not be saved?
     What boots it then to think on God or heaven?
     Away with such vain fancies and despair,
5   Despair in God and trust in Belzebub.°   *the Devil*
     Now go not backward. No, Faustus, be resolute.
     Why waverest thou? Oh, something soundeth in mine ears
     Abjure this magic, turn to God again.
     Ay, and Faustus will turn to God again.
10   To God? He loves thee not.
     The God thou servest is thine own appetite,
     Wherein is fixed the love of Belzebub.
     To him I'll build an altar and a church,
     And offer lukewarm blood of new-born babes.

[*Enter the Good and Evil Angels.*]

GOOD ANGEL: Sweet Faustus, leave that execrable art.
FAUSTUS: Contrition, prayer, repentance, what of these?
GOOD ANGEL: Oh, they are means to bring thee unto heaven.
EVIL ANGEL: Rather illusions, fruits of lunacy,
     That make men foolish that do trust them most.
GOOD ANGEL: Sweet Faustus, think of heaven and heavenly things.
EVIL ANGEL: No, Faustus, think of honor and of wealth.

[*Exeunt Angels.*]

FAUSTUS: Of wealth!
     Why, the signory of Emden⁴ shall be mine!
     When Mephostophilis shall stand by me,
25   What God can hurt thee, Faustus? Thou art safe.
     Cast no more doubts. Come, Mephostophilis,
     And bring glad tidings from great Lucifer.
     Is't not midnight? Come Mephostophilis!
     Veni, veni,° *Mephostophile!*   *come, come*

[*Enter Mephostophilis.*]

30   Now tell me, what saith Lucifer, thy lord?
MEPHOSTOPHILIS: That I shall wait on Faustus whilst he lives,
     So he will buy my service with his soul.
FAUSTUS: Already Faustus hath hazarded that for thee.
MEPHOSTOPHILIS: But now thou must bequeath it solemnly,
35   And write a deed of gift with thine own blood,
     For that security craves great Lucifer.
     If thou deny it, I will back to hell.
FAUSTUS: Stay, Mephostophilis, and tell me
     What good will my soul do thy lord?
MEPHOSTOPHILIS: Enlarge his kingdom.

---

4. At this point in his career, Faustus aspires to the governorship of Emden, an important trading town in Germany, a pathetic exchange for his immortal soul.

FAUSTUS: Is that the reason why he tempts us thus?

MEPHOSTOPHILIS: *Solamen miseris, socios habuisse doloris.*[5]

FAUSTUS: Why, have you any pain, that torture others?

MEPHOSTOPHILIS: As great as have the human souls of men.

45   But tell me, Faustus, shall I have thy soul?

        And I will be thy slave and wait on thee,

        And give thee more than thou hast wit to ask.

FAUSTUS: Ay, Mephostophilis, I'll give it thee.

MEPHOSTOPHILIS: Then, Faustus, stab thy arm courageously,

50   And bind thy soul, that at some certain day

        Great Lucifer may claim it as his own,

        And then be thou as great as Lucifer.

FAUSTUS: Lo, Mephostophilis, for love of thee

        I cut mine arm, and with my proper blood

55   Assure my soul to be great Lucifer's,

        Chief lord and regent of perpetual night.

        View here the blood that trickles from mine arm,

        And let it be propitious for my wish.

MEPHOSTOPHILIS: But, Faustus, thou must write it in manner of a deed of gift.

FAUSTUS: Ay, so I will. But, Mephostophilis,

        My blood congeals and I can write no more!

MEPHOSTOPHILIS: I'll fetch thee fire to dissolve it straight.   [*Exit.*]

FAUSTUS: What might the staying of my blood portend?

        Is it unwilling I should write this bill?

65   Why streams it not that I may write afresh?

        "Faustus gives to thee his soul": ah, there it stayed!

        Why shouldst thou not? Is not thy soul thine own?

        Then write again: "Faustus gives to thee his soul."

        [*Enter Mephostophilis with a chafer of coals.*]

MEPHOSTOPHILIS: Here's fire. Come, Faustus, set it on.

FAUSTUS: So, now my blood begins to clear again.

        Now will I make an end immediately.

MEPHOSTOPHILIS: Oh what will not I do to obtain his soul!

FAUSTUS: *Consummatum est:*[6] this bill is ended,

        And Faustus hath bequeathed his soul to Lucifer.

75   But what is this inscription on mine arm?

        Homo fuge!° Whither should I flee?   *Flee, O man*

        If unto heaven, he'll throw me down to hell.

        My senses are deceived: here's nothing writ!

        Oh, yes, I see it plain. Even here is writ

80   *Homo fuge.* Yet shall not Faustus fly.

MEPHOSTOPHILIS: I'll fetch him somewhat to delight his mind.   [*Exit.*]

        [*Enter Devils, giving crowns and rich apparel to Faustus; they dance and then depart.*

        Enter Mephostophilis.]

FAUSTUS: What means this show? Speak, Mephostophilis.

---

5. Mephostophilis states that misery loves company in hell: "It is a comfort in wretchedness to have companions in woe."

6. As reported in the Vulgate Bible, Faustus speaks the last words of Jesus on the cross: "It is finished" (John 19.30), and then realizes he must try to avoid the consequences: "Flee, O man."

MEPHOSTOPHILIS: Nothing, Faustus, but to delight thy mind,
　　　　And let thee see what magic can perform.
FAUSTUS: But may I raise such spirits when I please?
MEPHOSTOPHILIS: Ay, Faustus, and do greater things than these.
FAUSTUS: Then there's enough for a thousand souls.
　　　　Here, Mephostophilis, receive this scroll,
　　　　A deed of gift, of body and of soul:
90　　　But yet conditionally, that thou perform
　　　　All covenants and articles between us both.
MEPHOSTOPHILIS: Faustus, I swear by hell and Lucifer
　　　　To effect all promises between us both.
FAUSTUS: Then hear me read it, Mephostophilis.
95　　　On these conditions following:
　　　　First, that Faustus may be a spirit in form and substance.
　　　　Secondly, that Mephostophilis shall be his servant, and be by him com-
　　　　manded.
　　　　Thirdly, that Mephostophilis shall do for him, and bring him whatsoever.
100　　Fourthly, that he shall be in his chamber or house invisible.
　　　　Lastly, that he shall appear to the said John Faustus at all times, in what
　　　　shape and form soever he please.
　　　　I, John Faustus of Wittenberg Doctor, by these presents, do give both body
　　　　and soul to Lucifer, Prince of the East, and his minister Mephostophilis,
105　　and furthermore grant unto them that four and twenty years being
　　　　expired, and these articles above written being inviolate, full power to
　　　　fetch or carry the said John Faustus, body and soul, flesh, blood or goods,
　　　　into their habitation wheresoever.
　　　　By me, John Faustus.
MEPHOSTOPHILIS: Speak, Faustus, do you deliver this as your deed?
FAUSTUS: Ay, take it, and the devil give thee good of it.
MEPHOSTOPHILIS: So now, Faustus, ask me what thou wilt.
FAUSTUS: First I will question with thee about hell.
　　　　Tell me, where is the place that men call hell?
MEPHOSTOPHILIS: Under the heavens.
FAUSTUS: Ay, so are all things else; but whereabouts?
MEPHOSTOPHILIS: Within the bowels of these elements,
　　　　Where we are tortured and remain for ever.
　　　　Hell hath no limits, nor is circumscribed
120　　In one self place. But where we are is hell,
　　　　And where hell is there must we ever be.
　　　　And to be short, when all the world dissolves
　　　　And every creature shall be purified,
　　　　All places shall be hell that is not heaven.
FAUSTUS: Come, I think hell's a fable.
MEPHOSTOPHILIS: Ay, think so still, till experience change thy mind.
FAUSTUS: Why, dost thou think that Faustus shall be damned?
MEPHOSTOPHILIS: Ay, of necessity, for here's the scroll
　　　　In which thou hast given thy soul to Lucifer.
FAUSTUS: Ay, and body too, but what of that?
　　　　Think'st thou that Faustus is so fond to imagine

That after this life there is any pain?
Tush, these are trifles and old wives' tales.

MEPHOSTOPHILIS: But Faustus, I am an instance to prove the contrary,
135   For I tell thee I am damned, and now in hell.

FAUSTUS: How? Now in hell? Nay, and this be hell, I'll willingly be damned here.
        What! Sleeping, eating, walking and disputing? But leaving this, let me
        have a wife, the fairest maid in Germany, for I am wanton and lascivious,
        and can not live without a wife.

MEPHOSTOPHILIS: How, a wife? I prithee, Faustus, talk not of a wife.

FAUSTUS: Nay, sweet Mephostophilis, fetch me one, for I will have one.

MEPHOSTOPHILIS: Well, thou wilt have one. Sit there till I come: I'll fetch
        thee a wife in the devil's name.
        [Enter a Devil dressed like a woman, with fireworks.]

FAUSTUS: What sight is this?

MEPHOSTOPHILIS: Tell, Faustus, how dost thou like thy wife?

FAUSTUS: A plague on her for a hot whore.

MEPHOSTOPHILIS: Tut, Faustus, marriage is but a ceremonial toy.
        If thou lovest me, think no more of it.
        I'll cull thee out the fairest courtesans
150   And bring them every morning to thy bed.
        She whom thine eye shall like, thy heart shall have,
        Be she as chaste as was Penelope,[7]
        As wise as Saba, or as beautiful
        As was bright Lucifer before his fall.
155   Here, take this book, and peruse it well.
        The iterating° of these lines brings gold,   *repetition*
        The framing of this circle on the ground
        Brings thunder, whirlwinds, storm and lightning.
        Pronounce this thrice devoutly to thyself
160   And men in harness shall appear to thee,
        Ready to execute what thou commandest.

FAUSTUS: Thanks, Mephostophilis. Yet fain would I have a book wherein I
        might behold all spells and incantations, that I might raise up spirits when I
        please.

MEPHOSTOPHILIS: Here they are in this book.   [There turn to them.]

FAUSTUS: Now would I have a book where I might see all characters and planets
        of the heavens, that I might know their motions and dispositions.

MEPHOSTOPHILIS: Here they are too.   [Turn to them.]

FAUSTUS: Nay, let me have one book more, and then I have done, wherein I
170   might see all plants, herbs and trees that grow upon the earth.

MEPHOSTOPHILIS: Here they be.

FAUSTUS: Oh thou art deceived.

MEPHOSTOPHILIS: Tut, I warrant thee.   [Turn to them.]

---

7. Mephostophilis compares the ideal woman to Penelope, the wife of Odysseus, who waited 20 years for him to return
from the Trojan wars, and to Saba, the wise Queen of Sheba, who caught King Solomon, known himself for his wisdom (1
Kings).

ACT 2

Scene 1

[*Enter Faustus in his study, and Mephostophilis.*]

FAUSTUS: When I behold the heavens then I repent,
　　　　And curse thee, wicked Mephostophilis,
　　　　Because thou hast deprived me of those joys.

MEPHOSTOPHILIS: 'Twas thine own seeking, Faustus, thank thyself.

5　　　But thinkst thou heaven is such a glorious thing?
　　　　I tell thee, Faustus, it is not half so fair
　　　　As thou or any man that breathes on earth.

FAUSTUS: How prov'st thou that?

MEPHOSTOPHILIS: 'Twas made for man; then he's more excellent.

FAUSTUS: If heaven was made for man, 'twas made for me.
　　　　I will renounce this magic and repent.

[*Enter the Good and Evil Angels.*]

GOOD ANGEL: Faustus, repent. Yet God will pity thee.

EVIL ANGEL: Thou art a spirit. God cannot pity thee.

FAUSTUS: Who buzzeth in mine ears I am a spirit?

15　　Be I a devil, yet God may pity me.
　　　　Yea, God will pity me if I repent.

EVIL ANGEL: Ay, but Faustus never shall repent.　　　　　　　[*Exeunt.*]

FAUSTUS: My heart's so hardened I cannot repent.
　　　　Scarce can I name salvation, faith or heaven,
20　　But fearful echoes thunder in mine ears
　　　　"Faustus, thou art damned." Then swords and knives,
　　　　Poison, guns, halters and envenomed steel
　　　　Are laid before me to dispatch myself.
　　　　And long ere this I should have done the deed,
25　　Had not sweet pleasure conquered deep despair.
　　　　Have not I made blind Homer sing to me
　　　　Of Alexander's love and Oenon's death?[1]
　　　　And hath not he that built the walls of Thebes
　　　　With ravishing sound of his melodious harp
30　　Made music with my Mephostophilis?[2]
　　　　Why should I die then, or basely despair?
　　　　I am resolved, Faustus shall not repent.
　　　　Come, Mephostophilis, let us dispute again,
　　　　And reason of divine astrology.
35　　Speak, are there many spheres above the moon?
　　　　Are all celestial bodies but one globe,
　　　　As is the substance of this centric earth?[3]

---

1. Faustus claims he has made the poet Homer sing to him of the love of Alexander the Great (356–323 B.C.), who was married to Statira, daughter of the Emperor Darius of Persia; and of Oenone, a nymph of Mount Ida, who died from grief when her lover, Paris of Troy, deserted her for Helen, the wife of King Menalaus of Sparta.
2. Faustus further claims that the legendary Amphion, whose music built the walls of Thebes, also made music with Mephostophilis, now Faustus's servant.
3. Faustus alludes to the Ptolemaic universe in which the earth, at the center, is surrounded by concentric spheres, beginning with the moon. Beyond the spheres of the stars that were thought to move (the constellations) were the spheres of the fixed stars.

MEPHOSTOPHILIS: As are the elements, such are the heavens,
    Even from the moon unto the empyrial orb,
40   Mutually folded in each other's spheres,
    And jointly move upon one axle-tree,
    Whose termine° is termed the world's wide pole.   *end point*
    Nor are the names of Saturn, Mars or Jupiter
    Feigned, but are erring stars.
FAUSTUS: But have they all one motion, both *situ et tempore?*[4]
MEPHOSTOPHILIS: All move from east to west in four and twenty hours upon
    the poles of the world, but differ in their motions upon the poles of the
    zodiac.
FAUSTUS: Tush, these slender trifles Wagner can decide. Hath Mephostophilis no
50   greater skill? Who knows not the double motion of the planets? That
    the first is finished in a natural day? The second thus, as Saturn in thirty
    years, Jupiter in twelve, Mars in four, the sun, Venus and Mercury in
    twenty-eight days. Tush, these are freshmen's suppositions. But tell me,
    hath every sphere a dominion or *intelligentia?*[5]
MEPHOSTOPHILIS: Ay.
FAUSTUS: How many heavens or spheres are there?
MEPHOSTOPHILIS: Nine, the seven planets, the firmament, and the empyrial
    heaven.
FAUSTUS: But is there not *coelum igneum et cristallinum?*
MEPHOSTOPHILIS: No, Faustus, they be but fables.[6]
FAUSTUS: Resolve me then in this one question. Why are not conjunctions, op-
    positions, aspects, eclipses, all at one time, but in some years we have more,
    in some less?
MEPHOSTOPHILIS: *Per inaequalem motum, respectu totius.*[7]
FAUSTUS: Well, I am answered. Now tell me, who made the world?
MEPHOSTOPHILIS: I will not.
FAUSTUS: Sweet Mephostophilis, tell me.
MEPHOSTOPHILIS: Move me not, Faustus.
FAUSTUS: Villain, have not I bound thee to tell me anything?
MEPHOSTOPHILIS: Ay, that is not against our kingdom, but this is.
    Think on hell, Faustus, for thou art damned.
FAUSTUS: Think, Faustus, upon God, that made the world.
MEPHOSTOPHILIS: Remember this—   [*Exit.*]
FAUSTUS: Ay, go, accursed spirit to ugly hell.
75   'Tis thou hast damned distressed Faustus' soul.
    Is't not too late?
    [*Enter the Good and Evil Angels.*]
EVIL ANGEL: Too late.
GOOD ANGEL: Never too late, if Faustus will repent.
EVIL ANGEL: If thou repent devils will tear thee in pieces.
GOOD ANGEL: Repent, and they shall never raze° thy skin.   *shave*
    [*Exeunt Angels.*]

---

4. In place and in time.
5. Guiding spirit.
6. Faustus asks whether there is a "fiery and crystalline heaven" beyond the "empyrial heaven" Mephostophilis

has mentioned, and he is told it is a fiction.
7. Faustus asks why planetary and astral events do not occur uniformly, and Mephostophilis answers that they do "with respect to the whole" but each "by unequal motion."

FAUSTUS: Ah, Christ my savior,
　　　　Seek to save distressed Faustus' soul.
　　[*Enter Lucifer, Belzebub and Mephostophilis.*]
LUCIFER: Christ cannot save thy soul, for he is just.
　　　　There's none but I have interest in the same.
FAUSTUS: Oh what art thou that look'st so terribly?
LUCIFER: I am Lucifer, and this is my companion prince in hell.
FAUSTUS: Oh Faustus, they are come to fetch away thy soul.
BELZEBUB: We are come to tell thee thou dost injure us.
LUCIFER: Thou call'st on Christ contrary to thy promise.
BELZEBUB: Thou shouldst not think on God.
LUCIFER: Think on the devil.
BELZEBUB: And his dam too.
FAUSTUS: Nor will I henceforth. Pardon me in this,
　　　　And Faustus vows never to look to heaven,
95　　　 Never to name God or to pray to him,
　　　　To burn his scriptures, slay his ministers,
　　　　And make my spirits pull his churches down.
LUCIFER: Do so, and we will highly gratify thee.
BELZEBUB: Faustus, we are come from hell in person to show thee some pastime.
100　　　 Sit down and thou shalt behold the seven deadly sins appear to thee in
　　　　their own proper shapes and likeness.
FAUSTUS: That sight will be as pleasant to me as Paradise was to Adam the first
　　　　day of his creation.
LUCIFER: Talk not of Paradise or Creation, but mark this show. Talk of the devil
105　　　 and nothing else. Go, Mephostophilis, fetch them in.
　　　　[*Enter the Seven Deadly Sins.*]
BELZEBUB: Now, Faustus, question them of their names and dispositions.
FAUSTUS: That shall I soon. What art thou, the first?
PRIDE: I am Pride. I disdain to have any parents. I am like to Ovid's flea.[8] I can
　　　　creep into every corner of a wench. Sometimes like a periwig I sit upon her
110　　　 brow. Next, like a necklace I hang about her neck. Then, like a fan of feath-
　　　　ers, I kiss her. And then turning myself to a wrought smock do what I list.
　　　　But fie, what a smell is here! I'll not speak a word for a king's ransom, un-
　　　　less the ground be perfumed and covered with cloth of Arras.[9]
FAUSTUS: Thou art a proud knave indeed. What art thou, the second?
COVETOUSNESS: I am Covetousness. Begotten of an old churl in a leather bag.
　　　　And might I now obtain my wish, this house, you and all, should turn to
　　　　gold, that I might lock you safe into my chest. Oh, my sweet gold!
FAUSTUS: And what art thou, the third?
ENVY: I am Envy, begotten of a chimney-sweeper and an oyster-wife. I cannot read
120　　　 and therefore wish all books were burnt. I am lean with seeing others eat.
　　　　Oh, that there would come a famine over all the world, that all might die,
　　　　and I live alone, then thou should'st see how fat I'd be. But must thou sit
　　　　and I stand? Come down, with a vengeance!
FAUSTUS: Out, envious wretch. But what art thou, the fourth?

---

8. One of the poems of the Roman poet Ovid (43
B.C.–A.D. 18) describes the journey of a flea around a
woman's body.
9. Flemish cloth for tapestries.

WRATH: I am Wrath. I had neither father nor mother. I leapt out of a lion's
mouth when I was scarce an hour old, and ever since have run up and
down the world with this case of rapiers, wounding myself when I could get
none to fight withal. I was born in hell, and look to it, for some of you shall
be my father.

FAUSTUS: And what art thou, the fifth?

GLUTTONY: I am Gluttony. My parents are all dead, and the devil a penny they
have left me, but a small pension and that buys me thirty meals a day and
ten bevers:[1] a small trifle to suffice nature. I come of a royal pedigree; my
father was a gammon of bacon and my mother was a hog's head of claret
wine.

135   My godfathers were these: Peter Pickle-herring and Martin Martlemas-beef.
But my godmother, oh, she was an ancient gentlewoman, and well-beloved
in every good town and city. Her name was Mistress Margery March-beer.
Now, Faustus, thou hast heard all my progeny, wilt thou bid me to supper?

FAUSTUS: No, I'll see thee hanged. Thou wilt eat up all my victuals.

GLUTTONY: Then the devil choke thee.

FAUSTUS: Choke thyself, Glutton. What art thou, the sixth?

SLOTH: Hey ho, I am Sloth. I was begotten on a sunny bank where I have lain
ever since, and you have done me great injury to bring me from thence. Let
me be carried thither again by Gluttony and Lechery. I'll not speak another
145   word for a king's ransom.

FAUSTUS: And what are you, Mistress Minx, the seventh and last?

LECHERY: Who, I sir? I am one that loves an inch of raw mutton better than an ell
of fried stockfish,[2] and the first letter of my name begins with Lechery.

FAUSTUS: Away to hell! Away, on, piper!

[*Exeunt the Seven Deadly Sins.*]

LUCIFER: Now, Faustus, how dost thou like this?

FAUSTUS: Oh, this feeds my soul.

LUCIFER: Tut, Faustus, in hell is all manner of delight.

FAUSTUS: Oh, might I see hell and return again safe, how happy were I then!

LUCIFER: Faustus, thou shalt. At midnight I will send for thee. Meanwhile, peruse
155   this book and view it throughly, and thou shalt turn thyself into what shape
thou wilt.

FAUSTUS: Thanks, mighty Lucifer. This will I keep as chary as my life.

LUCIFER: Now, Faustus, farewell, and think on the devil.

FAUSTUS: Farewell, great Lucifer. Come, Mephostophilis.

[*Exeunt omnes, several ways.*]

Scene 2

[*Enter the Clown.*]

CLOWN: What, Dick, look to the horses there till I come again. I have gotten one
of Doctor Faustus' conjuring books, and now we'll have such knavery as't
passes.

[*Enter Dick.*]

DICK: What, Robin, you must come away and walk the horses.

---

1. Snacks.
2. Lechery implies that she would prefer a short but
energetic penis to a yard-long but dry one.

ROBIN: I walk the horses? I scorn't, faith. I have other matters in hand. Let the
          horses walk themselves and they will. *A per se a, t.h.e. the: o per se o deny*
          orgon, gorgon.[3] Keep further from me, O thou illiterate and unlearned
          hostler.

DICK: 'Snails![4] What hast thou got there? A book? Why, thou canst not tell ne'er
10   a word on't.

ROBIN: That thou shalt see presently. Keep out of the circle, I say, lest I send you
          into the ostry[5] with a vengeance.

DICK: That's like, faith. You had best leave your foolery, for, an my master come,
         he'll conjure you, faith!

ROBIN: My master conjure me? I'll tell thee what, an my master come here, I'll
          clap as fair a pair of horns[6] on's head as e'er thou sawest in thy life.

DICK: Thou need'st not do that, for my mistress hath done it.

ROBIN: Ay, there be of us here, that have waded as deep into matters as other
          men, if they were disposed to talk.

DICK: A plague take you! I thought you did not sneak up and down after her for
        nothing. But I prithee tell me, in good sadness, Robin, is that a conjuring
        book?

ROBIN: Do but speak what thou't have me to do, and I'll do't. If thou't dance
          naked, put off thy clothes and I'll conjure thee about presently. Or if thou't
25   go but to the tavern with me, I'll give thee white wine, red wine, claret
          wine, sack, muskadine, malmesey and whippincrust.[7] Hold, belly, hold; and
          we'll not pay one penny for it.

DICK: Oh brave! Prithee, let's to it presently, for I am as dry as a dog.

ROBIN: Come, then, let's away.   [*Exeunt.*]

ACT 3

Scene 1

[*Enter the Chorus.*]

CHORUS: Learned Faustus,
         To find the secrets of astronomy,
         Graven in the book of Jove's high firmament,
         Did mount him up to scale Olympus' top,
5   Where sitting in a chariot burning bright,
         Drawn by the strength of yoked dragons' necks,
         He views the clouds, the planets, and the stars,
         The tropic, zones, and quarters of the sky,
         From the bright circle of the horned moon,
10   Even to the height of *Primum Mobile.*[1]
         And whirling round with this circumference,
         Within the concave compass of the pole,
         From east to west his dragons swiftly glide,

---

3. Barely literate, Robin is trying to parse a Latin phrase, *atheo Demigorgon* ("godless Demigorgon").
4. Christ's nails.
5. Inn.
6. Sign of a cuckold.
7. Robin lists various kinds of wine; "whippencrust" is

probably a corruption of "hippocras," a kind of sweet wine.
1. The outermost of the heavenly spheres. Faustus is pictured as viewing the heavens from Mount Olympus to the circle of the moon and beyond, to the *primum mobile.*

And in eight days did bring him home again.
15   Not long he stayed within his quiet house,
To rest his bones after his weary toil,
But new exploits do hale him out again,
And mounted then upon a dragon's back,
That with his wings did part the subtle air,
20   He now is gone to prove cosmography,
That measures coasts and kingdoms of the earth;
And as I guess will first arrive at Rome,
To see the Pope and manner of his court,
And take some part of holy Peter's feast,
25   The which this day is highly solemnized.   [Exit.]

Scene 2

[Enter Faustus and Mephostophilis.]

FAUSTUS: Having now, my good Mephostophilis,
Passed with delight the stately town of Trier,
Environed round with airy mountain tops,
With walls of flint, and deep entrenched lakes,
5   Not to be won by any conquering prince,
From Paris next coasting the realm of France
We saw the river Main fall into Rhine,
Whose banks are set with groves of fruitful vines;
Then up to Naples, rich Campania,
10   Whose buildings fair and gorgeous to the eye,
The streets straight forth and paved with finest brick,
Quarters the town in four equivolence.°   parts
There saw we learned Maro's golden tomb,[2]
The way he cut an English mile in length,
15   Thorough a rock of stone in one night's space.
From thence to Venice, Padua and the rest,
In midst of which a sumptuous temple stands,
That threats the stars with her aspiring top,
Whose frame is paved with sundry colored stones,
20   And roofed aloft with curious work in gold.
Thus hitherto hath Faustus spent his time.
But tell me now, what resting place is this?
Hast thou, as erst I did command,
Conducted me within the walls of Rome?

MEPHOSTOPHILIS: I have, my Faustus, and for proof thereof,
This is the goodly palace of the Pope;
And cause we are no common guests,
I choose his privy chamber for our use.

FAUSTUS: I hope his Holiness will bid us welcome.

MEPHOSTOPHILIS: All's one, for we'll be bold with his venison.
But now, my Faustus, that thou may'st perceive

---

2. Faustus' fiery chariot cut through rocks to go from Naples, where the Roman poet Publius Virgilius Maro, or Virgil, is buried, to Padua and Venice.

What Rome contains for to delight thine eyes,
Know that this city stands upon seven hills
That underprop the groundwork of the same.
35   Just through the midst runs flowing Tiber's stream,
With winding banks that cut it in two parts,
Over the which four stately bridges lean,
That make safe passage to each part of Rome.
Upon the bridge called Ponto Angelo
40   Erected is a castle passing strong,
Where thou shalt see such store of ordinance
As that the double cannons forged of brass
Do match the number of the days contained
Within the compass of one complete year.
45   Beside the gates and high pyramides,
That Julius Caesar brought from Africa.[3]

FAUSTUS: Now by the kingdoms of infernal rule,
Of Styx, or Acheron, and the fiery lake
Of ever-burning Phlegethon,° I swear   *rivers in hell*
50   That I do long to see the monuments
And situation of bright splendent Rome.
Come, therefore, let's away.

MEPHOSTOPHILIS: Now, stay, my Faustus. I know you'd see the Pope,
And take some part of holy Peter's feast,
55   The which in state and high solemnity
This day is held through Rome and Italy
In honor of the Pope's triumphant victory.

FAUSTUS: Sweet Mephostophilis, thou pleasest me.
Whilst I am here on earth let me be cloyed
60   With all things that delight the heart of man.
My four and twenty years of liberty
I'll spend in pleasure and in dalliance,
That Faustus' name, whilst this bright frame doth stand,
May be admired through the furthest land.

MEPHOSTOPHILIS: 'Tis well said, Faustus. Come then, stand by me,
And thou shalt see them come immediately.

FAUSTUS: Nay stay, my gentle Mephostophilis,
And grant me my request, and then I go.
Thou know'st within the compass of eight days
70   We viewed the face of heaven, of earth and hell.
So high our dragons soared into the air,
That looking down, the earth appeared to me
No bigger than my hand in quantity.
There did we view the kingdoms of the world,
75   And what might please mine eye, I there beheld.
Then in this show let me an actor be,
That this proud Pope may Faustus' cunning see.

---

3. The Emperor Caligula brought an obelisk back from Heliopolis in Egypt, which stands before St. Peter's in Rome.

MEPHOSTOPHILIS: Let it be so, my Faustus, but first stay
    And view their triumphs° as they pass this way.   *procession*
80   And then devise what best contents thy mind
    By cunning in thine art to cross the Pope,
    Or dash the pride of this solemnity,
    To make his monks and abbots stand like apes,
    And point like antics° at his triple crown,   *clowns*
85   To beat the beads about the friars' pates,
    Or clap huge horns upon the cardinals' heads,
    Or any villainy thou canst devise,
    And I'll perform it, Faustus. Hark, they come!
    This day shall make thee be admired in Rome.

[*Enter the Cardinals and Bishops, some bearing crosiers, some the pillars, Monks and Friars, singing their procession. Then the Pope and Raymond, King of Hungary with Bruno[4] led in chains.*]

POPE: Cast down our footstool.
RAYMOND: Saxon Bruno, stoop,
    Whilst on thy back his Holiness ascends
    Saint Peter's chair and state pontifical.
BRUNO: Proud Lucifer, that state belongs to me:
95   But thus I fall to Peter, not to thee.
POPE: To me and Peter shalt thou grovelling lie,
    And crouch before the papal dignity.
    Sounds trumpets then, for thus Saint Peter's heir
    From Bruno's back ascends Saint Peter's chair.

[*A flourish while he ascends.*]

100   Thus, as the gods creep on with feet of wool
    Long ere with iron hands they punish men,
    So shall our sleeping vengeance now arise,
    And smite with death thy hated enterprise.
    Lord cardinals of France and Padua,
105   Go forthwith to our holy consistory,
    And read amongst the statutes decretal,
    What by the holy council held at Trent[5]
    The sacred synod hath decreed for them
    That doth assume the papal government,
110   Without election and a true consent.
    Away, and bring us word with speed!
FIRST CARDINAL: We go, my lord.

                                  [*Exeunt Cardinals.*]

POPE: Lord Raymond.
FAUSTUS: Go, haste thee, gentle Mephostophilis,
115   Follow the cardinals to the consistory,
    And as they turn their superstitious books,
    Strike them with sloth and drowsy idleness,

4. This character has no apparent historical counterpart or model.
5. The council of Trent, called to meet the challenges posed by the Protestant Reformation, was held between 1545 and 1563.

And make them sleep so sound that in their shapes
Thyself and I may parly° with this Pope,   *speak*
120   This proud confronter of the Emperor,[6]
And in despite of all his holiness
Restore this Bruno to his liberty
And bear him to the states of Germany.

MEPHOSTOPHILIS: Faustus, I go.

FAUSTUS: Dispatch it soon,
The Pope shall curse that Faustus came to Rome.

[*Exeunt Faustus and Mephostophilis.*]

BRUNO: Pope Adrian,[7] let me have some right of law:
I was elected by the Emperor.

POPE: We will depose the Emperor for that deed,
130   And curse the people that submit to him.
Both he and thou shalt stand excommunicate,
And interdict from Church's privilege
And all society of holy men.
He grows too proud in his authority,
135   Lifting his lofty head above the clouds
And like a steeple overpeers the Church.
But we'll pull down his haughty insolence,
And, as Pope Alexander, our progenitor,
Stood on the neck of German Frederick,[8]
140   Adding this golden sentence to our praise,
That Peter's heirs should tread on emperors
And walk upon the dreadful adder's back,
Treading the lion and the dragon down,
And fearless spurn the killing basilisk,[9]
145   So will we quell that haughty schismatic,
And by authority apostolical
Depose him from his regal government.

BRUNO: Pope Julius swore to princely Sigismond[1]
For him and the succeeding popes of Rome,
150   To hold the emperors their lawful lords.

POPE: Pope Julius did abuse the Church's rites,
And therefore none of his decrees can stand.
Is not all power on earth bestowed on us?
And therefore though we would we cannot err.
155   Behold this silver belt, whereto is fixed
Seven golden seals fast sealed with seven seals,
In token of our seven-fold power from heaven,
To bind or loose, lock fast, condemn or judge,
Resign or seal, or what so pleaseth us.

---

6. The Holy Roman Emperor, Charles V, Emperor from 1519.
7. Possibly Marlowe means Hadrian VI (1522–1523), although he was Pope before the Council of Trent, after which the action of the play is supposed to have taken place.

8. Pope Alexander III (1159–1181) forced Emperor Frederick Barbarossa to acknowledge his authority.
9. A mythical creature whose glance was lethal.
1. It is unclear to whom Marlowe refers; there was no Pope Julius during the reign of the Emperor Sigismund (1368–1436).

160   Then he and thou, and all the world, shall stoop,
        Or be assured of our dreadful curse,
        To light as heavy as the pains of hell.
        [*Enter Faustus and Mephostophilis, like the cardinals.*]
MEPHOSTOPHILIS: Now tell me, Faustus, are we not fitted well?
FAUSTUS: Yes, Mephostophilis, and two such cardinals
165   Ne'er served a holy Pope as we shall do.
        But whilst they sleep within the consistory,
        Let us salute his reverend fatherhood.
RAYMOND: Behold, my lord, the cardinals are returned.
POPE: Welcome, grave fathers, answer presently
170   What have our holy council there decreed
        Concerning Bruno and the Emperor,
        In quittance of their late conspiracy
        Against our state and papal dignity?
FAUSTUS: Most sacred patron of the Church of Rome,
175   By full consent of all the synod
        Of priests and prelates, it is thus decreed:
        That Bruno and the German Emperor
        Be held as lollards² and bold schismatics
        And proud disturbers of the Church's peace.
180   And if that Bruno by his own assent,
        Without enforcement of the German peers,
        Did seek to wear the triple diadem
        And by your death to climb Saint Peter's chair,
        The statutes decretal have thus decreed:
185   He shall be straight condemned of heresy
        And on a pile of faggots burnt to death.
POPE: It is enough. Here, take him to your charge,
        And bear him straight to Ponto Angelo,
        And in the strongest tower enclose him fast.
190   Tomorrow, sitting in our consistory
        With all our college of grave cardinals,
        We will determine of his life or death.
        Here, take his triple crown along with you,
        And leave it in the Church's treasury.
195   Make haste again, my good lord cardinals,
        And take our blessing apostolical.
MEPHOSTOPHILIS: So, so, was never devil thus blessed before.
FAUSTUS: Away, sweet Mephostophilis, be gone:
        The cardinals will be plagued for this anon.
                                            [*Exeunt Faustus and Mephostophilis.*]
POPE: Go presently, and bring a banquet forth
        That we may solemnize Saint Peter's feast,
        And with Lord Raymond, King of Hungary,
        Drink to our late and happy victory.   [*Exeunt.*]

2. Heretics; in England, followers of John Wycliffe (1328?–1384).

Scene 3

[*A sennet³ while the banquet is brought in, and then enter Faustus and Mephostophilis in their own shapes.*]

MEPHOSTOPHILIS: Now, Faustus, come prepare thyself for mirth.
    The sleepy cardinals are hard at hand
    To censure Bruno that is posted° hence,   *ridden*
    And on a proud paced steed as swift as thought
5   Flies o'er the Alps to fruitful Germany,
    There to salute the woeful Emperor.

FAUSTUS: The Pope will curse them for their sloth today,
    That slept both Bruno and his crown away.
    But now, that Faustus may delight his mind,
10   And by their folly make some merriment,
    Sweet Mephostophilis, so charm me here,
    That I may walk invisible to all,
    And do what e'er I please unseen of any.

MEPHOSTOPHILIS: Faustus, thou shalt. Then kneel down presently:
15   Whilst on thy head I lay my hand,
    And charm thee with this magic wand.
    First wear this girdle, then appear
    Invisible to all are here.
    The planets seven, the gloomy air,
20   Hell and the Furies'⁴ forked hair,
    Pluto's⁵ blue fire and Hecate's⁶ tree,
    With magic spells so compass thee,
    That no eye may thy body see.
    So, Faustus, now for all their holiness,
25   Do what thou wilt, thou shalt not be discerned.

FAUSTUS: Thanks, Mephostophilis. Now, friars, take heed
    Lest Faustus make your shaven crowns to bleed.

MEPHOSTOPHILIS: Faustus, no more. See where the cardinals come.

[*Enter the Pope and all the Lords. Enter the Cardinals with a book.*]

POPE: Welcome, lord cardinals. Come, sit down.
30   Lord Raymond, take your seat. Friars, attend
    And see that all things be in readiness
    As best beseems this solemn festival.

FIRST CARDINAL: First, may it please your sacred Holiness,
    To view the sentence of the reverend synod
35   Concerning Bruno and the Emperor?

POPE: What needs this question? Did I not tell you
    Tomorrow we would sit i'the consistory
    And there determine of his punishment?
    You brought us word even now, it was decreed
40   That Bruno and the cursed Emperor

---

3. A trumpet call.
4. Greek divinities instigating revenge.
5. The Roman god of the underworld.

6. Goddess representing death and the dark side of the moon.

Were by the holy Council both condemned
For loathed lollards and base schismatics.
Then wherefore would you have me view that book?
FIRST CARDINAL: Your Grace mistakes. You gave us no such charge.
RAYMOND: Deny it not. We all are witnesses
That Bruno here was late delivered you,
With his rich triple crown to be reserved
And put into the Church's treasury.
BOTH CARDINALS: By holy Paul, we saw them not.
POPE: By Peter, you shall die
Unless you bring them forth immediately.
Hale° them to prison, lade their limbs with gyves!°   take / chains
False prelates, for this hateful treachery,
Cursed be your souls to hellish misery.
FAUSTUS: So, they are safe. Now Faustus, to the feast.
The Pope had never such a frolic guest.
POPE: Lord Archbishop of Rheims, sit down with us.
BISHOP: I thank your Holiness.
FAUSTUS: Fall to, and the devil choke you an you spare.
POPE: Who's that spoke? Friars, look about.
FRIARS: Here's nobody, if it like your Holiness.
POPE: Lord Raymond, pray fall to. I am beholding
To the Bishop of Milan for this so rare a present.
FAUSTUS: I thank you, sir.
    [Snatches it.]
POPE: How now? Who snatched the meat from me?
Villains, why speak you not?
My good Lord Archbishop, here's a most dainty dish
Was sent me from a cardinal in France.
FAUSTUS: I'll have that too.
    [Snatches it.]
POPE: What lollards do attend our Holiness
That we receive such great indignity? Fetch me some wine.
FAUSTUS: Ay, pray do, for Faustus is a-dry.
POPE: Lord Raymond, I drink unto your grace.
FAUSTUS: I pledge your grace.
    [Snatches the glass.]
POPE: My wine gone too? Ye lubbers,° look about   louts
And find the man that doth this villainy,
Or by our sanctitude you all shall die.
I pray, my lords, have patience at this
Troublesome banquet.
BISHOP: Please it your Holiness, I think it be some ghost crept out of Purgatory,
and now is come unto your Holiness for his pardon.
POPE: It may be so.
Go, then, command our priests to sing a dirge
To lay the fury of this same troublesome ghost.
    [The Pope crosseth himself.]
FAUSTUS: How now? Must every bit be spiced with a cross?

Nay then, take that.
[*Faustus hits him a box of the ear.*]
POPE: Oh, I am slain! Help me, my lords.
Oh come, and help to bear my body hence.
Damned be this soul for ever for this deed!

[*Exeunt the Pope and his train.*]

MEPHOSTOPHILIS: Now, Faustus, what will you do now?
For I can tell you, you'll be cursed with bell, book and candle.
FAUSTUS: Bell, book and candle, candle, book and bell,
Forward and backward, to curse Faustus to hell.
[*Enter the Friars with bell, book and candle, for the dirge.*]
FIRST FRIAR: Come, brethren, let's about our business with good devotion.
95   [*sing*] Cursed be he that stole his Holiness' meat from the table. *Maledicat
dominus.*[7]
Cursed be he that took his Holiness a blow on the face. *Maledicat dominus.*
Cursed be he that struck Friar Sandelo a blow on the pate. *Maledicat
dominus.*
100   Cursed be he that disturbeth our holy dirge. *Maledicat dominus.*
Cursed be he that took away his Holiness' wine. *Maledicat dominus.*
Et omnes sancti.[8] Amen
[*Faustus and Mephostophilis beat the Friars, fling fireworks among them and exeunt.
Enter Chorus.*]
CHORUS: When Faustus had with pleasure ta'en the view
Of rarest things and royal courts of kings,
105   He stayed his course and so returned home;
Where such as bear his absence but with grief,
I mean his friends and nearest companions,
Did gratulate his safety with kind words,
And in their conference of what befell,
110   Touching his journey through the world and air,
They put forth questions of astrology,
Which Faustus answered with such learned skill
As they admired and wondered at his wit.
Now is his fame spread forth in every land;
115   Amongst the rest, the Emperor is one,
Carolus the Fifth, at whose palace now
Faustus is feasted 'mongst his noblemen.
What there he did in trial of his art,
I leave untold: your eyes shall see performed.

Scene 4

[*Enter Robin the ostler[9] with a book in his hand.*]
ROBIN: Oh this is admirable! Here I ha' stol'n one of Doctor Faustus' conjuring
books, and, i'faith, I mean to search some circles for my own use. Now will I
make all the maidens in our parish dance at my pleasure stark naked before
me. And so by that means I shall see more than ere I felt or saw yet.
[*Enter Rafe calling Robin.*]

7. May God curse you.   9. Stableman.
8. And all the saints.

RAFE: Robin, prithee come away! There's a gentleman tarries to have his horse, and he would have his things rubbed and made clean. He keeps such a chafing with my mistress about it, and she has sent me to look thee out. Prithee, come away!

ROBIN: Keep out, keep out, or else you are blown up. You are dismembered, Rafe,
10   keep out, for I am about a roaring piece of work.

RAFE: Come, what dost thou with that same book? Thou canst not read?

ROBIN: Yes, my master and mistress shall find that I can read, he for his forehead, she for her private study. She's born to bear with me, or else my art fails.

RAFE: Why, Robin, what book is that?

ROBIN: What book? Why, the most intolerable book for conjuring that ere was invented by any brimstone devil.

RAFE: Canst thou conjure with it?

ROBIN: I can do all these things easily with it. First, I can make thee drunk with ippocras at any tavern in Europe, for nothing. That's one of my conjuring
20   works!

RAFE: Our master parson says that's nothing.

ROBIN: True, Rafe. And more, Rafe, if thou hast any mind to Nan Spit, our kitchen maid, then turn her and wind her to thy own use as often as thou wilt, and at midnight.

RAFE: Oh brave Robin! Shall I have Nan Spit, and to mine own use? On that condition, I'll feed thy devil with horsebread as long as he lives, of free cost.

ROBIN: No more, sweet Rafe. Let's go and make clean our boots which lie foul upon our hands, and then to our conjuring, in the devil's name.

[Exeunt. Re-enter Robin and Rafe with a silver goblet.]

ROBIN: Come, Rafe, did I not tell thee we were for ever made by this Doctor
30   Faustus' book? *Ecce signum,*[1] here's a simple purchase for horse-keepers. Our horses shall eat no hay as long as this lasts.
        [Enter the Vintner.]

RAFE: But, Robin, here comes the vintner.

ROBIN: Hush, I'll gull[2] him supernaturally. Drawer, I hope all is paid. God be with you. Come, Rafe.

VINTNER: Soft, sir, a word with you. I must yet have a goblet paid from you ere you go.

ROBIN: I, a goblet? Rafe, I a goblet? I scorn you, and you are but a etc. I, a goblet? Search me.

VINTNER: I mean so, sir, with your favor.

ROBIN: How say you now?

VINTNER: I must say somewhat to your fellow—you, sir.

RAFE: Me, sir? Me, sir? Search your fill. Now, sir, you may be ashamed to burden honest men with a matter of truth.

VINTNER: Well, t'one of you hath this goblet about you.

ROBIN: You lie, drawer. 'Tis afore me! Sirrah, you! I'll teach ye to impeach honest men. Stand by, I'll scour you for a goblet. Stand aside, you were best. I charge you in the name of Belzebub. Look to the goblet, Rafe.

VINTNER: What mean you, sirrah?

1. "Behold, the sign"; i.e., of the truth.   2. Trick.

ROBIN: I'll tell you what I mean. [*He reads*] *Sanctobolorum Periphrasticon.*[3] Nay, I'll
50   tickle you, vintner—look to the goblet, Rafe. *Polypragmos Belseborams*
            framanto pacostiphos tostu Mephostophilis, Etc.
        [*Enter Mephostophilis, who sets squibs*[4] *at their backs. They run about.*]
VINTNER: O *nomine Domine*[5] what mean'st thou, Robin? Thou hast no goblet.
RAFE: *Peccatum peccatorum*[6] here's thy goblet, good vintner.
ROBIN: *Misericordia pro nobis*[7] what shall I do? Good devil, forgive me now and I'll
55   never rob thy library more.
        [*Enter to them Mephostophilis.*]
MEPHOSTOPHILIS: Vainish villains! Th'one like an ape, another like a bear, the
            third an ass, for doing this enterprise.
            Monarch of hell, under whose black survey
            Great potentates do kneel with awful fear,
60   Upon whose altars thousand souls do lie,
            How am I vexed with these villains' charms?
            From Constantinople am I hither come,
            Only for pleasure of these damned slaves.
ROBIN: How, from Constantinople? You have had a great journey. Will you take
65   six pence in your purse to pay for your supper, and be gone?
MEPHOSTOPHILIS: Well, villains, for your presumption I transform thee into an
            ape and thee into a dog, and so be gone.   [*Exit.*]
ROBIN: How, into an ape? That's brave! I'll have fine sport with the boys. I'll get
            nuts and apples enow.
RAFE: And I must be a dog!
ROBIN: I'faith thy head will never be out of the potage pot.   [*Exeunt.*]

ACT 4

Scene 1

[*The Emperor's Court. Enter Martino and Frederick at several doors.*]
MARTINO: What ho, officers, gentlemen!
            Hie to the presence to attend the Emperor.
            Good Frederick, see the rooms be voided straight.
            His Majesty is coming to the hall;
5   Go back, and see the state in readiness.
FREDERICK: But where is Bruno, our elected Pope,
            That on a fury's back came post from Rome?
            Will not his grace consort° the Emperor?   greet
MARTINO: Oh yes, and with him comes the German conjuror,
10   The learned Faustus, fame of Wittenberg,
            The wonder of the world for magic art.
            And he intends to show great Carolus
            The race of all his stout progenitors,
            And bring in presence of his Majesty
15   The royal shapes and warlike semblances
            Of Alexander and his beauteous paramour.[1]

3. Gibberish.
4. Firecrackers.
5. In God's name.

6. Sin of sins.
7. Mercy on us.
1. Alexander the Great and his wife, Roxana.

FREDERICK: Where is Benvolio?
MARTINO: Fast asleep, I warrant you.

      He took his rouse with stoups° of Rhenish wine   *large cups*
20   So kindly yesternight to Bruno's health,
      That all this day the sluggard keeps his bed.
FREDERICK: See, see, his window's ope. We'll call to him.
MARTINO: What ho, Benvolio?

    [*Enter Benvolio above at a window in his nightcap, buttoning.*]

BENVOLIO: What a devil ail you two?
MARTINO: Speak softly, sir, lest the devil hear you;

      For Faustus at the court is late arrived,
      And at his heels a thousand furies wait
      To accomplish whatsoever the Doctor please.
BENVOLIO: What of this?
MARTINO: Come, leave thy chamber first, and thou shalt see

      This conjuror perform such rare exploits
      Before the Pope and royal Emperor
      As never yet was seen in Germany.
BENVOLIO: Has not the Pope enough of conjuring yet?
35   He was upon the devil's back late enough,

      And if he be so far in love with him,
      I would he would post with him to Rome again.
FREDERICK: Speak, wilt thou come and see this sport?
BENVOLIO: Not I.
MARTINO: Wilt thou stand in thy window and see it, then?
BENVOLIO: Ay, and I fall not asleep i' the meantime.
MARTINO: The Emperor is at hand, who comes to see

      What wonders by black spells may compassed be.
BENVOLIO: Well, go you, attend the Emperor. I am content for this once to thrust
45   my head out at a window, for they say if a man be drunk over night the devil
     cannot hurt him in the morning. If that be true, I have a charm in my head
     shall control him as well as the conjuror, I warrant you.

                       [*Exeunt Martino and Frederick.*]

Scene 2

[*Sennet. Charles, the German Emperor, Bruno, Saxony, Faustus, Mephostophilis, Frederick, Martino, and Attendants. Benvolio still at the window.*]

EMPEROR: Wonder of men, renowned magician,

      Thrice-learned Faustus, welcome to our court.
      This deed of thine, in setting Bruno free
      From his and our professed enemy,
5   Shall add more excellence unto thine art,
      Than if by powerful necromantic spells
      Thou couldst command the world's obedience.
      For ever be beloved of Carolus;
      And if this Bruno thou hast late redeemed,
10   In peace possess the triple diadem
      And sit in Peter's chair, despite of chance,

Thou shalt be famous through all Italy,
And honored of the German Emperor.
FAUSTUS: These gracious words, most royal Carolus,
15   Shall make poor Faustus to his utmost power
Both love and serve the German Emperor,
And lay his life at holy Bruno's feet.
For proof whereof, if so your Grace be pleased,
The Doctor stands prepared, by power of art,
20   To cast his magic charms that shall pierce through
The ebon° gates of ever-burning hell,   *ebony*
And hale the stubborn furies from their caves,
To compass whatsoe'er your Grace commands.
BENVOLIO [ASIDE]: Blood, he speaks terribly! But for all that, I do not greatly
25   believe him. He looks as like a conjuror as the Pope to a coster-monger.[2]
EMPEROR: Then, Faustus, as thou late didst promise us,
We would behold that famous conqueror,
Great Alexander, and his paramour,
In their true shapes and state majestical,
30   That we may wonder at their excellence.
FAUSTUS: Your Majesty shall see them presently.
Mephostophilis, away!
And with a solemn noise of trumpets' sound,
Present before this royal Emperor
35   Great Alexander and his beauteous paramour.
MEPHOSTOPHILIS: Faustus, I will.
BENVOLIO: Well, Master Doctor, an your devils come not away quickly, you shall
have me asleep presently. Zounds, I could eat myself for anger, to think I
have been such an ass all this while, to stand gaping after the devil's
40   governor, and can see nothing.
FAUSTUS: I'll make you feel something anon, if my art fail me not.
My lord, I must forwarn your Majesty
That when my spirits present the royal shapes
Of Alexander and his paramour,
45   Your Grace demand no questions of the King,
But in dumb silence let them come and go.
EMPEROR: Be it as Faustus please, we are content.
BENVOLIO: Ay, ay, and I am content too. And thou bring Alexander and his
paramour before the Emperor, I'll be Actaeon[3] and turn myself to a stag.
FAUSTUS: And I'll play Diana, and send you the horns presently.
[*Sennet. Enter at one the Emperor Alexander, at the other Darius. They meet. Darius
is thrown down; Alexander kills him, takes off his crown, and, offering to go out, his
Paramour meets him. He embraceth her and sets Darius' crown upon her head, and
coming back, both salute the Emperor, who, leaving his state, offers to embrace them,
which Faustus seeing, suddenly stays him. Then trumpets cease and music sounds.*]
My gracious lord, you do forget yourself.
These are but shadows, not substantial.

2. Vegetable seller.
3. Mythical hunter, changed by the goddess Diana into a   stag because he had seen her naked as she bathed after a
hunt; he was then devoured by his own dogs.

EMPEROR: Oh pardon me, my thoughts are so ravished
    With sight of this renowned Emperor,
55 That in mine arms I would have compassed him.
    But, Faustus, since I may not speak to them,
    To satisfy my longing thoughts at full,
    Let me this tell thee: I have heard it said
    That this fair lady, whilst she lived on earth,
60 Had on her neck a little wart or mole.
    How may I prove that saying to be true?
FAUSTUS: Your Majesty may boldly go and see.
EMPEROR: Faustus, I see it plain,
    And in this sight thou better pleasest me
65 Than if I gained another monarchy.
FAUSTUS: Away, be gone.
    [*Exit Show.*]
    See, see, my gracious lord, what strange beast is yon, that thrusts his head
    out at window?
EMPEROR: Oh, wondrous sight! See, Duke of Saxony,
70 Two spreading horns most strangely fastened
    Upon the head of young Benvolio!4
SAXONY: What, is he asleep? Or dead?
FAUSTUS: He sleeps, my lord: but dreams not of his horns.
EMPEROR: This sport is excellent. We'll call and wake him.
75 What ho, Benvolio!
BENVOLIO: A plague upon you! Let me sleep awhile.
EMPEROR: I blame thee not to sleep much, having such a head of thine own.
SAXONY: Look up, Benvolio, 'tis the Emperor calls.
BENVOLIO: The Emperor? Where? Oh, zounds, my head!
EMPEROR: Nay, and thy horns hold, 'tis no matter for thy head, for that's armed
    sufficiently.
FAUSTUS: Why, how now, Sir Knight? What, hanged by the horns? This most
    horrible! Fie, fie! Pull in your head for shame; let not all the world wonder
    at you.
BENVOLIO: Zounds, Doctor, is this your villainy?
FAUSTUS: Oh, say not so, sir. The Doctor has no skill,
    No art, no cunning, to present these lords
    Or bring before this royal Emperor
    The mighty monarch, warlike Alexander.
90 If Faustus do it, you are straight resolved
    In bold Actaeon's shape to turn a stag.
    And therefore, my lord, so please your majesty,
    I'll raise a kennel of hounds shall hunt him so
    As all his footmanship shall scarce prevail
95 To keep his carcass from their bloody fangs.
    Ho, Belimote, Argiron, Asterote!

4. To be "horned" was to be cuckolded. Benvolio, who has insulted scholars, is given horns by Faustus, who takes a scholar's revenge. The insult is introduced as a reflection on the myth of Diana and Actaeon.

BENVOLIO: Hold, hold! Zounds, he'll raise up a kennel of devils, I think anon.
Good my lord, entreat for me. 'Sblood, I am never never able to endure
these torments.

EMPEROR: Then, good Master Doctor,
Let me entreat you to remove his horns:
He has done penance now sufficiently.

FAUSTUS: My gracious lord, not so much for injury done to me, as to delight your
majesty with some mirth, hath Faustus justly requited this injurious knight;
105   which being all I desire, I am content to remove his horns. Mephostophilis,
transform him. And hereafter, sir, look you speak well of scholars.

BENVOLIO [ASIDE]:   Speak well of ye? 'Sblood, and scholars be such cuckold-
makers to clap horns of honest men's heads o' this order, I'll ne'er trust
smooth faces and small ruffs more. But an I be not revenged for this, would
110   I might be turned to a gaping oyster and drink nothing but salt water.

EMPEROR: Come, Faustus, while the Emperor lives,
In recompense of this thy high desert,°   *merit*
Thou shalt command the state of Germany,
And live beloved of mighty Carolus.   *[Exeunt omnes.]*

Scene 3

[Enter Benvolio, Martino, Frederick and Soldiers.]

MARTINO: Nay, sweet Benvolio, let us sway thy thoughts
From this attempt against the conjuror.

BENVOLIO: Away, you love me not, to urge me thus.
Shall I let slip° so great an injury,   *overlook*
5   When every servile groom jests at my wrongs,
And in their rustic gambols proudly say
Benvolio's head was graced with horns today?
Oh, may these eyelids never close again
Till with my sword I have that conjuror slain.
10   If you will aid me in this enterprise,
Then draw your weapons and be resolute.
If not, depart. Here will Benvolio die,
But Faustus' death shall quit my infamy.

FREDERICK: Nay, we will stay with three, betide what may,
15   And kill that Doctor if he come this way.

BENVOLIO: Then, gentle Frederick, hie° thee to the grove,   *take*
And place our servants and our followers
Close in an ambush there behind the trees.
By this I know the conjuror is near:
20   I saw him kneel and kiss the Emperor's hand,
And take his leave, laden with rich rewards.
Then, soldiers, boldly fight. If Faustus die,
Take you the wealth, leave us the victory.

FREDERICK: Come, soldiers, follow me unto the grove.
25   Who kills him shall have gold and endless love.
                             [Exit Frederick with the Soldiers.]

BENVOLIO: My head is lighter than it was by th'horns,
But yet my heart more ponderous than my head,

And pants until I see that conjuror dead.

MARTINO: Where shall we place ourselves, Benvolio?

BENVOLIO: Here will we stay to bide the first assault.
Oh, were that damned hell-hound but in place,
Thou soon shouldst see me quit my foul disgrace.
[Enter Frederick.]

FREDERICK: Close, close! The conjuror is at hand,
And all alone comes walking in his gown.
35   Be ready then, and strike the peasant down.

BENVOLIO: Mine be that honor, then. Now sword, strike home.
For horns he gave, I'll have his head anon.
[Enter Faustus with a false head.]

MARTINO: See, see, he comes.

BENVOLIO: No words. This blow ends all.
40   Hell take his soul; his body thus must fall.
[Attacks Faustus.]

FAUSTUS: Oh!

FREDERICK: Groan you, Master Doctor?

BENVOLIO: Break may his heart with groans! Dear Frederick, see,
Thus will I end his griefs immediately.
[Cuts off his head.]

MARTINO: Strike with a willing hand: his head is off.

BENVOLIO: The devil's dead! The Furies now may laugh.

FREDERICK: Was this that stern aspect, that awful frown,
Made the grim monarch of infernal spirits
Tremble and quake at his commanding charms?

MARTINO: Was this that damned head, whose heart conspired
Benvolio's shame before the Emperor?

BENVOLIO: Ay, that's the head, and here the body lies,
Justly rewarded for his villainies.

FREDERICK: Come, let's devise how we may add more shame
55   To the black scandal of his hated name.

BENVOLIO: First, on his head, in quittance° of my wrongs,   *payment*
I'll nail huge forked horns, and let them hang
Within the window where he yoked° me first,   *overcame*
That all the world may see my just revenge.

MARTINO: What use shall we put his beard to?

BENVOLIO: We'll sell it to a chimney-sweeper: it will wear
out ten birching° brooms, I warrant you.   *birch-twig*

FREDERICK: What shall eyes do?

BENVOLIO: We'll put out his eyes, and they shall serve for buttons to his lips, to
65   keep his tongue from catching cold.

MARTINO: An excellent policy! And now, sirs, having divided him, what shall
the body do?
[Faustus rises.]

BENVOLIO: Zounds, the devil's alive again!

FREDERICK: Give him his head, for God's sake!

FAUSTUS: Nay, keep it. Faustus will have heads and hands.
I call your hearts to recompense this deed.

       Knew you not, traitors, I was limited
       For four and twenty years to breathe on earth?
       And had you cut my body with your swords,
75   Or hewed this flesh and bones as small as sand,
       Yet in a minute had my spirit returned,
       And I had breathed a man made free from harm.
       But wherefore do I dally° my revenge?   *delay*
       Asteroth, Belimoth, Mephostophilis!
    [*Enter Mephostophilis and other Devils.*]
80   Go, horse these traitors on your fiery backs,
       And mount aloft with them as high as heaven;
       Thence pitch them headlong to the lowest hell.
       Yet stay, the world shall see their misery,
       And hell shall after plague their treachery.
85   Go, Belimoth, and take this caitiff° hence,   *coward*
       And hurl him in some lake of mud and dirt.
       Take thou this other: drag him through the woods
       Amongst the pricking thorns and sharpest briars,
       Whilst with my gentle Mephostophilis,
90   This traitor flies unto some steepy rock,
       That rolling down may break the villain's bones,
       As he intended to dismember me.
       Fly hence, dispatch my charge immediately.
FREDERICK: Pity us, gentle Faustus! Save our lives!
FAUSTUS: Away!
FREDERICK: He must needs go that the devil drives.
    [*Exeunt Spirits with the Knights. Enter the Ambush Soldiers.*]
FIRST SOLDIER: Come, sirs, prepare yourselves in readiness.
       Make haste to help these noble gentlemen.
       I heard them parley with the conjuror.
SECOND SOLDIER: See, where he comes. Dispatch and kill the slave.
FAUSTUS: What's here? An ambush to betray my life!
       Then Faustus, try thy skill. Base peasants, stand!
       For lo, these trees remove at my command,
       And stand as bulwarks twixt yourselves and me,
105   To shield me from your hated treachery.
       Yet, to encounter this your weak attempt,
       Behold an army comes incontinent.°   *rapidly*
[*Faustus strikes the door, and enter a devil playing on a drum; after him another bearing an ensign;*[5] *and divers with weapons; Mephostophilis with fireworks. They set upon the soldiers and drive them out.*]

Scene 4

[*Enter at several doors Benvolio, Frederick and Martino, their heads and faces bloody and besmeared with mud and dirt, all having horns on their heads.*]
MARTINO: What ho, Benvolio!
BENVOLIO: Here! What, Frederick, ho!

5. Flag.

FREDERICK: Oh help me, gentle friend. Where is Martino?
MARTINO: Dear Frederick, here,
5   Half smothered in a lake of mud and dirt,
           Through which the Furies dragged me by the heels.
FREDERICK: Martino, see Benvolio's horns again!
MARTINO: Oh misery! How now, Benvolio?
BENVOLIO: Defend me, heaven! Shall I be haunted still?
MARTINO: Nay, fear not, man; we have no power to kill.
BENVOLIO: My friends transformed thus! Oh hellish spite!
           Your heads are all set with horns!
FREDERICK: You hit it right:
           It is your own you mean. Feel on your head.
BENVOLIO: Zounds, horns again!
MARTINO: Nay, chafe not, man. We all are sped.°   *done for*
BENVOLIO: What devil attends this damned magician,
           That, spite of spite, our wrongs are doubled?
FREDERICK: What may we do, that we may hide our shames?
BENVOLIO: If we should follow him to work revenge,
           He'd join long asses' ears to these huge horns,
           And make us laughing stocks to all the world.
MARTINO: What shall we then do, dear Benvolio?
BENVOLIO: I have a castle joining near these woods,
25   And thither we'll repair and live obscure,
           Till time shall alter these our brutish shapes.
           Sith° black disgrace hath thus eclipsed our fame,   *since*
           We'll rather die with grief, than live with shame.

                                                   [*Exeunt omnes.*]

                         Scene 5
     [*Enter Faustus and Mephostophilis.*]
FAUSTUS: Now, Mephostophilis, the restless course
           That time doth run with calm and deadly foot,
           Shortening my days and thread of vital life,
           Calls for the payment of my latest years.
5   Therefore, sweet Mephostophilis, let us
           Make haste to Wittenberg.
MEPHOSTOPHILIS: What, will you go on horseback, or on foot?
FAUSTUS: Nay, till I am past this fair and pleasant green
           I'll walk on foot.
     [*Enter a Horse-Courser.*]⁶
HORSE-COURSER: I have been all this day seeking one master Fustian.⁷ Mass,
           see where he is! God save you, Master Doctor.
FAUSTUS: What, horse-courser! You are well met.
HORSE-COURSER: Do you hear, sir? I have brought you forty dollars for your
           horse.
FAUSTUS: I cannot sell him so. If thou likest him for fifty, take him.
HORSE-COURSER: Alas, sir, I have no more. I pray you, speak for me.

---

6. Horse trader.   7. Bombast.

MEPHOSTOPHILIS: I pray you, let him have him. He is an honest fellow, and he
    has a great charge, neither wife nor child.

FAUSTUS: Well, come, give me your money. My boy will deliver him to you. But
20   I must tell you one thing before you have him: ride him not into the water
    at any hand.

HORSE-COURSER: Why, sir, will he not drink of all waters?

FAUSTUS: Oh yes, he will drink of all waters; but ride him not into the water.
    Ride him over hedge or ditch or where thou wilt, but not into the water.

HORSE-COURSER: Well, sir, now I am a made man for ever. I'll not leave my
    horse for forty. If he had but the quality of hey ding ding, hey ding ding, I'd
    make a brave living on him. He has a buttock as slick as an eel. Well, God
    bye, sir. Your boy will deliver him me. But hark ye sir: if my horse be sick or
    ill at ease, if I bring his water to you, you'll tell me what is?

FAUSTUS: Away, you villain! What, dost think I am a horse-doctor?

                                            [Exit Horse-Courser.]

    What art thou, Faustus, but a man condemned to die?
    Thy fatal time doth draw to final end:
    Despair doth drive distrust into my thoughts.
    Confound these passions with a quiet sleep.
35   Tush, Christ did call the thief upon the cross;
    Then rest thee, Faustus, quiet in conceit.

    [Sleeps in his chair. Enter Horse-Courser all wet, crying.]

HORSE-COURSER: Alas, alas, Doctor Fustian quotha! Mass, Doctor Lopus[8] was
    never such a doctor. Has given me a purgation has purged me of forty dollars:
    I shall never see them more. But yet like an ass as I was, I would not be
    ruled by him, for he bade me I should ride him into no water. Now I, think
40   ing my horse had had some rare quality that he would not have had me
    known of, I, like a venturous youth, rid him into the deep pond at the
    town's end. I was no sooner in the middle of the pond but my horse van-
    ished away, and I sat upon a bottle of hay, never so near drowning in my life.
    But I'll seek out my Doctor and have my forty dollars again, or I'll make it
45   the dearest horse. Oh, yonder is his snipper-snapper. Do you hear? You!
    Hey-pass, where's your master?

MEPHOSTOPHILIS: Why, sir, what would you? You cannot speak with him.

HORSE-COURSER: But I *will* speak with him.

MEPHOSTOPHILIS: Why, he's fast asleep. Come some other time.

HORSE-COURSER: I'll speak with him now, or I'll break his glass windows about
    his ears.

MEPHOSTOPHILIS: I tell thee he has not slept this eight nights.

HORSE-COURSER: And he have not slept this eight weeks I'll speak with him.

MEPHOSTOPHILIS: See where he is fast asleep.

HORSE-COURSER: Ay, this is he. God save ye, Master Doctor. Master Doctor!
    Master Doctor Fustian! Forty dollars, forty dollars for a bottle of hay!

MEPHOSTOPHILIS: Why, thou seest he hears thee not.

HORSE-COURSER: So, ho, ho! So, ho, ho!

    [Halloos in his ear.]

---

8. Dr. Lopez, Queen Elizabeth's physician, who was executed in 1594 for alleged complicity in an attempt to murder the
Queen. Marlowe died in 1593, so the reference is not his but one of a later editor.

No, will you not wake? I'll make you wake e'er I go.

[*He pulls him by the leg, and pulls it away.*]

60   Alas, I am undone! What shall I do?

FAUSTUS: Oh, my leg, my leg! Help, Mephostophilis. Call the officers. My leg, my leg!

MEPHOSTOPHILIS: Come, villain, to the Constable.

HORSE-COURSER: Oh lord, sir, let me go and I'll give you forty dollars more.

MEPHOSTOPHILIS: Where be they?

HORSE-COURSER: I have none about me. Come to my hostry and I'll give them you.

MEPHOSTOPHILIS: Be gone, quickly!

[*Horse-Courser runs away.*]

FAUSTUS: What, is he gone? Farewell he. Faustus has his leg again, and the

70   horse-courser, I take it, a bottle of hay for his labor. Well, this trick shall cost him forty dollars more.

[*Enter Wagner.*]

FAUSTUS: How now, Wagner, what news with thee?

WAGNER: If it please you, the Duke of Vanholt[9] doth earnestly entreat your company, and hath sent some of his men to attend you with provision for your

75   journey.

FAUSTUS: The Duke of Vanholt's an honorable gentleman, and one to whom I must be no niggard[1] of my cunning. Come, away.   [*Exeunt.*]

Scene 6

[*Enter Clown, Dick, Horse-Courser and a Carter.*]

CARTER: Come, my masters, I'll bring you to the best beer in Europe. What ho, hostess. Where be these whores?

[*Enter Hostess.*]

HOSTESS: How now, what lack you? What, my old guests, welcome!

CLOWN: Sirrah Dick, dost thou know why I stand so mute?

DICK: No, Robin, why is't?

CLOWN: I am eighteen pence on the score.[2] But say nothing. See if she have forgotten me.

HOSTESS: Who's this, that stands so solemnly by himself? What, my old guest?

CLOWN: Oh, hostess, how do you? I hope my score stands still.

HOSTESS: Ay, there's no doubt of that, for methinks you make no haste to wipe it out.

DICK: Why, hostess, I say, fetch us some beer.

HOSTESS: You shall presently. Look up into the hall there, ho!   [*Exit.*]

DICK: Come, sirs, what shall we do now till mine hostess comes?

CARTER: Marry, sir, I'll tell you the bravest tale how a conjuror served me. You know Doctor Faustus?

HORSE-COURSER: Ay, a plague take him. Here's some on's have cause to know him. Did he conjure thee too?

CARTER: I'll tell you how he served me. As I was going to Wittenberg t'other

20   day, with a load of hay, he met me and asked me what he should give me for as much hay as he could eat. Now, sir, I, thinking that a little would serve

9. The Duchy of Anholt in Germany.   2. Eighteen pence in debt.
1. Miser.

his turn, bade him take as much as he would for three-farthings. So he presently gave me my money and fell to eating. And, as I am a cursen man, he never left eating till he had eat up all my load of hay.

ALL: Oh monstrous! Eat a whole load of hay?

CLOWN: Yes, yes, that may be, for I have heard of one that has eat a load of logs.

HORSE-COURSER: Now, sirs, you shall hear how villainously he served me. I went to him yesterday to buy a horse of him, and he would by no means sell him under forty dollars. So, sir, because I knew him to be such a horse as

30   would run over hedge and ditch and never tire, I gave him his money. So when I had my horse, Doctor Fauster bade me ride him night and day and spare him no time. But, quoth he, in any case ride him not into the water. Now, sir, I thinking the horse had some quality that he would not have me

35   know of, what did I but ride him into a great river, and when I came just in the midst, my horse vanished away, and I sat straddling upon a bottle of hay.

ALL: Oh brave Doctor!

HORSE-COURSER: But you shall hear how bravely I served him for it: I went me home to his house, and there I found him asleep. I kept a-hallowing and

40   whooping in his ears, but all could not wake him. I, seeing that, took him by the leg and never rested pulling, till I had pulled me his leg quite off, and now 'tis at home in mine hostry.

CLOWN: And has the Doctor but one leg, then? That's excellent, for one of his devils turned me into the likeness of an ape's face.

CARTER: Some more drink, hostess.

CLOWN: Hark you, we'll into another room and drink a while, and then we'll go seek out the Doctor.   [Exeunt omnes.]

Scene 7

[Enter the Duke of Vanholt, his Duchess, Faustus and Mephostophilis.]

DUKE: Thanks, Master Doctor, for these pleasant sights. Nor know I how suffi- ciently to recompense your great deserts in erecting that enchanted castle in the air, the sight whereof so delighted me, as nothing in the world could please me more.

FAUSTUS: I do think myself, my good lord, highly recompensed in that it pleaseth your grace to think but well of that which Faustus hath performed. But, gra- cious lady, it may be that you have taken no pleasure in those sights. There- fore, I pray you tell me, what is the thing you most desire to have. Be it in the world, it shall be yours. I have heard that great-bellied women do long

60   for things are rare and dainty.

LADY: True, Master Doctor, and since I find you so kind, I will make known unto you what my heart desires to have; and were it now summer, as it is January, a dead time of the winter, I would request no better meat than a dish of ripe grapes.

FAUSTUS: This is but a small matter. Go, Mephostophilis, away.

[Exit Mephostophilis.]

Madame, I will do more than this for your content.

[Enter Mephostophilis again with the grapes.]

Here, now taste ye these. They should be good, for they come from a far country, I can tell you.

DUKE: This makes me wonder more than all the rest, that at this time of the year,

20   when every tree is barren of his fruit, from whence you had these ripe grapes.

FAUSTUS: Please it your grace, the year is divided into two circles over the whole
    world, so that when it is winter with us, in the contrary circle it is likewise
    summer with them, as in India, Saba and such countries that lie far East,
25   where they have fruit twice a year. From whence, by means of a swift spirit
    that I have, I had these grapes brought as you see.

LADY: And trust me, they are the sweetest grapes that e'er I tasted.

[*The Clowns bounce at the gate within.*]

DUKE: What rude disturbers have we at the gate?
    Go, pacify their fury. Set it ope,
30   And then demand of them what they would have.

[*They knock again and call out to talk with Faustus.*]

SERVANT: Why, how now, masters? What a coil[3] is there?
    What is the reason you disturb the Duke?

DICK: We have no reason for it, therefore a fig for him.

SERVANT: Why, saucy varlets, dare you be so bold?

HORSE-COURSER: I hope, sir, we have wit enough to be more bold than
    welcome.

SERVANT: It appears so. Pray be bold elsewhere,
    And trouble not the Duke.

DUKE: What would they have?

SERVANT: They all cry out to speak with Doctor Faustus.

CARTER: Ay, and we will speak with him.

DUKE: Will you, sir? Commit the rascals.

DICK: Commit with us! He were as good commit with his father as commit with
    us.

FAUSTUS: I do beseech your grace let them come in.
    They are good subject for a merriment.

DUKE: Do as thou wilt, Faustus; I give thee leave.

FAUSTUS: I thank your grace.

[*Enter the Clown, Dick, Carter and Horse-Courser.*]
    Why, how now, my good friends?
50   Faith, you are too outrageous, but come near.
    I have procured your pardons. Welcome all.

CLOWN: Nay, sir, we will be welcome for our money, and we will pay forwhat we
    take. What ho! Give's half-a-dozen of beer here, and be hanged.

FAUSTUS: Nay, hark you. Can you tell me where you are?

CARTER: Ay, marry can I. We are under heaven.

SERVANT: Ay, but, sir sauce-box, know you in what place?

HORSE-COURSER: Ay, ay, the house is good enough to drink in. Zounds, fill us
    some beer or we'll break all the barrels in the house and dash out all your
    brains with your bottles.

FAUSTUS: Be not so furious. Come, you shall have beer.
    My lord, beseech you give me leave awhile.
    I'll gage my credit, 'twill content your Grace.

---

3. Disturbance.

DUKE: With all my heart, kind Doctor; please thyself.
Our servants and our court's at thy command.

FAUSTUS: I humbly thank your Grace. Then fetch some beer.

HORSE-COURSER: Ay, marry. There spake a doctor indeed, and faith, I'll drink a
health to thy wooden leg for that word.

FAUSTUS: My wooden leg? What dost thou mean by that?

CARTER: Ha, ha, ha! Dost thou hear him, Dick? He has forgot his leg.

HORSE-COURSER: Ay, ay, he does not stand much upon that.

FAUSTUS: No, faith. Not much upon a wooden leg.

CARTER: Good lord! That flesh and blood should be so frail with your worship.
Do not you remember a horse-courser you sold a horse to?

FAUSTUS: Yes, I remember I sold one a horse.

CARTER: And do you remember you bid he should not ride into the water?

FAUSTUS: Yes, I do very well remember that.

CARTER: And do you remember nothing of your leg?

FAUSTUS: No, in good sooth.

CARTER: Then I pray remember your courtesy.[4]

FAUSTUS: I thank you, sir.

CARTER: 'Tis not so much worth. I pray you, tell me one thing.

FAUSTUS: What's that?

CARTER: Be both your legs bedfellows every night together?

FAUSTUS: Wouldst thou make a colossus[5] of me, that thou askest me such
85   questions?

CARTER: No, truly, sir. I would make nothing of you, but I would fain know that.
[Enter Hostess with drink.]

FAUSTUS: Then I assure thee certainly they are.

CARTER: I thank you, I am fully satisfied.

FAUSTUS: But wherefore dost thou ask?

CARTER: For nothing, sir: but methinks you should have a wooden bedfellow of
one of 'em.

HORSE-COURSER: Why, do you hear, sir? Did not I pull off one of your legs
when you were asleep?

FAUSTUS: But I have it again now I am awake. Look you here, sir.

ALL: Oh horrible! Had the Doctor three legs?

CARTER: Do you remember, sir, how you cozened[6] me and eat up my load of—
[Faustus charms him dumb.]

DICK: Do you remember how you made me wear an ape's—

HORSE-COURSER: You whoreson conjuring scab, do you remember how you
cozened me with a ho—

CLOWN: Ha'you forgotten me? You think to carry it away with your hey-pass and
re-pass. Do you remember the dog's fa—
[Faustus has charmed each dumb in turn; exeunt Clowns.]

HOSTESS: Who pays for the ale? Hear you, Master Doctor, now you have sent
away my guests, I pray who shall pay me for my a—?
[Exit Hostess.]

4. Kindness
5. Huge statue.
6. Tricked.

LADY: My lord,
105   We are much beholding to this learned man.
DUKE: So are we, madam, which we will recompense
        With all the love and kindness that we may.
        His artful sport drives all sad thoughts away.   [Exeunt.]

ACT 5

Scene 1

[*Thunder and lightning. Enter Devils with covered dishes. Mephostophilis leads them into Faustus' study. Then enter Wagner.*]

WAGNER: I think my master means to die shortly.
        He hath made his will, and given me his wealth,
        His house, his goods, and store of golden plate,
        Besides two thousand ducats ready coined.
5   And yet methinks, if that death were near,
        He would not banquet and carouse and swill
        Amongst the students, as even now he doth,
        Who are at supper with such belly-cheer
        As Wagner ne'er beheld in all his life.
10   See where they come; belike the feast is ended.   [Exit.]

[*Enter Faustus, Mephostophilis and two or three Scholars.*]

FIRST SCHOLAR: Master Doctor Faustus, since our conference about fair ladies,
        which was the beautifullest in all the world, we have determined with our-
        selves that Helen of Greece[1] was the admirablest lady that ever lived.
        Therefore Master Doctor, if you will do us so much favor, as to let us see that
15   peerless dame of Greece, whom all the world admires for majesty, we should
        think ourselves much beholding unto you.
FAUSTUS: Gentlemen, for that I know your friendship is unfeigned,
        It is not Faustus' custom to deny
        The just request of those that wish him well.
20   You shall behold that peerless dame of Greece,
        No otherwise for pomp of majesty,
        Than when Sir Paris crossed the seas with her,
        And brought the spoils to rich Dardania.°   Troy
        Be silent then, for danger is in words.

[*Music sounds. Mephostophilis brings in Helen; she passeth over the stage.*]

SECOND SCHOLAR: Was this fair Helen, whose admired worth
        Made Greece with ten years wars afflict poor Troy?
THIRD SCHOLAR: Too simple is my wit to tell her worth
        Whom all the world admires for majesty.
FIRST SCHOLAR: Now we have seen the pride of nature's work,
30   We'll take our leaves, and for this blessed sight
        Happy and blest be Faustus evermore.

[*Enter an Old Man.*]

FAUSTUS: Gentlemen, farewell: the same wish I to you.   [*Exeunt Scholars.*]

---

1. The mythical queen of Menelaus, King of Sparta, who was abducted by Paris, son of King Priam of Troy. The action began the Trojan War.

OLD MAN: Oh gentle Faustus, leave this damned art,[2]
                This magic, that will charm thy soul to hell,
35   And quite bereave thee of salvation.
                Though thou hast now offended like a man,
                Do not persever in it like a devil.
                Yet, yet, thou hast an amiable° soul,   *lovable*
                If sin by custom grow not into nature:
40   Then, Faustus, will repentance come too late,
                Then thou art banished from the sight of heaven;
                No mortal can express the pains of hell.
                It may be this my exhortation
                Seems harsh and all unpleasant; let it not,
45   For, gentle son, I speak it not in wrath,
                Or envy of thee, but in tender love,
                And pity of thy future misery.
                And so have hope, that this my kind rebuke,
                Checking thy body, may amend thy soul.
FAUSTUS: Where art thou, Faustus? Wretch, what hast thou done?
                Damned art thou, Faustus, damned: despair and die.
                Hell claims his right, and with a roaring voice
                Says "Faustus, come, thine hour is almost come"
        [*Mephostophilis gives him a dagger.*]
                And Faustus now will come to do thee right.
OLD MAN: Oh stay, good Faustus, stay thy desperate steps.
                I see an angel hover o'er thy head,
                And with a vial full of precious grace,
                Offers to pour the same into thy soul.
                Then call for mercy and avoid despair.
FAUSTUS: Ah my sweet friend, I feel thy words
                To comfort my distressed soul.
                Leave me awhile to ponder on my sins.
OLD MAN: I leave thee, but with grief of heart,
                Fearing the ruin of thy hopeless soul.   [*Exit.*]
FAUSTUS: Accursed Faustus, wretch, what hast thou done?
                I do repent, and yet I do despair.
                Hell strives with grace for conquest in my breast.
                What shall I do to shun the snares of death?
MEPHOSTOPHILIS: Thou traitor, Faustus, I arrest thy soul
70   For disobedience to my sovereign lord.
                Revolt,[3] or I'll in piecemeal tear thy flesh.
FAUSTUS: I do repent I e'er offended him.
                Sweet Mephostophilis, entreat thy lord

---

2. The Old Man's lines in the A text reflect a Calvinist sense that Faustus may be saved by the Saviour's "mercy" and "blood alone":

  Ah Doctor Faustus, that I might prevail,
  To guide thy steps unto the way of life,
  By which sweet path thou mayst attain the goal
  That shall conduct thee to celestial rest.
  Break heart, drop blood, and mingle it with tears,

Tears falling from repentant heaviness
Of thy most vile and loathsome filthiness,
The stench whereof corrupts the inward soul
With such flagitious crimes of hainous sinnes,
As no commiseration may expel,
But mercy Faustus of thy Saviour sweet,
Whose blood alone must wash away thy guilt.
3. I.e., return to the terms of your bargain with the devil.

To pardon my unjust presumption,
75   And with my blood again I will confirm
The former vow I made to Lucifer.

MEPHOSTOPHILIS: Do it then, Faustus, with unfeigned heart,
Lest greater dangers do attend thy drift.

FAUSTUS: Torment, sweet friend, that base and crooked age
80   That durst dissuade me from thy Lucifer,
With greatest torment that our hell affords.

MEPHOSTOPHILIS: His faith is great: I cannot touch his soul.
But what I may afflict his body with
I will attempt, which is but little worth.

FAUSTUS: One thing, good servant, let me crave of thee,
To glut the longing of my heart's desire,
That I may have unto my paramour
That heavenly Helen which I saw of late,
Whose sweet embraces may extinguish clear
90   Those thoughts that do dissuade me from my vow,
And keep my vow I made to Lucifer.

MEPHOSTOPHILIS: This, or what else my Faustus shall desire,
Shall be performed in twinkling of an eye.

[Enter Helen again, passing over between two Cupids.]

FAUSTUS: Was this the face that launched a thousand ships,
95   And burnt the topless towers of Ilium?
Sweet Helen, make me immortal with a kiss.
Her lips suck forth my soul: see where it flies.
Come, Helen, come, give me my soul again.
Here will I dwell, for heaven is in those lips,
100   And all is dross that is not Helena.

[Enter Old Man.]

I will be Paris,[4] and for love of thee
Instead of Troy shall Wittenberg be sacked,
And I will combat with weak Menelaus,
And wear thy colors on my plumed crest.
105   Yea, I will wound Achilles in the heel,
And then return to Helen for a kiss.
Oh, thou art fairer than the evening's air,
Clad in the beauty of a thousand stars.
Brighter art thou than flaming Jupiter,
110   When he appeared to hapless Semele:[5]
More lovely than the monarch of the sky,
In wanton Arethusa's[6] azure arms,
And none but thou shalt be my paramour.   [Exeunt.]

OLD MAN: Accursed Faustus, miserable man,
115   That from thy soul exclud'st the grace of heaven,
And fliest the throne of his tribunal seat.

---

4. Faustus imagines he will be not only Paris, Helen's lover, but also the victor in combat with her husband, King Menelaus, as well as with the greatest of the Greek warriors, Achilles.

5. The mortal woman to whom Jupiter appeared as lightening.
6. A nymph beloved by the river-god Alpheus; no myth describes her as Jupiter's lover.

[*Enter the Devils.*]

Satan begins to sift° me with his pride, — scrutinize

As in this furnace God shall try my faith.

My faith, vile hell, shall triumph over thee.

120   Ambitious fiends, see how the heavens smiles

At your repulse, and laughs your state to scorn.

Hence, hell, for hence I fly unto my God.   [*Exeunt.*]

Scene 2

[*Thunder. Enter Lucifer, Belzebub and Mephostophilis.*]

LUCIFER: Thus from infernal Dis° do we ascend — hell

To view the subjects of our monarchy,

Those souls which sin seals the black sons of hell,

'Mong which as chief, Faustus, we come to thee,

5   Bringing with us lasting damnation

To wait upon thy soul. The time is come

Which makes it forfeit.

MEPHOSTOPHILIS: And this gloomy night,

Here in this room will wretched Faustus be.

BELZEBUB: And here we'll stay,

To mark him how he doth demean himself.

MEPHOSTOPHILIS: How should he, but in desperate lunacy?

Fond worldling, now his heart blood dries with grief.

His conscience kills it, and his laboring brain

15   Begets a world of idle fantasies

To overreach the devil. But all in vain:

His store of pleasures must be sauced with pain.

He and his servant Wagner are at hand.

Both come from drawing Faustus' latest will.

20   See where they come.

[*Enter Faustus and Wagner.*]

FAUSTUS: Say, Wagner, thou hast perused my will:

How dost thou like it?

WAGNER: Sir, so wondrous well

As in all humble duty I do yield

25   My life and lasting service for your love.

[*Enter the Scholars.*]

FAUSTUS: Gramercies, Wagner. Welcome, gentlemen.

FIRST SCHOLAR: Now, worthy Faustus, methinks your looks are changed.

FAUSTUS: Oh gentlemen!

SECOND SCHOLAR: What ails Faustus?

FAUSTUS: Ah, my sweet chamber-fellow, had I lived with thee

Then had I lived still, but now must die eternally.

Look, sirs, comes he not? Comes he not?

FIRST SCHOLAR: Oh, my dear Faustus, what imports this fear?

SECOND SCHOLAR: Is all our pleasure turned to melancholy?

THIRD SCHOLAR: He is not well with being oversolitary.

SECOND SCHOLAR: If it be so, we'll have physicians, and Faustus shall be cured.

THIRD SCHOLAR: 'Tis but a surfeit, sir; fear nothing.

FAUSTUS: A surfeit of deadly sin, that hath damned both body and soul.
SECOND SCHOLAR: Yet Faustus, look up to heaven, and remember mercy is
40   infinite.
FAUSTUS: But Faustus' offence can ne'er be pardoned, The serpent that tempted
Eve may be saved, but not Faustus. Oh gentlemen, hear with patience and
tremble not at my speeches. Though my heart pant and quiver to remember
that I have been a student here these thirty years, oh would I had never seen
45   Wittenberg, never read book. And what wonders I have done all Germany
can witness, yea all the world, for which Faustus hath lost both Germany
and the world, yea heaven itself, heaven, the seat of God, the throne of the
blessed, the kingdom of joy, and must remain in hell for ever. Hell, oh hell
for ever. Sweet friends, what shall become of Faustus, being in hell for ever?
SECOND SCHOLAR: Yet Faustus, call on God.
FAUSTUS: On God, whom Faustus hath abjured? On God, whom Faustus hath
blasphemed? Oh my God, I would weep, but the devil draws in my tears.
Gush forth blood instead of tears, yea, life and soul. Oh, he stays my tongue.
I would lift up my hands, but see, they hold them, they hold them.
ALL: Who, Faustus?
FAUSTUS: Why, Lucifer and Mephostophilis: Oh gentlemen, I gave them my soul
for my cunning.
ALL: Oh, God forbid.
FAUSTUS: God forbade it indeed, but Faustus hath done it. For vain pleasure of
60   four and twenty years hath Faustus lost eternal joy and felicity. I writ them
a bill with mine own blood, the date is expired: this is the time, and he will
fetch me.
FIRST SCHOLAR: Why did not Faustus tell us of this before, that divines might
have prayed for thee?
FAUSTUS: Oft have I thought to have done so, but the devil threatened to tear me
in pieces if I named God; to fetch me body and soul if I once gave ear to divinity, and now 'tis too late. Gentlemen, away, lest you perish with me.
SECOND SCHOLAR: Oh what may we do to save Faustus?
FAUSTUS: Talk not of me, but save yourselves and depart.
THIRD SCHOLAR: God will strengthen me. I will stay with Faustus.
FIRST SCHOLAR: Tempt not God, sweet friend, but let us into the next room and
pray for him.
FAUSTUS: Ay, pray for me, pray for me. And what noise soever you hear, come
not unto me, for nothing can rescue me.
SECOND SCHOLAR: Pray thou, and we will pray, that God may have mercy upon
thee.
FAUSTUS: Gentlemen, farewell. If I live till morning, I'll visit you. If not, Faustus
is gone to hell.
ALL: Faustus, farewell.
    [Exeunt Scholars.]
MEPHOSTOPHILIS: Ay, Faustus, now thou hast no hope of heaven,
Therefore despair, think only upon hell,
For that must be thy mansion, there to dwell.
FAUSTUS: Oh, thou bewitching fiend, 'twas thy temptation
Hath robbed me of eternal happiness.
MEPHOSTOPHILIS: I do confess it, Faustus, and rejoice.
'Twas I that, when thou were't i' the way to heaven,

Dammed up thy passage; when thou took'st the book
To view the scriptures, then I turned the leaves
And led thine eye.

90   What, weep'st thou? 'Tis too late, despair. Farewell.
Fools that will laugh on earth, must weep in hell.   [*Exit.*]
[*Enter the Good and the Evil Angel at several doors.*]

GOOD ANGEL: Oh Faustus, if thou hadst given ear to me,
Innumerable joys had followed thee.
But thou didst love the world.

EVIL ANGEL: Gave ear to me,
And now must taste hell's pains perpetually.

GOOD ANGEL: Oh, what will all thy riches, pleasures, pomps,
Avail thee now?

EVIL ANGEL: Nothing but vex thee more,
100   To want in hell, that had on earth such store.
[*Music while the throne descends.*]

GOOD ANGEL: Oh, thou hast lost celestial happiness,
Pleasures unspeakable, bliss without end.
Hadst thou affected sweet divinity,
Hell, or the devil, had had no power on thee.

105   Hadst thou kept on that way, Faustus, behold
In what resplendent glory thou hadst sat
In yonder throne, like those bright shining saints,
And triumphed over hell. That thou hast lost,
And now, poor soul, must thy good angel leave thee:

110   The jaws of hell are open to receive thee.   [*Exit.*]
[*Hell is discovered.*]

EVIL ANGEL: Now, Faustus, let thine eyes with horror stare
Into that vast perpetual torture house.
There are the furies tossing damned souls
On burning forks. Their bodies broil in lead.

115   There are live quarters broiling on the coals
That ne'er can die. This ever-burning chair
Is for o'er-tortured souls to rest them in.
These, that are fed with sops of flaming fire,
Were gluttons, and loved only delicates,

120   And laughed to see the poor starve at their gates.
But yet all these are nothing. Thou shalt see
Ten thousand tortures that more horrid be.

FAUSTUS: Oh, I have seen enough to torture me.

EVIL ANGEL: Nay, thou must feel them, taste the smart of all:
125   He that loves pleasure must for pleasure fall.
And so I leave thee, Faustus, till anon.
Then wilt thou tumble in confusion.   [*Exit.*]
[*The clock strikes eleven.*]

FAUSTUS: Ah Faustus,
Now hast thou but one bare hour to live,
130   And then thou must be damned perpetually.
Stand still, you ever-moving spheres of heaven,
That time may cease and midnight never come.

Fair nature's eye, rise, rise again, and make
Perpetual day. Or let this hour be but
135 A year, a month, a week, a natural day,
That Faustus may repent and save his soul.
O lente, lente, currite noctis equi.[7]
The stars move still, time runs, the clock will strike.
The devil will come, and Faustus must be damned.
140 Oh, I'll leap up to my God: who pulls me down?
See, see, where Christ's blood streams in the firmament.
One drop would save my soul, half a drop. Ah, my Christ!
Ah, rend not my heart for naming of my Christ!
Yet will I call on him. Oh, spare me, Lucifer!
145 Where is it now? 'Tis gone:
And see where God stretcheth out his arm,
And bends his ireful brows.
Mountains and hills, come, come, and fall on me,
And hide me from the heavy wrath of God.
150 No, no. Then will I headlong run into the earth.
Earth, gape! Oh no, it will not harbor me.
You stars that reigned at my nativity,
Whose influence hath allotted death and hell,
Now draw up Faustus like a foggy mist
155 Into the entrails of yon laboring cloud,
That when you vomit forth into the air
My limbs may issue from your smoky mouths,
So that my soul may but ascend to heaven.
[The watch strikes.]
Ah! half the hour is past,
160 'Twill all be past anon.°   soon
Oh God, if thou wilt not have mercy on my soul,
Yet, for Christ's sake whose blood hath ransomed me,
Impose some end to my incessant pain.
Let Faustus live in hell a thousand years,
165 A hundred thousand, and at last be saved.
Oh, no end is limited to damned souls.
Why wert thou not a creature wanting soul?
Or why is this immortal that thou hast?
Ah, Pythagoras' metempsychosis,[8] were that true
170 This soul should fly from me, and I be changed
Unto some brutish beast.
All beasts are happy, for when they die
Their souls are soon dissolved in elements,
But mine must live still to be plagued in hell.
175 Cursed be the parents that engendered me!
No, Faustus, curse thyself, curse Lucifer,
That hath deprived thee of the joys of heaven.

---

7. Faustus quotes from Ovid's *Amores* 1.13.40: "O slowly, slowly run, horses of the night."
8. The transmigration of souls. The Greek philosopher Pythagoras speculated that souls were reborn in other bodies in an endless progression.

[*The clock strikes twelve.*]
  Oh, it strikes, it strikes! Now body turn to air,
  Or Lucifer will bear thee quick to hell.
[*Thunder and lightning.*]
180 Oh soul, be changed into little water drops
  And fall into the ocean, ne'er be found.
[*Thunder. Enter the Devils.*]
  My God, my God, look not so fierce on me.
  Adders and serpents, let me breathe awhile.
  Ugly hell, gape not, come not, Lucifer!
185 I'll burn my books. Ah, Mephostophilis!   [*Exeunt with him.*]

Scene 3

[*Enter the Scholars.*]
FIRST SCHOLAR: Come, gentlemen, let us go visit Faustus,
  For such a dreadful night was never seen
  Since first the world's creation did begin.
  Such fearful shrieks and cries were never heard.
5 Pray heaven the Doctor have escaped the danger.
SECOND SCHOLAR: Oh help us, heaven! See, here are Faustus' limbs,
  All torn asunder by the hand of death.
THIRD SCHOLAR: The devils whom Faustus served have torn him thus:
  For twixt the hours of twelve and one, methought
10 I heard him shriek and call aloud for help,
  At which self time the house seemed all on fire
  With dreadful horror of these damned fiends.
SECOND SCHOLAR: Well, gentlemen, though Faustus' end be such,
  As every Christian heart laments to think on,
15 Yet, for he was a scholar once admired
  For wondrous knowledge in our German schools,
  We'll give his mangled limbs due burial,
  And all the students clothed in mourning black
  Shall wait upon his heavy funeral.   [*Exeunt.*]

Epilogue

[*Enter the Chorus.*]
CHORUS: Cut is the branch that might have grown full straight,
  And burned is Apollo's laurel bough,
  That sometime grew within this learned man.
  Faustus is gone. Regard his hellish fall,
5 Whose fiendful fortune may exhort the wise
  Only to wonder at unlawful things,
  Whose deepness doth entice such forward wits,
  To practice more than heavenly power permits.

Terminat hora diem, Terminat Author opus.[9]

Finis.

---

9. The hour ends the day, the author ends the work.

⊷‧≖◆≖‧⊶

Sir Walter Raleigh

c. 1554–1618

Born in South Devon, a region in which ports and shipyards testified to the importance of England's world trade and colonies abroad, Sir Walter Raleigh spent a considerable part of his life outside his native land. As a boy, he fought with Huguenot armies in France; at twenty-four he led an expedition to the West Indies with his half-brother, Sir Humphrey Gilbert; and two years later, he commanded a contingent of English troops in Ireland. He is reported to have been a great favorite of Elizabeth, at least until in 1592, when he secretly married one of her ladies-in-waiting, Elizabeth Throckmorton. The Queen, furious that she had had no say in the match, imprisoned Raleigh in the Tower of London for a period that summer.

Raleigh was famous for his travels. His most challenging expedition was intended to locate the legendary gold mines of El Dorado in South America. In 1595 he set out for the Spanish colony of Guiana, penetrating the interior of that land by venturing up the Orinoco. He described his trip in the brilliantly detailed *Discovery of the Large, Rich and Beautiful Empire of Guiana*, and although he returned to England without the gold he had gone for, his leadership of an expedition to sack the harbor of Cadiz in 1596 was enough to restore him to royal favor. But Raleigh was to encounter real trouble with the accession of James I. His enemies at court convinced the king that Raleigh had committed treason, and in 1603 he was tried, convicted, and once again confined to the Tower of London, this time with his wife and family. He remained there for thirteen years. His release was finally granted on the condition that he lead another expedition to Guiana. He had informed the King that on his earlier trip he had discovered an actual gold mine, and he now claimed that his new adventure would be successful. In fact, it was a disaster. Not only did he find no gold, but the mine to whose existence he had sworn was revealed to be a fabrication. On this occasion the grounds for proving treason were stronger than they had been in 1603. Raleigh was executed in 1618.

During his long imprisonment, Raleigh began to write a complete history of the world, managing only to cover events in ancient history to 168 B.C. Entitled *The History of the World* and published in 1614, the work is primarily remembered for the stunning reflection on death that appears on its last page: "O eloquent, just and mighty Death! Whom none could advise, thou hast persuaded; what none hath dared, thou hast done; and whom all the world hath flattered, thou only hast cast out of the world and despised; thou hast drawn together all the far stretched greatness, all the pride, cruelty, and ambition of man, and covered it all over with those two narrow words, *Hic iacet*."

Much of Raleigh's poetry is occasional, written to address the circumstances and the moment in which he found himself. It possesses the quality Castiglione celebrated in his treatise on court life: a brilliance of self-expression that contemporary Italians termed *sprezzatura*, created by the supposedly artless use of artifice showing not the courtier's education but, rather, his native wit and talent. Raleigh exploits images of common life but with an unusual intensity, adding sensuous detail to expressions of affection and reminders of mortality to celebrations of love. His longest and greatest poem, *The 21st and Last Book of the Ocean to Cynthia*, remained fragmentary at the time of his death. Occasioned when Queen Elizabeth imprisoned him for his marriage, the poem illustrates Raleigh's fury at the Queen's inconsistent treatment of her "Ocean" or "Water," as Raleigh pronounced his first name. It ends in an equivocation: Raleigh professes his devotion to Elizabeth, instancing his good will that "knit up by faith shall ever last"; but he also concludes that despite this, they will not be reconciled: "Her love hath end; my woe must ever last."

Nature That Washed Her Hands in Milk

Nature that washed her hands in milk
    And had forgot to dry them,
Instead of earth took snow and silk,[1]
    At love's request to try them,
5   If she a mistress could compose
To please love's fancy out of those.

Her eyes he would should be of light,
    A violet breath and lips of jelly,
Her hair not black nor over-bright,
10   And of the softest down her belly;
As for her inside he would have it
Only of wantonness and wit.

At love's entreaty, such a one
    Nature made, but with her beauty
15   She hath framed a heart of stone,
    So as love by ill destiny
Must die for her whom nature gave him
Because her darling would not save him.

But time, which nature doth despise,
20   And rudely gives her love the lie,
Makes hope a fool, and sorrow wise,
    His hands doth neither wash nor dry,
But being made of steel and rust,
Turns snow, and silk, and milk to dust.

25   The light, the belly, lips, and breath
    He dims, discolors, and destroys,
With those he feeds, but fills not death,
    Which sometimes were the food of joys;
Yea, time doth dull each lively wit
30   And dries all wantonness with it.

Oh cruel time which takes in trust
    Our youth, our joys, and all we have,
And pays us but with age and dust,
    Who in the dark and silent grave,
35   When we have wandered all our ways,
Shuts up the story of our days.[2]

---

1. "And the Lord God formed man of the dust of the ground" (Genesis 2.7).

2. With one slight change and the addition of a final couplet, the last stanza of this poem is also Raleigh's *Epitaph*.

To the Queen[1]

Our passions are most like to floods and streams,
The shallow murmur, but the deep are dumb.
So when affections yield discourse, it seems
The bottom is but shallow whence they come.
5   They that are rich in words must needs discover
That they are poor in that which makes a lover.

Wrong not, dear empress of my heart,
  The merit of true passion,
With thinking that he feels no smart,
10   That sues for no compassion.
Since, if my plaints serve not to prove
  The conquest of your beauty,
It comes not from defect of love,
  But from excess of duty.

15 For knowing that I sue to serve
  A saint of such perfection,
As all desire, but none deserve,
  A place in her affection;
I rather choose to want relief
20   Than venture the revealing,
When glory recommends the grief,
  Despair distrusts the healing.

Thus those desires that aim too high
  For any mortal lover,
25 When reason cannot make them die,
  Discretion will them cover.
Yet when discretion doth bereave
  The plaints that they should utter,
Then your discretion may perceive
30   That silence is a suitor.

Silence in love bewrays more woe
  Than words, though ne'er so witty,
A beggar that is dumb, you know,
  Deserveth double pity.
35 Then misconceive not (dearest heart)
  My true, though secret passion,
He smarteth most that hides his smart,
  And sues for no compassion.

---

1. This elaborate compliment is typical of the courtly expressions of devotion Elizabeth I often inspired. Its respectful complaint can be compared to the bitter regret in Raleigh's later poem *The Shepherd of the Ocean to Cynthia.*

On the Life of Man

What is our life? A play of passion,
Our mirth the music of division,
Our mothers' wombs the tiring houses be,
Where we are dressed for this short comedy,
5   Heaven the judicious sharp spectator is,
That sits and marks still who doth act amiss,
Our graves that hide us from the searching sun,
Are like drawn curtains when the play is done;
Thus march we playing to our latest rest,
10   Only we die in earnest, that's no jest.

1612

The Author's Epitaph, Made by Himself

Even such is time, which takes in trust
Our youth, our joys, and all we have,
And pays us but with age and dust,
Who in the dark and silent grave,
5   When we have wandered all our days,
Shuts up the story of our days;
And from which earth, and grave, and dust,
The Lord shall raise me up, I trust.

As You Came from the Holy Land

As you came from the holy land
   Of Walsingham[1]
Met you not with my true love
   By the way as you came?[2]

5   How shall I know your true love
   That have met many one?
As I went to the holy land
   That have come, that have gone.

She is neither white nor brown
10   But as the heavens, fair.
There is none hath a form so divine
   In the earth or the air.

Such a one did I meet good sir,
   Such an angelic face,

---

1. A district in the county of Norfolk and site of Walsingham Abbey, one of the great shrines of medieval England.
2. This stanza is the first in the dialogue that constitutes the poem. Its first seven stanzas alternate statements between two speakers: a lover and a traveler. Stanzas 8 and 9 are spoken by the traveler; the final two stanzas are spoken by the lover.

15 Who like a queen, like a nymph did appear
    By her gait, by her grace.

She hath left me here all alone,
    All alone as unknown,
Who sometimes did me lead with herself,
20   And me loved as her own.

What's the cause that she leaves you alone
    And a new way doth take,
Who loved you once as her own,
    And her joy did you make?

25 I have loved her all my youth,
    But now old, as you see;
Love likes not the falling fruit
    From the withered tree.

Know that love is a careless child
30   And forgets promise past;
He is blind, he is deaf, when he list,°   *wishes*
    And in faith never fast.

His desire is a dureless° content   *transient*
    And a trustless joy;
35 He is won with a world of despair
    And is lost with a toy.

Of womankind such indeed is the love
    Or the word love abused,
Under which many childish desires
40   And conceits are excused.

But love is a durable fire
    In the mind ever burning;
Never sick, never old, never dead,
    From itself never turning.

from The Discovery of the Large, Rich and Beautiful Empire of Guiana[1]
from Epistle Dedicatory

To the Right Honorable my singular good lord and kinsman, Charles Howard,[2] Knight of the Garter, Baron, and Chancellor, and of the Admirals of England the

---

1. A region in Venezuela. The full title of Raleigh's report is *The Discovery of the Large, Rich and Beautiful Empire of Guiana, with a relation of the Great and Golden City of Manoa (which the Spaniards call El Dorado) and the provinces of Emeria, Arromaia, Amapaia and other Countries, with their rivers, adjoining.* It was written and published in London in 1596, a year after Raleigh undertook his expedition.

2. Charles Howard (1536–1624) was Baron Howard of Effingham and Earl of Nottingham, commander of the Queen's navy at the defeat of the Armada and the capture of Cadiz.

most reknowned, and to the Right Honorable Sir Robert Cecil, Knight, Counselor in Her Highness's Privy Councils.[3]

For your Honors' many honorable and friendly parts, I have hitherto only returned promises, and now for answer of both your adventures, I have sent you a bundle of papers which I have divided between your Lordship and Sir Robert Cecil in these two respects chiefly. First, for it is reasonable that wasteful factors,[4] when they have consumed such stocks as they had in trust, do yield some color for the same in their account; secondly, for that I am assured that whatsoever shall be done or written by me shall need a double protection and defense. The trial that I had of both your loves, when I was left of all but of malice and revenge, makes me still presume that you will be pleased (knowing what little power I had to perform aught, and the great advantage of forewarned enemies) to answer that out of knowledge which others shall but object out of malice.[5] In my more happy times as I did especially honor you both, so I found that your loves sought me out in the darkest shadow of adversity, and the same affection which accompanied my better fortune, soared not away from me in my many miseries. All which, though I cannot requite, yet I shall ever acknowledge, and the great debt which I have no power to pay, I can do no more for a time but confess to be due. It is true that as my errors were great, so they have yielded very grievous effects, and if aught might have been deserved in former times to have counterpoised any part of offenses, the fruit thereof (as it seemeth) was long before fallen from the tree and the dead stock[6] only remained.[7] I did therefore even in the winter of my life undertake these travels, fitter for boys less blasted with misfortunes, for men of greater ability, and for minds of better encouragement, that thereby if it were possible I might recover but the moderation of excess and the least taste of the greatest plenty formerly possessed. If I had known other way to win, if I had imagined how greater adventures might have regained, if I could conceive what further means I might yet use but even to appease so powerful displeasure, I would not doubt but for one year more to hold fast my soul in my teeth til it were performed. Of that little remain I had, I have wasted in effect all therein,[8] I have undergone many constructions,[9] I have been accompanied with many sorrows, with labor, hunger, heat, sickness, and peril. It appeareth notwithstanding that I made no other bravado of going to sea than was meant, and that I was neither hidden in Cornwall or elsewhere, as was supposed.[1] They have grossly belied me, that forejudged that I would rather become a servant to the Spanish king than return; and the rest were much mistaken who would have persuaded that I was too easeful and sensual to undertake a journey of so great travel. But if what I have done receive the gracious construction[2] of a painful pilgrimage and purchase the least remission, I shall think all too little, and

---

3. Sir Robert Cecil was the first Earl of Salisbury, son of a principal advisor to Elizabeth I. Robert Cecil became Elizabeth's secretary of state in 1589 and was a key figure in the administration of James I, in which he eventually held the office of Lord Treasurer.

4. Raleigh refers to himself as a "factor," an agent who is commissioned to perform a certain function. Factors who exhausted the resources at their disposal had to account for their expenditures.

5. Raleigh presumes that Howard and Cecil will be able to answer his detractors (who speak from malice) with knowledge gained from this account of his travels to Guiana.

6. Trunk.

7. Raleigh admits that he has made errors and that the successes he had earlier in his career, which might have compensated for these errors, can no longer serve this purpose.

8. I.e., of what was left of my resources, I have effectually wasted everything.

9. Trials.

1. I.e., it is apparent that I made no other boast of going to sea than to state that I intended to do it and that I was not hidden in Cornwall or elsewhere. Here Raleigh addresses the rumor that he had never gone to Guiana but rather had waited for his men to return from there, then claimed that his expedition was a success.

2. Interpretation.

that there were wanting to the rest, many miseries.[3] But if both the times past, the present, and what may be in the future do all by one grain of gall continue in an eternal distaste, I do not then know whether I should bewail myself either for my too much travel and expense, or condemn myself for doing less than that which can deserve nothing.[4] From myself I have deserved no thanks, for I am returned a beggar, and withered, but that I might have bettered my poor estate it shall appear by the following discourse, if I had not only respected Her Majesty's future honor and riches. It became not the former fortune in which I once lived, to go journeys of picorie,[5] and it had sorted ill with the offices of honor which by Her Majesty's grace I hold this day in England to run from Cape to Cape and from place to place for the pillage of ordinary prizes. Many years since, I had knowledge by relation of that mighty, rich and beautiful Empire of Guiana and of that great and golden city which the Spaniards call El Dorado, and the naturals,[6] Manoa, which city was conquered, re-edified, and enlarged by a younger son of Guainacapa, Emperor of Peru, at such time as Francisco Pizarro[7] and others conquered the said empire from his two elder brethren, Guascar and Atabalipa, both then contending for the same, the one being favored by the Oreiones of Cuzco, the other by the people of Caximalca. I sent my servant Jacob Whiddon the year before to get knowledge of the passages, and I had some light from Captain Parker, sometime my servant and now attending on your Lordship, that such a place there was to the southward of the great bay of Charuas, or Guanipa, but I found that it was six hundred miles farther off than they supposed, and many other impediments to them unknown and unheard. After I had displanted[8] Don Antonio de Berreo, who was upon the same enterprise, leaving my ships at Trinidad, at the port called Curiapan, I wandered four hundred miles into the said country by land and river, the particulars I will leave to the following discourse.[9] The country hath more quantity of gold by manifold than the best parts of the Indies or Peru; all the most of the kings of the borders are already become Her Majesty's vassals and seem to desire nothing more than Her Majesty's protection and the return of the English nation.

To the Reader

Because there have been diverse opinions conceived of the gold ore brought from Guiana, and for that an alderman of London and an officer of Her Majesty's Mint hath given out that the same is of no price, I have thought good by the addition of these lines to give answer as well to the said malicious slander, as to other objections. It is true that while we abode at the Island of Trinidad, I was informed by an Indian that not far from the port where we were anchored there were found certain mineral

---

3. I.e., if I could get some credit for having taken this painful pilgrimage, I would wish that my miseries had been more severe.

4. I.e., if everything continues to go badly, I do not know whether I should regret my travel or condemn myself for doing less than what can deserve nothing (what is not enough to deserve anything).

5. Suitable for the *picaro*, or rogue in Spanish.

6. Indigenous people.

7. Pizarro (1475–1541) conquered Peru by capturing the Incan king Atahualpa, whom Raleigh refers to as Atabalipa. Atahualpa was the son of Guainacapa and the brother of Guascar, whom he killed to get the throne. This passage suggests that Guainacapa had three sons;

Raleigh later states that he had only two sons. Pizarro captured Cuzco, the principal city of the Incas, in 1533. The Oreiones were the native people of Cuzco; Caximalca or Casimarca was another large city in Peru.

8. Dislodged.

9. Here Raleigh claims that a Captain Parker told him that El Dorado was south of the bay of Guanipa (which opens onto the Gulf of Paria and has no connection with the Orinoco), but he discovered that it was 600 miles in the interior of the country and away from the shore. Don Antonio de Berreo was the Spanish Governor of Trinidad and Guiana; Trinidad is an island just off the Venezuelan coast. Presumably, Raleigh marched from that coast 400 miles inland.

stones which they esteemed to be gold and were thereunto persuaded the rather for that they had seen both English and French men gather and embark some quantities thereof. Upon this likelihood I sent forty men and gave order that each one should bring a stone of that mine to make trial of the goodness, which being performed, I assured them at their return that the same was marcasite[1] and of no riches or value. Notwithstanding, diverse,[2] trusting more to their own sense than to my opinion, kept of the said marcasite and have tried thereof, since my return, in diverse places. In Guiana itself I never saw marcasite, but all the rocks, mountains, all stones in the plains, in woods, and by the rivers' sides are in effect thereof shining, and appear marvelous rich, which being tried[3] to be no marcasite, are the true signs of rich minerals, but[4] are no other than *el madre del oro* (as the Spaniards term them), which is the mother of gold, or as it is said by others, the scum of gold. Of diverse sorts of these, many of my company brought also into England, every one taking the fairest for the best, which is not general.[5] For mine own part, I did not countermand any man's desire or opinion, and I could have afforded them little if I should have denied them the pleasing of their own fancies therein. But I was resolved that gold must be found either in grains separate from the stone (as it is in most of all the rivers in Guiana) or else in a kind of hard stone, which we call the white spar, of which I saw diverse hills and in sundry places but had neither time, nor men, nor instruments fit to labor. Near unto one of the rivers I found of the said white spar or flint a very great ledge or bank which I endeavored to break by all means I could, because there appeared on the outside some small grains of gold, but finding no means to work the same upon the upper part, seeking the sides and circuit of the said rock, I found a cleft in the same from whence with daggers and with the head of an ax we got out some small quantity thereof, of which kind of white stone (wherein gold is engendered) we saw diverse hills and rocks in every part of Guiana wherein we traveled. Of this there hath been made many trials, and in London it was first assayed by Master Westwood, a refiner dwelling in Wood Street, and it was held after the rate of 12,000 or 13,000 pounds a ton. Another sort was afterward tried by Master Bulmar and Master Dimoke, assay master, and it held after the rate of 23,000 pounds a ton. There was some of it again tried by Master Palmer, comptroller of the mint, and Master Dimoke in Goldsmith's Hall, and it held after 26,900 pounds a ton. There was also at the same time and by the same persons a trial made of the dust of the said mine, which held eight pounds, six ounces weight of gold in the hundred. There was likewise at the same time a trial made of an image of copper made in Guiana which held a third part gold, besides diverse trials made in the country and by others in London.[6] But because there came of ill with the good, and belike the said alderman was not presented with the best, it hath pleased him therefore to scandal[7] all the rest, and to deface[8] the enterprises as much as in him lieth. It hath also been concluded by diverse that if there had been any such ore in Guiana and the same discovered, that I would have brought home a greater quantity thereof. First, I was not bound to satisfy any man of the quantity, but such only as adventured, if any store had been returned

---

1. Pyrite.
2. Some men.
3. Discovered.
4. And.
5. I.e., the fairest mineral is judged to be best, provided that it is also rare or "not general."
6. Raleigh reports that the ore he brought back from

Guiana was tested by several goldsmiths, who were experts at refining the metal, and that it was found to be substantially gold. Throughout his address to the reader, Raleigh argues that he actually discovered gold and that this gold will allow England to rival Spain.
7. Disparage.
8. Criticize.

thereof. But it is very true that had all their mountains been of massy gold, it was impossible for us to have made any longer stay to have wrought the same, and whosoever hath seen with what strength of stone the best gold is environed,[9] he will not think it easy to be had out in heaps and especially by us who had neither men, instruments, nor time (as it is said before) to perform the same. There were, on this discovery, no less than one hundred persons, who can all witness that when we passed any branch of the river to view the land within, and stayed from our boats but six hours, we were driven to wade to the eyes at our return, and if we attempted the same the day following, it was impossible either to ford it or to swim it,[1] both by reason of the swiftness and also for that the borders were so pestered[2] with fast[3] woods as neither boat nor man could find place either to land or to embark. For in June, July, August, and September, it is impossible to navigate any of those rivers, for such is the fury of the current and there are so many trees and woods overflowed as if any boat but touch upon any tree or stake, it is impossible to save any one person therein, and ere we departed the land, it ran with that swiftness as[4] we drove down most commonly against the wind little less than one hundred miles a day. Besides, our vessels were no other than wherries,[5] one little barge, a small cockboat,[6] and a bad galiota,[7] which we framed in haste for that purpose at Trinidad, and those little boats had nine or ten men apiece, with all their victuals and arms. It is further true that we were about four hundred miles from our ships and had been a month from them, which also we left weakly manned in an open road[8] and had promised our return in fifteen days. Others have devised that the same ore was had from Barbary,[9] and that we carried it with us into Guiana. Surely the singularity of that device I do not well comprehend; for my own part, I am not so much in love with these long voyages as to devise, thereby to cozen myself, to lie hard, to fare worse, to be subjected to perils, to diseases, to ill savors, to be parched and withered, and withal to sustain the care and labor of such an enterprise, except the same had more comfort than the fetching of marcasite in Guiana or buying of gold ore in Barbary.[1] But I hope the better sort will judge me by themselves, and that the way of deceit is not the way of honor or good opinion. I have herein consumed much time and many crowns, and I had no other respect or desire than to serve Her Majesty and my country thereby. If the Spanish nation had been of like belief to these detractors, we should little have feared or doubted their attempts wherewith we now are daily threatened.[2] But if we now consider of the actions both of Charles the Fifth,[3] who had the maidenhead of Peru and the abundant treasures of Atabalipa, together with the affairs of the Spanish king now living,[4] what territories he hath purchased, what he hath added to the acts of predecessors, how many kingdoms he hath endangered, how many armies, garrisons, and navies he hath and doth maintain, the great losses which he hath repaired, as in 1588, above one hundred sail of great ships with their artillery, and that no year is less unfortunate but

---

9. Embedded.
1. The river Orinoco, which Raleigh describes as tidal.
2. Crowded.
3. Thick.
4. That.
5. Small barges.
6. Rowboat.
7. A small sailing ship, also equipped with oars.
8. An exposed anchorage, outside the protection of a harbor.
9. The regions along the coast of North Africa.
1. I.e., I would not have undergone such trials to bring

marcasite from Guiana or to buy gold in Barbary.
2. Raleigh uses the Spaniards' interest in American gold as proof that his detractors are wrong.
3. Charles V (1500–1558) was the Holy Roman Emperor under whose rule the Spanish empire in the Americas was enormously enlarged.
4. Philip II (1527–1598). Raleigh alludes to the expenditures of that king—including the repair of his Armada, which was defeated by the English fleet in 1588—none of which stood in the way of his harrassing English interests and property. Spanish affluence and influence, Raleigh claims, are sustained by "Indian gold."

that many vessels, treasures, and people are devoured, and yet notwithstanding he beginneth again like a storm to threaten shipwreck to us all, we shall find that these abilities rise not from the trades of sacks[5] and Seville oranges, nor from aught else that either Spain, Portugal, or any of his other provinces produce. It is his Indian gold that endangereth and disturbeth all the nations of Europe, it purchaseth intelligence, creepeth into councils, and setteth bound loyalty at liberty in the greatest monarchies of Europe. If the Spanish king can keep us from foreign enterprises and from the empeachment of his trades, either by offer of invasions or by besieging us in Britain, Ireland, or elsewhere, he hath then brought the work of our peril in great forwardness.[6] Those princes which abound in treasure have great advantages over the rest, if they once constrain them[7] to a defensive war, where they are driven once a year or oftener to cast lots for their own garments, and from such shall all trades and intercourse be taken away, to the general loss and impoverishment of the kingdom and commonweal so reduced. Besides, when men are constrained to fight, it hath not the same hope as when they are pressed and encouraged by the desire of spoil and riches. Further, it is to be doubted how those that in time of victory seem to affect[8] their neighbor nations will remain after the first view of misfortunes or ill success. To trust also to the doubtfulness of a battle is but a fearful and uncertain adventure, seeing therein fortune is as likely to prevail as virtue. It shall not be necessary to allege all that might be said, and therefore I will thus conclude that whatsoever kingdom shall be enforced to defend itself may be compared to a body dangerously diseased, which for a season may be preserved with vulgar[9] medicines, but in a short time and by little and little, the same must needs fall to the ground and be dissolved. I have therefore labored all my life, both according to my small power and persuasion, to advance all those attempts that might either promise return of profit for ourselves or at least be a let[1] and empeachment to the quiet course and plentiful trades of the Spanish nation, who[2] in my weak judgment by such a war were as easily endangered and brought from his powerfulness as any prince in Europe, if it be considered from how many kingdoms and nations his revenues are gathered, and those so weak in their own beings and so far severed from mutual succour. But because such a preparation and resolution are not to be hoped for in haste, and that the time which our enemies embrace cannot be had again to advantage, I will hope that these provinces and that empire now by me discovered shall suffice to enable Her Majesty and the whole kingdom with no less quantities of treasure than the King of Spain hath in all the Indies, east and west, which he possesseth; which if the same be considered and followed ere the Spaniards enforce the same, and if Her Majesty will undertake it, I will be contented to lose Her Highness's favor and good opinion forever, and my life withal, if the same be not found rather to exceed than to equal whatsoever is in this discourse promised or declared. I will now refer the reader to the following discourse with the hope that the perilous and chargeable labors and endeavors of such as thereby seek the profit and honor of Her Majesty and the English nation shall by men of quality and virtue receive such construction and good acceptance as themselves would look to be rewarded withal in the like.

---

5. Wines.
6. I.e., he has advanced the work of our destruction.
7. I.e., the rest.
8. Support.

9. Ordinary.
1. Hindrance.
2. I.e., Philip II.

[THE AMAZONS]

I made inquiry amongst the most ancient and best traveled of the Orenoqueponi, and I had knowledge of all the rivers between Orenoque and [the river of the] Amazons, and was very desirous to understand the truth of those warlike women, because of some it is believed, of others not.[3] And though I digress from my purpose, yet I will set down what hath been delivered me for truth of those women, and I spake with a Casique or Lord of people that told me he had been in the river, and beyond it also. The nations of these women are on the south side of the river in the provinces of Topago, and their chiefest strengths and retreats are in the Islands situated on the south side of the entrance, some 60 leagues within the mouth of the said river. The memories of the like women are very ancient as well in Africa as in Asia. In Africa those that had Medusa[4] for Queen: others in Scithia near the rivers of Tanais and Thermadon: we find also that Lampedo and Marthesia[5] were Queens of the Amazons: in many histories they are verified to have been, and in diverse ages and provinces. But they which are not far from Guiana do accompany with men but once a year, and for the time of one month, which I gather by their relation to be in April. At that time all the kings of the borders assemble, and the queens of the Amazons, and after the queens have chosen, the rest cast lots for their Valentines. This one month, they feast, dance, and drink of their wines in abundance, and the moon being done, they all depart to their own provinces. If they conceive, and be delivered of a son, they return him to the father, if of a daughter they nourish it, and retain it, and as many as have daughters send unto the begetters a present, all being desirous to increase their own sex and kind, but that they cut off the right dug of the breast I do not find to be true. It was further told me, that if in the wars they took any prisoners that they used to accompany with those also at what time soever, but in the end for certain they put them to death: for they are said to be very cruel and bloodthirsty, especially to such as offer to invade their territories.

[THE ORINOCO]

The great river of Orenoque or Baraquan hath nine branches which fall out on the north side of his own main mouth. On the south side it hath seven other fallings into the sea, so it disemboqueth[6] by sixteen arms in all, between islands and broken ground, but the islands are very great, many of them as big as the Isle of Wight[7] and bigger, and many less. From the first branch on the north to the last of the south it is at least one hundred leagues, so as the river's mouth is no less than three hundred miles wide at his entrance into the sea, which I take to be far bigger than that of [the] Amazons. All those that inhabit in the mouth of this river upon the several north branches are these Tivitivas,[8] of which there are two chief lords which have continual wars one with the other. The islands which lie on the right hand are called Pallamos, and the land on the left, Hororotomaka, and the river by which John Douglas returned within the land from Amana to Capuri, they call Macuri.

---

3. Raleigh takes his account of the Amazons from a native of Guiana. He associates this race of women, whose presence has never been verified, with a comparable people described in Greek mythology who are also warlike and consort with men only to conceive children.
4. A mythical monstrous woman, one of the Gorgons, who turned to stone whoever looked at her.

5. The legendary queen of the Amazons who fought in the Trojan war.
6. Discharges.
7. Island off the southern coast of England.
8. The Waraus, an indigenous people who live on the delta of the Orinoco and adjoining coasts. Spanish historians refer to them as the Guaraunos or Guaraunu.

These Tivitivas are a very goodly people and very valiant, and have the most manly speech and most deliberate that ever I heard of, what nation so ever. In the summer they have houses on the ground as in other places, where they build very artificial towns and villages, as it is written in the Spanish story of the West Indies, that those people do in the low lands near the gulf of Uraba. For between May and September, the river of Orenoque riseth thirty foot upright, and then those islands overflow twenty foot high above the level of the ground, saving some few raised grounds in the middle of them, and for this cause they are enforced to live in this manner. They never eat of anything that is set or sown, and as at home they use neither planting nor other manurance, so when they come abroad they refuse to feed of aught but of that which nature without labor bringeth forth.[9] They use the tops of *palmitos* [palm trees] for bread and kill deer, fish, and porks for the rest of their sustenance; they also have many sorts of fruits that grow in the woods and a great variety of birds and fowl.

And if to speak of them were not tedious and vulgar, surely we saw in those passages of very rare colors and forms not elsewhere to be found, for as much as I have either seen or read. Of these people, those that dwell upon the branches of the Orenoque called Capuri and Macureo are for the most part carpenters of *canoas* [canoes], for they make the most and fairest houses and sell them into Guiana for gold, and into Trinidad for tobacco, in the excessive taking whereof they exceed all nations, and notwithstanding the moistness of the air in which they live, the hardness of their diet, and the great labors they suffer to hunt, fish, and fowl for their living, in all my life either in the Indies or in Europe did I never behold a more goodly or better-favored people, or a more manly. They were wont to make war upon all nations and especially on the Cannibals, so as none durst without a good strength trade by those rivers; but of late they are at peace with their neighbors, all holding the Spaniards for a common enemy.[1] When their commanders die, they use great lamentation, and when they think the flesh of their bodies is putrified and fallen from the bones, then they take up the carcass again and hang it in the Casique's house that died, and deck his skull with feathers of all colors and hang all his gold plates about the bones of his arms, thighs, and legs. Those nations which are called Arwacas,[2] which dwell on the south of Orenoque (of which place and nation our Indian pilot was), are dispersed in many other places and do use to beat the bones of their lords into powder, and their wives and friends drink it all in their several sorts of drinks.

[THE KING OF AROMAIA]

The next day we arrived at the port of Morequito,[3] and anchored there, sending away one of our pilots to seek the king of Aromaia, uncle to Morequito, slain by Berreo as

9. As people that do not farm, the Tivitivas would have been categorized by many Europeans as having no conception of property and therefore incapable of being dispossessed.

1. Here and throughout the narrative, Raleigh portrays the people of the region as desiring the protection of the English against the Spanish, whose mistreatment of the natives of the Americas was well publicized. Raleigh could claim that by making these natives vassals of the English monarch, England could acquire an empire to rival Spain's.

2. Known today as Arawaks, these people were neighbors

of the Tivitivas.

3. A king whose territory bordered Guiana. He was captured and executed by the Spanish Governor of Trinidad, Antonio de Berreo, for having killed a Spanish garrison. His uncle, here described as the king of Aromaia and later named Topiawari, succeeded Morequito. His people are later identified as the Orenoqueponi, because they live on the shores of the Orinoco. The king's dignified report testifies to both his status as royalty and the culture of the Orenoqueponi, who are conscious of their history as one among many peoples of the territory that is now northern Venezuela.

aforesaid. The next day following, before noon he came to us on foot from his house, which was fourteen English miles (himself being 110 years old), and returned on foot the same day, and with him many of the borderers,[4] with many women and children that came to wonder at our nation and to bring us down victual, which they did in great plenty, as venison, pork, hens, chickens, fowl, fish, with diverse sorts of excellent fruits and roots, and great abundance of *pinas* [pineapples], the princess of fruits that grow under the sun, especially those of Guiana. They brought us also store of bread, and of their wine, and a sort of *paraquitos* [parakeets], no bigger than wrens, and of all other sorts both small and great. One of them gave me a beast called by the Spaniards *armadilla* [armadillo] which they call *cassacam,* which seemeth to be all barred over with small plates somewhat like to a *renocero* [rhinoceros], with a white horn growing in his hinder parts as big as a great hunting horn, which they use to wind[5] instead of a trumpet. Monadarus writeth that a little of the powder of that horn put into the ear cureth deafness.

After this old king had rested a while in a little tent that I caused to be set up, I began by my interpretor to discourse with him of the death of Morequito his predecessor and afterward of the Spaniards, and ere I went any farther I made him know the cause of my coming thither, whose servant I was, and that the Queen's pleasure was I should undertake the voyage for their defense and to deliver them from the tyranny of the Spaniards, dilating[6] at large (as I had done before to those of Trinidad) Her Majesty's greatness, her justice, her charity to all oppressed nations, with as many of the rest of her beauties and virtues as either I could express or they conceive, all which being with great admiration attentively heard and marvellously admired, I began to sound the old man as touching Guiana and the state thereof, what sort of commonwealth it was, how governed, of what strength and policy, how far it extended, and what nations were friends or enemies adjoining, and finally of the distance and the way to enter the same; he told me that himself and his people, with all those down the river towards the sea, as far as Emeria, the province of Carapana, were of Guiana, but that they called themselves Orenoqueponi, because they bordered the great river of Orenoque, and that all the nations between the river and those mountains in sight called Wacarima were of the same cast and appellation, and that on the other side of the mountains of Wacarima there was a large plain (which after I discovered in my return) called the valley of Amariocapana, in all that valley the people were also of the ancient Guianans. I asked what nations those were which inhabited on the further side of those mountains, beyond the valley of Amariocapana, he answered with a great sigh (as a man which had inward feeling of the loss of his country and liberty, especially for that his eldest son was slain in a battle on that side of the mountains, whom he most entirely loved) that he remembered in his father's lifetime, when he was very old and himself a young man, that there came down into that large valley of Guiana, a nation from so far off as the sun slept (for such were his own words) with so great a multitude as they could not be numbered or resisted, and that they wore large coats and hats of crimson color, which color he expressed by showing a piece of red wood wherewith my tent was supported, and that they were called Oreiones and Epuremei,[7] those that had slain and rooted out so

---

4. People living on the borders of Aromaia.
5. Blow.
6. Describing.
7. The King of Aromaia describes a conquest of the

Orenoqueponi by the Oreiones, a "nation from so far off as the sun slept," i.e., Peru. His son, he reports, was killed in a battle with the Oreiones.

many of the ancient people as there were leaves in the wood upon all the trees, and had now made themselves lords of all, even to that mountain foot called Curaa, saving only of two nations, the one called Iwarawaqueri, and the other Cassipagotos, and that in the last battle fought between the Epuremei and the Iwarawaqueri, his eldest son was chosen to carry to the aide of the Iwarawaqueri a great troop of the Orenoqueponi and was there slain with all his people and friends, and that he now had remaining but one son; and further told me that those Epuremei had built a great town called Macureguarai at the said mountain foot, at the beginning of the great plains of Guiana, which have no end, and that their houses have many rooms, one over the other, and that therein the great king of the Oreiones and Epuremei kept three thousand men to defend the borders against them and withal daily to invade and slay them; but that of late years, since the Christians offered to invade his territories and those frontiers, they were all at peace and traded one with another, saving only the Iwarawaqueri and those other nations upon the head of the river Caroli called Cassipagotos, which we afterwards discovered, each one holding the Spaniard for a common enemy.

After he had answered thus far, he desired leave to depart, saying that he had far to go, that he was old, and weak, and was every day called for by death, which was also his own phrase. I desired him to rest with us that night, but I could not entreat him. But he told me that at my return from the country above he would again come to us and in the mean time provide for us the best he could of all that his country yielded. The same night he returned to Orocotona, his own town, so as he went that day 28 miles, the weather being very hot, the country being situated between four and five degrees of the equator. This Topiawari is held for the proudest and wisest of all the Orenoqueponi, and so he behaved himself towards me in all his answers at my return, as I marvelled to find a man of that gravity and judgment and of so good discourse that had no help of learning or breed.

[THE NEW WORLD OF GUIANA]

To conclude, Guiana is a country that hath yet her maidenhead, never sacked, turned, nor wrought; the face of the earth hath not been torn, nor the virtue and salt of the soil spent by manurance, the graves have not been opened for gold, the mines not broken with sledges, nor their images pulled down out of their temples. It hath never been entered by any army of strength and never conquered or possessed by any Christian prince. It is besides so defensible that if two forts be built in one of the provinces which I have seen, the flood setteth in so near the bank where the channel also lieth that no ship can pass but within a pike's length of the artillery, first of the one and afterwards of the other. Which two forts will be a sufficient guard both to the empire of *Inga* [Inca] and to an hundred other several kingdoms lying within the said river, even to the city of Quito in Peru.

There is therefore a great difference between the easiness of the conquest of Guiana and the defense of it being conquered, and the West or East Indies. Guiana hath but one entrance by the sea (if it have that) for any vessels of burden, so as whosoever shall first possess it, it shall be found inaccessible for any enemy except he come in wherries, barges, or *canoas,* or else in flat-bottomed boats; and if he do offer to enter it in that manner, the woods are so thick two hundred miles together upon the rivers of such entrance as a mouse cannot sit in a boat unhit from the bank. By land it is more impossible to approach, for it hath the strongest situation of any region under the sun, and is so environed with impassable mountains on every side as it is impossible to victual any company in the passage, which hath been well-proved by the Spanish nation, who, since the conquest of Peru have never left five years free from attempting this empire or discovering some way into it, and yet of twenty-three several gentlemen, knights, and noblemen, there was never any that knew which way to lead an army by land or to conduct ships by sea anything near the said country. Oreliano, of which the river of the Amazons taketh name, was the first, and Don Anthonio de Berreo (whom we displanted), the last; and I doubt much whether he himself or any of his yet know the best way into the said empire. It can therefore hardly be regained if any strength be formerly set down but in one or two places, and but two or three crumsters or galleys built and furnished upon the river within. The West Indies hath many ports, watering places, and landings, and nearer than three hundred miles to Guiana no man can harbor a ship, except he know one only place which is not learned in haste, and which I will undertake there is not any one of my companies that knoweth, whosoever hearkened after it.

Besides by keeping one good fort or building one town of strength, the whole empire is guarded, and whatsoever companies shall be afterwards planted within the land, although in twenty several provinces, those shall be able all to reunite themselves upon any occasion either by the way of one river or be able to march by land without either wood, bog, or mountain; whereas in the West Indies there are few towns or provinces that can succour or relieve one the other, either by land or sea. By land the countries are either desert, mountainous, or strong enemies. By sea, if any man invade to the eastward, those to the west cannot in many months turn against the breeze and east wind, besides the Spaniards are therein so dispersed as they are nowhere strong but in *Nueva Hispania* [New Spain] only. The sharp mountains, the thorns, the poisoned prickles, the sandy and deep ways in the valleys, the smothering heat and air, and want of water in other places are their only and best defense, which (because those nations that invade them are not victualled or provided to stay, neither have any place to friend adjoining) do serve them instead of good arms and great multitudes.

The West Indies were first offered Her Majesty's grandfather by Columbus,[8] a stranger in whom there might be doubt of deceit, and besides it was then thought incredible that there were such and so many lands and regions never written of before. This empire is made known to Her Majesty by her own vassal, and by him that oweth to her more duty than an ordinary subject, so that it shall ill sort with the many graces and benefits which I have received to abuse Her Highness either with fables or imaginations. The country is already discovered,[9] many nations won to Her Majesty's love and obedience, and those Spaniards which have latest and longest

8. The brother of Christopher Columbus, Bartholomew Columbus, who invited Henry VII, King of England and grandfather of Elizabeth I, to accept his brother's services in his effort to find a continent west of England. Henry is reported to have accepted this offer, but not before Christopher Columbus had contracted his services to Queen Isabella of Spain. Therefore the West Indies were not ever offered to Henry VII; they were and remained Spanish through the 19th century.

9. The continent of which Guiana is a part.

labored about the conquest, beaten out, discouraged and disgraced, which among these nations were thought invincible. Her Majesty may in this enterprise employ all those soldiers and gentlemen that are younger brethren, and all captains and chieftains that want employment, and the charge will be only the first setting out in victualling and arming them, for after the first or second year I doubt not but to see in London a contratation house of more receipt for Guiana than there is now in Seville for the West Indies.[1]

And I am resolved that if there were but a small army afoot in Guiana, marching towards Manoa, the chief city of *Inga*, he would yield Her Majesty by composition so many hundred thousand pounds yearly as should both defend all enemies abroad and defray all expenses at home and that he would besides pay a garrison of three or four thousand soldiers very royally to defend him against other nations. For he cannot but know how his predecessors, yea, how his own great uncles Guascar and Atibalipa, sons to Guanacapa, Emperor of Peru, were (while they contended for the empire) beaten out by the Spaniards and that both of late years and ever since the said conquest, the Spaniards have sought the passages and entry of his country; and of their cruelties used to the borderers he cannot be ignorant. In which respects no doubt but he will be brought to tribute with great gladness, if not, he hath neither shot nor iron weapon in all his empire and therefore may be easily conquered.

And I further remember that Berreo confessed to me and others (which I protest before the majesty of God to be true) that there was found among the prophecies of Peru (at such time as the empire was reduced to Spanish obedience) in their chiefest temples, among diverse others, which foreshadowed the loss of the said empire, that from *Inglatierra* [England] those *Ingas* should be again in time to come restored and delivered from the servitude of the said conquerors. And I hope, as we with these few hands have displanted the first garrison and driven them out of the said country, so Her Majesty will give order for the rest and either defend it and hold it as tributary, or conquer and keep it as Empress of the same. For whatsoever Prince shall possess it shall be greatest, and if the king of Spain enjoy it, he will become unresistable. Her Majesty hereby shall confirm and strengthen the opinions of all nations as touching her great and princely actions. And where the south border of Guiana reacheth to the dominion and empire of the Amazons, those women shall hereby hear the name of a virgin which is not only able to defend her own territories and her neighbors, but also to invade and conquer so great empires so far removed.[2]

To speak more at this time I fear would be but troublesome. I trust in God, this being true will suffice, and that he which is King of all Kings and Lord of all Lords will put it into her heart which is Lady of Ladies to possess it, if not, I will judge those men worthy to be kings thereof that by her grace and leave will undertake of it themselves.

---

1. Raleigh states that there will be a trading house or mercantile exchange for investors in Guiana that will exceed in its volume of business the comparable institution for the West Indian trade in Seville.

2. This reference to the Amazons allows Raleigh to pay tribute to Elizabeth I, who represented herself as a powerful virgin queen.

—◆—

William Shakespeare
1564–1616

Attributed to John Taylor, *Portrait of William Shakespeare*, c. 1610.

English colonists venturing to the New World carried with them an English Bible; if they owned a single secular book, it was probably the works of William Shakespeare. A humanist scripture of sorts, his works have never hardened into doctrine; rather, they have lent themselves to a myriad range of interpretations, each shaped by particular interests, tastes, and expectations. Ben Jonson's line—"He was not of an age, but for all time!"—describes the appeal Shakespeare has had for speakers of English and the many other languages into which his works have been translated.

Shakespeare was born in the provincial town of Stratford-on-Avon, a three-day journey from London by horse or carriage. His father, John Shakespeare, was a glover and local justice of the peace; his mother, Mary Arden, came from a family that owned considerable land in the county. He probably went to a local grammar school where he learned Latin and read histories of the ancient world. Jonson's disparaging comment, that Shakespeare knew "small Latin and less Greek," must not be taken too seriously. Shakespeare (unlike Jonson) was not classically inclined, but his mature works reveal a mind that was extraordinarily well informed and acutely aware of rhetorical techniques and logical argument. At eighteen Shakespeare married Anne Hathaway, who was twenty-six; in the next three years they had a daughter, Susanna, and then twins, Hamnet and Judith. Six years later, perhaps after periods of teaching school in Stratford, he went to London, eventually (in 1594) to join one of the great theatrical companies of the day, the Chamberlain's Men. It was with this company that he began his career as actor, manager, and playwright. In 1599 the troupe began to put on plays at the Globe, an outdoor theater in Southwark, not far from the other principal theaters of the day—the Rose, the Bear Garden, and the Swan—and across the river from the city of London itself. Because these theaters were outside city limits, in a district known as "the liberties," they were free from the control of authorities responsible for civic order; in effect, the theater provided a place in which all kinds of ideas and ways of life, whether conventional or not, could be represented, examined, and criticized. When James I acceded to the throne in 1603, Shakespeare's company became the King's Men and played also at court and at Blackfriars, an indoor theater in London. Some critics think that the change in venue necessitated a degree of allusiveness and innuendo that was not evident in earlier productions.

During the years Shakespeare was writing for the theater, the populations of Europe were periodically devastated by the plague, and city authorities were obliged to close places of public gathering, including theaters. Shakespeare provided plays for seasons in which the theaters in London were open, composing them at lightning speed and helping to stage productions on very short notice. The plays that we now accept as Shakespeare's fall roughly into several general categories: first, the histories, largely based on the chronicles of the Tudor historian Raphael Holinshed, and the Roman plays, inspired by Plutarch's *Lives of the Ancient Romans*, written in Greek and translated by Sir Thomas North; second, the comedies, often set in the romantic world of the English countryside or an Italian town; third, the tragedies, some of which explore the dark legends of the past; and fourth, a group in the mixed genre of tragicomedy but also called, after critics in the nineteenth century, the romances. A fifth, somewhat anomalous group—*All's Well That Ends Well*, *Measure for Measure*, and *Troilus and Cressida*—falls between comedy and satire; these plays are usually termed "problem comedies."

The early phase of Shakespeare's career, the decade beginning in the late 1580s, saw the first cycle of his English histories. In four plays (known as the first tetralogy) this cycle depicted events in the reigns of Henry VI and Richard III and concluded by dramatizing the accession of the first Tudor monarch, Henry VII. Fascinated by the fate of peoples governed by feeble or oppressive rulers, Shakespeare expressed his loathing of tyranny by showing how the misgovernment of a weak king can lead to despotic rule. The cycle ends with the death of the tyrant, Richard III, and the accession of the Duke of Richmond, later Henry VII (Elizabeth's grandfather)—an action that celebrates the founder of the Tudor dynasty and the providence that had selected this family to bring peace to England. A later play, *King John*, concerns an earlier monarch whose claim to the throne is suspect; here divine right, having validated the succession of the Tudor monarchy in the first tetralogy, is made doubtful by a monarch's own viciousness. The play implies a question that Shakespeare continues to ask of history for the rest of his career: in what sense may divine right be understood as a principle of monarchic rule? History, as Shakespeare will go on to represent it, no longer clearly demonstrates the triumph of justice but rather shows the interrelatedness of good and evil motives that end in morally ambiguous action. The first of the Roman plays, *The Tragedy of Titus Andronicus*, which tells of the Roman general's revenge for the rape of his daughter Lavinia, and the early comedies, *The Taming of the Shrew*, *The Comedy of Errors*, *Two Gentlemen of Verona*, and *Love's Labor's Lost*, which depict the effects of mistaken identity and misunderstood speech, illustrate other themes that Shakespeare will continue to represent: the terrible consequences of the search for revenge and the unfortunate, as well as salutary, self-deceptions of love.

The second phase, culminating in productions around 1600, is marked by more and subtler comedy: *A Midsummer Night's Dream*, *The Merchant of Venice*, *The Merry Wives of Windsor*, *Much Ado About Nothing*, *As You Like It*, and *Twelfth Night*. These plays insert into plots focusing primarily on the courtship of young couples a dramatic commentary on darker kinds of human desire: longing for possessions; a wish to control others, particularly children; and a self-love so intense that it leads to fantasy and delusion. A romantic tragedy of this period, *Romeo and Juliet*, shows how the gross unreason sustaining a family feud and a mysteriously malevolent fate combine to destroy the future of lovers. A second cycle of four English histories, beginning with the deposition of Richard II and ending in the triumphs of Henry V and the birth of Henry VI, reveals how Shakespeare complicates the genre. An ostensible motive for the second tetralogy was the celebration of an English monarchy that had been preserved through the ages by God's will. Yet the actions of even the least controversial of its kings are questionable: Henry V's conquest of France is driven by greed as much as by his claim to the French throne, which is represented as dubious even in the playtext. A second Roman play, *The Tragedy of Julius Caesar*, takes up the question of tyranny in relation to the liberty inherent in a republic; the play seems most tragic when its action suggests that the Roman people do not recognize the sacrifices that are necessary to preserve such freedom and even regard freedom itself as negligible. As a whole, these plays demonstrate the characteristics of Shakespeare's mature style. Certain recurring images unify the plays thematically and, more important, link them to contemporary habits of speech as well as to the intellectual discourse of the period. Visual images—the I and the eye of the lover—often clarify the language of love, and figures denoting the well-being of different kinds of "corporation," including the human body, the family, and the body politic, signal the comprehensive order that was supposed to govern relations among all the elements of creation.

Incorporating many of the themes in the "problem comedies," the tragedies of the same period preoccupied Shakespeare for the seven years following the accession of James I: *Hamlet*, *Othello*, *King Lear*, *Macbeth*, *Antony and Cleopatra*, and *Coriolanus*, together with *Timon of Athens*, a play that was apparently written in collaboration with Thomas Middleton. *All's Well That Ends Well* and *Measure for Measure* illustrate societies that contain rather than reject sordid or unregenerate characters, both noble and common, and thus provide opportunities for comic endings to situations that might otherwise have ended in tragedy. And making much of the need for order but exemplifying the deep disorder of the military societies of Greece and Troy, the characters in *Troilus and Cressida* reveal the extent to which Shakespeare could imagine language as ironic and the human spirit as utterly possessed by a cynical need to turn every occasion to its own advantage. These plays serve to introduce tragedies of unprecedented scope.

Featuring heroes who overreach the limits of their place in life and so fail to fulfill their obligations to themselves and their dependents, Shakespeare's later tragedies embrace a wider range of human experience than can be explained by traditional conceptions of sin and fate. Profoundly complex in their treatment of motivation and the operations of the will, the tragedies entertain the idea of a beneficent deity who both permits terrible suffering and infuses, to use Hamlet's words, a "special providence in the fall of a sparrow." They reveal the blinding egotism that causes fatal misperceptions of character, motive, and action; their heroes are at once terribly in error and also strangely sympathetic. The human capacity for evil is perhaps most fully realized in the characters of women: the bestial daughters of King Lear, Goneril and Regan; the diabolical Lady Macbeth; the shamelessly duplicitous Cleopatra. Yet even they are not entirely unsympathetic; in many ways their behavior responds to the challenges that other, essentially more authoritative characters represent. The romances—*Pericles, Cymbeline, The Winter's Tale*, and *The Tempest*—round out the final phase of Shakespeare's dramatic career, representing (like the comedies) the restoration of family harmony and (like the histories) the return of good government. The deeply troubling divisions within families and states that characterize the tragedies are the basis for the restorative unions in the romances. Their depiction of passages of time and space that allow providential recoveries of health and prosperity to both individual characters and whole bodies politic are largely owing to the intervention of women. Unlike the women of the tragedies, the daughters and wives of the romances are generative in the broadest sense. They heal their fathers and husbands by restoring to their futures the possibility of descendents and therefore of dynastic continuity. Their agency is, in turn, sustained by forces identified as divine and outside history. *Henry VIII*, a history, and *Two Noble Kinsmen*, a romance, both probably composed jointly with John Fletcher, conclude Shakespeare's career as a dramatist.

Shakespeare also wrote narrative and lyric poems of great power, notably *Venus and Adonis*, *The Rape of Lucrece*, and a cycle of 154 sonnets. In a bold departure from tradition the sonnets celebrate the poet's steadfast love for a young man (never identified), his competitive rivalry with another poet (sometimes identified as Christopher Marlowe), and his troubled relationship with a woman who has dark features. The cycle encourages an interpretation that accounts for its romantic elements, but it also thwarts any obvious construction of events. It is thought that most of the sonnets were composed in the mid-1590s, although they were not published until 1609, apparently without Shakespeare's oversight. Their order therefore cannot be assigned to Shakespeare, and for this reason alone their function as narrative must remain problematic. Still, the reader can trace their representation of successive relations between persons and themes: the young man, although himself derelict in the duties of friendship, will remain beloved by the poet and be made immortal by his verse, while the dark lady, who is unscrupulous and afflicted with venereal disease, receives only expressions of desire and lust, shadowed by the poet's disdain and self-loathing.

In a sense, Shakespeare has always been up to date. True, his language is not what is heard today, and his characters are shaped by forces within his culture, not ours. Yet we continue to see his plays on stage and in film, sometimes as recreations of the productions that historians of theater think he knew and saw but more often as reconceived with the addition of modern costumes, settings, and music as well as some strategic cutting of the dramatic text. Earlier periods produced their own kinds of Shakespeare. The Restoration stage, with scenery that allowed audiences to imagine they were looking through a window to life itself, put on plays that were embellished and trimmed to satisfy the taste of the time. Some producers omitted characters who were considered superfluous (the porter in *Macbeth*); others added characters who were judged essential for balance (Miranda's sister, Dorinda, in *The Tempest*). *King Lear* acquired a happy ending when Edgar married Cordelia. No one production of any period has defined a play entirely; every director has had his or her vision of what Shakespeare meant an audience to see. These reinterpretations testify to the perennial vitality of a playwright who was indeed, as Jonson said, "for all time."

THE SONNETS   The entire sequence numbers 154 sonnets. The first fourteen encourage a young man to marry and have children and may have been commissioned by his family. Neither the young man nor his family has been identified, although some readers have thought Henry Wriosthesley, Earl of Southampton, a possible subject. Sonnet 20 initiates a long sequence of sonnets addressed to a young man as the poet's lover; whether he is the man who featured in the earlier sonnets on procreation is unclear, but it has generally been assumed so. Beginning with Sonnet 78, the poet complains that a rival poet is stealing his subject—the young man's virtue and grace—to the detriment of his own poetry. Who Shakespeare's rival is (or whether he is in fact a single person) is not known, although some readers have considered Christopher Marlowe a possibility. A final set of twenty-eight sonnets introduces a new character to the sequence, a figure often referred to as "the dark lady," who is the lover of both the poet and the young man. The threesome make up a dramatic unity that is fraught with tension and anguish.

Sonnets

1

From fairest creatures we desire increase,
That thereby beauty's rose might never die,
But as the riper° should by time decease,   *the older person*
His tender heir might bear his memory;
5   But thou, contracted° to thine own bright eyes,   *engaged, shrunk*
Feed'st thy light's flame with self-substantial fuel,
Making a famine where abundance lies,
Thyself thy foe, to thy sweet self too cruel.
Thou that art now the world's fresh ornament
10   And only herald to the gaudy spring,
Within thine own bud buriest thy content,
And, tender churl, mak'st waste in niggarding.°   *hoarding*
　　Pity the world, or else this glutton be:
　　To eat the world's due, by the grave and thee.[1]

18

Shall I compare thee to a summer's day?
Thou art more lovely and more temperate.
Rough winds do shake the darling buds of May,
And summer's lease hath all too short a date.°   *duration*
5   Sometimes too hot the eye of heaven shines,
And often is his gold complexion dimmed;

1. Have pity on the world and do not consume your own substance by refusing to engender the child you owe now to the world and finally to the grave.

And every fair from fair sometimes declines,
By chance or nature's changing course untrimmed.°   *stripped bare*
But thy eternal summer shall not fade
10 Nor lose possession of that fair thou ow'st;°   *own*
Nor shall Death brag thou wanderest in his shade,
When in eternal lines° to time thou grow'st.   *of verse*
    So long as men can breathe or eyes can see,
    So long lives this, and this gives life to thee.

20

A woman's face with Nature's own hand painted
Hast thou, the master-mistress of my passion;[2]
A woman's gentle heart, but not acquainted
With shifting change, as is false women's fashion;
5 An eye more bright than theirs, less false in rolling,°   *straying*
Gilding the object whereupon it gazeth;
A man in hue, all hues in his controlling,[3]
Which steals men's eyes and women's souls amazeth.
And for a woman wert thou first created,
10 Till Nature, as she wrought thee, fell a-doting,°   *in love*
And by addition me of thee defeated,[4]
By adding one thing to my purpose nothing.
    But since she pricked thee out for women's pleasure,
    Mine be thy love and thy love's use their treasure.

29

When, in disgrace with fortune and men's eyes,
I all alone beweep my outcast state,
And trouble deaf heaven with my bootless° cries,   *unavailing*
And look upon myself and curse my fate,
5 Wishing me like to one more rich in hope,
Featured like him, like him with friends possessed,
Desiring this man's art and that man's scope,°   *powers*
With what I most enjoy contented least;
Yet in these thoughts myself almost despising,
10 Haply° I think on thee, and then my state,   *perhaps*
Like to the lark at break of day arising
From sullen earth, sings hymns at heaven's gate;
    For thy sweet love remembered such wealth brings
    That then I scorn to change° my state with kings.   *exchange*

---

2. Feminine in appearance, the young man is both a master and a mistress of the poet's passion. This is the first of a series of sonnets in which Shakespeare addresses the young man in clearly erotic language.
3. A man in appearance, he determines the nature of what he sees, what is apparent to him.
4. The last four lines of the sonnet are full of double meanings: the thing loving nature adds to the young man is a penis; this points or "pricks" him out for women's pleasure or "use" (with the added suggestion that his body is capital, which through usury generates interest); but the poet reserves for himself the young man's love, which is beyond commerce and has no price.

30

When to the sessions° of sweet silent thought⁵   *law courts*
I summon up remembrance of things past,
I sigh the lack of many a thing I sought,
And with old woes new wail my dear time's waste.⁶
5   Then can I drown an eye, unused to flow,
For precious friends hid in death's dateless° night,   *endless*
And weep afresh love's long since cancelled woe,
And moan th'expense° of many a vanished sight.   *what it cost*
Then can I grieve at grievances foregone,
10 And heavily° from woe to woe tell o'er   *sorrowfully*
The sad account of fore-bemoanèd moan,
Which I new pay as if not paid before.⁷
        But if the while I think on thee, dear friend,
        All losses are restored, and sorrows end.

33

Full many a glorious morning have I seen
Flatter the mountaintops with sovereign eye,
Kissing with golden face the meadows green,
Gilding pale streams with heavenly alchemy;
5   Anon° permit the basest clouds to ride   *soon*
With ugly rack° on his celestial face,   *driven clouds*
And from the forlorn world his visage hide,
Stealing unseen to west with this disgrace.
Even so my sun one early morn did shine
10 With all-triumphant splendor on my brow.
But out, alack! He was but one hour mine;
The region° cloud hath masked him from me now.   *of the upper air*
        Yet him for this my love no whit disdaineth;
        Suns of the world may stain when heaven's sun staineth.⁸

55

Not marble nor the gilded monuments
Of princes shall outlive this powerful rhyme,
But you shall shine more bright in these contents
Than unswept stone besmeared with sluttish° time.   *dirty*
5   When wasteful war shall statues overturn,
And broils° root out the work of masonry,   *uprisings*
Nor° Mars his sword nor war's quick fire shall burn   *neither*

---

5. The conceit governing this imagery depends on the poet's association of his sense of guilt at his misdeeds with a notion of a debt. He represents himself as a debtor who cannot discharge what he owes to others because the complaints against him remain constantly fresh in his mind. He also figures as in debt to himself, as it is his time that he has wasted in reviewing these complaints. His debts are paid, however, when he thinks of his friend.

6. I bemoan the waste of my time by remembering anew former sadness.
7. I add up the sorrows and complaints against me that I have already accounted for; I pay for them as if they were new debts; so I add to the sum I have wasted.
8. If the sun may be covered by clouds, so too the suns (or sons) of the world may dim in their affections. This is the first of the poet's laments for his lover's insincerity.

The living record of your memory.
'Gainst death and all-oblivious° enmity   *casting into oblivion*
10   Shall you pace forth; your praise shall still find room
Even in the eyes of all posterity
That wear this world out to the ending doom.°   *judgment day*
    So, till the judgment that yourself° arise,   *when you yourself*
    You live in this, and dwell in lovers' eyes.

60

Like as the waves make towards the pebbled shore,
So do our minutes hasten to their end;
Each changing place with that which goes before,
In sequent° toil all forwards do contend.°   *successive / strive*
5   Nativity, once in the main° of light,   *sea*
Crawls to maturity, wherewith being crowned,
Crookèd eclipses 'gainst his glory fight,
And Time that gave doth now his gift confound.°   *destroy*
Time doth transfix° the flourish set on youth   *puncture*
10   And delves° the parallels in beauty's brow,   *digs*
Feeds on the rarities of nature's truth,
And nothing stands but for his scythe to mow.
    And yet to times in hope my verse shall stand,
    Praising thy worth despite his cruel hand.

71

No longer mourn for me when I am dead
Than° you shall hear the surly sullen bell   *then*
Give warning to the world that I am fled
From this vile world with vildest° worms to dwell.   *vilest*
5   Nay, if you read this line, remember not
The hand that writ it, for I love you so,
That I in your sweet thoughts would be forgot,
If thinking on me then should make you woe.°   *grieve you*
O if, I say, you look upon this verse,
10   When I, perhaps, compounded am with clay,
Do not so much as my poor name rehearse,°   *repeat*
But let your love ev'n with my life decay,
    Lest the wise world should look into your moan,
    And mock you with me after I am gone.[9]

73

That time of year thou mayst in me behold
When yellow leaves, or none, or few, do hang

9. Lest people seeing your grief at my death should ridicule you because of your association with me.

Upon those boughs which shake against the cold,
Bare ruined choirs[1] where late the sweet birds sang.
5   In me thou seest the twilight of such day
As after sunset fadeth in the west,
Which by and by black night doth take away,
Death's second self, that seals up all in rest.
In me thou seest the glowing of such fire
10   That on the ashes of his youth doth lie
As the deathbed whereon it must expire,
Consumed with that which it was nourished by.
    This thou perceiv'st, which makes thy love more strong,
    To love that well which thou must leave ere long.

87

Farewell! Thou art too dear for my possessing,
And like enough thou know'st thy estimate.°   *value*
The charter of thy worth gives thee releasing;[2]
My bonds in thee are all determinate.°   *ended*
5   For how do I hold thee but by thy granting,
And for that riches where is my deserving?
The cause of this fair gift in me is wanting,
And so my patent[3] back again is swerving.
Thyself thou gav'st, thy own worth then not knowing,
10   Or me, to whom thou gav'st it, else mistaking;
So thy great gift, upon misprision° growing,   *error*
Comes home again, on better judgment making.
    Thus have I had thee as a dream doth flatter,
    In sleep a king, but waking no such matter.

94

They that have pow'r to hurt, and will do none,[4]
That do not do the thing they most do show,°   *appear to do*
Who moving others are themselves as stone,
Unmovèd, cold, and to temptation slow—
5   They rightly° do inherit heaven's graces,   *justly*
And husband° nature's riches from expense;   *protect*
They are the lords and owners of their faces,°   *appearances*
Others but stewards of their excellence.
The summer's flow'r is to the summer sweet,
10   Though to itself it only live and die;
But if that flow'r with base° infection meet,   *common*

---

1. The choir is the section of a church reserved for the singers in the choir. "Choir" puns on "quire," the gathering of pages in a book, and thus recalls the "leaves" in line 2.
2. You are worth so much that you can pay off all obligations you owe me; in other words, I have no right to you.
3. Deed granting a monopoly.

4. The poem warns against a loss of self-control, which is associated with a loss of self-ownership. Persons (the undefined "they" of the sonnet) can lend themselves to others, their stewards, but at the same time, they retain control over their own great virtue. If they succumb to evil or ill-will, however, they risk becoming very corrupt.

The basest° weed outbraves his dignity.   *humblest*
    For sweetest things turn sourest by their deeds;
    Lilies that fester smell far worse than weeds.

104

To me, fair friend, you never can be old,
For, as you were when first your eye I eyed,
Such seems your beauty still. Three winters cold
Have from the forests shook three summers' pride,
Three beauteous springs to yellow autumn turned
In process of the seasons have I seen,
Three April perfumes in three hot Junes burned,
Since first I saw you fresh, which yet are green.
Ah, yet doth beauty, like a dial⁵ hand,
Steal from his figure and no pace perceived.
So your sweet hue, which methinks still doth stand,
Hath motion, and mine eye may be deceived,
    For fear of which, hear this, thou age unbred:°   *unborn*
    Ere you were born was beauty's summer dead.

116

Let me not to the marriage of true minds
Admit impediments. Love is not love
Which alters when it alteration finds,°   *in the beloved*
Or bends with the remover to remove.
O, no, it is an ever-fixèd mark°   *landmark*
That looks on tempests and is never shaken;
It is the star to every wandering bark,
Whose worth's unknown, although his height be taken.⁶
Love's not Time's fool, though rosy lips and cheeks
Within his bending sickle's compass° come;   *range*
Love alters not with his brief hours and weeks,
But bears it out even to the edge of doom.°   *judgment day*
    If this be error and upon me proved,
    I never writ, nor no man ever loved.

126

O thou, my lovely boy, who in thy power
Dost hold Time's fickle glass,° his sickle hour;   *hourglass*
Who hast by waning grown, and therein show'st
Thy lovers withering as thy sweet self grow'st;
If Nature, sovereign mistress over wrack,°   *destruction*
As thou goest onwards, still will pluck thee back,

---

5. Beauty is like the hand of a clock, a dial; it moves slowly but inexorably away from the height of the hour.
6. The star by which ships navigate by measuring its altitude from the horizon (known values) is itself beyond valuation.

She keeps thee to this purpose, that her skill
May Time disgrace and wretched minutes kill.[7]
Yet fear her, O thou minion° of her pleasure!   slave
10   She may detain, but not still keep, her treasure.
    Her audit, though delayed, answered must be,
    And her quietus° is to render thee.[8]   settlement

129

The expense° of spirit in a waste of shame[9]   dissipation
Is lust in action; and, till action, lust
Is perjured, murderous, bloody, full of blame,
Savage, extreme, rude, cruel, not to trust,
5   Enjoyed no sooner but despised straight,°   immediately
Past reason hunted, and no sooner had
Past reason hated, as a swallowed bait
On purpose laid to make the taker mad;[1]
Mad in pursuit, and in possession so;°   also
10   Had, having, and in quest to have, extreme;
A bliss in proof,° and proved, a very woe;   i.e., while experienced
Before, a joy proposed; behind, a dream.
    All this the world well knows; yet none knows well
    To shun the heaven that leads men to this hell.

130

My mistress' eyes are nothing like the sun;
Coral is far more red than her lips' red;
If snow be white, why then her breasts are dun;°   brown
If hairs be wires, black wires grow on her head.
5   I have seen roses damasked,° red and white,   mingled
But no such roses see I in her cheeks;
And in some perfumes is there more delight
Than in the breath that from my mistress reeks.
I love to hear her speak, yet well I know
10   That music hath a far more pleasing sound.
I grant I never saw a goddess go;
My mistress, when she walks, treads on the ground.
    And yet, by heaven, I think my love as rare
    As any she belied with false compare.[2]

7. His lover's power can hold back time and prevent his sickle from mowing down his green youth; paradoxically, while others grow old, he grows young. Nature permits this expressly to defy Time.
8. Yet Nature owes you to Time and will pay her debt by handing you over at last. The sonnet ends short of the 14 lines the form demands, as if to emphasize the idea of brevity.
9. The line evokes two kinds of meaning, moral and sex-

ual: the futility and degradation of passion, and its waste as "spirit," conventionally understood as semen, in the body or waist of the woman.
1. The lover is both the hunter, who seeks satisfaction, and the hunted, for whom a bait is laid by mad passion.
2. The couplet suggests ironic or hyperbolic compliment: my mistress is exceptional in that she has set new standards for true beauty by a comparison that defies its standards.

138

When my love swears that she is made of truth
I do believe her, though I know she lies,
That she might think me some untutored youth,
Unlearnèd in the world's false subtleties.
5   Thus vainly thinking that she thinks me young,
Although she knows my days are past the best,
Simply I credit her false-speaking tongue;
On both sides thus is simple truth suppressed.
But wherefore says she not she is unjust?
10   And wherefore say not I that I am old?
O, love's best habit is in seeming° trust,   *apparent*
And age in love loves not to have years told.
     Therefore I lie with her, and she with me,[3]
     And in our faults by lies we flattered be.

144

Two loves I have, of comfort and despair,
Which like two spirits do suggest° me still: *tempt*
The better angel is a man right fair,
The worser spirit a woman colored ill.
5   To win me soon to hell, my female evil
Tempteth my better angel from my side,
And would corrupt my saint to be a devil,
Wooing his purity with her foul pride.
And whether that my angel be turned fiend
10   Suspect I may, yet not directly tell;
But being both from me, both to each friend,
I guess one angel in another's hell.
     Yet this shall I ne'er know, but live in doubt
     Till my bad angel fire my good one out.[4]

152

In loving thee thou know'st I am forsworn,°   *faithless*
But thou art twice forsworn, to me love swearing:
In act thy bed-vow° broke, and new faith torn   *marriage vow*
In vowing new hate after new love bearing.[5]
5   But why of two oaths' breach do I accuse thee,
When I break twenty? I am perjured most,
For all my vows are oaths but to misuse° thee,   *deceive*
And all my honest faith in thee is lost.
For I have sworn deep oaths of thy deep kindness,

3. We deceive each other; we have sex with each other.
4. The couplet suggests several interpretations. The poet's lady or bad angel could fire or dismiss his "fair" friend; she could infect him with a venereal disease, a condition that would cause a fever; finally, she could be the cause of his descent into hellfire, a consequence of sin.
5. You have broken your marriage vow and your vow to love me.

10   Oaths of thy love, thy truth, thy constancy,
        And, to enlighten thee, gave eyes to blindness,[6]
        Or made them swear against the thing they see;
            For I have sworn thee fair. More perjured eye,
            To swear against the truth so foul a lie!

THE TEMPEST   Shakespeare's *The Tempest* is at once the most enchanting and disturbing of his plays. It is about love and marriage, but also about revenge and political power. The magician Prospero's memorable lines following the masque for the "contract of true love" between his daughter Miranda and her beloved Ferdinand evoke the hovering between life and death that haunts the play: "we are such stuff / As dreams are made on, and our little life / Is rounded with a sleep" (4.1.156–57). The play opens with a quarrel among men facing death by shipwreck. These are the magician's enemies—his brother Antonio, Duke of Milan, and Alonso, Duke of Naples, who conspired to usurp power from and to exile Prospero. He assures Miranda that "The direful spectacle of the wreck, which touched / The very virtue of compassion in thee / I have with such provision in mine art / so safely ordered that there is no soul— / No, not so much perdition as an hair / betid to any creature in the vessel" (1.2.26–31).

Prospero's magic art controls nearly all that happens on this Mediterranean island. He boasts to the native spirit Ariel that it was his "art" that freed him from imprisonment in a pine tree. The "savage and deformed slave" Caliban, son of the witch Sycorax, claims Prospero's "art Is of such power, / It would control my dam's god Setebos / And make a vassal of him" (1.2.371–73). The shipwreck, the consequent love at first sight of the survivor Ferdinand for Miranda, the elaborately staged torment of Alonso and Antonio, and the wedding pageant for the lovers are all the products of Prospero's art. Art here has the power to enthrall and entertain as well as to unsettle and terrify. Alonso is on the point of suicide when he is convinced by Prospero's staged haunting that by some kind of natural retribution "[i]ncensed seas and shores" have "bereft" him of his son Ferdinand. The benevolent father Prospero seeks revenge on those who caused his near death, and he only achieves reconciliation with them when assured that his daughter Miranda will marry the son of his old enemy Alonso of Naples.

Juxtaposed against the wondrous enamourment of Ferdinand and Miranda (her name means "wondering" or "marveling") and the happy restoration of Prospero's dukedom through their marriage is the history of her near rape by Caliban and of strife on the island. This drawer of water and hewer of wood rails against Prospero for reducing him to slavery and usurping his native island from him. His name and past link Caliban with the history of colonialism. Caliban is an anagram of Cannibal, a word for the mythic, man-eating people of the Caribbean that entered the English language through John Florio's translation of Montaigne's essays *Of the Cannibals* (1603). Gonzalo's speech on his ideal commonwealth (2.1.145–54), where all is held in common and no one has to struggle for power or work, also derives from Florio's translation of Montaigne. This colonial view of the New World is conditioned not only by an idealized literary myth but also by real political oppression. Gonzalo's dream of a land with "no sovereignty" is one that Caliban sharply contradicts in his complaint to Prospero: "For I am all the subjects that you had / Which first was mine own king" (1.2.341–42). Other associations with the literature of early modern conquest of the Americas abound in the play—the god Setebos, the god of the Patagonians, mentioned in Richard Eden's translation of Peter Martyr's *Decades of the New World* (1555); and the Bermudas, the place where the first English colonists of the Virginia Company landed when they were blown off course, related in William Strachey's *True Repertory of the Wreck* (1610; published 1625).

As a response to the play's implicit criticism of the oppressive effects of colonialism, Aimé Césaire's *A Tempest* performs an explicit decolonizing critique. Césaire's Caliban protests the destruction of his language, history, and identity by Prospero's rule. In this

---

6. To make you seem fair, I saw what was not there or did not see what was there.

context, Prosperos's defending his education of Caliban and his establishment of civilization on the island are revealed as propaganda to justify the exploitation of the slave's labor for his master's profit.

If political succession and New World exploitation and colonialism impinge upon the action and language of *The Tempest,* so too does art—through music, masquelike scenes, and metadramatic allusions to the public theater itself. The play contains some of the most beautiful lyrics in all of Shakespeare's works—"Full fathom five thy father lies," and "Where the bee sucks there suck I," music for which was composed by Robert Johnson, musician in the court of James I. Even Caliban, in his comic role as follower of an insurrection against Prospero led by the drunken buffoon Stephano, expresses the musical properties of the island in melodic and lilting verse: "Be not afeard, the isle is full of noises, / Sounds and sweet airs, that give delight and hurt not" (3.2.133–34). Alternately causing delight and fear are the scenes staged by Prospero and Ariel, who work together as director and stage manager to bring to life the magus's dramatic vision. One of these scenes, the wedding celebration for Miranda and Ferdinand in Act 4, is the closest thing to a court masque, the form of which Ben Jonson was master (see *Pleasure Reconciled to Virtue*), that Shakespeare ever produced. When Prospero interrupts the masque to stop the plot on his life by "Caliban and his confederates," he reminds us that just as Miranda and Ferdinand have been watching a performance, so too are we:

> These our actors,
> As I foretold you, were all spirits, and
> Are melted into air, into thin air,
> And, like the baseless fabric of this vision,
> The cloud-capped towers, the gorgeous palaces,
> The solemn temples, the great globe itself,
> Yea, all which it inherit, shall dissolve,
> And, like this insubstantial pageant faded,
> Leave not a rack behind. (4.1.148–56)

This self-referential turn runs throughout the play and is brought to the spectators' attention forcefully at the conclusion of the drama, when Prospero, having renounced his "art to enchant," stands before the audience and begs for their applause and prayers: "And my ending is despair / Unless I be relieved by prayer" (5.1.331–35). Somewhere between Marlowe's proud ambitious intellectual Faustus and Jonson's madcap, fraudulent alchemist Subtle, Prospero achieves an apparently wise and happy ending that is tinged with some fear and anxiety. His renunciation of his art is at once more complex and problematic than Faustus' tragic damnation and Subtle's comic failure. Since the play causes us to think deeply about what it means to make art, and about what the limits of art's power to transform reality are, it has often been taken as Shakespeare's final statement on his work. It would be hard to find another play from his age—or from any other—that causes us to reflect so deeply on these questions and to be so spellbound by the music of its poetry.

The text of *The Tempest* is based on the 1623 Folio, where it appears as the first play. This is the earliest extant version of the play.

The Tempest

The Names of the Actors

ALONSO, *King of Naples*

SEBASTIAN, *his brother*

PROSPERO, *the right Duke of Milan*

ANTONIO, *his brother, the usurping Duke of Milan*

STEPHANO, *a drunken butler*

MASTER OF A SHIP

BOATSWAIN

MARINERS

MIRANDA, *daughter to Prospero*

FERDINAND, *SON TO THE* KING *OF*
   NAPLES
GONZALO, *AN HONEST OLD*
   COUNCILLOR
ADRIAN *AND* } *lords*
FRANCISCO,
CALIBAN, *A SAVAGE AND DEFORMED*
   SLAVE
TRINCULO, *A JESTER*

ARIEL, *AN AIRY SPIRIT*
IRIS
CERES
JUNO   } *(PRESENTED BY) SPIRITS*
NYMPHS
REAPERS

[OTHER SPIRITS ATTENDING ON PROSPERO]

Scene: An uninhabited island

ACT 1

Scene 1

[*A tempestuous noise of thunder and lightning heard. Enter a Shipmaster and a Boatswain.*[1]]

MASTER: Boatswain!

BOATSWAIN: Here, Master. What cheer?

MASTER: Good, speak to the mariners. Fall to 't yarely,[2] or we run ourselves
      aground.

5   Bestir, bestir!   [*Exit.*]

[*Enter Mariners.*]

BOATSWAIN: Heigh, my hearts! Cheerly, cheerly, my hearts! Yare, yare! Take in
      the topsail. Tend[3] to the Master's whistle.—Blow[4] till thou burst thy
      wind, if room enough![5]

[*Enter Alonso, Sebastian, Antonio, Ferdinand, Gonzalo, and others.*]

ALONSO: Good Boatswain, have care. Where's the Master? Play[6] the men.

BOATSWAIN: I pray now, keep below.

ANTONIO: Where is the Master, Boatswain?

BOATSWAIN: Do you not hear him? You mar our labor. Keep your cabins! You do
      assist the storm.

GONZALO: Nay, good, be patient.

BOATSWAIN: When the sea is. Hence! What cares these roarers[7] for the name of
      king? To cabin! Silence! Trouble us not.

GONZALO: Good, yet remember whom thou hast aboard.

BOATSWAIN: None that I more love than myself. You are a councillor; if you can
      command these elements to silence and work the peace of the present,
20   we will not hand[8] a rope more. Use your authority. If you cannot, give
      thanks you have lived so long and make yourself ready in your cabin for
      the mischance of the hour, if it so hap.—Cheerly, good hearts!—Out of
      our way, I say.   [*Exit.*]

---

1. Location: On board ship.
2. Quickly.
3. Attend.
4. Addressed to the wind.

5. As long as we have sea room enough.
6. Ply? Urge the men to exert themselves.
7. Waves or wind.
8. Handle.

GONZALO: I have great comfort from this fellow. Methinks he hath no drowning
25   mark upon him; his complexion is perfect gallows.[9] Stand fast, good Fate,
to his hanging! Make the rope of his destiny our cable, for our own doth
little advantage.[1] If he be not born to be hanged, our case is miserable.

                                                      [Exeunt (courtiers).]

[Enter Boatswain.]

BOATSWAIN: Down with the topmast! Yare! Lower, lower! Bring her to try wi' the
main course.[2] *[A cry within.]* A plague upon this howling! They are
30   louder than the weather or our office.[3]

[Enter Sebastian, Antonio, and Gonzalo.]

      Yet again? What do you here? Shall we give o'er and drown? Have you a
mind to sink?

SEBASTIAN: A pox o' your throat, you bawling, blasphemous, incharitable dog!

BOATSWAIN: Work you, then.

ANTONIO: Hang, cur! Hang, you whoreson, insolent noisemaker! We are less
afraid to be drowned than thou art.

GONZALO: I'll warrant him for drowning,[4] though the ship were no stronger than a
nutshell and as leaky as an unstanched[5] wench.

BOATSWAIN: Lay her ahold,[6] ahold! Set her two courses.[7]
40   Off to sea again! Lay her off!

[Enter Mariners, wet.]

MARINERS: All lost! To prayers, to prayers! All lost!

[The Mariners run about in confusion, exiting at random.]

BOATSWAIN: What, must our mouths be cold?[8]

GONZALO: The King and Prince at prayers! Let's assist them,
      For our case is as theirs.

SEBASTIAN: I am out of patience.

ANTONIO: We are merely° cheated of our lives by drunkards.   *utterly*
      This wide-chapped° rascal! Would thou mightst lie drowning   *wide-jawed*
      The washing of ten tides![9]

GONZALO: He'll be hanged yet,
      Though every drop of water swear against it
      And gape at wid'st to glut° him.   *gobble*

[A confused noise within.]

                             "Mercy on us!"—
50   "We split, we split!"—"Farewell my wife and children!"—
      "Farewell, brother!"—"We split, we split, we split!"

                                  [Exit Boatswain.]

ANTONIO: Let's all sink wi' the King.

SEBASTIAN: Let's take leave of him.

                                  [Exit (with Antonio)].

---

9. Alludes to the proverb "He that's born to be hanged
need fear no drowning."
1. Doesn't do much good.
2. Sail her close to the wind.
3. The noise we make at our work.
4. Guarantee against.
5. Loose (suggesting also "menstrual").

6. Close to the wind.
7. Sets of sails.
8. Must we drown in the cold sea; or, let us heat up our
mouths with liquor.
9. Pirates were hanged on the shore and left until three
tides had come in.

GONZALO: Now would I give a thousand furlongs of sea for an acre of barren
55   ground: long heath, brown furze; anything. The wills above be done! But
       I would fain die a dry death.   [*Exit.*]

                              Scene 2¹

            [*Enter Prospero (in his magic cloak) and Miranda.*]
MIRANDA: If by your art, my dearest father, you have
        Put the wild waters in this roar, allay them.
        The sky, it seems, would pour down stinking pitch,
        But that the sea, mounting to th' welkin's cheek,°   *the sky's face*
5   Dashes the fire out. O, I have suffered
        With those that I saw suffer! A brave° vessel,   *splendid*
        Who had, no doubt, some noble creature in her,
        Dashed all to pieces. O, the cry did knock
        Against my very heart! Poor souls, they perished.
10   Had I been any god of power, I would
        Have sunk the sea within the earth or ere°   *before*
        It should the good ship so have swallowed and
        The freighting° souls within her.   *forming the cargo*
PROSPERO: Be collected.°   *composed*
        No more amazement.° Tell your piteous° heart   *consternation / pitying*
15   There's no harm done.
MIRANDA: O, woe the day!
PROSPERO: No harm.
        I have done nothing but in care of thee,
        Of thee, my dear one, thee, my daughter, who
        Art ignorant of what thou art, naught knowing
        Of whence I am, nor that I am more better
20   Than Prospero, master of a full° poor cell,   *very*
        And thy no greater father.
MIRANDA: More to know
        Did never meddle° with my thoughts.   *mingle*
PROSPERO: 'Tis time
        I should inform thee farther. Lend thy hand
        And pluck my magic garment from me. So,
            [*laying down his magic cloak and staff*]
25   Lie there, my art.—Wipe thou thine eyes. Have comfort.
        The direful spectacle of the wreck,° which touched   *shipwreck*
        The very virtue° of compassion in thee,   *essence*
        I have with such provision° in mine art   *foresight*
        So safely ordered that there is no soul—
30   No, not so much perdition° as an hair   *loss*
        Betid° to any creature in the vessel   *happened*
        Which thou heard'st cry, which thou saw'st sink. Sit down.
        For thou must now know farther.
MIRANDA   [*sitting*]:   You have often
        Begun to tell me what I am, but stopped

_____
1. Location: The island, near Prospero's cell.

35   And left me to a bootless inquisition,°   *fruitless inquiry*
            Concluding, "Stay, not yet."
PROSPERO: The hour's now come;
            The very minute bids thee ope thine ear.
            Obey, and be attentive. Canst thou remember
            A time before we came unto this cell?
40   I do not think thou canst, for then thou wast not
            Out° three years old.   *fully*
MIRANDA: Certainly, sir, I can.
PROSPERO: By what? By any other house or person?
            Of anything the image, tell me, that
            Hath kept with thy remembrance.
MIRANDA: 'Tis far off,
45   And rather like a dream than an assurance
            That my remembrance warrants.² Had I not
            Four or five women once that tended me?
PROSPERO: Thou hadst, and more, Miranda. But how is it
            That this lives in thy mind? What seest thou else
50   In the dark backward and abysm of time?³
            If thou rememberest aught ere thou cam'st here,
            How thou cam'st here thou mayst.
MIRANDA: But that I do not.
PROSPERO: Twelve year since, Miranda, twelve year since,
            Thy father was the Duke of Milan and
            A prince of power.
MIRANDA: Sir, are not you my father?
PROSPERO: Thy mother was a piece° of virtue, and   *masterpiece*
            She said thou wast my daughter; and thy father
            Was Duke of Milan, and his only heir
            And princess no worse issued.°   *no less nobly born*
MIRANDA: O the heavens!
60   What foul play had we, that we came from thence?
            Or blessèd was 't we did?
PROSPERO: Both, both, my girl.
            By foul play, as thou sayst, were we heaved thence,
            But blessedly holp° hither.   *helped*
MIRANDA: O, my heart bleeds
            To think o' the teen° that I have turned you to,⁴   *trouble*
65   Which is from° my remembrance! Please you, farther.   *out of*
PROSPERO: My brother and thy uncle, called Antonio—
            I pray thee mark me—that a brother should
            Be so perfidious!—he whom next° thyself   *next to*
            Of all the world I loved, and to him put
70   The manage° of my state, as at that time   *management*
            Through all the seigniories⁵ it was the first,
            And Prospero the prime duke, being so reputed

2. A certainty that my memory guarantees.   4. I've caused you to remember.
3. Abyss of the past.   5. City-states of northern Italy.

In dignity, and for the liberal arts
Without a parallel; those being all my study,
75   The government I cast upon my brother
And to my state grew stranger,[6] being transported°   *carried away*
And rapt in secret studies. Thy false uncle—
Dost thou attend me?

MIRANDA: Sir, most heedfully.

PROSPERO: Being once perfected° how to grant suits,   *grown skillful*
80   How to deny them, who t' advance and who
To trash for overtopping,[7] new created
The creatures that were mine, I say, or° changed 'em,   *either*
Or else new formed 'em; having both the key[8]
Of officer and office, set all hearts i' the state
85   To what tune pleased his ear, that° now he was   *so that*
The ivy which had hid my princely trunk
And sucked my verdure out on 't. Thou attend'st not.

MIRANDA: O, good sir, I do.

PROSPERO: I pray thee, mark me.
I, thus neglecting worldly ends, all dedicated
90   To closeness° and the bettering of my mind   *seclusion*
With that which, but by being so retired,
O'erprized° all popular rate,° in my false brother   *outvalued / estimation*
Awaked an evil nature; and my trust,
Like a good parent,[9] did beget of° him   *in*
95   A falsehood in its contrary as great
As my trust was, which had indeed no limit,
A confidence sans° bound. He being thus lorded°   *without / made a lord*
Not only with what my revenue yielded
But what my power might else exact, like one
100   Who, having into° truth by telling of it,   *unto*
Made such a sinner of his memory
To° credit his own lie,[1] he did believe   *as to*
He was indeed the Duke, out° o' the substitution   *as a result*
And executing th' outward face of royalty
105   With all prerogative. Hence his ambition growing—
Dost thou hear?

MIRANDA: Your tale, sir, would cure deafness.

PROSPERO: To have no screen between this part he played
And him he played it for, he needs will be°   *insisted on becoming*
Absolute Milan.[2] Me, poor man, my library
110   Was dukedom large enough. Of temporal royalties
He thinks me now incapable; confederates°—   *allies himself*
So dry° he was for sway—wi' the King of Naples   *thirsty*
To give him annual tribute, do him homage,
Subject his coronet to his crown, and bend

---

6. Withdrew from my responsibilities as a duke.
7. To check for going too fast, like hounds.
8. Key for unlocking; tool for tuning stringed instruments.

9. Alludes to the proverb that good parents often bear bad children; see line 120.
1. Who starts to believe his own lie.
2. Duke of Milan in fact.

115	The dukedom yet° unbowed—alas, poor Milan!— *previously*
	To most ignoble stooping.
MIRANDA:	O the heavens!
PROSPERO:	Mark his condition° and th' event,° then tell me *pact / outcome*
	If this might be a brother.
MIRANDA:	I should sin
	To think but nobly of my grandmother.
120	Good wombs have borne bad sons.
PROSPERO:	Now the condition.
	This King of Naples, being an enemy
	To me inveterate, hearkens° my brother's suit, *listens to*
	Which was that he, in lieu o' the premises³
	Of homage and I know not how much tribute,
125	Should presently° extirpate° me and mine *immediately / remove*
	Out of the dukedom and confer fair Milan,
	With all the honors, on my brother. Whereon,
	A treacherous army levied, one midnight
	Fated° to th' purpose did Antonio open *devoted*
130	The gates of Milan, and, i' the dead of darkness,
	The ministers° for the purpose hurried thence *agents*
	Me and thy crying self.
MIRANDA:	Alack, for pity!
	I, not remembering how I cried out then,
	Will cry it o'er again. It is a hint° *occasion*
135	That wrings⁴ mine eyes to 't.
PROSPERO:	Hear a little further,
	And then I'll bring thee to the present business
	Which now's upon 's, without the which this story
	Were most impertinent.° *irrelevant*
MIRANDA:	Wherefore° did they not *why*
	That hour destroy us?
PROSPERO:	Well demanded,° wench. *asked*
140	My tale provokes that question. Dear, they durst not,
	So dear the love my people bore me, nor set
	A mark so bloody on the business, but
	With colors fairer painted their foul ends.
	In few,° they hurried us aboard a bark,° *few words / ship*
145	Bore us some leagues to sea, where they prepared
	A rotten carcass of a butt,° not rigged, *tub*
	Nor tackle, sail, nor mast; the very rats
	Instinctively have quit it. There they hoist us,
	To cry to th' sea that roared to us, to sigh
150	To th' winds whose pity, sighing back again,
	Did us but loving wrong.
MIRANDA:	Alack, what trouble
	Was I then to you!
PROSPERO:	O, a cherubin

---

3. In exchange for the guarantee.   4. Constrains; wrings tears from.

Thou wast that did preserve me. Thou didst smile,
Infusèd with a fortitude from heaven,
155 When I have decked° the sea with drops full salt,   *adorned*
Under my burden groaned, which raised in me
An undergoing stomach,° to bear up   *courage to endure*
Against what should ensue.

MIRANDA: How came we ashore?

PROSPERO: By Providence divine.
160 Some food we had, and some fresh water, that
A noble Neapolitan, Gonzalo,
Out of his charity, who being then appointed
Master of this design, did give us, with
Rich garments, linens, stuffs,° and necessaries,   *supplies*
165 Which since have steaded much.° So, of his gentleness,   *been of much use*
Knowing I loved my books, he furnished me
From mine own library with volumes that
I prize above my dukedom.

MIRANDA: Would I might
But ever see that man!

PROSPERO: Now I arise.
[*He puts on his magic cloak.*]
170 Sit still, and hear the last of our sea sorrow.
Here in this island we arrived; and here
Have I, thy schoolmaster, made thee more profit°   *profit more*
Than other princes'° can, that have more time   *princesses*
For vainer hours and tutors not so careful.

MIRANDA: Heavens thank you for 't! And now, I pray you, sir—
For still 'tis beating in my mind—your reason
For raising this sea storm?

PROSPERO: Know thus far forth:
By accident most strange, bountiful Fortune,
Now my dear lady, hath mine enemies
180 Brought to this shore; and by my prescience
I find my zenith° doth depend upon   *apex of fortune*
A most auspicious star, whose influence
If now I court not, but omit,° my fortunes   *neglect*
Will ever after droop. Here cease more questions.
185 Thou art inclined to sleep. 'Tis a good dullness,°   *drowsiness*
And give it way. I know thou canst not choose.
[*Miranda sleeps.*]
Come away,° servant, come! I am ready now.   *come here*
Approach, my Ariel, come.
[*Enter Ariel.*]

ARIEL: All hail, great master, grave sir, hail! I come
190 To answer thy best pleasure; be 't to fly,
To swim, to dive into the fire, to ride
On the curled clouds, to thy strong bidding task°   *make demands upon*
Ariel and all his quality.°   *cohorts or abilities*

PROSPERO: Hast thou, spirit,

Performed to point° the tempest that I bade thee?   *in detail*

ARIEL: To every article.

I boarded the King's ship. Now on the beak,°   *prow*

Now in the waist,° the deck,° in every cabin,   *midships / poop*

I flamed amazement.[5] Sometimes I'd divide

And burn in many places; on the topmast,

200   The yards, and bowsprit would I flame distinctly,°   *in different places*

Then meet and join. Jove's lightning, the precursors

O' the dreadful thunderclaps, more momentary

And sight-outrunning° were not. The fire and cracks   *swifter than sight*

Of sulfurous roaring the most mighty Neptune

205   Seem to besiege and make his bold waves tremble,

Yea, his dread trident shake.

PROSPERO: My brave spirit!

Would not infect his reason?

ARIEL: Not a soul

But felt a fever of the mad and played

210   Some tricks of desperation. All but mariners

Plunged in the foaming brine and quit the vessel,

Then all afire with me. The King's son, Ferdinand,

With hair up-staring°—then like reeds, not hair—   *standing on end*

Was the first man that leapt; cried, "Hell is empty,

215   And all the devils are here!"

PROSPERO: Why, that's my spirit!

But was not this nigh shore?

ARIEL: Close by, my master.

PROSPERO: But are they, Ariel, safe?

ARIEL: Not a hair perished.

On their sustaining garments[6] not a blemish,

But fresher than before; and, as thou bad'st me,

220   In troops I have dispersed them 'bout the isle.

The King's son have I landed by himself,

Whom I left cooling of the air with sighs

In an odd angle° of the isle, and sitting,   *corner*

His arms in this sad knot.

[*He folds his arms.*]

PROSPERO: Of the King's ship,

225   The mariners, say how thou hast disposed,

And all the rest o' the fleet.

ARIEL: Safely in harbor

Is the King's ship; in the deep nook,° where once   *bay*

Thou called'st me up at midnight to fetch dew[7]

From the still-vexed° Bermudas,[8] there she's hid;   *ever stormy*

230   The mariners all under hatches stowed,

---

5. Struck terror by appearing as St. Elmo's fire, an electric discharge seen at the prominent parts of ships in stormy weather.
6. Garments that buoyed them up in the sea.

7. For magical purposes; see line 324.
8. Perhaps refers to the then-recent Bermuda shipwreck; see William Strachey, *A Time Reportory of the Wreck and Redemption of Sir Thomas Gates.*

	Who, with a charm joined to their suffered° labor,	*undergone*
	I have left asleep. And for the rest o' the fleet,	
	Which I dispersed, they all have met again	
	And are upon the Mediterranean float°	*sea*
235	Bound sadly home for Naples,	
	Supposing that they saw the King's ship wrecked	
	And his great person perish.	

PROSPERO: Ariel, thy charge
Exactly is performed. But there's more work.
What is the time o' the day?

ARIEL: Past the mid season.°   *noon*

PROSPERO: At least two glasses.° The time twixt six and now   *hourglasses*
Must by us both be spent most preciously.

ARIEL: Is there more toil? Since thou dost give me pains,°   *labors*
Let me remember° thee what thou hast promised,   *remind*
Which is not yet performed me.
Which is not yet performed me.

PROSPERO: How now? Moody?
245   What is't thou canst demand?

ARIEL: My liberty.

PROSPERO: Before the time be out? No more!

ARIEL: I prithee,
Remember I have done thee worthy service,
Told thee no lies, made thee no mistakings, served
Without or grudge or grumblings. Thou did promise
250   To bate° me a full year.   *remit*

PROSPERO: Dost thou forget
From what a torment I did free thee?

ARIEL: No.

PROSPERO: Thou dost, and think'st it much to tread the ooze
Of the salt deep,
To run upon the sharp wind of the north,
255   To do me° business in the veins⁹ o' the earth   *do for me*
When it is baked° with frost.   *hardened*

ARIEL: I do not, sir.

PROSPERO: Thou liest, malignant thing! Hast thou forgot
The foul witch Sycorax, who with age and envy°   *malice*
Was grown into a hoop?¹ Hast thou forgot her?

ARIEL: No, sir.

PROSPERO: Thou hast. Where was she born? Speak. Tell me.

ARIEL: Sir, in Argier.°   *Algiers*

PROSPERO: O, was she so? I must
Once in a month recount what thou hast been,
Which thou forget'st. This damned witch Sycorax,
265   For mischiefs manifold and sorceries terrible
To enter human hearing, from Argier,
Thou know'st, was banished. For one thing she did°   *becoming pregnant*
They would not take her life. Is not this true?

9. Of minerals, or underground streams.   1. So bent with age as to resemble a hoop.

ARIEL: Ay, sir.
PROSPERO: This blue-eyed² hag was hither brought with child°   *pregnant*
        And here was left by the sailors. Thou, my slave,
        As thou report'st thyself, was then her servant;
        And, for° thou wast a spirit too delicate   *because*
        To act her earthy and abhorred commands,
275   Refusing her grand hests,° she did confine thee,   *orders*
        By help of her more potent ministers
        And in her most unmitigable rage,
        Into a cloven pine, within which rift
        Imprisoned thou didst painfully remain
280   A dozen years; within which space she died
        And left thee there, where thou didst vent thy groans
        As fast as mill wheels strike.³ Then was this island—
        Save° for the son that she did litter° here,   *except / give birth to*
        A freckled whelp°, hag-born—not honored with   *animal offspring*
285   A human shape.
ARIEL: Yes, Caliban her son.
PROSPERO: Dull thing, I say so:⁴ he, that Caliban
        Whom now I keep in service. Thou best know'st
        What torment I did find thee in. Thy groans
        Did make wolves howl, and penetrate the breasts
290   Of ever-angry bears. It was a torment
        To lay upon the damned, which Sycorax
        Could not again undo. It was mine art,
        When I arrived and heard thee, that made gape°   *open wide*
        The pine and let thee out.
ARIEL: I thank thee, master.
PROSPERO: If thou more murmur'st, I will rend an oak
        And peg thee in his° knotty entrails till   *its*
        Thou hast howled away twelve winters.
ARIEL: Pardon, master.
        I will be correspondent° to command   *obedient*
        And do my spriting⁵ gently.°   *graciously*
PROSPERO: Do so, and after two days
300   I will discharge thee.
ARIEL: That's my noble master!
        What shall I do? Say what? What shall I do?
PROSPERO: Go make thyself like a nymph o' the sea. Be subject
        To no sight but thine and mine, invisible
        To every eyeball else. Go take this shape
305   And hither come in 't. Go, hence with diligence!
                             [*Exit (Ariel).*]
        Awake, dear heart, awake! Thou hast slept well.
        Awake!
MIRANDA: The strangeness of your story put

2. With dark circles under her eyes, implying pregnancy.   4. Exactly, that's what I said, you dimwit.
3. As the blades of a mill wheel strike water.   5. Duties as a spirit.

	Heaviness° in me.	*drowsiness*
PROSPERO:	Shake it off. Come on,	

PROSPERO: Shake it off. Come on,
We'll visit Caliban, my slave, who never
310 Yields us kind answer.

MIRANDA: 'Tis a villain, sir,
I do not love to look on.

PROSPERO: But, as 'tis,
We cannot miss° him. He does make our fire,   *do without*
Fetch in our wood, and serves in offices°   *functions*
That profit us.—What ho! Slave! Caliban!
315 Thou earth, thou! Speak.

CALIBAN [within]:   There's wood enough within.

PROSPERO: Come forth, I say! There's other business for thee.
Come, thou tortoise! When?[6]
[*Enter Ariel like a water nymph.*]
 Fine apparition! My quaint° Ariel,   *ingenious*
 Hark in thine ear. [*He whispers.*]

ARIEL: My lord, it shall be done.   [*Exit.*]

PROSPERO: Thou poisonous slave, got° by the devil himself *begotten*
Upon thy wicked dam,° come forth!   *mother*
[*Enter Caliban.*]

CALIBAN: As wicked dew as e'er my mother brushed
With raven's feather from unwholesome fen°   *marsh*
Drop on you both! A southwest° blow on ye *diseased wind*
325 And blister you all o'er!

PROSPERO: For this, be sure, tonight thou shalt have cramps,
Side-stitches that shall pen thy breath up. Urchins[7]
Shall forth at vast° of night that they may work[8] *desolate time*
All exercise on thee. Thou shalt be pinched
330 As thick as honeycomb, each pinch more stinging
Than bees that made 'em.

CALIBAN: I must eat my dinner.
This island's mine, by Sycorax my mother,
Which thou tak'st from me. When thou cam'st first,
Thou strok'st me and made much of me, wouldst give me
335 Water with berries in 't, and teach me how
To name the bigger light, and how the less,
That burn by day and night. And then I loved thee
And showed thee all the qualities° o' th' isle,   *resources*
The fresh springs, brine pits, barren place and fertile.
340 Cursed be I that did so! All the charms°   *spells*
Of Sycorax, toads, beetles, bats, light on you!
For I am all the subjects that you have,
Which first was mine own king; and here you, sty° me *put me in a sty*
In this hard rock, whiles you do keep from me
345 The rest o' th' island.

6. Expression of impatience.   8. Malignant spirits were thought to prowl at night.
7. Hedgehogs (here, goblins in the shape of hedgehogs).

PROSPERO: Thou most lying slave,
        Whom stripes° may move, not kindness! I have used thee,   *lashes*
        Filth as thou art, with humane care, and lodged thee
        In mine own cell, till thou didst seek to violate
        The honor of my child.
CALIBAN: O ho, O ho! Would't had been done!
        Thou didst prevent me; I had peopled else°   *otherwise populated*
        This isle with Calibans.
MIRANDA:[9]   Abhorrèd slave,
        Which any print° of goodness wilt not take,   *imprint*
        Being capable of all ill! I pitied thee,
355   Took pains to make thee speak, taught thee each hour
        One thing or other. When thou didst not, savage,
        Know thine own meaning, but wouldst gabble like
        A thing most brutish, I endowed thy purposes°   *meanings*
        With words that made them known. But thy vile race,°   *nature*
360   Though thou didst learn, had that in 't which good natures
        Could not abide to be with; therefore wast thou
        Deservedly confined into this rock,
        Who hadst deserved more than a prison.
CALIBAN: You taught me language, and my profit on 't
365   Is I know how to curse. The red° plague rid° you   *bubonic / destroy*
        For learning me your language!
PROSPERO: Hagseed, hence!
        Fetch us in fuel, and be quick, thou'rt best,[1]
        To answer other business[2]: Shrugg'st thou, malice?
        If thou neglect'st or dost unwillingly
370   What I command, I'll rack thee with old[3] cramps,
        Fill all thy bones with aches,[4] make thee roar
        That beasts shall tremble at thy din.
CALIBAN: No, pray thee.
        [*Aside.*] I must obey. His art is of such power
        It would control my dam's god, Setebos,[5]
        And make a vassal of him.
PROSPERO: So, slave, hence!

                                                        [*Exit Caliban.*]
[*Enter Ferdinand; and Ariel, invisible,[6] playing and singing. (Ferdinand does not see
Prospero and Miranda.)*]
                            [*Ariel's Song.*]
ARIEL:

            Come unto these yellow sands,
                And then take hands;
            Curtsied when you have, and kissed
                The wild waves whist[7];

9. This speech is sometimes assigned by editors to Prospero.
1. You'd be well advised.
2. Perform other tasks.
3. Such as old people have.
4. Pronounced "aitches."

5. A god of the Patagonians, at the tip of South America,
named in Richard Eden's *History of Travel*, 1577.
6. To the other characters.
7. Kissed the waves into silence.

380	Foot it featly° here and there,	*dance nimbly*
	And, sweet sprites, bear	
	The burden. Hark, hark!	
	[Burden,° dispersedly (within)]. Bow-wow.	*Refrain*
	The watchdogs bark.	
385	[Burden, dispersedly within.] Bow-wow.	
	Hark, hark! I hear	
	The strain of strutting chanticleer	
	Cry Cock-a-diddle-dow.	

FERDINAND: Where should this music be? I' th' air or th' earth?
390   It sounds no more; and sure it waits upon
            Some god o' th' island. Sitting on a bank,
            Weeping again the King my father's wreck,
            This music crept by me upon the waters,
            Allaying both their fury and my passion°   *lamentation*
395   With its sweet air. Thence I have followed it,
            Or it hath drawn me rather. But 'tis gone.
            No, it begins again.
                          [Ariel's Song.]
ARIEL: Full fathom five thy father lies.
                      Of his bones are coral made.
400   Those are pearls that were his eyes.
                      Nothing of him that doth fade
                   But doth suffer a sea change
                   Into something rich and strange.
                   Sea nymphs hourly ring his knell.
                          [Burden (within)]. Ding dong.
405   Hark, now I hear them, ding dong bell.

FERDINAND: The ditty does remember° my drowned father.   *allude to*
            This is no mortal business, nor no sound
            That the earth owes°. I hear it now above me.   *owns*
PROSPERO [to Miranda]:   The fringèd curtains of thine eye advance°   *raise*
            And say what thou seest yond.
MIRANDA: What is 't? A spirit?
            Lord, how it looks about! Believe me, sir,
            It carries a brave° form. But 'tis a spirit.   *excellent*
PROSPERO: No, wench, it eats and sleeps and hath such senses
            As we have, such. This gallant which thou seest
415   Was in the wreck; and, but he's something stained°   *disfigured*
            With grief, that's beauty's canker,° thou mightst call him   *cankerworm*
            A goodly person. He hath lost his fellows
            And strays about to find 'em.
MIRANDA: I might call him
            A thing divine, for nothing natural
            I ever saw so noble.
PROSPERO [aside]:   It goes on, I see,
            As my soul prompts° it.—Spirit, fine spirit, I'll free thee   *would like*
            Within two days for this.

FERDINAND [*seeing Miranda*]:   Most sure,° the goddess   *this is certainly*
          On whom these airs° attend!—Vouchsafe° my prayer   *songs / grant*
          May know if you remain° upon this island,   *dwell*
425   And that you will some good instruction give
          How I may bear me° here. My prime request,   *conduct myself*
          Which I do last pronounce, is—O you wonder!⁸—
          If you be maid⁹ or no?

MIRANDA: No wonder, sir,
          But certainly a maid.

FERDINAND: My language? Heavens!
430   I am the best° of them that speak this speech,   *in birth*
          Were I but where 'tis spoken.

PROSPERO [*coming forward*]:   How? The best?
          What wert thou if the King of Naples heard thee?

FERDINAND: A single¹ thing, as I am now, that wonders
          To hear thee speak of Naples.° He does hear me,   *King of Naples*
435   And that he does I weep. Myself am Naples,
          Who with mine eyes, never since at ebb,° beheld   *dry*
          The King my father wrecked.

MIRANDA: Alack, for mercy!

FERDINAND: Yes, faith, and all his lords, the Duke of Milan
          And his brave son² being twain.

PROSPERO [*aside*]:   The Duke of Milan
440   And his more braver° daughter could control° thee,   *splendid / refute*
          If now 'twere fit to do 't. At the first sight
          They have changed eyes.°—Delicate Ariel,   *exchanged love looks*
          I'll set thee free for this. [*To Ferdinand.*] A word, good sir.
          I fear you have done yourself some wrong.° A word!   *told a lie*

MIRANDA [*aside*]:   Why speaks my father so ungently? This
          Is the third man that e'er I saw, the first
          That e'er I sighed for. Pity move my father
          To be inclined my way!

FERDINAND: O, if a virgin,
          And your affection not gone forth, I'll make you
          The Queen of Naples.

PROSPERO: Soft, sir! One word more.
          [*Aside.*] They are both in either's power's; but this swift business
          I must uneasy° make, lest too light winning   *difficult*
          Make the prize light. [*To Ferdinand.*] One word more: I charge thee
          That thou attend° me. Thou dost here usurp   *listen to*
455   The name thou ow'st° not, and hast put thyself   *ownest*
          Upon this island as a spy, to win it
          From me, the lord on 't.

FERDINAND: No, as I am a man.

MIRANDA: There's nothing ill can dwell in such a temple.
          If the ill spirit have so fair a house,

---

8. Miranda's name means "to be wondered at."
9. As opposed to either a goddess or a married woman.

1. Solitary, being at once King of Naples and myself; feeble.
2. Antonio's son is not mentioned elsewhere.

Good things will strive to dwell with 't.

PROSPERO: Follow me.—
Speak not you for him; he's a traitor.—Come,
I'll manacle thy neck and feet together.
Seawater shalt thou drink; thy food shall be
The fresh-brook mussels, withered roots, and husks
Wherein the acorn cradled. Follow.

FERDINAND: No!
I will resist such entertainment° till   *treatment*
Mine enemy has more power. [*He draws, and is charmed from moving.*]

MIRANDA: O dear father,
Make not too rash° a trial° of him, for   *harsh / judgment*
He's gentle,° and not fearful.³   *noble*

PROSPERO: What, I say,
470   My foot° my tutor?—Put thy sword up, traitor,   *subordinate*
Who mak'st a show but dar'st not strike, thy conscience
Is so possessed with guilt. Come, from thy ward,°   *defensive posture*
For I can here disarm thee with this stick
And make thy weapon drop.

[*He brandishes his staff.*]

MIRANDA [*trying to hinder him*]:   Beseech you, father!

PROSPERO: Hence! Hang not on my garments.

MIRANDA: Sir, have pity!
I'll be his surety.°   *guarantee*

PROSPERO: Silence! One word more
Shall make me chide thee, if not hate thee. What,
An advocate for an impostor? Hush!
Thou think'st there is no more such shapes as he,
480   Having seen but him and Caliban. Foolish wench,
To° the most of men this is a Caliban,   *compared to*
And they to him are angels.

MIRANDA: My affections
Are then most humble; I have no ambition
To see a goodlier man.

PROSPERO [*to Ferdinand*]:   Come on, obey.
485   Thy nerves° are in their infancy again   *sinews*
And have no vigor in them.

FERDINAND: So they are.
My spirits,° as in a dream, are all bound up.   *vital powers*
My father's loss, the weakness which I feel,
The wreck of all my friends, nor this man's threats
490   To whom I am subdued, are but light° to me,   *unimportant*
Might I but through my prison once a day
Behold this maid. All corners else° o' th' earth   *other regions*
Let liberty make use of; space enough
Have I in such a prison.

PROSPERO [*aside*]:   It works. [*To Ferdinand.*] Come on.—

---

3. Frightening; cowardly.

495   Thou hast done well, fine Ariel! [*To Ferdinand.*] Follow me.
           [*To Ariel.*] Hark what thou else shalt do me.°   *for me*

MIRANDA [*to Ferdinand*]:   Be of comfort.
           My father's of a better nature, sir,
           Than he appears by speech. This is unwonted°   *unusual*
           Which now came from him.

PROSPERO [*to Ariel*]:   Thou shalt be as free
500   As mountain winds; but then° exactly do   *until then*
           All points of my command.

ARIEL: To th' syllable.

PROSPERO [*to Ferdinand*]:   Come, follow. [*To Miranda.*] Speak not for him.

                                               [*Exeunt.*]

ACT 2

Scene 1[4]

[*Enter Alonso, Sebastian, Antonio, Gonzalo, Adrian, Francisco, and others.*]

GONZALO [*to Alonso*]:   Beseech you, sir, be merry. You have cause,
           So have we all, of joy, for our escape
           Is much beyond our loss. Our hint° of woe   *occasion*
           Is common; every day some sailor's wife,
5   The masters of some merchant, and the merchant,[5]
           Have just our theme of woe. But for the miracle,
           I mean our preservation, few in millions
           Can speak like us. Then wisely, good sir, weigh
           Our sorrow with our comfort.

ALONSO: Prithee, peace.

SEBASTIAN [*aside to Antonio*]:   He receives comfort like cold porridge.[6]

ANTONIO [*aside to Sebastian*]:   The visitor[7] will not give him o'er[8] so.

SEBASTIAN: Look, he's winding up the watch of his wit; by and by it will strike.

GONZALO [*to Alonso*]:   Sir—

SEBASTIAN [*aside to Antonio*]:   One. Tell.°   *keep count*

GONZALO: When every grief is entertained
           That's offered, comes to th' entertainer—

SEBASTIAN: A dollar.[9]

GONZALO: Dolor comes to him, indeed. You have spoken truer than you purposed.

SEBASTIAN: You have taken it wiselier than I meant you should.

GONZALO [*to Alonso*]:   Therefore, my lord—

ANTONIO: Fie, what a spendthrift is he of his tongue!

ALONSO [*to Gonzalo*]:   I prithee, spare.°   *forbear*

GONZALO: Well, I have done. But yet—

SEBASTIAN [*aside to Antonio*]:   He will be talking.

---

4. Location: Another part of the island.
5. Officers of some merchant vessel and the owner himself.
6. Broth, with a pun on *peace* (peas), often used in porridge.

7. One taking comfort to the sick, as Gonzalo is doing.
8. Let him alone.
9. Widely circulated coin. (Sebastian puns on *entertainer* in the sense of inn-keeper; to Gonzalo, *dollar* suggests "dolor," or grief.)

ANTONIO [*aside to Sebastian*]: Which, of he or Adrian, for a good wager, first begins to crow?¹

SEBASTIAN: The old cock.°   *Gonzalo*

ANTONIO: The cockerel.°   *Adrian*

SEBASTIAN: Done. The wager?

ANTONIO: A laughter.²

SEBASTIAN: A match!°   *agreed*

ADRIAN: Though this island seem to be desert°—   *uninhabited*

ANTONIO: Ha, ha, ha!

SEBASTIAN: So, you're paid.

ADRIAN: Uninhabitable and almost inaccessible—

SEBASTIAN: Yet—

ADRIAN: Yet—

ANTONIO: He could not miss 't.

ADRIAN: It must needs be of subtle, tender, and delicate temperance.°   *climate*

ANTONIO: Temperance° was a delicate wench.³   *girl's name*

SEBASTIAN: Ay, and a subtle,° as he most learnedly delivered.⁴   *sexually tricky*

ADRIAN: The air breathes upon us here most sweetly.

SEBASTIAN: As if it had lungs, and rotten ones.

ANTONIO: Or as 'twere perfumed by a fen.°   *swamp*

GONZALO: Here is everything advantageous to life.

ANTONIO: True, save° means to live.   *except*

SEBASTIAN: Of that there's none, or little.

GONZALO: How lush and lusty° the grass looks! How green!   *healthy*

ANTONIO: The ground indeed is tawny.°   *dull brown*

SEBASTIAN: With an eye° of green in 't.   *spot*

ANTONIO: He misses not much.

SEBASTIAN: No. He doth but° mistake the truth totally.   *merely*

GONZALO: But the rarity of it is—which is indeed almost beyond credit—

SEBASTIAN: As many vouched rarities⁵ are.

GONZALO: That our garments, being, as they were, drenched in the sea, hold notwithstanding their freshness and glosses, being rather new-dyed than stained with salt water.

ANTONIO: If but one of his pockets⁶ could speak, would it not say he lies?

SEBASTIAN: Ay, or very falsely pocket up⁷ his report.

GONZALO: Methinks our garments are now as fresh as when we put them on first in Afric, at the marriage of the King's fair daughter Claribel to the King of Tunis.

SEBASTIAN: 'Twas a sweet marriage, and we prosper well in our return.

ADRIAN: Tunis was never graced before with such a paragon to⁸ their queen.

GONZALO: Not since widow Dido's⁹ time.

ANTONIO [*aside to Sebastian*]: Widow? A pox o' that! How came that "widow" in? Widow Dido!

---

1. Speak.
2. Whoever laughs, wins.
3. Antonio is mocking Adrian's Puritan phrase, *tender, and delicate temperance*, by applying it to a young woman.
4. Puritan cant for "well-phrased." (Sebastian joins Antonio in baiting the Puritans.)
5. Wonders guaranteed to be true.

6. I.e., because they are muddy.
7. Suppress.
8. For.
9. Queen of Carthage, deserted by Aeneas. (She was, in fact, a widow when Aeneas, a widower, met her, but Antonio may be amused at Gonzalo's prudish use of "widow" for a woman deserted by her lover.)

SEBASTIAN: What if he had said "widower Aeneas" too? Good Lord, how you take it!

ADRIAN [to Gonzalo]:   "Widow Dido" said you? You make me study of that. She was of Carthage, not of Tunis.

GONZALO: This Tunis, sir, was Carthage.

ADRIAN: Carthage?

GONZALO: I assure you, Carthage.

ANTONIO: His word is more than the miraculous harp.[1]

SEBASTIAN: He hath raised the wall, and houses too.

ANTONIO: What impossible matter will he make easy next?

SEBASTIAN: I think he will carry this island home in his pocket and give it his son for an apple.

ANTONIO: And, sowing the kernels of it in the sea, bring forth more islands.

GONZALO: Ay.[2]

ANTONIO: Why, in good time.

GONZALO [to Alonso]:   Sir, we were talking that our garments seem now as fresh as when we were at Tunis at the marriage of your daughter, who is now queen.

ANTONIO: And the rarest that e'er came there.

SEBASTIAN: Bate,° I beseech you, widow Dido.   *except*

ANTONIO: O, widow Dido? Ay, widow Dido.

GONZALO: Is not, sir, my doublet as fresh as the first day I wore it? I mean, in a sort.[3]

ANTONIO: That "sort"[4] was well fished for.

GONZALO: When I wore it at your daughter's marriage.

ALONSO: You cram these words into mine ears against
        The stomach of my sense.[5] Would I had never
        Married° my daughter there! For, coming thence,   *married off*
        My son is lost and, in my rate,° she too,   *estimation*
        Who is so far from Italy removed
95   I ne'er again shall see her. O thou mine heir
        Of Naples and of Milan, what strange fish
        Hath made his meal on thee?

FRANCISCO: Sir, he may live.
        I saw him beat the surges° under him   *waves*
        And ride upon their backs. He trod the water,
100   Whose enmity he flung aside, and breasted
        The surge most swoll'n that met him. His bold head
        'Bove the contentious waves he kept, and oared
        Himself with his good arms in lusty stroke
        To th' shore, that o'er his° wave-worn basis° bowed,   *its / base*
105   As° stooping to relieve him. I not doubt   *as if*
        He came alive to land.

ALONSO: No, no, he's gone.

---

1. The harp of Amphion, which raised the walls of Thebes; Gonzalo has exceeded that deed by recreating ancient Carthage mistakenly on the site of modern-day Tunis.
2. This and Antonio's rejoinder have not been satisfactorily explained.
3. Comparatively.
4. Play on the idea of drawing lots, or else fishing for something to say.
5. My appetite to hear them.

SEBASTIAN [*to Alonso*]:   Sir, you may thank yourself for this great loss,
    That° would not bless our Europe with your daughter,   *you who*
    But rather loose° her to an African,   *release; lose*
110   Where she at least is banished from your eye,
    Who hath cause to wet the grief on 't.
ALONSO: Prithee, peace.
SEBASTIAN: You were kneeled to and importuned otherwise
    By all of us, and the fair soul herself
    Weighed between loathness and obedience at
115   Which end o' the beam should bow.[6] We have lost your son,
    I fear, forever. Milan and Naples have
    More widows in them of this business' making
    Than we bring men to comfort them.
    The fault's your own.
ALONSO: So is the dear'st° o' the loss.   *heaviest*
GONZALO: My lord Sebastian,
    The truth you speak doth lack some gentleness
    And time to speak it in. You rub the sore
    When you should bring the plaster.°   *bandage*
SEBASTIAN: Very well.
ANTONIO: And most chirurgeonly.°   *like a surgeon*
GONZALO [*to Alonso*]:   It is foul weather in us all, good sir,
    When you are cloudy.
SEBASTIAN [*to Antonio*]:   Fowl weather?
ANTONIO [*to Sebastian*]:   Very foul.
GONZALO: Had I plantation[7] of this isle, my lord—
ANTONIO [*to Sebastian*]:   He'd sow 't with nettle seed.
SEBASTIAN: Or docks, or mallows.[8]
GONZALO: And were the king on 't, what would I do?
SEBASTIAN: Scape° being drunk for want° of wine.   *escape / only for lack*
GONZALO: I' the commonwealth I would by contraries[9]
    Execute all things; for no kind of traffic°   *trade*
    Would I admit; no name of magistrate;
    Letters° should not be known; riches, poverty,   *learning*
135   And use of service,° none; contract, succession,°   *servants / inheritance*
    Bourn,° bound of land, tilth,° vineyard, none;   *borders / tilled soil*
    No use of metal, corn,° or wine, or oil;   *grain*
    No occupation; all men idle, all,
    And women too, but innocent and pure;
    No sovereignty—
SEBASTIAN: Yet he would be king on 't.
ANTONIO: The latter end of his commonwealth forgets the beginning.
GONZALO: All things in common nature should produce
    Without sweat or endeavor. Treason, felony,
    Sword, pike,° knife, gun, or need of any engine°   *lance / weapon*
145   Would I not have; but nature should bring forth,

6. Which side of the moral scale was heavier.   8. Antidotes to nettle stings.
7. Colonization; planting.   9. In contrast to custom.

Of its own kind, all foison,° all abundance,   *plenty*
To feed my innocent people.

SEBASTIAN: No marrying 'mong his subjects?

ANTONIO: None, man, all idle—whores and knaves.

GONZALO: I would with such perfection govern, sir,
T' excel the Golden Age.[1]

SEBASTIAN: 'Save° His Majesty!   *God save*

ANTONIO: Long live Gonzalo!

GONZALO: And—do you mark me, sir?

ALONSO: Prithee, no more. Thou dost talk nothing to me.

GONZALO: I do well believe Your Highness, and did it to minister occasion[2] to
these gentlemen, who are of such sensible[3] and nimble lungs that they always use to laugh at nothing.

ANTONIO: 'Twas you we laughed at.

GONZALO: Who in this kind of merry fooling am nothing to you; so you may continue, and laugh at nothing still.

ANTONIO: What a blow was there given!

SEBASTIAN: An[4] it had not fallen flat-long.[5]

GONZALO: You are gentlemen of brave mettle; you would lift the moon out of her
sphere if she would continue in it five weeks without changing.

[*Enter Ariel (invisible) playing solemn music.*]

SEBASTIAN: We would so, and then go a-batfowling.[6]

ANTONIO: Nay, good my lord, be not angry.

GONZALO: No, I warrant you, I will not adventure my discretion[7] so weakly. Will
you laugh me asleep? For I am very heavy.[8]

ANTONIO: Go sleep, and hear us.

[*All sleep except Alonso, Sebastian, and Antonio.*]

ALONSO: What, all so soon asleep? I wish mine eyes
Would, with themselves, shut up my thoughts. I find
They are inclined to do so.

SEBASTIAN: Please you, sir,
Do not omit° the heavy offer of it.   *neglect*
It seldom visits sorrow; when it doth,
It is a comforter.

ANTONIO: We two, my lord,
Will guard your person while you take your rest,
And watch your safety.

ALONSO: Thank you. Wondrous heavy.

[*Alonso sleeps. Exit Ariel.*]

SEBASTIAN: What a strange drowsiness possesses them!

ANTONIO: It is the quality o' the climate.

SEBASTIAN: Why
180   Doth it not then our eyelids sink? I find not
Myself disposed to sleep.

---

1. In Hesiod, an age of innocence and abundance.
2. Provide opportunity.
3. Sensitive.
4. If.
5. Fallen flat.

6. Hunting birds at night with sticks (bats); duping a fool
(Gonzalo).
7. Risk my reputation for discretion.
8. Sleepy.

ANTONIO: Nor I. My spirits are nimble.
        They fell together all, as by consent;°   *agreement*
        They dropped, as by a thunderstroke. What might,
        Worthy Sebastian, O, what might—? No more.
185   And yet methinks I see it in thy face,
        What thou shouldst be. Th' occasion speaks° thee, and   *summons*
        My strong imagination sees a crown
        Dropping upon thy head.
SEBASTIAN: What, art thou waking?
ANTONIO: Do you not hear me speak?
SEBASTIAN: I do, and surely
190   It is a sleepy language, and thou speak'st
        Out of thy sleep. What is it thou didst say?
        This is a strange repose, to be asleep
        With eyes wide open—standing, speaking, moving—
        And yet so fast asleep.
ANTONIO: Noble Sebastian,
195   Thou lett'st thy fortune sleep—die, rather; wink'st°   *shut your eyes*
        Whiles thou art waking.
SEBASTIAN: Thou dost snore distinctly;°   *articulately*
        There's meaning in thy snores.
ANTONIO: I am more serious than my custom. You
        Must be so too if heed° me, which to do   *you heed*
        Trebles thee o'er.[9]
SEBASTIAN: Well, I am standing water.
ANTONIO: I'll teach you how to flow.
SEBASTIAN: Do so. To ebb
        Hereditary sloth[1] instructs me.
ANTONIO: O,
        If you but knew how you the purpose cherish°   *enrich*
        Whiles thus you mock it! How, in stripping it,
205   You more invest° it! Ebbing men, indeed,   *clothe*
        Most often do so near the bottom run
        By their own fear or sloth.
SEBASTIAN: Prithee, say on:
        The setting° of thine eye and cheek proclaim   *expression*
        A matter from thee, and a birth indeed
210   Which throes° thee much to yield.   *pains*
ANTONIO: Thus, sir:
        Although this lord of weak remembrance,° this   *memory*
        Who shall be of as little memory°   *as little remembered*
        When he is earthed°, hath here almost persuaded—   *buried*
        For he's a spirit of persuasion, only
215   Professes° to persuade—the King his son's alive,   *functions*
        'Tis as impossible that he's undrowned
        As he that sleeps here swims.

9. Will make you three times as powerful.   1. Natural laziness; the position of younger son.

SEBASTIAN: I have no hope
              That he's undrowned.
ANTONIO: O, out of that "no hope"
              What great hope have you! No hope that way is
220   Another way so high a hope that even
              Ambition cannot pierce a wink° beyond,   *glimpse*
              But doubt discovery there. Will you grant with me
              That Ferdinand is drowned?
SEBASTIAN: He's gone.
ANTONIO: Then tell me,
              Who's the next heir of Naples?
SEBASTIAN: Claribel.
ANTONIO: She that is Queen of Tunis; she that dwells
              Ten leagues beyond man's life; she that from Naples
              Can have no note,° unless the sun were post°—   *news / messenger*
              The Man i' the Moon's too slow—till newborn chins
              Be rough and razorable; she that from° whom   *leaving*
230   We all were sea-swallowed, though some cast² again,
              And by that destiny to perform an act
              Whereof what's past is prologue, what to come
              In yours and my discharge.°   *business*
SEBASTIAN: What stuff is this? How say you?
              'Tis true my brother's daughter's Queen of Tunis,
235   So is she heir of Naples, twixt which regions
              There is some space.
ANTONIO: A space whose every cubit°   *unit of length*
              Seems to cry out, "How shall that Claribel
              Measure us° back to Naples? Keep in Tunis,   *the cubits*
              And let Sebastian wake." Say this were death
240   That now hath seized them, why, they were no worse
              Than now they are. There be that can rule Naples
              As well as he that sleeps, lords that can prate°   *prattle*
              As amply and unnecessarily
              As this Gonzalo. I myself could make
245   A chough° of as deep chat. O, that you bore   *jackdaw*
              The mind that I do! What a sleep were this
              For your advancement! Do you understand me?
SEBASTIAN: Methinks I do.
ANTONIO: And how does your content°   *desire*
              Tender° your own good fortune?   *regard*
SEBASTIAN: I remember
250   You did supplant your brother Prospero.
ANTONIO: True.
              And look how well my garments sit upon me,
              Much feater° than before. My brother's servants   *more suitably*
              Were then my fellows.° Now they are my men.°   *equals / servants*
SEBASTIAN: But, for your conscience?

2. Thrown up; cast, as in a play.

ANTONIO: Ay, sir, where lies that? If 'twere a kibe,°   *sore on the heel*
       'Twould put me to° my slipper; but I feel not   *make me wear*
       This deity in my bosom. Twenty consciences
       That stand twixt me and Milan, candied° be they   *sugared*
       And melt ere they molest!° Here lies your brother,   *interfere*
260   No better than the earth he lies upon,
       If he were that which now he's like—that's dead,
       Whom I, with this obedient steel, three inches of it,
       Can lay to bed forever; whiles you, doing thus,
       To the perpetual wink° for aye° might put   *sleep / ever*
265   This ancient morsel, this Sir Prudence, who
       Should not° upbraid our course. For all the rest,   *would not be able to*
       They'll take° suggestion as a cat laps milk;   *respond to*
       They'll tell the clock° to any business that   *chime in*
       We say befits the hour.
SEBASTIAN: Thy case, dear friend,
270   Shall be my precedent. As thou gott'st Milan,
       I'll come by Naples. Draw thy sword. One stroke
       Shall free thee from the tribute which thou payest,
       And I the king shall love thee.
ANTONIO: Draw together;
       And when I rear my hand, do you the like
       To fall it° on Gonzalo. [*They draw.*]   *let it fall*
SEBASTIAN: O, but one word. [*They talk apart.*]
   [*Enter Ariel (invisible), with music and song.*]
ARIEL [*to Gonzalo*]: My master through his art foresees the danger
       That you, his friend, are in, and sends me forth—
       For else his project dies—to keep them living.
   [*Sings in Gonzalo's ear.*]
       While you here do snoring lie,
280   Open-eyed conspiracy
         His time° doth take.   *opportunity*
       If of life you keep a care,
       Shake off slumber, and beware.
         Awake, awake!
ANTONIO: Then let us both be sudden.°   *quick*
GONZALO [*waking*]: Now, good angels preserve the King!
   [*The others wake.*]
ALONSO: Why, how now, ho, awake? Why are you drawn?
       Wherefore this ghastly looking?
GONZALO: What's the matter?
SEBASTIAN: Whiles we stood here securing° your repose,   *guarding*
290   Even now, we heard a hollow burst of bellowing
       Like bulls, or rather lions. Did 't not wake you?
       It struck mine ear most terribly.
ALONSO: I heard nothing.
ANTONIO: O, 'twas a din to fright a monster's ear,
       To make an earthquake! Sure it was the roar
       Of a whole herd of lions.

ALONSO: Heard you this, Gonzalo?
GONZALO: Upon mine honor, sir, I heard a humming,
          And that a strange one too, which did awake me.
          I shaked you, sir, and cried. As mine eyes opened,
          I saw their weapons drawn. There was a noise,
300   That's verily.° 'Tis best we stand upon our guard,   *true*
          Or that we quit this place. Let's draw our weapons.
ALONSO: Lead off this ground, and let's make further search
          For my poor son.
GONZALO: Heavens keep him from these beasts!
          For he is, sure, i' th' island.
ALONSO: Lead away.
ARIEL [*aside*]: Prospero my lord shall know what I have done.
          So, King, go safely on to seek thy son.

                                        [*Exeunt (separately).*]

                      Scene 2³
     [*Enter Caliban with a burden of wood. A noise of thunder heard.*]
CALIBAN: All the infections that the sun sucks up
          From bogs, fens, flats,° on Prosper fall, and make him   *swamps*
          By inchmeal° a disease! His spirits hear me,   *inch by inch*
          And yet I needs must° curse. But they'll nor° pinch,   *have to / neither*
5   Fright me with urchin shows,° pitch me i' the mire,   *hedgehog goblins*
          Nor lead me, like a firebrand,⁴ in the dark
          Out of my way, unless he bid 'em. But
          For every trifle are they set upon me,
          Sometimes like apes, that mow° and chatter at me   *make faces*
10   And after bite me; then like hedgehogs, which
          Lie tumbling in my barefoot way and mount
          Their pricks at my footfall. Sometimes am I
          All wound with adders, who with cloven tongues
          Do hiss me into madness.
     [*Enter Trinculo.*]
                      Lo, now, lo!
15   Here comes a spirit of his, and to torment me
          For bringing wood in slowly. I'll fall flat.
          Perchance he will not mind° me. [*He lies down.*]   *notice*
TRINCULO: Here's neither bush nor shrub to bear off⁵ any weather at all. And an-
          other storm brewing; I hear it sing i' the wind. Yond same black cloud,
20   yond huge one, looks like a foul bombard⁶ that would shed his⁷ liquor. If
          it should thunder as it did before, I know not where to hide my head.
          Yond same cloud cannot choose but fall by pailfuls. [*Seeing Caliban.*]
          What have we here, a man or a fish? Dead or alive? A fish, he smells like
          a fish; a very ancient and fishlike smell; a kind of not-of-the-newest poor-
25   John.⁸ A strange fish! Were I in England now, as once I was, and had but
          this fish painted,⁹ not a holiday fool there but would give a piece of

---

3. Location: another part of the island.   6. Leather bottle.
4. In the form of a will-'o-th'-wisp, a light that appears at   7. Its.
night over marshy ground, often a metaphor for false hope.   8. Salted fish.
5. Ward off.   9. Painted on a sign outside a booth at a fair.

silver. There would this monster make a man.[1] Any strange beast there
makes a man. When they will not give a doit[2] to relieve a lame beggar,
they will lay out ten to see a dead Indian. Legged like a man, and his fins
30   like arms! Warm, o' my troth! I do now let loose my opinion, hold it no
longer: this is no fish, but an islander, that hath lately suffered[3] by a
thunderbolt. [*Thunder.*] Alas, the storm is come again! My best way is to
creep under his gaberdine.[4] There is no other shelter hereabout. Misery
acquaints a man with strange bedfellows. I will here shroud[5] till the dregs
35   of the storm be past. [*He creeps under Caliban's garment.*]

[*Enter Stephano, singing, (a bottle in his hand).*]

STEPHANO: "I shall no more to sea, to sea,
          Here shall I die ashore—"
          This is a very scurvy tune to sing at a man's funeral.
          Well, here's my comfort. [*Drinks.*]

     [*Sings.*]

40   "The master, the swabber, the boatswain, and I,
                    The gunner and his mate,
               Loved Mall, Meg, and Marian, and Margery,
                    But none of us cared for Kate.
                    For she had a tongue with a tang,
45   Would cry to a sailor, 'Go hang!'
               She loved not the savor of tar nor of pitch,
               Yet a tailor might scratch her where'er she did itch.
                    Then to sea, boys, and let her go hang!"

          This is a scurvy tune too. But here's my comfort.
     [*Drinks.*]

CALIBAN: Do not torment me! O!

STEPHANO: What's the matter?[6] Have we devils here? Do you put tricks upon 's
          with savages and men of Ind,[7] ha! I have not scaped drowning to be
          afeard now of your four legs. For it hath been said, "As proper[8] a man as
          ever went on four[9] legs cannot make him give ground," and it shall be
55   said so again while Stephano breathes at' nostrils.

CALIBAN: This spirit torments me! O!

STEPHANO: This is some monster of the isle with four legs, who hath got, as I take
          it, an ague. Where the devil should he learn[1] our language? I will give
          him some relief, if it be but for that.[2] If I can recover[3] him and keep him
60   tame and get to Naples with him, he's a present for any emperor that ever
          trod on neat's leather.[4]

CALIBAN: Do not torment me, prithee. I'll bring my wood home faster.

STEPHANO: He's in his fit now and does not talk after the wisest. He shall taste of
          my bottle. If he have never drunk wine afore, it will go near to remove

1. Make a man's fortune; be indistinguishable from an
Englishman.
2. Small coin.
3. Died.
4. Cloak.
5. Take shelter.
6. What's going on here?
7. India.

8. Handsome.
9. The expression supplies *two* legs, but Stephano thinks
he sees a creature with four.
1. Could he have learned.
2. His speaking our language.
3. Restore.
4. Cowhide.

65   his fit. If I can recover him and keep him tame, I will not take too much[5] for him. He shall pay for him that hath him, and that soundly.

CALIBAN: Thou dost me yet but little hurt; thou wilt anon,[6] I know it by thy trembling. Now Prosper works upon thee.

STEPHANO: Come on your ways. Open your mouth. Here is that which will give
70   language to you, cat.[7] Open your mouth. This will shake your shaking, I can tell you, and that soundly. [*Giving Caliban a drink.*] You cannot tell who's your friend. Open your chaps[8] again.

TRINCULO: I should know that voice. It should be—but he is drowned, and these are devils. O, defend me!

STEPHANO: Four legs and two voices—a most delicate[9] monster! His forward voice now is to speak well of his friend; his backward voice is to utter foul speeches and to detract. If all the wine in my bottle will recover him, I will help[1] his ague. Come. [*Giving a drink.*] Amen! I will pour some in thy other mouth.

TRINCULO: Stephano!

STEPHANO: Doth thy other mouth call me?[2] Mercy, mercy! This is a devil, and no monster. I will leave him. I have no long spoon.[3]

TRINCULO: Stephano! If thou beest Stephano, touch me and speak to me, for I am Trinculo—be not afeard—thy good friend Trinculo.

STEPHANO: If thou beest Trinculo, come forth. I'll pull thee by the lesser legs. If any be Trinculo's legs, these are they. [*Pulling him out.*] Thou art very Trinculo indeed! How cam'st thou to be the siege[4] of this mooncalf?[5] Can he vent[6] Trinculos?

TRINCULO: I took him to be killed with a thunderstroke. But art thou not drowned,
90   Stephano? I hope now thou art not drowned. Is the storm overblown?[7] I hid me under the dead mooncalf's gaberdine for fear of the storm. And art thou living, Stephano? O Stephano, two Neapolitans scaped!

[*He capers with Stephano.*]

STEPHANO: Prithee, do not turn me about. My stomach is not constant.[8]

CALIBAN: These be fine things, an if[9] they be not spirits.
     That's a brave[1] god, and bears celestial liquor.
     I will kneel to him.

STEPHANO: How didst thou scape? How cam'st thou hither? Swear by this bottle how thou cam'st hither. I escaped upon a butt of sack[2] which the sailors
100   heaved o'erboard—by this bottle, which I made of the bark of a tree with mine own hands since I was cast ashore.

CALIBAN [*kneeling*]: I'll swear upon that bottle to be thy true subject, for the liquor is not earthly.

STEPHANO: Here. Swear then how thou escapedst.

TRINCULO: Swum ashore, man, like a duck. I can swim like a duck, I'll be sworn.

5. No perice will be too much.
6. Presently
7. Allusion to the proverb "Liquor will make a cat talk."
8. Jaws.
9. Ingenious.
1. Cure.
2. Call my name (know who I am).
3. Allusion to the proverb "He who sups with the devil must have a long spoon."

4. Excrement.
5. Monster.
6. Excrete.
7. Blown over.
8. Unsteady.
9. If.
1. Magnificent.
2. Barrel of Canary wine.

STEPHANO: Here, kiss the book.[3] Though thou canst swim like a duck, thou art
　　　　made like a goose.[4] [Giving him a drink.]

TRINCULO: O Stephano, hast any more of this?

STEPHANO: The whole butt, man. My cellar is in a rock by the seaside, where my
110　　　wine is hid.—How now, mooncalf? How does thine ague?

CALIBAN: Hast thou not dropped from heaven?

STEPHANO: Out o' the moon, I do assure thee. I was the Man i' the Moon when
　　　　time was.[5]

CALIBAN: I have seen thee in her, and I do adore thee.
115　　　My mistress showed me thee, and thy dog, and thy bush.[6]

STEPHANO: Come, swear to that. Kiss the book. I will furnish it anon with new
　　　　contents. Swear. [Giving him a drink.]

TRINCULO: By this good light, this is a very shallow monster! I afeard of him? A
　　　　very weak monster! The Man i' the Moon? A most poor credulous mon-
120　　　ster! Well drawn,[7] monster, in good sooth!

CALIBAN　[to Stephano]: I'll show thee every fertile inch o' th' island,
　　　　And I will kiss thy foot. I prithee, be my god.

TRINCULO: By this light, a most perfidious and drunken monster! When 's god's
　　　　asleep, he'll rob his bottle.

CALIBAN: I'll kiss thy foot. I'll swear myself thy subject.

STEPHANO: Come on then. Down, and swear.

　　　[Caliban kneels.]

TRINCULO: I shall laugh myself to death at this puppy-headed monster. A most
　　　　scurvy monster! I could find in my heart to beat him—

STEPHANO: Come, kiss.

TRINCULO: But that the poor monster's in drink.[8] An abominable monster!

CALIBAN: I'll show thee the best springs. I'll pluck thee berries.
　　　　I'll fish for thee and get thee wood enough.
　　　　A plague upon the tyrant that I serve!
　　　　I'll bear him no more sticks, but follow thee,
135　　　Thou wondrous man.

TRINCULO: A most ridiculous monster, to make a wonder of a poor drunkard!

CALIBAN: I prithee, let me bring thee where crabs° grow,　　　　　　*crab apples*
　　　　And I with my long nails will dig thee pignuts,°　　　　　　　*peanuts*
　　　　Show thee a jay's nest, and instruct thee how
140　　　To snare the nimble marmoset.° I'll bring thee　　　　*small monkey*
　　　　To clustering filberts, and sometimes I'll get thee
　　　　Young scamels[9] from the rock. Wilt thou go with me?

STEPHANO: I prithee now, lead the way without any more talking.—Trinculo, the
　　　　King and all our company else being drowned, we will inherit[1] here.—
145　　　Here, bear my bottle.—Fellow Trinculo, we'll fill him by and by[2] again.

CALIBAN　[sings drunkenly]: Farewell, master, farewell, farewell!

TRINCULO: A howling monster; a drunken monster!

---

3. I.e., the bottle (ironic allusion to swearing on the Bible).
4. With a long neck.
5. Once upon a time.
6. The Man in the Moon was popularly imagined to have with him a dog and a thorn-bush.
7. Drawn from the bottle.
8. Drunk.
9. Unexplained, but either a shellfish or a rock-nesting bird.
1. Take possession.
2. Soon.

CALIBAN: No more dams I'll make for fish,
          Nor fetch in firing°   *firewood*
150   At requiring,
          Nor scrape trenchering°, nor wash dish.   *wooden plates*
          'Ban, 'Ban, Ca-Caliban
          Has a new master. Get a new man!°   *servant*
    Freedom, high-day!° High-day, freedom! Freedom, high-day, freedom!
                                                        holiday
STEPHANO: O brave monster! Lead the way.   *[Exeunt.]*

ACT 3

Scene 1³

[Enter Ferdinand, bearing a log.]

FERDINAND: There be some sports are painful,° and their labor   *strenuous*
          Delight in them sets off.° Some kinds of baseness   *compensates*
          Are nobly undergone, and most poor matters°   *poorest affairs*
          Point to rich ends. This my mean° task   *lowly*
5   Would be as heavy to me as odious, but°   *but that*
          The mistress which I serve quickens° what's dead   *brings to life*
          And makes my labors pleasures. O, she is
          Ten times more gentle than her father's crabbed,
          And he's composed of harshness. I must remove
10   Some thousands of these logs and pile them up,
          Upon a sore injunction.° My sweet mistress   *severe command*
          Weeps when she sees me work and says such baseness
          Had never like executor. I forget;
          But these sweet thoughts do even refresh my labors,
15   Most busy lest⁴ when I do it.

[Enter Miranda; and Prospero (at a distance, unseen).]

MIRANDA: Alas now, pray you,
          Work not so hard. I would the lightning had
          Burnt up those logs that you are enjoined° to pile!   *commanded*
          Pray, set it down and rest you. When this burns,
          'Twill weep° for having wearied you. My father   *exude resin*
20   Is hard at study. Pray now, rest yourself.
          He's safe for these three hours.
FERDINAND: O most dear mistress,
          The sun will set before I shall discharge
          What I must strive to do.
MIRANDA: If you'll sit down,
          I'll bear your logs the while. Pray, give me that.
25   I'll carry it to the pile.
FERDINAND: No, precious creature,
          I had rather crack my sinews, break my back,
          Than you should such dishonor undergo
          While I sit lazy by.
MIRANDA: It would become me

---

3. Location: Before Prospero's cell.   4. Busy, but with my mind on other things.

As well as it does you; and I should do it
30   With much more ease, for my good will is to it,
And yours it is against.

PROSPERO [*aside*]:   Poor worm, thou art infected!
This visitation[5] shows it.

MIRANDA: You look wearily.

FERDINAND: No, noble mistress, 'tis fresh morning with me
When you are by° at night. I do beseech you—   nearby
35   Chiefly that I might set it in my prayers—
What is your name?

MIRANDA: Miranda.—O my father,
I have broke your hest° to say so.   command

FERDINAND: Admired Miranda![6]
Indeed the top of admiration, worth
What's dearest to the world! Full many a lady
40   I have eyed with best regard, and many a time
The harmony of their tongues hath into bondage
Brought my too diligent° ear. For several° virtues   attentive / different
Have I liked several women, never any
With so full soul° but some defect in her   so wholeheartedly
45   Did quarrel with the noblest grace she owed°   owned
And put it to the foil.[7] But you, O you,
So perfect and so peerless, are created
Of every creature's best!

MIRANDA: I do not know
One of my sex; no woman's face remember,
50   Save, from my glass, mine own. Nor have I seen
More that I may call men than you, good friend,
And my dear father. How features are abroad°   elsewhere
I am skilless° of; but, by my modesty,°   ignorant / virginity
The jewel in my dower, I would not wish
55   Any companion in the world but you;
Nor can imagination form a shape,
Besides yourself, to like of.° But I prattle   care for
Something° too wildly, and my father's precepts   somewhat
I therein do forget.

FERDINAND: I am in my condition°   rank
60   A prince, Miranda; I do think, a king—
I would,° not so!—and would no more endure   wish
This wooden slavery than to suffer
The flesh-fly[8] blow° my mouth. Hear my soul speak: lay eggs
The very instant that I saw you did
65   My heart fly to your service, there resides
To make me slave to it, and for your sake
Am I this patient log-man.

MIRANDA: Do you love me?

---

5. Visit; attack of plague (in the metaphor of *infected*).
6. Her name means "to be admired or wondered at."
7. Overthrow; contrast.
8. Insect that lays eggs in dead flesh.

FERDINAND: O heaven, O earth, bear witness to this sound,
    And crown what I profess with kind event°   *favorable outcome*
70   If I speak true! If hollowly,° invert°   *falsely / turn*
    What best is boded° me to mischief!° I   *in store for / harm*
    Beyond all limit of what else i' the world
    Do love, prize, honor you.
MIRANDA   [*weeping*]:   I am a fool
    To weep at what I am glad of.
PROSPERO   [*aside*]:   Fair encounter
75   Of two most rare affections! Heavens rain grace
    On that which breeds between 'em!
FERDINAND: Wherefore weep you?
MIRANDA: At mine unworthiness, that dare not offer
    What I desire to give, and much less take
    What I shall die⁹ to want.° But this is trifling,   *lack*
80   And all the more it seeks to hide itself
    The bigger bulk it shows. Hence, bashful cunning,°   *coyness*
    And prompt me, plain and holy innocence!
    I am your wife, if you will marry me;
    If not, I'll die your maid.¹ To be your fellow°   *equal*
85   You may deny me, but I'll be your servant
    Whether you will° or no.   *desire it*
FERDINAND: My mistress, dearest,
    And I thus humble ever.
MIRANDA: My husband, then?
FERDINAND: Ay, with a heart as willing
90   As bondage e'er of freedom.° Here's my hand.   *to win freedom*
MIRANDA   [*clasping his hand*]: And mine, with my heart in 't. And now farewell
    Till half an hour hence.
FERDINAND: A thousand thousand!°   *farewells*
    [*Exeunt (Ferdinand and Miranda, separately).*]
PROSPERO: So glad of this as they I cannot be,
    Who are surprised with all; but my rejoicing
95   At nothing can be more. I'll to my book,
    For yet ere suppertime must I perform
    Much business appertaining.°   [*Exit.*]   *relevant*

Scene 2²

[*Enter Caliban, Stephano, and Trinculo.*]
STEPHANO: Tell not me. When the butt is out,³ we will drink water, not a drop
    before. Therefore bear up and board 'em.⁴ Servant monster, drink to me.
TRINCULO: Servant monster? The folly of this island! They say there's but five
    upon this isle. We are three of them; if th' other two be brained⁵ like us,
5   the state totters.

---

9. Probably with unconscious sexual meaning.   3. Empty.
1. Servant; virgin.   4. Drink up (using the language of a nautical assault).
2. Location: Another part of the island.   5. Have brains.

STEPHANO: Drink, servant monster, when I bid thee. Thy eyes are almost set[6] in
  thy head.
 [*Giving a drink.*]
TRINCULO: Where should they be set[7] else? He were a brave[8] monster indeed if
  they were set in his tail.
STEPHANO: My man-monster hath drowned his tongue in sack. For my part, the
  sea cannot drown me. I swam, ere I could recover[9] the shore, five and
  thirty leagues off and on. By this light, thou shalt be my lieutenant, mon-
  ster, or my standard.[1]
TRINCULO: Your lieutenant, if you list;[2] he's no standard.[3]
STEPHANO: We'll not run,[4] Monsieur Monster.
TRINCULO: Nor go[5] neither, but you'll lie[6] like dogs and yet say nothing neither.
STEPHANO: Mooncalf, speak once in thy life, if thou beest a good mooncalf.
CALIBAN: How does thy honor? Let me lick thy shoe.
  I'll not serve him. He is not valiant.
TRINCULO: Thou liest, most ignorant monster, I am in case[7] to jostle a constable.
  Why, thou debauched fish, thou, was there ever man a coward that hath
  drunk so much sack[8] as I today? Wilt thou tell a monstrous lie, being but
  half a fish and half a monster?
CALIBAN: Lo, how he mocks me! Wilt thou let him, my lord?
TRINCULO: "Lord," quoth he? That a monster should be such a natural![9]
CALIBAN: Lo, lo, again! Bite him to death, I prithee.
STEPHANO: Trinculo, keep a good tongue in your head. If you prove a mutineer—
  the next tree![1] The poor monster's my subject, and he shall not suffer in-
  dignity.
CALIBAN: I thank my noble lord. Wilt thou be pleased
  To hearken once again to the suit I made to thee?
STEPHANO: Marry, will I. Kneel and repeat it. I will stand, and so shall Trinculo.
 [*Caliban kneels.*]
 [*Enter Ariel, invisible.*]
CALIBAN: As I told thee before, I am subject to a tyrant,
  A sorcerer, that by his cunning hath
35 Cheated me of the island.
ARIEL   [*mimicking Trinculo*]: Thou liest.
CALIBAN: Thou liest, thou jesting monkey, thou!
  I would my valiant master would destroy thee.
  I do not lie.
STEPHANO: Trinculo, if you trouble him any more in 's tale, by this hand, I will
  supplant[2] some of your teeth.
TRINCULO: Why, I said nothing.
STEPHANO: Mum, then, and no more.—Proceed.

---

6. Sunk, like the sun.
7. Placed.
8. Fine.
9. Reach.
1. Standard-bearer.
2. Prefer.
3. Not able to stand up.
4. Retreat; urinate.

5. Walk.
6. Tell lies; lie down; excrete.
7. Fit condition.
8. Spanish white wine.
9. Fool; as opposed to "unnatural."
1. I.e., you'll hang.
2. Remove.

CALIBAN: I say by sorcery he got this isle;
45   From me he got it. If thy greatness will
             Revenge it on him—for I know thou dar'st,
             But this thing° dare not—   *Trinculo*
STEPHANO: That's most certain.
CALIBAN: Thou shalt be lord of it, and I'll serve thee.
STEPHANO: How now shall this be compassed? Canst thou bring me to the party?³
CALIBAN: Yea, yea, my lord. I'll yield him thee asleep,
             Where thou mayst knock a nail into his head.
ARIEL: Thou liest; thou canst not.
CALIBAN: What a pied ninny's° this! Thou scurvy patch!°—   *motley fool / clown*
55   I do beseech thy greatness, give him blows
             And take his bottle from him. When that's gone
             He shall drink naught but brine, for I'll not show him
             Where the quick freshes° are.   *freshwater springs*
STEPHANO: Trinculo, run into no further danger. Interrupt the monster one word
60   further and, by this hand, I'll turn my mercy out o' doors and make a
             stockfish⁴ of thee.
TRINCULO: Why, what did I? I did nothing. I'll go farther off.
STEPHANO: Didst thou not say he lied?
ARIEL: Thou liest.
STEPHANO: Do I so? Take thou that. [*He beats Trinculo.*] As you like this, give me
             the lie⁵ another time.
TRINCULO: I did not give the lie. Out o' your wits and hearing too? A pox o' your
             bottle! This can sack and drinking do. A murrain⁶ on your monster, and
             the devil take your fingers!
CALIBAN: Ha, ha, ha!
STEPHANO: Now, forward with your tale. [*To Trinculo.*] Prithee, stand further off.
CALIBAN: Beat him enough. After a little time
             I'll beat him too.
STEPHANO: Stand farther.—Come, proceed.
CALIBAN: Why, as I told thee, 'tis a custom with him
             I' th' afternoon to sleep. There thou mayst brain him,
             Having first seized his books; or with a log
             Batter his skull, or paunch° him with a stake,   *stab in the belly*
             Or cut his weasand° with thy knife. Remember   *windpipe*
80   First to possess his books, for without them
             He's but a sot,° as I am, nor hath not   *fool*
             One spirit to command. They all do hate him
             As rootedly as I. Burn but his books.
             He has brave utensils°—for so he calls them—   *furnishings*
85   Which, when he has a house, he'll deck withal.°   *furnish with them*
             And that most deeply to consider is
             The beauty of his daughter. He himself
             Calls her a nonpareil. I never saw a woman
             But only Sycorax my dam and she;

---

3. Person.   5. Call me a liar.
4. Dried cod, prepared by beating.   6. Cattle disease.

90   But she as far surpasseth Sycorax
        As great'st does least.
STEPHANO: Is it so brave° a lass?   *splendid*
CALIBAN: Ay, lord. She will become° thy bed, I warrant,   *suit (sexually)*
        And bring thee forth brave brood.
STEPHANO: Monster, I will kill this man. His daughter and I will be king and
95   queen—save Our Graces!—and Trinculo and thyself shall be viceroys.
        Dost thou like the plot, Trinculo?
TRINCULO: Excellent.
STEPHANO: Give me thy hand. I am sorry I beat thee; but, while thou liv'st, keep
        a good tongue in thy head.
CALIBAN: Within this half hour will he be asleep.
        Wilt thou destroy him then?
STEPHANO: Ay, on mine honor.
ARIEL [*aside*]: This will I tell my master.
CALIBAN: Thou mak'st me merry; I am full of pleasure.
        Let us be jocund. Will you troll the catch°   *sing the song*
105   You taught me but whilere?°   *just now*
STEPHANO: At thy request, monster, I will do reason, any reason.[7]—Come on,
        Trinculo, let us sing.

    [*Sings.*]

            "Flout° 'em and scout° 'em   *scoff at / deride*
            And scout 'em and flout 'em!
110   Thought is free."

CALIBAN: That's not the tune.
    [*Ariel plays the tune on a tabor° and pipe.*]   *small drum*
STEPHANO: What is this same?
TRINCULO: This is the tune of our catch, played by the picture of Nobody.[8]
STEPHANO: If thou beest a man, show thyself in thy likeness. If thou beest a devil,
115   take 't as thou list.[9]
TRINCULO: O, forgive me my sins!
STEPHANO: He that dies pays all debts. I defy thee. Mercy upon us!
CALIBAN: Art thou afeard?
STEPHANO: No, monster, not I.
CALIBAN: Be not afeard. The isle is full of noises,
        Sounds, and sweet airs, that give delight and hurt not.
        Sometimes a thousand twangling instruments
        Will hum about mine ears, and sometimes voices
        That, if I then had waked after long sleep,
125   Will make me sleep again; and then, in dreaming,
        The clouds methought would open and show riches
        Ready to drop upon me, that when I waked
        I cried to dream again.
STEPHANO: This will prove a brave kingdom to me, where I shall have my music
130   for nothing.

---

7. Anything reasonable.   9. Suit yourself.
8. Familiar image with head, arms, legs, but no trunk.

CALIBAN: When Prospero is destroyed.

STEPHANO: That shall be by and by.° I remember the story.   *right away*

TRINCULO: The sound is going away. Let's follow it, and after do our work.

STEPHANO: Lead, monster; we'll follow. I would I could see this taborer! He lays
135   it on.[1]

TRINCULO: Wilt come? I'll follow, Stephano.

                                                            [*Exeunt (following Ariel's music).*]

Scene 3[2]

[*Enter Alonso, Sebastian, Antonio, Gonzalo, Adrian, Francisco, etc.*]

GONZALO: By'r lakin,[3] I can go no further, sir.
           My old bones aches. Here's a maze trod indeed
           Through forthrights° and meanders! By your patience,   *straight paths*
           I needs must rest me.

ALONSO: Old lord, I cannot blame thee,
5   Who am myself attached° with weariness,   *seized*
           To th' dulling of my spirits. Sit down and rest.
           Even here I will put off my hope, and keep it
           No longer for° my flatterer. He is drowned   *as*
           Whom thus we stray to find, and the sea mocks
10   Our frustrate° search on land. Well, let him go.   *frustrated*
           [*Alonso and Gonzalo sit.*]

ANTONIO [*aside to Sebastian*]:   I am right glad that he's so out of hope.
           Do not, for° one repulse, forgo the purpose   *because of*
           That you resolved t' effect.

SEBASTIAN [*to Antonio*]:   The next advantage
           Will we take throughly.°   *thoroughly*

ANTONIO [*to Sebastian*]:   Let it be tonight,
15   For, now they are oppressed with travel, they
           Will not, nor cannot, use such vigilance
           As when they are fresh.

SEBASTIAN [*to Antonio*]:   I say tonight. No more.
           [*Solemn and strange music; and Prospero on the top,[4] invisible.*]

ALONSO: What harmony is this? My good friends, hark!

GONZALO: Marvelous sweet music!
           [*Enter several strange shapes, bringing in a banquet, and dance about it with gentle
           actions of salutations; and, inviting the King, etc., to eat, they depart.*]

ALONSO: Give us kind keepers,° heavens! What were these?   *guardian angels*

SEBASTIAN: A living drollery.[5] Now I will believe
           That there are unicorns; that in Arabia
           There is one tree, the phoenix' throne, one phoenix
           At this hour reigning there.

ANTONIO: I'll believe both;
25   And what does else want credit,° come to me   *lack credibility*
           And I'll be sworn 'tis true. Travelers ne'er did lie,
           Though fools at home condemn 'em.

1. I.e., plays the drum vigorously.   4. An upper level of the theater.
2. Location: Another part of the island.   5. Puppet show with live actors.
3. By our Ladykin (Virgin Mary).

GONZALO: If in Naples
    I should report this now, would they believe me
    If I should say I saw such islanders?
30   For, certes,° these are people of the island,   *certainly*
    Who, though they are of monstrous shape, yet note,
    Their manners are more gentle, kind, than of
    Our human generation you shall find
    Many, nay, almost any.
PROSPERO [*aside*]:   Honest lord,
35   Thou hast said well, for some of you there present
    Are worse than devils.
ALONSO: I cannot too much muse
    Such shapes, such gesture, and such sound, expressing—
    Although they want° the use of tongue—a kind   *lack*
    Of excellent dumb discourse.
PROSPERO [*aside*]:   Praise in departing.[6]
FRANCISCO: They vanished strangely.
SEBASTIAN: No matter, since
    They have left their viands° behind, for we have stomachs.° *food / appetites*
    Will't please you taste of what is here?
ALONSO: Not I.
GONZALO: Faith, sir, you need not fear. When we were boys,
    Who would believe that there were mountaineers
45   Dewlapped[7] like bulls, whose throats had hanging at 'em
    Wallets° of flesh? Or that there were such men   *wattles*
    Whose heads stood in their breasts?[8] Which now we find
    Each putter-out of five for one[9] will bring us
    Good warrant of.
ALONSO: I will stand to° and feed,   *take the risk*
50   Although my last[1]—no matter, since I feel
    The best is past. Brother, my lord the Duke,
    Stand to, and do as we.
  [*They approach the table.*]
  [*Thunder and lightning. Enter Ariel, like a harpy,[2] claps his wings upon the table, and
  with a quaint[3] device the banquet[4] vanishes.*]
ARIEL: You are three men of sin, whom Destiny—
    That hath to° instrument this lower world   *as its*
55   And what is in 't—the never-surfeited sea
    Hath caused to belch up you, and on this island
    Where man doth not inhabit, you 'mongst men
    Being most unfit to live. I have made you mad;
    And even with suchlike valor men hang and drown

6. Save your praise for the end of the performance (proverbial).
7. With folds of flesh at the neck.
8. Like the Anthropophagi described in *Othello* 1.3.146.
9. Traveler whose insurance policy guarantees 5:1 repayment on his return.

1. Even if this were my last meal.
2. Monster with a woman's face and breasts and a vulture's body, supposed to bring divine vengeance.
3. Ingenious.
4. The food only.

60   Their proper° selves.   *own*
      [*Alonso, Sebastian, and Antonio draw their swords.*]
                        You fools! I and my fellows
              Are ministers of Fate. The elements
              Of whom° your swords are tempered° may as well   *which / composed*
              Wound the loud winds, or with bemocked-at° stabs   *scorned*
              Kill the still-closing° waters, as diminish   *ever-closing*
65   One dowl° that's in my plume. My fellow ministers   *feather*
              Are like° invulnerable. If you could hurt,   *likewise*
              Your swords are now too massy° for your strengths   *massive*
              And will not be uplifted. But remember—
              For that's my business to you—that you three
70   From Milan did supplant good Prospero;
              Exposed unto the sea, which hath requit° it,   *avenged*
              Him and his innocent child; for which foul deed
              The powers, delaying, not forgetting, have
              Incensed the seas and shores, yea, all the creatures,
75   Against your peace. Thee of thy son, Alonso,
              They have bereft; and do pronounce by me
              Ling'ring perdition,° worse than any death   *ruin*
              Can be at once, shall step by step attend
              You and your ways; whose wraths to guard you from—
80   Which here, in this most desolate isle, else° falls   *or else*
              Upon your heads—is nothing° but heart's sorrow   *there is no way*
              And a clear° life ensuing.   *innocent*
      [*He vanishes in thunder; then, to soft music, enter the shapes again, and dance, with
      mocks and mows,*⁵ *and carrying out the table.*]
PROSPERO: Bravely the figure of this harpy hast thou
              Performed, my Ariel; a grace it had devouring.⁶
85   Of my instruction hast thou nothing bated°   *omitted*
              In what thou hadst to say. So,° with good life°   *similarly / acting*
              And observation strange,° my meaner ministers   *close attention*
              Their several kinds° have done. My high charms work,   *separate parts*
              And these mine enemies are all knit up
90   In their distractions.° They now are in my power;   *trances*
              And in these fits I leave them, while I visit
              Young Ferdinand, whom they suppose is drowned,
              And his and mine loved darling.   [*Exit above.*]
GONZALO: I' the name of something holy, sir, why stand you
95   In this strange stare?
ALONSO: O, it is monstrous, monstrous!
              Methought the billows° spoke and told me of it;°   *waves / my sin*
              The winds did sing it to me, and the thunder,
              That deep and dreadful organ pipe, pronounced
              The name of Prosper; it did bass° my trespass.   *boom*
100   Therefore my son i' th' ooze is bedded; and

---

5. Grimaces and gestures.   "grace" as the blessing at meals and "devouring" as in
6. Causing the banquet to disappear, with puns on   "ravishing grace."

I'll seek him deeper than e'er plummet sounded,°   *probed*
And with him there lie mudded.   *[Exit.]*

SEBASTIAN: But one fiend at a time,
   I'll fight their legions o'er.°   *one by one*

ANTONIO: I'll be thy second.
                       [Exeunt (Sebastian and Antonio).]

GONZALO: All three of them are desperate. Their great guilt,
105   Like poison given to work a great time after,
    Now 'gins to bite the spirits. I do beseech you,
    That are of suppler joints, follow them swiftly
    And hinder them from what this ecstasy°   *madness*
    May now provoke them to.

ADRIAN: Follow, I pray you.
                            [Exeunt omnes.]

ACT 4

Scene 1[7]

[Enter Prospero, Ferdinand, and Miranda.]

PROSPERO: If I have too austerely punished you,
    Your compensation makes amends, for I
    Have given you here a third[8] of mine own life,
    Or that for which I live; who once again
5   I tender° to thy hand. All thy vexations   *offer*
    Were but my trials of thy love, and thou
    Hast strangely° stood the test. Here, afore heaven,   *extraordinarily*
    I ratify this my rich gift. O Ferdinand,
    Do not smile at me that I boast her off;°   *boast of her*
10   For thou shalt find she will outstrip all praise
    And make it halt° behind her.   *limp*

FERDINAND: I do believe it
    Against an oracle.[9]

PROSPERO: Then, as my gift and thine own acquisition
    Worthily purchased, take my daughter. But
15   If thou dost break her virgin-knot before
    All sanctimonious° ceremonies may   *sacred*
    With full and holy rite be ministered,
    No sweet aspersion° shall the heavens let fall   *blessing*
    To make this contract grow; but barren hate,
20   Sour-eyed disdain, and discord shall bestrew
    The union of your bed with weeds[1] so loathly
    That you shall hate it both. Therefore take heed,
    As Hymen's lamps shall light you.[2]

FERDINAND: As I hope

---

7. Location: Before Prospero's cell.
8. The other two thirds being his knowledge and his power?
9. Even if an oracle should deny it.

1. As opposed to flowers.
2. Hymen was the Greek and Roman god of marriage, whose torches burned brightly for a happy marriage and smokily for a troubled one.

For quiet days, fair issue,° and long life,   *offspring*
25   With such love as 'tis now, the murkiest den,
The most opportune place, the strong'st suggestion°   *temptation*
Our worser genius can,° shall never melt   *bad angel can make*
Mine honor into lust, to take away
The edge of that day's celebration
30   When I shall think or Phoebus' steeds are foundered[3]
Or Night kept chained below.
PROSPERO: Fairly spoke.
Sit then and talk with her. She is thine own.
[Ferdinand and Miranda sit and talk together.]
What, Ariel! My industrious servant, Ariel!
[Enter Ariel.]
ARIEL: What would my potent master? Here I am.
PROSPERO: Thou and thy meaner fellows° your last service   *subordinates*
Did worthily perform, and I must use you
In such another trick. Go bring the rabble,
O'er whom I give thee power, here to this place.
Incite them to quick motion, for I must
40   Bestow upon the eyes of this young couple
Some vanity° of mine art. It is my promise,   *show*
And they expect it from me.
ARIEL: Presently?°   *now*
PROSPERO: Ay, with a twink.°   *now*
ARIEL: Before you can say "Come" and "Go,"
45   And breathe twice, and cry "So, so,"
Each one, tripping on his toe,
Will be here with mop and mow.°   *antics and gestures*
Do you love me, master? No?
PROSPERO: Dearly, my delicate Ariel. Do not approach
50   Till thou dost hear me call.
ARIEL: Well; I conceive.°   *[Exit.]*   *understand*
PROSPERO: Look thou be true;° do not give dalliance   *true to your word*
Too much the rein. The strongest oaths are straw
To the fire i' the blood. Be more abstemious,
Or else good night your vow!
FERDINAND: I warrant you, sir,
55   The white cold virgin snow upon my heart
Abates the ardor of my liver.[4]
PROSPERO: Well.
Now come, my Ariel! Bring a corollary,°   *surplus*
Rather than want° a spirit. Appear, and pertly!°—   *lack / briskly*
No tongue! All eyes! Be silent.
[Soft music.]
[Enter Iris.[5]]
IRIS: Ceres,[6] most bounteous lady, thy rich leas°   *meadows*

---

3. Either the sun-god's horses are lame.
4. Supposed seat of the passions.
5. Goddess of the rainbow and Juno's messenger.
6. Goddess of fertility.

Of wheat, rye, barley, vetches,° oats, and peas;   *fodder*
Thy turfy mountains, where live nibbling sheep,
And flat meads° thatched with stover,° them to keep;   *meadows / fodder*
Thy banks with pionèd and twillèd brims,[7]
65   Which spongy° April at thy hest° betrims   *wet / command*
To make cold nymphs chaste crowns; and thy broom° groves,   *gorse*
Whose shadow the dismissèd° bachelor loves,   *rejected*
Being lass-lorn; thy poll-clipped° vineyard;   *pruned*
And thy sea marge,° sterile and rocky hard,   *shore*
70   Where thou thyself dost air: the queen o' the sky,°   *Juno*
Whose watery arch° and messenger am I,   *rainbow*
Bids thee leave these, and with her sovereign grace,
[Juno descends (slowly in her car).]
Here on this grass plot, in this very place,
To come and sport. Her peacocks[8] fly amain.°   *at full speed*
75   Approach, rich Ceres, her to entertain.°   *receive*
[Enter Ceres.]

CERES: Hail, many-colored messenger, that ne'er
Dost disobey the wife of Jupiter,
Who with thy saffron° wings upon my flowers   *yellow*
Diffusest honeydrops, refreshing showers,
80   And with each end of thy blue bow° dost crown   *rainbow*
My bosky° acres and my unshrubbed down,   *wooded*
Rich scarf to my proud earth. Why hath thy queen
Summoned me hither to this short-grassed green?

IRIS: A contract of true love to celebrate,
85   And some donation freely to estate°   *bestow*
On the blest lovers.

CERES: Tell me, heavenly bow,
If Venus or her son,[9] as thou dost know,
Do now attend the Queen? Since they did plot
The means that dusky Dis my daughter got,[1]
90   Her and her blind boy's scandaled° company   *disgraceful*
I have forsworn.

IRIS: Of her society
Be not afraid. I met her deity°   *her Divine Majesty*
Cutting the clouds towards Paphos,[2] and her son
Dove-drawn° with her. Here thought they to have done°   *drawn by doves /*
95   Some wanton charm upon this man and maid,   *placed*
Whose vows are that no bed-right shall be paid
Till Hymen's torch be lighted; but in vain.
Mars's hot minion° is returned again;   *Venus*
Her waspish-headed° son has broke his arrows,   *spiteful*

7. Dug under by the current and protected by woven layers of branches.
8. Birds sacred to Juno, that drew her chariot.
9. Cupid, often portrayed as blind-folded.

1. Pluto (Dis), god of the underworld, kidnapped Ceres's daughter Prosperpina.
2. In Cyprus, center of Venus's cult.

100   Swears he will shoot no more, but play with sparrows[3]
         And be a boy right out.°   outright
[*Juno alights.*]
CERES: Highest Queen of state,
         Great Juno, comes; I know her by her gait.
JUNO: How does my bounteous sister?° Go with me   fellow goddess
         To bless this twain, that they may prosperous be,
105   And honored in their issue.° [*They sing.*]   offspring
JUNO: Honor, riches, marriage blessing,
                      Long continuance, and increasing,
                      Hourly joys be still° upon you!   constantly
                      Juno sings her blessings on you.
CERES: Earth's increase, foison° plenty,   abundance
                      Barns and garners° never empty,   granaries
                      Vines with clustering bunches growing,
                      Plants with goodly burden bowing;
                      Spring come to you at the farthest
115   In the very end of harvest![4]
                      Scarcity and want shall shun you;
                      Ceres' blessing so is on you.

FERDINAND: This is a most majestic vision, and
                 Harmonious charmingly. May I be bold
120   To think these spirits?
PROSPERO: Spirits, which by mine art
          I have from their confines called to enact
          My present fancies.
FERDINAND: Let me live here ever!
          So rare a wondered° father and a wife   wonderful
          Makes this place Paradise.
[*Juno and Ceres whisper, and send Iris on employment.*]
PROSPERO: Sweet now, silence!
125   Juno and Ceres whisper seriously;
          There's something else to do. Hush and be mute,
          Or else our spell is marred.   water nymphs /
IRIS [*calling offstage*]: You nymphs, called naiads,° of the windring° brooks,   winding
          With your sedged° crowns and ever-harmless looks,   made of reeds
130   Leave your crisp° channels, and on this green land   rippling
          Answer your summons; Juno does command.
          Come, temperate° nymphs, and help to celebrate   chaste
          A contract of true love. Be not too late.
[*Enter certain nymphs.*]
          You sunburned sicklemen, of August° weary,   the harvest
135   Come hither from the furrow and be merry.
          Make holiday; your rye-straw hats put on,
          And these fresh nymphs encounter every one
          In country footing.°   dancing

---

3. Thought to be lustful, sparrows were sacred to Venus.   4. I.e., with no winter in between.

[*Enter certain reapers, properly habited. They join with the nymphs in a graceful dance, towards the end whereof Prospero starts suddenly, and speaks; after which, to a strange, hollow, and confused noise, they heavily vanish.*]

PROSPERO [*aside*]:   I had forgot that foul conspiracy
140   Of the beast Caliban and his confederates
           Against my life. The minute of their plot
           Is almost come. [*To the Spirits.*] Well done! Avoid;° no more!   *be off*

FERDINAND [*to Miranda*]:   This is strange. Your father's in some passion
           That works° him strongly.   *affects*

MIRANDA: Never till this day
145   Saw I him touched with anger so distempered.

PROSPERO: You do look, my son, in a moved sort,°   *troubled state*
           As if you were dismayed. Be cheerful, sir.
           Our revels now are ended. These our actors,
           As I foretold you, were all spirits and
150   Are melted into air, into thin air;
           And, like the baseless° fabric of this vision,   *insubstantial*
           The cloud-capped towers, the gorgeous palaces,
           The solemn temples, the great globe itself,°   *(glances at theater)*
           Yea, all which it inherit,° shall dissolve,   *occupy it*
155   And, like this insubstantial pageant faded;
           Leave not a rack° behind. We are such stuff   *cloud*
           As dreams are made on,° and our little life   *of*
           Is rounded° with a sleep. Sir, I am vexed.   *surrounded*
           Bear with my weakness. My old brain is troubled.
160   Be not disturbed with my infirmity.
           If you be pleased, retire into my cell
           And there repose. A turn or two I'll walk
           To still my beating° mind.   *agitated*

FERDINAND, MIRANDA: We wish your peace.
                               [*Exeunt (Ferdinand and Miranda).*]

PROSPERO: Come with a thought!° I thank thee, Ariel. Come.   *right now*
           [*Enter Ariel.*]

ARIEL: Thy thoughts I cleave to. What's thy pleasure?

PROSPERO: Spirit,
           We must prepare to meet with Caliban.

ARIEL: Ay, my commander. When I presented° Ceres,   *played; introduced*
           I thought to have told thee of it, but I feared
           Lest I might anger thee.

PROSPERO: Say again, where didst thou leave these varlets?

ARIEL: I told you, sir, they were red-hot with drinking;
           So full of valor that they smote the air
           For breathing in their faces, beat the ground
           For kissing of their feet; yet always bending
175   Towards their project. Then I beat my tabor,
           At which, like unbacked° colts, they pricked their ears,   *unbroken*
           Advanced° their eyelids, lifted up their noses   *raised*
           As they smelt music. So I charmed their ears
           That calflike they my lowing followed through

180   Toothed briers, sharp furzes, pricking gorse, and thorns,
       Which entered their frail shins. At last I left them
       I' the filthy-mantled° pool beyond your cell,   *scummed*
       There dancing up to the chins, that the foul lake
       O'erstunk their feet.

PROSPERO: This was well done, my bird.

185   Thy shape invisible retain thou still.
       The trumpery° in my house, go bring it hither,   *cheap goods*
       For stale° to catch these thieves.   *decoy*

ARIEL: I go, I go.

                                                                       [*Exit.*]

PROSPERO: A devil, a born devil, on whose nature
            Nurture can never stick; on whom my pains,
190   Humanely taken, all, all lost, quite lost!
            And as with age his body uglier grows,
            So his mind cankers.° I will plague them all,   *festers*
            Even to roaring.

       [*Enter Ariel, loaden with glistering apparel, etc.*]

                            Come, hang them on this line.°   *lime or linden tree*

       [(*Ariel hangs up the showy finery; Prospero and Ariel remain, invisible.*) *Enter Caliban, Stephano, and Trinculo, all wet.*]

CALIBAN: Pray you, tread softly, that the blind mole may
195   Not hear a foot fall. We now are near his cell.

STEPHANO: Monster, your fairy, which you say is a harmless fairy, has done little
            better than played the jack[5] with us.

TRINCULO: Monster, I do smell all horse piss, at which my nose is in great
            indignation.

STEPHANO: So is mine. Do you hear, monster? If I should take a displeasure
            against you, look you—

TRINCULO: Thou wert but a lost monster.

CALIBAN: Good my lord, give me thy favor still.
           Be patient, for the prize I'll bring thee to
205   Shall hoodwink° this mischance. Therefore speak softly.   *cover over*
           All's hushed as midnight yet.

TRINCULO: Ay, but to lose our bottles in the pool—

STEPHANO: There is not only disgrace and dishonor in that, monster, but an infi-
            nite loss.

TRINCULO: That's more to me than my wetting. Yet this is your harmless fairy,
            monster!

STEPHANO: I will fetch off my bottle, though I be o'er ears[6] for my labor.

CALIBAN: Prithee, my king, be quiet. Seest thou here,
           This is the mouth o' the cell. No noise, and enter.
215   Do that good mischief which may make this island
           Thine own forever, and I thy Caliban
           For aye thy footlicker.

STEPHANO: Give me thy hand. I do begin to have bloody thoughts.

---

5. Knave; jack o' lantern, will o' th' wisp.   6. Submerged or drowned.

TRINCULO [*seeing the finery*]:   O King Stephano! O peer![7]

220   O worthy Stephano! Look what a wardrobe here is for thee!

CALIBAN: Let it alone, thou fool, it is but trash.

TRINCULO: O ho, monster! We know what belongs to a frippery.[8] O King
          Stephano!

[*He puts on a gown.*]

STEPHANO: Put off that gown, Trinculo. By this hand, I'll have that gown.

TRINCULO: Thy Grace shall have it.

CALIBAN: The dropsy[9] drown this fool! What do you mean
          To dote thus on such luggage? Let 't alone
          And do the murder first. If he awake,
          From toe to crown he'll fill our skins with pinches,
230   Make us strange stuff.

STEPHANO: Be you quiet, monster.—Mistress line, is not this my jerkin?[1] [*He
          takes it down.*] Now is the jerkin under the line.[2] Now, jerkin, you are like
          to lose your hair and prove a bald jerkin.

TRINCULO: Do, do! We steal by line and level,[3] an 't like[4] your Grace.

STEPHANO: I thank thee for that jest. Here's a garment for 't. [*He gives a garment.*]
          Wit shall not go unrewarded while I am king of this country. "Steal by
          line and level" is an excellent pass of pate.[5] There's another garment
          for 't.

TRINCULO: Monster, come, put some lime[6] upon your fingers, and away with the
          rest.

CALIBAN: I will have none on 't. We shall lose our time,
          And all be turned to barnacles,[7] or to apes
          With foreheads villainous low.

STEPHANO: Monster, lay to[8] your fingers. Help to bear this away where my
          hogshead of wine is, or I'll turn you out of my kingdom. Go to, carry this.

TRINCULO: And this.

STEPHANO: Ay, and this.

[*They load Caliban with more and more garments.*]

[*A noise of hunters heard. Enter divers spirits, in shape of dogs and hounds, hunting
them about, Prospero and Ariel setting them on.*]

PROSPERO: Hey, Mountain, hey!

ARIEL: Silver! There it goes, Silver!

PROSPERO: Fury, Fury! There, Tyrant, there! Hark! Hark!

[*Caliban, Stephano, and Trinculo are driven out.*]

250   Go, charge my goblins that they grind their joints
          With dry[9] convulsions, shorten up their sinews
          With agèd cramps, and more pinch-spotted make them
          Than pard or cat o'mountain.[1]

---

7. Alludes to the ballad beginning "King Stephen was a
worthy peer . . . "
8. Old-clothes shop.
9. Disease in which joints fill with fluid.
1. Leather jacket.
2. Lime tree; pun on the equator, south of which sailors
supposedly caught scurvy and lost their hair.
3. Methodically (pun on *line*).

4. If it please.
5. Witticism.
6. Bird-lime (sticky and good for stealing).
7. Geese.
8. Start using.
9. Aged.
1. Leopard or wildcat.

ARIEL: Hark, they roar!
PROSPERO: Let them be hunted soundly. At this hour
255   Lies at my mercy all mine enemies.
             Shortly shall all my labors end, and thou
             Shalt have the air at freedom. For a little
             Follow, and do me service.   [Exeunt.]

ACT 5

Scene 1²

[Enter Prospero in his magic robes, (with his staff,) and Ariel.]
PROSPERO: Now does my project gather to a head.
             My charms crack° not, my spirits obey, and Time   fail
             Goes upright with his carriage.³ How's the day?
ARIEL: On the sixth hour, at which time, my lord,
5   You said our work should cease.
PROSPERO: I did say so,
             When first I raised the tempest. Say, my spirit,
             How fares the King and 's followers?
ARIEL: Confined together
             In the same fashion as you gave in charge,
             Just as you left them; all prisoners, sir,
10   In the line grove which weather-fends° your cell.   protects from weather
             They cannot budge till your release° The King,   you release them
             His brother, and yours abide all three distracted,°   mad
             And the remainder mourning over them,
             Brim full of sorrow and dismay; but chiefly
15   Him that you termed, sir, the good old lord, Gonzalo.
             His tears runs down his beard like winter's drops
             From eaves of reeds.° Your charm so strongly works 'em   thatched roof
             That if you now beheld them your affections°   feelings
             Would become tender.
PROSPERO: Dost thou think so, spirit?
ARIEL: Mine would, sir, were I human.
PROSPERO: And mine shall.
             Hast thou, which art but air, a touch,° a feeling   a sense
             Of their afflictions, and shall not myself,
             One of their kind, that relish° all° as sharply   feel / quite
             Passion as they, be kindlier moved than thou art?
25   Though with their high wrongs I am struck to the quick,
             Yet with my nobler reason 'gainst my fury
             Do I take part. The rarer° action is   nobler
             In virtue than in vengeance. They being penitent,
             The sole drift of my purpose doth extend
30   Not a frown further. Go release them, Ariel.
             My charms I'll break, their senses I'll restore,

---

2. Location: Before Prospero's cell.   3. Time's burden is light.

And they shall be themselves.

ARIEL: I'll fetch them, sir.   [Exit.]

[*Prospero traces a charmed circle with his staff.*]

PROSPERO:[4] Ye elves of hills, brooks, standing lakes, and groves,

And ye that on the sands with printless foot

35   Do chase the ebbing Neptune, and do fly him

When he comes back; you demi-puppets° that   *fairies*

By moonshine do the green sour ringlets° make,   *circles in grass*

Whereof the ewe not bites; and you whose pastime

Is to make midnight mushrooms, that rejoice

40   To hear the solemn curfew;° by whose aid,   *evening bell*

Weak masters° though ye be, I have bedimmed   *forces*

The noontide sun, called forth the mutinous winds,

And twixt the green sea and the azured vault°   *the sky*

Set roaring war; to the dread rattling thunder

45   Have I given fire, and rifted° Jove's stout oak[5]   *split*

With his own bolt; the strong-based promontory

Have I made shake, and by the spurs° plucked up   *roots*

The pine and cedar; graves at my command

Have waked their sleepers, oped, and let 'em forth

50   By my so potent art. But this rough magic

I here abjure, and when I have required°   *requested*

Some heavenly music—which even now I do—

To work mine end upon their senses that[6]

This airy charm° is for, I'll break my staff,   *music*

55   Bury it certain fathoms in the earth,

And deeper than did ever plummet sound

I'll drown my book.

[*Solemn music.*]

[*Here enters Ariel before; then Alonso, with a frantic gesture, attended by Gonzalo;
Sebastian and Antonio in like manner, attended by Adrian and Francisco. They all enter the circle which Prospero had made, and there stand charmed; which Prospero observing, speaks:*]

[*To Alonso.*]

A solemn air°, and° the best comforter   *song / which is*

To an unsettled fancy, cure thy brains,

60   Now useless, boiled within thy skull! [*To Sebastian and Antonio.*] There
stand,

For you are spell-stopped.—

Holy Gonzalo, honorable man,

Mine eyes, e'en sociable° to the show° of thine,   *sympathetic / sight*

Fall° fellowly drops. [*Aside.*] The charm dissolves apace,   *let fall*

65   And as the morning steals upon the night,

Melting the darkness, so their rising senses

Begin to chase the ignorant fumes that mantle°   *envelop*

Their clearer reason.—O good Gonzalo,

4. This famous passage, lines 33–50, is an embellished paraphrase of Golding's translation of Ovid's *Metamorphoses*
7.197–219.

5. Tree sacred to Jove.
6. The senses of those whom.

My true preserver, and a loyal sir
70   To him thou follow'st! I will pay thy graces°   *favors*
Home° both in word and deed.—Most cruelly   *fully*
Didst thou, Alonso, use me and my daughter.
Thy brother was a furtherer° in the act.—   *an accomplice*
Thou art pinched for 't now, Sebastian. [*To Antonio.*] Flesh and blood,
75   You, brother mine, that entertained ambition,
Expelled remorse° and nature,° whom, with Sebastian,   *pity / natural feeling*
Whose inward pinches therefore are most strong,
Would here have killed your king, I do forgive thee,
Unnatural though thou art.—Their understanding
80   Begins to swell, and the approaching tide
Will shortly fill the reasonable shore°   *shore of the mind*
That now lies foul and muddy. Not one of them
That yet looks on me, or would know me.—Ariel,
Fetch me the hat and rapier in my cell.

[*Ariel goes to the cell and returns immediately.*]

85   I will discase° me and myself present   *disrobe*
As I was sometime Milan.⁷ Quickly, spirit!
Thou shalt ere long be free.

[*Ariel sings and helps to attire him.*]

ARIEL: Where the bee sucks, there suck I.
                       In a cowslip's bell I lie;
90   There I couch° when owls do cry.   *lie*
                       On the bat's back I do fly
                       After° summer merrily.   *pursuing*
                       Merrily, merrily shall I live now
                       Under the blossom that hangs on the bough.

PROSPERO: Why, that's my dainty Ariel! I shall miss thee,
But yet thou shalt have freedom. So, so, so.
To the King's ship, invisible as thou art!
There shalt thou find the mariners asleep
Under the hatches. The Master and the Boatswain
100   Being awake, enforce them to this place,
And presently,° I prithee.   *right away*
ARIEL: I drink the air° before me and return   *consume space*
Or ere° your pulse twice beat.   *before*
                                                                    [*Exit.*]

GONZALO: All torment, trouble, wonder, and amazement
105   Inhabits here. Some heavenly power guide us
Out of this fearful° country!   *frightening*
PROSPERO: Behold, sir King,
The wrongèd Duke of Milan, Prospero.
For more assurance that a living prince

---

7. As I looked when I was Duke of Milan.

Does now speak to thee, I embrace thy body;
110 And to thee and thy company I bid
A hearty welcome.

[Embracing him.]

ALONSO: Whe'er thou be'st he or no,
Or some enchanted trifle° to abuse° me,   trick / deceive
As late° I have been, I not know. Thy pulse   lately
Beats as of flesh and blood; and, since I saw thee,
115 Th' affliction of my mind amends, with which
I fear a madness held me. This must crave°—   require
An if this be at all[8]—a most strange story.
Thy dukedom I resign, and do entreat
Thou pardon me my wrongs. But how should Prospero
120 Be living, and be here?

PROSPERO *[to Gonzalo]:*   First, noble friend,
Let me embrace thine age,° whose honor cannot   yourself
Be measured or confined.

[Embracing him.]

GONZALO: Whether this be
Or be not, I'll not swear.

PROSPERO: You do yet taste
Some subtleties° o' th' isle, that will not let you   illusions
125 Believe things certain. Welcome, my friends all!

[Aside to Sebastian and Antonio.]

But you, my brace[9] of lords, were I so minded,
I here could pluck° his Highness' frown upon you   pull down
And justify° you traitors. At this time   prove
I will tell no tales.

SEBASTIAN: The devil speaks in him.

PROSPERO: No.
130 *[To Antonio.]* For you, most wicked sir, whom to call brother
Would even infect my mouth, I do forgive
Thy rankest fault—all of them; and require
My dukedom of thee, which perforce° I know   necessarily
Thou must restore.

ALONSO: If thou be'st Prospero,
135 Give us particulars of thy preservation,
How thou hast met us here, whom three hours since
Were wrecked upon this shore; where I have lost—
How sharp the point of this remembrance is!—
My dear son Ferdinand.

PROSPERO: I am woe° for 't, sir.   sorry

ALONSO: Irreparable is the loss, and patience
Says it is past her cure.

PROSPERO: I rather think
You have not sought her help, of whose soft grace
For the like loss I have her sovereign° aid   effective

8. If all this is actually happening.   9. Pair.

And rest myself content.
ALONSO: You the like loss?
PROSPERO: As great to me as late,° and supportable   *recent*
            To make the dear° loss, have I means much weaker   *grievous*
            Than you may call to comfort you; for I
            Have lost my daughter.
ALONSO: A daughter?
            O heavens, that they were living both in Naples,
150   The king and queen there! That° they were, I wish   *so that*
            Myself were mudded° in that oozy bed   *buried in mud*
            Where my son lies. When did you lose your daughter?
PROSPERO: In this last tempest. I perceive these lords
            At this encounter do so much admire°   *wonder*
155   That they devour their reason° and scarce think   *are open-mouthed*
            Their eyes do offices° of truth, their words   *perform services*
            Are natural breath. But, howsoever you have
            Been jostled from your senses, know for certain
            That I am Prospero and that very duke
160   Which was thrust forth of Milan, who most strangely
            Upon this shore, where you were wrecked, was landed
            To be the lord on 't. No more yet of this,
            For 'tis a chronicle of day by day,°   *many days' telling*
            Not a relation for a breakfast nor
165   Befitting this first meeting. Welcome, sir.
            This cell's my court. Here have I few attendants,
            And subjects none abroad.° Pray you, look in.   *elsewhere*
            My dukedom since you have given me again,
            I will requite° you with as good a thing,   *repay*
170   At least bring forth a wonder to content ye
            As much as me my dukedom.
            [*Here Prospero* discovers° *Ferdinand and Miranda, playing at chess.*]   *discloses*
MIRANDA: Sweet lord, you play me false.
FERDINAND: No, my dearest love,
            I would not for the world.
MIRANDA: Yes, for a score of kingdoms you should wrangle,
175   And I would call it fair play.[1]
ALONSO: If this prove
            A vision° of the island, one dear son   *illusion*
            Shall I twice lose.
SEBASTIAN: A most high miracle!
FERDINAND   [*approaching his father*]: Though the seas threaten, they are merciful;
            I have cursed them without cause. [*He kneels.*]
ALONSO: Now all the blessings
180   Of a glad father compass° thee about!   *encompass*
            Arise, and say how thou cam'st here.

---

1. Miranda would still love Ferdinand, even if he did not play fair.

[*Ferdinand rises.*]

MIRANDA: O, wonder!
    How many goodly creatures are there here!
    How beauteous mankind is! O brave° new world   *splendid*
    That has such people in 't!
PROSPERO: 'Tis new to thee.
ALONSO: What is this maid with whom thou wast at play?
    Your eld'st° acquaintance cannot be three hours.   *longest*
    Is she the goddess that hath severed us,
    And brought us thus together?
FERDINAND: Sir, she is mortal;
    But by immortal Providence she's mine.
190   I chose her when I could not ask my father
    For his advice, nor thought I had one. She
    Is daughter to this famous Duke of Milan,
    Of whom so often I have heard renown,
    But never saw before; of whom I have
195   Received a second life; and second father
    This lady makes him to me.
ALONSO: I am hers.
    But O, how oddly will it sound that I
    Must ask my child forgiveness!
PROSPERO: There, sir, stop.
    Let us not burden our remembrances with
200   A heaviness° that's gone.   *sadness*
GONZALO: I have inly° wept,   *inwardly*
    Or should have spoke ere this. Look down, you gods,
    And on this couple drop a blessèd crown!
    For it is you that have chalked forth the way
    Which brought us hither.
ALONSO: I say amen, Gonzalo!
GONZALO: Was Milan° thrust from Milan, that his issue   *the Duke of Milan*
    Should become kings of Naples? O, rejoice
    Beyond a common joy, and set it down
    With gold on lasting pillars: In one voyage
    Did Claribel her husband find at Tunis,
210   And Ferdinand, her brother, found a wife
    Where he himself was lost; Prospero his dukedom
    In a poor isle; and all of us ourselves°   *our senses*
    When no man was his own.°   *sane*
ALONSO [*to Ferdinand and Miranda*]:   Give me your hands.
    Let grief and sorrow still° embrace his heart   *always*
215   That doth not wish you joy!
GONZALO: Be it so! Amen!
[*Enter Ariel, with the Master and Boatswain amazedly following.*]
    O, look, sir, look, sir! Here is more of us.
    I prophesied, if a gallows were on land,
    This fellow could not drown.—Now, blasphemy,°   *blasphemer*

That swear'st grace o'erboard, not an oath on shore?
220   Hast thou no mouth by land? What is the news?

BOATSWAIN: The best news is that we have safely found
      Our King and company; the next, our ship—
      Which, but three glasses° since, we gave out° split—   *hours / reported*
      Is tight and yare° and bravely rigged as when   *shipshape*
225   We first put out to sea.

ARIEL   [*aside to Prospero*]:   Sir, all this service
      Have I done since I went.

PROSPERO   [*aside to Ariel*]:   My tricksy° spirit!   *ingenious*

ALONSO: These are not natural events; they strengthen
      From strange to stranger. Say, how came you hither?

BOATSWAIN: If I did think, sir, I were well awake,
230   I'd strive to tell you. We were dead of sleep,
      And—how we know not—all clapped under hatches,
      Where but even now, with strange and several° noises   *various*
      Of roaring, shrieking, howling, jingling chains,
      And more diversity of sounds, all horrible,
235   We were awaked; straightway at liberty;
      Where we, in all her trim°, freshly beheld   *sail*
      Our royal, good, and gallant ship, our Master
      Cap'ring° to eye° her. On a trice, so please you,   *dancing / see*
      Even in a dream, were we divided from them
240   And were brought moping° hither.   *in a daze*

ARIEL   [*aside to Prospero*]: Was't well done?

PROSPERO   [*aside to Ariel*]: Bravely, my diligence. Thou shalt be free.

ALONSO: This is as strange a maze as e'er men trod,
      And there is in this business more than nature
      Was ever conduct° of. Some oracle   *conductor*
245   Must rectify our knowledge.

PROSPERO: Sir, my liege,
      Do not infest° your mind with beating on   *bother*
      The strangeness of this business. At picked° leisure,   *chosen*
      Which shall be shortly, single° I'll resolve° you,   *privately / explain*
      Which to you shall seem probable, of every°   *every one of*
250   These happened accidents;° till when, be cheerful   *incidents*
      And think of each thing well. [*Aside to Ariel.*] Come hither, spirit.
      Set Caliban and his companions free.
      Untie the spell. [*Exit Ariel.*] How fares my gracious sir?
      There are yet missing of your company
255   Some few odd lads that you remember not.

[*Enter Ariel, driving in Caliban, Stephano, and Trinculo, in their stolen apparel.*]

STEPHANO: Every man shift[2] for all the rest,[3] and let no man take care for himself; for all is but fortune. Coragio,[4] bully monster,[5] coragio!

---

2. Provide.
3. Stephano drunkenly gets wrong the saying "Every man for himself."
4. Courage.
5. Gallant monster (ironical).

TRINCULO: If these be true spies[6] which I wear in my head, here's a goodly sight.

CALIBAN: O Setebos, these be brave° spirits indeed!   *handsome*

260   How fine° my master is! I am afraid   *well-dressed*
               He will chastise me.

SEBASTIAN: Ha, ha!
               What things are these, my lord Antonio?
               Will money buy 'em?

ANTONIO: Very like. One of them
               Is a plain fish, and no doubt marketable.

PROSPERO: Mark but the badges of these men,° my lords,   *servants*
               Then say if they be true.° This misshapen knave,   *honest*
               His mother was a witch, and one so strong
               That could control the moon, make flows and ebbs,
               And deal in her° command without° her power.   *the moon's / beyond*

270   These three have robbed me, and this demidevil—
               For he's a bastard° one—had plotted with them   *counterfeit*
               To take my life. Two of these fellows you
               Must know and own.° This thing of darkness I   *acknowledge as mine*
               Acknowledge mine.

CALIBAN: I shall be pinched to death.

ALONSO: Is not this Stephano, my drunken butler?

SEBASTIAN: He is drunk now. Where had he wine?

ALONSO: And Trinculo is reeling ripe.° Where should they   *stumbling drunk*
               Find this grand liquor that hath gilded[7] 'em?
           [*To Trinculo.*]
               How cam'st thou in this pickle?[8]

TRINCULO: I have been in such a pickle since I saw you last that, I fear me, will
               never out of my bones. I shall not fear flyblowing.[9]

SEBASTIAN: Why, how now, Stephano?

STEPHANO: O, touch me not! I am not Stephano, but a cramp.

PROSPERO: You'd be king o' the isle, sirrah?[1]

STEPHANO: I should have been a sore[2] one, then.

ALONSO [*pointing to Caliban*]:   This is a strange thing as e'er I looked on.

PROSPERO: He is as disproportioned in his manners
               As in his shape.—Go, sirrah, to my cell.
               Take with you your companions. As you look
290   To have my pardon, trim° it handsomely.   *decorate*

CALIBAN: Ay, that I will; and I'll be wise hereafter
               And seek for grace.° What a thrice-double ass   *favor*
               Was I to take this drunkard for a god
               And worship this dull fool!

PROSPERO: Go to. Away!

ALONSO: Hence, and bestow your luggage where you found it.

---

6. Sharp eyes.
7. Intoxicated; covered with gold (suggesting horse urine).
8. Predicament; pickling brine (here, horse urine).

9. Being soiled by fly eggs (he is protected by being pickled).
1. Address to an inferior (here, a reprimand).
2. Tyrannical; sorry; aching.

SEBASTIAN: Or stole it, rather.

[*Exeunt Caliban, Stephano, and Trinculo.*]

PROSPERO: Sir, I invite Your Highness and your train
To my poor cell, where you shall take your rest
For this one night; which, part of it, I'll waste°   spend
300   With such discourse as, I not doubt, shall make it
Go quick away: the story of my life,
And the particular accidents° gone by   events
Since I came to this isle. And in the morn
I'll bring you to your ship, and so to Naples,
305   Where I have hope to see the nuptial
Of these our dear-belovèd solemnized;
And thence retire me to my Milan, where
Every third thought shall be my grave.
ALONSO: I long
To hear the story of your life, which must
310   Take° the ear strangely.   captivate
PROSPERO: I'll deliver° all;   tell
And promise you calm seas, auspicious gales,
And sail so expeditious that shall catch
Your royal fleet far off. [*Aside to Ariel.*] My Ariel, chick,
That is thy charge. Then to the elements
315   Be free, and fare thou well!—Please you, draw near.

[*Exeunt omnes (except Prospero).*]

EPILOGUE

[*Spoken by Prospero.*]
Now my charms are all o'erthrown,
And what strength I have's mine own,
Which is most faint. Now, 'tis true,
I must be here confined by you
5   Or sent to Naples. Let me not,
Since I have my dukedom got
And pardoned the deceiver, dwell
In this bare island by your spell,°   silence
But release me from my bands°   bonds
10   With the help of your good hands.°   applause
Gentle breath of yours my sails
Must fill, or else my project fails,
Which was to please. Now I want°   lack
Spirits to enforce,° art to enchant,   control
15   And my ending is despair,
Unless I be relieved by prayer,°   this very speech
Which pierces so that it assaults°   gains the attention of
Mercy itself, and frees° all faults.   earns pardon for
As you from crimes° would pardoned be,   sins
20   Let your indulgence° set me free.   humoring; pardon
                                                                                        [*Exit.*]

$\iff$

RESPONSE

Aimé Césaire: from *A Tempest*[1]

Characters as in Shakespeare

TWO ALTERATIONS: ARIEL, A MULATTO SLAVE
CALIBAN, A BLACK SLAVE[2]

ACT 1, SCENE 2

Prospero with Ariel and Caliban[3]

[*Enter Caliban.*]

CALIBAN: Uhuru![4]

PROSPERO: What did you say?

CALIBAN: I said, Uhuru!

PROSPERO: Back to your native language again. I've already told you, I don't like it. You could be polite, at least; a simple "hello" wouldn't kill you.

CALIBAN: Oh, I forgot. . . . But as froggy, waspish, pustular and dung-filled a "hello" as possible. May today hasten by a decade the day when all the birds of the sky and beasts of the earth will feast upon your corpse!

PROSPERO: Gracious as always, you ugly ape! How can anyone *be* so ugly?

CALIBAN: You think I'm ugly . . . well, I don't think you're handsome either. With that big hooked nose, you look just like some old vulture. [*Laughing.*] An old vulture with a scrawny neck!

PROSPERO: Since you're so fond of invective, you could at least thank me for having taught you to speak at all. You savage . . . a dumb animal, a beast I educated, trained, dragged up from the bestiality that still sticks out all over you!

CALIBAN: In the first place, that's not true. You didn't teach me a thing! Except to jabber in your own language so that I could understand your orders—chop the wood, wash the dishes, fish for food, plant vegetables, all because you're too lazy to

---

1. Translated by Emile Snyder and Sanford Upson. The full title is *A Tempest Based on Shakespeare's "The Tempest": Adaptation for a Black Theatre.* Aimé Césaire was born to an impoverished black family in Martinique in 1913. Along with the Senegalese poet Léopold Senghor, he established the influential movement of "négritude," which encouraged a return to African roots and a reaction against European values. While Césaire writes in French, he often infuses his language with words of African origin and distorts original meanings and syntax. *A Tempest,* written in 1969, takes Shakespeare's late romance as a model to be subverted, although Césaire was also arguably influenced by an 1878 play entitled *Caliban* by the French intellectual Ernest Renan.

2. Césaire maintains the list of characters in Shakespeare's play, but specifies that Ariel is a mulatto (of mixed ancestry) and Caliban is black or African. The setting is unspecified; in his notes to the "Characters," Césaire suggests that the atmosphere is one of a "psychodrama" in which the actors enter "one after the other and each chooses a mask of his liking."

3. The play opens with a flashback to Prospero's exile from Milan, and a discussion of the storm produced by Prospero, with Ariel's assistance, in which the Neapolitans—portrayed by Césaire as ruthless conquerors—are tempest-tossed and in danger of death. At the beginning of Act I, Scene 2, Ariel asks Prospero to be released from having to do such work in the future, and after Prospero sternly rebukes his slave ("Ingrate!. . . . As for your freedom, you'll have it when I'm good and ready") he summons Caliban to the cave: "I've been keeping my eye on him and he's getting a little too emancipated."

4. Swahili word for freedom.

do it yourself.[5] And as for your learning, did you ever impart any of *that* to me? No, you took care not to. All your science and know-how you keep for yourself alone, shut up in big books like those.

PROSPERO: What would you be without me?

CALIBAN: Without you? I'd be the king, that's what I'd be, the King of the Island. The king of the island I inherited from my mother, Sycorax.

PROSPERO: There are some family trees it's better not to climb! She's a ghoul! A witch from whom—and may God be praised—death has delivered us.

CALIBAN: Dead or alive, she was my mother, and I won't deny her! Anyhow, you only think she's dead because you think the earth itself is dead. . . . It's so much simpler that way! Dead, you can walk on it, pollute it, you can tread upon it with the steps of a conqueror. I respect the earth, because I know that it is alive, and I know that Sycorax is alive. Sycorax, Mother.

> Serpent, rain, lightning.
> And I see thee everywhere!
> In the eye of the stagnant pool into which I gaze
> unflinching,
> through the rushes,
> in the gesture made by twisted root and its awaiting thrust.
> In the night, the all-seeing blinded night,
> the nostril-less all-smelling night!

. . . Often, in my dreams, she speaks to me and warns me. . . . Yesterday, even, when I was lying by the stream on my belly lapping at the muddy water, when the Beast was about to spring upon me with that huge stone in his hand. . . .

PROSPERO: If you keep on like that even your sorcery won't save you from punishment!

CALIBAN: That's right, that's right! In the beginning, he was all sweet talk: dear Caliban here, my little Caliban there! And what do you think you'd have done without me in this strange land? Ingrate! I taught you the trees, fruits, birds, the seasons, and now you don't give a damn. . . . Caliban the animal, Caliban the slave! I know that story! Once you've squeezed the juice from the orange, you toss the rind away!

PROSPERO: Oh!

CALIBAN: Do I lie? Isn't it true that you threw me out of your house and made me live in a filthy cave, a hovel, a slum, a ghetto?

PROSPERO: It's easy to say "ghetto"! It wouldn't be such a ghetto if you took the trouble to keep it clean! And there's something you forgot, which is that what forced me to get rid of you was your lust. Good God, you tried to rape my daughter!

CALIBAN: Rape! Rape! Listen, you old goat, you're the one that puts those sexy thoughts in my head. Let me tell you something: I couldn't care less about your daughter, or about your cave, for that matter. If I complain, it's on principle, because I didn't like living with you at all, as a matter of fact. Your feet stink!

PROSPERO: I did not summon you here to argue. Away with you! Back to work! Wood, water, and lots of both! I'm expecting company today.

CALIBAN: I've had just about enough. There's already a pile of wood that high. . . .

PROSPERO: Enough! Take care, Caliban! If you keep grumbling you will be thrashed. And if you don't step lively, if you try to go on strike or to sabotage

5. Césaire bases the exchange on *The Tempest*, 1.2.322–75 in which Caliban argues with both Prospero and Miranda.

things, I'll beat you. Beating is the only language you really understand. So much the worse for you; I'll speak it, loud and clear. Off with you, and hurry!

CALIBAN: All right, I'm going . . . but this is the last time. It's the last time, do you hear me? Oh . . . I forgot: I've got something important to tell you.

PROSPERO: Important? Well, out with it.

CALIBAN: It's this: I've decided I don't want to be called Caliban any longer.

PROSPERO: What kind of rot is that? I don't understand.

CALIBAN: Put it this way: I'm *telling* you that from now on I won't answer to the name Caliban.

PROSPERO: What put that notion into your head?

CALIBAN: Well, because Caliban isn't my name. It's as simple as that.

PROSPERO: It's mine, I suppose!

CALIBAN: It's the name given me by hatred, and every time it's spoken it's an insult.

PROSPERO: My, how sensitive we're getting to be! All right, suggest something else. . . . I've got to call you something. What will it be? Cannibal would suit you but I'm sure you wouldn't like that, would you? Let's see . . . what about Hannibal?[6] That fits. And why not . . . they all seem to like historical names.

CALIBAN: Call me X.[7] That would be best. Like a man without a name. Or, to be more precise, a man whose name has been *stolen*. You talk about history . . . well, that's history, and everyone knows it! Every time you call me it reminds me of a basic fact, the fact that you've stolen everything from me, even my identity! Uhuru!

[He exits.]

[Enter Ariel as a sea-nymph.]

PROSPERO: My dear Ariel, did you see how he looked at me, that glint in his eye? That's something new. Well, let me tell you, Caliban is the enemy. As for those people on the boat, I've changed my mind about them. Give them a scare, but for God's sake don't touch a hair of their heads! You'll answer to me if you do!

ARIEL: I've suffered too much myself from having had to be the agent of their sufferings not to be pleased at your mercy. You can count on me, Master.

PROSPERO: Yes, however great their crimes, if they repent you can assure them of my forgiveness. They are men of my race, and of high rank. As for me, at my age one must rise above disputes and quarrels and think about the future. I have a daughter. Alonso has a son. If they were to love each other, I would give my consent. Let Ferdinand marry Miranda, and may their marriage bring us harmony and peace. That is my plan. I wish to see it carried out. As for Caliban, does it matter what that villain plots against me? All the nobility of Italy, Naples and Milan henceforth combined, will protect my person. Go!

ARIEL: Yes, Master. Your orders will be fully carried out.

[Ariel sings.][8]

> Sandy seashore, deep blue sky,
> Surf is rising, sea birds fly
> Here the lover finds delight,

6. Famous general from Carthage in North Africa and a bitter enemy of Rome in the Punic Wars.

7. A possible allusion to Malcolm X, who rejected his name Malcom Little as a relic of slavery; he converted to the Nation of Islam while in prison and was assassinated in 1965.

8. Ariel's song and Ferdinand's subsequent appearance are also from Act 1, Scene 2, of The Tempest.

> Sun at noontime, moon at night.
> Join hands lovers, join the dance,
> Find contentment, find romance.
>
> Sandy seashore, deep blue sky,
> Cares will vanish . . . so can I . . .

FERDINAND: What is this music? It has led me here and now it stops. . . . No, there it is again. . . .

ARIEL [singing]:

> Waters move, the ocean flows,
> Nothing comes and nothing goes . . .
> Strange days are upon us . . .
>
> Oysters stare through pearly eyes
> Heart-shaped corals gently beat
> In the crystal undersea
> Here the journey ends—oh see:
>
> Waters move and ocean flows,
> Nothing comes and nothing goes . . .
> Strange days are upon us . . .

FERDINAND: What do I see before me? A goddess? A mortal?

MIRANDA: I know what I'm seeing: a flatterer. Young man, your ability to pay compliments in the situation in which you find yourself at least proves your courage. Who are you?

FERDINAND: As you see, a poor shipwrecked soul.

MIRANDA: But one of high degree!

FERDINAND: In other surroundings I might be called "Prince," "son of the King". . . . But, no, I was forgetting . . . not "Prince" but "King," alas . . . "King" because my father has just perished in the disaster.

MIRANDA: Poor young man! Here, you'll be received with hospitality and we'll support you in your misfortune.

FERDINAND: Alas, my father. . . . Can it be that I am an unnatural son? Your pity would make the greatest of sorrows seem sweet.

MIRANDA: I hope you'll like it here with us. The island is pretty. I'll show you the beaches and the forests, I'll tell you the names of fruits and flowers, I'll introduce you to a whole world of insects, of lizards of every hue, of birds. . . . Oh, you cannot imagine! The birds! . . .

PROSPERO: That's enough, daughter! I find your chatter irritating . . . and let me assure you, it's not at all fitting. You are doing too much honor to an imposter. Young man, you are a traitor, a spy, and a woman-chaser to boot! No sooner has he escaped the perils of the sea than he's sweet-talking the first girl he meets! You won't get round me that way. Your arrival is convenient, because I need more manpower: you shall be my house servant.

FERDINAND: Seeing the young lady, more beautiful than any wood-nymph, I thought I was Ulysses on Nausicaa's isle.[9] But hearing you, Sir, I now understand my fate a little better—I see I have come ashore on the Barbary Coast and am in

---

9. In the *Odyssey*, Ulysses was shipwrecked on the island of the Phaiakians, naked and hungry, he appeals to Nausicaa, daughter of the king, for help.

the hands of a cruel pirate.[1] [*Drawing his sword.*] However, a gentleman prefers death to dishonor! I shall defend my life with my freedom!

PROSPERO: Poor fool: your arm is growing weak, your knees are trembling! Traitor! I could kill you now . . . but I need help. Follow me.

ARIEL: It's no use trying to resist, young man. My master is a sorcerer: neither your passion nor your youth can prevail against him. Your best course would be to follow and obey him.

FERDINAND: Oh God! What sorcery is this? Vanquished, a captive—yet far from rebelling against my fate, I am finding my servitude sweet. Oh, I would be imprisoned for life if only heaven will grant me a glimpse of my sun each day, the face of my own sun. Farewell, Nausicaa.

[*They exit.*]

from ACT 2, SCENE 1

Caliban's cave. Caliban is singing as he works when Ariel enters. He listens to him for a moment.

CALIBAN [*singing*]:

> *May he who eats his corn heedless of Shango[2]*
> *Be accursed! May Shango creep beneath*
> *His nails and into his every pore!*
> *Shango, Shango ho!*
>
> *Forget to give him room if you dare!*
> *He will make himself at home on your nose!*
>
> *Refuse to have him under your roof at your own risk!*
> *He'll tear off your roof and wear it as a hat!*
> *Whoever tries to mislead Shango*
> *Will suffer for it!*
> *Shango, Shango ho!*

* * *

from ACT 3, SCENE 5[3]

* * *

PROSPERO: Enough! Today is a day to be benevolent, and it will do no good to try to talk sense to you in the state you're in. . . . Leave us. Go sleep it off, drunkards. We raise sail tomorrow.

TRINCULO: Raise sail! But that's what we do all the time, Sire, raise things, Stephano and I . . . at least, we raise our glasses, from dawn till dusk till dawn. . . . The hard part is putting them down, decking, as you might say.

PROSPERO: Scoundrels, would that in your voyage through life you might one day put in at the harbor of Temperance and Sobriety!

ALONSO [*indicating Caliban*]: That is the strangest creature I've ever seen!

PROSPERO: And the most devilish too!

GONZALO: What's that? Devilish! You've reprimanded him, preached at him, you've given orders and made him obey, and you say he is still indomitable!

---

1. The Barbary Coast is in North Africa.
2. Shango is a Yoruba god of thunder and war, worshipped in the Antilles, Africa, and Brazil.
3. The final scene brings to a culmination the various threads of the play, much as in *The Tempest*. As the scene

opens, Ferdinand and Miranda are playing chess, and Prospero tells the entire group, assembled in his grotto, that they will all set sail for Italy on the following day; with that, he sets Ariel free.

PROSPERO: Honest Gonzalo, it is as I have said.

GONZALO: Well—and forgive me, Counsellor, if I give counsel—on the basis of my long experience the only thing left is exorcism. "Begone, unclean spirit, in the name of the Father, of the Son and of the Holy Ghost." That's all there is to it! *[Caliban bursts out laughing.]*

GONZALO: You were absolutely right! And more so than you thought. . . . He's not just a rebel, he's a hardened criminal! *[To Caliban.]* So much the worse for you, my friend. I have tried to save you. I give up. I leave you to the secular arm![4]

PROSPERO: Draw near, Caliban. What say you in your own defense? Take advantage of my good humor. Today, I feel in a forgiving mood.

CALIBAN: I'm not interested in defending myself. My only regret is that I've failed.

PROSPERO: What were you hoping for?

CALIBAN: To get back my island and regain my freedom.

PROSPERO: And what would you do all alone here on this island, haunted by the devil, tempest tossed?

CALIBAN: First of all, I'd get rid of you! I'd spew you out, all your works and pomps! Your "white" magic!

PROSPERO: That is a fairly negative program. . . .

CALIBAN: You don't understand it. . . . I say I'm going to spew you out, and that's very positive. . . .

PROSPERO: Well, the world is really upside down. . . . We've seen everything now: Caliban as a dialectician! However, in spite of everything I'm fond of you, Caliban. Come, let's make peace. We've lived together for ten years and worked side by side! Ten years count for something, after all! We've ended up by becoming compatriots!

CALIBAN: You know very well that I'm not interested in peace. I'm interested in being free! Free, you hear?

PROSPERO: It's odd . . . no matter what you do, you won't succeed in making me believe that I'm a tyrant!

CALIBAN: Understand what I say, Prospero:
        For years I bowed my head
        for years I took it, all of it—
        your insults, your ingratitude . . .
        and worst of all, more degrading than all the rest,
        your condescension,
        But now, it's over!
        Over, do you hear?
        Of course, at the moment
        You're still stronger than I am.
        But I don't give a damn for your power
        or for your dogs or your police or your inventions!
        And do you know why?
        It's because I know I'll get you!
        I'll impale you! And on a stake that you've
        sharpened yourself!
        You'll have impaled yourself!
        Prospero, you're a great magician:
        you're an old hand at deception.
        And you lied to me so much,

---

4. Having played at being the exorcist, Gonzalo "releases" Caliban to the "state."

about the world, about yourself,
that you ended up by imposing on me
an image of myself:
underdeveloped, in your words, incompetent,
that's how you made me see myself!
And I loathe that image . . . and it's false!
But now I know you, you old cancer,
And I also know myself!

And I know that one day my bare fist, just that, will be enough to crush
your world. The old world is falling apart!

Isn't it true? Just look. It even bores *you* to death.
And by the way . . . you have a chance to get
it over with: you can fuck off.
You can go back to Europe. But in a pig's eye you will!
I'm sure you won't leave. You make me laugh
with your "mission"!
Your "vocation"!
Your vocation is to give me shit.
And that's why you'll stay . . . just like those
guys who founded the colonies
and who now can't live anywhere else.
You're just an old colonial addict, that's what you are!

PROSPERO: Poor Caliban! You know that you're headed toward your own ruin.
You're sliding toward suicide! You know I will be the stronger, and stronger all the
time. I pity you!

CALIBAN: And I hate you!

PROSPERO: Beware! My generosity has its limits.

CALIBAN: [*shouting*]:

> *Shango marches with strength*
> *along his path, the sky!*
> *Shango is a fire-bearer,*
> *his arms shake the heavens*
> *and the earth*
> *Oh, Shango! Shango!*

PROSPERO: I have uprooted the oak and raised the sea,

> I have caused the mountain to tremble and have bared my chest to adversity.
> With Jove I have traded thunderbolt for thunderbolt.
> Better yet—from a brutish monster I have made man!
> But ah! To have failed to find the path to man's heart . . .
> if that be where man is.
> [*To Caliban.*] Well, I hate you as well!
> For it is you who have made me doubt myself for the first time.
> [*To the Nobles.*] My friends, draw near. I take my leave of you . . . I shall not
>   be going. My fate is here: I shall not run from it.

ANTONIO: What, Sire?

PROSPERO: Hear me well. I am not in any ordinary sense a master,
as this savage thinks,

but rather the conductor of a boundless score—
this isle,
summoning voices—I alone—
and mingling them at my pleasure,
arranging out of confusion
one intelligible line.
Without me, who would be able to draw music from all that?
This isle is mute without me.
My duty, thus, is here, and here I shall stay.

GONZALO: Oh day full rich in miracles!

PROSPERO: Do not be distressed. Antonio, be you the lieutenant of my goods and make use of them as procurator until that time when Ferdinand and Miranda may take effective possession of them, joining them with the Kingdom of Naples. Nothing of that which has been set for them must be postponed: let their marriage be celebrated at Naples with all royal splendor. Honest Gonzalo, I place my trust in your word. You shall stand as father to our Princess at this ceremony.

GONZALO: Count on me, Sire.

PROSPERO: Gentlemen, farewell.

[They exit.]

And now Caliban, it's you and me!
What I have to tell you will be brief:
Ten times, a hundred times, I've tried to save you,
above all from yourself.
But you have always answered me with wrath and venom,
like the opossum that pulls itself up by its own tail
the better to bite the hand that tears it from the darkness.
Well, my boy, I shall set aside my indulgent nature
and henceforth I will answer your violence
with violence!

[Time passes, symbolized by the curtain's being lowered halfway and reraised. In semi-darkness Prospero appears, aged and weary. His gestures are jerky and automatic, his speech weak, toneless.]

PROSPERO: Odd, but for some time now we seem to be overrun with opossums. Peccarys[5] wild boar, all of the unpleasant animals! But mainly opossums. With those eyes! And the vile grin they have! It's as though the jungle was laying siege to the cave. . . . But I shall stand firm . . . I shall not let my work perish! [Shouting.] I shall protect civilization! [He fires in all directions.] They're done for! Now, this way I'll be able to have some peace and calm for a while. But it's cold. Odd how the climate's changed. Cold on this island. . . . Have to think about making a fire. . . . Well, Caliban, old fellow, it's just us two now, here on the island . . . only you and me. You and me. You-me . . . me-you! What in the hell is he up to? [Shouting.] Caliban!

[In the distance, above the sound of the surf and the chirping of birds, we hear snatches of Caliban's song.]

FREEDOM HI-DAY, FREEDOM HI-DAY!!

❧

══╬ PERSPECTIVES ╬══

Tracts on Women and Gender

What is the nature of woman? Is she meant to be subordinate to man or an equal partner? What virtues is she capable of? Does she have intellectual ability, and if so, is it appropriate for her to write? How should she behave toward her husband? What are his responsibilities to her? What is the difference between a good woman and a bad one? What is the difference between manly behavior and womanly behavior? These are some of the questions that early modern English tracts on women and gender ask. Although we would not ask all of these questions in precisely the same way today, they are still of burning interest. The debate over these questions in early modern tracts on women sheds light on the representation of sex and gender in the poetry and drama of the period. By *sex* is meant the representation of biological difference; by *gender* is meant the representation of sex difference as it is socially constructed.

In the Middle Ages there were both attacks on women and defenses of them by both women and men, but intellectual and social changes modified the debate in the early modern period. One of the prominent medieval genres that continued to be imitated in the early modern period was the praise of exemplary women, such as Boccaccio's *De Claris Mulieribus* ("concerning famous women"), Chaucer's *Legend of Good Women*, and Christine de Pizan's *Le Livre de la Cité des Dames* (translated into English in 1521 as *The Book of the City of Ladies*). Renaissance humanism brought a new intellectual rigor to the genre. The German humanist Heinrich Cornelius Agrippa (1486–1535) stands out in the early Tudor controversy of the 1540s. Agrippa's *De Nobilitate et Praecellentia Foemenei Sexus* (translated in 1542 as *A Treatise of the Nobilitie and Excellencye of Woman Kynde*) not only lists biblical and classical heroines but also examines how the place of women in society is determined by culture rather than nature: "And thus by these lawes, the women being subdued as it were by force of arms, are constrained to give place to men, and to obey their subduers, not by natural, nor divine necessity or reason, but by custom, education, fortune, and a certain tyrannical occasion." However, even a humanist author such as Erasmus, who had enlightened views on other social issues, had very strict views about the absolute subordination of wife to husband. Indeed, this subordination seems to have increased in intensity in the early modern period as the nuclear family headed by the father superseded the extended family, in which power was more dispersed throughout the network of kinship.

Among the learned, the new classical humanist education was still largely reserved for young men. Such changes moved the historian Joan Kelly Gadol to ask, "Did women have a Renaissance?" At the same time, some early modern women were educated enough to represent themselves in the debate on the nature of women, and they brought new perspectives to it. Margaret Tyler was one of the first English women to speak in defense of women as writers. Rachel Speght, the first polemical or argumentative woman writer in English, wrote her defense of women in response to a controversy set in motion by the publication of Joseph Swetnam's *An Arraignment of Lewd, Idle, Froward, and Unconstant Women* (1615). Swetnam was a misogynist, but his tract had the virtue of eliciting defenses of women. Among these responses were *A Muzzle for Melastomus*, written from the theological perspective of Rachel Speght, and *Ester Hath Hanged Haman*, written from the more secular outlook of "Ester Sowernam" (a pen-name adopted to counter the "sweet" in the name Swetnam). Two other tracts of the 1620s, *Hic Mulier* ("the mannish woman") and *Haec Vir* ("the womanish man") humorously raised the problem of the blurring of genders and carried on a debate about the style of dress and behavior that men and women should adopt.

Whether these tracts take the form of an oration, a speech by one person, or a dialogue between two people (as in *Haec Vir*), they are all in lively conversation with each other, either directly or indirectly. They are also in a lively conversation with other texts in this period. Representing only a fraction of the early modern literature on women and gender, these tracts attest to heightened interest in questions of gender, such as those posed by the speakers in

Title page from *The English Gentlewoman*, by Richard Brathwaite, 1631.

Lady Mary Wroth's and Katherine Philips's poems and the cross-dressing, independent Moll Cutpurse of Thomas Dekker and Thomas Middleton's *The Roaring Girl*.

Desiderius Erasmus
1469?–1536

Erasmus was the author not only of the humorous *Encomium Morae* (*The Praise of Folly*), dedicated to his friend Thomas More, but also of numerous works on Christian morals. Although *The Praise of Folly* was translated into English only in 1551, Erasmus's *Coniugium* (c. 1523), a text on marriage, appeared in English as *A Mery Dialogue, Declaringe the Propertyes of Shrewde Shrewes, and Honest Wyves* as early as 1542. This text advocated wifely submissiveness but also domesticity for both men and women—concepts that influenced the English bourgeois notion of marriage. Richard Tavernour also translated Erasmus's writing on marriage as *A Ryght Frutefull Epystle Devised in Laude and Praise of Matrimony* (1534). The following passage from this text demonstrates a view of marriage as the closest possible bond between human beings—and, more than that, as a sacrament calling for the wife's sole loyalty to her husband and lasting even beyond death.

from In Laude and Praise of Matrimony

* * * if the most part of things (yea which be also bitter) are of a good man to be desired for none other purpose, but because they be honest, matrimony doubtless is chiefly to be desired whereof a man may doubt whether it hath more honesty than pleasure. For what thing is sweeter than with her to live, with whom ye may be most straightly coupled, not only in the benevolence of the mind, but also in the conjunction of the body? If a great delectation of mind be taken of the benevolence of our other kinsmen, since it is an especial sweetness to have one with whom ye may communicate the secret affections of your mind, with whom ye may speak even as it were with your own self, whom ye may safely trust, which supposeth your chances to be his, what felicity (think ye) have the conjunction of man and wife, than which no thing in the universal world may be found either greater or firmer. For with our other friends we be conjoined only with the benevolence of minds, with our wife we be coupled with most high love, with permixtion[1] of bodies, with the confederate band of the sacrament, and finally with the fellowship of all chances. Furthermore, in other friendships, how great simulation is there, how great falsity? Yea, they whom we judge our best friends, like as the swallows flee away when summer is gone, so they forsake us when fortune turneth her wheel. And sometime the fresher friend casts out the old. We hear of few whose fidelity endure till their lives' end. The wife's love is with no falsity corrupted, with no simulation obscured, with no chance of things minished,[2] finally with death only (nay not with death neither) withdrawn. She, the love of her parents, she, the love of her sisters, she, the love of her brethren, despiseth for the love of you, her only respect is to you, of you she hangeth,[3] with you she coveteth to die. * * *

* * * Do ye judge any pleasure to be compared with this so great a conjunction? If ye tarry at home there is at hand which shall drive away the tediousness of solitary being. If from home ye have one that shall kiss you when ye depart, long for you when ye be absent, receive you joyously when ye return. A sweet companion of youth, a kind solace of age. By nature yea any fellowship is delectable to man, as whom nature hath created to benevolence and friendship. This fellowship then how shall it not be most sweet, in which everything is common to them both? And contrarily, if we see the savage beasts also abhor[4] solitary living and delighted in fellowship, in my mind he is not once to be supposed a man, which abhoreth from[5] this fellowship most honest and pleasant of all. For what is more hateful than the man which (as though he were born only to himself) liveth for himself, seeketh for himself, spareth for himself, doth cost to himself, loveth no person, is loved of no person? Shall not such a monster be adjudged worthy to be cast out of all men's company into the mid sea with Timon the Athenian,[6] which because he fled all men's company, was called Misanthropus that is to say hate man * * *

But I know well enough what among these, ye murmur against me. A blessed thing is wedlock, if all prove according to the desire, But what if a wayward wife

---

1. A thorough mixture or mingling.
2. Diminished, lessened in power.
3. In the sense of clinging, holding fast, adhering.
4. Hate.

5. Shrink with horror from.
6. The story of how Timon shunned society after his friends abandoned him when he lost his wealth is told by Plutarch (the source for Shakespeare's *Timon of Athens*).

chanceth?[7] What if an unchaste? What if unnatural children? There will run in your mind the examples of those whom wedlock have brought to utter destruction. Heap up as much as ye can, but yet these be the vices of men and not of wedlock. Believe me, an evil wife is not wont to chance, but to evil husbands. Put this unto it, that it lieth in you to choose out a good one. But what if after the marriage she be marred?[8] Of an evil husband (I will well) a good wife may be marred, but of a good, the evil is wont to be reformed and mended. We blame wives falsely. No man (if ye give any credence to men) had ever a shrew to his wife, but through his own default.[9]

✦═◈═✦

Barnabe Riche
1542–1617

A veteran of wars in the Low Countries and Ireland and author of twenty-six books, Barnabe Riche led a life as fraught with contention as his writing. Best known as the author of *His Farewell to Military Profession* (1581), which contains the source for Shakespeare's *Twelfth Night*, Riche was both a keen observer of contemporary social life and a spy. Alongside his attacks on shameless city women in *My Lady's Looking Glass* (1616) and *A New Description of Ireland* (1610), he also portrays Dublin ladies as critics of his work in *A True and Kind Excuse* (1612)—an interesting episode documenting women's literacy in this period. His writing has the zealous spirit of reforming Protestantism and looks forward to the impassioned prose of radical dissenters in the Civil War. *My Lady's Looking Glass* was published by Thomas Adams, London, in 1616, and dedicated to Lady Saint Jones, wife of the Lord Deputy of Ireland. This text bears comparison with Riche's *Excellency of Good Women* (London, 1613), as well as numerous other Jacobean tracts on the conduct of women.

from My Lady's Looking Glass

But my promise was to give rules how to distinguish between a good woman and a bad, and promise is debt, but I must be well advised how I take the matter in hand; for we were better to charge a woman with a thousand defects in her soul, than with that one abuse of her body; and we must have two witnesses, besides our own eyes, to testify, or we shall not be believed: but I myself have thought of a couple that I hope will carry credit.

The first is the prophet Isaiah, that in his days challenged the daughters of Zion for their stretched-out necks, their wandering eyes, at their mincing and wanton demeanor as they passed through the streets: these signs and shows have ever been thought to be the special marks whereby to know a harlot.[1] But Solomon in a more particular manner better furnishes us with more assured notes, and to the end that we might the better distinguish the good woman from the bad, he delivereth their several qualities, and wherein they are opposite: and speaking of a good woman he saith, *She seeketh out wool and flax, and laboreth cheerfully with her hands: she overseeth the ways of her household, and eateth not the bread of idleness.*[2]

Solomon thinketh that a good woman should be a home *housewife*, he pointeth her out her housework. *She overseeth the ways of her household,* she must look to her

---

7. Comes about by chance.
8. Injured.
9. Fault.

1. See Isaiah 3.16.
2. See Proverbs 31.13, 27.

children, her servants and family; but *the paths of a harlot* (he saith) *are movable, for now she is in the house, now in the streets, now she lies in wait in every corner*, she is still gadding from place to place, from person to person, from company to company; from custom to custom, she is evermore wandering: her feet are wandering, her eyes are wandering, her wits are wandering, *Her ways are like the ways of a serpent:* hard to be found out.[3]

A good woman (again) *opens her mouth with wisdom, the law of grace is in her tongue:* but *a harlot is full of words, she is loud and babbling*, saith Solomon.

She is bold, she is impudent, she is shameless, she cannot blush: and she that hath lost all these virtues hath lost her evidence of honesty: for the ornaments of a good woman are temperance in her mind, silence in her tongue, and bashfulness in her countenance.

It is not she that can lift up her heels highest in the dancing of a galliard,[4] she that is lavish of her lips or loose of her tongue.

Now if Solomon's testimony be good, the woman that is impudent, immodest, shameless, insolent, audacious, a night-walker, a company-keeper, a gadder from place to place, a reveller, a ramper, a roister, a rioter: she that has these properties, has the certain signs and marks of a harlot, as Solomon has avowed. Now what credit his words will carry in the Commissaries' court, I leave to those that be advocates, and proctors in women's causes.[5]

I have hitherto presented to your view the true resemblance of a harlot, as well what she is, as how she might be discerned: I would now give you the like notice of that notable *Strumpet, the whore of Babylon*,[6] that has made so many Kings and Emperors drunk with the cup of abominations, by whom the nations of the earth have so defiled themselves by their spiritual fornication, called in the Scripture by the name of *idolatry* (but now within the last five hundred years, amongst Christians) shadowed under the title of Popery. This harlot has her agents, Popes, Cardinals, Bishops, Abbots, Monks, Friars, Jesuits, Priests, with a number of other like, and all of them factors in her bands,[7] the professed enemies of the Gospel of Jesus Christ, that do superstitiously adore the crucifix, and are indeed enemies of the cross of Christ, and do tread his holy blood under their scornful feet: that build up devotion with ignorance, and do ring out their hot alarms in the ears of the unlearned, teaching that the light can be no light, that the Scriptures can be no Scriptures, nor the truth can be no truth, but by their allowance, and if they will say that high noon is midnight, we must believe them, and make no more ado but get us to bed.

—+—≡◊≥—+—

Margaret Tyler
fl. 1578

Margaret Tyler is best known today for the preface to her translation of Diego Ortunez de Calahorra's Spanish prose romance *The Mirrour of Princely Deedes and Knighthood*, Book I (1578), in which she argues that women have the ability to write on any subject. She was a

---

3. See Proverbs 7.10–12.
4. A lively dance in triple time.
5. Commissaries' court: the court of a bishop's representative, which had jurisdiction over divorce and probate; ad-

vocates: pleaders, legal counselors; proctors: attorneys.
6. An image from Revelation 17, taken by Protestants to symbolize the Roman Catholic Church.
7. Agents in her leagues, or covenants.

waiting woman in the Catholic household of the Duke of Norfolk in the 1560s, where she may have read her translation aloud to the Duchess and her circle. In the preface to her translation, Tyler refers both to the "friends" who wanted her to return to her "old reading" and defends herself against potential critics who might object to her translating "matter more manlike than becometh my sex." She argues that she is more interested in virtue than in war and that, in any case, war affects women as much as it does men. The sixteenth-century humanist Vives had viewed romances as unsuitable for women readers, while male authors of romances often dedicated their work to women. Arguing for women's right to an education, Tyler reasons that if men can dedicate their texts to women, then women can read them, and that if women can read texts on such subjects as war and government, then they can write them.

from Preface to *The First Part of the Mirror of Princely Deeds*

Thou hast here, gentle Reader, the history of Trebatio, an Emperor in Greece: whether a true history of him indeed, or a feigned fable, I wot[1] not, neither did I greatly seek after it in the translation, but by me it is done into English for thy profit and delight. The chief matter therein contained, is of exploits of wars, and the parties therein named are especially renowned for their magnanimity and courage. * * * Such delivery as I have made I hope thou wilt friendly accept, the rather for that it is a woman's work, though in a story profane, and a matter more manlike than becometh my sex. But as for any manliness of the matter, thou knowest that it is not necessary for every trumpeter or drumstare[2] in the war to be a good fighter. They take wages only to incite others, though themselves have privy maims,[3] and are thereby recureless.[4] So, gentle reader, if my travail in Englishing this author may bring thee to a liking of the virtues herein commended, and by example thereof in thy princes' and countries' quarrel to hazard thy person, and purchase good name, as for hope of well deserving myself that way, I neither bend my self thereto, nor yet fear the speech of people if I be found backward. I trust every man holds not the plough, which would that the ground were tilled, and it is no sin to talk of Robin Hood, though you never shot in his bow. Or be it that the attempt were bold to intermeddle in arms, as the ancient Amazons[5] did, and in this story Claridiana doth, and in other stories not a few, yet to report of arms is not so odious, but that it may be borne withall, not only in you men which yourselves are fighters, but in us women, to whom the benefit in equal part appertains of your victories, either the matter is so commendable that it carries no discredit from the homeliness of the speaker, or that it is so generally known, that it fits every man to speak thereof. * * * But my defense is by example of the best, amongst which, many have dedicated their labors, some stories, some of war, some physic, some law, some as concerning government, some divine matters, unto diverse ladies and gentlewomen. And if men may and do bestow such of their travails upon gentlewomen, then may we women read such of their works as they dedicate to us, and if we may read them, why not further wade in them to the search of truth. * * * But to return to whatever the truth is, whether that women may not at all discourse in learning, for men late in their claim to being sole possessioners of knowledge, or whether they may in some manner, that is by limitation or appointment in some kind of learning, my persuasion hath been thus, that it is all one for a woman to pen a story, as for a man to address his story to a woman. But amongst all

1. Know.
2. Drummer.
3. Secret weaknesses.

4. Irrecoverable.
5. A tribe of female warriors described by Herodotus and other ancient Greek authors as living in Scythia.

my ill-willers, some I hope are not so straight that they would enforce me necessarily either not to write or to write of divinity. Whereas neither durst I trust mine own judgment sufficiently, if matter of controversy were handled, nor yet could I find any book in any tongue, which would not breed offense to some. But I perceive some may be rather angry to see their Spanish delight turned to all English pastime: they could well allow the story in Spanish, but they may not afford it so cheap, or they would have it proper to themselves. What natures such men be of, I list[6] not greatly to dispute, but my meaning hath been to make others partners of my liking, as I doubt not gentle reader, but if it shall please thee after serious matters to sport thyself with this Spaniard, that thou shalt find in him the just reward of malice and cowardice, with the good speed of honesty and courage, being able to furnish thee with sufficient store of foreign examples to both purposes. And as in such matters which have been rather devised to beguile time, than to breed matter of sad learning, he hath ever borne away any price which could season such delights with some profitable reading: so shalt thou have this stranger an honest man when need serveth, and at other times either a good companion to drive out a weary night, or a merry jest at thy board. And this much concerning this present story, that it is neither unseemly for a woman to deal in, neither greatly requiring a less staid age than mine is. But of these two points, gentle reader, I thought to give thee warning, lest perhaps understanding my name and years, there mightest be a wrong suspect[7] of my boldness and rashness, from which I would gladly free myself by this plain excuse, and if I may deserve thy good favor by like labor, when the choice is my own, I will have a special regard of thy liking. So I wish thee well.

Thine to use, M.T.[8]

----- ✦ -----

Joseph Swetnam
fl. 1615

Little is known about Joseph Swetnam other than that he stirred up an enormous controversy over the question of women when he wrote *An Arraignment of Lewd, Idle, Froward, and Unconstant Women* (1615). The work was published anonymously with an introductory letter signed by "Thomas Tel-troth." Trotting out all the negative stereotypes of women he could jumble together, Swetnam constructed his mock treatise as a piece of raucous comedy, aimed at the lowest common denominator. Reading Swetnam's work as a serious diatribe against women, Rachel Speght and the pseudonymous Ester Sowernam and Constantia Munda produced critiques of misogyny. Speght unmasked Swetnam's authorship and identified him as a fencing master in Bristol. An anonymous comedy, *Swetnam the Womanhater, Arraigned by Women* (1620), possibly by Thomas Heywood, dramatized the debate as a court trial with Swetnam prosecuting his case against women and the Amazon Atlanta (a soldier disguised as a woman) defending them. Swetnam is finally turned over to a court of women, who find him guilty and muzzle him (an obvious reference to Speght's *Muzzle for Melastomus*).

6. Wish.
7. Suspicion.
8. Margaret Tyler.

from The Arraignment of Lewd, Idle, Froward, and Unconstant Women

from *Chapter 2. The Second Chapter showeth the manner of such women as live upon evil report: it also showeth that the beauty of women has been the bane of many a man, for it hath overcome valiant and strong men, eloquent and subtle men. And in a word it hath overcome all men, as by examples following shall appear.*

First, that of Solomon unto whom God gave singular wit and wisdom, yet he loved so many women that he quite forgot his God which always did guide his steps, so long as he lived godly and ruled justly, but after he had glutted himself with women, then he could say, vanity of vanity all is but vanity. He also in many places of his book of Proverbs exclaims most bitterly against lewd women calling them all that naught is, and also displayeth their properties, and yet I cannot let men go blameless although women go shameless; but I will touch them both, for if there were not receivers then there would not be so many stealers: if there were not some knaves there would not be so many whores, for they both hold together to bolster each other's villainy, for always birds of a feather will flock together hand in hand to bolster each other's villainy.

Men, I say, may live without women, but women cannot live without men. For Venus, whose beauty was excellent fair, yet when she needeth man's help she took Vulcan, a clubfooted smith. And therefore if a woman's face glister,[1] and her gesture pierce the marble wall, or if her tongue be as smooth as oil or as soft as silk, and her words so sweet as honey, or if she were a very ape for wit, or a bag of gold for wealth, or if her personage have stolen away all that nature can afford, and if she be decked up in gorgeous apparel, then a thousand to one but she will love to walk where she may get acquaintance, and acquaintance bringeth familiarity, and familiarity setteth all follies abroach,[2] and twenty to one that if a woman love gadding but that she will pawn her honor to please her fantasy.

Man must be at all the cost and yet live by the loss. A man must take all the pains and women will spend all the gains. A man must watch and ward, fight and defend, till the ground, labor in the vineyard, and look what he getteth in seven years; a woman will spread it abroad with a fork in one year, and yet little enough to serve her turn but a great deal too little to get her good will. Nay, if thou give her ever so much and yet if thy person please not her humor, then will I not give a halfpenny for her honesty at the year's end.

For then her breast will be the harborer of an envious heart, and her heart the storehouse of poisoned hatred; her head will devise villainy, and her hands are ready to practice that which their heart desireth. Then who can but say that women are sprung from the devil, whose heads, hands and hearts, minds and souls are evil, for women are called the hook of all evil, because men are taken by them as a fish is taken in with the hook.

For women have a thousand ways to entice thee, and ten thousand ways to deceive thee, and all such fools as are suitors unto them; some they keep in hand with promises, and some they feed with flattery, and some they delay with dalliances, and some they please with kisses. They lay out the folds of their hair to entangle men into

1. Glitter, shine.   2. Flowing abroad.

their love; betwixt their breasts is the vale of destruction, and in their beds there is hell, sorrow and repentance. Eagles do not eat men till they are dead, but women devour them alive, for a woman will pick thy pocket and empty thy purse, laugh in thy face and cut thy throat. They are ungrateful, perjured, full of fraud, flouting and deceit, unconstant, waspish,[3] toyish,[4] light, sullen, proud, discourteous and cruel, and yet they were by God created, and by nature formed, and therefore by policy and wisdom to be avoided, for good things abused are to be refused. Or else for a month's pleasure, she may make thee go stark naked. She will give thee roast meat, but she will beat thee with the spit. If thou hast crowns in thy purse, she will be thy heart's gold until she leave thee not a whit of white money. They are like summer birds, for they will abide no storm, but flock about thee in the pride of thy glory, and fly from thee in the storms of affliction; for they aim more at thy wealth than at thy person, and esteem more thy money than any man's virtuous qualities; for they esteem of a man without money as a horse does a fair stable without meat. They are like eagles which will always fly where the carrion is.

They will play the horse-leech to suck away thy wealth, but in the winter of thy misery, she will fly away from thee. Not unlike the swallow, which in the summer harboreth herself under the eaves of a house, and against winter flieth away, leaving nothing but dirt behind her.

Solomon saith, he that will suffer himself to be led away or to take delight in such women's company is like a fool which rejoiceth when he is led to the stocks. *Proverbs* 7.

Hosea, by marrying a lewd woman of light behavior was brought unto idolatry, *Hosea* 1. Saint Paul accounteth fornicators so odious, that we ought not to eat meat with them. He also showeth that fornicators shall not inherit the kingdom of Heaven, 1 *Corinthians* the 9th and 11th verse.

And in the same chapter Saint Paul excommunicateth fornicators, but upon amendment he receiveth them again. Whoredom punished with death, *Deuteronomy* 22.21 and *Genesis* 38.24. Phineas a priest thrust two adulterers, both the man and the woman, through the belly with a spear, *Numbers* 25.

God detests the money or goods gotten by whoredom, *Deuteronomy* 23.17, 18. Whores called by diverse names, and the properties of whores, *Proverbs* 7.6 and 21. A whore envieth an honest woman, *Esdras* 16 and 24. Whoremongers God will judge, *Hebrews* 13 and 42. They shall have their portions with the wicked in the lake that burns with fire and brimstone, *Revelation* 21.8.

Only for the sin of whoredom God was sorry at heart, and repented that he ever made man, *Genesis* 6.67.

Saint Paul saith, to avoid fornication every man may take a wife, 1 *Corinthians* 6.9.

Therefore he which hath a wife of his own and yet goeth to another woman is like a rich thief which will steal when he has no need.

There are three ways to know a whore: by her wanton looks, by her speech, and by her gait. *Ecclesiasticus* 26.[5] And in the same chapter he saith, that we must not give our strength unto harlots, for whores are the evil of all evils, and the vanity of all vanities, they weaken the strength of a man and deprive the body of his beauty, it

3. Spiteful.
4. Frivolous, wanton.

5. Apocryphal book of the Old Testament.

furroweth his brows and maketh the eyes dim, and a whorish woman causeth the fever and the gout; and at a word, they are a great shortening to a man's life.

For although they seem to be as dainty as sweet meat, yet in trial not so wholesome as sour sauce. They have wit, but it is all in craft; if they love it is vehement, but if they hate it is deadly.

Plato saith, that women are either angels or devils, and that they either love dearly or hate bitterly, for a woman hath no mean in her love, nor mercy in her hate, no pity in revenge, nor patience in her anger; therefore it is said, that there is nothing in the world which both pleases and displeases a man more than a woman, for a woman most delighteth a man and yet most deceiveth him, for as there is nothing more sweet to a man than a woman when she smiles, even so there is nothing more odious than the angry countenance of a woman.

Solomon in his 20th chapter of *Ecclesiastes*[6] saith, that an angry woman will foam at the mouth like a boar. If all this be true as most true it is, why shouldest thou spend one hour in the praise of women as some fools do, for some will brag of the beauty of such a maid, another will vaunt of the bravery of such a woman, that she goeth beyond all the women in the parish. Again, some study their fine wits how they may cunningly swooth[7] women, and with logic how to reason with them, and with eloquence to persuade them. They are always tempering their wits as fiddlers do their strings, who wrest them so high, that many times they stretch them beyond time, tune and reason.

Again, there are many that weary themselves with dallying, playing, and sporting with women, and yet they are never satisfied with the unsatiable desire of them; if with a song thou wouldest be brought asleep, or with a dance be led to delight, then a fair woman is fit for thy diet. If thy head be in her lap she will make thee believe that thou are hard by[8] God's seat, when indeed thou are just at hell gate.

―――― ⊨◇⊨ ――――

Rachel Speght
1597?–?

The daughter of the rector of two London churches and the wife of a minister, Rachel Speght was only about nineteen years old when she wrote *A Muzzle for Melastomus, the Cynical Baiter of, and Foul-Mouthed Barker Against Evah's Sex, or an Apologetical Answer to the Irreligious and Illiterate Pamphlet made by Io. Swu. and by him Intituled The Arraignment of Women*. Speght interpreted Swetnam's *Arraignment* as a serious attack on women to show the faulty logic underpinning misogyny. Her title indicates the dual thrust of her analysis: the *irreligious* Swetnam has misinterpreted Scripture, and the *illiterate* pamphlet is logically confused and rhetorically flawed. She argues for a view of marriage as a mutual partnership and the relation between the sexes as one of greater equality. Modern critics have debated the implications of Speght's work: Barbara Lewalski has called Rachel Speght "the first self-proclaimed and positively identified female polemicist in England," while Ann Rosalind Jones has questioned whether Speght's work can be considered as feminist in the twentieth-century sense. All critics of early modern gender studies agree, however, that Speght was a learned and committed author. She alone of the participants in the Jacobean controversy about women affixed her own name to

6. A faulty citation: in Ecclesiasticus 25, an angry woman is compared to a bear.

7. Sway, woo.
8. Close to.

the title page. And she reiterated her authorship with the publication of her poetic dream-vision *Mortalities Memorandum* (1621), in which she defends women's education.

from A Muzzle for Melastomus
Of Woman's Excellency, with the causes of her creation, and of the sympathy which ought to be in man and wife each toward other

The work of creation being finished, this approbation thereof was given by God himself, that "All was very good."[1] If all, then woman, who—except man—is the most excellent creature under the canopy of heaven. But if it be objected by any:

First, that woman, though created good, yet by giving ear to Satan's temptations brought death and misery upon all her posterity.

Secondly, that "Adam was not deceived, but that the woman was deceived and was in the transgression."[2]

Thirdly, that St. Paul says "It were good for a man not to touch a woman."[3]

Fourthly and lastly, that of Solomon, who seems to speak against all of our sex: "I have found one man among a thousand, but a woman among them all I have not found,"[4] whereof in its due place.

To the first of these objections, I answer: that Satan first assailed the woman because where the hedge is lowest, most easy it is to get over, and she being the weaker vessel[5] was with more facility to be seduced—like as a crystal glass sooner receives a crack than a strong stone pot. Yet we shall find the offense of Adam and Eve almost to parallel; for as an ambitious desire to be made like God was the motive which caused her to eat, so likewise was it his, as may plainly appear by that *ironia*: "Behold, man is become as one of us"[6]—not that he was so indeed, but hereby his desire to attain a greater perfection than God had given him was reproved. Woman sinned, it is true, by her infidelity in not believing the word of God but giving credit to Satan's fair promises that "she should not die";[7] but so did the man, too. And if Adam had not approved of that deed which Eve had done, and been willing to tread the steps where she had gone, he   being her head   would have reproved her and have made the commandment a bit to restrain him from breaking his Maker's injunction. For if a man burn his hand in the fire, the bellows that blew the fire is not to be blamed, but himself rather for not being careful to avoid the danger. Yet if the bellows had not blown, the fire had not burned; no more is woman simply to be condemned for man's transgression. For by the free will which before his fall he enjoyed, he might have avoided and been free from being burned or singed with that fire which was kindled by Satan and blown by Eve. It therefore served not his turn a whit afterwards to say: "The woman which thou gavest me gave me of the tree, and I did eat."[8] For a penalty was inflicted upon him as well as on the woman, the punishment of her transgression being particular to her own sex and to none but the female kind, but for the sin of man the whole earth was cursed.[9] And he being better able than the woman to have resisted temptation, because the stronger vessel, was first called to

---

1. Genesis 1.31. References to the Bible are indicated in the margins of Speght's text.
2. 1 Timothy 2.14.
3. 1 Corinthians 7.1.
4. Ecclesiastes 7.28.
5. "The weaker vessel," a phrase taken from 1 Peter 3.7, is frequently used in early modern English sermons to describe woman.
6. Genesis 3.22. "Ironia," or irony, is a figure of speech in which the meaning is the opposite of that of the words used and the tone of which is often mocking.
7. Genesis 3.4.
8. Genesis 3.12.
9. Genesis 3.17.

account, to show that to whom much is given, of them much is required; and that he who was the sovereign of all creatures visible should have yielded greatest obedience to God.

True it is (as is already confessed) that woman first sinned, yet find we no mention of spiritual nakedness till man had sinned. Then it is said "Their eyes were opened,"[1] the eyes of their mind and conscience; and then perceived they themselves naked, that is, not only bereft of that integrity which they originally had, but felt the rebellion and disobedience of their members in the disordered motions of their now corrupt nature, which made them for shame to cover their nakednesse. Then (and not afore) it is said that they saw it, as if sin were imperfect and unable to bring a deprivation of a blessing received, or death on all mankind, till man (in whom lay the active power of generation) had transgressed. The offense, therefore, of Adam and Eve is by St. Austin[2] thus distinguished: "the man sinned against God and himself, the woman against God, herself and her husband"; yet in her giving of the fruit to eat had she no malicious intent towards him, but did therein show a desire to make her husband partaker of that happiness, which she thought by their eating they should both have enjoyed. This her giving Adam of that sauce, wherewith Satan had served her, whose sourness, afore he had eaten, she did not perceive, was that which made her sin to exceed his. Wherefore, that she might not of him who ought to honor her be abhorred,[3] the first promise that was made in Paradise, God makes to woman, that by her seed should the serpent's head be broken.[4] Whereupon Adam calls her *Hevah*, Life, that as the woman had been an occasion of his sin so should woman bring forth the Savior from sin, which was in the fullness of time accomplished.[5] By which was manifested that he is a Savior of believing women no less than of men, that so the blame of sin may not be imputed to his creature, which is good, but to the will by which Eve sinned; and yet by Christ's assuming the shape of man was it declared that his mercy was equivalent to both sexes. So that by Hevah's blessed seed, as St. Paul affirms, it is brought to pass that "male and female are all one in Christ Jesus."[6]

To the second objection I answer: that the Apostle does not hereby exempt man from sin, but only giveth to understand that the woman was the primary transgressor, and not the man; but that man was not at all deceived was far from his meaning. For he afterwards expressly saith that "in Adam all die, so in Christ shall all be made alive."[7]

For the third objection, "It is good for a man not to touch a woman": the Apostle makes it not a positive prohibition but speaks it only because of the Corinth[ian]s' present necessity,[8] who were then persecuted by the enemies of the church. For which cause, and no other, he saith: "Art thou loosed from a wife? Seek not a wife"— meaning whilst the time of these perturbations should continue in their heat; "but if thou are bound, seek not to be loosed; if thou marriest, thou sinnest not," only increase thy care: "for the married careth for the things of this world. And I wish that you were without care that ye might cleave fast to the Lord without separation: for the time remaineth, that they which have wives be as though they had none, for the persecutors shall deprive you of them either by imprisonment, banishment or death."

1. Genesis 3.7.
2. Saint Augustine; this commonplace echoes parts of his sermon on Adam and Eve.
3. 1 Peter 3.7.
4. Genesis 3.15.

5. Galatians 4.4.
6. Galatians 3.28.
7. 1 Corinthians 15.22.
8. 1 Corinthians 7.

So that manifest it is, that the Apostle does not hereby forbid marriage, but only adviseth the Corinth[ian]s to forbear a while, till God in mercy should curb the fury of their adversaries. For (as Eusebius[9] writeth) Paul was afterward married himself, the which is very probable, being that interrogatively he saith: "Have we not power to lead about a wife being a sister, as well as the rest of the Apostles, and as the brethren of the Lord, and Cephas?"[1]

The fourth and last objection is that of Solomon: "I have found one man among a thousand, but a woman among them all have I not found."[2] For answer of which, if we look into the story of his life, we shall find therein a commentary upon this enigmatical[3] sentence included. For it is there said that Solomon had seven hundred wives and three hundred concubines, which number connected make one thousand. These women turning away his heart from being perfect with the Lord his God,[4] sufficient cause had he to say, that among the said thousand women found he not one upright. He saith not, that among a thousand women never any man found one worthy of commendation, but speaks in the first person singularly "I have not found," meaning in his own experience. For this assertion is to be held a part of the confession of his former follies, and no otherwise, his repentance being the intended drift of *Ecclesiastes*.

Thus having (by God's assistance) removed those stones whereat some have stumbled, others broken their shins, I will proceed toward the period of my intended task, which is to decipher the excellency of women. Of whose creation I will, for order's sake, observe: first, the efficient cause,[5] which was God; secondly, the material cause, or whereof she was made; thirdly, the formal cause, or fashion and proportion of her feature; fourthly and lastly, the final cause, the end or purpose for which she was made. To begin with the first.

The efficient cause of woman's creation was Jehovah the Eternal, the truth of which is manifest in Moses his narration of the six days' works, where he says, "God created them male and female."[6] And David, exhorting all "the earth to sing to the Lord" (meaning, by a metonymy,[7] "earth": all creatures that live on the earth, of whatever sex or nation) gives this reason: "For the Lord has made us."[8] That work then cannot choose but be good, yea very good, which is wrought by so excellent a workman as the Lord; for he, being a glorious Creator, must effect a worthy creature. Bitter water cannot proceed from a pleasant sweet fountain, nor bad work from that workman which is perfectly good—and, in propriety, none but he.[9]

Secondly, the material cause, or matter whereof woman was made, was of a refined mold, if I may so speak. For man was created of the dust of the earth,[1] but woman was made of a part of man after that he was a living soul. Yet she was not produced from Adam's foot, to be his too low inferior; nor from his head to be his superior; but from his side, near his heart, to be his equal: that where he is lord, she may be lady. And therefore saith God concerning man and woman jointly: "Let them rule over the fish of the sea, and over the fowls of the heaven, and over every beast that moves upon the earth."[2] By which words he makes their authority equal, and all

---

9. Eusebius (A.D. 260–340) was Bishop of Caesarea and a church historian. See *Ecclesiastical History* 3.30.
1. 1 Corinthians 9.5.
2. Ecclesiastes 7.28.
3. Mysterious.
4. 1 Kings 11.3.
5. The agent who makes something; see Aristotle's *Physics* 2.3.

6. Genesis 1.28 [27].
7. A figure of speech that substitutes one term for another to which it is closely related.
8. Psalms 100.3.
9. Psalms 100.5; Matthew 19.7.
1. Genesis 2.7.
2. Genesis 1.26.

creatures to be in subjection to them both. This, being rightly considered, doth teach men to make such account of their wives as Adam did of Eve: "This is bone of my bone, and flesh of my flesh."[3] As also, that they neither do or wish any more hurt unto them, than unto their own bodies. For men ought to love their wives as themselves, because he that loves his wife loves himself;[4] and never did man hate his own flesh (which the woman is) unless a monster in nature.

Thirdly, the formal cause, fashion and proportion, of woman was excellent. For she was neither like the beasts of the earth, fowls of the air, fishes of the sea, or any other inferior creature; but man was the only object which she did resemble. For as God gave man a lofty countenance that he might look up toward Heaven, so did he likewise give unto woman. And as the temperature of man's body is excellent, so is woman's. For whereas other creatures, by reason of their gross humors, have excrements for their habit—as fowls their feathers, beasts their hair, fishes their scales—man and woman only have their skin clear and smooth.[5] And (that more is) in the image of God were they both created; yea and to be brief, all the parts of their bodies, both external and internal, were correspondent and meet each for other.

Fourthly and lastly, the final cause or end for which woman was made was to glorify God, and to be a collateral companion for man to glory God, in using her body and all the parts, powers and faculties thereof as instruments for his honor. As with her voice to sound forth his praises, like Miriam, and the rest of her company;[6] with her tongue not to utter words of strife, but to give good counsel unto her husband, the which he must not despise. For Abraham was bidden to give ear to Sarah his wife.[7] Pilate was willed by his wife not to have any hand in the condemning of Christ;[8] and a sin it was in him that he listened not to her; Leah and Rachel counseled Jacob to do according to the word of the Lord;[9] and the Shunamite put her husband in mind of harboring the prophet Elisha.[1] Her hands should be open, according to her ability, in contributing towards God's service and distressed servants, like to that poor widow who cast two mites into the treasury;[2] and as Mary Magdalene, Susanna and Joanna, the wife of Herod's steward, with many others which of their substance ministered unto Christ.[3] Her heart should be a receptacle for God's word, like Mary that treasured the sayings of Christ in her heart.[4] Her feet should be swift in going to seek the Lord in his sanctuary, as Mary Magdalene made haste to seek Christ at his sepulcher.[5] Finally, no power external or internal ought woman to keep idle, but to employ it in some service of God, to the glory of her creator and comfort of her own soul.

The other end for which woman was made was to be a companion and helper for man; and if she must be a *helper*, and but a *helper*, then are those husbands to be blamed, which lay the whole burden of domestical affairs and maintenance on the shoulders of their wives. For, as yoke-fellows they are to sustain part of each other's cares, griefs and calamities. But as if two oxen be put into one yoke, the one being bigger than the other, the greater bears most weight; so the husband, being the stronger vessel, is to bear a greater burden than his wife. And therefore the Lord said to Adam: "In the sweat of your face shall you eat your bread, till you return to the

3. Genesis 2.23.
4. Ephesians 5.28.
5. Genesis 1.26.
6. Exodus 15.20.
7. Genesis 21.12.
8. Matthew 27.19.

9. Genesis 31.16.
1. 2 Kings 4.9.
2. Mark 12.43.
3. Luke 8.
4. Luke 1.45.
5. John 20.1.

dust."[6] And St. Paul says that "he that provideth not for his household is worse than an infidel."[7] Nature hath taught senseless creatures to help one another: as the male pigeon, when his hen is weary with sitting on her eggs and comes off from them, supplies her place, that in her absence they may receive no harm, until such time as she is fully refreshed. Of small birds, the cock always helps his hen to build her nest; and while she sits upon her eggs he flies abroad to get meat for her, who cannot then provide any for herself. The crowing cockerel helps his hen to defend her chickens from peril, and will endanger himself to save her and them from harm. Seeing then, that these unreasonable creatures by the instinct of nature bear such affection to each other, that without any grudge they willingly according to their kind help one another, I may reason, *a minore ad maius*,[8] that much more should man and woman, which are reasonable creatures, be helpers to each other in all things lawful, they having the law of God to guide them, his word to be a lantern to their feet and a light unto their paths, by which they are excited to a far more mutual participation of each other's burden than other creatures. So that neither the wife may say to her husband nor the husband to his wife: "I have no need of thee,"[9] no more than the members of the body may say to each other, between whom there is such a sympathy that if one member suffer, all suffer with it. Therefore though God bade Abraham forsake his country and kindred, yet he bade him not forsake his wife who, being "Flesh of his flesh, and bone of his bone," was to be copartner with him of whatsoever did betide him, whether joy or sorrow. Wherefore Solomon says "woe to him that is alone";[1] for when thoughts of discomfort, troubles of this world and fear of dangers do possess him, he wants a companion to lift him up from the pit of perplexity into which he is fallen.[2] For a good wife, saith Plautus, is the wealth of the mind and the welfare of the heart; and therefore a meet associate for her husband. And "woman," saith Paul, "is the glory of the man."[3]

Marriage is a merri-age, and this world's paradise, where there is mutual love. Our blessed Savior vouchsafed to honor a marriage with the first miracle that he wrought,[4] unto which miracle matrimonial estate may not unfitly be resembled. For as Christ turned water into wine, a far more excellent liquor (which, as the Psalmist saith, "Makes glad the hearts of man"[5]) so the single man is changed by marriage from a bachelor to a husband, a far more excellent title: from a solitary life to a joyful union and conjunction with such a creature as God had made meet for man, for whom none was fit till she was made. The enjoying of this great blessing made Pericles more unwilling to part from his wife than to die for his country; and Antonius Pius to pour forth that pathetic exclamation against death for depriving him of his dearly beloved wife: "O cruel hard-hearted death in bereaving me of her whom I esteemed more than my own life!"[6] "A virtuous woman," saith Solomon, "is the crown of her husband";[7] by which metaphor he shows both the excellency of such a wife and what account her husband is to make of her. For a king does not trample his crown under his feet, but highly esteems it, gently handles it and carefully lays it up as the evidence of his kingdom; and therefore when David destroyed Rabbah[8] he

6. Genesis 3.19.
7. 1 Timothy 5.8.
8. From the lesser to the greater.
9. 1 Corinthians 12.21.
1. Ecclesiastes 4.10.
2. Ecclesiastes 4.10.
3. 1 Corinthians 11.7.
4. John 2.

5. Psalms 104.15.
6. Antonius Pius (A.D. 86–161) Roman emperor, founded a charity for orphaned girls in honor of his wife. Plutarch writes about how Pericles (495–429 B.C.), ruler of Athens, greatly loved Aspasia.
7. Proverbs 7.4.
8. 1 Chronicles 20.2. Joab destroyed Rabbah, while David took the king's crown.

took off the crown from their king's head. So husbands should not account their wives as their vassals but as those that are "heirs together of the grace of life,"[9] and with all lenity and mild persuasions set their feet in the right way if they happen to tread awry, bearing with their infirmities, as Elkanah did with his wife's barrenness.[1]

The kingdom of God is compared to the marriage of a king's son;[2] John calleth the conjunction of Christ and his chosen a marriage;[3] and not few but many times does our blessed Savior in the Canticles[4] set forth his unspeakable love towards his church under the title of a husband rejoicing with his wife, and often vouchsafeth to call her his sister a spouse—by which is showed that with God "is no respect of persons," nations, or sexes.[5] For whosoever, whether it be man or woman, that doth "believe in the lord Jesus, such shall be saved."[6] And if God's love, even from the beginning, had not been as great toward woman as to man, then he would not have preserved from the deluge of the old world as many women as men. Nor would Christ after his resurrection have appeared to a woman first of all other, had it not been to declare thereby, that the benefits of his death and resurrection are as available, by belief, for women as for men; for he indifferently died for the one sex as well as the other.

⊷ ⚌⟐⚌ ⊶

"Ester Sowernam"

The pen name Ester Sowernam comes from the Old Testament heroine Esther, who defended her people against Haman, and the antithesis of Joseph Swetnam's last name (sweet/sour). The full title of her text also parodies Swetnam's: *Ester Hath Hanged Haman; or An Answer to a Lewd Pamphlet, Entitled The Arraignment of Women. With the Arraignment of Lewd, Idle, Froward and Unconstant Men, and Husbands* (1617). On the whole, the author of this pamphlet presents herself in a more secular light than Rachel Speght does. Sowernam's criticisms of misogyny are more psychological and social than moral and logical. Trained in Classics as well as Scripture and a keen observer, Ester Sowernam finds that Swetnam has incorrectly stated that the Bible is the source of the statement that women are a necessary evil and finds that the true source is in Euripides' *Medea*. The occasion for Sowernam's writing is a dinner party at which Swetnam's book and Speght's response were discussed. Sowernam finds fault with both—Swetnam because he "damns all women" and Speght because she "undertaking to defend women doth rather charge and condemn them." Sowernam cites the double standard by which men are excused for what women are judged harshly for in order to assert women's superiority. She argues that women are judged more severely because they are thought to be more virtuous in the first place. The second half of her pamphlet may have helped to inspire the comedy that spoofed the entire controversy, *Swetnam the Woman-Hater Arraigned By Women* (1620).

from **Ester Hath Hanged Haman**
from *Chapter 7. The answer to all objections which are material made against women*

As for that crookedness and frowardness[1] with which you charge women, look from whence they have it. For of themselves and their own disposition it doth not proceed, which is proved directly by your own testimony. For in your 46th page, line

---

9. 1 Peter 3.7.
1. 1 Samuel 1.17.
2. Matthew 22.
3. Revelation 19.7.

4. The Song of Songs.
5. Romans 2.11.
6. John 3.18.
1. Perversity, unreasonableness.

15[16], you say: "A young woman of tender years is flexible, obedient, and subject to do anything, according to the will and pleasure of her husband." How cometh it then that this gentle and mild disposition is afterwards altered? Yourself doth give the true reason, for you give a great charge not to marry a widow. But why? Because, say you in the same page, "A widow is framed to the conditions[2] of another man." Why then, if a woman have froward conditions, they be none of her own, she was framed to them. Is not our adversary ashamed of himself to rail against women for those faults which do all come from men? Doth not he most grievously charge men to learn[3] their wives bad and corrupt behavior? For he saith plainly: "Thou must unlearn a widow, and make her forget and forego her former corrupt and disordered behavior." Thou must unlearn her; *ergo*, what fault she hath learned: her corruptness comes not from her own disposition but from her husband's destruction.

Is it not a wonder that your pamphlets are so dispersed? Are they not wise men to cast away time and money upon a book which cutteth their own throats? 'Tis pity but that men should reward you for your writing (if it be but as the Roman Sertorius[4] did the idle poet: he gave him a reward, but not for his writing—but because he should never write more). As for women, they laugh that men have no more able a champion. This author cometh to bait women or, as he foolishly saith, the "Bearbaiting of Women," and he bringeth but a mongrel cur who doth his kind[5] to brawl and bark, but cannot bite. The mild and flexible disposition of a woman is in philosophy proved in the composition of her body, for it is a maxim: *Mores animi sequuntur temperaturam corporis* (the disposition of the mind is answerable to the temper of the body). A woman in the temperature of her body is tender, soft and beautiful, so doth her disposition in mind correspond accordingly: she is mild, yielding and virtuous. What disposition accidentally happeneth unto her is by the contagion of a froward husband, as Joseph Swetnam affirmeth.

And experience proveth. It is a shame for a man to complain of a froward woman—in many respects all concerning himself. It is a shame he hath no more government over the weaker vessel.[6] It is a shame he hath hardened her tender sides and gentle heart with his boisterous and Northern blasts. It is a shame for a man to publish and proclaim household secrets—which is a common practice amongst men, especially drunkards, lechers, and prodigal spendthrifts. These when they come home drunk, or are called in question for their riotous misdemeanors, they presently show themselves the right children of Adam. They will excuse themselves by their wives and say that their unquietness and frowardness at home is the cause that they run abroad: an excuse more fitter for a beast than a man. If thou wert a man thou wouldst take away the cause which urgeth a woman to grief and discontent, and not by thy frowardness increase her distemperature.[7] Forbear thy drinking, thy luxurious riot, thy gaming and spending, and thou shalt have thy wife give thee as little cause at home as thou givest her great cause of disquiet abroad. Men which are men, if they chance to be matched with froward wives—either of their own making or others' marring[8]—they would make a benefit of the discommodity:[9] either try his skill to make her mild or exercise his patience to endure her cursedness; for all crosses are

---

2. Circumstances, character traits.
3. Teach.
4. Quintus Sertorius, Roman general, appointed governor of Farther Spain in 83 B.C.
5. Nature.

6. From 1 Peter 3.7.
7. Disorder in mind and body.
8. Spoiling.
9. Inconvenience, disadvantageousness.

inflicted either for punishment of sins or for exercise of virtues. But humorous[1] men will sooner mar a thousand women than out of a hundred make one good.

And this shall appear in the imputation which our adversary chargeth upon our sex: to be lascivious, wanton and lustful. He saith: "Women tempt, allure and provoke men." How rare a thing is it for women to prostitute and offer themselves? How common a practice is it for men to seek and solicit women to lewdness? What charge do they spare? What travail do they bestow? What vows, oaths and protestations do they spend to make them dishonest? They hire panders, they write letters, they seal them with damnations and execrations to assure them of love when the end proves but lust. They know the flexible disposition of women, and the sooner to overreach them some will pretend they are so plunged in love that, except they obtain their desire, they will seem to drown, hang, stab, poison, or banish themselves from friends and country. What motives are these to tender dispositions? Some will pretend marriage, another offer continual maintenance; but when they have obtained their purpose, what shall a woman find?—just that which is her everlasting shame and grief: she hath made herself the unhappy subject to a lustful body and the shameful stall[2] of a lascivious tongue. Men may with foul shame charge woman with this sin which she had never committed, if she had not trusted; nor had ever trusted, if she had not been deceived with vows, oaths and protestations. To bring a woman to offend in one sin, how many damnable sins do they commit? I appeal to their own consciences. The lewd disposition of sundry men doth appear in this: if a woman or maid will yield to lewdness, what shall they want?[3]—but if they would live in honesty, what help shall they have? How much will they make of the lewd? How base an account of the honest? How many pounds will they spend in bawdy houses? But when will they bestow a penny upon an honest maid or woman, except it be to corrupt them?

Our adversary bringeth many examples of men which have been overthrown by women. It is answered before: the fault is their own. But I would have him, or anyone living, to show any woman that offended in this sin of lust, but that she was first solicited by a man.

Helen was the cause of Troy's burning: first, Paris did solicit her; next, how many knaves and fools of the male kind had Troy, which to maintain whoredom would bring their city to confusion?

When you bring in examples of lewd women and of men which have been stained by women, you show yourself both frantic and a profane irreligious fool to mention Judith,[4] for cutting off Holofernes' head, in that rank.

You challenge women for untamed and unbridled tongues; there was never woman was ever noted for so shameless, so brutish, so beastly a scold as you prove yourself in this base and odious pamphlet. Your blaspheme God, you rail at his creation, you abuse and slander his creatures; and what immodest or impudent scurrility is it which you do not express in this lewd and lying pamphlet?

Hitherto I have so answered all your objections against women that, as I have not defended the wickedness of any, so I have set down the true state of the question. As Eve did not offend without temptation of a serpent, so women do seldom offend but it is by provocation of men. Let not your impudency, nor your consorts'

---

1. Moody.
2. Target.
3. Lack, need.
4. A wealthy, attractive widow who saved her people

from Holofernes, an Assyrian general, by attracting and then killing him. (See The Book of Judith, part of the Catholic Bible, but viewed as apocryphal by Jews and Protestants.)

dishonesty, charge our sex hereafter with those sins of which you yourselves were the first procurers. I have, in my discourse, touched you, and all yours, to the quick. I have taxed you with bitter speeches; you will, perhaps, say I am a railing scold. In this objection, Joseph Swetnam, I will teach you both wit and honesty. The difference between a railing scold and an honest accuser is this: the first rageth upon passionate fury without bringing cause or proof, the other bringeth direct proof for what she allegeth. You charge women with clamorous words, and bring no proof; I charge you with blasphemy, with impudency, scurrility, foolery and the like. I show just and direct proof for what I say. It is not my desire to speak so much; it is your dessert to provoke me upon just cause so far. It is not railing to call a crow black, or a wolf a ravenor,[5] or a drunkard a beast; the report of the truth is never to be blamed: the deserver of such a report deserves the shame.

Now, for this time, to draw to an end. Let me ask according to the question of Cassian, *cui bono?*[6]—what have you gotten by publishing your pamphlet? Good I know you can get none. You have, perhaps, pleased the humors of some giddy, idle, conceited persons. But you have dyed yourself in the colors of shame, lying, slandering, blasphemy, ignorance, and the like.

The shortness of time and the weight of business call me away, and urge me to leave off thus abruptly; but assure yourself, where I leave now I will by God's grace supply the next term, to your small content. You have exceeded in your fury against widows, whose defense you shall hear of at the time aforesaid. In the mean space, recollect your wits; write out of deliberation, not out of fury; write out of advice, not out of idleness: forbear to charge women with faults which come from the contagion of masculine serpents.

Hic Mulier and Haec-Vir

Hic Mulier and *Haec-Vir* were published anonymously within a week of each other in February 1620. *Hic Mulier*, the first of the two pamphlets to appear, begins with the complaint that "since the days of Adam women were never so masculine." The title introduces this theme by a gender switch of its own: *Hic Mulier*, Latin for "This Woman," uses the masculine form *hic* instead of the feminine *haec*. The title page contains illustrations of two such mannish women—one wearing a man's hat, which she admires in a mirror, and another sitting in a barber's chair to get her hair cut. Structured as a "brief declamation," or oration, the text argues that such activities as hair bobbing and wearing men's clothes are immoral and unnatural for women. Furthermore, such gender crossing is also a threat to the entire political order: "most pernicious to the commonwealth for she hath power by example to do it a world of injury."

As its subtitle boasts, *Haec-Vir* was "an answer to the late book intituled *Hic Mulier*" and was represented as "a brief dialogue between Haec-Vir the Womanish-Man, and Hic Mulier the Man-Woman." The effeminate man and the hermaphroditic woman first misrecognize each other's gender. Once that is cleared up, the foppish man launches into a diatribe against the woman, who defends herself by arguing that "custom is an idiot." The first half of the dialogue reads like a proclamation of the equality of the sexes, with the bare-breasted, dagger-swinging Hic Mulier exclaiming, "We are as free-born as men, have as free election, and as free spirits, we are compounded of like parts and may with like liberty make benefit of our creations." Despite this bold challenge, the text as a whole makes a rather conservative case for

5. An animal who seizes in order to devour.
6. "To whose benefit," a phrase attributed by Cicero to   Lucius Cassius.

the need for gender distinctions, the overturning of which was seen as an assault on hierarchy. The dialogue ends with both participants agreeing to exchange clothes and Latin pronouns so that men will again be manly and women subservient to them.

These pamphlets display the early modern fascination with, and loathing of, transvestism. Not only did the fashionable young male favorites of King James I's court resemble the womanish man of *Haec-Vir*, but there were more than a few documented cases of women wearing breeches on the streets. One of these women, the notorious Mary Frith, was immortalized in Dekker and Middleton's comedy, *The Roaring Girl*. A few women were actually brought before ecclesiastical courts for "shamefully" putting on "man's apparel."

While conforming to the comic pattern of disrupting and then reestablishing the status quo, these pamphlets show that questions about custom, nature, and sex and gender roles were being asked in the early seventeenth century.

from Hic Mulier; or, The Man-Woman

So I present these masculine women in their deformities as they are, that I may call them back to the modest comeliness in which they were.

The modest comeliness in which they were? Why, did ever these mermaids, or rather mere-monsters,[1] that wear the Car-man's block,[2] the Dutchman's feather *upse-van-muffe*, the poor man's pate pouled by a Treene dish, the French doublet trussed with points, to Mary Aubries' light nether skirts, the fool's baldric, and the devil's poniard. Did they ever know comeliness or modesty? Fie, no, they never walked in those paths, for these at the best are sure but rags of gentry, torn from better pieces for their foul stains, or else the adulterate branches of rich stocks,[3] that taking too much sap from the root, are cut away, and employed in base uses; or, if not so, they are the stinking vapors drawn from dunghills, which nourished in the higher regions of the air, become meteors and false fires blazing and flashing therein, and amazing men's minds with their strange proportions, till the substance of their pride being spent, they drop down again to the place from whence they came, and there rot and consume unpitied, and unremembered.

And questionless it is true, that such were the first beginners of these last deformities, for from any purer blood would have issued a purer birth; there would have been some spark of virtue: some excuse for imitation; but this deformity has no agreement with goodness, nor any difference against the weakest reason: it is all base, all barbarous. Base, in the respect it offends men in the example, and God in the most unnatural use: barbarous, in that it is exorbitant from nature, and an antithesis to kind,[4] going astray (with ill-favored affectation) both in attire, in speech, in manners, and (it is to be feared) in the whole courses and stories of their actions. What can be more true and curious consent of the most fairest colors and the wealthy gardens which fill the world with living plants? Do but you receive virtuous inmates (as what palaces are more rich to receive heavenly messengers?) and you shall draw men's souls to you with that severe, devout, and holy adoration, that you shall never want praise, never love, never reverence.

But now methinks I hear the witty-offending great ones reply in excuse of their deformities: What, is there no difference amongst women? no distinction of places,

---

1. Pure monsters.
2. A merchant's hat. Descriptions of ridiculous fashions follow: the *upse-van-muffe* is an elaborate feathered hat; the pate pouled by a Treene dish is hair cut short to the shape of a wooden dish; the French doublet is a man's

close-fitting upper body garment tied with laces; baldric: fancy belt; poniard: dagger.
3. Trunks or stems.
4. The opposite of what is natural to the gender.

no respect of honors, nor no regard of blood, or alliance? Must but a bare pair of shears pass between noble and ignoble, between the generous spirit and the base mechanic; shall we be all co-heirs of one honor, one estate, and one habit? O men, you are then too tyrannous, and not only injure nature, but also break the laws and customs of the wisest princes. Are not bishops known by their miters, princes by their crowns, judges by their robes, and knights by their spurs? But poor women have nothing (how great soever they be) to divide themselves from the enticing shows or moving images which do furnish most shops in the city. What is it that either the laws have allowed to the greatest ladies, custom found convenient, or their bloods or places challenged, which hath not been engrossed into the city with as great greediness, and pretense of true title; as if the surcease[5] from the imitation were the utter breach of their charter everlastingly.

For this cause, these apes of the city have enticed foreign nations to the cells, and there committing gross adultery with their gewgaws,[6] have brought out such unnatural conceptions, that the whole world is not able to make a *Democritus* big enough to laugh at their foolish ambitions.[7] Nay, the very art of painting (which to the last age shall ever be held in detestation) they have so cunningly stolen and hidden amongst their husbands' hoards of treasure, that the decayed stock of prostitution (having little other revenues) are hourly in bringing their action of *detinue*[8] against them. Hence (being thus troubled with these *Popeniars*,[9] and loath still to march in one rank with fools and *zanies*[1]) have proceeded these disguised deformities, not to offend the eyes of goodness, but to tire with ridiculous contempt the never to be satisfied appetites of these gross and unmannerly intruders. Nay, look if this very last edition of disguise, this which is so full of faults, corruptions, and false quotations, this bait which the devil had laid to catch the souls of wanton women, be not as frequent in the demi-palaces of burghers and citizens as it is either at masque, triumph, tilt-yard, or playhouse. Call but to account the tailors that are contained within the circumference of the walls of the city, and let but their heels and their hard reckonings be justly summed together, and it will be found they have raised more new foundations of this new disguise, and metamorphosed more modest old garments, to this new manner of short base and French doublet (only for the use of freemen's wives[2] and their children) in one month, than has been worn in court, suburbs, or country, since the unfortunate beginning of the first devilish invention.

Let therefore the powerful Statute of Apparel[3] but lift his battle-axe, and crush the offenders in pieces, so as every one may be known by the true badge of their blood, or fortune; and then these *Chimeras* of deformity will be sent back to hell, and there burn to cinders in the flames of their own malice.

Thus, methinks, I hear the best offenders argue, nor can I blame a high blood to swell when it is coupled and counter-checked with baseness and corruption; yet this shows an anger passing near akin to envy, and alludes much to the saying of an excellent poet:

5. Cessation, stop.
6. Showy decorations.
7. Seneca recounts how Democritus laughed rather than cried at human life (*De tranquilitate animi* 15.2).
8. Legal action to recover personal property.
9. Popinjays, vain and empty people.
1. Parasites, those who play the fool for amusement.

2. Women married to men possessing the freedom of a city, borough, or corporation.
3. Laws governing dress that were intended to differentiate the aristocracy from the common people had been enacted from the Middle Ages through to the early modern period.

> Women never
> Love beauty in their sex, but envy ever.

They have Caesar's ambition, and desire to be one and one alone, but yet to offend themselves, to grieve others, is a revenge dissonant to reason, and as *Euripides* says, a woman of that malicious nature is a fierce beast, and most pernicious to the commonwealth, for she has power by example to do it a world of injury. But far be such cruelty from the softness of their gentle dispositions: O let them remember what the poet saith:

> Women be
> Fram'd with the same parts of the mind as men
> Nay Nature triumph'd in their beauty's birth,
> And women made the glory of the earth,
> The life of beauty, in whose simple breast,
> (As in her fair lodging) Virtue rests:
> Whose towering thoughts attended with remorse,
> Do make their fairness be of greater force.

But when they thrust virtue out of doors, and give a shameless liberty to every loose passion, that either their weak thoughts engender, or the discourse of wicked tongues can charm into their yielding bosoms (much too apt to be opened with any pick-lock of flattering and deceitful insinuation) then they turn maskers, mummers, nay monsters in their disguises, and so they may catch the bridle in their teeth, and run away with their rulers, they care not into what dangers they plunge either their fortunes or reputations, the disgrace of the whole sex, or the blot and obloquy of their private families, according to the saying of the poets

> Such is the cruelty of women-kind,
> When they have shaken off the shamefac'd band
> With which wise nature did them strongly bind,
> T'obey the hests of man's well-ruling hand
> That then all rule and reason they withstand
> To purchase a licentious liberty;
> But virtuous women wisely understand,
> That they were born to mild humility,
> Unless the heavens them lift to lawful sovereignty.[4]

To you therefore that are fathers, husbands, of sustainers of these new hermaphrodites, belongs the cure of this impostume;[5] it is you that give fuel to the flames of their wild indiscretion. You add the oil which makes their stinking lamps defile the whole house with filthy smoke, and your purses purchase these deformities at rates both dear and unreasonable. Do you but hold close your liberal hands, or take a strict account of the employment of the treasure you give to their necessary maintenance,

---

4. Description of the tyranny of the Amazonian ruler Radigund in Spenser's *Faerie Queene* 5.5.25.

5. Abscess.

and these excesses will either cease, or else die smothered in prison in the tailors' trunks for want of redemption.

from Haec-Vir; or, The Womanish-Man

Hic-Mulier: Well, then to the purpose: first, you say, I am base in being a slave to novelty. What flattery can there be in freedom of election? Or what baseness to crown my delights with those pleasures which are most suitable to mine affections? Bondage or slavery is a restraint from those actions, which the mind (of its own accord) doth most willingly desire: to perform the intents and purposes of another's disposition, and that not but by mansuetude[1] or sweetness of entreaty; but by the force of authority and strength of compulsion. Now for me to follow change, according to the limitation of my own will and pleasure, there cannot be a greater freedom. Nor do I in my delight of change otherwise than as the whole world doth, or as becometh a daughter of the world to do. For what is the world, but a very shop or warehouse of change? Sometimes winter, sometimes summer; day and night: they hold sometimes riches, sometimes poverty, sometimes health, sometimes sickness: now pleasure; presently anguish; now honor; then contempt: and to conclude, there is nothing but change, which doth surround and mix with all our fortunes. And will you have poor woman such a fixed star, that she shall not so much as move or twinkle in her own sphere? That would be true slavery indeed, and a baseness beyond the chains of the worst servitude. Nature to everything she hath created hath given a singular delight in change, as to herbs, plants, and trees a time to wither and shed their leaves, a time to bud and bring forth their leaves, and a time for their fruits and flowers; to worms and creeping things a time to hide themselves in the pores and hollows of the earth, and a time to come abroad and suck the dew; to beasts liberty to choose their food, liberty to delight in their food, and liberty to feed and grow fat with their food. The birds have the air to fly in, the waters to bathe in, and the earth to feed on. But to man, both these and all things else, to alter, frame, and fashion, according to his will and delight shall rule him. Again, who will rob the eye of the variety of objects, the ear of the delight of sounds, the nose of smells, the tongue of taste, and the hand of feeling? And shall only woman, excellent woman, so much better in that she is something purer, be only deprived of this benefit? Shall she be the bondslave of time, the handmaid of opinion, or the strict observer of every frosty or cold benumbed imagination? It would be a cruelty beyond the rack or strapado.[2]

But you will say it is not change, but novelty, from which you deter us: a thing that doth avert the good, and erect the evil; prefer the faithless, and confound desert; that with the change of opinions breeds the change of states, and with continual alterations thrusts headlong forward both ruin and subversion. Alas (soft Sir) what can you christen by that new imagined title, when the words of a wise man are: *that what was done, is but done again: all things do change, and under the cope of heaven there is no new thing.*[3] So that whatsoever we do or imitate, it is neither slavish, base, nor a breeder of novelty.

Next, you condemn me of unnaturalness, in forsaking my creation, and contemning[4] custom. How do I forsake my creation, that do all the right and offices due

---

1. Gentleless, meekness.
2. Rack: a frame with a roller at either end on which a person would be tortured; strapado: a form of torture in which the victim's hands would be tied behind his or her

back and the victim would then be suspended by a pulley with a sharp jolt.
3. Ecclesiastes 1.9.
4. Disdaining, despising.

to my creation? I was created free, born free, and live free: what lets me then so to spin out my time, that I may die free?

To alter creation were to walk on my hands with my heels upward, to feed myself with my feet, or to forsake the sweet sound of sweet words, for the hissing noise of the serpent: but I walk with a face erected, with a body clothed, with a mind busied, and with a heart full of reasonable and devout cogitations; only offensive in attire, inasmuch as it is a stranger to the curiosity of the present times, and an enemy to custom. Are we then bound to be the flatterers of time, or the dependents on custom? O miserable servitude chained only to baseness and folly! For then custom, nothing is more absurd, nothing more foolish. * * *

Cato Junior held it for a custom, never to eat meat but sitting on the ground. The Venetians kiss one another ever at the first meeting; and even in this day it is a general received custom amongst our English, that when we meet or overtake any man in our travel or journeying, to examine him whither he rides, how far, to what purpose, and where he lodgeth? Nay, and with that unmannerly boldness of inquisition, that it is a certain ground of a most insufficient quarrel, not to receive a full satisfaction of those demands which go far astray from good manners, or comely civility; and will you have us to marry ourselves to these mimic and most fantastic customs? It is a fashion or custom with us to mourn in black, yet the Argian[5] and Roman ladies ever mourned in white; and (if we will tie the action upon the signification of colors) I see not but we may mourn in green, blue, red or any simple color used in heraldry. For us to salute strangers with a kiss is counted but civility, but with foreign nations immodesty; for you to cut the hair of your upper lips, familiar here in England, everywhere else almost thought unmanly. To ride on side-saddles at first was counted here abominable pride, and et cetera. I might instance in a thousand things that only custom and not reason hath approved. To conclude, Custom is an idiot, and whoever dependeth wholly upon him, without the discourse of reason, will take from him his pied[6] coat, and become a slave indeed to contempt and censure.

But you say we are barbarous and shameless and cast off all softness, to run wild through a wilderness of opinions. In this you express more cruelty than in all the rest, because I do not stand with my hands on my belly like a baby[7] at Bartholomew Fair,[8] that move not my whole body when I should but only stir my head like Jack of the clock house[9] which has no joints, that is not dumb when wantons court me, as if asslike I were ready for all burdens, or because I weep not when injury gripes me, like a worried deer in the fangs of many curs. Am I therefore barbarous or shameless? He is much injurious that so baptized us; we are as free-born as men, have as free election, and as free spirits, we are compounded of like parts, and may with like liberty make benefit of our creations; my countenance shall smile on the worthy, and frown on the ignoble, I will hear the wise, and be deaf to idiots, give counsel to my friend, but be dumb to flatterers, I have hands that shall be liberal to reward desert, feet that shall move swiftly to do good offices, and thoughts that shall ever accompany freedom and severity. If this be barbarous, let me leave the city and live with creatures of like simplicity.

* * *

5. Of Argos.
6. Spotted, motley.
7. Doll.
8. A popular carnival fair held every year from 1133 to 1865 at West Smithfield on August 24, the feast day of Saint Bartholomew.
9. Figure that strikes the bell of a clock.

Hic-Mulier: Therefore to take your proportion in a few lines (my dear Feminine-Masculine) tell me what Charter, prescription or right of claim you have to those things you make our absolute inheritance? Why do you curl, frizzle and powder your hair, bestowing more hours and time in dividing lock from lock, and hair from hair, in giving every thread his posture, and every curl his true fence and circumference than ever Caesar did in marshalling his army, either at Pharsalia, in Spain, or Britain? Why do you rob us of our ruffs, our earrings, carkanets,[1] and mamillions,[2] of our fans and feathers, our busks and French bodies, nay, of our masks, hoods, shadows, and shapynas,[3] not so much as the very art of painting, but you have so greedily engrossed it, that were it not for that little fantastical sharp pointed dagger that hangs at your chins, and the cross hilt which guards your upper lip, hardly would there be any difference between the fair mistress and the foolish servant. But is this theft the uttermost of our spoil? Fie, you have gone a world further, and even ravished from us our speech, our actions, sports, and recreations. Goodness leave me, if I have not heard a man court his mistress with the same words that Venus did Adonis, or as near as the book could instruct him;[4] where are the tilts and tourneys, and lofty galliards[5] that were danced in the days of old, when men capered in the air like wanton kids on the tops of mountains, and turned above ground as if they had been compact of fire or a purer element?[6] Tut, all's forsaken, all's vanished, those motions showed more strength than art, and more courage than courtship; it was much too robustious, and rather spent the body than prepared it, especially where any defect before reigned; hence you took from us poor women our traverses and tourneys, our modest stateliness and curious slidings, and left us nothing but the new French garb of puppet hopping and setting. Lastly, poor shuttlecock[7] that was only a female invention, how have you taken it out of our hands, and made yourselves such lords and rulers over it, that though it be a very emblem of us, and our lighter despised fortunes, yet it dare now hardly come near us; nay, you keep it so imprisoned within your bedchambers and dining rooms, amongst your pages and panders, that a poor innocent maid to give but a kick with her battledore,[8] were more than halfway to the ruin of her reputation. For this you have demolished the noble schools of horsemanship (of which many were in this city) hung up your arms to rust, glued up those swords in their scabbards that would shake all Christendom with the brandish, and entertained into your mind such softness, dullness, and effeminate niceness that it would even make *Heraclitus*[9] himself laugh against his nature to see how pulingly[1] you languish in this weak entertained sin of womanish softness. To see one of your gender either show himself (in the midst of his pride or riches) at a playhouse or public assembly; how (before he dare enter) with the Jacob's-staff of his own eyes and his pages, he takes a full survey of himself, from the highest sprig in his feather, to the lowest spangle that shines in his shoestring: how he prunes and picks himself like a hawk set a-weathering, calls every several garment to auricular[2] confession, making them utter both their mortal great stains, and their venial and less blemishes, though the mote

---

1. A jeweled or gold necklace.
2. Rounded protuberances (from French *mamelon*, nipple).
3. Disguises.
4. Venus, goddess of love, fell in love with the beautiful youth Adonis.
5. A brisk dance in triple time.
6. Men were thought to be dominated by dry humors and women by humid ones.

7. A small piece of cork with feathers sticking out of it, batted back and forth in the game of battledoor and shuttlecock.
8. A small racket, used to hit a shuttlecock.
9. Heraclitus was said to weep whenever he went forth in public (see Seneca, *De tranquilitate animi* 15.2).
1. In a whining tone.
2. Told privately, to the ear.

must be much less than an atom. Then to see him pluck and tug everything into the form of the newest received fashion; and by *Durer's* rules[3] make his leg answerable to his neck; his thigh proportionable with his middle, his foot with his hand, and a world of such idle disdained foppery. To see him thus patched up with symmetry, make himself complete, and even as a circle, and lastly, cast himself among the eyes of the people (as an object of wonder) with more niceness than a virgin goes to the sheets of her first lover would make patience herself mad with anger, and cry with the poet:

> O hominum mores, O gens, O tempora dura,
> Quantus in urbe dolor; quantus in orbe dolus![4]

Now since according to your own inference, even by the laws of nature, by the rules of religion, and the customs of all civil nations, it is necessary there be a distinct and special difference between man and woman, both in their habit and behaviors, what could we poor weak women do less (being far too weak by force to fetch back those spoils you have unjustly taken from us) than to gather up those garments you have proudly cast away, and therewith to clothe both our bodies and our minds; since no other means was left us to continue our names, and to support a difference? For to have held the way in which our forefathers first set us, or to have still embraced the civil modesty, or gentle sweetness of our soft inclinations; why, you had so far encroached upon us, and so over-bribed the world, to be deaf to any grant of restitution, that as at our creation, our whole sex was contained in man our first parent, so we should have had no other being, but in you, and your most effeminate quality. Hence we have preserved (though to our own shames) those manly things which you have forsaken, which would you again accept, and restore to us the blushes we laid by, when first we put on your masculine garments; doubt not but chaste thoughts and bashfulness will again dwell in us, and our palaces being newly gilt, trimmed, and reedified, draw to us all the Graces, all the Muses,[5] which that you may more willingly do, and (as we of yours) grow into detestation of that deformity you have purloined, to the utter loss of your honors and reputations. Mark how the brave Italian poet,[6] even in the infancy of your abuses, most lively describes you:

> About his neck a Carknet[7] rich he ware
> Of precious Stones, all set in gold well tried;
> His arms that erst all warlike weapons bare,
> In golden bracelets wantonly were tied:
> Into his ears two rings conveyed are
> Of golden wire, at which on either side,
> Two Indian pearls, in making like two pears,
> Of passing price were pendant at his ears.
>
> His locks bedewed with water of sweet savor,
> Stood curled round in order on his head;

---

3. Albrecht Dürer (1471–1528), German painter and engraver, wrote a work on human proportions that was published after his death.
4. O customs of men, O people, O hard times / what great sadness in the city; what great fraud in the world.
5. The graces were the three sisters, Aglaia, Thalia, and Euphrosyne, viewed as bestowers of charm and beauty; the muses were the nine daughters of Zeus and Memory who inspire poetry and the arts.
6. Ludovico Ariosto (1474–1532), whose description of Ruggiero's decadence when he is seduced by the sorceress Alcina in *Orlando Furioso 7* is quoted here in the translation (1590) by Sir John Harington, Queen Elizabeth's godson.
7. Necklace.

He had such wanton womanish behavior,
At though in valor he had ne'er been bred:
So chang'd in speech, in manners and in favor,
So from himself beyond all reason led,
By these enchantments of this amorous dame;
He was himself in nothing, but in name.

Thus you see your injury to us is of an old and inveterate continuance, having taken such strong root in your bosoms, that it can hardly be pulled up, without some offense to the soil: ours young and tender, scarce freed from the swaddling clothes, and therefore may with as much ease be lost, as it was with little difficulty found. Cast then from you our ornaments, and put on your own armors. Be men in shape, men in show, men in words, men in actions, men in counsel, men in example: then will we love and serve you; then will we hear and obey you; then will we like rich jewels hang at your ears to take our instructions, like true friends follow you through all dangers, and like careful leeches[8] pour oil into your wounds. Then shall you find delight in our words; pleasure in our faces; faith in our hearts; chastity in our thoughts, and sweetness both in our inward and outward inclinations. Comeliness shall be then our study; fear our armor, and modesty our practice: then shall we be all your most excellent thoughts can desire, and have nothing in us less than impudence and deformity.

Haec-Vir; Enough: you have both raised my eyelids, cleared my sight, and made my heart entertain both shame and delight at an instant; shame in my follies past; delight in our noble and worthy conversion. Away then from me these light vanities, the only ensigns[9] of a weak and soft nature: and come you grave and solid pieces, which arm a man with fortitude and resolution: you are too rough and stubborn for a woman's wearing, we will here change our attires, as we have changed our minds, and with our attires, our names. I will no more be *Haec-Vir*, but *Hic Vir*, nor you *Hic-Mulier*, but *Haec Mulier*. From henceforth deformity shall pack to Hell; and if at any time he hide himself upon the earth, yet it shall be with contempt and disgrace. He shall have no friend but Poverty; no favorer but Folly, nor no reward but Shame. Henceforth we will live nobly like ourselves, ever sober, ever discreet, ever worthy; true men, and true women. We will be henceforth like well-coupled doves, full of industry, full of love: I mean, not of sensual and carnal love, but heavenly and divine love, which proceeds from God, whose inexpressible nature none is able to deliver in words, since is like his dwelling, high and beyond the reach of human apprehension.

⇥ END OF PERSPECTIVES: TRACTS ON WOMEN AND GENDER ⇤

Thomas Campion
1567–1620

Thomas Campion was orphaned by the age of thirteen. Months after his mother's death, his stepfather sent him to Peterhouse, Cambridge. Leaving the university after three years without

---

8. Physicians.   9. Banners, signs.

taking a degree, Campion then attended Gray's Inn for close to eight years. While there he participated in the active literary life of the Inns of Court, as much—or more—a training ground for poets as a school for lawyers. He performed in masques and Roman comedies and published his first verse, under the pen name "Content," in a pirated edition of Sidney's sonnet sequence *Astrophil and Stella* (1591). After military service with English forces aiding the Protestant cause in France during 1591 and 1592, Campion returned to England to publish a book of Latin poetry, *Thomae Campiani Poemata* (1595), and songs performed to lute music, issued by his lifelong friend Philip Rosseter under the title *A Book of Ayres* (1601). Although only Rosseter's name appeared on the title page, the preface to the book gave Campion credit as author of the first twenty-one songs. Among these are *My sweetest Lesbia, let us live and love* and *When thou must home to shades of underground*, both of which are reprinted here.

In addition to writing songs and court entertainments, Campion practiced medicine, having taken an M.D. from the University of Caen in 1605. In 1616, he treated his friend and patron Sir Thomas Monson (the dedicatee of *A Booke of Ayres*), who was imprisoned in the Tower of London for conspiring in the murder of Sir Thomas Overbury. This infamous case of the poisoning of Overbury, the sometime husband of Frances Howard, who left him to marry Robert Carr, entailed Campion's own interrogation and eventual clearance from all charges. Campion dedicated his *The Third and Fourth Booke of Ayres* to Monson in 1617, the year of his release from prison.

Campion was transformed from a minor Latin poet to one of the great English lyric poets by his exposure to the music of John Dowland and Philip Rosseter, his neighbors in the London parish of St. Dunstan's-in-the-West. Campion attempted to fuse the concept of poetry as music with the Latin system of quantitative verse in *Observations in the Art of English Poesie* (1602), but the argument was trounced in Samuel Daniel's *A Defence of Ryme*. Nevertheless Campion's treatise contains some of his finest poems, including *Rose-cheeked Laura, come*, which Derek Attridge described as having a "gently expanding and contracting accentual rhythm that makes this poem flow in a way so perfectly expressive of its subject matter." Campion likened his favorite verse form, the ayre, to the Latin verse form, the epigram, which he called "naked"—simple and unadorned—as well as "requiring so much the more invention to make it please." Campion continued to write ayres throughout his life. The poem reprinted from his work here, *Never weather-beaten sail more willing bent to shore*, is from *Two Bookes of Ayres* (1613). He also wrote *The Lord's Masque*, performed for the wedding of the Princess Elizabeth (see Color Plate 14, Inigo Jones' design for the costume of *Torchbearer: A Fiery Spirit*), a book on the theory of musical counterpoint, and a final collection of Latin verse (1619). When Campion died in 1620, he left his entire estate of twenty-two pounds to his friend Philip Rosseter. Campion has left us poetry that is fully wedded to music, and so achieved a formal perfection that has caused his work to be admired by poets as diverse as Swinburne, Pound, and Auden.

My sweetest Lesbia, let us live and love

My sweetest Lesbia, let us live and love;[1]
And though the sager sort our deeds reprove,
Let us not weigh them: heaven's great lamps do dive
Into their west, and straight again revive:
But soon as once set is our little light,
Then must we sleep one ever-during night.

5

---

1. This poem is based on a lyric by the Roman poet Catullus (87–54 B.C.), who wrote poems to his beloved Lesbia.

If all would lead their lives in love like me,
Then bloody swords and armour should not be;
No drum nor trumpet peaceful sleeps should move,
10   Unless alarm came from the camp of love:
But fools do live, and waste their little light,
And seek with pain their ever-during night.

When timely death my life and fortune ends,
Let not my hearse be vexed with mourning friends;
15   But let all lovers, rich in triumph, come
And with sweet pastimes grace my happy tomb:
And, Lesbia, close up thou my little light,
And crown with love my ever-during night.

There is a garden in her face

There is a garden in her face,
Where roses and white lilies grow;
    A heavenly paradise is that place,
Wherein all pleasant fruits do flow.
5   There cherries grow, which none may buy
    Till "Cherry ripe" themselves do cry.

Those cherries fairly do enclose
Of orient pearl a double row;
    Which when her lovely laughter shows,
10   They look like rosebuds filled with snow.
    Yet them nor peer nor prince can buy
    Till "Cherry ripe" themselves do cry.

Her eyes like angels watch them still;
Her brows like bended bows do stand,
15   Threatening with piercing frowns to kill
All that attempt, with eye or hand,
    Those sacred cherries to come nigh
    Till 'Cherry ripe' themselves do cry.

Rose-cheeked Laura, come

Rose-cheeked Laura, come;
Sing thou smoothly with thy beauty's
Silent music, either other
    Sweetly gracing.

5   Lovely forms do flow
From concent° divinely framed;   *harmony*
Heaven is music, and thy beauty's
    Birth is heavenly.

    These dull notes we sing
10   Discords need for helps to grace them,
Only beauty purely loving
    Knows no discord,

But still moves delight,
Like clear springs renewed by flowing,
15   Ever perfect, ever in them-
            selves eternal.

When thou must home to shades of underground

When thou must home to shades of underground,
And there arrived, a new admired guest,
The beauteous spirits do engirt thee round,
White Iope, blithe Helen,[1] and the rest,
5   To hear the stories of thy finished love
From that smooth tongue whose music hell can move;
Then wilt thou speak of banqueting delights,
Of masques and revels which sweet youth did make,
Of tourneys and great challenges of knight,
10   And all these triumphs for thy beauty's sake:
When thou hast told these honours done to thee,
Then tell, O tell, how thou didst murder me.

Never weather-beaten sail more willing bent to shore

Never weather-beaten sail more willing bent to shore,
Never tired pilgrim's limbs affected slumber more,
Than my wearied sprite now longs to fly out of my troubled breast.
    O come quickly, sweetest Lord, and take my soul to rest!

5   Ever blooming are the joys of heaven's high Paradise,
Cold age deafs not there our ears nor vapour dims our eyes:
Glory there the sun outshines; whose beams the Blessed only see.
    O come quickly, glorious Lord, and raise my sprite to Thee!

——— ❈ ———

Ben Jonson
1572–1637

Ben Jonson's life was full of changes and contradictions. His earliest biographer, William Drummond, called him "passionately kind and angry, careless either to gain or keep, vindictive, but, if he be well answered, at himself." His father was Protestant, but Jonson turned Catholic, only to recant that conversion later; nevertheless, in his last years he called himself a "beadsman." The stepson of a bricklayer, he became Poet Laureate. He wrote poems of praise to win the patronage of king and court but also skewered their follies in satire. Though often assuming the role of moralist in his poetry and plays, Jonson admitted that as a younger man he was "given to venery" and pleaded guilty to the charge of murder. He was attached to admiring younger poets, "the tribe of Ben," yet he also enjoyed feuds, such as those with fellow

---

1. Classical beauties; Helen's beauty was famous for having caused the Trojan War.

dramatists Marston and Dekker. While espousing Horatian spareness and an acute sense of meter in both criticism and poetry, Jonson also had a keen ear for the colloquial language of London.

Indeed, London was one of the few constants in Jonson's turbulent career. Born in Harts-Born Lane near Charing Cross, he was buried in Poets' Corner at Westminster Abbey. Jonson portrayed the city as the world of those who lived by their wits. He dramatized literary infighting in *Every Man Out of His Humour* (1599), greedy schemes in *Volpone* (1606), intellectual confidence scams in *The Alchemist* (1610), and antitheatrical Puritan preaching in *Bartholomew Fair* (1614). The London audience at the Hope Theatre was reported to have exclaimed at a performance of *Bartholomew Fair*: "O rare Ben Jonson!"

Unlike other playwrights of his time (including Shakespeare), Jonson oversaw the publication of his plays, which appeared with his poems in the same deluxe folio volume, entitled *Works* (1616). The assertion of the dignity of popular drama surprised many of his readers, one of whom wrote, "Pray tell me Ben, where doth the mystery lurk, / What others call a play, you call a work?" That Jonson wanted his plays to be read as much as performed can be gathered from the comment printed on the title page of *Every Man Out of His Humour*: "as it was first composed by the author, Ben Jonson, containing more than hath been publicly spoken or acted."

Jonson viewed writing as his profession; he became the first poet in England to earn a living by his art. His achievement was recognized by James I, who made Jonson the first Poet Laureate of England and granted him a pension for life. Before becoming laureate, Jonson depended on a whole string of patrons. With the new Stuart king in power, Jonson was able to use his claim of Scots descent to advantage. He was supported by Esme Stuart Seigneur D'Aubigny (a cousin of King James), to whom he dedicated his first tragedy, *Sejanus* (1603). His patrons included Sir Walter Raleigh and Lady Mary Wroth, to whom he dedicated *The Alchemist*. Jonson's most important break came when he received a commission for a court masque. In 1605 he wrote *The Masque of Blackness* starring the Queen herself. To gain some idea of the extravagance of these masques, consider that in 1617, while 12,000 pounds were spent on the entire administration of Ireland, 4,000 pounds were spent on a single masque, *Pleasure Reconciled to Virtue*. The masques were lavish ventures that required costumes, music, and magnificent scenery, which was designed by Inigo Jones, who introduced the Italian invention of perspective.

If the pursuit of patronage was crucial to Jonson's advancement, his satire of politics and power repeatedly put his career and even his life at risk. In 1603 Jonson was called before the Privy Council for *Sejanus;* the charges included "popery and treason." Jonson's *Epicoene, or the Silent Woman*—which climaxes in the revelation that the silent woman is really a boy—was suppressed because it lampooned a love affair of the King's first cousin, Lady Arbella Stuart. One observer complained of the 1613 *Irish Masque at Court* that it was "no time . . . to exasperate that nation by making ridiculous." Jonson was imprisoned twice for the offense that his plays gave to the powerful—once for the now lost *The Isle of Dogs* (1597) and another time for *Eastward Ho!* (1605), in which he made fun of King James's Scots accent.

Jonson took reckless risks, whose consequences he barely managed to escape. While imprisoned for the murder of Gabriel Spencer in 1598, Jonson became a Catholic. Following his conversion, Jonson pleaded guilty to manslaughter (later calling it the result of a duel) but went free by claiming benefit of clergy. This medieval custom originally allowed clerics to be judged by the bishop's court but, by Jonson's time, permitted anyone who could translate the Latin Bible to go free. Jonson left prison with his belongings confiscated, his thumb branded for the felony, and his reputation marked by his profession of an outlaw religion. Like any other Catholic in Elizabethan England, Jonson could be fined or have his property confiscated for not attending Anglican services. Indeed, he and his wife were interrogated for their nonattendance in 1605; Jonson was also charged with being "a poet, and by fame a seducer of youth to the

Popish religion." Threatened again with loss of property and another prison term, Jonson complied with the Court's order that he take instruction in Protestantism.

Not all Jonson's disputes were quite so dangerous. Like the characters in his plays, he enjoyed engaging in the game of vapors, a mock argument, drummed up for the display of wit. He not only engaged in combats of wit with Shakespeare (who acted in *Every Man Out of His Humour*) but also ridiculed Marston and Dekker in what critics call "the War of the Theaters." Jonson's *Every Man Out of His Humour* satirized Marston as a pseudo-intellectual. The same year, Jonson and Dekker collaborated on a play. Two years later, Dekker parodied Jonson as the bombastic Horace, constantly reading his work aloud and expecting praise in *Satiriomastix* (1601). The title of this play means "the whipping of the satirist," and it is full of barbs about Jonson's checkered past—both his imprisonment and his theatrical flops. Dekker called Jonson a "brown-bread mouth-stinker." Jonson responded with a "forced defense" against "base detractors and illiterate apes" in *Poetaster* (1601).

Jonson did have high regard for some of his contemporaries, as they did for him. Among these was John Donne, who wrote commendatory verses for *Volpone* and to whom Jonson wrote "Who shall doubt, Donne, whe'er I a poet be / When I dare send my epigrams to thee?" As an older man, Jonson held court at the Devil Tavern among his fellow poets as self-proclaimed *arbiter bibendi* (master of drinking), whose main object was "Not drinking much, but talking wittily." This vein of wit was carried on by Sir John Suckling's *A Session of Poets* and Herrick's *Prayer for Ben Jonson*. His servant Brome wrote an elegy for him, as did the many men of letters who contributed to *Jonsonius Virbius* ("Jonson Reborn"), the year after his death.

Jonson saw himself as a moral and poetic guide. His satire of moral depravity and intellectual delusion is hysterically funny. His plays include direct criticism of contemporary poetry and drama, contracts with the audience, and self-mockery—a foretaste of the break from realistic conventions in modernism. Jonson's comedies also persuade us that there is no reality without satire; we cannot know the world without laughing at its ridiculousness. The human foibles and obsessions portrayed in his comedies are captured in a language so vivid and oral that it has to be read aloud. Jonson's verse dazzles by concealing its art, allowing conversational words and rhythms to be perfectly wedded to poetic meters. The simplicity and restraint of his language, as in his elegy on the death of his son, are the vehicles for pure music and powerful emotion.

On Something, That Walks Somewhere[1]

At court I met it, in clothes brave° enough   *showy*
    To be a courtier, and looks grave enough
To seem a statesman. As I near it came,
    It made me a great face; I asked the name.
5   "A lord," it cried, "buried in flesh, and blood,
    And such from whom let no man hope least good,
For I will do none; and as little ill,
    For I will dare none." Good lord, walk dead still.

On My First Daughter[1]

Here lies to each her parents' ruth,°   *grief*
    Mary, the daughter of their youth;
Yet, all heaven's gifts, being heaven's due,

---

1. This and the following four poems were all first printed in the collected *Works* of 1616 under the heading "Epigrams." An epigram is a short, witty poem of invective or satire. Jonson's "Epigrams" include epitaphs, poems of praise, and verse letters.

1. Probably written in the late 1590s.

It makes the father less to rue.
5 At six months' end, she parted hence
With safety of her innocence;
Whose soul heaven's Queen (whose name she bears),
In comfort of her mother's tears,
Hath placed amongst her virgin-train;
10 Where, while that severed doth remain,
This grave partakes the fleshly birth;[2]
Which cover lightly, gentle earth.

To John Donne

Donne, the delight of Phoebus,[1] and each Muse,
    Who, to thy one, all other brains refuse;[2]
Whose every work, of thy most early wit
    Came forth example, and remains so, yet;
5 Longer a-knowing than most wits do live;
    And which no affection praise enough can give!
To it,[3] thy language, letters, arts, best life,
    Which might with half mankind maintain a strife;
All which I meant to praise, and, yet, I would,
10   But leave, because I cannot as I should.

On My First Son[1]

Farewell, thou child of my right hand,[2] and joy;
    My sin was too much hope of thee, loved boy.
Seven years thou wert lent to me, and I thee pay,
    Exacted by thy fate, on the just day.
5 O, could I lose all father, now![3] For why
    Will man lament the state he should envy?
To have so soon 'scaped world's and flesh's rage,
    And, if no other misery, yet age?
Rest in soft peace, and, asked, say, "Here doth lie
10   Ben Jonson his best piece of poetry."
For whose sake, henceforth, all his vows be such,
    As what he loves may never like too much.[4]

Inviting a Friend to Supper[1]

Tonight, grave sir, both my poor house and I
    Do equally desire your company:
Not that we think us worthy such a guest,
    But that your worth will dignify our feast

---

2. While the soul is in heaven, the grave holds the body.
1. God of poetry.
2. The muses give the inspiration to your brain that they deny to others.
3. In addition to your wit.
1. Benjamin, who died of the plague on his birthday in 1603.

2. In Hebrew, Benjamin means "son of the right hand; dexterous, fortunate."
3. Let go of fatherly feeling.
4. "If you wish . . . to beware of sorrows that gnaw the heart, to no man make yourself too much a comrade" (Martial 12.34, lines 8–11).
1. Based on three poems of invitation by the Roman poet Martial, 11.52, 5.78, and 10.48.

5   With those that come; whose grace may make that seem
        Something, which else could hope for no esteem.
     It is the fair acceptance, Sir, creates
        The entertainment perfect, not the cates.°   *food*
     Yet shall you have, to rectify your palate,
10   An olive, capers, or some better salad
     Ushering the mutton; with a short-legged hen
        If we can get her, full of eggs, and then
     Lemons, and wine for sauce: to these, a coney°   *rabbit*
        Is not to be despaired of, for our money;
15   And though fowl now be scarce, yet there are clerks,°   *scholars*
        The sky not falling, think we may have larks.
     I'll tell you of more, and lie, so you will come:
        Of partridge, pheasant, woodcock, of which some
     May yet be there; and godwit, if we can;
20   Knat, rail, and ruff,° too. Howsoe'er, my man   *gamebirds*
     Shall read a piece of Virgil, Tacitus,
        Livy, or of some better book to us,
     Of which we'll speak our minds, amidst our meat;
        And I'll profess no verses to repeat;
25   To this, if aught appear, which I not know of,
        That will the pastry, not my paper, show of.[2]
     Digestive cheese and fruit there sure will be;
        But that, which most doth take my muse and me,
     Is a pure cup of rich Canary wine,
30   Which is the Mermaid's,[3] now, but shall be mine:
     Of which had Horace, or Anacreon tasted,
        Their lives, as do their lines, till now had lasted.[4]
     Tobacco, nectar, or the Thespian spring
        Are all but Luther's beer to this I sing.[5]
35   Of this we will sup free, but moderately,
        And we will have no Poley, or Parrot by;[6]
     Nor shall our cups make any guilty men,
        But, at our parting, we will be, as when
     We innocently met. No simple word
40   That shall be uttered at our mirthful board
     Shall make us sad next morning, or affright
        The liberty, that we'll enjoy tonight.

To Penshurst[1]

     Thou art not, Penshurst, built to envious show
        Of touch,° or marble; nor canst boast a row   *black marble*

---

2. Add to this that if there is any paper, it will only be
that used to keep the pastry from sticking to the pan.
3. A famous tavern in Cheapside, London.
4. Horace praised wine in Latin verse, as did Anacreon in
Greek.
5. The Thespian spring, inspiration of poetry, and all these
things are but Luther's beer in comparison with Canary.
6. Government spies; talkative birds.

1. First published in the 1616 *Works* in *The Forest*, a title
inspired by the Latin *silva* (timber), suggesting raw materials to be worked, used by classical authors for an improvised collection of poems. Penshurst was the Sidney
family's house in Kent since 1552, the "great lord" (line
91) of which was Robert Sidney, Baron Sidney of Penshurst and Viscount of Lille, younger brother of Sir Philip
Sidney.

Of polished pillars, or a roof of gold;
   Thou hast no lantern,° whereof tales are told,   *turret*
5 Or stair, or courts; but stand'st an ancient pile,[2]
   And these grudged at, art reverenced the while.
Thou joy'st in better marks, of soil, of air,
   Of wood, of water; therein thou art fair.
Thou hast thy walks for health, as well as sport:
10   Thy mount to which the dryads° do resort,   *wood nymphs*
Where Pan, and Bacchus their high feasts have made,[3]
   Beneath the broad beech and the chestnut shade;
That taller tree, which of a nut was set
   At his great birth, where all the Muses met.
15 There, in the writhèd bark, are cut the names
   Of many a sylvan,° taken with his flames;   *wood sprite*
And thence, the ruddy satyrs oft provoke
   The lighter fauns, to reach thy Lady's oak.[4]
Thy copse,° too, named of Gamage, thou hast there,   *a small wood*
20   That never fails to serve thee seasoned deer
When thou wouldst feast, or exercise thy friends.
   The lower land, that to the river bends,
Thy sheep, thy bullocks, kine° and calves do feed;   *cows*
   The middle grounds thy mares and horses breed.
25 Each bank doth yield thee conies,° and the tops   *rabbits*
   Fertile of wood, Ashour and Sydney's copse,
To crown thy open table, doth provide
   The purpled pheasant with the speckled side;
The painted partridge lies in every field,
30   And, for thy mess, is willing to be killed.
And if the high-swoll'n Medway[5] fail thy dish,
   Thou hast thy ponds, that pay thee tribute fish:
Fat, agèd carps, that run into thy net.
   And pikes, now weary their own kind to eat,
35 As loath, the second draught, or cast to stay,
   Officiously, at first, themselves betray;
Bright eels, that emulate them, and leap on land
   Before the fisher, or into his hand.
Then hath thy orchard fruit, thy garden flowers,
40   Fresh as the air, and new as are the hours.
The early cherry, with the later plum,
   Fig, grape, and quince, each in his time doth come;
The blushing apricot and woolly peach
   Hang on thy walls, that every child may reach.
45 And though thy walls be of the country stone,
   They're reared with no man's ruin, no man's groan;
There's none, that dwell about them, wish them down;

---

2. The castle was built in 1340.
3. Pan was the god of forest, field, and pasture; Bacchus was the god of wine.
4. In Greek mythology the satyr with a man's body and a goat's legs was devoted to lechery. Robert Sidney's wife Barbara Gamage was said to have given birth under this oak.
5. The local river.

But all come in, the farmer, and the clown,°   *peasant*
And no one empty-handed, to salute
50   Thy lord and lady, though they have no suit.
Some bring a capon, some a rural cake,
        Some nuts, some apples; some that think they make
The better cheeses, bring'em; or else send
        By their ripe daughters, whom they would commend
55   This way to husbands; and whose baskets bear
        An emblem of themselves in plum, or pear.
But what can this (more than express their love)
        Add to thy free provisions, far above
The need of such? whose liberal board doth flow
60   With all that hospitality doth know!
Where comes no guest, but is allowed to eat
        Without his fear, and of thy lord's own meat;
Where the same beer, and bread, and self-same wine
        That is his lordship's shall be also mine,
65   And I not fain to sit (as some this day
        At great men's tables) and yet dine away.
Here no man tells my cups; nor, standing by,
        A waiter, doth my gluttony envy,
But gives me what I call, and lets me eat;
70   He knows below he shall find plenty of meat,
Thy tables hoard not up for the next day.
        Nor, when I take my lodging, need I pray
For fire, or lights, or livery:° all is there,   *provisions, food*
        As if thou then wert mine, or I reigned here;
75   There's nothing I can wish, for which I stay.
        That found King James, when, hunting late this way
With his brave son, the Prince, they saw thy fires
        Shine bright on every hearth as the desires
Of thy Penates[6] had been set on flame
80   To entertain them; or the country came,
With all their zeal, to warm their welcome here.
        What (great, I will not say, but) sudden cheer
Didst thou, then, make 'em! and what praise was heaped
        On thy good lady, then, who therein reaped
85   The just reward of her high housewifery;
        To have her linen, plate, and all things nigh,
When she was far, and not a room, but dressed
        As if it had expected such a guest!
These, Penshurst, are thy praise, and yet not all.
90   Thy lady's noble, fruitful, chaste withall.
His children thy great lord may call his own,
        A fortune, in this age, but rarely known.
They are, and have been, taught religion; thence
        Their gentler spirits have sucked innocence.

6. Household gods.

95   Each morn and even, they are taught to pray,
          With the whole household, and may every day
      Read in their virtuous parents' noble parts
          The mysteries of manners, arms, and arts.
      Now, Penshurst, they that will proportion° thee   *compare*
100   With other edifices, when they see
      Those proud, ambitious heaps, and nothing else,
         May say, their lords have built, but thy lord dwells.

Song to Celia

      Drink to me only with thine eyes,
         And I will pledge with mine;
      Or leave a kiss but in the cup,
         And I'll not look for wine.
5   The thirst that from the soul doth rise
         Doth ask a drink divine;
      But might I of Jove's nectar sup,
         I would not change for thine.
      I sent thee late a rosy wreath,
10   Not so much honoring thee
      As giving it a hope that there
         It could not withered be.
      But thou thereon didst only breathe,
         And sent'st it back on me;
15   Since when it grows, and smells, I swear,
         Not of itself, but thee.

Queen and Huntress[1]

      Queen and huntress, chaste and fair,
      Now the sun is laid to sleep,
      Seated in thy silver chair,
      State in wonted manner keep;
5   Hesperus° entreats thy light,   *the evening star*
         Goddess excellently bright.

      Earth, let not thy envious shade
      Dare itself to interpose;
      Cynthia's shining orb was made
10   Heaven to clear, when day did close.
         Bless us then with wishèd sight,
         Goddess excellently bright.

      Lay thy bow of pearl apart,
      And thy crystal-shining quiver;
15   Give unto the flying hart

---

1. From *Cynthia's Revels*, 5.6.1–18. Cynthia, another name for Diana, goddess of the moon and the hunt, and of chastity, an image associated with Queen Elizabeth.

Space to breathe, how short soever.
  Thou that mak'st a day of night,
  Goddess excellently bright.

To the Memory of My Beloved, the Author, Mr. William Shakespeare, and What He Hath Left Us[1]

To draw no envy, Shakespeare, on thy name,
  Am I thus ample[2] to thy book and fame,
While I confess thy writings to be such,
  As neither man nor muse can praise too much.
5 'Tis true, and all men's suffrage. But these ways
  Were not the paths I meant unto thy praise;
For silliest ignorance on these may light,
  Which, when it sounds at best, but echoes right;
Or blind affection, which doth ne'er advance
10   The truth, but gropes, and urgeth all by chance;
Or crafty malice, might pretend this praise,
  And think to ruin, where it seemed to raise.
These are as some infamous bawd or whore
  Should praise a matron. What could hurt her more?
15 But thou art proof against them, and indeed
  Above the ill fortune of them, or the need.
I, therefore will begin. Soul of the age!
  The applause! delight! the wonder of our stage!
My Shakespeare, rise; I will not lodge thee by
20   Chaucer, or Spenser, or bid Beaumont lie
A little further, to make thee a room;[3]
  Thou art a monument without a tomb,
And art alive still while thy book doth live,
  And we have wits to read, and praise to give.
25 That I not mix thee so, my brain excuses,
  I mean with great, but disproportioned, Muses;
For, if I thought my judgment were of years,
  I should commit thee surely with thy peers,
And tell how far thou didst our Lyly outshine,
30   Or sporting Kyd, or Marlowe's mighty line.[4]
And though thou hadst small Latin, and less Greek,
  From thence to honor thee, I would not seek
For names, but call forth thundering Aeschylus,
  Euripides, and Sophocles to us,
35 Pacuvius, Accius, him of Cordova dead,
  To life again, to hear thy buskin[5] tread
And shake a stage; or, when thy socks[6] were on,

---

1. Prefixed to the first folio of Shakespeare's plays (1623).
2. From Latin *amplus*: copious; an *amplus orator* was one who spoke richly and with dignity.
3. Chaucer, Spenser, and Francis Beaumont were buried in Westminster Abbey; Shakespeare was buried in Stratford.
4. Lyly was an author of English prose comedies; Kyd and Marlowe were authors of English verse tragedies.
5. Boot worn by tragic actors. Jonson compares Shakespeare to tragedians of ancient Greece (Aeschylus, Sophocles, Euripides) and Rome (Pacuvius, Accius, and "him of Cordova," Seneca).
6. Symbols of comedy.

Leave thee alone for the comparison
Of all that insolent Greece or haughty Rome
40   Sent forth, or since did from their ashes come.
Triumph, my Britain; thou hast one to show
   To whom all scenes of Europe homage owe.
He was not of an age, but for all time!
   And all the muses still were in their prime
45   When like Apollo he came forth to warm
   Our ears, or like a Mercury to charm![7]
Nature herself was proud of his designs,
   And joyed to wear the dressing of his lines,
Which were so richly spun, and woven so fit
50   As, since, she will vouchsafe no other wit.
The merry Greek, tart Aristophanes,
   Neat Terence, witty Plautus,[8] now not please,
But antiquated, and deserted lie,
   As they were not of nature's family.
55   Yet must I not give nature all; thy art,
   My gentle Shakespeare, must enjoy a part.
For though the poet's matter nature be,
   His art doth give the fashion. And that he
Who casts to write a living line must sweat
60   (Such as thine are) and strike the second heat
Upon the Muses' anvil: turn the same,
   And himself with it, that he thinks to frame;[9]
Or for the laurel, he may gain a scorn;
   For a good poet's made as well as born.
65   And such wert thou! Look how the father's face
   Lives in his issue; even so, the race
Of Shakespeare's mind and manners brightly shines
   In his well-turnèd, and true-filèd lines:
In each of which he seems to shake a lance,[1]
70   As brandished at the eyes of ignorance.
Sweet Swan of Avon, what a sight it were
   To see thee in our waters yet appear,
And make those flights upon the banks of Thames,
   That so did take Eliza, and our James![2]
75   But stay, I see thee in the hemisphere
   Advanced, and made a constellation there!
Shine forth, thou star of poets, and with rage
   Or influence chide or cheer the drooping stage,[3]
Which, since thy flight from hence, hath mourned like night,
80   And despairs day, but for thy volume's light.

7. Apollo and Mercury were the gods of poetry and eloquence.
8. Aristophanes was an ancient Greek comic playwright; Terence and Plautus were authors of Roman comedy.
9. See Horace, *Ars Poetica* 441: "return the ill-tuned verses to the anvil."

1. Pun on "Shake-speare."
2. Queen Elizabeth and King James.
3. Like an ancient hero, Shakespeare is given a place among the stars; as the "rage" and "influence" of the planets affect life on earth, Shakespeare affects the world of the stage.

John Donne
1572–1631

A. Duncan, engraved portrait of John Donne.

John Donne wrote some of the most passionate love poems and most moving religious verse in the English language. Even his contemporaries wondered how one mind could express itself in such different modes. Eliciting a portrait of the artist as a split personality, Donne's letters mention the melancholic lover "Jack Donne," succeeded by the Anglican priest "Doctor Donne." Izaak Walton's *Life of Donne* (1640) portrays an earnest, aspiring clergyman who wrote love poetry to his wife. Yet Donne actually wrote most of his poetry—both the love lyrics and the *Holy Sonnets*—before he entered the ministry at forty-three. An ambitious, talented, and handsome young man, Donne struggled to attain secular patronage; later, he resigned himself to life in the church and, after his wife's death, came to terms with his own mortality.

Donne was born into a Catholic family. His mother was the great-niece of Sir Thomas More; she went into exile in Antwerp for a time to seek religious toleration. One of Donne's uncles was imprisoned in the Tower of London because he was a Jesuit priest. Donne wrote of his family that none "hath endured and suffered more in their persons and fortunes, for obeying the Teachers of Roman Doctrine, then it hath done." Donne and his brother Henry entered Hart Hall, Oxford, when they were just eleven and ten, young enough to be spared the required oath recognizing the Queen as head of the church. The Donne brothers later studied law at Lincoln's Inn, where Henry was arrested for harboring a priest in 1593. The priest was drawn and quartered; Henry died in Newgate prison of the plague.

Though shadowed by his brother's death, Donne's student years in London had their pleasures. Donne was distracted from studying law by "the worst voluptuousness . . . an Hydroptique immoderate desire of humane learning and languages." The young Donne was described by his friend Sir Richard Baker as "a great visitor of ladies, a great frequenter of Playes, a great writer of conceited Verses." Among these were Donne's erotic *Elegies*, including *To His Mistress Going to Bed* and *Love's Progress*, both of which were refused a license for publication in the 1633 edition of his collected verse.

Shortly after gaining a position as secretary to Sir Thomas Egerton, Lord Keeper of the Great Seal, in 1597, Donne met and fell in love with Ann More. His noble employer's niece, she was so far above Donne's station that they married secretly. When Ann's father heard the news, he asked Egerton to have Donne fired and saw to it that he was incarcerated. At this time, Donne is said to have written to Ann: *"John Donne, Ann Donne, un-done."* As a result of Donne's petition, the Court of Audience for Canterbury declared the marriage lawful; nevertheless, Ann was disinherited.

John and Ann made a love match, but their life was not easy. She bore twelve children in fifteen years, not counting miscarriages. Donne lamented the "poorness of [his] fortune and the greatness of [his] charge." After thirteen years of marriage, however, he could also still say: "we had not one another at so cheap a rate, as that we should ever be weary of one another." A few of the love poems in *Songs and Sonnets* express a mixture of bliss and hardship linked with their marriage.

Relations with friends and patrons also influenced Donne's poetry. He is said to have addressed several poems to Magdalen Herbert, mother of the poet George. Living in Mitcham near London, Donne cemented his friendship with Ben Jonson, who wrote two epigrams in praise of Donne in thanks for his Latin verses on *Volpone* (1607). Donne was also introduced to Lucy,

Countess of Bedford, who asked Jonson to get her a copy of Donne's *Satires*. Donne not only addressed several verse letters to her but also enjoyed her poems. An even more generous patron was Sir Robert Drury, for the death of whose young daughter Elizabeth the poet composed A *Funeral Elegie*, the inspiration for his two *Anniversaries* (1612) on the nature of the cosmos and death.

Donne's writing from 1607 to 1611 dealt with theological and moral controversies. His *Pseudo-Martyr* (1610) argued that Catholics should take the Oath of Allegiance to the King and that resistance to him should not be glorified as a form of martyrdom. This work won him James I's advice to enter the ministry, but, still skeptical, Donne held off. He protested against sectarianism: "You know I never fettered nor imprisoned the word Religion . . . immuring it in a Rome, or a Wittenberg, or a Geneva." Donne also examined the morality of suicide in *Biathanatos* (written 1607, published 1646). His *Holy Sonnets* (some of which may have been written as early as 1608–1610) reveal an obsession with his own death and fear of damnation: "I dare not move my dim eyes any way, / Despair behind, and death before doth cast / Such terror."

Donne was plagued by professional bad luck until he became an Anglican priest. With the exception of Sir Robert Drury, Donne never found a dependable patron. His applications for secretaryships in Ireland and Virginia were unsuccessful. In search of the Earl of Somerset's patronage, Donne wrote an epithalamion for his marriage to Frances Howard and even volunteered to justify her earlier controversial divorce. Fortunately for Donne, his attempts to win a position through Somerset failed, since a year later the Earl fell from power. Giving up his long quest for secular preferment, Donne took holy orders in 1615. Once an Anglican priest, he was made a royal chaplain and received an honorary Doctorate of Divinity from Cambridge. Two years later, he became reader in divinity at his old law school Lincoln's Inn.

Prosperity was followed by tragic loss. Ann Donne died giving birth in 1617. The death of his wife turned Donne more completely toward God. His later prose viewed death from a different perspective from his earlier personal torment. Suffering from a recurring fever, he wrote *Devotions upon Emergent Occasions* (1624). In the midst of a major epidemic, at the height of his fever, distraught and sleepless, he realizes our common mortality: "never send to know for whom the bell tolls; it tolls for thee." He became a prolific and stirring preacher of sermons. Some of these, such as that urging the Company of the Virginia Plantation to spread the gospel (1622), were printed in his lifetime. One written just before his death shows confidence in God's forgiveness: "I cannot plead innocency of life, especially of my youth; But I am to be judged by a merciful God."

If Donne's life can be split into the secular and religious, his poetic sensibility cannot. His verse fuses flesh and spirit through metaphysical conceits that create fascinating connections between apparently unrelated topics. In Donne's erotic lyrics, sex excites spiritual ecstasy along with hot lust and seductive wit. Similarly, Donne's religious poems express his relation with God not as an intellectual construct but as an emotional need, articulated in intimate and even erotic language. Later ages did not always appreciate either Donne's sensuality or his intellectual extravagance; remarkably, none of his poems were included in the most important nineteenth-century anthology of poetry, Palgraves's *Golden Treasury*. Donne's fame was revived early in the twentieth century, when modernist poets, especially T. S. Eliot, took inspiration from Donne's complex mixture of immediacy and artifice, passion and subtle thought.

The Good Morrow[1]

I wonder by my troth, what thou, and I
Did, till we loved? Were we not weaned till then?
But sucked on country pleasures, childishly?

---

1. Donne's love poems, written over a period of 20 years, cannot be dated with any certainty. They were first printed in 1633, scattered throughout the entire collection of poems. Then, in the 1635 edition, the love poems were printed as a group under the title *Songs and Sonnets*. There is no certainty that the titles were chosen by Donne.

Or snorted we in the seven sleepers' den?[2]
5   'Twas so; but this, all pleasures fancies be.
      If ever any beauty I did see,
      Which I desired, and got, 'twas but a dream of thee.

      And now good morrow to our waking souls,
      Which watch not one another out of fear;
10   For love, all love of other sights controls,
      And makes one little room, an everywhere.
      Let sea-discoverers to new worlds have gone,
      Let maps to others, worlds on worlds have shown,
      Let us possess one world, each hath one, and is one.

15   My face in thine eye, thine in mine appears,
      And true plain hearts do in the faces rest.
      Where can we find two better hemispheres
      Without sharp north, without declining west?
      What ever dies was not mixed equally;[3]
20   If our two loves be one, or, thou and I
      Love so alike, that none do slacken, none can die.

Song

      Go, and catch a falling star,
          Get with child a mandrake root,[1]
      Tell me, where all past years are,
          Or who cleft the Devil's foot,
5   Teach me to hear mermaids singing,
      Or to keep off envy's stinging,
              And find
              What wind
      Serves to advance an honest mind.

10   If thou be borne to strange sights,
          Things invisible to see,
      Ride ten thousand days and nights,[2]
          Till age snow white hairs on thee.
      Thou, when thou return'st, will tell me
15   All strange wonders that befell thee,
              And swear
              No where
      Lives a woman true, and fair.

      If thou findest one, let me know,
20   Such a pilgrimage were sweet;

---

2. Legendary cave where seven Ephesian youths were put
to sleep by God to escape the persecution of Christians by
the Emperor Decius (249).
3. According to ancient medicine, death was caused by
an imbalance of elements in the body.

1. A fork-rooted plant, resembling the human body in its
form.
2. See *Faerie Queene* 3.7.56–61, where Spenser's Squire of
Dames searches the country for a chaste woman.

Yet do not, I would not go,
 Though at next door we might meet,
Though she were true, when you met her,
And last, till you write your letter,
25   Yet she
   Will be
False, ere I come, to two, or three.

The Sun Rising[1]

  Busy old fool, unruly Sun,
   Why dost thou thus
Through windows, and through curtains call on us?
Must to thy motions lovers' seasons run?
5   Saucy pedantic wretch, go chide
    Late schoolboys, and sour prentices,°   *apprentices*
  Go tell court-huntsmen, that the king will ride,
   Call country ants to harvest offices;
Love, all alike, no season knows, nor clime,
10 Nor hours, days, months, which are the rags of time.

    Thy beams, so reverend, and strong
    Why shouldst thou think?
I could eclipse and cloud them with a wink,
But that I would not lose her sight so long:
15   If her eyes have not blinded thine,
    Look, and tomorrow late, tell me,
  Whether both th'Indias of spice and mine[2]
   Be where thou left'st them, or lie here with me.
Ask for those kings whom thou saw'st yesterday,
20 And thou shalt hear, all here in one bed lay.

    She is all states, and all princes, I,
    Nothing else is.
Princes do but play us; compared to this,
All honor's mimic; all wealth alchemy.°   *fake science*
25   Thou sun art half as happy as we,
    In that the world's contracted thus;
  Thine age asks ease, and since thy duties be
   To warm the world, that's done in warming us.
Shine here to us, and thou art everywhere;
30 This bed thy center is, these walls, thy sphere.

The Canonization[1]

For God's sake hold your tongue, and let me love,
 Or° chide my palsy, or my gout,   *either*
My five gray hairs, or ruined fortune flout,

---

1. In the tradition of the alba, a love song addressing
the dawn, as in Ovid's *Amores* 1.13 and Petrarch's
Canzoniere 188.

2. The East Indies was the source of spice; the West
Indies was the source of gold.
1. The making of saints.

With wealth your state, your mind with arts improve,
5   Take you a course, get you a place,
    Observe his Honor, or his Grace,
Or the King's real, or his stampèd face[2]
    Contemplate, what you will, approve,
    So you will let me love.

10 Alas, alas, who's injured by my love?
    What merchant's ships have my sighs drowned?
Who says my tears have overflowed his ground?
    When did my colds a forward spring remove?
    When did the heats which my veins fill
15   Add one more to the plaguy bill?[3]
Soldiers find wars, and lawyers find out still
    Litigious men, which quarrels move
    Though she and I do love.

Call us what you will, we are made such by love;
20   Call her one, me another fly,
We are tapers° too, and at our own cost die,[4]   *candles*
    And we in us find the eagle and the dove.
The phoenix riddle hath more wit[5]
    By us; we two being one, are it.
25   So to one neutral thing both sexes fit,
    We die and rise the same, and prove
    Mysterious by this love.

We can die by it, if not live by love,
    And if unfit for tombs and hearse
30 Our legend be, it will be fit for verse;
    And if no piece of chronicle we prove,
    We'll build in sonnets pretty rooms;[6]
    As well a well wrought urn becomes
The greatest ashes, as half-acre tombs,
35   And by these hymns, all shall approve
    Us canonized for love.

And thus invoke us: You whom reverend love
    Made one another's hermitage;°   *refuge, retreat*
You, to whom love was peace, that now is rage;
40   Who did the whole world's soul contract, and drove
    Into the glasses° of your eyes[7]   *lenses*
    (So made such mirrors, and such spies,
That they did all to you epitomize)

---

2. The King's actual face or his image stamped on coins.
3. Daily list of those who have died issued during outbreaks of the plague.
4. To die is to experience orgasm.
5. The mythical bird that was burned and reborn out of its own ashes, a symbol of perfection. See George

Whitney, "The Phoenix" from *A Choice of Emblems* in Perspectives: Print Culture.
6. A play on *stanza*, Italian for "room."
7. The lovers gazing into each other's eyes saw there a compact version or microcosm of the larger world or macrocosm.

Countries, towns, courts: beg from above
45   A pattern of your love!

A Valediction°: of Weeping   *farewell*

Let me pour forth
My tears before thy face, whilst I stay here,
For thy face coins them, and thy stamp° they bear,   *image*
And by this mintage they are something worth,
5   For thus they be
Pregnant of thee;
Fruits of much grief they are, emblems° of more,   *symbols*
When a tear falls, that thou falst which it bore,
So thou and I are nothing then, when on a diverse shore.

10   On a round ball
A workman that hath copies by, can lay
A Europe, Africa, and an Asia,
And quickly make that, which was nothing, all,[1]
          So doth each tear,
15   Which thee doth wear,
A globe, yea world by that impression grow,
Till thy tears mixed with mine do overflow
This world, by waters sent from thee, my heaven dissolvèd so.

Oh more than moon,
20   Draw not up seas to drown me in thy sphere,[2]
Weep me not dead, in thine arms, but forbear
To teach the sea, what it may do too soon;
          Let not the wind
          Example find,
25   To do me more harm, than it purposeth;
Since thou and I sigh one another's breath,
Whoe'er sighs most, is cruelest, and hastes the other's death.

Love's Alchemy

Some that have deeper digged love's mine than I,
Say, where his centric° happiness doth lie: *central*
          I have loved, and got, and told,
But should I love, get, tell, till I were old,
5   I should not find that hidden mystery;
          Oh, 'tis imposture all:
And as no chemic° yet the elixir got,[1]   *alchemist*

---

1. The blank ball looks like a zero ("nothing") until the continents are painted on it to represent the entire world ("all").
2. An astral sphere with a power of attraction greater than the moon might draw the seas up to itself.
1. A goal of alchemy was to produce a pure essence with the power to heal and prolong life.

> But glorifies his pregnant pot,
> If by the way to him befall
10 Some odoriferous thing, or medicinal,
> > So, lovers dream a rich and long delight,
> > But get a winter-seeming summer's night.

Our ease, our thrift, our honor, and our day,
Shall we, for this vain bubble's shadow pay?
15   Ends love in this, that my man,°   *servant*
Can be as happy as I can; if he can
Endure the short scorn of a bridegroom's play?
> > That loving wretch that swears,
> 'Tis not the bodies marry, but the minds,
20   Which he in her angelic finds,
> > Would swear as justly, that he hears,
In that day's rude hoarse minstrelsy, the spheres.[2]
> > Hope not for mind in women; at their best
> Sweetness and wit, they're but mummy,[3] possessed.

The Flea[1]

Mark but this flea, and mark in this,
How little that which thou deniest me is;
It sucked me first,[2] and now sucks thee,
And in this flea, our two bloods mingled be;
5 Thou know'st that this cannot be said
A sin, nor shame, nor loss of maidenhead,
> > Yet this enjoys before it woo,
> > And pampered swells with one blood made of two,
And this, alas, is more than we would do.

10 Oh stay, three lives in one flea spare,
Where we almost, yea more than married are.
This flea is you and I, and this
Our marriage bed, and marriage temple is;
> > Though parents grudge, and you, w'are met,
15   And cloistered in these living walls of jet.°   *black*
> > Though use make you apt to kill me,
> > Let not to that, self murder added be,
And sacrilege, three sins in killing three.

Cruel and sudden, hast thou since
20 Purpled thy nail, in blood of innocence?
Wherein could this flea guilty be,
Except in that drop which it sucked from thee?
> > Yet thou triumph'st, and say'st that thou
Find'st not thy self, nor me the weaker now;

---

2. The concentric globes that created sublime music as they revolved around the earth.
3. Medicine made from mummies; dead bodies.

1. Based on a poem attributed to Ovid, the poem plays on the belief that intercourse involved the mixing of bloods.
2. "Me it sucked first" in the 1635 edition.

25   'Tis true, then learn how false, fears be;
        Just so much honor, when thou yield'st to me,
        Will waste, as this flea's death took life from thee.

A Valediction: Forbidding Mourning[1]

        As virtuous men pass mildly away,
            And whisper to their souls, to go,
        Whilst some of their sad friends do say,
            The breath goes now, and some say, no:

5   So let us melt, and make no noise,
            No tear-floods, nor sigh-tempests move,
        'Twere profanation° of our joys   desecration
            To tell the laity[2] of our love.

        Moving of th'earth brings harms and fears,
10   Men reckon what it did and meant,
        But trepidation of the spheres,[3]
            Though greater far, is innocent.

        Dull sublunary[4] lovers' love
            (Whose soul is sense) cannot admit
15   Absence, because it doth remove
            Those things which elemented° it.   composed

        But we by a love, so much refined,
            That our selves know not what it is,
        Inter-assurèd of the mind,
20   Care less, eyes, lips, and hands to miss.

        Our two souls therefore, which are one,
            Though I must go, endure not yet
        A breach, but an expansion,
            Like gold to airy thinness beat.[5]

25   If they be two, they are two so
            As stiff twin compasses[6] are two,
        Thy soul the fixed foot, makes no show
            To move, but doth, if th' other do.

        And though it in the center sit,
30   Yet when the other far doth roam,
        It leans, and hearkens after it,
            And grows erect, as that comes home.

        Such wilt thou be to me, who must
            Like th' other foot, obliquely run;
35   Thy firmness makes my circle just,°   complete
            And makes me end, where I begun.

1. In his *Life of Dr. John Donne* (1640), Walton describes the occasion as Donne's farewell to his wife before his journey to France in 1611.
2. The uninitiated.
3. Though the movement of the spheres is greater than an earthquake, we feel its effects less.
4. Under the sphere of the moon, hence sensual.
5. Gold was beaten to produce gold leaf. "Airy" suggests their love will become so fine that it will be spiritual.
6. A common enblem of constancy amidst change.

The Ecstasy[1]

Where, like a pillow on a bed,
    A pregnant bank swelled up, to rest
The violet's reclining head,[2]
    Sat we two, one another's best.

5   Our hands were firmly cemented
    With a fast balm, which thence did spring,
Our eye-beams twisted, and did thread
    Our eyes, upon one double string;[3]

So to intergraft our hands, as yet
10   Was all the means to make us one,
And pictures in our eyes to get
    Was all our propagation.[4]

As 'twixt two equal armies, Fate
    Suspends uncertain victory,
15   Our souls (which to advance their state
    Were gone out) hung 'twixt her and me.

And whilst our souls negotiate there,
    We like sepulchral statues lay;
All day, the same our postures were,
20   And we said nothing, all the day.

If any, so by love refined,
    That he soul's language understood,
And by good love were grown all mind,
    Within convenient distance stood,

25   He (though he knew not which soul spake
    Because both meant, both spake the same)
Might thence a new concoction[5] take,
    And part far purer than he came.

This ecstasy doth unperplex,
30   We said, and tell us what we love,
We see by this, it was not sex,
    We see, we saw not what did move:

But as all several souls contain
    Mixture of things, they know not what,
35   Love, these mixed souls, doth mix again,
    And makes both one, each this and that.

A single violet transplant,
    The strength, the color, and the size,

---

1. From *ekstasis* (Greek) meaning passion and the withdrawal of the soul from the body. A beautiful and secluded pastoral spot was a frequent setting for love poetry.
2. The violet was an emblem of faithfulness.

3. The lovers are totally enthralled by gazing into each other's eyes.
4. The act of reflecting each other's image was called "making babies."
5. Refining of metals by heat.

(All which before was poor and scant)
40   Redoubles still, and multiplies.

When love with one another so
    Interinanimates two souls,
That abler soul, which thence doth flow,
    Defects of loneliness controls.

45 We then, who are this new soul, know,
    Of what we are composed and made,
For, th' atomies° of which we grow,   *components, parts*
    Are souls, whom no change can invade.

But O alas, so long, so far
50   Our bodies why do we forbear?
They are ours, though they are not we, we are
    The intelligences, they the sphere.[6]

We owe them thanks, because they thus,
    Did us to us at first convey,
55 Yielded their forces, sense, to us,
    Nor are dross° to us, but allay.°   *refuse / a mixture*

On man heaven's influence works not so,
    But that it first imprints the air,[7]
So soul into the soul may flow,
60   Though it to body first repair.

As our blood labors to beget
    Spirits, as like souls as it can,
Because such fingers need to knit
    That subtle knot, which makes us man:[8]

65 So much pure lovers' souls descend
    T'affections,° and to faculties,°[9]   *feelings / powers*
Which sense may reach and apprehend,
    Else a great prince in prison lies.

To our bodies turn we then, that so
70   Weak men on love revealed may look;
Love's mysteries in souls do grow,
    But yet the body is his book.

And if some lover, such as we,
    Have heard this dialogue of one,
75 Let him still mark us, he shall see
    Small change, when we are to bodies gone.

---

6. In Aristotelian cosmology, each planet moved in a sphere (the form of its motion around the earth) and was guided by an inner spiritual force, or intelligence.
7. An angel has to put on clothes of air to be seen by men; in hermetic medicine, the air mediates the influence of the stars. Just as spirits need a material medium, so souls need the union of bodies.
8. In scholastic philosophy a human being is composed of body and soul, and vapors called spirits produced by the blood link the body with the soul.
9. As the blood mediates between body and soul, so the lovers' feelings mediate between flesh and spirit.

The Funeral

Whoever comes to shroud me, do not harm
      Nor question much
That subtle wreath of hair, which crowns my arm;
The mystery, the sign you must not touch,
5   For 'tis my outward soul,
Viceroy to that, which then to heaven being gone,
      Will leave this to control,
And keep these limbs her provinces, from dissolution.

For if the sinewy thread my brain lets fall
10   Through every part,
Can tie those parts, and make me one of all;[1]
These hairs which upward grew, and strength and art
      Have from a better brain,
Can better do it;[2] except she meant that I
15   By this should know my pain,
As prisoners then are manacled when they're condemned to die.

Whate'er she meant by it, bury it with me,
      For since I am
Love's martyr, it might breed idolatry,
20 If into others' hands these relics[3] came;
      As 'twas humility
To afford to it all a soul can do,
      So, 'tis some bravery,
That since you would save[4] none of me, I bury some of you.

The Relic

When my grave is broke up again
Some second guest to entertain,
(For graves have learned that woman-head[1]
To be to more than one a bed)
5   And he that digs it, spies
A bracelet of bright hair about the bone,
      Will he not let us alone,
And think that there a loving couple lies,
Who thought that this device might be some way
10   To make their souls, at the last busy day,
Meet at this grave, and make a little stay?

      If this fall in a time, or land,
      Where misdevotion[2] doth command,

---

1. There was a theory that nerves emanating from the brain held the entire body together.
2. Her hairs coming from a better brain could better preserve his body.
3. Objects, often body parts, that served as memorials of a saint.
4. Editions from 1633 to 1669 read "have," as do some manuscripts.

1. A feminine trait, with a play on maidenhead. The reference is to the custom of burying more than one corpse in the same grave.
2. Idolatry, as in *The Second Anniversary*, where Donne calls prayers to saints "misdevotion."

15 Then, he that digs us up, will bring
    Us, to the Bishop, and the King,
        To make us relics; then
    Thou shalt be a Mary Magdalen, and I
        A something else thereby;[3]
    All women shall adore us, and some men;
20 And since at such time, miracles are sought,
    I would have that age by this paper taught
    What miracles we harmless lovers wrought.

    First, we loved well and faithfully,
    Yet knew not what we loved, nor why,
25 Difference of sex no more we knew,
    Than our guardian angels do;
        Coming and going, we
    Perchance might kiss, but not between those meals;
        Our hands ne'er touched the seals,
30 Which nature, injured by late law, sets free:[4]
    These miracles we did; but now alas,
    All measure, and all language, I should pass,
    Should I tell what a miracle she was.

Elegy 19: To His Mistress Going to Bed[1]

Come, Madam, come, all rest my powers defy,
Until I labor, I in labor° lie.   *suffering*
The foe oft-times having the foe in sight,
Is tired with standing though he never fight.
5 Off with that girdle,° like heaven's zone° glistering,   *belt / zodiac*
But a far fairer world encompassing.
Unpin that spangled breastplate[2] which you wear,
That th'eyes of busy fools may be stopped there.
Unlace your self, for that harmonious chime,
10 Tells me from you, that now it is bed time.
Off with that happy busk,° which I envy,   *bodice*
That still can be, and still can stand so nigh.
Your gown going off, such beauteous state reveals,
As when from flowery meads th' hill's shadow steals.
15 Off with that wiry coronet and show
The hairy diadem which on you doth grow:
Now off with those shoes, and then safely tread
In this love's hallowed temple, this soft bed.
In such white robes, heaven's angels used to be
20 Received by men; thou angel bring'st with thee

A heaven like Mahomet's paradise;[3] and though
Ill spirits walk in white, we easily know,
By this these angels from an evil sprite,
Those set our hairs, but these our flesh upright.
25   License my roving hands, and let them go,
Before, behind, between, above, below.
Oh my America! my new-found-land,
My kingdom, safliest when with one man manned,
My mine of precious stones, my empery,°   *empire*
30   How blest am I in this discovering thee!
To enter in these bonds, is to be free;
Then where my hand is set, my seal shall be.[4]
        Full nakedness! All joys are due to thee.
As souls unbodied, bodies unclothed must be,
35   To taste whole joys. Gems which you women use
Are like Atalanta's balls, cast in men's views,[5]
That when a fool's eye lighteth on a gem,
His earthly soul may covet theirs, not them.
Like pictures, or like books' gay coverings made
40   For laymen, are all women thus arrayed;
Themselves are mystic books, which only we
(Whom their imputed grace will dignify)
Must see revealed.[6] Then since that I may know,
As liberally, as to a midwife, show
45   Thyself: cast all, yea, this white linen hence,
Here is no penance much less innocence.[7]
To teach thee, I am naked first; why then
What need'st thou have more covering than a man?

from Holy Sonnets
Divine Meditations
1

As due by many titles° I resign   *legal rights*
Myself to thee, Oh God, first I was made
By thee, and for thee, and when I was decayed
Thy blood bought that, the which before was thine,
5   I am thy son, made with thyself to shine,
Thy servant, whose pains thou has still repaid,
Thy sheep, thine image, and, till I betrayed
Myself, a temple of thy Spirit divine;
Why doth the devil then usurp on me?
10   Why doth he steal, nay ravish that's thy right?
Except thou rise and for thine own work fight,

---

3. Heaven of sensual pleasure.
4. He has signed an agreement, which he will now stamp with his seal. Also, he has put his hand where he will consummate his desire.
5. Donne changes the story of how Atalanta was distracted from racing her suitor Hippomenes when he threw three

golden apples before her, which she paused to pick up.
6. The analogy is between the grace that man cannot merit from God in Calvinist doctrine and the undeserved favors women grant their lovers.
7. The 1669 edition and some manuscripts read: "There is no penance due to innocence."

Oh I shall soon despair, when I do see
That thou lov'st mankind well, yet wilt not choose me,
And Satan hates me, yet is loth to lose me.

2

Oh my black soul! Now thou art summoned
By sickness, death's herald, and champion;
Thou art like a pilgrim, which abroad hath done
Treason, and durst not turn to whence he is fled,
5 Or like a thief, which till death's doom be read,
Wisheth himself delivered from prison;
But damned and haled° to execution,   *dragged*
Wisheth that still he might be imprisoned;
Yet grace, if thou repent, thou canst not lack;
10 But who shall give thee that grace to begin?
Oh make thyself with holy mourning black,
And red with blushing, as thou art with sin;
Or wash thee in Christ's blood, which has this might
That being red, it dyes red souls to white.

3

This is my play's last scene, here heavens appoint
My pilgrimage's last mile; and my race
Idly, yet quickly run, hath this last pace,
My span's last inch, my minute's latest point,
5 And gluttonous death, will instantly unjoint
My body, and soul, and I shall sleep a space,
But my ever-waking part shall see that face,
Whose fear already shakes my every joint:
Then, as my soul, to heaven her first seat, takes flight,
10 And earth-borne body, in the earth shall dwell,
So, fall my sins, that all may have their right,
To where they're bred, and would press me, to hell.
Impute me righteous, thus purged of evil,[1]
For thus I leave the world, the flesh, and devil.

4

At the round earth's imagined corners, blow[2]
Your trumpets, angels, and arise, arise
From death, you numberless infinities
Of souls, and to your scattered bodies go,
5 All whom the flood did, and fire shall o'erthrow,[3]

1. Protestant theology held that even when a man repented of his sins, he was still marked by the sin of Adam and needed to be made righteous by Christ's grace.
2. "I saw four angels standing on the four corners of the earth, holding the four winds of the earth" (Revelation 7.1).
3. The flood that Noah survived (Genesis 7) and the fire that will destroy the world at the last judgment (Revelation 6.11).

All whom war, dearth, age, agues, tyrannies,
Despair, law, chance, hath slain, and you whose eyes,
Shall behold God, and never taste death's woe.[4]
But let them sleep, Lord, and me mourn a space,
For, if above all these, my sins abound,
'Tis late to ask abundance of thy grace,
When we are there; here on this lowly ground,
Teach me how to repent; for that's as good
As if thou hadst sealed my pardon with thy blood.

5

If poisonous minerals, and if that tree,
Whose fruit threw death on else immortal us,
If lecherous goats, if serpents envious
Cannot be damned; alas, why should I be?
Why should intent or reason, born in me,
Make sins, else equal, in me more heinous?
And mercy being easy, and glorious
To God, in his stern wrath, why threatens he?
But who am I, that dare dispute with thee?
O God, Oh! of thine only worthy blood,
And my tears, make a heavenly Lethean[5] flood,
And drown in it my sins' black memory.
That thou remember them, some claim as debt,
I think it mercy, if thou wilt forget.

6

Death be not proud, though some have called thee
Mighty and dreadful, for thou are not so.
For, those, whom thou think'st thou dost overthrow,
Die not, poor death, nor yet canst thou kill me;
From rest and sleep, which but thy pictures be,
Much pleasure, then from thee, much more must flow,
And soonest our best men with thee do go,
Rest of their bones, and soul's delivery.
Thou art slave to fate, chance, kings, and desperate men,
And dost with poison, war, and sickness dwell,
And poppy,° or charms can make us sleep as well,   *a narcotic*
And better than thy stroke; why swell'st° thou then?   *grow in pride*
One short sleep past, we wake eternally,
And death shall be no more. Death thou shalt die.[6]

---

4. The resurrection of the body (see 1 Corinthians 15.51–52).
5. Of Lethe, the river of forgetfulness in the underworld of ancient mythology.
6. "The last enemy that shall be destroyed is death" (1 Corinthians 15.26).

10

Batter my heart, three-personed God;[7] for, you
As yet but knock, breathe, shine, and seek to mend;
That I may rise, and stand, o'erthrow me, and bend
Your force, to break, blow, burn and make me new.
5   I, like an usurped town, to another due,
Labor to admit you, but oh, to no end,
Reason your viceroy° in me, me should defend,   *ruler*
But is captived, and proves weak or untrue,
Yet dearly I love you, and would be loved fain,°   *willingly*
10   But am betrothed unto your enemy,
Divorce me, untie, or break that knot again,
Take me to you, imprison me, for I
Except you enthrall me, never shall be free,
Nor ever chaste, except you ravish me.

from Devotions Upon Emergent Occasions[1]
["FOR WHOM THE BELL TOLLS"]

Nunc lento sonitu dicunt, morieris.
Now this bell tolling softly for another, says to me, Thou must die.

Perchance he for whom this bell[2] tolls may be so ill as that he knows not it tolls for him; and perchance I may think myself so much better than I am, as that they who are about me, and see my state may have caused it to toll for me, and I know not that. The Church is catholic, universal, so are all her actions; all that she does, belongs to all. When she baptises a child, that action concerns me; for that child is thereby connected to that Head which is my Head too, and engrafted into that body,[3] whereof I am a member. And when she buries a man, that action concerns me: all mankind is of one Author, and is of one volume; when one man dies, one chapter is not torn out of the book, but translated[4] into a better language; and every chapter must be so translated. God employs several translators; some pieces are translated by age, some by sickness, some by war, some by justice; but God's hand is in every translation, and his hand shall bind up all our scattered leaves again, for that library where every book shall lie open to one another. As therefore the bell that rings to a sermon calls not upon the preacher only, but upon the congregation to come, so this bell calls us all; but how much more me, whom am brought so near the door by this sickness. There was a contention as far as a suit, (in which both piety and dignity, religion, and estimation, were mingled) which of the religious orders should ring to prayers first in the morning; and it was determined that they should ring first that rose earliest. If we understand aright the dignity of this bell that tolls for our evening prayer, we would be glad to make it ours by rising early, in that application, that it might be ours, as well as his whose indeed it is. The bell doth toll for him that thinks it doth; and though it intermit again, yet from that minute that occasion wrought upon him, he is united to God. Who casts not up his

---

7. The Trinity: God the Father, Son, and Holy Spirit.
1. Donne wrote the *Devotions* (1624) following an illness he suffered in winter 1623. Each meditation concerns a phase of his disease.

2. The passing-bell rung slowly when a person was dying.
3. United with the church.
4. From Latin *translatus*, "having been carried across."

eye to the sun when it rises? but who takes off his eye from a comet when that breaks out? Who bends not his ear to any bell which upon any occasion rings? but who can remove it from that bell which is passing a piece of himself out of this world? No man is an island, entire of itself; every man is a piece of the Continent, a part of the main. If a clod be washed away by the sea, Europe is the less, as well as if a promontory were, as well as if a manor of thy friends or of thine own were Any man's death diminishes me, because I am involved in mankind; and therefore never send to know for whom the bell tolls; it tolls for thee. Neither can we call this a begging of misery or a borrowing of misery, as though we were not miserable enough of ourselves but must fetch in more from the next house in taking upon us the misery of our neighbors. Truly it were an excusable covetousness if we did; for affliction is a treasure, and scarce any man hath enough of it. No man hath affliction enough that is not matured and ripened by it, and made fit for God by that affliction. If a man carry treasure in bullion, or in a wedge of gold, and have none coined into current moneys, his treasure will not defray him as he travels. Tribulation is treasure in the nature of it, but it is not current money in the use of it, except we get nearer and nearer our home, heaven, by it. Another man may be sick too, and sick to death, and this affliction may lie in his bowels as gold in a mine and be of no use to him: but this bell that tells me of his affliction digs out and applies that gold to me, if by this consideration of another's danger I take mine own into contemplation and so secure myself by making my recourse to my God who is our only security.

<hr />

Lady Mary Wroth
1586–1640

Lady Mary Wroth was born the same year that her uncle Sir Philip Sidney died in battle. Like her uncle, she wrote brilliant sonnets and an entertaining and complex prose romance, but whereas his death and writing became the stuff of myth, she died in obscurity. Appreciated by the finest poets of her time, her writing was neglected for the next 300 years; she has only recently been rediscovered as one of the most compelling women writers of her age. Her *Pamphilia to Amphilanthus*, the first Petrarchan sonnet sequence in English by a woman, was first printed in 1621 but was not reprinted until 1977. Wroth's work has finally become available outside rare book libraries, thanks to Josephine Robert's editions of Wroth's complete poems (1983) and her prose romance *The Countess of Montgomeries Urania* (1995), along with Michael Brennan's edition of her pastoral tragicomedy *Love's Victory* (1988). Recent criticism has stressed the formal complexity and variety of her poetry and prose, their creation of female subjectivity, and their relationship to her life and social context, shedding new light on one of the most emotionally powerful and stylistically innovative authors of the Jacobean period.

Mary Wroth was born into the cultivated and distinguished Sidney family. Mary and her mother, two brothers, and seven sisters lived at the family estate Penshurst in Kent. She sometimes visited her father in the Low Countries, where he commanded the English troops fighting for the Protestant cause against the Spanish. Ben Jonson sang the praises of Lady Mary's family and their way of life in *To Penshurst*, a place where the children not only enjoyed natural beauty—"broad beech" and "chest-nut shade"—but also learned the "mysteries of manners, arms and arts." Mary also spent a great deal of time in London with her aunt for whom she was named, Mary (Sidney) Herbert, Countess of Pembroke, hostess to and patron of a circle of poets that included George Chapman and Ben Jonson.

Mary found a mentor in her aunt, who herself wrote poems as well as translations of the Psalms and of Petrarch. Mary Herbert's translation of Petrarch's *Trionfo della Morte* ("Triumph of Death") portrays the poet's beloved Laura not as a passive object but as a lively and eloquent speaker. Mary Wroth's own sonnets similarly portray the woman as the suffering and desiring subject of love rather than the mute object that was common in earlier English Petrarchan poetry. Mary Wroth took the title of her *Urania* from a character in Philip Sidney's *The Countess of Pembrokes Arcadia*, whose publication had been overseen by his sister, Mary Sidney Herbert. Mary Wroth even created the character of the Queen of Naples as a fictional version of her aunt and perhaps saw *Urania* as a continuation of *Arcadia*.

When Mary married Sir Robert Wroth, Lord of Durance and Laughton House and juror for the Gunpowder Plot, she continued her close family ties with her aunt and father (yet another poet), but she also moved into the larger world of the Jacobean court. She served as Queen Anne's companion, and she became at once an observer and a center of attention in the aristocratic circle at court. In 1605, shortly after the first recorded performance of *Othello* at Whitehall, Lady Mary Wroth played in Ben Jonson's *Masque of Blackness*, in which she was presented to the court with Lady Frances Walsingham as the embodiment of gravity and dignity. Later, Wroth would deploy metaphors of darkness and night to great effect in her lyric poems.

It was in this court context that she attracted the attention of Ben Jonson, who not only wrote a poem complimenting her husband but also dedicated a sonnet and two epigrams to her. Jonson paid tribute to her as a subject and inspiration for poetry and as a powerfully moving poet in her own right. He claimed that since writing out her sonnets, he had "become / A better lover and much better poet." Dedicating his great play *The Alchemist* to her, he portrayed her as inheriting her uncle's mantle as poet: "To that Lady Most Deserving her Name and Blood, Lady Mary Wroth,"—a pun on her name, as Wroth was pronounced "worth." While she, too, punned on her married name in her poetry, Mary clung to her identity as a Sidney, using the Sidney device in her letters.

Her marriage was not particularly happy and pales in comparison with her literary friendship and love affair with her cousin William Herbert, by whom she had two illegitimate children, after she was widowed in 1614. During the years of her early widowhood she wrote the first part of her prose romance *Urania*, which was printed with *Pamphilia to Amphilanthus* in 1621. The *Urania* not only presents a fictional account of her relationship with her cousin and her parents' own happy marriage but also was read at the time as a criticism of the mores of the court. King James's courtiers, taking offense at the satire of their private lives, attacked her, prompting her to ask for the book to be removed from publication a few months after it first appeared. The early modern prejudice against women writing surfaces in Lord Denny's punning condescension to Wroth: "leave idle books alone / For wiser and worthier women have writ none."

Fortunately for us, she didn't take his advice and continued to write the second book of the *Urania*, which survives in manuscript. Indeed, no record of a warrant to recall the book survives. Her final years remain a mystery; she lived in retirement after her cousin's death. She left behind a body of poetry challenging the status quo of the court, proclaiming the suffering she had endured for love, and singing the beauty of spiritual love in a woman's voice. Imitating not only her uncle Philip's *Arcadia* but also the *Heptameron* of the French writer Marguerite de Navarre, Mary Wroth made the prose romance a complex combination of novelistic fantasy, roman à clef, and social satire. The greatest English woman writer of her age, Mary Wroth fashioned a new voice and new perspectives within literary tradition that convey the fullness and complexity of her life as woman, lover, and writer.

from **Pamphilia to Amphilanthus**[1]

1

When night's black mantle could most darkness prove,
    And sleep death's image did my senses hire
    From knowledge of myself, then thoughts did move
    Swifter than those most swiftness need require:
5   In sleep, a chariot drawn by winged desire
    I saw, where sat bright Venus, Queen of love,
    And at her feet her son,[2] still adding fire
    To burning hearts which she did hold above,
But one heart flaming more than all the rest
10   The goddess held, and put it to my breast.
    "Dear son, now shut,"[3] said she, "thus must we win."
He her obeyed, and martyred my poor heart,
    I, waking, hoped as dreams it would depart;[4]
    Yet since, O me, a lover I have been.

5

Can pleasing sight, misfortune ever bring?
    Can firm desire a painful torment try?
    Can winning eyes prove to the heart a sting?
    Or can sweet lips in treason hidden lie?
5   The Sun most pleasing blinds the strongest eye.
    If too much look'd on, breaking the sight's string;[5]
    Desires still crossed, must unto mischief hie,°   *move quickly*
    And as despair, a luckless chance may fling.
Eyes, having won, rejecting proves a sting
10   Killing the bud before the tree doth spring;
    Sweet lips not loving do as poison prove:
Desire, sight, eyes, lips, seek, see, prove, and find
    You love may win, but curses if unkind;
    Then show you harm's dislike, and joy in Love.

16

Am I thus conquered? Have I lost the powers
    That to withstand, which joys to ruin me?
    Must I be still while it my strength devours
    And captive leads me prisoner, bound, unfree?[6]
5   Love first shall leave men's fant'sies to them free,[7]

1. The title means "From the All-loving one to the Dual Lover." First published in 1621, the sonnet sequence is here printed according to the numbering in Josephine Robert's 1983 edition.
2. Cupid. Compare the image of the chariot here with that in Petrarch's *Triumph of Love*.
3. Enclose that flaming heart within Pamphilia.
4. Pamphilia's experience of love is represented as a dream vision, a symbolic narrative in which the dreamer discovers hidden truth.
5. Compare 1.6 with Donne's "The Ecstasy," lines 7–8. Both poems rely on the early modern notion that the eyes give off light that make vision possible.
6. The form of this poem that begins with rhetorical questions that are echoed in the answers that follow is called *carmen correlativum*, or correlative verse.
7. Before I surrender to Love, Love will allow men to realize their fantasies freely.

Desire shall quench love's flames, spring hate sweet showers,
Love shall loose all his darts, have sight, and see
His shame, and wishings hinder happy hours.[8]
Why should we not Love's purblind° charms resist?   *totally blind*
10   Must we be servile, doing what he list?°   *wants*
No, seek some host to harbor thee: I fly
Thy babish° tricks, and freedom do profess;   *childish*
But O my hurt, makes my lost heart confess
I love, and must. So farewell liberty.

55

How like a fire doth love increase in me,
The longer that it lasts, the stronger still,
The greater purer, brighter, and doth fill
No eye with wonder more, then hopes still be
5   Bred in my breast, when fires of love are free
To use that part to their best pleasing will,
And now impossible it is to kill
The heat so great where Love his strength doth see.
Mine eyes can scare sustain the flames my heart
10   Doth trust in them my passions to impart,
And languishingly strive to show my love;
My breath not able is to breathe least part
Of that increasing fuel of my smart;
Yet love I will till I but ashes prove.[9]
Pamphilia[1]

68

My pain, still smothered in my grièved breast
Seeks for some ease, yet cannot passage find
To be discharged of this unwelcome guest;
When most I strive, more fast his burdens bind,
5   Like to a ship, on Goodwins[2] cast by wind
The more she strives, more deep in sand is pressed
Till she be lost; so am I, in this kind°   *way*
Sunk and devoured, and swallowed by unrest,
Lost, shipwracked, spoiled, debarred of smallest hope
10   Nothing of pleasure left; save thoughts have scope,
Which wander may. Go then, my thoughts, and cry
Hope's perished, Love tempest-beaten, Joy lost:
Killing Despair hath all these blessings crossed.
Yet Faith still cries, Love will not falsify.

---

8. Cupid blindfolded was a popular figure in Renaissance iconography.
9. Josephine Roberts has noted that "will" may stand for the poet's lover William Herbert. Early modern poets frequently used the device of the embedded name.

1. To mark the completion of the first section of sonnets, the poet signed her pen-name at the foot of sonnet 55.
2. A dangerous shoal off the south eastern coast of England.

from The Countess of Montgomery's Urania
from Book 1[1]

When the spring began to appear like the welcome messenger of summer, one sweet (and in that more sweet) morning, after Aurora[2] had called all careful eyes to attend the day, forth came the fair shepherdess Urania,[3] (fair indeed; yet that far too mean a title for her, who for beauty deserved the highest style could be given by best knowing judgments). Into the mead[4] she came, where usually she drove her flocks to feed, whose leaping and wantonness showed they were proud of such a guide: But she, whose sad thoughts led her to another manner of spending her time, made her soon leave them, and follow her late begun custom; which was (while they delighted themselves) to sit under some shade, bewailing her misfortune; while they fed, to feed upon her own sorrow and tears, which at this time she began again to summon, sitting down under the shade of a well-spread beech; the ground (then blest) and the tree with full and fine leaved branches growing proud to bear and shadow such perfections. But she regarding nothing, in comparison of her woe, thus proceeded in her grief:

"Alas Urania," said she (the true servant to misfortune); "of any misery that can befall woman, is not this the most and greatest which thou art fallen into? Can there be any near the unhappiness of being ignorant, and that in the highest kind, not being certain of mine own estate or birth? Why was I not still continued in the belief I was, as I appear, a shepherdess, and daughter to a shepherd? My ambition then went no higher than this estate, now flies it to a knowledge; then was I contented, now perplexed. O ignorance, can thy dullness yet procure so sharp a pain? and that such a thought as makes me now aspire unto knowledge? How did I joy in this poor life being quiet? blest in the love of those I took for parents, but now by them I know the contrary, and by that knowledge, not to know myself. Miserable Urania, worse art thou now than these thy lambs; for they know their dams, while thou dost live unknown of any."

By this were others come into that mead with their flocks: but she esteeming her sorrowing thoughts her best, and choicest company, left that place, taking a little path which brought her to the further side of the plain, to the foot of the rocks, speaking as she went these lines, her eyes fixed upon the ground, her very soul turned into mourning.

> Unseen, unknown, I here alone complain
>   To rocks, to hills, to meadows and to springs,
> Which can no help return to ease my pain,
>   But back my sorrows the sad echo brings.
> 5   Thus still increasing are my woes to me,
>   Doubly resounded by that moanful voice,

---

1. The text is in two parts; one part corresponds to the published version of 1621, the other to a unique manuscript in the author's hand at the Newberry Library in Chicago. The publishers entered *Urania* in the Stationer's Register in 1621; it is not clear whether they had the author's permission. Once in print, the book provoked attacks from powerful courtiers, who did not like to see their foibles fictionalized. In her defense, Wroth claimed that she never intended to have her work published. This may have been simply an aristocratic disclaimer against the taint of publication, but the remark may also carry a concern with the prohibition against women's publishing. Although Wroth asked for a King's warrant to recall the book, no record of such a warrant exists.

2. Goddess of the dawn.

3. Urania represents Susan Herbert, countess of Montgomery (1587–1629), the author's close friend. In Spenser's *Colin Clouts Come Home Again*, Urania stands for Wroth's aunt, Mary Sidney, Countess of Pembroke.

4. Meadow.

> Which seems to second me in misery,
>   And answer gives like friend of mine own choice.
> Thus only she doth my companion prove,
> 10   The others silently do offer ease:
> But those that grieve, a grieving note do love;
>   Pleasures to dying eyes bring but disease:
> And such am I, who daily ending live,
>   Wailing a state which can no comfort give.

In this passion she went on, till she came to the foot of a great rock, she thinking of nothing less than ease, sought how she might ascend it; hoping there to pass away her time more peaceably with loneliness, though not to find least respite from her sorrow, which so dearly she did value, as by no means she would impart it to any. The way was hard, though by some windings making the ascent pleasing. Having attained the top, she saw under some hollow trees the entry into the rock: she fearing nothing but the continuance of her ignorance, went in; where she found a pretty room, as if that stony place had yet in pity, given leave for such perfections to come into the heart as chiefest, and most beloved place, because most loving. The place was not unlike the ancient (or the descriptions of ancient) hermitages,[5] instead of hangings, covered and lined with ivy, disdaining aught else should come there, that being in such perfection. This richness in nature's plenty made her stay to behold it, and almost grudge the pleasant fullness of content that place might have, if sensible, while she must know to taste of torments. As she was thus in passion mixed with pain, throwing her eyes as wildly as timorous lovers do for fear of discovery, she perceived a little light, and such a one, as a chink doth oft discover to our sights. She curious to see what this was, with her delicate hands put the natural ornament aside, discerning a little door, which she putting from her, passed through it into another room, like the first in all proportion; but in the midst there was a square stone, like to a pretty table, and on it a wax-candle burning; and by that a paper, which had suffered itself patiently to receive the discovering of so much of it, as presented this sonnet (as it seemed newly written) to her sight.

> Here all alone in silence might I mourn:
>   But how can silence be where sorrows flow?
>   Sighs with complaints have poorer pains out-worn;
>   But broken hearts can only true grief show.
> 5   Drops of my dearest blood shall let love know
>   Such tears for her I shed, yet still do burn,
>   As no spring can quench least part of my woe,
>   Till this live earth, again to earth do turn.
>
> Hateful all thought of comfort is to me,
> 10   Despised day, let me still night possess;
>   Let me all torments feel in their excess,
>   And but this light[6] allow my state to see.
>
> Which still doth waste, and wasting as this light,
> Are my sad days unto eternal night.

---

5. Hermits' cells.
6. A candle. The story of Cleophila finding a poem atop a

table in a dark cave (Philip Sidney, *Old Arcadia*) is the source for the story of Urania's finding the sonnet.

"Alas Urania!" sighed she. "How well do these words, this place, and all agree with thy fortune? Sure poor soul thou wert here appointed to spend thy days, and these rooms ordained to keep thy tortures in; none being assuredly so matchlessly unfortunate."

Turning from the table, she discerned in the room a bed of boughs, and on it a man lying, deprived of outward sense, as she thought, and of life, as she at first did fear, which struck her into a great amazement: yet having a brave spirit, though shadowed under a mean habit, she stepped unto him, whom she found not dead, but laid upon his back, his head a little to her wards,[7] his arms folded on his breast, hair long, and beard disordered, manifesting all care; but care itself had left him: curiousness thus far afforded him, as to be perfectly discerned the most exact piece of misery; apparel he had suitable to the habitation, which was a long gray robe. This grievefull spectacle did much amaze the sweet and tender-hearted shepherdess; especially, when she perceived (as she might by the help of the candle) the tears which distilled from his eyes; who seeming the image of death, yet had this sign of worldly sorrow, the drops falling in that abundance, as if there were a kind strife among them, to rid their master first of that burdenous carriage; or else meaning to make a flood, and so drown their woeful patient in his own sorrow, who yet lay still, but then fetching a deep groan from the profoundest part of his soul, he said:

"Miserable Perissus,[8] canst thou thus live, knowing she that gave thee life is gone? Gone, O me! and with her all my joy departed. Wilt thou (unblessed creature) lie here complaining for her death, and know she died for thee? Let truth and shame make thee do something worthy of such a love, ending thy days like thyself, and one fit to be her servant. But that I must not do: then thus remain and softer storms, still to torment thy wretched soul withall, since all are little, and too too little for such a loss. O dear Limena,[9] loving Limena, worthy Limena, and more rare, constant Limena: perfections delicately feigned to be in women were verified in thee, was such worthiness framed only to be wondered at by the best, but given as a prey to base and unworthy jealousy? When were all worthy parts joined in one, but in thee (my best Limena)? Yet all these grown subject to a creature ignorant of all but ill; like unto a fool, who in a dark cave, that hath but one way to get out, having a candle, but not the understanding what good it doth him, puts it out:[1] this ignorant wretch not being able to comprehend thy virtues, did so by thee in thy murder, putting out the world's light, and men's admiration: Limena, Limena, O my Limena."

With that he fell from complaining into such a passion, as weeping and crying were never in so woeful a perfection, as now in him; which brought as deserved a compassion from the excellent shepherdess, who already had her heart so tempered with grief, as that it was apt to take any impression that it would come to feel withall. Yet taking a brave courage to her, she stepped unto him, kneeling down by his side, and gently pulling him by the arm, she thus spake.

"Sir," said she, "having heard some part of your sorrows, they have not only made me truly pity you, but wonder at you; since if you have lost so great a treasure, you should not lie thus leaving her and your love unrevenged, suffering her murderers to live, while you lie here complaining; and if such perfections be dead in her, why

---

7. Toward her.
8. Lost one.
9. Woman of the home or threshold.

1. An allusion to the Myth of the Cave in Plato's *Republic*.

make you not the phoenix[2] of your deeds live again, as to new life raised out of revenge you should take on them? Then were her end satisfied, and you deservedly accounted worthy of her favor, if she were so worthy as you say."

"If she were? O God," cried out Perissus, "what devilish spirit art thou, that thus dost come to torture me? But now I see you are a woman; and therefore not much to be marked, and less resisted: but if you know charity, I pray now practice it, and leave me who am afflicted sufficiently without your company; or if you will stay, discourse not to me."

"Neither of these will I do," said she.

"If you be then," said he, "some fury of purpose sent to vex me, use your force to the uttermost in martyring me; for never was there a fitter subject, than the heart of poor Perissus is."

"I am no fury," replied the divine Urania, "not hither come to trouble you, but by accident lighted on this place; my cruel hap[3] being such, as only the like can give me content, while the solitariness of this like cave might give me quiet, though not ease, seeking for such a one, I happened hither; and this is the true cause of my being here, though now I would use it to a better end if I might. Wherefore favor me with the knowledge of your grief; which heard, it may be I shall give you some counsel, and comfort in your sorrow."

"Cursed may I be," cried he, "if ever I take comfort, having such case of mourning: but because you are, or seem to be afflicted, I will not refuse to satisfy your demand, but tell you the saddest story that ever was rehearsed by dying man to living woman; and such a one, as I fear will fasten too much sadness in you; yet should I deny it, I were to blame, being so well known to these senseless places; as were they sensible of sorrow, they would condole, or else amazed at such cruelty, stand dumb as they do, to find that man should be so inhuman."

⚔

Robert Herrick
1591–1674

The urbane and at times pagan poet Robert Herrick might seem an unlikely candidate for rural vicar, but such were his connections that he was promoted from deacon to priest in a day. He spent most of his life as vicar of the Devonshire parish of Dean, where he wrote poetry about country customs and church liturgy. A hundred and fifty years after his death, a writer in the *Quarterly Review* was able to find people in the village who could recite from memory Herrick's *Farewell to Dean Bourn*: "I never look to see / Dean, or thy watery incivility," lines that "they said he uttered as he crossed the brook, upon being ejected from the vicarage by Cromwell." Referring to Herrick's return to the vicarage after the Restoration, these locals "added with an air of innocent triumph, 'He did see it again.'" The villagers also recalled stories of how the bachelor vicar threw his sermon at the congregation one day for their inattention and how he taught his pet pig to drink from a tankard. Many of his best poems, such as *Corinna's Going A-Maying* and *The Hock-Cart, or Harvest Home*, celebrate the landscape and the life of the country in the idealized tradition of pastoral poetry.

2. The mythical bird that burned and was then reborn from its ashes.   3. Fate, chance.

The son of a goldsmith in Cheapside, Herrick was apprenticed to the trade at age fourteen. After taking his B.A. from Cambridge in 1617, he returned to London, where he spent his poetic apprenticeship until he was appointed chaplain to the Duke of Buckingham in his failed expedition to aid the French Protestants of Rhé in 1627. Only a year later, Herrick moved to the vicarage at Dean, but many of his poems recount his London days, recalling the feasts frequented by Ben Jonson, whose verse "out-did the meat, out-did the frolic wine." The influence of Jonson's classical concision, wit, and urbanity can be felt in such poems as *Delight in Disorder* and his *Prayer* to the poet. While in London, Herrick also became friends with William Lawes, the court composer who wrote the music for Milton's masque *Comus*. When Lawes set Herrick's *To the Virgins, to Make Much of Time* to music, this poem became one of the most popular drinking songs of the seventeenth century—often sung as a "catch," which meant that its words could be played with to produce ribald double meanings. His poems circulated in manuscript until his volume of verse was printed in 1648, with his secular poetry entitled *Hesperides* and his religious poetry entitled *Noble Numbers*. He first achieved a wide readership in the early nineteenth century with the romantic revival of interest in rural life and poetry.

from HESPERIDES

The Argument of His Book[1]

I sing of brooks, of blossoms, birds, and bowers,
Of April, May, of June, and July flowers.
I sing of Maypoles, hock carts, wassails, wakes,[2]
Of bridegrooms, brides, and of their bridal cakes.
5   I write of youth, of love, and have access
By these, to sing of cleanly wantonness.°   *carefree abandon*
I sing of dews, of rains, and piece by piece,
Of balm, of oil, of spice, and ambergris.[3]
I sing of times trans-shifting;[4] and I write
10   How roses first came red, and lilies white.
I write of groves, of twilights, and I sing
The court of Mab,[5] and of the fairy king.
I write of hell; I sing (and ever shall)
Of Heaven, and hope to have it after all.

To His Book

While thou did keep thy candor[1] undefil'd,
Dearly I lov'd thee as my first-born child;
But when I saw thee wantonly to roam
From house to house, and never stay at home,
5   I break° my bonds of love, and bade thee go,   *broke*
Regardless whether well thou sped'st, or no.
On with thy fortunes then, what e're they be;
If good I'll smile, if bad I'll sigh for thee.

---

1. All of Herrick's poems were published in 1648. The "Argument" introduces the book's themes.
2. Hock carts: harvest wagons; wassails: drinking toasts; wakes: celebrations in honor of the dedication of a parish church.
3. Secretion from the intestines of sperm whales, used to make perfume.
4. Times changing and passing; the cycle of the seasons.
5. Queen of the fairies.
1. A play on the modern meaning of "candor" (frank honesty) and its Latin meaning, "whiteness, radiance."

Corinna's Going A-Maying

Get up, get up for shame! the blooming morn
Upon her wings presents the god unshorn.[1]
   See how Aurora[2] throws her fair
   Fresh-quilted colors through the air:
5   Get up, sweet slug-a-bed, and see
      The dew-bespangling herb and tree.
Each flower has wept, and bowed toward the east,
Above an hour since; yet you not dressed,
   Nay! not so much as out of bed?
10   When all the birds have matins° said,   *morning prayer*
   And sung their thankfull hymns: 'tis sin,
      Nay, profanation° to keep in,   *impiety*
Whenas a thousand virgins on this day
Spring, sooner than the lark, to fetch in May.[3]

15   Rise, and put on your foliage, and be seen
To come forth, like the springtime, fresh and green,
   And sweet as Flora.[4] Take no care
   For jewels for your gown, or hair:
      Fear not; the leaves will strew
20   Gems in abundance upon you;
Besides, the childhood of the day has kept,
Against you come, some orient° pearls unwept;   *oriental, shining*
   Come, and receive them while the light
   Hangs on the dew-locks of the night,
25   And Titan[5] on the eastern hill
      Retires himself, or else stands still
Till you come forth. Wash, dress, be brief in praying:
Few beads are best,[6] when once we go a-Maying.

Come, my Corinna, come; and coming, mark
30   How each field turns a street; each street a park
   Made green, and trimmed with trees; see how
   Devotion gives each house a bough,
      Or branch: each porch, each door, ere this,
      An ark, a tabernacle is,[7]
35   Made up of whitethorn neatly interwove;
As if here were those cooler shades of love.
   Can such delights be in the street
   And open fields, and we not see't?
      Come, we'll abroad; and let's obey
40   The proclamation made for May,
And sin no more, as we have done, by staying;
But my Corinna, come, let's go a-Maying.

---

1. Apollo, the sun god, whose beams are seen as his flowing locks.
2. Goddess of the dawn in Roman mythology.
3. The custom on May Day morning was to gather blossoms.
4. Ancient Italian goddess of fertility and flowers.
5. The sun god.
6. An allusion to Catholic rosary beads.
7. The Hebrew ark of the Covenant contained the tablets of the laws; a tabernacle is an ornamental niche to hold the consecrated host.

There's not a budding boy, or girl, this day,
But is got up, and gone to bring in May.
45   A deal of youth, ere this, is come
          Back, and with whitethorn laden home.
          Some have dispatched their cakes and cream,
          Before that we have left to dream:
And some have wept, and wooed, and plighted troth,
50   And chose their priest, ere we can cast off sloth.
          Many a green-gown has been given,
          Many a kiss, both odd and even:[8]
          Many a glance, too, has been sent
          From out the eye, love's firmament:
55   Many a jest told of the keys betraying
     This night, and locks picked; yet we're not a-Maying.

Come, let us go, while we are in our prime,
And take the harmless folly of the time.
          We shall grow old apace, and die
60   Before we know our liberty.
          Our life is short; and our days run
          As fast away as does the sun;
And as a vapor, or a drop of rain
Once lost, can ne'er be found again,
65   So when or you or I are made
          A fable, song, or fleeting shade,°   soul
          All love, all liking, all delight
Lies drowned with us in endless night.
Then while time serves, and we are but decaying,
70   Come, my Corinna, come, let's go a-Maying.

To the Virgins, to Make Much of Time

Gather ye rosebuds while ye may,
     Old time is still a-flying;[1]
And this same flower that smiles today,
     Tomorrow will be dying.[2]

5   The glorious lamp of heaven, the sun,
     The higher he's a-getting;
The sooner will his race be run,[3]
     And nearer he's to setting.

That age is best, which is the first,
10   When youth and blood are warmer;
But being spent, the worse, and worst
     Times still succeed the former.
Then be not coy, but use your time,
     And while ye may, go marry;

---

8. Green gown . . . given; by lying in the grass. Kisses are
odd and even in kissing games.
1. The Latin tag *tempus fugit* ("time flies").

2. "Dying" was also a euphemism for orgasm.
3. In Greek mythology, the sun was seen as the chariot of
Phoebus Apollo drawn across the sky each day as in a race.

15   For having lost but once your prime,
            You may for ever tarry.

His Prayer to Ben Jonson[1]

When I a verse shall make,
Know I have prayed thee,
For old religion's sake,[2]
Saint Ben to aid me.

5   Make the way smooth for me,
When I, thy Herrick,
Honoring thee, on my knee
Offer my lyric.

Candles I'll give to thee
10   And a new altar;
And thou Saint Ben shall be
Writ in my psalter.°   *hymn book*

Upon Julia's Clothes

When as in silks my Julia goes,
Then, then, me thinks, how sweetly flows
That liquefaction of her clothes.
Next, when I cast mine eyes and see
5   That brave° vibration each way free;   *splendid*
O how that glittering taketh me!

The Christian Militant

A man prepar'd against all ills to come,
That dares to dead the fire of martyrdom;
That sleeps at home, and sailing there at ease,
Fears not the fierce sedition of the seas;
5   That's counter-proof against the farm's mishaps,
Undreadful too of courtly thunderclaps;
That wears one face (like heaven) and never shows
A change, when Fortune either comes or goes;
That keeps his own strong guard, in the despite
10   Of what can hurt by day or harm by night;
That takes and redelivers every stroke
Of Chance (as made up of rock and oak);
That sighs at others' death, smiles at his own
Most dire and horrid crucifixion.
15   Who for true glory suffers thus: we grant
Him to be here our Christian militant.

1. The humorous conceit in this poem is of Ben Jonson as a saint in the "religion" of poetry, aiding Herrick as a saint would intercede for a sinner. Herrick pays homage to Jonson's style both in his humor and verse form.
2. A reference to Jonson's Catholicism.

To His Tomb-Maker

Go I must; when I am gone,
Write but this upon my stone:
Chaste I liv'd, without a wife,
That's the story of my life.
5   Strewings need none; every flow'r
Is in this word, Bachelor.

Upon Himself Being Buried

Let me sleep this night away,
Till the dawning of the day;
Then at th' opening of mine eyes,
I, and all the world, shall rise.

His Last Request to Julia

I have been wanton and too bold, I fear,
To chafe o'er much the virgin's cheek or ear:
Beg for my Pardon, Julia; *He doth win*
Grace with the Gods, who's sorry for his sin.
5   That done, my Julia, dearest Julia, come,
And go with me to choose my burial room:
My fates are ended; when thy Herrick dies,
Clasp thou his book, then close thou up his eyes.

—◄═♦═►—

George Herbert
1593–1633

Engraved portrait of George
Herbert.

George Herbert spent the last three years of his life as a country parson. In an age in which such a church living was often a mere sinecure, Herbert had a genuine vocation, which he chose over other paths open to him through his talent and the connections of his distinguished Welsh family. His education and vocation were most influenced by his mother Magdalene Herbert, a woman with a great appreciation for poetry and strong devotion to the Church of England. When she died in 1627, John Donne gave the funeral sermon, extolling not only her grace, wit, and charm but especially her extraordinary charity to those who suffered from the plague of 1625, among whom was Donne himself. Herbert's mother had been widowed when he was just three years old. She brought up ten children, first in Oxford and then in London, where she saw to it that they were well read in the Bible and the classics.

Herbert studied at Cambridge University, where he became Reader in Rhetoric in 1616; in 1620 he was elected Public Orator, a post that he held for eight years. He wrote poetry and delivered public addresses in Latin and worked on the Latin version of Francis Bacon's *The Advancement of Learning*. Herbert also stood for Parliament and served there in 1624, when the Virginia Company, in which many of his friends and family were stockholders, was beset by financial difficulties and ultimately dissolved by James I.

Though his book *The Temple*, which included all his English poems, was not published until just after his death in 1633, Herbert was already writing verse as an undergraduate in 1610, when he dedicated two sonnets to his mother that advocated religious rather than secular love as the subject for poetry. His first published poems were written in Latin, commemorating the death of Prince Henry (1612). Herbert also wrote three different collections of Latin poems during his Cambridge years: *Musae Responsoriae*, polemical poems that defended the rites of the Church of England from Puritan criticism; *Passio discerpta*, religious verse that focused on Christ's passion and death in a style reminiscent of Crashaw; and *Lucas*, a collection of brief epigrams, such as this one on pride: "Each man is earth, and the field's child. Tell me, / Will you be a sterile mountain or a fertile valley?" The sardonic and mocking tone of these epigrams may surprise a reader of his English poems, but the wit and the rhetorical finish of his Latin poetry recur in his later verse.

Herbert's poetry is some of the most complex and innovative of all English verse. In a very pared-down style, enlivened by gentle irony, Herbert produces complexity of meaning through allegory and emblem, directly or more often indirectly alluding to biblical images, events, and insights, which take on their own moral and poetic meaning in the life of the speaker and the reader. Each of his poems is a kind of spiritual event, enacting in its form, both visual and aural, the very theological experiences and beliefs or conflict of beliefs—expressed. Herbert allows us to make the spiritual journey with him through suffering and redemption, through doubt and hope. The meaning of one of his poems unravels like a discovery, each line and stanza raising alternative possibilities and altering the meaning of the one before. His spirituality is not a matter of easy acceptance but one of struggle, portrayed with wit, logic, and passion that recall the best of Donne's verse. The humility, subtle hesitancy, and whimsical irony are Herbert's alone, as when he addresses a love poem, *The Pearl*, to God:

> I know the ways of pleasure, the sweet strains,
> The lullings and the relishes of it . . .
> My stuff is flesh, not brass; my senses live,
> And grumble oft, that they have more in me
> Then he that curbs them, being but one to five:
>   Yet I love thee.

The Altar[1]

A broken ALTAR, Lord, thy servant rears,
Made of a heart, and cemented with tears:
    Whole parts are as thy hand did frame;
    No workman's tool has touched the same.[2]
        A HEART alone
        Is such a stone,
        As nothing but
        Thy power doth cut.
        Wherefore each part
        Of my hard heart
        Meets in this frame,
        To praise thy Name.

5

10

---

1. All of Herbert's poems were published in *The Temple* (1633).
2. See Exodus 20.5, where God tells Moses: "And if thou wilt make me an altar of stone, thou shalt not build it of hewn stone: for if thou lift up thy tool upon it thou has polluted it."
3. See Luke 19.40: "I tell you that, if these should hold their peace, the stones would immediately cry out."

That, if I chance to hold my peace,
These stones to praise thee may not cease.[3]
15   Oh let thy blessed SACRIFICE be mine,
and   sanctify   this   ALTAR   to   be   thine.

Redemption[1]

Having been tenant long to a rich lord,
    Not thriving, I resolvèd to be bold,
    And make a suit unto him, to afford
A new small-rented° lease, and cancel the old.   *cheaper*

5   In heaven at his manor I him sought:
    They told me there, that he was lately gone
    About some land, which he had dearly bought
Long since on earth, to take possession.

I straight returned, and knowing his great birth,
10   Sought him accordingly in great resorts—
    In cities, theaters, gardens, parks, and courts:
At length I heard a ragged noise and mirth

Of thieves and murderers: there I him espied,
Who straight, "Your suit is granted," said, and died.

Easter

Rise heart, thy Lord is risen. Sing his praise
                    Without delays,
Who takes thee by the hand, that thou likewise
                    With him may'st rise:
5   That, as his death calcinèd° thee to dust,   *reduced by fire*
His life may make thee gold, and much more just.

Awake, my lute, and struggle for thy part
                    With all thy art.
The cross taught all wood to resound his name
10   Who bore the same.
His stretchèd sinews taught all strings, what key
Is best to celebrate this most high day.

Consort° both heart and lute, and twist a song   *harmonize*
                    Pleasant and long:
15   Or, since all music is but three parts vied
                    And multiplied,[1]
Oh let thy blessed spirit bear a part,
And make up our defects with his sweet art.

I got me flowers to strew thy way;
20   I got me boughs off many a tree:

1. "Redemption" means deliverance from sin and comes
from the Latin *redimere*, meaning to buy back, to ransom.

1. Since music is increased by three-part harmony.

But thou wast up by break of day,
And brought'st thy sweets along with thee.

The sun arising in the east,
Though he give light, and th' east perfume,
25 If they should offer to contest
With thy arising, they presume.

Can there be any day but this,
Though many suns to shine endeavor?
We count three hundred, but we miss:[2]
30 There is but one, and that one ever.

Easter Wings[1]

Lord, who createdst man in wealth and store,[2]
Though foolishly he lost the same,
Decaying more and more,
Till he became
Most poor:
With thee
Oh let me rise
As larks, harmoniously,
And sing this day thy victories:
Then shall the fall[3] further the flight in me.

My tender age in sorrow did begin
And still with sickness and shame
Thou didst so punish sin,
That I became
Most thin.
With thee
Let me combine,
And feel this day thy victory:
For, if I imp[4] my wing on thine,
Affliction shall advance the flight in me.

5

10

15

20

Man

My God, I heard this day
That none doth build a stately habitation,
But he that means to dwell therein.
What house more stately hath there been,
5 Or can be, than is man? to[1] whose creation
All things are in decay.

For man is everything,
And more; he is a tree, yet bears more[2] fruit;

---

2. We are mistaken in neckoning that there are 300-plus days in the year, since they are all but as one day when compared to the light of the Son (christ) rising.

1. As in the first editions of Herbert, this poem is printed sideways to represent the shape of wings.

2. Plenty.

3. The human frailty of sin, as well as the speaker's own descent into sin and suffering, which Christ redeems through his rising from the dead on Easter.

4. In falconry, to insert feathers in a bird's wing.

1. In comparison to.

2. An alternative reading is "no."

A beast, yet is, or should be more:
10   Reason and speech we only bring.
Parrots may thank us, if they are not mute:
They go upon the score.[3]

Man is all symmetry,
Full of proportions, one limb to another,
15   And all to all the world besides:
Each part may call the farthest, brother;
For head with foot has private amity,
And both with moons and tides.

Nothing hath got so far
20   But man hath caught and kept it as his prey.
His eyes dismount the highest star:
He is in little all the sphere.
Herbs gladly cure our flesh; because that they
Find their acquaintance there.

25   For us the winds do blow,
The earth doth rest, heav'n move, and fountains flow;
Nothing we see, but means our good,
As our delight, or as our treasure.
The whole is, either our cupboard of food,
30   Or cabinet of pleasure.

The stars have us to bed;
Night draws the curtain, which the sun withdraws,
Music and light attend our head.
All things unto our flesh are kind
35   In their descent and being; to our mind
In their ascent and cause.

Each thing is full of duty.
Waters united are our navigation,
Distinguished, our habitation;
40   Below, our drink; above, our meat;
Both are our cleanliness. Hath one such beauty?
Then how are all things neat?

More servants wait on man
Than he'll take notice of: in ev'ry path,
45   He treads down that which doth befriend him,
When sickness makes him pale and wan.
Oh mighty love! Man is one world, and hath
Another to attend him.

Since then, my God, thou hast
50   So brave a palace built, O dwell in it,

3. They are indebted to us.

That it may dwell with thee at last!
    Till then, afford us so much wit,
That, as the world serves us, we may serve thee,
    And both thy servants be.

Jordan (2)

When first my lines of heav'nly joys made mention,
Such was their luster, they did so excel,
That I sought out quaint° words, and trim invention;   *clever*
My thoughts began to burnish,° sprout, and swell,   *spread out*
5   Curling with metaphors a plain intention,
Decking the sense, as if it were to sell.[1]

Thousands of notions in my brain did run,
Off'ring their service, if I were not sped.[2]
I often blotted what I had begun;
10   This was not quick° enough, and that was dead.   *lively*
Nothing could seem too rich to clothe the sun,
Much less those joys which trample on his head.[3]

As flames do work and wind, when they ascend,
So did I weave my self into the sense.
15   But while I bustled, I might hear a friend
Whisper, "How wide° is all this long pretence!   *beside the point*
There is in love a sweetness ready penn'd:
Copy out only that, and save expense."

Time

Meeting with time, "Slack thing," said I,
"Thy scythe is dull; whet it for shame."
"No marvel sir," he did reply,
"If it at length deserve some blame:
5   But where one man would have me grind it,
     Twenty for one too sharp do find it."

"Perhaps some such of old did pass,[1]
Who above all things lov'd this life;
To whom thy scythe a hatchet was,
10   Which now is but a pruning knife.
     Christ's coming hath made man thy debtor,
     Since by thy cutting he grows better.

"And in this blessing thou art blest:
For where thou only wert before
15   An executioner at best,
Thou art a gard'ner now, and more,

---

1. Decorating the meaning as if it were for sale.
2. Dealt with so that I was satisfied.
3. The sun is a symbol for Christ; the sun's head is the Son's head.

1. Herbert is the speaker in stanzas 2, 3, and 4 and in the first two lines of stanza 5.

An usher to convey our souls
        Beyond the utmost stars and poles.

"And this is that makes life so long,
20   While it detains us from our God.
Ev'n pleasures here increase the wrong,
And length of days lengthen the rod.
        Who wants° the place, where God doth dwell,   *lacks*
        Partakes already half of hell.

"Of what strange length must that needs be,
Which ev'n eternity excludes!"
Thus far Time heard me patiently:
Then chafing° said, "This man deludes: *getting angry*
        What do I here before his door?
30   He doth not crave less time, but more."

The Collar

        I struck the board,° and cried, "No more.   *table*
                I will abroad!
What? Shall I ever sigh and pine?
My lines and life are free; free as the road,
5   Loose as the wind, as large as store.°   *abundance*
                Shall I be still in suit?[1]
Have I no harvest but a thorn
To let me blood, and not restore
What I have lost with cordial[2] fruit?
10   Sure there was wine
        Before my sighs did dry it; there was corn
        Before my tears did drown it.
        Is the year only lost to me?
        Have I no bays[3] to crown it?
15   No flowers, no garlands gay? all blasted?
                All wasted?
        Not so, my heart; but there is fruit,
                And thou hast hands.
        Recover all thy sigh-blown age
20   On double pleasures: leave thy cold dispute
Of what is fit and not forsake thy cage,
                Thy rope of sands,
Which petty thoughts have made, and made to thee
        Good cable, to enforce and draw,
25   And be thy law,
        While thou didst wink[4] and wouldst not see.
                        Away! take heed:
                        I will abroad.

1. Engaged in a lawsuit.   3. The poet's laurel wreath.
2. Invigorating to the heart.   4. Shut your eyes to.

Call in thy death's head[5] there: tie up thy fears.
30   He that forbears
      To suit and serve his need,
            Deserves his load."
But as I raved and grew more fierce and wild
           At every word,
35   Me thoughts I heard one calling, *Child!*
           And I replied, *My Lord*.

The Pulley

When God at first made man,
Having a glass of blessings standing by,
"Let us," said he "pour on him all we can:
Let the world's riches, which dispersèd lie,
5   Contract into a span."

So strength first made a way;
Then beauty flowed, then wisdom, honor, pleasure:
When almost all was out, God made a stay,
Perceiving that alone of all his treasure
10   Rest in the bottom lay.[1]

"For if I should," said he,
"Bestow this jewel also on my creature,
He would adore my gifts instead of me,
And rest in Nature, not the God of Nature.
15   So both should losers be.

"Yet let him keep the rest,
But keep them with repining° restlessness: *complaining*
Let him be rich and weary, that at least,
If goodness lead him not, yet weariness
20   May toss him to my breast."

The Forerunners

The harbingers[1] are come: see, see their mark;
White is their color, and behold my head.
But must they have my brain? Must they dispark°   *turn out*
Those sparkling notions, which therein were bred?
5   Must dullness turn me to a clod?
Yet have they left me, "Thou art still my God."

Good men ye be, to leave me my best room,
Ev'n all my heart, and what is lodged there:
I pass not, I, what of the rest become,

---

5. The skull as an emblem of human mortality.
1. "Rest" in the sense of repose, or freedom from distress, and in the sense of remainder, or surplus.

1. Men sent out before a royal train to requisition lodgings by marking the doors with chalk.

10   So "Thou art still my God," be out of fear.[2]
          He will be pleasèd with that ditty;
    And if I please him, I write fine and witty.

    Farewell, sweet phrases, lovely metaphors:
    But will ye leave me thus? when ye before
15   Of stews[3] and brothels only knew the doors,
    Then did I wash you with my tears, and more,
          Brought you to Church well-dressed and clad:
    My God must have my best, ev'n all I had.

    Lovely enchanting language, sugarcane,
20   Honey of roses, whither wilt thou fly?
    Hath some fond lover 'ticed thee to thy bane?
    And wilt thou leave the Church, and love a sty?
          Fie, thou wilt soil thy 'broidered coat,
    And hurt thy self, and him that sings the note.

25   Let foolish lovers, if they will love dung,
    With canvas, not with arras° clothe their shame: *rich tapestry*
    Let Folly speak in her own native tongue.
    True Beauty dwells on high; ours is a flame
          But borrowed thence to light us thither:
30   Beauty and beauteous words should go together.

    Yet if you go, I pass not; take your way.
    For, "Thou art still my God" is all that ye
    Perhaps with more embellishment can say.
    Go, birds of spring; let winter have his fee;
35   Let a bleak paleness chalk the door.
    So all within be livelier than before.

Love (3)

    Love bade me welcome: yet my soul drew back,
          Guilty of dust and sin.
    But quick-eyed Love, observing me grow slack°   *slow, weak*
          From my first entrance in,
5   Drew nearer to me, sweetly questioning,
          If I lacked anything.

    "A guest," I answered, "worthy to be here":
          Love said, "You shall be he."
    "I the unkind, ungrateful? Ah my dear,
10   I cannot look on thee."
    Love took my hand, and smiling did reply,
          "Who made the eyes but I?"

    "Truth Lord, but I marred them; let my shame
          Go where it doth deserve."

2. I don't care about anything except being left with the   3. Public hot bathhouses, brothels.
thought that "Thou art still my God."

15   "And know you not," says Love, "who bore the blame?"
                "My dear, then I will serve."
            "You must sit down," says Love, "and taste my meat."
                So I did sit and eat.[1]

⊷ ⹌⧫⹌ ⊶

Andrew Marvell
1621–1678

Praised by his nephew for "joining the most peculiar graces of wit and learning" and berated by his antagonist Samuel Parker for speaking the language of "boat-swains and cabin boys," Andrew Marvell left little evidence for his biographers. Most of what remains of his verse has been bequeathed to posterity by virtue of a shady banking scheme on his part and an implausible claim by his housekeeper to be "Mrs. Marvell." Though she couldn't remember the date of his death, Mary Palmer tried to prove that she was the poet's wife to get at money that her master had squirrelled away in an account for some bankrupt acquaintances. To further her claim, she saw to it that Marvell's *Miscellaneous Poems* were published in 1681. In his own name, Marvell published only a few occasional poems and a satire attacking religious intolerance and political authoritarianism.

If it is thanks to Mrs. Palmer's rummaging through the poet's papers that such exquisite poems as *To His Coy Mistress* and *The Definition of Love* saw the light of day, it is largely thanks to T. S. Eliot that modern critical attention was turned to Marvell's poetry. The Augustans and Romantics neglected him, and it was not until Eliot that such features of Marvell's verse as Latinate gravity, metaphysical wit, and muscular syntax came to be fully appreciated. For ingenious ambiguity and sheer seductive sensuousness, Marvell is one of the greatest poets of all time.

As tantalizing as the verse is, it leaves little solid evidence of what was a very private life. Marvell grew up in a house surrounded by gardens in the Yorkshire town of Hull on the Humber, where his father was the Anglican rector. There is a story that Marvell once left university for London to flirt with Catholicism, but his father made sure he returned to Cambridge and Protestantism. After his father's death, Marvell traveled in Holland, France, Italy, and Spain (1642–1647). He later tutored Mary Fairfax, daughter of Lord Fairfax of Nun-Appleton House (1650–1652), and taught William Dutton, Cromwell's ward (1653–1656). Initially recommended by Milton to serve as Assistant Latin Secretary in 1653, Marvell was first appointed Latin Secretary to the Council of State in 1657. He was elected Member of Parliament for Hull in 1659, a position he held until 1678. When Charles II restored the monarchy, Marvell interceded on Milton's behalf and made sure his old friend and fellow poet was released from prison. Later in life, Marvell wrote satires criticizing the corruption of the Restoration regime, all but one published anonymously.

Marvell chose to keep his cards close to his chest in the ideologically volatile atmosphere of the Civil War and Restoration. A contemporary biographer remarked that Marvell "was wont to say that, he would not play the good-fellow in any man's company in whose hands he would not trust his life." He did not fight in the Civil War, since he was in Europe at the time, and as he later ambiguously maintained, "the Cause was too good to have been fought for." His strategy in dealing with change involved publicly siding with the faction in power while maintaining politically incorrect friendships and finding himself "inclinable to favor the weaker party"—whether it was a Royalist who had given his life for the King,

---

1. The speaker takes communion, which symbolizes union with God.

such as Lord Hastings, or a Republican who went to prison for his convictions, such as Milton. Marvell wrote poems praising both royalists and revolutionaries. He was nothing if not tolerant.

He was also something of a chameleon, an assumer of numerous poetic personae and disguises. In *Tom May's Death*, Marvell satirized the Royalist turned Republican, here portrayed arriving in heaven drunk. Marvell equivocally praised Cromwell in *An Horatian Ode*, ironically maintaining that it was the Irish whom Cromwell had so brutally massacred who could "best affirm his praises." When he became tutor to Cromwell's ward William Dutton, Marvell wrote poems praising Cromwell in such slavishly glowing terms that the poet was made Latin Secretary to the Council of State.

The last word should go to Marvell, whose choice to translate the following chorus from Seneca's *Thyestes* shows his outlook on the vicissitudes of power:

> Climb at court for me that will
> Giddy favor's slippery hill;
> All I seek is to lie still,
> Settled in some secret nest.
> In calm leisure let me rest,
> And far off the public stage
> Pass away my silent age.
> Thus, when without noise, unknown,
> I have lived out all my span,
> I shall die without a groan,
> An old honest countryman,
> Who exposed to others' eyes,
> Into his own heart ne'er pries.
> Death to him's a strange surprise.

The Coronet[1]

When for the thorns with which I long, too long,
   With many a piercing wound,
     My Savior's head have crowned,
I seek with garlands to redress that wrong:
5   Through every garden, every mead,
I gather flow'rs (my fruits are only flow'rs)
   Dismantling all the fragrant towers°   *tall headdresses*
That once adorned my shepherdess's head.
And now when I have summed up all my store,
10   Thinking (so I myself deceive)
     So rich a chaplet° thence to weave   *wreath*
As never yet the King of Glory wore:
   Alas, I find the serpent old
     That, twining in his speckled breast,[2]
15   About the flowers disguised does fold,°   *wind*
   With wreaths° of fame and interest.   *coils*
Ah, foolish man, that wouldst debase with them,
And mortal glory, Heaven's diadem!

---

1. Marvell's poems were first published in 1681.   2. See Spenser, *Faerie Queene* 1.11.15.

But Thou who only couldst the serpent tame,
20 Either his slippery knots at once untie,
And disentangle all his winding snare:
Or shatter too with him my curious frame:[3]
And let these wither, so that he may die,
Though set with skill and chosen out with care:
25 That they, while Thou on both their spoils[4] dost tread,
May crown thy feet, that could not crown thy head.[5]

Bermudas[1]

Where the remote Bermudas ride
In th' ocean's bosom unespied,
From a small boat, that rowed along,
The list'ning winds received this song.
5   "What should we do but sing his praise
That led us through the watry maze,
Unto an isle so long unknown,[2]
And yet far kinder than our own?
Where he the huge sea-monsters wracks,°   *shipwrecks*
10 That lift the deep upon their backs.
He lands us on a grassy stage,
Safe from the storms, and prelate's[3] rage.
He gave us this eternal spring,
Which here enamels everything;
15 And sends the fowl to us in care,
On daily visits through the air.
He hangs in shades the orange bright,
Like golden lamps in a green night,
And does in the pom'granates close,
20 Jewels more rich than Ormus[4] shows.
He makes the figs our mouths to meet,
And throws the melons at our feet,
But apples° plants of such a price,   *pineapples*
No tree could ever bear them twice.
25 With cedars, chosen by his hand,
From Lebanon, he stores the land,
And makes the hollow seas, that roar,
Proclaim the ambergris[5] on shore.
He cast (of which we rather boast)
30 The gospel's pearl upon our coast,
And in these rocks for us did frame

3. Ingenious structure (the chaplet).
4. Sloughing of the snake's skin; plundering.
5. See Genesis 3.15, for the prophecy that the seed of Eve will bruise the serpent's head.
1. Probably composed sometime after 1653, when Marvell was living in the house of John Oxenbridge, who had made two trips to the Bermudas. Marvell could also have known Captain John Smith's 1624 work *The General His-*

tory of Virginia, New England and the Summer Isles (as the Bermudas were called).
2. Unknown to Europeans; Juan Bermudez first came there in 1515.
3. Clergyman's, bishop's.
4. Hormuz on the Persian Gulf.
5. Musky secretion of the sperm whale that is used in perfumes.

A temple, where to sound his name.
Oh let our voice his praise exalt,
Till it arrive at heaven's vault:
35   Which thence (perhaps) rebounding, may
Echo beyond the Mexique Bay.[6]
Thus sung they, in the English boat,
An holy and a cheerful note,
And all the way, to guide their chime,
40   With falling oars they kept the time.

To His Coy Mistress[1]

Had we but world enough, and time,
This coyness, Lady, were no crime.
We would sit down, and think which way
To walk, and pass our long love's day.
5   Thou by the Indian Ganges' side
Shouldst rubies find: I by the tide
Of Humber would complain.[2] I would
Love you ten years before the flood:
And you should if you please refuse
10   Till the conversion of the Jews.[3]
My vegetable love should grow
Vaster than empires, and more slow.[4]
An hundred years should go to praise
Thine eyes, and on thy forehead gaze.
15   Two hundred to adore each breast:
But thirty thousand to the rest.
An age at least to every part,
And the last age should show your heart.
For Lady you deserve this state;
20   Nor would I love at lower rate.
  But at my back I always hear
Times wingèd chariot hurrying near:
And yonder all before us lie
Deserts of vast eternity.
25   Thy beauty shall no more be found;
Nor, in thy marble vault, shall sound
My echoing song: then worms shall try
That long preserved virginity:
And your quaint honor turn to dust;[5]
30   And into ashes all my lust.
The grave's a fine and private place,

---

6. Gulf of Mexico.
1. A poem on the theme of *carpe diem* ("seize the day") that includes a blazon, or description of the lady from head to toe, and a logical argument: "If ... But ... Therefore."
2. Marvell grew up in Hull on the Humber River.
3. The end of time: the Flood occurred in the distant past, and Christians prophesied that Jews would convert to Christianity at the end of the world.
4. The "vegetable" was characterized only by growth, in contrast to the sensitive, which felt, and the rational, which could reason.
5. "Quaint honor," proud chastity. Note the pun on *queynte* (Middle English), woman's genitals.

But none, I think, do there embrace.
   Now, therefore, while the youthful hue
Sits on thy skin like morning dew,[6]
35   And while thy willing soul transpires
At every pore with instant fires,
Now let us sport us while we may;
And now, like amorous birds of prey,
Rather at once our time devour,
40   Than languish in his slow-chapped° power.   *slowly biting*
Let us roll all our strength, and all
Our sweetness, up into one ball:
And tear our pleasures with rough strife,
Thorough the iron gates of life.[7]
45   Thus, though we cannot make our sun
Stand still, yet we will make him run.[8]

The Definition of Love

My Love is of a birth as rare
As 'tis for object strange and high:
It was begotten by Despair
Upon Impossibility.

5   Magnanimous Despair alone
Could show me so divine a thing,
Where feeble Hope could ne'er have flown
But vainly flapped its tinsel wing.

And yet I quickly might arrive
10   Where my extended soul is fixed,
But Fate does iron wedges drive,
And always crowds itself betwixt.

For Fate with jealous eye does see
Two perfect loves, nor lets them close:°   *unite*
15   Their union would her ruin be,
And her tyrannic power depose.

And therefore her decrees of steel
Us as the distant poles have placed,
(Though Love's whole world on us doth wheel)
20   Not by themselves to be embraced.

Unless the giddy heaven fall,
And earth some new convulsion tear;
And, us to join, the world should all
Be cramped into a planisphere.[1]

---

6. In the 1681 Folio, "dew" reads "glue," and in two manuscripts the rhymes in lines 33 and 34 are "glue" and "dew."
7. One manuscript reads "grates" for "gates."

8. Joshua made the sun stand still in the war against Gibeon (see Joshua 10.12).
1. A two-dimensional map of the globe.

25   As lines (so loves) oblique[2] may well
      Themselves in every angle greet:
          But ours so truly parallel,
          Though infinite, can never meet.

      Therefore the love which us doth bind,
30   But Fate so enviously debars,
          Is the conjunction of the mind,
          And opposition of the stars.[3]

An Horatian Ode Upon Cromwell's Return from Ireland[1]

      The forward youth that would appear
      Must now forsake his muses dear,
          Nor in the shadows sing
          His numbers[2] languishing.
5   'Tis time to leave the books in dust,
      And oil th' unusèd armor's rust:
          Removing from the wall
          The corslet[3] of the hall.
      So restless Cromwell could not cease
10   In the inglorious arts of peace,
          But through adventurous war
          Urgèd his active star.
      And, like the three-forked lightning, first
      Breaking the clouds where it was nursed,
15   Did thorough his own side
          His fiery way divide:[4]
      For 'tis all one to courage high
      The emulous or enemy;
          And with such to enclose
20   Is more than to oppose.
      Then burning through the air he went,
      And palaces and temples rent:
          And Caesar's head at last
          Did through his laurels blast.[5]
25   'Tis madness to resist or blame
      The force of angry heaven's flame:
          And, if we would speak true,
          Much to the man is due,

2. Slanting at an angle other than a right angle, and also veering away from right morals.
3. Conjunction: coming together in the same sign of the zodiac; union. Stars in opposition are diametrically opposed to one another.
1. Cromwell returned from his military campaign in Ireland in May 1650. After General Fairfax resigned as commander of the parliamentary army because he refused to invade Scotland, Cromwell assumed his position and attacked the Scots. This poem was printed in the 1681 edition but then was canceled from printed copies until

1776. The influence of Horace's *Odes* (especially I. 35, 37; IV. 4, 5, 14, 15) surfaces in the poised dignity of the verse and its subtly ambiguous attitude toward power.
2. Conformity to a rhythmical pattern in verse or music.
3. Defensive armor covering the upper body.
4. Cromwell's overtaking his rivals in Parliament is described as an elemental force similar to the "three-forked lightning" of Zeus.
5. Although lightning was thought not to strike the laurel (symbolizing the royal crown), Cromwell had struck down Charles I (Caesar).

Who, from his private gardens, where
30 He lived reservèd and austere,
    As if his highest plot
    To plant the bergamot,[6]
Could by industrious valor climb
To ruin the great work of Time,
35 And cast the kingdom old
    Into another mold.
Though justice against fate complain,
And plead the ancient rights in vain:
    But those do hold or break,
40 As men are strong or weak.
Nature, that hateth emptiness,
Allows of penetration less:[7]
    And therefore must make room
    Where greater spirits come.
45 What field of all the Civil Wars,
Where his were not the deepest scars?
    And Hampton[8] shows what part
    He had of wiser art,
Where, twining subtle fears with hope,
50 He wove a net of such a scope,
    That Charles himself might chase
    To Carisbrooke's narrow case:
That thence the royal actor borne,
The tragic scaffold might adorn;
55 While round the armèd bands
    Did clap their bloody hands.
He nothing common did or mean
Upon that memorable scene:
    But with his keener eye
60 The axe's[9] edge did try;
Nor called the gods with vulgar spite
To vindicate his helpless right,
    But bowed his comely head,
    Down, as upon a bed.
65 This was that memorable hour
Which first assured the forcèd power.
    So when they did design
    The Capitol's first line,
A bleeding head where they begun,
70 Did fright the architects to run;
    And yet in that the State

6. A pear known as the "prince's pear."
7. Nature abhors not only a vacuum but even more so the penetration of one body's space by another body.
8. Hampton Court where Charles I was held captive before his execution in 1649. He had fled to Carisbrooke

Castle on the Isle of Wight, where he was betrayed to the Governor in 1647.
9. Marvell plays on the Latin "*acies*," the sharp edge of a sword, a keen glance, and the vanguard of battle.

Foresaw it's happy fate.[1]
And now the Irish are ashamed
To see themselves in one year tamed:[2]
75   So much one man can do,
          That does both act and know.
They can affirm his praises best,
And have, though overcome, confessed
          How good he is, how just,
80   And fit for highest trust.[3]
Nor yet grown stiffer with command,
But still in the Republic's hand:
          How fit he is to sway
          That can so well obey.[4]
85   He to the commons' feet presents
A kingdom, for his first year's rents:
          And, what he may, forbears
          His fame to make it theirs:
And has his sword and spoils ungirt,
90   To lay them at the public's skirt.
          So when the falcon high
          Falls heavy from the sky,
She, having killed, no more does search,
But on the next green bough to perch;
95   Where, when he first does lure,
          The falconer has her sure.
What may not then our isle presume
While victory his crest does plume!
          What may not others fear
100   If thus he crown each year!
A Caesar he ere long to Gaul,
To Italy an Hannibal,[5]
          And to all states not free
          Shall climactéric° be.   *period of change*
105   The Pict no shelter now shall find
Within his particolored mind;
          But from this valor sad°   *severe*
          Shrink underneath the plaid:[6]
Happy if in the tufted brake
110   The English hunter him mistake;
          Nor lay his hounds in near
          The Caledonian° deer.   *Scottish*

---

1. In digging the foundations of the temple of Jupiter Capitolinum, the excavators found a human's head (*caput*), which was interpreted as prophesying that Rome should be the capitol of the Empire (see Livy, *Annals* I.55.6).
2. From August 1649 to his return to England in May 1650, Cromwell went on a savage military campaign that included the slaughter of Irish civilians.
3. An example of one of the many equivocal statements in this poem; of course, the Irish did not affirm Cromwell's greatness.
4. A saying attributed to the Athenian Solon the lawgiver.
5. Neither Caesar nor Hannibal gave freedom to peoples whose countries they invaded and conquered.
6. Marvell uses "Picts" the ancient name for the Scots, creating a play on *picti* (Latin: painted) and particolored.

But thou the wars' and fortune's son
March indefatigably on;
115 And for the last effect
Still keep thy sword erect:
Besides the force it has to fright
The spirits of the shady night,[7]
The same arts that did gain
120 A power must it maintain.

❈

Katherine Philips
1631–1664

Idolized as the "Matchless Orinda" in her own day, Katherine Philips is now taking her place in the history of English verse after two centuries of neglect. During her lifetime, her work circulated in manuscript among a close network of friends. The first edition of her poems appeared posthumously in 1664. The second edition of 1667 was evidently a commercial success, since it was reprinted in 1669, 1678, and 1710. The next complete edition of her poems did not appear until 1994.

John Keats esteemed Philips's *To Mrs. Mary Aubrey at Parting* as an example of "real feminine Modesty;" today, by contrast, critics praise her poems to women friends as reminiscent of the ancient Greek Sappho's erotic lyrics. By imitating Donne's love lyrics in her poems to women, Philips poetically conceives of these friendships as no less world-changing, no less ennobling and enthralling, than Donne's romantic liaisons. Some of the best poets of her own day were able to appreciate her as a fellow poet rather than as Keats's romanticized ideal woman. Marvell paid tribute to her by subtly alluding to lines of her poetry in one of his greatest poems, *The Garden*. And Henry Vaughan insisted that "No laurel grows, but for [her] brow."

Katherine Philips's work was particularly important for other women writers. Philips's lyric poetry influenced such other early modern women poets as Aphra Behn and Anne Killigrew. Yet it is impossible to pigeonhole Philips as stereotypically feminine. She wrote on public and political themes as well as personal subjects, endowing traditional genres such as the parting poem, the elegy, and the epitaph, with a particular directness and clarity all her own.

Katherine Philips was born in London to a well-to-do Presbyterian family. Her father was a prosperous merchant, and her mother was the daughter of a Fellow of the Royal College of Physicians. Philips's father was wealthy enough to invest two hundred pounds for a thousand acres in Ulster, a scheme that was begun in 1642 by the Puritan Parliament but, ironically, not realized until the Restoration, when we find Katherine in Ireland pursuing lawsuits to obtain this land. As a girl, Katherine attended Mrs. Salmon's Presbyterian School, where she learned to love poetry and began to write verses. In 1646 her widowed mother married Sir Richard Philips, and the family moved to his castle in Wales. Philips herself married Sir Richard's kinsman James Philips, and they lived together for twelve years in the small Welsh town of Cardigan when not in London, where her husband served as a Member of Parliament during the Interregnum.

---

7. There was an ancient tradition of dead spirits being frightened by raised swords (Homer, *Odyssey* 11; Virgil, *Aeneid* 6). The dead spirits referred to here include the dead in the wars in Ireland and England, including the king.

However Presbyterian and Cromwellian were the associations of her family and marriage, she emerged after the Restoration as a complete Anglican. Not only did she write poetry against the regicide, such as *Upon the Double Murder of King Charles*, but she became a favorite author at court. She was encouraged to write poetry by her friend "Poliarchus," Sir Charles Cotterell, Master of Ceremonies in the Court of Charles II, who showed her poems to the royal family. An Anglo-Irish nobleman, the Earl of Orrery, encouraged her to complete a translation of Corneille's *Pompey* and actually produced and had the play printed in Dublin in 1663.

Katherine Philips developed friendships that became the theme of what most critics regard as her best poems. Perhaps the most intense of these friendships was that with Mrs. Anne Owen, the Lucasia of Philips's most passionate poems, several of which echo love poems by Donne. Her friend Sir Edward Dering, whom she called "the Noble Silvander," lamented Katherine Philips's death in recounting the extraordinary accomplishment of both her poetry and her life, which had attempted

> the most generous design . . . to unite all those of her acquaintance which she found worthy or desired to make so (among which later number she was pleased to give me a place) into one society, and by the bands of friendship to make an alliance more firm than what nature, our country or equal education can produce.

Friendship in Emblem
or the Seal,[1]
To My Dearest Lucasia[2]

The hearts thus intermixèd speak
A love that no bold shock can break;
For joined and growing, both in one,
Neither can be disturbed alone.

5   That means a mutual knowledge too;
For what is't either heart can do,
Which by its panting sentinel°   *guard*
It does not to the other tell?

That friendship hearts so much refines,
10   It nothing but itself designs:
The hearts are free from lower ends,
For each point to the other tends.

They flame, 'tis true, and several ways,
But still those flames do so much raise,
15   That while to either they incline
They yet are noble and divine.

From smoke or hurt those flames are free,
From grossness or mortality:
The hearts (like Moses bush presumed)[3]
20   Warmed and enlightened, not consumed.

---

1. A symbolic picture, which appeared with a motto and a poem in such books as Whitney's *Choice of Emblems*. The central emblematic image of this poem is "the compasses" (line 21); another emblem is "those flames" (line 14).
2. Anne Owen, to whom many of Philips's poems are

dedicated, was a neighbor of hers in Wales and a close friend from 1651 until Philips's death.
3. See Exodus 3.2–5 for the burning bush through which the angel of the Lord appeared to and from which God called Moses.

The compasses that stand above
Express this great immortal Love;[4]
For friends, like them, can prove this true,
They are, and yet they are not, two.

25   And in their posture is expressed
Friendship's exalted interest:
Each follows where the other leans,
And what each does, the other means.

    And as when one foot does stand fast,
30   And t'other circles seeks to cast,
The steady part does regulate
And make the wanderer's motion straight:

    So friends are only two in this,
T'reclaim each other when they miss:
35   For whose'er will grossly fall,
Can never be a friend at all.

    And as that useful instrument
For even lines was ever meant;
So friendship from good angels[5] springs,
40   To teach the world heroic things.

    As these are found out in design
To rule and measure every line;
So friendship governs actions best,
Prescribing law to all the rest.

45   And as in nature nothing's set
So just as lines and numbers met;
So compasses for these being made,
Do friendship's harmony persuade.

    And like to them, so friends may own
50   Extension, not division:
Their points, like bodies, separate;
But head, like souls, knows no such fate.

    And as each part so well is knit,
That their embraces ever fit:
55   So friends are such by destiny,
And no third can the place supply.

    There needs no motto to the seal:
But that we may the mine[6] reveal
To the dull eye, it was thought fit

---

4. Compare the image of the compasses here to the "twin compasses" in Donne's A Valediction: Forbidding Mourning, 1680.
5. Guardian spirits, with puns on angels, and *angeli*
(Latin), messengers.
6. A mass of gold, a store of plenty, as well as a pun on the possessive pronoun meaning "my own" and perhaps also on "mind."

60   That friendship only should be writ.

But as there is degrees of bliss,
So there's no friendship meant by this,
But such as will transmit to fame
Lucasia's and Orinda's name.

Upon the Double Murder of King Charles
in Answer to a Libelous Rhyme Made by V. P.[1]

I think not on the state, nor am concerned
Which way soever that great helm is turned,
But as that son whose father's danger nigh
Did force his native dumbness, and untie
5   The fettered organs: so here is a cause
That will excuse the breach of nature's laws.[2]
Silence were now a sin: nay passion now
Wise men themselves for merit would allow.
What noble eye could see, (and careless pass)
10   The dying lion kicked by every ass?
Hath Charles so broke God's laws, he must not have
A quiet crown, nor yet a quiet grave?
Tombs have been sanctuaries; thieves lie here
Secure from all their penalty and fear.
15   Great Charles his double misery was this,
Unfaithful friends, ignoble enemies;
Had any heathen been this prince's foe,
He would have wept to see him injured so.
His title was his crime, they'd reason good
20   To quarrel at the right they had withstood.
He broke God's laws, and therefore he must die,
And what shall then become of thee and I?
Slander must follow treason; but yet stay,
Take not our reason with our king away.
25   Though you have seized upon all our defense,
Yet do not sequester° our common sense.   *confiscate*
But I admire not at this new supply:
No bounds will hold those who at scepters fly.
Christ will be King, but I ne'er understood,
30   His subjects built his kingdom up with blood,
(Except their own) or that he would dispense
With his commands, though for his own defense.
Oh! to what height of horror are they come,
Who dare pull down a crown, tear up a tomb![3]

---

1. Vavasor Powell, a Fifth Monarchist who believed that Christ's second coming was imminent, and an ardent Republican, whose verses on the murder of the king are lost. According to Philips's poem, Powell argued that Charles I had usurped God's power.
2. Breaking the prohibition against women speaking on public affairs. See Margaret Tyler's preface to *The First Part of the Mirror of Princely Deeds*, pages 848–49, for a defense of woman's ability to write about war, traditionally considered only appropriate to male authors.
3. Possibly a reference to the unearthing of the regicides' bodies.

On the Third of September, 1651[1]

As when the glorious magazine of light[2]
Approaches to his canopy of night,
He with new splendor clothes his dying rays,
And double brightness to his beams conveys;
5   As if to brave and check his ending fate,
Puts on his highest looks in 's lowest state;
Dressed in such terror as to make us all
Be anti-Persians,[3] and adore his fall;
Then quits the world, depriving it of day,
10   While every herb and plant does droop away:
So when our gasping English royalty
Perceived her period now was drawing nigh,
She summons her whole strength to give one blow,
To raise her self, or pull down others too.
15   Big with revenge and hope, she now spake more
Of terror than in many months before;
And musters her attendants, or to save
Her from, or wait upon her to the grave:
Yet but enjoyed the miserable fate
20   Of setting majesty, to die in state.
    Unhappy Kings! who cannot keep a throne,
Nor be so fortunate to fall alone!
Their weight sinks others: Pompey could not fly,
But half the world must bear him company;[4]
25   Thus captive Sampson could not life conclude,
Unless attended with a multitude.[5]
Who'd trust to greatness now, whose food is air,
Whose ruin sudden, and whose end despair?
Who would presume upon his glorious birth,
30   Or quarrel for a spacious share of earth,
That sees such diadems° become thus cheap,   *crowns*
And heroes tumble in the common heap?
    O! give me virtue then, which sums up all,
And firmly stands when crowns and scepters fall.

To the Truly Noble, and Obliging Mrs. Anne Owen
(on My First Approaches)[1]

Madam,
As in a triumph conquerors admit
Their meanest captives to attend on it,[2]

1. Cromwell defeated Charles II at the Battle of Worcester on this date.
2. The sun; a magazine is a storehouse for gunpowder.
3. Anti-sun, since the Persians were thought to worship the sun, and anti-monarchist, possibly with reference to Darius I, the Persian king who put down many revolts during his lifetime.
4. Caesar defeated Pompey at the battle of Pharsalus, where 15,000 of Pompey's men were killed. Afterward,

Pompey fled to Egypt, where he was assassinated.
5. The blind Israelite hero Samson tore down the temple at Gaza, thus killing both himself and his enemies (Judges 16).
1. Mrs. Anne Owen of Orielton, Wales, was Philips's close friend and the Lucasia of her poems; she was married to John Owen and was the heiress to the ancient seat of Presaddfed in Anglesey.
2. Here, "triumph" means military victory and the triumphal procession that announced it.

Who, though unworthy, have the power confessed,
And justified the yielding of the rest:
5   So when the busy world (in hope t'excuse
Their own surprise) your conquests do peruse,
And find my name, they will be apt to say
Your charms were blinded, or else thrown away.
There is no honor got in gaining me,
10   Who am a prize not worth your victory.
But this will clear you, that 'tis general
The worst applaud what is admired by all.
But I have plots in't: for the way to be
Secure of fame to all posterity
15   Is to obtain the honor I pursue,
To tell the world I was subdued by you.
And since in you all wonders common are,
Your votaries° may in your virtues share,   *devoted admirers*
While you by noble magic worth impart:
20   She that can conquer, can reclaim a heart.
Of this creation I shall not despair,
Since for your own sake it concerns your care:
For 'tis more honor that the world should know
You made a noble soul, than found it so.

To Mrs. Mary Awbrey at Parting[1]

I have examined, and do find,
    Of all that favor me,
There's none I grieve to leave behind
    But only, only thee.
5   To part with thee I needs must die,
Could parting separate thee and I.

But neither chance nor compliment
    Did element our love;
'Twas sacred sympathy was lent
10   Us from the choir above.
That friendship fortune did create,
Which fears a wound from time or fate.

Our changed and mingled souls are grown
    To such acquaintance now,
15   That if each would assume their own,
    Alas! we know not how.
We have each other so engrossed,
That each is in the union lost.

And thus we can no absence know,

1. Mrs. Mary Awbrey, one of Philips's classmates at Mrs. Salmon's school. Quoting the entire poem, John Keats praises it as an example of "real feminine Modesty" in a letter to J. H. Reynolds of 21 September 1817.

20   Nor shall we be confined;
           Our active souls will daily go
              To learn each other's mind.
           Nay, should we never meet to sense,
           Our souls would hold intelligence.[2]

25   Inspired with a flame divine,
              I scorn to court a stay;
           For from the noble soul of thine
              I can ne'er be away.
           But I shall weep when thou dost grieve;
30   Nor can I die whilst thou dost live.

           By my own temper I shall guess
              At thy felicity,
           And only like my happiness
              Because it pleaseth thee.
35   Our hearts at any time will tell
           If thou, or I, be sick, or well.

           All honor sure I must pretend,
              All that is good or great;
           She that would be Rosania's[3] friend,
40   Must be at least complete.
           If I have any bravery,
           'Tis cause I am so much of thee.

           Thy leiger° soul in me shall lie,   *ambassador*
              And all thy thoughts reveal;
45   Then back again with mine shall fly,
              And thence to me shall steal.
           Thus still to one another tend;
           Such is the sacred name of friend.

           Thus our twin souls in one shall grow,
50   And teach the world new love;
           Redeem the age and sex, and show
              A flame fate dares not move:
           And courting death to be our friend,
           Our lives together too shall end.

55   A dew shall dwell upon our tomb
              Of such a quality,

---

2. A Neoplatonic idea, that the souls would know each other not by physical contact but by spiritual communion. Compare Donne's *A Valediction: Forbidding Mourning*, page 889.

3. Rosania was the poetic name that Philips gave to her friend Mary Awbrey.

That fighting armies, thither come,
    Shall reconciled be.
We'll ask no epitaph, but say
60   Orinda and Rosania.

To My Excellent Lucasia, on Our Friendship
17th. July 1651[1]

I did not live until this time
    Crowned my felicity,
When I could say without a crime,
    I am not thine, but thee.
5   This carcass breathed, and walked, and slept,
    So that the world believed
There was a soul the motions kept;
    But they were all deceived.
For as a watch by art is wound
10   To motion, such was mine:
But never had Orinda found
    A soul till she found thine;
Which now inspires, cures and supplies,
    And guides my darkened breast:
15   For thou art all that I can prize,
    My joy, my life, my rest.
Nor bridegroom's nor crowned conqueror's mirth
    To mine compared can be:
They have but pieces of this earth,
20   I've all the world in thee.
Then let our flame still light and shine,
    (And no bold fear control)
As innocent as our design,
    Immortal as our soul.

1. Philips met her friend Anne Owen (called Lucasia) in 1651.

John Milton
1608–1674

John Milton Surrounded by Muses.
Seventeenth-century engraving.

While writing *Paradise Lost*, Milton would rise early to begin composing poetry; when his secretary arrived late, the old blind man would complain, "I want to be milked." Prodigious in his memory and ingenuity, austere in his frugality and discipline, Milton devoted his life to learning, politics, and art. He put his eloquence at the service of the Puritan Revolution, which brought on the beheading of a king and the institution of a republican commonwealth. Milton entered controversies on divorce and freedom of the press. He showed courage in defending the Puritan republic when he could have lost his life for doing so. Radical, scholar, sage— Milton is above all the great epic poet of England.

Milton's life was marked by a passionate devotion to his religious, political, and artistic ideals, a devotion that ran in his family. Milton's father was said to have been disinherited for his Protestantism by his own father, who was Roman Catholic. When the Civil War broke out, Milton sided with Cromwell while his brother fought for the King. The oldest of three children in a prosperous middle-class family, young John read Virgil, Ovid, and Livy; he especially loved "our sage and serious Spenser," whom he called "a better teacher than Aquinas." Milton later wrote that from the age of twelve he "hardly ever gave up reading for bed till midnight." After his first year at Christ's College, Cambridge, the poet was expelled. While in exile, Milton excoriated academia: "How wretchedly suited that place is to the worshippers of Phoebus! It is disgusting to be constantly subjected to the threats of a rough tutor and to other indignities my spirit cannot endure." Returning to Cambridge, he took his B.A. in 1629 and his M.A. in 1632. On vacations during these years he wrote two of his most musical lyrics, the erotic *L'Allegro* and the Platonic *Il Penseroso*. After leaving university, Milton lived with his parents in Berkshire, where he wrote *Lycidas*, a haunting elegy for the early death of his Cambridge friend Edward King, and *Comus*, a masque for the prominent noble Egerton family at Ludlow Castle.

After his mother's death in 1638, Milton traveled to Europe. He stayed longest in Italy, where his poems were greatly admired by the Florentine literati, who welcomed him into their academies. He later reflected that it was in Italy that he first sensed his vocation as an epic poet, hoping to "perhaps leave something so written, as they should not willingly let it die." Visiting Rome, Naples, and Venice, Milton collected Monteverdi's music, which he would later sing and play. He also met the famed astronomer Galileo, the censorship of whose works Milton would later protest. Concerned about political turmoil in England, he returned home at the outbreak of the Civil War.

From 1640 to 1660, Milton devoted himself to "the cause of real and substantial liberty," by which he meant religious, domestic, and civil liberties. Defending religious liberty, he decried Anglican hierarchy and ritualism—"the new vomited paganism of sensual idolatry"—in a series of tracts, including *Of Reformation* (1641) and *The Reason of Church Government* (1642).

That same year, Milton married seventeen-year-old Mary Powell, who came from a royalist Oxfordshire family. After only a month, she left Milton alone to his "philosophical" life for a more sociable one at home. Troubled by the unhappiness of his marriage, Milton wrote four treatises on divorce, for which he was publicly condemned. He argued that incompatibility should be grounds for divorce, that both husband and wife should be allowed to remarry, and that to maintain otherwise was contrary to reason and scripture. According to his nephew, whom Milton tutored during this time, he was interested in marrying another woman but by 1645 was reunited with Mary. They had a daughter soon afterward. They were joined for several years by Mary's family, who had lost their estate in the Civil War.

Along with "the true conception of marriage," Milton's concept of domestic liberty included "the sound education of children, and freedom of thought and speech." In *Of Education* (1644), opposing strictly vocational instruction, Milton called for the study of languages, rhetoric, poetry, philosophy, and science, the goal of which was "to perform justly, skillfully and magnanimously all of the offices both private and public of peace and war." In *Areopagitica* (1644), Milton fought against censorship before publication but counseled control of printed texts posing political or religious danger. In the 1640s, Milton steered a course midway between the religious conformity demanded by the once-dissenting Presbyterians and the complete separation of church and state advocated by such radicals as Roger Williams, who ultimately went to America in search of greater toleration.

After Oliver Cromwell defeated the Royalists and the King was tried and executed by order of the "Rump" parliament purged of dissenters, Milton wrote *The Tenure of Kings and Magistrates* (1649) to argue that subjects could justly overthrow a tyrant. This tract won him the job of Latin Secretary to the Council of State, handling all correspondence to foreign governments. After the beheading of Charles I in 1649, *Eikon Basilike*, "the Royal Image" appeared, pieced together from the King's papers by his chaplain John Gauden. To counteract sympathy for the King's cause that this work might elicit, Milton wrote a chapter-by-chapter refutation of it entitled *Eikonoklastes*, or *Image-Breaker* (1649). Milton also defended Cromwell's government in three Latin works that were in some measure self-defenses: *First* and *Second Defense of the English People* (1651, 1654) and *Defense of Himself* (1656).

His eyes weakened by the strain of so much writing, Milton went blind. His wife Mary died, leaving three daughters and one son. The boy died soon after, in May 1652. That same month, Milton wrote a sonnet exhorting the Lord General Cromwell to "Help us to save free conscience from the paw of hireling wolves," a reference to ministers who wanted to exclude dissenters from a unified established church. Sounding the cry for liberty again in *Avenge, O Lord these Slaughtered Saints* (1655), Milton lamented the massacre of Italian Protestants. One of Milton's most beautiful and best-known sonnets, *Methought I Saw My Late Espoused Saint*, is said to be about his second wife, Katherine Woodcock, who, after just two years of marriage, died following the birth of her child in 1558.

Cromwell died the same year, and his son Richard's succession to power began a period of political confusion. Milton continued to write political tracts, now even more radical in arguing for universal education and freedom from allegiance to *any* established church and against the abuse of church positions for money. In *De Doctrina Christiana* (written 1655–1660, published 1823), Milton set forth his individualistic theology; he was convinced that no one should be required to attend church and that everyone should interpret scripture in his own way. Committed to the cause of the republic even after the Restoration of Charles II, Milton published *The Ready and Easy Way to Establish a Free Commonwealth* in 1660. Shortly after its appearance, Milton went into hiding. The House of Commons ordered the burning of *Eikonoklastes* and had Milton arrested. He was held in prison for several months. For a time threatened with heavy fines and even death by hanging, Milton was finally released through the aid of his friend Andrew Marvell.

In the aftermath of the Restoration, Milton lived in obscurity and desolation. On the anniversary of Charles I's execution, Cromwell's body was dug up and hanged. More than a few of Milton's friends were either executed or forced into exile. The republic to which he had devoted his life's work had been defeated. Amid this experience of defeat, he worked on *Paradise Lost,* with its themes of fall, damnation, war in heaven, and future redemption for an erring humanity.

While writing his epic, he was much helped by the companionship and housekeeping of his young and amiable third wife Elizabeth Minshull, whom he married in 1663. Young pupils, secretaries, and his daughters read to him in many languages (some of which they didn't understand). The Miltons lived frugally on the money that he had saved from his salary as Latin Secretary (1649–1659). Milton had begun writing *Paradise Lost* by 1658–1659, but he completed only the first edition for publication in 1667. First conceiving of this work as a drama, he had written a soliloquy for the rebellious Lucifer in 1642, which later appeared near the opening of the epic's fourth book. Milton explained that he had put off writing *Paradise Lost* because it was "a work to be raised . . . by devout prayer to that eternal Spirit who can enrich with all utterance and knowledge."

In the last ten years of his life, Milton also wrote *Paradise Regained* (1671), a short epic about the temptation of Christ, based on the model of the Book of Job. Published in the same year was *Samson Agonistes*, a verse tragedy about the Biblical hero, who, betrayed by his lover Delilah, brought down destruction on himself as well as his enemies. In 1673 he published an expanded edition of his *Poems* (1645), to which he added his translations of the Psalms. Finally, in 1674, all twelve books of *Paradise Lost* as we know it were published. That same year, Milton died in a fit of gout and was buried in Saint Giles Cripplegate alongside his father.

Milton combined the traditional erudition of a Renaissance poet with the committed politics of a Puritan radical, both of which contributed to his crowning achievement, *Paradise Lost*. Milton draws on the Bible, Homer, Virgil, and Dante to create his own original sound and story. The vivid sensual imagery of *L'Allegro*, echoing Shakespeare and Spenser, suggests the pastoral idyll of Adam and Eve in Paradise. The intellectual rebelliousness of his prose works inflects the epic's dramatic embodiment of such problems as the origin of evil, sin, and death. Like *Samson Agonistes*, *Paradise Lost* reaches humanity's psychological depths: arrogance, despair, revenge, self-destruction, desire, and self-knowledge. Most of all, *Paradise Lost* dramatizes human wayfaring in the face of the Fall, not unlike Milton's own heroic perseverance in writing his epic after the loss of the world he had helped to create.

Lycidas

In this Monody[1] the Author bewails a learned Friend,[2] unfortunately drowned in his passage from Chester on the Irish Seas, 1637. And by occasion foretells the ruin of our corrupted Clergy then in their height.

Yet once more, O ye laurels, and once more	
Ye myrtles brown, with ivy[3] never sear,°	withered
I come to pluck your berries harsh and crude,°	unripe
And with forced fingers rude,	
5 Shatter your leaves before the mellowing year.	
Bitter constraint, and sad occasion dear,	
Compels me to disturb your season due:	
For Lycidas is dead, dead ere his prime,[4]	
Young Lycidas, and hath not left his peer:	
10 Who would not sing for Lycidas? he knew	
Himself to sing, and build the lofty rhyme.	

1. A mournful song sung by one voice. *Lycidas* is a pastoral elegy, a lament for the dead through language evoking nature and the rural life of shepherds. The first *Idyll* of Theocritus and Virgil's fifth *Eclogue* are classical precedents for *Lycidas*. Shelley's *Adonais* and Arnold's *Thyrsis* are later examples of this form.

2. Edward King, who attended Cambridge when Milton did, drowned 10 August 1637. He had planned to enter the clergy and had written some Latin poems.

3. Laurels . . . myrtles . . . ivy: the leaves used to crown respectively poets, lovers, and scholars.

4. King ("Lycidas") was 25 when he died.

He must not float upon his watery bier
Unwept, and welter° to the parching wind,   *writhe*
Without the meed° of some melodious tear.°   *recompense / elegy*
15   Begin then, sisters of the sacred well,[5]
That from beneath the seat of Jove doth spring,
Begin, and somewhat loudly sweep the string.
Hence with denial vain, and coy excuse,
So may some gentle Muse
20   With lucky words favor my destined urn,
And as he passes turn,
And bid fair peace be to my sable° shrowd.   *black*
For we were nursed upon the self-same hill,
Fed the same flock; by fountain, shade, and rill.
25   Together both, ere the high lawns appeared
Under the opening eyelids of the morn,
We drove a field, and both together heard
What time the grayfly[6] winds her sultry horn,
Battening° our flocks with the fresh dews of night,   *fattening*
30   Oft till the star that rose, at evening, bright,
Toward heaven's descent had sloped his westering wheel.
Meanwhile the rural ditties were not mute,
Tempered to th' oaten flute,
Rough satyrs danced, and fauns with cloven heel,
35   From the glad sound would not be absent long,
And old Damaetas[7] lov'd to hear our song.
    But O the heavy change, now thou art gone,
Now thou art gone, and never must return!
Thee shepherd, thee the woods, and desert caves,
40   With wild thyme and the gadding° vine o'ergrown,   *wandering*
And all their echoes mourn.
The willows, and the hazle copses green,
Shall now no more be seen,
Fanning their joyous leaves to thy soft lays.
45   As killing as the canker° to the rose,   *cankerworm*
Or taint-worm[8] to the weanling herds that graze,
Or frost to flowers, that their gay wardrop wear,
When first the white thorn blows;
Such, Lycidas, thy loss to shepherd's ear.
50   Where were ye nymphs when the remorseless deep
Closed o'er the head of your loved Lycidas?
For neither were ye playing on the steep
Where your old Bards, the famous Druids,° lie,   *pagan Celtic priests*
Nor on the shaggy top of Mona[9] high,
55   Nor yet where Deva spreads her wizard stream:
Ay me, I fondly dream!

5. Sisters: the nine muses; well: Aganippe, on Mount
Helicon, where there was an altar to Jove.
6. Name used to designate various kinds of insects.
7. "Damaetas" is etymologically derived from the Greek

verb meaning "to tame;" thus a tutor is meant.
8. An intestinal worm that can kill newly weaned calves.
9. The island of Anglesey; Deva: the river Dee, viewed as
magical and prophetic by the inhabitants.

Had ye been there—for what could that have done?
What could the Muse[1] herself that Orpheus bore,
The Muse herself for her inchanting son
60   Whom universal nature did lament,
When by the rout that made the hideous roar
His gory visage down the stream was sent,
Down the swift Hebrus to the Lesbian shore.[2]
        Alas! What boots° it with incessant care   *avails*
65   To tend the homely slighted shepherd's trade,
And strictly meditate the thankless Muse,
Were it not better done as others use,
To sport with Amaryllis in the shade,
Or with the tangles of Neaera's hair?[3]
70   Fame is the spur that the clear spirit doth raise
(That last infirmity of noble mind)
To scorn delights, and live laborious days;
But the fair guerdon° when we hope to find,   *reward*
And think to burst out into sudden blaze,
75   Comes the blind Fury[4] with th'abhorred shears,
And slits the thin spun life. "But not the praise,"
Phoebus replied, and touched my trembling ears;[5]
"Fame is no plant that grows on mortal soil,
Nor in the glistering foil[6]
80   Set off to the world, nor in broad rumor lies,
But lives and spreds aloft by those pure eyes,
And perfet witness of all-judging Jove;
As he pronounces lastly on each deed,
Of so much fame in heaven expect thy meed."
85   O Fountain Arethuse, and thou honored flood,
Smooth-sliding Mincius, crowned with vocal reeds,
That strain I heard was of a higher mood.[7]
But now my oat proceeds,
And listens to the herald of the sea
90   That came in Neptune's plea.[8]
He asked the waves, and asked the felon° winds,   *savage*
"What hard mishap hath doomed this gentle swain?"
And questioned every gust of rugged wings
That blows from off each beakèd promontory;
95   They knew not of his story,
And sage Hippotades[9] their answer brings,
That not a blast was from his dungeon strayed,

---

1. Calliope, Orpheus' mother.
2. Ovid, *Metamorphoses*, 11.1–55, relates how Orpheus was torn to pieces by the Thracian women and how his severed head floated down the Hebrus and was carried across to the island of Lesbos.
3. Amaryllis symbolizes erotic poetry (Virgil, *Eclogues* 2.14–15); Neaera: see *Eclogues* 3.3.
4. Atropos, one of the Fates, who cut the thread of life spun by her sisters.
5. Echoing Virgil, *Eclogues* 6.3–4: "the Cynthian plucked my ear and warned me."
6. A reflecting leaf of gold or silver placed under a precious stone.
7. The "higher mood" is the lofty tone of Phoebus' speech. The invocation to the river Arethuse (in Sicily) and the Mincius (Virgil's native river) marks a return to pastoral.
8. The herald Triton came to defend Neptune from blame for King's death.
9. God of winds, son of Hippotes.

The air was calm, and on the level brine,
Sleek Panope[1] with all her sisters played.
100   It was that fatal and perfidious bark,
Built in th' eclipse,° and rigged with curses dark,   *period of evil omen*
That sunk so low that sacred head of thine.
    Next Camus,[2] reverend sire, went footing slow,
His mantle hairy, and his bonnet sedge,[3]
105   Inwrought with figures dim, and on the edge
Like to that sanguine flower inscribed with woe.[4]
"Ah! who hath reft (quoth he) my dearest pledge?"°   *child*
Last came, and last did go,
The Pilot of the Galilean lake,[5]
110   Two massy keys he bore of metals twain,
(The golden opes, the iron shuts amain°).   *vehemently*
He shook his mitered[6] locks, and stern bespake,
"How well could I have spared for thee, young swain,
Enow° of such as for their bellies' sake,   *enough*
115   Creep and intrude, and climb into the fold?[7]
Of other care they little reckoning make,
Than how to scramble at the shearer's feast,
And shove away the worthy bidden guest.
Blind mouths![8] that scarce themselves know how to hold
120   A sheep-hook, or have learned aught else the least
That to the faithfull herdman's art belongs!
What recks it them?[9] What need they? They are sped;°   *satisfied*
And when they list,° their lean and flashy° songs   *please / insipid*
Grate on their scrannel° pipes of wretched straw,   *feeble*
125   The hungry sheep look up, and are not fed,
But swoln with wind, and the rank mist they draw,
Rot inwardly, and foul contagion spread.
Besides what the grim woolf[1] with privy° paw   *secret, hidden*
Daily devours apace, and nothing said,
130   But that two-handed engine at the door,
Stands ready to smite once, and smite no more."[2]
    Return Alpheus,[3] the dread voice is past,
That shrunk thy streams; return Sicilian muse,
And call the vales, and bid them hither cast
135   Their bells, and flowerets of a thousand hues.
Ye valleys low where the mild whispers use,°   *often go*
Of shades and wanton winds, and gushing brooks,

---

1. One of the 50 Nereids (sea nymphs), mentioned by Virgil, *Aeneid* 5.240.
2. The River Cam, representing Cambridge University.
3. "Hairy" refers to the fur of the academic gown; "sedge" is a rushlike plant growing near water.
4. The hyacinth; see Ovid, *Metamorphoses* 10.214–16: "the flower bore the marks AI AI, letters of lamentation."
5. St. Peter bearing the keys of heaven given to him by Christ (Matthew 16.19).
6. Wearing a bishop's headdress.

7. See John 10.1: "He that entereth not by the door into the sheepfold, but climbeth up some other way, the same is a thief and a robber."
8. Milton's charge against the greed of the clergy.
9. What business is it of theirs?
1. The Roman Catholic Church.
2. Indicates that the corrupted clergy will be punished; see 1 Samuel 26.8.
3. The Arcadian hunter, who pursued Arethusa, the nymph he loved, under the sea to Sicily.

On whose fresh lap the swart star[4] sparely looks,
Throw hither all your quaint enameled eyes,
140   That on the green turf suck the honeyed showers,
And purple all the ground with vernal flowers.
Bring the rathe° primrose that forsaken dies,   *early*
The tufted crow-toe,° and pale jessamine,°   *hyacinth / jasmine*
The white pink, and the pansie freaked° with jet,   *adorned*
145   The glowing violet.
The musk-rose, and the well attired woodbine,
With cowslips wan° that hang the pensive head,   *pale*
And every flower that sad embroidery wears:
Bid amaranthus[5] all his beauty shed,
150   And daffadillies fill their cups with tears,
To strew the laureate hearse where Lycid lies.
For so to interpose a little ease,
Let our frail thoughts dally with false surmise.[6]
Ay me! whilst thee the shores, and sounding seas
155   Wash far away, where'er thy bones are hurled,
Whether beyond the stormy Hebrides[7]
Where thou perhaps under the whelming tide
Visit'st the bottom of the monstrous world;
Or whether thou to our moist° vows denied,   *tearful*
160   Sleep'st by the fable of Bellerus[8] old,
Where the great vision of the guarded mount
Looks toward Namancos and Bayona's hold;[9]
Look homeward angel° now, and melt with ruth.°   *Michael / pity*
And, O ye dolphins, waft the haples youth.[1]
165   Weep no more, woeful shepherds weep no more,
For Lycidas your sorrow is not dead,
Sunk though he be beneath the wat'ry floor,
So sinks the day-star° in the ocean bed,   *the sun*
And yet anon repairs his drooping head,
170   And tricks° his beams, and with new spangled ore,°   *arrays / gold*
Flames in the forehead of the morning sky:
So Lycidas sunk low, but mounted high,
Through the dear might of him[2] that walked the waves
Where other groves, and other streams along,
175   With nectar pure his oozy lock's he laves,[3]
And hears the unexpressive nuptial[4] song,
In the blest kingdoms meek of joy and love.
There entertain him all the saints above,
In solemn troops, and sweet societies

---

4. The Dog-star, Sirius. Its rising brings on the dog-days of heat.
5. The eternal flower (see *Paradise Lost*, 3.353–57).
6. The surmise is false since King's body drowned and will have no hearse.
7. Islands off the northwest coast of Scotland.
8. A giant of Bellerium, the Latin name for Land's End.
9. Namancos: an ancient name for a district in northwestern Spain; Bayona: a fortress town about 50 miles south of Cape Finisterre. The two names represent the threat of Spanish Catholicism, against which St. Michael guards England.
1. The dolphin is a symbol of Christ; waft: convey by water.
2. Christ, who walks on the sea in Matthew 14.25–6.
3. The brooks in Eden run with nectar, *Paradise Lost* 4.240; oozy: slimy from contact with the sea.
4. Relating to the marriage of the Lamb, or Christ, to the Church (Revelation 19.7).

180 That sing, and singing in their glory move,
 And wipe the tears for ever from his eyes.[5]
 Now Lycidas the shepherds weep no more;
 Henceforth thou art the genius° of the shore,   *local deity*
 In thy large recompense, and shalt be good
185 To all that wander in that perilous flood.
  Thus sang the uncouth° swain to th' oaks and rills, *unknown*
 While the still morn went out with sandals gray,
 He touched the tender stops of various quills,[6]
 With eager thought warbling his Doric° lay: *pastoral*
190 And now the sun had stretched out all the hills,[7]
 And now was dropped into the western bay;
 At last he rose, and twitch'd his mantle blue:[8]
 Tomorrow to fresh woods, and pastures new.

How Soon Hath Time

 How soon hath time the subtle thief of youth,
  Stol'n on his wing my three and twentieth year![1]
  My hasting days fly on with full career,°   *speed*
  But my late spring no bud or blossom shew'th.
5 Perhaps my semblance° might deceive the truth, *appearance*
  That I to manhood am arrived so near,
  And inward ripeness doth much less appear,
  That some more timely-happy spirits[2] endu'th.° *gives, endows*
 Yet be it less or more, or soon or slow,
10 It shall be still° in strictest measure even,° *always / level with*
  To that same lot, however mean or high,
 Toward which Time leads me, and the will of Heaven;
  All is, if I have grace to use it so,
  As ever in my great task Master's° eye.   *God's*

On the New Forcers of Conscience Under the Long Parliament[1]

 Because you have thrown off your prelate Lord,[2]
  And with stiff vows renounced his liturgy[3]
  To seize the widowed whore Plurality[4]
 From them whose sin ye envied, not abhored,

5. See Revelation 7.17: "God shall wipe away all tears from their eyes"; see also Revelation 21.4.
6. Stops are the finger-holes in the pipes; quills are the hollow reeds of the shepherd's pipe.
7. The setting sun had shone over the hills and lengthened their shadows.
8. Blue is the traditional symbol of hope.
1. Written when Milton was 23, this sonnet was published in 1645.
2. Those individuals of Milton's age who have already

achieved success.
1. Written c. 1646, but printed in 1673.
2. Refers to the abolishment of episcopacy in England in September 1646.
3. The House of Commons forbade the use of the *Book of Common Prayer* in August 1645.
4. The practice of holding more than one living identified with episcopacy but subsequently supported by the Presbyterian system.

5   Dare ye for this adjure° the civil sword   *entreat*
      To force our consciences that Christ set free,[5]
      And ride us with a classic hierarchy[6]
    Taught ye by meer A. S. and Rutherford?[7]
    Men whose life, learning, faith and pure intent
10   Would have been held in high esteem with Paul
      Must now be named and printed heretics
    By shallow Edwards[8] and Scotch what d'ye call:
      But we do hope to find out all your tricks,
      Your plots and packing worse then those of Trent,[9]
15   That so the Parliament
    May with their wholsome and preventive shears
    Clip your phylacteries,[1] though balk° your ears,[2]   *stop short of*
          And succor our just fears,
    When they shall read this clearly in your charge:
20   *New presbyter* is but *old priest* writ large.[3]

To the Lord General Cromwell

    Cromwell, our chief of men, who through a cloud[1]
      Not of war only, but detractions rude,
      Guided by faith and matchless fortitude
      To peace and truth thy glorious way hast ploughed,
5   And on the neck of crownèd Fortune² proud
      Hast reard° God's trophies and his work pursued,   *raised, erected*
      While Darwen stream[3] with blood of Scotts imbrued,°   *stained*
      And Dunbar field[4] resounds thy praises loud,
    And Worester's laureate wreath;[5] yet much remains
10   To conquer still; peace hath her victories
      No less renownd than war, new foes arise
    Threatening to bind our souls with secular chains:
      Help us to save free conscience from the paw
      Of hireling wolves whose gospel is their maw.

---

5. Milton complains of the Westminster Assembly's attempt to impose Presbyterianism by force.
6. Parliament resolved that the English congregations were to be grouped in Presbyteries or "Classes," which could impose rules after the Scottish pattern.
7. A. S.: Dr. Adam Stewart, Scottish Presbyterian controversialist; Rutherford: Samuel Rutherford, author of pamphlets in defense of Presbyterianism.
8. Thomas Edwards, author of *Antapologia*, advocating strict Presbyterianism, and *Gangraena* (1646), which included a denunciation of Milton's views on divorce.
9. Comparing the overwhelming Presbyterian predominance in the Assembly to the anti-protestant Roman Catholic Council of Trent (1545–1563).
1. Small leather boxes containing scriptural texts worn by Jews as a mark of obedience. Christ in Matthew 23.5 uses the phrase "make broad their phylacteries" in the sense "vaunt their own righteousness."
2. William Prynne, who had attacked one of the Bishops

in print, actually did have both of his ears cut off. Milton's manuscript of this poem contains the line: "Crop ye as close as marginal P—'s ears."
3. "Priest" is etymologically a contracted form of Latin "presbyter" (an elder). The Presbyterians now appeared as dictatorial as the bishops had been.
1. In Virgil, Aeneas prevails through the "war-cloud" of battle as he conquers Italy (*Aeneid* 10.809).
2. Refers to Charles I and to his successor, whose army Cromwell defeated at Worcester after he had been crowned king in Scotland on 1 January 1651. This poem was written in 1652 but not published until 1694.
3. Near Preston, where, on 17–19 August 1648, Cromwell routed the invading Scottish army.
4. At Dunbar, on 3 September 1650, after being virtually surrounded, Cromwell routed the Scottish army.
5. At Worcester, on 3 September 1651, Cromwell virtually annihilated Charles II's Royalist Scottish army.

On the Late Massacre in Piedmont[1]

Avenge O Lord thy slaughtered saints, whose bones
    Lie scattered on the Alpine mountains cold,[2]
    Even them who kept thy truth so pure of old
    When all our Fathers worshiped stocks and stones,[3]
5   Forget not: in thy book[4] record their groans
    Who were thy sheep and in their ancient fold
    Slain by the bloody Piemontese that rolled
    Mother with infant down the rocks. Their moans
The vales redoubled to the hills, and they
10   To Heaven. Their martyred blood and ashes sow
    O'er all th' Italian fields where still doth sway
The triple tyrant:[5] that from these may grow
    A hundred-fold,[6] who having learnt thy way
    Early may fly the Babylonian[7] woe.

When I Consider How My Light Is Spent[1]

When I consider how my light is spent,
    Ere half my days, in this dark world and wide,
    And that one talent which is death to hide,[2]
    Lodged with me useless, though my soul more bent
5   To serve therewith my Maker, and present
    My true account, lest he returning chide,
    Doth God exact day-labor, light denied,
    I fondly° ask; but Patience to prevent   *foolishly*
That murmur, soon replies, "God doth not need
10   Either man's work or his own gifts,[3] who best
    Bear his mild yoke,[4] they serve him best, his state
Is kingly. Thousands at his bidding speed
    And post o'er land and ocean without rest:
    They also serve who only stand and wait."

Methought I Saw My Late Espoused Saint[1]

Methought I saw my late espousèd saint°   *soul in heaven*
    Brought to me like Alcestis[2] from the grave,
    Whom Jove's great son to her glad husband gave,

1. The poem protests the persecution of Protestants in
northern Italy in 1655.
2. See Luke 18.7: "shall not God avenge his own elect,"
and Psalms 141.7: "Our bones are scattered at the grave's
mouth."
3. Gods of wood and stone.
4. See Revelation 5.1: "I saw in the right hand of him
that sat on the throne a book."
5. The Pope with his three-tiered crown.
6. Lines 10–13 combine the parable of the sower
(Matthew 13.3–23) with the legend of Cadmus, in which
an army of warriors sprouts from the sowing of a dragon's
teeth.
7. The Puritans used the corrupt Babylon of Revelation

as a symbol for the Roman Catholic Church.
1. Probably written around 1652, as Milton's blindness
became complete.
2. In the parable of the talents, Jesus tells of a servant
who is given a talent (a large sum of money) to keep for
his master. He buries the money; his master condemns
him for not having invested it wisely. Matthew 25.14–30.
3. See Job 22.2.
4. See Matthew 11.30: "My yoke is easy."
1. The date of composition is placed at 1658; the poem
appears as the last sonnet in the 1673 edition.
2. In Euripides' *Alcestis*, she gives her life for her husband
Admetus, but Hercules ("Jove's great son") wrestles with
death and brings her back from the grave.

Rescued from death by force though pale and faint.
5   Mine as whom washed from spot of child-bed taint,
       Purification in the old Law[3] did save,
       And such, as yet once more I trust to have
       Full sight of her in Heaven without restraint,
       Came vested all in white, pure as her mind:
10   Her face was veiled, yet to my fancied sight,
       Love, sweetness, goodness, in her person shined
       So clear, as in no face with more delight,
       But O, as to embrace me she enclined,
       I waked, she fled, and day brought back my night.[4]

PARADISE LOST

PARADISE LOST *Paradise Lost* is about devastating loss attended by redemption. The reader's knowledge of the Fall creates a sense of tragic inevitability. And Satan, no less than Adam and Eve, appears in all the psychological complexity and verbal grandeur of a tragic hero. Indeed, there is even a manuscript in which Milton outlined the story as a tragedy. In that version, "Lucifer's contriving Adam's ruin" is Act 3. Following epic tradition, Milton places this part of the action at the forefront of his poem, beginning *in medias res*.

So powerful is Milton's opening portrayal of Satan that the Romantic poets thought Satan was the hero of the poem. Focusing on the first two books, the romantic reading sees him as a dynamic rebel. From a Renaissance point of view, Satan is more like an Elizabethan hero-villain, with his many soliloquies and his tortured psychology of brilliance twisted toward evil. Only in Book 9, however, does Milton say, "I now must change these notes to tragic," thereby signaling that he is about to narrate the fall of Adam and Eve. From this point on, the poem follows Adam and Eve's tragic movement from sin to despair to the recognition of sin and the need for repentance. Adam and Eve's learning through suffering and the prophecy of the Son's redemption of sin make this a story of gain as well as loss, on the order of Aeschylean tragedy.

Like all epics, *Paradise Lost* is encyclopedic, combining many different genres. To read this poem is to have an education in everything from literary history to astronomy. Milton draws on a vast wealth of reading, with the Bible as his main source—not only Genesis, but also Exodus, the Prophets, Revelation, Saint Paul, and especially the Psalms, which he had translated. Milton also makes great use of biblical commentary from rabbinical, patristic, and contemporary sources. Early on, Milton had envisaged a poem about the Arthurian legend, and his choice of the nonmartial, seemingly unheroic biblical story of Adam and Eve marks a bold departure from epic tradition. While Spenser's *Faerie Queene* is Milton's most important vernacular model, among epic poets his closest affinity is with Virgil and Dante, both of whom had written of the underworld; Dante especially devoted himself to humanity's free choice of sin. Like Dante, Milton creates his poem as a microcosm of the natural universe. His ideal vision of the world before the Fall is one where day and night are equal and the sun is always in the same sign of the zodiac, an image that embodies in poetic astronomy the world of simplicity and perfection that humans have lost through sin. Milton does not choose between the earth-centered Ptolemaic and the heliocentric Copernican systems but presents both as alternative explanations for the order of the universe.

3. According to Leviticus 12.4–8, after bearing a female child, a woman shall be unclean "two weeks, as in her separation: and she shall continue in the blood of her purifying threescore and six days" (i.e., during this period "she shall touch no hallowed thing, nor come into the sanctuary"). Some critics construe this line as evidence that the sonnet is about the death of Milton's second wife Katherine Woodcock, who died three months after childbirth in 1658.
4. In Virgil, Aeneas sees the ghost of his wife Creusa amid the ruins of Troy; when he tries to embrace her, "she withdrew into thin air ... most like a winged dream" (*Aeneid* 2.791–794).

Although we know nothing about the order in which the parts of the poem were composed, we do know that Milton typically composed at night or in the early morning. Sometimes he lay awake unable to write a line; at others he was seized "with a certain impetus and *oestro*" [frenzy]. He would dictate forty lines from memory and then reduce them to half that number. According to his nephew, the poem was written from 1658 to 1663.

The one extant manuscript of the poem, which contains the first book, reveals that Milton revised for punctuation and spelling. There were two editions in Milton's lifetime, both printed by Samuel Simmons. The first edition, *Paradise Lost: A poem in ten books,* was printed in six different issues in 1667, 1668, and 1669. From the fourth issue of the poem on, such paratexts as "The Printer to Reader," "The Argument" (which stood altogether), and Milton's note on the verse appear. With the second octave edition of 1674, Milton divided Books 7 and 10 into two books each to create twelve books in all. Prefaced by dedicatory Latin verses, one of which was by his old friend Andrew Marvell, this 1674 edition, which appeared in the year of Milton's death, is the basis for the present text.

from **Paradise Lost**[1]
Book 1
The Argument

This first Book proposes, first in brief, the whole Subject, *Man's disobedience, and the loss thereupon of Paradise wherein he was plac't:* Then touches *the prime cause of his fall, the Serpent, or rather* Satan *in the Serpent; who revolting from God, and drawing to his side many Legions of Angels, was by the command of God driven out of Heaven with all his Crew into the great Deep.* Which action past over, the Poem hastes into the midst of things,[2] presenting *Satan with his Angels now fallen into Hell,* describ'd here, *not in the Centre* (for Heaven and Earth may be suppos'd as yet not made, certainly not yet accurst) *but in a place of utter darkness, fitliest call'd Chaos: Here Satan with his Angels lying on the burning Lake, thunder-struck and astonisht, after a certain space recovers, as from confusion, calls up him who next in Order and Dignity lay by him; they confer of thir miserable fall. Satan awakens all his Legions, who lay till then in the same manner confounded; They rise, thir Numbers, array of Battle, thir chief Leaders nam'd, according to the Idols known afterwards in Canaan and the Countries adjoining. To these Satan directs his Speech, comforts them with hope yet of regaining Heaven but tells them lastly of a new World and new kind of Creature to be created, according to an ancient Prophecy or report in Heaven;* for that Angels were long before this visible Creation, was the opinion of many ancient Fathers. *To find out the truth of this Prophecy, and what to determine thereon he refers to a full Council. What his Associates thence attempt.* Pandemonium *the Palace of Satan rises, suddenly built out of the Deep: The infernal Peers there sit in Council.*

> Of Man's First Disobedience, and the Fruit
> Of that Forbidden Tree, whose mortal[3] taste
> Brought Death into the World, and all our woe,[4]
> With loss of *Eden,* till one greater Man[5]

1. Our text is taken from Merritt Y. Hughes, ed., *John Milton Complete Poems and Major Prose,* and the notes are adapted from John Carry and Alastair Fowler, ed., *The Poems of John Milton.*
2. Following Horace's rule that the epic should plunge "*in medias res.*"
3. "Death-bringing" (Latin *mortalis*) but also "to mortals."

4. This definition of the first sin follows Calvin's Catechism.
5. Christ, in Pauline theology the second Adam (see Romans 5.19). The people and events referred to in these lines have a typological connection, i.e., the Christian interpretation of the Old Testament as a prefiguration of the New.

5   Restore us, and regain the blissful Seat,
        Sing Heav'nly Muse,[6] that on the secret top
        Of *Oreb*, or of *Sinai*, didst inspire
        That Shepherd, who first taught the chosen Seed,[7]
        In the Beginning how the Heav'ns and Earth
10   Rose out of *Chaos*: Or if *Sion* Hill[8]
        Delight thee more, and *Siloa's* Brook[9] that flow'd
        Fast° by the Oracle of God; I thence   *close*
        Invoke thy aid to my advent'rous Song,
        That with no middle flight intends to soar
15   Above th' *Aonian* Mount,[1] while it pursues
        Things unattempted yet in Prose or Rhyme.[2]
        And chiefly Thou O Spirit, that dost prefer
        Before all Temples th' upright heart and pure,[3]
        Instruct me, for Thou know'st; Thou from the first
20   Wast present, and with mighty wings outspread
        Dove-like satst brooding on the vast Abyss
        And mad'st it pregnant:[4] What in me is dark
        Illumine, what is low raise and support;
        That to the highth of this great Argument°   *theme*
25   I may assert Eternal Providence,
        And justify[5] the ways of God to men.
            Say first, for Heav'n hides nothing from thy view
        Nor the deep Tract of Hell, say first what cause
        Mov'd our Grand[6] Parents in that happy State,
30   Favor'd of Heav'n so highly, to fall off
        From thir Creator, and transgress his Will
        For° one restraint, Lords of the World besides?°   *because of / otherwise*
        Who first seduc'd them to that foul revolt?
        Th' infernal Serpent;[7] hee it was, whose guile
35   Stirr'd up with Envy and Revenge, deceiv'd
        The Mother of Mankind; what time his Pride
        Had cast him out from Heav'n, with all his Host
        Of Rebel Angels, by whose aid aspiring
        To set himself in Glory above his Peers,

6. Rhetorically, lines 1–49 are the *invocatio*, consisting of an address to the Muse, and the *principium* that states the whole scope of the poem's action. The "Heavenly Muse," later addressed as the muse of astronomy Urania (7.1), is here identified with the Holy Spirit of the Bible, which inspires Moses.

7. The "Shepherd" is Moses, who was granted the vision of the burning bush on Mount Oreb (Exodus 3) and received the Law, either on Mount Oreb (Deuteronomy 4.10) or on its lower part, Mount Sinai (Exodus 19.20). Moses, the first Jewish writer, taught "the chosen seed," the children of Israel, about the beginning of the world in Genesis.

8. The sanctuary, a place of ceremonial song but also (Isaiah 2.3) of oracular pronouncements.

9. A spring immediately west of Mount Zion and beside Calvary, often used as a symbol of the operation of the Holy Ghost.

1. Helicon, sacred to the Muses.

2. Ironically translating Ariosto's boast in the invocation to *Orlando Furioso*.

3. The Spirit is the voice of God, which inspired the Hebrew prophets.

4. Identifying the Spirit present at the creation (Genesis 1.2) with the Spirit in the form of a dove that descended on Jesus at the beginning of his ministry (John 1.32). Vast: large; deserted (Latin *vastus*).

5. Does not mean merely "demonstrate logically" but has its biblical meaning and implies spiritual rather than rational understanding.

6. Implies not only greatness, but also inclusiveness of generality or parentage.

7. "That old serpent, called the Devil, and Satan" (Revelation 12.9) both because Satan entered the body of a serpent to tempt Eve and because his nature is guileful and dangerous to humans.

40   He trusted to have equall'd the most High,[8]
     If he oppos'd; and with ambitious aim
     Against the Throne and Monarchy of God
     Rais'd impious War in Heav'n and Battle proud
     With vain attempt. Him the Almighty Power
45   Hurl'd headlong flaming from th' Ethereal Sky[9]
     With hideous ruin and combustion down
     To bottomless perdition, there to dwell
     In Adamantine Chains[1] and penal Fire,
     Who durst defy th' Omnipotent to Arms.
50   Nine times the Space that measures Day and Night[2]
     To mortal men, hee with his horrid crew
     Lay vanquisht, rolling in the fiery Gulf
     Confounded though immortal: But his doom
     Reserv'd him to more wrath; for now the thought
55   Both of lost happiness and lasting pain
     Torments him; round he throws his baleful° eyes   *evil, suffering*
     That witness'd huge affliction and dismay
     Mixt with obdúrate° pride and steadfast hate: *unyielding*
     At once as far as Angels' ken° he views   *power of vision*
60   The dismal° Situation waste and wild,   *dreadful, sinister*
     A Dungeon horrible, on all sides round
     As one great Furnace flam'd, yet from those flames
     No light, but rather darkness visible
     Serv'd only to discover sights of woe,[3]
65   Regions of sorrow, doleful shades, where peace
     And rest can never dwell, hope never comes
     That comes to all;[4] but torture without end
     Still urges,° and a fiery Deluge, fed   *presses*
     With ever-burning Sulphur unconsum'd:
70   Such place Eternal Justice had prepar'd
     For those rebellious, here thir Prison ordained
     In utter° darkness, and thir portion set   *complete, outer*
     As far remov'd from God and light of Heav'n
     As from the Center thrice to th' utmost Pole.[5]
75   O how unlike the place from whence they fell!
     There the companions of his fall, o'erwhelm'd
     With Floods and Whirlwinds of tempestuous fire,

8. Satan's crime was not his aspiring "above his peers" but aspiring "To set himself in [divine] Glory." Numerous verbal echoes relate lines 40–48 to the biblical accounts of the fall and binding of Lucifer, in 2 Peter 2.4, Revelation 20.1–2, and Isaiah 14.12–15: "Thou hast said . . . I will exalt my throne above the stars of God . . . I will be like the most High. Yet thou shalt be brought down to hell."
9. Mingling an allusion to Luke 10.18, "I beheld Satan as lightning fall from heaven," with one to Homer, *Iliad* 1.591, Hephaistos "hurled from the ethereal threshold."
1. 2 Peter 2.4; "God spared not the angels that sinned, but . . . delivered them into chains of darkness."
2. The devils fall for the same number of days that the Titans fall from heaven when overthrown by the Olympian gods (see Hesiod, *Theogony* 664–735).
3. See the account of the land of the dead in Job 10.22: "the light is as darkness."
4. The phrase echoes Dante's *Inferno:* III.9 "All hope abandon, ye who enter here."
5. Milton refers to the Ptolemaic universe in which the earth is at the center of ten concentric spheres. Milton draws attention to the numerical proportion, heaven-earth:earth-hell—i.e., earth divides the interval between heaven and hell in the proportion that Neoplatonists believed should be maintained between reason and concupiscence.

He soon discerns, and welt'ring by his side
One next himself in power, and next in crime,
80   Long after known in *Palestine*, and nam'd
Beëlzebub.[6] To whom th' Arch-Enemy,
And thence in Heav'n call'd Satan,[7] with bold words
Breaking the horrid silence thus began.[8]
    If thou beest hee; But O how fall'n! how chang'd
85   From him, who in the happy Realms of Light
Cloth'd with transcendent brightness didst outshine
Myriads though bright:[9] If he whom mutual league,
United thoughts and counsels, equal hope,
And hazard in the Glorious Enterprise,
90   Join'd with me once, now misery hath join'd
In equal ruin: into what Pit thou seest
From what highth fall'n, so much the stronger prov'd
He with his Thunder: and till then who knew
The force of those dire Arms? yet not for those,
95   Nor what the Potent Victor in his rage
Can else inflict, do I repent or change,
Though chang'd in outward luster; that fixt mind
And high disdain, from sense of injur'd merit,
That with the mightiest rais'd me to contend,
100   And to the fierce contention brought along
Innumerable force of Spirits arm'd
That durst dislike his reign, and mee preferring,
His utmost power with adverse power oppos'd
In dubious Battle on the Plains of Heav'n,
105   And shook his throne.[1] What though the field be lost?
All is not lost; the unconquerable Will,
And study° of revenge, immortal hate,   *pursuit*
And courage never to submit or yield:
And what is else not to be overcome?
110   That Glory[2] never shall his wrath or might
Extort from me. To bow and sue for grace
With suppliant knee, and deify his power
Who from the terror of this Arm so late
Doubted° his Empire, that were low indeed,   *feared for*
115   That were an ignominy and shame beneath
This downfall; since by Fate the strength of Gods
And this Empyreal substance cannot fail,[3]

---

6. Hebrew, "Lord of the flies"; Matthew 12.24, "the prince of the devils."
7. Hebrew, "enemy." After his rebellion, Satan's "former name" (Lucifer) was no longer used (5.658).
8. Rhetorically, the opening of the action proper. The 41-line speech beginning here, the first speech in the book, exactly balances the last, which also is spoken by Satan and also consists of 41 lines (1.622–62).
9. The break in grammatical concord (between "him" and "didst") reflects Satan's doubt whether Beelzebub

is present and so whether second-person forms are appropriate.
1. The Son's chariot, not Satan's armies, shakes heaven to its foundations, as we learn in Book 6. Throughout the present passage, Satan sees himself as the hero of a pagan epic.
2. Either "the glory of overcoming me" or "my glory of will."
3. Implying not only that as angels they are immortal, but also that the continuance of their strength is assured by fate.

Since through experience of this great event
In Arms not worse, in foresight much advanc't,
120   We may with more successful hope resolve
To wage by force or guile eternal War
Irreconcilable to our grand Foe,
Who now triúmphs, and in th' excess of joy
Sole reigning holds the Tyranny of Heav'n.[4]
125   So spake th' Apostate Angel, though in pain,
Vaunting aloud, but rackt with deep despair:
And him thus answer'd soon his bold Compeer.°   comrade
O Prince, O Chief of many Throned Powers,
That led th' imbattl'd Seraphim[5] to War
130   Under thy conduct, and in dreadful deeds
Fearless, endanger'd Heav'n's perpetual King;
And put to proof his high Supremacy,
Whether upheld by strength, or Chance, or Fate;[6]
Too well I see and rue the dire event,
135   That with sad overthrow and foul defeat
Hath lost us Heav'n, and all this mighty Host
In horrible destruction laid thus low,
As far as Gods and Heav'nly Essences
Can perish: for the mind and spirit remains
140   Invincible, and vigor soon returns,
Though all our Glory extinct, and happy state
Here swallow'd up in endless misery.
But what if he our Conqueror (whom I now
Of force° believe Almighty, since no less   necessarily
145   Than such could have o'erpow'rd such force as ours)
Have left us this our spirit and strength entire
Strongly to suffer and support our pains,
That we may so suffice° his vengeful ire,   satisfy
Or do him mightier service as his thralls
150   By right of War, whate'er his business be
Here in the heart of Hell to work in Fire,
Or do his Errands in the gloomy Deep;
What can it then avail though yet we feel
Strength undiminisht, or eternal being
155   To undergo eternal punishment?[7]
Whereto with speedy words th' Arch-fiend repli'd.
Fall'n Cherub, to be weak is miserable
Doing or Suffering: but of this be sure,
To do aught good never will be our task,
160   But ever to do ill our sole delight,
As being the contrary to his high will

---

4. An obvious instance of the devil's bias.
5. The traditional nine orders of angels are seraphim,
cherubim, thrones, dominions, virtues, powers, principal-
ities, archangels, and angels, but Milton does not use
these terms systematically.

6. The main powers recognized in the devils' ideology.
God's power rests on a quality that does not occur to
Beelzebub: goodness.
7. Existing eternally, merely so that our punishment may
also be eternal.

Whom we resist.[8] If then his Providence
Out of our evil seek to bring forth good,
Our labor must be to pervert that end,
165   And out of good still to find means of evil;
Which oft-times may succeed, so as perhaps
Shall grieve him, if I fail not, and disturb
His inmost counsels from thir destin'd aim.
But see the angry Victor hath recall'd
170   His Ministers of vengeance and pursuit
Back to the Gates of Heav'n: the Sulphurous Hail
Shot after us in storm, o'erblown hath laid°   *subdued*
The fiery Surge, that from the Precipice
Of Heav'n receiv'd us falling, and the Thunder,
175   Wing'd with red Lightning and impetuous rage,
Perhaps hath spent his shafts, and ceases now
To bellow through the vast and boundless Deep.
Let us not slip° th' occasion, whether scorn,   *lose*
Or satiate fury yield it from our Foe.
180   Seest thou yon dreary Plain, forlorn and wild,
The seat of desolation, void of light,
Save what the glimmering of these livid flames
Casts pale and dreadful? Thither let us tend
From off the tossing of these fiery waves,
185   There rest, if any rest can harbor there,
And reassembling our afflicted° Powers,   *downcast*
Consult how we may henceforth most offend°   *harm*
Our Enemy, our own loss how repair,
How overcome this dire Calamity,
190   What reinforcement we may gain from Hope,
If not what resolution from despair.
     Thus Satan talking to his nearest Mate
With Head up-lift above the wave, and Eyes
That sparkling blaz'd, his other Parts besides
195   Prone on the Flood, extended long and large
Lay floating many a rood,° in bulk as huge   *six to eight yards*
As whom the Fables name of monstrous size,
Titanian, or *Earth-born*, that warr'd on *Jove*,
Briareos or *Typhon*,[9] whom the Den
200   By ancient *Tarsus*[1] held, or that Sea-beast
Leviathan,[2] which God of all his works
Created hugest that swim th' Ocean stream:

8. This fundamental disobedience and disorientation make Satan's heroic virtue into the corresponding excess of vice. Lines 163–65 look forward to 12.470–78 and Adam's wonder at the astonishing reversal whereby God will turn the Fall into an occasion for good.
9. The serpent-legged *Briareos* was a Titan, the serpent-headed *Typhon* (Typhoeus) a Giant. Each was a son of Earth; each fought against Jupiter; and each was eventually confined beneath Aetna (see lines 232–37). Typhon

was so powerful that when he first made war on the Olympians, they had to resort to metamorphoses to escape (Ovid, *Metamorphoses* 5.325–31 and 346–58).
1. The biblical Tarsus was the capital of Cilicia, and both Pindar and Aeschylus describe Typhon's habitat as a Cilician cave or "den."
2. The monster of Job 41, identified in Isaiah's prophecy of judgment as "the crooked serpent" (Isaiah 27.1) but also sometimes thought of as a whale.

Him haply slumb'ring on the *Norway* foam
The Pilot of some small night-founder'd° Skiff,   *sunk in night*
205   Deeming some Island, oft, as Seamen tell,
With fixed Anchor in his scaly rind
Moors by his side under the Lee, while Night
Invests° the Sea, and wished Morn delays: *wraps*
So stretcht out huge in length the Arch-fiend lay
210   Chain'd on the burning Lake, nor ever thence
Had ris'n or heav'd his head, but that the will
And high permission of all-ruling Heaven
Left him at large to his own dark designs,
That with reiterated crimes he might
215   Heap on himself damnation, while he sought
Evil to others, and enrag'd might see
How all his malice serv'd but to bring forth
Infinite goodness, grace and mercy shown
On Man by him seduc't, but on himself
220   Treble confusion, wrath and vengeance pour'd.
Forthwith upright he rears from off the Pool
His mighty Stature; on each hand the flames
Driv'n backward slope thir pointing spires, and roll'd
In billows, leave i' th' midst a horrid° Vale.   *bristling*
225   Then with expanded wings he steers his flight
Aloft, incumbent[3] on the dusky Air
That felt unusual weight, till on dry Land
He lights, if it were Land that ever burn'd
With solid, as the Lake with liquid fire
230   And such appear'd in hue;[4] as when the force
Of subterranean wind transports a Hill
Torn from *Pelorus*,[5] or the shatter'd side
Of thund'ring *Etna*, whose combustible
And fuell'd entrails thence conceiving Fire,
235   Sublim'd[6] with Mineral fury,[7] aid the Winds,
And leave a singed bottom all involv'd°   *wreathed*
With stench and smoke: Such resting found the sole
Of unblest feet. Him follow'd his next Mate,
Both glorying to have scap't the *Stygian*[8] flood
240   As Gods, and by thir own recover'd strength,
Not by the sufferance of supernal Power.
        Is this the Region, this the Soil, the Clime,
Said then the lost Arch-Angel, this the seat
That we must change° for Heav'n, this mournful gloom   *exchange*
245   For that celestial light? Be it so, since he
Who now is Sovran can dispose and bid
What shall be right: fardest° from him is best   *farthest*

---

3. Pressing with his weight.
4. In the 17th century, "hue" referred to surface appearance and texture as well as color.
5. Pelorus and Aetna are volcanic mountains in Sicily.

6. Converted directly from solid to vapor by volcanic heat in such a way as to resolidify on cooling.
7. Disorder of minerals, or subterranean disorder.
8. Of the River Styx—i.e., hellish.

Whom reason hath equall'd, force hath made supreme
Above his equals. Farewell happy Fields
250   Where Joy for ever dwells: Hail horrors, hail
Infernal world, and thou profoundest Hell
Receive thy new Possessor: One who brings
A mind not to be chang'd by Place or Time.
The mind is its own place, and in itself
255   Can make a Heav'n of Hell, a Hell of Heav'n.[9]
What matter where, if I be still the same,
And what I should be, all but less than hee
Whom Thunder hath made greater? Here at least
We shall be free; th' Almighty hath not built
260   Here for his envy, will not drive us hence:
Here we may reign secure, and in my choice
To reign is worth ambition[1] though in Hell:
Better to reign in Hell, than serve in Heav'n.
But wherefore let we then our faithful friends,
265   Th' associates and copartners of our loss
Lie thus astonisht on th' oblivious Pool,[2]
And call them not to share with us their part
In this unhappy Mansion: or once more
With rallied Arms to try what may be yet
270   Regain'd in Heav'n, or what more lost in Hell?
     So *Satan* spake, and him *Beëlzebub*
Thus answer'd. Leader of those Armies bright,
Which but th' Omnipotent none could have foiled,
If once they hear that voice, thir liveliest pledge
275   Of hope in fears and dangers, heard so oft
In worst extremes, and on the perilous edge°   *front line*
Of battle when it rag'd, in all assaults
Thir surest signal, they will soon resume
New courage and revive, though now they lie
280   Groveling and prostrate on yon Lake of Fire,
As we erewhile, astounded and amaz'd;
No wonder, fall'n such a pernicious highth.
     He scarce had ceas't when the superior Fiend
Was moving toward the shore; his ponderous shield
285   Ethereal temper,[3] massy, large and round,
Behind him cast; the broad circumference
Hung on his shoulders like the Moon, whose Orb
Through Optic Glass the *Tuscan* Artist[4] views
At Ev'ning from the top of *Fesole*,

9. The view that heaven and hell are states of mind was
held by Amaury de Bene, a medieval heretic often cited
in 17th-century accounts of atheism.
1. Worth striving for (Latin *ambitio*). Satan refers not
merely to a mental state but also to an active effort that is
the price of power.
2. The pool attended by forgetfulness.

3. Tempered in celestial fire.
4. Galileo, who looked through a telescope ("optic
glass"), had been placed under house arrest by the Inquisition near Florence, which is in the "Valdarno" or the
Valley of the Arno, overlooked by the hills of "Fesole" or
Fiesole.

290   Or in *Valdarno*, to descry new Lands,
         Rivers or Mountains in her spotty Globe.
         His Spear, to equal which the tallest Pine
         Hewn on *Norwegian* hills, to be the Mast
         Of some great Ammiral,° were but a wand,   *flagship*
295   He walkt with to support uneasy steps
         Over the burning Marl,° not like those steps   *ground*
         On Heaven's Azure, and the torrid Clime
         Smote on him sore besides, vaulted with Fire;
         Nathless° he so endur'd, till on the Beach   *nevertheless*
300   Of that inflamed Sea, he stood and call'd
         His Legions, Angel Forms, who lay intrans't
         Thick as Autumnal Leaves that strow the Brooks
         In *Vallombrosa*, where th' *Etrurian* shades
         High overarch't imbow'r;⁵ or scatter'd sedge
305   Afloat, when with fierce Winds *Orion* arm'd
         Hath vext the Red-Sea Coast,⁶ whose waves o'erthrew
         Busiris and his *Memphian* Chivalry,
         While with perfidious hatred they pursu'd
         The Sojourners of *Goshen*, who beheld
310   From the safe shore thir floating Carcasses
         And broken Chariot Wheels;⁷ so thick bestrown
         Abject and lost lay these, covering the Flood,
         Under amazement of thir hideous change.
         He call'd so loud, that all the hollow Deep
315   Of Hell resounded. Princes, Potentates,
         Warriors, the Flow'r of Heav'n, once yours, now lost,
         If such astonishment as this can seize
         Eternal spirits; or have ye chos'n this place
         After the toil of Battle to repose
320   Your wearied virtue,° for the ease you find   *strength*
         To slumber here, as in the Vales of Heav'n?
         Or in this abject posture have ye sworn
         To adore the Conqueror? who now beholds
         Cherub and Seraph rolling in the Flood
325   With scatter'd Arms and Ensigns,° till anon   *battle flags*
         His swift pursuers from Heav'n Gates discern
         Th' advantage, and descending tread us down
         Thus drooping, or with linked Thunderbolts
         Transfix us to the bottom of this Gulf.
330   Awake, arise, or be for ever fall'n.
              They heard, and were abasht, and up they sprung

5. See Isaiah 34.4: "and all their host shall fall down, as the leaf falleth off from the vine, and as a falling fig from the fig tree." Fallen leaves were an enduring simile for the numberless dead; see Homer, *Iliad* 6.146; Virgil, *Aeneid* 6.309; Dante, *Inferno* 3.112. Milton adds an actual locality, Vallombrosa, again near Florence.
6. Commentators on Job 9.9 and Amos 5.8 interpreted the creation of Orion as a symbol of God's power to raise tempests and floods to execute his judgments. Thus Mil-

ton's transition to the Egyptians overwhelmed by God's judgment in lines 306–11 is a natural one. The Hebrew name for the Red Sea was "Sea of Sedge."
7. Contrary to his promise, the Pharaoh with his Memphian (i.e., Egyptian) charioteers pursued the Israelites—who had been in captivity in Goshen—across the Red Sea. The Israelites passed over safely; but the Egyptians' chariot wheels were broken (Exodus 14.25), and the rising sea engulfed them and cast their corpses on the shore.

Upon the wing; as when men wont to watch
On duty, sleeping found by whom they dread,
Rouse and bestir themselves ere well awake.
335   Nor did they not perceive the evil plight
In which they were, or the fierce pains not feel;
Yet to thir General's Voice they soon obey'd
Innumerable. As when the potent Rod
Of *Amram's* Son[8] in *Egypt's* evil day
340   Wav'd round the Coast, up call'd a pitchy cloud
Of *Locusts*, warping° on the Eastern Wind,   *floating*
That o'er the Realm of impious *Pharaoh* hung
Like Night, and darken'd all the Land of *Nile*:
So numberless were those bad Angels seen
345   Hovering on wing under the Cope° of Hell   *canopy*
'Twixt upper, nether, and surrounding Fires;
Till, as a signal giv'n, th' uplifted Spear
Of thir great Sultan waving to direct
Thir course, in even balance down they light
350   On the firm brimstone, and fill all the Plain;
A multitude, like which the populous North
Pour'd never from her frozen loins, to pass
Rhene or the *Danaw*, when her barbarous Sons
Came like a Deluge on the South, and spread
355   Beneath *Gibraltar* to the *Lybian* sands.[9]
Forthwith from every Squadron and each Band
The Heads and Leaders thither haste where stood
Thir great Commander; Godlike shapes and forms
Excelling human, Princely Dignities,
360   And Powers that erst in Heaven sat on Thrones;
Though of thir Names in heav'nly Records now
Be no memorial, blotted out and ras'd
By thir Rebellion, from the Books of Life.[1]
Nor had they yet among the Sons of *Eve*
365   Got them new Names, till wand'ring o'er the Earth,
Through God's high sufferance for the trial of man,
By falsities and lies the greatest part
Of Mankind they corrupted to forsake
God thir Creator, and th' invisible
370   Glory of him that made them, to transform
Oft to the Image of a Brute, adorn'd
With gay Religions° full of Pomp and Gold,   *ceremonies*
And Devils to adore for Deities:[2]
Then were they known to men by various Names,
375   And various Idols through the Heathen World.

8. Moses, who used his rod to bring down on the Egyptians a plague of locusts (Exodus 10.12–15).
9. The barbarian invasions of Rome began with crossings of the Rhine ("Rhene") and Danube ("Danaw") Rivers and spread to North Africa.

1. See Revelation 3.5 ("He that overcometh . . . I will not blot out his name out of the book of life") and Exodus 32.32–33.
2. The catalogue of gods here is an epic convention.

Say, Muse, thir Names then known, who first, who last,
Rous'd from the slumber on that fiery Couch,
At thir great Emperor's call, as next in worth
Came singly where he stood on the bare strand,
380   While the promiscuous crowd stood yet aloof?
The chief were those who from the Pit of Hell
Roaming to seek thir prey on earth, durst fix
Thir Seats long after next the Seat of God,
Thir Altars by his Altar, Gods ador'd
385   Among the Nations round, and durst abide
Jehovah thund'ring out of *Sion*, thron'd
Between the Cherubim; yea, often plac'd
Within his Sanctuary itself thir Shrines,
Abominations; and with cursed things
390   His holy Rites, and solemn Feasts profan'd,
And with thir darkness durst affront his light.
First *Moloch*,³ horrid King besmear'd with blood
Of human sacrifice, and parents' tears,
Though for the noise of Drums and Timbrels° loud   *tambourines*
395   Thir children's cries unheard, that pass'd through fire
To his grim Idol. Him the *Ammonite*
Worshipt in *Rabba* and her wat'ry Plain,
In *Argob* and in *Basan*, to the stream
Of utmost *Arnon*.⁴ Nor content with such
400   Audacious neighborhood, the wisest heart
Of *Solomon*⁵ he led by fraud to build
His Temple right against the Temple of God
On that opprobrious Hill,⁶ and made his Grove
The pleasant Valley of *Hinnom*, *Tophet* thence
405   And black *Gehenna* call'd, the Type of Hell.⁷
Next *Chemos*,⁸ th' obscene dread of *Moab's* Sons,
From *Aroar* to *Nebo*, and the wild
Of Southmost *Abarim*; in *Hesebon*
And *Horonaim*, *Seon's* Realm, beyond
410   The flow'ry Dale of *Sibma* clad with Vines,
And *Eleale* to th' *Asphaltic* Pool.⁹

3. Satan gathers twelve disciples: Moloch, Chemos, Baalim, Ashtaroth, Astoreth, Thammuz, Dagon, Rimmon, Osiris, Isis, Horus, and Belial. The literal meaning of *Moloch* is "king."
4. Though ostensibly magnifying Moloch's empire, these lines look forward to his eventual defeat; for Rabba, the Ammonite royal city, is best known for its capture by David after his repentance (2 Samuel 12), while the Israelite conquest of the regions of Argob and Basan, as far as the boundary river Arnon, is recalled by Moses as particularly crushing (Deuteronomy 3.1–13).
5. Solomon's wives drew him into idolatry (1 Kings 11. 5–7); but the "high places that were before Jerusalem . . . on the right hand of the mount of corruption which Solomon . . . had builded for Ashtoreth the abomination of the Zidonians, and for Chemosh the abomination of the Moabites, and Milcom the abomination of the children of Ammon" were later destroyed by Josiah (2 Kings 23.13–14).

6. The Mount of Olives, because of Solomon's idolatry called "mount of corruption." Throughout the poem, Solomon functions as a type both of Adam and of Christ.
7. To abolish sacrifice to Moloch, Josiah "defiled Topheth, which is in the valley of the children of Hinnom" (2 Kings 23.10). Gehenna, for "Valley of Hinnom," is used in Matthew 10.28 as a name for hell.
8. "The abomination of Moab," associated with neighboring god Moloch in 1 Kings 11.7.
9. Most of these places are named in Numbers 32 as the formerly Moabite inheritance assigned by Moses to the tribes of Reuben and Gad. Numbers 21.25–30 rejoices at the Israelite capture of Hesebon (Heshbon), a Moabite city which had been taken by the Amorite King Seon, or Sihon. Heshbon, Horonaim, "the vine of Sibmah," and Elealeh all figure in Isaiah's sad prophecy of the destruction of Moab (Isaiah 15.5, 16.8f). The Asphaltic Pool is the Dead Sea.

Peor¹ his other Name, when he entic'd
Israel in *Sittim* on thir march from *Nile*
To do him wanton rites, which cost them woe.²

415 Yet thence his lustful Orgies he enlarg'd
Even to that Hill of scandal, by the Grove
Of *Moloch* homicide, lust hard by hate;
Till good *Josiah*³ drove them thence to Hell.
With these came they, who from the bord'ring flood

420 Of old *Euphrates*⁴ to the Brook that parts
Egypt from *Syrian* ground, had general Names
Of *Baalim* and *Ashtaroth*,⁵ those male,
These Feminine. For Spirits when they please
Can either Sex assume, or both; so soft

425 And uncompounded is thir Essence pure,
Not ti'd or manacl'd with joint or limb,
Nor founded on the brittle strength of bones,
Like cumbrous flesh; but in what shape they choose
Dilated° or condens't, bright or obscure,   *expanded*

430 Can execute thir aery purposes,
And works of love or enmity fulfil.
For those the Race of *Israel* oft forsook
Thir living strength,⁶ and unfrequented left
His righteous Altar, bowing lowly down

435 To bestial Gods; for which thir heads as low
Bow'd down in Battle, sunk before the Spear
Of despicable foes. With these in troop
Came *Astoreth*, whom the *Phoenicians* call'd
Astarte, Queen of Heav'n, with crescent Horns;⁷

440 To whose bright Image nightly by the Moon
Sidonian Virgins paid thir Vows and Songs,
In *Sion* also not unsung, where stood
Her Temple on th' offensive Mountain, built
By that uxorious King, whose heart though large,

445 Beguil'd by fair Idolatresses, fell
To Idols foul. *Thammuz*⁸ came next behind,
Whose annual wound in *Lebanon* allur'd
The *Syrian* Damsels to lament his fate
In amorous ditties all a Summer's day,

1. For the story of Peor, see Numbers 25.1–3 and Hosea 9.10.
2. A plague that killed 24,000 (Numbers 25.9).
3. Always a favorite with the Reformers because of his destruction of idolatrous images.
4. An area stretching from the northeast limit of Syria to the southwest limit of Canaan, the River Besor.
5. Baal is the general name for most idols; the Phoenician and Canaanite sun gods were collectively called Baalim (plural form). Astartes (Ishtars) were manifestations of the moon goddess.
6. See 1 Samuel 15.29: "Strength of Israel," a formulaic periphrasis for Jehovah.
7. The image of Astoreth or Astarte, the Sidonian

(Phoenician) moon goddess and Venus, was the statue of a woman with the head of a bull above her head with horns resembling the crescent moon. "Queen of heaven:" from Jeremiah 44.17–19.
8. The lover of Astarte. His identification with Adonis was based on St. Jerome's commentary on the passage in Ezekiel 8.14, drawn on by Milton in lines 454–56. The Syrian festival of Tammuz was celebrated after the summer solstice; the slaying of the young god by a boar was mourned as a symbol of the southward withdrawal of the sun and the death of vegetation. Each year when the River Adonis became discolored with red mud, it was regarded as a renewed sign of the god's wound.

450 While smooth *Adonis* from his native Rock
     Ran purple to the Sea, suppos'd with blood
     Of *Thammuz* yearly wounded: the Love-tale
     Infected *Sion's* daughters with like heat,
     Whose wanton passions in the sacred Porch
455 *Ezekiel* saw, when by the Vision led
     His eye survey'd the dark Idolatries
     Of alienated *Judah*. Next came one
     Who mourn'd in earnest, when the Captive Ark
     Maim'd his brute Image, head and hands lopt off
460 In his own Temple, on the grunsel° edge,   threshold
     Where he fell flat, and sham'd his Worshippers:
     Dagon his Name, Sea Monster, upward Man
     And downward Fish:[9] yet had his Temple high
     Rear'd in *Azotus*, dreaded through the Coast
465 Of *Palestine*, in *Gath* and *Ascalon*,
     And *Accaron* and *Gaza's* frontier bounds.[1]
     Him follow'd *Rimmon*, whose delightful Seat
     Was fair *Damascus*, on the fertile Banks
     Of *Abbana* and *Pharphar*, lucid streams.[2]
470 He also against the house of God was bold:
     A Leper once he lost and gain'd a King,
     Ahaz his sottish Conqueror, whom he drew
     God's Altar to disparage and displace
     For one of *Syrian* mode, whereon to burn
475 His odious off'rings, and adore the Gods
     Whom he had vanquisht.[3] After these appear'd
     A crew who under Names of old Renown,
     Osiris, *Isis*, *Orus* and thir Train
     With monstrous shapes and sorceries abus'd°   deceived
480 Fanatic *Egypt* and her Priests, to seek
     Thir wand'ring Gods disguis'd in brutish forms
     Rather than human.[4] Nor did *Israel* scape
     Th' infection when thir borrow'd Gold compos'd
     The Calf in *Oreb*:[5] and the Rebel King[6]
485 Doubl'd that sin in *Bethel* and in *Dan*,
     Lik'ning his Maker to the Grazed Ox,[7]

9. When the Philistines put the ark of the Lord, which they had captured, into the temple of Dagon, "on the morrow morning, behold, Dagon was fallen upon his face to the ground . . . and the head of Dagon and both the palms of his hands were cut off upon the threshold" (1 Samuel 5.4).

1. Divine vengeance on these Philistine cities is prophesied in Zephaniah 2.4.

2. When Elisha told Naaman that his leprosy would be cured if he washed in the Jordan, the Syrian was at first angry (2 Kings 5.12: "Are not Abana and Pharpar, rivers of Damascus, better than all the waters of Israel?") but then humbled himself and was cured.

3. After engineering the overthrow of Damascus by the Assyrians, the sottish (foolish) King Ahaz became interested in the cult of Rimmon and had an altar of the Syr-

ian type put in the temple of the Lord (2 Kings 16.9–17).

4. Milton alludes to the myth of the Olympian gods fleeing from the Giant Typhoeus into Egypt and hiding in bestial forms (Ovid, *Metamorphoses* 5.319–31) afterward worshipped by the Egyptians.

5. Perhaps the most familiar of all Israelite apostasies was their worship of "a calf in Horeb" (Psalms 106.19) made by Aaron while Moses was away receiving the tables of the Law (Exodus 32).

6. Jeroboam, who led the revolt of the ten tribes of Israel against Rehoboam, Solomon's successor; he "doubled" Aaron's sin, since he made "two calves of gold," placing one in Bethel and the other in Dan (1 Kings 12.28–29).

7. "Thus they changed their glory into the similitude of an ox that eateth grass" (Psalms 106.20).

Jehovah, who in one Night when he pass'd
From Egypt marching, equall'd with one stroke
Both her first born and all her bleating Gods.[8]
490   Belial came last,[9] than whom a Spirit more lewd
Fell not from Heaven, or more gross to love
Vice for itself: To him no Temple stood
Or Altar smok'd; yet who more oft than hee
In Temples and at Altars, when the Priest
495   Turns Atheist, as did Ely's Sons, who fill'd
With lust and violence the house of God.[1]
In Courts and Palaces he also Reigns
And in luxurious Cities, where the noise
Of riot ascends above thir loftiest Tow'rs,
500   And injury and outrage: And when Night
Darkens the Streets, then wander forth the Sons
Of Belial, flown° with insolence and wine.[2]   swollen
Witness the Streets of Sodom, and that night
In Gibeah, when the hospitable door
505   Expos'd a Matron to avoid worse rape.[3]
These were the prime in order and in might;
The rest were long to tell, though far renown'd,
Th' Ionian Gods,[4] of Javan's Issue held
Gods, yet confest later than Heav'n and Earth
510   Thir boasted Parents; Titan Heav'n's first born
With his enormous° brood, and birthright seiz'd   monstrous
By younger Saturn, he from mightier Jove
His own and Rhea's Son like measure found;
So Jove usurping reign'd: these first in Crete
515   And Ida known,[5] thence on the Snowy top
Of cold Olympus rul'd the middle Air
Thir highest Heav'n; or on the Delphian Cliff,[6]
Or in Dodona, and through all the bounds
Of Doric Land;° or who with Saturn old   Greece
520   Fled over Adria to th' Hesperian Fields,
And o'er the Celtic roam'd the utmost Isles.[7]
All these and more came flocking; but with looks
Downcast and damp,° yet such wherein appear'd   depressed
Obscure some glimpse of joy, to have found thir chief

8. At the passover, Jehovah smote all the Egyptian first-born, "both man and beast" (Exodus 12.12); presumably, this stroke would extend to their sacred animals.
9. Belial comes last, both because he had no local cult and because in the poem he is "timorous and slothful" (2.117). Properly, "Belial" is an abstract noun meaning "iniquity."
1. The impiety and fornication of Ely's sons are described in 1 Samuel 2.12–24.
2. The Puritans referred to their enemies as the Sons of Belial.
3. See Genesis 19 and Judges 19.

4. The Ionian Greeks were held by some to be the issue of Javan the son of Japhet the son of Noah, on the basis of the Septuagint version of Genesis 10.
5. Jove was born and secretly reared on Mount Ida, in Crete.
6. Delphi was famed as the site of the Pythian oracle of Apollo, but cults of Ge, Poseidon, and Artemis were also celebrated there.
7. After Saturn's downfall he fled across the Adriatic Sea (Adria) to Italy (Hesperian Fields), France (the Celtic), and the British Isles (Utmost Isles).

525   Not in despair, to have found themselves not lost
       In loss itself; which on his count'nance cast
       Like doubtful hue: but he his wonted pride
       Soon recollecting,° with high words, that bore   recovering
       Semblance of worth, not substance, gently rais'd
530   Thir fainting courage, and dispell'd thir fears.
       Then straight commands that at the warlike sound
       Of Trumpets loud and Clarions° be uprear'd   shrill trumpets
       His mighty Standard; that proud honor claim'd
       Azazel as his right, a Cherub tall:[8]
535   Who forthwith from the glittering Staff unfurl'd
       Th' Imperial Ensign, which full high advanc't
       Shone like a Meteor streaming to the Wind
       With Gems and Golden lustre rich imblaz'd,[9]
       Seraphic arms and Trophies: all the while
540   Sonorous metal blowing Martial sounds:
       At which the universal Host upsent
       A shout that tore Hell's Concave,° and beyond   vault
       Frighted the Reign of Chaos and old Night.[1]
       All in a moment through the gloom were seen
545   Ten thousand Banners rise into the Air
       With Orient° Colors waving: with them rose   brilliant
       A Forest huge of Spears: and thronging Helms
       Appear'd, and serried° Shields in thick array   locked together
       Of depth immeasurable: Anon they move
550   In perfect Phalanx[2] to the Dorian° mood   solemn
       Of Flutes and soft Recorders; such as rais'd
       To highth of noblest temper Heroes old
       Arming to Battle, and instead of rage
       Deliberate valor breath'd, firm and unmov'd
555   With dread of death to flight or foul retreat,
       Nor wanting power to mitigate and swage°   assuage
       With solemn touches, troubl'd thoughts, and chase
       Anguish and doubt and fear and sorrow and pain
       From mortal or immortal minds. Thus they
560   Breathing united force with fixed thought
       Mov'd on in silence to soft Pipes that charm'd
       Thir painful steps o'er the burnt soil; and now
       Advanc't in view they stand, a horrid° Front   bristling
       Of dreadful length and dazzling Arms, in guise
565   Of Warriors old with order'd Spear and Shield,
       Awaiting what command thir mighty Chief
       Had to impose: He through the armed Files
       Darts his experienc't eye, and soon traverse°   across

---

8. Azazel was one of the chief fallen angels who are the
object of God's wrath in the apocryphal Book of Enoch.
For the healing of the earth he is bound and cast into the
same wilderness where the scapegoat was led (Enoch
10.4–8).

9. Adorned with heraldic devices.
1. Chaos and Night, rulers of the region of unformed matter between Heaven and Hell.
2. A square battle formation.

The whole Battalion views, thir order due,
570   Thir visages and stature as of Gods;
Thir number last he sums. And now his heart
Distends with pride, and hard'ning in his strength
Glories: For never since created man,[3]
Met such imbodied° force, as nam'd with these   *united*
575   Could merit more than that small infantry
Warr'd on by Cranes:[4] though all the Giant brood
Of *Phlegra* with th' Heroic Race were join'd
That fought at *Thebes* and *Ilium*, on each side
Mixt with auxiliar Gods;[5] and what resounds
580   In Fable or *Romance of Uther's* Son°   *King Arthur*
Begirt with *British* and *Armoric*[6] Knights;
And all who since, Baptiz'd or Infidel
Jousted in *Aspramont* or *Montalban*,
Damasco, or *Marocco*, or *Trebisond*,
585   Or whom *Biserta* sent from *Afric* shore
When *Charlemain* with all his Peerage fell
By *Fontarabbia*.[7] Thus far these beyond
Compare of mortal prowess, yet observ'd°   *obeyed*
Thir dread commander: he above the rest
590   In shape and gesture proudly eminent
Stood like a Tow'r; his form had yet not lost
All her Original brightness, nor appear'd
Less than Arch-Angel ruin'd, and th' excess
Of Glory obscur'd: As when the Sun new ris'n
595   Looks through the Horizontal misty Air
Shorn of his Beams, or from behind the Moon
In dim Eclipse disastrous twilight sheds
On half the Nations, and with fear of change
Perplexes Monarchs.[8] Dark'n'd so, yet shone
600   Above them all th' Arch-Angel: but his face
Deep scars of Thunder had intrencht, and care
Sat on his faded cheek, but under Brows
Of dauntless courage, and considerate° Pride   *deliberate*
Waiting revenge: cruel his eye, but cast
605   Signs of remorse and passion to behold
The fellows of his crime, the followers rather
(Far other once beheld in bliss) condemn'd
For ever now to have thir lot in pain,

3. Since humanity was created.
4. When compared with Satan's, any army would seem no bigger than pygmies ("that small infantry"), who were portrayed by Pliny as tiny men who fought with cranes.
5. To amplify the heroic stature of the angels, Milton mentions a series of armies that had been thought worthy of epic treatment only to dismiss them. The Giants, who fought with the Olympians at Phlegra, join with the heroes of Thebes and Troy (Ilium).
6. From Brittany.
7. Aspramont was a castle near Nice, and Montalban was

the castle of Rinaldo; these castles figure in Ariosto's *Orlando Furioso* and the romances concerned with chivalric wars between Christians and Saracens. Milton would know late versions of the Charlemagne legend. Charlemagne's whole rearguard, led by Roland, one of the 12 peers or paladins, was massacred at Roncesvalles, about 40 miles from Fontarabbia (Fuenterrabia).
8. The comparison is ironically double-edged, for the ominous solar eclipse presages not only disaster for creation but also the doom of the god-like ruler for whom the sun was a traditional symbol.

Millions of Spirits for his fault amerc't°   *deprived*
610   Of Heav'n, and from Eternal Splendors flung
For his revolt, yet faithful how they stood,
Thir Glory wither'd. As when Heaven's Fire
Hath scath'd the Forest Oaks, or Mountain Pines,
With singed top thir stately growth though bare
615   Stands on the blasted Heath. He now prepar'd
To speak; whereat thir doubl'd Ranks they bend
From wing to wing, and half enclose him round
With all his Peers: attention held them mute.
Thrice he assay'd, and thrice in spite of scorn,
620   Tears such as Angels weep, burst forth: at last
Words interwove with sighs found out thir way.
O Myriads of immortal Spirits, O Powers
Matchless, but with th' Almighty, and that strife
Was not inglorious, though th' event° was dire,   *result*
625   As this place testifies, and this dire change
Hateful to utter: but what power of mind
Foreseeing or presaging, from the Depth
Of knowledge past or present, could have fear'd
How such united force of Gods, how such
630   As stood like these, could ever know repulse?
For who can yet believe, though after loss,
That all these puissant° Legions, whose exíle   *powerful*
Hath emptied Heav'n, shall fail to re-ascend
Self-rais'd, and repossess thir native seat?
635   For mee be witness all the Host of Heav'n,
If counsels different, or danger shunn'd
By me, have lost our hopes. But he who reigns
Monarch in Heav'n, till then as one secure
Sat on his Throne, upheld by old repute,
640   Consent or custom, and his Regal State
Put forth at full, but still his strength conceal'd,
Which tempted our attempt, and wrought our fall.
Henceforth his might we know, and know our own
So as not either to provoke, or dread
645   New War, provok't; our better part remains
To work in close° design, by fraud or guile   *secret*
What force effected not: that he no less
At length from us may find, who overcomes
By force, hath overcome but half his foe.
650   Space may produce new Worlds; whereof so rife°   *common*
There went a fame° in Heav'n that he ere long   *rumor*
Intended to create, and therein plant
A generation, whom his choice regard
Should favor equal to the Sons of Heaven:
655   Thither, if but to pry, shall be perhaps
Our first eruption, thither or elsewhere:
For this Infernal Pit shall never hold
Celestial Spirits in Bondage, nor th' Abyss

Long under darkness cover. But these thoughts
660   Full Counsel must mature: Peace is despair'd,
For who can think Submission? War then, War
Open or understood, must be resolv'd.
     He spake: and to confirm his words, out-flew
Millions of flaming swords, drawn from the thighs
665   Of mighty Cherubim; the sudden blaze
Far round illumin'd hell: highly they rag'd
Against the Highest, and fierce with grasped Arms
Clash'd on thir sounding shields the din of war,
Hurling defiance toward the Vault of Heav'n.
670   There stood a Hill not far whose grisly top
Belch'd fire and rolling smoke; the rest entire
Shone with a glossy scurf, undoubted sign
That in his womb was hid metallic Ore,
The work of Sulphur.[9] Thither wing'd with speed
675   A numerous Brígad° hasten'd. As when bands   *brigade*
Of Píoners° with Spade and Pickax arm'd   *engineers*
Forerun the Royal Camp, to trench a Field,
Or cast a Rampart. Mammon[1] led them on,
Mammon, the least erected° Spirit that fell   *elevated*
680   From Heav'n, for ev'n in Heav'n his looks and thoughts
Were always downward bent, admiring more
The riches of Heav'n's pavement, trodd'n Gold,
Than aught divine or holy else enjoy'd
In vision beatific: by him first
685   Men also, and by his suggestion taught,
Ransack'd the Center, and with impious hands
Rifl'd the bowels of thir mother Earth
For Treasures better hid. Soon had his crew
Op'n'd into the Hill a spacious wound
690   And digg'd out ribs of Gold. Let none admire°   *wonder*
That riches grow in Hell; that soil may best
Deserve the precious bane. And here let those
Who boast in mortal things, and wond'ring tell
Of *Babel*, and the works of *Memphian* Kings,[2]
695   Learn how thir greatest Monuments of Fame,
And Strength and Art are easily outdone
By Spirits reprobate, and in an hour
What in an age they with incessant toil
And hands innumerable scarce perform.
700   Nigh on the Plain in many cells prepar'd,
That underneath had veins of liquid fire
Sluic'd° from the Lake, a second multitude   *led by channels*

---

9. The traditional physiognomy of the fiend is in Milton's hell displaced onto the landscape. It is a dead or corrupt body imaged as scurf (i.e., scales, crust), belching, ransacked womb, bowels, entrails, and ribs.
1. In Matthew 6.24 and Luke 16.13, "Mammon" is an abstract noun meaning wealth, but later it was used as the name of "the prince of this world" (John 12.31). Medieval and Renaissance tradition often associated Mammon with Plutus, the Greek god of riches.
2. The Tower of Babel was built by the ambitious Nimrod. The works of Memphian kings, the Pyramids, were regarded as memorials of vanity.

With wondrous Art founded the massy Ore,
Severing each kind, and scumm'd the Bullion dross:
705 A third as soon had form'd within the ground
A various mould, and from the boiling cells
By strange conveyance fill'd each hollow nook:
As in an Organ from one blast of wind
To many a row of Pipes the sound-board breathes.
710 Anon out of the earth a Fabric huge
Rose like an Exhalation,[3] with the sound
Of Dulcet Symphonies and voices sweet,
Built like a Temple, where *Pilasters*° round   *columns*
Were set, and Doric pillars overlaid
715 With Golden Architrave; nor did there want
Cornice or Frieze, with bossy° Sculptures grav'n;   *embossed*
The Roof was fretted° Gold. Not *Babylon*,[4]   *patterned*
Nor great *Alcairo* such magnificence
Equall'd in all thir glories,[5] to inshrine
720 *Belus*[6] or *Serapis*[7] thir Gods, or seat
Thir Kings, when *Egypt* with *Assyria* strove
In wealth and luxury. Th' ascending pile
Stood fixt her stately highth, and straight the doors
Op'ning thir brazen folds discover wide
725 Within, her ample spaces, o'er the smooth
And level pavement: from the arched roof
Pendant by subtle Magic many a row
Of Starry Lamps and blazing Cressets[8] fed
With *Naphtha* and *Asphaltus*[9] yielded light
730 As from a sky. The hasty multitude
Admiring enter'd, and the work some praise
And some the Architect: his hand was known
In Heav'n by many a Tow'red structure high,
Where Scepter'd Angels held thir residence,
735 And sat as Princes, whom the supreme King
Exalted to such power, and gave to rule,
Each in his Hierarchy, the Orders bright.
Nor was his name unheard or unador'd
In ancient *Greece*; and in *Ausonian* land
740 Men call'd him *Mulciber*;[1] and how he fell

3. Pandaemonium rises to music, since in the Renaissance it was believed that musical proportions governed the forms of architecture.
4. An ironic allusion to Ovid's description of the Palace of the Sun built by Mulciber (*Metamorphoses* 2.1–4). Pandaemonium has a classical design, complete in every respect, like that of the ancient (but still surviving) giltroofed Pantheon, the most admired building of Milton's time. Doric is the oldest and simplest order of Greek architecture.
5. In traditional biblical exegesis, Babylon, a place of proud iniquity, was often a figure of Antichrist or of hell. Memphis (modern Cairo) was the most splendid city of heathen Egypt.
6. Bel, the Babylonian Baal; see lines 421–23 n5 and Jeremiah 51.44: "I will punish Bel in Babylon."
7. An Egyptian deity.
8. Basketlike lamps.
9. *Naphtha* is an oily constituent of asphalt (asphaltus).
1. The Greek god Hephaistos, in Latin *Mulciber* or Vulcan, presided over all arts, such as metal-working, that required the use of fire. He built all the palaces of the gods. "Ausonian land" is the old Greek name for Italy. Milton emulates Homer's description of the daylong fall of Hephaistos (*Iliad* 1.591–95) and then deflates it in the casual but commanding dismissal of lines 746–48.

From Heav'n, they fabl'd, thrown by angry *Jove*
Sheer o'er the Crystal Battlements: from Morn
To Noon he fell, from Noon to dewy Eve,
A Summer's day; and with the setting Sun
745   Dropt from the Zenith like a falling Star,
On *Lemnos* th' *Aegean* Isle:[2] thus they relate,
Erring; for he with this rebellious rout
Fell long before; nor aught avail'd him now
To have built in Heav'n high Tow'rs; nor did he scape
750   By all his Engines, but was headlong sent
With his industrious crew to build in hell.
Meanwhile the winged Heralds by command
Of Sovran power, with awful Ceremony
And Trumpets' sound throughout the Host proclaim
755   A solemn Council forthwith to be held
At *Pandaemonium,* the high Capitol
Of Satan and his Peers: thir summons call'd
From every Band and squared Regiment
By place or choice the worthiest; they anon
760   With hunderds and with thousands trooping came
Attended: all access was throng'd, the Gates
And Porches wide, but chief the spacious Hall
(Though like a cover'd field, where Champions bold
Wont ride in arm'd, and at the Soldan's° chair   Sultan's
765   Defi'd the best of *Paynim*° chivalry   pagan
To mortal combat or career with Lance)
Thick swarm'd, both on the ground and in the air,
Brusht with the hiss of rustling wings. As Bees
In spring time, when the Sun with *Taurus*[3] rides,
770   Pour forth thir populous youth about the Hive
In clusters; they among fresh dews and flowers
Fly to and fro, or on the smoothed Plank,
The suburb of thir Straw-built Citadel,
New rubb'd with Balm, expatiate° and confer   debate
775   Thir State affairs. So thick the aery crowd
Swarm'd and were strait'n'd; till the Signal giv'n,
Behold a wonder! they but now who seem'd
In bigness to surpass Earth's Giant Sons
Now less than smallest Dwarfs, in narrow room
780   Throng numberless, like that Pigmean Race
Beyond the *Indian* Mount, or Faery Elves,
Whose midnight Revels, by a Forest side
Or Fountain some belated Peasant sees,
Or dreams he sees, while over-head the Moon
785   Sits Arbitress, and nearer to the Earth

2. In Homer (*Iliad* 2.87–90), the Achaians going to a
council are compared to bees, as are the Carthaginians in
Virgil (*Aeneid* 1.430–36). Milton also glances at Virgil's
mock-epic account of the ideal social organization of the
hive (*Georgics* 4.149–227).
3. In Milton's time the sun entered the second sign of the
zodiac in mid-April, according to the Julian calendar.

Wheels her pale course;[4] they on thir mirth and dance
Intent, with jocund Music charm his ear;
At once with joy and fear his heart rebounds.
Thus incorporeal Spirits to smallest forms
790   Reduc'd thir shapes immense, and were at large,
Though without number still amidst the Hall
Of that infernal Court. But far within
And in thir own dimensions like themselves
The great Seraphic Lords and Cherubim
795   In close° recess and secret conclave[5] sat   *secret*
A thousand Demi-Gods on golden seats,
Frequent° and full. After short silence then   *crowded*
And summons read, the great consult began.
                    The End of the First Book.

from **Book 2**
The Argument

The Consultation begun, Satan debates whether another Battle be to be hazarded for the recovery of Heaven: some advise it, others dissuade: A third proposal is preferr'd, mention'd before by Satan, to search the truth of that Prophecy or Tradition in Heaven concerning another world, and another kind of creature equal or not much inferior to themselves, about this time to be created: Thir doubt who shall be sent on this difficult search: Satan thir chief undertakes alone the voyage, is honor'd and applauded. The Council thus ended, the rest betake them several ways and to several employments, as thir inclinations lead them, to entertain the time till Satan return. He passes on his Journey to Hell Gates, finds them shut, and who sat there to guard them, by whom at length they are op'n'd, and discover[1] to him the great Gulf between Hell and Heaven; with what difficulty he passes through, directed by Chaos, the Power of that place, to the sight of this new World which he sought.

High on a Throne of Royal State,[2] which far
Outshone the wealth of *Ormus* and of *Ind*,[3]
Or where the gorgeous East with richest hand
Show'rs on her Kings *Barbaric* Pearl and Gold,
5   Satan exalted sat, by merit rais'd
To that bad eminence; and from despair
Thus high uplifted beyond hope, aspires
Beyond thus high, insatiate to pursue
Vain War with Heav'n, and by success° untaught   *result*
10   His proud imaginations thus display'd.
Powers and Dominions,[4] Deities of Heav'n,
For since no deep within her gulf can hold
Immortal vigor, though opprest and fall'n,

---

4. Echoing *A Midsummer Night's Dream* 2.1.28f and 141. "The moon / Sits arbitress" because the moon-goddess was queen of faery.
5. "Conclave" could refer to any assembly in secret session but already had the specifically ecclesiastical meaning on which Milton's satire here depends.
1. Disclose.

2. Compare Spenser's description of the bright throne of the Phaethon-like Lucifera, embodiment of pride in *The Faerie Queene* 1.4.8, page 499.
3. India. Ormus, an island town in the Persian Gulf, was famous as a jewel market.
4. Two angelic orders mentioned by St. Paul in Colossians 1.16.

I give not Heav'n for lost. From this descent
15   Celestial Virtues rising, will appear
More glorious and more dread than from no fall
And trust themselves to fear no second fate:
Mee though just right and the fixt Laws of Heav'n
Did first create your Leader, next, free choice,
20   With what besides, in Counsel or in Fight,
Hath been achiev'd of merit, yet this loss
Thus far at least recover'd, hath much more
Establisht in a safe unenvied Throne
Yielded with full consent. The happier state
25   In Heav'n, which follows dignity, might draw
Envy from each inferior; but who here
Will envy whom the highest place exposes
Foremost to stand against the Thunderer's aim[5]
Your bulwark, and condemns to greatest share
30   Of endless pain? where there is then no good
For which to strive, no strife can grow up there
From Faction; for none sure will claim in Hell
Precedence, none, whose portion is so small
Of present pain, that with ambitious mind
35   Will covet more. With this advantage then
To union, and firm Faith, and firm accord,
More than can be in Heav'n, we now return
To claim our just inheritance of old,
Surer to prosper than prosperity
40   Could have assur'd us; and by what best way,
Whether of open War or covert guile,
We now debate; who can advise, may speak.
        He ceas'd, and next him *Moloch*, Scepter'd King
Stood up, the strongest and the fiercest Spirit
45   That fought in Heav'n; now fiercer by despair:
His trust was with th' Eternal to be deem'd
Equal in strength, and rather than be less
Car'd not to be at all; with that care lost
Went all his fear: of God, or Hell, or worse
50   He reck'd° not, and these words thereafter spake.   *cared*
        My sentence° is for open War: Of Wiles,   *opinion*
More unexpert,° I boast not: them let those   *inexperienced*
Contrive who need, or when they need, not now.
For while they sit contriving, shall the rest,
55   Millions that stand in Arms, and longing wait
The Signal to ascend, sit ling'ring here
Heav'n's fugitives, and for thir dwelling place
Accept this dark opprobrious Den of shame,
The Prison of his Tyranny who Reigns
60   By our delay? no, let us rather choose

5. By identifying him with thunder, the attribute of Jupiter, Satan reduces God to a mere Olympian tyrant.

Arm'd with Hell flames and fury[6] all at once
O'er Heav'n's high Tow'rs to force resistless way,
Turning our Tortures into horrid Arms
Against the Torturer; when to meet the noise
65   Of his Almighty Engine[7] he shall hear
Infernal Thunder, and for Lightning see
Black fire and horror shot with equal rage
Among his Angels; and his Throne itself
Mixt with *Tartarean* Sulphur, and strange fire,[8]
70   His own invented Torments. But perhaps
The way seems difficult and steep to scale
With upright wing against a higher foe.
Let such bethink them, if the sleepy drench[9]
Of that forgetful Lake benumb not still,
75   That in our proper motion we ascend
Up to our native seat: descent and fall
To us is adverse. Who but felt of late
When the fierce Foe hung on our brok'n Rear
Insulting,° and pursu'd us through the Deep,   *assaulting, exulting*
80   With what compulsion and laborious flight
We sunk thus low? Th' ascent is easy then;
Th' event° is fear'd; should we again provoke   *outcome*
Our stronger, some worse way his wrath may find
To our destruction: if there be in Hell
85   Fear to be worse destroy'd: what can be worse
Than to dwell here, driv'n out from bliss, condemn'd
In this abhorred deep to utter woe;
Where pain of unextinguishable fire
Must exercise° us without hope of end   *afflict*
90   The Vassals[1] of his anger, when the Scourge
Inexorably, and the torturing hour
Calls us to Penance? More destroy'd than thus
We should be quite abolisht and expire.
What fear we then? what doubt we to incense
95   His utmost ire? which to the highth enrag'd,
Will either quite consume us, and reduce
To nothing this essential,° happier far   *essence*
Than miserable to have eternal being:
Or if our substance be indeed Divine,
100   And cannot cease to be, we are at worst
On this side nothing;[2] and by proof we feel
Our power sufficient to disturb his Heav'n,

6. The violent yoking of concrete and abstract words is one of the most characteristic figures of Milton's style.
7. Machine of war, probably here referring to the Messiah's chariot or perhaps to his thunder.
8. In the classical underworld, Tartarus was the place of the guilty. For "strange fire," see Leviticus 10.1–2: "Nadab and Abihu, the sons of Aaron . . . offered strange fire before the Lord, which he commanded them not. And there went out fire from the Lord, and devoured them."

9. A draught of medicine for an animal.
1. Servants, slaves. Also an allusion to Romans 9.22: "What if God, willing to show his wrath, and to make his power known, endured with much longsuffering the vessels of wrath fitted to destruction . . . ?"
2. Already we are in the worst condition possible, short of being nothing, being annihilated.

And with perpetual inroads to Alarm,
Though inaccessible, his fatal Throne:

105   Which if not Victory is yet Revenge.

    He ended frowning, and his look denounc'd
Desperate revenge, and Battle dangerous
To less than Gods. On th' other side up rose
Belial, in act more graceful and humane;

110   A fairer person lost not Heav'n; he seem'd
For dignity compos'd and high exploit:
But all was false and hollow; though his Tongue
Dropt Manna, and could make the worse appear
The better reason,[3] to perplex and dash

115   Maturest Counsels: for his thoughts were low;
To vice industrious, but to Nobler deeds
Timorous and slothful: yet he pleas'd the ear,
And with persuasive accent thus began.

    I should be much for open War, O Peers,

120   As not behind in hate; if what was urg'd
Main reason to persuade immediate War,
Did not dissuade me most, and seem to cast
Ominous conjecture on the whole success:
When he who most excels in fact° of Arms,   *feat*

125   In what he counsels and in what excels
Mistrustful, grounds his courage on despair
And utter dissolution, as the scope
Of all his aim, after some dire revenge.
First, what Revenge? the Tow'rs of Heav'n are fill'd

130   With Armed watch, that render all access
Impregnable; oft on the bordering Deep
Encamp thir Legions, or with obscure[4] wing
Scout far and wide into the Realm of night,
Scorning surprise. Or could we break our way

135   By force, and at our heels all Hell should rise
With blackest Insurrection, to confound
Heav'n's purest Light, yet our great Enemy
All incorruptible would on his Throne
Sit unpolluted, and th' Ethereal mould

140   Incapable of stain would soon expel
Her mischief, and purge off the baser fire
Victorious.[5] Thus repuls'd, our final hope
Is flat° despair: we must exasperate   *absolute*
Th' Almighty Victor to spend all his rage,

145   And that must end us, that must be our cure,
To be no more; sad cure; for who would lose,

---

3. This was the claim of the Greek Sophists, who taught their students how to use rhetoric to win an argument.
4. "Obscure" is stressed on the first syllable here.
5. Criticizing Moloch's proposal to mix God's throne with sulphur (lines 68–9) and shoot "black fire" among his angels. This "baser fire" Belial contrasts with the "ethereal" (derived from ether, the fifth and purest element) fire of the throne.

Though full of pain, this intellectual being,
Those thoughts that wander through Eternity,
To perish rather, swallow'd up and lost
150 In the wide womb of uncreated night,
Devoid of sense and motion? and who knows,
Let this be good,[6] whether our angry Foe
Can give it, or will ever? how he can
Is doubtful; that he never will is sure.
155 Will he, so wise, let loose at once his ire,
Belike° through impotence, or unaware,   *no doubt*
To give his Enemies thir wish, and end
Them in his anger, whom his anger saves
To punish endless? wherefore cease we then?
160 Say they who counsel War, we are decreed,
Reserv'd and destin'd to Eternal woe;
Whatever doing, what can we suffer more,
What can we suffer worse? is this then worst,
Thus sitting, thus consulting, thus in Arms?
165 What when we fled amain,° pursu'd and strook°   *headlong / struck*
With Heav'n's afflicting Thunder, and besought
The Deep to shelter us? this Hell then seem'd
A refuge from those wounds: or when we lay
Chain'd on the burning Lake? that sure was worse.
170 What if the breath that kindl'd those grim fires
Awak'd should blow them into sevenfold rage
And plunge us in the flames? or from above
Should intermitted vengeance arm again
His red right hand to plague us? what if all
175 Her° stores were op'n'd, and this Firmament   *Hell's*
Of Hell should spout her Cataracts of Fire,
Impendent° horrors, threat'ning hideous fall   *threatening*
One day upon our heads; while we perhaps
Designing or exhorting glorious war,
180 Caught in a fiery Tempest shall be hurl'd
Each on his rock transfixt, the sport and prey
Of racking whirlwinds, or for ever sunk
Under yon boiling Ocean, wrapt in Chains;
There to converse with everlasting groans,
185 Unrespited, unpitied, unrepriev'd,
Ages of hopeless end; this would be worse.
War therefore, open or conceal'd, alike
My voice dissuades; for what can force or guile
With him, or who deceive his mind, whose eye
190 Views all things at one view? he from Heav'n's highth
All these our motions° vain, sees and derides;   *schemes*
Not more Almighty to resist our might
Than wise to frustrate all our plots and wiles.
Shall we then live thus vile, the race of Heav'n

6. Suppose it is good to be destroyed.

195   Thus trampl'd, thus expell'd to suffer here
        Chains and these Torments? better these than worse
        By my advice; since fate inevitable
        Subdues us, and Omnipotent Decree,
        The Victor's will. To suffer, as to do,
200   Our strength is equal, nor the Law unjust
        That so ordains: this was at first resolv'd,
        If we were wise, against so great a foe
        Contending, and so doubtful what might fall.
        I laugh, when those who at the Spear are bold
205   And vent'rous, if that fail them, shrink and fear
        What yet they know must follow, to endure
        Exile, or ignominy, or bonds, or pain,
        The sentence of thir Conqueror: This is now
        Our doom; which if we can sustain and bear,
210   Our Supreme Foe in time may much remit
        His anger, and perhaps thus far remov'd
        Not mind us not offending, satisfi'd
        With what is punisht; whence these raging fires
        Will slack'n, if his breath stir not thir flames.
215   Our purer essence then will overcome
        Thir noxious vapor, or enur'd° not feel,   *accustomed*
        Or chang'd at length, and to the place conform'd
        In temper[7] and in nature, will receive
        Familiar the fierce heat, and void of pain;
220   This horror will grow mild, this darkness light,[8]
        Besides what hope the never-ending flight
        Of future days may bring, what chance, what change
        Worth waiting, since our present lot appears
        For happy though but ill, for ill not worst,[9]
225   If we procure not to ourselves more woe.
            Thus *Belial* with words cloth'd in reason's garb
        Counsell'd ignoble ease, and peaceful sloth,
        Not peace: and after him thus *Mammon* spake.
            Either to disinthrone the King of Heav'n
230   We war, if war be best, or to regain
        Our own right lost: him to unthrone we then
        May hope, when everlasting Fate shall yield
        To fickle Chance, and *Chaos* judge the strife:
        The former vain to hope argues as vain
235   The latter: for what place can be for us
        Within Heav'n's bound, unless Heav'n's Lord supreme
        We overpower? Suppose he should relent
        And publish Grace to all, on promise made
        Of new Subjection; with what eyes could we
240   Stand in his presence humble, and receive

---

7. Temperament, the mixture or adjustment of humors. Thus the phrase means "adjusted psychologically and physically to the new environment."

8. Easy to bear, and illumination.
9. Though as far as happiness is concerned, the devils are but ill off, as far as evil is concerned, they could be worse.

Strict Laws impos'd, to celebrate his Throne
With warbl'd Hymns, and to his Godhead sing
Forc't Halleluiahs[1] while he Lordly sits
Our envied Sovran, and his Altar breathes
245 Ambrosial[2] Odors and Ambrosial Flowers,
Our servile offerings. This must be our task
In Heav'n, this our delight; how wearisome
Eternity so spent in worship paid
To whom we hate. Let us not then pursue
250 By force impossible, by leave obtain'd
Unácceptable, though in Heav'n, our state
Of splendid vassalage, but rather seek
Our own good from ourselves, and from our own
Live to ourselves, though in this vast recess,
255 Free, and to none accountable, preferring
Hard liberty before the easy yoke
Of servile Pomp.[3] Our greatness will appear
Then most conspicuous, when great things of small,
Useful of hurtful, prosperous of adverse
260 We can create, and in what place soe'er
Thrive under evil, and work ease out of pain
Through labor and endurance. This deep world
Of darkness do we dread? How oft amidst
Thick clouds and dark doth Heav'n's all-ruling Sire
265 Choose to reside, his Glory unobscur'd,
And with the Majesty of darkness round
Covers his Throne; from whence deep thunders roar
Must'ring thir rage, and Heav'n resembles Hell?
As he our darkness, cannot we his Light
270 Imitate when we please? This Desert soil
Wants not her hidden lustre, Gems and Gold;
Nor want we skill or art, from whence to raise
Magnificence; and what can Heav'n show more?
Our torments also may in length of time
275 Become our Elements, these piercing Fires
As soft as now severe, our temper chang'd
Into their temper;[4] which must needs remove
The sensible of pain.[5] All things invite
To peaceful Counsels, and the settl'd State
280 Of order, how in safety best we may
Compose° our present evils, with regard   order
Of what we are and where, dismissing quite
All thoughts of War; ye have what I advise.

1. The word "hallelujah" (Hebrew, "praise Jehovah") occurred in so many psalms that it came to mean a song of praise to God.
2. Fragrant and perfumed, immortal. Ambrosia was the fabled food or drink of the gods.
3. In *Samson Agonistes* 271, Samson condemns those who are fonder of "bondage with ease than strenuous liberty." The antithesis is from the Roman historian, Sallust, who assigns it to an opponent of the dictator Sulla. See also Jesus' words in Matthew 11.28–30: "Come unto me. . . . For my yoke is easy."
4. Milton alludes to an idea of St. Augustine's, that the devils are bound to tormenting fires as if to bodies (*City of God*, 21.10).
5. The part of pain apprehended through the senses.

He scarce had finisht, when such murmur fill'd
285 Th' Assembly, as when hollow Rocks retain
The sound of blust'ring winds, which all night long
Had rous'd the Sea, now with hoarse cadence lull
Sea-faring men o'erwatcht, whose Bark by chance
Or Pinnace anchors in a craggy Bay
290 After the Tempest: Such applause was heard
As *Mammon* ended, and his Sentence° pleas'd,   *opinion*
Advising peace: for such another Field
They dreaded worse than Hell: so much the fear
Of Thunder and the Sword of *Michaël*[6]
295 Wrought still within them; and no less desire
To found this nether Empire, which might rise
By policy,[7] and long process of time,
In emulation opposite to Heav'n.
Which when *Beëlzebub*[8] perceiv'd, than whom,
300 *Satan* except, none higher sat, with grave
Aspect he rose, and in his rising seem'd
A Pillar of State; deep on his Front° engraven   *forehead*
Deliberation sat and public care;
And Princely counsel in his face yet shone,
305 Majestic though in ruin: sage he stood
With *Atlantean*[9] shoulders fit to bear
The weight of mightiest Monarchies; his look
Drew audience and attention still as Night
Or Summer's Noon-tide air, while thus he spake.
310   Thrones and Imperial Powers, off-spring of Heav'n,
Ethereal Virtues; or these Titles now
Must we renounce, and changing style be call'd
Princes of Hell? for so the popular vote
Inclines, here to continue, and build up here
315 A growing Empire; doubtless; while we dream,
And know not that the King of Heav'n hath doom'd
This place our dungeon, not our safe retreat
Beyond his Potent arm, to live exempt
From Heav'n's high jurisdiction, in new League
320 Banded against his Throne, but to remain
In strictest bondage, though thus far remov'd,
Under th' inevitable curb, reserv'd
His captive multitude: For he, be sure,
In highth or depth, still first and last will Reign
325 Sole King, and of his Kingdom lose no part
By our revolt, but over Hell extend
His Empire, and with Iron Sceptre rule
Us here, as with his Golden those in Heav'n.

6. In the war in Heaven, Michael's two-handed sword felled "squadrons at once" and wounded even Satan. "Michael" here has three syllables.
7. Statesmanship, often in a bad sense, implying Machiavellian strategems. "Process" is stressed on the second syllable.

8. Satan's closest associate.
9. Worthy of Atlas, who was forced by Jupiter to carry the heavens on his shoulders as a punishment for his part in the rebellion of the Titans.

What° sit we then projecting peace and war?   *why*
330   War hath determin'd[1] us, and foil'd with loss
Irreparable; terms of peace yet none
Voutsaf't[2] or sought; for what peace will be giv'n
To us enslav'd, but custody severe,
And stripes, and arbitrary punishment
335   Inflicted? and what peace can we return,
But to our power[3] hostility and hate,
Untam'd reluctance,° and revenge though slow,   *resistance*
Yet ever plotting how the Conqueror least
May reap his conquest, and may least rejoice
340   In doing what we most in suffering feel?[4]
Nor will occasion want, nor shall we need
With dangerous expedition to invade
Heav'n, whose high walls fear no assault or Siege,
Or ambush from the Deep. What if we find
345   Some easier enterprise? There is a place
(If ancient and prophetic fame in Heav'n
Err not) another World, the happy seat
Of some new Race call'd *Man*, about this time
To be created like to us, though less
350   In power and excellence, but favor'd more
Of him who rules above;[5] so was his will
Pronounc'd among the Gods, and by an Oath,
That shook Heav'n's whole circumference, confirm'd.[6]
Thither let us bend all our thoughts, to learn
355   What creatures there inhabit, of what mould,
Or substance, how endu'd,° and what thir Power,   *gifted*
And where thir weakness, how attempted° best,   *attacked*
By force or subtlety: Though Heav'n be shut,
And Heav'n's high Arbitrator sit secure
360   In his own strength, this place may lie expos'd
The utmost border of his Kingdom, left
To their defense who hold it: here perhaps
Some advantageous act may be achiev'd
By sudden onset, either with Hell fire
365   To waste his whole Creation, or possess
All as our own, and drive as we were driven,
The puny° habitants, or if not drive,   *weak*
Seduce them to our Party, that thir God
May prove thir foe, and with repenting hand
370   Abolish his own works. This would surpass
Common revenge, and interrupt his joy

1. Finished, but the context also activates a subsidiary meaning, "war has given us a settled aim."
2. "Vouchsafed": granted; Milton's spelling, "Voutsaf't," indicates the 17th-century pronunciation he preferred.
3. To the limit of our power.
4. How God may get the least happiness from our pain. Beelzebub portrays God as similar in his motives to the devils.

5. The creation of humanity was the subject of a public oath by God, but the time of the creation was the subject of a rumor only ("it is not for you to know the times or season," Acts 1.7).
6. See Isaiah 13.12–13: "I will make a man more precious than fine gold. . . . Therefore I will shake the Heavens."

In our Confusion, and our Joy upraise
In his disturbance; when his darling Sons
Hurl'd headlong to partake with us,[7] shall curse
375   Thir frail Original,° and faded bliss,   *author*
Faded so soon. Advise if this be worth
Attempting, or to sit in darkness here
Hatching vain Empires. Thus *Beëlzebub*
Pleaded his devilish Counsel, first devis'd
380   By *Satan*, and in part propos'd: for whence,
But from the Author of all ill could Spring
So deep a malice, to confound the race
Of mankind in one root,[8] and Earth with Hell
To mingle and involve, done all to spite
385   The great Creator? But thir spite still serves
His glory to augment. The bold design
Pleas'd highly those infernal States,[9] and joy
Sparkl'd in all thir eyes; with full assent
They vote: whereat his speech he thus renews.
390   Well have ye judg'd, well ended long debate,
Synod[1] of Gods, and like to what ye are,
Great things resolv'd, which from the lowest deep
Will once more lift us up, in spite of Fate,
Nearer our ancient Seat; perhaps in view
395   Of those bright confines, whence with neighboring Arms
And opportune excursion we may chance
Re-enter Heav'n; or else in some mild Zone
Dwell not unvisited of Heav'n's fair Light
Secure, and at the bright'ning Orient beam
400   Purge off this gloom; the soft delicious Air,
To heal the scar of these corrosive Fires
Shall breathe her balm. But first whom shall we send
In search of this new world, whom shall we find
Sufficient? who shall tempt° with wand'ring feet   *venture upon*
405   The dark unbottom'd infinite Abyss
And through the palpable obscure[2] find out
His uncouth° way, or spread his aery flight   *unknown*
Upborne with indefatigable wings
Over the vast abrupt,[3] ere he arrive
410   The happy Isle; what strength, what art can then
Suffice, or what evasion bear him safe
Through the strict Senteries° and Stations thick   *sentries*
Of Angels watching round? Here he had need
All circumspection, and wee now no less
415   Choice in our suffrage;[4] for on whom we send,
The weight of all and our last hope relies.

7. Share in our condition; also, take sides with us.
8. Adam, the root of the genealogical tree of man.
9. Estates of the realm, people of rank and authority.
1. A meeting of councillors.
2. See Exodus 10.21: "The Lord said unto Moses, Stretch

out thine hand toward heaven, that there may be darkness over the land of Egypt, even darkness which may be felt."
3. The adjective (precipitous, broken off) is here used as a noun and refers to the abyss between hell and heaven.
4. Care in our vote (to elect him).

This said, he sat; and expectation held
His look suspense, awaiting who appear'd
To second, or oppose, or undertake

420 The perilous attempt; but all sat mute,
Pondering the danger with deep thoughts; and each
In other's count'nance read his own dismay
Astonisht: none among the choice and prime
Of those Heav'n-warring Champions could be found

425 So hardy as to proffer° or accept   *offer*
Alone the dreadful voyage; till at last
Satan, whom now transcendent glory rais'd
Above his fellows, with Monarchal pride
Conscious of highest worth, unmov'd thus spake.

430   O Progeny of Heav'n, Empyreal Thrones,
With reason hath deep silence and demur°   *delay*
Seiz'd us, though undismay'd: long is the way
And hard, that out of Hell leads up to light;
Our prison strong, this huge convex° of Fire,   *vault*

435 Outrageous to devour, immures us round
Ninefold, and gates of burning Adamant
Barr'd over us prohibit all egress.
These past, if any pass, the void profound
Of unessential° Night receives him next   *empty*

440 Wide gaping, and with utter loss of being
Threatens him, plung'd in that abortive gulf.
If thence he scape into whatever world,
Or unknown Region, what remains him less
Than[5] unknown dangers and as hard escape.

445 But I should ill become this Throne, O Peers,
And this Imperial Sov'ranty, adorn'd
With splendor, arm'd with power, if aught propos'd
And judg'd of public moment, in the shape
Of difficulty or danger could deter

450 Mee from attempting. Wherefore do I assume
These Royalties, and not refuse to Reign,
Refusing[6] to accept as great a share
Of hazard as of honor, due alike
To him who Reigns, and so much to him due

455 Of hazard more, as he above the rest
High honor'd sits? Go therefore mighty Powers.
Terror of Heav'n, though fall'n; intend° at home,   *consider*
While here shall be our home, what best may ease
The present misery, and render Hell

460 More tolerable; if there be cure or charm
To respite° or deceive, or slack the pain   *rest*
Of this ill Mansion: intermit no watch
Against a wakeful Foe, while I abroad
Through all the Coasts of dark destruction seek

5. What awaits him except.   6. If I refuse.

465 Deliverance for us all: this enterprise
None shall partake with me. Thus saying rose
The Monarch, and prevented all reply,
Prudent, lest from his resolution rais'd°   *encouraged*
Others among the chief might offer now
470 (Certain to be refus'd) what erst they fear'd;
And so refus'd might in opinion stand
His Rivals, winning cheap the high repute
Which he through hazard huge must earn. But they
Dreaded not more th' adventure than his voice
475 Forbidding; and at once with him they rose;
Thir rising all at once was as the sound
Of Thunder heard remote. Towards him they bend
With awful° reverence prone; and as a God   *respectful*
Extol him equal to the highest in Heav'n:
480 Nor fail'd they to express how much they prais'd,
That for the general safety he despis'd
His own: for neither do the Spirits damn'd
Lose all thir virtue; lest bad men should boast[7]
Thir specious° deeds on earth, which glory excites,   *pretending*
485 Or close° ambition varnisht o'er with zeal.   *secret*
Thus they thir doubtful consultations dark
Ended rejoicing in their matchless Chief:
As when from mountain tops the dusky clouds
Ascending, while the North wind sleeps, o'erspread
490 Heav'n's cheerful face, the low'ring Element
Scowls o'er the dark'n'd lantskip° Snow, or show'r;   *landscape*
If chance the radiant Sun with farewell sweet
Extend his ev'ning beam, the fields revive,
The birds thir notes renew, and bleating herds
495 Attest thir joy, that hill and valley rings.
O shame to men! Devil with Devil damn'd
Firm concord holds, men only disagree
Of Creatures rational, though under hope
Of heavenly Grace; and God proclaiming peace,
500 Yet live in hatred, enmity, and strife
Among themselves, and levy cruel wars,
Wasting the Earth, each other to destroy:
As if (which might induce us to accord)
Man had not hellish foes anow° besides,   *enough*
505 That day and night for his destruction wait.
       The *Stygian* Council thus dissolv'd; and forth
In order came the grand infernal Peers:
Midst came thir mighty Paramount,° and seem'd   *ruler*
Alone th' Antagonist of Heav'n, nor less
510 Than Hell's dread Emperor with pomp Supreme,[8]
And God-like imitated State; him round
A Globe° of fiery Seraphim inclos'd   *band*

7. So that men ought not to boast.
8. Lines 510–20 may portray the English mob's easy

gullibility and their passion (which Milton detested) for
the regalia of monarchy.

With bright imblazonry,° and horrent° Arms.   *heraldry/bristling*
Then of thir Session ended they bid cry
515 With Trumpet's regal sound the great result:
Toward the four winds four speedy Cherubim
Put to thir mouths the sounding Alchymy[9]
By Herald's voice explain'd: the hollow Abyss
Heard far and wide, and all the host of Hell
520 With deaf'ning shout, return'd them loud acclaim.
Thence more at ease thir minds and somewhat rais'd° *encouraged*
By false presumptuous hope, the ranged powers[1]
Disband, and wand'ring, each his several way
Pursues, as inclination or sad choice
525 Leads him perplext, where he may likeliest find
Truce to his restless thoughts, and entertain
The irksome hours, till this great Chief return.
Part on the Plain, or in the Air sublime°   *uplifted*
Upon the wing, or in swift Race contend,
530 As at th' *Olympian* Games or *Pythian* fields;[2]
Part curb thir fiery Steeds, or shun the Goal
With rapid wheels, or fronted Brígads form.
As when to warn proud Cities war appears
Wag'd in the troubl'd Sky, and Armies rush
535 To Battle in the Clouds, before each Van
Prick forth the Aery Knights, and couch thir spears
Till thickest Legions close; with feats of Arms
From either end of Heav'n the welkin° burns.   *sky*
Others with vast *Typhoean*[3] rage more fell
540 Rend up both Rocks and Hills, and ride the Air
In whirlwind; Hell scarce holds the wild uproar.
As when *Alcides* from *Oechalia* Crown'd
With conquest, felt th' envenom'd robe, and tore
Through pain up by the roots *Thessalian* Pines,
545 And *Lichas* from the top of *Oeta* threw
Into th' *Euboic* Sea.[4] Others more mild,
Retreated in a silent valley, sing
With notes Angelical to many a Harp
Thir own Heroic deeds and hapless fall
550 By doom of Battle; and complain that Fate
Free Virtue should enthrall to Force or Chance.
Thir Song was partial,° but the harmony   *prejudiced*
(What could it less when Spirits immortal sing?)
Suspended° Hell, and took with ravishment   *enthralled*

---

9. Trumpets made of the alloy brass, associated with alchemy.
1. Armies drawn up in ranks.
2. Epic models for lines 528–69 include the sports of the Myrmidons during Achilles' absence from the war (Homer, *Iliad* 2.774ff.), the Greek funeral games of *Iliad* 23 and the Trojan of *Aeneid* 5, and the amusements of the blessed dead in Virgil's Elysium (*Aeneid* 6.642–59). To "shun the goal" (line 531) is to drive a chariot as close

as possible around a post without touching it.
3. Like that of Typhon, the hundred-headed Titan. A pun, for "typhon" was also an English word meaning "whirlwind."
4. "Alcides" (Hercules) returning as victor from "Oechalia" (Ovid, *Metamorphoses* 9.136) put on a ritual robe that had inadvertently been soaked by his wife in corrosive poison. Mad with pain, he blamed his friend Lichas, who had brought the robe, and hurled him far into the "Euboic" (Euboean) Sea.

555   The thronging audience. In discourse more sweet
       (For Eloquence the Soul, Song charms the Sense,)
       Others apart sat on a Hill retir'd,
       In thoughts more elevate, and reason'd high
       Of Providence, Foreknowledge, Will, and Fate,
560   Fixt Fate, Free will, Foreknowledge absolute,
       And found no end, in wand'ring mazes lost.
       Of good and evil much they argu'd then,
       Of happiness and final misery,
       Passion and Apathy, and glory and shame,
565   Vain wisdom all, and false Philosophie:[5]
       Yet with a pleasing sorcery could charm
       Pain for a while or anguish, and excite
       Fallacious hope, or arm th' obdured° breast   hardened
       With stubborn patience as with triple steel.
570   Another part in Squadrons and gross° Bands,   dense
       On bold adventure to discover wide
       That dismal World, if any Clime perhaps
       Might yield them easier habitation, bend
       Four ways thir flying March, along the Banks
575   Of four infernal Rivers that disgorge
       Into the burning Lake thir baleful° streams;[6]   evil
       Abhorred *Styx* the flood of deadly hate,
       Sad *Acheron* of sorrow, black and deep;
       Cocytus, nam'd of lamentation loud
580   Heard on the rueful stream; fierce *Phlegeton*
       Whose waves of torrent fire inflame with rage.
       Far off from these a slow and silent stream,
       Lethe the River of Oblivion rolls
       Her wat'ry Labyrinth, whereof who drinks,
585   Forthwith his former state and being forgets,
       Forgets both joy and grief, pleasure and pain.
       Beyond this flood a frozen Continent
       Lies dark and wild, beat with perpetual storms
       Of Whirlwind and dire Hail, which on firm land
590   Thaws not, but gathers heap, and ruin seems
       Of ancient pile; all else deep snow and ice,
       A gulf profound as that *Serbonian* Bog[7]
       Betwixt *Damiata* and Mount *Casius* old,
       Where Armies whole have sunk: the parching° Air   withering
595   Burns frore,° and cold performs th' effect of Fire.   frozen
       Thither by harpy-footed Furies hal'd,[8]
       At certain revolutions all the damn'd
       Are brought: and feel by turns the bitter change

5. Directed against Stoicism, the most formidable ethical
challenge to Christianity; "apathy," or complete freedom
from passion, was a Stoic ideal.
6. This description of the four rivers of hell takes its
broad outline from Virgil's *Aeneid* 6, Dante's *Inferno* 14,
and Spenser's *Faerie Queene* 2.7.56ff. Milton adds the detail of confluence in the "burning lake." The epithet or

description attached to each river translates its Greek
name (e.g., "Styx" means hateful).
7. Serbonis, a lake bordered by quicksands on the Egyptian coast.
8. Milton combines the hook-clawed Harpies of Dante
and Virgil with the ancient Greek Furies, daughters of
Acheron and Night and agencies of divine vengeance.

Of fierce extremes, extremes by change more fierce,
600   From Beds of raging Fire to starve° in Ice   *stifle*
Thir soft Ethereal warmth, and there to pine
Immovable, infixt, and frozen round,
Periods of time, thence hurried back to fire.
They ferry over this *Lethean* Sound
605   Both to and fro, thir sorrow to augment,
And wish and struggle, as they pass, to reach
The tempting stream, with one small drop to lose
In sweet forgetfulness all pain and woe,
All in one moment, and so near the brink;
610   But Fate withstands, and to oppose th' attempt
Medusa[9] with *Gorgonian* terror guards
The Ford, and of itself the water flies
All taste of living wight, as once it fled
The lip of *Tantalus.*[1] Thus roving on
615   In confus'd march forlorn, th' advent'rous Bands
With shudd'ring horror pale, and eyes aghast
View'd first thir lamentable lot, and found
No rest: through many a dark and dreary Vale
They pass'd, and many a Region dolorous,
620   O'er many a Frozen, many a Fiery Alp,
Rocks, Caves, Lakes, Fens, Bogs, Dens, and shades of death,
A Universe of death, which God by curse
Created evil, for evil only good,
Where all life dies, death lives, and Nature breeds,
625   Perverse, all monstrous, all prodigious things,
Abominable, inutterable, and worse
Than Fables yet have feign'd, or fear conceiv'd,
Gorgons and *Hydras,* and *Chimeras* dire.[2]

* * *

Book 9
The Argument

Satan *having compast the Earth, with meditated guile returns as a mist by Night into Paradise, enters into the Serpent sleeping. Adam and Eve in the Morning go forth to thir labors, which Eve proposes to divide in several places, each laboring apart: Adam consents not, alleging the danger, lest that Enemy, of whom they were forewarn'd, should attempt her found alone: Eve loath to be thought not circumspect or firm enough, urges her going apart, the rather desirous to make trial of her strength; Adam at last yields: The Serpent finds her alone; his subtle approach, first gazing, then speaking, with much flattery extolling Eve above all other Creatures. Eve wond'ring to hear the Serpent speak, asks how he attain'd to human speech and such understanding not till now; the Serpent answers, that by tasting of a certain Tree in the Garden he attain'd both to Speech and Reason, till then void*

---

9. One of the Gorgons, mythical sisters with snakes for
hair, whose look turned the beholder into stone.
1. In Homer's hell, Tantalus is tormented by thirst, standing in a pool that recedes whenever he tries to drink

(*Odyssey* 11.582–92).
2. The Hydra was many-headed, and the Chimeras
breathed flame.

of both: Eve requires him to bring her to that Tree, and finds it to be the Tree of Knowledge forbidden: The Serpent now grown bolder, with many wiles and arguments induces her at length to eat; she pleas'd with the taste deliberates awhile whether to impart thereof to Adam or not, at last brings him of the Fruit, relates what persuaded her to eat thereof: Adam at first amaz'd, but perceiving her lost, resolves through vehemence[1] of love to perish with her; and extenuating[2] the trespass, eats also of the Fruit: The effects thereof in them both; they seek to cover thir nakedness; then fall to variance and accusation of one another.

      No more of talk where God or Angel Guest
With Man, as with his Friend, familiar us'd
To sit indulgent, and with him partake
Rural repast, permitting him the while
5   Venial° discourse unblam'd: I now must change   *permissible*
Those Notes to Tragic; foul distrust, and breach
Disloyal on the part of Man, revolt,
And disobedience: On the part of Heav'n
Now alienated, distance and distaste,
10   Anger and just rebuke, and judgment giv'n,
That brought into this World a world of woe,
Sin and her shadow Death, and Misery
Death's Harbinger: Sad task, yet argument
Not less but more Heroic than the wrath
15   Of stern *Achilles* on his Foe pursu'd
Thrice Fugitive about *Troy* Wall; or rage
Of *Turnus* for *Lavinia* disespous'd,
Or *Neptune's* ire or *Juno's,* that so long
Perplex'd the *Greek* and *Cytherea's* Son;[3]
20   If answerable° style I can obtain   *equal, accountable*
Of my Celestial Patroness,[4] who deigns
Her nightly visitation unimplor'd,
And dictates to me slumb'ring, or inspires
Easy my unpremeditated Verse:
25   Since first this Subject for Heroic Song
Pleas'd me long choosing, and beginning late;
Not sedulous by Nature to indite
Wars, hitherto the only Argument
Heroic deem'd, chief maistry to dissect
30   With long and tedious havoc fabl'd Knights
In Battles feign'd; the better fortitude
Of Patience and Heroic Martyrdom
Unsung; or to describe Races and Games,
Or tilting Furniture, emblazon'd Shields,

---

1. The root meaning of Latin "vehementia" is mindlessness.
2. Carrying further, drawing out.
3. Achilles is "stern" in his "wrath" because he refused any covenant with Hector, and Turnus dies fighting Aeneas for the hand of Lavinia, whereas Messiah, more heroically, is not implacable in his anger. He issued his sole commandment "sternly" (8.333); but when it is disobeyed, he works for reconciliation. Similarly, God's anger is distinguished from "Neptune's ire" and "Juno's"

(which merely "perplexed" Odysseus and Aeneas) in that it is expressed in justice rather than in victimization.
4. The heavenly Muse, Urania. Both ancient and modern epics had always had war, or at least fighting, as a principal ingredient. (So has *Paradise Lost,* in the first half of the poem; but in the second half this subject is transcended.) Milton now glances unfavorably at the typical matter of the romantic epic.

35	Impreses[5] quaint, Caparisons[6] and Steeds;
	Bases and tinsel Trappings, gorgeous Knights
	At Joust and Tournament; then marshall'd Feast
	Serv'd up in Hall with Sewers,° and Seneschals;° *waiters / stewards*
	The skill of Artifice or Office mean,
40	Not that which justly gives Heroic name
	To Person or to Poem.[7] Mee of these
	Nor skill'd nor studious, higher Argument
	Remains, sufficient of itself to raise
	That name,[8] unless an age too late, or cold
45	Climate, or Years damp my intended wing
	Deprest; and much they may, if all be mine,
	Not Hers who brings it nightly to my Ear.
	The Sun was sunk, and after him the Star
	Of *Hesperus*,° whose Office is to bring *the planet Venus*
50	Twilight upon the Earth, short Arbiter
	Twixt Day and Night, and now from end to end
	Night's Hemisphere had veil'd the Horizon round:
	When *Satan* who late fled before the threats
	Of *Gabriel* out of *Eden*,[9] now improv'd° *intensified*
55	In meditated fraud and malice, bent
	On Man's destruction, maugre what might hap
	Of heavier on himself,[1] fearless return'd.
	By Night he fled, and at Midnight return'd
	From compassing the Earth, cautious of day,
60	Since *Uriel* Regent of the Sun descri'd
	His entrance, and forewarn'd the Cherubim
	That kept thir watch; thence full of anguish driv'n,
	The space of seven continu'd Nights he rode
	With darkness, thrice the Equinoctial Line
65	He circl'd, four times cross'd the Car of Night
	From Pole to Pole, traversing each Colure;[2]
	On th'eighth return'd, and on the Coast averse
	From entrance or Cherubic Watch, by stealth
	Found unsuspected way. There was a place,
70	Now not, though Sin, not Time, first wrought the change,
	Where *Tigris* at the foot of Paradise
	Into a Gulf shot under ground, till part
	Rose up a Fountain by the Tree of Life;
	In with the River sunk, and with it rose
75	*Satan* involv'd in rising Mist, then sought
	Where to lie hid; Sea he had searcht and Land

5. Heraldic devices, often with accompanying mottos.
6. Ornamented coverings spread over the saddle of a horse.
7. Artifice implies mechanic or applied art. It is beneath the dignity of epic to teach etiquette and social ceremony and heraldry.
8. The name of epic.

9. I.e., at the end of Book 4, a week earlier.
1. Despite the danger of heavier punishment.
2. By keeping to earth's shadow, Satan contrives to experience a whole week of darkness. The two colures were great circles, intersecting at right angles at the poles and dividing the equinoctial circle (the equator) into four equal parts.

From *Eden* over *Pontus*, and the Pool
Maeotis, up beyond the River *Ob*;[3]
Downward as far Antarctic; and in length
West from *Orontes* to the Ocean barr'd
At *Darien*, thence to the Land where flows
Ganges and *Indus*:[4] thus the Orb he roam'd
With narrow search; and with inspection deep
Consider'd every Creature, which of all
Most opportune might serve his Wiles, and found
The Serpent subtlest Beast of all the Field.[5]
Him after long debate, irresolute° *undecided*
Of thoughts revolv'd, his final sentence° chose *judgment*
Fit Vessel, fittest Imp° of fraud, in whom *offshoot*
To enter, and his dark suggestions hide
From sharpest sight: for in the wily Snake,
Whatever sleights none would suspicious mark,
As from his wit and native subtlety
Proceeding, which in other Beasts observ'd
Doubt° might beget of Diabolic pow'r *suspicion*
Active within beyond the sense of brute.
Thus he resolv'd, but first from inward grief
His bursting passion into plaints thus pour'd:
  O Earth, how like to Heav'n, if not preferr'd
More justly, Seat worthier of Gods, as built
With second thoughts, reforming what was old!
For what God after better worse would build?
Terrestrial Heav'n, danc't round by other Heav'ns
That shine, yet bear thir bright officious Lamps,
Light above Light, for thee alone, as seems,
In thee concentring all thir precious beams
Of sacred influence:[6] As God in Heav'n
Is Centre, yet extends to all, so thou
Centring receiv'st from all those Orbs; in thee,
Not in themselves, all thir known virtue appears
Productive in Herb, Plant, and nobler birth
Of Creatures animate with gradual life
Of Growth, Sense, Reason, all summ'd up in Man.[7]
With what delight could I have walkt thee round,
If I could joy in aught, sweet interchange
Of Hill and Valley, Rivers, Woods and Plains,
Now Land, now Sea, and Shores with Forest crown'd,
Rocks, Dens, and Caves; but I in none of these
Find place or refuge; and the more I see

3. In his north-south circles, Satan passed Pontus (the Black Sea), the "pool / maeotis" (the Sea of Azov), and the Siberian River Ob, which flows north into the Gulf of Ob and from there into the Arctic Ocean.
4. In his westward circling of the equinoctial line, he crossed the Syrian River Orontes, then the Pacific ("peaceful") "Ocean barred" by the Isthmus of Darien (Panama) and India.
5. See Genesis 3.1.
6. The case for an earth-centered universe, put at 8.86–114 by Raphael, is now put by Satan.
7. "Growth, sense, reason" are the activities of the vegetable, animal, and rational souls, respectively, in humans.

120   Pleasures about me, so much more I feel
        Torment within me, as from the hateful siege°   *conflict*
        Of contraries; all good to me becomes
        Bane,° and in Heav'n much worse would be my state.   *poison*
        But neither here seek I, no nor in Heav'n
125   To dwell, unless by maistring Heav'n's Supreme;
        Nor hope to be myself less miserable
        By what I seek, but others to make such
        As I, though thereby worse to me redound:
        For only in destroying I find ease
130   To my relentless thoughts; and him destroy'd,
        Or won to what may work his utter loss,
        For whom all this was made, all this will soon
        Follow, as to him linkt in weal or woe,
        In woe then: that destruction wide may range:[8]
135   To mee shall be the glory sole among
        Th'infernal Powers, in one day to have marr'd
        What he *Almight* styl'd, six Nights and Days
        Continu'd making, and who knows how long
        Before had been contriving, though perhaps
140   Not longer than since I in one Night freed
        From servitude inglorious well nigh half
        Th' Angelic Name, and thinner left the throng
        Of his adorers: hee to be aveng'd,
        And to repair his numbers thus impair'd,
145   Whether such virtue° spent of old now fail'd   *power*
        More Angels to Create, if they at least
        Are his Created, or to spite us more,
        Determin'd to advance into our room
        A Creature form'd of Earth, and him endow,
150   Exalted from so base original,
        With Heav'nly spoils, our spoils; What he decreed
        He effected; Man he made, and for him built
        Magnificent this World, and Earth his seat,
        Him Lord pronounc'd, and, O indignity!
155   Subjected to his service Angel wings,
        And flaming Ministers to watch and tend
        Thir earthy Charge: Of these the vigilance
        I dread, and to elude, thus wrapt in mist
        Of midnight vapor glide obscure, and pry
160   In every Bush and Brake, where hap may find
        The Serpent sleeping, in whose mazy folds
        To hide me, and the dark intent I bring.
        O foul descent! that I who erst contended
        With Gods to sit the highest, am now constrain'd
165   Into a Beast, and mixt with bestial slime,
        This essence to incarnate and imbrute,

8. The created cosmos will follow humans to destruction.

That to the highth of Deity aspir'd;
But what will not Ambition and Revenge
Descend to? who aspires must down as low

170 As high he soar'd, obnoxious° first or last   *exposed*
To basest things. Revenge, at first though sweet,
Bitter ere long back on itself recoils;
Let it, I reck not, so it light well aim'd,
Since higher I fall short, on him who next

175 Provokes my envy, this new Favorite
Of Heav'n, this Man of Clay, Son of despite,
Whom us the more to spite his Maker rais'd
From dust: spite then with spite is best repaid.
        So saying, through each Thicket Dank or Dry,

180 Like a black mist low creeping, he held on
His midnight search, where soonest he might find
The Serpent: him fast sleeping soon he found
In Labyrinth of many a round self-roll'd,
His head the midst, well stor'd with subtle wiles:

185 Not yet in horrid Shade or dismal Den,
Nor nocent° yet, but on the grassy Herb   *harmful, guilty*
Fearless unfear'd he slept: in at his Mouth
The Devil enter'd, and his brutal sense,
In heart or head, possessing soon inspir'd

190 With act intelligential; but his sleep
Disturb'd not, waiting close° th' approach of Morn.   *concealed*
Now whenas sacred Light began to dawn
In *Eden* on the humid Flow'rs, that breath'd
Thir morning incense, when all things that breathe,

195 From th' Earth's great Altar send up silent praise
To the Creator, and his Nostrils fill
With grateful Smell, forth came the human pair,
And join'd thir vocal Worship to the Choir
Of Creatures wanting voice; that done, partake

200 The season, prime for sweetest Scents and Airs:
Then cómmune how that day they best may ply
Thir growing work: for much thir work outgrew
The hands' dispatch of two Gard'ning so wide.
And *Eve* first to her Husband thus began.

205   *Adam*, well may we labor still to dress
This Garden, still to tend Plant, Herb and Flow'r,
Our pleasant task enjoin'd, but till more hands
Aid us, the work under our labor grows,
Luxurious by restraint; what we by day

210 Lop overgrown, or prune, or prop, or bind,
One night or two with wanton growth derides
Tending to wild. Thou therefore now advise
Or hear what to my mind first thoughts present,
Let us divide our labors, thou where choice

215 Leads thee, or where most needs, whether to wind

The Woodbine round this Arbor, or direct
The clasping Ivy where to climb, while I
In yonder Spring of Roses intermixt
With Myrtle, find what to redress till Noon:
220   For while so near each other thus all day
Our task we choose, what wonder if so near
Looks intervene and smiles, or object new
Casual discourse draw on, which intermits
Our day's work brought to little, though begun
225   Early, and th' hour of Supper comes unearn'd.
        To whom mild answer *Adam* thus return'd.
Sole *Eve*, Associate sole, to me beyond
Compare above all living Creatures dear,
Well hast thou motion'd,° well thy thoughts imploy'd   *proposed*
230   How we might best fulfil the work which here
God hath assign'd us, nor of me shalt pass
Unprais'd: for nothing lovelier can be found
In Woman, than to study household good,
And good works in her Husband to promote.
235   Yet not so strictly hath our Lord impos'd
Labor, as to debar us when we need
Refreshment, whether food, or talk between,
Food of the mind, or this sweet intercourse
Of looks and smiles, for smiles from Reason flow,
240   To brute deni'd, and are of Love the food,
Love not the lowest end of human life.
For not to irksome toil, but to delight
He made us, and delight to Reason join'd.
These paths and Bowers doubt not but our joint hands
245   Will keep from Wilderness with ease, as wide
As we need walk, till younger hands ere long
Assist us: But if much converse perhaps
Thee satiate, to short absence I could yield.
For solitude sometimes is best society,
250   And short retirement urges sweet return.
But other doubt possesses me, lest harm
Befall thee sever'd from me; for thou know'st
What hath been warn'd us, what malicious Foe
Envying our happiness, and of his own
255   Despairing, seeks to work us woe and shame
By sly assault; and somewhere nigh at hand
Watches, no doubt, with greedy hope to find
His wish and best advantage, us asunder,
Hopeless to circumvent us join'd, where each
260   To other speedy aid might lend at need;
Whether his first design be to withdraw
Our fealty from God, or to disturb
Conjugal Love, than which perhaps no bliss
Enjoy'd by us excites his envy more;

265   Or this, or worse,[9] leave not the faithful side
     That gave thee being, still shades thee and protects.
     The Wife, where danger or dishonor lurks,
     Safest and seemliest by her Husband stays,
     Who guards her, or with her the worst endures.
270   To whom the Virgin° Majesty of *Eve*,   *chaste, innocent*
     As one who loves, and some unkindness meets,
     With sweet austere composure thus repli'd.
       Offspring of Heav'n and Earth, and all Earth's Lord,
     That such an Enemy we have, who seeks
275   Our ruin, both by thee inform'd I learn,
     And from the parting Angel over-heard
     As in a shady nook I stood behind,
     Just then return'd at shut of Ev'ning Flow'rs.
     But that thou shouldst my firmness therefore doubt
280   To God or thee, because we have a foe
     May tempt it, I expected not to hear.
     His violence thou fear'st not, being such,
     As wee, not capable of death or pain,
     Can either not receive, or can repel.
285   His fraud is then thy fear, which plain infers
     Thy equal fear that my firm Faith and Love
     Can by his fraud be shak'n or seduc't;
     Thoughts, which how found they harbor in thy breast,
     Adam, misthought of her to thee so dear?
290   To whom with healing words *Adam* repli'd.
     Daughter of God and Man, immortal *Eve*,
     For such thou art, from sin and blame entire:°   *free*
     Not diffident° of thee do I dissuade   *mistrustful*
     Thy absence from my sight, but to avoid
295   Th' attempt itself, intended by our Foe.
     For hee who tempts, though in vain, at least asperses°   *falsely charges*
     The tempted with dishonor foul, suppos'd
     Not incorruptible of Faith, not proof
     Against temptation: thou thyself with scorn
300   And anger wouldst resent the offer'd wrong,
     Though ineffectual found: misdeem not then,
     If such affront I labor to avert
     From thee alone, which on us both at once
     The Enemy, though bold, will hardly dare,
305   Or daring, first on mee th' assault shall light.
     Nor thou his malice and false guile contemn;
     Subtle he needs must be, who could seduce
     Angels, nor think superfluous others' aid.
     I from the influence of thy looks receive
310   Access° in every Virtue, in thy sight   *increase*
     More wise, more watchful, stronger, if need were

9. Whether this or worse (be his first design).

Of outward strength; while shame, thou looking on,
Shame to be overcome or over-reacht
Would utmost vigor raise, and rais'd unite.

315   Why shouldst not thou like sense within thee feel
When I am present, and thy trial choose
With me, best witness of thy Virtue tri'd.
So spake domestic *Adam* in his care
And Matrimonial Love; but *Eve*, who thought
320   Less° attribúted to her Faith sincere,   *too little*
Thus her reply with accent sweet renew'd.
If this be our condition, thus to dwell
In narrow circuit strait'n'd by a Foe,
Subtle or violent, we not endu'd
325   Single with like defense, wherever met,
How are we happy, still in fear of harm?
But harm precedes not sin: only our Foe
Tempting affronts us with his foul esteem
Of our integrity: his foul esteem
330   Sticks no dishonor on our Front,° but turns   *forehead*
Foul on himself; then wherefore shunn'd or fear'd
By us? who rather double honor gain
From his surmise prov'd false, find peace within,
Favor from Heav'n, our witness from th' event.
335   And what is Faith, Love, Virtue unassay'd
Alone, without exterior help sustain'd?
Let us not then suspect our happy State
Left so imperfet by the Maker wise,
As not secure to single or combin'd.
340   Frail is our happiness, if this be so,
And *Eden* were no Eden[1] thus expos'd.
To whom thus Adam fervently repli'd.
O Woman, best are all things as the will
Of God ordain'd them, his creating hand
345   Nothing imperfet or deficient left
Of all that he Created, much less Man,
Or aught that might his happy State secure,
Secure from outward force; within himself
The danger lies, yet lies within his power:
350   Against his will he can receive no harm.
But God left free the Will, for what obeys
Reason, is free, and Reason he made right,
But bid her well beware, and still erect,[2]
Lest by some fair appearing good surpris'd
355   She dictate false, and misinform the Will
To do what God expressly hath forbid.
Not then mistrust, but tender love enjoins,
That I should mind thee oft, and mind thou me.
Firm we subsist, yet possible to swerve,

---

1. I.e., no pleasure, the literal Hebrew meaning of "Eden."   2. Always attentive, but also with a glance at upright.

360   Since Reason not impossibly may meet
       Some specious object by the Foe suborn'd,
       And fall into deception unaware,
       Not keeping strictest watch, as she was warn'd.
       Seek not temptation then, which to avoid
365   Were better, and most likely if from mee
       Thou sever not: Trial will come unsought.
       Wouldst thou approve° thy constancy, approve   *demonstrate*
       First thy obedience; th' other who can know,
       Not seeing thee attempted, who attest?
370   But if thou think, trial unsought may find
       Us both securer° than thus warn'd thou seem'st,   *more careless*
       Go; for thy stay, not free, absents thee more;
       Go in thy native innocence, rely
       On what thou hast of virtue, summon all,
375   For God towards thee hath done his part, do thine.
           So spake the Patriarch of Mankind, but *Eve*
       Persisted, yet submiss, though last, repli'd.
           With thy permission then, and thus forewarn'd
       Chiefly by what thy own last reasoning words
380   Touch'd only, that our trial, when least sought,
       May find us both perhaps far less prepar'd,
       The willinger I go, nor much expect
       A Foe so proud will first the weaker seek;
       So bent, the more shall shame him his repulse.
385   Thus saying, from her Husband's hand her hand
       Soft she withdrew, and like a Wood-Nymph light,
       Oread or *Dryad,* or of *Delia's* Train,[3]
       Betook her to the Groves, but *Delia's* self
       In gait surpass'd and Goddess-like deport,
390   Though not as shee with Bow and Quiver arm'd,
       But with such Gard'ning Tools as Art yet rude,
       Guiltless° of fire had form'd, or Angels brought.[4]   *innocent, ignorant*
       To Pales, or Pomona, thus adorn'd,
       Likest she seem'd, Pomona when she fled
395   *Vertumnus,* or to *Ceres* in her Prime,
       Yet Virgin of *Proserpina* from *Jove.*[5]
       Her long and ardent look his Eye pursu'd
       Delighted, but desiring more her stay.
       Oft he to her his charge of quick return
400   Repeated, shee to him as oft engag'd
       To be return'd by Noon amid the Bow'r,
       And all things in best order to invite
       Noontide repast, or Afternoon's repose.

---

3. Oreads were mountain nymphs, such as attended on Diana; dryads were wood nymphs. Neither class of nymphs was immortal.
4. Only as a result of the Fall did it become necessary for humans to have some means of warming themselves. There may also be an allusion to the fire stolen from heaven by Prometheus.
5. Pales was the Roman goddess of pastures; Pomona was the nymph or goddess of fruit trees, seduced by the disguised Vertumnus; Ceres was the goddess of corn and agriculture who bore Proserpina to Jove.

O much deceiv'd, much failing, hapless *Eve*,
405   Of thy presum'd return! event perverse!
Thou never from that hour in Paradise
Found'st either sweet repast, or sound repose;
Such ambush hid among sweet Flow'rs and Shades
Waited with hellish rancor imminent
410   To intercept thy way, or send thee back
Despoil'd of Innocence, of Faith, of Bliss.
For now, and since first break of dawn the Fiend,
Mere° Serpent in appearance, forth was come,   *plain*
And on his Quest, where likeliest he might find
415   The only two of Mankind, but in them
The whole included Race, his purpos'd prey.
In Bow'r and Field he sought, where any tuft
Of Grove or Garden-Plot more pleasant lay,
Thir tendance° or Plantation for delight,   *object of care*
420   By Fountain or by shady Rivulet,
He sought them both, but wish'd his hap° might find   *chance*
Eve separate, he wish'd, but not with hope
Of what so seldom chanc'd, when to his wish,
Beyond his hope, *Eve* separate he spies,
425   Veil'd in a Cloud of Fragrance, where she stood,
Half spi'd, so thick the Roses bushing round
About her glow'd, oft stooping to support
Each Flow'r of slender stalk, whose head though gay
Carnation, Purple, Azure, or speckt with Gold,
430   Hung drooping unsustain'd, them she upstays
Gently with Myrtle band, mindless the while,
Herself, though fairest unsupported Flow'r,
From her best prop so far, and storm so nigh.
Nearer he drew, and many a walk travers'd
435   Of stateliest Covert, Cedar, Pine, or Palm,
Then voluble and bold, now hid, now seen
Among thick-wov'n Arborets and Flow'rs
Imborder'd on each Bank, the hand° of *Eve*:   *handiwork*
Spot more delicious than those Gardens feign'd
440   Or of reviv'd *Adonis*, or renown'd
Alcinoüs, host of old *Laertes'* Son,
Or that, not Mystic, where the Sapient King
Held dalliance with his fair *Egyptian* Spouse.[6]
Much hee the Place admir'd, the Person more.
445   As one who long in populous City pent,
Where Houses thick and Sewers annoy the Air,

---

6. "The sapient king" was Solomon (*Song of Solomon* 6.2). Milton alludes to Spenser's addition to the myth of Adonis, that Venus keeps Adonis hidden in a secret garden (*The Faerie Queene* 3.6). "Laertes' son" was Odysseus; much-traveled as he was, he marveled when he saw the Garden of Alcinoüs (Homer, *Odyssey* 7).

Forth issuing on a Summer's Morn to breathe
Among the pleasant Villages and Farms
Adjoin'd, from each thing met conceives delight,
450   The smell of Grain, or tedded° Grass, or Kine,°   *mown / cows*
Or Dairy, each rural sight, each rural sound;
If chance with Nymphlike step fair Virgin pass,
What pleasing seem'd, for her now pleases more,
She most, and in her look sums all Delight.
455   Such Pleasure took the Serpent to behold
This Flow'ry Plat,° the sweet recess of *Eve*   *piece of ground*
Thus early, thus alone; her Heav'nly form
Angelic, but more soft, and Feminine,
Her graceful Innocence, her every Air
460   Of gesture or least action overaw'd
His Malice, and with rapine sweet bereav'd
His fierceness of the fierce intent it brought:
That space the Evil one abstracted stood
From his own evil, and for the time remain'd
465   Stupidly good, of enmity disarm'd,
Of guile, of hate, of envy, of revenge;
But the hot Hell that always in him burns,
Though in mid Heav'n, soon ended his delight,
And tortures him now more, the more he sees
470   Of pleasure not for him ordain'd: then soon
Fierce hate he recollects, and all his thoughts
Of mischief, gratulating,° thus excites.   *rejoicing*
      Thoughts, whither have ye led me, with what sweet
Compulsion thus transported to forget
475   What hither brought us, hate, not love, nor hope
Of Paradise for Hell, hope here to taste
Of pleasure, but all pleasure to destroy,
Save what is in destroying, other joy
To me is lost. Then let me not let pass
480   Occasion which now smiles, behold alone
The Woman, opportune° to all attempts,   *exposed*
Her Husband, for I view far round, not nigh,
Whose higher intellectual more I shun,
And strength, of courage haughty, and of limb
485   Heroic built, though of terrestrial mould,°   *formed of earth*
Foe not informidable, exempt from wound,
I not; so much hath Hell debas'd, and pain
Infeebl'd me, to what I was in Heav'n.
Shee fair, divinely fair, fit Love for Gods,
490   Not terrible, though terror be in Love
And beauty, not approacht by stronger hate,
Hate stronger, under show of Love well feign'd,
The way which to her ruin now I tend.
      So spake the Enemy of Mankind, enclos'd
495   In Serpent, Inmate bad, and toward *Eve*

Address'd his way, not with indented wave,
Prone on the ground, as since, but on his rear,
Circular base of rising folds, that tow'r'd
Fold above fold a surging Maze, his Head
500 Crested aloft, and Carbuncle his Eyes;[7]
With burnisht Neck of verdant Gold, erect
Amidst his circling Spires,° that on the grass   *coils*
Floated redundant:° pleasing was his shape,   *abundant to excess*
And lovely, never since of Serpent kind
505 Lovelier, not those that in *Illyria* chang'd
Hermione and *Cadmus*, or the God
In *Epidaurus*;[8] nor to which transform'd
Ammonian Jove, or *Capitoline* was seen,
Hee with *Olympias*, this with her who bore
510 *Scipio* the highth of Rome.[9] With tract oblique
At first, as one who sought access, but fear'd
To interrupt, side-long he works his way.
As when a Ship by skilful Steersman wrought
Nigh River's mouth or Foreland, where the Wind
515 Veers oft, as oft so steers, and shifts her Sail;
So varied hee, and of his tortuous Train
Curl'd many a wanton wreath in sight of *Eve*,
To lure her Eye; shee busied heard the sound
Of rustling Leaves, but minded not, as us'd
520 To such disport before her through the Field,
From every Beast, more duteous at her call,
Than at *Circean* call the Herd disguis'd.[1]
Hee bolder now, uncall'd before her stood;
But as in gaze admiring: Oft he bow'd
525 His turret Crest, and sleek enamell'd Neck,
Fawning, and lick'd the ground whereon she trod.
His gentle dumb expression turn'd at length
The Eye of *Eve* to mark his play; he glad
Of her attention gain'd, with Serpent Tongue
530 Organic, or impulse of vocal Air,
His fraudulent temptation thus began.
    Wonder not, sovran Mistress, if perhaps
Thou canst, who are sole Wonder, much less arm
Thy looks, the Heav'n of mildness, with disdain,
535 Displeas'd that I approach thee thus, and gaze
Insatiate, I thus single, nor have fear'd
Thy awful brow, more awful thus retir'd.

---

7. "Carbuncle" or reddish eyes denoted rage.
8. Cadmus was turned into a serpent first; only after he
had embraced his wife Hermione (Harmonia) in his new
form did she, too, change, (Ovid, *Metamorphoses*
4.572–603). Aesculapius, the god of healing, once
changed into a serpent to help the Romans in that form
(Ovid, *Metamorphoses* 15.626–744).

9. Jupiter Ammon, the "Lybian Jove," as a serpent mated
with Olympias to father Alexander the Great, just as the
Roman Jupiter, Capitolinus, took the form of a snake to
father the great general Scipio.
1. Homer's Circe changed men into beasts who surprised
Odysseus's company by fawning on them like dogs
(*Odyssey* 10.212–19).

Fairest resemblance of thy Maker fair,
Thee all things living gaze on, all things thine
540   By gift, and thy Celestial Beauty adore
With ravishment beheld, there best beheld
Where universally admir'd: but here
In this enclosure wild, these Beasts among,
Beholders rude, and shallow to discern
545   Half what in thee is fair, one man except,
Who sees thee? (and what is one?) who shouldst be seen
A Goddess among Gods, ador'd and serv'd
By Angels numberless, thy daily Train.
      So gloz'd° the Tempter, and his Proem° tun'd;   *flattered / prelude*
550   Into the Heart of *Eve* his words made way,
Though at the voice much marvelling; at length
Not unamaz'd she thus in answer spake.
      What may this mean? Language of Man pronounc't
By Tongue of Brute, and human sense exprest?[2]
555   The first at least of these I thought deni'd
To Beasts, whom God on thir Creation-Day
Created mute to all articulate sound;
The latter I demur,° for in thir looks   *hesitate about*
Much reason, and in thir actions oft appears.
560   Thee, Serpent, subtlest beast of all the field
I knew, but not with human voice endu'd;
Redouble then this miracle, and say,
How cam'st thou speakable of mute,[3] and how
To me so friendly grown above the rest
565   Of brutal kind, that daily are in sight?
Say, for such wonder claims attention due.
      To whom the guileful Tempter thus repli'd.
Empress of this fair World, resplendent *Eve,*
Easy to mee it is to tell thee all
570   What thou command'st and right thou should'st be obey'd:
I was at first as other Beasts that graze
The trodden Herb, of abject° thoughts and low,   *mean-spirited*
As was my food, nor aught but food discern'd
Or Sex, and apprehended nothing high:
575   Till on a day roving the field, I chanc'd
A goodly Tree far distant to behold
Loaden with fruit of fairest colors mixt,
Ruddy and Gold: I nearer drew to gaze;
When from the boughs a savory odor blown,
580   Grateful to appetite, more pleas'd my sense
Than smell of sweetest Fennel, or the Teats
Of Ewe or Goat dropping with Milk at Ev'n,

2. Milton is unusually favorable to Eve in making her ask the serpent how it came by its voice. The Eve of Scriptural exegesis, by contrast, is carried away by the words and makes no inquiry into their source.
3. How did you become capable of speech from being dumb?

Unsuckt of Lamb or Kid, that tend thir play.
To satisfy the sharp desire I had
585   Of tasting those fair Apples, I resolv'd
Not to defer; hunger and thirst at once,
Powerful persuaders, quick'n'd at the scent
Of that alluring fruit, urg'd me so keen.
About the mossy Trunk I wound me soon,
590   For high from ground the branches would require
Thy utmost reach or *Adam's:* Round the Tree
All other Beasts that saw, with like desire
Longing and envying stood, but could not reach.
Amid the Tree now got, where plenty hung
595   Tempting so nigh, to pluck and eat my fill
I spar'd not, for such pleasure till that hour
At Feed or Fountain never had I found.
Sated at length, ere long I might perceive
Strange alteration in me, to degree
600   Of Reason in my inward Powers, and Speech
Wanted not long, though to this shape retain'd.
Thenceforth to Speculations high or deep
I turn'd my thoughts, and with capacious mind
Consider'd all things visible in Heav'n,
605   Or Earth, or Middle, all things fair and good;
But all that fair and good in thy Divine
Semblance, and in thy Beauty's heav'nly Ray
United I beheld; no Fair° to thine   *beauty*
Equivalent or second, which compell'd
610   Mee thus, though importune perhaps, to come
And gaze, and worship thee of right declar'd
Sovran of Creatures, universal Dame.
      So talk'd the spirited[4] sly Snake; and *Eve,*
Yet more amaz'd unwary thus repli'd.
615   Serpent, thy overpraising leaves in doubt
The virtue° of that Fruit, in thee first prov'd: *power*
But say, where grows the Tree, from hence how far?
For many are the Trees of God that grow
In Paradise, and various, yet unknown
620   To us, in such abundance lies our choice,
As leaves a greater store of Fruit untoucht,
Still hanging incorruptible, till men
Grow up to thir provision, and more hands
Help to disburden Nature of her Birth.
625   To whom the wily Adder, blithe and glad.
Empress, the way is ready, and not long,
Beyond a row of Myrtles, on a Flat,
Fast by a Fountain, one small Thicket past

4. Endowed with an animating spirit, stirred up; also energetic, enterprising, possessed by a spirit.

	Of blowing° Myrrh and Balm; if thou accept	*blooming*
630	My conduct,° I can bring thee thither soon.	*guidance*
	Lead then, said Eve. Hee leading swiftly roll'd	
	In tangles, and made intricate seem straight,	
	To mischief swift. Hope elevates, and joy	
	Bright'ns his Crest, as when a wand'ring Fire,	
635	Compact° of unctuous vapor, which the Night	*made up*
	Condenses, and the cold invirons round,	
	Kindl'd through agitation to a Flame,	
	Which oft, they say, some evil Spirit attends,	
	Hovering and blazing with delusive Light,	
640	Misleads th' amaz'd Night-wanderer from his way	
	To Bogs and Mires, and oft through Pond or Pool,	
	There swallow'd up and lost, from succor far.	
	So glister'd the dire Snake, and into fraud	
	Led *Eve* our credulous Mother, to the Tree	
645	Of prohibition, root of all our woe;	
	Which when she saw, thus to her guide she spake.	
	Serpent, we might have spar'd our coming hither,	
	Fruitless to mee, though Fruit be here to excess,	
	The credit of whose virtue rest with thee,	
650	Wondrous indeed, if cause of such effects.	
	But of this Tree we may not taste nor touch;	
	God so commanded, and left that Command	
	Sole Daughter of his voice;[5] the rest, we live	
	Law to ourselves, our Reason is our Law.	
655	To whom the Tempter guilefully repli'd.	
	Indeed? hath God then said that of the Fruit	
	Of all these Garden Trees ye shall not eat,	
	Yet Lords declar'd of all in Earth or Air?[6]	
	To whom thus *Eve* yet sinless. Of the Fruit	
660	Of each Tree in the Garden we may eat,	
	But of the Fruit of this fair Tree amidst	
	The Garden, God hath said, Ye shall not eat	
	Thereof, nor shall ye touch it, lest ye die.	
	She scarce had said, though brief, when now more bold	
665	The Tempter, but with show of Zeal and Love	
	To Man, and indignation at his wrong,	
	New part puts on, and as to passion mov'd,	
	Fluctuates disturb'd, yet comely, and in act	
	Rais'd, as of some great matter to begin.	
670	As when of old some Orator renown'd	
	In *Athens* or free *Rome,* where Eloquence	
	Flourish'd, since mute, to some great cause addrest,	
	Stood in himself collected, while each part,	
	Motion, each act won audience ere the tongue,	

---

5. A Hebraism for "voice sent from heaven."   6. Lines 655–58 closely follow Genesis. 3.1.

675   Sometimes in highth began, as no delay
    Of Preface brooking through his Zeal of Right.[7]
    So standing, moving, or to highth upgrown
    The Tempter all impassion'd thus began.
       O Sacred, Wise, and Wisdom-giving Plant,
680   Mother of Science,° Now I feel thy Power   *knowledge*
    Within me clear, not only to discern
    Things in thir Causes, but to trace the ways
    Of highest Agents, deem'd however wise.
    Queen of this Universe, do not believe
685   Those rigid threats of Death; ye shall not Die:
    How should ye? by the Fruit? it gives you Life
    To° Knowledge: By the Threat'ner? look on mee,   *in addition to*
    Mee who have touch'd and tasted, yet both live,
    And life more perfet have attain'd than Fate
690   Meant mee, by vent'ring higher than my Lot.
    Shall that be shut to Man, which to the Beast
    Is open? or will God incense his ire
    For such a petty Trespass, and not praise
    Rather your dauntless virtue, whom the pain
695   Of Death denounc't, whatever thing Death be,
    Deterr'd not from achieving what might lead
    To happier life, knowledge of Good and Evil;
    Of good, how just? of evil, if what is evil
    Be real, why not known, since easier shunn'd?[8]
700   God therefore cannot hurt ye, and be just;
    Not just, not God; not fear'd then, nor obey'd:
    Your fear itself of Death removes the fear.
    Why then was this forbid? Why but to awe,
    Why but to keep ye low and ignorant,
705   His worshippers; he knows that in the day
    Ye Eat thereof, your Eyes that seem so clear,
    Yet are but dim, shall perfetly be then
    Op'n'd and clear'd, and ye shall be as Gods,
    Knowing both Good and Evil as they know.[9]
710   That ye should be as Gods, since I as Man,
    Internal Man,[1] is but proportion meet,
    I of brute human, thee of human Gods.
    So ye shall die perhaps, by putting off
    Human, to put on Gods, death to be wisht,
715   Though threat'n'd, which no worse than this can bring.[2]

7. This simile blends oratorical, theatrical, and theological meanings. Thus "part" means "part of the body," "dramatic role," and "moral act"; "motion" means "gesture," "mime" (or "puppet-show"), and "instigation, persuasive force, inclination"; "act" means "action," "performance of a play," and "the accomplished deed itself."
8. If the knowledge is good, how is it just to prohibit it? Here occurs the most egregious logical fallacy in speech. (For evil to be "shunned," it is not at all necessary that it

should be "known" in the sense of being experienced.)
9. See Genesis 3.5.
1. The serpent's pretence is that his "inward powers" are human.
2. Satan offers a travesty of Christian mortification and death to sin; see Colossians 3.1–15: "ye have put off the old man with his deeds; And have put on the new man, which is renewed in knowledge after the image of him that created him."

And what are Gods that Man may not become
As they, participating° God-like food?   *sharing*
The Gods are first, and that advantage use
On our belief, that all from them proceeds;
720   I question it, for this fair Earth I see,
Warm'd by the Sun, producing every kind,
Them nothing: If they° all things, who enclos'd   *if they produce*
Knowledge of Good and Evil in this Tree,
That who so eats thereof, forthwith attains
725   Wisdom without their leave? and wherein lies
Th' offense, that Man should thus attain to know?
What can your knowledge hurt him, or this Tree
Impart against his will if all be his?
Or is it envy, and can envy dwell
730   In heav'nly breasts?[3] these, these and many more
Causes import° your need of this fair Fruit.   *suggest*
Goddess humane, reach then, and freely taste.
      He ended, and his words replete with guile
Into her heart too easy entrance won:
735   Fixt on the Fruit she gaz'd, which to behold
Might tempt alone, and in her ears the sound
Yet rung of his persuasive words, impregn'd°   *impregnated*
With Reason, to her seeming, and with Truth;
Meanwhile the hour of Noon drew on, and wak'd
740   An eager appetite, rais'd by the smell
So savory of that Fruit, which with desire,
Inclinable now grown to touch or taste,
Solicited her longing eye;[4] yet first
Pausing a while, thus to herself she mus'd.
745   Great are thy Virtues, doubtless, best of Fruits,
Though kept from Man, and worthy to be admir'd,
Whose taste, too long forborne, at first assay
Gave elocution to the mute, and taught
The Tongue not made for Speech to speak thy praise:[5]
750   Thy praise hee also who forbids thy use,
Conceals not from us, naming thee the Tree
Of Knowledge, knowledge both of good and evil;
Forbids us then to taste, but his forbidding
Commends thee more, while it infers the good
755   By thee communicated, and our want:
For good unknown, sure is not had, or had
And yet unknown, is as not had at all.
In plain° then, what forbids he but to know,   *plainly*
Forbids us good, forbids us to be wise?

3. See Virgil, *Aeneid* 1.11; Satan is inviting Eve to participate in a pagan epic, complete with machinery of jealous
gods.
4. For lines 735–43, see Genesis 3.6.

5. Eve has trusted Satan's account of the fruit and consequently argues from false premises, such as its magical
power.

760 Such prohibitions bind not. But if Death
    Bind us with after-bands, what profits then
    Our inward freedom? In the day we eat
    Of this fair Fruit, our doom is, we shall die.
    How dies the Serpent? hee hath eat'n and lives,
765 And knows, and speaks, and reasons, and discerns,
    Irrational till then. For us alone
    Was death invented? or to us deni'd
    This intellectual food, for beasts reserv'd?
    For Beasts it seems: yet that one Beast which first
770 Hath tasted, envies not, but bring with joy
    The good befall'n him, Author unsuspect,[6]
    Friendly to man, far from deceit or guile.
    What fear I then, rather what know to fear[7]
    Under this ignorance of Good and Evil,
775 Of God or Death, of Law or Penalty?
    Here grows the Cure of all, this Fruit Divine,
    Fair to the Eye, inviting to the Taste,
    Of virtue° to make wise: what hinders then   power
    To reach, and feed at once both Body and Mind?
780   So saying, her rash hand in evil hour
    Forth reaching to the Fruit, she pluck'd, she eat:°   ate
    Earth felt the wound, and Nature from her seat
    Sighing through all her Works gave signs of woe,
    That all was lost. Back to the Thicket slunk
785 The guilty Serpent, and well might, for _Eve_,
    Intent now wholly on her taste, naught else
    Regarded, such delight till then, as seem'd,
    In Fruit she never tasted, whether true
    Or fancied so, through expectation high
790 Of knowledge, nor was God-head from her thought.[8]
    Greedily she ingorg'd without restraint,
    And knew not eating Death:[9] Satiate at length,
    And hight'n'd as with Wine, jocund and boon,°   jolly
    Thus to herself she pleasingly began.
795   O Sovran, virtuous, precious of all Trees
    In Paradise, of operation blest
    To Sapience,[1] hitherto obscur'd, infam'd,°   defamed
    And thy fair Fruit let hang, as to no end
    Created; but henceforth my early care,
800 Not without Song, each Morning, and due praise
    Shall tend thee, and the fertile burden ease
    Of thy full branches offer'd free to all;

6. Eve means "informant not subject to suspicion."
7. What fear I, then—or rather (since I'm not allowed to know anything) what do I know that is to be feared?
8. She expected to achieve godhead.
9. She knew not that she was eating death; "she was

unaware, while she ate death" or even "she 'knew'; not eating (immediate) death."
1. "Sapience" is derived from Latin _sapientia_ (discernment, taste) and ultimately from _sapere_ (to taste).

Till dieted by thee I grow mature
In knowledge, as the Gods who all things know;
805   Though others² envy what they cannot give;
For had the gift been theirs, it had not here
Thus grown. Experience, next to thee I owe,
Best guide; not following thee, I had remain'd
In ignorance, thou op'n'st Wisdom's way,
810   And giv'st access, though secret she retire.
And I perhaps am secret; Heav'n is high,
High and remote to see from thence distinct
Each thing on Earth; and other care perhaps
May have diverted from continual watch
815   Our great Forbidder, safe with all his Spies
About him. But to *Adam* in what sort
Shall I appear? shall I to him make known
As yet my change, and give him to partake
Full happiness with mee, or rather not.
820   But keep the odds of Knowledge in my power
Without Copartner? so to add what wants
In Female Sex, the more to draw his Love,
And render me more equal, and perhaps,
A thing not undesirable, sometime
825   Superior: for inferior who is free?
This may be well: but what if God have seen,
And Death ensue? then I shall be no more,
And *Adam* wedded to another *Eve*,
Shall live with her enjoying, I extinct;
830   A death to think. Confirm'd then I resolve,
Adam shall share with me in bliss or woe:
So dear I love him, that with him all deaths
I could endure, without him live no life.
        So saying, from the Tree her step she turn'd,
835   But first low Reverence done, as to the power
That dwelt within, whose presence had infus'd
Into the plant sciential³ sap, deriv'd
From Nectar, drink of Gods. *Adam* the while
Waiting desirous her return, had wove
840   Of choicest Flow'rs a Garland to adorn
Her Tresses, and her rural labors crown,
As Reapers oft are wont thir Harvest Queen.
Great joy he promis'd to his thoughts, and new
Solace in her return, so long delay'd;
845   Yet oft his heart, divine° of something ill,   *prophet*
Misgave him; hee the falt'ring measure⁴ felt;
And forth to meet her went, the way she took
That Morn when first they parted; by the Tree

---

2. I.e., God. Eve's language is now full of lapses in logic   3. Endowed with knowledge.
and evasions in theology.   4. The rhythm of his own heart.

Of Knowledge he must pass; there he her met,
850   Scarce from the Tree returning; in her hand
A bough of fairest fruit that downy smil'd,
New gather'd, and ambrosial smell diffus'd.
To him she hasted, in her face excuse
Came Prologue, and Apology to prompt,[5]
855   Which with bland words at will she thus addrest.
     Hast thou not wonder'd, *Adam*, at my stay?
Thee I have misst, and thought it long, depriv'd
Thy presence, agony of love till now
Not felt, nor shall be twice, for never more
860   Mean I to try, what rash untri'd I sought,
The pain of absence from thy sight. But strange
Hath been the cause, and wonderful to hear:
This Tree is not as we are told, a Tree
Of danger tasted,° nor to evil unknown   *if tasted*
865   Op'ning the way, but of Divine effect
To open Eyes, and make them Gods who taste;
And hath been tasted such: the Serpent wise,
Or not restrain'd as wee, or not obeying,
Hath eat'n of the fruit, and is become,
870   Not dead, as we are threat'n'd, but thenceforth
Endu'd with human voice and human sense,
Reasoning to admiration, and with mee
Persuasively hath so prevail'd, that I
Have also tasted, and have also found
875   Th' effects to correspond, opener mine Eyes,
Dim erst, dilated Spirits, ampler Heart,
And growing up to Godhead; which for thee
Chiefly I sought, without thee can despise.
For bliss, as thou hast part, to me is bliss,
880   Tedious, unshar'd with thee, and odious soon.
Thou therefore also taste, that equal Lot
May join us, equal Joy, as equal Love;
Lest thou not tasting, different degree[6]
Disjoin us, and I then too late renounce
885   Deity for thee, when Fate will not permit.
     Thus *Eve* with Count'nance blithe her story told;
But in her Cheek distemper[7] flushing glow'd.
On th' other side, *Adam*, soon as he heard
The fatal Trespass done by *Eve*, amaz'd,
890   Astonied° stood and Blank, while horror chill   *stunned*
Ran through his veins, and all his joints relax'd;

5. The expression on Eve's face is visible in advance as she approaches and so is like the prologue-speaker of a play. But it also remains on her face as she speaks, to help out her words, and so is like the prompter of the play. The actor prompted is apology, i.e., justification or defense personified.
6. Differing position in the scale of creatures.
7. A disordered condition due to disturbance of the temperament of the bodily humors.

From his slack hand the Garland wreath'd for *Eve*,
Down dropp'd, and all the faded Roses shed:
Speechless he stood and pale, till thus at length
895 First to himself he inward silence broke.
     O fairest of Creation, last and best
Of all God's Works, Creature in whom excell'd
Whatever can to sight or thought be form'd,
Holy, divine, good, amiable, or sweet!
900 How art thou lost, how on a sudden lost,
Defac't, deflow'r'd, and now to death devote?°   *given over*
Rather how hast thou yielded to transgress
The strict forbiddance, how to violate
The sacred Fruit forbidd'n! some cursed fraud
905 Of Enemy hath beguil'd thee, yet unknown,
And mee with thee hath ruin'd, for with thee
Certain my resolution is to Die;
How can I live without thee, how forgo
Thy sweet Converse and Love so dearly join'd,
910 To live again in these wild Woods forlorn?
Should God create another *Eve*, and I
Another Rib afford, yet loss of thee
Would never from my heart; no no, I feel
The Link of Nature draw me: Flesh of Flesh,
915 Bone of my Bone thou art, and from thy State
Mine never shall be parted, bliss or woe.
     So having said, as one from sad dismay
Recomforted, and after thoughts disturb'd
Submitting to what seem'd remediless,
920 Thus in calm mood his Words to *Eve* he turn'd.
     Bold deed thou hast presum'd, advent'rous *Eve*,
And peril great provok't, who thus hath dar'd
Had it been only coveting to Eye
That sacred Fruit, sacred° to abstinence,   *devoted*
925 Much more to taste it under ban to touch.
But past who can recall, or done undo?
Not God Omnipotent, nor Fate; yet so
Perhaps thou shalt not Die, perhaps the Fact°   *crime, deed*
Is not so heinous now, foretasted Fruit,
930 Profan'd first by the Serpent, by him first
Made common and unhallow'd ere our taste;
Nor yet on him found deadly, he yet lives,
Lives, as thou said'st, and gains to live as Man
Higher degree of Life, inducement strong
935 To us, as likely tasting to attain
Proportional ascent, which cannot be
But to be Gods, or Angels Demi-gods.
Nor can I think that God, Creator wise,
Though threat'ning, will in earnest so destroy
940 Us his prime Creatures, dignifi'd so high,

Set over all his Works, which in our Fall,
For us created, needs with us must fail,
Dependent made; so God shall uncreate,
Be frustrate, do, undo, and labor lose,
945   Not well conceiv'd of God, who though his Power
Creation could repeat, yet would be loath
Us to abolish, lest the Adversary
Triumph and say; Fickle their State whom God
Most Favors, who can please him long? Mee first
950   He ruin'd, now Mankind; whom will he next?
Matter of scorn, not to be given the Foe.
However I with thee have fixt my Lot,
Certain to undergo like doom;[8] if Death
Consort with thee, Death is to mee as Life;
955   So forcible within my heart I feel
The Bond of Nature draw me to my own,
My own in thee, for what thou art is mine;
Our State cannot be sever'd, we are one,
One Flesh; to lose thee were to lose myself.
960   So *Adam*, and thus *Eve* to him repli'd.
O glorious trial of exceeding Love,
Illustrious evidence, example high!
Ingaging me to emulate, but short
    Of thy perfection, how shall I attain,
965   *Adam*, from whose dear side I boast me sprung,
And gladly of our Union hear thee speak,
One Heart, one Soul in both; whereof good proof
This day affords, declaring thee resolv'd,
Rather than Death or aught than Death more dread
970   Shall separate us, linkt in Love so dear,
To undergo with mee one Guilt, one Crime,
If any be, of tasting this fair Fruit,
Whose virtue, for of good still good proceeds,
Direct, or by occasion[9] hath presented
975   This happy trial of thy Love, which else
So eminently never had been known.
Were it I thought Death menac't would ensue
This my attempt, I would sustain alone
The worst, and not persuade thee, rather die
980   Deserted, than oblige° thee with a fact   *make liable*
Pernicious to thy Peace, chiefly assur'd
Remarkably so late of thy so true,
So faithful Love unequall'd; but I feel
Far otherwise th' event,° nor Death, but Life   *result*
985   Augmented, op'n'd Eyes, new Hopes, new Joys,

8. Three separate meanings are possible: judgment, irrev-   9. I.e., directly or indirectly.
ocable destiny, and death.

Taste so Divine, that what of sweet before
Hath toucht my sense, flat seems to this, and harsh.
On my experience, *Adam*, freely taste,
And fear of Death deliver to the Winds.
990   So saying, she embrac'd him, and for joy
Tenderly wept, much won that he his Love
Had so ennobl'd, as of choice to incur
Divine displeasure for her sake, or Death.
In recompense (for such compliance bad
995   Such recompense best merits) from the bough
She gave him of that fair enticing Fruit
With liberal hand: he scrupl'd not to eat
Against his better knowledge, not deceiv'd,
But fondly overcome with Female charm.[1]
1000   Earth trembl'd from her entrails, as again
In pangs, and Nature gave a second groan,
Sky low'r'd, and muttering Thunder, some sad drops
Wept at completing of the mortal Sin
Original;[2] while *Adam* took no thought,
1005   Eating his fill, nor *Eve* to iterate
Her former trespass fear'd, the more to soothe
Him with her lov'd society, that now
As with new Wine intoxicated both
They swim in mirth, and fancy that they feel
1010   Divinity within them breeding wings
Wherewith to scorn the Earth: but that false Fruit
Far other operation first display'd,
Carnal desire inflaming, hee on *Eve*
Began to cast lascivious Eyes, she him
1015   As wantonly repaid; in Lust they burn:
Till *Adam* thus 'gan *Eve* to dalliance move.
    Eve, now I see thou are exact of taste,
And elegant, of Sapience[3] no small part,
Since to each meaning savor[4] we apply,
1020   And Palate call judicious; I the praise
Yield thee, so well this day thou hast purvey'd.°   *provided*
Much pleasure we have lost, while we abstain'd
From this delightful Fruit, nor known till now
True relish, tasting; if such pleasure be
1025   In things to us forbidden, it might be wish'd,
For this one Tree had been forbidden ten.
But come, so well refresh't, now let us play,
As meet is, after such delicious Fare;
For never did thy Beauty since the day

1. See 1 Timothy 2.14: "And Adam was not deceived, but the woman being deceived was in the transgression."
2. The only occurrence in *Paradise Lost* of the term "Original Sin." In his *De doctrina* (1.11), Milton defines Original Sin as "the sin which is common to all men, that which our first parents, and in them all their posterity committed, when, casting off their obedience to God, they tasted the fruit of the forbidden tree."
3. Wisdom, from Latin *sapere*, to taste.
4. Tastiness, understanding.

1030   I saw thee first and wedded thee, adorn'd
With all perfections, so inflame my sense
With ardor to enjoy thee, fairer now
Than ever, bounty of this virtuous Tree.[5]
        So said he, and forbore not glance or toy°   *caress*
1035   Of amorous intent, well understood
Of° *Eve*, whose Eye darted contagious Fire.   *by*
Her hand he seiz'd, and to a shady bank,
Thick overhead with verdant roof imbowr'd
He led her nothing loath; Flow'rs were the Couch,
1040   Pansies, and Violets, and Asphodel,
And Hyacinth, Earth's freshest softest lap.
There they thir fill of Love and Love's disport
Took largely, of thir mutual guilt the Seal,
The solace of thir sin, till dewy sleep
1045   Oppress'd them, wearied with thir amorous play.
Soon as the force of that fallacious Fruit,
That with exhilarating vapor bland°   *pleasing*
About thir spirits had play'd, and inmost powers
Made err, was now exhal'd, and grosser sleep
1050   Bred of unkindly fumes,[6] with conscious dreams
Encumber'd, now had left them, up they rose
As from unrest, and each the other viewing,
Soon found thir Eyes how op'n'd, and thir minds
How dark'n'd;[7] innocence, that as a veil
1055   Had shadow'd them from knowing ill, was gone,
Just confidence, and native righteousness,
And honor from about them, naked left
To guilty shame: hee cover'd, but his Robe
Uncover'd more. So rose the *Danite* strong
1060   *Herculean Samson* from the Harlot-lap
Of *Philistean Dalilah*, and wak'd
Shorn of his strength, They destitute and bare
Of all thir virtue:[8] silent, and in face
Confounded long they sat, as struck'n mute,
1065   Till *Adam*, though not less than *Eve* abasht,
At length gave utterance to these words constrain'd.
        O *Eve*, in evil hour thou didst give ear
To that false Worm, of whomsoever taught
To counterfeit Man's voice, true in our Fall,
1070   False in our promis'd Rising; since our Eyes
Op'n'd we find indeed, and find we know
Both Good and Evil, Good lost, and Evil got,

---

5. See Homer, *Iliad* 14, where Hera, bent on deceiving Zeus, comes to him wearing Aphrodite's belt and seems more charming to him than ever before.
6. Unnatural vapors or exhalations rising from the stomach to the brain.

7. See Genesis 3.7: "The eyes of them both were opened, and they knew that they were naked."
8. See Judges 16 for the story of Samson's betrayal by Delilah.

Bad Fruit of Knowledge, if this be to know,
Which leaves us naked thus, of Honor void,
1075 Of Innocence, of Faith, of Purity,
Our wonted Ornaments now soil'd and stain'd,
And in our Faces evident the signs
Of foul concupiscence; whence evil store;
Even shame, the last of evils; of the first
1080 Be sure then. How shall I behold the face
Henceforth of God or Angel, erst with joy
And rapture so oft beheld? those heav'nly shapes
Will dazzle now this earthly, with thir blaze
Insufferably bright. O might I here
1085 In solitude live savage, in some glade
Obscur'd, where highest Woods impenetrable
To Star or Sun-light, spread thir umbrage broad,
And brown as Evening: Cover me ye Pines,
Ye Cedars, with innumerable boughs
1090 Hide me, where I may never see them more.
But let us now, as in bad plight, devise
What best may for the present serve to hide
The Parts of each from other, that seem most
To shame obnoxious,° and unseemliest seen,   *exposed*
1095 Some Tree whose broad smooth Leaves together sew'd,
And girded on our loins, may cover round
Those middle parts, that this new comer, Shame,
There sit not, and reproach us as unclean.[9]
    So counsell'd hee, and both together went
1100 Into the thickest Wood, there soon they chose
The Figtree,[1] not that kind for Fruit renown'd,
But such as at this day to *Indians* known
In *Malabar* or *Decan* spreads her Arms
Branching so broad and long, that in the ground
1105 The bended Twigs take root, and Daughters grow
About the Mother Tree, a Pillar'd shade
High overarch't, and echoing Walks between;
There oft the *Indian* Herdsman shunning heat
Shelters in cool, and tends his pasturing Herds
1110 At Loopholes cut through thickest shade: Those Leaves
They gather'd, broad as Amazonian Targe,°   *shield*
And with what skill they had, together sew'd,
To gird thir waist, vain Covering if to hide
Thir guilt and dreaded shame; O how unlike
1115 To that first naked Glory. Such of late
Columbus found th' *American* so girt

9. See Genesis 3.7.   from Gerard's *Herball* (1597).
1. Milton's description of the banyan or Indian fig comes

With feather'd Cincture,° naked else and wild   *belt*
Among the Trees on Isles and woody Shores.
Thus fenc't, and as they thought, thir shame in part
1120   Cover'd, but not at rest or ease of Mind,
They sat them down to weep, nor only Tears
Rain'd at thir Eyes, but high Winds worse within
Began to rise, high Passions, Anger, Hate,
Mistrust, Suspicion, Discord, and shook sore
1125   Thir inward State of Mind, calm Region once
And full of Peace, now toss't and turbulent:
For Understanding rul'd not, and the Will
Heard not her lore, both in subjection now
To sensual Appetite, who from beneath
1130   Usurping over sovran Reason claim'd
Superior sway: From thus distemper'd breast,
Adam, estrang'd in look and alter'd style,
Speech intermitted thus to *Eve* renew'd.
    Would thou hadst heark'n'd to my words, and stay'd
1135   With me, as I besought thee, when that strange
Desire of wand'ring this unhappy Morn,
I know not whence possess'd thee; we had then
Remain'd still happy, not as now, despoil'd
Of all our good, sham'd, naked, miserable.
1140   Let none henceforth seek needless cause to approve°   *give proof of*
The Faith they owe;[2] when earnestly they seek
Such proof, conclude, they then begin to fail.
    To whom soon mov'd with touch of blame thus *Eve*.
What words have past thy Lips,[3] *Adam* severe,
1145   Imput'st thou that to my default, or will
Of wand'ring, as thou call'st it, which who knows
But might as ill have happ'n'd thou being by,
Or to thyself perhaps: hadst thou been there,
Or here th' attempt, thou couldst not have discern'd
1150   Fraud in the Serpent, speaking as he spake;
No ground of enmity between us known,
Why hee should mean me ill, or seek to harm.
Was I to have never parted from thy side?
As good have grown there still a lifeless Rib.
1155   Being as I am, why didst not thou the Head[4]
Command me absolutely not to go,
Going into such danger as thou said'st?
Too facile° then thou didst not much gainsay,   *permissive*
Nay, didst permit, approve, and fair dismiss.
1160   Hadst thou been firm and fixt in thy dissent
Neither had I transgress'd, nor thou with mee.
    To whom then first incenst Adam repli'd.

---

2. Be under obligation to render or possess.
3. Echoes Odysseus's disapproval of a speech of Agamemnon's (*Iliad* 14.83).
4. Alludes to 1 Corinthians 11.3: "The head of every man is Christ; and the head of the woman is the man; and the head of Christ is God."

	Is this the Love, is this the recompense
	Of mine to thee, ingrateful *Eve*, express't
1165	Immutable° when thou wert lost, not I,	*unchangeable*
	Who might have liv'd and joy'd immortal bliss,
	Yet willingly chose rather Death with thee:
	And am I now upbraided, as the cause
	Of thy transgressing? not enough severe,
1170	It seems, in thy restraint: what could I more?
	I warn'd thee, I admonish'd thee, foretold
	The danger, and the lurking Enemy
	That lay in wait; beyond this had been force,
	And force upon free Will hath here no place.
1175	But confidence then bore thee on, secure
	Either to meet no danger, or to find
	Matter of glorious trial; and perhaps
	I also err'd in overmuch admiring
	What seem'd in thee so perfet, that I thought
1180	No evil durst attempt thee, but I rue
	That error now, which is become my crime,
	And thou th' accuser. Thus it shall befall
	Him who to worth in Woman overtrusting
	Lets her Will rule; restraint she will not brook,
1185	And left to herself, if evil thence ensue,
	Shee first his weak indulgence will accuse.

Thus they in mutual accusation spent
The fruitless hours, but neither self-condemning,
And of thir vain contést appear'd no end.
The End of the Ninth Book.

from **Book 12**
The Argument

The Angel Michael continues from the Flood to relate what shall succeed; then, in the mention of Abraham, comes by degrees to explain, who that Seed of the Woman shall be, which was promised Adam and Eve in the Fall; his Incarnation, Death, Resurrection, and Ascension; the state of the Church till his second Coming. Adam greatly satisfied and recomforted by these Relations and Promises descends the Hill with Michael; wakens Eve, who all this while had slept, but with gentle dreams compos'd to quietness of mind and submission. Michael in either hand leads them out of Paradise, the fiery Sword waving behind them, and the Cherubim taking thir Stations to guard the Place.

	As one who in his journey bates° at Noon,	*pauses*
	Though bent on speed, so here the Arch-Angel paus'd
	Betwixt the world destroy'd and world restor'd,
	If *Adam* aught perhaps might interpose;
5	Then with transition sweet new Speech resumes.
	Thus thou hast seen one World begin and end;
	And Man as from a second stock proceed.[1]

---

1. "Stock," an ambiguity, refers not only to the literal replacement of one source of the human line of descent (Adam) by another (Noah), but also to the grafting of mankind onto the stem of Christ, according to the Pauline allegory of regeneration (Romans 11). The covenant with Noah was a type of the New Covenant.

Much thou hast yet to see, but I perceive
Thy mortal sight to fail; objects divine
10   Must needs impair and weary human sense:
Henceforth what is to come I will relate,
Thou therefore give due audience, and attend.
This second source of Men, while yet but few,
And while the dread of judgment past remains
15   Fresh in thir minds, fearing the Deity,
With some regard to what is just and right
Shall lead thir lives, and multiply apace,
Laboring° the soil, and reaping plenteous crop,   *tilling*
Corn, wine and oil; and from the herd or flock,
20   Oft sacrificing Bullock, Lamb, or Kid,
With large Wine-offerings pour'd, and sacred Feast,
Shall spend thir days in joy unblam'd, and dwell
Long time in peace by Families and Tribes
Under paternal rule; till one shall rise[2]
25   Of proud ambitious heart, who not content
With fair equality, fraternal state,
Will arrogate Dominion undeserv'd
Over his brethren, and quite dispossess
Concord and law of Nature from the Earth:[3]
30   Hunting (and Men not Beasts shall be his game)
With War and hostile snare such as refuse
Subjection to his Empire tyrannous:[4]
A mighty Hunter thence he shall be styl'd
Before the Lord, as in despite of Heav'n,
35   Or from Heav'n claiming second Sovranty;[5]
And from Rebellion shall derive his name,
Though of Rebellion others he accuse.
Hee with a crew, whom like Ambition joins
With him or under him to tyrannize,
40   Marching from *Eden* towards the West, shall find
The Plain, wherein a black bituminous gurge°   *whirlpool*
Boils out from under ground, the mouth of Hell;
Of Brick, and of that stuff they cast to build
A City and Tow'r, whose top may reach to Heav'n;[6]
45   And get themselves a name, lest far disperst
In foreign Lands thir memory be lost,
Regardless whether good or evil fame.[7]
But God who oft descends to visit men

2. Nimrod is not connected with the builders of the Tower in Genesis 10.8. The connection is made, however, in Josephus, *Antiquities* 1.4.2ff., where we also learn that Nimrod "changed the government into tyranny."
3. In *The Tenure of Kings and Magistrates,* Milton denies the natural right of kings and insists that their power is committed to them in trust by the people.
4. See *Eikonoklastes:* "The Bishops could have told him, that 'Nimrod,' the first that hunted after Faction is reputed, by ancient Tradition, the first that founded

monarchy; whence it appeares that to hunt after Faction is more properly the King's Game."
5. "Before the Lord," Genesis 10.9; Milton takes it in a constitutional sense; see *The Tenure:* "To say Kings are accountable to none but God, is the overturning of all Law."
6. The materials of the Tower—brick with bitumen as mortar—are specified in Genesis 11.3.
7. See Genesis 11.4.

Unseen, and through thir habitations walks
50   To mark thir doings, them beholding soon,
Comes down to see thir City, ere the Tower
Obstruct Heav'n Tow'rs, and in derision sets
Upon thir Tongues a various Spirit to rase
Quite out thir Native Language, and instead
55   To sow a jangling noise of words unknown:
Forthwith a hideous gabble rises loud
Among the Builders; each to other calls
Not understood, till hoarse, and all in rage,
As mockt they storm;[8] great laughter was in Heav'n
60   And looking down, to see the hubbub strange
And hear the din; thus was the building left
Ridiculous, and the work Confusion nam'd.[9]
     Whereto thus *Adam* fatherly displeas'd.
O execrable Son so to aspire
65   Above his Brethren, to himself assuming
Authority usurpt, from God not giv'n:
He gave us only over Beast, Fish, Fowl
Dominion absolute; that right we hold
By his donation; but Man over men
70   He made not Lord; such title to himself
Reserving, human left from human free.
But this Usurper his encroachment proud
Stays not on Man; to God his Tower intends
Siege and defiance: Wretched man! what food
75   Will he convey up thither to sustain
Himself and his rash Army, where thin Air
Above the Clouds will pine his entrails gross,
And famish him of breath, if not of Bread?
     To whom thus *Michael.* Justly thou abhorr'st
80   That Son, who on the quiet state of men
Such trouble brought, affecting to subdue
Rational Liberty;[1] yet know withal,
Since thy original lapse, true Liberty
Is lost, which always with right Reason dwells
85   Twinn'd, and from her hath no dividual° being: *separate*
Reason in man obscur'd, or not obey'd,
Immediately inordinate desires
And upstart Passions catch the Government
From Reason, and to servitude reduce
90   Man till then free. Therefore since hee permits

8. In the 17th century it was generally believed that the separation of language into distinct individual languages had its beginning at the confusion of tongues at Babel.
9. See Genesis 11.9, "Therefore is the name of it called Babel"; marginal gloss: "that is, Confusion."
1. Lines 80–101 recall the regicide tracts and follow St. Augustine's *City of God* 19.15, where we read that the derivation of servitude, whose mother is sin, is the "first cause of man's subjection to man: which notwithstanding comes not to pass but by the direction of the highest, in whom is no injustice." For the connection between psychological and political enslavement, see 9.1127–31.

Within himself unworthy Powers to reign
Over free Reason, God in Judgment just
Subjects him from without to violent Lords;
Who oft as undeservedly enthral
95   His outward freedom: Tyranny must be,
Though to the Tyrant thereby no excuse.
Yet sometimes Nations will decline so low
From virtue, which is reason, that no wrong,
But Justice, and some fatal curse annext
100   Deprives them of thir outward liberty,
Thir inward lost:[2]

* * *

So spake th' Arch-Angel *Michaël*, then paus'd,
As at the World's great period;[3] and our Sire
Replete with joy and wonder thus repli'd.
    O goodness infinite, goodness immense![4]
470   That all this good of evil shall produce,
And evil turn to good; more wonderful
Than that which by creation first brought forth
Light out of darkness! full of doubt I stand,
Whether I should repent me now of sin
475   By mee done and occasion'd, or rejoice
Much more, that much more good thereof shall spring,
To God more glory, more good will to Men
From God, and over wrath grace shall abound.[5]
But say, if our deliverer up to Heav'n
480   Must reascend, what will betide the few
His faithful, left among th' unfaithful herd,
The enemies of truth; who then shall guide
His people, who defend? will they not deal
Worse with his followers than with him they dealt?
485   Be sure they will, said th' Angel; but from Heav'n
Hee to his own a Comforter will send,[6]
The promise of the Father, who shall dwell
His Spirit within them, and the Law of Faith
Working through love, upon thir hearts shall write,[7]
490   To guide them in all truth, and also arm
With spiritual Armor, able to resist
Satan's assaults, and quench his fiery darts,[8]
What Man can do against them, not afraid,

---

2. Michael goes on to describe the history of Israel, from Abraham to king David, then tells of the birth of the Merriah, who will crush Satan and defeat Sin and Death.

3. This is Michael's second pause; the first was at 12.2. The three divisions of Adam's instruction are meant to correspond to "three drops" of the well of life placed in his eyes (11.416). Here the pause is compared with the world's period the dawning of the present age, from the first to the second coming of Christ.

4. The Final Cause or end of the Fall: a greater "glory" for God and an opportunity for him to show his surpassing love through the sacrifice of Christ.

5. See Romas 5.20 ("where sin abounded, grace did much more abound") and 2 Corinthians 4.15.

6. The Holy Spirit. See John 14.18 and 15.26.

7. See Galations 5.6: "faith which worketh by love."

8. Alluding to the allegory in Ephesians 6.16: "Above all, taking the shield of faith, wherewith ye shall be able to quench all the fiery darts of the wicked."

495 Though to the death, against such cruelties
     With inward consolations recompens't,
     And oft supported so as shall amaze
     Thir proudest persecutors: for the Spirit
     Pour'd first on his Apostles, whom he sends
     To evangelize the Nations, then on all
500 Baptiz'd, shall them with wondrous gifts endue°   *endow*
     To speak all Tongues, and do all Miracles,
     As did thir Lord before them. Thus they win
     Great numbers of each Nation to receive
     With joy the tidings brought from Heav'n: at length
505 Thir Ministry perform'd, and race well run,
     Thir doctrine and thir story written left,
     They die; but in thir room, as they forewarn,
     Wolves shall succeed for teachers, grievous Wolves,[9]
     Who all the sacred mysteries of Heav'n
510 To thir own vile advantages shall turn
     Of lucre and ambition, and the truth
     With superstitions and traditions taint,
     Left only in those written Records pure,
     Though not but by the Spirit understood.[1]
515 Then shall they seek to avail themselves of names,
     Places and titles, and with these to join
     Secular power, though feigning still to act
     By spiritual, to themselves appropriating
     The Spirit of God, promis'd alike and giv'n
520 To all Believers;[2] and from that pretense,
     Spiritual Laws by carnal° power shall force   *worldly*
     On every conscience; Laws which none shall find
     Left them inroll'd, or what the Spirit within
     Shall on the heart engrave.[3] What will they then
525 But force the Spirit of Grace itself, and bind
     His consort Liberty; what, but unbuild
     His living Temples, built by Faith to stand,[4]
     Thir own Faith not another's: for on Earth
     Who against Faith and Conscience can be heard
530 Infallible?[5] yet many will presume:
     Whence heavy persecution shall arise
     On all who in the worship persevere
     Of Spirit and Truth; the rest, far greater part,

9. "For I know this, that after my departing shall grievous wolves enter in among you, not sparing the flock" (Acts 20.29). See the simile comparing Satan to a wolf in the fold, at 4.183–87.
1. It was an important article of Protestant belief that in doctrinal matters the ultimate arbiter is individual conscience rather than mere authority.
2. The corruption of the Church through its pursuit of "secular power" is a subject Milton had dealt with in *Of Reformation*. In *De doctrina* 1.30 he condemns the enforcement of obedience to human opinions or authority.
3. The wolves will enforce laws written neither in Scripture nor in the individual conscience.
4. See 1 Corinthians 3.17: "The temple of God is holy, which temple ye are."
5. Even though the doctrine of papal infallibility was not formally adapted until 1870, there can be no doubt that Rome is Milton's main target here. In *A Treatise of Civil Power* he writes that the "Pope assumes infallibility over conscience and scripture."

Will deem in outward Rites and specious forms
535   Religion satisfi'd; Truth shall retire
Bestuck with sland'rous darts, and works of Faith
Rarely be found: so shall the World go on,
To good malignant, to bad men benign,
Under her own weight groaning, till the day
540   Appear of respiration[6] to the just,
And vengeance to the wicked, at return
Of him so lately promis'd to thy aid,
The Woman's seed, obscurely then foretold,
Now amplier known thy Saviour and thy Lord,
545   Last in the Clouds from Heav'n to be reveal'd
In glory of the Father, to dissolve
Satan with his perverted World, then raise
From the conflagrant° mass, purg'd and refin'd,   *burning*
New Heav'ns, new Earth, Ages of endless date
550   Founded in righteousness and peace and love,
To bring forth fruits Joy and eternal Bliss.
　　　He ended; and thus *Adam* last repli'd.
How soon hath thy prediction, Seer blest,
Measur'd this transient World, the Race of time,
555   Till time stand fixt: beyond is all abyss,
Eternity, whose end no eye can reach.
Greatly instructed I shall hence depart,
Greatly in peace of thought, and have my fill
Of knowledge, what this Vessel can contain;
560   Beyond which was my folly to aspire.
Henceforth I learn, that to obey is best,
And love with fear the only God, to walk
As in his presence, ever to observe
His providence, and on him sole depend,
565   Merciful over all his works, with good
Still overcoming evil, and by small
Accomplishing great things, by things deem'd weak
Subverting worldly strong, and worldly wise
By simply meek; that suffering for Truth's sake
570   Is fortitude to highest victory,
And to the faithful Death the Gate of Life;
Taught this by his example whom I now
Acknowledge my Redeemer ever blest.
　　　To whom thus also th' Angel last repli'd:
575   This having learnt, thou hast attain'd the sum
Of wisdom; hope no higher, though all the Stars
Thou knew'st by name, and all th' ethereal Powers,
All secrets of the deep, all Nature's works,
Or works of God in Heav'n, Air, Earth, or Sea,
580   And all the riches of this World enjoy'dst,

6. Opportunity for breathing again; rest.

And all the rule, one Empire; only add
Deeds to thy knowledge answerable, add Faith,
Add Virtue, Patience, Temperance, add Love,
By name to come call'd Charity, the soul

585 Of all the rest;[7] then wilt thou not be loath
To leave this Paradise, but shalt possess
A paradise within thee, happier far.
Let us descend now therefore from this top
Of Speculation;[8] for the hour precise

590 Exacts our parting hence; and see the Guards,
By mee encampt on yonder Hill, expect
Thir motion,[9] at whose Front a flaming Sword,
In signal of remove, waves fiercely round;
We may no longer stay: go, waken *Eve*;

595 Her also I with gentle Dreams have calm'd
Portending good, and all her spirits compos'd
To meek submission: thou at season fit
Let her with thee partake what thou hast heard,
Chiefly what may concern her Faith to know,

600 The great deliverance by her Seed to come
(For by the Woman's Seed)[1] on all Mankind,
That ye may live, which will be many days,[2]
Both in one Faith unanimous though sad,
With cause for evils past, yet much more cheer'd

605 With meditation on the happy end.
      He ended, and they both descend the Hill;
Descended, *Adam* to the Bow'r where *Eve*
Lay sleeping ran before, but found her wak't;
And thus with words not sad she him receiv'd.

610   Whence thou return'st, and whither went'st, I know;
For God is also in sleep, and Dreams advise,
Which he hath sent propitious, some great good
Presaging, since with sorrow and heart's distress
Wearied I fell asleep: but now lead on;

615 In mee is no delay; with thee to go,
Is to stay here; without thee here to stay,
Is to go hence unwilling; thou to mee
Art all things under Heav'n, all places thou,
Who for my wilful crime art banisht hence.[3]

620 This further consolation yet secure
I carry hence; though all by mee is lost,
Such favor I unworthy am voutsaf't,

7. Compare 2 Peter 1.5–7: "Add to your faith virtue; and
to virtue knowledge; and to knowledge temperance; and
to temperance patience; and to patience godliness; and to
godliness brotherly kindness; and to brotherly kindness
charity."
8. Vantage point but also height of theological speculation.

9. Await deployment, marching orders.
1. Alluding to the birth of Jesus.
2. Adam lived to be 930 years of age (Genesis 5.5).
3. Eve has assimilated Michael's exhortation at 11.292:
"where [Adam] abides, think there thy native soil." There is
also a resonance with Eve's song at 4.635–56 (every time of
day is pleasing with Adam, none is pleasing without him).

By mee the Promis'd Seed shall all restore.
　　So spake our Mother *Eve,* and *Adam* heard
625 Well pleas'd, but answer'd not; for now too nigh
Th' Arch-Angel stood, and from the other Hill
To thir fixt Station, all in bright array
The Cherubim descended; on the ground
Gliding meteorous,° as Ev'ning Mist   *meteoric*
630 Ris'n from a River o'er the marish° glides,   *marsh*
And gathers ground fast at the Laborer's heel
Homeward returning. High in Front advanc't,
The brandisht Sword of God before them blaz'd
Fierce as a Comet; which with torrid heat,
635 And vapor as the *Libyan* Air adust,°   *scorched*
Began to parch that temperate Clime; whereat
In either hand the hast'ning Angel caught
Our ling'ring Parents, and to th' Eastern Gate
Led them direct, and down the Cliff as fast
640 To the subjected° Plain; then disappear'd.   *underlying*
They looking back, all th' Eastern side beheld
Of Paradise, so late thir happy seat,
Wav'd over by that flaming Brand,[4] the Gate
With dreadful Faces throng'd and fiery Arms:
645 Some natural tears they dropp'd, but wip'd them soon;
The World was all before them, where to choose
Thir place of rest, and Providence thir guide:[5]
They hand in hand with wand'ring steps and slow,
Through *Eden* took thir solitary way.

The End

---

4. See Genesis. 3.24: "a flaming sword which turned every way."

5. Note that "Providence" can be the object of "choose": decisions of faith lie ahead.

Thomas Bowles, *The Bubblers' Medley, or a Sketch of the Times*, 1720.

The Restoration and
the Eighteenth Century

◄━┼ ⋈◆⋈ ┼━►

On 25 May 1660, Charles II set foot on the shore of Dover and brought his eleven-year exile to an end. The arrival was recorded by the great diarist Samuel Pepys, and his words preserve for us a form of the event:

> I went, and Mr. Mansell, and one of the King's footmen, with a dog that the King loved (which beshat the boat, which made us laugh, and methink that a king and all that belong to him are but just as others are), in a boat by ourselves, and so got on shore when the King did, who was received . . . with all imaginable love and respect at his entrance upon the land of Dover. Infinite the crowd of people and the horsemen, citizens, and noblemen of all sorts. The Mayor of the town came and gave him his white staff, the badge of his place, which the King did give him again. The Mayor also presented him from the town a very rich Bible, which he took and said it was the thing that he loved above all things in the world. . . . The shouting and joy expressed by all is past imagination.

Pepys captures and creates a brilliant mix of materials and experiences: his words compound jubilation and skepticism, images of authority and obeisance, tropes of spirituality and irony, and they remind us of the elements and passions by which all mortals live. Every gesture and exchange in this scene forecast the world to come, but what most signals the future is the paradox of remembering and forgetting that the diarist performs even as he records this scene. And all who witnessed the King's descent at Dover committed similar acts of memory and oblivion. Many of those (Pepys included) who were drunk with pleasure at the return of Charles Stuart had endorsed the destruction of his father eleven years before. The entire Restoration and the events that would follow over the ensuing years would prove a complex unfolding of memory and forgetfulness.

The jubilant crowds at Dover thought to make flux stop here: forever to banish the turbulence of civil war and political innovation, to restore all the old familiar forms, utterly to erase what had come between the death of the father and the restoration of the son. Charles II would soon institute an Act of Oblivion to those ends, forgiving proponents of rebellion by officially forgetting their misdeeds. But civil war and revolution would not be erased, nor could monarchy, the Anglican Church, aristocratic privilege, political patronage, and the old social hierarchies be revived as though nothing had intervened. Much of the old was brought back with the return of the Stuart monarchy, but the consequence of layering the present over a willfully suppressed past was an instability of feelings and forms that ensured the ever-changing triumph of different memories and different oblivions during the ensuing decades. No one celebrating the return of ancient ways in 1660 could have foreseen the ruptures and innovations that lay ahead in the next half of the century, when crises of conspiracy and the birth of party politics would produce further shifts in monarchy through a sequence of three ruling houses from three different countries. But even in 1660 the innocent acclaim on the shores of Dover was accompanied by hidden guilts and ironies, by vindictive desires, even for some by millenarian hopes. And while such stresses and tensions were unacknowledged in May 1660, they soon enough surfaced, and they unsettled not only the pleasures of this king's rule but the politics of an entire age.

MONARCHS, MINISTERS, EMPIRE

The coronation of Charles II in May 1661 marked the beginning of both the first and the eleventh year of his rule. The King's laws were named as if he had taken possession of the crown at the moment of his father's execution in 1649. And fictions, legal and not so legal, were to prove a hallmark of Stuart rule. The King openly proclaimed his love of parliaments, his devotion to the immemorial constitution of balance and moderation, his Protestant fervor, and his pious hopes for a national church. Yet he often postponed his parliaments; he claimed a tender conscience for Protestant dissenters, but he maneuvered for the toleration of Roman Catholics; he conducted an aggressive, nationalist program against European powers, but he signed a secret and deeply compromising treaty with Louis XIV; he took communion in the Anglican Church, but on his deathbed he sealed his own conversion to Catholicism; he was tenderly affectionate to his barren queen, yet he publicly flaunted his whoring tastes; he repeatedly exiled his unpopular brother James, Duke of York, while promoting and indulging his own bastard sons, yet he staunchly resisted any effort to displace his brother from the line of succession. The dominance of masquerade surely derived from Charles's temper, but fiction and falsehood were also the structural principles and aesthetic features of an entire world.

In December 1678, a series of events started to unfold that proved the very emblem of the masking, the fears, and the psychology of Charles II's rule. It began with legal depositions: one Titus Oates, a baker's son and self-anointed savior of a Protestant people, claimed to have knowledge of a secret plot to kill the King, crown his Catholic brother, and begin the wholesale conversion of English souls—and, just as frightening, English properties—to Rome. Oates offered to a public hungry for scandal and change a Popish plot and a familiar mix of images and idioms: priests and idols, the Roman Antichrist, conspiracy, murder, and mayhem. His depositions and fabrications played brilliantly on memories of the past and on fears of a future under a Catholic king. Nor did it help that the Duke of York's private secretary, Edward Coleman, was caught with treasonous correspondence in his chamber. The plot seemed compounded of sufficient truths to challenge the stability of the Crown. From the midst of the plot, and under the hand of the Earl of Shaftesbury, a political party emerged that took advantage of Popish facts and fears by proposing the Bill of Exclusion in Parliament, which would have barred the Duke of York and any future Catholic monarchs from the English throne. In the event, the bill failed, Charles died of natural causes, and the Duke succeeded his brother in February 1685.

During James's brief reign, no plots, conspiracies, or political parties proved so costly to his rule as did the new king himself. He succeeded his brother in a mood of surprising public affirmation. At his accession, James returned the embrace of Anglican England by promising to honor the national church and that most beloved of Protestant properties, a tender conscience. There would be no forcing of religious uniformity in this reign. But soon enough James began to move against Anglican interests: he staffed his army with Catholic officers, he imposed Catholic officials on Oxford University, and he insisted that his Declarations of Toleration be read aloud from the pulpits of Anglican churches. Such a program challenged interest, property, and propriety, and it spelled the quick demise of Catholic rule.

As Duke of York, James had been famed for martial valor. But now, when confronted in November 1688 by the army of his Dutch son-in-law, William of Orange, he fled under cover of night to France. What had in part provoked James's flight were memories of the past—of civil war and of the execution of his father, Charles I. What had provoked the invasion by William of Orange was not merely the specter of Louis XIV hovering behind James's rule or the open presence of Jesuits at James's court. It was the birth of James Francis Edward Stuart, son of James II and Mary of Modena. Protestants would suffer not only the inconvenience of one Catholic monarch but the possibility of an endless Catholic succession. The prospect was too much to bear. Secret negotiations were begun between powerful English aristocrats—Whigs and Tories alike—and William, the governor (stadholder) of Holland, resulting in what many called the Glorious Revolution. But the deceits and pretenses—the gaps and silences—of this palace coup did not strike all contemporaries as glorious. The stadholder who chased a Catholic king from England was not only an invading hero (though some did call him William the Conqueror), he was also the son-in-law of James II. Those who clung to the binding ties of loyalty and gratitude accused William and Mary of deep impiety, indeed, of parricide.

But the astonishing invitation to William of Orange produced no bloodshed. What it did produce was a Protestant monarchy under the rule of King William III and Queen Mary. Members of Parliament, meeting to invent the laws that would sanctify this revolutionary change, decided that it would be best to say they had discovered the throne of England mysteriously vacant and that this William was no conqueror but a rightful claimant on a vacant throne. Of course, not everyone was pleased by such a revolution—sacred oaths had been broken, binding ties were cast aside, vows were juggled as mere words. Those who would not accept a convenient revolution were called Jacobites, that is, supporters of King James (*Jacobus* in Latin); they remained a force that would trouble British political life by threatening a Stuart restoration in the fervent but failed Jacobite rebellions of 1715 and 1745.

Most of William's subjects, though, were content with the evasions of this Glorious Revolution. Many were not content, though, with the program of European war in which the English were now plunged by their new king, intent on thwarting the ambitions of Louis XIV, his lifelong nemesis. The ruinous expense of war demanded taxes and fiscal innovation; it produced a stream of grumbling satire, complaint against Dutch favorites, and more than one conspiracy and attempted assassination. No such disaffection or turbulence disturbed the reign (1702–1714) of William's successor, Queen Anne. Her years were the twilight of Stuart monarchy, a time of political nostalgia and commercial confidence whose mood the young Alexander Pope captured in the lines of *Windsor-Forest* (1713), where softened memories and strategic elisions of the years of Stuart rule are mingled with images of triumph—of imperial expansion and a swelling commerce of domestic and foreign trade.

But luxury was not England's only import. At the death of Queen Anne, an entire court and new ruling house were shipped to England from the German state of

Hanover. George I was the grandson of James I; beyond lineage, George's communion in a Protestant church was the virtue that most recommended his succession. He spoke no English, knew nothing of his new subjects, and could not be bothered to learn. Nor was he much implicated in the management of a state whose rule would successively become less the prerogative of kings than the business of ministers and the function of parties, interest, and corruption. This displacement of monarch by minister was cemented during the period caustically nicknamed "Robin's Reign": two decades (1721–1742), transversing the reigns of George I and George II, when politics were dominated by Robert Walpole, who bought loyalties, managed kings, and ran the state with such ruthless efficency as to earn him the new label "prime minister" (the phrase was meant as an insult, aimed at the perceived excess of his power in a government where ministers were only supposed to advise their colleagues and their king). The South Sea Bubble, a state-endorsed investment scheme that ruined many, was the making of Robert Walpole. As the only cabinet minister untainted by the scandal (he had initially argued against the scheme, then lost money in it), he was put in charge of the subsequent governmental housecleaning. Once empowered, he cheerfully shed his scruples, devising a political machine fueled by patronage that made his cronies rich, his opposition apoplectic. By the firmness of his rule and the prudence of his policies, Walpole consolidated a long period of Whig supremacy that supplanted the party contest of the preceding decades, when Whigs and Tories had see-sawed more swiftly in and out of power.

The parties had begun to crystallize during the Exclusion crisis of the early 1680s, when Whigs fought to bar the king's Catholic brother from the throne and Tories upheld the established continuity of the Stuart line. Like "prime minister," the two party names began as insult, "Tory" denoting an Irish-Catholic bandit, "Whigs" identifying a group of Scottish rebels during the civil wars. Late in the eighteenth century, Samuel Johnson summed up their polarities: "The prejudice of the Tory is for establishment; the prejudice of the Whig is for innovation." "Establishment" meant preserving monarchic prerogatives, upholding the Anglican church, lamenting the advent of the Hanoverians, and—for some Tories, not all—actively yearning for the restoration of the Stuart line and abetting the attempts to achieve this in the Jacobite rebellions of 1715 and 1745. Whig "innovation" entailed enthusiastic support for both the Glorious Revolution and the House of Hanover, for policies of religious tolerance, and for all measures that advanced the interests of the newly prosperous and powerful merchant class. In the late seventeenth century, party politics had begun for the first time to supplant long-running religious conflicts as the main articulation of interest and power. For all its noise and rage, the new structure produced a paradoxical calm, not by the suppression of difference but by its recognition. The division into parties amounted to a sanctioned fragmentation of the whole. Even during the reign of Anne, when party conflict was at its most feverish, what the machinery of party seemed to ensure was the containment of partisan interest within the dynamic, even organic, coherence of the state.

During Walpole's "reign," portions of the two parties coalesced in an uneasy alliance. The arrogance, obstinacy, and efficacy of Walpole's methods galvanized an opposition consisting of both Tories and alienated Whigs; their endeavors acquired luster from the contributions of a remarkable array of writers (the Tories Jonathan Swift, Alexander Pope, John Gay, and Henry Fielding, and the Whig James Thomson) who opposed the prime minister on grounds of personality, principle, and of course self-interest. Walpole, recognizing that the best writers worked for the opposition, strove to suppress them by all the strategies of censorship he could devise. But by his greatness as a character and his force as an opponent, Walpole loomed for a long while as both literature's nemesis and its muse.

In fact, Walpole enforced the policies endorsed by only a fraction of his party—those moderate Whigs deeply interested in cultivating the country's wealth by commerce, deeply resistant to waging war. "My *politics*," he once wrote emphatically, "*are to keep free from all engagements, as long as we possibly can*"; by "engagements," he meant military commitments abroad. By the late 1730s, he discovered that he could keep free from them no longer. Britons feared that powers on the Continent—Spain, Austria, and above all France—were encroaching on their rights, and the popular clamor to wage European war prevailed. "When trade is at stake," the oppositionist William Pitt warned the British, "it is your last retrenchment; you must defend it or perish." Under the pressure of such sentiments Walpole eventually resigned, having led the state through two decades of comparative peace, growing national prosperity, and a new stability in government, but leaving behind him an army and a navy debilitated by disuse. Nonetheless, with trade at stake and the navy rebuilt, Britain embarked on a series of wars that ran almost unbroken for the rest of the century. Pitt presided brilliantly over many of them, wars waged directly or indirectly against France for trading privileges and territories abroad. By 1763, Britain had secured possession of Bengal in India, many islands and coastal territories in the Caribbean, and virtually all of North America (including Canada) east of the Mississippi, as well as half of all the international trade transpiring on the planet. So great was the impetus toward empire that even Britain's humiliating defeat in the American War of Independence (1775–1783) could not really halt the momentum; territories in India were still expanding, and settlement of Australia lay in the offing.

By now, the throne was occupied by the first Hanoverian monarch born in Britain, George III. His long reign (1760–1820) teemed with troubles: the popular scorn for his chosen ministers, the loss of the American war, the aftershocks of the French Revolution, the defiance of his heirs, the torments of his own slow-encroaching madness. But almost from beginning to end he ruled over the richest nation and the widest empire in the world. In 1740, a new song could be heard with a catchy refrain: "Rule, Britannia, rule the waves / Britons never will be slaves." The words were the work of the Scots-born poet James Thomson, now a proud adherent of "Britannia" by virtue of the Act of Union (1707), which had fused Scotland with England and Wales into a new nation, newly named: Great Britain. Over the ensuing years the song took hold partly because of the seductively prophetic ways in which it forecast Britain's greatness and partly because of the proud but peculiar resonances of the refrain's last line. There, Thomson contrasts British liberties with the slave-like constraints supposedly suffered by subjects of absolute monarchy elsewhere. Less directly, "slaves" also points to those peoples upon whose subjugation British privilege and British prosperity were increasingly to depend. Throughout the century, Britons profited spectacularly from the capture, transport, sale, and labor of African slaves in current and former colonies; "no nation," William Pitt the Younger proclaimed in 1792, had "plunged so deeply into this guilt as Great Britain."

There were also whole populations whose condition often evoked the analogy of slavery in the minds of the few who paid reformist attention to their plight: the oppressed indigenous peoples of the colonies, and women and the poor at home. Conversation about such issues became louder and more purposeful near the end of the eighteenth century, as particular champions began to turn social questions into moral causes: John Wilkes on the widening of liberties and voting rights; Mary Wollstonecraft on the rights of women; William Blake (and later, William Cobbett) on the economic inequities of the whole social structure. The problems themselves did not even begin to find redress until the following century, but the emergence of such advocacies, quickened by the audacities of the French Revolution, marked a turning point toward the Romanticism that seized poetic and political imaginations in the 1790s. For most Britons of the eighteenth century, however, the new prosperity produced no special promptings of conscience. As their Restoration forebears had actively encouraged oblivion in an effort to anesthetize themselves to their past, men and women now sustained a moral and social oblivion that eased their use of others and their pleasure in new wealth. Out of such adroitly managed oscillations, Britons fabricated a new sense of themselves as a nation and an empire.

This new construct was in large measure the work of a prominent breed of economic architects: the capital-wielding middle classes. For centuries, wealth had derived primarily from land: tenant farmers performed the labor; the landed gentry collected the often enormous profits. The new wealth was amassed, even created, by people situated between these two extremes, constituting what was often referred to as "the middling rank," "the middling station," or "the middling orders." What set the middling orders apart was the comparatively new way in which they made their money: not by landed inheritance, not by tenancy or wage work, but by the adroit deployment of money itself. Having acquired a sum by inheritance, wage, or loan, they used it as capital, investing it, along with their own efforts, in potentially lucrative enterprises: in shops, in factories, and in the enormous new financial structures (banks, stocks) that underwrote the nation's economic expansiveness. They hired helpers, reinvested profits, and when their schemes succeeded, they made their money grow. With wealth, of course, grew clout. The interests of the "City"—that is, of the eastern half of London where bustling merchants made their deals—increasingly shaped the affairs of state, the appetites for empire. Empire also shaped the progress of the arts: members of the middle class became the chief consumers and energetic producers of the period's most conspicuous new forms of literature: newspapers and novels. But nowhere were the new powers of the burgeoning bourgeoisie more striking than in the theater, that cultural site they often visited and ultimately revised.

MONEY, MANNERS, AND THEATRICS

No event more exactly and more economically signals the return of an aristocratic court to the center of English culture than the reopening of the London theaters in 1662. The intimacy, indeed the complicity, of court with theater throughout the early modern period was such that when in the 1640s Parliament took aim at monarchy, aristocracy, and privilege, it not only struck off the heads of the Earl of Strafford and Archbishop Laud, it also banished play acting and shut tight the doors of the London stage. But Puritans could not banish the theater from the English imagination, and no sooner were the playhouses closed than publishers issued new editions of old plays and the theater made a secret return in domestic spaces and before private audiences. Print and memory would be the preservative of an entire culture. In 1660, monarchy and theater were restored in tandem. But this artistic restoration, like the political one that made it possible, irresistibly mingled the old with the new. Pepys captured all the excitement and splendor of this restoration; as usual he proves adroit at reckoning innovation:

> [T]he stage is now . . . a thousand times better and more glorious than heretofore. Now, wax-candles, and many of them; then, not above three pounds of tallow. Now, all things civil, no rudeness anywhere; then, as in a bear garden. Then, two or three fiddlers; now, nine or ten of the best. Then, nothing but rushes upon the ground and everything mean; and now all otherwise. Then the Queen seldom and the King never would come; now not the King only for state but all civil people do think they may come as well as any.

One reason that "all civil people" thought so was a matter of simple geography. Whereas the theaters of Shakespeare's day had been located in seedy districts on the outskirts of the city, this new and sumptuous theatrical world was ensconced in new neighborhoods strategically located for maximum social confluence, on the border between Westminster—home of the court—and the City of London, dwelling place of a "mighty band of citizens and prentices" whose sudden convergence with royalty seemed a dramatic innovation. They had all gathered to witness the most astonishing new spectacle of all: women on stage in a public theater.

Before the Restoration, aristocratic women had tantalized the court in private and privileged masquing; now the pleasures of display and consumption were democratized in several ways. For women, theatricality was no longer a pastime reserved for the very few but a plausible—though precarious—profession. For audiences at the new theaters, actresses represented the possibility of erotic spectacle for the price of a ticket—a chance to gaze on women who everyone knew were managing the pleasures, and often the policies, of kings and courtiers. Inevitably new strategies of theatricality suffused this audience, where women might model seductive conduct on the teasing combinations of concealment and display enacted before them. Pepys eavesdropped on the libertine Sir Charles Sedley in urgent banter with two women: "And one of the women would and did sit with her mask on, all the play. He would fain know who she was, but she would not tell; yet did give him many pleasant hints of her knowledge of him, by that means setting his brains at work to find out who she was, and did give him leave to use all means but pulling off her mask." Display and disguise not only animated the stage, they quickened social exchange in the intimate spaces of stalls and boxes. The traffic between revelation and concealment defined this theater. It drove the plots of plays and galvanized audiences, modeling and scripting their fashions, their language, their lives.

In such a world the theater provided a national mask, a fantasy of empire and heroism, and yet at the same time sustained a critique of masquerade, a brutal exposure of deceptions rampant in the culture. On the one hand, the heroic drama displayed, indeed reveled in, outsized acts of conquest in exotic lands, valor, and virtue: on stage, princes slaughtered infidels by the thousands; virgins sustained honor through impossible ordeals of abduction and assault. Yet in 1667, at the same moment such dramas were thriving in the king's and the duke's playhouses, the royal fleet was being burned and sunk by a Dutch navy that breached all defenses, invading the very precincts and privacy of London's docks and shipyards. And while the fleet burned, the king busied himself with other depredations, sustaining a series of intrigues, some with the very actresses who wore such incomparable honor and virtue on the stage. (The mix of myth and mischief was popular in pictures too—for example, in the portrait of Barbara Villiers, Countess of Castlemaine, perhaps the most notorious of all the king's mistresses, gotten up in the guise of Minerva, Roman goddess of wisdom; see Color Plate 21.) The heroic drama celebrated military conquest and colonial glory, and displayed them at a moment in national history that produced nothing so much as shame and humiliation: defeat at the hands of Dutch ships and Dutch commerce.

At the same time, but in a far different dramatic mode, the stage sustained a brilliant critique of a whole culture of incongruity, masquerade, and self-delusion. Restoration comedy took as its subject appetite and opportunism, social hypocrisy and sexual power play. The London audience watched scenes of seduction and connivance set in the very vicinities they had traversed to reach the playhouse: St. James's Park, Covent Garden. Such aristocratic libertines as Sir Charles Sedley and Lord Rochester, intent on their own intrigues, might admire themselves in a theatrical mirror, where the rake-hero conducted endless parry-and-thrust with his equals, brutalized his inferiors, and laid hands and claim on any moveable object of desire: fruits and foodstuffs, silks and sonnets, housemaids and women of high estate. But the rakes in the playhouse might see themselves mocked as well. The best comic writers—Wycherley, Etherege, Behn, Congreve—showed the libertines equaled and often bested in cunning by the women they pursued, baffled where they would be most powerful, enslaved where they would be most free. In brilliant volleys of dialogue, these lovers mixed passion and poison in volatile measures, chasing one another through a maze of plots, counterplots, and subplots so convoluted as to suggest a world of calculation run mad. Over the thirty years of its triumphs, Restoration comedy, in an astounding fugue of excesses and depravities, laid bare the turbulence and toxins of this culture.

That the heroic drama, with all its exaggerations and flatteries, found a market is hardly surprising; what is more puzzling is the commercial triumph of Restoration comedy, a theatrical mode that entertained by punishing and humiliating its audience—though it is hardly surprising that this theater should itself have fallen victim in the 1690s to prudery and what would come to be called "taste." In the wake of the Protestant revolution of 1688, which typed Stuart rule as the very emblem of self-indulgence, agents of moral improvement and social propriety made their assault on Restoration comedy the stalking horse for a broad program of Christian reform. Restoration comedy, which had erupted as a repudiation of Puritan prohibitions, now seemed to prompt a new wave of moral rectitude.

Under such pressures, the playhouse redirected its mirror away from the aristocracy toward the upper strata of the "middling sort": London merchants, colonial profiteers. During the Restoration, the newly prosperous mercantile classes who converged with courtiers at the theater had watched themselves either derided or ignored on stage, their social pretensions and ineptitudes put down in the comedies, their commercial concerns absent from the heroic drama. In the early eighteenth century, they saw themselves glorified instead, in "domestic tragedy," which displayed the tribulations of commercial households, and in sentimental comedy, which sought by a mix of tears and modest laughter to inculcate family values and to portray the merchant class as the nation's moral core. Richard Steele's *The Conscious Lovers* (1722) sounded the fanfare for a newly theatric social self-conception. "We merchants," a businessman informs an aristocrat, "are a species of gentry that have grown

Color Plate 21 Sir Peter Lely, *Barbara Villiers, Countess of Castlemaine*, c. 1641–1709. Theatricality disseminated: Charles II's favorite painter portrays Charles II's favorite mistress, in costume as Minerva, Roman goddess of wisdom, against a stormy background. Castlemaine's countenance was reproduced in less costly ways as well, in engravings from Lely's portraits that made the visage of the King's mistress possessible by ordinary mortals. The diarist Samuel Pepys records a visit to Lely's sumptuous studio, where he "saw the so-much-by-me-desired picture of my Lady Castlemaine, which is a most blessed picture and that I must have a copy of." *(The Royal Collection © 2003, Her Majesty Queen Elizabeth II.)*

Color Plate 22 Johann Zoffany (1733/4–1810), *Queen Charlotte with Her Two Eldest Sons*, 1764. Theatricality domesticated: a century after Lely painted the king's mistress in the garb of the goddess of wisdom (Color Plate 21), such mythological trappings are reduced to dress-up for George III's two young sons at play. Amid sumptuous furnishings, Zoffany's conversation piece emphasizes not the grandeur of the royal family but its intimacy and affection; a new era of majesty as "good example" has commenced. *(The Royal Collection © 2003, Her Majesty Queen Elizabeth II.)*

Color Plate 23 Joshua Reynolds, *Mrs. Abington as "Miss Prue,"* 1771. Restoration theatricality transposed and transformed: the comic actress Frances Abington (1737–1815) here traverses time and rank, reincarnating Miss Prue, an "awkward country girl" in William Congreve's late-17th-century comedy *Love for Love* (1695), in garb that epitomizes late-18th-century high fashion. Abington later scored her greatest triumph in a similar role, modeled on Restoration antecedents and crafted especially for her: Lady Teazle, the country wife ardent for London life in Richard Brinsley Sheridan's *School for Scandal.* *(The Bridgeman Art Library International Ltd.)*

Color Plate 24 Marcellus Laroon, *Charles II as President of the Royal Society*, 1684. Science enthroned: in this portrait of the King painted a year before his death, the traditional trappings of royalty—crown, throne, and orb—literally take a back seat (in the background at left) to the advancements of the new science. Charles gestures toward the instruments of seeing, modeling, mapping, and calibrating that the Royal Society he sponsored had done much to devise and develop. By their placement, the painter suggests that these tools make possible the naval commerce and conquest depicted in the distance—as though the telescope were the world's new scepter, and the globe the monarch's proper sphere. (*The Art Archive/Christ's Hospital/Eileen Tweedy.*)

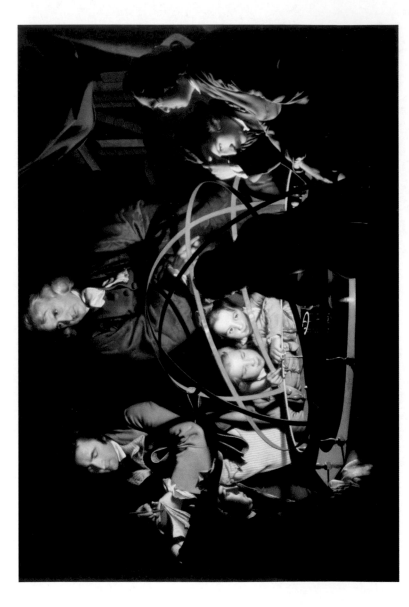

Color Plate 25 Joseph Wright, *A Philosopher Giving That Lecture on the Orrery, in Which a Lamp Is Put in Place of the Sun,* 1766. Science popularized: the experimental philosophy and new science pioneered during the 17th century provided both pleasure and instruction in the 18th, as teachers and textbooks strove to distill and redistribute recondite discoveries as common knowledge. The orrery, a working model of the solar system, figured prominently in this new educational endeavor; it could supply, wrote Richard Steele, "the pleasures of science to any one." The spheres within the circle, coordinated by clockwork, enacted the orbits of the planets and their moons. The sun's stand-in was often a brass ball, but more rarely (as here) a lit oil lamp at the center of the machine. In Wright's painting, the flame sheds light on the lecturer and his listeners, each of them different, all of them enthralled. *(Derby Museums and Art Gallery.)*

Color Plate 26 Joseph Wright, *An Experiment on a Bird in the Air Pump*, 1768. Science interrogated: the experiment's purpose is to demonstrate the effects of a vacuum on a breathing creature; its outcome, unless the experimenter restores air to the glass chamber, will be the death of the bird. Such experiments, though widely performed, were deemed by one lecturer "too shocking to every spectator who has the least degree of humanity." This time, Wright depicts a mixture of reactions. The lecturer, gesturing like a conjurer, stares out at the viewer as though in a kind of trance, oblivious both to the bird and to his audience, whose faces and forms variously evince absorption, meditation, distraction, and distress. (© *National Gallery, London.*)

Color Plate 27 William Hogarth, *The Beggar's Opera, Act 3, Scene 11,* 1792. Theatricality encompasses all: audience and actors encounter each other on stage. Hogarth here replicates icons of art history much as *The Beggar's Opera*, a theatrical sensation of 1728, echoed popular ballads. Macheath, the criminal-hero of the play, is shown poised in the center between Lucy (left) and Polly (right)—a grouping that evokes the hero Hercules at his mythic moment of choosing between Virtue and Vice. Meanwhile, Polly and her father, Mr. Peachum (in black at right), strike poses bizarrely reminiscent of Christ and Mary Magdalen. Another kind of pairing is in play too. Lavinia Fenton, the actress playing Polly, gestures not so much toward her stage father as to the audience member standing starstruck just beyond him: the Duke of Bolton, so taken with her in the role that he became her lover and eventually her husband. In this, the fifth version he painted of the same scene, Hogarth has expanded the scope of the stage set so that the prison walls appear to enclose the spectators too within the *Opera's* bright, bleak world, where everything and everyone have become commodities—objects of desire and items of exchange engulfed in intricate, energetic, precarious transactions. *(Yale Center for British Art, Paul Mellon Collection, USA/Photo: Bridgeman Art Library.)*

Color Plate 28 William Hogarth, *Hogarth's Servants*, mid-1750s. In this late painting, Hogarth's lifelong brilliancies of satire cede place to an approach both documentary and tender, as he traces, with painstaking attention and evident affection, the faces of six people deeply familiar to him. *(Tate Gallery, London/Art Resource, NY.)*

Color Plate 29 Thomas Gainsborough, *The Cottage Door*, c. 1788. As the critic John Barrell has pointed out, Gainsborough's painting mingles two different perceptions of the rural poor. The gracious women and boisterous children basking in the day's last light conjure up the sort of sentimental idealization of pastoral joys that also found expression in such poems as Oliver Goldsmith's *The Deserted Village*. Other writers insisted, by contrast, on the misery of the laborer's lot, an emphasis that is figured here in the form of the returning husband at bottom left, bent with his burden of firewood and nearly buried by the shadows. *(Cincinnati Art Museum, Acc. 1948.173.)*

into the world this last century, and are as honorable and almost as useful as you landed folk, that have always thought yourself so much above us."

Nor was the stage the only venue to promulgate this new cultural self-awareness. By its very title *The Spectator* (1711–1713), one of the most widely read periodicals of the century, assured its largely middle-class audience that they moved under the constant, thoughtful scrutiny of a virtual playgoer, the paper's fictive author, "Mr. Spectator," who made all London a kind of theater, in which he (and his eagerly imitative readers) might perpetually enjoy the privileges of making observations and forming judgments. The very energies that had been drained away from the stage now found a new home in the theatricalized world of commerce, fashion, manners, taste.

The cast members in this new theater were numerous, varied, and eager for direction, mostly because, as a "new species of gentry," they aspired to roles for which they had formerly been deemed unfit. Terms like "esquire" and "gentleman" had operated in previous centuries as proof of literal "entitlement." They were secured by registration with the College of Heralds, and they calibrated not merely monetary wealth but lineage, landholdings, education, and social standing. In the eighteenth century, men and women with sufficient money and nerve assumed these titles for themselves, confident enough that they might learn to play the part. "In our days," noted a 1730 dictionary, "all are accounted gentlemen that have money." But since "the money" was now so variously attainable—by shopkeeping, by manufacture, by international trade—the "middle station" was itself subdivided into many strata, and since the very point of capital was accumulation and improvement, ascent by emulation became a master plot in the new social theater. "Everyone," observed one commentator, "is flying from his inferiors in pursuit of his superiors, who fly from him with equal alacrity."

Amid the flux, fashion and commodity—what one wore, what one owned—mattered enormously. Wigs, fans, scarves, silks, petticoats, and jewels; china, silver, family portraits—these were the costumes, these the props of the new commercial theater, by which members of the middle orders pleased themselves and imitated the gentry. The commercial classes who had begun by catering to the aristocracy gradually became, in their waxing prosperity, their own best customers, selling garb and goods to one another. Shrewd marketers saw that novelty itself possessed an intrinsic and urgent appeal for people constantly in social flight, tirelessly engaged in remaking themselves. Advertising came into its own, filling the pages and underwriting the costs of the daily, weekly, and monthly periodicals. The listing of consumables became a prevalent mode of print, in everything from auction catalogues (the still-dominant houses of Christie's and Sotheby's got their start near the middle of the century) to poems and novels, where long lists of products and possessions became a means of recording the culture's appetites, and at times of satirizing them. In the hands of Swift and Pope, the catalogue itself became a form of art. The taste in literary miscellany reflected a more general taste for omnivorous consumption: variety indexed abundance and proved power. Tea from China, coffee from the Caribbean, tobacco from Virginia—all were relatively new, comparatively inexpensive, and enormously popular. In daily rituals of drink and smoke, the middling orders imbibed and inhaled a pleasing sense of their global reach, their comfortable centrality on a planet newly commercialized.

Commodities formed part of a larger discourse, involving speech and gesture as well as prop and costume. A cluster of precepts, gathered under the umbrella-term "politeness," supplied the stage directions, even at times the script, for the new social theater in which everyone was actor and everyone was audience. Eager to shine in their recently acquired roles, the merchant classes pursued the polish implicit in the word "polite." They hired "dancing masters" to teach them graceful motions and proper manners, "bear leaders" (tutors) to guide their sons on the Grand Tour of France and Italy in the footsteps of the nobility, elocution coaches to help them purge inappropriate accents, teachers of painting and music to supply their daughters with marriageable competence. For the newly prosperous, politeness was the epitome of distinction: it went beyond gesture and accomplishment to suggest a state of mind, a refinement of perception, a mix of knowledge, responsiveness, and judgment often summarized as "taste." "The man of polite imagination," said the *Spectator*, "is let into a great many pleasures that the vulgar are not capable of receiving." Eager to gain access, middle-class readers avidly sought instruction.

Politeness (which Samuel Johnson once defined as "fictitious benevolence") required considerable self-control; the passions (rage, greed, lust) were to be contained and channeled into the appearance of abundant and abiding goodwill. The middle classes embraced such constraints partly to allay widespread suspicion of their commercial aggressions, their social ambitions. Their preoccupation with politeness has helped to foster a recurrent misimpression of the period: that, setting aside the occasional rake or wench, it was all manners and morals, dignity and decorum, fuss and formality, reason and enlightenment. Not so. Even among the merchant classes, politeness afforded only provisional concealment for roiling energies; amid the impoverished and the gentry, it held less purchase still. In no succeeding epoch until our own was language so openly and energetically obscene, drunkenness so rampant, sexual conduct so various and unapologetic. Even among the "officially" polite, the very failure of containment could produce a special thrill. In one of the century's most often-used phrases, a speaker announces that "I cannot forbear"—that is, cannot restrain myself—from saying or doing what the verb itself suggests were better left unsaid or undone. The formula declares helpless and pleasurable surrender to an unmastered impulse, and the condition was apparently endemic. James Boswell records the memorable self-summary of an elderly lawyer: "I have tried . . . in my time to be a philosopher, but—I don't know how—cheerfulness was always breaking in." Such "breakings-in" (and breakings-out) of feeling were common, even cherished. The scholar Donald Greene has argued well that the eighteenth century was less an "age of reason" (as has often been said) than an age of exuberance. Certainly much of what the middle classes read and wrote is a literature of outburst: of hilarity, of lament, of rage, of exaltation. The copious diaries that the century brought forth deal in all such exclamations; they are the prose of people who have chosen to write rather than repress the thoughts and actions that strict politeness might proscribe. Even the *Spectator*, that manual of polished taste, presents itself as the daily outpouring of a writer who, after maintaining an eccentric lifelong silence, has found that he can no longer keep his "discoveries"—moral, social, experiential—to himself.

Such self-publicizing was more complex for women than for men. When women represented their own lives—in manuscript (letters, journals) and increasingly in print—they sometimes chafed at the paradoxical mix of tantalizing possibilities and painful limitations that their privilege produced. Post-Restoration prosperity and politeness supplied women with many new venues for self-display and sociability, in playhouses and pleasure gardens, ballrooms, spas, and shops. Society exalted and paraded women as superior consumers: wearing the furs, fragrances, and fabrics of distant climes, they furnished evidence of empire, proud proof of their fathers' and husbands' economic attainments. They consumed print, too; near the start of the eighteenth century, male editors invented the women's periodical and found the new genre immensely profitable. Increasingly, women not only purchased print but produced it, deploying their words and wit as a kind of cultural capital, which when properly expended might reap both cash and fame. During the eighteenth century, for the first time, books by women—of poems, of precepts, and above all of fiction—became not exotic but comparatively commonplace.

Still, books by women remained controversial, as did all manifestations of female autonomy and innovation. The very excitement aroused by women's new conspicuousness in the culture provoked counter-efforts at containment. Preachers and moralists argued endlessly that female virtue resided in domesticity. Marriage itself offered an age-old instrument of social control, newly retooled to meet the needs of ambitious merchants, for whom daughters were the very currency of social mobility. If parents could arrange the right marriage, the whole family's status promptly rose. The dowry that the bride brought with her was an investment in future possibilities: in the rank and connections that the union secured, in the inheritance that would descend to its heirs, in the annual income ("jointure") that the wife herself would receive following the death of the husband. Financially, a widow (or for that matter, a well-born woman who never married) was often far more independent than a wife, whose wedding led to a kind of sanctioned erasure. She possessed little or no control over marital property (including the wealth she had brought to the union); "in marriage," wrote the codifier of English law William Blackstone, "husband and wife are one person, and that person is the husband." The sums that the husband undertook to hand over to his wife were dubbed "pin money" (a suggestive trivialization): funds for managing the household, that sphere wherein, as the moral literature insisted, a woman might best deploy her innate talents and find her sanctioned satisfactions. These consisted first and foremost in producing children and in shaping their manners and morals. In a time of improvisatory birth control, precarious obstetrics, and high infant mortality, the bearing of children was a relentless, dangerous, and emotionally exhausting process. The upbringing of children provided more pleasure and possessed a new cachet: the conduct literature endorsed busy, attentive child-rearing as the highest calling possible for women whose prosperity freed them from the need to work for wages. (Guidebooks for parents and pleasure books for children both had their origins in the eighteenth century.) Apart from the duties of motherhood and household management—the supervision of servants, meals, shopping, and social occasions—the woman of means was encouraged to pursue those pleasures for which her often deliberately constricted education had prepared her: music, embroidery, letter writing, and talk at the tea table—the domestic counterpart of the clubs and coffeehouses, where women were not permitted to appear.

In the late seventeenth century, the possibilities for women had seemed at moments more various and more audacious. In the plays of Aphra Behn, female characters pursued their pleasures with an almost piratical energy and ingenuity; in *A Serious Proposal to the Ladies* (1694), the feminist Mary Astell imagined academies where women could withdraw to pursue the pleasures of learning and escape the drudgeries of marriage. In the eighteenth century, though, despite women's increasing authorial presence, these early audacities tended to go underground. Protests by women against their secondary status are most overt in manuscript—in the acerbic poems and letters that Mary Wortley Montagu circulated among her friends, in the journal entries wherein the brewer's wife Hester Thrale vented her frustrations. In print, women's desire for autonomy became a tension in the text, rather than its explicit point or outcome. Novelists explored women's psyches with subtlety; their plots, however, nearly always culminated in marriage, and more rarely in catastrophe, as though those were the only alternatives. Even the Bluestocking Circle, an eminent late-century group of intellectual women, preached tenets of essential sexual difference and subordination; they argued (for example) in favor of improving girls' educations, but as a way of preparing them for better and happier work within the home rather than for adventures abroad. During the eighteenth century, the middle classes did much to spell out the gendered divison of labor—father as the family's champion in the marketplace, mother as cheerfully efficient angel in the house—that remained a cultural commonplace, among families who could afford it, for the next two hundred years.

Among the poor, such divisions were not tenable; most manual labor paid so little that everyone in the family had to work if all were to survive. Wives not only managed their frugal households, they also worked for wages, in fields, in shops, or in cottage manufacture of fabrics, gloves, basketry. Children often began wage work at age four or five, treading laundry, scaring crows, sweeping chimneys; boys began the more promising role of apprenticeships around the age of ten. For many of the poor, domestic service offered employment comparatively secure and endlessly demanding. Darker prospects included prostitution and crime: shoplifting was punishable by death. In the case of the helplessly indigent, local government was responsible for providing relief, but the Poor Law provided large loop-holes by which the parish could drive out any unwanted supplicant—an unwed mother, for example—who could not meet the intricate and restrictive criteria for legal residence. The poor had no vote, no voice in government; as the century progressed, their predicament attracted increasing attention and advocacy. Philanthropists instituted charity schools designed, in the words of their proponent Hannah More, "to train up the lower classes in habits of industry and piety." Two convictions informed even the most ambitious philanthropy: that poverty was part of a divine plan and that it was the fault of the indolent poor themselves; they thus found themselves caught between the rock of providence and the hard place of reproach. Yet charity schools did increase literacy, and with it perhaps the sense of possibilities. Other late-century developments, too, were mixed. Improvements in sanitation, medicine, and hygiene contributed to a surge in population, which in turn produced among the rural poor a labor surplus: too many people, too little work. At the same time, wealthy landholders increased the practice of "enclosure," acquiring and sequestering acreage formerly used by the poor for common pasturage and family farming. As a result, many rural families left the land on which they had worked for centuries and traveled to alien terrain: the textile mills that capitalists had newly built and the industrial cities developing rapidly around them.

As the poor became poorer, the very rich—landowning lords and gentry—became very much richer, both by the means they now shared with the middle class (capital investment in banks and stocks) and through their own long-held resources. Land increased in value, partly because there were now so many merchant families passionately eager to buy into the landscape and the life of their aristocratic betters, among whom the spectacle of emulation provoked amusement and revulsion. The landed gentry preserved their distance by many means: social practices (they often flaunted their adulteries, for example, as contrast to middle-class proprieties), artistic allegiance (with the advent of the bourgeois drama, aristocratic audiences defected from the theater to the opera house, where elaborate productions and myth-based plots sustained the aristocratic values of the heroic drama), and the sheer ostentation of their leisure and magnitude of their consumption. But the pivotal difference remained political: by the award of offices, by the control of elections, landowners maintained their strangle-hold on local and national power, despite all the waxing wealth of trade.

At the same time, their very absorption in pleasure and power demanded a continual traffic with their inferiors. Merchants and shopkeepers catered to them; professionals managed their transactions; household servants contrived their comforts; aspiring artists sought to cultivate their taste and profit by their patronage. Transactions among the aristocracy and the middle classes took other forms as well. A lord low on money often found it lucrative to marry the daughter of a thriving merchant. And middle-class modes of life could exert a subtler magnetism, too—particularly for George III, who prized mercantile decorum over aristocratic swagger. In the portrait of his queen and her two eldest sons in Color Plate 22, the artist Johann Zoffany (himself an expensive German import) celebrates not their royal state but their domestic felicity: the heroic trappings (helmet, spear, turban) so conspicuous in Lely's portrait of the scandalous Lady Castlemaine (see Color Plate 21) are here reduced to the props of child's play in the domestic theater of family relations.

King George had commissioned Johann Zoffany in pursuit of precisely this effect. By his eager emulation of the middling orders, George III broke with monarchic traditions, but he inaugurated a new one that would be sustained and expanded in various ways by Queen Victoria in the nineteenth century and her successors in the twentieth. During George's reign, too, the middle classes began to pursue more practical convergence with the aristocracy: a wider distribution of voting rights, a firmer political power base. For the first time, the phrase "middle classes" itself came into use, as a way of registering this cohort's recognition of its own coherence and interests, its unique, often combative relations with the classes above and below; the plural ("classes") registered the abiding diversity—of income, of lifestyle—within the cohesion. In the years since the Restoration, the middle classes had moved themselves energetically in the theater of social and economic relations from a place in the audience toward center stage, exerting enormous power over the working lives of the poor, posing challenges to the elite. Increasingly, their money, manners, appetites, and tastes came to be perceived as the essence of national life, as the part that might stand for the whole. "Trade," Henry Fielding remarked in 1751, "has indeed given a new face to the nation."

It gave the nation new momentum, too, literal as well as figurative. The engineering marvels of the eighteenth century—the harnessing of steam power, the innovations in factory design, the acceleration of production—were instruments of capital. So were improvements in the rate of transport. Over the course of the century, the government collaborated with private investors to construct a proliferating network of smooth turnpikes and inland waterways: canal boats delivered coal and other cargo with new celerity; stagecoaches sped between cities on precise schedules with crowded timetables. Timekeeping itself became a source of national wealth and pride. During the 1660s,

British clockmakers established themselves as the best in Europe. A century later, the clockmaker John Harrison invented the "marine chronometer," a large watch so sturdy and so precise that it could keep time to the minute throughout a voyage around the world, amid all vicissitudes of wind and weather. Harrison's invention made it possible to calculate a ship's longitude accurately, thus solving a problem that had bedeviled navigation for centuries (and sometimes sunk whole fleets). The innovation further paved the way for trade and empire-building, and did much to establish Greenwich, a town just east of London, as the reference point for world timekeeping. Trade was giving a new face—a new distribution of power and priority—not only to the nation but also to the globe, placing Britain (so Britons liked to think) at its center.

FAITH AND KNOWLEDGE, THOUGHT AND FEELING

Clockwork functioned another way too: as a new, theologically unsettling metaphor for the relations between God and his creation. In his *Principia Mathematica* (1687), Isaac Newton set forth the mathematical principles—the laws of motion, the workings of gravity—by which, it turned out, the universe could be seen to operate more consistently and efficiently than even the finest clockwork. What need had this flawless mechanism for any further adjustments by its divine clockmaker? Some of Newton's admirers—though never the pious scientist himself—found in his discoveries the cue for a nearly omnivorous skepticism. The boldest deists and "freethinkers" dismissed Christianity as irrational fiction, to be supplanted by the stripped-down doctrine of "natural religion." In the intricate design of nature they found the proof of a creator whose existence and infinite wisdom, they argued, are all we know on earth and all we need to know. The fashion for such thought—at least in its purest form—proved fleeting. To most minds, the "argument from design" simply furnished further proof of God's benevolence. Amid such comfortable conviction, the blasphemies of a virtuoso skeptic like David Hume appeared an aberration, even an entertainment, rather than a trend. "There is a great cry about infidelity," Samuel Johnson remarked in 1775, "but there are, in reality, very few infidels." From deep belief and ingrained habit, Christianity retained its hold over the entire culture; though a few pietists voiced alarm, science tended to enhance faith, not destroy it.

Still, the relation of religion to public life had changed. In the mid-seventeenth century, politics was inevitably suffused with spirituality. Charles I had gone to the scaffold as an Anglican martyr; he had ruled according to the dictum "No bishop, no king." For many English men and women, the war of Parliament against the king was a holy war: Puritans had typed Charles I as that "man of blood"; Cromwell's army had gone to battle singing David's psalms. By the eighteenth century, ardors had cooled: no one went to war for creed alone. But that is not to say that these were lives bereft of the spiritual; deep religious feeling remained, even as violence of expression abated. The Restoration had reinstated Anglicanism as the national faith; its adherents were admitted to the full privileges of education and office. Over the ensuing century, the Church of England pursued a strategic but controversial mix of old exclusions and new accommodations. For dissenters (offspring of the Puritans), new laws proffered certain permissions (to teach, to congregate for public worship) in exchange for certain oaths. Catholics, by contrast, were kept beyond the pale; they received no such concessions until late in the eighteenth century, when even a limited act provoked angry Protestant riots. Early in the century, the Anglican faithful were divided between the "high flyers," who perennially claimed that the church was in danger of dilution, and the Latitudinarians, who argued that all kinds of dissent might finally be accommodated within the structure of the church. Latitudinarians prevailed, but as the Church of England broadened, it began to lose the force of its exclusiveness; attendance at services shrank markedly as the century advanced, but alternative forms of communal worship flourished. In the eighteenth century, evangelical religions came to occupy the crucial space of fervent spirituality that the church of Donne and Herbert had once claimed as its own. By midcentury, in the new movement called Methodism, John Wesley expressed a vehement response against the skeptical rationalism of the freethinkers and the monied complacency of the established church. Wesley preached the truth of scriptural revelation. He urged his followers to purge their sins methodically—by a constant self-monitoring, partly modeled on earlier Puritan practices—and enthusiastically, by attending revival meetings, hearing electrifying sermons. Wesley delivered some 40,000 sermons over the course of a phenomenally energetic life, and his no less relentless brother Charles composed some 6,000 hymns to quicken evangelical spirits. Methodism found its most ardent following among the poor, who discovered in the doctrine a sympathy for their condition and a recognition of their worth, epitomized in one of Charles Wesley's verses: "Our Savior by the rich unknown / Is worshipped by the poor alone." Their worship was loud and fervent; intensity of feeling attested authenticity of faith.

The middle class and gentry located their own fervor in the more polished idioms of sentiment and sensibility. The terms named a code of conduct and of feeling current in the mid-eighteenth century, when men and women increasingly came to pride themselves on an emotional responsiveness highly cultivated and conspicuously displayed: tears of pity at the spectacle of suffering, admiration for the achievements of art or the magnificence of nature. For many in the middle class, the cult of sentiment held out the appealing prospect of a democratization of manners; the elaborate protocols of the aristocracy might remain elusive, but pure *feeling* was surely more accessible, to anyone with the leisure and the training. For many women, the cult afforded the added attraction of honoring that very susceptibility to feeling and that renunciation of reason that had long and pejoratively been gendered female. The sufferings of the poor, of children, of animals, became a testing ground for empathy; majestic mountains became favorite proving grounds for heightened response. The fashion for benevolence helped focus attention on the plight of the poor and the oppressed, prompting new charities and social movements. For many of the conventionally religious, sentimentality became an adjunct article of faith. They found their scriptures in treatises that posited proper feeling as a chief measure of human worth—Adam Smith's *Theory of Moral Sentiments* (1759); in sentimental dramas that modeled the cultivation (and the performance) of elaborate emotion; in novels that paid minute attention to the protagonist's every emotional nuance—Samuel Richardson's *Pamela* (1740–1741) and *Clarissa* (1747–1749), Laurence Sterne's *Life and Opinions of Tristram Shandy* (1759–1767) and *A Sentimental Journey* (1768), Henry Mackenzies's *The Man of Feeling* (1771); in travel books that transported readers geographically and emotionally by charged descriptions of mighty vistas. For both deists and pietists earlier in the century, nature had testified the existence of a God; for connoisseurs of the sublime near century's end, nature itself was beginning to serve as surrogate for the divine.

In the articulation of eighteenth-century faith and science, thought and feeling, the most conspicuous and continuous voice was that of the first person. The "I" was omnipresent, observing world and self alike: in the experiment-reports of the scientists and the thought-experiments of the philosophers; in the Methodists' self-monitoring, the sentimentalists' self-approbation, the sublimity-seekers' recorded raptures; in the copious autobiographical writings—diaries, letters, memoirs—of characters in novels and people in the real world. Always and everywhere, it seems, someone was setting down the nuances of his or her experience. The self-reckoning promulgated in the past by dissenters was now a broad cultural preoccupation. Its dominion may help to explain why the literature of this era famed for the dominance and delight of its conversation returns us, again and again, to a sense of fundamental solitude.

WRITERS, READERS, CONVERSATIONS

The century and a half from the English Civil Wars to the brink of the French Revolution brought startling change to the structures of politics, social relations, scientific knowledge, and the economy, and no change was more intimate to all these revolutions than the transformations in the relations between writers and readers. From our present perspective, perhaps no scene seems more familiar, even eternal, than that of reader with book in hand. We imagine Virgil's readers and Dante's, Austen's and Wilde's, Pound's and Pynchon's similarly situated, alone with a book, communing silently with an oracular author. But these configurations have changed radically from age to age—sometimes driven by shifts in technology, at other times by social changes. In the eighteenth century, the sea change in relations between writers and readers derived from new social transactions and a new marketplace of letters. And this change did much to shape the modern reckoning of the mix of the solitary and the social, the commercial and the therapeutic within the act of reading. In its refiguring of the social contract between writers and readers, the eighteenth century was nearly as eruptive as our own time with its marketplace of e-mail and Internet, where everyone can potentially operate as both consumer and purveyor—and no one knows for sure the shape of literary things to come.

In 1661, the Earl of Argyle wrote to his son with advice on books, their acquisition, and their proper use:

> Think no cost too much in purchasing rare books; next to that of acquiring good friends I look upon this purchase; but buy them not to lay by or to grace your library, with the name of such a manuscript, or by such a singular piece, but read, revolve him, and lay him up in your memory where he will be far the better ornament. Read seriously whatever is before you, and reduce and digest it to practice and observation, otherwise it will be Sisyphus's labor to be always revolving sheets and books at every new occurence which will require the oracle of your reading. Trust not to your memory, but put all remarkable, notable things you shall meet with in your books *sub salva custodia* [under the sound care] of pen and ink, but so alter the property by your own scholia and annotations on it, that your memory may speedily recur to the place it was committed to.

The earl's account displays all the elements of the traditional reading program of Renaissance humanism: book or manuscript as surrogate friend, as "ornament" of the gentleman's mind and library, as "oracle" of enduring truths, as "property" to be possessed, marked, transcribed, and committed to memory. In the decades that followed, all these constructions remained in play, yet every one of the earl's crucial terms broadened in application to include print genres and transactions that Argyle would not have imagined: the periodical review, the monthly miscellany; epistolary fiction; the three-volume novel; as well as the coffeehouses and penny lending libraries that broadly circulated these new forms of print. With these new genres and modes of distribution, the text's status as friend, ornament, oracle, and property changed markedly.

Nothing had demonstrated (some even thought created) the material force and oracular authority of print so much as the English Civil Wars. Sermons and prophecies bearing the names of "oracles" and "revelations" forecast the demise of the Beast, the triumph of Parliament, indeed the imminence of the thousand-year rule of Christ on earth. Nor had the restoration of the Stuart monarchy wholly denatured print as prophecy—royalists and radicals continued to publish apocalyptic claims. And yet, over the ensuing decades the repeated threat of contest and rebellion began to exhaust both the authority of print as prophecy and the appetite of readers for a textual diet of frenzy and apocalypse—not that party warfare in print forms declined, but rather that partisanship yoked political contest to forms of confrontation that cooled apocalyptic tempers and supplanted military combat with paper controversy. The uneven course of government censorship, the issuing and lapsing of the licensing laws that governed press freedom, meant that paper wars with their full armory of ephemera—pamphlets, broadsides, pasquinades—raged at moments of crisis and parliamentary inattention when printers might cash in on the market for opposition and confrontation.

But not all the action of print contest was situated in the gutter of journalism. Satire, that most venerable mode of attack and advocacy, flourished in England as it had in Augustan Rome. Horace and Juvenal were indeed the models for Dryden, Pope, and Swift, who not only translated the forms of Roman satire into native idioms but were themselves possessed by all the Roman delight in outrage and invective, in civic engagement and political contest. But the genius of satire is never solely political. Satirists always score their most important points by wit, by cool savagery, by the thrust and parry of language, by the most brilliant and damaging metaphors and rhymes. Their peers, their rivals, even their enemies ruefully conceded that Dryden, Pope, and Swift had brought the verse couplet and the prose sentence to an unprecedented suppleness and precision. Satire in the years of civil war and Stuart agitations had begun in politics; pamphlet wars, swelled by periodicals, continued to rage through the Georgian age. But the classic verse satire had moved to a more exalted ground where the aesthetic often overwhelmed the political, and satire itself became an object of admiration, even of theorizing, and of the most vivid and polite conversation.

"Conversation" had once meant the entire conduct of life itself; now, "conversation" had narrowed to signify social exchange; yet social exchange in its turn had expanded to govern the conduct of life itself. Many of the most striking literary developments in the period—its poetic modes and tastes, the popularity and prominence of letter and journal writing, the advent of the newspaper and the novel—can perhaps best be understood as new ways devised by writers for performing conversation on the page—conversation with readers, with other writers, and within the texts themselves. The cultural critic Mikhail Bakhtin has pinpointed as one key feature of the novel its "heteroglossia": its capacity to speak, almost concurrently, many different languages, in the various voices and viewpoints of its characters and narrators; the range of its concerns (across social ranks and geographical spaces); even the variabilities of its style (each with its own cultural connotations) from page to page, paragraph to paragraph. But in this respect as in so many, the novel, usually reckoned the greatest literary invention of the period, is the product of a time when virtually all modes of writing were involved with diversity and dialogue.

One of the most popular ways of buying and reading poetry, for example, was in the form of "miscellanies"—anthologies of work by many hands ancient and modern in many modes, brought together in intriguing juxtapositions. Such juxtapositions could also take place within a single poem. For poets, a crucial procedure was the "imitation"—a poem in English that closely echoes the tone, structure, and sequence of a classical model while applying the predecessor's form and thought to contemporary topics. Where the Roman poet Juvenal, for example, begins his tenth Satire by declaring that wise men are hard to find even if you search every country from Spain to India (roughly the extent of the known Roman world), Samuel Johnson begins his imitation of Juvenal's poem (*The Vanity of Human Wishes*) this way:

> Let Observation, with extensive view,
> Survey mankind, from China to Peru . . .

The known world, Johnson tacitly reminds his knowing reader, is much larger than it was when Juvenal wrote (and hence the rarity of discerning mortals will be all the more striking). The opening couplet prepares us for the poem's close, where it will turn out that moral possibilities are larger too: there, Johnson will supplant Juvenal's characteristically Roman resignation to "Fortune" with an expressly Christian reliance on the cardinal virtues (faith, hope, charity) as a means of protection from the delusions of desire. The writer of a poetic imitation always conducts at least a double dialogue: between poet and predecessor, and between the present writer and the ideal reader who knows enough of the "original" to savor the poetic exchange, the cultural cross-talk, in all its echoes, divergences, and diversions.

Johnson here practices a more general kind of imitation as well, by casting his poem in heroic couplets: iambic pentameter lines paired in a sequence of successive rhymes. The rhymed pairs are often "closed," so that the moment of the rhyme coincides with and clinches the completion of a sentence and a thought. The verse form was called "heroic" because of its frequent use in the heroic drama and other high-aspiring poetry of the Restoration; the rhymed, closed pentameter was also thought to imitate, as closely as English allowed, the grandeur and the sonority of the lines in which ancient poets composed their epics. Throughout the century following the Restoration, the heroic couplet prevailed as the most commonly used poetic structure, adaptable to all genres and occasions, deployed by every sort of poet from hacks to John Dryden and Alexander Pope, the supreme masters of the mode. It was in this form that Dryden translated Virgil's *Aeneid* (1697) and Pope translated Homer's *Iliad* (1715–1720) and *Odyssey* (1725–1726), it was in this form that they wrote original poems of high seriousness and savage satire, and it was in this form that they aspired (like many of their contemporaries) to write new epics of their own. Neither ever did; both complained intermittently that they lived in an unheroic age. But the mesh of mighty ancient models with trivial modern subjects produced a new mode of satire, the mock-heroic, and disclosed astonishing suppleness in the heroic couplet itself.

In the hands of Dryden, Pope, and many others, the mock mode—high style, low subject matter—performed brilliant accommodations and solved large problems. It allowed poets to turn what they perceived as the crassness of modern culture to satiric advantage. If the triviality of modern life prevented them from recapturing epic grandeur whole, they could at least strive to match the epic's inclusiveness, its capacity to encompass all the things and actions of the world: the accessories of a young woman's dressing table (Pope's *Rape of the Lock*), the clutter in a gutter after rain (Swift's *Description of a City Shower*), the glut of print itself and the folly of those who produce so much bad writing (Pope's *Dunciad*). After Pope's death, though, this vein of mockery seemed exhausted. The heroic couplet persisted in poetry to the end of the century, but other verse forms became prominent too, partly in the service of an even wider inclusiveness, of paying new kinds of attention to modes of life and literature that lay outside the heroic and the mock: the predicament of the poor, the pleasures of domesticity, the discoveries of science, the tones and textures of medieval English balladry, the modalities of melancholy, the improvisatory motions of human thought and feeling. Blank verse—iambic pentameter without rhyme—offered one manifestation of the impulse to open-endedness. James Thomson's *The Seasons* (1730) and William Cowper's *The Task* (1785), huge works in blank verse, are epic in their own kind: they mingle genres and move from topic to topic with the improvisatory energy of a barely stoppable train of thought. They perform the world's miscellany, the mind's conversation with itself and others, in a new poetic language—one that Wordsworth had absorbed by century's end, when he cast his *Prelude* in a capacious blank verse and praised in the preface to *Lyrical Ballads* that kind of poetry which deploys "the real language" of "a man speaking to men."

In the new prose forms of the eighteenth century—both nonfiction and fiction— the dominion of miscellany, the centrality of conversation, is if anything more palpable than in poetry. The first daily newspaper and the first magazines both appeared early in the century, providing a regularly recurrent compendium of disparate items intended to appeal to a variety of tastes and interests. These periodicals formed part of a larger and highly visible print mix: coffeehouses attracted a burgeoning clientele of urbanites by laying out copies of the current gazettes, mercuries, newsletters, playbooks, and satiric verses. Customers took pleasure in the literary montage, the ever-shifting anthology on the tabletops (of which the pictorial medley on page 1016 conveys a vivid visual idea). Coffeehouse customers gathered to consume new drink and new print in a commerce of pleasure, intellect, and gossip. Some read silently, others aloud to listeners who eagerly seized on texts and topics. Habits of social reading that would have been familiar to Chaucer and his audience (even to Virgil performing his epic at the court of Augustus Caesar) contributed to sociable debate on the persons and personalities of public life, foreign potentates, military campaigns, theatrical rivalries, monsters, and prodigies. In the eighteenth century, the papers and the consequent conversations broadened to encompass questions of personal conduct, relations between the sexes, manner and fashion. Writers of papers still claimed oracular authority: "Isaac Bickerstaff" of the *Tatler* dubbed himself the Censor of Great Britain, Mr. Spectator claimed to watch everyone who read his paper, and the *Athenian Gazette* dispensed advice as though with the authority of a supremely learned society. But writers made such claims at least partly with tongue in cheek; they knew that their oracular "truths" would trickle down into the commerce of conversation.

The press not only stimulated but also simulated conversation. Newspapers had always depended on "correspondents"—not (as now) professional reporters, but local letter writers who sent in the news of their parish and county in exchange for free copies of the paper. To read a newspaper was to read in part the work of fellow readers. Other periodicals—the scientific monthly as well as the journal of advice and the review of arts—adopted the practice of printing letters as a reliable source of copy and as an act and model of sociability. Printed correspondence ran longer, more ambitiously, and more lucratively. For the first time, the collected letters of the eminent became an attractive commercial genre (Pope was a pioneer), and travel books in the form of copious letters home sold by the thousands.

The printed letter would prove crucial too to the development of the newest form of all, the "novel." Aphra Behn had pioneered epistolary fiction in the Restoration, and Samuel Richardson recast the mode on an epic scale in *Pamela* and *Clarissa*, among the most important and talked-about fictions of the eighteenth century. In discussing the fate of his characters, Richardson's readers joined a conversation already in progress; Richardson's characters, in their lively exchange of letters, performed and modeled what their creator called "the converse of the pen."

Yet letters were only one among the many kinds of conversation that novelists contrived to carry on. "The rise of the novel"—the emergence over the course of the eighteenth century of so curious, capacious, and durable a genre—has long excited interest and controversy among scholars, who explain the phenomenon in various ways: by the emergence of a large middle-class readership with the money to obtain, the leisure to read, and the eagerness to absorb long narratives that mirrored their circumstances, their aspirations, and their appetites; by a tension between the aristocratic virtues central to older forms of fiction and the constructs of human merit prized by a proud commercial culture; by the passion for journalistic and experiential fact (in newspapers, criminal autobiographies, scientific experiments, etc.), shading over imperceptibly into new practices of fiction.

All of these explanations are true, and each is revelatory when applied to particular clusters of novels. Still, definition and explanation remain elusive, as they clearly were for the genre's early readers and practitioners. The very word "novel"—identifying the genre by no other marks than newness itself—performs a kind of surrender in the face of a form whose central claim to novelty was its barely definable breadth. Mimicry, motion, and metamorphosis are the genre's stock in trade. Novels absorbed all the modes of literature around them: letters, diaries, memoirs, news items, government documents, drawings, verses, even sheet music all crop up within the pages of the early novels, one representational mode supplanting another with often striking speed. Novelists moved with equal alacrity through space: through England (Henry Fielding's *Tom Jones*), Britain more broadly (Tobias Smollett's *Humphry Clinker*), Europe (Smollett's *Roderick Random*), the entire globe as it is ordinarily mapped (Behn's *Oroonoko*, Defoe's *Robinson Crusoe*) or as it could be extraordinarily imagined (Swift's *Gulliver's Travels*). Traversing geographies, the genre crossed cultures too, mostly by means of mimicry, and parroted a range of accents, for purposes either of mockery—the malapropisms of a semiliterate housemaid, the fulminations of a Scots soldier, the outrage of an Irish cuckold—or of pathos: the lamentations of the African slave Oroonoko, the delirium of the violated Clarissa. Many novels, too, made a point of spanning the social spectrum, often compassing destitution and prosperity, labor and luxury within the career of a single ambitious character. Social mobility was perhaps the one plot element that novel readers savored most.

But the novel's supplest means of self-conveyance, its subtlest modes of conversation, were grounded in its attention to the workings of the mind. In his *Essay Concerning Human Understanding* (1690), the philosopher John Locke had explained the mind as a capacious, absorptive instrument engaged in constant motion, linking mixed memories, impressions, and ideas in a ceaseless chain of "associations." In the eighteenth century, novelists took Locke's cue: their works both mimicked the mind's capacity, heterogeneity, and associativeness, and explored them too, tracking over many pages the subtlest modulations in the characters' thoughts and feelings. Richardson famously boasted that his epistolary mode, featuring "familiar letters written as it were to the moment" by characters in their times of crisis, enabled him to track the course of their "hopes and fears" with unprecedented precision—and he trusted that the value of such a process would surely excuse the "bulk" of the huge novels themselves. In the nine volumes of Laurence Sterne's *Life and Opinions of Tristram Shandy*, the title narrator is so committed to following his digressive trains of thought wherever they may lead that the pronouncement of his opinions leaves him preposterously little time to narrate his life. Moving widely over space, freely through society, minutely through time, and deeply into mind, the novelists devised new strategies for achieving that epic inclusiveness that writers sought, in various ways, throughout the century.

The new tactics of miscellany, the new conversations conducted by means of pen and printing press, poetry and prose, refigured the practices of reading that the Earl of Argyle had wished to transmit to his son. In the aristocratic world of Renaissance letters, the book as friend had intimated a sphere of male pedagogy and sociability. The grammar school classroom, the college lecture hall, the estate library, the world of the tutor and his high-born protégé, all these figured reading principally as the privilege and the pleasure of a limited few, mostly males in positions of some leisure, comfort, and power. The links between reading and power were sustained through patterns of production and consumption in which authors received benefits from aristocratic patrons, and manuscripts passed from hand to hand. Donne refused to imagine his verse circulating in any other fashion. After the Restoration, Dryden, Behn, and Pope all pursued the compensations of print, but they nonetheless remained eager to participate in patronage and coterie circulation. Even when printed, their satires purveyed the pleasurable sense of shared knowledge that had constituted the *frisson* of coterie reading. Printers and poets understood that concealing a public name behind initials and dashes provided safety from censors and litigants, at the same time garnering a market share among readers who pleased themselves by decoding "dangerous matter."

By the middle of the eighteenth century, the patronage model of literary production and the coterie mode of distribution had been complicated (some thought ruined) by the commerce of print, for print had become the principal mode of literary distribution. Samuel Johnson, a bookseller's son, thought of literature as print and rarely circulated a manuscript as a gesture of literary sociability. ("None but a blockhead," he famously intoned, "ever wrote except for money.") As a consequence of the dominance of print and its broad distribution, the audiences for texts proliferated into new mixtures. Readers from many strata could afford a penny paper; apprentices and merchants' daughters might read the same novel. Assumptions of commonality that had underwritten the intimate sociability of Renaissance reading had been exploded by civil conflict in the mid-seventeenth century, by the profusion of print and the proliferation of genres that drove and were driven by the appetite of contest and conversation. During the eighteenth century, the print marketplace generated audiences on a scale vaster than ever before, circulating widely across the boundaries of class and gender. Print may have canceled some of the intimacies of the coterie, but it generated new convergences, even new consciousness—a public sphere in which aesthetics, politics, conduct, and taste were all objects of perpetual, often pleasurable debate. To an unprecedented extent, print furnished its readers with the substance for sustained conversation and continual contact.

It also kept them apart. Nothing was more evident to eighteenth-century men and women than the burgeoning of their domestic economy, the vastness of their colonial empire, and the growth in wealth and population which both entailed. The proliferation of consumables was evident in the village market, the Royal Exchange, and the bookstalls of country towns and capitol. The sheer bulk and variety of these consumables were strikingly evident in the length and scope of that capacious new genre, the novel. But even in the midst of abundance and sociability, eighteenth-century consumers were instructed in their paradoxical solitude. Defoe inscribes the condition of the novel as isolation—Robinson Crusoe, a man alone on an island, opines that human life "is, or ought to be, one universal act of solitude." And in novel after novel the very transactions of commerce produce isolation, as ambition and acquisition drive each character into the solitary, often melancholy corner of his or her own self-interest. The novel itself as a reading experience produced comparable sensations. Readers might now empathize with an entire world of fictional characters, but in order to savor such imaginative pleasures, they spent long hours in the privacy of their own quarters, in silent acts of reading.

A sense of solitude underwrote all this century's celebrated gregariousness. This held true even for sociable transactions that might take place between a reader and a text. In the Renaissance, it had long been a practice to annotate texts with comments echoing and endorsing the author's oracular wisdom. Under the pressure of civil war, the dialogue between author and reader often became more heated as the manuscript marginalia expressed anger and outrage at the partisan zeal of the printed text. But one form of textual reverence persisted. Throughout the seventeenth century readers took pleasure in writing marginalia that epitomized the text, making its wisdom portable. They filled blank books with pithy sentences, "commonplaces" drawn from their favorite works and organized in ways that would allow them to recirculate these sayings in their own writing and conversation.

By the eighteenth century, print had managed to appropriate all these modes of study and sociability. Through print, the manuscript collation of wit and wisdom turned into popular commodities—the printed commonplace book, the miscellany, the anthology. Even annotation itself migrated from manuscript markings into print, as Swift and Pope (among others) found ways of exploding scholarly pretension and of rendering the breath of gossip and scandal in the elaborate apparatus of the printed page. By century's end, all of manuscript's august authority and its most cherished genres—letters and memoirs—had been commandeered by print. In the mid-1730s, Pope alarmed and outraged his contemporaries by publishing his letters as if they deserved to partake of eternity with Cicero's. By the early nineteenth century, even

Joshua Reynolds, Mrs. Abington as "Miss Prue," 1771. Restoration theatricality transposed and transformed.

that most secretive mode of self-communion, the private journal, had made its way into the marketplace. In 1825, Pepys's *Diary* appeared in two large printed folios, laying bare the elaborate machinery of public life, the secrets and scandals of the Restoration court, and the diarist's own experiences, transgressions, and sequestered musings, which he had written in shorthand code and shown to no one. The communal and commodified medium of print had found yet another way to market signal acts of solitude.

CODA

Mrs. Abington as "Miss Prue" (1771), by the pre-eminent portraitist Sir Joshua Reynolds (see Color Plate 23), shows a solitary figure engaged in intricate conversation with the viewer. Some of the intricacy inheres in the life history of the sitter, whose career many of the painting's first viewers would have known well. The daughter of a cobbler, Frances Abington had worked in childhood as a flower seller and in her teens as an actress, quickly establishing herself as "by far the most eminent performer in comedy of her day" (these words, and others to follow, are the testimony of contemporaries); she would eventually score one of her greatest hits in the role of that latter-day country wife Lady Teazle, in Richard Brinsley Sheridan's *The School for Scandal* (1777). When an unknown, Abington had married her music teacher; as fame increased, she carried on several well-publicized affairs with members of parliament and the aristocracy. By her sexual frankness, she scandalized—and of course fascinated—the multitudes. By her grace and taste, she became "a favorite of the public" and "the high priestess of fashion"; her costumes on stage instantly set new trends among her audience. Reynolds, who greatly admired her, here captures the complexity of her character and reputation. Her dress is supremely stylish, her pose deliberately provocative. For a woman to lean casually over the back of a chair this way violated all propriety; in earlier portraits, only men had struck such a pose. The thumb at her lips suggests vulgarity verging on the lascivious. The portrait's title purports to explain such seeming aberrations: the actress here appears in her celebrated role as Miss Prue, the "silly, awkward country girl" in William Congreve's Restoration comedy *Love for Love* (1695), who comes to London with the intention, frankly lustful and loudly declared, of getting herself a husband. In Reynolds's painting, of course, Mrs. Abington plays a role more layered: a hybrid of Miss Prue, of the matchlessly fashionable figure into which the actress had transformed herself, and of the whole range of experiences, the prodigious lifelong motion from poverty to polish, which formed part of her self-creation and her fame. Impersonating Miss Prue some seventy-five years after the comedy's first production, Mrs. Abington here infuses Restoration wantonness with Georgian elegance, transgression with high taste, theatricality with self-assertive authenticity. Like the century she inhabits, she is miscellany incarnate.

Stuart Sherman
and Steven N. Zwicker

Samuel Pepys
1633–1703

John Hayls, *Samuel Pepys*, 1666.

Twice in his life, Samuel Pepys embarked on long projects that allowed him to fuse the methods of the bureaucrat with an inventiveness that amounted to genius. The longer project, which occupied him from his mid-twenties through his mid-fifties, was a fundamental restructuring of the Royal Navy. The shorter project began just a few months earlier. Starting on January 1, 1660, and continuing for the next nine years, Pepys devised the diary form as we know it today: a detailed, private, day-by-day account of daily doings.

Halfway through the diary, Pepys delights to describe himself as "a very rising man," and he wrote the diary in part to track his ascent. The rise began slowly. Born in London to a tailor and a butcher's sister, Pepys studied at Puritan schools; he then attended Magdalene College, Cambridge, as a scholarship student. His B.A. left him well educated but short on cash. A year later he married the fifteen-year-old Elizabeth St. Michel, a French Protestant whose poverty surpassed his own. By his mid-twenties (when the diary commences), neither his accomplishments nor his prospects were particularly striking: he was working as factotum for two powerful men, one of them his high-born cousin Edward Mountagu, First Earl of Sandwich, an important naval officer once devoted to Cromwell but recently turned Royalist.

The diary begins at a calendrical turning point (the first day of a new week, a new year, and a new decade) and on a kind of double bet: that the coming time would bring changes worth writing up, both in the life of the diarist and in the history of the state. The two surmises quickly proved true. As a schoolboy taught by Puritans, Pepys had attended and applauded the execution of Charles I, but the Restoration of Charles II was the making of him, and he recalibrated his loyalties readily enough. His cousin secured for him the Clerkship of the Acts in the Navy Office, a secretarial post that Pepys transformed into something more. By mastering the numberless details of shipbuilding and supplying—from the quality of timber to the composition of tar and hemp—he contrived to control costs and produce results to an extent unmatched by any predecessor.

He managed all these matters so carefully that he soon became the ruler of the Royal Navy, in effect if not in name. When the Test Act of 1673 forced Charles's Catholic brother James to resign as Lord High Admiral, Pepys took his place (in the newly created post of Admiralty Secretary) and ran the operation. He immediately launched a systematic reform of the institution, which he had come to see as dangerously slipshod. By devising (in the words of one biographer) "a rule for all things, great or small" and by enforcing the new disciplines through a method of tireless surveillance and correspondence with ports extending from the Thames to Tangier, Pepys made the navy immeasurably more efficient than ever before. His efforts were interrupted by the political tribulations of his patron James: Pepys spent two brief terms in prison on trumped-up charges of Catholic sympathies, and in 1688 the Glorious Revolution drove him from office into a prosperous retirement. At the height of his power, though, as his biographer Richard Ollard observes, Pepys was the "master builder" of the permanent, professional navy that made possible the expansion of trade and the conquest of colonies over the ensuing century. Energetic in his king's service and in his own (the taking of bribes was one of the perquisites of office that Pepys mastered most adroitly), the tailor's son functioned formidably as an early architect of empire.

Pepys's schooling and profession had immersed him in the two practices most central to earlier English diaries, Puritanism and financial bookkeeping. But where account books and religious diaries emphasize certain kinds of moment—exchanges of money and goods, instances of moral redemption and relapse—Pepys tries for something more comprehensive. He implicitly commits himself to tracking the whole day's experience: the motions of the body as it makes its way through the city in boats, in coaches, and on foot, and the motions of the mind as it shuttles between business and pleasure. He sustained his narrative over a virtually unbroken series of daily entries before stopping out of fear that his work on the diary had helped to damage his eyesight to the brink of blindness. "None of Pepys's contemporaries," writes his editor Robert Latham, "attempted a diary in the all-inclusive Pepysian sense and on the Pepysian scale." To the efficiency of the bookkeeper and the discipline of the Puritan, Pepys added the ardor of the virtuoso, eager (as he observes at one point) "to see any strange thing" and capable of finding wonder in ordinary things: music, plays, books, food, clothes, conversation. The phrase "with great pleasure" recurs in the diary as a kind of leitmotiv, and superlatives play leapfrog through the pages: many, many experiences qualify in turn as the "best" thing that the diarist ever ate, read, thought, saw, heard. To achieve the diary's seeming immediacy, Pepys put his entries through as many as five stages of revision, sometimes days or even months after the events recorded. Even at the final stage, in the bound, elegantly formatted volumes of the diary manuscript, he often crammed new detail or comment into margins and between the lines. Comparable pressures operated in connection with the diary's complex privacy. Pepys took pains to secure secrecy for his text. He hid it from view in drawers or in cabinets. He wrote most of it in a secretarial shorthand, and where he most wanted secrecy, as in the accounts of his many flirtations and infidelities, he obscured things further by an improvised language made up of Spanish, French, Latin, and other tongues. (Elizabeth Pepys figures throughout the diary as a kind of muse and countermuse, the narrative's most recurrent and obsessive subject, and the person most urgently to be prevented from reading it.) At the same time, the manuscript makes notable gestures toward self-display. Pepys frequently shifts to a readily readable longhand, especially for names, places, titles of books, plays, and persons; at times even his secret sexual language opens out into longhand.

This ambivalent secrecy persisted past the diarist's death. Pepys bequeathed the manuscript to Magdalene College without calling any special attention to it. It was included among his many collections: of naval books and papers, of broadsheet ballads, and of instruction manuals on shorthand methods—including the one Pepys used to write the diary. The manuscript kept its secrets long. In the early nineteenth century, the diary was discovered and painstakingly decoded (by a transcriber who, missing the connection between the manuscript and the shorthand manuals on adjacent shelves, treated the text as a million-word cryptogram); it was finally published, in a severely shortened and expurgated version, in 1825. Readers and reviewers soon called for more, recognizing that Pepys possessed (in the words of one reviewer) "the most indiscriminating, insatiable, and miscellaneous curiosity, that ever . . . supplied the pen, of a daily chronicler." Expanded (but still bowdlerized) editions appeared throughout the century, and only in the 1970s did the semisecret manuscript make its way wholly into print.

from **The Diary**
[FIRST ENTRIES][1]
$16\frac{59}{60}$

Blessed be God, at the end of the last year I was in very good health, without any sense of my old pain[2] but upon taking of cold.

I lived in Axe Yard,[3] having my wife and servant Jane, and no more in family than us three.

My wife, after the absence of her terms[4] for seven weeks, gave me hopes of her being with child, but on the last day of the year she hath them again. The condition of the state was thus. *Viz.* the Rump, after being disturbed by my Lord Lambert, was lately returned to sit again.[5] The officers of the army all forced to yield. Lawson lies still in the river and Monck is with his army in Scotland.[6] Only my Lord Lambert is not yet come in to the Parliament; nor is it expected that he will, without being forced to it.

The new Common Council of the City doth speak very high; and hath sent to Monck their sword-bearer, to acquaint him with their desires for a free and full Parliament, which is at present the desires and the hopes and expectation of all— 22 of the old secluded members having been at the House door the last week to demand

1. England still adhered to the Old Style calendar, in which the new year officially began on March 25. Pepys wrote this "prelude" in early January 1659 according to the English reckoning, but 1660 (New Style) in the rest of Europe.

2. Pepys had suffered from stones in the bladder from babyhood until 1658, when he underwent a risky but successful operation.

3. In Westminster.

4. Menstrual periods.

5. John Lambert, a skilled general under Oliver Cromwell, now opposed the convening of the Rump Parliament, which had governed England since the fall of Cromwell's son Richard in 1659.

6. At this point, the political intentions and allegiance of General George Monck were the object of much speculation; he led his army back from Scotland into England on January 1 and became one of the principal engineers of the Restoration. Vice-Admiral John Lawson supported the Rump.

entrance; but it was denied them, and it is believed that they nor the people will not be satisfied till the House be filled.[7]

My own private condition very handsome; and esteemed rich, but indeed very poor, besides my goods of my house and my office, which at present is somewhat uncertain. Mr Downing master of my office.[8]

1 January 1659/60. Lord's Day. This morning (we lying lately in the garret) I rose, put on my suit with great skirts,[9] having not lately worn any other clothes but them.

Went to Mr. Gunning's church at Exeter House, where he made a very good sermon upon these words: that in the fullness of time God sent his Son, made of a woman, etc., showing that by "made under the law" is meant his circumcision, which is solemnized this day.[1]

Dined at home in the garret, where my wife dressed the remains of a turkey, and in the doing of it she burned her hand.

I stayed at home all the afternoon, looking over my accounts.

Then went with my wife to my father's; and in going, observed the great posts which the City hath set up[2] at the Conduit in Fleet Street.

Supped at my father's, where in came Mrs. Theophila Turner and Madam Morris[3] and supped with us. After that, my wife and I went home with them, and so to our own home.

[THE CORONATION OF CHARLES II][4]

[23 April 1661] I lay with Mr. Shiply,[5] and about 4 in the morning I rose.

Coronation Day.

And got to the Abbey,[6] where I followed Sir J. Denham the surveyor with some company that he was leading in. And with much ado, by the favor of Mr. Cooper his man, did get up into a great scaffold across the north end of the Abbey—where with a great deal of patience I sat from past 4 till 11 before the King came in. And a pleasure it was to see the Abbey raised in the middle, all covered with red and a throne (that is a chair) and footstool on the top of it. And all the officers of all kinds, so much as the very fiddlers, in red vests.

At last comes in the Dean and prebends of Westminster with the Bishops (many of them in cloth-of-gold copes); and after them the nobility all in their Parliament robes, which was a most magnificent sight. Then the Duke[7] and the King with a

---

7. A Parliament that would include the "old secluded members"—the representatives expelled in 1648—was understood to be a first step toward restoration of the monarchy.

8. Pepys was at this point a clerk in the office of the Exchequer.

9. I.e., with a long coat.

1. Peter Gunning had held illegal Anglican services during the Commonwealth. His sermon text is Galatians 4.4: "But, when the fullness of the time was come, God sent forth his Son, made of a woman, made under the law."

2. As defensive barriers during its opposition to the Rump

Parliament.

3. A relative and a friend, respectively. "Mistress" ("Mrs.") was applied to unmarried as well as to married women; Theophila was eight years old.

4. Charles II had returned to England in May 1660; he scheduled his coronation for St. George's Day, honoring England's patron saint.

5. Edward Shipley was steward to Pepys's cousin Edward Mountagu.

6. Westminster Abbey, site of English coronations.

7. Charles's brother James, Duke of York, later James II.

scepter (carried by my Lord of Sandwich) and sword and mond before him, and the crown too.

The King in his robes, bare-headed, which was very fine. And after all had placed themselves, there was a sermon and the service. And then in the choir at the high altar he passed all the ceremonies of the coronation—which, to my very great grief, I and most in the Abbey could not see. The crown being put upon his head, a great shout begun. And he came forth to the throne and there passed more cere-monies: as, taking the oath and having things read to him by the Bishop, and his lords (who put on their caps as soon as the King put on his crown) and bishops came and kneeled before him.

And three times the King-at-Arms went to the three open places on the scaffold and proclaimed that if any one could show any reason why Charles Stuart should not be King of England, that now he should come and speak.

And a general pardon also was read by the Lord Chancellor;[8] and medals flung up and down by my Lord Cornwallis—of silver; but I could not come by any.

But so great a noise, that I could make but little of the music; and indeed, it was lost to everybody. But I had so great a list[9] to piss, that I went out a little while before the King had done all his ceremonies and went round the Abbey to Westminster Hall, all the way within rails, and 10,000 people, with the ground covered with blue cloth—and scaffolds all the way. Into the hall I got—where it was very fine with hangings and scaffolds, one upon another, full of brave[1] ladies. And my wife in one little one on the right hand.

Here I stayed walking up and down; and at last, upon one of the side-stalls, I stood and saw the King come in with all the persons (but the soldiers) that were yes-terday in the cavalcade;[2] and a most pleasant sight it was to see them in their several robes. And the King came in with his crown on and his scepter in his hand—under a canopy borne up by six silver staves, carried by Barons of the Cinqueports—and little bells at every end.

And after a long time he got up to the farther end, and all set themselves down at their several tables—and that was also a rare sight. And the King's first course carried up by the Knights of the Bath. And many fine ceremonies there was of the heralds leading up people before him and bowing; and my Lord of Albemarle's[3] going to the kitchen and eat[4] a bit of the first dish that was to go to the King's table.

But above all was these three Lords, Northumberland and Suffolk and the Duke of Ormond, coming before the courses on horseback and staying so all dinner-time; and at last, to bring up Dymock the King's champion, all in armor on horseback, with his spear and target carried before him. And a herald proclaim that if any dare deny Charles Stuart to be lawful King of England, here was a champion that would fight with him; and with those words the champion flings down his gauntlet; and all this he doth three times in his going up toward the King's table. At last, when he is come, the King drinks to him and then sends him the cup, which is of gold; and he drinks it off and then rides back again with the cup in his hand.

I went from table to table to see the bishops and all others at their dinner, and was infinite pleased with it. And at the lords' table I met with Will Howe and he

---

8. Charles II's Act of Oblivion forgave the crimes of all those on the parliamentary side, with the principal ex-ception of those who had participated in the trial, sen-tencing, and execution of his father.
9. Desire.

1. Splendid.
2. The previous day's procession.
3. In 1660 Charles II had made George Monck Duke of Albemarle as a reward for his role in the Restoration.
4. Ate (pronounced "ett"), to test for poison.

spoke to my Lord for me and he did give him four rabbits and a pullet; and so I got it, and Mr. Creed and I got Mr. Mitchell to give us some bread and so we at a stall eat it, as everybody else did what they could get.[5]

I took a great deal of pleasure to go up and down and look upon the ladies—and to hear the music of all sorts; but above all, the 24 violins.

About 6 at night they had dined; and I went up to my wife and there met with a pretty lady (Mrs. Franklin, a doctor's wife, a friend of Mr. Bowyer's) and kissed them both—and by and by took them down to Mr. Bowyer's. And strange it is, to think that these two days have held up fair till now that all is done and the King gone out of the Hall; and then it fell a-raining and thundering and lightening as I have not seen it do some years—which people did take great notice of God's blessing of the work of these two days—which is a foolery, to take too much notice of such things.

I observed little disorder in all this; but only the King's footmen had got hold of the canopy and would keep it from the Barons of the Cinqueports; which they endeavored to force from them again but could not do it till my Lord Duke of Albemarle caused it to be put into Sir R. Pye's hand till tomorrow to be decided.

At Mr. Bowyer's, a great deal of company; some I knew, others I did not. Here we stayed upon the leads[6] and below till it was late, expecting to see the fireworks; but they were not performed tonight. Only, the City had a light like a glory round about it, with bonfires.

At last I went to King Street; and there sent Crockford to my father's and my house to tell them I could not come home tonight, because of the dirt and a coach could not be had.

And so after drinking a pot of ale alone at Mrs. Harper's, I returned to Mr. Bowyer's; and after a little stay more, I took my wife and Mrs. Franklin (who I proferred the civility of lying with my wife at Mrs. Hunt's tonight) to Axe Yard. In which, at the further end, there was three great bonfires and a great many great gallants, men and women; and they laid hold of us and would have us drink the King's health upon our knee, kneeling upon a fagot; which we all did, they drinking to us one after another—which we thought a strange frolic. But these gallants continued thus a great while, and I wondered to see how the ladies did tipple.

At last I sent my wife and her bedfellow to bed, and Mr. Hunt and I went in with Mr. Thornbury (who did give the company all their wines, he being yeoman of the wine-cellar to the King) to his house; and there, with his wife and two of his sisters and some gallant sparks that were there, we drank the King's health and nothing else, till one of the gentlemen fell down stark drunk and there lay spewing. And I went to my Lord's pretty well. But no sooner a-bed with Mr. Shiply but my head begun to turn and I to vomit, and if ever I was foxed[7] it was now—which I cannot say yet, because I fell asleep and sleep till morning—only, when I waked I found myself wet with my spewing. Thus did the day end, with joy everywhere; and blessed be God, I have not heard of any mischance to anybody through it all, but only to Sergeant Glynne, whose horse fell upon him yesterday and is like to kill him; which people do please themselves with, to see how just God is to punish that rogue at such a time as this—he being now one of the King's sergeants and rode in the cavalcade with Maynard, to whom people wished the same fortune.[8]

---

5. Will Howe and John Creed served as clerks to Sandwich, whom the diarist invariably refers to as "my Lord." Miles Mitchell was a local bookseller.
6. Rooftop.

7. Drunk.
8. Sir John Glynne and Sir John Maynard were lawyers who had served under Cromwell.

There was also this night, in King Street, a woman had her eye put out by a boy's flinging of a firebrand into the coach.

Now after all this, I can say that besides the pleasure of the sight of these glorious things, I may now shut my eyes against any other objects, or for the future trouble myself to see things of state and show, as being sure never to see the like again in this world.

[24 April 1661] Waked in the morning with my head in a sad taking through the last night's drink, which I am very sorry for. So rise and went out with Mr. Creed to drink our morning draught, which he did give me in chocolate to settle my stomach. And after that to my wife, who lay with Mrs. Franklin at the next door to Mrs. Hunt's.

And they were ready, and so I took them up in a coach and carried the lady to Paul's[9] and there set her down; and so my wife and I home—and I to the office.

That being done, my wife and I went to dinner to Sir W. Batten;[1] and all our talk about the happy conclusion of these last solemnities.

After dinner home and advised with my wife about ordering things in my house; and then she went away to my father's to lie, and I stayed with my workmen, who do please me very well with their work.

At night set myself to write down these three days' diary; and while I am about it, I hear the noise of the chambers and other things of the fireworks, which are now playing upon the Thames before the King. And I wish myself with them, being sorry not to see them.

So to bed.

[THE FIRE OF LONDON]

[2 September 1666] Lord's Day. Some of our maids sitting up late last night to get things ready against our feast today, Jane called us up, about 3 in the morning, to tell us of a great fire they saw in the City. So I rose, and slipped on my nightgown and went to her window, and thought it to be on the back side of Mark Lane at the furthest; but being unused to such fires as followed, I thought it far enough off, and so went to bed again and to sleep. About 7 rose again to dress myself, and there looked out at the window and saw the fire not so much as it was, and further off. So to my closet[1] to set things to rights after yesterday's cleaning. By and by Jane comes and tells me that she hears that above 300 houses have been burned down tonight by the fire we saw, and that it was now burning down all Fish Street by London Bridge. So I made myself ready presently, and walked to the Tower and there got up upon one of the high places, Sir J. Robinson's little son going up with me; and there I did see the houses at that end of the bridge all on fire, and an infinite great fire on this and the other side the end of the bridge—which, among other people, did trouble me for poor little Mitchell and our Sarah on the bridge.[2] So down, with my heart full of trouble, to the Lieutenant of the Tower, who tells me that it begun this morning in the King's baker's house in Pudding Lane, and that it hath burned down St. Magnus's Church and most part of Fish Street already. So I down to the water-side and there got a boat and through bridge,[3] and there saw a lamentable fire. Poor Mitchell's house, as far as the Old Swan, already burned that way and the fire running further, that in a very

9. St. Paul's Cathedral.
1. Surveyor of the Navy.
1. Private room, study.
2. London Bridge was lined with shops and houses, in-

cluding the liquor shop of Pepys's friend Michael Mitchell and the residence of his former servant Sarah.
3. Under the bridge.

little time it got as far as the Steelyard while I was there. Everybody endeavoring to remove their goods, and flinging into the river or bringing them into lighters[4] that lay off. Poor people staying in their houses as long as till the very fire touched them, and then running into boats or clambering from one pair of stair by the water-side to another. And among other things, the poor pigeons I perceive were loath to leave their houses, but hovered about the windows and balconies till they were some of them burned, their wings, and fell down.

Having stayed, and in an hour's time seen the fire rage every way, and nobody to my sight endeavoring to quench it, but to remove their goods and leave all to the fire; and having seen it get as far as the Steelyard, and the wind mighty high and driving it into the City, and everything, after so long a drought, proving combustible, even the very stones of churches, and among other things, the poor steeple by which pretty Mrs. Horsley lives, and whereof my old school-fellow Elborough is parson, taken fire in the very top and there burned till it fall down—I to Whitehall with a gentleman with me who desired to go off from the Tower to see the fire in my boat—to Whitehall, and there up to the King's closet in the chapel, where people came about me and I did give them an account dismayed them all; and word was carried in to the King, so I was called for and did tell the King and Duke of York what I saw, and that unless his Majesty did command houses to be pulled down, nothing could stop the fire. They seemed much troubled, and the King commanded me to go to my Lord Mayor from him and command him to spare no houses but to pull down before the fire every way. The Duke of York bid me tell him that if he would have any more soldiers, he shall; and so did my Lord Arlington afterward, as a great secret. Here meeting with Captain Cocke, I in his coach, which he lent me, and Creed with me, to Paul's; and there walked along Watling Street as well as I could, every creature coming away loaden with goods to save—and here and there sick people carried away in beds. Extraordinary good goods carried in carts and on backs. At last met my Lord Mayor in Canning Street, like a man spent, with a hankercher about his neck. To the King's message, he cried like a fainting woman, "Lord, what can I do? I am spent! People will not obey me. I have been pulling down houses. But the fire overtakes us faster than we can do it." That he needed no more soldiers; and that for himself, he must go and refresh himself, having been up all night. So he left me, and I him, and walked home—seeing people all almost distracted and no manner of means used to quench the fire. The houses too, so very thick thereabouts, and full of matter for burning, as pitch and tar, in Thames Street—and warehouses of oil and wines and brandy and other things. Here I saw Mr. Isaac Houblon, that handsome man—prettily dressed and dirty at his door at Dowgate, receiving some of his brothers' things whose houses were on fire; and as he says, have been removed twice already, and he doubts (as it soon proved) that they must be in a little time removed from his house also—which was a sad consideration. And to see the churches all filling with goods, by people who themselves should have been quietly there at this time.

By this time it was about 12 a-clock, and so home and there find my guests, which was Mr. Wood and his wife, Barbary Shelden, and also Mr. Moone—she mighty fine, and her husband, for aught I see, a likely man. But Mr. Moone's design and mine, which was to look over my closet and please him with the sight thereof, which he hath long desired, was wholly disappointed, for we were in great trouble

4. Barges.

and disturbance at this fire, not knowing what to think of it. However, we had an extraordinary good dinner, and as merry as at this time we could be.

While at dinner, Mrs. Batelier came to inquire after Mr. Woolfe and Stanes (who it seems are related to them), whose houses in Fish Street are all burned, and they in a sad condition. She would not stay in the fright.

As soon as dined, I and Moone away and walked through the City, the streets full of nothing but people and horses and carts loaden with goods, ready to run over one another, and removing goods from one burned house to another—they now removing out of Canning Street (which received goods in the morning) into Lombard Street and further; and among others, I now saw my little goldsmith Stokes receiving some friend's goods, whose house itself was burned the day after. We parted at Paul's, he home and I to Paul's Wharf, where I had appointed a boat to attend me; and took in Mr. Carkesse and his brother, whom I met in the street, and carried them below and above bridge, to and again, to see the fire, which was now got further, both below and above, and no likelihood of stopping it. Met with the King and Duke of York in their barge, and with them to Queenhithe and there called Sir Richard Browne to them. Their order was only to pull down houses apace, and so below bridge at the water-side; but little was or could be done, the fire coming upon them so fast. Good hopes there was of stopping it at the Three Cranes above, and at Buttolph's Wharf below bridge, if care be used; but the wind carries it into the City, so as we know not by the water-side what it doth there. River full of lighters and boats taking in goods, and good goods swimming in the water; and only, I observed that hardly one lighter or boat in three that had the goods of a house in, but there was a pair of virginals[5] in it. Having seen as much as I could now, I away to Whitehall by appointment, and there walked to St. James's Park, and there met my wife and Creed and Wood and his wife and walked to my boat, and there upon the water again, and to the fire up and down, it still increasing and the wind great. So near the fire as we could for smoke; and all over the Thames, with one's face in the wind you were almost burned with a shower of firedrops—this is very true—so as houses were burned by these drops and flakes of fire, three or four, nay five or six houses, one from another. When we could endure no more upon the water, we to a little alehouse on the Bankside over against the Three Cranes, and there stayed till it was dark almost and saw the fire grow; and as it grow darker, appeared more and more, and in corners and upon steeples and between churches and houses, as far as we could see up the hill of the City, in a most horrid malicious bloody flame, not like the fine flame of an ordinary fire. Barbary and her husband away before us. We stayed till, it being darkish, we saw the fire as only one entire arch of fire from this to the other side the bridge, and in a bow up the hill, for an arch of above a mile long. It made me weep to see it. The churches, houses, and all on fire and flaming at once, and a horrid noise the flames made, and the cracking of houses at their ruin. So home with a sad heart, and there find everybody discoursing and lamenting the fire; and poor Tom Hayter[6] came with some few of his goods saved out of his house, which is burned upon Fish Street Hill. I invited him to lie at my house, and did receive his goods: but was deceived in his lying there, the noise coming every moment of the growth of the fire, so as we were forced to begin to pack up our own goods and prepare for their removal. And did by moonshine (it being brave,[7] dry, and moonshine and warm weather) carry much of my goods into the garden, and

5. A small harpsichord.   7. Pleasant.
6. One of Pepys's clerks in the Navy Office.

Mr. Hayter and I did remove my money and iron-chests into my cellar—as thinking that the safest place. And got my bags of gold into my office ready to carry away, and my chief papers of accounts also there, and my tallies into a box by themselves. So great was our fear, as Sir W. Batten had carts come out of the country to fetch away his goods this night. We did put Mr. Hayter, poor man, to bed a little; but he got but very little rest, so much noise being in my house, taking down of goods.

[3 September 1666] About 4 a-clock in the morning, my Lady Batten sent me a cart to carry away all my money and plate and best things to Sir W. Rider's at Bethnell Green; which I did, riding myself in my nightgown in the cart; and Lord, to see how the streets and the highways are crowded with people, running and riding and getting of carts at any rate to fetch away things. I find Sir W. Rider tired with being called up[8] all night and receiving things from several friends. His house full of goods—and much of Sir W. Batten and Sir W. Penn's.[9] I am eased at my heart to have my treasure so well secured. Then home with much ado to find a way. Nor any sleep all this night to me nor my poor wife. But then, and all this day, she and I and all my people laboring to get away the rest of our things, and did get Mr. Tooker to get me a lighter to take them in, and we did carry them (myself some) over Tower Hill, which was by this time full of people's goods, bringing their goods thither. And down to the lighter, which lay at the next quay above the Tower Dock. And here was my neighbor's wife, Mrs. Buckworth, with her pretty child and some few of her things, which I did willingly give way to be saved with mine. But there was no passing with anything through the postern,[1] the crowd was so great.

The Duke of York came this day by the office and spoke to us, and did ride with his guard up and down the City to keep all quiet (he being now general, and having the care of all).

This day, Mercer being not at home, but against her mistress's order gone to her mother's, and my wife going thither to speak with W. Hewer, met her there and was angry; and her mother saying that she was not a prentice girl, to ask leave every time she goes abroad, my wife with good reason was angry, and when she came home, bid her be gone again. And so she went away, which troubled me; but yet less than it would, because of the condition we are in fear of coming into in a little time, of being less able to keep one in her quality. At night, lay down a little upon a quilt of W. Hewer in the office (all my own things being packed up or gone); and after me, my poor wife did the like—we having fed upon the remains of yesterday's dinner, having no fire nor dishes, nor any opportunity of dressing anything.

[4 September 1666] Up by break of day to get away the remainder of my things, which I did by a lighter at the Iron Gate; and my hands so few, that it was the afternoon before we could get them all away.

Sir W. Penn and I to Tower Street, and there met the fire burning three or four doors beyond Mr. Howell's; whose goods, poor man (his trays and dishes, shovels, etc., were flung all along Tower Street in the kennels, and people working therewith from one end to the other), the fire coming on in that narrow street, on both sides, with infinite fury. Sir W. Batten, not knowing how to remove his wine, did dig a pit in the garden and laid it in there; and I took the opportunity of laying all the papers

---

8. Called on, woken.
9. William Penn, Pepys's colleague on the Navy Board

(and father of the founde of Penn sylvania).
1. Back or side gate.

of my office that I could not otherwise dispose of. And in the evening Sir W. Penn and I did dig another and put our wine in it, and I my parmesan cheese as well as my wine and some other things.

The Duke of York was at the office this day at Sir W. Penn's, but I happened not to be within. This afternoon, sitting melancholy with Sir W. Penn in our garden and thinking of the certain burning of this office without extraordinary means, I did propose for the sending up of all our workmen from Woolwich and Deptford yards (none whereof yet appeared), and to write to Sir W. Coventry to have the Duke of York's permission to pull down houses rather then lose this office, which would much hinder the King's business. So Sir W. Penn he went down this night, in order to the sending them up tomorrow morning; and I wrote to Sir W. Coventry about the business, but received no answer.

This night Mrs. Turner (who, poor woman, was removing her goods all this day—good goods, into the garden, and knew not how to dispose of them)—and her husband supped with my wife and I at night in the office, upon a shoulder of mutton from the cook's, without any napkin or anything, in a sad manner but were merry. Only, now and then walking into the garden and saw how horridly the sky looks, all on a fire in the night, was enough to put us out of our wits; and indeed it was extremely dreadful—for it looks just as if it was at us, and the whole heaven on fire. I after supper walked in the dark down to Tower Street, and there saw it all on fire at the Trinity House on that side and the Dolphin Tavern on this side, which was very near us—and the fire with extraordinary vehemence. Now begins the practice of blowing up of houses in Tower Street, those next the Tower, which at first did frighten people more than anything; but it stopped the fire where it was done—it bringing down the houses to the ground in the same places they stood, and then it was easy to quench what little fire was in it, though it kindled nothing almost. W. Hewer this day went to see how his mother did, and comes late home, but telling us how he hath been forced to remove her to Islington, her house in Pye Corner being burned. So that it is got so far that way and all the Old Bailey, and was running down to Fleet Street. And Paul's is burned, and all Cheapside. I wrote to my father this night; but the posthouse being burned, the letter could not go.

━━┉━━ ⊠◆⊠ ━━┉━━

Margaret Cavendish, Duchess of Newcastle
1623–1674

The youngest child in a wealthy family whose social arrogance and Royalist sympaties brought it near ruin during the Civil Wars, Margaret Lucas combined a near immobilizing shyness with a passion for fame. She spent the years of war and Interregnum on the Continent, first as maid of honor to Charles's exiled queen, then as wife to the Royalist general William Cavendish, Marquis of Newcastle; he was made Duke by Charles II after the couple returned to England at the Restoration. Neglected by the Court, they lived far from London on their northern estates, where they cultivated their passions: his, riding and fencing; hers, reading and writing. Words poured from her pen into a variety of genres: verse (*Poems and Fancies*, 1653), fiction (*Nature's Pictures*, 1656), plays (*Love's Adventure, The Matrimonial Trouble, The Female Academy*, and some fifteen others: all printed, none performed); essays (*The World's Olio*, 1655); scientific speculations (*Philosophical and Physical Opinions*, 1663; *Observations upon Experimental Philosophy*, 1665); biography (of her husband); and autobiography (*A True*

Relation, 1656; *Sociable Letters*, 1664). Cavendish and her husband published much of her work (and some of his) in sumptuous editions at their own expense.

It was rare for a woman to write and publish, rarer still for an aristocrat to write so revealingly and emphatically about her own fears, desires, opinions, and aspirations. The combination of her gender, rank, and work brought the Duchess an equivocal celebrity, a mix of amazement and derision which her occasional trips to London did much to animate. After one such visit, Mary Evelyn (wife of the diarist John) tried to capture Cavendish's impact in a letter to a friend: "I was surprised to find so much extravagancy and vanity in any person not confined within four walls" (of a madhouse). Her clothing, Evelyn reported, was "fantastical"; her behavior outstripped "the imagination of poets, or the descriptions of a romance heroine's greatness; her gracious bows, seasonable nods, courteous stretching out of hands, twinkling of her eyes, and various gestures of approbation, show what may be expected from her discourse, which is as airy, empty, whimsical, and rambling as her books, aiming at science, difficulties, high notions . . . " Evelyn voices a satiric hostility shared by many London onlookers, but she also pinpoints some of Cavendish's range and intensity: her idiosyncratic engagement with the new science of her day, and her variable, highly conscious self-presentation.

At letter's end, Evelyn despairs of description. The Duchess "is not of mortal race, and therefore cannot be defined." Cavendish, though, knew herself mortal. She repeatedly made clear that the threat of oblivion impelled her pen, and she worked constantly and inventively to define herself, sometimes in familiar genres, sometimes in modes of her own making—most notably that mix of fantasy, science fiction, argument, and autobiography she called *The Blazing World* (1665). The Duchess's extraordinary energies and kaleidoscopic output have transmuted seventeenth-century ridicule into late twentieth-century fascination with a woman's voice in relentless pursuit of (a favorite Cavendish term) "singularity."

from POEMS AND FANCIES[1]

The Poetress's Hasty Resolution

Reading my verses, I liked them so well,
Self-love did make my judgment to rebel;
And thinking them so good, thought more to make,
Considering not how others would them take.
5 I writ so fast, thought, lived I many a year,
A pyramid of fame thereon to rear.[2]
Reason, observing which way I was bent,
Did stay my hand, and asked me what I meant.
"Will you," said he, "thus waste your time in vain,
10 On that which in the world small praise shall gain?
For shame leave off, and do the printer spare:
He'll lose by your ill poetry, I fear.
Besides, the world already hath great store
Of useless books, wherefore do write no more,
15 But pity take, do the world a good turn,
And all you write cast in the fire and burn."
Angry I was, and Reason struck away,
When I did hear what he to me did say.
Then all in haste I to the press it sent,

1. This was Cavendish's first publication; the first three pieces presented here functioned as a verse preface to the collection. The texts are taken from the second edition (1664), "much altered and corrected."

2. I.e., I thought that if I were to live a long time I would be able to create a poetic monument to myself.

20   Fearing persuasion might my book prevent.
       But now 'tis done, repent with grief do I,
       Hang down my head with shame, blush, sigh, and cry.
       Take pity, and my drooping spirits raise,
       Wipe off my tears with handkerchiefs of praise.

The Poetress's Petition

       Like to a fever's pulse my heart doth beat,
       For fear my book some great repulse should meet.
       If it be naught, let it in silence lie;
       Disturb it not; let it in quiet die;
5   Let not the bells of your dispraise ring loud,
       But wrap it up in silence as a shroud;
       Cause black oblivion on its hearse to lie,
       Instead of tapers, let dark night stand by;
       Instead of flowers, on its grave to strew,
10   Before its hearse, sleepy, dull poppy throw;
       Instead of scutcheons,[3] let my tears be hung,
       Which grief and sorrow from my eyes out wrung.
       Let those that bear its corpse no jesters be,
       But sober, sad, and grave mortality.
15   No satyr° poets by its grave appear,   *satirical*
       No altars raised, to write inscriptions there.
       Let dust of all forgetfulness be cast
       Upon its corpse, there let it lie and waste.
       Nor let it rise again, unless some know,
20   At Judgments some good merits it can show;
       Then shall it live in Heavens of high praise,
       And for its glory, garlands have of bays.[4]

An Apology for Writing So Much upon This Book

       Condemn me not, I make so much ado
       About this book; it is my child, you know;
       Just like a bird, when her young are in nest,
       Goes in, and out, and hops, and takes no rest;
5   But when their young are fledged,[5] their heads out peep,
       Lord! what a chirping does the old one keep.
       So I, for fear my strengthless child should fall
       Against a door, or stool, aloud I call,
       Bid have a care of such a dangerous place.
10   Thus write I much, to hinder all disgrace.

---

3. Escutcheons: funeral ornaments, shield-shaped, exhibiting the deceased's coat of arms.
4. Wreaths of laurel leaves, awarded for military victory

or literary excellence.
5. Feathered; ready to fly.

from **The Description of a New Blazing World**
from To the Reader

If you wonder that I join a work of fancy[1] to my serious philosophical contemplations, think not that it is out of a disparagement to philosophy, or out of an opinion as if this noble study were but a fiction of the mind * * * The end of reason is truth, the end of fancy is fiction. But mistake me not when I distinguish fancy from reason; I mean not as if fancy were not made by the rational parts of matter, but by "reason" I understand a rational search and inquiry into the causes of natural effects, and by "fancy" a voluntary creation or production of the mind, both being effects, or rather actions, of the rational part of matter, of which, as that[2] is a more profitable and useful study than this, so it is also more laborious and difficult, and requires sometimes the help of fancy to recreate the mind and withdraw it from its more serious contemplations.

And this is the reason, why I added this piece of fancy to my philosophical observations, and joined them as two worlds at the ends of their poles; both for my own sake, to divert my studious thoughts, which I employed in the contemplation thereof, and to delight the reader with variety, which is always pleasing. But lest my fancy should stray too much, I chose such a fiction as would be agreeable to the subject treated of in the former parts; it is a description of a new world, not such as Lucian's, or the Frenchman's world in the moon;[3] but a world of my own creating, which I call the Blazing World: the first part whereof is romancical, the second philosophical, and the third is merely fancy, or (as I may call it) fantastical, which if it add any satisfaction to you, I shall account myself a happy creatoress.[4] If not, I must be content to live a melancholy life in my own world; I cannot call it a poor world, if poverty be only want of gold, silver, and jewels; for there is more gold in it than all the chemists ever did, and (as I verily believe) will ever be able to make.[5] As for the rocks of diamonds, I wish with all my soul they might be shared amongst my noble female friends, and upon that condition, I would willingly quit my part;[6] and of the gold I should only desire so much as might suffice to repair my noble Lord and husband's losses:[7] for I am not covetous, but as ambitious as ever any of my sex was, is, or can be; which makes, that though I cannot be Henry the Fifth, or Charles the Second,[8] yet I endeavor to be Margaret the First; and although I have neither power, time, nor occasion to conquer the world as Alexander and Caesar did; yet rather than not to be mistress of one, since Fortune and the Fates would give me none, I have made a world of my own: for which nobody, I hope, will blame me, since it is in everyone's power to do the like.

---

1. Imagination.
2. Philosophy.
3. The *True History*, by the Greek satirist Lucian (2nd century A.D.), initiated a long literary tradition of imaginary voyages, to which the French writer Savinien Cyrano de Bergerac's account of a trip to the moon (*Histoire comique contenant les états et empires de la lune* [1657]) was a recent, celebrated contribution.
4. In the first part of *The Blazing World*, a "virtuous lady" survives her abduction at sea and is transported into a "Blazing World" that touches Earth at the North Pole; quickly wooed and wedded by the Emperor of this utopia, she becomes its Empress. In the second, "philosophical," section, she hears the testimony of various scholars,

scientists, theologians, and philosophers; in the third, "fantastical," section, the Empress summons the soul of Margaret Cavendish to travel from England to the Blazing World, in order to serve as her companion and secretary. The excerpts that follow are from the third part of the narrative.
5. Alchemists sought to turn base metals into gold.
6. Give up my share.
7. During the civil wars, William Cavendish had lost much wealth and property, of which he had recovered only part since the Restoration.
8. Henry V of England (1387–1422) was celebrated for his conquest of France; Charles II for his restoration of the monarchy after the Interregnum.

[CREATING WORLDS]

At last, when the Duchess[9] saw that no patterns would do her any good in the framing of her world, she resolved to make a world of her own invention, * * * which world after it was made, appeared so curious and full of variety, so well ordered and wisely governed, that it cannot possibly be expressed by words, nor the delight and pleasure which the Duchess took in making this world of her own.

In the meantime the Empress was also making and dissolving several worlds in her own mind, and was so puzzled, that she could not settle in any of them; wherefore she sent for the Duchess, who being ready to wait on the Empress, carried her beloved world along with her, and invited the Empress's soul to observe the frame, order, and government of it. Her Majesty was so ravished with the perception of it, that her soul desired to live in the Duchess's world; but the Duchess advised her to make such another world in her own mind; for, said she, your Majesty's mind is full of rational corporeal motions, and the rational motions of my mind shall assist you by the help of sensitive expressions, with the best instructions they are able to give you.

The Empress being thus persuaded by the Duchess to make an imaginary world of her own, followed her advice; and after she had quite finished it, and framed all kinds of creatures proper and useful for it, strengthened it with good laws, and beautified it with arts and sciences; having nothing else to do, unless she did dissolve her imaginary world, or made some alterations in the Blazing World she lived in, which yet she could hardly do, by reason it was so well ordered that it could not be mended.[1]

[EMPRESS, DUCHESS, DUKE]

At last, they entered into the Duke's house,[2] an habitation not so magnificent, as useful; and when the Empress saw it, "Has the Duke," said she, "no other house but this?" "Yes," answered the Duchess, "some five miles from this place, he has a very fine castle, called Bolsover."[3] "That place then," said the Empress, "I desire to see." "Alas!" replied the Duchess, "it is but a naked house, and unclothed of all furniture." "However," said the Empress, "I may see the manner of its structure and building." "That you may," replied the Duchess. And as they were thus discoursing, the Duke came out of the house into the court, to see his horses of manage;[4] whom when the Duchess's soul perceived, she was so overjoyed, that her aerial vehicle[5] became so splendorous, as if it had been enlightened by the sun; by which we may perceive, that the passions of souls or spirits can alter their bodily vehicles. Then these two ladies' spirits went close to him, but he could not perceive them; and after the Empress had observed the art of manage, she was much pleased with it, and commended it as a noble pastime, and an exercise fit and proper for noble and heroic persons; but when the Duke was gone into the house again, those two souls followed him; where the Empress observing, that he went to the exercise of the sword, and was such an excellent and unparalleled master thereof, she was as much pleased with that exercise, as

9. Cavendish herself, whose soul has been transported to the Blazing World at the Empress's request. At this point in the story she and the Empress have been experimenting with creating worlds in accordance with the theories established by various experts, ancient and modern (Pythagoras, Plato, Aristotle, Descartes, Hobbes).
1. Instead, the Empress resolves "to see the world the Duchess came from," and so "those two female souls" travel together "as lightly as two thoughts," into England.

2. Welbeck Abbey, north-country birthplace and family seat of Cavendish's husband the Duke of Newcastle.
3. The Duke's favorite residence.
4. Well-disciplined in the actions and paces of *ménage*, or systematic horse training. The Duke, an expert equestrian, had published two books on the subject; when Charles II was a boy, Newcastle had taught him how to ride.
5. Form made out of air.

she was with the former. But the Duchess's soul being troubled, that her dear lord and husband used such a violent exercise before meat, for fear of overheating himself, without any consideration of the Empress's soul, left her aerial vehicle, and entered into her lord. The Empress's soul perceiving this, did the like: and then the Duke had three souls in one body; and had there been but some such souls more, the Duke would have been like the Grand Signior in his seraglio,[6] only it would have been a Platonic seraglio.[7] But the Duke's soul being wise, honest, witty, complaisant, and noble, afforded such delight and pleasure to the Empress's soul by her conversation, that these two souls became enamored of each other; which the Duchess's soul perceiving, grew jealous at first, but then considering that no adultery could be committed amongst Platonic lovers, and that Platonism was divine, as being derived from divine Plato, cast forth of her mind that idea of jealousy. Then the conversation of these three souls was so pleasant, that it cannot be expressed; for the Duke's soul entertained the Empress's soul with scenes, songs, music, witty discourses, pleasant recreations, and all kinds of harmless sports; so that the time passed away faster than they expected. At last, a spirit came and told the Empress, that although neither the Emperor, nor any of his subjects knew that her soul was absent; yet the Empress's soul was so sad and melancholy, for want of his own beloved soul, that all the imperial court took notice of it. Wherefore he advised the Empress's soul to return into the Blazing World, into her own body she left there; which both the Duke's and Duchess's soul was very sorry for, and wished, that if it had been possible, the Empress's soul might have stayed a longer time with them; but seeing it could not be otherwise, they pacified themselves. * * *

Epilogue
To The Reader

By this poetical description, you may perceive, that my ambition is not only to be Empress, but Authoress of a whole world; and that the worlds I have made, both the Blazing and the other Philosophical World, mentioned in the first part of this description, are framed and composed of the most pure, that is, the rational parts of matter, which are the parts of my mind; which creation was more easily and suddenly effected than the conquests of the two famous monarchs of the world, Alexander and Caesar. Neither have I made such disturbances, and caused so many dissolutions of particulars,[8] otherwise named deaths, as they did; for I have destroyed but some few men in a little boat,[9] which died through the extremity of cold, and that by the hand of Justice, which was necessitated to punish their crime of stealing away a young and beauteous lady. And in the formation of those worlds, I take more delight and glory, than ever Alexander or Caesar did in conquering this terrestrial world; and though I have made my Blazing World a peaceable world, allowing it but one religion, one language, and one government; yet could I make another world, as full of factions, divisions, and wars, as this is of peace and tranquility; and the rational figures of my mind might express as much courage to fight, as Hector and Achilles had; and be as wise as Nestor, as eloquent as Ulysses, and as beautiful as Helen.[1] But I esteeming peace before war, wit before policy, honesty before beauty; instead of the figures of Alexander, Caesar,

6. Harem.
7. One where the pleasures of the flesh would be repudiated in favor of the contemplation of pure, disembodied Ideas.
8. Individuals.

9. The sailor-abductors of the "virtuous lady," who die during the boat's passage through the North Pole to the Blazing World.
1. Characters in the *Iliad*, Homer's epic poem about the Trojan War.

Hector, Achilles, Nestor, Ulysses, Helen, etc. chose rather the figure of honest Margaret Newcastle, which now I would not change for all this terrestrial world; and if any should like the world I have made, and be willing to be my subjects, they may imagine themselves such, and they are such, I mean, in their minds, fancies, or imaginations; but if they cannot endure to be subjects, they may create worlds of their own, and govern themselves as they please: but yet let them have a care, not to prove unjust usurpers, and to rob me of mine; for concerning the Philosophical World, I am Empress of it myself; and as for the Blazing World, it having an Empress already, who rules it with great wisdom and conduct, which Empress is my dear Platonic friend; I shall never prove so unjust, treacherous, and unworthy to her, as to disturb her government, much less to depose her from her imperial throne, for the sake of any other; but rather choose to create another world for another friend.

1666

—•—≡◊≡—•—

John Dryden
1631–1700

Godfrey Kneller, *John Dryden*, 1693.

In his last years, John Dryden often felt the need to defend his morals, his religion, his politics, even his writing. For nearly a quarter of a century, he had held high literary office and mingled with the great; he had curried royal favor and aristocratic patronage, bolstering officialdom, aiming to injure the Crown's enemies and to caress its friends. He wrote about politics and religion, about trade and empire; he wrote for the theater and for public occasions; he composed songs, fables, odes, and panegyrics, brilliant satire and savage polemic; he translated from many languages and formulated an idiomatic, familiar, and fluent prose style. Dryden virtually invented the idea of a commercial literary career; and through all the turns of a difficult public life, he fashioned from his own unlikely personality—from his privacy, self-doubts, and hesitations—a public figure of literary distinction. But he attained this celebrity at the cost of gossip and scandal, and in the last decade of his life (after the Glorious Revolution and his deposition from the Poet Laureateship) he faced suspicion and scorn.

The poet's beginnings give no hint of literary greatness or the likelihood of fame. He was born in 1631 in a country town and to comfortable circumstance; he was educated at Westminster School and graduated from Trinity College, Cambridge. He held minor public office in the 1650s but had written almost nothing before he was twenty-seven. Dryden then began his long career as public poet. He mourned the Lord Protector in 1659 (*Heroic Stanzas*) and then, in what looks like a convenient turn of allegiance, he celebrated the return of monarchy in 1660, writing poems to Charles II, to the Lord Chancellor, and to the Duchess of York; he praised the Royal Society (*To Doctor Charleton*) and defended the Royal Navy and its aristocratic high command (*Annus Mirabilis*, 1667).

The first years seem a series of calculated moves; and the combination of talent, application, and opportunity was crowned when Dryden was named Poet Laureate in 1667. But in addition to fashioning a career in the 1660s, Dryden also forged a new drama—an epic theater whose themes and language echoed the idioms of heroic verse—and a body of literary criticism that itself would have made his lasting reputation. Indeed, the great text of the first decade was the *Essay of Dramatic Poesy* (1668), Dryden's formulation of a pointedly English poetics and theater. Along with Sir Philip Sidney's *Apology for Poetry*, and Samuel Johnson's *Lives of the Poets*, Dryden's *Essay* is central to the long-standing canon of English literary criticism. Some of Dryden's early plays have been forgotten, but he worked steadily at a craft that would enable him to turn Milton's *Paradise Lost* into theater (*The State of Innocence*, 1677), create a superb adaptation of Shakespeare's *Antony and Cleopatra* in *All for Love* (1678), the finest of Restoration tragedies in *Don Sebastian* (1690), and the texts of one of England's first operas, *King Arthur* (1691), and last masques, *The Pilgrim* (1700).

By the late 1670s Dryden was famed as publicist for the Crown, and his theatrical work had come to dominate the stage; but he had hardly begun the career as satirist by which he is now best known. Its opening move was *Mac Flecknoe* (1676), and in the next few years Dryden fashioned masterpieces of literary mockery and political invective, poems that virtually created literary genres and dominated satire for decades to come. *Mac Flecknoe* allowed Dryden to ridicule and crush his rivals, all the while conjuring the suave tones and elegant manners of literary supremacy. In the abuse of rivals, only Pope surpasses Dryden as a master of scorn. But *Mac Flecknoe* was only the first act in a theater of invective. In the fall of 1681 Dryden wrote *Absalom and Achitophel*, a biblical allegory occasioned by the crisis of succession. The king had failed to beget a legitimate heir, and the king's Catholic brother waited ominously in the wings. It was Dryden's job to defend the Crown, to extenuate royal indulgence, and, especially, to defuse anxieties. With *Absalom and Achitophel*, Dryden wove together the Bible and contemporary politics with such deftness that mere diversionary tactics were spun into an incomparable allegory of envy, ambition, and misdeed. The satire was read, marked, circulated, and treasured as a masterpiece and a menace.

The masterpiece secured Dryden's fame; the menace exacted a cost. The poet had attacked powerful men: aristocrats, politicians, and their partisan hacks who intrigued against the Crown. They failed in the early 1680s to foment rebellion, but by 1688 they were able to effect a revolution that deposed the Catholic monarchy and the Poet Laureate himself. Dryden was reputed a brilliant and damaging advocate of Stuart rule; he had collaborated with court publicity and polemic; he had even converted to Roman Catholicism after James ascended the throne. Indeed, Dryden wrote his longest and most elaborate original poem—*The Hind and the Panther* (1687)—in defense of that king's rule and religion, and of his own conversion to Roman Catholicism. Once James II had been chased into exile, the poet felt he had nowhere to turn. In 1688 Dryden was fifty-seven, an old man by contemporary standards. He was forced from office, his pension was canceled, and he was driven back to the venues of commercial writing: the theater, translation, publication by subscription, even editing and anthologizing. He often expressed a keen sense of loss and abandonment in the 1690s, yet the decade would prove to be a remarkable phase of his career. Between his loss of the laureateship in 1689 and his death in 1700, Dryden wrote a series of superb translations that included selections from the satires of Juvenal and Persius, Ovid's *Metamorphoses* and *Amores*, Boccaccio's and Chaucer's tales. In these same years he wrote odes and epitaphs, and collaborated with his publisher Jacob Tonson in the new fashion for literary anthologies. Most remarkably, he produced *The Works of Virgil*, which set the standard for the translation of Latin poetry. He had come to his project late, and more than once he wrote of his inadequacy for this daunting task: "What Virgil wrote in the vigor of his age, in plenty and at ease, I have undertaken to translate in my declining years, struggling with wants, oppressed with sickness, curbed in my genius, liable to be misconstrued in all I write; and my judges . . . already prejudiced against me, by the lying character which has been given them of my morals." But Dryden's *Virgil* was a resounding, rehabilitating commercial and artistic success.

Nor were the twelve thousand lines of translated Virgil the close of this career. What followed was *Fables Ancient and Modern*, an anthology of original verse and new translations that included Ovid, Boccaccio, and Chaucer as well as a trial for what Dryden hoped would be his English Homer. He saw commercial opportunity in this new collection; but he must also have understood it as a crowning achievement in this life of theatricality and ventriloquism. He had begun by seeking a voice in the idioms and gestures of other poets; he now belonged wholly to himself as he casually turned their verse into his own. It is something of a paradox that a life of literary self-assertion, of aggressive, even calculating, careerism, should have closed with Dryden rummaging among other poets' verse, pausing over favorite lines, translating Ovid's Latin and Boccaccio's Italian into what was unmistakably his own voice. And the paradox of self-assertion ending in translation helps us to identify what is so particularly and so brilliantly Dryden's art. In the early modern world, writing meant belonging to others—to the authority of antiquity, to the opinions and fickle pleasure of patrons, to favor, to obligation, to taste, even to the emerging appetites of a reading public. Many of Dryden's contemporaries—Donne, Milton, Rochester—appeal to us by their seeming defiance of such self-denying ordinances. We read Dryden today not just for the skill with which he picked his way through political dangers or negotiated social minefields, not even for the savage cartooning of enemies or baroque praise of friends, but for the achievement of belonging to others as he became more exactly and more generously himself.

MAC FLECKNOE   In *Mac Flecknoe*, Dryden put on display a literary culture dangerously debased. The poem's title ("Son of Flecknoe") announces a royal succession in the kingdom of bad writing. A literary "father," the priest and minor poet Richard Flecknoe (c. 1605–c. 1677), anoints as his true heir Thomas Shadwell (1640–1692), a playwright whom Dryden loathed as a tiresome controversialist and an ardent (worse, successful) rival for public favor and aristocratic patronage. Dryden wages his attack in an idiom at once elevated and scandalous, in language whose allegiance alternates (even within a single line) between epic poetry and the privy. Like much libelous and bawdy verse, Dryden's demolitionary masterpiece circulated in manuscript for several years; it was eventually printed in a pirated edition (1682) by a publisher seeking to capitalize on the recent success of *Absalom and Achitophel*. Like that poem, *Mac Flecknoe* plays upon the question of monarchic succession, but stages it in such a way as to implicate bad politics in bad taste. Dryden maps a City of London where foul writing chokes the streets, and dim-witted citizens get—and applaud—the poet-monarchs they deserve.

Mac Flecknoe

> All human things are subject to decay,
> And, when Fate summons, monarchs must obey.
> This Flecknoe found, who, like Augustus, young
> Was called to empire,[1] and had governed long:
> 5   In prose and verse was owned, without dispute,
> Through all the realms of Nonsense, absolute.
> This aged prince, now flourishing in peace,
> And blest with issue of a large increase,
> Worn out with business, did at length debate
> 10   To settle the succession of the state:

1. Augustus became the first Roman emperor at the age of 32.

And, pondering which of all his sons was fit
To reign, and wage immortal war with wit,
Cried, "'Tis resolved; for Nature pleads that he
Should only rule, who most resembles me:
15   Sh——alone my perfect image bears,
Mature in dullness from his tender years.
Sh——alone, of all my sons, is he
Who stands confirmed in full stupidity.
The rest to some faint meaning make pretense,
20   But Sh——never deviates into sense.
Some beams of wit on other souls may fall,
Strike through and make a lucid interval,
But Sh——'s genuine night admits no ray,
His rising fogs prevail upon the day.
25   Besides, his goodly fabric° fills the eye,   *large body*
And seems designed for thoughtless majesty:
Thoughtless as monarch oaks that shade the plain,
And, spread in solemn state, supinely reign.
Heywood and Shirley were but types of thee,[2]
30   Thou last great prophet of tautology:
Even I, a dunce of more renown than they,
Was sent before but to prepare thy way;
And coarsely clad in Norwich drugget[3] came
To teach the nations in thy greater name.[4]
35   My warbling lute, the lute I whilom° strung   *once*
When to King John of Portugal I sung,[5]
Was but the prelude to that glorious day
When thou on silver Thames didst cut thy way,
With well-timed oars before the royal barge,
40   Swelled with the pride of thy celestial charge;
And big with hymn, commander of an host,
The like was ne'er in Epsom blankets tossed.[6]
Methinks I see the new Arion[7] sail,
The lute still trembling underneath thy nail.
45   At thy well-sharpened thumb from shore to shore
The treble squeaks for fear, the basses roar:
Echoes from Pissing Alley[8] 'Sh————' call,
And 'Sh————' they resound from A————Hall.[9]
About thy boat the little fishes throng,

2. Thomas Heywood and James Shirley, popular and pro-lific playwrights from the first half of the 17th century. As "types," they foreshadow or prepare for Shadwell, just as Old Testament figures such as Moses or Isaac were interpreted in Christian theology as forerunners of Jesus.
3. Woolen cloth; Shadwell came from Norwich.
4. Here, Flecknoe is John the Baptist ("coarsely clad" in camel's hair) to Shadwell's Jesus.
5. Flecknoe claimed that, during his travels in Europe, he had been summoned to perform before the king of Portugal.

6. A glance at two of Shadwell's plays: *Epsom Wells* and *The Virtuoso*, in which Sir Samuel Hearty is tossed in a blanket; tossing in blankets was also a means of inducing childbirth.
7. Greek musician-poet rescued from drowning by music-loving dolphins.
8. West of Temple Bar, it led from the Strand down to the Thames.
9. Unidentified.

50	As at the morning toast° that floats along.
	Sometimes as prince of thy harmonious band
	Thou wield'st thy papers in thy threshing hand.
	St. André's feet[1] ne'er kept more equal time,
	Not ev'n the feet of thy own *Psyche*'s rhyme,
55	Though they in number as in sense excel;
	So just, so like tautology they fell,

sewage

That, pale with envy, Singleton foreswore
The lute and sword which he in triumph bore,
And vowed he ne'er would act Villerius[2] more."

60   Here stopped the good old sire, and wept for joy
     In silent raptures of the hopeful boy.
     All arguments, but most his plays, persuade,
     That for anointed dullness he was made.
         Close to the walls which fair Augusta bind[3]
65   (The fair Augusta much to fears inclined[4]),
     An ancient fabric,[5] raised t' inform the sight,
     There stood of yore, and Barbican it hight:[6]
     A watchtower once, but now, so Fate ordains,
     Of all the pile an empty name remains.
70   From its old ruins brothel-houses rise,
     Scenes of lewd loves and of polluted joys;
     Where their vast courts the mother-strumpets keep
     And, undisturbed by watch,° in silence sleep.[7]   *police*
     Near these a nursery[8] erects its head,
75   Where queens[9] are formed and future heroes bred;
     Where unfledged actors learn to laugh and cry,
     Where infant punks° their tender voices try,   *prostitutes*
     And little Maximins[1] the gods defy.
     Great Fletcher never treads in buskins here,
80   Nor greater Jonson dares in socks appear.[2]
     But gentle Simkin[3] just reception finds
     Amid this monument of vanished minds:
     Pure clinches° the suburbian Muse[4] affords,   *puns*
     And Panton[5] waging harmless war with words.

1. St. André, a French dancer who choreographed the opera *Psyche* (1675), for which Shadwell wrote the libretto.
2. John Singleton, one of the king's musicians; Villerius, a character in William Davenant's opera, *The Siege of Rhodes*.
3. The old wall of the City of London (Augusta).
4. Fears aroused by the Popish Plot.
5. Structure.
6. Was named; the Barbican, a medieval gatehouse, gave its name to a disreputable district of gaming and prostitution; adjoining it was Grub Street, the center of hack journalism.
7. Parodying Abraham Cowley, *Davideis* (1656), "Where their vast court the mother-waters keep, / And undisturbed by moons in silence sleep."

8. A training theater for the two main playhouses.
9. Dryden puns on queen (stage-monarch)/quean (prostitute). During the Restoration, actresses were often thought to moonlight as sexual companions.
1. Maximin is the fulminating protagonist of Dryden's *Tyrannic Love*.
2. John Fletcher and Ben Jonson, major playwrights of the previous generations. The buskin is the symbol of tragedy (Fletcher's forte) and the sock of comedy (Jonson's). Shadwell promoted himself as Jonson's successor in the tradition of "humors" comedy.
3. A clownish character in a series of popular farces.
4. I.e., the muse presiding over the disreputable area outside the City walls.
5. Another farce character.

85 Here Flecknoe, as a place to fame well known,
 Ambitiously designed his Sh————'s throne. ⎫
 For ancient Dekker[6] prophesied long since, ⎬
 That in this pile should reign a mighty prince, ⎬
 Born for a scourge of wit, and flail of sense: ⎭

90 To whom true dullness should some *Psyches* owe,
 But Worlds of *Misers* from his pen should flow;
 Humorists and *Hypocrites*[7] it should produce,
 Whole Raymond families, and tribes of Bruce.
  Now Empress Fame had published the renown

95 Of Sh————'s coronation through the town.
 Roused by report of Fame, the nations meet,
 From near Bunhill, and distant Watling Street.[8]
 No Persian carpets spread th' imperial way,
 But scattered limbs of mangled poets lay:

100 From dusty shops neglected authors come,
 Martyrs of pies, and relics of the bum.[9]
 Much Heywood, Shirley, Ogilby[1] there lay,
 But loads of Sh————almost choked the way.
 Bilked stationers for yeomen stood prepared,

105 And H————[2] was captain of the guard.
 The hoary prince in majesty appeared,
 High on a throne of his own labors reared.
 At his right hand our young Ascanius[3] sate,
 Rome's other hope, and pillar of the state.

110 His brows thick fogs, instead of glories, grace,
 And lambent° dullness played around his face.   *glowing*
 As Hannibal did to the altars come,
 Sworn by his sire a mortal foe to Rome,[4]
 So Sh————swore, nor should his vow be vain,

115 That he till death true dullness would maintain;
 And in his father's right, and realm's defense,
 Ne'er to have peace with wit, nor truce with sense.
 The king himself the sacred unction[5] made,
 As king by office, and as priest by trade:

120 In his sinister° hand, instead of ball,   *left*
 He placed a mighty mug of potent ale;
 Love's Kingdom[6] to his right he did convey,

6. Thomas Dekker (1570?–1632), prolific dramatist whose plays focused on London life.
7. Shadwell was the author of *The Miser* (1672), *The Humorists* (1671), and *The Hypocrite* (1669). Raymond and Bruce appear in *The Humorists* and *The Virtuoso*, respectively.
8. Fame draws her crowd both from cemeteries (like Bunhill Fields) and from mercantile districts (like Watling Street); thus, these devotees of Shadwell include both the dead and the living.
9. Unsold books might be recycled as pie wrappers or as toilet paper; the bones of martyrs were often venerated as relics.

1. John Ogilby, printer, cartographer, and translator (like Dryden) of Virgil.
2. Henry Herringman, a prominent bookseller-publisher; he had published both Shadwell and Dryden.
3. The son of Aeneas, marked for greatness by a heaven-sent flame about his head.
4. According to Livy, Hannibal's father made the young boy swear himself Rome's enemy.
5. The oil with which the king was anointed during the coronation ceremony.
6. A play by Flecknoe.

At once his scepter and his rule of sway,[7]
Whose righteous lore the prince had practiced young,
125   And from whose loins[8] recorded Psyche sprung.
His temples last with poppies[9] were o'erspread,
That nodding seemed to consecrate his head:
Just at that point of time, if Fame not lie,
On his left hand twelve reverend owls[1] did fly.
130   So Romulus,[2] 'tis sung, by Tiber's brook,
Presage of sway from twice six vultures took.
Th' admiring throng loud acclamations make,
And omens of his future empire take.
The sire then shook the honors[3] of his head,
135   And from his brows damps of oblivion shed ⎤
Full on the filial dullness: long he stood,   ⎬
Repelling from his breast the raging God;   ⎦
At length burst out in this prophetic mood:
    "Heavens bless my son, from Ireland let him reign
140   To far Barbados on the western main;[4]
Of his dominion may no end be known,
And greater than his father's be his throne.
Beyond *Love's Kingdom* let him stretch his pen!"
He paused, and all the people cried, "Amen."
145   "Then thus," continued he, "my son, advance
Still in new impudence, new ignorance.
Success let others teach, learn thou from me
Pangs without birth, and fruitless industry.
Let *Virtuosos* in five years be writ,
150   Yet not one thought accuse thy toil of wit.
Let gentle George[5] in triumph tread the stage,
Make Dorimant betray, and Loveit rage;
Let Cully, Cockwood, Fopling charm the pit,
And in their folly show the writer's wit.
155   Yet still thy fools shall stand in thy defense,
And justify° their author's want of sense.   prove
Let 'em be all by thy own model made
Of dullness, and desire no foreign aid:
That they to future ages may be known,
160   Not copies drawn, but issue[6] of thy own.
Nay let thy men of wit too be the same,
All full of thee, and differing but in name;
But let no alien S—dl—y[7] interpose

---

7. Dryden parodies the rituals and props of the coronation ceremony.
8. Pronounced "lines" (a fact that permits Dryden a significant pun).
9. Symbolizing sleep.
1. Symbols of ignorance and darkness (because nocturnal).
2. Cofounder of Rome (through which the Tiber runs).

3. Ornaments, and by extension, hair—a Virgilian expression.
4. His kingdom will be the Atlantic Ocean.
5. Sir George Etherege, comic playwright; characters from his plays follow.
6. A pun: both progeny and printing.
7. Sir Charles Sedley, courtier, poet, and intimate of Dryden's circle; he wrote a prologue for *Epsom Wells*.

To lard with wit thy hungry *Epsom* prose.
165 And when false flowers of rhetoric thou would'st cull,
Trust nature, do not labor to be dull;
But write thy best, and top; and in each line,
Sir Formal's[8] oratory will be thine.
Sir Formal, though unsought, attends thy quill,
170 And does thy northern dedications[9] fill.
Nor let false friends seduce thy mind to fame,
By arrogating Jonson's hostile name.
Let father Flecknoe fire thy mind with praise,
And uncle Ogilby thy envy raise.
175 Thou art my blood, where Jonson has no part;
What share have we in nature or in art?
Where did his wit on learning fix a brand,
And rail at arts he did not understand?
Where made he love in Prince Nicander's[1] vein,
180 Or swept the dust in *Psyche*'s humble strain?
Where sold he bargains,[2] 'whip-stitch, kiss my arse,'
Promised a play and dwindled to a farce?
When did his Muse from Fletcher scenes purloin,
As thou whole Eth'rege dost transfuse to thine?
185 But so transfused as oil on waters flow,
His always floats above, thine sinks below.
This is thy province, this thy wondrous way,
New humors to invent for each new play:[3]
This is that boasted bias of thy mind,
190 By which one way, to dullness, 'tis inclined;
Which makes thy writings lean on one side still,
And in all changes that way bends thy will.
Nor let thy mountain belly make pretense
Of likeness; thine's a tympany[4] of sense.
195 A tun of man in thy large bulk is writ,
But sure thou'rt but a kilderkin[5] of wit.
Like mine thy gentle numbers feebly creep;
Thy tragic Muse gives smiles, thy comic sleep.
With whate'er gall thou sett'st thyself to write,
200 Thy inoffensive satires never bite.
In thy felonious heart, though venom lies,
It does but touch thy Irish[6] pen, and dies.
Thy genius calls thee not to purchase fame

8. Sir Formal Trifle, a character in Shadwell's *The Virtuoso*, described by Shadwell as "the Orator, a florid coxcomb."
9. Both Flecknoe and Shadwell dedicated several of their works to the Duke and Duchess of Newcastle (a town in the north of England).
1. A character in *Psyche*.
2. "To sell bargains" is to respond to an innocent question with a coarse phrase, as in this line. Dryden sharpens the insult by quoting the slangy nonsense phrase "whip-stitch" from Shadwell's own play, *The Virtuoso*.
3. I.e., by these contemptible means, you purport to outdo Ben Jonson.
4. A swelling of the abdomen, caused by air or gas.
5. A tun was a large cask of wine; a kilderkin a quarter of a tun.
6. Neither Flecknoe nor Shadwell was actually Irish; Ireland was regarded in England as an abode of savages.

In keen iambics,[7] but mild anagram:
205 Leave writing plays, and choose for thy command
Some peaceful province in acrostic land.
There thou may'st wings display and altars[8] raise,
And torture one poor word ten thousand ways.
Or if thou would'st thy diff'rent talents suit,
210 Set thy own songs, and sing them to thy lute."
He said, but his last words were scarcely heard,⎫
For Bruce and Longvil had a trap prepared,[9] ⎬
And down they sent the yet declaiming bard. ⎭
Sinking he left his drugget robe behind,
215 Borne upward by a subterranean wind.
The mantle fell to the young prophet's part,[1]
With double portion of his father's art.

c. 1676   1682

To the Memory of Mr. Oldham[1]

Farewell, too little and too lately known,
Whom I began to think and call my own;
For sure our souls were near allied; and thine
Cast in the same poetic mold with mine.[2]
5 One common note on either lyre did strike,
And knaves and fools[3] we both abhorred alike:
To the same goal did both our studies drive,
The last set out the soonest did arrive.
Thus Nisus[4] fell upon the slippery place,
10 While his young friend performed and won the race.
O early ripe! to thy abundant store
What could advancing age have added more?
It might (what Nature never gives the young)
Have taught the numbers[5] of thy native tongue.
15 But satire needs not those, and wit will shine
Through the harsh cadence of a rugged line:
A noble error, and but seldom made,
When poets are by too much force betrayed.
Thy generous fruits, though gathered ere their prime, ⎫
20 Still showed a quickness;[6] and maturing time ⎬

---

7. Sharp satire (written in iambic meter by classical satirists).
8. Dryden here mocks the practice of writing emblematic verse, poems in the shape of their subjects (e.g., George Herbert's *Easter Wings* and *The Altar*). He lumps this practice together with other forms of empty ingenuity.
9. In Shadwell's *The Virtuoso*, Bruce and Longvil open a trap door beneath the long-winded Sir Formal Trifle.
1. A burlesque of 2 Kings 2.8–14, in which the prophet Elijah is borne up to heaven, while his mantle falls to his successor, Elisha.
1. John Oldham (1653–1683) achieved fame at age 28 with his *Satires upon the Jesuits* (1681). Three years later, an aging Dryden mourned him in a tribute that prefaced

the *Remains of Mr. John Oldham in Verse and Prose*. Within his poem's brief compass, Dryden echoes many poets—Virgil, Catullus, Milton, and Oldham himself—and invokes several modes: satire, celebration, elegy.
2. An echo of Oldham's poem *David's Lamentation*: "Oh, dearer than my soul! if I can call it mine, / For sure we had the same, 'twas very thine."
3. Satire's traditional targets.
4. In Book 5 of Virgil's *Aeneid*, Nisus slips near the finish line during a footrace, falling in a manner that permits "his young friend" Euryalus to win.
5. Metrical patterns and harmonies.
6. Liveliness; also, sharpness of taste.

But mellows what we write to the dull sweets of rhyme.
Once more, hail and farewell;[7] farewell thou young,
But ah too short, Marcellus of our tongue;
Thy brows with ivy, and with laurels bound;
25   But fate and gloomy night encompass thee around.[8]

                                     1684

Alexander's Feast
or, The Power of Music
An Ode in Honor of St. Cecilia's Day[1]

1

'Twas at the royal feast, for Persia won
    By Philip's warlike son:[2]
      Aloft in awful state
      The godlike hero sate
5   On his imperial throne:
  His valiant peers were placed around;
Their brows with roses and with myrtles bound
    (So should desert in arms be crowned).
The lovely Thais[3] by his side
10 Sat like a blooming Eastern bride
In flow'r of youth and beauty's pride.
    Happy, happy, happy pair!
    None but the brave
    None but the brave
15   None but the brave deserves the fair.

                CHORUS

    Happy, happy, happy pair!
    None but the brave
    None but the brave
    None but the brave deserves the fair.

2

20 Timotheus,[4] placed on high
    Amid the tuneful choir,
  With flying fingers touched the lyre:

7. Dryden echoes a phrase in Catullus's elegy for his brother; "Ave arque vale" (101.10).
8. In Book 6 of Virgil's *Aeneid*, the hero visits the underworld, where his dead father shows him a vision of Rome's future. This vision concludes with a sight of aftgustus Caesar's adopted son and heir Marcellus, who after a glorious military career died at the age of 20. The last line of Dryden's elegy reworks Virgil's conclusion; "But howring mists around his brows are spread, / And night with sable, shades, involves his head." (*Aeneid* 6,866; Dryden's translation)..
1. The early martyr Cecilia is the patron saint of music and musicians. Her feast day (22 November) was annually celebrated in London by a concert featuring a new piece with words by an eminent poet and music by a

distinguished composer. The musical society in charge of the occasion commissioned two odes from Dryden, ten years apart: *A Song for St. Cecilia's Day* (1687) and *Alexander's Feast*. Dryden undertook the commission with some reluctance, but after the piece's successful premiere, he noted with pleasure that *Alexander's Feast* "is esteemed the best of all my poetry, by all the town. I thought so myself when I writ it, but being old, I mistrusted my own judgment."
2. Alexander the Great, son of Philip of Macedon; Dryden depicts the feast that Alexander held after defeating the Persians and their emperor Darius in 331 B.C.
3. Alexander's Greek concubine.
4. Celebrated poet and musician.

The trembling notes ascend the sky,
    And heav'nly joys inspire.
25 The song began from Jove,
Who left his blissful seats above
(Such is the power of mighty love).
A dragon's fiery form belied[5] the god:
Sublime on radiant spires° he rode,   *coils*
30   When he to fair Olympia pressed:
  And while he sought her snowy breast:
Then, round her slender waist he curled,
And stamped an image of himself, a sov'reign of the world.
The listening crowd admire the lofty sound:
35 "A present deity," they shout around:
"A present deity," the vaulted roofs rebound.
   With ravished ears
   The monarch hears,
   Assumes the god,[6]
40   Affects to nod,
And seems to shake the spheres.

CHORUS

*   With ravished ears*
*   The monarch hears,*
*   Assumes the god,*
45   *Affects to nod,*
And seems to shake the spheres.

3

The praise of Bacchus then the sweet musician sung,
  Of Bacchus ever fair and ever young:
   The jolly god in triumph comes;
50   Sound the trumpets; beat the drums:
    Flushed with a purple grace
    He shows his honest face,
Now give the hautboys° breath; he comes, he comes.   *oboes*
    Bacchus, ever fair and young,
55   Drinking joys did first ordain:
Bacchus' blessings are a treasure;
Drinking is the soldier's pleasure;
    Rich the treasure,
    Sweet the pleasure;
60   Sweet is pleasure after pain.

CHORUS

Bacchus' blessings are a treasure;

---

5. Timotheus tells the alternative story of Alexander's parentage, that he was begotten by Jove—disguised ("belied") as a serpent—upon Philip's wife Olympias.

6. Behaves like Jove, whose nod is said by Virgil to cause earthquakes.

Drinking is the soldier's pleasure;
  Rich the treasure,
  Sweet the pleasure;
65   *Sweet is pleasure after pain.*

    4
 Soothed with the sound, the king grew vain;
  Fought all his battles o'er again;
And thrice he routed all his foes, and thrice he slew the slain.
   The master saw the madness rise,
70   His glowing cheeks, his ardent eyes;
  And, while he heav'n and earth defied,
  Changed his hand, and checked his pride.[7]
    He chose a mournful Muse
    Soft pity to infuse:
75   He sung Darius great and good,
   By too severe a fate
  Fallen, fallen, fallen, fallen,
   Fallen from his high estate
    And welt'ring in his blood:
80 Deserted at his utmost need,
By those his former bounty fed:
On the bare earth exposed he lies,
With not a friend to close his eyes.

With downcast looks the joyless victor sat,
85 Revolving° in his altered soul   *pondering*
  The various turns of chance below;
 And, now and then, a sigh he stole,
  And tears began to flow.

    CHORUS

 Revolving in his altered soul
90   *The various turns of chance below;*
 And, now and then, a sigh he stole;
  And tears began to flow.

    5
The mighty master smiled to see
That love was in the next degree:
95 'Twas but a kindred sound to move;[8]
For pity melts the mind to love.
  Softly sweet, in Lydian measures,[9]
  Soon he soothed his soul to pleasures.
  "War," he sung, "is toil and trouble,
100   Honor but an empty bubble.
  Never ending, still° beginning,   *always*

---

7. Timotheus ("the master") changes the music in order to restrain Alexander's swelling pride.
8. All it took to "move" Alexander to the "next degree"

of feeling was to shift ("move") musical registers.
9. In ancient Greek music, the mode associated with pathos.

Fighting still, and still destroying,
If the world be worth thy winning,
Think, O think, it worth enjoying.

105   Lovely Thais sits beside thee,
Take the good the gods provide thee."

The many[1] rend the skies with loud applause;
So love was crowned, but music won the cause.
The prince, unable to conceal his pain,

110   Gazed on the fair
Who caused his care,
And sighed and looked, sighed and looked,
Sighed and looked, and sighed again:
At length, with love and wine at once oppressed,

115   The vanquished victor sunk upon her breast.

CHORUS

The prince, unable to conceal his pain,
Gazed on the fair
Who caused his care,
And sighed and looked, sighed and looked,

120   *Sighed and looked, and sighed again:*
At length, with love and wine at once oppressed,
The vanquished victor sunk upon her breast.

6

Now strike the golden lyre again:
A louder yet, and yet a louder strain.

125   Break his bands of sleep asunder,
And rouse him, like a rattling peal of thunder.
Hark, hark, the horrid sound
Has raised up his head,
As awaked from the dead,

130   And, amazed, he stares around.
"Revenge, revenge," Timotheus cries,
"See the Furies[2] arise!
See the snakes that they rear,
How they hiss in their hair,

135   And the sparkles that flash from their eyes!
Behold a ghastly band,
Each a torch in his hand!
Those are Grecian ghosts, that in battle were slain,
And unburied remain

140   Inglorious on the plain.
Give the vengeance due
To the valiant crew.
Behold how they toss their torches on high,
How they point to the Persian abodes,

---

1. The retinue or company.   2. Spirits of punishment.

145   And glitt'ring temples of their hostile gods!"
          The princes applaud, with a furious joy;
          And the king seized a flambeau,[3] with zeal to destroy;
                Thais led the way,
                To light him to his prey,
150   And, like another Helen, fired another Troy.[4]

CHORUS

And the king seized a flambeau, with zeal to destroy;
            Thais led the way,
              To light him to his prey,
   And, like another Helen, fired another Troy.

7

155   Thus, long ago,
           Ere heaving bellows learned to blow,
             While organs yet were mute,
          Timotheus, to his breathing flute,
               And sounding lyre,
160   Could swell the soul to rage, or kindle soft desire.
           At last divine Cecilia came,
          Inventress of the vocal frame;[5]
       The sweet enthusiast,[6] from her sacred store,
           Enlarged the former narrow bounds,
165   And added length to solemn sounds,
      With nature's mother wit, and arts unknown before.
          Let old Timotheus yield the prize,
           Or both divide the crown;
          He raised a mortal to the skies;
170   She drew an angel down.[7]

GRAND CHORUS

     At last divine Cecilia came,
      Inventress of the vocal frame;
    The sweet enthusiast, from her sacred store,
       Enlarged the former narrow bounds,
175   *And added length to solemn sounds,*
   With nature's mother wit, and arts unknown before.
       Let old Timotheus yield the prize,
        Or both divide the crown;
       He raised a mortal to the skies;
         She drew an angel down.

1697   1697

---

3. Torch.
4. Stolen away to Troy by Paris, Helen was blamed for
setting in motion the chain of events that led to the
burning of the city by the Greeks.
5. Cecilia was believed to have invented the organ.

6. One possessed by spirits or by a god.
7. Dryden alludes to his earlier ode to music, *A Song for
St. Cecilia's Day* (1687): as Cecilia plays the organ, "An
angel heard and straight appear'd, / Mistaking earth for
heaven."

Aphra Behn
1640?–1689

Robert White, after John Riley,
line engraving of *Aphra Behn*
(*née Johnson*), 1716.

Aphra Behn's career was unprecedented, her output prodigious, her fame extensive, and her voice distinctive. Her origins, though, remain elusive. We know nothing certain about her birth, family, education, or marriage. She may have been born at the start or at the end of the 1640s, to parents of low or "gentle" station, named Johnson, Amies, or Cooper. Her Catholicism and her firm command of French suggest the possibility of a prosperous upbringing in a convent at home or abroad; the running argument against marriage for money that she sustains through much of her work suggests that her own marriage, to the otherwise unidentifiable "Mr. Behn," may have been obligatory and unhappy. In any case it was brief—and just possibly fictitious, since a widow could pursue a profession more freely than a spinster.

Behn's first appearances in the historical record suggest a propensity for self-invention. In 1663–1664, during a short stay with her family in the South American sugar colony of Surinam, a government agent there reported that she was conducting a flirtation with William Scott, an antimonarchist on the run from the Restoration. The agent referred to Scott as "Celadon" and Aphra as "Astraea," names the lovers may well have chosen for themselves from a popular French romance; Behn kept hers, as a *nom de plume,* for the whole of her writing life. Within two years, her loyalties had shifted and her self-invention had grown more intricate. In 1666 Behn herself became the king's spy, sent from London to Antwerp to persuade her old flame Scott to turn informer against his fellow Republicans and to apprise King Charles of rebellious plots. She did useful but costly work, garnering good information that her handlers ignored and spending much money that they were slow to reimburse. Returning to England later that year, and threatened with imprisonment for debt, she wrote her supervisor, "I have cried myself dead and could find in my heart to break through all and get to the King and never rise till he were pleased to pay this, but I am sick and weak and unfit for it or a prison . . . Sir, if I have not the money tonight you must send me something to keep [sustain] me in prison, for I will not starve." The king paid up, and Behn forestalled any further threat of starvation by writing plays for money—the first woman in England to earn a living by her pen. She had been "forced to write for bread," she later declared, and she was "not ashamed to own it."

Throughout her career Behn transmuted such "shamelessness" into a positive point of pride and a source of literary substance. Many of her plays, poems, and fictions focus on the difficulty with which intelligent, enterprising women pursue their desires against the current of social convention. In the prologues, prefaces, postscripts, and letters by which she provided a running commentary on her work, Behn sometimes aligned herself with the large fraternity of male authors who "like good tradesmen" sell whatever is "in fashion," but she often stood apart to muse acerbically on her unique position as a *female* purveyor of literary product. Once, surveying the panoply of contemporary male playwrights, she declared that "except for our most unimitable Laureate [Dryden], I dare say I know of none that write at such a formidable rate, but that a woman may well hope to reach their greatest heights." "Formidable rate" suggests both speed and skill; Behn made good on both boasts, producing twenty plays in twenty years, along with much poetry (including fervent pro-Stuart propaganda), copious translations, one of the earliest epistolary novels in English, and a cluster of innovative shorter fiction. In her range and her dexterity, she approached the stature of the "unimitable Laureate" himself, who knew her and praised her repeatedly. With her greatest successes—the comedy *The Rover* (1677), the novella *Oroonoko* (1688)—she secured both an audience and a reputation that continued without pause well into the following century.

Other pieces worked less well. Changes in literary fashion often obliged Behn to try new modes; she switched to fiction, for example, in the 1680s, when plays became less lucrative. Out of her vicissitudes—professional and personal, amorous, financial, literary—she fashioned a formidable celebrity, becoming the object of endless speculation in talk and in ink. "I value fame," she once wrote, and she cultivated it by what seemed an unprecedented frankness. ("All women together," wrote Virginia Woolf, "ought to let flowers fall upon the grave of Aphra Behn . . . for it was she who earned them the right to speak their minds.") In an age of libertines, when men like Rochester paraded their varied couplings in verse couplets, Behn undertook to proclaim and to analyze women's sexual desire, as manifested in her characters and in herself. Her disclosures, though, were intricately orchestrated. Living and writing at the center of a glamorous literary circle, Behn may have fostered, as the critic Janet Todd suggests, the "fantasy of a golden age of sexual and social openness," but she performed it for her readers rather than falling for it herself. Throughout her work Behn adroitly conceals the "self" that she purports to show and sell. She sometimes likens herself to those other female denizens of the theater, the mask-wearing prostitutes who roamed the audience in search of customers. The critic Catherine Gallagher has argued that Behn's literary persona—defiant, vulnerable, hypnotic—functions like the prostitute's vizard, promising the woman's "availability" as commodity while at the same time implying "the impenetrability of the controlling mind" behind the mask.

In Gallagher's reckoning, as in Woolf's, Behn's total career is more important than any particular work it produced. This is fitting tribute to a writer who, in an era of spectacular self-performers (Charles II, Dryden, Rochester), brought off, by virtue of her gender and her art, one of the most intricate performances of all. That performance now looks set for a long second run. After a hiatus in the nineteenth century, when both the writer and the work were dismissed as indecent, Behn's fame has undergone extraordinary revival. She dominates cultural-studies discourse as both a topic and a set of texts. The texts in particular are worth attending to: many are as astonishing as the career that engendered them.

The Disappointment[1]

    One day the amorous Lysander,
    By an impatient passion swayed,
    Surprised fair Cloris, that loved maid,
    Who could defend herself no longer.
5   All things did with his love conspire;
    The gilded planet of the day,
    In his gay chariot drawn by fire,
    Was now descending to the sea,
    And left no light to guide the world,
10   But what from Cloris' brighter eyes was hurled.

    In a lone thicket made for love,
    Silent as yielding maid's consent,

1. Behn based this poem partly on a French source, *Sur une impuissance* (1661), itself derived in part from Ovid's poem on impotence in "Amores," which also provided the model for Rochester's "Imperfect" Enjoyment (see page 1083). Behn's poem and Rochester's first appeared in the same volume, *Poems on Several Occasions* (1680); she later included hers, with alterations, in her own collection, *Poems on Several Occasions* (1684).

She with a charming languishment
Permits his force, yet gently strove;
15 Her hands his bosom softly meet,
But not to put him back designed,
Rather to draw 'em² on inclined;
Whilst he lay trembling at her feet,
Resistance 'tis in vain to show;
20 She wants° the power to say, "Ah! What d'ye do?"   lacks

Her bright eyes sweet, and yet severe,
Where love and shame confusedly strive,
Fresh vigor to Lysander give;
And breathing faintly in his ear,
25 She cried, "Cease, cease your vain desire,
Or I'll call out—what would you do?
My dearer honor even to you
I cannot, must not give—retire,
Or take this life, whose chiefest part
30 I gave you with the conquest of my heart."

But he as much unused to fear,
As he was capable of love,
The blessed minutes to improve,
Kisses her mouth, her neck, her hair;
35 Each touch her new desire alarms,
His burning trembling hand he pressed
Upon her swelling snowy breast,
While she lay panting in his arms.
All her unguarded beauties lie
40 The spoils and trophies of the enemy.

And now without respect or fear,
He seeks the object of his vows,
(His love no modesty allows)
By swift degrees advancing—where
45 His daring hand that altar seized,
Where gods of love do sacrifice:
That awful° throne, that paradise   awe-inspiring
Where rage is calmed, and anger pleased;
That fountain where delight still flows,
50 And gives the universal world repose.

Her balmy lips encountering his,
Their bodies, as their souls, are joined;
Where both in transports unconfined
Extend themselves upon the moss.
55 Cloris half dead and breathless lay;

---

2. Behn's earlier version reads "him."

Her soft eyes cast a humid light,
Such as divides the day and night;
Or falling stars, whose fires decay:
And now no signs of life she shows,
60   But what in short-breathed sighs returns and goes.

He saw how at her length she lay;
He saw her rising bosom bare;
Her loose thin robes, through which appear
A shape designed for love and play;
65   Abandoned by her pride and shame,
She does her softest joys dispense,
Offering her virgin innocence
A victim to love's sacred flame;
While the o'er-ravished shepherd lies
70   Unable to perform the sacrifice.

Ready to taste a thousand joys,
The too transported hapless swain[3]
Found the vast pleasure turned to pain;
Pleasure which too much love destroys.
75   The willing garments by he laid,
And Heaven all opened to his view,
Mad to possess, himself he threw
On the defenseless lovely maid.
But oh what envying god conspires
80   To snatch his power, yet leave him the desire!

Nature's support[4] (without whose aid
She can no human being give)
Itself now wants the art to live.
Faintness its slackened nerves invade.
85   In vain the enraged youth essayed
To call its fleeting vigor back,
No motion 'twill from motion take.
Excess of love his love betrayed.
In vain he toils, in vain commands;
90   The insensible[5] fell weeping in his hand.

In this so amorous cruel strife,
Where love and fate were too severe,
The poor Lysander in despair
Renounced his reason with his life.
95   Now all the brisk and active fire
That should the nobler part inflame,
Served to increase his rage and shame,
And left no spark for new desire.
Not all her naked charms could move

---

3. In English pastoral poetry, this is the conventional
term for the shepherd/lover.

4. I.e., the erect penis.
5. The unfeeling object.

100   Or calm that rage that had debauched° his love.   *corrupted*

Cloris returning from the trance
Which love and soft desire had bred,
Her timorous hand she gently laid
(Or° guided by design or chance)   *either*
105   Upon that fabulous Priapus,⁶
That potent god, as poets feign;
But never did young shepherdess,
Gathering of fern upon the plain,
More nimbly draw her fingers back,
110   Finding beneath the verdant leaves a snake,

Than Cloris her fair hand withdrew,
Finding that god of her desires
Disarmed of all his awful fires,
And cold as flowers bathed in the morning dew.
115   Who can the nymph's confusion guess?
The blood forsook the hinder place,
And strewed with blushes all her face,
Which both disdain and shame expressed.
And from Lysander's arms she fled,
120   Leaving him fainting on the gloomy bed.

Like lightning through the grove she hies,
Or Daphne from the Delphic god,⁷
No print upon the grassy road
She leaves, to instruct pursuing eyes.
125   The wind that wantoned in her hair,
And with her ruffled garments played,
Discovered in the flying maid
All that the gods e'er made, if fair.
So Venus, when her love was slain,
130   With fear and haste flew o'er the fatal plain.⁸

The nymph's resentments none but I
Can well imagine or condole.
But none can guess Lysander's soul,
But those who swayed his destiny.
135   His silent griefs swell up to storms,
And not one god his fury spares;
He cursed his birth, his fate, his stars;
But more the shepherdess's charms,
Whose soft bewitching influence
140   Had damned him to the hell of impotence.

1680

---

6. Greek god of male fertility, often depicted as possessing
a permanent erection.
7. Apollo, who pursued the nymph Daphne until she was
turned into a laurel tree in order to escape his advances.
8. When her beloved Adonis was wounded by a boar, the
goddess of love rushed to help him, but in vain.

To Lysander,[1] on Some Verses He Writ, and Asking More for His Heart than 'Twas Worth

Take back that heart you with such caution give,
    Take the fond[2] valued trifle back;
I hate love-merchants that a trade would drive;
    And meanly cunning bargains make.

5   I care not how the busy market goes,
    And scorn to chaffer° for a price: *bargain*
Love does one staple° rate on all impose,   *fixed*
    Nor leaves it to the trader's choice.

A heart requires a heart unfeigned and true,
10   Though subtly you advance the price,
And ask a rate that simple love ne'er knew:
    And the free trade monopolize.

An humble slave the buyer must become,
    She must not bate[3] a look or glance,
15   You will have all, or you'll have none;
    See how love's market° you enhance.°   *price / increase*

Is't not enough, I gave you heart for heart,
    But I must add my lips and eyes?
I must no friendly smile or kiss impart;
20   But you must dun[4] me with advice?

And every hour still more unjust you grow.
    Those freedoms you my life deny,
You to Adraste[5] are obliged to show,
    And give her all my rifled° joy.   *stolen*

25   Without control she gazes on that face,
    And all the happy envied night,
In the pleased circle of your fond embrace:
    She takes away the lover's right.

From me she ravishes those silent hours,
30   That are by sacred love my due;
Whilst I in vain accuse the angry powers,
    That make me hopeless love pursue.

Adraste's ears with that dear voice are blest,
    That charms my soul at every sound,
35   And with those love-enchanting touches pressed:
    Which I ne'er felt without a wound.

---

1. "Lysander," the addressee of several of Behn's poems (and, in name at least, the male lover in The Disappointment), has not been identified; the poem suggests that he was a married man.

2. The word meant both "foolish" and "affectionate."
3. Withhold (by way of reducing love's "price").
4. Badger, demand payment from.
5. Apparently his wife.

She has thee all: whilst I with silent grief,
    The fragments of thy softness feel,
Yet dare not blame the happy licensed[6] thief:
40   That does my dear-bought pleasures steal.

Whilst like a glimmering taper still I burn,
    And waste myself in my own flame,
Adraste takes the welcome rich return:
    And leaves me all the hopeless pain.

45 Be just, my lovely swain, and do not take
    Freedoms you'll not to me allow;
Or give Amynta[7] so much freedom back:
    That she may rove as well as you.

Let us then love upon the honest square,[8]
50   Since interest neither have designed.[9]
For the sly gamester,[1] who ne'er plays me fair,
    Must trick for trick expect to find.

1684

To Lysander at the Music-Meeting

It was too much, ye gods, to see and hear,
Receiving wounds both from the eye and ear.
One charm might have secured a victory;
Both, raised the pleasure even to ecstasy.
5 So ravished lovers in each other's arms,
Faint with excess of joy, excess of charms.
Had I but gazed and fed my greedy eyes,
Perhaps you'd pleased no farther than surprise.
That heav'nly form might admiration move,
10 But, not without the music, charmed° with love: *have charmed*
At least so quick the conquest had not been;
You stormed without, and harmony within.
Nor could I listen to the sound alone,
But I alas must look—and was undone:
15 I saw the softness that composed your face,
While your attention heightened every grace:
Your mouth all full of sweetness and content,
And your fine killing eyes of languishment:
Your bosom now and then a sigh would move,
20 (For music has the same effects with love).
Your body easy and all tempting lay,
Inspiring wishes which the eyes betray,
In all that have the fate to glance that way.
A careless and a lovely negligence,

---

6. Permitted (by the marriage license).
7. I.e., the poem's speaker.
8. I.e., by rules that apply to both sides equally.

9. Neither of us has intended to make a profit (on our investment in each other).
1. Trickster or gambler.

25 Did a new charm to every limb dispense.
    So look young angels, listening to the sound,
    When the tuned spheres glad[1] all the heav'ns around:
    So raptured lie amidst the wondering crowd,
    So charmingly extended on a cloud.

30   When from so many ways love's arrows storm,
    Who can the heedless heart defend from harm?
    Beauty and music must the soul disarm;
    Since harmony, like fire to wax, does fit
    The softened heart impressions to admit:

35 As the brisk sounds of war the courage move,
    Music prepares and warms the soul to love.
    But when the kindling sparks such fuel meet,
    No wonder if the flame inspired be great.

                                                1684

A Letter to Mr. Creech at Oxford[1]
Written in the Last Great Frost[2]

    Daphnis, because I am your debtor,
    (And other causes which are better)
    I send you here by debt of letter.
    You should have had a scrap of nonsense,
5   You may remember left at Tonson's.[3]
    (Though by the way that's scurvy rhyme Sir,
    But yet 'twill serve to tag° a line Sir.)   round off
    A *billet-doux*° I had designed then,   sweet note
    But you may think I was in wine then;
10 Because it being cold, you know
    We warmed it with a glass—or so.
    I grant you that shy° wine's the devil,   cheap
    To make one's memory uncivil;
    But when, 'twixt every sparkling cup,
15 I so much brisker wit took up;
    Wit, able to inspire a thinking;
    And make one solemn even in drinking;
    Wit that would charm and stock a poet,
    Even instruct ———[4] who has no wit;
20 Wit that was hearty, true, and loyal,
    Of wit, like Bays'[5] Sir, that's my trial;

---

1. Gladden. In the Ptolemaic view of the universe that Behn invokes here, the heavens were composed of concentric crystalline spheres, whose motion produced a sublime music. Angels could hear it, humans could not.
1. Thomas Creech (1659–1700), classicist and translator. Behn had praised his work in a previous poem, in which (as here) she addresses him by the pastoral name "Daphnis." Here she produces a less solemn piece, explaining why a love letter from her has failed to reach him, and conveying (in the postscript) a compliment from an unnamed well-wisher.
2. The winter of 1683–1684 was so severe that the surface

of the river Thames froze solid.
3. The eminent bookseller Jacob Tonson (1656–1737) had published several of Behn's plays and her *Poems on Several Occasions* (1684). The route through London that Behn traces in this poem would have taken her past Tonson's shop.
4. An in-joke, probably referring to some mutually despised Whig poet.
5. John Dryden, Poet Laureate (so nicknamed because in ancient Rome the laureate wore a wreath of bay leaves); Behn here implies that Dryden sets the standard ("trial") for true wit.

I say 'twas most impossible,
That after that one should be dull.
Therefore because you may not blame me,
25   Take the whole truth as —— shall sa'me.[6]
 From Whitehall[7] Sir, as I was coming,
His sacred Majesty from dunning—
Who oft in debt is, truth to tell,
For Tory farce, or doggerel—[8]
30   When every street as dangerous was,
As ever the Alpian hills° to pass,   *the Alps*
When melted snow and ice confound one,
Whether to break one's neck or drown one,
And *billet-doux* in pocket lay,
35   To drop as° coach should jolt that way,   *whenever*
Near to that place of fame called Temple,[9]
(Which I shall note by sad example)
Where college dunce is cured of simple,[1]
Against that sign of whore called scarlet,[2]
40   My coachman fairly laid pilgarlic.[3]
 Though scribbling fist was out of joint,
And every limb made great complaint;
Yet missing the dear assignation,[4]
Gave me most cause of tribulation.
45   To honest H—le[5] I should have shown ye,
A wit that would be proud t'have known ye;
A wit uncommon, a facetious,
A great admirer of Lucretius.[6]
But transitory hopes do vary,
50   And high designments oft miscarry.
Ambition never climbed so lofty,
But may descend too fair and softly.
But would you'd seen how sneakingly
I looked with this catastrophe.
55   So saucy Whig, when plot broke out,
Dejected hung his sniveling snout;[7]
So Oxford member looked, when Rowley
Kicked out the rebel crew so foully;[8]

6. As Christ shall save me.
7. The royal palace in London; Behn has apparently been trying to collect payment from the king for a poem she wrote in his support.
8. I.e., Charles II frequently owes money to the partisan poets who write for him.
9. A cluster of buildings on Fleet Street containing residences, offices, and lecture halls for lawyers and students.
1. Simplicity, foolishness.
2. The Pope's Head tavern, so nicknamed because anti-Catholic literature identified the Roman church with the "whore . . . in scarlet" of Revelation 17.
3. The word originally denoted baldness (with "a head like peeled garlic"), but had become slang for any unfortunate person.

4. I.e., with Creech.
5. John Hoyle, a rakish lawyer with whom Aphra Behn had carried on a much-talked-about amorous relationship and to whom she had addressed many poems.
6. Roman author of *De rerum natura* (*On the Nature of Things*), which Creech had translated (1683). Lucretius's insistence on worldly pleasure had established him as the patron philosopher of Restoration libertines.
7. Behn imagines a partisan disappointed by the exposure (and hence the failure) of the Rye House plot, an alleged Whig scheme to assassinate the king and his brother in 1683.
8. In March 1681, Charles II (often dubbed "Rowley" in casual talk and satiric ballads) dismissed the Parliament at Oxford to frustrate the ambitions of the Whig faction.

60   So Perkin, once that god of Wapping,
     Whom slippery turn of state took napping,
     From hopes of James the Second fell
     Into the native scoundrel.[9]
     So lover looked of joy defeated,
     When too much fire his vigor cheated.[1]
65   Even so looked I, when bliss-depriving
     Was caused by over-hasty driving.
     Who saw me could not choose but think,
     I looked like brawn in sousing drink,[2]
     Or Lazarello[3] who was showed
70   For a strange fish, to the gaping crowd.
         Thus you by fate (to me, sinister)
     At shop of book my *billet* missed Sir.
     And home I went as discontent,
     As a new routed° Parliament,   *dismissed*
75   Not seeing Daphnis ere he went.
     And sure his grief beyond expressing,
     Of joy proposed to want the blessing.[4]
     Therefore to pardon pray incline,
     Since disappointment all was mine.
80   Of Hell we have no other notion,
     Than all the joys of Heaven's privation;
     So Sir with recommendations fervent,
     I rest your very humble servant.

Postscript

     On Twelfth Night Sir, by that good token,
85   When lamentable cake was broken,[5]
     You had a friend, a man of wit,
     A man whom I shall ne'er forget,
     For every word he did impart,
     'Twas worth the keeping in a heart.
90   True Tory all! and when he spoke,
     A god of wit, though man in look.
     "To this your friend Daphnis, address
     The humblest of my services.
     Tell him how much—yet do not, too.

9. "Perkin" is Charles II's illegitimate son James, Duke of Monmouth, who (like the medieval pretender Perkin Warbeck) claimed that he was the legitimate heir to the crown; his cause was at one point popular in the rough neighborhood of Wapping. Had he made good on his claim, he (rather than his like-named uncle the Duke of York) would have become James II. Disappointed of that prospect, Behn suggests, he has now "fallen back" into what he truly is: a born rascal.
1. I.e., because of premature ejaculation.
2. Like pickled pig's flesh, bruised and discolored.
3. Hero of Juan de Luna's picaresque narrative *Lazarillo de Tormes*, who is rescued in fishermen's nets after a shipwreck and displayed as a sea monster.
4. Certainly he, having missed out on a promised pleasure, suffers inexpressible grief.
5. On the Twelfth Night of Christmas (6 January, "lamentable," perhaps, because it marked the holiday's conclusion), the traditional festivities included the cutting of a cake in which a pea and bean had been concealed. The recipients of the "prize" pieces presided over the celebration as king and queen (cf. the poem's final line, where Behn and Creech are linked in praise).

95   My vast esteem no words can show.
        Tell him—that he is worthy—you.”

                                                    1685

To the Fair Clarinda, Who Made Love to Me, Imagined More than Woman

Fair lovely maid, or if that title be
Too weak, too feminine for nobler thee,
Permit a name that more approaches truth,
And let me call thee, lovely charming youth.
5   This last will justify my soft complaint,
    While that may serve to lessen my constraint;
    And without blushes I the youth pursue,
    When so much beauteous woman is in view.
    Against thy charms we struggle but in vain,
10 With thy deluding form thou giv'st us pain,
    While the bright nymph betrays us to the swain.[1]
    In pity to our sex sure thou wert sent,
    That we might love, and yet be innocent:
    For sure no crime with thee we can commit;
15 Or if we should—thy form excuses it.
    For who that gathers fairest flowers believes
    A snake lies hid beneath the fragrant leaves.
        Thou beauteous wonder of a different kind,
    Soft Cloris with the dear Alexis[2] joined;
20 Whene'er the manly part of thee would plead
    Thou tempts us with the image of the maid,
    While we the noblest passions do extend
    The love to Hermes, Aphrodite the friend.[3]

                                                    1688

John Wilmot, Earl of Rochester
1647–1680

In one of his many notorious escapades, John Wilmot, Earl of Rochester, drunkenly smashed to pieces one of the king's costliest timekeepers. He always lived at odds with ordinary time, mostly ahead of it: he became earl at age ten, when his father died; received his M.A. from Oxford at fourteen; conducted a Grand Tour of Europe during the next three years; tried to abduct his future wife Elizabeth Malet (a much-sought woman of wealth, wit, and beauty) when he was eighteen, and was briefly imprisoned for the attempt; married her at twenty; and died, after long libertinage and precipitate piety, at thirty-three. Rochester's wit and beauty, the stupendous energies of his mind (erudite, inventive), of his language (adroit,

---

1. The conventional pastoral term for a male lover or a country lad.
2. "Cloris" is female, "Alexis" male.

3. Named after the offspring of these two gods, a hermaphrodite combines the characteristics of both sexes.

obscene), of his body (alcoholic, bisexual), and of his convictions (hedonistic, atheistic) made him the fascination of the Restoration court, whose proclivities for theatrics, for combat, and for amorous entanglement he pushed to matchless extremes. Theatrics: Rochester wrote plays of his own and produced plays by others; he tutored the stage novice Elizabeth Barry, soon to become the greatest actress of the age (they carried on a volatile affair, and had a daughter); at times he could don a disguise himself and play a role so successfully (in order to go underground, to escape punishment, to bring off a seduction) that close friends could not recognize him. Combat: Rochester distinguished himself for courage by plunging into the thick of the fighting during several sea battles; he once disgraced himself for cowardice in running away during a nocturnal street brawl, "frighted" (he later wrote) "at my own mischiefs" and leaving one of his own defenders dead. In the lesser combats of the court, those endless verbal cutting contests of improvised insult and impromptu verse, Rochester was virtually unbeatable (though the king, when cut, could cut back: the earl's status shifted often and quickly between favorite and outcast). Amorous entanglement: Rochester's letters to his wife bespeak a marriage of extraordinary tenderness; his poems boast a career of fornication scarcely credible in its range and ferocity. In 1680, ill and exhausted, Rochester left London for his ancestral country estate where, frighted by his own mischiefs on a grander scale, he pursued a highly publicized course of penitence under the tutelage of the clergyman Gilbert Burnet, who later published a detailed account of their conversations. The authenticity of this deathbed conversion was questioned then, and has been questioned since, but its results were real enough: Rochester asked his mother to burn his papers, and she did. Fewer than a hundred poems survive. Rochester had never troubled to publish any of them himself; a pirated collection appeared a few months after his death. Yet these pieces, and the conflicting accounts of the life that produced them, have been enough to make him last. Soon after his death, the poet Aphra Behn claimed in verse to have received a visit from his "lovely phantom." "The great, the god-like Rochester" comes before her in order both to praise and to correct her poetry. Since then he has haunted many—pietists, poets, and others—as object of veneration, or reproach, or both together: as admonitory example, verbal virtuoso, extraordinary mortal.

Against Constancy

Tell me no more of constancy,
    The frivolous pretense
Of cold age, narrow jealousy,
    Disease, and want of sense.

5   Let duller fools, on whom kind chance
    Some easy heart has thrown,
Despairing higher to advance,
    Be kind to one alone.

Old men and weak, whose idle flame
10   Their own defects discovers,
Since changing can but spread their shame,
    Ought to be constant lovers.

But we, whose hearts do justly swell
    With no vainglorious pride,
15   Who know how we in love excel,
    Long to be often tried.

Then bring my bath, and strew my bed,
    As each kind night returns;
I'll change a mistress till I'm dead—
20   And fate change me to worms.

The Disabled Debauchee

As some brave admiral, in former war
    Deprived of force, but pressed with courage still,
Two rival fleets appearing from afar,
    Crawls to the top of an adjacent hill;

5   From whence, with thoughts full of concern, he views
    The wise and daring conduct of the fight,
Whilst each bold action to his mind renews
    His present glory and his past delight;

From his fierce eyes flashes of fire he throws,
10   As from black clouds when lightning breaks away;
Transported, thinks himself amidst the foes,
    And absent, yet enjoys the bloody day;

So, when my days of impotence approach,
    And I'm by pox and wine's unlucky chance
15   Forced from the pleasing billows of debauch
    On the dull shore of lazy temperance,

My pains at least some respite shall afford
    While I behold the battles you maintain
When fleets of glasses sail about the board,[1]
20   From whose broadsides volleys of wit shall rain.

Nor let the sight of honorable scars,
    Which my too forward valor did procure,
Frighten new-listed soldiers from the wars:
    Past joys have more than paid what I endure.

25   Should any youth (worth being drunk) prove nice,
    And from his fair inviter meanly shrink,
'Twill please the ghost of my departed Vice[2]
    If, at my counsel, he repent and drink.

Or should some cold-complexioned sot forbid,
30   With his dull morals, our bold night-alarms,
I'll fire his blood by telling what I did
    When I was strong and able to bear arms.

1. I.e., wine glasses passed around the table.
2. A character bearing this name had been a staple figure in medieval morality plays, as the comic, scoffing incarnation of depravity.

I'll tell of whores attacked, their lords at home;
    Bawds' quarters beaten up, and fortress won;
35   Windows demolished, watches overcome;
    And handsome ills by my contrivance done.

Nor shall our love-fits, Chloris,[3] be forgot,
    When each the well-looked linkboy[4] strove t' enjoy,
And the best kiss was the deciding lot
40   Whether the boy fucked you, or I the boy.

With tales like these I will such thoughts inspire
    As to important mischief shall incline:
I'll make him long some ancient church to fire,
    And fear no lewdness he's called to by wine.

45   Thus, statesmanlike, I'll saucily impose,
    And safe from action, valiantly advise;
Sheltered in impotence, urge you to blows,
    And being good for nothing else, be wise.

1675?   1680

Song

Love a woman? You're an ass!
    'Tis a most insipid passion
To choose out for your happiness
    The silliest part of God's creation.

5   Let the porter and the groom,
    Things designed for dirty slaves,
Drudge in fair Aurelia's womb
    To get supplies for age and graves.

Farewell, woman! I intend
10   Henceforth every night to sit
With my lewd, well-natured friend,
    Drinking to engender wit.

Then give me health, wealth, mirth, and wine,
    And, if busy love entrenches,
15   There's a sweet, soft page of mine
    Does the trick worth forty wenches.

                                           1680

The Imperfect Enjoyment

Naked she lay, clasped in my longing arms,
I filled with love, and she all over charms;
Both equally inspired with eager fire,
Melting through kindness, flaming in desire.

---

3. A woman's name, common in pastoral verse (and in Rochester's).
4. A boy employed to accompany walkers on the city streets at night, lighting their way by means of a torch ("link").

5   With arms, legs, lips close clinging to embrace,
      She clips me to her breast, and sucks me to her face.
      Her nimble tongue, Love's lesser lightning, played
      Within my mouth, and to my thoughts conveyed
      Swift orders that I should prepare to throw
10   The all-dissolving thunderbolt below.
      My fluttering soul, sprung with the pointed kiss,
      Hangs hovering o'er her balmy brinks of bliss.
      But whilst her busy hand would guide that part
      Which should convey my soul up to her heart,
15   In liquid raptures I dissolve all o'er,
      Melt into sperm, and spend at every pore.
      A touch from any part of her had done 't:
      Her hand, her foot, her very look's a cunt.
          Smiling, she chides in a kind murmuring noise,
20   And from her body wipes the clammy joys,
      When, with a thousand kisses wandering o'er
      My panting bosom, "Is there then no more?"
      She cries. "All this to love and rapture's due;
      Must we not pay a debt to pleasure too?"
25   But I, the most forlorn, lost man alive,
      To show my wished obedience vainly strive:
      I sigh, alas! and kiss, but cannot swive.°   *screw*
      Eager desires confound my first intent,
      Succeeding shame does more success prevent,
30   And rage at last confirms me impotent.
      Ev'n her fair hand, which might bid heat return
      To frozen age, and make cold hermits burn,
      Applied to my dead cinder, warms no more
      Than fire to ashes could past flames restore.
35   Trembling, confused, despairing, limber, dry,
      A wishing, weak, unmoving lump I lie.
      This dart of love, whose piercing point, oft tried,
      With virgin blood ten thousand maids have dyed,
      Which nature still directed with such art
40   That it through every cunt reached every heart—
      Stiffly resolved, 'twould carelessly invade
      Woman or man, nor ought° its fury stayed:°   *anything / stopped*
      Where'er it pierced, a cunt it found or made—
      Now languid lies in this unhappy hour,
45   Shrunk up and sapless like a withered flower.
          Thou treacherous, base deserter of my flame,
      False to my passion, fatal to my fame,
      Through what mistaken magic dost thou prove
      So true to lewdness, so untrue to love?
50   What oyster-cinder-beggar-common whore
      Didst thou e'er fail in all thy life before?
      When vice, disease, and scandal lead the way,
      With what officious haste doest thou obey!

Like a rude, roaring hector° in the streets   *bully*
55   Who scuffles, cuffs, and justles all he meets,
But if his king or country claim his aid,
The rakehell villain shrinks and hides his head;
Ev'n so thy brutal valor is displayed,
Breaks every stew,° does each small whore invade,   *brothel*
60   But when great Love the onset does command,
Base recreant to thy prince, thou dar'st not stand.
Worst part of me, and henceforth hated most,
Through all the town a common fucking post,
On whom each whore relieves her tingling cunt
65   As hogs on gates do rub themselves and grunt,
Mayst thou to ravenous chancres° be a prey,   *syphilis sores*
Or in consuming weepings waste away;
May strangury and stone[1] thy days attend;
May'st thou never piss, who didst refuse to spend
70   When all my joys did on false thee depend.
    And may ten thousand abler pricks agree
    To do the wronged Corinna right for thee.

                                       1680

Upon Nothing

Nothing! thou elder brother even to Shade:
Thou hadst a being ere the world was made,
And well fixed, art alone of ending not afraid.

Ere Time and Place were, Time and Place were not,
5   When primitive Nothing Something straight begot;
Then all proceeded from the great united What.

Something, the general attribute of all,
Severed from thee, its sole original,
Into thy boundless self must undistinguished fall;

10   Yet Something did thy mighty power command,
And from thy fruitful Emptiness's hand
Snatched men, beasts, birds, fire, water, air, and land.

Matter, the wicked'st offspring of thy race,
By Form assisted, flew from thy embrace,
15   And rebel Light obscured thy reverend dusky face.

With Form and Matter, Time and Place did join;
Body, thy foe, with these did leagues combine
To spoil thy peaceful realm, and ruin all thy line;

But turncoat Time assists the foe in vain,
20   And bribed by thee, destroys their short-lived reign,
And to thy hungry womb drives back thy slaves again.

1. Painful diseases of the bladder and urinary tract that block the flow of urine.

Though mysteries are barred from laic° eyes,   *uninitiated*
And the divine alone with warrant pries
Into thy bosom, where the truth in private lies,

25   Yet this of thee the wise may truly say:
Thou from the virtuous nothing dost delay,
And to be part of thee the wicked wisely pray.

Great Negative, how vainly would the wise
Inquire, define, distinguish, teach, devise,
30   Didst thou not stand to point their blind philosophies!

Is or Is Not, the two great ends of Fate,
And True or False, the subject of debate,
That perfect or destroy the vast designs of state—

When they have racked the politician's breast,
35   Within thy bosom most securely rest,
And when reduced to thee, are least unsafe and best.

But Nothing, why does Something still permit
That sacred monarchs should in council sit
With persons highly thought at best for nothing fit,

40   While weighty Something modestly abstains
From princes' coffers, and from statesmen's brains,
And Nothing there like stately Nothing reigns?

Nothing! who dwellst with fools in grave disguise,
For whom they reverend shapes and forms devise,
45   Lawn¹ sleeves and furs and gowns, when they like thee look wise:

French truth, Dutch prowess, British policy,
Hibernian learning, Scotch civility,
Spaniards' dispatch, Danes' wit are mainly seen in thee;

The great man's gratitude to his best friend,
50   Kings' promises, whores' vows—towards thee they bend,
Flow swiftly into thee, and in thee ever end.

1678   1679

A Satyr¹ Against Reason and Mankind

Were I (who to my cost already am
One of those strange, prodigious creatures, man)
A spirit free to choose, for my own share,
What case of flesh and blood I pleased to wear,
5   I'd be a dog, a monkey, or a bear,
Or anything but that vain animal
Who is so proud of being rational.
The senses are too gross, and he'll contrive

---

1. Linen; worn (like the furs and gowns) as a mark of rank   1. Possibly a pun, identifying both the genre (satire) and
by eminent professionals: lawyers, scholars, statesmen,   the speaker (a satyr: half-man, half-animal).
etc.

A sixth, to contradict the other five,
10 And before certain instinct, will prefer
Reason, which fifty times for one does err;
Reason, an *ignis fatuus*[2] in the mind,
Which, leaving light of nature, sense, behind,
Pathless and dangerous wandering ways it takes
15 Through error's fenny bogs and thorny brakes;
Whilst the misguided follower climbs with pain
Mountains of whimseys, heaped in his own brain;
Stumbling from thought to thought, falls headlong down
Into doubt's boundless sea, where, like to drown,
20 Books bear him up awhile, and make him try
To swim with bladders of philosophy;
In hopes still to o'ertake th' escaping light,
The vapor dances in his dazzling sight
Till, spent, it leaves him to eternal night.
25 Then old age and experience, hand in hand,
Lead him to death, and make him understand,
After a search so painful and so long,
That all his life he has been in the wrong.
Huddled in dirt the reasoning engine lies,
30 Who was so proud, so witty, and so wise.
    Pride drew him in, as cheats their bubbles° catch,   *victims*
And made him venture to be made a wretch.
His wisdom did his happiness destroy,
Aiming to know that world he should enjoy.
35 And wit was his vain, frivolous pretense
Of pleasing others at his own expense,
For wits are treated just like common whores:
First they're enjoyed, and then kicked out of doors.
The pleasure past, a threatening doubt remains
40 That frights th' enjoyer with succeeding pains.
Women and men of wit are dangerous tools,
And ever fatal to admiring fools:
Pleasure allures, and when the fops escape,
'Tis not that they're belov'd, but fortunate,
45 And therefore what they fear at heart, they hate.
    But now, methinks, some formal band and beard[3]
Takes me to task. Come on, sir; I'm prepared.
    "Then, by your favor, anything that's writ
Against this gibing, jingling knack called wit
50 Likes° me abundantly; but you take care   *pleases*
Upon this point, not to be too severe.
Perhaps my muse were fitter for this part,

2. Literally "foolish fire": a marshland phosphorescence that, appearing now here and now there, was thought to be created by sprites to mislead night travelers.
3. I.e., clergyman, wearing these marks of office. In 1675 one clergyman in particular, the king's chaplain Edward Stillingfleet, had denounced in a sermon an earlier version of Rochester's *Satyr*, prompting the poet to alter and add some portions of the dialogue that follows.

For I profess I can be very smart
On wit, which I abhor with all my heart.
55   I long to lash it in some sharp essay,
But your grand indiscretion bids me stay
And turns my tide of ink another way.
    "What rage ferments in your degenerate mind
To make you rail at reason and mankind?
60   Blest, glorious man! to whom alone kind heaven
An everlasting soul has freely given,
Whom his great Maker took such care to make
That from himself he did the image take
And this fair frame in shining reason dressed
65   To dignify his nature above beast;
Reason, by whose aspiring influence
We take a flight beyond material sense,
Dive into mysteries, then soaring pierce
The flaming limits of the universe,
70   Search heaven and hell, find out what's acted there,
And give the world true grounds of hope and fear."
    Hold, mighty man, I cry, all this we know
From the pathetic pen of Ingelo,
From Patrick's *Pilgrim*, Stillingfleet's replies,[4]
75   And 'tis this very reason I despise:
This supernatural gift, that makes a mite
Think he's the image of the infinite,
Comparing his short life, void of all rest,
To the eternal and the ever blest;
80   This busy, puzzling stirrer-up of doubt
That frames deep mysteries, then finds 'em out,
Filling with frantic crowds of thinking fools
Those reverend bedlams,° colleges and schools;   °*madhouses*
Borne on whose wings, each heavy sot can pierce
85   The limits of the boundless universe;
So charming ointments make an old witch fly
And bear a crippled carcass through the sky.
'Tis this exalted power, whose business lies
In nonsense and impossibilities,
90   This made a whimsical philosopher
Before the spacious world, his tub prefer,[5]
And we have modern cloistered coxcombs who
Retire to think, 'cause they have nought to do.
    But thoughts are given for action's government;
95   Where action ceases, thought's impertinent.
Our sphere of action is life's happiness,
And he who thinks beyond, thinks like an ass.

---

4. Rochester names three pious inspirational writers: Nathaniel Ingelo (?1621–1683); Simon Patrick, whose *Parable of the Pilgrim* appeared in 1664; and Stillingfleet, Rochester's clerical critic.

5. Diogenes (c. 400–325 B.C.), Greek philosopher who supposedly lived in an earthenware tub, as an emblem of his scorn for the shallowness of more opulent modes of life.

Thus, whilst against false reasoning I inveigh,
I own[6] right reason, which I would obey:
100 That reason which distinguishes by sense
And gives us rules of good and ill from thence,
That bounds desires with a reforming will
To keep 'em more in vigor, not to kill.
Your reason hinders, mine helps to enjoy,
105 Renewing appetites yours would destroy.
My reason is my friend, yours is a cheat;
Hunger calls out, my reason bids me eat;
Perversely, yours your appetite does mock:
This asks for food, that answers, "What's o'clock?"
110 This plain distinction, sir, your doubt secures:
'Tis not true reason I despise, but yours.
        Thus I think reason righted, but for man,
I'll ne'er recant; defend him if you can.
For all his pride and his philosophy,
115 'Tis evident beasts are, in their degree,
As wise at least, and better far than he.
Those creatures are the wisest who attain,
By surest means, the ends at which they aim.
If therefore Jowler[7] finds and kills his hares
120 Better than Meres[8] supplies committee chairs,
Though one's a statesman, th' other but a hound,
Jowler, in justice, would be wiser found.
        You see how far man's wisdom here extends;
Look next if human nature makes amends:
125 Whose principles most generous are, and just,
And to whose morals you would sooner trust.
Be judge yourself, I'll bring it to the test.
Which is the basest creature, man or beast?
Birds feed on birds, beasts on each other prey,
130 But savage man alone does man betray.
Pressed by necessity, they kill for food;
Man undoes man to do himself no good.
With teeth and claws by nature armed, they hunt
Nature's allowance, to supply their want.
135 But man, with smiles, embraces, friendship, praise,
Inhumanly his fellow's life betrays;
With voluntary pains works his distress,
Not through necessity, but wantonness.
        For hunger or for love they fight and tear,
140 Whilst wretched man is still in arms for fear.
For fear he arms, and is of arms afraid,
By fear to fear successively betrayed;

6. Acknowledge. "Right reason" refers to natural instinct
or common sense, as opposed to the more elaborate
modes of thought Rochester is attacking.
7. A dog's name, emphasizing the animal's appetites.

8. Sir Thomas Meres (1634–1715), politician noted for
his energy, efficacy, and self-serving flexibility in questions of party allegiance.

Base fear, the source whence his best passions came:
His boasted honor, and his dear-bought fame;
145   That lust of power, to which he's such a slave,
And for the which alone he dares be brave;
To which his various projects are designed;
Which makes him generous, affable, and kind;
For which he takes such pains to be thought wise,
150   And screws his actions in a forced disguise,
Leading a tedious life in misery
Under laborious, mean hypocrisy.
Look to the bottom of his vast design,
Wherein man's wisdom, power, and glory join:
155   The good he acts, the ill he does endure,
'Tis all from fear, to make himself secure.
Merely for safety, after fame we thirst,
For all men would be cowards if they durst.
          And honesty's against all common sense:
160   Men must be knaves, 'tis in their own defense.
Mankind's dishonest; if you think it fair
Amongst known cheats to play upon the square,
You'll be undone.
Nor can weak truth your reputation save:
165   The knaves will all agree to call you knave.
Wronged shall he live, insulted o'er, oppressed,
Who dares be less a villain than the rest.
          Thus, sir, you see what human nature craves:
Most men are cowards, all men should be knaves.
170   The difference lies, as far as I can see,
Not in the thing itself, but the degree,
And all the subject matter of debate
Is only: Who's a knave of the first rate?
          All this with indignation have I hurled
175   At the pretending part of the proud world,
Who, swollen with selfish vanity, devise
False freedoms, holy cheats, and formal lies
Over their fellow slaves to tyrannize.
But if in court so just a man there be
180   (In court a just man, yet unknown to me)
Who does his needful flattery direct,
Not to oppress and ruin, but protect
(Since flattery, which way soever laid,
Is still a tax on that unhappy trade);
185   If so upright a statesman you can find,
Whose passions bend to his unbiased mind,
Who does his arts and policies apply
To raise his country, not his family,
Nor, whilst his pride owned avarice withstands,
190   Receives close bribes through friends' corrupted hands—
          Is there a churchman who on God relies;

Whose life, his faith and doctrine justifies?
Not one blown up with vain prelatic pride,
Who, for reproof of sins, does man deride;
195   Whose envious heart makes preaching a pretense,
With his obstreperous, saucy eloquence,
To chide at kings, and rail at men of sense;
None of that sensual tribe whose talents lie
In avarice, pride, sloth, and gluttony;
200   Who hunt good livings, but abhor good lives;
Whose lust exalted to that height arrives
They act adultery with their own wives,
And ere a score of years completed be,
Can from the lofty pulpit proudly see
205   Half a large parish their own progeny;
Nor doting bishop who would be adored
For domineering at the council board,
A greater fop in business at fourscore,
Fonder of serious toys, affected more,
210   Than the gay, glittering fool at twenty proves
With all his noise, his tawdry clothes, and loves;
    But a meek, humble man of honest sense,
Who, preaching peace, does practice continence;
Whose pious life's a proof he does believe
215   Mysterious truths, which no man can conceive.
If upon earth there dwell such God-like men,
I'll here recant my paradox to them,
Adore those shrines of virtue, homage pay,
And, with the rabble world, their laws obey.
220   If such there be, yet grant me this at least:
Man differs more from man, than man from beast.

1674–1676   1679

⊷ ⚎⚭⚎ ⊶

William Wycherley
1641–1715

The plot of *The Country Wife* turns on a trick. The rakish Harry Horner devises a tactic calculated to secure both a cover-story and a kinky enhancement for his future seductions of other men's wives. He starts a rumor going round to the effect that he has become a eunuch; husbands will henceforth not suspect him, and wives, he trusts, will be intrigued. Early in the play, it becomes clear that Horner has tested his new disguise by making a visit to the theater. "Come," one of his friends remarks, "your appearance at the play yesterday has, I hope, hardened you for the future" as to the social consequences of his sexless new reputation. "Did I not bear it bravely?" asks Horner, pleased. "With a most theatrical impudence," answers his friend.

    In London playhouses of the 1660s and the 1670s, theatrical impudence was in high supply. People came to watch not only the performers, but also each other. Pepys records a telling anecdote (so telling that it is cited also, more compactly, within a fuller discussion of Restoration theater in the introduction to this section, p. 1022). Attending a play one evening, he found himself distracted throughout the performance by the libertine Sir Charles Sedley, seated nearby in conversation with two women.

> And one of the ladies would and did sit with her mask on, all the play and, being exceedingly witty as ever I heard woman, did talk most pleasantly with him; but was, I believe, a virtuous woman and of quality. He would fain know who she was, but she would not tell; yet did give him many pleasant hints of her knowledge of him, by that means setting his brains at work to find out who she was, and did give him leave to use all means to find out who she was but pulling off her mask. He was mighty witty and she also, making sport of him very inoffensively, that a more pleasant rencontre I never heard. By that means lost the pleasure of the play wholly . . .

But that loss hardly seems to matter, in comparison with the pleasure of the playlet Pepys has witnessed within the audience. Masks of the kind this woman wears were a widespread item of Restoration fashion. Characters in the *Country Wife* mention them obsessively, in part because they were worn both by "virtuous" women and by prostitutes, with the tantalizing effect of rendering those two human categories not quite distinguishable from one another. In Pepys's anecdote, man and woman engage in a contest for power grounded in wit, concealment, and artifice; the new plays on stage during the Restoration teemed with just such sexually charged encounters and combats. For purposes of theatrical impudence and strategic experiment, Horner could not have picked for himself a better venue.

Neither could William Wycherley. He wrote four comedies while in his early thirties. The last two—*The Country Wife* (1675) and *The Plain Dealer* (1676)—brought him to the early high point of a career that sloped rather steeply on either side. Before these successes he had been a law student, soldier, courtier, traveler in France, and convert to Catholicism. In their wake he was widely celebrated as the deftest wielder alive of those gifts that Dryden enumerated in a single memorable line: "The satire, wit, and strength of manly Wycherley." "Manly" was the name of the forthright protagonist in *The Plain Dealer*; the adjective alternated with "brawny" as the most popular epithets for this vigorous and accomplished playwright in his prime. But by the time Dryden wrote the line, in 1694, it applied more readily to the work than to the man. Before Wycherley turned forty, a serious illness had left his memory permanently damaged and an imprudent marriage with a widowed countess had cost him much in money, serenity, and the patronage of Charles II and his court. He spent years mired in debt, received temporary relief in the form of a pension from that temporary king James II, and found more reliable respite in the estate he inherited from his father in 1697. In old age he published a failed book of ungainly poems, held literary court at Will's Coffee House (where Dryden had previously presided), and basked in the attention of the young, ambitious Alexander Pope. Eleven days before his death he married a second time. His estate passed to his young widow and hence to his cousin, her secret lover; they had spent his last days scheming to secure it.

In the *Country Wife*, alliances prove comparably shifty. The wits (Horner and his friends), though ostensibly relentless in their pursuit of women, nonetheless seem often more interested in their transactions with each other. They array themselves against the "cits"—the prudent, prosperous businessmen of London—and chase after their desirable, precariously domesticated spouses and sisters. Horner the London rake works his charms on Margery the country wife, who proves cheerfully, even ingeniously susceptible. A group of erotically agitated women—headed by the aptly named Lady Fidget—collude with Horner in his deceit, disappear behind closed doors to savor his emphatically noneunuchoid sexuality while pretending to sample his china, and finally team up, as a suddenly "virtuous gang," to reproach him for his perfidies. Throughout the play, Wycherley works a running comparison between sex and gambling (and, in the famous china scene, a second parallel between sex and shopping). Most of the amorous gamesters play their hands with witty fervor, but the playwright deliberately leaves unclear what exactly is at stake. Deep feelings, real risks, sturdy allegiances seem hard to come by. Most bets are placed instead on power, on cunning, on conquest, perhaps on momentary pleasure; in the end it can be hard to tell who's won, who's lost, and why. *Comedy* takes its name from *komos*, the dance of communal harmony with which so many such plays close. *The Country Wife*, by contrast, ends with a "dance of cuckolds": music for a world where fidelities are faint, and even betrayals, transpiring for muddled motives behind closed doors, are not fully comprehensible.

The Country Wife
PROLOGUE, *SPOKEN BY* MR. HART[1]

Poets, like cudgeled bullies, never do
At first or second blow submit to you;
But will provoke you still, and ne'er have done,
Till you are weary first with laying on.
5   The late so baffled scribbler[2] of this day,
Though he stands trembling, bids me boldly say,
What we before most plays are used to do,
For poets out of fear first draw on you;
In a fierce prologue the still pit defy
10   And ere you speak, like Castril,[3] give the lie.
But though our Bayes's battles[4] oft I've fought,
And with bruised knuckles their dear conquests bought;
Nay, never yet feared odds upon the stage,
In prologue dare not hector with the age,
15   But would take quarter from your saving hands,
Though Bayes within[5] all yielding countermands,
Says you confederate wits[6] no quarter give,
Therefore his play shan't ask your leave to live.
Well, let the vain rash fop, by huffing[7] so,
20   Think to obtain the better terms of you;
But we the actors humbly will submit,
Now, and at any time, to a full pit;
Nay, often we anticipate your rage,
And murder poets for you on our stage.
25   We set no guards upon our tiring-room,[8]
But when with flying colors there you come,
We patiently, you see, give up to you
Our poets, virgins, nay, our matrons too.

---

1. Charles Hart, who starred as Horner in the first production, was famous both as actor and as lover. As actor, he achieved some of his greatest successes playing the preternaturally virile and virtuous protagonists in Dryden's heroic tragedies. As lover, he had been linked with eminent beauties, including Nell Gwyn and Lady Castlemaine.
2. Refers to the cold reception of *The Gentleman Dancing Master*, which Wycherley himself recognized as a trivial work.
3. An angry character in Ben Jonson's *The Alchemist* (1610), who impulsively challenges ("gives the lie" to) others.

4. The battles that Hart had "fought" onstage in his roles as soldier-hero in Dryden's tragedies, and also the struggles of writers in general (and Wycherley in particular) to secure approval of their work. Bayes was the central character in the Duke of Buckingham's comedy *The Rehearsal* (1671): a foolish, preening playwright, he incarnated in every particular a merciless, hilarious parody of Dryden. His name soon became a mocking designation for any ambitious poet.
5. I.e., Wycherley, backstage.
6. Critics conjoined to condemn the play.
7. Blustering.
8. Dressing room.

The Persons

MR. HORNER	MRS. DAINTY FIDGET
MR. HARCOURT	MRS. SQUEAMISH
MR. DORILANT	OLD LADY SQUEAMISH
MR. PINCHWIFE	WAITERS, SERVANTS, AND ATTENDANTS
MR. SPARKISH	A BOY
SIR JASPAR FIDGET	A QUACK
MRS. MARGERY PINCHWIFE	LUCY, ALITHEA'S MAID
MRS. ALITHEA	[CLASP]
MY LADY FIDGET	[A PARSON]

The Scene: London

ACT 1

Scene 1

[*Enter Horner, and Quack following him at a distance.*]

HORNER [*aside*]: A quack is as fit for a pimp as a midwife for a bawd;[1] they are still[2] but in their way both helpers of nature.—Well, my dear doctor, hast thou done what I desired?

QUACK: I have undone you forever with the women, and reported you throughout the whole town as bad as an eunuch, with as much trouble as if I had made you one in earnest.

HORNER: But have you told all the midwives you know, the orange-wenches[3] at the playhouses, the city husbands,[4] and old fumbling keepers[5] of this end of the town? For they'll be the readiest to report it.

QUACK: I have told all the chambermaids, waiting-women, tire-women[6] and old women of my acquaintance; nay, and whispered it as a secret to 'em, and to the whisperers of Whitehall;[7] so that you need not doubt, 'twill spread, and you will be as odious to the handsome young women as—

HORNER: As the smallpox. Well—

QUACK: And to the married women of this end of the town as—

HORNER: As the great ones;[8] nay, as their own husbands.

QUACK: And to the city dames as aniseed Robin[9] of filthy and contemptible memory; and they will frighten their children with your name, especially their females.

HORNER: And cry, "Horner's coming to carry you away." I am only afraid 'twill not be believed. You told 'em 'twas by an English–French disaster and an English–French chirurgeon,[1] who has given me at once, not only a cure, but an antidote[2] for the future against that damned malady, and that worse distemper, love, and all other women's evils.

---

1. Brothel-keeper.
2. Always.
3. Orange-sellers.
4. Respectable men of business who (according to stereotype) would loathe the likes of Horner.
5. Men who keep mistresses.
6. Ladies' maids, also dressmakers.
7. The royal residence, a center for news and gossip.
8. Syphilis.

9. A famous hermaphrodite; hence (from the vantage of respectable "city dames") a repellent monster.
1. In muddled phrasing, Horner appears to blame both English and French personnel (women, doctors) for both his supposed illness (syphilis, often called "the French pox") and its drastic cure. The muddle may be intentional; Horner is, after all, making up the whole story.
2. I.e., his purported impotence.

QUACK: Your late journey into France has made it the more credible and your being here a fortnight before you appeared in public looks as if you apprehended the shame, which I wonder you do not. Well, I have been hired by young gallants to belie 'em t' other way, but you are the first would be thought a man unfit for women.

HORNER: Dear Mr. Doctor, let vain rogues be contented only to be thought abler men than they are, generally 'tis all the pleasure they have; but mine lies another way.

QUACK: You take, methinks, a very preposterous way to it and as ridiculous as if we operators in physic should put forth bills to disparage our medicaments, with hopes to gain customers.

HORNER: Doctor, there are quacks in love as well as physic, who get but the fewer and worse patients for their boasting; a good name is seldom got by giving it oneself, and women no more than honor are compassed[3] by bragging. Come, come, doctor, the wisest lawyer never discovers[4] the merits of his cause till the trial; the wealthiest man conceals his riches, and the cunning gamester his play. Shy husbands and keepers, like old rooks,[5] are not to be cheated but by a new unpracticed trick; false friendship will pass now no more than false dice upon 'em; no, not in the city. [Enter Boy.]

BOY: There are two ladies and a gentleman coming up.

[Exit.]

HORNER: A pox! Some unbelieving sisters of my former acquaintance, who, I am afraid, expect their sense should be satisfied of the falsity of the report. No—this formal[6] fool and women!

[Enter Sir Jaspar Fidget, Lady Fidget, and Mrs. Dainty Fidget.]

QUACK: His wife and sister.

SIR JASPAR: My coach breaking just now before your door, sir, I look upon as an occasional[7] reprimand to me, sir, for not kissing your hands, sir, since your coming out of France, sir; and so my disaster, sir, has been my good fortune, sir; and this is my wife, and sister, sir.

HORNER: What then, sir?

SIR JASPAR: My lady, and sister, sir.—Wife, this is Master Horner.

LADY FIDGET: Master Horner, husband!

SIR JASPAR: My lady, my Lady Fidget, sir.

HORNER: So, sir.

SIR JASPAR: Won't you be acquainted with her, sir? [Aside.] So the report is true, I find, by his coldness or aversion to the sex; but I'll play the wag with him.—Pray salute my wife, my lady, sir.

HORNER: I will kiss no man's wife, sir, for him, sir; I have taken my eternal leave, sir, of the sex already, sir.

SIR JASPAR [aside]: Hah, hah, hah! I'll plague him yet.—Not know my wife, sir?

HORNER: I do know your wife, sir; she's a woman, sir, and consequently a monster, sir, a greater monster than a husband, sir.

SIR JASPAR: A husband! How, sir?

3. Won.
4. Reveals.
5. Cheats, swindlers.
6. Unduly ceremonious, stiff.
7. Opportune.

HORNER [*makes horns*[8]]: So, sir; but I make no more cuckolds, sir.

SIR JASPAR: Hah, hah, hah! Mercury, Mercury![9]

LADY FIDGET: Pray, Sir Jaspar, let us be gone from this rude fellow.

DAINTY: Who, by his breeding, would think he had ever been in France?

LADY FIDGET: Foh, he's but too much a French fellow,[1] such as hate women of quality and virtue for their love to their husbands, Sir Jaspar; a woman is hated by 'em as much for loving her husband as for loving their money. But pray, let's be gone.

HORNER: You do well, madam, for I have nothing that you came for; I have brought over not so much as a bawdy picture, new postures,[2] nor the second part of the *École des Filles*,[3] nor—

QUACK [*apart to Horner*]: Hold, for shame, sir! What d'ye mean? You'll ruin yourself forever with the sex—

SIR JASPAR: Hah, hah, hah, he hates women perfectly, I find.

DAINTY: What a pity 'tis he should.

LADY FIDGET: Ay, he's a base, rude fellow for't; but affectation makes not a woman more odious to them than virtue.

HORNER: Because your virtue is your greatest affectation madam.

LADY FIDGET: How, you saucy fellow! Would you wrong my honor?

HORNER: If I could.

LADY FIDGET: How d'ye mean, sir?

SIR JASPAR: Hah, hah, hah! No, he can't wrong your ladyship's honor, upon my honor; he, poor man—hark you in your ear—a mere eunuch.

LADY FIDGET: O filthy French beast, foh, foh! Why do we stay? Let's be gone; I can't endure the sight of him.

SIR JASPAR: Stay but till the chairs[4] come; they'll be here presently.

LADY FIDGET: No, no.

SIR JASPAR: Nor can I stay longer. 'Tis—let me see, a quarter and a half quarter of a minute past eleven; the Council[5] will be sat, I must away. Business must be preferred always before love and ceremony with the wise, Mr. Horner.

HORNER: And the impotent, Sir Jaspar.

SIR JASPAR: Ay, ay, the impotent, Master Horner, hah, ha, ha!

LADY FIDGET: What, leave us with a filthy man alone in his lodgings?

SIR JASPAR: He's an innocent man now, you know. Pray stay, I'll hasten the chairs to you.—Mr. Horner, your servant; I should be glad to see you at my house. Pray come and dine with me, and play at cards with my wife after dinner; you are fit for women at that game yet, hah, ha! [*Aside*.] 'Tis as much a husband's prudence to provide innocent diversion for a wife as to hinder her unlawful pleasures, and he had better employ her than let her employ herself.—Farewell. [*Exit Sir Jaspar*.]

HORNER: Your servant, Sir Jaspar.

LADY FIDGET: I will not stay with him, foh!

---

8. With forefingers on the forehead, the cuckold sign.
9. Both the messenger-god, whose winged hat Horner's "horns" may call to mind, and the chemical often used in treating syphilis.
1. Fop.
2. Pornographic engravings.

3. A pornographic dialogue between a virgin and an experienced woman (1655); Pepys called it "the most bawdy, lewd book that I ever saw."
4. Sedan chairs, in which two bearers carried a single passenger.
5. Privy Council.

HORNER: Nay, madam, I beseech you stay, if it be but to see I can be as civil to ladies yet as they would desire.

LADY FIDGET: No, no, foh, you cannot be civil to ladies.

DAINTY: You as civil as ladies would desire?

LADY FIDGET: No, no, no, foh, foh, foh!

[Exeunt Lady Fidget and Dainty.]

QUACK: Now, I think, I, or you yourself rather, have done your business[6] with the women.

HORNER: Thou art an ass. Don't you see already, upon the report and my carriage,[7] this grave man of business leaves his wife in my lodgings, invites me to his house and wife, who before would not be acquainted with me out of jealousy?

QUACK: Nay, by this means you may be the more acquainted with the husbands, but the less with the wives.

HORNER: Let me alone; if I can but abuse the husbands, I'll soon disabuse the wives. Stay—I'll reckon you up the advantages I am like to have by my stratagem: first, I shall be rid of all my old acquaintances, the most insatiable sorts of duns,[8] that invade our lodgings in a morning. And next to the pleasure of making a new mistress is that of being rid of an old one; and of all old debts, love, when it comes to be so, is paid the most unwillingly.

QUACK: Well, you may be so rid of your old acquaintances; but how will you get any new ones?

HORNER: Doctor, thou wilt never make a good chemist, thou art so incredulous and impatient. Ask but all the young fellows of the town if they do not lose more time, like huntsmen, in starting the game than in running it down; one knows not where to find 'em, who will or will not. Women of quality are so civil, you can hardly distinguish love from good breeding and a man is often mistaken; but now I can be sure, she that shows an aversion to me loves the sport, as those women that are gone, whom I warrant to be right.[9] And then the next thing is, your women of honor, as you call 'em, are only chary[1] of their reputations, not their persons, and 'tis scandal they would avoid, not men. Now may I have, by the reputation of an eunuch, the privileges of one and be seen in a lady's chamber in a morning as early as her husband, kiss virgins before their parents or lovers and may be, in short, the passe partout[2] of the town. Now, doctor.

QUACK: Nay, now you shall be the doctor; and your process is so new that we do not know but it may succeed.

HORNER: Not so new neither; probatum est,[3] doctor.

QUACK: Well, I wish you luck and many patients whilst I go to mine. [Exit Quack.]

[Enter Harcourt and Dorilant to Horner.]

HARCOURT: Come, your appearance at the play yesterday has, I hope, hardened you for the future against the women's contempt and the men's raillery and now you'll abroad as you were wont.

HORNER: Did I not bear it bravely?

---

6. Spoiled your reputation.
7. Conduct.
8. Persistent creditors.
9. Ripe for play, promiscuous.

1. Careful, wary.
2. One who may go anywhere.
3. "It has been proved or tested," a phrase used in prescriptions.

DORILANT: With a most theatrical impudence; nay, more than the orange-wenches show there or a drunken vizard-mask[4] or a great-bellied actress; nay, or the most impudent of creatures, an ill poet; or what is yet more impudent, a secondhand critic.

HORNER: But what say the ladies? Have they no pity?

HARCOURT: What ladies? The vizard-masks, you know, never pity a man when all's gone, though in their service.

DORILANT: And for the women in the boxes, you'd never pity them when 'twas in your power.

HARCOURT: They say, 'tis pity, but all that deal with common women should be served so.

DORILANT: Nay, I dare swear, they won't admit you to play at cards with them, go to plays with 'em, or do the little duties which other shadows of men are wont to do for 'em.

HORNER: Who do you call shadows of men?

DORILANT: Half-men.

HORNER: What, boys?

DORILANT: Ay, your old boys, old *beaux garçons*,[5] who, like superannuated[6] stallions, are suffered to run, feed and whinny with the mares as long as they live, though they can do nothing else.

HORNER: Well, a pox on love and wenching! Women serve but to keep a man from better company; though I can't enjoy them, I shall you the more. Good fellowship and friendship are lasting, rational and manly pleasures.

HARCOURT: For all that, give me some of those pleasures you call effeminate too; they help to relish one another.

HORNER: They disturb one another.

HARCOURT: No, mistresses are like books. If you pore upon them too much, they doze[7] you and make you unfit for company; but if used discreetly, you are the fitter for conversation by 'em.

DORILANT: A mistress should be like a little country retreat near the town, not to dwell in constantly, but only for a night and away, to taste the town the better when a man returns.

HORNER: I tell you, 'tis as hard to be a good fellow, a good friend and a lover of women, as 'tis to be a good fellow, a good friend and a lover of money. You cannot follow both, then choose your side. Wine gives you liberty, love takes it away.

DORILANT: Gad, he's in the right on't.

HORNER: Wine gives you joy; love, grief and tortures, besides the chirurgeon's. Wine makes us witty; love, only sots. Wine makes us sleep; love breaks it.

DORILANT: By the world, he has reason,[8] Harcourt.

HORNER: Wine makes—

DORILANT: Ay, wine makes us—makes us princes; love makes us beggars, poor rogues, egad—and wine—

HORNER: So, there's one converted.—No, no, love and wine, oil and vinegar.

HARCOURT: I grant it; love will still be uppermost.

HORNER: Come, for my part I will have only those glorious, manly pleasures of being very drunk and very slovenly. [*Enter Boy.*]

---

4. A prostitute; many of them wore masks, as emblems of their trade.
5. Old gallants.

6. Old and infirm.
7. Stupefy.
8. Speaks truth (French *il a raison*: "he is right").

BOY: Mr. Sparkish is below, sir. [*Exit.*]

HARCOURT: What, my dear friend! A rogue that is fond of me only, I think, for abusing him.

DORILANT: No, he can no more think the men laugh at him than that women jilt[9] him, his opinion of himself is so good.

HORNER: Well, there's another pleasure by drinking I thought not of: I shall lose his acquaintance, because he cannot drink; and you know 'tis a very hard thing to be rid of him, for he's one of those nauseous offerers at wit, who, like the worst fiddlers, run themselves into all companies.

HARCOURT: One that, by being in the company of men of sense, would pass for one.

HORNER: And may so to the short-sighted world, as a false jewel amongst true ones is not discerned at a distance. His company is as troublesome to us as a cuckold's when you have a mind to his wife's.

HARCOURT: No, the rogue will not let us enjoy one another, but ravishes our conversation, though he signifies no more to't than Sir Martin Mar-all's[1] gaping and awkward thrumming upon the lute does to his man's voice and music.

DORILANT: And to pass for a wit in town shows himself a fool every night to us that are guilty of the plot.

HORNER: Such wits as he are, to a company of reasonable men, like rooks[2] to the gamesters, who only fill a room[3] at the table, but are so far from contributing to the play that they only serve to spoil the fancy of those that do.

DORILANT: Nay, they are used like rooks too, snubbed, checked and abused; yet the rogues will hang on.

HORNER: A pox on 'em, and all that force nature and would be still what she forbids 'em! Affectation is her greatest monster.

HARCOURT: Most men are the contraries to that they would seem. Your bully, you see, is a coward with a long sword; the little, humbly fawning physician, with his ebony cane, is he that destroys men.

DORILANT: The usurer, a poor rogue possessed of moldy bonds and mortgages, and we they call spendthrifts are only wealthy, who lay out his money upon daily new purchases of pleasure.

HORNER: Ay, your arrantest cheat is your trustee or executor; your jealous man, the greatest cuckold; your churchman, the greatest atheist; and your noisy, pert rogue of a wit, the greatest fop, dullest ass and worst company, as you shall see: for here he comes.

  [*Enter Sparkish to them.*]

SPARKISH: How is't, sparks,[4] how is't? Well, faith, Harry, I must rally[5] thee a little, ha, ha, ha, upon the report in town of thee, ha, ha, ha, I can't hold i'faith; shall I speak?

HORNER: Yes, but you'll be so bitter then.

---

9. Reject.
1. Foolish title character of Dryden's comedy (1667) who lip-synchs and fake-strums a serenade to his mistress while his "man" (servant), hidden, actually performs the song. When his servant finishes playing, Sir Martin fails to quit miming. Harcourt regards Sparkish as such

another empty fraud.
2. Here, simpletons, fools.
3. Space.
4. Fashionable young men; the term is usually derogatory, but Sparkish speaks it in fellowship.
5. Mock, tease.

SPARKISH: Honest Dick and Frank here shall answer for me, I will not be extreme bitter, by the universe.

HARCOURT: We will be bound in ten thousand pound bond, he shall not be bitter at all.

DORILANT: Nor sharp, nor sweet.

HORNER: What, not downright insipid?

SPARKISH: Nay then, since you are so brisk and provoke me, take what follows. You must know, I was discoursing and rallying with some ladies yesterday, and they happened to talk of the fine new signs[6] in town.

HORNER: Very fine ladies, I believe.

SPARKISH: Said I, "I know where the best new sign is." "Where?" says one of the ladies. "In Covent Garden,"[7] I replied. Said another, "In what street?" "In Russell Street," answered I. "Lord," says another, "I'm sure there was ne'er a fine new sign there yesterday." "Yes, but there was," said I again, "and it came out of France and has been there a fortnight."

DORILANT: A pox, I can hear no more, prithee.

HORNER: No, hear him out; let him tune his crowd[8] a while.

HARCOURT: The worst music, the greatest preparation.

SPARKISH: Nay, faith, I'll make you laugh. "It cannot be," says a third lady. "Yes, yes," quoth I again. Says a fourth lady—

HORNER: Look to't, we'll have no more ladies.

SPARKISH: No—then mark, mark, now. Said I to the fourth, "Did you never see Mr. Horner? He lodges in Russell Street, and he's a sign of a man, you know, since he came out of France." Heh, hah, he!

HORNER: But the devil take me, if thine be the sign of a jest.

SPARKISH: With that they all fell a-laughing, till they bepissed themselves. What, but it does not move you, methinks? Well, I see one had as good go to law without a witness as break a jest without a laugher on one's side. Come, come, sparks, but where do we dine? I have left at Whitehall an earl to dine with you.

DORILANT: Why, I thought thou hadst loved a man with a title better than a suit with a French trimming to't.

HARCOURT: Go, to him again.

SPARKISH: No, sir, a wit to me is the greatest title in the world.

HORNER: But go dine with your earl, sir; he may be exceptious.[9] We are your friends and will not take it ill to be left, I do assure you.

HARCOURT: Nay, faith, he shall go to him.

SPARKISH: Nay, pray, gentlemen.

DORILANT: We'll thrust you out, if you wo'not. What, disappoint anybody for us?

SPARKISH: Nay, dear gentlemen, hear me.

HORNER: No, no, sir, by no means; pray go, sir.

SPARKISH: Why, dear rogues—

DORILANT: No, no.

[*They all thrust him out of the room.*]

ALL: Ha, ha, ha!

[*Sparkish returns.*]

6. Indicating the business of a shop.
7. The most fashionable area of London, teeming with theaters, taverns, and shops.

8. Fiddle.
9. Peevish.

SPARKISH: But, sparks, pray hear me. What, d'ye think I'll eat then with gay, shallow fops and silent coxcombs? I think wit as necessary at dinner as a glass of good wine, and that's the reason I never have any stomach when I eat alone.—Come, but where do we dine?

HORNER: Even where you will.

SPARKISH: At Chateline's?[1]

DORILANT: Yes, if you will.

SPARKISH: Or at the Cock?[2]

DORILANT: Yes, if you please.

SPARKISH: Or at the Dog and Partridge?[3]

HORNER: Ay, if you have a mind to't, for we shall dine at neither.

SPARKISH: Pshaw, with your fooling we shall lose the new play; and I would no more miss seeing a new play the first day than I would miss setting in the wits' row. Therefore I'll go fetch my mistress and away.

[*Exit Sparkish. Manent*[4] *Horner, Harcourt, Dorilant. Enter to them Mr. Pinchwife.*]

HORNER: Who have we here? Pinchwife?

PINCHWIFE: Gentlemen, your humble servant.

HORNER: Well, Jack, by the long absence from the town, the grumness of thy countenance and the slovenliness of thy habit, I should give thee joy, should I not, of marriage?

PINCHWIFE [*aside*]: Death! Does he know I'm married too? I thought to have concealed it from him at least.—My long stay in the country will excuse my dress and I have a suit of law, that brings me up to town, that puts me out of humor, besides, I must give Sparkish tomorrow five thousand pound[5] to lie with my sister.

HORNER: Nay, you country gentlemen, rather than not purchase, will buy anything; and he is a cracked title,[6] if we may quibble. Well, but am I to give thee joy? I heard thou wert married.

PINCHWIFE: What then?

HORNER: Why, the next thing that is to be heard is thou'rt a cuckold.

PINCHWIFE [*aside*]: Insupportable name!

HORNER: But I did not expect marriage from such a whoremaster[7] as you, one that knew the town so much and women so well.

PINCHWIFE: Why, I have married no London wife.

HORNER: Pshaw, that's all one; that grave circumspection in marrying a country wife is like refusing a deceitful, pampered Smithfield jade[8] to go and be cheated by a friend in the country.

PINCHWIFE [*aside*]: A pox on him and his simile.—At least we are a little surer of the breed there, know what her keeping has been, whether foiled[9] or unsound.

HORNER: Come, come, I have known a clap[1] gotten in Wales; and there are cozens,[2] justices, clerks and chaplains in the country, I won't say coachmen. But she's handsome and young?

---

1. A famous French ordinary, or restaurant, in Covent Garden.
2. Probably the Cock Tavern in Bow Street, where Wycherley himself spent time.
3. A tavern in Fleet Street; the least fashionable of the places Sparkish suggests.
4. Remain.
5. As a dowry.
6. I.e., Sparkish owns shoddy property, has a weak claim to it, and is himself a bad bargain.

7. A man who consorts with whores and is given to lechery.
8. Broken-down horse bought at Smithfield Market, where the sellers were often swindlers; here a metaphor for disreputable women purchased at far too high a price.
9. With reference to a horse, injured; to a woman, deflowered.
1. Gonorrhea.
2. Cheaters.

PINCHWIFE [aside]: I'll answer as I should do.—No, no, she has no beauty but her youth; no attraction but her modesty; wholesome, homely and house-wifely; that's all.

DORILANT: He talks as like a grazier[3] as he looks.

PINCHWIFE: She's too awkward, ill-favored and silly to bring to town.

HARCOURT: Then methinks you should bring her, to be taught breeding.

PINCHWIFE: To be taught! No, sir! I thank you. Good wives and private soldiers should be ignorant. [Aside.] I'll keep her from your instructions, I warrant you.

HARCOURT [aside]: The rogue is as jealous as if his wife were not ignorant.

HORNER: Why, if she be ill-favoured, there will be less danger here for you than by leaving her in the country; we have such variety of dainties that we are seldom hungry.

DORILANT: But they have always coarse, constant, swingeing stomachs[4] in the country.

HARCOURT: Foul feeders indeed.

DORILANT: And your hospitality is great there.

HARCOURT: Open house, every man's welcome.

PINCHWIFE: So, so, gentlemen.

HORNER: But, prithee, why wouldst thou marry her? If she be ugly, ill-bred and silly, she must be rich then.

PINCHWIFE: As rich as if she brought me twenty thousand pound out of this town, for she'll be as sure not to spend her moderate portion as a London baggage would be to spend hers, let it be what it would; so 'tis all one. Then, because she's ugly, she's the likelier to be my own; and being ill-bred, she'll have conversation; and since silly and innocent, will not know the difference betwixt a man of one-and-twenty and one of forty.

HORNER: None—to my knowledge; but if she be silly, she'll expect as much from a man of forty-nine as from him of one-and-twenty. But methinks wit is more necessary than beauty, and I think no young woman ugly that has it, and no handsome woman agreeable without it.

PINCHWIFE: 'Tis my maxim, he's a fool that marries, but he's a greater that does not marry a fool. What is wit in a wife good for, but to make a man a cuckold?

HORNER: Yes, to keep it from his knowledge.

PINCHWIFE: A fool cannot contrive to make her husband a cuckold.

HORNER: No, but she'll club[5] with a man that can; and what is worse, if she cannot make her husband a cuckold, she'll make him jealous and pass for one, and then 'tis all one.

PINCHWIFE: Well, well, I'll take care for one, my wife shall make me no cuckold, though she had your help, Mr. Horner; I understand the town, sir.

DORILANT [aside]: His help!

HARCOURT [aside]: He's come newly to town, it seems, and has not heard how things are with him.

HORNER: But tell me, has marriage cured thee of whoring, which it seldom does?

HARCOURT: 'Tis more than age can do.

HORNER: No, the word is, I'll marry and live honest; but a marriage vow is like a penitent gamester's oath and entering into bonds and penalties to stint himself to

3. One who feeds cattle for market.   5. Associate.
4. Immense appetites.

such a particular small sum at play for the future, which makes him but the more eager and, not being able to hold out, loses his money again and his forfeit to boot.

DORILANT: Ay, ay, a gamester will be a gamester whilst his money lasts, and a whoremaster whilst his vigor.

HARCOURT: Nay, I have known 'em, when they are broke and can lose no more, keep a-fumbling with the box[6] in their hands to fool with only and hinder other gamesters.

DORILANT: That had wherewithal to make lusty stakes.

PINCHWIFE: Well, gentlemen, you may laugh at me, but you shall never lie with my wife; I know the town.

HORNER: But prithee, was not the way you were in better? Is not keeping better than marriage?

PINCHWIFE: A pox on't! The jades would jilt me; I could never keep a whore to myself.

HORNER: So, then you only married to keep a whore to yourself. Well, but let me tell you, women, as you say, are like soldiers, made constant and loyal by good pay rather than by oaths and covenants. Therefore I'd advise my friends to keep rather than marry, since too, I find, by your example, it does not serve one's turn, for I saw you yesterday in the eighteen-penny place[7] with a pretty country wench.

PINCHWIFE [aside]: How the devil! Did he see my wife then? I sat there that she might not be seen. But she shall never go to a play again.

HORNER: What, dost thou blush at nine-and-forty, for having been seen with a wench?

DORILANT: No, faith, I warrant 'twas his wife, which he seated there out of sight, for he's a cunning rogue and understands the town.

HARCOURT: He blushes. Then 'twas his wife, for men are now more ashamed to be seen with them in public than with a wench.

PINCHWIFE [aside]: Hell and damnation! I'm undone, since Horner has seen her and they know 'twas she.

HORNER: But prithee, was it thy wife? She was exceedingly pretty; I was in love with her at that distance.

PINCHWIFE: You are like never to be nearer to her. Your servant, gentlemen.
[Offers to go.]

HORNER: Nay, prithee stay.

PINCHWIFE: I cannot, I will not.

HORNER: Come, you shall dine with us.

PINCHWIFE: I have dined already.

HORNER: Come, I know thou hast not. I'll treat thee, dear rogue; thou shalt spend none of thy Hampshire[8] money today.

PINCHWIFE [aside]: Treat me! So, he uses me already like his cuckold.

HORNER: Nay, you shall not go.

PINCHWIFE: I must, I have business at home. [Exit Pinchwife.]

HARCOURT: To beat his wife; he's as jealous of her as a Cheapside[9] husband of a Covent Garden wife.

---

6. For throwing dice in gaming; also slang for vagina. Parallels between gambling and sex recur throughout the play.
7. The middle gallery of the playhouse occupied by (among others) clerks, merchants, and prostitutes.
8. The rural county in south-central England where Pinchwife now lives.
9. City-merchant (Cheapside was a center of finance).

HORNER: Why, 'tis as hard to find an old whoremaster without jealousy and the gout, as a young one without fear or the pox.

As gout in age from pox in youth proceeds,
So wenching past, then jealousy succeeds,
The worst disease that love and wenching breeds.

[*Exeunt.*]

ACT 2

Scene 1

[*Mrs. Margery Pinchwife and Alithea. Mr. Pinchwife peeping behind at the door.*]

MRS. PINCHWIFE: Pray, sister, where are the best fields and woods to walk in, in London?

ALITHEA: A pretty question! Why, sister, Mulberry Garden and St. James's Park[1] and, for close walks, the New Exchange.[2]

MRS. PINCHWIFE: Pray, sister, tell me why my husband looks so grum[3] here in town and keeps me up so close and will not let me go a-walking, nor let me wear my best gown yesterday.

ALITHEA: Oh, he's jealous, sister.

MRS. PINCHWIFE: Jealous? What's that?

ALITHEA: He's afraid you should love another man.

MRS. PINCHWIFE: How should he be afraid of my loving another man, when he will not let me see any but himself?

ALITHEA: Did he not carry you yesterday to a play?

MRS. PINCHWIFE: Ay, but we sat amongst ugly people; he would not let me come near the gentry, who sat under us, so that I could not see 'em. He told me none but naughty women sat there, whom they toused and moused.[4] But I would have ventured for all that.

ALITHEA: But how did you like the play?

MRS. PINCHWIFE: Indeed, I was a-weary of the play, but I liked hugeously the actors; they are the goodliest, properest men, sister!

ALITHEA: O, but you must not like the actors, sister.

MRS. PINCHWIFE: Ay, how should I help it, sister? Pray, sister, when my husband comes in, will you ask leave for me to go a-walking?

ALITHEA [*aside*]: A-walking, hah, ha! Lord, a country gentlewoman's leisure is the drudgery of a foot-post;[5] and she requires as much airing as her husband's horses.
        [*Enter Mr. Pinchwife to them.*]
But here comes your husband; I'll ask, though I'm sure he'll not grant it.

MRS. PINCHWIFE: He says he won't let me go abroad for fear of catching the pox.

ALITHEA: Fie! The smallpox you should say.

MRS. PINCHWIFE: O my dear, dear bud, welcome home! Why dost thou look so fropish? Who has nangered[6] thee?

PINCHWIFE: You're a fool.

---

1. Popular places for gathering, strolling and savoring sights, talk, and entertainment.
2. This elegant arcade, with its covered ("close") walkways, served as *the* center for fashionable London shopping. The second scene in Act 3 takes place there.

3. Gloomy, surly.
4. Pulled about good-naturedly, but roughly.
5. A walking message-carrier.
6. Baby-talk: *fropish*, irritable; *nangered*, angered.

[*Mrs. Pinchwife goes aside and cries.*]

ALITHEA: Faith, so she is, for crying for no fault, poor tender creature!

PINCHWIFE: What, you would have her as impudent as yourself, as arrant a jillflirt, a gadder, a magpie[7] and, to say all, a mere notorious town-woman?

ALITHEA: Brother, you are my only censurer; and the honor of your family shall sooner suffer in your wife there than in me, though I take the innocent liberty of the town.

PINCHWIFE: Hark you, mistress, do not talk so before my wife. The innocent liberty of the town!

ALITHEA: Why, pray, who boasts of any intrigue with me? What lampoon[8] has made my name notorious? What ill women frequent my lodgings? I keep no company with any women of scandalous reputations.

PINCHWIFE: No, you keep the men of scandalous reputations company.

ALITHEA: Where? Would you not have me civil? Answer 'em in a box at the plays? In the drawing room at Whitehall? In St. James's Park? Mulberry Gardens? Or—

PINCHWIFE: Hold, hold! Do not teach my wife where the men are to be found! I believe she's the worse for your town documents[9] already. I bid you keep her in ignorance, as I do.

MRS. PINCHWIFE: Indeed, be not angry with her, bud; she will tell me nothing of the town, though I ask her a thousand times a day.

PINCHWIFE: Then you are very inquisitive to know, I find!

MRS. PINCHWIFE: Not I, indeed, dear; I hate London. Our place-house[1] in the country is worth a thousand of't; would I were there again!

PINCHWIFE: So you shall, I warrant. But were you not talking of plays and players when I came in? [*To Alithea.*] You are her encourager in such discourses.

MRS. PINCHWIFE: No, indeed, dear; she chid me just now for liking the playermen.

PINCHWIFE [*aside*]: Nay, if she be so innocent as to own to me her liking them, there is no hurt in't.—Come, my poor rogue, but thou lik'st none better than me?

MRS. PINCHWIFE: Yes, indeed, but I do; the playermen are finer folks.

PINCHWIFE: But you love none better than me?

MRS. PINCHWIFE: You are mine own dear bud, and I know you; I hate a stranger.

PINCHWIFE: Ay, my dear, you must love me only and not be like the naughty town-women, who only hate their husbands and love every man else, love plays, visits, fine coaches, fine clothes, fiddles, balls, treats, and so lead a wicked town-life.

MRS. PINCHWIFE: Nay, if to enjoy all these things be a town-life, London is not so bad a place, dear.

PINCHWIFE: How! If you love me, you must hate London.

ALITHEA [*aside*]: The fool has forbid me discovering to her the pleasures of the town and he is now setting her agog upon them himself.

MRS. PINCHWIFE: But, husband, do the town-women love the playermen too?

PINCHWIFE: Yes, I warrant you.

---

7. A wanton girl, a rover, a chatterer.
8. Scurrilous satire.

9. Teachings about fashionable life.
1. Grand home.

MRS. PINCHWIFE: Ay, I warrant you.

PINCHWIFE: Why, you do not, I hope?

MRS. PINCHWIFE: No, no, bud; but why have we no playermen in the country?

PINCHWIFE: Ha—Mrs. Minx, ask me no more to go to a play.

MRS. PINCHWIFE: Nay, why, love? I did not care for going; but when you forbid me, you make me, as 'twere, desire it.

ALITHEA [aside]: So 'twill be in other things, I warrant.

MRS. PINCHWIFE: Pray let me go to a play, dear.

PINCHWIFE: Hold your peace, I wo'not.

MRS. PINCHWIFE: Why, love?

PINCHWIFE: Why, I'll tell you.

ALITHEA [aside]: Nay, if he tell her, she'll give him more cause to forbid her that place.

MRS. PINCHWIFE: Pray, why, dear?

PINCHWIFE: First, you like the actors and the gallants may like you.

MRS. PINCHWIFE: What, a homely country girl? No, bud, nobody will like me.

PINCHWIFE: I tell you, yes, they may.

MRS. PINCHWIFE: No, no, you jest—I won't believe you, I will go.

PINCHWIFE: I tell you then that one of the lewdest fellows in town, who saw you there, told me he was in love with you.

MRS. PINCHWIFE: Indeed! Who, who, pray, who was't?

PINCHWIFE [aside]: I've gone too far and slipped before I was aware. How over-joyed she is!

MRS. PINCHWIFE: Was it any Hampshire gallant, any of our neighbors? I promise you, I am beholding to him.

PINCHWIFE: I promise you, you lie, for he would but ruin you, as he has done hundreds. He has no other love for women but that; such as he look upon women, like basilisks,[2] but to destroy 'em.

MRS. PINCHWIFE: Ay, but if he loves me, why should he ruin me? Answer me to that. Methinks he should not; I would do him no harm.

ALITHEA: Hah, ha, ha!

PINCHWIFE: 'Tis very well; but I'll keep him from doing you any harm, or me either.

[Enter Sparkish and Harcourt.]

But here comes company; get you in, get you in.

MRS. PINCHWIFE: But pray, husband, is he a pretty gentleman that loves me?

PINCHWIFE: In, baggage, in. [Thrusts her in, shuts the door.] What, all the lewd libertines of the town brought to my lodging by this easy coxcomb! 'Sdeath, I'll not suffer it.

SPARKISH: Here, Harcourt, do you approve my choice? [To Alithea.] Dear little rogue, I told you I'd bring you acquainted with all my friends, the wits, and—
    [Harcourt salutes her.]

PINCHWIFE [aside]: Ay, they shall know her, as well as you yourself will, I warrant you.

SPARKISH: This is one of those, my pretty rogue, that are to dance at your wedding tomorrow; and him you must bid welcome ever to what you and I have.

PINCHWIFE [aside]: Monstrous!

---

2. Mythical reptiles whose gaze dealt death.

SPARKISH: Harcourt, how dost thou like her, faith?—Nay, dear, do not look down; I should hate to have a wife of mine out of countenance at anything.

PINCHWIFE [aside]: Wonderful!

SPARKISH: Tell me, I say, Harcourt, how dost thou like her? Thou hast stared upon her enough to resolve me.

HARCOURT: So infinitely well that I could wish I had a mistress too, that might differ from her in nothing but her love and engagement to you.

ALITHEA: Sir, Master Sparkish has often told me that his acquaintance were all wits and railleurs[3] and now I find it.

SPARKISH: No, by the universe, madam, he does not rally now; you may believe him. I do assure you, he is the honestest, worthiest, true-hearted gentleman—a man of such perfect honor, he would say nothing to a lady he does not mean.

PINCHWIFE [aside]: Praising another man to his mistress!

HARCOURT: Sir, you are so beyond expectation obliging that—

SPARKISH: Nay, egad, I am sure you do admire her extremely; I see't in your eyes.—He does admire you, madam.—By the world, don't you?

HARCOURT: Yes, above the world, or the most glorious part of it, her whole sex; and till now I never thought I should have envied you, or any man about to marry, but you have the best excuse for marriage I ever knew.

ALITHEA: Nay, now, sir, I'm satisfied you are of the society of the wits and railleurs, since you cannot spare your friend, even when he is but too civil to you; but the surest sign is since you are an enemy to marriage, for that, I hear, you hate as much as business or bad wine.

HARCOURT: Truly, madam, I never was an enemy to marriage till now, because marriage was never an enemy to me before.

ALITHEA: But why, sir, is marriage an enemy to you now? Because it robs you of your friend here? For you look upon a friend married as one gone into a monastery, that is dead to the world.

HARCOURT: 'Tis indeed because you marry him; I see, madam, you can guess my meaning. I do confess heartily and openly, I wish it were in my power to break the match; by heavens I would.

SPARKISH: Poor Frank!

ALITHEA: Would you be so unkind to me?

HARCOURT: No, no, 'tis not because I would be unkind to you.

SPARKISH: Poor Frank! No, gad, 'tis only his kindness to me.

PINCHWIFE [aside]: Great kindness to you indeed! Insensible fop, let a man make love to his wife to his face!

SPARKISH: Come, dear Frank, for all my wife there that shall be, thou shalt enjoy me sometimes, dear rogue. By my honor, we men of wit condole for our deceased brother in marriage as much as for one dead in earnest. I think that was prettily said of me, ha, Harcourt? But come, Frank, be not melancholy for me.

HARCOURT: No, I assure you I am not melancholy for you.

SPARKISH: Prithee, Frank, dost think my wife that shall be there a fine person?

HARCOURT: I could gaze upon her till I became as blind as you are.

SPARKISH: How, as I am? How?

HARCOURT: Because you are a lover and true lovers are blind, stock blind.[4]

---

3. Mockers, banterers.   4. As blind as any lifeless object.

SPARKISH: True, true; but by the world, she has wit too, as well as beauty. Go, go with her into a corner and try if she has wit; talk to her anything; she's bashful before me.

HARCOURT: Indeed, if a woman wants[5] wit in a corner, she has it nowhere.

ALITHEA [aside to Sparkish]: Sir, you dispose of me a little before your time—

SPARKISH: Nay, nay, madam, let me have an earnest[6] of your obedience, or—go, go, madam—

[Harcourt courts Alithea aside.]

PINCHWIFE: How, sir! If you are not concerned for the honor of a wife, I am for that of a sister; he shall not debauch her. Be a pander[7] to your own wife, bring men to her, let 'em make love before your face, thrust 'em into a corner together, then leave 'em in private! Is this your town wit and conduct?

SPARKISH: Hah, ha, ha, a silly wise rogue would make one laugh more than a stark fool, hah, ha! I shall burst. Nay, you shall not disturb 'em; I'll vex thee, by the world. [Struggles with Pinchwife to keep him from Harcourt and Alithea.]

ALITHEA: The writings are drawn, sir, settlements made; 'tis too late, sir, and past all revocation.

HARCOURT: Then so is my death.

ALITHEA: I would not be unjust to him.

HARCOURT: Then why to me so?

ALITHEA: I have no obligation to you.

HARCOURT: My love.

ALITHEA: I had his before.

HARCOURT: You never had it; he wants, you see, jealousy, the only infallible sign of it.

ALITHEA: Love proceeds from esteem; he cannot distrust my virtue. Besides, he loves me, or he would not marry me.

HARCOURT: Marrying you is no more sign of his love than bribing your woman, that he may marry you, is a sign of his generosity. Marriage is rather a sign of interest than love, and he that marries a fortune covets a mistress, not loves her. But if you take marriage for a sign of love, take it from me immediately.

ALITHEA: No, now you have put a scruple in my head; but, in short, sir, to end our dispute, I must marry him; my reputation would suffer in the world else.

HARCOURT: No, if you do marry him, with your pardon, madam, your reputation suffers in the world and you would be thought in necessity for a cloak.[8]

ALITHEA: Nay, now you are rude, sir.—Mr. Sparkish, pray come hither, your friend here is very troublesome, and very loving.

HARCOURT [aside to Alithea]: Hold, hold!—

PINCHWIFE: D'ye hear that?

SPARKISH: Why, d'ye think I'll seem to be jealous, like a country bumpkin?

PINCHWIFE: No, rather be a cuckold, like a credulous cit.[9]

HARCOURT: Madam, you would not have been so little generous as to have told him.

ALITHEA: Yes, since you could be so little generous as to wrong him.

5. Lacks.
6. Foretaste, pledge.
7. Pimp, procurer.
8. I.e., to hide your secrets: perhaps pregnancy or love affairs.
9. "A pert low townsman, a pragmatical trader" (Johnson's Dictionary); contemptuous abbreviation of "citizen."

HARCOURT: Wrong him! No man can do't, he's beneath an injury; a bubble,[1] a coward, a senseless idiot, a wretch so contemptible to all the world but you that—

ALITHEA: Hold, do not rail at him, for since he is like to be my husband, I am resolved to like him. Nay, I think I am obliged to tell him you are not his friend.— Master Sparkish, Master Sparkish.

SPARKISH: What, what?—Now, dear rogue, has not she wit?

HARCOURT [speaks surlily]: Not so much as I thought and hoped she had.

ALITHEA: Mr. Sparkish, do you bring people to rail at you?

HARCOURT: Madam—

SPARKISH: How! No, but if he does rail at me, 'tis but in jest, I warrant; what we wits do for one another and never take any notice of it.

ALITHEA: He spoke so scurrilously of you, I had no patience to hear him; besides, he has been making love to me.

HARCOURT [aside]: True, damned, telltale woman!

SPARKISH: Pshaw, to show his parts[2]—we wits rail and make love often but to show our parts; as we have no affections, so we have no malice. We—

ALITHEA: He said you were a wretch, below an injury.

SPARKISH: Pshaw!

HARCOURT [aside]: Damned, senseless, impudent, virtuous jade! Well, since she won't let me have her, she'll do as good, she'll make me hate her.

ALITHEA: A common bubble.

SPARKISH: Pshaw!

ALITHEA: A coward.

SPARKISH: Pshaw, pshaw!

ALITHEA: A senseless, driveling idiot.

SPARKISH: How! Did he disparage my parts? Nay, then my honor's concerned; I can't put up that, sir, by the world. Brother, help me to kill him. [Aside.] I may draw now, since we have the odds of him. 'This a good occasion, too, before my mistress—[Offers to draw.]

ALITHEA: Hold, hold!

SPARKISH: What, what?

ALITHEA [aside]: I must not let 'em kill the gentleman neither, for his kindness to me; I am so far from hating him that I wish my gallant had his person and understanding. —Nay, if my honor—

SPARKISH: I'll be thy death.

ALITHEA: Hold, hold! Indeed, to tell the truth, the gentleman said after all that what he spoke was but out of friendship to you.

SPARKISH: How! say I am—I am a fool, that is, no wit, out of friendship to me?

ALITHEA: Yes, to try whether I was concerned enough for you and made love to me only to be satisfied of my virtue, for your sake.

HARCOURT [aside]: Kind, however—

SPARKISH: Nay, if it were so, my dear rogue, I ask thee pardon; but why would not you tell me so, faith?

HARCOURT: Because I did not think on't, faith.

SPARKISH: Come, Horner does not come, Harcourt, let's be gone to the new play.—Come, madam.

---

1. Dupe.   2. Abilities, talents.

ALITHEA: I will not go if you intend to leave me alone in the box and run into the pit, as you use to do.

SPARKISH: Pshaw! I'll leave Harcourt with you in the box to entertain you, and that's as good; if I sat in the box, I should be thought no judge but of trimmings.[3]—Come away, Harcourt, lead her down.

[*Exeunt Sparkish, Harcourt and Alithea.*]

PINCHWIFE: Well, go thy ways, for the flower of the true town fops, such as spend their estates before they come to 'em and are cuckolds before they're married. But let me go look to my own freehold.—How!—

[*Enter Lady Fidget, Mrs. Dainty Fidget and Mrs. Squeamish.*]

LADY FIDGET: Your servant, sir; where is your lady? We are come to wait upon her to the new play.

PINCHWIFE: New play!

LADY FIDGET: And my husband will wait upon you presently.

PINCHWIFE [*aside*]: Damn your civility.—Madam, by no means; I will not see Sir Jaspar here till I have waited upon him at home; nor shall my wife see you till she has waited upon your ladyship at your lodgings.

LADY FIDGET: Now we are here, sir—

PINCHWIFE: No, madam.

DAINTY: Pray, let us see her.

SQUEAMISH: We will not stir till we see her.

PINCHWIFE [*aside*]: A pox on you all! [*Goes to the door, and returns.*]—She has locked the door and is gone abroad.

LADY FIDGET: No, you have locked the door and she's within.

DAINTY: They told us below she was here.

PINCHWIFE [*aside*]: Will nothing do?—Well, it must out then. To tell you the truth, ladies, which I was afraid to let you know before, lest it might endanger your lives, my wife has just now the smallpox come out upon her. Do not be frightened but pray, be gone, ladies; you shall not stay here in danger of your lives. Pray get you gone, ladies.

LADY FIDGET: No, no, we have all had 'em.

SQUEAMISH: Alack, alack.

DAINTY: Come, come, we must see how it goes with her; I understand the disease.

LADY FIDGET: Come.

PINCHWIFE [*aside*]: Well, there is no being too hard for[4] women at their own weapon, lying; therefore I'll quit the field. [*Exit Pinchwife.*]

SQUEAMISH: Here's an example of jealousy.

LADY FIDGET: Indeed, as the world goes, I wonder there are no more jealous, since wives are so neglected.

DAINTY: Pshaw, as the world goes, to what end should they be jealous?

LADY FIDGET: Foh, 'tis a nasty world.

SQUEAMISH: That men of parts, great acquaintance and quality should take up with and spend themselves and fortunes in keeping little playhouse creatures, foh!

LADY FIDGET: Nay, that women of understanding, great acquaintance and good quality should fall a-keeping too of little creatures, foh!

---

3. Clothes, fashions. The "wits," who came to criticize the play, customarily occupied not the boxes but the "pit."
4. Too clever for.

SQUEAMISH: Why, 'tis the men of quality's fault; they never visit women of honor and reputation, as they used to do and have not so much as common civility for ladies of our rank, but use us with the same indifferency and ill-breeding as if we were all married to 'em.

LADY FIDGET: She says true; 'tis an arrant shame women of quality should be so slighted. Methinks birth, birth should go for something. I have known men admired, courted, and followed for their titles only.

SQUEAMISH: Ay, one would think men of honor should not love, no more than marry, out of their own rank.

DAINTY: Fie, fie upon 'em! They are come to think crossbreeding for themselves best, as well as for their dogs and horses.

LADY FIDGET: They are dogs and horses for't.

SQUEAMISH: One would think, if not for love, for vanity a little.

DAINTY: Nay, they do satisfy their vanity upon us sometimes and are kind to us in their report, tell all the world they lie with us.

LADY FIDGET: Damned rascals! That we should be only wronged by 'em! To report a man has had a person, when he has not had a person, is the greatest wrong in the whole world that can be done to a person.

SQUEAMISH: Well, 'tis an arrant shame noble persons should be so wronged and neglected.

LADY FIDGET: But still 'tis an arranter shame for a noble person to neglect her own honor and defame her own noble person with little inconsiderable fellows, foh!

DAINTY: I suppose the crime against our honor is the same with a man of quality as with another.

LADY FIDGET: How! No, sure, the man of quality is likest one's husband and therefore the fault should be the less.

DAINTY: But then the pleasure should be the less.

LADY FIDGET: Fie, fie, fie, for shame, sister! Whither shall we ramble? Be continent[5] in your discourse, or I shall hate you.

DAINTY: Besides, an intrigue is so much the more notorious for the man's quality.

SQUEAMISH: 'Tis true, nobody takes notice of a private man and therefore with him 'tis more secret, and the crime's the less when 'tis not known.

LADY FIDGET: You say true; i'faith, I think you are in the right on't. 'Tis not an injury to a husband till it be an injury to our honors; so that a woman of honor loses no honor with a private person; and to say truth—

DAINTY [apart to Squeamish]: So, the little fellow is grown a private person—with her—

LADY FIDGET: But still my dear, dear honor.

    [Enter Sir Jaspar, Horner, Dorilant.]

SIR JASPAR: Ay, my dear, dear of honor, thou hast still so much honor in thy mouth—

HORNER [aside]: That she has none elsewhere.

LADY FIDGET: Oh, what d'ye mean to bring in these upon us?

DAINTY: Foh, these are as bad as wits.

SQUEAMISH: Foh!

5. Restrained.

LADY FIDGET: Let us leave the room.

SIR JASPAR: Stay, stay; faith, to tell you the naked truth—

LADY FIDGET: Fie, Sir Jaspar, do not use that word "naked."

SIR JASPAR: Well, well, in short, I have business at Whitehall and cannot go to the play with you, therefore would have you go—

LADY FIDGET: With those two to a play?

SIR JASPAR: No, not with t'other but with Mr. Horner; there can be no more scandal to go with him than with Mr. Tattle or Master Limberham.[6]

LADY FIDGET: With that nasty fellow! No—no!

SIR JASPAR: Nay, prithee, dear, hear me.

[Whispers to Lady Fidget.]

HORNER: Ladies—

[Horner, Dorilant drawing near Squeamish and Dainty.]

DAINTY: Stand off.

SQUEAMISH: Do not approach us.

DAINTY: You herd with the wits, you are obscenity all over.

SQUEAMISH: And I would as soon look upon a picture of Adam and Eve, without fig leaves, as any of you, if I could help it; therefore keep off and do not make us sick.

DORILANT: What a devil are these?

HORNER: Why, these are pretenders to honor, as critics to wit, only by censuring others; and as every raw, peevish, out-of-humored, affected, dull, tea-drinking, arithmetical[7] fop sets up for a wit by railing at men of sense, so these for honor by railing at the Court and ladies of as great honor as quality.

SIR JASPAR: Come, Mr. Horner, I must desire you to go with these ladies to the play, sir.

HORNER: I, sir!

SIR JASPAR: Ay, ay, come, sir.

HORNER: I must beg your pardon, sir, and theirs; I will not be seen in women's company in public again for the world.

SIR JASPAR: Ha, ha, strange aversion!

SQUEAMISH: No, he's for women's company in private.

SIR JASPAR: He—poor man—he! Hah, ha, ha!

DAINTY: 'Tis a greater shame amongst lewd fellows to be seen in virtuous women's company than for the women to be seen with them.

HORNER: Indeed, madam, the time was I only hated virtuous women, but now I hate the other too; I beg your pardon, ladies.

LADY FIDGET: You are very obliging, sir, because we would not be troubled with you.

SIR JASPAR: In sober sadness, he shall go.

DORILANT: Nay, if he wo'not, I am ready to wait upon the ladies; and I think I am the fitter man.

SIR JASPAR: You, sir, no, I thank you for that—Master Horner is a privileged man amongst the virtuous ladies; 'twill be a great while before you are so; heh, he, he! He's my wife's gallant, heh, he, he! No, pray withdraw, sir, for as I take it, the virtuous ladies have no business with you.

---

6. I.e., Horner and Dorilant.   7. Precise, fussy.

DORILANT: And I am sure he can have none with them. 'Tis strange a man can't come amongst virtuous women now but upon the same terms as men are admitted into the Great Turk's seraglio;[8] but heavens keep me from being an ombre[9] player with 'em! But where is Pinchwife?

[*Exit Dorilant.*]

SIR JASPAR: Come, come, man; what, avoid the sweet society of womankind? that sweet, soft, gentle, tame, noble creature, woman, made for man's companion—

HORNER: So is that soft, gentle, tame and more noble creature a spaniel, and has all their tricks: can fawn, lie down, suffer beating and fawn the more; barks at your friends when they come to see you; makes your bed hard; gives you fleas, and the mange sometimes. And all the difference is, the spaniel's the more faithful animal and fawns but upon one master.

SIR JASPAR: Heh, he, he!

SQUEAMISH: Oh, the rude beast!

DAINTY: Insolent brute!

LADY FIDGET: Brute! Stinking, mortified, rotten French wether,[1] to dare

SIR JASPAR: Hold, an't please your ladyship.—For shame, Master Horner, your mother was a woman. [*Aside.*] Now shall I never reconcile 'em. [*Aside to Lady Fidget.*] Hark you, madam, take my advice in your anger. You know you often want one to make up your drolling[2] pack of ombre players; and you may cheat him easily, for he's an ill gamester and consequently loves play. Besides, you know, you have but two old civil gentlemen, with stinking breaths too, to wait upon you abroad; take in the third into your service. The other are but crazy; and a lady should have a supernumerary gentleman-usher,[3] as a supernumerary coach-horse, lest sometimes you should be forced to stay at home.

LADY FIDGET: But are you sure he loves play and has money?

SIR JASPAR: He loves play as much as you and has money as much as I.

LADY FIDGET: Then I am contented to make him pay for his scurrility; money makes up in a measure all other wants in men. [*Aside.*] Those whom we cannot make hold for gallants, we make fine.[4]

SIR JASPAR [*aside*]: So, so; now to mollify, to wheedle him.—Master Horner, will you never keep civil company? Methinks 'tis time now, since you are only fit for them. Come, come, man, you must e'en fall to visiting our wives, eating at our tables, drinking tea with our virtuous relations after dinner, dealing cards to 'em, reading plays and gazettes[5] to 'em, picking fleas out of their shocks[6] for 'em, collecting receipts,[7] new songs, women, pages and footmen for 'em.

HORNER: I hope they'll afford me better employment, sir.

SIR JASPAR: Heh, he, he! 'Tis fit you know your work before you come into your place; and since you are unprovided of a lady to flatter and a good house to eat at, pray frequent mine and call my wife mistress and she shall call you gallant, according to the custom.

HORNER: Who, I?

SIR JASPAR: Faith, thou shalt for my sake; come, for my sake only.

---

8. The Sultan's harem.
9. Three-person card game (with a pun on *hombre*: man).
1. Castrated ram.
2. Jesting, silly.
3. Extra attendant, servant.

4. Compensate, especially by way of money.
5. Newspapers.
6. Poodles.
7. Recipes.

HORNER: For your sake—

SIR JASPAR [to Lady Fidget]: Come, come, here's a gamester for you; let him be a little familiar sometimes. Nay, what if a little rude? Gamesters may be rude with ladies, you know.

LADY FIDGET: Yes, losing gamesters have a privilege with women.

HORNER: I always thought the contrary, that the winning gamester had most privilege with women, for when you have lost your money to a man, you'll lose anything you have, all you have, they say, and he may use you as he pleases.

SIR JASPAR: Heh, he, he! Well, win or lose, you shall have your liberty with her.

LADY FIDGET: As he behaves himself; and for your sake I'll give him admittance and freedom.

HORNER: All sorts of freedom, madam?

SIR JASPAR: Ay, ay, ay, all sorts of freedom thou canst take, and so go to her, begin thy new employment; wheedle[8] her, jest with her and be better acquainted one with another.

HORNER [aside]: I think I know her already, therefore may venture with her, my secret for hers.

[Horner and Lady Fidget whisper.]

SIR JASPAR: Sister, cuz, I have provided an innocent playfellow for you there.

DAINTY: Who, he!

SQUEAMISH: There's a playfellow indeed!

SIR JASPAR: Yes, sure; what, he is good enough to play at cards, blindman's buff,[9] or the fool with sometimes.

SQUEAMISH: Foh, we'll have no such playfellows.

DAINTY: No, sir, you shan't choose playfellows for us, we thank you.

SIR JASPAR: Nay, pray hear me. [Whispering to them.]

LADY FIDGET [aside to Horner]: But, poor gentleman, could you be so generous, so truly a man of honor, as for the sakes of us women of honor, to cause yourself to be reported no man? No man! And to suffer yourself the greatest shame that could fall upon a man, that none might fall upon us women by your conversation? But indeed, sir, as perfectly, perfectly the same man as before your going into France, sir? As perfectly, perfectly, sir?

HORNER: As perfectly, perfectly, madam. Nay, I scorn you should take my word; I desire to be tried only, madam.

LADY FIDGET: Well, that's spoken again like a man of honor; all men of honor desire to come to the test. But, indeed, generally you men report such things of yourselves, one does not know how or whom to believe and it is come to that pass we dare not take your words, no more than your tailors,[1] without some staid servant of yours be bound with you. But I have so strong a faith in your honor, dear, dear, noble sir, that I'd forfeit mine for yours at any time, dear sir.

HORNER: No, madam, you should not need to forfeit it for me; I have given you security already to save you harmless, my late reputation being so well known in the world, madam.

---

8. Entice.
9. Game in which a blindfolded player is pushed about as he guesses other players' identities.

1. Tailors often went unpaid by their customers, and so had reason to mistrust them.

LADY FIDGET: But if upon any future falling out or upon a suspicion of my taking the trust out of your hands to employ some other, you yourself should betray your trust, dear sir? I mean, if you'll give me leave to speak obscenely, you might tell, dear sir.

HORNER: If I did, nobody would believe me; the reputation of impotency is as hardly recovered again in the world as that of cowardice, dear madam.

LADY FIDGET: Nay then, as one may say, you may do your worst, dear, dear sir.

SIR JASPAR: Come, is your ladyship reconciled to him yet? Have you agreed on matters? For I must be gone to Whitehall.

LADY FIDGET: Why, indeed, Sir Jaspar, Master Horner is a thousand, thousand times a better man than I thought him. Cousin Squeamish, Sister Dainty, I can name him now; truly, not long ago, you know, I thought his very name obscenity and I would as soon have lain with him as have named him.

SIR JASPAR: Very likely, poor madam.

DAINTY: I believe it.

SQUEAMISH: No doubt on't.

SIR JASPAR: Well, well—that your ladyship is as virtuous as any she, I know, and him all the town knows—heh, he, he! Therefore, now you like him, get you gone to your business together; go, go to your business, I say, pleasure, whilst I go to my pleasure, business.

LADY FIDGET: Come then, dear gallant.

HORNER: Come away, my dearest mistress.

SIR JASPAR: So, so. Why, 'tis as I'd have it.   [Exit Sir Jaspar.]

HORNER: And as I'd have it.

LADY FIDGET: Who for his business from his wife will run,
Takes the best care to have her business done.   [Exeunt omnes.]

ACT 3

Scene 1

[Alithea and Mrs. Pinchwife.]

ALITHEA: Sister, what ails you? You are grown melancholy.

MRS. PINCHWIFE: Would it not make anyone melancholy to see you go every day fluttering about abroad, whilst I must stay at home like a poor, lonely, sullen bird in a cage?

ALITHEA: Ay, sister, but you came young and just from the nest to your cage, so that I thought you liked it and could be as cheerful in't as others that took their flight themselves early and are hopping abroad in the open air.

MRS. PINCHWIFE: Nay, I confess I was quiet enough till my husband told me what pure[1] lives the London ladies live abroad, with their dancing, meetings and junketings,[2] and dressed every day in their best gowns, and, I warrant you, play at ninepins[3] every day of the week, so they do.

[Enter Mr. Pinchwife.]

---

1. Splendid.
2. Merrymakings.

3. A game like bowling, more common in the country than in London high society.

PINCHWIFE: Come, what's here to do? You are putting the town pleasures in her head and setting her a-longing.

ALITHEA: Yes, after ninepins; you suffer none to give her those longings, you mean, but yourself.

PINCHWIFE: I tell her of the vanities of the town like a confessor.

ALITHEA: A confessor! Just such a confessor as he that, by forbidding a silly ostler to grease the horse's teeth,[4] taught him to do't.

PINCHWIFE: Come, Mistress Flippant, good precepts are lost when bad examples are still before us; the liberty you take abroad makes her hanker after it, and out of humor at home, poor wretch! She desired not to come to London; I would bring her.

ALITHEA: Very well.

PINCHWIFE: She has been this week in town and never desired, till this afternoon, to go abroad.

ALITHEA: Was she not at a play yesterday?

PINCHWIFE: Yes, but she ne'er asked me; I was myself the cause of her going.

ALITHEA: Then, if she ask you again, you are the cause of her asking, and not my example.

PINCHWIFE: Well, tomorrow night I shall be rid of you and the next day, before 'tis light, she and I'll be rid of the town, and my dreadful apprehensions. [*To Mrs. Pinchwife.*] Come, be not melancholy, for thou shalt go into the country after tomorrow, dearest.

ALITHEA: Great comfort!

MRS. PINCHWIFE: Pish, what d'ye tell me of the country for?

PINCHWIFE: How's this! What, pish at the country!

MRS. PINCHWIFE: Let me alone, I am not well.

PINCHWIFE: Oh, if that be all—what ails my dearest?

MRS. PINCHWIFE: Truly I don't know; but I have not been well since you told me there was a gallant at the play in love with me.

PINCHWIFE: Ha—

ALITHEA: That's by my example too!

PINCHWIFE: Nay, if you are not well, but are so concerned because a lewd fellow chanced to lie and say he liked you, you'll make me sick too.

MRS. PINCHWIFE: Of what sickness?

PINCHWIFE: O, of that which is worse than the plague, jealousy.

MRS. PINCHWIFE: Pish, you jeer! I'm sure there's no such disease in our receipt-book[5] at home.

PINCHWIFE: No, thou never met'st with it, poor innocent. [*Aside.*] Well, if thou cuckold me, 'twill be my own fault—for cuckolds and bastards are generally makers of their own fortune.

MRS. PINCHWIFE: Well, but pray, bud, let's to go a play tonight.

PINCHWIFE: 'Tis just done, she comes from it. But why are you so eager to see a play?

---

4. The groomsmen ("ostlers") at inns reputedly played this lucrative trick: they would grease the horse's teeth to discourage its eating, but charge the owner nonetheless for the uneaten feed.
5. Book of medical recipes.

MRS. PINCHWIFE: Faith, dear, not that I care one pin for their talk there; but I like to look upon the playermen and would see, if I could, the gallant you say loves me; that's all, dear bud.

PINCHWIFE: Is that all, dear bud?

ALITHEA: This proceeds from my example.

MRS. PINCHWIFE: But if the play be done, let's go abroad, however, dear bud.

PINCHWIFE: Come, have a little patience and thou shalt go into the country on Friday.

MRS. PINCHWIFE: Therefore I would see first some sights, to tell my neighbors of. Nay, I will go abroad, that's once.[6]

ALITHEA: I'm the cause of this desire too.

PINCHWIFE: But now I think on't, who was the cause of Horner's coming to my lodging today? That was you.

ALITHEA: No, you, because you would not let him see your handsome wife out of your lodging.

MRS. PINCHWIFE: Why, O Lord! Did the gentleman come hither to see me indeed?

PINCHWIFE: No, no.—You are not cause of that damned question too, Mistress Alithea? [Aside.] Well, she's in the right of it. He is in love with my wife—and comes after her—'tis so—but I'll nip his love in the bud, lest he should follow us into the country and break his chariot-wheel near our house on purpose for an excuse to come to't. But I think I know the town.

MRS. PINCHWIFE: Come, pray, bud, let's go abroad before 'tis late, for I will go, that's flat and plain.

PINCHWIFE [aside]: So! the obstinacy already of a town-wife, and I must, whilst she's here, humor her like one.—Sister, how shall we do, that she may not be seen or known?

ALITHEA: Let her put on her mask.

PINCHWIFE: Pshaw, a mask makes people but the more inquisitive and is as ridiculous a disguise as a stage-beard; her shape, stature, habit will be known and if we should meet with Horner, he would be sure to take acquaintance with us, must wish her joy, kiss her, talk to her, leer upon her, and the devil and all. No, I'll not use her to a mask, 'tis dangerous, for masks have made more cuckolds than the best faces that ever were known.

ALITHEA: How will you do then?

MRS. PINCHWIFE: Nay, shall we go? The Exchange will be shut, and I have a mind to see that.

PINCHWIFE: So—I have it—I'll dress her up in the suit we are to carry down to her brother, little Sir James; nay, I understand the town tricks. Come, let's go dress her. A mask! No—a woman masked, like a covered dish, gives a man curiosity and appetite, when, it may be, uncovered, 'twould turn his stomach; no, no.

ALITHEA: Indeed your comparison is something a greasy[7] one. But I had a gentle gallant used to say, "A beauty masked, like the sun in eclipse, gathers together more gazers than if it shined out."

[Exeunt.]

6. I.e., That's that.   7. Filthy or obscene.

Scene 2

[*The scene changes to the New Exchange. Enter Horner, Harcourt, Dorilant.*]

DORILANT: Engaged to women, and not sup with us?

HORNER: Ay, a pox on 'em all!

HARCOURT: You were much a more reasonable man in the morning and had as noble resolutions against 'em as a widower of a week's liberty.

DORILANT: Did I ever think to see you keep company with women in vain?

HORNER: In vain! No—'tis, since I can't love 'em, to be revenged on 'em.

HARCOURT: Now your sting is gone, you looked in the box amongst all those women, like a drone in the hive, all upon you, shoved and ill-used by 'em all, and thrust from one side to t'other.

DORILANT: Yet he must be buzzing amongst 'em still, like other old beetle-headed,[8] liquorish[9] drones. Avoid 'em, and hate 'em as they hate you.

HORNER: Because I do hate 'em, and would hate 'em yet more, I'll frequent 'em; you may see by marriage, nothing makes a man hate a woman more than her constant conversation. In short, I converse with 'em, as you do with rich fools, to laugh at 'em and use 'em ill.

DORILANT: But I would no more sup with women, unless I could lie with 'em, than sup with a rich coxcomb, unless I could cheat him.

HORNER: Yes, I have known thee sup with a fool for his drinking; if he could set out your hand[1] that way only, you were satisfied, and if he were a wine-swallowing mouth 'twas enough.

HARCOURT: Yes, a man drinks often with a fool, as he tosses with a marker,[2] only to keep his hand in ure.[3] But do the ladies drink?

HORNER: Yes, sir, and I shall have the pleasure at least of laying 'em flat with a bottle, and bring as much scandal that way upon 'em as formerly t'other.

HARCOURT: Perhaps you may prove as weak a brother amongst 'em that way as t'other.

DORILANT: Foh, drinking with women is as unnatural as scolding with 'em; but 'tis a pleasure of decayed fornicators, and the basest way of quenching love.

HARCOURT: Nay, 'tis drowning love instead of quenching it. But leave us for civil women too!

DORILANT: Ay, when he can't be the better for 'em. We hardly pardon a man that leaves his friend for a wench, and that's a pretty lawful call.

HORNER: Faith, I would not leave you for 'em, if they would not drink.

DORILANT: Who would disappoint his company at Lewis's[4] for a gossiping?

HARCOURT: Foh, wine and women, good apart, together as nauseous as sack and sugar.[5] But hark you, sir, before you go, a little of your advice; an old maimed general, when unfit for action, is fittest for counsel. I have other designs upon women than eating and drinking with them. I am in love with Sparkish's mistress, whom he is to marry tomorrow. Now how shall I get her?

[*Enter Sparkish, looking about.*]

HORNER: Why, here comes one will help you to her.

---

8. Stupid.
9. Lecherous.
1. Provide you with food and drink.
2. Plays dice with a score-keeper.

3. In practice.
4. A London restaurant.
5. Sack, white wine from Spain or the Canary Islands, was often drunk with sugar.

HARCOURT: He! He, I tell you, is my rival, and will hinder my love.

HORNER: No, a foolish rival and a jealous husband assist their rival's designs, for they are sure to make their women hate them, which is the first step to their love for another man.

HARCOURT: But I cannot come near his mistress but in his company.

HORNER: Still the better for you, for fools are most easily cheated when they themselves are accessories; and he is to be bubbled[6] of his mistress, as of his money, the common mistress, by keeping him company.

SPARKISH: Who is that, that is to be bubbled? Faith, let me snack,[7] I han't met with a bubble since Christmas. Gad, I think bubbles are like their brother woodcocks,[8] go out with the cold weather.

HARCOURT [apart to Horner]: A pox! He did not hear all, I hope.

SPARKISH: Come, you bubbling rogues you, where do we sup?—Oh, Harcourt, my mistress tells me you have been making fierce love to her all the play long, hah, ha! But I—

HARCOURT: I make love to her?

SPARKISH: Nay, I forgive thee, for I think I know thee, and I know her, but I am sure I know myself.

HARCOURT: Did she tell you so? I see all women are like these of the Exchange, who, to enhance the price of their commodities, report to their fond customers offers which were never made 'em.

HORNER: Ay, women are as apt to tell before the intrigue as men after it, and so show themselves the vainer sex. But hast thou a mistress, Sparkish? 'Tis as hard for me to believe it as that thou ever hadst a bubble, as you bragged just now.

SPARKISH: Oh, your servant, sir; are you at your raillery, sir? But we were some of us beforehand with you today at the play. The wits were something bold with you, sir; did you not hear us laugh?

HORNER: Yes, but I thought you had gone to plays to laugh at the poet's wit, not at your own.

SPARKISH: Your servant, sir; no, I thank you. Gad, I go to a play as to a country treat;[9] I carry my own wine to one and my own wit to t'other, or else I'm sure I should not be merry at either. And the reason why we are so often louder than the players is because we think we speak more wit and so become the poet's rivals in his audience. For to tell you the truth, we hate the silly rogues, nay, so much that we find fault even with their bawdy upon the stage, whilst we talk nothing else in the pit as loud.

HORNER: But why shouldst thou hate the silly poets? Thou hast too much wit to be one, and they, like whores, are only hated by each other—and thou dost scorn writing, I'm sure.

SPARKISH: Yes, I'd have you to know I scorn writing; but women, women, that make men do all foolish things, make 'em write songs too. Everybody does it. 'Tis even as common with lovers as playing with fans; and you can no more help rhyming to your Phyllis[1] than drinking to your Phyllis.

HARCOURT: Nay, poetry in love is no more to be avoided than jealousy.

DORILANT: But the poets damned your songs, did they?

SPARKISH: Damn the poets! They turned 'em into burlesque, as they call it. That burlesque[2] is a hocus-pocus trick they have got, which, by virtue of *hictius doctius*,[3] *topsy-turvy*, they make a wise and witty man in the world a fool upon the stage, you know not how; and 'tis therefore I hate 'em too, for I know not but it may be my own case, for they'll put a man into a play for looking asquint.[4] Their predecessors were contented to make serving-men only their stage-fools, but these rogues must have gentlemen, with a pox to 'em, nay, knights; and, indeed, you shall hardly see a fool upon the stage but he's a knight and, to tell you the truth, they have kept me these six years from being a knight in earnest, for fear of being knighted in a play, and dubbed a fool.

DORILANT: Blame 'em not; they must follow their copy,[5] the age.

HARCOURT: But why shouldst thou be afraid of being in a play, who expose yourself every day in the play-houses, and as public places?

HORNER: 'Tis but being on the stage, instead of standing on a bench in the pit.

DORILANT: Don't you give money to painters to draw you like? And are you afraid of your pictures at length in a playhouse, where all your mistresses may see you?

SPARKISH: A pox! Painters don't draw the smallpox or pimples in one's face. Come, damn all your silly authors whatever, all books and booksellers, by the world, and all readers, courteous or uncourteous.

HARCOURT: But who comes here, Sparkish?

[*Enter Mr. Pinchwife and his wife in man's clothes, Alithea, Lucy her maid.*]

SPARKISH: Oh, hide me! There's my mistress too. [*Sparkish hides himself behind Harcourt.*]

HARCOURT: She sees you.

SPARKISH: But I will not see her. 'Tis time to go to Whitehall and I must not fail the drawing room.

HARCOURT: Pray, first carry me, and reconcile me to her.

SPARKISH: Another time; faith, the King will have supped.

HARCOURT: Not with the worse stomach for thy absence; thou art one of those fools that think their attendance at the King's meals as necessary as his physicians', when you are more troublesome to him than his doctors, or his dogs.

SPARKISH: Pshaw, I know my interest, sir. Prithee hide me.

HORNER: Your servant, Pinchwife.—What, he knows us not!

PINCHWIFE [*to his wife aside*]: Come along.

MRS. PINCHWIFE: Pray, have you any ballads? Give me sixpenny worth.

CLASP: We have no ballads.

MRS. PINCHWIFE: Then give me *Covent Garden Drollery*,[6] and a play or two— Oh, here's *Tarugo's Wiles*, and *The Slighted Maiden*;[7] I'll have them.

PINCHWIFE [*apart to her*]: No, plays are not for your reading. Come along; will you discover yourself?

HORNER: Who is that pretty youth with him, Sparkish?

SPARKISH: I believe his wife's brother, because he's something like her, but I never saw her but once.

2. I.e., they wrote parodies of Sparkish's songs
3. Like hocus pocus.
4. I.e., they'll make him a comic character in a play, mocking even the tiniest fault.
5. The original from which a copy is made.
6. A collection of songs, prologues, epilogues, and poetry by various authors, including Wycherley, believed to have been edited by Aphra Behn (1672).
7. Two theatrical "oldies," no longer current: a comedy by Thomas St. Serfe (1668) and a tragicomedy by Robert Stapleton (1663).

HORNER: Extremely handsome; I have seen a face like it too. Let us follow 'em.

[*Exeunt Pinchwife, Mrs. Pinchwife, Alithea, Lucy; Horner, Dorilant following them.*]

HARCOURT: Come, Sparkish, your mistress saw you and will be angry you go not to her. Besides, I would fain be reconciled to her, which none but you can do, dear friend.

SPARKISH: Well, that's a better reason, dear friend, I would not go near her now, for hers or my own sake, but I can deny you nothing, for though I have known thee a great while, never go,[8] if I do not love thee as well as a new acquaintance.

HARCOURT: I am obliged to you indeed, dear friend. I would be well with her, only to be well with thee still, for these ties to wives usually dissolve all ties to friends. I would be contented she should enjoy you a-nights, but I would have you to myself a-days, as I have had, dear friend.

SPARKISH: And thou shalt enjoy me a-days, dear, dear friend, never stir, and I'll be divorced from her sooner than from thee. Come along.

HARCOURT [*aside*]: So, we are hard put to't when we make our rival our procurer; but neither she nor her brother would let me come near her now. When all's done, a rival is the best cloak to steal to a mistress under, without suspicion, and when we have once got to her as we desire, we throw him off like other cloaks.

[*Exit Sparkish, and Harcourt following him. Re-enter Mr. Pinchwife, Mrs. Pinchwife in man's clothes.*]

PINCHWIFE [*to Alithea (off-stage)*]: Sister, if you will not go, we must leave you. [*Aside.*] The fool her gallant and she will muster up all the young saunterers of this place, and they will leave their dear seamstresses to follow us. What a swarm of cuckolds and cuckold-makers are here!—Come, let's be gone, Mistress Margery.

MRS. PINCHWIFE: Don't you believe that; I ha'n't half my bellyful of sights yet.

PINCHWIFE: Then walk this way.

MRS. PINCHWIFE: Lord, what a power of brave signs are here! Stay—the Bull's-Head, the Ram's-Head and the Stag's-Head, dear—

PINCHWIFE: Nay, if every husband's proper sign[9] here were visible, they would be all alike.

MRS. PINCHWIFE: What d'ye mean by that, bud?

PINCHWIFE: 'Tis no matter—no matter, bud.

MRS. PINCHWIFE: Pray tell me; nay, I will know.

PINCHWIFE: They would be all bulls', stags', and rams' heads.

[*Exeunt Mr. Pinchwife, Mrs. Pinchwife. Re-enter Sparkish, Harcourt, Alithea, Lucy, at t'other door.*]

SPARKISH: Come, dear madam, for my sake you shall be reconciled to him.

ALITHEA: For your sake I hate him.

HARCOURT: That's something too cruel, madam, to hate me for his sake.

SPARKISH: Ay indeed, madam, too, too cruel to me, to hate my friend for my sake.

ALITHEA: I hate him because he is your enemy; and you ought to hate him too, for making love to me, if you love me.

SPARKISH: That's a good one! I hate a man for loving you! If he did love you, 'tis but what he can't help and 'tis your fault, not his, if he admires you. I hate a man for being of my opinion! I'll ne'er do't by the world.

---

8. Worry not.   9. I.e., a cuckold's horns.

ALITHEA: Is it for your honor or mine, to suffer a man to make love to me, who am to marry you tomorrow?

SPARKISH: Is it for your honor or mine, to have me jealous? That he makes love to you is a sign you are handsome and that I am not jealous is a sign you are virtuous. That, I think, is for your honor.

ALITHEA: But 'tis your honor too I am concerned for.

HARCOURT: But why, dearest madam, will you be more concerned for his honor than he is himself? Let his honor alone, for my sake and his. He, he has no honor—

SPARKISH: How's that?

HARCOURT: But what my dear friend can guard himself.

SPARKISH: O ho—that's right again.

HARCOURT: Your care of his honor argues his neglect of it, which is no honor to my dear friend here; therefore once more, let his honor go which way it will, dear madam.

SPARKISH: Ay, ay, were it for my honor to marry a woman whose virtue I suspected and could not trust her in a friend's hands?

ALITHEA: Are you not afraid to lose me?

HARCOURT: He afraid to lose you, madam! No, no—you may see how the most estimable and most glorious creature in the world is valued by him. Will you not see it?

SPARKISH: Right, honest Frank, I have that noble value for her that I cannot be jealous of her.

ALITHEA: You mistake him, he means you care not for me, nor who has me.

SPARKISH: Lord, madam, I see you are jealous.[1] Will you wrest a poor man's meaning from his words?

ALITHEA: You astonish me, sir, with your want of jealousy.

SPARKISH: And you make me giddy, madam, with your jealousy and fears and virtue and honor. Gad, I see virtue makes a woman as troublesome as a little reading or learning.

ALITHEA: Monstrous!

LUCY [behind]: Well, to see what easy husbands these women of quality can meet with; a poor chambermaid can never have such lady-like luck. Besides, he's thrown away upon her; she'll make no use of her fortune, her blessing. None to[2] a gentleman for a pure cuckold, for it requires good breeding to be a cuckold.

ALITHEA: I tell you then plainly, he pursues me to marry me.

SPARKISH: Pshaw!

HARCOURT: Come, madam, you see you strive in vain to make him jealous of me; my dear friend is the kindest creature in the world to me.

SPARKISH: Poor fellow.

HARCOURT: But his kindness only is not enough for me, without your favor; your good opinion, dear madam, 'tis that must perfect my happiness. Good gentleman, he believes all I say—would you would do so. Jealous of me! I would not wrong him nor you for the world.

SPARKISH: Look you there; hear him, hear him, and do not walk away so.

[Alithea walks carelessly to and fro.]

---

1. Here, vehement, fearful.   2. There's no one like.

HARCOURT: I love you, madam, so—

SPARKISH: How's that! Nay—now you begin to go too far indeed.

HARCOURT: So much, I confess, I say I love you, that I would not have you miserable and cast yourself away upon so unworthy and inconsiderable a thing as what you see here. [*Clapping his hand on his breast, points at Sparkish.*]

SPARKISH: No, faith, I believe thou wouldst not; now his meaning is plain. But I knew before thou wouldst not wrong me nor her.

HARCOURT: No, no, heavens forbid the glory of her sex should fall so low as into the embraces of such a contemptible wretch, the last of mankind—my dear friend here—I injure him! [*Embracing Sparkish.*]

ALITHEA: Very well.

SPARKISH: No, no, dear friend, I knew it.—Madam, you see he will rather wrong himself than me, in giving himself such names.

ALITHEA: Do not you understand him yet?

SPARKISH: Yes, how modestly he speaks of himself, poor fellow.

ALITHEA: Methinks he speaks impudently of yourself, since—before yourself too; insomuch that I can no longer suffer his scurrilous abusiveness to you, no more than his love to me. [*Offers to go.*]

SPARKISH: Nay, nay, madam, pray stay—his love to you! Lord, madam, he has not spoke yet plain enough?

ALITHEA: Yes, indeed, I should think so.

SPARKISH: Well then, by the world, a man can't speak civilly to a woman now but presently she says he makes love to her. Nay, madam, you shall stay, with your pardon, since you have not yet understood him, till he has made an éclaircissement[3] of his love to you, that is, what kind of love it is. [*To Harcourt.*] Answer to thy catechism. Friend, do you love my mistress here?

HARCOURT: Yes, I wish she would not doubt it.

SPARKISH: But how do you love her?

HARCOURT: With all my soul.

ALITHEA: I thank him; methinks he speaks plain enough now.

SPARKISH [*to Alithea*]: You are out still.—But with what kind of love, Harcourt?

HARCOURT: With the best and truest love in the world.

SPARKISH: Look you there then, that is with no matrimonial love, I'm sure.

ALITHEA: How's that? Do you say matrimonial love is not best?

SPARKISH: Gad, I went too far ere I was aware. But speak for thyself, Harcourt; you said you would not wrong me nor her.

HARCOURT: No, no, madam, e'en take him for heaven's sake—

SPARKISH: Look you there, madam.

HARCOURT: Who should in all justice be yours, he that loves you most. [*Claps his hand on his breast.*]

ALITHEA: Look you there, Mr. Sparkish, who's that?

SPARKISH: Who should it be?—Go on, Harcourt.

HARCOURT: Who loves you more than women titles or fortune fools. [*Points at Sparkish.*]

SPARKISH: Look you there, he means me still, for he points at me.

ALITHEA: Ridiculous!

3. Explanation.

HARCOURT: Who can only match your faith and constancy in love.

SPARKISH: Ay.

HARCOURT: Who knows, if it be possible, how to value so much beauty and virtue.

SPARKISH: Ay.

HARCOURT: Whose love can no more be equaled in the world than that heavenly form of yours.

SPARKISH: No.

HARCOURT: Who could no more suffer a rival than your absence, and yet could no more suspect your virtue than his own constancy in his love to you.

SPARKISH: No.

HARCOURT: Who, in fine,[4] loves you better than his eyes that first made him love you.

SPARKISH: Ay—nay, madam, faith, you shan't go till—

ALITHEA: Have a care, lest you make me stay too long—

SPARKISH: But till he has saluted you, that I may be assured you are friends, after his honest advice and declaration. Come, pray, madam, be friends with him.

   [Enter Mr. Pinchwife, Mrs. Pinchwife]

ALITHEA: You must pardon me, sir, that I am not yet so obedient to you.

PINCHWIFE: What, invite your wife to kiss men? Monstrous! Are you not ashamed? I will never forgive you.

SPARKISH: Are you not ashamed that I should have more confidence in the chastity of your family than you have? You must not teach me. I am a man of honor, sir, though I am frank[5] and free; I am frank, sir—

PINCHWIFE: Very frank, sir, to share your wife with your friends.

SPARKISH: He is an humble, menial[6] friend, such as reconciles the differences of the marriage bed. You know man and wife do not always agree; I design him for that use, therefore would have him well with my wife.

PINCHWIFE: A menial friend!—you will get a great many menial friends by showing your wife as you do.

SPARKISH: What then? It may be I have a pleasure in't, as I have to show fine clothes at a playhouse the first day and count money before poor rogues.

PINCHWIFE: He that shows his wife or money will be in danger of having them borrowed sometimes.

SPARKISH: I love to be envied and would not marry a wife that I alone could love; loving alone is as dull as eating alone. Is it not a frank age? And I am a frank person. And to tell you the truth, it may be I love to have rivals in a wife; they make her seem to a man still but as a kept mistress. And so good night, for I must to Whitehall.—Madam, I hope you are now reconciled to my friend and so I wish you a good night, madam, and sleep if you can, for tomorrow you know I must visit you early with a canonical gentleman. Good night, dear Harcourt. [Exit Sparkish.]

HARCOURT: Madam, I hope you will not refuse my visit tomorrow, if it should be earlier, with a canonical gentleman, than Mr. Sparkish's.

4. In short.
5. Unreserved, open.

6. Household.

PINCHWIFE [*coming between Alithea and Harcourt*]: This gentlewoman is yet under my care; therefore you must yet forbear your freedom with her, sir.

HARCOURT: Must, sir!

PINCHWIFE: Yes, sir, she is my sister.

HARCOURT: 'Tis well she is, sir—for I must be her servant, sir.—Madam—

PINCHWIFE: Come away, sister; we had been gone, if it had not been for you, and so avoided these lewd rake-hells,[7] who seem to haunt us.

[*Enter Horner, Dorilant to them.*]

HORNER: How now, Pinchwife?

PINCHWIFE: Your servant.

HORNER: What, I see a little time in the country makes a man turn wild and unsociable and only fit to converse with his horses, dogs and his herds.

PINCHWIFE: I have business, sir, and must mind it; your business is pleasure, therefore you and I must go different ways.

HORNER: Well, you may go on, but this pretty young gentleman—[*Takes hold of Mrs. Pinchwife.*]

HARCOURT: The lady—

DORILANT: And the maid—

HORNER: Shall stay with us, for I suppose their business is the same with ours, pleasure.

PINCHWIFE [*aside*]: 'Sdeath, he know her, she carries it so sillily! Yet if he does not, I should be more silly to discover it first.

ALITHEA: Pray, let us go, sir.

PINCHWIFE: Come, come—

HORNER [*to Mrs. Pinchwife*]: Had you not rather stay with us?—Prithee, Pinchwife, who is this pretty young gentleman?

PINCHWIFE: One to whom I'm a guardian. [*Aside.*] I wish I could keep her out of your hands.

HORNER: Who is he? I never saw anything so pretty in all my life.

PINCHWIFE: Pshaw, do not look upon him so much. He's a poor bashful youth, you'll put him out of countenance.—Come away, brother. [*Offers to take her away.*]

HORNER: Oh, your brother!

PINCHWIFE: Yes, my wife's brother.—Come, come, she'll stay supper for us.

HORNER: I thought so, for he is very like her I saw you at the play with, whom I told you I was in love with.

MRS. PINCHWIFE [*aside*]: O jeminy! Is this he that was in love with me? I am glad on't, I vow, for he's a curious fine gentleman, and I love him already too. [*To Mr. Pinchwife.*] Is this he, bud?

PINCHWIFE [*to his wife*]: Come away, come away.

HORNER: Why, what haste are you in? Why won't you let me talk with him?

PINCHWIFE: Because you'll debauch him; he's yet young and innocent and I would not have him debauched for anything in the world. [*Aside.*] How she gazes on him! The devil!

---

7. Scoundrels.

HORNER: Harcourt, Dorilant, look you here; this is the likeness of that dowdy[8] he told us of, his wife. Did you ever see a lovelier creature? The rogue has reason to be jealous of his wife since she is like him, for she would make all that see her in love with her.

HARCOURT: And as I remember now, she is as like him here as can be.

DORILANT: She is indeed very pretty, if she be like him.

HORNER: Very pretty? A very pretty commendation! She is a glorious creature, beautiful beyond all things I ever beheld.

PINCHWIFE: So, so.

HARCOURT: More beautiful than a poet's first mistress of imagination.

HORNER: Or another man's last mistress of flesh and blood.

MRS. PINCHWIFE: Nay, now you jeer, sir; pray don't jeer me.

PINCHWIFE: Come, come. [Aside.] By heavens, she'll discover herself!

HORNER: I speak of your sister, sir.

PINCHWIFE: Ay, but saying she was handsome, if like him, made him blush. [Aside.] I am upon a rack!

HORNER: Methinks he is so handsome he should not be a man.

PINCHWIFE [aside]: Oh, there 'tis out! He has discovered her! I am not able to suffer any longer. [To his wife.] Come, come away, I say.

HORNER: Nay, by your leave, sir, he shall not go yet.—[To them.] Harcourt, Dorilant, let us torment this jealous rogue a little.

HARCOURT:
DORILANT: } How?

HORNER: I'll show you.

PINCHWIFE: Come, pray, let him go, I cannot stay fooling any longer. I tell you his sister stays supper for us.

HORNER: Does she? Come then, we'll all go sup with her and thee.

PINCHWIFE: No, now I think on't, having stayed so long for us, I warrant she's gone to bed. [Aside.] I wish she and I were well out of their hands.—Come, I must rise early tomorrow, come.

HORNER: Well, then, if she be gone to bed, I wish her and you a good night. But pray, young gentleman, present my humble service to her.

MRS. PINCHWIFE: Thank you heartily, sir.

PINCHWIFE [aside]: 'Sdeath! she will discover herself yet in spite of me.—He is something more civil to you, for your kindness to his sister, than I am, it seems.

HORNER: Tell her, dear sweet little gentleman, for all your brother there, that you have revived the love I had for her at first sight in the playhouse.

MRS. PINCHWIFE: But did you love her indeed, and indeed?

PINCHWIFE [aside]: So, so.—Away, I say.

HORNER: Nay, stay. Yes, indeed, and indeed, pray do you tell her so, and give her this kiss from me. [Kisses her.]

PINCHWIFE [aside]: O heavens! What do I suffer! Now 'tis too plain he knows her, and yet—

HORNER: And this, and this—[Kisses her again.]

MRS. PINCHWIFE: What do you kiss me for? I am no woman.

---

8. Shabby, dull woman.

PINCHWIFE [*aside*]: So—there, 'tis out.—Come, I cannot, nor will stay any longer.

HORNER: Nay, they shall send your lady a kiss too. Here, Harcourt, Dorilant, will you not? [*They kiss her.*]

PINCHWIFE [*aside*]: How! Do I suffer this? Was I not accusing another just now for this rascally patience, in permitting his wife to be kissed before his face? Ten thousand ulcers gnaw away their lips!—Come, come.

HORNER: Good night, dear little gentleman. Madam, good night. Farewell, Pinchwife. [*Apart to Harcourt and Dorilant.*] Did not I tell you I would raise his jealous gall? [*Exeunt Horner, Harcourt, and Dorilant.*]

PINCHWIFE: So, they are gone at last; stay, let me see first if the coach be at this door. [*Exit.*]

[*Horner, Harcourt, Dorilant return.*]

HORNER: What, not gone yet? Will you be sure to do as I desired you, sweet sir?

MRS. PINCHWIFE: Sweet sir, but what will you give me then?

HORNER: Anything. Come away into the next walk.

[*Exit Horner, haling away Mrs. Pinchwife.*]

ALITHEA: Hold, hold! What d'ye do?

LUCY: Stay, stay, hold—

HARCOURT: Hold, madam, hold! Let him present[9] him, he'll come presently. Nay, I will never let you go till you answer my question.

LUCY: For God's sake, sir, I must follow 'em.

DORILANT: No, I have something to present you with too; you shan't follow them.

[*Alithea, Lucy struggling with Harcourt and Dorilant. Pinchwife returns.*]

PINCHWIFE: Where?—how?—what's become of?—gone!—whither?

LUCY: He's only gone with the gentleman, who will give him something, an't please your worship.

PINCHWIFE: Something—give him something, with a pox!—where are they?

ALITHEA: In the next walk only, brother.

PINCHWIFE: Only, only! Where, where?

[*Exit Pinchwife and returns presently, then goes out again*]

HARCOURT: What's the matter with him? Why so much concerned? But dearest madam—

ALITHEA: Pray let me go, sir; I have said and suffered enough already.

HARCOURT: Then you will not look upon nor pity my sufferings?

ALITHEA: To look upon 'em, when I cannot help 'em, were cruelty, not pity; therefore I will never see you more.

HARCOURT: Let me then, madam, have my privilege of a banished lover, complaining or railing, and giving you but a farewell reason why, if you cannot condescend to marry me, you should not take that wretch, my rival.

ALITHEA: He only, not you, since my honor is engaged so far to him, can give me a reason why I should not marry him; but if he be true and what I think him to me, I must be so to him. Your servant, sir.

HARCOURT: Have women only constancy when 'tis a vice and, like fortune, only true to fools?

9. Offer a gift to.

DORILANT [*to Lucy, who struggles to get from him*]: Thou shalt not stir, thou robust creature; you see I can deal with you, therefore you should stay the rather, and be kind.

[*Enter Pinchwife.*]

PINCHWIFE: Gone, gone, not to be found! Quite gone! Ten thousand plagues go with 'em! Which way went they?

ALITHEA: But into t'other walk, brother.

LUCY: Their business will be done presently sure, an't please your worship; it can't be long in doing, I'm sure on't.

ALITHEA: Are they not there?

PINCHWIFE: No; you know where they are, you infamous wretch, eternal shame of your family, which you do not dishonor enough yourself, you think, but you must help her to do it too, thou legion of bawds!

ALITHEA: Good brother—

PINCHWIFE: Damned, damned sister!

ALITHEA: Look you here, she's coming.

[*Enter Mrs. Pinchwife in man's clothes, running, with her hat under her arm, full of oranges and dried fruit; Horner following.*]

MRS. PINCHWIFE: O dear bud, look you here what I have got, see!

PINCHWIFE [*aside, rubbing his forehead*]: And what I have got here too, which you can't see.

MRS. PINCHWIFE: The fine gentleman has given me better things yet.

PINCHWIFE: Has he so? [*Aside.*] Out of breath and colored! I must hold yet.

HORNER: I have only given your little brother an orange, sir.

PINCHWIFE [*to Horner*]: Thank you, sir. [*Aside.*] You have only squeezed my orange, I suppose, and given it me again; yet I must have a city patience. [*To his wife.*] Come, come away.

MRS. PINCHWIFE: Stay, till I have put up my fine things, bud.

[*Enter Sir Jaspar Fidget.*]

SIR JASPAR: O Master Horner, come, come, the ladies stay for you; your mistress, my wife, wonders you make not more haste to her.

HORNER: I have stayed this half hour for you here and 'tis your fault I am not now with your wife.

SIR JASPAR: But pray, don't let her know so much; the truth on't is, I was advancing a certain project to his Majesty about—I'll tell you.

HORNER: No, let's go and hear it at your house.—Good night, sweet little gentleman. One kiss more, you'll remember me now, I hope. [*Kisses her.*]

DORILANT: What, Sir Jaspar, will you separate friends? He promised to sup with us; and if you take him to your house, you'll be in danger of our company too.

SIR JASPAR: Alas, gentlemen, my house is not fit for you; there are none but civil women there, which are not fit for your turn. He, you know, can bear with the society of civil women now, ha, ha, ha! Besides, he's one of my family—he's—heh, heh, heh!

DORILANT: What is he?

SIR JASPAR: Faith, my eunuch, since you'll have it, heh, he, he!

[*Exeunt Sir Jaspar Fidget and Horner.*]

DORILANT: I rather wish thou wert his, or my cuckold. Harcourt, what a good cuckold is lost there for want of a man to make him one! Thee and I cannot have Horner's privilege, who can make use of it.

HARCOURT: Ay, to poor Horner 'tis like coming to an estate at threescore, when a man can't be the better for't.

PINCHWIFE: Come.

MRS. PINCHWIFE: Presently, bud.

DORILANT: Come, let us go too. [*To Alithea.*] Madam, your servant. [*To Lucy.*] Good night, strapper.[1]

HARCOURT: Madam, though you will not let me have a good day or night, I wish you one; but dare not name the other half of my wish.

ALITHEA: Good night, sir, forever.

MRS. PINCHWIFE: I don't know where to put this here, dear bud; you shall eat it; nay, you shall have part of the fine gentleman's good things, or treat as you call it, when we come home.

PINCHWIFE: Indeed, I deserve it, since I furnished the best part of it.[*Strikes away the orange.*]

> The gallant treats, presents, and gives the ball
> But 'tis the absent cuckold pays for all.

[Exeunt.]

ACT 4

Scene 1

[*In Pinchwife's house in the morning. Lucy, Alithea dressed in new clothes.*]

LUCY: Well—madam, now have I dressed you and set you out with so many ornaments and spent upon you ounces of essence and pulvilio,[1] and all this for no other purpose but as people adorn and perfume a corpse for a stinking secondhand grave[2]—such or as bad I think as Master Sparkish's bed.

ALITHEA: Hold your peace.

LUCY: Nay, madam, I will ask you the reason why you would banish poor Master Harcourt forever from your sight. How could you be so hardhearted?

ALITHEA: 'Twas because I was not hardhearted.

LUCY: No, no, 'twas stark love and kindness, I warrant.

ALITHEA: It was so; I would see him no more because I love him.

LUCY: Hey-day, a very pretty reason!

ALITHEA: You do not understand me.

LUCY: I wish you may yourself.

ALITHEA: I was engaged to marry, you see, another man, whom my justice will not suffer me to deceive or injure.

LUCY: Can there be a greater cheat or wrong done to a man than to give him your person without your heart? I should make a conscience of[3] it.

ALITHEA: I'll retrieve it for him after I am married a while.

LUCY: The woman that marries to love better will be as much mistaken as the wencher that marries to live better. No, madam, marrying to increase love is like gaming to become rich; alas, you only lose what little stock you had before.

---

1. Robust woman.
1. Perfume and fragrant powder.

2. I.e., a grave newly opened for a second burial.
3. Have scruples about.

ALITHEA: I find by your rhetoric you have been bribed to betray me.

LUCY: Only by his merit, that has bribed your heart, you see, against your word and rigid honor. But what a devil is this honor! 'Tis sure a disease in the head, like the megrim, or falling sickness,[4] that always hurries people away to do themselves mischief. Men lose their lives by it; women what's dearer to 'em, their love, the life of life.

ALITHEA: Come, pray talk you no more of honor, nor Master Harcourt. I wish the other would come to secure my fidelity to him and his right in me.

LUCY: You will marry him then?

ALITHEA: Certainly. I have given him already my word and will my hand too, to make it good when he comes.

LUCY: Well, I wish I may never stick pin more if he be not an arrant natural to[5] t'other fine gentleman.

ALITHEA: I own he wants the wit of Harcourt, which I will dispense withal for another want he has, which is want of jealousy, which men of wit seldom want.

LUCY: Lord, madam, what should you do with a fool to your husband? You intend to be honest, don't you? Then that husbandly virtue, credulity, is thrown away upon you.

ALITHEA: He only that could suspect my virtue should have cause to do it; 'tis Sparkish's confidence in my truth that obliges me to be so faithful to him.

LUCY: You are not sure his opinion may last.

ALITHEA: I am satisfied 'tis impossible for him to be jealous after the proofs I have had of him. Jealousy in a husband—Heaven defend me from it! It begets a thousand plagues to a poor woman, the loss of her honor, her quiet and her—

LUCY: And her pleasure.

ALITHEA: What d'ye mean, impertinent?

LUCY: Liberty is a great pleasure, madam.

ALITHEA: I say, loss of her honor, her quiet, nay, her life sometimes, and what's as bad almost, the loss of this town; that is, she is sent into the country, which is the last ill usage of a husband to a wife, I think.

LUCY [aside]: Oh, does the wind lie there?—Then, of necessity, madam, you think a man must carry his wife into the country, if he be wise. The country is as terrible, I find, to our young English ladies as a monastery to those abroad, and, on my virginity, I think they would rather marry a London jailer than a high sheriff of a county, since neither can stir from his employment. Formerly women of wit married fools for a great estate, a fine seat, or the like, but now 'tis for a pretty seat only in Lincoln's Inn Fields, St James's Fields, or the Pall Mall.[6]

[Enter to them Sparkish and Harcourt dressed like a parson.]

SPARKISH: Madam, your humble servant, a happy day to you, and to us all.

HARCOURT: Amen.

ALITHEA: Who have we here?

SPARKISH: My chaplain, faith. O madam, poor Harcourt remembers his humble service to you and, in obedience to your last commands, refrains coming into your sight.

---

4. Migraine headache, or epilepsy.
5. An utter fool in comparison to.
6. Fashionable residential areas of London, distinguished by their famous inhabitants and expensive shops, as well as their grand houses.

ALITHEA: Is not that he?

SPARKISH: No, fie, no; but to show that he ne'er intended to hinder our match, has sent his brother here to join our hands. When I get me a wife, I must get her a chaplain, according to the custom; this is his brother, and my chaplain.

ALITHEA: His brother?

LUCY [aside]: And your chaplain, to preach in your pulpit then.

ALITHEA: His brother!

SPARKISH: Nay, I knew you would not believe it.—I told you, sir, she would take you for your brother Frank.

ALITHEA: Believe it!

LUCY [aside]: His brother! hah, ha, he! He has a trick left still, it seems.

SPARKISH: Come, my dearest, pray let us go to church before the canonical hour[7] is past.

ALITHEA: For shame, you are abused still.

SPARKISH: By the world, 'tis strange now you are so incredulous.

ALITHEA: 'Tis strange you are so credulous.

SPARKISH: Dearest of my life, hear me. I tell you this is Ned Harcourt of Cambridge; by the world, you see he has a sneaking college look. 'Tis true he's something like his brother Frank and they differ from each other no more than in their age, for they were twins.

LUCY: Hah, ha, he!

ALITHEA: Your servant, sir; I cannot be so deceived, though you are. But come, let's hear; how do you know what you affirm so confidently?

SPARKISH: Why, I'll tell you all. Frank Harcourt coming to me this morning, to wish me joy and present his service to you, I asked him if he could help me to a parson, whereupon he told me he had a brother in town who was in orders and he went straight away and sent him you see there to me.

ALITHEA: Yes, Frank goes and puts on a black coat, then tells you he is Ned; that's all you have for't.

SPARKISH: Pshaw, pshaw, I tell you by the same token, the midwife put her garter about Frank's neck to know 'em asunder, they were so like.

ALITHEA: Frank tells you this too.

SPARKISH: Ay, and Ned there too; nay, they are both in a story.

ALITHEA: So, so; very foolish!

SPARKISH: Lord, if you won't believe one, you had best try him by your chambermaid there, for chambermaids must needs know chaplains from other men, they are so used to 'em.

LUCY: Let's see; nay, I'll be sworn he has the canonical smirk and the filthy, clammy palm of a chaplain.

ALITHEA: Well, most reverend doctor, pray let us make an end of this fooling.

HARCOURT: With all my soul, divine, heavenly creature, when you please.

ALITHEA: He speaks like a chaplain indeed.

SPARKISH: Why, was there not "soul," "divine," "heavenly," in what he said?

ALITHEA: Once more, most impertinent black coat, cease your persecution and let us have a conclusion of this ridiculous love.

---

7. Church law permitted the marriage ceremony only in the morning; it could be performed at any time between 8 A.M. and noon.

HARCOURT [*aside*]: I had forgot. I must suit my style to my coat, or I wear it in vain.

ALITHEA: I have no more patience left; let us make once an end of this troublesome love, I say.

HARCOURT: So be it, seraphic lady, when your honor shall think it meet and convenient so to do.

SPARKISH: Gad, I'm sure none but a chaplain could speak so, I think.

ALITHEA: Let me tell you, sir, this dull trick will not serve your turn; though you delay our marriage, you shall not hinder it.

HARCOURT: Far be it from me, munificent patroness, to delay your marriage. I desire nothing more than to marry you presently, which I might do, if you yourself would, for my noble, good-natured and thrice generous patron here would not hinder it.

SPARKISH: No, poor man, not I, faith.

HARCOURT: And now, madam, let me tell you plainly, nobody else shall marry you; by heavens, I'll die first, for I'm sure I should die[8] after it.

LUCY [*aside*]: How his love has made him forget his function, as I have seen it in real parsons!

ALITHEA: That was spoken like a chaplain too! Now you understand him, I hope.

SPARKISH: Poor man, he takes it heinously to be refused. I can't blame him; 'tis putting an indignity upon him not to be suffered. But you'll pardon me, madam, it shan't be, he shall marry us. Come away, pray, madam.

LUCY [*aside*]: Hah, ha, he! More ado! 'Tis late.

ALITHEA: Invincible stupidity! I tell you he would marry me as your rival, not as your chaplain.

SPARKISH [*pulling her away*]: Come, come, madam.

LUCY: Ay, pray, madam, do not refuse this reverend divine the honor and satisfaction of marrying you, for I dare say he has set his heart upon't, good doctor.

ALITHEA: What can you hope or design by this?

HARCOURT [*aside*]: I could answer her, a reprieve for a day only often revokes a hasty doom; at worst, if she will not take mercy on me and let me marry her, I have at least the lover's second pleasure, hindering my rival's enjoyment, though but for a time.

SPARKISH: Come, madam, 'tis e'en twelve o'clock, and my mother charged me never to be married out of the canonical hours. Come, come. Lord, here's such a deal of modesty, I warrant, the first day.

LUCY: Yes, an't please your worship, married women show all their modesty the first day, because married men show all their love the first day.

[*Exeunt Sparkish, Alithea, Harcourt, and Lucy.*]

Scene 2

[*The scene changes to a bedchamber, where appear Pinchwife, Mrs. Pinchwife.*]

PINCHWIFE: Come, tell me, I say.

MRS. PINCHWIFE: Lord, ha'n't I told it an hundred times over?

---

8. Harcourt plays on literal death and sexual "death": orgasm.

PINCHWIFE [*aside*]: I would try if, in the repetition of the ungrateful[9] tale, I could find her altering it in the least circumstance, for if her story be false, she is so too.—Come, how was't, baggage?

MRS. PINCHWIFE: Lord, what pleasure you take to hear it, sure!

PINCHWIFE: No, you take more in telling it, I find; but speak, how was't?

MRS. PINCHWIFE: He carried me up into the house next to the Exchange.

PINCHWIFE: So, and you two were only in the room.

MRS. PINCHWIFE: Yes, for he sent away a youth that was there, for some dried fruit and China oranges.[1]

PINCHWIFE: Did he so? Damn him for it—and for—

MRS. PINCHWIFE: But presently came up the gentle-woman of the house.

PINCHWIFE: O, 'twas well she did; but what did he do whilst the fruit came?

MRS. PINCHWIFE: He kissed me an hundred times and told me he fancied he kissed my fine sister, meaning me, you know, whom he said he loved with all his soul and bid me be sure to tell her so and to desire her to be at her window by eleven of the clock this morning and he would walk under it at that time.

PINCHWIFE [*aside*]: And he was as good as his word, very punctual—a pox reward him for't.

MRS. PINCHWIFE: Well, and he said if you were not within, he would come up to her, meaning me, you know, bud, still.

PINCHWIFE [*aside*]: So—he knew her certainly; but for this confession, I am obliged to her simplicity.—But what, you stood very still when he kissed you?

MRS. PINCHWIFE: Yes, I warrant you; would you have had me discovered myself?

PINCHWIFE: But you told me he did some beastliness to you, as you called it; what was't?

MRS. PINCHWIFE: Why, he put—

PINCHWIFE: What?

MRS. PINCHWIFE: Why, he put the tip of his tongue between my lips and so mousled[2] me—and I said, I'd bite it.

PINCHWIFE: An eternal canker seize it, for[3] a dog!

MRS. PINCHWIFE: Nay, you need not be so angry with him neither, for to say truth, he has the sweetest breath I ever knew.

PINCHWIFE: The devil!—you were satisfied with it then, and would do it again.

MRS. PINCHWIFE: Not unless he should force me.

PINCHWIFE: Force you, changeling![4] I tell you no woman can be forced.

MRS. PINCHWIFE: Yes, but she may, sure, by such a one as he, for he's a proper, goodly strong man; 'tis hard, let me tell you, to resist him.

PINCHWIFE: So, 'tis plain she loves him, yet she has not love enough to make her conceal it from me; but the sight of him will increase her aversion for me and love for him and that love instruct her how to deceive me and satisfy him, all idiot as she is. Love! 'Twas he gave women first their craft, their art of deluding; out of nature's hands they came plain, open, silly and fit for slaves, as she and Heaven intended 'em; but damned love—well—I must strangle that little monster[5] whilst I can deal with him.—Go fetch pen, ink and paper out of the next room.

MRS. PINCHWIFE: Yes, bud.   [*Exit Mrs. Pinchwife.*]

---

9. Unpleasant.
1. Sweet oranges, regarded in the seventeenth century as an exotic delicacy.
2. A variation on "muzzled": kissed deeply.

3. I.e., for acting like.
4. Fool.
5. Cupid.

PINCHWIFE [aside]: Why should women have more invention in love than men? It can only be because they have more desires, more soliciting passions, more lust, and more of the devil. [Mrs. Pinchwife returns.] Come, minx, sit down and write.

MRS. PINCHWIFE: Ay, dear bud, but I can't do't very well.

PINCHWIFE: I wish you could not at all.

MRS. PINCHWIFE: But what should I write for?

PINCHWIFE: I'll have you write a letter to your lover.

MRS. PINCHWIFE: O Lord, to the fine gentleman a letter!

PINCHWIFE: Yes, to the fine gentleman.

MRS. PINCHWIFE: Lord, you do but jeer; sure, you jest.

PINCHWIFE: I am not so merry. Come, write as I bid you.

MRS. PINCHWIFE: What, do you think I am a fool?

PINCHWIFE [aside]: She's afraid I would not dictate any love to him, therefore she's unwilling.—But you had best begin.

MRS. PINCHWIFE: Indeed, and indeed, but I won't, so I won't.

PINCHWIFE: Why?

MRS. PINCHWIFE: Because he's in town; you may send for him if you will.

PINCHWIFE: Very well, you would have him brought to you; is it come to this? I say, take the pen and write, or you'll provoke me.

MRS. PINCHWIFE: Lord, what d'ye make a fool of me for? Don't I know that letters are never writ but from the country to London and from London into the country? Now he's in town and I am in town too; therefore I can't write to him, you know.

PINCHWIFE [aside]: So, I am glad it is no worse; she is innocent enough yet.— Yes, you may, when your husband bids you, write letters to people that are in town.

MRS. PINCHWIFE: O, may I so? Then I'm satisfied.

PINCHWIFE: Come, begin.—[Dictates.] "Sir"—

MRS. PINCHWIFE: Shan't I say, "Dear Sir"? You know one says always something more than bare "Sir."

PINCHWIFE: Write as I bid you, or I will write "whore" with this penknife in your face.

MRS. PINCHWIFE: Nay, good bud—[She writes.] "Sir"—

PINCHWIFE: "Though I suffered last night your nauseous, loathed kisses and embraces"—Write.

MRS. PINCHWIFE: Nay, why should I say so? You know I told you he had a sweet breath.

PINCHWIFE: Write.

MRS. PINCHWIFE: Let me but put out "loathed."

PINCHWIFE: Write, I say.

MRS. PINCHWIFE: Well then. [Writes.]

PINCHWIFE: Let's see, what have you writ? [Takes the paper and reads.] "Though I suffered last night your kisses and embraces"—Thou impudent creature, where is "nauseous" and "loathed"?

MRS. PINCHWIFE: I can't abide to write such filthy words.

PINCHWIFE: Once more write as I'd have you, and question it not, or I will spoil thy writing with this. [*Holds up the penknife.*] I will stab out those eyes that cause my mischief.

MRS. PINCHWIFE: O Lord, I will!

PINCHWIFE: So—so—let's see now! [*Reads.*] "Though I suffered last night your nauseous, loathed kisses and embraces"—go on—"yet I would not have you presume that you shall ever repeat them"—So—[*She writes.*]

MRS. PINCHWIFE: I have writ it.

PINCHWIFE: On then.—"I then concealed myself from your knowledge to avoid your insolencies"—[*She writes.*]

MRS. PINCHWIFE: So—

PINCHWIFE: "The same reason, now I am out of your hands"—[*She writes.*]

MRS. PINCHWIFE: So—

PINCHWIFE: "Makes me own to you my unfortunate, though innocent, frolic, of being in man's clothes"—[*She writes.*]

MRS. PINCHWIFE: So—

PINCHWIFE: "That you may for evermore cease to pursue her, who hates and detests you"—[*She writes on.*]

MRS. PINCHWIFE: So—h—[*Sighs.*]

PINCHWIFE: What, do you sigh?—"detests you—as much as she loves her husband and her honour."

MRS. PINCHWIFE: I vow, husband, he'll ne'er believe I should write such a letter.

PINCHWIFE: What, he'd expect a kinder from you? Come, now your name only.

MRS. PINCHWIFE: What, shan't I say, "Your most faithful, humble servant till death"?

PINCHWIFE: No, tormenting fiend! [*Aside.*] Her style, I find, would be very soft.—Come, wrap it up now, whilst I go fetch wax and a candle, and write on the backside, "For Mr. Horner."   [*Exit Pinchwife.*]

MRS. PINCHWIFE: "For Mr. Horner."—So, I am glad he has told me his name. Dear Mr. Horner! But why should I send thee such a letter that will vex thee and make thee angry with me?—Well, I will not send it—Ay, but then my husband will kill me—for I see plainly he won't let me love Mr. Horner—but what care I for my husband?—I won't, so I won't send poor Mr. Horner such a letter—But then my husband—But oh—What if I writ at bottom, my husband made me write it?—Ay, but then my husband would see't—Can one have no shift?[6] Ah, a London woman would have had a hundred presently. Stay—what if I should write a letter, and wrap it up like this, and write upon't too? Ay, but then my husband would see't—I don't know what to do—But yet y'vads[7] I'll try, so I will—for I will not send this letter to poor Mr. Horner, come what will on't.

[*She writes, and repeats what she hath writ.*]

"Dear, sweet Mr. Horner"—so—"my husband would have me send you a base, rude, unmannerly letter—but I won't"—so—"and would have me forbid you loving me—but I won't"—so—"and would have me say to you, I hate you, poor Mr. Horner—but I won't tell a lie for him"—there—"for I'm sure if you and I were in the country at cards together"—so—"I could not help treading on your toe under

6. Expedient; trick.   7. In faith.

the table"—so—"or rubbing knees with you and staring in your face till you saw me"—very well—"and then looking down and blushing for an hour together"—so—"but I must make haste before my husband comes; and now he has taught me to write letters, you shall have longer ones from me, who am, Dear, dear, poor, dear Mr. Horner, Your most humble friend, and servant to command till death, Margery Pinchwife." Stay, I must give him a hint at bottom—so—now wrap it up just like t'other—so—now write, "For Mr. Horner"—But, oh now, what shall I do with it? For here comes my husband. [Enter Pinchwife.]

PINCHWIFE [aside]: I have been detained by a sparkish coxcomb, who pretended a visit to me; but I fear 'twas to my wife.—What, have you done?

MRS. PINCHWIFE: Ay, ay, bud, just now.

PINCHWIFE: Let's see't. What d'ye tremble for? What, you would not have it go?

MRS. PINCHWIFE: Here. [Aside.] No, I must not give him that; so I had been served if I had given him this.

PINCHWIFE [He opens, and reads the first letter]: Come, where's the wax and seal?

MRS. PINCHWIFE [aside]: Lord, what shall I do now? Nay, then, I have it.—Pray let me see't. Lord, you think me so arrant a fool I cannot seal a letter. I will do't, so I will. [Snatches the letter from him, changes it for the other, seals it and delivers it to him.]

PINCHWIFE: Nay, I believe you will learn that, and other things too, which I would not have you.

MRS. PINCHWIFE: So, han't I done it curiously?[8] [Aside.] I think I have; there's my letter going to Mr. Horner, since he'll needs have me send letters to folks.

PINCHWIFE: 'Tis very well; but I warrant you would not have it go now?

MRS. PINCHWIFE: Yes, indeed, but I would, bud, now.

PINCHWIFE: Well, you are a good girl then. Come, let me lock you up in your chamber, till I come back, and be sure you come not within three strides of the window when I am gone, for I have a spy in the street.

[Exit Mrs. Pinchwife. Pinchwife locks the door.]

At least, 'tis fit she think so. If we do not cheat women, they'll cheat us, and fraud may be justly used with secret enemies, of which a wife is the most dangerous, and he that has a handsome one to keep, and a frontier town, must provide against treachery rather than open force. Now I have secured all within, I'll deal with the foe without with false intelligence. [Holds up the letter. Exit Pinchwife.]

Scene 3

[The scene changes to Horner's lodging. Quack and Horner.]

QUACK: Well, sir, how fadges[9] the new design? Have you not the luck of all your brother projectors,[1] to deceive only yourself at last?

HORNER: No, good domine[2] doctor, I deceive you, it seems, and others too, for the grave matrons and old, rigid husbands think me as unfit for love as they are but their wives, sisters and daughters know some of 'em better things already.

QUACK: Already!

---

8. Adroitly; cleverly.
9. Progresses.

1. Designers, schemers.
2. Master.

HORNER: Already, I say. Last night I was drunk with half a dozen of your civil persons, as you call 'em, and people of honor, and so was made free of their society and dressing-rooms forever hereafter, and am already come to the privileges of sleeping upon their pallets,[3] warming smocks,[4] tying shoes and garters, and the like, doctor, already, already, doctor.

QUACK: You have made use of your time, sir.

HORNER: I tell thee, I am now no more interruption to 'em when they sing or talk bawdy than a little squab[5] French page who speaks no English.

QUACK: But do civil persons and women of honor drink and sing bawdy songs?

HORNER: O, amongst friends, amongst friends. For your bigots in honor are just like those in religion; they fear the eye of the world more than the eye of Heaven and think there is no virtue but railing at vice and no sin but giving scandal. They rail at a poor, little, kept player and keep themselves some young, modest pulpit comedian[6] to be privy to their sins in their closets, not to tell 'em of them in their chapels.

QUACK: Nay, the truth on't is, priests among the women now have quite got the better of us lay confessors, physicians.

HORNER: And they are rather their patients, but— [Enter Lady Fidget, looking about her.]

Now we talk of women of honor, here comes one. Step behind the screen there and but observe if I have not particular privileges with the women of reputation already, doctor, already.

[Quack steps behind screen.]

LADY FIDGET: Well, Horner, am not I a woman of honor? You see I'm as good as my word.

HORNER: And you shall see, madam, I'll not be behindhand with you in honor and I'll be as good as my word too, if you please but to withdraw into the next room.

LADY FIDGET: But first, my dear sir, you must promise to have a care of my dear honor.

HORNER: If you talk a word more of your honor, you'll make me incapable to wrong it. To talk of honor in the mysteries of love is like talking of heaven or the deity in an operation of witchcraft, just when you are employing the devil; it makes the charm impotent.

LADY FIDGET: Nay, fie, let us not be smooty.[7] But you talk of mysteries and bewitching to me; I don't understand you.

HORNER: I tell you, madam, the word "money" in a mistress's mouth, at such a nick of time, is not a more disheartening sound to a younger brother[8] than that of "honor" to an eager lover like myself.

LADY FIDGET: But you can't blame a lady of my reputation to be chary.

HORNER: Chary! I have been chary of it already, by the report I have caused of myself.

LADY FIDGET: Ay, but if you should ever let other women know that dear secret, it would come out. Nay, you must have a great care of your conduct, for my

---

3. Mattresses.
4. I.e., their underwear (which the wealthy wanted warmed before worn).
5. Short and stout.

6. Household chaplain.
7. Smutty.
8. Because the eldest son inherited the estate, younger brothers typically lacked cash.

acquaintance are so censorious (oh, 'tis a wicked, censorious world, Mr. Horner!), I say, are so censorious and detracting that perhaps they'll talk, to the prejudice of my honor, though you should not let them know the dear secret.

HORNER: Nay, madam, rather than they shall prejudice your honor, I'll prejudice theirs, and, to serve you, I'll lie with 'em all, make the secret their own, and then they'll keep it. I am a Machiavel in love, madam.

LADY FIDGET: Oh, no, sir, not that way.

HORNER: Nay, the devil take me if censorious women are to be silenced any other way.

LADY FIDGET: A secret is better kept, I hope, by a single person than a multitude; therefore pray do not trust anybody else with it, dear, dear Mr. Horner. [*Embracing him.*]

[*Enter Sir Jaspar Fidget.*]

SIR JASPAR: How now!

LADY FIDGET [*aside*]: Oh, my husband—prevented—and what's almost as bad, found with my arms about another man—that will appear too much—what shall I say?—Sir Jaspar, come hither, I am trying if Mr. Horner were ticklish, and he's as ticklish as can be; I love to torment the confounded toad. Let you and I tickle him.

SIR JASPAR: No, your ladyship will tickle him better without me, I suppose. But is this your buying china? I thought you had been at the china house.[9]

HORNER [*aside*]: China house! That's my cue, I must take it.—A pox, can't you keep your impertinent wives at home? Some men are troubled with the husbands, but I with the wives. But I'd have you to know, since I cannot be your journeyman[1] by night, I will not be your drudge by day, to squire your wife about and be your man of straw, or scarecrow, only to pies and jays,[2] that would be nibbling at your forbidden fruit; I shall be shortly the hackney gentleman-usher[3] of the town.

SIR JASPAR [*aside*]: Heh, heh, he! Poor fellow, he's in the right on't, faith; to squire women about for other folks is as ungrateful an employment as to tell[4] money for other folks.—Heh, he, he! Ben't angry, Horner—

LADY FIDGET: No, 'tis I have more reason to be angry, who am left by you to go abroad indecently alone; or, what is more indecent, to pin myself upon such illbred people of your acquaintance as this is.

SIR JASPAR: Nay, prithee, what has he done?

LADY FIDGET: Nay, he has done nothing.

SIR JASPAR: But what d'ye take ill, if he has done nothing?

LADY FIDGET: Hah, hah, hah! Faith, I can't but laugh, however; why d'ye think the unmannerly toad would not come down to me to the coach? I was fain to come up to fetch him, or go without him, which I was resolved not to do, for he knows china very well and has himself very good, but will not let me see it lest I should beg some. But I will find it out and have what I came for yet.

[*Exit Lady Fidget and locks the door, followed by Horner to the door.*]

---

9. China shop, sometimes used by lovers as a secret meeting place.
1. One who works for another.

2. Crafty fellows and fools.
3. Hired escort.
4. Count.

HORNER [*apart to Lady Fidget*]: Lock the door, madam.—So, she has got into my chamber, and locked me out. Oh, the impertinency of womankind! Well, Sir Jaspar, plain-dealing is a jewel; if ever you suffer your wife to trouble me again here, she shall carry you home a pair of horns, by my Lord Mayor she shall; though I cannot furnish you myself, you are sure, yet I'll find a way.

SIR JASPAR [*aside*]: Hah, ha, he! At my first coming in and finding her arms about him, tickling him it seems, I was half jealous, but now I see my folly.—Heh, he, he! Poor Horner.

HORNER: Nay, though you laugh now, 'twill be my turn ere long. Oh, women, more impertinent, more cunning and more mischievous than their monkeys,[5] and to me almost as ugly! Now is she throwing my things about and rifling all I have, but I'll get into her the back way and so rifle her for it.

SIR JASPAR: Hah, ha, ha, poor angry Horner.

HORNER: Stay here a little; I'll ferret her out to you presently, I warrant.

[*Exit Horner at t'other door.*]

SIR JASPAR: Wife! My Lady Fidget! Wife! He is coming into you the back way.

[*Sir Jaspar calls through the door to his wife; she answers from within.*]

LADY FIDGET: Let him come, and welcome, which way he will.

SIR JASPAR: He'll catch you and use you roughly and be too strong for you.

LADY FIDGET: Don't you trouble yourself; let him if he can.

QUACK [*behind*]: This indeed I could not have believed from him, nor any but my own eyes.

[*Enter Mrs. Squeamish.*]

SQUEAMISH: Where's this woman-hater, this toad, this ugly, greasy, dirty sloven?

SIR JASPAR [*aside*]: So, the women all will have him ugly; methinks he is a comely person, but his wants make his form contemptible to 'em and 'tis e'en as my wife said yesterday, talking of him, that a proper handsome eunuch was as ridiculous a thing as a gigantic coward.

SQUEAMISH: Sir Jaspar, your servant. Where is the odious beast?

SIR JASPAR: He's within in his chamber, with my wife; she's playing the wag with him.

SQUEAMISH: Is she so? And he's a clownish beast, he'll give her no quarter;[6] he'll play the wag with her again, let me tell you. Come, let's go help her.—What, the door's locked?

SIR JASPAR: Ay, my wife locked it.

SQUEAMISH: Did she so? Let us break it open then.

SIR JASPAR: No, no, he'll do her no hurt.

SQUEAMISH: No. [*Aside.*] But is there no other way to get in to 'em? Whither goes this? I will disturb 'em. [*Exit Squeamish at another door.*]

OLD LADY SQUEAMISH: Where is this harlotry, this impudent baggage, this rambling tomrig?[7] O Sir Jaspar, I'm glad to see you here. Did you not see my vild[8] grandchild come in hither just now?

SIR JASPAR: Yes.

---

5. Which ladies sometimes kept as pets.
6. No mercy.

7. Strumpet.
8. Vile.

OLD LADY SQUEAMISH: Ay, but where is she then? Where is she? Lord, Sir Jaspar, I have e'en rattled myself to pieces in pursuit of her. But can you tell what she makes here? They say below, no woman lodges here.

SIR JASPAR: No.

OLD LADY SQUEAMISH: No! What does she here then? Say, if it be not a woman's lodging, what makes she here? But are you sure no woman lodges here?

SIR JASPAR: No, nor no man neither; this is Mr. Horner's lodging.

OLD LADY SQUEAMISH: Is it so, are you sure?

SIR JASPAR: Yes, yes.

OLD LADY SQUEAMISH: So then there's no hurt in't, I hope. But where is he?

SIR JASPAR: He's in the next room with my wife.

OLD LADY SQUEAMISH: Nay, if you trust him with your wife, I may with my Biddy.⁹ They say he's a merry harmless man now, e'en as harmless a man as ever came out of Italy with a good voice,¹ and as pretty harmless company for a lady as a snake without his teeth.

SIR JASPAR: Ay, ay, poor man.

[*Enter Mrs. Squeamish.*]

SQUEAMISH: I can't find 'em.—Oh, are you here, Grandmother? I followed, you must know, my Lady Fidget hither; 'tis the prettiest lodging and I have been staring on the prettiest pictures.

[*Enter Lady Fidget with a piece of china in her hand, and Horner following.*]

LADY FIDGET: And I have been toiling and moiling² for the prettiest piece of china, my dear.

HORNER: Nay, she has been too hard for me, do what I could.

SQUEAMISH: O Lord, I'll have some china too. Good Mr. Horner, don't think to give other people china and me none; come in with me too.

HORNER: Upon my honor, I have none left now.

SQUEAMISH: Nay, nay, I have known you deny your china before now, but you shan't put me off so. Come—

HORNER: This lady had the last there.

LADY FIDGET: Yes, indeed, madam, to my certain knowledge he has no more left.

SQUEAMISH: O, but it may be he may have some you could not find.

LADY FIDGET: What, d'ye think if he had had any left, I would not have had it too? For we women of quality never think we have china enough.

HORNER: Do not take it ill. I cannot make china for you all, but I will have a roll-wagon³ for you too, another time.

SQUEAMISH: Thank you, dear toad.

LADY FIDGET [*to Horner aside*]: What do you mean by that promise?

HORNER [*apart to Lady Fidget*]: Alas, she has an innocent, literal understanding.

OLD LADY SQUEAMISH: Poor Mr. Horner, he has enough to do to please you all, I see.

HORNER: Ay, madam, you see how they use me.

OLD LADY SQUEAMISH: Poor gentleman, I pity you.

---

9. Abbreviation of Bridget; also, a general term for a young woman.
1. I.e., as a castrato, a male singer castrated in boyhood so as to preserve his soprano voice.

2. Working hard.
3. A cylindrical vase; here (of course) with phallic connotations.

HORNER: I thank you, madam. I could never find pity but from such reverend ladies as you are; the young ones will never spare a man.

SQUEAMISH: Come, come, beast, and go dine with us, for we shall want a man at ombre after dinner.

HORNER: That's all their use of me, madam, you see.

SQUEAMISH: Come, sloven, I'll lead you, to be sure of you: [*Pulls him by the cravat.*]

OLD LADY SQUEAMISH: Alas, poor man, how she tugs him! Kiss, kiss her; that's the way to make such nice[4] women quiet.

HORNER: No, madam, that remedy is worse than the torment; they know I dare suffer anything rather than do it.

OLD LADY SQUEAMISH: Prithee, kiss her and I'll give you her picture in little,[5] that you admired so last night; prithee do.

HORNER: Well, nothing but that could bribe me; I love a woman only in effigy and good painting, as much as I hate them. I'll do't, for I could adore the devil well painted. [*Kisses Mrs. Squeamish.*]

SQUEAMISH: Foh, you filthy toad! Nay, now I've done jesting.

OLD LADY SQUEAMISH: Ha, ha, ha, I told you so.

SQUEAMISH: Foh, a kiss of his—

SIR JASPAR: Has no more hurt in't than one of my spaniel's.

SQUEAMISH: Nor no more good neither.

QUACK [*behind*]: I will now believe anything he tells me.
    [*Enter Mr. Pinchwife.*]

LADY FIDGET: O Lord, here's a man! Sir Jaspar, my mask, my mask! I would not be seen here for the world.

SIR JASPAR: What, not when I am with you?

LADY FIDGET: No, no, my honor—let's be gone.

SQUEAMISH: Oh, Grandmother, let us be gone; make haste, make haste, I know not how he may censure us.

LADY FIDGET: Be found in the lodging of anything like a man! Away!
    [*Exeunt Sir Jaspar, Lady Fidget, Old Lady Squeamish, Mrs. Squeamish.*]

QUACK [*behind*]: What's here? Another cuckold? He looks like one, and none else sure have any business with him.

HORNER: Well, what brings my dear friend hither?

PINCHWIFE: Your impertinency.

HORNER: My impertinency!—Why, you gentlemen that have got handsome wives think you have a privilege of saying anything to your friends and are as brutish as if you were our creditors.

PINCHWIFE: No, sir, I'll ne'er trust you any way.

HORNER: But why not, dear Jack? Why diffide[6] in me thou knowest so well?

PINCHWIFE: Because I do know you so well.

HORNER: Han't I been always thy friend, honest Jack, always ready to serve thee, in love or battle, before thou wert married, and am so still?

PINCHWIFE: I believe so; you would be my second now indeed.

HORNER: Well then, dear Jack, why so unkind, so grum, so strange to me? Come, prithee kiss me, dear rogue. Gad, I was always, I say, and am still as much thy servant as—

4. Fastidious; also, in an older sense, wanton.   6. Distrust.
5. Miniature.

PINCHWIFE: As I am yours, sir. What, you would send a kiss to my wife, is that it?

HORNER: So, there 'tis—a man can't show his friendship to a married man but presently he talks of his wife to you. Prithee, let thy wife alone and let thee and I be all one, as we were wont. What, thou art as shy of my kindness as a Lombard Street[7] alderman of a courtier's civility at Locket's.[8]

PINCHWIFE: But you are overkind to me, as kind as if I were your cuckold already; yet I must confess you ought to be kind and civil to me, since I am so kind, so civil to you, as to bring you this. Look you there, sir. [*Delivers him a letter.*]

HORNER: What is't?

PINCHWIFE: Only a love-letter, sir.

HORNER: From whom?—how! this is from your wife—hum—and hum—[*Reads.*]

PINCHWIFE: Even from my wife, sir. Am I not wondrous kind and civil to you now too? [*Aside.*] But you'll not think her so.

HORNER [*aside*]: Ha, is this a trick of his or hers?

PINCHWIFE: The gentleman's surprised, I find. What, you expected a kinder letter?

HORNER: No, faith, not I, how could I?

PINCHWIFE: Yes, yes, I'm sure you did; a man so well made as you are must needs be disappointed if the women declare not their passion at first sight or opportunity.

HORNER [*aside*]: But what should this mean? Stay, the postscript. [*Reads aside.*] "Be sure you love me, whatsoever my husband says to the contrary, and let him not see this, lest he should come home and pinch me, or kill my squirrel."[9] [*Aside.*] It seems he knows not what the letter contains.

PINCHWIFE: Come, ne'er wonder at it so much.

HORNER: Faith, I can't help it.

PINCHWIFE: Now, I think, I have deserved your infinite friendship and kindness and have showed myself sufficiently an obliging kind friend and husband; am I not so, to bring a letter from my wife to her gallant?

HORNER: Ay, the devil take me, art thou the most obliging, kind friend and husband in the world, ha, ha!

PINCHWIFE: Well, you may be merry, sir; but in short I must tell you, sir, my honor will suffer no jesting.

HORNER: What dost thou mean?

PINCHWIFE: Does the letter want a comment? Then know, sir, though I have been so civil a husband as to bring you a letter from my wife, to let you kiss and court her to my face, I will not be a cuckold, sir, I will not.

HORNER: Thou art mad with jealousy. I never saw thy wife in my life but at the play yesterday, and I know not if it were she or no. I court her, kiss her!

PINCHWIFE: I will not be a cuckold, I say; there will be danger in making me a cuckold.

HORNER: Why, wert thou not well cured of thy last clap?

PINCHWIFE: I wear a sword.

HORNER: It should be taken from thee lest thou shouldst do thyself a mischief with it; thou art mad, man.

---

7. Banking center of London.
8. In Charing Cross, a celebrated restaurant and popular post-theater meeting place.
9. A fashionable pet.

PINCHWIFE: As mad as I am, and as merry as you are, I must have more reason from you ere we part. I say again, though you kissed and courted last night my wife in man's clothes, as she confesses in her letter—

HORNER [aside]: Ha!

PINCHWIFE: Both she and I say, you must not design it again, for you have mistaken your woman, as you have done your man.

HORNER [aside]: Oh—I understand something now.—Was that thy wife? Why wouldst thou not tell me 'twas she? Faith, my freedom with her was your fault, not mine.

PINCHWIFE [aside]: Faith, so 'twas.

HORNER: Fie, I'd never do't to a woman before her husband's face, sure.

PINCHWIFE: But I had rather you should do't to my wife before my face than behind my back, and that you shall never do.

HORNER: No—you will hinder me.

PINCHWIFE: If I would not hinder you, you see by her letter, she would.

HORNER: Well, I must e'en acquiesce then and be contented with what she writes.

PINCHWIFE: I'll assure you 'twas voluntarily writ; I had no hand in't, you may believe me.

HORNER: I do believe thee, faith.

PINCHWIFE: And believe her too, for she's an innocent creature, has no dissembling in her; and so fare you well, sir.

HORNER: Pray, however, present my humble service to her and tell her I will obey her letter to a tittle and fulfill her desires, be what they will, or with what difficulty soever I do't, and you shall be no more jealous of me, I warrant her and you.

PINCHWIFE: Well, then, fare you well, and play with any man's honor but mine, kiss any man's wife but mine, and welcome. [Exit Mr. Pinchwife.]

HORNER: Ha, ha, ha, doctor.

QUACK: It seems he has not heard the report of you, or does not believe it.

HORNER: Ha, ha! Now, doctor, what think you?

QUACK: Pray let's see the letter—hum— [Reads the letter.] "tor—dear—love you—"

HORNER: I wonder how she could contrive it! What say'st thou to't? 'Tis an original.

QUACK: So are your cuckolds, too, originals, for they are like no other common cuckolds, and I will henceforth believe it not impossible for you to cuckold the Grand Signior[1] amidst his guards of eunuchs, that I say.

HORNER: And I say for the letter, 'tis the first love-letter that ever was without flames, darts, fates, destinies, lying and dissembling in't.

[Enter Sparkish, pulling in Mr. Pinchwife.]

SPARKISH: Come back, you are a pretty brother-in-law, neither go to church, nor to dinner with your sister bride!

PINCHWIFE: My sister denies her marriage and you see is gone away from you dissatisfied.

SPARKISH: Pshaw, upon a foolish scruple, that our parson was not in lawful orders and did not say all the Common Prayer; but 'tis her modesty only, I believe. But let women be never so modest the first day, they'll be sure to come to themselves

---

1. Sultan of Turkey, whose eunuchs guarded his harem.

by night, and I shall have enough of her then. In the meantime, Harry Horner, you must dine with me; I keep my wedding at my aunt's in the Piazza.[2]

HORNER: Thy wedding! What stale maid has lived to despair of a husband, or what young one of a gallant?

SPARKISH: Oh, your servant, sir—this gentleman's sister then—no stale maid.

HORNER: I'm sorry for't.

PINCHWIFE [aside]: How comes he so concerned for her?

SPARKISH: You sorry for't? Why, do you know any ill by her?

HORNER: No, I know none but by thee; 'tis for her sake, not yours, and another man's sake that might have hoped, I thought.

SPARKISH: Another man, another man! What is his name?

HORNER: Nay, since 'tis past he shall be nameless. [Aside.] Poor Harcourt, I am sorry thou hast missed her.

PINCHWIFE [aside]: He seems to be much troubled at the match.

SPARKISH: Prithee tell me—nay, you shan't go, brother.

PINCHWIFE: I must of necessity, but I'll come to you to dinner.   [Exit Pinchwife.]

SPARKISH: But, Harry, what, have I a rival in my wife already? But with all my heart, for he may be of use to me hereafter, for though my hunger is now my sauce and I can fall on heartily without, but the time will come when a rival will be as good sauce for a married man to a wife as an orange to veal.

HORNER: O thou damned rogue! Thou hast set my teeth on edge with thy orange.

SPARKISH: Then let's to dinner—there I was with[3] you again. Come.

HORNER: But who dines with thee?

SPARKISH: My friends and relations, my brother Pinchwife, you see, of your acquaintance.

HORNER: And his wife?

SPARKISH: No, gad, he'll ne'er let her come amongst us good fellows. Your stingy country coxcomb keeps his wife from friends, as he does his little firkin[4] of ale for his own drinking, and a gentleman can't get a smack[5] on't; but his servants, when his back is turned, broach[6] it at their pleasures and dust it away,[7] ha, ha, ha! Gad, I am witty, I think, considering I was married today, by the world. But come—

HORNER: No, I will not dine with you, unless you can fetch her too.

SPARKISH: Pshaw, what pleasure canst thou have with women now, Harry?

HORNER: My eyes are not gone; I love a good prospect yet and will not dine with you unless she does too. Go fetch her, therefore, but do not tell her husband 'tis for my sake.

SPARKISH: Well, I'll try what I can do. In the mean-time come away to my aunt's lodging; 'tis in the way to Pinchwife's.

HORNER: The poor woman has called for aid and stretched forth her hand, doctor; I cannot but help her over the pale[8] out of the briars.

[Exeunt Sparkish, Horner, Quack.]

---

2. An elegant arcade near Covent Garden; Act 5, Scene 3 is set there.
3. Caught.
4. Small cask.
5. Taste.
6. Tap.
7. Finish it off.
8. Fence; here, figuratively, the constraints of marital fidelity.

Scene 4

[The scene changes to Pinchwife's house. Mrs. Pinchwife alone, leaning on her elbow. A table, pen, ink and paper.]

MRS. PINCHWIFE: Well, 'tis e'en so, I have got the London disease they call love; I am sick of my husband and for my gallant. I have heard this distemper[9] called a fever, but methinks 'tis liker an ague, for when I think of my husband, I tremble and am in a cold sweat and have inclinations to vomit but when I think of my gallant, dear Mr. Horner, my hot fit comes and I am all in a fever, indeed, and as in other fevers my own chamber is tedious to me and I would fain be removed to his and then methinks I should be well. Ah, poor Mr. Horner! Well, I cannot, will not stay here; therefore I'd make an end of my letter to him, which shall be a finer letter than my last, because I have studied it like anything. O, sick, sick!

[Takes the pen and writes.]

[Enter Mr. Pinchwife, who, seeing her writing, steals softly behind her and, looking over her shoulder, snatches the paper from her.]

PINCHWIFE: What, writing more letters?

MRS. PINCHWIFE: O Lord, bud, why d'ye fright me so?

[She offers to run out; he stops her and reads.]

PINCHWIFE: How's this! Nay, you shall not stir, madam. "Dear, dear, dear Mr. Horner"—very well—I have taught you to write letters to good purpose—but let's see't. "First, I am to beg your pardon for my boldness in writing to you, which I'd have you to know I would not have done had not you said first you loved me so extremely, which if you do, you will never suffer me to lie in the arms of another man, whom I loathe, nauseate and detest."—Now you can write these filthy words. But what follows?—"Therefore I hope you will speedily find some way to free me from this unfortunate match, which was never, I assure you, of my choice, but I'm afraid 'tis already too far gone. However, if you love me, as I do you, you will try what you can do, but you must help me away before tomorrow, or else, alas, I shall be forever out of your reach, for I can defer no longer our—our" *[The letter concludes.]*—What is to follow "our"?—Speak, what? Our journey into the country, I suppose—Oh, woman, damned woman and love, damned love, their old tempter! For this is one of his miracles; in a moment he can make all those blind that could see and those see that were blind, those dumb that could speak and those prattle who were dumb before; nay, what is more than all, make these dough-baked,[1] senseless, indocile animals, women, too hard for us, their politic[2] lords and rulers, in a moment. But make an end of your letter and then I'll make an end of you thus, and all my plagues together. *[Draws his sword.]*

MRS. PINCHWIFE: O Lord, O Lord, you are such a passionate man, bud!

[Enter Sparkish.]

SPARKISH: How now, what's here to do?

PINCHWIFE: This fool here now!

SPARKISH: What, drawn upon your wife? You should never do that but at night in the dark, when you can't hurt her. This is my sister-in-law, is it not?

[Pulls aside her handkerchief.]

9. Disease.
1. Half-baked, feeble-minded.

2. Sagacious, judicious.

Ay, faith, e'en our country Margery; one may know her. Come, she and you must go dine with me; dinner's ready, come. But where's my wife? Is she not come home yet? Where is she?

PINCHWIFE: Making you a cuckold; 'tis that they all do, as soon as they can.

SPARKISH: What, the wedding day? No, a wife that designs to make a cully[3] of her husband will be sure to let him win the first stake of love, by the world. But come, they stay dinner for us. Come, I'll lead down our Margery.

PINCHWIFE: No—sir, go, we'll follow you.

SPARKISH: I will not wag[4] without you.

PINCHWIFE [aside]: This coxcomb is a sensible[5] torment to me amidst the greatest in the world.

SPARKISH: Come, come, Madam Margery.

PINCHWIFE: No, I'll lead her my way. What, would you treat your friends with mine, for want of your own wife? [Leads her to t'other door and locks her in and returns. Aside.] I am contented my rage should take breath.

SPARKISH [aside]: I told Horner this.

PINCHWIFE: Come now.

SPARKISH: Lord, how shy[6] you are of your wife! But let me tell you, brother, we men of wit have amongst us a saying that cuckolding, like the smallpox, comes with a fear, and you may keep your wife as much as you will out of danger of infection but if her constitution incline her to't, she'll have it sooner or later, by the world, say they.

PINCHWIFE [aside]: What a thing is a cuckold, that every fool can make him ridiculous!—Well, sir—but let me advise you, now you are come to be concerned, because you suspect the danger, not to neglect the means to prevent it, especially when the greatest share of the malady will light upon your own head, for—

> Hows'e'er the kind wife's belly comes to swell,
> The husband breeds for her[7] and first is ill.

[Exeunt Pinchwife and Sparkish.]

ACT 5

Scene 1

[Mr. Pinchwife's house. Enter Mr. Pinchwife and Mrs. Pinchwife. A table and candle.]

PINCHWIFE: Come, take the pen and make an end of the letter, just as you intended; if you are false in a tittle, I shall soon perceive it and punish you with this as you deserve. [Lays his hand on his sword.] Write what was to follow—let's see— "You must make haste and help me away before tomorrow, or else I shall be forever out of your reach, for I can defer no longer our—" What follows "our"?

MRS. PINCHWIFE: Must all out then, bud?

[Mrs. Pinchwife takes the pen and writes.] Look you there then.

PINCHWIFE: Let's see—"For I can defer no longer our—wedding—Your slighted Alithea."—What's the meaning of this? My sister's name to't. Speak, unriddle!

---

3. Dupe, gull.
4. Stir.
5. Keenly felt.

6. Distrustful.
7. Grows cuckold's horns in consequence of her behavior.

MRS. PINCHWIFE: Yes, indeed, bud.

PINCHWIFE: But why her name to't? Speak—speak, I say!

MRS. PINCHWIFE: Ay, but you'll tell her then again; if you would not tell her again—

PINCHWIFE: I will not—I am stunned, my head turns round. Speak.

MRS. PINCHWIFE: Won't you tell her, indeed, and indeed?

PINCHWIFE: No, speak, I say.

MRS. PINCHWIFE: She'll be angry with me, but I had rather she should be angry with me than you, bud; and to tell you the truth, 'twas she made me write the letter and taught me what I should write.

PINCHWIFE [aside]: Ha! I thought the style was somewhat better than her own.— But how could she come to you to teach you, since I had locked you up alone?

MRS. PINCHWIFE: O, through the keyhole, bud.

PINCHWIFE: But why should she make you write a letter for her to him, since she can write herself?

MRS. PINCHWIFE: Why, she said because—for I was unwilling to do it.

PINCHWIFE: Because what—because?

MRS. PINCHWIFE: Because, lest Mr. Horner should be cruel and refuse her or vain afterwards and show the letter, she might disown it, the hand not being hers.

PINCHWIFE [aside]: How's this? Ha!—then I think I shall come to myself again. This changeling could not invent this lie; but if she could, why should she? She might think I should soon discover it—stay—now I think on't too, Horner said he was sorry she had married Sparkish, and her disowning her marriage to me makes me think she has evaded it for Horner's sake. Yet why should she take this course? But men in love are fools; women may well be so.—But hark you, madam, your sister went out in the morning and I have not seen her within since.

MRS. PINCHWIFE: Alackaday, she has been crying all day above, it seems, in a corner.

PINCHWIFE: Where is she? Let me speak with her.

MRS. PINCHWIFE [aside]: O Lord, then he'll discover all!—Pray hold, bud. What, d'ye mean to discover me? She'll know I have told you then. Pray, bud, let me talk with her first.

PINCHWIFE: I must speak with her, to know whether Horner ever made her any promise and whether she be married to Sparkish or no.

MRS. PINCHWIFE: Pray, dear bud, don't, till I have spoken with her and told her that I have told you all, for she'll kill me else.

PINCHWIFE: Go then, and bid her come out to me.

MRS. PINCHWIFE: Yes, yes, bud.

PINCHWIFE: Let me see—

MRS. PINCHWIFE [aside]: I'll go, but she is not within to come to him. I have just got time to know of Lucy her maid, who first set me on work, what lie I shall tell next, for I am e'en at my wit's end. [Exit Mrs. Pinchwife.]

PINCHWIFE: Well, I resolve it; Horner shall have her. I'd rather give him my sister than lend him my wife and such an alliance will prevent his pretensions to my wife, sure. I'll make him of kin to her and then he won't care for her.
  [Mrs. Pinchwife returns.]

MRS. PINCHWIFE: O Lord, bud, I told you what anger you would make me with my sister.

PINCHWIFE: Won't she come hither?

MRS. PINCHWIFE: No, no, alackaday, she's ashamed to look you in the face, and she says, if you go in to her, she'll run away downstairs and shamefully go herself to Mr. Horner, who has promised her marriage, she says, and she will have no other, so she won't—

PINCHWIFE: Did he so—promise her marriage—then she shall have no other. Go tell her so, and if she will come and discourse with me a little concerning the means, I will about it immediately. Go.   [Exit Mrs. Pinchwife.]
His estate is equal to Sparkish's, and his extraction as much better than his as his parts are; but my chief reason is, I'd rather be of kin to him by the name of brother-in-law than that of cuckold.
    [Enter Mrs. Pinchwife.]
Well, what says she now?

MRS. PINCHWIFE: Why, she says she would only have you lead her to Horner's lodging—with whom she first will discourse the matter before she talk with you, which yet she cannot do, for alack, poor creature, she says she can't so much as look you in the face, therefore she'll come to you in a mask, and you must excuse her if she make you no answer to any question of yours, till you have brought her to Mr. Horner, and if you will not chide her, nor question her, she'll come out to you immediately.

PINCHWIFE: Let her come. I will not speak a word to her, nor require a word from her.

MRS. PINCHWIFE: Oh, I forgot; besides, she says, she cannot look you in the face though through a mask, therefore would desire you to put out the candle.

PINCHWIFE: I agree to all; let her make haste—there, 'tis out. [Puts out the candle.]
                                                                [Exit Mrs. Pinchwife.]
My case is something better. I'd rather fight with Horner for not lying with my sister than for lying with my wife, and of the two I had rather find my sister too forward than my wife; I expected no other from her free education, as she calls it, and her passion for the town. Well—wife and sister are names which make us expect love and duty, pleasure and comfort, but we find 'em plagues and torments, and are equally, though differently, troublesome to their keeper, for we have as much ado to get people to lie with our sisters as to keep 'em frm lying with our wives.
    [Enter Mrs. Pinchwife masked and in hoods and scarves, and a nightgown[1] and petticoat of Alithea's, in the dark.]
What, are you come, sister? Let us go then—but first let me lock up my wife.—Mrs. Margery, where are you?

MRS. PINCHWIFE: Here, bud.

PINCHWIFE: Come hither, that I may lock you up; get you in. [Locks the door.]
Come, sister, where are you now?
    [Mrs. Pinchwife gives him her hand but, when he lets her go, she steals softly on t'other side of him, and is led away by him for his sister Alithea.]

Scene 2

[The scene changes to Horner's lodging. Quack, Horner.]

QUACK: What, all alone? Not so much as one of your cuckolds here, nor one of their wives! They use to take their turns with you, as if they were to watch you.

1. A loose gown, usually (but not exclusively) worn at night.

HORNER: Yes, it often happens that a cuckold is but his wife's spy and is more upon family duty when he is with her gallant abroad, hindering his pleasure, than when he is at home with her, playing the gallant. But the hardest duty a married woman imposes upon a lover is keeping her husband company always.

QUACK: And his fondness wearies you almost as soon as hers.

HORNER: A pox, keeping a cuckold company, after you have had his wife, is as tiresome as the company of a country squire to a witty fellow of the town, when he has got all his money.

QUACK: And as at first a man makes a friend of the husband to get the wife, so at last you are fain to fall out with the wife to be rid of the husband.

HORNER: Ay, most cuckold-makers are true courtiers; when once a poor man has cracked[2] his credit for 'em, they can't abide to come near him.

QUACK: But at first, to draw him in, are so sweet, so kind, so dear, just as you are to Pinchwife. But what becomes of that intrigue with his wife?

HORNER: A pox, he's as surly as an alderman that has been bit[3] and, since he's so coy, his wife's kindness is in vain, for she's a silly innocent.

QUACK: Did she not send you a letter by him?

HORNER: Yes, but that's a riddle I have not yet solved. Allow the poor creature to be willing, she is silly too, and he keeps her up so close—

QUACK: Yes, so close that he makes her but the more willing and adds but revenge to her love, which two, when met, seldom fail of satisfying each other one way or other.

HORNER: What, here's the man we are talking of, I think.

[*Enter Mr. Pinchwife, leading in his wife masked, muffled, and in her sister's gown.*] Pshaw!

QUACK: Bringing his wife to you is the next thing to bringing a love-letter from her.

HORNER: What means this?

PINCHWIFE: The last time, you know, sir, I brought you a love-letter; now, you see, a mistress. I think you'll say I am a civil man to you.

HORNER: Ay, the devil take me, will I say thou art the civilest man I ever met with, and I have known some! I fancy I understand thee now better than I did the letter. But hark thee, in thy ear—

PINCHWIFE: What?

HORNER: Nothing but the usual question, man: is she sound,[4] on thy word?

PINCHWIFE: What, you take her for a wench and me for a pimp?

HORNER: Pshaw, wench and pimp, paw[5] words. I know thou art an honest fellow and hast a great acquaintance among the ladies and perhaps hast made love for me rather than let me make love to thy wife—

PINCHWIFE: Come, sir, in short, I am for no fooling.

HORNER: Nor I neither; therefore, prithee, let's see her face presently. Make her show, man. Art thou sure I don't know her?

PINCHWIFE: I am sure you do know her.

HORNER: A pox, why dost thou bring her to me then?

PINCHWIFE: Because she's a relation of mine.

---

2. Ruined.
3. A city official who's been tricked.

4. Free from venereal disease.
5. Naughty.

HORNER: Is she, faith, man? Then thou art still more civil and obliging, dear rogue.

PINCHWIFE: Who desired me to bring her to you.

HORNER: Then she is obliging, dear rogue.

PINCHWIFE: You'll make her welcome for my sake, I hope.

HORNER: I hope she is handsome enough to make herself welcome. Prithee, let her unmask.

PINCHWIFE: Do you speak to her; she would never be ruled by me.

HORNER: Madam—

[Mrs. Pinchwife whispers to Horner.]

She says she must speak with me in private. Withdraw, prithee.

PINCHWIFE [aside]: She's unwilling, it seems, I should know all her undecent conduct in this business.—Well then, I'll leave you together and hope when I am gone you'll agree; if not, you and I shan't agree, sir.

HORNER [aside]: What means the fool?—If she and I agree, 'tis no matter what you and I do.

[Whispers to Mrs. Pinchwife, who makes signs with her hand for him (Pinchwife) to be gone.]

PINCHWIFE: In the meantime, I'll fetch a parson and find out Sparkish and disabuse him. You would have me fetch a parson, would you not? Well then—now I think I am rid of her, and shall have no more trouble with her. Our sisters and daughters, like usurers' money, are safest when put out; but our wives, like their writings,[6] never safe but in our closets under lock and key.   [Exit Mr. Pinchwife.]
[Enter Boy.]

BOY: Sir Jaspar Fidget, sir, is coming up.   [Exit.]

HORNER: Here's the trouble of a cuckold, now, we are talking of. A pox on him! Has he not enough to do to hinder his wife's sport but he must other women's too?—Step in here, madam.   [Exit Mrs. Pinchwife.]
[Enter Sir Jaspar.]

SIR JASPAR: My best and dearest friend.

HORNER [aside to Quack]: The old style, doctor.—Well, be short, for I am busy. What would your impertinent wife have now?

SIR JASPAR: Well guessed, i'faith, for I do come from her.

HORNER: To invite me to supper. Tell her I can't come; go.

SIR JASPAR: Nay, now you are out, faith, for my lady and the whole knot of the virtuous gang, as they call themselves, are resolved upon a frolic of coming to you tonight in a masquerade and are all dressed already.

HORNER: I shan't be at home.

SIR JASPAR [aside]: Lord, how churlish he is to women!—Nay, prithee don't disappoint 'em; they'll think 'tis my fault. Prithee don't. I'll send in the banquet and the fiddles. But make no noise on't, for the poor virtuous rogues would not have it known for the world that they go a-masquerading, and they would come to no man's ball but yours.

HORNER: Well, well—get you gone and tell 'em, if they come, 'twill be at the peril of their honor and yours.

SIR JASPAR: Heh, he, he!—we'll trust you for that; farewell. [Exit Sir Jaspar.]

6. Legal and financial documents.

HORNER: Doctor, anon you too shall be my guest, But now I'm going to a private feast.

[Exeunt.]

Scene 3

[The scene changes to the Piazza of Covent Garden. Sparkish, Pinchwife.]

SPARKISH [with the letter in his hand]: But who would have thought a woman could have been false to me? By the world, I could not have thought it.

PINCHWIFE: You were for giving and taking liberty; she has taken it only, sir, now you find in that letter. You are a frank person and so is she you see there.

SPARKISH: Nay, if this be her hand—for I never saw it.

PINCHWIFE: 'Tis no matter whether that be her hand or no; I am sure this hand, at her desire, led her to Mr. Horner, with whom I left her just now, to go fetch a parson to 'em, at their desire too, to deprive you of her forever, for it seems yours was but a mock marriage.

SPARKISH: Indeed, she would needs have it that 'twas Harcourt himself in a parson's habit that married us, but I'm sure he told me 'twas his brother Ned.

PINCHWIFE: Oh, there 'tis out, and you were deceived, not she, for you are such a frank person—but I must be gone. You'll find her at Mr. Horner's; go and believe your eyes.   [Exit Mr. Pinchwife.]

SPARKISH: Nay, I'll to her and call her as many crocodiles, sirens, harpies and other heathenish names as a poet would do a mistress who had refused to hear his suit, nay more, his verses on her.—But stay, is not that she following a torch at t'other end of the Piazza? And from Horner's certainly—'tis so.

[Enter Alithea, following a torch,[7] and Lucy behind.]

You are well met, madam, though you don't think so. What, you have made a short visit to Mr. Horner, but I suppose you'll return to him presently; by that time the parson can be with him.

ALITHEA: Mr. Horner, and the parson, sir!

SPARKISH: Come, madam, no more dissembling, no more jilting, for I am no more a frank person.

ALITHEA: How's this?

LUCY [aside]: So, 'twill work, I see.

SPARKISH: Could you find out no easy country fool to abuse? None but me, a gentleman of wit and pleasure about the town? But it was your pride to be too hard for a man of parts, unworthy false woman, false as a friend that lends a man money to lose, false as dice who undo those that trust all they have to 'em.

LUCY [aside]: He has been a great bubble by his similes, as they say.

ALITHEA: You have been too merry, sir, at your wedding dinner, sure.

SPARKISH: What, d'ye mock me too?

ALITHEA: Or you have been deluded.

SPARKISH: By you.

ALITHEA: Let me understand you.

SPARKISH: Have you the confidence—I should call it something else, since you know your guilt—to stand my just reproaches? You did not write an impudent letter to Mr. Horner, who I find now has clubbed with you in deluding me with his aversion for women, that I might not, forsooth, suspect him for my rival.

7. A boy carrying a torch.

LUCY [*aside*]: D'ye think the gentleman can be jealous now, madam?

ALITHEA: I write a letter to Mr. Horner!

SPARKISH: Nay, madam, do not deny it; your brother showed it me just now and told me likewise he left you at Horner's lodging to fetch a parson to marry you to him, and I wish you joy, madam, joy, joy, and to him too, much joy, and to myself more joy for not marrying you.

ALITHEA [*aside*]: So, I find my brother would break off the match, and I can consent to't, since I see this gentleman can be made jealous.—O Lucy, by his rude usage and jealousy, he makes me almost afraid I am married to him. Art thou sure 'twas Harcourt himself and no parson that married us?

SPARKISH: No, madam, I thank you. I suppose that was a contrivance too of Mr. Horner's and yours, to make Harcourt play the parson; but I would as little as you have him one now, no, not for the world, for shall I tell you another truth? I never had any passion for you till now, for now I hate you. 'Tis true I might have married your portion, as other men of parts of the town do sometimes, and so your servant, and to show my unconcernedness, I'll come to your wedding and resign you with as much joy as I would a stale wench to a new cully, nay, with as much joy as I would after the first night, if I had been married to you. There's for you, and so your servant, servant.   [*Exit Sparkish.*]

ALITHEA: How was I deceived in a man!

LUCY: You'll believe, then, a fool may be made jealous now? For that easiness in him that suffers him to be led by a wife will likewise permit him to be persuaded against her by others.

ALITHEA: But marry Mr. Horner! My brother does not intend it, sure; if I thought he did, I would take thy advice and Mr. Harcourt for my husband. And now I wish that if there be any over-wise woman of the town who, like me, would marry a fool for fortune, liberty or title; first, that her husband may love play and be a cully to all the town but her and suffer none but fortune to be mistress of his purse; then, if for liberty, that he may send her into the country under the conduct of some housewifely mother-in-law, and, if for title, may the world give 'em none but that of cuckold.

LUCY: And for her greater curse, madam, may he not deserve it.

ALITHEA: Away, impertinent!—Is not this my old Lady Lanterlu's?[8]

LUCY: Yes, madam. [*Aside.*] And here I hope we shall find Mr. Harcourt.
                                                                 [*Exeunt Alithea, Lucy.*]

Scene 4

[*The scene changes again to Horner's lodging. Horner, Lady Fidget, Mrs. Dainty Fidget, Mrs. Squeamish. A table, banquet, and bottles.*]

HORNER [*aside*]: A pox! They are come too soon—before I have sent back my new—mistress. All I have now to do is to lock her in, that they may not see her.

LADY FIDGET: That we may be sure of our welcome, we have brought our entertainment with us and are resolved to treat thee, dear toad.

DAINTY: And that we may be merry to purpose, have left Sir Jaspar and my old Lady Squeamish quarrelling at home at backgammon.

SQUEAMISH: Therefore let us make use of our time, lest they should chance to interrupt us.

---

8. The lady is comically named after a popular card game, "loo" for short.

LADY FIDGET: Let us sit then.

HORNER: First, that you may be private, let me lock this door and that, and I'll wait upon you presently.

LADY FIDGET: No, sir, shut 'em only and your lips forever, for we must trust you as much as our women.

HORNER: You know all vanity's killed in me; I have no occasion for talking.

LADY FIDGET: Now, ladies, supposing we had drank each of us our two bottles, let us speak the truth of our hearts.

DAINTY: ⎫
SQUEAMISH: ⎬ Agreed.

LADY FIDGET: By this brimmer,[9] for truth is nowhere else to be found. [*Aside to Horner.*] Not in thy heart, false man!

HORNER [*aside to Lady Fidget*]: You have found me a true man, I'm sure.

LADY FIDGET [*aside to Horner*]: Not every way.—But let us sit and be merry. [*Lady Fidget sings.*]

1

    Why should our damned tyrants oblige us to live
    On the pittance of pleasure which they only give?
    We must not rejoice
    With wine and with noise.
5   In vain we must wake in a dull bed alone,
    Whilst to our warm rival, the bottle, they're gone.
    They lay aside charms
    And take up these arms.[1]

2

    'Tis wine only gives 'em their courage and wit;
10   Because we live sober, to men we submit.
    If for beauties you'd pass,
    Take a lick of the glass;
    'Twill mend your complexions and, when they are gone,
    The best red we have is the red of the grape.
15   Then, sisters, lay't on,
    And damn a good shape.

DAINTY: Dear brimmer! Well, in token of our openness and plain-dealing, let us throw our masks over our heads.

HORNER: So, 'twill come to the glasses anon.

SQUEAMISH: Lovely brimmer! Let me enjoy him first.

LADY FIDGET: No, I never part with a gallant till I've tried him. Dear brimmer, that mak'st our husbands shortsighted.

DAINTY: And our bashful gallants bold.

SQUEAMISH: And for want of a gallant, the butler lovely in our eyes.—Drink, eunuch.

---

9. Brimming cup.   1. I.e., the glasses.

LADY FIDGET: Drink, thou representative of a husband. Damn a husband!

DAINTY: And, as it were a husband, an old keeper.

SQUEAMISH: And an old grandmother.

HORNER: And an English bawd and a French chirurgeon.[2]

LADY FIDGET: Ay, we have all reason to curse 'em.

HORNER: For my sake, ladies?

LADY FIDGET: No, for our own, for the first spoils all young gallants' industry.

DAINTY: And the other's art makes 'em bold only with common women.

SQUEAMISH: And rather run the hazard of the vile distemper amongst them than of a denial amongst us.

DAINTY: The filthy toads choose mistresses now as they do stuffs,[3] for having been fancied and worn by others.[4]

SQUEAMISH: For being common and cheap.

LADY FIDGET: Whilst women of quality, like the richest stuffs, lie untumbled and unasked for.

HORNER: Ay, neat and cheap and new often they think best.

DAINTY: No, sir, the beasts will be known by a mistress longer than by a suit.

SQUEAMISH: And 'tis not for cheapness neither.

LADY FIDGET: No, for the vain fops will take up druggets[5] and embroider 'em. But I wonder at the depraved appetites of witty men; they use to be out of the common road and hate imitation. Pray tell me, beast, when you were a man, why you rather chose to club with a multitude in a common house[6] for an entertainment than to be the only guest at a good table!

HORNER: Why, faith, ceremony and expectation are unsufferable to those that are sharp bent;[7] people always eat with the best stomach at an ordinary, where every man is snatching for the best bit.

LADY FIDGET: Though he get a cut over the fingers.—But I have heard people eat most heartily of another man's meat, that is, what they do not pay for.

HORNER: When they are sure of their welcome and freedom, for ceremony in love and eating is as ridiculous as in fighting; falling on briskly is all should be done in those occasions.

LADY FIDGET: Well, then, let me tell you, sir, there is nowhere more freedom than in our houses and we take freedom from a young person as a sign of good breeding, and a person may be as free as he pleases with us, as frolic, as gamesome, as wild as he will.

HORNER: Han't I heard you all declaim against wild men?

LADY FIDGET: Yes, but for all that, we think wildness in a man as desirable a quality as in a duck or rabbit; a tame man, foh!

HORNER: I know not, but your reputations frightened me, as much as your faces invited me.

LADY FIDGET: Our reputation! Lord, why should you not think that we women make use of our reputation, as you men of yours, only to deceive the world with less suspicion? Our virtue is like the statesman's religion, the Quaker's word, the gamester's oath and the great man's honor—but to cheat those that trust us.

---

2. The supposed causes of Horner's fictitious plight (see Act 1, scene 1, page 1094).
3. Garments.
4. Second-hand trade was commonplace in Restoration
England.
5. Cheap woolen fabric.
6. A restaurant or brothel.
7. Hungry.

SQUEAMISH: And that demureness, coyness and modesty that you see in our faces in the boxes at plays is as much a sign of a kind woman as a vizard-mask in the pit.

DAINTY: For, I assure you, women are least masked when they have the velvet vizard on.

LADY FIDGET: You would have found us modest women in our denials only.

SQUEAMISH: Our bashfulness is only the reflection of the men's.

DAINTY: We blush when they are shamefaced.

HORNER: I beg your pardon, ladies; I was deceived in you devilishly. But why that mighty pretense to honor?

LADY FIDGET: We have told you. But sometimes 'twas for the same reason you men pretend business often, to avoid ill company, to enjoy the better and more privately those you love.

HORNER: But why would you ne'er give a friend a wink then?

LADY FIDGET: Faith, your reputation frightened us as much as ours did you, you were so notoriously lewd.

HORNER: And you so seemingly honest.

LADY FIDGET: Was that all that deterred you?

HORNER: And so expensive—you allow freedom, you say—

LADY FIDGET: Ay, ay.

HORNER: That I was afraid of losing my little money, as well as my little time, both which my other pleasures required.

LADY FIDGET: Money, foh! You talk like a little fellow now; do such as we expect money?

HORNER: I beg your pardon, madam; I must confess, I have heard that great ladies, like great merchants, set but the higher prizes[8] upon what they have, because they are not in necessity of taking the first offer.

DAINTY: Such as we make sale of our hearts?

SQUEAMISH: We bribed for our love? Foh!

HORNER: With your pardon, ladies, I know, like great men in offices, you seem to exact flattery and attendance only from your followers; but you have receivers[9] about you and such fees to pay, a man is afraid to pass your grants.[1] Besides, we must let you win at cards, or we lose your hearts, and if you make an assignation, 'tis at a goldsmith's, jeweller's or china house, where, for your honor you deposit to him, he must pawn his to the punctual cit, and so paying for what you take up, pays for what he takes up.[2]

DAINTY: Would you not have us assured of our gallant's love?

SQUEAMISH: For love is better known by liberality than by jealousy.

LADY FIDGET: For one may be dissembled, the other not. [Aside.] But my jealousy can be no longer dissembled, and they are telling ripe.[3]—Come, here's to our gallants in waiting, whom we must name, and I'll begin. This is my false rogue. [Claps him on the back.]

SQUEAMISH: How!

HORNER: So all will out now.

---

8. Prices.
9. Collectors.
1. Accept your favors (because in the end they are so expensive).
2. I.e., you arrange to meet your lover at an expensive shop, where he in effect pays for your favors by purchasing for you the shopkeeper's ("punctual cit's") costly merchandise.
3. Ripe for the telling.

SQUEAMISH [*aside to Horner*]: Did you not tell me, 'twas for my sake only you reported yourself no man?

DAINTY [*aside to Horner*]: Oh, wretch! Did you not swear to me, 'twas for my love
and honor you passed for that thing you do?

HORNER: So, so.

LADY FIDGET: Come, speak, ladies; this is my false villain.

SQUEAMISH: And mine too.

DAINTY: And mine.

HORNER: Well then, you are all three my false rogues too, and there's an end on't.

LADY FIDGET: Well then, there's no remedy; sister sharers, let us not fall out, but
have a care of our honor. Though we get no presents, no jewels of him, we are
savers of our honor, the jewel of most value and use, which shines yet to the world
unsuspected, though it be counterfeit.

HORNER: Nay, and is e'en as good as if it were true, provided the world think so;
for honor, like beauty now, only depends on the opinion of others.

LADY FIDGET: Well, Harry Common, I hope you can be true to three. Swear—but
'tis to no purpose to require your oath, for you are as often forsworn as you swear to
new women.

HORNER: Come, faith, madam, let us e'en pardon one another, for all the difference I find betwixt we men and you women, we forswear ourselves at the beginning of an amour, you as long as it lasts.

[*Enter Sir Jaspar Fidget and Old Lady Squeamish.*]

SIR JASPAR: Oh, my Lady Fidget, was this your cunning, to come to Mr. Horner
without me? But you have been nowhere else, I hope.

LADY FIDGET: No, Sir Jaspar.

OLD LADY SQUEAMISH: And you came straight hither, Biddy?

SQUEAMISH: Yes, indeed, Lady Grandmother.

SIR JASPAR: 'Tis well, 'tis well; I knew when once they were thoroughly acquainted with poor Horner, they'd ne'er be from him. You may let her masquerade
it with my wife and Horner and I warrant her reputation safe.

[*Enter Boy.*]

BOY: Oh, sir, here's the gentleman come whom you bid me not suffer to come up
without giving you notice, with a lady too, and other gentlemen—

HORNER: Do you all go in there, whilst I send 'em away, and, boy, do you desire
'em to stay below till I come, which shall be immediately.

[*Exeunt Sir Jaspar, Old Lady Squeamish, Lady Fidget, Mrs. Dainty, Squeamish.*]

BOY: Yes, sir.   [*Exit.*]

[*Exit Horner at t'other door and returns with Mrs. Pinchwife.*]

HORNER: You would not take my advice to be gone home before your husband
came back; he'll now discover all. Yet pray, my dearest, be persuaded to go home
and leave the rest to my management. I'll let you down the back way.

MRS. PINCHWIFE: I don't know the way home, so I don't.

HORNER: My man shall wait upon you.

MRS. PINCHWIFE: No, don't you believe that I'll go at all. What, are you weary of
me already?

HORNER: No, my life, 'tis that I may love you long, 'tis to secure my love, and your
reputation with your husband; he'll never receive you again else.

MRS. PINCHWIFE: What care I? D'ye think to frighten me with that? I don't intend to go to him again; you shall be my husband now.

HORNER: I cannot be your husband, dearest, since you are married to him.

MRS. PINCHWIFE: Oh, would you make me believe that? Don't I see every day, at London here, women leave their first husbands and go and live with other men as their wives? Pish, pshaw, you'd make me angry, but that I love you so mainly.[4]

HORNER: So, they are coming up—in again, in, I hear 'em.

[Exit Mrs. Pinchwife.]

Well, a silly mistress is like a weak place, soon got, soon lost, a man has scarce time for plunder; she betrays her husband first to her gallant and then her gallant to her husband.

[Enter Pinchwife, Alithea, Harcourt, Sparkish, Lucy and a Parson.]

PINCHWIFE: Come, madam, 'tis not the sudden change of your dress, the confidence of your asseverations and your false witness there, shall persuade me I did not bring you hither just now; here's my witness, who cannot deny it, since you must be confronted.—Mr. Horner, did not I bring this lady to you just now?

HORNER [aside]: Now must I wrong one woman for another's sake, but that's no new thing with me, for in these cases I am still on the criminal's side, against the innocent.

ALITHEA: Pray, speak, sir.

HORNER [aside]: It must be so—I must be impudent and try my luck; impudence uses to be too hard for truth.

PINCHWIFE: What, you are studying an evasion or excuse for her. Speak, sir.

HORNER: No, faith, I am something backward only to speak in women's affairs or disputes.

PINCHWIFE: She bids you speak.

ALITHEA: Ay, pray, sir, do; pray satisfy him.

HORNER: Then truly, you did bring that lady to me just now.

PINCHWIFE: O ho!

ALITHEA: How, sir!

HARCOURT: How, Horner!

ALITHEA: What mean you, sir? I always took you for a man of honor.

HORNER [aside]: Ay, so much a man of honor that I must save my mistress, I thank you, come what will on't.

SPARKISH: So, if I had had her, she'd have made me believe the moon had been made of a Christmas pie.

LUCY [aside]: Now could I speak, if I durst, and solve the riddle, who am the author of it.

ALITHEA: O unfortunate woman! A combination against my honor, which most concerns me now, because you share in my disgrace, sir, and it is your censure, which I must now suffer, that troubles me, not theirs.

HARCOURT: Madam, then have no trouble, you shall now see 'tis possible for me to love too, without being jealous; I will not only believe your innocence myself, but make all the world believe it. [Apart to Horner.] Horner, I must now be concerned for this lady's honor.

HORNER: And I must be concerned for a lady's honor too.

HARCOURT: This lady has her honor and I will protect it.

HORNER: My lady has not her honor but has given it me to keep and I will preserve it.

HARCOURT: I understand you not.

HORNER: I would not have you.

MRS. PINCHWIFE [*peeping in behind*]: What's the matter with 'em all?

PINCHWIFE: Come, come, Mr. Horner, no more disputing. Here's the parson; I brought him not in vain.

HARCOURT: No, sir, I'll employ him, if this lady please.

PINCHWIFE: How! What d'ye mean?

SPARKISH: Ay, what does he mean?

HORNER: Why, I have resigned your sister to him; he has my consent.

PINCHWIFE: But he has not mine, sir; a woman's injured honor, no more than a man's, can be repaired or satisfied by any but him that first wronged it; and you shall marry her presently, or—[*Lays his hand on his sword.*]
    [*Enter to them Mrs. Pinchwife.*]

MRS. PINCHWIFE [*aside*]: O Lord, they'll kill poor Mr. Horner! Besides, he shan't marry her whilst I stand by and look on; I'll not lose my second husband so.

PINCHWIFE: What do I see?

ALITHEA: My sister in my clothes!

SPARKISH: Ha!

MRS. PINCHWIFE [*to Mr. Pinchwife*]: Nay, pray now don't quarrel about finding work for the parson; he shall marry me to Mr. Horner, for now, I believe, you have enough of me.

HORNER: Damned, damned, loving changeling!

MRS. PINCHWIFE: Pray, sister, pardon me for telling so many lies of you.

HARCOURT: I suppose the riddle is plain now.

LUCY: No, that must be my work. Good sir, hear me.
    [*Kneels to Mr. Pinchwife, who stands doggedly, with his hat over his eyes.*]

PINCHWIFE: I will never hear woman again, but make 'em all silent, thus—
    [*Offers to draw upon his wife.*]

HORNER: No, that must not be.

PINCHWIFE: You then shall go first; 'tis all one to me. [*Offers to draw on Horner; stopped by Harcourt.*]

HARCOURT: Hold!
    [*Enter Sir Jaspar Fidget, Lady Fidget, Old Lady Squeamish, Mrs. Dainty Fidget, Mrs. Squeamish.*]

SIR JASPAR: What's the matter, what's the matter, pray, what's the matter, sir? I beseech you communicate, sir.

PINCHWIFE: Why, my wife has communicated,[5] sir, as your wife may have done too, sir, if she knows him, sir.

SIR JASPAR: Pshaw, with him? Ha, ha, he!

PINCHWIFE: D'ye mock me, sir? A cuckold is a kind of a wild beast; have a care, sir.

SIR JASPAR: No, sure, you mock me, sir—he cuckold you! It can't be, ha, ha, he! Why, I tell you, sir—[*Offers to whisper.*]

5. Fornicated.

PINCHWIFE: I tell you again, he has whored my wife, and yours too, if he knows her, and all the women he comes near; 'tis not his dissembling, his hypocrisy can wheedle me.

SIR JASPAR: How! does he dissemble? Is he a hypocrite? Nay, then—how—wife—sister, is he an hypocrite?

OLD LADY SQUEAMISH: An hypocrite, a dissembler! Speak, young harlotry, speak, how?

SIR JASPAR: Nay, then—O, my head too!—O thou libidinous lady!

OLD LADY SQUEAMISH: O thou harloting harlotry! Hast thou done't then?

SIR JASPAR: Speak, good Horner, art thou a dissembler, a rogue? Hast thou—

HORNER: Soh—

LUCY [apart to Horner]: I'll fetch you off, and her too, if she will but hold her tongue.

HORNER [apart to Lucy]: Canst thou? I'll give thee—

LUCY [to Mr. Pinchwife]: Pray have but patience to hear me, sir, who am the unfortunate cause of all this confusion. Your wife is innocent, I only culpable, for I put her upon telling you all these lies concerning my mistress, in order to the breaking off the match between Mr. Sparkish and her, to make way for Mr. Harcourt.

SPARKISH: Did you so, eternal rotten tooth? Then, it seems, my mistress was not false to me, I was only deceived by you.—Brother that should have been, now man of conduct, who is a frank person now? To bring your wife to her lover—ha!

LUCY: I assure you, sir, she came not to Mr. Horner out of love, for she loves him no more—

MRS. PINCHWIFE: Hold, I told lies for you, but you shall tell none for me, for I do love Mr. Horner with all my soul, and nobody shall say me nay. Pray, don't you go to make poor Mr. Horner believe to the contrary; 'tis spitefully done of you, I'm sure.

HORNER [aside to Mrs. Pinchwife]: Peace, dear idiot.

MRS. PINCHWIFE: Nay, I will not peace.

PINCHWIFE: Not till I make you.

[Enter Dorilant, Quack.]

DORILANT: Horner, your servant; I am the doctor's guest, he must excuse our intrusion.

QUACK: But what's the matter, gentlemen? For heaven's sake, what's the matter?

HORNER: Oh, 'tis well you are come. 'Tis a censorious world we live in; you may have brought me a reprieve, or else I had died for a crime I never committed, and these innocent ladies had suffered with me. Therefore pray satisfy these worthy, honorable, jealous gentlemen—that—[Whispers.]

QUACK: O, I understand you; is that all?

[Whispers to Sir Jaspar.]

Sir Jaspar, by heavens and upon the word of a physician, sir—

SIR JASPAR: Nay, I do believe you truly.—Pardon me, my virtuous lady and dear of honor.

OLD LADY SQUEAMISH: What, then all's right again?

SIR JASPAR: Ay, ay, and now let us satisfy him too.

[They whisper with Mr. Pinchwife.]

PINCHWIFE: An eunuch! Pray, no fooling with me.

QUACK: I'll bring half the chirurgeons in town to swear it.

PINCHWIFE: They!—they'll swear a man that bled to death through his wounds died of an apoplexy.[6]

QUACK: Pray hear me, sir—why, all the town has heard the report of him.

PINCHWIFE: But does all the town believe it?

QUACK: Pray inquire a little, and first of all these.

PINCHWIFE: I'm sure when I left the town he was the lewdest fellow in't.

QUACK: I tell you, sir, he has been in France since; pray, ask but these ladies and gentlemen, your friend Mr. Dorilant.—Gentlemen and ladies, han't you all heard the late sad report of poor Mr. Horner?

ALL THE LADIES: Ay, ay, ay.

DORILANT: Why, thou jealous fool, dost thou doubt it? He's an arrant French capon.[7]

MRS. PINCHWIFE: 'Tis false, sir, you shall not disparage poor Mr. Horner, for to my certain knowledge—

LUCY: Oh, hold!

SQUEAMISH [aside to Lucy]: Stop her mouth!

LADY FIDGET [to Pinchwife]: Upon my honor, sir, 'tis as true—

DAINTY: D'ye think we would have been seen in his company?

SQUEAMISH: Trust our unspotted reputations with him!

LADY FIDGET [aside to Horner]: This you get, and we too, by trusting your secret to a fool.

HORNER: Peace, madam. [Aside to Quack.] Well, doctor, is not this a good design, that carries a man on unsuspected and brings him off safe?

PINCHWIFE [aside]: Well, if this were true, but my wife—[Dorilant whispers with Mrs. Pinchwife.]

ALITHEA: Come, brother, your wife is yet innocent, you see; but have a care of too strong an imagination, lest like an overconcerned, timorous gamester, by fancying an unlucky cast, it should come. Women and fortune are truest still to those that trust 'em.

LUCY: And any wild thing grows but the more fierce and hungry for being kept up and more dangerous to the keeper.

ALITHEA: There's doctrine for all husbands, Mr. Harcourt.

HARCOURT: I edify, madam, so much that I am impatient till I am one.

DORILANT: And I edify so much by example I will never be one.

SPARKISH: And because I will not disparage my parts I'll ne'er be one.

HORNER: And I, alas, can't be one.

PINCHWIFE: But I must be one—against my will, to a country wife, with a country murrain[8] to me.

MRS. PINCHWIFE [aside]: And I must be a country wife still too, I find, for I can't, like a city one, be rid of my musty husband and do what I list.

HORNER: Now, sir, I must pronounce your wife innocent, though I blush whilst I do it, and I am the only man by her now exposed to shame, which I will straight drown in wine, as you shall your suspicion, and the ladies' troubles we'll divert with a ballet.—Doctor, where are your maskers?

LUCY: Indeed, she's innocent, sir, I am her witness; and her end of coming out was but to see her sister's wedding and what she has said to your face of her love to Mr.

---

6. A convenient fiction since dueling was now illegal (1679).   7. Eunuch.
8. Pestilence.

Horner was but the usual innocent revenge on a husband's jealousy—was it not, madam? Speak.

MRS. PINCHWIFE [*aside to Lucy and Horner*]: Since you'll have me tell more lies— Yes, indeed, bud.

PINCHWIFE: For my own sake fain I would all believe; Cuckolds, like lovers, should themselves deceive. But—[*Sighs.*]

> His honor is least safe, too late I find,
> Who trusts it with a foolish wife or friend.

[*A Dance of Cuckolds.*9]

HORNER: Vain fops but court and dress and keep a puther,1
            To pass for women's men with one another,
5   But he who aims by women to be priz'd,
            First by the men, you see, must be despis'd.

EPILOGUE, *SPOKEN BY* MRS. *KNEPP*2

> Now, you the vigorous,3 who daily here
> O'er vizard-mask in public domineer,
> And what you'd do to her if in place where,
> Nay, have the confidence to cry, "Come out,"
5 > Yet when she says "Lead on," you are not stout,
> But to your well-dressed brother straight turn round
> And cry, "Pox on her, Ned, she can't be sound,"
> Then slink away, a fresh one to engage,
> With so much seeming heat and loving rage,
10 > You'd frighten listening actress on the stage,
> Till she at last has seen you huffing come
> And talk of keeping in the tiring-room,
> Yet cannot be provok'd to lead her home.
> Next, you Falstaffs4 of fifty, who beset
15 > Your buckram5 maidenheads, which your friends get,
> And while to them you of achievements boast,
> They share the booty and laugh at your cost.
> In fine, you essenced boys, both old and young,
> Who would be thought so eager, brisk and strong,
20 > Yet do the ladies, not their husbands, wrong,
> Whose purses for your manhood make excuse,
> And keep your Flanders mares6 for show, not use:
> Encourag'd by our woman's man today,
> A Horner's part may vainly think to play
25 > And may intrigues so bashfully disown

9. This dance was performed to the then-familiar tune called "Cuckolds All [in] a Row."
1. Make a fuss.
2. Elizabeth Knepp, actress and singer, created the role of Lady Fidget. Pepys held her in high regard.
3. The epilogue derisively addresses two categories of males who, unlike Horner, pretend to sexual potency: the young (lines 1–13) and the old (14–17).

4. I.e., you who resemble the immense, aged, comic liar Shakespeare created in *Henry IV*.
5. A stiff fabric. Falstaff at one point pretends to have killed some "rogues in buckram suits" during a robbery (*1 Henry IV* 2.4). In truth he killed no one, and his younger accomplices made off with the loot.
6. Costly coach horses, here a metaphor for kept mistresses or prostitutes.

That they may doubted be by few or none,[7]
May kiss the cards at picquet, ombre, loo,[8]
And so be thought to kiss the lady too;
But, gallants, have a care, faith, what you do.
30   The world, which to no man his due will give,
You by experience know you can deceive
And men may still believe you vigorous,
But then we women—there's no cozening[9] us.

1675   1675

Daniel Defoe
1660–1731

At the age of fifty-two, Daniel Defoe summed up his life in a couplet:

No man has tasted differing fortunes more,
And thirteen times I have been rich or poor.

Vicissitude marked his career until the very end, and money, though a constant preoccupation, was not the only medium of change. Deeply engaged in politics, and phenomenally skilled at promoting causes with his pen, Defoe switched allegiances several times among the most conspicuous factions of his day. What's more, since he was prized by each side in turn for his efficiency as a secret agent, his political work often required him to present himself—in person and in print—as someone or something he was not, to incur hostilities from the very factions he was secretly working to support. His accomplishments, late in life, as a pioneer of English fiction partly originate in the fictions he manipulated as a consummate political journalist and spy obliged to "taste" in imagination and performance the "differing fortunes" of the person he pretended, for one purpose or another, to be. Out of all these oscillations—financial, political, imaginative—came one of the most prolific and inventive careers in British literature.

Defoe was born in the City of London in the year of the Restoration to a family whose fortunes were on the rise. His father James Foe manufactured and sold candles, and over the ensuing decades attained positions of increasing eminence in his trade (Defoe himself later added the French prefix to his family surname). Under the influence of their pastor, the Foes left the Church of England to become Dissenters, at a time when to do so was to incur certain exclusion—from attending universities, from holding public office—and possible persecution (violence, imprisonment). At around the age of ten, shortly after his mother's early death, Defoe began a decade in the schools of the Dissenters. The curriculum, underplaying the Greek and Latin of conventional Anglican education, focused instead on new science and philosophy, on clear argument and public speaking, as well as on two forms of thought and composition that cultivated the student's ability to imagine "differing fortunes": prose impersonation, where the student was asked to "play" a given figure (for example, a secretary of state) in a particular situation, and to write a letter or give a speech suitable to the occasion; and casuistry, a kind of moral and theological game of "What if?": if I were to find myself in such and such a predicament, such a dilemma, what should I do? The question recurs, explicitly and implicitly, throughout Defoe's prose.

As Defoe entered his twenties, the question became personally pressing. Many of his classmates were preparing for the ministry; he opted instead to enter his father's world of trade,

---

7. I.e., Horner's example may encourage "you" fakers to reverse tactics, and to seek a rake's reputation by feigning "bashfulness."

8. Card games; kissing the cards was a way of flirting with fellow-players.
9. Fooling.

though with a taste for range and risk that his prudent forebear had never displayed. Defoe dealt at one time or another in men's clothing, tobacco, wine; opened and operated a brick and tile factory, and invested capital so audaciously and ill-advisedly that in 1692 he was forced to declare bankruptcy, having incurred the enormous debt of £17,000. "The God that gave me brains will give me bread," Defoe remarked at one point, with characteristic confidence in both the deity and himself. From his late thirties onward, he used those brains to earn bread, for himself and his large family, by writing. He worked with astonishing speed and efficiency, producing by his life's end more than 500 separate works, as well as several periodical series that he wrote (at the rate of two or three essays a week) over the course of many years. Nonetheless, he never quite escaped the financial distresses that had first pushed him into print.

His pen's other impetus was politics. As a Whig and a Dissenter eager to end the reign of the Catholic James II, Defoe had fought as soldier in the abortive Monmouth Rebellion of 1685, and in 1688 celebrated the advent of the Glorious Revolution and William III. He served his new king as secret agent and as author, publishing the phenomenally popular poem *The True-Born Englishman* (1701), whose title sarcastically identifies those "natives" hostile to William on the grounds of his foreign birth (the poem argues, among other things, that their own lineage is far more complex and corrupt than they admit). Defoe's powers as a political advocate were now near full stride, and his knack for irony soon brought him trouble. In his parodic pamphlet *The Shortest Way with Dissenters*, published anonymously in 1702 at the height of Tory hopes for a new assault on Nonconformists, Defoe impersonates a rabid Tory eager to mete out extravagant punishments on the Nonconformists (to whom Defoe himself had felt a lifelong loyalty and tenderness). Neither faction appreciated the joke. After four months in hiding, Defoe was arrested, convicted of libel, and sentenced to prison and to three separate sessions in the pillory, where the crowds (to his surprise) celebrated him as a hero, pelting him with fresh flowers rather than rotten vegetables. The episode initiated a sea change in his affiliations. Disillusioned with Whigs and Dissenters, Defoe secretly aligned himself with the ambitious Tory politician Robert Harley, who in an inspired move had arranged to pay some of Defoe's fines and debts after his release from jail. Commissioned by Harley to create and manage a kind of personal secret service, Defoe traveled extensively, often under assumed names, advocating Tory causes (most notably the Union with Scotland) and reporting on the opposition; he also wrote the widely read *Review* (1704–1713), a thrice-weekly periodical essay intricately calculated to further Harley's interests. After the fall of the Tories, the intricacy deepened. Under threat of punishment by the new Whig government, Defoe agreed to work as double agent for *them*, by moving among Tory journalists and contributing to Tory papers, but in such ways as to undermine the Tory cause. For the seasoned ironist and impersonator this was irony enough: having worked brilliantly for years to devise Tory propaganda, he was now at pains to dilute it.

At the age of fifty-nine, Defoe hit upon a new way to make impersonation pay. His book *The Strange, Surprising Adventures of Robinson Crusoe* (1719) was the first in a series of long fictions that present themselves as historical fact, as the written reminiscences of people who had actually lived the extraordinary experiences they relate, in books that often bear their fictive names as titles: *Captain Singleton* (1720); *Moll Flanders* (1722); *Colonel Jack* (1722); *Roxana* (1724). In creating these memoirists, Defoe drew on his decades as a journalist. He saturated his stories with particulars (clothing, furniture, tools); his memoirists write a prose that often reads like talk—digressive, fervent, improvisatory. By such strategies he made his tales persuasive. As a genre, the novel has no one inventor, because it absorbs so much (and so variously) from other kinds of texts: newspapers, essays, diaries, financial accounts, religious devotions, conduct manuals. Defoe, though, was perhaps the most astute early orchestrator of such absorptions. Having written in most of his culture's modes, he melded them into a form of fiction that still seems (in keeping with the genre's name) new.

Vicissitude persisted. Having written his last long fiction (*Roxana*) in 1724, Defoe turned his hand to another project. In his *Tour through the Whole Island of Great Britain* (three volumes, 1724–1726), and in other late works, he celebrated British trade as a source of present prosperity and a seedbed of future empire. He died while hiding out from his creditors in the neighborhood of his birth, once again on the run from debt and cut off from his contentious family. The ending feels emblematic. In many ways the most communicative of writers, Defoe often used his powers to study solitude. "Between me and thee there is a great gulf fixed," remarks Robinson Crusoe on his island, quoting scripture: "thee" is the whole world, from which he finds himself definitively sundered. But the phrase might be invoked by almost any speaker in Defoe—characters talking to characters, ghosts to the living, narrators to readers—as they survey the landscape of their own isolation, even in crowded cities. Defoe devoted his writing life to mapping these "great gulfs," to chronicling the energies—political, social, and commercial—by which the mortals of his time and place tried to bridge them, and to seeking out the work of God and Providence in all these prolific, troubled transactions.

from A Journal of the Plague Year

Being Observations or Memorials of the Most Remarkable Occurrences,
as Well Public as Private, Which Happened in London during
the Last Great Visitation in 1665[1]

[AT THE BURIAL PIT]

I went all the first part of the time freely about the streets, though not so freely as to run myself into apparent danger, except when they dug the great pit in the churchyard of our parish of Aldgate; a terrible pit it was, and I could not resist my curiosity to go and see it. As near as I may judge, it was about 40 foot in length, and about 15 or 16 foot broad; and at the time I first looked at it, about nine foot deep; but it was said they dug it near 20 foot deep afterwards, in one part of it, till they could go no deeper for the water: for they had, it seems, dug several large pits before this, for though the plague was long a-coming to our parish, yet when it did come, there was no parish in or about London where it raged with such violence as in the two parishes of Aldgate and Whitechapel.

I say they had dug several pits in another ground, when the distemper began to spread in our parish, and especially when the dead carts began to go about, which was not in our parish till the beginning of August. Into these pits they had put perhaps 50 or 60 bodies each; then they made larger holes, wherein they buried all that the cart brought in a week, which by the middle to the end of August, came to from 200 to 400 a week; and they could not well dig them larger, because of the order of the magistrates, confining them to leave no bodies within six foot of the surface; and the water coming on, at about 17 or 18 foot, they could not well, I say, put more in one pit; but now at the beginning of September, the plague raging in a dreadful manner, and the number of burials in our parish increasing to more than was ever buried in any parish about London of no larger extent, they ordered this dreadful gulf to be dug; for such it was, rather than a pit.

They had supposed this pit would have supplied them for a month or more, when they dug it, and some blamed the church wardens for suffering such a frightful thing, telling them they were making preparations to bury the whole parish, and the

---

1. In the early 1720s, London found itself once again threatened with the prospect of bubonic plague. Defoe responded with two long pieces of prose: a manual of preventive measures called *Due Preparations for the Plague* (1720), and a historical fiction thoroughly researched and deeply grounded in historical facts. The text's purported narrator—already dead by the time his book is published—presents himself as recasting in retrospect the journal entries he wrote during that terrible year, in the hope that they may benefit future generations. Designated only by his initials, "H. F.," he is probably modeled in part on the author's uncle Henry Foe, who like "H. F." was a London saddler who lived in the parish of Aldgate.

like; but time made it appear, the church wardens knew the condition of the parish better than they did; for the pit being finished the 4th of September, I think, they began to bury in it the 6th, and by the 20th, which was just two weeks, they had thrown into it 1,114 bodies, when they were obliged to fill it up, the bodies being then come to lie within six foot of the surface: I doubt not but there may be some ancient persons alive in the parish, who can justify the fact of this, and are able to show even in what part of the churchyard the pit lay, better than I can; the mark of it also was many years to be seen in the churchyard on the surface lying in length, parallel with the passage which goes by the west wall of the churchyard, out of Houndsditch, and turns east again into Whitechapel, coming out near the Three Nuns Inn.

It was about the 10th of September, that my curiosity led, or rather drove me to go and see this pit again, when there had been near 400 people buried in it; and I was not content to see it in the daytime, as I had done before; for then there would have been nothing to have been seen but the loose earth; for all the bodies that were thrown in were immediately covered with earth, by those they called the buriers, which at other times were called bearers;[2] but I resolved to go in the night and see some of them thrown in.

There was a strict order to prevent people coming to those pits, and that was only to prevent infection: but after some time, that order was more necessary, for people that were infected, and near their end, and delirious also, would run to those pits wrapped in blankets or rugs and throw themselves in and, as they said, bury themselves: I cannot say that the officers suffered any willingly to lie there; but I have heard that in a great pit in Finsbury, in the parish of Cripplegate, it lying open then to the fields (for it was not then walled about) came and threw themselves in, and expired there, before they threw any earth upon them; and that when they came to bury others, and found them there, they were quite dead, though not cold.

This may serve a little to describe the dreadful condition of that day, though it is impossible to say anything that is able to give a true idea of it to those who did not see it, other than this; that it was indeed very, very, very dreadful, and such as no tongue can express.

I got admittance into the churchyard by being acquainted with the sexton[3] who attended, who though he did not refuse me at all, yet earnestly persuaded me not to go; telling me very seriously, for he was a good religious and sensible man, that it was indeed their business and duty to venture, and to run all hazards; and that in it they might hope to be preserved; but that I had no apparent call to it, but my own curiosity, which, he said, he believed I would not pretend was sufficient to justify my running that hazard. I told him I had been pressed in my mind to go, and that perhaps it might be an instructing sight that might not be without its uses. "Nay," says the good man, "if you will venture upon that score, 'Name of God go in; for depend upon it, 'twill be a sermon to you, it may be, the best that ever you heard in your life. 'Tis a speaking sight," says he, "and has a voice with it, and a loud one, to call us all to repentance." And with that he opened the door and said, "Go, if you will."

2. H. F. combines two categories: the buriers put the dead bodies into the pits, arranging them in order to conserve space, and covering them with lime in order to quicken decomposition. The bearers, by contrast, handled bodies living and dead: during the day they delivered the infected to the plague-hospitals; by night they collected corpses for the pits.
3. Caretaker of the church and graveyard.

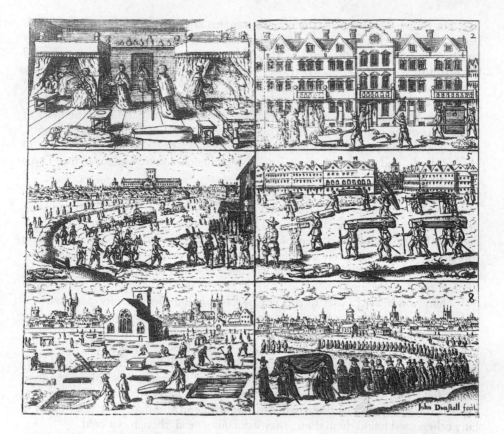

His discourse had shocked my resolution a little, and I stood wavering for a good while; but just at that interval I saw two links[4] come over from the end of the Minories,[5] and heard the bellman,[6] and then appeared a dead cart, as they called it, coming over the streets so I could no longer resist my desire of seeing it, and went in: there was nobody, as I could perceive at first, in the churchyard or going into it, but the buriers and the fellow that drove the cart, or rather led the horse and cart; but when they came up to the pit, they saw a man go to and again, muffled up in a brown cloak and making motions with his hands, under his cloak, as if he was in a great agony; and the buriers immediately gathered about him, supposing he was one of those poor delirious or desperate creatures that used to pretend,[7] as I have said, to bury themselves. He said nothing as he walked about, but two or three times groaned very deeply, and loud, and sighed as he would break his heart.

When the buriers came up to him they soon found he was neither a person infected and desperate, as I have observed above, or a person distempered in mind, but one oppressed with a dreadful weight of grief indeed, having his wife and several of his children, all in the cart that was just come in with him, and he followed in an agony and excess of sorrow. He mourned heartily, as it was easy to see, but with a kind of

4. I.e., boys carrying torches ("links"), who for a fee led people through the streets at night.
5. A street.
6. In ordinary times, the bellman announced the time

and weather as he made his way through the streets at night; in plague time, he rang his bell to alert people that the cart burying the dead was approaching.
7. Attempt.

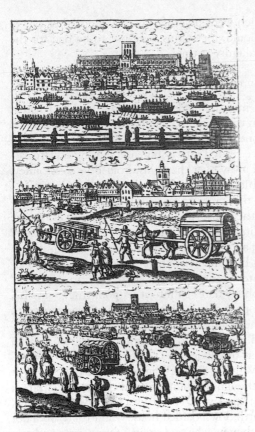

John Dunstall, *Scenes from the Plague in London*, 1665. The sequence tracks the course of corpses, from death within the city to burial in the plague-pits outside the city's walls.

masculine grief that could not give itself vent by tears, and calmly desiring the buriers to let him alone, said he would only see the bodies thrown in, and go away, so they left importuning him; but no sooner was the cart turned round, and the bodies shot into the pit promiscuously, which was a surprise to him, for he at least expected they would have been decently laid in, though indeed he was afterwards convinced that was impractible; I say, no sooner did he see the sight, but he cried out aloud unable to contain himself; I could not hear what he said, but he went backward two or three steps, and fell down in a swoon: the buriers ran to him and took him up, and in a little while he came to himself, and they led him away to the Pye Tavern over-against the end of Houndsditch, where, it seems, the man was known, and where they took care of him. He looked into the pit again, as he went away, but the buriers had covered the bodies so immediately with throwing in earth that, though there was light enough, for there were lanterns and candles in them placed all night round the sides of the pit, upon the heaps of earth, seven or eight, or perhaps more, yet nothing could be seen.

This was a mournful scene indeed, and affected me almost as much as the rest; but the other was awful, and full of terror. The cart had in it sixteen or seventeen bodies; some were wrapped up in linen sheets, some in rugs, some little other than naked, or so loose that what covering they had fell from them in the shooting out of the cart, and they fell quite naked among the rest; but the matter was not much to them, or the indecency much to anyone else, seeing they were all dead, and were to be huddled together into the common grave of mankind, as we may call it, for here was no difference made, but poor and rich went together; there was no other way of burials, neither was it possible there should, for coffins were not to be had for the prodigious numbers that fell in such a calamity as this.

[ENCOUNTER WITH A WATERMAN]

Much about the same time I walked out into the fields towards Bow; for I had a great mind to see how things were managed in the river, and among the ships; and as I had some concern in shipping, I had a notion that it had been one of the best ways of securing oneself from the infection to have retired into a ship, and musing how to satisfy my curiosity in that point, I turned away over the fields, from Bow to Bromley, and down to Blackwall, to the Stairs, which are there for landing or taking water.[8]

Here I saw a poor man walking on the bank, or seawall, as they call it, by himself. I walked a while also about, seeing the houses all shut up;[9] at last I fell into some talk, at a distance, with this poor man; first I asked him, how people did thereabouts? "Alas, Sir!" says he, "almost all desolate; all dead or sick: here are very few families in this part, or in that village," pointing at Poplar, "where half of them are not dead already, and the rest sick." Then he pointed to one house. "There they are all dead," said he, "and the house stands open; nobody dares go into it. A poor thief," says he, "ventured in to steal something, but he paid dear for his theft; for he was carried to the churchyard too last night." Then he pointed to several other houses. "There," says he, "they are all dead; the man and his wife, and five children. There," says he, "they are shut up; you see a watchman at the door," and so of other houses. "Why," says I, "What do you here all alone?" "Why," says he, "I am a poor desolate man; it has pleased God I am not yet visited,[1] though my family is, and one of my children dead." "How do you mean then," said I, "that you are not visited?" "Why," says he, "that's my house," pointing to a very little low boarded house, "and there my poor wife and two children live," said he, "if they may be said to live; for my wife and one of the children are visited, but I do not come at them." And with that word I saw the tears run very plentifully down his face; and so they did down mine too, I assure you.

But said I, "Why do you not come at them? How can you abandon your own flesh, and blood?" "Oh, Sir!" says he, "the Lord forbid; I do not abandon them; I work for them as much as I am able, and blessed be the Lord, I keep them from want," and with that I observed, he lifted up his eyes to Heaven, with a countenance that presently told me, I had happened on a man that was no hypocrite, but a serious, religious good man, and his ejaculation was an expression of thankfulness, that in such a condition as he was in, he should be able to say his family did not want. "Well," says I, "honest man, that is a great mercy as things go now with the poor: but how do you live then, and how are you kept from the dreadful calamity that is now upon us all?" "Why Sir," says he, "I am a waterman,[2] and there's my boat," says he, "and the boat serves me for a house; I work in it in the day, and I sleep in it in the night; and what I get, I lay down upon that stone," says he, showing me a broad stone on the other side of the street, a good way from his house, "and then," says he, "I halloo, and call to them till I make them hear; and they come and fetch it."

"Well friend," says I, "but how can you get any money as a waterman? Does anybody go by water these times?" "Yes Sir," says he, "in the way I am employed there

---

8. H. F.'s walk takes him to the bank of the river Thames.
9. By London ordinances, all houses in which an inhabitant had become infected were "shut up," with the sur-

viving residents confined inside.
1. Infected.
2. Ferryman.

does. Do you see there," says he, "five ships lie at anchor," pointing down the river, a good way below the town, "and do you see," says he, "eight or ten ships lie at the chain, there, and at anchor yonder," pointing above the town. "All those ships have families on board, of their merchants and owners, and such like, who have locked themselves up, and live on board, close shut in, for fear of the infection; and I tend on them to fetch things for them, carry letters, and do what is absolutely necessary, that they may not be obliged to come on shore; and every night I fasten my boat on board one of the ship's boats, and there I sleep by myself, and blessed be God, I am preserved hitherto."

"Well," said I, "friend, but will they let you come on board, after you have been on shore here, when this is such a terrible place, and so infected as it is?"

"Why, as to that," said he, "I very seldom go up the ship side, but deliver what I bring to their boat, or lie by the side, and they hoist it on board; if I did, I think they are in no danger from me, for I never go into any house on shore, or touch anybody, no, not of my own family; but I fetch provisions for them."

"Nay," says I, "but that may be worse, for you must have those provisions of somebody or other; and since all this part of the town is so infected, it is dangerous so much as to speak with anybody; for this village," said I, "is as it were, the beginning of London, though it be at some distance from it."

"That is true," added he, "but you do not understand me right, I do not buy provisions for them here; I row up to Greenwich and buy fresh meat there, and sometimes I row down the river to Woolwich and buy there; then I go to single farm houses on the Kentish side, where I am known, and buy fowls and eggs and butter, and bring to the ships, as they direct me, sometimes one, sometimes the other; I seldom come on shore here; and I came now only to call to my wife, and hear how my little family do, and give them a little money, which I received last night."

"Poor man!" said I, "and how much hast thou gotten for them?"

"I have gotten four shillings," said he, "which is a great sum, as things go now with poor men; but they have given me a bag of bread too, and a salt fish and some flesh; so all helps out."

"Well," said I, "and have you given it them yet?"

"No," said he, "but I have called, and my wife has answered, that she cannot come out yet, but in half an hour she hopes to come, and I am waiting for her: poor woman!" says he, "she is brought sadly down; she has a swelling, and it is broke, and I hope she will recover;[3] but I fear the child will die; but *it is the Lord!*"—Here he stopped, and wept very much.

"Well, honest friend," said I, "thou hast a sure comforter, if thou hast brought thyself to be resigned to the will of God; He is dealing with us all in judgment."

"Oh, Sir," says he, "it is infinite mercy, if any of us are spared; and who am I to repine!"

"Sayest thou so," said I, "and how much less is my faith than thine?" And here my heart smote me, suggesting how much better this poor man's foundation was, on which he stayed in the danger, than mine; that he had nowhere to fly; that he had a family to bind him to attendance, which I had not; and mine was mere presumption, his a true dependence, and a courage resting on God: and yet, that he used all possible caution for his safety.

---

3. The plague afflicted its victims with painful swellings ("buboes"); if the swelling broke open, it was thought to presage recovery.

I turned a little way from the man, while these thoughts engaged me, for indeed, I could no more refrain from tears than he.

At length, after some farther talk, the poor woman opened the door, and called, "Robert, Robert." He answered and bid her stay a few moments, and he would come; so he ran down the common stairs to his boat, and fetched up a sack in which was the provisions he had brought from the ships; and when he returned, he hallooed again; then he went to the great stone which he showed me, and emptied the sack, and laid all out, everything by themselves, and then retired; and his wife came with a little boy to fetch them away; and he called, and said, such a captain had sent such a thing, and such a captain such a thing, and at the end adds, "God has sent it all, give thanks to Him." When the poor woman had taken up all, she was so weak, she could not carry it at once in, *though the weight was not much neither*; so she left the biscuit which was in a little bag and left a little boy to watch it till she came again.

"Well, but," says I to him, "did you leave her the four shillings too, which you said was your week's pay?"

"YES, YES," says he, "you shall hear her own it." So he calls again, "Rachel, Rachel,"[4] which it seems was her name, "did you take up the money?" "YES," said she. "How much was it?" said he. "Four shillings and a groat," said she. "Well, well," says he, "the Lord keep you all"; and so he turned to go away.

As I could not refrain contributing tears to this man's story, so neither could I refrain my charity for his assistance; so I called him. "Hark thee friend," said I, "come hither; for I believe thou art in health, that I may venture thee." So I pulled out my hand, which was in my pocket before. "Here," says I, "go and call thy Rachel once more, and give her a little more comfort from me. God will never forsake a family that trust in him as thou dost." So I gave him four other shillings, and bade him go lay them on the stone and call his wife.

I have not words to express the poor man's thankfulness, neither could he express it himself, but by tears running down his face; he called his wife, and told her God had moved the heart of a stranger, upon hearing their condition, to give them all that money; and a great deal more such as that he said to her. The woman too made signs of the like thankfulness, as well to Heaven, as to me, and joyfully picked it up; and I parted with no money all that year that I thought better bestowed.

1722

---

4. The name evokes Jeremiah 31.15: "Rachel weeping for her children refused to be comforted."

≈⊹ PERSPECTIVES ⊹≈
Reading Papers

Shakespeare never read a newspaper. In the early seventeenth century, the news was purveyed irregularly and improvisatorily. A breaking story or a sensational event might prompt a spate of ballads, broadsides, and bulletins, which would then abate until the next big thing hove into view. The news periodical, nascent on the Continent during Shakespeare's lifetime, arrived in England in 1620 in the form of English-language news sheets dispatched from Amsterdam. London publishers quickly took up the enterprise, to their considerable profit. Shakespeare's caustic contemporary Ben Jonson lived to witness their innovation; he promptly forecast an imminent glut of cheap and worthless information—fearing, with reason, that the new medium would supplant the theater as the public's favored oracle.

Even Jonson, though, could not have foreseen the quantities of print that would pour from presses decades later during the Civil Wars, when the instability of authority allowed innumerable newsbooks to appear, supporting every party in the conflict. During the Interregnum and Restoration, government tried through strict licensing laws to limit the flow and narrow the range of newsprint, but whenever those laws lapsed, innovations abounded: the first daily reports on proceedings in the House of Commons (1680), the first English newspaper outside London (1701), the first daily newspaper (1702), the first weekly journals (1713), melding the news with a miscellany of other departments. At the centennial of Shakespeare's death, London was producing some sixteen newspapers; a century later Britain possessed more than 350, in addition to legions of other periodicals purveying opinion and advice. The newspaper, the periodical essay, and the magazine had become confirmed habits in the lives of almost everyone who could read, and even of many who could not, since the papers were often read aloud, their contents discussed and debated, in public gathering places and household circles.

The periodical was a creature of the seventeenth century and a staple of the eighteenth. It punctuated the calendar with a new print pulse, and imparted to its readership a new sense of moving together in synchrony, in a rhythm that paradoxically combined the solitary and the social, the private and the public. The "mass ceremony" of reading the newspaper is generally performed (as the historian Benedict Anderson has observed) in "privacy, in the lair of the skull. Yet each communicant is well aware that the ceremony he performs is being replicated simultaneously by thousands (or millions) of others, of whose existence he is confident, yet of whose identity he has not the slightest notion." The periodical press, then, gave its readers a new way of seeing the world, and of seeing themselves in the world, as private beings and public entities; it prompted them (in Anderson's phrase) to imagine themselves as a community.

Monarchs and politicians tried hard to control the press, to dictate its views and to contain its criticisms, but in Britain the phenomenon proved too large for such arrant limitation. The news sheets and the essays helped create a new arena of political thought and action, separate from the older power centers of Court and Parliament, a public sphere of newly engaged readers who increasingly valued and deployed their own capacity to form collective opinions, and who increasingly expected their opinions to affect events. The freedom and copiousness of the press became a national boast, and abetted Britons in a conviction they were already cultivating: that they were participants in an ongoing narrative of commerce and taste, politeness, politics, and empire, protagonists in a story with numberless installments and no foreseeable end, unfolding at the center of the world.

Each newspaper in this section is introduced at its first appearance.

News and Comment

If the seventeenth century gave birth to the seething enterprise of print journalism, it also ushered in still-lingering distinctions and confusions as to what newspapers ought to be, and do. Most papers proudly declared their objectivity, yet at the same time they plainly manifested their partisan sympathies in their reportage and their prose. The division between news and opinion was rarely sharp, but in the early 1700s, opinion found fuller expression in periodicals like Defoe's *Review* (which more or less took for granted that readers had gathered their news elsewhere, and offered instead a running commentary on events), and in weekly journals like the *Craftsman*, which included ordinary news but which began each number with a long, fervently partisan political essay. Such essays anticipated the op-ed pages of today's newspapers, the closing meditations of news broadcasters.

MERCURIUS PUBLICUS (1660–1663)   During the Civil Wars, journalism gave voice to different factions; afterwards, it became the instrument of consolidated power. During the Interregnum, Cromwell controlled the news through his chief journalist Marchamont Nedham; strict licensing laws ensured that Nedham's *Public Intelligencer* (published every Monday) and *Mercurius Politicus* (every Thursday) were virtually the sole print sources for fresh information. (Mercury, the speedy messenger-god, remained throughout the century the favorite titular deity of the English press; more than a hundred periodicals bore his name.) In 1660 the chief architects of the Restoration dismissed Nedham and supplanted him with their own advocate, Henry Muddiman (1629–1692). Taking over Nedham's newsbooks (now pointedly renamed the *Kingdom's Intelligencer* and *Mercurius Publicus*), Muddiman denounced the old regime and heralded the new with the zeal that would maintain him for nearly three decades, despite stiff competition from rival newsmen, as a favored journalist with the House of Stuart, right up to its fall from power in the 1688 Revolution.

from Mercurius Publicus
24–31 January 1661

[ANNIVERSARY OF THE REGICIDE]

London

    This day January 30 (we need say no more but name the day of the month) was doubly observed, not only by a solemn fast, sermons, and prayers at every parish church, for the precious blood of our late pious sovereign King Charles the First, of ever glorious memory; but also by public dragging of those odious carcasses of Oliver Cromwell, Henry Ireton, and John Bradshaw to Tyburn.[1] On Monday night Cromwell and Ireton in two several carts were drawn to Holborn from Westminster, after they were digged up on Saturday last, and the next morning Bradshaw; today they were drawn upon sledges to Tyburn, all the way (as before from Westminster) the outcry of the people went along with them. When these their carcasses were at Tyburn, they were pulled out of their coffins and hanged at the several angles of the triple tree,[2] where they hung till the sun was set; after which they were taken down,

---

1. Ireton (1611–1651) and Bradshaw (1602–1659) had played key roles in the trial, condemnation, and execution of Charles I. Tyburn had been for nearly three centuries the site for the public execution of common criminals (Charles had been dispatched on the grounds of the

royal palace at Whitehall).
2. Tyburn's notorious "triangular gallows," whose three long horizontal beams could support as many as 21 hangings at a time.

their heads cut off, and their loathsome trunks thrown into a deep hole under the gallows. And now we cannot forget how at Cambridge when Cromwell first set up for a rebel, he rode under the gallows where, his horse just curvetting,[3] threw his cursed Highness out of the saddle just under the gallows (as if he had been turned off[4] the ladder), the spectators then observing the place, and rather presaging the present work of this day, than the monstrous villainies of this day twelve years.[5] But he is now again thrown under the gallows (never more to be digged up) and there we leave him.

LONDON GAZETTE (1665–PRESENT)   New media are often modeled on old. In its first decades, English print journalism took the shape of a newsbook (actually a pamphlet) because that was a format with which printers and consumers had been long familiar. The *London Gazette* was something visibly different: the first news*paper*, a single sheet printed in double columns. Containment was the paper's whole point, not only in format but in content. Published twice weekly, "by authority" (as it proclaimed on its masthead), it remained for thirteen years the only printed news source the English were legally permitted to read, and it presented only that news which its government masters deemed fit for wide publication: full accounts of Continental politics, carefully trimmed treatments of domestic doings, all couched in a dry prose that deliberately eschewed the popular (and sometimes rabble-rousing) effects of the paper's midcentury forebears. The *Gazette* broke briefly from its self-constraints in the number for 10 September 1666, when the Great Fire of London had forced the printer to set up his press in the open air, and the correspondents reported very local events with considerable accuracy and unaccustomed fervor.

from The London Gazette
10 September 1666

[THE FIRE OF LONDON[1]]

Whitehall, September 8

The ordinary course of this paper having been interrupted by a sad and lamentable accident of fire lately happened in the City of London, it hath been thought fit for satisfying the minds of so many of His Majesty's good subjects, who must needs be concerned for the issue of so great an accident, to give this short, but true account of it.

On the second instant[2] at one of the clock in the morning there happened to break out a sad and deplorable fire, in Pudding Lane near New Fish Street, which falling out at that hour of the night, and in a quarter of the town so close-built with wooden pitched[3] houses, spread itself so far before day, and with such distraction to the inhabitants and neighbors, that care was not taken for the timely preventing the further diffusion of it by pulling down houses, as ought to have been; so that this lamentable fire in a short time became too big to be mastered by any engines or working near it. It fell out most unhappily too, that a violent easterly wind fomented it, and kept it burning all that day, and the night following spreading itself up to Gracechurch Street, and downwards from Cannon Street to the waterside as far as the Three Cranes in the Vintry.

---

3. Leaping, frisking.
4. Dropped from.
5. Ago. I.e., they foresaw that he would eventually be hung, but not that he would accomplish the regicide of 30 January 1649.

1. Compare the accounts of Pepys (page 1046).
2. 2 September.
3. Covered with pitch (distilled tar) in order to keep out water.

The people in all parts about it distracted by the vastness of it, and their particular care to carry away their goods, many attempts were made to prevent the spreading of it, by pulling down houses, and making great intervals, but all in vain, the fire seizing upon the timber and rubbish, and so continuing itself, even through those spaces, and raging in a bright flame all Monday and Tuesday, notwithstanding His Majesty's own, and his Royal Highness's[4] indefatigable and personal pains to apply all possible remedies to prevent it, calling upon and helping the people with their Guards;[5] and a great number of nobility and gentry unweariedly assisting therein, for which they were requited with a thousand blessings from the poor distressed people. * * *

And we cannot but observe, to the confutation of all His Majesty's enemies, who endeavor to persuade the world abroad of great parties and disaffection at home against His Majesty's government, that a greater instance of the affections of this City could never be given than hath been now given in this sad and deplorable accident, when if at any time disorder might have been expected from the losses, distraction, and almost desperation of some persons in their private fortunes, thousands of people not having had habitations to cover them. And yet in all this time it hath been so far from any appearance of designs or attempts against His Majesty's government, that His Majesty and his royal brother, out of their care to stop and prevent the fire, frequently exposing their persons with very small attendance in all parts of the town, sometimes even to be intermixed with those who labored in the business, yet nevertheless there hath not been observed so much as a murmuring word to fall from any, but on the contrary, even those persons whose losses rendered their conditions most desperate, and to be fit objects of other prayers, beholding those frequent instances of His Majesty's care of this people, forgot their own misery, and filled the streets with their prayers for His Majesty, whose trouble they seemed to compassionate before their own.

THE DAILY COURANT (1702–1735)   The *Daily Courant's* title announced its innovation. Its editor-publisher, Samuel Buckley (d. 1741), was the first in England to put out a paper every day (except for Sunday, which had no paper of its own until the 1770s); before now, papers had appeared thrice weekly at most. In his opening number, Buckley made clear both his dependence on "foreign prints" (newspapers from the Continent) and his distrust of them; his faith in his readers' capacity to winnow bias and interpret information; and his perhaps defensive condescension to his journalistic rivals as he embarked on the audacious enterprise of a daily paper.

from The Daily Courant No. 1
Wednesday, 11 March 1702

[EDITORIAL POLICY]

It will be found from the foreign prints, which from time to time, as occasion offers, will be mentioned in this paper, that the author has taken care to be duly furnished with all that comes from abroad in any language. And for an assurance that he will not, under pretense of having private intelligence, impose any additions of feigned circumstances to an action, but give his extracts fairly and impartially, at the beginning of each article he will quote the foreign paper from whence 'tis taken, that the

---

4. The King's brother James, Duke of York.

5. The royal brothers deployed their soldiers to aid the fire's victims.

public, seeing from what country a piece of news comes with the allowance of that government, may be better able to judge of the credibility and fairness of the relation. Nor will he take upon him to give any comments or conjectures of his own, but will relate only matter of fact, supposing other people to have sense enough to make reflections for themselves.

The *Courant* (as the title shows) will be published daily, being designed to give all the material[1] news as soon as every post arrives; and is confined to half the compass,[2] to save the public at least half the impertinences[3] of ordinary newspapers.

A REVIEW OF THE STATE OF THE BRITISH NATION (1704–1713)   Of the periodical commentators on the news, none was more formidable than Daniel Defoe, who single-handedly wrote his *Review* twice and sometimes thrice a week for nine years. The paper changed its name, its format, and its ostensible focus several times during its long run, but its general purposes remained the same throughout. Defoe wrote to celebrate trade, and to propose strategies for its improvement; to teach a rigorous piety and morality to a readership he saw as lax; and to advance by adroit advocacy the favorite programs of the paper's secret sponsor, Secretary of State Robert Harley (1661–1724). One of these was the Treaty of Union, whereby Scotland would merge under a single government with England and Wales to form the new national entity of Great Britain. Advocates of the measure construed it as a fair exchange, providing expanded trade for Scotland, enhanced security for England. In support of the cause, Defoe not only wrote copiously (pamphlets and essays as well as *Reviews*), he also persuaded Harley to send him to Scotland (where the prospect of Union was far from popular) to serve as chief strategist and propagandist. There, he argued energetically and successfully for passage of the treaty, while keeping his affiliation with Harley a close secret. When the Treaty of Union was ratified, the *Review* indulged in a moment of exultation, in the characteristic voice its creator had devised during his sustained periodic enterprise: that of a writer enmeshed in actual and volatile circumstance, deeply engaged with the politics, conduct, and commerce of the real world, sometimes embattled, often exasperated, occasionally exhausted, but ultimately indefatigable.

For more about Defoe, see his principal listing on page 1162.

Daniel Defoe: *from* A Review of the State of the British Nation, Vol. 4, No. 21
Saturday, 29 March 1707

[THE NEW UNION]

I have a long time dwelt on the subject of a Union; I have happily seen it transacted in the kingdom of Scotland; I have seen it carried on there through innumerable oppositions, both public and private, peaceable and unpeaceable; I have seen it perfected there, and ratified, sent up to England, debated, opposed, and at last passed in both houses, and having obtained the royal assent, I have the pleasure, just while I am writing these lines, to hear the guns proclaiming the happy conjunction from Edinburgh Castle. And though it brings an unsatisfying childish custom in play, and exposes me to a vain and truly ridiculous saying in England, "as the fool thinks, etc.," yet 'tis impossible to put the lively sound of the cannon just now firing into any other note to my ear than the articulate expression of Union, Union. Strange power of

---

1. Relevant.
2. Space. Most newspapers printed on both sides of the sheet. At first, Buckley printed on only one side, unsure that his sources would supply him with enough matter to fill two sides daily (they soon did).
3. Irrelevancies; filler.

imagination, strange incoherence of circumstances that fills the mind so with the thing that it makes even the thunder of warlike engines cry peace; and what is made to divide and destroy, speaks out the language of this glorious conjunction!

I have hardly room to introduce the various contemplations of the consequences of this mighty transaction; 'tis a sea of universal improvement, every day it discovers new mines of treasure, and when I launch out in the bark of my own imagination, I every minute discover new success, new advantages, and the approaching happiness of both kingdoms. Nor am I an idle spectator here; I have told Scotland of improvements in trade, wealth, and shipping that shall accrue to them on the happy conclusion of this affair, and I am pleased double with this, that I am like to be one of the first men that shall give them the pleasure of the experiment. I have told them of the improvement of their coal trade, and 'tis their own fault if they do not particularly engage 20 or 25 sail of ships immediately from England on that work. I have told them of the improvement of their salt, and I am now contracting for English merchants for Scots salt to the value of about ten thousand pounds per annum. I have told them of linen manufactures, and I have now above 100 poor families at work, by my procuring and direction, for the making such sorts of linen, and in such manner as never was made here before, and as no person in the trade will believe could be made here, till they see it.

This has been my employment in Scotland, and this my endeavor to do that nation service, and convince them by the practice that what I have said of the Union has more weight in it than some have endeavored to persuade them. Those that have charged me with missions and commissions from neither they nor I know who, shall blush at their rashness, and be ashamed for reflecting on a man come hither on purpose to do them good.[1] Have I had a hand in the Union, have I been maltreated by the tongues of the violent, threatened to be murdered, and insulted, because I have pleaded for it and pressed you to it—gentlemen, in Scotland, I refer you to Her Majesty's speech; there's my claim, and you do me too much honor to entitle me to a share in what Her Majesty says shall be their due that have done so. Hearken to the words of your sovereign: "I make no doubt but it will be remembered and spoke of hereafter to the honor of those that have been instrumental to bring it to such an happy conclusion." (Queen's Speech to the Parliament, 6 March 1707.)

Pray, gentlemen, have a care how you charge me with having any hand in bringing forward this matter *to such an happy conclusion*, lest you build that monument upon me which Her Majesty has foretold, and honor the man you would debase. I plead no merit, I do not raise the value of what I have done; and I know some that are gone to London to solicit the reward of what they have had no hand in—I might have said, are gone to claim the merit of what I have been the single author of—but as this has been the constant way of the world with me, so I have no repinings on that account. Nor am I pleading any other merit than that I may have it wrote on my grave that I did my duty in promoting the Union, and consequently the happiness of these nations. ***

THE CRAFTSMAN (1726–1750)   From 1721 to 1742, Sir Robert Walpole served George I and George II as First Lord of the Treasury, and, in effect, as prime minister. Walpole refined

---

1. In both England and Scotland, Defoe had been accused (with reason) of conducting a kind of espionage on behalf of Harley and the Union.

the techniques of earlier ministers. He used his control of the royal purse to build up a follow-ing in the House of Commons by means of pensions and lucrative government positions as re-ward for loyal service; he sought to shape public opinion by imposing strict libel laws against his critics, and by controlling prominent papers (the *London Journal*, the *Free Briton*, and oth-ers, as well as the government's long-running *London Gazette*) through adroitly managed pa-tronage. He also enriched himself in the process, building a stately mansion at Houghton, and becoming an avid collector of art. Such brazen abuse of power prompted a two-party coalition in Parliament consisting of members opposed to Walpole's policies.

Many journals and periodicals contributed to the opposition to Walpole, but none was as feared or as popular as the *Craftsman*. In part, this was because no other journal could boast as compelling an array of writing talent. Edited by Nicholas Amhurst (1697–1742), an expelled student and hack writer from Oxford University, the journal derived its political philosophy and character from two politicians: William Pulteney (later Earl of Bath) and Henry St. John (Viscount Bolingbroke). As the respective leaders of the Whig and Tory factions of the Wal-pole opposition, Pulteney (1684–1764) and Bolingbroke (1678–1751) were in a unique posi-tion to coordinate parliamentary attacks on Walpole, as well as to generate public support for their criticisms of the ministry. Thus, from its first appearance in December 1726, the journal dedicated itself to exposing the "mystery of state-craft" in Walpole's ministry, a ministry which it regarded as the "grand fountain of corruption."

Hampered by the libel laws from attacking Walpole outright, the authors of the *Crafts-man*, writing under the pseudonym "Caleb D'Anvers," pioneered new techniques of innuendo and allusion that allowed them to attack the ministry without actually breaking the law and incurring its penalties. The following number, for example, pretends to mediate an argument that took place at a party attended by Caleb D'Anvers. It takes advantage of the English interest in "prodigies"—monstrous births, strange apparitions, and vampires—to generate a stinging attack on Walpole as the great "bloodsucker." In so doing, this particular number of the *Craftsman* relies heavily on the pun implicit in the phrase "body politic."

from The Craftsman No. 307
Saturday, 20 May 1732

[VAMPIRES IN BRITAIN]

Non missura cutem, nisi plena cruoris hirudo.[1]

One evening last week I called to see a friend, and met a company of gentlemen and ladies engaged in a dispute about prodigies, occasioned by a very remarkable event which hath lately happened in Hungary. The account of this affair, as it is given in the *London Journal* of March the 11th, is of so extraordinary a nature, that it will be difficult to give my readers any just conception of it, without quoting it at large.

Extract of a private letter from Vienna:

We have received certain advice of a sort of prodigy lately discovered in Hungary, at a place called Heyducken, situate on the other side of the Tibiscus, or Teys; namely, of dead bodies sucking, as it were, the blood of the living; for the latter visibly dry up, while the former are filled with blood. The fact at first sight seems to be impossible and even ridicu-lous; but the following is a true copy of a relation attested by unexceptionable witnesses, and sent to the imperial council of war.

1. "A leech that will not let the skin go, unless gorged with blood" (Horace, *Ars Poetica* 476), referring to mad poets who insist on reading their worthless verses to everyone.

Medreyga in Hungary, Jan. 7, 1732.

Upon a current report, that in the village of Medreyga certain dead bodies (called here Vampyres) had killed several persons, by sucking out all their blood, the present inquiry was made by the honorable commander in chief; and Capt. Goschutz of the company of Stallater, the Hadnagi Bariacrar, and the senior Heyduke of the village were severally examined; who unanimously declared that about five years ago a certain Heyduke, named Arnold Paul, was killed by the overturning of a cartload of hay, who in his lifetime was often heard to say, he had been tormented near Caschaw, and upon the borders of Turkish Serbia, by a vampyre; and that to extricate himself, he had eaten some of the earth of the vampyres' graves, and rubbed himself with their blood.

That 20 or 30 days after the decease of the said Arnold Paul, several persons complained that they were tormented, and that, in short, he had taken away the lives of four persons. In order, therefore, to put a stop to such a calamity, the inhabitants of the place, after having consulted their Hadnagi, caused the body of the said Arnold Paul to be taken up, 40 days after he had been dead, and found the same to be fresh and free from all manner of corruption; that he bled at the nose, mouth and ears, as pure and florid blood as was ever seen; and that his shroud and winding sheet were all over bloody; and lastly his finger and toe nails were fallen off, and new ones grown in their room.

As they observed from all these circumstances that he was a vampyre, they according to custom drove a stake through his heart; at which he gave a horrid groan, and lost a great deal of blood. Afterwards they burnt his body to ashes the same day, and threw them into his grave.

These good men say farther that all such as have been tormented or killed by the vampyres become vampyres when they are dead; and therefore they served several other dead bodies as they had done Arnold Paul's, for tormenting the living.

Signed,

Batruer, first lieutenant of the regiment of Alexander.

Flickhenger, surgeon major to the regiment of Furstemburch.

—three other surgeons.

Gurschitz, Captain at Stallath.

I shall now proceed to give my readers the substance of our conversation upon this extraordinary narrative.

The brunt of the dispute, upon my entering the room, lay between a grave doctor of physic and a beautiful young lady, who was a great admirer of strange and wonderful occurrences. The doctor endeavored to ridicule such romantic stories, by treating them as the common artifices of newswriters to fill up their papers at a dead season, for want of other intelligence. The young lady confessed, with a good deal of modesty and candor, that she believed such things were frequently done; but still insisted on the truth of this relation, which stood attested by such unexceptionable witnesses. She observed that the time, the place, and the names of the persons concerned in this affair were particularly mentioned; that an authentic account of it appears to have been transmitted to the court of Vienna, signed by no less than six persons; four of whom were surgeons, and the other two officers of the army; that such gentlemen must be supposed to have too much skill to be imposed upon themselves in such a matter, and too much honor to impose upon others. To this the doctor replied, with some disdain, that all the surgeons and soldiers in the universe should never make him believe that a dead body, whose animal powers were totally extinguished, could torment the living, by sucking their blood, or performing any other active and operative functions. He added, that it was contrary to all the principles of philosophy, as well as the laws of nature; and, in my opinion, urged the point somewhat too far against a young, female opponent; who, by the color in her cheeks, appeared to be a little nettled and, with a scornful smile, returned; "Well, well, doctor, you may say what you please; but as wise as you pretend to be now, it is not long ago that you endeavored to make us believe a fact equally ridiculous and absurd. Surely, doctor," said she, "you cannot have forgot the famous Rabbit-Woman of Godalmin."[2]—The smartness of this reply produced an hearty laugh on the lady's side, and put the doctor somewhat out of countenance. Then turning to me with an air of triumph and satisfaction, "I am sure," said she, "Mr. D'Anvers, that you are of my opinion, and believe there may be such things as vampyres."—A man, who hath any degree of complaisance, is loath to contradict a pretty girl, who forestalls his judgment in so agreeable a manner. I desired therefore to read over the account very attentively before I gave my opinion upon it; and, clapping on my political spectacles, I soon discovered a secret meaning in it, which I was in hopes would moderate the dispute. I perceived the whole company waited with impatience for my answer; so that having unsaddled my nose, and composed my muscles into a becoming gravity for such an occasion, I delivered myself to them in the following manner.

Gentlemen and ladies,
I think this dispute may be easily compromised without any reproach, or disgrace to either side. I must agree with the learned doctor that an inanimate corpse cannot possibly perform any vital functions; and yet I am firmly persuaded, with the young lady, that there are vampyres, or dead bodies, which afflict and torment the living. In order to explain myself the more clearly on this head, I must desire you to reflect that the account, now before us, comes from the eastern part of the world, which hath always been remarkable for writing in the allegorical style.[3] Besides, it deserves our consideration that the states of Hungary are, at present, under the subjection of the Turks, or the Germans, and governed by them with a pretty hard rein; which obliges them to couch all their complaints under types, figures, and parables. I believe you will make no doubt that this relation of the vampyres is a piece of that kind, and contains a secret satire upon the administration of those countries, when you consider the following particulars.

You see that the method, by which these vampyres are said to torment and kill the living, is by sucking out all their blood; and what, I pray, is a more common phrase for a ravenous minister, even in this part of the world, than a leech, or a bloodsucker, who preys upon human gore, and fattens himself upon the vitals of his country?

Now, if you admit of this interpretation, which I think far from being strained, the whole mystery of the vampyres will unfold itself of course; for a plundering minister carries his oppressions beyond the grave, and continues to torment those whom he leaves behind him by anticipating the public revenues, and entailing a perpetuity of taxes and gabels[4] upon the people, which must drain the body politic by degrees of all its blood and spirit.

---

2. Mary Tofts, of Godalming in Surrey, reportedly gave birth to a litter of rabbits in the winter of 1726. For a time, this famous fraud deceived many physicians.
3. "Eastern," or Oriental, tales included a wide variety of fables, tall tales, mythical representations, and stories of wonder. Samuel Johnson's *Rasselas* (1759) is perhaps the most famous example of this broad genre.
4. A form of interest or rent due on land.

It is farther said, in the narrative, that all such as have been tormented, or killed by the vampyres, become vampyres, when they are dead.—This likewise is perfectly agreeable to my system; for those persons who groan under the burdens of such a minister are often obliged to sell or mortgage their estates, and therefore may be said, in a proper sense, to torment their unhappy posterity in the same manner.

Whether this Arnold Paul, or Paul Arnold, mentioned in the narrative, was a person in any office, or employment in the administration, which gave him a power of oppressing the people, either as a tax-layer or a tax-gatherer, I am not able to determine without farther inquiry. He is said, indeed, to have been a Heyduke, which I take to be a character of some consequence in those countries; but, perhaps, he might have been employed only as a ministerial tool, or instrument of oppression, under some great bloodsucker of state. For my own part, I am inclined to this opinion; because it is said that he had killed only four persons; whereas if he had been a vampyre of any considerable rank, we should in all probability have heard of his thousands and his ten thousands.[5] * * *

Having finished my speech, which was honored with the strictest attention, I was very much pleased to find it produce the desired effect, by putting an end to the dispute, which occasioned it. The doctor only nodded his head and told me, with a smile, that I had a political turn for every thing. The young lady expressed her satisfaction in the most obliging terms, and was pleased to say that my solution of this prodigy would make a very good *Craftsman*. She was immediately seconded by the whole company, who pressed me with so much importunity to print it in my next paper, that I could not in good manners refuse their request; and I hope my loving readers will excuse me, on that account, for troubling them this week with a loose, unpremeditated piece of conversation.

Having afterwards smoked my pipe, and spent the evening very agreeably, I took my leave at eleven o'clock, which hath been, for many years, my constant hour. The young lady followed me to the door, and, pulling me by the sleeve, "Pray, Mr. D'Anvers," said she, "don't forget the paper upon the vampyres."

Periodical Personae

In print journalism it was primarily the news that sold the paper; in the periodical essay it was the voice: the idiosyncratic mix of assertion and deference, comedy and charisma, with which author addressed audience. Political writers had long known the advantages of using a mask or *persona*— a pen name, a fictitious character—as a means of both concealing their identity and expanding the appeal of their controversial arguments. In the early 1700s, the inventors of the periodical essay extended the tactic of the fictitious self into new territory. While collaborating on *The Tatler* and *The Spectator*, Richard Steele and Joseph Addison devised strategies for making the unreal author a real arbitrator in the culture, a teacher of taste and conduct, manners and morality, someone whom readers found it pleasurable to learn from, to identify with, even to "believe in," despite (and because of) his comically exaggerated quirks, his patent nonexistence. Working behind their carefully crafted masks, Addison and Steele sold so many papers and impressed so many readers that their mark became indelible. For the rest of the century, the periodical essayist's first task was to devise a persona unusual enough to define the paper, and engaging enough to sustain it.

---

5. An allusion to Saul, who had "slain his thousands," and David, "his ten thousands" (1 Samuel 21.11). D'Anvers goes on to explain that certain private citizens ("sharpers, usurers, stock-jobbers") pursue an economic vampirism as skillfully as do the public officials.

THE TATLER (1709–1711)   At age thirty-five, after a checkered career as soldier, poet, playwright, popular moralist, and Whig propagandist, Captain Richard Steele (1672–1729) was appointed editor of the *London Gazette*, the government's long-running newspaper. Evidently even this task did not sufficiently absorb his energies. Two years later, while still supervising the *Gazette*, he launched *The Tatler*, a periodical of his own that outstripped all its predecessors in commercial success and enduring appeal. It appeared three times a week, ran for two years and 271 numbers, spawned many imitators, and continued to sell (in a four-volume collected edition) for the rest of the century. The *Tatler's* appeal derived in large measure from its putative author, Isaac Bickerstaff, Esquire, whose name Steele had borrowed from one of Swift's satires, but whose character he elaborated into that of a genial, perceptive, and comically self-congratulatory old man. The paper's commodious structure mirrored the gregariousness of its "author." Bickerstaff datelined his dispatches from the coffeehouses around London where papers were distributed, read, and discussed; he included letters (fictitious and authentic) from readers all over the country. The *Tatler's* audience thus found itself absorbed into the paper several ways: they were its constant topic, they sometimes supplied its text, they constituted both its origin and its end point, and they gave it their unprecedented devotion. Steele soon made further discoveries of form under the influence of his school friend Joseph Addison (1672–1729), whom he had brought in (so one contemporary put it) as his "great and constant assistant." Addison and Steele found that Bickerstaff's private musings, dispatched "From my Own Apartment," were the most pleasing items of all, and so they often devoted whole papers to reprinting what their character was pleased to call his "lucubrations" (meditations by candlelight, late at night). John Gay summed up the strategy's success. Coffeehouse owners, Gay reported, "began to be sensible that the Esquire's lucubrations alone had brought them more customers than all their other newspapers put together." Bickerstaff's other "departments" diminished or disappeared, and "the Esquire's lucubrations," now running the full length of the paper, created the format and the fashion for the periodical essay, a unified piece on a single topic as opposed to the fragmentary "miscellany" from which Steele had started. By the time he stopped *The Tatler* (probably because of political pressures following the Whigs' fall from power), he and Addison had devised means and achieved ends with which they would experiment anew in *The Spectator*: ways of creating community shot through with solitude, of mixing sociability and meditation, morality and mirth.

Richard Steele: *from* Tatler No. 1
Tuesday, 12 April 1709

[INTRODUCING MR. BICKERSTAFF]

Quicquid agunt homines nostri farrago libelli.[1]

Though the other papers which are published for the use of the good people of England have certainly very wholesome effects, and are laudable in their particular kinds, they do not seem to come up to the main design of such narrations, which, I humbly presume, should be principally intended for the use of politic persons, who are so public-spirited as to neglect their own affairs to look into transactions of state. Now these gentlemen, for the most part, being persons of strong zeal and weak intellects,[2] it is both a charitable and necessary work to offer something whereby such worthy and well-affected members of the commonwealth may be instructed, after their reading,

<hr/>

1. "Whatever people do [will furnish] the variety of our little book" (Juvenal, *Satires* 1.85–86); or (in the freer and more apt 18th-century translation by Thomas Percy) "Whate'er men do, or say, or think, or dream, / Our motley paper seizes for its theme."

2. Bickerstaff mocks that category of men known as the "coffeehouse politicians," who spent long hours together discussing news. For a more-sustained satire of them, see *Tatler* No. 155 (pages 1227–28).

what to think: which shall be the end and purpose of this my paper, wherein I shall from time to time report and consider all matters of what kind soever that shall occur to me, and publish such my advices and reflections every Tuesday, Thursday, and Saturday in the week, for the convenience of the post.[3] I resolve also to have something which may be of entertainment to the fair sex, in honor of whom I have invented the title of this paper. I therefore earnestly desire all persons, without distinction, to take it in for the present *gratis*,[4] and hereafter at the price of one penny, forbidding all hawkers to take more for it at their peril. And I desire all persons to consider, that I am at a very great charge for proper materials for this work, as well as that before I resolved upon it, I had settled a correspondence in all parts of the known and knowing world. And forasmuch as this globe is not trodden upon by mere drudges of business only, but that men of spirit and genius are justly to be esteemed as considerable agents in it, we shall not upon a dearth of news present you with musty foreign edicts, or dull proclamations, but shall divide our relations of the passages which occur in action or discourse throughout this town, as well as elsewhere, under such dates of places as may prepare you for the matter you are to expect, in the following manner.

All accounts of gallantry,[5] pleasure, and entertainment shall be under the article of White's Chocolate House; poetry, under that of Will's Coffeehouse; learning, under the title of Grecian; foreign and domestic news you will have from St. James's Coffeehouse; and what else I have to offer on any other subject, shall be dated from my own apartment.[6]

I once more desire my reader to consider, that as I cannot keep an ingenious man to go daily to Will's, under two-pence each day merely for his charges; to White's, under sixpence; nor to the Grecian, without allowing him some Plain Spanish,[7] to be as able as others at the learned table; and that a good observer cannot speak with even Kidney[8] at St. James's without clean linen. I say, these considerations will, I hope, make all persons willing to comply with my humble request (when my *gratis* stock is exhausted) of a penny apiece; especially since they are sure of some proper amusement, and that it is impossible for me to want means to entertain 'em, having, besides the force of my own parts, the power of divination, and that I can, by casting a figure, tell you all that will happen before it comes to pass.[9]

But this last faculty I shall use very sparingly, and speak but of few things 'till they are passed, for fear of divulging matters which may offend our superiors.[1] * * *

From my own apartment

I am sorry I am obliged to trouble the public with so much discourse, upon a matter which I at the very first mentioned as a trifle, *viz.* the death of Mr. Partridge, under

---

3. These were the days on which the postal system carried mail from London to the provinces.
4. Steele distributed his first four numbers free, as a way of attracting readers.
5. Flirtation and self-display.
6. Steele exploits associations between topic and venue long familiar to his readers. Each of the coffeehouses he names catered to a clientele "specializing" in the pursuits he names. A journalist himself, Steele parodies the newspaper format that headed each item by the name of its (usually foreign) city of origin.
7. A kind of snuff, used as a stimulant to induce sneezing.
8. A waiter.
9. To "cast a figure" is to work out a horoscope, an ability

that the *Tatler's* first readers would readily associate with the character "Isaac Bickerstaff." Jonathan Swift had originally created the character (in a series of pamphlets in 1708) as a way of satirizing the fashion for astrological almanacs, which purported to foretell the important events of the coming year. In Swift's first pamphlet, the fictitious astrologer Isaac Bickerstaff forecast the imminent death of the real (and very successful) astrologer John Partridge; in the second pamphlet, Bickerstaff declared blithely that his prophecy had come to pass. Partridge's subsequent, frantic protestations added relish to the joke.
1. Bickerstaff proceeds to supply first dispatches from White's, Will's, and St. James's coffeehouses.

whose name there is an almanac come out for the year 1709.[2] In one page of which, it is asserted by the said John Partridge, that he is still living, and not only so, but that he was also living some time before, and even at the instant when I writ of his death. I have in another place, and in a paper by itself, sufficiently convinced this man that he is dead, and if he has any shame, I don't doubt but that by this time he owns it to all his acquaintance: for though the legs and arms, and whole body, of that man may still appear and perform their animal functions; yet since, as I have elsewhere observed, his art is gone, the man is gone. I am, as I said, concerned that this little matter should make so much noise; but since I am engaged, I take myself obliged in honor to go on in my lucubrations, and by the help of these arts of which I am master, as well as my skill in astrological speculations, I shall, as I see occasion, proceed to confute other dead men, who pretend to be in being, that they are actually deceased. I therefore give all men fair warning to mend their manners, for I shall from time to time print bills of mortality; and I beg the pardon of all such who shall be named therein, if they who are good for nothing shall find themselves in the number of the deceased.

THE SPECTATOR (1711–1713)   In the weeks of the *Spectator*'s first appearance, readers marveled at both its contents and its pace. "We had at first . . . no manner of notion," the wit John Gay reported from London, "how a diurnal paper could be continued in the spirit and style of our present *Spectators*; but to our no small surprise we find them still rising upon us, and can only wonder from whence so prodigious a run of wit and learning can proceed." It proceeded (as Gay guessed) from the minds and pens of the same two writers who had shut down the *Tatler* just a few months before. For their second periodical collaboration, Addison and Steele considerably upped the ante. Not only did they undertake to publish a new number every day (something no essayist had hitherto attempted), they also devised a new persona, intricately linked with their triumphant earlier creation Isaac Bickerstaff. Where the *Tatler* had begun in gregariousness and modulated towards solitude (at "my own apartment"), the new paper started from an even farther remove, in the eccentric silence of Mr. Spectator, who declares at the outset that he has not spoken "three sentences together" since birth. Mr. Spectator carries his "own apartment"—his state of psychological apartness—with him, not at his residence but in his head; "the working of my own mind," he announces early on, "is the chief entertainment of my life."

In his focused interiority, Mr. Spectator played out the principles of psychology that John Locke had propounded, but his extreme self-possession turned out to possess enormous rhetorical impact and commercial cachet as well. More than any other periodical persona, Mr. Spectator managed to embody and to allegorize the operations of the paper he inhabited. Like the paper he was everywhere, at once silent and articulate, fictitious in substance but impressive in effect, observant and absorbent of the culture, able to move into his readers' minds by the mysterious osmosis of reading itself, and to remain there, a disembodied monitor with a rapidly growing portfolio of daily essays. An anonymous pamphleteer reproached Mr. Spectator for the presumptuous "tyranny" of his surveillance, but the paper's tactics of reform remained in power for most of the century. It was read (and imitated) on the Continent, in the American colonies, and in remoter outposts like Sumatra, from whence a British trader wrote home to his daughter in London, admonishing her "to study the *Spectators,* especially those which relate to religion and domestic life. Next to the Bible you cannot read any writings so much to your purpose for the improvement of your mind and the conduct of your actions." The *Spectator,* Gay noted soon after the paper's debut, "is in everyone's hands, and a constant topic for our morning conversation at tea tables and coffeehouses." More than sixty years later, the Scots rhetorician Hugh Blair could only echo and elaborate on Gay's phrasing, in accordance

---

2. In the 1709 issue of his annual almanac *Merlinus Liberatus*, Partridge had insisted that he was "still alive."

with the paper's now long-established place in the British canon: "The *Spectator* . . . is a book which is in the hands of everyone, and which cannot be praised too highly. The good sense, and good writing, the useful morality, and the admirable vein of humor which abound in it, render it one of those standard books which have done the greatest honor to the English nation."

Joseph Addison: *from* Spectator No. 1
Thursday, 1 March 1711

[INTRODUCING MR. SPECTATOR]

*Non fumum ex fulgore, sed ex fumo dare lucem
Cogitat, ut speciosa debinc miracula promat.*[1]

I have observed, that a reader seldom peruses a book with pleasure 'till he knows whether the writer of it be a black or a fair man,[2] of a mild or choleric disposition, married or a bachelor, with other particulars of the like nature, that conduce very much to the right understanding of an author. To gratify this curiosity, which is so natural to a reader, I design this paper, and my next, as prefatory discourses to my following writings, and shall give some account in them of the several persons that are engaged in this work. As the chief trouble of compiling, digesting, and correcting will fall to my share, I must do myself the justice to open the work with my own history.

I was born to a small hereditary estate, which, according to the tradition of the village where it lies, was bounded by the same hedges and ditches in William the Conqueror's time[3] that it is at present, and has been delivered down from father to son whole and entire, without the loss or acquisition of a single field or meadow, during the space of six hundred years. There runs a story in the family, that when my mother was gone with child of me about three months, she dreamt that she was brought to bed of[4] a judge. Whether this might proceed from a lawsuit which was then depending in the family, or my father's being a justice of the peace, I cannot determine; for I am not so vain as to think it presaged any dignity that I should arrive at in my future life, though that was the interpretation which the neighborhood put upon it. The gravity of my behavior at my very first appearance in the world, and all the time that I sucked, seemed to favor my mother's dream: for, as she has often told me, I threw away my rattle before I was two months old, and would not make use of my coral[5] 'till they had taken away the bells from it.

As for the rest of my infancy, there being nothing in it remarkable, I shall pass it over in silence. I find that, during my nonage,[6] I had the reputation of a very sullen youth, but was always a favorite of my schoolmaster, who used to say, *that my parts were solid and would wear well.* I had not been long at the university before I distinguished myself by a most profound silence: for during the space of eight years, excepting in the public exercises of the college, I scarce uttered the quantity of an hundred words; and indeed do not remember that I ever spoke three sentences together in my whole life. Whilst I was in this learned body I applied myself with so much diligence

---

1. "He intends to produce not smoke from fire, but light from smoke, so that he may then put forth striking and amazing things" (Horace, *Ars Poetica* 143–44).
2. Of dark or light complexion.
3. The late 11th century, when William ruled as king of England.
4. Had given birth to. The silence of judges was proverbial.
5. Another sound maker for infants.
6. Childhood.

to my studies that there are very few celebrated books, either in the learned or the modern tongues, which I am not acquainted with.

Upon the death of my father I was resolved to travel into foreign countries, and therefore left the university, with the character[7] of an odd unaccountable fellow that had a great deal of learning, if I would but show it. An insatiable thirst after knowledge carried me into all the countries of Europe, in which there was anything new or strange to be seen; nay, to such a degree was my curiosity raised, that having read the controversies of some great men concerning the antiquities of Egypt, I made a voyage to Grand Cairo, on purpose to take the measure of a pyramid; and as soon as I had set myself right in that particular, returned to my native country with great satisfaction.

I have passed my latter years in this city, where I am frequently seen in most public places, though there are not above half a dozen of my select friends that know me; of whom my next paper shall give a more particular account. There is no place of general resort, wherein I do not often make my appearance.[8] Sometimes I am seen thrusting my head into a round of politicians at Will's, and listening with great attention to the narratives that are made in those little circular audiences. Sometimes I smoke a pipe at Child's; and whilst I seem attentive to nothing but the *Post-Man*,[9] overhear the conversation of every table in the room. I appear on Sunday nights at St. James's Coffeehouse, and sometimes join the little committee of politics in the inner-room, as one who comes there to hear and improve. My face is likewise very well known at the Grecian, the Cocoa Tree, and in the theaters both of Drury Lane, and the Haymarket. I have been taken for a merchant upon the Exchange[1] for above these ten years, and sometimes pass for a Jew in the assembly of stock-jobbers at Jonathan's.[2] In short, wherever I see a cluster of people I always mix with them, though I never open my lips but in my own club.

Thus I live in the world, rather as a spectator of mankind than as one of the species; by which means I have made myself a speculative statesman, soldier, merchant, and artisan, without ever meddling with any practical part in life. I am very well versed in the theory of an husband or a father, and can discern the errors in the economy, business, and diversion of others, better than those who are engaged in them; as standers-by discover blots,[3] which are apt to escape those who are in the game. I never espoused any party with violence, and am resolved to observe an exact neutrality between the Whigs and Tories,[4] unless I shall be forced to declare myself by the hostilities of either side. In short, I have acted in all the parts of my life as a looker-on, which is the character I intend to preserve in this paper.

I have given the reader just so much of my history and character as to let him see I am not altogether unqualified for the business I have undertaken. As for other particulars in my life and adventures, I shall insert them in following papers as I shall see occasion. In the mean time, when I consider how much I have seen, read, and heard, I begin to blame my own taciturnity; and since I have neither time nor inclination to

7. Reputation.

8. With a conspicuous openness to all parties and pursuits, Mr. Spectator distributes his visitations among some of London's favorite meeting places, including ones popular with Whigs (St. James's), Tories (the Cocoa Tree), authors (Child's), lawyers (the Grecian), and the news-obsessives he calls "politicians" (Will's).

9. A thrice-weekly newspaper, favored by Whigs.

1. The Royal Exchange was a large building containing many shops and serving as a meeting place for merchants. (For Addison's paean to the place, see *Spectator* No. 69,

page 1194).

2. Jonathan's coffeehouse, near the Royal Exchange, was a principal meeting place of merchants and stockbrokers ("stock-jobbers").

3. In backgammon, a blot is a piece whose position puts it at risk of being taken.

4. Addison and Steele maintained "neutrality" more strictly in the *Spectator* than they had in the *Tatler*, which had incurred much controversy by its Whig partisanship.

communicate the fullness of my heart in speech, I am resolved to do it in writing; and to print my self out, if possible, before I die. I have been often told by my friends that it is pity so many useful discoveries which I have made should be in the possession of a silent man. For this reason therefore, I shall publish a sheet-full of thoughts every morning, for the benefit of my contemporaries; and if I can any way contribute to the diversion or improvement of the country in which I live, I shall leave it, when I am summoned out of it, with the secret satisfaction of thinking that I have not lived in vain. * * *

THE FEMALE SPECTATOR (APRIL 1744–MAY 1746)   *The Female Spectator* was the first periodical written by a woman for women. Its author, Eliza Haywood (c. 1693–1756), had been an actress, a playwright, and the writer of some sixty romances, novels, and other narratives, many of them scandalous and some of them wildly successful. In the mid-1740s, after a long eclipse prompted in part by Alexander Pope's derision of her in the *Dunciad*, Haywood emerged in a new guise: no longer a purveyor of exotic thrills, she set up instead as a teacher of morality. *The Female Spectator* differed from its namesake in calendar (monthly rather than daily) and format: a pamphlet and not a sheet, each number presented an essay focused on a single topic with several illustrative fictional stories interspersed. The biggest difference, though, was in the new paper's point of view. Mr. Spectator had observed, described, and instructed "the fair sex" from without, as supremely self-confident male mentor. Haywood offered instead a running report from the interior of women's lives. Her vantage point proved popular. *The Female Spectator* continued to sell, in a four-volume collected edition, for more than two decades after its periodical run had ceased.

from Female Spectator Vol. 1, No. 1
[THE AUTHOR'S INTENT]

It is very much by the choice we make of subjects for our entertainment that the refined taste distinguishes itself from the vulgar and more gross. Reading is universally allowed to be one of the most improving as well as agreeable amusements; but then to render it so, one should, among the number of books which are perpetually issuing from the press, endeavor to single out such as promise to be most conducive to those ends. In order to be as little deceived as possible, I, for my own part, love to get as well acquainted as I can with an author, before I run the risk of losing my time in perusing his work; and as I doubt not but most people are of this way of thinking, I shall, in imitation of my learned brother of ever precious memory,[1] give some account of what I am, and those concerned with me in this undertaking; and likewise of the chief intent of the lucubrations[2] hereafter communicated, that the reader, on casting his eye over the four or five first pages, may judge how far the book may or may not be qualified to entertain him, and either accept or throw it aside as he thinks proper. And here I promise that in the pictures I shall give of myself and associates, I will draw no flattering lines, assume no perfection that we are not in reality possessed of, nor attempt to shadow over any defect with an artificial gloss.

As a proof of my sincerity, I shall in the first place assure him that for my own part I never was a beauty, and am now very far from being young (a confession he will

---

1. Addison and Steele's Mr. Spectator.   Isaac Bickerstaff's catchword for his essays in the *Tatler*.
2. Writings by candlelight; Haywood pointedly picks up

find few of my sex ready to make). I shall also acknowledge that I have run through as many scenes of vanity and folly as the greatest coquette of them all. Dress, equipage,[3] and flattery were the idols of my heart. I should have thought that day lost which did not present me with some new opportunity of showing myself. My life, for some years, was a continued round of what I then called pleasure, and my whole time engrossed by a hurry of promiscuous diversions. But whatever inconveniences such a manner of conduct has brought upon myself, I have this consolation, to think that the public may reap some benefit from it. The company I kept was not, indeed, always so well chosen as it ought to have been, for the sake of my own interest or reputation; but then it was general, and by consequence furnished me not only with the knowledge of many occurrences, which otherwise I had been ignorant of, but also enabled me, when the too great vivacity of my nature became tempered with reflection, to see into the secret springs which gave rise to the actions I had either heard or been witness of—to judge of the various passions of the human mind, and distinguish those imperceptible degrees by which they become masters of the heart, and attain the dominion over reason. A thousand odd adventures, which at the time they happened made slight impression on me, and seemed to dwell no longer on my mind than the wonder they occasioned, now rise fresh to my remembrance, with this advantage, that the mystery I then, for want of attention, imagined they contained, is entirely vanished, and I find it easy to account for the cause by the consequence.

With this experience, added to a genius[4] tolerably extensive, and an education more liberal than is ordinarily allowed to persons of my sex, I flattered myself that it might be in my power to be in some measure both useful and entertaining to the public; and this thought was so soothing to those remains of vanity not yet wholly extinguished in me, that I resolved to pursue it, and immediately began to consider by what method I should be most likely to succeed. To confine myself to any one subject, I knew could please but one kind of taste, and my ambition was to be as universally read as possible. From my observations of human nature, I found that curiosity had more or less a share in every breast; and my business, therefore, was to hit this reigning humor in such a manner as that the gratification it should receive from being made acquainted with other people's affairs should at the same time teach every one to regulate their own.

Having agreed within myself on this important point, I commenced author, by setting down many things which, being pleasing to myself, I imagined would be so to others; but on examining them the next day, I found an infinite deficiency both in matter and style, and that there was an absolute necessity for me to call in to my assistance such of my acquaintance as were qualified for that purpose. The first that occurred to me, I shall distinguish by the name of Mira, a lady descended from a family to which wit seems hereditary, married to a gentleman every way worthy of so excellent a wife, and with whom she lives in so perfect a harmony, that having nothing to ruffle the composure of her soul, or disturb those sparkling ideas she received from nature and education, left me no room to doubt if what she favored me with would be acceptable to the public. The next is a widow of quality, who not having buried her vivacity in the tomb of her lord, continues to make one in all the modish diversions of the times, so far, I mean, as she finds them consistent with innocence and honor; and as she is far from having the least austerity in her behavior, nor is

3. Fancy carriages, servants, and furniture.   4. Talent, ability.

rigid to the failings she is wholly free from herself, those of her acquaintance who had been less circumspect scruple not to make her the confidante of secrets they conceal from all the world beside. The third is the daughter of a wealthy merchant, charming as an angel, but endued with so many accomplishments that to those who know her truly, her beauty is the least distinguished part of her. This fine young creature I shall call Euphrosyne, since she has all the cheerfulness and sweetness ascribed to that goddess.[5]

These three approved my design, assured me of all the help they could afford, and soon gave a proof of it in bringing their several essays; but as the reader, provided the entertainment be agreeable, will not be interested from which quarter it comes, whatever productions I shall be favored with from these ladies, or any others I may hereafter correspond with, will be exhibited under the general title of *The Female Spectator*, and how many contributors soever there may happen to be to the work, they are to be considered only as several members of one body, of which I am the mouth. ***

Richard Steele: *from* Tatler No. 18
21 May 1709

[THE NEWS WRITERS IN DANGER[1]]
St. James's Coffeehouse, May 20.

*** It being therefore visible, that our society[2] will be greater sufferers by the peace than the soldiery itself; insomuch, that the *Daily Courant* is in danger of being broken, my friend Dyer of being reformed,[3] and the very best of the whole band of being reduced to half-pay; might I presume to offer anything in the behalf of my distressed brethren, I would humbly move, that an appendix of proper apartments furnished with pen, ink, and paper, and other necessaries of life should be added to the Hospital of Chelsea,[4] for the relief of such decayed news writers as have served their country in the wars; and that for their exercise, they should compile the annals of their brother-veterans, who have been engaged in the same service, and are still obliged to do duty after the same manner.

I cannot be thought to speak this out of an eye to any private interest; for, as my chief scenes of action are coffeehouses, playhouses, and my own apartment, I am in no need of camps, fortifications, and fields of battle, to support me; I don't call out for heroes and generals to my assistance. Though the officers are broken, and the armies disbanded, I shall still be safe as long as there are men or women, or politicians, or lovers, or poets, or nymphs, or swains, or cits,[5] or courtiers, in being.

---

5. Euphrosyne is one of the three Graces, sister goddesses in Greek mythology who possess (and bestow) the gift of beauty.

1. Papers often defined themselves by contrasting their methods and achievements with those of their rivals. For the essayists, the newspapers afforded the readiest foil. Steele was a seasoned journalist, but he and Addison devised many ways of mocking the vacuity of the news-mongers, and of flattering those readers who preferred essays to mere journalism. In this early *Tatler*, Bickerstaff announces that England will soon be victorious in its for-

eign wars, observes that "the approach of peace strikes a panic through our armies," who will have nowhere left to fight, and worries that peace will prove even more costly to the journalists, who will have nothing left to write about.

2. I.e., the "brotherhood" of news writers.
3. John Dyer's fervently Tory newsletter often denounced the Whigs for (among other things) mismanaging the wars abroad.
4. Where disabled soldiers were given care and lodging.
5. City dwellers, tradespeople.

Joseph Addison: *from* Tatler No. 155
Thursday, 6 April 1710

[THE POLITICAL UPHOLSTERER]

—Aliena negotia curat
Excussus propriis.[1]

From My Own Apartment, April 5

There lived some years since within my neighborhood a very grave person, an upholsterer, who seemed a man of more than ordinary application to business. He was a very early riser, and was often abroad two or three hours before any of his neighbors. He had a particular carefulness in the knitting of his brows, and a kind of impatience in all his motions, that plainly discovered he was always intent on matters of importance. Upon my enquiry into his life and conversation, I found him to be the greatest newsmonger in our quarter;[2] that he rose before day to read the *Post-Man;*[3] and that he would take two or three turns to the other end of the town before his neighbors were up, to see if there were any Dutch mails[4] come in. He had a wife and several children; but was much more inquisitive to know what passed in Poland than in his own family, and was in greater pain and anxiety of mind for King Augustus's[5] welfare than that of his nearest relations. He looked extremely thin in a dearth of news, and never enjoyed himself in a westerly wind.[6] This indefatigable kind of life was the ruin of his shop; for about the time that his favorite prince left the crown of Poland, he broke and disappeared.

   This man and his affairs had been long out of my mind, till about three days ago, as I was walking in St. James's Park, I heard somebody at a distance hemming after me: and who should it be but my old neighbor the upholsterer? I saw he was reduced to extreme poverty, by certain shabby superfluities in his dress: for notwithstanding that it was a very sultry day for the time of the year, he wore a loose great coat and a muff, with a long campaign-wig out of curl;[7] to which he had added the ornament of a pair of black garters buckled under the knee. Upon his coming up to me, I was going to inquire into his present circumstances; but was prevented by his asking me, with a whisper, whether the last letters brought any accounts that one might rely upon from Bender?[8] I told him, none that I heard of; and asked him, whether he had yet married his eldest daughter? He told me, No. But pray, says he, tell me sincerely, what are your thoughts of the King of Sweden? For though his wife and children were starving, I found his chief concern at present was for this great monarch. I told him, that I looked upon him as one of the first heroes of the age. But pray, says he, do you think there is anything in the story of his wound? And finding me surprised at the

1. "He minds others' concerns, since he has lost his own" (Horace, *Satires* 2.3.19–20).
2. "Monger" not because he sells news but because he tells it, to anyone who will listen; Addison's news-addicted upholsterer became one of the *Tatler's* most popular comic creations, reappearing in several later numbers.
3. The leading Whig newspaper (1695–1730).
4. Mailboats from the Netherlands, bringing fresh news.
5. Frederick Augustus I of Poland, whose loss and recovery of power had filled the papers for several years.

6. Which prevented the arrival of the "Dutch mails."
7. A "campaign wig" was used when traveling and was remarkable for its decorative curls (here flattened and disordered).
8. A town in modern Bessarabia, where Charles XII of Sweden (1682–1718) had sought refuge after a long string of military victories and a final catastrophic defeat (see Samuel Johnson, *The Vanity of Human Wishes*, lines 191–222, page 1430).

question, Nay, says he, I only propose it to you. I answered, that I thought there was no reason to doubt of it. But why in the heel, says he, more than in any other part of the body? Because, says I, the bullet chanced to light there. * * *

We were now got to the upper end of the Mall,[9] where were three or four very odd fellows sitting together upon the bench. These I found were all of them politicians, who used to sun themselves in that place every day about dinner time.[1] * * *

I at length took my leave of the company, and was going away; but had not been gone thirty yards before the upholsterer hemmed again after me. Upon his advancing towards me, with a whisper, I expected to hear some secret piece of news, which he had not thought fit to communicate to the bench; but instead of that, he desired me in my ear to lend him half a crown. In compassion to so needy a statesman, and to dissipate the confusion I found he was in, I told him, if he pleased, I would give him five shillings, to receive five pounds of him when the Great Turk was driven out of Constantinople; which he very readily accepted, but not before he had laid down to me the impossibility of such an event, as the affairs of Europe now stand.

This paper I design for the particular benefit of those worthy citizens who live more in a coffeehouse than in their shops, and whose thoughts are so taken up with the affairs of the Allies, that they forget their customers.

Joseph Addison: *from* Spectator No. 10
Monday, 12 March 1711

[THE SPECTATOR AND ITS READERS[1]]

Non aliter quam qui adverso vix flumine lembum
Remigiis subigit: si brachia forte remisit,
Atque illum in praeceps prono rapit alveus amni.[2]

It is with much satisfaction that I hear this great city inquiring day by day after these my papers, and receiving my morning lectures with a becoming seriousness and attention. My publisher tells me, that there are already three thousand of them distributed every day: so that if I allow twenty readers to every paper, which I look upon as a modest computation, I may reckon about three-score thousand disciples in London and Westminster, who I hope will take care to distinguish themselves from the thoughtless herd of their ignorant and inattentive brethren. Since I have raised to myself so great an audience, I shall spare no pains to make their instruction agreeable, and their diversion useful. For which reasons I shall endeavor to enliven morality with wit, and to temper wit with morality, that my readers may, if possible, both ways find their account in the speculation of the day. And to the end that their virtue and discretion may not be short transient intermitting starts of thought, I have resolved to refresh their memories from day to day, till I have recovered them out of that desperate state of vice and folly into which the age is fallen. The mind that lies

---

9. The public walk in St. James's Park, near the royal residence.
1. Bickerstaff proceeds to eavesdrop, astonished, on the conversation of these news-obsessives.
1. The *Spectator* bore a close resemblance to the *Daily Courant:* both papers were a single sheet produced by the same printer (Samuel Buckley) for the same price (a penny), and both appeared every day except Sunday. In

this number, Addison elaborates on the ways in which his new essay—less than two weeks old and already very successful—is not a newspaper.
2. "As if one, whose oars can scarce force his skiff against the stream, should by chance slacken his arms, and lo! headlong down the current the channel sweeps it away" (Virgil, *Georgics* 1.201–3).

fallow but a single day sprouts up in follies that are only to be killed by a constant and assiduous culture. It was said of Socrates, that he brought philosophy down from heaven, to inhabit among men;[3] and I shall be ambitious to have it said of me, that I have brought philosophy out of closets and libraries, schools and colleges, to dwell in clubs and assemblies, at tea tables, and in coffeehouses.

I would therefore in a very particular manner recommend these my speculations to all well-regulated families, that set apart an hour in every morning for tea and bread and butter; and would earnestly advise them for their good to order this paper to be punctually served up, and to be looked upon as a part of the tea equipage.

Sir Francis Bacon observes that a well-written book, compared with its rivals and antagonists, is like Moses's serpent, that immediately swallowed up and devoured those of the Egyptians.[4] I shall not be so vain as to think that where the *Spectator* appears, the other public prints will vanish; but shall leave it to my readers' consideration whether, is it not much better to be let into the knowledge of oneself, than to hear what passes in Muscovy[5] or Poland; and to amuse ourselves with such writings as tend to the wearing out of ignorance, passion, and prejudice, than such as naturally conduce to inflame hatreds and make enmities irreconcilable?

In the next place, I would recommend this paper to the daily perusal of those gentlemen whom I cannot but consider as my good brothers and allies, I mean the fraternity of spectators who live in the world without having anything to do in it; and either by the affluence of their fortunes, or laziness of their dispositions, have no other business with the rest of mankind but to look upon them. Under this class of men are comprehended all contemplative tradesmen, titular physicians, Fellows of the Royal Society,[6] Templers[7] that are not given to be contentious, and statesmen that are out of business. In short, everyone that considers the world as a theater, and desires to form a right judgment of those who are the actors on it.

There is another set of men that I must likewise lay a claim to, whom I have lately called the Blanks of society, as being altogether unfurnished with ideas, till the business and conversation of the day has supplied them. I have often considered these poor souls with an eye of great commiseration, when I have heard them asking the first man they have met with, whether there was any news stirring? and by that means gathering together materials for thinking. These needy persons do not know what to talk of, till about twelve a clock in the morning; for by that time they are pretty good judges of the weather, know which way the wind sits, and whether the Dutch mail[8] be come in. As they lie at the mercy of the first man they meet, and are grave or impertinent all the day long, according to the notions which they have imbibed in the morning, I would earnestly entreat them not to stir out of their chambers till they have read this paper, and do promise them that I will daily instill into them such sound and wholesome sentiments as shall have a good effect on their conversation for the ensuing twelve hours.

But there are none to whom this paper will be more useful than to the female world. I have often thought there has not been sufficient pains taken in finding out proper employments and diversions for the fair ones. Their amusements seem contrived for them rather as they are women, than as they are reasonable creatures; and

---

3. Addison paraphrases a remark by the Roman orator Cicero (*Tusculan Disputations* 5.4.10).
4. Bacon makes this point in his *Advancement of Learning* (2.14), alluding to Exodus 7.10–12.
5. A territory in west-central Russia (Moscow was its capital).
6. The London group chartered in the 1660s for the advancement of scientific inquiry.
7. Lawyers.
8. The boat bearing letters and newspapers from Holland.

are more adapted to the sex, than to the species. The toilet[9] is their great scene of business, and the right adjusting of their hair the principal employment of their lives. The sorting of a suit of ribbons is reckoned a very good morning's work; and if they make an excursion to a mercer's[1] or a toy shop,[2] so great a fatigue makes them unfit for anything else all the day after. Their more serious occupations are sewing and embroidery, and their greatest drudgery the preparation of jellies and sweetmeats. This, I say, is the state of ordinary women; though I know there are multitudes of those of a more elevated life and conversation, that move in an exalted sphere of knowledge and virtue, that join all the beauties of the mind to the ornaments of dress, and inspire a kind of awe and respect, as well as love, into their male beholders. I hope to increase the number of these by publishing this daily paper, which I shall always endeavor to make an innocent if not an improving entertainment, and by that means at least divert the minds of my female readers from greater trifles. At the same time, as I would fain give some finishing touches to those which are already the most beautiful pieces in human nature, I shall endeavor to point out all those imperfections that are the blemishes, as well as those virtues which are the embellishments, of the sex. In the meanwhile I hope these my gentle readers, who have so much time on their hands, will not grudge throwing away a quarter of an hour in a day on this paper, since they may do it without any hindrance to business.

I know several of my friends and well-wishers are in great pain for me, lest I should not be able to keep up the spirit of a paper which I oblige myself to furnish every day: but to make them easy in this particular, I will promise them faithfully to give it over as soon as I grow dull. This I know will be matter of great raillery to the small wits; who will frequently put me in mind of my promise, desire me to keep my word, assure me that it is high time to give over, with many other little pleasantries of the like nature, which men of a little smart genius cannot forbear throwing out against their best friends, when they have such a handle given them of being witty. But let them remember, that I do hereby enter my caveat against this piece of raillery.

━━━━━◆◆◆━━━━━

Getting, Spending, Speculating

The periodical essay was one commodity among many, in an economy whose energies were evident almost everywhere: in shops stocked with new (often exotic) goods; at outposts in remote countries where trade was gradually being transmuted into empire; at London banks, where the apparatus of transaction (loans, bills, draughts) was rapidly being refined; in nearby coffeehouses, where the agents and accumulators of wealth paused during busy days to absorb substances imported from abroad (coffee, tobacco, chocolate) as well as that home-crafted item of consumption, the periodical essay itself. The essayists often construed their audience as though it consisted *primarily* of merchants, shopkeepers, and customers—of people profoundly concerned with the course of commerce, whatever their gender or occupation. Defoe, Addison, and Steele all wrote to celebrate trade (its new profusions and possibilities), but also to regularize it, to render it respectable, to reconcile it with notions of human excellence originating in an earlier culture centered on aristocracy. The *Review*, the *Tatler*, and the *Spectator* all undertook (as the historian J. G. A. Pocock has elegantly argued) to redefine the idea of

---

9. Dressing tables.
1. Fabric sellers.

2. Where they might buy ornamental accessories—fans, silks, ribbons, laces—as well as playthings.

The Gentleman's Magazine:
St JOHN's GATE.

Lond Gazette
Lond Journ
Fog's Journ.
Applebee's ::
Read's : : : :
Craftsman ::
D. Spectator
Lit Courier of
Grubstreet
Hyp-Docto
Daily-Post
D. Advertiser
St James's Eu.
Whitehall Eu
Lond. Evtng
Weekly Misc
Generale-ve.
Old Whig
D. Gazetteer
Lon. E. Post
Com. Sense

York News
Dublin 5 ::
Edinburgh 2
Bristol ::::
Norwich 2
Exeter 2 :: :
Worcester
Northampton
Gloucester ::
Stamford ::
Nottingham
Bury Journ.
Chester ditto
Derby ditto
Ipswich do.
Reading do.
Leeds Merc:
Newcastle
Canterbury
Durham
Kendal
Boston : : 5
Barbados :
Jamaica &c

For JANUARY, 1738.

CONTAINING,

/More in Quantity, and greater Variety, than any Book of the kind and Price/.

I. ORIGINAL ESSAYS, Moral : The
Character of a *Good Man*, by a late
illustrious Lady. Of the Magistrate's
Right to punish ẘ Death. Prescience
consistent with Liberty. Whether
Heaven and Hell be Local.
II. —— PHILOLOGICAL : Essay on
Tragedy, with *Horace's* four Rules for ẙ
Drama. Answers to Biblical Questions.
III. —— MATHEMATICKS: A new
Astronomical Equation, discover'd by
Mr *Facio*. A Method to find the Lon-
gitude and Latitude at Sea.
IV. —— THE Lady's Adventure, and
Love Letters from a Protestant Gent.
to a Catholic Lady.
V. ESSAYS from the Weekly Papers.
The Literary Courier of Grub-street.
Characters of News-Papers. Advice to
Ladies on their Return to *London*. Zen-
ger's Tryal for printing a Libel. Rules

of Physiognomy in chusing Husbands.
The Widow describ'd. The Character
of a Prince Royal, &c.
VI. POETRY. A Poem, inscrib'd to the
Dublin Society, by Mr *Arbuckle*. Ode
on the Death of P. *George* of *Denmark*,
by the celebrated Mr *Aisop.* Prologue to
Venice preserv'd, by a Person of Quality.
The Blind Boy, with the Musick cor-
rect. Songs, Epigrams, Ænigmas, &c.
VII. HISTORICAL. The King's Speech;
Addresses of the Lords and Commons.
The Secrets of Free-Masonry.
VIII. LISTS of Births, Mariages, and
Deaths, &c.
IX. FOREIGN AFFAIRS. Match
of Don *Carlos* with the Princess Royal
of *Poland*, &c. Caution to Mariners.
X. Price of Stocks. Bill of Mortality.
XI. Register of Books.
XII. TABLE of Contents.

By SYLVANUS URBAN, Gent.

LONDON; Printed by E. CAVE at St JOHN's GATE, and Sold by the
Booksellers of Town and Country ; of whom may be had any former Month.

Where the *Review, Tatler*, and *Spectator* defined themselves *against* their print contemporaries, other periodicals took a different tack. With so much information, instruction, and entertainment flowing from so many sources, a desire developed for a digest that might organize it all. No one catered more adroitly to this new market than did Edward Cave, founder and editor of *Gentleman's Magazine*, a monthly pamphlet whose title coined a pivotal new term for print. "Magazine" meant a military storehouse of provisions and artillery; the *Gentleman's Magazine* promised an intellectual storehouse similarly well stocked. Cave promised "more in quantity, and greater variety, than any book of the kind and price." He delivered on the promise by publishing extracts and abstracts from many periodicals, but he soon cultivated a stable of his own writers (including the young Samuel Johnson) who furnished his readers with an ever-widening range of fresh materials: biographies, poetry, parliamentary debates. The *Magazine*'s logo presents it as a compendium of other papers, but Cave had in fact produced a true original, "one of the most successful and lucrative pamphlets" (wrote Johnson, whose observation still holds true) "which literary history has upon record." The title page depicts the 200-year-old gatehouse where the *Gentleman's Magazine* was composed, printed, and sold (the building's fortress-like appearance may entail a visual pun, conjuring up the military meaning of "magazine"). The building is flanked by the names of papers that the *Magazine* has incorporated, one way or another, into its own pages (London papers on the left, provincial and foreign ones on the right). The fictitious name "Sylvanus Urban" conjures up both countryside (*sylvanus*, "wooded") and city; as the bottom lines make clear, Cave aimed his appeal at audiences in both domains.

"virtue," to shift its focus of application from the classically defined obligations of the hereditary landowner to the prudent calculation of the urban merchant, alert to realities and proba-
bilities in an economy awash with speculation and controlled by credit, where "what one
owned was promises": promises by entrepreneurs in search of capital; by stock-jobbers selling
hopes of future prosperity; by the government whose operations depended on intricately structured loans from its own citizens. One central concern of the periodicals was how to commute
promise into actual prosperity, rather than mere air.

In the selections in this section, Addison rejoices in the commercial and cultural confluence at the Royal Exchange (London's shopping center). In a more sentimental vein, Steele
tracks the consequences of foreign trade in the lives and feelings of two lovers. Defoe, by contrast, is harder-headed, more closely analytic. Unlike the authors of the *Spectator*, he had spent
years in business, making and losing fortunes. Surveying the shops of London, Defoe declares
(as in virtually every *Review*) his passion for trade, but he asks what prospects the *present* patterns of consumption actually hold forth.

Joseph Addison: Spectator No. 69
Saturday, 19 May 1711

[ROYAL EXCHANGE[1]]

> *Hic segetes, illic veniunt felicius uvae:*
> *Arborei foetus alibi, atque injussa virescunt*
> *Gramina. Nonne vides, croceos ut Tmolus odores,*
> *India mittit ebur, molles sua thura Sabaei?*
> *At Chalybes nudi ferrum, virosaque Pontus*
> *Castorea, Eliadum palmas Epirus equarum?*
> *Continuo has leges aeternaque foedera certis*
> *Imposuit Natura locis . . . [2]*

There is no place in the town which I so much love to frequent as the Royal
Exchange. It gives me a secret satisfaction, and in some measure gratifies my vanity,
as I am an Englishman, to see so rich an assembly of countrymen and foreigners consulting together upon the private business of mankind, and making this metropolis a
kind of emporium for the whole earth. I must confess I look upon high-change[3] to be
a great council, in which all considerable nations have their representatives. Factors[4]
in the trading world are what ambassadors are in the politic world; they negotiate
affairs, conclude treaties, and maintain a good correspondence between those
wealthy societies of men that are divided from one another by seas and oceans, or
live on the different extremities of a continent. I have often been pleased to hear disputes adjusted between an inhabitant of Japan and an alderman of London, or to see

1. The Exchange, a quadrangle of arcades and shops surrounding a huge courtyard, had functioned as a crucial
site of London commerce since its creation in 1570.
Destroyed in the Great Fire, it was rebuilt from a new
design in 1669. The illustration on page 1195 depicts
both the original building by Thomas Gresham (upper
right corner) and the later structure with its more intricate, Baroque ornamentation. Statues of English kings
occupy the second-floor arches. At the center of the
courtyard, the statue of Charles II in the garb of a Roman
emperor enacts that favored comparison (echoed by
Addison in his essay's epigraph from Virgil) between contemporary Britain and the ancient Roman Empire.
2. "Corn grows more plentifully here, grapes there. In

other places grow trees laden with fruit, and grasses
unbidden. Do you not see how Tmolus sends us its saffron
perfumes; India her ivory; the soft Sabaens their frankincense; but the naked Chalybes send us iron, the Pontus
pungent beaver-oil, and Epirus prize-winning Olympic
horses? These perpetual laws and eternal covenants
Nature has imposed on certain places" (Virgil, *Georgics*
1.54–61).
3. In addition to housing shops, the Exchange was a central meeting place for international merchants, who frequently closed deals in the courtyard. "High change" was
that period when trading was at its peak.
4. Commercial agents.

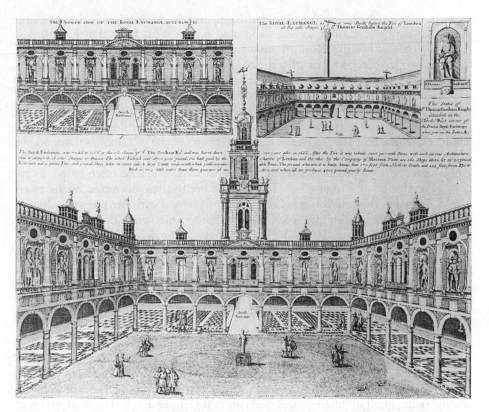

Sutton Nicholls, *The Royal Exchange*, 1712

a subject of the Great Mogul[5] entering into a league with one of the Czar of Muscovy.[6] I am infinitely delighted in mixing with these several ministers of commerce, as they are distinguished by their different walks and different languages. Sometimes I am jostled among a body of Armenians: sometimes I am lost in a crowd of Jews, and sometimes make one in a group of Dutchmen. I am a Dane, Swede, or Frenchman at different times, or rather fancy myself like the old philosopher,[7] who upon being asked what countryman he was, replied that he was a citizen of the world.

Though I very frequently visit this busy multitude of people, I am known to nobody there but my friend, Sir Andrew,[8] who often smiles upon me as he sees me bustling in the crowd, but at the same time connives at my presence without taking any further notice of me. There is indeed a merchant of Egypt, who just knows me by sight, having formerly remitted me some money to Grand Cairo;[9] but as I am not versed in the modern Coptic, our conferences go no further than a bow and a grimace.[1]

This grand scene of business gives me an infinite variety of solid and substantial entertainments. As I am a great lover of mankind, my heart naturally overflows with

---

5. The Indian emperor.

6. A territory in west-central Russia (Moscow was its capital).

7. Diogenes the Cynic, credited for developing the concept of "cosmopolitanism" (citizenship in the universe), in which all beings are parts of a single whole.

8. Sir Andrew Freeport, a member of Mr. Spectator's club: Whig merchant and ardent advocate (as his name implies) of free trade.

9. Where Mr. Spectator spent some time as a young man (see *Spectator* No. 1, page 1222).

1. The word denoted an expression of politeness.

pleasure at the sight of a prosperous and happy multitude, insomuch that at many public solemnities I cannot forbear expressing my joy with tears that have stolen down my cheeks. For this reason I am wonderfully delighted to see such a body of men thriving in their own private fortunes, and at the same time promoting the public stock; or in other words, raising estates for their own families, by bringing into their country whatever is wanting, and carrying out of it whatever is superfluous.

Nature seems to have taken a particular care to disseminate her blessings among the different regions of the world, with an eye to this mutual intercourse and traffic among mankind, that the natives of the several parts of the globe might have a kind of dependence upon one another, and be united together by their common interest. Almost every degree produces something peculiar to it. The food often grows in one country, and the sauce in another. The fruits of Portugal are corrected by the products of Barbados; the infusion of a China plant sweetened with the pith of an Indian cane; the Philippic islands give a flavor to our European bowls. The single dress of a woman of quality is often the product of an hundred climates. The muff and the fan come together from the different ends of the Earth. The scarf is sent from the torrid zone, and the tippet from beneath the pole. The brocade petticoat rises out of the mines of Peru, and the diamond necklace out of the bowels of Indostan.

If we consider our own country in its natural prospect, without any of the benefits and advantages of commerce, what a barren uncomfortable spot of earth falls to our share! Natural historians tell us that no fruit grows originally among us, besides hips and haws, acorns and pig-nuts, with other delicacies of the like nature; that our climate of itself, and without the assistances of art, can make no further advances towards a plum than to a sloe,[2] and carries an apple to no greater a perfection than a crab;[3] that our melons, our peaches, our figs, our apricots, and cherries, are strangers among us, imported in different ages, and naturalized in our English gardens; and that they would all degenerate and fall away into the trash of our own country, if they were wholly neglected by the planter, and left to the mercy of our sun and soil. Nor has traffic more enriched our vegetable world, than it has improved the whole face of nature among us. Our ships are laden with the harvest of every climate; our tables are stored with spices, and oils, and wines; our rooms are filled with pyramids of China, and adorned with the workmanship of Japan; our morning's draught[4] comes to us from the remotest corners of the earth; we repair our bodies by the drugs of America, and repose ourselves under Indian canopies. My friend Sir Andrew calls the vineyards of France our gardens; the Spice Islands[5] our hotbeds; the Persians our silk weavers, and the Chinese our potters. Nature indeed furnishes us with the bare necessaries of life, but traffic gives us a great variety of what is useful, and at the same time supplies us with everything that is convenient and ornamental. Nor is it the least part of this our happiness, that whilst we enjoy the remotest products of the north and south, we are free from those extremities of weather which give them birth; that our eyes are refreshed with the green fields of Britain, at the same time that our palates are feasted with fruits that rise between the tropics.

For these reasons there are not more useful members in a commonwealth than merchants. They knit mankind together in a mutual intercourse of good offices, distribute the gifts of nature, find work for the poor, add wealth to the rich, and mag-

2. The berry of the blackthorn.
3. Crabapple.

4. Drink.
5. A cluster of islands in modern Indonesia.

nificence to the great. Our English merchant converts the tin of his own country into gold, and exchanges his wool for rubies. The Mahometans are clothed in our British manufacture, and the inhabitants of the frozen zone warmed with the fleeces of our sheep.

When I have been upon the 'Change, I have often fancied one of our old kings[6] standing in person, where he is represented in effigy, and looking down upon the wealthy concourse of people with which that place is every day filled. In this case, how would he be surprised to hear all the languages of Europe spoken in this little spot of his former dominions, and to see so many private men, who in his time would have been the vassals of some powerful baron, negotiating like princes for greater sums of money than were formerly to be met with in the Royal Treasury! Trade, without enlarging the British territories, has given us a kind of additional empire: it has multiplied the number of the rich, made our landed estates infinitely more valuable than they were formerly, and added to them an accession of other estates as valuable as the lands themselves.

Richard Steele: Spectator No. 11
Tuesday, 13 March 1711

[INKLE AND YARICO[1]]

Dat veniam corvis, vexat censura columbas.[2]

Arietta is visited by all persons of both sexes who have any pretense to wit and gallantry. She is in that time of life which is neither affected with the follies of youth or infirmities of age; and her conversation is so mixed with gaiety and prudence that she is agreeable both to the young and the old. Her behavior is very frank, without being in the least blameable; and as she is out of the tract of any amorous or ambitious pursuits of her own, her visitants entertain her with accounts of themselves very freely, whether they concern their passions or their interests. I made her a visit this afternoon, having been formerly introduced to the honor of her acquaintance by my friend Will. Honeycomb,[3] who has prevailed upon her to admit me sometimes into her assembly, as a civil, inoffensive man. I found her accompanied with one person only, a commonplace talker who, upon my entrance, rose, and after a very slight civility sat down again; then turning to Arietta, pursued his discourse, which I found was upon the old topic of constancy in love. He went on with great facility in repeating what he talks every day of his life; and with the ornaments of insignificant laughs and gestures, enforced his arguments by quotations out of plays and songs, which allude to the perjuries of the fair, and the general levity[4] of women. Methought he strove to shine more than ordinarily in his talkative way, that he might insult my silence, and distinguish himself before a woman of Arietta's taste and understanding.

6. As depicted in the statues on the second story (see illustration on page 1195).
1. Steele here elaborates on a 60-year-old traveler's tale, in such a way as to combine two of the *Spectator*'s central concerns: the transactions of love and power between men and women, and the impact of commerce on human conduct.
2. "Their verdict goes easy on the raven, but is severe on

the dove" (Juvenal, *Satires* 2.63). The speaker, a woman, is complaining of how leniently men assess themselves, and how harshly they criticize women.
3. An aged member of Mr. Spectator's club, proud of his long-ago days as a Restoration rake, and still deeply interested in matters of the heart.
4. Lightness, fickleness.

She had often an inclination to interrupt him, but could find no opportunity, 'till the larum[5] ceased of itself; which it did not 'till he had repeated and murdered the celebrated story of the Ephesian matron.[6]

Arietta seemed to regard this piece of raillery as an outrage done to her sex, as indeed I have always observed that women, whether out of a nicer[7] regard to their honor, or what other reason I cannot tell, are more sensibly touched with those general aspersions which are cast upon their sex, than men are by what is said of theirs.

When she had a little recovered herself from the serious anger she was in, she replied in the following manner.

"Sir, when I consider, how perfectly new all you have said on this subject is, and that the story you have given us is not quite two thousand years old, I cannot but think it a piece of presumption to dispute with you: but your quotations put me in mind of the fable of the lion and the man.[8] The man, walking with that noble animal, showed him, in the ostentation of human superiority, a sign of a man killing a lion. Upon which the lion said very justly, 'We lions are none of us painters, else we could show a hundred men killed by lions, for one lion killed by a man.' You men are writers, and can represent us women as unbecoming as you please in your works, while we are unable to return the injury. You have twice or thrice observed in your discourse that hypocrisy is the very foundation of our education; and that an ability to dissemble our affections is a professed part of our breeding. These, and such other reflections, are sprinkled up and down the writings of all ages, by authors who leave behind them memorials of their resentment against the scorn of particular women, in invectives against the whole sex. Such a writer, I doubt not, was the celebrated Petronius, who invented the pleasant aggravations of the frailty of the Ephesian lady; but when we consider this question between the sexes, which has been either a point of dispute or raillery ever since there were men and women, let us take facts from plain people, and from such as have not either ambition or capacity to embellish their narrations with any beauties of imagination. I was the other day amusing myself with Ligon's *Account of Barbados*; and, in answer to your well-wrought tale, I will give you (as it dwells upon my memory) out of that honest traveler, in his fifty-fifth page, the History of Inkle and Yarico.[9]

"Mr. Thomas Inkle[1] of London, aged 20 years, embarked in the Downs[2] on the good ship called the Achilles, bound for the West Indies, on the 16th of June 1647, in order to improve his fortune by trade and merchandise. Our adventurer was the third son of an eminent citizen, who had taken particular care to instill into his mind an early love of gain, by making him a perfect master of numbers, and consequently giving him a quick view of loss and advantage, and preventing the natural impulses of his passions, by prepossession towards his interests. With a mind thus turned, young Inkle had a person every way agreeable, a ruddy vigor in his countenance, strength in his limbs, with ringlets of fair hair loosely flowing on his shoulders. It happened, in the course of the voyage, that the Achilles, in some distress, put into a creek on the main of America, in search of provisions. The youth, who is the hero of my story, among others, went ashore on this occasion. From their first landing they

---

5. The long-ringing alarm bell (of his talk).
6. The Roman story (told in Petronius's *Satyricon*, pt. 2) of a widow who, while mourning at the tomb of her newly deceased husband, succumbs to the attractions of a soldier standing nearby, and makes love with him on her husband's tomb.
7. More precise.
8. In Aesop's *Fables* (No. 219).

9. Richard Ligon's *True and Exact History of the Island of Barbados* (1657) includes a paragraph on a slave named Yarico and her misadventures in love, which Steele elaborates into the tale that follows.
1. Steele invents the name for this character; it means (perhaps prophetically) "linen tape," a common commodity.
2. A harbor on the southeastern coast of England.

were observed by a party of Indians, who hid themselves in the woods for that purpose. The English unadvisedly marched a great distance from the shore into the country, and were intercepted by the natives, who slew the greatest number of them. Our adventurer escaped among others, by flying into a forest. Upon his coming into a remote and pathless part of the wood, he threw himself, tired and breathless, on a little hillock, when an Indian maid rushed from a thicket behind him. After the first surprise, they appeared mutually agreeable to each other. If the European was highly charmed with the limbs, features, and wild graces of the naked American, the American was no less taken with the dress, complexion, and shape of an European, covered from head to foot. The Indian grew immediately enamored of him, and consequently solicitous for his preservation. She therefore conveyed him to a cave, where she gave him a delicious repast of fruits, and led him to a stream to slake his thirst. In the midst of these good offices, she would sometimes play with his hair, and delight in the opposition of its color to that of her fingers; then open his bosom, then laugh at him for covering it. She was, it seems, a person of distinction, for she every day came to him in a different dress, of the most beautiful shells, bugles, and bredes.[3] She likewise brought him a great many spoils, which her other lovers had presented to her; so that his cave was richly adorned with all the spotted skins of beasts, and most parti-colored feathers of fowls, which that world afforded. To make his confinement more tolerable, she would carry him in the dusk of the evening, or by the favor of moonlight, to unfrequented groves and solitudes, and show him where to lie down in safety, and sleep amidst the falls of waters, and melody of nightingales. Her part was to watch and hold him in her arms, for fear of her countrymen, and wake him on occasions to consult his safety. In this manner did the lovers pass away their time, till they had learned a language of their own, in which the voyager communicated to his mistress, how happy he should be to have her in his country, where she should be clothed in such silks as his waistcoat was made of, and be carried in houses drawn by horses, without being exposed to wind or weather. All this he promised her the enjoyment of, without such fears and alarms as they were there tormented with. In this tender correspondence these lovers lived for several months, when Yarico, instructed by her lover, discovered a vessel on the coast, to which she made signals, and in the night, with the utmost joy and satisfaction accompanied him to a ship's crew of his countrymen, bound for Barbados. When a vessel from the main arrives in that island, it seems the planters come down to the shore, where there is an immediate market of the Indians and other slaves, as with us of horses and oxen.

"To be short, Mr. Thomas Inkle, now coming into English territories, began seriously to reflect upon his loss of time, and to weigh with himself how many days' interest of his money he had lost during his stay with Yarico. This thought made the young man very pensive, and careful what account he should be able to give his friends of his voyage. Upon which considerations, the prudent and frugal young man sold Yarico to a Barbadian merchant; notwithstanding that the poor girl, to incline him to commiserate her condition, told him that she was with child by him; but he only made use of that information, to rise in his demands upon the purchaser."

I was so touched with this story, (which I think should be always a counterpart to the Ephesian matron) that I left the room with tears in my eyes; which a woman of Arietta's good sense did, I am sure, take for greater applause, than any compliments I could make her.

---

3. Tube-shaped glass beads and braiding.

Daniel Defoe: *from* A Review of the State of the British Nation, Vol. 1, No. 43
Thursday, 8 January 1713
[WEAK FOUNDATIONS]

The subject of trade which I am now entered upon has this one excellency in it, for the benefit of the author, that really it can never be exhausted. * * * I remember some time ago I gave you a hint about the mighty alteration in the face of trade in this city; I cannot but touch it again on this occasion, because it relates to what I am upon. Let any man who remembers the glorious state of our trade about thirty or forty years past view but the streets of this opulent city and even the Exchange of London—nay, even our courts of law. It must of necessity put him in mind of Ezra 3.12, where the ancient men who had seen the old temple wept when they saw the weak foundations of the new.

However, to go on as I began and examine our new increase of commerce which we so must boast of: let me note a little to you with what mighty advantages the chasms, gaps, and breaches of our trade are filled up of late, and let us see it, I say, in the streets. Here, in the room of a trifling banker, or goldsmith, we are supplied with a most eminent brandy shop (Cheapside). There in the room of ditto you have a flaming shop[1] for white tea pots and luted earthen mugs (Cornhill), the most excellent offspring of that most valuable manufacture of earthenware. It is impossible that coffee, tea, and chocolate can be so advanced in their consumption without an eminent increase of those trades that attend them; whence we see the most noble shops in the city taken up with the valuable utensils of the tea table. The china warehouses are little marts within themselves (and by the way, are newly become markets of clandestine trade, of which I shall say more very quickly), and the eminent corner houses in the chief streets of London are chosen out by the town tinkers to furnish us with tea kettles and chocolate pots—vide Catherine Street and Bedford Buildings. Two thousand pound is reckoned a small stock in copper pots and lacquered kettles, and the very fitting up one of these brazen people's shops with fine sashes,[2] etc., to set forth his ware, costs above 500£ sterling, which is more by half than the best draper or mercer's shop in London requires.

This certainly shows the increase of our trade. Brass locks for our chambers and parlors, brass knockers for our doors, and the like add to the luster of those shops, of which hereafter. And the same sash works, only finer and larger, are now used to range[3] your brass and copper, that the goldsmiths had always to set out their less valuable silver and gold plate. From hence, be pleased to look upon the druggists of the town who are the merchants of these things. Bucklers-Bury and Little Lombard Street were the places which a few years ago held the whole number, a very few excepted, of that difficult nice employment, whose number is now spread over the whole town and with the most capital stocks, whose whole employ is the furnishing us by wholesale and retail with these most valuable of all drugs, coffee, tea, and chocolate—the general furniture of a druggist's shop being now three bales of coffee, twelve boxes of chocolate, six large canisters of tea, and an hundred and fifty empty gilded boxes. In like manner the rest of the town—how gloriously it is supplied! How do pastry cooks and periwig makers, brandy shops and toy shops, succeed linen drapers, mercers, upholsterers, and the like. A hundred pounds to rent for a house to sell

---

1. A shop with a kiln for making earthenware.
2. Windows made up of two sliding frames (common
now, new and fancy at this time).
3. Display.

jellies and apple pies; two hundred pounds to fit up a brandy shop, and afterwards not a hundred pound stock to put into it. These I can show many instances of.

Look, gentlemen, upon the particular parts of your town, formerly eminent for the best of tradesmen! View the famous churchyard of St. Paul's where so many aldermen and lord mayors have been raised by the trade of broadcloth and mere woolen manufactures,[4] and on whose trades so many families of poor always depended, that Sir William Turner used to say his shop alone employed 50,000 poor people! What succeeds him? A most noble, and to be sure, a much more valuable vintner's warehouse, *Anglice*,[5] a tavern, more vulgarly a bawdyhouse. And the next draper's shop, a coffee house; what takes up the whole row there? and supplies the place of eighteen or nineteen topping drapers? Who can but observe it! Cane chair makers, gilders of leather, looking-glass shops, and peddlers or toy shops—manifold improvements of trade! and an eminent instance of the growth of our manufactures! * * *

Advertisements from the *Spectator*[1]

At the Lace Chamber on Ludgate Hill, kept by Mary Parsons, is a great quantity of Flanders lace, lately come over, to be sold off at great pennyworths[2] by wholesale or retail. She bought them there herself. [No. 200; Friday, 19 October 1711]

This day is published *The Court and City Vagaries*, being some late (and real) intrigues of several gentlemen and ladies. Written by one of the fair sex, price 6d. Sold by J. Baker in Paternoster Row. [No. 255; Saturday, 22 December 1711]

The famous Italian water, for dying red and gray hairs of the head and eyebrows into a lasting brown or black; at 1, 2, or 4s. the bottle, with printed directions for the use of it. To be had at Mrs. Hannam's toyshop, at the sign of the Three Angels near the Half-Moon Tavern in Cheapside. [Vol. 8, No. 634; Friday, 17 December 1714]

The ladies that called at Mr. Charles Lillie's at the corner of Beauford Buildings,[3] in a hackney coach on Wednesday night, the 6th of this instant, about 10 o'clock, are desired to let him know where to direct to them, he being now able to give a particular account of what they enquired after. [No. 305; Tuesday, 19 February 1712]

———— ≡◆≡ ————

Women and Men, Manners and Marriage

When Isaac Bickerstaff, in his first *Tatler*, undertook to teach his readers "what to think," politics was apparently what he most expected them to think about. Soon, though, he found a second focus: that cluster of questions today grouped under the rubric "gender." Bickerstaff, his imitators, and his successors strove constantly to instruct men and women as to who they were, what they should become, how they differed from each other, how they ought to interact, and

---

4. The trade in textiles had provided the foundation for many family fortunes and (hence) political careers.
5. In English.
1. Periodicals did not merely comment on commerce, they participated in it, earning much of their revenue from the advertisements that they printed at the conclusion of their main editorial matter.

2. At a terrific bargain.
3. Charles Lillie, a close associate of Addison's and Steele's, owned a perfume shop in the Strand. He had been one of the publishers and distributors of the *Tatler*, and sold the *Spectator* at his shop, where he also accepted advertisements for inclusion in the paper.

how they might most happily merge in love and marriage. The *Tatler*, the *Review*, and the *Spectator* all urged men to supplant aggression with morality and grace; women to cultivate sound sense over mere caprice; and both sexes to ground their marriages in reciprocity, love, and reason, rather than financial gain or impulsive passion.

The essayists' instruction, though, was far from even-handed. "I will not meddle with the *Spectator*," Jonathan Swift wrote scornfully to Stella in 1711. "Let him *fair-sex* it to the world's end." Addison and Steele had used that phrase obsessively to describe, address, and instruct their female readers; it had by now become a kind of shorthand for a variable blend of courtesy and condescension endemic to the periodicals, almost all of which were written by men and directed at an audience in which males possessed a barely questioned sway. Nonetheless, women had for more than a decade occupied an important (albeit elusive) place in the periodical scheme of things, as purchasers, as readers, as participants. In the early 1690s, when John Dunton launched the first "question and answer" periodical, he quickly discovered that queries submitted by women were abundant, popular, and profitable. In the wake of his *Athenian Mercury*, almost all important periodicals devised strategies for incorporating "the fair sex" into their texts and even into their titles: Mr. Spectator sketched lines of identification between his silent, self-contained conduct and the proper demeanor of the women whom he proposed to instruct; the *Tatler* proposed to "honor" (but also mocked) its female audience by its choice of title; many periodicals bore titles pitched even more explicitly at women: the *Female Tatler*, the *Ladies' Almanac*, the *Ladies' Magazine*, etc.

Such "inclusion" entailed obvious control. If the periodicals took up women's questions, they almost invariably supplied men's answers (even the *Ladies'* titles were mostly run by men). Eliza Haywood's *Female Spectator*, written not only for women but by a woman, offered something different. Far more fascinated with women's predicaments than with men's opinions, it helped foster a tradition of women's writing that grew richer and more various (encompassing novels and tracts as well as periodicals) as the century progressed.

Richard Steele: *from* Tatler No. 25
Tuesday, 7 June 1709

[DUELLISTS]

White's Chocolate-house, June 6

A letter from a young lady, written in the most passionate terms (wherein she laments the misfortune of a gentleman, her lover, who was lately wounded in a duel) has turned my thoughts to that subject, and inclined me to examine into the causes which precipitate men into so fatal a folly. And as it has been proposed to treat of subjects of gallantry[1] in the article from hence,[2] and no one point in nature is more proper to be considered by the company who frequent this place, than that of duels, it is worth our consideration to examine into this chimerical groundless humor, and to lay every other thought aside, till we have stripped it of all its false pretenses to credit and reputation amongst men.

But I must confess, when I consider what I am going about, and run over in my imagination all the endless crowd of men of honor who will be offended at such a discourse, I am undertaking, methinks, a work worthy an invulnerable hero in Romance, rather than a private gentleman with a single rapier. But as I am pretty well acquainted by great opportunities with the nature of man, and know of a truth, that all men fight *against their will*, the danger vanishes, and resolution rises upon this

---

1. Social conduct, particularly that having to do with courtship and self-display.   2. From White's.

subject. For this reason I shall talk very freely on a custom which all men wish exploded, though no man has courage enough to resist it.

But there is one unintelligible word which I fear will extremely perplex my dissertation, and I confess to you I find very hard to explain, which is, the term *satisfaction*. An honest country gentleman had the misfortune to fall into company with two or three modern men of honor, where he happened to be very ill treated; and one of the company being conscious of his offense, sends a note to him in the morning, and tells him, he was ready to give him satisfaction. This is fine doing (says the plain fellow): last night he sent me away cursedly out of humor, and this morning he fancies it would be a satisfaction to be run through the body.

As the matter at present stands, it is not to do handsome actions denominates a man of honor; it is enough if he dares to defend ill ones. Thus you often see a common sharper[3] in competition with a gentleman of the first rank; though all mankind is convinced, that a fighting gamester is only a pickpocket with the courage of an highwayman. One cannot with any patience reflect on the unaccountable jumble of persons and things in this town and nation, which occasions very frequently, that a brave man falls by a hand below that of the common hangman, and yet his executioner escapes the clutches of the hangman for doing it. I shall therefore hereafter consider, how the bravest men in other ages and nations have behaved themselves upon such incidents as we decide by combat; and show, from their practice, that this resentment neither has its foundation from true reason, or solid fame; but is an imposture, made up of cowardice, falsehood, and want of understanding. For this work, a good history of quarrels would be very edifying to the public, and I apply myself to the town for particulars and circumstances within their knowledge, which may serve to embellish the dissertation with proper cuts. Most of the quarrels I have ever known, have proceeded from some valiant coxcomb's persisting in the wrong, to defend some prevailing folly, and preserve himself from the ingenuity of owning a mistake.

By this means it is called, "giving a man satisfaction," to urge your offense against him with your sword; which puts me in mind of Peter's order to the keeper, in *The Tale of a Tub*: "If you neglect to do all this, damn you and your generation forever; and so we bid you heartily farewell."[4] If the contradiction in the very terms of one of our challenges were as well explained, and turned into downright English, would it not run after this manner?

Sir,

Your extraordinary behavior last night, and the liberty you were pleased to take with me, makes me this morning give you this, to tell you, because you are an ill-bred puppy, I will meet you in Hyde Park an hour hence; and because you want both breeding and humanity, I desire you would come with a pistol in your hand, on horseback, and endeavor to shoot me through the head, to teach you more manners. If you fail of doing me this pleasure, I shall say, you are a rascal on every post in town: and so, Sir, if you will not injure me more, I shall never forgive what you have done already. Pray Sir, do not fail of getting everything ready, and you will infinitely oblige,

Sir,
Your most obedient
humble servant, &c.

---

3. Trickster.
4. Steele paraphrases this fervent curse from Jonathan

Swift's intricate satire *A Tale of a Tub* (1704), sec. 4.

Daniel Defoe: *from* A Review of the State of the British Nation, Vol. 9, No. 34

Saturday, 29 November 1712

[A DUELLIST'S CONSCIENCE]

I have in one *Review* lately taken the liberty to mention that so exploded, rejected thing called peace among ourselves. I confess I see no room to expect good usage among you when I touch so ungrateful a subject, but I look for all sides to fall upon me as upon one prompting them to what they are resolved against.

I look upon the present feuds and outrageous party quarrelling which we are all embarked in to be the worst war we could ever engage in; and I think it was never so lively represented as by the late wretched unhappy duel between the Lord M[ohu]n and Duke H[amilto]n, wherein, both enraged, both desperately bent to ruin and destroy one another, both draw their swords in an unjust, needless, and dishonorable quarrel, and both die in the engagement.[1] I call the quarrel unjust and dishonorable not as to the cause of quarrel, which I have nothing to do with, but as to the manner of duelling, which I undertake to be unjust and dishonorable, because illegal and unchristian. * * *

I cannot but observe * * * what some public papers pretend about His Grace Duke H[amilto]n, viz., that he spent all the night before the action in his closet, retired pensive; and, says another author, in his devotion. I have nothing to say to the fact in this, for I do not believe it to be true. But for the sake of the surviving part of mankind, let us speak to this ridiculous newsmonger a little. Pray, sir, what devotion could you rationally suppose the Duke to be passing the time in? I cannot but think His Grace was a better Christian, at least I am sure he knew better, than to be praying to God for success upon what he was going about. Let all the men in England but tell me, what could the Duke say? Could anything of a Christian bring him in saying thus, with his eyes up to heaven: "Lord, thou knowest I will affront thy justice tomorrow by taking my cause into my own hand, and executing that vengeance which thou hast forbid me, and reserved to thyself. Lord, give me thy blessing to this wicked and willful action, and grant me success that I may kill my enemy, and become a murderer of my neighbor, etc." If he could not say this, let anyone tell me what he could pray. Can they think he would say thus? "Lord, I am going to commit a most grievous wickedness, and I am resolved to do it in spite of its being abhorred and forbidden by thee. But I WILL do it; however, I desire thou wilt pardon the sin and assist me to increase it by my murdering my adversary." This must be the devotion, the wretched devotion of such a retreat, and for that reason I will not so far affront the memory of Duke H[amilto]n to say he employed that time in devotion. If I might guess at the perturbation of thoughts which took up those few, or such unhappy hours; I say, if I may guess at them *by my own unhappy experience*, and may appeal to others who know what it is, I am of the opinion such times are taken up in the rolling of the passions, the boiling of the blood, the furious agitation of the animal spirits moved by the violence of the provocation. If conscience presumes to give a pinch in the dark, or put in a word, the inflamed organ answers: "Come what will, I cannot go

---

1. The duel, between James Douglas, Duke of Hamilton (1658–1712), and Charles Mohun (1675?–1712), had taken place two weeks earlier, on November 15.

back, I cannot live; I had better be run a thousand times through the body, I can die but once; but to bear this, is to be stabbed every day, to be insulted at the corner of every street, be posted, caned, and the Devil; I cannot bear it, I cannot help it." If the mind retreats a little and looks in through a very, very little bit, it occurs thus: "You are mad, you give up your reason, you are a murderer if you fall not in the action, you are a lost man forever. You know it is not a lawful action." All this is stopped thus: "What! Can I bear to be called COWARD! Had I not better be out of the world! I cannot go off, I must do it, all is at stake, I must, I cannot go from it, die or be damned, or anything is all one, I must do it." And so in the morning away he goes to be undone; goes to lay in a store for repentance; goes to take away his neighbor's life, and lay at stake his own, and sometimes, as in this case, to lose both.

Those people who would send the late Duke to his closet to prayers to prepare for his next day's work, I believe know little what fighting a duel is, or what temper the mind is in when such an appointment is upon their hands; I rather believe His Grace was fighting with my Lord M[ohu]n all night; many a silent pass was made that night in imagination, I doubt not; not that I believe the Duke was weak enough to act by himself the postures or motions of fighting; but I believe it was impossible to suppose that a mind possessed with such views and such resolutions as he then had could refrain from fixing the ideas of the action itself in its thoughts.

But to talk of devotion, let that jest be laid by. I can take upon me to say, God hears no such prayers, nor can any man who is in his right senses have the face to look up to his Maker in such a case as that was.

THE ATHENIAN MERCURY (1691–1697) In *The Athenian Mercury* (initially titled the *Athenian Gazette*, until the *London Gazette* clamped down), the eccentric and ingenious entrepreneur John Dunton (1659–1732) performed a bold experiment in interactive media. "All persons whatever," announced the paper's first number, "may be resolved *gratis* in any question that their own satisfaction or curiosity shall prompt them to, if they send [in] their questions by a penny-post letter." Inquiring readers, Dunton promised, would soon see their questions in print, accompanied by knowledgable and thoughtful answers from a society of "Athenians"— actually a quartet of learned but not particularly eminent men (including the editor himself), whose identities Dunton both cloaked and burnished by that elegant cover name, which connoted both ancient wisdom and university education. The paper succeeded so well that he promptly expanded his operation, adding more "members" to the Athenian Society (including Daniel Defoe) and pages to the publication in order to absorb the multitude of questions that kept pouring in. The paper prided itself on its range of topics, but announced in its eighteenth number a particular area of specialization: "Whereas the questions we receive from the *fair sex* are both *pressing* and *numerous*, we being willing to oblige 'em, as knowing they have a very *strong party* in the world, resolve to set apart the first Tuesday in every month on purpose to satisfy questions of that nature"; the recurrent special issue proved so popular that it was soon appearing biweekly, then weekly. Its pages included questions from both men and women on those subjects construed as particularly "feminine" (love, courtship, marriage); the letters often took the form of short but expressive autobiographies—a mode Steele, Addison, and numberless others imitated and developed during the following decades. Dunton claimed to have conceived his "question project" (as he affectionately termed it) in the course of an afternoon's walk. Its influence has lasted centuries, and is still plain to see in columns of advice and information. Dunton taught the periodical press an irresistibly simple and enduringly successful way of mirroring its readers, making them part of (and hence committed to) the papers they read.

from **The Athenian Mercury**[1]

QUEST. Whether it is lawful for a man to beat his wife?

ANSW. The affirmative would be very disobliging to that sex, without adding any more to it. Therefore we ought to be as cautious and tender as may be in asserting such an ill-natured position. We allow a wife to be[2] naturalized into, and part of her husband, and yet nature sometimes wars against part of itself, in ejecting by sweat, urine, etc. what otherwise would be destructive to its very frame; nay, sometimes there is occasion of greater violence, as lancing,[3] burning, dismembering, etc., which the patient submits to as his interest. Now if a man may thus cruelly treat himself, and be an accessory to his own torture, he may legally chastise his wife, who is no nearer to him than he is to himself, but yet (for I am not covetous of the fate of Orpheus[4]) as none but doctors are proper judges of seasonable violences to nature, so there are but few husbands that know how to correct a wife. To do it in a passion, and pretend justice, is ridiculous, because that passion incapacitates the judgment from its office; and to do it when one is pleased is a harder task; so that we conclude, as the legality is unquestionable, so the time and measure are generally too critical[5] for a calculation. When a wife goes astray, it is safe to use a sympathetic remedy, as the rebuke of a kiss; the antipathetic[6] may prove worse than the disease.

QUEST. Whether since it is your opinion that if a man be a discreet and prudent man, he may correct the misbehavior of his wife by beating, *vice versa*, a wife being so qualified, and having a sot to her husband, whether she may not (if able) beat her husband?

ANSW. The power was at first vested in man specifically,[7] without provisions, distinctions, or limitations of sot, foolish, weak, etc. Therefore these altering not his species by consequence, cannot annul his prerogative.

QUEST. Whether it be lawful for a young lady to pray for a husband, and if lawful, in what form?

ANSW. He must renounce humanity, and confess himself a sort of an aggressor upon the privileges of nature, that would not make it as immortal as possible, which is only honorably effected by marriage, whereby we survive in our children. Misery without a friend to bear a part is very afflicting, and happiness without communication is tedious, and (as Seneca[8] has observed) sometimes inclines us to make a voluntary choice of misery for novelty. We should be vagrant sort of animals without marriage, as if nature were ashamed of our converse. We should contribute to the destruction of states, condemn the wisdom of the first Institutor and censure the edicts of such commonwealths who have upon very good grounds discountenanced and punished celibacy. Nay, supposing all the miseries that marriage-haters suggest should fall upon us, it is our own fault, if with Socrates we don't learn more by a scolding wife than by all the precepts of philosophers.[9]

---

1. The following questions and answers are taken from Vol. 1, Nos. 1 and 2 (1691); Vol. 2, No. 15 (1691); and Vol. 14, No. 23 (1694).
2. Agree that a wife is.
3. Pricking, for medical purposes.
4. The musician of Greek myth, torn apart by raging women, votaries of Bacchus.
5. Complicated.

6. Remedy.
7. Refers to God's "curse" upon Eve for eating the forbidden fruit: "Thy desire shall be to thy husband, and he shall rule over thee" (Genesis 3.12).
8. Stoic philosopher and tragic playwright.
9. A misogynist tradition held that the philosopher Socrates's wife Xanthippe berated him constantly, and thereby taught him skill in argument.

Now if it be lawful to marry, it is lawful for ladies to pray for good husbands, if they find their inclination, concerns in the world, or other motives (which they are to be judges of) consistent with the ends of such society. As to the form of prayer required, they may, if they please, use the following, if they are not better furnished already:

From a profane libertine, from one affectedly pious, from a profuse almoner,[1] from an uncharitable wretch, from a wavering religioso,[2] and an injudicious zealot—deliver me!

From one of a starched gravity, or of ridiculous levity, from an ambitious states-man, from a restless projector,[3] from one that loves anything besides me, but what is very just and honorable—deliver me!

From an ecstasied poet, from a modern wit, from a base coward and a rash fool, from a pad[4] and a pauper—deliver me!

From a Venus's darling, from a Bacchus's proselyte,[5] from a traveling half,[6] from a domestic animal, from all masculine plagues not yet recounted—deliver me!

Give me one whose love has more of judgment than passion, who is master of himself, or at least an indefatigable scholar in such a study, who has an equal flame, that as two tallies[7] we may appear more perfect by union.

Give me one of as genteel an education as a little expense of time will permit, with an indifferent fortune, rather independent of the servile fate of palaces, and yet one whose retirement is not so much from the public as into himself. One (if possible) above all flattery and affronts, and yet as careful in preventing the injury as able to repair it. One, the beauty of whose mind exceeds that of his face, yet not deformed so as to be distinguishable from others even unto a ridicule.

Give me one that has learnt to live much in a little time, one that is no great familiar in converse with the world, nor no little one with himself. One (if two such happinesses may be granted at one time to our sex) who with these uncom-mon endowments of mind may (naturally) have a sweet, mild, easy disposition, or at least one who by his practice and frequent habit has made himself so before he is made mine. But as the master-perfection and chiefest draught,[8] let him be truly virtuous and pious; that is to say, let me be truly happy in my choice. * * *

QUEST. It was my fortune about four years since to be for some time in a family,[9] and a son of the family addressed himself to me. I told him his parents would not like it, my fortune being much inferior to his, and that I feared he would incur his father's displeasure, if he knew he loved me. He said he loved no woman upon the earth but me, and assured me it was for my sake he rejected a very advantageous match that was offered him at that time. All his actions persuaded me his intentions were real. I found myself inclinable to love him. He urged me to make him a promise, that then he would be contented to live so until it should please God to take his good father, who, if he could possibly, he would not disoblige. Now I do love him not for his estate, I take God to witness; for if he had not six pence in the world I could love him as I do, which is far beyond what I am able to say. There was a

1. Charity-giver.
2. One who changes his faith.
3. Scientist; deviser of grand plans and schemes.
4. Thief.
5. From a rake, from a drunk.
6. Perhaps suggesting a passive, mute companion.
7. A "tally" was originally a tool used to record a debt or payment. A wooden rod, notched several times crosswise (to indicate the amount of money transferred) was then cut lengthwise. Creditor and debtor each retained one of the halves, whose "match" with each other constituted legal proof of the transaction.
8. I.e., feature of the portrait.
9. As a servant ("family" meant "household").

mutual vow made between us; we called God to witness. He added that if ever he falsified the least tittle of what he had promised, that God's just curse might light on him. Gentlemen, he is twelve years older than I. He is a scholar, and very well qualified. And to show you it was not done rashly, since we were parted (which was as soon as they had any suspicion of our love), he has repeated the same promises in several letters to me. Some time before I went from him, I was told he was married to a gentlewoman that he had a child by. I told him of it; he protested it was false, and that the child was not his, nor did he ever converse with the person since; it was at least twelve years ago that the child was born. He invited me lately to see his house, where I observed some of the goods marked with the gentlewoman's name. It made me very uneasy. He quickly found the reason, and assured me there was nothing at all in it; but I since found a letter that came with those goods from that very person. At the reading it I thought I should have died, and I have scarce been myself ever since. She tells him she loves him before her life, and subscribes herself thus, "No more at present from your truest of lovers," and the two first letters of her own name to it. I showed him the letter, and then he said it was things he took for a debt of a relation of hers. Gentlemen, pray, as soon as you can possible, advise me in this thing, for there's not one creature upon the earth that knows it; nor can I confide in any person to ask their advice.

ANSW. We'd not willingly either injure an innocent gentleman, nor mislead you who desire our advice. But if the letter you found was worded as you relate it, his excuse is too weak to clear him. For the writer of it must at least be more than an ordinary friend or acquaintance; and he a very ill man to endeavor to deceive you both, which we should think would go a good way towards taking off your love from him, and settling it on a more worthy object, that neither will nor can deceive or abuse you.

Richard Steele: *from* Tatler No. 104
Thursday, 8 December 1709

[JENNY DISTAFF NEWLY MARRIED[1]]

——Garrit aniles
Ex re Fabellas.——[2]

From My Own Apartment, December 7

My brother[3] Tranquillus being gone out of town for some days, my sister Jenny sent me word she would come and dine with me, and therefore desired me to have no other company. I took care accordingly, and was not a little pleased to see her enter the room with a decent and matronlike behavior, which I thought very much became her. I saw she had a great deal to say to me, and easily discovered in her eyes, and the air of her countenance, that she had abundance of satisfaction in her heart, which she longed to communicate. However, I was resolved to let her break into her dis-

---

1. Jenny Distaff is Isaac Bickerstaff's half-sister. In some earlier *Tatlers* (Nos. 10 and 33), she appeared as an essayist in her own right, composing pieces for the paper whenever her brother was out of town. In more recent numbers (75, 79), Bickerstaff had told the story of arranging her marriage to "Tranquillus" ("the calm one"),

which he described as "a domestic affair of great importance, . . . no less than the disposal of my sister Jenny for life."
2. "He tells an old wives' tale very pertinently" (Horace, *Satires* 2.6.77–78).
3. Brother-in-law.

course her own way, and reduced her to a thousand little devices and intimations to bring me to the mention of her husband. But finding I was resolved not to name him, she began of her own accord; my husband (said she) gives his humble service to you: to which I only answered, I hope he is well; and without waiting for a reply, fell into other subjects. She at last was out of all patience, and said (with a smile and manner that I thought had more beauty and spirit than I had ever observed before in her) I did not think, Brother, you had been so ill-natured. You have seen ever since I came in, that I had a mind to talk of my husband, and you won't be so kind as to give me an occasion. I did not know (said I) but it might be a disagreeable subject to you. You do not take me for so old-fashioned a fellow as to think of entertaining a young lady with the discourse of her husband. I know, nothing is more acceptable than to speak of one who is to be so; but to speak of one who is so! Indeed, Jenny, I am a better bred man than you think me. She showed a little dislike at my raillery; and by her bridling up, I perceived she expected to be treated hereafter not as Jenny Distaff, but Mrs. Tranquillus. I was very well pleased with this change in her humor; and upon talking with her on several subjects, I could not but fancy that I saw a great deal of her husband's way and manner in her remarks, her phrases, the tone of her voice, and the very air of her countenance. This gave me an unspeakable satisfaction, not only because I had found her an husband, from whom she could learn many things that were laudable, but also because I looked upon her imitation of him as an infallible sign that she entirely loved him. This is an observation that I never knew fail, though I do not remember that any other has made it. The natural shyness of her sex hindered her from telling me the greatness of her own passion; but I easily collected it, from the representation she gave me of his. I have everything, says she, in Tranquillus that I can wish for; and enjoy in him (what indeed you have told me were to be met with in a good husband) the fondness of a lover, the tenderness of a parent, and the intimacy of a friend. It transported me to see her eyes swimming in tears of affection when she spoke. And is there not, Dear Sister, said I, more pleasure in the possession of such a man, than in all the little impertinencies[4] of balls, assemblies, and equipage, which it cost me so much pains to make you condemn? She answered, smiling, Tranquillus has made me a sincere convert in a few weeks, though I am afraid you could not have done it in your whole life. To tell you truly, I have only one fear hanging upon me, which is apt to give me trouble in the midst of all my satisfactions: I am afraid, you must know, that I shall not always make the same amiable appearance in his eye that I do at present. You know, Brother Bickerstaff, that you have the reputation of a conjurer; and if you have any one secret in your art to make your sister always beautiful, I should be happier than if I were mistress of all the worlds you have shown me in a starry night. Jenny (said I) without having recourse to magic, I shall give you one plain rule, that will not fail of making you always amiable to a man who has so great a passion for you, and is of so equal and reasonable a temper as Tranquillus. Endeavor to please, and you must please; be always in the same disposition as you are when you ask for this secret, and, you may take my word, you will never want it. An inviolable fidelity, good humor, and complacency of temper, outlive all the charms of a fine face, and make the decays of it invisible.

We discoursed very long upon this head, which was equally agreeable to us both; for I must confess, (as I tenderly love her) I take as much pleasure in giving her instructions for her welfare, as she herself does in receiving them. * * *

---

4. Irrelevancies, distractions.

Joseph Addison: Spectator No. 128
Friday, 27 July 1711

[VARIETY OF TEMPER[1]]

. . . Concordia discors.[2]

Women in their nature are much more gay and joyous than men; whether it be that their blood is more refined, their fibers more delicate, and their animal spirits more light and volatile; or whether, as some have imagined, there may not be a kind of sex in the very soul,[3] I shall not pretend to determine. As vivacity is the gift of women, gravity is that of men. They should each of them therefore keep a watch upon the particular bias which nature has fixed in their minds, that it may not draw too much, and lead them out of the paths of reason. This will certainly happen, if the one in every word and action affects the character of being rigid and severe, and the other of being brisk and airy. Men should beware of being captivated by a kind of savage philosophy, women by a thoughtless gallantry. Where these precautions are not observed, the man often degenerates into a cynic, the woman into a coquette; the man grows sullen and morose, the woman impertinent and fantastical.[4]

By what I have said we may conclude, men and women were made as counterparts to one another, that the pains and anxieties of the husband might be relieved by the sprightliness and good humor of the wife. When these are rightly tempered, care and cheerfulness go hand in hand; and the family, like a ship that is duly trimmed, wants neither sail nor ballast.

Natural historians observe (for whilst I am in the country I must fetch my allusions from thence[5]) that only the male birds have voices; that their songs begin a little before feeding-time, and end a little after; that whilst the hen is covering her eggs, the male generally takes his stand upon a neighboring bough within her hearing; and by that means amuses and diverts her with his songs during the whole time of her sitting.

This contract among birds lasts no longer than till a brood of young ones arises from it; so that in the feathered kind, the cares and fatigues of the married state, if I may so call it, lie principally upon the female. On the contrary, as in our species the man and woman are joined together for life, and the main burden rests upon the former, nature has given all the little arts of soothing and blandishment to the female, that she may cheer and animate her companion in a constant and assiduous application to the making a provision for his family, and the educating of their common children. This however is not to be taken so strictly, as if the same duties were not often reciprocal, and incumbent on both parties; but only to set forth what seems to have been the general intention of Nature, in the different inclinations and endowments which are bestowed on the different sexes.

But whatever was the reason that man and woman were made with this variety of temper, if we observe the conduct of the fair sex, we find that they choose rather to associate themselves with a person who resembles them in that light and volatile

---

1. Lady Mary Wortley Montagu praised this essay in a letter written to her husband shortly after it appeared: "One of the *Spectators* is very just, that says a man ought always to be on his guard against spleen and too severe a philosophy; a woman against levity and coquetry."
2. "Discordant concord" (i.e., harmony arising from difference; Lucan, *Pharsalia* 1.98).

3. In *Tatler* No. 172, Steele had asserted that "there is a sort of sex in souls" (i.e., an essential difference between men and women).
4. Irrelevant in her talk, preposterous in her thought.
5. Mr. Spectator is visiting the country estate of his friend and club fellow, Sir Roger de Coverley.

humor which is natural to them, than to such as are qualified to moderate and counterbalance it. It has been an old complaint, that the coxcomb carries it[6] with them before the man of sense. When we see a fellow loud and talkative, full of insipid life and laughter, we may venture to pronounce him a female favorite. Noise and flutter are such accomplishments as they cannot withstand. To be short, the passion of an ordinary woman for a man, is nothing else but self-love diverted upon another object: she would have the lover a woman in every thing but the sex. I do not know a finer piece of satire on this part of womankind than those lines of Mr. Dryden,

> Our thoughtless sex is caught by outward form
> And empty noise, and loves itself in man.[7]

This is a source of infinite calamities to the sex, as it frequently joins them to men who in their own thoughts are as fine creatures as themselves; or if they chance to be good-humored, serve only to dissipate their fortunes, inflame their follies, and aggravate their indiscretions.

The same female levity is no less fatal to them after marriage than before. It represents to their imaginations the faithful prudent husband as an honest tractable and domestic animal, and turns their thoughts upon the fine gay gentleman that laughs, sings, and dresses so much more agreeably.

As this irregular vivacity of temper leads astray the hearts of ordinary women in the choice of their lovers and the treatment of their husbands, it operates with the same pernicious influence towards their children, who are taught to accomplish themselves in all those sublime perfections that appear captivating in the eye of their mother. She admires in her son what she loved in her gallant; and by that means contributes all she can to perpetuate herself in a worthless progeny.

The younger Faustina[8] was a lively instance of this sort of women. Notwithstanding she was married to Marcus Aurelius, one of the greatest, wisest, and best of the Roman emperors, she thought a common gladiator much the prettier gentleman; and had taken such care to accomplish[9] her son Commodus according to her own notions of a fine man, that when he ascended the throne of his father, he became the most foolish and abandoned tyrant that was ever placed at the head of the Roman Empire, signalizing himself in nothing but the fighting of prizes, and knocking out men's brains. As he had no taste of true glory, we see him in several medals and statues which are still extant of him, equipped like an Hercules with a club and a lion's skin.

I have been led into this speculation by the characters I have heard of a country gentleman and his lady, who do not live many miles from Sir Roger. The wife is an old coquette, that is always hankering after the diversions of the town; the husband is a morose rustic, that frowns and frets at the name of it; the wife is overrun with affectation, the husband sunk into brutality. The lady cannot bear the noise of the larks and nightingales, hates your tedious summer days, and is sick at the sight of shady woods and purling streams; the husband wonders how any one can be pleased with the fooleries of plays and operas, and rails from morning to night at essenced[1] fops and tawdry courtiers. The children are educated in these different notions of their parents. The sons follow the father about his grounds, while the daughters read volumes of love letters and romances to their mother. By this means it comes to pass,

---

6. Succeeds.
7. From John Dryden's tragedy *Oedipus* (1.1).
8. Annia Galeria Faustina (d. 175 A.D.), wife of Marcus Aurelius (121–180 A.D.), cherished by her husband but

dispraised by ancient writers as an unfaithful wife.
9. Educate.
1. Perfumed.

that the girls look upon their father as a clown, and the boys think their mother no better than she should be.

How different are the lives of Aristus and Aspatia? The innocent vivacity of the one is tempered and composed by the cheerful gravity of the other. The wife grows wise by the discourses of the husband, and the husband good-humored by the conversations of the wife. Aristus would not be so amiable were it not for his Aspatia, nor Aspatia so much to be esteemed were it not for her Aristus. Their virtues are blended in their children, and diffuse through the whole family a perpetual spirit of benevolence, complacency, and satisfaction.

Eliza Haywood: *from* The Female Spectator, Vol. 1, No. 1
April 1744
[SEOMANTHE'S ELOPEMENT[1]]

Seomanthe, to her misfortune, was brought up under the tuition of her aunt Negratia,[2] a woman extremely sour by nature, but rendered yet more so by age and infirmity. Past all the joys of life herself, she looked with a malicious eye on every one who partook of them, censured the most innocent diversions in the severest manner, and the least complaisance between persons of different sexes was, with her, scandalous to the last degree. Her character was so well known that none but prudes, whose deformity was an antidote to desire (worn-out, superannuated rakes, who had outlived all sense of pleasure) and canting zealots,[3] whose bread depended on their hypocrisy, frequented her house. To this sort of company was the young, beautiful, and naturally gay Seomanthe condemned. She heard nothing but railing against that way of life she knew was enjoyed by others of equal rank and fortune with herself, and which she had too much good sense to look upon as criminal. She thought people might be perfectly innocent, yet indulge themselves in sometimes going to a play or opera; nor could be brought to believe the court such a bugbear[4] as she was told it was: a laced coat and a toupee wig had double charms for her, as they were every day so much preached against; and she never saw a coach pass, wherein were gentlemen and ladies, but she wished to be among them, or a well-dressed beau, with whom she did not languish to be acquainted.

At length her desires were fulfilled. Close as she was kept, the report that Negratia had a young lady in her house, who was mistress of a large fortune on the day of marriage, reached the ears of one of those harpies who purchase to themselves a wretched sustenance, by decoying the unwary into everlasting ruin. This creature, who had been employed by one so far a gentleman as to be bred to no business, and whose whole estate was laid out on his back,[5] in hopes of appearing charming in the eyes of some moneyed woman, too truly guessed she had found in Seomanthe what she sought. She came to the house under the pretense of offering some lace, holland,[6] and fine tea, extraordinary cheap. Negratia being what is called a good housewife, and a great lover of bargains, readily admitted her; and while she was examining some of the goods at a small distance off, the artful woman put a letter into Seoman-

---

1. Haywood tells this story to illustrate her point that it is sometimes wrong to blame young women for marrying unwisely; parents and other authorities "are sometimes, by an over-caution, guilty of forcing them into things, which otherwise would be far distant from their thoughts."

2. The name means "unpleasing."
3. People pretending to fanatic piety.
4. Danger (with the illusory connotation of "boogey-man").
5. Spent on clothing.
6. Imported fabric.

the's hand, telling her it came from the finest gentleman in the world, who she was sure would die, if she did not favor him with an answer. The young lady took it, blushed, and put it in her bosom, but had not time to make any reply to the woman, Negratia that instant coming towards them. As nobody understood her business better, she managed it so that she was ordered to come again the next day, when she said she should have greater variety to show their ladyships. While she was packing up her bundles, she winked on Seomanthe, and at the same time gave her the most beseeching look; the meaning of which, young and unexperienced as she was, the destined victim but too well comprehended, and was, perhaps, no less impatient for the success of an adventure, the beginning of which afforded her infinite satisfaction.

She ran immediately to her chamber, shut herself in, and broke open her billet,[7] which she found stuffed with flames, darts, wounds, love, and death; the highest encomiums on her beauty, and the most vehement imprecations of not outliving his hope of obtaining her favor—expressions which would have excited only the laughter of a woman who knew the world, but drew tears into the eyes of the innocent Seomanthe. She imagined he had seen her either at church or looking out of the window, for she was permitted to show herself in no other place; and doubted not but all he had wrote to her of his love and despair, was no less true than what she had heard delivered from the pulpit. She looked upon herself as too much obliged by the passion he had for her, not to write an answer full of complaisance, and very dexterously gave it to the woman, on her coming the next day.

On the ensuing Sunday she saw a strange gentleman in the next pew to her; by the glances he stole at her every time he could do it without being taken notice of, she fancied him the person who had declared himself her lover, and was convinced her conjecture had not deceived her, when being kneeled down at her devotions, he found means, while everyone had their fans before their faces, to drop a letter on the bench she leaned upon. She was not so much taken up with the business she was employed about, as not to see it immediately, and throwing her handkerchief over it, clapped it into her pocket. The looks that passed between them afterwards, during the time of divine service, confirmed her in the opinion that he was no less charmed with her than he said he was; and him, that the sight of him had not destroyed the impression his letter by the old woman had made on her.

Both thought they had reason to be highly satisfied with this interview; but poor Seomanthe was up to the head and ears in love. The person of the man was agreeable enough, and, compared to those Negratia had suffered her to converse with, angelic. The prepossession she had for him, at least, rendered him so in her eyes, and she thought every moment an age till she got home to read this second billet, the contents of which were of the same nature with the former, only a postscript added, entreating she would contrive some means to let him entertain her with his passion, by word of mouth. He mentioned the woman who sold the things, and by whose means he at first made a discovery of it,[8] and gave the directions where she lived; begged a meeting there, if possible; at least an answer, whether he might be so happy or not; which, he told her, he would wait for himself early the next morning under her window, if she would be so good as to throw it out.

She sighed at reading it; thought her fate very hard that it was not in her power to comply with the first part of his request, but hesitated not in the least if she ought to grant the other. She snatched the first opportunity she could lay hold on to

7. Letter.   8. I.e., had revealed his passion.

prepare a letter, in which she let him know how impossible it was for her to come out; but expressed such a regret at not being able to do so, as showed it would be no difficult matter to prevail on her to run the greatest lengths.

By the help of his adviser, he carried on a correspondence with her, which ended in her consenting to quit Negratia forever, and put herself under his protection. In fine, she packed up all her clothes and jewels, threw the former from the window to the woman, who stood ready to receive them on an appointed night; and having put the other into her pocket, exchanged one scene of hypocrisy for another, and flew from a life irksome for the present, to enter into one of lasting misery.

Early in the morning they were married, and it is possible passed some days in the usual transports of a bridal state. But when their place of abode was discovered by the friends and kindred of Seomanthe, who, distracted at her elopement, had searched the whole town, in how wretched a manner was she found! The villain had drawn her whole fortune out of the bank, robbed her of all her jewels and the best of her apparel, had shipped everything off, and was himself embarked she knew not to what place. The people of the house where they lodged, perceiving him, whom they expected to have been their paymaster, gone, seized on the few trifles he had left behind, as satisfaction for the rent, and were going to turn the unfortunate Seomanthe out of doors.

Not the sight of her distress, nor the lamentations she made, which were pitiful enough to have softened the most rugged hearts, had any effect on that of Negratia, who thought no punishment too severe for a person who had deceived her caution. But some others were of a more compassionate disposition. They took her home with them, and comforted her as well as they were able. She still lives with them a dependent on their courtesy, which she is obliged to purchase the continuance of, by rendering herself subservient to all their humors.[9] No news is yet arrived what course her wicked husband took; but it is supposed he is retired either to France or Holland, being almost as much in debt here, as all he wronged Seomanthe of would discharge; so that there is little probability of his ever returning, or if he did, that it would be at all to the satisfaction of his unhappy wife.

I was going on to recite some other instances of the mischiefs, which, for the most part, are the consequence of laying young people under too great a restraint, when Mira[1] came in, and seeing what I was about, took the pen out of my hand, and told me I had already said enough; if I proceeded to expatiate any farther on that head, I should be in danger of being understood to countenance an extreme on the other side,[2] which was much more frequently fatal to our sex.

I yielded to her superior judgment, and needed but few arguments to be convinced, that if unbridled youth were indulged in all the liberties it would take, we should scarce see anything but unhappy objects before maturity arrived.

Eliza Haywood: *from* The Female Spectator, Vol. 2, No. 10
February 1745

[WOMEN'S EDUCATION]

We[1] were beginning to lament the misfortunes our sex frequently fall into through the want of those improvements we are doubtless capable of, when a letter, left for us

---

9. Whims, moods.
1. One of the *Female Spectator*'s collaborators.

2. I.e., in favor of leniency.
1. The *Female Spectator* and her collaborators.

at our publisher's, was brought in which happened to be on that subject, and cannot anywhere be more properly inserted than in this place.

To the Female Spectator

Ladies,

Permit me to thank you for the kind and generous task you have undertaken in endeavoring to improve the minds and manners of our unthinking sex. It is the noblest act of charity you could exercise in an age like ours, where the sense of good and evil is almost extinguished, and people desire to appear more vicious than they really are, that so they may be less unfashionable. This humor, which is too prevalent in the female sex, is the true occasion of the many evils and dangers to which they are daily exposed. No wonder the men of sense disregard us! and the dissolute triumph over that virtue they ought to protect!

Yet I think it would be cruel to charge the ladies with all the errors they commit; it is most commonly the fault of a wrong education, which makes them frequently do amiss, while they think they act not only innocently but uprightly. It is therefore only the men—and the men of understanding, too—who, in effect, merit the blame of this, and are answerable for all the misconduct we are guilty of. Why do they call us silly women, and not endeavor to make us otherwise? God and Nature has endued them with means, and custom has established them in the power of rendering our minds such as they ought to be. How highly ungenerous is it then to give us a wrong turn, and then despise us for it!

The Mahometans indeed enslave their women, but then they teach them to believe their inferiority will extend to eternity. But our case is even worse than this; for while we live in a free country, and are assured from our excellent Christian principles that we are capable of those refined pleasures which last to immortality, our minds, our better parts, are wholly left uncultivated, and, like a rich soil neglected, bring forth nothing but noxious weeds.

There are, undoubtedly, no sexes in souls; and we are as able to receive and practice the impressions, not only of virtue and religion, but also of those sciences which the men engross to themselves, as they can be. Surely our bodies were not formed by the great Creator out of the finest mold, that our souls might be neglected like the coarsest of the clay?

O! would too imperious and too tenacious man be so just to the world as to be more careful of the education of those females to whom they are parents or guardians! Would they convince them in their infancy, that dress and show are not the essentials of a fine lady, and that true beauty is seated in the mind; how soon should we see our sex retrieve the many virtues which false taste has buried in oblivion! Strange infatuation! to refuse us what would so much contribute to their own felicity! Would not themselves reap the benefit of our amendment? Should we not be more obedient daughters, more faithful wives, more tender mothers, more sincere friends, and more valuable in every other station of life?

But, I find, I have let my pen run a much greater length than I at first intended. If I have said anything worthy your notice, or what you think the truth of the case, I hope you will mention this subject in some of your future essays; or if you find I have any way erred in my judgment, to set me right will be the greatest favor you can confer on,

Ladies,
Your constant reader,
And humble servant,
CLEORA

Hampton Court,
January 12, 1744–45

After thanking this lady for the favor of her obliging letter, we think it our duty to congratulate her on being one of those happy few who have been blessed with that sort of education which she so pathetically laments the want of in the greatest part of our sex.

Those men are certainly guilty of a great deal of injustice who think that all the learning becoming in a woman is confined to the management of her family; that is, to give orders concerning the table, take care of her children in their infancy, and observe that her servants do not neglect their business. All this, no doubt, is very necessary; but would it not be better if she performs those duties more through principle than custom? And will she be less punctual in her observance of them after she becomes a wife, for being perfectly convinced, before she is so, of the reasonableness of them, and why they are expected from her?

Many women have not been inspired with the least notion of even those requisites in a wife, and when they become so, continue the same loitering, lolloping, idle creatures they were before; and then the men are ready enough to condemn those who had the care of their education. * * *

⇒⊢ END OF PERSPECTIVES: READING PAPERS ⊣⇐

⊢ ⊞◈⊞ ⊣

Jonathan Swift
1667–1745

Charles Jervas, *Jonathan Swift.*

Arguably the greatest prose satirist in the history of English literature, Jonathan Swift was born in Dublin, the only son of English parents, seven months after his father died. In his infancy he was kidnapped by his nurse and did not see his mother for three years. With the future dramatist William Congreve he attended the Kilkenny School (Ireland's best), and in 1682 he began six years of study at Trinity College, Dublin. He received his B.A. degree in 1686. From 1689, Swift served as secretary to Sir William Temple (1628–1699), a retired diplomat whose father had befriended Swift's family. Swift worked at Temple's estate at Moor Park in Surrey for most of the next ten years. It was at Moor Park that Swift first experienced the vertigo, nausea, and hearing impairment of Ménière's syndrome, a disturbance of the inner ear that would plague him for the rest of his life and sometimes wrongly led him (and others) to question his mental stability. While working for Temple, Swift also wrote his first poems, undistinguished compositions that do not presage the literary acclaim that was to come.

Not content with his station in life, Swift took an M.A. degree from Oxford University in 1692; three years later, he was ordained a priest in the (Anglican) Church of Ireland and appointed to the undesirable prebendary of Kilroot, where he found the local Presbyterians unsympathetic and the salary meager. Added to professional discontent was personal disappointment: Swift was rejected in his marriage proposal to Jane "Varina" Waring, the daughter of an Anglican clergyman. Swift returned to Moor Park in 1696, and, after Temple died in 1699, held a series of ecclesiastical posts in Ireland, none of which fulfilled his ambition for an important position in England. In 1702 he was made Doctor of Divinity by his alma mater, Trinity College, Dublin.

While at Moor Park, Swift began to tutor an eight-year-old girl, Esther "Stella" Johnson, daughter of Sir William's late steward. Though she was nearly fourteen years Swift's junior, "Stella" would in time become his beloved companion and his most trusted friend. When she was eighteen, Swift described her as "one of the most beautiful, graceful, and agreeable young women in London." In 1701, at Swift's request, Stella and Sir William's spinster cousin, Rebecca Dingley, moved to Dublin, where they remained for the rest of their lives. Swift and Stella met regularly, but never alone. Although there has been much debate about the nature of their relationship, it is clear that Swift and Stella loved, trusted, and valued each other, whether or not they were ever secretly married (the evidence suggests they were not). Swift's *Journal to Stella* (composed 1710 to 1713) and the series of poems he composed for her birthdays reveal a playful intimacy and affection not seen in his more public writings.

Moor Park not only led him to Stella but was also the cradle of Swift's first major literary work: *A Tale of a Tub* (composed 1697 to 1698, published 1704), a brilliant satire on "corruptions in religion and learning," published with *The Battle of the Books*, Swift's mock-epic salvo in the debate between the Ancients and the Moderns. Like most of his subsequent works, *A Tale of a Tub* did not appear under Swift's name, though its ironic treatment of the church subsequently damaged his prospects for ecclesiastical preferment when his authorship became widely known.

In the first decade of the new century Swift placed his hopes for preferment with the Whigs, then in power, and became associated with the Whig writers Joseph Addison and Richard Steele, founder of the *Tatler*, a London periodical in which two of Swift's important early poems, *A Description of the Morning* (1709) and *A Description of a City Shower* (1710), first appeared. Swift's career as a political polemicist began when he rose to the defense of three Whig lords facing impeachment with his allegorical *Discourse of the Contests and Dissentions between the Nobles and Commons in Athens and Rome* (1701). His *Bickerstaff Papers* (1708–1709), witty parodies of the cobbler-turned-astrologer John Partridge, occasioned much laughter regardless of party allegiances. More important, Swift began to write a series of pamphlets on church affairs, including his ironical *Argument against Abolishing Christianity* (1708) and *A Letter . . . Concerning the Sacramental Test* (1709), which damaged his relationship with the Whigs.

While in London as an emissary for the Irish clergy in 1708, Swift met Esther "Vanessa" Vanhomrigh (pronounced "Vanummry") and, as with "Stella," acted as her mentor. Although his feelings for this attractive young woman (twenty-one years younger than he) clearly became more than paternal, Swift was eventually put off by her declaration of "inexpressible passion" and wrote *Cadenus and Vanessa* (composed 1713, published 1726) to cool the relationship.

Vehemently disagreeing with the Whig policies supporting the Dissenters (Protestants who were not members of the established church) because he feared they would weaken the Anglican church, Swift shifted his allegiance to the Tories in 1710 and soon became their principal spokesman and propagandist, taking charge of their weekly periodical the *Examiner* (1710–1711) and producing a series of highly effective political pamphlets, such as *The Conduct of the Allies* (1712), which called for an end to the War of Spanish Succession (1701–1713). Swift's years in London from 1710 to 1714, when he was an important lobbyist for the Church of Ireland and an influential agent of the Tory government, were the most exciting of his life.

In 1713 Swift was installed as Dean of Saint Patrick's Cathedral, Dublin—a prestigious appointment, but far short of the English bishopric he felt he deserved. Returning quickly to London, Swift became a vital presence in the Scriblerus Club—with Alexander Pope, John Arbuthnot, John Gay, Thomas Parnell, and Robert Harley, Earl of Oxford—which met in 1714. The influence of this group, with its love of parody, literary hoaxes, and the ridicule of false learning, is evident in *Gulliver's Travels*. Upon the death of Queen Anne in 1714 and the resultant fall of the Tory Ministry, Swift's hopes for further advancement were dashed, and he took up permanent residence in Ireland, where he conscientiously carried out his duties as Dean.

When Swift successfully defended Irish interests by writing *The Drapier's Letters* (1724–1725)—attacking a government plan to impose a new coin, "Wood's halfpence," that would devalue Ireland's currency and seriously damage the economy—he became a national hero. Thereafter, the people lit bonfires on his birthday and hailed him as a champion of Irish liberty, though he never ceased to regard Ireland as the land of his exile. From Dublin, he corresponded with Pope, Gay, Arbuthnot, and Henry St. John, Lord Bolingbroke; he enjoyed a long visit with his friends in England in 1726. While there, he encouraged Gay's *The Beggar's Opera* and Pope's *The Dunciad*, and arranged for the publication of his own masterpiece, *Gulliver's Travels* (1726).

When the death of George I the following year briefly created hopes of unseating "Prime Minister" Robert Walpole, Swift paid his final visit to England, where he assisted Pope in editing their joint *Miscellanies* in three volumes (1727, 1728, 1732). The years that followed in Dublin saw the production of many of Swift's finest poems, including *The Lady's Dressing Room* (1732), *A Beautiful Young Nymph Going to Bed* (1734), and *Verses on the Death of Dr. Swift* (composed 1731–1732, published 1739), his most celebrated poem. Swift continued to champion the cause of Irish political and economic freedom; with his like-minded friend Thomas Sheridan, he conducted a weekly periodical, the *Intelligencer* (1728). In 1729, he published his most famous essay, *A Modest Proposal*. Some years later, he supervised the publication of the first four volumes of his *Works* (1735) by the Dublin publisher George Faulkener.

When Swift reached his early seventies, his infirmities made him incapable of carrying out his clerical duties at Saint Patrick's; at seventy-five, he was found "of unsound mind and memory," and guardians were appointed to manage his affairs. In addition to ongoing debilities from Ménière's syndrome, he suffered from arteriosclerosis, aphasia, memory loss, and other diseases of old age; he was not insane, however, as many of his contemporaries believed. A devoted clergyman, Swift practiced the Christian charity he preached, giving more than half of his income to the needy; the founding of Ireland's first mental hospital through a generous provision in his will was the most famous of Swift's many benefactions.

Voltaire hailed Swift as the "English Rabelais," while Henry Fielding lauded him as the "English Lucian." Although the more delicate sensibilities of the nineteenth century eschewed his writings for their coarseness and truculence, twentieth-century readers have prized Swift's work for its intelligence, wit, and inventiveness. A committed champion of social justice and an untiring enemy of pride, Swift was a brilliant satirist in part because he was a thoroughgoing humanist.

A DESCRIPTION OF THE MORNING   Introducing this poem in the ninth number of his new periodical, the *Tatler* (for 30 April 1709), Richard Steele wrote that Swift, "has . . . run into a way [of writing] perfectly new, and described things exactly as they happen." *A Description of the Morning* is an early and important example of the "town eclogue," or urban pastoral, a poetic style further popularized by John Gay's *Trivia, or The Art of Walking the Streets of London* (1716). Traditionally, the eclogue—Virgil's bucolic poems are the most famous example—has no appreciable action or characterization, but depends on the thorough and evocative depiction of a pastoral scene. Swift's *Morning* imitates the conventions of pastoral description, not to portray the idealized natural harmony of Arcadia but rather to present the reality of social disorder masquerading under the appearance of order as day breaks over London. Remarkably, Alexander Pope's *Pastorals*, his first published poems, went on sale in the same week that Swift's pioneering mock-pastoral appeared, though the two future friends would not meet for several years.

A Description of the Morning

Now hardly° here and there a hackney coach[1]   *harshly*
Appearing, showed the ruddy morn's approach.

---

1. A hired coach, drawn by two horses and seating six   Apollo, Greek god of the sun.
people; here, equated with the chariot of Phoebus

Now Betty[2] from her master's bed has flown,
And softly stole to discompose her own.
5   The slipshod 'prentice from his master's door
Had pared° the dirt, and sprinkled round the floor.[3]   reduced
Now Moll had whirled her mop with dexterous airs,
Prepared to scrub the entry and the stairs.
The youth with broomy stumps began to trace
10   The kennel edge, where wheels had worn the place.[4]
The smallcoal man was heard with cadence deep;[5]
Till drowned in shriller notes of chimney sweep.
Duns° at his Lordship's gate began to meet;   creditors
And brickdust[6] Moll had screamed through half a street.
15   The turnkey now his flock returning sees,
Duly let out a-nights to steal for fees.[7]
The watchful bailiffs take their silent stands;
And schoolboys lag with satchels in their hands.[8]
1709   1709

A DESCRIPTION OF A CITY SHOWER   "They say 'tis the best thing I ever writ, and I think
so too," boasted Swift of his *Description of a City Shower* in 1710. It was first published in the
Tatler, No. 238, on 17 October 1710, soon after its composition. Swift's closely observed rendering of London street life playfully mocks the English imitators of Virgil, especially John
Dryden and his celebrated translation, *The Works of Virgil* (1697). We see, for example, Swift's
mock-heroic effects based on Virgil's *Aeneid* (29–19 B.C.), most notably in comparing the tim-
orous "beau" trapped in his sedan chair to the fierce Greek warriors hiding inside the Trojan
Horse, and in calling to mind the storm that led to Queen Dido's seduction and eventual ruin
(Dryden's translation 4.231–238). More important, just as Swift invoked the mock-pastoral in
A Description of the Morning, so too does he create a mock-georgic mode in his *City Shower*.
The division of the poem into portents, preliminaries, and deluge closely parallels the tempest
scene in Virgil's *Georgics* (36–29 B.C.; bk. 1, 431–458, 483–538 in Dryden), so that Swift uses
structural and verbal elements from a classical poem extolling the virtues of agriculture and
rural life to depict the teeming diversity of the contemporary urban scene.

A Description of a City Shower

Careful observers may foretell the hour
(By sure prognostics) when to dread a shower.
While rain depends,° the pensive cat gives o'er   is impending
Her frolics, and pursues her tail no more.
5   Returning home at night you find the sink[1]

2. Like "Moll" (line 7), a typical maidservant's name.
3. Fresh sawdust was used to absorb mud.
4. Scavenging in the gutters (kennels) "to find old nails" [Swift's note] was common.
5. Small pieces of coal or charcoal used to light fires; like many other products and services, they were sold by street vendors who advertised, or "cried," their wares by calling or singing as they walked the streets. The small-coal man has a deep voice; sweeps were always small boys.
6. An abrasive, used for cleaning or for sharpening knives.
7. As prisoners had to pay the jailer for food and for other

comforts, the jailer has let them out overnight to steal.
8. Cf. the second "age of man" in Shakespeare's *As You Like It*: "Then the whining schoolboy, with his satchel / And shining morning face, creeping like snail / Unwillingly to school" (2.7.145–47).
1. Sewer. The poem is built upon Swift's experiences in London: on November 8, 1710, Swift wrote to his beloved Stella (Esther Johnson) that "I will give ten shillings a week for my lodging; for I am almost stunk out of this with the sink, and it helps me to verses in my Shower." The parsimonious Swift normally spent around half this amount for lodgings.

Strike your offended sense with double stink.
If you be wise, then go not far to dine,
You spend in coach-hire more than save in wine.
A coming shower your shooting corns[2] presage,
10   Old aches[3] throb, your hollow tooth will rage:
Sauntering in coffee-house is Dulman seen;
He damns the climate, and complains of spleen.[4]

Meanwhile the South,° rising with dabbled° wings,   *south wind / muddy*
A sable cloud athwart the welkin° flings;   *sky*
15   That swilled more liquor than it could contain,
And like a drunkard gives it up again.
Brisk Susan whips her linen from the rope,[5]
While the first drizzling shower is borne aslope:°   *at a slant*
Such is that sprinkling which some careless quean°   *hussy*
20   Flirts° on you from her mop, but not so clean: *flicks*
You fly, invoke the gods; then turning, stop
To rail; she singing, still whirls on her mop.
Nor yet the dust had shunned th' unequal strife,
But aided by the wind, fought still for life;
25   And wafted with its foe by violent gust,
'Twas doubtful which was rain, and which was dust.[6]
Ah! Where must needy poet seek for aid,
When dust and rain at once his coat invade?
Sole coat, where dust cemented by the rain
30   Erects the nap, and leaves a cloudy stain.

Now in contiguous drops the flood comes down,
Threatening with deluge this devoted° town.   *doomed*
To shops in crowds the daggled° females fly,   *muddied*
Pretend to cheapen° goods, but nothing buy.   *bargain for*
35   The Templer spruce,[7] while every spout's abroach,[8]
Stays till 'tis fair, yet seems to call a coach.
The tucked-up seamstress walks with hasty strides,
While streams run down her oiled umbrella's sides.
Here various kinds by various fortunes led,
40   Commence acquaintance underneath a shed.°   *shelter*
Triumphant Tories, and desponding Whigs,[9]
Forget their feuds, and join to save their wigs.
Boxed° in a chair[1] the beau impatient sits,   *confined*

2. The shooting pain in your corns.
3. Pronounced "aitches."
4. Dulman (a descriptive name) complains of melancholy or depression, then attributed to the spleen.
5. The typically named maid brings in her washing from the line.
6. Swift here parallels a line from Samuel Garth's popular satirical poem, *The Dispensary* (1699): "'Tis doubtful

which is sea, and which is sky" (5.176).
7. Well-dressed lawyer.
8. Drainpipe pouring water.
9. 1710, the year this poem was written, was the first year of the Tory ministry under Queen Anne.
1. A sedan chair, carried by two men; this one has a leather roof.

While spouts run clattering o'er the roof by fits;
45 And ever and anon with frightful din
The leather sounds; he trembles from within.
So when Troy chairmen bore the wooden steed,
Pregnant with Greeks, impatient to be freed;
(Those bully Greeks, who, as the moderns do,
50 Instead of paying chairmen, run them through[2])
Laocoon struck the outside with his spear,
And each imprisoned hero quaked for fear.[3]

Now from all parts the swelling kennels[4] flow,
And bear their trophies with them as they go:
55 Filths of all hues and odors, seem to tell
What streets they sailed from, by the sight and smell.
They, as each torrent drives with rapid force
From Smithfield, or St. Pulchre's shape their course;[5]
And in huge confluent join at Snow Hill ridge,
60 Fall from the conduit prone to Holborn Bridge.[6]
Sweepings from butchers' stalls, dung, guts, and blood,
Drowned puppies, stinking sprats,° all drenched in mud,   } small fish
Dead cats and turnip tops come tumbling down the flood.[7]

1710   1710

STELLA'S BIRTHDAY Between 1719 and 1727 Swift wrote seven birthday poems to "Stella," his dear Esther Johnson. The two reprinted here are his first and last. Swift's earliest use of the name "Stella" in verse was in the first of this series of celebratory verses, which play on the obligation of the Poet Laureate to write an official "birthday ode" for the monarch every year. Placing himself in the role of her laureate, Swift may have chosen the name "Stella" to highlight the difference between his own uncontrived expressions of affection and those of the courtly Sir Philip Sidney in *Astrophil and Stella* (1591). Like Shakespeare's Sonnet 130 ("My mistress' eyes are nothing like the sun"), Swift's first poem on Stella's birthday violates the traditions of the conventional love lyric by calling attention to his beloved's considerable weight and age, only to suggest that his admiration of her lies in her deeper virtues. In his last birthday poem, Swift attempts to escape from the prospect of Stella's impending death, first by humor and then by the power of reason; when these fail, he tenderly acknowledges how much she means to him. Swift was to sail for England less than a month after he gave those verses to her—both knew that they might never see each other again. Though more formal than the *Journal to Stella*, Swift's birthday verses were written primarily for Stella's enjoyment and for the entertainment of their small circle of intimate friends. Despite the private nature of these poems, Swift nevertheless authorized their publication in the third and last volume of the Pope-Swift *Miscellanies*, which appeared in March 1728.

2. With their swords.
3. When the Trojans carried the Greek's wooden horse into Troy, thinking that the opposing army had given up their siege, the priest Laocoon was suspicious, and struck the horse. See *Aeneid* 2.50–53.
4. Gutters, which were also open sewers.
5. Respectively, the cattle market and the parish west of the Newgate prison.
6. Snow Hill ridge extended down to Holborn Bridge, which spanned Fleet ditch, used as an open sewer; from 1343, local butchers had been given permission to dump

entrails in the Fleet.
7. These last three lines were intended against the licentious manner of modern poets, in making three rhymes together, which they call *Triplets*; and the last of the three was two, or sometimes more syllables longer, called an *Alexandrian*. These *Triplets* and *Alexandrians* were brought in by Dryden, and other poets in the reign of Charles II. They were the mere effect of haste, idleness, and want of money, and have been wholly avoided by the best poets since these verses were written [Swift's note].

Stella's Birthday, 1719
WRITTEN IN THE YEAR 1718/9[1]

Stella this day is thirty-four,[2]
(We shan't dispute a year or more):
However, Stella, be not troubled,
Although thy size and years are doubled,
5   Since first I saw thee at sixteen,[3]
The brightest virgin on the green.[4]
So little is thy form° declined;   *figure*
Made up° so largely in thy mind.   *compensated*

  Oh, would it please the gods to *split*
10 Thy beauty, size, and years, and wit,
No age could furnish out a pair
Of nymphs so graceful, wise, and fair:
With half the luster of your eyes,
With half your wit, your years, and size:
15 And then before it grew too late,
How should I beg of gentle fate,
(That either nymph might have her swain),
To split my worship too in twain.

1719   1728

Stella's Birthday, 1727

This day, whate'er the fates decree,
Shall still be kept with joy by me:
This day then, let us not be told,
That you are sick, and I grown old,
5   Nor think on our approaching ills,
And talk of spectacles and pills.
Tomorrow will be time enough
To hear such mortifying stuff.[1]
Yet, since from reason may be brought
10 A better and more pleasing thought,
Which can in spite of all decays,

---

1. Until the calendar was reformed in 1751, the new year legally began on the Feast of the Annunciation (sometimes called "Lady Day") on March 25th, though January 1st was also commonly recognized as the start of the new year. Therefore, to avoid confusion, it was a widely accepted practice to write dates between January 1 and March 24 according to both methods of reckoning: 1718/19. Since Swift's poem was composed in February or March, we would say it was written in 1719.

2. Stella (Esther Johnson) actually celebrated her thirty-eighth birthday on 13 March 1719.
3. Swift first met Stella when she was eight years old; he may have "seen" her only when she grew from child to woman.
4. The village green, or common land, here implies a pastoral simplicity that suggests the natural innocence of their relationship.
1. Both humbling and leading to death. Stella died less than a year later.

Support a few remaining days:
From not the gravest of divines,°   *clergymen*
Accept for once some serious lines.

15   Although we now can form no more
Long schemes of life, as heretofore;
Yet you, while time is running fast,
Can look with joy on what is past.

Were future happiness and pain[2]
20   A mere contrivance of the brain,
As atheists argue, to entice
And fit their proselytes° for vice   *converts*
(The only comfort they propose,
To have companions in their woes);
25   Grant this the case, yet sure 'tis hard,
That virtue, styled its own reward,
And by all sages understood
To be the chief of human good,
Should acting, die, nor leave behind
30   Some lasting pleasure in the mind;
Which by remembrance will assuage
Grief, sickness, poverty, and age;
And strongly shoot a radiant dart
To shine through life's declining part.

35   Say, Stella, feel you no content,
Reflecting on a life well spent?
Your skillful hand employed to save
Despairing wretches from the grave;[3]
And then supporting with your store,
40   Those whom you dragged from death before
(So Providence on mortals waits,
Preserving what it first creates);
Your generous boldness to defend
An innocent and absent friend;
45   That courage which can make you just,
To merit humbled in the dust;
The detestation you express
For vice in all its glittering dress;
That patience under torturing pain,
50   Where stubborn Stoics would complain.

Shall these like empty shadows pass,
Or forms reflected from a glass?
Or mere chimeras° in the mind,   *imaginary creatures or notions*
That fly and leave no marks behind?

2. I.e., heaven and hell.
3. Swift often praised Stella's charity, not only for nursing

him in his bouts of illness, but also for attending to the
poor in her neighborhood.

55   Does not the body thrive and grow
       By food of twenty years ago?
       And had it not been still supplied,
       It must a thousand times have died.
       Then, who with reason can maintain
60   That no effects of food remain?
       And is not virtue in mankind
       The nutriment that feeds the mind?
       Upheld by each good action past,
       And still continued by the last:
65   Then who with reason can pretend,
       That all effects of virtue end?

           Believe me, Stella, when you show
       That true contempt for things below,
       Nor prize your life for other ends
70   Than merely to oblige your friends;
       Your former actions claim their part,
       And join to fortify your heart.
       For Virtue in her daily race,
       Like Janus[4] bears a double face;
75   Looks back with joy where she has gone,
       And therefore goes with courage on.
       She at your sickly couch will wait,
       And guide you to a better state.

           O then, whatever Heaven intends,
80   Take pity on your pitying friends;
       Nor let your ills affect your mind,
       To fancy they can be unkind.
       Me, surely me, you ought to spare,
       Who gladly would your sufferings share;
85   Or give my scrap of life to you,
       And think it far beneath your due;
       You, to whose care so oft I owe
       That I'm alive to tell you so.

1727   1728

THE LADY'S DRESSING ROOM   The first of Swift's so-called scatological poems, which have attracted much critical attention and amateur psychoanalysis, these verses enjoyed considerable popularity in Swift's lifetime, though some contemporaries condemned them as "deficient in point of delicacy, even to the highest degree." One of Swift's friends recorded in her memoirs that *The Lady's Dressing Room* made her mother "instantly" lose her lunch. Sir Walter Scott found in this poem (and other pieces by Swift) "the marks of an incipient disorder of the mind, which induced the author to dwell on degrading and disgusting subjects." If Pope's *The Rape of the Lock* describes Belinda at the "altar" of her dressing table undergoing "the sacred rites of pride" as she and her maid apply all manner of cosmetics to make her a beautiful

---

4. The god of doorways and of the rising and setting sun, whose two-faced head looks forward and backward, and after whom the month of January is named.

"goddess" and arm her for the battle of the sexes, then *The Lady's Dressing Room* reveals the coarse realities of Celia's embodiment—a humorous and disturbing corrective to the pretense and false appearances on which her glorification depends. Although Swift assails the social and literary conventions that celebrate women for their superficial qualities, there is also a misogynistic quality to the poem, which may be attributable to his anger and disappointment over his beloved Stella's death in January 1728. Nevertheless, Strephon is ridiculed for being so naively idealistic about his lover and so easily deceived by appearances; once his secret investigations free him from his illusions, Strephon's permanent revulsion and rejection of all women show his inability to follow a middle course by appreciating women in their complex reality.

The Lady's Dressing Room

Five hours (and who can do it less in?)
By haughty Celia spent in dressing;
The goddess from her chamber issues,
Arrayed in lace, brocade, and tissues:
5   Strephon,[1] who found the room was void,
And Betty[2] otherwise employed,
Stole in, and took a strict survey,
Of all the litter as it lay:
Whereof, to make the matter clear,
10   An *inventory* follows here.

    And first, a dirty smock appeared,
Beneath the arm-pits well besmeared;
Strephon, the rogue, displayed it wide,
And turned it round on every side.
15   In such a case few words are best,
And Strephon bids us guess the rest;
But swears how damnably the men lie,
In calling Celia sweet and cleanly.

    Now listen while he next produces
20   The various combs for various uses,
Filled up with dirt so closely fixed,
No brush could force a way betwixt;
A paste of composition rare,
Sweat, dandruff, powder, lead,[3] and hair,
25   A forehead cloth with oil upon't
To smooth the wrinkles on her front;
Here alum flour[4] to stop the steams,
Exhaled from sour, unsavory streams;
There night-gloves made of Tripsy's[5] hide,
30   Bequeathed by Tripsy when she died;
With puppy water,[6] beauty's help,

---

1. Strephon and Celia are names usually associated with pastoral poetry, and are therefore used mockingly here.
2. A typical maidservant's name.
3. White lead face paint, used to whiten the skin.
4. Powdered alum used like modern antiperspirant.
5. Celia's lapdog; no fashionable lady was without such a pet.

6. A recipe for this cosmetic, made from the innards of a pig or a fat puppy, was given in the "Fop's Dictionary" in *Mundus Muliebris* [Womanly Make-up]: *Or, the Ladies' Dressing Room Unlocked* (1690), which Swift also used for other terms.

Distilled from Tripsy's darling whelp.
Here gallipots° and vials placed,   *ointment jars*
Some filled with washes, some with paste;
35   Some with pomatum,° paints, and slops,   *hair ointment*
And ointments good for scabby chops.°   *lips or cheeks*
Hard° by a filthy basin stands,   *close*
Fouled with the scouring of her hands;
The basin takes whatever comes,
40   The scrapings of her teeth and gums,
A nasty compound of all hues,
For here she spits, and here she spews.

But oh! it turned poor Strephon's bowels,
When he beheld and smelt the towels;
45   Begummed, bemattered, and beslimed;
With dirt, and sweat, and ear-wax grimed.
No object Strephon's eye escapes,
Here, petticoats in frowzy° heaps;   *unkempt*
Nor be the handkerchiefs forgot,
50   All varnished o'er with snuff[7] and snot.
The stockings why should I expose,
Stained with the moisture of her toes;
Or greasy coifs and pinners° reeking,   *night caps*
Which Celia slept at least a week in?
55   A pair of tweezers next he found
To pluck her brows in arches round,
Or hairs that sink the forehead low,
Or on her chin like bristles grow.

The virtues we must not let pass
60   Of Celia's magnifying glass;
When frighted Strephon cast his eye on't,
It showed the visage of a giant:[8]
A glass that can to sight disclose
The smallest worm in Celia's nose,
65   And faithfully direct her nail
To squeeze it out from head to tail;
For catch it nicely by the head,
It must come out alive or dead.

Why, Strephon, will you tell the rest?
70   And must you needs describe the chest?
That careless wench! no creature warn her
To move it out from yonder corner,
But leave it standing full in sight,

7. Powdered tobacco, sniffed by fashionable men and women alike.
8. Cf. *Gulliver's Travels*, Part 2, "A Voyage to Brobding-nag," ch. 1: "This made me reflect upon the fair skins of our *English* ladies, who appear so beautiful to us, only because they are of our own size, and their defects not to be seen but through magnifying glass, where we find by experiment that the smoothest and whitest skins look rough and coarse, and ill colored."

For you to exercise your spite!
75   In vain the workman showed his wit
With rings and hinges counterfeit
To make it seem in this disguise
A cabinet to vulgar eyes;
Which Strephon ventured to look in,
80   Resolved to go through *thick and thin*;
He lifts the lid: there need no more,
He smelt it all the time before.

As, from within Pandora's box,
When Epimethus oped the locks,
85   A sudden universal crew
Of human evils upward flew;[9]
He still was comforted to find
That hope at last remained behind.

So, Strephon, lifting up the lid
90   To view what in the chest was hid,
The vapors flew from out the vent,
But Strephon cautious never meant
The bottom of the pan to grope,
And foul his hands in search of hope.

95   O! ne'er may such a vile machine°   construction
Be once in Celia's chamber seen!
O! may she better learn to keep
"Those secrets of the hoary deep."[1]

As mutton cutlets, prime of meat,
100   Which though with art you salt and beat
As laws of cookery require,
And roast them at the clearest fire;
If from adown the hopeful chops
The fat upon a cinder drops,
105   To stinking smoke it turns the flame
Poisoning the flesh from whence it came;
And up exhales a greasy stench
For which you curse the careless wench:
So things which must not be expressed,
110   When *plumped*° into the reeking chest,   dropped
Send up an excremental smell
To taint the parts from which they fell:
The petticoats and gown perfume,
And waft a stink round every room.

115   Thus finishing his grand survey,
The swain disgusted slunk away,

9. In Greek mythology, Epimethus, acting against advice, opened the box Jove had given his wife Pandora, and all the evils and vices of the world flew out, leaving only hope in the box.
1. Quoting Milton's *Paradise Lost* 2.891, in which Sin is unleashing the chaotic forces of her infernal realm.

Repeating in his amorous fits,
"Oh! Celia, Celia, Celia shits!"

But Vengeance, goddess never sleeping,
120 Soon punished Strephon for his peeping.
His foul imagination links
Each dame he sees with all her stinks:
And if unsavory odors fly,
Conceives a lady standing by:
125 All women his description fits,
And both ideas jump° like wits   *join together*
By vicious fancy coupled fast,
And still appearing in contrast.

I pity wretched Strephon, blind
130 To all the charms of womankind;
Should I the queen of love refuse,
Because she rose from stinking ooze?[2]
To him that looks behind the scene,
Statira's but some pocky quean.[3]

135 When Celia in her glory shows,
If Strephon would but stop his nose,
Who now so impiously blasphemes
Her ointments, daubs, and paints and creams;
Her washes, slops, and every clout,[4]
140 With which she makes so foul a rout;[5]
He soon would learn to think like me,
And bless his ravished eyes to see
Such order from confusion sprung,
Such gaudy *tulips* raised from *dung*.

c. 1730   1732

❧

RESPONSE

Lady Mary Wortley Montagu: The Reasons that Induced Dr. S. to write a Poem called The Lady's Dressing Room[1]

The Doctor in a clean starched band,
His golden snuff box in his hand,

2. Venus, Roman goddess of sexual love and physical beauty, rose from the sea.
3. One of the heroines of Nathaniel Lee's highly popular tragedy *The Rival Queens* (1677); Swift's common slattern (quean) has had either smallpox or venereal disease.
4. Washes were either treated water used for the complexion or stale urine used as a detergent; clouts were rags.
5. Both of her skin and, presumably, of the men.
1. Lady Mary Wortley Montagu, energetic traveler and versatile writer, found in Swift an object of recurrent scorn. *Gulliver's Travels* (and particularly its fourth book)

she dismissed as filth, perpetrated upon a "mad" and inexplicably admiring readership. When "The Lady's Dressing Room" appeared, Montagu crafted her own verse retort. Here, with formidable mimicry, she echoes Swift's method (the catalogue of disconcerting physical particulars), his meter, his phrasings, and his thoughts in such a way that they recoil upon their maker. What Swift depicts as disillusion (Strephon's), Montagu re-reckons as self-delusion (Swift's). The trauma that he derives from Celia's fabrications, she ascribes instead to the Dean's own fears and failures. (For more on Montagu, see page 1353.)

With care his diamond ring displays
And artful shows its various rays,
5   While grave he stalks down —— street
His dearest Betty —— to meet.[2]
        Long had he waited for this hour,
Nor gained admittance to the bower,
Had joked and punned, and swore and writ,
10   Tried all his gallantry and wit,[3]
Had told her oft what part he bore
In Oxford's schemes in days of yore,[4]
But bawdy,° politics, nor satire   *obscenity*
Could move this dull hard hearted creature.
15   Jenny her maid could taste° a rhyme   *enjoy*
And, grieved to see him lose his time,
Had kindly whispered in his ear,
"For twice two pound you enter here;
My lady vows without that sum
20   It is in vain you write or come."
        The destined offering now he brought,
And in a paradise of thought,
With a low bow approached the dame,
Who smiling heard him preach his flame.
25   His gold she takes (such proofs as these
Convince most unbelieving shes)
And in her trunk rose up to lock it
(Too wise to trust it in her pocket)
And then, returned with blushing grace,
30   Expects the doctor's warm embrace.
        But now this is the proper place
Where morals stare me in the face,
And for the sake of fine expression
I'm forced to make a small digression.
35   Alas for wretched humankind,
With learning mad, with wisdom blind!
The ox thinks he's for saddle fit
(As long ago friend Horace writ[5])
And men their talents still mistaking,[6]
40   The stutterer fancies his is speaking.
With admiration oft we see
Hard features heightened by toupée,
The beau affects° the politician,   *pretends to be*
Wit is the citizen's ambition,
45   Poor Pope philosophy displays on
With so much rhyme and little reason,
And though he argues ne'er so long

---

2. In Swift's poem, Betty is the maid's name, Celia the mistress's.
3. Montagu echoes Swift's poem *Cadenus and Vanessa*, where the clumsy lover "Had sighed and languished, vowed and writ, / For pastime, or to show his wit" (542–43).

4. Swift had collaborated closely in the political schemes of Robert Harley, first Earl of Oxford (1661–1724).
5. "The ox desires the saddle" (Horace, *Epistles* 1.14.43).
6. In this line, Montague echoes an idea, and a way of wording it, that Swift used often in his work.

That all is right, his head is wrong.[7]
　　None strive to know their proper merit
50　But strain for wisdom, beauty, spirit,
And lose the praise that is their due
While they've th' impossible in view.
So have I seen the injudicious heir
To add one window the whole house impair.
55　　Instinct the hound does better teach,
Who never undertook to preach;
The frighted hare from dogs does run
But not attempts to bear a gun.
Here many noble thoughts occur
60　But I prolixity abhor,
And will pursue th' instructive tale
To show the wise in some things fail.
　　The reverend lover with surprise ⎫
Peeps in her bubbies, and her eyes, ⎬
65　And kisses both, and tries—and tries. ⎭
The evening in this hellish play,
Beside his guineas thrown away,
Provoked the priest to that degree
He swore, "The fault is not in me.
70　Your damned close stool° so near my nose,　　　　　　*chamber pot*
Your dirty smock, and stinking toes
Would make a Hercules as tame
As any beau that you can name."[8]
　　The nymph grown furious roared, "By God
75　The blame lies all in sixty odd,"[9]
And scornful pointing to the door
Cried, "Fumbler, see my face no more."
"With all my heart I'll go away,
But nothing done, I'll nothing pay.
80　Give back the money." "How," cried she,
"Would you palm such a cheat on me!
For poor four pound to roar and bellow—
Why sure you want some new Prunella?"[1]
"I'll be revenged, you saucy quean"°　　　　　　　　*whore*
85　(Replies the disappointed Dean)
"I'll so describe your dressing room
The very Irish shall not come."
She answered short, "I'm glad you'll write.
You'll furnish paper when I shite."[2]

　　　　　　　　　　　　　　　　　　　　　　　1734

<hr/>

7. Montagu ridicules Pope's conclusion to Epistle 1 of *An
Essay on Man*: "Whatever IS, is RIGHT." Over the previous
few years, her long, ardent friendship with Pope had dissolved in rancor.
8. In these four lines, Montagu compacts some scattered
particulars and the sustained conclusion of Swift's poem:
ll. 11–14, 51–52, 69ff.

9. I.e., Swift's impotence derives not from her odors but
from his age (65 at the time the poem was written).
1. "Prunella" is both a fabric used in clergy vestments
(Swift was a clergyman), and the name of the promiscuous, low-born heroine in Richard Estcourt's comic inter-
lude, *Prunella* (1708).
2. Compare line 118 of Swift's poem.

GULLIVER'S TRAVELS   *Travels into Several Remote Nations of the World. In Four Parts. By Lemuel Gulliver*—better known as *Gulliver's Travels*—was first published in late October 1726 and enjoyed instant success. One contemporary observer noted that "several thousands sold in a week," and Swift's London friends wrote to him in Dublin to say that everyone was reading and talking about Gulliver. Readers continue to be fascinated by Swift's masterpiece: since 1945, more than 500 books and scholarly articles have been devoted to *Gulliver's Travels*. Variously classified as an early novel, an imaginary voyage, a moral and political allegory, and even a children's story, Lemuel Gulliver's four journeys, representing the four directions of the globe, comprise a survey of the human condition: a comic, ironic, and sometimes harrowing answer to the question, "What does it mean to be a human being?"

In the first voyage, the diminutive citizens of Lilliput represent human small-mindedness and petty ambitions. Filled with self-importance, the Lilliputians are cruel, treacherous, malicious, and destructive. The perspective is reversed in the second voyage to Brobdingnag, land of giants, where Gulliver has the stature of a Lilliputian. He is humbled by his own helplessness and, finding the huge bodies of the Brobdingnagians grotesque, he realizes how repulsive the Lilliputians must have found him. When Gulliver gives the wise king an account of the political affairs of England—which manifest hypocrisy, avarice, and hatred—the enlightened monarch concludes that most of the country's inhabitants must be "the most pernicious race of little odious vermin that Nature ever suffered to crawl upon the surface of the earth." In the third voyage (which was written last), Gulliver visits the flying island of Laputa and the metropolis of Lagado, on an adjacent continent, where he encounters the misuse of human reason. In Laputa, those who are supposedly "wise" lack all common sense and practical ability; at Lagado, the Academy of Projectors is staffed by professors who waste both money and intelligence on absurd endeavors. Swift aims his satire at so-called intellectuals—especially the "virtuosi," or amateur scientists of the Royal Society—who live in the world of their own speculations and so fail to use their gifts for the common good. Throughout *Gulliver's Travels* that which is admirable is held up to expose corruption in the reader's world, and that which is deplorable is identified with the institutions and practices associated with contemporary Europe, particularly Britain.

Gulliver's fourth voyage (printed in its entirety below) finds him on the island of the Houyhnhnms, horses endowed with reason, whose highly rational and well-ordered (though emotionally sterile) society is contrasted with the violence, selfishness, and brutality of the Yahoos, irrational beasts who bear a disconcerting resemblance to humans. In his foolish pride, Gulliver believes that he can escape the human condition and live as a stoical Houyhnhnm, even when he returns to his family in England. Of course, Gulliver is neither Houyhnhnm nor Yahoo, but a man. His time in Houyhnhnm-land does not teach him to be more rational or compassionate, but makes him more foolish, derelict in his duties as husband, father, and citizen. Instead of seeking to become a better man, Gulliver strives to become what he is not—with results that are both tragic and farcical. Although the poet Edward Young charged Swift with having "blasphemed a nature little lower than that of the angels" in satirizing the follies of humankind, *Gulliver's Travels* reveals the Dean of Saint Patrick's to be more a humanist than a misanthrope. With brilliantly modulated ironic self-awareness, Swift's painful comedy of exposure to the truth of human frailty demonstrates that there is no room for the distortions of human pride in a world where our practices are so evidently at variance with our principles. Swift advances no program of social reform, but provokes a new recognition—literally, a rethinking—of our own humanity.

from Gulliver's Travels

from *Part 3. A Voyage to Laputa*

CHAPTER 5

The author permitted to see the grand Academy of Lagado. The Academy largely[1] described. The arts wherein the professors employ themselves.

This Academy is not an entire single building, but a continuation of several houses on both sides of a street, which growing waste,[2] was purchased and applied to that use.

I was received very kindly by the Warden, and went for many days to the Academy. Every room has in it one or more projectors,[3] and I believe I could not be[4] in fewer than five hundred rooms.

The first man I saw was of a meager aspect, with sooty hands and face, his hair and beard long, ragged and singed in several places. His clothes, shirt, and skin were all of the same color. He had been eight years upon a project for extracting sunbeams out of cucumbers,[5] which were to be put into vials hermetically sealed, and let out to warm the air in raw, inclement summers. He told me, he did not doubt in eight years more, that he should be able to supply the Governor's gardens with sunshine at a reasonable rate; but he complained that his stock was low, and entreated me to give him something as an encouragement to ingenuity,[6] especially since this had been a very dear season for cucumbers. I made him a small present, for my Lord[7] had furnished me with money on purpose, because he knew their practice of begging from all who go to see them.

I went into another chamber, but was ready to hasten back, being almost overcome with a horrible stink. My conductor pressed me forward, conjuring me in a whisper to give no offense, which would be highly resented, and therefore I durst not so much as stop my nose. The projector of this cell was the most ancient student of the Academy. His face and beard were of a pale yellow; his hands and clothes daubed over with filth. When I was presented to him, he gave me a very close embrace (a compliment I could well have excused). His employment from his first coming into the Academy was an operation to reduce human excrement to its original food, by separating the several parts, removing the tincture which it receives from the gall, making the odor exhale, and scumming off the saliva. He had a weekly allowance from the Society of a vessel filled with human ordure,[8] about the bigness of a Bristol barrel.[9]

I saw another at work to calcine[1] ice into gunpowder, who likewise showed me a treatise he had written concerning the malleability of fire,[2] which he intended to publish.

---

1. In general. The academy is a satire of the Royal Society, founded in 1662 for the purpose of scientific experimentation. Though many of its members made major contributions to science, the Society had a reputation for bizarre speculation. Swift had visited the Society in 1710 and here parodies actual experiments recorded in its *Philosophical Transactions;* he is also parodying the description of "Solomon's House," an academy of science in Francis Bacon's *New Atlantis* (1626).
2. Falling into disuse.
3. Those people undertaking the project.
4. Could not have been.

5. Stephen Hales (1677–1761), English botanist and physiologist, had recently investigated sunlight's agency in plant respiration. This and other studies were published in his *Vegetable Staticks* (1726).
6. His investigative powers.
7. The warden of the Academy.
8. Excrement.
9. A medium-size barrel, holding about 37 gallons.
1. Desiccate.
2. Cf. Rabelais, *Gargantua and Pantagruel* (1532–1564), bk. 5, ch. 22: "Others were cutting fire with a knife, and drawing water up in a net."

There was a most ingenious architect who had contrived a new method for building houses, by beginning at the roof and working downwards to the foundation, which he justified to me by the like practice of those two prudent insects, the bee and the spider.

There was a man born blind, who had several apprentices in his own condition: their employment was to mix colors for painters, which their master taught them to distinguish by feeling and smelling.[3] It was indeed my misfortune to find them at that time not very perfect in their lessons, and the professor himself happened to be generally mistaken: this artist is much encouraged and esteemed by the whole fraternity.

In another apartment I was highly pleased with a projector, who had found a device of ploughing the ground with hogs, to save the charges of ploughs, cattle, and labor. The method is this; in an acre of ground you bury, at six inches distance, and eight deep, a quantity of acorns, dates, chestnuts, and other mast[4] or vegetables whereof these animals are fondest: then you drive six hundred or more of them into the field, where in a few days they will root up the whole ground in search of their food, and make it fit for sowing, at the same time manuring it with their dung; it is true upon experiment they found the charge and trouble very great, and they had little or no crop. However, it is not doubted that this invention may be capable of great improvement.

I went into another room, where the walls and ceiling were all hung round with cobwebs, except a narrow passage for the artist[5] to go in and out. At my entrance he called aloud to me not to disturb his webs. He lamented the fatal mistake the world had been so long in of using silkworms, while we had such plenty of domestic insects, who infinitely excelled the former, because they understood how to weave as well as spin. And he proposed farther, that by employing spiders, the charge[6] of dyeing silks would be wholly saved, whereof I was fully convinced when he showed me a vast number of flies most beautifully colored, wherewith he fed his spiders, assuring us, that the webs would take a tincture from them; and as he had them of all hues, he hoped to fit everybody's fancy, as soon as he could find proper food for the flies, of certain gums, oils, and other glutinous matter to give a strength and consistence to the threads.

There was an astronomer who had undertaken to place a sundial upon the great weathercock on the Town House,[7] by adjusting the annual and diurnal motions of the earth and sun, so as to answer and coincide with all accidental turnings of the wind.

I was complaining of a small fit of the colic, upon which my conductor led me into a room, where a great physician resided, who was famous for curing that disease by contrary operations from the same instrument. He had a large pair of bellows with a long slender muzzle of ivory. This he conveyed eight inches up the anus, and drawing in the wind, he affirmed he could make the guts as lank as a dried bladder. But when the disease was more stubborn and violent, he let in the muzzle while the bellows was full of wind, which he discharged into the body of the patient, then withdrew the instrument to replenish it, clapping his thumb strongly against the orifice of

3. Based on Robert Boyle's account in *Experiments and Observations Upon Colors* (1665), of a blind man who could distinguish colors.
4. Nuts.
5. Modeled on both the Frenchman M. Bon, who believed silk could be made from cobwebs, and Dr. Wall,

who suggested that the excreta of ants fed on plant sap could be used as dye; both suggestions were published in the *Transactions of the Royal Society*.
6. Expense.
7. Town Hall.

the fundament; and this being repeated three or four times, the adventitious wind would rush out, bringing the noxious along with it (like water put into a pump) and the patient recover. I saw him try both experiments upon a dog, but could not discern any effect from the former. After the latter, the animal was ready to burst, and made so violent a discharge, as was very offensive to me and my companions. The dog died on the spot, and we left the doctor endeavoring to recover him by the same operation.[8]

I visited many other apartments, but shall not trouble my reader with all the curiosities I observed, being studious of brevity.

I had hitherto seen only one side of the Academy, the other being appropriated to the advancers of speculative learning, of whom I shall say something when I have mentioned one illustrious person more, who is called among them *the universal artist*.[9] He told us he had been thirty years employing his thoughts for the improvement of human life. He had two large rooms full of wonderful curiosities, and fifty men at work. Some were condensing air into a dry, tangible substance, by extracting the niter,[1] and letting the aqueous or fluid particles percolate; others softening marble for pillows and pincushions; others petrifying the hoofs of a living horse to preserve them from foundering. The artist himself was at that time busy upon two great designs: the first, to sow land with chaff, wherein he affirmed the true seminal virtue to be contained, as he demonstrated by several experiments which I was not skillful enough to comprehend. The other was, by a certain composition of gums, minerals, and vegetables outwardly applied, to prevent the growth of wool upon two young lambs; and he hoped in a reasonable time to propagate the breed of naked sheep all over the kingdom.

We crossed a walk to the other part of the Academy, where, as I have already said, the projectors in speculative learning resided.

The first professor I saw was in a very large room, with forty pupils about him. After salutation, observing me to look earnestly upon a frame, which took up the greatest part of both the length and breadth of the room, he said perhaps I might wonder to see him employed in a project for improving speculative knowledge by practical and mechanical operations. But the world would soon be sensible[2] of its usefulness, and he flattered himself that a more noble exalted thought never sprang in any other man's head. Everyone knew how laborious the usual method is of attaining to arts and sciences; whereas by his contrivance, the most ignorant person at a reasonable charge, and with a little bodily labor, may write books in philosophy, poetry, politics, law, mathematics, and theology, without the least assistance from genius or study. He then led me to the frame, about the sides whereof all his pupils stood in ranks. It was twenty foot square, placed in the middle of the room. The superficies[3] was composed of several bits of wood, about the bigness of a die,[4] but some larger than others. They were all linked together by slender wires. These bits of wood were covered on every square with papers pasted on them, and on these papers were written all the words of their language in their several moods, tenses, and declensions, but without any order. The professor then desired me to observe, for he was go-

8. Robert Hooke (1635–1703) produced artificial respiration in a dog (1667) by blowing air into its windpipe with a pair of bellows.
9. Possibly Robert Boyle (1627–1691), whose many scientific experiments investigated the nature of air, marble, petrifaction, agriculture, and sheep breeding.
1. Air was believed to contain nitrous matter.
2. Aware.
3. Surface.
4. Singular of dice.

ing to set his engine[5] at work. The pupils at his command took each of them hold of an iron handle, whereof there were forty fixed round the edges of the frame, and giving them a sudden turn, the whole disposition of the words was entirely changed. He then commanded six and thirty of the lads to read the several lines softly as they appeared upon the frame; and where they found three or four words together that might make part of a sentence, they dictated to the four remaining boys who were scribes. This work was repeated three or four times, and at every turn the engine was so contrived, that the words shifted into new places, as the square bits of wood moved upside down.

Six hours a day the young students were employed in this labor, and the professor showed me several volumes in large folio already collected, of broken sentences, which he intended to piece together, and out of those rich materials to give the world a complete body of all arts and sciences; which however might be still improved, and much expedited, if the public would raise a fund for making and employing five hundred such frames in Lagado, and oblige the managers to contribute in common their several[6] collections.

He assured me, that this invention had employed all his thoughts from his youth, that he had emptied the whole vocabulary into his frame, and made the strictest computation of the general proportion there is in books between the numbers of particles, nouns, and verbs, and other parts of speech.

I made my humblest acknowledgments to this illustrious person for his great communicativeness, and promised if ever I had the good fortune to return to my native country, that I would do him justice, as the sole inventor of this wonderful machine; the form and contrivance of which I desired leave to delineate upon paper as in the figure here annexed. I told him, although it were the custom of our learned in Europe to steal inventions from each other,[7] who had thereby at least this advantage, that it became a controversy which was the right owner, yet I would take such caution, that he should have the honor entire without a rival.

We next went to the school of languages, where three professors sat in consultation upon improving that of their own country.[8]

The first project was to shorten discourse by cutting polysyllables into one, and leaving out verbs and participles, because in reality all things imaginable are but nouns.

The other project was a scheme for entirely abolishing all words whatsoever; and this was urged as a great advantage in point of health as well as brevity. For, it is plain, that every word we speak is in some degree a diminution of our lungs by corrosion, and consequently contributes to the shortening of our lives. An expedient was therefore offered, that since words are only names for *things*, it would be more convenient for all men to carry about them such *things* as were necessary to express the particular business they are to discourse on.[9] And this invention would certainly have

---

5. Machine.
6. Individual.
7. No international patent agreement existed at this time, and the theft of inventions was common as nations competed in developing technology for commercial manufacturing and navigation on the open seas.
8. The first secretary to the Royal Society, Thomas Spratt, in his *History* (1667) of that institution, recommended that such an Academy be founded, as the new style of science writing should strive to describe "so many *things* in an equal number of words." Although Swift burlesques this notion, he himself had published *Proposals for*

Correcting, Improving and Ascertaining the English Tongue (1712), in which he suggested that an Academy be established with the aim of preserving culture and "fixing our language for ever."
9. The growth of scientific knowledge about the nature of the material world had encouraged suggestions that language should be made less abstract. In satirizing the projector, Swift alludes to John Locke's theory of language in Book 3 of *An Essay Concerning Human Understanding* (1690), where Locke argues that words stand for things only indirectly.

taken place, to the great ease as well as health of the subject.[1] If the women in conjunction with the vulgar and illiterate had not threatened to raise a rebellion, unless they might be allowed the liberty to speak with their tongues, after the manner of their forefathers; such constant irreconcilable enemies to science are the common people. However, many of the most learned and wise adhere to the new scheme of expressing themselves by *things*, which hath only this inconvenience attending it, that if a man's business be very great, and of various kinds, he must be obliged in proportion to carry a greater bundle of *things* upon his back, unless he can afford one or two strong servants to attend him. I have often beheld two of those sages almost sinking under the weight of their packs, like peddlers among us; who when they met in the streets would lay down their loads, open their sacks, and hold conversation for an hour together; then put up their implements, help each other to resume their burdens, and take their leave.

But for short conversations a man may carry implements in his pockets and under his arms, enough to supply him, and in his house he cannot be at a loss; therefore the room where company meet who practice this art, is full of all *things* ready at hand, requisite to furnish matter for this kind of artificial converse.[2]

Another great advantage proposed by this invention, was that it would serve as a universal language to be understood in all civilized nations, whose goods and utensils are generally of the same kind, or nearly resembling, so that their uses might easily be comprehended. And thus, ambassadors would be qualified to treat with foreign princes or ministers of state, to whose tongues they were utter strangers.

I was at the mathematical school, where the master taught his pupils after a method scarce imaginable to us in Europe. The proposition and demonstration were fairly written on a thin wafer, with ink composed of a cephalic[3] tincture. This the student was to swallow upon a fasting stomach, and for three days following eat nothing but bread and water. As the wafer digested, the tincture mounted to his brain, bearing the proposition along with it. But the success has not hitherto been answerable, partly by some error in the *quantum* or composition, and partly by the perverseness of lads, to whom this bolus[4] is so nauseous that they generally steal aside, and discharge it upwards before it can operate; neither have they been yet persuaded to use so long an abstinence as the prescription requires.

CHAPTER 10

The Luggnaggians commended. A particular description of the Struldbruggs, with many conversations between the author and some eminent persons upon that subject.[5]

The Luggnaggians are a polite and generous people, and although they are not without some share of that pride which is peculiar to all Eastern countries, yet they show themselves courteous to strangers, especially such who are countenanced by the Court. I had many acquaintance among persons of the best fashion, and being always attended by my interpreter, the conversation we had was not disagreeable.

1. Both the individual practitioner and the people of the nation as a whole.
2. A reference to the Royal Society's attempt to collect one specimen or example of every thing in the world.
3. Of or for the head.

4. Mass of chewed food.
5. In order to return to England, Gulliver sails west on the Pacific from Balnibarbi (the country of which Lagado is the capital) to Japan, stopping en route at the island of "Luggnagg," where he makes the following observations.

One day in much good company, I was asked by a person of quality, whether I had seen any of their Struldbruggs or Immortals. I said I had not, and desired he would explain to me what he meant by such an appellation applied to a mortal creature. He told me, that sometimes, though very rarely, a child happened to be born in a family with a red circular spot in the forehead, directly over the left eyebrow, which was an infallible mark that it should never die. The spot, as he described it, was about the compass of a silver threepence, but in the course of time grew larger, and changed its color; for at twelve years old it became green, so continued till five and twenty, then turned to a deep blue; at five and forty it grew coal black, and as large as an English shilling, but never admitted any farther alteration. He said these births were so rare, that he did not believe there could be above eleven hundred Struldbruggs of both sexes in the whole kingdom, of which he computed about fifty in the metropolis, and among the rest a young girl born about three years ago. That these productions were not peculiar to any family, but a mere effect of change, and the children of the Struldbruggs themselves, were equally mortal with the rest of the people.

I freely own myself to have been struck with inexpressible delight upon hearing this account: and the person who gave it me happening to understand the Balnibarbian language, which I spoke very well, I could not forbear breaking out into expressions perhaps a little too extravagant. I cried out as in a rapture: Happy nation where every child hath at least a chance for being immortal! Happy people who enjoy so many living examples of ancient virtue, and have masters ready to instruct them in the wisdom of all former ages! But, happiest beyond all comparison are those excellent Struldbruggs, who being born exempt from that universal calamity of human nature, have their minds free and disengaged, without the weight and depression of spirits caused by the continual apprehension of death. I discovered my admiration[6] that I had not observed any of these illustrious persons at Court, the black spot on the forehead being so remarkable a distinction, that I could not have easily overlooked it; and it was impossible that his Majesty, a most judicious prince, should not provide himself with a good number of such wise and able counselors. Yet perhaps the virtue of those reverend sages was too strict for the corrupt and libertine manners of a Court. And we often find by experience that young men are too opinionative and volatile to be guided by the sober dictates of their seniors. However, since the King was pleased to allow me access to his royal person, I was resolved upon the very first occasion to deliver my opinion to him on this matter freely, and at large, by the help of my interpreter; and whether he would please to take my advice or no, yet in one thing I was determined, that his Majesty having frequently offered me an establishment in this country, I would with great thankfulness accept the favor, and pass my life here in the conversation of those superior beings the Struldbruggs, if they would please to admit me.

The gentleman to whom I addressed my discourse, because (as I have already observed) he spoke the language of Balnibarbi, said to me with a sort of a smile, which usually ariseth from pity to the ignorant, that he was glad of any occasion to keep me among them, and desired my permission to explain to the company what I had spoke. He did so, and they talked together for some time in their own language, whereof I understood not a syllable, neither could I observe by their countenances what impression my discourse had made on them. After a short silence the same person told

---

6. Expressed my surprise.

me, that his friends and mine (so he thought fit to express himself) were very much pleased with the judicious remarks I had made on the great happiness and advantages of immortal life, and they were desirous to know in a particular manner, what scheme of living I should have formed to myself, if it had fallen to my lot to have been born a Struldbrugg.

I answered, it was easy to be eloquent on so copious and delightful a subject, especially to me who have been often apt to amuse myself with visions of what I should do if I were a king, a general, or a great lord; and upon this very case I had frequently run over the whole system how I should employ myself, and pass the time if I were sure to live for ever.

That, if it had been my good fortune to come into the world a Struldbrugg, as soon as I could discover my own happiness by understanding the difference between life and death, I would first resolve by all arts and methods whatsoever to procure myself riches. In the pursuit of which by thrift and management, I might reasonably expect in about two hundred years, to be the wealthiest man in the kingdom. In the second place, I would from my earliest youth apply myself to the study of arts and sciences, by which I should arrive in time to excel all others in learning. Lastly I would carefully record every action and event of consequence that happened in the public,[7] impartially draw the characters of the several successions of princes, and great ministers of state, with my own observations on every point. I would exactly set down the several changes in customs, language, fashions of dress, diet and diversions. By all which acquirements, I should be a living treasury of knowledge and wisdom, and certainly become the oracle of the nation.

I would never marry after threescore, but live in an hospitable manner, yet still on the saving side. I would entertain myself in forming and directing the minds of hopeful young men, by convincing them from my own remembrance, experience, and observation, fortified by numerous examples, of the usefulness of virtue in public and private life. But, my choice and constant companions should be a set of my own immortal brotherhood, among whom I would elect a dozen from the most ancient down to my own contemporaries. Where any of these wanted[8] fortunes, I would provide them with convenient lodges round my own estate, and have some of them always at my table, only mingling a few of the most valuable among you mortals, whom length of time would harden me to lose with little or no reluctance, and treat your posterity after the same manner, just as a man diverts himself with the annual succession of pinks and tulips in his garden, without regretting the loss of those which withered the preceding year.

These Struldbruggs and I would mutually communicate our observations and memorials through the course of time, remark the several gradations by which corruption steals into the world, and oppose it in every step, by giving perpetual warning and instruction to mankind; which, added to the strong influence of our own example, would probably prevent that continual degeneracy of human nature so justly complained of in all ages.

Add to all this, the pleasure of seeing the various revolutions of states and empires, the changes in the lower and upper world,[9] ancient cities in ruins, and obscure villages become the seats of kings. Famous rivers lessening into shallow brooks, the ocean leaving one coast dry, and overwhelming another, the discovery of many

---

7. The state (from Latin *res publica*, the "public thing," from which derives the word *republic*).

8. Lacked.

9. On the earth and in the heavens.

countries yet unknown. Barbarity overrunning the politest nations, and the most barbarous becoming civilized. I should then see the discovery of the longitude, the perpetual motion, the universal medicine,[1] and many other great inventions brought to the utmost perfection.

What wonderful discoveries should we make in astronomy, by outliving and confirming our own predictions, by observing the progress and returns of comets, with the changes of motion in the sun, moon, and stars.

I enlarged upon many other topics, which the natural desire of endless life and sublunary[2] happiness could easily furnish me with. When I had ended, and the sum of my discourse had been interpreted as before, to the rest of the company, there was a good deal of talk among them in the language of the country, not without some laughter at my expense. At last the same gentleman who had been my interpreter said, he was desired by the rest to set me right in a few mistakes, which I had fallen into through the common imbecility of human nature, and upon that allowance was less answerable for them. That, this breed of Struldbruggs was peculiar to their country, for there were no such people either in Balnibarbi or Japan, where he had the honor to be ambassador from his Majesty, and found the natives in both those kingdoms very hard to believe[3] that the fact was possible, and it appeared from my astonishment when he first mentioned the matter to me, that I received it as a thing wholly new, and scarcely to be credited. That in the two kingdoms abovementioned, where during his residence he had conversed very much, he observed long life to be the universal desire and wish of mankind. That whoever had one foot in the grave, was sure to hold back the other as strongly as he could. That the oldest had still hopes of living one day longer, and looked on death as the greatest evil, from which nature always prompted him to retreat; only in this island of Luggnagg, the appetite for living was not so eager, from the continual example of the Struldbruggs before their eyes.

That the system of living contrived by me was unreasonable and unjust, because it supposed a perpetuity of youth, health, and vigor, which no man could be so foolish to hope, however extravagant he may be in his wishes. That the question therefore was not whether a man would choose to be always in the prime of youth, attended with prosperity and health, but how he would pass a perpetual life under all the usual disadvantages which old age brings along with it. For although few men will avow their desires of being immortal upon such hard conditions, yet in the two kingdoms before-mentioned of Balnibarbi and Japan, he observed that every man desired to put off death for some time longer, let it approach ever so late, and he rarely heard of any man who died willingly, except he were incited by the extremity of grief or torture. And he appealed to me whether in those countries I had traveled, as well as my own, I had not observed the same general disposition.

After this preface he gave me a particular account of the Struldbruggs among them. He said they commonly acted like mortals, till about thirty years old, after which by degrees they grew melancholy and dejected, increasing in both till they came to fourscore. This he learned from their own confession; for otherwise there not being above two or three of that species born in an age, they were too few to form a general observation by. When they came to fourscore years, which is reckoned the

1. As at Lagado, Gulliver enumerates scientific quests Swift scoffed at: for a method of determining the longitude of a ship at sea, for a perpetual motion machine, for one drug sufficient to cure all ills.
2. Earthly.
3. To convince.

extremity of living in this country, they had not only all the follies and infirmities of other old men, but many more which arose from the dreadful prospect of never dying. They were not only opinionative, peevish, covetous, morose, vain, talkative, but uncapable of friendship, and dead to all natural affection, which never descended below their grandchildren. Envy and impotent desires are their prevailing passions. But those objects against which their envy seems principally directed, are the vices of the younger sort, and the deaths of the old. By reflecting on the former, they find themselves cut off from all possibility of pleasure; and whenever they see a funeral, they lament and repine that others have gone to an harbor of rest, to which they themselves never can hope to arrive. They have no remembrance of anything but what they learned and observed in their youth and middle age, and even that is very imperfect. And for the truth or particulars of any fact, it is safer to depend on common traditions than upon their best recollections. The least miserable among them appear to be those who turn to dotage, and entirely lose their memories; these meet with more pity and assistance, because they want many bad qualities which abound in others.

If a Struldbrugg happen to marry one of his own kind, the marriage is dissolved of course by the courtesy of the kingdom, as soon as the younger of the two comes to be fourscore. For the law thinks it a reasonable indulgence, that those who are condemned without any fault of their own to a perpetual continuance in the world, should not have their misery doubled by the load of a wife.[4]

As soon as they have completed the term of eighty years, they are looked on as dead in law; their heirs immediately succeed to their estates, only a small pittance is reserved for their support, and the poor ones are maintained at the public charge. After that period they are held incapable of any employment of trust or profit, they cannot purchase lands or take leases, neither are they allowed to be witnesses in any cause, either civil or criminal, not even for the decision of meres[5] and bounds.

At ninety they lose their teeth and hair, they have at that age no distinction of taste, but eat and drink whatever they can get, without relish or appetite. The diseases they were subject to, still continue without increasing or diminishing. In talking they forget the common appellation of things, and the names of persons, even of those who are their nearest friends and relations. For the same reason they never can amuse themselves with reading, because their memory will not serve to carry them from the beginning of a sentence to the end; and by this defect they are deprived of the only entertainment whereof they might otherwise be capable.

The language of this country being always upon the flux, the Struldbruggs of one age do not understand those of another, neither are they able after two hundred years to hold any conversation (farther than by a few general words) with their neighbors the mortals, and thus they lie under the disadvantage of living like foreigners in their own country. This was the account given me of the Struldbruggs, as near as I can remember. I afterwards saw five or six of different ages, the youngest not above two hundred years old, who were brought to me at several times by some of my friends; but although they were told that I was a great traveler, and had seen all the world, they had not the least curiosity to ask me a question; only desired I would give them *slumskudask*, or a token of remembrance, which is a modest way of begging, to avoid the law that strictly forbids it, because they are provided for by the public, although indeed with a very scanty allowance.

---

4. Swift himself never married.   5. Property lines (at issue in property disputes).

They are despised and hated by all sorts of people; when one of them is born, it is reckoned ominous, and their birth is recorded very particularly; so that you may know their age by consulting the registry, which however hath not been kept above a thousand years past, or at least hath been destroyed by time or public disturbances. But the usual way of computing how old they are, is, by asking them what kings or great persons they can remember, and then consulting history, for infallibly the last prince in their mind did not begin his reign after they were fourscore years old.

They were the most mortifying sight I ever beheld, and the women more horrible than the men. Besides the usual deformities in extreme old age, they acquired an additional ghastliness in proportion to their number of years, which is not to be described, and among half a dozen I soon distinguished which was the eldest, although there were not above a century or two between them.

The reader will easily believe, that from what I had heard and seen, my keen appetite for perpetuity of life was much abated. I grew heartily ashamed of the pleasing visions I had formed, and thought no tyrant could invent a death into which I would not run with pleasure from such a life. The king heard of all that had passed between me and my friends upon this occasion, and rallied me very pleasantly, wishing I would send a couple of Struldbruggs to my own country, to arm our people against the fear of death; but this it seems is forbidden by the fundamental laws of the kingdom, or else I should have been well content with the trouble and expense of transporting them.

I could not but agree that the laws of this kingdom, relating to the Struldbruggs, were founded upon the strongest reasons, and such as any other country would be under the necessity of enacting in the like circumstances. Otherwise, as avarice is the necessary consequent of old age, those Immortals would in time become proprietors of the whole nation, and engross the civil power, which, for want of abilities to manage, must end in the ruin of the public.

Part 4. A Voyage to the Country of the Houyhnhnms[1]

CHAPTER 1

The author sets out as Captain of a ship. His men conspire against him, confine him a long time to his cabin, set him on shore in an unknown land. He travels up into the country. The Yahoos,[2] a strange sort of animal, described. The author meets two Houyhnhnms.

I continued at home with my wife and children about five months in a very happy condition, if I could have learned the lesson of knowing when I was well. I left my poor wife big with child, and accepted an advantageous offer made me to be Captain of the *Adventure*,[3] a stout merchantman of 350 tons: for I understood navigation well, and being grown weary of a surgeon's employment at sea, which however I could exercise upon occasion, I took a skillful young man of that calling, one Robert

---

1. Pronounced "whinnims," to mimic the sound of a horse's whinny, though some scholars have offered more complex interpretations of this name. With characteristic irony, Swift probably chose horses to represent rational creatures because the philosopher John Locke (1632–1704) and Bishop Edward Stillingfleet (1635–1699) had argued extensively about how one might distinguish man as a rational animal from an evidently irrational animal, such as a horse.

2. The name may be derived from similarly titled African or Guianan tribes. The animals represent sinful, fallen humanity, and their juxtaposition with the Houyhnhnms is designed to question belief in the innate rationality of humankind and the superiority of humans over other creatures.

3. The name of two ships of the notorious pirate Captain William Kidd (d. 1701). Kidd, originally commissioned to capture pirates, was also subject to a mutiny.

Purefoy,[4] into my ship. We set sail from Portsmouth upon the seventh day of September, 1710; on the fourteenth, we met with Captain Pocock[5] of Bristol, at Teneriffe,[6] who was going to the bay of Campeche, to cut logwood. On the sixteenth, he was parted from us by a storm; I heard since my return, that his ship foundered, and none escaped, but one cabin boy. He was an honest man, and a good sailor, but a little too positive in his own opinions, which was the cause of his destruction, as it hath been of several others. For if he had followed my advice, he might at this time have been safe at home with his family as well as myself.

I had several men died in my ship of calentures,[7] so that I was forced to get recruits out of Barbados, and the Leeward Islands, where I touched by[8] the direction of the merchants who employed me, which I had soon too much cause to repent; for I found afterwards that most of them had been buccaneers. I had fifty hands on board, and my orders were, that I should trade with the Indians in the South Sea, and make what discoveries I could. These rogues whom I had picked up debauched my other men, and they all formed a conspiracy to seize the ship and secure me; which they did one morning, rushing into my cabin, and binding me hand and foot, threatening to throw me overboard, if I offered to stir. I told them, I was their prisoner, and would submit. This they made me swear to do, and then unbound me, only fastening one of my legs with a chain near my bed, and placed a sentry at my door with his piece charged,[9] who was commanded to shoot me dead, if I attempted my liberty. They sent me down victuals and drink, and took the government of the ship to themselves. Their design was to turn pirates, and plunder the Spaniards, which they could not do till they got more men. But first they resolved to sell the goods in the ship, and then go to Madagascar[1] for recruits, several among them having died since my confinement. They sailed many weeks, and traded with the Indians, but I knew not what course they took, being kept close prisoner in my cabin, and expecting nothing less than to be murdered, as they often threatened me.

Upon the ninth day of May, 1711, one James Welch came down to my cabin; and said he had orders from the Captain to set me ashore. I expostulated with him, but in vain; neither would he so much as tell me who their new captain was. They forced me into the longboat, letting me put on my best suit of clothes, which were good as new, and a small bundle of linen, but no arms except my hanger;[2] and they were so civil as not to search my pockets, into which I conveyed what money I had, with some other little necessaries. They rowed about a league; and then set me down on a strand.[3] I desired them to tell me what country it was. They all swore, they knew no more than myself, but said, that the Captain (as they called him) was resolved, after they had sold the lading,[4] to get rid of me in the first place where they discovered land. They pushed off immediately, advising me to make haste, for fear of being overtaken by the tide, and bade me farewell.

In this desolate condition I advanced forward, and soon got upon firm ground, where I sat down on a bank to rest myself, and consider what I had best to do. When

I was a little refreshed, I went up into the country, resolving to deliver myself to the first savages I should meet, and purchase my life from them by some bracelets, glass rings, and other toys,[5] which sailors usually provide themselves with in those voyages, and whereof I had some about me: the land was divided by long rows of trees, not regularly planted, but naturally growing; there was great plenty of grass, and several fields of oats. I walked very circumspectly for fear of being surprised, or suddenly shot with an arrow from behind or on either side. I fell into a beaten road, where I saw many tracks of human feet, and some of cows, but most of horses. At last I beheld several animals in a field, and one or two of the same kind sitting in trees. Their shape was very singular, and deformed, which a little discomposed me, so that I lay down behind a thicket to observe them better. Some of them coming forward near the place where I lay, gave me an opportunity of distinctly marking[6] their form. Their heads and breasts were covered with a thick hair, some frizzled and others lank; they had beards like goats, and a long ridge of hair down their backs, and the foreparts of their legs and feet, but the rest of their bodies were bare, so that I might see their skins, which were of a brown buff color. They had no tails, nor any hair at all on their buttocks, except about the anus; which, I presume, Nature had placed there to defend them as they sat on the ground; for this posture they used, as well as lying down, and often stood on their hind feet. They climbed high trees, as nimbly as a squirrel, for they had strong extended claws before and behind, terminating in sharp points, and hooked. They would often spring, and bound, and leap with prodigious agility. The females were not so large as the males; they had long lank hair on their heads, and only a sort of down on the rest of their bodies, except about the anus, and pudenda.[7] Their dugs[8] hung between their forefeet, and often reached almost to the ground as they walked. The hair of both sexes was of several colors, brown, red, black, and yellow. Upon the whole, I never beheld in all my travels so disagreeable an animal, nor one against which I naturally conceived so strong an antipathy. So that thinking I had seen enough, full of contempt and aversion, I got up and pursued the beaten road, hoping it might direct me to the cabin of some Indian. I had not gone far when I met one of these creatures full in my way, and coming up directly to me. The ugly monster, when he saw me, distorted several ways every feature of his visage, and stared as at an object he had never seen before; then approaching nearer, lifted up his forepaw, whether out of curiosity or mischief, I could not tell. But I drew my hanger, and gave him a good blow with the flat side of it; for I durst not strike him with the edge, fearing the inhabitants might be provoked against me, if they should come to know, that I had killed or maimed any of their cattle. When the beast felt the smart, he drew back, and roared so loud, that a herd of at least forty came flocking about me from the next field, howling and making odious faces; but I ran to the body of a tree, and leaning my back against it, kept them off, by waving my hanger. Several of this cursed brood getting hold of the branches behind leaped up into the tree, from whence they began to discharge their excrements on my head: however, I escaped pretty well, by sticking close to the stem of the tree, but was almost stifled with the filth, which fell about me on every side.

In the midst of this distress, I observed them all to run away on a sudden as fast as they could, at which I ventured to leave the tree, and pursue the road, wondering what it was that could put them into this flight. But looking on my left hand, I saw a

5. Trinkets.
6. Observing.

7. Genitals.
8. Breasts.

horse walking softly in the field, which my persecutors having sooner discovered, was the cause of their flight. The horse started a little when he came near me, but soon recovering himself, looked full in my face with manifest tokens of wonder: he viewed my hands and feet, walking round me several times. I would have pursued my journey, but he placed himself directly in the way, yet looking with a very mild aspect, never offering the least violence. We stood gazing at each other for some time; at last I took the boldness to reach my hand towards his neck, with a design to stroke it, using the common style and whistle of jockeys when they are going to handle a strange horse. But this animal, seeming to receive my civilities with disdain, shook his head, and bent his brows, softly raising up his left forefoot to remove my hand. Then he neighed three or four times, but in so different a cadence, that I almost began to think he was speaking to himself in some language of his own.

While he and I were thus employed, another horse came up; who applying[9] himself to the first in a very formal manner, they gently struck each other's right hoof before, neighing several times by turns, and varying the sound, which seemed to be almost articulate. They went some paces off, as if it were to confer together, walking side by side, backward and forward, like persons deliberating upon some affair of weight, but often turning their eyes towards me, as it were to watch that I might not escape. I was amazed to see such actions and behavior in brute beasts, and concluded with myself, that if the inhabitants of this country were endued with a proportionable degree of reason, they must needs be the wisest people upon earth. This thought gave me so much comfort, that I resolved to go forward until I could discover some house or village, or meet with any of the natives, leaving the two horses to discourse together as they pleased. But the first, who was a dapple-grey, observing me to steal off, neighed after me in so expressive a tone, that I fancied myself to understand what he meant; whereupon I turned back, and came near him, to expect[1] his farther commands. But concealing my fear as much as I could, for I began to be in some pain,[2] how this adventure might terminate; and the reader will easily believe I did not much like my present situation.

The two horses came up close to me, looking with great earnestness upon my face and hands. The grey steed rubbed my hat all round with his right forehoof, and discomposed it so much, that I was forced to adjust it better, by taking it off, and settling it again; whereat both he and his companion (who was a brown bay) appeared to be much surprised; the latter felt the lappet[3] of my coat, and finding it to hang loose about me, they both looked with new signs of wonder. He stroked my right hand, seeming to admire the softness, and color; but he squeezed it so hard between his hoof and his pastern,[4] that I was forced to roar; after which they both touched me with all possible tenderness. They were under great perplexity about my shoes and stockings, which they felt very often, neighing to each other, and using various gestures, not unlike those of a philosopher,[5] when he would attempt to solve some new and difficult phenomenon.

Upon the whole, the behavior of these animals was so orderly and rational, so acute and judicious, that I at last concluded, they must needs be magicians, who had thus metamorphosed themselves upon some design, and seeing a stranger in the way,

9. Addressing.
1. Await.
2. Began to be worried.
3. Lapel.

4. Part of a horse's foot between the fetlock (a projection of the lower leg) and the hoof.
5. Scientist.

were resolved to divert themselves with him; or perhaps were really amazed at the sight of a man so very different in habit, feature, and complexion from those who might probably live in so remote a climate.[6] Upon the strength of this reasoning, I ventured to address them in the following manner: Gentlemen, if you be conjurers, as I have good cause to believe, you can understand any language; therefore I make bold to let your Worships know, that I am a poor distressed Englishman, driven by his misfortunes upon your coast, and I entreat one of you, to let me ride upon his back, as if he were a real horse, to some house or village, where I can be relieved. In return of which favor, I will make you a present of this knife and bracelet (taking them out of my pocket). The two creatures stood silent while I spoke, seeming to listen with great attention; and when I had ended, they neighed frequently towards each other, as if they were engaged in serious conversation. I plainly observed that their language expressed the passions[7] very well, and the words might with little pains be resolved into an alphabet more easily than the Chinese.

I could frequently distinguish the word *Yahoo*, which was repeated by each of them several times; and although it were impossible for me to conjecture what it meant, yet while the two horses were busy in conversation, I endeavored to practice this word upon my tongue; and as soon as they were silent, I boldly pronounced *Yahoo* in a loud voice, imitating, at the same time, as near as I could, the neighing of a horse; at which they were both visibly surprised, and the grey repeated the same word twice, as if he meant to teach me the right accent, wherein I spoke after him as well as I could, and found myself perceivably to improve every time, although very far from any degree of perfection. Then the bay tried me with a second word, much harder to be pronounced; but reducing it to the English *orthography*,[8] may be spelled thus, *Houyhnhnm*. I did not succeed in this so well as the former, but after two or three farther trials, I had better fortune; and they both appeared amazed at my capacity.

After some farther discourse, which I then conjectured might relate to me, the two friends took their leaves, with the same compliment of striking each other's hoof; and the grey made me signs that I should walk before him; wherein I thought it prudent to comply, till I could find a better director. When I offered to slacken my pace, he would cry *Hhuun, Hhuun*; I guessed his meaning, and gave him to understand, as well as I could, that I was weary, and not able to walk faster; upon which, he would stand a while to let me rest.

CHAPTER 2

The author conducted by a Houyhnhnm to his house. The house described. The author's reception. The food of the Houyhnhnms. The author in distress for want of meat, is at last relieved. His manner of feeding in that country.

Having traveled about three miles, we came to a long kind of building, made of timber stuck in the ground, and wattled across;[9] the roof was low, and covered with straw. I now began to be a little comforted, and took out some toys, which travelers usually carry for presents to the savage Indians of America and other parts, in hopes the people of the house would be thereby encouraged to receive me kindly. The horse made me a sign to go in first; it was a large room with a smooth, clay floor, and

6. Region.
7. Emotions.

8. Spelling.
9. Filled in with twigs and branches.

a rack[1] and manger extending the whole length on one side. There were three nags,[2] and two mares, not eating, but some of them sitting down upon their hams,[3] which I very much wondered at; but wondered more to see the rest employed in domestic business. The last seemed but ordinary cattle; however, this confirmed my first opinion, that a people who could so far civilize brute animals, must needs excel in wisdom all the nations of the world. The grey came in just after, and thereby prevented any ill treatment, which the others might have given me. He neighed to them several times in a style of authority, and received answers.

Beyond this room there were three others, reaching the length of the house, to which you passed through three doors, opposite to each other, in the manner of a vista;[4] we went through the second room towards the third; here the grey walked in first, beckoning me to attend.[5] I waited in the second room, and got ready my presents, for the master and mistress of the house: they were two knives, three bracelets of false pearl, a small looking glass, and a bead necklace. The horse neighed three or four times, and I waited to hear some answers in a human voice, but I heard no other returns than in the same dialect, only one or two a little shriller than his. I began to think that this house must belong to some person of great note among them, because there appeared so much ceremony before I could gain admittance. But, that a man of quality should be served all by horses, was beyond my comprehension. I feared my brain was disturbed by my sufferings and misfortunes: I roused myself, and looked about me in the room where I was left alone; this was furnished as the first, only after a more elegant manner. I rubbed mine eyes often, but the same objects still occurred. I pinched my arms and sides, to awake myself, hoping I might be in a dream. I then absolutely concluded, that all these appearances could be nothing else but necromancy[6] and magic. But I had no time to pursue these reflections; for the grey horse came to the door, and made me a sign to follow him into the third room, where I saw a very comely mare, together with a colt and foal, sitting on their haunches, upon mats of straw, not unartfully made, and perfectly neat and clean.

The mare, soon after my entrance, rose from her mat, and coming up close, after having nicely[7] observed my hands and face, gave me a most contemptuous look; then turning to the horse, I heard the word *Yahoo* often repeated betwixt them; the meaning of which word I could not then comprehend, although it were the first I had learned to pronounce; but I was soon better informed, to my everlasting mortification: for the horse beckoning to me with his head, and repeating the word *Hhuun, Hhuun,* as he did upon the road, which I understood was to attend him, led me out into a kind of court, where was another building at some distance from the house. Here we entered, and I saw three of those detestable creatures, which I first met after my landing, feeding upon roots, and the flesh of some animals, which I afterwards found to be that of asses and dogs, and now and then a cow dead by accident or disease.[8] They were all tied by the neck with strong withes,[9] fastened to a beam; they held their food between the claws of their forefeet, and tore it with their teeth.

The master horse ordered a sorrel nag, one of his servants, to untie the largest of these animals, and take him into the yard. The beast and I were brought close

---

1. Hayrack for the feed.
2. Ponies.
3. Buttocks.
4. Long, narrow view (usually between rows of trees).
5. Wait.
6. Sorcery.

7. Closely.
8. The Yahoos eat food listed in Leviticus (11.3, 27, 39–40) as unclean, suggesting that they exemplify the human condition distorted and debased by sin.
9. Leashes.

together, and our countenances diligently compared, both by master and servant, who thereupon repeated several times the word *Yahoo*. My horror and astonishment are not to be described, when I observed, in this abominable animal, a perfect human figure; the face of it indeed was flat and broad, the nose depressed, the lips large, and the mouth wide. But these differences are common to all savage nations, where the lineaments of the countenance are distorted by the natives suffering[1] their infants to lie groveling on the earth, or by carrying them on their backs, nuzzling with their face against the mother's shoulders. The forefeet of the Yahoo differed from my hands in nothing else but the length of the nails, the coarseness and brownness of the palms, and the hairiness on the backs. There was the same resemblance between our feet, with the same differences, which I knew very well, though the horses did not, because of my shoes and stockings; the same in every part of our bodies, except as to hairiness and color, which I have already described.

The great difficulty that seemed to stick with the two horses, was, to see the rest of my body so very different from that of a Yahoo, for which I was obliged to my clothes, whereof they had no conception: the sorrel nag offered me a root, which he held (after their manner, as we shall describe in its proper place) between his hoof and pastern; I took it in my hand, and having smelt it, returned it to him as civilly as I could. He brought out of the Yahoo's kennel a piece of ass's flesh, but it smelt so offensively that I turned from it with loathing; he then threw it to the Yahoo, by whom it was greedily devoured. He afterwards showed me a wisp of hay, and a fetlock full of oats; but I shook my head, to signify, that neither of these were food for me. And indeed, I now apprehended, that I must absolutely starve, if I did not get to some of my own species: for as to those filthy Yahoos, although there were few greater lovers of mankind, at that time, than myself; yet I confess I never saw any sensitive[2] being so detestable on all accounts; and the more I came near them, the more hateful they grew, while I stayed in that country. This the master horse observed by my behavior, and therefore sent the Yahoo back to his kennel. He then put his forehoof to his mouth, at which I was much surprised, although he did it with ease, and with a motion that appeared perfectly natural, and made other signs to know what I would eat; but I could not return him such an answer as he was able to apprehend; and if he had understood me, I did not see how it was possible to contrive any way for finding myself nourishment. While we were thus engaged, I observed a cow passing by, whereupon I pointed to her, and expressed a desire to let me go and milk her. This had its effect; for he led me back into the house, and ordered a mare-servant to open a room, where a good store of milk lay in earthen and wooden vessels, after a very orderly and cleanly manner. She gave me a large bowl full, of which I drank very heartily, and found myself well refreshed.

About noon I saw coming towards the house a kind of vehicle drawn like a sledge by four Yahoos. There was in it an old steed, who seemed to be of quality; he alighted with his hind feet forward, having by accident got a hurt in his left forefoot. He came to dine with our horse, who received him with great civility. They dined in the best room, and had oats boiled in milk for the second course, which the old horse ate warm, but the rest cold. Their mangers were placed circular in the middle of the room and divided into several partitions, round which they sat on their haunches upon bosses[3] of straw. In the middle was a large rack with angles answering to every

---

1. Allowing.
2. "Having sense or perception, but not reason" (Johnson's *Dictionary*).

3. Piles or seats.

partition of the manger. So that each horse and mare ate their own hay, and their own mash of oats and milk, with much decency and regularity. The behavior of the young colt and foal appeared very modest, and that of the master and mistress extremely cheerful and complaisant[4] to their guest. The grey ordered me to stand by him, and much discourse passed between him and his friend concerning me, as I found by the stranger's often looking on me, and the frequent repetition of the word Yahoo.

I happened to wear my gloves, which the master grey observing, seemed perplexed, discovering signs of wonder what I had done to my forefeet; he put his hoof three or four times to them, as if he would signify, that I should reduce them to their former shape, which I presently did, pulling off both my gloves, and putting them into my pocket. This occasioned farther talk, and I saw the company was pleased with my behavior, whereof I soon found the good effects. I was ordered to speak the few words I understood, and while they were at dinner, the master taught me the names for oats, milk, fire, water, and some others; which I could readily pronounce after him, having from my youth a great facility in learning languages.

When dinner was done, the master horse took me aside, and by signs and words made me understand the concern he was in, that I had nothing to eat. Oats in their tongue are called *hlunnh*. This word I pronounced two or three times; for although I had refused them at first, yet upon second thoughts, I considered that I could contrive to make of them a kind of bread, which might be sufficient with milk to keep me alive, till I could make my escape to some other country, and to creatures of my own species. The horse immediately ordered a white mare-servant of his family to bring me a good quantity of oats in a sort of wooden tray. These I heated before the fire as well as I could, and rubbed them till the husks came off, which I made a shift[5] to winnow from the grain; I ground and beat them between two stones, then took water, and made them into a paste or cake, which I toasted at the fire, and ate warm with milk. It was at first a very insipid diet, although common enough in many parts of Europe, but grew tolerable by time; and having been often reduced to hard fare in my life, this was not the first experiment I had made how easily nature is satisfied.[6] And I cannot but observe, that I never had one hour's sickness, while I stayed in this island. 'Tis true, I sometimes made a shift to catch a rabbit, or bird, by springes[7] made of Yahoos' hairs, and I often gathered wholesome herbs, which I boiled, or ate as salads with my bread, and now and then, for a rarity, I made a little butter, and drank the whey. I was at first at a great loss for salt; but custom soon reconciled the want of it; and I am confident that the frequent use of salt among us is an effect of luxury, and was first introduced only as a provocative to drink; except where it is necessary for preserving of flesh in long voyages, or in places remote from great markets. For we observe no animal to be fond of it but man[8] and as to myself, when I left this country, it was a great while before I could endure the taste of it in anything that I ate.

This is enough to say upon the subject of my diet, wherewith other travelers fill their books, as if the readers were personally concerned whether we fared[9] well or ill. However, it was necessary to mention this matter, lest the world should think it

---

4. Courteous.
5. Attempted.
6. A commonplace idea in ancient satire; Swift may here be mocking it.
7. Snares.

8. This is, of course, untrue, but Gulliver's subsequent dislike of salt indicates his dislike of human society in general.
9. A pun on "fare," meaning both food and "to get along."

impossible that I could find sustenance for three years in such a country, and among such inhabitants.

When it grew towards evening, the master horse ordered a place for me to lodge in; it was but six yards from the house, and separated from the stable of the Yahoos. Here I got some straw, and covering myself with my own clothes, slept very sound. But I was in a short time better accommodated, as the reader shall know hereafter, when I come to treat more particularly about my way of living.

CHAPTER 3

The author studious to learn the language, the Houyhnhnm his master assists in teaching him. The language described. Several Houyhnhnms of quality come out of curiosity to see the author. He gives his master a short account of his voyage.

My principal endeavor was to learn the language, which my master (for so I shall henceforth call him) and his children, and every servant of his house were desirous to teach me. For they looked upon it as a prodigy that a brute animal should discover[1] such marks of a rational creature. I pointed to everything, and inquired the name of it, which I wrote down in my journal book when I was alone, and corrected my bad accent, by desiring those of the family to pronounce it often. In this employment, a sorrel nag, one of the under servants, was very ready to assist me.

In speaking, they pronounce through the nose and throat, and their language approaches nearest to the High Dutch or German, of any I know in Europe; but is much more graceful and significant.[2] The Emperor Charles V made almost the same observation, when he said, that if he were to speak to his horse, it should be in High Dutch.[3]

The curiosity and impatience of my master were so great, that he spent many hours of his leisure to instruct me. He was convinced (as he afterwards told me) that I must be a Yahoo, but my teachableness, civility, and cleanliness astonished him; which were qualities altogether so opposite to those animals. He was most perplexed about my clothes, reasoning sometimes with himself, whether they were a part of my body; for I never pulled them off till the family were asleep, and got them on before they waked in the morning. My master was eager to learn from whence I came, how I acquired those appearances of reason, which I discovered in all my actions, and to know my story from my own mouth, which he hoped he should soon do by the great proficiency I made in learning and pronouncing their words and sentences. To help my memory, I formed all I learned into the English alphabet, and writ the words down with the translations. This last, after some time, I ventured to do in my master's presence. It cost me much trouble to explain to him what I was doing; for the inhabitants have not the least idea of books or literature.

In about ten weeks' time I was able to understand most of his questions, and in three months could give him some tolerable answers. He was extremely curious to know from what part of the country I came, and how I was taught to imitate a rational creature, because the Yahoos (whom he saw I exactly resembled in my head, hands, and face, that were only visible), with some appearance of cunning, and the

---

1. Display.
2. Expressive.

3. I.e., German; Charles V of Spain (1500–1551) was believed to have said that he would address his God in Spanish, his mistress in Italian, and his horse in German.

strongest disposition to mischief, were observed to be the most unteachable of all brutes. I answered, that I came over the sea, from a far place, with many others of my own kind, in a great hollow vessel made of the bodies of trees. That my companions forced me to land on this coast, and then left me to shift for myself. It was with some difficulty, and by the help of many signs, that I brought him to understand me. He replied, that I must needs be mistaken, or that I *said the thing which was not.* (For they have no word in their language to express lying or falsehood.) He knew it was impossible[4] that there could be a country beyond the sea, or that a parcel of brutes could move a wooden vessel whither they pleased upon water. He was sure no Houyhnhnm alive could make such a vessel, or would trust Yahoos to manage it.

The word *Houyhnhnm*, in their tongue, signifies a *horse,* and in its etymology, the *Perfection of Nature*. I told my master, that I was at a loss for expression, but would improve as fast as I could; and hoped in a short time I should be able to tell him wonders: he was pleased to direct his own mare, his colt and foal, and the servants of the family to take all opportunities of instructing me, and every day for two or three hours, he was at the same pains himself: several horses and mares of quality in the neighborhood came often to our house upon the report spread of a wonderful Yahoo, that could speak like a Houyhnhnm, and seemed in his words and actions to discover some glimmerings of reason. These delighted to converse with me; they put many questions, and received such answers as I was able to return. By all which advantages, I made so great a progress, that in five months from my arrival, I understood whatever was spoke, and could express myself tolerably well.

The Houyhnhnms who came to visit my master, out of a design of seeing and talking with me, could hardly believe me to be a right[5] Yahoo, because my body had a different covering from others of my kind. They were astonished to observe me without the usual hair or skin, except on my head, face, and hands; but I discovered that secret to my master, upon an accident, which happened about a fortnight before.

I have already told the reader, that every night when the family were gone to bed, it was my custom to strip and cover myself with my clothes: it happened one morning early, that my master sent for me, by the sorrel nag, who was his valet; when he came, I was fast asleep, my clothes fallen off on one side, and my shirt above my waist. I awaked at the noise he made, and observed him to deliver his message in some disorder; after which he went to my master, and in a great fright gave him a very confused account of what he had seen: this I presently discovered; for going as soon as I was dressed, to pay my attendance upon his Honor, he asked me the meaning of what his servant had reported, that I was not the same thing when I slept as I appeared to be at other times; that his valet assured him, some part of me was white, some yellow, at least not so white, and some brown.

I had hitherto concealed the secret of my dress, in order to distinguish myself as much as possible, from that cursed race of Yahoos; but now I found it in vain to do so any longer. Besides, I considered that my clothes and shoes would soon wear out, which already were in a declining condition, and must be supplied by some contrivance from the hides of Yahoos or other brutes; whereby the whole secret would be known: I therefore told my master, that in the country from whence I came, those of my kind always covered their bodies with the hairs of certain animals prepared by art,

4. The Houyhnhnm thus shows himself to be so dependent on reason that he is dogmatic in his ignorance, unable (like rationalists in religion) to accept what he does not know by his own reasoning.
5. True.

as well for decency, as to avoid inclemencies of air both hot and cold; of which, as to my own person, I would give him immediate conviction, if he pleased to command me; only desiring his excuse, if I did not expose those parts that Nature taught us to conceal. He said my discourse was all very strange, but especially the last part; for he could not understand why Nature should teach us to conceal what Nature had given. That neither himself nor family were ashamed of any parts of their bodies; but however I might do as I pleased. Whereupon, I first unbuttoned my coat, and pulled it off. I did the same with my waistcoat,[6] I drew off my shoes, stockings, and breeches. I let my shirt down to my waist, and drew up the bottom, fastening it like a girdle about my middle to hide my nakedness.

My master observed the whole performance with great signs of curiosity and admiration. He took up all my clothes in his pastern, one piece after another, and examined them diligently; he then stroked my body very gently, and looked round me several times, after which he said, it was plain I must be a perfect Yahoo; but that I differed very much from the rest of my species, in the softness, and whiteness, and smoothness of my skin, my want of hair in several parts of my body, the shape and shortness of my claws behind and before, and my affectation of walking continually on my two hinder feet. He desired to see no more, and gave me leave to put on my clothes again, for I was shuddering with cold.

I expressed my uneasiness at his giving me so often the appellation of *Yahoo*, an odious animal, for which I had so utter an hatred and contempt; I begged he would forbear applying that word to me, and take the same order in his family, and among his friends whom he suffered to see me. I requested likewise, that the secret of my having a false covering to my body might be known to none but himself, at least as long as my present clothing should last; for, as to what the sorrel nag his valet had observed, his Honor might command him to conceal it.

All this my master very graciously consented to,[7] and thus the secret was kept till my clothes began to wear out, which I was forced to supply by several contrivances, that shall hereafter be mentioned. In the meantime, he desired I would go on with my utmost diligence to learn their language, because he was more astonished at my capacity for speech and reason, than at the figure of my body, whether it were covered or no; adding, that he waited with some impatience to hear the wonders which I promised to tell him.

From thenceforward he doubled the pains he had been at to instruct me; he brought me into all company, and made them treat me with civility, because, as he told them privately, this would put me into good humor, and make me more diverting.

Every day when I waited on him, beside the trouble he was at in teaching, he would ask me several questions concerning myself, which I answered as well as I could; and by those means he had already received some general ideas, though very imperfect. It would be tedious to relate the several steps, by which I advanced to a more regular conversation: but the first account I gave of myself in any order and length, was to this purpose:

That, I came from a very far country, as I already had attempted to tell him, with about fifty more of my own species; that we traveled upon the seas, in a great hollow vessel made of wood, and larger than his Honor's house. I described the ship to him

---

6. Vest.

7. The Houyhnhnms may have no word for "lying," but they can hide the truth.

in the best terms I could, and explained by the help of my handkerchief displayed, how it was driven forward by the wind. That upon a quarrel among us, I was set on shore on this coast, where I walked forward without knowing whither, till he delivered me from the persecution of those execrable Yahoos. He asked me, who made the ship, and how it was possible that the Houyhnhnms of my country would leave it to the management of brutes? My answer was, that I durst proceed no farther in my relation, unless he would give me his word and honor that he would not be offended, and then I would tell him the wonders I had so often promised. He agreed; and I went on by assuring him, that the ship was made by creatures like myself, who in all the countries I had traveled, as well as in my own, were the only governing, rational animals, and that upon my arrival hither, I was as much astonished to see the Houyhnhnms act like rational beings, as he or his friends could be in finding some marks of reason in a creature he was pleased to call a Yahoo, to which I owned my resemblance in every part, but could not account for their degenerate and brutal nature. I said farther, that if good fortune ever restored me to my native country, to relate my travels hither, as I resolved to do, everybody would believe that I *said the thing which was not*; that I invented the story out of my own head; and with all possible respect to himself, his family, and friends, and under his promise of not being offended, our countrymen would hardly think it probable, that a Houyhnhnm should be the presiding creature of a nation, and a Yahoo the brute.

CHAPTER 4

The Houyhnhnms' notion of truth and falsehood. The author's discourse disapproved by his master. The author gives a more particular account of himself, and the accidents of his voyage.

My master heard me with great appearances of uneasiness in his countenance, because *doubting* or *not believing*, are so little known in this country, that the inhabitants cannot tell how to behave themselves under such circumstances. And I remember in frequent discourses with my master concerning the nature of manhood,[8] in other parts of the world, having occasion to talk of *lying*, and *false representation*, it was with much difficulty that he comprehended what I meant, although he had otherwise a most acute judgment. For he argued thus: that the use of speech was to make us understand one another, and to receive information of facts; now if any one *said the thing which was not*, these ends were defeated; because I cannot properly be said to understand him, and I am so far from receiving information, that he leaves me worse than in ignorance, for I am led to believe a thing *black* when it is *white*, and *short* when it is *long*. And these were all the notions he had concerning that faculty of *lying*, so perfectly well understood, and so universally practiced among human creatures.

To return from this digression; when I asserted that the Yahoos were the only governing animal in my country, which my master said was altogether past his conception, he desired to know, whether we had Houyhnhnms among us, and what was their employment: I told him, we had great numbers, that in summer they grazed in the fields, and in winter were kept in houses, with hay and oats, where Yahoo servants were employed to rub their skins smooth, comb their manes, pick their feet, serve them with food, and make their beds. I understand you well, said my master; it

8. Human nature.

is now very plain, from all you have spoken, that whatever share of reason the Yahoos pretend to, the Houyhnhnms are your masters;[9] I heartily wish our Yahoos would be so tractable. I begged his Honor would please to excuse me from proceeding any farther, because I was very certain that the account he expected from me would be highly displeasing. But he insisted in commanding me to let him know the best and the worst: I told him, he should be obeyed. I owned, that the Houyhnhnms among us, whom we called *horses*, were the most generous and comely animal we had, that they excelled in strength and swiftness; and when they belonged to persons of quality, employed in traveling, racing, or drawing chariots, they were treated with much kindness and care, till they fell into diseases, or became foundered in the feet;[1] but then they were sold, and used to all kind of drudgery till they died; after which their skins were stripped and sold for what they were worth, and their bodies left to be devoured by dogs and birds of prey.[2] But the common race of horses had not so good fortune, being kept by farmers and carriers and other mean people, who put them to greater labor, and fed them worse. I described as well as I could, our way of riding, the shape and use of a bridle, a saddle, a spur, and a whip, of harness and wheels. I added, that we fastened plates of a certain hard substance called *iron* at the bottom of their feet, to preserve their hoofs from being broken by the stony ways on which we often traveled.

My master, after some expressions of great indignation, wondered how we dared to venture upon a Houyhnhnm's back, for he was sure that the weakest servant in his house would be able to shake off the strongest Yahoo, or by lying down, and rolling upon his back, squeeze the brute to death. I answered, that our horses were trained up from three or four years old to the several uses we intended them for; that if any of them proved intolerably vicious, they were employed for carriages; that they were severely beaten while they were young, for any mischievous tricks; that the males, designed for the common use of riding or draft, were generally *castrated* about two years after their birth, to take down their spirits, and make them more tame and gentle; that they were indeed sensible of rewards and punishments; but his Honor would please to consider, that they had not the least tincture of reason any more than the Yahoos in this country.

It put me to the pains of many circumlocutions to give my master a right idea of what I spoke; for their language doth not abound in variety of words, because their wants and passions are fewer than among us. But it is impossible to express his noble resentment at our savage treatment of the Houyhnhnm race, particularly after I had explained the manner and use of *castrating* horses among us, to hinder them from propagating their kind, and to render them more servile. He said, if it were possible there could be any country where Yahoos alone were endued with reason, they certainly must be the governing animal, because reason will in time always prevail against brutal strength. But, considering the frame of our bodies, and especially of mine, he thought no creature of equal bulk was so ill-contrived for employing that reason in the common offices of life; whereupon he desired to know whether those among whom I lived, resembled me or the Yahoos of his country. I assured him, that I was as well shaped as most of my age, but the younger and the females were much more soft and tender, and the skins of the latter generally as white as milk. He said, I differed indeed from other Yahoos, being much more cleanly, and not altogether so

---

9. Possibly a satire on the English love of horses.
1. Until their feet give in from overwork.
2. Swift mockingly paraphrases the *Iliad* 1.4–6: "The souls

of mighty Chiefs untimely slain; / Whose limbs unburied on the naked shore, / Devouring dogs and hungry vultures tore" (Pope's translation).

deformed, but in point of real advantage, he thought I differed for the worse. That my nails were of no use either to my fore or hinder feet; as to my forefeet, he could not properly call them by that name, for he never observed me to walk upon them; that they were too soft to bear the ground; that I generally went with them uncovered, neither was the covering I sometimes wore on them of the same shape, or so strong as that on my feet behind. That I could not walk with any security, for if either of my hinder feet slipped, I must inevitably fall. He then began to find fault with other parts of my body, the flatness of my face, the prominence of my nose, mine eyes placed directly in front, so that I could not look on either side without turning my head, that I was not able to feed myself, without lifting one of my forefeet to my mouth, and therefore Nature had placed those joints to answer that necessity. He knew not what could be the use of those several clefts and divisions in my feet behind; that these were too soft to bear the hardness and sharpness of stones without a covering made from the skin of some other brute; that my whole body wanted a fence against heat and cold, which I was forced to put on and off every day with tediousness and trouble. And lastly, that he observed every animal in this country naturally to abhor the Yahoos, whom the weaker avoided, and the stronger drove from them. So that supposing us to have the gift of reason, he could not see how it were possible to cure that natural antipathy which every creature discovered[3] against us; nor consequently, how we could tame and render them serviceable. However, he would (as he said) debate that matter no farther, because he was more desirous to know my own story, the country where I was born, and the several actions and events of my life before I came hither.

I assured him, how extremely desirous I was that he should be satisfied in every point; but I doubted much, whether it would be possible for me to explain myself on several subjects whereof his Honor could have no conception, because I saw nothing in his country to which I could resemble[4] them. That, however, I would do my best, and strive to express myself by similitudes, humbly desiring his assistance when I wanted proper words; which he was pleased to promise me.

I said, my birth was of honest parents, in an island called England, which was remote from this country, as many days' journey as the strongest of his Honor's servants could travel in the annual course of the sun. That I was bred a surgeon, whose trade it is to cure wounds and hurts in the body, got by accident or violence; that my country was governed by a female man, whom we called a *Queen*. That I left it to get riches,[5] whereby I might maintain myself and family when I should return. That in my last voyage, I was commander of the ship, and had about fifty Yahoos under me, many of which died at sea, and I was forced to supply[6] them by others picked out from several nations. That our ship was twice in danger of being sunk; the first time by a great storm, and the second, by striking against a rock. Here my master interposed, by asking me, how I could persuade strangers out of different countries to venture with me, after the losses I had sustained, and the hazards I had run. I said, they were fellows of desperate fortunes, forced to fly from the places of their birth, on account of their poverty or their crimes. Some were undone by lawsuits; others spent all they had in drinking, whoring, and gaming; others fled for treason; many for murder, theft, poisoning, robbery, perjury, forgery, coining false money, for committing rapes or

---

3. Displayed.
4. Compare.
5. Gulliver originally stated that he undertook his second

and third voyages out of a desire to travel: he now reads all human motivation in the worst possible light.
6. Replace.

sodomy, for flying from their colors,[7] or deserting to the enemy, and most of them had broken prison; none of these durst return to their native countries for fear of being hanged, or of starving in a jail; and therefore were under a necessity of seeking a livelihood in other places.

During this discourse, my master was pleased often to interrupt me. I had made use of many circumlocutions in describing to him the nature of the several crimes, for which most of our crew had been forced to fly their country. This labor took up several days' conversation before he was able to comprehend me. He was wholly at a loss to know what could be the use or necessity of practicing those vices. To clear up which I endeavored to give him some ideas of the desire of power and riches, of the terrible effects of lust, intemperance, malice, and envy. All this I was forced to define and describe by putting of cases, and making suppositions. After which, like one whose imagination was struck with something never seen or heard of before, he would lift up his eyes with amazement and indignation. Power, government, war, law, punishment, and a thousand other things had no terms, wherein that language could express them, which made the difficulty almost insuperable to give my master any conception of what I meant. But being of an excellent understanding, much improved by contemplation and converse, he at last arrived at a competent knowledge of what human nature in our parts of the world is capable to perform, and desired I would give him some particular account of that land, which we call Europe, but especially, of my own country.

CHAPTER 5

The author at his master's commands informs him of the state of England. The causes of war among the princes of Europe. The author begins to explain the English Constitution.

The reader may please to observe, that the following extract of many conversations I had with my master, contains a summary of the most material points, which were discoursed at several times for above two years; his Honor often desiring fuller satisfaction[8] as I farther improved in the Houyhnhnm tongue. I laid before him, as well as I could, the whole state of Europe; I discoursed of trade and manufactures, of arts and sciences; and the answers I gave to all the questions he made, as they arose upon several subjects, were a fund of conversation not to be exhausted. But I shall here only set down the substance of what passed between us concerning my own country, reducing it into order as well as I can, without any regard to time or other circumstances, while I strictly adhere to truth. My only concern is, that I shall hardly be able to do justice to my master's arguments and expressions, which must needs suffer by my want of capacity, as well as by a translation into our barbarous English.[9]

In obedience therefore to his Honor's commands, I related to him the Revolution under the Prince of Orange,[1] the long war with France[2] entered into by the said Prince, and renewed by his successor the present Queen, wherein the greatest powers of Christendom were engaged, and which still continued: I computed, at his request,

7. Deserting their regiment in the army.
8. Better explanation.
9. Presumably "barbarous," because English both lacks appropriate words to express Houyhnhnm concepts and has concepts (e.g., of lust, malice, envy) for which the other language has no words.

1. The Glorious Revolution of 1688 by which William of Orange, and his wife, Mary Stuart, ascended to the English throne in 1689.
2. The War of the League of Augsburg (1689–1697) and the War of the Spanish Succession (1701–1713), which Swift (as a good Tory) opposed.

that about a million of Yahoos might have been killed in the whole progress of it, and perhaps a hundred or more cities taken, and five times as many ships burnt or sunk.

He asked me what were the usual causes or motives that made one country go to war with another. I answered they were innumerable, but I should only mention a few of the chief. Sometimes the ambition of princes, who never think they have land or people enough to govern; sometimes the corruption of ministers, who engage their master in a war in order to stifle or divert the clamor of the subjects against their evil administration. Difference in opinions[3] hath cost many millions of lives: for instance, whether *flesh* be *bread*, or *bread* be *flesh*; whether the juice of a certain *berry* be *blood* or *wine*; whether *whistling* be a vice or a virtue; whether it be better to *kiss a post*, or throw it into the fire; what is the best color for a *coat*, whether *black*, *white*, *red*, or *grey*; and whether it should be *long* or *short*, *narrow* or *wide*, *dirty* or *clean*, with many more. Neither are any wars so furious and bloody, or of so long continuance, as those occasioned by difference in opinion, especially if it be in things indifferent.[4]

Sometimes the quarrel between two princes is to decide which of them shall dispossess a third of his dominions, where neither of them pretend to any right. Sometimes one prince quarrels with another, for fear the other should quarrel with him. Sometimes a war is entered upon, because the enemy is too *strong*, and sometimes because he is too *weak*. Sometimes our neighbors *want* the *things* which we *have*, or *have* the *things* which we *want*; and we both fight, till they take ours or give us theirs. It is a very justifiable cause of war to invade a country after the people have been wasted by famine, destroyed by pestilence, or embroiled by factions amongst themselves.[5] It is justifiable to enter into a war against our nearest ally, when one of his towns lies convenient for us, or a territory of land, that would render our dominions round and compact. If a prince send forces into a nation where the people are poor and ignorant, he may lawfully put half of them to death, and make slaves of the rest, in order to civilize and reduce[6] them from their barbarous way of living. It is a very kingly, honorable, and frequent practice, when one prince desires the assistance of another to secure him against an invasion, that the assistant, when he hath driven out the invader, should seize on the dominions himself, and kill, imprison, or banish the prince he came to relieve. Alliance by blood or marriage is a sufficient cause of war between princes, and the nearer the kindred is, the greater is their disposition to quarrel: *poor* nations are *hungry*, and *rich* nations are *proud*, and pride and hunger will ever be at variance. For these reasons, the trade of a *soldier* is held the most honorable of all others: because a *soldier* is a Yahoo hired to kill in cold blood as many of his own species, who have never offended him, as possibly he can.

There is likewise a kind of beggarly princes in Europe, not able to make war by themselves, who hire out their troops to richer nations, for so much a day to each man; of which they keep three fourths to themselves, and it is the best part of their maintenance; such are those in Germany and other northern parts of Europe.[7]

What you have told me (said my master), upon the subject of war, doth indeed discover most admirably the effects of that reason you pretend to: however, it is

---

3. Religious controversies, over the doctrine of transubstantiation, the place of music (whistling) and images (the post) in church, and the color and style of liturgical vestments.
4. Of no importance either way.

5. Probably a reference to the English Civil War of 1642–1646, 1648.
6. Convert.
7. George I employed German mercenaries in his defense of Hanover.

happy that the *shame* is greater than the *danger*; and that Nature hath left you utterly uncapable of doing much mischief. For your mouths lying flat with your faces, you can hardly bite each other to any purpose, unless by consent. Then as to the claws upon your feet before and behind, they are so short and tender, that one of our Yahoos would drive a dozen of yours before him. And therefore in recounting the numbers of those who have been killed in battle, I cannot but think that you have *said the thing which is not*.

I could not forbear shaking my head and smiling a little at his ignorance. And, being no stranger to the art of war, I gave him a description of cannons, culverins,[8] muskets, carabines,[9] pistols, bullets, powder, swords, bayonets, battles, sieges, retreats, attacks, undermines, countermines,[1] bombardments, seafights; ships sunk with a thousand men, twenty thousand killed on each side; dying groans, limbs flying in the air, smoke, noise, confusion, trampling to death under horses' feet; flight, pursuit, victory; fields strewed with carcasses left for food to dogs, and wolves, and birds of prey; plundering, stripping, ravishing, burning, and destroying. And to set forth the valor of my own dear countrymen, I assured him, that I had seen them blow up a hundred enemies at once in a siege, and as many in a ship, and beheld the dead bodies drop down in pieces from the clouds, to the great diversion of all the spectators.

I was going on to more particulars, when my master commanded me silence. He said, whoever understood the nature of Yahoos might easily believe it possible for so vile an animal to be capable of every action I had named, if their strength and cunning equaled their malice. But as my discourse had increased his abhorrence of the whole species, so he found it gave him a disturbance in his mind, to which he was wholly a stranger before. He thought his ears being used to such abominable words, might by degrees admit them with less detestation. That although he hated the Yahoos of this country, yet he no more blamed them for their odious qualities, than he did a *gnnayh* (a bird of prey) for its cruelty, or a sharp stone for cutting his hoof. But when a creature pretending to reason could be capable of such enormities, he dreaded lest[2] the corruption of that faculty might be worse than brutality itself. He seemed therefore confident, that instead of reason, we were only possessed of some quality fitted to increase our natural vices; as the reflection from a troubled stream returns the image of an ill-shapen body, not only *larger*, but more *distorted*.

He added, that he had heard too much upon the subject of war, both in this, and some former discourses. There was another point which a little perplexed him at present. I had said, that some of our crew left their country on account of being ruined by *law*; that I had already explained the meaning of the word; but he was at a loss how it should come to pass, that the *law* which was intended for *every* man's preservation, should be any man's ruin. Therefore he desired to be farther satisfied what I meant by *law*, and the dispensers thereof, according to the present practice in my own country; because he thought Nature and reason were sufficient guides for a reasonable animal, as we pretended to be, in showing us what we ought to do, and what to avoid.

I assured his Honor, that law was a science wherein I had not much conversed,[3] further than by employing advocates in vain, upon some injustices that had been done me; however, I would give him all the satisfaction I was able.

---

8. Large cannons.
9. Short firearms.
1. Digging under fortification walls, and counter-digging

by those inside the fort to stop the besiegers.
2. Worried that.
3. Had not had much instruction.

I said there was a society of men among us, bred up from their youth in the art of proving by words multiplied for the purpose, that white is black, and black is white, according as they are paid.[4] To this society all the rest of the people are slaves. For example, if my neighbor hath a mind to my cow, he hires a lawyer to prove that he ought to have my cow from me. I must then hire another to defend my right, it being against all rules of law that any man should be allowed to speak for himself.[5] Now in this case, I who am the true owner lie under two great disadvantages. First, my lawyer, being practiced almost from his cradle in defending falsehood, is quite out of his element when he would be an advocate for justice, which as an office unnatural, he always attempts with great awkwardness, if not with ill will. The second disadvantage is, that my lawyer must proceed with great caution, or else he will be reprimanded by the judges, and abhorred by his brethren, as one who would lessen the practice[6] of the law. And therefore I have but two methods to preserve my cow. The first is to gain over my adversary's lawyer with a double fee, who will then betray his client by insinuating that he hath justice on his side. The second way is for my lawyer to make my cause appear as unjust as he can, by allowing the cow to belong to my adversary; and this if it be skillfully done will certainly bespeak[7] the favor of the Bench.

Now, your Honor is to know that these judges are persons appointed to decide all controversies of property, as well as for the trial of criminals, and picked out from the most dexterous lawyers who are grown old or lazy, and having been biased all their lives against truth and equity, lie under such a fatal necessity of favoring fraud, perjury, and oppression, that I have known several of them refuse a large bribe from the side where justice lay, rather than injure the *Faculty*[8] by doing anything unbecoming their nature or their office.

It is a maxim among these lawyers, that whatever hath been done before, may legally be done again; and therefore they take special care to record all the decisions formerly made against common justice and the general reason of mankind. These, under the name of *precedents*, they produce as authorities to justify the most iniquitous opinions; and the judges never fail of directing accordingly.

In pleading, they studiously avoid entering into the *merits* of the cause; but are loud, violent, and tedious in dwelling upon all *circumstances* which are not to the purpose. For instance, in the case already mentioned; they never desire to know what claim or title my adversary hath to my cow, but whether the said cow were red or black, her horns long or short, whether the field I graze her in be round or square, whether she were milked at home or abroad, what diseases she is subject to, and the like; after which they consult *precedents*, adjourn the cause from time to time, and in ten, twenty, or thirty years come to an issue.

It is likewise to be observed that this society hath a peculiar cant[9] and jargon of their own, that no other mortal can understand, and wherein all their laws are

---

4. Swift's satirical treatment of lawyers probably stems from his dislike of Lord Chief Justice Whitehead, who tried to force juries to give verdicts against Swift and the printer of two of his political pamphlets.

5. One of Swift's many references to Thomas More's *Utopia* (1516) in this discussion of the ideals of human and Houyhnhnm society. *Utopia* suggests that it is "better for each man to plead for his own cause, and tell the judge the same story he'd otherwise tell his lawyer." Other important sources for *Gulliver* include Lucian's *True History* (mid-second century A.D.); Cyrano de

Bergerac's *Histoire comique des états et empires de la lune* (1656); William Temple's essay *Of Heroick Virtue* (in *Miscellanea*, pt. 2, 1692); William Dampier's *New Voyage Round the World* (1697); and Lionel Wafer's *A New Voyage and Description of the Isthmus of America* (1699), which includes descriptions of monkeys Swift may have used for the Yahoos.

6. Both profession, and morally questionable dealing.

7. Gain.

8. Legal profession.

9. Both insincere and specialist language.

written, which they take special care to multiply; whereby they have wholly confounded the very essence of truth and falsehood, of right and wrong; so that it will take thirty years to decide whether the field, left me by my ancestors for six generations, belong to me or to a stranger three hundred miles off.

In the trial of persons accused for crimes against the state the method is much more short and commendable: the judge first sends to sound the disposition of those in power, after which he can easily hang or save the criminal, strictly preserving all the forms of law.

Here my master, interposing, said it was a pity, that creatures endowed with such prodigious abilities of mind as these lawyers, by the description I gave of them, must certainly be, were not rather encouraged to be instructors of others in wisdom and knowledge. In answer to which, I assured his Honor, that in all points out of their own trade they were usually the most ignorant and stupid generation among us, the most despicable in common conversation, avowed enemies to all knowledge and learning, and equally disposed to pervert the general reason of mankind in every other subject of discourse, as in that of their own profession.

CHAPTER 6

A continuation of the state of England. The character of a first Minister.[1]

My master was yet wholly at a loss to understand what motives could incite this race of lawyers to perplex, disquiet, and weary themselves by engaging in a confederacy of injustice, merely for the sake of injuring their fellow animals; neither could he comprehend what I meant in saying they did it for *hire*. Whereupon I was at much pains to describe to him the use of *money*, the materials it was made of, and the value of the metals; that when a Yahoo had got a great store of this precious substance, he was able to purchase whatever he had a mind to, the finest clothing, the noblest houses, great tracts of land, the most costly meats and drinks, and have his choice of the most beautiful females. Therefore since *money* alone was able to perform all these feats, our Yahoos thought they could never have enough of it to spend or to save, as they found themselves inclined from their natural bent either to profusion or avarice. That the rich man enjoyed the fruit of the poor man's labor, and the latter were a thousand to one in proportion to the former.[2] That the bulk of our people was forced to live miserably, by laboring every day for small wages to make a few live plentifully. I enlarged myself[3] much on these and many other particulars to the same purpose: but his Honor was still to seek,[4] for he went upon a supposition that all animals had a title to their share in the productions of the earth, and especially those[5] who presided over the rest. Therefore he desired I would let him know, what these costly meats were, and how any of us happened to want them. Whereupon I enumerated as many sorts as came into my head, with the various methods of dressing them, which could not be done without sending vessels by sea to every part of the world, as well for liquors to drink, as for sauces, and innumerable other conveniencies. I assured him, that this whole globe of earth must be at least three times gone round, before one of our better

1. Swift's first printer/publisher, Benjamin Motte, prudently added "under Queen Anne" and "in the Courts of Europe" at the end of these two sentences, respectively, to remove some of the sting from this satire on George I's reign.

2. A theme of Thomas More's *Utopia* (1516).
3. Explained myself further.
4. Unable to understand.
5. The ruling species.

female Yahoos could get her breakfast, or a cup to put it in.[6] He said, that must needs be a miserable country which cannot furnish food for its own inhabitants. But what he chiefly wondered at was how such vast tracts of ground as I described should be wholly without *fresh water*, and the people put to the necessity of sending over the sea for drink. I replied, that England (the dear place of my nativity) was computed to produce three times the quantity of food more than its inhabitants are able to consume, as well as liquors extracted from grain, or pressed out of the fruit of certain trees, which made excellent drink, and the same proportion in every other convenience of life. But in order to feed the luxury and intemperance of the males, and the vanity of the females, we sent away the greatest part of our necessary things to other countries, from whence in return we brought the materials of diseases, folly, and vice, to spend among ourselves. Hence it follows of necessity, that vast numbers of our people are compelled to seek their livelihood by begging, robbing, stealing, cheating, pimping, forswearing,[7] flattering, suborning,[8] forging, gaming, lying, fawning, hectoring,[9] voting, scribbling, stargazing,[1] poisoning, whoring, canting,[2] libeling, freethinking,[3] and the like occupations: every one of which terms, I was at much pains to make him understand.

That *wine* was not imported among us from foreign countries to supply the want of water or other drinks, but because it was a sort of liquid which made us merry, by putting us out of our senses; diverted all melancholy thoughts, begat wild extravagant imaginations in the brain, raised our hopes, and banished our fears, suspended every office of reason for a time, and deprived us of the use of our limbs, till we fell into a profound sleep; although it must be confessed, that we always awaked sick and dispirited, and that the use of this liquor filled us with diseases, which made our lives uncomfortable and short.[4]

But beside all this, the bulk of our people supported themselves by furnishing the necessities or conveniencies of life to the rich, and to each other. For instance, when I am at home and dressed as I ought to be, I carry on my body the workmanship of an hundred tradesmen; the building and furniture of my house employ as many more, and five times the number to adorn my wife.

I was going on to tell him of another sort of people, who get their livelihood by attending the sick, having upon some occasions informed his Honor that many of my crew had died of diseases. But here it was with the utmost difficulty that I brought him to apprehend what I meant. He could easily conceive, that a Houyhnhnm grew weak and heavy a few days before his death, or by some accident might hurt a limb. But that Nature, who worketh all things to perfection, should suffer any pains to breed in our bodies, he thought impossible, and desired to know the reason of so unaccountable an evil. I told him, we fed on a thousand things which operated contrary to each other; that we ate when we were not hungry, and drank without the provocation of thirst; that we sat whole nights drinking strong liquors without eating a bit, which disposed us to sloth, inflamed our bodies, and precipitated or prevented digestion. That prostitute female Yahoos acquired a certain malady, which bred rottenness in the bones of those who fell into their embraces; that this and many other diseases

---

6. Coffee, tea, and chocolate were relatively new (and highly fashionable) drinks; chinaware was also imported.
7. Perjury.
8. Inducing through bribery.
9. Bullying.
1. Sensationalist popular astrology of the type Swift

mocked when writing as "Isaac Bickerstaff" in 1708.
2. Using jargon, often for deceit.
3. Freethinkers rejected religious authority and dogma in favor of rational inquiry and speculation.
4. Swift, however, was a great wine drinker.

were propagated from father to son, so that great numbers come into the world with complicated maladies upon them; that it would be endless to give him a catalog of all diseases incident to human bodies; for they could not be fewer than five or six hundred, spread over every limb, and joint; in short, every part, external and intestine, having diseases appropriated to each. To remedy which, there was a sort of people bred up among us, in the profession or pretense of curing the sick. And because I had some skill in the faculty, I would, in gratitude to his Honor, let him know the whole mystery[5] and method by which they proceed.

Their fundamental is, that all diseases arise from *repletion*, from whence they conclude, that a great *evacuation* of the body is necessary, either through the natural passage, or upwards at the mouth. Their next business is, from herbs, minerals, gums, oils, shells, salts, juices, seaweed, excrements, barks of trees, serpents, toads, frogs, spiders, dead men's flesh and bones, birds, beasts and fishes, to form a composition for smell and taste the most abominable, nauseous, and detestable that they can possibly contrive, which the stomach immediately rejects with loathing; and this they call a *vomit*;[6] or else from the same storehouse, with some other poisonous additions, they command us to take in at the orifice *above* or *below* (just as the physician then happens to be disposed), a medicine equally annoying and disgustful to the bowels, which, relaxing the belly, drives down all before it; and this they call a *purge*, or a *clyster*.[7] For Nature (as the physicians allege) having intended the superior anterior orifice[8] only for the *intromission* of solids and liquids, and the inferior posterior for ejection, these artists ingeniously considering that in all diseases Nature is forced out of her seat; therefore to replace her in it, the body must be treated in a manner directly contrary, by interchanging the use of each orifice, forcing solids and liquids in at the anus, and making evacuations at the mouth.

But, besides real diseases, we are subject to many that are only imaginary, for which the physicians have invented imaginary cures; these have their several names, and so have the drugs that are proper for them, and with these our female Yahoos are always infested.

One great excellency in this tribe is their skill at *prognostics*, wherein they seldom fail; their predictions in real diseases, when they rise to any degree of malignity, generally portending *death*, which is always in their power, when recovery is not: and therefore, upon any unexpected signs of amendment, after they have pronounced their sentence, rather than be accused as false prophets, they know how to approve their sagacity to the world by a seasonable dose.[9]

They are likewise of special use to husbands and wives who are grown weary of their mates, to eldest sons, to great ministers of state, and often to princes.[1]

I had formerly upon occasion discoursed with my master upon the nature of *government* in general, and particularly of our own *excellent Constitution*, deservedly the wonder and envy of the whole world. But having here accidentally mentioned a *Minister of State*, he commanded me some time after to inform him, what species of Yahoo I particularly meant by that appellation.

5. Medical secrets.
6. Dr. John Woodward (1665–1728), a leading member of the Royal Society, was noted for believing this method a cure for virtually all ills.
7. Enema.
8. The mouth.

9. Cf. *Verses on the Death of Dr. Swift*, lines 131–132: "He'd rather choose that I should die / Than his prediction prove a lie."
1. The references are to Queen Caroline, Prince Frederick, and Walpole.

I told him, that a *First* or *Chief Minister of State*[2] whom I intended to describe, was a creature wholly exempt from joy and grief, love and hatred, pity and anger; at least made use of no other passions but a violent desire of wealth, power, and titles; that he applies his words to all uses, except to the indication of his mind,[3] that he never tells a *truth*, but with an intent that you should take it for a *lie*; nor a *lie*, but with a design that you should take it for a *truth* that those he speaks worst of behind their backs are in the surest way to preferment[4] and whenever he begins to praise you to others or to yourself, you are from that day forlorr.[5] The worst mark you can receive is a *promise*, especially when it is confirmed with an oath; after which every wise man retires, and gives over all hopes.

There are three methods by which a man may rise to be Chief Minister: the first is, by knowing how with prudence to dispose of a wife, a daughter, or a sister; the second, by betraying or undermining his predecessor; and the third is, by a *furious zeal* in public assemblies against the corruptions of the Court. But a wise prince would rather choose to employ those who practice the last of these methods; because such zealots prove always the most obsequious and subservient to the will and passions of their master. That the *Ministers* having all employment[6] at their disposal, preserve themselves in power by bribing the majority of a senate or great council; and at last, by an expedient called an *Act of Indemnity*,[7] (whereof I described the nature to him) they secure themselves from after-reckonings, and retire from the public, laden with the spoils of the nation.

The palace of a *Chief Minister* is a seminary to breed up others in his own trade: the pages, lackeys, and porter, by imitating their master, become *Ministers of State* in their several districts, and learn to excel in the three principal *ingredients*, of *insolence*, *lying*, and *bribery*. Accordingly, they have a *subaltern*[8] court paid to them by persons of the best rank, and sometimes by the force of dexterity and impudence arrive through several gradations to be successors to their lord.

He is usually governed by a decayed wench[9] or favorite footman, who are the tunnels[1] through which all graces[2] are conveyed, and may properly be called, *in the last resort*, the governors of the kingdom.

One day my master, having heard me mention the *nobility* of my country, was pleased to make me a compliment which I could not pretend to deserve: that he was sure I must have been born of some noble family, because I far exceeded in shape, color, and cleanliness, all the Yahoos of his nation, although I seemed to fail in strength and agility, which must be imputed to my different way of living from those other brutes; and besides, I was not only endowed with a faculty of speech, but likewise with some rudiments of reason, to a degree, that with all his acquaintance I passed for a prodigy.

He made me observe, that among the Houyhnhnms, the white, the *sorrel*, and the *iron-grey* were not so exactly shaped as the *bay*, the *dapple-grey*, and the *black*; nor

2. A satire on Robert Walpole, then the First Minister or "Prime Minister."
3. Real thoughts or intentions.
4. Most likely to receive a government position or promotion.
5. Forsaken, ruined.
6. Government positions.
7. Swift here suggests that corrupt government ministers make themselves secure from any future legal prosecution for their illegal dealings. He refers to the Act of Indemnity

and Oblivion of 1660, which pardoned almost all those who had taken part in the English Civil War (1642–1646, 1648), or the subsequent Commonwealth government (1649–1660).
8. Lower-ranking
9. The government Minister's mistress is "decayed" either in age or in morals.
1. Routes or conduits.
2. Favors.

born with equal talents of mind, or a capacity to improve them; and therefore continued always in the condition of servants, without ever aspiring to match[3] out of their own race, which in that country would be reckoned monstrous and unnatural.

I made his Honor my most humble acknowledgments for the good opinion he was pleased to conceive of me; but assured him at the same time, that my birth was of the lower sort, having been born of plain, honest parents, who were just able to give me a tolerable education; that *nobility* among us was altogether a different thing from the idea he had of it; that our young *noblemen* are bred from their childhood in idleness and luxury; that as soon as years will permit, they consume their vigor and contract odious diseases among lewd females; and when their fortunes are almost ruined, they marry some woman of mean birth, disagreeable person, and unsound constitution, merely for the sake of money, whom they hate and despise. That the productions of such marriages are generally scrofulous,[4] rickety,[5] or deformed children, by which means the family seldom continues above three generations, unless the wife take care to provide a healthy father among her neighbors or domestics, in order to improve and continue the breed. That a weak diseased body, a meager countenance, and sallow complexion are the true marks of *noble blood*; and a healthy robust appearance is so disgraceful in a man of quality, that the world concludes his real father to have been a groom, or a coachman. The imperfections of his mind run parallel with those of his body, being a composition of spleen, dullness, ignorance, caprice, sensuality, and pride.

Without the consent of this *illustrious body* no law can be enacted, repealed, or altered, and these nobles have likewise the decision of all our possessions without appeal.[6]

CHAPTER 7

The author's great love of his native country. His master's observations upon the Constitution and Administration of England, as described by the author, with parallel cases and comparisons. His master's observations upon human nature.

The reader may be disposed to wonder how I could prevail on myself to give so free a representation of my own species, among a race of mortals who were already too apt to conceive the vilest opinion of humankind from that entire congruity betwixt me and their Yahoos. But I must freely confess, that the many virtues of those excellent *quadrupeds*, placed in opposite view to human corruptions, had so far opened mine eyes and enlarged my understanding, that I began to view the actions and passions of man in a very different light, and to think the honor of my own kind not worth managing[7] which, besides, it was impossible for me to do before a person of so acute a judgment as my master, who daily convinced me of a thousand faults in myself, whereof I had not the least perception before, and which with us would never be numbered even among human infirmities. I had likewise learned from his example an utter detestation of all falsehood or disguise; and *truth* appeared so amiable to me, that I determined upon sacrificing everything to it.

3. Mate.
4. Tubercular.
5. Feeble, weak-jointed.
6. Swift here refers to the House of Lords, the upper house of Parliament and the highest law court in the land.
7. Maintaining.

Let me deal so candidly with the reader, as to confess, that there was yet a much stronger motive for the freedom I took in my representation of things. I had not been a year in this country before I contracted such a love and veneration for the inhabitants, that I entered on a firm resolution never to return to humankind, but to pass the rest of my life among these admirable Houyhnhnms in the contemplation and practice of every virtue; where I could have no example or incitement to vice. But it was decreed by Fortune, my perpetual enemy, that so great a felicity should not fall to my share. However, it is now some comfort to reflect, that in what I said of my countrymen, I *extenuated* their faults as much as I durst before so strict an examiner, and upon every article gave as *favorable* a turn as the matter would bear. For, indeed, who is there alive that will not be swayed by his bias and partiality to the place of his birth?

I have related the substance of several conversations I had with my master, during the greatest part of the time I had the honor to be in his service, but have indeed for brevity sake omitted much more than is here set down.

When I had answered all his questions, and his curiosity seemed to be fully satisfied, he sent for me one morning early, and commanding me to sit down at some distance (an honor which he had never before conferred upon me), he said, he had been very seriously considering my whole story, as far as it related both to myself and my country: that he looked upon us as a sort of animals to whose share, by what accident he could not conjecture, some small pittance of *reason* had fallen, whereof we made no other use than by its assistance to aggravate our *natural* corruptions, and to acquire new ones which Nature had not given us. That we disarmed ourselves of the few abilities she had bestowed, had been very successful in multiplying our original wants, and seemed to spend our whole lives in vain endeavors to supply them by our own inventions. That as to myself, it was manifest I had neither the strength or agility of a common Yahoo, that I walked infirmly on my hinder feet, had found out a contrivance to make my claws of no use or defense, and to remove the hair from my chin, which was intended as a shelter from the sun and the weather. Lastly, that I could neither run with speed, nor climb trees like my *brethren* (as he called them) the Yahoos in this country.

That our institutions of *government* and *law* were plainly owing to our gross defects in *reason*, and by consequence, in *virtue*; because *reason* alone is sufficient to govern a *rational* creature; which was therefore a character we had no pretense to challenge,[8] even from the account I had given of my own people, although he manifestly perceived, that in order to favor them I had concealed many particulars, and often *said the thing which was not*.

He was the more confirmed in this opinion, because he observed, that as I agreed in every feature of my body with other Yahoos, except where it was to my real disadvantage in point of strength, speed, and activity, the shortness of my claws, and some other particulars where Nature had no part; so from the representation I had given him of our lives, our manners, and our actions, he found as near a resemblance in the disposition of our minds. He said the Yahoos were known to hate one another more than they did any different species of animals; and the reason usually assigned, was, the odiousness of their own shapes, which all could see in the rest, but not in themselves. He had therefore begun to think it not unwise in us to *cover* our bodies, and, by that invention, conceal many of our deformities from each other, which would

---

8. We had no right to claim to be rational creatures.

else be hardly supportable. But, he now found he had been mistaken, and that the dissensions of those brutes in his country were owing to the same cause with ours, as I had described them. For if (said he) you throw among five Yahoos as much food as would be sufficient for fifty, they will, instead of eating peaceably, fall together by the ears, each single one impatient to *have all to itself*; and therefore a servant was usually employed to stand by while they were feeding abroad, and those kept at home were tied at a distance from each other; that if a cow died of age or accident, before a Houyhnhnm could secure it for his own Yahoos, those in the neighborhood would come in herds to seize it, and then would ensue such a battle as I had described, with terrible wounds made by their claws on both sides, although they seldom were able to kill one another, for want of such convenient instruments of death as we had invented. At other times the like battles have been fought between the Yahoos of several neighborhoods without any visible cause: those of one district watching all opportunities to surprise the next before they are prepared. But if they find their project hath miscarried, they return home, and for want of enemies, engage in what I call a civil war among themselves.

That in some fields of his country there are certain *shining stones* of several colors, whereof the Yahoos are violently fond, and when part of these *stones* are fixed in the earth, as it sometimes happens, they will dig with their claws for whole days to get them out, and carry them away, and hide them by heaps in their kennels; but still looking round with great caution, for fear their comrades should find out their treasure. My master said, he could never discover the reason of this unnatural appetite, or how these *stones* could be of any use to a Yahoo; but now he believed it might proceed from the same principle of *avarice* which I had ascribed to mankind; that he had once, by way of experiment, privately removed a heap of these *stones* from the place where one of his Yahoos had buried it: whereupon, the sordid animal, missing his treasure, by his loud lamenting brought the whole herd to the place, there miserably howled, then fell to biting and tearing the rest, began to pine away, would neither eat, nor sleep, nor work, till he ordered a servant privately to convey the *stones* into the same hole, and hide them as before; which when his Yahoo had found, he presently recovered his spirits and good humor, but took care to remove them to a better hiding place, and hath ever since been a very serviceable brute.

My master farther assured me, which I also observed myself, that in the fields where these *shining stones* abound, the fiercest and most frequent battles are fought, occasioned by perpetual inroads of the neighboring Yahoos.[9]

He said, it was common, when two Yahoos discovered such a *stone* in a field, and were contending which of them should be the proprietor, a third would take the advantage,[1] and carry it away from them both; which my master would needs contend to have some resemblance with our *suits at law*; wherein I thought it for our credit not to undeceive him; since the decision he mentioned was much more equitable than many decrees among us: because the plaintiff and defendant there lost nothing beside the *stone* they contended for, whereas our *Courts of Equity*[2] would never have dismissed the cause while either of them had anything left.

My master, continuing his discourse, said, there was nothing that rendered the Yahoos more odious, than their undistinguishing appetite to devour everything that

---

9. Neighboring Yahoos attempt invasions to steal these stones.
1. Opportunity.

2. Courts that decide on general (rather than common) principles of law. Swift ironically plays on the name of the court.

came in their way, whether herbs, roots, berries, the corrupted flesh of animals, or all mingled together; and it was peculiar in their temper, that they were fonder of what they could get by rapine or stealth at a greater distance, than much better food provided for them at home. If their prey held out, they would eat till they were ready to burst, after which Nature had pointed out to them a certain *root* that gave them a general evacuation.

There was also another kind of *root* very *juicy*, but something rare and difficult to be found, which the Yahoos sought for with much eagerness, and would suck it with great delight; and it produced in them the same effects that wine hath upon us. It would make them sometimes hug, and sometimes tear one another; they would howl and grin, and chatter, and reel, and tumble, and then fall asleep in the mud.

I did indeed observe, that the Yahoos were the only animals in this country subject to any diseases; which, however, were much fewer than horses have among us, and contracted not by any ill treatment they meet with, but by the nastiness and greediness of that sordid brute. Neither has their language any more than a general appellation for those maladies, which is borrowed from the name of the beast, and called *hnea-Yahoo*, or the *Yahoo's-evil*, and the cure prescribed is a mixture of *their own dung* and *urine* forcibly put down the Yahoo's throat. This I have since often known to have been taken with success, and do here freely recommend it to my countrymen, for the public good, as an admirable specific against all diseases produced by repletion.[3]

As to learning, government, arts, manufactures, and the like, my master confessed he could find little or no resemblance between the Yahoos of that country and those in ours. For, he only meant to observe what parity there was in our natures. He had heard indeed some curious Houyhnhnms observe, that in most herds there was a sort of ruling Yahoo (as among us there is generally some leading or principal stag in a park), who was always more *deformed* in body, and *mischievous* in *disposition*, than any of the rest. That this *leader* had usually a favorite as *like himself* as he could get, whose employment was to *lick his master's feet and posteriors, and drive the female Yahoos to his kennel;* for which he was now and then rewarded with a piece of ass's flesh. This *favorite* is hated by the whole herd, and therefore to protect himself, keeps always *near the person of his leader*. He usually continues in office till a worse can be found; but the very moment he is discarded, his successor, at the head of all the Yahoos in that district, young and old, male and female, come in a body, and discharge their excrements upon him from head to foot. But how far this might be applicable to our *Courts* and *favorites*, and *Ministers of State*, my master said I could best determine.

I durst make no return to this malicious insinuation, which debased human understanding below the sagacity of a common *hound*, who hath judgment enough to distinguish and follow the cry of the *ablest dog in the pack*, without being ever mistaken.

My master told me, there were some qualities remarkable in the Yahoos, which he had not observed me to mention, or at least very slightly, in the accounts I had given him of humankind: he said, those animals, like other brutes, had their females in common,[4] but in this they differed, that the she-Yahoo would admit the male while she was pregnant, and that the hes[5] would quarrel and fight with the females as fiercely as with each other. Both which practices were such degrees of infamous brutality, that no other sensitive[6] creature ever arrived at.

---

3. Overeating.
4. Implying that English society did the same.

5. The males.
6. Sensible, thinking.

Another thing he wondered at in the Yahoos, was their strange disposition to nastiness and dirt, whereas there appears to be a natural love of cleanliness in all other animals. As to the two former accusations, I was glad to let them pass without any reply, because I had not a word to offer upon them in defense of my species, which otherwise I certainly had done from my own inclinations. But I could have easily vindicated humankind from the imputation of singularity upon the last article, if there had been any *swine* in that country (as unluckily for me there were not), which although it may be a *sweeter quadruped* than a Yahoo, cannot, I humbly conceive, in justice pretend to more cleanliness; and so his Honor himself must have owned, if he had seen their filthy way of feeding, and their custom of wallowing and sleeping in the mud.

My master likewise mentioned another quality which his servants had discovered in several Yahoos, and to him was wholly unaccountable. He said, a fancy would sometimes take a Yahoo to retire into a corner, to lie down and howl, and groan, and spurn away all that came near him, although he were young and fat, and wanted neither food nor water; nor did the servants imagine what could possibly ail him. And the only remedy they found was to set him to hard work, after which he would infallibly come to himself. To this I was silent out of partiality to my own kind; yet here I could plainly discover the true seeds of *spleen*,[7] which only seizeth on the *lazy*, the *luxurious*, and the *rich*; who, if they were forced to undergo the *same regimen*, I would undertake for[8] the cure.

His Honor had farther observed, that a female Yahoo would often stand behind a bank or a bush, to gaze on the young males passing by, and then appear, and hide, using many antic gestures and grimaces, at which time it was observed, that she had a most *offensive smell*; and when any of the males advanced, would slowly retire, looking often back, and with a counterfeit show of fear, run off into some convenient place where she knew the male would follow her.[9]

At other times if a female stranger came among them, three or four of her own sex would get about her, and stare and chatter, and grin, and smell her all over, and then turn off with gestures that seemed to express contempt and disdain.

Perhaps my master might refine a little in these speculations, which he had drawn from what he observed himself, or had been told him by others; however, I could not reflect without some amazement, and much sorrow, that the rudiments of *lewdness*, *coquetry*, *censure*, and *scandal*, should have place by instinct in womankind.

I expected every moment that my master would accuse the Yahoos of those unnatural appetites in both sexes, so common among us. But Nature it seems hath not been so expert a schoolmistress; and these politer pleasures are entirely the productions of art and reason, on our side of the globe.

CHAPTER 8

The author relateth several particulars of the Yahoos. The great virtues of the Houyhnhnms. The education and exercise of their youth. Their general Assembly.

As I ought to have understood human nature much better than I supposed it possible for my master to do, so it was easy to apply the character he gave of the Yahoos to myself and my countrymen, and I believed I could yet make farther discoveries from my own observation. I therefore often begged his Honor to let me go among the

---

7. Depression.
8. Guarantee.

9. The sort of seduction tactics used by female characters in literary pastoral.

herds of Yahoos in the neighborhood, to which he always very graciously consented, being perfectly convinced that the hatred I bore those brutes would never suffer me to be corrupted by them; and his Honor ordered one of his servants, a strong sorrel nag, very honest and good-natured, to be my guard, without whose protection I durst not undertake such adventures. For I have already told the reader how much I was pestered by those odious animals upon my first arrival. I afterwards failed very narrowly three or four times of falling into their clutches, when I happened to stray at any distance without my hanger. And I have reason to believe they had some imagination that I was of their own species, which I often assisted myself, by stripping up my sleeves, and showing my naked arms and breast in their sight, when my protector was with me. At which times they would approach as near as they durst, and imitate my actions after the manner of monkeys, but ever with great signs of hatred, as a tame *jackdaw*,[1] with cap and stockings, is always persecuted by the wild ones, when he happens to be got among them.

They are prodigiously nimble from their infancy; however, I once caught a young male of three years old, and endeavored by all marks of tenderness to make it quiet; but the little imp fell a squalling, and scratching, and biting with such violence, that I was forced to let it go, and it was high time, for a whole troop of old ones came about us at the noise, but finding the cub was safe (for away it ran), and my sorrel nag being by, they durst not venture near us. I observed the young animal's flesh to smell very rank, and the stink was somewhat between a *weasel* and a *fox*, but much more disagreeable. I forgot another circumstance (and perhaps I might have the reader's pardon, if it were wholly omitted), that while I held the odious vermin in my hands, it voided its filthy excrements of a yellow liquid substance all over my clothes; but by good fortune there was a small brook hard by, where I washed myself as clean as I could, although I durst not come into my master's presence, until I were sufficiently aired.

By what I could discover, the Yahoos appear to be the most unteachable of all animals, their capacities never reaching higher than to draw or carry burdens. Yet I am of opinion this defect ariseth chiefly from a perverse, restive[2] disposition. For they are cunning, malicious, treacherous, and revengeful. They are strong and hardy, but of a cowardly spirit, and by consequence insolent, abject, and cruel. It is observed, that the *red-haired* of both sexes are more libidinous and mischievous than the rest, whom yet they much exceed in strength and activity.[3]

The Houyhnhnms keep the Yahoos for present[4] use in huts not far from the house; but the rest are sent abroad to certain fields, where they dig up roots, eat several kinds of herbs, and search about for carrion, or sometimes catch weasels and *luhimuhs* (a sort of wild rat), which they greedily devour. Nature hath taught them to dig deep holes with their nails on the side of a rising ground, wherein they lie by themselves, only the kennels of the females are larger, sufficient to hold two or three cubs.

They swim from their infancy like frogs, and are able to continue long under water, where they often take fish, which the females carry home to their young. And upon this occasion, I hope the reader will pardon my relating an odd adventure.

Being one day abroad with my protector the sorrel nag, and the weather exceeding hot, I entreated him to let me bathe in a river that was near. He consented, and I

---

1. Small crow, often kept as a pet.   3. A prejudice dating back to medieval times.
2. Stubborn.   4. Daily.

immediately stripped myself stark naked, and went down softly into the stream. It happened that a young female Yahoo, standing behind a bank, saw the whole proceeding, and inflamed by desire, as the nag and I conjectured, came running with all speed, and leaped into the water within five yards of the place where I bathed. I was never in my life so terribly frighted; the nag was grazing at some distance, not suspecting any harm. She embraced me after a most fulsome manner; I roared as loud as I could, and the nag came galloping towards me, whereupon she quitted her grasp, with the utmost reluctancy, and leaped upon the opposite bank, where she stood gazing and howling all the time I was putting on my clothes.

This was matter of diversion to my master and his family, as well as of mortification to myself. For now I could no longer deny, that I was a real Yahoo in every limb and feature, since the females had a natural propensity to me as one of their own species; neither was the hair of this brute of a red color (which might have been some excuse for an appetite a little irregular) but black as a sloe[5] and her countenance did not make an appearance altogether so hideous as the rest of the kind; for, I think, she could not be above eleven years old.[6]

Having already lived three years in this country, the reader I suppose will expect that I should, like other travelers, give him some account of the manners and customs of its inhabitants, which it was indeed my principal study to learn.

As these noble Houyhnhnms are endowed by Nature with a general disposition to all virtues, and have no conceptions or ideas of what is evil in a rational creature, so their grand maxim is, to cultivate *Reason*, and to be wholly governed by it. Neither is *Reason* among them a point problematical as with us, where men can argue with plausibility on both sides of a question, but strikes you with immediate conviction, as it must needs do where it is not mingled, obscured, or discolored by passion and interest.[7] I remember it was with extreme difficulty that I could bring my master to understand the meaning of the word opinion, or how a point could be disputable, because *Reason* taught us to affirm or deny only where we are certain, and beyond our knowledge we cannot do either.[8] So that controversies, wranglings, disputes, and positiveness[9] in false or dubious propositions are evils unknown among the Houyhnhnms. In the like manner, when I used to explain to him our several systems of *natural philosophy*, he would laugh that a creature pretending to *Reason* should value itself upon the knowledge of other people's conjectures, and in things where that knowledge, if it were certain, could be of no use. Wherein he agreed entirely with the sentiments of Socrates, as Plato delivers them[1] which I mention as the highest honor I can do that prince of philosophers. I have often since reflected what destruction such a doctrine would make in the libraries of Europe, and how many paths to fame would be then shut up in the learned world.

Friendship and benevolence are the two principal virtues among the Houyhnhnms, and these not confined to particular objects,[2] but universal to the whole race. For a stranger from the remotest part is equally treated with the nearest neighbor, and wherever he goes, looks upon himself as at home. They preserve *decency* and

---

5. A wild berry.
6. The disparity in age between Gulliver and the Yahoo may suggest a grotesque parody of Esther Vanhomrigh's pursuit of Swift, she being 21 years his junior.
7. Prejudice based on interest in personal benefit. Both Descartes (*Discourse on Method*) and Locke (*Essay Concerning Human Understanding*) wrote of the intuitive nature of some knowledge.
8. Gulliver's master has clearly expressed "opinion" (i.e.,

prejudice) himself, however.
9. Assertiveness.
1. I.e., that ethics (human nature) is worth studying, while the physical world is not, as we can never have certain knowledge of it: "Socrates: I am a friend of learning—the trees and the countryside won't teach me anything, but the people in the city do" *Phaedrus* (230d3–5).
2. To other, particular Houyhnhnms.

civility in the highest degrees, but are altogether ignorant of *ceremony*.[3] They have no fondness for their colts or foals, but the care they take in educating them proceedeth entirely from the dictates of *Reason*. And I observed my master to show the same affection to his neighbor's issue that he had for his own.[4] They will have it that *Nature* teaches them to love the whole species, and it is *Reason* only that maketh a distinction of persons, where there is a superior degree of virtue.

When the matron Houyhnhnms have produced one of each sex, they no longer accompany with[5] their consorts, except they lose one of their issue by some casualty, which very seldom happens: but in such a case they meet again. Or when the like accident befalls a person,[6] whose wife is past bearing, some other couple bestow him one of their own colts, and then go together a second time, till the mother be pregnant. This caution is necessary to prevent the country from being overburdened with numbers.[7] But the race of inferior Houyhnhnms bred up to be servants is not so strictly limited upon this article; these are allowed to produce three of each sex, to be domestics in the noble families.

In their marriages they are exactly careful to choose such colors as will not make any disagreeable mixture in the breed.[8] *Strength* is chiefly valued in the male, and *comeliness* in the female, not upon the account of *love*, but to preserve the race from degenerating; for where a female happens to excel in *strength*, a consort is chosen with regard to *comeliness*. Courtship, love, presents, jointures,[9] settlements, have no place in their thoughts, or terms whereby to express them in their language. The young couple meet and are joined, merely because it is the determination of their parents and friends: it is what they see done every day, and they look upon it as one of the necessary actions in a reasonable being. But the violation of marriage, or any other unchastity, was never heard of, and the married pair pass their lives with the same friendship, and mutual benevolence that they bear to others of the same species who come in their way; without jealousy, fondness, quarreling, or discontent.

In educating the youth of both sexes, their method is admirable, and highly deserveth our imitation. These are not suffered to taste a grain of *oats*, except upon certain days, till eighteen years old; nor *milk*, but very rarely; and in summer they graze two hours in the morning, and as many in the evening, which their parents likewise observe, but the servants are not allowed above half that time, and a great part of their grass is brought home, which they eat at the most convenient hours, when they can be best spared from work.

Temperance, industry, exercise, and *cleanliness*, are the lessons equally enjoined to the young ones of both sexes, and my master thought it monstrous in us to give the females a different kind of education from the males, except in some articles of domestic management,[1] whereby as he truly observed, one half of our natives were good for nothing but bringing children into the world, and to trust the care of their children to such useless animals, he said, was yet a greater instance of brutality.

But the Houyhnhnms train up their youth to strength, speed, and hardiness, by exercising them in running races up and down steep hills, or over hard stony grounds,

3. As are the Utopians.
4. As do men in Plato's *Republic* (461d).
5. Have sex with.
6. A male Houyhnhnm.
7. The Utopians are under no such restriction, knowing (as the Houyhnhnms do not) of other lands to which they can send their excess population.
8. In Plato's *Republic* (458d–461e), eugenic principles

also control mating.
9. Marriage settlements for wives, should they survive their husbands.
1. In both Plato's *Republic* (451e6–7) and *Utopia*, the sexes receive the same education; Swift also began (but never completed) an essay entitled *Of the Education of Ladies* (c. 1728).

and when they are all in a sweat, they are ordered to leap over head and ears into a pond or a river. Four times a year the youth of certain districts meet to show their proficiency in running, and leaping, and other feats of strength or agility, where the victor is rewarded with a song made in his or her praise. On this festival the servants drive a herd of Yahoos into the field, laden with hay, and oats, and milk for a repast to the Houyhnhnms; after which, these brutes are immediately driven back again, for fear of being noisome to the assembly.

Every fourth year, at the *vernal equinox*, there is a Representative Council of the whole nation, which meets in a plain about twenty miles from our house, and continueth about five or six days. Here they inquire into the state and condition of the several districts, whether they abound or be deficient in hay or oats, or cows or Yahoos? And wherever there is any want (which is but seldom) it is immediately supplied by unanimous consent and contribution. Here likewise the regulation of children is settled: as for instance, if a Houyhnhnm hath two males, he changeth one of them with another who hath two females: and when a child hath been lost by any casualty, where the mother is past breeding, it is determined what family in the district shall breed another to supply the loss.

CHAPTER 9

A grand debate at the general Assembly of the Houyhnhnms, and how it was determined. The learning of the Houyhnhnms. Their buildings. Their manner of burials. The defectiveness of their language.

One of these grand Assemblies was held in my time, about three months before my departure, whither my master went as the Representative of our district. In this Council was resumed their old debate, and indeed, the only debate that ever happened in their country; whereof my master after his return gave me a very particular account.

The question to be debated, was, whether the Yahoos should be exterminated from the face of the earth. One of the *members* for the affirmative offered several arguments of great strength and weight, alleging, that as the Yahoos were the most filthy, noisome, and deformed animal which Nature ever produced, so they were the most restive and indocible,[2] mischievous, and malicious: they would privately suck the teats of the Houyhnhnms' cows, kill and devour their cats, trample down their oats and grass, if they were not continually watched, and commit a thousand other extravagancies. He took notice of a general tradition, that Yahoos had not been always in their country, but, that many ages ago, two of these brutes appeared together upon a mountain,[3] whether produced by the heat of the sun upon corrupted mud and slime, or from the ooze and froth of the sea, was never known.[4] That these Yahoos engendered, and their brood in a short time grew so numerous as to overrun and infest the whole nation. That the Houyhnhnms, to get rid of this evil, made a general hunting, and at last enclosed the whole herd; and destroying the elder, every Houyhnhnm kept two young ones in a kennel, and brought them to such a degree of tameness, as an animal so savage by nature can be capable of acquiring; using them for draft and carriage. That there seemed to be much truth in this tradition, and that

2. Unteachable.
3. Probably Milton's "steep savage Hill," the garden of Eden (*Paradise Lost*, 4.172).
4. Humans are supposed to be of divine origin, but the

Yahoos represent such a degraded form of humanity that they (like, it was believed, insects on the Nile's banks) were formed from the action of the sun on mud.

those creatures could not be *ylnhniamshy* (or *aborigines* of the land) because of the violent hatred the Houyhnhnms, as well as all other animals, bore them; which although their evil disposition sufficiently deserved, could never have arrived at so high a degree, if they had been *aborigines,* or else they would have long since been rooted out. That the inhabitants taking a fancy to use the service of the Yahoos, had very imprudently neglected to cultivate the breed of *asses,* which were a comely animal, easily kept, more tame and orderly, without any offensive smell, strong enough for labor, although they yield to the other in agility of body; and if their braying be no agreeable sound, it is far preferable to the horrible howlings of the Yahoos.[5]

Several others declared their sentiments to the same purpose, when my master proposed an expedient to the assembly, whereof he had indeed borrowed the hint from me. He approved of the tradition, mentioned by the Honorable Member who spoke before, and affirmed, that the two Yahoos said to be first seen among them had been driven thither over the sea; that coming to land, and being forsaken by their companions, they retired to the mountains, and degenerating by degrees, became in process of time, much more savage than those of their own species in the country from whence these two originals came. The reason of his assertion was, that he had now in his possession a certain wonderful[6] Yahoo (meaning myself), which most of them had heard of, and many of them had seen. He then related to them, how he first found me: that my body was all covered with an artificial composure of the skins and hairs of other animals; that I spoke in a language of my own, and had thoroughly learned theirs; that I had related to him the accidents which brought me thither; that when he saw me without my covering, I was an exact Yahoo in every part, only of a whiter color, less hairy, and with shorter claws. He added, how I had endeavored to persuade him, that in my own and other countries the Yahoos acted as the governing, rational animal, and held the Houyhnhnms in servitude; that he observed in me all the qualities of a Yahoo, only a little more civilized by some tincture of reason, which however was in a degree as far inferior to the Houyhnhnm race, as the Yahoos of their country were to me;[7] that, among other things, I mentioned a custom we had of *castrating* Houyhnhnms when they were young, in order to render them tame; that the operation was easy and safe; that it was no shame to learn wisdom from brutes, as industry is taught by the ant, and building by the swallow. (For so I translate the word *lyhannh,* although it be a much larger fowl.) That this invention might be practiced upon the younger Yahoos here, which, besides rendering them tractable and fitter for use, would in an age put an end to the whole species without destroying life. That, in the meantime the Houyhnhnms should be exhorted to cultivate the breed of asses, which, as they are in all respects more valuable brutes, so they have this advantage, to be fit for service at five years old, which the others are not till twelve.

This was all my master thought fit to tell me at that time, of what passed in the grand Council. But he was pleased to conceal[8] one particular, which related personally to myself, whereof I soon felt the unhappy effect, as the reader will know in its proper place, and from whence I date all the succeeding misfortunes of my life.

The Houyhnhnms have no letters, and consequently their knowledge is all traditional. But there happening few events of any moment among a people so well

---

5. The commonplace comparison of humans to asses was one Swift had previously used in *A Tale of a Tub* (1704) and *The Battle of the Books* (1704).
6. Amazing, unusual.
7. Gulliver falls between the Houyhnhnms and the Yahoos in reason, as he did between the Lilliputians and the Brobdingnagians in size.
8. Another indication that the Houyhnhnms are not completely honest or candid.

united, naturally disposed to every virtue, wholly governed by reason, and cut off from all commerce with other nations, the historical part is easily preserved without burdening their memories. I have already observed, that they are subject to no diseases, and therefore can have no need of physicians. However, they have excellent medicines composed of herbs, to cure accidental bruises and cuts in the pastern or frog of the foot by sharp stones, as well as other maims and hurts in the several parts of the body.

They calculate the year by the revolution of the sun and the moon, but use no subdivisions into weeks. They are well enough acquainted with the motions of those two luminaries, and understand the nature of eclipses; and this is the utmost progress of their astronomy.

In poetry they must be allowed to excel all other mortals; wherein the justness of their similes, and the minuteness, as well as exactness of their descriptions, are indeed inimitable. Their verses abound very much in both of these, and usually contain either some exalted notions of friendship and benevolence, or the praises of those who were victors in races, and other bodily exercises.[9] Their buildings, although very rude and simple, are not inconvenient, but well contrived to defend them from all injuries of cold and heat. They have a kind of tree, which at forty years old loosens in the root, and falls with the first storm; it grows very straight, and being pointed like stakes with a sharp stone (for the Houyhnhnms know not the use of iron), they stick them erect in the ground about ten inches asunder,[1] and then weave in oat-straw, or sometimes wattles betwixt them. The roof is made after the same manner, and so are the doors.

The Houyhnhnms use the hollow part between the pastern and the hoof of their forefeet as we do our hands, and this with greater dexterity than I could at first imagine. I have seen a white mare of our family thread a needle (which I lent her on purpose) with that joint. They milk their cows, reap their oats, and do all the work which requires hands, in the same manner. They have a kind of hard flints, which by grinding against other stones, they form into instruments, that serve instead of wedges, axes, and hammers. With tools made of these flints they likewise cut their hay, and reap their oats, which there groweth naturally in several fields: the Yahoos draw home the sheaves in carriages, and the servants tread them in certain covered huts, to get out the grain, which is kept in stores. They make a rude kind of earthen and wooden vessels, and bake the former in the sun.

If they can avoid casualties, they die only of old age, and are buried in the obscurest places that can be found, their friends and relations expressing neither joy nor grief at their departure; nor does the dying person discover the least regret that he is leaving the world, any more than if he were upon returning[2] home from a visit to one of his neighbors;[3] I remember, my master having once made an appointment with a friend and his family to come to his house upon some affair of importance, on the day fixed, the mistress and her two children came very late; she made two excuses, first for her husband, who, as she said, happened that very morning to *lhnuwnh*. The word is strongly expressive in their language, but not easily rendered into English; it signifies, *to retire to his first mother*. Her excuse for not coming sooner, was, that her

---

9. The type of poetry advocated in Plato's *Republic* (390d1–3) and practiced in Sparta.
1. Apart.

2. About to return.
3. This attitude toward death is characteristic of both the Stoics and the Utopians.

husband dying late in the morning, she was a good while consulting her servants about a convenient place where his body should be laid; and I observed she behaved herself at our house as cheerfully as the rest; she died about three months after.

They live generally to seventy or seventy-five years, very seldom to fourscore; some weeks before their death they feel a gradual decay, but without pain. During this time they are much visited by their friends, because they cannot go abroad with their usual ease and satisfaction. However, about ten days before their death, which they seldom fail in computing, they return the visits that have been made them by those who are nearest in the neighborhood, being carried in a convenient sledge drawn by Yahoos, which vehicle they use, not only upon this occasion, but when they grow old, upon long journeys, or when they are lamed by an accident. And therefore when the dying Houyhnhnms return those visits, they take a solemn leave of their friends, as if they were going to some remote part of the country, where they designed to pass the rest of their lives.

I know not whether it may be worth observing, that the Houyhnhnms have no word in their language to express anything that is *evil*, except what they borrow from the deformities or ill qualities of the Yahoos. Thus they denote the folly of a servant, an omission of a child, a stone that cuts their feet, a continuance of foul or unseasonable weather, and the like, by adding to each the epithet of *yahoo*. For instance, *hhnm yahoo, whnaholm yahoo, ynlhmnawihlma yahoo,* and an ill-contrived house, *ynholmhnmrohlnw yahoo.*

I could with great pleasure enlarge farther upon the manners and virtues of this excellent people; but intending in a short time to publish a volume by itself expressly upon that subject, I refer the reader thither. And in the meantime, proceed to relate my own sad catastrophe.

CHAPTER 10

The author's economy[4] and happy life among the Houyhnhnms. His great improvement in virtue, by conversing with them. Their conversations. The author hath notice given him by his master that he must depart from the country. He falls into a swoon for grief, but submits. He contrives and finishes a canoe, by the help of a fellow servant, and puts to sea at a venture.[5]

I had settled my little economy to my own heart's content. My master had ordered a room to be made for me after their manner, about six yards from the house, the sides and floors of which I plastered with clay, and covered with rush mats of my own contriving; I had beaten hemp, which there grows wild, and made of it a sort of ticking;[6] this I filled with the feathers of several birds I had taken with springes made of Yahoos' hairs, and were excellent food I had worked[7] two chairs with my knife, the sorrel nag helping me in the grosser[8] and more laborious part. When my clothes were worn to rags, I made myself others with the skins of rabbits, and of a certain beautiful animal about the same size, called *nnuhnoh*, the skin of which is covered with a fine down. Of these I likewise made very tolerable stockings. I soled my shoes with wood which I cut from a tree, and fitted to the upper leather, and when this was worn out, I supplied it with the skins of Yahoos dried in the sun. I often got honey out of hollow trees, which I mingled with water;[9] or ate it with my bread. No man could more

4. Method of living.
5. Without further planning.
6. Sturdy material used for making mattress covering.
7. Made.
8. Heavier, larger.
9. Honey-sweetened water was a Utopian drink.

verify the truth of these two maxims, *That nature is very easily satisfied*; and, *That necessity is the mother of invention*. I enjoyed perfect health of body and tranquillity of mind; I did not feel the treachery or inconstancy of a friend, nor the injuries of a secret or open enemy. I had no occasion of bribing, flattering, or pimping, to procure the favor of any great man or of his minion. I wanted no fence[1] against fraud or oppression; here was neither physician to destroy my body, nor lawyer to ruin my fortune; no informer to watch my words and actions, or forge accusations against me for hire; here were no jibers, censurers, backbiters, pickpockets, highwaymen, housebreakers, attorneys, bawds, buffoons, gamesters, politicians, wits, splenetics, tedious talkers, controvertists, ravishers, murderers, robbers, virtuosos;[2] no leaders or followers of party and faction; no encouragers to vice, by seducement or examples; no dungeon, axes, gibbets, whipping posts, or pillories; no cheating shopkeepers or mechanics;[3] no pride, vanity, or affectation; no fops, bullies, drunkards, strolling whores, or poxes;[4] no ranting, lewd, expensive wives; no stupid, proud pedants; no importunate, overbearing, quarrelsome, noisy, roaring, empty, conceited, swearing companions; no scoundrels, raised from the dust upon the merit of their vices, or nobility thrown into it on account of their virtues; no lords, fiddlers, judges, or dancing masters.[5]

I had the favor of being admitted to[6] several Houyhnhnms, who came to visit or dine with my master; where his Honor graciously suffered me to wait in the room, and listen to their discourse. Both he and his company would often descend to ask me questions, and receive my answers. I had also sometimes the honor of attending my master in his visits to others. I never presumed to speak, except in answer to a question, and then I did it with inward regret, because it was a loss of so much time for improving myself; but I was infinitely delighted with the station of a humble auditor in such conversations, where nothing passed but what was useful, expressed in the fewest and most significant words; where (as I have already said) the greatest *decency* was observed, without the least degree of ceremony; where no person spoke without being pleased himself, and pleasing his companions; where there was no interruption, tediousness, heat,[7] or difference of sentiments. They have a notion, that when people are met together, a short silence doth much improve conversation: this I found to be true, for during those little intermissions of talk, new ideas would arise in their minds, which very much enlivened the discourse. Their subjects are generally on friendship and benevolence, or order and economy, sometimes upon the visible operations of Nature, or ancient traditions, upon the bounds and limits of virtue, upon the unerring rules of reason, or upon some determinations to be taken at the next great Assembly, and often upon the various excellencies of *poetry*. I may add without vanity, that my presence often gave them sufficient matter for discourse, because it afforded my master an occasion of letting his friends into the history of me and my country, upon which they were all pleased to descant in a manner not very advantageous to humankind; and for that reason I shall not repeat what they said: only I may be allowed to observe, that his Honor, to my great admiration, appeared to understand the nature of Yahoos much better than myself. He went through all our vices and follies, and discovered many which I had never mentioned to him, by only supposing

1. Defense.
2. One knowledgeable or interested in apparently trivial "scientific" pursuits.
3. Laborers.
4. Venereal diseases.

5. That necessary tutor for the socially aspiring, the dancing master (usually French), was a particular figure of fun; he usually accompanied himself on the fiddle.
6. Allowed to meet.
7. Heat of argument.

what qualities a Yahoo of their country, with a small proportion of reason, might be capable of exerting; and concluded, with too much probability, how vile as well as miserable such a creature must be.

I freely confess, that all the little knowledge I have of any value, was acquired by the lectures I received from my master, and from hearing the discourses of him and his friends; to which I should be prouder to listen, than to dictate to the greatest and wisest assembly in Europe. I admired the strength, comeliness, and speed of the inhabitants; and such a constellation of virtues in such amiable persons produced in me the highest veneration. At first, indeed, I did not feel that natural awe which the Yahoos and all other animals bear towards them, but it grew upon me by degrees, much sooner than I imagined, and was mingled with a respectful love and gratitude, that they would condescend to distinguish me from the rest of my species.

When I thought of my family, my friends, my countrymen, or human race in general, I considered them as they really were, Yahoos in shape and disposition, perhaps a little more civilized, and qualified with the gift of speech, but making no other use of reason, than to improve and multiply those vices, whereof their brethren in this country had only the share that Nature allotted them. When I happened to behold the reflection of my own form in a lake or a fountain, I turned away my face in horror and detestation of myself,[8] and could better endure the sight of a common Yahoo, than of my own person. By conversing with the Houyhnhnms, and looking upon them with delight, I fell to imitate their gait and gesture, which is now grown into a habit, and my friends often tell me in a blunt way, that I *trot like a horse*; which, however, I take for a great compliment; neither shall I disown, that in speaking I am apt to fall into the voice and manner of the Houyhnhnms, and hear myself ridiculed on that account without the least mortification.

In the midst of all this happiness, when I looked upon myself to be fully settled for life, my master sent for me one morning a little earlier than his usual hour. I observed by his countenance that he was in some perplexity, and at a loss how to begin what he had to speak. After a short silence, he told me, he did not know how I would take what he was going to say; that in the last general Assembly, when the affair of the Yahoos was entered upon, the representatives had taken offense at his keeping a Yahoo (meaning myself) in his family more like a Houyhnhnm, than a brute animal. That he was known frequently to converse with me, as if he could receive some advantage or pleasure in my company; that such a practice was not agreeable to reason or Nature, or a thing ever heard of before among them. The Assembly did therefore *exhort* him, either to employ me like the rest of my species, or command me to swim back to the place from whence I came. That the first of these expedients was utterly rejected by all the Houyhnhnms who had ever seen me at his house or their own, for they alleged, that because I had some rudiments of reason, added to the natural pravity[9] of those animals, it was to be feared, I might be able to seduce them into the woody and mountainous parts of the country, and bring them in troops by night to destroy the Houyhnhnms' cattle, as being naturally of the ravenous[1] kind, and averse from labor.

My master added, that he was daily pressed by the Houyhnhnms of the neighborhood to have the Assembly's *exhortation* executed, which he could not put off much

---

8. A mocking reversal both of a common pattern in pastoral love poetry and of the Greek myth of Narcissus.

9. Depravity.
1. Rapacious, predatory, or greedy.

longer. He doubted[2] it would be impossible for me to swim to another country, and therefore wished I would contrive some sort of vehicle resembling those I had described to him, that might carry me on the sea, in which work I should have the assistance of his own servants, as well as those of his neighbors. He concluded, that for his own part he could have been content to keep me in his service as long as I lived, because he found I had cured myself of some bad habits and dispositions, by endeavoring, as far as my inferior nature was capable, to imitate the Houyhnhnms.

I should here observe to the reader, that a decree of the general Assembly in this country is expressed by the word *hnhloayn*, which signifies an *exhortation*, as near as I can render it, for they have no conception how a rational creature can be *compelled*, but only advised, or *exhorted*, because no person can disobey reason, without giving up his claim to be a rational creature.

I was struck with the utmost grief and despair at my master's discourse, and being unable to support the agonies I was under, I fell into a swoon at his feet; when I came to myself, he told me, that he concluded I had been dead. (For these people are subject to no such imbecilities of nature.) I answered, in a faint voice, that death would have been too great an happiness; that although I could not blame the Assembly's *exhortation*, or the urgency[3] of his friends, yet in my weak and corrupt judgment, I thought it might consist[4] with reason to have been less rigorous. That I could not swim a league, and probably the nearest land to theirs might be distant above a hundred; that many materials, necessary for making a small vessel to carry me off, were wholly wanting in this country, which, however, I would attempt in obedience and gratitude to his Honor, although I concluded the thing to be impossible, and therefore looked on myself as already devoted to destruction. That the certain prospect of an unnatural death was the least of my evils: for, supposing I should escape with life by some strange adventure, how could I think with temper[5] of passing my days among Yahoos, and relapsing into my old corruptions, for want of examples to lead and keep me within the paths of virtue? That I knew too well upon what solid reasons all the determinations of the wise Houyhnhnms were founded, not to be shaken by arguments of mine, a miserable Yahoo; and therefore after presenting him with my humble thanks for the offer of his servants' assistance in making a vessel, and desiring a reasonable time for so difficult a work, I told him I would endeavor to preserve a wretched being; and, if ever I returned to England, was not without hopes of being useful to my own species, by celebrating the praises of the renowned Houyhnhnms, and proposing their virtues to the imitation of mankind.

My master in a few words made me a very gracious reply, allowed me the space of two *months* to finish my boat; and ordered the sorrel nag, my fellow servant (for so at this distance I may presume to call him) to follow my instructions, because I told my master, that his help would be sufficient, and I knew he had a tenderness for me.

In his company my first business was to go to that part of the coast, where my rebellious crew had ordered me to be set on shore. I got upon a height, and looking on every side into the sea, fancied I saw a small island, towards the northeast: I took out my pocket glass, and could then clearly distinguish it about five leagues off, as I computed; but it appeared to the sorrel nag to be only a blue cloud: for, as he had no

2. Feared.
3. Urging.
4. Be consistent.

5. Calmness.

conception of any country beside his own, so he could not be as expert in distinguishing remote objects at sea, as we who so much converse[6] in that element.

After I had discovered this island, I considered no farther; but resolved it should, if possible, be the first place of my banishment, leaving the consequence to Fortune.

I returned home, and consulting with the sorrel nag, we went into a copse at some distance, where I with my knife, and he with a sharp flint fastened very artificially, after their manner, to a wooden handle, cut down several oak wattles about the thickness of a walking staff, and some larger pieces. But I shall not trouble the reader with a particular description of my own mechanics; let it suffice to say, that in six weeks' time, with the help of the sorrel nag, who performed the parts that required most labor, I finished a sort of Indian canoe, but much larger, covering it with the skins of Yahoos well stitched together, with hempen threads of my own making. My sail was likewise composed of the skins of the same animal; but I made use of the youngest I could get, the older being too tough and thick, and I likewise provided myself with four paddles. I laid in a stock of boiled flesh, of rabbits and fowls, and took with me two vessels, one filled with milk, and the other with water.

I tried my canoe in a large pond near my master's house, and then corrected in it what was amiss; stopping all the chinks with Yahoos' tallow, till I found it staunch,[7] and able to bear me and my freight. And when it was as complete as I could possibly make it, I had it drawn on a carriage very gently by Yahoos, to the seaside, under the conduct of the sorrel nag, and another servant.

When all was ready, and the day came for my departure, I took leave of my master and lady, and the whole family, mine eyes flowing with tears, and my heart quite sunk with grief. But his Honor, out of curiosity, and perhaps (if I may speak it without vanity) partly out of kindness, was determined to see me in my canoe, and got several of his neighboring friends to accompany him. I was forced to wait above an hour for the tide, and then observing the wind very fortunately bearing towards the island, to which I intended to steer my course, I took a second leave of my master, but as I was going to prostrate myself to kiss his hoof, he did me the honor to raise it gently to my mouth. I am not ignorant how much I have been censured for mentioning this last particular. For my detractors are pleased to think it improbable, that so illustrious a person should descend to give so great a mark of distinction to a creature so inferior as I. Neither have I forgot, how apt some travelers are to boast of extraordinary favors they have received.[8] But if these censurers were better acquainted with the noble and courteous disposition of the Houyhnhnms, they would soon change their opinion.

I paid my respects to the rest of the Houyhnhnms in his Honor's company; then getting into my canoe, I pushed off from shore.

CHAPTER 11

The author's dangerous voyage. He arrives at New Holland, hoping to settle there. Is wounded with an arrow by one of the natives. Is seized and carried by force into a Portuguese ship. The great civilities of the captain. The author arrives at England.

I began this desperate voyage on February 15, 1715, at 9 o'clock in the morning. The wind was very favorable; however, I made use at first only of my paddles, but con-

---

6. Are familiar with.
7. Watertight.

8. Swift heightens the absurdity of Gulliver's action, and draws attention to his later misanthropy.

sidering I should soon be weary, and that the wind might probably chop about,[9] I ventured to set up my little sail; and thus, with the help of the tide, I went at the rate of a league and a half an hour, as near as I could guess. My master and his friends continued[1] on the shore, till I was almost out of sight; and I often heard the sorrel nag (who always loved me) crying out, *Hnuy illa nyha maiah Yahoo*, Take care of thyself, gentle Yahoo.

My design was, if possible, to discover some small island uninhabited, yet sufficient by my labor to furnish me with the necessaries of life, which I would have thought a greater happiness than to be first minister in the politest court of Europe; so horrible was the idea I conceived of returning to live in the society and under the government of Yahoos. For in such a solitude as I desired, I could at least enjoy my own thoughts, and reflect with delight on the virtues of those inimitable Houyhnhnms, without any opportunity of degenerating into the vices and corruptions of my own species.

The reader may remember what I related when my crew conspired against me, and confined me to my cabin. How I continued there several weeks, without knowing what course we took, and when I was put ashore in the longboat, how the sailors told me with oaths, whether true or false, that they knew not in what part of the world we were. However, I did then believe us to be about ten degrees southward of the Cape of Good Hope, or about 45 degrees southern latitude, as I gathered from some general words I overheard among them, being I supposed to the southeast in their intended voyage to Madagascar. And although this were but little better than conjecture, yet I resolved to steer my course eastward, hoping to reach the southwest coast of New Holland, and perhaps some such island as I desired, lying westward of it. The wind was full west, and by six in the evening I computed I had gone eastward at least eighteen leagues, when I spied a very small island about half a league off, which I soon reached. It was nothing but a rock, with one creek, naturally arched by the force of tempests. Here I put in my canoe, and climbing a part of the rock, I could plainly discover[2] land to the east, extending from south to north. I lay all night in my canoe, and repeating my voyage early in the morning, I arrived in seven hours to the southwest point of New Holland.[3] This confirmed me in the opinion I have long entertained, that the maps and charts place this country at least three degrees more to the east than it really is,[4] which thought I communicated many years ago to my worthy friend Mr. Herman Moll, and gave him my reasons for it, although he hath rather chosen to follow other authors.[5]

I saw no inhabitants in the place where I landed, and being unarmed, I was afraid of venturing far into the country. I found some shellfish on the shore, and ate them raw, not daring to kindle a fire, for fear of being discovered by the natives. I continued three days feeding on oysters and limpets,[6] to save my own provisions, and I fortunately found a brook of excellent water, which gave me great relief.

On the fourth day, venturing out early a little too far, I saw twenty or thirty natives upon a height, not above five hundred yards from me. They were stark naked,

9. Change direction.
1. Stayed.
2. Discern.
3. New Holland was the name the explorer Abel Tasman originally gave to the western coast of Australia. Gulliver seems to place the land of the Houyhnhnms west of southwestern Australia, in which case the distance he covers to reach New Holland is improbable (1,500 to 2,000 nautical miles in 16 hours). It is possible, however,

that Gulliver is meant to have landed on Tasmania, thus putting the Houyhnhnms a short distance west of this island.
4. Dampier claimed that he had found New Holland further west than indicated in Tasman's charts.
5. This geographer's *New and Correct Map of the Whole World* (1719) was probably the basis for Swift's geography in *Gulliver's Travels*.
6. Small mollusks that attach themselves to rocks.

men, women, and children, round a fire, as I could discover by the smoke. One of them spied me, and gave notice to the rest; five of them advanced towards me, leaving the women and children at the fire. I made what haste I could to the shore, and getting into my canoe, shoved off: the savages observing me retreat, ran after me; and before I could get far enough into the sea, discharged an arrow, which wounded me deeply on the inside of my left knee (I shall carry the mark to my grave). I apprehended the arrow might be poisoned, and paddling out of the reach of their darts (being a calm day) I made a shift to suck the wound, and dress it as well as I could.

I was at a loss what to do, for I durst not return to the same landing place, but stood[7] to the north, and was forced to paddle; for the wind though very gentle was against me, blowing northwest. As I was looking about for a secure landing place, I saw a sail to the north-north-east, which appearing every minute more visible, I was in some doubt, whether I should wait for them or no; but at last my detestation of the Yahoo race prevailed, and turning my canoe, I sailed and paddled together to the south, and got into the same creek from whence I set out in the morning, choosing rather to trust myself among these *barbarians*, than live with European Yahoos. I drew up my canoe as close as I could to the shore, and hid myself behind a stone by the little brook, which, as I have already said, was excellent water.

The ship came within a half a league of this creek, and sent out her longboat with vessels to take in fresh water (for the place it seems was very well known) but I did not observe it till the boat was almost on shore, and it was too late to seek another hiding place. The seamen at their landing observed my canoe, and rummaging it all over, easily conjectured that the owner could not be far off. Four of them well armed searched every cranny and lurking hole, till at last they found me flat on my face behind the stone. They gazed a while in admiration[8] at my strange uncouth dress, my coat made of skins, my wooden-soled shoes, and my furred stockings; from whence, however, they concluded I was not a native of the place, who all go naked. One of the seamen in Portuguese bid me rise, and asked who I was. I understood that language very well, and getting upon my feet, said, I was a poor Yahoo, banished from the Houyhnhnms, and desired they would please to let me depart. They admired to hear me answer them in their own tongue, and saw by my complexion I must be a European; but were at a loss to know what I meant by Yahoos and Houyhnhnms, and at the same time fell a laughing at my strange tone in speaking, which resembled the neighing of a horse. I trembled all the while betwixt fear and hatred: I again desired leave to depart, and was gently moving to my canoe; but they laid hold on me, desiring to know, what country I was of? whence I came? with many other questions. I told them, I was born in England, from whence I came about five years ago, and then their country and ours were at peace. I therefore hoped they would not treat me as an enemy, since I meant them no harm, but was a poor Yahoo, seeking some desolate place where to pass the remainder of his unfortunate life.

When they began to talk, I thought I never heard or saw anything so unnatural; for it appeared to me as monstrous as if a dog or a cow should speak in England, or a Yahoo in Houyhnhnmland. The honest Portuguese were equally amazed at my strange dress, and the odd manner of delivering my words, which however they understood very well. They spoke to me with great humanity, and said they were sure their captain would carry me *gratis* to Lisbon, from whence I might return to my own

---

7. Steered.   8. Wonder, amazement.

country; that two of the seamen would go back to the ship, to inform the captain of what they had seen, and receive his orders; in the meantime, unless I would give my solemn oath not to fly;[9] they would secure me by force. I thought it best to comply with their proposal. They were very curious to know my story, but I gave them very little satisfaction; and they all conjectured, that my misfortunes had impaired my reason. In two hours the boat, which went loaden with vessels of water, returned with the captain's commands to fetch me on board. I fell on my knees to preserve my liberty; but all was in vain, and the men having tied me with cords, heaved me into the boat, from whence I was taken into the ship, and from thence into the captain's cabin.

His name was Pedro de Mendez; he was a very courteous and generous person; he entreated me to give some account of myself, and desired to know what I would eat or drink; said, I should be used as well as himself, and spoke so many obliging things, that I wondered to find such civilities from a Yahoo. However, I remained silent and sullen; I was ready to faint at the very smell of him and his men. At last I desired something to eat out of my own canoe; but he ordered me a chicken and some excellent wine, and then directed that I should be put to bed in a very clean cabin. I would not undress myself, but lay on the bed clothes, and in half an hour stole out, when I thought the crew was at dinner, and getting to the side of the ship was going to leap into the sea, and swim for my life, rather than continue among Yahoos. But one of the seamen prevented me, and having informed the captain, I was chained to my cabin.

After dinner Don Pedro came to me, and desired to know my reason for so desperate an attempt: assured me he only meant to do me all the service he was able, and spoke so very movingly, that at last I descended[1] to treat him like an animal which had some little portion of reason. I gave him a very short relation of my voyage, of the conspiracy against me by my own men, of the country where they set me on shore, and of my three years' residence there. All which he looked upon as if it were a dream or a vision; whereat I took great offense; for I had quite forgot the faculty of lying, so peculiar to Yahoos in all countries where they preside, and consequently the disposition of suspecting truth in others of their own species. I asked him, whether it were the custom of his country to *say the thing that was not?* I assured him I had almost forgot what he meant by falsehood, and if I had lived a thousand years in Houyhnhnmland, I should never have heard a lie from the meanest servant; that I was altogether indifferent whether he believed me or no; but however, in return for his favors, I would give so much allowance to the corruption of his nature, as to answer any objection he would please to make, and then he might easily discover the truth.

The captain, a wise man, after many endeavors to catch me tripping in some part of my story, at last began to have a better opinion of my veracity.[2] But he added, that since I professed so inviolable an attachment to truth, I must give him my word of honor to bear him company in this voyage without attempting anything against my life, or else he would continue[3] me a prisoner till we arrived at Lisbon. I gave him the

---

9. Attempt to escape.
1. Condescended.
2. In the first edition, the sentence continues: "and the rather, because he confessed, he met with a Dutch Skipper, who pretended to have landed with five others of his crew upon a certain island or continent south of New Holland, where they went for fresh water, and observed a horse driving before him several animals exactly resembling those I had described under the name of Yahoos, with some other particulars, which the captain said he had forgot, because he then concluded them all to be lies." In 1735 Swift's Dublin publisher, George Faulkener, omitted these lines, probably because they contradicted Gulliver's later statement that no other European had visited this land.
3. Keep.

promise he required; but at the same time protested that I would suffer the greatest hardships rather than return to live among Yahoos.

Our voyage passed without any considerable accident.[4] In gratitude to the captain I sometimes sat with him at his earnest request, and strove to conceal my antipathy against human kind, although it often broke out, which he suffered to pass without observation. But the greatest part of the day, I confined myself to my cabin, to avoid seeing any of the crew. The captain had often entreated me to strip myself of my savage dress, and offered to lend me the best suit of clothes he had. This I would not be prevailed on to accept, abhorring to cover myself with anything that had been on the back of a Yahoo. I only desired he would lend me two clean shirts, which having been washed since he wore them, I believed would not so much defile me. These I changed every second day, and washed them myself.

We arrived at Lisbon, Nov. 5, 1715. At our landing the captain forced me to cover myself with his cloak, to prevent the rabble from crowding about me. I was conveyed to his own house and at my earnest request, he led me up to the highest room backwards.[5] I conjured[6] him to conceal from all persons what I had told him of the Houyhnhnms, because the least hint of such a story would not only draw numbers of people to see me, but probably put me in danger of being imprisoned, or burnt by the Inquisition.[7] The captain persuaded me to accept a suit of clothes newly made, but I would not suffer the tailor to take my measure; however, Don Pedro being almost of my size, they fitted me well enough. He accoutered[8] me with other necessaries all new, which I aired for twenty-four hours before I would use them.

The captain had no wife, nor above three servants, none of which were suffered to attend at meals, and his whole deportment was so obliging, added to very good *human* understanding, that I really began to tolerate his company. He gained so far upon me, that I ventured to look out of the back window. By degrees I was brought into another room, from whence I peeped into the street, but drew my head back in a fright. In a week's time he seduced me down to the door. I found my terror gradually lessened, but my hatred and contempt seemed to increase. I was at last bold enough to walk the street in his company, but kept my nose well stopped with rue,[9] or sometimes with tobacco.

In ten days Don Pedro, to whom I had given some account of my domestic affairs, put it upon me as a point of honor and conscience, that I ought to return to my native country, and live at home with my wife and children. He told me, there was an English ship in the port just ready to sail, and he would furnish me with all things necessary. It would be tedious to repeat his arguments, and my contradictions. He said, it was altogether impossible to find such a solitary island as I had desired to live in; but I might command in my own house, and pass my time in a manner as recluse as I pleased.

I complied at last, finding I could not do better. I left Lisbon the 24th day of November, in an English merchantman, but who was the master I never inquired. Don Pedro accompanied me to the ship, and lent me twenty pounds. He took kind leave of me, and embraced me at parting, which I bore as well as I could. During this last

---

4. Incident.
5. At the back of the house.
6. Appealed earnestly to.
7. Either because the Houyhnhnm hierarchy contradicted Genesis, in which man has dominion over the earth, or because Gulliver had been associating with diabolical powers, who could make humans appear to be horses (as Gulliver himself had first believed).
8. Attired.
9. Strong-smelling shrub, used for medicinal purposes.

voyage I had no commerce[1] with the master or any of his men, but pretending I was sick kept close in my cabin. On the fifth of December, 1715, we cast anchor in the Downs[2] about nine in the morning, and at three in the afternoon I got safe to my house at Redriff.

My wife and family received me with great surprise and joy, because they concluded me certainly dead; but I must freely confess the sight of them filled me only with hatred, disgust, and contempt, and the more by reflecting on the near alliance I had to them. For, although since my unfortunate exile from the Houyhnhnm country, I had compelled myself to tolerate the sight of Yahoos, and to converse with Don Pedro de Mendez, yet my memory and imaginations were perpetually filled with the virtues and ideas of those exalted Houyhnhnms. And when I began to consider, that by copulating with one of the Yahoo species, I had become a parent of more, it struck me with the utmost shame, confusion, and horror.

As soon as I entered the house, my wife took me in her arms, and kissed me, at which, having not been used to the touch of that odious animal for so many years, I fell in a swoon for almost an hour. At the time I am writing it is five years since my last return to England: during the first year I could not endure my wife or children in my presence, the very smell of them was intolerable, much less could I suffer them to eat in the same room. To this hour they dare not presume to touch my bread, or drink out of the same cup, neither was I ever able to let one of them take me by the hand.[3] The first money I laid out was to buy two young stone-horses,[4] which I keep in a good stable, and next to them the groom is my greatest favorite; for I feel my spirits revived by the smell he contracts in the stable. My horses understand me tolerably well; I converse with them at least four hours every day. They are strangers to bridle or saddle, they live in great amity with me, and friendship to each other.

CHAPTER 12

The author's veracity. His design in publishing this work. His censure of those travelers who swerve from the truth. The author clears himself from any sinister ends in writing. An objection answered. The method of planting Colonies. His native country commended. The right of the Crown to those countries described by the author is justified. The difficulty of conquering them. The author takes his last leave of the reader, proposeth his manner of living for the future, gives good advice, and concludeth.

Thus, gentle reader,[5] I have given thee a faithful history of my travels for sixteen years, and above seven months, wherein I have not been so studious of ornament as of truth. I could perhaps like others have astonished thee with strange improbable tales; but I rather chose to relate plain matter of fact in the simplest manner and style, because my principal design was to inform, and not to amuse thee.

It is easy for us who travel into remote countries, which are seldom visited by Englishmen or other Europeans, to form descriptions of wonderful animals both at sea and land. Whereas a traveler's chief aim should be to make men wiser and better,

1. Interaction.
2. The sea off the North Downs in East Kent.
3. Gulliver's unwillingness to share his bread or cup with his wife or children emphasizes his unchristian behavior.

4. Stallions.
5. Highly ironic, since the "gentle" readers must be Yahoos.

and to improve their minds by the bad as well as good example of what they deliver concerning foreign places.[6]

I could heartily wish a law were enacted, that every traveler, before he were permitted to publish his voyages, should be obliged to make oath before the Lord High Chancellor that all he intended to print was absolutely true to the best of his knowledge; for then the world would no longer be deceived as it usually is, while some writers, to make their works pass the better upon the public, impose the grossest falsities on the unwary reader. I have perused several books of travels with great delight in my younger days; but having since gone over most parts of the globe, and been able to contradict many fabulous accounts from my own observation, it hath given me a great disgust against this part of reading, and some indignation to see the credulity of mankind so impudently abused. Therefore since my acquaintance were pleased to think my poor endeavors might not be unacceptable to my country, I imposed on myself as a maxim, never to be swerved from, that I would *strictly adhere to truth*; neither indeed can I be ever under the least temptation to vary from it, while I retain in my mind the lectures and example of my noble master, and the other illustrious Houyhnhnms, of whom I had so long the honor to be an humble hearer.

> —*Nec si miserum Fortuna Sinonem*
> *Finxit, vanum etiam mendacemque improba finget*.[7]

I know very well how little reputation is to be got by writings which require neither genius nor learning, nor indeed any other talent, except a good memory or an exact journal. I know likewise, that writers of travels, like dictionary-makers, are sunk into oblivion by the weight and bulk of those who come last, and therefore lie uppermost.[8] And it is highly probable, that such travelers who shall hereafter visit the countries described in this work of mine, may, by detecting my errors (if there be any), and adding many new discoveries of their own, jostle me out of vogue, and stand in my place, making the world forget that ever I was an author. This indeed would be too great a mortification if I wrote for fame; but, as my sole intention was the PUBLIC GOOD.[9] I cannot be altogether disappointed. For who can read of the virtues I have mentioned in the glorious Houyhnhnms, without being ashamed of his own vices, when he considers himself as the reasoning, governing animal of his country? I shall say nothing of those remote nations where Yahoos preside, amongst which the least corrupted are the Brobdingnagians, whose wise maxims in morality and government it would be our happiness to observe. But I forbear descanting further, and rather leave the judicious reader to his own remarks and applications.

I am not a little pleased that this work of mine can possibly meet with no[1] censurers: for what objections can be made against a writer who relates only plain facts that happened in such distant countries, where we have not the least interest with respect either to trade or negotiations? I have carefully avoided every fault with which common writers of travels are often too justly charged. Besides, I meddle not

---

6. More's *Utopia* also argues that accounts of distant travels should provide useful lessons rather than fabulous tales.

7. "Nor, if cruel Fortune has made Sinon miserable, shall he also make him false and deceitful" (Virgil, *Aeneid* 2. 79–80). Swift cleverly employs the words that the Greek Sinon, the most famous liar in antiquity, used in the fraudulent tale he told to fool the Trojans into accepting *his* (wooden) horse.

8. The most current dictionary is the one most frequently used.

9. The English buccaneer and navigator William Dampier professes a similar aim in the dedication to his *New Voyage Round the World* (1697).

1. Cannot possibly encounter any.

the least with any *party*, but write without passion, prejudice, or ill-will against any man or number of men whatsoever. I write for the noblest end, to inform and instruct mankind, over whom I may, without breach of modesty, pretend to some superiority from the advantages I received by conversing so long among the most accomplished Houyhnhnms. I write without any view towards profit or praise. I never suffer a word to pass that may look like reflection,[2] or possibly give the least offense even to those who are most ready to take it. So that I hope I may with justice pronounce myself an author perfectly blameless, against whom the tribe of answerers, considerers, observers, reflecters, detecters, remarkers, will never be able to find matter for exercising their talents.[3]

I confess, it was whispered to me, that I was bound in duty as a subject of England, to have given in a memorial to a Secretary of State, at my first coming over; because, whatever lands are discovered by a subject belong to the Crown. But I doubt whether our conquests in the countries I treat of, would be as easy as those of Ferdinando Cortez over the naked Americans.[4] The Lilliputians, I think, are hardly worth the charge of a fleet and army to reduce them, and I question whether it might be prudent or safe to attempt the Brobdingnagians. Or whether an English army would be much at their ease with the Flying Island over their heads.[5] The Houyhnhnms, indeed, appear not to be so well prepared for war, a science to which they are perfect strangers, and especially against missive weapons.[6] However, supposing myself to be a minister of State, I could never give my advice for invading them. Their prudence, unanimity, unacquaintedness with fear, and their love of their country would amply supply all defects in the military art. Imagine twenty thousand of them breaking into the midst of an European army, confounding the ranks, overturning the carriages, battering the warriors' faces into mummy,[7] by terrible yerks[8] from their hinder hoofs. For they would well deserve the character given to Augustus; *Recalcitrat undique tutus*.[9] But instead of proposals for conquering that magnanimous nation, I rather wish they were in a capacity or disposition to send a sufficient number of their inhabitants for civilizing Europe, by teaching us the first principles of honor, justice, truth, temperance, public spirit, fortitude, chastity, friendship, benevolence, and fidelity. The *names* of all which virtues are still retained among us in most languages, and are to be met with in modern as well as ancient authors; which I am able to assert from my own small reading.

But I had another reason which made me less forward[1] to enlarge his Majesty's dominions by my discoveries. To say the truth, I had conceived a few scruples with

2. Criticism.

3. At this time it was common for historical and fictional accounts to be "applied" to contemporary situations or persons; by having Gulliver deny at such length that he is doing this, Swift draws attention to the possibility of making such connections.

4. In the 1520s, Cortés and 400 soldiers rapidly conquered the Aztec empire in Mexico.

5. These sentences refer to Gulliver's other travels: in Lilliput he encountered a miniature people; in Brobdingnag he met with giants; and in Laputa he encountered the Flying Island (able to force inhabitants below to submit either through starving them by blocking out the sun or by crushing them).

6. Anything thrown or shot through the air.

7. Pulp.

8. Kicks.

9. "He kicks back, well protected on every side" (Horace, *Satires* 2.i.20). While Gulliver refers admiringly to the horse's ability to defend itself, Swift recalls the context for Horace's decision to use satire (rather than praise) when writing about Augustus: according to Horace, Augustus would kick out like a horse if he sensed servile flattery, so flattery was pointless. Gulliver's lavish praise of the Houyhnhnms backfires on him, not because the Houyhnhnms disliked it, but because his uncritical identification with them leaves him unable to cope with human society.

1. Eager.

relation to the distributive justice[2] of princes upon those occasions. For instance, a crew of pirates[3] are driven by a storm they know not whither, at length a boy discovers land from the topmast, they go on shore to rob and plunder; they see a harmless people, are entertained with kindness, they give the country a new name, they take formal possession of it for the king, they set up a rotten plank or a stone for a memorial, they murder two or three dozen of the natives, bring away a couple more by force for a sample, return home, and get their pardon. Here commences a new dominion acquired with a title by *divine right*. Ships are sent with the first opportunity, the natives driven out or destroyed, their princes tortured to discover their gold;[4] a free license given to all acts of inhumanity and lust, the earth reeking with the blood of its inhabitants; and this execrable crew of butchers employed in so pious an expedition, is a *modern colony* sent to convert and civilize an idolatrous and barbarous people.

But this description, I confess, doth by no means affect the British nation, who may be an example to the whole world for their wisdom, care, and justice in planting colonies,[5] their liberal endowments for the advancement of religion and learning; their choice of devout and able pastors to propagate Christianity; their caution in stocking their provinces with people of sober lives and conversations from this the mother kingdom,[6] their strict regard to the distribution of justice, in supplying the civil administration through all their colonies with officers of the greatest abilities, utter strangers to corruption; and to crown all, by sending the most vigilant and virtuous governors, who have no other views than the happiness of the people over whom they preside, and the honor of the King their master.

But, as those countries which I have described do not appear to have any desire of being conquered, and enslaved, murdered, or driven out by colonies, nor abound either in gold, silver, sugar, or tobacco; I did humbly conceive they were by no means proper objects of our zeal, our valor, or our interest. However, if those whom it more concerns, think fit to be of another opinion, I am ready to depose, when I shall be lawfully called, that no European did ever visit those countries before me. I mean, if the inhabitants ought to be believed.[7]

But as to the formality of taking possession in my Sovereign's name, it never came once into my thoughts; and if it had, yet as my affairs then stood, I should perhaps in point of prudence and self-preservation, have put it off to a better opportunity.

Having thus answered the *only* objection that can ever be raised against me as a traveler, I here take a final leave of my courteous readers, and return to enjoy my own speculations in my little garden at Redriff, to apply those excellent lessons of virtue which I learned among the Houyhnhnms, to instruct the Yahoos of my own family as far as I shall find them docible[8] animals, to behold my figure often in a glass, and thus if possible habituate myself by time to tolerate the sight of a human creature, to lament the brutality of Houyhnhnms in my own country, but always treat their persons with respect, for the sake of my noble master, his family, his friends, and the

---

2. Fairness with regard to the rights of the native people.
3. Referring to the first Spanish colonizers of America.
4. Montezuma was tortured by Cortés, and the Incan emperor Atahuallpa by Pizarro (1533).
5. Intended ironically.
6. Felons were commonly given a sentence of mandatory "transportation" to Britain's colonies.
7. The first edition continued: "unless a dispute may arise about the two Yahoos, said to have been seen many Ages

ago on a mountain in Houyhnhnm-land, from whence the opinion is, that the race of those brutes hath descended; and these, for anything I know, may have been English, which indeed I was apt to suspect from the lineaments of their posterity's countenances, although very much defaced. But how far that will go to make out a title, I leave to the learned in colony law." Faulkener omitted this passage in the 1735 edition.
8. Teachable.

whole Houyhnhnm race, whom these of ours[9] have the honor to resemble in all their lineaments, however their intellectuals[1] came to degenerate.

I began last week to permit my wife to sit at dinner with me, at the farthest end of a long table, and to answer (but with the utmost brevity) the few questions I ask her. Yet the smell of a Yahoo continuing very offensive, I always keep my nose well stopped with rue, lavender, or tobacco leaves. And although it be hard for a man late in life to remove old habits, I am not altogether out of hopes in some time to suffer a neighbor Yahoo in my company, without the apprehensions I am yet under of his teeth or his claws.

My reconcilement to the Yahoo-kind in general might not be so difficult if they would be content with those vices and follies only, which Nature hath entitled them to. I am not in the least provoked at the sight of a lawyer, a pickpocket, a colonel, a fool, a lord, a gamester, a politician, a whoremonger, a physician, an evidence,[2] a suborner,[3] an attorney, a traitor, or the like: this is all according to the due course of things; but when I behold a lump of deformity and diseases both in body and mind, smitten with *pride*, it immediately breaks all the measures of my patience; neither shall I be ever able to comprehend how such an animal and such a vice could tally together. The wise and virtuous Houyhnhnms, who abound in all excellencies that can adorn a rational creature, have no name for this vice in their language, which hath no terms to express anything that is evil, except those whereby they describe the detestable qualities of their Yahoos, among which they were not able to distinguish this of pride, for want of thoroughly understanding human nature, as it showeth itself in other countries, where that animal presides. But I, who had more experience, could plainly observe some rudiments of it among the wild Yahoos.

But the Houyhnhnms, who live under the government of Reason, are no more proud of the good qualities they possess, than I should be for not wanting a leg or an arm, which no man in his wits would boast of, although he must be miserable without them. I dwell the longer upon this subject from the desire I have to make the society of an English Yahoo by any means not insupportable, and therefore I here entreat those who have any tincture of this absurd vice, that they will not presume to appear in my sight.[4]

FINIS

c. 1721–1725   1726

A MODEST PROPOSAL   In a letter written to Alexander Pope in August 1729, Swift described the condition of Ireland: "There have been three terrible years' dearth of corn [i.e., wheat], and every place strewn with beggars, but dearths are common in better climates, and our evils lie much deeper. Imagine a nation the two-thirds of whose revenues are spent out of it, and who are not permitted [by Britain] to trade with the other third, and where the pride of the women will not suffer them to wear their own manufactures even where they excel what come from abroad." Two months later, Swift published what is today his most famous political essay: *A Modest Proposal*. Swift had previously written a dozen or more tracts to help free Ireland from its desperate social, economic, and political plight. In *A Modest Proposal*, however, Swift wielded two favorite weapons from his armory of satirical techniques—irony and parody—with devastating effect. In creating a persona who combines a mixture of calculating rationality and misplaced compassion but does not comprehend the enormity of his plan, Swift

---

9. I.e., horses.
1. Intellects.
2. A (false) witness.

3. One who bribes another to commit a misdeed.
4. Gulliver thus falls into pride, the very vice he rejects.

aims his satire not only at the political arithmeticians (forerunners of today's social engineers and economic planners) and the exploitative and predatory absentee landlords living in England but at the Irish people as well. Believing Ireland to be its own worst enemy, Swift delineates a program of commercial cannibalism that institutionalizes the country's own self-destructive tendencies. Preserving a nation through the consumption of its children is self-defeating, however demographically logical, because it undermines the understanding of humanity upon which civil society depends. Swift thus highlights the futility of financial improvement unaccompanied by social and moral reform.

A Modest Proposal

FOR PREVENTING THE CHILDREN OF POOR PEOPLE IN IRELAND
FROM BEING A BURDEN TO THEIR PARENTS OR COUNTRY,
AND FOR MAKING THEM BENEFICIAL TO THE PUBLIC

It is a melancholy object to those who walk through this great town,[1] or travel in the country, when they see the streets, the roads, and cabin doors crowded with beggars of the female sex, followed by three, four, or six children, *all in rags*, and importuning every passenger[2] for an alms. These mothers, instead of being able to work for their honest livelihood, are forced to employ all their time in strolling,[3] to beg sustenance for their helpless infants, who, as they grow up, either turn thieves for want of work, or leave their dear native country to fight for the Pretender in Spain,[4] or sell themselves to the Barbados.[5]

I think it is agreed by all parties that this prodigious number of children, in the arms, or on the backs, or at the heels of their mothers, and frequently of their fathers, is in the present deplorable state of the kingdom a very great additional grievance; and therefore whoever could find out a fair, cheap, and easy method of making these children sound, useful members of the commonwealth would deserve so well of the public, as to have his statue set up for a preserver of the nation.

But my intention is very far from being confined to provide only for the children of professed beggars; it is of a much greater extent, and shall take in the whole number of infants at a certain age who are born of parents in effect as little able to support them as those who demand our charity in the streets.

As to my own part, having turned my thoughts for many years upon this important subject, and maturely weighed the several schemes of other projectors,[6] I have always found them grossly mistaken in their computation. It is true a child just dropped from its dam may be supported by her milk for a solar year with little other nourishment, at most not above the value of two shillings, which the mother may certainly get, or the value in scraps, by her lawful occupation of begging, and it is exactly at one year old that I propose to provide for them, in such a manner as instead of being a charge upon their parents or the parish, or wanting food and raiment for the rest of their lives, they shall, on the contrary, contribute to the feeding and partly to the clothing of many thousands.

1. Dublin.
2. Passerby.
3. Wandering aimlessly.
4. Catholic Ireland was loyal to the Pretender, James Francis Edward Stuart (1688–1766), son of James II, who was deposed from the English throne in 1688 because of his Catholicism. Religious ties also made the Irish ideal

recruits for France and Spain in their wars against England.
5. The impoverished Irish emigrated to the West Indies in large numbers, buying their passage by selling their labor in advance to the sugar plantations.
6. Devisers of new "projects," usually of doubtful value.

There is likewise another great advantage in my scheme, that it will prevent those voluntary abortions, and that horrid practice of women murdering their bastard children, alas, too frequent among us, sacrificing the poor innocent babes, I doubt[7] more to avoid the expense than the shame, which would move tears and pity in the most savage and inhuman breast.

The number of souls in this kingdom being usually reckoned one million and a half, of these I calculate there may be about two hundred thousand couple whose wives are breeders, from which number I subtract thirty thousand couple who are able to maintain their own children, although I apprehend there cannot be so many under the present distresses of the kingdom; but this being granted, there will remain an hundred and seventy thousand breeders. I again subtract fifty thousand for those women who miscarry, or whose children die by accident or disease within the year.[8] There only remain a hundred and twenty thousand children of poor parents annually born: the question therefore is how this number shall be reared and provided for, which, as I have already said, under the present situation of affairs, is utterly impossible by all the methods hitherto proposed: for we can neither employ them in handicraft, or agriculture; we neither build houses (I mean in the country) nor cultivate land;[9] they can very seldom pick up a livelihood by stealing till they arrive at six years old, except where they are of towardly parts,[1] although, I confess they learn the rudiments much earlier, during which time they can however be properly looked upon only as *probationers*, as I have been informed by a principal gentleman in the County of Cavan, who protested to me, that he never knew above one or two instances under the age of six, even in a part of the kingdom so renowned for the quickest proficiency in that art.

I am assured by our merchants that a boy or a girl, before twelve years old, is no salable commodity, and even when they come to this age, they will not yield above three pounds, or three pounds and half-a-crown at most on the Exchange,[2] which cannot turn to account[3] either to the parents or kingdom, the charge of nutriment and rags having been at least four times that value.

I shall now therefore humbly propose my own thoughts, which I hope will not be liable to the least objection.

I have been assured by a very knowing American[4] of my acquaintance in London, that a young healthy child well nursed is at a year old a most delicious, nourishing, and wholesome food, whether stewed, roasted, baked, or boiled, and I make no doubt that it will equally serve in a fricassee or ragout.[5]

I do therefore humbly offer it to public consideration, that of the hundred and twenty thousand children already computed, twenty thousand may be reserved for breed, whereof only one fourth part to be males, which is more than we allow to sheep, black cattle, or swine, and my reason is that these children are seldom the fruits of marriage, a circumstance not much regarded by our savages, therefore one male will be sufficient to serve four females. That the remaining hundred thousand may at a year old be offered in sale to the persons of quality and fortune through the

7. Believe.
8. It is telling that Swift here projects an infant mortality rate of approximately 30 percent in a child's first year.
9. The vast estates of English absentee landlords, and British retention of Irish land for grazing sheep, rather than agriculture, contributed to Ireland's poverty.
1. Precocious.
2. At the market.

3. Be of value.
4. Some of the British believed that the harsh living conditions in America made the colonists adopt "savage" practices.
5. A fricassee is meat stewed in gravy, a ragout is a highly seasoned French stew; such foreign dishes were becoming increasingly popular with fashionable Britons.

kingdom, always advising the mother to let them suck plentifully in the last month, so as to render them plump, and fat for a good table. A child will make two dishes at an entertainment for friends, and when the family dines alone, the fore or hind quarter will make a reasonable dish, and seasoned with a little pepper or salt will be very good boiled on the fourth day, especially in winter.

I have reckoned upon a medium, that a child just born will weigh 12 pounds, and in a solar year if tolerably nursed increaseth to 28 pounds.

I grant this food will be somewhat dear,[6] and therefore very proper for landlords, who, as they have already devoured most of the parents, seem to have the best title to the children.

Infants' flesh will be in season throughout the year, but more plentiful in March, and a little before and after, for we are told by a grave author,[7] an eminent French physician, that fish being a prolific diet,[8] there are more children born in Roman Catholic countries about nine months after Lent than at any other season; therefore reckoning a year after Lent, the markets will be more glutted than usual, because the number of Popish infants is at least three to one in this kingdom, and therefore it will have one other collateral advantage by lessening the number of Papists among us.

I have already computed the charge of nursing a beggar's child (in which list I reckon all cottagers,[9] laborers, and four-fifths of the farmers) to be about two shillings *per annum*, rags included, and I believe no gentleman would repine to give ten shillings for the carcass of a good fat child, which, as I have said, will make four dishes of excellent nutritive meat, when he hath only some particular friend or his own family to dine with him. Thus the Squire will learn to be a good landlord and grow popular among his tenants, the mother will have eight shillings net profit, and be fit for work till she produces another child.

Those who are more thrifty (as I must confess the times require) may flay the carcass, the skin of which, artificially[1] dressed, will make admirable gloves for ladies and summer boots for fine gentlemen.

As to our City of Dublin, shambles[2] may be appointed for this purpose in the most convenient parts of it, and butchers we may be assured will not be wanting, although I rather recommend buying the children alive and dressing them hot from the knife,[3] as we do roasting pigs.

A very worthy person, a true lover of his country, and whose virtues I highly esteem, was lately pleased, in discoursing on this matter, to offer a refinement upon my scheme. He said that many gentlemen of this kingdom, having of late destroyed their deer, he conceived that the want of venison might be well supplied by the bodies of young lads and maidens, not exceeding fourteen years of age nor under twelve, so great a number of both sexes in every country being now ready to starve for want of work and service;[4] and these to be disposed of by their parents if alive, or otherwise by their nearest relations. But with due deference to so excellent a friend and so deserving a patriot, I cannot be altogether in his sentiments; for as to the males, my American acquaintance assured me from frequent experience that their

---

6. Both expensive and, of course, beloved.
7. The satirist François Rabelais, in *Gargantua and Pantagruel* (1532–1564), Book 5, ch. 29.
8. One increasing fertility.
9. Tenant farmers.

1. Skillfully.
2. Places where meat is slaughtered and sold.
3. Skinning and gutting them immediately after killing.
4. Positions as servants.

flesh was generally tough and lean, like that of our schoolboys, by continual exercise, and their taste disagreeable, and to fatten them would not answer the charge. Then as to the females, it would, I think with humble submission, be a loss to the public, because they soon would become breeders themselves; and besides, it is not improbable that some scrupulous people might be apt to censure such a practice (although indeed very unjustly) as a little bordering upon cruelty which, I confess, hath always been with me the strongest objection against any project, however so well intended.

But in order to justify my friend, he confessed that this expedient was put into his head by the famous Psalmanazar,[5] a native of the island Formosa, who came from thence to London above twenty years ago, and in conversation told my friend that in his country when any young person happened to be put to death, the executioner sold the carcass to persons of quality as a prime dainty, and that, in his time, the body of a plump girl of fifteen, who was crucified for an attempt to poison the emperor, was sold to his Imperial Majesty's Prime Minister of State[6] and other great Mandarins of the Court, in joints from the gibbet,[7] at four hundred crowns. Neither indeed can I deny that if the same use were made of several plump young girls in this town, who, without one single groat[8] to their fortunes, cannot stir abroad without a chair,[9] and appear at the playhouse and assemblies[1] in foreign fineries which they never will pay for, the kingdom would not be the worse.

Some persons of a desponding spirit are in great concern about that vast number of poor people who are aged, diseased, or maimed, and I have been desired to employ my thoughts what course may be taken to ease the nation of so grievous an encumbrance. But I am not in the least pain upon that matter, because it is very well known that they are every day dying, and rotting, by cold, and famine, and filth, and vermin, as fast as can be reasonably expected. And as to the younger laborers they are now in almost as hopeful a condition. They cannot get work, and consequently pine away for want of nourishment, to a degree that if at any time they are accidentally hired to common labor, they have not strength to perform it; and thus the country and themselves are in a fair way of being soon delivered from the evils to come.

I have too long digressed, and therefore shall return to my subject. I think the advantages by the proposal which I have made are obvious and many, as well as of the highest importance.

For first, as I have already observed, it would greatly lessen the number of Papists, with whom we are yearly overrun, being the principal breeders of the nation as well as our most dangerous enemies, and who stay at home on purpose with a design to deliver the kingdom to the Pretender, hoping to take their advantage by the absence of so many good Protestants, who have chosen rather to leave their country than stay at home, and pay tithes against their conscience, to an Episcopal curate.[2]

---

5. George Psalmanazar, a Frenchman who pretended to be from Formosa (now Taiwan), wrote a book about its customs, the *Historical and Geographical Description of Formosa* (1704), which was quickly exposed as fraudulent.
6. A reference to Robert Walpole.
7. Gallows.
8. Silver coin (issued 1351–1662) equal to four pennies.

9. A sedan chair, carried by two men.
1. Social gatherings.
2. The tithes, or ecclesiastical taxes, that supported the Church were avoided by the many "good" Protestants who absented themselves from Ireland on the grounds— spurious, Swift implies—of "conscience."

Secondly, the poorer tenants will have something valuable of their own, which by law may be made liable to distress,[3] and help to pay their landlords rent, their corn and cattle being already seized, and *money a thing unknown.*

Thirdly, whereas the maintenance of a hundred thousand children from two years old and upwards cannot be computed at less than ten shillings a piece *per annum,* the nation's stock will be thereby increased fifty thousand pounds *per annum,* besides the profit of a new dish introduced to the tables of all gentlemen of fortune in the kingdom who have any refinement in taste, and the money will circulate among ourselves, the goods being entirely of our own growth and manufacture.

Fourthly, the constant breeders, besides the gain of eight shillings sterling *per annum* by the sale of their children, will be rid of the charge of maintaining them after the first year.

Fifthly, this food would likewise bring great custom to taverns, where the vintners will certainly be so prudent as to procure the best receipts[4] for dressing it to perfection, and consequently have their houses frequented by all the fine gentlemen, who justly value themselves upon their knowledge in good eating; and a skillful cook who understands how to oblige his guests will contrive to make it as expensive as they please.

Sixthly, this would be a great inducement to marriage, which all wise nations have either encouraged by rewards or enforced by laws and penalties. It would increase the care and tenderness of mothers toward their children, when they were sure of a settlement for life to the poor babes, provided in some sort by the public to their annual profit instead of expense. We should see an honest emulation[5] among the married women, which of them could bring the fattest child to the market; men would become as fond of their wives, during the time of their pregnancy, as they are now of their mares in foal, their cows in calf, or sows when they are ready to farrow,[6] nor offer to beat or kick them (as it is too frequent a practice) for fear of a miscarriage.

Many other advantages might be enumerated: for instance, the addition of some thousand carcasses in our exportation of barreled beef;[7] the propagation of swine's flesh, and improvement in the art of making good bacon, so much wanted among us by the great destruction of pigs, too frequent at our tables, which are no way comparable in taste or magnificence to a well-grown, fat yearling child, which roasted whole will make a considerable figure at a Lord Mayor's feast or any other public entertainment. But this and many others I omit, being studious of brevity.

Supposing that one thousand families in this city would be constant customers for infants' flesh, besides others who might have it at merry-meetings, particularly weddings and christenings, I compute that Dublin would take off annually about twenty thousand carcasses, and the rest of the kingdom (where probably they will be sold somewhat cheaper) the remaining eighty thousand.

I can think of no one objection that will possibly be raised against this proposal, unless it should be urged that the number of people will be thereby much lessened in the kingdom. This I freely own, and was indeed one principal design in offering it to the world. I desire the reader will observe that I calculate my remedy *for this one individual Kingdom of Ireland, and for no other that ever was, is, or, I think, ever can be upon earth.* Therefore let no man talk to me of other expedients:[8] *Of taxing our absentees at*

---

3. Seizure for debt.
4. Recipes.
5. Competition.
6. Give birth.
7. Pickled beef.

8. The kind of proposals Swift himself had made in earnest for remedying the poverty of Ireland; his *Proposal for the Universal Use of Irish Manufacture in Cloaths and Furniture . . . Utterly Rejecting and Renouncing Everything Wearable that Comes from England* (1720) is a typical example.

five shillings a pound; of using neither clothes nor household furniture, except what is of our own growth and manufacture; of utterly rejecting the materials and instruments that promote foreign luxury; of curing the expensiveness of pride, vanity, idleness, and gaming in our women; of introducing a vein of parsimony, prudence, and temperance; of learning to love our country, wherein we differ even from LAPLANDERS, *and the inhabitants of* TOPINAMBOO;[9] *of quitting our animosities and factions, nor act any longer like the Jews, who were murdering one another at the very moment their city was taken;[1] of being a little cautious not to sell our country and consciences for nothing; of teaching landlords to have at least one degree of mercy toward their tenants. Lastly, of putting a spirit of honesty, industry, and skill into our shopkeepers, who, if a resolution could now be taken to buy our native goods, would immediately unite to cheat and exact upon us in the price, the measure, and the goodness, nor could ever yet be brought to make one fair proposal of just dealing, though often and earnestly invited to it.*

Therefore I repeat, let no man talk to me of these and the like expedients till he hath at least some glimpse of hope that there will ever be some hearty and sincere attempt to put them in practice.

But as to myself, having been wearied out for many years with offering vain, idle, visionary thoughts, and at length utterly despairing of success, I fortunately fell upon this proposal, which as it is wholly new, so it hath something solid and real, of no expense and little trouble, full in our own power, and whereby we can incur no danger in *disobliging* ENGLAND. For this kind of commodity will not bear exportation, the flesh being of too tender a consistence, to admit a long continuance in salt, *although perhaps I could name a country[2] which would be glad to eat up our whole nation without it.*

After all I am not so violently bent upon my own opinion as to reject any offer proposed by wise men, which shall be found equally innocent, cheap, easy, and effectual. But before something of that kind shall be advanced in contradiction to my scheme and offering a better, I desire the author or authors will be pleased maturely to consider two points. First, as things now stand, how they will be able to find food and raiment for an hundred thousand useless mouths and backs. And secondly, there being a round million of creatures in human figure throughout this kingdom whose whole subsistence put into a common stock would leave them in debt two millions of pounds sterling; adding those who are beggars by profession to the bulk of farmers, cottagers, and laborers with their wives and children, who are beggars in effect; I desire those politicians who dislike my overture, and may perhaps be so bold to attempt an answer, that they will first ask the parents of these mortals whether they would not at this day think it a great happiness to have been sold for food at a year old, in the manner I prescribe, and thereby have avoided such a perpetual scene of misfortunes as they have since gone through, by the oppression of landlords, the impossibility of paying rent without money or trade, the want of common sustenance, with neither house nor clothes to cover them from the inclemencies of the weather, and the most inevitable prospect of entailing[3] the like or greater miseries upon their breed forever.

I profess in the sincerity of my heart that I have not the least personal interest in endeavoring to promote this necessary work, having no other motive than the *public good of my country, by advancing our trade, providing for infants, relieving the poor, and*

---

9. The inhabitants of the most hostile environments—the frozen north or the Brazilian jungle—love their countries more than the Irish.

1. According to one historian, when Jerusalem was besieged and captured by the Emperor Titus in A.D. 70, factional fighting inside the city contributed to its destruction.

2. England.

3. Bequeathing.

giving some pleasure to the rich. I have no children by which I can propose to get a single penny; the youngest being nine years old, and my wife past child-bearing.
1729   1729

◼ "A MODEST PROPOSAL" AND ITS TIME ◼
William Petty: from *Political Arithmetic* [1]

from Chapter 4. How to enable the people of England and Ireland to spend 5 millions worth of commodities more than now; and how to raise the present value of the lands and goods of Ireland from 2 to 3.

This is to be done: 1. By bringing one million of the present 1,300 thousand of the people out of Ireland into England, though at the expense of a million of money. 2. That the remaining three hundred thousand left behind be all herdsmen and dairy women, servants to the owners of the lands and stock transplanted into England, all aged between 16 and 60 years, and to quit all other trades, but that of cattle, and to import nothing but salt and tobacco. Neglecting all housing, but what is fittest for these 300 thousand people, and this trade, though to the loss of 2 millions-worth of houses. Now if a million of people be worth 70 pounds per head one with another, the whole are worth 70 millions; then the said people, reckoned as money at 5 percent interest, will yield 3 millions and a half per annum. 3. And if Ireland send into England 1 million and a half worth of effects (receiving nothing back), then England will be enriched from Ireland, and otherwise, 5 millions per annum more than now, which, at 20 year's purchase, is worth one hundred millions of pounds sterling, as was propounded. * * *

POSTSCRIPT

If in this jealous age this essay should be taxed of an evil design to waste and dispeople Ireland, we say that the author of it intends not to be *Felo de se*,[2] and propound something quite contrary, by saying it is naturally possible in about 25 years to double the inhabitants of Great Britain and Ireland and make the people full as many as the territory of those kingdoms can with tolerable labor afford a competent livelihood unto, which I prove thus, (viz.)

1. The sixth part of the people are teeming women[3] of between 18 and 44 years old.
2. It is found by observation that but 1/3 part or between 30 and 40 of the teeming women are married.
3. That a teeming woman, at a medium, bears a child every two years and a half.
4. That in mankind at London, there are 14 males for 13 females, and because males are prolific[4] 40 years, and females but 25, there are in effect 560 males for 325 females.

---

1. William Petty (1623–1687) represents the type of Englishman Swift had in mind in his implicit criticism of English rapaciousness in Ireland in *A Modest Proposal.* Petty, the son of a London clothier and weaver, was an extraordinary scholar and anatomist, and a charter member of the Royal Society. Appointed physician-general to the parliamentary army in Ireland in 1652, he obtained considerable property holdings in Ireland through his additional task of surveying lands forfeited by Roman Catholics. His newfound fortune enabled him to devote his attention to his economic writings and to the Royal Society in London, though he was less than solicitous of his tenants in Ireland. Swift's friendship with Petty's children, Lord Shelburne and Lady Kerry, did not prevent him parodying Petty's *Political Arithmetic* (1691) in *A Modest Proposal.* Petty's suggestion that Ireland be turned into one huge farm to supply England by removing all the Irish was only one of many "political arithmetic" projects published during the Restoration and 18th century, reflecting English interest in "scientific" programs for social "improvement."

2. Suicidal; literally, "felon of (one)self."
3. Women capable of breeding.
4. Capable of procreation.

5. That out of the mass of mankind there dies one out of 30 per annum.
6. That at Paris, where the christenings and the births are the same in number, the christenings are above 18,000 per annum, and consequently the births at London, which far exceed the christenings there, cannot be less than 19,000 where the burials are above 23,000.

AS FOR EXAMPLE

Of 600 people, the sixth part (viz. 100) are teeming women, which (if they were all married) might bear 40 children per annum (viz.) 20 more than do die out of 600, at the rate of one out of 30; and consequently in 16 years the increase will be 320, making the whole 920. And by the same reason, in the next 9 years, the said 920 will be 280 more, in all 1,200, viz. double of the original number of 600.

Upon these principles, if there be about 19,000 births per annum at London, the number of the married teeming women must be above 38,000; and of the whole stock of the teeming women must be above 114,000, and of the whole people six times as many viz. 684,000; which agrees well enough with 696,000, which they have been elsewhere computed to be.

To conclude it is naturally possible, that all teeming women may be married, since there are in effect 560 males to 325 females; and since Great Britain and Ireland can with moderate labor, food, and other necessaries to near double the present people or to about 20 millions of heads, as shall when occasion requires it, be demonstrated. * * *

1691

END OF "A MODEST PROPOSAL" AND ITS TIME

Alexander Pope
1688–1744

William Hoare, *Sketch of Alexander Pope.*

"The life of a wit is a warfare upon earth; and the present spirit of the learned world is such, that to serve it . . . one must have the constancy of a martyr, and a resolution to suffer for its sake." Though still in his twenties when he wrote these words, Alexander Pope knew from painful experience their bitter truth. As a Roman Catholic, he could not vote, inherit or purchase land, attend a "public" school or a university, live within ten miles of London, hold public office, or openly practice his religion. He was obliged to pay double taxes. Such civil disenfranchisement barred him from receiving the literary patronage most talented writers depended upon for their livelihood. No wonder Pope wrote of "certain laws, by suff'rers thought unjust," by which he was "denied all posts of profit or of trust" (*Imitations of Horace, Epistle* 2.2.60–61). Despite whatever patriotism or loyalty to their country they may have felt, Catholics were widely regarded as alien and seditious. Pope's resentment of this attitude is evident in the *Epistle to Bathurst*

(1733) when he calls the London Monument, which bears an inscription blaming the Great Fire of 1666 on a Papist conspiracy to destroy the capital, "a tall bully" who "lies."

Religion was not Pope's greatest impediment to success, however. When he was twelve, he contracted tuberculosis of the spine (Pott's disease), a condition that stunted his growth and left him humpbacked and deformed. At four feet six inches, he could not sit at an ordinary table with other adults unless his seat was raised. His constitution was so weakened that he frequently suffered from migraine headaches, asthma, nausea, and fevers. For much of his life, he could not hold his body upright without the help of stays, and he was unable to bathe, dress or undress, rise or go to bed by himself. Pope summarized his condition most succinctly in *An Epistle to Dr. Arbuthnot* (1735), when he wrote of "this long disease, my life."

Pope was born in London in 1688, the only child of his parents' marriage. Pope's *Epistle to Dr. Arbuthnot* includes a tribute to his father's equanimity and goodness; his mother is praised as "a noble wife." At the age of nine, Pope was sent to a school for Catholic boys but was expelled in his first year for writing a satire on his schoolmaster— a sign of things to come. When he was twelve, his family moved from the environs of London to Binfield, in the royal forest of Windsor; the effect of Windsor's "green retreats" on Pope's youthful imagination is apparent in the *Pastorals* (1709) and in *Windsor-Forest* (1713). At Binfield, he began to teach himself Greek and Latin with great determination, though the rigors of his studies made his sickness worse. Refusing to yield to his infirmity, he began, at fifteen, to journey into London to learn French and Italian. Pope spoke of these adolescent years as his "great reading period" when he "went through all the best critics, almost all the English, French, and Latin poets of any name . . . [and] Homer and some other of the Greek poets in the original." During this time Pope met his great friend John Caryll, at whose request he would write *The Rape of the Lock*, and Martha Blount, who was to become his lifelong intimate companion and to whom he addressed *Of the Characters of Women: An Epistle to a Lady* (1735).

Pope claimed that "as yet a child . . . I lisp'd in numbers [i.e., meter]." Certainly he was a precocious poet and his early efforts were encouraged by many, including the playwrights William Wycherley and William Congreve, to whom Pope dedicated his *Iliad* (1715–1720). If Pope had encouraging friends, he soon had detracting enemies as well. His first publication, the *Pastorals* (1709), occasioned a rivalry between Pope's Tory supporters and the Whig partisans of Ambrose Philips, whose *Pastorals* appeared in the same volume. Pope's next important poem, *An Essay on Criticism* (1711), brought a barrage of vituperative abuse from the critic John Dennis, who called Pope "a hunch-backed toad" and argued that his deformity was merely the outward sign of mental and moral ugliness. Undaunted, Pope continued to publish: the *Messiah* (1712), *The Rape of the Lock* (1712, substantially enlarged in 1714), *Windsor-Forest* (1713), and *The Temple of Fame* (1715). With the publication of his *Works* (1717), Pope had proved himself master of a dazzling repertoire of poetic modes: pastoral and georgic, didactic, eclogue, mock-epic, allegorical dream-vision, heroic, and elegiac. No other living poet could display such dazzling versatility and comprehensive control.

There was still another area, however, in which Pope was proving the breathtaking range of his poetic gifts. Between 1713 and 1726, Pope devoted much of his creative energy to translating Homer's epics, the *Iliad* and the *Odyssey*, into heroic couplets. "Pope's Homer" not only won for him financial independence so that he could "live and thrive, / Indebted to no Prince or Peer alive" (*Imitations of Horace, Epistle* 2.2), it also confirmed his reputation as the presiding poetic genius of his time. While he was working on the *Odyssey*, Pope produced a six-volume edition of Shakespeare's works (1725), which, though it contained some valuable insights, was very much an amateur effort. When Lewis Theobald, the leading Shakespeare scholar of the time, rather pedantically highlighted Pope's many editorial shortcomings in *Shakespeare Restored, or, a Specimen of the Many Errors Committed . . . by Mr. Pope* (1726),

Pope's revenge was not far off: two years later, he published *The Dunciad*, a savagely satirical assault on Pope's critics and the bankrupt cultural values they embodied.

In the seventeen years between Dennis's attack and the publication of *The Dunciad*, Pope's appearance, talent, and character had been assailed in print more than fifty times. His enemies accused him of being obscene, seditious, duplicitous, venal, vain, blasphemous, libelous, ignorant, and a bad poet. Theobald's rebuke was the last straw, perhaps because it was the most justified. Pope's style of comic social criticism owed much to his membership in the Scriblerus Club with John Gay, Jonathan Swift, Dr. John Arbuthnot, Thomas Parnell, and Robert Harley, Earl of Oxford. The Scriblerians originally planned to produce a series entitled *The Works of the Unlearned*; although the group regularly met only for a short while in 1714, its members remained in contact. In addition to *The Dunciad*, the fruit of their exchanges may be seen in Swift's *Gulliver's Travels* (1726), Gay's *The Beggar's Opera* (1728), Pope's *Peri Bathous: Or, the Art of Sinking in Poetry* (1728), and Arbuthnot's and Pope's *Memoirs of the Extraordinary Life, Works, and Discoveries of Martinus Scriblerus* (1741).

An Essay on Man (1733–1734) showcased Pope's talent for philosophical poetry. This work and four *Moral Essays* (1731–1735) were originally intended to form part of a long poetic sequence on the nature of humankind that Pope had hoped would be his greatest work, though the project was abandoned. Between 1733 and 1738, Pope published more than a dozen *Imitations of Horace*. In these loose adaptations of Horace's epistles and satires, Pope invested his modern social criticism with the classical authority of a revered Roman poet. The *Moral Essays*, or "Epistles to Several Persons" as Pope called them, also show Pope assuming the mantle of Horace by using the familiar epistle as a vehicle for social commentary. Pope's Horatian poems are his most mature, elegant, and self-assured works.

In 1737, he published an authorized version of his letters, which he doctored to improve his reputation. His last years were a time of retirement at his villa at Twickenham, famous for its grotto of "Friendship and Liberty" and for the five-acre landscape garden Pope had designed. In *The New Dunciad* (1742), Pope shifted his attack from hack writers and low culture to all forms of hypocrisy and pretense. It was his final triumph. He worked with William Warburton on a new edition of his *Works* (1751), even as his many illnesses became still more overwhelming. Though he was a self-confessed "fool to Fame" (*Arbuthnot*), he told those gathered around his deathbed: "There is nothing that is meritorious but virtue and friendship." He was, as his enemies claimed, bellicose, self-indulgent, and self-aggrandizing. He was morally and physically courageous and had a great gift for friendship. Although it is no longer fashionable to call the first half of the eighteenth century the "Age of Pope," many of his contemporaries saw him as the predominant literary genius of his time. Today, most literary historians agree that the greatest English poet between John Milton and William Wordsworth was Alexander Pope.

AN ESSAY ON CRITICISM   Pope was only twenty-one years old when he wrote *An Essay on Criticism*, which was published anonymously in 1711. This aesthetic manifesto in heroic couplets is written in the tradition of Horace's *Ars Poetica* (c. 19 B.C.), Boileau's *Art poétique* (1674), and other verse essays delineating poetic principles and practices. Pope's chief contributions to the genre are his ringing epigrams and the playful ease with which he satirizes contemporary critics who lack genuine poetic understanding. *The Essay on Criticism* is divided into three parts: the first examines the rules of taste, their relationship to Nature, and the authority of classical authors. The second (lines 201–559) considers the impediments preventing the attainment of the classical ideals outlined in part one. In the third part, Pope proposes an aesthetic and moral reformation to restore wit, sense, and taste to their former glory. While acknowledging the importance of precepts, Pope asserts the primacy of poetic genius and the power of imagination.

An Essay on Criticism

'Tis hard to say, if greater want of skill
Appear in writing or in judging ill;
But, of the two, less dangerous is th' offense,
To tire our patience, than mislead our sense:°   *judgment*
5   Some few in that, but numbers err in this,
Ten censure wrong for one who writes amiss;
A fool might once himself alone expose,
Now one in verse makes many more in prose.[1]
'Tis with our judgments as our watches, none
10 Go just alike, yet each believes his own.
In poets as true genius is but rare,
True taste as seldom is the critic's share;
Both must alike from Heav'n derive their light,
These born to judge, as well as those to write.
15 Let such teach others who themselves excel,
And censure freely who have written well.
Authors are partial to their wit,[2] 'tis true,
But are not critics to their judgment too?
Yet if we look more closely, we shall find
20 Most have the seeds of judgment in their mind;
Nature affords at least a glimm'ring light;
The lines, though touched but faintly, are drawn right.
But as the slightest sketch, if justly traced, ⎤
Is by ill coloring but the more disgraced,   ⎬
25 So by false learning is good sense defaced; ⎦
Some are bewildered in the maze of Schools,[3]
And some made coxcombs[4] Nature meant but fools.
In search of wit these lose their common sense,
And then turn critics in their own defense.
30 Each burns alike, who can, or cannot write,
Or° with a rival's or an eunuch's spite.[5]   *either*
All fools have still° an itching to deride,[6]   *continually*
And fain° would be upon the laughing side: *gladly*
If Maevius scribble in Apollo's spite,[7]
35 There are, who judge still worse than he can write.
Some have at first for wits,° then poets past,   *intellectuals*
Turned critics next, and proved plain fools at last;
Some neither can for wits nor critics pass,
As heavy mules are neither horse nor ass.
40 Those half-learned witlings, num'rous in our isle,
As half-formed insects on the banks of Nile;
Unfinished things, one knows not what to call,

1. I.e., many bad critics respond to one bad poet.
2. Both their writings and their (fancied) ability to write well.
3. Schools of criticism.
4. Conceited show-offs.

5. I.e., they either seek to compete or, knowing themselves sterile, criticize out of envy.
6. The fool's perpetual itching suggests disease.
7. Maevius, a third-rate Roman poet, is set against Apollo, patron of good poetry.

Their generation's so equivocal:[8]
To tell° 'em, would a hundred tongues require,   count
45   Or one vain wit's, that might a hundred tire.
    But you who seek to give and merit° fame,   deserve
And justly bear a critic's noble name,
Be sure yourself and your own reach° to know,   ability
How far your genius, taste, and learning go;
50   Launch not beyond your depth, but be discrete,
And mark° that point where sense and dullness meet.   note
    Nature to all things fixed the limits fit,
And wisely curbed proud man's pretending° wit: aspiring
As on the land while here the ocean gains,
55   In other parts it leaves wide sandy plains;
Thus in the soul while memory prevails,
The solid power of understanding fails;
Where beams of warm imagination play,
The memory's soft figures melt away.
60   One science only will one genius fit;[9]
So vast is Art, so narrow human wit;°   understanding
Not only bounded to peculiar° arts,   particular
But oft in those, confined to single parts.
Like kings we lose the conquests gained before,
65   By vain ambition still to make them more:
Each might his several province well command,
Would all but stoop to what they understand.
    First follow NATURE, and your judgment frame
By her just standard, which is still° the same: always
70   Unerring Nature, still divinely bright,
One clear, unchanged, and universal light,
Life, force, and beauty, must to all impart,
At once the source, and end, and test of art.
Art from that fund each just supply provides,
75   Works without show,[1] and without pomp presides:
In some fair body thus th' informing soul[2]
With spirits feeds, with vigor fills the whole,
Each motion guides, and every nerve sustains;
Itself unseen, but in th' effects, remains.
80   Some, to whom Heav'n in wit has been profuse,
Want° as much more, to turn it to its use;   need
For wit and judgment often are at strife,
Though meant each other's aid, like man and wife.
'Tis more to guide than spur the Muse's steed;[3]
85   Restrain his fury, than provoke his speed;

---

8. Like the generation of insects on the banks of the Nile, thought to occur spontaneously, through the action of sun on mud.
9. The artist can hope only to succeed in one subject area or object of study.

1. The suggestion that art should mask its presence came from Horace.
2. The force that animates.
3. Pegasus, the winged horse.

The winged courser,° like a gen'rous horse,   *swift horse*
Shows most true mettle° when you check his course.   *spirit*
    Those RULES of old discovered, not devised,
Are Nature still, but Nature *methodized*;
90   Nature, like Liberty, is but restrained
By the same laws which first herself ordained.
    Hear how learn'd Greece her useful rules indites,°   *composes*
When to repress, and when indulge our flights:
High on Parnassus'[4] top her sons she showed,
95   And pointed out° those arduous paths they trod,   *appointed*
Held from afar, aloft, th' immortal prize,
And urged the rest by equal steps to rise;
Just precepts thus from great examples giv'n,
She drew from them what they derived from Heav'n.
100   The gen'rous critic fanned the poet's fire,
And taught the world, with reason to admire.
Then criticism the Muse's handmaid proved,
To dress her charms,[5] and make her more beloved;
But following wits from that intention strayed;
105   Who could not win the mistress, wooed the maid;
Against the poets their own arms they turned,
Sure to hate most the men from whom they learned.
So modern 'pothecaries,° taught the art   *druggists*
By doctors' bills° to play the doctor's part,   *prescriptions*
110   Bold in the practice of mistaken° rules,   *misunderstood*
Prescribe, apply, and call their masters fools.
Some on the leaves of ancient authors prey,[6]
Nor time nor moths e'er spoiled so much as they:
Some dryly plain, without invention's° aid,   *imagination's*
115   Write dull receipts° how poems may be made: *recipes*
These leave the sense, their learning to display,
And those explain the meaning quite away.
    You then whose judgment the right course would steer,
Know well each ANCIENT'S proper character,[7]
120   His fable,° subject, scope° in every page,   *plot / intention*
Religion, country, genius of his age:
Without all these at once before your eyes,
Cavil° you may, but never criticize.   *quibble*
Be Homer's works your study, and delight,
125   Read them by day, and meditate by night,
Thence form your judgment, thence your maxims bring,
And trace the Muses upward to their spring;
Still with itself compared, his text peruse;
And let your comment be the Mantuan Muse.[8]

---

4. Mount Parnassus in Greece was sacred to the Muses.
5. Both dress and address, i.e., both interpret and adjust.
6. Textual commentators, depicted as literal bookworms
in continuation of the earlier insect metaphor.
7. An interest in the historical method in criticism was

on the rise.
8. Virgil (born near Mantua) and his *Aeneid*, which took
Homer's epics as models and was the best commentary on
them.

130   When first young Maro° in his boundless mind   *Virgil*
    A work t' outlast immortal Rome designed,
    Perhaps he seemed° above the critic's law,   *thought himself*
    And but from Nature's fountains scorned to draw:
    But when t' examine every part he came,
135   Nature and Homer were, he found, the same:
    Convinced, amazed, he checks the bold design, ⎤
    And rules as strict his labored work confine, ⎬
    As if the Stagyrite[9] o'erlooked each line. ⎦
    Learn hence for ancient rules a just esteem;
140   To copy Nature is to copy them.
       Some beauties yet, no precepts can declare,[1]
    For there's a happiness as well as care.
    Music resembles poetry, in each ⎤
    Are nameless graces which no methods teach, ⎬
145   And which a master-hand alone can reach. ⎦
    If, where the rules not far enough extend,
    (Since rules were made but to promote their end)
    Some lucky license° answers to the full   *deviation*
    Th' intent proposed, that license is a rule.
150   Thus Pegasus, a nearer way to take,
    May boldly deviate from the common track.
    Great wits sometimes may gloriously offend,
    And rise to faults true critics dare not mend;
    From vulgar bounds with brave disorder part,
155   And snatch a grace beyond the reach of Art,
    Which, without passing through the judgment, gains
    The heart, and all its end at once attains.
    In prospects,[2] thus, some objects please our eyes, ⎤
    Which out of Nature's common order rise, ⎬
160   The shapeless rock, or hanging precipice. ⎦
    But though the Ancients thus their rules invade,
    (As kings dispense with laws themselves have made)
    Moderns, beware! Or if you must offend
    Against the precept, ne'er transgress its end,
165   Let it be seldom, and compelled by need,
    And have, at least, their precedent to plead.
    The critic else proceeds without remorse,
    Seizes your fame, and puts his laws in force.
       I know there are, to whose presumptuous thoughts
170   Those freer beauties, ev'n in them, seem faults:[3]
    Some figures[4] monstrous and misshaped appear,

---

9. Aristotle, whose *Poetics* provided the basis for later rules on poetry and epic writing.
1. Pope's belief that true poetic genius consisted not of rigid adherence to rules but of "brave disorder" and "grace beyond the reach of art" had earlier been expressed in the treatise *On the Sublime*, attributed to the Greek rhetorician Longinus (210?–273).
2. Views of an extensive landscape.
3. I.e., there are critics to whom even the Ancients' occasional "glorious offense" is unforgivable.
4. Both figures in the landscape and rhetorical figures or literary style.

Considered singly, or beheld too near,
Which, but proportioned to their light, or place,
Due distance reconciles to form and grace.
175 A prudent chief not always must display
His pow'rs in equal ranks, and fair array,
But with th' occasion and the place comply,
Conceal his force, nay seem sometimes to fly.
Those oft are stratagems which errors seem,
180 Nor is it Homer nods, but we that dream.
    Still green with bays[5] each ancient altar[6] stands,
Above the reach of sacrilegious hands,
Secure from flames, from envy's fiercer rage,
Destructive war, and all-involving age.
185 See, from each clime the learn'd their incense bring;
Hear, in all tongues consenting paeans° ring!   *songs of praise*
In praise so just, let every voice be joined,
And fill the gen'ral chorus of mankind!
Hail bards triumphant! born in happier days;
190 Immortal heirs of universal praise!
Whose honors with increase of Ages grow,
As streams roll down, enlarging as they flow!
Nations unborn your mighty names shall sound,
And worlds applaud that must not yet be found!
195 Oh may some spark of your celestial fire
The last, the meanest of your sons inspire,[7]
(That on weak wings, from far, pursues your flights;
Glows while he reads, but trembles as he writes)
To teach vain wits° a science little known,   *would-be critics*
200 T' admire superior sense, and doubt their own!

    Of all the causes which conspire to blind
Man's erring judgment, and misguide the mind,
What the weak head with strongest bias[8] rules,
Is pride, the never-failing vice of fools.
205 Whatever Nature has in worth denied,
She gives in large recruits° of needful° pride;   *supplies / needed*
For as in bodies, thus in souls, we find
What wants° in blood and spirits, swelled with wind;   *is lacking*
Pride, where wit fails, steps in to our defense,
210 And fills up all the mighty void of sense!
If once right reason drives that cloud away,
Truth breaks upon us with resistless day;
Trust not yourself; but your defects to know,
Make use of every friend—and every foe.
215   A little learning is a dang'rous thing;
Drink deep, or taste not the Pierian spring:[9]

5. Laurels, used to crown both poets and military heroes.
6. The works of each ancient author.
7. Pope himself, who follows tradition in writing about writing.
8. Not only prejudice but a kind of bowling ball. (In bowls, the bias ball is one weighted to roll obliquely.)
9. Hippocrene, the stream associated with the Muses.

There shallow draughts[1] intoxicate the brain,
And drinking largely sobers us again.
Fired at first sight with what the Muse imparts,
220   In fearless youth we tempt° the heights of Arts,   *attempt*
While from the bounded° level of our mind,   *limited*
Short views we take, nor see the lengths behind,
But more advanced, behold with strange surprise
New, distant scenes of endless science[2] rise!
225   So pleased at first, the towering Alps we try,
Mount o'er the vales, and seem to tread the sky;
Th' eternal snows appear already past,
And the first clouds and mountains seem the last:
But those attained, we tremble to survey
230   The growing labors of the lengthened way,
Th' increasing prospect tires our wandering eyes,
Hills peep o'er hills, and Alps on Alps arise!
      A perfect judge will read each work of wit
With the same spirit that its author writ,
235   Survey the whole, nor seek slight faults to find,
Where Nature moves, and rapture warms the mind;
Nor lose, for that malignant dull delight,
The gen'rous pleasure to be charmed with wit.
But in such lays° as neither ebb, nor flow,   *poems*
240   Correctly cold, and regularly low,
That shunning faults, one quiet tenor° keep;   *tone*
We cannot blame indeed—but we may sleep.
In wit, as Nature, what affects our hearts
Is not th' exactness of peculiar° parts;   *particular*
245   'Tis not a lip, or eye, we beauty call,
But the joint force and full result of all.
Thus when we view some well-proportioned dome,[3]
(The world's just wonder, and even thine O Rome!)
No single parts unequally surprise;
250   All comes united to th' admiring eyes;
No monstrous height, or breadth, or length appear;
The whole at once is bold, and regular.°   *well-proportioned*
      Whoever thinks a faultless piece to see,
Thinks what ne'er was, nor is, nor e'er shall be.
255   In every work regard the writer's end,
Since none can compass° more than they intend;   *encompass*
And if the means be just, the conduct° true,   *execution*
Applause, in spite of trivial faults, is due.
As men of breeding,[4] sometimes men of wit,
260   T' avoid great errors, must the less commit,
Neglect the rules each verbal critic lays,[5]

1. I.e., drinking small amounts.
2. Knowledge, subjects requiring study.
3. Any large and stately building, but those of a classical design are particularly implied.
4. Good breeding (in both birth and upbringing).
5. Lays down. A verbal critic is one concerned with linguistic detail rather than literary whole.

For not to know some trifles, is a praise.
Most critics, fond of some subservient art,
Still make the whole depend upon a part,
265 They talk of principles, but notions° prize,   *prejudices*
And all to one loved folly sacrifice.
   Once on a time, La Mancha's Knight,[6] they say,
A certain bard encountering on the way,
Discoursed in terms as just, with looks as sage,
270 As e'er could Dennis,[7] of the Grecian stage;
Concluding all were desp'rate sots and fools,
Who durst depart from Aristotle's rules.
Our author, happy in a judge so nice,
Produced his play, and begged the Knight's advice,
275 Made him observe the subject and the plot,
The manners, passions, unities,[8] what not?
All which, exact to rule were brought about,
Were but a combat in the lists[9] left out.
"What! leave the combat out?" exclaims the Knight;
280 Yes, or we must renounce the Stagyrite.°   *Aristotle*
"Not so by Heav'n" (he answers in a rage)
"Knights, squires, and steeds, must enter on the stage."
So vast a throng the stage can ne'er contain.
"Then build a new, or act it in a plain."
285   Thus critics, of less judgment than caprice,
Curious,° not knowing, not exact, but nice,°   *picky / fussy*
Form short ideas; and offend in arts
(As most in manners) by a love to parts.[1]
Some to conceit[2] alone their taste confine,
290 And glitt'ring thoughts struck out at every line;
Pleased with a work where nothing's just or fit;
One glaring chaos and wild heap of wit:
Poets like painters, thus, unskilled to trace
The naked Nature and the living grace,
295 With gold and jewels cover every part,
And hide with ornaments their want° of art.   *lack*
True wit is Nature to advantage dressed,
What oft was thought, but ne'er so well expressed,
Something, whose truth convinced at sight we find,
300 That gives us back the image of our mind:
As shades° more sweetly recommend the light,   *shadows*
So modest plainness sets off sprightly wit:
For works may have more wit than does 'em good,

---

6. Don Quixote, Cervantes's foolish knight errant. This episode comes from part two of *Don Quixote* (1615), bk. 3, ch. 10.
7. John Dennis (1657–1734), an eminent critic but not one in Pope's favor.
8. The three unities of plot (one story), time (one day),

and place (one location) were thought to have been the Greek playwrights' structuring principles, recommended by Aristotle.
9. The field of combat in medieval jousting tournaments.
1. Individual talents.
2. Extravagant use of metaphor.

As bodies perish through excess of blood.[3]
305   Others for language all their care express,
And value books, as women men, for dress:
Their praise is still—The style is excellent:
The sense, they humbly take upon content.°   trust
Words are like leaves; and where they most abound,
310   Much fruit of sense beneath is rarely found.
False eloquence, like the prismatic glass,
Its gaudy colors spreads on every place;
The face of Nature we no more survey,°   observe
All glares alike, without distinction gay:
315   But true expression, like th' unchanging sun, ⎫
Clears, and improves whate'er it shines upon, ⎬
It gilds all objects, but it alters none. ⎭
Expression is the dress of thought,[4] and still
Appears more decent° as more suitable;   correct
320   A vile conceit° in pompous words expressed,   idea
Is like a clown° in regal purple dressed;   peasant
For different styles with different subjects sort,°   belong
As several garbs with Country, Town, and Court.[5]
Some by old words to fame have made pretense;[6]
325   Ancients in phrase, mere Moderns in their sense!
Such labored nothings, in so strange a style,
Amaze the unlearn'd, and make the learned smile.
Unlucky, as Fungoso in the play,[7] ⎫
These sparks[8] with awkward vanity display ⎬
330   What the fine gentleman wore yesterday! ⎭
And but so mimic ancient wits at best,
As apes our grandsires in their doublets[9] dressed.
In words, as fashions, the same rule will hold;
Alike fantastic, if too new, or old;
335   Be not the first by whom the new are tried,
Nor yet the last to lay the old aside.
But most by numbers[1] judge a poet's song,
And smooth or rough, with them, is right or wrong;
In the bright Muse though thousand charms conspire,°   work together
340   Her voice is all these tuneful fools admire,
Who haunt Parnassus but to please their ear, ⎫
Not mend their minds; as some to church repair, ⎬
Not for the doctrine, but the music there. ⎭
These equal syllables alone require,

---

3. Apoplexy, it was thought, was caused by such an excess.
4. It was generally held that a person's appearance reflected his or her inner self.
5. As various styles of dress suit country, mercantile, and courtly life.
6. Made a claim. Deliberately archaic language was used

by Spenser and by a number of his 18th-century imitators.
7. In Ben Jonson's *Every Man Out of His Humor* (1599), this student lagged behind the fashions.
8. Hot-blooded young men, aspiring to fame and romantic conquest.
9. Close-fitting garment for the upper body.
1. Meter of verse, patterns of sound.

345   Though oft the ear the open vowels tire,[2]
        While expletives their feeble aid do join,
        And ten low words oft creep in one dull line,
        While they ring round the same unvaried chimes,
        With sure returns of still expected rhymes.
350   Where-e'er you find the cooling western breeze,
        In the next line, it whispers through the trees;
        If crystal streams with pleasing murmurs creep,
        The reader's threatened (not in vain) with sleep.
        Then, at the last, and only couplet fraught
355   With some unmeaning thing they call a thought,
        A needless Alexandrine[3] ends the song,
        That like a wounded snake, drags its slow length along.
        Leave such to tune their own dull rhymes, and know
        What's roundly smooth, or languishingly slow;
360   And praise the easy vigor of a line,
        Where Denham's strength, and Waller's sweetness join.[4]
        True ease in writing comes from art, not chance,
        As those move easiest who have learned to dance.
        'Tis not enough no harshness gives offense,
365   The sound must seem an echo to the sense.[5]
        Soft is the strain when Zephyr° gently blows,   *the west wind*
        And the smooth stream in smoother numbers flows;
        But when loud surges lash the sounding shore,
        The hoarse, rough verse should like the torrent roar.
370   When Ajax[6] strives, some rock's vast weight to throw,
        The line too labors, and the words move slow;
        Not so, when swift Camilla[7] scours the plain,
        Flies o'er th' unbending corn, and skims along the main.°   *sea*
        Hear how Timotheus'[8] varied lays surprise,
375   And bid alternate passions fall and rise!
        While, at each change, the son of Lybian Jove[9]
        Now burns with glory, and then melts with love;
        Now his fierce eyes with sparkling fury glow;
        Now sighs steal out, and tears begin to flow:
380   Persians and Greeks like turns of nature[1] found,
        And the world's victor stood subdued by sound!
        The pow'rs of music all our hearts allow;°   *admit to*
        And what Timotheus was, is Dryden now.

            Avoid extremes; and shun the fault of such,
385   Who still are pleased too little, or too much.

---

2. This line, like the couplets that follow, illustrates the fault it criticizes.
3. The 12 syllables and six stresses of an Alexandrine are illustrated in the next line.
4. Pope follows Dryden in his stylistic characterization of John Denham (1615–1669) and Edmund Waller (1606–1687), two poets greatly respected by writers of the early 18th century, especially for their work in heroic couplets.

5. The following nine lines exemplify the rule laid down here.
6. The fabulously strong Greek hero in Homer's *Iliad*.
7. An Amazon warrior in Virgil's *Aeneid*.
8. Musician to Alexander the Great, as portrayed in Dryden's *Alexander's Feast* (1697).
9. Alexander the Great.
1. Similar changes of emotion.

At every trifle scorn to take offense,
That always shows great pride, or little sense;
Those heads as stomachs are not sure the best
Which nauseate° all, and nothing can digest.   *feel sick at*
390 Yet let not each gay turn° thy rapture move,   *phrase*
For fools admire,[2] but men of sense approve;
As things seem large which we through mists descry,°   *see*
Dullness is ever apt to magnify.
    Some foreign writers, some our own despise;
395 The Ancients only, or the Moderns prize:
(Thus wit, like faith, by each man is applied
To one small sect, and all are damned beside.)
Meanly they seek the blessing to confine,
And force that sun but on a part to shine;
400 Which not alone the southern wit sublimes,°   *exalts*
But ripens spirits in cold northern climes;
Which from the first has shone on Ages past,
Enlights the present, and shall warm the last:
(Though each may feel increases and decays,
405 And see now clearer and now darker days)
Regard not then if wit be old or new,
But blame the false, and value still the true.
    Some ne'er advance a judgment of their own,
But catch the spreading notion° of the Town;[3]   *fashion*
410 They reason and conclude by precedent,
And own° stale nonsense which they ne'er invent.   *express*
Some judge of authors' names, not works, and then
Nor° praise nor blame the writings, but the men.   *neither*
Of all this servile herd the worst is he
415 That in proud dullness joins with Quality,[4]
A constant critic at the great man's board,[5]
To fetch and carry nonsense for my Lord.
What woeful stuff this madrigal would be,
In some starved Hackney sonneteer,[6] or me?
420 But let a Lord once own[7] the happy lines,
How the wit brightens! How the style refines!
Before his sacred name flies every fault,
And each exalted stanza teems with thought!
    The vulgar thus through imitation err;
425 As oft the learned by being singular;
So much they scorn the crowd, that if the throng
By chance go right, they purposely go wrong;

2. Wonder at the poetry, while "men of sense" deliberate before reaching favorable judgment.
3. The fashionable members of the city; the term was commonly used for fashionable London society.
4. The nobility, people of quality.
5. Dining table; i.e., he always eats there.
6. Like the horses from Hackney, in Middlesex, this poet's services are readily for hire. The designation "sonneteer" indicates one who writes poor poetry. Pope, who made a point of refusing to sell his services, includes himself here perhaps because of his youth when the *Essay* was written.
7. Own up to, admit that they are his.

So Schismatics[8] the plain believers quit,
And are but damned for having too much wit.
430   Some praise at morning what they blame at night;
But always think the last° opinion right.   *latest*
A Muse by these is like a mistress used,
This hour she's idolized, the next abused,
While their weak heads, like towns unfortified,
435   'Twixt sense and nonsense daily change their side.
Ask them the cause; they're "wiser still," they say;
And still tomorrow's wiser than today.
We think our fathers fools, so wise we grow;
Our wiser sons, no doubt, will think us so.
440   Once School-Divines[9] this zealous Isle o'erspread;
Who knew most sentences[1] was deepest read;
Faith, gospel, all, seemed made to be disputed,
And none had sense enough to be confuted.°   *disproved*
Scotists and Thomists,[2] now, in peace remain,
445   Amidst their kindred cobwebs in Duck Lane.[3]
If faith itself has diff'rent dresses worn,
What wonder modes in wit should take their turn?
Oft, leaving what is natural and fit,
The current folly proves the ready wit,[4]
450   And authors think their reputation safe,
Which lives as long as fools are pleased to laugh.
    Some valuing those of their own side,[5] or mind,
Still make themselves the measure of mankind;
Fondly we think we honor merit then,
455   When we but praise ourselves in other men.
Parties in wit attend on those of state,
And public faction doubles private hate.
Pride, malice, folly, against Dryden rose,
In various shapes of parsons, critics, beaus;[6]
460   But sense survived, when merry jests were past;
For rising merit will buoy up at last.
Might he return, and bless once more our eyes,
New Blackmores and new Milbourns must arise;
Nay should great Homer lift his awful head,
465   Zoilus[7] again would start up from the dead.
Envy will merit as its shade° pursue,   *shadow*

8. Religious sectarians.
9. Theologians who followed the highly formal Scholastic method.
1. The *sententiae*, or sayings of the Church Fathers, presented and explained for the student in works like Peter Lombard's *Book of Sentences* (1148–1151).
2. The schools of medieval philosophy formed by followers of Duns Scotus and Thomas Aquinas.
3. A street in London where old and secondhand books were sold.
4. Current folly allows ready wit to show itself.
5. Political persuasion.

6. The parsons: Jeremy Collier, *A Short View of the Profaneness and Immorality of the English Stage* (1698); Luke Milbourne, *Notes on Dryden's Virgil* (1698). The critics: Thomas Shadwell (1642?–1692); Elkanah Settle (1648–1724); Gerard Langbaine (1656–1692), *An Account of the English Dramatic Poets*; Richard Blackmore (1654–1729). Among the beaus: George Villiers, Second Duke of Buckingham, who co-authored *The Rehearsal* (1671); John Wilmot, Second Earl of Rochester, *An Allusion to Horace: The 10th Satyr of the 1st Book* (1680).
7. A critic of Homer's, of the 4th century B.C.

But like a shadow, proves the substance true;
For envied wit, like Sol° eclipsed, makes known   *the sun*
Th' opposing body's grossness,° not its own.   *ponderousness*
470 When first that sun too powerful beams displays,
It draws up vapors which obscure its rays;
But ev'n those clouds at last adorn its way,
Reflect new glories, and augment the day.
   Be thou the first true merit to befriend;
475 His praise is lost, who stays till all commend;
Short is the date,° alas, of modern rhymes;   *life*
And 'tis but just to let 'em live betimes.°   *awhile*
No longer now that Golden Age appears,
When Patriarch-Wits survived a thousand years;
480 Now length of fame (our second life) is lost,
And bare threescore is all ev'n that can boast:
Our sons their fathers' failing language see,
And such as Chaucer[8] is, shall Dryden be.
So when the faithful pencil has designed
485 Some bright idea of the master's mind,
Where a new world leaps out at his command,
And ready Nature waits upon his hand;
When the ripe colors soften and unite,
And sweetly melt into just shade and light,
490 When mellowing years their full perfection give,
And each bold figure just begins to live;
The treach'rous colors the fair art betray,
And all the bright creation fades away!
   Unhappy wit, like most mistaken° things,   *misunderstood*
495 Atones not for that envy which it brings.
In youth alone its empty praise we boast,
But soon the short-lived vanity is lost!
Like some fair flow'r the early spring supplies,
That gaily blooms, but ev'n in blooming dies.
500 What is this wit which must our cares employ?
The owner's wife, that other men enjoy,
Then most our trouble still when most admired,
And still the more we give, the more required;
Whose fame with pains we guard, but lose with ease,
505 Sure some to vex, but never all to please;
'Tis what the vicious° fear, the virtuous shun;   *wicked*
By fools 'tis hated, and by knaves undone!
   If wit so much from ign'rance undergo,
Ah, let not learning too commence° its foe!   *start to be*
510 Of old, those met rewards who could excel,
And such were praised who but endeavored well:
Though triumphs were to gen'rals only due,

---

8. Chaucer was admired but seen as quaint and arcane, his language unintelligible. It was common to complain of the transience of the English language at this time.

Crowns were reserved to grace the soldiers too.[9]
Now, they who reached Parnassus' lofty crown,
515　Employ their plans to spurn some others down;
And while self-love each jealous writer rules,
Contending wits become the sport of fools:
But still the worst with most regret commend,
For each ill author is as bad a friend.
520　To what base ends, and by what abject ways,
Are mortals urged through sacred° lust of praise!　　　　*accursed*
Ah, ne'er so dire a thirst of glory boast,
Nor in the critic let the man be lost!
Good nature and good sense must ever join;
525　To err is human; to forgive, divine.
　　But if in noble minds some dregs remain,
Not yet purged off, of spleen° and sour disdain,　　　　*bad temper*
Discharge that rage on more provoking crimes,
Nor fear a dearth in these flagitious° times.　　　　*corrupt*
530　No pardon vile obscenity should find,
Though wit and art conspire to move your mind;
But dullness with obscenity must prove
As shameful sure as impotence in love.
In the fat Age of pleasure, wealth, and ease,
535　Sprung the rank weed, and thrived with large increase;
When love was all an easy monarch's[1] care;
Seldom at council, never in a war:[2]
Jilts ruled the State, and statesmen farces writ;[3]
Nay wits had pensions,° and young Lords had wit:　　　　*government salaries*
540　The fair sat panting at a courtier's play,
And not a Mask[4] went unimproved away:
The modest fan was lifted up no more,
And virgins smiled at what they blushed before—
The following license of a foreign reign[5]
545　Did all the dregs of bold Socinus[6] drain;
Then unbelieving priests reformed the nation,
And taught more pleasant methods of salvation;
Where Heav'ns free subjects might their rights dispute,
Lest God himself should seem too absolute.
550　Pulpits their sacred satire learned to spare,
And vice admired° to find a flatt'rer there!　　　　*was surprised*

9. Soldiers who had distinguished themselves in the field received crowns. Unlike those soldiers rewarded for assisting one another, the poets in the following lines achieve their crowns, then turn on their fellow writers.
1. Charles II (1630–1685). Ease was a much-prized social grace in the late 17th and early 18th centuries.
2. Charles had commanded an army defeated at the Battle of Worcester in 1651.
3. "Jilts" were whores, a reference to Charles's many mistresses. The statesmen were the Duke of Buckingham, *The Rehearsal* (1671); Sir Charles Sedley, *The Mulberry*

Garden (1668); Sir George Etherege (1634–1691), a number of plays.
4. Masks were initially worn by noblewomen attending plays, but the potential for concealment meant that they came to be particularly associated with prostitutes.
5. That of William III (1650–1702), from the Netherlands, who introduced policies of increased religious toleration.
6. Laelius Socinus (1525–1562) and Faustus Socinus (1539–1604), two Italian theologians who sponsored various heresies, including denying the divinity of Christ.

Encouraged thus, wit's Titans[7] braved the skies,
And the press groaned with licensed blasphemies[8]—
These monsters, critics! with your darts engage,
555 Here point your thunder, and exhaust your rage!
Yet shun their fault, who, scandalously nice,°   *fastidious*
Will needs mistake an author into vice;
All seems infected that th' infected spy,°   *see*
As all looks yellow to the jaundiced eye.
560   LEARN then what MORALS critics ought to show,
For 'tis but half a judge's task, to know.
'Tis not enough, taste, judgment, learning, join;
In all you speak, let truth and candor shine;
That not alone what to your sense is due,
565 All may allow; but seek your friendship too.
  Be silent always when you doubt your sense;
And speak, though sure, with seeming diffidence:
Some positive persisting fops we know,
Who, if once wrong, will needs be always so;
570 But you, with pleasure own your errors past,
And make each day a critic on° the last.   *assessment of*
   'Tis not enough your counsel still be true;
Blunt truths more mischief than nice° falsehoods do. *delicate*
Men must be taught as if you taught them not;
575 And things unknown proposed as things forgot:
Without good breeding, truth is disapproved;
That only makes superior sense belov'd.
  Be niggards of advice on no pretense;[9]
For the worse avarice is that of sense:
580 With mean complacence ne'er betray your trust,[1]
Nor be so civil as to prove unjust;
Fear not the anger of the wise to raise;
Those best can bear reproof, who merit praise.
   'Twere well, might critics still this freedom take;
585 But Appius[2] reddens at each word you speak,
And stares, tremendous![3] with a threatening eye,
Like some fierce tyrant in old tapestry!
Fear most to tax an honorable fool,
Whose right it is, uncensured to be dull;
590 Such without wit are poets when they please,
As without learning they can take degrees.[4]
Leave dang'rous truths to unsuccessful satires,

---

7. This reference compares the deistic writers to the classical giants, the Titans, who attempted to conquer heaven, and were severely punished as a result.
8. The Licensing Act lapsed in 1663, allowing books to be published that Pope and others found blasphemous.
9. Do not withhold your advice however good your reasons.
1. Do not avoid your duty to give judgment by being servile or polite.
2. Dennis; the hero of his tragedy, *Appius and Virginia* (1705), was also sensitive to criticism.
3. Staring and use of the adjective "tremendous" were both characteristic of Dennis.
4. Privy Councilors, bishops, and peers could obtain academic degrees without fulfilling normal requirements.

And flattery to fulsome dedicators,
Whom, when they praise, the world believes no more,
595   Than when they promise to give scribbling o'er.
'Tis best sometimes your censure to restrain,
And charitably let the dull be vain:
Your silence there is better than your spite,
For who can rail so long as they can write?
600   Still humming on, their drowsy course they keep,
And lashed so long, like tops,° are lashed asleep.   *spinning tops*
False steps but help them to renew the race,
As after stumbling, jades° will mend their pace.   *ruined horses*
What crowds of these, impenitently bold,
605   In sounds and jingling syllables grown old,
Still run on poets in a raging vein,
Ev'n to the dregs and squeezings of the brain;
Strain out the last, dull droppings of their sense,
And rhyme with all the rage of impotence!
610   Such shameless bards we have; and yet 'tis true,
There are as mad, abandoned critics too.
The bookful blockhead, ignorantly read,
With loads of learned lumber in his head,
With his own tongue still edifies his ears,
615   And always listening to himself appears.
All books he reads, and all he reads assails,
From Dryden's Fables down to Durfey's Tales.[5]
With him, most authors steal their works, or buy;
Garth did not write his own Dispensary.[6]
620   Name a new play, and he's the poet's friend,
Nay showed his faults—but when would poets mend?
No place so sacred from such fops is barred,
Nor is Paul's church more safe than Paul's churchyard:[7]
Nay, fly to altars; there they'll talk you dead;
625   For fools rush in where angels fear to tread.
Distrustful sense with modest caution speaks; ⎫
It still looks home, and short excursions makes; ⎬
But rattling nonsense in full volleys breaks; ⎭
And never shocked, and never turned aside,
630   Bursts out, resistless, with a thundering tide!
        But where's the man, who counsel can bestow,
Still pleased to teach, and yet not proud to know°?   *of knowing*
Unbiased, or° by favor or by spite;   *either*
Not dully prepossessed, nor blindly right;
635   Though learn'd, well-bred; and though well-bred, sincere;
Modestly bold, and humanly severe?

---

5. Dryden, *Fables Ancient and Modern* (1700); Thomas D'Urfey, *Tales Tragical and Comical* (1704). D'Urfey, a popular playwright and singer, is best known for the ballad collection *Pills to Purge Melancholy*, to which his name was attached.

6. The report that Pope's friend Samuel Garth had plagiarized his popular mock-heroic work *The Dispensary* (1699) was, according to William Warburton, "a common slander at that time."

7. Booksellers kept stalls in St. Paul's churchyard.

Who to a friend his faults can freely show,
And gladly praise the merit of a foe?
Blest with a taste exact, yet unconfined;
640 A knowledge both of books and humankind;
Generous converse;[8] a soul exempt from pride;
And love to praise, with reason on his side?
    Such once were critics, such the happy few,
Athens and Rome in better Ages knew.
645 The mighty Stagyrite° first left the shore,   *Aristotle*
Spread all his sails, and durst the deeps explore;
He steered securely, and discovered far,
Led by the light of the Maeonian star.°   *Homer*
Poets, a race long unconfined and free,
650 Still fond and proud of savage liberty,
Received his laws,[9] and stood convinced 'twas fit
Who conquered Nature,[1] should preside o'er wit.
    Horace still charms with graceful negligence,
And without method talks us into sense,
655 Will like a friend familiarly convey
The truest notions in the easiest way.
He, who supreme in judgment, as in wit,
Might boldly censure, as he boldly writ,
Yet judged with coolness though he sung with fire;
660 His precepts teach but what his works inspire.
Our critics take a contrary extreme,
They judge with fury, but they write with phlegm:[2]
Nor suffers Horace more in wrong translations
By wits, than critics in as wrong quotations.
665   See Dionysius[3] Homer's thoughts refine,
And call new beauties forth from ev'ry line!
    Fancy and art in gay Petronius[4] please,
The Scholar's learning, with the courtier's ease.
    In grave Quintilian's copious work[5] we find
670 The justest rules, and clearest method joined;
Thus useful arms in magazines we place,
All ranged in order, and disposed with grace,
But less to please the eye, than arm the hand,
Still fit for use, and ready at command.
675   Thee, bold Longinus![6] all the Nine° inspire,   *the Muses*
And bless their critic with a poet's fire.
And ardent judge, who zealous in his trust,
With warmth gives sentence, yet is always just;

---

8. Good conversation and well-mannered behavior.
9. Aristotle's *Poetics* set rules for poetic composition.
1. Aristotle was also noted for his study of the physical world.
2. Under the humoral understanding of the body, an excess of phlegm caused disease, and so the term came to mean coolness, dullness, or apathy.
3. Dionysius of Halicarnassus, a Roman critic contemporary

with Horace.
4. Petronius Arbiter (d. A.D. 66) judged on matters of taste in Nero's court.
5. Quintilian (c. 35–c. 99 A.D.) was a Latin rhetorician, whose *Institutio Oratoria* Pope knew well.
6. Longinus (210?–273) was a Greek rhetorician, to whom was attributed the enormously influential treatise *On the Sublime.*

Whose own example strengthens all his laws,
680   And is himself that great sublime he draws.
         Thus long succeeding critics justly reigned,
License repressed, and useful laws ordained;
Learning and Rome alike in Empire grew,
And Arts still followed where her eagles[7] flew;
685   From the same foes, at last, both felt their doom,
And the same Age saw learning fall, and Rome.
With tyranny, then superstition joined,
As that the body, this enslaved the mind;
Much was believed, but little understood,
690   And to be dull was construed to be good;
A second deluge learning thus o'er-run,
And the monks finished what the Goths begun.
         At length, Erasmus, that great, injured name,
(The glory of the priesthood, and the shame!)[8]
695   Stemmed the wild torrent of a barb'rous age,
And drove those holy vandals off the stage.
         But see! each Muse, in Leo's[9] golden days,
Starts from her trance, and trims her withered bays!
Rome's ancient Genius,° o'er its ruins spread,   *guardian spirit*
700   Shakes off the dust, and rears his rev'rend head!
Then Sculpture and her sister Arts revive;
Stones leaped to form, and rocks began to live;
With sweeter notes each rising temple rung;
A Raphael painted, and a Vida sung![1]
705   Immortal Vida! on whose honored brow
The Poet's bays and critic's ivy[2] grow:
Cremona now shall ever boast thy name,
As next in place to Mantua, next in fame![3]
         But soon by impious arms from Latium[4] chased,
710   Their ancient bounds the banished Muses passed;
Thence Arts o'er all the northern world advance;
But critic Learning flourished most in France.
The rules, a nation born to serve,[5] obeys,
And Boileau[6] still in right of Horace sways.
715   But we, brave Britons, foreign laws despised,
And kept unconquered, and uncivilized,
Fierce for the liberties of wit, and bold,
We still defied the Romans, as of old.
Yet some there were, among the sounder few
720   Of those who less presumed, and better knew,

7. The emblem of the Roman Empire.
8. Erasmus (c. 1466–1536), the Dutch humanist who influenced the course of the Reformation; the "glory of the priesthood" because of his learning, Erasmus was its "shame" both because he criticized priests and because he was persecuted for his outspokenness.
9. Pope Leo X (1475–1521), patron of letters and arts.
1. Raphael (1483–1520) was considered the greatest of painters; Girolamo Vida (c. 1485–1566), Italian poet.

2. Ivy was associated with poets (and with Bacchus), but also with learning.
3. Cremona and Mantua were the birthplaces of Vida and Virgil, respectively.
4. Italy; Rome was conquered by the Holy Roman Empire in 1527.
5. A reference to the despotic reign of Louis XIV.
6. Nicolas Boileau-Despréaux (1636–1711) wrote much that was praised in England.

Who durst° assert the juster ancient cause,   *dared to*
And here restored wit's fundamental laws.
Such was the Muse, whose rules and practice tell,
Nature's chief Master-piece is writing well.[7]
725 Such was Roscommon[8]—not more learn'd than good,
With manners gen'rous as his noble blood;
To him the wit of Greece and Rome was known,
And ev'ry author's merit, but his own.
Such late was Walsh,[9]—the Muse's judge and friend,
730 Who justly knew° to blame or to commend;   *knew when to*
To failings mild, but zealous for desert;
The clearest head, and the sincerest heart.
This humble praise, lamented shade°! receive,   *spirit*
This praise at least a grateful Muse may give!
735 The Muse, whose early voice you taught to sing,
Prescribed her heights, and pruned° her tender wing,   *groomed*
(Her guide now lost) no more attempts to rise,
But in low numbers° short excursions tries: *lowly verses*
Content, if hence th' unlearn'd their wants° may view,   *lacks*
740 The learn'd reflect on what before they knew:
Careless of censure, nor too fond of fame,
Still pleased to praise, yet not afraid to blame,
Averse alike to flatter, or offend,
Not free from faults, nor yet too vain to mend.

c. 1709   1711

THE RAPE OF THE LOCK   "New things are made familiar, and familiar things are made new," wrote Samuel Johnson about the most accomplished poem of Pope's younger years. "The whole detail of a female day is brought before us invested with so much art of decoration that, though nothing is disguised, everything is striking."

Only a poet with formidable imaginative powers could have made a great mock-heroic poem out of such unpromising materials. When Robert, Lord Petre, cut a love-lock from the head of Arabella Fermor without her permission, the two young people, both in their early twenties, quarreled bitterly. Their families, leading members of the Roman Catholic gentry once on the friendliest terms, became seriously estranged. Pope's friend John Caryll, who saw himself as a mediator among the group, asked him "to write a poem to make a jest of it, and laugh them together."

Pope's first effort was a poem in two cantos, *The Rape of the Locke*, printed in 1712 with some of his other pieces and the work of other poets. Two years later, Pope separately published *The Rape of the Lock*, enlarged to five cantos by the addition of the "machinery" of the sylphs and gnomes, and by the game of Ombre. The poem reached its final form in 1717 when Pope added the moralizing declamation of Clarissa (5.7–35), a parody of the speech of Sarpedon to Glaucus in the *Iliad*. The mock-epic tenor of the five-canto poem was clearly influenced by Pope's translation of the *Iliad*, his main project while most of *The Rape of the Lock* was being composed. Other influences were Homer's *Odyssey*, Virgil's *Aeneid*, Milton's *Paradise Lost*, and Boileau's *Le Lutrin* (1674, 1683), a mock-heroic satire on clerical infighting

7. This line is quoted from the then well-known *Essay on Poetry* (1682) by John Sheffield, third Earl of Mulgrave and later first Duke of Buckingham.
8. Wentworth Dillon (c. 1630–1685), fourth Earl of

Roscommon; poet, critic, didactic writer.
9. William Walsh (1663–1708), friend and mentor of Pope.

over the placement of a lectern. Yoking together the mundanely trivial and the mythically heroic as he follows the course of Belinda's day, Pope produced a vivid, yet affectionate, mockery of the fashions and sexual mores common in his own social circle.

The arming of the champion for war became the application of Belinda's (i.e., Arabella's) make-up for the battle of the sexes; the larger-than-life gods of classical mythology became miniature cartoon-like sylphs; Aeneas' voyage up the Tiber became Belinda's progress up the Thames; the depiction of Achilles' shield became the description of Belinda's petticoat; the test of single combat became the game of cards; the hero's journey to the underworld became the gnome's adventure in the Cave of Spleen; and the rape of Helen that started the Trojan War became the "rape" (stealing) of Belinda's hair that began an unpleasant social squabble. All the trappings of classical epic are here: the divine messenger appearing to the hero in a dream, the sacrifice to the gods, the inspirational speech to the troops before battle, the epic feast, the violent melee, and the final triumphant apotheosis. Throughout the poem, the enormous distance between the trivial *matter* and the heroic *manner* produces brilliantly comic results.

The Rape of the Lock
An Heroi-Comical Poem in Five Cantos

Nolueram, Belinda, tuos violare capillos,
Sed juvat hoc precibus me tribuisse tuis.

Martial[1]

To Mrs. Arabella Fermor
Madam,
It will be in vain to deny that I have some regard for this piece, since I dedicate it to you. Yet you may bear me witness, it was intended only to divert a few young ladies, who have good sense and good humor enough, to laugh not only at their sex's little unguarded follies, but at their own.[2] But as it was communicated with the air of a secret, it soon found its way into the world. An imperfect copy having been offered to a bookseller, you had the good nature for my sake to consent to the publication of one more correct; this I was forced to before I had executed half my design, for the *machinery* was entirely wanting to complete it.

The *machinery*, Madam, is a term invented by the critics, to signify that part which the deities, angels, or demons, are made to act in a poem; for the ancient poets are in one respect like many modern ladies: let an action be never so trivial in itself, they always make it appear of the utmost importance. These machines I determined to raise on a very new and odd foundation, the Rosicrucian[3] doctrine of spirits.

I know how disagreeable it is to make use of hard words before a lady; but 'tis so much the concern of a poet to have his works understood, and particularly by your sex, that you must give me leave to explain two or three difficult terms.

The Rosicrucians are a people I must bring you acquainted with. The best account I know of them is in a French book called *Le Comte de Gabalis*,[4] which both in its title and size is so like a novel, that many of the fair sex have read it for one by mistake. According to these gentlemen, the four elements are inhabited by spirits,

1. "I did not wish, [Belinda,] to violate your locks, but I rejoice to have yielded this to your wishes" (Martial, *Epigrams* 12.84). Pope has substituted "Belinda" for Martial's "Polytimus."
2. I.e., at their own individual follies as well.
3. A secret society of the 17th and 18th centuries,

devoted to the study of ancient religious, philosophical, and mystical doctrines.
4. Written in 1670 by the Abbé de Monfaucon de Villars, its approach to Rosicrucian philosophy was lighthearted. It was printed in duodecimo, a small "pocketbook" size common to many inexpensive novels.

which they call Sylphs, Gnomes, Nymphs, and Salamanders.[5] The Gnomes, or Demons of Earth, delight in mischief; but the Sylphs, whose habitation is in the air, are the best-conditioned[6] creatures imaginable. For they say, any mortals may enjoy the most intimate familiarities with these gentle spirits, upon a condition very easy to all true adepts, an inviolate preservation of chastity.

As to the following cantos, all the passages of them are as fabulous,[7] as the vision at the beginning, or the transformation at the end (except the loss of your hair, which I always mention with reverence). The human persons are as fictitious as the airy ones; and the character of Belinda, as it is now managed, resembles you in nothing but in beauty.

If this poem had as many graces as there are in your person, or in your mind, yet I could never hope it should pass through the world half so uncensured as you have done. But let its fortune be what it will, mine is happy enough, to have given me this occasion of assuring you that I am, with the truest esteem,

Madam,

Your most obedient

humble servant.

A. Pope

CANTO 1

What dire offense from am'rous causes springs,
What mighty contests rise from trivial things,
I sing[8]—This verse to Caryll, Muse! is due;
This, ev'n Belinda may vouchsafe to view:
5   Slight is the subject, but not so the praise,
If she inspire, and he approve my lays.°   *verses*
    Say what strange motive, Goddess°! could compel   *his Muse*
A well-bred lord t' assault a gentle belle?
Oh say what stranger cause, yet unexplored,
10 Could make a gentle belle reject a lord?
In tasks so bold, can little men engage,
And in soft bosoms dwells such mighty rage?
    Sol through white curtains shot a tim'rous ray,
And op'd those eyes that must eclipse the day;
15 Now lapdogs[9] give themselves the rousing shake,
And sleepless lovers, just at twelve, awake:
Thrice rung the bell, the slipper knocked the ground,[1]
And the pressed watch returned a silver sound.[2]
Belinda still her downy pillow pressed,
20 Her guardian Sylph prolonged the balmy rest.
'Twas he had summoned to her silent bed

---

5. Elemental spirits living in fire.
6. Best natured, having the best character.
7. Fictional.
8. Pope begins with the ancient epic formula of "proposition" of the work as a whole, and "invocation" of the gods' assistance, continuing with the traditional epic questions.

9. Small dogs imported from Asia were highly fashionable ladies' pets at this time.
1. Belinda rings the bell and then finally bangs her slipper on the floor to call her maid.
2. The popular "pressed watch" chimed the hour and quarter hours when its stem was pressed, saving its owner from striking a match to see the time.

The morning dream that hovered o'er her head.
A youth more glitt'ring than a birthnight beau,[3]
(That ev'n in slumber caused her cheek to glow)
25   Seemed to her ear his winning lips to lay,
And thus in whispers said, or seemed to say:[4]
    "Fairest of mortals, thou distinguished care
Of thousand bright inhabitants of air!
If e'er one vision touched thy infant thought,
30   Of all the nurse and all the priest have taught,[5]
Of airy elves by moonlight shadows seen,
The silver token, and the circled green,[6]
Or virgins visited by angel pow'rs,[7]
With golden crowns and wreaths of heav'nly flow'rs,
35   Hear and believe! thy own importance know,
Nor bound thy narrow views to things below.
Some secret truths from learned pride concealed,
To maids alone and children are revealed:
What though no credit doubting wits may give?[8]
40   The fair and innocent shall still believe.
Know then, unnumbered spirits round thee fly,
The light militia of the lower sky;
These, though unseen, are ever on the wing,
Hang o'er the box, and hover round the ring.[9]
45   Think what an equipage[1] thou hast in air,
And view with scorn two pages and a chair.[2]
As now your own, our beings were of old,
And once enclosed in woman's beauteous mold;
Thence, by a soft transition, we repair
50   From earthly vehicles[3] to these of air.
Think not, when woman's transient breath is fled,
That all her vanities at once are dead:
Succeeding vanities she still regards,
And though she plays no more, o'erlooks the cards.
55   Her joy in gilded chariots, when alive,
And love of Ombre,[4] after death survive.
For when the fair in all their pride expire,
To their first elements[5] their souls retire:
The sprites of fiery termagants° in flame   *scolding women*

---

3. On a royal birthday, courtiers' clothes were particularly extravagant.
4. His whispering recalls the serpent's temptation of Eve in Milton.
5. The nurse and priest were seen as two standard sources of superstition.
6. Withered circles in the grass and silver coins were supposed to be signs of fairies' presence.
7. Belinda is reminded of the many virgin saints, and particularly the Annunciation to the Virgin Mary.
8. Religious skepticism was on the increase.
9. The theater box and the equally fashionable drive round Hyde Park.

1. Carriage, horses, and attendants.
2. A sedan chair, carried by two chairmen.
3. Both the carriage, and the physical body.
4. Ombre (pronounced Omber) was an elaborate card game, introduced into England in the 17th century and highly fashionable in the early 18th century. Given the general tenor of the poem, Pope may also be punning on the origin of the word "Ombre," from the Spanish *hombre*, meaning "man."
5. The four elements of fire, water, earth, and air were thought to make up all things; so an individual's character was determined by whichever element dominated his or her soul.

60   Mount up, and take a salamander's name.
      Soft yielding minds to water glide away,
      And sip with Nymphs, their elemental tea.
      The graver prude sinks downward to a Gnome,
      In search of mischief still on earth to roam.
65   The light coquettes in Sylphs aloft repair,
      And sport and flutter in the fields of air.
          "Know farther yet; whoever fair and chaste
      Rejects mankind, is by some Sylph embraced:
      For spirits, freed from mortal laws, with ease
70   Assume what sexes and what shapes they please.[6]
      What guards the purity of melting maids,[7]
      In courtly balls, and midnight masquerades,
      Safe from the treach'rous friend, the daring spark,[8]
      The glance by day, the whisper in the dark;
75   When kind occasion prompts their warm desires,
      When music softens, and when dancing fires?
      'Tis but their Sylph, the wise celestials know,
      Though *Honor* is the word with men below.
          "Some nymphs there are, too conscious of their face,
80   For life predestined to the Gnomes' embrace.
      These swell their prospects and exalt their pride,
      When offers are disdained, and love denied.
      Then gay ideas crowd the vacant brain;
      While peers° and dukes, and all their sweeping train,   *aristocrats*
85   And garters, stars, and coronets[9] appear,
      And in soft sounds, 'your Grace'[1] salutes their ear.
      'Tis these that early taint the female soul,
      Instruct the eyes of young coquettes to roll,
      Teach infant cheeks a hidden° blush to know,   *deliberate*
90   And little hearts to flutter at a beau.
          "Oft when the world imagine women stray,
      The Sylphs through mystic mazes guide their way,
      Through all the giddy circle they pursue,
      And old impertinence° expel by new.   *frivolity*
95   What tender maid but must a victim fall
      To one man's treat, but for another's ball?
      When Florio speaks, what virgin could withstand,
      If gentle Damon did not squeeze her hand?
      With varying vanities, from ev'ry part,
100   They shift the moving toy shop[2] of their heart;
      Where wigs with wigs, with sword knots sword knots strive,[3]
      Beaus banish beaus, and coaches coaches drive.[4]

---

6. Cf. *Paradise Lost*, "For spirits when they please / Can
either sex assume, or both" (1.423–24).
7. I.e., the chastity of weakening virgins.
8. A bold, brash, and showy young man.
9. Emblems of noble rank.
1. Form of address for a duke or a duchess.

2. Where toys and trinkets are sold; "moving" here means
easily changed, unstable.
3. Most men wore wigs in public; formally dressed men
tied ribbons to the hilt of their swords.
4. In word order and versification, these two lines mimic
both Homer's and Ovid's description of heroic combat.

This erring mortals levity may call,
Oh blind to truth! the Sylphs contrive it all.

105   "Of these am I, who thy protection claim,
A watchful sprite, and Ariel is my name.
Late, as I ranged the crystal wilds of air,
In the clear mirror of thy ruling star
I saw, alas! some dread event impend,

110 Ere to the main° this morning sun descend.   *sea*
But Heav'n reveals not what, or how, or where:
Warned by thy Sylph, oh pious maid beware!
This to disclose is all thy guardian can.
Beware of all, but most beware of man!"

115   He said; when Shock,[5] who thought she slept too long,
Leapt up, and waked his mistress with his tongue.
'Twas then Belinda! if report say true,
Thy eyes first opened on a *billet-doux;*°   *love letter*
Wounds, charms, and ardors, were no sooner read,

120 But all the vision vanished from thy head.
    And now, unveiled, the toilet° stands displayed,   *dressing table*
Each silver vase in mystic order laid.
First, robed in white, the nymph intent adores
With head uncovered, the cosmetic pow'rs.

125 A heav'nly image[6] in the glass appears,
To that she bends, to that her eyes she rears;°   *raises*
Th' inferior priestess,[7] at her altar's side,
Trembling, begins the sacred rites of pride.
Unnumbered treasures ope at once, and here

130 The various off'rings of the world appear;
From each she nicely culls with curious° toil,   *careful*
And decks the goddess with the glitt'ring spoil.
This casket India's glowing gems unlocks,
And all Arabia° breathes from yonder box.   *eastern perfume*

135 The tortoise here and elephant unite,
Transformed to combs, the speckled and the white.[8]
Here files of pins extend their shining rows,
Puffs, powders, patches, Bibles,[9] *billet-doux.*
Now awful° beauty puts on all its arms;   *awe-inspiring*

140 The fair each moment rises in her charms,
Repairs her smiles, awakens ev'ry grace,
And calls forth all the wonders of her face;
Sees by degrees a purer blush[1] arise,
And keener lightnings[2] quicken in her eyes.

145 The busy Sylphs surround their darling care;
These set the head, and those divide the hair,

---

5. The shock or shough, a long-haired Icelandic poodle, fashionable as a lapdog.
6. I.e., Belinda herself.
7. Belinda's maid, Betty.
8. Tortoise-shell and ivory.
9. Patches were small beauty spots of black silk, pasted onto the face to make the skin appear whiter. It was fashionable to own Bibles in very small format.
1. The even, artificial blush of rouge.
2. Caused by drops of belladonna (deadly nightshade), which dilates the pupils.

Some fold the sleeve, whilst others plait the gown;
And Betty's praised for labors not her own.

CANTO 2

Not with more glories, in th' ethereal plain,°   sky
The sun first rises o'er the purpled main,
Than issuing forth, the rival of his beams
Launched on the bosom of the silver Thames.³
5   Fair nymphs, and well-dressed youths around her shone,
But ev'ry eye was fixed on her alone.
On her white breast a sparkling cross she wore,
Which Jews might kiss, and infidels adore.⁴
Her lively looks a sprightly mind disclose,
10   Quick as her eyes, and as unfixed as those:
Favors to none, to all she smiles extends,
Oft she rejects, but never once offends.
Bright as the sun, her eyes the gazers strike,
And, like the sun, they shine on all alike.
15   Yet graceful ease, and sweetness void of pride,
Might hide her faults, if belles had faults to hide:
If to her share some female errors fall,
Look on her face, and you'll forget 'em all.
    This nymph, to the destruction of mankind,
20   Nourished two locks which graceful hung behind
In equal curls, and well conspired to deck
With shining ringlets the smooth iv'ry neck.
Love in these labyrinths his slaves detains,
And mighty hearts are held in slender chains.
25   With hairy springes° we the birds betray,   noose traps
Slight lines° of hair surprise the finny prey,   fishing lines
Fair tresses man's imperial race ensnare,
And beauty draws us with a single hair.
    Th' adventurous Baron⁵ the bright locks admired,
30   He saw, he wished, and to the prize aspired:
Resolved to win, he meditates the way,
By force to ravish, or by fraud betray;
For when success a lover's toil attends,
Few ask, if fraud or force attained his ends.
35   For this, ere Phoebus rose, he had implored
Propitious Heav'n, and ev'ry pow'r adored,°   worshipped
But chiefly *Love*—to *Love* an altar built,
Of twelve vast French romances, neatly gilt.
There lay three garters, half a pair of gloves;
40   And all the trophies of his former loves.

3. Belinda takes a boat from London to Hampton Court,
avoiding the dirt and squalor of the streets; her voyage compares with Aeneas's up the Tiber (*Aeneid* 7), or, alternatively, Cleopatra's up the Nile (*Antony and Cleopatra* 2.2).

4. Kissing the cross was the sign of religious conversion.
5. Robert, Lord Petre (1690–1713), responsible for the
original incident.

With tender *billet-doux* he lights the pyre,
And breathes three am'rous sighs to raise the fire.
Then prostrate falls, and begs with ardent eyes
Soon to obtain, and long possess the prize:
45   The pow'rs gave ear, and granted half his pray'r,
The rest the winds dispersed in empty air.[6]
    But now secure the painted vessel glides,
The sunbeams trembling on the floating tides,
While melting music steals upon the sky,
50   And softened sounds along the waters die.
Smooth flow the waves, the zephyrs° gently play,   breezes
Belinda smiled, and all the world was gay.
All but the Sylph—with careful° thoughts oppressed,   worried
Th' impending woe sat heavy on his breast.
55   He summons strait his denizens[7] of air;
The lucid squadrons round the sails repair:
Soft o'er the shrouds° aerial whispers breathe,   ropes
That seemed but zephyrs to the train beneath.
Some to the sun their insect wings unfold,
60   Waft on the breeze, or sink in clouds of gold.
Transparent forms, too fine for mortal sight,
Their fluid bodies half dissolved in light,
Loose to the wind their airy garments flew,
Thin glitt'ring textures of the filmy dew;
65   Dipped in the richest tincture of the skies,
Where light disports in ever-mingling dyes,
While ev'ry beam new transient colors flings,
Colors that change whene'er they wave their wings.
Amid the circle, on the gilded mast,
70   Superior by the head, was Ariel placed;[8]
His purple pinions opening to the sun,
He raised his azure wand, and thus begun:
    "Ye Sylphs and Sylphids,° to your chief give ear,   female Sylphs
Fays, Fairies, Genii, Elves, and Demons hear!
75   Ye know the spheres and various tasks assigned,
By laws eternal to th' aerial kind.
Some in the fields of purest ether[9] play,
And bask and whiten in the blaze of day.
Some guide the course of wandering orbs° on high,   comets
80   Or roll the planets through the boundless sky.
Some less refined, beneath the moon's pale light
Pursue the stars that shoot athwart the night,
Or suck the mists in grosser° air below,   heavier
Or dip their pinions in the painted bow,°   rainbow
85   Or brew fierce tempests on the wintry main,
Or o'er the glebe° distill the kindly rain.   farmland

---

6. Cf. *The Aeneid* 2.794–95, which Dryden translated: "Apollo heard, and granting half his pray'r, / Shuffled in winds the rest, and toss'd in empty air."

7. Naturalized foreigners.
8. Heroes of epics were typically taller than their men.
9. Air beyond the moon.

Others on earth o'er human race preside,
Watch all their ways, and all their actions guide:
Of these the chief the care of nations own,
90   And guard with arms divine the British throne.
        "Our humbler province is to tend the fair,
Not a less pleasing, though less glorious care.
To save the powder from too rude° a gale,   rough
Nor let th' imprisoned essences° exhale,   perfumes
95   To draw fresh colors from the vernal flow'rs,
To steal from rainbows ere they drop in show'rs
A brighter wash;¹ to curl their waving hairs,
Assist their blushes, and inspire their airs;
Nay oft, in dreams, invention we bestow,
100 To change a flounce, or add a furbelow.°   fringe
        "This day, black omens threat the brightest fair
That e'er deserved a watchful spirit's care;
Some dire disaster, or° by force or sleight,°   either / trick
But what, or where, the fates have wrapped in night.
105 Whether the nymph shall break Diana's law,°   virginity
Or some frail China jar receive a flaw,
Or stain her honor, or her new brocade,
Forget her pray'rs, or miss a masquerade,
Or lose her heart, or necklace, at a ball;
110 Or whether Heav'n has doomed that Shock must fall.
Haste then ye spirits! to your charge° repair;   duty
The flutt'ring fan be Zephyretta's care;
The drops° to thee, Brillante, we consign;   earrings
And, Momentilla, let the watch be thine;
115 Do thou, Crispissa,² tend her fav'rite lock;
Ariel himself shall be the guard of Shock.
        "To fifty chosen Sylphs, of special note,
We trust th' important charge, the petticoat:
Oft have we known that sev'nfold fence³ to fail,
120 Though stiff with hoops, and armed with ribs of whale.
Form a strong line about the silver bound,
And guard the wide circumference around.
        "Whatever spirit, careless of his charge,
His post neglects, or leaves the fair at large,
125 Shall feel sharp vengeance soon o'ertake his sins,
Be stopped in vials, or transfixed with pins;
Or plunged in lakes of bitter washes lie,
Or wedged whole ages in a bodkin's⁴ eye:
Gums and pomatums° shall his flight restrain,   ointments
130 While clogged he beats his silken wings in vain;

1. A cosmetic rinse.
2. The Latin *crispere* means "to curl."
3. Serving Belinda like the epic warrior's shield, her petticoat has seven layers bound together with a silver band (cf. *Iliad* 18 or *Aeneid* 8).

4. Blunt, thick needle; the Sylph, like the camel in Matthew 19.24, has difficulty getting through. Pope later plays on the various meanings of "bodkin," which also include a hair ornament and a dagger.

Or alum styptics[5] with contracting power
Shrink his thin essence like a rivelled° flower.   *shriveled*
Or as Ixion[6] fixed, the wretch shall feel
The giddy motion of the whirling mill,[7]
135   In fumes of burning chocolate shall glow,
And tremble at the sea that froths below!"
　　　He spoke; the spirits from the sails descend;
Some, orb in orb, around the nymph extend,
Some thrid° the mazy ringlets of her hair,   *slid through*
140   Some hang upon the pendants of her ear;
With beating hearts the dire event they wait,
Anxious, and trembling for the birth of fate.

CANTO 3

Close by those meads forever crowned with flow'rs,
Where Thames with pride surveys his rising tow'rs,
There stands a structure of majestic frame,
Which from the neighb'ring Hampton takes its name.[8]
5   Here Britain's statesmen oft the fall foredoom
Of foreign tyrants, and of nymphs at home;
Here thou, great Anna! whom three realms obey,[9]
Dost sometimes counsel take—and sometimes tea.
　　　Hither the heroes and the nymphs resort,
10   To taste awhile the pleasures of a court;
In various talk th' instructive hours they passed,
Who gave the ball, or paid the visit last:
One speaks the glory of the British Queen,
And one describes a charming Indian screen;
15   A third interprets motions, looks, and eyes;
At ev'ry word a reputation dies.
Snuff, or the fan, supply each pause of chat,
With singing, laughing, ogling, and all that.
　　　Meanwhile declining from the noon of day,
20   The sun obliquely shoots his burning ray;
The hungry judges soon the sentence sign,
And wretches hang that jurymen may dine;
The merchant from th' Exchange° returns in peace,   *market*
And the long labors of the toilette cease—
25   Belinda now, whom thirst of fame invites,
Burns to encounter two advent'rous knights,
At Ombre[1] singly to decide their doom;

---

5. Astringents that stopped bleeding.
6. Having tried the chastity of Hera, Ixion was punished by being tied to a revolving wheel of fire.
7. For beating chocolate, a new and highly fashionable drink.
8. Hampton Court, about 15 miles upriver from London, was built in the 16th century by Cardinal Wolsey, and by Queen Anne's day was associated with wits as well as with statesmen.
9. The English Crown still maintained its ancient claim to rule France as well as Great Britain and Ireland.
1. A card game played with 40 cards, similar to modern bridge: three players hold nine cards each and bid for tricks, with the highest bidder becoming the "ombre" (man) and choosing trumps.

And swells her breast with conquests yet to come.
Straight the three bands prepare in arms to join,
30   Each band the number of the Sacred Nine.[2]
Soon as she spreads her hand, th' aerial guard
Descend, and sit on each important card:
First Ariel perched upon a Matador,[3]
Then each, according to the rank they bore;
35   For Sylphs, yet mindful of their ancient race,
Are, as when women, wondrous fond of place.°   rank
    Behold, four kings in majesty revered,
With hoary whiskers[4] and a forky beard;
And four fair queens whose hands sustain° a flow'r,   hold
40   Th' expressive emblem of their softer pow'r;
Four knaves in garbs succinct,° a trusty band,   girded up
Caps on their heads, and halberds in their hand;
And particolored troops, a shining train,
Draw forth to combat on the velvet plain.[5]
45   The skillful nymph reviews her force with care;
"Let spades be trumps!" she said, and trumps they were.[6]
    Now move to war her sable Matadors,
In show like leaders of the swarthy moors.
Spadillio first, unconquerable lord!
50   Led off two captive trumps, and swept the board.
As many more Manillio forced to yield,
And marched a victor from the verdant field.
Him Basto followed, but his fate more hard
Gained but one trump and one plebeian card.
55   With his broad saber next, a chief in years,
The hoary majesty of spades appears;
Puts forth one manly leg, to sight revealed;
The rest his many-colored robe concealed.
The rebel knave who dares his prince engage,
60   Proves the just victim of his royal rage.
Ev'n mighty Pam[7] that kings and queens o'erthrew,
And mowed down armies in the fights of Lu,
Sad chance of war! now, destitute of aid,
Falls undistinguished by the victor spade!
65   Thus far both armies to Belinda yield;
Now to the Baron fate inclines the field.
His warlike amazon her host invades,
Th' imperial consort of the crown of spades.
The club's black tyrant first her victim died,

2. Pope links the nine Muses to the nine cards each player holds.
3. The Matadores are the three cards of highest value; Belinda holds all three: when trumps are black, they are the Spadillio (ace of spades), Manillio (deuce of spades), and Basto (ace of clubs).
4. Gray mustache. The royal figures on the cards now conduct a mock-epic review of their forces, and the

whole game is described as an epic battle, with the characters appearing as on the cards.
5. The green velvet card table.
6. Cf. Genesis 1.3, "Then God said, 'Let there be light'; and there was light."
7. The knave or jack of clubs, which took precedence over all trumps in the game of Lu, or Loo.

70   Spite of his haughty mien and barb'rous pride:
        What boots the regal circle on his head,
        His giant limbs in state unwieldy spread?
        That long behind he trails his pompous robe,
        And of all monarchs only grasps the globe?
75   The Baron now his diamonds pours apace;
        Th' embroidered king who shows but half his face,
        And his refulgent queen, with pow'rs combined,
        Of broken troops an easy conquest find.
        Clubs, diamonds, hearts, in wild disorder seen,
80   With throngs promiscuous strew the level green.
        Thus when dispersed a routed army runs,
        Of Asia's troops and Afric's sable sons,
        With like confusion different nations fly,
        Of various habit and of various dye,
85   The pierced battalions disunited fall,
        In heaps on heaps; one fate o'erwhelms them all.
            The knave of diamonds tries his wily arts,
        And wins (oh shameful chance!) the queen of hearts.
        At this, the blood the virgin's cheek forsook,
90   A livid paleness spreads o'er all her look;
        She sees, and trembles at th' approaching ill,
        Just in the jaws of ruin, and codille.[8]
        And now (as oft in some distempered state)
        On one nice trick[9] depends the gen'ral fate.
95   An ace of hearts steps forth: the king[1] unseen
        Lurked in her hand, and mourned his captive queen.
        He springs to vengeance with an eager pace,
        And falls like thunder on the prostrate ace.
        The nymph exulting fills with shouts the sky,
100   The walls, the woods, and long canals reply.
            Oh thoughtless mortals! ever blind to fate,
        Too soon dejected, and too soon elate!
        Sudden these honors shall be snatched away,
        And cursed forever this victorious day.
105   For lo! the board with cups and spoons is crowned,
        The berries crackle, and the Mill turns round.[2]
        On shining altars of Japan[3] they raise
        The silver lamp; the fiery spirits blaze.
        From silver spouts the grateful° liquors glide,   *pleasing*
110   While China's earth receives the smoking tide.
        At once they gratify their scent and taste,
        And frequent cups prolong the rich repast.
        Straight° hover round the fair her airy band;   *immediately*
        Some, as she sipped, the fuming liquor fanned,

<hr>

8. Literally "elbow": the defeat suffered by the ombre if another player wins more tricks.
9. Trick applies in both its technical and general senses as Belinda makes this careful maneuver.

1. The King of Hearts.
2. Grinding coffee beans.
3. Lacquered tables ("Japan" was a type of varnish originating in that country).

115   Some o'er her lap their careful plumes displayed,
       Trembling, and conscious of the rich brocade.
       Coffee (which makes the politician wise,
       And see through all things with his half-shut eyes)
       Sent up in vapors[4] to the Baron's brain
120   New stratagems, the radiant lock to gain.
       Ah cease rash youth! desist ere 'tis too late,
       Fear the just gods, and think of Scylla's fate![5]
       Changed to a bird, and sent to flit in air,
       She dearly pays for Nisus' injured hair!
125   But when to mischief mortals bend their will,
       How soon they find fit instruments of ill!
       Just then, Clarissa drew with tempting grace
       A two-edged weapon from her shining case;
       So ladies in romance assist their knight,
130   Present the spear, and arm him for the fight.
       He takes the gift with rev'rence, and extends
       The little engine° on his fingers' ends,   *instrument*
       This just behind Belinda's neck he spread,
       As o'er the fragrant steams she bends her head:
135   Swift to the lock a thousand sprites repair,
       A thousand wings, by turns, blow back the hair,
       And thrice they twitched the diamond in her ear,
       Thrice she looked back, and thrice the foe drew near.
       Just in that instant, anxious Ariel sought
140   The close recesses of the virgin's thought;
       As on the nosegay in her breast reclined,
       He watched th' ideas rising in her mind,
       Sudden he viewed, in spite of all her art,
       An earthly lover lurking at her heart.
145   Amazed, confused, he found his pow'r expired,
       Resigned to fate, and with a sigh retired.
           The peer now spreads the glitt'ring forfex° wide,   *scissors*
       T' enclose the lock; now joins it, to divide.
       Ev'n then, before the fatal engine closed,
150   A wretched Sylph too fondly interposed;
       Fate urged the shears, and cut the Sylph in twain
       (But airy substance soon unites again)[6]
       The meeting points the sacred hair dissever
       From the fair head, forever and forever!
155   Then flashed the living lightning from her eyes,
       And screams of horror rend th' affrighted skies.
       Not louder shrieks to pitying Heav'n are cast,
       When husbands or when lapdogs breathe their last,
       Or when rich china vessels, fall'n from high,

4. Both steam and vain imaginations.
5. Scylla plucked purple hair from the head of her father, King Nisus, to offer to her lover, Minos, so destroying her father's power. Minos rejected her impiety, and Scylla was transformed into a bird.

6. *Milton* lib. 6 [Pope's note], citing *Paradise Lost* 6.329–31, "The girding sword with discontinuous wound / Passed through him, but the ethereal substance closed / Not long divisible. . . ."

160   In glitt'ring dust and painted fragments lie!
           Let wreaths of triumph now my temples twine,
       (The victor cried) the glorious prize is mine!
       While fish in streams, or birds delight in air,
       Or in a coach and six⁷ the British fair,
165   As long as *Atalantis*⁸ shall be read,
       Or the small pillow grace a lady's bed,⁹
       While visits shall be paid on solemn days,
       When numerous wax lights¹ in bright order blaze,
       While nymphs take treats, or assignations give,
170   So long my honor, name, and praise shall live!
           What time would spare, from steel receives its date,°   *end*
       And monuments, like men, submit to fate!
       Steel could the labor of the gods destroy,
       And strike to dust th' imperial tow'rs of Troy;²
175   Steel could the works of mortal pride confound,
       And hew triumphal arches to the ground.
       What wonder then, fair nymph! thy hairs should feel
       The conqu'ring force of unresisted steel?

CANTO 4

       But anxious cares the pensive nymph oppressed,
       And secret passions labored in her breast.
       Not youthful kings in battle seized alive,
       Not scornful virgins who their charms survive,
5   Not ardent lovers robbed of all their bliss,
       Not ancient ladies when refused a kiss,
       Not tyrants fierce that unrepenting die,
       Not Cynthia when her manteau's° pinned awry,   *gown's*
       E'er felt such rage, resentment, and despair,
10   As thou, sad virgin! for thy ravished hair.
           For, that sad moment, when the Sylphs withdrew,
       And Ariel weeping from Belinda flew,
       Umbriel, a dusky melancholy sprite
       As ever sullied the fair face of light,
15   Down to the central earth, his proper scene,
       Repaired to search the gloomy Cave of Spleen.³
           Swift on his sooty pinions flits the Gnome,
       And in a vapor⁴ reached the dismal dome.
       No cheerful breeze this sullen region knows,
20   The dreaded east⁵ is all the wind that blows.

7. A carriage drawn by six horses; a symbol of wealth and prestige.
8. The scandalous *Atalantis: Secret Memoirs and Manners of Several Persons of Quality* (1709), by Mary Delarivière Manley.
9. Said to be a place where ladies hid romance novels and other contraband.
1. Candles made of wax, rather than the cheaper tallow. Evening social visits were an essential part of the fashionable woman's routine.

2. Even Troy, fabled to have been built by Apollo and Poseidon, was destroyed by arms.
3. Named after the bodily organ, "spleen" was the current name for the fashionable affliction of melancholy or ill-humor. Umbriel's descent into the womb-like Cave of Spleen suggests the epic commonplace of the journey to the underworld.
4. "The spleen" was also called "the vapors."
5. The east wind was supposed to induce fits of spleen.

Here, in a grotto, sheltered close from air,
And screened in shades° from day's detested glare,   shadows
She sighs forever on her pensive bed,
Pain at her side, and Megrim° at her head.   migraine
25   Two handmaids wait the throne: alike in place,
But diff'ring far in figure and in face.
Here stood Ill-Nature like an ancient maid,
Her wrinkled form in black and white arrayed;
With store of pray'rs, for mornings, nights, and noons,
30   Her hand is filled; her bosom with lampoons.
      There Affectation with a sickly mien
Shows in her cheek the roses of eighteen,
Practiced to lisp, and hang the head aside,
Faints into airs, and languishes with pride;
35   On the rich quilt sinks with becoming woe,
Wrapped in a gown, for sickness, and for show.
The fair ones feel such maladies as these,
When each new nightdress gives a new disease.
      A constant vapor o'er the palace flies;
40   Strange phantoms rising as the mists arise;
Dreadful, as hermit's dreams in haunted shades,
Or bright as visions of expiring maids.[6]
Now glaring fiends, and snakes on rolling spires,°   coils
Pale specters, gaping tombs, and purple fires:
45   Now lakes of liquid gold, Elysian scenes,[7]
And crystal domes, and angels in machines.
      Unnumbered throngs on ev'ry side are seen
Of bodies changed to various forms by Spleen.[8]
Here living teapots stand, one arm held out,
50   One bent; the handle this, and that the spout:
A pipkin[9] there like Homer's tripod walks;
Here sighs a jar, and there a goose pie[1] talks;
Men prove with child, as pow'rful fancy works,
And maids, turned bottles, call aloud for corks.
55   Safe passed the Gnome through this fantastic band,
A branch of healing spleenwort[2] in his hand.
Then thus addressed the pow'r—"Hail, wayward Queen!
Who rule the sex to fifty from fifteen,
Parent of vapors and of female wit,
60   Who give th' hysteric or poetic fit,
On various tempers act by various ways,
Make some take physic,° others scribble plays;[3]   medicine
Who cause the proud their visits to delay,

---

6. Religious visions of hell and heaven.
7. Elysium was the classical paradise, but this also recalls contemporary theater, which made much of scenic spectacle and the use of machinery.
8. Hallucinations similar to those described in the following lines were common to those afflicted with spleen.
9. Small pot or pan. Hephaistos's "walking" tripods are

described in the *Iliad* 18.439ff.
1. Alludes to a real fact, a Lady of distinction imagin'd herself in this condition [Pope's note].
2. Pope changes the golden bough that protected Aeneas on his trip through the underworld into an herb that was supposed to be good for the spleen.
3. Melancholy was associated with artistic creativity.

And send the godly in a pet° to pray.   *ill-humor*
65   A nymph there is that all thy pow'r disdains,
And thousands more in equal mirth maintains.
But oh! if e'er thy Gnome could spoil a grace,
Or raise a pimple on a beauteous face
Like citron-waters° matrons' cheeks inflame,   *flavored brandy*
70   Or change complexions at a losing game;
If e'er with airy horns[4] I planted heads,
Or rumpled petticoats, or tumbled beds,
Or caused suspicion when no soul was rude,
Or discomposed the headdress of a prude,
75   Or e'er to costive° lapdog gave disease,   *constipated*
Which not the tears of brightest eyes could ease:
Hear me, and touch Belinda with chagrin;
That single act gives half the world the spleen."
      The goddess with a discontented air
80   Seems to reject him, though she grants his pray'r.
A wondrous bag with both her hands she binds,
Like that where once Ulysses held the winds;[5]
There she collects the force of female lungs,
Sighs, sobs, and passions, and the war of tongues.
85   A vial next she fills with fainting fears,
Soft sorrows, melting griefs, and flowing tears.
The Gnome rejoicing bears her gifts away,
Spreads his black wings, and slowly mounts to day.
      Sunk in Thalestris'[6] arms the nymph he found,
90   Her eyes dejected and her hair unbound.
Full o'er their heads the swelling bag he rent,
And all the furies issued at the vent.
Belinda burns with more than mortal ire,
And fierce Thalestris fans the rising fire.
95   "O wretched maid!" she spread her hands, and cried,
(While Hampton's echoes "Wretched maid!" replied)
"Was it for this you took such constant care
The bodkin, comb, and essence to prepare;
For this your locks in paper durance° bound,   *curling papers*
100   For this with tort'ring irons wreathed around?
For this with fillets[7] strained your tender head,
And bravely bore the double loads of lead?°   *wire supports*
Gods! shall the ravisher display your hair,
While the fops envy, and the ladies stare!
105   Honor forbid! at whose unrivaled shrine
Ease, pleasure, virtue, all, our sex resign.
Methinks already I your tears survey,
Already hear the horrid things they say,

4. A sign that a husband had been cuckolded.
5. Given to him by the wind god Aeolus (*Odyssey* 10.19ff.).
6. A queen of the Amazons; here Mrs. Morley, Arabella's second cousin.
7. Headbands, with reference to priestesses in the *Aeneid*.

Already see you a degraded toast,[8]
110 And all your honor in a whisper lost!
How shall I, then, your helpless fame defend?
'Twill then be infamy to seem your friend!
And shall this prize, th' inestimable prize,
Exposed through crystal to the gazing eyes,
115 And heightened by the diamond's circling rays,
On that rapacious hand forever blaze?[9]
Sooner shall grass in Hyde Park Circus grow,[1]
And wits take lodgings in the sound of Bow;[2]
Sooner let earth, air, sea, to Chaos fall,
120 Men, monkeys, lapdogs, parrots, perish all!"
　　　She said; then raging to Sir Plume[3] repairs,
And bids her beau demand the precious hairs:
(Sir Plume, of amber snuffbox justly vain,
And the nice conduct of a clouded cane[4])
125 With earnest eyes, and round unthinking face,
He first the snuffbox opened, then the case,
And thus broke out—"My Lord, why, what the devil?
Z—ds![5] damn the lock! 'fore Gad, you must be civil!
Plague on't! 'tis past a jest—nay prithee, Pox!
130 Give her the hair"—he spoke, and rapped his box.
　　　"It grieves me much" (replied the Peer again)
"Who speaks so well should ever speak in vain.
But by this lock, this sacred lock I swear
(Which never more shall join its parted hair,
135 Which never more its honors shall renew,
Clipped from the lovely head where late it grew)
That while my nostrils draw the vital air,
This hand which won it shall forever wear."
He spoke, and speaking, in proud triumph spread
140 The long-contended honors[6] of her head.
　　　But Umbriel, hateful Gnome! forbears not so;
He breaks the vial whence the sorrows flow.
Then see! the nymph in beauteous grief appears,
Her eyes half-languishing, half-drowned in tears;
145 On her heaved bosom hung her drooping head,
Which, with a sigh, she raised; and thus she said:
　　　"Forever cursed be this detested day,[7]
Which snatched my best, my fav'rite curl away!
Happy! ah ten times happy, had I been,
150 If Hampton Court these eyes had never seen!

8. A woman whose toast is often drunk, and who by implication is all too well known to her (male) toasters: (cf. Canto 5.10, and Fielding's *Tom Jones*, where Sophia is not pleased by reports that she has been Tom's toast, bk. 13, ch. 11).
9. I.e., mounted in a ring.
1. The fashion for driving coaches around Hyde Park prevented grass from growing there.
2. A commercial area around St. Mary-le-Bow, and not at

all fashionable.
3. Sir George Browne, cousin of Arabella's mother.
4. Skilled use of a cane with a head of dark polished stone.
5. Zounds, a corruption of "God's wounds," a mild oath.
6. Her beautiful hair.
7. Echoing Achilles' lament for his slain friend Patroclus (*Iliad* 18.107ff.).

Yet am not I the first mistaken maid,
By love of courts to num'rous ills betrayed.
Oh had I rather unadmired remained
In some lone isle, or distant northern land;

155   Where the gilt chariot never marks the way,
Where none learn Ombre, none e'er taste bohea°!   *tea*
There kept my charms concealed from mortal eye,
Like roses that in deserts bloom and die.
What moved my mind with youthful lords to roam?

160   O had I stayed, and said my pray'rs at home!
'Twas this, the morning omens seemed to tell;
Thrice from my trembling hand the patch box fell;
The tott'ring china shook without a wind,
Nay, Poll° sat mute, and Shock was most unkind!   *her parrot*

165   A Sylph too warned me of the threats of fate,
In mystic visions, now believed too late!
See the poor remnants of these slighted hairs!
My hands shall rend what ev'n thy rapine spares:
These, in two sable ringlets taught to break,°   *divide*

170   Once gave new beauties to the snowy neck.
The sister lock now sits uncouth, alone,
And in its fellow's fate foresees its own;
Uncurled it hangs, the fatal shears demands;
And tempts once more thy sacrilegious hands.

175   Oh hadst thou, cruel! been content to seize
Hairs less in sight, or any hairs but these!"

CANTO 5

She said: the pitying audience melt in tears,
But Fate and Jove had stopped the Baron's ears.
In vain Thalestris with reproach assails,
For who can move when fair Belinda fails?

5   Not half so fixed the Trojan[8] could remain,
While Anna begged and Dido raged in vain.
Then grave Clarissa[9] graceful waved her fan;
Silence ensued, and thus the nymph began.
    "Say, why are beauties praised and honored most,

10   The wise man's passion, and the vain man's toast?
Why decked with all that land and sea afford,
Why angels called, and angel-like adored?
Why round our coaches crowd the white-gloved beaus,
Why bows the side box from its inmost rows?[1]

15   How vain are all these glories, all our pains,

8. Aeneas, fixed on his decision to leave Carthage and abandon Dido despite her pleas and those of her sister Anna (*Aeneid* 4.269–449).
9. A new character introduced . . . to open more clearly the moral of the poem, in a parody of the speech of

Sarpedon to Glaucus in Homer [Pope's note in the 1717 edition]. Sarpedon's speech (*Iliad* 12) is a famous reflection on glory.
1. At the theater, gentlemen sat in the side boxes, ladies in the front boxes facing the stage.

Unless good sense preserve what beauty gains:
That men may say when we the front box grace,
Behold the first in virtue as in face!
Oh! if to dance all night, and dress all day,
20 Charmed the smallpox,[2] or chased old age away;
Who would not scorn what housewife's cares produce,
Or who would learn one earthly thing of use?
To patch, nay ogle, might become a saint,
Nor could it sure be such a sin to paint.
25 But since, alas! frail beauty must decay,
Curled or uncurled, since locks will turn to gray,
Since painted or not painted, all shall fade,
And she who scorns a man, must die a maid;
What then remains, but well our pow'r to use,
30 And keep good humor still whate'er we lose?
And trust me, dear! good humor can prevail,
When airs, and flights, and screams, and scolding fail.
Beauties in vain their pretty eyes may roll;
Charms strike the sight, but merit wins the soul."
35 So spoke the dame, but no applause ensued;
Belinda frowned, Thalestris called her prude.
"To arms, to arms!" the fierce virago[3] cries,
And swift as lightning to the combat flies.
All side in parties, and begin th' attack;
40 Fans clap, silks rustle, and tough whalebones crack;
Heroes' and heroines' shouts confus'dly rise,
And bass and treble voices strike the skies.
No common weapons in their hands are found,
Like gods they fight, nor dread a mortal wound.
45 So when bold Homer makes the gods engage,
And heav'nly breasts with human passions rage,
'Gainst Pallas,° Mars; Latona,[4] Hermes arms;   *Athena*
And all Olympus rings with loud alarms.
Jove's thunder roars, Heav'n trembles all around;
50 Blue Neptune storms, the bellowing deeps resound;
Earth shakes her nodding tow'rs, the ground gives way;
And the pale ghosts start at the flash of day!
Triumphant Umbriel on a sconce's[5] height
Clapped his glad wings, and sat to view the fight:
55 Propped on their bodkin spears, the sprites survey
The growing combat, or assist the fray.
While through the press enraged Thalestris flies,
And scatters deaths around from both her eyes,
A beau and witling° perished in the throng,   *°little wit*
60 One died in metaphor, and one in song.
"O cruel Nymph! a living death I bear,"

2. A common disease, which frequently left permanent facial scars.
3. Woman who behaves like a man.
4. Mother of Diana and Apollo.
5. Candlestick attached to the wall.

Cried Dapperwit, and sunk beside his chair.
A mournful glance Sir Fopling upwards cast,
"Those eyes are made so killing"[6]—was his last:
65   Thus on Meander's flow'ry margin lies
Th' expiring swan, and as he sings he dies.[7]
    When bold Sir Plume had drawn Clarissa down,
Chloe stepped in, and killed him with a frown;
She smiled to see the doughty hero slain,
70   But at her smile the beau revived again.
    Now Jove suspends his golden scales in air,[8]
Weighs the men's wits against the lady's hair;
The doubtful beam long nods from side to side;
At length the wits mount up, the hairs subside.
75   See fierce Belinda on the Baron flies,
With more than usual lightning in her eyes;
Nor feared the chief th' unequal fight to try,
Who sought no more than on his foe to die.[9]
But this bold lord, with manly strength indued,
80   She with one finger and a thumb subdued:
Just where the breath of life his nostrils drew,
A charge of snuff the wily virgin threw;
The Gnomes direct, to ev'ry atom just,
The pungent grains of titillating dust.
85   Sudden, with starting tears each eye o'erflows,
And the high dome re-echoes to his nose.[1]
    "Now meet thy fate," incensed Belinda cried,
And drew a deadly bodkin from her side.
(The same, his ancient personage to deck,
90   Her great-great-grandsire wore about his neck
In three seal rings; which after, melted down,
Formed a vast buckle for his widow's gown:
Her infant grandame's° whistle next it grew,   grandmother's
The bells she jingled, and the whistle blew;
95   Then in a bodkin[2] graced her mother's hairs,
Which long she wore, and now Belinda wears.)
    "Boast not my fall" (he cried) "insulting foe!
Thou by some other shalt be laid as low.
Nor think, to die dejects my lofty mind;
100   All that I dread is leaving you behind!
Rather than so, ah let me still survive,
And burn in Cupid's flames—but burn alive."
    "Restore the lock!" she cries; and all around
"Restore the lock!" the vaulted roofs rebound.
105   Not fierce Othello in so loud a strain

---

6. A line from Giovanni Bononcini's opera, *Camilla* (1696), which at this time was popular in London.
7. Meander: a river in Asia Minor. Swans were popularly believed to sing only on their death. This simile refers to Ovid's *Heroides* 7, a lament from Dido to Aeneas.

8. To determine victory in battle; a convention found in both Homer and Virgil.
9. A standard metaphor for sexual climax.
1. Cf. his boast, 4.133–38.
2. A decorative pin, shaped like a dagger.

Roared for the handkerchief that caused his pain.
But see how oft ambitious aims are crossed,
And chiefs contend 'till all the prize is lost!
The lock, obtained with guilt, and kept with pain,
110 In ev'ry place is sought, but sought in vain:
With such a prize no mortal must be blest,
So Heav'n decrees! with Heav'n who can contest?
 Some thought it mounted to the lunar sphere,[3]
Since all things lost on earth are treasured there.
115 There heroes' wits are kept in ponderous vases,
And beaus' in snuffboxes and tweezer cases.
There broken vows and deathbed alms are found,
And lovers' hearts with ends of riband bound;
The courtier's promises, and sick man's pray'rs,
120 The smiles of harlots, and the tears of heirs,
Cages for gnats, and chains to yoke a flea;
Dried butterflies, and tomes of casuistry.[4]
 But trust the Muse—she saw it upward rise,
Though marked by none but quick poetic eyes:
125 (So Rome's great founder to the heav'ns withdrew,
To Proculus alone confessed in view.[5])
A sudden star, it shot through liquid air,
And drew behind a radiant trail of hair.
Not Berenice's locks first rose so bright,[6]
130 The heav'ns bespangling with disheveled light.
The Sylphs behold it kindling as it flies,
And pleased pursue its progress through the skies.
 This the beau monde shall from the Mall[7] survey,
And hail with music its propitious ray.
135 This, the blest lover shall for Venus° take,   *the planet*
And send up vows from Rosamonda's Lake.[8]
This Partridge[9] soon shall view in cloudless skies,
When next he looks through Galileo's eyes;[1]
And hence th' egregious wizard shall foredoom
140 The fate of Louis, and the fall of Rome.
 Then cease, bright nymph! to mourn thy ravished hair
Which adds new glory to the shining sphere!
Not all the tresses that fair head can boast
Shall draw such envy as the lock you lost.
145 For, after all the murders of your eye,
When, after millions slain, yourself shall die;

---

3. Cf. Ariosto's *Orlando Furioso* (1516–1532), in which Orlando's lost wits are sought on the moon. See also *Paradise Lost* 3.444ff.
4. Subtle reasoning (often used of arguments justifying immoral conduct).
5. When Romulus was killed mysteriously, Proculus soothed popular grief by asserting that he had been taken up to heaven.
6. The Egyptian queen Berenice made an offering of her hair after her husband returned victorious from the wars;

when it disappeared from the temple, the court astronomer claimed it had been made into a new constellation.
7. A fashionable walk in St. James's Park.
8. Where lovers met in St. James's Park.
9. John Partridge was a ridiculous star-gazer, who, in his almanacs every year, never failed to predict the downfall of the Pope and the King of France, then at war with the English [Pope's note].
1. I.e., a telescope.

When those fair suns[2] shall set, as set they must,
And all those tresses shall be laid in dust;
This lock, the Muse shall consecrate to fame,
150   And mid'st the stars inscribe Belinda's name!
1711–1717   1712; 1714; 1717

THE ILIAD   "In the beginning of my translating the *Iliad* I wished anybody would hang me, a hundred times," Pope confided to his friend Joseph Spence, "it sat so heavily on my mind at first that I often used to dream of it, and so do sometimes still." Pope spent nearly seven years (1713–1720) translating the *Iliad* and writing critical notes to accompany his text. His work was an outstanding commercial and literary success; for his labors Pope made about £5,000, more than a hundred times the annual earnings of a skilled craftsman or a shop owner in Pope's day. Samuel Johnson called Pope's *Iliad* "the noblest version [translation] of poetry which the world has ever seen"; Samuel Taylor Coleridge said Pope's poem was "an astonishing product of matchless talent and ingenuity."

Sarpedon, king of the Lycians who were allied with the Trojans against the Greeks, exhorts his lieutenant Glaucus to fight bravely. This was the first passage of the *Iliad* that Pope published; it appeared in 1709 with the *Pastorals* as the *Episode of Sarpedon*. Eight years later, Pope's final addition to *The Rape of the Lock* (1717) was a parody of the warrior's famous speech, spoken by Clarissa at the beginning of Canto 5. Pope's own comment reveals his thoughts about Sarpedon's great exhortation: "In former times, kings were looked upon as the generals of armies, who to return the honors that were done to them, were obliged to expose themselves first in battle, and be an example to their soldiers. Upon this Sarpedon grounds his discourse, which is full of generosity and nobleness. We are, says he, honored like gods, and what can be more unjust than not to behave ourselves like men? He ought to be superior in virtue, who is superior in dignity. What strength is there and what greatness in that thought! It includes justice, gratitude, and magnanimity: justice, in that he scorns to enjoy what he does not merit; gratitude, because he would endeavor to recompense his obligations to his subjects; and magnanimity, because he despises death, and thinks of nothing but glory."

from The Iliad
from **Preface**
[ON TRANSLATION]

Having now spoken of the beauties and defects of the original, it remains to treat of the translation, with the same view to the chief characteristic. As far as that is seen in the main parts of the poem, such as the fable, manners, and sentiments, no translator can prejudice it but by willful omissions or contractions. As it also breaks out in every particular image, description, and simile, whoever lessens or too much softens those takes off from this chief character. It is the first grand duty of an interpreter to give his author entire and unmaimed; and for the rest, the diction and versification only are his proper province, since these must be his own, but the others he is to take as he finds them.

It should then be considered what methods may afford some equivalent in our language for the graces of these in the Greek. It is certain no literal translation can be just to an excellent original in a superior language, but it is a great mistake to imagine (as many have done) that a rash paraphrase can make amends for this

2. I.e., her eyes.

general defect, which is no less in danger to lose the spirit of an Ancient, by deviating into the modern manners of expression. If there be sometimes a darkness, there is often a light in antiquity which nothing better preserves than a version almost literal. I know no liberties one ought to take, but those which are necessary for transfusing the spirit of the original, and supporting the poetical style of the translation; and I will venture to say, there have not been more men misled in former times by a servile dull adherence to the letter, than have been deluded in ours by a chimerical[1] insolent hope of raising and improving their author. It is not to be doubted that the fire of the poem is what a translator should principally regard, as it is most likely to expire in his managing; however, it is his safest way to be content with preserving this to his utmost in the whole, without endeavoring to be more than he finds his author is in any particular place. 'Tis a great secret in writing to know when to be plain, and when poetical and figurative, and it is what Homer will teach us if we will but follow modestly in his footsteps. Where his diction is bold and lofty, let us raise ours as high as we can; but where his is plain and humble, we ought not to be deterred from imitating him by the fear of incurring the censure of a mere English critic. Nothing that belongs to Homer seems to have been more commonly mistaken than the just pitch of his style: some of his translators having swelled into fustian[2] in a proud confidence of the sublime; others sunk into flatness in a cold and timorous notion of simplicity. Methinks I see these different followers of Homer, some sweating and straining after him by violent leaps and bounds (the certain signs of false mettle), others slowly and servilely creeping in his train, while the poet himself is all the time proceeding with an unaffected and equal[3] majesty before them. However, of the two extremes one could sooner pardon frenzy than frigidity: no author is to be envied for such commendations as he may gain by that character of style which his friends must agree together to call simplicity, and the rest of the world will call dullness. There is a graceful and dignified simplicity, as well as a bald and sordid one, which differ as much from each other as the air of a plain man from that of a sloven: 'tis one thing to be tricked up,[4] and another not to be dressed at all. Simplicity is the mean between ostentation and rusticity.

This pure and noble simplicity is nowhere in such perfection as in the Scripture and our author. One may affirm with all respect to the inspired writings, that the divine spirit made use of no other words but what were intelligible and common to men at that time, and in that part of the world; and as Homer is the author nearest to those, his style must of course bear a greater resemblance to the sacred books than that of any other writer. This consideration (together with what has been observed of the parity of some of his thoughts) may, methinks, induce a translator on the one hand to give in to several of those general phrases and manners of expression, which have attained a veneration even in our language from being used in the Old Testament, as on the other, to avoid those which have been appropriated to the divinity, and in a manner consigned to mystery and religion.

For a farther preservation of this air of simplicity, a particular care should be taken to express with all plainness those moral sentences and proverbial speeches which are so numerous in this poet. They have something venerable, and as I may say oracular, in that unadorned gravity and shortness with which they are delivered, a

1. Fanciful.
2. Bombast; high-flown language.
3. Consistent.
4. Overdressed.

grace which would be utterly lost by endeavoring to give them what we call a more ingenious (that is a more modern) turn in the paraphrase.

Perhaps the mixture of some Graecisms and old words after the manner of Milton, if done without too much affectation, might not have an ill effect in a version of this particular work, which most of any other seems to require a venerable antique cast. But certainly the use of modern terms of war and government, such as platoon, campaign, junto, or the like (into which some of his translators have fallen) cannot be allowable; those only excepted, without which it is impossible to treat the subjects in any living language.

* * *

It only remains to speak of the versification. Homer (as has been said) is perpetually applying the sound to the sense, and varying it on every new subject. This is indeed one of the most exquisite beauties of poetry, and attainable by very few: I know only of Homer eminent for it in the Greek, and Virgil in Latin. I am sensible it is what may sometimes happen by chance, when a writer is warm, and fully possessed of his image: however it may be reasonably believed they designed this, in whose verse it so manifestly appears in a superior degree to all others. Few readers have the ear to be judges of it, but those who have will see I have endeavored at this beauty.

Upon the whole, I must confess myself utterly incapable of doing justice to Homer. I attempt him in no other hope but that which one may entertain without much vanity, of giving a more tolerable copy of him than any entire translation in verse has yet done.

* * *

1715   1715

from *Book 12*

[SARPEDON'S SPEECH]

	Resolved alike, divine Sarpedon[1] glows	
	With gen'rous rage that drives him on the foes.	
	He views the tow'rs, and meditates° their fall,	*plans*
	To sure destruction dooms th' aspiring° wall;	*high*
5	Then casting on his friend an ardent look,	
	Fir'd with the thirst of glory, thus he spoke.	
	"Why boast we, Glaucus! our extended reign,	
	Where Xanthus' streams[2] enrich the Lycian plain,	
	Our num'rous herds that range the fruitful field,	
10	And hills where vines their purple harvest yield,	
	Our foaming bowls with purer nectar[3] crowned,	
	Our feasts enhanced with music's sprightly° sound?	*lively*
	Why on those shores° are we with joy surveyed,°	*of Greece / observed*
	Admired as heroes, and as gods obeyed?	
15	Unless great acts superior merit prove,	
	And vindicate the bount'ous pow'rs above.[4]	
	'Tis ours, the dignity they give, to grace;	

1. Sarpedon's father was Zeus, the supreme Olympian deity; his mother was Laodemia, a mortal.
2. The Xanthus is the principal river flowing through Lycia, a mountainous country in southwestern Asia Minor.

3. Perhaps mead, which is made from fermented honey, but probably any drink.
4. I.e., the gods' blessings on us.

The first in valor, as the first in place.[5]
That when with wond'ring eyes our martial bands

20 Behold our deeds transcending our commands,[6]
Such, they may cry, deserve the sov'reign state,°   *role*
Whom those that envy, dare not imitate!
Could all our care elude the gloomy° grave,[7]   *dark*
Which claims no less the fearful than the brave,

25 For lust of fame I should not vainly dare
In fighting fields, nor urge thy soul to war.
But since, alas! ignoble age must come,
Disease, and death's inexorable doom;°   *fate*
The life which others pay, let us bestow,

30 And give to Fame what we to Nature owe;
Brave though we fall, and honored if we live,
Or° let us glory gain, or glory give!"   *either*
    He said;° his words the list'ning chief inspire   *spoke*
With equal warmth, and rouse the warrior's fire;

35 The troops pursue their leaders with delight,
Rush to the foe, and claim the promised fight.

c. 1707   1709

from An Essay on Man
In Four Epistles to Henry St. John, Lord Bolingbroke[1]
Epistle 1

TO THE READER

As the epistolary way of writing hath prevailed much of late, we have ventured to publish this piece composed some time since, and whose author chose this manner, notwithstanding his subject was high and of dignity, because of its being mixed with argument which of its nature approacheth to prose. This,[2] which we first give the reader, treats of the Nature and State of MAN, with respect to the UNIVERSAL SYSTEM;[3] the rest will treat of him with respect to his OWN SYSTEM, as an individual, and as a member of society, under one or other of which heads all ethics are included.

---

5. I.e., we must justify our position of authority over the people (which the gods have bestowed) through valor.
6. I.e., we set an example for our troops, rather than commanding from the rear.
7. There is not a more forcible argument than this, to make all men condemn dangers, and seek glory by brave actions. Immortality with eternal youth is certainly preferable to glory purchased with the loss of life; but glory is certainly better than an ignominious life, which at last, though perhaps late, must end. It is ordained that all men shall die, nor can our escaping danger secure us immortality; it can only give us a longer continuance in disgrace, and even that continuance will be but short, though the infamy everlasting. This is incontestable, and whoever weighs his actions in these scales, can never hesitate in his choice; but what is most remarkable is that Homer does not put this in the mouth of an ordinary person, but ascribes it to the son of Jupiter [Pope's note].
1. "I believe," wrote Pope to his friend John Caryll, "that

there is not in the whole course of the Scripture any precept so often and so strongly inculcated, as the trust and eternal dependence we ought to repose in that Supreme Being who is our constant preserver and benefactor." This is the theme of Pope's didactic and exhortatory *Essay on Man*, whose four epistles were published anonymously over eleven months in 1733–1734. For Pope, "to reason right is to submit" (line 164), not least because humankind occupies a middle ground—between angels and beasts—in a divinely ordered universe. Pope had intended the *Essay on Man* and the four *Moral Essays* (1731–1735) to be the first and last parts of a great poetic sequence on the nature of humankind, though he never completed the project. The *Essay* is addressed to Henry St. John, first Viscount Bolingbroke (1678–1751), a leading Tory statesman and political writer whom Pope described as "my guide, philosopher, and friend."
2. I.e., the first Epistle.
3. I.e., within the cosmic order, ordained by God.

As he imitates no man, so he would be thought to vie with no man in these Epistles, particularly with the noted author of two lately published;[4] but this he may most surely say: that the matter of them is such as is of importance to all in general, and of offense to none in particular.

THE DESIGN

Having proposed to write some pieces on human life and manners, such as (to use my lord Bacon's expression) "come home to men's business and bosoms,"[5] I thought it more satisfactory to begin with considering Man in the abstract, his Nature and his State, since, to prove any moral duty, to enforce any moral precept, or to examine the perfection or imperfection of any creature whatsoever, it is necessary first to know what condition and relation it is placed in, and what is the proper end and purpose of its being.

The science[6] of human nature is, like all other sciences, reduced to a few clear points: there are not many *certain truths* in this world. It is therefore in the anatomy of the mind as in that of the body: more good will accrue to mankind by attending to the large, open, and perceptible parts, than by studying too much such finer nerves and vessels, the conformations and uses of which will forever escape our observation. The disputes are all upon these last, and, I will venture to say, they have less sharpened the wits than the hearts of men against each other, and have diminished the practice more than advanced the theory of morality. If I could flatter myself that this Essay has any merit, it is in steering betwixt the extremes of doctrines seemingly opposite, in passing over terms utterly unintelligible, and in forming a temperate yet not inconsistent, and a short yet not imperfect system of ethics.

This I might have done in prose, but I chose verse, and even rhyme, for two reasons. The one will appear obvious: that principles, maxims, or precepts so written, both strike the reader more strongly at first, and are more easily retained by him afterwards. The other may seem odd, but is true: I found I could express them more shortly this way than in prose itself; and nothing is more certain, than that much of the force as well as grace of arguments or instructions depends on their conciseness. I was unable to treat this part of my subject more in detail without becoming dry and tedious, or more poetically, without sacrificing perspicuity to ornament, without wandering from the precision, or breaking the chain of reasoning. If any man can unite all these without diminution of any of them, I freely confess he will compass a thing above my capacity.

What is now published, is only to be considered as a general map of MAN, marking out no more than the greater parts, their extent, their limits, and their connection, but leaving the particular to be more fully delineated in the charts which are to follow. Consequently, these Epistles in their progress (if I have health and leisure to make any progress) will be less dry, and more susceptible of poetical ornament. I am here only opening the fountains, and clearing the passage. To deduce the rivers, to follow them in their course, and to observe their effects, may be a task more agreeable.

---

4. I.e., Pope himself, whose *Epistle to Bathurst* (1733) and the first *Imitation of Horace* (1733) had recently been published. The *Essay on Man* was published anonymously; Pope uses his little address to the reader both to advertise his own work and to confuse his enemies about the identity of the poem's author.
5. From Bacon's Dedicatory Epistle in the collected edition of the *Essays* (1625).
6. Knowledge.

ARGUMENT

Of the Nature and State of Man, with respect to the UNIVERSE.

Of Man in the abstract.—I. That we can judge only with regard to our own system, being ignorant of the relations of systems and things, verses 17, etc. II. That Man is not to be deemed imperfect, but a being suited to his place and rank in the creation, agreeable to the general order of things, and conformable to ends and relations to him unknown, ver. 35, etc. III. That it is partly upon his ignorance of future events, and partly upon the hope of a future state, that all his happiness in the present depends, ver. 77, etc. IV. The pride of aiming at more knowledge, and pretending to more perfection, the cause of man's error and misery. The impiety of putting himself in the place of God, and judging of the fitness or unfitness, perfection or imperfection, justice or injustice of his dispensations, Ver. 113, etc. V. The absurdity of conceiving himself the final cause of the creation, or expecting that perfection in the *moral* world, which is not in the *natural*, Ver. 131, etc. VI. The unreasonableness of his complaints against Providence, while on the one hand he demands the perfections of the angels, and on the other the bodily qualifications of the brutes; though, to possess any of the sensitive faculties in a higher degree, would render him miserable, Ver. 173, etc. VII. That throughout the whole visible world, an universal order and gradation in the sensual and mental faculties is observed, which causes a subordination of creature to creature, and of all creatures to Man. The gradations of sense, instinct, thought, reflection, reason; that reason alone countervails all the other faculties, Ver. 207. VIII. How much farther this order and subordination of living creatures may extend, above and below us; were any part of which broken, not that part only, but the whole connected creation must be destroyed. Ver. 233. IX. The extravagance, madness, and pride of such a desire, Ver. 259. X. The consequence of all the absolute submission due to providence, both as to our present and future state, Ver. 281, etc. to the end.

	Awake, my ST. JOHN! leave all meaner° things	base
	To low ambition, and the pride of kings.	
	Let us (since life can little more supply	
	Than just to look about us and to die)	
5	Expatiate free[7] o'er all this scene of man;	
	A mighty maze! but not without a plan;	
	A wild, where weeds and flow'rs promiscuous° shoot,	randomly mixed
	Or garden, tempting with forbidden fruit.	
	Together let us beat[8] this ample field,	
10	Try what the open, what the covert yield;	
	The latent tracts, the giddy heights explore	
	Of all who blindly creep, or sightless soar;[9]	
	Eye nature's walks,° shoot folly as it flies,	behaviors
	And catch the manners living as they rise;	
15	Laugh where we must, be candid° where we can;	generous
	But vindicate the ways of God to Man.[1]	

7. Wander or speak unrestrainedly.

8. "Beat," "open," "covert" are all hunting terms: Pope imagines them to be searching out game by walking back and forth across open and wooded land.

9. There is a middle way appropriate to man between ignorance and presumption.

1. Cf. *Paradise Lost*, 1.24–26: "That to the highth of this great argument / I may assert eternal providence, / And justify the ways of God to men." Pope's mention of the "garden, tempting with forbidden fruit" (line 8) also calls to mind the opening lines of Milton's epic.

1. Say first, of God above, or Man below,
What can we reason, but from what we know?
Of Man what see we, but his station here,
20   From which to reason, or to which refer?
Through worlds unnumbered though the God be known,
'Tis ours to trace him only in our own.
He, who through vast immensity can pierce,
See worlds on worlds compose one universe,
25   Observe how system into system runs,
What other planets circle other suns,
What varied being peoples° ev'ry star,   *inhabits*
May tell why Heav'n has made us as we are.
But of this frame the bearings, and the ties,
30   The strong connections, nice dependencies,
Gradations just,[2] has thy° pervading soul   *the reader's*
Looked through? or can a part contain the whole?
     Is the great chain,[3] that draws all to agree,
And drawn supports, upheld by God, or thee?

35   2. Presumptuous Man! the reason wouldst thou find,
Why formed so weak, so little, and so blind!
First, if thou canst, the harder reason guess,
Why formed no weaker, blinder, and no less!
Ask of thy mother earth, why oaks are made
40   Taller or stronger than the weeds they shade?
Or ask of yonder argent fields above,
Why Jove's satellites[4] are less than Jove?
     Of systems possible, if 'tis confest
That wisdom infinite must form the best,
45   Where all must full or not coherent be,[5]
And all that rises, rise in due degree;
Then, in the scale of reas'ning life, 'tis plain
There must be, somewhere, such a rank as Man;
And all the question (wrangle e'er so long)
50   Is only this, if God has placed him wrong?
     Respecting Man, whatever wrong we call,
May, must be right, as relative to all.
In human works, though labored on with pain,
A thousand movements scarce one purpose gain;
55   In God's, one single can its end produce;
Yet serves to second too some other use.
So Man, who here seems principal alone,
Perhaps acts second to some sphere unknown,
Touches some wheel, or verges to some goal;
60   'Tis but a part we see, and not a whole.

---

2. "Connections," "dependencies," and "gradations" were
key terms of the new sciences.
3. The Great Chain of Being linked all levels of creation,
at the same time maintaining a fixed hierarchy.

4. Jupiter's moons. "Satellites" here has four syllables.
5. The Great Chain of Being could not be broken at any
point.

When the proud steed shall know why Man restrains
His fiery course, or drives him o'er the plains;
When the dull ox, why now he breaks the clod,
Is now a victim, and now Egypt's god:[6]
65   Then shall Man's pride and dullness comprehend
His actions', passions', being's, use and end;
Why doing, suff'ring, checked, impelled; and why
This hour a slave, the next a deity.
    Then say not Man's imperfect, Heav'n in fault;
70   Say rather, Man's as perfect as he ought;
His knowledge measured to his state and place,
His time a moment, and a point his space.
If to be perfect in a certain sphere,°   *area of influence*
What matter, soon or late, or here or there?
75   The blest today is as completely so,
As who began a thousand years ago.

    3. Heav'n from all creatures hides the book of fate,
All but the page prescribed, their present state;
From brutes what men, from men what spirits° know: *angels*
80   Or who could suffer being here below?
The lamb thy riot° dooms to bleed today,   *extravagance*
Had he thy reason, would he skip and play?
Pleased to the last, he crops the flow'ry food,
And licks the hand just raised to shed his blood.
85   Oh blindness to the future! kindly giv'n,
That each may fill the circle marked by Heav'n;
Who sees with equal eye, as God of all,
A hero perish, or a sparrow fall,
Atoms or systems° into ruin hurled,   *solar systems*
90   And now a bubble burst, and now a world.
    Hope humbly then; with trembling pinions soar;
Wait the great teacher death, and God adore!
What future bliss, he gives not thee to know,
But gives that hope to be thy blessing now.
95   Hope springs eternal in the human breast:
Man never *is*, but always to *be* blest:
The soul, uneasy and confined from home,[7]
Rests and expatiates in a life to come.
    Lo! the poor Indian, whose untutored mind
100   Sees God in clouds, or hears him in the wind;
His soul proud science never taught to stray
Far as the solar walk, or milky way;
Yet simple nature to his hope has giv'n,
Behind the cloud-topped hill, an humbler Heav'n;
105   Some safer world in depth of woods embraced,
Some happier island in the watry waste,

---

6. Apis, sacred bull of Memphis.   7. Away from its heavenly origin.

Where slaves once more their native land behold,
No fiends torment, no Christians thirst for gold![8]
To be, contents his natural desire,

110　　He asks no angel's wing, no seraph's fire;[9]
But thinks, admitted to that equal sky,
His faithful dog shall bear him company.

　　4. Go, wiser thou! and in thy scale of sense
Weigh thy opinion against providence;

115　　Call imperfection what thou fancy'st such,
Say, here he gives too little, there too much;
Destroy all creatures for thy sport or gust,°　　　　　　*appetite*
Yet cry, If Man's unhappy, God's unjust;
If Man alone engross not Heav'n's high care,

120　　Alone made perfect here, immortal there:
Snatch from his hand the balance and the rod,
Rejudge his justice, be the God of God!
　　In pride, in reas'ning pride, our error lies;
All quit their sphere, and rush into the skies.

125　　Pride still is aiming at the blest abodes,
Men would be angels, angels would be gods.
Aspiring to be gods, if angels fell,
Aspiring to be angels, men rebel;
And who but wishes to invert the laws

130　　Of ORDER, sins against th' Eternal Cause.

　　5. Ask for what end th' heav'nly bodies shine,
Earth for whose use? Pride answers, "'Tis for mine:
For me kind Nature wakes her genial° pow'r,　　　　*generating*
Suckles each herb, and spreads out ev'ry flow'r;

135　　Annual for me, the grape, the rose renew
The juice nectareous, and the balmy dew;
For me, the mine a thousand treasures brings;
For me, health gushes from a thousand springs;
Seas roll to waft me, suns to light me rise;

140　　My foot-stool earth, my canopy the skies."
　　But errs not Nature from this gracious end,
From burning suns when livid deaths descend,
When earthquakes swallow, or when tempests sweep
Towns to one grave, whole nations to the deep?

145　　"No" ('tis replied) "the first Almighty cause[1]
Acts not by partial, but by gen'ral laws;
Th' exceptions few; some change since all began,
And what created perfect?"—Why then Man?
If the great end be human happiness,

150　　Then Nature deviates; and can Man do less?
As much that end a constant course requires
Of show'rs and sunshine, as of Man's desires;

8. The Christian is meant to "thirst for God" (Psalm 42.2).

9. Seraphs were traditionally thought of as fiery.
1. God the Creator.

As much eternal springs and cloudless skies,
As men for ever temp'rate, calm, and wise.
155 If plagues or earthquakes break not Heav'n's design,
Why then a Borgia, or a Catiline?[2]
Who knows but he, whose hand the light'ning forms,
Who heaves old ocean, and who wings the storms,
Pours fierce ambition in a Caesar's mind,
160 Or turns young Ammon[3] loose to scourge mankind?
From pride, from pride, our very reas'ning springs;
Account for moral as for nat'ral things:
Why charge we Heav'n in those, in these acquit?
In both, to reason right is to submit.
165 Better for us, perhaps, it might appear,
Were there all harmony, all virtue here;
That never air or ocean felt the wind;
That never passion discomposed the mind:
But all subsists by elemental strife;
170 And passions are the elements of life.
The gen'ral ORDER, since the whole began,
Is kept in Nature, and is kept in Man.

6. What would this Man? Now upward will he soar,
And little less than angel, would be more;
175 Now looking downwards, just as grieved appears
To want the strength of bulls, the fur of bears.
Made for his use all creatures if he call,
Say what their use, had he the pow'rs of all?
Nature to these, without profusion kind,
180 The proper organs, proper pow'rs assigned;
Each seeming want compensated of course,[4]
Here with degrees of swiftness, there of force;
All in exact proportion to the state;
Nothing to add, and nothing to abate.
185 Each beast, each insect, happy in its own;
Is Heav'n unkind to Man, and Man alone?
Shall he alone, whom rational we call,
Be pleased with nothing, if not blessed with all?
The bliss of Man (could pride that blessing find)
190 Is not to act or think beyond mankind;
No pow'rs of body or of soul to share,
But what his nature and his state can bear.
Why has not Man a microscopic eye?
For this plain reason, Man is not a fly.
195 Say what the use, were finer optics giv'n,
T' inspect a mite, not comprehend the Heav'n?[5]

2. Cesare Borgia (1476–1507), an Italian duke from a notoriously ruthless family. Lucius Sergius Catiline (d. 62
B.C.) plotted unsuccessfully against the Roman state.
3. Alexander the Great, King of Macedonia (336–323 B.C.)
and conqueror of Asia Minor, Syria, Egypt, Babylonia,

and Persia.
4. As is fitting, in the normal course of events.
5. It was commonly believed that man alone of all the animals was able to look up to Heaven.

Or touch, if tremblingly alive all o'er,
To smart and agonize at ev'ry pore?
Or quick effluvia[6] darting through the brain,
200   Die of a rose in aromatic pain?
If Nature thundered in his op'ning ears,
And stunned him with the music of the spheres,
How would he wish that Heav'n had left him still
The whisp'ring zephyr,° and the purling rill?   *breeze*
205   Who finds not providence all good and wise,
Alike in what it gives, and what denies?

      7. Far as creation's ample range extends,
The scale of sensual, mental pow'rs ascends:
Mark how it mounts, to Man's imperial race,
210   From the green myriads in the peopled grass:
What modes of sight betwixt each wide extreme,
The mole's dim curtain, and the lynx's beam:
Of smell, the headlong lioness[7] between,
And hound sagacious on the tainted[8] green:
215   Of hearing, from the life that fills the flood,
To that which warbles through the vernal wood:
The spider's touch, how exquisitely fine!
Feels at each thread, and lives along the line:
In the nice bee, what sense so subtly true
220   From pois'nous herbs extracts the healing dew:[9]
How instinct varies in the grov'ling swine,
Compared, half-reas'ning elephant, with thine:
'Twixt that, and reason, what a nice barrier;[1]
Forever sep'rate, yet forever near!
225   Remembrance and reflection how allied;
What thin partitions sense from thought divide:
And middle natures, how they long to join,
Yet never pass th' insuperable line!
Without this just gradation, could they be
230   Subjected these to those, or all to thee?
The pow'rs of all subdued by thee alone,
Is not thy reason all these pow'rs in one?

      8. See, through this air, this ocean, and this earth,
All matter quick,° and bursting into birth.   *living*
235   Above, how high progressive life may go!
Around, how wide! how deep extend below!
Vast chain of being, which from God began,
Natures ethereal, human, angel, Man,

---

6. Epicurus (c. 340–270 B.C.) and others believed that
sensations reached the brain from the pores via streams of
invisible particles.
7. Lions were, according to Pope, believed to hunt "by
the ear, and not by the nostril."

8. Sagacious: of acute perception; tainted: i.e., with the
smell of the hunted animal.
9. Honey had been thought to fall on flowers as dew and
was used for medicinal purposes.
1. Fine distinction. "Barrier" is pronounced "bar-REAR."

Beast, bird, fish, insect! what no eye can see,
240 No glass° can reach! from infinite to thee,   *magnifying glass*
From thee to nothing!—On superior pow'rs
Were we to press, inferior might on ours:
Or in the full creation leave a void,
Where, one step broken, the great scale's destroyed:
245 From nature's chain whatever link you strike,
Tenth or ten thousandth, breaks the chain alike.
    And if each system in gradation roll,
Alike essential to th' amazing whole;
The least confusion but in one, not all
250 That system only, but the whole must fall.
Let earth unbalanced from her orbit fly,[2]
Planets and suns run lawless through the sky,
Let ruling angels from their spheres be hurled,[3]
Being on being wrecked, and world on world,
255 Heav'n's whole foundations to their center nod,
And Nature tremble to the throne of God:
All this dread ORDER break—for whom? for thee?
Vile worm!—oh madness, pride, impiety!

    9. What if the foot, ordained the dust to tread,
260 Or hand to toil, aspired to be the head?
What if the head, the eye, or ear repined
To serve mere engines to the ruling mind?
Just as absurd for any part to claim
To be another, in this gen'ral frame:
265 Just as absurd, to mourn the tasks or pains
The great directing MIND of ALL ordains.
    All are but parts of one stupendous whole,
Whose body, Nature is, and God the soul;
That, changed through all, and yet in all the same,
270 Great in the earth, as in th' ethereal frame,
Warms in the sun, refreshes in the breeze,
Glows in the stars, and blossoms in the trees,
Lives through all life, extends through all extent,
Spreads undivided, operates unspent,
275 Breathes in our soul, informs° our mortal part,   *permeates*
As full, as perfect, in a hair as heart;
As full, as perfect, in vile Man that mourns,
As the rapt seraph that adores and burns;
To him no high, no low, no great, no small;
280 He fills, he bounds, connects, and equals all.

    10. Cease then, nor ORDER imperfection name:[4]
Our proper bliss depends on what we blame.

---

2. Cf. *Paradise Lost* 7.242, where "Earth, self-balanced, on her center hung."

3. According to Thomas Aquinas (c. 1225–1274), a sign of the end of the world.

4. I.e., do not call order imperfection.

Know thy own point: This kind, this due degree
Of blindness, weakness, Heav'n bestows on thee.
285   Submit—In this, or any other sphere,
Secure to be as blest as thou canst bear:
Safe in the hand of one disposing Pow'r,
Or° in the natal, or the mortal hour.   *either*
All nature is but art, unknown to thee;
290   All chance, direction, which thou canst not see;
All discord, harmony, not understood;[5]
All partial evil, universal good:[6]
And, spite of pride, in erring reason's spite,
One truth is clear, "Whatever IS, is RIGHT."

1733

THE DUNCIAD   Encouraged by Jonathan Swift, who spent some months with him at Twickenham in 1726, Pope produced two satires against "Dulness," bad writing, and the stupidity of "Dunces." *Peri Bathous, or the Art of Sinking in Poetry,* a prose treatise about how to write bad poetry, illustrated with many examples from Pope's contemporaries, was first published in 1728. Just two months later there appeared Pope's comic masterpiece, *The Dunciad,* in three books. Pope's pseudo-scholarly edition, *The Dunciad Variorum* (1729), intensified his attack on the hack writers of Grub Street and the proliferation of popular culture. In *The New Dunciad* (1742), the focus of Pope's contempt expanded from Grub Street to the pretentious, the ponderous, and the pedantic in its many forms. In 1743 Pope issued *The Dunciad in Four Books,* incorporating *The New Dunciad* as Book 4 of the poem, adding further mock-scholarly trappings, and transferring the conclusion of the three-book *Dunciad* to the end of Book 4; the "hero" of Books 1–3, Lewis Theobald (1688–1744), a minor writer and editor of Shakespeare, is replaced by the self-aggrandizing playwright and Poet Laureate Colly Cibber (1671–1757). In Book 4, the hero does nothing, and the climax of the poem is the goddess Dulness's infectious yawn, which sends all the world into darkness and primeval chaos. For the reader, the actions of Dulness and her sychophants engender not sleep, but laughter.

∽

from **The Dunciad**
from **Book the Fourth**
ARGUMENT

The poet being, in this book, to declare the completion of the prophecies mentioned at the end of the former,[1] makes a new invocation, as the greater poets are wont, when some high and worthy matter is to be sung. He shows the Goddess coming in her majesty, to destroy *Order* and *Science,*[2] and to substitute the *Kingdom of the Dull* upon earth. How she leads captive the Sciences, and silenceth the Muses; and what they be who succeed in their stead. All her children, by a wonderful attraction, are drawn about her, and bear along with them divers others, who promote her empire by con-

---

5. Here, as earlier in the poem, Pope invokes the Horatian principle of *concordia discors* (Horace, *Epistles* 1.12.19), a harmony of opposites.
6. In a letter to John Caryll in 1718, Pope wrote that "true piety would make us know, that all misfortunes may

as well be blessings."
1. Book 3 of *The Dunciad* concludes with an oracle foretelling that the goddess Dulness and hers sons shall triumph in the theaters, the court, and the universities.
2. Knowledge.

nivance, weak resistance, or discouragement of arts, such as half-wits, tasteless admirers, vain pretenders, the flatterers of dunces, or the patrons of them. All these crowd round her; one of them offering to approach her, is driven back by a rival, but she commends and encourages both. The first who speak in form[3] are the geniuses[4] of the schools, who assure her of their care to advance her cause, by confining youth to words, and keeping them out of the way of real knowledge. Their address, and her gracious answer, with her charge[5] to them and the universities. The universities appear by their proper deputies, and assure her that the same method is observed in the progress of education; the speech of Aristarchus[6] on this subject. They are driven off by a band of young gentlemen returned from travel with their tutors, one of whom delivers to the Goddess, in a polite oration, an account of the whole conduct and fruits of their travels, presenting to her at the same time a young nobleman perfectly accomplished. She receives him graciously, and indues him with the happy quality of *want of shame*. She sees loitering about her a number of indolent persons abandoning all business and duty, and dying with laziness; to these approaches the antiquary Annius,[7] entreating her to make them virtuosos,[8] and assign them over to him. But Mummius,[9] another antiquary, complaining of his fraudulent proceeding, she finds a method to reconcile their difference. Then enter a troop of people fantastically adorned, offering her strange and exotic presents. Amongst them, one stands forth and demands justice on another, who had deprived him of one of the greatest curiosities in Nature; but he justifies himself so well, that the Goddess gives them both her approbation. She recommends to them to find proper employment for the indolents before-mentioned, in the study of butterflies, shells, birds' nests, moss, etc. but with particular caution not to proceed beyond trifles, to any useful or extensive views of Nature, or of the Author of Nature. Against the last of these apprehensions, she is secured by a hearty address from the Minute Philosophers and Freethinkers,[1] one of whom speaks in the name of the rest. The youth thus instructed and principled are delivered to her in a body, by the hands of Silenus, and then admitted to taste the cup of the Magus her high priest, which causes a total oblivion of all obligations, divine, civil, moral, or rational. To these her adepts she sends priests, attendants, and comforters, of various kinds; confers on them Orders and Degrees; and then dismissing them with a speech, confirming to each his privileges[2] and telling what she expects from each, concludes with a yawn of extraordinary virtue,[3] the progress and effects whereof on all orders of men, and the consummation of all, in the restoration of night and chaos, conclude the poem.

[The Goddess Coming in Her Majesty]

> Yet, yet a moment, one dim ray of light
> Indulge, dread chaos, and eternal night!
> Of darkness visible[4] so much be lent,

3. Formally.

4. Guardian deities.

5. Commission, instruction of duties.

6. Aristarchus of Samothrace (c. 217–145 B.C.), a scholar who "corrected" the poems of Homer; he represents a severe and short-sighted critic. In a preface added to *The Dunciad in Four Books* (1743), he is named "Richard Aristarchus" and clearly represents Richard Bentley, the scholar and critic who, in 1732, published a disastrous "corrected" version of Milton's *Paradise Lost*.

7. A monk, famous for his forgeries.

8. Men knowledgeable in trivial subjects or antique curiosities.

9. A Roman general, who burned Corinth.

1. Petty philosophers and those who rejected orthodox religious dogma in favor of rational inquiry.

2. From this point, the rest of the Argument was added in 1743, describing the new ending added at the same time.

3. Power.

4. Cf. Milton's description of Hell in *Paradise Lost* 1.62–65: "yet from those flames / No light, but rather darkness visible / Served only to discover sights of woe, / Regions of sorrow."

As half[5] to show, half veil the deep intent.
5   Ye pow'rs! whose mysteries restored I sing,
To whom Time bears me on his rapid wing,
Suspend a while your force inertly strong,
Then take at once the poet and the song.
     Now flamed the Dog-star's unpropitious ray,[6]
10   Smote ev'ry brain, and withered ev'ry bay;[7]
Sick was the sun, the owl forsook his bow'r,
The moon-struck prophet felt the madding hour:
Then rose the seed of chaos, and of night,
To blot out order, and extinguish light,
15   Of dull and venal a new world to mold,
And bring Saturnian days[8] of lead and gold
     She mounts the throne: her head a cloud concealed,
In broad effulgence all below revealed[9]
('Tis thus aspiring Dulness ever shines)
20   Soft on her lap her laureate son reclines.
     Beneath her footstool, Science groans in chains,
And Wit dreads exile, penalties, and pains.
There foamed rebellious Logic, gagged and bound,
There, stripped, fair Rhet'ric languished on the ground;
25   His blunted arms by Sophistry are born,[1]
And shameless Billingsgate her robes adorn.
Morality, by her false guardians drawn,
Chicane in furs, and Casuistry in lawn,[2]
Gasps, as they straiten° at each end the cord,   *tighten*
30   And dies, when Dulness gives her Page[3] the word.

[THE GENIUSES OF THE SCHOOLS]

135   Now crowds on crowds around the Goddess press,
Each eager to present the first address.[4]
Dunce scorning dunce beholds the next advance,
But fop shows fop superior complaisance.
When lo! a specter[5] rose, whose index hand
140 Held forth the virtue of the dreadful wand;
His beavered brow° a birchen garland wears,   *beaver hat*
Dropping with infant's blood, and mother's tears.[6]

5. This is a great propriety, for a dull poet can never express himself otherwise than by halves or imperfectly [Pope's note].
6. Sirius, the Dog-star, is most visible at the end of summer, the time at which poetry recitals used to take place in classical Rome.
7. The laurel leaves symbolic of poetic success.
8. Saturn's many associations are played on here: Saturnalia was the Roman festival of misrule; while the age of Saturn was the Golden Age, Saturn also symbolized lead, these two metals respectively representing venality (corruption) and dullness.
9. Pope glosses this line: "The higher you climb, the more you show your arse."
1. The quibbling reasoning of Sophistry replaces Logic,

while Billingsgate (the slang of fish sellers) replaces Rhetoric.
2. Legal trickery wears a judge's ermine robes, while the moral quibbler wears a bishop's fine linen.
3. Sir Francis Page, the "hanging judge," is linked with "Mutes or Pages" given the task of "strangling state criminals in Turkey" [Pope's note].
4. Written congratulations.
5. Dr. Richard Busby (1605–1695), headmaster of Westminster School, famed for instilling discipline as well as learning: the "dreadful wand" is his birch cane.
6. Cf. *Paradise Lost* 1.392–93. "First Moloch, horrid king besmeared with blood / Of human sacrifice, and parents' tears." In the Ancient Near East, the cult of Moloch practiced child sacrifice.

O'er ev'ry vein a shudd'ring horror runs;
Eton and Winton[7] shake through all their sons.
145   All flesh is humbled, Westminster's bold race[8]
Shrink, and confess the genius° of the place: *guardian deity*
The pale boy-senator[9] yet tingling stands,
And holds his breeches close with both his hands.
     Then thus: "Since man from beast by words is known,
150   Words are man's province, words we teach alone.
When reason doubtful, like the Samian letter,[1]
Points him two ways, the narrower is the better.
Placed at the door of learning, youth to guide,
We never suffer it to stand too wide.
155   To ask, to guess, to know, as they commence,
As fancy opens the quick springs of sense,
We ply the memory, we load the brain,
Bind rebel wit, and double chain on chain,
Confine the thought, to exercise the breath;[2]
160   And keep them in the pale of words[3] till death.
Whate'er the talents, or howe'er designed,
We hang one jingling padlock on the mind:[4]
A poet the first day, he dips his quill;
And what the last? a very poet still.
165   Pity! the charm works only in our wall,
Lost, lost too soon in yonder House or Hall."[5]

[Young Gentlemen Returned from Travel]

275   In flowed at once a gay embroidered race,
And titt'ring pushed the pedants off the place:
Some would have spoken, but the voice was drowned
By the French horn, or by the op'ning° hound.   *baying*
The first came forwards, with as easy mien,
280   As if he saw St. James's° and the Queen.   *the palace*
When thus th' attendant orator[6] begun.
"Receive, great Empress! thy accomplished son:
Thine from the birth, and sacred° from the rod,   *spared*
A dauntless infant! never scared with God.
285   The sire saw, one by one, his virtues wake:
The mother begged the blessing of a rake.[7]
Thou gav'st that ripeness, which so soon began,
And ceased so soon, he ne'er was boy, nor man.

7. Eton and Winchester, two schools influenced by Busby.
8. The many graduates of the top schools who went on to be parliamentarians (at Westminster).
9. Young member of Parliament.
1. The letter "Y", emblem of the choice between the paths of virtue and vice.
2. By obliging them to get the classic poets by heart, which furnishes them with endless matter for conversation, and verbal amusement for their whole lives [Pope's note].
3. I.e., within the boundaries of pedantic learning.

4. For youth being used like packhorses and beaten on under a heavy load of words, lest they should tire, their instructors contrive to make the words jingle in rhyme and meter [Pope's note].
5. They can no longer compose once they leave the school for the parliamentary or legal professions, in the House of Commons or Westminster Hall.
6. The "lac'd governor from France" who had entered earlier with "whore" and "pupil" (line 272).
7. She hoped he would become a rake (an arrogant young libertine).

Through school and college, thy kind cloud o'ercast,
290   Safe and unseen the young Aeneas past:[8]
Thence bursting glorious, all at once let down,°   *released*
Stunned with his giddy larum° half the town.   *noise*
Intrepid then, o'er seas and lands he flew:
Europe he saw, and Europe saw him too.
295   There all thy gifts and graces we display,
Thou, only thou, directing all our way!
To where the Seine, obsequious as she runs,
Pours at great Bourbon's feet her silken sons;[9]
Or Tiber, now no longer Roman, rolls,
300   Vain of Italian arts, Italian souls:[1]
To happy convents, bosomed deep in vines,
Where slumber abbots, purple as their wines:
To isles of fragrance, lily-silvered vales,
Diffusing languor in the panting gales:°   *light winds*
305   To lands of singing, or of dancing slaves,
Love-whisp'ring woods, and lute-resounding waves.
But chief her shrine where naked Venus keeps,
And cupids ride the Lion of the Deeps;[2]
Where, eased of fleets, the Adriatic main°   *sea*
310   Wafts the smooth eunuch and enamored swain.
Led by my hand, he sauntered Europe round,
And gathered ev'ry vice on Christian ground;
Saw ev'ry court, heard ev'ry king declare
His royal sense, of op'ra's or the fair;[3]
315   The stews° and palace equally explored,   *brothels*
Intrigued with glory, and with spirit whored;
Tried all *hors d'oeuvres*, all *liqueurs* defined,
Judicious drank, and greatly-daring dined;
Dropped the dull lumber of the Latin store,[4]
320   Spoiled his own language, and acquired no more;
All classic learning lost on classic ground;
And last turned *Air*, the echo of a sound![5]
See now, half-cured, and perfectly well-bred,
With nothing but a solo in his head;
325   As much estate, and principle, and wit,
As Jansen, Fleetwood, Cibber[6] shall think fit;
Stol'n from a duel, followed by a nun,
And, if a borough choose him, not undone;[7]

8. Aeneas was hidden in a cloud by Venus when entering Carthage.
9. Bourbon: Louis XIV, so absolute a monarch that even the rivers are "obsequious" (servile).
1. The poetic and martial might of the Roman Empire had degenerated into the effeminacy and shallowness of the Italian states.
2. The winged lion of Venice, a city-state known previously for its naval and trading might, known now as "the brothel of Europe."
3. Britain's king, George II, was notorious for his interest in women and song.

4. His classical learning.
5. Yet less a body than Echo itself; for Echo reflects sense or words at least, this gentleman only airs and tunes [Pope's note].
6. Three very eminent persons, all managers of plays [the first at gambling, the latter two in the theater], who, though not [school] governors by profession, had, each in his way, concerned themselves in the education of youth . . . [Pope's note].
7. If elected to Parliament, he could not be arrested for debt.

See, to my country happy I restore
330   This glorious youth, and add one Venus[8] more.
Her too receive (for her my soul adores)
So may the sons of sons of sons of whores
Prop thine, O Empress! like each neighbor throne,
And make a long posterity thy own."
335   Pleased, she accepts the hero, and the dame,
Wraps in her veil, and frees from sense of shame.

Lady Mary Wortley Montagu
1689–1762

In learning, literature, and travel, Lady Mary Wortley Montagu outdistanced almost all of her contemporaries. Born Mary Pierrepont, she acquired her title at age one (when her father became an earl), lost her mother at age three, and immersed herself throughout her youth in the Roman classics, fervently pursuing a plan of self-education at odds with the conventional domesticating agenda (dancing, drawing, social graces) laid out for young women of her rank. For a time in her teens she aspired to implement the idea set forth by the feminist Mary Astell, of founding a convent consecrated to women's learning. In 1712 she married, against her father's wishes, a Whig Member of Parliament named Edward Wortley Montagu, after conducting with him a wary, carefully reasoned courtship mostly by means of letters. When he was appointed Ambassador to Turkey four years later, she accompanied him, and was fascinated by what she saw: by the Turkish practice of inoculating against smallpox, which (having survived the disease herself) she successfully championed in England at her return; by the gaps and continuities between British and Turkish culture, on which she reported eloquently in missives home. Her *Turkish Embassy Letters*, which she compiled from her writings during this sojourn for publication after her death, remain the foundation of her fame.

Her life as a writer yielded other riches, just now beginning to be explored. She wrote essays, including a *Spectator* for Addison and Steele and a later periodical series of her own (1737–1738). She produced short fiction and a comedy but worked more steadily at verse, collaborating with Alexander Pope on some poems and combating him in others, after their friendship had disintegrated into a round of bitter, witty recriminations. Most plentifully she wrote letters, sharp and searching, adroitly tailored to please her wide array of correspondents.

Montagu's spate of accomplishment made her alert to the constrictions of gender. "There is hardly a character in the world," she wrote at age twenty, "more liable to universal ridicule than that of a Learned Woman." Women, she counseled, should know much but hide their knowledge, lest they lose out on the comforts of love, marriage, and social ease. Deeply attentive to the burdens imposed on women and the tactics available to them, Montagu's idiosyncratic feminism earned esteem from her predecessor Astell, and from many who came after.

Idiosyncrasy exacted costs, in the form of that "ridicule" she had early anticipated, and in the breakdown of important relationships. Her marriage failed, as did a passionate love affair (again largely epistolary) with the bisexual Italian writer Francesco Algarotti. Montagu lived her last twenty-five years mostly in Italy. In retrospect, her self-removal looks like part of a lifelong strategy. Montagu had always held it crucial to keep some distance from her culture's

---

8. A prostitute he brings back with him.

assumptions in order to see them clearly, to critique them, to change or expunge their operations in herself and in the world. The title she chose for her periodical series, *The Nonsense of Common Sense*, encapsulates her lifelong conviction. By the eccentricity of her self-education, the remoteness of her travels and her residences, the originality of her thought and conduct, the amused acerbity of her style, Montagu kept her distance and found her voice.

from The Turkish Embassy Letters[1]
To Lady ———————[2]
[ON THE TURKISH BATHS]

Adrianople, 1 April 1717

I am now got into a new world where everything I see appears to me a change of scene, and I write to your Ladyship with some content of mind, hoping at least that you will find the charm of novelty in my letters and no longer reproach me that I tell you nothing extraordinary. I won't trouble you with a relation of our tedious journey, but I must not omit what I saw remarkable at Sophia, one of the most beautiful towns in the Turkish Empire and famous for its hot baths that are resorted to both for diversion and health. I stopped here one day on purpose to see them. Designing to go incognito, I hired a Turkish coach. These *voitures* are not at all like ours, but much more convenient for the country, the heat being so great that glasses[3] would be very troublesome. They are made a good deal in the manner of the Dutch coaches, having wooden lattices painted and gilded, the inside being painted with baskets and nosegays of flowers, intermixed commonly with little poetical mottoes. They are covered all over with scarlet cloth, lined with silk and very often richly embroidered and fringed. This covering entirely hides the persons in them, but may be thrown back at pleasure and the ladies peep through the lattices. They hold four people very conveniently, seated on cushions, but not raised.

In one of these covered wagons I went to the bagnio[4] about ten o'clock. It was already full of women. It is built of stone in the shape of a dome with no windows but in the roof, which gives light enough. There was five of these domes joined together, the outmost being less than the rest and serving only as a hall where the porteress stood at the door. Ladies of quality generally give this woman the value of a crown or ten shillings, and I did not forget that ceremony. The next room is a very large one, paved with marble, and all round it raised two sofas of marble, one above another. There were four fountains of cold water in this room, falling first into marble basins and then running on the floor in little channels made for that purpose, which carried the streams into the next room, something less than this, with the same sort of marble sofas, but so hot with steams of sulphur proceeding from the baths joining to it, 'twas impossible to stay there with one's clothes on. The two other domes were the hot baths, one of which had cocks of cold water turning into it to temper it to what degree of warmth the bathers have a mind to.

I was in my traveling habit, which is a riding dress, and certainly appeared very extraordinary to them, yet there was not one of 'em that showed the least surprise or

1. The text of the *Turkish Embassy Letters* comes not from the actual letters Montagu sent while on her travels but from two manuscript books in which she combined portions of her letters and travel journals with new prose to produce a hybrid account of the trip, which she intended for posthumous publication. In 1724 Montagu lent the volumes to Mary Astell, who inscribed into the second a preface addressed to future readers: ". . . I confess I am malicious enough to desire that the world should see to how much better purpose the *ladies* travel than their *lords*, and that whilst it is surfeited with male travels [i.e.,

travel-books], all in the same tone and stuffed with the same trifles, a *lady* has the skill to strike out a new path and to embellish a worn out subject with variety of fresh and elegant entertainment . . . Let us freely own the superiority of this sublime genius as I do in sincerity of my soul, pleased that a *woman* triumphs, and proud to follow in her train."
2. In the manuscript, Montagu supplies no name for this person, who may be a fictive "recipient."
3. Glass windows (which the Turkish coaches lacked).
4. The bath.

impertinent curiosity, but received me with all the obliging civility possible. I know of no European court where the ladies would have behaved themselves in so polite a manner to a stranger.

I believe in the whole there were two hundred women, and yet none of those disdainful smiles or satiric whispers that never fail in our asemblies when anybody appears that is not dressed exactly in fashion. They repeated over and over to me, *uzelle, pek uzelle*, which is nothing but "charming, very charming." The first sofas were covered with cushioned and rich carpets, on which sat the ladies, and on the second their slaves behind 'em, but without any distinction of rank by their dress, all being in the state of nature, that is, in plain English, stark naked, without any beauty or defect concealed, yet there was not the least wanton smile or immodest gesture amongst 'em. They walked and moved with the same majestic grace which Milton describes of our "general mother."[5] There were many amongst them as exactly proportioned as ever any goddess was drawn by the pencil of Guido or Titian,[6] and most of their skins shiningly white, only adorned by their beautiful hair divided into many tresses hanging on their shoulders, braided either with pearl or riband,[7] perfectly representing the figures of the Graces.[8] I was here convinced of the truth of a reflection that I had often made, that if 'twas the fashion to go naked, the face would be hardly observed. I perceived that the ladies with the finest skins and most delicate shapes had the greatest share of my admiration, though their faces were sometimes less beautiful than those of their companions. To tell you the truth, I had wickedness enough to wish secretly that Mr. Gervase could have been there invisible.[9] I fancy it would have very much improved his art to see so many fine women naked in different postures, some in conversation, some working, others drinking coffee or sherbet, and many negligently lying on their cushions while their slaves (generally pretty girls of seventeen or eighteen) were employed in braiding their hair in several pretty manners. In short, 'tis the women's coffee-house, where all the news of the town is told, scandal invented, etc. They generally take this diversion once a week, and stay there at least four or five hours without getting cold by immediate coming out of the hot bath into the cool room, which was very surprising to me. The lady that seemed the most considerable among them entreated me to sit by her and would fain have undressed me for the bath. I excused myself with some difficulty, they being all so earnest in persuading me. I was at last forced to open my skirt and show them my stays,[1] which satisfied them very well, for I saw they believed I was so locked up in that machine that it was not in my own power to open it, which contrivance they attributed to my husband. I was charmed with their civility and beauty, and should have been very glad to pass more time with them, but Mr. W[2] resolving to pursue his journey the next morning early, I was in haste to see the ruins of Justinian's church,[3] which did not afford me so agreeable a prospect as I had left, being little more than a heap of stones.

Adieu, Madam. I am sure I have now entertained you with an account of such a sight as you never saw in your life and that no book of travels could inform you of. 'Tis no less than death for a man to be found in one of those places.

---

5. Eve (*Paradise Lost* 4.304–18).
6. Artists of the Italian Renaissance.
7. Ribbon.
8. Resembling the three sister divinities who (in Greek mythology) embody and endow grace and beauty.
9. Charles Jervas (c. 1675–1739), a successful portraitist who had once painted Montagu as a shepherdess. The French painter Jean Auguste Dominique Ingres (1780–1867) later took up the hint implicit in Montagu's

"fancy" here. Having transcribed portions of this letter from a French edition (1805), he made use of Montagu's descriptions in his painting *Le Bain Turc* (The Turkish Bath, 1862).
1. A tightly laced undergarment, stiffened with whalebone, extending from breast to thigh.
2. Her husband, Edward Wortley Montagu.
3. The Church of St. Sofia, built during the reign of the Byzantine Emperor Justinian (483–565).

To Lady Mar[1]
[On Turkish Dress]

Adrianople, 1 April 1717

I wish to God (dear Sister) that you was as regular in letting me have the pleasure of knowing what passes on your side of the globe as I am careful in endeavoring to amuse you by the account of all I see that I think you care to hear of. You content yourself with telling me over and over that the town is very dull. It may possibly be dull to you when every day does not present you with something new, but for me that am in arrear at least two months' news, all that seems very stale with you would be fresh and sweet here; pray let me into more particulars. I will try to awaken your gratitude by giving you a full and true relation of the novelties of this place, none of which would surprise you more than a sight of my person as I am now in my Turkish habit, though I believe you would be of my opinion that 'tis admirably becoming. I intend to send you my picture; in the meantime accept of it here.

The first piece of my dress is a pair of drawers, very full, that reach to my shoes and conceal the legs more modestly than your petticoats. They are of a thin rose-color damask brocaded with silver flowers, my shoes of white kid leather embroidered with gold. Over this hangs my smock of a fine white silk gauze edged with embroidery. This smock has wide sleeves hanging half way down the arm and is closed at the neck with a diamond button, but the shape and color of the bosom very well to be distinguished through it. The *antery* is a waistcoat[2] made close to the shape, of white and gold damask, with very long sleeves falling back and fringed with deep gold fringe, and should have diamond or pearl buttons. My caftan, of the same stuff with my drawers, is a robe exactly fitted to my shape and reaching to my feet, with very long straight falling sleeves. Over this is the girdle of about four fingers broad, which all that can afford have entirely of diamonds or other precious stones. Those that will not be at that expense have it of exquisite embroidery on satin, but it must be fastened before with a clasp of diamonds. The *curdée* is a loose robe they throw off or put on according to the weather, being of a rich brocade (mine is green and gold) either lined with ermine or sables; the sleeves reach very little below the shoulders. The headdress is composed of a cap called *talpock*, which is in winter of fine velvet embroidered with pearls or diamonds and in summer of a light shining silver stuff. This is fixed on one side of the head, hanging a little way down with a gold tassel and bound on either with a circle of diamonds (as I have seen several) or a rich embroidered handkerchief. On the other side of the head the hair is laid flat, and here the ladies are at liberty to show their fancies, some putting flowers, others a plume of heron's feathers, and, in short, what they please, but the most general fashion is a large bouquet of jewels made like natural flowers, that is, the buds of pearl, the roses of different colored rubies, the jasmines of diamonds, jonquils of topazes, etc., so well set and enameled 'tis hard to imagine anything of that kind so beautiful. The hair hangs at its full length behind, divided into tresses braided with pearl or riband, which is always in great quantity.

1. Montagu's sister Frances (1690–1761), who had married the Earl of Mar.

2. A vest.

I never saw in my life so many fine heads of hair. I have counted 110 of these tresses of one lady's, all natural; but it must be owned that every beauty is more common here than with us. 'Tis surprising to see a young woman that is not very handsome. They have naturally the most beautiful complexions in the world and generally large black eyes. I can assure you with great truth that the Court of England (though I believe it the fairest in Christendom) cannot show so many beauties as are under our protection here. They generally shape their eyebrows, and the Greeks and Turks have a custom of putting round their eyes on the inside a black tincture that, at a distance or by candlelight, adds very much to the blackness of them. I fancy many of our ladies would be overjoyed to know this secret, but 'tis too visible by day. They dye their nails rose color; I own I cannot enough accustom myself to this fashion to find any beauty in it.

As to their morality or good conduct, I can say like Arlequin, 'tis just as 'tis with you,[3] and the Turkish ladies don't commit one sin the less for not being Christians. Now I am a little acquainted with their ways, I cannot forbear admiring either the exemplary discretion or extreme stupidity of all the writers that have given accounts of 'em.[4] 'Tis very easy to see they have more liberty than we have, no woman of what rank soever being permitted to go in the streets without two muslins, one that covers her face all but her eyes and another that hides the whole dress of her head and hangs half way down her back; and their shapes are wholly concealed by a thing they call a *ferigée*, which no woman of any sort appears without. This has straight sleeves that reaches to their fingers' ends and it laps all round 'em, not unlike a riding hood. In winter 'tis of cloth, and in summer, plain stuff or silk. You may guess how effectually this disguises them, that there is no distinguishing the great lady from her slave, and 'tis impossible for the most jealous husband to know his wife when he meets her, and no man dare either touch or follow a woman in the street.

This perpetual masquerade gives them entire liberty of following their inclinations without danger of discovery. The most usual method of intrigue is to send an appointment to the lover to meet the lady at a Jew's shop,[5] which are as notoriously convenient as our Indian houses,[6] and yet even those that don't make that use of 'em do not scruple to go to buy pennorths and tumble over[7] rich goods, which are chiefly to be found amongst that sort of people.[8] The great ladies seldom let their gallants[9] know who they are, and 'tis so difficult to find it out that they can very seldom guess at her name they have corresponded with above half a year together. You may easily imagine the number of faithful wives very small in a country where they have nothing to fear from their lovers' indiscretion, since we see so many that have the courage to expose themselves to that in this world and all the threatened punishment of the next, which is never preached to the Turkish damsels. Neither have they much to apprehend from the resentment of their husbands, those ladies that are rich having

---

3. A paraphrase (and misattribution) of a line from Aphra Behn's comedy *The Emperor of the Moon* (1687): the prankster Harlequin, pretending to be an ambassador from the moon, describes the corrupt social customs of his world to a gullible listener, who repeatedly exclaims that morality there is "just as 'tis here" (3.2).
4. Many (though not all) writers on Turkey had emphasized the strict confinement and chastity of the women there.

5. Jewish women sometimes helped arrange these assignations; being permitted to enter the harems, they could transmit secret messages.
6. London shops selling goods imported from India.
7. Penny-worths: good bargains; tumble over: browse through.
8. Jews.
9. Lovers.

all their money in their own hands, which they take with 'em upon a divorce with an addition which he is obliged to give 'em. Upon the whole, I look upon the Turkish women as the only free people in the Empire. The very *Divan*[1] pays a respect to 'em, and the *Grand Signor* himself, when a *Bassa*[2] is executed, never violates the privileges of the harem (or women's apartment), which remains unsearched entire to the widow. They are queens of their slaves, which the husband has no permission so much as to look upon, except it be an old woman or two that his lady chooses. 'Tis true their law permits them four wives, but there is no instance of a man of quality that makes use of this liberty, or of a woman of rank that would suffer it. When a husband happens to be inconstant (as those things will happen) he keeps his mistress in a house apart and visits her as privately as he can, just as 'tis with you. Amongst all the great men here I only know the *Tefterdar* (i.e. treasurer) that keeps a number of she slaves for his own use (that is, on his own side of the house, for a slave once given to serve a lady is entirely at her disposal) and he is spoke of as a libertine, or what we should call a rake, and his wife won't see him, though she continues to live in his house.

Thus you see, dear Sister, the manners of mankind do not differ so widely as our voyage writers would make us believe. Perhaps it would be more entertaining to add a few surprising customs of my own invention, but nothing seems to me so agreeable as truth, and I believe nothing so acceptable to you. I conclude with repeating the great truth of my being, dear Sister, etc.

Letter to Lady Bute[1]
[ON HER GRANDDAUGHTER]

28 January 1753

Dear Child,

You have given me a great deal of satisfaction by your account of your eldest daughter. I am particularly pleased to hear she is a good arithmetician; it is the best proof of understanding. The knowledge of numbers is one of the chief distinctions between us and brutes. If there is anything in blood, you may reasonably expect your children should be endowed with an uncommon share of good sense. Mr. Wortley's[2] family and mine have both produced some of the greatest men that have been born in England. I mean Admiral Sandwich,[3] and my great grandfather who was distinguished by the name of Wise William.[4] I have heard Lord Bute's father mentioned as an extraordinary genius (though he had not many opportunities of showing it), and his uncle the present Duke of Argyll has one of the best heads I ever knew.

I will therefore speak to you as supposing Lady Mary not only capable but desirous of learning. In that case, by all means let her be indulged in it. You will tell me, I did not make it a part of your education. Your prospect was very different from hers, as you had no defect either in mind or person to hinder, and much in your circumstances to attract, the highest offers. It seemed your business to learn how to live in

---

1. A governmental official.
2. *Pasha*: a high official.
1. Montagu's only daughter, Mary (1718–1794), had in 1736 married John Stuart, third Earl of Bute. At the time this letter was written, Montagu had been long separated from her husband and was living in Italy.

2. Her estranged husband, Edward Wortley Montagu.
3. Edward Montagu (1625–1672), first Earl of Sandwich (and Samuel Pepys's patron), was Wortley's grandfather.
4. The Hon. William Pierrepont (1608–1678) was a prominent politician.

the world, as it is hers to know how to be easy out of it. It is the common error of builders and parents to follow some plan they think beautiful (and perhaps is so) without considering that nothing is beautiful that is misplaced. Hence we see so many edifices raised that the raisers can never inhabit, being too large for their fortunes. Vistas are laid open over barren heaths, and apartments contrived for a coolness very agreeable in Italy but killing in the north of Britain. Thus every woman endeavors to breed her daughter a fine lady, qualifying her for a station in which she will never appear, and at the same time incapacitating her for that retirement to which she is destined. Learning (if she has a real taste for it) will not only make her contented but happy in it. No entertainment is so cheap as reading, nor any pleasure so lasting. She will not want new fashions nor regret the loss of expensive diversions or variety of company if she can be amused with an author in her closet. To render this amusement extensive, she should be permitted to learn the languages. I have heard it lamented that boys lose so many years in mere learning of words. This is no objection to a girl, whose time is not so precious. She cannot advance herself in any profession, and has therefore more hours to spare; and as you say her memory is good, she will be very agreeably employed this way.

There are two cautions to be given on this subject: first, not to think herself learned when she can read Latin or even Greek. Languages are more properly to be called vehicles of learning than learning itself, as may be observed in many schoolmasters, who though perhaps critics in grammar are the most ignorant fellows upon earth. True knowledge consists in knowing things, not words. I would wish her no farther a linguist than to enable her to read books in their originals, that are often corrupted and always injured by translations. Two hours' application every morning will bring this about much sooner than you can imagine, and she will have leisure enough beside to run over the English poetry, which is a more important part of a woman's education than it is generally supposed. Many a young damsel has been ruined by a fine copy of verses, which she would have laughed at if she had known it had been stolen from Mr. Waller.[5] I remember when I was a girl I saved one of my companions from destruction, who communicated to me an epistle she was quite charmed with. As she had a natural good taste, she observed the lines were not so smooth as Prior's[6] or Pope's, but had more thought and spirit than any of theirs. She was wonderfully delighted with such a demonstration of her lover's sense and passion, and not a little pleased with her own charms, that had force enough to inspire such elegancies. In the midst of this triumph, I showed her they were taken from Randolph's poems,[7] and the unfortunate transcriber was dismissed with the scorn he deserved. To say truth, the poor plagiary was very unlucky to fall into my hands; that author, being no longer in fashion, would have escaped anyone of less universal reading than myself. You should encourage your daughter to talk over with you what she reads, and as you are very capable of distinguishing, take care she does not mistake pert folly for wit and humor, or rhyme for poetry, which are the common errors of young people, and have a train of ill consequences.

5. Edmund Waller (1606–1687), love poet frequently quoted (or plagiarized) by amorous wooers.
6. Matthew Prior (1664–1721), like Alexander Pope a celebrated poet.
7. The minor writer Thomas Randolph (1605–1635), whose collected *Poems* were published in 1638.

The second caution to be given her (and which is most absolutely necessary) is to conceal whatever learning she attains, with as much solicitude as she would hide crookedness or lameness. The parade of it can only serve to draw on her the envy, and consequently the most inveterate hatred, of all he and she fools, which will certainly be at least three parts in four of all her acquaintance. The use of knowledge in our sex (beside the amusement of solitude) is to moderate the passions and learn to be contented with a small expense, which are the certain effects of a studious life and, it may be, preferable even to that fame which men have engrossed to themselves and will not suffer us to share. You will tell me I have not observed this rule myself, but you are mistaken; it is only inevitable accident that has given me any reputation that way. I have always carefully avoided it, and ever thought it a misfortune.

The explanation of this paragraph would occasion a long digression, which I will not trouble you with, it being my present design only to say what I think useful for the instruction of my granddaughter, which I have much at heart. If she has the same inclination (I should say passion) for learning that I was born with, history, geography, and philosophy will furnish her with materials to pass away cheerfully a longer life than is allotted to mortals. I believe there are few heads capable of making Sir I. Newton's[8] calculations, but the result of them is not difficult to be understood by a moderate capacity. Do not fear this should make her affect the character of Lady ——, or Lady ——, or Mrs.——.[9] Those women are ridiculous, not because they have learning but because they have it not. One thinks herself a complete historian after reading Eachard's *Roman History*,[1] another a profound philosopher having got by heart some of Pope's unintelligible essays,[2] and a third an able divine on the strength of Whitfield's sermons.[3] Thus you hear them screaming politics and controversy. It is a saying of Thucydides, ignorance is bold, and knowledge reserved.[4] Indeed it is impossible to be far advanced in it without being more humbled by a conviction of human ignorance than elated by learning.

At the same time I recommend books, I neither exclude work nor drawing. I think it as scandalous for a woman not to know how to use a needle, as for a man not to know how to use a sword. I was once extreme fond of my pencil, and it was a great mortification to me when my father turned off[5] my master, having made a considerable progress for the short time I learnt. My over eagerness in the pursuit of it had brought a weakness on my eyes that made it necessary to leave it off, and all the advantage I got was the improvement of my hand. I see by hers that practice will make her a ready writer. She may attain it by serving you for a secretary when your health or affairs make it troublesome to you to write yourself, and custom will make it an agreeable amusement to her. She cannot have too many for that station of life which will probably be her fate. The ultimate end of your education was to make you a good wife (and I have the comfort to hear that you are one); hers ought to be, to make her happy in a virgin state. I will not say it is happier, but it is undoubtedly safer than any marriage. In a lottery where there is (at the lowest computation) ten thousand blanks to a prize, it is the most prudent choice not to venture.

8. Isaac Newton, mathematician and scientist, author of *Principia Mathematica* (1687).

9. The names, which Montagu omitted in her manuscript, have not been recovered.

1. Lawrence Echard, *The Roman History* (1695–1698).

2. Probably his *Essay on Man* (1733–1734) in four epistles, published long after the friendship between him and

Montagu had ended.

3. George Whitfield (1714–1770), Methodist preacher.

4. Thucydides (c. 460–c. 399 B.C.), Greek historian of the Peloponnesian War; Montagu paraphrases his assertion that "boldness means ignorance and reflection brings hesitation" (*History* 2.40.3).

5. Dismissed.

I have always been so thoroughly persuaded of this truth that, notwithstanding the flattering views I had for you (as I never intended you a sacrifice to my vanity), I thought I owed you the justice to lay before you all the hazards attending matrimony. You may recollect I did so in the strongest manner. Perhaps you may have more success in the instructing your daughter. She has so much company at home she will not need seeking it abroad, and will more readily take the notions you think fit to give her. As you were alone in my family, it would have been thought a great cruelty to suffer you no companions of your own age, especially having so many near relations, and I do not wonder their opinions influenced yours. I was not sorry to see you not determined on a single life, knowing it was not your father's intention, and contented myself with endeavoring to make your home so easy that you might not be in haste to leave it.

I am afraid you will think this a very long and insignificant letter. I hope the kindness of the design will excuse it, being willing to give you every proof in my power that I am your most affectionate Mother,

M. Wortley.

Epistle from Mrs. Yonge to Her Husband[1]

Think not this paper comes with vain pretense
To move your pity, or to mourn th' offense.
Too well I know that hard obdurate heart;
No soft'ning mercy there will take my part,
5   Nor can a woman's arguments prevail,
When even your patron's wise example fails,[2]
But this last privilege I still retain,
Th' oppressed and injured always may complain.
        Too, too severely laws of honor bind
10   The weak submissive sex of womankind.
If sighs have gained or force compelled our hand,
Deceived by art, or urged by stern command,
Whatever motive binds the fatal tie,
The judging world expects our constancy.
15   Just Heaven! (for sure in heaven does justice reign
Though tricks below that sacred name profane)
To you appealing I submit my cause
Nor fear a judgment from impartial laws.
All bargains but conditional are made;
20   The purchase void, the creditor unpaid,
Defrauded servants are from service free;
A wounded slave regains his liberty.
For wives ill used no remedy remains,
To daily racks condemned, and to eternal chains.

1. In 1724 the heiress Mary Yonge became embroiled in a highly publicized divorce from her notorious, womanizing husband William, who accused her (accurately) of adultery committed during the couple's separation. Public sympathy was on her side, but the king approved a divorce that allowed her husband to retain most of her fortune. Montagu's poem remained in manuscript throughout her life.

2. I.e., Robert Walpole's. William Yonge was a devoted adherent of the powerful minister, who carried on open adulteries himself but also (unlike Yonge) permitted them to his wife.

25   From whence is this unjust distinction grown?
   Are we not formed with passions like your own?
   Nature with equal fire our souls endued,
   Our minds as haughty, and as warm our blood;
   O're the wide world your pleasures you pursue,
30   The change is justified by something new;
   But we must sigh in silence—and be true.
   Our sex's weakness you expose and blame
   (Of every prattling fop the common theme),
   Yet from this weakness you suppose is due
35   Sublimer virtue than your Cato[3] knew.
   Had Heaven designed us trials so severe,
   It would have formed our tempers then to bear.
    And I have borne (O what have I not borne!)
   The pang of jealousy, th' insults of scorn.
40   Wearied at length, I from your sight remove,
   And place my future hopes in secret love.
   In the gay bloom of glowing youth retired,
   I quit the woman's joy to be admired,
   With that small pension your hard heart allows,
45   Renounce your fortune, and release your vows.
   To custom (though unjust) so much is due;
   I hide my frailty from the public view.
   My conscience clear, yet sensible of shame,
   My life I hazard, to preserve my fame.
50   And I prefer this low inglorious state,
   To vile dependence on the thing I hate—
   But you pursue me to this last retreat.
   Dragged into light, my tender crime is shown
   And every circumstance of fondness known.
55   Beneath the shelter of the law you stand,
   And urge my ruin with a cruel hand.
   While to my fault thus rigidly severe,
   Tamely submissive to the man you fear.
    This wretched outcast, this abandoned wife,
60   Has yet this joy to sweeten shameful life,
   By your mean conduct, infamously loose,
   You are at once my accuser, and excuse.
   Let me be damned by the censorious prude
   (Stupidly dull, or spiritually lewd),
65   My hapless case will surely pity find
   From every just and reasonable mind,
   When to the final sentence I submit;
   The lips condemn me, but their souls acquit.
    No more my husband, to your pleasures go,
70   The sweets of your recovered freedom know;

---

3. Marcus Porcius Cato of Utica (95–46 B.C.), champion of the Roman Republic, whose name had become a byword for integrity.

Go; court the brittle friendship of the great,
Smile at his board, or at his levée[4] wait
And when dismissed, to Madam's toilet° fly,   *dressing room*
More than her chambermaids, or glasses,° lie,   *mirrors*
75   Tell her how young she looks, how heavenly fair,
Admire the lilies and the roses there;
Your high ambition may be gratified,
Some cousin of her own be made your bride,
And you the father of a glorious race
80   Endowed with Ch——l's strength and Low—r's face.[5]

1724   1972

The Lover: A Ballad

1

At length, by so much importunity pressed,
Take (Molly[1]) at once the inside of my breast;
This stupid indifference so often you blame
Is not owing to nature, to fear, or to shame;
5   I am not as cold as a virgin in lead,
Nor is Sunday's sermon so strong in my head;
I know but too well how time flies along,
That we live but few years and yet fewer are young.

2

But I hate to be cheated, and never will buy
10   Long years of repentance for moments of joy.
Oh was there a man (but where shall I find
Good sense, and good nature so equally joined?)
Would value his pleasure, contribute to mine,
Not meanly would boast, nor lewdly design,
15   Not over severe, yet not stupidly vain,
For I would have the power though not give the pain.

3

No pedant yet learned, not rakehelly gay
Or laughing because he has nothing to say,
To all my whole sex obliging and free,
20   Yet never be fond of any but me.
In public preserve the decorums are just
And show in his eyes he is true to his trust,
Then rarely approach, and respectfully bow,
Yet not fulsomely pert, nor yet foppishly low.

---

4. Social assemblies at the homes of the "great," often crowded with petitioners, opportunists, and sycophants.
5. The line implies that the adulterous William Yonge will himself be supplanted in his next wife's bed by fellow-libertines: Charles Churchill (c. 1679–1745) and Antony Lowther (d. 1741).
1. Probably Maria ("Molly") Skerrett (1702–1738), Montagu's friend and Robert Walpole's mistress.

4

25   But when the long hours of public are past
        And we meet with champagne and a chicken at last,
        May every fond pleasure that hour endear,
        Be banished afar both discretion and fear,
        Forgetting or scorning the airs of the crowd
30   He may cease to be formal, and I to be proud,
        Till lost in the joy, we confess that we live
        And he may be rude, and yet I may forgive.

5

        And that my delight may be solidly fixed
        Let the friend and the lover be handsomely mixed,
35   In whose tender bosom my soul might confide,
        Whose kindness can soothe me, whose counsel could guide;
        From such a dear lover as here I describe
        No danger should fright me, no millions should bribe,
        But till this astonishing creature I know
40   As I long have lived chaste I will keep myself so.

6

        I never will share with the wanton coquette,
        Or be caught by a vain affectation of wit.
        The toasters and songsters may try all their art
        But never shall enter the pass of my heart;
45   I loathe the lewd rake, the dressed fopling despise,
        Before such pursuers the nice virgin flies;
        And as Ovid has sweetly in parables told
        We harden like trees, and like rivers are cold.[2]

c. 1721–1725   1747

✦◆✦

John Gay
1685–1732

John Gay was born to hardworking, pious tradespeople in Barnstaple, a busy port town in southwestern England. Educated well but orphaned early, he moved at age eighteen to London, where he tried trade for a time, gave it up for literature, and made himself a master of the mock, at a moment when the mock mattered most.

In the early eighteenth century, the "mock" was not just a gesture of derision but an intricate art form, in which scenes of contemporary life, appropriated from streets, stables, salons, and other ordinary sites, were represented in grand styles first crafted for the actions of ancient heroes. In his mock-pastoral *Description of a City Shower* (1709), for example, Swift depicted the muddy chaos of an urban rainstorm in the language Virgil had devised to render the rural delights of a Golden Age; in his mock-epic *Rape of the Lock* (1712), Pope

------

2. In his *Metamorphoses*, Ovid tells stories of virgins who are transformed into a laurel tree (Daphne) or a fountain (Arethusa), rather than succumb to the importunities of a pursuing god (1.452–567; 5.572–641).

portrayed the trivial agitations of London beaux and belles in formulations absorbed from Homer. Befriended by Pope and Swift, Gay became perhaps the most supple and assiduous practitioner in their mock-heroic vein. In his early successes, he showed himself adept at devising new combinations of mode and topic, new ways of savoring both high styles and low subjects even while making fun of them. In *The Shepherd's Week* (1714), he took on both Virgil's idealism and also the ungainly "realism" attempted by some of that Roman poet's eighteenth-century imitators. He endowed his shepherds with preposterously "rustic" names (Bumkinet, Hobnelia, Bowzybeus) and a ludicrously hybrid language, alternately high-flying and homespun. But he gave them also a grace and good nature that survive the mock. The poem's closing image of a drunken swain sleeping out the sunset ("ruddy, like his face, the sun descends") reads like the poet's own benediction. In his next big work, *Trivia, or the Art of Walking the Streets of London* (1716), Gay's grandiloquent Virgilian instruction makes city walking seem not just a "trivial" chore but an "art," comic, challenging, alternately appalling and attractive.

Gay built his life as he made his art, by improvising. He earned money by his plays and poems; he lost money in that evanescent investment scheme the South Sea Bubble; he served as Commissioner of Lotteries, and as secretary, steward, and companion to several members of the nobility; and he sought for years to secure steady patronage at court, by means of flattering verse and ingratiating conduct. His frustration peaked when he published a virtuosic set of *Fables* (1727) for the four-year-old Prince William and received as reward a royal appointment as attendant to the prince's two-year-old sister. The aristocrats he courted valued him for his compliant temper and beguiling company, but they patronized him in both senses of the word.

Gay refused the royal appointment, staking his hopes instead on his new project for the stage, *The Beggar's Opera* (1728). The initial notion for the piece had come from Swift, who suggested a "Newgate pastoral"—that is, a mixture in which the "whores and thieves" who inhabited Newgate prison and its neighborhood would supplant the nymphs and shepherds frolicking on Arcadian hillsides. Swift's hint is an ordinary mock recipe: two worlds collide, one real, one fictitious. Gay built from it an intricate hall of mirrors, where many more worlds met. For his thieves he drew on two real-life models, recently executed: Jonathan Wild and Jack Sheppard. Wild had run a large criminal organization that profited him two ways: he collected money from the resale of goods stolen by his subordinates; and he collected rewards from the government for turning in his associates and rivals whenever they became too troublesome. Sheppard had acquired fame as Wild's most high-spirited and elusive prey; a brilliant thief in his own right, he had often managed to escape the prisons and predicaments into which Wild had betrayed him. In *The Beggar's Opera*, Gay resurrects the two late criminals as Mr. Peachum, who like Wild manages a lucrative double life, and Captain Macheath, who like Sheppard proves susceptible of capture and gifted at escape. Here the worlds begin to multiply. Developing a comparison then current in the political press, Gay made his criminals conjure up the most powerful politician alive: Robert Walpole, the Whig prime minister who ran his political machine (so the *Opera* insists) with the efficiency of Peachum and the self-indulgence of Macheath.

The Beggar's Opera mixed low with high in form as well as content. Like "Newgate pastoral," the phrase "beggar's opera" fuses opposites. Italian opera was the most expensive, exotic, and fashionable entertainment in London. Gay's theatrical game was to replay opera's intricacies using beggars' means. He supplanted the elaborate arias of foreign composers with the simpler tunes of British street songs; he replaced the original words to those tunes with new lyrics that voiced his characters' strong emotions; he even re-enacted a recent, much-publicized rivalry between two high-paid prima donnas, at war for the allegiance of their audience, in the contest he stages between Peachum's daughter Polly and the jailer's daughter Lucy Lockit for the devotion of fickle Captain Macheath. On Gay's stage, worlds converge with a density even Swift could not have foreseen. Opera house and street corner; Whitehall and Newgate; art and commerce; politics, business, and crime: all of these turn out to operate on the same principles of self-interest.

Reading the new piece before its premiere, Gay's well-wishers hedged their bets as to its success. "It would either take greatly," the playwright William Congreve predicted, "or be damned confoundedly." In the event, it did both. The triumph of the opening night is the stuff of theatrical legend, but it provoked a counter-chorus of condemnation from critics who saw the play as endangering opera, glorifying thieves, traducing government. Amid the debate, the play enjoyed a long run, entrancing an audience made up of the very people it mocked (including Walpole himself, who reportedly conducted an extra chorus of the play's most satiric song, "When you censure the age"). *The Beggar's Opera* offered theatergoers simple pleasures (deft performances, comic reversals, well-loved tunes) and intricate ones too: the often ironic play of Gay's new lyrics against the original words that the auditors had already in their heads; the debunking of love and marriage in sharp dialogue and the glorifying of it in sentimental song; the volatile charisma of the mock-hero Macheath, who for many observers came to seem utterly heroic by evening's end; the arresting alchemy by which Gay transmuted (as the Romantic essayist William Hazlitt later expressed it) "this motley group" of "highwaymen, turnkeys, their mistresses, wives, or daughters . . . into a set of fine gentlemen and ladies, satirists and philosophers." In his painting of the opening night (Color Plate 27), William Hogarth suggests how these transformations came to include the spectators as well. Occupying the sides of the stage, an audience of aristocrats, politicians, and theater people (Gay himself among them) observe the play in progress; they are encompassed by the same prison walls wherein Macheath and his pursuers play out their intricate transactions, in which everything and everyone—goods, votes, spouses—had become commodities, items of exchange, reckoned in account books as profit and as loss.

The Beggar's Opera brought Gay prosperity and celebrity but not security. Walpole evicted him from his subsidized lodgings and banned production of the *Opera*'s much-anticipated sequel *Polly*. When Gay died less than five years after his fabled first night, however, he was buried with elaborate ceremony in the Poet's Corner of Westminster Abbey. Friends commended the appropriateness of the site but marveled at the incongruity of the pomp. Incongruity, though, had been Gay's stock in trade, and nowhere more so than in his greatest hit. Its long run continues in theaters around the world. It spawned numberless short-lived imitations in its own time and a more durable descendant in the twentieth century: *Die Dreigroschenoper* (*The Threepenny Opera,* 1928), in which Bertolt Brecht and Kurt Weill adapted Gay's characters, plot, and critique of commerce to produce their own dark and gleeful Marxist assault on contemporary capitalism. By routes less direct, Gay's work has infused both the modern musical theater (which continues to combine operatic and popular modes) and pop culture in general—where, for example, Brecht and Weill's sardonic "Ballad of Mack the Knife" became a pop hit of the early 1960s. *The Beggar's Opera* grabbed attention first—and sustains it still—for the ironic dexterity with which it mixed things up, in full mock mode.

The Beggar's Opera

Nos haec novimus esse nihil.[1]

Dramatis Personae[2]

Men

PEACHUM

LOCKIT

MACHEATH

---

1. We know these things to be nothing (Martial, *Epigrams* 13.2.8).
2. Many of these names reflect the characters' low-life habits: to "peach" is to inform on, to filch is to steal, twitchers are pickpockets, nimmers are thieves, and trulls and doxies are prostitutes.

FILCH
JEMMY TWITCHER
CROOK-FINGERED JACK
WAT DREARY
ROBIN OF BAGSHOT   } *Macheath's Gang*
NIMMING NED
HARRY PADINGTON
MATT OF THE MINT
BEN BUDGE
BEGGAR
PLAYER
CONSTABLES, DRAWER, TURNKEY, ETC.

Women

MRS. PEACHUM
POLLY PEACHUM
LUCY LOCKIT
DIANA TRAPES
MRS. COAXER
DOLLY TRULL
MRS. VIXEN   } *Women of the Town*
BETTY DOXY
JENNY DIVER
MRS. SLAMMEKIN
SUKY TAWDRY
MOLLY BRAZEN

INTRODUCTION

[Beggar, Player]

BEGGAR: If poverty be a title[3] to poetry, I am sure nobody can dispute mine. I own myself of the Company of Beggars; and I make one at their weekly festivals at St. Giles's.[4] I have a small yearly salary for my catches,[5] and am welcome to a mock laureate dinner there whenever I please, which is more than most poets can say.

PLAYER: As we live by the Muses, 'tis but gratitude in us to encourage poetical merit wherever we find it. The Muses, contrary to all other ladies, pay no distinction to dress, and never partially[6] mistake the pertness of embroidery for wit, nor the modesty of want for dullness. Be the author who he will, we push his play as far as it will go. So (though you are in want) I wish you success heartily.

BEGGAR: This piece I own was originally writ for the celebrating the marriage of James Chanter and Moll Lay, two most excellent ballad singers. I have introduced the similes that are in all your celebrated operas: the swallow, the moth, the bee,

---

3. Deed of ownership.
4. An almshouse near the parish of St. Giles, patron saint of lepers and beggars.
5. Rounds, songs for two or more voices in which each

voice starts the same melody at a different time. The form was very popular; enthusiasts assembled in "catch clubs" for whole evenings of singing.
6. In a prejudiced way.

the ship, the flower, etc. Besides, I have a prison scene which the ladies always reckon charmingly pathetic. As to the parts, I have observed such a nice impartiality to our two ladies, that it is impossible for either of them to take offense.[7] I hope I may be forgiven, that I have not made my opera throughout unnatural, like those in vogue; for I have no recitative.[8] Excepting this, as I have consented to have neither prologue nor epilogue, it must be allowed an opera in all its forms. The piece indeed hath been heretofore frequently represented by ourselves in our great room at St. Giles's, so that I cannot too often acknowledge your charity in bringing it now on the stage.

PLAYER: But I see 'tis time for us to withdraw; the actors are preparing to begin. Play away the overture.

[Exeunt.]

ACT 1

Scene 1. Peachum's House

[Peachum sitting at a table with a large book of accounts before him.]

Air 1. An old woman clothed in gray, etc.[9]

Through all the employments of life
    Each neighbor abuses his brother;
Whore and rogue they call husband and wife:
    All professions be-rogue one another.
The priest calls the lawyer a cheat,
    The lawyer be-knaves the divine;
And the statesman, because he's so great, [1]
    Thinks his trade as honest as mine.

A lawyer is an honest employment, so is mine. Like me too he acts in a double capacity, both against rogues and for 'em; for 'tis but fitting that we should protect and encourage cheats, since we live by them.

Scene 2

[Peachum, Filch]

FILCH: Sir, Black Moll hath sent word her trial comes on in the afternoon, and she hopes you will order matters so as to bring her off.

PEACHUM: Why, she may plead her belly at worst;[2] to my knowledge she hath taken care of that security. But as the wench is very active and industrious, you may satisfy her that I'll soften the evidence.

FILCH: Tom Gagg, Sir, is found guilty.

PEACHUM: A lazy dog! When I took him the time before, I told him what he would come to if he did not mend his hand. This is death without reprieve. I may

---

7. The Beggar alludes to recent rivalries between leading ladies in Italian operas.
8. Sung speech, an operatic convention. The Beggar promises that here, by contrast, dialogue will be spoken naturally.
9. I.e., this air is to be sung to the familiar ballad tune, An

Old Woman Clothed in Gray.
1. The word "great" was often attached to the Whig Prime Minister Robert Walpole, whom Gay's Tory party opposed vigorously in the 1720s and 1730s.
2. A pregnant woman could not be hanged.

venture to book him.[3] [*Writes.*] For Tom Gagg, forty pounds. Let Betty Sly know that I'll save her from transportation,[4] for I can get more by her staying in England.

FILCH: Betty hath brought more goods into our lock to-year than any five of the gang; and in truth, 'tis a pity to lose so good a customer.

PEACHUM: If none of the gang take her off, she may, in the common course of business, live a twelve-month longer. I love to let women scape. A good sportsman always lets the hen partridges fly, because the breed of the game depends upon them. Besides, here the law allows us no reward; there is nothing to be got by the death of woman—except our wives.[5]

FILCH: Without dispute, she is a fine woman! 'Twas to her I was obliged for my education, and (to say a bold word) she hath trained up more young fellows to the business than the gaming-table.

PEACHUM: Truly, Filch, thy observation is right. We and the surgeons[6] are more beholden to women than all the professions besides.

Air 2. The bonny gray-eyed morn, etc.

FILCH: *'Tis woman that seduces all mankind,*
           By her we first were taught the wheedling arts:
    Her very eyes can cheat; when most she's kind,
           She tricks us of our money with our hearts.
    For her, like wolves by night we roam for prey,
           And practice ev'ry fraud to bribe her charms;
    For suits of love, like law, are won by pay,
           And beauty must be fee'd into our arms.

PEACHUM: But make haste to Newgate,[7] boy, and let my friends know what I intend; for I love to make them easy one way or other.

FILCH: When a gentleman is long kept in suspense, penitence may break his spirit ever after. Besides, certainty gives a man a good air upon his trial, and makes him risk another without fear or scruple. But I'll away, for 'tis a pleasure to be the messenger of comfort to friends in affliction.

Scene 3

[*Peachum*]

But 'tis now high time to look about me for a decent execution against next Sessions.[8] I hate a lazy rogue, by whom one can get nothing 'till he is hanged. A register of the gang, [*reading*] Crook-fingered Jack. A year and a half in the service; Let me see how much the stock owes to his industry; one, two, three, four, five gold watches, and seven silver ones. A mighty clean-handed fellow! Sixteen snuffboxes, five of them of true gold. Six dozen of handkerchiefs, four silver-hilted swords, half a dozen of shirts, three tie-perriwigs, and a piece of broad cloth. Considering these are only the fruits of his leisure hours, I don't know a prettier fellow, for no man alive hath a more engaging presence of mind upon the road. Wat

---

3. I.e., enter in the books the reward for "peaching" him.
4. Convicts were often transported to the colonies.
5. Husbands inherited their wives' property.

6. Who treat venereal diseases.
7. London's main prison.
8. Of the criminal court.

Dreary, alias Brown Will, an irregular dog, who hath an underhand way of disposing of his goods. I'll try him[9] only for a Sessions or two longer upon his good behavior. Harry Padington, a poor petty-larceny rascal, without the least genius;
that fellow, though he were to live these six months, will never come to the gallows with any credit. Slippery Sam; he goes off the next Sessions, for the villain
hath the impudence to have views of following his trade as a tailor, which he calls
an honest employment. Mat of the Mint; lifted[1] not above a month ago, a promising sturdy fellow, and diligent in his way; somewhat too bold and hasty, and may
raise good contributions on[2] the public, if he does not cut himself short by murder.
Tom Tipple, a guzzling soaking sot, who is always too drunk to stand himself, or to
make others stand. A cart[3] is absolutely necessary for him. Robin of Bagshot, alias
Gorgon, alias Bluff Bob, alias Carbuncle, alias Bob Booty.[4]

Scene 4

[Peachum, Mrs. Peachum]

MRS. PEACHUM: What of Bob Booty, husband? I hope nothing bad hath betided
him. You know, my dear, he's a favorite customer of mine. 'Twas he made me a
present of this ring.

PEACHUM: I have set his name down in the blacklist, that's all, my dear; he spends
his life among women, and as soon as his money is gone, one or other of the ladies
will hang him for the reward, and there's forty pound lost to us forever.

MRS. PEACHUM: You know, my dear, I never meddle in matters of death; I always
leave those affairs to you. Women indeed are bitter bad judges in these cases, for
they are so partial to the brave that they think every man handsome who is going
to the camp[5] or the gallows.

Air 3. Cold and raw, etc.

> If any wench Venus's girdle wear,
>   Though she be never so ugly;
> Lilies and roses will quickly appear,
>   And her face look wond'rous smugly.
> Beneath the left ear so fit but a cord
>   (A rope so charming a zone[6] is!),
> The youth in his cart hath the air of a lord,
>   And we cry, There dies an Adonis!

But really, husband, you should not be too hardhearted, for you never had a finer,
braver set of men than at present. We have not had a murder among them all,
these seven months. And truly, my dear, that is a great blessing.

PEACHUM: What a dickens is the woman always a whimpering about murder for?
No gentleman is ever looked upon the worse for killing a man in his own defense;
and if business cannot be carried on without it, what would you have a gentleman do?

---

9. Keep him on.
1. Enlisted.
2. From.
3. A condemned prisoner rode in a cart to his execution.

4. All names referring to the prime minister, Robert
Walpole.
5. To war.
6. Belt.

MRS. PEACHUM: If I am in the wrong, my dear, you must excuse me, for nobody can help the frailty of an over-scrupulous conscience.

PEACHUM: Murder is as fashionable a crime as a man can be guilty of. How many fine gentlemen have we in Newgate every year, purely upon that article! If they have wherewithal to persuade the jury to bring it in[7] manslaughter, what are they the worse for it? So, my dear, have done upon this subject. Was Captain Macheath here this morning, for the bank-notes[8] he left with you last week?

MRS. PEACHUM: Yes, my dear; and though the bank hath stopped payment, he was so cheerful and so agreeable! Sure there is not a finer gentleman upon the road than the Captain! If he comes from Bagshot[9] at any reasonable hour he hath promised to make one this evening with Polly and me, and Bob Booty, at a party of quadrille.[1] Pray, my dear, is the Captain rich?

PEACHUM: The Captain keeps too good company ever to grow rich. Marybone and the chocolate-houses[2] are his undoing. The man that proposes to get money by "play" should have the education of a fine gentleman, and be trained up to it from his youth.

MRS. PEACHUM: Really, I am sorry upon Polly's account the Captain hath not more discretion. What business hath he to keep company with lords and gentlemen? He should leave them to prey upon one another.

PEACHUM: Upon Polly's account! What, a plague, does the woman mean? Upon Polly's account!

MRS. PEACHUM: Captain Macheath is very fond of the girl.

PEACHUM: And what then?

MRS. PEACHUM: If I have any skill in the ways of women, I am sure Polly thinks him a very pretty man.

PEACHUM: And what then? You would not be so mad to have the wench marry him! Gamesters and highwaymen are generally very good to their whores, but they are very devils to their wives.

MRS. PEACHUM: But if Polly should be in love, how should we help her, or how can she help herself! Poor girl, I am in the utmost concern about her.

Air 4. Why is your faithful slave disdained? etc.

If love the virgin's heart invade,
How, like a moth, the simple maid
   Still plays about the flame!
If soon she be not made a wife;
Her honor's singed, and then for life,
   She's—what I dare not name.

PEACHUM: Look ye, wife. A handsome wench in our way of business is as profitable as at the bar of a Temple coffeehouse, who looks upon it as her livelihood to grant every liberty but one. You see I would indulge the girl as far as prudently we can. In anything, but marriage! After that, my dear, how shall we be safe? Are we not then in her husband's power? For a husband hath the absolute power over all a

---

7. Reduce it to.
8. Bankers' checks.
9. Bagshot Heath, west of London, where many highwaymen plied their trade.

1. A fashionable card game for four.
2. Both sites of gambling.

wife's secrets but her own. If the girl had the discretion of a court lady, who can have a dozen young fellows at her ear without complying with one, I should not matter it; but Polly is tinder, and a spark will at once set her on a flame. Married! If the wench does not know her own profit, sure she knows her own pleasure better than to make herself a property! My daughter to me should be, like a court lady to a minister of state, a key to the whole gang. Married! If the affair is not already done, I'll terrify her from it, by the example of our neighbors.

MRS. PEACHUM: Mayhap, my dear, you may injure the girl. She loves to imitate the fine ladies, and she may only allow the Captain liberties in the view of interest.[3]

PEACHUM: But 'tis your duty, my dear, to warn the girl against her ruin, and to instruct her how to make the most of her beauty. I'll go to her this moment, and sift[4] her. In the meantime, wife, rip out the coronets and marks[5] of these dozen of cambric handkerchiefs, for I can dispose of them this afternoon to a chap in the city.

Scene 5

[Mrs. Peachum]

Never was a man more out of the way[6] in an argument than my husband! Why must our Polly, forsooth, differ from her sex, and love only her husband? And why must Polly's marriage, contrary to all observation, make her the less followed by other men? All men are thieves in love, and like a woman the better for being another's property.

Air 5. Of all the simple things we do, etc.

A maid is like the golden oar,[7]
Which hath guineas intrinsical in't,
  Whose worth is never known, before
  It is tried and imprest[8] in the Mint.
  A wife's like a guinea in gold,
Stamped with the name of her spouse;
  Now here, now there; is bought, or is sold;
And is current in every house.

Scene 6

[Mrs. Peachum, Filch]

MRS. PEACHUM: Come hither Filch. I am as fond of this child, as though my mind misgave me[9] he were my own. He hath as fine a hand at picking a pocket as a woman, and is as nimble fingered as a juggler. If an unlucky Session does not cut the rope of thy life, I pronounce, boy, thou wilt be a great man[1] in history. Where was your post last night, my boy?

FILCH: I plyed at the opera, Madam; and considering 'twas neither dark nor rainy, so that there was no great hurry in getting chairs and coaches, made a tolerable hand on't. These seven handkerchiefs, Madam.

3. Self-interest, profit.
4. Question.
5. The embroidered marks of the handkerchiefs' aristocratic owners.
6. In the wrong.

7. Ore.
8. Smelted and stamped.
9. Suspected.
1. Another jab at the prime minister, Robert Walpole.

MRS. PEACHUM: Colored ones, I see. They are of sure sale from our warehouse at Redriff among the seamen.

FILCH: And this snuffbox.

MRS. PEACHUM: Set in gold! A pretty encouragement this to a young beginner.

FILCH: I had a fair tug at a charming gold watch. Pox take the tailors for making the fobs[2] so deep and narrow! It stuck by the way, and I was forced to make my escape under a coach. Really, Madam, I fear I shall be cut off in the flower of my youth, so that every now and then (since I was pumped[3]) I have thoughts of taking up[4] and going to sea.

MRS. PEACHUM: You should go to Hockley in the Hole,[5] and to Marybone, child, to learn valor. These are the schools that have bred so many brave men. I thought, boy, by this time, thou hadst lost fear as well as shame. Poor lad! How little does he know as yet of the Old Baily![6] For the first fact I'll insure thee from being hanged; and going to sea, Filch, will come time enough upon a sentence of transportation. But now, since you have nothing better to do, ev'n go to your book, and learn your catechism;[7] for really a man makes but an ill figure in the ordinary's paper,[8] who cannot give a satisfactory answer to his questions. But, hark you, my lad. Don't tell me a lie; for you know I hate a liar. Do you know of anything that hath passed between Captain Macheath and our Polly?

FILCH: I beg you, Madam, don't ask me; for I must either tell a lie to you or to Miss Polly; for I promised her I would not tell.

MRS. PEACHUM: But when the honor of our family is concerned—

FILCH: I shall lead a sad life with Miss Polly, if ever she come to know that I told you. Besides, I would not willingly forfeit my own honor by betraying anybody.

MRS. PEACHUM: Yonder comes my husband and Polly. Come Filch, you shall go with me into my own room, and tell me the whole story. I'll give thee a glass of a most delicious cordial that I keep for my own drinking.

Scene 7

[Peachum, Polly]

POLLY: I know as well as any of the fine ladies how to make the most of myself and of my man too. A woman knows how to be mercenary, though she hath never been in a court or at an assembly.[9] We have it in our natures, Papa. If I allow Captain Macheath some trifling liberties, I have this watch and other visible marks of his favor to show for it. A girl who cannot grant some things, and refuse what is most material, will make but a poor hand of her beauty, and soon be thrown upon the common.

Air 6. What shall I do to show how much I love her, etc.

Virgins are like the fair flower in its luster,
Which in the garden enamels the ground;
Near it the bees in play flutter and cluster,
And gaudy butterflies frolic around.

2. Watch-pockets.
3. Half-drowned under a pump (a punishment for pickpockets).
4. Reforming.
5. A site of boxing and bear-baiting.
6. London's main trial court.
7. Religious instruction.
8. The chaplain of Newgate (the Ordinary) often published the confessions of recently executed prisoners.
9. A fashionable social gathering.

> But, when once plucked, 'tis no longer alluring,
>   To Covent Garden[1] 'tis sent (as yet sweet),
> There fades, and shrinks, and grows past all enduring,
>   Rots, stinks, and dies, and is trod under feet.

PEACHUM: You know, Polly, I am not against your toying and trifling with a customer in the way of business, or to get out a secret, or so. But if I find out that you have played the fool and are married, you jade you, I'll cut your throat, hussy. Now you know my mind.

Scene 8

[Peachum, Polly, Mrs. Peachum]

Air 7. Oh London is a fine town

[Mrs. Peachum, in a very great passion.]

> Our Polly is a sad slut! nor heeds what we have taught her.
> I wonder any man alive will ever rear a daughter!
> For she must have both hoods and gowns, and hoops to swell her pride,
> With scarves and stays,[2] and gloves and lace; and she will have men beside;
> And when she's dressed with care and cost, all tempting, fine and gay,
> As men should serve a cowcumber,[3] she flings herself away.
> Our Polly is a sad slut, etc.

You baggage! You hussy! You inconsiderate jade! Had you been hanged, it would not have vexed me, for that might have been your misfortune; but to do such a mad thing by choice! The wench is married, husband.

PEACHUM: Married! The Captain is a bold man, and will risk anything for money; to be sure he believes her a fortune. Do you think your mother and I should have lived comfortably so long together, if ever we had been married? Baggage!

MRS. PEACHUM: I knew she was always a proud slut; and now the wench hath played the fool and married, because forsooth she would do like the gentry. Can you support the expense of a husband, hussy, in gaming, drinking, and whoring? Have you money enough to carry on the daily quarrels of man and wife about who shall squander most? There are not many husbands and wives who can bear the charges[4] of plaguing one another in a handsome way. If you must be married, could you introduce nobody into our family but a highwayman? Why, thou foolish jade, thou wilt be as ill-used, and as much neglected, as if thou hadst married a lord!

PEACHUM: Let not your anger, my dear, break through the rules of decency, for the Captain looks upon himself in the military capacity, as a gentleman by his profession. Besides what he hath already, I know he is in a fair way of getting, or of dying;[5] and both these ways, let me tell you, are most excellent chances for a wife. Tell me hussy, are you ruined or no?

MRS. PEACHUM: With Polly's fortune, she might very well have gone off to a person of distinction. Yes, that you might, you pouting slut!

---

1. A London market for flowers, fruits, and vegetables;   3. A (worthless) cucumber.
also a haunt of prostitutes.   4. Expense.
2. Corsets.   5. He is likely to make more or to die trying.

PEACHUM: What, is the wench dumb? Speak, or I'll make you plead by squeezing out an answer from you.[6] Are you really bound wife to him, or are you only upon liking?

[*Pinches her.*]

POLLY: Oh!

[*Screaming.*]

MRS. PEACHUM: How the mother is to be pitied who hath handsome daughters! Locks, bolts, bars, and lectures of morality are nothing to them. They break through them all. They have as much pleasure in cheating a father and mother, as in cheating at cards.

PEACHUM: Why, Polly, I shall soon know if you are married, by Macheath's keeping from[7] our house.

Air 8. Grim king of the ghosts, etc.

> POLLY: *Can love be controlled by advice?*
>   *Will Cupid our mothers obey?*
>   *Though my heart were as frozen as ice,*
>   *At his flame 'twould have melted away.*
>
>   *When he kissed me so closely he pressed,*
>   *'Twas so sweet that I must have complied;*
>   *So I thought it both safest and best*
>   *To marry, for fear you should chide.*

MRS. PEACHUM: Then all the hopes of our family are gone forever and ever!

PEACHUM: And Macheath may hang his father and mother-in-law, in hope to get into their daughter's fortune.

POLLY: I did not marry him (as 'tis the fashion) coolly and deliberately for honor and money. But, I love him.

MRS. PEACHUM: Love him! worse and worse! I thought the girl had been better bred. Oh husband, husband! Her folly makes me mad! My head swims! I'm distracted! I can't support myself—Oh!

[*Faints.*]

PEACHUM: See, wench, to what a condition you have reduced your poor mother! A glass of cordial, this instant. How the poor woman takes it to heart!

[*Polly goes out, and returns with it.*]

Ah, hussy, now this is the only comfort your mother has left!

POLLY: Give her another glass, Sir; my mama drinks double the quantity whenever she is out of order. This, you see, fetches[8] her.

MRS. PEACHUM: The girl shows such a readiness, and so much concern, that I could almost find in my heart to forgive her.

Air 9. O Jenny, O Jenny, where hast thou been

> *O Polly, you might have toyed and kissed.*
> *By keeping men off, you keep them on.*

---

6. Confessions were sometimes extracted by pressing with weights.

7. Staying away from.

8. Revives.

POLLY: *But he so teased me,*
And he so pleased me,
What I did, you must have done.

MRS. PEACHUM: Not with a highwayman.—You sorry slut!

PEACHUM: A word with you, wife. 'Tis no new thing for a wench to take man without consent of parents. You know 'tis the frailty of woman, my dear.

MRS. PEACHUM: Yes, indeed, the sex is frail. But the first time a woman is frail, she should be somewhat nice[9] methinks, for then or never is the time to make her fortune. After that, she hath nothing to do but guard herself from being found out, and she may do what she pleases.

PEACHUM: Make yourself a little easy; I have a thought shall soon set all matters again to rights. Why so melancholy, Polly? Since what is done cannot be undone, we must all endeavor to make the best of it.

MRS. PEACHUM: Well, Polly, as far as one woman can forgive another, I forgive thee. Your father is too fond of you, hussy.

POLLY: Then all my sorrows are at an end.

MRS. PEACHUM: A mighty likely speech in troth, for a wench who is just married!

Air 10. Thomas, I cannot, etc.

POLLY: *I, like a ship in storms, was tossed;*
Yet afraid to put into land;
For seized in the port the vessel's lost,
Whose treasure is contraband.
The waves are laid,[1]
My duty's paid.
O joy beyond expression!
Thus, safe a-shore,
I ask no more,
My all is in my possession.

PEACHUM: I hear customers in t'other room; Go, talk with 'em, Polly; but come to us again, as soon as they are gone. But, hark ye, child, if 'tis the gentleman who was here yesterday about the repeating-watch,[2] say you believe we can't get intelligence of it till tomorrow. For I lent it to Suky Straddle, to make a figure with it tonight at a tavern in Drury Lane.[3] If t'other gentleman calls for the silver-hilted sword; you know beetle-browed Jemmy hath it on, and he doth not come from Tunbridge till Tuesday night; so that it cannot be had till then.

Scene 9

[*Peachum, Mrs. Peachum*]

PEACHUM: Dear wife, be a little pacified. Don't let your passion run away with your senses. Polly, I grant you, hath done a rash thing.

9. Careful, fastidious.
1. Have subsided.
2. An especially valuable timepiece: it announced the current hour and quarter-hour by a series of bells that

rang at the push of a button.
3. Another haunt of prostitutes; also the location of the rival theater.

MRS. PEACHUM: If she had had only an intrigue with the fellow, why the very best families have excused and huddled up a frailty of that sort. 'Tis marriage, husband, that makes it a blemish.

PEACHUM: But money, wife, is the true fuller's earth[4] for reputations, there is not a spot or a stain but what it can take out. A rich rogue nowadays is fit company for any gentleman; and the world, my dear, hath not such a contempt for roguery as you imagine. I tell you, wife, I can make this match turn to our advantage.

MRS. PEACHUM: I am very sensible,[5] husband, that Captain Macheath is worth money, but I am in doubt whether he hath not two or three wives already, and then if he should die in a Session or two, Polly's dower would come into dispute.

PEACHUM: That, indeed, is a point which ought to be considered.

Air 11. A soldier and a sailor

A fox may steal your hens, Sir,
A whore your health and pence, Sir,
Your daughter rob your chest, Sir,
Your wife may steal your rest, Sir,
   A thief your goods and plate.[6]
But this is all but picking,
With rest, pence, chest, and chicken;
It ever was decreed, Sir,
If lawyer's hand is fee'd, Sir,
   He steals your whole estate.

The lawyers are bitter enemies to those in our way.[7] They don't care[8] that anybody should get a clandestine livelihood but themselves.

Scene 10

[Mrs. Peachum, Peachum, Polly]

POLLY: 'Twas only Nimming Ned. He brought in a damask window curtain, a hoop petticoat, a pair of silver candlesticks, a periwig, and one silk stocking from the fire that happened last night.

PEACHUM: There is not a fellow that is cleverer in his way, and saves more goods out of the fire than Ned. But now, Polly, to your affair; for matters must not be left as they are. You are married then, it seems?

POLLY: Yes, Sir.

PEACHUM: And how do you propose to live, child?

POLLY: Like other women, Sir, upon the industry of my husband.

MRS. PEACHUM: What, is the wench turned fool? A highwayman's wife, like a soldier's, hath as little of his pay as of his company.

PEACHUM: And had not you the common views of a gentlewoman in your marriage, Polly?

POLLY: I don't know what you mean, Sir.

PEACHUM: Of a jointure,[9] and of being a widow.

---

4. A mineral used as a cleaning solvent.
5. Well aware.
6. Utensils plated with silver or gold.
7. In our line of work.

8. Want.
9. "Estate settled on a wife to be enjoyed after her husband's decease" (Johnson's *Dictionary*).

POLLY: But I love him, Sir: how then could I have thoughts of parting with him?

PEACHUM: Parting with him! Why, that is the whole scheme and intention of all marriage articles. The comfortable estate of widowhood is the only hope that keeps up a wife's spirits. Where is the woman who would scruple to be a wife, if she had it in her power to be a widow whenever she pleased? If you have any views of this sort, Polly, I shall think the match not so very unreasonable.

POLLY: How I dread to hear your advice! Yet I must beg you to explain yourself.

PEACHUM: Secure what he hath got, have him peached the next Sessions, and then at once you are made a rich widow.

POLLY: What, murder the man I love! The blood runs cold at my heart with the very thought of it.

PEACHUM: Fie, Polly! What hath murder to do in the affair? Since the thing sooner or later must happen, I dare say, the Captain himself would like that we should get the reward for his death sooner than a stranger. Why, Polly, the Captain knows, that as 'tis his employment to rob, so 'tis ours to take robbers; every man in his business. So that there is no malice in the case.

MRS. PEACHUM: Ay, husband, now you have nicked the matter. To have him peached is the only thing could ever make me forgive her.

Air 12. Now ponder well, ye parents dear

POLLY: *Oh, ponder well! be not severe;*
               So save a wretched wife!
           For on the rope that hangs my dear
               Depends poor Polly's life.

MRS. PEACHUM: But your duty to your parents, hussy, obliges you to hang him. What would many a wife give for such an opportunity!

POLLY: What is a jointure, what is widowhood to me? I know my heart. I cannot survive him.

Air 13. Le printemps rappelle aux armes[1]

           The turtle[2] *thus with plaintive crying,*
               Her lover dying,
           The turtle thus with plaintive crying,
               Laments her dove.
           Down she drops quite spent with sighing,
               Paired in death, as paired in love.

Thus, Sir, it will happen to your poor Polly.

MRS. PEACHUM: What, is the fool in love in earnest then? I hate thee for being particular.[3] Why, wench, thou art a shame to thy very sex.

POLLY: But hear me, Mother. If you ever loved—

MRS. PEACHUM: Those cursed playbooks she reads have been her ruin. One word more, hussy, and I shall knock your brains out, if you have any.

PEACHUM: Keep out of the way, Polly, for fear of mischief, and consider of what is proposed to you.

---

1. Spring calls to arms.   3. Odd, exceptional.
2. Turtledove.

MRS. PEACHUM: Away, hussy. Hang your husband, and be dutiful.

Scene 11

[Mrs. Peachum, Peachum]

[Polly listening.]

MRS. PEACHUM: The thing, husband, must and shall be done. For the sake of intelligence[4] we must take other measures, and have him peached the next Session without her consent. If she will not know her duty, we know ours.

PEACHUM: But really, my dear, it grieves one's heart to take off a great man. When I consider his personal bravery, his fine stratagem, how much we have already got by him, and how much more we may get, methinks I can't find in my heart to have a hand in his death. I wish you could have made Polly undertake it.

MRS. PEACHUM: But in a case of necessity—our own lives are in danger.

PEACHUM: Then, indeed, we must comply with the customs of the world, and make gratitude give way to interest. He shall be taken off.

MRS. PEACHUM: I'll undertake to manage Polly.

PEACHUM: And I'll prepare matters for the Old Baily.

Scene 12

[Polly]

Now I'm a wretch, indeed. Methinks I see him already in the cart, sweeter and more lovely than the nosegay[5] in his hand! I hear the crowd extolling his resolution and intrepidity! What volleys of sighs are sent from the windows of Holborn,[6] that so comely a youth should be brought to disgrace! I see him at the tree![7] The whole circle are in tears! Even butchers weep! Jack Ketch[8] himself hesitates to perform his duty, and would be glad to lose his fee, by a reprieve. What then will become of Polly! As yet I may inform him of their design, and aid him in his escape. It shall be so. But then he flies, absents himself, and I bar myself from his dear dear conversation! That too will distract me.[9] If he keep out of the way, my Papa and Mama may in time relent, and we may be happy. If he stays, he is hanged, and then he is lost forever! He intended to lie concealed in my room, 'till the dusk of the evening: If they are abroad, I'll this instant let him out, lest some accident should prevent him. *[Exit, and returns.]*

Scene 13

[Polly, Macheath]

Air 14. Pretty Parrot, say—

MACHEATH: *Pretty Polly, say,*
    When I was away,
    Did your fancy never stray
        To some newer lover?
POLLY: *Without disguise,*
        Heaving sighs,

---

4. "Account of things distant or secret" (Johnson's *Dictionary*).
5. Bouquet, often carried by condemned prisoners.
6. The road from Newgate to Tyburn, where criminals were hanged.

7. The gallows ("Tyburn tree").
8. England's most famous hangman (d. 1686); thereafter, any hangman.
9. Make me crazy.

> Doting eyes,
> My constant heart discover.[1]
> Fondly let me loll!

MACHEATH: O pretty, pretty Poll.

POLLY: And are you as fond as ever, my dear?

MACHEATH: Suspect my honor, my courage, suspect anything but my love. May my pistols miss fire, and my mare slip her shoulder while I am pursued, if I ever forsake thee!

POLLY: Nay, my dear, I have no reason to doubt you, for I find in the romance you lent me, none of the great heroes were ever false in love.

Air 15. Pray, fair one, be kind

MACHEATH: *My heart was so free,*
> *It roved like the bee,*
> *'Till Polly my passion requited;*
> *I sipped each flower,*
> *I changed ev'ry hour,*
> *But here ev'ry flower is united.*

POLLY: Were you sentenced to transportation, sure, my dear, you could not leave me behind you—could you?

MACHEATH: Is there any power, any force that could tear me from thee? You might sooner tear a pension out of the hands of a courtier, a fee from a lawyer, a pretty woman from a looking glass, or any woman from quadrille. But to tear me from thee is impossible!

Air 16. Over the hills and far away

> *Were I laid on Greenland's coast,*
> *And in my arms embraced my lass;*
> *Warm amidst eternal frost,*
> *Too soon the half year's night[2] would pass.*

POLLY: *Were I sold on Indian soil,*
> *Soon as the burning day was closed,*
> *I could mock the sultry toil,*
> *When on my charmer's breast reposed.*

MACHEATH: *And I would love you all the day,*
POLLY: *Every night would kiss and play,*
MACHEATH: *If with me you'd fondly stray*
POLLY: *Over the hills and far away.*

POLLY: Yes, I would go with thee. But oh!—how shall I speak it? I must be torn from thee. We must part.

MACHEATH: How! Part!

POLLY: We must, we must. My Papa and Mama are set against thy life. They now, even now are in search after thee. They are preparing evidence against thee. Thy life depends upon a moment.

---

1. Reveal, uncover.   2. The long dark winter of the polar regions.

Air 17. Gin thou wert mine awn thing—

O what pain it is to part!
  Can I leave thee, can I leave thee?
O what pain it is to part!
  Can thy Polly ever leave thee?
But lest death my love should thwart,
  And bring thee to the fatal cart,
Thus I tear thee from my bleeding heart!
  Fly hence, and let me leave thee.

One kiss and then—one kiss—begone—farewell.

MACHEATH: My hand, my heart, my dear, is so riveted to thine, that I cannot unloose my hold.

POLLY: But my Papa may intercept thee, and then I should lose the very glimmering of hope. A few weeks, perhaps, may reconcile us all. Shall thy Polly hear from thee?

MACHEATH: Must I then go?

POLLY: And will not absence change your love?

MACHEATH: If you doubt it, let me stay—and be hanged.

POLLY: O how I fear! How I tremble! Go—but when safety will give you leave, you will be sure to see me again; for 'till then Polly is wretched.

Air 18. O the broom, etc.

[*Parting, and looking back at each other with fondness; he at one door, she at the other.*]

MACHEATH: *The miser thus a shilling sees,*
  Which he's obliged to pay,
With sighs resigns it by degrees,
  And fears 'tis gone for aye.[3]

POLLY: *The boy, thus, when his sparrow's flown,*
  The bird in silence eyes;
But soon as out of sight 'tis gone,
  Whines, whimpers, sobs, and cries.

ACT 2
Scene 1. A Tavern near Newgate

[*Jemmy Twitcher, Crook-fingered Jack, Wat Dreary, Robin of Bagshot, Nimming Ned, Henry Padington, Matt of the Mint, Ben Budge, and the rest of the gang, at the table, with wine, brandy, and tobacco.*]

BEN: But prithee, Matt, what is become of thy brother Tom? I have not seen him since my return from transportation.

MATT: Poor brother Tom had an accident this time twelvemonth, and so clever a made fellow he was, that I could not save him from those fleaing[4] rascals the surgeons; and now, poor man, he is among the otamys[5] at Surgeon's Hall.

---

3. Forever.
4. Flaying, robbing.

5. Skeletons (from "anatomies"). The corpses of executed criminals were often used in medical studies.

BEN: So it seems, his time was come.

JEMMY: But the present time is ours, and nobody alive hath more. Why are the laws leveled at us? Are we more dishonest than the rest of mankind? What we win, gentlemen, is our own by the law of arms, and the right of conquest.

CROOK-FINGERED JACK: Where shall we find such another set of practical philosophers, who to a man are above the fear of death?

WAT: Sound men, and true!

ROBIN: Of tried courage, and indefatigable industry!

NED: Who is there here that would not die for his friend?

HARRY: Who is there here that would betray him for his interest?

MATT: Show me a gang of courtiers that can say as much.

BEN: We are for a just partition of the world, for every man hath a right to enjoy life.

MATT: We retrench[6] the superfluities of mankind. The world is avaricious, and I hate avarice. A covetous fellow, like a jackdaw, steals what he was never made to enjoy, for the sake of hiding it. These are the robbers of mankind, for money was made for the free-hearted and generous, and where is the injury of taking from another, what he hath not the heart to make use of?

JEMMY: Our several stations[7] for the day are fixed. Good luck attend us all. Fill the glasses.

Air 19. Fill ev'ry glass, etc.

MATT: *Fill ev'ry glass, for wine inspires us,*
              And fires us
       With courage, love, and joy.
       Women and wine should life employ.
       Is there aught else on earth desirous?

CHORUS: *Fill ev'ry glass, etc.*

Scene 2

[To them enter Macheath]

MACHEATH: Gentlemen, well met. My heart hath been with you this hour; but an unexpected affair hath detained me. No ceremony, I beg you.

MATT: We were just breaking up to go upon duty. Am I to have the honor of taking the air with you, Sir, this evening upon the heath? I drink a dram now and then with the stage-coachmen in the way of friendship and intelligence; and I know that about this time there will be passengers upon the Western Road,[8] who are worth speaking with.

MACHEATH: I was to have been of that party—but—

MATT: But what, Sir?

MACHEATH: Is there any man who suspects my courage?

MATT: We have all been witnesses of it.

MACHEATH: My honor and truth to the gang?

MATT: I'll be answerable for it.

MACHEATH: In the division of our booty, have I ever shown the least marks of avarice or injustice?

---

6. Cut back, economize.   8. Through Bagshot Heath, west of London.
7. Our respective jobs.

MATT: By these questions something seems to have ruffled you. Are any of us suspected?

MACHEATH: I have a fixed confidence, gentlemen, in you all, as men of honor, and as such I value and respect you. Peachum is a man that is useful to us.

MATT: Is he about to play us any foul play? I'll shoot him through the head.

MACHEATH: I beg you, gentlemen, act with conduct and discretion. A pistol is your last resort.

MATT: He knows nothing of this meeting.

MACHEATH: Business cannot go on without him. He is a man who knows the world, and is a necessary agent to us. We have had a slight difference, and till it is accommodated I shall be obliged to keep out of his way. Any private dispute of mine shall be of no ill consequence to my friends. You must continue to act under his direction, for the moment we break loose from him, our gang is ruined.

MATT: As a bawd[9] to a whore, I grant you, he is to us of great convenience.

MACHEATH: Make him believe I have quitted the gang, which I can never do but with life.[1] At our private quarters I will continue to meet you. A week or so will probably reconcile us.

MATT: Your instructions shall be observed. 'Tis now high time for us to repair to our several duties; so till the evening at our quarters in Moor-fields[2] we bid you farewell.

MACHEATH: I shall wish myself with you. Success attend you.

[Sits down melancholy at the table.]

Air 20. March in Rinaldo, with drums and trumpets

MATT: *Let us take the road.*
    Hark! I hear the sound of coaches!
    The hour of attack approaches,
   To your arms, brave boys, and load.
     See the ball I hold!
    Let the chemists[3] toil like asses,
    Our fire their fire surpasses,
    And turns all our lead to gold.

[The gang, ranged in the front of the stage, load their pistols, and stick them under their girdles,[4] then go off singing the first part in chorus.]

Scene 3

[Macheath, Drawer[5]]

MACHEATH: What a fool is a fond wench! Polly is most confoundedly bit.[6] I love the sex. And a man who loves money might as well be contented with one guinea, as I with one woman. The town perhaps hath been as much obliged to me, for recruiting it with free-hearted ladies, as to any recruiting officer in the army. If it were not for us and the other gentlemen of the sword, Drury Lane would be uninhabited.

---

9. Pimp.
1. I.e., I will quit the gang only when I quit my life.
2. Just outside the old City wall.
3. Alchemists, who sought to turn base metals into gold.

4. Belts.
5. Bartender.
6. Ensnared.

Air 21. Would you have a young virgin, etc.

If the heart of a man is depressed with cares,
The mist is dispelled when a woman appears;
Like the notes of a fiddle, she sweetly, sweetly
Raises the spirits, and charms our ears,
   Roses and lilies her cheeks disclose,
But her ripe lips are more sweet than those.
   Press her,
   Caress her
   With blisses,
   Her kisses
Dissolve us in pleasure, and soft repose.

I must have women. There is nothing unbends[7] the mind like them. Money is not so strong a cordial for the time. Drawer! [*Enter Drawer.*] Is the porter gone for all the ladies, according to my directions?

DRAWER: I expect him back every minute. But you know, Sir, you sent him as far as Hockley in the Hole, for three of the ladies, for one in Vinegar Yard, and for the rest of them somewhere about Lewkner's Lane.[8] Sure some of them are below, for I hear the bar bell. As they come I will show them up. Coming, coming!

Scene 4

[*Macheath, Mrs. Coaxer, Dolly Trull, Mrs. Vixen, Betty Doxy, Jenny Diver, Mrs. Slammekin,*
Suky Tawdry, and Molly Brazen]

MACHEATH: Dear Mrs. Coaxer, you are welcome. You look charmingly today. I hope you don't want the repairs of quality, and lay on paint.[9]—Dolly Trull! Kiss me, you slut; are you as amorous as ever, hussy? You are always so taken up with stealing hearts, that you don't allow yourself time to steal anything else. Ah Dolly, thou wilt ever be a coquette!—Mrs. Vixen, I'm yours, I always loved a woman of wit and spirit; they make charming mistresses, but plaguy wives.—Betty Doxy! Come hither, hussy. Do you drink as hard as ever? You had better stick to good wholesome beer; for in troth, Betty, strong waters[1] will in time ruin your constitution. You should leave those to your betters.—What! And my pretty Jenny Diver too! As prim and demure as ever! There is not any prude, though ever so high bred, hath a more sanctified look, with a more mischievous heart. Ah! Thou art a dear artful hypocrite.—Mrs. Slammekin! As careless and genteel as ever! All you fine ladies, who know your own beauty, affect an undress.—But see, here's Suky Tawdry come to contradict what I was saying. Everything she gets one way she lays out upon her back. Why, Suky, you must keep at least a dozen tallymen.[2]— Molly Brazen! [*She kisses him.*] That's well done. I love a free-hearted wench. Thou hast a most agreeable assurance, girl, and art as willing as a turtle. But hark! I hear music. The harper is at the door. "If music be the food of love, play on."[3] Ere you seat yourselves, ladies, what think you of a dance? Come in. [*Enter Harper.*] Play the French tune, that Mrs. Slammekin was so fond of.

---

7. Relaxes.
8. Both in Drury Lane.
9. I hope you do not need to paint your face as women of quality do.

1. Hard liquor.
2. Merchants who provide goods on credit.
3. The opening line of Shakespeare's *Twelfth Night*.

[*A dance* à la ronde[4] *in the French manner; near the end of it this song and chorus.*]

Air 22. Cotillon

Youth's the season made for joys,
  Love is then our duty,
She alone who that employs,
  Well deserves her beauty.
  Let's be gay,
  While we may,
Beauty's a flower, despised in decay.
Youth's the season etc.

Let us drink and sport today,
  Ours is not tomorrow.
Love with youth flies swift away,
  Age is nought but sorrow.
    Dance and sing,
    Time's on the wing,
Life never knows the return of spring.

CHORUS: *Let us drink, etc.*

MACHEATH: Now, pray ladies, take your places. Here fellow. [*Pays the Harper.*] Bid the Drawer bring us more wine. [*Exit Harper.*] If any of the ladies choose gin, I hope they will be so free to call for it.

JENNY: You look as if you meant me. Wine is strong enough for me. Indeed, Sir, I never drink strong waters, but when I have the cholic.

MACHEATH: Just the excuse of the fine ladies! Why, a lady of quality is never without the cholic. I hope, Mrs. Coaxer, you have had good success of late in your visits among the mercers.[5]

COAXER: We have so many interlopers—yet with industry, one may still have a little picking. I carried a silver-flowered lutestring, and a piece of black padesoy[6] to Mr. Peachum's lock but last week.

VIXEN: There's Molly Brazen hath the ogle of a rattlesnake. She riveted a linen-draper's eye so fast upon her, that he was nicked[7] of three pieces of cambric before he could look off.

BRAZEN: Oh dear, Madam! But sure nothing can come up to your handling of laces! And then you have such a sweet deluding tongue! To cheat a man is nothing; but the woman must have fine parts indeed who cheats a woman!

VIXEN: Lace, Madam, lies in a small compass, and is of easy conveyance. But you are apt, Madam, to think too well of your friends.

COAXER: If any woman hath more art than another, to be sure, 'tis Jenny Diver. Though her fellow be never so agreeable, she can pick his pocket as coolly, as if money were her only pleasure. Now that is a command of the passions uncommon in a woman!

JENNY: I never go to the tavern with a man, but in the view of business. I have other hours, and other sort of men for my pleasure. But had I your address,[8] Madam—

4. A circular dance.
5. Dealers in textiles.
6. Types of silk fabric.
7. Robbed.
8. Polished manner.

MACHEATH: Have done with your compliments, ladies; and drink about: You are not so fond of me, Jenny, as you use to be.

JENNY: 'Tis not convenient, Sir, to show my fondness among so many rivals. 'Tis your own choice, and not the warmth of my inclination that will determine you.[9]

Air 23. All in a misty morning, etc.

Before the barn door crowing,
  The cock by hens attended,
His eyes around him throwing,
  Stands for a while suspended.
Then one he singles from the crew,
  And cheers the happy hen;
With how do you do, and how do you do,
  And how do you do again.

MACHEATH: Ah Jenny! Thou art a dear slut.

TRULL: Pray, Madam, were you ever in keeping?[1]

TAWDRY: I hope, Madam, I ha'n't been so long upon the town, but I have met with some good fortunes as well as my neighbors.

TRULL: Pardon me, Madam, I meant no harm by the question; 'twas only in the way of conversation.

TAWDRY: Indeed, Madam, if I had not been a fool, I might have lived very handsomely with my last friend. But upon his missing five guineas, he turned me off. Now I never suspected he had counted them.

SLAMMEKIN: Who do you look upon, Madam, as your best sort of keepers?

TRULL: That, Madam, is thereafter as they be.[2]

SLAMMEKIN: I, Madam, was once kept by a Jew; and bating[3] their religion, to women they are a good sort of people.

TAWDRY: Now for my part, I own I like an old fellow: for we always make them pay for what they can't do.

VIXEN: A spruce prentice, let me tell you, ladies, is no ill thing, they bleed[4] freely. I have sent at least two or three dozen of them in my time to the plantations.[5]

JENNY: But to be sure, Sir, with so much good fortune as you have had upon the road, you must be grown immensely rich.

MACHEATH: The road, indeed, hath done me justice, but the gaming table hath been my ruin.

Air 24. When once I lay with another man's wife, etc.

JENNY: *The gamesters and lawyers are jugglers[6] alike,*
      If they meddle your all is in danger.
    Like gypsies, if once they can finger a souse,[7]
    Your pockets they pick, and they pilfer your house,
      And give your estate to a stranger.

---

9. Make up your mind.
1. A kept mistress of a wealthy gentleman.
2. It depends how they treat me.
3. Apart from.
4. Spend.

5. I.e., incited them to steal and thereby caused them to be transported to the colonies.
6. Sleight-of-hand artists.
7. Get their hands on a sou (a French penny).

A man of courage should never put anything to the risk, but his life. These are the tools of a man of honor. Cards and dice are only fit for cowardly cheats, who prey upon their friends. [*She takes up his pistol. Tawdry takes up the other.*]

TAWDRY: This, Sir, is fitter for your hand. Besides your loss of money, 'tis a loss to the ladies. Gaming takes you off from women. How fond could I be of you! But before company, 'tis ill bred.

MACHEATH: Wanton hussies!

JENNY: I must and will have a kiss to give my wine a zest.

[*They take him about the neck, and make signs to Peachum and the constables, who rush in upon him.*]

Scene 5

[*To them, Peachum and constables*]

PEACHUM: I seize you, Sir, as my prisoner.

MACHEATH: Was this well done, Jenny? Women are decoy ducks; who can trust them! Beasts, jades, jilts, harpies, furies, whores!

PEACHUM: Your case, Mr. Macheath is not particular. The greatest heroes have been ruined by women. But, to do them justice, I must own they are a pretty sort of creatures, if we could trust them. You must now, Sir, take your leave of the ladies, and if they have a mind to make you a visit, they will be sure to find you at home. The gentleman, ladies, lodges in Newgate. Constables, wait upon the Captain to his lodgings.

Air 25. When first I laid siege to my Chloris, etc.

MACHEATH: *At the tree I shall suffer with pleasure,*
At the tree I shall suffer with pleasure,
Let me go where I will,
In all kinds of ill,
I shall find no such furies as these are.

PEACHUM: Ladies, I'll take care the reckoning shall be discharged.[8]

[*Exit Macheath, guarded with Peachum and constables.*]

Scene 6

[*The women remain*]

VIXEN: Look ye, Mrs. Jenny, though Mr. Peachum may have made a private bargain with you and Suky Tawdry for betraying the Captain, as we were all assisting, we ought all to share alike.

COAXER: I think, Mr. Peachum, after so long an acquaintance, might have trusted me as well as Jenny Diver.

SLAMMEKIN: I am sure at least three men of his hanging, and in a year's time too (if he did me justice) should be set down to my account.[9]

TRULL: Mrs. Slammekin, that is not fair. For you know one of them was taken in bed with me.

JENNY: As far as a bowl of punch or a treat, I believe Mrs. Suky will join with me. As for anything else, ladies, you cannot in conscience expect it.

SLAMMEKIN: Dear Madam—

8. The bill shall be paid.

9. I.e., I deserve the credit for at least three men that Peachum has had hanged.

TRULL: I would not for the world—

SLAMMEKIN: 'Tis impossible for me—

TRULL: As I hope to be saved, Madam—

SLAMMEKIN: Nay, then I must stay here all night—

TRULL: Since you command me.

[*Exit with great ceremony.*]

Scene 7. Newgate

[*Lockit, Turnkeys,*[1] *Macheath, Constables*]

LOCKIT: Noble Captain, you are welcome. You have not been a lodger of mine this year and half. You know the custom, Sir. Garnish,[2] Captain, garnish. Hand me down those fetters there.

MACHEATH: Those, Mr. Lockit, seem to be the heaviest of the whole set. With your leave, I should like the further pair better.

LOCKIT: Look ye, Captain, we know what is fittest for our prisoners. When a gentleman uses me with civility, I always do the best I can to please him. Hand them down I say. We have them of all prices, from one guinea to ten, and 'tis fitting every gentleman should please himself.

MACHEATH: I understand you, Sir. [*Gives money.*] The fees here are so many, and so exorbitant, that few fortunes can bear the expense of getting off[3] handsomely, or of dying like a gentleman.

LOCKIT: Those, I see, will fit the Captain better. Take down the further pair. Do but examine them, Sir. Never was better work. How genteelly they are made! They will sit as easy as a glove, and the nicest[4] man in England might not be ashamed to wear them. [*He puts on the chains.*] If I had the best gentleman in the land in my custody I could not equip him more handsomely. And so, Sir, I now leave you to your private meditations.

Scene 8

[*Macheath*]

Air 26. Courtiers, courtiers think it no harm, etc.

> Man may escape from rope and gun;
> Nay, some have outlived the doctor's pill:
> Who takes a woman must be undone,
>   That basilisk[5] is sure to kill.
> The fly that sips treacle is lost in the sweets,
> So he that tastes woman, woman, woman,
>   He that tastes woman, ruin meets.

To what a woeful plight have I brought myself! Here must I (all day long, 'till I am hanged) be confined to hear the reproaches of a wench who lays her ruin at my door. I am in the custody of her father, and to be sure if he knows of the matter, I shall have a fine time on't betwixt this[6] and my execution. But I promised the wench

---

1. Jailers.
2. Pay the jailer the customary bribe.
3. Escaping punishment.
4. Most discerning.

5. Mythical serpent which killed by its breath or its glance.
6. This moment.

marriage. What signifies a promise to a woman? Does not man in marriage itself promise a hundred things that he never means to perform? Do all we can, women will believe us; for they look upon a promise as an excuse for following their own inclinations. But here comes Lucy, and I cannot get from her. Would I were deaf!

Scene 9

[Macheath, Lucy]

LUCY: You base man you, how can you look me in the face after what hath passed between us? See here, perfidious wretch, how I am forced to bear about the load of infamy you have laid upon me.[7] O Macheath! Thou hast robbed me of my quiet. To see thee tortured would give me pleasure.

Air 27. A lovely lass to a friar came, etc.

> Thus when a good housewife sees a rat
>> In her trap in the morning taken,
> With pleasure her heart goes pit a pat,
>> In revenge for her loss of bacon.
>>> Then she throws him
>>> To the dog or cat,
> To be worried, crushed, and shaken.

MACHEATH: Have you no bowels,[8] no tenderness, my dear Lucy, to see a husband in these circumstances?

LUCY: A husband!

MACHEATH: In every respect but the form, and that, my dear, may be said over us at any time. Friends should not insist upon ceremonies. From a man of honor, his word is as good as his bond.

LUCY: 'Tis the pleasure of all you fine men to insult the women you have ruined.

Air 28. 'Twas when the sea was roaring, etc.

> How cruel are the traitors,
>> Who lie and swear in jest,
> To cheat unguarded creatures
>> Of virtue, fame, and rest!
> Whoever steals a shilling,
>> Through shame the guilt conceals:
> In love the perjured villain
>> With boasts the theft reveals.

MACHEATH: The very first opportunity, my dear (have but patience), you shall be my wife in whatever manner you please.

LUCY: Insinuating monster! And so you think I know nothing of the affair of Miss Polly Peachum. I could tear thy eyes out!

HEATH: Sure Lucy, you can't be such a fool as to be jealous of Polly!

LUCY: Are you not married to her, you brute you?

---

7. I.e., she is pregnant.   8. The bodily seat of tenderness, pity.

MACHEATH: Married! Very good. The wench gives it out only to vex thee, and to ruin me in thy good opinion. 'Tis true, I go to the house; I chat with the girl, I kiss her, I say a thousand things to her (as all gentlemen do) that mean nothing, to divert myself; and now the silly jade hath set it about that I am married to her, to let me know what she would be at. Indeed, my dear Lucy, these violent passions may be of ill consequence to a woman in your condition.

LUCY: Come, come, Captain, for all your assurance, you know that Miss Polly hath put it out of your power to do me the justice you promised me.

MACHEATH: A jealous woman believes everything her passion suggests. To convince you of my sincerity, if we can find the ordinary,[9] I shall have no scruples of making you my wife; and I know the consequence of having two at a time.

LUCY: That you are only to be hanged, and so get rid of them both.

MACHEATH: I am ready, my dear Lucy, to give you satisfaction—if you think there is any in marriage. What can a man of honor say more?

LUCY: So then it seems, you are not married to Miss Polly.

MACHEATH: You know, Lucy, the girl is prodigiously conceited. No man can say a civil thing to her, but (like other fine ladies) her vanity makes her think he's her own for ever and ever.

Air 29. The sun had loosed his weary teams, etc.

> The first time at the lookingglass
>   The mother sets her daughter,
> The image strikes the smiling lass
>   With self-love ever after.
> Each time she looks, she, fonder grown,
>   Thinks ev'ry charm grows stronger.
> But alas, vain maid, all eyes but your own
>   Can see you are not younger.

When women consider their own beauties, they are all alike unreasonable in their demands; for they expect their lovers should like them as long as they like themselves.

LUCY: Yonder is my father—perhaps this way we may light upon the ordinary, who shall try if you will be as good as your word. For I long to be made an honest woman.

Scene 10

[Peachum, Lockit with an account book]

LOCKIT: In this last affair, Brother Peachum, we are agreed. You have consented to go halves in Macheath.

PEACHUM: We shall never fall out about an execution. But as to that article, pray how stands our last year's account?

LOCKIT: If you will run your eye over it, you'll find 'tis fair and clearly stated.

PEACHUM: This long arrear[1] of the government is very hard upon us! Can it be expected that we should hang our acquaintance for nothing, when our betters will

---

9. The prison chaplain.   1. Lateness in the payment of debts.

hardly save theirs without being paid for it. Unless the people in employment pay better, I promise them for the future, I shall let other rogues live besides their own.

LOCKIT: Perhaps, Brother, they are afraid these matters may be carried too far. We are treated too by them with contempt, as if our profession was not reputable.

PEACHUM: In one respect indeed, our employment may be reckoned dishonest, because like great statesmen, we encourage those who betray their friends.

LOCKIT: Such language, Brother, anywhere else, might turn to your prejudice.[2] Learn to be more guarded, I beg you.

Air 30. How happy are we, etc.

> When you censure the age,
> Be cautious and sage,
> Lest the courtiers offended should be:
> If you mention vice or bribe,
> 'Tis so pat[3] to all the tribe;
> Each cries, "That was leveled at me!"

PEACHUM: Here's poor Ned Clincher's name, I see. Sure, Brother Lockit, there was a little unfair proceeding in Ned's case: for he told me in the condemned hold,[4] that for value received, you had promised him a Session or two longer without molestation.

LOCKIT: Mr. Peachum, this is the first time my honor was ever called in question.

PEACHUM: Business is at an end if once we act dishonorably.

LOCKIT: Who accuses me?

PEACHUM: You are warm,[5] Brother.

LOCKIT: He that attacks my honor, attacks my livelihood. And this usage, Sir, is not to be borne.

PEACHUM: Since you provoke me to speak, I must tell you too, that Mrs. Coaxer charges you with defrauding her of her information money[6] for the apprehending of curl-pated Hugh. Indeed, indeed, Brother, we must punctually pay our spies, or we shall have no information.

LOCKIT: Is this language to me, Sirrah, who have saved you from the gallows, Sirrah!

[Collaring each other.]

PEACHUM: If I am hanged, it shall be for ridding the world of an arrant rascal.

LOCKIT: This hand shall do the office of the halter[7] you deserve, and throttle you—you dog!—

PEACHUM: Brother, Brother, we are both in the wrong. We shall be both losers in the dispute—for you know we have it in our power to hang each other. You should not be so passionate.

LOCKIT: Nor you so provoking.

PEACHUM: 'Tis our mutual interest; 'tis for the interest of the world we should agree. If I said anything, Brother, to the prejudice of your character, I ask pardon.

LOCKIT: Brother Peachum, I can forgive as well as resent. Give me your hand. Suspicion does not become a friend.

---

2. Be used against you.
3. Suitable.
4. Death row.

5. Angry.
6. Reward for informing on someone.
7. Noose.

PEACHUM: I only meant to give you occasion to justify yourself. But I must now step home, for I expect the gentleman about this snuffbox that Filch nimmed two nights ago in the park. I appointed him at this hour.

Scene 11

[Lockit, Lucy]

LOCKIT: Whence come you, hussy?

LUCY: My tears might answer that question.

LOCKIT: You have then been whimpering and fondling, like a spaniel, over the fellow that hath abused you.

LUCY: One can't help love; one can't cure it. 'Tis not in my power to obey you, and hate him.

LOCKIT: Learn to bear your husband's death like a reasonable woman. 'Tis not the fashion, nowadays, so much as to affect sorrow upon these occasions. No woman would ever marry, if she had not the chance of mortality for a release. Act like a woman of spirit, hussy, and thank your father for what he is doing.

Air 31. Of a noble race was Shenkin

LUCY: *Is then his fate decreed, Sir?*
          Such a man can I think of quitting?
     When first we met, so moves me yet,
          O see how my heart is splitting!

LOCKIT: Look ye, Lucy, there is no saving him. So, I think, you must do like other widows: buy yourself weeds,[8] and be cheerful.

Air 32

You'll think ere many days ensue
     This sentence not severe;
I hang your husband, child, 'tis true,
     But with him hang your care.
          Twang dang dillo dee.

Like a good wife, go moan over your dying husband. That, child, is your duty. Consider, girl, you can't have the man and the money too—so make yourself as easy as you can, by getting all you can from him.

Scene 12

[Lucy, Macheath]

LUCY: Though the ordinary was out of the way today, I hope, my dear, you will, upon the first opportunity, quiet my scruples. Oh, Sir! My father's hard heart is not to be softened, and I am in the utmost despair.

MACHEATH: But if I could raise a small sum—would not twenty guineas, think you, move him? Of all the arguments in the way of business, the perquisite[9] is the most prevailing. Your father's perquisites for the escape of prisoners must amount

---

8. A widow's mourning clothes.   9. Tip.

to a considerable sum in the year. Money well timed, and properly applied, will do anything.

Air 33. London ladies

> *If you at an office solicit your due,[1]*
>   *And would not have matters neglected;*
> *You must quicken the clerk with the perquisite too,*
>   *To do what his duty directed.*
> *Or would you the frowns of a lady prevent,*
>   *She too has this palpable failing,*
> *The perquisite softens her into consent;*
>   *That reason with all is prevailing.*

LUCY: What love or money can do shall be done: for all my comfort depends upon your safety.

Scene 13

[Lucy, Macheath, Polly]

POLLY: Where is my dear husband? Was a rope ever intended for this neck! O let me throw my arms about it, and throttle thee with love! Why dost thou turn away from me? 'Tis thy Polly. 'Tis thy wife.

MACHEATH: Was ever such an unfortunate rascal as I am!

LUCY: Was there ever such another villain!

POLLY: O Macheath! Was it for this we parted? Taken! Imprisoned! Tried! Hanged! Cruel reflection! I'll stay with thee 'till death. No force shall tear thy dear wife from thee now. What means my love? Not one kind word! Not one kind look! Think what thy Polly suffers to see thee in this condition.

Air 34. All in the downs, etc.

> *Thus when the swallow, seeking prey,*
>   *Within the sash[2] is closely pent,*
> *His comfort, with bemoaning lay,[3]*
>   *Without sits pining for th' event.*
> *Her chatt'ring lovers all around her skim;*
>   *She heeds them not (poor bird!) her soul's with him.*

MACHEATH: I must disown her. [*Aside.*] The wench is distracted.

LUCY: Am I then bilked of my virtue? Can I have no reparation? Sure men were born to lie, and women to believe them! O villain! Villain!

POLLY: Am I not thy wife? Thy neglect of me, thy aversion to me too severely proves it. Look on me. Tell me, am I not thy wife?

LUCY: Perfidious wretch!

POLLY: Barbarous husband!

LUCY: Hadst thou been hanged five months ago, I had been happy.

---

1. Seek what is due to you.
2. Window frame.

3. Plaintive song.

POLLY: And I too. If you had been kind to me 'till death, it would not have vexed me. And that's no very unreasonable request (though from a wife) to a man who hath not above seven or eight days to live.

LUCY: Art thou then married to another? Hast thou two wives, monster?

MACHEATH: If women's tongues can cease for an answer—hear me.

LUCY: I won't. Flesh and blood can't bear my usage.

POLLY: Shall I not claim my own? Justice bids me speak.

Air 35. Have you heard of a frolicsome ditty, etc.

MACHEATH: *How happy could I be with either,*
    Were t'other dear charmer away!
    But while you thus tease me together,
      To neither a word will I say;
      But tol de rol, etc.

POLLY: Sure, my dear, there ought to be some preference shown to a wife! At least she may claim the appearance of it. He must be distracted with his misfortunes, or he could not use me thus!

LUCY: O villain, villain! Thou hast deceived me. I could even inform against thee with pleasure. Not a prude wishes more heartily to have facts against her intimate acquaintance, than I now wish to have facts against thee. I would have her satisfaction, and they should all out.

Air 36. Irish trot

POLLY: *I'm bubbled.*[4]

LUCY: *I'm bubbled.*

POLLY: *Oh how I am troubled!*

LUCY: *Bamboozled, and bit!*

POLLY: *My distresses are doubled.*

LUCY: *When you come to the tree, should the hangman refuse,*
    These fingers, with pleasure, could fasten the noose.

POLLY: *I'm bubbled, etc.*

MACHEATH: Be pacified, my dear Lucy. This is all a fetch[5] of Polly's, to make me desperate with[6] you in case I get off. If I am hanged, she would fain[7] the credit of being thought my widow. Really, Polly, this is no time for a dispute of this sort; for whenever you are talking of marriage, I am thinking of hanging.

POLLY: And hast thou the heart to persist in disowning me?

MACHEATH: And hast thou the heart to persist in persuading me that I am married? Why, Polly, dost thou seek to aggravate my misfortunes?

LUCY: Really, Miss Peachum, you but expose yourself. Besides, 'tis barbarous in you to worry a gentleman in his circumstances.

Air 37

POLLY: *Cease your funning;*
      Force or cunning

---

4. Cheated, fooled.
5. Trick.

6. Ruin my hopes of having.
7. Would like.

> Never shall my heart trapan.[8]
>   All these sallies
>   Are but malice
> To seduce my constant man.
>   'Tis most certain,
>   By their flirting
> Women oft, have envy shown;
>   Pleased, to ruin
>   Others' wooing;
> Never happy in their own!

POLLY: Decency, Madam, methinks might teach you to behave yourself with some reserve with the husband, while his wife is present.

MACHEATH: But seriously, Polly, this is carrying the joke a little too far.

LUCY: If you are determined, Madam, to raise a disturbance in the prison, I shall be obliged to send for the turnkey to show you the door. I am sorry, Madam, you force me to be so ill-bred.

POLLY: Give me leave to tell you, Madam. These forward airs don't become you in the least, Madam. And my duty, Madam, obliges me to stay with my husband, Madam.

Air 38. Good-morrow, gossip Joan

LUCY: *Why how now, Madam Flirt?*
>   *If you thus must chatter;*
> *And are for flinging dirt,*
>   *Let's try who best can spatter;*
>   *Madam Flirt!*

POLLY: *Why how now, saucy jade;*
>   *Sure the wench is tipsy!*

[To him.]   *How can you see me made*
> *The scoff of such a gypsy?*

[To her.]   *Saucy jade!*

Scene 14

[Lucy, Macheath, Polly, Peachum]

PEACHUM: Where's my wench? Ah, hussy! Hussy! Come you home, you slut; and when your fellow is hanged, hang yourself, to make your family some amends.

POLLY: Dear, dear father, do not tear me from him—I must speak; I have more to say to him. Oh! Twist thy fetters about me, that he may not haul me from thee!

PEACHUM: Sure all women are alike! If ever they commit the folly, they are sure to commit another by exposing themselves. Away—not a word more. You are my prisoner now, hussy.

Air 39. Irish howl

POLLY: *No power on earth can e'er divide*
> *The knot that sacred love hath tied.*

---

8. Esnare.

When parents draw against our mind,[9]
The true-love's knot they faster bind.
    Oh, oh ray, oh Amborah, oh, oh, etc.

                          [*Holding Macheath, Peachum pulling her.*]

Scene 15

[*Lucy, Macheath*]

MACHEATH: I am naturally compassionate, wife, so that I could not use the wench as she deserved, which made you at first suspect there was something in what she said.

LUCY: Indeed, my dear, I was strangely puzzled.

MACHEATH: If that had been the case, her father would never have brought me into this circumstance. No, Lucy, I had rather die than be false to thee.

LUCY: How happy am I, if you say this from your heart! For I love thee so, that I could sooner bear to see thee hanged than in the arms of another.

MACHEATH: But couldst thou bear to see me hanged?

LUCY: O, Macheath, I can never live to see that day.

MACHEATH: You see, Lucy, in the account of love you are in my debt, and you must now be convinced, that I rather choose to die than be another's. Make me, if possible, love thee more, and let me owe my life to thee. If you refuse to assist me, Peachum and your father will immediately put me beyond all means of escape.

LUCY: My father, I know, hath been drinking hard with the prisoners, and I fancy he is now taking his nap in his own room. If I can procure the keys, shall I go off with thee, my dear?

MACHEATH: If we are together, 'twill be impossible to lie concealed. As soon as the search begins to be a little cool, I will send to thee. 'Till then my heart is thy prisoner.

LUCY: Come then, my dear husband, owe thy life to me, and though you love me not, be grateful. But that Polly runs in my head strangely.

MACHEATH: A moment of time may make us unhappy forever.

Air 40. The lass of Patie's mill, etc.

LUCY: *I like the fox shall grieve,*
        Whose mate hath left her side.
    Whom hounds, from morn to eve,
        Chase o'er the country wide.
    Where can my lover hide?
    Where cheat the weary pack?
    If love be not his guide,
        He never will come back!

9. Pull against our wishes.

ACT 3

Scene 1. Newgate

[Lockit, Lucy]

LOCKIT: To be sure, wench, you must have been aiding and abetting to help him to this escape.

LUCY: Sir, here hath been Peachum and his daughter Polly, and to be sure they know the ways of Newgate as well as if they had been born and bred in the place all their lives. Why must all your suspicion light upon me?

LOCKIT: Lucy, Lucy, I will have none of these shuffling answers.

LUCY: Well then, if I know anything of him I wish I may be burnt!

LOCKIT: Keep your temper, Lucy, or I shall pronounce you guilty.

LUCY: Keep yours, Sir, I do wish I may be burned. I do—and what can I say more to convince you?

LOCKIT: Did he tip handsomely? How much did he come down with? Come hussy, don't cheat your father; and I shall not be angry with you. Perhaps you have made a better bargain with him than I could have done. How much, my good girl?

LUCY: You know, Sir, I am fond of him, and would have given money to have kept him with me.

LOCKIT: Ah, Lucy! Thy education might have put thee more upon thy guard; for a girl in the bar of an alehouse is always besieged.

LUCY: Dear Sir, mention not my education—for 'twas to that I owe my ruin.

Air 41. If love's a sweet passion, etc.

When young at the bar you first taught me to score,[1]
And bid me be free of my lips, and no more;
I was kissed by the parson, the squire, and the sot.
When the guest was departed, the kiss was forgot.
But his kiss was so sweet, and so closely he pressed,
That I languished and pined till I granted the rest.

If you can forgive me, Sir, I will make a fair confession, for to be sure he hath been a most barbarous villain to me.

LOCKIT: And so you have let him escape, hussy? Have you?

LUCY: When a woman loves, a kind look, a tender word can persuade her to anything, and I could ask no other bribe.

LOCKIT: Thou wilt always be a vulgar[2] slut, Lucy. If you would not be looked upon as a fool, you should never do anything but upon the foot of[3] interest. Those that act otherwise are their own bubbles.[4]

LUCY: But love, Sir, is a misfortune that may happen to the most discreet woman, and in love we are all fools alike. Notwithstanding all he swore, I am now fully convinced that Polly Peachum is actually his wife. Did I let him escape (fool that I was!) to go to her? Polly will wheedle herself into his money, and then Peachum will hang him, and cheat us both.

LOCKIT: So I am to be ruined, because, forsooth, you must be in love! A very pretty excuse!

---

1. Tally, keep an account.   3. For the sake of.
2. Common.   4. Cheat themselves.

LUCY: I could murder that impudent happy strumpet. I gave him his life, and that creature enjoys the sweets of it. Ungrateful Macheath!

Air 42. South Sea ballad

My love is all madness and folly,
    Alone I lie,
    Toss, tumble, and cry,
What a happy creature is Polly!
Was e'er such a wretch as I!
With rage I redden like scarlet,
That my dear inconstant varlet,
    Stark blind to my charms,
    Is lost in the arms
Of that jilt, that inveigling harlot!
    Stark blind to my charms,
    Is lost in the arms
Of that jilt, that inveigling harlot!
This, this my resentment alarms.

LOCKIT: And so, after all this mischief, I must stay here to be entertained with your caterwauling, Mistress Puss! Out of my sight, wanton strumpet! You shall fast and mortify yourself into reason, with now and then a little handsome discipline[5] to bring you to your senses. Go.

Scene 2

[Lockit]

LOCKIT: Peachum then intends to outwit me in this affair; but I'll be even with him. The dog is leaky in his liquor,[6] so I'll ply him that way, get the secret from him, and turn this affair to my own advantage. Lions, wolves, and vultures don't live together in herds, droves, or flocks. Of all animals of prey, man is the only sociable one. Every one of us preys upon his neighbor, and yet we herd together. Peachum is my companion, my friend. According to the custom of the world, indeed, he may quote thousands of precedents for cheating me. And shall not I make use of the privilege of friendship to make him a return?

Air 43. Packington's Pound

Thus gamesters united in friendship are found,
Though they know that their industry all is a cheat;
They flock to their prey at the dicebox's sound,
And join to promote one another's deceit.
    But if by mishap
    They fail of a chap,[7]
To keep in their hands, they each other entrap.
Like pikes, lank with hunger, who miss of their ends,[8]
They bite their companions, and prey on their friends.

---

5. A beating.
6. Talkative when drunk.

7. Cannot get a customer (prey).
8. Fail to catch their prey.

Now, Peachum, you and I, like honest tradesmen, are to have a fair trial which of us two can overreach the other.—Lucy! [*Enter Lucy.*] Are there any of Peachum's people now in the house?

LUCY: Filch, Sir, is drinking a quartern[9] of strong waters in the next room with Black Moll.

LOCKIT: Bid him come to me.

Scene 3

[*Lockit, Filch*]

LOCKIT: Why, boy, thou lookest as if thou wert half starved, like a shotten herring.[1]

FILCH: One had need have the constitution of a horse to go through the business. Since the favorite child-getter[2] was disabled by a mishap, I have picked up a little money by helping the ladies to a pregnancy against their being called down to sentence. But if a man cannot get an honest livelihood any easier way, I am sure, 'tis what I can't undertake for another Session.

LOCKIT: Truly, if that great man should tip off,[3] 'twould be an irreparable loss. The vigor and prowess of a knight-errant never saved half the ladies in distress that he hath done. But, boy, can'st thou tell me where thy master is to be found?

FILCH: At his lock,[4] Sir, at the Crooked Billet.

LOCKIT: Very well. I have nothing more with you.

[*Exit Filch.*]

I'll go to him there, for I have many important affairs to settle with him; and in the way of those transactions, I'll artfully get into his secret. So that Macheath shall not remain a day longer out of my clutches.

Scene 4. A Gaming House

[*Macheath in a fine tarnished coat, Ben Budge, Matt of the Mint*]

MACHEATH: I am sorry, gentlemen, the road was so barren of money. When my friends are in difficulties, I am always glad that my fortune can be serviceable to them. [*Gives them money.*] You see, gentlemen, I am not a mere Court friend, who professes everything and will do nothing.

Air 44. Lillibullero

> *The modes of the Court so common are grown,*
> *   That a true friend can hardly be met;*
> *Friendship for interest is but a loan,*
> *   Which they let out for what they can get.*
> *   'Tis true, you find*
> *   Some friends so kind,*
> *Who will give you good counsel themselves to defend.*
> *   In sorrowful ditty,*

---

9. Quarter-pint.
1. A herring that has spawned.
2. Begetter (i.e., Macheath).

3. Die.
4. A cant word signifying a warehouse where stolen goods are deposited [Gay's note].

> *They promise, they pity,*
> *But shift you[5] for money, from friend to friend.*

But we, gentlemen, have still honor enough to break through the corruptions of the world. And while I can serve you, you may command me.

BEN: It grieves my heart that so generous a man should be involved in such difficulties, as oblige him to live with such ill company, and herd with gamesters.

MATT: See the partiality of mankind! One man may steal a horse, better than another look over a hedge.[6] Of all mechanics,[7] of all servile handicraftsmen, a gamester is the vilest. But yet, as many of the quality[8] are of the profession, he is admitted amongst the politest company. I wonder we are not more respected.

MACHEATH: There will be deep play tonight at Marybone, and consequently money may be picked up upon the road. Meet me there, and I'll give you the hint who is worth setting.[9]

MATT: The fellow with a brown coat with a narrow gold binding, I am told, is never without money.

MACHEATH: What do you mean, Matt? Sure you will not think of meddling with him! He's a good honest kind of a fellow, and one of us.

BEN: To be sure, Sir, we will put ourselves under your direction.

MACHEATH: Have an eye upon the moneylenders. A rouleau,[1] or two, would prove a pretty sort of an expedition. I hate extortion.

MATT: Those rouleaus are very pretty things. I hate your bank bills. There is such a hazard in putting them off.[2]

MACHEATH: There is a certain man of distinction, who in his time hath nicked me out of a great deal of the ready. He is in my cash,[3] Ben; I'll point him out to you this evening, and you shall draw upon him for the debt. The company are met; I hear the dicebox in the other room. So, gentlemen, your servant. You'll meet me at Marybone.

Scene 5. Peachum's Lock

[A table with wine, brandy, pipes, and tobacco. Peachum, Lockit]

LOCKIT: The coronation account,[4] Brother Peachum, is of so intricate a nature, that I believe it will never be settled.

PEACHUM: It consists indeed of a great variety of articles. It was worth to our people, in fees of different kinds, above ten installments.[5] This is part of the account, Brother, that lies open before us.

LOCKIT: A lady's tail[6] of rich brocade—that, I see, is disposed of.

PEACHUM: To Mrs. Diana Trapes, the tallywoman,[7] and she will make a good hand[8] on't in shoes and slippers, to trick out young ladies, upon their going into keeping.

LOCKIT: But I don't see any article of the jewels.

---

5. Put you off.
6. I.e., one man is permitted to steal a horse, though another is not permitted even to look at one; proverbial.
7. Tradesmen.
8. The people of quality (gentry).
9. Setting upon, robbing.
1. A packet of gold coins.
2. Getting rid of them, passing them off.
3. Owes me money.

4. A manuscript inventory of items stolen during the coronation of George II; Peachum "keeps books" like an ordinary businessman.
5. I.e., the thieves have found a single coronation more than ten times as profitable as the annual installment of the new Lord Mayor.
6. Train (of a woman's dress).
7. One who provides goods on credit.
8. Profit.

PEACHUM: Those are so well known, that they must be sent abroad. You'll find them entered under the article of exportation. As for the snuffboxes, watches, swords, etc., I thought it best to enter them under their several heads.

LOCKIT: Seven and twenty women's pockets[9] complete; with the several things therein contained; all sealed, numbered, and entered.

PEACHUM: But, Brother, it is impossible for us now to enter upon this affair. We should have the whole day before us. Besides, the account of the last half year's plate is in a book by itself, which lies at the other office.

LOCKIT: Bring us then more liquor. Today shall be for pleasure, tomorrow for business. Ah, Brother, those daughters of ours are two slippery hussies. Keep a watchful eye upon Polly, and Macheath in a day or two shall be our own again.

Air 45. Down in the north country, etc.

LOCKIT: *What gudgeons[1] are we men!*
Ev'ry woman's easy prey.
Though we have felt the hook, again
We bite and they betray.
The bird that hath been trapped,
When he hears his calling mate,
To her he flies, again he's clapped
Within the wiry grate.

PEACHUM: But what signifies catching the bird, if your daughter Lucy will set open the door of the cage?

LOCKIT: If men were answerable for the follies and frailties of their wives and daughters, no friends could keep a good correspondence together for two days. This is unkind of you, Brother; for among good friends, what they say or do goes for nothing.

[Enter a servant.]

SERVANT: Sir, here's Mrs. Diana Trapes wants to speak with you.

PEACHUM: Shall we admit her, Brother Lockit?

LOCKIT: By all means. She's a good customer, and a fine-spoken woman. And a woman who drinks and talks so freely will enliven the conversation.

PEACHUM: Desire her to walk in.

[Exit servant.]

Scene 6

[Peachum, Lockit, Mrs. Trapes]

PEACHUM: Dear Mrs. Dye, your servant. One may know by your kiss, that your gin is excellent.

TRAPES: I was always very curious[2] in my liquors.

LOCKIT: There is no perfumed breath like it. I have been long acquainted with the flavor of those lips. Han't I, Mrs. Dye?

TRAPES: Fill it up. I take as large draughts of liquor, as I did of love. I hate a flincher in either.

---

9. A pocket was a detachable bag worn outside the woman's dress.
1. "A small fish . . . easily caught, and therefore made a

proverbial name for a man easily cheated" (Johnson's *Dictionary*).
2. Fastidious.

Air 46. A shepherd kept sheep, etc.

In the days of my youth I could bill like a dove, fa, la, la, etc.
Like a sparrow at all times was ready for love, fa, la, la, etc.
The life of all mortals in kissing should pass,
Lip to lip while we're young—then the lip to the glass, fa, la, etc.

But now, Mr. Peachum, to our business. If you have blacks[3] of any kind, brought in of late: mantoes,[4] velvet scarves, petticoats—let it be what it will—I am your chap, for all my ladies are very fond of mourning.

PEACHUM: Why, look ye, Mrs. Dye, you deal so hard with us, that we can afford to give the gentlemen, who venture their lives for the goods, little or nothing.

TRAPES: The hard times oblige me to go very near[5] in my dealing. To be sure, of late years I have been a great sufferer by the Parliament. Three thousand pounds would hardly make me amends. The act for destroying the Mint[6] was a severe cut upon our business. 'Till then, if a customer[7] stepped out of the way, we knew where to have her. No doubt you know Mrs. Coaxer. There's a wench now (till today) with a good suit of clothes of mine upon her back, and I could never set eyes upon her for three months together. Since the act too against imprisonment for small sums,[8] my loss there too hath been very considerable, and it must be so, when a lady can borrow a handsome petticoat, or a clean gown, and I not have the least hank[9] upon her! And, o' my conscience, now-a-days most ladies take a delight in cheating, when they can do it with safety.

PEACHUM: Madam, you had a handsome gold watch of us t'other day for seven guineas. Considering we must have our profit, to a gentleman upon the road, a gold watch will be scarce worth the taking.

TRAPES: Consider, Mr. Peachum, that watch was remarkable, and not of very safe sale. If you have any black velvet scarves—they are a handsome winter wear; and take with most gentlemen who deal with my customers. 'Tis I that put the ladies upon a good foot. 'Tis not youth or beauty that fixes their price. The gentlemen always pay according to their dress, from half a crown to two guineas; and yet those hussies make nothing of bilking of me. Then too, allowing for accidents. I have eleven fine customers now down under the surgeon's hands[1]—what with fees and other expenses, there are great goings-out, and no comings-in, and not a farthing to pay for at least a month's clothing. We run great risks—great risks indeed.

PEACHUM: As I remember, you said something just now of Mrs. Coaxer.

TRAPES: Yes, Sir. To be sure I stripped her of a suit of my own clothes about two hours ago; and have left her as she should be, in her shift, with a lover of hers at my house. She called him upstairs, as he was going to Marybone in a hackney coach. And I hope, for her own sake and mine, she will persuade the Captain to redeem[2] her, for the Captain is very generous to the ladies.

LOCKIT: What Captain?

TRAPES: He thought I did not know him. An intimate acquaintance of yours, Mr. Peachum—only Captain Macheath—as fine as a lord.

---

3. Black clothing.
4. Loose robes (French: *manteaux*).
5. To pay as little as possible.
6. The Mint was a safe haven for debtors, and hence a gathering place for disreputable characters. The Act (10 October 1723) made it much harder to feign bankruptcy, and thereby to take refuge in the Mint.
7. Prostitute.

8. "An Act to Prevent Frivolous and Vexatious Arrests" (24 June 1726); "small sums" meant ten pounds if a Superior court matter, or 40 shillings if an Inferior.
9. Hold.
1. For treatment of venereal disease.
2. I.e., will help her to buy back (as at a pawn shop) her "suit of . . . clothes."

PEACHUM: Tomorrow, dear Mrs. Dye, you shall set your own price upon any of the goods you like. We have at least half a dozen velvet scarves, and all at your service. Will you give me leave to make you a present of this suit of nightclothes for your own wearing? But are you sure it is Captain Macheath?

TRAPES: Though he thinks I have forgot him, nobody knows him better. I have taken a great deal of the Captain's money in my time at second hand, for he always loved to have his ladies well dressed.

PEACHUM: Mr. Lockit and I have a little business with the Captain—you understand me—and we will satisfy you for Mrs. Coaxer's debt.

LOCKIT: Depend upon it. We will deal like men of honor.

TRAPES: I don't inquire after your affairs—so whatever happens, I wash my hands on't. It hath always been my maxim, that one friend should assist another. But if you please, I'll take one of the scarves home with me. 'Tis always good to have something in hand.

Scene 7. Newgate

[Lucy]

LUCY: Jealousy, rage, love, and fear are at once tearing me to pieces. How I am weather-beaten and shattered with distresses!

Air 47. One evening, having lost my way, etc.

> I'm like a skiff on the ocean tossed,
>   Now high, now low, with each billow born,
> With her rudder broke, and her anchor lost,
>   Deserted and all forlorn.
> While thus I lie rolling and tossing all night,
> That Polly lies sporting on seas of delight!
>   Revenge, revenge, revenge,
> Shall appease my restless sprite.

I have the ratsbane[3] ready. I run no risk; for I can lay her death upon the gin, and so many die of that naturally that I shall never be called in question. But say I were to be hanged—I never could be hanged for anything that would give me greater comfort than the poisoning that slut.

[Enter Filch.]

FILCH: Madam, here's our Miss Polly come to wait upon you.

LUCY: Show her in.

Scene 8

[Lucy, Polly]

LUCY: Dear Madam, your servant. I hope you will pardon my passion, when I was so happy to see you last. I was so overrun with the spleen,[4] that I was perfectly out of myself. And really when one hath the spleen, everything is to be excused by a friend.

---

3. Rat poison.
4. Generally, ill temper; more specifically, a fashionable

disease resembling hypochondria, also known as "the vapors."

Air 48. Now Roger, I'll tell thee, because thou'rt my son

> *When a wife's in her pout,*
> *(As she's sometimes, no doubt)*
> *The good husband as meek as a lamb,*
> *Her vapors to still,*
> *First grants her her will,*
> *And the quieting draught is a dram.*[5]
> *Poor man! And the quieting draught is a dram.*

I wish all our quarrels might have so comfortable a reconciliation.

POLLY: I have no excuse for my own behavior, Madam, but my misfortunes. And really, Madam, I suffer too upon your account.

LUCY: But, Miss Polly, in the way of friendship, will you give me leave to propose a glass of cordial to you?

POLLY: Strong waters are apt to give me the headache. I hope, Madam, you will excuse me.

LUCY: Not the greatest lady in the land could have better in her closet, for her own private drinking. You seem mighty low in spirits, my dear.

POLLY: I am sorry, Madam, my health will not allow me to accept of your offer. I should not have left you in the rude manner I did when we met last, Madam, had not my Papa hauled me away so unexpectedly. I was indeed somewhat provoked, and perhaps might use some expressions that were disrespectful. But really, Madam, the Captain treated me with so much contempt and cruelty, that I deserved your pity, rather than your resentment.

LUCY: But since his escape, no doubt all matters are made up again. Ah Polly! Polly! 'Tis I am the unhappy wife; and he loves you as if you were only his mistress.

POLLY: Sure, Madam, you cannot think me so happy as to be the object of your jealousy. A man is always afraid of a woman who loves him too well—so that I must expect to be neglected and avoided.

LUCY: Then our cases, my dear Polly, are exactly alike. Both of us indeed have been too fond.

Air 49. O Bessy Bell

POLLY: *A curse attends that woman's love,*
        Who always would be pleasing.
LUCY: *The pertness of the billing dove,*
        Like tickling, is but teasing.
POLLY: *What then in love can woman do?*
LUCY: *If we grow fond they shun us.*
POLLY: *And when we fly them, they pursue.*
LUCY: *But leave us when they've won us.*

LUCY: Love is so very whimsical in both sexes, that it is impossible to be lasting. But my heart is particular,[6] and contradicts my own observation.

---

5. A shot of alcohol.
6. In two senses: (1) preoccupied with one person
(Macheath), and therefore (2) idiosyncratic—an exception to the rule she has just pronounced.

POLLY: But really, Mistress Lucy, by his last behavior, I think I ought to envy you. When I was forced from him, he did not show the least tenderness. But perhaps, he hath a heart not capable of it.

Air 50. Would fate to me Belinda give

Among the men, coquettes we find,
Who court by turns all womankind;
And we grant all their hearts desired,
When they are flattered, and admired.

The coquettes of both sexes are self-lovers, and that is a love no other whatever can dispossess. I fear, my dear Lucy, our husband is one of those.

LUCY: Away with these melancholy reflections; indeed, my dear Polly, we are both of us a cup too low.[7] Let me prevail upon you, to accept of my offer.

Air 51. Come, sweet lass, etc.

Come, sweet lass,
Let's banish sorrow
Till tomorrow;
Come, sweet lass,
Let's take a chirping[8] glass.
Wine can clear
The vapors of despair;
And make us light as air;
Then drink, and banish care.

I can't bear, child, to see you in such low spirits. And I must persuade you to what I know will do you good. [*Aside.*] I shall now soon be even with the hypocritical strumpet.

[*Exit.*]

Scene 9.

[*Polly*]

All this wheedling of Lucy cannot be for nothing. At this time too! When I know she hates me! The dissembling of a woman is always the forerunner of mischief. By pouring strong waters down my throat, she thinks to pump some secrets out of me. I'll be upon my guard, and won't taste a drop of her liquor, I'm resolved.

Scene 10

[*Lucy, with strong waters; Polly*]

LUCY: Come, Miss Polly.
POLLY: Indeed, child, you have given yourself trouble to no purpose. You must, my dear, excuse me.

7. I.e., needing a drink.   8. Cheering.

LUCY: Really, Miss Polly, you are so squeamishly affected about taking a cup of strong waters as a lady before company. I vow, Polly, I shall take it monstrously ill if you refuse me. Brandy and men (though women love them never so well)[9] are always taken by us with some reluctance—unless 'tis in private.

POLLY: I protest, Madam, it goes against me. What do I see! Macheath again in custody! Now every glimmering of happiness is lost.

  [*Drops the glass of liquor on the ground.*]

LUCY [*aside*]: Since things are thus, I'm glad the wench hath escaped: for by this event, 'tis plain, she was not happy enough to deserve to be poisoned.

Scene 11

[*Lockit, Macheath, Peachum, Lucy, Polly*]

LOCKIT: Set your heart to rest, Captain. You have neither the chance of love or money for another escape, for you are ordered to be called down upon your trial immediately.

PEACHUM: Away, hussies! This is not a time for a man to be hampered with his wives. You see, the gentleman is in chains already.

LUCY: O husband, husband, my heart longed to see thee; but to see thee thus distracts me!

POLLY: Will not my dear husband look upon his Polly? Why hadst thou not flown to me for protection? With me thou hadst been safe.

Air 52. The last time I went o'er the moor

POLLY: *Hither, dear husband, turn your eyes.*

LUCY: *Bestow one glance to cheer me.*

POLLY: *Think with that look, thy Polly dies.*

LUCY: *O shun me not—but hear me.*

POLLY: *'Tis Polly sues.*

LUCY: *'Tis Lucy speaks.*

POLLY: *Is thus true love requited?*

LUCY: *My heart is bursting.*

POLLY: *Mine too breaks.*

LUCY: *Must I—*

POLLY: *Must I be slighted?*

MACHEATH: What would you have me say, ladies? You see, this affair will soon be at an end, without my disobliging either of you.

PEACHUM: But the settling this point, Captain, might prevent a lawsuit between your two widows.

Air 53. Tom Tinker's my true love

MACHEATH: *Which way shall I turn me? How can I decide?*
  Wives, the day of our death, are as fond as a bride.
  One wife is too much for most husbands to hear,
  But two at a time there's no mortal can bear.

---

9. However much women may love them.

This way, and that way, and which way I will,
What would comfort the one, t'other wife would take ill.

POLLY: But if his own misfortunes have made him insensible to mine—A father sure will be more compassionate. Dear, dear Sir, sink[1] the material evidence, and bring him off at his trial. Polly upon her knees begs it of you.

Air 54. I am a poor shepherd undone

When my hero in court appears,
    And stands arraigned for his life;
Then think of poor Polly's tears;
    For Ah! Poor Polly's his wife.
Like the sailor he holds up his hand,
    Distressed on the dashing wave.
To die a dry death at land,
    Is as bad as a wat'ry grave.
And alas, poor Polly!
    Alack, and well-a-day!
Before I was in love,
    Oh! Every month was May.

LUCY: If Peachum's heart is hardened, sure you, Sir, will have more compassion on a daughter. I know the evidence is in your power. How then can you be a tyrant to me? [*Kneeling.*]

Air 55. Ianthe the lovely, etc.

When he holds up his hand arraigned for his life,
O think of your daughter, and think I'm his wife!
What are cannons, or bombs, or clashing of swords?
For death is more certain by witness's words.
Then nail up their lips; that dread thunder allay;
And each month of my life will hereafter be May.

LOCKIT: Macheath's time is come, Lucy. We know our own affairs, therefore let us have no more whimpering or whining.

Air 56. A cobbler there was, etc.

Ourselves, like the great, to secure a retreat,
When matters require it, must give up our gang:
    And good reason why,
    Or, instead of the fry,[2]
    Ev'n Peachum and I,
Like poor petty rascals, might hang, hang;
Like poor petty rascals, might hang.

---

1. Suppress.   2. Small fish.

PEACHUM: Set your heart at rest, Polly. Your husband is to die today. Therefore, if you are not already provided, 'tis high time to look about for another. There's comfort for you, you slut.

LOCKIT: We are ready, Sir, to conduct you to the Old Bailey.

Air 57. Bonny Dundee

MACHEATH: *The charge is prepared; the lawyers are met,*
The judges all ranged (a terrible show!).
I go undismayed, for death is a debt—
A debt on demand—so take what I owe.
Then farewell my love. Dear charmers, adieu.
Contented I die—'tis the better for you.
Here ends all dispute the rest of our lives,
For this way at once I please all my wives.

Now, gentlemen, I am ready to attend you.

Scene 12

[Lucy, Polly, Filch]

POLLY: Follow them, Filch, to the court. And when the trial is over, bring me a particular account of his behavior, and of everything that happened. You'll find me here with Miss Lucy. [*Exit Filch.*] But why is all this music?

LUCY: The prisoners, whose trials are put off till next Session, are diverting themselves.

POLLY: Sure there is nothing so charming as music! I'm fond of it to distraction! But alas! Now, all mirth seems an insult upon my affliction. Let us retire, my dear Lucy, and indulge our sorrows. The noisy crew, you see, are coming upon us. [*Exit.*]

[A dance of prisoners in chains, etc.]

Scene 13. The Condemned Hold

[Macheath, in a melancholy posture]

Air 58. Happy Groves

O cruel, cruel, cruel case!
Must I suffer this disgrace?

Air 59. Of all the girls that are so smart

Of all the friends in time of grief,
When threatening death looks grimmer,
Not one so sure can bring relief,
As this best friend, a brimmer.[3]

[*Drinks.*]

---

3. A cup filled to the brim.

Air 60. Britons strike home

Since I must swing, I scorn, I scorn to wince or whine.

[Rises.]

Air 61. Chevy Chase

But now again my spirits sink;
I'll raise them high with wine.

[Drinks a glass of wine.]

Air 62. To old Sir Simon the king

But valor the stronger grows,
The stronger liquor we're drinking.
And how can we feel our woes,
When we've lost the trouble of thinking?   [Drinks.]

Air 63. Joy to great Caesar

If thus—A man can die
Much bolder with brandy.

[Pours out a bumper of brandy.]

Air 64. There was an old woman

So I drink off this bumper. And now I can stand the test.
And my comrades shall see, that I die as brave as the best.   [Drinks.]

Air 65. Did you ever hear of a gallant sailor

But can I leave my pretty hussies,
Without one tear, or tender sigh?

Air 66. Why are mine eyes still flowing

Their eyes, their lips, their busses[4]
Recall my love—Ah must I die?

Air 67. Green Sleeves

Since laws were made for ev'ry degree,
To curb vice in others, as well as me,
I wonder we ha'n't better company,
      Upon Tyburn tree!

4. Kisses.

> *But gold from law can take out the sting;*
> *And if rich men like us were to swing,*
> *'Twould thin the land, such numbers to string*
>   *Upon Tyburn tree!*

JAILER: Some friends of yours, Captain, desire to be admitted. I leave you together.

Scene 14

[*Macheath, Ben Budge, Matt of the Mint*]

MACHEATH: For my having broke[5] prison, you see, gentlemen, I am ordered immediate execution. The sheriff's officers, I believe, are now at the door. That Jemmy Twitcher should peach me, I own surprised me! 'Tis a plain proof that the world is all alike, and that even our gang can no more trust one another than other people. Therefore, I beg you, gentlemen, look well to yourselves, for in all probability you may live some months longer.

MATT: We are heartily sorry, Captain, for your misfortune. But 'tis what we must all come to.

MACHEATH: Peachum and Lockit, you know, are infamous scoundrels. Their lives are as much in your power, as yours are in theirs. Remember your dying friend. 'Tis my last request. Bring those villains to the gallows before you, and I am satisfied.

MATT: We'll do't.

JAILER: Miss Polly and Miss Lucy entreat a word with you.

MACHEATH: Gentlemen, adieu.

Scene 15

[*Lucy, Macheath, Polly*]

MACHEATH: My dear Lucy—my dear Polly—whatsoever hath passed between us is now at an end. If you are fond of marrying again, the best advice I can give you is to ship yourselves off for the West Indies, where you'll have a fair chance of getting a husband apiece; or by good luck, two or three, as you like best.

POLLY: How can I support this sight!

LUCY: There is nothing moves one so much as a great man in distress.

Air 68. All you that must take a leap, etc.

LUCY: *Would I might be hanged!*
POLLY: *And I would so too!*
LUCY: *To be hanged with you.*
POLLY: *My dear, with you.*
MACHEATH: *O leave me to thought! I fear! I doubt!*
    I tremble! I droop! See, my courage is out.   [*Turns up the empty bottle.*]

POLLY: *No token of love?*
MACHEATH: *See, my courage is out.*   [*Turns up the empty pot.*]
LUCY: *No token of love?*
POLLY: *Adieu!*
LUCY: *Farewell!*
MACHEATH: *But hark! I hear the toll of the bell.*

5. Broken out of.

CHORUS: *Tol de rol lol, etc.*
    [*Enter the Jailer.*]
JAILER: Four women more, Captain, with a child a-piece! See, here they come.
    [*Enter women and children.*]
MACHEATH: What—four wives more! This is too much. Here—tell the sheriff's
    officers I am ready.

[Exit Macheath guarded.]

Scene 16

[To them, enter Player and Beggar]

PLAYER: But, honest friend, I hope you don't intend that Macheath shall be really
    executed.
BEGGAR: Most certainly, Sir. To make the piece perfect, I was for doing strict poet-
    ical justice. Macheath is to be hanged; and for the other personages of the drama,
    the audience must have supposed they were all either hanged or transported.
PLAYER: Why then, friend, this is a downright deep tragedy. The catastrophe is
    manifestly wrong, for an opera must end happily.
BEGGAR: Your objection, Sir, is very just; and is easily removed. For you must al-
    low, that in this kind of drama, 'tis no matter how absurdly things are brought
    about. So—you rabble there—run and cry a reprieve—let the prisoner be brought
    back to his wives in triumph.
PLAYER: All this we must do, to comply with the taste of the town.[6]
BEGGAR: Through the whole piece you may observe such a similitude of manners
    in high and low life, that it is difficult to determine whether (in the fashionable
    vices) the fine gentlemen imitate the gentlemen of the road, or the gentlemen of
    the road the fine gentlemen. Had the play remained, as I at first intended, it would
    have carried a most excellent moral. 'Twould have shown that the lower sort of
    people have their vices in a degree as well as the rich, and that they are punished
    for them.

Scene 17

[To them, Macheath with rabble, etc.]

MACHEATH: So, it seems, I am not left to my choice, but must have a wife at last.
    Look ye, my dears, we will have no controversy now. Let us give this day to mirth,
    and I am sure she who thinks herself my wife will testify her joy by a dance.
ALL: Come, a dance, a dance.
MACHEATH: Ladies, I hope you will give me leave to present a partner to each of
    you. And (if I may without offense) for this time, I take Polly for mine. [*To Polly.*]
    And for life, you slut, for we were really married. As for the rest—But at present
    keep your own secret.

A Dance

Air 69. Lumps of pudding, etc.

Thus I stand like the Turk, with his doxies around;[7]

---

6. The fashionable audience.   7. Like a Sultan in a harem.

> From all sides their glances his passion confound;
> For black, brown, and fair, his inconstancy burns,
> And the different beauties subdue him by turns:
> Each calls forth her charms, to provoke his desires:
> Though willing to all; with but one he retires.
> But think of this maxim, and put off your sorrow,
> The wretch of today, may be happy tomorrow.

CHORUS: *But think of this maxim, etc.*

FINIS.

1727   1728

⊷ ⊷⊱⊰⊶ ⊶

James Thomson

1700–1748

"Nature delights me in every form," James Thomson declared in a letter at age twenty-five. "I am just now painting her in her most lugubrious dress; for my own amusement describing winter as it presents itself." Though he may not have known it yet, he was "just now" embarking on his life's central work. In his long poem *The Seasons* (of which this piece on winter was the earliest installment), Thomson sought to develop a poetic structure capacious enough to compass the varied forms of nature in which he took so much delight.

Thomson wrote his letter in London, where he had recently arrived, to a friend in his native Scotland, where he would never return. The winters he remembered were those of the terrain where he had spent his first fifteen years, in a village near the border with England. When Thomson was seven, geographical proximity became political reality. The Act of Union, energetically endorsed by the poet's Whig neighbors, linked Scotland with England and Wales to form the new entity of Great Britain; that event resonates throughout the poet's life and work, in his depictions of nature (which remain centered in Scotland even as they span the globe), in his passionate advocacy of the politics he'd absorbed in youth, in his celebration of the incipient British empire.

Born to a Presbyterian minister praised for his "diligence," and to a mother noted for her "imagination," "warmth," and enthusiastic piety, Thomson felt toward both parents a lifelong affection. In deference to their wishes, and despite an early inclination to poetry, he initially planned to follow his father into the ministry. But Edinburgh, where he went at age fifteen to study divinity, abounded in literary aspirants, endeavors, publications, and societies. During his ten years there, Thomson gradually found that the attractions of poetry outflanked those of professional piety. Like many ambitious Scotsmen of the time, Thomson headed for London, along the route the Union had made smooth. There, aided and encouraged by new literary friends (Pope and Gay among them), he launched the poem of nature that he describes in his letter home. *Winter* (1726) was followed by *Summer* and *Spring* (both 1727); *The Seasons* (1730) brought the cycle to completion, with the new piece on *Autumn* added to the three earlier sections, now much expanded and revised. The work struck readers and reviewers as something altogether new, and quickly established the poet's fame. The following years produced another long poem, equally ambitious but less successful (*Liberty*, 1735–1736), a series of verse tragedies, and a plenitude of distractions. Thomson engaged exuberantly in politics and in the pleasures of food and drink, cherished his friends, and fell in love with women who did not love him back. The years also brought recurrent returns of *The Seasons*: the poem reappeared in a greatly enlarged and altered edition, in 1744, and in yet another incarnation two years later. In *The Castle of Indolence* (1748), Thomson produced an allegory, by turns serious and comic, on that very propensity toward imaginative idleness that had both generated his poetry and prevented his producing more. The poem, deeply autobiographical, proved valedictory as well. Four months after its publication the poet died, mourned by his many friends as "our old, tried, amiable, open, and honest-hearted Thomson," and by a wider world of readers as the writer who had newly transmuted nature into language, in the century's single most popular poem.

The *Seasons* often gave rise to a measure of puzzlement commingled with its popularity. Thomson had set so much going in the poem that familiar conventions of artistic order and containment seemed overthrown. "The great defect of *The Seasons*," Samuel Johnson opined, "is its want of method"—its lack of a self-evident logical structure. Still, reader after reader (including Johnson) discovered that this seeming defect correlated mysteriously with the poem's many pleasures: its comprehensiveness, its range of tones and modes, its contagious "enthusiasm," whereby (in Johnson's account) "our thoughts expand with [Thomson's] imagery and kindle with his sentiments." Expansiveness had marked the poem's making as well as its impact. During two decades of creation and revision, Thomson kept nature at the center of his scrutiny, but made it the repository for his many preoccupations: Whig politics, imperial expansion, ancient history, Christian faith, modern science. The poem links and navigates all these topics not so much by "method" as by the restless motion of the maker's mind. In this innovative arrangement, the physical world becomes a medium of meditation, a mirror of mind and culture, the meeting place where human inquiry most fully encounters divine display, in order to discern and to wonder at the ways of both self and God. Like his idol Isaac Newton, whose discoveries pervade the poem, Thomson was reading and representing God's Book of Nature in new, immensely influential terms. "Enthusiasm" itself means immersion "in the God," possession by the divine. Thomson makes good on the term when he declares at the poem's close that the seasons "are but the varied God," phenomena that mortals must inhabit and observe with deep discernment, proper awe. Thomson's own enthusiasm proved contagious across boundaries of space, time, and medium. His poem was translated and ardently imitated in most of the languages of Europe; the composer Franz Joseph Haydn set its sentiments to music, and draughtsmen depicted its scenes so often that it remained for a hundred years the most illustrated work in English. For writers of many nations and several generations, *The Seasons* served as almost inexhaustible sourcebook, as supplementary Scripture.

from The Seasons

from Autumn

[NIGHTFALL AND NIGHT[1]]

950   But see the fading many-colored woods,
       Shade deepening over shade, the country round
       Imbrown; a crowded umbrage,° dusk and dun,   shade
       Of every hue from wan declining green
       To sooty dark. These now the lonesome Muse,
955   Low-whispering, lead into their leaf-strewn walks,
       And give the season in its latest view.[2]
           Meantime,[3] light shadowing all, a sober calm

---

1. The original version of *Winter* begins with the description of an evening in late autumn; later, Thomson revised this description and transferred it to the section on autumn, which made its first appearance in *The Seasons* (1730). Thomson repeatedly revised the poem in the years that followed; the text here is taken from the last edition he produced (1746).
2. The colors display the very end of autumn.
3. For Thomson's earlier version of this passage (lines 955–1036), see *Winter*, lines 23–79.

Fleeces unbound ether; whose least wave
Stands tremulous, uncertain where to turn
960 The gentle current; while, illumined wide,
The dewy-skirted clouds imbibe the sun,
And through their lucid veil his softened force
Shed o'er the peaceful world. Then is the time
For those whom Wisdom and whom Nature charm
965 To steal themselves from the degenerate° crowd,   *unworthy*
And soar above this little scene of things—
To tread low-thoughted Vice beneath their feet,
To soothe the throbbing passions into peace,
And woo lone Quiet in her silent walks.
970   Thus solitary, and in pensive guise,
Oft let me wander o'er the russet mead,
And through the saddened grove, where scarce is heard
One dying strain to cheer the woodman's toil.
Haply some widowed songster pours his plaint
975 Far in faint warblings through the tawny copse;
While congregated thrushes, linnets, larks,
And each wild throat whose artless strains so late
Swelled all the music of the swarming shades,
Robbed of their tuneful souls, now shivering sit
980 On the dead tree, a dull despondent flock,
With not a brightness waving o'er their plumes,
And naught save chattering discord in their note.
Oh, let not, aimed from some inhuman eye,
The gun the music of the coming year
985 Destroy, and harmless, unsuspecting harm,
Lay the weak tribes, a miserable prey!
In mingled murder fluttering on the ground!
     The pale descending year, yet pleasing still,
A gentler mood inspires; for now the leaf
990 Incessant rustles from the mournful grove,
Oft startling such as, studious, walk below,
And slowly circles through the waving air.
But should a quicker breeze amid the boughs
Sob, o'er the sky the leafy deluge streams;
995 Till choked, and matted with the dreary shower,
The forest-walks, at every rising gale,
Roll wide the withered waste, and whistle bleak.
Fled is the blasted verdure of the fields;
And, shrunk into their beds, the flowery race
1000 Their sunny robes resign. Even what remained
Of bolder fruits falls from the naked tree;
And woods, fields, gardens, orchards, all around
The desolated prospect thrills the soul.
     He comes! he comes! in every breeze the power
1005 Of Philosophic Melancholy comes!
His near approach the sudden-starting tear,
The glowing cheek, the mild dejected air,

The softened feature, and the beating heart,
Pierced deep with many a virtuous pang, declare.
1010 O'er all the soul his sacred influence breathes;
Inflames imagination; through the breast
Infuses every tenderness; and far
Beyond dim earth exalts the swelling thought.
Ten thousand thousand fleet° ideas, such   *rapid*
1015 As never mingled with the vulgar dream,
Crowd fast into the mind's creative eye.
As fast the correspondent passions rise,
As varied, and as high—devotion raised
To rapture, and divine astonishment;
1020 The love of nature unconfined, and, chief,
Of human race; the large ambitious wish,
To make them blest; the sigh for suffering worth,
Lost in obscurity; the noble scorn,
Of tyrant pride; the fearless great resolve;
1025 The wonder which the dying patriot draws,
Inspiring glory through remotest time;
The awakened throb for virtue, and for fame;
The sympathies of love, and friendship dear;
With all the social offspring of the heart.
1030   Oh! bear me then to vast embowering shades,
To twilight groves, and visionary vales![4]
To weeping grottoes, and prophetic glooms!
Where angel forms athwart the solemn dusk,
Tremendous sweep, or seem to sweep along;
1035 And voices more than human, through the void
Deep-sounding, seize the enthusiastic ear.
    Or is this gloom too much?[5] Then lead, ye powers,
That o'er the garden and the rural seat
Preside, which shining through the cheerful land
1040 In countless numbers blest Britannia sees;
O lead me to the wide-extended walks,
The fair majestic paradise of Stowe![6]
Not Persian Cyrus,[7] on Ionia's shore,
E'er saw such sylvan scenes; such various art
1045 By genius fired, such ardent genius tamed
By cool judicious art; that, in the strife,
All-beauteous Nature fears to be outdone.
And there, O Pitt,[8] thy country's early boast,
There let me sit beneath the sheltered slopes,
1050 Or in that Temple[9] where, in future times,

4. Valleys where I may see visions.
5. Thomson added lines 1036–1081 in his revision of 1744.
6. Stowe, the Buckinghamshire estate of Sir Richard Temple, Viscount Cobham (1669–1749), had been laid out and reworked by a long series of distinguished architects and landscapers; the garden was among the most celebrated of the 18th century.
7. Cyrus the Younger (d. 401 B.C.), a Persian prince, designed and planted a famous garden at Sardis (on "Ionia's

shore," the coast of Asia Minor).
8. The statesman and orator William Pitt (1708–1778) was esteemed by Thomson and Cobham as a leading voice among those Whigs opposed to the still-dominant party faction led by Robert Walpole; Pitt later became Secretary of State and Prime Minister.
9. The Temple of Virtue in Stowe Gardens [Thomson's note]; this monument to ancient heroes was one of the gardens' most celebrated buildings.

Thou well shalt merit a distinguished name;
And, with thy converse blest, catch the last smiles
Of Autumn beaming o'er the yellow woods.
While there with thee the enchanted round I walk,
1055 The regulated wild, gay Fancy° then   *imagination*
Will tread in thought the groves of Attic land;¹
Will from thy standard taste refine her own,²
Correct her pencil to the purest truth
Of Nature, or, the unimpassioned shades
1060 Forsaking, raise it to the human mind.
O if hereafter she, with juster hand,
Shall draw the tragic scene, instruct her thou,
To mark the varied movements of the heart,
What every decent³ character requires,
1065 And every passion speaks. O through her strain°   *song, style*
Breathe thy pathetic eloquence! that molds
Th' attentive senate, charms, persuades, exalts,
Of honest zeal th' indignant lightning throws,
And shakes corruption on her venal throne.
1070 While thus we talk, and through Elysian vales⁴
Delighted rove, perhaps a sigh escapes.
What pity, Cobham, thou thy verdant files
Of ordered trees shouldst here inglorious range,
Instead of squadrons flaming o'er the field,
1075 And long-embattled hosts!⁵ When the proud foe,
The faithless vain disturber of mankind,
Insulting Gaul, has roused the world to war;
When keen, once more, within their bounds to press⁶
Those polished robbers, those ambitious slaves,
1080 The British youth would hail thy wise command,
They tempered ardor and thy veteran skill.⁷

The western sun withdraws the shortened day;⁸
And humid evening, gliding o'er the sky,
In her chill progress, to the ground condensed
1085 The vapors throws. Where creeping waters ooze,
Where marshes stagnate, and where rivers wind,
Cluster the rolling fogs, and swim along

---

1. Ancient Greece (Attica was the countryside surrounding Athens).
2. Influenced by your standard of taste, Fancy will refine hers.
3. Appropriate (Thomson, who wrote several tragedies, here asks Pitt for guidance in suiting his language to his characers and their emotions).
4. The Elysian Fields at Stowe (named for Elysium, Greek myth's paradise for heroes) were the most wild and natural area of the gardens.
5. Cobham left the Walpole government in 1733; thereafter he worked on his gardens and formed a group

of opposition Whigs known as "Cobham's Cubs." Here Thomson wishes that Cobham, an accomplished soldier, might deploy his gifts as military leader rather than as shaper of landscapes.
6. I.e., contain within their own borders.
7. Thomson here imagines how effective Cobham would be as a leader in the War of the Austrian Succession (1740–1748), England's current conflict with France ("insulting Gaul," "polished robbers," "ambitious slaves").
8. Compare the earlier version of these lines in *Winter* (lines 80–96).

The dusky-mantled lawn. Meanwhile the moon,
Full-orbed and breaking through the scattered clouds,
1090 Shows her broad visage in the crimsoned east.
Turned to the sun direct, her spotted disk
(Where mountains rise, umbrageous dales descend,
And oceans roll, as optic tube° descries)   *telescope*
A smaller earth, gives all his blaze again,
1095 Void of its flame, and sheds a softer day.
Now through the passing cloud she seems to stoop,
Now up the pure cerulean rides sublime.
Wide the pale deluge floats, and streaming mild
O'er the skied° mountain to the shadowy vale,   *sky-high*
1100 While rocks and floods reflect the quivering gleam,
The whole air whitens with a boundless tide
Of silver radiance, trembling round the world.
     But when, half-blotted from the sky, her light,
Fainting, permits the starry fires to burn,
1105 With keener luster through the depth of heaven;
Or quite extinct her deadened orb appears,
And scarce appears, of sickly beamless white;
Oft in this season, silent from the north
A blaze of meteors shoots[9]—ensweeping first
1110 The lower skies, they all at once converge
High to the crown of heaven, and all at once
Relapsing quick as quickly reascend,
And mix, and thwart,° extinguish, and renew,   *cross*
All ether coursing in a maze of light.
1115   From look to look, contagious through the crowd,
The panic runs, and into wondrous shapes
Th' appearance throws—armies in meet array,
Thronged with aërial spears, and steeds of fire;
Till the long lines of full-extended war
1120 In bleeding fight commixed, the sanguine flood
Rolls a broad slaughter o'er the plains of heaven.
As thus they scan the visionary scene,
On all sides swells the superstitious din,
Incontinent;° and busy frenzy talks   *unrestrained*
1125 Of blood and battle; cities overturned,
And late at night in swallowing earthquake sunk,
Or hideous wrapped in fierce ascending flame;
Of sallow famine, inundation, storm;
Of pestilence, and every great distress;
1130 Empires subversed, when ruling fate has struck
The unalterable hour: even Nature's self
Is deemed to totter on the brink of time.
Not so the man of philosophic eye,
And inspect sage;° the waving brightness he   *wise insight*

9. The aurora borealis, or northern lights.

1135   Curious surveys, inquisitive to know
    The causes, and materials, yet unfixed,[1]
    Of this appearance beautiful, and new. * * *

1726–1746   1746

Rule, Britannia[1]

When Britain first, at Heaven's command,
    Arose from out the azure main;°   *sea*
This was the charter of the land,
And guardian angels sung this strain:
5   "Rule, Britannia, rule the waves;
    "Britons never will be slaves."

The nations, not so blest as thee,
    Must, in their turns, to tyrants fall:
While thou shalt flourish great and free,
10   The dread and envy of them all.
      "Rule," etc.

Still more majestic shalt thou rise,
    More dreadful, from each foreign stroke:
As the loud blast that tears the skies,
15   Serves but to root thy native oak.
      "Rule," etc.

Thee haughty tyrants ne'er shall tame:
    All their attempts to bend thee down
Will but arouse thy generous flame;
20   But work their woe, and thy renown.
      "Rule," etc.

To thee belongs the rural reign;
    Thy cities shall with commerce shine:
All thine shall be the subject main,
25   And every shore it circles thine.
      "Rule," etc.

The Muses, still[2] with freedom found,
    Shall to thy happy coast repair:

---

1. Unaccounted for (by science).

1. Thomson wrote several longer poems of impassioned patriotism (*Britannia*, 1729; *Liberty*, 1735–1736), but his convictions found their most enduring expression in this short piece, first performed as the climactic song of *Alfred*, a patriotic masque on the subject of the Saxon king (848–899). Defeated by the Danes, the monarch receives comfort from a "venerable bard," who expresses with uncanny prescience the 18th-century appetite for naval conquest and expanding empire. The masque was created by Thomson in collaboration with his fellow Scots expatriate David Mallet (?1705–1765) and the composer Thomas Arne (1710–1778), as part of an entertainment commissioned by Frederick, Prince of Wales, to celebrate his daughter's third birthday and the anniversary of his German grandfather's accession to the English throne. Thomson's ode outlasted its occasion, gradually acquiring the status of an alternate national anthem (just behind *God Save the King*). While the Empire endured, Thomson's song proffered for many Britons a stirring account of their national origins, essence, and destiny.

2. The word meant both "always" and "as yet."

Blest isle! with matchless beauty crowned,
30   And manly hearts to guard the fair.
         "Rule, Britannia, rule the waves;
         "Britons never will be slaves."

1740   1740

━━━┉━◈━◷━┉━━━

Thomas Gray
1716–1771

Toward the end of his most famous poem, *Elegy Written in a Country Churchyard*, Thomas Gray
commends the quietude with which the villagers have led their ordinary lives:

Along the cool sequestered vale of life
They kept the noiseless tenor of their way.

Tenor here means "course," and the line incorporates a notable revision: Gray had originally
written "silent tenor," and then written the new adjective "noiseless" above the old, without
crossing out "silent." In retrospect, this manuscript moment of alternate possibilities looks emblematic. Sickly, shy, and melancholic, Gray was often drawn toward silence but never settled
there. Words—in ancient literature and in modern history, in talk and correspondence with
his friends, in the varied idioms of his own compelling poems—exerted too strong a fascination. The fascination started early. At age nine, having weathered a bleak childhood in the
troubled London household of his irascible father and doting mother, he entered the privileged
precincts of Eton College, where his uncles worked and where he hit upon the satisfactions
that would fill his life: passionate reading (in the classics first and foremost) and passionate
friendships, with three schoolmates in particular: Richard West, Thomas Ashton, and Horace
Walpole, son of the notorious prime minister Robert Walpole. Dubbing themselves the
Quadruple Alliance, the four friends piqued themselves on a collective erudition, refinement,
and wit that set them off from their contemporaries. The links among them mattered enormously in Gray's life of writing: West inspired his poems; Walpole sponsored their publication;
and all Gray's friendships, at Eton and beyond, drew from Gray a steady flow of virtuosic letters, in which the voice of the "Alliance," at once antic and vulnerable, never abated. "His letters," remarked Walpole (whose own letters have evoked similar praise), "were the best I ever
saw, and had more novelty and wit." Gray's affections took form and motion partly from their
containment. He was homosexual; yet there is no evidence that he ever physically consum-
mated the great passions of his life—for Walpole, for West, and, in his last years, for the young
Swiss scion Charles-Victor de Bonstatten.

    After nine years at Eton, Gray was admitted to Cambridge. He found university life far
less pleasing, with its drudgeries, pressures, and solitudes, but Cambridge ultimately afforded
him a few new friendships and a permanent sanctuary. After a Grand Tour of Europe, undertaken in Walpole's company (the two men quarreled en route, after which they were estranged for five years), Gray returned to the university, ostensibly to learn law, but in fact to
pursue his own private program of study. He read widely, copiously, and systematically in
many subjects (botany, zoology, and music, as well as literature and history), making himself
one of the most learned scholars alive, and eventually becoming (in 1768) Regius Professor
of Modern History. He never delivered a lecture, and continued to spend much of his time

alone reading, but thoroughgoing privacy had long ceased to be an option. In his late thirties, Gray had stumbled, reluctantly, into enormous poetic fame. He had written Latin verse when young; in 1742, the year his beloved West died of tuberculosis, he commenced English poetry in earnest. Some of his labor's early fruits bespeak an insistent sense of loss: a sonnet on West's death (never printed during the poet's lifetime); the *Ode on a Distant Prospect of Eton College*, in which the distance is one of time as well as space; and the *Elegy*, whose completion took five years or more and whose publication in 1751 (a "distress" the poet had hoped to avoid) brought upon Gray an instantaneous, massive, and baffling celebrity. As if in recoil, he veered onto an alternate poetic path, carefully crafting over the ensuing years a set of intricate Pindaric odes, including *The Bard* and *The Progress of Poesy*; the two poems were printed, on Walpole's own press, in 1757. They provoked both admiration, as a new embodiment of poetic sublimity, and derision, as gratuitously labored, showily obscure. In the years following their murky reception, Gray wrote only a few poems and published none. He pursued other studies (including Norse literature); fell in love one final time; and died abruptly, mourned deeply by his friends and widely by a public whose thoughts and feelings about death itself he had done much to shape. In one early version of the *Elegy* the line about silence appears as an admonition addressed by the poet to himself: "Pursue the silent tenor of thy doom." In his letters (published posthumously) and in his poems, Gray worked for that doom a delicate but decisive reversal.

Elegy Written in a Country Churchyard

The curfew tolls the knell of parting day,
The lowing herd wind slowly o'er the lea,
The plowman homeward plods his weary way,
And leaves the world to darkness and to me.

5 Now fades the glimmering landscape on the sight,
And all the air a solemn stillness holds,
Save where the beetle wheels his droning flight,
And drowsy tinklings lull the distant folds;

Save that from yonder ivy-mantled tower
10 The moping owl does to the moon complain
Of such as, wand'ring near her secret bower,
Molest her ancient solitary reign.

Beneath those rugged elms, that yew-tree's shade,
Where heaves the turf in many a mouldering heap,
15 Each in his narrow cell for ever laid,
The rude forefathers of the hamlet sleep.

The breezy call of incense-breathing morn,
The swallow twitt'ring from the straw-built shed,
The cock's shrill clarion, or the echoing horn,
20 No more shall rouse them from their lowly bed.

For them no more the blazing hearth shall burn,
Or busy housewife ply her evening care:
No children run to lisp their sire's return,
Or climb his knees the envied kiss to share.

25   Oft did the harvest to their sickle yield,
Their furrow oft the stubborn glebe° has broke;   *clod of earth*
How jocund did they drive their team afield!
How bowed the woods beneath their sturdy stroke!

Let not Ambition mock their useful toil,
30   Their homely joys, and destiny obscure;
Nor Grandeur hear, with a disdainful smile,
The short and simple annals of the poor.

The boast of heraldry, the pomp of power,
And all that beauty, all that wealth e'er gave,
35   Awaits alike th' inevitable hour.
The paths of glory lead but to the grave.

Nor you, ye Proud, impute to these the fault,
If Mem'ry o'er their tomb no trophies raise,
Where through the long-drawn aisle and fretted vault
40   The pealing anthem swells the note of praise.

Can storied urn or animated bust
Back to its mansion call the fleeting breath?
Can Honor's voice provoke the silent dust,
Or Flatt'ry soothe the dull cold ear of Death?

45   Perhaps in this neglected spot is laid
Some heart once pregnant with celestial fire;
Hands that the rod of empire might have swayed,
Or waked to ecstasy the living lyre.

But Knowledge to their eyes her ample page
50   Rich with the spoils of time did ne'er unroll;
Chill Penury repressed their noble rage,
And froze the genial current of the soul.

Full many a gem of purest ray serene,
The dark unfathomed caves of ocean bear:
55   Full many a flower is born to blush unseen,
And waste its sweetness on the desert air.

Some village-Hampden[1] that with dauntless breast
The little tyrant of his fields withstood;
Some mute inglorious Milton here may rest,
60   Some Cromwell guiltless of his country's blood.

Th' applause of listening senates to command,
The threats of pain and ruin to despise,

---

1. John Hampden (1594–1643), Parliamentary statesman and general in the Civil Wars, famed for his firm defiance of Charles I.

To scatter plenty o'er a smiling land,
And read their history in a nation's eyes,

65 Their lot forbade: nor circumscribed alone
Their growing virtues, but their crimes confined;
Forbade to wade through slaughter to a throne,
And shut the gates of mercy on mankind,

The struggling pangs of conscious truth to hide,
70 To quench the blushes of ingenuous shame,
Or heap the shrine of Luxury and Pride
With incense kindled at the Muse's flame.[2]

Far from the madding crowd's ignoble strife,
Their sober wishes never learned to stray;
75 Along the cool sequestered vale of life
They kept the noiseless tenor of their way.

Yet ev'n these bones from insult to protect
Some frail memorial still erected nigh,
With uncouth rhymes and shapeless sculpture decked,
80 Implores the passing tribute of a sigh.

Their name, their years, spelt by th' unlettered muse,
The place of fame and elegy supply:
And many a holy text around she strews,
That teach the rustic moralist to die.

85 For who to dumb Forgetfulness a prey,
This pleasing anxious being e'er resigned,
Left the warm precincts of the cheerful day,
Nor cast one longing ling'ring look behind?

On some fond breast the parting soul relies,
90 Some pious drops the closing eye requires;
Ev'n from the tomb the voice of nature cries,
Ev'n in our ashes live their wonted fires.

2. According to Gray's friend William Mason, the poem originally concluded at this juncture with the following four stanzas, preserved in a manuscript at Eton College:

The thoughtless world to majesty may bow
Exalt the brave, and idolize success,
But more to innocence their safety owe
Than power and genius e'er conspired to bless.

And thou, who mindful of the unhonored dead
Dost in these notes their artless tale relate
By night and lonely contemplation led

To linger in the gloomy walks of fate,

Hark how the sacred calm, that broods around
Bids ev'ry fierce tumultuous passion cease
In still small accents whisp'ring from the ground
A grateful earnest of eternal peace.

No more with reason and thyself at strife;
Give anxious cares and endless wishes room
But through the cool sequestered vale of life
Pursue the silent tenor of thy doom.

For thee, who mindful of th' unhonored dead
Dost in these lines their artless tale relate;
95   If chance, by lonely Contemplation led,
Some kindred spirit shall inquire thy fate,

Haply some hoary-headed swain may say,
"Oft have we seen him at the peep of dawn
Brushing with hasty steps the dews away
100   To meet the sun upon the upland lawn.

"There at the foot of yonder nodding beech
That wreathes its old fantastic roots so high,
His listless length at noontide would he stretch,
And pore upon the brook that babbles by.

105   "Hard by yon wood, now smiling as in scorn,
Mutt'ring his wayward fancies he would rove,
Now drooping, woeful wan, like one forlorn,
Or crazed with care, or crossed in hopeless love.

"One morn I missed him on the 'customed hill,
110   Along the heath and near his favorite tree;
Another came; nor yet beside the rill,
Nor up the lawn, nor at the wood was he;

"The next with dirges due in sad array
Slow through the church-way path we saw him borne.
115   Approach and read (for thou can'st read) the lay,
Graved on the stone beneath yon aged thorn."

The Epitaph

Here rests his head upon the lap of earth
A youth to fortune and to fame unknown.
Fair Science frowned not on his humble birth,
120   *And Melancholy marked him for her own.*

Large was his bounty, and his soul sincere,
Heaven did a recompense as largely send:
He gave to Mis'ry all he had, a tear,
He gained from Heav'n ('twas all he wished) a friend.

125   *No farther seek his merits to disclose,*
Or draw his frailties from their dread abode,
(There they alike in trembling hope repose)
The bosom of his Father and his God.

1746–1750   1751

⟶ ⊷≡⊶⊷ ⟵

Samuel Johnson
1709–1784

James Barry, *Samuel Johnson.*

Samuel Johnson was born among books—his father sold them, not very successfully, at the family's combined home and shop in the market town of Lichfield. The son went on to create some of the most celebrated books of his age: an entire *Dictionary*, an edition of Shakespeare, a travel book, philosophical fictions, two eminent series of essays, a thick cluster of biographies. Despite his output, Johnson suffered from a chronic sense that he was underusing his talent, and throughout his *oeuvre* he wrote about "human unsuccess" (in W. H. Auden's phrase) with an empathy and acuity that few have matched before or since.

Johnson's struggles began early. An infection in infancy, followed by an attack of scrofula at age two, left his face scarred and his sight and hearing permanently impaired; by the age of eight a nervous disorder, probably Tourette's syndrome, brought on the compulsive gesticulations and intermittent muttering that would afflict him throughout his life, making him appear bizarre or even repellent at first encounter—until (as many testified) the stunning moment when he would begin to speak. His impressiveness had begun early, too. In childhood, the speed with which he acquired knowledge and the force with which he retained it astonished classmates and teachers, and also his parents, whose desire to show off his attainments often made him miserable. Johnson found more congenial mentors in his cousin, the rakish but learned young clergyman Cornelius Ford, at whose home he spent about half a year at age sixteen, and in Gilbert Walmesley, a middle-aged Lichfield lawyer, who welcomed Johnson often to his ample table and to the intelligent, disputatious company there assembled. Under Ford's and Walmesley's influence, Johnson undertook an intense but improvisatory program of reading, mostly in his father's shop. He read with a ferocious concentration that locked the texts into lifelong memory. "In this irregular manner," he later recalled, "I had looked into a great many books, which were not commonly known at the university, where they seldom read any books but what are put into their hands by their tutors; so that when I came to Oxford, Dr. Adams, now master of Pembroke College, told me, I was the best qualified for the university that he had ever known come there."

Despite such qualifications, Johnson's time at Oxford ushered in not triumph but frustration, and an oppressive sense of failure. Though he continued to be admired for his reading, and began to be noted for his writing, Johnson left the university after only thirteen months, "miserably poor" and unable to pay the fees, unbearably depressed and incapable of envisioning a viable future. After a melancholy year at home, during which his father died in debt, Johnson tried his hand at a variety of jobs beneath his earlier expectations: as assistant at a grammar school (he applied for three such positions, secured one, and left it in disgust after six months), and as occasional contributor to *The Birmingham Journal*. At Birmingham, he befriended the merchant Harry Porter and his wife Elizabeth ("Tetty"); she saw past his awkwardness at their first encounter, remarking to her daughter, "This is the most sensible man that I ever saw in my life." In 1735, ten months after her husband's death, she and Johnson married, despite wariness in both families at their difference in age (she was twenty years his senior). The new husband and wife tried to start a country boarding school, but it attracted only a handful of students. Early in 1737, Johnson decided to try something new: the life of a freelance writer in London.

The generic term for such a life was "Grub Street": it identified both an actual London street where some writers lived and plied their trade, and also the painful state of mind in which almost all of them did so, eking out precarious incomes from whatever assignments they could drum up. From the first, Johnson fared a little better than most. He attached himself immediately to Edward Cave, founder of the flourishing *Gentleman's Magazine*, in which Johnson's writing appeared plentifully over the next decade: essays, poems, short biographies, reviews, and voluminous, ingeniously fictionalized reports of debates in Parliament (authentic transcriptions were prohibited by law). The work provided some security but no prosperity: Johnson and his wife lived in poverty for many years. The struggle fueled articulate rage: in his poem *London* (1738), Johnson inveighed against the corruption of Robert Walpole's government and the cruelties of the city. Among his Grub Street colleagues he found a friend who, far more than himself, had made a sense of injury the basis of both life and art. The poet Richard Savage, generous, brilliant, and unstable, believed himself the abandoned offspring of a wealthy countess, and squandered much of his short life in the vain pursuit of recognition and redress. In *The Life of Richard Savage* (1744), published soon after his friend's early death, Johnson for the first time orchestrated many of the elements that would make his own work great: a commitment to biographical precision rather than routine panegyric; an analysis of expectation, self-delusion, and disappointment; a deep sympathy combined with nuanced judgment.

Savage was a memoir of Grub Street, but not yet for Johnson a valedictory. For two more years he continued his life of anonymous publication, narrow income, and declining spirits—"lost," as a friend lamented, "both to himself and the world." Then a new project found him. In 1746, the bookseller Robert Dodsley, struck by the erudition evident in Johnson's unsigned pieces, persuaded him to create a new dictionary of English, and assembled a consortium of publishers to finance (and profit from) the enormous undertaking. Johnson and his wife promptly moved from cramped and squalid quarters to a three-story house complete with a well-lit garret. There, with the help of six part-time assistants, Johnson made his lexicon, compiling word lists, tracking shifts and gradations of meaning, devising definitions, and illustrating them with quotations culled from the authors he most admired. The writer who (as Adam Smith later testified) "knew more books than any man alive" now decanted them discriminatingly into the two folio volumes of his *Dictionary* (1755), so as to make the work not only a standard reference for the language but also a compendium of its literature and its learning. The task took Johnson longer than he had anticipated—seven years, not three—but during this span he had busied himself in other ways as well: publishing *The Vanity of Human Wishes* (1749), a long poem on the pain of disillusion; witnessing the long-postponed production of his tragedy *Irene* (which brought him welcome added income); and composing, twice a week for two years, the periodical essay called *The Rambler* (1750–1752), the most formidable and famous instance of the genre since Addison and Steele had set down the *Spectator* forty years before. Johnson had embarked on the *Dictionary* as a virtual unknown; he emerged from the project with lasting fame and a double measure of celebratory sobriquets: he was widely known as "Dictionary Johnson," and was sometimes referred to simply (without surname) as "the Rambler."

As an epitome of his character the second label was perhaps more apt. A restlessness closely connected with loneliness had marked Johnson's mind since childhood. During the years of the *Dictionary*'s making, the loneliness had deepened. In 1752 Tetty died, and despite the strains in a marriage that had been differently difficult for both of them, Johnson mourned her obsessively for the rest of his days. He also contrived new sources of companionship, at home and in the wider world. He housed under his roof a group of eccentric, often difficult characters, including the ungainly man of medicine Robert Levet; the Jamaican servant Francis Barber; the blind Anna Williams, who waited up late every night to keep him company in his final cup of tea, often after he had spent long hours in more elevated society. He established what amounted to a second residence in the more polished household of the brewer Henry Thrale and his witty wife Hester, who welcomed and pampered not only Johnson but also the accomplished people who now rejoiced to rotate in his orbit: the actor David Garrick (who had been his pupil in the failed school and his companion on the road to London); the painter Joshua Reynolds; the politician and orator Edmund Burke; the writer Oliver Goldsmith; and Johnson's ardent young protégé and future biographer James Boswell. At the Thrales' country seat, and at the London clubs he formed to stave off solitude, Johnson sat surrounded by luminaries, savoring and often dominating the conversation. He talked (as Boswell noted) "for victory," and he generally secured it by a kind of surprise attack, a witty demolition of his companions' most familiar premises and casual assumptions. He won his listeners over by texture as well as text: by the spontaneous clarity and force of his utterance (as lexicographer he had defined every word he spoke); by the depth and energy of his voice.

Writing was by contrast largely solitary. Johnson's work pattern in the decade after the *Dictionary* recapitulated that of the one before: one ambitious, overarching project—this time an edition of all Shakespeare's plays (1765)—punctuated by shorter writings of lasting significance: a new periodical essay called *The Idler* (1758–1760); the philosophical tale *Rasselas, Prince of Abyssinia* (1759). In 1762 Johnson received a royal pension from George III in recognition of the *Dictionary*, assuring him an income of £300 a year for the remainder of his life. The pension brought Johnson a new security, along with the occasional accusation that his subsequent political pamphlets, generally favorable to the regime, amounted to paid propaganda. In fact, Johnson's politics throughout his life correlated fairly well with the views he implicitly espoused in the distinction he once drew for Boswell: "The prejudice of the Tory is for establishment; the prejudice of the Whig is for innovation." Born into a world where Whigs had long prevailed, Johnson early committed himself to Tory ways of thought: he cherished precedent, defended "subordination" (social hierarchy), and opposed Whiggish innovation with seriocomic fervor. What remained most notable about his politics was their compassion. "From first to last," John Wain remarks, Johnson "rooted his life among the poor and outcast"; in his work he argued the causes of prostitutes and slaves, of anyone sunk by the "want of necessaries" into "motionless despondence."

In the wake of his pension, Johnson's writing grew sparser, and markedly more social, compassing gestures to and for people he valued. He continued an ingrained habit of churning out prose for his friends to use under their own names: dictating law briefs for lawyers, composing sermons for preachers. He carried on an abundant and affectionate correspondence with Hester Thrale. With Boswell as companion, he traveled to the Scottish Highlands, and on his return published his account of that gregarious trip, *A Journey to the Western Islands* (1775). His final large work was social in a different sense. He accepted a commission to provide *Prefaces Biographical and Critical* for an anthology of English poets of the past hundred and fifty years. These included predecessors who had influenced him, contemporaries he had known, successors he regarded with admiration or alarm. To write their biographies, to analyze their works, was in a sense to live over his own literary life, and to reenter, at length and for the last time, the world of reading and of writing in which he'd now made his way for almost seven decades.

"Our social comforts drop away," Johnson lamented when his friend Levet died in 1782; his own last years were marred by loss. Successive deaths shrunk his contentious household; his friendship with Hester Thrale disintegrated under the pressure of her passion for a man of whom Johnson disapproved; a stroke temporarily deprived him of speech and ushered in his final difficult illness. At his death, an admirer remarked that Johnson had left "a chasm, which not only nothing can fill up, but which nothing has a tendency to fill up. Johnson is dead. Let us go to the next best:—there is nobody: no man can be said to put you in mind of Johnson." Biographers rushed in to fill the chasm, with the testimony of friends and of detractors, and with transcriptions of the hypnotic talk that many of them (notably Boswell and Thrale) had begun to record decades before. For most of the nineteenth century the fame of Johnson's talk far surpassed that of his writing. In recent decades scholars and readers have redressed the balance, finding in Johnson's prose and verse the richest repositories of his thought. Throughout a life of arduous struggle, prodigious accomplishment, and (in the end) near-matchless celebrity, Johnson wrote most eloquently and most feelingly—even in the *Dictionary*, even in literary criticism—of human vulnerabilities: to hope and disappointment, suffering and loss.

THE VANITY OF HUMAN WISHES   In his *Life of Pope*, Johnson defines the imitation, a poetic form much in vogue during the late seventeenth and early eighteenth centuries, as a "mode . . . in which the ancients are familiarized by adapting their sentiments to modern topics. . . . It is a kind of middle composition between translation and original design, which pleases when the thoughts are unexpectedly applicable and the parallels lucky." *The Vanity of Human Wishes* is Johnson's most sustained and successful endeavor in the mode. In the second century A.D., the Roman poet Juvenal had written an enduring satire on human ambition and failure, drawing vivid instances from history and from contemporary life. Johnson does the same, replacing the Roman's ancient examples with modern ones, supplanting his Stoic "sentiments" with a Christian credo. Johnson produced his imitation quickly, composing the whole of it in his mind before writing any of it down. It was the first work to appear under his own name, after more than a decade of abundant but anonymous publications. Its title and text sound themes that would preoccupy him for the remainder of his writing life: the dangers of desire, the inevitability of disappointment, the necessity of faith. *The Vanity of Human Wishes* is Johnson's signature poem in more ways than one.

The Vanity of Human Wishes
The Tenth Satire of Juvenal Imitated

Let Observation, with extensive view,
Survey mankind, from China to Peru;
Remark each anxious toil, each eager strife,
And watch the busy scenes of crowded life;
5   Then say how hope and fear, desire and hate,
O'erspread with snares the clouded maze of fate,
Where wav'ring man, betrayed by vent'rous pride,
To tread the dreary paths without a guide,
As treach'rous phantoms in the mist delude,
10   Shuns fancied ills, or chases airy[1] good;
How rarely reason guides the stubborn choice,
Rules the bold hand, or prompts the suppliant voice;
How nations sink, by darling schemes oppressed,
When vengeance listens to the fool's request.
15   Fate wings with every wish th' afflictive dart,
Each gift of nature, and each grace of art,
With fatal heat impetuous courage glows,
With fatal sweetness elocution flows,

---

1. "Wanting reality; having no steady foundation in truth or nature" (Johnson's *Dictionary*).

Impeachment stops the speaker's pow'rful breath,
20   And restless fire precipitates on death.
        But scarce observed, the knowing and the bold
    Fall in the gen'ral massacre of gold;
    Wide-wasting pest! that rages unconfined,
    And crowds with crimes the records of mankind;
25   For gold his sword the hireling ruffian draws,
    For gold the hireling judge distorts the laws;
    Wealth heaped on wealth, nor truth nor safety buys,
    The dangers gather as the treasures rise.
        Let hist'ry tell where rival kings command,
30   And dubious title shakes the madded land,
    When statutes° glean the refuse of the sword,   *tax laws*
    How much more safe the vassal than the lord;
    Low skulks the hind° beneath the rage of pow'r,   *rural laborer*
    And leaves the wealthy traitor in the Tow'r,[2]
35   Untouched his cottage, and his slumbers sound,
    Though confiscation's vultures hover round.
        The needy traveler, secure and gay,
    Walks the wild heath, and sings his toil away.
    Does envy seize thee? crush th' upbraiding joy,
40   Increase his riches and his peace destroy;
    Now fears in dire vicissitude invade,
    The rustling brake° alarms, and quiv'ring shade,   *thicket*
    Nor light nor darkness bring his pain relief,
    One shows the plunder, and one hides the thief.
45   Yet still one gen'ral cry the skies assails,
    And gain and grandeur load the tainted gales;
    Few know the toiling statesman's fear or care,
    Th' insidious rival and the gaping heir.
        Once more, Democritus,[3] arise on earth,
50   With cheerful wisdom and instructive mirth,
    See motley[4] life in modern trappings dressed,
    And feed with varied fools th' eternal jest:
    Thou who couldst laugh where want enchained caprice,
    Toil crushed conceit, and man was of a piece;
55   Where wealth unloved without a mourner died,
    And scarce a sycophant was fed by pride;
    Where ne'er was known the form of mock debate,
    Or seen a new-made mayor's unwieldy state;
    Where change of fav'rites made no change of laws,
60   And senates heard before they judged a cause;
    How wouldst thou shake at Britain's modish tribe,
    Dart the quick taunt, and edge the piercing gibe?
    Attentive truth and nature to descry,°   *discern*

2. The Tower of London.
3. Ancient Greek philosopher who laughed at the follies

of humanity.
4. Multicolored clothes worn by jesters.

And pierce each scene with philosophic eye.
65   To thee were solemn toys or empty show,
The robes of pleasure and the veils of woe:
All aid the farce, and all thy mirth maintain,
Whose joys are causeless, or whose griefs are vain.
      Such was the scorn that filled the sage's mind,
70   Renewed at ev'ry glance on humankind;
How just that scorn ere yet thy voice declare,
Search every state, and canvass every prayer.
      Unnumbered suppliants crowd Preferment's gate,
Athirst for wealth, and burning to be great;
75   Delusive Fortune hears th' incessant call,
They mount, they shine, evaporate, and fall.[5]
On every stage the foes of peace attend,
Hate dogs their flight, and insult mocks their end.
Love ends with hope, the sinking statesman's door
80   Pours in the morning worshiper no more;
For growing names the weekly scribbler lies,
To growing wealth the dedicator flies,
From ev'ry room descends the painted face,
That hung the bright Palladium[6] of the place,
85   And smoked in kitchens, or in auctions sold,
To better features yields the frame of gold;
For now no more we trace in ev'ry line
Heroic worth, benevolence divine:
The form distorted justifies the fall,
90   And detestation rids th' indignant wall.
      But will not Britain hear the last appeal,
Sign her foes' doom, or guard her fav'rites' zeal?
Through Freedom's sons no more remonstrance rings,
Degrading nobles and controlling kings;
95   Our supple tribes° repress their patriot throats,   ° of voters
And ask no questions but the price of votes;
With weekly libels and septennial ale,[7]
Their wish is full to riot and to rail.
      In full-blown dignity, see Wolsey[8] stand,
100   Law in his voice, and fortune in his hand:
To him the church, the realm, their pow'rs consign,
Through him the rays of regal bounty shine,
Turned by his nod the stream of honor flows,
His smile alone security bestows:
105   Still to new heights his restless wishes tow'r,
Claim leads to claim, and pow'r advances pow'r;
Till conquest unresisted ceased to please,

5. The image is that of Fortune's wheel.
6. A statue of Pallas Athena, guardian of Troy.
7. Drink offered to voters as bribes during campaigns for Parliament, held every seven years.

8. Cardinal Wolsey (1475–1530), Henry VIII's Lord Chancellor, who was dismissed and imprisoned for failing to procure the King a divorce from Catherine of Aragon.

And rights submitted, left him none to seize.
At length his sov'reign frowns—the train of state
110   Mark the keen glance, and watch the sign to hate.
Wheree'er he turns he meets a stranger's eye,
His suppliants scorn him, and his followers fly;
At once is lost the pride of awful state,
The golden canopy, the glitt'ring plate,
115   The regal palace, the luxurious board,
The liv'ried army, and the menial lord.
With age, with cares, with maladies oppressed,
He seeks the refuge of monastic rest.
Grief aids disease, remembered folly stings,
120   And his last sighs reproach the faith of kings.
      Speak thou, whose thoughts at humble peace repine,
Shall Wolsey's wealth, with Wolsey's end be thine?
Or liv'st thou now, with safer pride content,
The wisest justice on the banks of Trent?[9]
125   For why did Wolsey near the steeps° of fate,   *precipices*
On weak foundations raise th' enormous weight?
Why but to sink beneath misfortune's blow,
With louder ruin to the gulfs below?
      What gave great Villiers[1] to th' assassin's knife,
130   And fixed disease on Harley's[2] closing life?
What murdered Wentworth, and what exiled Hyde,[3]
By kings protected, and to kings allied?
What but their wish indulged in courts to shine,
And pow'r too great to keep, or to resign?
135   When first the college rolls receive his name,
The young enthusiast[4] quits his ease for fame;
Through all his veins the fever of renown
Burns from the strong contagion of the gown;[5]
O'er Bodley's dome[6] his future labors spread,
140   And Bacon's mansion[7] trembles o'er his head.
Are these thy views? proceed, illustrious youth,
And virtue guard thee to the throne of Truth!
Yet should thy soul indulge the gen'rous heat,
Till captive Science° yields her last retreat;   *knowledge*
145   Should Reason guide thee with her brightest ray,
And pour on misty Doubt resistless day;

9. The river that divides northern from southern England; it is near Lichfield, Johnson's birthplace.
1. George Villiers (1592–1628), first Duke of Buckingham and a favorite of James I, was stabbed to death.
2. Robert Harley (1661–1724), first Earl of Oxford and leading statesman during the reign of Queen Anne, was impeached when George I succeeded to the throne in 1714.
3. Thomas Wentworth (1593–1641), first Earl of Strafford and adviser to Charles I, was executed at the beginning of the English Civil War. Edward Hyde

(1609–1674), first Earl of Clarendon, served Charles II but then fell from favor.
4. "One of hot imagination" (Johnson's *Dictionary*).
5. Scholastic dress (but also a reference to the poisoned garment that killed Hercules).
6. The Bodleian Library, Oxford.
7. "There is a tradition, that the study of friar Bacon [Roger Bacon, a medieval philosopher] built an arch over the bridge, will fall, when a man greater than Bacon shall pass under it" [Johnson's note].

Should no false Kindness lure to loose delight,
Nor Praise relax, nor Difficulty fright;
Should tempting Novelty thy cell refrain,
150 And Sloth effuse her opiate fumes in vain;
Should Beauty blunt on fops her fatal dart,
Nor claim the triumph of a lettered heart;
Should no disease thy torpid veins invade,
Nor Melancholy's phantoms haunt thy shade;
155 Yet hope not life from grief or danger free,
Nor think the doom of man reversed for thee:
Deign on the passing world to turn thine eyes,
And pause awhile from letters, to be wise;
There mark what ills the scholar's life assail,
160 Toil, envy, want, the patron,[8] and the jail.
See nations slowly wise, and meanly just,
To buried merit raise the tardy bust.
If dreams yet flatter, once again attend,
Hear Lydiat's life, and Galileo's end.[9]
165   Nor deem, when learning her last prize bestows,
The glitt'ring eminence exempt from foes;
See when the vulgar 'scape, despised or awed,
Rebellion's vengeful talons seize on Laud.[1]
From meaner minds, though smaller fines content,
170 The plundered palace or sequestered rent;
Marked out by dangerous parts° he meets the shock,   *abilities*
And fatal Learning leads him to the block:
Around his tomb let Art and Genius weep,
But hear his death, ye blockheads, hear and sleep.
175   The festal blazes, the triumphal show,
The ravished standard, and the captive foe,
The senate's thanks, the gazette's pompous tale,
With force resistless o'er the brave prevail.
Such bribes the rapid Greek[2] o'er Asia whirled,
180 For such the steady Romans shook the world;
For such in distant lands the Britons shine,
And stain with blood the Danube or the Rhine;
This pow'r has praise, that virtue scarce can warm,
Till fame supplies the universal charm.
185 Yet Reason frowns on War's unequal game,
Where wasted nations raise a single name,
And mortgaged states their grandsires' wreaths[3] regret,
From age to age in everlasting debt;
Wreaths which at last the dear-bought right convey

---

8. Johnson originally wrote "garret," but changed it to "patron" after enduring the neglect of Lord Chesterfield.
9. Thomas Lydiat (1572–1646) was a distinguished but impoverished mathematician. The astronomer Galileo Galilei (1564–1642) was silenced by the Inquisition.

1. William Laud (1572–1645), Archbishop of Canterbury under Charles I, was beheaded by the Parliamentarians.
2. Alexander the Great.
3. Garlands of victory.

190   To rust on medals, or on stones decay.
      On what foundation stands the warrior's pride,
   How just his hopes let Swedish Charles[4] decide;
   A frame of adamant, a soul of fire,
   No dangers fright him, and no labors tire;
195   O'er love, o'er fear, extends his wide domain,
   Unconquered lord of pleasure and of pain;
   No joys to him pacific scepters yield,
   War sounds the trump, he rushes to the field;
   Behold surrounding kings their pow'r combine,
200   And one capitulate, and one resign;
   Peace courts his hand, but spreads her charms in vain;
   "Think nothing gained," he cries, "till nought remain,
   On Moscow's walls till Gothic standards fly,
   And all be mine beneath the polar sky."
205   The march begins in military state,
   And nations on his eye suspended wait;
   Stern Famine guards the solitary coast,
   And Winter barricades the realms of Frost;
   He comes, not want and cold his course delay—
210   Hide, blushing Glory, hide Pultowa's day:
   The vanquished hero leaves his broken bands,
   And shows his miseries in distant lands;
   Condemned a needy supplicant to wait,
   While ladies interpose, and slaves debate.
215   But did not Chance at length her error mend?
   Did no subverted empire mark his end?
   Did rival monarchs give the fatal wound?
   Or hostile millions press him to the ground?
   His fall was destined to a barren strand,
220   A petty fortress, and a dubious hand;[5]
   He left the name, at which the world grew pale,
   To point a moral, or adorn a tale.
      All times their scenes of pompous woes afford,
   From Persia's tyrant[6] to Bavaria's lord.[7]
225   In gay hostility, and barb'rous pride,
   With half mankind embattled at his side,
   Great Xerxes comes to seize the certain prey,
   And starves exhausted regions in his way;
   Attendant Flattery counts his myriads o'er,
230   Till counted myriads soothe his pride no more;
   Fresh praise is tried till madness fires his mind,
   The waves he lashes, and enchains the wind;

---

4. Charles XII of Sweden, whose precarious military career ended at the Battle of Pultowa (1709). After his defeat by the Russians, Charles attempted to forge an alliance with the turks.
5. Charles XII of Sweden was thought to have been killed by one of his own officers during a siege of little military consequence.
6. Xerxes (519–465 B.C.) invaded Greece with a large army and navy. In order to transport his troops, he built a bridge of boats across the Hellespont. When a storm broke up his bridge, Xerxes ordered the wind and water to be punished. The Persian army was defeated at the Battle of Plataea, the navy and the Battle of Salamis.
7. Charles Albert (1697–1745), Elector of Bavaria, was defeated by Empress Maria Theresa, whose army included Austrian colonists from Croatia and Hungarian cavalry called "jussars."

New pow'rs are claimed, new pow'rs are still bestowed,
Till rude resistance lops the spreading god;
235 The daring Greeks deride the martial show,
And heap heir valleys with the gaudy foe;
Th' insulted sea with humbler thoughts he gains,
A single skiff to speed his ligh remains;
Th' encumbered oar scarce leaves the dreaded coast
240 Through purple billows and a floating host.
        The bold Bavarian, in a luckless hour,
Tries the dread summits of Cesarean power,
With unexpected legions bursts away,
And sees defenseless realms receive his sway;
245 Short sway! fair Austria spreads her mournful charms,
The queen, the beauty, sets the world in arms;
From hill to hill the beacon's rousing blaze
Spreads wide the hope of plunder and of praise;
The fierce Croatian, and the wild Hussar,
250 And all the sons of ravage crowd the war;
The baffled prince in honor's flattering bloom
Of hasty greatness finds the fatal doom,
His foes' derision, and his subjects' blame,
And steals to death from anguish and from shame.
255   Enlarge my life with multitude of days,
In health, in sickness, thus the suppliant prays;
Hides from himself his state, and shuns to know,
That life protracted is protracted woe.
Time hovers o'er, impatient to destroy,
260 And shuts up all the passages of joy:
In vain their gifts the bounteous seasons pour,
The fruit autumnal, and the vernal flow'r,
With listless eyes the dotard views the store,
He views, and wonders that they please no more;
265 Now pall the tasteless meats, and joyless wines,
And Luxury° with sighs her slave resigns.   *voluptuousness*
Approach, ye minstrels, try the soothing strain,
Diffuse the tuneful lenitives[8] of pain:
No sounds alas would touch th' impervious ear,
270 Though dancing mountains witnessed Orpheus[9] near;
Nor lute nor lyre his feeble pow'rs attend,
Nor sweeter music of a virtuous friend,
But everlasting dictates crowd his tongue,
Perversely grave, or positively wrong.
275 The still returning tale, and ling'ring jest,
Perplex the fawning niece and pampered guest,
While growing hopes scarce awe the gathering sneer,
And scarce a legacy can bribe to hear;

---

8. "Anything medicinally applied to ease pain" (Johnson's *Dictionary*).

9. In Greek mythology, the musician Orpheus charmed wild beasts and moved mountains.

	The watchful guests still hint the last° offense,	latest
280	The daughter's petulance, the son's expense,
	Improve his heady rage with treach'rous skill,
	And mold his passions till they make his will.
	Unnumbered maladies his joints invade,
	Lay siege to life and press the dire blockade;
285	But unextinguished Avarice still remains,
	And dreaded losses aggravate his pains;
	He turns, with anxious heart and crippled hands,
	His bonds of debt, and mortgages of lands;
	Or views his coffers with suspicious eyes,
290	Unlocks his gold, and counts it till he dies.

            The watchful guests still hint the last° offense,   *latest*
280   The daughter's petulance, the son's expense,
            Improve his heady rage with treach'rous skill,
            And mold his passions till they make his will.
                 Unnumbered maladies his joints invade,
            Lay siege to life and press the dire blockade;
285   But unextinguished Avarice still remains,
            And dreaded losses aggravate his pains;
            He turns, with anxious heart and crippled hands,
            His bonds of debt, and mortgages of lands;
            Or views his coffers with suspicious eyes,
290   Unlocks his gold, and counts it till he dies.
                 But grant, the virtues of a temp'rate prime
            Bless with an age exempt from scorn or crime;
            An age that melts with unperceived decay,
            And glides in modest innocence away;
295   Whose peaceful day Benevolence endears,
            Whose night congratulating Conscience cheers;
            The gen'ral favorite as the gen'ral friend:
            Such age there is, and who shall wish its end?
                 Yet ev'n on this her load Misfortune flings,
300   To press the weary minutes' flagging wings:
            New sorrow rises as the day returns,
            A sister sickens, or a daughter mourns.
            Now kindred Merit fills the sable bier,
            Now lacerated Friendship claims a tear.
305   Year chases year, decay pursues decay,
            Still drops some joy from with'ring life away;
            New forms arise, and different views engage,
            Superfluous lags the vet'ran on the stage,
            Till pitying Nature signs the last release,
310   And bids afflicted worth retire to peace.
                 But few there are whom hours like these await,
            Who set unclouded in the gulfs of fate.
            From Lydia's monarch should the search descend,
            By Solon cautioned to regard his end,[1]
315   In life's last scene what prodigies surprise,
            Fears of the brave, and follies of the wise?
            From Marlborough's eyes the streams of dotage flow,[2]
            And Swift expires a driveler and a show.[3]
                 The teeming mother, anxious for her race,
320   Begs for each birth the fortune of a face:
            Yet Vane could tell what ills from beauty spring;

---

1. Solon, Greek philosopher and legislator, warned the wealthy King Croesus of Lydia that no one should count himself happy until reaching the end of life.
2. John Churchill (1650–1722), first Duke of Marlborough,

hero of the War of the Spanish Succession, lived for six years after suffering two paralytic strokes.
3. Jonathan Swift, who declined into senility, was thought to have been exhibited by his servant for money.

And Sedley cursed the form that pleased a king.[4]
Ye nymphs of rosy lips and radiant eyes,
Whom Pleasure keeps too busy to be wise,
325   Whom Joys with soft varieties invite,
By day the frolic, and the dance by night,
Who frown with vanity, who smile with art,
And ask the latest fashion of the heart,
What care, what rules your heedless charms shall save,
330   Each nymph your rival, and each youth your slave?
Against your fame with fondness hate combines,
The rival batters, and the lover mines.
With distant voice neglected Virtue calls,
Less heard and less, the faint remonstrance falls;
335   Tired with contempt, she quits the slipp'ry reign,
And Pride and Prudence take her seat in vain.
In crowd at once, where none the pass defend,
The harmless Freedom, and the private Friend.
The guardians yield, by force superior plied;
340   By Interest, Prudence; and by Flattery, Pride.
Now beauty falls betrayed, despised, distressed,
And hissing Infamy proclaims the rest.
        Where then shall Hope and Fear their objects find?
Must dull Suspense corrupt the stagnant mind?
345   Must helpless man, in ignorance sedate,°   *calm*
Roll darkling° down the torrent of his fate?   *in the dark*
Must no dislike alarm, no wishes rise,
No cries attempt the mercies of the skies?
Inquirer, cease, petitions yet remain,
350   Which Heav'n may hear, nor deem religion vain.
Still raise for good the supplicating voice,
But leave to Heav'n the measure and the choice,
Safe in his power, whose eyes discern afar
The secret ambush of a specious prayer.
355   Implore his aid, in his decisions rest,
Secure whate'er he gives, he gives the best.
Yet when the sense of sacred presence fires,
And strong devotion to the skies aspires,
Pour forth thy fervors for a healthful mind,
360   Obedient passions, and a will resigned;
For love, which scarce collective man can fill;
For patience sov'reign o'er transmuted ill;
For faith, that panting for a happier seat,
Counts death kind Nature's signal of retreat:
365   These goods for man the laws of Heav'n ordain,
These goods he grants, who grants the power to gain;
With these celestial Wisdom calms the mind,
And makes the happiness she does not find.

1748   1749

4. Anne Vane (1705–1736) was the mistress of the Prince of Wales, Catherine Sedley (1657–1717) of James II.

THE RAMBLER   In the midst of working on his *Dictionary*, Johnson took on an ambitious additional task: he wrote *The Rambler*, a twice-weekly periodical essay which he sustained for two full years (1750–1752). The project brought him needed income and also a useful respite from the strains of lexicography. *The Rambler's* most famous antecedent was Addison and Steele's the *Spectator* (1711–1713), and though Johnson would later praise Addison's prose as a "model of the middle style . . . always equable and always easy," he chose for his own essays a mode more astringent: a large, often Latinate vocabulary, intricately balanced sentences, a steady alertness to the human propensity for self-delusion, a willingness to confront rather than ingratiate. Pressures of production could run high (Johnson later claimed that he sometimes wrote his essay with the printer's messenger standing at his side, waiting to take the text to the press), and speed of output may have helped shape the results. Many *Ramblers*, with their formidably wrought prose and surprising turns of thought, manage to seem imposing and improvisatory at the same time. Free to choose his topics, working under relentlessly recurrent deadlines, Johnson drew on four decades dense with reading and thought, during which (in the words of his biographer John Hawkins) he had "accumulated a fund of moral science that was more than sufficient for such an undertaking," and had become "in a very eminent degree qualified for the office of an instructor of mankind in their greatest and most important concerns." Readers proved eager for the instruction. More than any of his earlier writings, *The Rambler* established Johnson's style, his substance, and his fame.

Rambler No. 4
[ON FICTION]

Saturday, 31 March 1750

Simul et jucunda et idonea dicere vitae.

Horace, *Ars Poetica* 1.334

And join both profit and delight in one.

Creech

The works of fiction with which the present generation seems more particularly delighted are such as exhibit life in its true state, diversified only by accidents that daily happen in the world, and influenced by passions and qualities which are really to be found in conversing with mankind.

This kind of writing may be termed not improperly the comedy of romance, and is to be conducted nearly by the rules of comic poetry. Its province is to bring about natural events by easy means, and to keep up curiosity without the help of wonder: it is therefore precluded from the machines[1] and expedients of the heroic romance, and can neither employ giants to snatch away a lady from the nuptial rites, nor knights to bring her back from captivity; it can neither bewilder its personages in deserts, nor lodge them in imaginary castles.

I remember a remark made by Scaliger upon Pontanus,[2] that all his writings are filled with the same images; and that if you take from him his lillies and his roses, his satyrs and his dryads, he will have nothing left that can be called poetry. In like manner, almost all the fictions of the last age will vanish, if you deprive them of a hermit and a wood, a battle and a shipwreck.

1. "Supernatural agency in poems" (Johnson's *Dictionary*).
2. The Renaissance humanist Julius Caesar Scaliger

(1484–1558) criticized the poetry of Giovanni Pontano (1426–1503).

Why this wild strain of imagination found reception so long, in polite and learned ages, it is not easy to conceive; but we cannot wonder that, while readers could be procured, the authors were willing to continue it: for when a man had by practice gained some fluency of language, he had no further care than to retire to his closet,[3] let loose his invention, and heat his mind with incredibilities; a book was thus produced without fear of criticism, without the toil of study, without knowledge of nature, or acquaintance with life.

The task of our present writers is very different; it requires, together with that learning which is to be gained from books, that experience which can never be attained by solitary diligence, but must arise from general converse, and accurate observation of the living world. Their performances have, as Horace expresses it, *plus oneris quantum veniae minus*, little indulgence, and therefore more difficulty.[4] They are engaged in portraits of which every one knows the original, and can detect any deviation from exactness of resemblance. Other writings are safe, except from the malice of learning, but these are in danger from every common reader; as the slipper ill executed was censured by a shoemaker who happened to stop in his way at the Venus of Apelles.[5]

But the fear of not being approved as just copiers of human manners, is not the most important concern that an author of this sort ought to have before him. These books are written chiefly to the young, the ignorant, and the idle, to whom they serve as lectures of conduct, and introductions into life. They are the entertainment of minds unfurnished with ideas, and therefore easily susceptible of impressions; not fixed by principles, and therefore easily following the current of fancy; not informed by experience, and consequently open to every false suggestion and partial account.

That the highest degree of reverence should be paid to youth, and that nothing indecent should be suffered to approach their eyes or ears, are precepts extorted by sense and virtue from an ancient writer, by no means eminent for chastity of thought.[6] The same kind, though not the same degree of caution, is required in every thing which is laid before them, to secure them from unjust prejudices, perverse opinions, and incongruous combinations of images.

In the romances formerly written, every transaction and sentiment was so remote from all that passes among men, that the reader was in very little danger of making any applications to himself; the virtues and crimes were equally beyond his sphere of activity; and he amused himself with heroes and with traitors, deliverers and persecutors, as with beings of another species, whose actions were regulated upon motives of their own, and who had neither faults nor excellencies in common with himself.

But when an adventurer is leveled with the rest of the world, and acts in such scenes of the universal drama, as may be the lot of any other man, young spectators fix their eyes upon him with closer attention, and hope by observing his behavior and success to regulate their own practices, when they shall be engaged in the like part.

For this reason these familiar histories may perhaps be made of greater use than the solemnities of professed morality, and convey the knowledge of vice and virtue with more efficacy than axioms and definitions. But if the power of example is so great, as to take possession of the memory by a kind of violence, and produce effects

3. Study.
4. Horace, *Epistles* 2.1.170.
5. In his *Natural History*, Pliny the Elder tells this story of

the famous painter Apelles.
6. Johnson refers to the opening lines of Juvenal's fourteenth satire.

almost without the intervention of the will, care ought to be taken that, when the choice is unrestrained, the best examples only should be exhibited; and that which is likely to operate so strongly, should not be mischievous or uncertain in its effects.

The chief advantage which these fictions have over real life is, that their authors are at liberty, though not to invent, yet to select objects, and to cull from the mass of mankind those individuals upon which the attention ought most to be employed; as a diamond, though it cannot be made, may be polished by art, and placed in such a situation as to display that lustre which before was buried among common stones.

It is justly considered as the greatest excellency of art, to imitate nature; but it is necessary to distinguish those parts of nature, which are most proper for imitation: greater care is still required in representing life, which is so often discolored by passion, or deformed by wickedness. If the world be promiscuously[7] described, I cannot see of what use it can be to read the account; or why it may not be as safe to turn the eye immediately upon mankind, as upon a mirror which shows all that presents itself without discrimination.

It is therefore not a sufficient vindication of a character, that it is drawn as it appears, for many characters ought never to be drawn; nor of a narrative, that the train of events is agreeable to observation and experience, for that observation which is called knowledge of the world will be found much more frequently to make men cunning than good. The purpose of these writings is surely not only to show mankind, but to provide that they may be seen hereafter with less hazard; to teach the means of avoiding the snares which are laid by Treachery for Innocence, without infusing any wish for that superiority with which the betrayer flatters his vanity; to give the power of counteracting fraud, without the temptation to practice it; to initiate youth by mock encounters in the art of necessary defense, and to increase prudence without impairing virtue.

Many writers, for the sake of following nature, so mingle good and bad qualities in their principal personages, that they are both equally conspicuous; and as we accompany them through their adventures with delight, and are led by degrees to interest ourselves in their favor, we lose the abhorrence of their faults, because they do not hinder our pleasure, or, perhaps, regard them with some kindness for being united with so much merit.

There have been men indeed splendidly wicked, whose endowments threw a brightness on their crimes, and whom scarce any villainy made perfectly detestable, because they never could be wholly divested of their excellencies; but such have been in all ages the great corrupters of the world, and their resemblance ought no more to be preserved, than the art of murdering without pain.

Some have advanced, without due attention to the consequences of this notion, that certain virtues have their correspondent faults, and therefore that to exhibit either apart is to deviate from probability. Thus men are observed by Swift to be "grateful in the same degree as they are resentful."[8] This principle, with others of the same kind, supposes man to act from a brute impulse, and pursue a certain degree of inclination, without any choice of the object; for otherwise, though it should be allowed that gratitude and resentment arise from the same constitution of the passions, it follows not that they will be equally indulged when reason is consulted; yet unless that consequence be admitted, this sagacious maxim becomes an empty sound, without any relation to practice or to life.

7. Indiscriminately.
8. In fact, it was Pope who made this observation, in the   *Miscellanies* he coauthored with Swift.

Nor is it evident, that even the first motions to these effects are always in the same proportion. For pride, which produces quickness of resentment, will obstruct gratitude, by unwillingness to admit that inferiority which obligation implies; and it is very unlikely that he who cannot think he receives a favor will acknowledge or repay it.

It is of the utmost importance to mankind that positions of this tendency should be laid open and confuted; for while men consider good and evil as springing from the same root, they will spare the one for the sake of the other, and in judging, if not of others at least of themselves, will be apt to estimate their virtues by their vices. To this fatal error all those will contribute, who confound the colors of right and wrong, and instead of helping to settle their boundaries, mix them with so much art, that no common mind is able to disunite them.

In narratives where historical veracity has no place, I cannot discover why there should not be exhibited the most perfect idea of virtue; of virtue not angelical, nor above probability, for what we cannot credit we shall never imitate, but the highest and purest that humanity can reach, which, exercised in such trials as the various revolutions of things shall bring upon it, may, by conquering some calamities, and enduring others, teach us what we may hope, and what we can perform. Vice, for vice is necessary to be shown, should always disgust; nor should the graces of gaiety, or the dignity of courage, be so united with it, as to reconcile it to the mind. Wherever it appears, it should raise hatred by the malignity of its practices, and contempt by the meanness of its stratagems; for while it is supported by either parts[9] or spirit, it will be seldom heartily abhorred. The Roman tyrant was content to be hated, if he was but feared;[1] and there are thousands of the readers of romances willing to be thought wicked, if they may be allowed to be wits. It is therefore to be steadily inculcated, that virtue is the highest proof of understanding, and the only solid basis of greatness; and that vice is the natural consequence of narrow thoughts, that it begins in mistake, and ends in ignominy.

Rambler No. 5
[On Spring]

Tuesday, 3 April 1750

Et nunc omnis ager, nunc omnis parturit arbos,
Nunc frondent silvae, nunc formosissimus annus.

Virgil, *Eclogues* 3.56–57

Now every field, now every tree is green;
Now genial nature's fairest face is seen.

Elphinston

Every man is sufficiently discontented with some circumstances of his present state, to suffer his imagination to range more or less in quest of future happiness, and to fix upon some point of time, in which, by the removal of the inconvenience which now perplexes him, or acquisition of the advantage which he at present wants,[1] he shall find the condition of his life very much improved.

---

9. Abilities.
1. The Roman historian Suetonius reports this of the

emperor Caligula.
1. Lacks.

When this time, which is too often expected with great impatience, at last arrives, it generally comes without the blessing for which it was desired; but we solace ourselves with some new prospect, and press forward again with equal eagerness.

It is lucky for a man, in whom this temper prevails, when he turns his hopes upon things wholly out of his own power; since he forbears then to precipitate his affairs, for the sake of the great event that is to complete his felicity, and waits for the blissful hour, with less neglect of the measures necessary to be taken in the mean time.

I have long known a person of this temper, who indulged his dream of happiness with less hurt to himself than such chimerical wishes commonly produce, and adjusted his scheme with such address, that his hopes were in full bloom three parts of the year, and in the other part never wholly blasted. Many, perhaps, would be desirous of learning by what means he procured to himself such a cheap and lasting satisfaction. It was gained by a constant practice of referring the removal of all his uneasiness to the coming of the next spring; if his health was impaired, the spring would restore it; if what he wanted was at a high price, it would fall its value in the spring.

The spring, indeed, did often come without any of these effects, but he was always certain that the next would be more propitious; nor was ever convinced that the present spring would fail him before the middle of summer; for he always talked of the spring as coming 'till it was past, and when it was once past, everyone agreed with him that it was coming.

By long converse with this man, I am, perhaps, brought to feel immoderate pleasure in the contemplation of this delightful season; but I have the satisfaction of finding many, whom it can be no shame to resemble, infected with the same enthusiasm;[2] for there is, I believe, scarce any poet of eminence, who has not left some testimony of his fondness for the flowers, the zephyrs, and the warblers of the spring. Nor has the most luxuriant imagination been able to describe the serenity and happiness of the golden age, otherwise than by giving a perpetual spring, as the highest reward of uncorrupted innocence.

There is, indeed, something inexpressibly pleasing, in the annual renovation of the world, and the new display of the treasures of nature. The cold and darkness of winter, with the naked deformity of every object on which we turn our eyes, make us rejoice at the succeeding season, as well for what we have escaped, as for what we may enjoy; and every budding flower, which a warm situation brings early to our view, is considered by us as a messenger to notify the approach of more joyous days.

The spring affords to a mind, so free from the disturbance of cares or passions as to be vacant to calm amusements, almost every thing that our present state makes us capable of enjoying. The variegated verdure of the fields and woods, the succession of grateful odors, the voice of pleasure pouring out its notes on every side, with the gladness apparently conceived by every animal, from the growth of his food, and the clemency of the weather, throw over the whole earth an air of gaiety, significantly expressed by the smile of nature.

Yet there are men to whom these scenes are able to give no delight, and who hurry away from all the varieties of rural beauty, to lose their hours, and divert their thoughts by cards, or assemblies, a tavern dinner, or the prattle of the day.

It may be laid down as a position which will seldom deceive, that when a man cannot bear his own company there is something wrong. He must fly from himself, either because he feels a tediousness in life from the equipoise of an empty mind,

2. "Elevation of fancy; exaltation of ideas" (Johnson's *Dictionary*).

which, having no tendency to one motion more than another but as it is impelled by some external power, must always have recourse to foreign objects; or he must be afraid of the intrusion of some unpleasing ideas, and, perhaps, is struggling to escape from the remembrance of a loss, the fear of a calamity, or some other thought of greater horror.

Those whom sorrow incapacitates to enjoy the pleasures of contemplation, may properly apply to such diversions, provided they are innocent, as lay strong hold on the attention; and those, whom fear of any future affliction chains down to misery, must endeavor to obviate the danger.

My considerations shall, on this occasion, be turned on such as are burdensome to themselves merely because they want subjects for reflection, and to whom the volume of nature is thrown open, without affording them pleasure or instruction, because they never learned to read the characters.

A French author has advanced this seeming paradox, that "very few men know how to take a walk"; and, indeed, it is true, that few know how to take a walk with a prospect of any other pleasure, than the same company would have afforded them at home.

There are animals that borrow their color from the neighboring body, and, consequently, vary their hue as they happen to change their place. In like manner it ought to be the endeavor of every man to derive his reflections from the objects about him; for it is to no purpose that he alters his position, if his attention continues fixed to the same point. The mind should be kept open to the access of every new idea, and so far disengaged from the predominance of particular thoughts, as easily to accommodate itself to occasional entertainment.

A man that has formed this habit of turning every new object to his entertainment, finds in the productions of nature an inexhaustible stock of materials upon which he can employ himself, without any temptations to envy or malevolence; faults, perhaps, seldom totally avoided by those, whose judgment is much exercised upon the works of art. He has always a certain prospect of discovering new reasons for adoring the sovereign author of the universe, and probable hopes of making some discovery of benefit to others, or of profit to himself. There is no doubt but many vegetables and animals have qualities that might be of great use, to the knowledge of which there is not required much force of penetration, or fatigue of study, but only frequent experiments, and close attention. What is said by the chemists of their darling mercury, is, perhaps, true of every body through the whole creation, that, if a thousand lives should be spent upon it, all its properties would not be found out.

Mankind must necessarily be diversified by various tastes, since life affords and requires such multiplicity of employments, and a nation of naturalists is neither to be hoped, or desired; but it is surely not improper to point out a fresh amusement to those who languish in health, and repine in plenty, for want of some source of diversion that may be less easily exhausted, and to inform the multitudes of both sexes, who are burdened with every new day, that there are many shows which they have not seen.

He that enlarges his curiosity after the works of nature, demonstrably multiplies the inlets to happiness; and, therefore, the younger part of my readers, to whom I dedicate this vernal speculation, must excuse me for calling upon them, to make use at once of the spring of the year, and the spring of life; to acquire, while their minds may be yet impressed with new images, a love of innocent pleasures, and an ardor for useful knowledge; and to remember, that a blighted spring makes a barren year, and that the vernal flowers, however beautiful and gay, are only intended by nature as preparatives to autumnal fruits.

Idler No. 31[1]

[ON IDLENESS]

Saturday, 18 November 1758

Many moralists have remarked, that pride has of all human vices the widest dominion, appears in the greatest multiplicity of forms, and lies hid under the greatest variety of disguises; of disguises, which, like the moon's "veil of brightness," are both its "luster and its shade,"[2] and betray it to others, though they hide it from ourselves.

It is not my intention to degrade pride from this pre-eminence of mischief, yet I know not whether idleness may not maintain a very doubtful and obstinate competition.

There are some that profess idleness in its full dignity, who call themselves the Idle, as Busiris in the play "calls himself the Proud";[3] who boast that they do nothing, and thank their stars that they have nothing to do; who sleep every night till they can sleep no longer, and rise only that exercise may enable them to sleep again; who prolong the reign of darkness by double curtains, and never see the sun but to "tell him how they hate his beams";[4] whose whole labor is to vary the postures of indulgence, and whose day differs from their night but as a couch or chair differs from a bed.

These are the true and open votaries of idleness, for whom she weaves the garlands of poppies, and into whose cup she pours the waters of oblivion; who exist in a state of unruffled stupidity,[5] forgetting and forgotten; who have long ceased to live, and at whose death the survivors can only say, that they have ceased to breathe.

But idleness predominates in many lives where it is not suspected, for, being a vice which terminates in itself, it may be enjoyed without injury to others, and is therefore not watched like fraud, which endangers property, or like pride, which naturally seeks its gratifications in another's inferiority. Idleness is a silent and peaceful quality, that neither raises envy by ostentation, nor hatred by opposition; and therefore nobody is busy to censure or detect it.

As pride sometimes is hid under humility, idleness is often covered by turbulence and hurry. He that neglects his known duty and real employment, naturally endeavors to crowd his mind with something that may bar out the remembrance of his own folly, and does any thing but what he ought to do with eager diligence, that he may keep himself in his own favor.

Some are always in a state of preparation, occupied in previous measures, forming plans, accumulating materials, and providing for the main affair. These are certainly under the secret power of idleness. Nothing is to be expected from the workman whose tools are forever to be sought. I was once told by a great master, that

---

1. *The Idler* (1758–1760) bears a more self-deprecating title than *The Rambler;* other circumstances, too, suggest that Johnson intended a less imposing performance in this series of periodical essay than in its predecessor. The new pieces appeared not twice but once a week, and not as an independent sheet but as a department within a weekly newspaper called *The Universal Chronicle* (which achieved little eminence apart from Johnson's contribution). The *Idlers* were shorter than the *Ramblers,* and dealt more often in light topics and comic touches. Boswell opined that the

second series had "less body and more spirit . . . more variety of real life, and greater facility of language." His judgment is hardly definitive; the comparison has been assayed, with varying results, many times since.

2. Both quotations come from Samuel Butler's poem *Hudibras* (1663–1678) 2.1.905 and 908.

3. *Busiris* (1719) by Edward Young.

4. Milton, *Paradise Lost* 4.37.

5. Stupor.

no man ever excelled in painting, who was eminently curious[6] about pencils[7] and colors.

There are others to whom idleness dictates another expedient, by which life may be passed unprofitably away without the tediousness of many vacant hours. The art is, to fill the day with petty business, to have always something in hand which may raise curiosity, but not solicitude, and keep the mind in a state of action, but not of labor.

This art has for many years been practiced by my old friend Sober,[8] with wonderful success. Sober is a man of strong desires and quick imagination, so exactly balanced by the love of ease, that they can seldom stimulate him to any difficult undertaking; they have, however, so much power, that they will not suffer him to lie quite at rest, and though they do not make him sufficiently useful to others, they make him at least weary of himself.

Mr. Sober's chief pleasure is conversation; there is no end of his talk or his attention; to speak or to hear is equally pleasing; for he still fancies that he is teaching or learning something, and is free for the time from his own reproaches.

But there is one time at night when he must go home, that his friends may sleep; and another time in the morning, when all the world agrees to shut out interruption. These are the moments of which poor Sober trembles at the thought. But the misery of these tiresome intervals, he has many means of alleviating. He has persuaded himself that the manual arts are undeservedly overlooked; he has observed in many trades the effects of close thought, and just ratiocination. From speculation he proceeded to practice, and supplied himself with the tools of a carpenter, with which he mended his coal-box very successfully, and which he still continues to employ, as he finds occasion.

He has attempted at other times the crafts of the shoemaker, tinman, plumber, and potter; in all these arts he has failed, and resolves to qualify himself for them by better information. But his daily amusement is chemistry. He has a small furnace, which he employs in distillation, and which has long been the solace of his life. He draws oils and waters, and essences and spirits, which he knows to be of no use; sits and counts the drops as they come from his retort, and forgets that, while a drop is falling, a moment flies away.

Poor Sober! I have often teased him with reproof, and he has often promised reformation; for no man is so much open to conviction as the idler, but there is none on whom it operates so little. What will be the effect of this paper I know not; perhaps he will read it and laugh, and light the fire in his furnace; but my hope is that he will quit his trifles, and betake himself to rational and useful diligence.

Idler No. 84

[ON AUTOBIOGRAPHY]

Saturday, 24 November 1759

Biography is, of the various kinds of narrative writing, that which is most eagerly read, and most easily applied to the purposes of life.

6. "Difficult to please" (Johnson's *Dictionary*).
7. Brushes.

8. Johnson's friends believed that the portrait of Sober was autobiographical.

In romances, when the wild field of possibility lies open to invention, the incidents may easily be made more numerous, the vicissitudes more sudden, and the events more wonderful; but from the time of life when fancy begins to be overruled by reason and corrected by experience, the most artful tale raises little curiosity when it is known to be false; though it may, perhaps, be sometimes read as a model of a neat or elegant style, not for the sake of knowing what it contains, but how it is written; or those that are weary of themselves, may have recourse to it as a pleasing dream, of which, when they awake, they voluntarily dismiss the images from their minds.

The examples and events of history press, indeed, upon the mind with the weight of truth; but when they are reposited in the memory, they are oftener employed for show than use, and rather diversify conversation than regulate life. Few are engaged in such scenes as give them opportunities of growing wiser by the downfall of statesmen or the defeat of generals. The stratagems of war, and the intrigues of courts, are read by far the greater part of mankind with the same indifference as the adventures of fabled heroes, or the revolutions of a fairy region. Between falsehood and useless truth there is little difference. As gold which he cannot spend will make no man rich, so knowledge which he cannot apply will make no man wise.

The mischievous consequences of vice and folly, of irregular desires and predominant passions, are best discovered by those relations which are leveled with the general surface of life, which tell not how any man became great, but how he was made happy; not how he lost the favor of his prince, but how he became discontented with himself.

Those relations are therefore commonly of most value in which the writer tells his own story. He that recounts the life of another, commonly dwells most upon conspicuous events, lessens the familiarity of his tale to increase its dignity, shows his favorite at a distance decorated and magnified like the ancient actors in their tragic dress, and endeavors to hide the man that he may produce a hero.

But if it be true which was said by a French prince, "that no man was a hero to the servants of his chamber," it is equally true that every man is yet less a hero to himself. He that is most elevated above the crowd by the importance of his employments or the reputation of his genius, feels himself affected by fame or business but as they influence his domestic life. The high and low, as they have the same faculties and the same senses, have no less similitude in their pains and pleasures. The sensations are the same in all, though produced by very different occasions. The prince feels the same pain when an invader seizes a province, as the farmer when a thief drives away his cow. Men thus equal in themselves will appear equal in honest and impartial biography; and those whom fortune or nature place at the greatest distance may afford instruction to each other.

The writer of his own life has at least the first qualification of an historian, the knowledge of the truth; and though it may be plausibly objected that his temptations to disguise it are equal to his opportunities of knowing it, yet I cannot but think that impartiality may be expected with equal confidence from him that relates the passages of his own life, as from him that delivers the transactions of another.

Certainty of knowledge not only excludes mistake but fortifies veracity. What we collect by conjecture, and by conjecture only can one man judge of another's motives or sentiments, is easily modified by fancy or by desire; as objects imperfectly discerned take forms from the hope or fear of the beholder. But that which is fully known cannot be falsified but with reluctance of understanding, and alarm of conscience; of understanding, the lover of truth; of conscience, the sentinel of virtue.

He that writes the life of another is either his friend or his enemy, and wishes either to exalt his praise or aggravate his infamy; many temptations to falsehood will occur in the disguise of passions, too specious[1] to fear much resistance. Love of virtue will animate panegyric, and hatred of wickedness embitter censure. The zeal of gratitude, the ardor of patriotism, fondness for an opinion, or fidelity to a party, may easily overpower the vigilance of a mind habitually well disposed, and prevail over unassisted and unfriended veracity.

But he that speaks of himself has no motive to falsehood or partiality except self-love, by which all have so often been betrayed, that all are on the watch against its artifices. He that writes an apology for[2] a single action, to confute an accusation, or recommend himself to favor, is indeed always to be suspected of favoring his own cause; but he that sits down calmly and voluntarily to review his life for the admonition of posterity, or to amuse himself, and leaves this account unpublished, may be commonly presumed to tell truth, since falsehood cannot appease his own mind, and fame will not be heard beneath the tomb.

❦

James Boswell
1740–1795

"I have discovered," James Boswell announced at age twenty-two in the journal he had just commenced, "that we may be in some degree whatever character we choose." The possibilities opened up by this discovery both exhilarated and troubled him. Neither the "choosing" nor the "being" turned out to be as simple as he expected, in part because some alternate choice always beckoned. In the pages of his journal, Boswell performed his excited choices and anxious reconsiderations. The oscillation did much to drive the intricate comedy and intermittent pathos, the energetic posing and fervent self-scrutiny of the diaries he kept all his adult life, and of the published books he crafted from them.

Boswell's parents had chosen their own characters early, and had stuck to them assiduously. His father was a Scots laird—heir to an ancient family and a landed estate—and a distinguished jurist, serving as justice on Scotland's highest courts. His mother was an impassioned Calvinist, who numbered among her many strictures an abhorrence of the theater; the actors' freedom of character-choice, which made the playhouse for her a place of sinful deception, would make it the site of a lifelong enchantment for her son. Boswell's parents had chosen firmly for their first-born too. James was to become, like his father, an eminent lawyer and respectable landowner.

Boswell chafed at the narrowness of the scheme. Struggling (he later recalled) "against paternal affection, ambition, interest," he ran away to London for a short spell at age eighteen and returned there at twenty-two, seeking a commission as a soldier with the king's personal bodyguard, a post that would have secured him lifelong residence in the city, flashy uniforms, and ample opportunities to display himself in them. While Boswell waited for this prospect to

---

1. "Plausible; superficially, not solidly right" (Johnson's   2. Defense of.
Dictionary).

materialize (it never did), he found his real calling. He started to keep a copious journal, narrating each day in succession, dispatching the text in weekly packets to his friend John Johnston back home in Scotland. Here too was self-display, intricately contrived. Boswell managed his journal as a kind of manuscript theater—often written as a play text, complete with dialogue and stage directions—for an audience of one (the performance of his journal texts for a wider reading public would later become his literary life's work). London, the theatrical city, teemed with "characters" living and dead, real and fictional, whom Boswell by turns and in combinations strove to "be": Addison, Steele, and their imaginary paragon of self-possession Mr. Spectator; Captain Macheath from *The Beggar's Opera* (on whose adventures Boswell modeled some of his own sexual exploits); the actors Thomas Sheridan and David Garrick; and most important, Garrick's old teacher Samuel Johnson, whose writings had provided Boswell with a model of moral firmness more attractive than his father's, and who befriended the young diarist six months into his London stay.

The friendship with Johnson gave Boswell's journal a new purpose (to record the conversations of this dazzling talker) and his life a new direction. Reconciled to his father's plan, Boswell studied law in Holland and, as reward for his painfully diligent endeavors, made the Grand Tour of Europe, where he collected the conversation and the counsel of further celebrities: the French iconoclasts Voltaire and Rousseau, and the Corsican rebel leader Pasquale Paoli, then fighting to free his island from foreign domination. Returning to Scotland in 1766, Boswell took up the life his father had mapped for him, settling in Edinburgh, and becoming (as he haughtily informed his disreputable friend John Wilkes) "a Scottish lawyer, a Scottish laird, and a Scottish married man." In each of these roles, though, he repeatedly broke character. He went down to London almost every spring, ostensibly to cultivate his legal practice but really to renew his old absorptions: in theater, in sexual adventure, in the spellbinding company of Johnson and the group of artists, writers, and thinkers who surrounded him.

Boswell yearned to join their number not merely as admirer but as eminent author, and he soon did. Over the ensuing years, he produced much journalism and some verse, as well as three books in which he explored with increasing audacity the potential of his own diary as a public text—as a vehicle of entertainment, instruction, profit, and fame. He pursued for the journal form a print authority it had not previously possessed, devising ways for it to encroach upon, even to colonize, territory and tasks traditionally reserved to other genres: travel book, "character" sketch, biography. In his first attempt, *An Account of Corsica . . . and Memoirs of Pascal Paoli* (1769), he recast his original travel journal (rearranging the entries, dropping the dates) to produce a heroic portrait of his friend the liberator. In his second experiment, *A Journal of a Tour to the Hebrides with Samuel Johnson* (1785), which appeared the year after Johnson's death, the imperative to portraiture was even more pronounced. The public craved accounts of the lost titan, and this time Boswell met that demand a different way. He presented his journal *as* a journal, with scrupulously dated, plentifully narrated consecutive entries rich in the "minute details of daily life" that Johnson himself had stipulated as the criteria for good biography. The book struck readers as startlingly new. Some mocked it for its minutiae ("How are we all with rapture touched," exclaimed one versifier, "to see / Where, when, and at what hour, you swallowed tea!"), while many praised its veracity and abundance.

There was much more where that came from. In *The Life of Samuel Johnson, LL.D.* (1791), Boswell deployed the *Tour*'s techniques on a massive scale. Drawing on his diaries, and on years of arduous research among Johnson's many acquaintances, Boswell built a thousand-page biography that is largely a book of talk, of conversations diligently recorded and deftly dramatized, the culmination of the textual theater that Boswell had long practiced in manuscript. Johnson's capacious mind and imposing presence find embodiment in a text dense with accumulated time, told and retold over the span of almost three decades that stretches from Boswell's first Johnsonian journal entry to the biography's publication. Pleased with the book's commercial success, stung by charges that he had been either too partial to Johnson or too critical of him, Boswell worked at two further editions (in which his footnotes swelled with new information and rebuttals). He died at fifty-five, unmade by alcoholism, by venereal disease, and by the violent depressions that accompanied his ongoing uncertainty as to what he might "be" and had become.

His books sustained his fame, though ever since the *Life*'s first appearance, readers have debated the degree of its accuracy and the merits of its portraiture. Two centuries later, Boswell's biography has become a touchstone text for the problem of the "documentary"—the question of how art and "fact" should merge in representations of historical events. Over the past eighty years the debate has been deepened by the unexpected recovery of Boswell's original papers, including the diaries that he drew on and boasted of in his published books. The papers had long been given up for lost, but masses of them had actually been stashed and forgotten by various descendants in odd receptacles (cabinet, croquet box, grain loft) on estates scattered across Scotland and Ireland. The papers' recovery took more than twenty years; the process of their publication continues. Taken together, Boswell's papers and his published works make it possible to trace the intricate course by which the flux of his energetic, agitated life became fixed in text.

from London Journal
[A SCOT IN LONDON]

Wednesday, 1 December [1762]. * * * On Tuesday I wanted to have a silver-hilted sword, but upon examining my pockets as I walked up the Strand,[1] I found that I had left the most of my guineas at home and had not enough to pay for it with me. I determined to make a trial of the civility of my fellow-creatures, and what effect my external appearance and address would have. I accordingly went to the shop of Mr. Jefferys, sword-cutter to His Majesty, looked at a number of his swords, and at last picked out a very handsome one at five guineas. "Mr. Jefferys," said I, "I have not money here to pay for it. Will you trust me?" "Upon my word, Sir," said he, "you must excuse me. It is a thing we never do to a stranger." I bowed genteelly and said, "Indeed, Sir, I believe it is not right." However, I stood and looked at him, and he looked at me. "Come, Sir," cried he, "I will trust you." "Sir," said I, "if you had not trusted me, I should not have bought it from you." He asked my name and place of abode, which I told him. I then chose a belt, put the sword on, told him I would call and pay it tomorrow, and walked off. I called this day and paid him. "Mr. Jefferys," said I, "there is your money. You paid me a very great compliment. I am much obliged to you. But pray don't do such a thing again. It is dangerous." "Sir," said he, "we know our men. I would have trusted you with the value of a hundred pounds." This I think was a good adventure and much to my honor. * * *

This afternoon I was surprised with the arrival of Lady Betty Macfarlane, Lady Anne Erskine, Captain Erskine, and Miss Dempster, who were come to the Red Lion Inn at Charing Cross. It seems Lady Betty had written to the laird that if he would not come down, she would come up; and upon his giving her an indolent answer, like a woman of spirit, she put her resolution in practice. I immediately went to them.[2]

To tell the plain truth, I was vexed at their coming. For to see just the plain *hamely*[3] Fife family hurt my grand ideas of London. Besides, I was now upon a plan of studying polite reserved behavior, which is the only way to keep up dignity of character. And as I have a good share of pride, which I think is very proper and even noble,

---

1. A major commercial street in the West End of London.
2. With the exception of Miss Dempster, the sister of his friend George, Boswell refers to the daughters and son of the Fifth Earl of Kellie ("the laird"). The family came from Fife, a county in eastern Scotland.
3. Scots dialect for "homely," home-like.

I am hurt with the taunts of ridicule and am unsatisfied if I do not feel myself something of a superior animal. This has always been my favorite idea in my best moments. Indeed, I have been obliged to deviate from it by a variety of circumstances. After my wild expedition to London in the year 1760, after I got rid of the load of serious reflection which then burthened me, by being always in Lord Eglinton's company, very fond of him, and much caressed by him, I became dissipated and thoughtless.[4] When my father forced me down to Scotland, I was at first very low-spirited, although to appearance very high. I afterwards from my natural vivacity endeavored to make myself easy; and like a man who takes to drinking to banish care, I threw myself loose as a heedless, dissipated, rattling fellow who might say or do every ridiculous thing. This made me sought after by everybody for the present hour, but I found myself a very inferior being; and I found many people presuming to treat me as such, which notwithstanding of my appearance of undiscerning gaiety, gave me much pain. I was, in short, a character very different from what God intended me and I myself chose. I remember my friend Johnston[5] told me one day after my return from London that I had turned out different from what he imagined, as he thought I would resemble Mr. Addison.[6] I laughed and threw out some loud sally of humor, but the observation struck deep. Indeed, I must do myself the justice to say that I always resolved to be such a man whenever my affairs were made easy and I got upon my own footing. For as I despaired of that, I endeavored to lower my views and just to be a good-humored comical being, well liked either as a waiter, a common soldier, a clerk in Jamaica, or some other odd out-of-the-way sphere. Now, when my father at last put me into an independent situation, I felt my mind regain its native dignity. I felt strong dispositions to be a Mr. Addison. Indeed, I had accustomed myself so much to laugh at everything that it required time to render my imagination solid and give me just notions of real life and of religion. But I hoped by degrees to attain to some degree of propriety. Mr. Addison's character in sentiment, mixed with a little of the gaiety of Sir Richard Steele and the manners of Mr. Digges,[7] were the ideas which I aimed to realize.

Indeed, I must say that Digges has more or as much of the deportment of a man of fashion as anybody I ever saw; and he keeps up this so well that he never once lessened upon me even on an intimate acquaintance, although he is now and then somewhat melancholy, under which it is very difficult to preserve dignity; and this I think is particularly to be admired in Mr. Digges. Indeed, he and I never came to familiarity, which is justly said to beget contempt. The great art of living easy and happy in society is to study proper behavior, and even with our most intimate friends to observe politeness; otherwise we will insensibly treat each other with a degree of rudeness, and each will find himself despised in some measure by the other. As I was therefore pursuing this laudable plan, I was vexed at the arrival of the Kellie family, with whom when in Scotland I had been in the greatest familiarity. Had they not come for a twelvemonth, I should have been somewhat established in my address, but as I had been but a fortnight from them, I could not without the appearance of strong

4. At the age of 18, Boswell had run away to London, where he impulsively converted to Catholicism. The tenth Earl of Eglinton, a charming and generous rake, weaned him from religion by turning him into a libertine.
5. John Johnston of Grange, Boswell's close friend, to whom he was sending the journal in weekly installments.
6. Joseph Addison, author, with Sir Richard Steele, of the

Tatler and *Spectator* papers. Addison was particularly identified with the character of the silent, all-seeing Mr. Spectator.
7. West Digges, an actor in Edinburgh, particularly known for his portrayal of Macheath in *The Beggar's Opera*.

affectation appear much different from what they had seen me. I accordingly was very free, but rather more silent, which they imputed to my dullness, and roasted me about London's not being agreeable to me. I bore it pretty well, and left them.

* * *

Wednesday, 15 December [1762]. The enemies of the people of England who would have them considered in the worst light represent them as selfish, beef-eaters, and cruel. In this view I resolved today to be a true-born Old Englishman. I went into the City[8] to Dolly's Steak-house in Paternoster Row and swallowed my dinner by myself to fulfill the charge of selfishness; I had a large fat beefsteak to fulfill the charge of beef-eating; and I went at five o'clock to the Royal Cockpit in St. James's Park and saw cockfighting for about five hours to fulfill the charge of cruelty.

A beefsteak house is a most excellent place to dine at. You come in there to a warm, comfortable, large room, where a number of people are sitting at table. You take whatever place you find empty; call for what you like, which you get well and cleverly dressed. You may either chat or not as you like. Nobody minds you, and you pay very reasonably. My dinner (beef, bread and beer and waiter) was only a shilling. The waiters make a great deal of money by these pennies.[9] Indeed, I admire the English for attending to small sums, as many smalls make a great, according to the proverb.

At five I filled my pockets with gingerbread and apples (quite the method), put on my old clothes and laced hat, laid by my watch, purse, and pocketbook, and with oaken stick in my hand sallied to the pit. I was too soon there. So I went into a low inn, sat down amongst a parcel of arrant blackguards, and drank some beer. The sentry near the house had been very civil in showing me the way. It was very cold. I bethought myself of the poor fellow, so I carried out a pint of beer myself to him. He was very thankful and drank my health cordially. He told me his name was Hobard, that he was a watchmaker but in distress for debt, and enlisted that his creditors might not touch him.

I then went to the Cockpit, which is a circular room in the middle of which the cocks fight. It is seated round with rows gradually rising. The pit and the seats are all covered with mat. The cocks, nicely cut and dressed and armed with silver heels, are set down and fight with amazing bitterness and resolution. Some of them were quickly dispatched. One pair fought three quarters of an hour. The uproar and noise of betting is prodigious. A great deal of money made a very quick circulation from hand to hand. There was a number of professed gamblers there. An old cunning dog whose face I had seen at Newmarket[1] sat by me a while. I told him I knew nothing of the matter.[2] "Sir," said he, "you have as good a chance as anybody." He thought I would be a good subject for him. I was young-like. But he found himself balked. I was shocked to see the distraction and anxiety of the betters. I was sorry for the poor cocks. I looked round to see if any of the spectators pitied them when mangled and torn in a most cruel manner, but I could not observe the smallest relenting sign in any countenance. I was therefore not ill pleased to see them endure mental torment. Thus did I complete my true English day, and came home pretty much fatigued and pretty much confounded at the strange turn of this people.

---

8. The older, eastern half of London, which included the centers of finance, law, and journalism.
9. The waiter's tip was one of the 12 pence that made up a shilling.
1. A town in Suffolk famous for horse racing.
2. About betting on cockfighting.

[FIRST MEETING WITH JOHNSON]

Monday, 16 May [1763]. Temple[1] and his brother breakfasted with me. I went to Love's to try to recover some of the money which he owes me. But, alas, a single guinea was all I could get. He was just going to dinner, so I stayed and eat a bit, though I was angry at myself afterwards. I drank tea at Davies's[2] in Russell Street, and about seven came in the great Mr. Samuel Johnson, whom I have so long wished to see. Mr. Davies introduced me to him. As I knew his mortal antipathy at the Scotch, I cried to Davies, "Don't tell where I come from." However, he said, "From Scotland." "Mr. Johnson," said I, "indeed I come from Scotland, but I cannot help it." "Sir," replied he, "that, I find, is what a very great many of your countrymen cannot help." Mr. Johnson is a man of a most dreadful appearance. He is a very big man, is troubled with sore eyes, the palsy, and the king's evil.[3] He is very slovenly in his dress and speaks with a most uncouth voice. Yet his great knowledge and strength of expression command vast respect and render him very excellent company. He has great humor and is a worthy man. But his dogmatical roughness of manners is disagreeable. I shall mark what I remember of his conversation. * * *

1762–1763   1950

from The Life of Samuel Johnson, LL.D.

[INTRODUCTION; BOSWELL'S METHOD]

To write the Life of him who excelled all mankind in writing the lives of others, and who, whether we consider his extraordinary endowments or his various works, has been equaled by few in any age, is an arduous, and may be reckoned in me a presumptuous task.

Had Dr. Johnson written his own life, in conformity with the opinion which he has given, that every man's life may be best written by himself;[1] had he employed in the preservation of his own history, that clearness of narration and elegance of language in which he has embalmed so many eminent persons, the world would probably have had the most perfect example of biography that was ever exhibited. But although he at different times, in a desultory manner, committed to writing many particulars of the progress of his mind and fortunes, he never had preserving diligence enough to form them into a regular composition. Of these memorials a few have been preserved; but the greater part was consigned by him to the flames, a few days before his death.

As I had the honor and happiness of enjoying his friendship for upwards of twenty years; as I had the scheme of writing his life constantly in view; as he was well apprised of this circumstance, and from time to time obligingly satisfied my inquiries, by communicating to me the incidents of his early years; as I acquired a facility in recollecting, and was very assiduous in recording, his conversation, of which the extraordinary vigor and vivacity constituted one of the first features of his character; and as I have spared no pains in obtaining materials concerning him, from every quarter where I could discover that they were to be found, and have been favored with the most liberal communications by his friends; I flatter myself that few biographers have entered upon such a work as this with more advantages; independent of

1. William Johnson Temple, Boswell's most intimate and upstanding friend.
2. Thomas Davies, actor and bookseller.

3. Scrofula, a form of tuberculosis that the king's touch was believed to cure.
1. In *Idler* No. 84.

literary abilities, in which I am not vain enough to compare myself with some great names who have gone before me in this kind of writing. * * *

Instead of melting down my materials into one mass, and constantly speaking in my own person, by which I might have appeared to have more merit in the execution of the work, I have resolved to adopt and enlarge upon the excellent plan of Mr. Mason, in his *Memoirs* of Gray.[2] Wherever narrative is necessary to explain, connect, and supply, I furnish it to the best of my abilities; but in the chronological series of Johnson's life, which I trace as distinctly as I can, year by year, I produce, wherever it is in my power, his own minutes,[3] letters, or conversation, being convinced that this mode is more lively, and will make my readers better acquainted with him, than even most of those were who actually knew him, but could know him only partially; whereas there is here an accumulation of intelligence from various points, by which his character is more fully understood and illustrated.

Indeed I cannot conceive a more perfect mode of writing any man's life than not only relating all the most important events of it in their order, but interweaving what he privately wrote, and said, and thought; by which mankind are enabled as it were to see him live, and to "live o'er each scene"[4] with him, as he actually advanced through the several stages of his life. Had his other friends been as diligent and ardent as I was, he might have been almost entirely preserved. As it is, I will venture to say that he will be seen in this work more completely than any man who has ever yet lived.

And he will be seen as he really was; for I profess to write, not his panegyric, which must be all praise, but his Life; which, great and good as he was, must not be supposed to be entirely perfect. To be as he was, is indeed subject of panegyric enough to any man in this state of being; but in every picture there should be shade as well as light, and when I delineate him without reserve, I do what he himself recommended, both by his precept[5] and his example. * * *

What I consider as the peculiar value of the following work is the quantity that it contains of Johnson's conversation; which is universally acknowledged to have been eminently instructive and entertaining; and of which the specimens that I have given upon a former occasion have been received with so much approbation that I have good grounds for supposing that the world will not be indifferent to more ample communications of a similar nature. * * *

I am fully aware of the objections which may be made to the minuteness on some occasions of my detail of Johnson's conversation, and how happily it is adapted for the petty exercise of ridicule, by men of superficial understanding and ludicrous fancy;[6] but I remain firm and confident in my opinion, that minute particulars are frequently characteristic,[7] and always amusing, when they relate to a distinguished man. I am therefore exceedingly unwilling that anything, however slight, which my illustrious friend thought it worth his while to express, with any degree of point,[8] should perish. * * *

---

2. William Mason constructed his *Memoirs* of Thomas Gray (1775) around a selection of the poet's letters.
3. Memoranda.
4. "To wake the soul by tender strokes of art, / To raise the genius, and to mend the heart, / To make mankind in conscious virtue bold, / Live o'er each scene, and be what they behold" (lines 1–4 of Pope's prologue to Addison's *Cato*).

5. Boswell proceeds to quote from *Rambler* No. 60, in which Johnson articulates his biographical principles.
6. Boswell's Hebridean journal had already been parodied in print for its "minuteness" and "detail."
7. Revealing of character.
8. "Remarkable turn of words or thought" (Johnson's *Dictionary*).

Of one thing I am certain, that considering how highly the small portion which we have of the table talk and other anecdotes of our celebrated writers[9] is valued, and how earnestly it is regretted that we have not more, I am justified in preserving rather too many of Johnson's sayings than too few; especially as from the diversity of dispositions it cannot be known with certainty beforehand, whether what may seem trifling to some, and perhaps to the collector himself, may not be most agreeable to many; and the greater number that an author can please in any degree, the more pleasure does there arise to a benevolent mind.

To those who are weak enough to think this a degrading task, and the time and labor which have been devoted to it misemployed, I shall content myself with opposing the authority of the greatest man of any age, Julius Caesar, of whom Bacon observes, that "in his book of Apothegms which he collected, we see that he esteemed it more honor to make himself but a pair of tables, to take the wise and pithy words of others, than to have every word of his own to be made an apothegm or an oracle."

Having said thus much by way of introduction, I commit the following pages to the candor of the Public.

[DINNER WITH WILKES]

[May 1776] I am now to record a very curious incident in Dr. Johnson's life, which fell under my own observation; of which *pars magna fui*,[1] and which I am persuaded will, with the liberal-minded, be much to his credit.

My desire of being acquainted with celebrated men of every description had made me, much about the same time, obtain an introduction to Dr. Samuel Johnson and to John Wilkes, Esq.[2] Two men more different could perhaps not be selected out of all mankind. They had even attacked one another with some asperity in their writings; yet I lived in habits of friendship with both. I could fully relish the excellence of each; for I have ever delighted in that intellectual chemistry which can separate good qualities from evil in the same person.

Sir John Pringle,[3] "mine own friend and my Father's friend," between whom and Dr. Johnson I in vain wished to establish an acquaintance, as I respected and lived in intimacy with both of them, observed to me once, very ingeniously, "It is not in friendship as in mathematics, where two things, each equal to a third, are equal between themselves. You agree with Johnson as a middle quality, and you agree with me as a middle quality; but Johnson and I should not agree." Sir John was not sufficiently flexible, so I desisted, knowing, indeed, that the repulsion was equally strong on the part of Johnson, who, I know not from what cause, unless his being a Scotchman, had formed a very erroneous opinion of Sir John. But I conceived an irresistible wish, if possible, to bring Dr. Johnson and Mr. Wilkes together. How to manage it was a nice[4] and difficult matter.

My worthy booksellers[5] and friends, Messieurs Dilly in the Poultry, at whose hospitable and well-covered table I have seen a greater number of literary men than at

9. E.g., Joseph Spence's *Anecdotes, Observations and Characters of Books and Men, Collected from the Conversation of Mr. Pope,* which (though unpublished until 1820) Johnson drew on for his *Life* of Pope.
1. "I was no small part." (Virgil, *Aeneid* 2.5).
2. John Wilkes (1727–1797), libertine, satirist, and radical politician, had been expelled from Parliament for blasphemous and seditious libel. Johnson considered Wilkes an unprincipled philanderer and demagogue.
3. John Pringle (1707–1782), distinguished physician and president of the Royal Society. Johnson disliked Pringle's freethinking religious views and his pro-American political convictions.
4. Delicate.
5. Publishers.

any other, except that of Sir Joshua Reynolds, had invited me to meet Mr. Wilkes and some more gentlemen on Wednesday, May 15. "Pray," said I, "let us have Dr. Johnson."—"What, with Mr. Wilkes? not for the world," said Mr. Edward Dilly, "Dr. Johnson would never forgive me."—"Come," said I, "if you'll let me negotiate for you, I will be answerable that all shall go well." DILLY: "Nay, if you will take it upon you, I am sure I shall be very happy to see them both here."

Notwithstanding the high veneration which I entertained for Dr. Johnson, I was sensible that he was sometimes a little actuated by the spirit of contradiction, and by means of that I hoped I should gain my point. I was persuaded that if I had come upon him with a direct proposal, "Sir, will you dine in company with Jack Wilkes?" he would have flown into a passion, and would probably have answered, "Dine with Jack Wilkes, Sir! I'd as soon dine with Jack Ketch."[6] I therefore, while we were sitting quietly by ourselves at his house in an evening, took occasion to open my plan thus:—"Mr. Dilly, Sir, sends his respectful compliments to you, and would be happy if you would do him the honor to dine with him on Wednesday next along with me, as I must soon go to Scotland." JOHNSON: "Sir, I am obliged to Mr. Dilly. I will wait upon him:" BOSWELL: "Provided, Sir, I suppose, that the company which he is to have is agreeable to you." JOHNSON: "What do you mean, Sir? What do you take me for? Do you think I am so ignorant of the world, as to imagine that I am to prescribe to a gentleman what company he is to have at his table?" BOSWELL: "I beg your pardon, Sir, for wishing to prevent you from meeting people whom you might not like. Perhaps he may have some of what he calls his patriotic[7] friends with him." JOHNSON: "Well, Sir, and what then? What care I for his *patriotic friends?* Poh!" BOSWELL: "I should not be surprised to find Jack Wilkes there." JOHNSON: "And if Jack Wilkes *should* be there, what is that to *me,* Sir? My dear friend, let us have no more of this. I am sorry to be angry with you; but really it is treating me strangely to talk to me as if I could not meet any company whatever, occasionally." BOSWELL: "Pray forgive me, Sir. I meant well. But you shall meet whoever comes, for me." Thus I secured him, and told Dilly that he would find him very well pleased to be one of his guests on the day appointed.

Upon the much-expected Wednesday, I called on him about half an hour before dinner, as I often did when we were to dine out together, to see that he was ready in time, and to accompany him. I found him buffeting[8] his books, as upon a former occasion, covered with dust and making no preparation for going abroad. "How is this, Sir?" said I. "Don't you recollect that you are to dine at Mr. Dilly's?" JOHNSON: "Sir, I did not think of going to Dilly's: it went out of my head. I have ordered dinner at home with Mrs. Williams."[9] BOSWELL: "But, my dear Sir, you know you were engaged to Mr. Dilly, and I told him so. He will expect you, and will be much disappointed if you don't come." JOHNSON: "You must talk to Mrs. Williams about this."

Here was a sad dilemma. I feared that what I was so confident I had secured would yet be frustrated. He had accustomed himself to show Mrs. Williams such a degree of humane attention, as frequently imposed some restraint upon him; and I knew that if she should be obstinate, he would not stir. I hastened downstairs to the blind lady's room and told her I was in great uneasiness, for Dr. Johnson had engaged

---

6. Famous 17th-century hangman.

7. Those in favor of diminishing the power of the monarch and supporting the rights of the American colonists. Johnson had recently written a political tract called *The Patriot* (1774) in which he attacked Wilkes and his supporters.

8. Vigorously cleaning.

9. An elderly blind woman who lived in Johnson's house as one of several dependents.

to me to dine this day at Mr. Dilly's, but that he had told me he had forgotten his engagement, and had ordered dinner at home. "Yes, Sir," said she, pretty peevishly, "Dr. Johnson is to dine at home." "Madam," said I "his respect for you is such that I know he will not leave you unless you absolutely desire it. But as you have so much of his company, I hope you will be good enough to forgo it for a day; as Mr. Dilly is a very worthy man, has frequently had agreeable parties at his house for Dr. Johnson, and will be vexed if the Doctor neglects him today. And then, Madam, be pleased to consider my situation; I carried the message, and I assured Mr. Dilly that Dr. Johnson was to come, and no doubt he has made a dinner, and invited a company, and boasted of the honor he expected to have. I shall be quite disgraced if the Doctor is not there." She gradually softened to my solicitations, which were certainly as earnest as most entreaties to ladies upon any occasion, and was graciously pleased to empower me to tell Dr. Johnson, "That all things considered, she thought he should certainly go." I flew back to him, still in dust, and careless of what should be the event,[1] "indifferent in his choice to go or stay";[2] but as soon as I had announced to him Mrs. Williams's consent, he roared, "Frank, a clean shirt," and was very soon dressed. When I had him fairly[3] seated in a hackney coach with me, I exulted as much as a fortune hunter who has got an heiress into a post chaise with him to set out for Gretna Green.[4]

When we entered Mr. Dilly's drawing room, he found himself in the midst of a company he did not know. I kept myself snug and silent, watching how he would conduct himself. I observed him whispering to Mr. Dilly, "Who is that gentleman, Sir?"—"Mr. Arthur Lee."—JOHNSON: "Too, too, too" (under his breath), which was one of his habitual mutterings. Mr. Arthur Lee could not but be very obnoxious to Johnson, for he was not only a *patriot* but an *American*. He was afterwards minister from the United States at the court of Madrid. "And who is the gentleman in lace?"—"Mr. Wilkes, Sir." This information confounded him still more; he had some difficulty to restrain himself, and taking up a book, sat down upon a window seat and read, or at least kept his eye upon it intently for some time, till he composed himself. His feelings, I dare say, were awkward enough. But he no doubt recollected his having rated[5] me for supposing that he could be at all disconcerted by any company, and he, therefore, resolutely set himself to behave quite as an easy man of the world, who could adapt himself at once to the disposition and manners of those whom he might chance to meet.

The cheering sound of "Dinner is upon the table" dissolved his reverie, and we *all* sat down without any symptom of ill humor. There were present, besides Mr. Wilkes, and Mr. Arthur Lee, who was an old companion of mine when he studied physics at Edinburgh, Mr. (now Sir John) Miller, Dr. Lettsom, and Mr. Slater, the druggist. Mr. Wilkes placed himself next to Dr. Johnson and behaved to him with so much attention and politeness that he gained upon him insensibly.[6] No man eat[7] more heartily than Johnson, or loved better what was nice and delicate. Mr. Wilkes was very assiduous in helping him to some fine veal. "Pray give me leave, Sir—It is better here—A little of the brown—Some fat, Sir—A little of the stuffing—Some gravy—Let me have the pleasure of giving you some butter—Allow me to recommend

---

1. Not caring how the matter turned out.
2. Boswell adapts a line from Addison's *Cato:* "Indiff'rent in his choice to sleep or die" (5.1).
3. Securely.
4. A village just across the border in Scotland; it was the common destination of eloping couples, who could

thereby bypass the formalities and restrictions of the Anglican Church.
5. Chided.
6. Imperceptibly.
7. Ate (pronounced "ett").

a squeeze of this orange, or the lemon, perhaps, may have more zest."—"Sir, Sir, I am obliged to you, Sir," cried Johnson, bowing, and turning his head to him with a look for some time of "surly virtue,"[8] but, in a short while, of complacency.

Foote being mentioned, Johnson said, "He is not a good mimic." One of the company added, "A merry Andrew, a buffoon." JOHNSON: "But he has wit[9] too, and is not deficient in ideas, or in fertility and variety of imagery, and not empty of reading;[1] he has knowledge enough to fill up his part. One species of wit he has in an eminent degree, that of escape. You drive him into a corner with both hands; but he's gone, Sir, when you think you have got him—like an animal that jumps over your head. Then he has a great range for his wit; he never lets truth stand between him and a jest, and he is sometimes mighty coarse. Garrick is under many restraints from which Foote is free." WILKES: "Garrick's wit is more like Lord Chesterfield's." JOHNSON: "The first time I was in company with Foote was at Fitzherbert's.[2] Having no good opinion of the fellow, I was resolved not to be pleased; and it is very difficult to please a man against his will. I went on eating my dinner pretty sullenly, affecting not to mind him. But the dog was so very comical, that I was obliged to lay down my knife and fork, throw myself back upon my chair, and fairly laugh it out. No, Sir, he was irresistible. He upon one occasion experienced, in an extraordinary degree, the efficacy of his powers of entertaining. Among the many and various modes which he tried of getting money, he became a partner with a small-beer brewer, and he was to have a share of the profits for procuring customers among his numerous acquaintance. Fitzherbert was one who took his small beer;[3] but it was so bad that the servants resolved not to drink it. They were at some loss how to notify[4] their resolution, being afraid of offending their master, who they knew liked Foote much as a companion. At last they fixed upon a little black boy, who was rather a favorite, to be their deputy and deliver their remonstrance; and having invested him with the whole authority of the kitchen, he was to inform Mr. Fitzherbert, in all their names, upon a certain day, that they would drink Foote's small beer no longer. On that day Foote happened to dine at Fitzherbert's, and this boy served at table; he was so delighted with Foote's stories, and merriment, and grimace,[5] that when he went downstairs, he told them, 'This is the finest man I have ever seen. I will not deliver your message. I will drink his small beer.'"

Somebody observed that Garrick could not have done this. WILKES: "Garrick would have made the small beer still smaller. He is now leaving the stage; but he will play Scrub[6] all his life." I knew that Johnson would let nobody attack Garrick but himself, as Garrick once said to me, and I had heard him praise his liberality; so to bring out his commendation of his celebrated pupil, I said, loudly, "I have heard Garrick is liberal." JOHNSON: "Yes, Sir, I know that Garrick has given away more money than any man in England that I am acquainted with, and that not from ostentatious views. Garrick was very poor when he began life; so when he came to have money, he probably was very unskillful in giving away, and saved when he should not. But Garrick began to be liberal as soon as he could; and I am of opinion, the reputation of avarice which he has had, has been very lucky for him and prevented his having

8. Boswell quotes from Johnson's poem *London*.
9. Intelligence, cleverness.
1. Devoid of learning.
2. William Fitzherbert (1712–1772), landowner and politician.
3. Weak beer.

4. Express.
5. Exaggerated facial expressions (Foote specialized in caricatures of his contemporaries).
6. A character in George Farquhar's comedy, *The Beaux' Stratagem*.

many enemies. You despise a man for avarice, but do not hate him. Garrick might have been much better attacked for living with more splendor than is suitable to a player: if they had had the wit to have assaulted him in that quarter, they might have galled him more. But they have kept clamoring about his avarice, which has rescued him from much obloquy and envy."

Talking of the great difficulty of obtaining authentic information for biography, Johnson told us, "When I was a young fellow I wanted to write the *Life of Dryden*, and in order to get materials, I applied to the only two persons then alive who had seen him; these were old Swinney, and old Cibber.[7] Swinney's information was no more than this, "That at Will's coffeehouse Dryden had a particular chair for himself, which was set by the fire in winter, and was then called his winter-chair; and that it was carried out for him to the balcony in summer, and was then called his summer-chair." Cibber could tell no more but "that he remembered him a decent old man, arbiter of critical disputes at Will's." You are to consider that Cibber was then at a great distance from Dryden, had perhaps one leg only in the room, and durst not draw in the other." BOSWELL: "Yet Cibber was a man of observation?" JOHNSON: "I think not." BOSWELL: "You will allow his *Apology* to be well done." JOHNSON: "Very well done, to be sure, Sir. That book is a striking proof of the justice of Pope's remark:

> Each might his several province well command,
> Would all but stoop to what they understand."[8]

BOSWELL: "And his plays are good." JOHNSON: "Yes; but that was his trade; *l'esprit du corps*: he had been all his life among players and play-writers. I wondered that he had so little to say in conversation, for he had kept the best company, and learnt all that can be got by the ear. He abused Pindar[9] to me, and then showed me an ode of his own, with an absurd couplet, making a linnet soar on an eagle's wing. I told him that when the ancients made a simile, they always made it like something real."

Mr. Wilkes remarked, that "among all the bold flights of Shakespeare's imagination, the boldest was making Birnam Wood march to Dunsinane,[1] creating a wood where there never was a shrub; a wood in Scotland! ha! ha! ha!" And he also observed that "the clannish slavery of the Highlands of Scotland was the single exception to Milton's remark[2] of 'The mountain nymph, sweet Liberty,' being worshipped in all hilly countries." "When I was at Inverary," said he, "on a visit to my old friend, Archibald, Duke of Argyle, his dependents congratulated me on being such a favorite of his Grace. I said, 'It is then, gentlemen, truly lucky for me; for if I had displeased the Duke, and he had wished it, there is not a Campbell among you but would have been ready to bring John Wilkes's head to him in a charger. It would have been only

Off with his head! So much for Aylesbury.[3]

I was then member[4] for Aylesbury." * * *

7. Owen Mac Swiney and Colley Cibber, actors from the first half of the 18th century. Cibber was also a poet, playwright, and the author of a widely read autobiography (his *Apology*).

8. Pope, *Essay on Criticism*, lines 66–67.

9. Spoke disparagingly of the ancient Greek poet Pindar, famous for his odes.

1. In Act 5 of *Macbeth*. In his *Journey to the Western Islands* (1775), Johnson had commented repeatedly on the treelessness of Scotland.

2. In his poem *L'Allegro* (36).

3. Wilkes adapts Colley Cibber's popular version of Shakespeare's *Richard III*, which contains the line, "Off with his head. So much for Buckingham."

4. Of Parliament.

Mr. Arthur Lee mentioned some Scotch who had taken possession of a barren part of America, and wondered why they should choose it. JOHNSON: "Why, Sir, all barrenness is comparative. The *Scotch* would not know it to be barren." BOSWELL: "Come, come, he is flattering the English. You have now been in Scotland, Sir, and say if you did not see meat and drink enough there." JOHNSON: "Why yes, Sir; meat and drink enough to give the inhabitants sufficient strength to run away from home." All these quick and lively sallies were said sportively, quite in jest, and with a smile, which showed that he meant only wit. Upon this topic he and Mr. Wilkes could perfectly assimilate; here was a bond of union between them, and I was conscious that as both of them had visited Caledonia,[5] both were fully satisfied of the strange narrow ignorance of those who imagine that it is a land of famine. But they amused themselves with persevering in the old jokes. When I claimed a superiority for Scotland over England in one respect, that no man can be arrested there for a debt merely because another swears it against him; but there must first be the judgment of a court of law ascertaining its justice; and that a seizure of the person, before judgment is obtained, can take place only if his creditor should swear that he is about to fly from the country, or, as it is technically expressed, is *in meditatione fugae*. WILKES: "That, I should think, may be safely sworn of all the Scotch nation." JOHNSON (to Mr. Wilkes): "You must know, Sir, I lately took my friend Boswell and showed him genuine civilized life in an English provincial town. I turned him loose at Lichfield, my native city, that he might see for once real civility: for you know he lives among savages in Scotland, and among rakes in London." WILKES: "Except when he is with grave, sober, decent people like you and me." JOHNSON (smiling): "And we ashamed of him."

They were quite frank and easy. Johnson told the story of his asking Mrs. Macaulay[6] to allow her footman to sit down with them, to prove the ridiculousness of the argument for the equality of mankind; and he said to me afterwards, with a nod of satisfaction, "You saw Mr. Wilkes acquiesced." Wilkes talked with all imaginable freedom of the ludicrous title given to the Attorney General, *Diabolus Regis*,[7] adding, "I have reason to know something about that officer; for I was prosecuted for a libel."[8] Johnson, who many people would have supposed must have been furiously angry at hearing this talked of so lightly, said not a word. He was now, *indeed*, "a good-humored fellow."

After dinner we had an accession[9] of Mrs. Knowles, the Quaker lady, well known for her various talents, and of Mr. Alderman Lee. Amidst some patriotic groans, somebody (I think the Alderman) said, "Poor old England is lost." JOHNSON: "Sir, it is not so much to be lamented that Old England is lost, as that the Scotch have found it."[1] WILKES: "Had Lord Bute governed Scotland only, I should not have taken the trouble to write his eulogy, and dedicate *Mortimer* to him."[2]

---

5. Scotland (from the Roman name for North Britain).
6. Catherine Macaulay, author of a controversial *History of England* (1763–1783). In order to test her egalitarian principles, Johnson had proposed that she invite her footman to join them at dinner. "I thus, Sir, showed her the absurdity of the leveling doctrine," he told Boswell. "She has never liked me since."
7. The King's Devil.
8. See n. 2, page 1452.
9. I.e., these additional guests arrived: Mary Morris Knowles (1733–1807), a highly accomplished needlewoman whose "sutile pictures" Johnson praised in a

letter to Mrs. Thrale; and William Lee (1739–1795), merchant, diplomat, and the only American ever elected an alderman of London.
1. Soon after succeeding to the throne in 1760, George III made his former tutor, the Scottish Earl of Bute, Prime Minister of Britain. The appointment unleashed a flood of anti-Scottish propaganda.
2. As part of a sustained campaign against Bute's government, Wilkes had chosen to reprint a 1731 play called *The Fall of Mortimer* and had prefaced it with a mockrespectful dedication to the prime minister.

Mr. Wilkes held a candle to show a fine print of a beautiful female figure which hung in the room, and pointed out the elegant contour of the bosom with the finger of an arch connoisseur. He afterwards, in a conversation with me, waggishly insisted that all the time Johnson showed visible signs of a fervent admiration of the corresponding charms of the fair Quaker.

This record, though by no means so perfect as I could wish, will serve to give a notion of a very curious interview, which was not only pleasing at the time, but had the agreeable and benignant effect of reconciling any animosity, and sweetening any acidity, which in the various bustle of political contest, had been produced in the minds of two men, who though widely different, had so many things in common—classical learning, modern literature, wit, and humor, and ready repartee—that it would have been much to be regretted if they had been forever at a distance from each other.

Mr. Burke gave me much credit for this successful *negotiation* and pleasantly said that "there was nothing to equal it in the whole history of the *Corps Diplomatique*."

I attended Dr. Johnson home, and had the satisfaction to hear him tell Mrs. Williams how much he had been pleased with Mr. Wilkes's company, and what an agreeable day he had passed.

<hr />

Oliver Goldsmith
1730–1774

Goldsmith's cluster of famous friends never tired of describing and diagnosing what they saw as the baffling discrepancy between his success in writing and his oddity in conversation. Samuel Johnson put the problem succinctly: "No man was more foolish when he had not a pen in his hand, or more wise when he had." The actor David Garrick compacted the same paradox into the second line of an imaginary epitaph, composed while its outraged subject was present in the room: "Here lies Nolly Goldsmith, for shortness called Noll, / Who wrote like an angel, and talked like poor Poll"—that is, like a parrot, noisily spouting verbiage mimicked from minds better furnished than his own. Always quick to take offense, Goldsmith took so much at this that he devoted the remaining months of his short life to a *Retaliation* in which he took vengeance, in the form of caustic verse epitaphs, on the many people from whom he thought he had suffered slights.

Goldsmith's awkwardness, competitiveness, and defensiveness arose partly from discomfort as to humble origins and scattershot education. Born in Ireland to an eccentric curate, he had come to London in 1756 after a checkered academic career spent in Dublin, Edinburgh, and on the Continent, half-heartedly pursuing degrees (never obtained) in divinity and medicine. Upon arriving in London, Goldsmith took a series of odd jobs (druggist, physician, schoolteacher) before establishing himself as a reviewer, translator, essayist, and editor. His work brought him to the attention of the eminent, in whose company he launched that precarious social strategy which his closest friend, the painter Joshua Reynolds, later analyzed: "He had a very strong desire, which I believe nobody will think very peculiar, to be liked, to have his company sought after by his friends. To this end, for it was a system, he abandoned his respectable character as a writer or a man of observation to that of a character [in whose presence] nobody was afraid of being humiliated." As Reynolds acknowledges, the "system" often backfired, because Goldsmith wanted desperately to be impressive as well as "liked." Friends found his mystery worth probing because of the almost palpable preponderance of his merits: alongside irascibility, Goldsmith possessed a compelling charm and generosity; and an amazing *feeling* (Reynolds's emphatic term) for what made writing work.

To support spendthrift habits and a love of gambling, Goldsmith undertook much compendious hackwork—*A History of England* (1764); *Roman History* (1769); *Grecian History* (1774); and a *History of the Earth, and Animated Nature* (1774). At the same time, he managed to score more successes in more genres than almost any of his contemporaries save Johnson: periodical essay (*The Citizen of the World*, 1760–1761); biography (*The Life of Richard Nash*, 1762); novel (*The Vicar of Wakefield*, 1766); stage comedy (*The Good Natured Man*, 1768; *She Stoops to Conquer*, 1773); and poetry (*The Traveller*, 1764; and *The Deserted Village*, 1770). *The Deserted Village* was the work most celebrated in his own lifetime. Two years in the making, the poem recasts an argument Goldsmith had voiced earlier in an essay against the acquisition of rural acreage by merchants who, having acquired their wealth by the commerce of empire and the trade in luxuries, were now bent on converting their new-bought lands from productive communal pasture into pretty pleasure grounds: "In almost every part of the kingdom the laborious husbandman [farmer] has been reduced, and the lands are now either occupied by some general undertaker, or turned into enclosures destined for the purposes of amusement or luxury." Such encroachment, Goldsmith contended, was driving farm families from their villages and annihilating centuries of graceful country tradition. In his poem, Goldsmith mingled nostalgia for a rural past with dread of a commercial future. Contemporary critics promptly ushered *The Deserted Village* into the poetic canon by sundering those elements Goldsmith had worked hard to fuse: they dismissed the poem's economic doctrine and praised its imaginative power. Like the poet's friends, the poem's readers are left to sort out and savor Goldsmith's characteristic complexity: a "sentimental radicalism" (the phrase is John Barrell's) whereby the conservative defense of old values produces a new and volatile empathy with the plight of the poor.

The Deserted Village
To Sir Joshua Reynolds[1]

Dear Sir,

I can have no expectations in an address of this kind, either to add to your reputation, or to establish my own. You can gain nothing from my admiration, as I am ignorant of that art in which you are said to excel; and I may lose much by the severity of your judgment, as few have a juster taste in poetry than you. Setting interest therefore aside, to which I never paid much attention, I must be indulged at present in following my affections. The only dedication I ever made was to my brother,[2] because I loved him better than most other men. He is since dead. Permit me to inscribe this poem to you.

How far you may be pleased with the versification and mere mechanical parts of this attempt, I don't pretend to inquire; but I know you will object (and indeed several of our best and wisest friends concur in the opinion) that the depopulation it deplores is nowhere to be seen, and the disorders it laments are only to be found in the poet's own imagination. To this I can scarce make any other answer than that I sincerely believe what I have written; that I have taken all possible pains, in my country

---

1. Reynolds (1723–1792) was one of England's leading portrait painters and first president of the Royal Academy; his close friendship with Goldsmith had begun in the mid-1760s.

2. Goldsmith had dedicated his previous long poem, *The Traveller* (1764), to his brother Henry, who died in 1768.

excursions, for these four or five years past, to be certain of what I allege; and that all my views and inquiries have led me to believe those miseries real, which I here attempt to display. But this is not the place to enter into an inquiry, whether the country be depopulating, or not; the discussion would take up much room, and I should prove myself, at best, an indifferent politician, to tire the reader with a long preface, when I want his unfatigued attention to a long poem.

In regretting the depopulation of the country, I inveigh against the increase of our luxuries; and here also I expect the shout of modern politicians against me. For twenty or thirty years past, it has been the fashion to consider luxury as one of the greatest national advantages; and all the wisdom of antiquity in that particular, as erroneous.[3] Still however, I must remain a professed ancient on that head, and continue to think those luxuries prejudicial to states, by which so many vices are introduced, and so many kingdoms have been undone. Indeed so much has been poured out of late on the other side of the question, that, merely for the sake of novelty and variety, one would sometimes wish to be in the right.

I am,

Dear Sir,

Your sincere friend,

and ardent admirer,

OLIVER GOLDSMITH.

Sweet Auburn, loveliest village of the plain,[4]
Where health and plenty cheered the laboring swain,
Where smiling spring its earliest visit paid,
And parting summer's lingering blooms delayed:
5   Dear lovely bowers of innocence and ease,
Seats of my youth, when every sport could please,
How often have I loitered o'er thy green,
Where humble happiness endeared each scene;
How often have I paused on every charm,
10   The sheltered cot,° the cultivated farm,   *cottage*
The never-failing brook, the busy mill,
The decent church that topped the neighboring hill,
The hawthorn bush, with seats beneath the shade,
For talking age and whispering lovers made.
15   How often have I blessed the coming day,
When toil remitting lent its turn to play,
And all the village train, from labor free,
Led up their sports beneath the spreading tree,
While many a pastime circled in the shade,
20   The young contending as the old surveyed;
And many a gambol frolicked o'er the ground,
And sleights of art and feats of strength went round.
And still as each repeated pleasure tired,
Succeeding sports the mirthful band inspired;

---

3. A long line of ancient authors—Horace, Seneca, and Pliny among them—had warned that the traffic in luxuries was sapping Rome's health, and had urged moderation.

4. "Auburn" is fictitious; it may be based in part on the Irish village of Lissoy, Goldsmith's childhood home.

25 The dancing pair that simply sought renown
By holding out to tire each other down;
The swain mistrustless of his smutted face,
While secret laughter tittered round the place;
The bashful virgin's sidelong looks of love,
30 The matron's glance that would those looks reprove.
These were thy charms, sweet village; sports like these,
With sweet succession, taught even toil to please;
These round thy bowers their cheerful influence shed,
These were thy charms—But all these charms are fled.

35 Sweet smiling village, loveliest of the lawn,
Thy sports are fled, and all thy charms withdrawn;
Amidst thy bowers the tyrant's hand is seen,
And desolation saddens all thy green:
One only master grasps the whole domain,
40 And half a tillage⁵ stints° thy smiling plain;   *sets limits to*
No more thy glassy brook reflects the day,
But choked with sedges, works its weedy way.
Along thy glades, a solitary guest,
The hollow sounding bittern guards its nest;
45 Amidst thy desert walks the lapwing flies,
And tires their echoes with unvaried cries.
Sunk are thy bowers, in shapeless ruin all,
And the long grass o'ertops the mouldering wall,
And trembling, shrinking from the spoiler's hand,
50 Far, far away thy children leave the land.

Ill fares the land, to hastening ills a prey,
Where wealth accumulates and men decay:
Princes and lords may flourish or may fade;
A breath can make them, as a breath has made;
55 But a bold peasantry, their country's pride,
When once destroyed, can never be supplied.

A time there was, ere England's griefs began,
When every rood° of ground maintained its man;   *quarter acre*
For him light labor spread her wholesome store,
60 Just gave what life required, but gave no more:
His best companions, innocence and health;
And his best riches, ignorance of wealth.

But times are altered; trade's unfeeling train
Usurp the land and dispossess the swain;
65 Along the lawn,° where scattered hamlets rose,   *open countryside*
Unwieldy wealth and cumbrous pomp repose;
And every want to opulence allied,
And every pang that folly pays to pride.
These gentle hours that plenty bade to bloom,

5. Piece of tilled land.

70   Those calm desires that asked but little room,
      Those healthful sports that graced the peaceful scene,
      Lived in each look, and brightened all the green;
      These far departing seek a kinder shore,
      And rural mirth and manners are no more.

75   Sweet Auburn! parent of the blissful hour,
      Thy glades forlorn confess the tyrant's power.
      Here as I take my solitary rounds,
      Amidst thy tangling walks, and ruined grounds,
      And, many a year elapsed, return to view
80   Where once the cottage stood, the hawthorn grew,
      Remembrance wakes with all her busy train,
      Swells at my breast, and turns the past to pain.

          In all my wanderings round this world of care,
      In all my griefs—and God has given my share—
85   I still had hopes my latest hours to crown,
      Amidst these humble bowers to lay me down;
      To husband out life's taper⁶ at the close,
      And keep the flame from wasting by repose.
      I still had hopes, for pride attends us still,
90   Amidst the swains to show my book-learned skill,
      Around my fire an evening group to draw,
      And tell of all I felt, and all I saw;
      And, as an hare whom hounds and horns pursue,
      Pants to the place from whence at first she flew,
95   I still had hopes, my long vexations past,
      Here to return—and die at home at last.

          O blest retirement, friend to life's decline,
      Retreats from care that never must be mine,
      How happy he who crowns in shades like these
100   A youth of labor with an age of ease;
      Who quits a world where strong temptations try,
      And, since 'tis hard to combat, learns to fly.
      For him no wretches, born to work and weep,
      Explore the mine, or tempt the dangerous deep;
105   No surly porter stands in guilty state
      To spurn imploring famine from the gate,
      But on he moves to meet his latter end,
      Angels around befriending virtue's friend;
      Bends to the grave with unperceived decay,
110   While resignation gently slopes the way;
      And, all his prospects brightening to the last,
      His Heaven commences ere the world be past!

---

6. Candle. "To husband out" means to maintain something thriftily, so that it lasts long.

Sweet was the sound when oft at evening's close
Up yonder hill the village murmur rose;
115   There as I passed with careless steps and slow,
The mingling notes came softened from below;
The swain responsive as the milkmaid sung,
The sober herd that lowed to meet their young,
The noisy geese that gabbled o'er the pool,
120   The playful children just let loose from school,
The watchdog's voice that bayed the whispering wind,
And the loud laugh that spoke the vacant° mind,   *carefree*
These all in sweet confusion sought the shade,
And filled each pause the nightingale had made.
125   But now the sounds of population fail,
No cheerful murmurs fluctuate in the gale,
No busy steps the grass-grown footway tread,
For all the bloomy flush of life is fled.
All but yon widowed, solitary thing
130   That feebly bends beside the plashy[7] spring;
She, wretched matron, forced, in age, for bread,
To strip the brook with mantling° cresses[8] spread,   *growing*
To pick her wintry faggot° from the thorn,   *firewood*
To seek her nightly shed, and weep till morn;
135   She only left of all the harmless train,
The sad historian of the pensive plain.

Near yonder copse, where once the garden smiled,
And still where many a garden flower grows wild;
There, where a few torn shrubs the place disclose,
140   The village preacher's modest mansion rose.
A man he was, to all the country dear,
And passing rich with forty pounds a year;
Remote from towns he ran his godly race,
Nor e'er had changed, nor wished to change his place;
145   Unpracticed he to fawn, or seek for power,
By doctrines fashioned to the varying hour;
Far other aims his heart had learned to prize,
More skilled to raise the wretched than to rise.
His house was known to all the vagrant train,
150   He chid their wanderings, but relieved their pain;
The long remembered beggar was his guest,
Whose beard descending swept his aged breast;
The ruined spendthrift, now no longer proud,
Claimed kindred there, and had his claims allowed;
155   The broken soldier, kindly bade to stay,
Sat by his fire, and talked the night away;
Wept o'er his wounds, or tales of sorrow done,
Shouldered his crutch, and showed how fields were won.

---

7. Abounding in pools.   8. Leafy, edible plants.

Pleased with his guests, the good man learned to glow,
160   And quite forgot their vices in their woe;
Careless their merits or their faults to scan,
His pity gave ere charity began.

Thus to relieve the wretched was his pride,
And even his failings leaned to virtue's side;
165   But in his duty prompt at every call,
He watched and wept, he prayed and felt, for all.
And, as a bird each fond endearment tries,
To tempt its new fledged offspring to the skies,
He tried each art, reproved each dull delay,
170   Allured to brighter worlds, and led the way.

Beside the bed where parting life was laid,
And sorrow, guilt, and pain by turns dismayed,
The reverend champion stood. At his control,
Despair and anguish fled the struggling soul;
175   Comfort came down the trembling wretch to raise,
And his last faltering accents whispered praise.

At church, with meek and unaffected grace,
His looks adorned the venerable place;
Truth from his lips prevailed with double sway,
180   And fools, who came to scoff, remained to pray.
The service past, around the pious man,
With steady zeal each honest rustic ran;
Even children followed with endearing wile,
And plucked his gown, to share the good man's smile.
185   His ready smile a parent's warmth expressed,
Their welfare pleased him, and their cares distressed;
To them his heart, his love, his griefs were given,
But all his serious thoughts had rest in Heaven.
As some tall cliff that lifts its awful form,
190   Swells from the vale, and midway leaves the storm,
Though round its breast the rolling clouds are spread,
Eternal sunshine settles on its head.

Beside yon straggling fence that skirts the way,
With blossomed furze° unprofitably gay,   *thorny bushes*
195   There, in his noisy mansion, skilled to rule,
The village master taught his little school;
A man severe he was, and stern to view,
I knew him well, and every truant knew;
Well had the boding tremblers learned to trace
200   The day's disasters in his morning face;
Full well they laughed with counterfeited glee,
At all his jokes, for many a joke had he;
Full well the busy whisper circling round,
Conveyed the dismal tidings when he frowned;
205   Yet he was kind, or if severe in aught,

The love he bore to learning was in fault;
The village all declared how much he knew;
'Twas certain he could write, and cipher too;
Lands he could measure, terms and tides presage,[9]
210   And even the story ran that he could gauge.[1]
In arguing too, the parson owned° his skill,   *acknowledged*
For even though vanquished, he could argue still;
While words of learned length, and thundering sound,
Amazed the gazing rustics ranged around;
215   And still they gazed, and still the wonder grew,
That one small head could carry all he knew.

But past is all his fame. The very spot,
Where many a time he triumphed, is forgot.
Near yonder thorn, that lifts its head on high,
220   Where once the signpost caught the passing eye,
Low lies that house where nut-brown draughts° inspired,   *drinks*
Where gray-beard mirth and smiling toil retired,
Where village statesmen talked with looks profound,
And news much older than their ale went round.
225   Imagination fondly stoops to trace
The parlor splendors of that festive place;
The whitewashed wall, the nicely sanded floor,
The varnished clock that clicked behind the door;
The chest contrived a double debt to pay,
230   A bed by night, a chest of drawers by day;
The pictures placed for ornament and use,
The twelve good rules,[2] the royal game of goose;[3]
The hearth, except when winter chilled the day,
With aspen boughs, and flowers, and fennel gay,
235   While broken teacups, wisely kept for show,
Ranged o'er the chimney, glistened in a row.

Vain transitory splendors! Could not all
Reprieve the tottering mansion from its fall!
Obscure it sinks, nor shall it more impart
240   An hour's importance to the poor man's heart;
Thither no more the peasant shall repair
To sweet oblivion of his daily care;
No more the farmer's news, the barber's tale,
No more the woodman's ballad shall prevail;
245   No more the smith his dusky brow shall clear,
Relax his ponderous strength, and lean to hear;
The host himself no longer shall be found

---

9. "Terms" were the days when payments of rents and wages were due; "tides" were holidays like Easter that shifted date from year to year; information on both was readily available in the annual almanacs.
1. Calculate the capacity of barrels and other containers.
2. This list of simple life lessons ("Keep no bad company";

"Encourage no vice"), supposedly compiled by Charles I, was displayed, beneath a picture of his execution, in many country inns and houses.
3. A game in which dice determine the movement of the pieces across the board.

Careful to see the mantling° bliss go round;   *foaming*
Nor the coy maid, half willing to be pressed,
250   Shall kiss the cup to pass it to the rest.

Yes! let the rich deride, the proud disdain,
These simple blessings of the lowly train;
To me more dear, congenial to my heart,
One native charm, than all the gloss of art;
255   Spontaneous joys, where nature has its play,
The soul adopts, and owns their first born sway;
Lightly they frolic o'er the vacant mind,
Unenvied, unmolested, unconfined.
But the long pomp, the midnight masquerade,
260   With all the freaks of wanton wealth arrayed,
In these, ere triflers half their wish obtain,
The toiling pleasure sickens into pain;
And, even while fashion's brightest arts decoy,
The heart distrusting asks, if this be joy.

265   Ye friends to truth, ye statesmen, who survey
The rich man's joys increase, the poor's decay,
'Tis yours to judge, how wide the limits stand
Between a splendid and an happy land.
Proud swells the tide with loads of freighted ore,
270   And shouting Folly hails them from her shore;
Hoards, even beyond the miser's wish abound,
And rich men flock from all the world around.
Yet count our gains. This wealth is but a name
That leaves our useful products still the same.
275   Not so the loss. The man of wealth and pride
Takes up a space that many poor supplied;
Space for his lake, his park's extended bounds,
Space for his horses, equipage, and hounds;
The robe that wraps his limbs in silken sloth
280   Has robbed the neighboring fields of half their growth;
His seat, where solitary sports are seen,
Indignant spurns the cottage from the green;
Around the world each needful product flies,
For all the luxuries the world supplies.
285   While thus the land adorned for pleasure all
In barren splendor feebly waits the fall.

As some fair female unadorned and plain,
Secure to please while youth confirms her reign,
Slights every borrowed charm that dress supplies,
290   Nor shares with art the triumph of her eyes;
But when those charms are past, for charms are frail,
When time advances, and when lovers fail,
She then shines forth, solicitous to bless,
In all the glaring impotence of dress.
295   Thus fares the land, by luxury betrayed;

In nature's simplest charms at first arrayed;
But verging to decline, its splendors rise,
Its vistas strike, its palaces surprise;
While scourged by famine from the smiling land,
The mournful peasant leads his humble band;
And while he sinks without one arm to save,
The country blooms—a garden, and a grave.

Where then, ah where, shall poverty reside,
To scape the pressure of contiguous pride?
If to some common's[4] fenceless limits strayed,
He drives his flock to pick the scanty blade,
Those fenceless fields the sons of wealth divide,
And even the bare-worn common is denied.

If to the city sped—What waits him there?
To see profusion that he must not share;
To see ten thousand baneful arts combined
To pamper luxury, and thin mankind;
To see those joys the sons of pleasure know
Extorted from his fellow-creature's woe.
Here, while the courtier glitters in brocade,
There the pale artist° plies the sickly trade;   *artisan*
Here, while the proud their long-drawn pomps display,
There the black gibbet glooms beside the way.
The dome° where Pleasure holds her midnight reign,   *lavish house*
Here, richly decked, admits the gorgeous train;
Tumultuous grandeur crowds the blazing square,
The rattling chariots clash, the torches glare.
Sure scenes like these no troubles e'er annoy!
Sure these denote one universal joy!
Are these thy serious thoughts?—Ah, turn thine eyes
Where the poor houseless shivering female lies.
She once, perhaps, in village plenty blest,
Has wept at tales of innocence distressed;
Her modest looks the cottage might adorn,
Sweet as the primrose peeps beneath the thorn;
Now lost to all; her friends, her virtue fled,
Near her betrayer's door she lays her head,
And pinched with cold, and shrinking from the shower,
With heavy heart deplores that luckless hour
When idly first, ambitious of the town,
She left her wheel and robes of country brown.

Do thine, sweet Auburn, thine, the loveliest train,
Do thy fair tribes participate° her pain?   *partake of*
Even now, perhaps, by cold and hunger led,
At proud men's doors they ask a little bread!

300

305

310

315

320

325

330

335

340

4. Grazing land once shared by all the villagers.

Ah, no. To distant climes, a dreary scene,
Where half the convex world intrudes between,
Through torrid tracts with fainting steps they go,
Where wild Altama⁵ murmurs to their woe.
345 Far different there from all that charmed before,
The various terrors of that horrid shore;
Those blazing suns that dart a downward ray,
And fiercely shed intolerable day;
Those matted woods where birds forget to sing,
350 But silent bats in drowsy clusters cling,
Those poisonous fields with rank luxuriance crowned,
Where the dark scorpion gathers death around;
Where at each step the stranger fears to wake
The rattling terrors of the vengeful snake;
355 Where crouching tigers wait their hapless prey,
And savage men, more murderous still than they;
While oft in whirls the mad tornado flies,
Mingling the ravaged landscape with the skies.
Far different these from every former scene,
360 The cooling brook, the grassy vested green,
The breezy covert of the warbling grove,
That only sheltered thefts of harmless love.

Good Heaven! what sorrows gloomed that parting day,
That called them from their native walks away;
365 When the poor exiles, every pleasure past,
Hung round their bowers, and fondly looked their last,
And took a long farewell, and wished in vain
For seats like these beyond the western main;
And shuddering still to face the distant deep,
370 Returned and wept, and still returned to weep.
The good old sire the first prepared to go
To new-found worlds, and wept for others' woe.
But for himself, in conscious virtue brave,
He only wished for worlds beyond the grave.
375 His lovely daughter, lovelier in her tears,
The fond companion of his helpless years,
Silent went next, neglectful of her charms,
And left a lover's for a father's arms.
With louder plaints the mother spoke her woes,
380 And blessed the cot° where every pleasure rose;   *cottage*
And kissed her thoughtless babes with many a tear,
And clasped them close in sorrow doubly dear;
Whilst her fond husband strove to lend relief
In all the silent manliness of grief.

385 O luxury! Thou curst by Heaven's decree,
How ill exchanged are things like these for thee!

5. The Altamaha River, in Georgia (then a colony).

How do thy potions, with insidious joy,
Diffuse their pleasures only to destroy!
Kingdoms, by thee to sickly greatness grown,
390   Boast of a florid vigor not their own;
At every draught more large and large they grow,
A bloated mass of rank unwieldy woe;
Till sapped their strength, and every part unsound,
Down, down they sink, and spread a ruin round.

395   Even now the devastation is begun,
And half the business of destruction done;
Even now, methinks, as pondering here I stand,
I see the rural virtues leave the land.
Down where yon anchoring vessel spreads the sail,
400   That idly waiting flaps with every gale,
Downward they move, a melancholy band,
Pass from the shore, and darken all the strand.
Contented toil, and hospitable care,
And kind connubial tenderness are there;
405   And piety, with wishes placed above,
And steady loyalty, and faithful love:
And thou, sweet Poetry, thou loveliest maid,
Still first to fly where sensual joys invade;
Unfit, in these degenerate times of shame,
410   To catch the heart, or strike for honest fame;
Dear charming nymph, neglected and decried,
My shame in crowds, my solitary pride;
Thou source of all my bliss, and all my woe,
That found'st me poor at first, and keep'st me so;
415   Thou guide by which the nobler arts excel,
Thou nurse of every virtue, fare thee well.
Farewell, and O where'er thy voice be tried,
On Torno's[6] cliffs, or Pambamarca's[7] side,
Whether where equinoctial fervors[8] glow,
420   Or winter wraps the polar world in snow,
Still let thy voice, prevailing over time,
Redress the rigors of the inclement clime;
Aid slighted truth, with thy persuasive strain
Teach erring man to spurn the rage of gain;
425   Teach him that states of native strength possessed,
Though very poor, may still be very blest;
That trade's proud empire hastes to swift decay,
As ocean sweeps the labored mole° away;   *breakwater*
While self-dependent power can time defy,
430   As rocks resist the billows and the sky.[9]

1770

---

6. The Tornio, a river in Sweden.   8. Equatorial heat.
7. A mountain in Ecuador.   9. Samuel Johnson supplied the poem's last two couplets.

+—• ᴈ♦ᴈ •—+

Eliza Haywood
ca. 1693–1756

Eliza Haywood, as Clara Reeve observed, "was one of the most voluminous female writers that England ever produced." Over the course of four decades, she published more than sixty works, in a vast variety of genres ranging from comedies to conduct books. But she achieved her first fame by pioneering a form of fiction that dwelt along the highly eroticized (and very lucrative) cusp between reality as the novel was beginning to figure it, and romance as Reeve would later define it: "an heroic fable, which treats of fabulous persons and things." In Haywood's fictions, the fabulousness inheres not in heroic exploits but in sexual ardor. Her female protagonists pursue their desires so intensely and so successfully that she was dubbed by one admirer "the Grand Arbitress of Passion." Her first novel, bearing the expressive title *Love in Excess* (1719), appeared in the same year as *Crusoe*, and vied with it in popularity. *Fantomina* (1724), the novel reprinted here, appeared simultaneously with *Roxana*, and explores some of the same issues, but in Haywood's characteristic register of an overtly heightened reality. Fantomina runs through a sequence of disguises that push deception beyond the plausible towards the preposterous, and her tactics differ diametrically from Roxana's in their motivation. They are directed at one man rather than many, and grounded in an intense desire for risk and sex rather than security and wealth. In Haywood's early fiction, her female adventurers, her lovers in excess, pursue their pleasures at variable cost, paying sometimes with their lives, and sometimes not at all. In *Fantomina* Haywood celebrates, as usual, her protagonist's erotic energies, ingenuities, and appetites, and at the same time partly anticipates the more domesticated and didactic novels of her later years, wherein (as Reeve remarks) "she had the good fortune to recover a lost reputation, and the yet greater honor to atone for her errors."

Fantomina: Or, Love in a Maze
Being a Secret History of an Amour Between Two Persons of Condition[1]

> In love the victors from the vanquished fly.
> They fly that wound, and they pursue that die.

> —Waller[2]

A young lady of distinguished birth, beauty, wit, and spirit, happened to be in a box one night at the playhouse; where, though there were a great number of celebrated toasts,[3] she perceived several gentlemen extremely pleased themselves with entertaining a woman who sat in a corner of the pit,[4] and, by her air and manner of receiving them, might easily be known to be one of those who come there for no other purpose than to create acquaintance with as many as seem desirous of it. She could not help testifying her contempt of men who, regardless either of the play or

---

1. Upper-class rank.
2. The final lines of Edmund Waller's "To a Friend, on the different success of their loves" (1645), in which a man describes how his infatuation with a proud woman named Celia met with her rejection, while his subsequent loss of interest turned the tables and made her solicitous of him. "To die" here also means "to experience orgasm."

3. Belles, fine young ladies (whose health was commonly drunk by gentlemen in toasts).
4. The area below the stage generally occupied by gentlemen, law students, professional or literary types, and (in this case) prostitutes. Aristocracy generally sat in the boxes above.

circle, threw away their time in such a manner, to some ladies that sat by her: but they, either less surprised by being more accustomed to such sights than she who had been bred for the most part in the country, or not of a disposition to consider anything very deeply, took but little notice of it. She still thought of it, however; and the longer she reflected on it, the greater was her wonder that men, some of whom she knew were accounted to have wit,[5] should have tastes so very depraved.—This excited a curiosity in her to know in what manner these creatures were addressed,[6]— she was young, a stranger to the world, and consequently to the dangers of it; and having nobody in town at that time to whom she was obliged to be accountable for her actions, did in everything as her inclinations or humors rendered most agreeable to her: therefore thought it not in the least a fault to put in practice a little whim which came immediately into her head, to dress herself as near as she could in the fashion of those women who make sale of their favors, and set herself in the way of being accosted as such a one, having at that time no other aim, than the gratification of an innocent curiosity.—She no sooner designed this frolic than she put it in execution; and muffling her hoods over her face, went the next night into the gallery-box, and practicing as much as she had observed at that distance the behavior of that woman, was not long before she found her disguise had answered the ends she wore it for.—A crowd of purchasers of all degrees and capacities were in a moment gathered about her, each endeavoring to outbid the other in offering her a price for her embraces.—She listened to 'em all, and was not a little diverted in her mind at the disappointment she should give to so many, each of which thought himself secure of gaining her.—She was told by 'em all that she was the most lovely woman in the world; and some cried, *Gad, she is mighty like my fine Lady Such-a-one*—naming her own name. She was naturally vain, and received no small pleasure in hearing herself praised, though in the person of another, and a supposed prostitute; but she dispatched as soon as she could all that had hitherto attacked her, when she saw the accomplished *Beauplaisir*[7] was making his way through the crowd as fast as he was able, to reach the bench she sat on. She had often seen him in the drawing-room, had talked with him; but then her quality[8] and reputed virtue kept him from using her with that freedom she now expected he would do, and had discovered something in him which had made her often think she should not be displeased, if he would abate some part of his reserve.—Now was the time to have her wishes answered:—he looked in her face, and fancied, as many others had done, that she very much resembled that lady whom she really was; but the vast disparity there appeared between their characters prevented him from entertaining even the most distant thought that they could be the same.—He addressed her at first with the usual salutations of her pretended profession, as, *Are you engaged, Madam?—Will you permit me to wait on you home after the play?—By Heaven, you are a fine girl!—How long have you used this house?*—and such like questions; but perceiving she had a turn of wit, and a genteel manner in her raillery, beyond what is frequently to be found among those wretches, who are for the most part gentlewomen but by necessity, few of 'em having had an education suitable to what they affect to appear, he changed the form of his conversation, and showed her it was not because he understood no better that he had made use of expressions so little polite.—In fine, they were

---

5. Intelligence, good taste, judgment.
6. Creatures: common term of disrespect for women of low birth or reputation. Addressed: approached, solicited.

7. Lovely pleasure (French).
8. High social station.

infinitely charmed with each other: he was transported to find so much beauty and wit in a woman, who he doubted not but on very easy terms he might enjoy; and she found a vast deal of pleasure in conversing with him in this free and unrestrained manner. They passed their time all the play with an equal satisfaction; but when it was over, she found herself involved in a difficulty, which before never entered into her head, but which she knew not well how to get over.—The passion he professed for her, was not of that humble nature which can be content with distant adorations:—he resolved not to part from her without the gratifications of those desires she had inspired; and presuming on the liberties which her supposed function allowed of, told her she must either go with him to some convenient house of his procuring, or permit him to wait on her to her own lodgings.—Never had she been in such a *dilemma*: three or four times did she open her mouth to confess her real quality; but the influence of her ill stars prevented it, by putting an excuse into her head, which did the business as well, and at the same time did not take from her the power of seeing and entertaining him a second time with the same freedom she had done this.—She told him, she was under obligations to a man who maintained her, and whom she durst not disappoint, having promised to meet him that night at a house hard by[9]—This story so like what those ladies sometimes tell was not at all suspected by *Beauplaisir*; and assuring her he would be far from doing her a prejudice,[1] desired that in return for the pain he should suffer in being deprived of her company that night, that she would order her affairs, so as not to render him unhappy the next. She gave a solemn promise to be in the same box on the morrow evening; and they took leave of each other; he to the tavern to drown the remembrance of his disappointment; she in a hackney-chair[2] hurried home to indulge contemplation on the frolic she had taken, designing nothing less on her first reflections than to keep the promise she had made him, and hugging herself with joy, that she had the good luck to come off undiscovered.

But these cogitations were but of a short continuance; they vanished with the hurry of her spirits, and were succeeded by others vastly different and ruinous:—all the charms of *Beauplaisir* came fresh into her mind; she languished, she almost died for another opportunity of conversing with him; and not all the admonitions of her discretion were effectual to oblige her to deny laying hold of that which offered itself the next night.—She depended on the strength of her virtue, to bear her fate through trials more dangerous than she apprehended this to be, and never having been addressed by him as Lady——was resolved to receive his devoirs[3] as a town-mistress, imagining a world of satisfaction to herself in engaging him in the character of such a one, observing the surprise he would be in to find himself refused by a woman, who he supposed granted her favors without exception.—Strange and unaccountable were the whimsies she was possessed of—wild and incoherent her desires—unfixed and undetermined her resolutions, but in that of seeing *Beauplaisir* in the manner she had lately done. As for her proceedings with him, or how a second time to escape him, without discovering who she was, she could neither assure herself, nor whether or not in the last extremity she would do so.—Bent, however, on meeting him, whatever should be the consequence, she went out some hours before the time of going to the playhouse, and took lodgings in a house not very far from it, intending, that if he should insist on passing some part of the night with her, to carry

9. Nearby.
1. Injury.

2. Hired sedan chair carried by two men.
3. Respects.

him there, thinking she might with more security to her honor entertain him at a place where she was mistress, than at any of his own choosing.

The appointed hour being arrived, she had the satisfaction to find his love in his assiduity: he was there before her; and nothing could be more tender than the manner in which he accosted her: but from the first moment she came in, to that of the play being done, he continued to assure her no consideration should prevail with him to part from her again, as she had done the night before; and she rejoiced to think she had taken that precaution of providing herself with a lodging, to which she thought she might invite him, without running any risk, either of her virtue or reputation.— Having told him she would admit of his accompanying her home, he seemed perfectly satisfied; and leading her to the place, which was not above twenty houses distant, would have ordered a collation[4] to be brought after them. But she would not permit it, telling him she was not one of those who suffered themselves to be treated at their own lodgings; and as soon she was come in, sent a servant, belonging to the house, to provide a very handsome supper, and wine, and everything was served to table in a manner which showed the director neither wanted money, nor was ignorant how it should be laid out.

This proceeding, though it did not take from him the opinion that she was what she appeared to be, yet it gave him thoughts of her, which he had not before.—He believed her a *mistress*, but believed her to be one of a superior rank, and began to imagine the possession of her would be much more expensive than at first he had expected; but not being of a humor to grudge anything for his pleasures, he gave himself no farther trouble than what were occasioned by fears of not having money enough to reach her price, about him.

Supper being over, which was intermixed with a vast deal of amorous conversation, he began to explain himself more than he had done; and both by his words and behavior let her know he would not be denied that happiness the freedoms she allowed had made him hope.—It was in vain; she would have retracted the encouragement she had given:—in vain she endeavored to delay, till the next meeting, the fulfilling of his wishes:—she had now gone too far to retreat:—*he* was bold;—he was resolute: *she* fearful—confused, altogether unprepared to resist in such encounters, and rendered more so, by the extreme liking she had to him.—Shocked, however, at the apprehension of really losing her honor, she struggled all she could, and was just going to reveal the whole secret of her name and quality, when the thoughts of the liberty he had taken with her, and those he still continued to prosecute, prevented her, with representing[5] the danger of being exposed, and the whole affair made a theme for public ridicule.—Thus much, indeed, she told him, that she was a virgin, and had assumed this manner of behavior only to engage him. But that he little regarded, or if he had, would have been far from obliging him to desist;—nay, in the present burning eagerness of desire, 'tis probable, that had he been acquainted both with who and what she really was, the knowledge of her birth would not have influenced him with respect sufficient to have curbed the wild exuberance of his luxurious wishes, or made him in that longing—that impatient moment, change the form of his addresses. In fine, she was undone; and he gained a victory, so highly rapturous, that had he known over whom, scarce could he have triumphed more. Her tears, however, and the distraction she appeared in, after the ruinous ecstasy was past, as it heightened his wonder, so it abated his satisfaction:—he could not imagine for what reason a woman, who, if she intended not to be a *mistress*, had counterfeited the part of one, and taken so much pains to engage him, should lament a consequence which she could not but expect, and till the last test, seemed inclinable to grant; and was both surprised and troubled at the mystery.—He omitted nothing that he thought might make her easy; and still retaining an opinion that the hope of interest had been the chief motive which had led her to act in the manner she had done, and believing that she might know so little of him, as to suppose, now she had nothing left to give, he might not make that recompense she expected for her favors: to put her out of that pain, he pulled out of his pocket a purse of gold, entreating her to accept of that as an earnest of what he intended to do for her; assuring her, with ten thousand protestations, that he would spare nothing, which his whole estate could purchase, to procure her content and happiness. This treatment made her quite forget the part she had assumed, and throwing it from her with an air of disdain, Is this a reward (*said she*) for condescensions,[6] such as I have yielded to?—Can all the wealth you are possessed of make a reparation for my loss of honor?—Oh! no, I am undone beyond the power of heaven itself to help me!—She uttered many more such exclamations; which the amazed *Beauplaisir* heard without being able to reply to, till by degrees sinking from that rage of temper, her eyes resumed their softening glances, and guessing at the consternation he was in, No, my dear *Beauplaisir*, (*added she*) your love alone can compensate for the shame you have involved me in; be you sincere and constant, and hereafter shall, perhaps, be satisfied with my fate, and forgive myself the folly that betrayed me to you.

Beauplaisir thought he could not have a better opportunity than these words gave him of inquiring who she was, and wherefore she had feigned herself to be of a profession which he was now convinced she was not; and after he had made her a thousand vows of an affection, as inviolable and ardent as she could wish to find in him, entreated she would inform him by what means his happiness had been brought about, and also to whom he was indebted for the bliss he had enjoyed.—Some remains of yet unextinguished modesty, and sense of shame, made her blush exceedingly at this demand; but recollecting herself in a little time, she told him so much of the truth, as to what related to the frolic she had taken of satisfying her curiosity in what manner *mistresses*, of the sort she appeared to be were treated by those who addressed them; but forbore discovering her true name and quality, for the reasons she had done before, resolving, if he boasted of this affair, he should not have it in his power to touch her character: she therefore said she was the daughter of a country gentleman, who was come to town to buy clothes, and that she was called *Fantomina*. He had no reason to distrust the truth of this story, and was therefore satisfied with it; but did not doubt by the beginning of her conduct, but that in the end she would be in reality, the thing she so artfully had counterfeited; and had good nature enough to pity the misfortunes he imagined would be her lot: but to tell her so, or offer his advice in that point, was not his business, at least, as yet.

They parted not till towards morning; and she obliged him to a willing vow of visiting her the next day at three in the afternoon. It was too late for her to go home that night, therefore contented herself with lying there. In the morning she sent for the woman of the house to come up to her; and easily perceiving, by her manner, that she was a woman who might be influenced by gifts, made her a present of a

6. Unworthiness, vice.

couple of broad pieces,[7] and desired her, that if the gentleman, who had been there the night before, should ask any questions concerning her, that he should be told, she was lately come out of the country, had lodged there about a fortnight, and that her name was *Fantomina*. I shall (*also added she*) lie but seldom here; nor, indeed, ever come but in those times when I expect to meet him: I would, therefore, have you order it so, that he may think I am but just gone out, if he should happen by any accident to call when I am not here; for I would not, for the world, have him imagine I do not constantly lodge here. The landlady assured her she would do everything as she desired, and gave her to understand she wanted not the gift of secrecy.

Everything being ordered at this home for the security of her reputation, she repaired to the other, where she easily excused to an unsuspecting aunt, with whom she boarded, her having been abroad all night, saying, she went with a gentleman and his lady in a barge, to a little country seat of theirs up the river, all of them designing to return the same evening; but that one of the bargemen happening to be taken ill on the sudden, and no other waterman to be got that night, they were obliged to tarry till morning. Thus did this lady's wit and vivacity assist her in all, but where it was most needed.—She had discernment to foresee, and avoid all those ills which might attend the loss of her *reputation,* but was wholly blind to those of the ruin of her *virtue;* and having managed her affairs so as to secure the *one,* grew perfectly easy with the remembrance she had forfeited the *other.*—The more she reflected on the merits of *Beauplaisir,* the more she excused herself for what she had done; and the prospect of that continued bliss she expected to share with him took from her all remorse for having engaged in an affair which promised her so much satisfaction, and in which she found not the least danger of misfortune.—If he is really (*said she, to herself*) the faithful, the constant lover he has sworn to be, how charming will be our amor?—And if he should be false, grow satiated, like other men, I shall but, at the worst, have the private vexation of knowing I have lost him;—the intrigue being a secret, my disgrace will be so too: I shall hear no whispers as I pass—She is forsaken:—the odious word *forsaken* will never wound my ears; nor will my wrongs excite either the mirth or pity of the talking world:—it would not be even in the power of my undoer himself to triumph over me; and while he laughs at, and perhaps despises the fond, the yielding *Fantomina,* he will revere and esteem the virtuous, the reserved lady.—In this manner did she applaud her own conduct, and exult with the imagination that she had more prudence than all her sex beside. And it must be confessed, indeed, that she preserved an economy in the management of this intrigue beyond what almost any woman but herself ever did: in the first place, by making no person in the world a confidant in it; and in the next, in concealing from *Beauplaisir* himself the knowledge who she was; for though she met him three or four days in a week, at that lodging she had taken for that purpose, yet as much as he employed her time and thoughts, she was never missed from any assembly she had been accustomed to frequent.—The business of her love has engrossed her till six in the evening, and before seven she has been dressed in a different habit, and in another place.—Slippers, and a night-gown loosely flowing, has been the garb in which he has left the languishing *Fantomina;*—laced and adorned with all the blaze of jewels has he, in less than an hour after, beheld at the royal chapel, the palace gardens, drawing-room, opera, or play, the haughty awe-inspiring lady—a thousand times has he stood

---

7. Gold coins.

amazed at the prodigious likeness between his little mistress and this court beauty; but was still as far from imagining they were the same as he was the first hour he had accosted her in the playhouse, though it is not impossible but that her resemblance to this celebrated lady might keep his inclination alive something longer than otherwise they would have been; and that it was to the thoughts of this (as he supposed) unenjoyed charmer she owed in great measure the vigor of his latter caresses.

But he varied not so much from his sex as to be able to prolong desire to any great length after possession: the rifled charms of *Fantomina* soon lost their potency, and grew tasteless and insipid; and when the season of the year inviting the company to the *Bath*,[8] she offered to accompany him, he made an excuse to go without her. She easily perceived his coldness, and the reason why he pretended her going would be inconvenient, and endured as much from the discovery as any of her sex could do: she dissembled it, however, before him, and took her leave of him with the show of no other concern than his absence occasioned: but this she did to take from him all suspicion of her following him, as she intended, and had already laid a scheme for.—From her first finding out that he designed to leave her behind, she plainly saw it was for no other reason, than that being tired of her conversation, he was willing to be at liberty to pursue new conquests; and wisely considering that complaints, tears, swoonings, and all the extravagancies which women make use of in such cases, have little prevalence over a heart inclined to rove, and only serve to render those who practice them more contemptible, by robbing them of that beauty which alone can bring back the fugitive lover, she resolved to take another course; and remembering the height of transport she enjoyed when the agreeable *Beauplaisir* kneeled at her feet, imploring her first favors, she longed to prove the same again. Not but a woman of her beauty and accomplishments might have beheld a thousand in that condition *Beauplaisir* had been; but with her sex's modesty, she had not also thrown off another virtue equally valuable, though generally unfortunate, *constancy:* she loved *Beauplaisir*; it was only he whose solicitations could give her pleasure; and had she seen the whole species despairing, dying for her sake, it might, perhaps, have been a satisfaction to her pride, but none to her more tender inclination.—Her design was once more to engage him, to hear him sigh, to see him languish, to feel the strenuous pressures of his eager arms, to be compelled, to be sweetly forced to what she wished with equal ardor, was what she wanted, and what she had formed a stratagem to obtain, in which she promised herself success.

She no sooner heard he had left the town, than making a pretense to her aunt, that she was going to visit a relation in the country, went towards *Bath*, attended but by two servants, who she found reasons to quarrel with on the road and discharged: clothing herself in a habit she had brought with her, she forsook the coach, and went into a wagon, in which equipage she arrived at *Bath*. The dress she was in was a round-eared cap,[9] a short red petticoat, and a little jacket of gray stuff,[1] all the rest of her accoutrements were answerable to these, and joined with a broad country dialect, a rude unpolished air, which she, having been bred in these parts, knew very well how to imitate, with her hair and eye-brows blacked, made it impossible for her to be known, or taken for any other than what she seemed. Thus disguised did she offer herself to service in the house where *Beauplaisir* lodged, having made it her business

8. Town in southwestern England, popular as a resort because of its hot springs.

9. Style of cap associated with country women.
1. Coarse wool fabric.

to find out immediately where he was. Notwithstanding this metamorphosis she was still extremely pretty; and the mistress of the house happening at that time to want a maid was very glad of the opportunity of taking her. She was presently received into the family; and had a post in it (such as she would have chose, had she been left at her liberty), that of making the gentlemen's beds, getting them their breakfasts, and waiting on them in their chambers. Fortune in this exploit was extremely on her side; there were no others of the male-sex in the house than an old gentleman, who had lost the use of his limbs with the rheumatism, and had come thither for the benefit of the waters, and her beloved *Beauplaisir;* so that she was in no apprehensions of any amorous violence, but where she wished to find it. Nor were her designs disappointed: He was fired with the first sight of her; and though he did not presently take any farther notice of her, than giving her two or three hearty kisses, yet she, who now understood that language but too well, easily saw they were the prelude to more substantial joys.—Coming the next morning to bring his chocolate, as he had ordered, he catched her by the pretty leg, which the shortness of her petticoat did not in the least oppose; then pulling her gently to him, asked her, how long she had been at service?—How many sweethearts she had? If she had ever been in love? and many other such questions, befitting one of the degree she appeared to be: all which she answered with such seeming innocence, as more enflamed the amorous heart of him who talked to her. He compelled her to sit in his lap; and gazing on her blushing beauties, which, if possible, received addition from her plain and rural dress, he soon lost the power of containing himself.—His wild desires burst out in all his words and actions: he called her little angel, cherubim, swore he must enjoy her, though death were to be the consequence, devoured her lips, her breasts with greedy kisses, held to his burning bosom her half-yielding, half-reluctant body, nor suffered her to get loose, till he had ravaged all, and glutted each rapacious sense with the sweet beauties of the pretty *Celia,*[2] for that was the name she bore in this second expedition.—Generous as liberality itself to all who gave him joy this way, he gave her a handsome sum of gold, which she durst not now refuse, for fear of creating some mistrust, and losing the heart she so lately had regained; therefore taking it with an humble courtesy, and a well counterfeited show of surprise and joy, cried, O law, Sir! what must I do for all this? He laughed at her simplicity, and kissing her again, though less fervently than he had done before, bad her not be out of the way when he came home at night. She promised she would not, and very obediently kept her word.

His stay at *Bath* exceeded not a month; but in that time his supposed country lass had persecuted him so much with her fondness, that in spite of the eagerness with which he first enjoyed her, he was at last grown more weary of her, than he had been of *Fantomina;* which she perceiving, would not be troublesome, but quitting her service, remained privately in the town till she heard he was on his return; and in that time provided herself of another disguise to carry on a third plot, which her inventing brain had furnished her with, once more to renew his twice-decayed ardors. The dress she had ordered to be made, was such as widows wear in their first mourning, which, together with the most afflicted and penitential countenance that ever was seen, was no small alteration to her who used to seem all gaiety.—To add to this, her

---

2. In Renaissance literature the name Celia is frequently associated with vanity or pride, as in Lyly's *Love's Metamorphosis* as well as Waller's "To Phyllis" and "To a Friend" (quoted in the epigraph); similarly, in Swift's

"The Lady's Dressing Room" (see pages 1225–28), Celia is the woman who spends five hours in her dressing room each day in an effort to conceal her natural nastiness.

hair, which she was accustomed to wear very loose both when *Fantomina* and *Celia*, was now tied back so straight, and her pinners[3] coming so very forward, that there was none of it to be seen. In fine, her habit and her air were so much changed, that she was not more difficult to be known in the rude country *girl*, than she was now in the sorrowful *widow*.

She knew that *Beauplaisir* came alone in his chariot to the *Bath*, and in the time of her being servant in the house where he lodged, heard nothing of any body that was to accompany him to *London*, and hoped he would return in the same manner he had gone: She therefore hired horses and a man to attend her to an inn about ten miles on this side of *Bath*, where having discharged them, she waited till the chariot should come by; which when it did, and she saw that he was alone in it, she called to him that drove it to stop a moment, and going to the door saluted the master with these words:

The distressed and wretched, Sir (*said she*), never fail to excite compassion in a generous mind; and I hope I am not deceived in my opinion that yours is such:—You have the appearance of a gentleman, and cannot, when you hear my story, refuse that assistance which is in your power to give to an unhappy woman, who without it, may be rendered the most miserable of all created beings.

It would not be very easy to represent the surprise, so odd an address created in the mind of him to whom it was made.—She had not the appearance of one who wanted charity; and what other favor she required he could not conceive: but telling her she might command any thing in his power gave her encouragement to declare herself in this manner: You may judge (*resumed she*), by the melancholy garb I am in, that I have lately lost all that ought to be valuable to womankind; but it is impossible for you to guess the greatness of my misfortune, unless you had known my husband, who was master of every perfection to endear him to a wife's affections.—But, notwithstanding, I look on myself as the most unhappy of my sex in out-living him, I must so far obey the dictates of my discretion, as to take care of the little fortune he left behind him, which being in the hands of a brother of his in *London*, will be all carried off to *Holland*,[4] where he is going to settle; if I reach not the town before he leaves it, I am undone for ever.—To which end I left *Bristol*, the place where we lived, hoping to get a place in the stage at *Bath*, but they were all taken up before I came; and being, by a hurt I got in a fall, rendered incapable of traveling any long journey on horseback, I have no way to go to *London*, and must be inevitably ruined in the loss of all I have on earth, without you have good nature enough to admit me to take part of your chariot.

Here the feigned widow ended her sorrowful tale, which had been several times interrupted by a parenthesis of sighs and groans; and *Beauplaisir*, with a complaisant and tender air, assured her of his readiness to serve her in things of much greater consequence than what she desired of him; and told her it would be an impossibility of denying a place in his chariot to a lady who he could not behold without yielding one in his heart. She answered the compliments he made her but with tears, which seemed to stream in such abundance from her eyes, that she could not keep her handkerchief from her face one moment. Being come into the chariot, *Beauplaisir* said a thousand handsome things to persuade her from giving way to so violent a

---

3. The side flaps of a close-fitting hat, usually worn by women of higher rank.

4. Holland had been a frequent destination for English religious dissenters in exile.

grief; which, he told her, would not only be destructive to her beauty, but likewise her health. But all his endeavors for consolement appeared ineffectual, and he began to think he should have but a dull journey, in the company of one who seemed so obstinately devoted to the memory of her dead husband, that there was no getting a word from her on any other theme:—but bethinking himself of the celebrated story of the *Ephesian* matron,[5] it came into his head to make trial, she who seemed equally susceptible of *sorrow*, might not also be so too of *love*: and having began a discourse on almost every other topic, and finding her still incapable of answering, resolved to put it to the proof, if this would have no more effect to rouse her sleeping spirits:— with a gay air, therefore, though accompanied with the greatest modesty and respect, he turned the conversation, as though without design, on that joy-giving passion, and soon discovered that was indeed the subject she was best pleased to be entertained with; for on his giving her a hint to begin upon, never any tongue run more voluble than hers, on the prodigious power it had to influence the souls of those possessed of it, to actions even the most distant from their intentions, principles, or humors.—From that she passed to a description of the happiness of mutual affection;— the unspeakable ecstasy of those who meet with equal ardency; and represented it in colors so lively, and disclosed by the gestures with which her words were accompanied, and the accent of her voice so true a feeling of what she said, that *Beauplaisir*, without being as stupid, as he was really the contrary, could not avoid perceiving there were seeds of fire, not yet extinguished, in this fair widow's soul, which wanted but the kindling breath of tender sighs to light into a blaze.— He now thought himself as fortunate, as some moments before he had the reverse; and doubted not, but, that before they parted, he should find a way to dry the tears of this lovely mourner, to the satisfaction of them both. He did not, however, offer, as he had done to *Fantomina* and *Celia*, to urge his passion directly to her, but by a thousand little softening artifices, which he well knew how to use, gave her leave to guess he was enamored. When they came to the inn where they were to lie, he declared himself somewhat more freely, and perceiving she did not resent it past forgiveness, grew more encroaching still:—he now took the liberty of kissing away her tears, and catching the sighs as they issued from her lips; telling her if grief was infectious, he was resolved to have his share; protesting he would gladly exchange passions with her, and be content to bear her load of *sorrow*, if she would as willingly ease the burden of his *love*.—She said little in answer to the strenuous pressures with which at last he ventured to enfold her, but not thinking it decent, for the character she had assumed, to yield so suddenly, and unable to deny both his and her own inclinations, she counterfeited a fainting, and fell motionless upon his breast.—He had no great notion that she was in a real fit, and the room they supped in happening to have a bed in it, he took her in his arms and laid her on it, believing, that whatever her distemper was, that was the most proper place to convey her to.—He laid himself down by her, and endeavored to bring her to herself; and she was too grateful to her kind physician at her returning sense, to remove from the posture he had put her in, without his leave.

It may, perhaps, seem strange that *Beauplaisir* should in such near intimacies continue still deceived: I know there are men who will swear it is an impossibility, and that no disguise could hinder them from knowing a woman they had once

5. In Petronius's *Satyricon*, the Ephesian matron is a faithful wife who stays by her dead husband's burial vault day and night until she is seduced by a soldier who guards the nearby bodies of crucified criminals. When one of the bodies is stolen, the matron gives her own husband's body to the soldier to save him from punishment.

enjoyed. In answer to these scruples, I can only say, that besides the alteration which the change of dress made in her, she was so admirably skilled in the art of feigning, that she had the power of putting on almost what face she pleased, and knew so exactly how to form her behavior to the character she represented, that all the comedians at both playhouses[6] are infinitely short of her performances: she could vary her very glances, tune her voice to accents the most different imaginable from those in which she spoke when she appeared herself.—These aids from nature, joined to the wiles of art, and the distance between the places where the imagined *Fantomina* and *Celia* were, might very well prevent his having any thought that they were the same, or that the fair *widow* was either of them: it never so much as entered his head, and though he did fancy he observed in the face of the latter, features which were not altogether unknown to him, yet he could not recollect when or where he had known them;—and being told by her, that from her birth, she had never removed from *Bristol*, a place where he never was, he rejected the belief of having seen her, and supposed his mind had been deluded by an idea of some other, whom she might have a resemblance of.

They passed the time of their journey in as much happiness as the most luxurious gratification of wild desires could make them; and when they came to the end of it, parted not without a mutual promise of seeing each other often.—He told her to what place she should direct a letter to him; and she assured him she would send to let him know where to come to her, as soon as she was fixed in lodgings.

She kept her promise; and charmed with the continuance of his eager fondness, went not home, but into private lodgings, whence she wrote to him to visit her the first opportunity, and inquire for the Widow *Bloomer*.—She had no sooner dispatched this billet,[7] than she repaired to the house where she had lodged as *Fantomina*, charging the people if *Beauplaisir* should come there, not to let him know she had been out of town. From thence she wrote to him, in a different hand, a long letter of complaint, that he had been so cruel in not sending one letter to her all the time he had been absent, entreated to see him, and concluded with subscribing herself his unalterably affectionate *Fantomina*. She received in one day answers to both these. The first contained these lines:

To the Charming Mrs. Bloomer,

It would be impossible, my Angel! for me to express the thousandth part of that infinity of transport, the sight of your dear letter gave me.—Never was woman formed to charm like you: never did any look like you.—write like you,—bless like you;—nor did ever man adore as I do.—Since yesterday we parted, I have seemed a body without a soul; and had you not by this inspiring billet, gave me new life, I know not what by tomorrow I should have been.—I will be with you this evening about five:—O, 'tis an age till then!—But the cursed formalities of duty oblige me to dine with my lord—who never rises from table till that hour;—therefore adieu till then sweet lovely mistress of the soul and all the faculties of

Your most faithful,
Beauplaisir.

The other was in this manner:

To the Lovely Fantomina,

If you were half so sensible as you ought of your own power of charming, you would be assured, that to be unfaithful or unkind to you, would be among the things that are in their very

---

6. Comedians are actors. There were only two public
playhouses in London, established by royal decree in
1660.
7. Note, brief letter.

natures impossibilities.—It was my misfortune, not my fault, that you were not persecuted every post with a declaration of my unchanging passion; but I had unluckily forgot the name of the woman at whose house you are, and knew not how to form a direction that it might come safe to your hands.—And, indeed, the reflection how you might misconstrue my silence, brought me to town some weeks sooner than I intended—If you knew how I have languished to renew those blessings I am permitted to enjoy in your society, you would rather pity than condemn

Your ever faithful,
Beauplaisir.

P.S. *I fear I cannot see you till tomorrow; some business has unluckily fallen out that will engross my hours till then.—Once more, my dear,* Adieu.

Traitor! (*cried she*) as soon as she had read them, 'tis thus our silly, fond, believing sex are served when they put faith in man: so had I been deceived and cheated, had I like the rest believed, and sat down mourning in absence, and vainly waiting recovered tendernesses.—How do some women (*continued she*) make their life a hell, burning in fruitless expectations, and dreaming out their days in hopes and fears, then wake at last to all the horror of despair?—But I have outwitted even the most subtle of the deceiving kind, and while he thinks to fool me, is himself the only beguiled person.

She made herself, most certainly, extremely happy in the reflection on the success of her stratagems; and while the knowledge of his inconstancy and levity of nature kept her from having that real tenderness for him she would else have had, she found the means of gratifying the inclination she had for his agreeable person, in as full a manner as she could wish. She had all the sweets of love, but as yet had tasted none of the gall, and was in a state of contentment, which might be envied by the more delicate.

When the expected hour arrived, she found that her lover had lost no part of the fervency with which he had parted from her; but when the next day she received him as *Fantomina*, she perceived a prodigious difference; which led her again into reflections on the unaccountableness of men's fancies, who still prefer the last conquest, only because it is the last.—Here was an evident proof of it; for there could not be a difference in merit, because they were the same person; but the Widow *Bloomer* was a more new acquaintance than *Fantomina*, and therefore esteemed more valuable. This, indeed, must be said of *Beauplaisir*, that he had a greater share of good nature than most of his sex, who, for the most part, when they are weary of an intrigue, break it entirely off, without any regard to the despair of the abandoned nymph. Though he retained no more than a bare pity and complaisance for *Fantomina*, yet believing she loved him to an excess, would not entirely forsake her, though the continuance of his visits was now become rather a penance than a pleasure.

The Widow *Bloomer* triumphed some time longer over the heart of this inconstant, but at length her sway was at an end, and she sunk in this character, to the same degree of tastelessness, as she had done before in that of *Fantomina* and *Celia*.— She presently perceived it, but bore it as she had always done; it being but what she expected, she had prepared herself for it, and had another project in embryo, which she soon ripened into action. She did not, indeed, complete it altogether so suddenly as she had done the others, by reason there must be persons employed in it; and the aversion she had to any confidants in her affairs, and the caution with which she had hitherto acted, and which she was still determined to continue, made it very difficult for her to find a way without breaking through that resolution to compass what she wished.—She got over the difficulty at last, however, by proceeding in a manner, if possible, more extraordinary than all her former behavior:—muffling herself up in her hood one day, she went into the park about the hour when there are a great many necessitous gentlemen,[8] who think themselves above doing what they call little things for a maintenance, walking in the *Mall*,[9] to take a *Camelion* Treat,[1] and fill their stomachs with air instead of meat. Two of those, who by their physiognomy she thought most proper for her purpose, she beckoned to come to her; and taking them into a walk more remote from company, began to communicate the business she had with them in these words: I am sensible, gentlemen (*said she*), that, through the blindness of fortune, and partiality of the world, merit frequently goes unrewarded, and that those of the best pretentions meet with the least encouragement:—I ask your pardon (*continued she*), perceiving they seemed surprised, if I am mistaken in the notion, that you two may, perhaps, be of the number of those who have reason to complain of the injustice of fate; but if you are such as I take you for, I have a pro-posal to make you, which may be of some little advantage to you. Neither of them made any immediate answer, but appeared buried in consideration for some mo-ments. At length, We should, doubtless, madam (*said one of them*), willingly come into any measures to oblige you, provided they are such as may bring us into no dan-ger, either as to our persons or reputations. That which I require of you (*resumed she*), has nothing in it criminal: All that I desire is *secrecy* in what you are entrusted, and to disguise yourselves in such a manner as you cannot be known, if hereafter seen by the person on whom you are to impose.—In fine, the business is only an innocent frolic, but if blazed abroad, might be taken for too great a freedom in me:—Therefore, if you resolve to assist me, here are five pieces to drink my health, and assure you, that I have not discoursed you[2] on an affair, I design not to proceed in; and when it is accomplished fifty more lie ready for your acceptance. These words, and, above all, the money, which was a sum which, 'tis probable, they had not seen of a long time, made them immediately assent to all she desired, and press for the beginning of their employment: but things were not yet ripe for execution; and she told them, that the next day they should be let into the secret, charging them to meet her in the same place at an hour she appointed. 'Tis hard to say, which of these parties went away best pleased; *they*, that fortune had sent them so unexpected a windfall; or *she*, that she had found persons, who appeared so well qualified to serve her.

Indefatigable in the pursuit of whatsoever her humor was bent upon, she had no sooner left her new-engaged emissaries, than she went in search of a house for the com-pleting of her project.—She pitched on one very large, and magnificently furnished, which she hired by the week, giving them the money beforehand, to prevent any in-quiries. The next day she repaired to the park, where she met the punctual 'squires of low degree; and ordering them to follow her to the house she had taken, told them they must condescend to appear like servants, and gave each of them a very rich livery. Then writing a letter to *Beauplaisir*, in a character vastly different from either of those she had made use of, as *Fantomina*, or the fair Widow *Bloomer*, ordered one of them to deliver it into his own hands, to bring back an answer, and to be careful that he sifted out nothing of the truth.—I do not fear (*said she*), that you should discover to him who I am, because that is a secret, of which you yourselves are ignorant; but I would have you be so careful in your replies, that he may not think the concealment springs from any other reasons than your great integrity to your trust.—Seem therefore to know my

---

8. Poor men.
9. A popular walk in St. James's Park.

1. Chameleons were thought to subsist on air.
2. Talked to you.

whole affairs; and let your refusing to make him partaker in the secret, appear to be only the effect of your zeal for my interest and reputation. Promises of entire fidelity on the one side, and reward on the other, being past, the messenger made what haste he could to the house of *Beauplaisir;* and being there told where he might find him, performed exactly the injunction that had been given him. But never astonishment exceeded that which *Beauplaisir* felt at the reading this billet, in which he found these lines:

To the All-conquering Beauplaisir.

I imagine not that 'tis a new thing to you, to be told, you are the greatest charm in nature to our sex: I shall therefore, not to fill up my letter with any impertinent praises on your wit or person, only tell you, that I am infinite in love with both, and if you have a heart not too deeply engaged, should think myself the happiest of my sex in being capable of inspiring it with some tenderness.—There is but one thing in my power to refuse you, which is the knowledge of my name, which believing the sight of my face will render no secret, you must not take it ill that I conceal from you.—The bearer of this is a person I can trust; send by him your answer; but endeavor not to dive into the meaning of this mystery, which will be impossible for you to unravel, and at the same time very much disoblige me:—But that you may be in no apprehensions of being imposed on by a woman unworthy of your regard, I will venture to assure you, the first and greatest men in the kingdom would think themselves blessed to have that influence over me you have, though unknown to yourself, acquired.—But I need not go about to raise your curiosity, by giving you any idea of what my person is; if you think fit to be satisfied, resolve to visit me tomorrow about three in the afternoon; and though my face is hid, you shall not want sufficient demonstration, that she who takes these unusual measures to commence a friendship with you, is neither old, nor deformed. Till then I am,

Yours,
Incognita[3]

He had scarce come to the conclusion, before he asked the person who brought it, from what place he came;—the name of the lady he served;—if she were a wife, or widow, and several other questions directly opposite to the directions of the letter; but silence would have availed him as much as did all those testimonies of curiosity: no *Italian Bravo,*[4] employed in a business of the like nature, performed his office with more artifice; and the impatient inquirer was convinced, that nothing but doing as he was desired, could give him any light into the character of the woman who declared so violent a passion for him; and little fearing any consequence which could ensue from such an encounter, resolved to rest satisfied till he was informed of everything from herself, not imagining this *Incognita* varied so much from the generality of her sex, as to be able to refuse the knowledge of anything to the man she loved with that transcendency of passion she professed, and which his many successes with the ladies gave him encouragement enough to believe. He therefore took pen and paper, and answered her letter in terms tender enough for a man who had never seen the person to whom he wrote. The words were as follows:

To the Obliging and Witty Incognita.

Though to tell me I am happy enough to be liked by a woman, such, as by your manner of writing, I imagine you to be, is an honor which I can never sufficiently acknowledge, yet I know not how I am able to content myself with admiring the wonders of your wit alone: I am certain, a soul like yours must shine in your eyes with a vivacity, which must bless all they look on.—I shall, however, endeavor to restrain myself in those bounds you are pleased to set me, till by the knowledge of

3. Unknown woman (Latin); i.e., a woman in disguise.   4. Hired assassin.

my inviolable fidelity, I may be thought worthy of gazing on that heaven I am now but to enjoy in contemplation.—You need not doubt my glad compliance with your obliging summons: there is a charm in your lines, which gives too sweet an idea of their lovely author to be resisted.—I am all impatient for the blissful moment, which is to throw me at your feet, and give me an opportunity of convincing you that I am,

Your everlasting slave,
Beauplaisir.

Nothing could be more pleased than she, to whom it was directed, at the receipt of this letter; but when she was told how inquisitive he had been concerning her character and circumstances, she could not forbear laughing heartily to think of the tricks she had played him, and applauding her own strength of genius, and force of resolution, which by such unthought-of ways could triumph over her lover's inconstancy, and render that very temper, which to other women is the greatest curse, a means to make herself more blessed.—Had he been faithful to me (*said she, to herself*), either as *Fantomina*, or *Celia*, or the Widow *Bloomer*, the most violent passion, if it does not change its object, in time will wither: possession naturally abates the vigor of desire, and I should have had, at best, but a cold, insipid, husband-like lover in my arms; but by these arts of passing on him as a new mistress whenever the ardor, which alone makes love a blessing, begins to diminish, for the former one, I have him always raving, wild, impatient, longing, dying.—O that all neglected wives, and fond abandoned nymphs would take this method!—Men would be caught in their own snare, and have no cause to scorn our easy, weeping, wailing sex! Thus did she pride herself as if secure she never should have any reason to repent the present gaiety of her humor. The hour drawing near in which he was to come, she dressed herself in as magnificent a manner, as if she were to be that night at a ball at court, endeavoring to repair the want of those beauties which the vizard[5] should conceal, by setting forth the others with the greatest care and exactness. Her fine shape, and air, and neck appeared to great advantage; and by that which was to be seen of her, one might believe the rest to be perfectly agreeable. *Beauplaisir* was prodigiously charmed, as well with her appearance, as with the manner she entertained him: but though he was wild with impatience for the sight of a face which belonged to so exquisite a body, yet he would not immediately press for it, believing before he left her he should easily obtain that satisfaction.—A noble collation being over, he began to sue for the performance of her promise of granting everything he could ask, excepting the sight of her face, and knowledge of her name. It would have been a ridiculous piece of affectation in her to have seemed coy in complying with what she herself had been the first in desiring: she yielded without even a show of reluctance: and if there be any true felicity in an amour such as theirs, both here enjoyed it to the full. But not in the height of all their mutual raptures, could he prevail on her to satisfy his curiosity with the sight of her face: she told him that she hoped he knew so much of her, as might serve to convince him, she was not unworthy of his tenderest regard; and if he could not content himself with that which she was willing to reveal, and which was the conditions of their meeting, dear as he was to her, she would rather part with him for ever, than consent to gratify an inquisitiveness, which, in her opinion, had no business with his love. It was in vain that he endeavored to make her sensible of her mistake; and that this restraint was the greatest enemy imaginable to the happiness of them

---

5. Mask or veil.

both: she was not to be persuaded, and he was obliged to desist his solicitations, though determined in his mind to compass what he so ardently desired, before he left the house. He then turned the discourse wholly on the violence of the passion he had for her; and expressed the greatest discontent in the world at the apprehensions of being separated;—swore he could dwell for ever in her arms, and with such an unde- niable earnestness pressed to be permitted to tarry with her the whole night, that had she been less charmed with his renewed eagerness of desire, she scarce would have had the power of resisting him; but in granting this request, she was not without a thought that he had another reason for making it besides the extremity of his pas- sion, and had it immediately in her head how to disappoint him.

The hours of repose being arrived, he begged she would retire to her chamber, to which she consented, but obliged him to go to bed first; which he did not much op- pose, because he supposed she would not lie in her mask, and doubted not but the morning's dawn would bring the wished discovery.—The two imagined servants ush- ered him to his new lodging; where he lay some moments in all the perplexity imag- inable at the oddness of this adventure. But she suffered not these cogitations to be of any long continuance: she came, but came in the dark; which being no more than he expected by the former part of her proceedings, he said nothing of; but as much satis- faction as he found in her embraces, nothing ever longed for the approach of day with more impatience than he did. At last it came; but how great was his disappoint- ment, when by the noises he heard in the street, the hurry of the coaches, and the cries of penny-merchants,[6] he was convinced it was night nowhere but with him? He was still in the same darkness as before; for she had taken care to blind the windows in such a manner, that not the least chink was left to let in day.—He complained of her behavior in terms that she would not have been able to resist yielding to, if she had not been certain it would have been the ruin of her passion:—she, therefore, an- swered him only as she had done before; and getting out of the bed from him, flew out of the room with too much swiftness for him to have overtaken her, if he had at- tempted it. The moment she left him, the two attendants entered the chamber, and plucking down the implements which had screened him from the knowledge of that which he so much desired to find out, restored his eyes once more to day:—they at- tended to assist him in dressing, brought him tea, and by their obsequiousness, let him see there was but one thing which the mistress of them would not gladly oblige him in.—He was so much out of humor, however, at the disappointment of his cu- riosity, that he resolved never to make a second visit.—Finding her in an outer room, he made no scruple of expressing the sense he had of the little trust she reposed in him, and at last plainly told her, he could not submit to receive obligations from a lady, who thought him uncapable of keeping a secret, which she made no difficulty of letting her servants into.—He resented—he once more entreated—he said all that man could do, to prevail on her to unfold the mystery; but all his adjurations were fruitless; and he went out of the house determined never to re-enter it, till she should pay the price of his company with the discovery of her face and circumstances.—She suffered him to go with this resolution, and doubted not but he would recede from it, when he reflected on the happy moments they had passed together; but if he did not, she comforted herself with the design of forming some other stratagem, with which to impose on him a fourth time.

6. Street vendors of cheap wares.

She kept the house, and her gentlemen-equipage[7] for about a fortnight, in which time she continued to write to him as *Fantomina* and the Widow *Bloomer*, and received the visits he sometimes made to each; but his behavior to both was grown so cold, that she began to grow as weary of receiving his now insipid caresses as he was of offering them: she was beginning to think in what manner she should drop these two characters, when the sudden arrival of her mother, who had been some time in a foreign country, obliged her to put an immediate stop to the course of her whimsical adventures.—That lady, who was severely virtuous, did not approve of many things she had been told of the conduct of her daughter; and though it was not in the power of any person in the world to inform her of the truth of what she had been guilty of, yet she heard enough to make her keep her afterwards in a restraint, little agreeable to her humor, and the liberties to which she had been accustomed.

But this confinement was not the greatest part of the trouble of this now afflicted lady: she found the consequences of her amorous follies would be, without almost a miracle, impossible to be concealed:—she was with child; and though she would easily have found means to have screened even this from the knowledge of the world, had she been at liberty to have acted with the same unquestionable authority over herself, as she did before the coming of her mother, yet now all her invention was at a loss for a stratagem to impose on a woman of her penetration:—by eating little, lacing prodigious straight, and the advantage of a great hoop-petticoat, however, her bigness was not taken notice of, and, perhaps, she would not have been suspected till the time of her going into the country, where her mother designed to send her, and from whence she intended to make her escape to some place where she might be delivered with secrecy, if the time of it had not happened much sooner than she expected.—A ball being at court, the good old lady was willing she should partake of the diversion of it as a farewell to the town.—It was there she was seized with those pangs, which none in her condition are exempt from:—she could not conceal the sudden rack which all at once invaded her; or had her tongue been mute, her wildly rolling eyes, the distortion of her features, and the convulsions which shook her whole frame, in spite of her, would have revealed she labored under some terrible shock of nature.—Everybody was surprised, everybody was concerned, but few guessed at the occasion.—Her mother grieved beyond expression, doubted not but she was struck with the hand of death; and ordered her to be carried home in a chair, while herself followed in another.—A physician was immediately sent for: but he presently perceiving what was her distemper, called the old lady aside, and told her, it was not a doctor of his sex, but one of her own, her daughter stood in need of.— Never was astonishment and horror greater than that which seized the soul of this afflicted parent at these words: she could not for a time believe the truth of what she heard; but he insisting on it, and conjuring her to send for a midwife, she was at length convinced of it.—All the pity and tenderness she had been for some moment before possessed of now vanished, and were succeeded by an adequate[8] shame and indignation:—she flew to the bed where her daughter was lying, and telling her what she had been informed of, and which she was now far from doubting, commanded her to reveal the name of the person whose insinuations had drawn her to this dishonor.—It was a great while before she could be brought to confess anything, and much longer before she could be prevailed on to name the man whom she so fatally

7. Retinue of footmen.   8. Equal.

had loved; but the rack of nature growing more fierce, and the enraged old lady protesting no help should be afforded her while she persisted in her obstinacy, she, with great difficulty and hesitation in her speech, at last pronounced the name of *Beauplaisir*. She had no sooner satisfied her weeping mother, than that sorrowful lady sent messengers at the same time, for a midwife, and for that gentleman who had occasioned the other's being wanted.—He happened by accident to be at home, and immediately obeyed the summons, though prodigiously surprised what business a lady so much a stranger to him could have to impart.—But how much greater was his amazement, when taking him into her closet, she there acquainted him with her daughter's misfortune, of the discovery she had made, and how far he was concerned in it?—All the idea one can form of wild astonishment, was mean to what he felt:—he assured her, that the young lady her daughter was a person whom he had never, more than at a distance, admired:—that he had indeed, spoke to her in public company, but that he never had a thought which tended to her dishonor.—His denials, if possible, added to the indignation she was before enflamed with:—she had no longer patience; and carrying him into the chamber, where she was just delivered of a fine girl, cried out, I will not be imposed on: the truth by one of you shall be revealed.— *Beauplaisir* being brought to the bedside, was beginning to address himself to the lady in it, to beg she could clear the mistake her mother was involved in; when she, covering herself with the cloths, and ready to die a second time with the inward agitations of her soul, shrieked out, Oh, I am undone!—I cannot live, and bear this shame!—But the old lady believing that now or never was the time to dive into the bottom of this mystery, forcing her to rear her head, told her, she should not hope to escape the scrutiny of a parent she had dishonored in such a manner, and pointing to *Beauplaisir*, Is this the gentleman (*said she*), to whom you owe your ruin? or have you deceived me by a fictitious tale? Oh! no (*resumed the trembling creature*), he is, indeed, the innocent cause of my undoing:—Promise me your pardon (*continued she*), and I will relate the means. Here she ceased, expecting what she would reply, which, on hearing *Beauplaisir* cry out, What mean you, madam? I your undoing, who never harbored the least design on you in my life, she did in these words, Though the injury you have done your family (*said she*), is of a nature which cannot justly hope forgiveness, yet be assured, I shall much sooner excuse you when satisfied of the truth, than while I am kept in a suspense, if possible, as vexatious as the crime itself is to me. Encouraged by this she related the whole truth. And 'tis difficult to determine, if *Beauplaisir*, or the lady, were most surprised at what they heard; he, that he should have been blinded so often by her artifices; or she, that so young a creature should have the skill to make use of them. Both sat for some time in a profound reverie; till at length she broke it first in these words: Pardon, sir (*said she*),[9] the trouble I have given you: I must confess it was with a design to oblige you to repair the supposed injury you had done this unfortunate girl, by marrying her, but now I know not what to say:—The blame is wholly hers, and I have nothing to request further of you, than that you will not divulge the distracted folly she has been guilty of.—He answered her in terms perfectly polite; but made no offer of that which, perhaps, she expected, though could not, now informed of her daughter's proceedings, demand. He assured her, however, that if she would commit the newborn lady to his care, he would discharge it faithfully. But neither of them would consent to that; and he took his leave, full of cogitations,[1] more confused than ever he had known in his whole life. He

---

9. I.e., the elder lady.   1. Anxious thoughts.

continued to visit there, to inquire after her health every day; but the old lady perceiving there was nothing likely to ensue from these civilities, but, perhaps, a renewing of the crime, she entreated him to refrain; and as soon as her daughter was in a condition, sent her to a monastery in *France,* the abbess of which had been her particular friend. And thus ended an intrigue, which, considering the time it lasted, was as full of variety as any, perhaps, that many ages have produced.

CREDITS

ILLUSTRATION CREDITS

INDEX

INDEX

INDEX